INTERNATIONAL LITERARY MARKET PLACE 1981–82

R. R. BOWKER COMPANY
New York & London, 1981

Published by R. R. Bowker Company (a Xerox Publishing Company)
1180 Avenue of the Americas
New York, N.Y. 10036

Copyright © 1981 by Xerox Corporation

All rights reserved.
Reproduction of this work, in whole or in part,
without written permission of the publisher is prohibited.

International Standard Book Number 0-8352-1345-5
International Standard Serial Number 0074-6827
Library of Congress Catalog Card Number 77-70295

Printed and bound in the United States of America

The publishers do not assume and hereby
disclaim any liability to any party for
any loss or damage caused by errors or
omissions in *International Literary
Market Place*, whether such errors or
omissions result from negligence,
accident or any other cause.

Computer typeset by Millford Reprographics International Ltd, Luton, England.

INTERNATIONAL LITERARY MARKET PLACE 1981–82

Contents

The material for each country is grouped under a series of sub-headings to the main country heading. These subheadings appear always in the same order, and the omission of any of them from a particular country implies that no information is available. The headings are as follows:

General Information (language, population, currency, etc)
Book Trade Organizations
Book Trade Reference Books and Journals
Publishers
Remainder Dealers
Literary Agents
Book Clubs
Major Booksellers
Major Libraries
Library Associations
Library Reference Books and Journals
Literary Associations and Societies
Literary Periodicals
Literary Prizes
Translation Agencies and Associations

Preface	vii
Abbreviations	viii
Afghanistan	1
Albania	1
Algeria	1
Angola	2
Argentina	2
Australia	9
Austria	23
Bahamas	31
Bahrain	31
Bangladesh	31
Barbados	32
Belgium	32
Belize	45
Benin	45
Bermuda	46
Bolivia	46
Botswana	47
Brazil	47
Brunei	57
Bulgaria	57
Burma	59
Burundi	60
United Republic of Cameroun	60
Central African Republic	61
Chad	61
Chile	61
People's Republic of China	63
China (Taiwan)	63
Colombia	64
Popular Republic of Congo	67
Costa Rica	67
Cuba	68
Cyprus	69
Czechoslovakia	69
Denmark	73
Dominican Republic	79
Ecuador	80
Egypt	81
El Salvador	82
Ethiopia	83
Fiji	84
Finland	84
France	87
French Guiana	113
French Polynesia	113
Gabon	113
The Gambia	114
German Democratic Republic	114
Federal Republic of Germany	118
Ghana	169
Gibraltar	170
Greece	170
Guatemala	173
Guinea	173
Guyana	174
Haiti	174
Honduras	174
Hong Kong	175
Hungary	176
Iceland	179
India	180
Indonesia	198
Iran	200
Iraq	201
Republic of Ireland	202
Israel	205
Italy	211
Ivory Coast	222
Jamaica	223
Japan	224
Jordan	233
Kampuchea	234
Kenya	234
Democratic People's Republic of Korea	235
Republic of Korea	236
Kuwait	238
Laos	239
Lebanon	239
Lesotho	240
Liberia	240
Libya	241
Liechtenstein	241
Luxembourg	241
Macau	242
Democratic Republic of Madagascar	242
Malawi	243
Malaysia	244
Mali	246
Malta	246
Isle of Man	247
Martinique	247
Mauritania	247
Mauritius	247
Mexico	248
Monaco	253
Mongolian People's Republic	253
Montserrat	253
Morocco	253
Mozambique	254
Namibia	254
Nepal	255
Netherlands	255
Netherlands Antilles	268
New Caledonia	268
New Zealand	268
Nicaragua	273
Niger	274
Nigeria	274
Norway	278
Pakistan	281
Panama	284
Papua New Guinea	285
Paraguay	285
Peru	286
Philippines	287
Poland	290
Portugal	295
Puerto Rico	298
Qatar	300
Réunion	300
Romania	300
Rwanda	302
Saudi Arabia	302
Senegal	303
Seychelles	304
Sierra Leone	304
Republic of Singapore	304
Somalia	307
Republic of South Africa	307
Spain	314
Sri Lanka	325
Sudan	326
Suriname	327
Swaziland	327
Sweden	327
Switzerland	336
Syria	352
Tanzania	353
Thailand	354
Togo	356
Trinidad and Tobago	356
Tunisia	357
Turkey	357
Uganda	359
Union of Soviet Socialist Republics	360
United Arab Emirates	363
United Kingdom	364
Upper Volta	416
Uruguay	416
Vatican City State	418
Venezuela	418
Socialist Republic of Viet Nam	420
Western Samoa	421
People's Democratic Republic of Yemen	421
Yemen Arab Republic	421
Yugoslavia	421
Zaire	426
Zambia	428
Zimbabwe	428

INTERNATIONAL SECTION	431
Copyright Conventions	431
International Organizations	431
International Bibliography	436
International Literary Prizes	439
The ISBN System	444
BOOK TRADE CALENDAR	448
INDEX	454

Preface

The annual appearance of a new edition of the *International Literary Market Place* is due once again to the collaborative effort of an experienced team who between them have made many thousand amendments. As the book becomes increasingly well known the rate of response grows. Rapidly to analyse and extract the information, supplementing it from catalogues and various other sources, requires unusual skill and accuracy. In addition to the careful processing of replies from existing entrants, several hundred new entries have been prepared, while firms no longer in existence, and non-repliers who can no longer be traced, have been removed.

As usual, Linda Redman has coped superbly with the internal organization of the project, answering countless queries and keeping the work on schedule. Pat Brown, Dennis Corbyn, Rosemary Harley and Martha Ross have dealt with individual sections of the book with a sharp eye for detail, and Derek French has given technical advice and updated the General Information, adding explanatory notes where necessary.

In conclusion I make my annual request to users of this directory for suggestions for its improvement. New ideas are always given careful consideration and should be sent to the editorial office at Bowker Publishing Co, Erasmus House, High Street, Epping, Essex, England CM16 4BU.

PETER FOUND
Editor

Abbreviations

*	questionnaire not returned for this edition
AB	aktiebolag (= limited company)
AG	Aktiengesellschaft (= public limited company)
Apdo	apartado (= post-box)
ApS	anpartsselskab (= private limited company)
A/S	(Norwegian) aksjeselskap, (Swedish) aktieselskab, (= limited company)
ASBL	association sans but lucratif (= non-profit-making society)
Ave	(English, French) avenue, (Portuguese, Spanish) avenida
Bldg	building
Blvd	(Bulgarian, Romanian) bulevard, (English, French) boulevard
BP	boîte postale (= post-box)
BV	besloten vennootschap (= private limited company)
C	compagnía (= company)
CA	compañía anónima (= public limited company)
CFA	Communauté financière africaine
CFP	comptoirs français du Pacifique
Cia	companhia (= company)
Cía	compañía (= company)
Cie	compagnie (= company)
Co	(English) company, (German) Kompanie
CP	(Italian) casetta postale, (Portuguese) caixa postal, (= post-box)
CV	commanditaire vennootschap (= limited partnership)
Dir	director
eV	eingetragener Verein (= registered society)
GmbH	Gesellschaft mit beschränkter Haftung (= private limited company)
Inc	incorporated
Jl	jalan (= street)
KG	Kommanditgesellschaft (= partnership)
KK	kabushiki kaisha (= public limited company)
Lda	limitada (= limited)
Ltd	limited
Ltda	limitada (= limited)
Man Dir	managing director
Nachf	Nachfolger(s) (= successor(s))
nám	náměstí (= square)
NV	naamloze vennootschap (= public limited company)
of	oficina (= office)
Off	office
Oy	osakeyhtiö (= limited company)
Pl	(Bulgarian) ploshtad, (English, French) place, (Polish) plac, (Russian) ploshchad', (Spanish) plaza
PL	postilokero (= post-box)
Pty	proprietary
PVBA	personenvennootschap met beperkte aansprakelijkheid (= private limited company)
Pvt	private
qqv	quae vide (= which see)
qv	quod vide (= which see)
Rd	road
SA	(French) société anonyme, (Portuguese) sociedade anônima, (Spanish) sociedad anónima (= public limited company)
Sàrl	société à responsabilité limitée (= private limited company)
SCA	sociedad en comandita por acciónes (= limited partnership)
S de RL	sociedad de responsabilidad limitada (= private limited company)
Sdn Bhd	sendirian berhad (= private limited company)
SL	sociedad de responsabilidad limitada (= private limited company)
SpA	società per azioni (= public limited company)
SPRL	société de personnes à responsabilité limitée (= private limited company)
SRL	(Italian) società à responsabilità limitata, (Spanish) sociedad de responsabilidad limitada, (= private limited company)
St	street
Str	(Danish) straede, (Dutch) straat, (German) Strasse, (Italian) strada, (Romanian) stradă (= street)
Sq	square
Tel	telephone number
u	utca (= street)
UCC	Universal Copyright Convention
ul	(Bulgarian) ulitsa, (Czech) ulice, (Polish) ulica, (Romanian) ulită, (Russian) ulitsa, (Serbocroatian, Slovak, Slovene) ulica (= street)
VEB	volkseigener Betrieb (= people's enterprise)
VZW	vereniging zonder winstoogmerk (= non-profit-making society)

A limited company is a corporation owned by shareholders (or stockholders) who may contribute capital to the company but are not otherwise generally liable for its debts.

A public company may invite anyone to become a shareholder, and its shares (or stock) are usually traded on a stock exchange. A private, or proprietary, company has a restricted number of shareholders and its shares are not traded on a stock exchange.

The owners of a partnership are generally liable for its debts, but a limited partnership has some owners who only contribute capital and are not otherwise liable for debts.

Afghanistan

General Information

Note: No replies were received to questionnaires sent to Afghanistan for this edition of *International Literary Market Place*. The information given in the 1980 edition has been repeated here but should be treated with caution.

Language: Pushtu and Persian
Religion: Sunni Muslim with approximately 1 million Shiite Muslim
Population: 15.1 million
Literacy rate (1975): 12.2% of population aged 6 or more (26.8% of urban population, 19.5% of rural)
Bank Hours: 0800-1200, 1300-1600 Saturday-Wednesday; 0800-1300 Thursday
Shop Hours: Winter: 0900-1300, 1400-1700 Saturday-Thursday; Summer: 0800-1300, 1500-1800 Saturday-Thursday
Currency: 100 puls = 1 afghani
Copyright: Florence (see International section)

Publishers

Afghan Kitab*, Kabul
Subject: Translations

Book Publishing Institute*, Herat
Subjects: Fiction, History, Religion
Founded: 1970 (by cooperation of Government Press and citizens of Herat)

Franklin Book Programs Inc*, PO Box 332, Kabul

Government Press*, Kabul
Subjects: Afghan history & literature, Textbooks, Newspapers, Magazines, Journals
Founded: 1870
Miscellaneous: Under supervision of Ministry of Information and Culture

Historical Society of Afghanistan*, Kabul
Dir: M Yakub Wahidi
Founded: 1931
Subjects: Afghan History and Culture
Publications: Afghanistan (in English, French and German); *Aryana* (in Dari and Pashtu), both quarterly

Kabul University, Institute of Geography*, Kabul
Subject: Maps

Ministry of Culture and Information, Book Publishing Department*, Kabul

Ministry of Education, Department of Educational Publications*, Kabul
Subjects: Primary & Secondary Textbooks in Pushtu and Dari

Pushtu Toulana, Afghan Academy*, Kabul
Subjects: Pushtu Language

Major Booksellers

Behzad Bookshop*, Welayat Ave, Kabul

Behzad Bookstore*, Shop No 122, Chahra-hi-Malikasghar, Kabul

Royal Afghanistan Press Department*, Kabul

University of Kabul Bookstores*, Ali-Abad, Kabul

Zuri Book Shop*, Shir Shah Meena, Kabul *also* Charahi-Sadarat, Kabul

Major Libraries

Institute of Education Library, Kabul University*, Kabul

Ministry of Education Library*, Kabul

Library of the **National Bank***, Kabul

Library of the **Press Department***, Kabul

Public Library*, Kabul

Library of the **Royal Palace***, Kabul

University Library*, Kabul

Library Associations

Anjuman Kitab-Khana-I-Afghanistan*, PO Box 3142, Kabul
Afghan Library Association
Publication: Afghan Library Association Bulletin

Library Journals

Afghan Library Association Bulletin, Anjuman-Kitab-Khani-I-Afghanistan, PO Box 3142, Kabul

Albania

General Information

Language: Albanian
Religion: Muslim, but Albania proclaimed an atheist state in 1967
Population: 2.6 million
Currency: 100 qintars = 1 lek
Export/Import Information: Importation of books is through State Trading Organization, Nah Shperndarjes Të (or NST) Librit, Blvd e Pezës, Tirana. Correspondence should be in Italian or French. Copies of correspondence to Albanian Legation in Rome. Import licences and strict exchange controls

Book Trade Organizations

Drejtoria Quëndrore e Përhapjes dhe e Propagandimit të Librit*, Tirana
Central Administration for the Dissemination and Propagation of the Book

Union of Writers and Artists of Albania*, 37Z Baboci St, Tirana
Chairman: Dritero Agolli
Publications: Nëndori, Drita

Book Trade Journals

The Albanian Book, National Library, Tirana

Articles from Albanian Periodicals, National Library, Tirana

Bibliografia kombëtare e Republikës Popullore të Shqipërisë (Albanian National Bibliography), Botim i Bibliotekës Kombëtare, Tirana

Libri (The Book), Rruga Konferenca e Pezës, Tirana

Publishers

'8' Nentori Publishing House*, Tirana
Subjects: Books and journals on Albania; documents and publications of the Albanian Party of Work

N I S H Shtypshkronjave 'Mihal Duri'*, Tirana
Subjects: Government Publications, Education, Politics, Law

Naim Frasheri*, Tirana
Subject: Books in foreign languages

Ndërmarrja e Botimeve Ushtarake*, Tirana
Subjects: Military, Technology

Major Booksellers

Nah Shperndarjes Të Librit (NST)*, Blvd e Pezës, Tirana
State trading organization controlling importation of books

Ndërmarrja e Librit*, Konfercenca e Pezës, Tirana Tel: 3323 Cable Add: Ndlibri Tirana
Distributor of books, journals and newspapers published in Albania in Albanian and foreign languages

Major Libraries

Biblioteka Kombëtare*, Tirana Tel: 5887
National Library
Dir: Marika Vegli

Biblioteka **Shkencore e Universitetit Shtetëror të Tiranës***, Tirana
Scientific Library of the State University of Tirana

Shkodër Public Library*, Shkodër

Library Associations

Council of Libraries*, Rruga 'Abdi Toptani', No 3, Tirana
President: M Domi

Literary Periodicals

Drita (The Light), Union of Writers and Artists of Albania, 37 Z Baboci St, Tirana

Nëndori (November), Union of Writers and Artists of Albania, 37 Z Baboci St, Tirana

Shejzat (Pleiades) (Albanian language and literature), Piazza della Balduina 59, I-00136 Rome, Italy

Algeria

General Information

Language: Arabic and French, the language for commerce
Religion: Muslim
Population: 18.5 million
Literacy Rate (1971): 26.4%
Bank Hours: Winter: 0745-1100, 1415-1700 Monday-Friday; Summer: 0715-1100, 1500-1730 Monday-Friday
Shop Hours: 0900-1200, 1500-1900 Monday-Saturday
Currency: 100 centimes = 1 Algerian dinar
Export/Import Information: Books not

textbooks dutied 11.11%; children's picture books, 37.50%. Advertising matter other than single copies, 25%. Global Sole Production Tax levied on duty paid. Books may be imported or exported only by or with permission of SNED State Monopoly, 3 blvd Zirout Yousef, BP 49, Alger Strasbourg. There are also quota restrictions. Permission to import usually entitles holder to obtain necessary foreign exchange; strict controls are in effect
Copyright: UCC (see International section)

Book Trade Organizations

Syndicat des Librairies d'Algérie*, 18 ave de la Marne, Algiers
Association of Algerian Booksellers

Book Trade Journals

Bibliographie de l'Algérie, National Library, ave du Docteur Fanon, Algiers (The national bibliography, published bi-annually)

Publishers

Editions Populaires de l'**Armée***, 2 rue de Normandie, Algiers Tel: 620613
Telex: 52039
Man Dir: T Senhadji
Subjects: General Fiction, General Nonfiction, Belles Lettres, Poetry, History, Africana, Religion, Social Science
Miscellaneous: Distributed by SNED

Government Printer*, 7-13a ave Abdelkador Benbarek, Algiers

Société nationale d'Edition et de Diffusion (SNED), 3 blvd Zirout Youcef, BP 49, Algiers Tel: 639670 Cable Add: Sneda Alger Telex: 53845 Sneda Dz
Dir-General: Sid Ahmed Baghli; *Editorial:* A Madoui; *Publishing:* H Nia
Subjects: General Fiction, General Nonfiction, Belles Lettres, Poetry, Biography, History, Africana, Philosophy, Religion, Juveniles, Arabic language & literature, English language, Dictionaries, Paperbacks, General & Social Science, University & Secondary Textbooks, Scientific & Technical, Sport, Travel
Bookshops: At above address, also 32 others throughout Algeria
1978-79: 140 titles *Founded:* 1966

Major Booksellers

Librairie '**Maison des Livres**'*, 12 rue Ali Boumendjel, Algiers

Librairie **S N E D** (Societe nationale d'Edition et de Diffusion)*, 13 blvd Zirout Youcef, Algiers
Sole importer, exporter and distributor of books and periodicals

Librairie du **Tiers Monde***, Pl Emir Abdelkader, Algiers

Major Libraries

Archives nationales*, Palais du Gouvernement, Esplanade d'Afrique, Algiers

Bibliothèque municipale*, Hôtel de Ville, Constantine

Bibliothèque nationale*, ave du Docteur Fanon, Algiers Tel: 630632
Dir: Mahmoud Agha Bouayed
Publication: Bibliographie de l'Algérie (in Arabic and French, twice a year)

Ecole nationale polytechnique, Bibliothèque*, ave Pasteur, El-Harrach, Algiers

Bibliothèque universitaire, **Université d'Alger***, 2 rue Didouche Mourad, Algiers Tel: 640215
Librarian: Zoulikha Bekadour

Bibliothèque de l'**Université de Constantine***, Route de Ain el Bey, Constantine Tel: 931125
Librarian: Sari Mahmoud

Université d'Oran, Bibliothèque*, rue du Colonel Lofti, Oran

Library Associations

Institut de Bibliothéconomie et des Sciences Documentaires, Université d'Alger, Algiers
Institute of Library Management and Documentary Science

Library Reference Books

Books

Bibliographie de l'Algérie (in Arabic and French, twice a year), Bibliothèque nationale, ave du Docteur Fanon, Algiers

Literary Associations and Societies

Union des Ecrivains algériens*, 12 rue Ali Boumendjel, Algiers
Union of Algerian Writers

Literary Prizes

Union des Ecrivains algériens*
Awards annual literary prize for fiction, 10,000 Algerian dinars. Enquiries to Union des Ecrivains algériens, 12 rue Ali Boumendjel, Algiers

Angola

General Information

Language: Portuguese, Bantu languages
Religion: Christian, Animist
Population: 6.7 million
Currency: 100 centavos = 1 kwanza
Export/Import Information: No tariff on books and advertising. Very restricted issuance of import licences. Advertising matter is currently given considerably lower priority. Exchange controls.

Publishers

Nova Editorial **Angolana** SARL*, CP 1225, Luanda
Man Dir: Pombo Fernandes
Subjects: General Books, Educational Books
Founded: 1935

Industrias ABC*, CP 1245, Luanda
Subjects: General Nonfiction, Directories
Bookshop: Address as above

Lello & Cia Lda*, CP 1245, Luanda
Bookshop: CP 1300, Luanda
Subjects: General Fiction & Nonfiction, Secondary & Primary Textbooks

Major Booksellers

Argente, Sentos & Cia Lda*, CP 1314, Luanda

Industrias ABC*, CP 1245, Luanda

Lello & Cia Lda*, CP 1300, Luanda

Livraria **Magalhães** Sarl, CP 70, Lobito Tel: 2241/2/3 Cable Add: Aljoma

Major Libraries

Biblioteca Nacional de Angola, CP 2915, Luanda Tel: 37317
Director: Rui Augusto Baptista Frende
Publication: Novas

Universidade de Luanda Biblioteca*, CP 815, Luanda Tel: 764
Librarian: A C Ferraz Correia

Library Journals

Novas (News), National Library, CP 2915, Luanda

Argentina

General Information

Language: Spanish
Religion: Roman Catholic
Population: 26.1 million
Literacy Rate (1970): 92.6%
Bank Hours: 1200-1600 Monday-Friday
Shop Hours: 0900-1900 Monday-Saturday
Currency: 100 centavos = 1 peso
Export/Import Information: No tariffs on books except children's picture books 5%, no VAT on books. Most advertising matter (more than one copy) subject to 130% duty. Added taxes of 7% on all imports. Import licences required, goods require prior deposit of 40%. Limited foreign exchange led to cancellation of most importation in 1975.
Copyright: UCC, Berne, Buenos Aires (see International section)

Book Trade Organizations

Cámara Argentina de Editores de Libros*, Maipú 359 — 2° piso of 31, Buenos Aires Tel: 451322
President: Hector Oscar Tucci
Association of Argentine Book Publishers

Cámara Argentina de Editoriales Tecnicas*, Venezuela 668, Buenos Aires
Argentinian Association of Technical Publishers

Cámara Argentina de Publicaciones*, Montevideo 48, 4° piso, Buenos Aires
President: Fernando Vidal Buzzi
Argentine Publications Association

Cámara Argentina del Libro*, Ave Belgrano 1580, 6° piso, 1093 Buenos Aires Tel: 388383
Secretary: A Sisco
Argentine Book Association

Federación Argentina de Librerías, Papelerías y Actividades Afines*, España 848, Losario, Santa Fé
Federation of Bookstores, Stationers and Related Activities

S A D E (Sociedad Argentina de Escritores)*, Uruguay 1371, 1016 Buenos Aires Tel: 413520/420773
Dir: Horatio E Tarri
Publication: Boletín de la SADE (bi-monthly)
Association of Argentine Writers

Sociedad General de Autores de la Argentina*, Pacheco de Melo 1818-20, Buenos Aires Tel: 444518
Publications: Boletín Social (quarterly), *Argentores* (monthly)
Argentine Society of Authors

Publishers

Editorial **Abaco** de Rodolfo Depalma SRL, Tucumán 1429 4°D, 1050 Buenos Aires Tel: 40165
Man Dir & Editorial: Rodolfo Depalma; *Sales:* James Farbinger; *Production:* Marcos José Azubel; *Psychology Section:* Daniel P Gómez Dupertuis
Branch Off: Centenera 461, Buenos Aires
Subjects: Law, Economics, Sociology, Philosophy, History, Psychology
Founded: 1975

Editorial **Abeledo** Perrot SAEeI*, Lavalle 1280-1328, 1048 Buenos Aires Tel: 352848
Man Dirs: Juan Carlos Abeledo, Emilio José Perrot; *Sales Dir:* Carlos Alberto Pazos
Subject: Law
Founded: 1901
Bookshop: Lavalle 1280-1328, 1048 Buenos Aires

Ediciones **Acervo** de Argentina SRL, Casillas 81 y 82, Sucursal 2-B (Congreso), 1402 Buenos Aires (Located at: Virrey Cevallos 645, P Baja, 1077 Capital Federal) Tel: 374141 Telex: 18522 Cecba Ar 028
Editorial: José Gamarra Alcalde
Parent Company: Ediciones Acervo, Spain (qv)
Subjects: Politics, Religion, Crime, Science Fiction, Fiction, General
1978: 78 titles *1979:* 56 titles

Editorial **Acme** SA*, Santa Magdalena 633, 1008 Buenos Aires Tel: 461662
Man Dir: Emilio I González
Subjects: General Fiction, Belles Lettres, Poetry, Biography, History, How-to, Juveniles, Paperbacks, Technical, University & Primary Textbooks
Founded: 1949

Aguilar Argentina SA de Ediciones, Ave Córdoba 2100, 1120 Buenos Aires Tel: 466400/466559
Man Dir: Antonio Sempere; *Sales Dir:* Manuel Rodríguez
Parent Company: Aguilar SA de Ediciones, Spain (qv)
Branch Off: Deán Funes 501, Córdoba
Subjects: Philosophy, Literature, Art, Psychology, Economics, Technical, Juveniles
Founded: 1946

Librería **Akadia** Editorial*, Luis María Drago 389, 1414 Buenos Aires Tel: 549037
Man Dir: José F Patlallan
Subject: Medicine
Bookshop: At above address
Founded: 1967

Editorial **Albatros** SRL*, Lavalle 3975, 1190 Buenos Aires Tel: 861215
Man Dir: Roberto R Canevaro
Subjects: Agriculture, Animal Care & Breeding, Technical, How-to, Social Sciences, Medicine, University Textbooks
Founded: 1967

Editorial **Alfa** Argentina SA*, Defensa 599, 3er piso, 1065 Buenos Aires Tel: 331199/341473
Man Dir: Leonardo Milla; *Manager:* Héctor Allegrini
Subjects: General Fiction, Literature, Philosophy, Psychology, University Textbooks
Founded: 1971

Editorial Rodolfo **Alonso** SRL*, Sánchez de Bustamante 923, 1173 Buenos Aires Tel: 891346
Man Dir: Rodolfo Alonso; *Sales Manager:* Raquel Rebaudi Basavilbaso
Subjects: General Fiction & Nonfiction
1978: 8 titles *Founded:* 1968

América Norildis Editores SA*, Belgrano 624, 11 piso, Buenos Aires Tel: 349903
Man Dir & Editorial: Fernando Videl Buzzi; *Sales & Publicity:* Federico Alberto Catalano; *Production:* Jorge Draoz Bodi; *Rights & Permissions:* Teresa Vernengo
Associate Companies: Editorial Crea SA (qv), Editorial Huemul (qv)
Subjects: Secondary and University Textbooks, Fiction, Literature
Founded: 1970

Editorial **Américalee** SRL, Andonaegui 1138, 1027 Buenos Aires Tel: 511491
Man Dir: Héctor E Landolfi; *Sales Dir:* Josefa A S de Landolfi
Subjects: Technical Sciences, Sports, Cooking
1980: 26 titles *Founded:* 1939

Editorial **Americana***, Brasil 675, 1154 Buenos Aires Tel: 238862
Man Dir: Manuel Rey Tosar
Subjects: History, Politics, Social Sciences, Arts, Fiction

Amorrortu Editores SA*, Icalma 2001, Esq José A Salmún Feijóo, 1274 Buenos Aires Tel: 282630/282818
Man Dir: Horacio de Amorrortu
Subjects: Anthropology & Religion, Economy, Philosophy, Psychology, Sociology, Argentine current affairs
Founded: 1967

Ediciones **Andromeda***, Mexico 625 – 1° piso, 1097 Buenos Aires Tel: 308280
Man Dir, Rights & Permissions: Carlos Samonta; *Editorial:* Jorge A Sanchez
Subjects: General Fiction, Literature
Founded: 1975

Arbó SACeI, Ave Martín García 653, 1268 Buenos Aires Tel: 3620643/3620747
Man Dir: Orestes Arbo; *Technical Dir:* J M Barcala; *Production:* Ariel Arbó; *Publicity:* Clotilde E H de Arbó
Subjects: Science & Technology
Founded: 1912

Asociación Educacionista Argentina, see Editorial Stella

Editorial **Astrea** de Alfredo y Ricardo Depalma SRL*, Lavalle 1208, 1048 Buenos Aires Tel: 351880
Man Dir: Alfredo Depalma; *Sales Dir:* Ricardo Depalma
Associate Company: Ediciones La Bastilla (qv)
Subjects: Law, Sociology, Politics, History, Philosophy, Economics
Bookshop: Librería Astrea, Lavalle 1208, 1367 Buenos Aires
Founded: 1968

Editorial El **Ateneo**, Pedro García SA, Patagones 2463, 1282 Buenos Aires Tel: 942/9002/9152/9052/9102 Cable Add: Ateneo
Dirs: Pedro García, Eustasio A García, Jorge I Letemeudía
Subjects: Medicine, Agronomy, Veterinary Science, Economics, Technical, Education, Business, University Textbooks
Bookshop: Florida 336, 340 & 344, 1005 Buenos Aires Tel: (46) 6801/6805
Founded: 1912

Editorial **Atlántida** SA, Florida 643, 1005 Buenos Aires Tel: 315416 Cable Add: Ediatlán Telex: 121163 AR
Man Dir: Alfredo J Vercelli; *Sales Dir:* Fernando A Parodi
Subject: Juveniles, Textbooks
Bookshop: Florida 643, 1005 Buenos Aires
1978: 95 titles *1979:* 39 titles *Founded:* 1918

Asociación Ediciones La **Aurora***, Doblas 1753, 1424 Buenos Aires Tel: 9215817/9224937
Dir: Pablo A La Moglie; *Editorial, Rights & Permissions:* Marcelo Pérez Rivas; *Sales Dir:* Mario C Ale
Subjects: Literature, History, Philosophy, Religion, Theology, Sociology, Psychology, Linguistics, Children's books
Bookclubs: Club del Libro Nuevo, Doblas 1753, 1424, Buenos Aires (qv)
Bookshop: Librería La Aurora, Corrientes 728, 1043 Buenos Aires
1978: 25 titles *Founded:* 1923

B A E S A (Buenos Aires Edita SA)*, Cordoba 1249, Buenos Aires

Editorial Com Ind **Barry**, SRL*, Talcahuano 860, 1013 Buenos Aires Tel: 447075

Ediciones la **Bastilla***, Lavalle 1208, 1048 Buenos Aires Tel: 351880
Man Dir: Alfredo Depalma; *Sales Dir:* Ricardo Depalma
Associate Company: Editorial Astrea de Alfredo y Ricardo Depalma SRL (qv)
Subjects: Politics, History
Founded: 1972

Asociacion **Bautista** Argentina de Publicaciones*, Rivadavia 3464, 1203 Buenos Aires Tel: 888938, 888924
Man Dir: Hans Iver Jorgensen; *Assistant Manager:* Emanuel Benavídez; *Editorial Dir:* Arnoldo Canclini
Branch Offs: San Martín 1572, 2000 Rosario, Santa Fe; Tucumán 351, 5000 Córdoba; San Martín 2242, 5500 Mendoza
Subject: Religion
Founded: 1906

SA Editorial **Bell**, Otamendi 215-17, 1405 Buenos Aires Tel: 901076/77/78 Cable Add: Edibell
Man Dir: Hugo O Varela; *Sales Dir:* C E Lippold; *Publicity Dir:* S Frasso; *Advertising Dir:* Susana Tubal; *Rights & Permissions:* Mario Martínez
Subjects: How-to, General Science, Technical, Sports
Founded: 1927

Editorial **Beta** SRL*, Tacuarí 237, 1071 Buenos Aires Tel: 389586
Man Dir: Miguel Angel Bini
Subjects: Medicine, Psychology, University Textbooks
Founded: 1948

Bias Editora*, Lavalle 1294, 1048 Buenos Aires Cable Add: Biasedita
Man Dir: Ival Rocca; *Editorial:* Ignacio Javier Barrio; *Sales:* Rodolfo Esteban Amigorana; *Production:* Francisco Spatafora; *Publicity:* Jorge O'Connor
Subjects: Law, Economics
Bookshop: Bias Editora (Libros Jurídicos), Lavalle 1294, 1048 Buenos Aires Tel: 354161
Founded: 1966

Librería **Bonum** SACI, Maipú 859, 1006 Buenos Aires Tel: 3929763 Cable Add: Bonum
Man Dir & Sales: Antonio Gremmelspacher
Subjects: Religion, Textbooks, Music, Philosophy, Psychology
Founded: 1960

Ediciones **Botella** al Mar*, Viamonte 2754- 1° "5", 1213 Buenos Aires Tel: 898073

ARGENTINA

Editorial **Bruguera** Argentina, Hipólito Irigoyen 646-650, Buenos Aires Tel: 301932/309255
Man Dir: Jorge Merlini
Parent Company: Editorial Bruguera SA, Spain (qv)

Editorial **Calicanto***, Suipacha 831-3°'C', 1008 Buenos Aires Tel: 317028
Man Dir: Eduardo Irazabal
Subjects: Literature & Criticism
Founded: 1975

Editorial **Cangallo** SACI, Ave Belgrano 609, 1092 Buenos Aires Tel: 338848/330204/332453/305930
Man Dir: Norberto del Hoyo
Subjects: Law, Economics, Business, University Textbooks
Bookshop: Ave Belgrano 609, 1092 Buenos Aires
1980: 46 titles *Founded:* 1968

Editorial **Cartago***, Viamonte 2617, 5° piso, of D, 1056 Buenos Aires Tel: 472783
Subjects: Politics, Economics, History

Editorial **Caymi***, 15 de Noviembre 1149, 1130 Buenos Aires Tel: 232474
Subjects: Popular Science & Medicine, Yoga, Judo & Karate, Magic & Fortune-Telling, Occultism, Sexology, Science Fiction, Spanish & South American Classics

Celcius — J J Vallory*, Ave Belgrano 2815 - 1, Buenos Aires Tel: 932469/939414
Subjects: Medicine, Politics, History
1978: 4 titles

Centro Editor de America Latina SA*, Cangallo 1228, 2° D, 1038 Buenos Aires Tel: 359449/350142 Cable Add: Centroedit
Man Dir: José Boris Spivacow; *Sales Dir:* Aldo Antonio Sangoi
Subjects: Literature, Biography, History, Art, Psychology, How-to, Juveniles, General Science, Social Science, Educational Materials
Founded: 1966

El **Cid** Editor SRL, Alsina 500, 1087 Buenos Aires Tel: 330071/349267/83795
President: Dr Eduardo Varela-Cid; *General Manager:* Julio A Oliva; *Sales:* Carlos Hurs; *Production:* Nilda Montesi
Subsidiary Companies: El Cid Editor CA, Apdo 60010, Caracas 1060, Venezuela; El Cid Editor SAE, Spain (qv)
Bookshop: Ciudad Educativa SAIC (Antigua Librería del Colegio), Alsina 500, 1087 Buenos Aires

Editorial **Científica Argentina***, Paraguay 1300, Buenos Aires Tel: 443562
Man Dir: Fernando Duelo Cavero
Subjects: Argentine history, Pedagogy, Various

Editorial **Ciordia** SRL*, Ave Belgrano 2271, 1094 Buenos Aires Tel: 481681
Man Dir: Eduardo B Ciordia; *Sales Dirs:* Manuel Ciordia, Carlos Danzini
Subjects: Literature, Philosophy, Psychology, University & Secondary Textbooks
Founded: 1938

Editorial **Claretiana***, Lima 1360, (1138) Buenos Aires Tel: 279250 Cable Add: Editorial Claretiana
Man Dir, Editorial, Rights & Permissions: Domingo A Beltrani; *Sales:* Eduardo Righetti; *Publicity:* José Luis Pérez
Subject: Religion
1978: 26 titles *Founded:* 1956

Editorial **Claridad** SA*, San José 1627, Buenos Aires Tel: 235573 Cable Add: Claridad Baires
Man Dir: Dr Elio M A Colle; *Sales Manager:* José Zamora

Subject: General Literature
Founded: 1922

Editora **Close Up** SA*, Thames 2450, 1425 Buenos Aires Tel: 7742961

Club de Lectores, Ave de Mayo 624, 1084 Buenos Aires Tel: 343955
Man Dir: Juan Manuel Fontenla; *Sales:* Carlos A Alvano; *Publicity:* María Inés Fontenla
Subjects: History, Philosophy, Religion, Psychology, Social Science, University Textbooks
1980: 176 titles *Founded:* 1938

Libreria del **Colegio** SA, Humberto 1° 545, 1103 Buenos Aires Tel: 337867
Subjects: Educational Books, Textbooks

Colmegna SA*, San Martín 2546, 3000 Santa Fe Tel: 23102
Man Dir, Editorial, Sales: Nestor Lammertyn
Subjects: Literature, History, Poetry
Bookshop: San Martín 2546, 3000 Santa Fe
Founded: 1889

Editorial **Columba** SA, Sarmiento 1889-5°, 1044 Buenos Aires Tel: 454297
Man Dir: Ramón Columba
Subjects: Classics in translation, Twentieth century themes
Founded: 1953

Compañia Impresora Argentina SA*, Alsina 2049, 1090 Buenos Aires Tel: 472308

Editorial **Conjunta** SRL*, Fr J S M de Oro 2587, 1425 Buenos Aires Tel: 7741734

Ediciones **Contabilidad** Moderna SACIC*, Independencia 3277/81, 1225 Buenos Aires Tel: 934918/19
Man Dir: Juan Carlos García Stella; *Sales Manager:* Oscar B Himschoot
Subject: Business
Founded: 1943

Editorial **Contempora** SRL, Sarmiento 643, of 522, 1382 Buenos Aires Tel: 451793/45275
Subjects: Architecture, Gardening

Ediciones **Corregidor** SAICI & E*, Hipolito Irigoyen 1287, 1086 Buenos Aires Tel: 468148
Dir: Manuel Pampín
Subject: General Literature
Founded: 1972

Cosmopolita SRL, Chile 474, 1098 Buenos Aires Tel: 348925
Man Dir: Eva Ruth F de Rapp
Subjects: Technical, Agriculture
Founded: 1940

Editorial **Crea** SA, Ave Belgrana 624 — 11° piso, 1092 Buenos Aires Tel: 307891/9
President: Sergio A Dellaccha; *General Dir:* Edoardo Pierozzi; *Man Dir:* Osvaldo Pierdominici; *Sales, Publicity:* Luis Alvarez; *Rights & Permissions:* Teresa Vernengo
Associate Company: Editorial Huemul SA (qv)
Subjects: Fiction, Secondary & Primary Textbooks
Founded: 1961

Editorial **Crespillo** SA*, Defensa 485, 1065 Buenos Aires Tel: 347384
Subjects: History, Arts, Maps

Depalma SRL, Talcahuano 494, 1013 Buenos Aires Tel: 407306
Man Dir: Roque Depalma; *Sales Dir:* Alberto E Barón
Subjects: Law, History, Social Science, Business, University Texts
Bookshop: Talcahuano 494, 1013 Buenos Aires
1978: 64 titles *Founded:* 1944

Editorial **Difusión** SA, Sarandí 1065, Buenos Aires Tel: 9410118
Man Dir: Luis Luchia Puig; *Sales Dir:* Domingo Palombella
Subjects: Literature, Philosophy, Religion, Juveniles, Education, Textbooks
Founded: 1936

Distasa*, Córdoba 2064, Buenos Aires
Associated Companies: See under Alianza Editorial SA, Spain

Ediciones **Dronte** Argentina SRL*, Juàn de Garay 1323, Buenos Aires Tel: 267207/268015
Man Dir: Nestor Ricardo Gutierrez
Founded: 1972

E C A (Ediciones Culturales Argentinas)*, Ave Alvear 1690, 1014 Buenos Aires Tel: 444124
Man Dir: Luis Ricardo Furlan
Subjects: Argentine Literature, Publications of the Ministry of Culture & Education
Founded: 1961

E U D E B A (Editorial Universitaria de Buenos Aires)*, Rivadavia 1571-73, 1033 Buenos Aires Tel: 371527
Man Dir: Capt de Navio Francisco Suarez Battan; *Sales Dir:* Eduardo Suarez Corrado; *Advertising Dir:* Miguel A Molaccino
Branch Offs: Córdoba (Argentina), México
Subjects: Literature, Biography, History, Art, Philosophy, Reference, Religion, Medicine, Psychology, Science & Technology, Social Sciences, Juveniles, Manuals, University & Secondary Textbooks
Founded: 1959

Edicient SAIC*, Pte Luis Saenz Peña 1021, 1110 Buenos Aires Tel: 235115
President: Rubén S Coda; *Technical Dir:* Roberto J Fillmann; *Sales Dir:* Julio A Casati; *Publicity:* Horacio A Andrada
Subjects: Technical, Electronics

Editorial **Sudamericana** SA, Humberto 1° 545, 1103 Buenos Aires Tel: 304232/337867 Cable Add: Librecol
President: Edith K de Lopez Llovet; *Man Dir:* Jaime Rodrigué; *Editorial:* Enrique Pezzoni; *Sales Dir:* Francisco La Falce; *Publicity Dir:* Maria Eugenia Ramos Mejía; *Rights & Permissions:* Gloria L Llovet de Rodrigué
Associate Companies: Edhasa, Spain (qv); Editorial Hermes, Mexico (qv)
Subjects: General Fiction & Nonfiction, Literature, Biography, History, Philosophy, Psychology
Founded: 1939

Editorial **Universidad** SRL*, Corrientes 1250 - 4° 'J', 1043 Buenos Aires Tel: 356490/6850
Subject: Textbooks

Editorial **Universitaria** de Buenos Aires*, Ave Rivadavia 1571/73, 1033 Buenos Aires Tel: 385478
Subject: Textbooks

Emecé Editores SA, Carlos Pellegrini 1069 9°, 1009 Buenos Aires Tel: 314710/314906/317327 Cable Add: Emece/Baires Telex: 17736 Emece Ar
President: Dr Bonifacio del Carril; *Administration:* Marcos I Fantin; *Sales Dirs:* Oscar Guerrieri, Eduardo Fantin; *Publicity Dir:* Jose A Mateo; *Rights & Permissions:* Jorge O Naveiro, José A Mateo; *Editorial:* Jorge O Naveiro, Carlos V Frias, Bonifacio P del Carril; *Production:* Francisco F Del Carril
Orders to: Emece Distribuidora SA, Alsina 2062, 1090 Buenos Aires
Subsidiary Companies: Emecé Distribuidora SA, Alsina 2062, 1090 Buenos Aires

Associate Companies: Ultramar Editores SA, Mallorca 49, Barcelona 29, Spain; Riomar Editora y Distribuidora, Atenas 42, Mexico 6 DF
Book Club: Club 'El Libro del Mes' (qv)
Subjects: General Fiction, Non-fiction, Biography, Essays, Mystery, History, Art, Poetry
1978: 110 titles *1979:* 108 titles *Founded:* 1939

Espacio Editora SA, Costa Rica 5595, 1414 Buenos Aires Tel: 7718231
President: Guillermo Raúl Kliczkowski; *Editorial:* Hugo Alberto Kliczkowski; *Sales:* Inés A de Gomez; *Production:* Silvia Leonor Wladimirski; *Publicity:* Mirta Adriana Kracoff; *Rights & Permissions:* Silvia Leonor Wladimirski
Associate Company: Sociedad Ambiente (at above address)
Subjects: Architecture, Design, History, Ecology, Urban Planning
1978: 17 titles *1979:* 23 titles *Founded:* 1977

Angel **Estrada** y Cía SA, Bolivar 462-66, 1066 Buenos Aires Tel: 336521/27
Man Dir: Angel M de Estrada
Subjects: How-to, Primary & Secondary Textbooks, Books for Infants, Teaching Guides, Atlas
1980: 80 titles *Founded:* 1869

Fabril Editora SA*, Armenia 2097 – 3°, 1289 Buenos Aires Tel: 213601
Subjects: General Nonfiction, Textbooks, Reference Books, Arts, Humanities

Ediciones Librerías **Fausto**, Ave Corrientes 1316, 1043 Buenos Aires Tel: 453914/456266
Manager: Rafael Zorrilla
Bookshops: see under Booksellers (Librerías Fausto, Martín Fierro)

Ediciones de la **Flor** SRL, Uruguay 252 — 1° B, 1015 Buenos Aires
Tel: 405795/492291
Man Dir: Daniel Divinsky; *Sales Dir:* Elisa Miler; *Publicity & Advertising Dir:* Ricardo Perugerría; *Rights & Permissions:* Ivonne G de Losada
Subjects: Fiction, Literature, History, Psychology, Juveniles, Humour
1978: 18 titles *1979:* 26 titles *Founded:* 1967

Ediciones **Formentor** SRL*, Ave Belgrano 1462, 1093 Buenos Aires Tel: 371657/382769
Man Dir: Ruben Duran; *Sales Dir:* Enrique Celis
Subjects: Literature, Philosophy, Religion, Social Sciences, Psychology, Engineering, University Textbooks
Founded: 1971

Editorial **Freeland***, Casilla de Correo 5093, Buenos Aires Tel: 457845
Man Dir: Jorge Enrique Freeland
Subjects: Fiction, History
Founded: 1953

Editorial **Galerna** SA, Charcas 3741, 1425 Buenos Aires Tel: 711739 Cable Add: Galerna
Dirs: Julio Martín Alonso, Hugo B Levin
Subsidiary Company: Librería Piloto (foreign sales & bibliographic service)
Subjects: Literature, History, Social Sciences, Paperbacks, Patagonia
Bookshops: Librerías Galerna, Tucumán 1425, Buenos Aires
Founded: 1967

Fernando **García Cambeiro**, Ave de Mayo 560, 1380 Buenos Aires Tel: 332713
Man Dir: Fernando García Cambeiro
Subjects: Essays on Latin American Writers
1979: 1 title *1980:* 1 title

Librería y Papelería Casa **García** SA*, C Pellegrini 41, Resistencia Chaco Tel: 5930
Man Dir: José García Pulido; *Sales Dir:* Luis Aguirre
Subjects: Fiction, Poetry, General Literature & Literary Criticism, History, Geography, Politics
Bookshop: C Pellegrini 41, Resistencia Chaco
Founded: 1939

Editorial **Géminis** SRL, Barcena 2105 — 8° B, 1431 Buenos Aires Tel: 513491
Executive President: Leonor de Pirro de Baran; *Editorial:* Walter J Baran; *Sales:* Norma Richard; *Production:* Mario di Bartolo
1978: 2 titles *1979:* 5 titles

Ediciones G **Gili** SA*, Cochambra 154-158, Buenos Aires
Parent Company: Editorial Gustavo Gili SA, Spain (qv)

Editorial **Glem** SACIF*, Ave Caseros 2056, 1264 Buenos Aires Tel: 266641
President: José Alfredo Tucci; *Vice-President:* Héctor Oscar Tucci; *Dir:* Eduardo Anibal Tucci
Subjects: Technical, Psychology
Founded: 1933

Editorial y Librería **Goncourt**, Ave Callao 1519, 1024 Buenos Aires Tel: 449743
Man Dir: Jaime Fariña
Subjects: Fiction & Non-fiction
Bookshop: Callao 1519, 1024 Buenos Aires
1979: 95 titles *Founded:* 1952

Goyanarte Editor SA*, Esmeralda 923 – 3° 'B', 1007 Buenos Aires Tel: 320023/8362
Telex: Bs As Booth NBR 9 Finazzi 32.0023
Man Dir: César Amadeo López; *Sales Dir:* Hugo Hanuel Vázquez
Subject: Fiction
Founded: 1969 (as Juan Goyanarte Editore)

Gram Editora*, Cochabamba 1652, 1148 Buenos Aires Tel: 268397
Dir: Manuel Herrero Montes
Subjects: Educational Books, Religion
1978: 6 titles *1979:* 12 titles *Founded:* 1925

Editorial Juan Carlos **Granda***, Corrientes 1243, 1043 Buenos Aires Tel: 356114

Granica Editor SA*, Lavalle 1634, 3° piso, 1048 Buenos Aires Tel: 461456
Man Dir: Juan Granica
Subjects: Fiction, Art, Social Sciences, Juveniles, University Textbooks
Founded: 1971

Librería & Editorial Alfa **Graziano** SACI*, Sarmiento 1343, 1° piso, 1041 Buenos Aires
Tel: 495349
Man Dir: Mauricio Domingo Graziano
Bookshop: Sarmiento 1343, 1041 Buenos Aires
Subjects: Medicine, Law, Social Sciences, Economics, General Culture

Grijalbo SA*, Belgrano 1256, 1093 Buenos Aires
Parent Company: Editorial Grijalbo SA (Mexico)
Subjects: Fiction & Nonfiction

Editorial **Guadalupe**, Mansilla 3865, 1425 Buenos Aires Tel: 846066
Man Dir: José Gallinger; *Sales Dir:* Alberto Klein; *Publicity Dir:* Roberto Bossio; *Production, Rights & Permissions:* Manuel de Gracia
Subjects: Pedagogy, Social Sciences, Religion, Literature
Bookshops: Librería Guadalupe, Mansilla 3865, 1425 Buenos Aires; Librería Verbo Divino, Deán Funes 165, Local 27, Córdoba
Founded: 1942

Libreria **Hachette** SA,
Rivadavia 739-43, 1002 Buenos Aires
Tel: 348481 Cable Add: Aglibrairi Baires
Telex: 17479 Hacba Ar
President: Juan A Musset; *Vice-President:* Carmen P de Picó; *Commercial Manager:* José Manuel Caneda
Subjects: History, Travel, Literature, Philosophy
Bookshop: Librería Hachette, Rivadavia 739-743, 1002 Buenos Aires Tel: 348481
1978: 14 titles

Editorial **Hemisferio** Sur SA, Pasteur 743, 1028 Buenos Aires Tel: 489825, 488454
Man Dirs: Juan Angel Peri, Adolfo Luis Peña
Associate Companies: Editorial Agropecuaria Hemisferio Sur SRL, Alzaibar 1328, Montevideo, Uruguay; Librería Agropecuaria SA, Pasteur 743, 1028 Buenos Aires, Argentina
Subjects: Agriculture, Veterinary Science, Natural Science
1978: 30 titles *Founded:* 1966

Editorial **Hobby***, Constitución 2348, Buenos Aires Tel: 9414255
Man Dir: Marcelo Oscar Castroman; *Sales Manager:* Norberto Luis Carca
Subjects: Technical
Founded: 1936

Editorial **Huemul** SA, Benito Perez Galdós 52, 1155 Buenos Aires Tel: 275492
President: Fernando Vidal Buzzi; *Vice-President:* Juan Carlos Pellegrini
Associate Company: América Norildis Editores SA, Editorial Crea SA (qv)
Subjects: Secondary & Primary Textbooks
Founded: 1961

Librería **Huemul**, Ave Santa Fe 2237, 1123 Buenos Aires Tel: 831666
Man Dir, Editorial: Antonio Rego; *Sales, Publicity, Rights & Permissions:* Carlos L Sánchez
Subjects: University, Secondary & Primary Textbooks, Children's Books
Bookshop: Ave Santa Fe 2237, 1123 Buenos Aires
1978: 12 titles *Founded:* 1954

Editorial **Humanitas**, Carlos Calvo 644, 1102 Buenos Aires Tel: 7821449 (Orders to: Tres Américas, Alsina 722, Buenos Aires)
Dir: Sela Sierra de Villaverde; *Sales:* Osvaldo R Dubini; *Publicity:* Mauricio Faistman
Subjects: Social Sciences, Psychology, Education, Psychological Textbooks
1978: 6 titles *1979:* 8 titles *Founded:* 1955

Instituto de Publicaciones Navales*, Córdoba 354, 1054 Buenos Aires Tel: 310042

Editorial **Inter-Médica** SAICI, Junín 917 — 1°, Casilla de Correo 4625, Buenos Aires
Tel: 833234/833148/855572
President: Jorge Modyeievsky; *Vice-President:* Sonia M B de Modyeievsky
Subjects: Medicine, Dentistry, General Science, University Textbooks
1978: 8 titles *Founded:* 1959

Intersea*, México 924, Buenos Aires

Biblioteca Popular **Judía***, Casilla de Correo 20, Suc 53, 1453 Buenos Aires (Located at: Larrea 744, 1030 Buenos Aires) Tel: 486213 Cable Add: Worldgress Baires
Editorial: Roberto Brzostowski
Subjects: Jewish History & Biography, Jewish Latinamerican Conference publications

Ediciones & Librería **Jurídica***, Calle 45, No 532, 1900 La Plata Tel: 41427
Subject: Law

Editorial **Juventud** Argentina*, Defensa 355, 1065 Buenos Aires Tel: 333756
Parent Company: Editorial Juventud SA, Spain (qv)
Subjects: History, Juveniles, Fiction, Maps

Editorial **Kapelusz** SA, Moreno 372, 1091 Buenos Aires Tel: 346451/59, 3928905 Cable Add: Kapelusz Telex: 18342 Ekasa Ar
Man Dir: Hober González; *Editorial, Rights & Permissions:* Diego S Guidotti; *Sales:* Hernando Ferreres; *Publicity & Public Relations:* Atilio A Veronelli
Subjects: Psychology, Pedagogy, Juveniles, Primary, Secondary & University Textbooks
Bookshop: Corrientes 999, Buenos Aires
1978: 92 titles *1979:* 56 titles *Founded:* 1905

Editorial **Kier** SACIFI, Ave Santa Fe 1260, 1059 Buenos Aires Tel: 410507/418243
President: Alfonso Florencio Pibernus; *Vice President:* José Grigna; *Man Dir:* Héctor Pibernus; *Sales Dir:* Alberto Pibernus
Subjects: Eastern Religions, Astrology, Tarots, Occultism, Rosicrucianism, Medicine
Bookshop: Santa Fe 1260, 1059 Buenos Aires
1978: 132 titles *Founded:* 1907

Editorial **Labor** Argentina SA*, Venezuela 617, 1095 Buenos Aires Tel: 334135
Man Dir: Pedro Clotas Cierco
Parent Company: Editorial Labor, Spain (qv)

Ediciones **Larousse** Argentina SA*, Valentin Gómez 3530, 1191 Buenos Aires
Tel: 876671 Telex: 0121783 Cable Add: Editlarousse
President: Georges Lucas
Subjects: Dictionaries, Encyclopaedias

Luis **Lasserre** y Cía, SACIFI*, Alsina 1666, 1088 Buenos Aires Tel: 405803/451693
Subjects: Textbooks, Public Health, Maps

Latina SCA*, Ave de Mayo 953 - 11°, 1084 Buenos Aires Tel: 389108/4631
Editorial: Juan Carlos Orgueira; *Sales:* Nelson Guillermo Cositorto
Subjects: Pre-school books, Juveniles
1978: 4 titles *Founded:* 1971

Editorial Victor **Lerú** SA, Don Bosco 3834, 1206 Buenos Aires (Located at: Casilla 2793, Correo central, 1000 Buenos Aires) Tel: 8116098/6198/8978
Man Dir: Victor Nep; *Sales Dir:* León Nep
Orders to: Editorial Victor Lerú SA, Casilla 2793, Correo central, 1000 Buenos Aires
Subjects: Art, Architecture, Technology, Primary, Secondary & University Textbooks, Music, Dictionaries, History
Founded: 1944
ISBN Publisher's Prefix: 84-8205

La **Ley** SA Editora e Impresora, Tucumán 1471, 1050 Buenos Aires Tel: 403421
President: Dr Carlos María Oliva Vélez; *Director-General:* Enrique J Algorta Gaona; *Editorial:* José María A Lebrón; *Commercial Manager:* Dr Raúl A Delucchi; *Production:* Raimundo Roldán
Branch Offs: In all Argentinian provinces, and in Asunción and the Republic of Paraguay
Subjects: Law, Economics, Philosophy, History
Founded: 1935

Carlos **Lohlé** SA, Tacuarí 1516, Casilla de Correo 3097, 1000 Buenos Aires Tel: 279969
President: Carlos F P Lohlé; *Man Dir:* Francisco M Lohlé
Subjects: Literature, Poetry, Philosophy, Religion, Psychology, Social Science
Founded: 1953

López Libreros y Editores, Junín 901, 1113 Buenos Aires Tel: 837744
Man Dir: Dr Pablo A López; *Sales Manager:* R Enrique Lohrmann
Subject: Medicine
Founded: 1927

Editorial **Losada** SA, Alsina 1131, 1088 Buenos Aires Tel: 387267/389902 Cable Add: Edilosada
President: Gonzalo Pedro Losada; *Man Dir:* Carlo Alberto Aramburu; *Sales Dir:* Manuel Taboada
Branch Offs: Moneda 1576, Santiago, Chile; Calle 18A, No 7-37, Bogotá, Colombia; Jirón Contumaza 1050, Lima, Peru; Maldonado 1092, Montevideo, Uruguay
Subjects: Fiction & Nonfiction, Classics, Poetry, Literary Studies, Philosophy, Psychology, Biography, History, Pedagogy, Secondary Textbooks
Founded: 1938

Ediciones **Macchi***, Alsina 1535 PB, 1088 Buenos Aires Tel: 460594
Man Dir: Raúl Luis Macchi; *Sales Dir:* Julio Ricardo Mora
Subjects: Economic Sciences
Bookshop: Córdoba 2015, 1120 Buenos Aires
Founded: 1947

Macondo Ediciones SRL, Lavalle 1882 — 1° piso, 1051 Buenos Aires Tel: 458535
Man Dir: Dr Samuel Tarnopolsky; *Editorial, Publicity, Rights & Permissions:* Haydée M Jofre Barroso; *Sales, Production:* José Antonio Serrano
Subjects: Belles Lettres, Science, Economics, Politics, Fiction, Science Fiction, Poetry
1978: 18 titles *1979:* 15 titles *Founded:* 1976
ISBN Publisher's Prefix: 84-89000

Marymar Ediciones SA, Chile 1432, 1098 Buenos Aires Tel: 380391
President: Isay Klasse; *Man Dir:* Hildegard Kupfer; *Dir of Production:* Saúl Cherny
Subjects: Social, Political & General Science, Economics, Philosophy, Architecture, Technology, Music, Cinema, History, Teaching, Library Science, Ecology, Fiction & Classics, Psychology
1978: 35 titles *Founded:* 1960

Librería y Editorial La **Médica***, Córdoba 2901, 2000 Rosario Tel: 397858
Man Dir: Cataline C de Radeff; *Sales Dir:* Ruben T Radeff, Ricardo A Radeff, Roberto A Radeff
Subject: Medicine
Miscellaneous: Major Distributor of Schoolbooks and General literature

Editorial **Médica** Panamericana SA, Viamonte 2164, 1056 Buenos Aires Tel: 479063/4
Man Dir, Editorial: Roberto Brik; *Sales:* Hector Brik; *Production:* Daniel Brik; *Publicity:* Hugo A Brik
Branch Offs: Santa Yzabel 267, Sao Paulo, Brazil; Carrera 7a No 40-20, Bogotá, Colombia; Marcoleta 328, Santiago de Chile; Ave del Generalísimo 30 — piso 14°, Madrid 16, Spain; Herschel 153, Mexico 5, DF; Centro Andres Bello — 6° piso of 64E, Caracas, Venezuela
Subjects: Medicine, Dentistry, Rehabilitation, Nursing
1980: 500 titles *Founded:* 1953

Editorial Librería **Mitre** SRL*, Bartólome Mitre 2063, 1039 Buenos Aires Tel: 495856
Man Dir: Rodolfo Amura
Subject: Technical (especially Mechanics)
1978: 5 titles *Founded:* 1949

Editorial **Mundi** SAIC y F, Casilla Correo 47, Suc 53, 1453 Capital Federal Tel: 839339, 839663
Production, Publicity, Rights & Permissions: Elena Garcia Mila
Subjects: Dentistry, Medicine
1978: 15 titles *1979:* 8 titles *Founded:* 1939

Editorial **Mundo** Técnico SRL, Montevideo 205 — 6° K, 1019 Buenos Aires
Tel: 350738 Cable Add: Muntex
Man Dir: Gustavo A Marini; *Sales Dir:* Juan C García Venturini
Literary Rep: International Editors' Co, Buenos Aires
Subjects: Technical, Engineering, Atlases, How-to, School Dictionaries & Textbooks
1978: 15 titles *Founded:* 1972

Librería y Editorial **Nigar** SRL*, Humberto 1° 667, 1103 Buenos Aires Tel: 331794

Editorial **Norte** SAIC*, José Mármol 2131, 1255 Buenos Aires Tel: 9239507

Editorial **Nova** SACI*, Perú 858, 1068 Buenos Aires Tel: 348698
Man Dir: Horacio D Rolando; *Publicity & Sales Dir:* María del Pilar Lopez Soto de Rolando
Subjects: Literature, Biography, History, Art, Philosophy, Religion, Medicine, Psychology, Education, University & Secondary Textbooks
Founded: 1945

Ediciones **Nueva Visión** SAIC, Tucumán 3748, 1189 Buenos Aires Tel: 895050
Man Dir: Jorge José Grisetti; *Sales Manager:* Anibal Victor Giacone
Subjects: Social Sciences, Psychology, Architecture, Art, Theatre
Founded: 1954

La **Obra**, Ave Santa Fe 3478 — 1°, 1425 Capital Federal Tel: 974291
Dir: Carlos G Salas; *Commercial Manager:* Hugo Mario Botti
Subject: Primary Textbooks

Ediciones **Orion***, Ägüero 1412 5°, 1425 Buenos Aires Tel: 8214101
Subjects: General Fiction & Nonfiction

Editorial **Paidós**, Defensa 599 — 1°, 1065 Buenos Aires Tel: 332275
Man Dir, Rights & Permissions: Enrique Butelman; *Sales Dir:* Renato Modai
Subjects: Social Sciences, Psychology, Medicine, Philosophy, Religion, History, Biography, Literature, University Textbooks
Bookshop: Librería Paidós, Las Heras and Canning
Founded: 1945

Ediciones **Pannedille***, Chacabuco 129, Buenos Aires Tel: 354957
Man Dir: Oscar Buonano
Subjects: History, Law, Technical
Founded: 1970

Casa **Pardo** SAC*, Defensa 1170, 1065 Buenos Aires Tel: 346676 Cable Add: Pardoroman
Dir: Roman José Pardo
Founded: 1892
Subjects: General Literature, Humanism
Miscellaneous: Company are exporters

Ediciones **Paulinas***, Nazca 4249, Buenos Aires Tel: 5723926/5724810 Cable Add: Paulinas
Man Dir: Lucía Monterumici; *Sales Dir:* Paulina Tibaldo
Branch Offs: Buenos Aires 837, Rosario; San Jerónimo 2136, Sante Fé; 24 de Setiembre 512, Tucumán; San Martín 980, Mendoza; Antártida Argentina 178, Resistencia; Calle 49, No 744, La Plata (all in Argentina)
Subjects: Education, Religion
Founded: 1940

A **Peña** Lillo SA*, H Yrigoyen 1394-1086, Buenos Aires Tel: 370994
Man Dir: Arturo Peña Lillo; *Sales Dir:* María Luisa Comellí; *Production &*

Publicity: Laura Peña
Orders to: Rivadavia 739, Buenos Aires
(Librería Hachette SA)
Associate Company: Librería Hachette SA
Subjects: History, Political Science,
Economics, Sociology, Literature
Founded: 1956
ISBN Publisher's Prefix: 84-8203
Miscellaneous: Firm is an importer and exporter

Ediciones **Periféria** SRL*, Cangallo 1730 —
6° of 68, 1037 Buenos Aires Tel: 450574
Subjects: Social Sciences, University Textbooks
Founded: 1971

Editorial Argentina **Plaza & Janés** SA*,
Lambaré 893, Buenos Aires Tel:
866769/866785
Man Dir: Jorge Perez; *Sales Dir:* Ernesto Pena
Subjects: General Fiction & Nonfiction

Editorial **Pleamar***, Corrientes 1994 — 1°,
Buenos Aires
Man Dir: Andrés Alfonso Bravo
Subjects: Political & Social Science
Founded: 1965

Editorial **Plus Ultra** SAI & C*, Viamonte
1755, 1055 Buenos Aires Tel:
446605/446694/446788 Cable Add:
Plusultra
Man Dirs: Rafael Román, Lorenzo
Marengo, Diego Mazzitelli; *Editorial:* Carlos
Alberto Loprete; *Sales:* Ricardo Errea;
Production: Francisco Barbati; *Publicity:*
Fernando Sorrentino
Subjects: Literature, History, Law,
Textbooks, Economics, Philosophy, Politics,
Sociology, Psychology, Pedagogy, Children's Books
Bookshops: Viamonte 1755, 1055 Buenos
Aires; Riobamba 265, 1025 Buenos Aires
Founded: 1964

Pomaire SA*, Lavalle 1634 – 3° 'G', 1048
Buenos Aires Tel: 490669
Man Dir: Oscar Molina
Parent Company: Editorial Pomaire,
Spain (qv)
Subject: Fiction

Prolam SRL (Ediciones Economia y
Empresa)*, México 625, Buenos Aires
Tel: 308280
Man Dir: Beatriz E P de Lambruschini
Subjects: Economics, Business, Science & Technology
Founded: 1958

Editorial **Proyección** SRL*, Yapeyú 321,
Buenos Aires Tel: 8115086
Man Dirs: Ernesto Portela, Noe Bursuck;
Sales Dir: Carlos Garcia Iribarren
Subject: Political Science
Founded: 1968

Ediciones **Quevedo** Sacif, Hipólito Vrigoyen
4245, 1212 Capital Federal Tel: 8112816
President: Oscar Luis Jorge Quevedo;
Editorial: Oscar del Carmen Quevedo; *Sales:*
Carlos Caballero; *Production:* Alejandro
Carlos Quevedo; *Rights & Permissions:*
Pablo Daniel Quevedo
Subjects: General Culture, Geography,
Atlases, Cooking, Juvenile, Teaching, Poetry
relating to Gauchos
1978: 5 titles *1979:* 14 titles *Founded:* 1965

Ricordi Americana SAEC*, Cangallo 1558,
1037 Buenos Aires Tel: 409841/3 Cable
Add: Ricordamericana Telex: 122580
Man Dir: Renzo Valcarenghi; *Manager:*
Egilberto Chiti; *Editorial, Sales:* Ernesto Larcade
Associate Companies: Ricordi Brasileira,
Sao Paulo, Brazil; G & C Ricordi, Italy (qv);
G & C Ricordi, Mexico

Subjects: Music, Musical Teaching Methods
Founded: 1924

Ruy Diaz SAEIC, Juan B Alberdi 3067,
1406 Buenos Aires Tel: 6126508/6125339
Cable Add: Ediruy
Man Dir: Rafael Zuccotti
Branch Off: Casilla de Correo 45, Su
cursal 6, 1406 Buenos Aires
Subjects: Educational, Atlases, Dictionaries
1978: 4 titles *Founded:* 1966

Editorial **Santiago** Rueda SRL*, Sarmiento
680 - 1°, 1041 Buenos Aires Tel:
491874/497860
Man Dir: Enrique S Rueda
Subject: Literature
Founded: 1940

Schapire Editor SRL*, Uruguay 1249, 1016
Buenos Aires Tel: 440765
Man Dir: Miguel Schapire
Subjects: Literature, Biography, History,
Art, Psychology, Social Science, Juveniles
Founded: 1935

Selcon SAEC & I (Selección Contable),
Sarandí 1067, 1222 Buenos Aires
Tel: 9410118
Man Dir: Luis Luchia Puig; *Sales &
Advertising Dir:* Domingo Palombella
Subjects: Business, Economics
Founded: 1942

Santiago **Sentis** Melendo*, Rivadavia 4076,
1205 Buenos Aires

Ediciones **Siglo XX** SAC & I*, Maza 177,
1206 Buenos Aires Tel: 882758 Cable Add:
Sigloveinte
Man Dir: Isidoro Wainer; *Sales Dir:* Carlos Zorrilla
Bookshop: At above address
Subjects: General Fiction & Nonfiction
Founded: 1943

Editorial **Sigmar** SACI, Belgrano 1580 —
7°, 1093 Buenos Aires Tel: 373045/384474
Cable Add: Sigmar
Man Dir: Sigfrido Chwat
Subject: Juveniles
1979: 37 titles *Founded:* 1941

Ediciones del **Sol** SA*, Ave Roque Saénz
Peña 974, 8° piso B, Buenos Aires
Tel: 350473
Man Dir: Adolfo Colombres; *Sales Dir:*
Manuel Valiz
Subjects: Fiction, General Literature, Social Sciences
Founded: 1973

Editorial **Sopena** Argentina SACI e I,
Echeverría 5037-39, Buenos Aires Tel:
309748/340748/345930
Executive President: Marta Sopena de
Olsen; *Director-General:* Carlos D Olsen;
Sales: Hipólito O Dhers
Subjects: Dictionaries, Language &
Linguistics, Literature & Criticism, Spanish
& Hispano-American classics, Chess, Health
& Beauty, Practical Guides, Contemporary
Politics, History, Children's Anthologies, all
mainly paperback

Editorial **Stella***, Viamonte 1984, 1056
Buenos Aires Tel: 460346
Asociación Educacionista Argentina
Subjects: Non-fiction, Textbooks

Studia Croatica*, Carlos Pelegrini 743.P.3,
Buenos Aires Tel: 3927254

Editorial **Sur** SA*, Viamonte 494 - 8°, 1053
Buenos Aires Tel: 325148

T E A (Tipográfica Editora Argentina),
Lavalle 1430, 1048 Buenos Aires
Tel: 405668
Man Dir: Pedro San Martín; *Sales Dir:*
María Teresa San Martín
Subjects: History, Social Science, Law,

Economics, Philosophy
Founded: 1946

Instituto Torcuato di **Tella**, 11 de
Septiembre 2139, 1428 Buenos Aires Tel:
7848264/7815013/7815015/7848225
Dir: Javier Villanueva
Subjects: Social Sciences, Economics,
History, Political Science, Epistemology and
Methodology of the Social Sciences
1978: 5 titles *Founded:* 1958

Ediciones **Theoria** SRL*, Rivadavia 1255, 4°
piso of 407, Casilla de Correo 5096, 1033
Buenos Aires Tel: 380131
Man Dir: Jorge O Orús; *Sales Dir:* José Luis Menéndez
Subjects: Literature, Biography, History,
Religion
1978: 8 titles *Founded:* 1954

Editorial **Tiempo** Contemporaneo*,
Viamonte 1453, 10° piso of 66, 1055 Buenos
Aires Tel: 459640
Man Dir: Alberto Mario Serebresky; *Sales
Dir:* José Fuster
Subjects: General Fiction, History,
Philosophy, Psychology, Technical,
Medicine, Social Sciences, University Textbooks
Founded: 1969

Ediciones **Tiempo de Hoy***, Casilla de
Correo 66, Sucursal 32, 1432 Buenos Aires
Dir: Juan Carlos Nigro
Miscellaneous: Firm runs a writers'
workshop, *Taller Literario*, offering tuition
in writing techniques, and also provides a
review service, API (see under Literary Associations)

Ediciones **Tres Tiempos** SRL, Ave Belgrano
225, 1092 Buenos Aires Tel:
342913/347184/338785
Man Dirs: José C Orríes e Ibars, Canio
Carmelo Cillo; *Assistant Manager:* José Luis
Tato; *Editor:* Susana Margulies; *Production
Dir:* Ana Barkacs van Gyarmath; *Sales Dirs:*
Lidia N de Guastavino, Raúl Villar;
Advertising & Promotion: Florinda Mintz;
Rights & Permissions: Teresa Cillo;
Imports/Exports: Alejandro Luis Calegari
Orders to: Belgrano 225, 3° 23
Branch Off: Moreno 3201, Buenos Aires
Tel: 936498
Subjects: Anthropology, Architecture and
Urbanism, Arts, Cinematography and
Theatre, Demography, Ecology, Economics,
Education, Philosophy, Psychology,
Management, Technology, Sciences, Social
& Political Sciences, Novels, Fiction & Poetry
1978: 103 titles *1979:* 208 titles *Founded:* 1975

Editorial **Troquel** SA, San José 157-159,
1076 Buenos Aires Tel: 380118/380349
Cable Add: Troquelsa
President: Armando Silvio Ressia; *Sales
Manager:* Oscar Gonzalez
Subjects: General Literature, Technology, Textbooks
Founded: 1954

Turismo Editorial*, Corrientes 369, Buenos Aires

Turner Ediciones SRL, Alsina 1535 — 8°
piso of 803, Buenos Aires 1088 Tel: 466477
Man Dir: Mary C Turner
Subjects: Reference, Bibliography
1978: 2 titles *1979:* 2 titles

Javier **Vergara** Editor SRL*, Juncal 691 – 9°
y 10°, 1062 Buenos Aires Tel: 312624
Dir: Javier Vergara; *Rights:* Gabriela Cruz de Vergara
Branch Offs: Cardenal Reig 18,
Barcelona 14, Spain Tel: 3347754;
Fresas 158, México 12 D F, Mexico

8 ARGENTINA

Tel: 5756071; Ave Bulnes 80, Santiago, Chile Tel: 65921
Subjects: General Fiction, Non-fiction, Science Fiction
1978: 50 titles Founded: 1975

Victor P de **Zavalía**, Editor*, Alberti 835, 1223 Buenos Aires Tel: 9421274/9423046
Man Dir: Ricardo L de Zavalía; Sales Dir: Araceli L de Zavalía
Bookshop: Law School of the University of Buenos Aires
Subjects: Law
1978: 8 titles Founded: 1950

Literary Agents

International Editors' Co*, Nicolás Costa, Cabildo 1156, Buenos Aires Tel: 734613
Cable Add: Lifeplay
Also office in Spain (qv)

Lawrence **Smith**, Ave de los Incas, 3110 Buenos Aires 1426 Tel: 7845012 Cable Add: Litagent Baires

Book Clubs

Círculo de Lectores Argentina SA, Paraguay 858 PB, 1057 Buenos Aires

Club del Libro Nuevo*, Doblas 1753, 1424 Buenos Aires
Owned by: Asociación Ediciones La Aurora, Buenos Aires (qv)

Club 'El **Libro** del Mes'*, Alsina 2041, 1090 Buenos Aires
Owned by: Emecé Editores SA, Buenos Aires (qv)

Major Booksellers

Librería **A B C**, Florida 725, 1005 Buenos Aires Tel: 316848
Branches at: Avda Córdoba 685, 1054 Buenos Aires; Avda Libertador 13777, 1646 Martinez, Buenos Aires

American Books*, Tucumán 994 — 1°, Buenos Aires Tel: 353704

El **Ateneo***, Florida 336, 340 & 344, 1005 Buenos Aires Tel: 466801

Bias Editora (Libros Jurídicos)*, Lavalle 1294, 1048 Buenos Aires Tel: 354161

Distribuidora **Cuspide***, Suipacha 764, 1008 Buenos Aires Tel: 3921727/3928868/3927434

Librería **Española***, Florida 943, 1005 Buenos Aires Tel: 323214/325850

Librerías **Fausto**, Ave Corrientes 1311, 1043 Buenos Aires Tel: 401222
Also at: Ave Santa Fé 1715, 1060 Buenos Aires Tel: 412708

Librería 'Martín **Fierro**', Corrientes 1264, 1043 Buenos Aires Tel: 350444

Ediciones **Garriga** Argentinas SA*, Talcahuano 897, Buenos Aires Tel: 443562

Librería Alfa **Graziano***, Sarmiento 1343, 1041 Buenos Aires Tel: 495349

Librería **Hachette**, Rivadavia 739-743, 1002 Buenos Aires Tel: 348481

Carlos **Hirsch** SRL, Florida 165, Galería Güemes — 4°, 1333 Buenos Aires Tel: 332391/331787/307122

Librería **Huemul**, Ave Santa Fe 2237, 1123 Buenos Aires Tel: 831666

Librería **Kier**, Ave Santa Fe 1260, 1059 Buenos Aires Tel: 410507/418243

Librerías **MacKern** SA*, Lavalle 1765, Buenos Aires Tel: 460737

H F **Martínez** de Murguía*, Ave Córdoba 2270, Buenos Aires Tel: 486173

Librería **Morena***, Rivera Indarte 62, Ave Gral Paz 1, Ave Gral Paz 162, Córdoba Tel: 43600

Librería La **Nena***, Callao 410, Buenos Aires Tel: 450271/463562

Librería **Norte***, Las Heras 2225, Buenos Aires Tel: 843944

Nueva Visión*, Viamonte 500, Buenos Aires Tel: 326434

Librería General de Tomas **Pardo***, Maipú 618, Buenos Aires Tel: 3920496

Pigmalión*, Corrientes 515, Buenos Aires Tel: 494621

Librerías **Premier***, Corrientes 1583, Talcahuano 459, Callao 1180, Buenos Aires

Librería **Rodríguez***, Sarmiento 835, Buenos Aires Tel: 358125

Librería **Ross***, Córdoba 1347, Rosario Tel: 65378

Librería **Santa** Fe*, Santa Fe 2386, 1123 Buenos Aires Tel: 835746
Also: Santa Fe 2928, 1125 Buenos Aires Tel: 8219442

Librería **Sarmiento**, Libertad 1214-20, 1012 Buenos Aires Tel: 414792

Tres **Américas** Libros, Alsina 722, 1087 Buenos Aires Tel: 339072/339082 Telex: 18593 Tresa Ar

Major Libraries

Biblioteca del **Banco** Central de la República Argentina*, Reconquista 266, Buenos Aires
Library of the Central Bank

Biblioteca Nacional, México 564, 1097 Buenos Aires Tel: 347370

Biblioteca Nacional de Maestros*, Pizzurno 935, Buenos Aires
National Teachers' Library

Biblioteca Publico Central*, Calle 47, No 510, La Plata

Biblioteca de la Asociación Argentina de Cultura Inglesa*, Juncal 851, Buenos Aires

British Council Library, see Biblioteca de la Asociación Argentina de Cultura Inglesa

Biblioteca del **Congreso** de la Nación*, Rivadavia 1850, Buenos Aires
National Library of Congress

Biblioteca **Lincoln***, Florida 935, Buenos Aires

Biblioteca Pública Gratuita de 'La **Prensa**'*, Rivadavia 552, Buenos Aires

Instituto Bibliotecológico, **Universidad de Buenos Aires***, Casilla de Correo 901, 1000 Buenos Aires (Located at: Azcuénaga 280, Buenos Aires)

Biblioteca de la **Universidad del Salvador***, Callao 542, Buenos Aires

Biblioteca Mayor de la **Universidad Nacional de Córdoba**, Calle Obispo Trejo y Sanabria 242, Córdoba
Principal Library of the National University of Córdoba
Dir: Professor Joaquín García
Publications: Informativo (irregular), Monographs

Biblioteca Pública de la **Universidad Nacional de La Plata**, Plaza Rocha 137, La Plata, Provincia de Buenos Aires Tel: 24109
Dir: Mrs Haydée Cervantes de Artola
Publications: Bulletin Informaciones

Library Associations

A B G R A (Asociación de Bibliotecarios Graduados de la República Argentina), Casilla de Correo 68 — suc 1, 1401 Ciudad de Buenos Aires
Association of Graduate Librarians of Argentina
Executive Secretary: Elida S Iriondo
Publications: Documentos Ocasionales, Reuniones Nacionales de Bibliotecarios (Documentos de Base; Actas); Memoria annual, Bibliotecologia y Documentacion

Asociación Argentina de Bibliotecas y Centros de Información Cientificos y Tecnicos*, Santa Fe 1145, Buenos Aires Tel: 411405
Executive Secretary: Olga E Veronelli

Asociación de Ex-Alumnos de la Escuela Nacional de Bibliotecarios*, c/o Biblioteca Nacional, México 564, Buenos Aires

Dirección de **Bibliotecas Municipales***, Talcahuano 1261, Buenos Aires

Centro De Documentación Bibliotecológica*, Universidad Nacional del Sur, Ave Alem 1253, Bahía Blanca
Centre for Library Science Documentation
Dir: Atilio Peralta
Publications: Bibliografía Bibliotecológica Argentina, Quien es Quien en la Bibliotecología Argentina, Guía de las Bibliotecas Universitarias Argentinas, Documentacion Bibliotecologica, Indices de Revistas de Bibliotecología

Colegio de Bibliotecarios de la Provincia de Buenos Aires*, Calle 48 — No 633 — piso 3 of 315, 1900 La Plata

Instituto de Bibliografía del Ministerio de Educación de la Provincia de Buenos Aires*, Calle 47, No 510, 6 piso, 1900 La Plata
Dir: María del Carmen Crespi de Bustos
Publications: Bibliografía Argentina de Historia, Boletín de Información Bibliográfica

Library Reference Books and Journals

Books

Bibliografía Bibliotecológica Argentina (Argentine Library Science Bibliography), Centre for Library Science Documentation, Ave Alem 1253, Bahía Blanca

Guía de las Bibliotecas Universitarias Argentinas (Guide to Argentine University Libraries), Centre for Library Science Documentation, Ave Alem 1253, Bahía Blanca

Journals

Boletín Informativo (Information Bulletin), Association of Graduate Librarians of Argentina, Casilla de Correo 68 — suc 1, 1401 Ciudad de Buenos Aires

Literary Associations and Societies

Academia Argentina de Letras*, Sánchez de Bustamante 2663, Buenos Aires
Secretary: Juan Carlos Ghiano
Publications: Boletín de la Academia Argentina de Letras (quarterly)
Library Publications: Serie de Clásicos Argentinos, Serie de Estudios Académicos, Serie de Discursos Académicos, Serie de Acuerdos acerca del Idioma, Boletín, Serie Estudios Lingüísticos y Filológicos

The **Dickens** Fellowship*, Basavilbaso 12A, Buenos Aires
Honarary Secretary: Miguel Alfredo Olivera

Instituto de Literatura*, Calle 47, No 625, La Plata
Dir: Arturo Cambours
Publications: Investigaciones, Boletín

P E N Club de la Argentina*, Calle de Basavilbaso 1396, 1006 Buenos Aires
President of the Advisory Council: D Miguel Alfredo Olivera
Publications: Boletín and books

Literary Periodicals

Boletín, Argentine Academy of Letters, Sánchez de Bustamante 2663, Buenos Aires

Boletín, Association of Argentine Writers, Uruguay 1371, 1016 Buenos Aires

Comentario, Tucuman 2137 y San Martin 663, Buenos Aires

Criterio, Alsina 840, Buenos Aires

Davar, Sociedad Hebraica Argentina, Sarmiento 2233, Buenos Aires

Historium, Paraná 464, Buenos Aires

Igitur Revista Literaria, Republica de Israel 115, Córdoba

Sur, Viamonte 494, 8° piso, Buenos Aires

Literary Prizes

Argentine National Prize for Literature*
For best works of prose and Poetry. Awarded every three years. Enquiries to Argentinian Ministry of Education and Culture, General Directorate of Culture, Ave Alvear 1630, Buenos Aires

Alfredo A **Bianchi** Essay Prize*
For the best scholarly essay on any subject. Awarded annually. Enquiries to Association of Argentine Writers, Uruguay 1371, 1016 Buenos Aires

Buenos Aires Literary Prizes*
For the best works written or published during the year in Buenos Aires. Awards are given for fiction; essay (including biography and literary criticism); poetry. Awarded annually. Enquiries to Buenos Aires Municipality, Secretariat of Culture and Social Activities, Ave de Mayo 525, Buenos Aires

Carlos **Casavalle** Prize*
Awarded in turn for the best book published in Argentina in the following categories: fiction; poetry and drama; essay, including scientific writing. Awarded annually. Enquiries to Argentine Book Association, Ave Belgrano 1580, 6° piso, 1093 Buenos Aires

Premio **Emecé** Annual Prize
Established 1954. For the best novel or short story in the Spanish language by an unpublished writer. 1979 award to Luis Casnati for *Historias de mi sangre*. Enquiries to Emecé Editores SA, Carlos Pellegrini 1069 9°, 1009 Buenos Aires

First Book Prize*
For the first literary work written by an author under 30. Awarded annually. Enquiries to Argentine Book Association, Paraguay 610, 7° piso, Buenos Aires

Kraft Prize*
For the best unpublished novel, particularly by young and unknown authors. Awarded biennially. Enquiries to Guillermo Kraft Publishing Ltd, Moreno 872, Buenos Aires

Fernando **Moreno** Poetry Prize*
For outstanding work in Poetry. Enquiries to Association of Argentine Writers, Uruguay 1371, 1016 Buenos Aires

Premio de '**La Nación**' Prize*
Given by the newspaper 'La Nación' for different types of literature. Enquiries to 'La Nación', Florida 343/San Martín, Buenos Aires CF

Pablo **Rojas** Paz Prize*
For the best unpublished biography. Enquiries to Association of Argentine Writers, Uruguay 1371, 1016 Buenos Aires

Ricardo **Rojas** Prize*
For prose work (imaginative writing, criticism, essay). Awarded biennially. Enquiries to Buenos Aires Municipality, Secretariat of Culture and Social Activities, Ave de Mayo 525, Buenos Aires

Medalla de Oro de la **S A D E** (Sociedad Argentina de Escritores)*
Annual prize for the total output of an author. Enquiries to Association of Argentine Writers, Uruguay 1371, 1016 Buenos Aires

Sarmiento Prize*
For the best book of prose written during the year. Awarded annually. Enquiries to Association of Argentine Writers, Uruguay 1371, 1016 Buenos Aires

Australia

General Information

Language: English
Religion: Predominantly Protestant
Population: 14.2 million
Bank Hours: 1000-1500 Monday-Thursday; 1000-1700 Friday
Shop Hours: 0900-1700 Monday-Friday; usually 0900-1200 Saturday
Currency: 100 cents = 1 Australian dollar
Export/Import Information: No tariffs on books. Advertising catalogues other than single copies or less than 1 kg gross weight dutied 35%. Most books, especially of literary or educational nature, free of sales tax. No import licences for books; no seditious literature permitted
Copyright: UCC, Berne (see International section)

Book Trade Organizations

Association of Australian University Presses, Australian National University Press, PO Box 4, Canberra, ACT 2600
President: B Clouston
Incorporating Australian National University Press, Deakin University Press, Melbourne University Press, Sydney University Press, University of Queensland Press, University of Western Australia Press, University of New South Wales Press (qqv under Publishers)

Association of British Book Publishers Representatives in Australia*, 18-20 Collins St, Melbourne, Victoria 3000

Australian Book Publishers Association, 163 Clarence St, Sydney, NSW 2000 Tel: (02) 292570
Dir: Sandra Forbes
Publication: Directory of Members

Australian Booksellers Association*, Box 3254, GPO Sydney, NSW 2001 Tel: (02) 2325311

Australian Copyright Council, 24 Alfred St, Milsons Point, NSW 2061 Tel: 921151
Chairman: G C O'Donnell (at above address)

Australian Independent Publishers' Association*, PO Box 4059, Mail Exchange, Melbourne, Victoria 3001
Secretary: Sally Milner

Australian Society of Authors, 24 Alfred St, Milsons Point, NSW 2061
Executive Secretary: Deirdre Hill
Publication: The Australian Author (quarterly)

Australian Society of Indexers, Unit 4, 2 Erne St, Mont Albert, Victoria 3129
Secretary: Miss J Hagger
Affiliated to The Society of Indexers, UK (qv)

Australian Standard Book Numbering Agency, National Library of Australia, Parkes Pl, Canberra, ACT 2600 Tel: (062) 621111
Administrator: Mrs Cornell Platzer

Australian Writers' Guild, Suite 505, Fifth Floor, 83 York St, Sydney, NSW 2000 Tel: (02) 291402
General Secretary: Angela Wales

Book Trade Group (New South Wales)*, c/o Evan Grigor, Granada Publishing Australia Pty Ltd, 717 York St, Sydney, NSW 2000

Book Trade Group (Queensland)*, Barker, Conlan and Ferret Pty Ltd, Brisbane, Queensland 4000

Book Trade Group Secretary (Victoria)*, PO Box 4065, Mail Exchange, Melbourne, Victoria 3001 Tel: (03) 3599535
Secretary: Deborah Dare

Children's Book Council of Australia*, GPO 2428V, Melbourne, Victoria 3001
Secretary: Philip Sydenham
Branches in Australian Capital Territory, New South Wales, South Australia, Tasmania, Victoria, Western Australia

Christian Bookselling Association of Australia, 47 Gawler Place, Adelaide, South Australia 5000
Secretary: Laurie Russell

Copyright Agency Ltd, PO Box 440, Milsons Point, NSW 2061 (Located at: Suite 301, 30 Glen St, Milsons Point) Tel: 4362820

Committee for **Freelance Writing***, The Secretary, PO Box 139, Caulfield South, Vic 3162

Galley Club of Sydney*, PO Box 91, Cammeray, NSW 2062

I B I S Information Services Ltd, PO Box 995, Sydney, NSW 2001
Secretary: Robert Howells

Imprint Society*, 125 Bank St, South Melbourne, Victoria 3205 Tel: 6999474
Secretary: Ian Green

Literature Board of the Australia Council, PO Box 302, 168 Walker St, North Sydney, NSW 2060 Tel: 9222122
Director: Dr Michael Costigan

AUSTRALIA

National Book Council*, 4th Floor, 71 Collins St, Melbourne, Victoria 3000 Tel: (03) 638043
Executive Director: Stuart Edwards

New South Wales Booksellers' Association, 66 King St, Sydney 2000
Secretary: Ms Jean Abbey

Public Lending Right Committee of Australia Council, Box 302, PO North Sydney, NSW 2060 (Located at: 4th Fl, Northside Gdns, 168 Walker St, North Sydney) Tel: (02) 9222122 Cable Add: Ozart Sydney Telex: 26023
Administrator, PLR: K L Waddell

Queensland Booksellers' Association*, Treasury Book Store, 14 Queen St, Brisbane 4000
Secretary: G Bott

Society of Editors*, c/o PO Box 176, Carlton South, Victoria 3053
Secretary: Christine Nicol

Society of Women Writers, PO Box 1388, Sydney, NSW 2001

South Australia Booksellers' Association*, Adelaide University Bookshop Pty Ltd, GPO Box 498, Adelaide 5001
President: R M Amundsen

Standard Book Numbering Agency, see Australian Standard Book Numbering Agency

Tasmanian Booksellers' Association, GPO Box 170, Launceston, Tasmania 7250
President: R F Tilley; *Secretary:* Y G Tilley

United States Book Association, PO Box 226, Artarmon, NSW 2064
Secretary: B Wilder

Victoria Booksellers' Association*, Collins Book Depot Pty Ltd, 86 Bourke St, Melbourne 3000
President: M G Zifcak

Western Australian Booksellers' Association*, c/o Child Education Services, 13A Havelock St, West Perth, Western Australia 6005
Secretary: M Walton

Book Trade Reference Books and Journals

Books

Australian and Pacific Book Prices Current, OP Books Pty Ltd, PO Box 591, Brookvale, NSW 2100

Australian Book Publishers' Association: Guide to Book Outlets in Australia, Meldrum, Johnston and Weston, 163 Clarence St, Sydney, NSW 2000

Australian Books in Print, D W Thorpe Pty Ltd, 384 Spencer St, Melbourne, Victoria 3003

Books Australia (annual catalogue), PO Box 41, Glebe, NSW 2037

Current Australian Serials; a select list, National Library of Australia, Parkes Pl, Canberra, ACT 2600

Directory of Australian Booksellers, Australian Book Trade Advisory Committee, 163 Clarence St, Sydney, NSW

Journals

Australian Author, Australian Society of Authors, 24 Alfred St, Milsons Point, NSW 2061

Australian Book Review, 46 Porter St, Prahran, Vic 3181

Australian Books, National Library of Australia, Parkes Pl, Canberra, ACT 2600

Australian Bookseller & Publisher, D W Thorpe Pty Ltd, 384 Spencer St, Melbourne, Victoria 3003

Australian Government Publications, National Library of Australia, Parkes Pl, Canberra, ACT 2600

Australian National Bibliography, National Library of Australia, Parkes Pl, Canberra, ACT 2600

The Indexer, c/o Hazel K Bell, 139 The Ryde, Hatfield, Herts AL9 5DP, UK (Journal of Australian, American and British Societies of Indexers)

Weekly Book Newsletter, D W Thorpe Pty Ltd, 384 Spencer St, Melbourne, Victoria 3003

Publishers

A D I S Press Australasia Pty Limited, PO Box 132, Balgowlah, NSW 2093 (Located at: 404 Sydney Road, Balgowlah, NSW 2093) Tel: 9492022 Cable Add: Adinfo Sydney Telex: Adis AA25868
Chief Editorial Office: 15 Rawene Rd, PO Box 34-030 Birkenhead, Auckland 10, New Zealand Tel: 486125 Telex: Adis NZ21334
Publisher: William W Hughes; *Editor-in-Chief:* Graeme S Avery; *Sales, Publicity:* Gervan McCune; *General Manager:* David R Bleakley
Orders to: ADIS Press Australasia Pty Ltd, 404 Sydney Road, Balgowlah, NSW 2093
Associate Companies: ADIS Press International Ltd, Unit 5b, Fifth Floor, Gardena Court, Kennedy Terrace, Kennedy Rd, Hong Kong; ADIS Press USA Inc, 488 Madison Avenue, New York, NY 10022, USA; ADIS Press, Hummelsbuetteler Kirchenweg 36, 2000 Hamburg 63, Federal Republic of Germany
Subject: Medicine
1978: 6 titles *Founded:* 1960
ISBN Publisher's Prefix: 0-9599827, 0-909337

A N Z, an imprint of Australia & New Zealand Book Co Pty Ltd (qv)

A P C O L, an imprint of Alternative Publishing Co-operative Ltd (qv)

Acme Books*, 188 Weston St, Brunswick 3057 Tel: (03) 3873525
Publisher: Jim Hart

Addison-Wesley Publishing Co, A1/6-8 Byfield St, North Ryde, NSW 2113 Tel: (02) 8882733 Cable Add: Adiwes Sydney
General Manager, Rights & Permissions: W Douglas; *Editorial:* James F Robins; *Sales:* Geoffrey Hasler (college and general), John Munro (school and juveniles); *Production:* Kenneth Markillie
Parent Company: Addison-Wesley Publishing Company, Reading, Mass, USA
Associate Company: Addison-Wesley Publishers Ltd, UK (qv for other associates)
Subjects: Educational Books, Scientific and Technical Books, Juveniles
1978: 37 titles

Adelaide University Union Press, PO Box 498, Adelaide 5001 Tel: 2234366 Telex: Univad AA89141
Chief Executive: Ray Amundsen
Subjects: Poetry, Politics, Literature, Critiques
1979: 4 titles *1980:* 6 titles *Founded:* 1976
ISBN Publisher's Prefix: 0-9598309

Algona Publications Pty Ltd*, PO Box 52, Montrose, Victoria 3765 Tel: 7283348
Chief Executives: John R Brownlie, Gloria E Harman
Subjects: Australian flora, fauna, history and landscape for travellers
1978: 3 titles *1979:* 1 title *Founded:* 1970
ISBN Publisher's Prefix: 0-909594

Allara Publishing, 47 Deakin St, East Bentleigh 3165
ISBN Publisher's Prefix: 0-85887

George **Allen & Unwin** Australia Pty Ltd, PO Box 764, North Sydney, NSW 2065 Tel: 9226399 Cable Add: Deucalion Sydney Telex: 24331 Gaua
Man Dir: P A Gallagher; *Sales:* Roger Ward
Warehouse and Distribution: Bookstocks Pty Ltd, Cnr Bridge Rd & Jersey St, Hornsby, NSW 2077
Parent Company: George Allen & Unwin Ltd, UK (qv)
Associate Company: Allen & Unwin Inc, 9 Winchester Terrace, Winchester, Mass 01890, USA
Subjects: Academic, Social Science, General Nonfiction
1978: 50 titles *Founded:* 1976
ISBN Publisher's Prefix: 0-86861

Alpha Books*, 280 Pitt St, Sydney 2000 Tel: (02) 265154
Head of Company: A W Sheppard

Alternative Publishing Co-operative Ltd, 10 Shepherd St, Chippendale, Sydney 2008 Tel: (02) 2113837/591937
Chairman: Greg Crough; *Editorial, Sales, Production, Publicity, Rights & Permissions:* D K Cleaver
Imprints: APCOL
Branch Off: 4 Longbourne, North Clayton 3168
Subjects: Reference, High-priced Paperbacks, Psychology, University & Secondary Textbooks, History, Political Science, Sociology, Economics
1978: 4 titles *1979:* 9 titles *Founded:* 1975

Angus & Robertson Publishers, Unit 4, 31 Waterloo Rd, North Ryde, NSW 2113 Tel: (02) 8872233 Cable Add: Fragment, Sydney Telex: 26452
Chief Executive: Richard Walsh; *Publishing Manager:* Jennifer Rowe; *Marketing Manager:* Norm Lurie; *Production Manager:* Judith Clegg; *Publicity Manager:* Alan Davidson; *Rights & Permissions:* Gwenda Jarred
Subsidiary Companies: Angus & Robertson (South-East Asia) Ltd, Singapore (qv); Angus & Robertson (South-East Asia) Ltd, 135-C Dolores St, Pasay City, Metro Manila, Philippines; Angus & Robertson (UK) Ltd, UK (qv)
Branch Offs: 627 Rathdowne St, North Carlton, Victoria 3054; 53 Victoria St, Balmoral, Queensland 4171; 25 Central Ave, Hallett Cove, South Australia 5158
Subjects: General Fiction, Belles Lettres, Poetry, Biography, History, How-to, Art, Reference, Juveniles, Low- & High-Priced Paperbacks, Medicine, Psychology, General & Social Science, University
1979: 223 titles *Founded:* 1884
Miscellaneous: Firm is a division of Ipec Holdings Ltd, 31 Bligh St, Sydney
ISBN Publisher's Prefix: 0-207

Ansay Pty Ltd, PO Box 90, 2040 Leichardt, NSW (Located at: 19-25 Beeson St, Leichhardt 1) Tel: 5602044 Cable Add: Cowboy Sydney
Man Dir: Philip Lindsay; *Editorial, Production:* H E Lindsay; *Sales, Rights & Permissions:* P S Lindsay; *Publicity:* C Rijks
Parent Companies: A L Lindsay & Co Pty Ltd, Lindsays Leichardt Pty Ltd

Imprint: Dollar Books
Subjects: Fiction, Educational
1978: 12 titles *1979:* 4 titles *Founded:* 1972
ISBN Publisher's Prefix: 0-909245

Antipodean Publishers Pty Ltd*, 7 Lanceley Pl, PO Box 277, Artarmon, NSW 2064 Tel: (02) 4392616
Subjects: Australiana, History, Psychological books by Australian authors
ISBN Publisher's Prefix: 0-86944

Apple Paperbacks, an imprint of Widescope International Publishers Pty Ltd (qv)

Edward **Arnold** (Australia) Pty Ltd, 373 Bay St, PO Box 146, Port Melbourne, Victoria 3207 Tel: (03) 641346 Cable Add: Edarnold Telex: 35974 AA
Man Dir: Robert J Blackmore; *Editorial, Permissions:* Colin P Jevons; *Sales:* Terry M Coyle
Parent Company: Edward Arnold (Publishers) Ltd, UK (qv)
Subjects: All categories, specializing in University and Secondary Textbooks
1978: 22 titles *Founded:* 1966, changed name 1975
ISBN Publisher's Prefix: 0-7131

Ashton Scholastic, PO Box 579, Gosford, NSW 2250 Tel: (043) 621401 Cable Add: Tonash Sydney Telex: 24881
Shipping Add: Railway Crescent, Lisarow, via Gosford
Man Dir: Ken A Jolly; *Publishing, Rights & Permissions:* Ruth A Hamilton; *Marketing Manager:* Geoffrey S Gribble; *National Sales Co-ordinator:* Gavin S Shepherd; *Publicity:* Derek A Harling
Parent Company: Scholastic Magazines Inc, 50 West 44th St, New York, NY 10036, USA
Imprints: Core Libraries, Impact, Read It Again, Visuals of the Australian Environment, Community Language Children's Books, Real Life
Branch Offs: 260 Auburn Road, Hawthorn, Victoria 3122; 2nd Fl, Teachers Bldg, 495 Boundary St, Spring Hill, Queensland 400; 254 Halifax St, Adelaide, South Australia 5000; PO Box 250, Wembley, Western Australia 6014
Subjects: Juveniles, Paperbacks, Secondary & Primary Textbooks, Educational Materials
Book Clubs: Arrow; Lucky; Teacher's Bookshelf; Teenage
Bookshop: Oldmeadow Booksellers (Australia) Pty Ltd, 18 Helen St, West Heidelberg, Victoria 3081
1978: 5 titles *1979:* 5 titles *Founded:* 1968
ISBN Publisher's Prefix: 0-86896

Associated Book Publishers (Aust) Ltd, 301 Kent St, Sydney, NSW 2000 Tel: (02) 291791 Cable Add: Asbook Sydney
Man Dir: W Mackarell; *Legal Division Dir:* D S Lees; *Trade Division Manager:* J E Coxhill
Parent Company: Associated Book Publishers Ltd, UK (qv)
Subsidiary Companies: Atlantic Forlib Pty Ltd; The Law Book Co Ltd (qv); Methuen of Australia Pty Ltd (qv); Associated Book Publishers (New Zealand) Ltd, New Zealand (qv)
Branch Offs: 610-612 Church St, Richmond, Vic 3121; IOOF House, Cnr Allenby and Leichhardt Sts, North Brisbane, Queensland 4000; 6 Sherwood Court, Perth, WA 6000
Subjects: See subsidiary companies

Australasian Book Society Ltd*, PO Box A 161, Sydney South, NSW 2000 Tel: (02) 613229
Man Dir: N Zusman; *Sales, Publicity, Advertising, Rights & Permissions:* D Cleaver
Subjects: General Fiction, High-priced Paperbacks, Social Science
Founded: 1951
ISBN Publisher's Prefix: 0-909916

Australasian Publishing Co Pty Ltd, Corner Bridge Rd and Jersey St, Hornsby, NSW 2077 Tel: 4762000 Cable Add: Publishing Hornsby Telex: AA23274
Man Dir: A S M Harrap; *Sales Dir:* G A Rutherford; *Publicity:* John Cody, Mrs R Onslow; *Rights & Permissions, Production:* A S M Harrap
Branch Offs: 83 Glen Eira Rd, Ripponlea, Victoria 3183; 303 Adelaide St, Brisbane, Queensland 4000; 33 Pirie St, Adelaide, South Australia 5000
Subjects: General Fiction, Belles Lettres, Juveniles, Education, General Science
ISBN Publisher's Prefix: 0-900882

Australia & New Zealand Book Co Pty Ltd, PO Box 459, Brookvale, NSW 2100 (Located at: 23 Cross St, Brookvale, NSW 2100) Tel: (02) 9382244 Cable Add: Anzbook Sydney
Chairman: Geoffrey M King; *Man Dir, Rights & Permissions:* G Ross King; *Publishing Dir:* Peter Benjamin; *Marketing Dir:* Wendy Livingston
Parent Company: G M King Investments Pty Ltd
Imprint: ANZ
Branch Offs: Brisbane and Melbourne, Australia; Auckland, New Zealand
Subjects: Science, Technical, Medical, General Nonfiction, Arts and Crafts, Sports
1978: 10 titles *1979:* 16 titles *Founded:* 1964
ISBN Publisher's Prefix: 0-85552

Australian Academy of Science, PO Box 783, Canberra City, ACT 2601 Tel: 486011
Orders to: Canberra Ho, Marcus Clarke St, Canberra City, ACT 2601
Subjects: Scientific and Educational Books
ISBN Publisher's Prefix: 0-85847

The **Australian Council** for Educational Research Ltd, PO Box 210, Hawthorn, Victoria 3122 (Located at: Radford House, Frederick St, Hawthorn) Tel: 8181271 Cable Add: Aceres
Man Dir: Dr J P Keeves; *Sales Dir:* Eric McIlroy; *Publicity:* P Jeffery; *Editorial, Production, Rights & Permissions:* Don Maguire
Subjects: Education, Textbooks, Educational materials
Founded: 1930
Bookshop: Frederick St, Hawthorn, Victoria 3122
ISBN Publisher's Prefix: 0-85563

Australian Encyclopaedia Pty Ltd, see The Grolier Society of Australia Pty Ltd

Australian Government Publishing Service, PO Box 84, Canberra, ACT 2600 (Located at: 109 Canberra Ave, Griffith, ACT 2603) Tel: (062) 954711 Telex: AA62013
Warehouse & Shipping Add: Wentworth Ave, Kingston, ACT 2604
Chief Executive: P E Westaway; *Director, Publishing, Rights & Permissions:* B P Shurman; *Government Printer:* C J Thompson; *Editorial:* M J Greenane; *Production:* J A Wainwright; *Sales, Publicity:* K G Blair
Parent Company: Branch of the Department of Administrative Services
Subjects: Australian Government Publications. Also sales agent for publications of Canadian Government; New Zealand Government Printer; HMSO (UK); FAO, UNESCO, WHO (United Nations)
Bookshops: 12 Pirie Street, Adelaide; 294 Adelaide Street, Brisbane; 70 Alinga St, Canberra; 162 Macquarie Street, Hobart; 347 Swanston Street, Melbourne; 200 St George's Terrace, Perth; 309 Pitt Street, Sydney
1978: approx 3400 *Founded:* 1970
ISBN Publisher's Prefix: 0-642

Australian Institute of Aboriginal Studies, PO Box 553, Canberra City 2601 Tel: (062) 461111 Cable Add: Abinst
Warehouse: Acton Ho, Acton ACT 2601
Principal: Dr P J Ucko; *Executive Officer, Publications and Rights & Permissions:* Graham Pike
Subjects: Anthropology, Archaeology, Ethnology, Ethnomusicology, Linguistics, Human Biology, Prehistory, Material culture, Aboriginal art, Education
ISBN Publisher's Prefix: 085575

Australian Institute of Criminology, PO Box 28, Woden, ACT 2606 (Located at: 10-18 Colbee Court, Phillip, ACT 2606) Tel: 822111 Cable Add: Austcrim
Dir: William Clifford; *Editorial:* Peter Kay
Subject: Criminology
1978: 3 titles *1979:* 4 titles *Founded:* 1976
ISBN Publisher's Prefix: 0-642

Australian National University Press, PO Box 4, Canberra, ACT 2600 Tel: (062) 492812 Cable Add: Natuniv Press, Canberra
Shipping Add: Old Administration Area, Australian National University, Canberra, ACT
Dir: B Clouston; *Editor:* P Croft; *Sales, Publicity & Advertising:* B Clouston; *Rights & Permissions:* P Croft
Subjects: Belles Lettres, Poetry, Biography, Geography, History, Reference, Social Science, Earth Sciences, University Textbooks, High-priced Paperbacks
1979: 93 titles *Founded:* 1965
ISBN Publisher's Prefix: 0-7081

Australian Universities Press Pty Ltd*, Offset Ho, 169-171 Philip St, Waterloo, NSW 2017 Tel: (02) 695633/4
Man Dir: R G Hackett
Subjects: Cookery Books, Australiana, Children's Books
ISBN Publisher's Prefix: 0-7249

Bacchus Books*, 4A Alfred St, Woolwich, NSW 2110 Tel: (02) 892764
Man Dir: Boo Johnson
Orders to: Rical Enterprises Pty Ltd, GPO Box 2510, Sydney, NSW 2001
Subjects: Australia, Nonfiction, Humour
ISBN Publisher's Prefix: 0-908003

S John **Bacon** Pty Ltd, 13 Windsor Ave, PO Box 345, Mt Waverley, Victoria 3149 Tel: (03) 2773944 Cable Add: Interbac, Melbourne
Dirs: Mary Bacon, Joan Diemar, Neville Cuthbert; *Editorial:* Bert Eadon; *Sales & Marketing:* Michael T Baker
Subsidiary Company: Lantern House Pty Ltd
Subjects: Theology, Christian Education, Devotional Music, Primary and Secondary Educational Books and Aids, Children's Books
Founded: 1938
ISBN Publisher's Prefix: 0-85579

Books for Pleasure, an imprint of Lansdowne Press (qv)

Bookwise (Australia) Pty Ltd*, 104 Sussex St, Sydney 2000 Tel: 296437 Cable Add: Bookwise Sydney Telex: Naku AA 25691
Man Dir: John Redrup; *Editorial, Sales, Production:* Arthur Vella; *Publicity, Rights & Permissions:* Max Herford
Branch Off: 10/247 Riversdale Rd, Hawthorn, Vic 3123
Subjects: Oriental Arts, Social Sciences, Languages, Cooking and Quality Non-fiction generally
1978: 4 titles *Founded:* 1957
ISBN Publisher's Prefix: 0-8120

12 AUSTRALIA

Boolarong Publications, PO Box 106, Spring Hill, Queensland 4000 (Located at: 18 Little Edward St, Brisbane, Queensland 4000) Tel: 2214872 Cable Add: Pressetch
Man Dir, Sales, Publicity, Rights & Permissions: L T Padman; *Editorial:* Mrs E M Bagnall; *Production:* G A Peake
Parent Company: Boolarong Investments Pty Ltd, 8 Henry St, Ascot, Queensland 4007
Subjects: Art, Historical, Biographies, Children's Books
1978: 3 titles *1979:* 4 titles *Founded:* 1977
ISBN Publisher's Prefix: 0-908175

Michael **Booth** Publications, PO Box 66, Carnegie, Victoria 3163 Tel: 509 2333
Chief Executive: Michael Booth
Imprint: Tallboy Publications
Subject: Overland travel through Asia
1978: 1 title *Founded:* 1978
ISBN Publisher's Prefix: 0-959595902

David **Boyce** Publishing & Associates, PO Box Q187 Queen Victoria Building, Sydney, NSW (Located at: 2-4 Bellvue St, Surry Hills, NSW) Tel: 2111906/2112962
Man & Sales Dir: David Boyce; *Editorial and Rights & Permissions:* Fenella Souter; *Production:* Jan Kenyon; *Advertising Manager:* Kate Fraser
Subjects: Automotive Technical
1978: 2 titles *1979:* 2 titles *Founded:* 1975
ISBN Publisher's Prefix: 0-909682

Butterworths Pty Ltd, 586 Pacific Highway, Chatswood, NSW 2067 Tel: (02) 4123444 Telex: 22033
Man Dir: D J Jackson; *Editorial:* K Siebel; *Sales:* D Brown; *Production:* B Coats; *Rights & Permissions:* K Siebel
Parent Company: Butterworth & Co (Publishers) Ltd, UK (qv)
Branch Offs: 233 Macquarie St, Sydney NSW 2000; 343 Little Collins St, Melbourne, Vic 3000; Commonwealth Bank Bldg, King George Sq, Brisbane Q 4000; 45 St George's Terr, Perth WA 6000; Lensworth Chambers, 84 Flinders St, Adelaide, SA 5000; Canberra House, Canberra ACT 2600
Bookshops: At some Branch Office addresses
Subjects: Law, Business, Medicine, Science, Technology, Textbooks
1978: 57 titles *1979:* 39 titles *Founded:* 1910
ISBN Publisher's Prefix: 0-409

C S I R O (Commonwealth Scientific and Industrial Research Organization), 314 Albert St, PO Box 89, East Melbourne, Victoria 3002 Tel: (03) 4191333 Telex: AA30236
Shipping Add: 19 Rokeby St, Collingwood, Victoria 3066
Publisher: B J Walby; *Sales and Publicity:* Ros McLeod; *Production:* Paul Lynch
Subjects: Engineering, Science & Technology
Founded: 1926
ISBN Publisher's Prefix: 0-643

Cambridge University Press (Australia) Pty Ltd, 296 Beaconsfield Parade, Middle Park, Victoria 3206 Tel: 5340457 Cable Add: Cantabaust
Man Dir: B W Harris
Subjects: Education, University, Secondary & Primary Textbooks
Miscellaneous: Firm is a branch of Cambridge University Press, UK (qv)
ISBN Publisher's Prefix: 0-521

Carroll's Pty Ltd, 566 Hay St, GPO Box M-954, Perth, Western Australia 6001 Tel: (09) 3256377 Cable Add: Carroll's Perth Telex: AA92842
Man Dir, Rights & Permissions, Editorial: Mark R Saunders; *Production:* Maxwell J McNamara; *Publicity:* Mark R Saunders
Branch Off: 17 Mobbs Lane, Carlingford, NSW 2118
Subjects: Secondary & Primary Textbooks, Children's books, General Books
1980: 89 titles *Founded:* 1904

Bookshop: 566 Hay St, Perth, Western Australia 6001
ISBN Publisher's Prefix: 0-909994

Cassell Australia Ltd, 44 Waterloo Rd, North Ryde, NSW 2113 Tel: 8887422 Cable Add: Pachamac Sydney Telex: AA21206
Man Dir: D C Field; *Publicity:* Eleanor Brasch
Parent Company: Cassell Ltd, UK (qv)
Branch Off: 30-36 Curzon St, North Melbourne, Victoria 3051
Subjects: General Fiction, Biography, Education, Travel, History, Agriculture, Textbooks
1979: 62 titles
ISBN Publisher's Prefix: 0-7269

Cat and Fiddle Press*, PO Box 153B, Hobart, Tasmania 7001 (Located at: 81 Murray St, Hobart, Tasmania 7000) Tel: (02) 346175
Dirs: Cedric Pearce, Chris Pearce, I P Pearce
Subjects: General, Fiction

Centre Publications, PO Box 114, Saint Kilda, Melbourne 3182 (Located at: 25 Chapel St, Saint Kilda, Melbourne 3182) Tel: (03) 514608
Man Dir: Paul Sumner
Parent Company: Yoco Pty Ltd, PO Box 114, Saint Kilda, Melbourne 3182
Associate Companies: The Helen Vale Foundation (qv); The Yoga Education Centre (at above address)
Subjects: Education, Health
1978: 2 titles *1979:* 2 titles *Founded:* 1974

Challenge, an imprint of Sapphire Books Pty Ltd (qv)

Chatto, Bodley Head & Jonathan Cape Australia Pty Ltd*, Suite 816, 121 Walker St, North Sydney, NSW 2060 Tel: 9294660 Telex: 24059
Man Dir: John Cody
Orders to: Australasian Publishing Co, Corner Bridge Rd and Jersey St, Hornsby, NSW 2077
Parent Company: Chatto, Bodley Head & Jonathan Cape Ltd, UK (qv)
Subjects: Fiction, Nonfiction, Reference, History, Childrens, Australiana
Founded: 1977

Cheshire, an imprint of Longman Cheshire Pty Ltd (qv)

Chevalier Press*, PO Box 312, Moorabbin, Victoria 3189
Branch Off: PO Box 13, Kensington, NSW 2033
1978: 2 titles *1979:* 5 titles

Childerset Pty Ltd, 67 Katrina St, Blackburn North, 3130 Melbourne Tel: (03) 8775121 Cable Add: Childerset Melbourne Telex: 33571
Man Dir: Haworth H Bartram; *Sales, Publicity, Rights & Permissions:* Denise Burt; *Production:* Veronica Capper
Subjects: Juveniles, Educational Materials, Children's Picture Books, Foreign Language Picture Books, Classroom Pictures
1978: 42 titles *1979:* 10 titles *Founded:* 1970
ISBN Publisher's Prefix: 0-909404

Churchill-Livingstone, imprint of Longman Cheshire Pty Ltd (qv)

Circus Books, now Schwartz Publishing Group (Victoria) Pty Ltd (qv)

Clearway, an imprint of Sapphire Books Pty Ltd (qv)

R J **Cleary** Pty Ltd, PO Box 939, Darlinghurst, NSW 2010 (Located at: 84 Oxford Towers, Waine St, Sydney) Tel: (02) 263750 Cable Add: Clearpub Sydney Telex: 27031

Man Dir: R J Cleary
Subjects: Biography, History, How-to, Reference, Juveniles, High-priced Paperbacks, Australiana, Series Books, Part-Works, Primary and Secondary Textbooks, Educational Materials, Children's Activities, Special Projects
1979: 100 titles *1980:* 100 titles *Founded:* 1969
ISBN Publisher's Prefix: 0-85567

The **Clifford** Press, PO Box 120, Hawthorn, Victoria 3122 Tel: 810231
Shipping Add: 597 Burwood Rd, Hawthorn, Victoria
General Secretary: C K Moss; *Rights & Permissions, Publicity, Business Manager:* Alma M Widdicombe
Subjects: Religion, Juveniles, Educational Materials
Founded: 1956
ISBN Publisher's Prefix: 0-85044

Cole Publications*, 3 Creswick St, Hawthorn, Victoria 3122 Tel: 8185640
Man Dir: Cole Turnley
Parent Company: Alterns Pty Ltd, same address
Subjects: Juveniles, Technical, Humour
Founded: 1868
ISBN Publisher's Prefix: 0-909900

Collier Macmillan Australia, 44 Waterloo Rd, North Ryde, NSW 2113
Parent Company: Cassell Ltd, UK (qv)

William **Collins** Pty Ltd, 55 Clarence St, Sydney, NSW 2000 Tel: (02) 2902066 Cable Add: Folio Sydney Telex: 26292 Folio
Warehouse and Shipping Add: Yarrawa Rd, Moss Vale, NSW 2577
Chairman: K W Wilder; *Paperback Sales Dir:* A J Horgan; *Special Projects Dir, Rights & Permissions:* A S Rein; *Editorial:* Anne Ingram, Mrs E Bradhurst; *Production Dir:* J Hooker; *Publicity & Advertising:* Mrs J Garvan; *Foreign Rights:* Mrs B Potts; *Marketing Dir:* I L Morton
Parent Company: William Collins Sons & Co Ltd, UK (qv)
Branch Offs: 62 Merivale St, South Brisbane, Qld 4101; 25 Trent St, Burwood, Vic 3125; 7-9 Maple Ave, Forestville, SA 5034; Boag St, Morley, WA 6062
Subjects: General Fiction, Biography, History, How-to, Music, Art, Philosophy, Reference, Religion, Juveniles, Low- & High-priced Paperbacks, University, Secondary & Primary Textbooks
1978: 40 titles *Founded:* 1872

Community Language Children's Books, imprint of Ashton Scholastic (qv)

Compendium Pty Ltd*, RSD Birregurra South, Victoria 3242 Tel: (052) 334574
Editorial Dir, Rights & Permissions: Gregory Ket; *Sales Dir:* Penny Lane
Subjects: General, Technical, Children's
Founded: 1974
ISBN Publisher's Prefix: 0-9598495

Contempa Publications*, PO Box 68, Clifton Hill 3060 Tel: (03) 3876859
Manager: Phillip Edmonds
Subject: Poetry

Core Libraries, an imprint of Ashton Scholastic (qv)

Croft Press, see Gryphon Books Pty Ltd

Currawong Press Pty Ltd, PO Box 233, Milson's Point, NSW 2061 Tel: 9223404
Chief Executive: Phillip Mathews
Subjects: Books of general appeal, mainly by Australian writers, and mainly Non-fiction
Founded: 1946
Miscellaneous: Publishers of *The Australian Language, Australian Children's Dictionary*
ISBN Publisher's Prefix: 0-85041

Currency Press Pty Ltd, 87 Jersey Rd, Woollahra, NSW 2025 Tel: (02) 324481 Cable Add: Dramabooks, Sydney
Editorial, Rights & Permissions: Mrs K Parsons
Orders to: Cambridge University Press, 296 Beaconsfield Parade, Middle Park, Victoria
Subject: Drama, Films
1978: 27 titles *Founded:* 1971
ISBN Publisher's Prefix: 0-86937 (Currency Methuen), 0-86819

John **Currey** O'Neil Publishers Pty Ltd, 2B Frederick St, Windsor, Victoria 3181 Tel: 514251/5294259 Telex: 36472 AA
Man Dir: John Currey; *General Manager:* Geoff Currey
Associate Companies: Lloyd O'Neil Pty Ltd (qv); George Philip and O'Neil Pty Ltd
Subjects: Australian History, Art and General Nonfiction, Natural History
1978/79: 12 titles
ISBN Publisher's Prefix: 0-85902

Curriculum Development Centre, PO Box 52, Dickson, ACT 2603 Tel: 433042 Telex: Education Canberra
Man Dir: Dr Malcolm Skilbeck; *Editorial, Rights & Permissions:* Chris Makepeace
Subjects: Educational
ISBN Publisher's Prefix: 0-642

Cypress Books*, PO Box 6, Box Hill, Vic 3128 (Located at: 5 Bentley St, Surry Hills, Vic 3127) Tel: (03) 894908
Dir & Editorial: Harley Forster
Subject: Australian History

D J Davies*, 18 South Valley Rd, Highton 3216 Tel: (052) 436862
Man Dir: David J Davies

Dollar Books, an imprint of Ansay Pty Ltd (qv)

Doubleday Australia Pty Ltd, PO Box 184, Lane Cove, NSW 2066 (Located at: 14 Mars Rd, Lane Cove, NSW 2066) Tel: 4270377 Telex: 20901 Dubday
Man Dir: Peter B Madgwick; *Editorial, Rights & Permissions:* Nevill Drury; *Publishing Manager:* Robert F Stafford; *Book Club Editorial:* Suzanne Delmont; *Book Club Marketing:* John D Madgwick
Divisions: Tudor Distributors, 2A Woodcock Place, Lane Cove, NSW 2066 (distributor and wholesaler of books in Australia); Book Club Associates (operates book clubs in Australia)
Parent Company: Doubleday & Co Inc, New York, USA
Subsidiary Company: Doubleday New Zealand Ltd, New Zealand (qv)
Branch Offs: Unit 1, 57 Parkhurst Drive, Knoxfield, Vic 3180; 8 Taylors Rd, Morningside, Auckland 3, New Zealand
Subjects: General and Biographical Australian Nonfiction
Book Clubs: Doubleday Australia Pty Ltd, Book Club Associates Division (see Book Club section for individual clubs)
1978: 8 titles *1979:* 10 titles
ISBN Publisher's Prefix: 0-86824

Dove Communications Pty Ltd, PO Box 51, Caulfield East, Victoria 3145 (Located at: 203 Darling Rd, East Malvern, Victoria) Tel: (03) 2119177 Cable Add: Dovcom
Man Dir: J Garry Eastman; *Sales & Editorial:* David C Lovell
Subjects: Catholic theology, Religion, Moral Philosophy, Education
1978: 16 titles *1979:* 16 titles *Founded:* 1972
ISBN Publisher's Prefix: 0-85924

Drummond Publishing, associate company of Primary Education (Publishing) Pty Ltd (qv)

E J Dwyer (Australia) Pty Ltd*, PO Box 492, Darlinghurst, NSW 2010 (Located at: Kippax and Waterloo Streets, Surry Hills, Sydney, NSW 2010) Tel: (02) 2114533 Telex: 26883
Subjects: Educational, Religion, Nonfiction
ISBN Publisher's Prefix: 0-85574

Educational Material Aid, 10 South St, Strathfield, NSW 2135 Tel: 767962
Dir: Yvonne McBurney
Subjects: Australian History and Novels designed to improve reading skills
Bookshop: 10 South St, Strathfield, NSW 2135
1979: 2 titles *1980:* 3 titles *Founded:* 1976
ISBN Publisher's Prefix: 0-908053

Edwards & Shaw Pty Ltd*, 184 Sussex St, Sydney, NSW 2000 Tel: (02) 29 6489
Dirs: Eric Edwards, Roderick Malcolm Shaw; *Rights & Permissions:* Eric Edwards; *Publicity:* R M Shaw
Subjects: Poetry, Belles Lettres
1978: 1 title
ISBN Publisher's Prefix: 0-85551

Encyclopaedia Britannica (Australia) Inc, Britannica House, 44 Miller Street, North Sydney, NSW 2060 Tel: (02) 9224799 Telex: Enbrit AA 23044
President: H W Deweese
Parent Company: Encyclopaedia Britannica Inc, USA
Associate Company: Encyclopaedia Britannica International Ltd, UK (qv for other associate companies)
Subjects: Educational Reference, Dictionaries, Geography, Biography, Art, Science, Suitable for levels from Kindergarten to Tertiary Education, Audio Visual material and teaching aids
ISBN Publisher's Prefix: 0-909263

Era Publications, 7 Silver Crescent, Grange, South Australia 5022 Tel: (08) 3566212
Chief Executives: Rodney David Martin, Sandra Dorothy Martin
Parent Company: R D Martin Pty Ltd (at above address)
Imprint: Play to Learn
Subjects: Children's Picture Books, Educational Aids Material
1979: 2 titles *Founded:* 1972
ISBN Publisher's Prefix: 0-908507

John **Ferguson** Pty Ltd, 133 Macquarie St, Sydney, NSW 2000 Tel: 272841
Man Dir: John R Ferguson; *Editorial:* Annette Robinson; *Production:* Elisa Clarke
Orders to: McGraw-Hill Book Co P/L, 4 Barcoo St, Roseville East, NSW 2069
Subjects: Australian General & Historical
1979: 10 titles *Founded:* 1975
ISBN Publisher's Prefix: 0-909134

Fine Arts Press Pty Ltd, 34 Glenview St, Gordon, NSW 2072 Tel: 4984656/4987452 Cable Add: Imprint Sydney
Publisher: Sam Ure Smith
Subjects: Australiana and the Fine Arts, *Art and Australia* (quarterly). Also produce books for other publishers
1979: 2 titles
ISBN Publisher's Prefix: 0-86917

Gazelle Publications Pty Ltd*, PO Box 43, Sth Yarra, Victoria 3141 (Located at: 59 E Station St, Bennettswood, Melbourne, Victoria 3125) Tel: 2889363
Man Dir: John R Brook; *Editorial:* Brian L Blackwell
Subjects: Fiction and Nonfiction (mostly paperbacks)
1978: 4 titles *Founded:* 1977

Georgian House Pty Ltd, 296 Beaconsfield Parade, Middle Park, Victoria 3206 Tel: 5340457
Man Dir: Brian W Harris
Subjects: General Australian Literature
Founded: 1943
ISBN Publisher's Prefix: 0-85585

Golden Press Pty Ltd*, 2-12 Tennyson Rd, Gladesville, NSW 2111 Tel: (02) 890421 Cable Add: Goldpress Telex: AA20514
Man Dir: Hugh Richardson; *Editorial & Rights & Permissions:* Robert Coupe; *Marketing Manager:* Peter Arentz; *Export Manager:* Charles Stempf; *Production:* Dennis Creer
Subsidiary Company: Shakespeare Head Press, Australia (qv)
Branch Off: 16 Copsey Place, Avondale, Auckland, New Zealand
Subjects: Biography, History, How-to, Juveniles, Secondary & Primary Textbooks, Australiana, Nonfiction
1978: 17 titles
Miscellaneous: Associated imprints include Whitman, Australia Pty Ltd
ISBN Publisher's Prefix: 0-85558

Granada Publishing Australia Pty Ltd*, PO Box Q164, Queen Victoria Bldgs, Sydney, NSW 2000 Tel: (02) 295239 Cable Add: Granada
Dirs: W M Blanshard, W Carr, A R H Birch, E G Grigor, G Wallis-Smith; *Sales:* E G Grigor; *Publicity:* Bev Weynton
Subjects: General Books, Science, Technical Books, Yachting, Education, Juveniles, Fiction, Paperbacks
Miscellaneous: Firm is a branch of Granada Publishing, UK (qv)

Greenhouse Publications*, 'Winooka' Riverview, Calder Highway, Kyneton, 3444 Victoria Tel: (054) 222425
Man Dir: Sally R Milner
Subjects: Technical, Sociology, Educational, Children's
Founded: 1975

The **Grolier** Society of Australia Pty Ltd, PO Box 410 Crows Nest, NSW 2065 (Located at: 1 Campbell St, Artarmon, NSW 2064) Tel: (02) 4392355 Cable Add: Grolier Sydney Telex: 26584
Man Dir, Rights & Permissions: D Ashley-Wilson; *Editorial, Production:* R Appleton; *Publicity:* K Brown
Parent Company: Grolier Inc, New York, USA
Associate Companies: Grolier Inc, Canada, Latin America, UK, Europe, Africa, Far East, New Zealand; Franklin Watts Inc, USA and UK (qv)
Subsidiary Company: Australian Encyclopaedia Pty Ltd, Sydney
Subjects: Reference, Educational
Founded: 1960

Gryphon Books Pty Ltd, 106 Napier St, South Melbourne, Vic 3205 Tel: 6994541
Man Dir, Editorial, Rights & Permissions: Richard Griffin; *Sales, Publicity:* Lyn Bevan; *Production:* William Pate
Subsidiary Company: Pegasus Books (at above address)
Associate Company: Croft Press, 59 Osborne St, South Yarra, Vic 3141
Subjects: Limited Editions of Illustrated Books
1978-79: 10 titles *Founded:* 1977

Guyra Publishing Co Pty Ltd*, 25 Lang St, South Yarra, 3141 Victoria
Subjects: Pictorial Diaries of Australia, Sepik Art of New Guinea

Paul **Hamlyn** Pty Ltd, now Lansdowne Press (qv)

Harcourt Brace Jovanovich Group (Australia) Pty Ltd, PO Box 300, North Ryde, NSW 2113 (Located at: Unit E, Centrecourt, 25-27 Paul St, North Ryde, NSW 2113) Tel: 8883655 Cable Add: Jovan Telex: AA23394

Man Dir: Barry Dingley; *Editorial:* Grant Walker; *Sales:* Don Duff; *Marketing:* Don Conson; *Publicity:* Janet Taylor
Parent Company: Harcourt Brace Jovanovich Inc, 757 Third Ave, New York NY 10017, USA
Associate Companies: Academic Press Inc (London) Ltd, UK (qv); Academic Press Inc, 111 Fifth Ave, New York, NY 10003, USA; Benefic Press, 1900N Narragansett, Chicago, Illinois 60639, USA; Grune & Stratton Inc, 111 Fifth Ave, New York, NY 10003, USA; Harcourt Brace Jovanovich Ltd, UK (qv); Instructor Publications Inc, Instructor Park, Dansville, NY 14437; Johnson Reprint Corporation, 111 Fifth Ave, New York, NY 10003, USA
Branch Off: 7C/622 St Kilda Rd, Melbourne, Vic 3004
Subjects: Educational, Science, Technical, Medicine, Reprints, Trade, Audiovisual software

Hargreen Publishing Co, PO Box 4582, Melbourne, Vic 3001 (Located at: 43 Walsh St, West Melbourne, Vic 3003) Tel: 3299714
Chief Executive: Michael Haratsis, Senior; *Editorial, Production, Rights & Permissions:* Tim Morfesse; *Sales, Publicity:* Michael Haratsis, Junior
Parent Company: M and M A H Nominees Pty Ltd
Subjects: Educational and Reference
1978: 3 titles *1979:* 6 titles *Founded:* 1972
ISBN Publisher's Prefix: 0-9596696

Harper & Row (Australasia) Pty Ltd, Cnr Reserve Rd and Campbell St, PO Box 226, Artarmon, NSW 2064 Tel: 4396155 Cable Add: Bookserv
Man Dir: M L Watson; *Publishing & Marketing:* Brian Wilder; *Trade Sales:* Harry Howell; *College Sales:* Adrian McComb
Parent Company: Harper & Row Inc, New York, NY 10022, USA
Associate Companies: Editora Harper & Row do Brasil Ltda, Sao Paulo (qv), Harper & Row Ltd, UK (qv), Harper & Row Latinoamericana-Harla, Mexico (qv)

The **Hawthorn** Press Pty Ltd, Viewfield, Mt Macedon Rd, Mt Macedon, Victoria 3441 Tel: (054) 261516
Man Dir, Editorial, Production, Publicity: John Gartner; *Sales Dir:* Zelma Gartner
Subsidiary Company: The Hawthorn Publishing Co Pty Ltd (at above address)
Subjects: Belles Lettres, Poetry, Biography, History, Reference, Religion, Political, Philately, Numismatics, Ships
1978: 21 titles *1979:* 26 titles *Founded:* 1945
ISBN Publisher's Prefix: 0-7256

William **Heinemann** Australia Pty Ltd, 60 Inkerman St, St Kilda, Victoria 3182 Tel: 5340383 Cable Add: Sunlocks
Parent Company: William Heinemann Ltd, UK (qv)
Man Dir: John Burchall; *Sales Manager:* R Hellier
Subjects: General Fiction, Belles Lettres, Poetry, Biography, Juveniles, High-priced Paperbacks, History
1978: 4 titles *Founded:* 1948
ISBN Publisher's Prefix: 0-85561

Heinemann Educational Australia Pty Ltd, 85 Abinger St, PO Box 133, Richmond, Victoria 3121 Tel: (03) 4293622 Cable Add: Hebooks Melb Telex: Heaust 35347
Man Dir: Nicholas J Hudson; *Editorial:* John Kerr; *Sales Dir:* Jim Warburton; *Production:* Roger Seddon; *Publicity:* Julie Morgan; *Rights:* Jenny Atherton; *Permissions:* Jenni Dean
Parent Company: Heinemann Educational Books Ltd, UK (qv)
Branch Offs: PO Box 1050, North Sydney, NSW 2060; PO Box 365, West End, Queensland 4101
Subjects: Educational (mainly Secondary, some Primary and Tertiary), General (Drama, Politics, Law)
1978-79: 24 titles *Founded:* 1967
ISBN Publisher's Prefix: 0-85859

Heritage, an imprint of Lansdowne Press (qv)

Hicks Smith & Sons Pty Ltd, now Methuen Australia Pty Ltd (qv)

Hill of Content Publishing Co Ltd*, 86 Bourke St, Melbourne, Vic 3000 Tel: (03) 6622711 Cable Add: Colbook
Man Dir, Rights & Permissions: M G Zifcak; *Editorial:* L Gregory; *Sales:* P Shaw
Orders to: 33 Lonsdale St, Melbourne, Vic 3000
Associated Company: Collins Booksellers Pty Ltd (qv under Booksellers)
Subjects: Australiana, Archive series, Australian Literature, Educational, Politics
1979: 15 titles *Founded:* 1965
ISBN Publisher's Prefix: 0-85572

Hodder & Stoughton (Australia) Pty Ltd, 2 Apollo Pl, Lane Cove 2066 Tel: (428) 1022 Cable Add: Expositor Telex: AA24858
Man Dir: Edward Coffey; *Publishing Director, Children's Editor, Production:* Margaret Hamilton; *General Editor:* Marilyn Stacy; *Sales & Marketing:* Michael Johnson (Hardback), Stuart Smith (Paperback); *Publicity, Rights & Permissions:* Rita Spencer
Parent Company: Hodder & Stoughton Ltd, UK (qv)
Branch Offs: 5 Yertchuk Ave, Ashwood 3147; Cnr Elizabeth & Albert Sts, Brisbane 4000; Rm 1, 1121 Hay St, West Perth 6005; 95 Currie St, Adelaide 5000
Subjects: General, Fiction, Children's Books, History, Education, Dictionaries, Religion, General Science, Travel, How-to
1980: 21 titles
ISBN Publisher's Prefix: 0-340

Holt-Saunders Pty Ltd, 9 Waltham St, PO Box 154, Artarmon, NSW 2064 Tel: (02) 4393633 Cable Add: Aytcholt, Sydney Telex: 21217
Chairman of Dirs: A R Taylor; *General Managers:* L Giles (School), P Evans (College), T MacLennan (Professional); *Advertising Manager:* S Stanton; *Production:* D Huffell
Associate Company: Holt-Saunders Ltd, UK (qv for other associates)
Branch Off: 10 Moa St, Otahuhu, Auckland, New Zealand
Subject: Education
1978: 20 titles *1979:* 29 titles *Founded:* 1967
ISBN Publishers' Prefix: 0-003

Horwitz Grahame Books Pty Ltd, Horwitz Cammeray Centre, 506 Miller St, PO Box 306, Cammeray, NSW 2062 Tel: (02) 9296144 Cable Add: Horbooks Sydney Telex: Horwtz AA27833
Shipping Add: c/o Frank Cridland Pty Ltd, 154 Sussex St, Sydney, NSW 2000 (exclusive of Grahame Book Company Orders)
Man Dir: L J Moore; *Rights & Permissions:* Miss B Benjamin
Branch Off: c/o U Spalinger and Co Ltd, PO Box 765, General Post Office, Hong Kong
Subjects: General Fiction, Biography, History, How-to, Reference, Low- & High-priced Paperbacks, Secondary & Primary Textbooks, Educational Materials
Bookshops: Grahame Book Co, Bankstown Square, Bankstown 2200; Grahame Book Co, Corner Pitt & Hunter Streets, Sydney 2000; Grahame Bookshop, 17 Alfred St, Circular Quay, Sydney 2000; Grahame Book Co, MLC Building, Miller St, North Sydney 2060; Grahame Bookshop, Imperial Centre, Gosford 2250 (all in Australia)
1978: over 400 titles *Founded:* 1921
Miscellaneous: The Horwitz Group includes Martin Educational, Horwitz Publications, Scripts Publications (all at 506 Miller St, Cammeray, NSW 2062); Grahame Book Co Pty Ltd, Grahame Library & Subscription Service (a Division of Horwitz Grahame Books Pty Ltd) (both at 35-51 Mitchell St, North Sydney, NSW 2060)
ISBN Publisher's Prefixes: 0-7252 (Scripts), 0-7253 (Martin Educational), 0-7255 (Horwitz)

Hutchinson Group (Australia) Ltd, PO Box 2031, Richmond South 3121 (Located at: 30-32 Cremorne St, Richmond, Victoria 3121) Tel: (03) 4283511 Cable Add: Kahminyah Telex: AA37972
Man Dir: Otto Hofner; *Sales Dir:* Paul Jaboor; *Man Editor, Rights & Permissions:* Elizabeth Douglas; *Publicity Manager:* Christine Moone
Associate Company: The Hutchinson Publishing Group Ltd, UK (qv)
Branch Offs: 330-370 Wattle St, Ultimo, NSW 2007 (02) 2113233 Cable Add: Kahminyah Sydney; PO Box 151 Broadway 2007; 236 Elizabeth St, Brisbane 4000, Queensland; 3 Norman Rd, Roleystone, Western Australia
Subjects: Biography, History, How-to, Reference, Juveniles
1978: 28 titles *1979:* 20 titles
ISBN Publisher's Prefix: 0-09

Hyland House Publishing Pty Ltd, 10 Hyland St, South Yarra, Victoria 3141 Tel: 263813
Editorial, Rights & Permissions: Anne Godden; *Sales, Production, Publicity:* Al Knight
Orders to: Book Collective Pty Ltd, 590 Little Bourke St, Melbourne, Victoria 3000
Subjects: General Australian
1978: 6 titles *1979:* 12 titles *Founded:* 1977
ISBN Publisher's Prefix: 0-908090

Impact, an imprint of Ashton Scholastic (qv)

Inkata Press Pty Ltd, 4 Longbourne Ave, North Clayton, Victoria 3168 Tel: 5600272 Cable Add: Inkata Melbourne
Man Dir: C H Jerram; *Editor:* Patricia Sellar
Subsidiary Company: Meredith Marketing
Subjects: Science, Technology, Natural History
1978: 3 titles *1979:* 7 titles *Founded:* 1968
ISBN Publisher's Prefix: 0-909605

Island Press, PO Box R217, Royal Exchange, Sydney, NSW 2000
Man Dir: Philip Hammial
Subject: Poetry
1978: 4 titles *1979:* 4 titles *Founded:* 1973
ISBN Publisher's Prefix: 0-909771

Jacaranda Wiley Ltd, GPO Box 859, Brisbane 4001 (Located at: 65 Park Road, Milton, Queensland 4064) Tel: (07) 362755 Cable Add: Japress Telex: AA 41845
Shipping Add: 172 Robinson Road, Geebung, Queensland 4034
Man Dir: John Collins; *Publishing Manager:* Colin Cunnington; *Marketing Managers:* John Braithwaite (school, general), John Collins (college); *Production:* Alan Robbie; *Business Manager:* Quentin Smith; *Advertising:* Tom Costin; *Rights & Permissions:* Sheree Cavaye
Orders to: 65 Park Rd, Milton, Queensland 4064
Parent Company: John Wiley & Sons Inc, Publishers, 605 Third Avenue, New York, NY 10016, USA

Associate Companies: Editorial Limusa SA, Mexico (qv); Livros Tecnicos e Cientificos Editora SA, Brazil (qv); Wiley Eastern Ltd, India (qv); John Wiley & Sons Ltd, UK (qv); John Wiley & Sons Canada Ltd
Subsidiary Companies: Jacaranda Wiley (Hong Kong) Ltd, 19D, 257 Gloucester Rd, Causeway Bay, Hong Kong; Niugini Press Pty Ltd, PO Box 15, Port Moresby, Papua New Guinea
Imprints: The Jacaranda Press, Niugini Press, John Wiley & Sons
Branch Offs: 9 Massey St, Gladesville, NSW 2111; 303 Wright Street, Adelaide, SA 5000; 83 Palmerston Crescent, South Melbourne, Vic 3205; 142 Colin Street, West Perth, WA 6005 (all in Australia); 4 Kirk St, Grey Lynn, Auckland 2, New Zealand; PO Box 15, Port Moresby, Papua New Guinea
Subjects: Preschool, Primary, Secondary and Tertiary Textbooks, Atlases, Educational Multimedia Materials, General
1980: 112 titles *Founded:* 1954
ISBN Publisher's Prefix: 0-7016 (The Jacaranda Press, Niugini Press), 0-471 (John Wiley & Sons)

Kelly Books, PO Box 313, Prahran, Victoria (Located at: 590 Little Bourke St, Melbourne) Tel: (03) 679249/(02) 293911

Kookaburra Technical Publications Pty Ltd, PO Box 648, Dandenong, Vic 3175 Tel: 5600841
Man Dir, Production: Geoff Pentland; *Editorial:* Miss J Martin; *Sales:* Mr F Parks
Branch Offs: 214 Kenmark Rd, Newark, Delaware 19713, USA; 1204 Campbell St, Joliet, Illinois 60435, USA
Subject: Aviation history
1978: 3 titles *1979:* 3 titles *Founded:* 1964
ISBN Publisher's Prefix: 0-85880

L & S Publishing Co Pty Ltd, 99 Argus Street, Cheltenham, Melbourne, Victoria 3192 Tel: (03) 5506311 Cable Add: Scholib Melbourne Telex: AA 33626
A Division of L & S Educational Group
Man Dir, Rights & Permissions: Ian Stevenson; *Manager & Sales:* Brian Barratt; *Publicity, Advertising and Production:* Malcolm MacArthur
Branch Offs: Brisbane, Sydney, Orange, Canberra
Company Divisions: L & S Educational Equipment Pty Ltd, L & S School Library Service Pty Ltd, L & S Textbook & Stationery Co Pty Ltd; L & S Design Development & Export Co, L & S Map & Globe Co Pty Ltd; L & S Education & Music Centre Pty Ltd
Subjects: Secondary & Primary Textbooks, Educational Materials
1979: 28 titles *Founded:* 1963
ISBN Publisher's Prefix: 0-86898

Ladybird, an imprint of Penguin Books Australia Ltd (qv)

Allen **Lane**, an imprint of Penguin Books Australia Ltd (qv)

Lansdowne Editions, an imprint of Lansdowne Press (qv)

Lansdowne Press, 176 Creek Rd, Dee Why West, NSW 2099 Tel: (02) 9822344 Cable Add: Pleasbooks Sydney Telex: AA21546
Chief Executive: Laurie Muller; *Publishing, Production:* Warwick Jacobson; *Advertising:* Arthur Severn; *Export Sales:* National branch offices (qv)
Remainder Division: Universal Books (qv)
Parent Company: The Rigby Group (at above address)
Imprints: Books for Pleasure, Heritage, Lansdowne Editions, Lansdowne Press, Summit Books, Universal Books
Branch Offs (Australia): 14 Lansdowne St, East Melbourne, Victoria 3002; 375 Montague Rd, West End, Queensland 4101
Branch Offs (Overseas): Rigby International Ltd, 31 Airedale St, Auckland, New Zealand; Mereweather Press Inc, 598 Madison Ave, New York, NY 10022, USA; Rigby International Pty Ltd, 6th Floor, Imperial Bldgs, 56 Kingsway, London WC2, UK
Subjects: General, Children's Books, Australiana, Art, Maps, Road Guides
Miscellaneous: Formerly Paul Hamlyn Pty Ltd
ISBN Publisher's Prefix: 0-7296 (Books for Pleasure), 0-7018 (Lansdowne), 0-7271 (Summit)

The **Law** Book Co Ltd, 31 Market St, Sydney, NSW 2000 Tel: (02) 2901299 Cable Add: Asbook Telex: Asbook 27995
Man Dir: D S Lees; *Sales:* G M Smith; *Marketing Manager:* J K Leonard; *Rights & Permissions:* D S Lees; *Production:* P Finneran
Parent Company: Associated Book Publishers (Australia) Ltd (qv for associate companies)
Branch Offs: 389 Lonsdale St, Melbourne, Victoria 3000; 239 George St, Brisbane, Queensland 4000; 6 Sherwood Court, Perth, WA 6000
Subjects: Law, Accountancy, Commerce
1978: 32 titles *1979:* 44 titles
ISBN Publisher's Prefix: 0-455

Libra Books Pty Ltd, GPO Box 10, Hobart, Tasmania 7001 Tel: (002) 251479
Chief Executive, Editorial: B M Wicks; *Sales:* Sue Doobov
Orders to: PO Box 1901, Canberra, ACT 2601
Subjects: Horse racing and breeding, Legal indexes
Founded: 1972
ISBN Publisher's Prefix: 0-909619

Lonely Planet Publications Pty Ltd, PO Box 88, South Yarra, Victoria 3141 Tel: (03) 4295268
Man Dir: Tony Wheeler; *Editorial:* Maureen Wheeler; *Sales:* Andy Nielson; *Production:* Jim Hart
Branch Off: 15 Heatherway, Crowthorne, Berks RG11 6HG, UK
Subject: Travel guides
1978: 7 titles *1979:* 6 titles *Founded:* 1973
ISBN Publisher's Prefixes: 0-9598080, 0-908086

Longman Cheshire Pty Ltd, Longman Cheshire House, 346 St Kilda Rd, Melbourne, Victoria 3004 Tel: 699 1522 Cable Add: Miscellany Melbourne Telex: AA 33501
Parent Company: Longman Group Ltd, UK (qv)
Man Dir: W P Kerr; *Editorial:* N J Ryan; *Sales Manager:* F R Priatel; *Rights & Permissions:* Mrs E Moody, N J Ryan; *Production:* P H R Hylands; *Publicity:* M Maslin
Orders to: Penguin Books Australia, 487 Maroondah Highway, Ringwood, Victoria 3134
Imprints: Cheshire, Churchill-Livingstone, Oliver & Boyd
Branch Offs: 33 Cooper St, Surry Hills, NSW 2010; 139 Merivale St, South Brisbane, Queensland 4101; 105 Gouger St, Adelaide, SA 5000; CWA Ho, 1174 Hay St, West Perth, WA 6005
Subjects: Educational (Primary, Secondary, Tertiary, Medical Textbooks)
1978: 43 titles *1979:* 61 titles *Founded:* 1976 (formed by merger of Longman Australia Pty Ltd and Cheshire Publishing Pty Ltd)
ISBN Publisher's Prefixes: 0-582, 0-7015

Lothian Publishing Company Pty Ltd, 4-12 Tattersalls Lane, Melbourne, Victoria 3000 Tel: (03) 6634976 Cable Add: Thorough Telex: Tcloth AA30333
Man Dir: Louis A Lothian; *Sales Director:* Peter H Lothian; *Publicity:* Sue Armstrong
Associate Company: Thomas C Lothian Pty Ltd (at above address)
Branch Offs: 146 Sussex Street, Sydney, NSW 2000; c/o All Book Agencies, 11 Bishop Street, Kelvin Grove, Q'ld 4059; 139 Gilles St, Adelaide, SA 5000; c/o Graden Enterprises, 56 Twelfth Ave, Armadale, WA 6112; New Zealand: 88 Nelson Street, Auckland 1, NZ
Subjects: How-to, Juveniles, Agriculture, Local history, Non-fiction
1978: 7 titles *1979:* 8 titles *Founded:* 1910
ISBN Publisher's Prefix: 0-85091

Lowden Publishing Co, Lowdens Rd, Kilmore, Victoria 3601 Tel: (057) 821118 Cable Add: Lowden, Kilmore
Man Dir: Jim Lowden
Subjects: Biography, History, Reference, Religion, Transport
1979: 6 titles *1980:* 6 titles *Founded:* 1969
ISBN Publisher's Prefix: 0-909706

M C A, an imprint of Macmillan Co of Australia Pty Ltd (qv)

McGraw-Hill Book Co Australia Pty Ltd, 4 Barcoo St, Roseville East, NSW 2069 Tel: (02) 4064288 Telex: 20849
Man Dir, Rights & Permissions: D J Pegrem; *General Manager Service:* J H Fowlstone; *Production:* M Bagnato
Parent Company: McGraw-Hill Inc, USA
Subjects: Technology, Management, Educational, Professional & Reference, General Interest, Secondary Textbooks
1978: 39 titles *1979:* 54 titles
ISBN Publisher's Prefix: 0-07

The **Macmillan** Co of Australia Pty Ltd, 107 Moray St, Locked Bag 12, South Melbourne, Victoria 3205 Tel: (03) 6998922 Cable Add: Scriniaire Melbourne Telex: AA34454
Man Dir: Brian Stonier; *Editorial* (General Books): John Ross, (Educational): John Rolfe; *Sales* (General Books): Peter Phillips, (Educational): Trevor Paparella; *Production:* George Smith; *Publicity* (General Books): Garth Britton, (Educational): Colin Wood; *Rights & Permissions* (General Books): John Ross; (Educational): Ann Paterson, (Serialization): Garth Britton
Parent Company: Macmillan London Ltd, UK
Associated Companies: Refer to Macmillan London Ltd, UK (qv)
Subsidiary Company: Sun Books Pty Ltd, Australia (qv)
Imprints: MCA, SUN
Branch Offs: Unit 4, 6 George Pl, Artarmon, NSW 2064; PO Box 587, South Brisbane, Queensland 4101; 9 Hackney Rd, Hackney, South Australia 5069; 44 Irvine Rd, Bayswater, WA 6053
Subjects: General Fiction, Biography, History, Music, Art, Religion, Juveniles, Paperbacks, Engineering, General & Social Sciences, University, Secondary & Primary Textbooks
Bookshops: Mary Martin Bookshop Pty Ltd, 68 Grenfell St, Adelaide South Australia; Canberra Arcade, Alinga St, Canberra, ACT; 269 Swanston St, Melbourne, Victoria; York St, Sydney, New South Wales
1978: 140 titles *1979:* 201 titles *Founded:* 1965
ISBN Publisher's Prefix: 0-333

McNamara's Books, an imprint of Second Back Row Press Pty Ltd (qv)

McPhee Gribble Publishers Pty Ltd, 203 Drummond St, Carlton, Victoria 3053 Tel: (03) 3477428 Telex: AA 33626
Principals: H J McPhee, D M Gribble
Subject: Nonfiction Paperbacks, Children's Fiction and Nonfiction, Australian Fiction
1978: 8 titles *Founded:* 1975
ISBN Publisher's Prefix: 0-86914

Martin Educational, see Horwitz Grahame Books Pty Ltd

Martindale Press, associate company of A H & A W Reed Pty Ltd (qv)

Mead & Beckett Publishing, 139 Macquarie St, Sydney, NSW 2000 Tel: 277251 Cable Add: Meadbeck Sydney Telex: AA23406
Chief Executives: Barbara Beckett, Rod Mead
Parent Company: Mead & Beckett Pty Ltd (at above address)
Subjects: Hardback popular illustrated General Books, mostly adult and mostly about Australia
1978: 10 titles *1979:* 9 titles *Founded:* 1978
Miscellaneous: Co-publishers and packagers

Melbourne University Press, PO Box 278, Carlton South, Victoria 3053 Tel: (03) 3473455 Cable Add: Mupress
Shipping Add: 138 Cardigan St, Carlton, Victoria 3053
Dir: P A Ryan; *Rights & Permissions:* Miss S A Hardiman; *Production:* P Jones
Branch Off: A W Sheppard, Room 43, 4th Floor, 104 Bathurst St, Sydney, NSW 2000
Subjects: Belles Lettres, Poetry, Biography, History, Music, Art, Philosophy, Reference, Paperbacks, Medicine, Psychology, Engineering, General & Social Sciences, University & Secondary Textbooks
Bookshop: University Bookroom, University of Melbourne, PO Box 278, Carlton South, Victoria 3053
1978: 31 titles *1979:* 29 titles *Founded:* 1922
ISBN Publisher's Prefix: 0-522

Methuen Australia Pty Ltd, Saint Martins Tower, 31 Market St, Sydney, NSW 2000 Tel: (02) 2902999 Cable Add: Sydney Asbook
(For personnel see Associated Book Publishers (Aust) Ltd)
Parent Company: Associated Book Publishers (Australia) Ltd (qv for associate companies)
Branch Offs: Cnr Allenby and Leichhardt St, Brisbane, Queensland 4000; 610-612 Church St, Richmond, Vic 3121
Subjects: Education, General, Juveniles
ISBN Publisher's Prefix: 0-454

Minerva's Express*, PO Box 71, Beaconsfield 2014 Tel: 6988013
Man Dir: D Hunter; *Editorial, Production:* J Power; *Sales, Publicity, Rights & Permissions:* P Henderson
Subject: Photographic Dictionary/Travel Aid in 12 languages
1979: 4 titles *Founded:* 1979

Modern Teaching Aids Pty Ltd, 26-28 Chard Rd, PO Box 608, Brookvale 2100 Tel: 9392355 Telex: Teaid 27109
Branch Off: Evandale Rd, Malvern 3144
Subject: Educational Books

Mullaya Publications*, 17 Griott St, PO Box 54, Canterbury, Victoria 3126 Tel: 839300
Man Dir: M C Sayers
Subjects: History, Biography
Founded: 1972
ISBN Publisher's Prefix: 0-85914

Nadjuri Australia, PO Box 102, Stansbury, SA 5582 Tel: (088) 524281
Manager, Editor: Nancy Robinson-Whittle
Subjects: Social & Folk History, Social Issues, Crafts
1978-79: 4 titles *Founded:* 1976
ISBN Publisher's Prefix: 0-909

National Library of Australia, Parkes Pl, Parkes, Canberra, ACT 2600 Tel: (062) 621111 Cable Add: Natlibaust Canberra Telex: 62100
Dir: A T Bolton; *Editor:* Ms J Stewart; *Publications Officer:* D Brown
Orders to: Australia and New Zealand Book Co Pty Ltd, 23 Cross St, Brookvale, NSW 2100
Subjects: National bibliographical publications, publications based on materials in the Library's collections
1979: 96 titles *Founded:* 1960
ISBN Publisher's Prefix: 0-642

Thomas **Nelson** Australia, 19-39 Jeffcott St, West Melbourne, Victoria 3003 Tel: 329 5199 Cable Add: Thonelson Melbourne Telex: 33088
Man Dir: B Rivers; *Trade Editorial:* R Sessions; *Educational Editorial:* R Andersen; *Trade Sales:* J Attenborough; *Mass Market Paperback Sales:* J Smith; *Educational Sales:* D Nancarrow; *Production:* K Yendell; *Trade Publicity:* D Goss; *Educational Publicity:* E Curtain; *Paperback Publicity:* M Adams; *Rights & Permissions:* E McDonald
Parent Company: International Thomson Organisation Ltd (Canada)
Associated Companies: Bowmar/Noble Inc, USA; Hamish Hamilton Ltd, UK (qv); Michael Joseph Ltd, UK (qv); Thomas Nelson & Sons (Canada) Ltd, Canada; Thomas Nelson & Sons Ltd, UK (qv); Sphere Books Ltd, UK (qv); Pelham Books Ltd, UK (qv); The Rainbird Publishing Group Ltd, UK (qv); TBL Book Services Ltd, UK; Thomas Nelson (Nigeria) Ltd, Nigeria (qv)
Branch Offs: 7th Floor, Dunstan Ho, 236 Elizabeth St, Brisbane 4000; 89-97 Jones St, Ultimo 2007; Rooms 305-306, Orlit Ho, 95 Currie St, Adelaide 5000
Subjects: Fiction, General Non-fiction, Juveniles, Mass Market Paperbacks, History, Gardening; Educational: Reading programmes, Primary and Secondary Texts
1978: 66 titles *1979:* 107 titles
ISBN Publisher's Prefix: 0-17

New Australian Library Pty Ltd*, 104 George St, Hornsby NSW 2077 Tel: 01061/4762282 Telex: 21332
Subjects: Books by the World's most read authors (including Paperback); Publishers and Distributors of Part Works

New South Wales University Press Ltd, PO Box 1, Kensington, NSW 2033 Tel: (02) 6630351 ext 3503/3547/3587
General Manager: D S Howie
Subjects: Biography, History, How-to, Philosophy, Reference, Engineering, General & Social Science, University and College Textbooks
Bookshop: College Shop, George St, Sydney
1980: 18 titles *Founded:* 1961
ISBN Publisher's Prefix: 0-86840

Nimaroo Publishers, PO Box 2046, Wollongong 2500 Tel: (042) 292297
Manager & Publicity: Stephen Standish; *Editorial:* P Balnaves; *Sales:* T Balnaves; *Production:* M Standish; *Rights & Permissions:* N Standish
Branch Off: 2/42 Park St, Como 6152, Western Australia
Subjects: Commercial, Scientific
1978: 2 titles *1979:* 3 titles *Founded:* 1978
ISBN Publisher's Prefix: 0-9596525

Van **Nostrand** Reinhold Australia Pty Ltd, 17 Queen St, PO Box 53, Mitcham, Victoria 3132 Tel: (03) 8741469 Telex: AA35877
Man Dir: Mark A Tucker
Parent Company: Litton Educational Publishing Inc, New York, USA
Associate Companies: American Book Co, New York, USA; D Van Nostrand Co, USA; Delmar Publishers, Albany, New York, USA; McCormick-Mathers Publishing Co, New York, USA; Van Nostrand Reinhold Co, UK (qv), USA, Canada
Subjects: Educational, Art and Craft, General Interest
1978: 9 titles *Founded:* 1967
ISBN Publisher's Prefix: 0-442

Anne **O'Donovan** Pty Ltd*, 203 Drummond St, Carlton, Vic 3053 Tel: (03) 3470313
Man Dir: Anne O'Donovan
Subject: Adult Non-fiction
1979: 2 titles *Founded:* 1978
ISBN Publisher's Prefix: 0-908476

Oliver & Boyd, an imprint of Longman Cheshire Pty Ltd (qv)

Lloyd **O'Neil** Pty Ltd, 19 Hornby Street, Windsor, Victoria 3181 Tel: 511325 Cable Add: Windsorpub Windsor Telex: Hornby AA36472
Chairman: Lloyd O'Neil; *Man Dir:* Sue Donovan
Associated Companies: John Currey O'Neil Publishers Pty Ltd (qv); George Philip and O'Neil Pty Ltd; Blond Pty Ltd
Subjects: Educational, Primary & Secondary Atlases, Australiana
ISBN Publisher's Prefix: 0-85550

Outback Press Pty Ltd, now Schwartz Publishing Group (Victoria) Pty Ltd (qv)

Oxford University Press, GPO Box 2784Y, Melbourne, Victoria 3001 (Located at: 7 Bowen Crescent, Melbourne, Victoria) Tel: (03) 263748 Cable Add: Oxonian Melbourne Telex: 35330
General Manager: David Cunningham; *Sales:* James Walker; *Publicity:* Mandy Parry-Jones
Parent Company: Oxford University Press, UK (qv)
Subjects: Nonfiction, Juveniles
ISBN Publisher's Prefix: 0-19

Pacific Publications (Australia) Pty Ltd, GPO Box 3408, Sydney, NSW 2001 (Located at: 76 Clarence Street, Sydney, 2000) Tel: (02) 296693 Cable Add: Pacpub Telex: 21242
Manager: John Berry; *Editor-in-Chief:* John McDonald
Parent Company: The Herald and Weekly Times of Melbourne
Branch Off: Pacific Publications, Herald & Weekly Times Bldg, 61 Flinders Lane, Melbourne, Victoria
Subjects: Pacific Island Subjects — General & Reference, Australian Agricultural/Technical Handbooks, *Pacific Islands Yearbook*, *Papua New Guinea Handbook*
Founded: 1930
ISBN Publisher's Prefix: 0-85807

Pan Books (Australia) Pty Ltd, 1 Castlereagh St, Sydney, NSW 2000 Tel: (02) 2328150 Telex: 70157
Chief Executive: Lyndsay Brown
Orders to: William Collins Book Distributors Pty Ltd, 55 Clarence St, Sydney, NSW 2000
Parent Company: Pan Books Ltd, UK (qv)
Imprints: Picador, Piccolo
Subjects: Fiction, General Literature, Children's Books, Reference, Technical, Educational
Founded: 1979
ISBN Publisher's Prefix: 0-330

Pegasus Books, see Gryphon Books Pty Ltd

Pelican, an imprint of Penguin Books Australia Ltd (qv)

Penguin Books Australia Ltd, 487 Maroondah Highway, PO Box 257, Ringwood, Victoria 3134 Tel: (03) 8703444 Cable Add: Penguinook Melbourne Telex: AA32458
Man Dir: T D Glover; *Publishing Dir:* B Johns
Associate Companies: Penguin Books Ltd, UK (qv); Viking-Penguin Inc, USA; Penguin Books (NZ) Ltd, NZ; Penguin Books Canada Ltd, Canada
Imprints: Allen Lane, Pelican, Puffin, Ladybird
Subjects: Low & high-priced Paperbacks, Juveniles
1978: 30 titles *1979:* 20 titles
ISBN Publisher's Prefix: 0-14

Pergamon Press (Australia) Pty Ltd, 19A Boundary St, Rushcutters Bay, NSW 2011 Tel: (02) 318211 Telex: Pergap AA27458
Dirs: Jerry Mayer (Managing), I R Maxwell (Chairman), R McLeod; *Editorial:* Gillian Hewitt, Beverley Barnes; *Sales Manager:* Ken Woods; *Publicity:* Dana Lundmark; *Rights & Permissions:* Jerry Mayer
Sales Offs: Melbourne, Sydney
Subjects: Reference, Medicine, Psychology, Engineering, General & Social Science, University, Secondary & Primary Textbooks, Educational Materials, High-priced Paperbacks
1978: 26 titles *1979:* 23 titles *Founded:* 1968
ISBN Publisher's Prefix: 0-80

Picador, an imprint of Pan Books (Australia) Pty Ltd (qv)

Piccolo, an imprint of Pan Books (Australia) Pty Ltd (qv)

Pinchgut Press, 6 Oaks Ave, Cremorne, NSW 2090 Tel: 905548
Chief Executives: Marjorie Pizer, Anne Spencer Parry
Subjects: Poetry, Fiction
1978: 1 title *1979:* 2 titles *Founded:* 1947
ISBN Publisher's Prefix: 09598913

Pioneer Design Studio Pty Ltd, North Rd, Lilydale, Victoria 3140 Tel: (03) 735 5020
Man Dir: Derrick I Stone; *General Manager:* Carolyn R Stone
Subjects: History, Nature, Gardening
1979-80: 3 titles

Pitman Publishing Pty Ltd, 158 Bouverie St, Carlton, Victoria 3053 Tel: (03) 3473055 Cable Add: Fono Telex: 30107
Man Dir: Philip Harris; *Editorial & Rights & Permissions:* Tudor Day; *Marketing:* Sandy Grant; *Sales:* Sylvia Hobbs; *Production:* Brian Howlett; *Publicity & Advertising:* Peta Landman
Associate Company: Pitman Publishing Ltd, UK (qv)
Subjects: How-to, Music, Art, High-priced Paperbacks, Medicine, Engineering, Social Science, University, Secondary & Primary Textbooks, Educational Materials, General
1978: 53 titles *1979:* 39 titles *Founded:* 1913
ISBN Publisher's Prefix: 0-85896

Play to Learn, an imprint of Era Publications (qv)

The **Polding** Press, 343 Elizabeth St, Melbourne, Victoria 3000 Tel: (03) 671740/675157
Chief Executive: John A Phillips SJ; *Sales Dir:* Marie-Thérèse Hilton
Subjects: Biography, History, Religion, High-priced Paperbacks, Secondary Textbooks
Bookshop: Central Catholic Library Bookshop, 343 Elizabeth St, Melbourne, Victoria 3000
1979: 3 titles *1980:* 6 titles *Founded:* 1968

Miscellaneous: Promotional and Wholesale marketing consortium formed in 1976 with Chevalier Press, Sydney, and Spectrum Publications, Melbourne, handling 90 titles

Prentice-Hall of Australia Pty Limited, 7 Grosvenor Place, Brookvale, NSW 2100 Tel: (02) 9391333 Cable Add: Prenhall Sydney
Man Dir: Patrick F Gleeson; *Editorial:* Charles Lucas; *Australian Marketing Manager:* James McGrath; *Publicity:* W Evans; *Rights & Permissions:* Mary Ward
Parent Company: Prentice Hall International, UK (qv for other associates)
Branch Off: 209 Glenhuntly Rd, Elsternwick, Vic 3185
Subjects: Elementary, Secondary and University Textbooks, Trade, Professional Reference, Art, Technical, Management, Medicine, Business, Nursing
ISBN Publisher's Prefix: 0-7248

Primary Education (Publishing) Pty Ltd, PO Box 150, East Melbourne, Victoria 3002 (Located at: 2 The Crofts, Richmond, Victoria 3121) Tel: 4294822 Telex: 35347
Publishers: Don Drummond, Sheila Drummond
Associate Companies & Imprints: Drummond Publishing; Primary Education Pty Ltd
Subjects: Education, Teacher reference, Politics
1978: 15 titles *1979:* 20 titles *Founded:* 1975
ISBN Publisher's Prefix: 0-909081

Prism Books (Poetry Society of Australia), Box N110 Grosvenor Street PO, Sydney 2000, NSW Tel: (02) 9602304
Business Manager: Robert Adamson
Subjects: Art, Poetry (Commercial & Collector's Editions), Art, Music, Photography
1978: 2 titles *1979:* 5 titles *Founded:* 1952
ISBN Publisher's Prefix: 0-909081

Puffin, an imprint of Penguin Books Australia Ltd (qv)

Quartet Books Australia Pty Ltd, 10 Hyland St, South Yarra, Victoria 3141 Tel: 263813 Telex: AA30934
Editorial, Rights & Permissions: Anne Godden; *Sales, Production, Publicity:* Al Knight
Orders to: Book Collective Pty Ltd, 590 Little Bourke St, Melbourne, Victoria 3000
Subjects: General Australian
1978: 6 titles *1979:* 6 titles *Founded:* 1978
ISBN Publisher's Prefix: 0-908128

Ragman Productions*, PO Box 54, Clifton Hill, Victoria 3068 (Located at: 24 Urquhart St, Northcote, Victoria 3070) Tel: (03) 4893925
Owner, Editorial, Rights & Permissions: Robert Kenny; *Sales, Publicity:* Retta Hemensley; *Production:* D O'Layshon
Imprint: Rigmarole of the Hours
Subjects: Innovative Fiction, Literary Criticism, Poetry
1978: 4 titles *1979:* 3 titles *Founded:* 1974
ISBN Publisher's Prefix: 0-909229

Reader's Digest Services Pty Ltd, GPO Box 4353, Sydney (Located at: 26-32 Waterloo St, Surry Hills, NSW 2010) Tel: (02) 6990111 Cable Add: Readigest Sydney
Man Dir: M Maton; *Editorial:* Barbara Ker Wilson (Condensed Books), Nelson Kenny (Other Books); *Product Managers:* Richard Watson (Condensed Books), Sandra Step (Other Books)
Subjects: Condensed books, Reference, Educational, General
ISBN Publisher's Prefix: 0-909486

Read It Again, an imprint of Ashton Scholastic (qv)

Real Life, an imprint of Ashton Scholastic (qv)

A H & A W Reed Pty Ltd, PO Box 126, Terry Hills, NSW 2084 Tel: (02) 4502555 Cable Add: Reedkoala Terrey Hills Telex: AA 27212 Reedoz
Man Dir, Rights & Permissions: Mrs E J Reed; *Marketing Dir:* K White; *Publisher & Editorial:* W A Reed; *Production:* B E Robson
Parent Company: A H & A W Reed Ltd, New Zealand (qv)
Associate Company: Martindale Press Pty Ltd
Subjects: Books on Australia, General Non-fiction
1978: 120 titles *1979:* 120 titles *Founded:* 1964
ISBN Publisher's Prefix: 0-589

Review Publications Pty Ltd, 1 Sterling St, Dubbo, NSW 2830 Tel: (068) 823283
Man Dir: William Hornadge
Subjects: Philatelic catalogues and handbooks, Australian history
1978: 14 titles *1979:* 13 titles *Founded:* 1947
ISBN Publisher's Prefix: 0-909895

Richmond Hill Press, 195 Bridge Rd, Richmond, Vic 3121 Tel: (03) 4295575
Man Dir, Editorial: John Curtain; *Sales, Publicity:* Peter Steer; *Production:* Michelle Johnston
Subjects: Limited Editions, Natural History, Australiana, Art
1978: 2 titles *1979:* 5 titles *Founded:* 1978
ISBN Publisher's Prefix: 0-908157

Rigby Publishers Ltd*, PO Box 104, Norwood, South Australia 5067 Tel: (08) 2235566 Cable Add: Rigbylim Telex: 88090
Chief Executive: Neil Balnaves; *Editorial:* M F Page, J D Gilder, Mrs D Adamek; *Marketing Manager:* Paul Harris; *Rights & Permissions:* J Hart; *Export:* M F Page
Orders to: 30 North Terrace, Kent Town, South Australia 5067
Parent Company: The Rigby Group, 176 Creek Rd, Dee Why West, NSW 2099
Branch Offs (Australia): 14 Lansdowne St, East Melbourne, Victoria 3002; 375 Montague Rd, West End, Queensland 4101
Branch Offs (Overseas): Rigby International Ltd, 31 Airedale St, Auckland, New Zealand; Mereweather Press Inc, 598 Madison Ave, New York, NY 10022, USA; Rigby International Pty Ltd, 6th Floor, Imperial Bldgs, 56 Kingsway, London WC2, UK
Subjects: General Fiction, Australiana, History, How-to, Art, Reference, Juveniles, Low- and High-priced Paperbacks, Secondary & Primary Textbooks, Educational Materials
Bookshop: Rigby Ltd, 24 James Pl, Adelaide, South Australia 5000
1978: 280 titles *Founded:* 1859
ISBN Publisher's Prefix: 0-85179, 0-7270

Rigmarole of the Hours, an imprint of Ragman Productions (qv)

Robin Books, PO Box 355, Wynyard, Tasmania 7321 Tel: (004) 422025
Man Dir, Editorial, Sales, Rights & Permissions: Barney Roberts; *Production, Publicity:* Bruce McM Roberts
Subjects: Poetry, Short Stories
1978: 1 title *1979:* 1 title *Founded:* 1976
ISBN Publisher's Prefix: 0-908030

Roebuck Books*, Dr J S Cumpston, 42 Araba St, Aranda, ACT 2614 Tel: 513284
Man Dir: J S Cumpston
Subject: Australian History
1978: 5 titles *Founded:* 1970

ISBN Publisher's Prefixes: 0-9500858, 0-909434

Sapphire Books Pty Ltd, PO Box 222, Strathfield, NSW 2135 (Located at: 21 Redmyre Rd, Strathfield, NSW 2135) Tel: 7641115/7631577
Man Dir: J Franklin
Imprints: Challenge, Clearway
Subjects: School textbooks, Study guides
1980: 44 titles *Founded:* 1971
ISBN Publisher's Prefixes: 0-909286, 0-85861

Schwartz Publishing Group (Victoria) Pty Ltd, 126 Wellington Parade, East Melbourne, Victoria 3002 Tel: (03) 4198644 Cable Add: Circus Melbourne Telex: Circus AA37222
Man Dir, Editor-in-Chief: Morry Schwartz; *Publicity Dir:* Margaret Gee
Imprint: Unicorn Books
Subjects: Fiction, Non-fiction
1980: 30 titles *Founded:* 1979
ISBN Publisher's Prefix: 0-86753 (Schwartz), 0-86757 (Unicorn)

Science Research Associates Pty Ltd, 82-84 Waterloo Rd, North Ryde, NSW 2113 Tel: (02) 8887833 Cable Add: Sciresant North Ryde Telex: AA70185
Man Dir, Rights & Permissions: R J Barton; *Editorial:* R W Duncan; *Sales:* C Trew; *Advertising:* R W Duncan; *Production:* W Kavanagh
Associate Company: Science Research Associates Ltd, UK (qv for other associates)
Subjects: Primary, Secondary, Tertiary & Other Textbooks, Multimedia Learning Systems
ISBN Publisher's Prefix: 0-574

Scripts Publications, see Horwitz Grahame Books Pty Ltd

Second Back Row Press Pty Ltd, PO Box 43, Leura, NSW 2060
Man Dirs: Tom Whitton, Wendy Whitton
Imprints include: McNamara's Books (social & political reprints)
Subjects: Alternative Lifestyles, Technology, Politics, Education, Juveniles
1978: 4 titles *1979:* 7 titles *Founded:* 1973
ISBN Publisher's Prefix: 0909-325

Shakespeare Head Press*, 2-12 Tennyson Rd, Gladesville, NSW 2111 Tel: (89) 0421 Cable Add: Goldpress
Man Dir: Hugh Richardson; *Marketing Manager:* P Arentz; *Editorial and Rights & Permissions:* R Coupe
Parent Company: Golden Press Pty Ltd (qv)
Subjects: Secondary & Primary Textbooks
1978: 7 titles
ISBN Publisher's Prefix: 0-85558

Sorrett Publishing Pty Ltd*, 1227 Malvern Rd, PO Box 94, Malvern 3144 Tel: (03) 205486
Man Dir: Ian Coghill
Subjects: General, Secondary Textbooks, Educational Materials
Founded: 1972
ISBN Publisher's Prefix: 0-909752

South Head Press, Market Place, Berrima, NSW 2577 Tel: (048) 771384
Man Dir: Grace Perry; *Sales & Publicity:* John Millet
Subjects: Poetry & Criticism
Founded: 1964
ISBN Publisher's Prefix: 0-901760

Spectrum Publications Pty Ltd, PO Box 75, Richmond, Victoria 3121 (Located at: 127 Burnley Street, Richmond) Tel: 4291404
Man Dir: H Rohr; *Editorial:* Irene Aili; *Sales:* M Peters; *Publicity:* Henry Rohr
Subjects: Religion, Australiana, Art
1978: 7 titles *1979:* 8 titles
ISBN Publisher's Prefix: 0-909837

Sugar and Snails Books, see Women's Movement Children's Literature Co-op Ltd

Summit Books, an imprint of Lansdowne Press (qv)

Sun Books Pty Ltd, 107 Moray St, South Melbourne, Victoria 3205 Tel: (03) 6998922 Cable Add: Sunbooks Telex: AA 34454
Man Dir: Brian Stonier; *Sales Dir, Rights & Permissions:* Peter Phillips
Parent Company: The Macmillan Co of Australia Pty Ltd (qv)
Subjects: General Fiction, Poetry, Biography, History, Music, Art, Philosophy, Reference, Low- & High-priced Paperbacks
1978: 50 titles *1979:* 60 titles
ISBN Publisher's Prefix: 0-7251

Sydney University Press, Press Bldg, University of Sydney, Sydney, NSW 2006 Tel: (02) 6604997 Cable Add: Sydpress
Dir: Malcolm Titt; *Deputy Director (Design & Production):* David New; *Editor:* Lesley Glaysher
Subjects: Scholarly Books, University Textbooks
1978: 19 titles *1979:* 18 titles *Founded:* 1964
ISBN Publisher's Prefix: 0-424

Tallboy Publications, an imprint of Michael Booth Publications (qv)

D W **Thorpe** Pty Ltd, 384 Spencer St, Melbourne, Victoria 3003 Tel: (03) 3295288 (3 lines) Cable Add: Bookstat
Man Dir, Production, Rights & Permissions, Editorial: Joyce Nicholson; *General Manager, Sales, Advertising Manager:* Pat White
Subject: Reference
1978: 3 titles *1979:* 8 titles *Founded:* 1921
ISBN Publisher's Prefix: 0-909532

Transworld Publishers (Australia) Pty Ltd*, 3 Bowen Crescent, Melbourne, Victoria 3004 Tel: (03) 263679 Cable Add: Transcable Telex: 33808
Sales & Marketing Dir: A Boardman
Associate Company: Transworld Publishers Ltd, UK (qv for other associates)
Subjects: Paperbacks, General, Fiction, Educational, Juveniles

Turton and Armstrong, 21 Lister St, Wahroonga, NSW 2076 Tel: 485524
Publisher: Paul Armstrong
Associate Company: Westbooks Pty Ltd (qv)
Subjects: Industrial Archaeology, Special Interest, Technical
1979: 4 titles *1980:* 4 titles *Founded:* 1977
ISBN Publisher's Prefix: 0-908031

Unicorn Books, an imprint of Schwartz Publishing Group (Victoria) Pty Ltd (qv)

Universal Books, an imprint of Lansdowne Press (qv)

University of New South Wales, now New South Wales University Press (qv)

University of Queensland Press, PO Box 42, St Lucia, Queensland 4067 Tel: (072) 3772127 Telex: Unnqld Press AA40315
Manager: Frank W Thompson; *Editorial:* Merril E Yule, D'Arcy Randall; *Sales:* Malcolm Beazley; *Publicity & Advertising:* Kym Madden; *Rights & Permissions:* Merril E Yule; *Production:* Cyrelle Birt
Subjects: Belles Lettres, Poetry, Biography, History, Music, Art, Philosophy, Reference, Religion, Low- & High-priced Paperbacks, Medicine, Psychology, Engineering, General & Social Science, University & Secondary Textbooks, Educational Materials
Bookshop: University Bookshop, University of Queensland, St Lucia, Queensland 4067
1979: 60 titles *1980:* 60 titles *Founded:* 1948
ISBN Publisher's Prefix: 0-7022

University of Western Australia Press, Nedlands, Western Australia 6009 Tel: (092) 3803182 Cable Add: Uniwest Perth
Manager, Rights & Permissions, Production: V S Greaves; *Editorial:* F A Brodalka, Mrs N Zeffertt; *Sales, Promotion:* A Kane
Subjects: Literary Criticism, Biological Sciences, Biography, History, Music, Art, Philosophy, Reference, Religion, Social Sciences, University & Secondary Textbooks
1978: 21 titles *1979:* 30 titles *Founded:* 1954
ISBN Publisher's Prefix: 0-85564

V C T A Publishing Pty Ltd*, 304 Nicholson St, Fitzroy, Victoria 3065 Tel: 4191066
Director: John Brooke; *Editorial:* Ian Horton
Parent Company: Victorian Commercial Teachers' Association
Subjects: Educational textbooks and teacher guides in Accountancy, Economics, Commercial and Legal Studies, Consumer Education, Secretarial Studies, General Business Education
1978: approx 27 titles *Founded:* 1953
ISBN Publisher's Prefix: 0-86859

The Helen **Vale** Foundation, PO Box 114, Saint Kilda, Melbourne, Victoria 3182 (Located at: 12 Chapel St, East Saint Kilda, Melbourne 3182) Tel: (03) 519861
Executive Dir: Kenneth J Ingbritsen
Associate Company: Centre Publications (qv)
Subjects: Education, Health
1979: 2 titles *Founded:* 1970
ISBN Publisher's Prefix: 0-909698

Visa Books, an imprint of Widescope International Publishers Pty Ltd (qv)

Visuals of the Australian Environment, an imprint of Ashton Scholastic (qv)

Was Is Press, PO Box 2, Moreland 3058 Tel: (03) 3863166
Proprietor: Yvonne Rousseau

Wentworth Books Pty Ltd, 48 Cooper St, Surry Hills, NSW 2010 Tel: 697286
Dirs: Walter W Stone, Walter P Stone
Associate Companies: Stone Printing Co Pty Ltd, Wentworth Press Pty Ltd
Subjects: Australian History, Literature, Biography, Educational, Bibliography
ISBN Publisher's Prefix: 0-85587

Westbooks Pty Ltd, 16 Gt Northern Hwy, Midland, Western Australia 6056 Tel: (09) 2745288
Dirs: Rayma and David Turton (Westbooks), Paul Armstrong (Turton & Armstrong)
Orders to: 44 Irvine St, Bayswater, Western Australia 6053
Associate Company: Turton & Armstrong (qv)
Subjects: Educational, Technical, Juvenile, Industrial Archaeology
Bookshops (specialist children's): 16 Gt Northern Hwy, Midland, Western Australia 6056; 4/29 Bayview Terrace, Claremont, Western Australia 6010; 14 Knuckey St, Darwin, Northern Territory 5790

Whitcombe & Tombs Pty Ltd, 159-163 Victoria Rd, Marrickville, NSW 2204 Tel: (02) 5609888 Cable Add: Whitcombes Sydney
Publishing Dir: J Smytheman; *Editorial, Rights & Permissions:* J Pagan
Parent Company: Whitcoulls Ltd, New Zealand (qv)
Subjects: General Fiction, Belles Lettres, Poetry, Biography, History, Music, Art, Juveniles, High-priced Paperbacks, Engineering, General & Social Science, University, Secondary & Primary Textbooks, Educational Materials

Bookshops: Whitcombe & Tombs, Sydney, NSW; Richmond, Melbourne, Victoria and West Perth, Western Australia
Founded: 1882
ISBN Publisher's Prefix: 0-7233

Whitman, Australia Pty Ltd, see Golden Press Pty Ltd

Widescope International Publishers Pty Ltd*, PO Box 339, Camberwell, Victoria 3124 (Located at: 7 Cato St, Hawthorn East, Victoria 3124) Tel: (03) 207909 Cable Add: Widescope Melbourne Telex: AA 36035
Man Dir: Geoffrey M Gold
Imprints: Apple Paperbacks, Visa Books
Subjects: Politics, Sociology, History, Biography, Media and Communications, Sport, Economics, Health and Sexuality, Culture, Fiction
1978: 25 titles *1979:* 25 titles *Founded:* 1974
ISBN Publisher's Prefix: 0-86932

Wild & Woolley Pty Ltd, PO Box 41, Glebe, NSW 2037 (Located at: 260 Kent St, Sydney, NSW 2000) Tel: (02) 2901411 Telex: Baabaa 70936
Man Dir: Pat Woolley; *Sales, Rights & Permissions:* Shar Adams
Associate Companies: Books Australia, Allbooks
Branch Off: PO Box 67427, Los Angeles, Ca 90067, USA
Subjects: Fiction, Cartoons, Art, Politics
1979: 2 titles *1980:* 5 titles *Founded:* 1974
ISBN Publisher's Prefix: 0-909331

John **Wiley** & Sons, see Jacaranda Wiley Ltd

Wobbledagger, 5/1 Parkview Rd, Manly, NSW 2095 Tel: 2901411
Man Dirs: Ian Hoyle, Sally Hoyle
Subjects: Children's Books
Founded: 1977

Women's Movement Children's Literature Co-op Ltd, PO Box 119, Mooroolbark, 3138 Victoria Tel: 7283291
Chief Executive: Robyn Wallace; *All other offices:* Noelle McCracken
Subsidiary Company: Sugar and Snails Books
Subjects: Counter-sexist children's books, Fiction and Non-Fiction
1979: 4 titles *1980:* 4 titles *Founded:* 1974
ISBN Publisher's Prefix: 0-908092

Wren Publishing Pty Ltd*, Palmer St, South Melbourne, 3205 Victoria
Man Dir, Editorial, Sales Production: Dennis Wren; *Publicity, Rights & Permissions:* Dee Wren
Orders to: Hibbins Taylor & Co Pty Ltd, 69 Stanley St, West Melbourne, 3003 Victoria
Subjects: History, Travel, Fiction, Juveniles
Founded: 1971
ISBN Publisher's Prefix: 0-85885

Remainder Dealers

Universal Books, 176 South Creek Rd, Dee Why West, NSW 2099 Tel: (02) 9822344
Manager: Duncan Wade
Parent Company: Lansdowne Press (qv)

Literary Agents

Dorothy **Blewett** Associates*, 50 View Hill Crescent, Eltham, Victoria 3095

Charter Books Pty Ltd*, Foveaux House, 63 Foveaux St, Surry Hills, NSW 2101
Contact: Bruce Semler, Malcolm Newell or Donald McLean

Curtis Brown (Australia) Pty Ltd, 86 William St, Paddington, Sydney, NSW 2021 Tel: 318301/336161 Cable Add: Browncurt Sydney
Contacts: Tim Curnow, Barbara Mobbs

Hampton Press Features Syndicate*, 5 Dick St, Henley, NSW 2111
Man Dir: Michael Hervey

Yaffa Syndicate Pty Ltd*, 432-436 Elizabeth St, Surry Hills, NSW 2010 Tel: (02) 699 7861 Telex: AA 21887

Book Clubs

Arrow, PO Box 579, Gosford, NSW 2250
Owned by: Ashton Scholastic (qv)

Australasian Book Society Ltd*, PO Box A161, Sydney South, NSW 2000

Australian Jewish Book Club Pty Ltd
Owned by: Outback Press Pty Ltd (qv)

Doubleday Australia Pty Ltd, Book Club Associates Division, 14 Mars Rd, Lane Cove, NSW 2066
Man Dir: Peter B Madgwick; *Editorial:* Suzanne Delmont; *Marketing:* John D Madgwick
Includes: Doubleday Book Club, The Literary Guild, Doubleday History Book Club, Reader's Choice (Australiana Book Club), Twentieth Century Classics

Doubleday Book Club, see Doubleday Australia Pty Ltd, Book Club Associates Division

Doubleday History Book Club, see Doubleday Australia Pty Ltd, Book Club Associates Division

The **Literary Guild**, see Doubleday Australia Pty Ltd, Book Club Associates Division

Lucky, PO Box 579, Gosford, NSW 2250
Owned by: Ashton Scholastic (qv)

Reader's Choice (Australiana Book Club), see Doubleday Australia Pty Ltd, Book Club Associates Division

Reader's Digest Condensed Book Services Pty Ltd, Box 4353 GPO, Sydney, NSW 2001
Editor: Barbara Ker Wilson

Teacher's Bookshelf, PO Box 579, Gosford, NSW 2250
Owned by: Ashton Scholastic (qv)

Teenage, PO Box 579, Gosford, NSW 2250
Owned by: Ashton Scholastic (qv)

Twentieth Century Classics, see Doubleday Australia Pty Ltd, Book Club Associates Division

Major Booksellers

Abbey's Bookshop, 477 George St, Sydney, NSW 2000 Tel: (02) 291093
Manager: Peter Milne

Angus & Robertson Bookshops*, 209 Pitt St, Sydney, NSW 2000 Tel: (02) 2314066. This is the head office; there are about 60 branches

Australian Government Publications*, Mt Newman House, 200 St George's Terrace, Perth, Western Australia 6000 Tel: (093) 224737

Birchalls, 118-120 Brisbane St, PO Box 170, Launceston, Tasmania 7250 Tel: 313011
Manager: Raymond F Tilley
Parent Company: A W Birchall & Sons Pty Ltd (at above address)
Australia's oldest (founded 1844) and Tasmania's largest bookseller

Collins Booksellers Pty Ltd, 86 Bourke St, Melbourne, Victoria 3000 Tel: (03) 6622711. This is the head office; there are 21 branches
Manager: Michael C Zifcak

Dymock's Book Arcade Ltd, 424 George St, Sydney, NSW 2000 Tel: (02) 2334111 (several branches)
Manager: S A Morehouse

Foreign Language Bookshop, 94 Elizabeth St, Melbourne, Victoria 3000 Tel: (03) 6542883
Manager: A Zoureff

Grahame Book Co, Pitt and Hunter Streets, Sydney, NSW 2000 Tel: (02) 2321966 (several branches)
Division of Horwitz Grahame Books Pty Ltd (qv)

Language Book Centre, 127 York St, Sydney 2000 Tel: 296643
Manager: Hanni Bääske

Queensland Book Depot, 61-63 Adelaide St, Brisbane, Queensland 4000 Tel: (072) 312331. This is the head office; there are 10 branches

Rigby Bookshops, 24 James Pl, Adelaide, South Australia 5000 Tel: (08) 2235566
Division of Rigby Ltd (qv)

John **Scott** Educational Books Supply*, PO Box 312B, Abbotsford, Victoria 3067 Tel: 417041

University Co-op Bookshop Ltd, 76-84 Bay St, Broadway, NSW 2007 Tel: (02) 2122211 (several branches) Telex: AA21968

Whitcombe & Tombs Pty Ltd, 159-163 Victoria Rd, Marrickville, NSW 2204 Tel: 5609888; 81 York St, Sydney Tel: 294743; 142 Colin St, West Perth, Western Australia 6005 Tel: 217044; 120 Chestnut St, Richmond, Victoria Tel: 421226

Major Libraries

Australian Archives, Commonwealth Government Centre, Chiefly Sq, Sydney, NSW 2000
Publications: Inventories, Guides (irregular)

Australian National University Library, PO Box 4, Canberra, ACT 2600 Tel: (062) 495111 Cable Add: Natuni Telex: AA 62760

The **Barr Smith** Library, The University of Adelaide, Adelaide, South Australia, 5001 Tel: (08) 2234333 Telex: Univad AA89141
Librarian: I D Raymond

C S I R O (Commonwealth Scientific and Industrial Research Organization), Central Information, Library and Editorial Section, Bureau of Scientific Services, PO Box 89, East Melbourne, Victoria 3002 (Located at: 314 Albert St, East Melbourne) Tel: (03) 4191333 Telex: 30236
Officer-in-Charge: P J Judge; *Editor-in-Chief:* B J Walby; *Chief Librarian:* P H Dawe; *Manager, Information Service:* C Garrow
Publications: CSIRO Index, Australian Science Index, Australian Renewable Energy Resources Index, Australian Sheep and Wool Information Service, Scientific Serials in Australian Libraries (microfiche), *Scientific and Technical Research Centres in Australia, Australian Scientific Societies and Professional Associations, CSIRO-SDI User Manual, Technical Communications, CILES Biennial Report*

Commonwealth Patents, Trade Marks and Designs Offices Library, Scarborough House, Phillip, PO Box 200, Woden, ACT 2606

AUSTRALIA

High Court of Australia Library*, Taylor Sq, Darlinghurst, Sydney, NSW 2010 Tel: 2381423
Librarian: Mark Powell

The **Library Board of Western Australia**, Henley House, 102 Beaufort St, Perth, WA 6000 Tel: (09) 3287466 Telex: Wainf 92231
State Librarian: Robert Sharman

National Library of Australia, Parkes Pl, Canberra, ACT 2600 Tel: (062) 621111 Cable Add: Natlibaust Canberra Telex: 62100
Director of Publications: A T Bolton
Publications include: Australian National Bibliography (four times monthly), *Current Australian Serials* (irregular)

The **State Library of New South Wales**, Macquarie St, Sydney, NSW 2000 Tel: (02) 2211388
State Librarian: R F Doust
Publications include: Annual Report, New South Wales Official Publications Received in the State Library, Public Libraries Division: Newsletter

State Library of Queensland, William St, Brisbane, Queensland 4000
Includes the Oxley Library
Librarian: S L Ryan
Publications include: Annual Statistical Bulletin of Queensland Public Libraries Services, 1968- ; *Queensland Government Publications,* 1977- (quarterly); *Directory of State and Public Library Service in Queensland* (annual); *The Development of State Libraries and their effect on the Public Library Movement in Australia, 1809-1964; Selected Serials Resources for Queensland Public Libraries* (annual, quarterly supplements)

State Library of South Australia, North Terrace, Adelaide, South Australia 5000 Tel: 2238911 Telex: 82074
Formerly Public Library of South Australia
Publications: South Australiana (twice yearly), *Pinpointer* (two-monthly), *Index to Australian Book Reviews* (quarterly), *Annual Report*

State Library of Tasmania, 91 Murray St, Hobart, Tasmania 7000 Tel: (002) 308033 Telex: 58222
Taking in Tasmanian Public Library
State Librarian: W L Brown
Publication: Annual report

State Library of Victoria, 328 Swanston St, Melbourne, Victoria 3000 Tel: (03) 6699888

University of Melbourne Library*, Parkville, Victoria 3052

University of New South Wales Library, PO Box 1, Kensington, NSW 2033 Tel: 6630351
Librarian: A R Horton
Publications: Annual Report, Staff Papers

University of Queensland Library, St Lucia, Queensland, Australia 4067 Tel: (07) 3772304
University Librarian: F D O Fielding
Publication: Annual Report

University of Sydney Library*, Sydney, NSW 2006 Tel: (02) 692 1122 Telex: 20056

University of Western Australia Library, Nedlands, Western Australia 6009 Tel: 3803838 Cable Add: Uniwest Telex: Uniwa 92992

Library Associations

Australian Advisory Council on Bibliographical Services (AACOBS), National Library, Canberra, ACT 2600
Chairman: The Hon Sir Peter Crisp
Publications include: Library Services for Australia: the Work of AACOBS (annual)

Australian Law Librarians' Group*, c/o Margaret McAleese, Law Librarian, Australian National University, PO Box 4, Canberra, ACT 2600
Convener: Margaret McAleese

Australian Library Promotion Council, Executive Director, 328 Swanston St, Melbourne, Victoria 3000 Tel: (03) 635994
Honorary Secretary: Joyce Nicholson
Publications: Australian Library News (10 issues per year), *Bookmark* (Annual Directory/Diary)

Australian Library Technicians' Association*, GPO Box 313B, Melbourne, Vic 3001
President: Joe Lynam; *Secretary:* Lorraine Conway (at above address)

Australian School Library Association, PO Box 266, Goulburn, NSW 2580 Tel: (048) 212325
Executive Secretary: Bill Sommerville
Publications: School Libraries in Australia (official journal; irregular)

Australian Society of Archivists*, PO Box 83, O'Connor, ACT 2601
President: Mr G L Fisher; *Secretary:* Ms D Wheeler (at above address)

Bibliographical Society of Australia and New Zealand, see entry under Literary Associations and Societies

International Association of Music Libraries, Australia/New Zealand Branch (IAMLANZ)*, Victorian College for the Arts, 234 Saint Kilda Rd, Melbourne, Victoria 3004
President: Kenneth A R Horn; *Secretary:* Ian G Miller (at above address)
Publication: Continuo

L A S I E Australia Co Ltd, PO Box 602, Lane Cove, NSW 2066 Tel: 9382722/55
The Library Automated Systems Information Exchange
President: Dorothy G Peake; *Executive Officer:* Arne Pedersen
Publication: LASIE (Information Bulletin)

Library Association of Australia, 35 Clarence St, Sydney, NSW 2000
Executive Director: Gordon Bower
Publications: Australian Library Journal, Incite, Handbook, Directory of Special Libraries in Australia, Australian Academic and Research Libraries, Australian Special Libraries News, Orana, Cataloguing Australia, List of Translators and Translation Services in Australia, Conference Proceedings, The Variety of Librarianship: Essays in Honour of John Wallace Metcalfe, Libraries, Information and Education

The **Library Automated Systems** Information Exchange, see LASIE

Medical Librarians' Group*, Central Library, Australian Department of Health, PO Box 100, Woden, ACT 2606
Convener: Mrs S Liki (at above address)

Public Lending Right Committee*, The Administrator, Australia Council, PO Box 302, North Sydney, NSW 2060 Tel: 9222122

State Librarians' Council, c/o State Library of Tasmania, 91 Murray St, Hobart, Tasmania 7000
Chairman: W L Brown

Library Reference Books and Journals

Books

Directory of Public Reference and Lending Libraries in Australia, Library Association of Australia, 35 Clarence St, Sydney, NSW 2000

Directory of Special Libraries in Australia, Library Association of Australia, 35 Clarence St, Sydney, NSW 2000

Library Association of Australia: Handbook, Library Association of Australia, 35 Clarence St, Sydney, NSW 2000

Journals

Acquisitions Newsletter (five or six times yearly), Sales and Subscriptions Unit, National Library of Australia, Parkes Pl, Canberra, ACT 2600

Archives and Manuscripts, A Lemon (Editor), 704 Toorak Rd, Malvern, Victoria 3144

Australian Academic and Research Library, 35 Clarence St, Sydney, NSW 2000

Australian Library Journal, Library Association of Australia, 35 Clarence St, Sydney, NSW 2000

Australian Library News, Australian Library Promotion Council, c/o State Library of Victoria, 328 Swanston St, Melbourne, Victoria 3000

Australian Library Technicians Association (ALTA) News (6 issues a year), 55 Radnor St, Camberwell, Victoria 3124

Australian School Librarian (quarterly), PO Box 280, East Melbourne, Vic 3001

Australian Special Libraries News, Library Association of Australia, Special Libraries Section, 32 Belvoir St, Surry Hills, NSW 2010

Biblia (monthly), Library Board of Western Australia, 102 Beaufort St, Perth, WA

Cataloguing Australia (quarterly), c/o School of Librarianship, University of New South Wales, Kensington, NSW 2033

Library Services for Australia: the Work of AACOBS (annual), Australian Advisory Council on Bibliographical Services (AACOBS), National Library, Canberra, ACT 2600

Orana (Children's Libraries Newsletter), Library Association of Australia, 35 Clarence St, Sydney, NSW 2000

School Libraries in Australia, Australian School Library Association, PO Box 266, Goulburn, NSW 2580

School Library Bulletin (quarterly), Education Department, Library Branch, 449 Swanston St, Melbourne, Victoria 3000

Teacher-Librarian (quarterly), PO Box 21, Waverley, NSW 2024

Literary Associations and Societies

Australian Literature Society, PO Box 55, Barooga, NSW 3644
Secretary: Mrs Alvie Egan

Bibliographical Society of Australia and New Zealand, 117 St Georges Rd, North Fitzroy, Victoria 3068
Secretary: Trevor Mills
Publications include: Bulletin (twice yearly); *Broadsheet* (irregular)

Book Collectors' Society of Australia, 64 Young St, Cremorne, NSW 2090 Tel: 902184
President: Walter Stone (at above address)
Publications: Biblionews, Australian Notes and Queries (periodical)

Bread and Cheese Club, 51 Elizabeth St, Newport, Victoria 3015 Tel: 3913039
Secretary: Dr Cyril Goode

Combined Literary Societies (Australia)*, PO Box 272, East Melbourne, Victoria 3002
Secretary: Miss F N Breen

The **Dickens** Fellowship*
29 Henley Beach Rd, Henley Beach, Adelaide, SA 5022
Honorary Secretary: G J Rowe
Also at:
Brisbane: Unit No 3, 12 Sydney St, New Farm, Queensland 4005
Honorary Secretary: Mrs G M Taylor
Melbourne: Flat 143, 200 Dorcas St, South Melbourne 3205, Victoria
Honorary Secretary: Mrs Barbara Barrett

Fellowship of Australian Writers NSW, GPO Box 3448, Sydney, NSW 2001
Secretary: Betty Cummins
Publication: Bulletin (bi-monthly)
Fifteen regional branches in suburbs of Sydney and country towns

International **P E N** (Melbourne Centre)*, 17-1 Domain Park, 193 Domain Rd, South Yarra, Victoria 3141
Secretary: Jean Gittins

International **P E N** (Sydney Centre)*, Secretary, 422/290 Jersey Rd, Woollahra, NSW 2025 Tel: 325668
Secretary: Susan Yorke
Publication: Newsletter (quarterly)

Poetry Society of Australia*, Box N110 Grosvenor Street PO, Sydney 2000, NSW
Joint Secretaries: Robert and Debra Adamson
Publication: New Poetry (quarterly).
Publishes poems, articles, reviews, notes and comments, interviews, photographs

Society of Australian Writers, Australia House, Strand, London, UK
Secretary: Alessandra Miach

Literary Periodicals

A U M L A, a journal of literary criticism, philology and linguistics (text in English and French), Australasian Universities Language and Literature Association, James Cook University of North Queensland, Townsville, Queensland 4811

The Australian Author, Australian Society of Authors, c/o 24 Alfred St, Milsons Point, NSW 2061

Australian Literary Studies, Department of English, University of Queensland, Saint Lucia, Queensland 4067

Australian Writers and Their Work, Oxford University Press, 7 Bowen Crescent, Melbourne, Victoria 3000

Index to Australian Book Reviews (quarterly), State Library of South Australia, North Terrace, Adelaide, South Australia 5000

Meanjin Quarterly, a magazine of literature, art and discussion, University of Melbourne, Parkville, Victoria 3052

New Poetry, Box 110, George St North PO, Sydney, NSW 2001

Overland, GPO Box 98a, Melbourne, Victoria 3001

Poetry Australia, 350 Lyons Rd, Five Dock, NSW 2046

Quadrant, Box C344, Clarence St Post Office, Sydney, NSW 2000

Reading Time, Children's Book Council of Australia, New South Wales Branch, PO Box 159, Curtin, ACT 2605

Southerly, a review of Australian literature (English Association, Sydney Branch), Department of English, University of Sydney, Sydney, NSW 2006

Westerly, English Department, University of Western Australia, Nedlands, Western Australia 6009

Literary Prizes

A N Z Local History Award
Awarded by the Australian and New Zealand Bank, $500, plus commended prizes, for a book of Australian local or regional history published during the year (ending 31 December). Administered by Victorian Fellowship of Australian Writers. Entries close 31 December. Enquiries to J Hamilton, 1/317 Barkers Rd, Kew, Victoria 3101

'Age' Book of the Year
Awarded by 'The Age', $3,000 for an Australian book of outstanding literary merit which best expresses Australia's identity or character. Can include fiction, poetry and scholarly writing. Enquiries to 'The Age', 250 Spencer St, Melbourne, Victoria 3000

The **Alice** Literary Award
Presented by The Society of Women Writers (Australia) biennially for a distinguished and long-term contribution to literature by an Australian woman. First award 1978 was to Eleanor Dark. Enquiries to Hilarie Lindsay, Chief Executive, The Society of Women Writers (Australia), GPO Box 1388, Sydney, NSW 2001

Angus & Robertson Writers' Fellowship
For a manuscript or book project of outstanding originality, preferably by a new author. Contract with advance of $2,000. Enquiries to The Publisher, Angus & Robertson Publishers, PO Box 290, North Ryde, NSW 2113 Tel: 8872233

Australian Industry Awards for Young Writers
Awarded by BHP, Shell, Ford and the 'Herald' for poetry, stories, essays, scripts and collections; for young writers 15-21 years, varying conditions (plus 21-25 years for 'Herald' story award). It includes BHP-FAW Young Poets Publishing Project. Administered by Victorian Fellowship of Australian Writers. Enquiries to J Hamilton, 1/317 Barkers Rd, Kew, Victoria 3101

Australian Literature Society Gold Medal
Awarded for the best literary work published in Australia each year. Originated by Colonel, the Honourable R A Crouch. Enquiries to Secretary, Australian Literature Society, Alvie Egan, c/o PO Box 55, Barooga, NSW 3644

Australian Natives' Association Literature Award
Founded in 1978 as an award for a book on an Australian theme. Prize $300. Administered by Victorian Fellowship of Australian Writers. Enquiries to J Hamilton, 1/317 Barkers Rd, Kew, Victoria 3101

Book Design Awards
Awarded annually by the Australian Book Publishers' Association. Closing date is 30 November and books must have been published during the previous calendar year. There is an entry fee of $10 per book and any type of book can be submitted, as judging is in several categories. Books must be contracted and designed in Australia, but may be printed anywhere. Enquiries to Director, ABPA, 163 Clarence St, Sydney, NSW 2000

Bookman of the Year Award*
Awarded by the National Book Council to a person who has made a substantial contribution to the promotion of books, but who might not necessarily be expected to be eligible for many of the other awards listed in this section. Enquiries to National Book Council, 4th Floor, 71 Collins St, Melbourne, Victoria 3000

Christopher **Brennan** Award, see FAW-Christopher Brennan Award

Bronze Swagman Award
Awarded annually for Bush Verse. Bronze statuette of The Swagman, sculpted by Daphne Mayo, valued at $500, and a Winton opal, valued at $50. Closes May 31st. Enquiries to Winton Tourist Promotion Association, PO Box 44, Winton, Queensland 4735

'Canberra Times' Short Story Award*
$2,000 and $700 awards for a short story. Enquiries to 'Canberra Times', PO Box 443, Canberra City, ACT 2601

Ronald **Carson-Gold** Memorial Short Story Competition
Awarded annually. Closes 23 April. Short Story by Australian with Australian setting. 1st Prize $600, 2nd Prize $300, 3rd Prize $100. Administered by the Union Fidelity Trust. Enquiries to Carson-Gold Short Story Competition, PO Box 339, Toowong, Brisbane, Queensland 4066

Children's Book of the Year Awards*
Awarded annually by the Children's Book Council of Australia. The awards now fall into three sections: Book of the Year — primarily for literary merit but quality of production considered; Picture Book of the Year — for younger children; Best Illustrated Book of the Year. For the first Section the Literature Board makes $2,500 available of which at least $1,500 must go to the winner, who also receives the medal. The Picture Book Award does not carry any monetary prize: the Council's medal is presented to the artist. The award for illustrators is $2,500 and is from the Visual Art Board. The award is to the artist for the best illustrated book entered in any section: a minor portion may be given to the runner up. Authors and illustrators entered for awards must be Australian citizens, or resident in Australia for five of the last ten years, or provide evidence of intention to reside permanently in Australia. Closing date is 31 December, for books published during that year. Entries must be sent by publishers to the State Children's Book Council which is providing the executive for that particular year. Enquiries to L Rees, 50 Booroondara St, Reid, ACT
or Library Services, 35 Mitchell St, North Sydney, NSW 2060

Tom **Collins** Poetry Prize
Administered by Western Australia FAW. For West Australian residents. Prizes $100 and two at $50. First awarded in 1977. Annual closing date: mid-January. Enquiries to Secretary, Western Australia FAW, Tom Collins House, 9 Servetus St, Swanbourne, WA 6010

James **Cook** Australian Literary Studies Award
Not less than $500 from the Townsville

Foundation for Australian Literary Studies at the James Cook University of North Queensland. The award is made to the author of the best book dealing with any aspect of Australian life. The book must have been published in Australia, even though printed elsewhere. The publication may be in any field of writing — fiction, poetry, drama, letters, biographical or historical. Closing date is 28 February. Enquiries to the Vice-Chancellor of the University, Townsville, PO, James Cook University, Queensland 4811

C J **Dennis** Award
$1,000, originally for a book about Australian flora and/or fauna, but not necessarily for that category in future. Award provided by Victorian Government and administered by Victorian Fellowship of Australian Writers. Enquiries to J Hamilton, 1/317 Barkers Rd, Kew, Victoria 3101

Anne **Elder** Poetry Fund Award
$500 for a first book of poetry. Administered by Victorian Fellowship of Australian Writers. Enquiries to J Hamilton, 1/317 Barkers Rd, Kew, Victoria 3101

F A W-**Barbara Ramsden** Award
Awarded by the Victorian Fellowship of Australian Writers to both the author and to the editor of an outstanding work of quality writing and presentation published each year. It is the Fellowship's major national award for quality writing and was founded by public subscription to honour Barbara Ramsden, MBE, a publisher's editor of distinction. The winning author and editor are each presented with a plaquette specially designed by sculptor Andor Meszaros, depicting the origin of art. More than one work may be submitted by any publisher, author or publisher's editor in Australia. The 'editor' is to be that person the publisher regards as responsible for editing the work. Entries close 31 December. Enquiries to J Hamilton, 1/317 Barkers Rd, Kew, Victoria 3101

F A W-**Christopher Brennan** Award
Formerly called the Robert Frost Award. Awarded to a poet in Australia whose work, particularly if sustained, achieves distinction. Entries not required. Administered by the Victorian Fellowship of Australian Writers. Enquiries to J Hamilton, 1/317 Barkers Rd, Kew, Victoria 3101

F A W-**John Shaw Neilson** Poetry Award
Awarded by the Victorian Fellowship of Australian Writers. Closing date 31 December. Any kind of poem is acceptable with a minimum of 14 lines. Merit will be the criterion. First prize at least $150. Enquiries to J Hamilton, 1/317 Barkers Rd, Kew, Victoria 3101

F A W **Regional Branch** Awards
Various FAW regional branches such as Parramatta, Ballarat, Eastwood, Geelong, Latrobe Valley and North Central hold occasional or regular awards, usually in the area of stories and poetry, for small cash prizes and sometimes publication. They are sometimes open within the State or the Nation

Ford Award, see Australian Industry Awards for Young Writers

Miles **Franklin** Award
Awarded annually for a published novel portraying Australian life in any of its phases. Entrants must submit one copy of the published work to each of the five judges, and also one copy to the Permanent Trustee Co Ltd, within two months of its publication. Closing date is 31 January. For 1980 the award was $2,500. Enquiries to The Manager, Permanent Trustee Co Ltd, Box 4270, GPO Sydney, NSW 2001

Robert **Frost** Award, now called FAW-Christopher Brennan Award (qv)

Gemini Awards*
Awarded by the Toowoomba Arts Festival, a prize of $100 for a short story. Enquiries to the Secretary, Gemini, PO Box 634, Toowoomba, Queensland 4350

Mary **Gilmore** Award*
Awarded annually on themes of significance to the life and aspirations of the Australian people. Subject matter — novel, short story, children's book, etc — varies year by year. $2,000 and a Mary Gilmore medallion will be awarded. Closing date is August. Enquiries to The Secretary, Mary Gilmore Award, Room 75, Trades Hall, Goulburn St, Sydney, NSW 2000

Grenfell 'Henry Lawson' Festival Prizes*
Awarded annually in June with engraved bronze statuettes created by Sydney sculptor Alan Ingham, and cash. Awards are made for prose, verse, art and the words and music of an Australian popular song. Prose (a short story up to 4,000 words); Verse (up to 60 lines). Enquiries to Honorary Secretary, PO Box 77, Grenfell, NSW 2810

The Grace **Leven** Prize for Poetry
Instituted under the Will of William Baylebridge, the Australian poet, who died in 1942. This Prize of $200 is offered annually for 'the best volume of poetry published during the twelve months immediately preceding the year in which the award is made'. Competitors must be either Australian born, and writing as Australians, or they must be naturalized in Australia and have lived in that country for at least ten years. The volume chosen may have been published in any country, but copies of it must be freely obtainable in Australia. Enquiries to Perpetual Trustee Co Ltd, 39 Hunter St, Sydney, NSW 2000

The '**Herald**' Short Story Award, see Australian Industry Awards for Young Writers

Jessie **Litchfield** Memorial Award
A cash prize of $300 and a bronze plaque awarded annually by the Bread and Cheese Club, Melbourne, to encourage writers who, in the opinion of the Committee, may make a contribution to Australian literature. Entry forms available on request accompanied by return postage. Enquiries to Dr Cyril Goode, Bread and Cheese Club, 51 Elizabeth St, Newport, Victoria 3015

Literature Board of the Australia Council
The Literature Board supports the writing of all forms of creative literature, including novels, short stories, poetry and plays. Aid is also given to some nonfiction (especially biography, autobiography, history and the humanities). All individual applicants must use the Literature Board's application form. Annual closing dates: Fellowships, 31 May; Special Purpose Grants, 31 March. Enquiries to the Secretary, Literature Board, Australia Council, PO Box 302, North Sydney 2060

Alan **Marshall** Award
For the best unpublished manuscript that tells a good story in any literary form. Prize currently $500. Administered by Victorian Fellowship of Australian Writers. Enquiries to J Hamilton, 1/317 Barkers Rd, Kew 3101, Victoria

National Book Council Awards*
Awarded by the National Book Council, first prize $3,000 ($600 to publisher) for book of highest literary merit, 2nd prize $2,000 ($400 to publisher) for book of highest literary merit in a category other than that of the book winning first prize. Enquiries to Executive Secretary, 4th Floor, 71 Collins St, Melbourne, Victoria 3000

John Shaw **Neilson** Poetry Award, see FAW-John Shaw Neilson Poetry Award

New Zealand Anzac Fellowships
The New Zealand Government offers several Fellowships each year to Australians. Awards are tenable for periods of between 3 and 12 months and candidates should preferably be under 45. Enquiries to Secretary, Department of Education, PO Box 826, Woden, ACT 2606

Banjo **Paterson** Awards
Competition run in conjunction with the Biennial Orange Festival of Arts (March/April 1981, 1983). One-act play and poetry competition. Enquiries to The Honorary Secretary, Festival of Arts Committee, Civic Centre, Byng St, PO Box 763, Orange, NSW 2800

Barbara **Ramsden** Award, see FAW-Barbara Ramsden Award

Shell Book of the Year Award, see Australian Industry Awards for Young Writers

South Australia Biennial Literature Prize
Two awards for literature were given by the South Australian Government in 1980. Each award was of $3,000, the first for a South Australian regional history or biography, the second (for writers who have had no more than two books published) for a work of poetry, fiction or drama. Enquiries to Arts Development Division, Department for the Arts, PO Box 2308, Adelaide, SA 5001

South Australian Government Literature Prize*
For a regional history or biography. $3,000, biennial. For a published work of poetry, fiction or drama. $3,000, biennial. Enquiries to Arts Development Division, Premier's Department, Box 2343, GPO, Adelaide 5001

State of Victoria Short Story Awards
Awarded annually; prizes of $700, $250 and $200 to an Australian writer for an original short story. There will also be other awards, e.g. of $50 each for unpublished writers. Stories should be unpublished and not exceed 4,000 words. More than one entry may be submitted in all sections. Closing date 31 December. Administered by Victorian Fellowship of Australian Writers. A stamped addressed envelope should be enclosed. Enquiries to J Hamilton, 1/317 Barkers Rd, Kew, Victoria 3101.

Townsville Foundation for Australian Literary Studies Award
For the best book dealing with any aspect of Australian life. 1980 award of $1,000. Enquiries to the Vice-Chancellor of the University, Townsville, Post Office, James Cook University, Queensland 4811

Warana Writers' Awards
Awarded annually by the Fellowship of Australian Writers (Queensland Branch) for poetry, feature article and short story. Closes 25 August. Enquiries to Mrs Jean Scott, PO Box 339, Toowong, Brisbane, Queensland 4066

Con **Weickhardt** Award
Awarded for a published work of biography, autobiography or a memoir. $500, administered by the Victorian Fellowship of Australian Writers. Closing date 31 December. Enquiries to the Secretariat, 1/317 Barkers Rd, Kew, Victoria 3101

Patricia **Weickhardt** Award
Cash prize to an aboriginal writer. Administered by Victorian Fellowship of Australian Writers. Enquiries to J Hamilton, 1/317 Barkers Rd, Kew, Victoria 3101

Patrick **White** Award*
Patrick White has applied his Nobel Prize money to establish a trust to make grants to Australian writers, to help relieve financial need of older writers of distinction. Submissions are not required. Enquiries to J Allison, Woollahra Municipal Library, Woollahra, NSW

Sir Thomas **White** Memorial Prize*
Annual award of the Society of Australian Writers (UK). Categories vary from year to year. Award is approximately $500. Enquiries to Secretary, Society of Australian Writers, Australia House, Strand, London, UK

Wilke Literary Award
For a book printed in Australia in field of Australiana. $100. Administered by the Victorian Fellowship of Australian Writers. Enquiries to J Hamilton, 1/317 Barkers Rd, Kew, Victoria 3101

Austria

General Information

Language: German (English widely spoken)
Religion: Predominantly Roman Catholic
Population: 7.5 million
Bank Hours: 0800-1530 Monday-Wednesday, Friday; 0800-1730 Thursday
Shop Hours: 0800-1800 Monday-Friday; 0800-1200 or 1300 Saturday
Currency: 100 groschen = 1 schilling
Export/Import Information: Member of the European Free Trade Association. Import licences not required for books. No exchange controls.
Copyright: UCC, Berne, Florence (see International section)

Book Trade Organizations

Bundesgremium des Handels mit Büchern, Kunstblättern und Musikalien, Zeitungen und Zeitschriften, A-1011 Vienna, Bauernmarkt 13 Tel: (0222) 635763
Federal Group for Traders in Books, Prints and Sheet Music, Newspapers and Periodicals

Hauptverband der graphischen Unternehmungen Österreichs*, A-1010 Vienna 1, Grünangergasse 4
Austrian Graphical Association

Hauptverband des österreichischen Buchhandels, A-1010 Vienna 1, Grünangergasse 4 Tel: (0222) 521535 Cable Add: Buchverein, Vienna
Austrian Publishers' and Booksellers' Association
Secretary: Dr Gerhard Prosser
Miscellaneous: A number of subsidiary organizations are administered from the same office, e.g. Verband der Antiquare (qv), Österreichischer Verlegerverband (qv), Standard Book Numbering Agency (qv)
Publications: Anzeiger des österreichischen Buchhandels (bi-monthly); *Adressbuch des österreichischen Buchhandels (Directory); Das österreichische Buch* (catalogue) (annual); *Bücher: Das Lesemagazin für Sie* (catalogue) (annual)

Landesgremium Kärnten des Handels mit Büchern, Kunstblättern, Musikalien, Zeitungen und Zeitschriften*, A-9020 Klagenfurt, Bahnhofstr 40-42 Tel: 04222/80411
Carinthian Regional Group of Traders in Books, Art Prints, Sheet Music, Periodicals and Newspapers

Landesgremium Niederösterreich des Handels mit Büchern, Kunstblättern, Musikalien, Zeitungen und Zeitschriften*, A-1014 Vienna, Herrengasse 10 Tel: 636691
Lower Austria Regional Group of Traders in Books, Art Prints and Sheet Music, Periodicals and Newspapers

Landesgremium Oberösterreich des Handels mit Büchern, Kunstblättern, Musikalien, Zeitungen und Zeitschriften, A-4010 Linz, Hessenpl 3 Tel: 78444/328
Upper Austria Regional Trade Association of Traders in Books, Art Prints, Sheet Music, Periodicals and Newspapers

Landesgremium Salzburg des Handels mit Büchern, Kunstblättern, Musikalien, Zeitungen und Zeitschriften, A-5027 Salzburg, Julius-Raab-Platz 1 Tel: 71571/251 Telex: 3633
Salzburg Regional Group of Traders in Books, Prints, Sheet Music, Periodicals and Newspapers

Landesgremium Steiermark des Handels mit Büchern, Kunstblättern, Musikalien, Zeitungen und Zeitschriften*, A-8010 Graz, Burggasse 11 Tel: 76411
Styrian Regional Group of Traders in Books, Prints, Sheet Music, Periodicals and Newspapers

Landesgremium Tirol des Handels mit Büchern, Kunstblättern, Musikalien, Zeitungen und Zeitschriften, A-6020 Innsbruck, Meinhardstr 14/IV Tel: 35651/290
Tyrol Regional Group of Traders in Books, Art Prints, Sheet Music, Periodicals and Newspapers

Landesgremium Vorarlberg des Handels mit Büchern und Musikalien, A-6800 Feldkirch, Wichnergasse 9 Tel: (05522) 2251148
Vorarlberg Regional Group of Traders in Books and Sheet Music
Man Dir: Heribert Eggler; *Secretary:* Dr Manfred Fiel

Landesgremium Wien des Handels mit Büchern, Kunstblättern, Musikalien, Zeitungen und Zeitschriften*, A-1040 Vienna, Schwarzenbergpl 14 Tel: 657671
Vienna Regional Group of Traders in Books, Prints, Sheet Music, Periodicals and Newspapers

Literar-Mechana, Wahrnehmungsgesellschaft für Urheberrechte mbH, A-1060 Vienna VI, Linke Wienzeile 18 Tel: (0222) 572161
Organization for Copyright Protection
Man Dir: Franz Leo Popp

Musikverleger Union Österreich, A-1030 Vienna, Baumannstr 8-10
Union of Austrian Music Publishers

Österreichischer Schriftstellerverband, A-1050 Vienna V, Kettenbrückeng 11 Tel: (0222) 564151
Austrian Writers' Association
General Secretary: Wilhelm Meissel

Österreichischer Verlegerverband, A-1010 Vienna, Grünangergasse 4 Tel: (0222) 521535
Association of Austrian Publishers
President: Dieter Reisser; *Secretary-General:* Dr Gerhard Prosser

Staatlich Genehmigte Gesellschaft der Autoren, Komponisten und Musikverleger (AKM) reg Gen mbH, A-1030 Vienna III, Baumannstr 8-10 Tel: (0222) 731555
National Licensing Society of Authors, Composers and Music Publishers
President: Prof Dr Marcel Rubin

Staatlich genehmigte Literarische Verwertungsgesellschaft (LVG) reg Gen mbH, A-1060 Vienna VI, Linke Wienzeile 18 Tel: (0222) 572161
National Licensing Society for Literary Exploitation
President: Milo Dor; *Man Dir:* Franz Leo Popp

Standard Book Numbering Agency, c/o Dr G Prosser, Hauptverband des Österreichischen Buchhandels, A-1010 Vienna 1, Grünangergasse 4 Tel: (0222) 521535

Verband der Antiquare Österreichs, A-1010 Vienna, Grünangergasse 4 Tel: (0222) 521535
Austrian Antiquarian Booksellers' Association
President: Dkfm Werner Taeuber; *Secretary-General:* Dr Gerhard Prosser

Verband der Bühnenverleger Österreichs*, A-1120 Vienna, Kiningergasse 6 Tel: 8367103
Association of Austrian Theatrical Publishers

Verband österreichischer Kommissionäre, Grossbuchhändler und Auslieferer, A-1010 Vienna, Grünangergasse 4 Tel: (0222) 521535
Association of Austrian Agents, Book Wholesalers and Distributors
President: Dr Harry Lechner; *Secretary-General:* Dr Gerhard Prosser

Book Trade Reference Books and Journals

Books

Adressbuch des österreichischen Buch-Kunst-Musikalien-und Zeitschriftenhandels (Directory of Austrian Book, Art, Music and Magazine Trade), Austrian Publishers' and Booksellers' Associations, A-1010 Vienna, Grünangergasse 4

(See also reference books listed under Federal Republic of Germany)

Journals

Anzeiger des österreichischen Buchhandels (Austrian Book Trade Gazette), Austrian Publishers' and Booksellers' Association, A-1010 Vienna, Grünangergasse 4

Anzeiger des Verbandes der Antiquare Österreichs (Austrian Antiquarian Booksellers' Association Gazette), Austrian Publishers' and Booksellers' Association, A-1010 Vienna, Grünangergasse 4

Buch und Bildung (Book and Education), Holzwarth & Berger, A-1010 Vienna, Borseplatz 6

Österreichische Bibliographie (Austrian Bibliography), Austrian Publishers' and Booksellers' Association, A-1010 Vienna, Grünangergasse 4

Wiener Bücherbriefe (Viennese Book Letters), Druck- und Verlagsanstalt Forum Verlag, A-1050 Vienna, Sonnenhofgasse 8

Zeit im Buch (Today in the Book), A-1010 Vienna, Stephans-Platz 6

Publishers

Adyar-Verlag, A-8011 Graz, Wartingergasse 31, Postfach 655 Tel: (0316) 657055
Man Dir: Norbert Lauppert
Subjects: Specialist Publishing House for Theosophical Literature: The Occult, Mysticism, Yoga, Eastern Religions
1978: 3 titles *1979:* 3 titles *Founded:* 1947
ISBN Publisher's Prefix: 3-85005

Akademische Druck- und Verlagsanstalt, A-8011 Graz, Auersperggasse 12, Ruf 31 1-65, Postfach 598 Tel: 31165 Cable Add: Adeva Graz Telex: 032234 Grade A
Owner: Elsy Struzl; *Man Dir:* Hans Kögeler; *Editorial:* Dr Hans Biedermann, Dr Karl Gratzl, Dr Manfred Kramer, Inge Schwarz
Subjects: Reference, Bibliographies, Scholarly Reprints, Facsimile Editions, University Textbooks
Founded: 1949
ISBN Publisher's Prefix: 3-201

Aktuell-Verlag*, Neidhardgasse 18, A-3400 Klosterneuburg Tel: 6939 Cable Add: Aktuellverlag klosterneaburg
Publisher: Hademar Bankhofer; *Editorial:* Hans Lichtblau; *Sales:* Erich Bruckberger
1978: 3 titles

Amalthea-Verlag*, A-1030 Vienna 3, Am Heumarkt 19 Tel: (0222) 723560
Dir: Dr Herbert Fleissner
Subjects: Belles Lettres, Art, Music, Fiction
Founded: 1917
Miscellaneous: Firm is a member of Verlagsgruppe Langen-Müller/Herbig, Federal Republic of Germany (qv)

Jörn **Andreas** Verlag*, Hans-Seebach-Str 10, A-5020 Salzburg 06222/21310
Subjects: Popular Scientific and other Factbooks

Andreas und Andreas Verlagsbuchhandel*, A-5020 Salzburg, Hans-Seebach Str 10 Tel: 21318 Cable Add: Andreasverlag Salzburg Telex: 063212
Publishers: Wolf-Dietrich Andreas, Ingrid Andreas; *Dir:* Franz Pemwieser
Branch Offs: Oskar Andreas Nachfolger Herzog & Co, Reise- und Versandbuchhandel, A-1170 Vienna, Parhamerpl 9; Andreas & Andreas Verlagsbuchhandel Zweigniederlassing, D-8228 Freilassing, Ludwig Zellerstr 40, Federal Republic of Germany; Andreas und Andreas Verlagsanstalt, FL-9490 Vaduz, Liechtenstein
Subjects: General Fiction
Founded: 1956
ISBN Publisher's Prefix: 3-85012

Ferdinand **Berger** und Söhne, A-3580 Horn, Wiener Str 21-23, Postfach 14 Tel: 02982/2318 Cable Add: Berger Horn Telex: 078/77123
Subjects: Folk History, Art History, Anthropology, Archaeology, Reference, Natural Sciences, Periodicals
Founded: 1868

Bergland Verlag, A-1051 Vienna, Spengergasse 39 Tel: 555641
Man Dir: Friedrich Geyer

Verlag 'Das **Bergland-Buch**' (R Kiesel GmbH), A-5021 Salzburg, Rainerstr 19 Postfach 175 Tel: (06222) 73587 Cable Add: Berglandbuch Salzburg Telex: 06/3588
Man Dir: Gerald Nowothy; *Publicity:* Anna Hofbauer
Orders to: Dr Franz Hain, A-1220 Vienna (for Austria)
Subjects: General Fiction, History, General Science, Sport, *Tieck* books
1979: 24 titles *1980:* 21 titles *Founded:* 1929
ISBN Publisher's Prefix: 3-7023

Verlag Alexander **Bernhardt**, A-6134 Vomperberg Tel: (5242) 2131
Associate Company: Verlag der Stiftung Gralsbotschaft, Federal Republic of Germany (qv)
Subject: Philosophy
Founded: 1945

Annette **Betz** Verlag, Postfach 60, A-1095 Vienna (Located at: Alser Strasse 24, A-1095 Vienna) Tel: (0222) 425684
Man Dir: Dr Otto Mang
Parent Company: Verlag Carl Überreuter (qv)
Associate Company: Meyster Verlag, Federal Republic of Germany (qv)
Subjects: Juveniles
Founded: 1962
ISBN Publisher's Prefix: 3-7631

Bibliographisches Institut GmbH, Vienna, see Bibliographisches Institut AG, Federal Republic of Germany

Bilderbuchstudio Neugebauer*, A-4822 Bad Goisern, Haus 8 Tel: (06135) 7164 Cable Add: Neugebauer Press Bad Goisern
Parent Company: Hermann Schroedel Verlag AG, Switzerland (qv)
Associate Company: Neugebauer Press Verlag, address as above
Subjects: Art, Juveniles

Verlag Hermann **Böhlaus** Nachf GmbH*, A-1061 Vienna, Schmalzhofgasse 4, Postfach 167 Tel: (0222) 574783/4
Man Dir: Dr Dietrich Rauch; *Editorial:* Dr Peter Rauch; *Sales Dir:* Otto Sprung; *Production:* Heinz Müller; *Publicity:* Renate Redl; *Rights & Permissions:* Robert Reula
Associate Company: Verlagsbuchhandlung Hermann Böhlaus Nachfolger GmbH, Graz, Kroisbach, Ob Plaffenweg 39
Branch Off: Böhlau Verlag, D-5 Cologne 60, Schwerinstr 40, Federal Republic of Germany (qv)
Subjects: Theatre, Biography, History, Music, Art and the Arts generally, Philosophy, Religion, Psychology, General & Social Science, University Textbooks, Economics, Education, Law, Linguistics
Founded: 1947
Bookshop: Antiquariat Böhlau, A-1061 Vienna, Schmalzhofgasse 4
ISBN Publisher's Prefix: 3-205

Bohmann Druck und Verlag AG*, A-1010 Vienna 1, Canovagasse 5 Tel: 658685 Telex: 12312
Dir: Dr Rudolf Bohmann
Subjects: Trade, Technical, Industrial
Founded: 1936
ISBN Publisher's Prefix: 3-7002

Verlag Dr Gerda **Borotha-Schoeler**, A-1190 Vienna, Glatzgasse 4 Tel: 3494382/3490365
Orders to: Lechner & Sohn, A-1010 Vienna, Seilerstätte 5
Subject: General Knowledge

Wilhelm **Braumüller** Universitätsverlag GmbH, A-1092 Vienna, Servitengasse 5 Tel: 348124 Cable Add: Braumüller
Man Dir: Albert F Reiterer
Subjects: History, Philosophy, Psychology, General Nonfiction, Juveniles, Agriculture, Literature, Education, Social Science, Economics, Periodicals
1978: 39 titles *1979:* 40 titles *Founded:* 1783
ISBN Publisher's Prefix: 3-7003

Galerie und Werkstatt **Breitenbrunn**, A-7091 Breitenbrunn/Neusiedlersee, Eisenstädterstr 8 Tel: (0043) 2683/5268
Dirs: Fria Elfen, Wil Frenken
Branch Off: Stechbahn 28, D-4190 Kleve, Federal Republic of Germany
Subjects: Hand-Printed Books, Special Books of Various Kinds, Bibliophile Texts and Documents

Verlagsbuchhandlung Julius **Breitschopf**, A-1170 Vienna, Bergsteiggasse 5
Tel: 437203/4 Cable Add: Breitschopfbuch Vienna Telex: 074539
Associate Companies: Julius Breitschopf KG, Verlags buchhandlung, Federal Republic of Germany (qv); Moderne Jugend Heute GmbH (at above address)
Subjects: Picture Books, Juveniles
Bookshops: A-1090 Vienna 9, Nussdorferstr 62; A-1170 Vienna 17, Kalvarienborgstr 30
Founded: 1937
ISBN Publisher's Prefix: 3-7004

Verlag **Carinthia**, A-9010 Klagenfurt, Völkermarkter Ring 25, Postfach 197
Tel: (04222) 83651 Telex: 042204
Subjects: Fiction, Art, Religion
1978: 29 titles

Codices Selecti, A-8010 Graz, Auersperggasse 12, Postfach 598 Tel: (0316) 31165/31
Subject: Facsimile Editions

Compass Verlagsgesellschaft Rudolf Hanel und Sohn, A-1013 Vienna 1, Wipplingerstr 32, Postfach 49 Tel: 636616/17/18 Cable Add: Compass Vienna
Man Dir: Werner Futter
Subjects: Austrian Industrial, Financial & Commercial Directories, Economics, Reference, Business
1980-81: 5 titles *Founded:* 1867
ISBN Publisher's Prefix: 3-85041

Cura Verlag GmbH, A-1030 Vienna, Beatrixgasse 32, Postfach 49 Tel: 736480
Man Dir: Dr Anton Plattner
Subjects: Belles Lettres, Educational, Household, Religious, Reference, *Selbsthilfen* series
1978: 6 titles *1979:* 6 titles
ISBN Publisher's Prefix: 3-7027

Denzel Verlag Auto-und Wander Führer*, A-6020 Innsbrück, Maximilianstr 9
Tel: (05222) 26880
Subjects: Geography, Atlases, Travel
Founded: 1952

Verlag Franz **Deuticke**, A-1011 Vienna 1, Helferstorferstr 4, Postfach 761 Tel: (0222) 634345/636429
Man Dir: Dr Peter Deuticke
Subjects: Nonfiction, Technical, Psychology, General Science, University & Secondary Textbooks, Earth Sciences (Geography, Cartography, Geology, Environmental Protection), Law
Bookshops: Buchhandlung Franz Deuticke, Antiquariat Franz Deuticke, A-1010 Vienna 1, Helferstorferstr 4
Founded: 1878
ISBN Publisher's Prefix: 3-7005

Ludwig **Doblinger** (Bernard Herzmansky) Musikverlag, A-1010 Vienna 1, Dorotheergasse 10, Postfach 882
Tel: 523504
Man Dir: Helmuth Pany
Subject: Music
Founded: 1876
ISBN Publisher's Prefix: 3-90035

Edition **Dumreicher**, an imprint of Rhombus-Verlag (qv)

Econ-Verlag GmbH*, A-1030 Vienna, Ziehrerpl 9 Tel: 724485
Subjects: Reference books on Culture, Science, Engineering, Economics

Wilhelm **Ennsthaler**, A-4400 Steyr, Stadtpl 26 Tel: (07252) 22053
Subjects: Belles Lettres, Poetry, History
Bookshop: A-4400 Steyr, Stadtpl 26
Founded: 1880
ISBN Publisher's Prefix: 3-85068

Europa Verlags-GmbH, A-1232 Vienna, Altmannsdorferstr 154-156 Tel: (0222) 672622 Cable Add: Europaverlag
Telex: 131326
Dir: Erich Pogats; *Editorial:* Dr Franz Haderer, Peter Aschner; *Sales, Publicity:* Christian Lunzer; *Production:* Georg Prechtl; *Rights & Permissions:* Anna Marchfeld
Subjects: Philosophy, Natural, Social & Political Science, Current Events, Literature, Economics, Law, Psychology, Belles Lettres
1978: 65 titles *1979:* 68 titles *Founded:* 1946
ISBN Publisher's Prefix: 3-203

Evangelischer Pressverband in Österreich*, A-1030 Vienna, Ungargasse 9
Tel: 725475/725461 Telex: 01/12818
Founded: 1925

Facultas Verlag*, A-1090 Vienna, Berggasse 4 Tel: 346198 Telex: 07-6529 ICPFA A
Subject: Sciences
1978: 7 titles

Forum Verlag GmbH*, A-1050 Vienna 5, Sonnenhofgasse 8 Tel: 526411
Man Dir: Dr Franz Hentschel
Subjects: General Fiction, General Science, Art, Juveniles
Founded: 1952
ISBN Publisher's Prefix: 3-7006

Freytag-Berndt und Artaria, Kartographische Anstalt, A-1071 Vienna 7, Schottenfeldgasse 62 Tel: (0222) 939501
Telex: 133526
Chairman: Dr W R Petrowitz, Harald Hochenegg
Orders to: Kohlmarkt 9, A-1010 Vienna; Wilhelm-Greil Str 15, A-6020 Innsbruck
Subjects: Geography, Atlases, Road maps

Georg **Fromme** und Co, A-1051 Vienna 5, Spengergasse 39 Tel: 555641 Telex: 011969
Man Dir: Friedrich Geyer
Subjects: Textbooks, General Science, Technology
1978-79: 30 titles *Founded:* 1748
ISBN Publisher's Prefix: 3-85086

Dr Heinrich **Fuchs**, Thimiggasse 82, A-1180 Vienna

Gerlach & Wiedling Buch und Kunstverlag*, A-1060 Vienna, Gumpendörferstr 51
Tel: 576326/27
Parent Company: Fa Hermann Waldbaur

Gerold & Co*, A-1011 Vienna, Graben 31
Tel: 522235/525739 Cable Add: Geroldbuch Vienna Telex: 847136157 Gerol A
Man Dirs: Dr Heinrich Neider, Hans Neusser
Subjects: Philosophy, Linguistics
Bookshop: A-1011 Vienna, Graben 31
ISBN Publisher's Prefix: 3-900190

Verlag für **Geschichte und Politik**, A-1030 Vienna, Neulinggasse 26/12 Tel: 726258/753106
Man Dir: Dr Karl Cornides; *Sales Dir:* Gerda Adler; *Publicity & Advertising:* Dr Erika Rüdegger
Associate Company: Verlag Oldenbourg, Vienna (qv)
Subjects: History, Sociology, Economics, Political Science
1978: 15 titles *1979:* 15 titles *Founded:* 1947
ISBN Publisher's Prefix: 3-7028

'Globus' Zeitungs-, Druck- und Verlagsanstalt GmbH, A-1206 Vienna 20, Höchstädtpl 3 Tel: 334501 Cable Add: Globusbuch Wien
General Manager: H Zaslawski
Subjects: Politics, Popular Sciences, Belles Lettres, Sports, Fiction, Newspapers
Founded: 1945
Miscellaneous: Firm are also general representatives and distributors

Alois **Göschl** & Co*, A-1190 Vienna 19, Trummelhofgasse 12 Tel: 321180
Proprietor: Hilde Göschl
Subjects: Health, Domestic Science, Juveniles
Founded: 1949

Dr Franz **Hain***, Dr Otto Neurath-Gasse 5, A-1220 Vienna Tel: (0222) 221624
Associate Companies: Verlag der Arche, Switzerland (qv); E Pfister GmbH, Federal Republic of Germany (qv); Sanssouci Verlag, Switzerland (qv)

Heimatland Verlag*, Obere Landstrasse 12, A-3500 Krems

Verlag **Herder** und Co*, Wollzeile 33, A-1011 Vienna 1, Postfach 248 Tel: (0222) 521413 Cable Add: Herderbuch Wien
Telex: 011046 (inland); 11046 (foreign)
Man Dir: Fritz Wieninger
Associate Companies: Verlag Herder KG, Freiburg im Breisgau, Federal Republic of Germany (qv); Herder AG, Basel, Switzerland (qv); A G Ploetz KG, Würzburg, Federal Republic of Germany
Bookshop: Herder und Co, Wollzeile 33, A-1011, Vienna
Subjects: Religion, Reference, Psychology, Philosophy, Juveniles, History
Founded: 1886
ISBN Publisher's Prefix: 3-210

Herold Druck- und Verlagsgesellschaft mbH, A-1081 Vienna 8, Strozzigasse 8, Postfach 321 Tel: (0222) 431551
Man Dir: J K Niedermaier
Associate Company: Herold Verlagsgesellschaft mbH, D-8000 Munich 90, Claude Lorrainstr 11, Federal Republic of Germany
Subjects: Art, History, Religion (Catholic)
Founded: 1893
ISBN Publisher's Prefix: 3-7008

Bernhard **Herzmansky**, see Ludwig Doblinger

Johannes **Heyn***, A-9020 Klagenfurt, Kraßniggstr 42 Tel: (04222) 72759/82522
Cable Add: Heyn Klagenfurt Telex: 042401
Man Dir: Kurt Zechner; *Sales:* Gerd Zechner
Subjects: General Fiction, Belles Lettres, Poetry, Biography, History, How-to, Music, Art, Reference, Juveniles, Low- & High-priced Paperbacks, General Science, University, Secondary & Primary Textbooks
Founded: 1868
Bookshop: Buchhandlung Johannes Heyn, A-9010 Klagenfurt, Kramergasse 2-4
ISBN Publisher's Prefix: 3-85366

Edition E **Hilger***, A-1010 Vienna, Dorotheergasse 2 Tel: (0222) 525315
Man Dir & Production: Ernst Hilger; *Sales & Publicity:* Gabriele Krombholz
Subjects: Collectors' Books, Art, Limited editions of original graphics
Founded: 1973

Ferdinand **Hirt** mbH & Co KG, A-1090 Vienna, Postfach 39 (Located at: Vienna, Widerhofergasse 8) Tel: (0222) 343558
Telex: 75014
Managers: Götz Hirt-Reger, Herwig Seebauer Sabine Hirt-Reger
Orders to: A-1080 Vienna, Lerchenfelder Str 138
Subjects: Science, Education, Academic, Geographical, Teachers' Training, Serials
Founded: 1965
ISBN Publisher's Prefix: 3-7019

Brüder **Hollinek** und Co GmbH, A-1130 Vienna, Gallgasse 40A Tel: 8257062
Man Dir: Dr R Hollinek; *Sales Dir:* Mag Ing R Hollinek; *Advertising Dir, Rights & Permissions:* E Kindler-Hollinek
Subsidiary Company: Druckerei Brüder Hollinek, A-2351 Wiener Neudorf
Subjects: Reference, Medicine, Law
Bookshop: A-1130 Vienna, Gallgasse 40A
Founded: 1872

Inn-Verlag, A-6021 Innsbruck, Roseggerstr 30, Postfach 516 Tel: (05222) 43240 Cable Add: Innverlag Innsbruck Telex: 05-3617 Innvlg A
Publisher: Käte Glotz-Hagleitner; *Sales:* Günther Glotz; *Production:* Klaus Hagleitner
Subjects: Technical Books, History, Sport, School Books
Bookshop: Kommissions-Reise & Versandbuchhandlung, Roseggerstr 30, A-6020 Innsbruck
1978: 19 titles *1979:* 20 titles *Founded:* 1947
ISBN Publisher's Prefix: 3-85123

Jasomirgott-Verlag, A-3400 Klosterneuburg, Leopoldstr 19 Tel: (02243) 7570
Man Dir: Herbert Neumaerker

Jugend und Volk Verlagsgesellschaft mbH, A-1014 Vienna, Tiefer Graben 7-9
Tel: 630771-0
Man Dir: Alfred Jelinek; *Sales Dir:* Friedrich Herda; *Production:* Helmut Leiter; *Marketing & Publicity Dir:* Hubert Hladej; *Rights and Permissions:* Friedrich Themel
Subsidiary Company: Jugend und Volk Verlag GmbH, Federal Republic of Germany (qv)
Subjects: Belles Lettres, Music, Art, Picture Books, Juveniles, High-priced Paperbacks, Psychology, Social Science, Education, Viennese Memorabilia, Secondary & Primary Textbooks, Educational Materials, Austrian post-war literature, Periodicals, Reprints
Bookshop: Bücher am Heidenschuss, A-1010 Vienna, Heidenschuss 2
1979: approx 270 titles *Founded:* 1921
ISBN Publisher's Prefix: 3-7141

Verlag **Jungbrunnen**, A-1011 Vienna 1, Rauhensteingasse 5, Postfach 583 Tel: (0222) 521299
Man Dir: Hans Matzenauer; *Editorial, Rights and Permissions:* Wolf Harranth
Subjects: Juveniles, Psychology, Education
1978-79: 10 titles *Founded:* 1923
ISBN Publisher's Prefix: 3-7026

Juridica-Verlag GmbH*, A-1070 Vienna, Wimbergergasse 33 Tel: 933292
Managers: Ing Werner Sopper, Karl Weidlich

Verlag A F **Koska**, A-1095 Vienna, Zimmermanngasse 1, Postfach 61
Tel: (0222) 424689, 432137
Manager: Prof Alfred F Koska

Verlag **Kremayr und Scheriau**, A-1120 Vienna, Niederhofstr 37 Tel: 834501 Telex: 131405
Man Dir: Heine Siegert
Orders to (Trade Dept): Zentralgesellschaft Dr Berger, A-1010 Vienna, Singerstrasse 12
Subjects: General Fiction, History, How-to, Music, Art, Juveniles
Book Club: Buchgemeinschaft Donauland
Bookshop: Buchhandlung ünd Zeitschriftenvertrieb Kremayr & Scheriau, A-1121 Vienna, Niederhofstr 37
1978: 15 titles *1979:* 11 titles *Founded:* 1950
Miscellaneous: Firm is part of Verlagsgruppe Bertelsmann, Federal Republic of Germany (qv)
ISBN Publisher's Prefix: 3-218

Kummerly und Frey Verlags GmbH, Nikolsdorferstr 8, A-1050 Vienna
Associate Companies: J Fink-Kummerly und Frey Verlag GmbH, Federal Republic of Germany (qv); Kummerly und Frey (Geographischer Verlag), Switzerland (qv)
Subjects: Maps, Travel

Elisabeth **Lafite***, A-1010 Vienna 1, Hegelgasse 13 Tel: 526869
Subjects: Music books and periodicals
Founded: 1962
ISBN Publisher's Prefix: 3-85151

Langenscheidt-Verlag GmbH*, A-1010 Vienna, Singerstr 12
Subject: Foreign Languages
Miscellaneous: Firm is a subsidiary of Langenscheidt KG, Federal Republic of Germany (qv)

Leykam AG, A-8011 Graz, Stempfergasse 3, Postfach 424 Tel: 0316 71691 Cable Add: Leykam Graz Telex: 031703
Man Dir: Dr Karl Schober
Subjects: Art, General Fiction, Textbooks
Bookshops: A-8605 Kapfenberg, Kol Wallischpl; A-8700 Leoben, Am Durchbruch 5; A-8940 Liezen, Hauptstr 29; A-8680 Mürzzuschlag, Toni Schruf-Str 12; A-8330 Feldbach, Grazerstr 9
1978: 17 titles *1979:* 18 titles *Founded:* 1585
ISBN Publisher's Prefix: 3-7011

Löcker Verlag, A-1010 Vienna, Annagasse 3A Tel: 520282
General Manager: Erhard Löcker; *Publicity, Rights & Permissions:* Dr Helga Kaschl
Orders to: Pichlers Witwe und Sohn, Altmannsdorferstr 154-156, A-1232 Vienna
1979: 6 titles *1980:* 8 titles *Founded:* 1974

Paul Mangold Verlag, A-8020 Graz, Josef Poschstr 117 Tel: (0316) 52536 Cable Add: Mangoldverlag
Man Dir: Paul Mangold
Subject: Juveniles
1978: 3 titles *1979:* 3 titles *Founded:* 1977
ISBN Publisher's Prefix: 3-900301

Manutiuspresse Wulf Stratowa Verlag*, A-1011 Vienna 1, Postfach 587
Subjects: Biography, Ethnology, Travel, Juveniles, Music, Theatre, Philosophy
ISBN Publisher's Prefix: 3-85171

Manz'sche Verlags- und Universitätsbuchhandlung, A-1014 Vienna, Kohlmarkt 16 Tel: 631785
Man Dirs: Dkfm Franz Stein, Dr Anton C Hilscher
Subjects: Law, Economics, University Textbooks, Educational Materials
Bookshop: Manz'sche Verlags-und Universitätsbuchhandlung, A-1014 Vienna, Kohlmarkt 16
1979: approx 100 titles *Founded:* 1849
ISBN Publisher's Prefix: 3-214

Verlag Wilhelm **Maudrich**, A-1097 Vienna 9, Lazarettg 1, Postfach 21 Tel: 425241 Cable Add: Mundrich Verlag Wien
Man Dir: Gerhard Grois; *Advertising Dir:* Elisabeth Bernard
Subjects: How-to, Medicine, Psychology, University Textbooks
Bookshop: Buchhandlung Wilhelm Maudrich, A-1097 Vienna, Spitalg 21a
Founded: 1909
ISBN Publisher's Prefix: 3-85175

Meyster Verlag, A-1095 Vienna, Alserstr 24, Postfach 60 Tel: 425684 Cable Add: Ueberreuter Vienna Telex: 07-4802
Man Dir: Dr Otto Mang; *Editorial:* Dieter Curths; *Sales:* Hermann Meyer; *Production:* Ing Günter Plass
Parent Company: Carl Überreuter Druck und Verlag in Salzer AG (qv)
Subsidiary Company: Meyster Verlag GmbH München, Federal Republic of Germany (qv)
Associate Company: Annette Betz Verlag (qv)
Subjects: Reference, Picture Books
1978: 11 titles *Founded:* 1977
ISBN Publisher's Prefix: 3-7057

Progress-Verlag Dr **Micolini's** Wtw*, A-8010 Graz, Glacisstr 57 Tel: (03122) 79508 Cable Add: Micolini Graz
Founded: 1934

Modulverlag GmbH, Seilergasse 16, A-1010 Vienna Telex: 112816 Aplan A
Subjects: Architecture, Design

Verlag Fritz **Molden**, A-1190 Vienna Grinzing, Sandgasse 33 Tel: (0222) 323151 Cable Add: Moldenverlag Vienna Telex: 074306
Publisher: Fritz P Molden; *Man Dir, Rights & Permissions:* Dr Hans-Peter Übleis; *Sales:* Klaus P Frank (Federal Republic of Germany), Josef Lukes (Austria, Switzerland); *Publicity:* Dr Arnica-Verena Langenmaier (Munich), Renate Wunderer (Vienna); *Advertising:* Gerhart Langthaler
Subsidiary Company: Buch ins Haus GmbH, Munich, Federal Republic of Germany
Associate Companies: Verlag Fritz Molden GmbH, Federal Republic of Germany (qv); Molden Press AG, Glarus, Switzerland; Buch in's Haus GmbH, Vienna; Molden Edition Graphische Kunst, Vienna; Verlag Fritz Molden, A-6020 Innsbruck, Maria Theresienstr 10; Fritz Molden Publishing Inc, 350 Fifth Ave, Suite 6312, New York, NY 10001, USA
Subjects: General Fiction, Biography, History, How-to, Music, Art, Travel, Paperbacks, General & Social Science
1980: 600 titles *Founded:* 1965
ISBN Publisher's Prefix: 3-217

Morawa & Co, A-1011 Vienna 1, Wollzeile 11
Associate Companies: Bayerische Verlagsanstalt Bamberg (BVB), Federal Republic of Germany (qv); Adolf Zwimpfer, CH-8954 Geroldswil ZH, Switzerland (qv)
Book Club: Welt im Heim Morawa & Co

Otto **Müller** Verlag KG, A-5021 Salzburg, Ernst-Thunstr 11, Postfach 167 Tel: 72152 Cable Add: Müller Verlag
Man Dir: Dr Richard Moissl; *Sales & Publicity:* Alexander Weiger
Subjects: Belles Lettres, Poetry, History, Religion, Psychology
1978: 16 titles *Founded:* 1937
ISBN Publisher's Prefix: 3-7013

Mundus, Österreichische Verlagsgesellschaft mbH, see Paul Zsolnay Verlag GmbH

Paul **Neff** Verlag KG, A-1060 Vienna 6, Gumpendorferstr 5 Tel: (0222) 574767 Cable Add: Neffverlag
Man Dir: Karl Andreas Edlinger
Associate Company: Paul Neff Verlag KG, Federal Republic of Germany (qv)
Subjects: General Fiction, Biography, Music, Art
Founded: 1829
ISBN Publisher's Prefix: 3-7014

Edition **Neue Mitte**, A-1033 Vienna, Postfach 12 (Located at: A-1030 Vienna, Landstrasser Hauptstrasse 13/43) Tel: (0222) 733703
Man Dir: Kurt Sattlberger
Subjects: Political/Social: especially, alternatives to Marxism, future political projections; periodical *Integral*, a tribune for ideological discussion in East and West
Founded: 1976
ISBN Publisher's Prefix: 85401

Neufeld-Verlag und Galerie, A-6890 Lustenau Tel: (0577) 3158 Cable Add: Neufeld
Editorial, Rights & Permissions: Kurt Prantl
Parent Company: Lopfe KG (address as above)
Associate Company: Neufeld-Verlag, Switzerland (qv)
Founded: 1962

Wolfgang **Neugebauer***, Wiss Verlagsbuchhandlung, Postfach 64, A-5033 Salzburg (Located at: Alpenstr 12, A-5033 Salzburg)
1978: 6 titles

Neugebauer Press Verlag für bibliophile Drucke*, A-4822 Bad Goisern, Haus 8 Tel: (06135) 7164 Cable Add: Neugebauer Press Bad Goisern
Parent Company: Hermann Schroedel Verlag AG, Switzerland (qv)
Associate Company: Bilderbuchstudio Neugebauer, at above address
Subject: Art
ISBN Publisher's Prefix: 3-85195

Wolfgang **Neugebauer***, A-5033 Salzburg, Postfach 64 Tel: (06222) 23136
Man Dir: Wolfgang Neugebauer
Subjects: Natural Sciences, Theology, Philosophy, Psychology, History, German Literature
Bookshops: Wolfgang Neugebauer, A-5033 Salzburg, Alpenstr 12
1978: 9 titles *Founded:* 1975
ISBN Publisher's Prefix: 3-85376

Verlag **Niederösterreichisches Pressehaus** mbH, A-3100 St Pölten, Gutenbergstr 12 Tel: 02742/51561 Telex: 015512
Man Dir, Sales & Editorial: Dr Ingeborg Ornazeder; *Publicity:* Franz Gloser; *Production:* Josef Schalk
Orders to: R Lechner und Sohn, Heizwerkstr 10, A-1232 Vienna
Subjects: History, Literature, Architecture, Art
Bookshop: Hippolyt-Buchhandlung, A-3100 St Pölten, Linzerstr 4
1978: 44 titles *Founded:* 1889
ISBN Publisher's Prefix: 3-85326

Obelisk-Verlag*, Falkstr 1, A-6020 Innsbruck Tel: (05222) 20733
Proprietor: Helga Buchroithner
Subjects: Geography, Ethnology, Travel, Guidebooks

Oberösterreichischer Landesverlag, A-4010 Linz, Landstr 41 Tel: (0732) 78121
Man Dir: Hubert Lehner
Subjects: Biography, History, Art, Religion
Bookshops: Linz, Landstr 41, Postfach 50; A-4810 Gmunden, Rodhauspl 1; A-4710 Grieskirchen, Stadtpl 42, Postfach 26; A-4910 Ried i Innkreis, Bahnhofstr 5-7, Postfach 116; A-4150 Rohrbach, Marktpl 28, Postfach 3; A-4690 Schwanenstadt, Stadtpl 45; A-4600 Wels, Bahnhofstr 16, Postfach 146; A-4820 Bad-Ischl, Pfarrgasse 11; A-4840 Vöcklabruck, Mühlbachgasse 4 (all in Austria)
1978: 21 titles *Founded:* 1872
ISBN Publisher's Prefix: 3-85214

Octopus Verlag, A-1236 Vienna, Postfach 53 Tel: (0222) 527146
Man Dir: Erich Skrleta
Subjects: Buddhism & Oriental Philosophies, Vienna
Bookshop: A-1010 Vienna, Fleischmarkt 16
1979: 4 titles *1980:* 5 titles *Founded:* 1973
ISBN Publisher's Prefix: 3-900290

Verlag **Oldenbourg**, A-1030 Vienna, Neulinggasse 26-12 Tel: 726258/753106
Man Dir: Dr Karl Cornides; *Sales Dir:* Gerda Adler; *Publicity & Advertising:* Dr Erika Rüdegger
Parent Company: R Oldenbourg Verlag GmbH, Federal Republic of Germany (qv)
Associate Company: Verlag für Geschichte & Politik (qv)
Subjects: History, Philosophy, Engineering, General & Social Science, University & Secondary Textbooks
1978: 32 titles *1979:* 41 titles *Founded:* 1957
ISBN Publisher's Prefix: 3-7029

Verlag **Orac**, A-1014 Vienna, Graben 17, Postfach 56 Tel: 528552
Man Dir, Sales, Production, Rights & Permissions: Dkfm Helmut Hanusch; *Editorial, Publicity:* Leo Mazakarini
Subjects: Economics, Jurisprudence, Management, Sport, General Nonfiction
Bookshop: address as above
1979: 60 titles *Founded:* 1946

Österreichische Verlagsanstalt GmbH, A-1051 Vienna, Spengergasse 39 Tel: 555641
Man Dir: Friedrich Geyer

Verlag der **österreichischen Akademie der Wissenschaften**, A-1010 Vienna, Dr Ignaz Seipelpl 2 Tel: (0222) 521586 Telex: 0112628
Publishing House of the Austrian Academy of Sciences
Man Dir: Brigitta Nowotny
Subjects: Archaeology, Architecture, Art, Belles Lettres, Biography, Byzantine and Oriental Studies, English Lang and Lit, History, Jurisprudence, Maps, Music, Numismatics, Philology & Dialect Studies, Philosophy, Psychology, Reference, Social Science, Theatre, Urbanism, Paperbacks
1978: 75 titles *1979:* 75 titles *Founded:* 1973
ISBN Publisher's Prefix: 3-7001

Verlag des **österreichischen Gewerkschaftsbundes** GmbH*, A-1232 Vienna 23, Altmannsdorfer Str 154-156
Tel: 67622
Man Dir: Erich Pogats
Founded: 1947

Österreichischer Agrarverlag, Druck- und Verlags- GmbH, A-1014 Vienna, Bankgasse 1-3, Postfach 136 Tel: 639676 Cable Add: Agrarverlag Telex: 074030
Man Dir: Dr Josef Enigl
Subjects: Agriculture, Fiction, Periodicals
1978: 17 titles *1979:* 23 titles *Founded:* 1945
ISBN Publisher's Prefix: 3-7040

Österreichischer Bundesverlag GmbH, A-1010 Vienna 1, Schwarzenbergstr 5
Tel: 522561 Cable Add: Bundesverlag Vienna
Orders to: Österreichischer Bundesverlag, A-2351 Wiener Neudorf, Postfach
Subjects: Belles Lettres, History, Juveniles, Textbooks, Reference, Educational Materials, Art, Music, General Fiction, General Science
1980: 100 titles *Founded:* 1772
Miscellaneous: Foundation administered by the State under the direction of Kommerzialrat Dkfm Kurt Biak

Österreichisches Katholisches Bibelwerk, A-3400 Klosterneuberg, Stiftspl 8, Postfach 48 Tel: (02243) 2938
Man Dir, Editorial, Rights & Permissions: Dr Norbert Höslinger; *Sales:* Gabriele Maroscher, Gerlinde Bieder; *Publicity:* Brigitta Witzmann
Subjects: Bibles, Pius Parsch Institute texts, Scriptural Studies
Bookshop: A-1010 Vienna, Sinperstr 7
1978: 8 titles *1979:* 7 titles *Founded:* 1966
Miscellaneous: Company is a member of AMB (qv under Federal Republic of Germany) and WCBFA (World Catholic Federation for the Biblical Apostolate)
ISBN Publisher's Prefix: 3-85396

Pinguin-Verlag, Pawlowski KG, A-6021 Innsbruck, Lindenbühelweg 2 Tel: (05222) 81183/83571 Telex: 053173 Cable Add: Pinguinverlag Innsbruck
Man Dirs: Olaf Pawlowski, Hella Pflanzer
Subjects: Art, Juveniles, Non-fiction, Reference Books, Calendars
Founded: 1945
ISBN Publisher's Prefix: 3-7016

Ernst **Ploetz***, A-9400 Wolfsberg
Subjects: Education, Child Welfare, Textbooks
ISBN Publisher's Prefix: 3-85232

Georg **Prachner**, A-1010 Vienna, Kärntnerstr 30 Tel: 528549
Man Dir: O G Prachner
Subjects: Architecture, Art, Belles Lettres, History, Fiction
Bookshop: A-1010 Vienna, Kärtnerstr 30

Prugg Verlag*, A-7000 Eisenstadt, Haydngasse 10 Tel: (02682) 2114
ISBN Publisher's Prefix: 3-85238

Universitätsverlag Anton **Pustet**, A-5021 Salzburg, Bergstrasse 12, Postfach 144 Tel: (06222) 73507/76392 Cable Add: Pustet Salzburg
Branch Off: D-8228 Freilassing, Postfach 498, Federal Republic of Germany
Subjects: Philosophy, Religion, Psychology, Education, Political Science, Law, Poetry and Iconographs of the University of Salzburg, Music
Founded: 1598
ISBN Publisher's Prefix: 3-7025

Verlag Dr Herta **Ranner**, A-1070 Vienna, Zeismannsbrunngasse 1

Felizian **Rauch** Verlagsbuchhandlung*, A-6010 Innsbruck, Innrain 6-8, Postfach 199 Tel: (05222) 23325 Cable Add: Bücherrauch Innsbruck
Subjects: Art, History, Religion, Philosophy
Founded: 1747
ISBN Publisher's Prefix: 3-85245

Residenz Verlag, A-5020 Salzburg, Gaisbergstr 6 Tel: (06222) 25771
Man Dir: Wolfgang Schaffler; *Editorial:* Dr Jochen Jung, Renate Buchmann, Dr Gündl Hradil; *Sales Manager:* Christl Sennewald; *Production:* Dr Barbara Brunner; *Publicity:* Erika Schafleitner; *Rights & Permissions:* Renate Buchmann
Subjects: Belles Lettres, Poetry, Music, Art, Architecture
Founded: 1956
ISBN Publisher's Prefix: 3-7017

Rhombus-Verlag, Edition Dumreicher*, A-1132 Vienna, Postfach Tel: (0222) 859027
Man Dir: Vintila Ivanceanu
Orders to: Mohr, A-1010 Vienna, Singerstr 12; Lang, D-1000 Berlin 15, Sächsischestr 7, Federal Republic of Germany
Imprint: Edition Dumreicher
Subject: Experimental modern literature
1978: 7 titles *1979:* 7 titles *Founded:* 1977
ISBN Publisher's Prefix: 3-85394

E **Rötzer** Verlag*, A-7001 Eisenstadt, Postfach 25 (Burgenland) Tel: (02682) 2473
Proprietor: Elfriede Weber
Subjects: Periodicals, Reference, Guidebooks

S N-Verlag, **Salzburger Nachrichten** Verlags GmbH & Co KG*, A-5020 Salzburg, Bergstr 14, Postfach 154 Tel: (06222) 775910
Subjects: Regional (Salzburg), Architecture, History, Music, Theatre

Verlag der **Salzburger Druckerei**, A-5020 Salzburg, Bergstr 12, Postfach 144
Tel: (06222) 73507, 76392
Subjects: Arts, Poetry, History and Chronicles of Salzburg
1978-79: 10 titles
ISBN Publisher's Prefix: 3-85338

Verlag für **Sammler***, A-8011 Graz, Kreuzgasse 45, Postfach 54 Tel: 348923
Subjects: History of Art, Culture, Manners & Morals, Folklore, Early History

Verlag **Sankt Gabriel**, A-2340 Mödling Tel: 02236/86351
Man Dir: P Alfons Jochum; *all other offices:* Direktor Leo Schuler
Parent Company: Missionshaus Sankt Gabriel, A-2340 Mödling
Associate Company: Steyler Verlag, Federal Republic of Germany (qv)
Subjects: Books for Children and Young People, Religious Knowledge, Practical Theology, Belles Lettres, Travel, Education
Bookshops: A-2340, Mödling; A-1010 Vienna
Founded: 1905
ISBN Publisher's Prefix: 3-85264

Verlag **Sankt Peter**, A-5010 Salzburg, Postfach 113 Tel: (06222) 4216682 Telex: 06/3094
Man Dir: R M Rinnerthaler
Subjects: Austrian Church Art, Austrian Guidebooks, Austrian History
1980: 100 titles *Founded:* 1946
ISBN Publisher's Prefix: 3-900173

Paul **Sappl**, Schulbuch- und Lehrmittelverlag*, A-6332 Kufstein, Eichelwang 406 Tel: (05372) 2835 Telex: 5119115
Branch Off: A-1050 Vienna, Stolberggasse 31-33
Subjects: School Books, Driving School Text Books
Founded: 1953

Dr A **Schendl** GmbH & Co KG, A-1041 Vienna, Karlsgasse 15, Postfach 29
Tel: (0222) 655593-96
Dirs: Dr Anna Schendl, Franz Ogg
Subjects: History, Ethnography, Geography, Folklore, Art, Literature, Music, Economy, Periodicals
1978: 6 titles *1979:* 5 titles

Schönbrunn-Verlag GmbH, A-1010 Vienna 1, Schulerstr 1-3 Tel: 526905
Subject: Art
Founded: 1946

Anton **Schroll** & Co, Buch und Kunstverlag, A-1051 Vienna 5, Spengergasse 39
Tel: 555641 Cable Add: Schrollverlag Vienna
Man Dir: Friedrich Geyer, Dieter Reisser
Branch Off: D-8000 Munich 95, Boostr 15, Federal Republic of Germany
Subjects: Belles Lettres, History, Art
1978: 20 titles *1979:* 20 titles *Founded:* 1889
ISBN Publisher's Prefix: 3-7031

Verlagsbüro Karl **Schwarzer***, A-1010 Vienna, Dorotheergasse 6-8 Tel: (0222) 521687
Man Dir: Karl Schwarzer
Subjects: Almanacs, Special Editions

Severin Presse, A-2346 Südstadt Vienna, Dobrastr 112, Postfach 15 Tel: (02236) 811744
Publisher: Peter Croy
Subject: Art (Original Engravings)

Josef Otto **Slezak**, A-1040 Vienna, Wiedner Hauptstr 42 Tel: (0222) 570259
Sales Managerial: Ilse Slezak
Subjects: Transport, especially historical accounts of railways and tramways in Austria and Europe generally
1978: 12 titles *1979:* 12 titles

Springer-Verlag KG, A-1011 Vienna, Mölkerbastei 5, Postfach 367 Tel: (0222) 639614 Cable Add: Springerbuch Wien Telex: 074506
Man Dir: Dr Wilhelm Schwabl; *Sales Manager:* Rudolf Siegle; *Promotion, Rights & Permissions:* Dr Erna Ungersbaeck; *Production Dir:* Bruno Skuhra
Associate Company: Springer-Verlag Inc, 175 Fifth Ave, New York, NY 10010, USA

Subjects: Medicine, Natural Sciences, Engineering, General & Social Science, Economics, Law, Philosophy, University Textbooks, Reference
Bookshop: Minerva Wissenschaftliche Buchhandlung GmbH, A-1010 Vienna, Schottengasse 7
1978: 66 titles *1979:* 63 titles *Founded:* 1924
ISBN Publisher's Prefix: 3-211

Dr Karl **Steinhauser***, A-2544 Leobersdorf, Südbahnstr 5
Subject: Arts

Leopold **Stocker** Verlag, A-8011 Graz, Bürgergasse 11, Postfach 438 Tel: (0316) 71636 Cable Add: Stockerverlag Graz
Publisher: Dr Ilse Dvorak-Stocker; *Editorial Sales, Publicity, Rights and Permissions:* Dr Peter Strallhofer
Branch Off: Agent in Vienna is: Rudolf Lechner & Sohn, Heizwerkstr 10, A-1232 Vienna
Subjects: Belles Lettres, Contemporary Literature, Hunting, Nature and Mountain Books, Specialist Books, Agricultural Textbooks and School Books
Founded: 1917

Verlag **Styria**, A-8010 Graz, Schönaugasse 64, Postfach 871 Tel: 775610 Cable Add: Styriaverlag Graz Telex: 031782 Kleine Zeitung
Man Dir, Editorial: Dr Gerhard Trenkler; *Sales:* Wolfgang Fath; *Production:* Hans Paar; *Publicity:* Peter Altenburg; *Rights & Permissions:* Margarethe Katholnig
Parent Company: Katholischer Pressverein
Branch Offs: Verlag Styria — Meloun & Co, D-5000 Cologne 51, Schillerstr 6, Postfach 511029, Federal Republic of Germany; Verlag Styria, Repräsentanz Wien, A-1010 Vienna, Lobkowitzpl 1
Subjects: Religion, History, Philosophy, Biography, Juveniles, Education, Books, Belles Lettres, Reference Books, Current Affairs
Bookshops: Buchhandlung Styria, A-1010 Vienna, Opernring 15; Buchhandlung Styria, A-8010 Graz, Albrechtgasse 5; Buchhandlung Ulrich Moser, A-8010 Graz, Herrengasse 23; Bücherbox, Goethestr 42, A-8010 Graz; Buchhandlung Styria, A-8750 Judenburg, Hauptplatz 1; Buchhandlung Styria, A-8720 Knittelfeld, Kapuzinerplatz 3, Postfach 72
1978: 80 titles *Founded:* 1869
ISBN Publisher's Prefix: 3222

Editio **Totius** Mundi E E Maenner*, A-1090 Vienna, Gussenbauergasse 5-9 Tel: 347346
Cable Add: Maennermundi
Subjects: Art, Maps, Textbooks

Rudolf **Trauner** Verlag*, A-4020 Linz, Baumbachstr 4a Tel: (0732) 78241-3
Man Dir: Rudolf Trauner
Branch Off: A-4020 Linz, Köglstr 14
Subjects: Popular Medicine, How-to, Art, Juveniles, Cookbooks, Sports, Maps, Nonfiction
1978: 7 titles *Founded:* 1946
ISBN Publisher's Prefix: 3-85320

Edition **Tusch**, A-1160 Vienna, Seitenberggasse 39 Tel: (0222) 452165
Cable Add: Editusch Wien Telex: 76262 Tusch A
Subject: Art

Verlagsanstalt **Tyrolia**, A-6020 Innsbruck, Exlgasse 20, Postfach 220 Tel: 81541 Cable Add: Tyrolia-Verlag Innsbruck Telex: 05/3620
Dirs: Dr Schiemer, Dr Kunzenmann
Subjects: Theology, School Books, Juveniles, Tour Guides, Illustrated Books, General Nonfiction
Bookshops: in Innsbruck, Ehrwald, Fulpmes, Imst, Landeck, Lienz, Mayrhofen, St Johann, Schwaz, Wattens, Vienna
1978: 49 titles *Founded:* 1888
ISBN Publisher's Prefix: 3-7022

Verlag Carl **Überreuter**, A-1095 Vienna, Alserstr 24, Postfach 60 Tel: (0222) 425684
Cable Add: Überreuter Vienna
Telex: 074802
Publisher: Thomas F Salzer, Andreas Salzer; *Man Dir:* Otto Mang; *Editorial:* Dr Marion Pongracz, Ingrid Weixelbaumer; *Sales, Publicity:* Thomas C Sacken
Subsidiary Companies: Annette Betz Verlag, Meyster Verlag, Austria (qqv); Meyster Verlag, Federal Republic of Germany (qv)
Branch Offs: A-2100 Korneuburg, Industriestr 1; D-6900 Heidelberg/Schlierbach, In der Aue 32A, Federal Republic of Germany
Subjects: Juveniles, Low-priced Paperbacks, Secondary & Primary Textbooks, Educational Materials
Founded: 1548
ISBN Publisher's Prefix: 3-8000

Universal Edition AG*, A-1015 Vienna, Bösendorfer Str 12, Postfach 3 Tel: 658695
Cable Add: Musikedition Wien Telex: 1397
Dirs: Dr J Juranek, S Harpner, A Schlee
Subjects: Music, Musicology
Founded: 1901

Urban und Schwarzenberg, A-1096 Vienna 9, Frankgasse 4, Postfach 102 Tel: (0222) 422731/2
Man Dir: Helmut Rieger
Subjects: Medicine, Psychology, Physics
Bookshop: At above address
Founded: 1866
Miscellaneous: Firm is a branch of Verlag Urban und Schwarzenberg, Federal Republic of Germany (qv)
ISBN Publisher's Prefix: 3-85327

Verband der wissenschaftlichen Gesellschaften Österreichs, A-1070 Vienna, Lindengasse 37 Tel: 0222/932166/934756
Telex: 134981 Vwgoe A
Man Dir: Dr Rainer Zitta
Orders to: Austria: Verband, Vienna; All other countries: Proost en Brandt, D-5000 Koeln 41 (Brannsfeld), Eupenerstr 92
1978: 29 titles *1979:* 29 titles *Founded:* 1954
ISBN Publisher's Prefix: 3-85369

Veritas-Verlag*, A-4010 Linz, Harrachstr 5, Postfach 403 Tel: 0732/71081
Man Dir: Karl Grüber
Branch Off: Veritas Passau, Theresienstr 42, D839 Passau
Subjects: Religion, Music, Art, Textbooks
Bookshop: Veritas, Singerstr 26, A-1010 Vienna
1978: 24 titles *Founded:* 1945
ISBN Publisher's Prefix: 3-85329

Vorarlberger Verlagsanstalt GmbH, A-6850 Dornbirn, Schwefel 81 Tel: (05572) 62864/64697
Subject: Literature

Universitätsverlag **Wagner** GmbH, A-6010 Innsbruck, Andreas-Hoferstr 13/1, Postfach 219 Tel: (05222) 27721 Cable Add: Universitätsverlag Wagner, A-6010 Innsbruck
Man Dir: Gottfried Grasl
Imprints: Universitätsverlag Wagner Innsbruck
Subjects: Scientific Works, Maps, Illustrated Motoring Guides, Literature, Colloquial Poetry
1978: 14 titles *1979:* 8 titles *Founded:* 1554
ISBN Publisher's Prefix: 3-7030

Weilburg-Verlag*, A-2500 Baden bei Wien, Am Fischertor 5 Tel: 02252/2906 Cable Add: Weilburg Verlag 2500 Baden
Subjects: Art Books, Lyrical Poetry, Numbered and Autographed Bibliophile Editions

Verlag Galerie **Welz** Salzburg, A-5010 Salzburg, Sigmund-Haffner-Gasse 16, Postfach 123 Tel: 41771
Publisher: Franz Eder; *Sales:* Hannes Lüftenegger
Subject: Art, Art Books, Art Prints, Art Post Cards, Art Posters

Wiener Dom-Verlag, A-1080 Vienna, Strozzigasse 8
General Manager: Kr J K Niedermaier
Subjects: Art, Education, History, General Science, Religion, Nonfiction
Founded: 1946
ISBN Publisher's Prefix: 0-85351

Wiener Urtext Edition-Musikverlag GmbH & Co KG*, A-1010 Vienna, Bösendorferstr 12 Tel: (publication) 658695, (sales) 657651
Cable Add: Musikedition Telex: 1397
Man Dir: Stefan G Harpner; *Sales Dir:* Vladimir Prusa; *Publicity & Advertising:* Friederike Zimmermann
Parent Company: Verlag B Schotts Söhne, Federal Republic of Germany (qv) and Universal Edition AG, Vienna, Austria
Subject: Music, especially *original scores* of Bach, Beethoven, Brahms, Chopin, Haydn, Mozart, Schubert, Schumann. All accompanying texts are in German and English
1978: 55 titles *Founded:* 1972

J **Wimmer** Druckerei und Zeitungshaus GmbH & Co*, A-4010 Linz, Promenade 23, Postfach 269
Subjects: Juveniles, Geography, History, Commerce, Art

Alfred **Winter** Verlag*, Gstöttengutstr 47, A-5020 Salzburg Tel: (06222) 35314
General Manager: Alfred Winter; *Reader:* Volker E Horn
Founded: 1974
Subjects: Belles Lettres, Folklore, Local History and Geography, Art Books
ISBN Publisher's Prefix: 3-85380

Kunstverlag **Wolfrum**, A-1010 Vienna 1, Augustinerstr 10 Tel: 525398/524178 Cable Add: Witwolf Vienna
Man Dir: Hubert Wolfrum
Subjects: Art, Art Reproductions, Calendars
Bookshop: A-1010 Vienna, Augustinerstr 10
Founded: 1919
ISBN Publisher's Prefix: 3-900178

Wort und Welt Verlag*, A-6020 Innsbruck, Heiliggeiststr 21 Tel: (05222) 25923 Cable Add: Wortwelt Innsbruck
Publisher: Professor Dr Walter Miess; *Editorial:* Günther Schick; *Publicity:* Ingrid Obermayr
Orders to: Thaurdruck, A-6065 Thaur bei Innsbruck
Branch Off: D-8031 Puchheim, Munich, Postfach 1169, Federal Republic of Germany
Subjects: Humour, Textbooks, Art, Belles Lettres, Factbooks
1978: 11 titles *1979:* 9 titles *Founded:* 1972
ISBN Publisher's Prefix: 3-85373

Paul **Zsolnay** Verlag GmbH, A-1041 Vienna, Prinz-Eugen-Str 30 Tel: (0222) 657661
Cable Add: Zsolnayverlag Wien Telex: 01-31515 (ruleso) Lechner
Dirs: Hans W Polak, August Langer; *Sales Manager:* Wolfgang Dechant; *Editor:* Alexandra Auer; *Production:* Peter Baumgartner; *Rights & Permissions:* Olga Kaindl
Parent Company: Heinemann & Zsolnay Ltd, see The Heinemann Group of Publishers, UK
Associate Companies: Mundus, Österreichische Verlagsgesellschaft mbH, A-1041 Vienna 4, Prinz-Eugen-Str 30,

Austria; Paul Zsolnay Verlag, Federal Republic of Germany (qv)
Branch Off: Büro München, Hildegart Eichholz, Über der Klause 7a, D-8000 Munich 90, Federal Republic of Germany
Subjects: General Fiction, Belles Lettres, Poetry, Biography, History, How-to, Music, Juveniles, Social & Political Science, Art, Medicine, Sports
1979: 36 titles *Founded:* 1923
ISBN Publisher's Prefix: 3-552

Book Clubs

A B C Buchklub GmbH & Co KG*, A-1010 Vienna 1, Schubertring 3

Ing Johann **Brunner***, A-4400 Steyr, Rooseveltstr 2b

Bücherbund Buch- und Schallplattenhandel Verlagsgesellschaft mbH*, A-1150 Vienna 14, Thaliastr 68

Buchhandlung b Theater a d Wien*, Stein & Co, A-1060 Vienna VI, Linke Wienzelle 6-8

Rudolf **Buchner***, A-8280 Fürstenfeld, Hauptstr 13

Deutsche Buch-Gemeinschaft C A Koch's Verlag Nachfolger*, Zweigniederlassung Wien, A-1010 Vienna I, Wipplingerstr 23

Buchgemeinschaft **Donauland**, A-1120 Vienna, Niederhofstr 37 Tel: 834501 Telex: 131405
Owned by: Kremayr & Scheriau

Erster Moderner Lesezirkel Kreith & Schram*, A-1070 Vienna, VII, Mariahilfer Str 54 Tel: 935550

Erster Wiener Lesezirkel Gebrüder Kreith*, A-1070 Vienna, VII, Mariahilfer Str 54 Tel: 935550

Festungsverlag*, A-5020 Salzburg, Mirabellpl 7

Reinfried **Fuchsbichler***, A-8021 Graz, Annenstr 53 and Querg. 1-3, Postfach 1026

Gertraude **Just***, A-3100 St Pölten, Kremsergasse 41

Eduard **Kaiser***, Verlag Buchgemeinde Alpenland OGH, A-9020 Klagenfurt, Brunnengasse 3, Postfach 30

Jos A **Kienreich***, A-8011 Graz, Sackstr 6, Postfach 428

Friedrich **Meixner***, A-8600 Bruck/M, Herzog-Ernst-Str 18, Postfach 123

Morawa & Co*, A-1011 Vienna I, Wollzeile 11/4

Osterreichischer Buchklub der Jugend, A-1041 Vienna, Mayerhofgasse 6 Tel: (0222) 651754

Elisabeth **Reiter***, A-6600 Reutte, Attlmayrstr 10

A & G **Tengler***, A-6010 Innsbruck, Bürgerstr 28, Postfach 214

Volksbuchverlag GmbH*, A-1232 Vienna, Altmannsdorferstr 154

Anna **Weber***, A-3500 Krems, Schmidgasse 13, Postfach 87 Tel: 02732/2857

Welt im Heim Morawa & Co*, A-1011 Vienna I, Wollzeile 11/4 Postfach 606
Owned by: Morawa & Co

Herta **Winter***, A-8490 Radkersburg, Langg 21

Major Booksellers

Hans **Fürstelberger**, A-4010 Linz, Landstr 49 Tel: (0732) 73177

Gerold & Co*, A-1011 Vienna, Graben 31 Tel: 522235/525739 Telex: 847136157 Gerol A (export and library supplier)
Man Dirs: Dr Heinrich Neider, Hans Neusser

Anna **Hadwiger***, A-1010 Vienna, Johannesgasse 4 Tel: (0222) 524772/3 (wholesaler)

Dr Franz **Hain***, A-1220 Vienna, Dr Otto Neurath-Gasse 5 Tel: (0222) 221624 (wholesaler)

A L **Hasbach**, A-1010 Vienna, Wollzeile 9 Tel: 528876/528932
Manager: Dr Herbert Borufka

Leopold **Heidrich**, A-1010 Vienna, Plankengasse 7 Tel: 523701 (wholesaler)

Gebhard **Heinzle's** Erben*, A-6700 Bludenz, Josef-Wolf-Platz 2 Tel: (05552) 2066 (export and library supplier)

Herder und Co*, A-1011 Vienna, Wollzeile 33 Tel: (0222) 521413

Johannes **Heyn***, A-9020 Klagenfurt, Krassnigstr 42 Tel: (04222) 82024 (export and library supplier)

Buchhandlung Karl **Hofbauer**, A-8430 Leibnitz, Hauptpl 31, Postfach 68 Tel: (03452) 27-93 and 21-77

Eduard **Hollriegl**, A-5020 Salzburg, Sigmund-Haffner-Gasse 10 Tel: (06222) 41146/52651 (export and library supplier)

Jos A **Kienreich***, Sackstrasse 6, A-8011 Graz
(export and library supplier)

Walter **Krieg***, Kärntnerstr 4, A-1010 Vienna Tel: (0222) 521193 (export and library supplier)

Franz **Leo** & Comp KG*, Universitätsbuchhandlung, A-1010 Vienna, Lichtensteg 1 Tel: (0222) 631451 (export and library supplier)

Manz'sche Verlags und Universitätsbuchhandlung, A-1014 Vienna, Kohlmarkt 16 Tel: (0222) 631785 (export and library supplier)

Wilhelm **Maudrich**, Buchhandlung und Verlag für medizinische Wissenschaften, A-1097 Vienna, Spitalg 21a Tel: (0222) 424712 (export and library supplier)

Robert **Mohr***, A-1010 Vienna, Singerstr 12 Tel: (0222) 525711 (wholesaler)

Marie **Mora** OHG*, A-5010 Salzburg, Residenzplatz 2 Tel: (06222) 43620 (export and library supplier)

Buchhandlung W **Neugebauer** GmbH und Co KG, A-4010 Linz, Landstr 1, Taubenmarkt Tel: (0732) 71766 (export and library supplier)

Max **Pock**, Universitätsbuchhandlung*, A-8010 Graz, Hauptplatz 1 Tel: (03122) 75254/79042 Telex: 03-1873 (export and library supplier)

Georg **Prachner** KG, A-1010 Vienna, Kärntnerstr 30 Tel: 528549
Manager: O G Prachner

Schottentor*, A-1014 Vienna, Schottengasse 9

Styria*, A-8010 Graz, Albrechtgasse 5 Tel: 0316/79355; A-1010 Vienna, Opernring 15 Tel: 0222/577196

Tyrolia*, A-6010 Innsbruck, Maria Theresienstr 15 Tel: (05222) 24944

Urban und Schwarzenberg, A-1096 Vienna 9, Frankgasse 4, Postfach 102 Tel: (0222) 422731/2

Wagner'sche Universitätsbuchhandlung, Museumstr 4, A-6021 Innsbruck Tel: (05222) 22316 Telex: 053793 (export and library supplier)
Dir: Ernst Angerer

Rupertusbuchhandlung Augustin **Weis** und Söhne KG, A-5024 Salzburg, Dreifaltigkeitsg 12, Linzer Gasse 29 Tel: (06222) 71661 (export and library supplier)

Fachbuchhandlung für **Wirtschaft und Recht**, A-1181 Vienna, Währinger Str 122 Tel: (0222) 348391 (export and library supplier)
Proprietor: Eleonore Stropek

Kunstverlag **Wolfrum**, A-1010 Vienna, Augustinstr 10 Tel: (0222) 524178/525398 Cable Add: Witwolf Wien (export and library supplier of art books)
Manager: Erich Pospisil

Zentralgesellschaft für buchgewerbliche und graphische Betriebe*, A-1010 Vienna, Singerstr 12 Tel: (0222) 526136 (wholesaler)
Proprietor: Dr Gottfried Berger

Major Libraries

Archiv der Universität Wien*, Vienna 1

Bibliothek des **Benediktinerklosters** Melk in Niederösterreich, A-3390 Melk Tel: (02752) 2312/21
Library of the Melk Benedictine Monastery in Lower Austria
Librarian: P Gottfried Glassner

Administrative Bibliothek und österreichische Rechtsdokumentation im **Bundeskanzeramt***, A-1010 Vienna, Herrengasse 23
Administrative Library and Law Documentation of the Chancellery

Bibliothek des **Kriegsarchivs Wien**, A-1070 Vienna, Stiftgasse 2
Library of the War Archives Dept of the Austrian State Archives
Librarian: Dr Edith Wohlgemuth

Bibliothek der **Österreichischen Akademie der Wissenschaften**, A-1010 Vienna, Dr Ignaz Seipelpl 2
Library of the Austrian Academy of Science

Österreichische Nationalbibliothek, A-1014 Vienna, Josefspl 1 Tel: (0222) 521684/525255
Austrian National Library

Bucherei des **Österreichischen Patentamtes**, A-1014 Vienna, Kohlmarkt 8-10
Library of the Austrian Patent Office
Publications: Österreichisches Patentblatt, Österreichischer Markenanzeiger, Patentschriften

Österreichisches Staatsarchiv, A-1010 Vienna 1, Minoritenpl 1
Austrian State Archives
Publication: Mitteilungen des Österreichischen Staatsarchivs

Universitätsbibliothek Graz, Universitätspl 3, Graz Tel: (0316) 31581/2 Telex: 031662
Librarian: Dr Franz Kroller
Publications: Jahresbericht; Fachliche Benützungsanleitungen für die Bibliotheken der Universität Graz, Heft 1 (1973); Bibliographische Informationen, 1 (1974); Schriftenreihe EDV-Projekt, 1 (1978); Grazer Zeitschriften-Verzeichnis, 1 (1974)

Universitätsbibliothek Innsbruck, A-6010 Innsbruck, Innrain 50 Tel: (05222) 33601 Telex: 53708

Universitätsbibliothek Wien, A-1010 Vienna, Dr-Karl-Lueger-Ring 1 Tel: (0222) 43002376/43002371

Wiener Stadt- und Landesarchiv*, A-1082 Vienna, Magistratsabteilung 8, 1 Rathaus
Vienna Municipal Archives

Wiener Stadt und Landesbibliothek, A-1082 Vienna, Rathaus Tel: (0222) 42800/9
Vienna Municipal and County Library
Dir: Dr Franz Patzer

Library Associations

Dokumentationsstelle für neuere österreichische Literatur, A-1060 Vienna, Gumpendorferstr 15/1/13 Tel: (0222) 561249
Documentation Centre for Modern Austrian Literature
General Secretary: Dr Heinz Lunzer
Publication: Zirkular

Österreichische Gesellschaft für Dokumentation und Information, c/o Austrian Standards Institute, A-1021 Vienna, Leopoldsgasse 4, Postfach 130
Austrian Society for Documentation and Information
Executive Secretary: B Hofer
Publication: ÖGDI-Mitteilungen

Österreichisches Institut für Bibliotheksforschung, Dokumentations- und Informationswesen*, A-1014 Vienna, Josefsplatz 1
Austrian Institute for Library Research, Documentation and Information
Secretary-General: Prof Dr Josef Mayerhöfer
Publication: Biblos

Verband österreichischer Archivare, c/o A-1010 Vienna, Minoritenpl 1
Association of Austrian Archivists
Publication: Scrinium (twice yearly)

Verband österreichischer Volksbüchereien und Volksbibliothekare, A-1080 Vienna, Lange Gasse 37 Tel: (0222) 439722
Association of Austrian Public Libraries
Man Chairman: Dr R Müller

Vereinigung österreichischer Bibliothekare, A-1014 Vienna, Josefspl 1 (Österreichische National-Bibliothek) Tel: 521684
Association of Austrian Librarians
President: Franz Kroller; *Secretary:* Manfred Lube
Publication: Mitteilungen (quarterly)

Library Reference Books and Journals

Books

Dokumentation und Information in Österreich (Documentation and Information in Austria), Brüder Hollinek, A-1030 Vienna, Landstrasser Hauptstr 163

Handbuch österreichischer Bibliotheken (Handbook of Austrian Libraries), Austrian National Library, A-1014 Vienna, Josefspl 1

Journals

Biblos, Austrian journal for book and library personnel, documentation, bibliography and bibliophily (text in English and German), c/o Austrian National Library, A-1014 Vienna, Josefspl 1

Mitteilungen der Vereinigung österreichischer Bibliothekare (Bulletin of the Association of Austrian Librarians), c/o Austrian National Library, A-1014 Vienna, Josefspl 1

ÖGDI-Mitteilungen (ÖGDI Bulletin) (Österreichische Gesellschaft für Dokumentation und Information), c/o Austrian Productivity Centre, A-1014 Vienna, Renngasse 5

Scrinium, Association of Austrian Archivists, c/o A-1010 Vienna, Minoritenpl 1

Literary Associations and Societies

Österreichische Exlibris-Gesellschaft, A-1040 Vienna, Johann Strauss-Gasse 28-18
Austrian Book-plate-collectors' Society
Chairman: Professor Dr Gustav Dichler
Publications: Jahrbuch, Mitteilungen, books on the art of the bookplate and on bookplate-collecting

Österreichische Gesellschaft für Literatur, A-1010 Vienna, Herrengasse 5
Austrian Literary Society
President: Dr W Kraus

Österreichisches Institut für Bibliographie*, Vienna 1, Rathauspl 4
Dir: Dr Oskar Langer

Österreichischer P E N-Club, Concordia Haus, A-1010 Vienna 1, Bankgasse 8
Secretary: Franz Richter

Wiener Bibliophilen-Gesellschaft*, A-1090 Vienna IX, Leichtensteinstr 61
Vienna Booklovers' Society
Chairman: Sekt Chef Dr Walter Sturminger

Wiener Goethe-Verein, A-1010 Vienna, Reitschulgasse 2
President: Dr Conrad H Lester; *Vice-President:* Dr Herbert Zeman
Publication: Jahrbuch (yearbook)

Literary Periodicals

Blätter für Volksliteratur (Popular Literature Magazine), Verein der Freunde der Volksliteratur, Graz, Naglergasse 22

Eröffnungen (Communications), magazine for literature and pictorial art (text mainly in German, occasionally in English or Slovene), Hubert Fabian Kulterer, A-1120 Vienna, Unter-Meidlinger Str 16-18

Eselsohr (Dog's Ear), G Pilz, A-4320 Perg, Stifterstr 4a

Literatur und Kritik (Literature and Criticism), Otto Müller Verlag, A-5021 Salzburg, Ernst-Thunstr 11

Literaturspiegel (Mirror to Literature), Vienna 4, Schleifmühlgasse 23-29

Manuskripte (Manuscripts); journal for literature, art, criticism, A-8010 Graz, Forum Stadtpark 1 Tel: (03122) 77734

Modern Austrian Literature (text and summaries in English and German), Arthur Schnitzler International Research Association, c/o Donald G Daviau, Editor, Department of German, University of California, Riverside, California 92502

Moderne Literatur (Modern Literature), Zeitschriftenverlag, Vienna, Favoritenstr 235/26

Das Pult (The Desk); literature, art, criticism, Klaus Sandler, A-3100 St Pölten, Schiessfach 12

Schrifttumsspiegel (Mirror to Literature), Gesellschaft für Ganzhehsforschung, A-1191 Vienna, Franz Klein Gasse 1

Sprachkunst (Art of Language) (text in English, French, German and Russian); contributions to the study of literature, Verlag der österreichischen Akademie der Wissenschaften, A-1010 Vienna, Dr Ignaz Seipelpl 2

Literary Prizes

Austrian literary prizes are generally not associated with a single work, and are not often awarded in a lump sum, because of the high taxes authors have to pay. In addition to those cited below, each province has its own prize

Austrian Appreciation Prize for Literature for Children and Young People
Conferred on an author in appreciation of his life's work. Presented in 1980 for the first time in a three-yearly cycle. Enquiries to Bundesministerium für Unterricht und Kunst, A-1014 Vienna, Postfach 65, Sektion V/Abteilung 3A

'Encouragement Prize'*
40,000 Schillings, awarded by jury. Submissions accepted. Enquiries to Bundesministerium für Unterricht und Kunst, A-1014 Vienna, Postfach 65, Sektion V/Abteilung 3A

'Encouragement Prizes' for Books for Children and Young People
There are six categories (small children, children reading levels 1-4 and levels 5-8, books for young people, translation and illustration) total sum 150,000 Schillings. All awarded by a jury. Submissions accepted. Enquiries to Bundesministerium für Unterricht und Kunst, A-1014 Vienna, Postfach 65, Sektion V/Abteilung 3A

Great Austrian State Prize*
150,000 Schillings, for life's work. Awarded by Österreichischer Kunstsenat. No applications. Enquiries to Bundesministerium für Unterricht und Kunst, A-1014 Vienna, Postfach 65, Sektion V/Abteilung 3A

New Writers Stipendium for Literature*
Four given each year. 6,000 Schillings each month for twelve months, awarded by jury. Submissions accepted. Enquiries to Bundesministerium för Unterricht und Kunst, A-1014 Vienna, Postfach 65, Sektion V/Abteilung 3A

'Recognition Prize'*
75,000 Schillings. Awarded by jury. No applications. Enquiries to Bundesministerium für Unterricht und Kunst, A-1014 Vienna, Postfach 65, Sektion V/Abteilung 3A

State Stipendium for Literature*
Eight given each year. 6,000 Schillings each month for twelve months, awarded by jury. Submissions accepted. Enquiries to Bundesministerium für Unterricht und Kunst, A-1014 Vienna, Postfach 65, Sektion V/Abteilung 3A

Vienna Art Foundation (Wiener Kunstfonds)*
Prizes totalling 20,000 Schillings. Enquiries to Zentralsparkasse der Gemeinde Wien, A-1030 Vienna, Vordere Zollamtstr 13

Vienna Prize for children's and young people's literature
Awarded annually by the City of Vienna for a distinguished book for children and young people, including illustration. Enquiries to Bundesministerium für Unterricht und Kunst,

A-1014 Vienna, Postfach 65, Sektion V/Abteilung 3A

Anton **Wildgans** Prize of Austrian Industry Awarded annually, at the beginning of the autumn, to an Austrian lyric poet, dramatist, novelist or essayist, young or middle aged. The author must be an Austrian citizen, writing in German, who lives either in Austria or abroad. Maximum prize 50,000 Schillings. Awarded by a committee. No applications. 1979 prize went to Matthias Mander. Enquiries to Vereinigung österreichischer Industrieller, A-1031 Vienna

Translation Agencies and Associations

Vienna **Übersetzungsbüro** und Sprachinstitut*, A-1010 Vienna, Universitätsstr 11

Bahamas

General Information

Language: English
Religion: Largest of 12 denominations are Baptist, Roman Catholic and Anglican
Population: 225,000
Bank Hours: 0930-1500 Monday-Thursday; 0930-1700 Friday
Shop Hours: 0900-1700 Monday-Saturday; noon closing on Friday
Currency: 100 cents = 1 Bahamian dollar
Export/Import Information: No tariffs on books and advertising matter. No import licences required. No exchange controls
Copyright: Berne, UCC (see International section)

Publishers

Bright Advertising and Publishing Ltd*, PO Box N4181, Nassau

Etienne **Dupuch** Jr Publications Ltd*, PO Box N7513, Nassau
Subjects: Journals, Maps, Educational Colouring Books

Major Booksellers

Bahamas Anglo American Book Store*, PO Box N9046, 9 Nassau Arcade, Hoffer Bldg, Bay St Tel: 50388

Bahamas Book & Bible House*, PO Box N356 Tel: 23032

Calypso Distributors Ltd*, PO Box ES 6220, Chesapeake Rd Tel: 28986 (wholesaler)

Christian Book Shop*, PO Box N4924, Shirley & Hall Lane Tel: (809) 325 8744
Manager: David Duame

The **Island** Shop*, PO Box N3947, Bay St Tel: 24183/21588

Lee's Book Centre, Bank Lane, PO Box N-8196, Nassau Tel: 22128
Manager: Maria Lee

Tryma Book Shop*, PO Box N1243, Independence Shopping Centre Tel: 57478

United Book Shop & Stationers, PO Box ES6220, Oakes Field Shopping Centre Tel: 50316; Madeira St Shopping Centre Tel: 28597/28986 Cable Add: Fantasia
President: Sigmund A Pritchard

Major Libraries

Archival Institution, Public Records Office, Ministry of Education and Culture, PO Box N3913, Nassau Tel: (809) 3223045

College of the Bahamas Library, PO Box N4912, Nassau Tel: 36456/7
Librarian: Paul G Boultbee
Publication: Bahamas Reference Collection: a Bibliography (1980, with annual supplements)

John **Harvard** Lending Library*, PO Box F40, Freeport, Grand Bahama

Nassau Public Library*, PO Box N3210, Nassau

Bahrain

General Information

Language: Arabic (English used commercially)
Religion: Muslim, officially
Population: 345,000
Literacy Rate (1971): 40.2%
Bank Hours: 0730-1200 Saturday-Wednesday; 0730-1100 Thursday
Bazaar Hours: 0800-1200, 1530-1830 Saturday-Thursday (few shops open Friday morning)
Currency: 1000 fils = 1 Bahrain dinar
Export/Import Information: Generally books dutied at 10%, most schoolbooks free of duty; none on advertising matter. No import licence required but no obscene literature permitted and for books (not for advertising) a Chamber of Commerce certificate is mandatory. No exchange controls

Major Booksellers

Al-**Aadab** Bookshop*, PO Box 384, Manama

Bahrain Bookshop*, PO Box 443, Manama Tel: 54415

Family Bookshop (Bahrain) WLL, PO Box 1, Manama Tel: 254288 Telex: 8444 Fambah Bn

Islamic Cultural Bookshop*, PO Box 873, Manama

National Bookshop and Branches*, PO Box 594, Manama

Literary Associations and Societies

Bahrain Writers and Literators Association*, PO Box 1010, Manama
Secretary: Ibrahim Abdullah Ghuloom

Bangladesh

General Information

Language: Bengali (English widely used commercially)
Religion: Muslim
Population: 84.7 million
Bank Hours: 0930-1330 Monday-Thursday; 0900-1100 Friday and Saturday
Shop Hours: 0900-2100 Monday-Friday; 0900-1400 Saturday
Currency: 100 paise = 1 taka
Export/Import Information: No tariff on books and advertising matter. Import licences required for all imports
Copyright: UCC

Book Trade Organizations

Bangladesh Pustak Prokashak o Bikreta Samity*, c/o Rahman Brothers, 5/1 Gopinath Datta, Kabiraj St (Babu Bazar), Dacca Tel: 282633

Bangladesh Publishers' & Booksellers' Association
Secretary: Azhirul Islam Khan

National Book Centre of Bangladesh, 67a Purana Paltan, Dacca 2

Book Trade Journals

Boi (Text in Bengali), National Book Centre of Bangladesh, 67a Purana Paltan, Dacca 2

Publishers

Adeylebros & Co*, 60 Patuatuly, Dacca 1

Anwari Publications*, 5/1 Simson Rd, Dacca 1

Banga Sahitya Bhavan*, 144 Government New Market, Dacca

Bangladesh Books International Ltd*, PO Box 377, Dacca (Located at: 1, RK Mission Rd/Hatkhola, Dacca 3) Tel: 245265/7 ext 19 Cable Add: Bhabooks Dacca
Man Dir: Manzurul Islam
Subjects: Educational, Academic, Reference, General
Founded: 1975

Biswakosh*, 316 Government New Market, Dacca

Boighar*, 149 Government New Market, Dacca

Chalantika*, 177 Government New Market, Dacca

Continental Publications*, 18 Dhanmandi Hawkers Market, Dacca 5
Subjects: Science, Technical

Crescent Publishers*, 77 Patuatuly, Dacca 1

Lekha Prokashani*, 18 Pyaridas Rd, Dacca 1

Mullick Bros*, 3/1 Bangla Bazar, Dacca
Subjects: Education, Secondary & Primary Textbooks

Pak Kitab Ghar*, 39 Patuatuly, Dacca

Paramount Book Corporation*, Ashraf Chamber, 66 Bangladesh Ave, Dacca
Administrator: D H Khondker
Subject: Literature

Rahman Brothers*, Educational Publishers, 5/1 Gopinath Datta, Kabiraj St (Babu Bazar), Dacca Tel: 282633

U P L, see University Press Ltd

University Press Ltd (UPL), PO Box 88, Dacca 2 (Located at: Red Cross Bldg, 114 Motijheel CA, Dacca) Tel: 242457/232950/255789 Cable Add: Dunipress
Chief Executive: Mohiuddin Ahmed; *Sales:* Abdul Halim; *Production:* Haribur Rahman
Subjects: Children's Education, Academic, General, Bangladesh: special area studies
1978: 50 titles *1979:* 60 titles *Founded:* 1975

Major Booksellers

Adeyle Brothers*, 60 Patnatully, Dacca

Ali Publications*, 77 Patnatully, Dacca

Dacca Book Mart*, 38 Banglabazar, Dacca

Golden Book House*, 38 Banglabazar, Dacca

Green Book House Limited*, 85 Motighlel, Dacca

Hakkim's Bookshop*, 33 Banglabazar, Dacca

Hamidia Library*, 65 Chawk Circular Rd, Dacca

Islamia Library*, 41/42 Islampur Rd, Dacca

Mohammadi Library*, Chawk Circular Rd, Dacca

Mullick Brothers*, 3/1 Banglabazar Dacca

Oriental Book Service*, c/o Bangladesh Books International Ltd, PO Box 377, Dacca

Provincial Book Depot*, Dacca Stadium, Dacca

Provincial Library*, 109-A Sarat Gupta Rd, Narinda, Dacca

Puthigar Limited*, 74 Farashgunj, Dacca

Major Libraries

Bangladesh Institute of Development Studies Library*, Adamjee Ct, Motij Heel Commercial Area, Dacca 2 Tel: 257360

British Council Library*, 5 Fuller Rd, Ramna, Dacca 2 POB 161
Librarian: G F Rowbotham

Dacca University Library*, Dacca 2

Central Public Library, Dacca*, Shahbagh, Dacca 2

University of Rajshahi Library*, Rajshahi

Library Associations

Bangladesh Granthagar Samity*, c/o Library, Bangladesh University of Engineering and Technology, Dacca 2
Library Association of Bangladesh
Secretary: Abu Bakr Siddique
Publication: Eastern Librarian (three times a year)

Directorate of Archives and Libraries*, 103 Elephant Rd, Dacca 5
Director: Dr K M Karim
Publications: Bangladesh National Bibliography (annually), *Article index* published in the daily newspapers, *Bulletin of the Dissertations on Social Science*

Library Journals

Bangladesh National Bibliography, Directorate of Archives and Libraries, 103 Elephant Rd, Dacca 5

Eastern Librarian (text in English), Library Association of Bangladesh, c/o Library, Bangladesh University of Engineering and Technology, Dacca 2

Literary Associations and Societies

Dacca Centre for International **P E N** Madhura*, House 3, Road 13, Dhanmondi RA, Dacca 9
Secretary: Sanaul Huq

Society of Arts, Literature and Welfare*, Society Park, K C Dey Rd, Chittagong
General Secretary: Musharraf Hussain

Literary Prizes

Bengali Academy Literary Awards*
For an overall contribution to Bengali literature in the following categories: novel, short story, children's literature, poetry, essay, drama, literary research. Awarded annually. Enquiries to Bengali Academy, Burdwan House, Dacca

Barbados

General Information

Language: English
Religion: Anglican
Population: 265,000
Literacy Rate (1946): 89.8%
Bank Hours: 0800-1300 Monday-Thursday; 0800-1300, 1500-1750 Friday
Shop Hours: 0800-1600 Monday-Friday; 0800-1200 Saturday
Currency: 100 cents = 1 Barbados dollar
Export/Import Information: No tariff on books; advertising matter, 45%. Import licence covering exchange required; no obscene literature permitted

Publishers

Caribbean Universities Press, 8 Rock Dundo Heights, Lodge Hill, Eagle Hall 15
Parent Company: Ginn & Co Ltd, UK (qv)
Manager: Alan Pittam
Subjects: Academic, Education, Caribbean History, Journal of Caribbean History

The **C E D A R** Press*, Publishing House of the Caribbean Conference of Churches, PO Box 616, Bridgetown
Editor: Dr David Mitchell; *Acting Publisher:* Mrs Muriel Forde
Subjects: Religion, Sociology, Education, Music, Agriculture, Communication, Politics, Caribbean History, Identity and Culture
1978: 4 titles

P P C Ltd*, Eldino, Gills Rd, St Michael Tel: 75505

Yoruba* Publishing and Typesetting, Mottley Ho, Coleridge St, Bridgetown Tel: 63927

Major Booksellers

Christian Literature Crusade, St Michael Plaza, St Michael's Row, Bridgetown Tel: 65675
Manager: Phyllis Trim

Cloister Book Store Ltd, Hincks St, Bridgetown Tel: 62662

Roberts Stationery Ltd, 9 High, Bridgetown Tel: 65500
Manager: T A L Roberts

Sandy Beach Book Store*, Worthing Plaza and Shopping Centre, Bridgetown Tel: 89432

Wayfarer Book Store Ltd, Trident Ho, Broad St, Bridgetown Tel: 73760 (4 other branches)

Major Libraries

Public Library, Coleridge St, Bridgetown
Publication: National Bibliography of Barbados

University of the West Indies*, Main Library, Cave Hill Campus, PO Box 64, Bridgetown
Librarian: Michael Gill

Library Associations

Library Association of Barbados, PO Box 827E, Bridgetown Tel: 02191
Secretary: Judy Blackman
Publication: Bulletin (annual)

Library Journals

Bulletin of the Library Association of Barbados, PO Box 27E, Bridgetown

Belgium

General Information

Language: Dutch in the north, French in the south. Brussels is officially bilingual. (English widely used)
Religion: Predominantly Roman Catholic
Population: 9.8 million
Literacy Rate (1947): 96.7%
Bank Hours: Variable locally. Brussels: 0900-1300 Monday-Friday; 1400-1630 Monday and Friday; 1430-1530 Tuesday-Thursday. Antwerp: 0930-1500 Monday-Friday; 1630-1800 Friday
Shop Hours: Variable. Department stores: 0915-1800 Monday-Saturday; open until 2100 Friday
Currency: 100 centimes = 1 Belgian franc
Export/Import Information: Member of the European Economic Community. No tariff on books except children's picture books, 13% from non-EEC; advertising other than single copies generally 10.6% with sales tax of 14%. VAT on books and advertising 6%. No import licence required, just Model A form of notice of declaration of payment. No exchange controls
Copyright: UCC, Berne, Florence

Book Trade Organizations

Algemene Vlaamse Boekverkopersbond, Frankrijklei 93, B-2000 Antwerp
Flemish Booksellers' Association

Association belge des Editeurs de Langue française (ABELF), 111 ave du Parc, B-1060 Brussels
Belgian Association of Publishers of French Language Books
Dir: J de Raeymaeker

Bond Alleenverkopers van Nederlandstalige Boeken (BANB), Dr Desmethlaan 4, B-1980 Tervuren
Association of Wholesalers of Dutch Books in Belgium
Secretary: J van den Berg

Centrale de l'Industrie du Livre*, Galerie du Centre, Bloc 2, B-1000 Brussels
Central Office of the Book Industry

Cercle Belge de la Librairie, 5 rue du Luxembourg, BP 1, B-1040 Brussels) Tel: (02) 5112158
Belgian Booksellers' Association
President: P Heroufosse; *Secretary General:* R Lohest; *Administration:* R Mertens
Publications: Journal de la Librairie (10 a year) *Annuaire du CBL* (next edition 1981)

Fédération des Editeurs belges, 111 ave du Parc, B-1060 Brussels Tel: (02) 5382167
Belgian Publishers' Association
Dir: Julien de Raeymaeker

Standard Book Numbering Agency: for publications in Dutch see under Netherlands Book Trade Organizations, for publications in French see under French Book Trade Organisations

Syndicat belge de la Librairie ancienne et moderne*, 112 rue de Trèves, B-1040 Brussels
Belgian Association of Antiquarian and Modern Booksellers

Union des Industries graphiques et du Livre (UNIGRA)*, 76 rue Renkin, B-1030 Brussels
Book & Graphics Industries Union

Vereniging ter Bevordering van het Vlaamse Boekwezen, Frankrijklei 93, Bus 3, B-2000 Antwerp Tel: (031) 324684
Association for the Promotion of Flemish Books
Publication: Iijdingen

Vereniging van Uitgevers van Nederlandstalige Boeken, Frankrijklei 93, Bus 3, B-2000 Antwerp Tel: (031) 324684
Association of Publishers of Dutch Language Books
Secretary: A Wouters

Book Trade Reference Books and Journals

Books

Annuaire des Editeurs belges (Belgian Publishers' Annual), Belgian Publishers' Association, 111 ave du Parc, B-1060 Brussels

Cercle belge de la Librairie Annuaire (Annual), Belgian Booksellers' Association, 111 ave du Parc, B-1060 Brussels

L'Edition en Belgique (Publishing in Belgium), Belgian Publishers' Association, 111 ave du Parc, B-1060 Brussels

Lijstenbook (List of Booksellers), Association of Publishers of Dutch Language Books, Frankrijklei 93, Bus 3, B-2000 Antwerp

Liste des Sociétés savantes et littéraires de Belgique (List of Belgian Learned and Literary Societies), Service belge des Echanges Internationaux, 80-84 rue des Tanneurs, B-1000 Brussels

Livres belges (Books from Belgium), Belgian Publishers' Association, 111 ave du Parc, B-1060 Brussels

Journals

Belgica Selecta, Belgian Institute of Information, 3 rue Montoyer, B-1040 Brussels (lists new Belgian books)

Bibliographie de Belgique (Bibliography of Belgium), Koninklijke Bibliotheek Albert 1er, Keizerlaan 4, B-1000 Brussels

Boekengids (Guide to Books), Katholiek Centrum voor Lectuurinformatie en Bibliotheekvoorziening, Raapstr 4, Antwerp

Bulletin, Belgian Commission of Bibliography, 80-84 rue des Tanneurs, B-1000 Brussels

Journal de la Librairie (Book Trade Journal), Belgian Booksellers' Association, 111 ave du Parc, B-1060 Brussels

Livre et l'Estampe (The Book and the Print) (text in French), Royal Society of Bibliophiles and Iconophiles of Belgium, 4 blvd de l'Empereur, B-1000 Brussels

Répertoire annuel des principaux Travaux bibliographiques récents (Annual Catalogue of the Principal Recent Bibliographical Works), Belgian Commission of Bibliography, 80-84 rue des Tanneurs, B-1000 Brussels

Tijdingen (News), Association of Publishers of Dutch Language Books, Frankrijklei 93, Bus 3, B-2000 Antwerp

Travailleur du Livre (Worker with Books), Central Office of the Book Industry, Galerie du Centre, Bloc 2, B-1000 Brussels

Publishers

3 Arches, see Trois Arches

Editions **A B C** Jeunesse SARL*, 160 ave Gabriel E Lebon, B-1150 Brussels Tel: (02) 7346601
Publisher: Emile D Probst
Subject: Juveniles

Acco SV, Tiensestr 134-136, B-3000 Louvain Tel: (016) 233520 Telex: 62547
Dir: H Van Slambrouck
Orders to: ACCO-Uitgeverij, at above address
Subjects: Classic Languages and Culture, Linguistics, Economics, Law, Social Sciences, Education, Pedagogy, Mathematics, General Science, History, Physiotherapy, Psychology, Medicine, Religion, Philosophy, Criminology, Ethics
1978: 140 titles *1979:* 142 titles *Founded:* 1960
ISBN Publisher's Prefix: 90-334

Acta Medica Belgica ASBL, 43 rue des Champs Elysées, B-1050 Brussels Tel: (02) 6480468
Subject: Medicine
Founded: 1945

Agence belge des grandes Editions SA, 146 Blvd Adolphe Max, B-1000 Brussels Tel: (02) 2191872 Cable Add: Belgeditions
Man Dir: Monique de Smet
Subjects: Medicine, Educational Materials, Encyclopaedias, Games, Sports
Founded: 1928

Bibliotheca **Alphonsiana** VZW*, Dekenstr 28, B-3000 Louvain Tel: (016) 23470
Subjects: Religion, Juveniles, Textbooks
Founded: 1927

Altiora NV, Abdijstr 1, B-3281 Averbode Tel: (013) 771751/4 Telex: 39104
Dirs: F Nauwelaerts, J Volkaerts; *Editor:* N C Vrancky; *Production:* I Willems
Subjects: Education, Juveniles, Religion, Periodicals
1978: 90 titles

Angelet, Potterie Rei 69, B-8000 Bruges Tel: (050) 335186
Dir: P Angelet
Subjects: Juveniles, Music
Founded: 1969

Editions Jacques **Antoine** SPRL, 55-57 rue des Éperonniers, B-1000 Brussels Tel: (02) 5124337
Dir: J Antoine; *Sales, Publicity, Rights & Permissions:* Milly Colmant
Subjects: Literature, Linguistics, Arts
1978: 8 titles *1979:* 13 titles *Founded:* 1968

Antwerpse Lloyd NV, see Editions du Lloyd Anversois SA

Editions **Arcade-Fonds Mercator**, Lange Nieuwstr 76, B-2000 Antwerp Tel: (02) 3435183 Cable Add: Arcadebel Telex: 24381 Arcade B
Man Dir: J Martens; *Sales Dir:* C Hoessels
Associate Company: Fonds Mercator (qv)
Branch Off: 299 ave Van Volxem, Brussels
Subject: Art
Founded: 1952
ISBN Publisher's Prefix: 2-8005

Editions **Arscia** SA*, rue de l'Etuve, B-1000 Brussels Tel: (02) 5114272
Dir: C Pirson
Subject: Belles Lettres
Founded: 1957

SC **Artis-Historia**, 19 rue Général Gratry, B-1040 Brussels Tel: (02) 7362000
Dir Secretary General: J M Ugeux
Subjects: Geography, History, Ethnography, Nature, Art, Travel
Bookshops: 70 throughout Belgium
Founded: 1949, companies merged to form Artis-Historia in 1976

Editions **Arts et Voyages**, 88 ave de Tervueren, B-1040 Brussels Tel: (02) 7343560/7343582
Man Dir: Lucien de Meyer; *Rights & Permissions:* Dominique Schoofs
Associate Company: Editions d'Art Lucien de Meyer (qv)
Subjects: Art, Literature, History, Juveniles, Management, Sports
Founded: 1954
ISBN Publisher's Prefix: 2-8016

Assimil, Uitgaven Nelis PVBA, Steenstr 5-7, B-1000 Brussels Tel: (02) 5114502
Man Dir: R Nelis; *Commercial Dir:* A Van Damme
Subjects: Bibliography, Languages (Teach Yourself)
ISBN Publisher's Prefix: 90-70077

Editions de **Association des Consommateurs** ASBL, see Uitgaven van de Verbruikersunie VZW

Association des Sociétés scientifiques médicales belges (ASBL)*, 43 rue des Champs Elysées, B-1050 Brussels Tel: (02) 6480468
Subjects: Medicine, Journals
Founded: 1945

ASTRID, see H-K de Jaeger Publications

Atlantis NV*, Kruishoftstr 205, B-2610 Wilrijk Tel: (031) 280986 Telex: 33164
Dir: A Jonckx

Parent Company: Beckers Groep (qv)
Subjects: Education, Pedagogy, Sports, Games, Juveniles, Journals
Founded: 1970
ISBN Publisher's Prefix: 90-6181

Audivox, Rubenslei 23, B-2000 Antwerp Tel: (031) 328465
Dir: W Gonnissen
Founded: 1953
Subjects: School Text Books
Miscellaneous: also Booksellers and Importers of Educational Books (Wholesale)

Aurelia Books*, Bonekruidlaan 30, B-1020 Brussels Tel: (02) 2678126 Telex: 63 009 Aurgam B
Dir: J Bauwens; *Editorial:* Jo Stevens; *Sales:* M Drieskens; *Production:* Jan Van Lier; *Publicity:* Jan Bauwens
Subjects: Training of Nurses, School Books, Flemish Folklore, Popular Devotion
Book Club: ABC (Aurelia Book Club)
Founded: 1972

De **Backer** Publishers PVBA*, Penitentenstr 14, B-9000 Ghent Tel: (091) 231013
Dir: Chr de Backer
Subjects: Bibliography, Languages, History of Pharmacy, History, Travel, Medicine, Literature, Music
Founded: 1972

Maison d'Editions **Baha'ies** ASBL, rue du Trône 205, 1050 Brussels Tel: (02) 6470749
Subject: Bahai
Founded: 1970

Banana Press NV*, Rozenlaan 10, B-2080 Kapellen (Bos) Tel: (031) 667171
Dir: W Beckers
Parent Company: Beckers Groep (qv)
Subjects: Bibliography, Languages, Education, Pedagogy, Sport, Games, Literature
Founded: 1972
ISBN Publisher's Prefix: 90-6180

Barbiaux (Drukkerij G — Uitgeverij de Garve) PVBA*, Groene Poortdreef 27, B-8200 St-Michiels, Bruges Tel: (050) 318283
Dir: W Barbiaux
Subjects: Law, Political, Administrative & Social Sciences, Mathematics, General Science, Music
Founded: 1909

Beckers Groep*, Brasschaatsteenweg 200, B-2180 Kalmthout Tel: 667171 Cable Add: Walbeck
Man Dir: R Peeters; *Literary Agent:* A van Hageland
Subsidiary Companies: Atlantis NV, Banana Press (qqv), De Beurs NV, Gutenberg, Rubens
Subjects: General Fiction, Belles Lettres, Poetry, Biography, History, Juveniles, High-priced Paperbacks
Book Clubs: Atlanta NV

Beckers SA Editions*, Brasschaatsteenweg 200, B-2180 Kalmthout Tel: (031) 667171
Owned by: Beckers Groep

Belgisch Instituut voor Voorlichting en Documentatie (INBEL), see Institut belge d'Information et de Documentation

Uitgeverij van **Belle** PVBA, Steenweg op Ninove 116, B-1080 Brussels Tel: (02) 5213417/5210221
Dir: R van Belle
Subjects: Geography, History, Ethnography, Travel, Juveniles, Sports
Founded: 1938

De **Beurs** NV, see Beckers Groep

Editions Gérard **Blanchart** & Cie SA, 15 ave Ernest Masoin, B-1090 Brussels Tel: (02) 4783706
Man Dir: Charles Blanchart
Subjects: Art, Religion, Educational Materials
Founded: 1930

Maison d'Edition A de **Boeck** SA, ave Louise 203 Bte 1, B-1050 Brussels Tel: 6407272
General Dir: Chr de Boeck; *Administrative Dir:* J van Nes
Subjects: Textbooks for primary and secondary schools, Higher education (educational psychology, methodology, social sciences, humanities), Technical and Professional textbooks (general and applied mechanics, machine tools)
1978: 70 titles *1979:* 77 titles *Founded:* 1883

Bordas-Dunod Bruxelles SA, 44 rue Otlet, B-1070 Brussels Tel: (02) 5238133 Telex: 24899 Bordun
Subjects: Textbooks, Education, Pedagogy, Sports, Mathematics, General Science, Geography, History, Juveniles, Paperbacks
Founded: 1969

Bourdeaux-Capelle SA, 69 rue Sax, B-5500 Dinant Tel: (082) 222283/222277
Dir: E Bourdeaux
Subjects: Bibliography, Languages, Journals
Founded: 1913

De **Branding** NV, Korte Winkelstr 13-15, B-2000 Antwerp Tel: (031) 332739
Dir: L Ruys
Subjects: Nautical
Bookshop: Belgisch Maritiem Centrum
Founded: 1956

Brepols IGP*, Baron F du Fourstr 8, B-2300 Turnhout Tel: (014) 415466/7 Telex: 34182
Chairman: Baron de Cartier de Marchienne; *Man Dir:* M Rolin
Branch Off: Éditions Brepols, 9 rue Huysmans, 75006 Paris, France
Subjects: Religion (Patristics, Bibles, Prayerbooks), History

Vanden **Broele** PVBA, Magdalenastr 41-47, B-8200 Bruges Tel: (050) 315074
Dir: E de Jonghe
Subjects: Law, Political, Administrative & Social Sciences, Popular Medicine
1978: 11 titles *1979:* 10 titles
ISBN Publisher's Prefix: 90-6267

A W **Bruna** & Zoon NV*, Antwerpsesteenweg 29a, B-2630 Aartselaar Tel: (031) 874018/9
Dir: J Raedschelders
Subjects: Juveniles, Literature, Paperbacks
Founded: 1966

Etablissements Emile **Bruylant** SA, 67 rue de la Régence, B-1000 Brussels Tel: (02) 5129845
Man Dirs: Angèle Van Sprengel, Jean Vandeveld
Subjects: Law, High-priced Paperbacks, General & Social Science, University Textbooks
Bookshop: Establissements Emile Bruylant, 67 rue de la Régence, B-1000 Brussels
1978: 35 titles *Founded:* 1838

J E **Buschmann** PVBA*, Italiëlei 26, B-2000 Antwerp Tel: (031) 323130/325235
Dir: J. Buschmann
Subjects: Arts, Geography, History, Ethnography, Travel, Journals
Miscellaneous: firm is both publisher and printer

Business Information Establishment SA*, 2 rue de la Résistance, B-4400 Herstal Tel: (041) 642174 Telex: 041118
Dir: P Lardinois
Subjects: Textbooks, Law, Political, Administrative & Social Sciences, Mathematics, General Science, Journals
Founded: 1968
ISBN Publisher's Prefix: 2-87000

C E D-Samsom NV*, 7 rue Philippe de Champagne, B-1000 Brussels Tel: (02) 5138570
Dir: O Chrispeels
Parent Company: NV ICU België (qv)
Bookshops: CED-Samsom, 7 rue Philippe de Champagne, Brussels
Subjects: General & Social Science, Documentation, Textbooks, Literature, Law, Psychology
Founded: 1964

Editions **C E F A** (Centre d'Éducation à la Famille et à l'Amour), 58 rue de la Prévoyance, B-1000 Brussels Tel: (02) 5131749
Man Dir: Pierre de Locht; *Sales:* Mrs André
Orders to: above address or Librairie Novissima, 33 rue de la Concorde, B-1050 Brussels
Subjects: The Family, Sexual Education, Religion
Bookshops: Librairie Novissima, 33 rue de la Concorde, B-1050 Brussels
1978: 7 titles *Founded:* 1961

Editions **Calozet** SPRL*, 40 rue des Chartreux, B-1000 Brussels Tel: (02) 5116026
Dir: J de Groef
Subjects: Mathematics, Cuisenaire Materials (educational)
Founded: 1874

Carmelitana VZW ('De Karmelieten')*, Burgstr 46, B-9000 Ghent Tel: (091) 255787
Dir: A Dupon
Subject: Religious books
ISBN Publisher's Prefix: 90-70092

Carto PVBA*, Gaucheretstr 139, B-1000 Brussels Tel: (02) 2161545 Cable Add: Cartopress
Man Dir: Wijnand Plaizier
Subsidiary Companies: Carpress, International Press Agency; European Cartographic Institute; Cremers Cartographic Institute (school maps)
Subjects: Geography, History, Secondary & Primary Textbooks, Educational Materials (Transparencies), Maps, Travel
Founded: 1950

Casterman, rue des Soeurs noires 28, B-7500 Tournai Tel: (069) 224141 Cable Add: Casteredim Tournai Telex: 57328
Man Dir: Louis-Robert Casterman; *Sales Dir:* Jean-Jacques Dursin; *Rights & Permissions:* Pierre Servais, Ivan Noerdinger
Branch Offs: 44 ave de Roodebeek, B-1040 Brussels; 66 rue Bonaparte, F-75006 Paris, France; De Morinel 25-29, NL-8251 HT Dronten, Netherlands
Subjects: General Fiction, Belles Lettres, Poetry, Biography, History, Music, Art, Philosophy, Reference, Religion, Juveniles, High-priced Paperbacks, Psychology, General & Social Science, University & Secondary Textbooks, Languages, Law, Geography, Sports, Travel, Medicine
1978: 220 titles *1979:* 180 titles *Founded:* 1780
ISBN Publisher's Prefix: 2-203 (French), 90-303 (Dutch)

Centre d'Education à la Famille et à l'Amour, see CEFA

Centre d'Etude et d'Edition Conjugale et Familiale ASBL*, 27 rue du Congrès, B-1000 Brussels Tel: (02) 2182482
Dir: J Hinnekens
Associate Companies: Les 'Feuilles Familiales' ASBL, Belgium (qv); NFF (Nouvelles Feuilles Familiales), Belgium (qv)
Subject: Marriage and the Family
Founded: 1947

Centre international d'Etudes de la Formation religieuse Lumen Vitae ASBL, see Editions Lumen Vitae ASBL

Centre national d'Etudes et de Recherches socio-économiques (CERSE) ASBL*, 9 rue Vilain XIIII 9, B-1050 Brussels Tel: (02) 6495817
President: R Gubbels
Subjects: Law, Political, Administrative & Social Sciences
Founded: 1963

Centre national de Recherches 'Primitifs Flamands' ASBL, 1 parc du Cinquantenaire, B-1040 Brussels Tel: (02) 7354160
Dir: R Sneyers; *Science Editor:* M Comblen; *Sales:* M Gierts; *Rights & Permissions:* R Sneyers
Subjects: Arts
Founded: 1950
ISBN Publisher's Prefix: 2-87033

Ceres*, Nukerkeplein 9, B-9681 Maarkedal Tel: (055) 211404
Dir: P de Riemaecker
Subjects: Geography, History, Ethnography, Travel
1978: 5 titles *Founded:* 1947

Chanlis, 17 B rue de Lennery, B-6430 Walcourt Tel: (071) 326394/611770
Man Dir: Pierre Magain; *Sales:* M Nowak
Subsidiary Company: Chanlis, Route de Mons 25A, B-6000 Charleroi
Subjects: Numismatics, Archaeology, Arts
Bookshop: Route de Mons 25A, B-6000 Charleroi
1979: 18 titles *Founded:* 1968
ISBN Publisher's Prefix: 2-87039

Editions Chantecler, Cleydaellaan 8, B-2630 Aartselaar, Antwerp Tel: (031) 878300 Telex: 31739 Zuidb
Man Dir: Joris Schaltin; *Editorial:* Emmanuel de Vocht; *Sales:* Jan Vande Velden; *Production:* Eric Feyten; *Rights & Permissions:* Wilfried Wuyts
Parent Company: Zuidnederlandse Uitgeverij (qv)
Subjects: Children's Fiction & Non-fiction
Founded: 1947

La Charte NV, Oude Gentweg 108, B-8000 Bruges Tel: (050) 331235
Dir: H Bogaerts
Subjects: Bibliography, Languages, Textbooks, Law, Political, Administrative & Social Sciences, Primary & Secondary Textbooks
Founded: 1948

De Clauwaert*, Koning Albertlaan 17, B-3040 Korbeek-Lo, Louvain Tel: (016) 462229
Man Dir: W Vanden Eynde; *Sales Dir:* J Raymaekers
Subjects: General Fiction, Belles Lettres, Secondary Textbooks
Founded: 1948
Miscellaneous: Firm is also a book club

Cogedi SA*, galerie des Princes 2-4, B-1000 Brussels Tel: (02) 5132038
Dir: Pierre Mardaga
Subjects: Education, Pedagogy, Psychology, Architecture
Founded: 1938

Compagnie belge d'Editions, now incorporated in Albert de Visscher Editeur (qv)

Editions Complexe (Diffusion-Promotion-Information), 24 rue de Bosnie, B-1060 Brussels Tel: (02) 5388843/6 Telex: 64507
Man Dir, Sales, Publicity: Danielle Vincken; *Man Dir, Editorial, Rights & Permissions:* André Versaille; *Production:* Pierre Borgers
Associate Company: Nouvelle Diffusion (at above address)
Subjects: Psychological, Socio-Political, Dialectics, History, Scientific, Ethnological series of books
1978: 20 titles *1979:* 13 titles *Founded:* 1973-74
Miscellaneous: Formerly Nouvelle Diffusion Complexe (founded 1971)
ISBN Publisher's Prefix: 2-87027

Contact NV*, Elsbos 33, B-2520 Edegem Tel: (031) 572024/573486
Dir: A J H Binneweg
Subjects: Arts, Textbooks, Education, Pedagogy, Sports, Games, Literature, Paperbacks
Founded: 1946
ISBN Publisher's Prefix: 90-254

Creadif*, 14 blvd de l'Empereur bte 3, B-1000 Brussels Tel: (02) 5114943
Dir: M Servais
Subjects: Geography, History, Ethnography, Travel, Economy, Commerce
Founded: 1974

Crédit Communal de Belgique—Centre Culturel, 44 blvd Pacheco, B-1000 Brussels Tel: (02) 2193200 Cable Add: Crédit Communal Brussels Cregem B 26354
Secretary General: C Swinnen
Subjects: History, Politics, Law, Music, Fine Arts
Founded: 1977
Miscellaneous: Incorporates Pro Civitate

Cremers (Schoollandkaarten) PVBA*, Gaucheretstr 139, B-1000 Brussels Tel: (02) 2161545 Cable Add: Cartopress
Dir: Wijnand Plaizier
Parent Company: Carto PVBA (qv)
Subjects: Textbooks, Geography, History, Ethnography, Travel, Journals
Founded: 1950

Crisp, 35 rue du Congrès, B-1000 Brussels Tel: (02) 2183226
Man Dir: J Gerard-Libois; *Editorial:* Xavier Mabille; *Publicity:* M Julin
Subjects: Political Science, Industry, Finance
Founded: 1958

Van Cromphout Frères & Soeurs Imprimerie*, 3 rue des Moulins, B-7860 Lessines Tel: (068) 332047/332182 Cable Add: Cromphout Lessines Telex: 32047
Man Dir: Robert Cromphout
Subjects: Education, Textbooks, Sports, Games, Pedagogy, Journals
Founded: 1853

Fondation Cultura-Stichting Cultura*, avenue de Broqueville 17, bte 11, B-1200 Brussels Tel: (02) 5136180 ext 431
Man Dir: Fernand Duffaut
Parent Company: Fonds Mercator SA (qv)
Subject: Art
Founded: 1958

Editions Culture et Civilisation, 115 ave Gabriel Lebon, B-1160 Brussels Tel: (02) 7345005 Cable Add: Jadam
Man Dir: Jos Adam
Subsidiary Company: Imprimerie Jos Adam, 115 ave Gabriel Lebon, B-1160 Brussels
Subjects: Biography, History, Geography, Ethnography, Travel, Music, Art, Philosophy, Reference, Religion, Medicine, Psychology, University Textbooks, Bibliography, Languages, Law, Social & General Sciences, Literature
Founded: 1960

De Dageraad PVBA*, Perenstr 13-15, B-2000 Antwerp Tel: (031) 356866
Dir: R van Hevel
Founded: 1971

Uitgeverij Dap-Reinart SV*, Industriepark B4, B-9140 Zele Tel: (052) 445171
Dir: A van Acker
Parent Company: Standaard Uitgeverij en Distributie BV, Netherlands (qv)
Subjects: Juveniles, Literature, Education, Law, Religion
Book Club: Dap-Reinart Uitgeven
Founded: 1946

Editions Daphne*, Mageleinstr 50, B-9000 Ghent Tel: (091) 253645
Man Dir: Albert Dubrulle
Subjects: Belles Lettres, Poetry, Music, Art, Education, Juveniles
Founded: 1945
ISBN Publisher's Prefix: 90-70090

Daphne Diffusion SPRL, Poortakkerstr 19, B-9820 Gent Tel: (091) 214591 Telex: 11659
Dir: F Dubrulle

Davidsfonds VZW, Blijde Inkomststr 79, B-3000 Louvain Tel: (016) 221801
Dir: F Valvekens
Subjects: Arts, Law, Political, Administrative & Social Sciences, Education, Pedagogy, Sports, Games, Juveniles, Religion, Philosophy, Literature, Journals
Founded: 1875
ISBN Publisher's Prefix: 90-6152

Maison d'Editions Cl Dejaie, 436 chaussée de Dinant, B-5150 Wepion Namur Tel: (081) 460516
Dir: M Cl M Dejaie
Subjects: Bibliography, Languages, Law, Political, Administrative & Social Sciences, Religion, Philosophy, Literature
1978: 8 titles *Founded:* 1972
ISBN Publisher's Prefix: 2-1491

Editions Delta, 92-94 sq Plasky, B-1040 Brussels Tel: (02) 7369060
Man Dir: Georges-Francis Seingry
Subjects: Reference books regarding EEC and other European Organizations
1978: 6 titles *1979:* 12 titles *Founded:* 1976
ISBN Publisher's Prefix: 2-8029

Deltas, an imprint of Zuidnederlandse Uitgeverij NV (qv)

Denis & Co PVBA*, Sterckshoffel 28-30, B-2100 Deurne Tel: (031) 213299/220804
Subjects: Art, Law, Education, History, Juveniles, Philosophy

Desclée, Editeurs*, 13 rue Barthélemy Frison, B-7500 Tournai Tel: (069) 226101 Cable Add: Desclée-Tournai Telex: Gedit 57251
Dir: J Desclée
Parent Company: Gedit SA (qv)
Associate Companies: Editions Desclée et Cie, France (qv); Editions Gamma (qv); Nouvelles Editions Mame, France (qv)
Subjects: Religion, Philosophy, Missals, Theology, Literature
Bookshop: At above address
Founded: 1872

Desclée de Brouwer SA*, 217b rue de la Loi, B-1040 Brussels Tel: (02) 352734/341169
Man Dir: Geoffroy de Halleux
Associate Companies: Desclée de Brouwer & Cie SA, France (qv); Desclée de Brouwer, Netherlands; Emmaus (qv)
Subsidiary Company: Orion (qv)
Branch Offs: Bilbao, Montreal, Utrecht
Subjects: Religion, Philosophy, Juveniles, Arts, Textbooks, Education, Sports, Games, Languages, Paperbacks
Founded: 1873

Desmet-Huysmans PVBA*, Dam 67, B-8500 Kortrijk Tel: (056) 217242
Man Dir: G Desmet

Editions Desoer SA*, 17 rue Ste Véronique, B-4000 Liège Tel: (041) 521175
Dir: J Quidonne
Subjects: Science, Medicine, Educational

Materials, Arts, Textbooks, Mathematics
Founded: 1750

F **Dessain** SPRL*, 7 rue Trappé, B-4000
Liège Tel: (041) 237882/3
Man Dir: Maximilien Dessain
Subjects: Religion, Mathematics, Textbooks,
Education, Pedagogy, Sports, Games,
General Science, Geography, History,
Ethnography, Travel
Founded: 1719

H **Dessain** NV, Regenboog 5-9, B-2800
Mechelen Tel: (015) 416986
Man Dir: Patrick Dessain
Subjects: Juveniles, Medicine, Music,
Religion, Reference, Geography, History,
Ethnography, Travel
Founded: 1854

A **Dewallens***, 212 chaussée de Bruxelles,
B-3020 Herent Tel: (016) 225857
Dir: A Dewallens
Subjects: Bibliography, Philology,
Languages, Education, Pedagogy, Sports,
Games, Journals
Founded: 1946

Editions Marcel **Didier** SA*, 1 pl de la
Maison Rouge, B-1020 Brussels Tel: (02)
4256602/4256753
Man Dir: Paul Didier
Associate Companies: Librairie Marcel
Didier, France (qv); Didier Canada,
Montreal
Subsidiary Company: Didier Nederland BV,
Postbus 5530, Amsterdam, Netherlands
Subjects: Reference, University, Secondary
& Primary Textbooks, Educational
Materials
Bookshop: Librairie Marcel Didier, 1 pl de
la Maison rouge, B-1020 Brussels Tel: (02)
4256753
1978: 17 titles Founded: 1932

Diligentia-Uitgeverij, Sint-Jozefstr 7, B-9040
Oostakker Tel: (091) 511281
Dir: Frank Vermeiren
Subject: Textbooks
Founded: 1908
ISBN Publisher's Prefix: 90-70021

Distri BD SPRL*, 47 rue de Namur, B-1000,
Brussels Tel: (02) 5129675
Dirs: Mrs Micheline Vandesande, Miss
Jacqueline Martin, André Leborgne
Orders to: 435 ave Van Volxem, B-1060
Belgium
Subject: Art
Founded: 1973

La **Documentation** Cistercienne, Abbaye
ND de St-Remy, B-5430 Rochefort Tel:
(084) 213181 Cable Add: Trappistes-
Rochefort
Dir: P Eug Manning
Subjects: Bibliography, Geography,
Literature, History (especially Medieval),
Heraldry
1978: 13 titles Founded: 1969

Edition **Doepgen** Verlag, PO Box 140, B-
4700 Eupen (Located at: Gospertstr 7,
Eupen) Tel: (87) 556042/556264
Chief Executive, Editorial, Publicity, Rights
& Permissions: Wolfgang Trees; Sales,
Production: Heinz Doepgen
Subjects: War and History (Aachen, Liège
and Maastricht regions)
Bookshops: At above address; Malmedyerstr
19, B-4780 Sint Vith
1978: 3 titles 1979: 10 titles Founded: 1978
Miscellaneous: Publishes in German
language for German-speaking part of
Belgium

Editions Irène **Dossche** SPRL*, 1256
chaussée de Mons, B-1070 Brussels Tel: (02)
5239564
Dir: Mme I Dossche
Subject: Arts
Founded: 1969

Editions et Imprimerie J **Duculot** SA, rue de
la Posterie, Parc industriel, B-5800
Gembloux Tel: (081) 610061 Telex: 59309
Duculo B
Administrator: Jean Verougstraete;
Publishing Dir, Sales, Publicity: Georges
David; Editorial, Rights & Permissions:
Christiane Lapp, Emmanuel Brutsaert;
Production: Jean Flament
Orders to: Presses de Belgique, rue du
Sceptre 25, B-1040 Brussels
Subsidiary Company: Editions J Duculot, 16
rue Séguier, F-75006, Paris, France
Subjects: Belles Lettres, General Literature,
Art, Religion, Juveniles, Linguistics, General
Science, University, Secondary & Primary
Textbooks, Guides, Regional Literature
1978: 55 titles 1979: 53 titles Founded: 1919
ISBN Publisher's Prefix: 2-8011

Editions Jean **Dupuis** SA*, 39 rue Destrée,
B-6001 Marcinelle-Charleroi Tel: (071)
364080 Telex: 51370
Dirs: Charles and Marcel Dupuis
Branch Off: Livornostr 97, B-1050 Brussels
Subjects: Art, How-to, Cinema, Paperbacks,
Juveniles, Comics
Bookshop: Editions Jean Dupuis, 39 rue
Destree, B-6001 Marcinelle-Charleroi
Founded: 1898
ISBN Publisher's Prefix: 2-8001

E P O, Lange Pastoorstraat 25, B-2600
Berchem Tel: (031) 396874
Man Dir: Marie-Paule Doumen; Editorial:
Hugo Durieux; Sales: Patrick van Buyten
Subjects: Literature, Politics
1978: 17 titles 1979: 9 titles Founded: 1974
ISBN Publisher's Prefix: 90-6445

Edi-Art*, 18 ave de Berchem Ste Agathe,
B-1080 Brussels Tel: (02) 4269270
Man Dir: J Freydiger
Founded: 1975

Editeurs de Litterature Biblique*, Ch de
Tubize 479, B-1420 Braine-L'Alleud
Tel: (02) 3545402
Man Dir: M Cl Kroeker
Subjects: Education, Juveniles, Philosophy,
Religion, Music, Pocketbooks
1978: 5 titles Founded: 1959

Editions interuniversitaires*, 14 boulevard
de l'Empereur, Bte 3, B-1000 Brussels Tel:
(02) 5114943
Dir: M Servais
Subjects: Geography, History, Ethnography,
Travel
Founded: 1974

Editions techniques et scientifiques SPRL,
35-43 rue Borrens, B-1050 Brussels Tel: (02)
6401040
Man Dir: G Louis
Subjects: General Technology, Law,
Mathematics, Science, Geography, History,
Ethnography, Travel, General
Founded: 1919

Editions universitaires SA*, 25 rue du
Sceptre, B-1040 Brussels Tel: (02)
6488026
Dir: L Honhon
Subjects: Textbooks, Law Political,
Administrative & Social Sciences,
Education, Pedagogy, Sports, Games,
Mathematics, General Science, Geography,
History, Ethnography, Travel, Religion,
Philosophy, Literature, Languages, Journals
Founded: 1944

Elsevier Séquoia, Leuvensesteenweg 325,
B-1940 Woluwe Tel: (02) 7209090 Cable
Add: Elsbook Bruxelles Telex: 21831 Elsbru
B
Man Dir: Jean-Jacques Schellens; Sales,
Publicity & Advertising: J Lamiroy;
Editorial: Claude van Godtsenhoven
Parent Company: Elsevier-NDU nv,
Netherlands (qv)
Associate Company: Elsevier Sequoia,
France (qv)
Subjects: Biography, History, Reference,
Juveniles, Art, Practical Guides, Nature,
Documentaries, Children's Books, Travel
1978: 34 titles 1979: 31 titles Founded: 1960
ISBN Publisher's Prefix: 2-8003

Emmaus-Desclée de Brouwer NV, Lieven
Bauwensstr 19, B-8200 Bruges Tel: (050)
318157 Telex: 81068
Dir: A Goyvaerts
Associate Company: Desclée de Brouwer
SA (qv)
Subjects: Textbooks, Religion, Philosophy,
Journals, Paperbacks
Founded: 1960
ISBN Publisher's Prefix: 90264

Editions **Erasme** (NV Scriptoria), Belgiëlei
147a, BP 212, B-2000 Antwerp Tel: (031)
395900 Telex: B Edista 31421
Man Dir: A Sap
Associate Companies: Standaard Uitgeverij,
Belgium (qv); Standaard Uitgeverij en
Distributie BV, Netherlands (qv)
Subjects: Medicine, Science, Reference,
Encyclopaedias, Arts, Textbooks, Juveniles
Founded: 1924
ISBN Publisher's Prefix: 90-020

Erel, St-Sebastiaanstr 16, B-8400 Ostend
Tel: (059) 701308
Dir: R Lanoye; Publicity: Monique Lanoye
Subjects: Arts, Bibliography, Languages,
Education, Pedagogy, Sports, Games,
Geography, History, Ethnography, Travel,
Literature, Journals
Bookshop: At above address
1978: 8 titles 1979: 9 titles Founded: 1946

Editions **Est-Ouest***, 66 rue St Bernard,
B-1060 Brussels Tel: (02) 5386177
Dir: C André
Subjects: Art, Travel, Belles Lettres,
Bibliography, Languages
Founded: 1939

Etablissements Généraux d'Imprimerie SA*,
14 blvd de l'Empereur, B-1000 Brussels
Tel: (02) 5118026
Man Dir: F Jacobs
Subject: Reference
Founded: 1831

Europa*, Botermarkt 10, B-3290 Diest
Tel: (013) 331187
Dir: R Peeters
Subjects: Arts, Geography, History,
Numismatics, Folklore
ISBN Publisher's Prefix: 90-6188

European Press Scientific Publisher*,
Kortrijksesteenweg 154, B-9000 Ghent Tel:
(091) 213000/10/08 Telex: Eupress 11008
Man Dir: R Desmet; Editorial, International
Books Department: M Guy
Branch Off: Citadellaan 36, B-9000 Ghent;
Borluutstraat, B-9000 Ghent; Postbus
Amsterdam, NL-3802 Amsterdam,
Netherlands
Subjects: Science (especially Medicine and
Pharmacology), Medical Periodicals,
Scientific Translations
1978: 6 titles

Europress NV*, Lousbergskaai 86A, B-9000
Ghent Tel: (091) 255701 Cable Add:
Europress Gent Telex: 11228 Volkge B
Man Dir, Publicity, Rights & Permissions:
S Vervloet; Editorial, Sales, Production:
J Van Haverbeke
Orders to: J Van Haverbeke, Forelstraat 22,
B-9000 Ghent
Subjects: Children's Books, Strip Cartoon
Books

Familia et Patria PVBA*, Kortemarkstr 26, B-8120 Handzame Tel: (051) 567336
Dir: M Mispelon
Subjects: Bibliography, Languages, Law, Political, Administrative & Social Sciences, Geography, History, Ethnography, Travel, Literature
Founded: 1966

Les '**Feuilles familiales**' ASBL*, 27 rue du Congrès, B-1000 Brussels Tel: (02) 2183482
Associate Companies: NFF (Nouvelles Feuilles Famiales) (qv); Centre d'Etude et d'Edition Conjugale et Familiale (qv)
Subjects: Marriage & Family Relations, Psychology, Educational, Religion
Founded: 1937

Fonds Mercator SA*, Lange Nieuwstr 76, B-2000 Antwerp Tel: (031) 319859
Publisher: Dr Jan Martens; *Dirs:* Christian Hoessels, Jos Jansen
Associate Company: Editions Arcade-Fonds Mercator (qv)
Subsidiary Company: Fondation Cultura (qv)
Subjects: Arts, Geography, History, Ethnography, Travel, Literature, Music
1978: 7 titles *Founded:* 1965

G A **Fonteyn** Medical Books NV, Fochplein 13, B-3000 Louvain Tel: (016) 222267 Telex: 26334
Man Dir: B Osaer
Subject: Medicine
Bookshop (specialist medical): at above address
Founded: 1836

Editions **Foyer** Notre-Dame, now incorporated in Editions Lumen Vitae

Editions de la **Francité** (Imprimeries Havaux)*, 37c rue A Levêque, B-1400 Nivelles Tel: (067) 226131
Dir: LL Havaux
Branch Off: 20 rue du Pouvre, 75001 Paris, France
Subjects: Arts, Bibliography, Languages, Textbooks, Education, Pedagogy, Sports, Games, Geography, History, Ethnography, Travel, Medicine, Literature, Religion, Philosophy, Journals, Paperbacks

G I A SA, 321 ave des Volontaires, B-1150 Brussels Tel: (02) 7620662
Art Director: J Carion; *Export:* M J Hellin
Subjects: Art, Medicine (*Savoir interpréter*)
Miscellaneous: Exporter of Belgian books

Editions **Gamma***, 11 rue Barthélemy Frison, B-7500 Tournai Tel: (069) 226105 Cable Add: Editions Gamma-Tournai Telex: Gedit 57251
Dir: J Desclée
Parent Company: Gedit SA (qv)
Associate Companies: Desclée, Editeurs (qv); Desclée et Cie, France (qv); Editions Gamma, France (qv); Nouvelles Editions Mame, France (qv)
Subjects: Education, How-to, Science & Technology, Textbooks, Sports, Games, Mathematics, Juveniles
Founded: 1962

De **Garve** PVBA*, Groene Poortdreef 27, B-8200 St-Michiels, Bruges Tel: (050) 318283/320707
Dir: W Barbiaux
Subjects: Bibliography, Languages, Textbooks, Law, Politics, Social Science, Mathematics, Physics, Technical, Music
Founded: 1909

Gedit SA*, 13 rue Barthélemy Frison, B-7500 Tournai Tel: (069) 226105 Cable Add: Gedit Tournai Telex: Gedit 57251
Dir: J Desclée
Subsidiary Companies: Desclée, Editeurs (qv); Editions Desclée et Cie, France (qv); Editions Gamma (qv); Editions Gamma, France (qv); Nouvelles Editions Mame, France (qv)
Subjects: General (also printers)
Founded: 1872

Editions **Gérard** et Cie SPRL, see Marabout SA

Girault **Gilbert** SPRL*, 50 rue de l'Association, B-1000 Brussels Tel: (02) 2171430
Subjects: Cartography
Founded: 1928, Reconstituted: 1956

Uitgeverij het **Gouden** Spoor*, Grotenhof 38, B-2510 Mortsel Tel: (03) 498415
Dir: M Saldien
Subjects: Juveniles, How-to, Medicine
Founded: 1951

De **Goudvink** NV*, Steenwinkelstr 644, B-2621 Schelle Tel: (031) 875318/9 Telex: 33866
Dirs: W L Detieger, W van den Hoek
Subjects: Arts, Education, Sport & Games, Geography, History, Ethnography, Travel, Juveniles
Founded: 1959
ISBN Publisher's Prefix: 90-270

Gutenberg, subsidiary of Beckers Groep (qv)

Hachette International, 715 chaussée de Waterloo, B-1180 Brussels Tel: (02) 3435600 Telex: 25028 Hachette Bru B
Man Dir: J Andrieu-Delille
Subject: General

Imprimeries **Havaux**, a division of Editions de la Francité (qv)

Imprimerie **Hayez** SPRL, 4 rue Fin, B-1080 Brussels Tel: (02) 4287112
Man Dir: Serge Hayez; *Sales Dir:* Frédéric Hayez
Subjects: Belles Lettres, Poetry, Philosophy, Religion, Medicine, General Science
Founded: 1780

Heibrand*, Hoevebosstr 1, B-2460 Kasterlee Tel: (014) 557328
Dir: R Lievens

Heideland PVBA*, Grote Markt 1, B-3500 Hasselt Tel: (011) 224505
Dir: L Nagels
Bookshop: Boekhandel Heideland, Hasselt (qv)
Subjects: Arts, Bibliography, Languages, Juveniles, Religion, Philosophy, Literature & Linguistics, Periodicals, Paperbacks, General
Founded: 1945

Heideland NV*, Grote Markt 1, B-3500 Hasselt Tel: (011) 224505
Dir: L Nagels
Subjects: Arts, Bibliography, Languages, Textbooks, Education, Sport & Games, Juveniles, Philosophy, Literature, Linguistics, General, Religion
Founded: 1945
ISBN Publisher's Prefix: 90-6440

Heideland-Orbis NV, Postbus 12/13, B-3500 Hasselt (Located at: Torenplein 6, B-3500 Hasselt) Tel: (011) 212112
Dirs: L Vandeschoor, F Smeets; *Editorial Manager:* H Fransen; *Sales Manager:* D Hilven; *Production & Rights:* J Cuyckens
Subjects: Encyclopaedias, Dictionaries, Language, Linguistics, Series, General
1978: 14 titles *1979:* 37 titles *Founded:* 1969
ISBN Publisher's Prefix: 90-291

Uitgeverij **Helios**, Kapelsestr 222, B-2080 Kapellen Tel: (031) 645320 Telex: 32242 Anvers Dnb B
Man Dirs: J Pelckmans, R Pelckmans
Associate Companies: Uitgeverij De Nederlandsche, Boekhandel (qv); Uitgeverij Opdebeek (qv); Uitgeverij Patmos (qv)
Subjects: General
Bookshop: Sint Jacobsmarkt 7, Antwerp
1978: 281 titles *1979:* 229 titles *Founded:* 1893
ISBN Publisher's Prefix: 90-333

Editions **Hemma**, 53 rue du Centre, BP 25 B-4081 Stoumont-Chevron Tel: (086) 433022 Cable Add: Hemma Telex: 41507
Dirs: Albert, Michel, Yvonne Hemmerlin
Subsidiary Company: Diffusion Hemma, 34-38 rue des Francs-Bourgeois, F-75003 Paris, France
Branch Off: Diffusion Hemma, 34 rue des Francs-Bourgeois, F-75003 Paris, France
Subjects: Juveniles, Educational Materials
1979: about 60 titles *Founded:* 1952
ISBN Publisher's Prefix: 2-8006

Hernieuwen-Uitgaven PVBA*, Noordstr 100, B-8800 Roeselare Tel: (051) 201541
Subjects: Juveniles, Religion, Philosophy

Drukkerij-Uitgeverij **Hertoghs***, Turnhoutsebaan 319, B-2110 Wijnegem Tel: (031) 536040
Dir: J Hertoghs
Subject: Textbooks
Founded: 1945

M van **Hove** DPN*, Dorpstr 11, B-2080 Kapellen, Antwerp Tel: (031) 642407
Dir: M van Hove
Subjects: Religion, Philosophy, General
Founded: 1966

Van **Hyfte**-De Coninck*, Lindenlaan 28A-30, B-9068 Ertvelde Tel: (091) 447200
Dir: M van Hyfte

NV **I C U-België***, Louizalaan 485, B-1050 Brussels Tel: (02) 6499026 Telex: 62067 Icubel
Parent Company: NV ICU, Netherlands (qv)
Subsidiary Companies: CED-Sansom nv (qv); CNES-Sansom; J B Wolters NV (qv)
Subjects: Publishing, text processing, planning and administration systems, training, consulting, films and AV packages, literature distribution, social and fiscal information

I N B E L, see Institut belge d'Information et de Documentation

I V A C, Amerikalei 26-28, B-2000 Antwerp Tel: (031) 162916 Telex: 31226 Bella B
Man Dir: Gilbert Gorissen
Subjects: Art, Education, History, General Science, Geography, Languages, Textbooks
Founded: 1949
Miscellaneous: A division of Bell Telephone Mfg Co SA

Uitgeverij J van **In**, Grote Markt 39, B-2500 Lier Tel: (031) 805511
Man Dir: Dr Laurent Woestenburg; *Editorial:* Ludo Camps; *Sales:* Jacques van Hellemont; *Production:* Ives Crokaerts; *Publicity:* Ludo Verscuren; *Rights & Permissions:* Dr Laurent Woestenburg
Parent Company: V N U NV, Netherlands (qv)
Subjects: Juveniles, University, Secondary & Primary Textbooks, Educational Materials, Law
Bookshop: At above address
1978: 115 titles *1979:* 75 titles *Founded:* 1833
ISBN Publisher's Prefix: 90-306

Infoboek, Roosterputstr 34, B-3990 Meerhout Tel: (014) 300477
Dir: W Verhaert
Subjects: Textbooks, Education, Sport & Games, Juveniles, Religion, Philosophy, Literature, Linguistics, Music
Founded: 1971

Institut belge d'Information et de Documentation (INBEL)*, Montoyerstr 3, B-1040 Brussels Tel: (02) 5126688 Telex: Inbel Bru 21716
Dir: F Coppieters
Subjects: Art, Bibliography, Law, Social Sciences, Literature, Periodicals
Founded: 1962

Institut national de Sténodactylographie*, rue de l'Union 23, B-1030 Brussels Tel: (02) 2176859
Dir: H Pringels
Subject: Textbooks relating to study of typing and shorthand-typing
Founded: 1897

Institut royal des Relations internationales, 88 ave de la Couronne, B-1050 Brussels Tel: (02) 6482000
Koninklijk Instituut voor Internationale Betrekkingen
Man Dir: Dr E Coppieters
Subjects: Political Science, Law, Economics, International Relations
1979: 6 titles *Founded:* 1947
Miscellaneous: Publishes periodical *Studia Diplomatica*

Uitgaven van **Interbankendienst** NV*, Keizerslaan 14, B-3000 Brussels Tel: (02) 5132553
Dir: L Dewincklear
Subjects: Law, Political & Social Science, Periodicals
Founded: 1968

International Publishers' Aid (IPA)*, Potterie Rei 69, BP 89, B-8000 Bruges Tel: (050) 335186
Man Dir: Pierre Angelet
Subject: Juveniles
Founded: 1969
Miscellaneous: Specialists in work to be jointly edited, jointly produced, in a number of languages

De **Internationale Pers**, Karel Govaertsstr 56-58, B-2100 Deurne Tel: (031) 213873
La Presse Internationale
Dir, Editorial, Publicity, Rights & Permissions: A J Walvisch; *Sales:* C J van Wolferen; *Production:* A Schödl
Subjects: Medicine, Juveniles, Periodicals
Founded: 1947

H-K de **Jaeger** Publications (ASTRID), K Astridlaan 89, B-9000 Ghent
Editor: H-K de Jaeger
Subject: ASTRID General Reference and Practical Information Science Series
1980: 1 title
ISBN Publisher's Prefix: 90-70078

J **Janssens**, Kruikstr 14, B-2000 Antwerp Tel: (031) 391220
Dir: J Janssens
Subjects: Arts, Education, Plays
Founded: 1876

Jecta*, A Gomandstr 24, B-1090 Brussels Tel: (02) 4268419
Dir: J Detremmerie
Subjects: Religion, Philosophy
Founded: 1961

Keesing — Internationale Drukkerij en Uitgeverij NV*, Keesinglaan 2-20, B-2100 Deurne Tel: (031) 243890 Cable Add: Systeka Telex: 32507
Dir: Mr Gillieron
Subjects: Education, Sport & Games, Medicine, Juveniles, Periodicals
Founded: 1911

Die **Keure** NV, Oude Gentweg 108, B-8000 Bruges Tel: (050) 331236
Dir: H Bogaerts
Subjects: Textbooks, Law, Political, Administrative & Social Sciences, Primary & Secondary Textbooks
Founded: 1948

NV Uitgeverij **Kluwer***, Santvoortbeeklaan 21-23, B-2100 Deurne Tel: (031) 247890/1/2
Dirs: R Roziers, J Wijnen
Subjects: Technical books and periodicals
Miscellaneous: Firm is part of Kluwer Group, Netherlands (qv)
Founded: 1954

Maarten **Kluwer's** Internationale Uitgeversonderneming NV, Somersstraat 13-15, B-2000 Antwerp Tel: (031) 312900
Dirs: M Kluwer, E Boerwinkel
Subjects: Textbooks, Law, Political & Social Science, Education, Technical, Periodicals
1978: 25 titles *Founded:* 1972
Miscellaneous: Wholesaler (Dutch books)

Koninklijk Instituut voor Internationale Betrekkingen, see Institut royale des Relations internationales

Kritak uitgeverij, Vesaliusstraat 1, B-3000 Leuven Tel: (016) 231264
Man Dirs: Rik Coolsaet, André Van Halewijck
Subjects: Politics, Social affairs, Literature, Comics
Bookshop: Vesaliusstraat 1, B-3000 Leuven
1978: 14 titles *1979:* 16 titles *Founded:* 1976
ISBN Publisher's Prefix: 90-6303

Editions **Labor**, 342 rue Royale, B-1030 Brussels Tel: (02) 2168750
Man Dir: Alexandre André; *all other offices:* J Fauconnier
Orders to: 156-158 chaussée de Haecht, B-1030 Brussels
Subjects: Belles Lettres, Poetry, Biography, History, Philosophy, Reference, Psychology, General & Social Science, University & Primary Textbooks, Pedagogy
1978: 40 titles *Founded:* 1927
ISBN Publisher's Prefix: 2-82590039

Imprimerie **Laconti** SA*, 51 rue Bonaventure, B-1090 Brussels Tel: (02) 4784835 Cable Add: Imprilaconti
Dir: C Volters
Subject: Art
Founded: 1935
ISBN Publisher's Prefix: 2-87008

Editions **Lampe** d'Or ASBL*, 23 ave Giele, B-1090 Brussels Tel: (02) 4279277
Man Dir: F M Van Dÿk
Subjects: Religion, Juveniles
Founded: 1955
ISBN Publisher's Prefix: 2-87001

Lannoo*, Kasteelstr 97, B-8880 Tielt Tel: (051) 402551 Cable Add: Lanoprint Telex: 81555
Man Dirs: Godfried Lannoo, Drs Johan Ducheyne
Subjects: Art, Philosophy, Religion, Juveniles, High-priced Paperbacks, Psychology, Education, Sports, Games, Travel
1978: 83 titles *Founded:* 1909
ISBN Publisher's Prefix: 90-209

Maison Ferdinand **Larcier** SA, 39 rue des Minimes, B-1000 Brussels Tel: (02) 5129679/5124712
Man Dir: Jean-Marie Ryckmans
Subjects: Social Science, Law (Belgian and International/European), Science & Technology, Periodicals: *Journal des Tribunaux* (weekly); *Journal des Tribunaux du Travail* (fortnightly); *Cahiers de droit européen* (6 issues a year)
1979: 17 titles *Founded:* 1839

Latomus ASBL, 60 rue Colonel Chaltin, B-1180 Brussels
Editorial: L Herrmann, M Renard; *Sales, Production, Publicity, Rights & Permissions:* G Cambier
Subjects: Bibliography, Philology, Roman Literature and History, Archaeology

1978: 5 titles *1979:* 9 titles *Founded:* 1937
ISBN Publisher's Prefix: 2-87031

Editions Paul **Legrain***, 72 rue Defacqz, B-1050 Brussels Tel: (02) 5387405
Dir: P Legrain
Subjects: Arts, Geography, History, Ethnography, Travel
Founded: 1946

Editions **Legrand***, rue Champs de Tignee, B-4511 Barchon Tel: (041) 628152 Telex: 41193 Apal B
Deputy Administrator: Ch Legrand, 42 Rue des Chateaux, B-4510 Saive
Subjects: Children's activities

Editions **Lesigne***, 171 ave du Prince Héritier, B-1200 Brussels Tel: (02) 7332097
Dir: P Moorkens
Subject: Textbooks

Uitgavenfonds Leon **Lesoli** V Z W*, Jan Palfijnstr 10, B-9000 Gent
Branch Off (Administration): Washuisstr 12-14, B-1000 Brussels Tel: (02) 5128778
Man Dir: Monique Laenen
Subject: Politics
1978: 8 titles *1979:* 2 titles *Founded:* 1973

Leuven University Press, Krakenstr 3, B-3000 Leuven
Dir: Guido Declercq
Subjects: Theology, Psychology, Pedagogy, Economics, Sociology, Political Studies, Music, Mathematics, Medicine, Philosophy, etc
1978: 16 titles *1979:* 19 titles *Founded:* 1971
ISBN Publisher's Prefix: 90-6186

Editions de la **Librairie encyclopédique**, 1593 chaussée de Waterloo, B-1180 Brussels Tel: (02) 5132467
Man Dir: A C Leyenberger
Subjects: History, Reference, Law, Economics, Political & Social Science
Bookshop: Librairie encyclopédique Exportation-Antiquariat (at above address)
Founded: 1939

Librairie générale SA*, 51 rue de Namur, B-1000 Brussels Tel: (02) 5123073 Telex: 61486 pauli b
Subjects: General Fiction, History, Music, Art, General Science
Associate Company: Librarie Pauli SA (qv)
Founded: 1919

Editeurs de **Littérature** biblique*, 479 chaussée de Tubize, B-1420 Braine-l'Alleud Tel: (02) 3845402
Biblical Publications
Dir: M Cl Kroeker
Subjects: Education, Pedagogy, Sport, Games, Juveniles, Religion, Philosophy, Music, Journals, Paperbacks
Founded: 1959

Editions du **Lloyd** Anversois SA (Antwerpse Lloyd NV), Eiermarkt 23, B-2000 Antwerp Tel: (031) 340550 Telex: 31446
Man Dir: M R Jaumotte
Subjects: Transport, Law, Maritime, Languages
Founded: 1904

Lombard SA*, ave Paul-Henri Spaak 1-11, B-1070 Brussels Tel: (02) 5225600 Cable Add: Lombarbel-Brussels Telex: 23097
Dir: G Leblanc; *Rights & Permissions:* Viviane Rousie
Subjects: Juveniles, Sports, Games, Education, Geography, History, Ethnography, Travel
Founded: 1946

Uitgeverij **Lotus**/Editions Lotus, Leopoldstraat 43, B-2000 Antwerp Tel: (031) 327010/327001
Man Dir: Andreas Ausloos; *Editorial (Dutch language books for children):* Jean-Pierre Zinje; *Publicity:* Andreas Ausloos

Orders to: (French language books) Garnier Frères, BP 168, 19 rue des plantes, F-75665 Paris; (Dutch language books, Belgium) Denis, Sterckshoflei 28-30, B-2100 Deurne; (Dutch language books, Netherlands) Centraal Boekhuis, Postbus 125, Erasmusweg 10, Culemborg
Subjects: Novels, Documentary Works, Juveniles
1978: 45 titles *1979:* 50 titles *Founded:* 1977
ISBN Publisher's Prefix: 90-6290 (Dutch language books); 2-87053 (French language books)

Editions **Lumen** Vitae ASBL*, 184 rue Washington, B-1050 Brussels Tel: (02) 3441882
International Centre for Religious Education
Man Dir: Jean Bouvy; *Sales Dir:* Albert Dreze
Subjects: Religion, High-priced Paperbacks, Psychology, Secondary & Primary Textbooks, Educational Materials
1978: 8 titles *Founded:* 1936

M I M, see Moderne Instructie Methoden

Magic-Strip SPRL, 46 blvd Maurice Lemonnier, B-1000 Brussels Tel: (02) 5115380
Dirs: Daniel Pasamonik, Didier Pasamonik; *Rights & Permissions:* Daniel Pasamonik
Subjects: Juveniles, Comic Books
Founded: 1979
ISBN Publisher's Prefix: 2-8035

Uitgeversmaatschappij A **Manteau** NV, Valkenburgstraat 51, B-2000 Antwerp Tel: (031) 371792 Telex: 33866
Man Dir: J Weverbergh; *Sales Dir:* W L Detiger
Associate Company: Elsevier-NDU nv, Netherlands (qv)
Subsidiary Company: A Manteau NV
Subjects: General Fiction, Belles Lettres, Poetry, Biography, Art, High-priced Paperbacks, Secondary Textbooks
1978: 116 titles *1979:* 85 titles *Founded:* 1932
ISBN Publisher's Prefix: 90-223

Les Nouvelles Editions **Marabout** SA*, 65 rue de Limbourg, B-4800 Verviers Tel: (087) 339135
Man Dir: Jean-Etienne Cohen-Seat; *Sales Dir:* Jacques Closset
Branch Off: 81 ave de Tervueren, B-1040 Brussels Tel: (02) 7359125; 34 avenue Marceau, F-75008 Paris Tel: 7237250
Subject: Paperbacks
Founded: 1977
Miscellaneous: Formerly Editions Gérard et Cie SPRL

Pierre **Mardaga** SA, 2-4 galerie des Princes, B-1000 Brussels Tel: (02) 5132038
Man Dir: Pierre Mardaga; *Rights & Permissions:* Pierre Mardaga, Gigi Dony
Subjects: Psychology, Social Science, Architecture
1980: 160 titles *Founded:* 1938
ISBN Publisher's Prefix: 2-87009

Maredsous ASBL*, 11 rue de Maredsous, B-5642 Denee Tel: (082) 699155
Dir: Père Léon-Nicolas Dayez
Subjects: Geography, History, Religion, Philosophy, General, Ethnography, Travel
Bookshop: Librairie de Maredsous, B-5642 Denee
Founded: 1924

Editions **Marie-Médiatrice** ASBL*, 172 ave Gevaert, B-1320 Genval Tel: (02) 6537613
Subjects: Juveniles, Religion, Paperbacks
Founded: 1941

Editions **Markus***, Schilsweg 23, B-4700 Eupen Tel: (087) 552108
Dir: M Schroder
Subjects: Bibliography, Languages, Textbooks, Geography, History, Ethnography, Travel, Religion, Philosophy, General

Frans **Masereel** Fonds VZW*, Raveschootstr 4, B-9000 Ghent Tel: (091) 253853
Dir: L Brabans
Subjects: History, Current Affairs
Founded: 1971

Les Ateliers d'Art graphique **Meddens** SA*, 141-143 ave de Scheut, B-1070 Brussels Tel: (02) 5227925
Dir: F Van Den Bremt
Subjects: Fine Arts, Geography, History, Music, Theology

Mercatorfonds SA, see Fonds Mercator SA

Mercatorfonds Arcade, see Editions Arcade-Fonds Mercator

Editeur Paul F **Merckx**, 145a ave des Statuaires, B-1180 Brussels Tel: (02) 3744156/3745158
Subjects: Art, Geography, History, Touring in Belgium
Founded: 1958

Mercurius PVBA*, Rodestr 44, B-2000 Antwerp Tel: (031) 333708/333762
Dir: K Schenck
Subjects: Geography, History, Ethnography, Travel
Founded: 1894

Editions d'Art Lucien de **Meyer** ASBL*, 88 ave de Tervueren, B-1040 Brussels Tel: (02) 7343560/7343582
Executives: As for Editions Arts et Voyages (qv)
Subject: Art
Founded: 1977

D **Meyers-Trefois***, Pontstr 50, B-9230 Melle, Ghent Tel: (091) 521081
Dir: D Meyers

Meysmans*, 23 rue de l'Union, B-1030 Brussels Tel: (02) 2176859
Dir: H Pringels
Subject: Textbooks
Founded: 1897

Michelin (Département Cartes & Guides) SA*, 33 quai de Willebroek, B-1020 Brussels Tel: (02) 2186100 ext 238 Cable Add: Pneumiclin
Dir: R Cammaerts
Subjects: Travel Guides, Maps
Founded: 1913

Moderne Instructie Methoden (MIM) PVBA*, Jules Moretuslei 760, B-2610 Wilrijk Tel: (031) 496271
Dir: M Callebaut
Subjects: Textbooks, Education, Sport & Games
Founded: 1971

Louis **Musin** Editeur, 99 ave de la Brabançonne, B-1040 Brussels Tel: (02) 7363727/7341276
Dir: L Musin
Subjects: Textbooks, Juveniles, Literature, Linguistics, History
1980: 124 titles *Founded:* 1960

N F F (Nouvelles Feuilles Familiales)*, 27 rue du Congrès, B-1000 Brussels Tel: (02) 2183482
Dir: Jean Hinnekens
Associate Companies: Centre d'Etude et d'Edition Conjugale et Familiale ASBL, (qv); Les 'Feuilles familiales' ASBL (qv)
Subjects: Marriage and Family Relations, Psychology, Educational, Religion, Pedagogy
Founded: 1937

NV Uitgeverij **Nauwelaerts** Edition SA, Mechelsestr 148, B-3000 Louvain Tel: (016) 229096
Man Dir: W Vandermeulen
Subjects: History, Philosophy, Theology, Medicine, Psychology, Social Science, Economics, University Textbooks, Educational Materials, Literature
Founded: 1938

Uitgeverij De **Nederlandsche Boekhandel**, Kapelsestr 222, B-2080 Kapellen Tel: (031) 645320 Telex: 32272 Anvers Dnb B
Man Dirs: J Pelckmans, R Pelckmans
Parent Company: Standaard Uitgeverij en Distributie BV, Netherlands (qv)
Associate Companies: Uitgeverij Helios (qv); Uitgeverij Opolebeek (qv); Uitgeverij Patmos (qv)
Subjects: History, Philosophy, Religion, Juveniles, Social Science, University, Secondary & Primary Textbooks
Bookshop: Sint Jacobsmarkt 7, B-2000 Antwerp
1978: 176 titles *Founded:* 1892
ISBN Publisher's Prefix: 90-289

Nici*, Lousbergkaai 32, B-900 Ghent Tel: (031) 252897
Dir: G Vander Rol

Nomath*, 65 rue de Maizeret, B-5134 Loyers Tel: (081) 588592
Dir: M van Cutsem
Subjects: Textbooks, Mathematics, Physics, Technical
Founded: 1967
ISBN Publisher's Prefix: 2-87002

Het **Noordnederlands** Boekbedrijf NV*, Paleisstr 23-25, B-2000 Antwerp Tel: (031) 374605/385506
Dir: F Doumh
Subjects: Bibliography, Philology, Languages, Textbooks, Law, Political & Social Sciences, Education, Sport & Games, Mathematics, Physics, Technical, Medicine, Juveniles, Religion, Philosophy, Literature, Linguistics, Music, Periodicals, General, Geography, History, Ethnography, Travel
Founded: 1951
ISBN Publisher's Prefix: 90-6154

Norma PVBA*, St Baafsplein 30, B-9000 Ghent Tel: (091) 252815
Subject: Textbooks
Founded: 1938

Nouvelle Diffusion, see Editions Complexe

Les **Nouvelles Editions Marabout** SA, see Marabout

Nouvelles Editions Vokaer SA, see Vokaer

Nouvelles Feuilles Familiales, see NFF

Uitgeverij S V **Ontwikkeling***, Leeuwerikstr 41, B-2000 Antwerp Tel: (031) 338659
Dir: R Binnemans
Subjects: Novels, Poetry, History, Textbooks
Bookshops: Boekhandel Ontwikkeling, Ommeganckstr 35-37, Antwerp; Boekhandel Ontwikkeling, Dés Boucherystr 18-20, Mechelen; Boekhandel Ontwikkeling, J Brochhovenstr 28, Deurne, Antwerp (all in Belgium)
Founded: 1923

Uitgeverij **Opdebeek**, Kapelsestr 222, B-2080 Kapellen Tel: (031) 645320 Telex: 32242 Anvers Dnb B
Dirs: J Pelckmans, R Pelckmans
Associate Companies: Uitgeverij Helios (qv); Uitgeverij De Nederlandsche Boekhandel (qv); Uitgeverij Patmos (qv)
Subject: Juveniles
Bookshop: Sint Jacobsmarkt 7, Antwerp

BELGIUM

1978: 17 titles *Founded:* 1953
ISBN Publisher's Prefix: 90-6162

Orbis Boekhandel NV, Vekestr 16-18,
B-2000 Antwerp Tel: (031) 318610
Dir: A Goyvaerts
Subjects: Geography, History, Ethnography,
Travel, Art, Religion
Founded: 1968
ISBN Publisher's Prefix: 90-6492

Ordina Editions, 5 rue Forgeur, B-4000
Liège Tel: (041) 323472
Man Dir: Georges Derouaux
Subject: Problems of population
1979: 3 titles *1980:* 4 titles *Founded:* 1974
ISBN Publisher's Prefix: 87040

Uitgeverij **Orientaliste** PVBA*, Klein
Dalenstr 42, B-3009 Winksele-Louvain
Tel: (016) 488102
Man Dir: E Peeters
Subjects: History, Philosophy, Religion,
Psychology, University Textbooks
Miscellaneous: Publish Oriental and foreign
language books

Uitgeverij **Orion**, Lieven Bauwensstraat 19,
B-8200 Bruges 2 Tel: 050 318157 Telex:
81068
Man Dir: A Goyvaerts; *Editorial, Rights &
Permissions:* F Bonneure
Parent Company: Desclée de Brouwer (qv)
Branch Off: B Gottmer, Nijmegen,
Netherlands
Subjects: General Fiction, Literature, Essays,
Poetry, Art, History, Hobbies
1979: 107 titles *Founded:* 1942
ISBN Publisher's Prefix: 90-264

De **Oude** Linden NV, Abdijstr 26, B-3180
Tongerlo-Westerlo Tel: (014) 544206
Dir: C van Heijst o praem
Subjects: Juveniles, Religion, Philosophy
Founded: 1962

Uitgeverij **Patmos**, Kapelsestr 222, B-2080
Kapellen Tel: (031) 645320 Telex: 32242
Anvers Dnb B
Dirs: J Pelckmans, R Pelckmans
Associate Companies: Uitgeverij Helis (qv);
Uitgeverij De Nederlandsche Boekhandel
(qv); Uitgeverij Opdebeek (qv)
Subjects: Education, Juveniles, Religion
Bookshop: Sint Jacobsmarkt 7, Antwerp
1978: 68 titles
ISBN Publisher's Prefix: 90-292

Pauli SA*, rue de Namur 51, B-1000
Brussels Tel: (02) 5123073 Telex: 61486
Pauli B
Associate Company: Librairie Générale SA
(qv)
Subjects: Geography, History, Ethnography,
Travel
Founded: 1930

Peeters SPRL*, BP 41, B-3000 Louvain
Tel: (016) 488102
Dir: Mme Peeters
Subjects: Periodicals, General
Founded: 1970

Pink Editions & Productions*,
Venusstr 18A, B-2000 Antwerp Tel: (031)
332273
Dir: R Lowet de Wotrenge
Founded: 1973
Subjects: Art, Bibliography

Uitgeverij **Plantyn** SA NV*,
Santvoortbeeklaan 21-23, B-2100 Deurne,
Antwerp Tel: (031) 247897
Dir: J Vrindts
Subjects: Education, all levels
Miscellaneous: Firm is a member of the
Kluwer Group, Deventer, Netherlands (qv)
Founded: 1950

La **Presse** Internationale, see De
Internationale Pers

Presses agronomiques de Gembloux ASBL*,
22 Ave de la Faculté d'Agronomie, B-5800
Gembloux Tel: (081) 611955
Dir: Mme C Dagnelie
Subjects: Agriculture, Botany, Chemistry,
Mathematics, Physics, Technical, Periodicals
Founded: 1965
ISBN Publisher's Prefix: 2-87016

Presses universitaires de Bruxelles ASBL, 42
ave Paul Heger, B-1050 Brussels Tel: (02)
6499780
President: Ed Burg; *Man Dir:* Marc Oostens;
Sales: Eric Suppes
Subjects: University Textbooks, especially
Philosophy, Medicine, Engineering,
Economics, General Science, Architecture
Bookshops: Librairie des Presses
Universitaires de Bruxelles, 42 ave Paul
Heger, B-1050 Brussels; 162 rue aux Laines,
B-1000 Brussels
1978: c. 60 titles *1979:* c. 40 titles *Founded:*
1958
ISBN Publisher's Prefix: 2-500

Presses universitaires de Liège ASBL,
Domaine du Sart Tilman, B-4000 Liège 1
Tel: (041) 562218
Dir: P Froidcoeur
Subjects: Law, Political & Social Sciences,
Medicine, General
Founded: 1920

Presses universitaires de Namur, Rempart de
la Vierge 8, B-5000 Namur Tel: (081) 29061
Telex: 59222 Facna B
Dir: P Pellemans; *Sales:* A Lambot;
Commercial: J C Leymarie
Subjects: Art, Biography, History,
Literature, Philosophy, Religion, Medicine,
General Scientific, Social Sciences,
University Textbooks, Quality Paperbacks
1978: 5 titles *1979:* 5 titles *Founded:* 1972
ISBN Publisher's Prefix: 2-87037

Het **Prisma** NV*, Corverstr 13, B-3700
Tongeren Tel: (012) 231325
Dir: G Michiels
Subject: Textbooks

Pro Civitate, now Crédit Communal de
Belgique—Centre Culturel

La **Procure**, 161 rue des Tanneurs, B-1000
Brussels Tel: (021) 5122672
Man Dir: J O Neukermans
Subjects: Travel, General & Political
Science, Educational Materials
Founded: 1881

Prodim SPRL*, Boulevard Général Jacques
184, B-1050 Brussels Tel: (02) 6405970
Production et Diffusion medico-techniques
Dir: P Nile
Subjects: Textbooks, Medicine, Science
Founded: 1968

Production et Diffusion medico-techniques
SPRL, see Prodim SPRL

Henri **Proost** & Co*, Everdongenlaan 23,
B-2300 Turnhout Tel: (014) 416911
Telex: 33185
Man Dir: Jef Proost; *Sales Dir:* Frans
Peeters
Subsidiary Company: Salamander Books
Ltd, UK (qv)
Subjects: Religion, Juveniles, Cookery,
Gardening, Travel, History

André De **Rache**, Editeur, 127 rue du
Château d'Eau, B-1180 Brussels Tel: (02)
3743950
Man Dir: A De Rache
Subjects: Belles Lettres, Poetry, Biography,
Art
Founded: 1954

Reader's Digest SA*, 12a Grande Place,
B-1000 Brussels Tel: (02) 4287100
Telex: 21876
Man Dir: P Kittel
Subjects: Education, Sport & Games,
Geography, History, Travel
Founded: 1967

Reinaert Uitgaven, see Dap-Reinaert
Uitgaven

La **Renaissance** du Livre SA, 12 pl du Petit-
Sablon, B-1000 Brussels Tel: (02)
5119914/5134751
Man Dir: Ch R Bousson
Subjects: Belles Lettres, History, Art,
Juveniles, Law, Business, Reference,
Educational Materials
Founded: 1923

Fondation André **Renard***, 9-11 pl St Paul,
B-4000 Liège Tel: (041) 237940
Dirs: R Gillon, G Vandersmissen,
M Hockers

La **Revue** nouvelle ASBL, 3-5 rue des
Moucherons, B-1000 Brussels Tel: (02)
5119862
Dir: Jean Delfosse
Subjects: Languages, Law, Economics,
Political & Social Sciences, Education,
Religion, Philosophy, Literature, Linguistics,
Bibliography
Founded: 1945

De **Riemaecker** Uitgeverij*, Kerkewijk 2,
B-9681 Nukerke Tel: (055) 211404
Dir: P de Riemaecker
Founded: 1947

Roeland Kamer Fonds VZW*,
Groenendaalsesteenweg 135, B-1990
Hoeilaart Tel: (02) 6572602
Man Dir: Rienk H Kamer

De **Roerdomp***, Vandereydtlaan 46, B-2160
Brecht Tel: (031) 138401
Dir: J Lombaerts
Subjects: Law, Political & Social Sciences,
Literature, Linguistics
Founded: 1967

Rossel Edition SA, 134 rue Royale, B-1000
Brussels Tel: (02) 2194190 Telex: 24298
Manager: J Gerlache; *Rights & Permissions:*
André-Paul Duchâteau
Associate Company: Rossel Edition,
France (qv)
Subjects: Education, Sports and Games,
Documentary Reports, Period History,
Juveniles; Periodicals
Founded: 1972

Roya Boudewijn*, Ravestraat 35, B-8000
Bruges Tel: (050) 331235

Rubens, see Beckers Groep

Saeftinge*, De Merodedreef 55, B-2180
Westerlo
Dir: J J A Verstappen
Subjects: Juveniles, Literature, Linguistics

Publications de **Saint-André**, allée de
Clerlande 1, B-1340 Ottignies Tel: (010)
417463
Subjects: Pastoral, Liturgical, Anthropology,
Contemporary Architecture (all periodicals)

Publications des Facultés universitaires **Saint
Louis**, 43 blvd du Jardin Botanique, B-1000
Brussels Tel: (02) 2177653
Man Dir: M van de Kerchove; *Sales,
Publicity:* M G Braive
Subjects: Humanities, Law, Economics
1978: 3 titles *1979:* 3 titles *Founded:* 1974
ISBN Publisher's Prefix: 2-8028

Samsom (CED), see CED-Samsom NV

Sanderus PVBA*, Rempardstr 36, B-9700
Oudenaarde Tel: (055) 311130
Dir: M van den Abeele
Subject: Textbooks
Founded: 1959

Schaubroeck PVBA*, Drapstr 23, B-9730 Nazareth Tel: (091) 854227
Dir: J Schaubroeck
Subjects: Law, Political & Social Sciences
Founded: 1911

Schott Frères SPRL (Éditeurs de Musique)*, 30 rue St-Jean, B-1000 Brussels Tel: (02) 5123980
Man Dir: Jean-Jacques Junne
Subject: Music
Founded: 1823

De **Schutter** SA*, Venusstraat 23, B-2000 Antwerp Tel: (031) 311750 Telex: 32339 Ds Ant
Subjects: Fine Art Reprints and Facsimiles

Editions **Sciences et Lettres** SA*, 13 rue de la Commune, B-4020 Liège Tel: (041) 426154
Man Dir: L Maraval
Subjects: History, Medicine, Psychology, University, Secondary & Primary Textbooks
Founded: 1946

Scribae-Uitgevers VZW, Postbus 50, B-2000 Antwerp 6 Tel: (031) 328483
Chief Executive, Rights & Permissions: Magda Heeffer; *Editorial:* George Leemans; *Publicity:* John Fennell
Subjects: Fiction, Short Stories, Plays, Poetry
1978: 6 titles *1979:* 7 titles *Founded:* 1978
ISBN Publisher's Prefix: 90-6387

De **Seizoenen** PVBA*, Prins Leopoldlei 60, B-2510 Mortsel Tel: (031) 496034
Dir: P Vanhout
Subject: Juveniles
Founded: 1958

Service SC, 232 blvd Em Bockstael, B-1020 Brussels Tel: (02) 4282627/4280520
Dirs: G Vanden Avyle, M Geets
Subjects: Law, Technical, Periodicals
Founded: 1949

Services interbancaires SA*, 14 boulevard de l'Empereur, B-2000 Brussels Tel: (02) 5132553
Dir: L Dewincklear
Subjects: Law, Political & Social Sciences, Periodicals
Founded: 1968

Uitgeverij De **Sikkel** NV, Nijverheidsweg 8, B-2140 Malle
Man Dir: Karel de Bock
Subjects: General Fiction, Belles Lettres, Art, History, General Science, Educational Materials
Founded: 1919
ISBN Publisher's Prefix: 90-260

Editions Le **Sillon** d'Or*, Grotenhof 38, B-2510 Mortsel Tel: (031) 498415
Dir: M Saldien
Subject: General
Founded: 1951

Simon Stevin NV, Zennestr 37, B-1000 Brussels Tel: (02) 5121085/5138295 Telex: 23602 Boetis
Dirs: J Van Hoorick, M Strens-Van Hoorick
Parent Company: N V Drukkerij De Bouwkroniek
Subjects: Law, Political & Social Sciences, Mathematics, Physics, Technical, Surveying, Architecture, Engineering Science, Periodicals
Founded: 1930

Sinite Parvulos VBVB, B-3581 Hamont-Achel Tel: (011) 641078
Dir: L van Gassel
Subjects: Devotional Literature and Miscellaneous

Sintal*, Dekenstr 28, B-3000 Louvain Tel: (016) 223470
Dir: J Devos
Subjects: Geography, History, Ethnography, Travel
Founded: 1928

Snoeck-Ducaju & Zoon NV, Begijnhoflaan 440, B-9000 Ghent Tel: (091) 234897
Dir: S Snoeck
Subjects: Snoeck's Literary Yearbook, Snoeck's almanakken
Founded: 1782

Société Biblique belge ASBL, 160 rue du Trône, B-1050 Brussels Tel: (02) 6401112/6401575
General Secretary: Rev R Catinus
Subjects: Editions of the Bible in many languages

Walter **Soethoudt***, Perenstr 15, B-2000 Antwerp Tel: (031) 367055
Dir: W Soethoudt
Subjects: Literature, Poetry, Paperbacks, General
Founded: 1964

Soledi (Imprimeur-Editeur) SA*, 37 rue de la Province, B-4020 Liège
Dir: P Mardaga
Subjects: Arts, Languages, Education, Philosophy, Architecture, Linguistics, General
Founded: 1919

Sonneville Press (Uitgeversmij) PVBA*, Orchideeënlaan 3, B-8200 St-Andries, Bruges Tel: (050) 321112
Dir: J Sonneville
Subjects: Arts, Law, Political & Social Sciences, Education, Sport & Games, Geography, History, Ethnography, Travel, Religion, Philosophy, Literature, Linguistics, Music, Periodicals, Paperbacks
Founded: 1966

Het **Spectrum** NV, Bijkhoevelaan 12, B-2110 Wijnegem Tel: (031) 539800 Telex: 33545 Spant B
Dirs: M Cornu, H C de Wit
Parent Company: Uitgeverij Het Spectrum BV, Netherlands (qv)
Subjects: Arts, Bibliography, Philology, Languages, Law, Political & Social Sciences, Education, Sport & Games, Mathematics, Physics, Technical, Geography, History, Ethnography, Travel, Medicine, Religion, Philosophy, Literature, Linguistics, Music, Periodicals, General
Founded: 1946

Le **Sphinx** SA*, 5 rue de Danemark, B-1060 Brussels Tel: (02) 5370437/5381044
Publisher: Marcel Leempoel
Subjects: General Fiction, Belles Lettres, General
Founded: 1951

Anciens Etablissements **Splichal** SA*, Apostoliekenstr 105, B-2300 Turnhout Tel: (014) 413861
Man Dir: L Verwaest
Subject: Religion
Founded: 1856

Standaard Uitgeverij (NV Scriptoria), Belgiëlei 147a, Postbus 212, B-2000 Antwerp Tel: (031) 395900 Telex: Edista 31421
Man Dir: A Sap
Associate Companies: Standaard Uitgeverij en Distributie BV, Netherlands (qv); Editions Erasme (qv)
Subjects: General Fiction, How-to, Politics, Economics, Law, Reference, General Science, Textbooks, Encyclopaedias, Juveniles
Bookshops: Owns chain of Standaard-Boekhandel shops in Belgium and Netherlands
Founded: 1924
ISBN Publisher's Prefix: 90-021

NV Uitgeverij **Stappaerts**, Letterkundestraat 138 A-B, B-2610 Wilrijk (Antwerp) Tel: (031) 288531 Telex: 71288
Man Dir: Jozee Stappaerts
Subject: Juveniles
1978: 78 titles *1979:* approx 45 titles
Founded: 1976

Steppe*, Aalstersesteenweg 99-101, B-9400 Ninove Tel: (054) 332591 Cable Add: Steppe-Ninove
Subjects: Textbooks, Mathematics, Physics, Technical

De **Ster** PVBA*, Lange Brilstr 9, B-2000 Antwerp Tel: (031) 322036
Dir: R De Smedt

E **Story**-Scientia PVBA, van Duysplein 8, B-9000 Ghent Tel: (091) 255757
Dirs: E Story, L Van Opdenbosch, J Story
Subjects: Science, Humanities, History, Business, Agriculture, Medicine, Law, Education, Economics, Psychology
Bookshop: At above address
Founded: 1960

De **Techniek***, J De Bomstr 61, B-2000 Antwerp Tel: (031) 378567
Dir: J Roggen
Subjects: Textbooks, Mathematics, Physics, Technical
Founded: 1926

Uitgeverij De **Tempel**, Tempelhof 37, B-8000 Bruges Tel: (050) 315505
Man Dir: Mrs M H Monseu
Subjects: Philosophy, Social Science (especially European unification), Archaeology
1978: 2 titles *1979:* 2 titles *Founded:* 1905

Imprimerie-Editions Georges **Thone** Sciences et Lettres*, 11-19 rue de la Commune, B-4020 Liège Tel: (041) 426154
Man Dir: L Maraval; *Sales, Publicity:* Mrs I Severyns; *Production, Rights & Permissions:* L Maraval
Parent Company: Imprimerie Georges Thone
Subjects: Scholastic Texts, Mathematics, Language, Chemistry, Law, Social History, Pedagogy, Education, Mechanics, Psysiology, Biology, Botany, Zoology, Science and Technology
Founded: 1908 ('Sciences et Lettres', 1946)

Toulon, Sportstr 35, B-8400 Ostend Tel: (059) 800927
Dir: P A Toulon
Subjects: Educational, Technical, Juveniles

Trois Arches, 496 ave Molière, B-1050 Brussels Tel: (02) 3447333/3587181
Also known as 3 Arches
Man Dir, Rights & Permissions: Hugues Boucher
Subjects: Literature, Fine Art, Architecture, Photography, Children's Books, Bibliography
1979: 2 titles *1980:* 3 titles *Founded:* 1975

Editions **U G A** (Uitgeverij voor Gemeente-Administratie)*, Stijn Streuvelslaan 73, B-8710 Kortrijk-Heule Tel: (056) 355881
Dir: L Deschildre
Branch Offs: 5 ave de Stassart, B-5000 Namur; 19 rue Guimard, Bte 2, B-1040 Brussels
Subjects: Administration, History, Social Science, Law, Language, Bibliography, Literature, Journals
Founded: 1948

U O P C, see Union et Orientation de Presse et de Culture

Uni-Oyez SA, see Oyez

Union et Orientation de Presse et de Culture (UOPC) SA*, 216 chaussée de Wavre, B-1040 Brussels Tel: (02) 6489689

Dir: Mme Lefebvre
Subjects: Religion, Philosophy
Founded: 1923

Universa PVBA, Hoenderstr 24, B-9200 Wetteren Tel: (091) 691563
Man Dir: A De Meester
Subjects: Textbooks, Geography, History, Ethnography, Travel, Music
Founded: 1958

Universitaire Boekhandel NV*, St-Amandstr 20, B-9000 Ghent Tel: (091) 231675/232311
Subject: Textbooks
Founded: 1964

Universitaire Pers Leuven, see Leuven University Press

Editions **Universitaires**, see under Editions

Presses **Universitaires** de Bruxelles, de Liège, de Namur, see under Presses

Publications des Facultés **Universitaires** Saint Louis, see under Saint Louis

Editions de l'**Université** de Bruxelles, Parc Léopold, 137A rue Belliard, B-1040 Brussels Tel: (02) 2307705
Man Dir: Mrs S Unger
Subjects: Humanities, Social Sciences, Science, Medicine; Periodicals
1978: 35 titles *1979:* 41 titles *Founded:* 1950
ISBN Publisher's Prefix: 2-8004

Vademecum de Pharmacie*, 3 pl Rotenberg, B-4700 Eupen Tel: (087) 553271
Man Dir: Paul Schiltz
Subjects: Reference, Medicine
Founded: 1963

Imprimerie H **Vaillant Carmanne** SA, rue Fond St-Servais 4, B-4000 Liège Tel: (041) 529616
Man Dir: G Dengis
Subjects: Science, Education, Political Science, Belles Lettres, Religion, Medicine, Law, History, Science, Technical
1978: 5 titles *Founded:* 1838

Vander Publishing, 148 Mechelsestraat, B-3000 Louvain Tel: (016) 229096
Man Dir: Willy Vandermeulen
Branch Offs: Brussels Tel: (322) 7620662
Subjects: Psychology, Engineering, General & Social Science, University Textbooks, Law, Economics, Politics, Medicine, Reference, Languages, Architecture, Periodicals
Founded: 1880
ISBN Publisher's Prefix: 2-8008

Librairie **Vanderlinden** SA*, 17 rue des Grands-Carmes, B-1000 Brussels Tel: (02) 5116140
Man Dir: J Vanderlinden
Bookshop: 17 rue des Grands-Carmes, B-1000 Brussels
Subjects: Art, General Fiction, Juveniles, Textbooks, Paperbacks, Science, Mathematics
Founded: 1897

L **Vanmelle** (Drukkerij) NV*, Lt Willemotlaan 80, B-9910 Mariakerke (Ghent) Tel: (091) 233586 Telex: 11850
Dir: L Vanmelle
Subjects: Textbooks, Juveniles

Uitgaven van de **Verbruikersunie** VZW (Editions de Association des Consommateurs ASBL), Hollandstr 13, B-1060 Brussels Tel: (02) 5374265 Telex: Test 26771 B
Dir: G Castelain
Subjects: Periodicals, Tests and Studies connected with consumers
Founded: 1957

Vereniging van de belgische medische Wetenschappelijke Genootschappen VZW, see Association des Sociétés scientifiques médicales belges ASBL

Editions **Verrycken**, Wiegstraat 30, B-2000 Antwerp Tel: (031) 323378
Man Dir, Editorial, Rights & Permissions: Christian Vandekerkhove; *Production:* E Droesbeke; *Sales, Publicity:* E Vandekerkhove
Orders to: Verrycken Booksellers (at above address)
Subjects: Philosophy, Medicine, Parapsychology, Occult
Bookshops: Librairie Verrycken, Wiegstraat 30, B-2000 Antwerp; Occult Bookshop, Hoogstraat 68, B-2000 Antwerp
1979: 4 titles *1980:* 6 titles *Founded:* 1976
ISBN Publisher's Prefix: 90-70181

De **Verzekeringswereld** PVBA*, Karel de Preterlei 146, B-2200 Borgehout Tel: (031) 365349
Dir: A Seghers
Subjects: Law, Political & Social Sciences
Founded: 1961

Les Editions **Vie** ouvrière ASBL, 4 rue d'Anderlecht, B-1000 Brussels Tel: (02) 5125090
Subjects: Religion, Juveniles, Psychology, Social Science, University & Secondary Textbooks, History, Economics
Founded: 1958
ISBN Publisher's Prefix: 2-87003

Albert de **Visscher** Editeur, Ave du Golf 31, B-1640 Rhode-St-Genèse Tel: (02) 3587423
Man Dir: Albert de Visscher
Subjects: Music, Art, Medicine, General Science
Founded: 1944

Vlaams Ekonomisch Verbond VZW, Brouwersvlier 15, Postbus 7, B-2000 Antwerp Tel: (031) 326861
Man Dir: R de Feyter; *Publicity:* M Paeleman
Subjects: Economics, Statistics
1978: 11 titles *1979:* 10 titles *Founded:* 1926

Vlaamse Bijbelstichting*, St Michielsstr 2, B-3000 Louvain Tel: 337468
Subjects: Religious Literature connected with Catholic Bible production in Belgium, the Netherlands, Austria, Switzerland and Federal Germany
Miscellaneous: Company is a member of AMB (qv under Federal Republic of Germany)

Vlaamse Toeristenbond VZW*, Sint-Jacobsmarkt 45, B-2000 Antwerp Tel: (031) 317680/313615
Dir: R Rombaut

De **Vlijt** NV, Nationalestr 46, B-2000 Antwerp Tel: (031) 312880
Dir: J Huybrechts
Subjects: Arts, Educational, History, Geography

Nouvelles Editions **Vokaer** SA, 131 rue de Birmingham, B-1070 Brussels Tel: (02) 5240070 Telex: 24326
Subjects: Arts, Geography, History, Tourism, Travel, General
Founded: 1969
ISBN Publisher's Prefix: 2-87012

Het **Volk** NV*, Forelstr 22, B-9000 Ghent Tel: (091) 255701
Dir: J van Haverbeke
Subject: Juveniles

C De **Vries** Brouwers PVBA, Haantjeslei 80, B-2000 Antwerp Tel: (031) 374180
Dir: I de Vries
Subjects: Education, Juveniles, History, Law
Founded: 1946

De **Vroente**, Bosakkersstr 10, B-2460 Kasterlee Tel: (014) 556160
Dir: S Debroey
Subjects: Arts, Textbooks, Education, Religion, Philosophy

PVBA Imprimerie-Editions **Vyncke**ature, Savaanstr 92, B-9000 Ghent Tel: (091) 253960
Dir: H Vyncke; all other offices: Frans Pauwels
Subjects: Textbooks (for technical schools), Periodicals (on textiles, industrial equipment, water sports)
1978: 3 titles *Founded:* 1922

Eugène **Wahle**, 14A rue du Mèry, B-4000 Liège Tel: (041) 322113
Subjects: History, Art, Archaeology
1978: 3 titles *1979:* 3 titles
ISBN Publisher's Prefix: 2-87011

Wastiau-Jeukens*, 9 rue de l'Industrie, B-1010 Brussels Tel: (02) 2303425
Dirs: R Wastiau, R Jeukens
Subjects: Arts, Literature, Linguistics
Founded: 1951
ISBN Publisher's Prefix: 2-87005

Wereldbibliotheek NV*, Leeuwerikstr 23, B-2000 Antwerp Tel: (031) 323642
Dir: L Reinalda
Subjects: Education, Sport & Games, Juveniles, General
Founded: 1947
ISBN Publisher's Prefix: 90-284

Maison d'Editions Ad **Wesmael-Charlier** SA*, 69 rue de Fer, B-5000 Namur Tel: (081) 220148
Subjects: Secondary & Primary Textbooks
Bookshops: At above address and 62 rue de la Loi, Brussels
Founded: 1790

Winkelhaak PVBA*, Perenstr 15, B-2000 Antwerp Tel: (031) 367055
Dir: R van Hevel
Founded: 1973

J B **Wolters** Leuven NV, Blijde Inkomststr 50, B-3000 Louvain Tel: (016) 233488 Telex: 24525
Man Dir: W Vanden Eynde
Parent Company: NV ICU-België (qv)
Subjects: Instruction and Education, Secondary & Primary Textbooks, Educational Materials
Founded: 1959
ISBN Publisher's Prefix: 90-309

Zuidnederlandse Uitgeverij NV, Cleydaellaan 8, B-2630 Aartselaar, Antwerp Tel: (031) 878300 Telex: 31739 Zuidb
Publishers: Emmanuel de Vocht, Joris Schaltin; *Sales:* Jan van de Velden; *Production:* Eric Feyten; *Rights & Permissions:* Wilfried Wuyts
Associated Companies: Centrale Uitgeverij, Netherlands; Editions Chantecler, France
Imprint: Deltas
Subjects: General Fiction and Nonfiction, Children's Books
Founded: 1946
ISBN Publisher's Prefix: 90-243

Literary Agents

Agence belge des grandes Editions SA*, 146 Blvd Adolphe Max, B-1000 Brussels Tel: (02) 2191872 Cable Add: Belgeditions

Firma **Denis** & Co PVBA*, Sterckshoflei 28-30, B-2100 Deurne

A van **Hageland**, Blutsdelle 10, B-1641 Alsemberg (Beersel) Tel: (02) 3582752
General Manager: Albert van Hageland. Represents authors, publishers and agencies in and for the Dutch and French territories.
Specialization: Fantasy and Science Fiction; Anthologies. Only printed works (no manuscripts)

Book Clubs

A B C (Aurelia Book Club)*, Bonekruidlaan 30, B-1020 Brussels
Owned by: Aurelia Books

L'**Académie** du Livre SA, 3 rue du Palais St Jacques, B-7500 Tournai Tel: (069) 226130
Owned by: CAL/Retz, France (qv)
Founded: 1963

Atlanta NV*, Brasschaatsteenweg 200, B-2180 Kalmthout Tel: (031) 667171
Owned by: Beckers Groep

Beckers NV Uitgeverij*, Brasschaatsteenweg 200, B-2180 Kalmthout Tel: (031) 667171
Owned by: Beckers Groep

Boekengilde de **Clauwaert***, Koning Albertlaan 17, B-3040 Korbeek-Lo, Louvain

Dap-Reinaert Uitgaven*, Industriepark B4, B-9140 Zele

Interbooks*, Holleweg 70, B-2550 Kontich Tel: (031) 570816/571395 Telex: 35521 Inbook B

Major Booksellers

Audivox, Rubenslei 23, B-2000 Antwerp Tel: (031) 328465
Wholesalers of Imported Educational Books, also publishers (qv)

Boekhandel **Belis-Vinck**, Lange Leemstr 41, B-2000 Antwerp Tel: (031) 327448

Librairie **Bellens***, 13 rue de la Wache, B-4000 Liège Tel: (041) 237860

Librairie **Castaigne***, 34 rue du Fosse-aux-Loups, B-1000 Brussels Tel: (02) 2170424

Librairie **Halbart***, 11 rue des Carmes, B-4000 Liège Tel: (041) 232125

Boekhandel **Heideland***, Grote Markt 1, B-3500 Hasselt Tel: (011) 224505

Office international de Librairie*, 30 ave Marnix, B-1050 Brussels Tel: (021) 5136675

Standaard Hoofdstadboekhandel, Adolf Maxlaan 146, B-1000 Brussels

E **Story**-Scientia PVBA, B-9000 Ghent, 8 P Van Duyseplein Tel: (091) 255757
Managers: E and J Story, L van Opdenbosch
(Also Importers)

Libris **Toison** d'Or SA*, 29 ave de la Toison d'Or, B-1060 Brussels Tel: (02) 5116400 Telex: 24084

U O P C*, 216 chaussée de Wavre, B-1040 Brussels Tel: (02) 6489689

Librairie **Vanderlinden***, 17 rue des Grands-Carmes, B-1000 Brussels Tel: (02) 5116140

Boekhandel het **Volk***, Forelstr 22, B-9000 Ghent

Major Libraries

Koninklijke Bibliotheek **Albert I**, Keizerslaan 4, B-1000 Brussels Tel: (02) 5136180

Archives générales du Royaume*, 2-6 rue de Ruysbroeck, B-1000 Brussels
National Archives

Deutsche Bibliothek — Goethe Institut Brüssel*, rue Belliard 58, B-1040 Brussels

Bibliothèque **Fonds** Quetelet, 6 rue de l'Industrie, Brussels Tel: (02) 5127950
Library of the Ministry of Economic Affairs
Librarian: J de Buck
Publications: Accroissements de la Bibliotheque Centrale (Fonds Quetelet), monthly

Institut royal des Sciences naturelles de Belgique, Service de Documentation, 31 rue Vautier, B-1040 Brussels

Katholieke Universiteit Leuven, Universiteitsbibliotheek, Mgr Ladeuzeplein 21, B-3000 Leuven Tel: (016) 238678 Telex: Kulbib 25715
University Library of Louvain
Librarian: W Dehennin

Bibliothèque centrale du **Ministère de l'Education** nationale*, 27 rue de Louvain, B-1000 Brussels

Bibliothèque Universitaire **Moretus Plantin***, 19 rue Grangagnage, B-5000 Namur
Librarian: R P Matagne

Bibliothèque du **Musée royal de Mariemont**, 100 chaussée de Mariemont, B-6510 Morlanwelz-Mariemont Tel: (064) 221243/226563
Librarian: M-B Delattre

Museum Plantin-Moretus, Vrijdagmarkt 22, B-2000 Antwerp Tel: (031) 322455/330688

Bibliothèque du **Parlement***, 2 Palais de la Nation, pl de la Nation, Brussels

Bibliotheek van de **Rijksuniversiteit te Gent**, Rozier 9, B-9000 Ghent Tel: (091) 233821/257571/257611 Telex: 11793 Ubgent B

Bibliotheek der Universitaire Faculteiten **Sint-Ignatius***, Prinsstr 13, B-2000 Antwerp

Stadsbibliotheek, Hendrik Conscienceplein 4, Antwerp Tel: (031) 323073
Municipal Library

Bibliothèque centrale de l'**Université Catholique de Leuven**, see Katholieke Universiteit Leuven

Bibliothèque générale de l'**Université de Liège**, Place Cockerill 1, B-4000 Liège Tel: (041) 420080
Librarian: Paul Goret

Bibliothèques de l'**Université libre de Bruxelles**, 50 ave Franklin D Roosevelt, B-1050 Brussels Tel: 6490030 Telex: 23654 Ulbipe B
Librarian: Paul Delsemme

Library Associations

Association belge de Documentation, BP 110, B-1040 Brussels 26
Belgian Association for Documentation
Secretary: J C Smeets
Publication: Cahiers de la Documentation

Association des Archivistes et Bibliothécaires de Belgique*, Koninklijke Bibliotheek Albert I, Keizerslaan 4, B-1000 Brussels
Belgian Association of Archivists and Librarians
General Secretary: Raphaël de Smedt
Publication: Archives et Bibliothèques de Belgique

Association des Bibliothécaires-Documentalistes de l'Institut d'Etudes sociales de l'Etat*, 24 rue de l'Abbaye, B-1050 Brussels Tel: 6493443
Association of Librarians and Documentalists of the State Institute of Social Studies
Secretary: Claire Gerard
Publication: Flash

Association des Bibliothécaires et du Personnel des Bibliothèques des Ministères de Belgique*, 22 rue des petits Carmes, B-1000 Brussels
Association of Librarians and Library Personnel in Belgian Government Departments
President: G Braive

Association nationale des Bibliothécaires d'Expression française*, 56 rue de la Station, B-5370 Havelange
National Association of French-speaking Librarians
Executive Secretary: J Peraux
Publications: Le Bibliothécaire: Revue d'Information culturelle et bibliographique

Centre national de Documentation scientifique et technique, 4 blvd de l'Empereur, B-1000 Brussels
Publications: Catalogue collectif belge et luxembourgeois des Périodiques étrangers en cours de publication: Inventaire des Centres Belges de Recherche disposant d'une Bibliothèque ou d'un Service de Documentation

Conseil national des Bibliothèques d'Hôpitaux*, Croix-Rouge de Belgique, 98 chaussée de Vleurgat, B-1050 Brussels
National Council of Hospital Libraries
Librarian/Secretary: Françoise Delsemme
Publications: Issues annual report, Proceedings of workshops, seminars; book selections for hospital patients

Fédération nationale des Bibliothèques Catholiques*, 21 rue du Marais, B-1000 Brussels
National Federation of Catholic Libraries

Institut belge d'Information et de Documentation (INBEL), 3 rue Montoyer, B-1040 Brussels Tel: (02) 5126688 Telex: Inbel Bru 21716
Dir: F Coppieters

Vereniging van Religieus-Wetenschappelijke Bibliothecarissen*, Minderbroederstr 5, B-3800 St Truiden
Association of Theological Librarians
Secretary: K Van de Casteele, Elsbos 16, B-2520 Edegem
Publication: VRB-Informatie (quarterly)

Vlaamse Vereniging van Bibliotheek-, Archief en Documentatie-Personeel*, Frans van Heymbeecklaan 4-6, Postbus 59, B-2100 Deurne Tel: (031) 252470
Flemish Association of Librarians, Archivists and Documentalists
General Secretary: J Bogaert
Publications: Bibliotheekgids (three monthly)

Library Reference Books and Journals

Books

Inventaire permanent des Institutions belges de Recherche disposant d'une Bibliothèque ou d'un Centre de Documentation (Directory of Belgian Research Libraries and Documentation Services), National Centre for Scientific and Technical Documentation, 4 blvd de l'Empereur, B-1000 Brussels

Journals

Archives et Bibliothèques de Belgique (Archief- en Bibliotheekwezen in België) (Archives and Libraries of Belgium), (text in Dutch, English, French German, Italian, Latin and Spanish), Belgian Association of Archivists and Librarians, 4 blvd de l'Empereur, B-1000 Brussels

Le Bibliothécaire (The Librarian), National Association of French-speaking Librarians, 56 rue de la Station, B-5370 Havelange

Bibliotheekgids (Library Guide), Flemish Association of Librarians, Archivists and Documentalists, Postbus 59, B-2100 Deurne

Bulletin de Documentation (Verkeersdocumentatie Bulletin) (Bulletin of Documentation), (text in Dutch, English, French and German), Ministère des Communications et des PTT, 62 rue de la Roi, B-1040 Brussels

Cahiers de la Documentation (Bladen voor de Documentatie) (Journal of Documentation), (text in Dutch, English, French), Belgian Association for Documentation, BP 110, B-1040 Brussels 26

Literary Associations and Societies

Académie royale de Langue et de Littérature françaises*, Palais des Académies, 1 rue Ducale, B-1000 Brussels
Permanent Secretary: Georges Sion
Publications: Bulletin, Annuaire, Mémoires

Académie royale des Sciences, des Lettres et des Beaux-Arts de Belgique, Palais des Académies, 1 rue Ducale, Brussels
Permanent Secretary: Maurice Leroy
Publications: Monthly Bulletin, Memoirs, Year Book

Association des Ecrivains belges de langue française, Maison des Ecrivains, 150 chaussée de Wavre, B-1050 Brussels Tel: (02) 5122968/5122863
Association of Belgian Writers in the French Language
Secretary-General: Philippe Delaby
Publications: Nos Lettres Informations (ten a year)

Commission belge de Bibliographie*, 80-84 rue des Tanneurs, B-1000 Brussels
Secretary: E Cosyns-Verhaegen
Publications: Bulletin (quarterly), *Bibliographia Belgica, Coll*

Icon, Lobergenbos 27, B-3200 Louvain
Association on marginal literature and art
Secretary: Jozef Peeters
Publication: Cahier Jean Ray (annual) in Dutch, English & French

The **Dickens** Fellowship*, Blvd Albert-Elisabeth 101, B-7000, Mons
Honorary Secretary: Georges C Haincourt

Koninklijke Academie voor Nederlandse Taal- en Letterkunde, Koningstr 18, B-9000 Ghent
Royal Academy of Dutch Language and Literature
Permanent Secretary: M Hoebeke

Koninklijke Academie voor Wetenschappen, Letteren en Schone Kunsten van België, Paleis der Academiën Hertogsstraat 1, B-1000 Brussels
Royal Academy of Science, Letters and Fine Arts
Permanent Secretary: G Verbeke
Publications: Proceedings, Memoirs, National Biography, Letters of Justus Lipsius, Year Book, Reports and Proposals, Special Editions

International **P E N Club, Belgian French Centre**, Ave du 11 novembre 76, BP 7, B-1040 Brussels
President: Baron de Radzitzky
General Secretary: Raymond Quinot

International **P E N Club, Flemish Centre**, Albert Heyrbautlaan 48, B-1710 Dilbeek
General Secretary: Willem M Roggeman
Publication: PEN-Club Tijdingen

Société belge des Auteurs, Compositeurs et Editeurs (SABAM), 75-77 rue d'Arlon, B-1040 Brussels Tel: (02) 2302660
Belgian Society of Authors, Composers and Publishers
President: Vic Legley; *Man Dirs:* Joseph Dethier, Ernest van der Eyken
Publication: Bulletin (quarterly)

Société de Langue et de Littérature wallones ASBL, Université de Liège, 7 pl du XX août, B-4000 Liège
Secretary: Jean Rathmès
Publications: Bulletin de la Société de Langue et de Littérature wallonnes, Dialectes de Wallonie (both periodically), Literary & Philological collections

Société royale des Bibliophiles et Iconophiles de Belgique, blvd de l'Empereur 4, B-1000 Brussels
Director: Eugéne Rouir

Vereeniging der Antwerpsche Bibliophielen, Museum Plantin-Moretus, Vrijdagmarkt 22, B-2000 Antwerp Tel: (031) 322455
Editorial Secretary: Dr L Voet
Publications: De Gulden Passer (annual)

Literary Periodicals

Dietsche Warande en Belfort, journal for literature, art and spiritual life, Standaard Boekhandel NV, Belgiëlei 147a, B-2000 Antwerp

Flambeau (Torch), Belgian review of political and literary questions, 75 ave Emile de Beco, Brussels 5

Livres et Disques (Books and Records), Centre d'Action culturelle de la Communauté d'Expression française, 12 rue Saintraint, B-5000 Namur

Mandragora, journal for literature and art, (text in Dutch), Acacalaan 58, B-9620 Zottegem

Marginales (Marginalia), review of ideas and letters, Albert Ayguesparse, 118 rue Marconi, B-1180 Brussels

Nieuw Vlaams Tijdschrift (New Flemish Journal), Leeuwerikstr 41, Antwerp

Revue générale belge (General Belgian Review), 21 rue de la Limité, B-1030 Brussels

Revue nouvelle (New Review), 305 ave van Volxem, B-1190 Brussels

Ruimten (text in Dutch and German), Antwerpsesteenweg 488, Hoboken, Antwerp

Scarabée, Centre européen de Diffusion de la Culture, 137 rue de Livourne, Brussels

Streven, Sanderusstr 5, B-2000 Antwerp

Trefpunt (Meeting-point), Blankenbergs Literair Archief Trefpunt, Kerkstr 41, Te Blankenberge

Literary Prizes

Goblet d'**Alviella** Prize
For the best work of a strictly scientific and objective character relating to the history of religions, published by a Belgian author. 40,000 francs. Awarded every five years. Winner for tenth period (1971-1975), Michel Malaise. Enquiries to Académie Royale de Belgique, Palais des Académies, 1 rue Ducale, B-1000 Brussels

Lode **Baekelmans** Prize
For the best literary work in Dutch — novel, poetry, play, radio play, essay, etc — dealing with the sea, sailors, navigation, the harbour, inland navigation or related topics. A prize of 40,000 francs is awarded every 3 years: the recipients must be Belgian nationals.
Enquiries to the Royal Academy of Dutch Language and Literature, Koningstr 18, B-9000 Ghent

Beernhaert Prize*
For the most outstanding work of a Belgian author written in French language. Awarded annually. Enquiries to Royal Academy of French Language and Literature, Palais des Académies, 1 rue Ducale, B-1000 Brussels

Belgian Government Prizes for Literature (Ministry of Flemish Culture)
Triennial State Prizes for prose, poetry, drama, essay and youth and children's literature, a triennial Great State Prize for a Literary Career. Each year two of these prizes may be awarded. The ordinary prizes amount to 200,000 francs and the Great State Prize to 400,000 francs. Enquiries to Ministerie van de Nederlandse Gemeenschap, Kolonliënstr 29-31, B-1000 Brussels

Belgian Government Prizes for Literature (Ministry of French Culture)
An annual State Prize for Literature, in turn awarded for prose, drama and poetry. A quinquennial State Prize for Critique and Essay and a quinquennial State Prize for a Literary Career are also awarded. The annual State Prize amounts to 125,000 francs, the Prize for Critique and Essay to 150,000 francs, and the State Prize for a Literary Career to 200,000 francs. An increase of these amounts is under consideration. Enquiries to Ministerie van Nationale Opvoeding en Nederlandse Cultuur, Kolonlënstr 29-31, B-1000 Brussels

Ernest **Bouvier-Parviliez** Prize*
For the entire work of a Belgian author written in French. Awarded every four years. Enquiries to Royal Academy of French Language and Literature, Palais des Académies, 1 rue Ducale, B-1000 Brussels

Adelson **Castiau** Prize
For the Belgian author of the best work on means of improving the moral, intellectual and physical conditions of the poor (works relating to the lower middle classes are also admissible). 40,000 francs. Awarded every three years. No prize awarded for thirty-fifth period (1975-1977). Last winner (1969-1971), Mme Nicole Lahaye. Enquiries to Académie Royale de Belgique, Palais des Académies, 1 rue Ducale, B-1000 Brussels

Felix **Denayer** Prize*
For a single work or the entire literary work of a Belgian written in French. Awarded annually. Enquiries to Royal Academy of French Language and Literature, Palais des Académies, 1 rue Ducale, B-1000 Brussels

Jules **Duculot** Prize
For a work in print or manuscript form, written in French, dealing with the history of philosophy. Awarded only to Belgians, or to foreigners holding an academic grade granted by a Belgian university. Printed work must have been published in the five years prior to the end of the relevant period. The prize is awarded for what appears the most deserving work, irrespective of whether it has been submitted for entry or not. 70,000 francs. Awarded every five years. Winner for the second period (1971-1975), Claude Troisfontaines. Enquiries to Académie Royale de Belgique, Palais des Académies, 1 rue Ducale, B-1000 Brussels

Charles **Duvivier** Prize
For the Belgian author of the best work on the history of Belgian or foreign law, or on the history of Belgian political, judicial or administrative institutions. 40,000 francs. Awarded every three years. Winner for twenty-fourth period (1976-1978), M Magits. Enquiries to Académie Royale de Belgique, Palais des Académies, 1 rue Ducale, B-1000 Brussels

Joseph **Gantrelle** Prize
For a work in classical philology. 40,000 francs. Awarded biennially to Belgian authors. Winner for forty-third period (1978-1979) Michel Dubuisson. Enquiries to Académie Royale de Belgique, Palais des Académies, 1 rue Ducale, B-1000 Brussels

Grand Franco-Belgian Literary Prize, see French literary prizes

Tobie **Jonckheere** Prize
For a work, in published or manuscript form, devoted to the educational sciences. 35,000 francs. Awarded every three years. Winner for eighth period (1977-1979), Mme M Lohle-Tart-Esser. Enquiries to Académie Royale de Belgique, Palais des Académies, 1 rue Ducale, B-1000 Brussels

Hubert **Krains** Prize*
Awarded biennially for the unpublished work of a writer below the age of 40. 20,000 francs. Founded by the Association of Belgian Writers in the French Language in memory of one of its presidents. Enquiries to Association des Ecrivains belges de langue française, Maison des Ecrivains, 150 chaussée de Wavre, B-1050 Brussels

Eugène **Lameere** Prize
For the best work in history teaching intended for use in primary or intermediate schools or teachers' training colleges in Belgium, in which pictures play an important rôle in the comprehension of the text. 45,000 francs. Awarded every five years. Winners for fourteenth period (1970-1975), Jean Georges and Jean Lefèvre. Enquiries to Académie Royale de Belgique, Palais des Académies, 1 rue Ducale, B-1000 Brussels

Malpertuis Prize*
For an outstanding contribution to Belgian literature in the field of drama, poetry, short story or essay written in French. Awarded biennially. Enquiries to the Royal Academy of French Language and Literature, Palais des Académies, 1 rue Ducale, B-1000 Brussels

Joseph-Edmond **Marchal** Prize
For the Belgian author of the best work, in print or in manuscript form, on national antiques or archaeology. 50,000 francs. Awarded every five years. Winners for twelfth period (1973-1977), Georges Rapsaet, Marie-Thérèse Rapsaet-Charlier, Monique Lesenne. Enquiries to Académie Royale de Belgique, Palais des Académies, 1 rue Ducale, B-1000 Brussels

Albert **Mockel** Grand Prize for Poetry*
For the best Belgian poet writing in French. Awarded every five years. Enquiries to Royal Academy of French Language and Literature, Palais des Académies, 1 rue Ducale, B-1000 Brussels

Emil **Polak** Prize*
For a distinguished literary work written in French, preferably by a poet. Awarded biennially. Enquiries to Royal Academy of French Language and Literature, Palais des Académies, 1 rue Ducale, B-1000 Brussels

Victor **Rossel** Prize
For the best novel, or collection of short stories, of the year written in French by a Belgian author. 125,000 francs. Awarded annually. Enquiries to 'Le Soir', 112 rue Royale, Brussels

Saint-Genois Prize
For the author of the best historical or literary work written in Dutch. 50,000 francs. Awarded every five years. Winner for seventeenth period (1970-1975), John Everaert. Enquiries to Académie Royale de Belgique, Palais des Académies, 1 rue Ducale, B-1000 Brussels

Suzanne **Tassier** Prize
For a Belgian woman who, following study at a Belgian university, has obtained at least a doctorate. The prize is awarded for a major scientific work, dealing with a subject from history, law, philology or the social sciences: failing a meritorious work from one of these branches, then for a subject from the natural sciences, medicine or mathematics. Preference will be given to a work of an historical nature, in its widest sense. 50,000 francs. Awarded every two years. Winner for the eleventh period (1977-1978), Mme A Van Neck. Enquiries to Académie Royale de Belgique, Palais des Académies, 1 rue Ducale, B-1000 Brussels

Auguste **Teirlinck** Prize
For a contribution to Flemish literature. 45,000 francs. Awarded every five years. Winner for sixteenth period (1970-1975), Marcel Janssens. Enquiries to Académie Royale de Belgique, Palais des Académies, 1 rue Ducale, B-1000 Brussels

Carton de **Wiart** Prize*
For a book in the field of literary history or on subjects which relate to Belgian life. Alternately awarded for a work in French and in Flemish. 10,000 francs. Awarded every five years. Enquiries to Belgian Ministry of National Education, 155 rue de la Loi, B$1040 Brussels

Translation Agencies and Associations

Centre belge de Traduction, 4 blvd de l'Empereur, B$1000 Brussels Tel: (02) 5136180 Ext 561 Telex: 21157
Dir: Mme I Clemens

Belize

General Information

Language: English (and Spanish)
Religion: Catholic and various Protestant denominations
Population: 153,000
Bank Hours: 0900-1500 Monday, Tuesday, Thursday, Friday; 0900-1130 Wednesday and Saturday
Shop Hours: 0730-1130, 1300-1600 Monday-Saturday (some open 1900-2100 evenings); generally early closing Wednesday
Currency: 100 cents = 1 Belize dollar
Export/Import Information: No tariff on books, but advertising 45% duty. General licence. Nominal exchange controls
Copyright: Berne, UCC (see International section)

Major Booksellers

Belize Book Shop (Anglican Diocese), Corner Regent St/Rectory Lane, Belize City Tel: (02) 2054 Cable Add: Literary
Manager: Shirley Smiling

Beuhler's Shoppe*, Fort George Hotel Lobby Tel: 3491

Cathedral Book Center, 144 North Front St, PO Box 426 Tel: 2757
Manager: Thomas Donovan

Christian Literature, Christian Literature Centre, PO Box 76 (Located at: 14 New Rd) Tel: 2993

The **Emporium***, 2 Bishop St Tel: 2566

Major Libraries

National Library Service, The Central Library, PO Box 287, Bliss Institute, Belize City Tel: 3367
Chief Librarian: L G Vernon

Library Association

Belize Library Association, Central Library, PO Box 287, Bliss Institute, Belize City

Benin

General Information

Language: French
Religion: equally divided among Muslim, Christian, and traditional religions
Population: 3.4 million
Bank Hours: 0800-1130, 1430-1530 Monday-Friday
Shop Hours: 0800-1200, 1430-1730 Monday-Saturday. Larger ones close Monday, some open for a few hours Sunday morning
Currency: franc CFA
Export/Import Information: 2% tariff on books of non-EEC origin; 7% on atlases. Advertising matter (unless single copy) 25%, or 37% from non-EEC countries. 5% C.I.F. price Amortization Tax; Stamp tax (4% of duty paid) and small additional taxes. Import licence required but issued automatically for imports from EEC countries. Exchange controls for non-franc zone.
Copyright: Berne (see International section)

Publishers

Government Printer*, BP 59, Porto Novo

Major Booksellers

Centre de Littérature Chrétienne*, BP 34, Cotonou

Librairie **A B M***, Cotonou

Librairie-Papetiere **A B M***, Porto Novo

Librairie **Drouot** (Ets Robert Drouot)*, BP 33, Cotonou Tel: 3451

La **Maison** du Livre*, BP 341, Cotonou

Librairie **Nationale** (Ministère Education National)*, Porto Novo

Librairie SA Gaston **Nègre***, BP 52, Cotonou

Librairie **Notre Dame***, Ave Clozel, BP 714, Cotonou

Librairie **Protestante***, Ave Proche, BP 34, Cotonou

46 BENIN — BOLIVIA

Major Libraries

Archives nationales de la République Populaire du Benin*, BP 3, Porto Novo
Director: A S Tidjari

Bibliothèque nationale*, BP 401, Porto Novo Tel: 212585
Publication: Bibliographie nationale (in preparation)

Bibliothèque de l'**Université du Benin***, BP 526, Cotonou

Bermuda

General Information

Language: English
Religion: Anglican
Population: 58,000
Literacy Rate (1960): 97.6%
Bank Hours: 0930-1500 Monday-Thursday; 0930-1500, 1630-1800 Friday
Shop Hours: 0900-1700 Monday-Saturday
Currency: 100 cents = 1 Bermuda dollar
Export/Import Information: No tariff on books and advertising matter. No import licence. Exchange controls on imports valued over $100
Copyright: Berne, UCC (see International section)

Publishers

Bermuda Press Ltd*, Reid St, Hamilton
Subject: Literature

Bermudian Publishing Co*, PO Box 283, Hamilton 5
Subjects: Law, Economics

Royal Gazette Ltd*, Reid St, Hamilton
Subject: Literature

Major Booksellers

Baxters*, Burnaby St, Hamilton Tel: 23292

Bermuda Book Store Ltd*, Queen St, Hamilton Tel: 53698

The **Bookmart**, Above Annex on Reid St, Hamilton 5 Tel: (809-29) 51647
Manager: Mrs E Lee Davidson

Major Libraries

Bermuda Archives, Par-la-Ville, Hamilton
Archivist: Helen E Rowe

Bermuda Library, Par-la-Ville, Hamilton 5-31 Tel: 52905
Librarian: Mary Skiffington

Bolivia

General Information

Language: Spanish
Religion: Roman Catholic
Population: 5.3 million
Literacy Rate (1976): 62.7% (84% of urban population, 47% rural)
Bank Hours: 0900-1200, 1400-1630 Monday-Friday
Shop Hours: 0900-1200, 1400-1800 Monday-Friday; 0900-1200 Saturday
Currency: 100 centavos = 1 peso Boliviano
Export/Import Information: Member of the Latin American Free Trade Association. No tariffs on books, except for 10% on luxury bindings. 10% ad valorem on children's picture books, 5% on atlases. Advertising matter dutied 10 pesos per kg gross weight and 5% ad valorem. 2% Services Rendered Tax on all. No import licences, except for textbooks, but no pornography allowed. No advertising that includes imitation money, stamps, etc allowed. No exchange controls
Copyright: Buenos Aires (see International section)

Book Trade Organization

Cámara Boliviana del Libro, Casilla 682, La Paz (Located at: Ave Camacho Esq Loayza 1377, Edf Saenz 6°, La Paz) Tel: 327039
Bolivian Booksellers' Association
President: Javier Gisbert

Book Trade Reference Books and Journals

Books

Informativo Amigol literario ('Literary Friend'), Los Amigos del Libro, Casilla 450, Cochabamba

Journals

Bibliografía Boliviana, Los Amigos del Libro, Casilla 450, Cochabamba

Boletin Bibliografico Boliviano (text in Spanish, summaries in English and Spanish), Ediciones ISLA, Casilla N4311, La Paz

Publishers

Ediciones los **Amigos del Libro**, Calle Mercado 1315, Casilla 4415, La Paz Tel: 22794 Cable Add: Amigol
Dir: Werner Guttentag; *Manager:* Peter Levy
Parent Company: Editorial los Amigos del Libro (qv)
Bookshop: Librería los Amigos del Libro: address as above
1978: 8 titles *1979:* 8 titles *Founded:* 1977

Editorial los **Amigos del Libro**, Casilla 450, Cochabamba Tel: 2920 Cable Add: Amigol
Man Dir: Werner Guttentag; *Sales Dir:* Peter Levy; *Foreign Sales Manager:* Eva Guttentag; *Production:* J Flores
Subsidiary Company: Ediciones los Amigos del Libro (qv)
Associate Company: Grijalbo Boliviana Ltda (qv)
Subjects: Bolivia, South America
Bookshops: Librería Universal Bookstore, Casilla 4415, La Paz; Librería Los Amigos del Libro, Mercado 1315, La Paz (and other branches)
1978: 48 titles *1979:* 50 titles *Founded:* 1945

Editorial **Difusión***, Casilla 1510, La Paz (Located at: Ave 16 Julio 1601, La Paz) Tel: 328126
Man Dir: Jorge F Catalano; *Publicity & Advertising:* Carmelo Andrade
Subjects: Bolivian literature & history, Politics, Social Studies
Bookshop: Librería Difusion, same address
1978: 75 titles *Founded:* 1960

Editorial y Librería **Don Bosco***, Ave 16 de Julio 1899, Casilla 4458, La Paz
Parent Company: Salesian Order, Rome, Italy
Associate Companies: Don Bosco der Gesellschaft der Salesianer, Federal Republic of Germany (qv); Ediciones Bosco, Spain (qv); Ecole Technique officielle Don Bosco, Rwanda (qv)
Subject: Religion
Bookshop: Address as above

Universidad Boliviana Tomás **Frías**, Div de Extensión Universitaria*, Casilla 36, Potosí
Subjects: Literature, History

Gisbert y Cia SA, Comercio 1270-80*, Casilla 195, La Paz Tel: 28484 Cable Add: Gisbercia
Dir: José Javier Gisbert
Subjects: Belles Lettres, History, Law, Textbooks

Grijalbo Bolivia Ltda, Apdo 4415, La Paz
Manager: Peter Levy
Parent Company: Ediciones Grijalbo SA, Spain (qv)

Librería y Editorial **Juventud***, Plaza Murillo 519, Casilla 1489, La Paz
Tel: 41694 Cable Add: Juventud
Man Dir: Rafael Urquizo; *Assistant Dir, Publicity:* Gustavo Urquizo; *Sales:* Jefe de Ventas, Nancy de Aramayo; *Production:* Rafael Urquizo Mendoza
Orders to: Casilla 1459, La Paz
Subsidiary Company: Empresa Editora Urquizo SA
Branch Off: Calle Mercado, Ayacucho
Subjects: Literature, Biography, History, Social Science, University, Secondary & Primary Textbooks; General Cultural Subjects
Bookshop: At above address
Founded: 1946

Universidad Mayor de San Andres*, Editorial Universitaria, Casilla 6548, La Paz

Major Booksellers

Librería Los **Amigos** del Libro, Calle Mercado 1315, Casilla 4415, La Paz Tel: 22794 (7 other branches)

Librería **Difusión***, Ave 16 de Julio 1601, Apdo 1510, La Paz Tel: 28126

Librería **Don Bosco***, Ave 16 de Julio 1899, Casilla 204, La Paz Tel: 22191

Gisbert y Cía SA*, Calle Comercio 1270-80, Casilla 195, La Paz Tel: 28484

Librería **Icthus***, Ave 16 de Julio 1800, Casilla 8353, La Paz Tel: 54007

Librería **Juventud***, Plaza Murillo 519, Casilla 1489, La Paz Tel: 341694

Librería **La Paz***, Ingavi esq Yanacocha, Casilla 539, La Paz Tel: 53323

Librería **Selecciones** SRL, Casilla 972, La Paz Tel: 324159

Alfonso **Tejerina** Ltda*, Comercio 1073, Casilla 834, La Paz

Major Libraries

Biblioteca y Archivo Nacional de Bolivia*, Calle Bolívar, Sucre

Biblioteca del **Congreso** Nacional*, Palacio Legislativo, La Paz

Biblioteca de la **Dirección de Cultura***, Alcaldía Municipal, Casilla 1856, La Paz
Library of Cultural Affairs Administration

Biblioteca Universitaria, Departamento de Bibliotecas **Universidad Boliviana** Tomás Frías*, CP 54, Potosí
Dir: Adolfo Vera del Carpio
Publications: Boletin de la Biblioteca Universitaria and occasional papers

Biblioteca Central de la **Universidad Mayor de San Andrés***, Ave Villazón 1995, Casilla 6548, La Paz

Biblioteca Central de la **Universidad Mayor de San Francisco Xavier***, Plaza 25 de Mayo, Apdo 212, Sucre

Biblioteca Central de la **Universidad Mayor de San Simón**, Oquendo esq Sucre, Cochabamba
Dir: Mario Estenssoro
Publication: Boletin Bibliografico

Library Associations

Asociación Boliviana de Bibliotecarios (A.B.B.), Casilla 992, Cochabamba
President: Dr Efraín Virreira Sánchez
Bolivian Library Association

Centro Nacional de Documentación Científica y Tecnológica, Casilla correo 3283, La Paz
Dir: Hugo Loaiza-Terán
National Scientific and Technological Documentation Centre

Centro Nacional de Documentación e Información Educativa*, c/o Ministerio de Educación y Cultura, La Paz
Dir: Rosa Melgar de Ipiña
National Centre of Documentation and Education Information

Literary Periodicals

Cultura Boliviana, Universidad Tecnica de Oruro, Departamento de Extension Cultural, Oruro

Presencia Literaria, Casilla 1913, La Paz

Literary Associations and Societies

P E N Club de Bolivia (Centro Internacional de Escritores)*, Calle Goitia 17, Casilla 149, La Paz
Secretary: Yolanda Bedregal de Cónitzer

Literary Prizes

Bolivian Grand Prize for Literature*
For an outstanding achievement in the field of literature. Enquiries to the Bolivian Government, La Paz

Premio Nacional de Cultura*
Enquiries to Ministerio de Educación, La Paz

Franjas Prizes*
For the best printing work done in Bolivia. Awarded annually. Enquiries to La Paz Municipal Mayor's Office, La Paz

Premio de Novela 'Erich Guttentag'
'Erich Guttentag' prize for novel of the year. First prize 25,000 Bolivian pesos, second prize 10,000 Bolivian pesos. Enquiries to Los Amigos del Libro, Casilla 450, Cochabamba

Franz Tamayo Prize*
For outstanding literary work. 25,000 Bolivian pesos, 15,000 pesos and 5,000 pesos. Awarded annually. Enquiries to La Paz Municipal Mayor's Office, La Paz

Botswana

General Information

Language: Setswana and English
Religion: Protestant
Population: 726,000
Bank Hours: 0830-1300 Monday-Friday; 0830-1100 Saturday
Shop Hours: 0800-1300, 1400-1700 or 1800 Monday-Saturday
Currency: 100 thebe = 1 pula
Export/Import Information: No tariffs on books or advertising matter. No import licence required; no obscene literature. Exchange controls

Book Trade Journals

The National Bibliography of Botswana, Botswana National Library Service, Private Bag 0036, Gaborone

Publishers

Government Printer, PO Box 87, Gaborone

Major Booksellers

Botswana Book Centre, PO Box 91, Gaborone Tel: 52931/2 Cable Add: Books
Manager: J D Jones
Parent Company: Ecumenical Literature Distribution Trust

Via Afrika Botswana Ltd*, PO Box 332, Gaborone

Major Libraries

Botswana National Archives, PO Box 239, Gaborone Tel: 55227

Botswana National Library Service, Private Bag 0036, Gaborone Tel: 52397/52288
Director of Library Services: G Seame

University College of Botswana Library, Private Bag 0022, Gaborone Tel: 51155
Telex: 2429 Bd
Publications: Annual Report, Accessions List

Library Association

Botswana Library Association, PO Box 1310, Gaborone
Secretary: Amos Thapisa

Brazil

General Information

Language: Portuguese (some English spoken)
Religion: Roman Catholic
Population: 115.4 million
Literacy Rate (1970): 66.2%
Bank Hours: Generally 1000-1600 Monday-Friday
Shop Hours: 0900-1700 Monday-Friday (many open much later); 0900-1230 or 1300 Saturday
Currency: 100 centavos = 1 cruzeiro
Export/Import Information: Member of the Latin American Free Trade Association. No tariffs on books and advertising, but 85% ad valorem on luxury bindings, 100% on children's picture books. Import licences and exchange controls. 100% import deposit held for 360 days.
Copyright: UCC, Berne, Buenos Aires, Florence (see International section)

Book Trade Organizations

Agência Brasileira do ISBN*, Biblioteca Nacional, Ave Rio Branco 219/39, 20000 Rio de Janeiro RJ

Associação Brasileira de Livreiros Antiquaries*, Rua Cosme Velho 800, Rio de Janeiro RJ
Brazilian Association of Antiquarian Booksellers

Associação Brasileira do Livro*, Ave 13 de Mayo 23 — 16° andar, Rio de Janeiro RJ
Tel: 2327173
Brazilian Booksellers' Association
Dir: Alberjano Torres

Câmara Brasileira do Livro, Ave Ipiranga 1267 — 10° andar, 01039 São Paulo 2 SP
Tel: 2297855/2295258
Brazilian Book Association
Superintendent: José Gorayeb

Instituto Nacional do Livro*, Edifício Venâncio V, Setor de Diversões Sul, 70000 Brasília DF Tel: 235628
National Book Institute
Dir: María Alice Barroso

Sindicato Nacional dos Editores de Livros, Ave Rio Branco 37 — 15° andar — salas 1503-6 e 1510-12, 20097 Rio de Janeiro RJ
Tel: 2336481/2335484 Cable Add: Sindelivros
Brazilian Publishers' Association
Man Dir: Maria H Geordane
Publications: Boletim Informativo (bi-monthly bulletin); *Guia das Editôras Brasileiras*; *Guia das Livrarías Brasileiras*

Standard Book Numbering Agency, see Agência Brasileira do ISBN

Book Trade Reference Books and Journals

Books

O Mundo do Edição Luso-Brasileira (The World of Publishing, Portugal and Brazil), Publicações Europa-Americana, Apdo 8, Mem Martins, Portugal

Journals

Bibliografia Brasileira (Brazilian Bibliography), National Book Institute. Edifício Venâncio V, Setor de Diversões Sul, 70000 Brasília

Bibliografia Classificada (Classified Bibliography), Centre of Investigation and Documentation, CP 23, Petropolis, Rio de Janeiro

Boletim Bibliográfico, National Library, Ave Rio Branco 219-39, Rio de Janeiro

Boletim Bibliográfico Brasileiro (Brazilian Bibliographical Bulletin), Estante Publicações, Ave Rio Branco 138, 11° andar, Rio de Janeiro

O Editor do Livros, Revistas e Jornais (The Publisher of Books, Reviews and Journals), Editôra Métodos Ltda, Rua da Lapa 180, sala 607, CP 15085, Rio de Janeiro GB

48 BRAZIL

El Libro (The Book), Equilar Editores, Castillan 5, São Paulo 17

Guia das Editôras Brasileiras, Brazilian Publishers' Association, Ave Rio Branco 37 — 15° andar — salas 1503-6 e 1510-12, 20097 Rio de Janeiro RJ

Guia das Livrarías Brasileiras, Brazilian Publishers' Association, Ave Rio Branco 37 — 15° andar — salas 1503-6 e 1510-12, 20097 Rio de Janeiro RJ

Livros Novos (New Books) (text in English and Portuguese), Atlantis Livros Ltda, CP 3752, 01000 São Paulo

Pregão de Livros ('Pawnbroker of Books'), J C Amaral Guimarães, Rua Conde de Sarzedas 246, 01512 São Paulo

Resumo Bibliográfico (Bibliographical Résumé), Brazilian Publishers' Association, Centro de Bibliotécnia, Ave Rio Branco 37, 15° andar, Salas 1503-6 & 1510-12, Rio de Janeiro RJ

Revisto do Livro (Review of Books), (text in Portuguese and Spanish), Ministerio da Educação e Cultura, of 3068, Brasília DF

Publishers

A G I R (Artes Graficas Industrias Reunidas SA), CP 3291, Rio de Janeiro RJ (Located at: Rua dos Invalidos 198, Rio de Janeiro) Tel: 2528261 Cable Add: Agirsa
Man Dir: Alfonso D Faveret; *Editorial:* Ernst Fromm
Branch Offs: São Paulo, Belo Horizonte
Subjects: Literature, Juveniles, Social Science, Religion
Bookshop: Livraria Agir Editôra, Rua México 98-B, Rio de Janeiro
1978: 7 titles *Founded:* 1944

Abril SA Cultural e Industrial*, Rua do Cortume 585, São Paulo SP Tel: (011) 2626222 Cable Add: Culturabril Telex: 23227
Man Dir: Roberto Civita; *Planning & Marketing Dir:* Jayme Almeida
Branch Offs: Rua do Passeio 56, 11° andar, Lapa 20021, Rio de Janeiro
Subjects: General Literature, Science
Book Club: Círculo do Livro SA (owned jointly with Bertelsmann Aktiengesellschaft, Federal Republic of Germany (qv))
Founded: 1950

Agents Editores Ltda, Rua Almirante Baltazar 349, São Cristovãovão, 20941 Rio de Janeiro RJ Tel: (021) 2845988/2640687/2649988 Cable Add: Agentsrio
Superintendent-Director: Francisco da Gama Lima Netto; *Editorial:* João Sergio Rao, Gabriel de Almeida
Subjects: Security in Technical and Scientific fields (including Security, Counter-surveillance, Criminal investigation, Intelligence)
1978: 6 titles *1979:* 6 titles *Founded:* 1977

Editôra Nova **Aguilar** S/A, Rua Maria Angélica 168, Lagoa, 22461 Rio de Janeiro RJ Tel: 2667474 Cable Add: Aguilar
President: Sergio Lacerda
Branch Off: Ave Jurema 767, 04079 São Paulo
Subjects: General Literature
Founded: 1958

Livraría Francisco **Alves** Editôra SA*, Rua Sete de Setembro 177, Centro, 20050 Rio de Janeiro RJ Tel: 2322009/2324064/2327188 Cable Add: Alvesia Telex: 2121637 Lfae Br
Man Dir: Paulo Roberto Rocco; *Editorial:* Carlos Leal; *Sales:* Harry Costa; *Publicity &

Public Relations: Mauro da Silveira Lobo
Parent Company: Companhia de Navegação Marítima Netumar, Ave Presidente Vargas 482-3° 18, 23 e 27 andar, 20071 Rio de Janeiro RJ, Brazil; Netumar International Inc, 67 Broad St, 28th floor, New York, NY, USA
Subsidiary Company: Hoje — Os Melhores Livros (The Book Digest Magazine), Rua Barão de Lucena 43, Botafogo, 22260 Rio de Janeiro RJ
Imprints include: São Paulo Editora
Branch Offs: Rua Pires de Mota 399, 01529 São Paulo SP; Rua da Bahia 1060, 30000 Belo Horizonte MG
Subjects University, High School and Primary Textbooks; Nonfiction, General Fiction, Crime etc.
Bookshops: Rua Farme de Amoedo 57, Ipanema; Rua do Ouvidor 166, Centro; Rua Sete de Setembro 177, Centro; Ave Amaral Peixoto 427, loja 121, Nova Iguaçu (all in Rio); Rua da Bahia 1060, Belo Horizonte
1978: 97 titles *Founded:* 1854

Editôra Das **Americas** SA Edameris, Rua Santa Isabel 152, V Buarque, 01221 São Paulo SP Tel: 2217573/2218482
Man Dir: Mário Fittipaldi
Subjects: Poetry, Fiction, Biography, Crime & Adventure

Organização **Andrei** Editôra SA*, Rua Conselheiro Nebias 1071, São Paulo SP Tel: 2207246 Cable Add: Carolandre
Dir: Edmondo L Andrei; *Sales Dir:* Alberto Mayer
Subjects: Medicine, Pharmacy, Veterinary Medicine
Founded: 1956

Antenna Edições Técnicas Ltda*, Ave Mal Floriano 143, 20080 Rio de Janeiro RJ Tel: (021) 2231799
Man Dir: Gilberto A Penna; *Publicity:* J F Kempner
Associate Company: Seleções Eletronicas Editôra Ltd (qv)
Branch Off: Rua Vitoria 195, São Paulo
Subjects: Electronics, Telecommunications
Bookshops: Lojas do Livro Eletrônico, Ave Mal Floriano 148, Rio de Janeiro; Rua Vitória 379-383, São Paulo
1978: 11 titles *Founded:* 1926
Miscellaneous: Firm has its own printing works

Ao Livro Técnico SA Industria a Comércio, CP 3655, 20000 Rio de Janeiro RJ (Located at: Rua Sá Freire 36-40, São Christovão, Rio de Janeiro) Tel: 2642474/2482566 Cable Add: Litecnico
Man Dir: Reynaldo Max Paul Bluhm; *Editorial:* Sebastião Feital; *Sales:* Reynaldo Bluhm; *Production:* Sebastiao Feital; *Publicity:* Carlos B Figueiredo; *Rights & Permissions:* Paulo E Bluhm
Orders to: Rua sa Freire 36-40, São Christovão, Rio de Janeiro 20000
Subsidiary Companies: AGIR-Litecnico Ltda; DISAL (Distribuidores Associados de Livros Ltda); LTC (Livros Tecnicos e Cientificos Editôra SA); A Nossa Livraría; A Nossa Livraría de Belo Horizonte Ltda
Subjects: Technical, Scientific, Children's books, Art, Language Textbooks, English Language Teaching, Schoolbooks
Bookshops: Ao Livro Técnico, Rua Miguel Couto 35, Loja C, Rio de Janeiro (for other branches see under Booksellers); Diálogo Livraria e Editôra Ltda, Rua da Conceição 204/6, Niterói, Rio de Janeiro; Agir Litécnico Ltda, C1S Quadra 104 — bloco C — lojas 18/19, 70342 Brasília DF; Livraria de Belo Horizonte Ltda, Rua Tupis 262, 30000 Belo Horizonte MG
1978: 52 titles *1979:* 88 titles *Founded:* 1946

Apec Editôra SA*, CP 15006, 20000 Rio de Janeiro RJ (Located at: Rua Sorocaba 316, Botafogo, Rio de Janeiro) Tel: 2663597/2663547/2664449/2664249 Cable Add: Editorapec
Branch Off: Ave Ipiranga 890, 1° andar, 3 piso, São Paulo
Subjects: Economics, Education, Law, History, Sociology, Reference Books

Aquarius Editôra e Distribuidora de Livros Ltda*, Rua Olavo Egidio 242, Santana, 02037 São Paulo SP Tel: 2902911/2994639
Man Dir: Alfredo Prata Ginja; *Sales:* Manuel Fonesca
1978: 15 titles *1979:* 38 titles *Founded:* 1976

Editôra **Artenova** Ltda, Rua Prefeito Olimpio de Mello 1774, Benfica, 20000 Rio de Janeiro RJ Tel: 2649198/2340965 Cable Add: Artnova
Man Dir: Alvaro Pacheco; *Editorial, Rights & Permissions:* Luzia Regina Alves; *Sales, Publicity:* Emilia Pacheco
Associate Companies: Artenova Filmes Ltda; Studio Artenova de Publicidade Ltda
Branch Off: Ave Augusto Pinto 122, Perdizes, São Paulo SP
Subjects: Literature, Sociology, Psychology, Occultism, Health, Cinema, History
Founded: 1971

Livraría Editôra **Artes** Medicas Ltda, Rua Dr Cesario Motta Jr 63, Vila Buorque, 01221 São Paulo SP Tel: Pabx 2219033 Cable Add: Leam
Man Dir: Henrique Hecht; *Editorial, Rights & Permissions:* M Hecht; *Sales:* C dos Santos; *Production:* W Steinhoff; *Publicity:* J Hecht
Subsidiary Companies: Editôra Artes Medicas Sul Ltda, Rua General Vitorino 277, 90000 Porto Alegre; Livraría Artes Medicas Norte Ltda, Recife
Subjects: Medicine, Dentistry
1978: 18 titles *1979:* 14 titles *Founded:* 1964

Livraria **Atheneu** Ltda, Rua Bambina 74 — lojas A/B, Botafogo, 22251 Rio de Janeiro RJ Tel: 2661295/2264793 Cable Add: Zigadag
Man Dir: Simão Rzezinski; *Editorial Dir, Rights & Permissions:* Paulo da Costa Rzezinski; *Sales Dir:* Peter Kümpfer; *Production Dir:* Moacyr Coelho
Branch Offs: Rua Senador Dantas 56B, Rio de Janeiro RJ; Rua Jesuino Pascoal 30, Santa Cecilia, São Paulo
Subjects: Medicine, Nursing, Psychology
Bookshops: 25 outlets
1978: 28 titles *1979:* 28 titles *Founded:* 1928

Editôra **Atica** SA*, CP 8656, 01507 São Paulo SP (Located at: Rua Barão de Iguape 110, Liberdade, São Paulo) Tel: 2789322 Cable Add: Bomlivro
President: Anderson Fernandes Dias
Branch Offs: Rua Barão de Ubá 173, Estácio, 20260 Rio de Janeiro
Subjects: University, Secondary & Primary Textbooks, Pre-school Books, Children's Books, Literature

Editôra **Atlas** SA, CP 7186, São Paulo SP (Located at: Rua Helvétia 574-578, São Paulo) Tel: 2219144 Cable Add: Atlasedita
Man Dir: Luiz Herrmann; *Editorial, Rights & Permissions:* J P Rossetti; *Sales, Publicity:* A B Brandão; *Production:* P Gerencer
Branch Offs: Rio de Janeiro, Brazília, Amazonas, Ceará, Goías, Paraná, Minas Gerais, Rio Grande do Sul, S Catarina
Subjects: Administration, Economics, Financial, Social Sciences
1978: 400 titles *Founded:* 1944

Atual Editôra Ltda*, Rua José Antonio Coelho 785, V Mariana, 04011 São Paulo SP Tel: 717795/5491720

Man Dirs: Gelson Iezzi, Osvaldo Dolce; *Editorial:* Gelson Iezzi; *Sales:* Osvaldo Dolce; *Production:* Iorge Fuzii; *Publicity, Rights & Permissions:* José Roberto Brauner
Associate Companies: Fimac—Distribuidora Livros Ltda, Rua da Bahia 478, Belo Horizonte MG; Editôra e Distribuidora Pre-Universitária Ltda, Rua do Príncipe 470, Recife PE
Subject: Didactics
Bookshop: Livraria Alberjano Torres Ltda, Rua Barão de Mesquita 28A, Rio de Janeiro RJ
1978: 15 titles *1979:* 15 titles *Founded:* 1973

Gráfica Editôra **Aurora** Ltda*, CP 7041, 20211 Rio de Janeiro RJ (Located at: Rua Frei Caneca 19, Centro, Rio de Janeiro) Tel: 2220654
Man Dir: Francesco Molinaro; *Sales Dir:* Natale A Molinaro; *Publicity Dir:* Solange de Paula; *Advertising Dir:* Socrates de Paula
Subjects: Secondary & Primary Textbooks, Literature, Pedagogy, How-to, Law, Business, Masonic themes
1978: 160 titles *Founded:* 1945
ISBN Publisher's Prefix: 85-30

Editôra **Beta** Ltda, Estrada do Gabinal 1521, Jacarepaguá, Rio de Janeiro RJ Tel: 3421818
Man Dir: Jacob Horowicz
Subjects: Law, Law Textbooks, Economics & Finance

Bloch Editores SA*, Rua Frei Caneca 511, Centro, 20211 Rio de Janeiro RJ Tel: 2321338/2831717
Publicity: Paulo Maia Poucinha
Subject: Textbooks

Editôra Edgard **Blücher** Ltda*, Rua Pedrosa Alvarenga 1245 — 2° andar — conj 22, 01000 São Paulo SP Tel: 648114/815613 Cable Add: Blucherlivro
Man Dir: Edgard Blücher
Subjects: Engineering, Science, Business, University Textbooks
Founded: 1966

Editôra do **Brasil** SA*, CP 4986, 01203 São Paulo SP (Located at: Rua Conselheiro Nébias 887-889, Campos Elíseos, São Paulo) Tel: 2211663/2220211/2220818 Cable Add: Editabras
Branch Off: Rua do Resende 89, Centro, 20231 Rio de Janeiro RJ
Subjects: Education, Reference, Juveniles, History, Psychology, Sociology

Editôra **Brasil-América** (EBAL) SA, Rua General Almério de Moura 302/320, São Cristóvão, 20921 Rio de Janeiro RJ Tel: 2646212 Cable Add: Ebalitada Telex: 21293
Man Dir: Adolfo Aizen; *Editorial:* Naumin Aizen; *Production:* Fernando Albagli
Subject: Children's Books
1978: 184 titles *1979:* 58 titles *Founded:* 1945

Editôra **Brasília**/Rio Ltda*, Rua Muniz Barreto 16, Botafogo, 20000 Rio de Janeiro RJ Tel: 2663428/2869394
Man Dir: Dr José Jobim; *Editorial:* Lygia M Jobim Silveira; *Rights & Permissions:* Gilda Oswaldo Cruz
Subjects: Brazilian Literature, Social Science, Law, Psychology, Pre-school & Juveniles, Fiction, Cinema, Cookery, Law, History
Founded: 1974

Brasilia Editôra Ltda*, Rua Cinco 15, Jardim da Penha, 29000 Vitória ES Tel: 2271962 Cable Add: Brasilivros
Subjects: Textbooks, Home Economics, Mathematics

Editôra **Brasiliense** SA*, CP 30644, 01042 São Paulo SP (Located at: Rua Barão de Itapetininga 93 — 12° andar, São Paulo) Tel: 345693/346268 Cable Add: Edibrasa
Man Dir, Editorial, Rights & Permissions: C G Prado; *Sales:* C C Guerrato; *Production:* A Orzari
Subjects: Social Sciences, Humanities, Literature, Education, Juveniles
Bookshop: address as above
Founded: 1943

Livraría e Editôra Juridica José **Bushatsky** Ltda*, CP 2826, 01007 São Paulo SP (Located at: Riachuelo 195, São Paulo) Tel: 344148/344149 Cable Add: Bushatsky
Man Dirs: José Bushatsky, Anna Bushatsky; *Sales, Publicity:* José Bushatsky; *Production:* Anna Bushatsky
Subject: Law
Bookshop: Ria Riachuelo 195, São Paulo
Founded: 1967

C E P A, see Centro Editor de Psicologia Aplicada Ltda

Cadernos Didáticos, Livros Cadernos Ltda*, Rua General Rocca 194, Tijuca, 20521 Rio de Janeiro RJ Tel: 2481211

Editôra **Campus** Ltda, Rua Japeri 35, Rio Comprido, 20261 Rio de Janeiro RJ Tel: 2848443/2842638
Man Dir, Editorial: Claudio M Rothmuller; *Sales, Publicity Dir:* Juarez Nery; *Production Dir:* Carlos Hamilton Rocha; *Rights & Permissions:* Emilia Fernandez
Parent Company: Elsevier-NDU nv, Netherlands (qv)
Subjects: Textbooks — all fields except Law and Medicine
1978: 14 titles *1979:* 26 titles *Founded:* 1976

Livraría Editôra **Cátedra** Ltda*, Rua Senador Dantas 20 — salas 806-7, Centro, 20031 Rio de Janeiro RJ Tel: 2227593
Subjects: Cookery, History, Children's Books, Reference Books, Sociology

Cedibra Editôra Brasileira Ltda, Rua Filomena Nunes 162, Olaria, 20000 Rio de Janeiro RJ Tel: 2807272 Cable Add: Edibras
Editorial: Rubens F Lucchetti; *Sales:* Marcelo Vital Brasil; *Production:* Albino M Marques; *Rights & Permissions:* Jan Rais
Subjects: Juveniles, Fiction, Paperbacks
1978: 1500 titles *1979:* 1500 titles *Founded:* 1952

Centro Editor de Psicologia Aplicada Ltda (CEPA)*, CP 15131, 20031 Rio de Janeiro RJ (Located at: Rua Senador Dantas 118 — salas 901-7, Centro, Rio de Janeiro) Tel: 2427638/2324983 Cable Add: Edicepa
Man Dir: Antonio Rodrigues
Subject: Psychology Textbooks and Tests
1978: 10 titles *1979:* 5 titles *Founded:* 1952

Editôra **Civilização** Brasileira SA*, Rua Muniz Barreto 91-93, 22251 Rio de Janeiro RJ Tel: 2869096 Cable Add: Civilização Rio
Man Dir: Enio Silveira; *Administrative Dir:* Joaquim Ignacio Baptista Cardoso; *Editorial Dir:* Enio Silveira
Branch Off: Rua das Palmeiras 260-262, São Paulo; Quadra 309, lojas 3 e 4, 70000 Brasília DF
Subjects: General Fiction, Belles Lettres, Poetry, Social Science
Founded: 1932

Editôra **Codecri** Ltda, Rua Saint Roman 142, Copacabana, 22071 Rio de Janeiro RJ Tel: 2875799
Man Dir: Sergio de Magalhães Gomes Jacuarire; *Editorial:* Alfredo Gonçalves Manso Filho; *Production:* Glauco Alexandre de Oliveira; *Publicity:* Douné Spínola

Subsidiary Company: Jornal Pasquim (at above address)
Subjects: Belles Lettres, Fiction, Dictionaries
Bookshop: Livraria do Pasquim, Ave Ataulfo de Paiva — loja 108, Leblon
1978: 20 titles *1979:* 35 titles *Founded:* 1976

Concordia SA—Artes Gráficas e Embalagens, CP 6150, 90000 Porto Alegre RS (Located at: Ave São Pedro 633 e 639, Porto Alegre) Tel: 422859 Cable Add: Concordia
Man Dir: Johanes Gedradt; *Sales, Publicity:* Luiz Ricardo Böttcher
Parent Company: Igreja Evangèlica Luterana do Brasil
Subject: Religion
1978: 10 titles *1979:* 20 titles *Founded:* 1923

Confraria dos Amigos do Livro Ltda*, Rua Maria Angélica 168, Lagoa, 22461 Rio de Janeiro RJ Tel: 2664928 Cable Add: Neofront Telex: 2122319 Enof Br
Man Dir, Sales & Publicity: Elson Mancen; *Editorial:* Sebastião Lacerda
Parent Company: Editôra Nova Fronteira SA (qv)
Subjects: Art books in special editions
Founded: 1976

Conquista, Empresa de Publicações Ltda, Ave 28 de Setembro 174, Vila Isabel, Rio de Janeiro RJ Tel: 2285709/2286752
Man Dir: Nilde Hersen da Costa
Subjects: Children's Books, Textbooks
1978: 20 titles *1979:* 24 titles *Founded:* 1951

Editôra e Gráfica Miguel **Couto** SA, Rua Capitão Carlos 68, Bonsucesso, 21040 Rio de Janeiro RJ Tel: 2807699
Man Dir: Paulo Kobler Pinto Lopes Sampaio; *Editorial:* Octacilio Ribeiro Lessa; *Sales:* José Geraldo Verginelli; *Production:* Victor Mauricio Notrica; *Publicity:* Alcides Lourenco Gomes; *Rights & Permissions:* Antenor Romanholo
Associate Companies: Curso Miguel Couto SA, Somatório Administração SA, Curso MCB
Subject: Textbooks
1978: 65 titles *1979:* 97 titles *Founded:* 1969

Editôra **Cultrix***, Rua Conselheiro Furtado 648 — 6° andar — sala 62, 01511 São Paulo SP Tel: 2784811
Man Dir: Diaulas Riedel
Subjects: General Literature, Social & General Science, Economics, Education, Philosophy, History, Children's Books, Psychology, Sociology
Founded: 1956

Editôra **Cultura Médica** Ltda*, CP 24052, 20550 Rio de Janeiroiro RJ (Located at: Rua São Francisco Xavier 111, Rio de Janeiro) Tel: 2349798/2484888
Man Dir, Editorial, Rights & Permissions: Ezequiel Feldman; *Sales, Publicity Dir:* Ivo Feldman; *Production:* João Emanuel Paes de Andrade
Orders to: Ave Heitor Beltão 61, Apto 801, Rio de Janeiro
Subject: Medicine
1978: 8 titles *1979:* 15 titles *Founded:* 1966

D I F E L, see Difusão Editorial SA

Difusão Editorial SA (DIFEL)*, Ave Vieira de Carvalho 40 — 5° andar, 01210 São Paulo SP Tel: 2236923/2234619
Man Dir: Fernando Baptista da Silva; *Sales Dir:* Fernando G Barros; *Rights & Permissions:* Karin M Winkler
Subjects: Sociology, History, Geography, General Fiction, Physical Fitness, Arts, Economics, Philosophy, Psychology, Religion
1978: 66 titles *Founded:* 1951

50 BRAZIL

Editôra **Documentário** Ltda*, Rua Muniz Barreto 12, 22251 Rio de Janeiro RJ Tel: (021) 2666648
Man Dir: Marcos Margulies; *Editorial Dir:* Mario Bendetson; *Production Dir:* Elias Salgado; *Rights & Permissions:* Esther Mellinger
Subjects: Psychology, Sociology, History & Art History, Languages, Publicity & Marketing, Dictionaries, Brazil, Judaism
1978: 38 titles *1979:* 15 titles *Founded:* 1973

Livraría **Duas Cidades** Ltda*, CP 433, 01220 São Paulo SP (Located at: Rua Bento Freitas 158, Vila Buarque, São Paulo) Tel: 375257
Man Dir: José Petronillo de Santa Cruz; *Sales Dir:* Mitsuro Nagata; *Publicity Dir:* Mara Valles
Branch Off: Ave Rio Branco 9, Sala 116, Centro 20090 Rio de Janeiro RJ
Subjects: Literature, Philosophy, Religion, Psychology, Social Science, University Textbooks
Founded: 1956

E B A L, see Editôra Brasil-América (EBAL) SA

E P U, see Editôra Pedagogica e Universitaria Ltda

E T A (Editôra Técnica de Aviação Ltda, Rua Real Grandeza 193 — lojas 15-16, Botafogo, 22281 Rio de Janeiro RJ Tel: 2468633
Man Dir: João Dutra de Medeiros
Subject: Aviation
1978: 26 titles *1979:* 29 titles *Founded:* 1969

Ebraesp Editorial Ltda, Rua Joaquim Floriano 488 — 6° andar, Itaim Bibi, 04534 São Paulo SP Tel: 2884904/2848164 Cable Add: Ebraesp
Man Dir, Editorial: Fernando Santos Burguete; *Production:* Antonio Baeza; *Publicity:* Heliodoro Teixeira Bastos; *Rights & Permissions:* Yolanda Lhullier Santos
Branch Off: Rua Marechal Floriano Peixoto 16 — sobreloja 207, Santos, 11100 São Paulo
Subjects: Philosophy, Anthropology, Communications
1978: 7 titles *1979:* 12 titles *Founded:* 1971

Edameris, see Editôra das Americas SA Edameris

Edart (São Paulo Livraría Editôra Ltda)*, CP 4108, 01224 São Paulo SP (Located at: Rua Jaguaribe 47, Vila Buarque, São Paulo) Tel: 2214399/2203962/2219933
Man Dir: Washington Luis José Helou; *Sales Dir:* Henrique Ademar Marques; *Publicity Dir:* Inácio Bueno; *Dir of Editions:* Antonio Orzari
Subjects: Medicine, Science, Technology, Psychology, History, Mathematics, How-to, Textbooks
Founded: 1966

Editôra **Interamericana** do Brasil Ltda, Rua Coronel Cabrita 8, São Cristovão, 20920 Rio de Janeiro RJ Tel: 2281693/2845645/2487969/2648617 Cable Add: Edinter Telex: 2123036
Man Dir: N B Cordeiro; *Editorial:* T M Ribas (Health Sciences), Estela Menezes (College); *Sales, Publicity:* G Chegure; *Production:* J Belmonte
Associate Company: CBS International Publishing (CIP), USA
Branch Offs: São Paulo, Porto Alegre, Salvador, Belo Horizonte, Recife, Curitiba, Belém
Subjects: Medicine and Related Sciences, Psychology, Business, Chemistry, Physical Education, Biology
1978: 16 titles *1979:* 33 titles *Founded:* 1972

Editôra **Moderna** Ltda, CP 45364, 04511 São Paulo SP (Located at: Rua Afonso Brás 431, 04511 São Paulo) Tel: 612235/2402637/5311730
Man Dir: Prof Ricardo Feltre
Branch Off: Rua dos Araújos 50, 20521 Rio de Janeiro RJ
Subjects: Textbooks, Social Science, Literature, Medicine
Founded: 1968

Cía Editôra **Nacional**, CP 7032, 01212 São Paulo SP (Located at: Rua dos Gusmões 639, Santa Ifigênia, São Paulo) Tel: (220) 1308/9881 Cable Add: Editora
Man Dir, Rights & Permissions: Ezio Távora dos Santos; *Editorial:* Carlos Rizzi; *Sales:* J R Breves; *Production:* Paulo Hiss; *Publicity:* L A Belia
Branch Offs: Benjamin Constant 30-32, Glória, 20241 Rio de Janeiro RJ; Rua dos Andradas 725, Porto Alegre; Dr José Mariano 94, Recife; Rua Sen Manuel Barata 122-130, Belém
Subjects: Pedagogy, History, Philosophy, Psychology, Technical, General & Social Science, Textbooks, Business, Fiction
Founded: 1925

Editôra **Pedagogica e Universitaria** Ltda (EPU), Praça Dom José Gaspar 106 — 3° andar — sobreloja 15, São Paulo SP
Subjects: Scientific, Technical
Founded: 1952

Seleções **Electrônicas Editôra** Ltda*, CP 771, 20221 Rio de Janeiro RJ (Located at: Ladeira do Faria 23, Rio de Janeiro) Tel: (021) 2232644
Man Dir: Maria B A Penna; *Editorial:* José F Kempner
Associate Company: Antenna Edições Técnicas Ltda (qv)
Subjects: Electronics, Radio and TV Technology, Electricity
Founded: 1960

Editôra **Espiritualista***, CP 7041, 20211 Rio de Janeiro RJ (Located at: Rua Frei Caneca 19, Centro, Rio de Janeiro) Tel: 2220654
Man Dir: Francesco Molinaro; *Sales Dir:* Natale A Molinaro; *Publicity & Advertising Dir:* Socrates de Paula
Subjects: Philosophy, Religion
1978: 150 titles *Founded:* 1945
ISBN Publisher's Prefix: 85-94

Exped-Expansaõ Editorial Ltda, Ave President Wilson 165 — 3° andar, Castelo, Rio de Janeiro RJ Tel: 2926116 Telex: (021) 23186
Dir: Ferdinando Bastos de Souza; *Editors:* Maria Alice Barroso, Terezinha Saraiva; *Sales:* Hélio Dias Carneiro Filho
Subjects: General Literature, Didactics, Reference Books
Founded: 1967

F E N A M E — Fundação Nacional de Material Escolar*, Rua Miguel Ângelo 96, Maria da Graça, Rio de Janeiro RJ Tel: 2617750/2614140
Man Dir: Milton Durço Pereira; *Editorial Dir:* Tania Jatobá de Matos Menezes; *Sales Dir:* Murilo Alves Nunes; *Production Dir:* Antonio José de Britto; *Publicity Dir:* Ivan Estelita Campos; *Rights & Permissions:* José Ribeiro de Castro Neto
Subject: Textbooks
Bookshops: About 250 outlets throughout Brazil
1978: 22 titles *1979:* 20 titles *Founded:* 1967

Editôra **F T D** SA*, CP 30402, 01519 São Paulo SP (Located at: Rua do Lavapés 1023, Cambuci, São Paulo) Tel: 2788264
President: João Tissi; *Man Dir:* Paulo Alves Ferraz
Branch Offs: Rua Agenor Meira 4/67, Bauru, São Paulo; Rua Lavras 235, Carmo Sion, Belo Horizonte MG; Rua Mal Deodoro 887, Curitiba PR; Ave Goiás 1146, Goiânia GO; Ave Rio Branco 185, Londrina PR; Ave Tiradentes 963, Maringa; Ave Joana Angélica 963, Salvador BA; Rua Prof Baltazar 12, Vitória ES; Rua André Cavalcanti 78, Rio de Janeiro GB; Rua Martins Junior 39, Recife PE; Ave do Imperador 1203, Fortaleza CE (all in Brazil)
Subject: Textbooks
Founded: 1897

Editôra **Forense**—Universitaria Ltda, CP 2284, 20020 Rio de Janeiro RJ (Located at: Ave Erasmo Braga 227 — 0° andar — grupo 309, Rio de Janeiro) Tel: 2526244/2831152/2831147

Editôra e Encadernadora **Formar** Ltda*, CP 13250, 03168 São Paulo SP (Located at: Rua dos Trilhos 1126, Mooca, São Paulo) Tel: 935133 Cable Add: Formar
Subjects: Education, Scientific & Technical, Cookery, History, Geography, Children's Books, Reference Books

Livraría **Freitas** Bastos SA*, Rua 7 de Setembro 127-129, Centro, 20050 Rio de Janeiro RJ Tel: 2220250/2228858/2228973 Cable Add: Etiel
Branch Off: Rua 15 de Novembro 62-66, São Paulo SP
Bookshop: Rua 7 de Setembro 111, Rio de Janeiro
Subject: Law

Fundação Instituto Brasileiro de Geografia e Estatística, Ave Brasil, 15671 Rio de Janeiro RJ Tel: 2304747/3917788
Dir: Paulo Roberto Salema G Ribeiro
Subjects: Statistics, Geography, Maps
Founded: 1936

Fundação Nacional de Material Escolar, see FENAME

Editôra Gustavo **Gili** do Brasil SA*, Rua Araripe Júnior 45, Andaraí, 20540 Rio de Janeiro RJ Tel: 2880881 Cable Add: Gustobras
Parent Company: Editorial Gustavo Gili SA, Spain (qv)
Subjects: Architecture, Engineering

Global Editôra e Distribuidora Ltda, CP 45329, 04011 São Paulo SP (Located at: Rua José Antonio Coelho 814, São Paulo) Tel: 5493137/5442917
Man Dir, Sales: Luis Alves Jr; *Editorial, Production, Publicity, Rights & Permissions:* José Carlos Rolo Venancio
Imprint: Parma
Subjects: Linguistics, Romance, Humour, UFOs, Politics, Economics, Poetry, History, Theatre, Health, Children
1978: 40 titles *1979:* 60 titles *Founded:* 1973

Editôra **Globo** SA, CP 1520, 90000 Porto Alegre RS (Located at: Ave Getúlio Vargas 1271, Porto Alegre) Tel: 331300 Cable Add: Dicionario
Editorial Dir, Rights & Permissions: José O Bertaso; *Sales Dirs:* Fernando José O Bertaso, Antonio C Leite
Parent Company: Livraría do Globo SA, Rua dos Andradas 1416, Pôrto Alegre
Subsidiary Company: Instituto Áudio-Visual e de Idiomas SA
Branch Off: Rua Gen Belford 190 — sobrelojas 201-2, Rocha, 20961 Rio de Janeiro RJ
Subjects: Education, Engineering, Dictionaries, Literature
1979: 43 titles *1980:* 55 titles *Founded:* 1954

Edições **Graal** Ltda, Rua Hermenegildo de Barros 31A, Glória, 20241 Rio de Janeiro RJ Tel: 2528582

Man & Editorial Dirs, and Rights & Permissions: André da Costa Santos, Paul Joseph Christoph Jr; *Sales Dir:* Francisco de Brito Magalhães Jr; *Production Dir:* Heyder Méndez de Matos; *Publicity Dir:* Maria Tereza Machado
Subjects: Social Sciences, Philosophy, Psychology, Social Medicine, Economics, History, Sociology
1978: 20 titles *1979:* 18 titles *Founded:* 1977

Ordem do **Graal** na Terra, CP 128, Embu, 06800 São Paulo SP (Located at: Ave 7 de Setembro 29200, Embu, São Paulo)
Man Dir: Harry von Sass
Subjects: Religion, Philosophy, History
Founded: 1947

Editorial **Grijalbo** Ltda*, Rua 7 de Abril 264 — loja B-2, 01044 São Paulo SP Tel: 369544
Man Dir: José Monfort
Parent Company: Editorial Grijalbo SA, Spain (qv)
Subjects: Law, Technical
Founded: 1958

Editôra **Ground Informação** Ltda, Rua Siqueira Campos 143, Sobreloja 56, Copacabana, Rio de Janeiro RJ Tel: 2367398
Man Dir: Mário Marcio de Castro
Subjects: Natural Foods and Medicines, Alternative Living, Acupuncture, Ecology
Bookshop: At above address
1978: 3 titles *1979:* 2 titles *Founded:* 1973

Editôra **Guanabara** Koogan SA, Travessa do Ouvidor 11, 20000 Rio de Janeiro RJ Tel: 2328020 Cable Add: Edigua
Man Dir: Joao Pedro Lorch; *Editorial:* E M Carneiro; *Sales:* R Berardinelli Filho; *Production:* M P Costa; *Rights and Permissions:* P M da Silveira Jr
Subjects: Medicine, Dentistry, Life Sciences

Livraría Pioneira Editôra Enio Matheus **Guazzelli** e Cia Ltda, Praça Dirceu de Lima 313, Casa Verde, 02515 São Paulo SP Tel: 2660926/2666507
Dir: Enio M Guazzelli; *Rights & Permissions:* Ricardo Guazzelli
Subjects: Social Sciences, Business and Management, Linguistics, Brazilian Studies, Architecture and Urbanism; General Subjects, Children's Books
Bookshop: At above address
1978: 36 titles *Founded:* 1960

H U C I T E C Ltda — Editôra de Humanismo, Ciência e Tecnologia*, Alameda Jau 404, Jardim Paulista, São Paulo SP Tel: (011) 2871825
Man Dirs: Adalgisa Pereira da Silva, Flávio George Aderaldo; *Editorial, Production, Rights & Permissions:* Flávio George Aderaldo; *Sales, Publicity:* Luiza Helena Alegro
Subjects: Textbooks, Education
1978: 50 titles *1979:* 50 titles *Founded:* 1971

Harbra, an imprint of Editôra Harper & Row do Brasil Ltda (qv)

Harla, an imprint of Editôra Harper & Row do Brasil Ltda (qv)

Editôra **Harper & Row** do Brasil Ltda*, CP 45312, 01000 Vila Mariana, São Paulo SP Tel: 703572/704891 Cable Add: Habra Sao Telex: (11) 25631 Ehrb
Man Dir, Editorial, Rights & Permissions: Francisco Gutiérrez; *Sales:* Luiz Carlos de Matos; *Production:* Ma Lucia S Leife; *Publicity:* Tania Castro
Parent Company: Harper & Row Inc, New York, NY 10022, USA
Associate Companies: Basic Books Inc, New York, USA; T Y Crowell, New York, USA; J B Lippincott, Philadelphia, USA; Harper & Row (Australasia) (qv); Harper & Row Ltd, UK (qv); Harper & Row Latinoamericana-Harla, Mexico (qv)
Imprints: Harbra, Harla
Subjects: University and High School Text Books in Science, Mathematics, Engineering, Social Science, Business, Medicine, General Interest Books
1978: 30 titles *1979:* 20 titles *Founded:* 1976

Hemus-Livraria Editôra Ltda, CP 9686, 01510 São Paulo SP (Located at: Rua da Glória 312, São Paulo) Tel: 2799911 Telex: 32005 Hlel Br
President: Eli Behar; *Man Dir:* Maxim Behar; *Financial Dir:* Uri Behar
Subjects: Technical & Engineering, Textbooks, Juveniles, Philosophy, Science Fiction, General Literature
1978: 82 titles *1979:* 73 titles *Founded:* 1965

Editôra de **Humanismo**, Ciência e Tecnologia, see HUCITEC Ltda

I B A M, see Instituto Brasileiro de Administraçao Municipal

I B E P, see Instituto Brasileiro de Edições Pedagógicas

I B I C T, see Instituto Brasileiro de Informação em Ciência e Tecnologia

I B R A S A (Instituição Brasileira de Difusão Cultural SA)*, CP 30927, 03047 São Paulo SP (Located at: Rua 21 de Abril 97, Brás, São Paulo) Tel: 939524
Man Dir: Jorge Leite
Orders to: IBREX Ltda, Rua 21 de Abril 101, CP 30927, São Paulo
Subjects: IBRASA Encyclopaedia, General Medical, Health & Sexuality, Parapsychology, Social Sciences, Psychology & Education, Philosophy, Politics, Economics, History, Exploration & Discovery, Modern Literature & Science
Founded: 1958

I P E A (Instituto de Planejamento Econômico e Social) Servico Editorial, CP 2672, Rio de Janeiro RJ (Located at: Ave President Antonio Carlos 51 — 13° andar, Centro, Rio de Janeiro) Tel: 2428098 Cable Add: Planipea Telex: 963
Man Dir, Editorial, Production: A F Vilar de Queiro; *Sales, Publicity:* Gilberto V de Carvalho
Subject: Economics
1979: 110 titles *Founded:* 1971

Livro **Ibero-Americano** Ltda, CP 816, 20241 Rio de Janeiro RJ (Located at: Rua Hermenegildo de Barros 40, Rio de Janeiro) Tel: 2325248/2528814/2329048 Cable Add: Nebrija
Man Dir: Ramón Martín González
Branch Offs: Rua Conselheiro Crispiniano 29, 1° pav, São Paulo SP; Rua do Rosário 99, 3° e 4° andares, Rio de Janeiro RJ
Subjects: History, Philosophy, Reference, Religion, Medicine, Psychology, Textbooks (all levels)
Founded: 1946

Impacto, Editorial e Serviços Ltda*, Ave Pres Vargas 534/1901, 20000 Rio de Janeiro RJ Cable Add: Jovinorio
Man Dir: Jovino de Oliveira; *Sales Dir:* João Silva
Subjects: General Literature, Tourism
Founded: 1974

Instituição Brasileira de Difusão Cultural SA, see IBRASA

Instituto Brasileiro de Administraçao Municipal (IBAM), Largo IBAM 1, 22282 Rio de Janeiro RJ Tel: 2666622 Cable Add: Ibambras
Superintendent-General: Diogo Lordello de Mello; *Editor:* Lucy Marques
Subjects: Law, Municipal Administration, Planning, O & M, Systems Analysis, Public Finance, Periodicals
Bookshop: at above address
1978: 12 titles *1979:* 6 titles *Founded:* 1952

Instituto Brasileiro de Edições Pedagógicas (IBEP)*, CP 5312, 03016 São Paulo SP (Located at: Rua Joli 294, Brás, São Paulo) Tel: 2912355
Branch Off: Ave Lóbo Júnior 1011, Penha, 21020 Rio de Janeiro RJ
Subjects: Textbooks, Reference Books

Fundação **Instituto Brasileiro de Geografia** e Estatística, see under Fundação

Instituto Brasileiro de Informação em Ciência e Tecnologia (IBICT), Rua General Argolo 90, São Cristovão, 20921 Rio de Janeiro RJ
Brazilian Institute for Information in Science and Technology
Dir: Paulo de Souza Moraes
Subjects: Social, Natural and General Sciences, Technology, Bibliographies, Periodical *Ciencia da Informação*

Instituto Campineiro de Ensino Agrícola, CP 1148, 13100 Campinas SP (Located at: Rua Antonio Lapa 78, Campinas) Tel: (0192) 516398/516198 Cable Add: Icampi
Man Dir: Gervásio Souza Cavalcanti; *Sales Dir:* Vicente Botacini
Subject: Agriculture
Founded: 1955

Instituto de Planejamento Econômico e Social, see IPEA Servicio Editorial

Livraría **Interciencia** Ltda, CP 1825, 20071 Rio de Janeiro RJ (Located at: Ave Pres Vargas 435 — 5° andar — sala 504, Centro, Rio de Janeiro) Tel: 2216850/2210993
Man Dir: Edson do Nascimento Pereira; *Rights & Permissions:* Joel José Gomes
Subject: Science in general
Bookshop: Livraría Interciencia Ltda, Ave Pres Vargas 435, Rio de Janeiro
Founded: 1969 (1975 as publisher)

Junta de Educação Religiosa e Publicações da Convenção Batista Brasileira*, CP 320, 20000 Rio de Janeiro RJ Tel: 2690772 Cable Add: Batistas
Superintendent-General: Prof H Victor Davis; *Editorial, Rights & Permissions:* Prof Darci Dusilek; *Sales, Publicity:* Prof Silvino Carlos Figueira Netto; *Production:* Dr Daniel dos Santos Nascimento
Subject: Religion
Bookshops: Rua do Rosário 141 s/Lj 201, Centro, 20041 Rio de Janeiro RJ (and others in Bandeira, Rio, Duque de Caxias, Niterói, Nova Iguaçu; Ave Visconde de São Lourenço 6, 40000 Salvador BA; Ave São João 816-820, 01000 São Paulo SP; SDS Bl G Lj 17, Conjunto Baracat, 70000 Brasília DF; Rua Barão de Intapemirin 208, 29000 Vitória ES
1978: 38 titles *1979:* 72 titles *Founded:* 1907

Norberto R **Keppe***, Ave Rebouças 3115, Pinheiros, 05401 São Paulo SP Tel: 8536755/8535551
Man Dir, Editorial: André R Keppe; *Sales Dir:* José Calderoni; *Production Dir:* Regina Bertazoni; *Publicity Dir:* Omnypolis Fozolino
Subjects: Psychoanalysis, Psychology, Medicine, General Science
1978: 3 titles *1979:* 3 titles *Founded:* 1977

Livraría **Kosmos** Editôra*, CP 3481, 20041 Rio de Janeiro RJ (Located at: Rua de Rosario 137, Centro, Rio de Janeiro) Tel: 2529534/2529552
Man Dirs: Walter and Stefan Geyerhahn
Subjects: Engineering, History, Linguistics, Music, Reference Books, Tourism
Founded: 1935

L I S A (Livros Irradiantes SA)*, CP 7873, 01532 São Paulo SP (Located at: Rua Castro Alves 139, Aclimação, São Paulo) Tel: 2788900/2797011/2797169 Cable Add: Lisalivros
Man Dir: Leonídio Balbino da Silva; *Sales Dir:* Francisco de Paula Oliveira Filho
Branch Off: Ave Presidente Vargas 446, Sala 1802, Centro, 20071 Rio de Janeiro RJ
Subjects: Textbooks, Reference, Education
Founded: 1965

L I T E C, see Livraría Editôra Tecnica Ltda

L T r Editôra Ltda*, Rua Jaguaribe 571-585, Vila Buarque, 01224 São Paulo SP Tel: 660458
Man Dir: Armando C Costa; *Editorial, Publicity:* Marinho; *Sales:* Armando C Costa Jr; *Production:* Arnaldo C Costa
Branch Off: Rua Anfilófio de Carvalho 29, Salas 607/8, Castelo, 20030 Rio de Janeiro RJ
Subject: Law
Founded: 1937

Editorial **Labor** do Brasil SA*, CP 1519, Rio de Janeiro RJ (Located at: Rua Buenos Aires 104, Rio de Janeiro) Tel: 2526554 Cable Add: Edilabor
Dir: Antonio Francisco Souza Filho
Parent Company: Editorial Labor, Spain (qv)
Branch Off: Mal Floriano 13 7 andar, Gonj 71/73 Porto Alegre; Rua Aurora 858 2 Conj 23, São Paulo
Subjects: Art, Medicine, Science, Engineering, Technology

Francisco J **Laissue**, Rua Gonçalves Diàs 75 — 1° andar — sala 3, Rio de Janeiro RJ Tel: 2226298
Man Dir: Francisco J Laissue
Subjects: Occult, The East, Religion, Philosophy
Founded: 1947

Editôra **Laudes** SA*, Ave Almirante Barroso 90 — 3° andar, Castelo, 20031 Rio de Janeiro RJ Tel: 2682796/2689981
Subjects: Textbooks, Brazilian Literature

Lex Editôra SA, CP 12888, 04106 São Paulo SP (Located at: Rua Machado de Assis 57, São Paulo) Tel: 5490122
Man Dir: Affonso Vitale Sobrinho; *Editorial:* Dra Dulce Eugênia de Oliveira; *Sales:* Oswaldo Messina Jr; *Production:* Paulo Celso Vitale
Branch Off: Rua Debret 23 conj 801, Rio de Janeiro
Subject: Law
1979: 10 titles *1980:* 11 titles *Founded:* 1937

Editôra **Liber Juris** Ltda, Rua da Assembléia 36 — 2° andar, Rio de Janeiro RJ Tel: (021) 2832446/2228742/2216664/2832696
Man Dir, Editorial, Production: Djalma de Magalhães; *Sales, Publicity:* André Luis Braga de Oliveira; *Rights & Permissions:* Djalma de Magalhães, Joao Manuel de Almeida
Parent Company: Livraría Cultural da Guanabara Ltda, Rua da Assembléia 38 — loja, Rio de Janeiro
Subject: Law
Bookshop: Livraría Cultural da Guanabara Ltda, Rua da Assembléia 38 — loja, Rio de Janeiro
1978: 8 titles *1979:* 5 titles *Founded:* 1972

Editôra **Lidador** Ltda, Rua Paulino Fernándes 58, Botafogo, 20000 Rio de Janeiro RJ Tel: 2667179/2664105/2867593
Publicity Manager: Ruy Carvalho
Subjects: Economics, Music, Occultism, Sociology, Dramatic Art

Waldyr **Lima** Editôra*, Rua Dr Bulhões 947, 20730 Rio de Janeiro RJ Tel: (021) 2691332/2893995
Director-General, Rights & Permissions: Waldyr Lima; *Editorial (Research & Planning Dir):* Lilian Moreira Neves; *Sales, Production, Publicity Dir:* Richard Noel Taylor
Subjects: Didactics, English as a foreign language
1978: 57 titles *1979:* 63 titles *Founded:* 1967

Editôra Max **Limonad** Ltda, Rua Quintino Bocaiuva 191 — 4° andar — sala 41, 01004 São Paulo SP Tel: 357393
Man Dir, Editorial: Sara Limonad
Subject: Law
1978: 5 titles *Founded:* 1944

Livraría Editôra Tecnica Ltda (LITEC)*, CP 30869, São Paulo SP (Located at: Rua dos Timbiras 257, São Paulo) Tel: 2208983
Man Dir: Adalbert Walter Miehe; *Sales Dir:* José Lopes
Subjects: Electronics, Technical
Founded: 1971

Livros Irradiantes SA, see LISA

Editôra **Logosófica**, Rua Coronel Oscar Porto 818, 04003 São Paulo SP Tel: 701476/706574
Man Dir, Editorial: José Antonio Antonini; *Sales:* Expedito Jorge Leite; *Production:* Antonio Francisco Ocãna
Orders to: Rua Luiz Machado Pedrosa 96, 01431 São Paulo SP
Subject: Logosophy
Bookshops: SHCG — Norte, Area de Escolas Q704, 70000 Brasília DF; Rua Piauí 742, 30000 Belo Horizonte MG; Rua Barão de Rio Branco 63 — sala 1902, 80000 Curitiba PR; Rua Nunes Machado 14 — sala 25, 88000 Florianópolis SC; Rua 17A, 959 Setor Aeroporto, 74000 Goiânia GO; Rua Domingos de Sá 373, 24220 Niterói RJ; Rua General Polidoro 36, 22280 Rio de Janeiro; Rua Capitão Domirifos 72, 38100 Uberaba MG; and others in Argentina, Mexico, Paraguay and Uruguay
1978: 4 titles *1979:* 2 titles *Founded:* 1964

Edições **Loyola** SA*, CP 42335, 04216 São Paulo SP (Located at: Rua 1822 No 347, Ipiranga, São Paulo) Tel: 639695/2746028
Subjects: Law, Education, Literature, Cinema, Economics, Philosophy, Psychology, Religion, Textbooks

Edições '**Lumen Christi**', CP 2666, 20000 Rio de Janeiro RJ (Located at: Rua Dom Gerardo 40, Rio de Janeiro) Tel: 2917122 Cable Add: Mosteiro Sanbento
Man Dir, Production, Publicity: D Hildebrando P Martins OSB; *Sales:* Nicolau Mueller OSB
Subjects: Liturgy, Theology, Spiritualism, Art
Bookshop: Edições 'Lumen Christi' (at above address)
1978: 6 titles *1979:* 6 titles *Founded:* 1935

Editôra **McGraw-Hill** do Brasil Ltda*, Alameda Juruá 434, Alphaville, KM 23 da Rodovia Castelo Branco, 06400 Barueri SP
Man Dir: Jan Rais
Associate Company: McGraw-Hill Book Co (UK) Ltd (qv for other associates)
Branch Off: Editôra McGraw-Hill Ltda, Rua Rosa, Damasceno 11, AB, Lisbon 2, Portugal
Subjects: Science & Technology
Founded: 1970

Editôra **Mandarino** Ltda, CP 11000, Rio de Janeiro RJ (Located at: Rua Marquês de Pombal 172, Rio de Janeiro) Tel: 2215016
Man Dir: Ernesto Emanuele Mandarino; *Editorial:* Elisa Maria Bruno; *Sales:* José Gabrielesco; *Production:* Ivan Giovanni Malgeri; *Publicity:* Niltom Mendes Mendonca
Associate Company: Publieco Promoçoes Ltda, Rua Marquês de Pombal 171, CP 11030, Rio de Janeiro
Subjects: Spiritualism, Magic, Afro-Brasilian Cults
1978: 30 titles *1979:* 12 titles *Founded:* 1970

Editôra **Manole** Ltda, CP 1489, 01327 São Paulo SP (Located at: Rua 13 de Maio 1026, São Paulo) Tel: 2870746
Man Dir, Editorial, Production, Rights & Permissions: Dinu Octau Manole; *Sales:* Glória Yasuda; *Publicity:* Ilma Manole
Subjects: Physiotherapy, Medicine, Psychology
1978: 65 titles *1979:* 47 titles *Founded:* 1969

Mapa Fiscal Editôra Ltda*, CP 30027, 01540 São Paulo SP (Located at: Rua Miguel Telles Jr 394, Cambucí, São Paulo) Tel: 2784011 Cable Add: Mapa Fiscal Telex: 1130323 Mfel Br
Man Dir: Jayro Gonçalves; *Editorial, Sales, Production, Publicity Dir:* Roberto Mateus Ordine
Branch Off: Rua do Russel 680 terreo, Praia do Russel, Rio de Janeiro
Subject: Tax laws
Bookshop: Rua Barão de Paranapiacaba 93 6° of 63, Rio de Janeiro
1978: 64 titles *1979:* 26 titles *Founded:* 1952

Livraría **Martins** Editôra SA*, Rua Rocha 274, Bela Vista, 01330 São Paulo SP Tel: 2880667
Branch Off: Rua Evaristo da Veiga 47, Rio de Janeiro GB
Subjects: Literature, Juveniles, Art, Social Sciences, Law, Economics, Geography, History

Editôra **Masson** do Brasil, Rua da Quitanda 20 — sala 301, 20011 Rio de Janeiro RJ Tel: 2638294
Associate Companies: Masson Editeur, France (qv); Masson Editores, Dakota 383, Colonia Napoles, Mexico 18 DF, Mexico; Toray Masson, Spain (qv); Masson Publishing USA Inc, 14 East 60th St, New York NY 10022, USA

Editôra **Meca** Ltda, Rua Araújo 81, Vila Buarque, São Paulo SP Tel: 2599049/2599034/2575346
Man Dir, Editorial, Production: Cosmo Juvela; *Sales:* Anna Maria Santos Brasil; *Publicity:* Eduardo Leonel; *Rights & Permissions:* Guarany Gallo
Subjects: General
1978: 4 titles *1979:* 2 titles *Founded:* 1970

Companhia **Melhoramentos** de São Paulo, CP 8120, 01000 São Paulo SP (Located at: Rua Tito 479, 05051, São Paulo) Tel: 2626866 Cable Add: Melhoraluz Telex: 1123151 Melp Br
General Manager: Dr Alfried Ploeger; *Editorial & Production Manager:* Alfredo Weiszflog
Branch Off: Rua Pinto Guedes 24, Tijuca, 20511 Rio de Janeiro RJ
Subjects: Children's Books, Dictionaries, Reference, General Literature
Bookshop: Livroluz, Largo do Arouche 167, São Paulo SP
1978: 170 titles *1979:* 176 titles *Founded:* 1915

Mestre Jou SA*, CP 24090, São Paulo SP (Located at: Rua Guaipa 518, Vila Leopoldina, São Paulo) Tel: 2602498/2611920 Cable Add: Mestrejou
Man Dir: Felipe Mestre Jou; *Sales, Publicity, Advertising & Rights Dir:* Antonio Bidin
Subjects: Literature, History, Philosophy,

Psychology, Medicine, Technical &
Engineering, Social Sciences
Bookshops: Rua Senador Dantas 19, S/206,
Rio de Janeiro; Rua Augusta 2843, Rua
Martins Fontes 99, Rua 7 de Abril 172 and
Rua Alvaro de Carvalho 111 (all in São
Paulo)
Founded: 1946
Miscellaneous: Firm is also an importer and
distributor for all Brazil

Editôra **Monterrey** Ltda*, Rua Visconde de
Pirajá 550 — 14° andar — sala 1401,
Ipanema, 22410 Rio de Janeiro RJ Tel:
2272795/2272602
Man Dir, Editorial: J Gueiros; *Sales:*
J Fernandez; *Production:* W Teixeira;
Publicity: C Marquez
Subject: Fiction
Founded: 1963

Editôra **Moraes** Ltda, Rua Ministro Godoy
1002, 05015 São Paulo SP Tel: (011)
8647849/628987/8641298/8641267
Man Dir: Orozimbo José de Moraes
Subjects: Education, Philosophy,
Psychology, Social Service, Literature,
Communications
Bookshop: Rua Curt Nimuendajú 19, 05015
São Paulo
1978: 40 titles *1979:* 25 titles *Founded:* 1969

Livraría **Nobel** SA Editôra, CP 2373, São
Paulo SP (Located at: Rua María Antonia
108, Vila Buarque, São Paulo) Tel: 2572144
Publicity: Ary Kuflik Benclowicz
Subjects: Textbooks, Agronomy,
Mathematics, Statistics, Science,
Engineering, Management & Economics,
Public Relations, Dictionaries, Veterinary,
Husbandry, Gardening, Literature
Bookshops: Rua Maria Antonia 108; Rua da
Consolacão 49, São Paulo
Miscellaneous: Also distributor
Founded: 1943

Noblet Editôra e Distribuidora Ltda, CP
15181, 01530 São Paulo SP (Located at:
Rua Almeida Torres 119/163, São Paulo)
Tel: 2786152 Cable Add: Altesse
Man Dir: Joseph Bekhor Abourbih;
Editorial: Yasukazu Hamazaki; *Production:*
Fausto Taoka; *Publicity:* Josette A H
Savatovsky
Subjects: Fiction, Periodicals
1978: 8 titles *1979:* 8 titles *Founded:* 1968

Editorial **Nórdica** Ltda, Ave NS
Copacabana 1189, 22070 Rio de Janeiro RJ
Tel: (021) 2872169 Cable Add: Nórdica
Telex: (021) 31810 Noca Br
Subjects: General Books, Juveniles,
Humour, Politics, Cinema, Cookery,
Economics, Sports, Occultism, Fiction

Editôra **Nova Aguilar** SA, Rua Maria
Angélica 168, 22461 Rio de Janeiro RJ Tel:
2667474 Cable Add: Aguilar
President: Sérgio Lacerda; *Editorial Dir:*
Pedro Paulo de Sena Madureira; *Sales:*
Elson M F da Rocha
Parent Company: Editôra Nova Fronteira
SA (qv)
Branch Off: Ave Jurema 767, 04079 São
Paulo
Subjects: Luxury editions of complete works
of important Brazilian, Portuguese and
International writers and poets
1978: 1 title *Founded:* 1958

Nova Epoca Editorial Ltda*, Ave Angélica
55, Santa Cecilia, 01228 São Paulo SP Tel:
679505
Man Dir: Maria Dorell; *Sales Dir:* Dr Mark
A Dorell; *Publicity Dir:* Poala Bassano;
Advertising Dir: Roberto Zaccola; *Rights &
Permissions:* Allan Delan
Subjects: General Fiction, Biography,
History, Philosophy, Reference Books,
Occultism
Founded: 1971

Editôra **Nova Fronteira**, Rua Maria
Angélica 168, 22461 Rio de Janeiro RJ Tel:
2667474 Cable Add: Neofront
President: Sérgio Lacerda; *Vice-President:*
Sebastião Lacerda; *Editorial Dir:* Pedro
Paul de Sena Madureira; *Sales:* Elson M F
da Rocha; *Production:* Beatriz Affonseca;
Publicity: Helena dos Guimarães Bastos;
Rights & Permissions: M A Bandeira
Subsidiary Companies: Nova Aguilar (qv);
Confraria dos Amigos do Livro (qv)
Branch Off: Ave Jurema 767, 04079 São
Paulo
Subjects: Fiction, Literature, Biography,
Psychology, History, Brazilian Problems,
Dictionaries
1978: 44 titles *1979:* 66 titles *Founded:* 1965

Livraría José **Olympio** Editôra SA*, CP
9018, 22251 Rio de Janeiro RJ (Located at:
Rua Marquês de Olinda 12, Botafogo, Rio
de Janeiro) Tel: 2660662/2665032 Cable
Add: Jolympio
Dir: Hênio Rodrigues de Souza; *Sales Dirs:*
Lidelmo Lima Terra, Harry de Almeida
Costa; *Foreign Rights:* Gilda O Cruz Lehner
Branch Offs: Rua dos Gusmões 100-104,
Santa Ifigênia, 01212 São Paulo SP; Rua
Januária 258, Belo Horizonte MG;
Comércio local da S Q Sul 108, Bloco D,
Loja 5, Brasília DF; Rua dos Andradas 717,
Porto Alegre RS; (all in Brazil)
Subjects: Juveniles, General Science, General
Fiction, Textbooks, Sports, Philosophy,
History, Humour, Music, Reference Books,
Psychology, Religion, Sociology
Founded: 1931

Pallas SA*, Editôra e Distribuidora, CP
7001, 21050 Rio de Janeiro RJ (Located at:
Rua Frederico de Albuquerque 44,
Higienopolis, Rio de Janeiro) Tel: 2700186
Man Dir: Martha Bozõti; *Editorial, Rights
& Permissions:* D Marques; *Sales:* A C
Fernandes
Subjects: Fiction, Social Sciences, National
Literature, Economics, Law, Psychology,
Occultism
Founded: 1975

Parma, an imprint of Global Editôra e
Distribuidora Ltda (qv)

Edições **Paulinas**, CP 12899, 04117 São
Paulo SP (Located at: Rua Dr Pinto Ferraz
183, São Paulo) Tel: 716302/702688 Cable
Add: Paulins Telex: 1130791 Ramc Br
Man Dir: Carlos D Vido; *Editorial:* Carlos
Vido; *Sales:* W P Bosio; *Production:* Vitt
Sarraceno; *Publicity:* W P Bosio; *Rights &
Permissions:* Carlos D Vido
Subjects: Religion, Philosophy, Biography,
Juveniles, Primary & Secondary Textbooks,
Theological, Biblical, Liturgical
Bookshops: Rua Dr Pinto Ferraz 183, and
three more in São Paulo; Rua México 111-B
and one more in Rio de Janeiro; one each in
Belo Horizonte, Brasília, Caxias do Sul,
Curitiba, Fortaleza, Goiânia, Maringá,
Niterói, Cuiabá, Porto Alegre, Recife,
Salvador, São Luís, Campo Grande
1978: 203 titles *1979:* 210 titles *Founded:*
1930

Editôra **Paz e Terra**, Rua Andrê Cavalcanti
86, Fátima, 20231 Rio de Janeiro RJ Tel:
2634399 Telex: 2122643
General Manager, Sales & Editorial:
Fernando Gasparian; *Production, Publicity,
Rights & Permissions Dir:* Vera Whately
Subjects: Brazilian Studies, Latin-American
Studies, Social Sciences, Philosophy,
Cinema, Theatre, Political Science,
Literature & Literary Theory
Bookshops: Livraría Argumento, Rua Oscar
Treire 608, São Paulo; Rua Dias Teneira
199, Rio de Janeiro
1978: 92 titles *1979:* 86 titles *Founded:* 1966

Editôra **Pensamento**, Rua Dr Mário Vicente
374, 04270 São Paulo Tel: 2741733
Man Dir: Diaulas Riedel
Subjects: Philosophy, Religion
Founded: 1908

Editôra **Perspectiva**, Ave Brigadeiro Luís
Antônio 3025, Jardim Paulista, 01401 São
Paulo SP Tel: 2888388/2886878
Man Dir: J Guinsburg
Subjects: Social Science, Humanities,
Cinema, Economics, Education, History,
Philosophy, Music, Psychology, Religion

Pink and Blue Editôra Ltda, Rua Jandaia
180, Bela Vista, 01320 São Paulo SP Tel:
325886/350036
Man Dir: Maria Cecília de sá Quartim
Barbosa; *Editorial Dir:* Francisco Quartim
Barbosa; *Sales Dir:* Lucia Barbosa Lemos;
Production Dirs: Genny M Ramalho, Maria
Eugenia C Obniski; *Publicity Dir:* Lucilia
Ribas Chaves; *Rights & Permissions:* Ana
Maria Quartim Barbosa
Subject: English as a foreign language,
primary & secondary stage
1978: 2 titles *1979:* 2 titles *Founded:* 1972

Pool Editorial Ltda, CP 650, 50000 Recife
PE (Located at: Rua Manoel Caetano 135,
Derby, Recife) Tel: 2215096/2215179 Cable
Add: Poolne Telex: 2273 Alpp Br
Man Dir, Editorial: Marco Aurèlio de
Alcântara; *Sales:* Leonio Souto Ribeiro;
Production: Manoel Alberto de Freitas;
Publicity: Maristela da Rocha Oliveira
Parent Company: Alcântara Promoções e
Publicidade Ltda (at above address)
Subsidiary Company: ANI — Agencia
Nordestina de Informações (at above
address)
Branch Off: Rua do Riachuelo 247 — apt
906, Fátima, Rio de Janeiro
Subjects: Politics, Economics, Poetry, Belles
Lettres
Bookshop: Livraría do Estacionamento
Periférico da Ilha Joana Bezerra, Recife
1978: 5 titles *1979:* 5 titles

Casa Editôra **Presbiteriana**, Rua
Comendador Norberto Jorge 40, Brooklin
Paulista, 04602 São Paulo SP Tel:
5431061/2236479
Man Dir: Rev Atael Fernando Costa
Subjects: History, Religion
Bookshop: Ave São João 439 — lojas 201-3,
São Paulo
1978: 5 titles *1979:* 6 titles *Founded:* 1942

Editôra **Primor** Ltda*, Ave Almirante
Barroso 63 — sala 2716, 20031 Rio de
Janeiro RJ Tel: (021) 2224122/2225977
Cable Add: Primor Telex: (021) 22150
Subsidiary Company: Gráfica Editôra
Primor SA (qv)
Subjects: Children's Books, Humour,
Tourism, Illustrated Fiction and Nonfiction,
International Co-Productions

Gráfica Editôra **Primor** SA*, Ave Almirante
Barroso 63 — sala 2716, 20031 Rio de
Janeiro RJ Tel: (5521) 3716622 Telex: (021)
22150
Man Dirs: Sergio Jacques Waissman, Simão
Waissman; *Editorial:* Jaime Rodrigues;
Sales, Publicity: Allen Josias; *Production:*
Miguel Lerner; *Rights & Permissions:* Sergio
Jacques Waissman
Parent Company: Editora Primor Ltda (qv)
Branch Offs: Rua Cons Carrão 191/7, 01328
São Paulo SP
Subjects: Didactics, Pre-school & Juvenile
Literature, Reference, Art, General Interest,
Notebooks, Illustrated books
1978: 9 titles *Founded:* 1969

Editôra de **Publiçações Científicas** Ltda*, Rua do Russel 404 — grupos 901-2 parte, Glória, 22210 Rio de Janeiro RJ Tel: 2654047/2654245/2258708/2451336
Man Dir: José Maria de Sousa e Melo; *Editorial:* Dr Ismar Chavés da Silveira; *Sales, Publicity:* Luiz Carlos Ávila de Souza; *Production:* Luiz Augusto Rodrigues
Associate Company: Editôra de Publicações Médicas Ltda (EPUME) (at above address)
Branch Off: Rua Borges Lagoa 126, São Paulo
Subject: General Medicine
Book Club: Estante do Livro Científico
1978: 3 titles *1979:* 5 titles *Founded:* 1959

Editôra **Raio X** Ltda*, Senador Dantas 117 — sala 640, 20000 Rio de Janeiro RJ
Subject: Literature in general

Distribuidora **Record** de Serviços de Imprensa SA, CP 884, 20291 Rio de Janeiro RJ (Located at: Rua Argentina 171, São Cristovão, Rio de Janeiro) Tel: 2842037 Cable Add: Recordist Telex: (21) 30501 Book Br
President & General Manager: Alfredo C Machado; *Vice-President:* Sergio C Machado
Branch Offs: Ave Erasmo Braza 255 — sala 304, Rio de Janeiro; Rua José Antônio Coelho 801, São Paulo SP; Ave Augusto de Lima 233, Belo Horizonte MG
Subjects: General Fiction & Nonfiction, Biography, History, Philosophy, Juveniles, Primary Textbooks
Bookshop: Livraría Record, Ave Copacabana 249, Rio de Janeiro
1978: 435 titles *1979:* 450 titles *Founded:* 1942

Editôra **Resenha** Tributaria Ltda*, Rua Cel Xavier de Toledo 210 — cj 74 — 7° andar, Centro, 01048 São Paulo SP Tel: 354445
Subjects: Law, Education

Editôra **Reverté** Ltda*, CP 23001, 20910 Rio de Janeiro RJ (Located at: Ave do Exército 49, São Cristovão, Rio de Janeiro) Tel: 2845244
Man Dir: E Rosel Albero
Associate Companies: See under Editorial Reverté SA, Spain (qv)

Editôra **Revista** dos Tribunais Ltda*, CP 8153, 01501 São Paulo SP (Located at: Rua Conde do Pinhai 78, Centro, São Paulo) Tel: 378689/379772
Man Dir: Nelson Palma Travassos; *Sales Dir:* Alvaro Malheiros
Subjects: Law, Economics, Philosophy, History, Reference Books, Sociology
Founded: 1955

Editôra **Rideel** Ltda, CP 12152, 02450 São Paulo SP (Located at: Alameda Afonso Schmidt 877, Santa Terezinha, São Paulo) Tel: 2908510/2902411/2987690/2981029 Telex: (011) 22262 Rdel Br
Man Dir, Editorial, Publicity, Rights & Permissions: Italo Amadio; *Sales:* Fiore Tadeu Marchesano; *Production:* Regina Maria Azevedo
Subjects: Reference, Medicine, Philology, History, Cooking, Infant/Juvenile Books, Sexual Education, Religion
1978: 54 titles *1979:* 63 titles *Founded:* 1971

Rio Grafica e Editôra SA*, Rua Itapiru 1209 — 5° andar, Rio Comprido, 20000 Rio de Janeiro RJ Tel: (021) 2342000 Telex: 021464
Subjects: Comic Books, Sports and Games; Activity Books

Editôra Ana **Rosa***, Rua Aurora 858 — 6° andar, São Paulo SP Tel: 2212211
Subjects: Fashion & Design

São Paulo Editôra, an imprint of Livraría Francisco Alves Editôra SA (qv)

Saraiva SA, Livreiros Editores, CP 2362, 01139 São Paulo SP (Located at: Ave do Emissario 1897, Barra Funda, São Paulo) Tel: 8268422 Cable Add: Academica Telex: (11) 25642 Edsa Br
Man Dirs: Ruy Gonçalves, J E Saraiva; *Dir:* P Saraiva; *Editorial:* A Faccioli, M Acquaviva, O Juarez; *Sales, Publicity:* N Lepera; *Production:* A Cardoso; *Rights & Permissions:* J E Saraiva
Branch Offs: Ave Marchal Rondon 2231, Rio de Janeiro; Rua Celia de Souza 571, Belo Horizonte
Subjects: Law, Education, Business Administration, Economics, Primary, Secondary School Texts
Bookshops: 21 branches throughout Brazil
1978: 329 titles *Founded:* 1917

Sarvier — Editôra de Livros Medicos Ltda*, CP 12927, 04012 São Paulo SP (Located at: Rua Dr Amancio de Carvalho 459, Vila Mariana, São Paulo) Tel: 713439
Man Dir: Cid A Balieiro
Subjects: Medicine, Dentistry
Founded: 1965

Scipione Autores Editores Ltda, Rua Princesa Leopoldina 431/445, Alto da Lapa, 05081 São Paulo SP Tel: 2605878/2612902
Man Dir, Editorial: Prof Dr Scipione di Pierro Netto; *Sales, Publicity:* Adonis Franco Martins; *Production:* José Augusto del Bianco; *Rights & Permissions:* Prof Dr Scipione di Pierro Netto, Luis Fernando di Pierro
Subsidiary Company: Módulus Orientação Pedagógica, Edição e Comercialização de Obras Didáticas Ltda (at above address)
Subject: Didactics
1978: 28 titles *1979:* 30 titles *Founded:* 1974

Seleções Editôra Ltda, see Eletrônicas Editôra Ltda

Edições **Símbolo**, Rua General Flores 518, 01129 São Paulo SP Tel: 2200267/2215833 Cable Add: Simbolgraf
Man Dir: Moysés Baumstein; *Editorial Dir:* Alberto Baumstein; *Sales Dir:* Messias Rodrigues Ferreira
Parent Company: Simbolo SA: Industrias Gráficas
Subjects: Literature, Social Literature, University Textbooks, Sociology, History, Politics, Jungian Psychology, Education, Communications
1979: 17 titles *1980:* 18 titles *Founded:* 1976

Livraría **Sulina** Editôra*, CP 357, 90000 Pôrto Alegre RS (Located at: Ave Borges de Medeiros 1030-36, Pôrto Alegre) Tel: 254765 Cable Add: Zipasul
President: Leopoldo Bernardo Boeck Jr; *Vice-President:* Vilson Nailor Noer
Parent Company: Organização Sulina de Representações S/A, Rua Cel Genuino 290, Pôrto Alegre (Distributor)
Subjects: Science, Technical, Law, Textbooks, Psychology
Bookshops: Above address and Rua Julio de Castilhos 1657, Caxias do Sul; Ave 7 de Setembro 1169, L 12 Bagé; Rua Marechal Floriano 1000, c 63 Sta Maria, and 5 other bookshops in Pôrto Alegre
1978: 42 titles *Founded:* 1946

Edições **Tabajara***, CP 1918, 90000 Pôrto Alegre RS (Located at: Rua dos Andradas 1774, Pôrto Alegre) Tel: 241073/247724
Assistant Manager: Maria Azambuja
Branch Off: Rua Santa Ifigênia 72, São Paulo
Subjects: Linguistics, Social & General Science, Mathematics, Sociology, Dramatic Art, Education, Textbooks

Livros **Tecnicos** e **Cientificos** Editôra SA, Ave Venezuela 163, 20220 Rio de Janeiro RJ Tel: 2238589 Cable Add: Litece
Man Dir: P Machado Alves; *Editorial, Production:* J R de Carvalho; *Sales, Publicity:* Novais de Paula; *Rights & Permissions:* S Felix
Orders to: A Mesma
Associate Companies: John Wiley & Sons, UK (qv for other associates)
Branch Off: Rua Dr V de Carvalho Pinto 301-7, São Paulo
Subjects: Scientific and Technical
1979: 70 titles *Founded:* 1968

Editôra **Tecnoprint** Ltda, CP 1880, 21040 Rio de Janeiro RJ (Located at: Rua Nova Jerusalém 345, Bonsucesso, Rio de Janeiro) Tel: 2606122/2804090 Cable Add: Ediouro
Subjects: Cookery, Textbooks, Sports, Children's Books, Reference Books, Paperbacks
Founded: 1939

Editôra da **U R G S** (Universidade Federal do Rio Grande do Sul), Rua Ramiro Barcelos 2.600 — 1° andar, 90000 Pôrto Alegre RS Tel: 315671
Dir: Blasio H Hickman
Subjects: General & Academic
1979: 112 titles

Editôra **Universidade de Brasília**, CP 040289, 70910 Brasília DF (Located at: Campus Universitário, Asa Norte Apt 15, Brasília) Tel: 2720000
President of Editorial Council: Prof Carlos Henrique Cardim; *Editorial, Sales:* Sérgio Sampaio; *Production:* Manuel M Cruz
Branch Offs: São Paulo, Rio de Janeiro
Subjects: Politics, General Non-fiction, Periodicals
Book Club: Clube do Livro Político

Editôra da **Universidade de São Paulo**, CP 11465, 05508 São Paulo SP (Located at: Edificio da Antiga Reitoria — 6° andar, Cidade Universitária 'Armando Salles Oliveira', Butantã, São Paulo) Tel: 2116988 Cable Add: Ruspaulo
President: Mario Guimarães Ferri
Subjects: Scholarly, General Nonfiction
Founded: 1964

Universidade Federal do Rio Grande do Sul, see Editôra da URGS

Livraría e Editôra **Universitária** de Direito Ltda*, Rua Benjamin Constant 171 — 1° andar — salas 1-5, 01005 São Paulo SP Tel: 356374/340314
Man Dir, Production: Armando Luiz Almeida Martins; *Editorial Dir:* Pedro Gellindo Sommavilla; *Sales Dir:* Armando des Santos Mesquita Martins
Subject: Legal works
1978: 16 titles *1979:* 8 titles *Founded:* 1968

Fundação Getúlio **Vargas**, CP 9052, 22253 Rio de Janeiro RJ (Located at: Praia de Botafogo 188, Rio de Janeiro) Tel: 2863344 Cable Add: Fugevar
Man Dir: Mauro Gama; *Sales Dir:* Jorge Rangel da Matta
Subjects: Administration, Economics, Business, Sociology, Psychology, Education, Marketing, Accounting

Editôra **Vecchi** SA*, Rua do Resende 144, Centro, 20231 Rio de Janeiro RJ Tel: 2444522 Cable Add: Vekieditora
Dir & Vice-President: Lotario Campello Vecchi
Subjects: Biography, Cookery, Philosophy, Reference Books, Occultism, Religion, Juveniles
Founded: 1913

Editôra **Verbo** Ltda*, CP 8811, 01526 São Paulo SP (Located at: Rua Bueno de Andrade 480-484, Liberdade, São Paulo) Tel: 2792776 Cable Add: Verbo
Subjects: Art, Social Science, Reference, Juveniles, Cinema, Education, Geography, History, Psychology, Religion

Vertente Editôra Ltda*, Rua Dr Homem de Melo 446, 05007 São Paulo SP Tel: 8641758/8640077
Man Dir: Wladyr Nader; *Production Dir:* Maria Teresa Teixeira Ribeiro
Subjects: Literature, The Humanities, Periodicals *Escrita* and *Escrita/Ensaic*
Bookshop: Escrita (at above address)
1978: 9 titles *1979:* 7 titles *Founded:* 1968

Editôra **Vigília** Ltda*, CP 2468, 30000 Belo Horizonte MG (Located at: Rua Felipe dos Santos 508, Bairro de Lourdes, Belo Horizonte) Tel: 3372744/3372363/3372834/3358720
Branch Off: Rua Pareto 23, Tijuca, 20550 Rio de Janeiro RJ
Subjects: Textbooks, Linguistics, Brazilian Literature, Religion

Editôra **Visão** Ltda, Rua Alfonso Celso 243, Vila Mariana, 04119 São Paulo SP Tel: 5494344 Cable Add: Revista Visão Telex: (011) 23552/30665 Sevl Br
Man Dir: Henry Maksoud; *Editorial Dir:* Isaac Jardanovski; *Sales Dir:* Paulino Da San Pancrazio; *Production Manager:* Antonio Lopes Colhado; *Publicity Manager:* Sylvio Tose; *Rights & Permissions:* Ayrton Pedro de Oliveira
Associate Company: Visão SA Editorial (at above address)
Branch Off: Conjunto Baracat — sala 301, Brasília DF
Subjects: Humanities, Economics, Finance, Agriculture, Cattle Breeding, Diet, Commerce, Hobbies, Tourism, Politics, Science, Technology
1978: 1 title *1979:* 1 title *Founded:* 1952

Vozes Editôra Ltda, CP 23, 25600 Rio de Janeiro RJ (Located at: Rua Frei Luís 100, Petrópolis, Rio de Janeiro) Tel: 435112 Cable Add: Vozes
Man Dir: Miguel Mourão de Castro
Branch Offs: Rua Senador Dantas 118-1, Rio de Janeiro; Rua Senador Feijó 168, São Paulo; Rua Tupis 85, Loja 10, Belo Horizonte; Rua Riachuelo 1280, Pôrto Alegre; CRL/Norte, Q704 Bloco A 15, Brasília DF; Rua Conselheiro Portela 354, Recife PE; Rua Alferes Poli 52, Curitiba PR
Subjects: Belles Lettres, Linguistics, Communications, Philosophy, Religion, Administration, Psychology, Sociology
Founded: 1901

Zahar Editores, CP 207, Rio de Janeiro GB (Located at: Rua México 31, Rio de Janeiro) Tel: 2215079
General Manager: Jorge Zahar; *Editorial:* Ana Cristina Zahar; *Sales Dir:* Jorge Zahar, Jr
Branch Off: Alameda Nothaman 1067, São Paulo
Subjects: Social Science, Psychology, Business & Economics
Founded: 1957

Zip Editôra Ltda, CP 35034, 20000 Rio de Janeiro RJ (Located at: Rua Filomena Nunes 162, Olaria, Rio de Janeiro) Tel: 2306470
Man Dir: Jan Rais; *Editorial:* Rubens Lucchetti; *Sales:* Marcolo Vital Brazil; *Production:* Nildo Vicente
Subjects: Juveniles, Fiction, Paperbacks
1979: 100 titles *Founded:* 1978

Literary Agents

Carmen **Balcells** Agencia Literaria, CP 33113, Rua Joaô Lira 97 — salas 203-202, Leblon, 22430 Rio de Janeiro RJ Tel: 2943248 Cable Add: Copyright Rio
Manager: Ana Maria Santeiro
Also office in Barcelona, Spain (qv)

Dr J E **Bloch** and Mrs Karin Schindler, Rua Oscar Freire 416 — apt 83, 01426 São Paulo SP Tel: 2823053 Cable Add: Copyright Sãopaulo

International Editors' Co*, Alameda IEU 402, São Paulo SP

Rômulo **Paes Barreto***, CP 16083, 20000 Rio de Janeiro RJ Tel: 2659478

Book Clubs

Círculo do Livro SA, CP 7413, São Paulo SP (Located at: Al Ministro Rocha Azevedo 346, São Paulo) Tel: 8818644 Cable Add: Cirlivro Telex: 1132900/1131747
Man Dir: Raymond Cohen
Owned by: Bertelsmann Aktiengesellschaft, Federal Republic of Germany (qv); Abril SA Cultural e Industrial (qv)

Estante do **Livro Científico***, Rua do Russel 404 — 9° andar, 22210 Rio de Janeiro RJ
Owned by: Editôra de Publicações Científicas Ltda (Rio de Janeiro) (qv)

Clube do **Livro Político***, CP 040289, 70910 Brasília DF (Located at: Campus Universitário, Asa Norte Apt 15, Brasília)
Owned by: Editôra Universidade de Brasília (qv)

Major Booksellers

Livraría **Agir**, Rua México 98 — loja B, Rio de Janeiro RJ Tel: 2401978

Ao Livro Técnico*, CP 3655, 20000 Rio de Janeiro RJ (Located at: Rua Miguel Couto 35 — loja C, Rio de Janeiro) Tel: 2639377
Branches in Brasília, Belo Horizonte, Minas Gerais, Rio de Janeiro, Niteroi, São Paulo
Also widespread wholesaler and distributors

Editôra **Brasiliense** SA*, Rua Barão de Itapetininga 93, São Paulo SP Tel: 367824

Livraría **Canuto** Ltda, Rua da Consolação 348 — 2° andar, São Paulo SP Tel: 2564564

Livraría **Científica Técnica***, Rua Riachuelo 453 — loja 4, 50000 Recife PE Tel: 24933

Livraría **Civilização** Brasileira*, Rua Bettencourt da Silva 12 — loja F, Rio de Janeiro RJ Tel: 2216980

Cultura 70 Livraría e Editôra SA*, Rua Barão de Itapetininga 93-99, 01042 São Paulo SP

Livraría **Duas Cidades***, CP 433, São Paulo SP (Located at: Rua Bento Freitas 158, São Paulo) Tel: 2204702

A Casa do Livro **Eldorado** Ltda, Ave Copacabana 1189, 22070 Rio de Janeiro RJ Tel: 2872147

Livraría **Freitas** Bastos*, Rua 7 de Setembro 111, Rio de Janeiro RJ Tel: 332999

Livraría do **Globo***, Rua dos Andradas 1416, Pôrto Alegre RS Tel: 24811

Librairie **Hachette** SA do Brasil*, Rua Décio Villares 278, Bairro Peixoto, Copacabana, Rio de Janeiro RJ

I B R E X - Distribuidora de Livros e Material de Escritório Ltda, Rua 21 de Abril 101, São Paulo SP Tel: 929639

Livro **Ibero-Americano***, Rua do Rosario 99 — 3-4° andares, Rio de Janeiro RJ Tel: 2212026
Also Publisher (qv)

Livraría **Kosmos***, CP 3481, Rio de Janeiro RJ (Located at: Rua do Rosario 137, Rio de Janeiro) Tel: 2529552

Livraría **L E R**, Rua México 31 — sobreloja, 20031 Rio de Janeiro RJ Tel: 2215073/74/75/76 Cable Add: Livreril
Also at Praça Olavo Bilac 28, Rio de Janeiro; Praça da República 71, 01045 São Paulo
Importer, Exporter & Distributor

L I T E C - Livraría Editôra Técnica Ltda, CP 30869, São Paulo SP (Located at: Rua dos Timbiras 257, São Paulo) Tel: (011) 2208983
Manager: A W Miehe

Livraría D **Landy**, Rua 7 de Abril 252 — 5° andar, São Paulo SP Tel: 2551953/2553272

Livraría **Leonardo da Vinci***, Ave Rio Branco 185 — loja 2, Rio de Janeiro RJ Tel: 2577192/2241329

Mestre Jou SA, Rua Guaipá 518, Vila Lepoldina, 05089 São Paulo SP Tel: 2602498/2611920
Firm is also an importer and distributor for all Brazil

Livraría **Nobel***, CP 2373, São Paulo SP (Located at: Rua de Consolação 49, São Paulo) Tel: 2593237

Livraría **Parthenón***, Rua Barão de Itapetininga 140 — 1° andar — sala 14, 01042 São Paulo SP Tel: 372623

Livraría Científica Ernesto **Reichman***, Rua Dom José de Barros 168 — 6° andar — conj 61-62, 01000 São Paulo SP Tel: 342340

Livraría **Sulina**, CP 357, Pôrto Alegre RS (Located at: Ave Borges de Medeiros 1030-36, Pôrto Alegre) Tel: 254755

Livraría **Triangulo** Ltda, CP 30317, 01042 São Paulo SP (Located at: Rua Barão de Itapetininga 255 — loja 23-24, São Paulo) Tel: 2310922/2553384

Major Libraries

Arquivo Nacional*, Praça da República 26, Rio de Janeiro RJ

Biblioteca Estadual*, Ave Presidente Vargas 1261, Rio de Janeiro RJ
State Library

Biblioteca Municipal Mário de Andrade, CP 8170, São Paulo SP (Located at: Rua da Consolação 94, São Paulo) Tel: 2394384/2565777
Dir: Maria Helena Guimarães da Costa e Silva

Biblioteca Nacional*, Ave Rio Branco 219-239, 20042 Rio de Janeiro RJ Tel: 2320520 Telex: 02122941 Bn Rj Br
Dir: Plinio Doyle

Biblioteca Publica do Estado do Rio de Janeiro*, Praça da República, Niterói, Rio de Janeiro RJ

Centro de Documentação e Informaçao da Camara dos Deputados, Coordenação de Publiçacoês, Praça dos Tres Poderes, Brasília DF
House of Representatives' Centre of Documentation & Information

BRAZIL

Biblioteca do **Ministerio das Relações Exteriores**, Esplanada dos Ministérios, 70170 Brasília DF   Tel: 2264305
Dir: Lilian Thome Andrade (Librarian)
Publications: Aquisiçoẽs (bi-monthly), *Aquisiçoẽs Bibliograficas* (annual), *Referência de Periodicos* (monthly)

Biblioteca da **Sociedade Brasileira** de Cultura Inglesa, CP 821, Rio de Janeiro RJ (Located at: Ave Graça Aranha 327 — 3° andar, Rio de Janeiro)
Librarian: Ilka Beauchamp

Universidade de Brasilia, Biblioteca Central*, Ag Postal 15, 70910 Brasilia DF   Tel: (061) 1083   Telex: 2720000, Ramal 2400

Divisão de Biblioteca e Documentação da **Universidade de São Paulo***, CP 8191, 05508 São Paulo SP (Located at: Cidade Universitaria, Butantan, São Paulo)
Library and Documentation Division of São Paulo University

Centro de Ciências da Saúde da **Universidade Federal do Rio de Janeiro**, Biblioteca Central — bloco L, Cidade Universitária, Ilha do Fundão, 20000 Rio de Janeiro RJ
Medical School Library of the University of Rio de Janeiro

Universidade Federal do Rio Grande do Sul, Biblioteca Central, Edificio da Reitoría-térreo, Ave Paulo Gama, 90000 Porto Alegre RS   Tel: (0512) 242431   Telex: 0511055
Librarian: H B Schreiner

Library Associations

Associação Brasileira de Bibliotecarios, now Profissional de Bibliotecários do Estado do Rio de Janeiro (qv)

Associação dos Arquivistas Brasileiros, Praia de Botafoga 186 — sala B-217, 22253 Rio de Janeiro RJ
Association of Brazilian Archivists
President: Regina Alves Vieira; *Secretary:* Maria Amélia Gomes Leite
Publication: Arquivo e Administração (4-monthly)

Associação Paulista de Bibliotecarios*, CP 343, 01327 São Paulo SP (Located at: Rua 13 de Maio 1100 — 3° andar, São Paulo)
Executive Secretary: Mirian L Honorato
Library Association of São Paulo

Associação Profissional de Bibliotecários do Estado do Rio de Janeiro (APBERJ), Rua Martins Torres 99, Santa Rosa, Niterói, 24000 Rio de Janeiro RJ
Brazilian Library Association
Previously known as Associação Brasileira de Bibliotecarios

Associação Rio-Grandense de Bibliotecarios, CP 2344, Pôrto Alegre, 90000 Rio Grande do Sul RS (Located at: Rua Dr Flores 245 — 7° andar — conj 902, Pôrto Alegre)
Library Association of the State of Rio Grande do Sul

Centro de Investigação e Documentação*, CP 23, Petropolis, Rio de Janeiro RJ

Comissao Brasileira de Documentação Agricola (CBDA)°, c/o Museu Paraense "Emilio Goeldi", CP 399, Belem, Pará PA
Secretary: Cely Farias Raphael
Headquarters of Brazilian Commission for Agricultural Documentation
Publication: Agricolas

Conselho Federal de Biblioteconomia (CFB), SCLRN 712-713 — bloco A — entr 31 sobreloja — sala 02, 70760 Brasília DF
Federal Council of Librarianship
President: Nancy Westphalen Corrêa

Federação Brasileira de Associações de Bibliotecários (FEBAB)*, Rua Avanhandava 40 — conj 110, 01306 São Paulo SP   Tel: 2579979
Brazilian Federation of Library Associations
President: Antonio Gabriel
Editor: Neusa Dias de Macedo
Publication: Revista Brasileira de Biblioteconomia e Documentação Jornal da FEBAB

Federação Brasileira de Associações de Bibliotecários — Comissão Brasileira de Documentação Jurídica (FEBAB/CBDJ), Rua Prof Antônio Maria Teixeira 120 — apt 802, Leblon, 22430 Rio de Janeiro RJ   Tel: 2592763
Brazilian Federation of Library Associations — Brazilian Committee of Legal Documentation
President: Nylma Thereza de Salles Velloso Amarante; *Executive Secretaries:* Tania Cordeiro Alvarez, Sérgio da Costa Velho
Publications: Many publications dealing with legal and related matters

Instituto Brasileiro de Informação em Ciência e Tecnologia (IBICT), Rua General Argolo 90, São Cristovão, 20921 Rio de Janeiro RJ   Tel: (021) 2423453/2425051
Brazilian Institute for Information in Science and Technology
Dir: Paulo de Souza Moraes
Publication: Ciência da Informação (bi-annual)

Library Reference Books and Journals

Books

Guia de Bibliografía Especializada (Guide to Specialist Libraries), Brazilian Library Association, Rua Martins Torres 99, Santa Rosa, Niterói, 24000 Rio de Janeiro (covers all Latin America)

Journals

Boletim Informativo (Information Bulletin), Library Association of São Paulo, Rua 13 de Maio 1100, 3° andar, São Paulo

Jornal, Library Association of São Paulo, Rua 13 de Maio 1100, 3° andar, São Paulo

Noticias (News), Brazilian Federation of Library Associations, Brazilian Committee of Legal Documentation, Rua Prof Antônio Maria Teixeira 120 — apt 802, Leblon, 22430 Rio de Janeiro

Revista Brasileira de Bibliteconomia e Documentação (Brazilian Review of Librarianship and Documentation), Brazilian Federation of Library Associations, Rua Prof Antônio Maria Teixeiro 120 — apt 802, Leblon, 22430 Rio de Janeiro

Literary Associations and Societies

Academia Amazonense de Letras*, Rua Ramos Ferreira 1009, Manaus, 69000 Amazonas AM
President: Dr Mario Y Monteiro; *Secretary:* Tânia Regina Mesquita
Publication: Revista

Academia Cachoeirense de Letras*, Praça Jerônimo Monteiro 105 — 2° andar, Cachoeiro de Itapemerim, Espírito Santo ES

Academia Catarinense de Letras*, Rua Tenente Silveira 6, Florianópolis, Santa Catarina SC
Secretary-General: Altino Flôres
Publication: Revista

Academia Cearense de Letras, Palácio Senador Alencar, Rua São Paulo 51, 60000 Fortaleza CE
Secretary-General: Raimundo Girâo
Publications: Revista da Academia Cearense de Letras, Coléção Dolor Barreira, Coléção Antonio Sales

Academia de Letras*, João Pessôa, Paraíba PB

Academia de Letras da Bahia*, CP 662, Bahia BA (Located at: Ave 7 de Setembro 283, Salvador, Bahia)
Secretary: Edith Mendes de Gama e Abreu
Publication: Revista (every 6 months)

Academia de Letras de Piauí*, Teresina, Piauí PI
Publication: Revista

Academia Feminina Espírito Santense de Letras*, Rua Bernardo Horta 30 — apdo 1, Jucutuara, Vitoria, Espírito Santo ES
Women's Academy of Letters

Academia Matogrossense de Letras*, Rua 13 de Junho 173, Cuiabá, Mato Grosso MT
President: José de Merquita
Publication: Revista

Academia Mineira de Letras*, Rua Carijos 150 — 6° andar, Belo Horizonte, Minas Gerais MG

Academia Paranaense de Letras, CP 8610, Curitiba, 80000 Paraná PR
President: Vasco José Taborda
Publications: Revista, and books

Academia Paulista de Letras, Largo do Arouche 312, São Paulo SP   Tel: 2212660/2239725
President: Francisco Marins
Publications: Revista da Academia Paulista de Letras, Biblioteca Academia Paulista de Letras

Academia Pernambucana de Letras*, CP 50000, Recife, Pernambuco PE (Located at: Ave Rui Barbosa 1596, Graças, Recife, Pernambuco)
President: Dr Mauro Mota; *Secretary:* Dr Andrade Lima Fılho
Publication: Revista

Academia Riograndense de Letras*, Rua Candido Silveira 43, Pôrto Alegre, Rio Grande do Sul RS
Publication: Revista

Academia de Letras 'Humberto de **Campos**'*, Rua 23 de Maio, Vila Velha, Espírito Santo ES

P E N Clube do Brasil (Associação Universal de Escritores)*, Praia do Flamengo 172 — 10° andar, Rio de Janeiro RJ
President: Professor Marcos Almir Madeira
Publications: Boletim, novels, poetry

Literary Periodicals

Escrita (Writing), Vertente Editôra Ltda, Rua Dr Homen de Melo 446, 05007 São Paulo SP

Jornal de Letras (Journal of Letters), Rua Barata Ribeiro 774 s/1-101, Copacabana-Rio, Estado da Guanabara

Opinião (Opinion), Ramos 78, Jardim Botanico, Rio de Janeiro

Verbum (The Word), Universidade Catolica, Rua Marques de São Vicente 209, Rio de Janeiro

Veritas (The Truth), Pontificia Universidade Catolica do Rio Grande do Sul, Ave Iparanga 6681, Pôrto Alegre

Literary Prizes

Graca **Aranha** Prize*
For the best Brazilian novel. Enquiries to PEN Clube do Brasil, Praia do Flamengo 172 — 10° andar, Rio de Janeiro RJ

Afonso **Arinos** Prize*
For the best work of fiction published or written during the two years preceding the year of award. Awarded annually. Enquiries to the Brazilian Academy, Ave Presidente Wilson 203, Rio de Janeiro

Olavo **Bilac** Prize*
For the best book of poetry. Awarded annually. Enquiries to the Brazilian Academy, Ave Presidente Wilson 203, Rio de Janeiro

Viriato **Correa** Prize*
To the author of the best unpublished book for children. Enquiries to National Book Institute, Edifício Venâncio V, Setor de Diversões Sul, 70000 Brasília DF

Folklore Prize
For outstanding research work on Brazilian folklore. 4,000 Cruzeiros. Awarded annually. Enquiries to Campaign for the Defence of Brazilian Folklore, Instituto Nacional de Folclore, Rua do Catete 179, 22220 Rio de Janeiro RJ

Fundepar Prize*
For best short stories in the Portuguese language. $17,000 distributed among the six winners. Awarded annually. Enquiries to Parana State Educational Foundation, CP 2854, 8000 Curitiba

Monteiro **Lobato** Prize*
For children's literature. Awarded annually. Enquiries to Brazilian Academy, Ave Presidente Wilson 203, Rio de Janeiro

Julia **Lopes** de Ameida Prize*
For the best unpublished or published literary work written by a woman, preferably for a novel or collection of short stories. Awarded annually. Enquiries to Brazilian Academy, Ave Presidente Wilson 203, Rio de Janeiro

Machado de Assis Prize*
For an outstanding Brazilian writer for the sum of his work. Awarded annually. One of Brazil's highest literary honours. Enquiries to Brazilian Academy, Ave Presidente Wilson 203, Rio de Janeiro

Odorico **Mendes** Prize*
For the best translation from foreign literature into the Portuguese language. Awarded annually. Enquiries to Brazilian Academy, Ave Presidente Wilson 203, Rio de Janeiro

National Book Institute Prizes*
For outstanding unpublished literary works of fiction, poetry, history and essays. In addition, one prize is awarded for the best unpublished work of children's literature and another for illustrations of books for children. Awarded annually. Enquiries to National Book Institute, Edifício Venâncio V, Setor de Diversões Sul, 70000 Brasília DF

National Cultural Awards*
For outstanding intellectual and artistic accomplishments in the fields of literature, theatre, sciences, social studies, music, cinematography and arts. Enquiries to Brazilian Government, Brasília

Silvio **Romero** Prize*
For best works in literary criticism and history of literature. Awarded annually. Enquiries to the Brazilian Academy, Ave Presidente Wilson 203, Rio de Janeiro

Luisa Claudio de **Sousa** Prize*
For the best book published in the previous year. Novels, plays, literary history and criticism works are considered. Awarded annually. Enquiries to PEN Clube do Brasil, Praia do Flamengo 172 — 10° andar, Rio de Janeiro RJ

José **Verissimo** Prize*
For the best essay and a work of scholarship. Awarded annually. Enquiries to Brazilian Academy, Ave Presidente Wilson 203, Rio de Janeiro

Brunei

General Information

Language: Malay and Chinese
Religion: Predominantly Muslim
Population: 201,000
Literacy Rate (1971): 63.9%
Bank Hours: 0900-1200, 1400-1500 Monday-Friday; 0900-1100 Saturday
Shop Hours: 0730-1930 or 2000 Monday-Saturday in Bandar Seri Begawan, Tuesday-Sunday in Seria, Wednesday-Monday in Kuala Belait
Currency: 100 cents = 1 Brunei dollar
Export/Import Information: No tariff on books. Advertising matter dutied at 25 cents per lb. No obscene literature allowed. Import licences not required. No exchange controls

Publishers

Leong Brothers*, 52 Jalan Bunga Kuning, PO Box 164, Seria Tel: Seria 22381 Cable Add: Leong

The **Star** Press*, Bandar Seri Begawan
Manager: F W Zimmermann
Founded: 1963

Major Booksellers

The **Brunei** Press*, Jalan Sungai, Kuala Belait
Stockists and dealers for books handled by the Strait Times Press, Singapore

Sharikat Toko Buku **Kwang Hwa**, PO Box 1211, Brunei (Located at: 308A Kiaw Lian Bldg, B S Begawan, Brunei) Tel: 24075
Manager: Frederick Yong

Rainbow Photo & Book Store, PO Box 153, 59 Jalan Pretty, Kuala Belait Tel: 34295

Rex Bookstore*, PO Box 500, Brunei Hotel, Jalan Chevalier Tel: 2060

Swan Book Store*, Shop No 2, Jalan Bunga Rambai, Kuala Belait Tel: 2639

Major Libraries

Language and Literature Bureau Library, Jalan Elizabeth II, Bandar Seri Begawan
Librarian: Thelma T Salazar

Bulgaria

General Information

Language: Bulgarian (English becoming common foreign language. Russian widely used)
Religion: Eastern Orthodox, Muslim
Population: 8.8 million
Literacy Rate (1965): 90.2% (94.8% Urban, 86.2% Rural)
Bank Hours: 0830-1145 Monday-Friday; 0800-1100 Saturday
Shop Hours: 0800-1300, 1600-1900 Monday-Saturday
Currency: 100 stotinki = 1 lev
Export/Import Information: Foreign trade is a state monopoly and tariffs are paid by enterprise involved. Books imported by the foreign trade organization 'Hemus', Russki blvd 6, Sofia. Exchange controls
Copyright: UCC, Berne (see International section)

Book Trade Organizations

Darzhavno Obedinenie 'Bulgarska Kniga'*, pl Slavejkov 11, Sofia Tel: 879111 Telex: 22927 Lpms
State Association 'Bulgarian Book'

Suyuz Knigoizdatelite i Knizharite*, vu Solum 4, Sofia
Union of Publishers and Booksellers

Union of Bulgarian Writers*, angel Kanchev 5, Sofia
President: Pantelev Zarev
Publications: Literaturen front, Septemvri, Obzor, Plamŭk, Savremennik, Slaveyche

Book Trade Reference Books and Journals

Books

Bulgarian Academic Books, Catalogue of the Books and Periodicals of the Bulgarian Academy of Sciences and the Academy of Agricultural Sciences in Bulgaria, Bulgarian Academy of Sciences, blvd Vitosha 39, Sofia

Bŭlgarski Knigi (Bulgarian Books), Jusautor, pl Slavejkov 11, Sofia

Journals

Bŭlgarski Knigopis (National Bibliography), Cyril and Methodius National Library, blvd Tolbuhin 11, Sofia

Publishers

Knigoizdatelstvo 'Georgi **Bakalov**'*, blvd Hristo Botev 3, Varna Tel: 25077
Subjects: Maritime, Economics

Izdatelstvo na **Bulgarskata Akademia** na Naukite*, ul Academician G Bonchev 1113, Sofia Tel: 724643
Publishing House of the Bulgarian Academy of Sciences
Subject: Science

Izdatelstvo na **Bulgarskata Komunisticheska Partiya**ature, blvd Lenin 47, Sofia Tel: 4631
Publishing House of the Bulgarian Communist Party
Subjects: Geodesy, Philosophy, Politics, Popular Sciences, Sociology, Political Economy

Bulgarski Houdozhnik*, ul Moskovska 37, Sofia Tel: 884480/884275
Dir: Prof Petr Tchuchovski
Subjects: Art, Archaeology, Juveniles
1978: 84 titles *Founded:* 1952

Bulgarski Pissatel*, ul 6 Septemvri 35, Sofia
Tel: 884734
Publishing House of the Union of Bulgarian Writers
Dir: Simeon Sultanov
Subjects: General Fiction, Belles Lettres

Izdatelstvo na **Bulgarskiya Zemedelski Naroden Suyuz***, ul Yanko Zabounov 1, Sofia Tel: 881951
Subjects: Social & Popular Politics, Agriculture, Fiction

Darzhavno Izdatelstov 'Christo G **Danov**'*, ul Petko Karavelov 17, 4000 Plovdiv Tel: 25232
Dir: Peter Anastassov: *Editorial:* Ivan Nikolov
Parent Company: Glavna Direkzia 'Knigoizdavane', pl Slaveikov 11, Sofia 1000
Subjects: Science, Agriculture, University Textbooks, Poetry, Fiction translations
Founded: 1855

Meditsina i Fizkultura*, pl Slaveikov 11, Sofia 1000 Tel: 879111
Subjects: Biology, Geography, Hygiene, Medicine, Sports

Darzhavno Izdatelstvo '**Muzica**'*, blvd Georgi Traykov 2a, Sofia Tel: 662031
Subjects: Music, Theory of Music

Narodna Kultura*, ul Gravril Genov 4, Sofia Tel: 862722
Subject: Belles Lettres

Narodna Mladezh*, ul Kaloyan 10, Sofia Tel: 8681
People's Youth Publishing House
Manager: Marko Nedyalkov
Subjects: Juveniles, Philosophy, Mathematics, General, Political & Social Science, Original and Translated Fiction

Darzhavno Izdatelstvo '**Narodna Prosveta**'*, ul Vasil Drumev 37, Sofia Tel: 442211
Dir: Paunka Gocheva
Subject: Educational

Izdatelstvo na **Natsionalniya Savet** na Otetchestveniya Front*, blvd Dandukov 32, Sofia Tel: 878481/882991
Publishing House of the National Council of the Fatherland Front
Subjects: History, Politics, Popular Sciences, Belles Lettres

Darzhavno Izdatelstvo **Nauka** i Izkustvo*, blvd Rousky 6, Sofia Tel: 875701
State Publishing House 'Science & Art'
Dir: Philip Genev
Subjects: History, Art, Music, Law, Philosophy, General & Social Science, Technology, Business, Languages
Founded: 1949

Izdatelstvo **Profizdat***, blvd Dondukov 82, Sofia Tel: 872501
Publishing House of the Central Council of Bulgarian Trade Unions
Manager: Ivan Daskalov
Subjects: General Fiction, Belles Lettres, Political Science, Philosophy, General & Social Science

Sinodalno Izdatelstvo*, ul Sveta Sofia 2, Sofia Tel: 883313
Synodal Publishing House
Subject: Liturgical Books

Sofia Press Agency*, ul Levski 1, Sofia
Tel: 885831/885832 Cable Add: Sofia Press Telex: 22622
General Dir: Kristo Santov
Subjects: General Fiction, Belles Lettres, Poetry, Biography, History, Political Science, Music, Art, Philosophy, Reference, Guides
Bookshop: Levski St 1, Sofia
Founded: 1967

Technica*, blvd Ruski 6, Sofia Tel: 875701
Subjects: Encyclopaedias and Dictionaries, Textbooks

Voenno Izdatelstvo*, ul Ivan Vazov 12, Sofia Tel: 878116
Subjects: History, Social Sciences, Military

Darzhavno Izdatelstvo **Zemizdat***, blvd Lenin 47, 1000 Sofia, PB 422 Tel: 4631
State Agricultural Publishing House
Dir: Yosif Grigorov
Subjects: General Science, Agriculture, Textbooks, Hobbies, Nonfiction
Founded: 1949

Literary Agents

Jusautor, pl Slavejkov 11, Sofia Tel: 884817 Cable Add: Jusautor Sofia
Dir General: Trayan Ivanov
Copyright Agency
The agency is the exclusive representative of Bulgarian authors of literary, scientific and art works, and also acts as an intermediary between foreign authors, publishers and agencies and Bulgarian users of their works

Major Booksellers

'**Hemus**' Foreign Trade Company*, pl Slavejkov 11, Sofia Tel: 870365 Telex: 22267 Hemkik

Major Libraries

Central Historical **Archives***, ul Zhdanov 5, Sofia

Central **Archives** of the People's Republic of Bulgaria*, ul Slavanjska 4, Sofia

Central Library, **Bulgarian Academy of Sciences***, 7 Noemvri 1, Sofia Tel: 877731
Librarian: Elena Savova
Publications: Collected Papers (irregular)

Centre for Pedagogical Information and Documentation*, Lenin 125, Sofia

Cyril and Methodius National Library*, blvd Tolbuhin 11, 1504 Sofia Tel: 882811
Dir: Ms K Kalajdzieva

Central Agricultural Library of the 'G **Dimitrov**' **Academy** of Agricultural Sciences*, Dr Cankov 6, Sofia

Central **Institute** for Scientific and Technical Information (of the State Committee for Science, Technical Progress and Higher Education)*, Chapaev 56, Sofia

Central Medical Library*, bul G Sofiiski 1, Sofia 1431
Dir: Mrs N Kudreva

Municipal Library*, ul Gurko 1, Sofia

National Library 'Ivan Vazov'*, Nikola Vaptzarov 17, 4000 Plovdiv Tel: 22915
Dir: Johan Lautliev

Sofia City and District State Archives*, ul Vitosha 2, Sofia
There are 26 District State Archives

Sofiiski Universitet 'Kliment Ohridsky' Biblioteka*, blvd Ruski 15, Sofia
University of Sofia Library

Central Library of the Higher **Technical Institutes***, Dr Cankov 2, Sofia

Central **Technical Library***, Gurko 16, Sofia

University of Sofia Library, see Sofiiski Universitet

Library Associations

Bulgarian Union of Public Libraries*, ul Alabin 31, Sofia

Sekciya na Bibliotechnite Rabotnitsi pri Centralniya Komitet na Profesionalniya Sŭyuz na Rabotnitsite ot **Poligraficheskata Promishlenost i Kulturnite Instituti***, c/o Cyril and Methodius National Library, blvd Tolbuhin 11, Sofia Tel: 882811
Section of the Librarians at the Professional Organization of the Workers in Polygraphics and Culture
President: Stefan Kánćev
Publications: Issues annual reports, and occasional publications jointly with the National Library, eg on IBY

Library Reference Books and Journals

Books

Biblioteki Bolgarii (Bulgarian Libraries), Cyril and Methodius National Library, blvd Tolbuhin 11, Sofia

Bibliotekoznanie, Bibliografiya, Knigoznanie Nauchna Informatsiya (Library Science, Bibliography, Scientific Information), Cyril and Methodius National Library, blvd Tolbuhin 11, Sofia

Journals

Bibliotekar (The Librarian), periodical for library work (Contents page in Bulgarian, English and Russian), Committee for Culture and Art and the Cyril and Methodius National Library, blvd Tolbuhin 11, Sofia

Statisticheski Danni za Bibliotekite v Bŭlgariya (Statistical Data on Libraries in Bulgaria), Cyril and Methodius National Library, blvd Tolbuhin 11, Sofia

Literary Associations and Societies

Bulgarian Academy of Sciences, Institute of Literature*, blvd Vitosha 39, Sofia C

Komitet za Izkoustvo i Koultoura*, blvd Stambolissky 18, Sofia
Committee for Arts and Culture

Society of Aesthetes, Art and Literary Critics*, pl Evtimij 48, Sofia
Secretary: Dr K Goranov

Literary Periodicals

Literatourna Missul (Literary Thought), (text in Bulgarian, contents page in English and French), Bulgarian Academy of Sciences, Institute of Literature, blvd Vitosha 39, Sofia C

Obzor (Survey), Bulgarian quarterly review of literature and the arts (text in English, Spanish and French), Union of Bulgarian Writers, Committee for Friendship and Cultural Relations with Foreign Countries, angel Kanchev 5, Sofia

Plamŭk (The Flame), literature, art, publicity, Union of Bulgarian Writers, angel Kanchev 5, Sofia

Literary Prizes

A competition for the best Bulgarian book published abroad is held at the annual Sofia International Book Fair

Bulgarian Publishing Award*
For the best artistic and technical achievements in the art of book publishing. Awarded annually. Enquiries to the Bulgarian People's Republic Council of Ministers, Committee for the Press and the Union of Bulgarian Artists, Sofia

Burma

General Information

Language: Burmese (English used for foreign correspondence)
Religion: Buddhism
Population: 32.2 million
Literacy Rate (1953): 69.1%
Bank Hours: 1000-1400 Monday-Friday; 1000-1200 Saturday
Shop Hours: Generally 0800-1700 Monday-Saturday
Currency: 100 pyas = 1 kyat
Export/Import Information: Burma has own complex tariff system, but duties are paid by State Trading Corporation No 9, 550-552 Merchant St, Rangoon, and Printing and Publishing Corporation, 228 Theinbyu St, Rangoon, principally. No tariffs on advertising. Books exempt from sales tax. Import licence required. Exchange controls; priorities apply
Copyright: No copyright conventions signed

Book Trade Organizations

Burmese Publishers' Union*, 146 Bogyoke Market, Rangoon

Publishers

Hanthawaddy Book House*, 157 Bo Aung Gyaw St, Rangoon
Subjects: Textbooks, Multilingual Dictionaries

Knowledge Printing & Publishing House*, 130 Bogyoke St, Yegyaw, Rangoon
Subjects: Art, Education, Politics, Religion, Sociology

Kyi-Pwar-Ye Book House*, 84th St, Letsegan Mandalay
Subjects: Travel, Arts, Religion, Juveniles

Sarpay Beikman Board*, 529 Merchant St, Rangoon Tel: 16611 Cable Add: Sarbeikman
Chairman: U Mya Maung; *Secretary:* U Aung Tun; *Sales, Publicity & Advertising:* U Tin Myint; *Editorial:* U Kyaw Khin
Subjects: Encyclopaedia, General Information, Culture, History, Applied Science, Agriculture, Law, Literature, Biography
Book Club: Sarpay Beikman Book Club, 529 Merchant St, Rangoon
Bookshop: 529 Merchant St, Rangoon
Founded: 1947

Shumawa Book House*, 146 Bogyoke Aung San Market, Rangoon
Bookshop: 1 Sandwith Rd, Rangoon
Subjects: Mechanical Engineering, Technical

Shwepyidan Printing & Publishing House*, 12(A) Hninban St, Yegwaw Quarter, Rangoon
Subjects: Politics, Law, Religion

Smart & Mookerdum*, 221 Sule Pagoda Rd, Rangoon
Subjects: Arts, Juveniles, Cookery, Popular Sciences

Than Myit Baho Publishing House*, 230 Anawyatha Rd, Rangoon
Subjects: Scientific, Technical

Thudhammawaddy Press*, 55-56 Moung Khine St, Rangoon
Subject: Religion

Universities Administration Office*, Prome Rd, University Post Office, Rangoon
Chief Editor, Translations and Publications Department: U Wun

Book Clubs

Sarpay Beikman Book Club*, 529 Merchant St, Rangoon

Major Booksellers

Ava Bookshop (Government Bookshop)*, 2 Sule Pagoda Rd, Rangoon

Chindwin Book Distributors*, 180 47th St, Rangoon

Gondu*, 209 33rd St, Rangoon

Hanthawaddy Bookshop*, 357 Bo Aung Gyaw St, Rangoon

Hna Lon Hla*, 5 100th St, PO Box 87, Kandawlay PO, Rangoon

Knowledge Book House*, 130 Bo Gyoke Aung San St, Rangoon

Pagan Publishing House*, 123 Myamagonyi St, Kandawlay, Rangoon

Sabe U*, 148-150 33rd St, Rangoon

Sarpay Beikman Bookshop*, 529 Merchant St, Rangoon

Sarpay Lawka*, 173 33rd St, Rangoon

Shumawa Publishing House*, 1 Sandwith Rd, Rangoon

Thwe Thauk*, 341 Bo Aung Gyaw St, Rangoon

Major Libraries

Arts & Science University Library*, University Estate, Mandalay

Institute of Economics Library*, University Estate, Rangoon

Institute of Education Library*, University Estate, Rangoon

Rangoon Institute of Technology Library, Gyogone, Insein PO, Rangoon
Librarian: Daw Myinet Myinet Khyne

International Institute of Advanced Buddhistic Studies Library*, Kaba-aye Pagoda Compound, Rangoon

Magwe College Library*, Magwe

National Library*, Town Hall, Rangoon

State Library*, Moulmein

Universities' Central Library*, University Estate, Rangoon

Library Associations

Burma Library Association*, c/o International Institute of Advanced Buddhistic Studies, Kaba Aya, Rangoon

Jubilee Library Association*, c/o Steel Road, Toungoo

Literary Associations and Societies

Department of Ancient Literature and Culture, **Ministry of Culture***, 1 Church Rd, Rangoon

Literary Prizes

National Literary Awards*
When the Burma Translation Society (now renamed Sarpay Beikman Board) was founded in 1947 it established the Best-Published-Novel-of-the-Year Prize. Min Aung won the prize for 1948 with his book *Mo Auk Mye Byin* (Land under the Sky). The prize money was K1000 (one thousand kyats).
The awards were gradually increased and in 1962 Sarpay Beikman was offering nine awards. They were for the best published novel of the year, the best collection of short stories, the best belles lettres, the best book of knowledge, the best book of poems, the best translation of a world classic, and the best published play of the year. In the absence of any official literary awards, the Sarpay Beikman literary awards were virtually honoured as national literary awards.
When Sarpay Beikman was taken over by the Revolutionary Government in August 1963 the Sarpay Beikman Literary Awards were transformed into National Literary Awards. More literary awards were gradually added and there are now 12 awards. The awards are for the best published novel of the year, the best collection of short stories, the best belles lettres, the best book of knowledge (arts), the best book of knowledge (science), the best book of poems, the best translation of a world classic, the best published play, the best book for children, the best book for youth, the best book on Burmese culture and the best book on political affairs. A panel of literary specialists is formed every two years by the State to adjudicate the published works.
Each national literary award now draws prize money of K5000. The awards are presented at a ceremony on Sarsodaw Day (Literary Day), which usually falls in December. Enquiries to the Secretary, Sarpay Beikman Board, 529 Merchant St, Rangoon

Sarpay Beikman Best Manuscripts Awards*
In order to discover new writers and to enable promising manuscripts to be published, Sarpay Beikman Board has established a competition for the Best-Manuscripts-of-the-Year-Awards since 1963. There are 11 prizes for the best manuscripts of the year: for novels, short stories, belles lettres, general knowledge (arts), general knowledge (science), plays, children's literature, literature for youth, Burmese cultural affairs, political affairs and translations of a prescribed literary material. There are first, second and third prizes for each award and prize moneys are K500, K300 and K200 respectively.
All prize-winning manuscripts (except translations) are published by Sarpay

Beikman. Only the manuscript which wins the first prize in translation is published by Sarpay Beikman. Payments for the manuscripts are made on royalty basis and are for the first publication rights only. Enquiries to the Secretary, Sarpay Beikman Board, 529 Merchant St, Rangoon

Burundi

General Information

Language: French and Kirundi (a Bantu language)
Religion: About half Roman Catholic; others follow traditional beliefs
Population: 4.3 million
Bank Hours: normally closed for cash transactions in afternoon but open for all other business morning and afternoon
Shop Hours: 0800-1200, 1400-1630 Monday-Friday; 0800-1200 Saturday
Currency: Burundi franc
Export/Import Information: advertising matter subject to 35% revenue duty. 3% ad valorem statistical tax on all imports. Import licence required over value of 20,000 Burundi francs

Publishers

Government Printer*, BP 1400, Bujumbura

Les Presses **Lavigerie***, 5 ave de l'Uprona, BP 1640, Bujumbura

Major Booksellers

Librairie A **Gennotte** & Fils*, BP 420, Bujumbura

Imparudi*, BP 509, Bujumbura

Librairie **Larousse** Centrafrique*, BP 509, Bujumbura

Librairie **Saint Paul***, BP 1360, Bujumbura

Major Libraries

Bibliothèque publique*, BP 960, Bujumbura

Ecole normale supérieure, Bibliothèque*, BP 1065, Bujumbura Tel: 3544
Librarian: Deogratias Ndayizeye
Publication: Pédagogie

Institut Murundi d'Information et de Documentation (IMIDOC)*, 7 ave Malfeyt, BP 902, Bujumbura

Bibliothèque de l'**Université du Burundi***, BP 1320, Bujumbura Tel: 5196/5446
Librarian: H Mununi

Literary Associations and Societies

Centre culturel du Burundi*, BP 1582, Bujumbura

United Republic of Cameroun

General Information

Language: French and English (officially bilingual)
Religion: Predominantly Roman Catholic in west and south, Muslim in centre and north
Population: 8.06 million
Bank Hours: East: 0800-1130, 1430-1530 Monday-Friday; West: 0800-1330 Monday-Friday
Shop Hours: 0800-1200, 1430-1730 (earlier closing in West) Monday-Friday; 0800-1200 Saturday
Currency: CFA franc
Export/Import Information: Member of Customs and Economic Union of Central Africa. No tariff on books, 7.5% fiscal, 30% customs, 10% VAT, 5% turnover tax on advertising matter. Import licence, entitling holder to provision for necessary foreign exchange, required if value of import is over 500,000 CFA francs
Copyright: UCC, Berne, Florence (see International section)

Book Trade Organizations

Association nationale des Poètes et Ecrivains camerounais (APEC), BP 2180, Yaoundé-Messa
National Association of Cameroun Poets and Writers
Secretary-General: R Philombe
Publication: Caméroun littéraire

Publishers

Editions **C L E**, BP 1501, Yaoundé
Tel: 223554 Cable/Telex: Cle Yaoundé
General Manager: Jean Dihang; *Sales Manager:* Nicolas Amougou
Subjects: General Fiction & Nonfiction, Belles Lettres, Poetry, Biography, History/Africana, How-to, Study Guides, Philosophy, Religion, Juveniles, Paperbacks, Medicine, General & Social Science, University & Secondary Textbooks
Founded: 1963
ISBN Publisher's Prefix: 2-7235

Centre d'Edition et de Production pour l'Enseignement et la Recherche (CEPER), Elig-Essono, BP 808, Yaoundé Tel: 221323
Cable Add: Cepmae Yaoundé Telex: 8338
Dir General: Michel Dzukou Tahouo; *Sales Manager:* Wilfred W Banmbuh; *Production Manager:* John Matute Ewoma-Esunge
Subjects: General Nonfiction, History/Africana, Paperbacks, Science & Technology, General & Social Science, University & Secondary Textbooks
Founded: 1967

Centre d'Edition et de Production de Manuels scolaires de l'UNESCO*, Yaoundé

Government Printer*, BP 1091, Yaoundé

Librairie/Imprimerie **Saint Paul***, Ave Monseigneur Vogt, BP 763, Yaoundé
Subjects: Religion, Christian tracts, Paperbacks, Secondary & Primary Textbooks
Bookshop: Librairie St Paul, BP 763, Yaoundé

Editions **Semences** Africaines*, BP 2180, Yaoundé-Messa
Man Dir, Production: Philippe-Louis Ombede; *Editorial, Rights & Permissions:* Martin King Mbida; *Sales:* Ateba Joseph Kono
Subjects: General Fiction, History, Africana, Religion, Paperbacks, Secondary & Primary Textbooks (in French and English only), Poetry, Theatre
Bookshop: address as above
1979: 6 titles *Founded:* 1976

Société Kenkoson d'Etudes Africaines*, BP 4064, Yaoundé
Chief Executive: Marie Salomé
Subjects: Academic, Law
Founded: 1975

Major Booksellers

Librairie '**Aux Frères Réunis**'*, BP 5346, Douala

Cameroun Book Centre*, 2C Nambeke St, PO Box 123, Victoria Tel: 332255

L'Imprimerie **Coulouma***, BP 134, Yaoundé

La Librairie L'**Equatoriale***, BP 324, Yaoundé

Librairie-Papeterie Moderne*, BP 495, Yaoundé

Librairie-Papeterie Protestante CEBEC*, BP 225, Douala

Presbyterian Book Depot and Printing Press Ltd (PRESBOOK)*, PO Box 13, Victoria, Cameroun Tel: Victoria 337214/335246 Telex: 5613 Kw
Branches: Presbook Mankon, PO Box 39, Bamenda; Presbook Kumbo, PO Box 4; Presbook Bura, PO Box 19; Presbook Kumba 87; Presbook Douala (Akwa)

Librairie **Saint Paul***, BP 763, Yaoundé

Major Libraries

Archives nationales du Cameroun*, BP 1053, Yaoundé

Bibliothèque nationale du Cameroun*, BP 1053, Yaoundé Tel: 220078

British Council Library*, BP 818, Yaoundé Tel: 221696

Centre culturel américain, Bibliothèque de Prêt, American Embassy, BP 817, Yaoundé
This is a lending library
Librarian: Emile Mongo-Bebey
Publications include: Selected bibliographies

Centre culturel français, Bibliothèque*, BP 513, Yaoundé Tel: 220533

Collège camerounais des Arts, des Sciences et de la Technologie, Bibliothèque*, Bamili, BP Bamenda

De **Sautoy** College Library, Pan African Institute for Development, PO Box 133, Buea, South-West Province Tel: 328216
Librarian: Eugene O Nwanosike

Université de Yaoundé, Bibliothèque*, BP 1312, Yaoundé Tel: 220744
Librarian: Peter Nkangafaok Chateh
Publications: Discours de la Rentrée Solennelle de l'Université (annual), *Newsletter de l'ABADCAM* (bi-monthly)

Library Associations

Association des Bibliothécaires, Archivistes, Documentalistes et Muséographes du Cameroun (ABADCAM)*, c/o P N Chateh, President, ABADCAM, Bibliothèque Universitaire, BP 1312, Yaoundé
Tel: 220744
Secretary General: Th Eno Belinga
Association of Librarians, Archivists, Documentalists and Museum Curators of Cameroun
Publications: Newsletter

Library Journal

Newsletter, Association of Librarians, Archivists, Documentalists and Museum Curators of Cameroun, c/o P N Chateh, President, Bibliothèque Universitaire, BP 1312, Yaoundé

Literary Associations and Societies

Forum littéraire camerounais*, BP 73, Yaoundé
Cameroun Literary Workshop
Publication: Ozila

Literary Periodicals

Abbia, Editions CLE, BP 1501 Yaoundé
An influential literary and cultural magazine edited by Bernard Fonlon; publication has been rather irregular during the past few years

Cameroun littéraire (Literary Cameroun) (text in English and French), National Association of Cameroun Poets and Writers, BP 2180, Yaoundé-Messa

Ozila, Cameroun Literary Workshop, BP 73, Yaoundé
A 'little magazine' edited by Jean-Pierre Togolo and published by the Cameroun Literary Workshop

Central African Republic

General Information

Language: French, Sangho
Religion: Christian and animist
Population: No reliable figures available; perhaps about 2 million
Bank Hours: 0700-1200 Monday-Saturday
Shop Hours: 0700 or 0800-1200 or 1230, 1430 or 1500-1830 or 1900 Tuesday-Saturday, mostly
Currency: CFA franc
Export/Import Information: Member of Customs and Economic Union of Central Africa. No tariff on books; advertising has 7.5% Fiscal Duty, 30% Customs Duty and 10% Turnover Tax. Import licence required but granted automatically for imports from EEC countries. Imports subject to quotas. Exchange controls outside franc zone
Copyright: Berne (see International Section)

Publishers

Government Printer (Imprimerie Centrale d'Afrique)*, BP 329, Bangui

Major Booksellers

Au Messager*, BP 823, Bangui
Librairie **Hachette***, BP 823, Bangui
Librairie évangélique*, BP 240, Bangui
Papeterie Centrale*, BP 1442, Bangui
'Papyrus'*, BP 920, Bangui

Major Libraries

Centre culturel français*, Bibliothèque, BP 971, Bangui Tel: 2927

Bibliothèque de l'**Université Jean-Bédel Bokassa**, BP 1450, Bangui Tel: 612000
National Library

Chad

General Information

Language: French
Religion: Muslim in north, Christian or animist in south
Population: 4.3 million
Bank Hours: 0700-1200 Monday-Saturday
Shop Hours: 0700 or 0800-1200 or 1230, 1430 or 1500-1900 Tuesday-Saturday
Currency: CFA franc
Export/Import Information: No tariff on books; total duty and taxes on advertising matter is 40%. Consumption tax on children's picture books and advertising 10%. Import licences required except for imports from the EEC and the Franc Zone. Import Turnover Tax of 10% on advertising.
Copyright: Berne (see International section)

Publishers

Government Printer*, BP 69, N'Djamena

Major Booksellers

Georges **Abtour** SA, Librairie-Papeterie*, BP 103, N'Djamena

Bielmas Librairie-Papeterie*, BP 71, N'Djamena

Librairie **Billeret***, BP 463, N'Djamena

Librairie évangélique*, BP 127, N'Djamena

Librairie **Notre Dame***, BP 7, N'Djamena Tel: 3330

Major Libraries

Bibliothèque paroissiale, Cathédrale Notre-Dame, BP 456, N'Djamena Tel: 3350
Parochial Library

Centre culturel américain, Bibliothèque*, BP 3, N'Djamena Tel: 2846

Centre culturel français, Bibliothèque*, BP 901, N'Djamena Tel: 2920

Centre de Documentation Pédagogique, Bibliothèque*, BP 731, N'Djamena
Tel: 2327

Bibliothèque de l'**Université du Tchad***, BP 1117, N'Djamena Tel: 2176

Chile

General Information

Language: Spanish
Religion: Roman Catholic
Population: 10.9 million
Literacy Rate (1970): 88.1% (92.4% Urban, 72.8% Rural)
Bank Hours: 0900-1400 Monday-Friday; 0900-1200 Saturday
Shop Hours (Santiago): 1500-1900 Monday; 1000-1900 Tuesday-Friday; 0900-1300 Saturday
Currency: 100 centavos = 1 peso
Export/Import Information: Member of Latin American Free Trade Association. Ad valorem duty for books generally 20% (children's picture books 40%, atlases 30%); advertising matter 40%. Advertising material dutiable if not sent in envelopes, no more than 2 lb. 6% Sales Tax on advertising.
Copyright: UCC, Berne, Buenos Aires (see International section)

Book Trade Organizations

Cámara Chilena del Libro*, Ave Bulnes 188, Casilla 2787, Santiago Tel: 81519
Chilean Publishers' Association
Secretary: A Neumann

Book Trade Reference Journal

Anuario de la prensa chilena (Yearbook of Chilean Publications), National Library, Ave Bernardo O'Higgins 651, Santiago

Publishers

Aguilar Chilena de Ediciones, subsidiary of Aguilar SA de Ediciones, Spain (qv)

Editorial Andrés **Bello**/Juridíca de Chile, Ave Ricardo Lyon 946, Casilla 4256, Santiago Tel: 40041 Cable Add: Edibel
General Manager: Carlos Ducci Claro;
Editorial: Mercedes Gaju Vallés;
Commercial: Francisco Hoyl Sotomayor;
Publicity: María Teresa Herreros
Subjects: Medicine, History, Social Science, Literature Law
Bookshop: Librería Andrés Bello, Huérfanos 1158, Santiago Tel: 722116
Book Club: Club de Lectores 'Andrés Bello'
1978: 80 titles *1979:* 127 titles *Founded:* 1947

Centro Latinoamericano de Demografía (CELADE), Edificio Naciones Unidas, Ave Dag Hammarskjöld, Casilla 91, Santiago Tel: 283206
Dir: Juan Carlos Elizaga
Branch Off: Apdo 5249, San José, Costa Rica
Subjects: Demography, Statistics, Sociology, Periodicals

Editorial Gustavo **Gili** Ltda*, Santa Beatriz 120, Santiago
Parent Company: Editorial Gustavo Gili SA, Spain (qv)

Grijalbo y Cía Ltda*, Casilla 180-d, Santiago
Parent Company: Editorial Grijalbo SA, Spain (qv)

Editorial **Jurídica** de Chile, see Editorial Andrés Bello

Editora Nacional Gabriela **Mistral** Ltda*, Ave Santa María 076, Santiago Tel: 779522
Man Dir: José Harrison de la Barra; *Sales & Publicity Dir:* Jorge Sims Sn Roman
Subjects: Literature, Biography, History, Philosophy, Reference, Religion, How-to, Art, Juveniles, Secondary & Primary Textbooks
Miscellaneous: Government-owned

Editorial **Mundo Nuevo***, Pasaje Matte 342 of 16, Santiago Tel: 381646
Manager: Servando Salgado R

Editorial **Nascimento** SA*, Chiloe 1433, Casilla 2298, Santiago Tel: 569405 Cable Add: Nascimento
Man Dir: Carlos George-Nascimento Marquez
Subjects: General Fiction & Nonfiction, Scholarly Books
Bookshop: Librería Nascimento, San Antonio 390 Tel: 32062
Founded: 1898

Editorial del **Pacifico** SA*, Alonso Ovalle 766, Casilla 3547, Santiago Tel: 397805/395317
General Manager: Arturo Valdes Phillips; *Editorial:* Lidio Ramirez Rivera; *Sales:* Jose de Gregorio Aroca; *Production:* Emilio Pot Von; *Publicity:* Mrs Magali Zamorano Castro; *Rights & Permissions:* Raul Zamora Messina
Associate Company: Ediciones Mar del Sur, Casilla 13844, Santiago
Subsidiary Company: Distribuidora Alonso Ovalle Ltda
Subjects: History, Politics, Economics, Literature, Educations, Primary, Secondary and University Textbooks
1978: 21 titles *Founded:* 1946

Ediciones **Paulinas***, Vicuña MacKenna 6299, Casilla 3429, Santiago Tel: 212832
Orders to: Centro Catequistico Paulino, Cienfuegos 60, Casilla 3429, Santiago Tel: 64650
Subjects: Catholic texts
Bookshop: Librería San Pablo, Ave Bernardo O'Higgins 1626, Santiago, Centro Catequistico Paulino, Cienfuegos 60, Santiago; Branches in Antofagasta, Concepción & Valparaiso

Pineda Libros*, Bandera 101, Casilla 13556, Santiago Tel: 721807
Man Dir: A Gonzalo Pineda
Subjects: Literature, History, Juveniles, Paperbacks
Bookshops: Pergola del Libro: Merced 838; Bandera 101 (both in Santiago)
Founded: 1944

Editorial **Pomaire** Ltda, Merced 152 P2, Santiago
Manager: Jorge Barros T
Parent Company: Editorial Pomaire, Spain (qv)

Editorial El **Sembrador**, Casilla 2037, Santiago (Located at: Sargento Aldea 1041, Santiago) Tel: 569454
Dir, Editorial: Isaías Gutiérrez V
Bookshop: Librería El Sembrador (at above address)

Editorial **Universitaria**, Maria Luisa Santander 0447, Casilla 10220, Santiago Tel: 234555 Cable Add: Edunsa
Man Dir: Eduardo Castro LeFort
Subjects: General Literature, General & Social Science, Technical, Textbooks
Founded: 1947

Ediciones **Universitarias** de Valparaiso, Casilla 1415, Valparaiso (Located at: Universidad Católica de Valparaiso, Dr Montt Saavedra 44, Valparaiso) Tel: 59105/52900 Telex: Ucval 30389
Man Dir, Editorial: Renato C Flores; *Production:* L A Briones Solis
Branch Off: Moneda 673, 8° piso, Santiago Tel: 383137
Subjects: General Literature, Social Sciences, Engineering, Education, Music & Arts, Textbooks, Children's Books
Founded: 1970

Empressa Editora **Zig-Zag** SA, Casilla 84-D, Santiago (Located at: Amapolas 2075, Santiago) Tel: 235766 Telex: 455 Sgo
General Manager: Rodrigo Castro Cuevas

Book Club

Club de Lectores 'Andrés **Bello**', Lyon 946, Casilla 4256, Santiago
Members: 20,000
Owned by: Editorial Andrés Bello
Specialization: Children's Books
Founded: 1979

Studio Book Club, Casilla 1227, Santiago (Located at: Andres de Fuenzalida 36, Santiago) Tel: 259432/465799 Cable Add: Studio Telex: 40084 Studi Cl
Members: 200
Owned by: Elise Friedler Librería Studio
See also under Booksellers

Major Booksellers

Librería Andrés **Bello**, Huérfanos 1158, Santiago Tel: 722116
Manager: Carlos Ducci Claro

Cooperativa del Libro*, José Miguel Infante 22, Santiago Tel: 461747

Librería y Editorial **Cultura***, Huérfanos 1179, Santiago Tel: 88830

Feria Chilena del Libro*, Huérfanos 1112, Santiago Tel: 721420

Librería **Tecno-Ciencia***, Huérfanos 972 of 409, Casilla 367, Santiago Tel: 64975

Librería **Universitaria***, Ave Bernardo O'Higgins 1050, Casilla 10220, Santiago Tel: 84135

Librería **Orellana***, Esmeralda 1148, Valparaiso Tel: 51821

Librería **Parera***, Condell 1202-1206, Valparaiso Tel: 57162

Librería **Pax**, Carlos Cesarman Ltda, Casilla 1499, Santiago (Located at: Calle Huérfanos 770, Santiago) Tel: 393822

Librería **San Pablo***, Ave Bernardo O'Higgins 1626, Casilla 3746, Santiago Tel: 89145

Librería El **Sembrador***, Pasaje Matte 342-344, Casilla 2037, Santiago Tel: 396675/35295 (two other branches in Santiago, and one in Arica)

Librería **Studio**, Andrés de Fuenzalida 36, Santiago Tel: 259432/465799 Cable Add: Studio Telex: 40084 Studi Cl
Manager: Elise Friedler Weiss
Branch in Valparaiso (Viña de Mar)

Major Libraries

Biblioteca Nacional, Ave Bernardo O'Higgins 651, Santiago Tel: 381151

Biblioteca Nacional de Chile de la Dirección de Bibliotecas, Archivos y Museos, Santiago
National Library of the Office of Libraries, Archives & Museums
Dir: Enrique Campos Menendez
Publications: Anuario Bibliográfico, Referencias Críticas de Autores Chilenos, Mapocho

Biblioteca del **Congreso** Nacional*, Huérfanos 1117 — 2° piso, Clasificador 1199, Santiago
Library of Congress
Dir: Jorge Ivan Hübner Gallo; *Librarian:* Jose Miguel Vicuña Lagarrigue
Publications include: Boletin bibliográfico; Efimeros

Biblioteca del **Instituto** Chileno-Británico de Cultura, Casilla 3900, Santiago Tel: 382156

Biblioteca Central de la **Universidad Católica de Chile***, Ave Bernardo O'Higgins 340, Santiago Tel: 224236
Dir: María Teresa Sanz
Publications: Bibliografía Eclesiástica Chilena; Presentación del trabajo escrito

Biblioteca de la **Universidad Católica de Valparaiso***, Casilla 4059, Valparaiso

Biblioteca Central de la **Universidad de Chile***, Calle Arturo Prat 23, Santiago

Biblioteca Central de la **Universidad de Concepción***, Casilla 1807, Concepción

Library Associations

Centro Nacional de Información y Documentación (CENID)*, Casilla 297-V, Santiago (Located at: Canada 308, Santiago)

Colegio de Bibliotecarios de Chile*, Diagonal Paraguay 383, Torre II, Departamento 122, Casilla 3741, Santiago
Chilean Library Association
President: Maria Teresa Sanz
Publications: Boletin del Colegio de Bibliotecarios de Chile, Noticias del Colegio, Indices de Publicaciones Periodicas en Bibliotecología

Library Reference Books and Journals

Books

Guía de Bibliotecas y Centros de Documentación de Chile (Guide to Chilean Libraries and Centres of Documentation), National Centre of Information and Documentation, Casilla 297-V, Correo 21, Santiago

Journals

Indices de Publicaciones Periodicas en Bibliotecología (Catalogue of Periodical Publications on Librarianship), Chilean Library Association, Diagonal Paraguay 383, Torre II, Departamento 122, Casilla 3741, Santiago

Literary Associations and Societies

Sociedad de Bibliófilos Chilenos*, Casilla 895, Santiago
Secretary: Ramón Eyzaguirre
Publication: El Bibliófilo Chileno (annual)

Literary Periodicals

El Bibliófilo Chileno (The Chilean Bibliophile), Society of Chilean Bibliophiles, Casilla 895, Santiago

Mapocho, Editorial Universitaria, Maria Luisa Santander 0447, Casilla 10220, Santiago

Revista Chilena de Literatura (Chilean Review of Literature), Editorial Universitaria, Maria Luisa Santander 0447, Casilla 10220, Santiago

Taller de Letras (Workshop of Letters), Editorial Universidad Católica, Diagonal Oriente 3300, Santiago

Literary Prizes

Andrés **Bello** Prize
Founded in 1979 to encourage new Chilean literature. A prize of $US5,000, and publication of the novel, to be awarded every two years commencing 1980. Enquiries to Editorial Andrés Bello, Lyon 946, Casilla 4256, Santiago

People's Republic of China

General Information

Language: Chinese: a single written language is used by speakers of several diverse spoken dialects. The most important spoken form is Mandarin, known in the People's Republic as *Putonghua* (= generally understood speech), which has been adopted as the national language of China. Other important spoken forms are Wu, Fukienese, Cantonese, Hakka and Amoy-Swatow
Religion: Atheistic state
Population: 933 million
Shop Hours: Generally 0900-1900 daily
Currency: 10 fen = 1 chiao; 10 chiao = 1 yuan
Export/Import Information: Foreign trade is a state monopoly. The foreign distributor for Chinese publications is Guozi Shudian, PO Box 399, Peking. The importing organization is Waiwen Shudian, PO Box 88, Peking

Book Trade Reference Journal

Quan guo xin shu mu bian ji bu (Chinese National Bibliography), Bei Zong Bu Hu Tong 33 Hao, Peking

Publishers

China Youth Publishing House*, Peking
Subjects: Literature, Journals
Founded: 1953

Chung Hua Book Co*, Peking
Subject: Chinese Classics

Commercial Press*, 36 Wang Fu Jing St, Peking
Subject: Foreign translations

Foreign Languages Press*, Peking 37
Subjects: Languages, Translations

Hsinhua New China Book Agency*, Peking
Subjects: All

National Minorities Publishing House*, Peking
Subject: Books in languages spoken by minorities in China

People's Literature Publishing House*, Peking and Shanghai

People's Sports Publishing House, Peking
Chief Executive: Xu Cai
Subjects: Sport books (including Chinese boxing, Washu), Periodicals

Publishing Department*, Peking
Special agency of the State Council; undertakes the major part of book publishing in China

Renmin-Jiyou-Chuban-She*, Peking
Subject: Education
People's Education Publishing Co

'Sanlian Shudian' Publishing House*, Peking
A state publishing house; general, political and literary

Workers' Press*, Peking
Publishing house of All China Federation of Trade Unions

Writers' Publishing House*, Peking
A state enterprise publishing reprints of Chinese literature

Youth Publishing House*, Peking

Major Booksellers

Guozi Shudian, China Publications Centre, PO Box 399, Peking (Located at: Chegongzhuang Xilu 21)
Distributor abroad for Chinese publications

Waiwen Shudian*, PO Box 88, 38 Suchou Hutung, Peking
Importer for foreign publications

Major Libraries

The Library of **Academia Sinica***, 9 Wang Fu Ta Chei, Peking

Beijing Tu Shu Guan, Peking 7
National Library of Peking
Director: Liu Ji-ping

Chekiang Library*, Hangchow

Chung-kuo k'o hsueh yuan t'u shu kuan*, 3 Wen-chin-chieh, Peking
Central Library of the China Academy of Sciences
Director: Tung Tseng-kung

Chungking Library*, Chungking

Chungshan Library of Kwangtung Province, Canton

Liaoning Library*, Shenyang (Mukden)

Nan-ching t'u shu kuan*, Nanking, Kiangsu Nanking Library

Pei-ching ta hsueh t'u shu kuan*, Peking
Peking University Library
Director: Guo Song-nian
Includes the Library School

Qinghua Daxue Tushuguan, Peking
Qinghua University Library

Shanghai Library, 325 Nanjing Rd, Shanghai
Director: Ku Ting-lung

Yunnan Provincial Library*, Kunming
Director: Mo Tien-Chuang

Literary Periodicals

Chinese Literature (English and French editions), Foreign Languages Press, Peking 37. Subscriptions to Guozi Shudian, PO Box 399, Peking

China (Taiwan)

General Information

Language: Chinese: a single written language is used by speakers of several diverse spoken dialects. The most important spoken form is Mandarin, known in Taiwan as *Kuo-Yü* (= national tongue). Other important spoken forms in Taiwan are Amoy-Swatow (also called Taiwanese) and Fukienese
Religion: Confucianism, Buddhism, Taoism, Christianity
Population: 7.6 million
Literacy Rate (1956): 45.5%
Bank Hours: 0900-1200 Monday-Friday; 0900-1530 Saturday
Shop Hours: 0800-1700 Monday-Saturday
Currency: 100 cents = 1 new Taiwan dollar
Export/Import Information: No tariffs on books and advertising. Import licences required; exchange available when licence presented at authorized bank
Copyright: No copyright conventions signed

Book Trade Reference Books and Journals

Books

Books on China 1980: A Cumulative List with Descriptions of Original and Reprinted Western-Language Titles Available from Taiwan, Chinese Materials Center Inc, PO Box 22048, Taipei, Taiwan

Journals

Chinese National Bibliography (text in Chinese and English), National Central Library, 43 Nan Hai Rd, Taipei

Shu mo chi kan (Bibliography quarterly), (text in Chinese), Student Book Co Ltd, 298 Roosevelt Rd, 3rd Section, Taipei

Publishers

Business Publications Ltd*, PO Box 58432, Taipei (Located at: Hui Feng Bldg 3rd/4th Fl, No 20 Lane 14 Chi Lin Rd, Taipei) Tel: 5216457/5218784 Cable Add: Andypandy Telex: 21032 Andy
Man Dir: Michelle Yang; *Editorial:* Nigel

White; *Sales, Publicity:* Hellen Tsai; *Production:* Dawn Chen; *Rights & Permissions:* Mark Van Roo
Associate Companies: Andy Pandy Pty Ltd (Hui Feng Bldg 3rd Fl); Business English Center (4th Fl)
Subjects: International Business, Business English Textbooks, Business Dictionary (English/Chinese), Periodical Magazine: *Current Business Affairs in Taiwan and International Trade*
Bookshop: (at above address)
1978: 5 titles *1979:* 10 titles *Founded:* 1978

Cheng Chung Book Co*, 20 Hengyang Rd, Taipei
Subjects: Academic

Ch'eng Wen Publishing Company, PO Box 22048, Taipei
Subjects: Scholarly, General Interest (in Chinese and English)

Chung Hwa Book Co Ltd, 94 Chungking S Rd, Section 1, Taipei 100 Tel: 3117365/3117344/3113541 Cable Add: 2821 Taipei
Man Dir: D S Hsiung; *Sales Dir:* C C Ku; *Publicity Dir:* Mrs S M Sun
Subjects: General Fiction, Belles Lettres, Poetry, Biography, History, How-to, Music, Art, Philosophy, Reference, Religion, Juveniles, Low- & High-priced Paperbacks, Medicine, Psychology, Engineering, General & Social Science, University, Secondary & Primary Textbooks, Educational Materials
1979: 235 titles *Founded:* 1911

Eastern Publishing Co Ltd*, 121 Chungking S Rd, Section 1, PO Box 7052, Taipei
Subjects: Geography, Atlases, Agriculture, General Technology

Far East Book Co, 66-1 (10th Floor) Chungking S Rd, Section 1, Taipei Tel: 3312022 Cable Add: 1418 Taipei
Manager: Peter Y K Pu
Subjects: Art, Education, History, Physics, Dictionaries, Shakespeare in translation

Fu-Hsing Book Co*, 44 Huai Ning St, Taipei
Subject: Textbooks

Great China Book Corporation*, 66 Chungking S Rd, Section 1, Taipei
Subject: Textbooks

Hua Kuo Publishing Co*, 6 Lane 180, Section 1, Ho-ping East Rd, Taipei
Publisher: T F Wang
Founded: 1950

San Min Book Co*, 77 Chung Ching S Rd, Section 1, Taipei
Subjects: History, Philosophy, Sociology

Tah Chung Book Co*, 37-1 Chung Shan N Rd, 2nd Section, Taipei
Subjects: Health, Music, Physics, Technical, Economics

World Book Co*, 99 Chungking S Rd, Section 1, Taipei

Yee Wen Publishing Co Ltd*, PO Box 969, Taipei
(Surburban Office Address: 14 Shiao-Chien St, Panchiao, Taipei, Taiwan 220) Tel: (02) 9616321

Major Booksellers

Chinese Materials Center Inc, PO Box 22048, Taipei
International distributor

J Cynthia Co Ltd*, PO Box 24-92, Taipei, Taiwan 106

Great Publications Co Ltd*, PO Box 58213, Taipei

H C Ling Book Store & Co Ltd*, PO Box 322, Taipei, Taiwan 100

Literature House Ltd, 6th Fl, 192 Ho-Ping East Rd — Sec 1, Taipei
Importer

Mei Ya Publications Inc (Sueling, Inc), PO Box 22555, Taipei Tel: 3923191
Specialize in College and University textbook reprints (all copyrighted)

The **National Book** Co*, 84-5 Sec 3, Sing Sung South Rd, Taipei

Southeast Book Co*, 105 Po Ali Rd, Taipei

Taipei Publications Trading Co, PO Box 59326, Taipei
Manager: Y C Huang

Win Join Book Co Ltd, PO Box 22, 32 Taipei (Located at; 105 Ho-Ping East Rd — Sec 1, Taipei) Tel: 3934063/3419646/3914280 Telex: 26985 Jetwin
Manager: Mrs M C Tasy Lin

Major Libraries

Fu Ssu-Nien Library Institute of History and Philology, Academia Sinica, Taipei

Kuomintang Central Committee Library*, Taipei

National Central Library, 43 Nan Hai Rd, Taipei Tel: 3147320/9 (Office of the Director); 3147322 (Reference Section)
Librarian: Chen-Ku Wang

National War College Library*, Yangmingshan, Taipei

Taipei Municipal Library*, Hsin I Rd, Section 4, Taipei

Taiwan Branch Library, National Central Library*, 1 Hsinshen South Rd, Section 1, Taipei, Taiwan 106
Librarian: Henry H S Jeng

Library Associations

Library Association of China, c/o National Central Library, 43 Nan Hai Rd, Taipei
Executive Dir: Karl M Ku
Publications: Library Association of China Newsletter (quarterly in Chinese); *Bulletin of the Library Association of China* (annually in Chinese)

Library Science Society, c/o Department of Library Science, National Taiwan University, Roosevelt Rd — 4th Section, Taipei
President: Prof Chien Hou
Publication: T'u-Shü-Kuan Hsüeh-K'an (Bulletin of Department of Library Science, National Taiwan University); Chinese, partly in English

Library Reference Journals

Chung-kuo t'u-shu-kuan hsueh-hui hui-pao (Bulletin of the Library Association of China), National Central Library, 43 Nan Hai Rd, Taipei

Journal of Library and Information Science, National Taiwan Normal University, Department of Social Education, Taipei

Literary Associations and Societies

China National Association of Literature and the Arts*, No 4, Lane 22, Ningpo St West, Taipei

National Council of Ethnographic Arts and Literature of China*, 11 Terrace 5, Lane 5, Section 3, Jan-Ai Rd, Taipei

Literary Periodicals

Counter Attack, National Institute for Compilation and Translation, 247 Keelung Rd, Taipei

Tamkang Review, a journal mainly devoted to comparative studies between Chinese and foreign literatures (text in English), Tamkang College, Graduate Institute of Western Languages and Literature, King-Hua St, Taipei

Yeh ko (Evensongs) (text in Chinese or English), Tamkang College, English Department Evening School, Evensongs Association, No 5, Lane 199, King-hua St, Taipei

Translation Agencies and Associations

National Institute for Compilation and Translation*, 247 Keelung Rd, Taipei
Dir: Tien-Ming Wang
Publication: Counter Attack

Colombia

General Information

Language: Spanish (English widely used in business)
Religion: Roman Catholic
Population: 25 million
Literacy Rate (1973): 80.8% (88.8% of urban population, 65.3% rural)
Bank Hours: 0900-1500 Monday-Friday
Shop Hours: 0900-1230, 1430-1830 Monday-Saturday
Currency: 100 centavos = 1 peso
Export/Import Information: Member of Latin American Free Trade Association. 7.5% value added taxes on all imports; no sales tax on books. Ad valorem: none generally on books except 50% on books bound in leather or similar materials, 50% on photonovels of thrillers, detective stories etc, and horoscopes, 10% on children's picture books, 10% on atlases. Advertising catalogues 45%. No import licence for books. Exchange licence from Banco de la Republica required
Copyright: UCC, Buenos Aires (see International section)

Book Trade Organizations

Asociación de Escritores de Colombia*, Carrera 5a No 8-47, Bogotá
Association of Colombian Writers

Asociación Nacional de Autores de Obras Didacticas (AUCOLDI)*, Calle 14 No 12-15, Of 508, Bogotá Tel: 349845
National Association of Authors of Textbooks and Teaching Materials

Cámara Colombiana de la Industria Editorial, Carrera 7a, No 17-51 Oficinas 409 y 410, Apdo 8998, Bogotá Tel: 821117/428403
Colombian Publishers' Association
Executive Secretary: Hipólito Hincapié
Publication: Libros Colombianos

Cámara Colombiana del Libro*, Carrera 50, 52-126 of 411, Medellín Tel: 425714; Carrera 54, 52-15P3 Tel: 457778
Colombian Book Association

Standard Book Numbering Agency, Centro Regional para el Fomento del Libro en America Latina y el Caribe, Apdo Aéreol 7438, Bogotá (Located at: Calle 70 No 9-52)

Book Trade Reference Books and Journals

Books

Guia de Editoriales, Distribuidores y Librerias de Bogotá, CERLAL, Calle 70 No 9-52, Apdo 17438, Bogotá

Journals

Anuario Bibliográfico Colombiano 'Rubén Pérez Ortiz' (Colombian Bibliographical Annual), Instituto Caro y Cuervo, Apdo Aéreo 51502, Bogotá

Bibliografia Oficial Colombiana (Official Colombian Bibliography), Escuela Interamericana de Bibliotecología, Universidad de Antioquia, Apdo Aéreo 1226, Medellín

Libros Colombianos (Colombian Books), Colombian Publishers' Association, Apdo 8998, Bogotá

Publishers

Aguilar Colombiana de Ediciones*, Calle 13 7-40, Bogotá Tel: 432046
Man Dir: Gustavo de Florza
Parent Company: Aguilar SA de Ediciones, Spain (qv)

Editorial **Bedout** SA*, Apdo Aéreo 760, Medellín (Located at: Calle 61 No 51-04, Medellín) Tel: 316900 Cable Add: Bedout
President: Manuel de Bedout del Valle; *Editorial:* Hernando Londoño Arango; *Sales Dir:* Miguel Angel Rojas; *Production:* Libardo Maya Upegui; *Publicity:* Fabio Arango Saraz
Branch Offs: Ave Jiménez 9-47, Bogatá DE, Plaza de Caicedo, Edificio Lloreda Of No 301, Cali; Calle 45 No 36-50, Barranquilla; Carrera 51 No 61-27, Medellín
Subjects: Literature, Social Science, Textbooks, Juveniles
1978: 90 titles *Founded:* 1889

Editorial **Bruguera** Colombiana Ltda*, Calle 18 No 8-64, Bogotá Tel: 429610
Man Dir: Antonio Mourin
Parent Company: Editorial Bruguera SA, Spain (qv)

Instituto **Caro y Cuervo**, Apdo Aéreo 51502, Bogotá Tel: 557753
Man Dir: José Manuel Rivas Sacconi
Subjects: Belles Lettres, Linguistics, Philology, Reference
Bookshops: Librería Yerbabuena, Carrera 11 No 64-37, Bogotá; Librería Cuervo, Calle 10 No 4-77, Bogotá
1978: 25 titles *Founded:* 1942

Carvajal SA, Apdo Aéreo 46, Cali Tel: 681111 Cable Add: Carvajales Cali Telex: 055555/055650
Subsidiary Company: Editorial Norma (qv)
Subjects: Children's Pop-ups, Juveniles, Textbooks, Magazines

Fundación **Centro** de Investigación ed Educación Popular (CINEP)*, Carrera 5 No 33 A 08, Apdo Aéreo 25916, Bogotá Tel: 324440/698160
Man Dir, Rights & Permissions: Alejandro Angulo Novoa; *Sales Manager:* Gilberto Gómez Arango; *Production, Publicity:* María Cecilía de Roux de Salazar
Subjects: Colombian Politics & Economics, Sociology
Founded: 1959

Editorial La **Chispa** Ltda, Calle 26 No 25-61, Bogotá Tel: 2694362
Man Dir, Editorial: Jacobo Naidorf; *Sales:* Guillermo Marin; *Production:* Gerardo Rivas; *Rights & Permissions:* Ana Arango, Jorge Osorio
Associate Company: Ediciones Tiempo Presento, Apdo 10717, Bogotá
Imprint: Lachispa
Subjects: Literature, Sciences
1979: 18 titles *Founded:* 1979

Colombiana de Ediciones SA **Colediciones**, Carrera 22 No 36-63 — 1° piso, Bogotá Tel: 2690670/2854312 Cable Add: Colediciones
Man Dir, Editorial, Rights & Permissions: Carlos Senior Pava; *Sales:* Harold Valencia Salinas; *Production:* Guillermo Cajale Santacoloma
Subsidiary Companies: Arte Libros Editores (at above address); Servicio de Documentacion (SD), Ave 22 No 37-90, Apdo 101, Bogotá
Associate Company: Librerías Unidas Ltda, Ave 22 No 37-90 — Apdo 101, Bogotá
Branch Off: Colediciones Medellin, Calle 48 No 67-152, Bogotá
Subjects: The Family, Spiritualism, Sociology
Bookshop: Librería Ancora, Ave 22 No 37-90, Apdo 101, Bogotá
1978: 50 titles *1979:* 60 titles *Founded:* 1978

Cultural Colombiana Ltda*, Calle 72 No 16-15/21, Apdo Aéreo 6307, Nacional 2169, Bogotá Tel: 355494/483311/483236 Cable Add: Culbiana
Man Dir: José Porto; *Editorial:* Jose Porto Vazquez; *Sales Dirs:* Hernando Salazar; *Production:* Maximilian Gomez
Associate Company: Cultural Colombiana de Occidente Ltda
Subjects: Primary & Secondary Textbooks
Bookshop: Carrera 9a, 16-72
1978: 83 titles *Founded:* 1951
ISBN Publishers Prefix: 84-8273

Edinorma Ltda y Cía SCA*, Calle 37 No 13-08, Apdo Aéreo 53550, Bogotá Tel: 2851600/853297 Cable Add: Edinorma
President: Alberto José Carvajal: *General Manager:* Humberto Serna Gómez; *Editorial Dir:* Daniel Ordóñez
Subjects: Textbooks, Children's Books, Juveniles, General Interest, Magazines

Fondo Educativo Interamericano SA*, Apdo Aéreo 29696, Bogotá Tel: 258839/2492088 Cable Add: Adiwes Bogota Telex: 45581
Man Dir: Luis Felipe Martínez
Associate Company: Addison-Wesley Publishers Ltd, UK (qv for other associates)
Subjects: University Textbooks, School Texts, Trade Books
1978: 20 titles *1979:* 120 titles *Founded:* 1970
Miscellaneous: This is the editorial department of Fondo Educativo Interamericano, of Panamá

Editorial **Ipler** Ltda, Carrera 11 No 71-75, Bogotá Tel: 2559916
Man Dir: C Abel Barahona Castro; *Editorial:* Olga Flor Barahona Castro; *Sales, Production:* Carmento Paipillo; *Publicity:* Maria Cecilia de Morales

Subject: Scientific Works
Founded: 1978

Editorial **Juventud** Ltda*, Calle 63-A No 10-30, Bogotá 2 Tel: 481634
Man Dir: Santiago Preckler
Parent Company: Editorial Juventud SA, Spain (qv)

Editorial **Labor** Colombiana Ltda*, Carrera 16 No 30-25, Bogotá Tel: 698301
Man Dir: Enrique Fajardo
Parent Company: Editorial Labor, Spain (qv)

Lachispa, an imprint of Editorial La Chispa Ltda

Legislación Económica Ltda*, Ave Las Americas 58-51, Apdo Aéreo 8646, Bogotá Tel: 2605200 Cable Add: Legislación
Man Dir: Tito Livio Caldas
Subsidiary Company: Legislación Económica Srl, URB Industrial la Urbina, Calle 8, Edifico Lec, Caracas, Venezuela
Subjects: Economics, Law, Commerce
Founded: 1952

Ediciones **Lerner** Ltda*, Ave Jiménez de Quesada 4-35 y Calle 8-A-No 68-A-41, Bogotá Tel: 430567/623-505/720/986 Cable Add: Edilerner Telex: 43195
Man Dir: Salomon Lerner Mutzmajer; *Editorial:* Jack A Grimberg; *Sales:* A Londono
Subjects: Literature, History, Medicine
Bookshop: address as above
Founded: 1959

Editorial **McGraw-Hill** Latinoamericana SA*, Calle 60 No 15-99, Apdo Aéreo 11255, Bogotá Tel: 2351952/2357741
Man Dir: Daniel Waingart; *Editorial:* Michael Bates
Subjects: Engineering, Technology, Biology, Physics, Chemistry, Mathematics, Psychology, Sociology, Textbooks

Editorial **Norma** y Cia SCA*, Calle 37 No 13-08, Apdo Aéreo 53550, Bogotá Tel: 453152/2851600 Cable Add: Edinorma Telex: 44855
Man Dir: Humberto Serna G; *Editorial:* D Ordonez, J Camacho; *Sales:* G Mateus C; *Production:* A Martinez (Infants and Juveniles), J Bonfante (School Textbooks)
Parent Company: Carvajal SA (qv)
Subsidiary Company: Publicar Ltda
Branch Offs: Bogotá, Cali, Medellín, Barranquilla, Cartagena, Manizales, Ibaqué, Neiva, Bucaramanga, Cúcuta
Subjects: General, Juveniles, Primary & Secondary Textbooks, Education
Founded: 1964

Papusa Ltda, Calle 26 No 13A-23 — piso 7, Bogotá Tel: 2825692 Telex: 0441302
Man Dir: Jaime Muñoz Polit; *Editorial:* Amanda Quijano; Ignacio Montealegre
Parent Company: Ediciones Libra SA, Matias Romero 1221, Mexico 12, DF
Subsidiary Companies: Dinalpusa; Janibi Editores: each at Matias Romero 1221, Mexico 12, DF
Associate Companies: Munoz Hnos SA, General Aguirre 166 y 10 de Agosto, Quito, Ecuador; Distribuidora Inca SA, Emilio Altahus, Lima, Peru
Subjects: Teaching of Music (Books, Periodicals)
Book Club: Guitarra Facil
1978: 12 titles *1979:* 15 titles *Founded:* 1977

Editorial **Pluma** Ltda, Apdo Aéreo 345, Bogotá (Located at: Carrera 22 No 35-45, Bogotá) Tel: 453458/853942
Man Dir: Ernesto Gamboa Morales; *Editorial:* Luis Guillermo Sorzano; *Sales:* Raul Kollmann; *Production:* Vilma Ripoll; *Publicity:* Amelia Sardo; *Rights &*

COLOMBIA

Permissions: Consuelo Herrera
Subsidiary Company: Robles
Iberoamericana de Ediciones, Peligros 2 —
8° piso, Madrid 14, Spain
Associate Company: Indice Ltda, Carrera 22
No 35-45, Bogotá
Subjects: Psychology, Sexology, Economics,
Politics, Literature
1978: 36 titles *1979:* 14 titles *Founded:* 1976

Editorial **Pomaire** SA*, Carrera 20 No 53-47, Apdo Aéreo 51042, Bogotá
Parent Company: Editorial Pomaire, Spain
(qv)

Editorial **Presencia** Ltda, Calle 23 No 24-50, Bogotá Tel: 2681634/2681817/2682241
Man Dir, Publicity: Alberto Umaña
Carrizosa; *Editorial:* Carlos Marulanda
Gomez; *Sales:* José Antonio Umaña;
Production: Luis Mendoza; *Rights &
Permissions:* Alberto Umaña
Subsidiary Companies: Ediciones
Contemporanea, Carrera 4A No 25B-12, Bogotá; El Mural, Carrera 4A No 25B-12, Bogotá

Siglo XXI Editores de Colombia Ltda*, Apdo Aéreo 19434, Bogotá
Man Dir: Alberto E Diaz
Parent Company: Siglo XXI de España, Editores SA, Spain (qv)
Associate Company: Siglo XXI Editores SA, Mexico (qv)
Subjects: Anthropology, Sociology, Psychology, History, Fiction, Linguistics, Art, Architecture, Politics, Philosophy
Founded: 1966

Editorial **Temis** Ltda*, Calle 13 No 6-45, Apdos 5941 y 12008, Bogotá 1 Tel: 2694721/2699235/2445297
Cable Add: Editemis
Man Dir: Jorge Guerrero; *Sales Dir:* Erwin Guerrero Pinzon
Subject: Law
Bookshop: Librería Temis Ltda, Calle 13, No 6-45, Bogotá
1978: 52 titles *Founded:* 1951
ISBN Publisher's Prefix: 84-8272

Ediciones **Tercer** Mundo Ltda*, Carrera 30 No 42-32, Apdo Aéreo 4817, Bogotá Tel: 695129/695149 Cable Add: Tercer Mundo
Man Dir: Luis Carlos Ibáñez
Subjects: General Literature, Social Science
Founded: 1961

Vertice Ltda, Apdo Aéreo 41137, Bogotá DE1 Tel: 2437113/2822748
General Manager: Jesus Antonio Villa
Parent Company: Calle 13 No 7-80 — of 629-30, Bogotá DE1
Subjects: History, Literature, Law, Agriculture, Art, Economics & Finance
Founded: 1980

Voluntad Editores Ltda y Cía SCA*, Carrera 13 No 38-99, Apartado 4692, Bogotá Tel: 325520 Cable: Voluntad
President: Samuel de Bedout; *Vice-president:* Gastón de Bedout; *Vice-president of Sales:* Luis Obregon; *Vice-president Finance:* Guillermo Fernandez
Branches: Barranquilla, Bucaramanga, Cartagena, Cali, Cúcuta, Manizales, Medellín, Montería, Ibaque, Valledupar, Tunja, Neiva, Pasto, Pereira, Villavicencio; Voluntad Publishers Inc, 7800 Shoal Creek Blvd, Austin, Texas, USA
Subjects: Kindergarten, Primary and Secondary Textbooks
Bookshops: Voluntad Editores Carrera 13, 38-99 Bogotá
1978: 290 titles *Founded:* 1930
ISBN Publisher's Prefix: 84-8270

Book Clubs

Circulo de Lectores*, Calle 57 No 6-35 — 4° piso, Bogotá Tel: 555676/555976

Guitarra Facil, Calle 26 No 13A-23 — piso 7, Bogotá Tel: 2825692
Owned by: Papusa Ltda (qv)

Major Booksellers

Librería **Aguirre***, Calle 53 No 49-123, Medellín Tel: 424268 Cable Add: Laguirre

Librería **América***, Calle 51 No 49-58, apdo 11-92, Medellín Tel: 412878

Librería **Buchholz***, Ave Jiménez 8-40, Bogotá Tel: 341309/415896/426350

Librería **Casa del Libro***, Calle 18 No 6-43, Bogotá Tel: 432668

Librería La **Gran Colombia***, Calle 18 No 6-30, Bogotá Tel: 421359/411755

Librería del **Ingeniero***, Ave Jiménez 7-45, Apartado aéreo 14825, Bogotá
Tel: 412507/823610/343260

Librería **Lerner***, Ave Jiménez 4-35, Bogotá Tel: 347826/430567

Librería **Central***, Calle 16 No 6-34, Bogotá Tel: 426767

Librería **Continental***, Carrera 50 No 52-06, Medellín Tel: 414948

Librería **Cultural Colombiana***, Calle 72 No 16-15, Bogotá Tel: 483236/483306
Also at Carrera 9a No 16-72, Bogotá

Librería **Nacional**, Carrera 5a No 11-50, Cali Tel: 731250

Librería **San Pablo***, Carrera 9 No 15-01, Bogotá Tel: 2433653/2345036
Also at Calle 57 No 13-71, Bogotá Tel: 494167

Librería del **Seminario***, Calle 57 No 49-44, Medellín, Antioquia Tel: 428374
Distributors

Librería **Temis** Ltda*, Calle 13 No 6-45, Bogotá Tel: 423035/413325

Librería **Tercer Mundo***, Carrera 30 No 42-32, Bogotá Tel: 695129/695149

Major Libraries

Biblioteca Luis-Angel **Arango***, Banco de la República, Calle 11 No 4-14, Bogotá
Tel: 439100

Archivo Nacional de Colombia, Biblioteca Nacional*, Calle 24 No 5-60 — 4° piso, Bogotá

Biblioteca Nacional de Colombia*, Calle 24 No 5-60, Apdo Aéreo 27600, Bogotá
Tel: 414029

Biblioteca y Centro Nacional de Documentación Pedagógica, Sección de Servicios Bibliotecarios*, Apdo Nacional 8475, Bogotá
National Centre of Educational Documentation

British Council Library*, Apdo Aéreo 4682, Bogotá (Located at: Calle 11 No 5-16, Bogotá 1) Tel: 2438181/2438184/2814922

Universidad de los Andes*, Calle 18-A Carrera 1-E, Bogotá

Universidad Nacional de Colombia, Biblioteca Central*, c/o Hugo Parra Acq Libr, Apdo Aéreo 14490, Bogotá DE

Library Associations

Asociación Colombiana de Bibliotecarios*, Calle 10 No 3-16, Apdo Aéreo 30883, Bogotá Tel: 825798
Colombian Library Association
Executive Secretary: Beatriz de Tabares
Publication: Boletín

Bibliotecarios Agricolas Colombianos*, c/o Biblioteca de Tibaitata, Apdo Aéreo 7984, Bogotá DE
Agricultural Librarians of Colombia
Secretary: Hector Galeano

Colegio de Bibliotecarios Colombianos*, Apdo Aéreo 3212, Bogotá
Association of Colombian Librarians
President: Martha Valencia H
Publication: Boletín Informativo

Departamento de Bibliotecas*, Universidad de Antioquia, Apdo Aéreo 1226, Medellín

Library Reference Books and Journals

Books

Bibliografía Bibliotecológica, Bibliográfica y de Obras de Referencia Colombianas (Bibliography of Library Science, Bibliography and Colombian Works of Reference), Universidad de Antioquia, Apdo Aéreo 1226, Medellín

Journals

Boletín (Bulletin), Colombian Library Association, Calle 10 No 3-16, Apdo Aéreo 30883, Bogotá

Boletin Cultural y Bibliografico (Cultural and Bibliographical Bulletin), Biblioteca Luis-Angel Arango, Banco de la República, Calle 11 No 4-14, Bogotá

Boletín Informativo (Information Bulletin), Association of Colombian Librarians, Apdo Aéreo 3212, Bogotá

Boletin Informativo y Bibliografico (Informative and Bibliographical Bulletin), Universidad de Narino, Biblioteca Central, Apdo Aéreo 505, Nacional 75, Narino

Literary Associations and Societies

Centro Filosófico-Literario*, Apdo Nacional 298, Manizales

P E N Internacional de Escritores de Colombia*, Apdo Aéreo 51557, Bogotá
President: José María Acosta Acosta;
Secretary: Hernando Torres Neira
PEN International of Colombian Writers

Literary Periodicals

Letras Nacionales (National Letters), Calle 17, 7-71, Of 401, Bogotá

Razón y Fábula (Reason and Fiction), Universidad de los Andes, Apdo Aéreo 4976, Bogotá

Literary Prizes

'Revista Vivencias' and the Instituto Colombiano de Cultura have annual prizes

Colombian Novel Contest Awards
For stimulating Colombian writers. 100,000 Colombian pesos. Awarded annually.
Enquiries to Universidad del Valle, Apdo Aéreo 2188, Cali

Cordoba Stories Prizes*
For stimulating and developing literary tastes. Diploma plus three prizes of 5,000, 3,000 and 2,000 Colombian pesos. Awarded annually. Enquiries to Cordoba Department, Secretary of Education, Montaria

National Story Prize*
For promoting literary development in Colombia. Diploma plus three prizes of 6,000 Colombian pesos, 3,000 pesos and 1,000 pesos. Awarded annually. Enquiries to University Day School of Colombia, Student Cultural Group 'El Candil', Carrera 16 No 24-25, Bogotá

Pamplona and its Culture Prize*
For stimulating a liking for reading in children. Awarded annually. Enquiries to Pedro de Orsua Public Library, Pamplona

José Ma **Vergara** y Vergara Prize*
For Colombian authors, to promote literary development. Diploma plus 10,000 Colombian pesos. Awarded annually. Enquiries to Colombian Ministry of National Education, Bogotá

Popular Republic of Congo

General Information

Language: French
Religion: Traditional animist religions, Roman Catholicism
Population: 1.46 million
Bank Hours: 0700-1130 Monday-Saturday
Shop Hours: 0700 or 0800-1200 or 1300, 1500-1700 or 1730 Tuesday-Friday; 0700 or 0800-1200 or 1300 Saturday
Currency: CFA franc
Export/Import Information: Member of Customs and Economic Union of Central Africa. 10% VAT on all goods, but goods for schools, the army, the police and health authorities are exempt. Import licences required for all goods. Favourable terms for imports from EEC countries
Copyright: Berne (see International section)

Publishers

Government Printer*, BP 58, Brazzaville

Société congolaise **Hachette***, BP 919, Brazzaville
Subjects: General Fiction, Belles Lettres, Education, Juveniles, Textbooks

Major Booksellers

Librairie **Hachette***, BP 2150, Brazzaville Tel: 2302

Librairie **Populaire***, BP 2212, Brazzaville

Maison de la Presse, Société congolaise Hachette*, BP 2150, Brazzaville

Office national des Librairies*, BP 577, Brazzaville

Major Libraries

Bibliothèque nationale populaire*, BP 114, Brazzaville Tel: 811287
Librarian: Francis Abaraka

Centre culturel français, Bibliothèque*, BP 2141, Brazzaville Tel: 3852

Ecole normale supérieure de l'Afrique centrale, Bibliothèque*, BP 237, Brazzaville Tel: 4454

Bibliothèque universitaire, **Université Marien Ngouabi**, BP 2025, Brazzaville Tel: 811430
Dir: François Wellot-Samba
Publications: Dimi; Annales; Repertoire d'auteurs congolais; Revue d'histoire anthropologie
Also other lists and catalogues

Library Associations

Direction générale des **Services** de Bibliothèques, Archives et Documentation*, BP 114, Brazzaville
General Management of Library, Archives and Documentation Services

Costa Rica

General Information

Language: Spanish
Religion: Roman Catholic
Population: 2.11 million
Literacy Rate (1973): 88.4%
Bank Hours: 0800-1100, 1330-1500 Monday-Friday; 0800-1100 Saturday
Shop Hours: 0800-1200, 1400-1800 Monday-Saturday (some close Saturday afternoon)
Currency: 100 centimos = 1 colon
Export/Import Information: Catalogues $0.03 per gross kg; other advertising material dutied at $1.50 per gross kg + 25% ad valorem. 10% Consumption Tax + 20% Exchange Surcharge on advertising. No import licences, but statistical recording prior to importation necessary. Imports over $300 must be registered with Banco Central to be eligible for foreign exchange allocation
Copyright: Berne, UCC, Buenos Aires (see International section)

Book Trade Reference Journal

Anuario bibliográfico costarricense (Costa Rican Annual Bibliography), Costa Rican Association of Librarians, Apdo 3308, San José

Publishers

Editorial **Costa Rica***, Apdo 10010, San José Tel: 234875/239303
Subject: Literature of Costa Rica
Founded: 1959

Editorial Universitaria Centroamericana (EDUCA), Apdo 64, Ciudad Universitaria 'Rodrigo Facio', San José (Located at San Pedro de Montes de Oca, San José) Tel: 258740/243727 Cable Add: Cosuca Educa
Editorial Dir, Publicity: Lic Julio Escoto;
Sales: Rodrigo Ortiz Astúa (International), Rodrigo Ortiz Astúa (National &
International); *Production:* Alvaro Gómez Astúa
Subjects: Science, Art, Philosophy
1978: 185 titles *Founded:* 1969
ISBN Publisher's Prefix: 84-8360

Instituto Centro Americano de Administración Pública (ICAP), Dpto de Publicaciones, Apdo 10025, San José
Dir: Carlos Cordero d'Aubuisson
Subject: Technical
Founded: 1954

Instituto Interamericano de Ciencias Agricolas (IICA)*, Dpto de Publicaciones, Turrialba

Librería Imprenta y Litografía **Lehmann** SA, Ave Central, Apdo 10011, San José
Tel: 231212 Telex: 2540 Lill Eh
Man Dir: Antonio Lehmann Struve;
Publicity: Orlando Mora
Subjects: General Fiction & Non-fiction
Bookshop: Librería Imprenta y Litografía Lehmann SA, Ave Central, Apdo 10011, San José Tel: 231212
Founded: 1894

Ministerio de Cultura*, Juventud y Deportes, Dpto de Publicaciones, Apdo 10227, San José
Subject: Literature in general
1978: 10 titles

Universal Librería, Imprenta y Fotolitografia (Carlos Federspiel & Co) SA*, Ave Fernández Guell 42-E, Apdo 1532, San José Tel: 222222
Subject: Textbooks

Editorial **Universidad** de Costa Rica, Universidad de Costa Rica, San José Tel: 247957
Dir: Mario Segura Vargas

Major Booksellers

Librería Universal Carlos **Federspiel***, Ave Fernández Guell 42-E, Apdo 1532, San José Tel: 222222

Librería Imprenta y Litografía **Lehmann** SA*, Ave Central, Apdo 10011, San José Tel: 231212

Librería **Trejos**, Calle 11-13, Ave Fernández Guell, Apdo 1313, San José Tel: 217055

Major Libraries

Biblioteca Nacional, Apdo 10008, San José (Located at: Calle 15 y 17, Ave 3 y 3 Bis, San José)
Dir: Carmen Quirós Saborío

Biblioteca del **Centro** Cultural Costarricense-Norteamericano, Apdo 1489, San José
International Communication Agency Library

Biblioteca de la **Universidad de Costa Rica***, Apdo 3862, Ciudad Universitaria Rodrigo Facio, San José Tel: 257372
Publications: Lista de tesis de grado de la Universidad de Costa Rica no 1- 1958-; *San Pedro de Montes de Oca* (Serie de bibliotecología, no 12-14, 19-20, 22-25)

Library Associations

Asociación Costarricense de Bibliotecarios*, Apdo 3308, San José
Secretary-General: Nelly Kopper
Costa Rican Association of Librarians
Publication: Boletín

Colegio de Bibliotecarios de Costa Rica*, C/o Lupita Rodriguez Mendez, Encargada de Biblioteca, Instituto de Fomento Asesoria Municipal, San José
Library Association of Costa Rica

Library Journals

Boletín (Bulletin), Costa Rican Association of Librarians, Apdo 3308, San José

Literary Prize

Aquileo T **Echeverria** Prize*
For Costa Rican citizens who have excelled in the fields of literature (novel, short story, poetry, essay, scientific literature); history; theatre; music; fine arts. 40,000 colones divided between the selected works. Total sum of awards cannot exceed 8,000,000 colones. Awarded annually. Enquiries to Costa Rican Ministry of Culture, Youth and Sport, General Directorate of Arts and Letters, San José

Cuba

General Information

Language: Spanish
Religion: Roman Catholic predominantly; no established church
Population: 9.7 million
Literacy Rate (1953): 75.8%
Bank Hours: 0800-1200, 1415-1615 Monday-Friday; 0800-1200 Saturday
Currency: 100 centavos = 1 peso
Export/Import Information: Control of all import and export by Ministry of Foreign Trade; books imported and exported by Ediciones Cubanas, Apdo 605, Havana. No commercial advertising permitted in Cuba; brochures etc must be sent to the appropriate foreign trade organization. Exchange controlled by National Bank of Cuba
Copyright: UCC, Florence (see International section)

Book Trade Organizations

Unión de Escritores y Artistas de Cuba*, Calle 17 No 351, Vedado, Havana
Union of Writers and Artists of Cuba
Administrative Secretary: Benvenido Suarez

Book Trade Reference Journals

Revolutionary Cuba; a bibliographical guide, University of Miami Press, Coral Gables, Florida, USA (annual)

Publishers

Casa de las **Américas***, G y Tercera, Vedado 3, Havana
Dir: Roberto Fernández Retamar
Subject: Latin American Literature, *Música* (monthly)
Founded: 1960

Editorial **Arte** y Literatura, Calle G No 505, Plaza de la Revolución, Havana
Dir: Abel E Prieto
Subjects: Art, Literature
1978: 86 titles *1979:* 83 titles *Founded:* 1967

Ediciones **C O R***, Revolutionary Orientation Commission of the Communist Party, Havana
Subject: Politics

Editorial **Ciencias Sociales***, Calle 14 No 4104e Mendoza y 43, Playa, Havana
Dir: Marcos Luit Lescailles
Subject: Social Sciences
1978: 152 titles

Editorial **Científico** Técnica*, Calle 2 No 58e 3 y 5, Vedado, Havana
Dir: Jorge Luis Victorero Gonta
Subjects: Science, Engineering
1978: 34 titles

Consejo Nacional de Cultura*, O'Reilly 126, Havana
President: Eduardo Muzio
Subjects: Art, Fiction, Periodicals

Editorial **Gente Nueva***, Calle 8 No 469e 19 y 21, Vedado, Havana
Dir: Elenia Rodríguez Oliva
Subject: Social Sciences
1978: 100 titles

Instituto Cubano del Libro*, Belascoaín 864, Apdo 6540, Havana
Dir: Rolando Rodríguez
Subject: Government Publications
Founded: 1967

Editorial **Letras Cubanas***, Calle G No 505e 21 y 23, Vedado, Havana
Dir: Pablo Pacheco López
Subject: Literature
1978: 86 titles

Editorial **Orbe***, Calle 17 No 1057e 12 y 14, Vedado, Havana
Dir: Humberto González Borduy
1978: 92 titles

Editorial **Oriente***, José Antonio Saco 356, Santiago
Dir: Reinaldo Cuesta Reina
1978: 34 titles

Editorial **Pueblo** y Educación*, Calle 15 No 604e B y C, Vedado, Havana
Dir: Ana María Santana Romero
Subject: Education
1978: 370 titles

Ediciones **Revolución***, Plaza Cívica, Havana
Subjects: Art, Culture

Universidad Central de la Villas, Carretera de Camajuani*, Km 10, Santa Clara
Subjects: Academic

Universidad de la Habana*, Apdo 3060, Havana 3 Tel: 325238/328815
Subjects: Academic
Founded: 1934

Major Booksellers

Ediciones **Cubanas**, Apdo 605, Havana (Located at: Empresa de Comercio Exterior de Publicaciones, O'Reilly 407, Havana)
The organization for book importation and exportation

Major Libraries

Academia de Ciencias de la República de Cuba*, Biblioteca Central, Capitolio Nacional, Havana

Archivo Histórico Municipal de la Habana*, Plaza de Catedral, Havana

Biblioteca Histórica Cubana y Americana*, Municipio de la Habana, Oficina del Historiador de la Ciudad, Havana

Biblioteca Nacional José Martí*, Plaza de la Revolución, Apdo Oficial 3, Havana
Tel: 73613
National Library
Publications: Revista de la Biblioteca Nacional José Martí; Boletín Bibliotecas; Bibliografía Cubana; Indice General de Publicaciones; Trabajos de Investigación

Biblioteca del **Colegio de Belén***, Apdo 221, Marianao, Havana

Biblioteca 'José Antonio **Echeverría**'*, Casa de las Americas, Tercera y G, Vedado, Havana

Biblioteca del **Instituto de Literatura** y Linguistica*, Salvador Allende 710, Havana

Biblioteca del **Instituto Pre-universitario** de la Habana*, Zulueta y San José, Havana
Library of the Pre-University Institute of Education

Biblioteca del **Museo de Zoologia***, 42 No 3307, Marianao 13, Havana

Biblioteca 'Manuel **Sanguily**'*, Ministerio de Relaciones Exteriores, Calzada y G, Vedado, Havana

Biblioteca General de la **Universidad Central** de las Villas*, Santa Clara, Las Villas

Biblioteca Central 'Rubén Martínez Villena' de la **Universidad de la Habana**, Havana

Biblioteca Central de la **Universidad de Oriente**, Carretera de Cuabitas, Santiago

Library Associations

Colegio Nacional de Bibliotecarios Universitarios*, c/o National Library, Plaza de la Revolucion, Havana
National Association of University Librarians

Library Reference Books and Journals

Books

Guía de Bibliotecas y Centros de Documentación de la República de Cuba (Guide to Libraries and Centres of Documentation of Cuba), National Library, Plaza de la Revolución, Apdo Oficial 3, Havana

Journals

Bibliotecas (Libraries), National Library, Plaza de la Revolución, Apdo Oficial 3, Havana

Cuba Bibliotecológica (Cuban Library Science), Colegio Nacional de Bibliotecarios Universitarios, c/o National Library, Plaza de la Revolución, Apdo Oficial 3, Havana

Revista de la Biblioteca Nacional José Marti (Review of the National Library), National Library, Plaza de la Revolución, Apdo Oficial 3, Havana

Literary Periodicals

Taller Literario (Literary Workshop), Universidad de Oriente, Escuela de Letras, Santiago de Cuba

Union, Union of Writers and Artists of Cuba, Calle 17 No 351, Vedado, Havana

Cyprus

General Information

Language: Greek and Turkish (English widely spoken)
Religion: Greek Orthodox and Muslim (among Turks)
Population: 616,000
Literacy Rate (1960): 74.5%
Bank Hours: 0830-1200 Monday-Saturday
Shop Hours: Winter: 0830-1300, 1430-1730 Monday-Friday; 0800-1300, Saturday Summer 0800-1300, 1600-1830 Monday-Friday; 0800-1300 Saturday
Currency: 1000 mils = 1 Cyprus pound
Export/Import Information: No tariffs on books or advertising matter. No import licence specially required. Exchange control administered by Central Bank of Cyprus
Copyright: Berne, Florence (see International section)

Book Trade Organisations

Cyprus Booksellers Association*, Hatzisavva Bldg, Evagora Ave, Box 1455, Nicosia Tel: 49500/62312
Secretary: Panikos Michaelides

Book Trade Reference Journals

O Kosmos Tou Kypriakou Vivliou (The World of Cypriot Books), (text in Greek), MAM, PO Box 1722, Nicosia

Publishers

M A M, PO Box 1722, Nicosia Tel: (21) 72744
Subjects: Various, specialising in publications about Cyprus and works by Cypriot authors
Bookshop: PO Box 1722, Nicosia
Miscellaneous: authorized distributors of Cyprus Government publications and works about Cyprus, and of publications by United Nations agencies and major international organizations

Major Booksellers

Arcane Bookshop, 15 Saripolou St, PO Box 373, Limassol Tel: (051) 63541

Hellenic Distribution Agency (Cyprus) Ltd*, 1-9 Kostis Palamas St, Nicosia Tel: (021) 73662

A Joannides & Co, 30-32 Athens St, PO Box 141, Limassol Tel: (051) 62204
Manager: A Joannides
Bookshops: 30-32 Athens St, Limassol; Archbishop Makarios III Ave 147, Limassol

K P Kyriakou (Books — Stationery) Ltd, PO Box 159, Limassol (Located at: 3 Grivas Digenis Ave, Panagides Bldg, Limassol) Tel: 68508 Cable Add: Cybooks Telex: 3392 Prc Cy
Man Dir: Kyriakos P Kyriakou

M A M, PO Box 1722, Nicosia Tel: (21) 72744
Specializes in publications about Cyprus and works by Cypriot authors. Authorized distributors of Cyprus Government publications and of publications of international organizations

K **Rustem** & Bro*, 24 Kyrenia St, Nicosia Tel: (021) 2681 Cable Add: Rustem Br 4
Iakovou **Yiannakis***, 22 Greg Xenopoulous St, Nicosia Tel: (021) 52197 Cable Add: Vivliopolis

Major Libraries

Library of the **Archbishopric***, PO Box 1130, Nicosia

British Council Library*, PO Box 1995, Nicosia (Located at: 3 Museum St, Nicosia) Tel: 42152/3

Library of the **Cyprus Museum**, PO Box 2024, Nicosia

Ministry of Education Library*, Didaskalikon Megaron, Archbishop Makarios III Ave, Nicosia

Municipal Library*, PO Box 41, Famagusta

Municipal Library*, Limassol

Library of the **Paedagogiki Academia***, Nicosia

Library of **Phaneromeni***, PO Box 1637, Nicosia

Sultan's Library, Evcaf, Nicosia

Turkish Public Library*, 49 Mecediye St, Nicosia

Library Association

Cyprus Library Association*, PO Box 1039, Nicosia Tel: 402310
Secretary: Paris G Rossos

Library Journals

Deltion Vivliothikarion (Library Bulletin), Cyprus Library Association, PO Box 1039, Nicosia

Czechoslovakia

General Information

Language: Czech in Bohemia and Moravia, Slovak and Hungarian in Slovakia. Russian is common second language
Religion: Roman Catholic and Protestant
Population: 15 million
Bank Hours: 0800-1400 Monday-Friday
Shop Hours: 0900-1200, 1400-1800 Monday-Friday; most open half day Saturdays
Currency: 100 haler = 1 koruna
Export/Import Information: Import policy administered by Federal Ministry of Foreign Trade. Appropriate corporations for book importation are Artia, Prague 1, Ve Smečkách 30, or Slovart, Bratislava, Gorkého 17. Exchange control administered by State Bank
Copyright: UCC, Berne (see International section)

Book Trade Organizations

Výtvarná služba **Českého fondu** výtvarných umělcu, sekce krásné knihy a grafiky*, Prague 1, Nové Město, třída Politických vězňu 7
Creative service of the Czech Fund for Creative Artists, Section for the Well-designed book and Prints

Ministerstvo kultury CSR, Odbor knižní kultury*, Prague 1, Staré Město, Na Perštýně 1
Czechoslovak Ministry of Culture, Department for Publishing and Book Trade

Slovenské ústredie knižnej kultúry*, Bratislava, nám SNP 12
Slovak Centre for Publishing and Book Trade

Společnost pro krásné písmo a typografii*, Prague 1, Malá Strana, Riční 5
Association of Design and Typography

Svaz českých spisovatelu*, 11147 Prague 1, Národní trída 11
Union of Czech Writers
Chairman: Dr Jan Kozak
Publication: Literáarní městčnik (literary monthly)

Zväz slovenských spisovateľov, 89008 Bratislava, ul Obrancov mieru 14
Union of Slovak Writers
Chairman: Andrej Plávka

Book Trade Reference Books and Journals

Book

Books in Czechoslovakia, a survey of Czech and Slovak publishers, book-museums and important libraries, Czechoslovak Ministry of Culture, Prague 1, Staré Město, Na Perštýně 1

Journals

Bibliografický katalog CSSR (Czech National Bibliography), consisting of: *Ceské knihy* (Czech Books), State Library of the CSSR, 11000 Prague 1, Klementinum 190 (weekly); *Slovenská národná bibliografia* (Slovak National Bibliography), Slovak National Library, 13601 Martin, Mudrónova 13 (monthly); *Ceské hudebniny* (Czech Music), State Library of the CSSR, 11000 Prague 1, Klementinum 190 (quarterly); *Slovenské hudebniny* (Slovak Music), State Library of the CSSR, 11000 Prague 1, Klementinum 190 (annual)

Czech Books in Print, Artia, 11127 Prague 1, Ve Smečkách 30, PO Box 790

Nové knihy (New Books), Prague 1, Vézeňská 5

Slovak Books in Print, Slovart Ltd, Foreign Trade Company, Bratislava, Gorkého 17

Věda a knihy (Science and Books), Academia, 11229 Prague 1, Vodicková 40

Publishers

Academia, 11229 Prague 1, Vodičkova 40 Tel: 246241/8 Cable Add: Academybooks Prague
Publishing House of the Czechoslovak Academy of Sciences
Man Dir: Radoslav Švec; *Export Manager:* Mrs Z Svobodová; *Publicity & Advertising:* J Vinkler; *Rights & Permissions:* L Zapletal
Subjects: History, Philosophy, Psychology, Economy, Archaeology, Linguistics, Mathematics, Physics, Chemistry,

CZECHOSLOVAKIA

Engineering, Geology; Monographs and University Textbooks
Bookshop: Prague 1, Vodickova 40
Founded: 1953

Albatros, Prague 1, Ná Perštyně 1
Tel: 245151/6, 247741/6, 248851/6
Telex: 121605 Alba C
Man Dir: Václav Mikeš; *Sales, Publicity & Advertising:* Jiří Lapáček
Subject: Books for Children and Young People
Book Club: KMC — Young Readers' Club
Founded: 1949

Alfa — Vydavateľstvo technickej a ekonomickej literatúry, 89331 Bratislava, Hurbanovo nám 3 Tel: 331441/5 Cable Add: Alfa Bratislava
Publishers of technical and economic literature
Dir: Rudolf Schallerz; *Sales Dir:* Jozef Bednárik
Subjects: Engineering, General & Social Science, Special Dictionaries, University & Secondary Textbooks
Bookshop: Bratislava, Palackého ul 1
1979: 337 titles *Founded:* 1952
Miscellaneous: Sole importers of scientific and technical books from Western countries in Slovakia

Artia, 11127 Prague 1, Ve Smečkách 30, PO Box 790 Tel: 246041 Cable Add: Artiapublish Telex: 121065/122775
Foreign language publishers
Man Dir: Dr V Silar; *Sales Dir:* J Ruźićka
Subjects: Art Books, Books on Nature, Children's Books
1978: 41 titles *Founded:* 1953

Avicenum, zdravotnické nakladatelství, 11802 Prague 1, Malostranské nám 28 Tel: 530640
Czechoslovak Medical Press
Subject: Medicine
Founded: 1953

Nakladatelství **Blok**, 60000 Brno, Rooseveltova 4
Dir: Ivo Odehnal
Subjects: Belles Lettres, Fiction, Regional Literature

Československý spisovatel, 11147 Prague 1, Národní 9 Tel: 266941 Cable Add: Spisovatel Prague
Dir: Ivan Skála
Subjects: General Fiction, Belles Lettres, Poetry, Biography, Philosophy, Juveniles
Book Club: Klub Přátel Poezie (Club of the Friends of Poetry)
Bookshops: Prague 1, Národní 9; Brno, Česká 7 (both in Czechoslovakia)
Founded: 1949

Nakladatelství **Dopravy** a spoju*, 11578 Prague 1, Hybernská ul 5, Nové Město
Publishing House of the Ministry of Transport and Communications
Dir: Bohumil Klail
Subjects: Science & Technology, Transport

Kartografie NP*, 17029 Prague 7, Kostelní 42 Cable Add: Kartografie Prague
Man Dir: Adolf Chmelař; *Editorial Dir:* Dr I Caslavka
Orders to: Artia, Foreign Trade Corporation 11127 Prague 1, Ve Sméckách 30
Subject: Cartography
Founded: 1971

Kruh*, 50021 Hradec Králové, Klicperova 197 Tel: 22076/225458
Eastern Bohemian Regional Publishing House
Dir: Dr Josef Kubíček
Subjects: General Fiction, Biography, History, Music, Art, Low- & High-priced Paperbacks, Regional Literature
Founded: 1966

Landwirtschaftlicher Staatsverlag (Agricultural Publishing House), see Státní zemědělské nakladtelství

Lidové nakladatelství*, 11565 Prague 1, Václavské nám 36 Tel: 226383/5 Cable Add: Lidové Nakladatelství Prague
Publishing House of the Union of Czechoslovak-Soviet Friendship
Dir: F J Kolár
Subjects: General Fiction, Belles Lettres, Poetry, Biography, History, Philosophy, Juveniles, Low-priced Paperbacks, Social Science
Founded: 1968 (formerly Svět Sovětu)

Madáh*, Bratislava, Martarovicova 10
Publishing House for Books and Journals in the Hungarian Language
Subject: Books in Hungarian

Melantrich, 11212 Prague 1, Václavské nám 36 Tel: 260341 Cable Add: Melantrich Telex: 121422
Publishing House of the Czechoslovak Socialist Party
Man Dir: O Balabán; *Sales Dir:* K Voleský; *Editorial:* Ph Dr K Houba; *Production:* M Nevole
Subjects: Belles Lettres, Poetry, Biography, Philosophy, High-priced Paperbacks, Textbooks
Bookshop: Na příkopě 3, Prague 1
1981: 37 titles *1982:* 39 titles *Founded:* 1898

Mladá fronta, 11222 Prague 1, Panská 8 Tel: 224141 Telex: 00245
Publishing House of the Czechoslovak Union of Youth
Dir: Dr Kornel Vavrinčík
Subjects: General Fiction, Belles Lettres, Poetry, Biography, History, How-to, Music, Art, Philosophy, Juveniles, Low-priced Paperbacks
Founded: 1945

Mladé letá*, 89426 Bratislava, nám SNP 12 Tel: 50475 Telex: 93421 Cable Add: Mladéletá Bratislava
Young Years: Slovak Publishing House of Children's Literature
Man Dir: Rudo Móric; *Editorial:* Dr Juraj Klaučo; *Sales Dir:* Vlasta Strnadová; *Production:* Jan Columby; *Publicity:* Silvia Kršková; *Rights & Permissions:* Eva Hornišová
Subjects: Juveniles, Reference
Book Club: club of Young Readers
Bookshop: Detská Kniha (The Child's Book), Bratislava, Hurbanovo nám 7
1978: 228 titles *Founded:* 1950

Nakladatelství a distribuce knih **Naše Vojsko***, 12812 Prague 2, Na Děkance 3 Tel: 547241/8
Publishing and Distribution House of Czechoslovak Army
Dir: Dr Lubomír Baroš
Subjects: General Fiction, Medicine, Technical, Paperbacks, Juveniles, Military Science, Psychology, History, Aviation, Book Industry
Founded: 1945

Nakladatelství **Obelisk***, Prague 1, Mikulandská 10
Publishing House of Czechoslovak Artists
Man Dir: Jiří Dvořák
Subject: Art

Obzor, vydavateľstvo knih a casopisov národní podnik*, 89336 Bratislava, ul Ceskoslovenskej armády 29a Tel: 53021/57251 Cable Add: Vydavatelstvo Obzor Bratislava
Horizon: Slovak Book & Periodical Publishing House for People's Education
Dir: Ján Mojžiš (acting)
Subjects: General Fiction, Non-fiction, Encyclopaedias, Law, General Science, Textbooks, Paperbacks, Educational, Maps
Founded: 1953

Odeon, nakladatelství krásné literatury a umění, 11587 Prague 1, Národní 36 Tel: 247141 Cable Add: Odeon Praha
Publishing House of Literature and Art
Dir: Josef Kulíček; *Assistant Dir:* Dr Edvard Vonka; *Editorial:* Karel Boušek; *Sales:* Dr M Burkon; *Production:* M Filipová; *Publicity:* J Janovský; *Rights & Permissions:* Dr V Vocetková
Subjects: General Fiction, Belles Lettres, Poetry, Biography, Art, Reproductions
Book Club: Odeon Book Club
Bookshop: Knihkupectví Odeon Na Florenci 3, 11586 Prague 1
1978: 140 titles *1979:* 150 titles *Founded:* 1953

Nakladatelství CSTV **Olympia**, 11588 Prague 1, Klimentská 1 Tel: 61639 Cable Add: Olympia Prague
Publishing House of Sports and Tourism
Man Dir: Ludvík Uhlíř; *Sales Dir:* M Karas; *Publicity & Advertising:* D Suchánková
Subjects: Sports, Travel, Juveniles, Albums
Bookshop: Prague 1, Hybernská 34
1978: 59 titles *Founded:* 1954
Miscellaneous: Formerly Sportovní a turistické nakladatelství

Opus Records and Publishing House, 89923 Bratislava, Dunajská 18 Tel: 53241/50783/52665 Telex: 92219
Man Dir: Dr Ivan Stanislav; *Editorial:* Marian Jurík; *Publicity:* Pavol Fellegi; *Rights & Permissions:* Dr Oldrich Horák
Subject: Music
1978: 41 titles (including sheet music)

Nakladatelství **Orbis**, dissolved in 1977, part of activity taken over by Nakladatelství a vydavatelství Panorama (qv); name Orbis now attached to Press Agency

Osveta, 03654 Martin, Osloboditelov 21
Dir: Ján Krajč
Subjects: Education, Popular Sciences, Tourism, Medicine
1979: 104 titles

Vydavateľstvo SFVU **Pallas***, 88209 Bratislava, Štúrova 1/b
Publishing House of the Slovak Fund of Fine Arts
Subjects: Art, Literature, Biography

Nakladatelství a vydavatelství **Panorama**, PO Box 75, 12072 Prague 2, Hálkova 1 Tel: 245449 Cable Add: Panorama Prague II Telex: 122657
Man Dir: Dr František Hanzlík
Subjects: Popular Science, Local History, Picture Books, Law, Concise Encyclopedias, Travels, Juveniles, Periodicals, Postcards, Applied Arts, Publicity Materials
Founded: 1978
Miscellaneous: Formerly Orbis, nakladatelsví a vydavatelství, Vinohradská tř 46, Prague 2

Panton, 11839 Prague 1, Ríční 12 Tel: 538151/5 Cable Add: Panton
Publishers of the Czech Music Fund — Prague
Man Dir: Miloš Konvalinka
Subjects: Music (Instruction, Works, Biography, General), Juveniles, Educational Materials
Bookshops: Prague 1, Jungmanova 30; Brno, Ceská 14; Bratislava, Sedlářská 10
Founded: 1958

Peace and Socialism International Publishers, 16616 Prague 6, Thakurova 3 Tel: 325731/325132 Cable Add: Cssr Prag Srozt
Subjects: International Communist and Working-Class Movement (in English, French, German, Russian, Spanish),

CZECHOSLOVAKIA 71

Periodicals, including *World Marxist Review* (in 37 languages), *Information Bulletin* (in English, French, German, Spanish)

Vydavateľstvo ROH 'Práca'*, 89717 Bratislava, Obrancov mieru 19 Tel: 330838/333779/332347/93283 Telex: 93329
Publishing House of the Revolutionary Trade Union Movement
Dir: Ján Duži
Subjects: Trade Unions (history and contemporary studies), Labour Problems, Social Security, Ergonomics, Labour Law, Work Safety, Needlework Handbooks, Economics
Bookshop: Knizna predajna PRACA, 89717 Bratislava, nám SNP 20
1978: 60 titles *Founded:* 1946

Práce*, 11258 Prague 1, Václavské nám 17, Nové Město
Publishing House of the Czech Trade Union Movement
Dir: Vilém Kún
Subjects: Belles Lettres, How-to, General, Social & Political Science, Juveniles, Law, Engineering, Fiction, Non-fiction
Book Club: ERB
Founded: 1945

Pragopress*, Prague Tel: 224651 Cable Add: Pragobublish Praha
Subjects: Reprints, Facsimilies

Nakladatelstvo Pravda*, CS-88205 Bratislava, Gunduličova ul 12 Tel: 335574
Dir: Viliam Kačer
Subjects: Fiction, Biography, History, Political Science, Philosophy, Social Science, Law, Economics
Book Club: ČKP (Členská knižnica pravdy)
Miscellaneous: Firm is the publishing house of the Central Committee of the Communist Party of Slovakia

Príroda, vydavateľ' stvo kníh a časopisov, 89417 Bratislava, Krížkova 9 Tel: 47241
Dir: Vincent Šugár; *Editorial:* Ján Braun
Subjects: Agriculture, Veterinary Science, Biology, Husbandry, Forestry, Nature Protection, Phytopathology, Beekeeping, Mechanisation of Agriculture
1979: 253 titles *Founded:* 1949

Nakladatelství Profil*, 70100 Ostrava 1, Cihlářská 51 Tel: 53559, 55129
Northern Moravian Publishing House
Dir: František Cečetka
Subjects: General Fiction, Belles Lettres, Poetry, Biography, History, Music, Art, Reference, Juveniles, Social Science, Psychology
Founded: 1957

Nakladatelství ruže*, 37196 Ceské Budějovice, Zižkovo nám 5
Tel: 2250/5620/7693
Southern Bohemian Publishing House
Dir: František Podlaha
Subjects: General Fiction, Belles Lettres, History, Juveniles, Low-priced Paperbacks, Regional Literature
Founded: 1960

S N T L Nakladatelství technické literatury, 11302 Prague 1, Spálená 51 Tel: 295880
Man Dir: Ing Jindřich Sucharda; *Editorial:* Dr V Šesták
Subjects: Engineering and Applied Technology, Science, Economics, Dictionaries, Reference, Periodicals
Book Club: Klub čtenáŕu technické literatury (Club for Readers of Technical Literature), Prague 1, Spálená 51
Bookshop: Středisko technické literatury (Centre of Technical Literature), Prague 1, Spálená 51
1978: 443 titles *Founded:* 1895

Severoceské nakladatelství*, 40021 Ústí nad Labem, Velká Hradební 33
North Bohemian Publishing House
Dir: Jan Stuchl
Subjects: General Fiction, Belles Lettres, Poetry, Biography, History, Music, Art, Philosophy, Juveniles, General Science, Low-priced Paperbacks, Regional Literature
Founded: 1961

Slovenská kartografia NP, 82717 Bratislava-Krasňany, Pekná cesta 17 Tel: 82001/82020
Slovak Cartographic Publishing House
Dir: P Kmetko; *Editorial:* Zd Matula; *Sales:* L Caníga
Orders to: Slovart AG, 80532 Bratislava, Gottwaldovo na'm 6
1978/79: 20 titles *Founded:* 1957

Slovenské pedagogické nakladatelstvo, Bratislava, Sasinkova 5 Tel: 64551/3 Cable Add: Spn Bratislava
Slovak Publishing House for Educational Literature
Man Dir: František Mráz
Subjects: History, Music, Art, Psychology, General Science, University, Secondary & Primary Textbooks, Education, Reference
1979: 500 titles *Founded:* 1920

Slovenské vydavateľ'stvo podohospodarskej literatúry*, 80000 Bratislava, Krizková 7
Slovak Publishing House of Literature on Agriculture
Subjects: Agriculture, Biology, Industry, Veterinary Science

Vydavateľstvo Slovenskej Akademie Vied, see VEDA

Slovenský spisovateľ, 89728 Bratislava, Leningradská 2 Tel: 333922
Publishing House of the Slovak Literary Fund
Man Dir: Vojtech Mihálik; *Editorial:* Vladimír Dudáš; *Sales, Production:* Rudolf Pernica; *Publicity:* Anna Sigmundová; *Rights & Permissions:* Olga Peťková
Orders to: 89728 Leningradská 2
Subjects: General Fiction, Belles Lettres, Poetry, Literary Theory and Criticism
Book Clubs: SPKK — Spoločnosť priateľ'ov' krásnych kníh; KMP — Kruh milovníkov poézie; NST — Nová sovietska tvorba; Vavrín
Bookshop: Dom knihy, 89728 Leningradská 2, Bratislava
1978: 119 titles *1979:* 118 titles *Founded:* 1950

Smena*, 89714 Bratislava, Pražská 11
Tel: 48539/48541 Cable Add: Bratislava, Smena, 09341
Publishing House of Slovak Central Committee of Socialist Youth Union
Dir: Rudolf Belan
Subjects: General Fiction, Belles Lettres, Poetry, Biography, History, Philosophy, Low- & High-priced Paperbacks, Psychology, Social Science, Juveniles, Hobbies
Book Club: Máj, Bratislava, Prazská 11
Founded: 1949

Sport*, 89344 Bratislava, Vajnorská 100
Dir: Ing František Mikloš
Subject: Sport
Miscellaneous: Firm is the publishing house of the Central Committee of the Slovak Physical Culture Organization

Statisticke a evidencni vydavatelství tiskopisu*, 11000 Prague 1, Malá strana, Trziste 9
Publishing House of Statistics and Data
Subject: Reference

Státní pedagogické nakladatelství, 11301 Prague 1, Ostrovní 30, 1 Nově Město Tel: 203787 Cable Add: Stapena Prague
State Publishing House for Educational Literature
Man Dir: Ing Josef Papež
Subjects: History, Juveniles, Medicine, Psychology, Engineering, Social Science, Secondary & Primary Textbooks, Pedagogical Journals, Reference
Founded: 1775

Státní zemědělské nakladatelství*, 11311 Prague 1, Nové Město, Václavské náměstí 47 Tel: 226641
Agricultural Publishing House
Man Dir: Karel Koukal
Subjects: Agriculture, Forestry, Veterinary Science, Agronomy, Hobbies

Středočeské nakladatelství knihkupectví*, 11000 Prague 1, U Prašné brány 3
Central Bohemian Publishing House & Bookshop
Dir: František Pěkný
Subjects: Regional Literature, Fiction, General, Belles Lettres

Supraphon, Prague 1, Palackého ul 1 Tel: 268141 Cable Add: Supraphon Praha
Telex: 121218 Sunp
Publishing House of Music, Recordings, Sheet Music and Musicological Literature
Man Dir: Viktor Kašák; *Foreign Connections, Rights & Permissions:* Pavel Smola; *Editorial:* Dr Olga Šotolová; *Commercial Director:* Karel Arbes
Subject: Music
Bookshops: 150 branches
1978: 13 titles, 212 music sheets *1979:* 15 titles, 184 music sheets *Founded:* 1946

Svepomoc*, 11000 Prague 1, Gorkého nám 10, Nové Město
Publishing House of the Central Cooperative Council

Svoboda*, 11303 Prague 1, Revoluční 15
Tel: 66851
Dir: Evžen Palonczy
Subjects: History, Philosophy, Politics, Belles-Lettres
Book Clubs: Friends of Antiquity, Svobodq
Miscellaneous: Firm is the publishing house of the Central Committee of the Communist Party of Czechoslovakia

Tatran*, 89134 Bratislava, Michalská 9 Tel: 30141/3
Slovak Publishing House of Belles Lettres
Man Dir: Dr Anton Markuš; *Sales, Publicity & Advertising:* Margita Lehocká; *Rights & Permissions:* LITA, Slovak Literary Agency, Bratislava, ul Ceskoslovenskej armády 31/III
Subjects: Belles Lettres, Poetry, Art, Low-priced Paperbacks
Book Club: Hviezdoslavova knižnica
Bookshop: Tatran, Bratislava, Michalská 9
Founded: 1947

V E D A, vydavateľ'stvo Slovenskej akadémie vied, 89530 Bratislava, Klemensova 19 Tel: 563219 Cable Add: Veda Bratislava
Publishing House of the Slovak Academy of Sciences
Man Dir: Ing Miroslav Murín; *Editorial:* Dr Ján Jankovič; *Publicity Manager:* Terézia Zelenáková
Subjects: Technical Sciences, Natural Sciences, Linguistics, History, Archaeology, Philosophy, Psychology, Encyclopedias, Dictionaries
Bookshop: Kníhkupectvo SAV, 89530 Bratislava, Dunajská 5
Founded: 1953

Východoslovenské vydavateľ'stvo np, 04011 Košice 1, Alejová 3 Tel: 66736/65205/65206
Slovak Publishing House
Man Dir: Mikuláš Jáger

CZECHOSLOVAKIA

Subjects: Belles Lettres, History, Political Science, Juveniles, Regional Literature
1978: 36 titles *1979:* 35 titles *Founded:* 1960

Vyšehrad*, Prague 1, ul 28, řijna 3
Publishing House of the Czech People's Party
Subjects: The Works of Christian Writers and Poets, Czech History, Philosophy, Social Sciences

Západočeské nakladatelství*, 30100 Plzeň, Moskevská 36
Western Bohemian Regional Publishing House
Dir: Václav Brašna
Subjects: General Fiction, Belles Lettres, History, Regional Literature, Juveniles

Literary Agents

D I L I A, 12824 Prague 2, Vyšehradská 28, Post Box 34 Tel: 296651/5 Cable Add: Dilia Prag Telex: 121367 Dili C
Theatrical and Literary Agency
Contact: Robert Jurák

L I T A, 89420 Bratislava, ul Cs Armády 37 Tel: 55007 Cable Add: LITA Bratislava
Slovak Literary Agency: copyright organization representing Slovak authors in foreign transactions
Contact: Judr Matej Andráš

Book Clubs

C K P (Clenská knižnica Pravdy), CS-88205 Bratislava, Gunduličová ul 12
Members: 43,500
Owned by: Nakladatelstvo Pravda, Bratislava
Founded: 1958

Club of Young Readers, 89426 Bratislava, nám SNP 12
Owned by: Mladé letá, Bratislava

E R B*, 11258 Prague 1, Václavské nám 17, Nové Město
Owned by: Práce, Prague

Friends of Antiquity*, 11303 Prague 1, Revoluční 15
Owned by: Svoboda

Hviezdoslavova knižnica*, 89134 Bratislava, Michalská 9
Owned by: Tatran (Slovak Publishing House of Belles Lettres), Bratislava

K M C*, Prague 1, ná Perštýně 1
Club for Young Readers
Owned by: Albatros, Prague
Subject: Juveniles

K M P (Kruh milovníkov poézie)*, 89728 Bratislava, Leningradská 2
Club for Poetry Lovers
Owned by: Slovenský spisovatel', Bratislava

Klub čtenářů technické literatury*, 11302 Prague 1, Spálená 51
Club for Readers of Technical Literature
Supervised by: SNTL-Nakladatelství technické literatury (qv)
Subjects: Engineering and Applied Technology, Science, Dictionaries, Applied Economics

Klub přátel poézie*, 11147 Prague 1, Národní 9
Club of the Friends of Poetry
Owned by: Československý spisovatel, Prague

Máj*, 89714 Bratislava, Pražská 11
Owned by: Smena, Bratislava

N S T (Nová sovietska tvorba)*, 89728 Bratislava, Leningradská 2
Owned by: Slovenský spisovatel', Bratislava

Odeon Book Club, 11697 Prague 1, Celetna 11
Members: 200,000
Owned by: Odeon, Prague
Subject: Fiction

S P K K (Spoločnost' priatel'ov' krásnych kníh)*, 89728 Bratislava, Leningradská 2
Society of Friends of Beautiful Books
Owned by: Slovenský spisovatel', Bratislava

Svoboda Book Club*, 11303 Prague 1, Revoluční 15 Tel: 66851
Owned by: Svaboda (Prague)
Subjects: History, Philosophy, Politics, Belles Lettres

Vavrín*, 89728 Bratislava, Leningradská 2
Owned by: Slovenský spisovatel', Bratislava

Major Booksellers

Artia*, 11127 Prague 1, Ve Smečkách 30, PO Box 790 Tel: 246041
Import/export organization

Slovart Ltd*, 80532 Bratislava, Gottwaldovo nam 48
Import/export organization

Kniha (The Book)*, Prague 2, Nové Město, 6 Zitna
The central purchasing place for single bookselling businesses in Czechoslovakia

Major Libraries

Státní knihovna **České socialistické republiky**, 11001 Prague 1, Klementinum 190 Tel: (Main switchboard) 266541/267241; (Dir) 225192
State Library of the Czech Socialist Republic

Základní knihovna — ústředí vědeckých informací **Československé akademie věd***, 88618 Bratislava, Klemensova 19 Tel: 56321/51733 Telex: 93464
Main Library — Scientific Information Centre of Czechoslovak Academy of Sciences

Knihovna Národního muzea, 11579 Prague 1, Václavské nám 68 Tel: 269451/9
National Museum Library
Dir: Dr Jaroslav Vrchotka CSc
Publication: Sbornik Národního muzea v Praze, řada C-literární historie (quarterly)

Matica Slovenská*, 03652 Martin, Mudroňova 13 Tel: 31346-9/32184 Telex: 121207
Slovak National Library

Městská knihovna v Praze, 11572 Prague 1, nám primátora Dr V Vacka 1
The City Library of Prague

Památník národního pisemnictví, Strahovská knihovna, 11838 Prague 1, Strahovské nádvoří 132 Tel: 538841
Museum of National Literature, Strahov Library

Slovenská technická knižnica, Bratislava, Gottwaldovo nám 19
Slovak Technical Library

Státní technická knihovna, 11307 Prague 1, nám primátora Dr V Vacka 5
State Technical Library

Státní technická knihovna v Brně*, Brno, Veveří 95
State Technical Library in Brno

Státní vědecka knihovna*, Olomouc, Bezručova 2
State Scientific Library

Státní vědecká knihovna, 60187 Brno, Leninova 5-7 Tel: 58321 Telex: 62299
State Research Library
Librarian: Jaromír Trautmann

Universitná knižnica*, Bratislava, Michalská 1
University Library

Knihovny fakult a ústavu **University Karlovy***, Prague
Libraries of Faculties and Institutes of Charles University

Library Associations

Slovenská knižničná*, Ministerstvo kultúry SSR, Bratislava, Suvorovová 2
Slovak Library Council
Chairman: Dr S Pasiar

Ústřední knihovnická rada ČSSR*, Prague 1, Valdštejnká 30
Central Library Council of the Czechoslovak Socialist Republic
Secretary: Jaroslav Lipovsky
Publication: Knihovnik

Zväz slovenských knihovníkov a informatikov*, 88517 Bratislava, Michalská 1 Tel: 331151 Telex: 093255
Association of Slovak Librarians and Information Scientists
Executive Secretary: Ing Štefan Kimlička
Publication: Zväzový bulletin

Library Reference Journals

Journals

Československá akademie věd. Ustřední archiv. Archivní zprávy (Czechoslovak Academy of Sciences. Central Archives. Archival Reports), Academia, 11229 Prague 1, Vodickova 40

Čitatel (The Reader) (text in Slovak, summaries in German and Russian), Slovak National Library, 03652 Martin, Mudroňova 13

Informačný bulletin (Information Bulletin), Association of Slovak Librarians and Information Scientists, 88517 Bratislava, Michalská 1

Literary Associations and Societies

Kruh priatelov detskej knihy*, 89426 Bratislava, nám SNP12
Association of Friends of Children's Books in Slovakia

Matice Moravská*, Brno, Gorkého 14
Moravian Society of History and Literature
Secretary: Dr Bedřich Čerešňák
Publication: Časopis matice Moravské (quarterly)

Společnost přátel knihy pro mládež*, 11000 Prague 1, Na Perštýně 1
Association of Friends of Children's Books
Publication: Bulletin (irregular)

Index-Společnost pro Československou literaturu v zahraničí*, Postfach 410511, D-5000 Cologne 41, Federal Republic of Germany
Society for the Promotion of Czechoslovak Literature Abroad

Spolek Českých bibliofilu*, Prague, Nové Město, Václavské nám 39
Association of Czech Bibliophiles

Literary Periodicals

Červený Květ (The Red Flower), literature and art, Ostrava 1, Tyrsová 9

Česká literatura (Czech Literature) (text in Czech, summaries in English, French, German and Russian), Academia, Publishing House of the Czechoslovak Academy of Sciences, 11229 Prague 1, Vodičkova 40

Literarní měsíčnik (Literary Monthly), Union of Czech Writers, 11147 Prague 1, Národní třída 11

Novinky literatury (Literary News), State Library, 11001 Prague 1, Klementinum 190

Sborník narodního muzea v Praže rada C: literarni historie (Magazine of the National Museum, Prague. Series 3: Literary History) (title also in Latin, summaries in English, French, German and Russian), National Museum, 11579 Prague 1, Václavské nám 68

Slovenská literatúra (Slovak Literature) (contents page and summaries in German and Russian), Slovak Academy of Sciences, Institute of Slovak Literature, Bratislava, Klemensová 27

Slovenské pohlady na literatúru a uměnie (Slovak View on Literature and Art), Slovenský spisovatel', 89728 Bratislava, Leningradská 2

Slowakei (Slovakia), literary, scientific and political review, Matus-Cernak-Institut, Kulturelles Zentrum der Slowaken in Deutschland, D-5000 Cologne 1, Postfach 100924, Federal Republic of Germany

Svědectví (Czech literary journal published abroad), 6 rue du Pont de Lodi, Paris 6e, and Vienna V, Margaretenpl 7

Svetova literatura, review of foreign literature, Odeon, 11587 Prague 1, Národní 36

Literary Prizes

Bratislava Literary Prize*
For the best literary work relating to the town of Bratislava written during the preceding five years. Awarded annually. Enquiries to Bratislava City Council, Bratislava

Brno Literary Prize*
For the best book written and published in Brno. Awarded annually. Enquiries to Brno City Council, Brno

Frano **Kral** Prize*
For existing works or for outstanding achievements in the field of juvenile literature. The executive body of Frano Kral Prize is the Slovak Literary Fund, the Circle of Friends of Juvenile Literature and publishing house Mladé leta. The prize is awarded annually. Enquiries to Ministry of Culture of the Slovak Socialist Republic, Suvorova 16, Bratislava

Marie **Majerove** Prize*
The highest award for a life's work in the fields of Czech literature and art for children and young people. Awarded every other year. Enquiries to Association of Friends of Children's Books, 11000 Prague 1, Na Perštýně 1

Maladá fronta Award*
For literary works of prose, poetry, journalism, popular science also translations, published by Mladá fronta during the preceding year. Awarded annually. Enquiries to Mladá fronta (Young Front) Publishing House, 11222 Prague 1, Panská 8

Mladé letá Prize*
For the best book of juvenile literature. Awarded annually. Enquiries to Mladé letá (Young Years) Publishing House, 89426 Bratislava, nám SNP 12

Naše vojsko Prizes*
For a political book, a book on military theory and a book of fiction Monetary prize is divided between the winners in each category. Enquiries to Nakladatelství a distribuce knih Nase Vojsko (Publishing and Distribution House of Czechoslovak Army), 12812 Prague 2, Na Dekance 3

Prague Literary Prize*
For the best creative work which has enriched human knowledge, contributed to the construction of socialism and furthered the development of culture in the City of Prague. Awarded annually. Enquiries to Prague City Council, Prague

Denmark

General Information

Language: Danish (English and German widely spoken)
Religion: Lutheran
Population: 5.1 million
Bank Hours: 0900 or 1000-1500 or 1600 Monday-Thursday; open until 1800 Friday
Shop Hours: 0800 or 0900-1700 or 1730 Monday-Thursday; open until 1900 or 2000 Friday; open until 1400 Saturday
Currency: 100 øre = 1 krone
Export/Import Information: Member of European Economic Community. No tariff on books except children's picture books 10.4% from non-EEC. Advertising matter 7.2% from non-EEC. VAT 15%. No import licences required. Importers must use longest of alternative credit terms in contract, otherwise no exchange controls
Copyright: UCC, Berne, Florence (see International section)

Book Trade Organizations

Bog- og Papirbranchens Kreditor-Udvalg, Kompagnistr 11, DK-1208 Copenhagen K
Committee of Inspection for the Book and Paper Trade

Dansk Boghandlermedhjaelperforening*, Siljangade 6, DK-2300 Copenhagen S
Danish Book Trade Employees' Association
Publication: Bogormen

Dansk Bogtjeneste*, Rostrup Bogmarked, Østergade 20, DK-7400 Herning
Danish Collective Book Advertising Organization
Chairman: Frits Rostrup

Dansk Forfatterforening, Forfatternes Hus, Nyhavn 21, DK-1051 Copenhagen K
Danish Authors' Society (also represents interests of Danish book illustrators)
Chairman: Hans Jørgen Lembourn
Publication: Forfatteren (8 a year)

Danske Antikvarboghandlerforening, Silkegade 11, DK-1113 Copenhagen K
Danish Antiquarian Booksellers' Association

Danske Boghandleres Bogimport A/S, Herlev Hovedgade 199, DK-2730 Herlev
Tel: (02) 918311
Danish Booksellers Book Import
Director: Hans Pedersen

Danske Boghandleres Importørforening (DANBIF), Blegdamsvej 28, DK-2200 Copenhagen N   Tel: (01) 141195
Danish Booksellers' Import Association
Chairman: Hans Jespersen

Danske Boghandleres Kommissionsanstalt (DBK)*, Siljangade 6, DK-2300 Copenhagen
Danish Booksellers Clearing House
Man Dir: Jorgen G Hensen

Den **Danske Boghandlerforening**, Boghandlernes Hus, Siljangade 6, DK-2300 Copenhagen S
Danish Booksellers' Association
Secretary: Elisabeth Brodersen
Publication: De Danske Bogmarked (with Danske Forlaeggerforening)

Den **Danske Forlaeggerforening**, Købmagergade 11, DK-1150 Copenhagen K
Tel: (01) 156688
Danish Publishers' Association
Dir: Erik V Krustrup
Publication: Det Danske Bogmarked (with Danske Boghandlerforening)

Fællesekspeditionen*, Njalsgade 19, DK-2300 Copenhagen S
Joint Trade Counter

Forening for Boghaandvaerk, Nørregade 26, DK-1165 Copenhagen K
Danish Book-craft Association
Publication: Bogvennen (yearbook)

Forening for Forlagsfolk, Erik Langkjaer Kommunetryk, 7 Sommerstedsgade, DK-1718 Copenhagen V   Tel: (451) 229725
Association of Young Publishers

Standard Book Numbering Agency, Bibliotekscentralen Dansk Bogfortegnelse, Telegrafvej 5, DK-2750 Ballerup
Administrator: Karen Lunde Christensen

Book Trade Reference Books and Journals

Book

Fortegnelse over Samhandels-Berettigede Boghandlere MV (Register of Licensed Booksellers etc), Danish Publishers' Association, Købmagergade 11, DK-1150 Copenhagen K

Journals

Bogormen (The Bookworm), journal for book trade employees, Danish Book Trade Employees' Association, Boghandlernes Hus, Siljangade 6, DK-2300 Copenhagen S

Bogvennen (The Book Lover), Brolaeggerstr 4, DK-1211 Copenhagen K, Danish Bookcraft Association, Nørregade 26, DK-1165 Copenhagen K

Dansk Bogfortegnelse (Danish National Bibliography), Bibliotekscentralen, Telegrafvej 5, DK-2750 Ballerup

Dansk Periodicafortegnelse (Danish National Bibliography, Serials), Bibliotekscentralen, Telegrafvej 5, DK-2750 Ballerup

Den Danske Bogmarked (The Danish Book Market), Danish Booksellers' Association, Boghandlernes Hus, Siljangade 6, DK-2300 Copenhagen S

DENMARK

Publishers

Akademisk Forlag, Store Kannikestr 6-8,
DK-1169 Copenhagen K Tel: (01) 119826
Man Dir: Der Holm Rasmussen
Subjects: History, Philosophy, High-priced
Paperbacks, Psychology, Engineering,
General Science, University Textbooks,
Educational Materials
1979: 120 titles *Founded:* 1962
ISBN Publisher's Prefix: 87-500

Arnkrone Forlaget A/S*, Fuglebækvej 4,
DK-2770 Kastrup Tel: (01) 507000
Man Dir: J Juul Rasmussen
Subjects: Art, Cultural History, Popular
Medicine
Founded: 1941
ISBN Publisher's Prefix: 87-87007

Aschehoug Dansk Forlag A/S,
Landemaerket 11, DK-1119 Copenhagen K
Tel: (01) 135130 Cable Add: Asdanfo
Man Dir: Erik Ipsen; *Rights & Permissions:*
Kaj Påskesen
Subsidiary Companies: J Fr Clausens
Forlag, Denmark (qv); H Hagerups Forlag,
Denmark (qv); H Hirschsprungs Forlag,
Denmark (qv)
Subjects: School Books, Textbooks
1978: 40 titles *1979:* 52 titles *Founded:* 1914
ISBN Publisher's Prefix: 87-11

H M Bergs Forlag ApS, Peder Skrams Gade
5, DK-1054 Copenhagen K Tel: (01) 135480
Man Dir: H M Berg
Subjects: General Non-fiction, Juveniles, Art
1978: 6 titles *1979:* 1 title *Founded:* 1965
ISBN Publisher's Prefix: 87-7228

Berlingske Forlag A/S, Antonigade 7,
DK-1147 Copenhagen K Tel: (01) 157575
Cable Add: Berlingske Telex: 27094
Publisher: Henrik Fonss
Subjects: Berlingske Encyclopaedic Series,
Dictionaries, Reference Books, Study Books
1978: 58 titles *1979:* 65 titles *Founded:* 1733
ISBN Publisher's Prefix: 87-19

Bibliotekscentralens Forlag, Telegrafvej 5,
DK-2750 Ballerup Tel: (02) 975555 Cable
Add: Danliber Telex: 35370
Man Dir: Leo Alster; *Editor:* Jørgen Richøj
Subjects: Literature about Librarians,
Bibliographical Manuals
1978: 12 titles *1979:* 6 titles *Founded:* 1939
ISBN Publisher's Prefix: 87-552

Bierman og Bierman A/S, Vestergade 120,
DK-7200, Grindsted Tel: (05)
320288/320481 Cable Add: Bierbook
Grindsted
Man Dir: H A Bierman
Subsidiary Companies: Bierman og
Fothergill ApS, Helleskraenten 33, DK-2860
Soborg; Chr Bakkes Eftf, Det Gamle
Antikvariat, Vestergade 120, DK-7200
Grindsted; Helle Samuels & Co Ltd, 32
Bodmin Road, Luton, Beds, UK
Subjects: Children's Books, Culture
Bookshop: At above address
1978: 3 titles *1979:* 2 titles *Founded:* 1968

Bogans Forlag*, Kastaniebakken 8,
DK-3540 Lynge Tel: (03) 188055
Owner: Evan Bogan
Subjects: Quality Paperbacks (factual,
general), Popular Science, Occult

Borgens Forlag A/S, Mynstersvej 19,
DK-1827 Copenhagen V Tel: (01) 312041
Man Dir: Jarl Borgen; *Dir and Editor-in-
Chief:* Ole Thestrup; *Sales Dir:* Else-Marie
Hyldekrog; *Rights and Permissions:* Mette
Nymark
Orders to: Fællesekspeditionen Njalsgade 19,
DK-2300 Copenhagen S Tel: (01) 541333
Subjects: General Fiction, Belles Lettres,
Poetry, Biography, Art, Philosophy,
Religion, Reference, Juveniles, Low- & High-
priced Paperbacks, Medicine, Psychology,
General & Social Science, Textbooks
1978: 255 titles *Founded:* 1948
ISBN Publisher's Prefix: 87-418

Børsen Forlaget A/S, Postboks 2103, DK-
1014 Copenhagen K (Located at:
Moentergade 19, DK-1014 Copenhagen)
Tel: (01) 157250
Publishing Manager: Ib Topholm; *Editorial:*
Jan Erik Olsen; *Sales Manager:* Peter
Rodbro; *Production:* Gitte Mortensen
Subject: Management
ISBN Publisher's Prefix: 87-7553

Branner og Korch's Forlag A/S, H C
Oerstedsvej 7B, DK-1879 Kastrup V Tel:
(01) 224511 Cable Add: Bookbranner
Man Dir: Torbar Schur
Subjects: General Fiction & Non-fiction,
Technical, Juveniles, Reference, Textbooks,
Politics
1978: 118 titles *1979:* 110 titles *Founded:*
1949
ISBN Publisher's Prefix: 87-411

Nyt Nordisk Forlag Arnold **Busck** A/S,
Købmagergade 49, DK-1150 Copenhagen K
Tel: (01) 111103 Cable Add: Bookbusck
Man Dirs: Helge Arnold Busck, Ole Arnold
Busck
Subsidiary Company: Det Schønbergske
Forlag, Denmark (qv)
Subjects: General Fiction, Biography,
History, How-to, Music, Art, Philosophy,
Reference, Religion, High-priced
Paperbacks, Medicine, Psychology, General
& Social Science, University, Secondary &
Primary Textbooks
Bookshops: Arnold Busck International
Booksellers, Købmagergade 49, DK-1150
Copenhagen K; Nordisk Boghandel,
Ostergade 16, DK-1100 Copenhagen K;
Arnold Busck Antiquarians, Fiolstr 24,
DK-1171 Copenhagen K
1978: 290 titles *Founded:* 1896
ISBN Publisher's Prefix: 87-17

Carit Andersens Forlag I/S*,
Amagertorv 31, DK-1160 Copenhagen K
Tel: (01) 123327
Owners: Poul Carit Andersen, Ulrik Boesen
Subjects: Travel, Limited Editions,
Handbooks, Psychology, Juveniles, Cookery

Carlsen if International Publishers A/S,
Postboks 6, Købmagergade 9, DK-1001
Copenhagen K Tel: (01) 143596 Cable Add:
Carlsenif Telex: 22426 Carl DK
Man Dir: Per Hjald Carlsen
Subsidiary Company: Carlsen Verlag
GmbH, Federal Republic of Germany (qv)
Subject: Children's Picture Books

J Fr **Clausens** Forlag, Landemaerket 11,
DK-1119 Copenhagen K Tel: (01) 135130
Man Dir: Erik Ipsen; *Editorial, Rights &
Permissions:* Kaj Påskesen
Parent Company: Aschehoug Dansk Forlag
(qv)
Subject: Practical Handbooks
1978: 37 titles *1979:* 40 titles
ISBN Publisher's Prefix: 87-11

Forlaget **Danmark** A/S*, Frederiksholms
Kanal 18, DK-1220 Copenhagen K Tel: (01)
129192
Man Dir: Erik Bastfeldt
Subjects: Handbooks, Encyclopaedias

Dansk Historisk Haandbogsforlag Ltd,
Klintevej 25, DK-2800 Lyngby Tel: (02)
888500 Telex: 37406
Owner, Man Dir: Henning Jensen
Subjects: Genealogy, Heraldry, Culture,
Local History
1978: 50 titles

Dansk Videnskabs Forlag ApS*, 32F
Lyngbyvej, DK-2100 Copenhagen Ö Tel:
(01) 297144/22
Danish Science Press Ltd
Chief Executive: H C Bjerg
Subjects: Scientific Works; Periodicals

Det **Danske Forlag**, Roskildevej 65,
DK-2620 Albertslund Tel: (02) 648765
Man Dir: N J Laursen
Orders to: Njalsgade 19, DK-2300
Copenhagen S
Subjects: Biography, History, Philosophy,
Reference, Juveniles, Low- & High-priced
Paperbacks, Psychology, General & Social
Science
1978: 19 titles *1979:* 2 titles *Founded:* 1941
ISBN Publisher's Prefix: 87-422

Christian **Ejlers'** Forlag A/S*, Brolaeggerstr
4, DK-1211 Copenhagen K Tel: (01) 122114
Man Dir: Christian Ejlers
Subjects: Educational & Academic, Art,
Bibliography
1978: 17 titles *Founded:* 1967
ISBN Publisher's Prefix: 87-7241

Chr **Erichsens** Forlag A/S,
Kronprinsensgade 1, DK-1114 Copenhagen
K Tel: (01) 159595 Cable Add: Bogerich
Man Dir: Mr Kay Holkenfeldt
Subjects: Fiction, Mysteries, How-to,
Juveniles, Handbooks
Founded: 1902
ISBN Publisher's Prefix: 87-555

F A D L Forlag (Foreningen af danske
Laegestuderendes Forlag)*, Blegdamsvej 84,
DK-2100 Copenhagen 0 Tel: (01) 262826
Telex: 16698
Man Dirs: Hans Jespersen, Steen Brynitz
Subjects: Medicine, Biology
Founded: 1964
ISBN Publisher's Prefix: 87-7437

Forlaget for **Faglitteratur** A/S, Vandkunsten
6, DK-1467 Copenhagen K Tel: (01) 137900
Subjects: Medicine, Technology
ISBN Publisher's Prefix: 87-573

Palle **Fogtdal** A/S*, Nørre Farimagsgade 49,
DK-1364 Copenhagen K Tel: (01) 126612
Chief Man Dir: Erik Skipper Larsen
Subjects: Home Decoration, DIY, Cooking,
Gardening, Motoring, Boating, Fashion,
Needlework
1978: 20 titles *Founded:* 1959

Forum Publishers Ltd, Åbenrå 31, DK-1124
Copenhagen K Tel: (01) 147714 Cable Add:
Forumbooks
Man Dir: Jokum Smith
Subjects: General, Scientific, Educational,
Juveniles, Mysteries, High-priced
Paperbacks
1978: 80 titles *1979:* 91 titles *Founded:* 1940
ISBN Publisher's Prefix: 87-553

Fremad*, Nørrebrogade 54, DK-2200
Copenhagen N Tel: (01) 394040 Cable
Add: Bogfremad
Man Dir: Mogens Bang; *Editorial:* Erik
Langkjaer
Subjects: General Fiction, Juveniles,
Textbooks, Cheap Editions of Travel Books
and International Novels, Periodicals
Bookshop: Boghandelen Fremad,
Nørrebrogade 54, DK-2200 Copenhagen N
Founded: 1912
ISBN Publisher's Prefix: 87-557

J **Frimodts** Forlag, Korskaervej 25, DK-7000
Fredericia Tel: (05) 926100
Man Dir: A Brendholdt
Associate Company: Lohses Forlag (qv)
Subjects: Religion, Fiction
1978: 3 titles
ISBN Publisher's Prefix: 87-7446

Forlaget **G M T**, Meilgaard, DK-8584
Tranehuse Tel: (06) 317511
Publishers: Hans Jørn Christensen, Erik Bjørn Olsen
Subjects: History, Aesthetics, Politics, Philosophy, Psychology, Sociology, General Fiction, Textbooks, Educational Materials
1979: 21 titles *Founded:* 1971
ISBN Publisher's Prefix: 87-7330

G E C **Gads** Forlag, Vimmelskaftet 32, DK-1161 Copenhagen K Tel: (01) 150558
Cable Add: Boggad
Man Dir: Kaj Lynnerup
Subjects: Religion, Psychology, General Science, Education, Textbooks, Art, Reference, Law, Management
Bookshop: G E C Gad Dansk og Udenlandsk Boghandel A/S, Vimmelskaftet 32, DK-1161 Copenhagen K
Founded: 1855
ISBN Publisher's Prefix: 87-12

Jul **Gjellerup** Forlagsaktieselskab, Rømersgade 11, DK-1362 Copenhagen K Tel: (451) 137801 Cable Add: Gjellerupbooks Telex: 19110 Gjbook Dk
The above-named publishing company comprises the management, and deals with contracts. For editorial, marketing and accounts see Gjellerups Forlag A/S
Man Dir: Svend E Pedersen
Subjects: Reference, University, Secondary & Primary Textbooks, Educational Materials
Bookshop: Jul Gjellerups Boghandel ApS, Sølvgade 87-89, DK-1307 Copenhagen K Tel: (01) 137233
1978: approx 300 titles *Founded:* 1884
ISBN Publisher's Prefix: 87-13

Gjellerups Forlag A/S, Rømersgade 11, DK-1362 Copenhagen K Tel: (451) 137801 Telex: 19110 Gjbook Dk
Joint Publishers: Harald Bertelsen (Editorial); Ulf Thomsen (Marketing)
Branch Off: 1 Maagaardsvej, Gerning, DK-8850 Bjerringbro
See also Jul Gjellerup Forlagsaktieselskab

Grafisk Forlag A/S, Klosterrisvej 7, DK-2100 Copenhagen O Tel: (01) 294000
Cable Add: Boggrafisk Telex: 16987
Man Dir: Birger Schmith; *Deputy Manager:* Ove Mølbeck
Subjects: General Fiction, Juveniles, Secondary & Primary Textbooks, Educational Materials, Foreign Language Easy Readers
1978: 81 titles *1979:* 72 titles *Founded:* 1941
ISBN Publisher's Prefix: 87-429

Grevas Forlag*, Skovfaldet 2 K, DK-8200 Århus N Tel: (06) 168387 Cable Add: Grevas Arhus
Man Dir: Eva Hemmer Hansen; *Sales Dir:* Luise Pihl
Subjects: General Fiction, Belles Lettres, Poetry, Biography, Art, Juveniles
Founded: 1966
ISBN Publisher's Prefix: 87-7235

Det **Grønlandske** Forlag, Postboks 1009, DK-3900 Godthåb, Greenland (Located at: Hans Egedesvej 21, DK-3900 Godthåb) Tel: 22122 Cable Add: Groefobo Telex: 90638
The Greenland Publishing House
Man Dir: Poul Bay
Subjects: Children's Books, Fiction
Bookshop: Atuagkat Bookstore, PO Box 1009, DK-3900 Godthåb, Greenland
1978: 47 titles *1979:* 60 titles *Founded:* 1956
ISBN Publisher's Prefix: 87-558

Gutenberghus Publishing Service, Vognmagergade 11, DK-1148 Copenhagen K Tel: (01) 151925 Cable Add: Gutenbergblade Telex: 16705
Dir: Peter Jerichow; *Editorial:* Carsten Jacobsen, Per Då, Jørgen Sonnergaard
Parent Company: Gutenberghus Group, Copenhagen
Associate Companies: Oy Kirjalito, Finland; Ehapa-Verlag GmbH, Federal Republic of Germany (qv); Hjemmet A/S, Norway (qv); Hemmets Journal AB (qv) and Forlaget Kärnan AB, Sweden; Egmont Publishing Ltd, UK
Subjects: Juveniles, Albums
Book Club: Walt Disney Wonderful World of Reading

Gyldendalske Boghandel — Nordisk Forlag A/S, Klareboderne 3, DK-1001 Copenhagen K Tel: (01) 110775 Cable Add: Gyldendalske Copenhagen Telex: 15887 Gyldaldk
Dirs: Kurt Fromberg, Mogens Knudsen, Ole Werner Thomsen, Eigil Winther, Ole Wivel; *Editorial:* Helge Dokkedal, Vagn Grosen, Karen Margrethe Henriksen, Peter Holst, Egon Schmidt; *Sales Manager:* Søren Melgaard; *Rights & Permissions:* Kirsten Franke, Per Finn Jacobsen; *Co-Productions Manager:* Eyvind Thorsen
Subsidiary Company: Forlaget Vindrose ApS (qv)
Subjects: General Fiction, Belles Lettres, Poetry, Biography, History, How-to, Music, Art, Philosophy, Reference, Juveniles, Low- & High-priced Paperbacks, Medicine, Psychology, General & Social Science, University, Secondary & Primary Textbooks, Educational Materials
Book Clubs: Gyldendals Bogklub, Gyldendals Børnebogklub, Samlerens Bogklub
Founded: 1770
ISBN Publisher's Prefix: 87-01

P **Haase** & Søns Forlag A/S, Løvstr 8, DK-1152 Copenhagen K Tel: (01) 115999
Cable Add: Boghaase
Man Dir: Niels Jørgen Haase; *Secretary:* Nina Jensen; *Treasurer:* Mogens Koreska; *Product Manager:* Preben Bentzen; *Editorial Manager:* Knud Andersen; *Sales & Marketing:* Steen Folkersen
Subsidiary Company: N J Haases Bookimport ApS; Rasmus Navers Forlag, Denmark (qv)
Subjects: Juveniles, University, Secondary & Primary Textbooks, Educational Materials
Bookshop: P Haase & Sons Boghandel A/S, Løvstr 8, DK-1152 Copenhagen K
1978: 132 titles *1979:* 127 titles *Founded:* 1877
ISBN Publisher's Prefix: 87-559

H **Hagerups** Forlag*, Landemaerket 11, DK-1119 Copenhagen K Tel: (01) 135130
Cable Add: Asdanfo
Man Dir: Erik Ipsen
Parent Company: Aschehoug Dansk Forlag A/S (qv)
Subjects: Juveniles, Secondary & Primary Textbooks
ISBN Publisher's Prefix: 87-11

Edition Wilhelm **Hansen***, Gothersgade 9-11, DK-1123 Copenhagen K Tel: (01) 117888 Cable Add: Musikhansen Telex: 19912 Musik Dk
Owners: Hanne and Lone Wilhelm Hansen
Subsidiary Company: AB Nordiska Musikforlaget (Edition Wilhelm Hansen, Stockholm), Sweden (qv)
Subjects: Music, Musicology, Art, Educational Materials
Miscellaneous: Also Literary Agent (Nordiska Teaterforlaget Edition Wilhelm Hansen)
Founded: 1857
ISBN Publisher's Prefix: 87-7455

Hernovs Forlag, Bredgade 14-16, DK-1260 Copenhagen K Tel: (01) 156284/156209/113930
Man Dir: Johs G Hernov; *Publicity Dir:* P Leslie Holst
Subsidiary Company: Johs G Hernov, Vinimport ApS
Subjects: General Fiction, Juveniles
Book Club: Hernovs Book Club (qv)
Founded: 1941
ISBN Publisher's Prefix: 87-7215

H **Hirschsprungs** Forlag, Landemaerket 11, DK-1119 Copenhagen K Tel: (01) 135130
Cable Add: Asdanfo
Man Dir: Erik Ipsen
Parent Company: Aschehoug Dansk Forlag (qv)
Subjects: School Books, Textbooks
ISBN Publisher's Prefix: 87-11

Hjorts Forlag ApS*, Hovedvagtsgade 8, DK-1103 Copenhagen K Tel: (01) 152292
Man Dir: Per Hjort
Subjects: Yachting, Needlework, How-to; Monthly magazines on Yachting and Needlework
ISBN Publisher's Prefix: 87-7300

Forlaget **Hönsetryk**, Godthåbsvej 15b, DK-3060 Espergaerde Tel: (03) 231074
Owner: Kirsten Hofstätter

Høst og Søns Forlag, Bredgade 35, DK-1260 Copenhagen K Tel: (01) 155051/153031
Cable Add: Bookhøst
Man Dir: Mogens C Lind; *Editorial:* Kirsten Skaarup
Subjects: Hobbies & Crafts, Languages, Books on Denmark, Juveniles, Reference
1978: approx 80 titles *Founded:* 1836
ISBN Publisher's Prefix: 87-14

Birgitte **Høvring's** Icelandic World Literature, Postboks 53, DK-3050 Humlebaek (Located at: Teglgårdsvej 531, DK-3050 Humlebaek) Tel: (03) 190926
Owner: Thorsteinn Stefánsson
1978: 1 title

Informations Forlag ApS, St Kongensgade 40, DK-1264 Copenhagen K Tel: (01) 141426 Telex: 22658
Man Dirs: Johs Feil, Asger Jepsen
Parent Company: Information Daily Newspaper
Subjects: Non-Fiction informative books on current issues, Politics, Fiction
1978: 16 titles *1979:* 25 titles *Founded:* 1975
ISBN Publisher's Prefix: 87-87498

A/S **Interpresse***, PO Box 11, DK-2880 Bagsvaerd (Located at: 32 Krogshoejvej, Bagsvaerd) Tel: 02985227
Cable Add: Stonepress Telex: 37416 Stenby Dk
Man Dir: Arne Stenby
Subjects: Juveniles, Comics
1978: 65 titles *1979:* 80 titles *Founded:* 1954
ISBN Publisher's Prefix: 87-7529

Jespersen og Pios Forlag*, Valkendorfsgade 22, DK-1151 Copenhagen K Tel: (01) 129642 Cable Add: Jespio
Man Dir: Iver Jespersen; *Rights & Permissions:* Elly Sandal
Subjects: General Fiction & Nonfiction, Juveniles, Paperbacks
Founded: 1865
ISBN Publisher's Prefix: 87-419

Lademann Ltd, Publishers, Linnesgade 25, DK-1361 Copenhagen K Tel: (01) 131650
Cable Add: Boglademann Telex: 19149
Publisher: J Lademann; *Dirs:* Frits Bülow Lehnsby, Georg Vejen, Niels Agner; *Rights & Permissions:* Kirsten Jacobsen
Subsidiary Companies: Hamlet Ltd; Kolon Ltd; Komma Ltd; Sesam Ltd; Albatros Ltd
Subjects: General

76 DENMARK

Book Clubs: Union Book Club, Union Crime Club, Union Novel Library, Union Harlekin Library, Danmark Book Club, Union Classics Library
1978: 280 titles *1979:* 280 titles *Founded:* 1954
ISBN Publisher's Prefix: 87-15

Lentz og Jenssens Forlag ApS, Torpetvej 9, DK-4100 Ringsted Tel: (03) 613161
Man Dir: Børge Lentz
Subjects: How-to, Reference, High-priced Paperbacks, Engineering, Secondary Textbooks, Sports
Founded: 1971
ISBN Publisher's Prefix: 87-7554

Lindhardt og Ringhof, Studiestr 14, DK-1455 Copenhagen Tel: (01) 111955
Cable Add: Eleteredit
Owners: Otto B Lindhardt, Gert Ringhof
Subjects: General Fiction, Biography, History, How-to, Philosophy, Paperbacks, Pre-school Materials
Book Club: Primavera (fiction)
1978: 38 titles *1979:* 40 titles *Founded:* 1971
ISBN Publisher's Prefix: 87-7560

Lohses Forlag, Korskaervej 25, DK-7000 Fredericia Tel: (05) 926100
Man Dir: A Brendholdt
Associate Company: J Frimodts Forlag (qv)
Subjects: Religion, Juveniles
1978: 18 titles *Founded:* 1868
ISBN Publisher's Prefix: 87-564

Mallings ApS, 638 Strandvejen, DK-2930 Klampenborg Tel: (01) 630773/260726
Cable Add: Mallingbook Telex: 15817 Jmco Dk
Man Dir, Editorial, Rights & Permissions: Joachim Malling; *Sales:* Hannah Malling; *Production:* Michael Malling; *Publicity:* Dorthe Malling
Subjects: Juveniles, Educational, Picture Books
1978: 26 titles *1979:* 31 titles *Founded:* 1975
ISBN Publisher's Prefix: 87-7333

Martins Forlag*, Kompagnistrade 34.4.sal, DK-1208 Copenhagen K Tel: (01) 146665
Owner: Erik Halkier
Subjects: General Fiction, Nonfiction, Juveniles
ISBN Publisher's Prefix: 87-566

Medicinsk Forlag ApS, Tranevej 2, DK-3650 Ölstykke Tel: (03) 176592
Man Dir: Anni Lindelöv
Subjects: Medical, Scientific, Literature

Forlaget **Modtryk** AMBA, Anholtsgade 4-6, DK-8000 Aarhus C Tel: (0045) 6127912/6137674 Telex: 4556785 Mod
Man Dir: Frands Mortensen; *Editorial:* Jan Knus; *Sales:* Niels Jørgen Jensen; *Production:* Kjeld Vindum; *Publicity:* Carsten Vengsgård; *Rights & Permissions:* Preben Bach
Parent Companies: Politisk Revy Skt, Pederstræde 28B, DK-1453 Copenhagen K; Værtshuset Aesken, Anholtsgade 8, DK-8000 Aarhus C
Subjects: Political Writings and Essays (especially in the field of the 'New Left' movement), Children's Books, Fiction
Book Club: Socialistisk Bogklub ApS
1978: 25 titles *1979:* 30 titles *Founded:* 1972
ISBN Publisher's Prefix: 87-458, 87-620, 87-817

Munksgaard, International Booksellers & Publishers Ltd, Nørre Søgade 35, DK-1370 Copenhagen K Tel: (01) 127030 Cable Add: Bogotto
Chairman of the Board: Per Saugman; *Man Dir:* Oluf V Møller; *Editorial:* Jørgen Bergmann, Peter Hartmann, Sven Erik Olsen; *Treasurer:* Jørgen Sandal
Subjects: Medicine, Nursing, Dentistry, Social Sciences, Psychology, Schoolbooks, Children's Books, Scientific Journals
Bookshop: Munksgaard Export & Subscription Service (at above address)
1979: 433 titles *Founded:* 1917

Rasmus Navers Forlag, Løvstr 8, DK-1152 Copenhagen K Tel: (01) 115999
Man Dir: Niels Jørgen Haase
Parent Company: P Haase & Søns Forlag A/S (qv)
Subjects: Humour, Art, Fiction

Nordisk Kolportage Forlag A/S*, Frederiksholms Kanal 18, DK-1220 Copenhagen K Tel: (01) 129192
Man Dir: Erik Bastfeldt
Subjects: Encyclopaedias, Handbooks

Nordisk Romanforlag A/S*, Frederiksholms Kanal 18, DK-1220 Copenhagen K Tel: (01) 111876
ISBN Publisher's Prefix: 87-7489

M **Normanns** Forlag A/S, Kastanievej 3, DK-5230 Odense M Tel: (09) 120697
Man Dir: Mogens Normann
Subjects: How-to, Secondary & Primary Textbooks
Founded: 1942
ISBN Publisher's Prefix: 87-7032

Jörgen **Paludans** Forlag A/S*, Fiolstr 32, DK-1171 Copenhagen K Tel: (01) 116042
Man Dir: Jörgen Paludan
Subjects: Non-fiction, Psychology, Sociology, History, Political Science, Economics, High-priced Paperbacks
ISBN Publisher's Prefix: 87-7230

Politikens Forlag A/S, Vestergade 26, DK-1456 Copenhagen K Tel: (01) 112122
Cable Add: Polbooks
Man Dir: Johannes Ravn; *Sales Dir:* Sören Seedorff
Subjects: General Nonfiction: Nature Study, History and Documentary, Sports, Games, Hobbies, Children's Folklore, Art, Literature, Music, Maps and Atlases, Travel, How-To
1978: 100 approx *Founded:* 1946
ISBN Publisher's Prefix: 87-567

C A **Reitzels** Forlag, Nørre Søgade 35, DK-1370 Copenhagen K Tel: (01) 117031
Man Dir: Jørgen Sandal
Subjects: General Science, Engineering, Textbooks
1978: 46 titles *1979:* 71 titles *Founded:* 1819
ISBN Publisher's Prefix: 87-421

Hans **Reitzels** Forlag A/S, Snaregade 4, DK-1205 Copenhagen K Tel: (01) 140451
Cable Add: Reitzelbooks
Man Dir: Hans Reitzel; *Editorial, Rights & Permissions:* Beate Lange
Subjects: Psychology, General & Social Science, University Textbooks, Philosophy, Reference, High-priced Paperbacks
1978: 56 titles *1979:* 54 titles *Founded:* 1949
ISBN Publisher's Prefix: 87-412

Rhodos, International Science and Art Publishers, Niels Brocks Gård, Strandgade 36, DK-1401 Copenhagen K Tel: (01) 543020 Cable Add: Sciencebooks
Man Dir: Niels Blaedel
Subjects: Art, Fiction, High-priced Paperbacks, General & Social Science, Handbooks, Encyclopedias
Founded: 1959
ISBN Publisher's Prefix: 87-7496

Rosenkilde og Bagger, Postboks 2184, DK-1017 Copenhagen K (Located at: Kron-Prinsens-Gade 3, Copenhagen) Tel: (01) 157044 Cable Add: Bogkunst
Man Dir: Finn Jacobsen
Subjects: Reprints, Facsimile Editions, High-priced Paperbacks, General Science

Bookshop: Rosenkilde og Bagger, Kron-Prinsens-Gade 3, PO Box 2184, DK-1017 Copenhagen K
1978: 21 titles *Founded:* 1941
ISBN Publisher's Prefix: 87-423

Samlerens Forlag A/S, Christian den Niendesgade 2, DK-1111 Copenhagen K Tel: (01) 131023
Man Dir: Børge Priskorn
Subjects: General Fiction & Nonfiction, History, Guides, Art, Social Science, Paperbacks, Domestic Crafts, Games, Sport
1978: 60 titles *1979:* 60 titles
ISBN Publisher's Prefix: 87-568

Det **Schoenbergske** Forlag A/S (Nyt Nordisk Forlag Arnold Busck A/S), Landemaerket 5, DK-1119 Copenhagen K Tel: (01) 113066 Cable Add: Schoenbook
Man Dir: Elsa Pedersen; *Library Dir:* Paul Monrad; *Sales Manager:* Max-Erik Reinhold
Subjects: General Fiction, Belles Lettres, Poetry, Biography, History, Art, Philosophy, Reference, Travel, Low- & High-priced Paperbacks, Psychology, Trade Books, University, Commercial School, Secondary & Primary Textbooks
1978: 44 titles *1979:* 60 titles *Founded:* 1857
ISBN Publisher's Prefix: 87-570

A/S J H **Schultz** Forlag, Møntergården, Møntergade 21, DK-1116 Copenhagen K Tel: (01) 121195 Cable Add: Bogschultz
Manager: H Borberg
Subjects: Nonfiction, Law, EEC publications, Medical books
1978: 76 titles *Founded:* 1661
ISBN Publisher's Prefix: 87-569

Scientology Publications Organization ApS, Store Kongensgade 55a, DK-1305 Copenhagen K Tel: (01) 145128 Telex: 16828 Pubsell Dk
Man Dir: Ivan Watson; *Sales Manager:* Neil Lumbsden; *Manufacturing Dir:* Marc Dumas; *Rights & Permissions:* Annette dél Francia
Branch Off: Pubs UK, St Mary's College, Falmer Rd, Rottingdean, Sussex, UK
Subjects: Philosophy, Religion, Management, Education
1978: 13 titles *Founded:* 1967
ISBN Publisher's Prefix: 87-87347

Skarv-Nature Publications ApS, Kongevejen 45, DK-2840 Holte Tel: (02) 424745
Man Dir: Soren Koustrup
Subjects: Nature & Wildlife Books, Modern Biology, Geography, Animal Behaviour, Ecology, Ornithology, Social Anthropology
1979: 25 titles *1980:* 28 titles *Founded:* 1976
ISBN Publisher's Prefix: 87-87581

A/S **Skattekartoteket**, Palaegade 4, DK-1261 Copenhagen K Tel: (01) 117874
Man Dir: Peter Taarnhøj
Subject: Taxation (national and international)
1978: 2 titles *1979:* 3 titles

Sommer og Sörensen Forlag ApS, Siljangade 3, DK-2300 Copenhagen S Tel: (01) 950945
Dirs: Erik Sommer, Aage Börglum Sörensen

A/S **Sparevirke**, Köbmagergade 62-64, DK-1150 Copenhagen K Tel: (01) 151811
Man Dir: T G Söndergaard
Subjects: Handbooks, School Books
Founded: 1979
ISBN Publisher's Prefix: 87-7538

Strandbergs Forlag*, Topstykket 17, DK-3460 Birkeröd Tel: (02) 816397
Owner: Hans Jörgen Strandberg
Subject: Cultural History

Strubes Forlag og Boghandel A/S*, 1 Söndergade, DK-4130 Gl Viby/Sjaelland Tel: (03) 394250 Cable Add: Strubebooks

Man Dirs: Jonna and Povl Strube
Subjects: Psychic & Occult, Philosophy, Art, Bibliophilic, Naval
Bookshop: at above address

Finn **Suenson** Forlag, Rosernörns Alle 18, DK-1970 Copenhagen V Tel: (01) 359888
Man Dir: Finn Suenson
Subjects: Handbooks, Reference, Politics, History
1979: 12 titles *1980:* 12 titles *Founded:* 1971
ISBN Publisher's Prefix: 87-201

Teknisk Forlag A/S*, Skelbaekgade 4, DK-1717 Copenhagen V Tel: (01) 216801 Cable Add: Technipress Telex: 16368 Tefko Dk
Man Dir: Peter Müller
Subjects: Engineering, Manuals, Directories, Guides
1978: 21 titles *Founded:* 1948
ISBN Publisher's Prefix: 87-571

Teknologisk Instituts Forlag, Gregersensvej, DK-2630 Tåstrup Tel: (02) 996611
Subjects: Technical, Special Literature and Handbooks for Crafts and Industries
1978: 20 titles *1979:* 28 titles
ISBN Publisher's Prefix: 87-7511

Thaning og Appels Forlag, H C Oerstedsvej 7b, DK-1879 Kastrup V Tel: (01) 224511
Man Dir: Thomas Blom
Subjects: General Fiction, Belles Lettres, Art, History, Philosophy, Science & Technical Education, Psychology, How-to; Paperbacks
1978: 43 titles *1979:* 44 titles *Founded:* 1866
ISBN Publisher's Prefix: 87-413

Ungdommens Forlag & Aamodts Forlag A/S*, Grundtvigsvej 37, DK-1864 Copenhagen K Tel: (01) 241500
Subjects: Special Literature, Juveniles
ISBN Publisher's Prefix: 87-7516

De **Unges** Forlag, Unitas Forlag*, Amaliegade 24, DK-1256 Copenhagen K Tel: (01) 159363
Subjects: Religion, Fiction
ISBN Publisher's Prefix: 87-7517

Forlaget **Vindrose** ApS, Nybrogade 14, DK-1203 Copenhagen K Tel: (01) 135000
Man Dir: Erik Vagn Jensen; *Editorial:* Line Schmidt-Madsen; *Production:* Susanne Heilesen; *Rights & Permissions:* Kirsten Franke
Parent Company: Gyldendalske Boghandel — Nordisk Forlag AS (qv)
Subjects: General Fiction, Belles Lettres, Poetry, Science, Social Science, High-priced paperbacks
Founded: 1980
ISBN Publisher's Prefix: 87-7456

Vinten's Forlag*, Amagertorv 31, DK-1160 Copenhagen K Tel: (01) 122121
Owner, Man Dir: Jeppe Vinten
Subjects: General Fiction, Belles Lettres, Art, Philosophy, Juveniles, Low- & High-priced Paperbacks, Psychology
1978: 31 titles *Founded:* 1950
ISBN Publisher's Prefix: 87-414

Wangels Forlag A/S, Postboks 1061, DK-1008 Copenhagen K (Located at: Gammeltorv 8, Copenhagen) Tel: (01) 156111
Man Dir: Benny Frederiksen
Subjects: General Fiction
Book Club: Danske Bogsamleres Klub
Founded: 1946
ISBN Publisher's Prefix: 87-7220

Wilkenschildts Forlag*, Gedevasevej 3, DK-3520 Farum Tel: (02) 951828
Owner: Ebbe Wilkenschildt
Subjects: Handbooks, Nonfiction

Winthers Forlag ApS, Naverland 1A, DK-2600 Glostrup Tel: (02) 960666 Cable Add: Winnpub
Man Dir: Per Andreassen; *Rights & Permissions:* Anni Groth
Subsidiary Companies: Wennerberg, Finland; Wennerbergs Förlags AB, Sweden
Subjects: General Fiction, Low-priced Paperbacks, Comics
Founded: 1945
ISBN Publisher's Prefix: 87-18

Wöldikes Forlag, Troels-Lundsvej 14, DK-2000 Copenhagen F Tel: (01) 748775
Owner & Man Dir: Arne Wöldike Schmith
Subjects: All types of books for the general trade market, Fiction & Nonfiction

Literary Agents

R P **Adam***, Brede Bovej 31, DK-2800 Lyngby, Copenhagen

A/S **Bookman**, Fiolstr 12, DK-1171 Copenhagen K Tel: (01) 145720 Cable Add: Bookman, Copenhagen
Miscellaneous: This company also acts as a Literary Agent in Sweden, Norway, Finland and Iceland for foreign authors

International Children's Book Service, Kildeskovsvej 21, DK-2820 Gentofte Tel: (01) 653032 Cable Add: Bookchild

Edith **Kiilerich**, Fiolstr 12, DK-1171 Copenhagen K
Miscellaneous: This company also acts as a Literary Agent in Sweden, Norway, Finland and Iceland for foreign authors

Preben **Klein**, PO Box 50, DK-3200 Helsinge
Also publishers representative

Albrecht **Leonhardt** ApS, Literary Agent, Studiestraede 35, DK-1455 Copenhagen K Tel: (01) 132523 Cable Add: Leolitag

Michaels og Licht, Osterbrogade 84, DK-2100 Copenhagen Tel: (01) 424608 Cable Add: Literagent
Chief executives: Ole Licht, Agnes Licht

Svend **Mondrup** International Literary Agency, Grenågade 12-14 — kldr, DK-1021 Copenhagen O Tel: (01) 149942/(01) 129666 Telex: 16600 Fotex Dk (attn Interlitagent Copenhagen)
Chief Executive: Svend Mondrup

Nordiska Teaterforlaget Edition Wilhelm Hansen, Gothersgade 9-11, DK-1123 Copenhagen Tel: (01) 117888
Branch Off: Norrlandsgatan 16, S-111 43 Stockholm, Sweden (qv)

Carl **Strakosch** & Olaf Nordgreen*, Nyhavn 5, DK-1051 Copenhagen K

Book Clubs

Danmark Book Club, Linnesgade 25, DK-1361 Copenhagen K
Owned by: Lademann Ltd, Publishers (Copenhagen)

Danske Bogsamleres Klub, Postboks 1061, DK-1008 Copenhagen K (Located at: Gammeltorv 8, Copenhagen)
Owned by: Wangels Forlag A/S (Copenhagen)

The **English Book** Club*, Raadhospladsen 55, DK-1500 Copenhagen
Owned by: Borge Boesen (qv under Booksellers)

Gyldendals Bogklub, 51 Pilestraede, DK-1001 Copenhagen K
Owned by: Gyldendalske Boghandel-Nordisk Forlag A/S (Copenhagen)
Subjects: Fiction and General Nonfiction
Associated Book Clubs: Gyldendals Børnebogklub, Samlerens Bogklub (qqv)

Gyldendals Børnebogklub, Pilestraede 51, DK-1001 Copenhagen K
Owned by: Gyldendalske Boghandel — Nordisk Forlag A/S (qv)

Hernovs Book Club, Bredgade 14-16, DK-1260 Copenhagen K
Owned by: Hernovs Forlag

Primavera, Studiestr 14, DK-1455 Copenhagen
Owned by: Lindhardt og Ringhof (Copenhagen)
Subject: Fiction

Det Bedste fra **Reader's Digest** A/S*, PO Box 1160, Oestergade 61, DK-1010 Copenhagen K

Samlerens Bogklub, Pilestraede 51, DK-1001 Copenhagen K
Owned by: Gyldendalske Boghandel-Nordisk Forlag A/S (Copenhagen)
Subjects: Fiction, Nonfiction, Political
Associated Book Clubs: Gyldendals Bogklub, Gyldendals Børnebogklub (qqv)

Socialistisk Bogklub ApS, Anholtsgade 4-6, DK-8000 Aarhus C
Owned by: Forlaget Modtryk AMBA (Aarhus)

Union Book Club, Linnesgade 25, DK-1361 Copenhagen K
Subjects: Fiction, Illustrated Nonfiction
Owned By: Lademann Ltd, Publishers (Copenhagen)

Union Classics Library, Linnesgade 25, DK-1361 Copenhagen K
Owned by: Lademann Ltd (Copenhagen)

Union Crime Club, Linnesgade 25, DK-1361 Copenhagen K
Owned by: Lademann Ltd, Publishers (Copenhagen)

Union Harlekin Library, Linnesgade 25, DK-1361 Copenhagen K
Owned by: Lademann Ltd (Copenhagen)

Union Novel Library, Linnesgade 25, DK-1361 Copenhagen K
Owned by: Lademann Ltd (Copenhagen)

Walt Disney Wonderful World of Reading*, Vognmagergade 11, DK-1148, Copenhagen K
Owned by: Gutenberghus (Copenhagen)

Major Booksellers

Akademisk Boghandel, Universitetsparken, DK-8000 Århus C Tel: (06) 128844
Manager: Erling Sieverts

Biblioteksboghandelen ApS*, Kultorvet 2, DK-1175 Copenhagen K

Bierman og Bierman, Book Import and Sale, Vestergade 120, DK-7200 Grindsted Tel: (05) 320288/320481

Borge **Boesen***, Raadhospladen 55, DK-1550 Copenhagen V Tel: (01) 132550
The English Bookshop
Man Dir: Borge Boesen

Clemens **Bøger** og Papir I/S, Skt Clemens Torv 17, DK-8000 Århus C

Boghallen*, Rådhuspladsen 37, DK-1585 Copenhagen V Tel: (01) 118511

Arnold **Busck** International Boghandel A/S, Købmagergade 49, DK-1150 Copenhagen K Tel: (01) 122453
Export Division (formerly Andr Fred Høst & Søn), Købmagergade 49, DK-1150 Copenhagen K Tel: (01) 122453 (Troels Bek)

78 DENMARK

Associate Company: Nordisk Boghandel, Østergade 16, DK-1100 Copenhagen K Tel: (01) 147007 (Mogens Staffeldt)

Dansk Central-Boghandel*, Nørregade 49, DK-1165 Copenhagen K

The **English Bookshop**, see Borge Boesen

G E C **Gad** Dansk og Udenlandsk Boghandel A/S, Vimmelskaftet 32, DK-1161 Copenhagen K Tel: (01) 150558

Gjellerups Boghandel ApS, Sølvgade 87-89, DK-1307 Copenhagen K Tel: (01) 137233 Telex: 19110 Gj Book Dk
Manager: Joergen F Lauridsen

Magasin du Nord A/S, Book Department, The English Bookshop, Kongens Nytorv 13, DK-1095 Copenhagen K Tel: (451) 114433 Cable Add: Magdunord Telex 15975

Munksgaard Export & Subscription Service, Nørre Søgade 35, DK-1370 Copenhagen K Tel: (01) 126970

Nordisk Boghandel*, Østergade 16, DK-1100 Copenhagen K

Erik **Paludans** Boghandel*, Fiolstr 10, DK-1171 Copenhagen K Tel: (01) 150675

Polyteknisk Boghandel og Forlag*, Anker Engelundsvej 1, DK-2800 Lyngby Tel: (02) 881488
Manager: Ove Dela

Universitetsbogladen (Panumbogladen/Naturfagsbogladen/Latinerbogladen), Blegdamsvej 3, DK-2200 Copenhagen N Tel: (01) 351643 Telex: 16698 Unbog Dk
Manager: Hans Jespersen
Branches: Blegdamsvej 3, DK-2200 Copenhagen N; Universitetsparken 13, DK-2100 Copenhagen O; Njalsgade 80, DK-2300 Copenhagen S

Major Libraries

Århus Kommunes Biblioteker*, Mølleparken, DK-8000 Århus C Tel: (06) 136622 Telex: 64850
Århus Public Library

Danmarks Tekniske Bibliotek*, Anker Engelunds Vej 1, DK-2800 Lyngby Tel: (02) 883088 Telex: 37148
National Technological Library of Denmark

Erhvervsarkivet-Statens Erhvervshistoriske Arkiv, Vester Allé 12, DK-8000 Århus C
Danish National Business History Archives

Gentofte Kommunebibliotek, Öregaards Allé 7, Hellerup, DK-2900 Copenhagen Tel: 45162/7500
Gentofte Municipal Library
Chief Librarian: Helge Stenkilde

Københavns Kommunes Biblioteker*, Kultorvet 2, DK-1175 Copenhagen K Tel: (01) 136070 Telex: 16648 Kkbhb Dk
Copenhagen Municipal Libraries

Københavns Stadsarkiv, Rådhuset, DK-1599 Copenhagen V
Copenhagen City Archives
Publication: Historiske Meddelelser om København (Historical Year-book)

Det **Kongelige Bibliotek**, Christians Brygge 8, DK-1219 Copenhagen K Tel: (01) 150111 Telex: 15009
Royal Library
National Librarian: Palle Birkelund
Publications: Contribution to the H C Andersen Bibliography; Bibliography of Old Norse-Icelandic Studies; Catalogue and Oriental Manuscripts, Xylographs, etc in Danish Collections; Discovery and Research in the Collections in the Royal Library

Det **Nordjyske Landsbibliotek**, Nytorv 26, DK-9000 Ålborg Tel: (08) 122277 Telex: 69605 Aalbib Dk
Central Library for the County of North Jutland
Librarian: Birger Knudsen

Odense Centralbibliotek*, DK-5000 Odense
Odense County Library

Odense Universitetsbibliotek, Campusvej 55, DK-5230 Odense M
Odense University Library

Rigsarkivet, Rigsdagsgården 9, DK-1218 Copenhagen K
National Record Office
Dir: Vaju Dybdahl

Statsbiblioteket, Universitetsparken, DK-8000 Århus C Tel: (06) 122022 Telex: 64515
State and University Library

Odense **Universitetsbibliotek**, see Odense

Universitetsbiblioteket, 1 afd, Fiolstraede 1, DK-1171 Copenhagen K Tel: (01) 130875
University Library: Humanities Department
Librarian: Torben Nielsen

Universitetsbiblioteket, 2 afd, Nørre allé 49, DK-2200 Copenhagen N Tel: (01) 396523 Telex: 15097 Ubisk Dk
University Library: Scientific and Medical Department
Chief Librarian: Kell Prehn

Library Associations

Arkivforeningen*, Rigsarkivet, Rigsdagsgården 9, DK-1218 Copenhagen K Tel: (01) 123878
Archives Society

Bibliotekarforbundet, Hyskenstr 2, DK-1207 Copenhagen K Tel: (01) 152811
Union of Librarians
Secretary: B Sørensen
Publication: Bibliotek 70

Bibliotekscentralen, Telegrafvej 5, DK-2750 Ballerup Tel: (02) 975555 Cable Add: Danliber Telex: 35370
Danish Library Bureau
Man Dir: Leo Alster; *Editor:* Jørgen Rishøj
Subjects: Literature about Libraries, Bibliographical Manuals and Material
Publications: Dansk Artikelindeks, Aviser og Tidsskrifter (Danish Index of Articles, Periodicals and Newspapers), *Dansk Bogfortegnelse* (The Danish National Bibliography, Books), *Dansk Periodicafortegnelse* (The Danish National Bibliography, Serials)

Danmarks Biblioteksforening, Trekronergade 15, DK-2500 Copenhagen Valby Tel: (01) 308682
Danish Library Association
Secretary: F Ettrup
Publications: Bogens Verden (Danish Library Journal); *Biblioteksvejviser* (Danish Library Guide); Biblioteksårborg (Danish Library Yearbook)

Danmarks Forskningsbiblioteksforening, The Royal Library, Christians Brygge 8, DK-1219, Copenhagen K Tel: (01) 150111
Danish Research Library Association: Section 1 Research Libraries; Section 2 Staff members of Danish Research Libraries
President: Palle Birkelund; *Secretary:* Dorte Bertram
Publication: DF-Revy

Danmarks Skolebibliotekarforening, Rønnevej 7, DK-6880 Tarm Tel: (07) 371788
Association of Danish School Librarians
Publication: Skole Biblioteket (The School Librarian), Kongshvilebakken 10-12, DK-2800 Lyngby

Danmarks Skolebiblioteksforening, Vejlemosevej 21, DK-2840 Holte Tel: (02) 424930
Association of Danish School Libraries
Chief Executive: Jørgen Christiansen;
Manager: Niels Jacobsen
Publication: Børn og Bøger; also books dealing with School Libraries and Youth Culture etc

Dansk Musikbiblioteksforening, The Secretary, The Royal Library, Music Department, Christians Brygge 8, 1219 Copenhagen K
Association of Danish Music Libraries (Danish section of AIBM/IAML)

Dansk Teknisk Litteraturselskab*, Anker Engelunds Vej 1, DK-2800 Lyngby
Danish Society for scientific and technological information and documentation

Foreningen af Medarbejdere ved Danmarks Forskningsbiblioteker, Det Kongelige Bibliotek, Christians Brygge 8, DK-1219 Copenhagen K Tel: (01) 150111
Association of Staff Members of Danish Research Libraries (section 2 of the Danish Research Library Association)
President: Mette Stockmarr; *Secretary:* Birgit Berg

Sammenslutningen af Danmarks Forskningsbiblioteker, Det Kongelige Bibliotek, Christians Brygge 8, DK-1219 Copenhagen K Tel: (01) 150111
Association of Danish Research Libraries (section 1 of the Danish Research Library Association)
President: Palle Birkelund; *Secretary:* Dorte Bertram

Library Reference Books and Journals

Books

Biblioteksårbog (Library Yearbook), Danish Library Association, Trekronergade 15, DK-2500 Copenhagen Valby

Biblioteksvejviser (Library Guide), Danish Library Association, Trekronergade 15, DK-2500 Copenhagen Valby

Public Libraries in Denmark, Det Danske Selskab, Kulturvet 2, DK-1175 Copenhagen K

Udenlandsk Bibliotekslitteratur i Danske Biblioteker (Foreign Library Literature in Danish Libraries), Bibliotekscentralen, Telegrafvej 5, DK-2750 Ballerup

Journals

Bibliotek 70 (Library 70), Union of Librarians, Hyskenstr 2, 4, DK-1207 Copenhagen K

Biblioteken (The Library), Biblioteksskole, Birketinget 6, DK-2300 Copenhagen S

Bogens Verden (Library Journal), magazine for Danish library employees, Danish Library Association, Trekronergade 15, DK-2500 Copenhagen Valby

DF-Revy, Danmarks Forskningsbiblioteksforening, Statsbiblioteket, Universitetsparken, DK-8000 Århus C

Information for Forskningsbiblioteker (Information for Research Librarians), The Royal Library, Christians Brygge 8, DK-1219 Copenhagen K

Meddelelser frä Rigsbibliotekaren (Communications from the State Librarians), The Royal Library, Christians Brygge 8, DK-1219 Copenhagen K

Restaurator, International journal for the preservation of library and archival material (text in English, French, German and Russian), Restaurator Press, PO Box 96, DK-1004 Copenhagen K

Skole Biblioteket (The School Librarian), Kongshvilebakken 10-12, DK-2800 Lyngby

Literary Associations and Societies

Bogvennerne*, Madvigs Allé 2, DK-1829 Copenhagen
Friends of the Book

Dansk Exlibris Selskab*, PO Box 1519, DK-2700 Copenhagen Brh
Danish Bookplate Society
Publication: Exlibris-Nyt

Nyt **Dansk Litteraturselskab**, Bibliotekscentralen, Telegrafvej 5, DK-2750 Ballerup
New Danish Society for Literature
Manager: Leo Alster
Aims: Publication/Republication of books in short supply in libraries
Special activity: Magnaprint (large print books for partially-sighted)
Members: public libraries only

Danske Sprog-og Litteraturselskab, Frederiksholms Kanal 18A, DK-1220 Copenhagen
Danish Language and Literature Society
Administrator: Dr Erik Dal

Kongelige Danske Videnskabernes Selskab, H C Andersens Boulevard 35, DK-1553 Copenhagen V Tel: (01) 113240
Royal Danish Academy of Sciences and Letters
President: P J Riis; *Secretary:* Christian Crone
Publications: Oversigt (annual) etc

Samfund til Udgivelse af Gammel Nordisk Litteratur, Kjaerstrupvej 33, DK-2500 Copenhagen Valby
Society for the Publication of Old Norse Literature
Secretary: Agnete Loth

Literary Periodicals

Bog-anmelderen (The Book Review), Bog-Anmelderens Tidsskrifter, Gammel Torv 16, DK-1457 Copenhagen

Børn og Bøger (Children and Books), Association of Danish School Libraries, Vejlemosevej 21, DK-2840 Holte

Exlibris-Nyt (Bookplate News), Danish Bookplate Society, PO Box 1519, DK-2700 Copenhagen Brh

Hvedekorn (Wheat Grain), Borgens Forlag, Mynstersvej 19, DK-1827 Copenhagen V

Language and Literature (text in English), Copenhagen University, English Institute, Lille Kirkestr 1, DK-1072 Copenhagen K

Orbis Litterarum, international review of literary studies (text mainly in English, occasionally in French and German), Munksgaard, Nørre Søgade 35, DK-1370 Copenhagen K

Literary Prizes

Emil **Aarestrup** Prize*
For a poet. DKr 2,500 and a medal. Awarded annually. Enquiries to Danish Ministry of Cultural Affairs, Nybrogade 2, Copenhagen K

Hans Christian **Andersen** Prize
For the best Danish book for children. Established in 1955 to commemorate the 150th anniversary of the birth of Andersen. Awarded annually. Enquiries to Nyt Nordisk Forlag Arnold Busck A/S, Købmagergade 49, DK-1150 Copenhagen K

Danish Academy Prize for Literature
For an outstanding work of literature. DKr 50,000. Awarded annually. Enquiries to The Danish Academy, Rungstedlund, 109 Rungsted Strandvej, DK-2960 Rungsted Kyst

Danish Authors' Colleagues Prize*
To a colleague who has published an interesting work. DKr 5,000. Awarded annually. Enquiries to Danish Authors' Society, Forfatternes Hus, Nyhavn 21, DK-1051 Copenhagen K

Danish Authors' Lyric Prize*
For poetry. DKr 5,000. Awarded annually. Enquiries to Danish Authors' Society, Forfatternes Hus, Nyhavn 21, DK-1051 Copenhagen K

Danish Critics Literary Prize*
For literary and art criticism. DKr 5,000. Awarded annually. Enquiries to Danish Publishers' Association, Købmagergade 11, DK-1150 Copenhagen K

Danish Prize for Children's Literature*
For the best Danish books for children and teenagers. Awarded annually. Enquiries to Danish Ministry of Cultural Affairs, Nybrogade 2, Copenhagen K

Johannes **Ewald** Prize*
For prose, poetry and dramatic works. DKr 2,000. Awarded annually. Enquiries to Danish Authors' Society, Forfatternes Hus, Nyhavn 21, DK-1051 Copenhagen K

Adam **Gottlob** Oehlenschläger Prize*
For outstanding Danish writers. DKr 2,000. Awarded annually. Enquiries to Danish Ministry of Cultural Affairs, Nybrogade 2, Copenhagen K

Søren **Gyldendal** Prize
For authors from any field whose work is of great literary value. DKr 20,000. Awarded annually. Enquiries to Gyldendalske Boghandel, Nordisk Forlag, Klareboderne 3, DK-1001 Copenhagen K

Holberg Medal*
For outstanding contributions to Danish literature. DKr 5,000 and a medal. Awarded annually. Enquiries to Danish Authors' Society, Forfatternes Hus, Nyhavn 21, DK-1051 Copenhagen K

Translation Agencies and Associations

Association of Translators*, Ribegade 8, Copenhagen

Danish Translations Centre (DTC), Risø Library, Risø National Laboratory, DK-4000 Roskilde Tel: (03) 371212 Telex: 43116 A Risoe

Translatørforeningen*, Bornholmsgade 1, DK-1266 Copenhagen K
Association of Danish Sworn Translators

Dominican Republic

General Information

Language: Spanish
Religion: Roman Catholic
Population: 5.12 million
Literacy Rate (1970): 68.5%
Bank Hours: 0830-1230 Monday-Friday; some open 0830-1130 Saturday
Shop Hours: 0800-1200, 1400 or 1500-1800 Monday-Friday; some open Saturday
Currency: 100 centavos = 1 peso oro (= $US1). US currency is widely used
Export/Import Information: Children's picture books dutiable at 25%, atlases 10%. Advertising catalogues 10% ad valorem. 35% VAT FOB Internal Tax, 20% Consumption Tax, and 4% surtax on all imports. No import licences required for books. Exchange licence and approval from Central Bank required
Copyright: Buenos Aires (see International section)

Publishers

Publicaciones **Ahora** C por A*, Ave San Martin 236, Apdo 1402, Santo Domingo Tel: 5655581 Cable Add: Ahora Dr Telex: 326438
Editorial: R Molina Morillo; *Sales:* Luis R Cordero; *Production:* José R Grau; *Publicity:* Manuel Fco Santana

Juan Max **Alemany***, E Henriquez 12, Santo Domingo

Editora **Alfa y Omega***, M Cabral 11, Santo Domingo

Blas de la Rosa*, Yolanda Guzmán 105, Santo Domingo

Editora El **Caribe**, Autop Duarte Km 7 1/2, Santo Domingo

Editora **Colonial***, Moca 27-B, Santo Domingo

Rafael **Corporan** de los Santos*, S. Valverde 44, Santo Domingo

Editora **Cosmos***, Calle N No. 13, Feria, Santo Domingo

Ediciones **Pedagógicas** Domincanas C por A*, Padre Billini 103, Apdo 1320, Santo Domingo Tel: 6889711
Man Dir: Miguel González Cano
Imprint: Escobo
Subjects: School Books and Educational Materials
Subsidiary Company: Editora Cultural Dominicana SA
Founded: 1962

Editora **Cultural Dominicana***, San Martín 236, Santo Domingo

Editora **Educativa Dominicana***, Mercedes 45, Santo Domingo

Editora **Internacional***, Moca 31, Santo Domingo

Editora y **Distribuidora** Nacional de Libros*, Arzobispo Nouel, 80 esqina Espaillat, Santo Domingo Tel: 98222 Cable Add: Edinalibros
President: Luis Franco
Subjects: History, Social Science, Law, Philosophy
Founded: 1964

Editorama, SA, Ave Tiradentes 56, Santo Domingo

Editorial Librería Dominicana*, Mercedes 45-49, Santo Domingo Tel: 96293/23893
Cable Add: Sirviendo
Dir: Julio Postigo
Subjects: General Literature, Religion, Law, Textbooks
Founded: 1937

Editora **Enriquillo***, I la Catolica 41, Santo Domingo

Escobo, an imprint of Ediciones Pedagógicas Dominicanas (qv)

P A **Gómez***, E Tejera 15, Santo Domingo

Editora **Horizontes** de América*, A Fleming 2, Santo Domingo

La **Información***, M Gómez 16, Santiago

Editora **Listín** Diario*, Paseo de los Periodistas 12, Santo Domingo

Editorial **Padilla***, San Fco Macorís 14, Santo Domingo
Bookshops: see under Booksellers

Editora Colegial **Quisqueyana** SA, Ave Tiradentes, Centro Comercial Naco, Santo Domingo Tel: 5661808/5654277/5671818
Subjects: Pre-school, Primary & Secondary Textbooks and Educational Materials
Bookshop: address as above

Editora La **Razon***, J Verne 14, Santo Domingo

Editorial **Stella***, Guayacanes 7, Santo Domingo

Ultima Hora*, Paseo de los Periodistas 12, Santo Domingo

Universidad Autónoma de Santo Domingo, Ciudad Universitaria, Apdo 1355, Santo Domingo Tel: 5331694 Cable Add: 3460182 Uniausd
Subjects: Academic

Universidad Católica Madre y Maestra, Departamento de Publicaciones, Autopista Duarte, Santiago de los Caballeros Tel: 5825105 Cable Add: Ucmm
Man Dir, Editorial: Danilo de los Santos
Subjects: General
1978: 10 titles *1979:* 11 titles *Founded:* 1967

Major Booksellers

Caribe Grolier Inc*, L de Castro 203
Tel: 6897373; Hostos 208 Tel: 6888544

Ediciones **Coquito***, E Tejera 19
Tel: 6883021

Casa **Cuello***, El Conde 33 Tel: 6896226/6874242

Disesa*, Hostos 202 Tel: 6897644/6823533; S Larga Tel: 6882163

Distribuidora Escolar SA*, Hostos 202 Tel: 6897644/6823533; S Larga 6882163

Encyclopaedia Britannica de Venezuela SA*, El Conde 35 Tel: 6829260

Papeleria **Fersobe** Hnos*, Ave Duarte 177 Tel: 6894744; Ave Mella 156 Tel: 6881848

Casa **Herrera***, Mercedes 125, Santo Domingo Tel: 97568

Febio **Herrera***, Bolivar 40 Tel: 6878677
Importer

Librería y Papeleria **Lope** de Vega*, L de Vega 55 Tel: 5658066

Mella*, Ave Duarte 27 Tel: 6886539

Niove*, 16 de Agosto 47 Tel: 6894088

Editorial **Padilla***, El Conde 511 Tel: 6820111/6880303
Branches: San Fco Macoris 14 Tel: 6823101; El Conde 109 Tel: 6880303

Editora Colegial **Quisqueyana** SA*, Tiradentes Tel: 5654277/5661808

Major Libraries

Archivo General de la Nación, Calle M E Diaz, Santo Domingo Tel: 5331608
National Archives

Biblioteca Dominicana*, Santo Domingo

Biblioteca Nacional*, César Nicolás Penson 91, Plaza de la Cultura, Santo Domingo
National Library

Biblioteca de la **Cámara** Oficial de Comercio, Agricultura e Industria del Distrito Nacional*, Arzobispo Nouel 52, Altos, Santo Domingo
Library of the Chamber of Commerce, Agriculture and Industry

Biblioteca Municipal de **Santo Domingo***, Padre Billini 18, Santo Domingo

Biblioteca de la **Secretaría de Estado de Relaciones Exteriores***, Estancia Ramfis, Santo Domingo
Library of the Secretariat of Foreign Affairs

Biblioteca de la **Universidad Autónoma** de Santo Domingo*, Ciudad Universitaria, Apdo 1355, Santo Domingo

Library Associations

Asociación Dominicana de Bibliotecarios (ASODOBI), Biblioteca Nacional, Santo Domingo Tel: 6884086
Dominican Association of Librarians
President: Prospero J Mella-Chavier;
Secretary-General: Verónica Regús de Tosca
Publication: El Papiro

Grupo Bibliografico Nacional de la Republica Dominicana*, c/o Emilio Rodriguez de Morizi, Director, Archivo General de la Nacion, Calle Chiclana de la Frontera, Santo Domingo

Servicio de Documentación y Biblioteca*, Palacio de Educación, Santo Domingo
Library and Documentation Service

Ecuador

General Information

Language: Spanish
Religion: Predominantly Roman Catholic
Population: 7.8 million
Literacy Rate (1962): 67.5% (88.1% Urban, 55.5% Rural)
Bank Hours: 0900-1200, 1500-1630 Monday-Friday
Shop Hours: 0830-1230, 1430-1830 Monday-Saturday. In Guayaquil, shops open in the afternoon Friday at 1530 and many are closed Saturday
Currency: 100 centavos = 1 sucre
Export/Import Information: Member of the Latin American Free Trade Association. Books and most advertising catalogues not dutiable. No import licences or exchange controls for books
Copyright: UCC, Buenos Aires (see International section)

Book Trade Organizations

Sociedad de Libreros del Ecuador*, Calle Bolivar 268 y Venezuela of 501, Quito
Booksellers' Society of Ecuador
Secretary: Eduardo Ruiz

Publishers

Fondo Editorial de **C I E S P A L** (Centro Internacional de Estudios Superiores de Comunicación para América Latina), Ave Diego de Almagro y Andrade Marín s/n, CP 584, Quito Tel: 544624/545831 Cable Add: Ciespal Telex: 2474 Ciespl Ed
Dirs: Marco Ordóñez Andrade; Galo Viteri Pinto (Orders)
Subjects: Social Communication, Development Planning, Research and Documentation; Periodicals
Founded: 1960

Cromograf SA*, Coronel 2207, PPB 4285, Guayaquil Tel: 346400 Cable Add: Cromograf Telex: 3387 Ariel Ed
Subjects: Juvenile/Children's Books; Paperbacks; Art Productions

Casa de la **Cultura** Ecuatoriana*, Ave 6 de Diciembre 332, Apdo 67, Quito
Tel: 230260 Cable Add: Casacultura
Branch Offs: Núcleo del Azuay, Apdo 4907, Cuenca; Núcleo del Guayas, Guayaquil
Subjects: General Fiction & Nonfiction, General Science (Ecuadorian authors only)
Founded: 1944

Editorial Interamericana del Ecuador CA*, Ave America 542, Quito
Manager: Manuel de Castillo
Associate Company: Holt-Saunders Ltd, UK (qv for other associates)

Editorial **Labor** del Ecuador SA*, Portoviejo 105 y 10 de Agosto, Edificio Carrera, CP-710A, Quito
Parent Company: Editorial Labor, Spain (qv)

Pontificia **Universidad Católica** de Ecuador*, 12 de Octubre 1076 y Carrion, Apdo 2184, Quito Tel: 529240
Subjects: Literature, Art, Natural Sciences, Law, Anthropology, Sociology, Politics, Economics, Theology, Philosophy, History, Archaeology

Universidad Central del Ecuador*, Dpto de Publicaciones, Servicio de Almacén Universitario, Ciudad Universitaria, Quito

Universidad de Guayaquil*, Dpto de Publicaciones, Biblioteca Gral, Apdo 3834, Guayaquil Tel: 392430
Man Dir: Constantino Vinueza M
Subjects: General Literature, History, Philosophy, Fiction
Founded: 1930
Bookshop: Librería Universitaria, Ciudad Universitaria, PO Box 3834, Guayaquil

Major Booksellers

Librería **Cervantes***, Vélez 416, Guayaquil
Tel: 15573

Librería **Cima***, Ave 10 de Agosto 285, Quito Tel: 233066

Librería **Científica***, Apdo 2905, Quito
Tel: 12556; Luque 223, Casilla 362, Guayaquil Tel: 14555

Librería **Española***, Venezuela 961 y Mejía, Casilla 356, Quito Tel: 212060; Librería Española Cía Ltda, Ave 10 de Agosto 1233, Casilla 356, Quito Tel: 543460

Librería Universitaria, García Moreno 739, Apdo 2982, Quito Tel: 212521
Dir: Ing Carlos E Wong Flores
Importer/Exporter

Una **Pequeña** Librería*, Ave 10 de Agosto 563, Quito Tel: 234296

Librería **Selecciones***, 9 de Octubre 735, Guayaquil; Calle Benalcázar 543, Quito

Su Librería*, Apdo 2556, Quito Tel: 210225

Major Libraries

Archivo Nacional de Historia*, Ave 6 de Diciembre 332, Apdo 67, Quito
National Historical Archives

Biblioteca Ecuatoriana 'Aurelio Espinosa Pólit'*, Apdo 160, Quito Tel: 530420

Biblioteca Nacional del Ecuador*, García Moreno y Sucre, Quito
National Library

Biblioteca de la **Casa de la Cultura Ecuatoriana***, Ave 6 de Diciembre 332, Apdo 67, Quito Tel: 230260
Library of Ecuadorian Culture

Museo y Biblioteca Municipal*, Ave 10 de Agosto y Calle Pedro Carbo, Guayaquil

Biblioteca de la **Universidad Central de Ecuador***, Ciudad Universitaria, Quito

Biblioteca General, **Universidad de Guayaquil***, Apdo 3834, Guayaquil

Library Association

Asociación Ecuatoriana de Bibliotecarios (AEB)*, Casa de la Cultura Ecuatoriana, Casilla 87, Quito Tel: 528840 Headquarters: 263474
Ecuadorian Library Association
Executive Secretary: Elizabeth Carrion
Publications: Unidad Bibliotecaria

Library Journal

Unidad Bibliotecaria, Ecuadorian Library Association, Casa de la Cultura Ecuatoriana, Casilla 87, Quito

Egypt

General Information

Language: Arabic (English and French widely used)
Religion: Muslim
Population: 39.6 million
Literacy rate (1976): 43.5% of population aged 10 or more
Bank Hours: Generally 0830-1230 Monday-Thursday; 1000-1200 Saturday
Shop Hours: 0830-1330, 1630-1900 Monday-Saturday
Currency: 100 piastres (1000 milliemes) = 1 Egyptian pound
Export/Import Information: No tariff on books, 25% on advertising in quantity. 10% Consolidation Duty, 1% statistical tax and small additional taxes apply. No import licences. Exchange control by Supreme Committee set up by Ministry of Finance, Economy and Foreign Trade. Banks authorized to execute foreign-exchange transactions. No longer government monopoly but some book importing done by Foreign Trade Company, Misr Import & Export Co, 6 Adly St, Cairo
Copyright: Berne, Florence (see International section)

Book Trade Organizations

Permanent Bureau of **Afro-Asian Writers***, 104 Kasr el-Aini St, Cairo

General Egyptian Book Organization*, Corniche el Nil, Boulac, Cairo Tel: 972649 Cable Add: Gebo Telex: 92252 Mena
Chairman: D M el Sheniti
See also entry under Publishers

The **Public Organization** for Books and Scientific Appliances*, Cairo University, Orman, Ghiza, Cairo
Chairman: Kamil Seddik

Standard Book Numbering Agency, c/o Dr S M El Sheniti, General Egyptian Book Organization, Corniche el Nil, Boulac, Cairo

Publishers

Al-Ahram Establishment, Al-Galaa St, Cairo Tel: 758333/745666/755500 Cable Add: Pyramidad Telex: 92001/92544
Book Club: Al-Ahram Establishment
Miscellaneous: Also translation agency, printer, distributor, importer, exporter

American University in Cairo Press, 113 Sharia Qasr el Aini, PO Box 25511, Cairo Tel: 29781 Cable Add: Victorious Telex: 92224 Aucai Un
Dir: John Rodenbeck
Subjects: Literature, Art, History, Africana, Anthropology, Arabic Language, Architecture, Coptology, Social Science, Textbooks, Guidebooks, Egypt and the Arab World, Religion, Natural Sciences, Reference Works, Periodicals
1978: 5 titles *1979:* 8 titles *Founded:* 1960

Al **Arab Publishing** House, 23 Faggalah St, Cairo Tel: 908025 Cable Add: Arabukshop Cairo
Man Dir: Prof Dr Saladin Boustany; *Sales Manager:* George G Eddé
Subjects: General Fiction, Belles Lettres, Poetry, Biography, History, Africana, Philosophy, Reference, Religion, Arabic Language & Literature, Arabic Manuscripts, Paperbacks, Social Science, University & Secondary Textbooks
Bookshop: 28 Faggalah St, Cairo
Founded: 1900

Cairo University Press*, Guiza-Orman, Giza, Cairo Tel: 846144
Subject: University Textbooks

E S D U C K, see The Egyptian Society for the Dissemination of Universal Culture and Knowledge

Les **Editions universitaires** d'Egypte*, 41 Sharia Sherif Pasha, Cairo
Subject: University Textbooks

The **Egyptian Society** for the Dissemination of Universal Culture and Knowledge (ESDUCK), PO Box 21, Cairo (Located at: 1081 Corniche el Nil St, Garden City, Cairo) Tel: 20295/25079 Cable Add: Esduck
Man Dir: Ibrahim Abdel Rahman; *Editorial:* Inas Effat; *Production:* Amira Farid; *Rights & Permissions:* Shewikar Zaki
Subjects: Trade Books, Textbooks, Children's Books, Reference
Founded: 1953
Miscellaneous: Co-publisher with local and American firms

General Egyptian Book Organization*, Corniche el Nil, Boulac, Cairo Tel: 972649 Cable Add: Gebo Telex: 92252
Chairman: D M el Sheniti
Foreign Distribution Centre: Samady & Salha Bldg, Syria St, Beyrouth, Lebanon
Subjects: Arab classic and modern books in all fields
Bookshops: International Book Centre, Cairo, 13 branches throughout Egypt
Founded: 1961
ISBN Publisher's Prefix: 977-201

The **General Organization** for Government Press Affairs*, 22 Al Nil St, Imbaba, Guiza, Cairo
This is the Government Printer

Government Printer, see The General Organization for Government Press Affairs

Dar Al **Hilal** Publishing Institution, 16 Sharia Mohammed Ezz El Arab, Cairo Tel: 20610 Cable Add: Al Mussawar Cairo Telex: 92703 Hilal Un
Chief Executive: Amina Al Said
Subjects: Fiction, Non-fiction, Periodicals

Dar Al **Maaref***, 1119 Corniche el Nil St, Cairo Tel: 59263/8 Cable Add: Damaref Telex: Un 92199
President: Anis Mansour; *Man Dir:* Dr M Fouad Ibrahim; *General Manager:* Dr Salib Botros; *Sales:* Camile Fahim Mossad
Subsidiary Company: Dar el-Maaref, Lebanon
Subjects: Academic, Scientific, General Islamic, Schoolbooks, Children's (in Arabic), University Textbooks (in English)
Bookshops: in Cairo, Alexandria, Assiut, Qena, Tanta, Shebin, El-Kom, Asswan
Founded: 1890
ISBN Publisher's Prefix: 977-247

Dar Al-Kitab Al-**Masri**, PO Box 156, Cairo Tel: 742168/744657/754301 Cable Add: Kitamisr Telex: 2336 Cairo
Man Dir: El-Zein Hassan
Parent Company: Dar Al-Kitab Allubnani, Lebanon (qv)
Branch Offs: Paris, Geneva, Madrid, Casablanca
Subjects: Islamic, Turath, Textbooks (in Arabic, English, French)
1978: 197 titles *1979:* 237 titles *Founded:* 1929

Middle East Book Centre*, 45 Sharia Kasr el-Nil, Cairo Tel: 910980
Man Dir: Dr A M Mosharrafa; *Sales Manager:* A Ismail
Subjects: General Fiction, Belles Lettres, Poetry, Biography, History, Africana, Philosophy, Religion, Arabic Language & Literature, Paperbacks, General & Social Science, University & Secondary Textbooks
Founded: 1954

Maktabet **Misr***, 3 Kamel Sidki St, PO Box 16, Cairo Tel: 908920
Misr Bookshop
Man Dir: Amir Said Gouda El Sahhar
Subjects: General Fiction, Belles Lettres, Poetry, Biography, History, Books in Arabic language, University & School Textbooks
Bookshop: Maktabet Misr, 3 Kamel Sidki St, Cairo
Founded: 1932

Dar al-**Nahda** al Arabia*, 32 Sharia Abdel-Khalek Sharwat St, Cairo
Subjects: Arabic Language & Literature
Bookshop: At above address

Editions le **Progrès***, 6 Sharia Sherif Pasha, Cairo
Man Dir: Wedi Choukri

The **Public Organization** for Books and Scientific Appliances, Cairo University*, Orman, Ghiza, Cairo

EGYPT — EL SALVADOR

Chairman: Kamil Seddik
Subject: University Textbooks
Founded: 1965

Senouhy Publishers*, 54 Sharia Abdel-Khalek, Sarwat, Cairo
Man Dir: Leila A Fadel
Subjects: General Nonfiction, Belles Lettres, Poetry, History, Africana, Religion
Founded: 1956

The **Sphinx**, Bookshop and Publishing House, 3 Shawarby St (Kasr El Nil) — 3rd Floor — Apartment 305, Cairo Tel: 744616 Cable Add: Bulhall Cairo Telex: 93927 Sfinx Un
Man Dir: Abd-el-Salam Hassan Sharara
Subjects: Educational and Academic Books
Founded: 1958

Literary Agent

The **Egyptian Society** for the Dissemination of Universal Culture and Knowledge (ESDUCK), PO Box 21, Cairo (Located at: 1081 Corniche el Nil St, Garden City, Cairo) Tel: 20295/25079 Cable Add: Esduck

Book Club

Al-**Ahram** Establishment*, Galaa St, Cairo
Owned by: Al Ahram Establishment (Publisher)

Major Booksellers

Al **Ahd** Al Gadeed Bookstore*, Farouk Zaky & Co, 4-5 Kamel Sidky St, Cairo Tel: 900290/905296

The **Anglo American** Bookshop*, 55 Algomhouria St, Cairo Tel: 905262

The **Anglo Egyptian** Bookshop, 165 Mohamed Farid St, Cairo Tel: 914337
Proprietor: Sobhy Grais

Al **Arab** Bookshop, 28 Faggalah St (del PL 480), Cairo Tel: 908025 Cable Add: Arabukshop Cairo
Manager: Saladin Boustany
Agent of the Library of Congress PL 480

Librairie **Hachette***, 45 bis rue Champolion, Cairo

Al **Ittihad** Bookstore*, Mohamed Abdel Mouty Ismail, 3 Kamel Sidky St, Al Ezbekia, Cairo Tel: 916403

Dar Al **Kutub** Al Hadeetha*, Tewfik Afeefi Amer & Co, 14 Al Goumhouria St, Abdeen, Cairo Tel: 916107

Lehnert & Landrock*, 44 Sherif St, PO Box 1013, Cairo

Livres de France*, Immeuble Immobilia, rue Kasr el Nil, Cairo

Misr Bookshop, 3 Kamel Sidki St, Faggalah, Cairo Tel: 908920 Cable Add: Dameltibaa Cairo
Manager: Amir Saïd El-Sahhar

Misr Import & Export Co*, 6 Adly St, Cairo
Importer/Exporter

Modern Cairo Bookshop*, 169 Tahreer St, Cairo

Saladdine Publications & Distributors, 28 Talaat Harb St, Abu Reijala Building, Cairo Tel: 52542

Ahmed **Shaker** Al Ansary*, Midan Birkit Al Ratly, Sikit Al Ratly No 3, Bab Al Sharea, Cairo Tel: 932895

Major Libraries

Alexandria Municipal Library*, 18 Sharia Menasce Moharrem Bey, Alexandria

American University in Cairo Library, 113 Sharia Kasr El-Aini, Cairo Tel: 22969

Al-**Azhar** University Library*, Cairo Tel: 904051

Dar-ul-Kutub*, Midan Ahmed Maher, Bab El-Khalq, Cairo
Egyptian National Library

Institut français d'Archéologie orientale*, Bibliothèque, 37 rue Mourira, Cairo

Institut d'Egypte Library*, 13 Sharia Sheikh Rhane, Cairo

Institute of Arab Research & Studies Library*, 1 Tolombat St, Cairo

Ministry of Justice Library*, Midan Lazoghli, Abassia, Cairo Tel: 831546

National Archives, Citadel, nr Military Museum, Cairo Tel: 921534

National Assembly Library*, Palace of the National Assembly, Cairo

National Information and Documentation Centre*, Sh Al-Tahrir, Dokki, Cairo

University of Alexandria Library*, 22 Al-Gueish Ave, Shatby, Alexandria Tel: 71675/8

University of Cairo Library*, Orman, Ghiza, Cairo Tel: 845186

Library Associations

Algamiia Almasriia Lilmaktabat Almadrasiia*, 35 Algalaa St, Cairo
Egyptian School Library Association
Publication: Sahifat al-Maktabát (Egyptian Library Journal)

Egyptian Association for Archives and Librarianship*, c/o Library of Fine Arts, 24 El Matbâa Al-Ahlia, Boulac, Cairo
Executive Secretary: Ahmed M Mansour
Publication: Alam al-Maktabát

National Information and Documentation Centre*, Al-Tahrir St, Dokki, Cairo

Library Reference Book and Journals

Book

Directory of Scientific and Technical Libraries, National Information and Documentation Centre, Sh-Al-Tahrir, Dokki, Cairo

Journals

Alam al-Maktabát (Library World), Egyptian Association for Archives and Librarianship, c/o Library of Fine Arts, 24 El Matbâa Al-Ahlia, Boulac, Cairo

Sahifat al-Maktabát (Egyptian Library Journal), Egyptian School Library Association, 35 Algalaa St, Cairo

Literary Associations and Societies

Atelier*, 1 Sharia St, Saba, Alexandria
Secretary-General: L Hergenstein
Society of Artists and Writers

High Council of Arts & Literature, 9 Sharia Hassan Sabri, Zamalek, Cairo
Secretary: Youssef Al Sibai

Literary Periodical

Lotus; Afro-Asian Writings, 104 Kasr el-Aini St, Cairo
Important quarterly review published for the Permanent Bureau of Afro-Asian Writers

Translation Agencies and Associations

Al-**Ahram**, Al-Galaa St, Cairo Tel: 755500/745666/758333 Cable Add: Pyramidad Telex: 92001-92544 Ahram UN

The **Egyptian Society** for the Dissemination of Universal Culture and Knowledge (ESDUCK)*, PO Box 21, Cairo (Located at: 1081 Corniche el Nil St, Cairo) Tel: 20295/25079

El Salvador

General Information

Language: Spanish
Religion: Roman Catholic
Population: 4.35 million
Literacy Rate (1975): 62.1% of population aged 10 or more
Bank Hours: 0830-1130, 1430-1600 Monday-Friday; 0900-1130 Saturday
Shop Hours: 0800-1200, 1400-1800 Monday-Friday; 0800-1200 Saturday
Currency: 100 centavos = 1 colon
Export/Import Information: Member of the Central American Common Market. Catalogues dutied at $0.03 per gross kg. No import licences but exchange licence from Exchange Control Department of Central Reserve Bank required, if goods coming from outside Central America. Commercial banks authorize certain import payments
Copyright: UCC, Buenos Aires, Florence (see International section)

Publishers

Editorial Universitaria de la Universidad de El Salvador*, Apdo Postal 1703, San Salvador (Located at: Ciudad Universitaria, San Salvador) Tel: 256604
Dir: Armando Herrara
Subjects: Scholarly Books, Textbooks, General Literature
Founded: 1923

Ministerio de Educación, Dirección de Publicaciones, Pasaje Contreras 145, San Salvador Tel: 254605/259092
Man Dir, Rights & Permissions: Jesús Romeo Galdámez; *Editorial:* José Reynaldo Echeverría; *Sales:* Arturo Martínez; *Production:* Ricardo Martínez; *Publicity:* Alfredo Campos
Orders to: Gerencia de Distribución, 9a Calle Oriente 104 y Ave España, San Salvador
Subjects: Literature, Art, Sociology, History, General Textbooks
Bookshop: 9a Calle Oriente 104 y Ave España, San Salvador
1980: 60 titles *Founded:* 1953

U C A Editores*, Apdo Postal (06) 668, San Salvador (Located at: Universidad Centroamericana José Simeón Cañas, Autopista Sur, Jardines de Guadalupe, San Salvador) Tel: 234491

Dir: Italo López Vallecillos
Subjects: Social Science, Religion, Economy and Scholarly Books
Founded: 1968

Major Booksellers

Librería Claudio **Bernard***, Calle Los Cedros 53, 100 metros al sur del IVU, San Salvador Tel: 256719

Clasicos Roxsil, 6a Ave Sur 1-6, Santa Tecla Tel: 281212
Manager: Rosa Victoria Serrano de López

Librería **Cultural** Salvadoreña SA de CV*, Calle Arce 423, San Salvador Tel: 27206/221307

Librería e Importadora **Neruda**, PO Box 1764, San Salvador (Located at: 29 Calle Poniente 222, Local No 6, San Salvador) Tel: 251566
Manager: José Reynaldo Echeverrío

Librería **Renacimiento** SA de CV*, Apdo Postal 852, San Salvador (Located at: Final Pasaje 5 No 126 y 2a diagonal, Urbanización La Esperanza, San Salvador) Tel: 254541/263198

Distribuidora **Salvadoreña***, Ave España 344, San Salvador Tel: 213438
Office: 9a Ave Norte 422, San Salvador Tel: 226983

Librería **Universitaria** de la Universidad de El Salvador, Apdo Postal 2028, San Salvador (Located at: Ciudad Universitaria, San Salvador) Tel: 258607/258022 ext 132

Librería **Universitaria** UCA*, Apdo Postal (06) 668, San Salvador (Located at: Universidad Centroamericana José Simeón Cañas, San Salvador) Tel: 240011 ext 193, 234491

Major Libraries

Biblioteca Nacional*, 8a Ave Norte y Calle Delgado, San Salvador Tel: 213249

Biblioteca de la **Universidad Centroamericana** José Simeón Cañas, Apdo Postal (06) 668, San Salvador (Located at: Autopista Sur, Jardines de Guadalupe, San Salvador) Tel: 240011
Dir: Mélida Arteaga

Biblioteca Central de la **Universidad de El Salvador***, Apdo Postal 143, San Salvador (Located at: Ciudad Universitaria, San Salvador) Tel: 258022 ext 115
Dir: Ana Aurora de Kapsalis
Publications: Boletín (monthly); *Lista de Adquisiciones Recientes* (monthly)

Library Associations

Asociación de Bibliotecarios de El Salvador*, Urbanización Gerardo Barrios Polígono, 'B' No 5, San Salvador Tel: 220409/253471
El Salvador Library Association
Secretary-General: Edgar Antonio Pérez Borja
Publication: Informa (Newsletter) (monthly)

Asociación General de Archivistas de El Salvador*, Apdo Postal No 664, Edificio Sede 8, Calle Oriente 314, San Salvador
Association of Archivists of El Salvador

Library Journal

Informa (Newsletter), El Salvador Library Association, Urbanización Gerardo Barrios Polígono, 'B' No 5, San Salvador

Literary Periodical

Guíon Literario (Literary Summary), Ministerio de Educación del Gobierno de El Salvador, Dirección General de Publicaciones, Pasaje Contreras 145, San Salvador

Ethiopia

General Information

Language: Amharic (English, French and Italian spoken)
Religion: Ethiopian Orthodox (allied to Coptic Church)
Population: 29 million
Bank Hours: 0900-1200, 1500-1700 Monday-Friday; 0900-1200 Saturday
Shop Hours: Addis Ababa: 0900-1300, 1500-2000 Monday-Saturday. Asmara: 0800-1300, 1600-2000 Monday-Friday
Currency: 100 cents = 1 birr
Export/Import Information: No tariff on books, but additional taxes of 15% CIF +1% and 1% cif +1% Advertising subject to 10% customs and same taxes. No import licence required but Exchange Payment Licence necessary
Copyright: No copyright conventions signed

Book Trade Reference Books and Journals

Book
List of Ethiopian Authors, Addis Ababa University Library, PO Box 1176, Addis Ababa

Journal
Ethiopian Publications (Ethiopian National Bibliography), Institute of Ethiopian Studies, Addis Ababa University, PO Box 1176, Addis Ababa

Publishers

Addis Ababa University Press*, PO Box 1176, Addis Ababa Tel: 119148 Cable Add: University Addis
Editor: Innes Marshall
Subjects: Public Health, Hydrology, Climatology, Botany, Ornithology, Conservation, Geology, Philosophy; University Textbooks, Reference; works in English language
1978: 3 titles *Founded:* 1968

The **Bible** Churchmen's Missionary Society*, PO Box 864, Asmara, Eritrea Tel: 114267
Dir: John Coracher
Subjects: General Fiction, Belles Lettres, Poetry, Biography, History, Africana, Religion, Juveniles, Amharic Language & Literature
Bookshop: PO Box 864, Asmara, Eritrea

Government Printer*, Government Printing Press, PO Box 980, Addis Ababa

Major Booksellers

Berhan Bookshop and Stationery*, PO Box 302, Addis Ababa

Bible Churchmen's Missionary Society*, PO Box 864 Asmara, Eritrea

The **City** Bookshop*, 9 Haile Selassie I Ave, PO Box 864, Asmara

E C A Bookshop Co-op Society*, PO Box 60100, Addis Ababa

International Press Agency*, G P Giannopoulos, PO Box 120, Addis Ababa

Menno Bookstore*, PO Box 1236, Addis Ababa

Major Libraries

Addis Ababa University Library*, PO Box 1176, Addis Ababa Tel: 115673

American Library*, PO Box 1014, Addis Ababa Tel: 113377

Asmara Public Library*, 20 Haile Selassie I Ave, Asmara

British Council Library, PO Box 1043, Addis Ababa (Located at: Artistic Bldg, Adua Ave, Addis Ababa) Tel: 110022/4 Cable Add: Britcoun

Ethiopian Manuscript Microfilm Library*, PO Box 30274, Addis Ababa
Publication: Bulletin (quarterly)

National Library and Archives of Ethiopia*, PO Box 717, Addis Ababa Tel: 442241

Organization for African Unity Library*, PO Box 3243, Addis Ababa Tel: 157700 Cable Add: Oau Telex: 21046

Polytechnic Institute Library*, PO Box 26, Bahar-Dar

U N Economic Commission for Africa Library*, PO Box 3001, Addis Ababa Tel: 447200

University of Asmara Library*, PO Box 1220, Asmara Tel: 113600

Library Associations

Ethiopian Library Association*, PO Box 30530, Addis Ababa Tel: 110844 ext 353
Publications: Ethiopian Library Association Bulletin; Directory of Ethiopian Libraries

Library Reference Books and Journals

Books
Directory of Ethiopian Libraries, Ethiopian Library Association, PO Box 30530, Addis Ababa

Journals
Bulletin, Ethiopian Library Association, PO Box 30530, Addis Ababa

Bulletin, Ethiopian Manuscript Microfilm Library, PO Box 30274, Addis Ababa

84 FIJI — FINLAND

Fiji

General Information

Language: English, Fijian, Hindi and Cantonese
Religion: Predominantly Protestant, with large minority of Hindus
Population: 607,000
Bank Hours: 1000-1500 Monday-Friday; 0930-1100 Saturday
Shop Hours: 0800-1630 or later Monday-Friday; early closing Wednesday or Saturday
Currency: 100 cents = 1 Fiji dollar
Export/Import Information: No tariffs on books and advertising. No import licences. Exchange control by central monetary authority; no specific exchange licence required and authorized banks perform transaction upon application
Copyright: Berne, UCC (see International section)

Book Trade Journals

Publications Bulletin, Government Printing and Stationery Department, Suva

Publishers

Home Products Ltd*, Garrick Bldg, Suva Tel: 25196

Indian Printing and Publishing Co*, PO Box 151, Suva
Man Dir: S M Bidesi Jr
Subjects: Law, Administration, Business Management

Lotu Pasifika Productions, PO Box 208, Suva Tel: 24314 Cable Add: Lotupak
Manager: Aisake M Raratabu
Subjects: Education, Religion, Poetry, Cookery
1978: 3 titles *1979:* 4 titles

Oceania Printers Ltd, PO Box 597, Suva Tel: 313044/313224
Subject: Literature

Sangam Sarada Printing Press*, PO Box 9, Nadi
Subjects: Literature, History, Geography

Tara Press*, Kings Rd, PO Box 923, Nasinu, Suva
Subjects: Literature, Music

Trans-Pacific Publishers*, PO Box 3083, Lami, Suva (Located at: Queens Rd, Lami, Suva) Tel: 361727

Major Booksellers

Desai Bookshops*, Head Office: Rajobhai Patel Rd, Suva Tel: 311188 (and 12 branches)

Suva Book Shop, Greig St, PO Box 153, Suva Tel: 311355
Manager: Harinivas Singh

Major Libraries

Library Service of Fiji, Western Regional Library, PO Box 150, Lautoka Tel: 60091/61866

National Archives of Fiji*, PO Box 2125, Government Buildings, Suva

Suva City Library, Victoria Arcade, Suva
Librarian: Edward David

Library Association

Fiji Library Association (FLA), c/o Honorary Secretary, PO Box 2292, Government Bldgs, Suva
Publication: Fiji Library Association Newsletter; Fiji Library Association Journal

Library Journal

Newsletter, Fiji Library Association, c/o Honorary Secretary, PO Box 2292, Government Bldgs, Suva

Finland

General Information

Language: Finnish and Swedish (officially bilingual); English and German spoken widely
Religion: Lutheran
Population: 4.7 million
Bank Hours: 0915-1615 Monday-Friday
Shop Hours: 0830-1700 or later Monday-Friday; 0830-1500 or 1600 Saturday
Currency: 100 pennia = 1 markka
Export/Import Information: Associate member of European Free Trade Association. Free trade agreed with European Economic Community. No tariff on books or advertising. 12.4% Turnover Tax, 3.1% Import Equalization Tax, 2-3% Port Charges. No import licences required
Copyright: UCC, Berne, Florence (see International section)

Book Trade Organizations

Kirja-ja Paperikauppiasliitto*, Pieni Roobertinkatu 13-B26, SF-00130 Helsinki 13 Tel: (90) 603479
Finnish Booksellers' Association
Chief Executive: Pentti Kuopio

Kirjapalvelu (Book Service)*, Kalevankatu 16, SF-00100 Helsinki 10
Advertising and Public Relations Organization

Standard Book Numbering Agency, Helsinki University Library, PL 312, SF-00170 Helsinki 17
Administrator: Dr Theo Aulo

Suomen Antikvariaattiyhdistys-Finska Antikvariatföreningen, P Makasiininkatu 6N, Magasinsgatan 6, SF-00130 Helsinki 13 Tel: 626352
Finnish Antiquarian Booksellers' Association

Suomen Kirjailijaliitto*, Runeberginkatu 32C, Helsinki
Association of Finnish Authors
Executive Secretary: Jarl Louhija
Publications: Suomen Runotar, Suomalaisetkertojat

Suomen Kustannusyhdistys, Bulevardi 6 A 10, SF-00120 Helsinki 12 Tel: 641644
Finnish Publishers' Association
Secretary-General: U Lappi

Suomen Nuortenkirjaneuvosto ry, Uudenkaupungintie 7 A 9, SF-00350 Helsinki 35
Finnish Section of the International Board on Books for Young People (IBBY)
President: Kaija Salonen, Haapaniemenkatu 16C, SF-00530 Helsinki 53
Secretary: Lilian Hakkarainen

Book Trade Reference Books and Journals

Book

Suomessa Ilmestyneen Kirjallisuuden Luettelo (Katalog över i Finland Utkommen Litteratur) (List of Books Published in Finland), Finnish Publishers' Association, Bulevardi 6 A 10, SF-00120, Helsinki 12

Journals

Kirja Ja Paperi (Book and Paper), Finnish Publishers' Association, Bulevardi 6 A 10, SF-00120, Helsinki 12

Kirjakauppalehti (Book Trade Journal), Finnish Publishers' Association, Bulevardi 6 A 10, SF-00120 Helsinki 12

Libristi (Journal for Booksellers' Assistants), PO Box 10242, Helsinki 10

Suomen Kirjallisuus (Finlands Litteratur) (The Finnish National Bibliography), Helsinki University Library, Unioninkatu 36, PO Box 312, SF-00171 Helsinki 17

Publishers

Akateeminen Kustannusliike Oy, Mikonk 20 B 12, SF-00100 Helsinki 10 Tel: (90) 174002
Manager: M O Mattila; *Sales:* Riitta Mattila
Subjects: Matriculation books, Religion, Fiction
Founded: 1927
ISBN Publisher's Prefix: 951-9023

Ekenäs Tryckeri AB, PO Box 36, SF-10600 Ekenäs (Located at: Stationsvägen 1, Ekenäs) Tel: (911) 12800 Telex: 13150 Vne Sf
Man Dir: Sven Sundström
Subjects: History, Politics
Bookshop: Ekenäs Bokhandel — Boktjänst AB (at above address)
1978: 3 titles *1979:* 12 titles *Founded:* 1881
ISBN Publisher's Prefix: 951-9000

Etelä-Suomen Kustannus Oy*, PO Box 15, Huoltomiehentie 1, SF-21420 Lieto
Tel: (921) 777502
Subjects: War, Reference, Science Fiction Paperbacks, Comics
ISBN Publisher's Prefix: 951-9064

Edition **Fazer**, PO Box 260, 00101 Helsinki 10 (Located at: Höyläämotie 16, 00380 Helsinki 38) Tel: (90) 558991 Cable Add: Musicfazer Telex: 121738 Mufa Sf
Man Dir (of Parent Company): John-Eric Westö; *Publishing Manager:* Liisa Aroheimo; *Rights & Permissions:* Mirjam Saksa
Parent Company: Oy Musiikki Fazer Musik AB, PO Box 260, 00101 Helsinki 10
Subjects: Music, Music Education
Bookshop: Aleksanterink 11, 00100 Helsinki 10
1978: 70 titles *1979:* 80 titles *Founded:* 1897
ISBN Publisher's Prefix: 951-757

Forsamlingsforbundets Forlags AB, PO Box 285, 00121 Helsinki 12 (Located at: Bangatan 29 A 1, 00120 Helsinki 12) Tel: 170221
Man Dir: Bjarne Boije; *Sales:* Aili Hellström; *Production:* Pia Hartman
Associate Company: Ab Fram (printing house), Vasaesplanaden 24, 65100 Vasa 10
Subject: Religion

Bookshop: Ab Gamlakarleby Bokhandel, Strandgatan 13, 67100 Karleby 10
1978: 19 titles *1979:* 15 titles *Founded:* 1920
ISBN Publisher's Prefix: 951-550

Government Printer*, Government Printing Centre, Valtion Painatuskeskus, Annankatu 44, Helsinki 10

K J Gummerus Osakeyhtiö, Alasinkatu 1-3, PO Box 130, SF-40101 Jyväskylä 10 Tel: (941) 272522 Cable Add: Gummerus Telex: 28289
Man Dir: Pekka Salojärvi; *Editorial:* Jussi Sorjonen; *Publishing Dir:* Olli Arrakoski; *Rights & Permissions:* Anna Thorwall
Subjects: Fiction, General Nonfiction, Philosophy, Psychology, Education, Juveniles, Paperbacks, Textbooks
Book Club: Uusi Kirjakerho Oy (partly owned)
Bookshops: Jyväskylä, Jämsä, Mänttä, Seinäjoki, Helsinki
1978: 240 titles *1979:* 260 titles *Founded:* 1872
ISBN Publisher's Prefix: 951-20

Karas-Sana Oy, PO Box 48, Vivamo, 08101 Lohja 10 Tel: (912) 87755
Man Dir, Rights & Permissions: Matti Valtonen; *Editorial:* Eva Mesiäinen; *Sales:* Jouni Ilmolahti
Parent Company: Kansan Raamattuseuran Säätio (at above address)
Subject: Christian Religion
1978: 13 titles *1979:* 18 titles *Founded:* 1974
ISBN Publisher's Prefix: 951-655

Arvi A **Karisto** Oy, Raatihoneenkatu 1, PO Box 102, SF-13101 Hämeenlinna 10 Tel: (917) 23551 Cable Add: Arvikaristo
Man Dir: Onni-Sakari Karisto; *Editorial:* Ilmari Lehmusvaara (Finnish Literature), Ritva Makelä (Foreign Literature); *Sales:* Leo Räiha; *Production:* Onni Helin; *Advertising:* Olli Tuomi; *Foreign Rights:* Ritva Mäkelä
Branch Off: Arvi A Karisto, Keskusk 3, Helsinki 10
Subjects: General Fiction and Non-fiction, Juvenile Fiction
Book Club: Uusi Kirjakerho Oy, PL 29, SF-00381 Helsinki 38 (owned jointly with Kirjayhtymä Oy (Helsinki), Weilin & Göös (Helsinki), K J Gummerus Osakeyhtiö (Jyväskylä)
1978: 160 titles *Founded:* 1900
ISBN Publisher's Prefix: 951-23

Kustannusliike **Kirjaneliö**, Töölönkatu 55, SF-00250 Helsinki 25 Tel: (90) 440 561
Orders to: Raamattutalo, PO Box 21, SF-76101 Pieksämäki 10
Subjects: Religion, Fiction, Juveniles
1979: 37 titles *Founded:* 1905
ISBN Publisher's Prefix: 951-600

Kirjayhtymä Oy*, Eerikinkatu 28, SF-00180 Helsinki 18 Tel: 602566 Cable Add: Kirjayhtymä
Man Dir: Pentti Nurmio; *Publishing Dir:* Keijo Immonen; *Marketing Dir:* Viljo Salin; *Publicity Manager:* Heikki Rönnqvist; *Rights & Permissions:* Mrs Salonen
Subjects: Fiction, Nonfiction, Textbooks
Book Club: Uusi Kirjakerho Oy (partly owned)
Founded: 1958
ISBN Publisher's Prefix: 951-26

Lasten Keskus Oy, Uudenmaankatu 4 A 5, SF-00120 Helsinki 12 Tel: (90) 643203 Cable Add: Lasten Keskus
Man Dir: Pertti Rosenholm; *Publishing Manager, Production, Rights & Permissions:* Juhani Järvelä; *Head Salesman, Publicity:* Anna-Maija Kurvinen
Associate Company: Yhteiskirjat, Kirstinkatu 1, SF-00530 Helsinki 53
Subjects: Juveniles, Books for Parents and Teachers, Religion (Luthcran)
Bookshop: Lasten Kirjakauppa (Children's Bookshop), Fredrikinkatu 61, SF-00100 Helsinki 10
1978: 22 titles *1979:* 39 titles *Founded:* 1974
ISBN Publisher's Prefix: 951-626

Otava Kustannusosakeyhtiö, Uudenmaankatu 8-12, PO Box 134, SF-00120 Helsinki 12 Tel: (3580) 647022 Cable Add: Otava Helsinki Telex: 124560
Chairman: Heikki A Reenpää; *Man Dir:* Olli Reenpää; *Literary Dirs:* Dr Paavo Haavikko (Fiction), Pentti Huovinen (Nonfiction & Encyclopaedias); *Dir of International Relations; Rights & Permissions:* Erkki Reenpää; *Export Manager:* Matti Käki
Subjects: General Fiction, Belles Lettres, Biography, History, How-to, Music, Art, Philosophy, Reference, Religion, Juveniles, Low- & High-priced Paperbacks, Textbooks, Educational Materials
Book Club: Suuri Suomalainen Kirjakerho Oy (partly owned)
Bookshops: 9 branches throughout Finland
1978: 789 titles *1979:* 743 titles *Founded:* 1890
ISBN Publisher's Prefix: 951-1

Rakennuskirja Oy, Bulevardi 3B, SF-00120 Helsinki 12 Tel: 645615
Building Book Ltd
Man Dir: Timo Olkkonen; *Marketing Manager:* Ilkka Kilpela
Parent Company: Rakennustietosäätio (Building Information Institute), Lonnrotinkatu 20B, 00120 Helsinki 12
Subject: Building
1978: 7 titles *1979:* 7 titles *Founded:* 1974
ISBN Publisher's Prefix: 951-682

Ristin Voitto ry, PO Box 75, SF-01301 Tikkurila Tel: 826377
President: Eino Vanhala; *Publishing Dir:* Valtter Luoto
Book Club: Ristin Voitto ry, PO Box 75, SF-01300 Tikkurila
Subjects: Christian Literature & Music
1979: 60 titles *Founded:* 1926
ISBN Publisher's Prefix: 951-605

Holger **Schildts** Förlagsaktiebolag, Annegatan 16, SF-90120 Helsinki 12 Tel: (90) 604892 Cable Add: Bokschildt
Man Dir: J af Hällström
Subjects: General Fiction, Belles Lettres, Poetry, Biography, History, Music, Art, Philosophy, University Textbooks, Reference, Juveniles, High-priced Paperbacks
1978: 132 titles *1979:* 95 titles *Founded:* 1913
ISBN Publisher's Prefix: 951-50

Söderström ja Co Förlagsaktiebolag, Murbacksgatan 6, SF-00210 Helsinki 21 Tel: 6923681 Cable Add: Söderströms
Man Dir: Göran Appelberg
Subjects: General Fiction, Belles Lettres, Poetry, Biography, History, How-to, Music, Art, Philosophy, Reference, Religion, Juveniles, Medicine, Psychology, General Science, University, Secondary & Primary Textbooks
1978: 302 titles *1979:* 319 titles *Founded:* 1891
ISBN Publisher's Prefix: 951-52

Suomalaisen Kirjallisuuden Seura, PO Box 259, SF-00171 Helsinki 17 (Located at: Hallituskatu 1, SF-00171 Helsinki 17) Tel: (90) 171229
Finnish Literature Society
Secretary-General/Director: Urpo Vento
Subjects: Folklore, Ethnology, Literary History, Linguistics
1978: 33 titles *1979:* 30 titles *Founded:* 1831
ISBN Publisher's Prefix: 951-717

Tammi Kustannusosakeyhtiö, Hämeentie 15, SF-00500 Helsinki 50 Tel: 716522 Cable Add: Tammi Helsinki
Man Dir: Jarl Hellemann; *Editorial:* Sirkka Kurki-Suonio; *Marketing Dir:* Sakari Lahtinen; *Rights & Permissions:* Ritva Urnberg
Subjects: General Fiction, Belles Lettres, Poetry, Biography, History, How-to, Music, Art, Philosophy, Reference, Juveniles, High-priced Paperbacks, Psychology, Engineering, Social Science, University Textbooks, Easy Readers
Book Club: Suuri Suomalainen Kirjakerho Oy (jointly owned)
1978: approx 350 titles *Founded:* 1943
ISBN Publisher's Prefix: 951-30

Tietoteos Publishing Co, PO Box 40, SF-02211 Espoo 21 (Located at: Yläportti 1 A, SF-02211 Espoo 21) Tel: 881133
Man Dir: Jyrki K Talvitie
Associate Company: Transpico Ltd (at above address)
Subjects: Technical Dictionaries, Travel Guides, Finnish Air Force History series, Stock Market Manual, General Technical
1978: 5 titles *1979:* 5 titles *Founded:* 1948
ISBN Publisher's Prefix: 951-9035

Kustannus Oy **Uusi Tie**, PO Box 54, SF-00601 Helsinki 60 (Located at: Oulunkyläntie 5, SF-00600 Helsinki 60) Tel: (90) 799244
Man Dir: Eino J Honkanen; *Sales:* Olavi Maijala
Subjects: Christian Religion, Theology
1978: 9 titles *1979:* 9 titles *Founded:* 1964
ISBN Publisher's Prefix: 951-619

Amer-yhtymä Oy **Weilin + Göös**, Ahertajantie 5, SF-02100 Espoo 10 Tel: 461322 Cable Add: Weilingöös Telex: 122597 Weigs Sf
Man Dir: Seppo Saario; *Publishing Dir:* Ville Repo; *Editorial:* Maarit Tyrkkö, Jaakko Manninen, Eero Syrjänen; *Rights & Permissions:* Tuula Kuusi
Subjects: General Fiction & Nonfiction, Belles Lettres, Poetry, Biography, History, Business, Reference, Juveniles, Economics, Textbooks, Educational Materials
Book Club: Uusi Kirjakerho Oy, PL29, SF-00381 Helsinki 38: owned jointly by Kirjayhtymä Oy (Helsinki), K J Gummerus Osakeyhtiö (Jyväskylä), Arvi A Karisto Osakeyhtiö (Hämeenlinna) and Weilin + Göös (Espoo)
Bookshop: Kirjakievari, Mannerheimintie 40, Helsinki 10
1978: 290 titles *Founded:* 1872
ISBN Publisher's Prefix: 951-35

Werner **Söderström** Osakeyhtiö (WSOY), Bulevardi 12, PO Box 222, SF-00121 Helsinki 12 Tel: (90) 643521 Cable Add: Wsoy Helsinki Telex: 122644 Wsoy sf
Man Dir: Hannu Tarmio; *Publishing Dir:* Keijo Ahti (Nonfiction, Encyclopaedias, Educational); *Assistant Literary Dir:* Matti Snell (Foreign Relations, Fiction and Nonfiction); *Assistant Dirs:* Petri Arpo (Educational); Asko Rysa (Juveniles); *Rights & Permissions:* Satu Suomala
Subjects: General Fiction, Nonfiction, Juveniles, Textbooks, Encyclopaedias, Audio-Visual Materials, Educational Materials
Book Club: Suuri Suomalainen Kirjakerho Oy (Great Finnish Book Club) (jointly owned)
1978: 865 titles *1979:* 965 titles *Founded:* 1878
ISBN Publisher's Prefix: 951-0

Yritystieto Oy — Foretagsdata HAb, PO Box 148, 00181 Helsinki 18 (Located at: Kalevankatu 45 A 1, 00181 Helsinki 18) Tel:

FINLAND

(90) 648292/648293 Cable Add: Hibernia
Telex: 121394 Tltx Sf for Hibernia
Publisher: Börje Thilman
Subjects: Business, Directories, Reference
1978: 3 titles *1979:* 4 titles *Founded:* 1972
ISBN Publisher's Prefix: 951-9102

Literary Agents

Edith **Kiilerich**, Fiolstr 12, DK-1171
Copenhagen K, Denmark
This company also acts as a literary agent in
Denmark, Norway, Sweden and Iceland for
foreign authors

Werner **Söderström** Osakeyhtiö (WSOY),
PL 222 Bulevardi 12, SF-00121 Helsinki 12

Book Clubs

Ristin Voitto ry, PO Box 75, SF-01300
Tikkurila

Suuri Suomalainen Kirjakerho Oy,
Hietalahdenranta 15A, SF-00180 Helsinki
18 Tel: 601466 Telex: 121394 Tltx Sf
Kirjakerho
Man Dir: Pertti Araviita
The Great Finnish Book Club Ltd
Owned by: Werner Söderström Osakeyhtiö
(Helsinki), Otava Kustannusosakeyhtiö
(Helsinki), Tammi Kustannusosakeyhtiö
(Helsinki)

Bokklubben **Tre Böcker***, 02510 Oitbacka
Subjects: Classics, Current Affairs,
Dictionaries, Encyclopaedias, Detective
fiction, Periodicals

Uusi Kirjakerho Oy, PO Box 29, SF-00381
Helsinki 38
Subjects: Bestselling Novels, General
Nonfiction, Encyclopaedias
Owned by: Kirjayhtymä Oy (Helsinki), K J
Gummerus Osakeyhtiö (Jyväskylä), Oy
Weilin & Göös Ab (Helsinki), Arvi A
Karisto Osakeyhtiö (Hämeenlinna)

Major Booksellers

Akateeminen Kirjakauppa, Keskuskatu 1,
SF-00100 Helsinki 10 Tel: (90) 651122
Cable Add: Akateeminen Telex: 124773
Chief Executive: Jorma Kaimio
Branch Offs: Rautatienkatu 11, SF-15101
Lahti; Kirkkokatu 29, SF-90100 Oulu 10

Gummeruksen Kirjakauppa, Kauppakatu
16, SF-40100 Jyväskylä 10 Tel: (941) 10760
Telex: 28289 Kjgoy Sf
Manager: Paavo Harju

Lappeenrannan Kirjakauppa Oy*, Valtakatu
36, SF-53100 Lappeenranta 10 Tel: (953)
15117

Pohjalainen Kirjakauppa Oy*, Kirkkokatu
17, SF-90100 Oulu 10 Tel: (981) 24133

Savolan Kirjakauppa Oy*, Tulliportinkatu
33, SF-70100 Kuopio 10 Tel: (971) 16611

Suomalainen Kirjakauppa Oy,
Aleksanterinkatu 23, SF-00100 Helsinki 10
Manager: Antti Remes
(7 other branches in Helsinki, and branches
in Kouvola, Oulu, Vaasa, Vantaa, Espoo,
Joensuu, Hämeenlinna, Lahti)

Tampereen Kirjakauppa Oy, Hämeenkatu
27, SF-33200 Tampere 20 Tel: (931) 28380
Telex: 22521 Tamki Sf

Turun Kansallinen*, PO Box 135, SF-20101
Turku 10 Tel: (921) 29451

Yliopistokirjakauppa Oy*, Fredrikinkatu
30A, SF-00120 Helsinki 12 Tel: (90) 640109

Major Libraries

Eduskunnan Kirjasto, SF-00102 Eduskunta
Library of Parliament

Helsingin Kaupunginkirjasto,
Rikhardinkatu 3, Helsinki 13
Helsinki City Library
Librarian: Hirn Sven

Helsingin Teknillisen Korkeakoulun
Kirjasto*, Otaniementie 9, SF-02150 Espoo
15
Helsinki University of Technology Library

Helsingin Yliopiston Kirjasto, Unioninkatu
36, PO Box 312, SF-00171 Helsinki 17 Tel:
(1911) 1912740 Telex: 12-1538 Hyk Sf
Helsinki University Library
Librarian: Prof Esko Häkli
Branches: Slavonic Library, Neitsytpolku
1B, PO Box 313, SF-00171 Helsinki 17 Tel:
661791; Science Library, Tukholmankatu 2,
SF-00250 Helsinki 25 Tel: 410566
Publications: Books from Finland; The
Finnish National Bibliography; Publications
of the University Library at Helsinki

Jyväskylän Yliopiston Kirjasto*,
Seminaarinkatu 15, SF-40100 Jyväskylä 10
Tel: (941) 291211 Telex: 28219
Jyväskylä University Library

Lääketieteellinen Keskuskirjasto*,
Haartmanink 4, SF-00290 Helsinki 29
Telex: 121498 Lkk Sf
Central Medical Library

Oulun Yliopiston Kirjasto, PO Box 186,
SF-90101 Oulu 10 (Located at: Kasarmintie
7, SF-90100 Oulu 10) Tel: (981) 223455
Telex: 32256 Oyk Sf
Oulu University Library

Sibelius-Akatemian Kirjasto*, Pohj
Rautatiek 9, Helsinki
Sibelius Academy Library

Statistics Library, PO Box 504, SF-00101
Helsinki 10 (Located at: Annakatu 44 — 2nd
floor, Helsinki) Telex: 122656
Library of the Central Statistical Office of
Finland
Chief Librarian: Hellevi Yrjölä

Tampereen Yliopiston Kirjasto, PL 617, SF-
33100 Tampere 10 (Located at: Tammelau
Puistokatu 38, Tampere) Tel: (931) 156111
Telex: 22263 Tayk Sf
Library of the University of Tampere

Turun Yliopiston Kirjasto, SF-20500 Turku
50
Turku University Library
Librarian: H Eskelinen

University Libraries, Finland, see under
town names

Valtionarkisto, PO Box 274, SF-00171
Helsinki 17
National Archives of Finland
Librarian: Elion Pispali

Library Associations

Arkistoyhdistys ry*, Rauhankatu 17,
SF-00170 Helsinki 17 Tel: (90) 176911
Archival Association
Secretary-Treasurer: Ritva Pesonen

Kirjastonhoitajien Keskusliitto-
Bibliotekariernas Centralforbund ry,
Tempplikatu 1 A, SF-00100 Helsinki 10
Central Federation of Librarians
Executive Secretary: Anna-Maija Hintikka

Kirjastovirkailijat-Biblioteksanstallda ry*,
c/o Helsinki University Library,
Unioninkatu 36, PO Box 312, SF-0017
Helsinki 17 Tel: (90) 1912737
Association for Non-Professional Staff of
Public and Research Libraries
Headquarters: Vipusentie 8, Helsinki
Tel: (90) 794276
Executive Secretary: Kirsti Tuominen
Publications: Volyymi

Suomen Kirjallisuuspalvelun Seura*, c/o
Helsinki University of Technology Library,
Otaniementie 9, SF-02150 Espoo 15
Finnish Association for Documentation

Suomen Kirjastonhoitajat — Finlands
Bibliotekarier ry*, Cygnaeuksenkatu 4 B 11,
SF-00100 Helsinki 10
Finnish Librarians
Executive Secretary: Kari Turunen

Suomen Kirjastoseura, Museokatu 18 A 4,
SF-00100 Helsinki 10 Tel: 492632
Finnish Library Association
Secretary General: Hilkka M Kauppi
Publication: Kirjastolehti (Library Journal)

Suomen Tieteellinen Kirjastoseura, c/o
Library of Parliament, SF-00102
Helsinki 10 Tel: 4323470 Telex: 121498
Lkk Sf
Finnish Research Library Association
Secretary: Jorma Hirsivuori

Tieteellisen Informoinnin Neuvosto, PO Box
312, SF-00171 Helsinki 17
Finnish Council for Scientific Information
and Research Libraries
Secretary: Marketta Lehto-Toivakka

Tieteellisten Kirjastojen Virkailijat —
Vetenskapliga Bibliotekens
Tjänstemannaförening ry, c/o Library of the
Soviet Institute, Armfeltintie 10, SF-00150
Helsinki 15
Association of Research and University
Librarians
Executive Secretary: Anneli Virtanen
Publications: Issues newsletter to members

Library Reference Books and Journals

Book

Suomen Erikoiskirjastojen Luettelo
(Directory of Special Libraries in Finland),
Finnish Association for Documentation, c/o
Helsinki University of Technology Library,
Otaniementie 9, SF-02150 Espoo 15

Journals

The Finnish National Bibliography, Helsinki
University Library, Unioninkatu 36, PO Box
312, SF-00171 Helsinki 17

Kirjastokalenteri (Library Calendar),
Finnish Library Association, Museokatu 18
A 4, SF-00100 Helsinki 10

Kirjastolehti (Library Journal), Finnish
Library Association, Museokatu 18 A 4,
SF-00100 Helsinki 10 (jointly with Central
Federation of Librarians)

Signum (text in Finnish and Swedish;
summaries in English), Finnish Research
Library Association, c/o Library of
Parliament, SF-00102 Helsinki 10

Volyymi (The Volume), Association for Non-
Professional Staff of Public and Research
Libraries, c/o Helsinki University Library,
Unioninkatu 36, PO Box 312, SF-00171
Helsinki 17

Literary Associations and Societies

Bibliofiilien Seura*, Lauttasaarentie 5 C 29, 00200 Helsinki 20
President: Onni M Turtiainen
Society of Bibliophiles

Finlands Svenska Författareförening, Runebergsgatan 32 C 27, 00100 Helsinki 10 Tel: (90) 446266
Association of Swedish Authors in Finland
Secretary: Mette C Jensen

Kirjallisuudentutkijain Seura*, Kotimaisen kirjallisuuden laitos, Fabianinkatu 33, 00170 Helsinki 17
Society of Literary Research Workers
Secretary: Pertti Lassila
Publication: Kirjallisuudentutkijain Seuran Vuosikirja (Annual of Literary Historians)

Suomalainen Tiedeakatemia, Snellmaninkatu 9-11, SF-00170 Helsinki 17 Tel: (90) 636800
Finnish Academy of Science and Letters
Secretary-General: Lauri A Vuorela
Publications: Annales Academiae Scientiarum Fennicae; F F Communications; Documenta Historica; Vuosikirja (Yearbook)

Suomalaisen Kirjallisuuden Seura, PO Box 259, SF-00171 Helsinki 17 (Located at: Hallituskatu 1, SF-00171 Helsinki 17) Tel: (90) 171229
Finnish Literature Society
Secretary-General/Director: Urpo Vento
Librarian: Rauni Puranen
Publications: Studia Fennica; Suomi; Tietolipas; Toimituksia; (irregular)

Suomen Arvostelijain Liitto*, Lönnrotinkatu 15 A7, SF-00120 Helsinki 12
Critics' Association of Finland

Svenska Litteratursällskapet i Finland, Snellmaninkatu 9-11, SF-00170 Helsinki 17 Tel: (90) 636738
Swedish Literary Society in Finland
Publication: Skrifter

Svenska Österbottens Litteraturförening*, Hrvrattsesplanaden 5, Vasa
Swedish Österbottens Literary Association

Literary Periodicals

Katsaus (Review) (text mainly in Finnish, occasionally in Swedish), Kulttuurikeskus Kriittisen Korkeakoulun Kannatusyhdistys ry, Lehtikuusentie 6, SF-00270 Helsinki 27

Parnasso, Hietalahdenranta 13, SF-00180 Helsinki 18

Skrifter (Writings), Swedish Literary Society in Finland, Snellmaninkatu 9-11, SF-00170 Helsinki 17

Virittäjä (The Kindler) (Summaries in English, French, or German), Society for the Study of the Mother Tongue, Fabianink 33, SF-00170 Helsinki 17

Literary Prizes

Helsinki Prize*
Awarded annually by the City of Helsinki to the artist of the year (author, musician or painter). Enquiries to Helsingin Kaupungin Kulttuuriasiainkeskus, Annankatu 30, SF-00100 Helsinki 10

Tauno Karilas Prize*
For the writer of the year's best Finnish book for children. Awarded annually. Enquiries to Finnish Section of the International Board on Books for Young People, Uudenkaupungintie 7 A 9, SF-00350 Helsinki 35

Rudolf Koivu Prize
For the best illustrated children's book. Awarded annually. Enquiries to Rudolf Koivu Foundation, c/o State Committee for Literature, Ministry of Education, Rauhankatu 4, SF-00170 Helsinki

Arvid Lydecken Prize*
For the writer of the year's best Finnish book for children. Awarded annually. Enquiries to Finnish Section of the International Board on Books for Young People, Uudenkaupungintie 7 A 9, SF-00350 Helsinki 35

State Prizes for Literature
Prizes for the best literary works. Awarded annually. Enquiries to State Committee for Literature, Ministry of Education, Rauhankatu 4, SF-00170 Helsinki

Anni Swan Prize*
For the best children's and/or young adults' book of the previous three years. Awarded every three years. Enquiries to Finnish Section of the International Board on Books for Young People, Uudenkaupungintie 7 A 9, SF-00350 Helsinki 35

Tampere Prize
For the best authors connected with the city of Tampere. Awarded annually. Enquiries to Tampere City Government, Tampere

Topelius Prize
For the writer of the year's best Finnish book for young adults. Awarded annually. Enquiries to Finnish Section of the International Board on Books for Young People, Uudenkaupungintie 7 A 9, SF-00350 Helsinki 35

Translation Agencies and Associations

Suomen Kääntäjäin Yhdists*, Oversättarförening ry, Fredrikinkatu 62 A 6, Helsinki 10
Finnish Translators' Association

France

General Information

Language: French
Religion: Roman Catholic predominantly
Population: 53.3 million
Bank Hours: 0900-1600 Monday-Friday
Shop Hours: 0900-1200, 1400-1800 Tuesday-Saturday
Department Stores: 0930-1830 Tuesday-Saturday; open Monday in Paris
Currency: 100 centimes = 1 franc
Export/Import Information: Member of the European Economic Community. No tariff on books, except children's picture books from non-EEC 13%. 1.8% on advertising. VAT on books 7%, 20% on most advertising matter. 2% Customs Stamp Tax (based on duty). Import licences not required. Nominal exchange controls over 1500-franc value. For imports over 50,000 francs, documents must be 'domiciliated' before any other transaction occurs. There is control of the book trade based on a number of legal and regulating provisions applying to the import of pirated publications, articles and writings that offend against morality, publications harmful to youth, writings forbidden by the Minister for the Interior, books, writings, printed matter, etc intended to provoke the crime of abortion; the customs official must submit articles subject to control for examination by the General Information Service of the Ministry of the Interior
Copyright: UCC, Berne, Buenos Aires, Florence (see International section)

Book Trade Organizations

Agence francophone pour la Numération internationale du Livre (AFNIL-ISBN), 117 blvd St-Germain, F-75279 Paris cedex 06
Secretary: Cécile Renault

Cercle de la Librairie (Syndicat des Industries et Commerces du Livre)*, 117 blvd St-Germain, F-75279 Paris cedex 06 Tel: 3292101
Booksellers' Circle of the Association of Book Trades and Industries
Man Dir: Michel Dupouey; *Director:* Patrick Lehideux
Publications: Bibliographie de la France; Notices établies par le Dépôt Légal (Copyright Depositions); *Les Livres de l'année—Biblio* ('Biblio' Books of the Year); *Les Livres Disponibles* (French Books in Print); *Le Répertoire International des Éditeurs et Diffuseurs de Langue Française* (International List of French Language Publishers and Distributors); *Répertoire des Livres au Format de Poche* (List of Paperback (or Pocket Edition) Books; *Livres et Matériel d'Enseignement* (Teaching Aids and Books); *Catalogue des Livres d'Étrennes* (Catalogue of New Year Gift Books); *Études et Statistiques sur le Livre français* (Statistics and Research on French Books); *Catalogue général des ouvrages parus en Langue française* (General Catalogue of Works which have appeared in the French Language)

Chambre syndicale des Editeurs d'Annuaires et de Publications similaires, Permanent Secretariat, Cercle de la Librairie, 117 blvd St-Germain, F-75006 Paris Tel: (01) 3232101
Association of Publishers of Directories and Similar Publications
President: Gérard Delaubier

Fédération française des Syndicats de Libraires, 117 blvd St-Germain, F-75279 Paris cedex 06
The French Booksellers' Association
Publication: Lettre du Libraire

Office de Promotion de L'Edition Française, 117 blvd Saint-Germain, F-75279 Paris cedex 06 Tel: 3266166
Man Dir: Gustave Girardot
Miscellaneous: Function of the office is to organise the national stands of all French publishing companies at international book fairs as well as specific exhibitions throughout the world. It represents all French publishing houses

Standard Book Numbering Agency, see Agence francophone pour la Numération internationale du Livre

Syndicat national de la Librairie ancienne et moderne, 117 blvd St-Germain, F-75279 Paris cedex 06
This is the National Association of Antiquarian and Modern Booksellers
Secretary: Gérard Fleury
Publications: Guide à l'Usage des Amateurs du Livre; Répertoire des Membres du Syndicat National de la Librairie Ancienne et Moderne; quarterly review *Le Bulletin du*

88 FRANCE

Bibliophile (in conjunction with l'Association Internationale de Bibliophile) Also second-hand Bookseller

Syndicat des Réprésentants littéraires français, 117 blvd St-Germain, F-75279 Paris cedex 06
Association of French Literary Agents

Syndicat national de l'Edition*, 117 blvd St-Germain, F-75279 Paris cedex 06 Tel: (01) 3292101
French Publishers' Association
Secretary: Michel Dupouey
Publications: Le Répertoire des Livres et Matériel d'Enseignement; Le Répertoire international des Editeurs et Diffuseurs de Langue française; Le Catalogue des Produits et Matériels audio visuels; La Classification décimale de Dewey; Le Catalogue des Livres au Format de Poche; Le Catalogue des Livres d'Etrennes; Les Livres disponibles (French Books in Print)

Syndicat national des Annuaires et Supports divers de Publicité*, 40 blvd Malesherbes, F-75008 Paris Tel: 7421248
National Federation of Yearbooks and Sundry Publicity Aids

Syndicat national des Importateurs et Exportateurs de Livres, 117 blvd St-Germain, F-75279 Paris cedex 06
National Federation of Book Importers and Exporters

U D E F, 117 blvd Saint-Germain, F-75279 Paris cedex 06 Tel: 3548714 Telex: Lifran 270838 F
Dir: P Monnet
This is the Union of French Publishers, with the aim of international promotion of books in the French language. It has five associated Groups: Groupe des Editeurs d'Art, Groupe des Editeurs de Poésie, Groupe des Editeurs d'Erudition, Groupe des Editeurs de Réligion, Groupe des Editeurs de Sport (Groups associated with Art, Poetry, Learning, Religion and Sport respectively
Founded: 1963

Union d'Editeurs Français, see U D E F

Unipress*, 14 rue de Bretagne, F-75140 Paris cedex 03
Non-profit-making organization, whose purpose is to extend knowledge of the French Press abroad

Book Trade Reference Books and Journals

Books

Catalogue de l'Edition française (Catalogue of French-language Publishing), 22 rue de Condé, F-75006 Paris

Etudes et Statistiques sur le Livre française (Studies and Statistics on the French Book), Cercle de la Librairie, 117 blvd St-Germain, F-75279 Paris cedex 06

Guide du Livre Ancien et du Livre d'occasion (Antique and second-hand book guide), Cercle de la Librairie, 117 blvd St-Germain, F-75279 Paris cedex 06

Répertoire des Livres au Format de Poche (Catalogue of Paperback Books), 117 blvd St-Germain, F-75279 Paris cedex 06

Répertoire international des Editeurs et Diffuseurs de Langue française (International List of French Language Publishers and Distributors), Cercle de la Librairie, 117 blvd St-Germain, F-75279 Paris cedex 06

Répertoire international des Librairies de Langue française (International List of French Language Bookshops), Cercle de la Librairie, 117 blvd Saint-Germain, F-75279 Paris cedex 06

Journals

Art et Métiers du Livre (Art and Crafts of the Book), Cercle de la Librairie, 117 blvd St-Germain, F-75279 Paris cedex 06

La Bibliographie de la France — Biblio (French National Bibliography), Cercle de la Librairie, 117 blvd St-Germain, F-75279 Paris cedex 06

Book Promotion News (French edition), Unesco, 7 pl de Fontenoy, F-75700 Paris

Bulletin, Association of Antiquarian and Modern Booksellers, 117 blvd St-Germain, F-75279 Paris cedex 06

Bulletin critique du Livre français (Critical Bulletin on French Books) (text in English and Spanish), Association pour la Diffusion de la Pensée française, 21 bis rue la Perouse, F-75116 Paris

Bulletin du Livre (Book Bulletin), 18 rue Dauphine, F-75006 Paris

Connaissance et Formation (Knowledge and Training), France Expansion, 336-340 rue St-Honoré, F-75001 Paris (trade journal for the educational market)

La Documentation française; 'Bibliographie sélective' des Publications officielles françaises (French Documentation; 'Selective Bibliography' of French Official Publications), Secrétariat général du Gouvernement, Paris

Documentation — technique, scientifique et commerciale (Documentation — Technical, Scientific and Commercial) (text and summaries in English, French and German), Librairie Lavoisier, 11 rue Lavoisier, F-75008 Paris

Francophonie-Edition; revue bibliographique de l'Edition de Langue française dans le Monde, France Expansion, 336-340 rue St-Honoré, F-75001 Paris

Liens, Editions du Cap, Palais de la Scala, Monte Carlo

Livres (Books), Institut national de Recherches et de la Documentation pédagogique, 29 rue d'Ulm, F-75230 Paris

Livres-Actualité (Books of the Day), Information Promotion et Culture Sàrl, 17 rue de la Félicité, Paris 17e

Livres de France, 18 rue Dauphine, F-75006 Paris

Les Livres de l'Année — Biblio; annual cumulation of *Bibliographie de la France — Biblio* (qv)

Les Livres disponibles (French Books in Print), Cercle de la Librairie, 117 blvd St-Germain, F-75279 Paris cedex 06

New French Books (English extracts from *Bulletin Critique du Livre français*), Association pour la Diffusion de la Pensée française, 21 bis rue la Perouse, F-75116 Paris

Officiel de la Librairie (Booksellers' Official Journal), French Booksellers' Association, 117 blvd St-Germain, F-75279 Paris cedex 06

Publishers

Edition No 1, 40 rue du Cherche Midi, F-75006, Paris Tel: 5440638
Man Dir: Bernard Fixot; *Rights & Permissions:* Léonello Brandolini
Parent Company: Librairie Hachette (qv)
Subjects: Novels, Children's, Sport
1978: 10 titles *1979:* 9 titles *Founded:* 1977
ISBN Publisher's Prefix: 2-86391

A R E D I P (Agence Recherches Droits Internationaux et Promotion)*, 23 rue Cambon, F-75001 Paris Tel: 2603633
Telex: 240620
President/Man Dir: André Limansky
Subject: Juveniles

Academy Editions, 70 rue des Saints-Pères, F-75007 Paris Tel: 2227897/5485010
Publisher: Dr Andreas Papadakis; *Dir:* Professor Philippe Sers
Parent Company: Academy Editions, UK (qv)
Subjects: Art, Architecture
1979: 12 titles *Founded:* 1978

Acropole, 4 ave Elysée-Reclus, F-75007 Paris
Parent Company: Ed Pierre Belfond (qv)

Agence Parisienne de Distribution Sarl, see Editions Techniques et Scientifiques Françaises (ETSF)

Editions Albin Michel, 22 rue Huyghens, F-75014 Paris Tel: (01) 3261350
President: Robert Esménard; *Man Dir:* Francis Esménard; *Sales Dir:* Georges Madamour; *Dir Foreign Department:* Ivan Nabokov; *Public Relations:* Raymonde Leroux; *Advertising:* Richard Ducousset; *Rights & Permissions:* Béatrix Blavier
Subjects: General Fiction, Science Fiction, Fine Arts, History, Philosophy, Reference, Religion, How-to, General & Social Science, Popular Music, The Occult
1978: 160 titles *Founded:* 1902
ISBN Publisher's Prefix: 2-226

Editions Alpina, 60 rue Mazarine, F-75006 Paris Tel: (01) 3298740
Man Dir: Alain Gründ
Subjects: Guide Books
Founded: 1928
Miscellaneous: Associate company of Librairie Gründ, Paris (qv)
ISBN Publisher's Prefix: 2-7000

Alsatia SA*, 10 rue Bartholdi, F-68001 Colmar Tel: 411450 Telex: Alco 88200 F 508
Man Dir: André Clemessy; *Sales, Publicity, Advertising, Rights & Permissions:* Auguste Rimelé
Subjects: Belles Lettres, Poetry, Biography, History, How-to, Religion, Low-priced Paperbacks, Medicine, Primary Textbooks, Educational Materials
Founded: 1896
Bookshops: Librairie Alsatia, 31 pl de la Cathédrale, F-67000 Strasbourg; Librairie Union, 4 pl de la Réunion, F-68000 Mulhouse; Librairie Union, 28 rue des Têtes, 68 Colmar; Librairie Union, 26 rue Charles de Gaulle, F-68130 Altkirch; Libraire Union, 3 rue St-Antoine, F-68500 Guebwiller
ISBN Publisher's Prefix: 2-7001

Editions Alta, 17 rue Jacob, F-75006, Paris Tel: 3290620
Man Dir: Sylvie Messinger
Parent Company: Editions Jean-Claude Lattès (qv)
Subjects: Novels, Sport, How-to, Non-fiction
Founded: 1977

Les **Amis de Milosz**, 6 rue José-Maria-de-Heredia, F-75007 Paris
Associate Company: Editions André Silvaire (qv)

Editions de l'**Amitié**, G-T Rageot, 21 rue Cassette, F-75006 Paris Tel: (01) 5480731
Man Dir: Jean Vilnet; *All other offices:* Mrs C Scob
Orders to: Librairie Hatier SA, 8 rue d'Assas, F-75006 Paris
Subject: Juvenile; mainly young people's fiction in the contemporary world, picture books
1978: 22 titles *1979:* 28 titles *Founded:* 1941
Miscellaneous: Editions de l'Amitié is an imprint of Librairie Hatier (qv)
ISBN Publisher's Prefix: 2-7002

L'**Amitié par le Livre**, F-25310 Blamont
Dir General: Henri Frossard
Subjects: Prose fiction, Poetry, Philosophy, Belles Lettres
Book Club: L'Amitié par le Livre
1978: 10 titles *1979:* 11 titles *Founded:* 1930
ISBN Publisher's Prefix: 2-7121

Editions **Amphora** SA, 14 rue de l'Odéon, F-75006 Paris Tel: (01) 3261087
Administration and Accounts: 51 blvd Saint-Michel, F-75005 Paris Tel: (01) 3253461
Man Dir: Roger Vaultier; *Editorial, Publicity:* Roland Antoine; *Sales, Production:* Michel Vaultier
Subjects: Sports and Leisure Activities
1978: 11 titles *Founded:* 1954
ISBN Publisher's Prefix: 2-85180

Annuaires Ravet **Anceau***, 42 rue Roger Salengro, F-59260 Hellemes-lez-Lille Tel: 567141
Man Dir: Daniel Melchior
Subjects: Professional Yearbooks/Directories
Founded: 1853

Editions **Anthropos** SA*, 12 ave du Maine, F-75015 Paris Tel: (01) 5484258/2227682
Man Dir: Serge Jonas
Subjects: History, Philosophy, Social Sciences, Anthropology, Economy etc
1978: 60 titles *Founded:* 1965
ISBN Publisher's Prefix: 2-7157

L'**Arbalète***, Marc Barbezat, F-69150 Décines-Charpieu Tel: 495101
Subjects: Literature, Art

Publications **Aredit***, 357 blvd de Gambetta, F-59200 Tourcoing Tel: 267981/295963 Telex: 130372F
Subjects: Picture-Strip Books in instalments on War, Adventure, Westerns, Romance, Schoolgirl interests

Arted (Editions d'Art)*, 6 ave du Coq, 75009 Paris Tel: (01) 8747184
Subjects: Fine Arts; Sculpture, Painting
ISBN Publisher's Prefix: 2-85067

Editions **Arthaud** SA*, 6 rue de Mézières, F-75006 Paris Tel: (01) 5443847 Cable Add: Artore Paris
President: Henri Flammarion; *Dir:* P-F Racine; *Rights & Permissions:* as for Flammarion (qv)
Parent Company: Flammarion et Cie (qv)
Subjects: Literature, Arts, History, Travel Books, Sailing, Mountaineering, Sports
Founded: 1890
ISBN Publisher's Prefix: 2-7003

Artisan du Livre (Guérin et Cie)*, 22 rue Guynemer and 2 rue de Fleurus, F-75006, Paris Tel: (01) 5483058
Subjects: Literary, Academic, Commentary on Classics, Music, Art etc

Arts et Métiers Graphiques*, 19 rue Racine, F-75006 Paris 6 Tel: (01) 3269220
Man Dir: Yves Rivière

Parent Company: Flammarion et Cie (qv)
Subject: Art
1977: 8 titles *Founded:* 1927
ISBN Publisher's Prefix: 2-7004

Compagnie Française des **Arts Graphiques** SA, 3 rue Duguay-Trouin, F-75006 Paris Tel: (01) 5487285
President: V P Victor-Michel
Subject: Art
Founded: 1939
ISBN Publisher's Prefix: 2-85001

L'**Asiathèque***, 6 rue Christine, F-75006 Paris Tel: (01) 3253437
Editorial, Production: Alain Thiollier; *Sales, Publicity:* Oscar Ferreyros
Subjects: Far East (language, literature, etc)
Bookshop: At above address
Founded: 1973

Editions **Assimil** SA, 13 rue Gay Lussac, PO Box 25, F-94430 Chennevières sur Marne Tel: 5768737 Cable Add: Publicode 777 Assimil Telex: 210311F
Dirs: J L Cherel, J le Gal; *Editorial:* J L Cherel; *Sales, Production, Publicity:* J le Gal
Subjects: The Teaching of Languages; Handbooks, Textbooks, Reference
Bookshop: 11 rue des Pyramides, F-75001 Paris
1978: 4 titles *1979:* 4 titles *Founded:* 1929
ISBN Publisher's Prefix: 2-7005

L'**Astrolabe**, La Librairie du Voyageur, 46 rue de Provence, F-75009 Paris Tel: 2854295/2811603
Man Dir: Jacques P Nobecourt; *Editorial:* Raymond M Chabaud; *Sales:* Odile Nobecourt
Subsidiary Company: Librairie Blondel La Rougery (qv)
Subjects: Travel, Geography, Cartography
1978: 2 titles *1979:* 3 titles *Founded:* 1974
ISBN Publisher's Prefix: 2-86230

Aubanel SA, 7 pl Saint-Pierre, F-84028 Avignon Tel: (90) 824626
Man Dir: Laurent Theodore-Aubanel
Subjects: General Fiction, Psychology, Secondary Textbooks, Latin, Regional History, Tourist Guides, Provençal interest
Founded: 1744
ISBN Publisher's Prefix: 2-7006

Editions **Aubier-Montaigne** SA, 13 quai Conti, F-75006 Paris Tel: (01) 3265559/6335917
Man Dir: Mrs M Aubier-Gabail; *Sales Manager, Rights & Permissions:* Patrice Mentha
Parent Company: Flammarion et Cie (qv)
Subjects: Belles Lettres, Poetry, History, Philosophy, Reference, Religion, Psychology, University Textbooks, Pedagogy, Sociology, Languages
1978: 40 titles *1979:* 43 titles *Founded:* 1924

Etudes **Augustiniennes**, see under Etudes

Editions d'**Aujourd'hui***, F-83120 Plan de La Tour Tel: (94) 437079
Man Dir: Odette Charrière
Subjects: Literature, Music, Drama, Cinema, Poetry, Fiction, Human Sciences, Folklore, Esoteric
1978: 50 titles *1979:* 50 titles *Founded:* 1974
ISBN Publisher's Prefix: 2-7307

Editions Philippe **Auzou**, see Editions Michel de Lile

L'**Avant-Scène** Théâtre, Cinéma et Opéra, 27 rue Saint-André des-Arts, F-75006 Paris Tel: (01) 3255229
Man Dir: C Dupeynon
Subjects: Theatre, Cinema, Opera, Ballet, Periodicals
1979: 150 titles *Founded:* 1949

Editions **B P I** (Bureau de Presse et d'Informations), 79 ave des Champs-Elysées, F-75008 Paris 8 Tel: 7236870
Man Dir: J Milinaire

Subjects: Science & Technical, Hotels and Restaurants, Surface Treatments

Editions **B R G M**, see Bureau de Recherches Géologiques et Minières

Editions J-B **Baillière**, 10 rue Thénard, F-75005 Paris Tel: 3292110 Telex: Livrcom 201326 F
Man Dir: M Roux Dessarps
Subjects: Technical texts for professional and instructional use in: all branches of Medical, Dental, Surgical care; Agriculture and Horticulture; various branches of Technology and Industry
Founded: 1819
ISBN Publisher's Prefix: 2-7008

André **Balland**, 33 rue St-André-des-Arts, F-75006 Paris Tel: (01) 3257440
Publisher: André Balland; *Sales:* Christian de Romanet; *Rights & Permissions:* Sabine Forest
Subjects: Fiction, Documentaries, Humour, Sexology
1978: 57 titles *Founded:* 1966
ISBN Publisher's Prefix: 2-7158

Baschet et Cie, Editeurs, an imprint of Editions de l'Illustration (qv)

Bayard-Presse SA, 17 rue de Babylone, F-75007 Paris Tel: (01) 2229315/5484417
President: Jean Gelamur
Associate Company: Le Centurion (qv)
Subjects: Juveniles, Religion, Literature
Founded: 1873
ISBN Publisher's Prefix: 2-7009

Editions **Beauchesne**, 72 rue des Saints-Pères, F-75007 Paris Tel: (01) 5488028
Dir: Miss M Cadic
Subjects: Religion and Theology, Social and Political Science, Humanities, Reference, Current Affairs, Spirituality, The Church Today, Holy Scripture, Biography, History, Literature, Essays
1978: 45 titles *1979:* 38 titles *Founded:* 1851
ISBN Publisher's Prefix: 2-7010

Editions Pierre **Belfond**, 3 bis passage de la Petite-Boucherie, F-75006 Paris Tel: (01) 3252760 Telex: 260717F
Chairmen: Pierre Belfond, Franca Belfond; *Rights & Permissions:* Véronique Garrigues
Subsidiary Companies: Nouvel Office d'Edition et de Diffusion (qv), Productions de Paris (both at 3 bis passage de la Petite-Boucherie, F-75006 Paris); Presses de la Renaissance (qv); Acropole (qv)
Subjects: General Fiction, Belles Lettres, Bibliophily, Poetry, Biography, History, Music, Art, Paperbacks
Founded: 1962

Editions le **Belier-Prisma** SA, see Editions Universitaires

Librairie Classique Eugène **Belin**, 8 rue Férou, F-75278 Paris cedex 06 Tel: (01) 3292142 Telex: Libelin 202978F
Man Dir & Chairman: Max Brossollet; *Editorial:* Marie-Claude Brossollet; *Documentation:* Soraya Eghbal-Dupouey; *Sales:* Maurice Farcy; *Publicity:* Jean Olivesi; *Production, Rights & Permissions:* Max Brossollet
Subjects: Secondary & Primary Textbooks, Educational Material, Literary & Scientific Magazines
Founded: 1777
ISBN Publisher's Prefix: 2-7011

Editions Les **Belles Images***, 53 rue St André-des-Arts, F-75006 Paris Tel: (01) 0338207 Telex: 202844F
Man Dir: Peter Watkins; *Sales:* Jacques-Edouard Tavernier
Imprints: Belles Images, Butterfly Books
Subjects: Children's Books, Posters and Puzzles, Educational Material
1978: 10 titles *Founded:* 1975

90 FRANCE

Société d'Edition 'Les **Belles Lettres**', 95 blvd Raspail, F-75006 Paris Tel: (01) 5487055
Man Dir: Pierre de Mijolla: *Editor:* Jean Malye
Subjects: Poetry, History, Philosophy, Literature, Religion, Scholarly, University Textbooks, Ancient History
1978: 60 titles *Founded:* 1919
Bookshop: Librairie Guillaume Budé, 95 blvd Raspail, F-75006 Paris
Miscellaneous: This Société now incorporates the formerly independent firm Cathasia
ISBN Publisher's Prefix: 2-251

Berg International Editeurs*, 19 blvd Saint-Michel, F-75005 Paris Tel: (01) 3258443
Cable Add: Bergedit Paris
Man Dir: Monique Gougaud
Subjects: Art, History, General & Social Science, Heraldry, Music, Reference, Religion
ISBN Publisher's Prefix: 2-900269

Berger-Levrault, 229 blvd Saint-Germain, F-75007 Paris Tel: (01) 7055614 Telex: 27797
Man Dir: Marc Friedel; *Editorial:* Didier Bonnet, Jean-Jacques Brisebarre, Hubert Cuny, Yves Robert; *Sales:* André Bourgeois; *Production:* Anne-Marie Veujoz; *Publicity:* Catherine Riand
Branch Off: 23 place Broglie, F-67000 Strasbourg
Subjects: Geography, History, Leisure, Art, Literature, Architecture
Bookshop: Librairie Berger-Levrault, pl Broglie, F-67000 Strasbourg
1978: 70 titles *Founded:* 1676
ISBN Publisher's Prefix: 2-7013

Société Internationale des Ecoles **Berlitz** SA*, 31 blvd des Italiens, F-75002 Paris Tel: (01) 7420509 Cable Add: Berliscool Paris
Subjects: Education, Textbooks
Founded: 1907
ISBN Publisher's Prefix: 2-7014

Atelier **Beyer***, 7 rue de Genève, F-68300 St-Louis Tel: (89) 677876
Sales Manager: Marie-France Durisch
Publisher: Jochen Beyer
Subject: Art

Bias (Société Nouvelle des Editions) SA, 26 rue Vauquelin, F-75005 Paris Tel: (01) 3376590
Man Dir: Georges Lauvaux; *Editorial, Production:* G Lauvaux; *Publicity & Advertising, Rights & Permissions:* Jean Lauvaux
Subjects: Stories, How-to and Information Books for all age juveniles; Travel, Hobbies, Popular Science & Technology
1978: 320 titles *1979:* 300 titles *Founded:* 1941
ISBN Publisher's Prefix: 2-7015

Société **Biblique** Française, 30 ave Lénine, BP 31, F-93380 Pierrefitte Tel: (01) 8223896
Subject: Bibles
ISBN Publisher's Prefix: 2-85300

Blondel La Rougery SA, 7 rue St-Lazare, F-75009 Paris Tel: (01) 8789554
Chairman: J Barbotte
Subjects: Maps & Charts, Science & Technical
Founded: 1902
ISBN Publisher's Prefix: 2-7016

Bloud et Gay (Librairie) SA, see Editions Desclée et Cie

Editions E de **Boccard**, 11 rue de Médicis, F-75006 Paris Tel: (01) 3260037
Subjects: Archaeology, History
ISBN Publisher's Prefix: 2-7018

Editions André **Bonne***, 15-17 rue Las-Cases, F-75007 Paris Tel: (01) 5510609/5515953
Man Dir: André Bonne; *Editorial Dir:* Robert de Chateaubriant
Subjects: General Fiction, Belles Lettres, Reference, Religion
Founded: 1861
ISBN Publisher's Prefix: 2-7019

Boosey & Hawkes*, Société des Grandes Editions Musicales, 4 rue Drouot, F-75009 Paris Tel: 1770-7344 Telex: Sonorous, Paris
Parent Company: Boosey & Hawkes, UK (qv)
Subject: Music

Editions **Bordas**, 37 rue Boulard, F-75686 Paris cedex 14 Tel: (01) 5392208; 17 rue Rémy Dumoncel, F-75686 Paris cedex 14 Tel: (01) 3201550 Telex: 270004
President: Jean-Manuel Bourgois; *Man Dir:* Jean-François Grollemund; *Editorial:* Michel Legrain (Business), Jean Lissarrague (Scientific/Technical), Dominique Desgranges (School); *Sales:* Dominique Desmottes, Fernand Joffre, Luc Tiberghien (Export); *Production:* Jacques Patry; *Publicity:* Philippe Fournier-Bourdier (Business), Jean Ganem (Scientific/Technical), Etienne Gotschaux (School); *Rights & Permissions:* Mireille Debenne (Business/School), Maryvonne Guérin (Scientific/Technical)
Orders to: 37 rue Boulard, F-75686 Paris cedex 14
Subsidiary Companies: Société Générale de Diffusion (SGED), BP 429, F-93104 Montreuil cedex; Société Gauthier-Villars, 70 rue de Saint-Mandé, F-93100 Montreuil; Société Bordas-Dunod-Bruxelles, Brussels, Belgium (qv); Bordas-Dunod-Montréal Inc, 350 Blvd Lebeau, Saint-Laurent, Montreal, Quebec, H4N 1W6 Canada; also Librairie de Montaigne, 24-26 blvd de l'Hôpital, F-75005, Paris; Librairie Dunod (see Bookshops)
Imprints: Bordas, Dunod, Gauthier-Villars, Pédagogie Moderne
Subjects: Educational (from Elementary to Higher Levels), General Non-fiction, Scientific, Technical, Reference (especially Dictionaries and Encyclopedias)
Book Club: Librairie de Montaigne
Bookshops: Librairie Dunod, 30 rue Saint-Sulpice, F-75006 Paris; Librairie Beranger, Liège, Belgium
1978: 200 titles *1979:* 240 titles *Founded:* 1946
ISBN Publisher's Prefix: 2-04

Editions **Bornemann**, 15 rue de Tournon, F-75006 Paris Tel: (01) 3260588
Manager: Maurice Bornemann
Subjects: Art, How-to, Sports, Nature, Easy Readers
Founded: 1829
ISBN Publisher's Prefix: 2-85182

Boscher-Chapron*, 10 rue du Docteur-Robin, 22600 Loudéac Tel: (96) 280127
Publisher/Author: Mrs J Chapron
Subjects: Educational, Juvenile; the 'Boscher' Method of Infant Teaching

Editions N **Boubée** et Cie*, 11 pl Saint-Michel, F-75006 Paris Tel: (01) 6330030
Subject: Biology
Founded: 1941
ISBN Publisher's Prefix: 2-85004

Christian **Bourgois***, Editeur, 8 rue Garancière, F-75006 Paris Tel: (01) 3291280 Telex: Precite 204807F
Subject: Literature
Miscellaneous: Member of the Presses de la Cité group (qv)
ISBN Publisher's Prefix: 2-267

Editions Colin **Bourrelier**, 103 blvd Saint-Michel, F-75240 Paris cedex 05
Subjects: Juvenile: formerly awarded French Youth Prize

Bréa Éditions, 24 ave Ledru-Rollin, F-75012 Paris Tel: 3452090 Telex: Brea 250303 Public Paris
Man Dir: Eric Brébant; *Commercial Manager:* Jean Arcache
Orders to: Weber Diffusion SA, 24-28 rue du Moulinet, F-75013 Paris Tel: 5803159
Subjects: Economics, Tourist Guides, Show Business series, Practical Information books
1980: 4 titles *Founded:* 1978

Editions **Brepols** SA*, 9 rue Huysmans, F-75006 Paris Tel: (01) 2224210
Subject: Religion
ISBN Publisher's Prefix: 2-85006

Michèle **Broutta** Oeuvres Graphiques Contemporaines, 31 rue des Bergers, F-75015 Paris Tel: (01) 5779371/5779379
Man Dir: Michèle Broutta
Subject: Art
1980: 14 titles *Founded:* 1970
ISBN Publisher's Prefix: 2-900332

Editions **Buchet/Chastel**, 18 rue de Condé, F-75006 Paris Tel: (01) 3544599/3545047; (sales) (01) 3269200 Cable Add: Buchet/Chastel Paris
Man Dir: Guy Buchet; *Editorial Dir:* Edmond Buchet; *Sales Dir:* René Charbonnier; *Publicity & Advertising:* Guy Buchet; *Rights & Permissions:* Anne Buchet
Subjects: General Fiction, Belles Lettres, Biography, History, Philosophy, Music, Religion, Social Science, Medicine
Founded: 1930
ISBN Publisher's Prefix: 2-7020

Bureau de Presse et d'Information, see B P I

Bureau de Recherches Géologiques et Minières, BP 6009, F-45018 Orléans cedex (Located at: 6-8 rue Chasseloup Laubat, F-75737 Paris cedex 15) Tel: (01) 7839400 Telex: brgm 270844 f
Subjects: Texts connected with mineralogical and geological research (principally in France and Francophone areas of world); Maps and Charts
1978: 105 titles
ISBN Publisher's Prefix: 2-7159

C A L/Retz* (Culture Art Loisirs/Retz), 114 ave des Champs Elysées, F-75391 Paris cedex 08 Tel: 3598650 Telex: 290049
Man Dir: François Richaudeau; *Sales:* Jacques Cabuj; *Rights & Permissions:* Simone Bulteau-Jumin
Subsidiary Companies: CAL, Pully, Switzerland; L'Académie du Livre SA, Belgium (Book Club only) (qv)
Subjects: History, Psychology, Social Science, Arts, Encyclopaedias
Book Club: CAL, 114 Champs Elysées, F-75008 Paris
Founded: 1957
ISBN Publisher's Prefix: 2-7140

C D R, see Centre de Documentation Universitaire

C E D S, see Centre d'Etudes et de Documentation Scientifiques

C E F A G, see Centre d'Etudes et Fabrication Arts Graphiques

C E L S E (Compagnie d'Editions Libres, Sociales et Economiques SA), 68 rue Cardinet, F-75017 Paris Tel: (01) 2674123
Subjects: Road Transport (Vocational Training, Economics, Administration, Management, Social Science, Vocabulary of International Transport), Railway Systems world-wide
ISBN Publisher's Prefix: 2-85009

C E P A D, see Cepadues Editions SA

C E P L (Centre d'Etude et de Promotion de la Lecture)*, 114 ave des Champs-Elysées, F-75008 Paris Tel: (01) 2251483

Subjects: Education, Popular Reference Works

C L D, BP 2, 42 ave des Platanes, F-37170 Chambray-Les-Tours Tel: (47) 282068
Man Dir: Jean-Pierre Normand; *Editorial:* Hélène Richard; *Sales and Rights & Permissions:* Jack Normand; *Production:* Pierre Proust; *Publicity:* Bernadette Dusseau
Subjects: Regional Interest, Folklore, History, Architecture, Religion, Tourism, Hunting
1978: 22 titles *1979:* 25 titles *Founded:* 1960

Editions du **C N R S** (Centre national de la recherche scientifique), 15 quai Anatole France, F-75700 Paris Tel: (01) 5559225 Telex: 260034
Man Dir: Henri Peronnin; *Sales:* Christian Debayle; *Publicity & Advertising:* Denis Cotard
Parent Company: Centre national de la recherche scientifique
Associate Company: CNRS Laboratoire Intergeo (qv)
Bookshop: Librairie des Editions du CNRS, 15 quai Anatole France, F-75700 Paris
Subjects: History, Geography, Literature, Linguistics, Music, Art, Philosophy, Reference, Religion, Medicine, Psychology, Engineering, Social Sciences, Education, Science & Technology, Law, Economics, Mathematics, Information Sciences, Electronics, Mechanics, Energy, Chemistry and Physics, Geology, Biology, Astronomy
1978: 151 titles *1979:* 151 titles *Founded:* 1939
ISBN Publisher's Prefix: 2-222

C N R S, Laboratoire Intergeo, see Intergeo

Editions **Cahiers d'Art**, 14 rue du Dragon, F-75006 Paris Tel: (01) 5487673
Man Dir: Yves de Fontbrune
Subject: Art
Founded: 1926
ISBN Publisher's Prefix: 2-85117

C R E R, see Coopérative Régionale de l'Enseignement Religieux

Les **Cahiers Fiscaux** Européens Sàrl, 51 ave Reine Victoria, F-06000 Nice Tel: (93) 810326
Parent Company: Société d'Etudes Juridiques Internationales et Fiscales (JURIF)
Subjects: European Taxation Systems, Fiscal Law, Economics, Social Science (embraced in 3 separate series and 1 periodical)
Founded: 1968

Editions **Calmann-Lévy** Sàrl, 3 rue Auber, F-75009 Paris Tel: (01) 0730802/0735389/7423833 Cable Add: Caledit
Man Dirs: Robert Calmann-Lévy, Alain Oulman; *Sales Dir:* Richard le Cocq; *Publicity & Advertising:* Michèle Truchan; *Rights & Permissions:* Thérèse Scaroni, Suzanne Lescoat
Subjects: General Fiction, Science Fiction, History, Biography, Philosophy, Psychology, Social Sciences, Economics, Practical, Memoirs, Humour, Sport
Founded: 1836
ISBN Publisher's Prefix: 2-7021

Camugli*, 6 rue de la Charité, Lyon Cedex 1 Tel: (78) 426550 Telex: Camugli 370897F

Editions **Capendu**, 3 rue des Haudriettes, F-75003 Paris Tel: (01) 2721319
Man Dir: J F Capendu
Subject: Juveniles
ISBN Publisher's Prefix: 2-85124

Editions André **Casteilla**, see Nouveautés de l'Enseignement

Editions **Casterman**, 66 rue Bonaparte, F-75006 Paris Tel: (01) 3252005 Telex: 200001 F Edicast
President: Louis-Robert Casterman; *Dir:* Gabriel Chamozzi; *Sales Dir:* Christophe Veyrin-Forrer, Claude Lelan; *Publicity & Advertising:* Christophe Veyrin-Forrer; *Rights & Permissions:* Pierre Servais
Parent Company: Editions Casterman, Belgium (qv)
Branch Offs: 28 rue des Soeurs noires, 7500 Tournai, Belgium; De Morinel 25-29, Dronten, Netherlands
Subjects: Children's Books and Albums, Picture Strips, Religion, Economics, Politics, Practical Living, Urban questions, Architecture, Painting, Photography, Cinema, Music, Poetry, Fiction, Records, Diaries
1978: 130 titles *Founded:* at Tournai, 1780; in Paris, 1857
ISBN Publisher's Prefix: 2-203

Editions **Catalanes** de Paris*, 18 rue Jobbé-Duval, F-75015 Paris Tel: (01) 2501643
Man Dir: Paul Kipfer; *Sales Dir:* Angelí Castanyer; *Publicity & Advertising, Rights & Permissions:* Romà Planas
Subjects: History, Low-priced Paperbacks, Social Science (in the Catalan language)
Founded: 1969

Catalogue de l'Edition Française*, 9 rue Séguier, F-75006 Paris Tel: (01) 3256170
Man Dir: Serge Ciregna
Subject: Bibliography

Cathasia, see Société d'Edition 'Les Belles Lettres'

Editions **Cedic**, 93 ave d'Italie, F-75013 Paris Tel: (01) 5896185/5802562
Man & Sales Dir: François Robineau; *Publicity, Advertising, Rights & Permissions:* François Robineau
Subjects: Low-priced Paperbacks, Biology, Biochemistry, Computer Science, Education, Mathematics, Physics, Secondary Textbooks, Languages
1979: 50 titles *Founded:* 1971
ISBN Publisher's Prefix: 2-7124

Editions **Cèdre***, 40 rue Grégoire-de-Tours, F-75006 Paris Tel: (01) 6339328
Man Dir: Bernard Dermineur
Subjects: History, Nonfiction, Encyclopaedias, Juveniles
Founded: 1976

Centre d'Etude et de Promotion de la Lecture, see C E P L

Editions du **Centre d'Etudes et de Documentation** Scientifiques (CEDS Editions)*, 95 bis Ave Foch, F-76290 Montivilliers Tel: (35) 300527 Telex: 190406F
Dir: Mme A Huard; *Literary Dir:* Dr G Mathieu
Subjects: Science & Technology, Nature & Health, Humour, Practical guides
ISBN Publisher's Prefix: 2-85256

Centre d'Etudes et Fabrication Arts Graphiques (CEFAG)*, 153 rue de Grenelle, F-75007 Paris Tel: (01) 7055105
Subjects: Religion, Audio Visual
Founded: 1958

Centre de Documentation Universitaire et Société d'Edition d'Enseignement Supérieur Réunis (CDU & SEDES)*, 5 pl de la Sorbonne, F-75005 Paris Tel: (01) 3252323
Subjects: History, Philosophy, Social Science, Science & Technology, Economics, Education, School Books, Fiction, Literature, Psychology, Maps
Founded: 1933
ISBN Publisher's Prefix: 2-202

Centre national d'Art et de Culture Georges Pompidou*, F-75191 Paris cedex 04 Tel: 2771233/2336178
President: Jean Millier; *Production:* Jean Seyrig; *Sales:* Marcel Lefranc
Orders to: Editions Flammarion, 27 rue Racine 75006, Paris (qv)
Subjects: Art (Modern Art, Contemporary Painting, Sculpture, Drawings, Photography); Industrial Design (Architecture, Environment, Urbanism); Musical and Acoustic Research (Modern Music, Music Composition); Various
ISBN Publisher's Prefix: 2-85850

Centre national de la Recherche Scientifique, see CNRS

Editions du **Centurion**, 17 rue de Babylone, F-75007 Paris Tel: (01) 2229315
Man Dir: Hervé Lauriot Prevost; *Editorial and Production:* Charles Ehlinger; *Sales:* Annie Valaise; *Publicity and Advertising:* Clotilde Manoury; *Rights and Permissions:* Magdeleine Leblanc
Orders to: Sofedis, 29 rue Saint Sulpice, F-75006 Paris
Parent Company: Bayard-Presse (qv)
Subjects: Religion, Juveniles, Social Sciences, General & Social Science, Paperbacks, How-to, Education
1978: 88 titles *1979:* 95 titles *Founded:* 1870
ISBN Publisher's Prefix: 2-227

Cepadues Editions (CEPAD) SA, 111 rue Nicolas Vauquelin, F-31300 Toulouse Tel: (61) 405736 Telex: message 520987F
Man Dir: Guy Collin
Subjects: Scientific, Technical, Data Processing
1978: 15 titles *1979:* 12 titles *Founded:* 1969
ISBN Publisher's Prefix: 2-85428

Editions **Cercle d'Art** SA, 90 rue du Bac, F-75007 Paris Tel: (01) 5442890
Man Dir: Charles Feld
Subjects: Art
1978: 8 titles *Founded:* 1950
ISBN Publisher's Prefix: 2-7022

Editions du **Cerf***, 29 blvd La Tour Maubourg, F-75007 Paris cedex 07 Tel: (01) 5503407 Cable Add: Edicerf
General Dir: M Houssin; *Man Dir:* J Kopf; *Editorial Dir:* F Refoulé; *Sales Dir:* J Mignon; *Publicity & Advertising:* Mrs L Rossi; *Rights & Permissions:* Mrs F de Chasse
Subjects: Religion, History, Philosophy, Juveniles, Social Science, Paperbacks, Reference, Textbooks, Crafts, Psychology, Economics
Founded: 1929
ISBN Publisher's Prefix: 2-204

Editions R **Chaix**, 1 rue de Fleurus, F-75006 Paris Tel: 5444111/5485124
Man Dir, Rights & Permissions: J-Y Vincent; *Editorial:* R Chaix; *Sales:* J Farge
Subjects: Leisure pursuits, Practical
Founded: 1977

Editions du **Chalet**, 77 rue de Vaugirard, F-75006 Paris Tel: 5487860
Subjects: Roman Catholic Devotional, Liturgical, Catechisms
Orders to: (France) Begedis, 77 rue de Vaugirard, F-75006 Paris Tel: 5487860; (Foreign) Arc-en-Ciel International, 11 rue Barthélemy Frison, B-7500 Tournai, Belgium
Associate Company: Editions Desclée et Cie (qv for other Associate Companies)
1979: 22 titles *Founded:* 1946
ISBN Publisher's Prefix: 2-7023

Editions **Champ Libre**, 13 rue de béarn, F-75003 Paris Tel: (01) 2722700/2723480
Subjects: Classics, History, Social Science, Literature, Modern Theory
1979: 10 titles *Founded:* 1970
ISBN Publisher's Prefix: 2-85184

Librairie des **Champs-Elysées** SA, 10 rue Marignan, F-75008 Paris Tel: (01) 3596616
Man Dir: Christian Poninski
Imprints: Le Masque, Club des Masques
Subjects: Several fiction series dealing exclusively with one theme; viz: Westerns; Science Fiction; Crime and Police Novels (Editions Le Masque, Club des Masques)
1979: 195 titles *Founded:* 1927
ISBN Publisher's Prefix: 2-7024

Chancerel Editions SA*, 4 rue Aumont Thiéville, F-75017 Paris Tel: (01) 7660302 Telex: 640093 CHANCED F
Chairman: Philippe Chancerel; *Publisher, Manager:* Jean-Marie Ide; *Sales:* Patrick Erhard; *Production:* Claude Blanc
Associate Company: Chancerel Publishers Ltd, UK (qv)
Subjects: Educational strip cartoons; Sport; Hobbies; Homecraft; (in French and other European languages)
1978: 15 titles *Founded:* 1960
ISBN Publishers' Prefix: 2-85429

Les Editions **Chantereine**, 13 rue Saint-Georges, F-75009 Paris Tel: 2806118
Subjects: Do-it-Yourself Encyclopaedia (6 vols), Terre Vivante Encyclopaedia (10 vols)

Editions du **Chat** Perché, an imprint of Flammarion et Cie

Editions du **Chêne**, 40 rue du Cherche-Midi, F-75006 Paris 6 Tel: (01) 2222852 Telex: 250302 Paris
Man Dir, Editorial, Rights & Permissions: Gérald Gassiot-Talabot; *Editorial Assistant:* Anne de Margerie
Orders to: Groupe International Hachette, 254 blvd Saint-Germain, F-75006 Paris
Parent Company: Librairie Hachette (qv)
Subjects: Ancient, Graphic and Contemporary Art, Architecture, Photography, Cinema, Documentaries
1978: 49 titles *1979:* 37 titles *Founded:* 1939
ISBN Publisher's Prefix: 2-85108

Le **Cherche-Midi**, Éditeur, 70 rue du Cherche-Midi, F-75006 Paris Tel: (01) 2227120
Dirs: Louis Aldebert, Jean Breton, Michel Breton, Jean Orizet; *Publicity:* Philippe Héraclès
Subjects: Belles Lettres, Poetry, Paperbacks
1978: 5 titles *Founded:* 1978
Miscellaneous: Managing company responsible for Editions Saint-Germain-des-Près SA (qv)

Editions du **Chiendent** Sarl, Marcevol Vinça F-66320 (Eastern Pyrenees) Tel: (68) 051263
Man Dir: Xavier d'Arthuys; *Sales:* Blandine Renaud; *Production:* Sophie d'Arthuys
Orders to: Blandine Renaud, 14 rue de Nanteuil, F-75015 Paris
Subjects: Four series deal generally with (1) people in conflict with events; (2) man's conflict with his apparent destiny; (3) Eastern Pyrenees regional; (4) writings by children
1980: 5 titles *Founded:* 1977
ISBN Publisher's Prefix: 2-85999001

Editions de **Chiré**, Chiré-en-Montreuil, F-86190 Vouillé Tel: (049) 518304
Man Dir: Jean Auguy; *Publicity Dir:* Jean Sechet
Branch Off: Duquesne Diffusion, 27 ave Duquesne, F-75007 Paris
Subjects: History, Social Science, Counter-revolution, Religion
1978: 7 titles *1979:* 5 titles *Founded:* 1966

Editions **Chiron***, 40 rue de Seine, F-75006 Paris Tel: (01) 6331893
Chairman: Denys Ferrando-Dufort; *Promotion & Marketing:* Henri Sinniger
Subjects: Education, Juveniles, Sports, Science & Technical

Founded: 1907
ISBN Publisher's Prefix: 2-7027

Chotard et Associés, Editeurs, 1 rue Garancière, F-75006 Paris Tel: (01) 2338065
Man Dir: Yvon Chotard; *Sales Dir:* Jacques Chapellon; *Rights & Permissions:* Anne Chotard
Parent Company: Editions France Empire (qv)
Orders to: 33 rue Beauregard, F-75002 Paris
Subjects: Psychology, Engineering, Technical, Economics, Marketing, Management, Social Science, University Textbooks, Educational Material
1978: 3 titles *1979:* 10 titles *Founded:* 1969
ISBN Publisher's Prefix: 2-7127

Editions de la **Chronique** des Lettres Françaises*, 33 rue de Verneuil, F-75007 Paris Tel: (01) 6477641
Editorial: Georges G Place; *Sales:* Mrs P Place
Orders to: 12 rue Pierre et Marie Curie, F-75005 Paris
Parent Company: Chronique des Lettres Françaises
Associate Company: Editions Jean-Michel Place (qv)
Subjects: Academic (Ancient and Modern), Bibliographies
Founded: 1922
ISBN Publisher's Prefix: 2-85185

Clé International, 11 rue Méchain, F-75014 Paris (Located at: 59-61 rue de la Santé, F-75013 Paris) Tel: 3376112
Man Dir: Jean-Claude Diemer; *Editorial, Production:* Anne Reberioux; *Sales, Rights & Permissions:* Jean-Claude Richard; *Publicity:* Martine Borgomano
Orders to: (outside France) as company address; (in France): Ed Fernand Nathan, 9 rue Méchain, F-75676 Paris cedex 14
Subjects: Books for the Foreign Market, especially connected with teaching French as a foreign language; also teaching French as a second language
1978: 29 titles *1979:* 28 titles *Founded:* 1973

Librairie Armand **Colin**, 103 blvd St-Michel, F-75005 Paris Tel: (01) 3291219 Telex: Acolin 201269 F
Man Dir: Jean-Max Leclerc; *Sales Dir:* Rémy Bourrelier; *Publicity & Advertising:* Yvette Dardenne; *Rights & Permissions:* Anne Nesteroff
Subjects: History, Philosophy, Psychology, Pedagogy, Geography, General Literature, General & Social Science, University, Secondary & Primary Textbooks, Educational Materials
1978-79: 150 titles *Founded:* 1870
ISBN Publisher's Prefix: 2-200

Editions **Comindus***, 1 rue Descombes, F-75017 Paris Tel: (01) 3807916
Subject: Trade Annuals
Miscellaneous: Associate company of SEAP (Société d'Edition d'Annuaires Professionnels), Paris

Compagnie d'Editions Libres, Sociales et Economiques, see C E L S E

Compagnie Française d'Editions SA*, 40 rue du Colisée, F-75008 Paris Tel: (01) 2961285
Subjects: Science & Technical

Le **Concours** Médical*, 37 rue de Bellefond, F-75009 Paris Tel: (01) 2850536
Subject: Medicine

Coopérative Régionale de l'Enseignement Religieux (CRER)*, 7 rue du Parvis St-Maurice, BP 230, F-49003 Angers cedex
Tel: 884695
Subject: Religion

Copernic, 13 rue Charles Lecocq, F-75737 Paris cedex 15 Tel: (01) 8888887
Man Dir: Jean-Claude Valla; *Sales:* Guy Devautoir; *Production, Rights & Permissions:* Gérard Landry; *Publicity:* Chantal de Chanterac
Associate Companies: Nouvelle École, Publeditec
Subjects: History, Documentary, Modern Thought, Philosophy/Religion, Myth and Fantasy
1978: 13 titles *1979:* 20 titles *Founded:* 1976
ISBN Publisher's Prefix: 2-85984

Courrier du Livre Sàrl*, 21 rue de Seine, F-75006 Paris Tel: (01) 3541891
Subjects: Philosophy, Religion, Ecology, Health and Nutrition, Organic Gardening, Yoga
ISBN Publisher's Prefix: 2-7029

Editions de la **Courtille***, 26 rue de Gramont, F-75002 Paris Tel: (01) 0738725/6 Telex: 27618
Man Dir: Denise Drouin; *Editorial:* André Rossel; *Sales, Rights & Permissions:* Denise Drouin; *Production:* André Casteilla; *Publicity:* Katia Favard
Associate Company: Editions Hier et Demain (qv)
Subjects: Biography, History, High-priced Paperbacks, Educational Materials, Collectors' Editions, Practical Guides, Encyclopedias
Founded: 1971
ISBN Publisher's Prefix: 2-1207

Editeurs **Crépin-Leblond** et Cie SA*, 12 rue Duguay-Trouin, F-75006 Paris Tel: (01) 5489350
Man Dir: Mrs A R Henry; *Sales:* Denise Bechu; *Publicity:* E-G Souquet
Subjects: Hunting, Shooting, Arms, Dogs, Horse-Riding, Nature
1979: 4 titles *Founded:* 1952
ISBN Publisher's Prefix: 2-7030

Editions **Cujas**, 4, 6 & 8 rue de la Maison Blanche, F-75013 Paris Tel: (01) 5889657/5888436
Man Dir: Pierre Joly; *Publicity Dir:* Jacqueline Joly
Subjects: Politics, Economics, Education, mainly in France and Francophone countries, Social Sciences
Bookshops: Librairie J Joly, 19 rue Cujas, F-75005 Paris; Cujas Librairie, 2 rue de Rouen, F-92000 Nanterre
1978: 25 titles *1979:* 30 titles *Founded:* 1946
ISBN Publisher's Prefix: 2-254

Culture Art Loisirs/Retz, see CAL/Retz

Editions d'Art — Christophe **Czwiklitzer***, 54 rue Bonaparte, F-75006 Paris Tel: 00331/5049665
Subjects: Bibliophile Editions; Monographs; Bibliographies; Original Graphics; Aesthetics

D A F S A, 125 rue Montmartre, F-75002 Paris Tel: (01) 2332123
Man Dir: Michel Vieillard
Subjects: Economics, Finance

Les Editions Roger **Dacosta**, 19 blvd Raspail, F-75007 Paris Tel: (01) 5441491
Man Dir: Jean Dacosta; *Sales Dir:* Mrs Stern
Subjects: Medicine, Medical History, Dentistry, Horse-riding, Hunting
1980: 19 titles
ISBN Publisher's Prefix: 2-85128

Jurisprudence Générale **Dalloz**, 11 rue Soufflot, F-75240 Paris Cedex 05 Tel: (01) 3295080
President, General Manager: Patrice Verge; *Man Dir, Rights & Permissions:* Georges Alapetite; *Financial Dir:* Raymond Sibille; *Editorial, Production:* M Dunes; *Sales:* M

Hapiot; *Publicity Dir:* A Stein
Bookshop: Dalloz, 14 rue Soufflot, F-75240 Paris cedex 05
Subjects: Law, Political Science, Reference, Business, Economics, Philosophy
1979: 120 titles *Founded:* 1845
ISBN Publisher's Prefix: 2-247

Editions **Dangles** SA, 18 rue Lavoisier, BP 36, F-45800 St Jean-de-Braye Tel: (01) 38864180
Man Dir, Editorial, Production, Publicity, Rights & Permissions: J-Y Anstet Dangles; *Sales:* Alain Queant
Subjects: Naturopathy, Esotericism and Spirit Life, Psychology, Physical Culture, Ecology
1978: 12 titles *1979:* 12 titles *Founded:* 1926
ISBN Publisher's Prefix: 2-7033

Editions **Dardalet** SA*, 22 rue René-Thomas, F-38000 Grenoble Tel: 961631
Subject: Juveniles

Dargaud Editeur, 12 Blaise Pascal, BP 155, F-92201 Neuilly sur Seine Tel: 7471133
Cable Add: Editfranc Neuilly Telex: 62631
Editorial: Michel Greg
Publisher: Georges Dargaud; *Rights & Permissions:* Anthéa Shackleton, Michel Lieuré
Subjects: Juveniles, Art, Strip Cartoons, Magazines
ISBN Publisher's Prefix: 2-205

Editions du **Dauphin**, 43-45 rue de la Tombe-Issoire, F-75014 Paris Tel: (01) 3277900/3275768
Publishing Manager: Anne Tromelin
Subjects: General Fiction, Poetry, Social Science, How-to, Dictionaries, Documentaries, Regional Studies
Founded: 1936
ISBN Publisher's Prefix: 2-7163

Éditions **De Vecchi** SA*, 20 rue de la Trémoille, F-75008 Paris Tel: 2255516
Man Dir: Robert Pinto; *Editorial:* Evelyne Level
Associate Companies: Giovanni De Vecchi Editore SpA, Italy (qv); Editorial De Vecchi SA, Spain (qv)
Subjects: Practical Guides on Legal Questions, Animals, Games, Leisure, Gardening, Health, Mystery, Cookery, History
Founded: 1971
ISBN Publisher's Prefix: 2-85177

Editions **Debard***, 17 rue du Vieux-Colombier, F-75006 Paris Tel: (01) 2225415
Subjects: Science & Technical, Encyclopaedias

Nouvelles Editions **Debresse***, 17 rue Duguay-Trouin, F-75006 Paris Tel: (01) 5481047
Man Dir: Pierre Moulin; *Editorial:* Paul Poncelet; *Sales:* Vincent Moulin; *Production, Publicity:* Josiane Muller
Subjects: General Fiction, Poetry, History, Social Science
Founded: 1933

Librairie Générale de l'Enseignement Mme **Decomble***, 4 rue Dante, Paris 5 Tel: (033) 0698
Man Dir and Other Offices: Mrs Decomble
Subject: Botany
1978: 13 titles *1979:* 13 titles *Founded:* 1903
Miscellaneous: General Educational Publisher
ISBN Publisher's Prefix: 2-85022

Défense de l'Occident, see Les Sept Couleurs

Editions **Delachaux** & Niestlé Spes, 32 rue de Grenelle, F-75007 Paris Tel: (01) 5483842
Parent Company: Editions Delachaux et Niestlé, Switzerland (qv)
Subjects: Religion, Medicine, Psychology, Education, Social & Natural Science, Juveniles, Technical, Mathematics, Architecture, Sports
Founded: 1860
ISBN Publisher's Prefix: 2-603

Librairie **Delagrave** Sàrl*, 15 rue Soufflot, F-75240 Paris cedex 05 Tel: (01) 3258866
Cable Add: Delagrave Paris Telex: 210311F Code 690
Manager: Fabrice Delagrave; *Sales Dir:* J Roustan; *Publicity:* F Simmonet; *Rights & Permissions:* Y Blaise
Subjects: Juveniles, General Science, University, Technical, Secondary & Primary Textbooks, Educational Materials, Languages
1978: 33 titles *Founded:* 1865
ISBN Publisher's Prefix: 2-206

Jean-Pierre **Delarge** SA, 10 rue Mayet, F-75006, Paris Tel: 7837070
Man Dir: Jean-Pierre Delarge; *Editorial:* Michel Gault; *Sales:* François Chagneau; *Rights & Permissions:* Chantal Galtier Roussel
Subjects: General Non-fiction; especially Popular Reference Works, Juveniles, Cookery, Reportage, Literature, History, Biography, Philosophy, Education, Religion, Games, Sports, Sociology; Paperbacks
1979: 60 titles *Founded:* 1942
ISBN Publisher's Prefix: 2-7113

Imprimeries **Delmas***, ave du Mirail, Artigues-près-Bordeaux, BP 14, F-33370 Tresses Tel: 863941
Subject: Literature
ISBN Publisher's Prefix: 2-7034

Editions J **Delmas** et Cie, 13 rue de l'Odéon, F-75006 Paris Tel: (01) 3250832
Man Dir: Jacques Delmas; *Sales, Rights & Permissions:* Jacques Delmas; *Publicity:* Evelyne Alaux
Subjects: Accountancy, Law, Finance, Management, Insurance, Data Processing, Social and Factory Legislation, Dictionaries
1978: 4 titles *Founded:* 1947
ISBN Publisher's Prefix: 7034

Editions Robert **Delpire** SA*, 9 rue Georges-Pitard, F-75015 Paris Tel: (01) 8426800
Subject: Art
ISBN Publisher's Prefix: 2-85107

Editions **Denoël** Sàrl, 19 rue de l'Université, F-75007 Paris Tel: (01) 2615085 Cable Add: EDEPEGE
Man Dir: Albert Blanchard; *Rights & Permissions:* Thérèse Mairesse
Parent Company: Editions Gallimard (qv)
Associate Company: Mercure de France (qv)
Subsidiary Company: Société Nouvelle des Editions Gonthier Sàrl (qv)
Subjects: General and Science Fiction, Art, Reference, Sports, Documents, Political Science, Economics, De Luxe Editions
1978: 133 titles
ISBN Publisher's Prefix: 2-207

Editions **Desclée** et Cie, 77 rue de Vaugirard, F-75006 Paris Tel: (01) 5487860 Telex: 202036 Blougay
Man Dir: Marcel Vervaet
Parent Company: Gedit SA, Tournai, Belgium (qv)
Associate Companies: Desclée Editeurs SA, Tournai, Belgium (qv); Editions Gamma, Paris (qv); Nouvelles Editions Mame, Paris (qv); Editions du Chalet, Paris (qv)
Subjects: History, Philosophy, Religion, Social Science
1978: 50 titles *1979:* 30 titles *Founded:* 1872
ISBN Publisher's Prefix: 2-7189

Desclée, De Brouwer SA, 76 bis rue des Saints-Pères, F-75007 Paris Tel: (01) 5440763 Cable Add: Dedebrouw
Man Dir, Publicity: François-Xavier de Guibert; *Editorial:* Jacques Deschanel; *Sales:* Michel Mugler; *Production:* Gerard Hoeltzel; *Rights & Permissions:* Yvonne Tomazi
Subjects: Belles Lettres, Religion and Theology, Juvenile and Educational, Music, Art, Medicine, Psychology, Psychiatry, Social Science, Low priced paperbacks
1977: 60 titles *Founded:* 1875
ISBN Publisher's Prefix: 2-220

Librairie **Desforges**, 27-29 quai des Grands-Augustins, F-75006 Paris Tel: (01) 3546054
Subjects: Technology, Commerce, Management, Education, Building, Pedagogy, Esoteric, Naturopathy

Dessain et Tolra, Lethielleux-Seneve Editorial Bouret, 10 rue Cassette, F-75006 Paris Tel: (01) 2229020
Man Dir: P Zech; *Rights & Permissions:* Mrs F Desgranchamps, Mrs F Houssin
Subjects: Children's and Young Adults' books, Handcrafts and Do-it-yourself, Pastoral works and Catechisms
ISBN Publisher's Prefix: 2-249

Librairie André **Desvigne***, 53-54 Quai Pierre Scize, F-69321 Lyon cedex 1 Tel: (078) 286374
President: André Desvigne
Orders to: Ed André Desvigne, 6 bis rue de l'Abbaye, Paris 6
Subject: School Books, Higher Grade education
ISBN Publisher's Prefix: 2-7037

Les Editions des **Deux Coqs d'Or**, 28 rue de la Boétie, F-75008 Paris Tel: (01) 2561052
Cable Add: Deucodo Paris Telex: 650780
Man Dirs: Philip A Jarvis, François Marhnezh; *Publicity & Advertising:* Claude Gille; *Rights & Permissions:* Monique Lanteline
Subjects: Art, How-to, Juveniles, Reference, Paperbacks
Founded: 1949
Book Clubs: Education et Culture; Presses d'Or
ISBN Publisher's Prefix: 2-7192

La Maison du **Dictionnaire**, see Maison

John **Didier** Editions, 1 rue des Chailles, F-92500 Rueil Malmaison Tel: 7514545
Telex: 250303 Service Didier Cable Add: Didier 92500 Rueil-Malmaison
Man Dir & Editor: John Didier; *Assistant Editor:* Barbara Lyon; *Sales Dir:* C Perrin; *Advertising Dir:* R Mercier; *Publicity Dir:* L Meynier; *Rights & Permissions:* Miss R Camus
Subjects: Fiction, Nonfiction, General Trade, Belles Lettres, Biography, History, Theses, How-to, Art, Philosophy, Religion, Juveniles
Bookshop: The American Bookshop (at above address)
Founded: 1962

Librairie Marcel **Didier** SA*, 15 rue Cujas, F-75005 Paris Tel: (01) 3292133
Associate Companies: Editions Marcel Didier SA, Belgium (qv); Didier Canada, Montreal
Subjects: Education, Audio Visual and Electronic Media
ISBN Publisher's Prefix: 2-208

Editions **Didier et Richard***, 9 Grande Rue, BP 137, F-38019 Grenoble cedex Tel: (076) 441286
Man Dir: Jacques Harel; *Sales:* F J Bach
Subjects: Cartography, Regional Literature
Bookshop: Librairie Didier et Richard (at above address)
Founded: 1924
ISBN Publisher's Prefix: 2-7038

Société Didot-Bottin SA, 28 rue du Docteur Finlay, F-75738 Paris cedex 15   Tel: (01) 5786166   Telex: 204286F
Bookshop: at above address
Subjects: Encyclopaedias and Annuals concerning Business, Trades, International Commerce and Touring, French Administration, Transport, Motor Cycling etc.
Founded: 1796
ISBN Publisher's Prefix: 2-7039

Editions la **Diffusion Scientifique***, 156 rue Lamarck, F-75018 Paris   Tel: (01) 6270160
Subject: Literature
ISBN Publisher's Prefix: 2-85012

Société de **Documentation** et d'Analyses Financières, see D A F S A

La **Documentation Française**, 29-31 quai Voltaire, F-75340 Paris cedex 07   Tel: (01) 2615010   Telex: 204826 DOCFRAN Paris
Publications of the General Secretary's Office of the French Government
Man Dir: Jean-Louis Cremieux-Brilhac; *Publicity:* Laura Esterhásy
Mail Order and Documentation requests to: 124 rue Henri Barbusse, F-93308 Aubervilliers cedex
Subjects: Reprints of documents and official reports bearing on French and Foreign Politics, Economics, Regional Administration, Environment, Social Problems, Science and Technology, Law, the Arts, Official Announcements;
40 Periodicals
Bookshops: 29-31 quai Voltaire, F-75007 Paris; 165 rue Garibaldi, F-69401 Lyons
Founded: 1945
Miscellaneous: Publishing House for the National Archives Administration, also comprises a library, a bookshop, a photographic library and an information service (all at the above address)
ISBN Publisher's Prefix: 2-86000

Doin Editeurs, 8 pl de l'Odéon, F-75006 Paris   Tel: (01) 3253402
Man Dir: M Abadie
Subjects: Medicine, Psychology, General & Social Science, University Textbooks
1978: 35 titles   *Founded:* 1874
ISBN Publisher's Prefix: 2-7040

Domino*, 22 rue de l'Echiquier, 75010 Paris   Tel: (01) 5230635
Dirs: Jean Chapelle, Humbert Rusconi

Doubleday-France, 9 rue du Pré-Aux-Clercs, Paris 7   Tel: 2611898/2611899   Cable Add: Doubday Paris
Business Manager: Véronique Poderzay; *Editorial:* Beverly Gordey; *Rights & Permissions:* Ruth Grossman
Parent Company: Doubleday & Co, Inc, 245 Park Ave, New York, NY 10017, USA
Associate Company: Doubleday & Co, Inc, UK (qv)
Founded: 1959 (Doubleday-France)

Draeger Editeur, 46 rue de Bagneux, F-92120 Montrouge   Tel: 6571154   Telex: 270294F
Man Dir: Claude Draeger
Subjects: Art, Architecture, Documents, Biography, De Luxe Editions
1977: 4 titles
ISBN Publisher's Prefix: 2-85119

Dragon's Dream Ltd, formerly of Paris, now in Netherlands (qv)

Droguet et Ardant, 41 rue Henri Giffard, BP 1010, F-87004 Limoges 57 cedex   Tel: (055) 374306   Telex: 580934
Man Dir: Robert Ardant; *Publicity Dir:* Suzanne Pasteau
Subjects: R C Devotional; the Mass, Bibles, Prayer Books, Catechisms
1978: 10 titles   *1979:* 12 titles
ISBN Publisher's Prefix: 2-7041

Librairie Générale de **Droit et de Jurisprudence**, 20 rue Soufflot, F-75005 Paris   Tel: (01) 0330719   Telex: 210023 Ogtel 741
Man Dirs: Françoise Marty, Jacqueline Hebert; *Sales Manager, Rights & Permissions:* Guy Hamonic
Subjects: Social Science, Law, University Textbooks, Jurisprudence
Bookshop: LGDJ, 24 rue Soufflot, Paris
Founded: 1836
ISBN Publisher's Prefix: 2-275

Dunod, see Bordas

Maison d'Editions J **Dupuis** Fils et Cie SA, 8 rue Bellini, F-75782 Paris cedex 16   Tel: (01) 7277280
Subjects: Juveniles, Literature

E P A, 83 rue de Rennes, F-75006 Paris   Tel: (01) 6090005   Telex: 202891F
Man Dir, Editorial, Sales, Publicity, Rights & Permissions: Arnauld de Fouchier; *Production:* Gilles Blanchet, Rosine Bélinguier; *Mail Order:* Christine Monjalous; *Press Agent:* Grita Chabasson
Orders to: E P A, 18 rue d'Issy, F-92100 Boulogne Billancourt
Parent Company: E T A I, 20-22 rue de la Saussière, F-92100 Boulogne Billancourt
Subjects: Aviation, Automobile, Railways, Military, Marine Interest, Photographic, Historical
Bookshops: 83 rue de Rennes, Paris 6; 92 rue Saint Lazare, Paris 9; 18 rue de l'Ancienne Préfecture, Lyon
1979: 25 titles   *1980:* 30 titles   *Founded:* 1953
ISBN Publisher's Prefix: 2-85120

Editions **E S F** (Editions Sociales Françaises)*, 17 rue Viète, F-75854 Paris cedex 17   Tel: (01) 9246876/2275383/2279016
President: Gérard Didier; *Man Dir:* Claude Chichet; *Sales Dir:* Michel Henry
Subsidiary Company: Entreprise Moderne d'Edition (qv)
Subjects: Education, Re-education, Pedagogy, Problems of Handicapped Children, Psychology, Social Problems and Legislation, Health and Nutrition
Bookshop: sales from SABRI, 292 rue Saint-Jacques, F-75005 Paris
1978: 20 titles   *Founded:* 1928
ISBN Publisher's Prefix: 2-7101

E T P (Editions Techniques Professionnelles et Régies Audiovisuelles)*, 31 ave Pierre-1er de Serbie, F-75784 Paris cedex 16   Tel: (01) 7236158/7236161
Subjects: Information Science in Business, Management and Marketing, International Relations

E T S F, see Editions Techniques et Scientifiques Françaises

E U R E D I F, see Eurédif

L'**Ecole**/L'Ecole des Loisirs, 11 rue de Sèvres, F-75006 Paris   Tel: (01) 2229410   Cable Add: Librecole
Man Dir: Jean Fabre; *Export Sales Manager:* H Doulmet; *Rights and Permissions, Publicity and Advertising:* Jean Delas
Subjects: Juveniles, High-priced Paperbacks, University, Secondary & Primary Textbooks, Educational Materials
1978: 90 titles
ISBN Publisher's Prefix: 2-211

Edhis, see Histoire Sociale

Les Editions **Edilec** SA*, 9 ave Robert Schuman, F-75007 Paris   Tel: 5556917/7055043   Telex: 22064F Ext 5506
Subjects: Encyclopaedias, Medicine, Psychology, Education, Law, Economics

Ediscience, see McGraw-Hill Inc

Edisud, La Calade, RN 7, F-13100 Aix-en-Provence   Tel: (42) 216144/216437
Man Dir: Charles-Yves Chaudoreille; *Sales, Production:* C-Y Chaudoreille; *Publicity:* Anne-Marie Paolantonacci; *Rights & Permissions:* A M Paolantonacci
Subjects: Ecology, Energy, Agriculture, History, Geography, Regional Interest (Provence), General Topics
1978: 10 titles   *1979:* 18 titles   *Founded:* 1971
ISBN Publisher's Prefix: 2-85744

Société **Editart** Quatre Chemins, 3 pl St-Sulpice, F-75006 Paris   Tel: (01) 3544073   Cable Add: Waledit
Dir: Mme A Gabrilovitch
Bookshop: Librairie des Quatre Chemins Editart (at above address)
Subject: Art
Founded: 1924

Les **Editeurs Français** Réunis*, 21 rue de Richelieu, F-75001 Paris   Tel: (01) 2961410
General Dir: Madeleine Braun; *Man Dir:* Mr Aragon; *Literary Dir:* Rouben Melik
Subjects: Belles Lettres, Theatre, Cinema, Poetry, Novels, History, Paperbacks, Fiction, Nonfiction, Art, Music
Founded: 1944
ISBN Publisher's Prefix: 2-201

Les **Editeurs Réunis***, 11 rue de la Montagne-Sainte-Geneviève, F-75005 Paris   Tel: (01) 6337446/0334381
Subjects: The company acts as sole agent for YMCA Press (qv), Bradda Books and Prideaux Press in publishing a very comprehensive list of Russian books in the original Russian

Editions **Maritimes** et d'Outre-Mer SA*, 17 rue Jacob, F-75006 Paris   Tel: (01) 3290620   Telex: 270461
Man Dir: Nicole Lattès
Subjects: General Fiction, Art, History, How-to, Education, Juveniles, Science and Technology, Geography, Ethnography, Marine, Colonial Literature
Founded: 1839
Bookshops: Librairie EMOM, 17 rue Jacob, F-75006 Paris
ISBN Publisher's Prefix: 2-7070

Editions **Modernes Média**, 21 rue du Cardinal-Lemoine, F-75005 Paris   Tel: (01) 3268384
Subjects: Philosophy, Linguistics, School Books, Pedagogy, Literature
ISBN Publisher's Prefix: 83398

Les **Editions Mondiales** SA*, 2 rue des Italiens, F-75009 Paris   Tel: (01) 8244621   Cable Add: Editomondiales
Dir: Cino del Duca
Subjects: General Fiction, How-to, History, Juveniles, Literature, Education, Philosophy, Languages
Founded: 1932
ISBN Publisher's Prefix: 2-7074

Les **Editions Sociales**, 146 rue du Faubourg-Poissonnière, F-75010 Paris   Tel: (01) 5261103   Telex: 226 Sogedil
Man Dir: Lucien Seve; *Editorial:* Richard Lagache, Nicole Chiaverini; *Publicity:* J da Costa; *Rights & Permissions:* Cecile Botlan
Orders to: Odeon Diffusion (at above address)
Subjects: Philosophy, Social Science, Politics, Literature, Education, Languages, Economics
Book Club: Livre Club Diderot
Bookshop: Les Librairies de la Renaissance; Librairie Racine, 24 rue Racine, F-75006 Paris

1978: 50 titles *1979:* 21 titles *Founded:* 1920
ISBN Publisher's Prefix: 2-209

Editions Sociales Françaises, see E S F

Editions Techniques SA, 123 rue d'Alésia, F-75680 Paris cedex 14 Tel: (01) 5392291 Telex: Editec 270737F; 18 rue Séguier, F-75006 Paris Tel: (01) 3292130
Man Dir: Philippe Durieux; *Assistant Dir:* Robert Turberg; *Export Sales Dir:* J P Chamoux
Subjects: Law, Medicine, Engineering, University Textbooks, Encyclopaedias
Founded: 1907
ISBN Publisher's Prefix: 2-7110

Editions Techniques des Industries de la Fonderie, see Fondeur d'aujourd'hui

Editions Techniques et Scientifiques Françaises, 2-12 rue de Bellevue, F-75940 Paris cedex 19 Tel: 2003305 Telex: PGV 230472F
Man Dir: Jean-Pierre Ventillard; *Editorial, Sales, Production, Publicity:* Christian Cheneau
Subjects: Technical books dealing with radio, television, electronics and associated themes: Periodicals on same subjects at popular and professional level
1978: 35 titles

Editions Techniques Professionnelles, see E T P

Les **Editions Universelles** Sàrl*, 140 blvd St-Germain, F-75006 Paris Tel: (01) 3267382
Subjects: Literature, Medicine, Philosophy

Editions Universitaires-Editions du Jour SA, now Editions Jean Pierre Delarge SA

Alfred **Eibel**, editeur, Les Argonautes, 9 rue Edouard Jacques, F-75014 Paris Tel: (01) 3214100
President & offices other than Sales: Alfred Eibel; *Sales:* Les Argonautes
Parent Companies: Alfred Eibel, Switzerland (qv); Alfred Eibel, 6 rue Henri Bocquillon, F-75015 Paris
Subsidiary Companies: Editions L'Age d'Homme, Switzerland (qv); Les Argonautes, Belgium; Agenzia Libraria Salvatore Fozzi, 72-76 Via Toscana, I-09100 Cagliari, Italy
Subjects: China, South-East Asia, Travel, Literature
1978: 10 titles *1979:* 4 titles *Founded:* 1974
ISBN Publisher's Prefix: 2-8274

Editions **Elsevier** Séquoia Sàrl, 1 rue du 29 Juillet, F-75001 Paris Tel: (01) 2601556
Man Dir: Georges Merlin
Parent Company: Elsevier-NDU nv, Netherlands (qv)
Associate Company: Elsevier Sequoia, Belgium (qv)
Subjects: History, Reference, Juveniles, Medicine and Health, Nature, Psychology, Travel, Family, Sports and Hobbies, Management, Education, Cookery
1980: 195 titles *Founded:* 1960
ISBN Publisher's Prefix: 2-8003

Editions **Encre**, 9 rue Duphot, F-75001 Paris Tel: 2969002
Man Dir: Michel Coquart; *Dir:* Gérard Sakon; *Sales:* Serge Beltz; *Production:* Jacques Lacogue; *Rights & Permissions:* Antonella Ortoli
Parent Company: Société IMC
Subsidiary Company: Encre-Dif, at above address
Subjects: General Literature, Fiction, Documentary and Reportage, How-To
1979: 54 titles *Founded:* 1978

Encyclopaedia Universalis France SA*, 10 rue Vercingétorix, F-750014 Paris Tel: 5394539/5396114 Cable Add: Encyversal Telex: 220064F Code 3121
President, Man Dir: Mr Baumberger; *Editorial:* Mr Bersani; *Sales:* Mr Nepveu; *Production:* Mr Schweizer; *Rights & Permissions:* Mr Rabilloud
Subjects: Encyclopedias, Atlases
1978: 2 titles *1979:* 4 titles *Founded:* 1967
Miscellaneous: Club Français du Livre (qv) and Encyclopaedia Britannica France are partners in the distribution of the Company's publications
ISBN Publisher's Prefix: 2-85229

Librairie Générale de l'**Enseignement** Sàrl, see Decomble

Editions **Entente**, 12 rue Honoré-Chevalier, F-75006 Paris Tel: (01) 2228070
Man Dir: Edouard Esmerian
Subjects: Ecology, Economics, Third World, Essays, Monographs on Minorities, Documentary Accounts, Novels etc
Bookshop: Librairie Entente, 12 rue Honoré Chevalier, F-75006 Paris
1980: 51 titles *Founded:* 1975
ISBN Publisher's Prefix: 2-7266

Entreprise Moderne d'Edition*, 17 rue Viète, F-75854 Paris cedex 17 Tel: 9246876
President: Gérard Didier; *Sales Manager:* Michel Henry
Parent Company: Editions E S F (qv)
Subjects: all aspects of Business Management; Personnel Training and Management; Data Processing; Technology; Periodicals
1979: 25 titles *Founded:* 1953
Miscellaneous: The merger between Entreprise Moderne and E S F dates from July 1979
ISBN Publisher's Prefix: 2-7043

Les Editions de l'**Epargne***, 174 blvd St-Germain, F-75280 Paris cedex 06 Tel: (01) 5482452
Man Dir: René Laurent
Subjects: Investment, Savings Banks, Economy and Finance, Family Budgets, aspects of Law, Penal Codes
ISBN Publisher's Prefix: 2-85015

Epi SA Editeurs, 76 bis rue des Saints-Pierres, F-75007 Paris Tel: (01) 5440763 Cable Add: Dedebrouw
Manager & Publicity Dir: François Xavier de Guibert; *Sales:* Michel Mugler; *Production:* Gerard Hoeltzel; *Rights & Permissions:* Yvonne Tomazi
Subjects: Social Science, Education, Juvenile, Yoga, Group Therapy, Psychology
1978-79: 80 titles *Founded:* 1947
ISBN Publisher's Prefix: 2-7045

Publications **Estoup et Roy** Sàrl, 47 rue du Château-des-Rentiers, F-75013 Paris Tel: (01) 5838550
Subject: Education
ISBN Publisher's Prefix: 2-85016

Etudes Augustiniennes, 3 rue de l'Abbaye, F-75006 Paris Tel: (01) 3548025
Man Dir: Georges Folliet
Subjects: Theology and Church History, especially in relation to Saint Augustine; the Works of Saint Augustine
1978: 7 titles *Founded:* 1954
ISBN Publisher's Prefix: 2-85121

Eurédif (Société Européenne d'Edition et de Diffusion), Tour Atlas, 10 Villa d'Este, F-75646 Paris cedex 13 Tel: 5838040

Man Dir: Guy Cécille
Subjects: General Fiction, Low-priced Paperbacks
1978: 600 titles *Founded:* 1969
ISBN Publisher's Prefix: 2-7167

L'**Expansion** Scientifique Française, 15 rue St-Benoît, F-75006 Paris Tel: (01) 2603950
Man Dir: Pierre Bergeaud
Subject: Medicine
Bookshop: Librairie des Facultés de Médécine et de Pharmacie, 174 blvd St-Germain, F-75006 Paris
1978: 40 titles *1979:* 40 titles *Founded:* 1925
ISBN Publisher's Prefix: 2-7046

Éditions **Eyrolles**, 61 blvd St-Germain, F-75240 Paris cedex 05 Tel: (01) 3292199
Man Dir: Claude Schoedler; *Editorial:* Lucien Tournier
Subsidiary Company: Les Editions d'Organisation (qv)
Subjects: Comprehensive series covering Physical Sciences, Earth Sciences, Electricity, Mechanics, Transport, Building and Architecture, Agriculture, Management and Industry, the Arts, Sports and Hobbies
Bookshop: Librairie Eyrolles, 61 blvd St-Germain, F-75240 Paris cedex 05
1978: 100 titles *1979:* 100 titles *Founded:* 1918
ISBN Publisher's Prefix: 2-212

Editions La **Farandole**, 146 rue du Faubourg Poissonnière, F-75010 Paris Tel: (01) 5261103
Man Dir: Ghilaine Povinha; *Editorial:* Michèle Courtois; *Sales:* Christian Boudeau; *Promotion:* José da Costa; *Publicity:* Katia Favard
Subject: Juveniles
Founded: 1955
ISBN Publisher's Prefix: 2-7047

Librairie Arthème **Fayard**, 6 rue Casimir-Delavigne, F-75006 Paris Tel: (01) 5443845
Man Dir: Alex Grall; *Sales Dir:* Bernard Clesca; *Publicity Dir:* Marylène Bellenger; *Advertising Dir:* Claude Danis; *Rights & Permissions:* Josette Wittorski
Subjects: General Fiction, Belles Lettres, Poetry, Biography, History, Religion, Music, Social Science
Founded: 1854
ISBN Publisher's Prefix: 2-213

Des **Femmes**, 2 rue de la Roquette, F-75011 Paris Tel: (01) 8051745
Subjects: General Fiction, Essays, Documents, Belles Lettres, Poetry, Biography, Juveniles, Low-priced Paperbacks
Bookshops: Librairie 'Des Femmes', 2 pl des Célestins, Lyon 2; Librairie 'Des Femmes', 35 rue Pavillon, F-13001 Marseille; Librairie 'Des Femmes', 68 rue des Sts-Pères, F-75007 Paris
1978: 120 titles *1979:* 150 titles *Founded:* 1974
ISBN Publisher's Prefix: 2-7210

Groupe **Femmes d'aujourd'hui***, 14 blvd de la Madeleine, F-75008 Paris Tel: (01) 2665715 Cable Add: Parisgraph Telex: 680200 Fer-Sen
Subjects: Domestic Crafts, Medicine, Bible
ISBN Publisher's Prefix: 2-87024

Editions du **Feu** Nouveau, 8 ave César-Caire, F-75380 Paris cedex 08 Tel: (01) 2257305
Subjects: Religion, Literature
Founded: 1946
ISBN Publisher's Prefix: 2-85017

Editions **Filipacchi***, 63 Champs Elysées,
F-75008 Paris Tel: (01) 3590179 Cable
Add: JazMag Telex: UEM 29294
Sales, Publicity, Rights & Permissions: Anne-
Marie Périer
Subjects: Art, General Fiction, How-to,
Juveniles; Paperbacks
Founded: 1970
ISBN Publisher's Prefix: 2-85018

Firmin-Didot et Cie*, 56 rue Jacob, F-75006
Paris Tel: (01) 5440026
Subjects: General Literature, History, Art,
Language
ISBN Publisher's Prefix: 2-7196

Editions **Fiscado***, 7 rue Godot-de-Mauroy,
F-75009 Paris Tel: (01) 0735004
Subject: Education

Librairie **Fischbacher**, International Art
Book Distribution (import-export), 33 rue de
Seine, F-75006 Paris Tel: (01) 3268487
Telex: Art & Edition 240896 (Garocie)
*Man Dir, Production, Publicity, Rights and
Permissions:* H Earle-Fischbacher; *Editorial:*
M C Galand; *Sales:* P Diani
Parent Company: Librairie Fischbacher SA
Subsidiary Companies: International Art
Books Distribution and Office of
Documentation Bibliographique et de
Diffusion
Subjects: Art, Primitive Art, Architecture,
Belles Lettres, Musicology, Philosophy,
History, Education, Religion, Juveniles
Bookshop: 33 rue de Seine, F-75006 Paris
1977: 2 titles *1978:* 2 titles
Founded: 1850
ISBN Publisher's Prefix: 2-7179

Flammarion et Cie, 26 rue Racine, F-75278
Paris cedex 06 Tel: (01) 3291220 Cable
Add: Flamedit Telex: flamedi 204034F
Chairman: Henri Flammarion; *Man Dir:*
Charles-Henri Flammarion; *Export
Manager:* G Vanhove; *Sales:* Alain
Flammarion; *Publicity:* Anne de Cazanove,
Charles Rubinsztein, Micheline Amar;
Advertising: Catherine Bachelez; *Rights &
Permissions:* Koukla Bonnier, Catherine
Cullaz
Orders to: Flammarion, 106-110 rue du Petit
Leroy, BP 403, F-94152 Rungis cedex
Subsidiary Companies: Editions Arthaud
SA, Editions Aubier-Montaigne SA, La
Maison Rustique SA, J'ai Lu, Arts et
Métiers Graphiques (qqv); Editions d'Art
Albert Skira SA, Switzerland (qv)
Imprints: Garnier-Flammarion, Père Castor,
Editions du Chat Perché
Subjects: General Fiction, Belles Lettres,
Poetry, History, How-to, Photography, Art,
Philosophy, Reference, Juveniles, Low- &
High-priced Paperbacks, Economics,
General & Social Science, University
Textbooks, Education, Medicine
Bookshops: Librairies Flammarion — 5 in
Paris, 3 in Lyons, 1 in Bordeaux, 1 in
Marseilles, 1 in Dijon. Also 7 in Montreal,
Canada
1978-79: approx 500 titles *Founded:* 1875
ISBN Publisher's Prefix: 2-08

Editions **Fleurus** SA*, 31 rue de Fleurus,
F-75280 Paris cedex 06 Tel: (01) 5484995
Telex: 21023 Ogtel Ref 557
Man Dir: Jacques Anfray; *Editorial:* Ms
M C Maine, Yves Jolly; *Sales Dir:* Jean Li
Sen Lie; *Production:* Gérard Piassale;
Publicity: Jean Ch Cornet; *Rights &
Permissions:* R J Pintigny
Parent Company: Fleurus-Presse, 31 rue de
Fleurus, Paris 6e
Subjects: Religion, Psycho-Sociological,
Illustrated Children's Albums, Picture strip
stories, Technical Manuals
Bookshop: Librarie du Soleil, 45 rue de
Vaugirard, Paris 6

Founded: 1944
ISBN Publisher's Prefix: 2-215

Editions **Fleuve** Noir*, 6 rue Garancière,
F-75278 Paris cedex 06 Tel: 3292161
Telex: Flenoir 204870 F
Man Dir: Armand de Caro; *Editorial Dir:*
Patrick Siry; *Sales Dir:* André de Caro;
Publicity Dir: Eugène Moineau; *Rights &
Permissions:* Jean-Marie Carpentier
Orders to: 35 rue Jean-Jacques Rousseau,
F-94200 Ivry
Subjects: General Fiction (especially Crime
and Science Fiction), Low-priced
Paperbacks
Founded: 1946
Miscellaneous: Firm is a member of the
Presses de La Cité group (qv)
ISBN Publisher's Prefix: 2-265

Fondeur d'Aujourd'hui, 12 ave Raphael,
F-75016 Paris Tel: 5047250
Man Dir: Pierre Brunschwig; *Editorial:* René
Chupeau; *Sales, Production, Publicity,
Rights & Permissions:* Mrs Zeilingher
Imprint: Editions Techniques des Industries
de la Fonderie
Subject: Foundry technique
Founded: 1950
ISBN Publisher's Prefix: 2-7119

Les Editions **Foucher***, 128 rue de Rivoli,
F-75001 Paris Tel: (01) 2363890
Founder-President: Ms Burgod-Foucher;
General Manager: Bernard Foulon; *Sales
Manager:* J C Richard
Subjects: Education, Medicine, Economics,
General & Social Science
Founded: 1934
ISBN Publisher's Prefix: 2-216

France-Caraïbes, an imprint of Editions
Louis Soulanges

Editions **France Empire**, 68 rue
Jean-Jacques Rousseau, F-75001 Paris
Tel: (01) 2365235/2332519 Telex: 680126
President, Man Dir: Yvon Chotard;
Editorial: Herve le Boterf; *Sales Dir:* Jacques
Chapellon; *Production:* Pierre Pousset;
Publicity: Christine Colinet; *Rights &
Permissions:* Anne Chotard, Dominique de
Saint-Ours
Subsidiary companies: Chotard et Associés,
Editeurs (qv); Sofedis, 29 rue Saint Sulpice,
Paris 6
Branch Off: 13 rue des Lombards, F-27000
Evreux
Subjects: Biography, History, Documentary,
Religion, Reference, Novels, Aviation,
Marine Interest
Book Clubs: Club du Roman Féminin; Club
du Livre de Guerre (both at 33 rue
Beauregard, F-75002 Paris)
Founded: 1945

France Expansion, 15 square de Vergennes,
F-75015 Paris Tel: (01) 8281013 Cable
Add: Francexpansion Paris Telex: Pubfran
202003 F
President: Jacques Dodeman; *Man Dir:*
Pascal Paradis; *Foreign Rights:* Régine Le
Meur
Subjects: Bibliography, Reference,
Humanities, Linguistics, Management,
Teaching French as Foreign Language,
Microfiche and Facsimile Editions
1978: 350 titles *Founded:* 1970

France-Loisirs*, 123 blvd de Crenelle,
F-75015 Paris Tel: (01) 5373565
Subjects: Juveniles, Literature, Art

Les Editions **Franciscaines** SA, 9 rue Marie-
Rose, F-75014 Paris 14e Tel: (01) 5407351
Imprint: Editions Franciscaines La Cordelle
Subjects: Saint Francis and the Franciscans
ISBN Publisher's Prefix: 2-85020

Le **François***, 91 blvd Saint-Germain,
F-75006 Paris Tel: (01) 3265545
Subject: History, Medicine, Science
ISBN Publishers' Prefix: 2-85085

Editions **Fréal***, 4 rue des Beaux Arts,
F-75006 Paris Tel: (01) 3265402
Subjects: Art, Architecture

Henri **Frossard**, see L'Amitié par le Livre

J **Gabalda** et Cie (Librairie Lecoffre) SA, 90
rue Bonaparte, F-75006 Paris Tel: (01)
3265355
Proprietor: J Gabalda
Subject: Religion, especially Biblical Studies
and Archaeology
Founded: 1845
ISBN Publisher's Prefix: 2-85021

Editions **Galilée**, 9 rue Linné, F-75005 Paris
Tel: (01) 3312384
Man Dir: Michel Delorme
Subjects: History, Philosophy, Art, Social
Science, Economics, Belles Lettres, Poetry,
How-to, University Textbooks
Founded: 1971
ISBN Publisher's Prefix: 2-7186

Editions **Gallimard***, 5 rue Sébastien-Bottin,
F-75007 Paris Tel: (01) 5443919 Cable
Add: Enerefene Paris 044 Telex: 204121
Gallim
Man Dir: Claude Gallimard; *Editorial:*
François Erval, Pierre Marchaad; *Rights
and Permissions:* Ania Chevallier, Monique
Poublan
Subjects: General Fiction, Belles Lettres,
Poetry, Biography, History, Music, Art,
Philosophy, Juveniles
Founded: 1911
Bookshop: Librairie Gallimard, 15 blvd
Raspail, F-75007 Paris
Subsidiaries: Editions Denoël (qv); Mercure
de France (qv)
ISBN Publisher's Prefix: 2-07

Editions **Gamma**, 77 rue de Vaugirard,
F-75006 Paris Tel: (01) 5487860 Telex:
202036 Blougay
Man Dir: Marcel Vervaet
Parent Company: Gedit SA Tournai,
Belgium (qv)
Associate Companies: Editions Desclée et
Cie, Editions du Chalet, Nouvelles Editions
Mame (all in France — qqv); Desclée
Editeurs, Editions Gamma (both in Belgium
— qqv)
Subjects: Science & Technology, Reference,
Social Science, Juveniles, School Books
1978: 70 titles *1979:* 75 titles *Founded:* 1964
ISBN Publisher's Prefix: 2-7130

Imprimerie Librairie **Gardet**, 16 rue du
Pâquier, F-74000 Annecy Tel: (50) 454437
Man Dir: Clément Gardet
Subjects: Arts, Crafts, Hobbies, Educational
1978: 3 titles *Founded:* 1836
ISBN Publisher's Prefix: 2-7049

Garnier-Flammarion, an imprint of
Flammarion et Cie

Éditions **Garnier** Frères, BP 168, F-75665
Paris cedex 14 (Located at: 19 rue des
Plantes, F-75014 Paris) Tel: (01) 5409815
Telex: 270105 F TXFRA/Ref 665
Man Dir: Bernard Vereano; *Sales Dir:*
Bertrand Cantegrit; *Rights & Permissions:*
Hubert Deveaux
Subjects: Literary Classics, Juvenile, Strip
Cartoons, Art, Travel Pictorial, History,
Dictionaries
Founded: 1833

Société **Gauthier-Villars***, 70 rue de Saint-
Mandé, F-93100 Montreuil
Parent Company: Editions Bordas,
France (qv)
Associate Companies: Société Générale de
Diffusion S G E D; Sté Bordas-Dunod,

Brussels (Belgium) (qv); Bordas-Dunod-Montreal, Canada (see Editions Bordas)

Les Editions **Gautier-Languereau**, 18 rue Jacob, F-75006 Paris Tel: (01) 3250751 Cable Add: Editlangue Telex: 641155 Elita G31
Man & Sales Dir: Bernard Moreau
Subjects: General Fiction, How-to, Juveniles
1979: 30 titles *Founded:* 1917
ISBN Publisher's Prefix: 2-217

Editions M Th **Genin**, see Librairies Techniques

Librairie Orientaliste Paul **Geuthner** SA, 12 rue Vavin, F-75006 Paris Tel: (01) 6347130 Cable Add: Liborient Paris
Man Dirs: Marie Schiffer, Marc Seidl-Geuthner
Subjects: Archaeology, Assyriology, Islam, Near & Far East, General Orientalia, Linguistics, Numismatics, Religion
1978: 20 titles *Founded:* 1902
Miscellaneous: Specialists in Oriental & North African subjects
ISBN Publisher's Prefix: 2-7053

Gibert Jeune Sàrl, 27 quai St-Michel, F-75005 Paris Tel: (01) 3545732
Subject: Education
ISBN Publisher's Prefix: 2-900002

Editions De **Gigord***, 15 rue Cassette, F-75006 Paris Tel: (01) 5485521
Subjects: General Fiction, Belles Lettres, Education, Religion, University & Secondary Textbooks
Founded: 1830
ISBN Publisher's Prefix: 2-7054

Société Nouvelle des Editions **Gonthier** Sàrl, 19 rue de l'Université, F-75007 Paris Tel: (01) 2615085 Cable Add: EDEPEGE
Man Dir: Albert Blanchard; *Rights & Permissions:* Thérèse Mairesse
Parent Company: Editions Denoël Sàrl (qv)
Subjects: Art, Philosophy, Education, Religion, Philology, Psychology, Sociology, Political Science & Economics, Women's Writing
1977: 17 titles *1978:* 25 titles *Founded:* 1964
ISBN Publisher's Prefix: 2-7197

Jacques **Grancher**, Editeur*, 98 rue de Vaugirard, F-75006 Paris Tel: 2226480/5447028 Cable Add: Sce de Vente/Libraries 5480317, 14 rue Littre, F-75006 Paris
Man Dir: Jacques Grancher
Subjects: Military Series (Uniforms, Arms), Memoirs (Art World), Health, Diet, Cookery Series
Founded: 1952
ISBN Publisher's Prefix: 2-7146

Grange Batelière SA*, 10 rue Chauchat, F-75009 Paris Tel: (01) 7709189 Cable Add: Edibatel Maine
Man Dir: Herman Grégoire; *Dir:* Italo Milani; *Publicity & Advertising:* Ms Lemoine
Subjects: Encyclopaedias, General Fiction, Belles Lettres
Founded: 1967
Miscellaneous: The company has sold its business goodwill to Editions Atlas and Alpha Editions
ISBN Publisher's Prefix: 2-255

Société des Editions **Grasset et Fasquelle**, 61 rue des Saints-Pères, F-75007 Paris Tel: (01) 5480771
Chairman: Jean-Claude Fasquelle; *Man Dir:* Claude Durand;
 Yves Berger, Françoise Verny; *Sales:* Gérard Porra; *Publicity and Advertising:* Monique Mayaud; *Production:* Jean Fournier; *Administrative Dir:* Philippe Méry; *Rights and Permissions:* Marie-Hélène d'Ovidio;
Public Relations: Claude Dalla-Torre
Subjects: General Fiction and Non-fiction, Belles Lettres, Poetry, Philosophy, Juveniles
Founded: 1908
ISBN Publisher's Prefix: 2-246

Jean **Grassin** Editeur, 50 rue Rodier, F-75009 Paris Tel: (01) 5269040
Man Dir: Jean Grassin
Orders to: Moulin de l'Ecluse, F-28210 Nogent-le-Roi Tel: 37 825154
Subjects: Literature, Poetry, History, Bibliophily
Book Club: Poètes Présents (Poets of Today) (qv)
Bookshop (and Gallery): Pl de Port-en-Dro, ave de l'Atlantique, F-56340 Carnac-Plage Tel: (97) 529363
1978: 34 titles *Founded:* 1957
ISBN Publisher's Prefix: 2-7055

Groupe Expansion, 67 ave de Wagram, BP 570, F-75017 Paris cedex 17 Tel: (01) 7581295 Telex: 650242 manxpan
President and Man Dir: Jean-Louis Servan-Schreiber; *General Manager:* Hubert Zieseniss; *Publicity Dir:* Philippe le Grix de la Salle; *International Advertising Dir:* Jacques Louvet
Subjects: Economics, Politics, Social Sciences, Education, Literature, Law, Architecture, Scientific and Technical

Librairie **Gründ**, 60 rue Mazarine, F-75006 Paris 6 Tel: (01) 3298740 Cable Add: Gründ Paris Telex: 270105 F TXFRA/ref 888
Man Dir: Michel Gründ; *Sales Dir:* Alain Gründ; *Rights & Permissions, Advertising:* P A Touttain
Associate Company: Editions Alpina (qv)
Subjects: Information and Reference books on Nature, Animals etc; Travel; Arts; How-to Books; Juvenile; 10-vol Benezit Biographical Dictionary of International Artists, Sculptors and Designers; Gift Books
1978: 23 titles *1979:* 47 titles *Founded:* 1880
ISBN Publisher's Prefix: 2-7000

Librairie **Guénégaud**, 10 rue de l'Odéon, F-75006 Paris Tel: 3260791
Man Dir: Mr Pénau
Subjects: History, Topography (France)
1980: 60 titles *Founded:* 1947
ISBN Publisher's Prefix: 2-85023

Guérin et Cie, see Artisan du Livre

Editions d'Art Albert **Guillot***, 4 rue de Sèze, F-69006 Lyon Tel: (078) 523133
Subject: Art
ISBN Publisher's Prefix: 2-85096

Groupe International **Hachette***, 254 blvd St-Germain, F-75007 Paris Tel: (01) 2603822 Telex: Gihac 270357 F and Hachetr 260624
Dir: Jean-Marie Lepargneur; *Sales Managers:* Jean-Claude Diemer (North), Gérard Choquet (South); *Publicity Manager:* Jacques Leblanc
Subjects: General Fiction, Art Books, Classics, Juveniles, History, Educational Materials

Librairie **Hachette***, 79 blvd St-Germain, F-75006 Paris Tel: (01) 3291224 Cable Add: Hachechi Paris 25 Telex: Hacsieg Paris 204434
Man Dir: Gerard Worms; *Export Manager:* Jean-Marie Lepargneur; *Foreign Rights:* Jean-Loup Chiflet
Branch Off: Hachette Inc, 2 Park Ave, New York, NY 10016
Subsidiary Companies:
Hachette/Enseignment (qv); Hachette Guides Bleus (qv); Hachette-Jeunesse (qv); Hachette Littérature (qv); Hachette Pratique (qv); Hachette Réalités (qv); Hachette-Sciences Humaines; Editions Stock (qv); Edition No 1 (qv)
Subjects: General Fiction, Nonfiction, History, How-to, Philosophy, Art, Travel, Reference, Education, Juveniles, Science, Paperbacks, Textbooks, Architecture, Bibliography, Engineering, Music, Politics, Social Science, Games, Sport, Languages, Economics
Bookshops: Bookshops throughout the world
Founded: 1826
ISBN Publisher's Prefix: 2-01

Hachette/Enseignement (Hachette Educational), 79 blvd Saint-Germain, BP 1506, F-75006 Paris Tel: 3291224 Cable Add: Hacheci-Paris 25 Telex: 26624 Hachepr Paris
Sales Manager: Jean-Claude Didelot
Parent Company: Librairie Hachette (qv)
Subjects: Pedagogic and para-pedagogic books on every subject and for every level from Nursery School to University

Hachette Guides Bleus, 284 blvd St-Germain, F-75007 Paris Tel: (01) 5556001
Publisher: Gérald Gassiot-Talabot; *Rights & Permissions:* Andrée Faure
Parent Company: Librairie Hachette (qv)
Subjects: Guides, Art

Hachette-Jeunesse, 79 blvd St-Germain, BP 1506, F-75006 Paris Tel: 3291224 Cable Add: Hacheci-Paris 25 Telex: Hacsieg-Paris 204434
Executives: Jean-Claude Dubost, Philippe Schuwer; *Rights and Permissions:* Françoise Laurent, Paule Tschudin
Parent Company: Librairie Hachette (qv)
Subjects: Illustrated Childrens' Books, Reference, How-to, Collections, Novels for the Young

Hachette-Littérature, 6 ave Pierre 1er de Serbie, F-75116 Paris Tel: 7236163
Man Dir: Michel Marcrette; *Rights & Permissions:* Andrée Faure
Parent Company: Librairie Hachette (qv)
Subjects: Reference Works, Science, Historical, Essays, Biographical, Documentation, Fiction
1978: 60 titles *1979:* 70 titles *Founded:* 1975

Hachette Pratique, 4 rue de Gallière, F-75116 Paris Tel: (01) 7236138
Publisher: Sylvie Diarte; *Rights and Permissions:* Andrée Faure
Subjects: How-to, Games, Sport, Cookery, Illustrated Books, Handicrafts

Hachette-Réalités, 284 blvd St-Germain, F-75007 Paris Tel: (01) 5556001 Telex: 26624 Hachepr-Paris
Publisher: Gérald Gassiot-Talabot; *Rights and Permissions:* Andrée Faure
Parent Company: Librairie Hachette (qv)
Subjects: Art, History, Reference
Founded: 1956

Editions Dominique **Halévy***, 26 pl Dauphine, F-75001 Paris Tel: (01) 3266127
Man Dir: Dominique Halévy
Subjects: Poetry, Juveniles
Founded: 1969
ISBN Publisher's Prefix: 2-85024

Le **Hameau**, Editeur, 15 rue Servandoni, F-75006 Paris Tel: 3290550
Man Dir, Rights & Permissions: Paule Truchaud; *Sales:* C Navelet; *Production:* C Noualhier; *Publicity:* A R L
Orders to: Le Hameau Diffusion, at above address
Subjects: Psychology, Psychoanalysis, Social Science, Medicine, Parapsychology, Fiction, Essays, Poetry
Bookshop: address as above
1978: 20 titles *Founded:* 1973
ISBN Publisher's Prefix: 2-7203

Librairie **Hatier** SA*, 8 rue d'Assas, F-75006 Paris Tel: (01) 5443838 Cable Add: Libhatier Paris Telex: 202 732
Man Dir: Michel Foulon; *Sales Dirs:* André Cazaux, Alain Jauson; *Rights & Permissions:* Marie-Blanche D'Ussel
Orders to: 8 rue d'Assas, F-75278 Paris cedex 06
Imprint: Editions de l'Amitié
Subjects: Children's Fiction, Travel, Tour Guides, Popular Natural History, Chess, Sport, How-to, DIY, Illustrated books
Bookshop: 59 blvd Raspail F-75006 Paris
Founded: 1880
ISBN Publisher's Prefix: 2-218

Pierre **Hautot** SA, 36 rue du Bac, F-75007 Paris Tel: (01) 2611015
Subject: Art
Founded: 1952

Fernand **Hazan** Editeur SA, 35-37 rue de Seine, F-75006 Paris Tel: (01) 3546872
Chairman: Blanche Hazan; *Man Dir:* Olivier Hazan
Subjects: Art, Reference, Juveniles, Paperbacks
Founded: 1945
Bookshop: Editions Fernand Hazan, 35-37 rue de Seine

Hermann (Editeurs des Sciences et des Arts) SA, 293 rue Lecourbe, F-75015 Paris Tel: (01) 5574540 Cable Add: Piby Paris Telex: Hermann Paris 200595
Man Dir: Pierre Berès; *Rights & Permissions:* Mrs A Rulleau
Branch Off: 6 rue de la Sorbonne, F-75005 Paris
Subjects: Science, Art, Medical and Technical, Textbooks, Reference, Paperbacks
Bookshop: 6 rue de la Sorbonne, F-75005, Paris
1978: 50 titles *Founded:* 1870
ISBN Publisher's Prefix: 2-7056

Editions de l'**Herne**, 41 rue de Verneuil, F-75007 Paris Tel: (01) 2612506
Chairman, Man Dir, Rights & Permissions: Constantin Tacou; *Editorial, Press Agent:* Miss Laurence Mauriac; *Sales:* Sodis; *Production, Publicity:* François Delaroière, Marie-Thérèse Marchand
Subjects: Belles Lettres, Poetry, Philosophy, Social Science, Politics, Art, Novels, Strategy
1978: 8 titles *Founded:* 1964
ISBN Publisher's Prefix: 5112

Editions d'Art Les **Heures Claires** SA*, 19 rue Bonaparte, F-75006 Paris Tel: (01) 3265475
Owner: Jean Estrade
Subject: Art
Founded: 1945
ISBN Publisher's Prefix: 2-85026

Editions **Hier et Demain***, 26 rue de Gramont, F-75002 Paris Tel: (01) 0738725/6 Telex: 27618
Man Dir: Denise Drouin; *Editorial:* André Rossel; *Sales, Rights & Permissions:* Denise Drouin; *Production:* Nicole Sabot; *Publicity:* Katia Favard
Associate Company: Editions de la Courtille, France (qv)
Subjects: Biography, History, High-priced Paperbacks, Educational Materials, Collectors' Editions, Practical Guides, Encyclopaedias
Founded: 1971
ISBN Publisher's Prefix: 2-7199, 2-7206

Editions d'**Histoire et d'Art**, J & R Wittman*, 32 ave du Président Wilson, F-75016 Paris Tel: (01) 7270431
Subjects: History, Art
Founded: 1933

Editions d'**Histoire Sociale** EDHIS*, 23 rue de Valois, F-75001 Paris Tel: (01) 2614778
Man Dir: Léon Centner
Subjects: Social History, Revolutions in France, Historical Documents
Bookshops: 23 rue de Valois, Paris; 144 Galerie de Valois, Paris 1e
1978: 37 titles *Founded:* 1967

Editions **Hommes et Techniques**, 2 rue Benoît Malon, BP 128, F-92154 Suresnes Tel: 7723132 Telex: 62785
Man Dir: Paul Guyot
Subjects: Business Management, Organizational Development
1978: 15 titles *1979:* 14 titles *Founded:* 1945

Pierre **Horay** Editeur, 22 bis passage Dauphine, F-75006 Paris Tel: (01) 3545390
Man Dir: Sophie Horay; *Editorial:* Jean-Jacques Lévêque; *Production:* Jean Paoli; *Rights & Permissions:* Colette Haro
Orders to: Editions Garnier, 19 rue des Plantes, F-75014 Paris
Subjects: General Fiction, Belles Lettres, Poetry, Biography, History, How-to, Music, Art, Juveniles, High-priced Paperbacks
1980: 15 titles *Founded:* 1946
ISBN Publisher's Prefix: 2-7058

Editions **Horizons** de France*, 34 rue de Laborde, F-75008 Paris Tel: (01) 5227634
Man Dir: Pierre Lagrange
Subjects: History, How-to, Art, Music, General and Social Sciences, Natural History
ISBN Publisher's Prefix: 2-85027

Les **Humanoïdes** Associés, 15-17 passage des Petites Ecuries, F-75010 Paris Tel: 2464538
Man Dir, Rights & Permissions: André Berthelot, Jean Pierre Dionnet, Isabelle Morin; *Editorial:* Philippe Manoeuvre; *Art Editor:* Janic Dionnet; *Publicity:* Dominique Bosch
Subjects: Fantasy Fiction, Strip Cartoons, Science Fiction
1978: 60 titles *Founded:* 1975
ISBN Publisher's Prefix: 2-902-123

La **Hune***, 170 blvd St-Germain, F-75006 Paris Tel: (01) 5483585
Subject: Art
Bookshop: Librairie La Hune, at same address

Idea Books Distribution SA*, 24 rue du 4 Septembre, F-75002 Paris Tel: (01) 628785; 48 rue de Montreuil, F-75011 Paris Tel: (01) 3404003 Cable Add: Idea Books-Paris
Publisher: Giampaolo Grazzini
Subject: Communications, Artbooks, Architecture, Visual Arts

Editions de l'**Illustration**, 13 rue St-Georges, F-75009 Paris 9 Tel: (01) 8785319
Man Dir: Roger Allegret
Imprints: Les Editions Chantereine (qv); Baschet et Cie, Editeurs
Subjects: History, Art, How-to, Encyclopaedias, Travel, Science, Geography
1978: 3 titles *1979:* 5 titles *Founded:* 1843
ISBN Publisher's Prefix: 2-7059

InterEditions Paris, 87 ave du Maine, F-75014 Tel: 3277450 Telex: 210311 Publi 147
Man Dir: Geoffrey M Staines; *Production:* Monika Neumann; *Rights & Permissions:* Anne Brassié
Orders to: Bordas SA, 37 rue Boulard, F-75680 Paris cedex 14
Parent Company: Inter-European Editions, Amsterdam, Netherlands
Subjects: Scientific texts related to teaching and/or research, especially Biology, Chemistry, Physics, Mathematics; Commerce
1978: 8 titles *1979:* 9 titles *Founded:* 1976
ISBN Publisher's Prefix: 7296

CNRS Laboratoire **Intergéo**, 191 rue Saint-Jacques, F-75005 Paris Tel: 6337431
Intergéo Laboratory of the French National Scientific Research Centre — CNRS
Man Dir: R Brunet
Parent Company: Centre National de la Recherche Scientifique (CNRS)
Associate Company: Editions CNRS (qv)
Subjects: Geography, Documentation
1978: 3 titles *1979:* 3 titles *Founded:* 1947
ISBN Publisher's Prefix: 2-901560

Librairie **Istra** Sàrl*, 93 rue Jeanne-d'Arc, F-75013 Paris Tel: (01) 5851660
Telex: 25884
Subjects: Economics, Education (Primary & Secondary)
Founded: 1928
ISBN Publisher's Prefix: 2-219

Groupe **J A** (Editions J A), 3 rue Roquépine, BP 250, F-75008 Paris Tel: 2656930 Cable Add: Grupjia Paris Telex: 280674
Man Dir and Editorial: Mme Ben Yahmed; *Rights & Permissions:* Mme Ben Yahmed, Mme R Prétat
Subjects: Geography, Tourism, Cartography, Art, History
1978: 15 titles *1979:* 14 titles *Founded:* 1968
ISBN Publisher's Prefix: 2-85258

Editions **J'ai Lu***, 31 rue de Tournon, F-75006 Paris Tel: (01) 3267759 Telex: Jailu 202765
Parent Company: Flammarion et Cie (qv)
Subjects: General Fiction, Belles Lettres, Low-priced Paperbacks
Founded: 1958

Editions **Jeune Afrique**, 3 rue Roquépine, F-75008 Paris Tel: (01) 2656930/2656931 Cable Add: Grupjia Paris Telex: Grupjia 280674
President: Bechir Ben Yahmed; *General Manager:* Danielle Ben Yahmed; *Literary Manager:* Michel Weber; *Commercial Manager:* Rolande Prétat; *Foreign Rights:* D Ben Yahmed, R Prétat; *Press/Publicity:* Anne Simon, R Prétat
Subjects: History, Biography, Geography and Travel, Political, Reference Works, Natural Sciences, Fine Arts
1978: 15 titles *1979:* 14 titles *Founded:* 1968
Miscellaneous: Firm publishes periodicals *Jeune Afrique, Annuaire de l'Afrique et du Moyen Orient, Marchés Nouveaux*
ISBN Publisher's Prefix: 2-85258

Journal des Notaires et des Avocats SA, 6 rue de Mézières, F-75006 Paris Tel: (01) 5481210
Subject: Law
ISBN Publisher's Prefix: 2-85028

Edition **Judogi***, 107 blvd Beaumarchais, F-75003 Paris Tel: (01) 2729559
Subject: Sports

Editions René **Julliard**, 8 rue Garancière, F-75008 Paris Tel: (01) 3291280 Cable Add: Edijulliard Paris 110
Man Dir: Bernard de Fallois; *Publicity Manager:* Nadia Leser; *Foreign Rights:* Loriane Bontion
Subjects: General Fiction, Belles Lettres, History, Political Science
Founded: 1931
Miscellaneous: Firm is a member of the Presses de la Cité group (qv)
ISBN Publisher's Prefix: 2-260

Editions **Jupiter** Sàrl*, 21-23 rue du Mont-Thabor, F-75001 Paris Tel: (01) 2607465/2607778
Dir: Pierre Legrand
Subjects: Law, Politics, Encyclopaedias
ISBN Publisher's Prefix: 2-7060

Jurif (Société d'Etudes Juridiques Internationales et Fiscales), see Cahiers Fiscaux Européens

Kent-Segep SA*, Editions-Publicité, 74 ave Kléber, F-75016 Paris Tel: (01) 5330080
Subject: Literature
1978: 1 title
ISBN Publisher's Prefix: 2-85029

Editions **Klincksieck**, 11 rue de Lille, F-75007 Paris Tel: (01) 2603825
Man Dir: Andrée Laurent-Klincksieck; *Publicity, Rights & Permissions:* Marie-Françoise Vauquelin
Subjects: Social Sciences, Philology, Linguistics, Archaeology, History, Belles Lettres, Aesthetics, Reference, General & Social Science
Bookshop: Librairie C Klincksieck, 11 rue de Lille, F-75007 Paris
1979: 70 titles *Founded:* 1842
ISBN Publisher's Prefix: 2-252

L J Productions*, 9 rue Méchain, F-75680 Paris cedex 14 Tel: (01) 5352816
Subjects: Juveniles, Games

Les Editions Robert **Laffont**, 6 pl St-Sulpice, F-75006 Paris Tel: (01) 3291233 Cable Add: Edilaf Paris 110 Telex: 25877
Man Dir: Robert Laffont
Associate Company: Les Editions Seghers (qv)
Subjects: General Fiction and Non-fiction, especially History, Documentary, Philosophy, Religion, Art, Music, Biography, Juveniles, Medicine, General & Social Science, Psychology, Hobbies, High-priced Paperbacks, Textbooks, Translations
Founded: 1941
ISBN Publisher's Prefix: 2-221

Lafolye et Lamarzelle Editeurs Sàrl*, 2 pl des Lices, F-56000 Vannes Tel: (097) 661198
Subject: Religion

Librairie Léonce **Laget**, 75 rue de Rennes, F-75006 Paris Tel: (01) 5489018 Cable Add: Liblaget Paris 110
Man Dir: Léonce Laget
Subjects: Art, History, Trades and Crafts
1978: 60 titles *1979:* 90 titles *Founded:* 1955
ISBN Publisher's Prefix: 2-85204

Editions **Lahumière**, 88 blvd de Courcelles, F-75017 Paris Tel: (01) 7630395/6224367
Publisher: Anne Margarète Lahumière
Subject: Art

Editions **Lamarre-Poinat** SA, 47 rue Saint André-des-Arts, F-75006 Paris Tel: (01) 3265838
Subject: Medicine
ISBN Publisher's Prefix: 2-85030

Lamy SA, 155 rue Legendre, F-75017 Paris cedex 17 Tel: (01) 6272890 Telex: 650790
President: Gérard Lamy; *Man Dir:* Bernard Nitot; *Sales:* Mr Laquieze; *Publicity:* Mr Chareton; *Public Relations:* Pierre-Yves Odinot
Subjects: Law (Social, Fiscal, Company, Transport, Transport Methods)
1979: 39 titles *Founded:* 1949

Librairie Fernand **Lanore** Sàrl, 1 rue Palatine, F-75006 Paris Tel: (01) 3256661
Dir: François Sorlot
Subjects: Belles Lettres, History, Philosophy, Secondary Textbooks, Education, Religion, Languages, Touring, Mountaineering
1978: 14 titles *1980:* 70 titles *Founded:* 1920

Editions J **Lanore** C L T*, Successeur de Laurens, 4 rue de Tournon, F-75006 Paris
Associate Company: Librairie-Editions J Lanore, 12 rue Oudinot, F-75007 Paris
Subjects: Pedagogy and Teaching Texts on Cookery and Catering, Dressmaking, Home Economy, Law, Technology, Careers
1978: 10 titles

Librairie **Larousse**, 17 rue du Montparnasse, F-75006 Paris Tel: (01) 5443817 Cable Add: Liblarous 43 Paris Telex: 250828
Man Dirs: Georges Lucas, Claude Moreau, Jean-Louis Moreau; *Foreign Trade Dir:* Francis Trébinjac; *Rights & Permissions:* E Faguer, Agence SEU, 95 rue de Rennes, F-75006 Paris
Subjects: Dictionaries, Encyclopaedias, Reference, Textbooks, Juveniles, Paperbacks, Technical, General & Social Science, Linguistics
Subsidiaries & Affiliates: Ediciones Larousse Argentina SA, Valentin Gomez 3530, Buenos Aires R 13, Argentina; Larousse-Belgique, 32 blvd du Jardin Botanique, B-1000 Brussels, Belgium; Editora Larousse do Brasil, Av Almte Barrosa, 63s/2609, Rio de Janeiro, Brazil; Editions Françaises Inc, 192 rue Dorchester, Quebec 2, Canada; Ediciones Larousse SA, Marsella 53, Esq Nápoles, Mexico City 6, Mexico; Larousse (Suisse) SA, 23 rue des Vollandes, CH-1211 Geneva 6, Switzerland; Larousse & Co Inc, 572 Fifth Ave, New York, NY, USA
1978: 148 titles *Founded:* 1852
ISBN Publisher's Prefix: 2-03

Editions Jean-Claude **Lattès**, 91 rue du Cherche-Midi, F-75006 Paris Tel: (01) 5443850
Man Dir: Jean-Claude Lattès; *Rights & Permissions:* Ursula Veit
Subjects: General Fiction & Nonfiction, Biography, Documents, Low-priced Paperbacks, Music
1978: 100 titles *Founded:* 1968

Editions Henri **Laurens** Successeurs Sàrl, see Editions J Lanore

Charles **Lavauzel**, BP 8, F-87350 Panazol Tel: (55) 341515
Man Dir: Jean Claude Mazaud; *Sales and Publicity:* Geneviève Giry; *Production:* Henri Chabrier
Subjects: Military History, Law, Horse-Riding
1978: 15 titles *1979:* 18 titles *Founded:* 1880
ISBN Publisher's Prefix: 2-7025

Diffusion Bernard **Laville***, 3 rue Garancière, F-75006 Paris Tel: (01) 6332930
Publisher: Bernard Laville; *Sales Manager:* Eric Prevost
Subjects: Fiction, Social Science, Politics, Juveniles, Religion, Art, Classics

Editions Guy **Le Prat**, 5 rue des Grands-Augustins, F-75006 Paris Tel: (01) 3265782
Man Dir: Guy Le Prat
Subjects: Reference, Leisure, Sports, Oriental and Occult, Natural Medicine, Environment, Ecology, Juvenile, Management, Investment, Glues/Adhesives, Fine Arts, Limited Editions; General Literature, Reprints, Paperbacks
1978: 5 titles *Founded:* 1825
Miscellaneous: Formerly Editions Delarue
ISBN Publisher's Prefix: 2-85205

Editions **Lechevalier** Sàrl*, 19 rue Augereau, F-75007 Paris Tel: (01) 5554369/5555510
Man Dir: Jacques Lechevalier
Subjects: Natural Sciences, Natural History, Biology, Entomology, Mycology, Ornithology, Silviculture, Botany, Zoology, Periodicals
1978: 4 titles *Founded:* 1875
ISBN Publisher's Prefix: 2-7205

Francis **Lefebvre***, 44 rue de Villiers, F-92300 Levallois-Perret Tel: 7581620
Dir: Francis Lefebvre
Subjects: Psychology, Educational Materials
Bookshop (affiliated): Librairie la Salamandre, 41 rue des Trois Frères, F-75018 Paris
ISBN Publisher's Prefix: 2-85115

Editions Robert **Léger** et Cie*, 27 rue de la Harpe, F-75005 Paris Tel: (01) 3540450
Subject: Arts

Editions André **Lesot** Sàrl*, 10 rue de l'Eperon, F-75006 Paris Tel: (01) 3265673
Subject: Science & Technical
ISBN Publisher's Prefix: 2-7062

Editions Olivier **Lesourd***, 252 Faubourg St-Honoré, F-75008 Paris Tel: (01) 9244070/2276930
Subject: Technical Reports (Energy)

Société Nouvelle des Editions **Letouzey** et Ané Sàrl, 87 blvd Raspail, F-75006 Paris Tel: (01) 5488014
Dir: J Letouzey
Subjects: Dictionaries, Religion, History
Founded: 1885
ISBN Publisher's Prefix: 2-7063

Lettres Modernes Minard, see Minard

Librairie Commerciale et Technique (Licet) Sàrl, 110 rue de Rivoli, F-75001 Paris Tel: (01) 2334488
Man Dir: Yves Defaucheux; *all other offices:* J P Le Gall
Orders to: 110 rue de Rivoli, Paris 1er
Subjects: Accountancy, Typewriting, Business Techniques, Economics, Law, English, Statistics, Data Processing
1978: 13 titles *1979:* 10 titles *Founded:* 1963
ISBN Publisher's Prefix: 2-85232

Librairie Générale de Droit et de Jurisprudence, see Droit et Jurisprudence

Librairie Générale Française SA, 14 rue de l'Ancienne-Comédie, F-75006 Paris Tel: (01) 3265393
Subject: Literature (Paperbacks)

Librairies Techniques SA, 27 pl Dauphine, F-75001 Paris Tel: (01) 3266090/3290771
Dir: Mme Argenson
Parent Company: Editions Techniques, 18 rue Séguier, F-75006 Paris
Branch Off: 26 rue Soufflot, F-75005 Paris
Subjects: Politics, Law, Commerce
1978: 36 titles *1979:* 41 titles
Miscellaneous: Firm incorporates Editions M Th Genin
ISBN Publisher's Prefix: 2-7111

Licet, see Librairie Commerciale et Technique

Editions de la **Licorne***, 95 rue La Boétie, F-75008 Paris Tel: (01) 3436443
Subject: Education

Editions **Lidis** SA, 23 rue des Grands-Augustins, F-75006 Paris Tel: (01) 3292188 Cable Add: Elidis Paris Telex: Elidis 270900 F
Man Dir, Rights & Permissions: Noël Schumann; *Editorial, Production:* Claire de la Pradelle; *Sales:* J Souci; *Publicity:* Sophie Schumann
Subsidiary Companies: Editions Lidis SA — Diffusion Benelux, 70 Chaussée de Charleroi, B-1060 Brussels, Belgium; La Diffusion, 23 rue des Grands Augustins, F-75006 Paris
Subjects: Encyclopaedias, Art
Book Club: Librairie Lidis, 208 rue de Rivoli, F-75001 Paris
1978: 2 titles *1979:* 2 titles *Founded:* 1955
ISBN Publisher's Prefix: 2-85032

Editions **Ligel**, 77 rue de Vaugirard, F-75006 Paris Tel: (01) 5487860
Man Dir: Henri Creff; *Deputy Director:* Jules Desmyetter
Subject: School Textbooks
Bookshop: 77 rue de Vaugirard, F-75006 Paris
Founded: 1909
ISBN Publisher's Prefix: 2-7064

Editions Michel de **Lile** et Philippe Auzou, 1 rue du Dahomey, F-75014 Paris Tel: (01) 5421877 Telex: Lile-Auzou Sofadif 220686 F
Man Dir: Michel de Lile
Subjects: Art Editions, Facsimile Reproductions
1978/79: 3 titles *1979/80:* 6 titles *Founded:* 1978

Office Central de **Lisieux** SA, see under Office Central

Editions **Lito**, 32 ave Oudinot, F-94340 Joinville le Pont Tel: 8832411 Cable Add: Litofrance Paris Telex: Edlit 680284
Man Dir, Rights & Permissions: Lennart Rosdahl; *Editorial, Publicity:* Janine Ancelet; *Sales:* Yvette Mallay
Parent Company: Lito Interco, 15 ave Guy Mocquet, 94340 Joinville le Pont
Subsidiary Companies: Lito Editrice, Via Palazzetto 15, I-10070 Mappano, Turin, Italy
Subjects: Children's Books, Puzzles, Teaching Aids, Cutouts and Stick-Ons, Transfers, Paperbacks
1978: 630 titles *Founded:* 1958
ISBN Publisher's Prefix: 2-244

Le **Livre de Paris***, 3-5 ave de Garlande, F-92221 Bagneux Tel: (01) 6571140
Subjects: Art, How-to, Juveniles
ISBN Publisher's Prefix: 2-245

Le **Livre de Poche**, 12 rue Francois 1er, F-75008 Paris Tel: (01) 3597959
Man Dir, Rights & Permissions: C Poninski
Subject: General Fiction
Founded: 1953

Lumiere Biblique, see Les Editions de la Source SA

M C L*, 22 rue Bergère, 75009 Paris Tel: (01) 7706183
Dirs: Jean Chapelle, Humbert Rusconi
Subjects: Occult, Medicine, Juveniles

Editions **M D I** (La Maison des Instituteurs), Parc des 10 Arpents, Dept 113, PO Box 39, F-78630 Orgeval Tel: 9756381 Telex: MDI Edit 698094F
Man Dir: Alexandre Schajer; *Export Dir:* Philippe Notté
Subjects: Juveniles, History, Geography, General Science, Secondary and Primary Textbooks, Educational Materials, Wall Maps
Founded: 1954
ISBN Publisher's Prefix: 2-223

McGraw-Hill Inc, 28 rue Beaunier, F-75014 Paris Tel: (01) 5409438 Telex: 250304
Man Dir, Rights & Permissions: Edgar S McLarin; *Editorial, Production:* Lidy Arslan
Parent Company: McGraw-Hill International, 1221 Ave of the Americas, New York, NY 10020, USA
Associate Companies: see McGraw-Hill, UK
Subjects: General Science, Technology, Economics, Finance, Humanities, Current Affairs
1979: 14 titles *1980:* 10 titles *Founded:* 1967
ISBN Publisher's Prefix: 2-7042

Maeght Editeur*, 13 rue de Téhéran, F-75008 Paris Tel: (01) 3876149 Cable Add: Galmaeght Paris 037 Telex: 28660
Dir: Jean Frémon; *Sales Manager:* François Bruller
Subject: Art
ISBN Publisher's Prefix: 2-85087

Les Editions **Magnard** Sàrl, 122 blvd St-Germain, F-75279 Paris cedex 06 Tel: (Management/Admin): (01) 3296420
Man Dir, Sales Dir: Louis Magnard; *Literary Dir:* Thérèse Roche-Magnard; *Export Manager:* Jean-Claude Brouillet, Rés Les Crêtes, Bat Géranium, Ave Marcel-Camusso, F-1360 La Ciotat
Subjects: Juveniles, University, Secondary & Primary Textbooks, Educational Materials
Bookshop: Librairie de France, 122 blvd Saint-Germain, F-75006 Paris
1978: over 1,000 titles *Founded:* 1934
Miscellaneous: awarders of the Jeune France Literary Prize (qv)
ISBN Publisher's Prefix: 2-210

La **Maison des Instituteurs**, see M D I

La **Maison du Dictionnaire**, 95 bis rue Legendre, F-75017 Paris Tel: 2294836 Telex: 270105 ref 355 txfra b rungi
Man Dirs: Michel Feutry
Subjects: Technical, Specialized and General Dictionaries in many languages
1978: 4 titles *1979:* 4 titles *Founded:* 1976
ISBN Publisher's Prefix: 2-85608

La **Maison** Rustique SA*, Librairie Agricole et Horticole, 26 rue Jacob, F-75006 Paris 6 Tel: (01) 3256700
Parent Company: Flammarion et Cie (qv)
Subjects: Natural Science, Horticulture, Agriculture, Forestry
Founded: 1836
ISBN Publisher's Prefix: 2-7066

Adrien **Maisonneuve**-Librairie d'Amérique et d'Orient, 11 rue St-Sulpice, F-75006 Paris Tel: (01) 3268635
Man Dir: Jean Maisonneuve
Subjects: History, Philosophy, Religion, Art, Social Science, Economics, Orientalia
Founded: 1926
ISBN Publisher's Prefix: 2-7200

Editions G P **Maisonneuve et Larose***, 15 rue Victor-Cousin, F-75005 Paris Tel: (02) 3543270
Man Dir: J-P Pinardon
Subjects: Scholarly, Social Science, Agriculture, Oriental & African Studies, Folklore
1978: 29 titles *Founded:* 1961
Miscellaneous: Firms merged in 1961. Founded 1853 and 1860, respectively
ISBN Publisher's Prefix: 2-7068

Librairie **Maloine**, 27 rue de l'École-de-Médecine, F-75006 Paris Tel: (01) 3256045 Telex: 203215F
Dir: Henry Grim; *Man Dir:* Antonin Philippart; *Publicity & Advertising:* Jean Philippart
Subjects: Medicine, Veterinary, Reference
1979: 132 titles *1980:* 143 titles *Founded:* 1881
ISBN Publisher's Prefix: 2-224

Nouvelles Editions **Mame*** (Division of SA Gedit), 77 rue de Vaugirard, F-75006 Paris Tel: 5487860 Telex: Blougay 202036
Man Dir: Marcel Vervaet; *Editorial, Sales, Production:* Louis de Bouville; *Publicity, Rights & Permissions:* Suzel Vervaet
Parent Company: Gedit SA, Tournai, Belgium (qv)
Associate Companies: Desclée Editeurs SA, Tournai, Belgium (qv); Editions Gamma, Paris, France (qv); Editions Desclée et Cie, Paris, France (qv)
Subjects: The Bible, Religious Literature, Catechism, Liturgy
ISBN Publisher's Prefix: 2-7289

Éditions **Marrimpouey** Jeune et Cie*, 2 pl de la Libération, F-64000 Pau
Subjects: Travel and customs in the South of France (especially Pyrenees and Basque regions); including works in the Gascon language

Editions **Martinsart***, 72 blvd de Sébastopol, F-75003, Paris Tel: 8875128
Subjects: Luxury and Semi-Luxury Editions, Collected Literary Works, Encyclopaedias

François **Maspero** Editeur, 1 pl Paul-Painlevé, F-75005 Paris Tel: (01) 6334116
Man Dir: François Maspero
Subjects: Belles Lettres, Poetry, History, Philosophy, Sociology, Political Economy, Low- & High-priced Paperbacks
1978: 80 titles *Founded:* 1959
ISBN Publisher's Prefix: 2-7071

Editions Charles **Massin** et Cie*, 2 rue de l'Echelle, F-75001 Paris Tel: (01) 2603005
Subjects: Architecture, Interior Decoration, Arts
Founded: 1910
ISBN Publisher's Prefix: 2-7072

Masson Editeur, 120 blvd St-Germain, F-75280 Paris cedex 06 Tel: (01) 3292160 Cable Add: Gemas Paris 025 Telex: Massoned 260946
Dir: Dr Jérôme Talamon; *Man Dirs:* P Lahaye, D de Costigliole; *Sales Dir:* F Clouzet; *Rights & Permissions:* Françoise Han
Associate Companies: Toray Masson, Spain (qv); Masson Publishing USA Inc, 111 West 57th St, New York, NY USA; Masson do Brasil, Rua da Quitanda 20, Sala 301, 20011 Rio de Janeiro, Brazil; Masson Editores, Mexico (qv)
Subjects: Medicine, Scientific, Technical, Social Science, Law, Economics
Founded: 1804
ISBN Publisher's Prefix: 2-225

Editions **Mazarine**, 34 ave Marceau, F-75008 Paris Tel: (01) 7237250
Man Dir: J-E Cohen-Seat; *Managing Editor:* Ronald Blunden; *Sales:* Martine Clairet; *Rights & Permissions:* Ronald Blunden
Subjects: General Literature; Novels, Belles Lettres, History, Current Events Reports
1979: 25 titles
ISBN Publisher's Prefix: 2-86374

Editions d'Art Lucien **Mazenod**, 33 rue de Naples, F-75008 Paris Tel: (01) 5222366 Cable Add: Mazeditio Telex: 270105 F TXFRA
Man Dir: Lucien Mazenod
Subjects: History, Art, Architecture
ISBN Publisher's Prefix: 2-85088

Editions **Mengès**, 13 Passage Landrieu, F-75007 Paris Tel: 5552667
Man Dirs: Bernard Blazin, Jean Paul Mengès; *Editorial, Production:* J P Mengès; *Sales, Publicity:* B Blazin; *Rights & Permissions:* M P Paillard
Subjects: Humour, Documentaries, Historical Novels, How-to, Illustrated Books
1978: 35 titles *1979:* 40 titles *Founded:* 1975
ISBN Publisher's Prefix: 2-85620

Mercure de France SA, 26 rue de Condé, F-75006 Paris Tel: (01) 3292113
Man Dir: Simone Gallimard; *Editorial Dir:* Michel Cournot; *Rights and Permissions:* Nicole Boyer
Parent Company: Editions Gallimard (qv)
Associate Company: Editions Denoël Sarl (qv)
Subjects: General Fiction, Belles Lettres, Poetry, History, Philosophy, Juveniles, Social Science, Psychology
1978: 72 titles *Founded:* 1891
ISBN Publisher's Prefix: 2-7152

Messageries Centrales du Livre*, 8 rue Garancière, F-75005 Paris
Subjects: Cartoon strips, Juveniles
Miscellaneous: Firm is a member of the Presses de la Cité group (qv)

Michelin et Cie (Services de Tourisme)*, 46 ave de Breteuil, F-75341 Paris cedex 07 Tel: (01) 5392500
Associate Company: Michelin Tyre Company Ltd, 81 Fulham Rd, London SW3 6RD, UK (qv)

Subjects: Travel Guides, Maps
1978: 4 titles

José **Millas-Martin***, 14 rue Le Bua, F-75020 Paris
ISBN Publisher's Prefix: 2-241

Lettres Modernes **Minard**, 73 rue du Cardinal Lemoine, F-75005 Paris Tel: (01) 3544609
Man Dir, Production: J Michel Minard; *Sales:* Librairie Minard Diffusion; *Rights & Permissions:* Danièle Morgat
Associate Company: Librairie Minard (qv)
Subjects: General Literature, University Studies and Theses, Critical Studies
Founded: 1954
ISBN Publisher's Prefix: 2-256

Librairie **Minard***, 73 rue du Cardinal Lemoine, F-75005 Paris Tel: (01) 3544609
Man Dir: Michel Minard; *Sales:* Librairie Minard Diffusion
Associate Company: Lettres Modernes Minard (qv)
Subjects: University Studies and Theses
1978: 5 titles
ISBN Publisher's Prefix: 2-85210

Les Editions de **Minuit** SA, 7 rue Bernard-Palissy, F-75006 Paris Tel: (01) 2223794
Man Dir: Jérôme Lindon
Orders to: Sodis, 128 Ave du Maréchal-de-Lattre de Tassigny, F-77400 Lagny
Subjects: General Fiction, Philosophy, Social Science, History, Literary Works
Bookshops: Librairie Autrement Dit, 73 blvd Saint-Michel, F-75005 Paris; 9 rue Bernard-Palissy, F-75006 Paris
1978: 25 titles *1979:* 20 titles *Founded:* 1942
ISBN Publisher's Prefix: 2-7073

Gérard **Monfort**, Saint-Pierre de Salerne, F-27800 Brionne Tel: (32) 448741
Man Dir: Gérard Monfort
Subjects: Literature, History, Art, Law, Archaeology, Ethnology
1979: 10 titles *1980:* 125 titles *Founded:* 1960

Editions du **Moniteur**, BP 49802, F-75066 Paris cedex 02 (Located at: 17 rue d'Uzes) Tel: 2334435 Telex: 680876F
President and Man Dir: Marc N Vigier; *Editorial:* Jean-Marc Pilpoul; *Sales:* Joseph Osman
Parent Company: C E P, 17 rue d'Uzes, F-75002 Paris
Subjects: Architecture, Building Construction, Public Works, Home Improvements, Laws and Regulations
Bookshops: Librarie du Moniteur, 15 rue d'Uzes, F-75002 Paris; 7 pl de l'Odéon, F-75006 Paris
1978: 28 titles *1979:* 52 titles
ISBN Publisher's Prefix: 2-86282

Editions **Montchrestien** Sàrl, 158-160 rue St-Jacques, F-75005 Paris Tel: (01) 3541710/3546270
Man Dir: Yves Ponssier
Subjects: Law, Economic and Political Science, Current Events
ISBN Publisher's Prefix: 2-7076

Publications Photo-Cinema Paul **Montel**, 189 rue St-Jacques, F-75005 Paris 5ème Tel: (01) 3294090
Man Dir: Pierre G Montel; *Editorial:* Yves Lorelle; *Sales:* Mr Sainsson; *Production:* Gérard Montel; *Publicity:* Xavier Bernard
Subjects: All aspects of photography and ciné-photography, filming; Periodicals
Founded: 1920
ISBN Publisher's Prefix: 2-7075

Montparnasse-Diffusion, see Alfred Eibel, Editeur

Editions de **Montsouris** SA*, 9 rue d'Alexandrie, F-75002 Paris Tel: (01) 5080190
Br Off: 176 rue de Paris, F-91300 Massy
Subjects: Science and Technical
ISBN Publisher's Prefix: 2-85035

Editions Albert **Morancé**, 1 rue Palatine, F-75006 Paris Tel: 6332455
Dirs: Mrs G-A Morancé, F Sorlot
Subjects: Fine Arts, Architecture
Founded: 1781
Book Club: Club du Livre d'Art
ISBN Publisher's Prefix: 2-85307

Editions Alain **Moreau**, 5 rue Eginhard, F-75004 Paris Tel: (01) 2725151
Editorial, Rights & Permissions, Sales: Alain Moreau
Orders to: Groupe International Hachette, 58 rue Jean Beluzen, F-92170 Vanves
Subjects: Social, Economic & Political Sciences, History
1978: 14 titles *Founded:* 1972
ISBN Publisher's Prefix: 2-85209

Morel Editeurs, les Imberts, F-84220 Gordes Tel: (90) 719175/718180
Dirs: Robert Morel
Associate Companies: Editions 'R' (qv) at same address; Editions Jeunesse Pratique; Le "A" (Periodical)
Subjects: Belles Lettres, Poetry, Music, Art, Religion, Paperbacks, Architecture, Gastronomy, Folklore, Juvenile, Humour
Founded: 1961
Bookshops: La Fête, 33 ave Victor Hugo, F-84400 Paris; Diffédit, 96 blvd du Montparnasse, Paris 15; Morel, 5 rue du Mail, Paris 2; Diffulivre, 27 route du Grand Mont, CH-1052 Mont-sur-Lausanne, Switzerland

Publications du **Musée de l'Affiche** et du Tract*, 20 rue des Ecoles, F-75005 Paris Tel: (01) 0334132
Subject: Encyclopaedias

Editions de la Réunion des **Musées Nationaux**, 10 rue de l'Abbaye, F-75006 Paris Tel: (01) 3292145
Subjects: Art, Guides, Science & Technology, Architecture
Founded: 1931
ISBN Publisher's Prefix: 2-7118

Editions du **Muséum** national d'Histoire naturelle, 38 rue Geoffroy Saint-Hilaire, F-75005 Paris Tel: (01) 3317124
Subjects: All aspects of Natural History

N O E, see Nouvel Office d'Edition

Fernand **Nathan** Editeur*, 9 rue Méchain, F-75014 Paris Tel: (01) 5898949 Cable Add: Nathaned Paris Telex: Nataned 24525 F
Dirs: Jean-Jacques Nathan, Pierre Nathan; *Publicity & Advertising:* André Broch
Subjects: History, How-to, Music, Art, Philosophy, Textbooks, Reference, Juveniles, Psychology, General & Social Science, Guides, Nature, Architecture, History, Education
Founded: 1881
ISBN Publisher's Prefix: 2-09

Librairie A-G **Nizet**, 3 bis pl de la Sorbonne, F-75005 Paris Tel: (01) 3547976
Man Dir: A G Nizet
Subjects: Belles Lettres, University Textbooks, Literary
1978/79: 56 titles *Founded:* 1922
ISBN Publisher's Prefix: 2-7078

F De **Nobele**, 35 rue Bonaparte, F-75006 Paris Tel: (01) 3260862 Cable Add: Denobelef Paris 110
Man Dir: F de Nobèle
Subjects: History of Art, Bibliography
1978: approx 70 titles *Founded:* 1880
ISBN Publisher's Prefix: 2-85189

Editions La **Noria***, 13 ave Théophile Gautier, F-75016 Paris Tel: (01) 2881983/2604429
Man Dir: Nicolas Munoz de la Mata
Subjects: Belles Lettres, Juveniles, Educational Materials
Founded: 1975

Nouveautés de l'Enseignement-éditions andré casteilla, 25 rue Monge, F-75005 Paris Tel: (01) 3545650
Commercial Manager: Mrs Casteilla
Subjects: Textbooks for Technical, Commercial and Secondary Education; Economy, Legislation, Careers, Philately
1980: 100 titles
ISBN Publisher's Prefix: 2-7135

Nouvel Office d'Edition et de Diffusion (Les Productions de Paris — NOE), 3 bis passage de la Petite Boucherie, F-75006 Paris Tel: (01) 3252760
Parent Company: Editions Pierre Belfond (qv)
Associate Company: Les Productions de Paris
Subjects: Novels, History, How-to, Juveniles, Paperbacks, Social Science, Belles Lettres
Founded: 1969
ISBN Publisher's Prefix: 2-7144

Nouvelle Cité, 131 rue Castagnary, F-75015 Paris Tel: (01) 8281894
Man Dir, Rights & Permissions: Jean-Michel Merlin; *Editorial, Production, Publicity:* Jean-Pierre Rosa; *Sales:* Michel Visart
Associate Companies: Citta Nuova, Italy (qv); Neue Stadt, Federal Republic of Germany (qv); Ciudad Nueva, Spain (qv); Niewe Stad, St Stephanusstraat 11, Nijmegen, Netherlands; Cidade Nova, Rua Pio XII, 274 Paraiso São Paulo, Brazil; New City, UK (qv)
Subjects: Spiritual themes, Testimonies, Essays
1978: 4 titles *1979:* 8 titles *Founded:* 1963
ISBN Publisher's Prefix: 2-85313

Nouvelles Editions Françaises, 13 rue St-Georges, F-75009 Paris Tel: (01) 8785319
Dir: Denis Baschet; *Man Dir:* Elaine Allegret; *Sales Dir:* Roger Allegret
Subject: Art
Founded: 1946
ISBN Publisher's Prefix: 2-7079

Nouvelles Editions Latines, 1 rue Palatine, F-75006 Paris Tel: (01) 0337742/3547742
Man Dir: Fernand Sorlot
Subjects: General Fiction, Belles Lettres, Poetry, History, Travel and Tourism, Religion
1978: 80 titles *Founded:* 1928
ISBN Publisher's Prefix: 2-7233

Nouvelles Editions Rationalistes SA, 16 rue de l'Ecole-Polytechnique, F-75005 Paris Tel: (01) 6330350
Subjects: Philosophy, Religion, History of Ideas, Rationalist Themes
Book Club: L'Oeil Ouvert, 16 rue de l'Ecole-Polytechnique

O R S T O M, see Office de la Recherche Scientifique

Office Central de Librairie Sàrl, 65 rue Claude-Bernard, F-75005 Paris Tel: (01) 7076210
Subject: Education
General Manager: François-Xavier de Guibert

Office Central de Lisieux SA*, 51 rue du Carmel, F-14100 Lisieux Tel: (31) 620188
Subject: Religion

102 FRANCE

Office de Documentation Bibliographique et de Diffusion, subsidiary of Librairie Fischbacher (qv)

Office de la Recherche Scientifique et Technique Outre Mer (ORSTOM), 24 rue Bayard, F-75008 Paris Tel: (01) 2253152
Cable Add: Orstom Paris
Man Dir: Professor G Camus
Publishing Dept and Orders to: Service des Publications, 70-74 route d'Alnay, F-93140, Bondy Tel: (847) 3195
Subjects: Scientific and Technical Texts, Social Sciences connected with the Tropical and Mediterranean Areas of the World
1978: 44 titles *1979:* 40-50 titles *Founded:* 1943
ISBN Publisher's Prefix: 2-7099

Opera Mundi SA, 100 ave Raymond Poincaré, F-75784 Paris cedex 16 Tel: (01) 5021820 Telex: Mundi Paris 611967
President: P Winkler; *Man Dir:* G Gauthier; *Dir:* C Ronsac
Subjects: Art, Social Science, History, General Fiction & Nonfiction, Juveniles

Editions **Ophrys**, 10 rue de Nesle, F-75006 Paris Tel: (01) 3268204
Man Dir: Mrs Jean; *Publicity & Advertising:* Mrs B Monnier
Subjects: Linguistics, Belles Lettres, History, Philosophy, Education, Economics, Sociology
Founded: 1934
Bookshops: Librairie Ophrys, 61 rue Monsieur le Prince, F-70006 Paris; Editions Ophrys succursale de Paris, 10 rue de Nesle, F-75006 Paris
ISBN Publisher's Prefix: 2-7080

Editions de l'**Orante***, 6 rue du Général-Bertrand, F-75007 Paris Tel: (01) 7835502
Man Dir: Simone Lafarge
Subjects: Belles Lettres, Poetry, History, Philosophy, Religion
Founded: 1940
ISBN Publisher's Prefix: 2-7031

Editions Oliver **Orban***, 7 rue Daunou, F-75002 Paris Tel: 2617601/2617804
Man Dir: Olivier Orban; *Editorial:* Françoise Roth, Anne Leclerc, Martine Laroche; *Rights & Permissions:* Marie-Ange Mosca
Subjects: General Fiction and Nonfiction
1978: 37 titles *Founded:* 1974
ISBN Publisher's Prefix: 2-85565

Les Editions d'**Organisation**, 5 rue Rousselet, F-75007 Paris 7 Tel: (01) 5671840 Telex: c/o Eyrotp 203385 F
Dir: Dominique Bidart
Trade Orders: 12 rue de Sommerard, F-75005 Paris Tel: 3292199
Parent Company: Editions Eyrolles (qv)
Subjects: Business Management & Organization generally; especially Data Processing, Personnel Training, Sociology, Industrial Law
Bookshop: 5 rue Rousselet, F-75007 Paris
1978: 30 titles *1979:* 35 titles *Founded:* 1953
ISBN Publisher's Prefix: 2-7081

Michel de l'**Ormeraie**, 4 rue Labrouste, F-75725 Paris cedex 15 Tel: 8284070
Man Dir, Editorial: Michel de l'Ormeraie; *Sales:* Hubert Germain; *Publicity:* Frédéric Mercier, Veronique Reiffers
Subjects: Exact Facsimiles (text and binding), of famous illustrated editions of French and other Literary Classics
Bookshop: Galerie Michel de l'Ormeraie, 17 rue Castagnary, F-75015 Paris
1980: 90 titles *Founded:* 1970
ISBN Publisher's Prefix: 2-85135

Editions Pierre Jean **Oswald***, 7 rue de l'Ecole Polytechnique, F-75005 Paris
Tel: (01) 0339007
Subjects: General Fiction, Poetry, Belles Lettres, Paperbacks, Music, Third World, Creative Literature
Founded: 1964
ISBN Publisher's Prefix: 2-7172

Les Editions **Ouvrières** SA*, 12 ave Soeur-Rosalie, F-75013 Paris Tel: (01) 3379385
Subjects: History, Religion, How-to, Education, Juveniles, Political & Social Science, Economics
Founded: 1939
ISBN Publisher's Prefix: 2-7082

Editions **P A C** (Presse-Auto-Conseil)*, 3 rue Saint Roch, F-75001 Paris Tel: 2615017
Man Dir, Rights and Permissions: Thierry Schimpff; *Publicity:* Catherine Schimpff
Subjects: Sport, Cinema, Crime Novels, Commentaries and Documentaries, Adventure Reports
1978: 32 titles *Founded:* 1975
ISBN Publisher's Prefix: 2-85336

P O F, see Publications Orientalistes de France

P U F, see Presses Universitaires de France

P U L, see Presses Universitaires de Lille

P Y C Edition*, 254 rue de Vaugirard, F-75740 Paris cedex 15 Tel: (01) 5322719
Subjects: Mechanical Engineering, Heating, Air Conditioning, Solar Energy, Refrigeration, Metallurgy, Welding

Les Editions du **Pacifique***, 26 rue des Carmes, F-75005 Paris Tel: (01) 3251022
Telex: 203913 f edpac
Man Dir: Didier Millet; *Assistant Editor:* Robert Cooley; *Marketing Dir:* Rose Desbois
Orders to: Groupe International Hachette, 254 blvd St-Germain, F-75007 Paris
Associate Company: Les Editions du Pacifique, French Polynesia (qv)
Subjects: General Nonfiction; Travel, Natural Sciences (for tropical environments), History, Gift Books
1977: 12 titles *1978:* 55 titles (Numbers refer to publications both in France and French Polynesia) *Founded:* 1971
ISBN Publisher's Prefix: 2-85700

Paris-Caraïbes, an imprint of Editions Louis Soulanges

Jean-Jacques **Pauvert** Editeur*, 8 rue de Nesle, F-75006 Paris Tel: (01) 6335640
Dir: Jean-Jacques Pauvert
Orders to: Distribution Hachette, 254 blvd St-Germain, F-75007 Paris
International orders to: Distribution Hachette, 58 rue Jean Bleuzen, F-92170 Vanves
Subjects: Fiction, Belles Lettres, Art, History, Reference, Social Science, Paperbacks, Poetry, Philosophy, Juveniles, Photography, Languages
Founded: 1945
ISBN Publisher's Prefix: 2-85092

Le **Pavillon**, Roger Maria Editeur*, 5 rue Rollin, F-75005 Paris Tel: (01) 3268429
Subjects: General Fiction, Belles Lettres, Philosophy, Religion, Social Science, History, Education
Founded: 1947
ISBN Publisher's Prefix: 2-85224

Editions **Payot**, 106 blvd St-Germain, F-75006 Paris 6 Tel: (01) 3297410
Man Dir: Jean-Luc Pidoux-Payot
Subjects: Biography, History, Philosophy, Reference, Religion, Ethnology, Anthropology, Low-priced Paperbacks, Education, General Science, Humanities, Psychology and Psychoanalysis, Linguistics
1977: 70 titles *1978:* 80 titles *Founded:* 1912
ISBN Publisher's Prefix: 2-228

Pédagogie Moderne, 39 rue Chanzy, F-75011 Paris Tel: 3716878
Man Dir, Rights & Permissions: Louis-J Bonnet; *Editorial:* Françoise Poquin; *Publicity:* Yvonne Cartier
Orders to: Diffusion Bordas, 39 rue Boulard, F-75680 Paris cedex 14
Parent Company: Groupe Bordas-Dunod, 17 rue Rémy Dumoncel, F-75680 Paris cedex 14
Subjects: Teaching Instruction (semi-scholastic)
1978: 21 titles *1979:* 27 titles *Founded:* 1931
ISBN Publisher's Prefix: 2-7294

Editions **Pédone**, 13 rue Soufflot, F-75005 Paris Tel: (01) 3540597
Man Dir: Denis Pédone
Subjects: Law, Engineering, Agriculture, Mining, Management, Economics, Book Industry
1978: 36 titles *1979:* 34 titles *Founded:* 1837
ISBN Publisher's Prefix: 2-233

Pensée Moderne Jacques Grancher, see Jacques Grancher

Père Castor, an imprint of Flammarion et Cie

Les **Périodiques** Parisiens*, 150 ave des Champs-Elysées, F-75008 Paris Tel: (01) 2255837
Subject: Annuals

Librairie Académique **Perrin**, 8 rue Garancière, F-75006 Paris Tel: (01) 3291280
Chairman: Claude Nielsen; *Publicity Manager:* Nadia Leser; *Foreign Rights:* Josiane Bontron
Subjects: Belles Lettres, History, Reference, Scholarly, Bibliography, Fiction, Arts, Religion
Founded: 1827
Miscellaneous: Member of Presses de la Cité group (qv)
ISBN Publisher's Prefix: 2-262

Editions G M **Perrin** SA*, 61 ave Ledru-Rollin, F-75012 Paris Tel: (01) 3437512
Subjects: Audio Visual & Electronic Media, Education, Science & Technical
Miscellaneous: Firm is a member of the Presses de la Cité group (qv)
ISBN Publisher's Prefix: 2-85084

Editions **Phébus**, 17 rue Pierre Lescot, F-75001 Paris Tel: 2602394
Man Dir: Jean-Pierre Sicre
Orders to: Diffusion Littera, 4 rue de Tournon, F-75006 Paris
Subjects: General Literature, Oriental (Eastern) Literature, Literary Criticism, Fine Arts
1979/80: 14 titles

Editions A & J **Picard** Sàrl, 82 rue Bonaparte, F-75006 Paris 6 Tel: (01) 3269673
Man Dirs: Jacques Picard, Chantal Pasini
Subjects: General, Art, Legal, Religious, Literary and Local History, Archaeology, Architecture, Reference, Education, Bibliography, Folklore, Philology, Textbooks, Musicology, Antiquarian Books
Founded: 1869
ISBN Publisher's Prefix: 2-7084

Editions **Pierron**, Terrain Industriel, 4 rue Gutenberg, F-57206 Sarreguemines Tel: (087) 951477, 951431 Telex: 860495 F
Dir: Jeannie Jung
Branch Off: Pierron Entreprise SA, 103 rue Foch, F-57206 Sarreguemines
Subjects: Education, Audio Visual Media, History

Editions Jean-Michel **Place**, 12 rue Pierre et Marie Curie, F-75005 Paris Tel: 6330511
Man Dir and other offices: Jean-Michel Place; *Publicity:* Leah Poller

Associate Company: Éditions de la Chronique des Lettres Françaises (qv)
Subjects: Literature and Literary Research; Bibliographies, Reference, Poetry, Fiction, Fascimile Reprints of various periodicals
Bookshop: 12 rue Pierre et Marie Curie, Paris
1980: 50 titles *Founded:* 1973
ISBN Publisher's Prefix: 2-85893

Editions **Plantyn** SA*, 1 pl Gabriel-Fauré, BP 803, F-74016 Annecy-le-Vieux Tel: (50) 572838
Subjects: Education, Science & Technical
Miscellaneous: Firm is a member of the Kluwer Group, Deventer, Netherlands (qv)
ISBN Publisher's Prefix: 2-7136

Librairie **Plon** SA, 8 rue Garancière, F-75006 Paris Tel: (01) 3291280 Cable Add: Ploédit Paris 110 Telex: 204807
Chairman: Claude Nielsen; *Foreign Rights:* Josiane Bontron
Subjects: General Fiction, History, Belles Lettres, Philosophy, How-to, Religion, Reference, Economics, Social Science, Scholarly, Arts, Maps, Travel, Anthropology, Trade Books
Founded: 1844
Miscellaneous: Member of Presses de la Cité group (qv)
ISBN Publisher's Prefix: 2-259

Presses **Pocket***, 8 rue Garancière, F-75006, Paris Tel: 3291280 Telex: Precite 204807 F
Subjects: Novels, Memoirs, War, Documentary, Science Fiction (all paperback)
Miscellaneous: Firm is a member of the Presses de la Cité group (qv)

Centre Georges **Pompidou** Edition, see Centre national d'art et de Culture Georges-Pompidou

Julien **Prélat** Sàrl, 17 rue du Petit-Pont, F-75005 Paris Tel: (01) 3547763
Management, Rights & Permissions: M Dargent, S Kolf; *Publicity & Advertising:* Mr Lizeux
Subjects: Textbooks and specialist books connected with odontology, stomatology; also general dentistry and medicine
1978: 17 titles *1979:* 13 titles *Founded:* 1946
Bookshops: Librairie Odonto Stomatologie, 17 rue du Petit-Pont, Paris 5e; Librairie Psychologique, 2 rue du Cardinal Lemoine, Paris 5e
Miscellaneous: Publishes two quarterly journals
ISBN Publisher's Prefix: 2-85039

Société Nouvelle **Présence Africaine***, 25 bis rue des Ecoles, F-75006 Paris Tel: (01) 0331374 Cable Add: Presafric Paris
Man Dir: Mrs Alioune Diop; *Publicity & Advertising, Rights & Permissions:* H G Jones
Subjects: General Fiction, Belles Lettres, Poetry, History, Philosophy, Reference, Religion, Low-priced Paperbacks, Primary Textbooks, Politics (all subjects pertain to Africa)
1977: 15 titles *1978:* 23 titles *Founded:* 1947
Bookshop: 25 bis rue des Ecoles
ISBN Publisher's Prefix: 2-7087

Presse-Auto-Conseil, see P A C

Les **Presses d'Ile-de-France** Sàrl, 12 rue de la Chaise, F-75007 Paris Tel: (01) 2223730
Man Dir: Guy Raclet; *Manager:* Jacqueline Preaudat
Orders to: Sofedis, 29 rue St-Sulpice, F-75007 Paris
Subject: Juveniles
ISBN Publisher's Prefix: 2-7088

Les **Presses de la Cité***, 8 rue Garancière, F-75006 Paris Tel: (01) 3291280 Cable Add: Svennil Paris
President and Distribution Dir: Claude Nielsen; *Publicity & Advertising:* Nadia Leser; *Rights & Permissions:* Josiane Bontron, Mrs Fréret
Subjects: General Fiction, History, How-to, Low- & High-priced Paperbacks
Founded: 1947
Presses de la Cité group: Librairie Plon (qv); G P Rouge et Or (qv); Solar (qv); Librairie Académique Perrin; Julliard (qv); Presses Pocket (qv); Fleuve Noir (qv); Messageries Centrales du Livre (qv); Editions Christian Bourgois (qv); Encyclopédie Internationale des Sciences & Techniques; 10/18; le Rocher; UGE
ISBN Publisher's Prefix: 2-258

Presses de la Fondation Nationale des Sciences Politiques, 27 rue St-Guillaume, F-75341 Paris cedex 07 Tel: 2603960
Man Dir, Rights and Permissions: Louis Bodin; *Editorial:* Mireille Perche; *Sales, Publicity:* Marc Rigle; *Production:* Josée Cabillon
Subjects: Research Works and Periodicals connected with the Social Sciences, especially Political, Historical, Sociological, Economics
1977: 12 titles *1978:* 13 titles *Founded:* 1975
ISBN Publisher's Prefix: 2-7246

Presses de la Renaissance, 198 blvd Saint-Germain, F-75007 Paris Tel: 5485982/5489687 Telex: 260717 orem 158
Man Dir, Sales: Fabienne Delmote; *Editorial:* Tony Cartano; *Rights & Permissions:* Françoise Triffaux
Parent Company: Pierre Belfond, Paris (qv)
Associate Companies: Nouvel Office d'Edition et de Diffusion (qv), Productions de Paris
Subjects: General Fiction, Biography, Documentary, Folklore, Science Fiction, Psychology and the Para-Normal, Animals; French Classics, and Foreign Classics in Translation
1978: 30 titles *1979:* 30 titles *Founded:* 1971
ISBN Publisher's Prefix: 85616

Les **Presses Monastiques**, see Zodiaque

Presses Universitaires de France (PUF), 108 blvd St-Germain, F-75279 Paris cedex 06
Tel: (01) 3291201
Registered Office: 17 rue Soufflot, F-75005 Paris; *General Management and Editorial:* 108 blvd Saint-Germain, F-75279 Paris; *Public Relations/Publicity:* 90 blvd Saint-Germain, F-75005 Paris
President: Pierre Angoulvent; *Dirs:* Robert Ruelle, Pierre Wittmann; *Sales Dir:* Jean-Pierre Giband; *Editorial:* Laurence Piel, Michel Prigent; *Publicity & Advertising:* Gabrielle Gelber; *Rights & Permissions:* Françoise Laye, Arlette Monsallier
Orders to: Bois de L'Epine, CE 1105, F-91002 Evry Cedex Tel: 0778205 Telex: PUF 600474 F
Subjects: Belles Lettres, Poetry, Biography, History, Music, Art, Philosophy, Reference, Religion, Engineering, Low- & High-priced Paperbacks, Psychology, Medicine, General, Social & Political Science, University Textbooks
1977: 450 titles *Founded:* 1921
Bookshops: Librairie générale des PUF, 49 blvd St-Michel, F-75005 Paris; Librairie Internationale, 17 rue Soufflot, F-75005 Paris

Presses Universitaires de Grenoble, Domaine Universitaire, BP 47X, F-38400 St Martin d'Hères Tel: (76) 548178 Telex: Unisog 980910
Manager: Philippe Hardouin; *Commercial Manager:* Jean-Claude Naar, Lydie Valero
Orders to: Sodis, 128 ave Marechal de Lattre de Tassigny F-77400 Lagny
Subjects: Architecture, Anthropology, Sociology, Law, Economics, Management, History, Statistics, Literature, Medicine, Data Processing, Physics, Politics
1978: 45 titles *1979:* 22 titles
ISBN Publisher's Prefix: 2-7061

Presses Universitaires de Lille (PUL), BP 149, F-59653 Villeneuve d'Ascq cedex Tel: (20) 911300
Man Dir: University President; *Editorial:* Y M Hilaire; *Production:* Ph Bonnefis; *Sales, Publicity, Rights & Permissions:* D Rosselle
Orders to: PUL, BP 149, F-59650 Villeneuve d'Ascq cedex
Subjects: Social Sciences and Humanities, French and Foreign Literature, History, Philosophy, Law, Philology, Psychology etc
1978: 20 titles *1979:* 18 titles *Founded:* 1972
ISBN Publisher's Prefix: 2-85939

Presses Universitaires de Lyon*, 86 rue Pasteur, F-69365 Lyon cedex 2 Tel: (78) 692048
Man Dir: Joël Saugnieux
Subjects: History, Economics, University Textbooks, Linguistics, Lyons Regional Interest, Religious History, Law
1978: 25 titles *Founded:* 1976
ISBN Publisher's Prefix: 2-7297

Editions Edouard **Privat** SA, 14 rue des Arts, F-31000 Toulouse 61 Tel: (61) 230926
Man Dir: Pierre Privat; *Literary, Production:* Dominique Autié; *Sales Dir:* Jean Sacrispeyre; *Publicity & Press Relations:* André Rimailho; *Rights & Permissions:* Noëlle Lever
Subjects: French regional history and culture; Education, Psychology, Sociology, Philosophy, Pedagogy
Founded: 1834
ISBN Publisher's Prefix: 2-7089

Les **Productions de Paris**, 3 bis passage de la Petite-Boucherie
Parent Company: Ed Pierre Belfond (qv)
Associate Company: Nouvel Office d'Edition (qv)

Publi-Union*, 10 rue Lyautey, F-75016 Paris Tel: (01) 9243610
Man Dir: Michel Wenlersse
Subjects: Law, Economics, Social Science, Education, Science & Technical
ISBN Publisher's Prefix: 2-85200

Publications Filmées d'Art et d'Histoire, 9-15 rue Carvès, F-92120 Montrouge
Tel: 6571413 (ext 78)
Man Dir: Marcel Hamelle; *Sales:* Georges Auger
Subjects: Books illustrated by slides on Art, History, and the Exploration of Space
1978: 4 titles
ISBN Publisher's Prefix: 2-85228

Publications Orientalistes de France (POF), 4 rue de Lille, F-75007 Paris Tel: (01) 2606705
Dir: Simone Maviel
Orders to: Ophrys, 10 rue de Nesles, F-75006 Paris
Subjects: Literature translated mainly from East European, Middle and Far East Languages; also Bibliographies, Vocabularies etc relating to these languages, Theatre, Economy; specialises in works covering all aspects of Eastern Europe and the Middle and Far East
1978: 23 titles *1979:* 17 titles
ISBN Publisher's Prefix: 2-7169

Editions **Pygmalion** — Gérard Watelet, 70 Ave de Breteuil, F-75007 Paris Tel: 5674077
Man Dir, Editorial: Gérard Watelet; *Sales, Rights & Permissions:* Luce Watelet

104 FRANCE

Subjects: General Literature, History, Archaeology, Art
1978: 25 titles *1979:* 25 titles *Founded:* 1977
ISBN Publisher's Prefix: 2-85704

Librairie Aristide **Quillet** SA*, 278 blvd St-Germain, F-75006 Paris Tel: (01) 5514810 Cable Add: Ariquillet Paris 44
Man Dir: Guy Rocaut; *Rights & Permissions:* Philippe Leturc
Subjects: Science & Technology, Dictionaries, Encyclopaedias
Founded: 1898
ISBN Publisher's Prefix: 2-85041

Editions **'R'***, Société Civile Typo, Graphique et Littéraire, 33 ave Victor Hugo, F-84400 Apt Tel: (90) 720598
Man Dir, Editorial, Rights & Permissions: Robert Morel; *Production, Publicity:* François Morel
Orders to: Morel, 5 rue du Mail, Paris 2 Tel: 2600738
Associate Companies: Morel Editeurs (qv), at same address; "R" Editore, Via Larga 9, Ortonovo (LS), Italy
Subjects: Rites, Myths and Symbols, Sorcery, Encylopaedia of Tarot, Fiction, Vocabulary Traditions and Images, Popular Literature
1978: 35 titles *Founded:* 1977

R E C T A Foldex*, 27 rue Trébois, F-92300 Levallois-Perret Tel: 2701203
Man Dir: Mrs Costard
Subject: Maps, Charts etc
Miscellaneous: RECTA = Réalisations, Études Cartographiques Touristiques et Administratives (Cartographic design and production in the touring and administrative fields)

R E M I, see Réalisations pour l'Enseignement Multilingue International

Editions R S T, see Editions Robert Steindecker

Société des Editions **Radio***, 9 rue Jacob, F-75006 Paris Tel: (01) 0331365
Subjects: Engineering (Books & Technical Journals), Mass Media
Founded: 1934
ISBN Publisher's Prefix: 2-7091

Editions **Ramsay**, 27 rue de Fleurus, F-75006 Paris Tel: 5445505
Man Dir: Jean-Pierre Ramsay; *Editorial:* Erick Orsenna, Gérard-H Goury, Sabine Delattre, Serge Bramly; *Production:* Nathalie Perrin; *Publicity:* Marie-Pierre de Rieux; *Rights and Permissions:* Monique Gonthier
Subjects: Novels, Documentary Books, Fine Editions, Essays, Science, History
Bookshop: 23 rue de Fleurus
1978: 42 titles *1979:* 50 titles *Founded:* 1976
ISBN Publisher's Prefix: 2-85956

Sélection du **Reader's Digest** Sàrl, 216 blvd St-Germain, F-75007, Paris Tel: 5443924 Cable Add: Readigest Paris
President, General Manager: Claude Pothier; *Editor-in-Chief:* Roland Harari; *Literary Manager:* Bernard Willerval; *Publicity:* Jean-Marie Vendroux
Subjects: General Fiction, History, How-to, Juveniles, Medicine, Science & Technology, Reference, Art, Architecture, Social Science, Economics

Réalisations pour l'Enseignement Multilingue International (REMI), 39 rue de l'Abbé-Grégoire, F-75006 Paris Tel: (01) 2227090
Man Dir: Mrs D Holtzer
Subjects: Foreign language courses for Primary schools (French, German, English); Elementary French readers
Founded: 1966
ISBN Publisher's Prefix: 2-85134

Retz, see CAL/Retz

Revisematic*, 61 rue Raymond Losserand, F-75014 Paris Tel: (01) 3060915
Subjects: Education, Science & Technical

Editions Scientifiques **Riber** Sàrl*, 54 rue du Vert-Bois, F-75003 Paris Tel: (01) 2775772
Subjects: Science & Technical
ISBN Publisher's Prefix: 2-7091

Franco Maria **Ricci**, Galerie 12, 12 Rue des Beaux-Arts, F-75006 Paris Tel: 6339631
Man Dir, Editorial, Production, Rights & Permissions: Franco Maria Ricci; *Sales:* Yves Dantoing
Orders to: Sofedis, 88 rue de Lille, F-75007
Parent Company: Franco Maria Ricci, Milan, Italy
Publishers Represented: Franco Maria Ricci, Deco Press
Subjects: Art Books, Bodoni Editions, Diderot Encyclopaedia, Bibliophile Editions, Graphic Design (Deco Press)
Book Clubs: Les Amis de Franco Maria Ricci
Bookshop: 12 rue des Beaux Arts, F-75006 Paris
1979: 11 titles *Founded:* 1974

Librairie Marcel **Rivière** et Cie*, 22 rue Soufflot, F-75005 Paris Tel: (01) 0330718
Dir: R Abranson
Subjects: History, Philosophy, Social Science, Economics, Scholarly Books, Politics, Management
Founded: 1902
ISBN Publisher's Prefix: 2-85229

Editions E **Robert**, L'École et la Famille, BP 4384, F-69241 Lyons cedex 1 (Located at: 28 rue du Bon-Pasteur, F-69001 Lyons) Tel: (78) 284889
Man Dir: Paul Chirat; *Sales, Publicity & Advertising:* Louis Chauffour
Subjects: Primary Textbooks, Educational Materials, Periodical
1980: 3 titles *Founded:* 1873
ISBN Publisher's Prefix: 2-7093

Dictionnaire Le **Robert**, see Société du Nouveau Littré (SNL)

Éditions **Rombaldi** SA*, 15-17 rue de Rome, F-75008 Paris Tel: (01) 2618401/2618425 Telex: rombald 641854 F
President: Pierre Godfroid; *Man Dir:* Michel Leroux; *Commercial Dirs:* Henri Kaufman, Hervé le Henaff; *Production Manager:* Henri Kaufman
Subjects: General Fiction, Belles Lettres, Encyclopaedias, History
Book Clubs: Bibliothèque Du Temps Présent and six others (sold by Ediclub Rombaldi, qv under Book Clubs)
Founded: 1920
ISBN Publisher's Prefix: 2-231

E S F **Rosenwald***, 15 rue St-Benoît, F-75006 Paris Tel: (01) 2225585
Subject: Annuals

Rossel Edition*, 73 rue d'Anjou, F-75008 Paris Tel: (01) 3874517
Associate Company: Rossel Edition, Belgium (qv)
Subjects: Juveniles, Sport, Novels, Guides, Gardening, Nature

Editions **Roudil***, 53 rue St-Jacques, F-75005 Paris Tel: (01) 0334797
Man Dir: Henry Roudil; *Sales Dir:* Lucien Drouot; *Publicity Dir:* Mr Roy; *Advertising Dir:* Mr Brajon; *Rights & Permissions:* Henry Roudil
Subjects: History, Philosophy, University & Secondary Textbooks, Fiction
Founded: 1954
ISBN Publisher's Prefix: 2-85044

Editions **Rouff** SA*, 36 rue du Vieux-Pont-de-Sèvres, F-92100 Boulogne-Billancourt Tel: 6090140
Subjects: Humour, Shooting, Periodicals
ISBN Publisher's Prefix: 2-85045

G P **Rouge et Or**, 8 rue Garancière, F-75006 Paris Tel: 3291280 Telex: Precite 204807 F
Subjects: Children's Literature
1978: 110 titles
Miscellaneous: Firm is a member of the Presses de la Cité group (qv)

La **Rougery**, see Blondel La Rougery SA

Publications **Roy**, now incorporated in Publications Estoup et Roy (qv)

Ruedo Ibérico*, 6 rue de Latran, F-75005 Paris Tel: (01) 3255649
Man Dir: Mr Martínez
Bookshop: 6 rue de Latran, F-75005 Paris
Subjects: Studies of Recent and Contemporary Spanish History, Spanish Politics, Social Science etc, General Fiction (many titles in Castilian)
Founded: 1962
ISBN Publisher's Prefix: 2-7153

S C E M I (Société Continentale d'Editions Modernes Illustrées) Sàrl*, 25 quai des Grands-Augustins, F-75006 Paris Tel: (01) 3260306
Subject: Encyclopaedias
ISBN Publisher's Prefix: 2-85046

S E C A (Société d'Exploitation et de Diffusion des Codes Rousseau Sàrl)*, 7 quai du Brise-Lames, F-85100 Sables-d'Olonne Tel: 327731
Subjects: Education, Juveniles, Audio Visual & Electronic Media
ISBN Publisher's Prefix: 2-7095

S E D E (Société d'Edition de Dictionnaires et d'Encyclopédies)*, 26 rue de Condé, F-75006 Paris Tel: (01) 3264781
Subject: Reference
Founded: 1949
ISBN Publisher's Prefix: 2-85151

S E D E S, see Centre de Documentation Universitaire

S I M E P SA, 38/46 rue de Bruxelles, BP 1214, F-69611 Villeurbanne, cedex Tel: 7/8899710
Name denotes Société d'Information medicale et d'Enseignement post-universitaire, Medical Information and Post-University Teaching Company
Chairman: Bernard Duportet; *Man Dir:* Micheline Duportet
Subject: Specialist texts on all aspects of medicine; Periodicals
1978: 130 titles *Founded:* 1965
ISBN Publisher's Prefix: 2-85334

S N L, see Société du Nouveau Littré

Editions **S O S** (Editions du Secours Catholique)*, 106 rue de Bac, F-75007 Paris Tel: (01) 5486066
Man Dir: Maurice Herr; *Publicity & Advertising:* Georges Fanucchi
Subjects: History, Philosophy, Religion, Social Science
Founded: 1949
ISBN Publisher's Prefix: 2-7185

S P E L D, 6 rue Victor-Cousin, F-75005 Paris
A group of French publishers specializing in Law, Economics, Politics

S R A (Société de Recherche appliquée à l'Education)*, 92 blvd de Latour-Maubourg, F-75007 Paris Tel: (01) 5517773
President: B de Luze
Parent Company: Science Research Associates Inc (USA)
Associate Companies: see Science Research

Associates (UK)
Subject: Primary & Secondary Education materials
1978: 1 title
ISBN Publisher's Prefix: 2-274

S U D E L (Société Universitaire d'Editions et de Librairie)*, 20 rue Corvisart, F-75640 Paris cedex 13 Tel: (01) 5354846
Subject: Education
ISBN Publisher's Prefix: 2-7162

Editions **Sageret***, 5 et 7 rue Plumet, F-75015 Paris Tel: (01) 5674674/5674682
Subject: Publishes a General Directory of Building and Public Works

Les Editions du **Sagittaire** — Union des Techniques d'Editions, 61 rue des Sts-Pères, F-75006 Paris Tel: (01) 2229976
Dirs: Jean-Claude Fasquelle
Subjects: Fiction, Biography, History, General Literature
Founded: 1929

Editions **Saint-Germain-des-Prés** SA, 70 rue du Cherche-Midi, F-75006 Paris Tel: (01) 2227120
Publicity: Philippe Héraclès
Holding Company: Le Cherche-Midi (qv)
1978: 75 titles *Founded:* 1969

Editions **Saint-Paul** SA, 6 rue Cassette, F-75006 Paris Tel: (01) 2221783 (Paris); 6422980 (Issy-les-Moulineaux)
Man Dir: M Dumas
Subsidiary Company: Editions Saint-Paul SA, Dept des Classiques Africains (qv)
Branch Off: 184 ave de Verdun, F-92130 Issy-les-Moulineaux
Subjects: Religion, Religious History, Biography, Africana
Bookshop: Librairie Saint-Paul, 6 rue Cassette, F-75006 Paris
1978: 8 titles *Founded:* 1873
ISBN Publisher's Prefix: 2-85049

Editions **Saint-Paul, Departement Les Classiques Africains**, 184 ave de Verdun, F-92130 Issy-les-Moulineaux Tel: 6422980
Parent Company: Editions Saint Paul
Subjects: Black Africa Literature, Daily Life, Tropical Medicine, School Books
Bookshop: Librairie Saint-Paul, 6 rue Cassette, F-75005 Paris
1978: 15 titles *1979:* 18 titles

Editions **Salvator** Sàrl, BP 1175, F-68053 Mulhouse cedex (Located at: 9 Pont d'Altkirch) Tel: (89) 451430
Orders to: Editions du Cerf (qv), Paris or to Salvator at above address
Subject: Religion
1978: 10 titles *Founded:* 1924
ISBN Publisher's Prefix: 2-7067

K G **Saur** Editeur Sàrl, rue de Bassano 38, F-75008 Paris Tel: 7235518

Schott Frères Sàrl, 35 rue Jean Moulin, F-94300 Vincennes Tel: 3743095

Scolavox, BP 429, F-86011 Poitiers Tel: 462766
Man Dir: Claude Moreau; *Sales Dir:* Albert Combe
Subjects: Poetry, Primary Textbooks, Educational Materials, including audio-visual slide programme
Founded: 1959
ISBN Publisher's Prefix: 2-85052

Editions du **Secours** Catholique, see S O S

La Société **Sécuritas** SA*, 2 rue de Châteaudun, F-75009 Paris Tel: (01) 8787206
Subjects: Science & Technical, Law, Economics, Social Science, Audio Visual & Electronic Media
ISBN Publisher's Prefix: 2-7097

Seditas (Société d'Editions et de Diffusion Tambourinaire-Sofradel), 186 rue du Faubourg-St-Honoré, F-75008 Paris Tel: (01) 5619600
Orders to: 41 rue Washington, F-75008 Paris
Subjects: Management, Scientific, Technical, Electronics
ISBN Publisher's Prefix: 2-85179

Les Editions **Seghers** SA, 6 pl St-Sulpice F-75006 Paris Tel: 3291233 Telex: Edilaf 250877
General Manager: Gérard Klein; *Rights & Permissions:* Béatrix Vernet
Orders to: Inter Forum, 13 rue de la Glacière, F-75013 Paris Telex: 250055
Associate Company: Les Editions Robert Laffont (qv)
Subjects: Belles Lettres, Poetry, History, Biography, Philosophy, Science & Technical, Music, Politics, Fantasy, Paperbacks
Founded: 1939
ISBN Publisher's Prefix: 2-232

Editions **Sélection** J Jacobs SA*, 66 rue Falguière, F-75015 Paris Tel: (01) 3203188
Subjects: Technology, Fine Arts, How-to series
ISBN Publisher's Prefix: 2-7174

Les Editions du **Sénevé***, 10 rue Cassette, F-75006 Paris Tel: (01) 2229020
Subjects: Art, Juveniles, Religion, Religious Educational Materials
Founded: 1947

Les **Sept Couleurs***, 13 rue des Montiboeufs, BP 9775962, F-75020 Paris cedex 20
Tel: 3314015
Man Dir: Maurice Bardèche
Orders to: Diffusion Sofedis, 29 rue St Sulpice, F-75006 Paris
Subsidiary Company: Défense de l'Occident Sarl, at above adddress
Subjects: Belles Lettres, Poetry, History, Social Science, Philology, Politics
Bookshop: Librairie Française, 27 rue de l'Abbé Grégoire, F-75006 Paris
Founded: 1948
ISBN Publisher's Prefix: 2-85147

Service Technique pour l'Education (Fonds Social Juif Unifié)*, 19 blvd Poissonnière, F-75002 Paris Tel: (01) 5084756
Man Dir: Mrs Krief
Subjects: General Fiction, Belles Lettres, Poetry, Biography, History, Music, Art, Philosophy, Reference, Religion, Juveniles, Educational Materials, Judaica
Founded: 1962
Bookshop: 19 blvd Poissonnière, F-75002 Paris

Editions du **Seuil**, 27 rue Jacob, F-75261 Paris cedex 06 Tel: (01) 3291215 Cable Add: Ediseuil Telex: 600605 F
Man Dir: Michel Chodkiewicz; *Editorial:* Anne Fréjer, Denis Roche, François Wahl, Bruno Flamand, Jean-Claude Guillebaud, Jean-Marie Borzeix; *Sales Dir:* Edouard de Andréis; *Production:* Anne Poulain; *Publicity:* Françoise Peyrot; *Rights & Permissions:* Jacqueline Lesschaeve
Subsidiary Company: Société d'Editions Scientifiques, Dimedia
Subjects: General Fiction, Literature, Poetry, Biography, History, How-to, Music, Art, Philosophy, Reference, Religion, Low- & High-priced Paperbacks, Psychology, General & Social Science, University Textbooks, Politics
Founded: 1935
ISBN Publisher's Prefix: 2-02

Editions **Siloé** Sàrl*, 8 pl St-Sulpice, F-75006 Paris Tel: (01) 3260057
Subject: Religion
ISBN Publisher's Prefix: 2-85054

Editions André **Silvaire**, 20 rue Domat, F-75005 Paris Tel: (01) 5513613
Associate Company: Les Amis de Milosz (qv)
Branch Off: 16 rue de Bellechasse, F-75007 Paris
Subjects: General Fiction, Belles Lettres, Poetry, Theatre, Philosophy, Social Sciences, Paperbacks, School Books
Bookshop: Librairie des Lettres, 16 rue de Bellechasse, F-75007 Paris
Founded: 1944
ISBN Publisher's Prefix: 2-85055

Sindbad, 1 et 3 rue Feutrier, F-75018 Paris Tel: (01) 2553523
Man Dir: Pierre Bernard; *Publicity & Advertising:* Fattauma Haniche; *Rights & Permissions:* Claudine Rulleau
Subjects: General Fiction, Belles Lettres, Poetry, History, Art, Philosophy, Reference, Religion, Social and Political Science connected with the Arabic, Persian and general Muslim worlds
1978: 14 titles *1980:* 50 titles *Founded:* 1972
ISBN Publisher's Prefix: 2-7274

Editions **Sirey**, 22 rue Soufflot, F-75005 Paris Tel: (01) 3540718
Dir: Patrice Vergé; *Dir:* Georges Alapetite; *Sales:* Alain Hapiot
Subjects: History, Philosophy, Social Science, Law, Business, University & Secondary Textbooks, Economics
1980: 290 titles *Founded:* 1791
ISBN Publisher's Prefix: 2-248

Société Continentale d'Editions Modernes Illustrées, see S C E M I

Société d'Edition d'Annuaires Professionnels, see S E A P

Société d'Edition de Dictionnaires et d'Encyclopédies, see S E D E

Société d'Edition d'Enseignement Supérieur, see Centre de Documentation Universitaire

Société d'Edition, de Publicité, de Radio et Télévision, see S E R T

Société d'Editions Scientifiques, Dimedia, subsidiary company of Editions du Seuil (qv)

Société de Recherche appliquée à l'Education, see S R A

Société d'Exploitation et de Diffusion des Codes Rousseau, see S E C A

Société d'Information médicale et d'enseignement post-universitaire, see S I M E P

Société du Nouveau Littré (SNL) Dictionnaire 'Le Robert', 107 ave Parmentier, F-75011 Paris Tel: (01) 3577313
President, Man Dir: Charles-Albert de Waziers; *Commercial Manager, Publicity:* Robert Crosa; *Technical Manager:* Jacques Pierre
Subject: Dictionaries
1980: 18 titles *Founded:* 1951
ISBN Publisher's Prefix: 2-85036

Société Encyclopédique Française (SEF), see SEF Philippe Daudy

Société Universitaire d'Editions et de Librairie, see S U D E L

Sodel (Editeur) SA, 336-340 rue St-Honoré, F-75001 Paris Tel: (01) 2603180
Subjects: Science & Technical
ISBN Publisher's Prefix: 2-7102

Sofiac (Société Française des Imprimeries Administratives Centrales), 8 rue de Furstenberg, F-75006 Paris Tel: (01) 3292129
General Manager: Pierre de Clerck
Subjects: Economics, Social Science,

Business Administration, Legal and Judicial, Accountancy
1978: 13 titles *1979:* 14 titles

Sofradel-Seditas, see Seditas

Sofradif Editions Philippe Auzou*, 1-1 bis rue du Dahomey, F-75011 Paris Tel: (01) 3714493
Publisher: Philippe Auzou; *Sales Manager:* Fred Frangeul
Subjects: Medicine, Law

Solar*, 8 rue Garancière, F-75006 Paris Tel: 329180 Telex: Precite 204807
Subjects: Practical Books, Cookery, Sport, Nature
Miscellaneous: Firm is a member of the Presses de la Cité group (qv)

Editions **Soleil Noir**, 2 rue Fléchier, F-75009 Paris Tel: (01) 2804702
Man Dir: François di Dio
Subjects: Poetry, Art, Social Science, General Fiction and Non-fiction
Founded: 1948
ISBN Publisher's Prefix: 2-85131

Editions d'Art Aimery **Somogy**, 91 rue de Seine, F-75006 Paris Tel: (01) 3268981 Telex: 204473
Man Dir: Aimery Somogy
Subject: Art
Founded: 1937
ISBN Publisher's Prefix: 2-85056

Editions **Sonzé***, 7 rue Alexandre-Cabanel, F-75015 Paris Tel: (01) 3064027
Subject: Education
ISBN Publisher's Prefix: 2-85057

Soprep (Editions de Bussac)*, 2 cours Sablon, F-63000 Clermont-Ferrand Tel: (073) 923278

Soprode*, 3 rue Crébillon, F-75006 Paris Tel: (01) 3260158
Man Dir: Bernard Laville
Subjects: Philosophy, Social Sciences, Literature, History
ISBN Publisher's Prefix: 2-85240

Editions Louis **Soulanges** 'Le Livre Ouvert', 20 rue de l'Odéon, F-75006 Paris Tel: (01) 3262538
Man Dir, Sales Dir, Publicity: Louis Drouot Soulanges
Imprints: Paris-Caraïbes, France-Caraïbes
Branch Off: 5-7 rue Abel Ferry, F-75016 Paris Tel: 5240609
Subjects: General Fiction, Philosophy, Reference, Religion, Juveniles
Founded: 1960

Les Editions de la **Source** SA*, 5 rue de la Source, F-75016 Paris Tel: (01) 5253007
Man Dir: Rev Father Dom André Gozier;
All Other Offices: Rev Father Dom Norbert Balladur
Orders to: Office Général du Livre, 14 bis rue Jean-Ferrandi F-75006, Paris
Imprints: Lumière Biblique series
Subjects: Religion; Doctrine, Theology, Holy Scripture, Monasticism and Monastic History
Bookshop: Librairie Sainte Marie, 5 rue de la Source, F-75016 Paris
Founded: 1927
ISBN Publisher's Prefix: 2-900005

Les Editions Internationales Alain **Stanké***, 6 rue Saint Florentin, F-75001 Paris Tel: 2602332 Telex: 05561358
Man Dir, Editorial: Alain Stanké; *Sales:* Eric Ghedin; *Production:* Annie Creton; *Publicity:* Claire Dayan; *Rights & Permissions:* Lyn Franklin
Subjects: Current Affairs, Biography, Fiction, How-to, Cookery, Art, Pocket Editions
1978: 42 titles *1979:* 50 titles *Founded:* 1975
ISBN Publisher's Prefix: 2-7604

Editions Robert **Steindecker** (Editions RST)*, 52 rue de Bassano, F-75008 Paris Tel: (01) 7201480
Man Dir: Robert Steindecker; *Sales Dir:* Guy Simbozel; *Publicity, Rights & Permissions:* Albert Monny
Subject: Juveniles
Founded: 1960
ISBN Publisher's Prefix: 2-7090

Editions **Stock**, 14 rue de l'Ancienne Comédie, F-75006 Paris Tel: (01) 3292125
President, Man Dir: Christian de Bartillat; *Assistant Dir:* Claude Daillencourt; *Sales Dir:* Christian Garraud; *Production:* Jacques Menard; *Publicity & Advertising:* Marie-Pierre Lassus-Debat; *Rights & Permissions:* Janine Noël
Parent Company: Librairie Hachette (qv)
Subjects: French and Foreign Literature, Human Sciences, Medicine, Juveniles, Theatre, Music, Cinema, Paperbacks
1978: 130 titles *1979:* 150 titles *Founded:* 1780
ISBN Publisher's Prefix: 2-234

Editions **Studia** SA*, 40 bis rue Maurice-Arnoux, F-92120 Montrouge Tel: 2533811
Subject: Education
ISBN Publisher's Prefix: 2-7104

Les Editions de la **Table** Ronde, 40 rue du Bac, F-75007 Paris Tel: (01) 2222891
Man Dir: Roland Laudenbach; *Publicity Dir:* Danielle Levêque; *Literary Dir:* Philippe de la Roche; *Rights & Permissions:* Mahaut Pascalis
Subjects: General Fiction, Belles Lettres, Poetry, Biography, History, Religion, Medicine, Psychology, Social Science
Founded: 1944
ISBN Publisher's Prefix: 2-7103

Les Presses de **Taizé***, F-71250 Taizé-Communauté (Saône et Loire) Tel: (85) 501414 Telex: Cotaize 800753F
Subject: Religious works
1978: 6 titles *Founded:* 1959

Librairie Jules **Tallandier**, 17 rue Rémy-Dumoncel, F-75677 Paris cedex 14 Tel: (01) 3277770
Subjects: General Fiction (especially Romantic), Art, Belles Lettres, Reference, History, Geography, Paperbacks
Founded: 1865
ISBN Publisher's Prefix: 2-235

Editions **Tardy** SA, 22 rue Joyeuse, BP 56, F-18002 Bourges Tel: 242986; 89 rue de Seine, F-75006 Paris Tel: (01) 3260058
Man Dir, Rights & Permissions: Pierre Tardy
Subjects: Religion, Catechisms, Parish Manuals, Religious Pedagogy
Founded: 1938
ISBN Publisher's Prefix: 2-7105

Editions **Taride** Sàrl*, 2 bis pl du Puits de l'Ermite, F-75005 Paris Tel: (01) 3364040
Cable Add: Cartaride Paris
Subjects: Geography, Travel
Founded: 1852
ISBN Publisher's Prefix: 2-7106

Claude **Tchou** Editeur, 6 rue du Mail, F-75002 Paris Tel: 2961693
Man Dir: Claude Tchou; *Rights & Permissions:* Agnes de Gorter
Subjects: General Fiction, Belles Lettres, Poetry, Biography, History, How-to, Music, Art, Juveniles, Reference, Paperbacks, Social Science, Geography, Psychology
Founded: 1963
ISBN Publisher's Prefix: 2-7107

Société des Éditions **Technip**, 27 rue Ginoux, F-75737 Paris cedex 15 Tel: (01) 5771108
Dir: Jacques Ledésert; *Man Dir:* Anna Beraud

Subjects: Petroleum Science & Technology
1978: 40 titles *Founded:* 1956
ISBN Publisher's Prefix: 2-7108

Technique et Documentation (Librairie Lavoisier)*, 11 rue Lavoisier, F-75008 Paris Tel: (01) 2657167
Subjects: Scientific and Technical covering: Engineering, Industrial Safety, Environment, Metallurgy, Hydraulics, Chemistry, Electro-Technology, Biology, Food Industry, Civil Engineering, Oceanography; Reference Works
ISBN Publisher's Prefix: 2-85206

Technique et Vulgarisation SA*, 21 rue Claude Bernard, F-75005 Paris Tel: (01) 5811131
Dirs: Laurent Heilmann, Charles Miguet
Subjects: Industrial, General Technology, Educational Materials, Engineering, Secondary & Primary Textbooks
1978: 23 titles *Founded:* 1946
ISBN Publisher's Prefix: 2-7109

Techniques de l'Ingénieur Sàrl, (Editorial), 21 rue Cassette, F-75006 Paris Tel: (01) 2223550; (Commercial Office) 123 rue d'Alésia, F-75678 Paris cedex 14 Tel: (01) 5392291
Man Dir: Jacques Debaene; *Editorial Manager:* Jean-Jacques Baron; *Publicity Manager:* Gérard Delepoulle (at Commercial Office address)
Subjects: Scientific, Technical
ISBN Publisher's Prefix: 2-85059

Editions **Techniques Professionels**, see ETP

Librairie Pierre **Tequi** et Editions Tequi, 82 rue Bonaparte, F-75006 Paris Tel: (01) 3260458
Head Office: Le Roc Saint Michel, F-53150 Saint-Ceneve Tel: (43) 010181
General Manager: Pierre Lemaire; *Literary Manager:* G Cerbelaud Salagnac; *Commercial Manager:* Mrs Pascal
Subjects: Education, Literature, Religion, Juveniles
1978-79: 35 titles
ISBN Publisher's Prefix: 2-85244

Editions **Tests***, 41 rue de la Grange-aux-Belles, F-75483 Paris cedex 10 Tel: (01) 2022910
Subjects: Science & Technical, Audio Visual & Electronic Media

Editions **Touret** SA*, 11 rue La Boétie, Paris 8eme
Paris office: 32 rue Baudin, 92400 Courbevoie Tel: 7881699
President & Director General: Denise Louvet; *Administration:* Raphaël Peres; *Editorial:* Michel Bizet; *Publicity:* Caroline Levy
Branch Off: Conty F80160 Tel: (22) 412324
Subjects: Children's and Young Peoples' books, Reading books, Colouring books, Cut-out books, Transfers
Founded: 1923
ISBN Publisher's Prefix: 2-7161

Editions de **Trévise**, 34 rue de Trévise, F-75009 Paris Tel: (01) 8246713/7703604
Man Dir: Gérald Gauthier; *Literary Dir:* Alexis Ovtchinnikoff
Subjects: History, Encyclopaedias, Art, Reference, Languages, Novels & Short Stories, General Non-fiction
Founded: 1956
ISBN Publisher's Prefix: 2-7112

Trianon Press*, 125 ave du Maine, F-75014 Paris Tel: (01) 3220917
Man Dir: Arnold D Fawcus
Subjects: Art, Art History (specialize in the works of William Blake, Ben Shann, Abbé Breuil)
Founded: 1947
ISBN Publisher's Prefix: 2-85172

U G E*, 10/18, 8 rue Garancière, F-75006
Paris Tel: 3291280 Telex: Precite 204807 F
Subjects: University and Political series
(various)
Miscellaneous: Member of the Presses de la
Cité group (qv)
ISBN Publisher's Prefix: 2-264

Union Latine d'Editions SA*, 5 rue de
Savoie, F-75006 Paris Tel: (01) 0330224
Subject: Collectors' editions
Book Clubs: Club Bibliophile de France SA,
5 rue de Savoie, F-75006 Paris
Founded: 1930
ISBN Publisher's Prefix: 2-85061

Presses **Universitaires** de France, de
Grenoble, de Lille, de Lyon, see Presses

Editions de **Vaillant** — IGO*, 126 La
Fayette, F-75010 Paris Tel: (01) 7709759
Telex: Edipif 64067
Subject: Juveniles

Vander-Oyez SA, 4 rue de Fleurus, F-75006
Paris Tel: 5484092
Man Dir: Mr Kaatee
Associate Company: Oyez SA, Belgium (qv)
Subjects: How-to, Medicine, Social Science,
Science & Technology, Economics,
Architecture, Languages, Humanities, Arts,
Agriculture, Mathematics, Education,
Philosophy, Psychology, Law, Sports
Founded: 1971
Miscellaneous: This Company incorporates
the former French firm Beatrice-
Nauwelaerts, taken over by Oyez, UK, in
1975
ISBN Publisher's Prefix: 2-85247

Editions de **Vecchi**, see De Vecchi

Editions Van de **Velde**, La Petite Plaine,
BP 22, Fondettes, F-37230 Luynes Tel: (47)
510623
Man Dir, Sales: Jean François Pitchal;
Editorial, Production: Francis Van de Velde;
Publicity: Sylvie Toussaint; *Rights &
Permissions:* Boris Cattier
Subject: Musical Instruction
1978: 8 titles *1979:* 10 titles *Founded:* 1898
ISBN Publisher's Prefix: 2-85868

Editions Francis Van de **Velde**, 12 rue Jacob,
F-75006 Paris Tel: (01) 3259343
Man Dir, Editorial: Francis Van de Velde;
Sales, Rights and Permissions: Alain
Gouiffes
Subject: Musicology

Editions de la Revue **Verve** Sàrl*, 4 rue
Férou, F-75006 Paris Tel: (01) 3267705
Dir: E Teriade
Subjects: Art, Special Editions
Founded: 1937
ISBN Publisher's Prefix: 2-900015

Veyrier, 12 rue de Nesle, F-75006 Paris Tel:
6332018/3258037
Man Dir: Henri Veyrier; *Editorial:* Jean-
Claude Hache; *Sales:* Jean-Pierre Appert
Orders to: Anagramme, at above address
Parent Company: Anagramme, at same
address
Subjects: Illustrated Books on Art, Cinema,
Paris, Fiction
Bookshops: 17 ter ave de Clichy, F-75018
Paris; 20 rue J H Fabre, Saint Ouen
1980: 120 titles *Founded:* 1973

Editions André **Vial***, 67 rue Madame,
F-75006 Paris Tel: (01) 2221315
Man Dir: André Vial
Subjects: Limited editions of illustrated
books
Founded: 1947
ISBN Publisher's Prefix: 2-85062

Editions **Vialetay** Sàrl*, 23 rue de l'Abbé-
Grégoire, F-75006 Paris Tel: (01) 2221276
Subject: Art
ISBN Publisher's Prefix: 2-85063

Editions **Vigot** Frères, 23 rue de l'Ecole-de-
Médecine, F-75006 Paris Tel: (01) 3295450
Man Dir: Daniel Vigot
Subjects: Medicine, General Science, Sports,
Veterinary
Bookshop: Librairie Vigot, at address above
1978: 30 titles *1979:* 50 titles
Founded: 1890
ISBN Publisher's Prefix: 2-7114

Editions **Vilo** SA, 25 rue Ginoux, F-75015
Paris Tel: (01) 5770805 Cable Add: Edivilo
Paris Telex: 200305 F
Man Dir: M Larfillon
Subjects: Art, History, Religion,
Architecture, Reference, Maps, Literature,
Aviation, Medicine, Non-fiction, Sports,
Languages, Tourism
ISBN Publisher's Prefix: 2-7191

Dominique **Vincent** et Cie*, 4 rue des Beaux-
Arts, F-75006 Paris Tel: (01) 3265402
Subjects: Science & Technical
ISBN Publisher's Prefix: 2-85064

Vingtième Siècle*, 13 rue de Nestle, F-75006
Paris Tel: (01) 3261823
Man Dir: I Potel

Editions La **Voix** de l'Ain*, 20 rue Lalande,
BP 88, F-01003 Bourg-en-Bresse Tel: (74)
215384
Subject: Religion

Librairie Philosophique J **Vrin**, 6 pl de la
Sorbonne, F-75005 Paris 5 Tel: (01)
3540347
Man Dir: Gérard Paulhac
Subjects: Philosophy, Reference, Religion,
Psychology, University Textbooks, History
1979: 50 titles *Founded:* 1920
Bookshops (new and second hand books):
Philosophy, Law, Religion at 6 Pl de la
Sorbonne, Paris; Literature, Art, History at
71 re St Jacques, Paris
ISBN Publisher's Prefix: 2-7116

Librairie **Vuibert** SA*, 63 blvd St-Germain,
F-75005 Paris Tel: (01) 3256100 Cable
Add: Vuibert Paris
President: Jean Adam; *Sales:* Serge Wils;
Production: Pierre Bonnefond; *Publicity,
Rights & Permissions:* Dominique Lallouette
Subjects: Mathematics, Physics, Chemistry,
Biology, Earth Sciences, Schoolbooks,
Children's Literature
Founded: 1877
ISBN Publisher's Prefix: 2-7117

Gerard **Watelet**, see Editions Pygmalion

Weber*, 90 rue de Rennes, F-75006 Paris
Tel: (01) 5481251 Cable Add: Webart-Paris
Subjects: Art, Architecture, Social Science,
Juveniles, Reference
Founded: 1967
ISBN Publisher's Prefix: 2-7190

Galerie Lucie **Weill***, Au Pont des Arts, 6
rue Bonaparte, F-75006 Paris Tel: 3547195
President: Lucie Weill
Subjects: Books with illustrations by famous
artists
Book Club: Nouveau Cercle Parisien du
Livre (qv)
Founded: 1930

Y M C A-Press*, 11 rue de la Montagne
Sainte-Geneviève, F-75005 Paris Tel: (01)
0337446
Imprint: Les Editeurs Réunis (qv) in
association with Bredda Books and Prideaux
Press
Subjects: Religion, Literature, Russian
books (in Russian)
ISBN Publisher's Prefix: 2-85065

Editions Philateliques **Yvert** et Tellier*, 35
bis rue de Provence, F-75009 Paris
Tel: 7706298
Subjects: General, Encyclopaedias, Sports

Zodiaque, la Pierre-qui-Vire, F-89830 St-
Léger-Vauban Tel: (86) 322123 Cable Add:
Zodiaque-89830 St Léger
Man Dir: José Surchamp
Distribution in France: Weber Diffusion, 28
rue du Moulinet, F-75013 Paris
Distribution outside France: Marcel Weber,
13 rue du Monthoux, CH-1211 Geneva 2,
Switzerland
Subjects: Ancient and Modern Art, Music
1978: 7 titles *1979:* 8 titles *Founded:* 1951

Literary Agents

Agence **Bataille***, 65 rue St André-des-Arts,
F-75006 Paris
Contact: Marie-Claude Bataille

Jean-Pierre **Boscq**, 65 rue du Faubourg St-
Honoré, F-75008 Paris

Mrs W A **Bradley***, 18 quai de Bethune,
F-75004 Paris Tel: (01) 3547514

Mlle Sabine **Delattre***, 9 rue Christine,
F-75006 Paris Tel: (01) 3262709

Mme Françoise **Germain**, 8 rue de la Paix,
F-75002 Paris Tel: (01) 2616814

Agence **Hoffman**, 77 blvd St-Michel,
F-75005 Paris Tel: (01) 3547115/3542327
Cable Add: Aghoff Paris Telex: 203605F
Contacts: Boris or Georges Hoffman

Mme Michelle **Lapautre**, 6 rue Jean Carriès,
F-75007 Paris Tel: (01) 7348241/7346450
Cable Add: Milalit Paris Telex:
210311F/939

Alice **Le Bayon***, 113 blvd St-Germain, Paris

Anne **Lenclud**, Pierre Lenclud, Agence
Renault-Lenclud, 18 rue Blanche, F-75009
Paris Tel: (01) 5262679

McKee et Mouche, 16 rue du Regard,
F-75006 Paris Tel: (01) 5484503/2224233

Matthias-Estienne*, 27 rue du Dragon,
F-75006 Paris Tel: 2222912

La **Nouvelle Agence**, 7 rue Corneille,
F-75006 Paris Tel: (01) 3258560
Contact: Mary Kling

Promotion Littéraire, 26 rue Chalgrin,
F-75116 Paris Tel: (01) 5004210 Cable
Add: Promolit Paris
Dir: Mariella Giannetti

Mme Janine **Quet***, Bureau littéraire, 20 rue
de la Michodière, F-75002 Paris Tel: (01)
0333850

Bureau littéraire international Marguerite
Scialtiel, 14 rue Chanoinesse, F-75004 Paris
Tel: (01) 3547116
Contact: Geneviève Ulmann

Mme Greta **Strassova**, 4 rue Gît-Le-Coeur,
F-75006 Paris Tel: (01) 6333457
Formerly Mme Héléna Strassova

W J **Taylor-Whitehead***, 60 rue Madame,
F-75006 Paris

Le **Téléscope**, 10 rue Mayet, F-75006 Paris
Tel: 7837070
Dir: Chantal Galtier Roussel

Mme Ellen **Wright***, 20 rue Jacob, F-75006
Paris

Book Clubs

Les **Amis** de Franco Maria Ricci, Galerie 12,
12 rue des Beaux-Arts, F-75006 Paris
Also associated with the Société des
Bibliophiles
Owned by: Franco Maria Ricci (qv)

L'**Amitié** par le Livre, F-25310 Blamont
Oldest book club and only one activated by voluntary effort

C A L (Culture Art Loisirs SA)*, 114 Champs Elysées, F-75008 Paris

Cercle du Bibliophile*, 22 rue de Cocherel, F-27 Evreux

Club Bibliophile de France SA*, 5 rue de Savoie, F-75002 Paris
Owned by: L'Union Latine d'Editions (Paris)
Subjects: Encyclopaedias, Collectors' editions

Club des Aventures de Guerre, 33 rue Beauregard, F-75002 Paris Tel: 2366965
Owned by: Editions France Empire

Club du Livre d'Art, 1 rue Palatine, F-75006 Paris
Owned by: Editions Albert Morancé

Club du Livre SA*, 28 rue Fortuny, F-75017 Paris Tel: 9248055
Man Dir: Philippe Lebaud
Subjects: Art, De Luxe Editions

Club du Livre technique*, 28 rue du Faubourg-Poissonnière, F-75000 Paris 10e

Club du Roman féminin, 33 rue Beauregard, F-75002 Paris Tel: 2366965
Owned by: Editions France Empire (qv)

Club Français des Bibliophiles*, 5 & 7 rue Baudoin, F-75013 Paris 13ème Tel: 583 4330
Subjects: Encyclopaedic Collections: The Sciences of Man, Sociology, Biography and Memoirs, Leisure, Touring, Sport

Club Français du Livre*, 7 & 9 rue Armand-Moisant, F-75015 Paris

Livre Club **Diderot**, 13 blvd Bourdon, F-75004 Paris Tel: (01) 8876519
Subjects: Political and Economic Science, History, Poetry, Literature
Owned by: Les Editions Sociales (qv)

Education et Culture, 28 rue de la Boétie, F-75008 Paris
Owned by: Les Editions des Deux Coqs d'Or

Libraire **Lidis**, 208 rue de Rivoli, F-75001 Paris
Owned by: Editions Lidis (qv)

Librairie **Montaigne**, c/o Editions Bordas (qv)

Nouveau Cercle parisien du Livre*, 6 rue Bonaparte, F-75006 Paris
President: Daniel S Sickles
Subjects: Illustrated Books
Club is associated with publisher Galerie Lucie Weill (qv)

L'**Oeil** Ouvert, 16 rue de l'Ecole Polytechnique, Paris 5
Owned by: Nouvelles Editions Rationalistes (qv)
Subject: Historical texts expressing rationalist thought

Opta Editions*, 39 rue d'Amsterdam, F-75008 Paris Tel: 5266004

Poètes Présents, 50 rue Rodier, F-75009 Paris
Owned by: Jean Grassin Editeur (qv)
Subject: Poetry

Presses d'Or, 28 rue de la Boétie, F-75008 Paris
Owned by: Les Editions des Deux Coqs d'Or (qv)

Ediclub **Rombaldi***, 222 blvd St-Germain, F-75007 Paris.
Selling organization for seven book clubs, including Bibliothèque du Temps Présent
Subjects: Mostly Fiction (mostly classics)

Société des Bibliophiles, associated with Book Club Les Amis de Franco Maria Ricci (qv)

Société Editions Internationales Sàrl*, 150 Champs Elysées, F-75008 Paris

Major Booksellers

Brentano's*, 37 ave de l'Opéra, F-75002 Paris

F N A C*, 136 rue de Rennes, F-75006 Paris Tel: (01) 2771133

Flammarion*, 19 pl Bellecour, F-69002 Lyon Tel: (078) 380157; 54 La Canebière, F-13231 Marseille cedex 1 Tel: (091) 542520 (for other bookshops see under entry in Publishers)

Librairie '**Furet du Nord**'*, 11 pl du Gnl de Gaulle, F-59000 Lille Tel: (020) 541234

Librairie Joseph **Gibert***, 26 blvd St Michel, F-75006 Paris Tel: (01) 3292141

Librairie **La Hune***, 170 blvd St-Germain, F-75006 Paris Tel: (01) 5483585

Librairie **Laffitte***, 156 La Canebière, F-13000 Marseille

Librairie **Maupetit***, 142 La Canebière, F-13232 Marseille

Librairie **Mollat**, 15 rue Vital-Carles, F-33080 Bordeaux cedex Tel: 448487 Telex: 541542 F

Librairie **Montparnasse** Edition*, 1 Quai de Conti, F-75006 Paris
Owned by: Alfred Eibel, éditeur (qv)

Presses universitaires de France*, 49 blvd St-Michel, F-75005 Paris Tel: (01) 3258340

Librairie de **Provence***, 31 cours Mirabeau, F-13100 Aix en Provence

Sodexport-Grem, 117 blvd Saint-Germain, F-75006 Paris
Association française pour la Diffusion du Livre Scientifique, Technique et Medical: exporters of scientific, technical and medical books
President: Mr Jean Adam Telex: Lifran 270838 F

Librairie **Sauramps***, Le Triangle, pl de la Comédie, F-34000 Montpellier Tel: (67) 588515

Librairie de l'**Université**, 17 rue de la Liberté, F-25025 Dijon cedex Tel: (80) 305117
Manager: Jacques Bazin

Major Librairies

Archives nationales, 60 rue des Francs-Bourgeois, F-75141 Paris cedex 03
Publications: National Archive Documents, which are distributed by La Documentation Française, Publisher (qv)

Bibliothèque de l'**Arsenal**, 1 rue de Sully, F-75004 Paris Tel: (01) 2774421
Chief Librarian: C Giteau

Bibliothèque mazarine, 23 quai de Conti, F-75006 Paris Tel: (01) 3548948
Chief Curator: Pierre Gasnault

Bibliothèque municipale*, 1 rue de la Bibliothèque, F-25000 Besançon Tel: (81) 812089

Bibliothèque municipale, blvd Maréchal Lyautey, BP 1095, RP, F-38021 Grenoble cedex Tel: 460156

Bibliothèque municipale de la Ville de Lyon, 30 blvd Vivier-Merle, F-69431 Lyon cedex 3 Tel: (078) 628520
Librarian: Jean-Louis Rocher

Bibliothèque nationale*, 58 rue de Richelieu, F-75084 Paris cedex 02 Tel: (01) 2666262
National Library
Publication: Bulletin de la Bibliothèque Nationale; Bulletin des Bibliothèques de France

Bibliothèque nationale et universitaire de Strasbourg*, 5 rue du Maréchal Joffre, BP 1029/F, F-67070 Strasbourg cedex Tel: (88) 360068 (main address and Management and Legal Section); 6 place de la République, BP 1029/F, F-67070 Strasbourg cedex Tel: (88) 360068 (Literature and Human Sciences Section); 3 bis rue du Maréchal Joffre, BP 1029/F, F-67070 Strasbourg cedex Tel: (88) 360068 (Section dealing with Alsace region affairs); 6 rue Kirschleger, F-67085 Strasbourg cedex Tel: (88) 362323 (Medical Section); 34 boulevard de la Victoire, BP 1037/F, F-67070 Strasbourg cedex Tel: (88) 613323 (Scientific and Technical Section)

Bibliothèque littéraire Jacques **Doucet**, 10 pl du Panthéon, F-75005 Paris Tel: (01) 3296100 (extensions 22, 56, 72)
Librarian: François Chapon
Publications: Exhibition Catalogues

Bibliothèque de l'**École** des Langues orientales, 2 rue de Lille, F-75007 Paris Tel: (01) 2603458/2616203
Dir: Mrs M Debout

Bibliothèque de l'**Institut de France**, 23 quai Conti, F-75006 Paris cedex Tel: (01) 3268540
Chief Curator: Mrs Hautecoeur

Bibliothèque du **Musée de l'Homme***, Palais de Chaillot, pl du Trocadéro, F-75116 Paris Tel: (01) 7045394
Librarian: Françoise Weil
Publication: Liste des Périodiques reçus regulièrement par la Bibliothèque du Musée de l'homme

Bibliothèque centrale du **Muséum national** d'Histoire naturelle, 38 rue Geoffroy Saint-Hilaire, F-75005 Paris 5 Tel: (01) 3317124/3319560

Bibliothèque de l'**Université de Strasbourg**, see Bibliothèque nationale

Bibliothèques des **Universités de Paris** (Paris University Libraries):

Bibliothèque d'**Art** et d'Archéologie, see Doucet

Bibliothèque de **Documentation** Internationale Contemporaine, Campus Universitaire, 2 rue de Rouen, F-92001 Nanterre cedex Tel: 7214022
Librarian: Véronique Blum

Bibliothèque d'Art et d'Archéologie (Fondation Jacques **Doucet**), 3 rue Michelet, F-75006 Paris Tel: 3543527
Dir: Denise Gazier

Bibliothèque de **Géographie**, 191 rue St-Jacques, F-75005 Paris Tel: (01) 3290147

Bibliothèque Interuniversitaire de **Médecine**, 12 rue de l'Ecole de Médecine, F-75270 Paris cedex 06 Tel: (01) 3541675/3292177 Telex: 20223714 U
Dir and Chief Curator: Ms Y Gueniot
Publications: Catalogue des Périodiques de la Bibliothèque (1976-1978), Catalogue des Congrès (1968)

Bibliothèque Interuniversitaire de **Pharmacie**, 4 ave de l'Observatoire, F-75270 Paris cedex 06 Tel: (01) 3291208 ext 238, 311, 241 Telex: 200707 f
Librarian: Paul Roux-Fouillet

Bibliothèque **Sainte-Geneviève***, 10 pl du Panthéon, F-75005 Paris Tel: (01) 3296100

Bibliothèque de la **Sorbonne***, 47 rue des Ecoles, F-75230 Paris cedex 05 Tel: (01) 3291213 (DAN 2194)
Chief Librarian: André Tuilier *Librarian:* Jacquette Reboul

The preceding seven libraries are Paris University Libraries

Service des Travaux Historiques de la **Ville de Paris** et Bibliothèque historique de la Ville de Paris*, 24 rue Pavée, F-75004 Paris Tel: (01) 2721018/2726836/2773975

Library Associations

The two following organizations administer the libraries and archives:

Direction des **Archives** de France, 60 rue des Francs-Bourgeois, F-75141 Paris cedex 03 Tel: 2771130

Service des Bibliothèques, Ministère des Universités, 61-65 rue Dutot, F-75732 Paris cedex 15
Chief Librarian: Andrée Carpentier
Publication: Bulletin des Bibliothèques de France

A B E F, see Association des Bibliothèques ecclésiastiques de France

Association de l'Ecole nationale supérieure de Bibliothécaires, 17-21 blvd du 11 Novembre 1918, F-69100 Villeurbanne Tel: (78) 524738
Association of the National School of Librarianship
General Secretary: P J Lamblin
Founded: 1967
Publication: Annuaire de l'Association de l'Ecole nationale supérieure de Bibliothécaires

Association de l'Institut national des Techniques de la Documentation*, 32 rue des Bluets, F-75011 La Garenne-Colombes
Association of the National Institute for Information Sciences
President: E Vallée

Association des Archivistes français, 60 rue des Francs-Bourgeois, F-75141 Paris cedex 03 Tel: 2771130
Association of French Archivists
President: Mr H Charnier; *Secretaries:* Mrs Rey, Miss Etienne
Publication: La Gazette des Archives (quarterly)

Association des Bibliothécaires français*, 65 rue de Richelieu, F-75002 Paris
Tel: 7429879
Association of French Librarians
President: Marc Chauveinc; *Executive Secretary:* Miss M Beaudiquez
Founded: 1906
Publication: Bulletin d'Information

Association des Bibliothèques ecclésiastiques de France (ABEF), 6 rue du Regard, F-75006 Paris
Executive Secretary: Paul-Marie Guillaume
Publication: Bulletin de Liaison de l'ABEF

Association des Diplômés de l'Ecole de Bibliothécaires-Documentalistes, Bibliothèque du Saulchoir, 43 bis rue la Glacière, F-75013 Paris Tel: 5870533
Association of Graduates of the School of Librarians and Documentalists
Executive Secretary: Miss A Piot
Publication: Bulletin d'Information

Association française des Documentalistes et Bibliothécaires spécialisés, 5 ave Franco-Russe, F-75007 Paris Tel: (01) 5555516
French Association of Information Scientists and Special Librarians
Publication: Documentaliste

Association nationale des Bibliothécaires Municipaux, c/o Mlle Pintaparis, Cité Administrative, 17 blvd Morland, F-75004 Paris
National Association of Municipal Librarians

Association pour la Mediathèque publique (AMP), Bibliothèque municipale, 37 rue Saint-Georges, F-59400 Cambrai

Centre d'Archives et de Documentation politiques et sociales*, 86 blvd Haussmann, F-75008 Paris
Centre for Political and Social Archives and Documentation
Publications: Informations politiques et sociales; Est et Ouest

Fédération des Amicales de Documentalistes et Bibliothécaires de l'Education nationale*, 29 rue d'Ulm, F-75007 Paris
Friendly Society of Documentalists and Librarians of National Education

Library Reference Books and Journals

Books

Les Bibliothèques (The Libraries), Presses Universitaires de France, 108 blvd St-Germain, F-75279 Paris cedex 06

Les Bibliothèques de France au Service de Public (Public Libraries in France), Ministère de l'Education nationale, Direction de Bibliothèque et de Lecture publique, 1 rue du Périgord, F-31000 Toulouse

Les Bibliothèques publiques en France, ENSB-Presses, 17-21 blvd du 11 novembre 1918, F-69100 Villeurbanne

Répertoire des Bibliothèques et Organismes de Documentation (Catalogue of Libraries and Documentation Organizations), National Library, 58 rue de Richelieu, F-75084 Paris cedex 02

Libraries in France, Clive Bingley Ltd, 1-19 New Oxford St, London WC1A 1NE, UK

Journals

Bulletin, Association of French Theological Libraries, 6 rue du Regard, F-75006 Paris

Bulletin d'Information (Information Bulletin), Association of French Librarians, 4 rue Louvois, F-75002 Paris

Bulletin de l'Unesco à l'intention des Bibliothèques (Unesco Bulletin for Libraries) (editions in English, French, Russian and Spanish), Unesco, pl de Fontenoy, F-75700 Paris

Bulletin de la Bibliothèque (Library Bulletin), Institut national de la Statistique et des Etudes économiques, 29 quai Branly, F-75000 Paris

Bulletin des Bibliothèques de France (Bulletin of French Libraries), Service des Bibliothèques, 61-65 rue Dutot, F-75732 Paris cedex 15

Documentaliste (Documentalist); review of documentary information and techniques, French Association of Information Scientists and Special Librarians, 61 rue du Cardinal-Lemoine, F-75005 Paris

La Gazette des Archives (Archives Gazette), Association of French Archivists, 60 rue des Francs-Bourgeois, F-75003 Paris

Informatique (Information Processing), Editions d'Informatique, 82 rue Lauriston, F-75116 Paris

Revue Bitrimestrielle (for specialist librarians), Inter-CDI, 7 Residence de Guinette, F-91150 Etampes

Literary Associations and Societies

Académie des Lettres et des Arts, (Société du Vieux Montmartre), c/o Musée de Montmartre, 12 rue Cortot, F-75018 Paris Tel: 6066111
President: Romain Delahalle

Académie Goncourt, Salons Drouant, pl Gaillon, Paris
President: Hervé Bazin

Académie Montaigne*, Le Doyenné, Sillé-le-Guillaume (Sarthe)
Secretary: Constant Hubert

Association des Ecrivains combattants*, 8 rue Roquépine, F-75008 Paris
Association of Armed Services Writers
Secretary: Maurice Ch Renard
Publication: Bulletin

Centre national des Académies et Associations littéraires et savantes des Provinces françaises*, Musée des Arts et Traditions populaires, route de Madrid, F-75016
National Centre of the Literary and Learned Academies and Associations of the French Provinces

Centre national des Lettres, 6 rue Dufrénoy, F-75116 Paris
Secretary-General: Jacques Charpillon

Jeunesses littéraires de France*, 117 blvd St-Germain, F-75279 Paris cedex 06
French Literary Youth

La Joie par les Livres, 4 rue de Louvois, F-75002 Paris
Joy through Books — an experimental library and a documentation centre on children's literature
Publications: La Revue des Livres pour Enfants and other special selections

Maison de Poésie (Fondation Emile Blémont)*, 11 bis rue Ballu, F-75009 Paris
President: Mrs George-Day

P E N Club Français, 6 rue François Miron, F-75004 Paris Tel: 2773787
President: René Tavernier; *General Secretary:* Dimitri Stoly-pine
Publication: News Bulletins to members as occasion arises

Société d'Etudes dantesques, Centre universitaire méditerranéen, 65 promenade des Anglais, F-06100 Nice Tel: 868156
President: Louis Gautier-Vignal (of The Society for Dantesque Studies)

Société d'Histoire littéraire de la France, 14 rue de l'Industrie, F-75013 Paris
French Literary History Association
President: R Pomeau
Publications: Revue d'Histoire littéraire de la France (alternate months); *Bibliographie de la Littérature française* (annually)

Société des anciens Textes Français*, 19 rue de la Sorbonne, F-75005 Paris
Society of Ancient French Texts
Sale of Publications from Ed A and J Picard (qv)
General Secretary: Professor J Monfrin

Société des Gens de Lettres*, Hôtel de Massa, 38 rue du Faubourg St Jacques, F-75014 Paris

110 FRANCE

Society of Men and Women of Letters
General Secretary: François Caradec

Société des Poètes français*, 38 rue du Faubourg St Jacques, F-75014 Paris
Secretary-General: Roland le Cordier;
Assistant Secretary-General: Brigitte Level
Publication: Bulletin Trimestriel

Société du Vieux Montmartre, see Académie des Lettres et des Arts

Syndicat des Critiques littéraires, 58 rue Claude Bernard, F-75005 Paris
Union of Literary Critics
Secretary: R André
Publication: Bulletin du Syndicat (quarterly)

Union des Ecrivains et Artistes latins*, 11 rue de l'Estrapade, F-75005 Paris
Association of Latin Writers and Artists
Secretary: Mr Decremps
Publications: France latine and books in Langue d'Oc

Literary Periodicals

Bulletin critique du livre français, Association pour la Diffusion de la Pensée Française, 9 rue Anatole de la Forge, F-75017 Paris

Bulletin des Lettres (Literary Report); review of criticism and of literary and bibliophilic information, Librairie Lardanchet, 10 rue du Président-Carnot, F-69002 Lyon

Critique (Criticism); general review of publications in France and abroad, Editions de Minuit, 7 rue Bernard Palissy, F-75006 Paris

Figaro littéraire (Literary Figaro), 14 Rond-Point des Champs-Elysées, Paris 8e

Information littéraire (Literary News), Editions J-B Baillière, 19 rue Hautefeuille, F-75006 Paris cedex 06

Lecture et Tradition (Reading and Tradition), Association pour la Diffusion de la Pensée Française, 9 rue Anatole de la Forge, F-75017 Paris

Lettres françaises (French Literature), 5 rue du Faubourg Poissonnière, Paris 9e

Lettres nouvelles (New Literature); literary review, 19 rue Aurelie, F-75007 Paris

Littérature (Literature), Larousse, 17 rue du Montparnasse, F-75280 Paris cedex 06

Magazine littéraire (Literary Magazine), Magazine-Expansion, 40 rue des Sts-Pères, Paris 7e

Nouvelles littéraires, Arts, Sciences, Spectacles (News of Literature, the Arts, Sciences, Entertainments), 146 rue Montmartre, Paris 2e

Parler (To Speak); literary review, Galerie 'Parti-Pris', 4 rue Alexandre Ier du Yougoslavie, Grenoble

Passerelle (Footbridge); literary review, Pierre Bearn, 60 rue Monsieur le Prince, F-75006 Paris

Quinzaine littéraire (Literary Fortnightly), 43 rue du Temple, F-75004 Paris 4

Revue de Littérature comparée (Review of Comparative Literature) (text in English, French, German, Italian and Spanish), Librairie Marcel Didier SA, 15 rue Cujas, F-75005 Paris

Strophes; literary review, Jean Fremon, 9 rue de Belfort, F-9200 Asnières

Literary Prizes

Academy of Thirteen Prize
Known as 'Prix le Boisson' and given for a work of prose or poetry. Sixteen bottles of famous wine. Awarded annually. Enquiries to Academy of Thirteen, 166 rue de la Burgonce, Niort, Deux-Sèvres

Francois-Joseph **Audiffred** Prize*
For a published work best qualified to inspire love of virtue, and to discourage egoism and envy; or to instil patriotism. Enquiries to Academy of Moral and Political Sciences, Institut de France, 23 quai de Conti, F-75006 Paris

Aujourd'hui Prize
For a historical or contemporary work on politics. Awarded annually. Enquiries to Secretariat, 12 rue du Quatre Septembre, F-75002 Paris

Joseph **Autran** Prize*
Awarded to a poet for the whole of his work. Enquiries to Société des Poètes Français, 38 rue du Faubourg St Jacques, F-75014 Paris

René **Bardet** Prize*
For a poetic work. Awarded every two years. Enquiries to French Academy, Institut de France, 23 quai de Conti, F-75006 Paris

André **Barre** Prize*
For the work with the most original thinking and clearest style. Enquiries to French Academy, Institut de France, 23 quai de Conti, F-75006 Paris

Alice Louis **Barthou** Prize*
To a woman of letters. For one work or all of her work. Awarded annually. Enquiries to French Academy, Institut de France, 23 quai de Conti, F-75006 Paris

Louis **Barthou** Prize*
To a writer whose work or life has served the best interests of France. Awarded annually. Enquiries to French Academy, Institut de France, 23 quai de Conti, F-75006 Paris

Max **Barthou** Prize*
To a writer under 30 years of age whose talent has been proven or who has shown great promise. Awarded annually. Enquiries to French Academy, Institut de France, 23 quai de Conti, F-75006 Paris

Charles **Blanc** Prize*
For a written work, preferably treating issues in art. Awarded annually. Enquiries to French Academy, Institut de France, 23 quai de Conti, F-75006 Paris

Emile **Blémont** Prize*
For poetry inspired by France or one of its regions. Monetary prize of 100 francs. Awarded annually. Enquiries to Maison de Poésie, 11 bis rue Ballu, F-75009 Paris

Pascal **Bonetti** Grand Prize*
Award of 1,000 francs for a poetic work of high quality, classical structure and lofty sentiments. Enquiries to Société des Poètes Français, 38 rue du Faubourg St Jacques, F-75014 Paris

Bordin Prize*
To encourage superior literature. Awarded annually. Enquiries to French Academy, Institut de France, 23 quai de Conti, F-75006 Paris

Broquette-Gonin Grand Prize*
To the author of a philosophical, political or literary work, inspiring the love of truth, beauty and virtue. Awarded annually. Enquiries to French Academy, Institut de France, 23 quai de Conti, F-75006 Paris

Louis **Castex** Prize*
For literary works such as reminiscences of important voyages or explorations. Works on discoveries in archaeology and ethnology are also considered. Awarded annually. Enquiries to French Academy, Institut de France, 23 quai de Conti, F-75006 Paris

Hercule **Catenacci** Prize*
To encourage the publication of de luxe illustrated books of poetry, literature, history, archaeology or music. Awarded annually. Enquiries to French Academy, Institut de France, 23 quai de Conti, F-75006 Paris

Chateauneuf-du-Pape Grand Prize
Instituted by the town of Chateauneuf-du-Pape and other cities in the same renowned area. Awarded every two years for a poetic work which, irrespective of subject, appears most deserving by virtue of its formal purity and lofty sentiments. 1,000 francs. Solely for a young poet. Enquiries to Société des Poètes Français, 38 rue du Faubourg St Jacques, F-75014 Paris

Honoré **Chavée** Prize*
To encourage work in linguistics and in particular research on romance languages. Awarded biennially. Enquiries to Academie des Inscriptions et Belles-Lettres, Institut de France, 23 quai de Conti, F-75006 Paris

Combat Prize*
For a published or unpublished novel. Awarded annually. Enquiries to Combat Newspaper, 18 rue du Croissant, F-75002 Paris

François **Coppée** Prize*
For the work of a poet, preferably just beginning his career. Awarded every two years. Enquiries to French Academy, Institut de France, 23 quai de Conti, F-75006 Paris

Courteline Prize*
For best humorous novel of the year by an author over 50. Awarded annually. Enquiries to Société de Gens de Lettres, Hotel de Massa, 38 rue du Faubourg St-Jacques, F-75014

Constant **Dauguet** Endowment*
To the author of the best work on morals, particularly from the Catholic point of view. Awarded annually. Enquiries to French Academy, Institut de France, 23 quai de Conti, F-75006 Paris

Albert **Dauzat** Prize*
Awarded for a poetic work extolling animals. Enquiries to Société des Poètes Français, 38 rue du Faubourg St Jacques, F-75014 Paris

Eve **Delacroix** Prize*
For a literary work, essay or novel expressing human dignity and responsibility of the writer to society. 5,000 francs. Awarded annually. Enquiries to Secretariat, 56 ave Foch, F-75016 Paris

Deldebat de Gonzalva Prize*
Given since 1941 (except 1948) to a small body of poems classical in form and noble in inspiration. Enquiries to Société des Poètes français, 38 rue du Faubourg St Jacques, F-75014 Paris

D'Erlanger Prize*
Given since 1921 for poem, 150 lines maximum, written by someone who has served in front line of combat. Enquiries to Société des Poètes français, 38 rue du Faubourg St Jacques, F-75014 Paris

Marceline **Desbordes-Valmore** Prize*
Founded 1937. To a member poetess in whom personality and talent are fully developed. Enquiries to Société des Poètes français, 38 rue du Faubourg St Jacques, F-75014 Paris

Deux Magots Prize*
For an avant-garde book by a young writer. Awarded annually. Enquiries to Café des Deux Magots, pl St-Germain-des-Prés, Paris

Dumas-Millier Prize*
To a writer over 45 whose work will be an honour to the French language and will contribute to the dissemination of French thought. Enquiries to French Academy, Institut de France, 23 quai de Conti, F-75006 Paris

Alfred **Dutens** Prize*
For the most useful work on linguistics. Awarded every ten years. Enquiries to Académie des Inscriptions et Belles Lettres, Institut de France, 23 quai de Conti, F-75270 Paris

Fabien Prize*
To the author who has made the best suggestions for improving the moral and material position of the largest class. Awarded annually. Enquiries to French Academy, Institut de France, 23 quai de Conti, F-75006 Paris

Fantasia Prize, see Jeune France Prize

Jules **Favre** Prize*
For a literary work by a woman, poetry or prose, dealing with moral, educational, philogical or historical questions. Awarded every two years. Enquiries to French Academy, Institut de France, 23 quai de Conti, F-75006 Paris

Fémina Prize*
Founded in 1904 by review 'Femina' to encourage writing and draw women of letters closer together. A jury of women of letters meets in Paris each December to select a literary work of imagination written in French, by man or woman, prose or poetry. 5,000 francs. Awarded annually. Enquiries to Secretary-General, 79 blvd St-Germain, F-75006 Paris

Fénéon Prize*
For outstanding published work of any kind by an author over 35. Awarded annually. Enquiries to Fénéon Foundation, 10 pl du Panthéon, F-75005 Paris

Jean **Finot** Prize*
For a work of a humanitarian social trend. Awarded every two years. Enquiries to Academy of Moral and Political Sciences, Institut de France, 23 quai de Conti, F-75006 Paris

Paul **Flat** Prize*
To the best critical work and the best novel published by a young writer (between 30 and 40 years of age). Awarded annually. Enquiries to French Academy, Institut de France, 23 quai de Conti, F-75006 Paris

Ernest **Fleury** Prize*
Instituted by Marthe-Claire Fleury in memory of her father, the poet Ernest Fleury. It is awarded for a work of quality, and of a high order of spirituality. Enquiries to Société des Poètes Français, 38 rue du Faubourg St Jacques, F-75014 Paris

Marshal **Foch** Prize*
For a book on the nation's defence by an officer, engineer, scholar or philosopher. Awarded biennially. Enquiries to French Academy, Institut de France, 23 quai de Conti, F-75006 Paris

Pascal **Fortuny** Prize*
To the author of a poem of 200 lines or less, preferably written in the classical form. Awarded annually. Enquiries to French Academy, Institut de France, 23 quai de Conti, F-75006 Paris

Fouraignan Prize*
Created in 1914 for volume of poems in 18th century style, inspired by current events. Enquiries to Société des Poètes Français, 38 rue du Faubourg St Jacques, F-75014 Paris

French Catholic Grand Prize for Literature*
For a recent book or the sum of the work of a Catholic writer. Awarded annually. Enquiries to 11 rue Pachot-Laine, F-93190 Livry-Gargan

French Grand Prize for Humour*
For the best humorous writing published during the year, preferably a novel. Awarded annually by the Academy of Humour. Enquiries to Society of Dramatic Authors and Composers, 11 bis rue Ballu, F-75009 Paris

Gegner Prize*
To a philosopher-writer whose works contribute to the science of philosophy. Awarded annually. Enquiries to Academy of Moral and Political Sciences, Institut de France, 23 quai de Conti, F-75006 Paris

Félix **Georges** Prize*
Created in 1949 to honour a poem in classical form. Enquiries to Société des Poètes français, 38 rue du Faubourg St Jacques, F-75014 Paris

Giles Prize*
For a work on China, Japan or the Far East. Awarded every two years to a French national only. Enquiries to Académie des Inscriptions et Belles Lettres, Institut de France, 23 quai de Conti, F-75270 Paris

Golden Feather of the 'Figaro littéraire*
For a novel by someone 'forgotten' by the other prize commissions. Awarded annually. Enquiries to 'Figaro littéraire', 14 Rond Point des Champs Elysées, F-75008 Paris

Goncourt Prize
Founded by J and E de Goncourt, 21 December 1903, the annual prize honours a prose work by a younger writer with originality of spirit and form. The novel is the preferred medium. The award is the same as when the prize was originated, 50 francs. In 1979 the prize was awarded to Antonine Maillet, for *Pélagie-la-Charrette* (Grasset). Enquiries to Académie Goncourt, Armand Lanoux, 7 route de Malnoue, F-77420 Champs du Marne

Grand Franco-Belgian Literary Prize*
Established 1956. For the sum of work of a Belgian author written in the French language, free from any political, religious or philosophical bias. Monetary prize of 2,000 French francs. Awarded annually. Enquiries to Association des Ecrivains d'Expression francaise de la Mer et de l'Outre-Mer (AEFMOM), 41 rue de la Bienfaisance, Paris 8, France

Grand Prize for Literature*
To a prose-writer or poet for one or more works showing inspiration and style. 10,000 francs. Awarded annually. Enquiries to French Academy, Institut de France, 23 quai de Conti, F-75006 Paris

Grand Prize for Poetry Criticism*
Awarded for a work or work of poetic criticism or exegesis. Enquiries to Société des Poètes Français, 38 rue du Faubourg St Jacques, F-75014 Paris

Grand Prize of French Poets*
Given since 1936. Enquiries to Société des Poètes français, 38 rue du Faubourg St Jacques, F-75014 Paris

Edmond **Haraucourt** Prize*
Replaces the J-M Renaitour Prize. Awarded annually for a complete poetic work, preferably in classical form. Enquiries to Société des Poètes Français, 38 rue du Faubourg St Jacques, F-75014 Paris

Marie **Havez-Planque** Prize*
One year for a collection of stories or news stories or for a psychological novel, the following year for a collection of classical poetry. Preferably to an author who has not yet been published. Awarded annually. Enquiries to French Academy, Institut de France, 23 quai de Conti, F-75006 Paris

Hermes Prize*
To a young writer who is publishing his first novel. 2,000 francs. Awarded annually. Enquiries to Higher School of Commerce of Paris, 79 ave de la République, F-75011 Paris

Emile **Hinzelin** Prize*
For a volume of verse or a play in verse following the rules of French prosody, and showing the author's love for France. Awarded annually. Enquiries to French Academy, Institut de France, 23 quai de Conti, F-75006 Paris

Clovis **Hugues** Prize*
Awarded to a poet whose work is inspired by the same sentiments of social brotherhood as moved Clovis Hugues. Enquiries to Société des Poètes Français, 38 rue du Faubourg St Jacques, F-75014 Paris

Interallié Prize
Awarded since 1930 for a high quality novel, preferably written by a journalist. Awarded annually. The winner for 1979 was François Cavanna for *Les Russkoffs*. Enquiries to Roger Giron (General Secretary), 72 blvd de La Tour-Maubourg, F-75007 Paris

Jean-Christophe Prize
For poetry, preferably of classical form. Offered by Mme Alice Cluchier in memory of the young tragedian, her son. Awarded to young poet for manuscript of 10 poems, judged likely to inspire love of art and beauty and having fidelity of recollection. Enquiries to Société des Poètes français, 38 rue du Faubourg St Jacques F-75014 Paris

Jeune France Prize
For the best unpublished book for young people. The book can cover any field. Awarded every two years. Enquiries to Les Editions Magnard Sàrl, 122 blvd Saint-Germain, F-75279 Paris cedex 06

Jeunesse et Poésie Prize
Awarded annually to a young poet. The 1979 winner was Catherine Terrand. Enquiries to L'Amitié par le Livre, F-25310, Blamont

Juteau-Duvigneaux Prize*
For works on morality, especially from the Catholic point of view. Awarded annually. Enquiries to French Academy, Institut de France, 23 quai de Conti, F-75006 Paris

La Fontaine Prize*
For a moral literary work. Awarded biennially. Enquiries to French Academy, Institut de France, 23 quai de Conti, F-75006 Paris

Paul **Labbé-Vauquelin** Prize*
Founded in 1924, and accorded to a collection of reflective poetry regionally inspired. Enquiries to Société des Poètes français, 38 rue du Faubourg St Jacques, F-75014 Paris

Georges **Lafenestre** Prize*
Given since 1938, it was founded by the family of Georges Lafenestre on the occasion of the poet's centenary and goes to an unpublished poem of high inspiration and classical form, 150 lines maximum. Enquiries to Société des Poètes français, 38 rue du Faubourg St Jacques, F-75014 Paris

Lambert Prize*
To men of letters or their widows (if they deserve public recognition). Awarded annually. Enquiries to French Academy, Institut de France, 23 quai de Conti, F-75006 Paris

Langlois Prize*
For the best translation in verse or prose of a Greek, Latin or other foreign work into the French language. Awarded annually. Enquiries to French Academy, Institut de France, 23 quai de Conti, F-75006 Paris

Eugène **Le Moël** Prize*
Founded in 1936 for a poem in any genre, but preferably inspired by Eugène Le Moël. Enquiries to Société des Poètes français, 38 rue de Faubourg St Jacques, F-75014 Paris

Sébastien-Charles **Leconte** Prize*
Given since 1935 to a poem of noble inspiration and strictly classical form, 150 line maximum. Enquiries to Société des Poètes français, 38 rue du Faubourg St Jacques, F-75014 Paris

Van **Lerberghe** Prize*
Founded in 1957 for French expression in poetry. 100 francs. Awarded annually. Enquiries to Maison de Poésie, 11 bis rue Ballu, F-75009 Paris

Literary Critics' Grand Prize
For the best work of literary criticism or literary history. Established 1959. 3,000 francs, awarded annually. Enquiries to Association of Literary Critics, 58 rue Claude Bernard, F-75005 Paris

Literary Prize of the Resistance
For a work contributing to the history and spirit of the Resistance. 10,000 francs. Awarded annually by the Resistance Action Committee. The 1979 prize was awarded to André Diligent for *Un Cheminot sans Importance*. Enquiries to Secretariat, 10 rue de Charenton, F-75012 Paris

Paul **Lofler** Prize*
Replaced the prize for the Sonnet in 1963. For the best regulated sonnet. Enquiries to Société des Poètes français, 38 rue du Faubourg St Jacques, F-75014 Paris

Jean **Mace** Prize*
For works of fiction or nonfiction either as published books or as manuscripts for readers aged fifteen to eighteen. Awarded annually. Enquiries to French Education League, 3 rue Recamier, F-75007 Paris

Maille-Latour-Landry Prize*
To a young writer who should be encouraged to follow a literary career. Awarded biennially. Enquiries to French Academy, Institut de France, 23 quai de Conti, F-75006 Paris

Maisondieu Prize*
To the author or founder of a work contributing to the betterment of the working classes. Awarded every two years. Enquiries to Academy of Moral and Political Sciences, Institut de France, 23 quai de Conti, F-75006 Paris

Fernand **Mazarde** Prize*
For criticism of poetry or a critical edition of poets or chronicle of poetry in reviews or publications. Created in 1955. Enquiries to Maison de Poésie, 11 bis rue Ballu, F-75009 Paris

Médicis Prize*
Awarded to an avant-garde novel, story or collection whose publication has not been accompanied by the celebrity or fame the author's talent deserves. Founded in 1958. Enquiries to 20 rue Cortot, F-75108 Paris

Narcisse **Michaut** Prize*
For the best piece of French literature. Awarded biennially. Enquiries to French Academy, Institut de France, 23 quai de Conti, F-75006 Paris

Louis P **Miller** Prize*
For works furthering the love of moral virtue, in particular remembrance and gratitude. Awarded annually. Enquiries to French Academy, Institut de France, 23 quai de Conti, F-75006 Paris

Marcelle **Millier** Prize*
To a female writer over 45 whose work will be an honour to French literature. Enquiries to French Academy, Institut de France, 23 quai de Conti, F-75006 Paris

Charles **Monselet** Prize*
For a poetical work on the glory of French cuisine. Founded in 1954. Enquiries to Société des Poètes français, 38 rue du Faubourg St Jacques, F-75104 Paris

Montyon Prize*
For literary works of high moral character. Awarded annually, Enquiries to French Academy, Institut de France, 23 quai de Conti, F-75006 Paris

National Grand Prize of Letters
To the French writer who has contributed most to French literature. 20,000 francs. Awarded annually. Enquiries to French Ministry of Cultural Affairs, Centre National des Lettres, 6 rue Dufrenoy, F-75116 Paris

Alfred **Née** Prize*
For a work showing originality of thought and style. Awarded annually. Enquiries to French Academy, Institut de France, 23 quai de Conti, F-75006 Paris

Novel Prize*
To a young prose-writer for an inspirational imaginative work. 20,000 francs. Awarded annually. Enquiries to French Academy, Institut de France, 23 quai de Conti, F-75006 Paris

Paris Grand Prize for Literature*
For different forms of literature such as novel, poetry, criticism, essay, history, philosophy. Awarded annually (each year for a different form). Enquiries to Paris City Council, Hôtel de Ville, F-75004 Paris

Paris Prize*
For a novel. Awarded annually. Enquiries to Academy of Letters and Arts, c/o Musée de Montmartre, 17 rue St-Vincent, F-75018 Paris

Petitdidier Prize*
To poets under 40, 300 francs. Awarded annually. Enquiries to Maison de Poésie, 11 bis rue Ballu, F-75009 Paris

De **Pimodan** Prize*
Given since 1926 to regional poet celebrating his land. Enquiries to Société des Poètes français, 38 rue du Faubourg St Jacques, F-75014 Paris

Charles **Pitou** Prize*
Founded 1928, reserved for poem in strictly classical form celebrating a French province, preferably Normandy. Enquiries to Société des Poètes français, 38 rue du Faubourg St Jacques, F-75014 Paris

Raymond **Poincaré** Prize*
For a literary work which creates a favourable climate for the army. Awarded to officers of the French army. 1,000 francs. Awarded annually. Enquiries to National Union of Reserve Officers, 17 ave de l'Opéra, F-75001 Paris

Racine Prize*
For a work on the life or works of Racine, containing previously unknown documents or new views. Awarded annually. Enquiries to Racine Society, BP 49 Neuilly Principal 92204, Neuilly, Seine

J-M **Renaitour** Prize, replaced by Edmond Haraucourt Prize (qv)

Théophraste **Rénaudot** Prize*
Founded by Gaston Picard in 1926. Same conditions as for Goncourt (qv). Enquiries to 62 rue de Vaugirard, Paris

Léon **Riotor** Prize*
Founded 1953, and honours a critical essay or poetical story. 100 francs. Awarded annually. Enquiries to Maison de Poésie, 11 bis rue Ballu, F-75009 Paris

Roberge Prizes*
One year to a young poet who has published no more than two volumes of verse. The following year to a young author who has published no more than two novels. Enquiries to French Academy, Institut de France, 23 quai de Conti, F-75006 Paris

Roucoules Foundation Grand Prize for Poetry*
10,000 francs. Awarded annually. Enquiries to French Academy, Institut de France, 23 quai de Conti, F-75006 Paris

Saintour Prize*
For works (lexicons, grammars, editions of criticism, commentaries, etc) on the study of the French language, in particular from the 16th century to the present. Awarded annually. Enquiries to French Academy, Institut de France, 23 quai de Conti, F-75006 Paris

Sobrier-Arnould Prize*
To the authors of the two best works in moral literature which are instructive to youth. Awarded annually. Enquiries to French Academy, Institut de France, 23 quai de Conti, F-75006 Paris

Paul **Teissonnière** Prize*
For the best liberal work (printed or manuscript) on a moral, philosophical or religious subject. Enquiries to French Academy, Institut de France, 23 quai de Conti, F-75006 Paris

Lucien **Tisserand** Prize*
To a novelist between 40 and 50 years of age who has proved his talent. Awarded annually. Enquiries to French Academy, Institut de France, 23 quai de Conti, F-75006 Paris

Maurice **Trubert** Prize*
For a prose or verse work taking into account classical traditions and presenting morality from a Catholic point of view. Author must be under 30. Awarded biennially. Enquiries to French Academy, Institut de France, 23 quai de Conti, F-75006 Paris

Antony **Valabrègue** Prize*
To a young poet who has published one volume of verse. Awarded biennially. Enquiries to French Academy, Institut de France, 23 quai de Conti, F-75006 Paris

Valentine Abraham **Verlain** Prize*
To a woman of letters or for a needy female artist. Awarded annually. Enquiries to French Academy, Institut de France, 23 quai de Conti, F-75006 Paris

Paul **Verlaine** Prize*
Founded 1950 for all kinds of poetry. 100 francs. Awarded annually. Enquiries to Maison de Poésie, 11 bis rue Ballu, F-75009 Paris

Gabriel **Vicaire** Prize*
Founded 1948 for traditional poetry. 100 francs. Awarded annually. Enquiries to Maison de Poésie, 11 bis rue Ballu, F-75009 Paris

Claire **Virenque** Prize*
To young authors. One year for a collection of poems, the next for a novel or biography showing Christian inspiration. Enquiries to French Academy, Institut de France, 23 quai de Conti, F-75006 Paris

Volney Prize*
For a work in comparative philology. Enquiries to Académie des Inscriptions et Belles-Lettres, Institut de France, 23 quai de Conti, F-75006 Paris

J J **Weiss** Prize*
For a prose work in the purest classic style on travel, literature, literary or dramatic criticism or politics. Awarded every two years. Enquiries to French Academy, Institut de France, 23 quai de Conti, F-75006 Paris

Valentine de **Wolmar** Prize*
For the most beautiful novel or collection of poetry. Awarded annually. Enquiries to French Academy, Institut de France, 23 quai de Conti, F-75006 Paris

Translation Agencies and Associations

Société française des Traducteurs (French Union of Translators), 1 rue de Courcelles, F-75008 Paris

French Guiana

General Information

Language: French
Religion: Roman Catholic
Population: 66,000
Literacy Rate (1967): 73.9%
Bank Hours: 0700-1130, 1400-1600 Monday-Friday
Shop Hours: 0800-1300, 1500-1800 Monday-Friday
Currency: French currency
Export/Import Information: Overseas department of France which is a member of the European Economic Community. Tariff as for France. See France for domiciliation of documents. No import licences required. Same exchange restrictions as France.
Copyright: Berne, UCC (see International Section)

Major Booksellers

Mme **Beaufort***, 16 rue du Lieutenant-Brassé, BP 505, Cayenne Tel: 98

La **Boutique** Bleue*, ave Pasteur, BP 243, Cayenne

Emilio **Gratien***, 25 ave du Général de Gaulle, Cayenne Tel: 280

Librairie-Papeterie Universelle*, 26 rue Lallouette, Cayenne Tel: 240

Major Libraries

Bibliothèque **Franconie***, 97300 Cayenne

Office de la Recherche Scientifique et Technique Outre-Mer*, Centre ORSTOM de Cayenne, Bibliothèque, BP 165, Cayenne
Office of Scientific and Technical Research Overseas

Literary Associations and Societies

Association des Amis du Livre (Association of Book Lovers)*, 97300 Cayenne

French Polynesia

General Information

Language: French is the commercial language
Religion: Roman Catholic
Population: 146,000
Literacy Rate (1962): 94.5%
Bank Hours: 0900-1100, 1400-1600 Monday-Friday; 0900-1100, 1400-1500 Saturday
Shop Hours: 0730-1100, 1330-1700 Monday-Friday; 0730-1130 Saturday
Currency: 100 centimes = 1 franc CFP
Export/Import Information: No tariff on books except 8% customs duty on children's picture books; advertising matter subject to 8% customs duty, 5% import duty, although catalogues generally considered printed books. Advertising subject to 20 francs per unit Statistical Tax. Miscellaneous tax of 2% of customs value on books and advertising. No import licence required. Exchange controls

Publishers

Les Editions du **Pacifique**, 10 ave Bruat, BP 1722, Papeete, Tahiti Tel: 26643 Telex: 293 fp tahiti
Man Dir: Didier Millet
Subjects: Travel Books, Natural Science (tropical environment), History, Nonfiction, Gift Books
1978: 12 titles (figures cover publications in both France and French Polynesia)
Founded: 1971
ISBN Publisher's Prefix: 2-85700

Major Booksellers

Librairie **Au Ping-Pong***, 6 rue du Commandant-Destremeau, Papeete, Tahiti Tel: 133

Librairie **Hachette Pacifique SA**, 10 ave Bruat, BP 334, Papeete, Tahiti Tel: 25610 Telex: Hachpac 293 FP
General Manager: Maurice Vasseur
Parent Company: Librairie Hachette, France (qv)
The following bookshops in French Polynesia are now under the management of Librairie Hachette Pacifique SA: Hachette Pacifique Bruat, Quartier-Latin, Hachette Vaïma, Kiosque Vaïma

La Boutique R **Klima**, La Boutique, BP 31, pl Notre-Dame, Papeete, Tahiti
Manager: Manuella Luciani

Librairie **Quartier-Latin**
Now under the Management of Librairie Hachette Pacifique SA (qv)

Librairie du **Sagittaire**
Now under the Management of Librairie Hachette Pacifique (qv)

Gabon

General Information

Language: French
Religion: About half Roman Catholic and half animist
Population: 538,000
Literacy Rate (1960-61): 14.8%
Currency: CFA franc
Export/Import Information: Member of the Customs and Economic Union of Central Africa. No tariff on books; 7.5% fiscal, 30% customs, 10% VAT, 5% tax turnover on advertising matter. Import licence required for all imports valued at 500,000 CFA francs or more
Copyright: Berne (see International Section)

Publishers

Government Printer (Imprimerie Centrale d'Afrique)*, BP 154, Libreville

Saint-Joseph*, BP 58, Libreville

Major Booksellers

Centre de Littérature Evangélique*, BP 206, Oyem

Librairie **Hachette***, BP 121, Libreville Tel: 733131 Telex: 5418 go

Librairie **Nouvelle***, BP 612, Libreville Tel: 3616

Librairie **Sogalivre***, BP 50, Port-Gentil Tel: 52319

Major Libraries

Archives et Bibliothèque nationale (National Library and Archives)*, BP 1188, Libreville Tel: 32543

Centre culturel américain*, Bibliothèque, BP 2237, Libreville Tel: 721558/722161

Centre culturel français St-Exupéry*, Bibliothèque, BP 2103, Libreville Tel: 721120

Centre **Bibliotheque** d'Information*, BP 3127, Libreville Tel: 21115

Collège Jésus Marie*, Bibliothèque, BP 120, Bitam Tel: 277

Ecole normale supérieure, Bibliothèque, BP 16030, Libreville
Teachers' Training College Library
Librarian: Miss M E Bouscarle

Institut polytechnique de l'Afrique centrale*, Bibliothèque, BP 1158, Libreville

Bibliothèque de l'**Université nationale** du Gabon*, BP 11132, Libreville Tel: 32506

Bibliothèque Centrale de l'**Université Omar Bongo**, BP 13131, Libreville Tel: 732956, 732979
Central Library of the Omar Bongo University, under the direction of the Ministry for Higher Teaching of Scientific Environmental Research and Nature Protection
Dir: Jean Gregoire Aboghe-Obyan
Publications: Liste des nouvelles acquisitions (six-monthly); *Liste des périodiques en cours* (annual); *Inventaire du fonds documentaire, par discipline* (annual)

The Gambia

General Information

Language: English
Religion: Muslim
Population: 569,000
Bank Hours: 0800-1300 Monday-Friday; 0800-1100 Saturday
Shop Hours: 0800-1200, 1400-1700 Monday-Thursday; 0800-1200, 1500-1700 Friday; 0800-1200 Saturday
Currency: 100 butut = 1 dalasi
Export/Import Information: No tariff on books; 25% on some advertising matter. 1% Import Tax on all. No import licence required. National Trading Corporation has no monopoly. Exchange controls

Publishers

The **Government Press**, Banjul

Major Booksellers

Jeng's Bookshop*, PO Box 234, Banjul

The **Gambia** Methodist Bookshop Ltd, PO Box 203, Banjul Tel: 8179

Major Libraries

Gambia National Library, Ministry of Education Youth and Sports, PMB, Banjul Tel: 8312
Chief Librarian: Sally P C N'Jie

Yundum College Library*, Yundum

German Democratic Republic

General Information

Language: German
Religion: About 60% Protestant, 8% Roman Catholic
Population: 17 million
Bank Hours: Generally 0800-1600 Monday-Friday; open Saturday morning
Shop Hours: Vary. Generally 0900 or 1000-1800 or 1900 Monday-Friday; open part day Saturday
Currency: 100 pfennige = 1 DDR mark or ostmark
Export/Import Information: Foreign trade is a state monopoly; books imported and exported by Buchexport, Leninstr 16, Postfach 160, DDR-701 Leipzig. Import licences required and Foreign Trade Bank handles all payments. No advertising materials to be sent to private individuals; for preparation of advertising, contact Interwerbung GmbH, Berlin
Copyright: UCC, Berne (see International section)

Book Trade Organizations

Börsenverein der Deutschen Buchhändler zu Leipzig, Gerichtsweg 26, DDR-7010 Leipzig Tel: 293851 Cable Add: Buchbörse
Association of German Democratic Republic Publishers and Booksellers in Leipzig
Publications: Börsenblatt für den Deutschen Buchhandel

Buchexport — Volkseigener Aussenhandelsbetrieb der Deutschen Demokratischen Republik, Leninstr 16, Postfach 160, DDR-7010 Leipzig Tel: 7661 Telex: 051678
GDR Peoples' Export Undertaking
Publications: Nova, Wissen und Können, Buch der Zeit, Land und Leute, DDR Gesamtkatalog, DDR Periodica. (See individual entries under Book Trade Reference Books and Journals).
The state organization for foreign trade. These catalogues contain particulars of the entire range of GDR publications.

Ministerrat der Deutschen Demokratischen Republik, Ministerium für Kultur, Hauptverwaltung Verlage und Buchhandel*, DDR-108 Berlin 8, Clara-Zetkin-Str 90
Council of Ministers of the German Democratic Republic, Ministry of Culture, Main Department — Publishing and Bookselling

Book Trade Reference Books and Journals

Books

Adressbuch des Volksbuchhandels der Deutschen Demokratischen Republik (Directory of the People's Booksellers of the GDR), Volksbuchhandel der DDR, Zentrale Zeitung, DDR-701 Leipzig, Friedrich-Ebert-Str 25

Die Deutsche Demokratische Republik, ein Land des Buches (The German Democratic Republic, A Country of the Book), Association of German Publishers and Booksellers in Leipzig, Gerichtsweg 26, DDR-701 Leipzig

Deutsches Bücherverzeichnis (5-year German Book List), Deutsche Bücherei, Deutscher Platz, DDR-701 Leipzig

LKG Lagerkatalog (LKG Stock Catalogue), Leipziger Kommissions- und Grossbuchhandel, Leninstr 16, DDR-701 Leipzig

Schriftenreihen aus den Verlagen der Deutschen Demokratischen Republik (Series from the Publishers of the GDR), Buchexport, Leninstr 16, DDR-701 Leipzig

Titel-Information (Title-Information), Leipziger Komissions- und Grossbuchhandel, Leninstr 16, DDR-701 Leipzig

Verlage der Deutschen Demokratischen Republik (Publishers of the GDR), Association of German Publishers and Booksellers in Leipzig, Gerichtsweg 26, DDR-701 Leipzig

Journals

Beiträge zur Literaturkunde (Contributions to Literary Knowledge); bibliography of selected newspaper and periodical contributions, VEB, Bibliographisches Institut, Gerichtsweg 26, DDR-701 Leipzig

Bibliographie der Bibliographien (Bibliography of Bibliographies), Deutsche Bücherei, Deutscher Platz, DDR-701 Leipzig

Bibliographie der Übersetzungen deutschsprachiger Werke (Bibliography of Translations of German Language Works), Deutsche Bücherei, Deutscher Platz, DDR-701 Leipzig

Bibliographie fremdsprachiger Germanica (Bibliography of Germanics in Foreign Languages), Deutsche Bücherei, Deutscher Platz, DDR-701 Leipzig

Börsenblatt für den deutschen Buchhandel (German Book Trade Journal), Association of German Publishers and Booksellers in Leipzig, Gerichtsweg 26, DDR-701 Leipzig

Buch der Zeit (Books of the Day), (text in English and German), Buchexport, Leninstr 16, DDR-701 Leipzig

Bücher aus der DDR (Books from the German Democratic Republic) Lists of new books and reprint editions on German Language and Literature, German history and culture etc. pub by Buchexport, Leninstr 16, DDR-701 Leipzig. Published every 3 months

DDR Gesamtkatalog (German Democratic Republic Complete Catalogue), Buchexport (qv under Book Trade Organisations), Leninstr 16, DDR-701 Leipzig
A general catalogue in two vols, it covers all titles published in one year and appears annually, at the start of the following year

Deutsche National-Bibliographie (German National Bibliography), Deutsche Bücherei, Deutscher Platz, DDR-701 Leipzig

Informationsblatt (Information Sheet), Library Association of the German Democratic Republic, Hermann-Matern-Str 57, DDR-104 Berlin

Jahresverzeichnis der Verlagsschriften (Annual List of Publications), Deutsche Bücherei, Deutscher Platz, DDR-701 Leipzig

Nova; forthcoming books (table of contents and subtitles in English, German and Russian), Buchexport, Leninstr 16, DDR-701 Leipzig. Two issues per month

Selecta; titles immediately available from the publishers of the DDR, Buchexport, Leninstr 16, DDR-701 Leipzig

Wissen und Können (To Know and Be Able), Buchexport, Leninstr 16, DDR-701 Leipzig. A series of 26 Catalogues covering every branch of knowledge under the headings: I — Social Sciences; II — Art and Literature; III — Natural Sciences; IV — Technical Science/Engineering; V — Agriculture and Forestry, Veterinary Science; VI — Medicine. The Catalogues list all books under the particular subject selected which are available for sale, in print or in course of preparation.
Publication of each list is annual.

Publishers

Akademie-Verlag, Leipziger Str 3-4, Postfach 1233, DDR-1080 Berlin Tel: 22360 Cable Add: Akademie-Verlag Berlin Telex: 114420 averl dd
Subjects: History, Philosophy, Literature, History of Art, Archaeology, Ethnography, Oriental, Biology, Geology, Mathematics, Physics, Chemistry, Medicine, Languages, Economics; Periodicals
1979: 350 titles *Founded:* 1946

Aufbau-Verlag Berlin und Weimar, Französische Str 32, Postfach 1217, DDR-1080 Berlin Tel: 2202421 Cable Add: Aufbau Verlag Berlin Telex: Berlin 112527
Associate Company: Verlag Rütten und Loening, German Democratic Republic
Subjects: General Fiction, Library of World Literature, Belles Lettres, Literary Criticism, Paperbacks, Periodicals
Founded: 1945

Johann Ambrosius **Barth** Verlagsbuchhandlung, Salomonstr 18b, Postfach 109, DDR-701 Leipzig Tel: 295245 Cable Add: Barth Leipzig
Man Dir: Klaus Wiecke
Orders to: LKG VA 221, Postfach 520, DDR-701 Leipzig
Subjects: Medicine, Dentistry, Stomatology, Psychology, Natural Science, Chemistry, Astronomy, Physics; Periodicals, Publications of the German Academy of Naturalists, *Leopoldina*
1978: 42 titles *Founded:* 1780

VEB Verlag für **Bauwesen**, Französische Str 13-14, Postfach 1232, DDR-1080 Berlin Tel: 20410 Cable Add: Bauwesenverlag Telex: 112229 Trave
Man Dir: Siegfried Seeliger; *Editorial:* Siegfried Schikora; *Sales:* Franz Rautenstrauch; *Production:* Günter Langer; *Publicity:* Marion Thiele
Subjects: Civil Engineering, Architecture and Building Construction, Materials and Mechanics; 10 Periodicals
1978: 60 titles (Figures include reprints)
Founded: 1960

VEB **Bibliographisches Institut**, Gerichtsweg 26, Postfach 130, DDR-7010 Leipzig Tel: 7801 Cable Add: Biblio Leipzig Telex: 512773
Man Dir: Helmut Bähring
Associate Companies: VEB Verlag für Buch und Bibliothekswesen (qv); VEB Max Niemeyer Verlag (qv); VEB Verlag Enzyklopädie (qv); all at above address
Subjects: General Dictionaries, Reference, Biography, Bibliographies, German Language, Library Science, Documentation, Literature, Languages, Periodicals
Founded: 1826

Hermann **Böhlaus** Nachfolger, Meyerstr 50a, DDR-53 Weimar Tel: 2071 Cable Add: Böhlauverlag DDR-53 Weimar
Man Dir: Dr Leiva Petersen
Subjects: History of Law, Literature & Art, Critical Editions & Yearbooks, Medieval History
1978: 30 titles *Founded:* 1624

VEB **Breitkopf und Härtel** Musikverlag, Karlstr 10, Postfach 147, DDR-7010 Leipzig Tel: 7351 Cable Add: Breitkopfs
Man Dir: Dr Gunter Hempel; *Sales Dir:* Werner Hennig
Subjects: Music: Vocal and Instrumental Music, Biographies, Reference, Musicology
Founded: 1719

VEB F A **Brockhaus** Verlag, Leipzig, Salomonstr 17, DDR-7010 Leipzig
Subjects: Picture-books (relating to the German Democratic Republic and other countries), Travel Books, Popular Scientific History and Reportage, Scientific and Technical Reference
1979: 33 titles

VEB Verlag für **Buch- und Bibliothekswesen**, Gerichtsweg 26, Postfach 130, DDR-7010 Leipzig Tel: 7801 Telex: 512773
Man Dir: Helmut Bähring
Associate Companies: VEB Verlag Enzyklopädie (qv); VEB Bibliographisches Institut (qv); VEB Max Niemeyer Verlag (qv); all at above address
Subjects: Bibliography, Book Industry, Reference, Periodicals

VEB **Deutscher Landwirtschaftsverlag**, Reinhardtstr 14, DDR-104 Berlin
Subject: Agriculture (instructional texts)
1978: 80 titles

VEB **Deutscher Verlag der Wissenschaften**, Johannes-Dieckmann-Str 10, Postfach 1216, DDR-108 Berlin Tel: 22900 Cable Add: Devauwe Berlin Telex: 112063 dvw dd
Subjects: History, Philosophy, Psychology; General, Natural & Social Sciences; Physics, Chemistry, Mathematics
1978: 67 titles

VEB **Deutscher Verlag für Grundstoffindustrie***, Karl-Heine-Str 27, DDR-7031 Leipzig Tel: 44441 Cable Add: Grundstoffverlag Leipzig
The German Democratic Republic Publishing House for the Raw Material Industry
Subjects: Geological Sciences, Coal, Energy, Mining of Ores, Metallurgy, Potash, Chemistry and Chemical Process Technology; also Popular Scientific Literature, Periodicals

VEB **Deutscher Verlag für Musik**, Karlstr 10, Postfach 147, DDR-7010 Leipzig Tel: 7351 Cable Add: Demusica Leipzig
Man Dir: Dr Gunter Hempel; *Sales Dir:* Werner Hennig
Subjects: Music: Vocal and Instrumental Music, Reference, Biographies, Children's and Young Peoples' Books on Music, Musicology, Facsimilies, Musical Belles Lettres
Founded: 1954

Dieterich'sche Verlagsbuchhandlung*, Mottelerstr 8, Postfach 88, DDR-7022 Leipzig
Associate Companies: Insel-Verlag (qv); Gustav Kiepenhauer Verlag (qv); Paul List Verlag (qv)
Subjects: World literature in translation
1978: 3 titles

Dietz Verlag, Wallstr 76-79, Postfach 273, DDR-1020 Berlin Tel: 270301
Subjects: Social Science, Economics, Philosophy, Politics, History, Memoirs, Periodicals
Founded: 1946

VEB Verlag **Enzyklopädie**, Gerichtsweg 26, Postfach 130, DDR-7010 Leipzig Tel: 7801 Telex: 512773
Man Dir: Helmut Bähring
Associate Companies: VEB Bibliographisches Institut (qv); VEB Verlag für Buch und Bibliothekswesen (qv); VEB Max Niemeyer Verlag (qv); all at above address
Subjects: Languages, Dictionaries, Foreign Language Textbooks, Handbook on the German Democratic Republic
Founded: 1956

Eulenspiegel Verlag für Satir und Humor*, Kronenstr 73-74, Postfach 1239, DDR-108 Berlin Tel: 2202126
Deputy Manager: Kurt Noack
Associate Company: Verlag Das Neue Berlin (qv)
Subjects: Humorous Publications generally: Satire, Caricature, Cartoons
1978: 73 titles

Evangelische Verlagsanstalt GmbH, Krautstr 52, Postfach 114, DDR-1017 Berlin Tel: 2700131
Dirs: Olkr von Brueck, Dr Forck
Subjects: Christian History, Devotional, Biblical Exegesis, Christian Fiction and Poetry, Biography, Art Books, Music; also Calendars, Periodicals
1978: 135 titles *1979:* 103 titles *Founded:* 1946

VEB **Fachbuchverlag**, Karl-Heine-Str 16, Postfach 67, DDR-7031 Leipzig Tel: 44021 Cable Add: Fachbuch Leipzig Telex: 51451 d d
Man Dir: Siegfried Hoffmann
Subjects: General Knowledge, Popular Science, Basic Technologies, Specific texts on variety of industries (e.g. food, leather, textiles etc), Periodicals
1980: 100 titles *1981:* 110 (projected) titles
Founded: 1949

VEB Gustav **Fischer** Verlag, Jena, Villengang 2, Postfach 176, DDR-690 Jena Tel: Jena 27332 Cable Add: Fischerbuch Telex: 05886176
Parent Company: Volkseigene Verlage für Medizin und Biologie, Berlin, Jena, Leipzig
Associate Companies: VEB Georg Thieme (qv); VEB Verlag Volk und Gesundheit (qv)
Subjects: Medicine, Veterinary, Biology; Periodicals
1978: 72 titles *1979:* 65 titles *Founded:* 1878

VEB **Fotokinoverlag**, Karl-Heine-Str 16, Postfach 67, DDR-7031 Leipzig Tel: 44021
Man Dir: Siegfried Hoffmann
Subjects: Photography, Film, Periodicals
1980: 29 titles *1981:* 26 (projected) titles
Founded: 1957

Verlag für die **Frau**, Friedrich-Ebert-Str 76-78, Postfach 1005/1025, DDR-7010 Leipzig
Woman's Publishing House
Subjects: Fashion, Family, Domestic Science, Periodicals

Akademische Verlagsgesellschaft **Geest und Portig** KG, Sternwarten Str 8, Postfach 106, DDR-701 Leipzig Tel: 293158/59/297535 Cable Add: Akabuch Leipzig
Man Dir: Ing Heinz Kratz
Associate Company: BSB B G Teubner Verlagsgesellschaft (qv)
Subjects: Chemistry, Physics, Mathematics, Engineering, History of Science, Geo-Sciences, Electro-Technology
Founded: 1906

Altberliner Verlag Lucie **Groszer**, Neue Schönhauser Str 8, Postfach 44, DDR-102 Berlin Tel: 2826749
Dir: Lucie Groszer; *Editorial:* Alfred Könner
Subject: Children's Books from infant age upwards
1978: 18 titles *1979:* 18 titles *Founded:* 1945

VEB Hermann **Haack**, Justus-Perthes-Str 3/9, Postfach 274, DDR-58 Gotha/Leipzig Tel: 3872-3874 Cable Add: Geokarbt Gotha Telex: 618583 telex hago dd
Imprint: Haack Gotha
Subjects: Maps, Atlases, Geographic and Cartographic Publications, Periodicals

Henschelverlag Kunst und Gesellschaft*, Oranienburger Str 67-68, Postfach 220, DDR-104 Berlin Tel: 28790 Cable Add: Henschelverlag Berlin
Dir: K Mittelstädt
Subjects: General Fiction, Film, Theatre, Music, Art, Architecture, Periodicals

GERMAN DEMOCRATIC REPUBLIC

VEB Hinstorff Verlag, Kröpeliner Str 25, Postfach 11, DDR-2500 Rostock Tel: 34441
Subjects: Contemporary Literature of the DDR, German Language Literature in Series, Scandinavian Literature in Translation, Literature in Low German, Homeland Literature and Studies, Maritime Literature
1980: 30-40 titles *Founded:* 1831

VEB Friedrich Hofmeister Musikverlag, Karlstr 10, Postschließfach 147, DDR-7010 Leipzig Tel: 7351
Man Dir: Dr Gunter Hempel; *Sales Dir:* Werner Hennig
Subjects: Vocal and Instrumental Music, Song Books, Bibliographies, Yearbooks
Founded: 1807

Insel-Verlag Anton Kippenberg*, Mottelerstr 8, Postfach 88, DDR-7022 Leipzig Tel: 592356 and 52857
Associate Companies: Insel-Verlag issues a common catalogue with: Gustav Kiepenhauer Verlag (qv); Dieterich'sche Verlagsbuchhandlung (qv); Paul List Verlag (qv)
Subjects: Literature, Art, Facsimile Editions, Classics of World Literature in Translation
1978: 29 titles *Founded:* 1899

Verlag **Junge Welt**, Postfach 43, DDR-1026 Berlin (Located at: Mauerstr 39/40, DDR-108 Berlin) Tel: 22330
Man Dir: Manfred Rucht
Subjects: Juvenile, Education, Science, Technical, Periodicals
1979: 32 titles *Founded:* 1952

Gustav **Kiepenheuer** Verlag, Mottelerstr 8, Postfach 88, DDR-7022 Leipzig
Associate Companies: Dieterich'sche Verlagsbuchhandlung (qv); Insel-Verlag (qv); Paul List Verlag (qv)
Subjects: Foreign Classics in Translation, Foreign Folklore, Far Eastern Studies, Quality German Literature
1978: 20 titles *Founded:* 1909

Der **Kinderbuchverlag** Berlin, Behrenstr 40-41, Postfach 1225, DDR-108 Berlin
Subject: Juveniles

Koehler und Amelang (VOB), Hainstr 2, DDR-701 Leipzig Tel: 282379
Associate Company: Union Verlag Berlin (VOB) (qv)
Branch Off: Talstr 3, DDR-701 Leipzig Tel: 209519
Subjects: Cultural History, Art History, Biographical
1978: 8 titles *1979:* 7 titles

VEB Verlag der Kunst, Spenerstr 21, DDR-8019 Dresden Tel: 34486
Subjects: Fine Arts, Reproductions

Edition **Leipzig**, Verlag für Kunst und Wissenschaft, Karl-Liebknecht-Str 77, DDR-703 Leipzig Tel: 32445 Cable Add: Edileip
Man Dir: Elmar Faber; *Sales Dir:* Fritz Becker
Subjects: Art, History of Civilization, Science, Scientific & Bibliophile Reprints
Founded: 1960

Paul **List** Verlag*, Paul-List-Str 22, Postfach 1062, DDR-701 Leipzig Tel: 35424
Associate Companies: Dieterich'sche Verlagsbuchhandlung (qv); Insel-Verlag (qv); Gustav Kiepenheuer Verlag (qv)
Subjects: Foreign Literature in translation
Founded: 1894

VEB Militärverlag der DDR, Storkower Str 158, Postfach 46551, DDR-1055 Berlin Tel: 4300618 Telex: 112673 mv
Subjects: Books, paperbacks and periodicals on military subjects; military theory, politics, history, specialised literature; Popular Science; Fiction, Periodicals
Founded: 1956

Mitteldeutscher Verlag Halle-Leipzig*, Thälmannplatz 2, Postfach 295, DDR-401 Halle/Saale Tel: 8730
Man Dir: Dr Eberhard Günther
Subjects: General Fiction & Non-fiction, Collected Works, Poetry, Essays, Literary Criticism, Belles Lettres, Biography, Novels
1978: 112 titles *1979:* 117 titles *Founded:* 1946

Buchverlag Der **Morgen**, Johannes-Dieckmann-Str 47, DDR-108 Berlin Tel: 2202181
Man Dir: Dr Wolfgang Tenzler
Subjects: General Fiction, Belles Lettres, Poetry, Biography, Political Monographs
Founded: 1958

Verlag der **Nation**, Friedrichstr 113, Postfach 74, DDR-104 Berlin Tel: 2825826
Dir: Günter Hofé
Subjects: Publications of the National Democratic Party of Germany, Current Politics, Biographical, Illustrated Texts, Historical Fiction, Belles Lettres, Cultural; Paperback Series
1978: 64 titles *Founded:* 1948

Verlag das **Neue Berlin***, Kronenstr 73/74, Postfach 1239, DDR-108 Berlin Tel: 2202126 Cable Add: Neuesberlinbuch Berlin
Associate Company: Eulenspiegel Verlag (qv)
Subjects: Crime Literature, Adventure, Science Fiction
1978: 50 titles

Verlag **Neues Leben**, Behrenstr 40-41, Postfach 1223, DDR-1080 Berlin Tel: 2032765 Cable Add: Neuesleben Berlin
Man Dir: Rudolf Chowanetz
Subjects: General Fiction and Nonfiction; Juveniles, Science Fiction: Paperbacks
1978: 221 titles *Founded:* 1946

VEB Max **Niemeyer** Verlag*, Gerichtsweg 26, Postfach 130, DDR-701 Leipzig Tel: 7801 Telex: 51773
Man Dir: Helmut Baehring
Associate Companies: VEB Verlag Enzyklopädie (qv); VEB Bibliographisches Institut (qv); VEB Verlag für Buch und Bibliothekswesen (qv); all at above address
Subjects: Philology, University Textbooks, Protestant Theology, Literature, Languages; Periodicals
Founded: 1869

Prisma-Verlag Zenner und Gürchott, Leibnizstr 10, Postfach 1461, DDR-7010 Leipzig Tel: 281411
Man Dir: Klaus Zenner; *Publicity Dir:* Fritz Gürchott
Subjects: Archaeology, Art and Cultural History, Fine Illustrated Editions, Historical Novels: many Non-fiction books have texts in German, English and Russian
1978: 6 titles *1979:* 9 titles *Founded:* 1957

Verlag Philipp **Reclam** jun, Nonnenstr 38, DDR-7031 Leipzig Tel: 44501 Cable Add: Reclam Leipzig
Man Dir: Hans Marquardt; *Sales Dir:* Gottfried Berthold; *Publicity & Advertising Dir:* Doris Lietz
Subjects: Reclam's Universal Library (a paperback series covering Belles Lettres, Philosophy, History, Aesthetics, Music, Biography), Literature, Original Graphics (woodcuts, etchings, lithographs)
1978: 110 titles *1979:* 122 titles *Founded:* 1828

Verlag **Rütten und Loening** Berlin, see Aufbau Verlag

Sankt-Benno Verlag GmbH, Verlag für katholisches Schrifttum, Thüringer Str 1-3, Postfach 98 and 112, DDR-7033 Leipzig Tel: 44161
Catholic Literature Publishing House
General Managers: Prelate Hermann J Weisbender, Franz J Cordier
Subjects: Religion, Philosophy, Music, Catholic Literature in German and Latin Languages; Periodicals
1978: 78 titles

VEB E A **Seemann** Buch- und Kunstverlag, Jacobstr 6, Postfach 846, DDR-701 Leipzig Tel: 7736 Cable Add: Kunstsemann
Subjects: Art, Reference

Seven Seas Publishers, Glinkastr 13-15, DDR-108 Berlin Tel: 2202851 Cable Add: Sevenseasberlin
Man Dir: Kay Pankey
Parent Company: Verlag Volk und Welt (qv)
Subjects: General Fiction, Poetry, Biography, History, High quality Paperbacks (in English), Secondary Textbooks
Founded: 1957

Sportverlag, Neustädtische Kirchstr 15, Postfach 1218, DDR-1086 Berlin Tel: 2202651 Cable Add: Sportverlag Berlin-DDR
Subjects: Sport, How-to
Founded: 1947

Staatsverlag der Deutschen Demokratischen Republik, Otto Grotewohl Str 17, DDR-1080 Berlin Tel: 2372502 (Publicity); 2372516 (Export); 2372498 (Sales)
The official State Publishing Company of the German Democratic Republic
Subjects: History, Social & Political Theory, Economics, Law, International Relations, Government Publications; Periodicals

VEB Verlag **Technik**, Oranienburger Str 13-14, Postfach 293, DDR-1020 Berlin Tel: 28700 Cable Add: Technikverlag Berlin Telex: Berlin 0112228 techn dd
Subjects: Science, Mechanical, Electrical and Electronics Engineering, Control Engineering and Automation, Cybernetics, Technical Dictionaries in numerous languages, Reference, University Textbooks, Periodical (in English, *Monthly Technical Review*)
1978: 42 titles *1979:* 43 titles *Founded:* 1946

BSB B G **Teubner** Verlagsgesellschaft, Sternwartenstr 8, DDR-701 Leipzig Postfach 930 Tel: 293158/59 Cable Add: Teubnerianum Leipzig
Man Dir: Ing Heinz Kratz
Associate Company: Akademische Verlagsgesellschaft Geest und Portig KG (qv)
Subjects: Mathematics, Physics, History of Science, Geo-sciences, Building Technology, Philology, Greek and Latin Languages
Founded: 1811

VEB Georg **Thieme**, Leipzig*, Verlag für Medizin und Naturwissenschaften, Hainstr 17-19, DDR-701 Leipzig Cable Add: Buchthieme Telex: 051533
Trade Dept: Villengang 2, DDR-69 Jena
Associate Companies: VEB Gustav Fischer Verlag (qv); VEB Verlag Volk und Gesundheit (qv)
Subjects: Medicine, Bio-Science, Periodicals
1978: 22 titles *Founded:* 1886

Transpress, VEB Verlag für Verkehrswesen, Französische Str 13-14, Postfach 1235, DDR-108 Berlin Tel: 20410 Cable Add: transpress Berlin Telex: 112229 travedd
Man Dir: Paul Kaiser

Subjects: Transport and Traffic (Railways, Shipping, Motor Traffic, Aviation), Post and Telecommunications, Philately, Numismatics, Popular Science; Periodicals
1978: 91 titles *Founded:* 1960

Union Verlag Berlin VOB*, Charlottenstr 79, DDR-108 Berlin Tel: 2202711
Dir: Dr sc phil Hubert Faensen
Associate Company: Koehler & Amelang (VOB), Leipzig (qv)
Branch Off: Talstr 3, DDR-701 Leipzig
Subjects: Political Science, Christian Literature, Belles Lettres, Christian Art, History of Philosophy and Religion
1978: 40 titles

Urania-Verlag, Salomonstr 26-28, Postfach 969, DDR-701 Leipzig Tel: 7426
Branch Offs: Jena and Berlin
Subjects: Popular Science, Non-fiction, Cultural History, Hobbies; Periodicals
1978: 37 titles

VEB Verlag **Volk und Gesundheit**, Neue Grünstr 18, Postfach 53, DDR-102 Berlin Tel: 2000621 Cable Add: Volksgesundheit Telex: 0114488
Trade Dept: Villengang 2, DDR-69 Jena
Parent Company: Volkseigene Verlag für Medizin und Biologie, Berlin, Jena, Leipzig
Associate Companies: VEB Gustav Fischer Verlag (qv); VEB Georg Thieme (qv)
Subjects: Scholarship, Medicine
1978: 104 titles *1979:* 98 titles *Founded:* 1952

Verlag **Volk und Welt**, Glinkastr 13-15, DDR-108 Berlin Tel: 2202851 Cable Add: Volkwelt Berlin
Company is subtitled Verlag für internationale Literatur (Publishing House for international literature)
Man Dir: Jürgen Gruner
Subsidiary Company: Seven Seas Publishers (qv)
Subjects: General Fiction and Nonfiction of other countries, worldwide, in German translation: Poetry, Reportage; Periodicals
Book Club: buchklub 65
1978: 153 titles *Founded:* 1947

Volk und Wissen Volkseigener Verlag Berlin, Krausenstr 50, Am Spittelmarkt, DDR-1080 Berlin Tel: 20430 Cable Add: Volkwissen Berlin Telex: 112181 vowiv dd
Subjects: Schoolbooks, Pedagogy, Illustrated Instructional Material, Literary History, Sports Training
Founded: 1945

Verlag Die **Wirtschaft**, Am Friedrichshain 22, DDR-1055 Berlin Tel: 43870 Cable Add: wirtschaftsplan Berlin Telex: Berlin 0112448
Subjects: Management, Economics, Statistics, Periodicals

Z A Reprints, see Zentralantiquariat der DDR

Verlag **Zeit** im Bild*, Julian-Grimau-Allee 10, DDR-801 Dresden
Manager: H Zumpe
Subjects: Politics, Foreign Languages, Economics, Periodicals

Zentralantiquariat der DDR — Reprintabteilung (ZA Reprints)*, Talstr 29, Postfach 1080, DDR-701 Leipzig 1 Tel: 293641-43, 295808
The Reprint Department of the Central Antiquarian and Second Hand Book Dealers' Office of the German Democratic Republic
Subjects: Special Editions, Reprints (generally of specialized texts), especially Near Eastern/Babylonic Cuneiform and History of Crime Series
1978: 89 titles

Literary Agents

Büro für Urheberrechte*, Clara-Zetkin-Str 105, DDR-108 Berlin
Copyright Office, Authors' manuscripts and publishing rights are submitted in the DDR without agents, however agreements with individuals and firms outside the DDR must be sanctioned and handled by the above Büro

Book Clubs

buchclub 65, Glinkastr 13-15, DDR-1080 Berlin Tel: 220851
Owned by: Verlag Volk und Welt (Berlin)
Founded: 1965

Buchklub der Schüler*, Clara-Zetkin-Str 90, DDR-108 Berlin

Major Booksellers

Volksbuchhandlung **Haus** des Buches*, Ernst-Thälmann-str 29, DDR-8010 Dresden

Volksbuchhandlung Edwin **Hoernle***, Ernst-Thälmann-Str 13, DDR-20 Neubrandenburg

Volksbuchhandlung Alexander von **Humboldt**, Am Platz der Einheit, DDR-15 Potsdam Tel: 22539/23574
Manager: Friedrich Richter

Humboldt-Buchhandlung*, Bahnhofstr 1, DDR-9001 Karl-Marx-Stadt

Ulrich v **Hutten** Volksbuchhandlung*, Karl-Marx Str 184, DDR-12 Frankfurt/Oder

Keysersche Buchhandlung*, Anger 11, DDR-50 Erfurt

Volksbuchhandlung Robert **Koch**, Universitätsring 7 and 10, DDR-40 Halle

L K G, see Leipziger Kommissions- und Grossbuchhandel

Leibniz-Volksbuchhandlung, Otto-Grotewohl-Str 3, DDR-27 Schwerin

Leipziger Kommissions- und Grossbuchhandel (LKG), Leninstr 16, DDR-701 Leipzig Tel: 70251
Dir: H Köhler
Leipzig Wholesale Booksellers and Distributors
Publications: LKG Lagerkatalog; Vorankündigungsdienst für den Buchhandel (Advance Information Service for the Book Trade)

Volksbuchhandlung Thomas **Mann**, Kollegiengasse, DDR-690 Jena

Buchhandlung für **Medizin***, Friedrichstr 128, DDR-1040 Berlin

Universitätsbuchhandlung*, Str der Freundschaft 77, DDR-22 Greifswald

Universitätsbuchhandlung*, Grimmaische Str 30, DDR-701 Leipzig

Universitätsbuchhandlung*, Kröpeliner Str 15, DDR-25 Rostock

Erich-**Weinert**-Buchhandlung, Wilhelm-Pieck-Allee 23-27, DDR-301 Magdeburg

Major Libraries

Ernst-Moritz-**Arndt** Universität Universitatsbibliothek, Rubenowstr 4, DDR-2200 Greifswald

Berliner Stadtbibliothek*, Breitestr 37, Berlin C2

Deutsche Bücherei, Deutscher Platz, DDR-7010 Leipzig Tel: 88120 Telex: 051562 dbuech dd
The German Library
Dir: Prof Dr Helmut Rötzsch
Publications: Deutsche Nationalbibliographie und Bibliographie des im Ausland erschienenen deutschsprachigen Schrifttums, Reihe A, B, C (German National Bibliography and Bibliography of German Language Literature appearing abroad Series A, B, C.); *Jahresverzeichnis der Verlagsschriften* (Annual List of Publications); *Deutsches Bücherverzeichnis* (5-Year German Book List); *Bibliographie der Übersetzungen deutschsprachiger Werke* (quarterly: Bibliography of Translations of German Language Works); *Bibliographie fremdsprachiger Germanica* (quarterly: Bibliography of Germanica in foreign languages); *Bibliographie der Bibliographien* (monthly: Bibliography of Bibliographies); *Jahresverzeichnis der Hochschulschriften der DDR, der BRD und Westberlins* (Annual List of Academy Texts appearing in the GDR, the FRG, and in West Berlin); *Deutsche Musikbibliographie* (monthly: German Bibliography of Music); *Jahresverzeichnis der Musikalien und Musikschriften* (Annual List of Musical Scores and Texts); *Bibliographie der Kunstblätter* (Bibliography of Art Prints); *Jahrbuch der Deutschen Bücherei* (Annual of the German Library); *Die Deutsche Bücherei im Bild* (The German Library in Pictures); *Wissenswertes über die Deutsche Bücherei* (Facts about the German Library); *Buch und Schrift von der Frühzeit bis zur Gegenwart* (Books and Print from the earliest times to the present day): also other regularly-appearing Bibliographies and Directories

Deutsche Staatsbibliothek, Unter den Linden 8, Postfach 1312, DDR-1086 Berlin Tel: 20780 Cable Add: Stabi Berlin
German State Library
Man Dir: Dr Friedhilde Krause
Publications: Berliner Titeldrucke, Jahreskatalog; Zentralkatalog der DDR, Zeitschriften und Serien des Auslandes; Beiträge zur Inkunabelkunde; Fontane-Blätter; Bibliographische Mitteilungen; Handschriften-Inventare; Kartographische Bestandsverzeichnisse; Ludwig van Beethoven (Konversationshefte: Band 1, 1972); *Heinz Wegehaupt: Alte deutsche Kinderbücher 1507-1850* (Bestandsverzeichnis 1979)

Humboldt Universität zu Berlin, Universitätsbibliothek, Clara-Zetkin-Str 27, DDR-1086 Berlin Tel: 2078356
Librarian: Dr Waltraud Irmscher

Karl-Marx-Universität*, Universitätsbibliothek, Beethovenstr 6, DDR-701 Leipzig Tel: 34391

Landwirtschaftliche Zentralbibliothek, Krausenstr 38-39, Postfach 1295, DDR-1086 Berlin
Agricultural Central Library

Nationale Forschungs- und Gedenkstätten der klassischen deutschen Literatur — Zentralbibliothek der deutschen Klassik, Platz der Demokratie 1, DDR-5300 Weimar
National Research and Memorial Foundation of Classical German Literature — Central Library of German Classicism

Wilhelm-Pieck-Universität **Rostock** Universitätsbibliothek*, Universitätsplatz 5, DDR-25 Rostock

Sächsische Landesbibliothek, Marienallee 12, DDR-806 Dresden Tel: 52677/576097
Dir: Prof Dr sc Burghard Burgemeister

Publications: Sächsische Bibliographie, Bibliographie Bildende Kunst, Bibliographie Illustrierter Bücher der DDR, Bibliographie Geschichte der Technik, Bibliographie Musik, Sozialistisches Musikschaffen in der Deutschen Demokratischen Republik — all Annual

Zentrales **Staatsarchiv**, Berliner Str 98-101, DDR-1500 Potsdam
The National Archives of the German Democratic Republic

Stadt- und Bezirksbibliothek Leipzig, Mozartstr 1, DDR-701 Leipzig Tel: 34216
Dir: Helga Laue

Universitäts- und Landesbibliothek Sachsen-Anhalt, August-Bebel-Str 13 & 50, DDR-4010 Halle/Saale Tel: 8950 Telex: 4252 mlb hal dd

Universitätsbibliothek, Goetheallee 6, DDR-69 Jena Tel: 8222239 Telex: 0588634
Dir: Prof Dr Lothar Bohmüller
Subjects: Various bibliographical works relating to Jena and the German Democratic Republic, and also to international themes; agricultural, historical, geographical, cultural

Universitätsbibliothek der Technischen Universität*, Mommsenstr 13, DDR-8027 Dresden

Zentralbibliothek der deutschen Klassik, Pl der Demokratie 1, DDR-53 Weimar
Tel: 3552 Telex: 618975 nfg dd

Library Associations

Bibliotheksverband der Deutschen Demokratischen Republik, Hermann-Matern-Str 57, DDR-1040 Berlin Tel: 2362845 Telex: 113247 zib dd
The Library Association of the German Democratic Republic
President: Gotthard Rückl; *Executive Secretary:* Wilfried Kern
Publications: Bibliotheksverband aktuell (Conference Reports, Publications relating to Librarianship — 6 times per year)
1979: 12 ttitles *Founded:* 1964

Zentralinstitut für Bibliothekswesen, Hermann-Matern Str 57, DDR-1040 Berlin
The Central Institute for Library Science
Publications: Bibliothekar; Mitteilungen und Materialien; Bibliothekswesen in der Deutschen Demokratischen Republik (Annual Report); *Berichte und Informationen zum Bibliothekswesen; Informationsdienst Bibliothekswesen; Beiträge zu Theorie und Praxis der Bibliotheksarbeit*

Zentralinstitut für Information und Dokumentation*, Köpenicker Str 80-82, DDR-102 Berlin Tel: 6576210 Telex: OWU 113070/113071 Cable Add: Zeniid Berlin
Central Institute for Information
Director: Mr Och

Library Reference Books and Journals

Books

Die Deutsche Bücherei im Bild (The German Library in Pictures), Deutsche Bücherei, Deutscher Platz, DDR-701 Leipzig

Die Entwicklung des Bibliothekswesens in der Deutschen Demokratischen Republik (The Development of Library Science in the DDR) (annual), Central Institute for Library Science, Hermann-Matern Str 57, DDR-104 Berlin

Jahrbuch der Bibliotheken, Archive und Informationsstellen der Deutschen Demokratischen Republik (Yearbook of the Libraries, Archives and Information Offices of the DDR), VEB Bibliographisches Institut, Gerichtsweg 26, Postfach 130, DDR-701 Leipzig

Sigel Liste der Bibliotheken der Deutschen Demokratischen Republik (Classification List of Libraries of the DDR), Deutsche Staatsbibliothek, Unter den Linden 8, DDR-108 Berlin

Wissenswertes über die Deutsche Bücherei (Facts About the German Library), Deutsche Bücherei, Deutscher Platz, DDR-701 Leipzig

Journals

Bibliothekar (Librarian) (text in German; contents page in English, French, German and Russian), Central Institute for Library Science, Hermann-Matern Str 57, DDR-104 Berlin

Informationsdienst Bibliothekswesen und Bibliographie der Literatur zum Bibliothekswesen (Information Service on Library Science and Bibliography of the Literature on Library Science), Central Institute for Library Science, Hermann-Matern Str 57, DDR-104 Berlin

Literatur zum Bibliothekswesen (Literature on Library Science), Central Institute for Library Science, Hermann-Matern Str 57, DDR-104 Berlin

Mitteilungen und Materialien (Communications and Materials), Central Institute for Library Science, Hermann-Matern Str 57, DDR-104 Berlin

Zentralblatt für Das Bibliothekswesen (Central Journal for Library Science) (text in German; contents page in English, French, German and Russian), VEB Bibliographisches Institut, Gerichtsweg 26, Postfach 130, DDR-701 Leipzig

Literary Associations and Societies

Institut für Literatur Johannes R **Becher***, Karl-Tauchnitzstr 8, Leipzig C1
Dir: Professor Max Walter Schulz

P E N Zentrum, Deutsche Demokratische Republik, Friedrichstr 194-199, DDR-108 Berlin
Secretary: Henryk Keisch

Literary Periodicals

Bücherkarren (Book-Cart), Verlag Volk und Welt, Glinkastr 13-15, DDR-108 Berlin

Deutsche Literaturzeitung (German Literature Newspaper), Akademie-Verlag, Leipziger Str 3-4, DDR-108 Berlin

Fontane-Blätter (Fontane Papers), Deutsche Staatsbibliothek, Theodor Fontane Archiv, Dortustr 30-34, Potsdam

Ich Schreibe (I Write), VEB Friedrich Hofmeister Musikverlag, Karlstr 10, Postschließfach 147, DDR-701 Leipzig

Kunst und Literatur (Art and Literature), Buchexport, Leninstr 16, Postfach 160, DDR-701 Leipzig

Literatur und Gesellschaft (Literature and Society), Buchexport, Leninstr 16, Postfach 160, DDR-701 Leipzig

Marginalien (Marginal Notes); journal for the art of the book and bibliophily, Aufbau-Verlag Berlin und Weimar, Französische Str 32, Postfach 1217, DDR-108 Berlin

Neue deutsche Literatur (New German Literature), Aufbau-Verlag Berlin und Weimar, Französische Str 32, Postfach 1217, DDR-108 Berlin

Sinn und Form (Sense and Form); contributions to literature, Deutsche Akademie der Künste, Rütten & Loening, Französische Str 32, Postfach 1217, DDR-108 Berlin

Weimarer Beträge (Weimar Contributions); journal for literature, aesthetics and culture, Aufbau-Verlag Berlin und Weimar, Französische Str 32, Postfach 1217, DDR-108 Berlin

Literary Prizes

Johannes R **Becher** Prize
Founded 1966. Awarded annually to beginners in the fields of prose, lyrical poetry and essay writing by the Institut für Literatur Johannes R Becher and the Mitteldeutscher Verlag. Enquiries to Institut für Literatur Johannes R Becher, Karl Fauchnitzstr 8, Leipzig C1

Federal Republic of Germany

General Information

Language: German
Religion: Protestant and Roman Catholic
Population: 62 million
Bank Hours: Vary. 0800 or 0830 or 0900-1400, or 0900-1200, 1400-1530 Monday-Friday; open until 1800 Thursday
Shop Hours: 0800 or 0830 or 0900-1800 Monday-Friday. Some have early closing one day a week. Open until 1330 or 1400 Saturday
Currency: 100 pfennige = 1 Deutsche mark
Export/Import Information: Member of the European Economic Community. No tariff on books except children's picture books 13% from non-EEC. None on advertising to be distributed free, if exporter's country grants reciprocal treatment, otherwise 9%. 11% Import Turnover Tax on books and advertising. No import licence required. No exchange controls
Copyright: UCC, Berne, Florence (see International section)

Book Trade Organizations

Adressbuchausschuss der deutschen Wirtschaft*, Adenauerallee 148, D-5300 Bonn 1 Tel: (02221) 104306 Telex: 886805 diht d
German Trade Directory Committee

Arbeitsgemeinschaft Buchgemeinschaften und verwandte Unternehmen im Börsenverein des Deutschen Buchhandels eV, Grosser Hirschgraben 17/21, D-6000 Frankfurt-am-Main 1 Tel: (0611) 1306310
Alliance of Book Clubs/Societies and related

FEDERAL REPUBLIC OF GERMANY

concerns in the German Publishers' and Booksellers' Association

Arbeitsgemeinschaft der Vertriebsfachverbände*, c/o Verband Deutscher Buch- Zeitungs- und Zeitschriften-Grossisten eV, Theodor-Heuss-Ring 32, D-5000 Cologne 1 Tel: (0221) 123803
Organization of the Distributive Trades Associations

Arbeitsgemeinschaft literarische und Sachbuchverlage*, Charlottenstr 21c, D-7000 Stuttgart 1 Tel: (0711) 245272
Dir: Dr Ferdinand Sieger
Alliance of Literary and Non-fiction Publishers

Arbeitsgemeinschaft rechts- und staatswissenschaftlicher Verleger*, Widenmayerstr 46/III, D-8000 Munich 22 Tel: (089) 479692
Economics and Legal Publishers Alliance

Arbeitsgemeinschaft von Jugendbuchverlegern in der Bundesrepublik Deutschland eV*, Otto Maier Verlag, Marktstr 22-26, D-7980 Ravensburg Tel: 862231
The Alliance of Publishers of Children's Books in the Federal Republic of Germany
Chairman: Christian Stottele

Arbeitsgemeinschaft wissenschaftliche Literatur eV, Postfach 21086, D-6000 Frankfurt am Main
Joint Association for Scientific Literature
Director: Peter Czerwonka

Arbeitskreis für Jugendliteratur eV*, Elisabethstr 15, D-8000, Munich 40
Youth Literature Committee (Section of IBBY)
Man Dir: R Majonica

Aussenhandels-Ausschuss*, Foreign Trade Committee of Börsenverein des deutschen Buchhandels e V (qv)

B A G Buchhändler-Abrechnungs-Gesellschaft mbH*, Grosser Hirschgraben 17-21, Postfach 2422, D-6000 Frankfurt 1
Booksellers' Clearing-House Company

Berliner Verleger- und Buchhändlervereinigung eV*, Lützowstr 105-107, D-1000 Berlin 30 Tel: (030) 2621040/2621049
Berlin Publishers' and Booksellers' Association

Börsenverein des deutschen Buchhandels eV*, Grosser Hirschgraben 17-19, Postfach 2404, D-6000 Frankfurt am Main 1 Tel: (0611) 13061 Cable Add: Börsenblatt Telex: 413573 buchv d
German Publishers' and Booksellers' Association; also has a Foreign Trade Committee (Aussenhandels-Ausschuss)
Secretary: F von Notz
Publications: Börsenblatt für den deutschen Buchhandel; Adressbuch für den deutschsprachigen Buchhandel; Deutsche Bibliographie; Neuerscheinungen-Sofortdienst (CIP); Archiv für die Geschichte des Buchwesens; Buch und Buchhandel in Zahlen; Die schönsten deutschen Bücher; Verzeichnis lieferbarer Bücher; Bibliothekswesen in Deutschland; LIT (a general magazine for those connected with the Book Trade); *How to obtain German books and periodicals*; and others

Bundesverband der deutschen Verlagsvertreter eV, Zeil 65-69, D-6000 Frankfurt am Main Tel: (0611) 288891
National Association of German Publishers' Representatives

Bundesverband der deutschen Versandbuchhändler eV*, Burchardstr 14, D-2000 Hamburg 1
National Federation of German Mail-order Booksellers

Bundesverband des werbenden Buch- und Zeitschriftenhandels eV*, Brusseler Str 96, D-5000 Cologne 1 Tel: 514774
National Federation of the Promotional Book and Periodical Trade
Publication: Der werbende Buch- und Zeitschriften Handel

Deutsches Jugendschriftenwerk, Kurt-Schumacher-Str 1, Frankfurt
German Young People's Writing

Hessischer Verleger- und Buchhändler-Verband eV*, Großer Hirschgraben 17-19, D-6000 Frankfurt am Main 1 Tel: (0611) 282643
Hessen Publishers' and Booksellers' Federation
Chairman: Dr Heribert Marré; *Manager:* Lisabeth Schubert

Informations-Zentrum Buch, Book Information Centre: an Association of prominent publishers who share information about their varied publishing programmes. Information can be obtained from any of the participating companies: Artemis/Winkler, Bouvier, Carl, Deutscher Taschenbuch Verlag, Duncker & Humblot, Ehrenwirth, W Fink, Frommann/Holzboog, Hanser, Herder, Hiersemann, Kiepenheuer & Witsch, Kindler, Klett, Klinkhardt, Kösel, W Kohlhammer, Metzler, M Niemeyer, Nymphenburger, Piper, Quelle & Meyer, Reclam, E Schmidt (qqv)

Interessengemeinschaft Musikwissenschaftlicher Herausgeber und Verleger (IHMV)*, Heinrich-Schütz-Allee 33, D-3500 Kassel-Wilhelmshöhe Tel: 30011/16
Association of Musicology Editors and Publishers

Landesverband der Buchhändler und Verleger in Niedersachsen eV, Hausmannstr 2, D-3000 Hanover 1 Tel: (0511) 14745
Provincial Federation of Booksellers and Publishers in Lower Saxony

Landesverband der Verleger und Buchhändler Bremen-Unterweser eV, Contrescarpe 17, D-2800 Bremen 1 Tel: 326949
Bremen (Lower Weser) Provincial Federation of Publishers and Booksellers

Landesverband der Verleger und Buchhändler Rheinland-Pfalz eV*, Schönbornstr 3, D-6500 Mainz 1 Tel: (06131) 27270
Rhineland-Palatinate Provincial Federation of Publishers and Booksellers

Landesverband der Verleger und Buchhändler Saar eV (LVBS)*, Eisenbahnstr 68, D-6600 Saarbücken Tel: (0681) 51471
Saar Provincial Federation of Publishers and Booksellers

Landesverband des werbenden Buch- und Zeitschriftenhandels eV*, Strohberg 38, D-7000 Stuttgart 1 Tel: (0711) 602088/604056
Provincial Federation of the Book and Periodical Trade of South-west Germany

Münchner Arbeitsgemeinschaft der Verlagshersteller*, Scharnitzer Str 58, D-8032 Gräfelfing Tel: 852238
Munich Association of Publishers' Production Managers

Norddeutscher Verleger- und Buchhändler-Verband eV*, Brahmsallee 24, D-2000 Hamburg 13 Tel: (040) 4103161
North German Publishers' and Booksellers' Federation

Standard Book Numbering Agency, c/o Wilfried H Schinzel, Büchhandler-Vereinigung GmbH, Postfach 2404, D-6000, Frankfurt am Main 1

Verband bayerischer Buch- und Zeitschriftenhändler eV*, Enzenspergerstr 9, D-8000 Munich 80 Tel: (089) 488533
Bavarian Booksellers' and Newsagents' Federation

Verband bayerischer Verlage und Buchhandlungen eV*, Enzenspergerstr 9, Postfach 800949, D-8000 Munich 80 Tel: (089) 484141
Bavarian Publishers' and Booksellers' Federation

Verband der Schulbuchverlage eV, Zeppelinallee 33, Postfach 900540, D-6000 Frankfurt-am-Main 1 Tel: (0611) 703075 Telex: vsib 416213
Association of Publishers of Schoolbooks
Chief Executive: Dipl-Volkswirt H P Vonhoff

Verband der Verlage und Buchhandlungen in Baden-Württemberg eV*, Leonhardspl 28, D-7000 Stuttgart 1 Tel: (0711) 245959
Federation of Publishers and Booksellers in Baden-Württemberg

Verband der Verlage und Buchhandlungen in Nordrhein-Westfalen eV, Marienstr 41, D-4000 Düsseldorf 1 Tel: (0211) 320951
Federation of Publishers and Booksellers in North Rhine-Westphalia

Verband des werbenden Buch- und Zeitschriftenhandels Gross-Berlin eV*, Leydenallee 70, D-1000 Berlin 41 Tel: (030) 720461
Greater Berlin Federation of the Promotional Book and Periodical Trade

Verband deutscher Adressbuchverleger eV*, Ritterstr 17-19, D-4000 Düsseldorf Tel: (0211) 320909
Association of German Directory Publishers

Verband deutscher Antiquare eV*, Zum Talblick 2, D-6264 Glashütten im Taunus bei Frankfurt am Main
German Antiquarian Booksellers' Association
President: Godebert M Reiss

Verband deutscher Bahnhofsbuchhändler*, Grosser Hirschgraben 19H, D-6000 Frankfurt am Main 1
Federation of German Station Booksellers

Verband deutscher Buch-Zeitungs- und Zeitschriften-Grossisten eV*, Theodor-Heuss-Ring 32, D-5000 Cologne 1 Tel: (0221) 123803 Telex: 08-885 203
Federation of German Wholesalers of Books, Newspapers and Periodicals
Chairman: Dr Eberhard Nolte; *Manager:* Dr Hans Ziebolz

Verband deutscher Bühnenverleger eV, Bundesallee 23, D-1000 Berlin 31 Tel: (030) 8618088
Federation of German Theatrical Publishers

Verband deutscher Schulbuchhändler eV, Marienstrasse 41, D-4000 Düsseldorf Tel: (0211) 320951
Federation of German School Book Dealers

Verband katholischer Verleger und Buchhändler eV, Lehenstr 31, D-7000 Stuttgart 1 Tel: 642061
Federation of Catholic Publishers and Booksellers
Manager: Wolfgang Grossmann

Verband norddeutscher Buch- und Zeitschriftenhändler eV*, An Der Rehbocksweide 22-24, D-3150 Hannoversch-Münden Tel: 4084/4089
Federation of North German Booksellers and Newsagents

Verband westdeutscher Buch- und Zeitschriftenhändler eV*, Dürener Str 251, D-5000 Cologne 41 Tel: (0221) 413704
West German Booksellers' and Newsagents' Federation

Verein für Verkehrsordnung im Buchhandel*, Frankfurt am Main 1, Postfach 2404, D-6000
Association for the Regulation of Dealing in the Book Trade

Vereinigung selbständiger Verlagsvertreter, Schatten und Gewand, D-7000 Stuttgart (Busnau) 80 Tel: (0711) 681457
Association of Self-Employed Publishers' Representatives

Verlegervereinigung Rechtsinformatik eV, Verlag Neue Wirtschafts-Briefe GmbH, Eschstr 16-22, D-4690 Herne Tel: 02323/54071 Telex: 8229870
Association of Publishers of Legal Documentation
Chairman: Dr Karl-Friedrich Peter

Book Trade Reference Books and Journals

Books

Adressbuch für den deutschsprachigen Buchhandel (Directory of German-speaking Book Trade) (including Austria, Switzerland, and German-speaking publishers and booksellers in other countries), German Publishers' and Booksellers' Association, Großer Hirschgraben 17-21, D-6000 Frankfurt am Main 1

Anschriften deutscher Buchhandlungen (Addresses of German Booksellers), Verlag der Schillerbuchhandlung Hans Banger, Mainzer Str 24, D-714 Marbach 2

Anschriften deutscher Verlage und ausländischer Verlage mit deutschen Auslieferungen (Addresses of German Publishers and Foreign Publishers with German Distribution), Verlag der Schillerbuchhandlung Hans Banger, Mainzer Str 24, D-7142 Marbach

Die Begegnung (The Meeting); authors, publishers, booksellers, Elwert & Meurer, Hauptstr 101, D-1000 Berlin 62

Bibliographie des Buchhandels (Bibliography of the Book Trade), Saur KG, Pössenbacherstr 2, D-8000 Munich 71

Buch und Buchhandel in Zahlen (Books and the Book Trade in Figures), German Publishers' and Booksellers' Association, Großer Hirschgraben 17-21, D-6000 Frankfurt am Main 1

Buchhändler Kalender (Booksellers' Calendar), Bibliographisches Institut AG, Dudenstr 6, Postfach 311, D-68 Mannheim

Deutsches Verlagsregister (German Publishers' List), Stamm-Verlag GmbH, Goldammerweg 16, D-4300 Essen 1

Freude mit Büchern (Joy with Books); the German book catalogue, Verlag Bücherschiff Walter Reutin, Rheinstr 122, Postfach 210947, D-7500 Karlsruhe

Handbuch des Buchhandels (Handbook of the Book Trade), Verlag für Buchmarktforschung, Beim Strohhause 34, D-2000 Hamburg 2

How to Obtain German Books and Periodicals, Börsenverein des deutschen Buchhandels eV, Postfach 2404, D-6000 Frankfurt am Main 1

Was erscheint wo. Verlage, Titel, Redaktionen (What Appears Where. Publishers, Titles, Editors), Team Verlag, Helmut Müller GmbH & Co KG, Rossertstr 9, Postfach 2661, D-6000 Frankfurt am Main

Journals

AGB-Titeldienst (AGB-Title Service); recently published German-language books, Amerika-Gedenk-Bibliothek, Arbeitsstelle für das Bibliothekswesen, Fehrbelliner Platz 3, D-1000 Berlin 31

Antiquariat (Second-hand Bookshop), Dr Lothar Rossipaul, Verlagsgesellschaft mbH, Finkenweg 6, D-7261 Stammheim/Calw, (monthly)

Börsenblatt für den deutschen Buchhandel (German Book Trade Journal), German Publishers' and Booksellers' Association, Grosser Hirschgraben 17-21, D-6000 Frankfurt am Main 1

Buch Aktuell (Contemporary Books), Westfalendamm 57, Postfach 1305, D-4600 Dortmund

Buch und Leser (Book and Reader), German Publishers' and Booksellers' Association, Grosser Hirschgraben 17-21, Postfach 2404, D-6000 Frankfurt am Main 1

Buchhändler Heute (Bookseller Today), Verlag Buchhändler Heute, Jahnstr 36, Düsseldorf, (monthly)

Buchmarkt (Book Market), the largest independent journal for the book trade in German-speaking areas, Rochusstr 34, Postfach 320545, D-4000 Düsseldorf

Buchreport (Book Report), Westfalendamm 57, Postfach 1305, D-4600 Dortmund

Deutsche Bibliographie (German National Bibliography), German Publishers' and Booksellers' Association, Großer Hirschgraben 17-21, D-6000 Frankfurt am Main 1

Dokumentation deutschsprachiger Verlage (Documentation of German-speaking Publishers), Günter Olzog Verlag, Thierschstr 11, D-8000 Munich 22

Goldmann's Mitteilungen für den Buchhandel (Goldmann's Communications for the Book Trade), Wilhelm Goldmann Verlag GmbH, Neumarkterstr 22, Postfach 800709, D-8000 Munich 80

LIT (bi-monthly general magazine for patrons of the Book Trade), Börsenverein des Deutschen Buchhandels eV, Grosser Hirschgraben 17/21, Postfach 2404, D-6000 Frankfurt am Main 1

Mitteilungsblatt für Dolmetscher und Übersetzer (Interpreters' and Translators' News Sheet), Federal German Association of Interpreters and Translators, Blaustr 1, D-6728 Germersheim (twice monthly)

Die Neuen Bücher (New Books), Dr Lothar Rossipaul, Verlagsgesellschaft mbH, Finkenweg 6, D-7261 Stammheim/Calw

Philobiblon; quarterly journal for books and graphic art, Dr Ernst Hauswedell & Co, Pöseldorfer Weg 1, D-2000 Hamburg 13

Taschenbücher, Halbjähriges Verzeichnis (Paperbacks, Half-yearly List), Verlag der Schillerbuchhandlung Hans Banger, Mainzer Str 24, D-7142 Marbach

Der Übersetzer (The Translator), Association of German-speaking Translators of Literary and Scientific Works, D-7400 Tübingen, Fürststr 17

Verzeichnis lieferbarer Bücher (German Books in Print), German Publishers' and Booksellers' Association, Großer Hirschgraben 17-21, D-6000 Frankfurt am Main 1

Welt der Bücher (World of Books), *Der werbende Buch- und Zeitschriftenhandel* (The Promotional Book and Periodical Trade), Bundesverband des werbenden Buch- und Zeitschriftenhandels eV, Brusseler Str 96, D-5000 Cologne 1

Publishers

Edition der **2**, see under der 2

A D A C Verlag, Baumgartnerstr 53, Postfach 700086, D-8000 Munich 70 Tel: (089) 12005 Cable Add: Adacverlag Telex: 52923135
Man Dir: Alfred Dietrich; *Editorial:* Bleinagel, Michael Dultz; *Sales Promotion:* Helmut Engerer; *Production:* Uto Rogner; *Advertising:* Horst Nitschke; *Rights & Permissions:* Alfred Dietrich
Subjects: Automobile Interest primarily: Touring, Holiday Guides, Car Buying, Repairs, Insurance, Driving Instruction etc Publishers of magazines *ADAC-Motorwelt* and *Deutsches Autorecht*
1978: 13 titles *1980:* 40 titles *Founded:* 1958
ISBN Publisher's Prefix: 3-87003

A D L A F, see Arbeitsgemeinschaft Deutsche Lateinamerika-Forschung

A E G - Telefunken Zentralabteilung Firmenverlag, Hohenzollerndamm 150, D-1000 Berlin 33 Tel: 8282133 Cable Add: Elektron Berlin Telex: 183581
Man Dir: Heinz Ketterer; *Editorial:* R Lutgens; *Sales, Publicity, Rights and Permissions:* Detlef Lorenz; *Production:* Reinhard Eckardt
Subjects: Electrical Engineering, Electronics
1978: 10 titles *1979:* 5 titles *Founded:* 1883
ISBN Publisher's Prefix: 3-87087

A M B (Arbeitsgemeinschaft mitteleuropäischer Bibelwerke), Association of Mid-European Biblical Presses, comprising Verlag Schweizerisches Katholisches Bibelwerk, Switzerland (qv), Vlaamse Bijbelstichting, Belgium (qv), Österreichisches Katholisches Bibelwerk, Austria (qv), and Verlag Katholisches Bibelwerk GmbH, Federal Republic of Germany (qv)

Aar-Verlag, Volkerstr 33, D-6200 Wiesbaden Tel: (06121) 88218
Proprietor: Iolanda Debus
Subject: General Literature
1978: 41 titles
ISBN Publisher's Prefix: 3-87945

Abakon Verlagsgesellschaft mbH, Luetzowstr 105, D-1000 Berlin 30 Tel: (030) 2611067 Telex: 182659
Man Dir, Rights & Permissions: Dr Achim Schneider
Orders to: Karl Halliant und Sohn, Luetzowstr 105, D-1000 Berlin 30
Imprints: Abakon; Edition Lichterfelde; Life Sciences Research Reports
Subjects: Science (in English language), Architecture, Art
1978: 11 titles *Founded:* 1975
ISBN Publisher's Prefix: 3-8200

Abakus Schallplatten Barbara Fietz, Haversbach 1, D-6331 Ulmtal-Allendorf Tel: (06478) 2250
Man Dirs: B and S Fietz; *Editorial, Sales, Publicity:* B Fietz; *Production:* S Frietz
Associate Companies: Ulmtal Musikverlags GmbH Ulmtal; Melos Musikverlag, Munich
Subjects: Song Books, Musical Scores,

Musical Instructional Books (all with Christian religious emphasis)
1978: 5 titles *1979:* 5 titles *Founded:* 1974

Accidentia Druck- und Verlagsgesellschaft mbH, Graf-Adolf-Str 112, D-4000 Düsseldorf Tel: (0211) 350271 Telex: 08581986
Man Dir: H Sontowski
Subjects: Photography, Travel Calendar
Founded: 1959
ISBN Publisher's Prefix: 3-920005

Achberger Verlag GmbH*, Esseratsweiler Nr 23, D-8991 Achberg Tel: 08380/515544
General Managers: Wilfried Heidt, Peter Schata
Subjects: Publications connected with the "Third Way" political alternative; publications of the Institute of Social Research, Achberg
Founded: 1973
ISBN Publisher's Prefix: 3-88103

Verlag Andreas **Achenbach***, Holzmühler Weg 63, Postfach 82, D-6304 Lollar Tel: (06406) 3639
Publisher: Andreas Achenbach; *Production:* Frederick Carl Schlotman; *Sales:* H F O Achenbach
Subjects: Social Science, Economics, Sport, Ethnology, Pedagogics
Founded: 1972
ISBN Publisher's Prefix: 3-87958

F A **Ackermanns** Kunstverlag, Wienerplatz 7-8, D-8000 Munich 80 Tel: (089) 488046 Cable Add: Kunstackermann Munich
Man Dir: Hubertus Weinert
Subjects: Art, Calendars, Photographic
1978: 70 titles *Founded:* 1874
ISBN Publisher's Prefix: 3-87002

Agis Verlag GmbH, Eberbachstr 7, Postfach 7, D-7570 Baden-Baden 19 Tel: (07221) 66810, (07222) 8321 Cable Add: Agis Baden-Baden
Man Dirs: Karl G Fischer, Karin Grochowiak
Subjects: Aesthetics, Cybernetics, Information Theory, Human and Natural Sciences, Philosophy
ISBN Publisher's Prefix: 3-87007

Agora-Verlag, Hanseatenweg 10, Postfach 210533, D-1000 Berlin 21 Tel: (030) 3913775 Cable Add: Agora
Man Dir, Production: Manfred Schlösser; *Sales & Publicity:* Monika Schlösser-Fischer
Subsidiary Company: Erato-Presse
Branch Off: Lucasweg 17, D-6100 Darmstadt
Subjects: Literary Criticism, Belles Lettres, Poetry, Juveniles, Music, Theatre, Literature by exiles
Founded: 1960
ISBN Publisher's Prefix: 3-87008

L B **Ahnert**-Verlag, Markt 9, Postfach 14, D-6360 Friedberg 3 Tel: (06031) 3131/60 Cable Add: Ahnert-Verlag Echzell Telex: 415961 pvlg d
Subjects: Sports, Horse Breeding, Nonfiction, Periodicals, Reproductions
ISBN Publisher's Prefix: 3-921142

Akademische Verlagsgesellschaft, Bahnhofstr 39, Postfach 1107, D-6200 Wiesbaden Tel: (06121) 39794 Cable Add: AKA Wiesbaden Telex: 4186451 avg d
Man Dir: Dr Claus Steiner; *Sales:* Gerhard Stahl; *Publicity:* Margret Nerger
Subsidiary Company: Akademische Verlagsgesellschaft Athenaion (qv)
Subjects: Educational, Data Processing, Life Science, Chemistry, Physics, Maths, Electrotechnology, Politics, Sociology; Periodicals
Founded: 1912
ISBN Publisher's Prefix: 3-400

Akademische Verlagsgesellschaft Athenaion, Bahnhofstr 39, Postfach 1107, D-6200 Wiesbaden Tel: (06121) 39794 Telex: 4186451 avg d
Parent Company: Akademische Verlagsgesellschaft, Wiesbaden (qv)
Subjects: Literary Science, Linguistics, with especial reference to English, German, Romance Languages; History of Culture, History of Germany; Periodicals
ISBN Publisher's Prefix: 3-7997

Alba Buchverlag GmbH und Co KG, Römerstr 9, Postfach 320108, D-4000 Düsseldorf 30 Tel: (0211) 482069
Man Dir, Rights & Permissions: Alf Teloeken; *Sales:* D Wiesent; *Production:* K Hartung; *Publicity:* Dip Kfm K Harrer
Associate Company: Alba Publikation Alf Teloeken GmbH und Co KG (qv)
Subjects: Model Railways, Transport, Modelling
1979: 83 titles *1980:* 120 titles *Founded:* 1951
ISBN Publisher's Prefix: 3-87094

Alba Publikation Alf Teloeken GmbH und Co KG, Römerstr 9, Postfach 320109, D-4000 Düsseldorf Tel: (0211) 482069
Man Dir, Rights & Permissions: Alf Teloeken; *Sales:* D Wiesent; *Production:* K Hartung; *Publicity:* Dip Kfm K Harrer
Associate Company: Alba Buchverlag GmbH und Co KG (qv)
Subjects: Model Railways, Transport, Modelling; Periodicals covering modelling and bus and rail transport

Verlag Karl **Albér** GmbH*, Hermann Herder Str 4, D-7800 Freiburg im Breisgau Tel: (0761) 273495 Telex: 07721440 vh d
Man Dir: Dr Meinolf Wewel
Orders to: Auslieferungsgemeinschaft Herder, Postfach D-7800 Freiburg im Breisgau Tel: 0761/27171
Parent Company: Verlag Herder (qv)
Subjects: Logic, History & Theory of Science, Philosophy, Psychology, Pedagogy, History, Law, Sociology, Political Science
1978: 25 titles *Founded:* 1939
ISBN Publisher's Prefix: 3-495

Alpha 9 GmbH, Eschborn, Postfach 3029, Königsbergerstr 9, D-6236 Eschborn II Tel: (06173) 62268/62368 Cable Add: alpha verlag eschborn
Subjects: Informative Books of Plates and Wall Calendars: speciality — book/calendar combinations

Alpha Literatur Verlag, August-Siebert-Str 9, D-6000 Frankfurt am Main 1 Tel: (0611) 555325 Telex: 414890
Man Dir: Dr G Philipps
Subjects: Poetry, Belles Lettres, Theatre

Alternative Verlag GmbH, Postfach 150230, D-1000 Berlin 15 (Located at: Konstanzer Str 11, D-1000 Berlin 31) Tel: (030) 8811570/8815550
Man Dir: H Brenner; *Sales & Advertising Dir:* Till Saver
Subjects: Literature, Social and Political Sciences, Philosophy, Literature, Theatre, Art
Founded: 1954

Amazonen Frauenverlag GmbH*, Kantstr 125, D-1000 Berlin 12
Subjects: Women's Cultural and Historical; Poster-Calendars; Female Homosexual Themes; Lesbians in the Women's Movement

Ambro Lacus, Buch- und Bildverlag W Kremnitz, see Lacus

Anabas-Verlag Günter Kämpf KG, Am unteren Hardthof, D-6300 Lahn-Giessen 1 Tel: 0641/72455

Man Dir: Günter Kämpf
Orders to: Sova Verlagsauslieferung, 44 Franziusstraße, D-6000 Frankfurt am Main; (West Berlin) — Zirk und Ellenrieder, Lützowstr 105/106, D-1000 Berlin 30
Subjects: Belles Lettres, Poetry, History, Art, High-priced Paperbacks, Educational Materials
1978: 8 titles *Founded:* 1966
ISBN Publisher's Prefix: 3-87038

Andres Kalender und Buch Verlag GmbH, Lenaustr 2, D-2000 Hamburg 76 Tel: (040) 255047/48 Telex: 02-173065 akb-d
Dirs: Klaus-Jürgen Breidenstein, Klaus-Jürgen Schlotte; *Editorial:* Eberhard Urban; *Publishing and Sales Manager:* Heinrich Jessen
Associate Company: Umschau Verlag Breidenstein GmbH (qv for other Associates)
Subjects: Calendars, Books
1980: 80 titles
ISBN Publisher's Prefix: 3-88231

Verlag Roland **Angst***, Achleitnerstrasse 1, D-8000 Munich 90 Tel: 640532
Publisher: Roland Angst
Subject: Modern Art

Neithard **Anrich** Verlag, Neunkirchen 5, D-6101 Modautal 3 Tel: (06254) 7229
Man Dir: Gerold Anrich
Subjects: Juveniles, History
Founded: 1970
ISBN Publisher's Prefix: 3-920110

Arani-Verlag GmbH, Kurfürstendamm 126, D-1000 Berlin 31, Postfach 310829 Tel: (030) 8911008
Publisher: Horst Meyer
Orders to: Libri VA, Postfach 3584, D-6000 Frankfurt-am-Main 3
Subjects: Belles Lettres, Poetry, History, books on Berlin
1978: 55 titles *Founded:* 1947
ISBN Publisher's Prefix: 3-7605

Ararat Verlag GmbH, Reinsburgstr 199, D-7000 Stuttgart 1 Tel: 654350; also Kottbusser Damm 79, D-1000 Berlin 61
Man Dir: Dr A I Dogan; *Marketing Manager:* Peter T Kampmann
Subjects: Turkish Literature in German translation; German-Turkish Twin-Language books, Turkish Literature Information Periodical
1979: 6 titles *1980:* 16 titles *Founded:* 1977
ISBN Publisher's Prefix: 3-921889

Verlag **Arbeiterbewegung und Gesellschaftswissenschaft**, Weidenhäuserstr 56, Postfach 564, D-3550 Marburg/Lahn Tel: (06421) 29983
Workers' Movement and Sociology Publishing Co
Man Dir: Karl-Heinz Flessenkemper; *Editors:* Wolfgang Abendroth, Frank Deppe, Georg Fülberth, Gerd Hardach, H-J Sandkühler
Subjects: Workers' Rights, Trade Unions, Social History
1978: 9 titles *Founded:* 1976
ISBN Publisher's Prefix: 921630

Arbeitsgemeinschaft Deutsche Lateinamerika-Forschung (ADLAF), Forschungsinstitut der Friedrich-Ebert-Stiftung, Godesberger Allee 149, D-5300 Bonn 2 Tel: (02221) 883668/883674 Telex: 885479 fest-d
German Association for Research on Latin America
Subjects: Embracing the work of 20 academic Member Institutes and more than 100 individual members in research areas of Archaeology, Ethnology, History, Literature, the Geo-Sciences, Economic and Social Sciences, Librarianship; also publish periodicals and Bibliographies

Arbeitsgemeinschaft mitteleuropäischer Bibelwerke, see AMB

Arbeitsgemeinschaft sozialistischer und demokratischer Verleger und Buchhändler (Co-operative of Socialist and Democratic Publishing Houses and Bookshops) comprises 18 Publishers, as follows: Verlag Marxistische Blätter GmbH, Frankfurt am Main (qv); Nachrichten-Verlags-GmbH, Frankfurt am Main (qv); Pahl-Rugenstein-Verlag, Cologne (qv); Röderberg-Verlag GmbH, Frankfurt am Main; Weltkreis-Verlags-GmbH, Dortmund (qv); Damnitz-Verlag, Munich (qv); Asso-Verlag, Oberhausen (qv); Stimme-Verlag GmbH, Mainz; Verlag Atelier im Bauernhaus, Fischerhude (qv); Institut für Marxistische Studien und Forschungen (IMSF), Frankfurt am Main (qv); Monitor-Verlag, Düsseldorf; W Runge-Verlag, Hamburg; Neue Kommentare, Frankfurt am Main; Rochus-Verlag, Düsseldorf; Plambeck und Co Druck und Verlag GmbH, Neuss (qv); Brücken-Verlag GmbH, Düsseldorf (qv)
Miscellaneous: the central marketing agency for this group is the Brücken-Verlag GmbH, Düsseldorf (qv)

Verlag Die **Arbeitswelt** GmbH, Grimmstr 27, D-1000 Berlin 61 Tel: (030) 6933069
Dirs: Ulrich Laube, Werner Jung
Subject: Politics (especially trade union studies)

Verlag für **Architektur**, Martiusstr 8, Postfach 104, D-8000 Munich 44 Tel: (089) 348074 Telex: 5215517
Branch Off: Zurich, Switzerland (qv)
Associate Companies: Artemis & Winkler Verlag, Munich (qv); Druckenmüller Verlag, Munich (qv); Artemis Verlag, Zurich, Switzerland (qv)
Subjects: Collected Works of Leading World Architects, Studio Paperback Series, Works on Town Planning, Pre-Fabrication etc

Arena-Verlag Georg Popp*, Talavera 7-11, D-8700 Würzburg 1 Tel: (0931) 43061 Postfach 5169 Telex: 068833
General Manager, Publicity and Advertising Manager, Rights & Permissions: Georg Popp; *Sales Dir:* Günter Reich
Associate Company: Georg Popp, Würzburg (qv)
Subjects: General Nonfiction, Juveniles, Young Adult, Low-price Paperbacks
Bookshop: Arena-Buchhandlung, Domstr 26, D-8700 Würzburg 1
1978: 53 titles *1979:* 60 titles *Founded:* 1949 (1969 acquisition of Westermann Jugendbuchverlag)
ISBN Publisher's Prefix: 3-401

Arkana-Verlag, Fritz-Frey Str 21, Postfach 105767, D-6900 Heidelberg 1 Tel: (06221) 499747 Cable Add: arkanaverlag
Man Dir: Dr Ewald Fischer
Associate Companies: Karl F Haug Verlag GmbH & Co (qv); Verlag für Medizin Dr E Fischer GmbH (qv)
Subjects: Fringe Medicine, Occult, the Arts
ISBN Publisher's Prefix: 3-920042

Verlag **Ars** Sacra Josef Müller, Friedrichstr 9, D-8000 Munich 43 Tel: (089) 393045 Cable Add: Arssacra Munich
Man Dir: Marcel Nauer
Subjects: Religion, Juveniles
1978: 40 titles *Founded:* 1896
ISBN Publisher's Prefix: 3-7607

Art Address Verlag Müller GmbH und Co KG, Gr Eschenheimer Str 16, D-6000 Frankfurt am Main Tel: (0611) 284486 Telex: 0411699 omf D
Man Dirs: J Müller, E Kohl
Subject: Art
Founded: 1949

Artemis und Winkler Verlag, Martiusstr 8, D-8000 Munich 40 Tel: (089) 348074 Cable Add: arte d Telex: 5215517
Man Dir: Dr Dieter Lutz; *Publicity Dir:* Anita Donat; *Advertising Dir:* Sunhild Pacheco; *Rights & Permissions:* Marianne Jahn
Orders to: Koch, Neff und Oetinger, Am Wallgraben 110, D-7000 Stuttgart 80
Associate Companies: Verlag für Architektur, Alfred Druckenmüller Verlag, (qqv, Federal Republic of Germany); Verlag für Architektur, Switzerland (qv)
Subsidiary Company: Winkler-Verlag (qv)
Subjects: (Artemis Verlag) Belles Lettres, The Humanities, Children's, Illustrated Books, History of Antiquity, Collected Works, Classics, Oriental Studies; (Winkler Verlag) India Paper Editions and Special Editions of World Literature, Special series of Classics, Works of Zola, Germanistics
ISBN Publisher's Prefix: 3-7608

Aschendorffsche Verlagsbuchhandlung*, Soesterstr 13, D-4400 Münster/Westfalen Postfach 1124 Tel: (0251) 6901 Cable Add: Verlag Aschendorff Münster Telex: 0892830
Man Dirs: Anton Wilhelm Hueffer, Maxfritz Hueffer
Subjects: History, Art History, Philosophy, Religion, Reference, Juveniles, Psychology, Law, Folklore, Social & Natural Science, Economics, Philology, Textbooks, Foreign Languages, Periodicals
Founded: 1720
ISBN Publisher's Prefix: 3-402

Aspekte Verlag GmbH*, Forsthausstr 9, D-6246 Glashütten 1 Tel: 06174/61116
Gen Man, Publicity, Rights & Permissions: Gerhard Hirschfeld; *Editorial & Advertising:* Stephan Bohnke; *Sales:* Annerose Bayer
Founded: 1965
Subjects: Sociology, Political Science, Economic Sciences, Psychology
ISBN Publisher's Prefix: 3-921096

Assimil-Verlag KG, Grimmstr 4, Postfach 230147, D-4000 Düsseldorf 23 Tel: (0211) 683191
Publisher: Franz Wilhelm Kreft
Parent Company: Assimil, France (qv)
Subjects: Language courses, Linguistics; also Records and Cassettes
ISBN Publisher's Prefix: 2-7005

Asso Verlag Anneliese Althoff*, Josefplatz 3, D-4200 Oberhausen Tel: (0208) 802356
Orders to: VVA Reinhard Mohn OHG, Carl-Bertelsmann-Str 161, D-4830 Gütersloh 1; (West Berlin): Lützowstr 105-106, D-1000 Berlin 30
Subjects: Contemporary Political Literature in prose, poetry, songs, graphics; Miners' Solidarity
1978: 5 titles
Miscellaneous: Member of Arbeitsgemeinschaft Sozialistischer und demokratischer Verleger und Buchhändler (qv for other members).

Verlag **Association** GmbH & Co*, Postfach 501525, D-2000 Hamburg 50 Tel: (040) 393245
Subjects: Politics, Socialism, Social History, Political Ecology

Ästhetik und Kommunikation Verlags-GmbH, Gneisenaustr 2, D-1000 Berlin 61 Tel: (030) 6912034/35
Man Dir, Editorial, Rights & Permissions: Eberhard Knödler-Bunte; *Sales:* Gudrun Fricke; *Production:* Richard Reitinger; *Publicity:* Gisela Kayser
Subjects: Contemporary Issues, Political Culture; Periodicals
1978: 3 titles *1979:* 8 titles *Founded:* 1969

Atelier-Handpresse Verlag H Hoffmann*, Blücherstr 23, Postfach 475, D-1000 Berlin 61 Tel: 6933080
Subjects: Prose/Lyrical Poetry with original graphics in hand-printed editions, First Editions, Calendars, Reprints

Verlag **Atelier im Bauernhaus**, in der Bredenau 5, D-2802 Fischerhude Tel: (04293) 671
Subjects: Regional Books; Prose and Poetry in Bibliophile Editions; Novels; Graphics
Miscellaneous: Member of Arbeitsgemeinschaft sozialistischer und demokratischer Verleger und Buchhändler (qv for other members)

Atelier Verlag Andernach (AVA)*, Antel 74, D-547 Andernach Tel: 44432
Man Dir & Rights & Permissions: Rosa Werf; *Publicity Dir:* Fritz Werf
Subjects: Belles Lettres, Poetry, Art
Founded: 1967
ISBN Publisher's Prefix: 3-921042

Athenaion, see Akademische Verlagsgesellschaft

Athenäum Verlag GmbH, Adelheidstr 2, Postfach 1220, D-6240 Königstein/TS Tel: (06174) 3026 Telex: 0410664
Publisher: Dietrich Pinkerneil; *Editorial:* Dr Beate Pinkerneil; *Sales:* Rudolf Klein; *Publicity:* J E Schmidt-Braül; *Rights & Permissions:* Hildegard Wilhöft
Subsidiary Companies: Anton Hain Verlag GmbH; Peter Hanstein Verlag GmbH; Scriptor Verlag GmbH (qqv)
Subjects: Philosophy, History, Textbooks, Paperbacks, Law, Linguistics, Pedagogy, Politics, Psychology, Social Science, Literary Criticism, Languages, Economics, General Non-fiction
1978: 77 titles *Founded:* 1949
ISBN Publisher's Prefix: 3-7610

Atlantis-Verlag GmbH & Co Kg, Erwinstr 58-60, Postfach 127, D-7800 Freiburg im Breisgau Tel: (0761) 71570
Man Dir: Georg Linke
Subjects: Poetry, Biography, History, Music, Art, Geography, Juveniles
Founded: 1930
Miscellaneous: Firm is a branch office of Atlantis Verlag AG, Zurich, Switzerland (qv)
ISBN Publisher's Prefix: 3-7611

Verlag Ludwig **Auer***, Heilig-Kreuz-Str 12, Postfach 239, D-8850 Donauwörth Tel: (0906) 3061 Cable Add: Auer Donauwörth Telex: 05-1845
Subjects: History, Religion, Education, Textbooks, Juveniles
Founded: 1875
ISBN Publisher's Prefix: 3-403

Aulis Verlag Deubner & Co KG, Antwerpener Str 6/12, D-5000 Cologne 1 Tel: (0221) 518051
Publisher: Karl-August Deubner; *Publicity Manager:* Monika Koster
Subjects: Non-fiction, Juveniles, Biology, Mathematics, Medicine, Physics, Psychology, Engineering, Maps, Geography, Education
ISBN Publisher's Prefix: 3-7614

Aurum Verlag GmbH & Co KG, Erwinstr 60, Postfach 5204, D-7800 Freiburg im Breisgau Tel: (0761) 71034
Publisher: Günther Berkau; *Editorial:* Dr Elisabeth Sicard
Orders to: Walter-Verlag GmbH, Erwinstr 58-60, Postfach 1708, D-7800 Freiburg im Breisgau Tel: (0761) 71050 Telex: 0772676
Associate Company: Hermann Bauer Verlag KG (qv)
Subjects: Psychology, Mysticism, Religion, Yoga, Meditation, Para-Medicine

FEDERAL REPUBLIC OF GERMANY 123

1978: 38 titles *1979:* 36 titles
ISBN Publisher's Prefix: 3-591

Aussaat-und-Schriftenmissions-Verlag GmbH, Wittensteinstr 110-114, Postfach 200735, D-5600 Wuppertal 2 Tel: (0202) 80075/76
Dir: Hans Steinacker, Werner Härtel; *Assistant Dir:* Manfred Gieche; *Editorial:* Alfred Salomon; *Production, Advertising:* Michael Lippkau
Orders to: Schriftenmissions-Verlag, Postfach 548, D-4390 Gladbeck
Subjects: Evangelical and Scriptural Texts, Religion, Education, Juveniles, Paperbacks
Bookshop: Rudolfstr 139, D-5600 Wuppertal 2
1978: 21 titles *1979:* 23 titles *Founded:* 1891
ISBN Publisher's Prefix: 3-7615

Verlag der **Autoren** GmbH & Co KG*, Staufenstr 46, D-6000 Frankfurt am Main Tel: (0611) 725222
Subjects: Texts for Theatre, Radio, Film and TV

Syndikat **Autoren-und Verlagsgesellschaft***, Savignystr 61-63, D-6000 Frankfurt am Main Tel: (0611) 751801/751781
Author/Publisher Syndicate Company
Orders to: VVA Reinhard Mohn OHG, Carl-Bertelsmann Str 161, D-4830 Gütersloh 1; (West Berlin): Lützowstr 105-106, D-1000 Berlin 30
Subjects: mostly serious Nonfiction; Literary Criticism, Art Theory, Psychology, Psychoanalysis, Ethnology, Social Theory and Social History, Political Economy etc

Auxilium Verlag*, Hasstr 7, D-8500 Nuremberg Tel: (0911) 313403
Subject: Educational Material
ISBN Publisher's Prefix: 3-920092

Axel-Juncker Verlag Jacobi KG, see Juncker

B L V Verlagsgesellschaft mbH, Lothstr 29, Postfach 400320, D-8000 Munich 40 Tel: (089) 38851 Cable Add: BLV Verlag Telex: 5215087
Man Dir: Dr A Egger; *Publishing Dir:* Dr Rudolf Schneider; *Editorial:* Wilhelm Eisenreich, Jürgen Kemmler; *International Relations Dir:* Curt Ablaßmayer; *Rights & Permissions:* Ursula Holkko, Monika Grill
Subjects: General Non-fiction: especially Nature, Sports, Field and Travel Guides, Horses, Hunting, Household and Garden, Geography, Bavaria; Technical books on Agriculture, Forestry, Environment, Biology, Nutrition; Education, School Textbooks
Founded: 1946
ISBN Publisher's Prefix: 3-405

B N V (Bohmann-Noltemeyer Verlag)*, Am Kronenburger Hof 9, Postfach 47, D-6901 Dossenheim Tel: (06221) 85755
Publisher: Werner Noltemeyer
Subjects: Engineering, Electronics, Technical

B S-Verlag Manfred Kerler, Marbacher Str 8, Postfach 450, D-7057 Winnenden-Stuttgart Tel: (07195) 8012
Subject: Transport

B V B, see Bayerische Verlagsanstalt Bamberg

J P **Bachem** Verlag GmbH, Ursulaplatz 1, D-5000 Cologne 1 Tel: (0221) 135041
Cable Add: Bachemhaus Cologne
Dirs: Dr Peter Bachem, Gerd Horbach
Subjects: Religion, Social Science, Economics, Biography, Popular Psychology, Books on Cologne and the Rhenish lands
Founded: 1818
ISBN Publisher's Prefix: 3-7616

Karl **Baedeker**, Rosastr 7, D-7800 Freiburg im Breisgau Tel: (0761) 32915 Cable Add: Baedeker Freiburg
Man Dir, Editorial, Production: Florian Baedeker; *Sales, Publicity:* Dr Volkmar Mair
Subsidiary Company: Baedekers Autoführer-Verlag (qv)
Branch Off: Mairs Geographischer Verlag, D-7302 Ostfildern
Subjects: Guide Books, Motoring Guides (in English and French), Facsimile early guidebooks
1980: 92 titles *Founded:* 1827
ISBN Publisher's Prefix: 3-87954

Baedekers Autoführer-Verlag GmbH, Marco-Polo-Str 1, Postfach, D-7302 Ostfildern 4 (Kemnat) bei Stuttgart Tel: (0711) 4502262 Cable Add: Baedeker Stuttgart Telex: 721796 mair d
Man Dirs: Karl Baedeker, Dr Volkmar Mair; *Editorial:* Dr Peter Baumgarten
Parent Company: Karl Baedeker (qv)
Subject: Travel Guides, Motoring Guides
1979: 12 titles *Founded:* 1951 (Stuttgart; originally 1827 Koblenz)
ISBN Publisher's Prefix: 3-87036

Hans A **Baensch**, see Mergus Verlag

Baha'i Verlag GmbH, Eppsteiner Str 89, D-6238 Hofheim-Langenhain Tel: (06192) 22921
Subject: The Baha'i Religion
1978: 5 titles *1979:* 6 titles
ISBN Publisher's Prefix: 3-87037

Friedrich **Bahn** Verlag GmbH, Zasiusstr 8, Postfach 1186, D-7550 Konstanz Tel: (07531) 23054/5
Man Dir: Herbert Denecke; *Manager, Rights & Permissions:* Herbert Denecke
Parent Company: Christliche Verlagsanstalt GmbH (qv)
Subjects: Children's Books, Christian Instruction, Christianity
1978: 6 titles *1979:* 8 titles *Founded:* 1891
ISBN Publisher's Prefix: 3-7621

Bärenreiter Verlag, Karl Vötterle KG*, Heinrich Schütz Allee 29-37, D-35 Kassel-Wilhelmshöhe Tel: (0561) 300117 Cable Add: Bärenreiter, Kassel Telex: 992376
Management: Wolfgang Matthei, Dr Wolfgang Rehm, Barbara Scheuch-Vötterle
Branch Offs: London, England; Tours, France; Basle, Switzerland
Subjects: Music, Calendars, Reproductions of Ancient Topographical Maps
Founded: 1924
ISBN Publisher's Prefix: 3-7618

Verlag **Bartels und Wernitz** KG*, Reinickendorfer Str 113, Postfach 650380, D-1000 Berlin 65 Tel: (030) 4611011 Cable Add: Bartelswernitz Westberlin Telex: 181331 bawer d
Man Dir: Harry Bartels; *Editorial:* Hans-Jürgen Ehrlich; *Sales & Advertising Dir:* Monika Schuchardt-Bartels
Orders to: Georg Lingenbrink, Postfach 3584, D-6000 Frankfurt am Main
Subjects: Sport (including training and history)
1978: 16 titles *Founded:* 1926
ISBN Publisher's Prefix: 3-87039

Otto Wilhelm **Barth**-Verlag KG, Stievestr 9, D-8000 Munich 19 Tel: (089) 172237 Telex: 5215282
Man Dir: Rudolf Streit-Scherz; *Editor:* Stephan Schuhmacher; *Sales:* E Send; *Production:* H Schneiter; *Publicity:* E Flückiger; *Rights & Permissions:* U Griessel
Parent Company: Scherz Verlag AG, Switzerland (qv)
Subjects: Philosophy and Religions of the East, Mysticism

1978: 22 titles *1979:* 26 titles *Founded:* 1924
ISBN Publisher's Prefix: 3-87041

Barudio & Hess Verlag, Neuhaus Str 8, D-6000 Frankfurt am Main Tel: (0611) 5972455
Man Dirs: Dr Gunter Barudio, Stephan Hess; *Editorial:* Barudio, Hess, Maschke; *Sales, Production, Rights & Permissions:* S Hess; *Publicity:* Hess, Schmidt
Subjects: Literature, Politics, Art, History, Economics
1978: 1 title *1979:* 5 titles *Founded:* 1978
ISBN Publisher's Prefix: 3-922182

Basis-Verlag, Postfach 645, D-1000 Berlin 15 (Located at: Gneisenaustr 2, Mehringhof, D-1000 Berlin 61) Tel: (0311) 7848433
Subjects: Juveniles, Comics, Education, Documentary
ISBN Publisher's Prefix: 3-88025

Friedrich **Bassermann**'sche Verlagsbuchhandlung im Falken-Verlag Erich Sicker KG*, Schöne Aussicht 21, Postfach 1120, D-6272 Niederhäusern Tel: (06127) 3011 Telex: 4186585
Subjects: Sports, Wilhelm-Busch-Edition
ISBN Publisher's Prefix: 3-87043

Bastei-Verlag Gustav H Lübbe*, Scheidtbachstr 23-31, Postfach 1170, D-5070 Bergisch Gladbach 3 Tel: (02202) 1211 Cable Add: Scheidtbachstr 23-31 Telex: 887922
Man Dir: Gustav Lübbe; *Manager:* Günther Jakel; *Editorial:* Rolf Schmitz; *Sales:* H-J Karl; *Production:* D Deichmann (Fiction); J Dippmann (Juveniles and Paperbacks); *Publicity:* L Becker-Voss, I Sellmann
Associate Company: Gustav Lübbe Verlag (qv)
Subjects: Paperbacks
Founded: 1953
ISBN Publisher's Prefix: 3-404

Ernst **Battenberg** Verlag, Prinzregentenstr 79, Postfach 800349, D-8000 Munich 80 Tel: (089) 4702066/67
Man Dir, Editorial, Sales, Rights & Permissions: Ernst Battenberg
Subjects: Art and Antiques, Numismatics, Heraldry, Orders and Decorations, Old Maps, Facsimile Editions
1978: 21 titles *1979:* 23 titles *Founded:* 1956
ISBN Publisher's Prefix: 3-87045

Hermann **Bauer** Verlag KG*, Staudingerstrasse 7, Postfach 167, D-7800 Freiburg Tel: 0761/43003 Telex: 0772821
Man Dir: Friedrich Kirner; *Editorial, Publicity, Rights & Permissions:* Gabriele Kirner; *Sales Manager:* Waltraud Kirner
Associate Company: Aurum Verlag GmbH & Co KG (qv)
Subjects: Astrology, Philosophy, Parapsychology, Yoga, Esoterica
1978: 12 titles
ISBN Publisher's Prefix: 3-7626

Bauverlag GmbH, Wittelsbacherstr 10, Postfach 1460, D-6200 Wiesbaden 1 Tel: (06121) 74951 Cable Add: Bauverlag Wiesbaden Telex: 4186792
Dir, Rights & Permissions: Reinhart Knapp; *Sales Dirs:* Eberhard Blottner, Karlheinz Gross; *Publicity & Advertising:* Eberhard Blottner
Subsidiary Companies: Verlag für Aufbereitung Schirmer & Zeh GmbH; Mauritius-Verlags-Messe- & Werbegesellschaft GmbH (both in Wiesbaden, Federal Republic of Germany)
Branch Off: Nikolsburger Str 11, D-1000 Berlin 31
Subjects: Civil Engineering, Architecture, Surveying, Town Planning, Building Materials, Dictionaries, Books and

124 FEDERAL REPUBLIC OF GERMANY

Periodicals in both German and English languages
1978: 82 titles *Founded:* 1929
ISBN Publisher's Prefix: 3-7625

Bayerische Verlagsanstalt Bamberg (B V B), Lange Str 22/24, D-8600 Bamberg
Tel: (0951) 25252 Telex: 06 62860 otvl
Man Dir: Kurt Kiening; *Other Offices:* Norbert Goebel
Associate Companies: Morawa & Co, Austria (qv); Adolf Zwimpfer, Switzerland (qv)
Subsidiary Company: Sankt Otto-Verlag GmbH, at address above
Subjects: Classics, World Literature Series, Poetry, Juveniles, Regional Literature
Bookshop: Goerres Buchhandlung at address above
1978: 15 titles *Founded:* 1949
ISBN Publisher's Prefix: 3-87052

Bayerischer Schulbuch-Verlag, Hubertusstr 4, Postfach 87, D-8000 Munich 19 Tel: (089) 174067/69 Telex: 526677
Dir: Heinz Klüter; *Sales Manager:* Hartmut Köppelmann
Orders to: BSV, Ohmstr 10, D-8047 Karlsfeld Tel: (08131) 95091 Telex: 526677 bsv d
Branch Off: Ohmstr 10, D-8047, Karlsfeld, Düsseldorf
Subjects: School textbooks on all subjects for teachers, and pupils of all ages; also Records, Audiovisual Materials, Periodicals
ISBN Publisher's Prefix: 3-7627

Bechtle*, Hubertusstr 4, D-8000 Munich 19
Tel: (089) 177041 Cable Add: Langenmüller Telex: 05215045
Dirs: Dr Herbert Fleissner, Otto Wolfgang Bechtle, Dr Friedrich Bechtle; *Man Dir:* Dr Georg Niebling
Orders to: VVA Reinhard Mohn, Carl-Bertelsmann-Str 161, D-4830 Gütersloh 1 Tel: (05241) 851 Telex: 0933827; (West Berlin) Halliant, Albrechtstr 17-19, D-1000 Berlin 42
Subjects: Poetry, Biography, History, Politics, High-priced Paperbacks, Series 'Bechtle Anekdoten'
Founded: 1868 (Book Department, 1949)
Miscellaneous: Firm is a member of Verlagsgruppe Langen Müller-Herbig (qv)
ISBN Publisher's Prefix: 3-7623

Verlag C H **Beck***, Wilhelmstr 9, Postfach 400340, D-8000 Munich 40 Tel: 381891
Telex: 05215085 beckd
Dirs: Dr Hans D Beck, Wolfgang Beck; *Editorial:* E Wieckenberg, Ursula Pietsch, Günther Schiwy, B Rüster; *Sales Dirs:* G Elze, E Hoppe; *Publicity Dir:* P Schunemann; *Rights & Permissions:* Eva von Freeden
Associate Companies: Franz Vahlen (qv); Biederstein Verlag (qv)
Branch Off: Palmengartenstr 14, D-6000 Frankfurt am Main
Subjects: Ancient and Modern History, Archaeology, Literary History, Linguistics, Social Sciences, Anthropology, Economics, Law, Popular Nonfiction, Art, Illustrated Books, Textbooks, Classics, Periodicals
1978: 520 titles *Founded:* 1763
ISBN Publisher's Prefixes: 3-406 (Beck), 3-8006 (Vahlen), 3-7642 (Biederstein)

Edition Monika **Beck***, Am Römer-Museum, D-665 Homburg-Schwarzenacker/Saar Tel: (06848) 554
Man Dir/Proprietor: Monika Beck; *Publicity Dir:* B O Beck
Branch Offs: Frankfurt, Kaiserslauten
Subjects: Bibliophile portfolios, First editions, Monograph portfolios
Founded: 1967
Bookclub: Kunstkreis für Bibliophile Mappen

Reinhard **Becker** Verlag, Friedrich-Ebert-Str 80, D-6520 Worms Tel: (06241) 51425
Man Dir, Editorial, Rights & Permissions: Reinhard Becker; *Sales:* Friedrich Becker; *Production:* Uschi Becker
Imprint: Edition Isis
Subjects: Current Events, Belles Lettres, Juveniles, Specialist Computer Operating Literature
Bookshop: Reinhard Becker Buchversand, at above address
1978: 5 titles *1979:* 10 titles *Founded:* 1977
ISBN Publisher's Prefix: 3-88325

M P **Belaieff**, see C F Peters Musikverlag Gmbh und Co KG

Chr **Belser** AG für Verlagsgeschäfte und Co KG, Falkertstr 73, Postfach 1002, D-7000 Stuttgart 1 Tel: (0711) 221359/221350
Cable Add: Belserverlag Telex: 0722334 belag d
Publishers: Hans Weitpert, Hilde Weitpert-Vogt; *General Manager:* Bernd Friedrich; *Managing Editor:* Michael Maegraith; *Sales Manager:* Herbert Lindauer; *Rights & Permissions:* Michael Maegraith, Elfriede Kurz
Subjects: Art, Architecture, Music, Biographies, Natural History, Non-fiction, Politics, Maps, Travel, Book/Record combinations, Periodical *Belser Kunst Quartal*
1979: 33 titles *Founded:* 1835
ISBN Publisher's Prefix: 3-7630

Beltz Verlag, Am Hauptbahnhof 10a Werderstr, Postfach 1120, D-6940 Weinheim Tel: (06201) 61041
Telex: 465500
Man Dir: Dr Manfred Beltz-Rubelmann; *Sales:* Brigitte Klempert, Hans-Joachim Bender, Anni Wetzel; *Publicity:* Gunter Holm
Subjects: Juveniles, Psychology, Social Science, Primary & University Textbooks
Founded: 1841
ISBN Publisher's Prefix: 3-407

Benziger Verlag*, Martinstr 16, D-5000 Cologne 1 Tel: (0221) 210925
Sales & Publicity: Klaus Opitz
Subjects: General Fiction, Juveniles, Education, Politics, Religion
Miscellaneous: Firm is a branch office of Benziger AG, Switzerland (qv)
ISBN Publisher's Prefix: 3-545

Johannes **Berchmans** Verlag GmbH, Münchhausenstr 4, D-8000 Munich 60 Tel: (089) 8114535
General Manager: Dr Erich Lampey
Subjects: Philosophy, Contemporary History
1978: 3 titles
ISBN Publisher's Prefix: 3-87056

Edition Sven Erik **Bergh**, formerly of Tübingen, see Edition Sven Erik Bergh im Europabuch AG, Switzerland

Berghaus Verlag, D-8347 Ramerding Tel: (08571) 8102
Man Dir: Ursel Bader
Imprint: Berghaus International
Subjects: Art, High-priced Paperbacks
1978: 32 titles *1979:* 16 titles *Founded:* 1960
ISBN Publisher's Prefix: 3-7635

J F **Bergmann**, Agnes-Bernauer-Platz 8, D-8000 Munich 21 Tel: (089) 563532 Cable Add: Bergmannverlag Munich
Telex: 529029
General Managers: Dr Heinz Goetze, Dr Konrad F Springer, Claus Michaletz
Subjects: General Science, Medicine, Economics
Founded: 1878
ISBN Publisher's Prefix: 3-8070

Bergverlag Rudolf Rother GmbH, Landshuter Allee 49, Postfach 67, D-8000 Munich 19 Tel: (089) 160081
Publisher: Rudolf Rother; *Sales:* Gertründ Stehberger
Subjects: Mountaineering and Ski-ing
Bookshop: at above address
1978: 25 titles *Founded:* 1920
ISBN Publisher's Prefix: 3-7633

Berlin Verlag, Pacelliallee 5, D-1000 Berlin 33 Tel: (030) 8326232; Ehrenbergstr 29, D-1000 Berlin 33 Tel: (030) 8313469/8326232
Proprietor, Publicity Manager: Arno Spitz
Subjects: International and Comparative Law, Economy, Politics, Bibliographic Guides to Social Science, Legal, Pedagogic Studies etc
1978: 37 titles *Founded:* 1962
ISBN Publisher's Prefix: 3-87061

Berliner Handpresse Wolfgang Joerg und Erich Schoenig, Kohlfurter Str 35, D-1000 Berlin 36 Tel: (030) 6148728/6142605/6141201
Publisher: Wolfgang Joerg
Subjects: General Fiction, Arts, First Editions, Children's Books
Founded: 1961

Berliner Union GmbH, Verlag für Wissenschaft & Technologie, 80 Hessbruehlstr 69, D-7000 Stuttgart Tel: (0711) 78631 Cable Add: Berlinunion
Dir: Dr Jürgen Gutbrod; *Editor:* Axel Schwelling; *Sales Dir:* Gerd W Ludwig; *Rights & Permissions:* Dr Alexander Schweickert
Parent Company: Unternehmensgruppe Verlag W Kohlhammer GmbH (qv)
Subjects: How-to, Reference, Engineering, Rubber Chemistry, Electronics, Electrical Engineering, Computer Programming, General Science
Founded: 1949
ISBN Publisher's Prefix: 3-408

Bernard & Graefe Verlag, Hubertusstr 5, Postfach 380180, D-8000 Munich Tel: (089) 174021/174022
Subjects: Military, History, Politics, Textbooks
Founded: 1918
ISBN Publisher's Prefix: 3-7637

C **Bertelsmann** GmbH, Neumarkterstr 18, D-8000 Munich 80 Tel: (089) 41730 Cable Add: Bertelsmann München Telex: 523259
Dir: Wolfgang Mertz
Parent Company: Verlagsgruppe Bertelsmann GmbH (qv)
Associate Companies: See Verlagsgruppe Bertelsmann GmbH
Subjects: General Fiction & Non-fiction, Juveniles, Arts, Biography, Current Events, Foreign Works in Translation
Founded: 1835
ISBN Publisher's Prefix: 3-570

Verlagsgruppe **Bertelsmann** GmbH, Carl-Bertelsmann-Str 270, D-4830 Gütersloh 1 Tel: (05241) 801 Cable Add: Bertelsmann Gütersloh Telex: 933646
The Bertelsmann Publishing Group
Chairman: Dr Ulrich Wechsler
Member Companies: Verlagsgruppe Bertelsmann International GmbH (qv); C Bertelsmann GmbH (qv); Blanvalet Verlag GmbH (qv); Verlag für Buchmarkt- und Medien-Forschung (qv); Kartographisches Institut Bertelsmann (qv); Lexikothek Verlag GmbH; Mosaik Verlag GmbH (qv); F G Neuer Verlag Gruenwald GmbH (qv); Orbis Verlag für Publizistik (Part-Works); Prisma Verlag GmbH (qv); Proschule Verlag GmbH (qv); RV Reise- und Verkehrsverlag (qv); Schulverlag Vieweg GmbH (qv); Literarischer Verlag Steinhausen GmbH (qv); Friedr Vieweg und Sohn GmbH (qv)

Book Clubs: Bertelsmann Lesering (qv); Europäische Bildungsgemeinschaft Verlags GmbH (qv); Europarings der Buch- und Schallplattenfreunde (qv), all Federal Republic of Germany; The Leisure Circle, UK (qv); Circulo de Leitores Lda, Portugal (qv); Circulo do Livro SA, Brazil (qv) (owned jointly with Abril SA Cultural e Industrial, Brazil (qv))
Founded: 1835
ISBN Publisher's Prefix: 3-570

Verlagsgruppe **Bertelsmann International** GmbH, Carl-Bertelsmann-Str 270, D-4830 Gütersloh Tel: (05241) 801 Telex: 933646
Dirs: Dr Jürgen Krämer, Dr Ulrich Wechsler
Parent Company: Verlagsgruppe Bertelsmann GmbH (qv)
Subjects: International Co-Productions, International Sales of Publishing Rights
Founded: 1977

Beton-Verlag (Concrete Publishing) GmbH, Düsseldorf Str 8, Postfach 110134, D-4000 Düsseldorf 11 Tel: (0211) 571068
General Manager: Emil Fuchs; *Editorial:* Dieter Bausch; *Publicity and Marketing:* Peter Fischer
Orders to: Abteilung Fachbuch at above address
Subjects: Structural Engineering, Technology and Architecture
Founded: 1958
ISBN Publisher's Prefix: 3-7640

Annette **Betz** Verlag, formerly of Munich, removed to Austria (qv)

Elke **Betzel** Verlag, Bertha von Suttner Ring 5a, D-6000 Frankfurt 78 Tel: (0611) 682600
Subjects: Artistic Philosophy, Author/Artist Co-operation, Poetry, Drama
Miscellaneous: Formerly Gruppe Hinterhaus

Beuroner Kunstverlag GmbH, D-7792 Beuron 1 Tel: (07466) 264 Cable Add: Beuroner Kunstverlag
Dir: Gabriel Gawletta; *Publicity Manager:* Siegfried Studer
Subjects: Calendars, Arts, Religion, Periodicals
Founded: 1898
ISBN Publisher's Prefix: 3-87071

Beuth Verlag GmbH, Burggrafenstr 4-10, D-1000 Berlin 30 Tel: (030) 26011 Telex: 183622 bvb d
Man Dirs: Hans Hermann Plischke, Dr-Ing Helmut Reihlen; *Sales Dir:* Werner Schmitz; *Publicity & Advertising Dir:* Albrecht Geuther
Branch Off: Kamekestr 2-8, D-5000 Cologne 1 Tel: (0221) 57131 Telex: 8881332 bvk d
Associate Company: VDI-Verlag GmbH (qv) D-4000 Düsseldorf 1
Subjects: Science & Technical, DIN (German Standards) Handbooks and Textbooks
1980: 2,200 titles *Founded:* 1924
ISBN Publisher's Prefix: 3-410

Bibellesebund eV, Höfel Nr 6, Postfach 1129, D-5277 Marienheide 1 Tel: (02264) 7575
Scripture Union of Germany
Man Dir: Karl Schäfer; *General Manager:* Helmut Klein
Parent Company: Scripture Union, UK (qv)
Subjects: Christian Literature for Juveniles and Adults
1978: 8 titles *Founded:* 1950
ISBN Publisher's Prefix: 3-87982

Bibliographisches Institut AG, Dudenstr 6, Postfach 311, D-6800 Mannheim 1 Tel: (0621) 39011 Cable Add: Biblio Telex: 04-62107 duden d
Man Dirs: Karl Felder, Claus Greuner, Dr Michael Wegner; *Sales:* Rosita Throm; *Sales Dir, Rights & Permissions:* Claus Greuner
Subsidiary Companies: Bibliographisches Institut AG, Zurich (qv); Bibliographisches Institut GmbH, Vienna; Südbuch Vertriebgesellschaft mbH, Mannheim
Subjects: Technology, Arts and Sciences, German Language, General Knowledge, Juveniles, Low-priced Paperbacks, General Science, University Textbooks, Encyclopaedias, Geography
Founded: 1826
Miscellaneous: Publishers of the Duden series of Dictionaries and Lexicons
ISBN Publisher's Prefix: 3-411

Biederstein Verlag, Wilhelmstr 9, D-8000 Munich 40 Tel: (089) 381891 Telex: 05-215085 beck d
Man Dir: Wolfgang Beck; *Sales:* Günter Elze; *Rights & Permissions:* Eva von Freeden
Parent Company: Verlag C H Beck (qv)
Subjects: General Fiction, Poetry, Biography, History, Natural Science
Founded: 1945
ISBN Publisher's Prefix: 3-7642

Birkhäuser Verlag, Olgastr 53, D-7000 Stuttgart 1
Parent Company: Birkhäuser Verlag, Switzerland (qv)

Georg **Bitter** Verlag, Herner Str 62, Postfach 248, D-4350 Recklinghausen Tel: (02361) 25888/21400
Man & Sales Dir: Dr Georg Bitter; *Editorial:* Hans-Sigismund von Buch; *Publicity & Advertising, Rights & Permissions:* Hildegard Schäfer
Subjects: Juveniles, Picture Books
1978: 16 titles *1979:* 18 titles *Founded:* 1968
ISBN Publisher's Prefix: 3-7903

Blanvalet Verlag, Neumarkterstr 16, Postfach 800360, D-8000 Munich 80 Tel: (089) 41730 Cable Add: Bertelsmann München Telex: 524631
Man Dir: Wolfgang Hertz
Parent Company: Verlagsgruppe Bertelsmann GmbH (qv)
Associate Companies: See Verlagsgruppe Bertelsmann
Subjects: Belles Lettres, Juveniles, Biographies
Founded: 1935
ISBN Publisher's Prefix: 3-7645

Blaukreuz-Verlag Wuppertal, Freiligrathstr 27, Postfach 201610 D-5600 Wuppertal 2 Tel: (0202) 621098
Publisher: Hans-Jürgen Weidtke
Parent Company: Blaues Kreuz in Deutschland eV, Wuppertal
Subjects: Alcoholism, Christian Books and Texts
1978: 10 titles *1979:* 18 titles
Miscellaneous: Firm is a contributor to the Telos (qv) series of evangelical paperbacks
ISBN Publisher's Prefix: 3-920106

Bleicher Verlags-KG, Holderäcker Str 14, Postfach 70, D-7016 Gerlingen Tel: (07156) 21033 Cable Add: Bleicherverlag
Publisher, Editorial, Rights & Permissions: Heinz M Bleicher; *Sales, Publicity:* Thomas Bleicher; *Production:* Rainer Abel
Subjects: General Fiction, Picture Books, Poster Books, Comic Verse, Periodicals
Founded: 1968
ISBN Publisher's Prefix: 3-921097

P Stephan **Blotzheim** Ostasiatischer Kunstverlag, see Ostasiatischer Kunstverlag

Böhlau-Verlag GmbH, Niehler Str 272-274, Postfach 600180, D-5000 Cologne 60 Tel: (0221) 765368 Cable Add: Böhlau, Cologne 60
Man Dir: Dr Günter J Henz
Associate Company: Verlag Böhlau, Austria (qv)
Subjects: History, Music, Art, Philosophy, Modern Philology, Theology, General & Social Science
Founded: 1951

Boje-Verlag, Holzstrasse 19, Postfach 1278, D-7000 Stuttgart 1 Tel: (0711) 247305/07 Cable Add: Bojeverlag
Proprietor: Hanns-Jörg Fischer; *Editorial:* Dr Doris Stephan; *Sales:* Michael Fischer; *Production:* Hildegard Schwarz; *Publicity:* Ursula Pfaffinger; *Rights & Permissions:* Erika Weiss
Subject: Juveniles
1978: 38 titles *1979:* 36 titles *Founded:* 1947
ISBN Publisher's Prefix: 3-414

Harald **Boldt** Verlag GmbH, Postfach 110, D-5407 Boppard am Rhein Tel: (06742) 2511
Man Dir, Publicity: Harald Boldt; *Sales Dir:* Heidrun Tschentke; *Production:* Peter Boldt; *Rights & Permissions:* Edith Boldt
Associated Company: Boldt Druck Boppard GmbH
Subjects: Biography, History, Reference, General & Social Science
1978: 26 titles *1979:* 36 titles *Founded:* 1951
ISBN Publisher's Prefix: 3-7646

Bollmann-Bildkarten-Verlag GmbH & Co KG, Lilienthalplatz 3, Postfach 1526, D-3300 Braunschweig Tel: (0531) 332069 Telex: 952546
Dir: Friedrich Bollmann
Subject: Maps

Verlag Aurel **Bongers** KG, Hubertusstr 13, Postfach 220, D-4350 Recklinghausen Tel: (02361) 26001/2 Cable Add: Bongers Recklinghausen
Proprietor, Publishing Dir, Rights & Permissions: Aurel Bongers Sr, Aurel Bongers Jr; *Sales Dir:* Renate Drygalla; *Publicity & Advertising Dir:* Aurel Bongers Jr
Subjects: Art (Modern and Classical Painting and Sculpture, Eastern Church Art), Archaeology, Calendars
1978: 8 titles *1979:* 9 titles *Founded:* 1931
ISBN Publisher's Prefix: 3-7647

Bonn Aktuell GmbH*, Pforzheimer Str 377, Postfach 310807, D-7000 Stuttgart 31 Tel: (0711) 881149
Publisher: Horst Poller
Subjects: Politics, Current Affairs
ISBN Publisher's Prefix: 3-87959

Verlag Adolf **Bonz** GmbH*, Kaisersbacher Str 4, D-7012 Fellbach-Oeffingen Tel: (0711) 511070 Cable Add: Bonz-Verlag
Man Dir: Wolfgang Reinecker
Subjects: Pedagogics, Psychology, Psychoanalysis, Social Science
Founded: 1876
ISBN Publisher's Prefix: 3-87089

Gebrüder **Borntraeger** Verlagsbuchhandlung, Johannesstr 3A, D-7000 Stuttgart 1 Tel: (0711) 623541/3
Man Dirs: Dr Erhard Naegele (Production), Klaus Obermiller (Sales)
Associate Company: E Schweizerbart'sche Verlagsbuchhandlung (qv)
Subjects: Geology, Geomorphology, Geography, Geophysics, Meteorology, Metallurgy, Botany, Biology, Oceanography, General Science
Founded: 1790
ISBN Publisher's Prefix: 3-443

Gustav **Bosse** Verlag, Von-der-Tann-Str 38, D-8400 Regensburg 1 Tel: (0941) 55455 Cable Add: Bosse Regensburg
Imprint: bmp (bosse musik paperback)
Subjects: Early Musical Training, New Religious Songs, Musicology, Musical

Pedagogy, "Contributions to the Musical History of the 19th Century"; Periodicals, Music Paperbacks
1978: 28 titles

Oscar **Brandstetter** Verlag, Stiftstr 30, Postfach 1708, D-6200 Wiesbaden Tel: (06121) 521002/3 Telex: 04186486 obra d
Man Dir: Martin Arndt; *Editorial:* Dr Antonin Kucera
Subjects: Language & Technical Dictionaries
1977-78: 6 titles *Founded:* 1862
ISBN Publisher's Prefix: 3-87097

Verlag G **Braun** GmbH, Karl-Friedrich-Str 14-18, Postfach 1709, D-7500 Karlsruhe Tel: (0721) 1651 Cable Add: Braunverlag Telex: 07826904
Man Dir: Dr Eberhard Knittel; *Dirs:* Karl Breh, Rolf Felz
Subjects: General Science, Medicine, Secondary Textbooks, Music, Paperbacks
ISBN Publisher's Prefix: 3-7650

Literarischer Verlag Helmut **Braun** KG*, Dünnwalder Mauspfad 390, D-5000 Cologne 80 Tel: (0221) 601457
Publisher: Helmut Braun; *Editor:* Berndt Mosblech, Dr Burghard Busse; *Press Chief:* Irene Peters
Orders to: VVA, Postfach 7779, D-4830 Gütersloh; (Berlin) Karl Halliant & Sohn, Albrechtstr 17-19, D-1000 Berlin 42
Subjects: General Fiction, Belles Lettres, Poetry, Juvenile
Founded: 1975
ISBN Publisher's Prefix: 3-88097

Verlag **Braun und Schneider***, Maximiliansplatz 9, D-8000 Munich 2 Tel: (089) 555580
Dirs: Dr Julius Schneider, Friedrich Schneider
Subjects: Juveniles, Paperbacks, Illustrated Books
Founded: 1843
ISBN Publisher's Prefix: 3-87099

Verlag die **Braunkohle**, see Droste Verlag

Werkstatt und Galerie **Breitenbrunn***, Stechbahn 28, D-4190 Kleve Tel: (0043) 2683/5268
A Branch Office of Galerie und Werkstatt Breitenbrunn, Austria (qv)
Dirs: Fria Elfen, Will Frenken
Subjects: Hand-Printed Books, Special Books of Various Kinds, Bibliophile Texts and Documents

Breitkopf und Härtel, Walkmühl-Str 52, Postfach 1707, D-6200 Wiesbaden 1 Tel: (06121) 402031 Cable Add: Breitkopfs Wiesbaden
Man Dirs: Lieselotte Sievers, Gottfried Möckel
Subjects: Music, Books, Education
1978: 30 book titles (plus sheet music)
Founded: 1719
ISBN Publisher's Prefix: 3-7651

Julius **Breitschopf** KG, Verlagsbuchhandlung, Schleisseimerstr 37B, D-8000 Munich 45 Tel: (089) 3514747
Subjects: Juveniles, Television Tie-in Books
Miscellaneous: Associate Company: Verlagsbuchhandlung Julius Breitschopf, A-1170 Vienna, Austria (qv)
ISBN Publishers' Prefix: 3-87254

Breklumer Verlag*, Bundesstr 5/Kirchenstr, Postfach Bredstedt 1220, D-2257 Breklum Tel: (04671) 2028 Cable Add: Breklumer Verlag Breklum
Publisher: Manfred Siegel
Subject: Religion
ISBN Publisher's Prefix: 3-7793

Brendow-Verlag*, Gutenbergstr 1, Postfach 1280, D-4130 Moers 1 Tel: (02841) 41036 Telex: 8121162
Dir: Gerhard Köller
Subjects: Evangelical Religious Literature; firm is a member of the Telos (qv) group of evangelical paperback publishers

Brigg Verlag GmbH (formerly Verlag die Brigg), Hermanstr 33, Postfach 112323, D-8900 Augsburg 11 Tel: (0821) 30008
Man Dir: Franz-Josef Büchler
Subjects: Fiction, Illustrated and Bibliophile Books, Travel, Children's Regional Books, Belles Lettres, Poetry, Music, Art, Juvenile, University Textbooks, Sport and Physical Fitness
1978: 10 titles *Founded:* 1950
ISBN Publisher's Prefix: 3-87101

F A **Brockhaus**, Leberberg 25, Postfach 1709, D-6200 Wiesbaden 1 Tel: (06121) 521054 Cable Add: Brockhausverlag Telex: 04186699
Dirs: Ulrich Porak; *Sales:* H-E Brandt, Gisela Reuter, Kurt Schreiner, Hansjorg Triebel; *Publicity:* Adelheid Schmitz-Valckenberg
Orders to: Publishing address; Hartwich for Berlin; Zentralgesellschaft, Vienna, for Austria; Schweizer Buchzentrum, Olten, for Switzerland
Subjects: Encyclopaedias, Language and other Dictionaries; Biography, History, General Science, Travel, Music, Schopenhauer, Nature, Animals; Fiction
1980: 16 titles *Founded:* 1805
ISBN Publisher's Prefix: 3-7653

R **Brockhaus** Verlag, Postfach 110197, D-5600 Wuppertall (Located at: Champagne 7, D-5657 Haan 2) Tel: (02104) 6311/12/13
Publisher: Dr Ulrich Brockhaus, *Editorial:* Doris Hoppler, Wolfgang Steinseifer, Elisabeth Wetter; *Sales:* Karl-Heinz Eisner, Raimond Schmidt
Associate Company: Theologischer Verlag Rolf Brockhaus (qv)
Subjects: Popular Christian Literature, Biographies, Fiction, Juveniles, Song Books, Bible Study
Founded: 1853
Bookshop: Christliche Buchhandlung R Brockhaus, Kleine Klotzbahn 8, D-5600 Wuppertal-Elberfeld
ISBN Publisher's Prefix: 3-417

Brönner Verlag Breidenstein GmbH, Stuttgarter Str 18-24, D-6000 Frankfurt am Main 1 Tel: (0611) 26001 Cable Add: Brönnerdruck Frankfurtmain Telex: 0411964
Dirs: Klaus-Jürgen Breidenstein, Klaus-Jürgen Schlotte; *Editorial:* Eberhard Urban; *Sales Manager:* Armin H Schwertfeger
Associate Company: Umschau Verlag Breidenstein GmbH (qv for other Associate Companies)
Subjects: Art, Calendars
1980: over 50 titles
ISBN Publisher's Prefix: 3-599

Broschek Druck GmbH & Co KG, Bargkoppelweg 61, D-2000 Hamburg 73
Publisher: Dr A Schneckenburger-Broschek
Subjects: Juveniles, Art History, Illustrated books
Founded: 1913
ISBN Publisher's Prefix: 3-87102

Broschek Verlag, Bargkoppelweg 61, D-2000 Hamburg 73 Tel: (040) 67961 Cable Add: Christians Druck
Orders to: Hans Christians Druckerei & Verlag (qv)
Subjects: Hamburg regional literature

Brücken-Verlag GmbH Literaturvertrieb Import-Export, Ackerstr 3, Postfach 1928, D-4000 Düsseldorf 1 Tel: (0211) 350473 Cable Add: Brücken-Verlag Telex: 8588674 brve
Dir: Erich Mayer; *Sales Managers:* Alfons Clemens, Gerd Fiegweil
Subjects: Textbooks, Literary Criticism, Reprints, Periodicals
Miscellaneous: This firm is the central marketing agency for the Arbeitsgemeinschaft sozialistischer und demokratischer Verleger und Buchhändler (qv for other members of organization)
ISBN Publisher's Prefix: 3-87106

Verlag F **Bruckmann** KG, Nymphenburger Str 86, Postfach 27, D-8000 Munich 20 Tel: (089) 12571 Cable Add: Bruckmannkoge Munich Telex: 0523739
Editor: Erhardt D Stiebner; *Publishing Manager:* F Andreae; *Editorial Manager:* Dr K Beth; *Sales:* H Ludwig; *Publicity:* Fritz Scheuer; *Production:* K Liese
Associate Company: Studio Bruckmann Kunst im Druck (qv)
Subjects: Art, Illustrated Books, Handbooks, Reference, History, Mountaineering, Bavaria
Founded: 1858
ISBN Publisher's Prefix: 3-7654

Studio **Bruckmann Kunst** im Druck Fine Art GmbH, Nymphenburger Str 86, Postfach 27, D-8000 Munich 19 Tel: (089) 12571 Cable Add: Bruckmannkoge Telex: 0523739
Editor: E D Stiebner; *Publishing Manager:* F Andreae; *Sales:* H Ludwig; *Publicity:* Fritz Scheuer; *Production:* K Liese
Associate Company: Verlag F Bruckmann KG (qv)
Subjects: Art; Special Editions
Founded: 1972
ISBN Publisher's Prefix: 3-7854

Brunnen-Verlag GmbH, Pestalozzistr 1, Postfach 5205, D-6300 Giessen Tel: (0641) 42029/42020
Man Dir: Wilfried Jerke; *Editorial:* Helmut Jablonski; *Rights and Permissions:* Rudolf Horn
Branch Off: CH-4001 Basel, Spalenberg 20, Switzerland (qv)
Subjects: Religion, Juveniles
1978: 40 titles *1979:* 40 titles *Founded:* 1919
ISBN Publisher's Prefix: 3-7655

Brunner Verlagsgesellschaft*, Hauptstr 4, D-8500 Nuremberg Tel: (0911) 831614
Man Dir: Monika Popp
Subjects: Children's Books
Founded: 1976
ISBN Publisher's Prefix: 3-88194

Brunnquell-Verlag der Bibel-und Missions-Stiftung Metzingen*, Karlstr 4, Postfach 99, D-7418 Metzingen Tel: (07123) 2280
Subject: Religion
ISBN Publisher's Prefix: 3-7656

Buch und Werburg — Helmut Krüger GmbH, see Krüger

C J **Bücher** GmbH, Borsigallee 17, D-6000 Frankfurt am Main 60 Tel: (0611) 422023
Parent Company: Verlag C J Bücher AG, Switzerland (qv)

Buchholz Verlag für Spiele und Freizeit, Bütehorn KG, Am Boksberg 2, D-3203 Sarstedt Tel: (05066) 5675 Telex: 0927142 kadis d
Games and Leisure Publishing Company
Production Manager: Mrs Buch
Subjects: Juveniles, How-to, Educational

Verlag für **Buchmarkt- und Medien-Forschung**, Faulbrunnstr 13, Postfach 5829, D-6200 Wiesbaden 1 Tel: (06121)

5341 Telex: 933868
And Carl-Bertelsmannstr 270, D-4830
Gütersloh Tel: (05241) 802580
Dir: Manfred Harnischfeger
Parent Company: Verlagsgruppe
Bertelsmann GmbH (qv)
Associate Companies: See Verlagsgruppe
Bertelsmann
Subjects: works connected with Book Trade,
Bibliographies, Periodicals
Founded: 1962

Verlag **Büchse** der Pandora GmbH, Postfach
2820, D-6330 Wetzlar (Located at: Alte
Chaussee 4, D-6334 Asslar-Werdorf) Tel:
(6443) 3361 Cable Add: 6334 Asslar-
Werdorf
Man Dir: Peter Grosshaus, Stefan Blankertz
Subjects: 20th century Literature, Pedagogy,
Philosophy, Art, Architecture, Anarchy
Bookshop (Associated): Buchladen
Galerie/Werkstatt, Obertorstr 22-24, D-6330
Wetzler
1980: 17 titles *Founded:* 1977
ISBN Publisher's Prefix: 3-88178

Bund-Verlag GmbH, Deutz-Kalker Str 46,
Postfach 210140, D-5000 Cologne 21 Tel:
(0221) 82821 Telex: 08873362
Man Dir: Tomas Kosta; *Sales:* Dr H Adam;
Production: Heinz Biermann; *Publicity:*
Waldemar Block; *Rights & Permissions:*
Gunther Heyder, Inge Stalker
Subjects: Trade Union Policy, Industrial
Law, Social Law and Studies, Legal Texts
and Commentaries, Economics, Politics,
Taxation and Finance, WSI Studies
(Industrial Series), Periodicals connected
with Social Services and Workers' Rights
Bookshops: Bund-Verlag GmbH
Buchhandlung at address above; Bund-
Verlag Buchhandlung, Wilhelm-Leuschner
Str 64, D-6000 Frankfurt-am-Main; Bund-
Verlag GmbH Buchhandlung,
Schwanthalerstr 64, D-8000 Munich 2
1979: 50 titles *1980:* 60 titles *Founded:* 1947
ISBN Publisher's Prefix: 3-7663

Burckhardthaus-Laetare Verlag GmbH,
Herzbachweg 2, D-6460 Gelnhausen Tel:
(06051) 891 Cable Add: Burckhardthaus
Dir: Heinz van Rissenbeck
Orders to: PO Box 1140, D-6460 Gelnhausen
Branch Offs: Burckhardthaus-
Buchhandlung, Stubenrauchstr 12, D-1000
Berlin 37
Subjects: Humanities, Arts, Textbooks,
Multimedia, Music, Education, Philosophy,
Psychology, Religion, Social Science, Games
Bookshops: Burckhardthaus-Buchhandlung,
Langgasse 2, D-6460 Gelnhausen;
Burckhardthaus-Buchhandlung, Teltower
Damm 9, D-1000 Berlin 37; Wichern-
Buchhandlung, PO Box 2025, D-6720
Speyer; Burckhardthaus-Buchhandlung
Hackhauser Hof, D-5650 Solingen 11
1980: 50 titles
ISBN Publisher's Prefix: 3-7664

Verlag Aenne **Burda**, Am Kestendamm 2,
Postfach 1160, D-7600 Offenburg Tel:
(0781) 871 Cable Add: burdamoden
offenburg Telex: 752804
Subjects: Hobbies, Cookery, Handicrafts;
Periodicals
1978: 70 titles
ISBN Publisher's Prefix: 3-920158

Burgert Handpresse, Lassenstr 22, D-1000
Berlin 33 Tel: (030) 8264348
Man Dir: Professor Hans-Joachim Burgert
Subjects: Early Lyrical Poetry, Limited
Editions (hand-printed with original
illustrations)
1978: 2 titles *1979:* 1 title *Founded:* 1962

Kartographischer Verlag **Busche** GmbH*,
Kaiserstr 129, Postfach 114, D-4600
Dortmund 1 Tel: (0231) 597088/89 Telex:
0822270
Man Dir: Günter Schiffmann; *Editorial:*
Alfred Heinemann; *Publicity & Advertising
Dir:* Herr Klaffka; *Rights & Permissions:*
Herr Schiffmann
Subjects: Street Maps, Atlases
1979-80: 56 titles *Founded:* 1972
ISBN Publisher's Prefix: 3-921143

Busse Kunstdokumentation GmbH, (Busse
Art Information) Parkstrasse 23, Postfach
1803, D-6200 Wiesbaden Tel: (0611) 553292
Managing Partner: Joachim Busse
Subjects: Art Reference Books, especially
*Internationales Handbuch aller Maler und
Bildhauer des 19 Jahrhunderts, Busse
Verzeichnis* (International Directory of all
Painters and Sculptors of the 19th Century,
Busse Index)
Founded: 1976

Bussesche Verlagshandlung GmbH,
Brüderstr 30, Postfach 1344, D-4900
Herford Tel: (05221) 72055 Cable Add:
Westverlag Herford Telex: 934717
Publishing Dir: K-H Zirkmann; *Commercial
Manager, Rights & Permissions:* Heinz
Zimmermann
Associate Companies: Westdeutsche
Verlagsanstalt GmbH, Postfach 3054,
D-4900 Herford; Buchdruckerei und Verlag
Busse, Postfach 3054, D-4900 Herford
Subjects: Leisure, Sport, Travel, Sailing,
Games and Hobbies, Orientalia
1978: 15 titles *1979:* 15 titles *Founded:* 1947
ISBN Publisher's Prefix: 3-87120

Verlag **Butzon und Bercker** GmbH, Neustr
7-13, Postfach 215, D-4178 Kevelaer 1
Tel: (02832) 6081 Telex: 812207 bb kev
Cable Add: Butzonbercker
Dirs: Edmund Bercker, Dr Edmund Bercker
Jr; *Editorial:* Josef Heckens; *Sales:* Walter
Roelofs; *Production:* Otto Paustian;
Publicity: Werner Krebber; *Rights &
Permissions:* Mrs I Eisenbach
Subjects: Catholic Religion and Theology,
Prayer and Meditation, Liturgy, Religious
Teaching Books for Children
1978: 40 titles *Founded:* 1870
ISBN Publisher's Prefix: 3-7666

Caann Verlag GmbH, Postfach 500148, D-
8000 Munich 71 Tel: (089) 1417239
Man Dir: Klaus Wagn
Subjects: Idea-books, Belles Lettres,
Philosophy, Psychology, Fiction, Nonfiction
Founded: 1969
ISBN Publisher's Prefix: 3-87121

Verlag Georg D W **Callwey**, Streitfeldstr 35,
Postfach 800409, D-8000 Munich 80 Tel:
(089) 433096 Cable Add: Callweyverlag
Telex: 5216752 cal v
Man Dir: Helmuth Baur; *Editorial:* Günther
Mehling, Dr Paulhans Peters; *Sales:* Traute
Geier; *Production:* Christian Pfeiffer-Belli;
Publicity: Ludger Marquardt
Subjects: Biography, History, Architecture,
History of Art, Handicrafts, Landscape
Architecture, Painting and Restoration,
Stonemasonry; Periodicals
1978: 29 titles *1979:* 28 titles *Founded:* 1884
ISBN Publisher's Prefix: 3-7667

Calwer Verlag, Scharnhäuser Str 44, D-7000
Stuttgart 70 Tel: (0711) 452019
Dir: Christof Munz; *Sales, Publicity, Rights
& Permissions:* Sibylle Fritz
Subjects: Reference, Encyclopaedias,
Dictionaries, Education, Audio-
visual/Visual Media, Religion, Periodicals
1978: 30 titles *1980:* 36 titles *Founded:* 1836
ISBN Publisher's Prefix: 3-7668

Campus Verlag GmbH, Schumannstr 65,
D-6000 Frankfurt am Main Tel: (0611)
751008
Man Dir: Frank Schwoerer; *Editor:*
Adalbert Hepp; *Advertising Dir:* Jochen
Woerner; *Editorial:* Klaus Bergmann, Beate
Koglin; *Rights & Permissions:* Ruth
Flickenstein
Subjects: Social Sciences, Psychology,
Pedagogics, Economics, Politics, History,
University Textbooks
1978: 102 titles *1979:* 128 titles *Founded:*
1972 (as Herder und Herder) renamed
Campus Verlag 1975
ISBN Publisher's Prefix: 3-593

Editio **Cantor**, Verlag für Medizin und
Naturwissenschaften KG, Zollenreuterstr 11,
Postfach 1310, D-7960 Aulendorf
Tel: (07525) 431/432/433 Cable Add:
Cantor Aulendorfwürtt Telex: 0732225
vebu d
Subjects: Medicine, Pharmacy, Periodicals
1978: 8 titles *Founded:* 1947
ISBN Publisher's Prefix: 3-87193

Verlag Hans **Carl** KG, Breite Gasse 58-60,
D-8500 Nuremberg 1 Tel: (0911) 203831
Cable Add: Carlverlag Telex: 623081
Man Dir, Editorial: Dr Tilman Schmitt;
Sales, Production: Raimund Schmitt;
Advertising Dir: Rudolf Weidinger;
Publicity Dir: Günter Schmiedel
Subjects: General Fiction, Belles Lettres,
Poetry, History, Art, Philosophy, General
Science, Biochemistry, University
Textbooks, Literature for Brewers
1978: 9 titles *Founded:* 1861
Bookshop: Fachbuchhandlung Hans Carl,
Breite Gasse 58-60, Postfach 9110, D-8500
Nuremberg 1
ISBN Publisher's Prefix: 3-418

Carlsen Verlag GmbH, Postfach 1169, D-
2057 Reinbek bei Hamburg (Located at:
Dieselstr 6, D-2057 Reinbek bei Hamburg)
Tel: (040) 7224051 Telex: 217879 carl d
President: Per Hjald Carlsen; *Man Dir:*
Herbert Voss; *Rights & Permissions:* Per
Hjald Carlsen
Parent Company: Carlsen if, Denmark (qv)
Subject: Juveniles
1978: 180 titles *1979:* 150 titles
Founded: 1953
ISBN Publisher's Prefix: 3-551

Ceres-Verlag Rudolf-August Oetker KG,
Brokstr 77, Postfach Bielefeld 85, D-4800
Bielefeld 1 Tel: (0521) 24024 Cable Add:
Ceres Telex: 0932324
Man Dirs: Ernst A Kobusch, Peter Ruhl;
Editorial: Gisela Knutzen, Ralph Plum;
Sales: Heinz Stühmer, Wolfgang Krauss;
Publicity: Heinz Stühmer, Ralph Plum
Parent Company: August Oetker, Bielefeld
Subjects: Cookery, Wines
1979: 8 titles *1980:* 13 titles *Founded:* 1951
ISBN Publisher's Prefix: 3-7670

Verlag **Chemie** GmbH, Pappelallee 3,
Postfach 1260/1280, D-6940
Weinheim/Bergstr Tel: (06201) 14031
Cable Add: Chemieverlag Weinheimbergstr
Telex: 465516
Man Dirs: Juergen Kreuzhage, Hans
Schermer; *Editorial:* Dr Hans Friedrich
Ebel, Dr Gerd Giesler, Dr Ulrich Herzfeld;
Production: Maximilian Montkowski; *Sales,
Publicity & Advertising:* Helmut Schmitzer;
Rights & Permissions: Kornelia Herbig,
Irmgard Doersam
Branch Offs: Verlag Chemie International
Inc, Plaza Centre, Suite E, 1020 NW 6th St,
Deerfield Beach, Florida 33441, USA; VC
Verlag Chemie AG, Basel, Switzerland (qv)
Subsidiary Companies: Physik Verlag
GmbH (qv); Spektrum der Wissenschaft
Verlags GmbH & Co, Pappelallee 3, D-6940
Weinheim
Subjects: Life Sciences, Physical Sciences
with emphasis on Chemistry & Chemical

Engineering; University Textbooks, Periodicals
1978: 60 titles *1979:* 60 titles *Founded:* 1921
Bookshop: Buchhandlung Chemie, D-6940 Weinheim/Bergstr, Boschstr 12, Postfach 1260/1280
ISBN Publisher's Prefix: 3-527

China Studien- und Verlagsgesellschaft mbH, Paul-Lincke-Ufer 39-40, D-1000 Berlin 36 Tel: (030) 6121056
Man Dirs: Uwe Marsen, Manfred Morgenstern; *Sales:* Uwe Marsen; *Publicity:* Peter Mischke; *Rights & Permissions:* Manfred Morgenstern
Associate Company: Guozi Shudian Distribution Centre
Branch Off: Berger Str 146, D-6000 Frankfurt 60
Subjects: Studies of Modern and Historical China, Dictionaries, Western Translations
1979: 4 titles *Founded:* 1979
ISBN Publisher's Prefix: 3-922373

Christian-Verlag*, Akademiestr 7, D-8000 Munich 40 Tel: (089) 398095
Man Dir: Christian Strasser
Subjects: Psychology, Educational Materials, Music, Art, Religion, High-priced Paperbacks, Social Science, General (illustrated) Nonfiction
Founded: 1949
ISBN Publisher's Prefix: 3-88472

Hans **Christians** Druckerei und Verlag*, Kleine Theaterstr 9-11, Postfach 301021, D-2000 Hamburg 36 Tel: (040) 341456
Cable Add: Christians Druck
General Manager: Jens Christians
Associate Company: Broschek Verlag (qv)
Subjects: General Fiction, Book Industry, History, Arts, Maps, Non-fiction
Founded: 1740
ISBN Publisher's Prefix: 3-7672

Christliche Verlagsanstalt GmbH, Zasiusstr 8, Postfach 1186, D-7750 Konstanz Tel: (07531) 23054/5
Man Dir: Herbert Denecke; *Manager, Rights & Permissions:* Herbert Denecke
Subsidiary Company: Friedrich Bahn Verlag (qv)
Subjects: Novels, Biography, Philosophy, Religion, Juveniles, Low- & High-priced Paperbacks, Psychology, Educational Materials
Bookshop: Buchhandlung der Christlichen Verlagsanstalt, Zasiusstr 8, D-7750 Konstanz
1978: 14 titles *1979:* 11 titles *Founded:* 1892/1933
ISBN Publisher's Prefix: 3-7673

Christliche Verlagsgesellschaft mbH, Moltekestr 1, Postfach 168, D-6340 Dillenburg 1 Tel: (02771) 34021/34022
Cable Add: Christlicher Verlag Dillenburg
Man Dirs: Dieter Boddenberg, Günther Kausemann; *Editorial, Publicity:* Dieter Boddenberg; *Sales:* Dieter Braas; *Production, Rights & Permissions:* Günther Kausemann
Subsidiary Company: Christliche Bücherstuben, at above address
Associate Company: Emmaus-Fernbibelschule Deutschland, at above address
Subjects: Working Texts for Scriptural Instruction, Evangelical Non-fiction
Bookshops: Marburger Tor 32, D-5900 Siegen 1; Alte Linner Str 124, D-4150 Krefeld 1; Moltekestr 1, D-6340 Dillenburg
1978: 6 titles *1979:* 8 titles *Founded:* 1957
ISBN Publisher's Prefix: 3-921292

Christliches Verlagshaus GmbH, Senefelderstr 109, D-7000 Stuttgart 1 Tel: (0711) 221301
Man Dir: Heinz Schäfer
Subjects: Religion (Juvenile & Young Adult); Paperbacks, Periodicals
1978: 40 titles *Founded:* 1872
ISBN Publisher's Prefix: 3-7675

Christophorus-Verlag Herder GmbH, Hermann-Herder-Str 4, D-7800 Freiburg im Breisgau Tel: (0761) 27171 Telex: 07721440
Man Dir: Benno Baldes
Parent Company: Verlag Herder KG (qv)
Subjects: Christian Religious for all ages, Leisure Crafts, Sheet Music
1978: 66 titles *Founded:* 1935
ISBN Publisher's Prefix: 3-419

Verlag Ernst **Chur***, Dedersberg 3, Postfach 2114, D-5372 Schleiden Tel: (02445) 7112
Cable Add: Dedersberg 3 D 5372 Schleiden
Man Dirs: Ernst & Gisela Chur
Subjects: Juveniles, Art, Periodicals
1978: 3 titles *Founded:* 1969
ISBN Publisher's Prefix: 3-87995

Cicero verlagsgesellschaft mbH*, Stuttgarter Str 82, D-7000 Stuttgart 30 Tel: (0711) 850829 Telex: 7252147 ciro d
Man Dir, Editorial, Sales, Rights & Permissions: F K Rothenbacher; *Production, Publicity:* H V Platen
Subjects: Art
Founded: 1970
ISBN Publisher's Prefix: 3-921165

Claassen-Verlag GmbH, Grupellostr 28, Postfach 9229, D-4000 Düsseldorf Tel: (0211) 360516 Cable Add: Claassen-Verlag Telex: 8587327
Publisher: Erwin Barth von Wehrenalp; *Sales Manager:* Herbert Borgartz; *Publicity Manager:* Michael Tochtermann
Subjects: General Fiction, Literary Criticism, Linguistics, Languages, Biography
Miscellaneous: Firm is member of Econ Verlagsgruppe (qv)
ISBN Publisher's Prefix: 3-546

Claudius Verlag GmbH, Birkerstr 22, D-8000 Munich 19 Tel: (089) 184031 Telex: 523718 epdm d
Dirs: Paul Rieger, Hans J Pfalzgraf; *Publicity:* Elfi Barth
Parent Company: Evangelischer Pressverband für Bayern eV (qv)
Associate Company: Verlag J Pfeiffer (qv)
Subjects: Juveniles, Religion, Paperbacks, Records, University Textbooks, Educational Materials
Founded: 1954
ISBN Publisher's Prefix: 3-532

Colloquium Verlag Otto H Hess, Unter den Eichen 93, D-1000 Berlin 45 Tel: (030) 8328085
Proprietors: Anja Hess, Otto H Hess; *Man Dir:* Otto H Hess; *Sales Dir:* Manfred Köppen; *Rights & Permissions:* Dr Gabriele Pangratz
Subsidiary Company: Zeitgeschichtlicher Buchversand GmbH, Unter den Eichen 93, D-1000 Berlin 45, (Mail-order Store)
Orders to: Koch, Neff, Oetinger & Co, Abt. Verlagsauslieferung, Am Wallgraben 110, D-7000 Stuttgart-Vaihingen
Subjects: Current Affairs, Latin-American Studies, History, Pedagogy, Biography, School TV, Research and General Knowledge, Politics
1978: 22 titles *1979:* 20 titles *Founded:* 1948
ISBN Publisher's Prefix: 3-7678

Verlag W A **Colomb***, D-7274 Haiterbach-Oberschwandorf
Editorial: Dr Hans Kittel
Parent Company: Verlag H Heenemann GmbH (qv)
Subjects: Specialist literature connected with enamels, coatings, corrosion protection

Columbus Verlag Paul Oestergaard GmbH, Columbus Haus, Postfach 1180, D-7056 Weinstadt-Beutelsbach Tel: (07151) 68011
Cable Add: Columbus-verlag
Telex: 0724382
Publishers: Peter Oestergaard, Rudi Heubach; *Sales:* Gerhard Reuschle
Subjects: Cartography, Globes, Reference
Founded: 1909
ISBN Publisher's Prefix: 3-87129

Concert Verlag G Kowalski, Ringstr 105, D-1000 Berlin 45 Tel: (030) 8331265 Cable Add: Championpress
Man Dir, Rights & Permissions: Gerhard Kowalski
Orders To: MGS, Postfach 1344, D-8032 Gräfelfing, Munich
Subjects: Music, Folklore, Freelight Stage Directories
Founded: 1974
Miscellaneous: Company also runs a Literary Agency (qv under Kowalski)
ISBN Publisher's Prefix: 3-921793

Verlag F **Coppenrath**, Martinistr 2, Postfach 3820, D-4400 Münster Tel: (0251) 42225
Cable Add: Martinistr 2 Telex: 892112 msfro d
Man Dir: Wolfgang Hölker; *Sales:* Manfred Goldschmidt; *Production:* Martina Walter; *Publicity:* Wolfgang Förster
Subsidiary Company: Verlag Wolfgang Hölker (qv)
Subjects: Arts and Design, General Non-fiction, Juvenile
1978: 16 titles *1979:* 19 titles *Founded:* 1768
ISBN Publisher's Prefix: 3-88547

Copress-Verlag, Schellingstr 39-43, Postfach 401280, D-8000 München 40 Tel: (089) 287202 Cable Add: Copress München
Telex: 524368
Man Dir: Oskar Müller; *Editorial:* Karl-Heinz Huba; *Sales:* Helmut Simler
Subjects: Juveniles, Education, Nonfiction, Games, Sports
ISBN Publisher's Prefix: 3-7679

Cornelsen und Oxford University Press GmbH*, Lützowstr 106, Postfach 3144, D-1000 Berlin 30 Tel: (030) 2621060/2621018 Telex: 184968 cvk b
Man Dirs: Peter Collier, Goetz Manth
Orders to: Cornelsen-Velhagen und Klasing VG (qv), Kammerratsheide 66, D-4800 Bielefeld 1
Parent Companies: Cornelsen-Velhagen und Klasing Verlag für Lehrmedien (Teaching Aids and Textbook Publisher) (qv); Oxford University Press, UK (qv)
Subjects: Secondary & Primary Textbooks in English Language Teaching
1978: 32 titles and 10 textbook series
Founded: 1971
ISBN Publisher's Prefix: 3-8109

Cornelsen-Velhagen und Klasing Verlagsgesellschaft*, Kammerratsheide 66, Postfach 8729, D-4800 Bielefeld 1 Tel: (0521) 700 Cable Add: Cevauka Bielefeld Telex: 932909 cvkbi d
Associate Company: Cornelsen und Oxford University Press
Subjects: Mainly Teaching Aids in National Sciences, Languages, History, Geography, Social Studies, Sexual Instruction

Cornelsen-Velhagen und Klasing GmbH & Co Verlag für Lehrmedien KG, Lützowstr 105-108, Postfach 3144, D-1000 Berlin 30 Tel: (030) 2621071 Cable Add: Cevaukamedien Telex: 184968
Man Dirs: Franz Cornelsen, Hans-H Kannegiesser, Manfred Lösing, Goetz Manth
Associate Companies: Cornelsen-Velhagen und Klasing VG (qv); Cornelsen und Oxford University Press GmbH (qv)
Subjects: Textbooks, Audio-Visual aids for all student levels and adults
Founded: 1968
ISBN Publisher's Prefix: 3-464

Corona Verlag KG, see Dipa-Verlag und Druck

Corvus Verlag, Kurfürstendamm 157, Postfach 311120, D-1000 Berlin Tel: (030) 8854041 Telex: 0184212
Subjects: Popular Non-fiction, Lexicons, Handbook to divining-rod practice, Special commissions in Book Production

J Cramer, in den Springäckern 2, D-3300 Braunschweig Tel: (0531) 65951
Associate Company: Strauss und Cramer GmbH, Hirschberg (Printers)
Subject: Botany (Specialized Technical, Reprints, Texts in English, Latin, French etc), Natural History
1978: 186 titles *1979:* 211 titles *Founded:* 1811
ISBN Publisher's Prefix: 3-7682

Verlag **D und C***, Verlag für zeitgeschichtliche Dokumente und Curiosa, Luitpoldstr 58, D-8520 Erlangen
Tel: (09131) 41505
Editorial: Hans Carl Hopferman; *Sales:* Martin Kirchner
Subject: History
ISBN Publisher's Prefix: 3-921295

D B V-Verlag*, Mühlenstr 9, Postfach 267, D-3508 Melsungen Tel: (05661) 6374
Founded: 1971
Subjects: Ornithology, Protection of Birds, Protection of the Environment/Nature
Periodical: Wir und die Vögel (The Birds and Ourselves)

d e b Verlag (das europäische buch Literaturvertrieb GmbH), Thielallee 34, D-1000 Berlin 33 Tel: (030) 8324051
Orders to: V V A, Postfach 7777, D-4830 Gütersloh
Dir: Tell Schwandt
Subjects: History, Philosophy, Politics, Economics, Marxism, Literature on Germanistics
1977: 10 titles
ISBN Publisher's Prefixes: 3-920303, 3-88436

D R W-Verlag Weinbrenner-KG, Fasanenweg 18, D-7022 Leinfelden-Echterdingen 1 Tel: (0711) 79891
Telex: 7255609 drw
Subsidiary Company: Verlagsanstalt Alexander Koch GmbH (qv)
Subjects: Forestry, Timber, Woodworking, Periodicals
ISBN Publisher's Prefix: 3-87181

D T V, see Deutscher Taschenbuch Verlag

D V A, see Deutsche Verlags-Anstalt GmbH

Damnitz Verlag GmbH, Hohenzollernstr 144, D-8000 Munich 40 Tel: (089) 301015/301016
Man Dir: Otto Schmidl; *Sales Dir:* Rita Grünauer; *Publicity Dir:* Liesl Neumann; *Advertising Dir, Rights & Permisions:* Otto Schmidl
Subjects: General Fiction, Belles Lettres, Poetry, Biography, How-to, Music, Art, Low-priced Paperbacks, Social Science
Founded: 1965
Miscellaneous: Member of Arbeitsgemeinschaft sozialistischer und demokratischer Verleger und Buchhandler (qv for other members)

Verlag **Darmstädter Blätter** Schwarz und Co, Haubachweg 5, D-6100 Darmstadt
Tel: (06151) 48196
Man Dir: Dr Günther Schwarz
Subjects: Semantics, Languages, Dictionaries, Philosophy, Reference, Psychology, Social Science, University, Secondary & Primary Textbooks, Judaica
1978: 27 titles *Founded:* 1967
ISBN Publisher's Prefix: 3-87139

Werner **Dausien***, Frankfurter Landstr 32, D-6450 Hanau am Main Tel: (06181) 82353/22316
Man Dir: Werner Dausien; *Editorial:* Gerlinde Schneider
Orders to: Burgallee 67, 6450 Hanau/M
Tel: (06181) 259052
Subsidiary Company: Verlag Müller & Kiepenheuer, German Federal Republic (qv)
Subjects: How-to, Music, Art, Reference, Juveniles, University Textbooks
Founded: 1949
Bookshop: Werner Dausien, Nürnberger-str 22, D-6450 Hanau am Main
ISBN Publisher's Prefix: 3-7684

R v **Decker's** Verlag G Schenck GmbH*, im Weiher 10, Postfach 102640, D-6900 Heidelberg Tel: (06221) 489250
Telex: 0461727 huehd
Dir: Dr Hans Windsheimer
Associate Companies: Kriminalistik Verlag (qv); C F Müller Juristischer Verlag GmbH (qv)
Subjects: Law, Economy, Admin, Post and Telecommunications, Defence, Defence Admin, Automation, Data Processing, Periodicals

Delius, Klasing und Co, Siekerwall 21, Postfach 4809, D-4800 Bielefeld 1,
Tel: (0521) 67015 Cable Add: Buchklasing
Telex: 0932934
Dirs: Konrad-Wilhelm Delius, Kurt Delius; *Production:* Leo Siebzehnrübl; *Publicity:* Wilhelm Meyerhenke; *Rights & Permissions:* Ilsemarie Steinbrinker
Subsidiary Company: Klasing und Co GmbH (qv)
Subjects: Yachting, Motor Boats, Seafaring and Navigation, Model Boat Building, Motor Cars, Surfing
Founded: 1911
ISBN Publisher's Prefix: 3-7688

Delphin Verlag GmbH, Herzog-Wilhelm-Str 22, D-8000 Munich 2 Tel: (089) 557697/8
Cable Add: Delphinverlag Telex: 522522
Man Dir: Martin Greil
Subsidiary Company: Delphin Verlag AG, Switzerland (qv)
Founded: 1963
ISBN Publisher's Prefix: 3-7735

Delp'sche Verlagsbuchhandlung, St Blasienstr 5, D-8000 Munich 40 Tel: (089) 358498 Telex: 61524
Man Dir: Heinrich Delp
Orders to: Delp, Kegstr 11, D-8532 Bad Windesheim
Subjects: Poetry, Art, Asiatica
1978: 8 titles *Founded:* 1961
ISBN Publisher's Prefix: 3-7689

edition **der 2** Gerald Fritsch und Stefan Fritsch Buchverlag GmbH, Merseburger Str 7, D-1000 Berlin 62 Tel: (030) 7849346
Dir: Gerald Fritsch
Branch Off: Wissenschaftliche Abt, Kurfürstendamm 65, D-1000 Berlin 15
Subjects: Belles Lettres, Fiction, Poetry, Essays
1979: 6 titles *1980:* 4 titles *Founded:* 1974
ISBN Publisher's Prefix: 3-921347

Engelbert **Dessart** Verlag KG, see Siebert und Engelbert Dessart Verlag GmbH

Dr Peter **Deubner** Verlag GmbH, Dürener Str 320, Postfach 410268, D-5000 Cologne 41 Tel: (0221) 436057/436058
Publisher: Dr Peter Deubner; *Dir:* Jürgen Wagner
Subject: Jurisprudence (especially Fiscal Law)
1978: 70 titles *Founded:* 1974

Verlag Harri **Deutsch**, Gräfstr 47, D-6000 Frankfurt am Main 90 Tel: (0611) 775021
Man Dir: Harri Deutsch; *All other offices:*
Dr Anton Reiter
Subsidiary Company: Verlag Harri Deutsch, Switzerland (qv)
Subjects: Natural Sciences, Technical, Textbooks, Reference, Mathematics, Economics, Foreign Languages, Agriculture, Paperbacks
Bookshop: Naturwissenschaftliche Fachbuchhandlung Harri Deutsch, Gräfstr 47, D-6000 Frankfurt am Main 90
1978: 40 titles *Founded:* 1960
ISBN Publisher's Prefix: 3-87144

Deutsche Bibelstiftung, Hauptstätterstr 51, Postfach 755, D-7000 Stuttgart 1 Tel: (0711) 247341 Cable Add: Bibelhaus Stuttgart
Telex: 721816 CSD
The German Bible Foundation
Man Dir: Dr Gernot Winter
Subject: Bibles
Founded: 1812
ISBN Publisher's Prefix: 3-4380

Deutsche Buch-Gemeinschaft C A Koch's Verlag Nachfolger*, Berliner Allee 6, Postfach 4131, D-6100 Darmstadt
Tel: (06151) 8661 Cable Add: Lesestunde
Man Dir: Ernst Leonhard
Associate Company: Deutsche Buch-Gemeinschaft CA Koch's Verlag Nachfolger, Austria (qv)
Subjects: General Fiction, Belles Lettres, Poetry, Biography, History, How-to, Music, Art, Philosophy, Reference, Juveniles
Book Club: Address as above
1978: 240 titles *Founded:* 1924

Deutsche Jugend-Presse-Agentur KG, see Dipa-Verlag und Druck

Deutsche Philips GmbH, see Philips GmbH

Deutsche Verlags-Anstalt GmbH (DVA), Neckarstr 121, Postfach 209, D-7000 Stuttgart 1, Tel: (0711) 2151392 Cable Add: deva Stuttgart Telex: 0722503
Man Dirs: Ulrich Frank-Planitz, Dr Hans Glücker; *Foreign Rights:* Mrs Märit Schütt
Subjects: Fiction, Poetry, Biography, History, Politics, Current Events, General Science, Humanities, Architecture; Scientific and Specialist Magazines
Bookshop: Buchversand Herbert Krebs GmbH, Postfach 209, D-7000 Stuttgart 1
1978: 68 titles *Founded:* 1848
ISBN Publisher's Prefix: 3-421

Deutscher Apotheker Verlag Dr Roland Schmiedel GmbH und Co, Birkenwaldstr 44, Postfach 40, D-7000 Stuttgart 1 Tel: (0711) 292559 Telex: 23636 dazd
Man Dirs: Dr Hanskarl Hornung, Hans Rotta
Associate Companies: Wissenschaftliche Verlagsgesellschaft mbH (qv); S Hirzel Verlag GmbH & Co, Stuttgart (qv); Franz Steiner Verlag GmbH, Wiesbaden; all in Federal Republic of Germany
Subjects: Pharmacy, Periodicals
Founded: 1861
Bookshop: Deutscher Apotheker Verlag, Sortiments-Abteilung, at Company address above
ISBN Publisher's Prefix: 3-7692

Deutscher Betriebswirte-Verlag GmbH, Bleichstr 20-22, Postfach 230, D-7562 Gernsbach 1 Tel: (07224) 3091 Cable Add: dbv Gernsbach Telex: 78915 dbv-d
Man Dirs: Dr Casimir Katz, Christel Katz
Subjects: Business Administration, Management, Marketing, Company Organization, Accounting, Personnel
Bookshops: DBV-Bücherstube, Kelterplatzzentrum, Gernsbach
1978: 10 titles *1979:* 15 titles *Founded:* 1926
ISBN Publisher's Prefix: 3-921099

Deutscher Eichverlag, Burgplatz 1, Postfach 3367, D-3300 Braunschweig
Parent Company: Friedr Vieweg und Sohn GmbH (qv)

Deutscher Fachschriften-Verlag Braun GmbH & Co KG, Felsenstr 23, Postfach 2120, D-6200 Wiesbaden-Dotzheim 1 Tel: (06121) 42785
Publisher: Dr Herbert Braun; *Publicity Manager, Rights & Permissions:* Friedrich Vohl
Subjects: Public Health, Law, Official Reports
ISBN Publisher's Prefix: 3-8078

Deutscher Fachverlag GmbH, renamed Lorch-Verlag GmbH (qv)

Deutscher Gemeindeverlag GmbH, Luxemburger Str 72, Postfach 100448, D-5000 Cologne 1 Tel: (0221) 426761 Telex: dgv köln 08882662
Parent Company: Verlag W Kohlhammer GmbH (qv)
Branch Offs: Hessbrühlstr 69, Postfach 800430, D-7000 Stuttgart 80; Alexanderstr 3, Postfach 1465, D-3000 Hanover Tel: (0511) 328721 Telex: dgv han 0922618
Jägersberg 17, Postfach 1865, D-2300 Kiel 1 Tel: (0431) 554857 Telex: dgv kiel 0292856
Philipp-Reis-Str 3, Postfach 421049, D-6500 Mainz 42 Tel: (06131) 59031/32 Telex: dgv mainz 04187768
Theresienstr, 124/1, Postfach 200625, D-8000 Munich 2 Tel: (089) 521359 Telex: dgv mu d 0523990
Postfach 2125, D-6200 Wiesbaden 1 Tel: (06131) 59031/32 Telex: dgv mainz 04187768
Subjects: The Company specialises in texts connected with local government and laws, environmental protection, social services etc., each of the above Branch Offices being responsible for texts appropriate to the particular region, with associated computer tape and microfilm services, periodicals
ISBN Publisher's Prefix: 3-555

Deutscher Instituts-Verlag GmbH*, Oberländer Ufer 84-88, Postfach 510670, D-5000 Cologne 51 Tel: (0221) 37041 Cable Add: Deutstitut Telex: 8882768
Man Dir, Rights and Permissions: Harald Schwer; *Editorial:* Wilhelm Weisser; *Sales:* Norbert Anselm; *Production:* Horst Schlechter; *Publicity:* Ludwig Matjasic
Parent Company: Institut der Deutschen Wirtschaft, Cologne (German Economics Institute)
Subsidiary Companies: Librex – Buchvertrieb der Deutschen Wirtschaft GmbH; Edition Agrippa GmbH
Subjects: Economic, Company and Educational Policy; Literature
1978: 65 titles *Founded:* 1951
ISBN Publisher's Prefix: 3-88054

Deutscher Kunstverlag GmbH, Vohburger Str 1, D-8000 Munich 21 Tel: (089) 564722
Man Dirs: Dr Michael Meier, Helmut Kaufmann
Orders to: Koch, Neft, Oetinger & Co, Postfach 800620, Am Wallgraben 110, D-7000 Stuttgart 80
Subjects: Art, Pictorial Guidebooks, Regional Art Books, Guides to Artistic Monuments, Egypotology, Catalogues, Yearbooks, Periodicals
1978: 17 titles *Founded:* 1921
ISBN Publisher's Prefix: 3-422

Deutscher Taschenbuch Verlag GmbH & Co KG*, Friedrichstr 1a, Postfach 400422, D-8000 Munich 40 Tel: (089) 397031 Telex: 05215396
Man Dir: Heinz Friedrich; *Editorial:* Maria Friedrich, Eberhard Gaupp, Dr Wolfram Goebel, Winfried Groth, Dr Walter Kumpmann; *Sales Dir:* Wolfgang Josephi; *Publicity & Advertising Dir:* Klaus Baeulke; *Rights & Permissions:* Konrad Jost
Subjects: General Fiction, Belles Lettres, Poetry, Biography, History, Music, Art, Philosophy, Reference, Religion, Juveniles, Medicine, Psychology, General and Social Science, Secondary & Primary Textbooks
Founded: 1961
ISBN Publisher's Prefix: 3-423

Deutscher Verlag für Kunstwissenschaft GmbH, Lindenstr 76, D-1000 Berlin 61 Tel: (030) 2512028 Cable Add: Kunstbrief Berlin
Man Dirs: Professors Dr Heinz Peters, Dr Peter Bloch, Dr Henning Bock
Associate Company: Gebr Mann Verlag (qv)
Subject: Art in Germany, Periodicals
1978: 2 titles *1979:* 5 titles *Founded:* 1964
ISBN Publisher's Prefix: 3-87157

Deutscher Wirtschaftsdienst John von Freyend GmbH, Fachverlag für Wirtschaft und Aussenhandel, Marienburger Str 22, D-5000 Cologne 51 Tel: (0221) 388011/388012 Cable Add: DWD
Sales, Rights & Permissions: Peter John von Freyend; *Editorial, Production:* Edelgard Reiche; *Publicity:* Karl Ludwig Ostermann
Subjects: Loose-leaf systems covering current international economic questions; Chamber of Commerce publications; Finance, Commercial Law
1978: 5 titles *1979:* 4 titles
ISBN Publisher's Prefix: 3-87156

Eugen **Diederichs** Verlag*, Brehmpl 1, Postfach 140163, D-4000 Düsseldorf 14; Bremer Str 5, Postfach 100526, D-5000 Cologne 1 Tel: (0211) 622035 (Düsseldorf); (0221) 137011 (Cologne)
Man Dirs: Dr Eugen Peter Diederichs, Ulf Diederichs; *Editorial:* Gabriele Pfau, Inge Diederichs, Christa Hinze; *Sales Dir:* Horst Biedermann; *Production:* Antje Ketteler; *Advertising & Publicity Dirs:* Ursula Albrecht, Eberhart May; *Rights & Permissions:* Christa Hinze
Orders to: Koch, Neff & Oetinger & Co, Am Wallgraben 110, D-7000 Stuttgart 80; (West Berlin) B A Claudius, Schillerstr 3, D-1000 Berlin 12
Subjects: Belles Lettres, Biography, History, Philosophy, Eastern Religion and Literature, Sociology; Illustrated collections of Folk and Fairy Tales from all countries
1978: 25 titles *Founded:* 1896
ISBN Publisher's Prefix: 3-424

Verlag Moritz **Diesterweg**/Otto Salle Verlag, Hochstr 31, D-6000 Frankfurt am Main 1 Tel: (0611) 13011 Telex: 413234 md d
Orders to: Koch, Neff & Oetinger & Co, Am Wallgraben 110, D-7000 Stuttgart 80
Man Dir: Dietrich Herbst; *Rights & Permissions:* Waltraud Soehnel
Subjects: Educational; Psychology, Social Science, University, Secondary & Primary Textbooks, Educational Materials
1978: 233 titles *Founded:* 1860
ISBN Publisher's Prefixes: 3-425 (Diesterweg), 3-7935 (Salle)

Verlag J H W **Dietz** Nachf GmbH, Godesberger Allee 143, Postfach 200189, D-5300 Bonn 2 Tel: (0228) 378021-378025
Orders to: Verlagsauslieferung Georg Lingenbrink, Postfach 3584, D-6000 Frankfurt am Main 1; (for Berlin) Zirk und Ellenrieder, Lützowstr 105 (bbz), D-1000 Berlin 30
Associate Company: Verlag Neue Gesellschaft GmbH (qv)
Subjects: History, Politics, Sociology, Economics, Legal, Reprints, Periodicals

Dipa-Verlag und Druck GmbH & Co, Deutsche Jugend-Presse-Agentur KG, Weberstr 69-71, D-6000 Frankfurt am Main 1 Tel: (0611) 556188
Man Dir: K-W Hesse (Am Röckerkopf 26, D-6238 Hofheim-Lorsbach Tel: (06192) 8210)
Subsidiary Company: Corona Verlag KG
Subjects: Biography, History, How-to, Music, Art, Reference, Psychology, Social Science, University Textbooks
1978: 76 titles *Founded:* 1948
ISBN Publisher's Prefix: 3-7638

Direkt Verlag*, Bremerstr 11, D-6236 Eschborn/Ts Tel: (06196) 46481
Owner, Rights & Permissions: Volker Abel
Founded: 1978
Subjects: Belles Lettres, Poetry, Social Subjects
1978: 2 titles *Founded:* 1972

Verlag **Dokumentation** Saur KG, now K G Saur Verlag KG (qv)

Don Bosco Verlag der Gesellschaft der Salesianer, Sieboldstr 11, D-8000 Munich 80 Tel: (089) 4138349
Dir: August Brecheisen; *Man Dir:* Johann Ernstberger; *Editorial:* Reinhold Storkenmaier; *Sales:* Johann Windmayer
Associate Companies: Editorial y Libreria Don Bosco, Bolivia (qv); Ecole Technique Don Bosco (Library), Rwanda (qv); Ediciones Don Bosco Spain (qv)
Subjects: Education, How-to, Religion, Textbooks
Founded: 1948
Bookshop: Sieboldstr 11, D-8000 Munich 80
Miscellaneous: The Don Bosco publishing companies and bookshops are departments of the Salesian Religious order, with headquarters in Rome
ISBN Publisher's Prefix: 3-7698

Dreisam-Verlag, Schwaighofstr 6, D-7800 Freiburg-im-Breisgau Tel: (0761) 77037
Subjects: Campaign literature to combat nuclear plants, military drafting; Civil Rights and student advice on dealing with authorities etc; Ecology, Socio-political, Literary Works (Prose and Poetry)
1978: 6 titles *1979:* 7 titles *Founded:* 1975
ISBN Publisher's Prefix: 3-921472

Galerie **Dreiseitel**, Richmondstr 25, D-5000 Cologne 1 Tel: (0221) 244165
Man Dir: H Dreiseitel
Subjects: Art, Illustrated Books (with original illustrations)
1978/9: 7 titles *Founded:* 1971

Cecilie **Dressler** Verlag*, Poppenbütteler Chaussee 55, Postfach 220, D-2000 Hamburg 65 Tel: (040) 6070484 Telex: 02174230
Man Dirs: Thomas Huggle, Uwe Weitendorf
Associate Company: Verlag Friedrich Oetinger (qv)
Subjects: Fiction, Juveniles, Paperbacks
Founded: 1928

Droemersche Verlagsanstalt Th Knaur Nachf, Rauchstr 9-11, Postfach 800480, D-8000 Munich 30 Tel: (089) 984984 Cable Add: Droemerverlag Telex: 522707
Man Dir: Willy Droemer; *Editorial:* Dr Dieter Harnack, Franz Nikolaus Mehling; *Sales Manager:* Ernst Linsmeier; *Publicity Manager:* Peter Breuer; *Rights & Permissions:* Alice Meyer
Subjects: General Fiction, Nonfiction, Dictionaries, Art, Juveniles, Reference, Paperbacks, Textbooks, Current Events, Architecture, Maps, Mathematics, Psychology
Founded: 1901
ISBN Publisher's Prefix: 3-426

Droste Verlag GmbH*, Pressehaus am Martin-Luther-Platz, Postfach 1122, D-4000 Düsseldorf 1 Tel: 8851 Cable Add: Drosteverlag Düsseldorf
Man Dir: Dr Joseph Schaffrath; *Publishing Dir:* Dr Manfred Lotsch; *Editorial:* Heidemarie Alertz; *Sales:* Klaus Ehrke; *Production, Publicity:* Helmut Schwanen
Subsidiary Companies: Verlag Die Braunkohle, Postfach 1122, D-4000 Düsseldorf 1; Wilhelm Knapp Verlag (qv)
Subjects: History, Current Affairs, Politics, Economics, Social Sciences, Art, Belles Lettres, Humour and Satire, Picture Books, Düsseldorf local interest books
Bookshop: Buchhandlung Droste, Pressehaus am Martin-Luther-Platz, Postfach 1122, D-4000 Düsseldorf 1
1978: 72 titles *1979:* 62 titles *Founded:* 1711
ISBN Publisher's Prefix: 3-7700

Druckenmüller Verlag*, Martiusstr 8, D-8000 Munich 40 Tel: (089) 348074 Telex: 5215517
Associate Companies: Artemis & Winkler Verlag, Munich (qv); Verlag für Architektur, Munich (qv); Artemis Verlag, Zürich, Switzerland (qv)
Subjects: Encyclopedia of Classical Antiquity, Classical Works, European Ancient History

Druffel-Verlag, Assenbucherstr 28, D-8131 Leoni am Starnbergersee Tel: (08151) 5326
Dir: Dr Gert Sudholt; *Publisher:* Ursula Sündermann;
Subjects: Popular German History (especially relative to World War II), German Politics, Controversial Reportage
ISBN Publisher's Prefix: 3-8061

Monika **Dülk** Verlag*, Kaiserdamm 12, D-1000 Berlin 19 Tel: (030) 322585
Subjects: City maps, Travel Guides

Horst-Werner **Dumjahn** Verlag, Parcusstr 9, Postfach 1746, D-6500 Mainz 1 Tel: 06131/21010
Man Dir and Other Offices: Horst-Werner Dumjahn
Orders to: Vereinigte Verlagsauslieferung (VVA), Postfach 7777, D-4830 Gütersloh
Subjects: Railways and Railway History (Federal German and other countries)
Bookshop: Versandbuchhandlung und Antiquariat Horst-Werner Dumjahn at above address (Antiquarian Bookshop and Despatch Office)
1978: 2 titles *1979:* 3 titles *Founded:* 1974
ISBN Publisher's Prefix: 3-921426

Wolfgang **Dummer** und Co, see Verlag Moderne Industrie

Ferd **Dümmlers** Verlag, Kaiserstr 31-37, Postfach 1480, D-5300 Bonn 1 Tel: (0228) 223031 Cable Add: Dümmlerbuch
Man Dir: Helmut Lehmann
Subjects: Schoolbooks and Pedagogic books for Schools of all levels, Technical and Specialised School Textbooks in Natural Sciences, Arts, Linguistics; also Sports, Hobbies, History, Politics, Periodicals
1979: 50 titles *Founded:* 1808
ISBN Publisher's Prefix: 3-427

Duncker und Humblot, Dietrich-Schäfer-Weg 9, Postfach 410329, D-1000 Berlin 41 Tel: (030) 7912026
Subjects: History, Philosophy, General & Social Science, Law, University Textbooks
1978: 220 titles *1979:* 240 titles *Founded:* 1798
ISBN Publisher's Prefix: 3-428

Dustri-Verlag Dr Karl Feistle, Bahnhofstrasse 5, Postfach 49, D-8024 Deisenhofen-Munich Tel: (089) 6132352
Dirs: Dr Karl Feistle, Hans-Peter Eckardt
Subjects: Medicine, Reference, Paperbacks, Periodicals

E O S Verlag, Erzabtei Sankt Ottilien, D-8917 Sankt Ottilen Tel: 08193/71261
Man Dir: Dr P Bernhard Sirch
Subjects: Religion, Theology, Spiritual Life, Travel, Children's Books
Bookshop: Klosterladen, D-8917 Sankt Ottillen
Founded: 1904
ISBN Publisher's Prefix: 3-88096, 3-920289

E R Verlags GmbH, see Symposium-Verlag

Ebeling Verlag GmbH, Langgasse 35, Postfach 2368, D-6200 Wiesbaden 1 Tel: (06121) 39081 Telex: 4186318
Subject: Art

Echter-Seelsorge Verlag*, Juliuspromenade 64, Postfach 5560, D-8700 Würzburg
Subjects: Exegesis, Bible Research, Spirituality, Books of Plates, Art Books, Stories, Periodicals

Econ Verlagsgruppe, Grupellostr 28, Postfach 9229, D-4000 Düsseldorf 1 Tel: (0211) 360516 Cable Add: Econ-Verlag Telex: 8587327
Publisher: Erwin Barth von Wehrenalp; *Sales & Marketing:* Herbert Borgartz; *Advertising & Promotion:* Michael Tochtermann
Subjects: Biography, History, Politics, Music, Art, Travel, Reference, Religion, Archaeology, Medicine, Psychology, General & Social Science, Audio-visual Teaching Aids, General Fiction
Miscellaneous: Group comprises Claassen Verlag GmbH (qv), Econ Verlag GmbH, Marion von Schröder Verlag GmbH (qv)
ISBN Publisher's Prefix: 3-430

Edition der 2, see der 2

Egoist-Verlag*, Postfach 910207, D-3000 Hanover 91 Tel: (0511) 451354
Man & Sales Dirs: E Kreutzburg, A Seide; *Publicity & Advertising Dir:* Herr Barth; *Rights & Permissions:* Herr Kreutzburg
Subjects: Modern Art, Design, Belles Lettres

Ehapa Verlag GmbH, Postfach 1215, D-7000 Stuttgart Tel: (0711) 790271 Cable Add: Ehapa Stuttgart Telex: 7255581 ehpd
Dir: Walter Berning; *Manager:* Adolf Kabatek; *Editorial:* A Kabatek (comics), W Berning (special magazines); *Sales:* M Klieber; *Production:* S Eberspächer; *Publicity:* U Marbach, M Grude; *Rights & Permissions:* Christine Wagner, A Kabatek, W Berning
Parent Company: Gutenberghus Publishing Service, Denmark (qv)
Associate Companies: Gutenberghus Bladene, Denmark; Hjemmet A/S, Norway; Hemmets Journal AB, Forlaget Kärnan AB, Sweden (qqv)
Subjects: Hobbies, Non-fiction, Comics, Cartoons, Periodicals relating to leisure pursuits and technology
Founded: 1951

Ehrenwirth Verlag GmbH, Postfach 860348, D-8000 Munich 86 (Located at: Vilshofenerstr 8) Tel: (089) 989025 Telex: 0529667
Publisher: Martin Ehrenwirth; *Man Dir:* Frank Auerbach; *Sales, Publicity & Advertising Dir:* Gebhard von Doering; *Editorial:* Perdita Pasche, Inge Jauss, Reinhard Stachwitz; *Rights & Permissions:* Frank Auerbach
Distribution: Verlegerdienst München, Postfach 1280, D-8031 Gilching
Subjects: General Fiction, Poetry, History, Biography, How-to, Natural Healing, Beekeeping, Reference, High-priced Paperbacks, Psychology, Social Science, University, Secondary and Primary Textbooks, Educational Materials

1978: 90 titles *1979:* 140 titles *Founded:* 1945
ISBN Publisher's Prefix: 3-431

Eldra Taschenbuchverlag, Postfach 950171, D-5000 Cologne 91 (Located at: Am Sommerberg 29, D-5064 Roesrath 3) Tel: (02205) 81849
Man Dir: A Osterhoff
Subjects: Epic, Lyrical and Dramatic Works in paperback form

Elitera-Verlag GmbH, see AEG-Telefunken

Ellenberg Verlag, Am Urbacher Wall 35, D-5000 90, also Postfach 100705, D-5000 Cologne 1 Tel: (02203) 22675
Man Dir: Dr Eduard Ellenberg
Parent Company: Ellenberg GmbH
Subsidiary Company: Theaterverlag Ellenberg
Subjects: Belles Lettres, Anthologies, Documentaries, Politics, Theology, History, Philosophy, Economics, Art, Science, Poetry, Novels, Theatre, Literature, other areas of Scholarship; Periodicals
1978: 28 titles *1979:* 26 titles *Founded:* 1974
ISBN Publisher's Prefix: 3-921369

Verlag Heinrich **Ellermann** KG, Romanstr 16, D-8000 Munich 19 Tel: (089) 133737 Cable Add: Ellerbuch, Munich
Man Dirs: Berthold und Christa Spangenberg; *Editorial, Sales, Production, Publicity, Rights & Permissions:* Christa Spangenberg
Orders to: Koch, Neff & Oetinger, Am Wallgraben 110, D-7000 Stuttgart Tel: (0711) 78601
Imprints: Edition Spangenberg
Subjects: Belles Lettres, Juveniles
1978: 19 titles *1979:* 20 titles *Founded:* 1934
ISBN Publisher's Prefix: 3-7707

Elpis Verlag GmbH, Husarenstr 35, D-6900 Heidelberg Tel: 46123
Man Dir and other offices: Dr Manfred Thiel
Subjects: Philosophy, Musical interest, Poetry
1979: 1 title *1980:* 3 titles *Founded:* 1977

Otto **Elsner** Verlagsgesellschaft mbH & Co KG*, Schöfferstr 15, Postfach 4039, D-6100 Darmstadt Tel: (06151) 891630
Man Dir: Dr Franz-G Rudl
Subjects: Belles Lettres, Poetry, Reference, Engineering, Transportation, University Textbooks
1978: 5 titles *Founded:* 1871
ISBN Publisher's Prefix: 3-87199

Elwert und Meurer GmbH*, Hauptstr 101, D-1000 Berlin 62 Tel: (030) 784001
Associate Company: Karl Ohm Verlag (qv)
Subjects: Cybernetics, Psychology, Philosophy, Law, Sociology, Politics
ISBN Publisher's Prefix: 3-7669

N G **Elwert** Verlag*, Reitgasse 7-9, Postfach 1128, D-3550 Marburg an der Lahn Tel: (06421) 25024 Cable Add: Elwert Marburg
Man Dir: Dr W Braun-Elwert
Subjects: History, Religion, Law, German Language & Literary History, Social Science
1978: 36 titles *Founded:* 1726
ISBN Publisher's Prefix: 3-7708

Encyclopaedia Britannica, Berliner Allee 47, Postfach 200209, D-4000 Düsseldorf Tel: (0211) 324945
Manager: R J Ellmers
Miscellaneous: Firm is an associate company of Encyclopaedia Britannica International Ltd, USA (see UK entry for other associates)

Friedemann von **Engel** Verlag*, Friedbergstr 5, D-1000 Berlin 19 Tel: (030) 3233145
Man Dir: F V Engel

Subsidiary Company: Globetrotter-Verlag, at same address
Subjects: Tips für Trips series of travel handbooks

Engelbert-Verlag Zimmermann KG, Widukindplatz 2, Postfach 120, D-5893 Balve/Sauerland Tel: (02375) 631 Cable Add: Gezet Balve Telex: 827755 gezi d
Publisher: Heinz Zimmermann; *Reader:* Alfons Schumacher; *Production:* Heinz Droste; *Sales Manager:* Helmut Levermann
Subjects: Juveniles, Popular Science, Information Books; General Fiction and Nonfiction
Founded: 1930
ISBN Publisher's Prefix: 3-536

Carl **Engels** Musikverlag, see P J Tonger

F **Englisch** Verlag GmbH, Webergasse 12, Postfach 2309, D-6200 Wiesbaden Tel: (06121) 39478/9 Telex: 4186741
Man Dir: F-I Englisch; *Editorial, Sales, Rights & Permissions:* R Fuhr; *Production, Publicity:* G Heigel
Orders to: Vereinigte Verlagsauslieferung (VVA), Reinhard Mohn OHG, Postfach 7777, D-4830 Gütersloh
Subjects: General Nonfiction, Folk and Myth, Facsimile editions
1978: 22 titles *1979:* 25 titles *Founded:* 1973
ISBN Publisher's Prefix: 3-88140

Ferdinand **Enke** Verlag, Herdweg 63, Postfach 1304, D-7000 Stuttgart 1 Tel: (0711) 20471 Cable Add: Enkebuch Telex: 721942
Man Dir: Dr med hc Günther Hauff, Dr Jur Albrecht Greuner, Frau Dr M Kuhlmann; *Sales Dir, Rights & Permissions:* Joachim Niendorf; *Publicity:* Jürgen Ritter
Subjects: Medicine, Psychology, Social Science, Veterinary, Geology, Chemistry, University Textbooks, Scientific Journals
Founded: 1837
ISBN Publisher's Prefix: 3-432

Ensslin Jugendbuchverlag, see Ensslin und Laiblin

Ensslin und Laiblin Verlag GmbH & Co KG, Harretstr 6, Postfach 754, D-7412 Eningen Tel: (07121) 8471/2/3 Cable Add: Buchhaus Reutlingen Telex: 0729733
Man Dir: Joachim Ulrich Hebsaker; *Editorial:* Grit Hebsaker, Lelo Cecilé Burkert; *Sales:* Gerda Uecker; *Production:* Bettina Drees; *Publicity:* Ellen Abel; *Rights & Permissions:* J U Hebsaker, Grit Hebsaker
Branch Off: Harretstr 6, D-7412 Eningen
Subjects: Children's Books
1979: 19 titles *1980:* 25 titles *Founded:* 1818
ISBN Publisher's Prefix: 3-7709

Hans P **Eppinger**, Brenzstr 16, D-7170 Schwäbisch Hall Tel: (0791) 53061 Cable Add: Eppinger-Verlag Schwäbisch Hall
Man Dir: Hans Paul Eppinger
Subjects: Belles Lettres, Picture Books, History, Anthropology, Juveniles
Founded: 1970
ISBN Publisher's Prefix: 3-87176

Horst **Erdmann** Verlag für Internationalen Kulturaustausch, Hartmayerstr 117, Postfach 1380, D-7400 Tübingen 1 Tel: (07071) 62061/2 Cable Add: Erdmannverlag Tübingen Telex: 7262741 erdm
Publicity & Sales Department: Milanweg 1, D-7400 Tübingen Tel: (07071) 64409
Man Dir: Horst J Erdmann; *Editorial and Production:* Dr Gernot Giertz; *Sales and Publicity:* Rosemarie Erdmann; *Rights & Permissions:* Margarete Graf
Orders to: VA Koch, Neff & Oetinger, Postfach 800620, D-7000 Stuttgart 80
Branch Off: Horst Erdmann Verlag & Co, Bachofenstr 10, CH-4000 Basel, Switzerland

Subjects: General Fiction, Belles Lettres, Poetry, Biography, History, How-to, Reference, Educational Materials
Founded: 1956
ISBN Publisher's Prefix: 3-7711

Verlag **Eremiten**-Presse Hülsmanns & Reske GmbH, Fortunastr 11, Eremiten-Haus, Postfach 170143, D-4000 Düsseldorf 1 Tel: (0211) 660590
Man Dirs: Dieter Huelsmanns, Friedolin Reske
Subjects: General Fiction, Belles Lettres, Poetry, Music, Art, High- & Low-priced Paperbacks
Founded: 1949
ISBN Publisher's Prefix: 3-87365

Edition **Eres** Horst Schubert Musikverlag, Feldhäuser Str 94, Postfach 1220, D-2804 Lilienthal-Bremen Tel: (04298) 1676
Man Dir: Horst Schubert
Subjects: Music, Art, High-priced Paperbacks, University, Secondary & Primary Textbooks, Educational Materials
Founded: 1946
ISBN Publisher's Prefix: 3-87204

Wilhelm **Ernst** und Sohn Verlag für Architektur und Technische Wissenschaften, Hohenzollerndamm 170, D-1000 Berlin 31 Tel: (030) 860376/7/8 Telex: 0184143 Cable Add: Ernstsohn Berlin
Dir: Karlheinz Grassmann; *Editorial, Rights & Permissions:* Rudi Groll; *Sales:* Wilhelm Schreiber, H-J Winterstein; *Production:* W Schreiber; *Publicity:* Bärbel Schneider
Branch Off: Flüggenstr 13, D-8000 Munich 19
Subjects: Technical, Architecture
Bookshops: Gropius, Technische Fachbuchhandlung, Hohenzollerndamm 170, D-1000 Berlin 31; Flüggenstr 13, D-8000 Munich 19
1978: 35 titles *1979:* 28 titles *Founded:* 1851
Miscellaneous: Member of ABV (Arbeitsgemeinschaft Baufachverlage)
ISBN Publisher's Prefix: 3-433

Erota-Press, see Odörfer-Verlags GmbH

Euphorion Verlag*, Egenolffstr 14, D-6000 Frankfurt am Main 1
Man Dir: H Imhoff; *Sales Manager:* Roderick Klein; *Publicity Dir:* Ulrich Raschke; *Rights and Permissions:* Peter Kochanski
Subjects: Belles Lettres, Poetry, Philosophy
Book Club: Freundeskreis des Euphorion Verlages, Neumannstr 13, D-6000 Frankfurt am Rhein 50
Founded: 1963

Verlag **Europa**-Lehrmittel, Nourney, Vollmer & Co OHG, Postfach 201815, D-5600 Wuppertal 2 (Located at: Kleiner Werth 50) Tel: (0202) 556070/593970
Managing Partner: Helmut Nourney; *General Manager:* Joachim Nourney
Subjects: Textbooks for School and Professional use: in Metallurgy, Automobile, Electrical, Electronics, Physics, Building, Timber, Economics
1978: 87 titles *1979:* 92 titles *Founded:* 1947
ISBN Publisher's Prefix: 3-8085

Das **Europäische** Buch, see D E B Verlag

Europäische Gemeinschaften (European Communities)*, Zitelmannstr 22, D-5300 Bonn Tel: 238041 Telex: 886648
Subjects: Monographs, Documents, Periodicals on European integration, Official and Business Reports, Studies of Competition, Industry and Agriculture, European Instructional and Information Literature, Periodical *EG Magazin*

Verlag **europäische Ideen***, Postfach 246, 1 Berlin 37 (Located at: Mühlenstrasse 17b) Tel: (030) 8111852
Subjects: Reprints of all the Works of Erich Mühsam, Anarchist, comprising some 33 titles, all of a socio-political nature

Europäische Verlagsanstalt GmbH*, Deutz-Kalker-Str 46, Postfach 210140, D-5000 Cologne 21 Tel: (0221) 82821 Telex: Bund d 8873362
Man Dir: Tomas Kosta; *Editorial:* Günther Heyder; *Sales Dir:* Karl-Ernst Sakobielski, Waldemar Block; *Rights & Permissions:* Lieselotte Vorwerk
Subjects: History, Philosophy, Psychology, Social Science, Judaica, Political Science, Economics, Trade Unions
Founded: 1946
ISBN Publisher's Prefix: 3-434

Europrisma-Verlag, Auf dem Gelling 7, D-5800 Hagen Tel: (02331) 46655
Dir: Stephan Ramrath

Verlag der **Evangelisch Lutherischen Mission**, Schenkstr 69, D-8520 Erlangen Tel: (09131) 33064
Publisher: Christoph Jahn; *Sales Manager:* Eva Mueller
Subjects: Juveniles, Calendars, Religion, Social Science, Paperbacks
1980: 20 titles
ISBN Publisher's Prefix: 3-87214

Verlag und Schriftenmission der **Evangelischer Gesellschaft** für Deutschland GmbH, Kaiserstr 78, D-5600 Wuppertal 11 Tel: (0202) 784018
Publishing House and Scriptural Mission of the German Evangelical Society
Man Dir: Ulrich Affeld; *Sales, Production, Publicity:* Herbert Becker
Subjects: Religious Literature; Telos and Junior Telos texts (see Miscellaneous)
1978: 8 titles *1979:* 10 titles *Founded:* 1954
Miscellaneous: Firm is a member of the Telos group (qv) publishing evangelical paperbacks
ISBN Publisher's Prefix: 3-87857

Evangelischer Missionsverlag, Postfach 1380, D-7015 Korntal-Münchingen 1 Tel: (0711) 831083
Man Dir: Erwin Scherer
Subjects: Religion, Juveniles, Educational Materials
Bookshop: Buchhandlung des Evangelischen Missionsverlag, D-7015 Korntal-Münchingen 1, Postfach 1380
Founded: 1920
ISBN Publisher's Prefix: 3-7714

Evangelischer Presseverband für Bayern eV, Birkerstr 22, D-8000 Munich 19 Tel: (089) 184031 Telex: 0523718
Bavarian Evangelical Press Union
Dirs: Paul Rieger, Hans-Joachim Pfalzgraf; *Publicity Manager:* Elfi Barth
Subsidiary Company: Claudius Verlag GmbH (qv)
Subjects: Evangelical Press Service, School Books, Song Books, Christian weekly periodical
Founded: 1932
ISBN Publisher's Prefix: 3-583

Evangelisches Verlagswerk GmbH, Leerbachstr 42, D-6000 Frankfurt-am-Main 1 Tel: (0611) 720379
Man Dir: Helga Müller-Römheld
Subject: Religion
1978: 6 titles *Founded:* 1947
ISBN Publisher's Prefix: 3-7715

Expanded Media Editions, Herwarthstr 27, D-5300 Bonn Tel: (02221) 655887
Editorial, Sales, Production, Publicity, Rights & Permissions: S Pociao; *Editorial, Production, Publicity:* Walter Hartmann

Associated Companies: see under Pro Media, Berlin (Major Booksellers)
Subjects: Belles Lettres, Poetry, Music, Art, High-priced Paperbacks
1978: 3 titles *Founded:* 1969
Bookshop: Pociao's Book Shop, Herwarthstr 27, D-5300 Bonn
ISBN Publisher's Prefix: 3-88030

Fackelträger-Verlag Schmidt-Küster GmbH*, Ricklinger Stadtweg 118, D-3000 Hanover 91 Tel: (0511) 454088
Man Dir: Hans Rauschning; *Sales:* Siegfried Liebrecht
Subjects: General Fiction, Poetry, Biography, History, How-to, Art, Juveniles
1978: 12 titles *Founded:* 1949
ISBN Publisher's Prefix: 3-7716

Fackelverlag G Bowitz GmbH*, Herdweg 29-31, Postfach 442, D-7000 Stuttgart 1 Tel: (0711) 20171 Cable Add: Fackelverlag Stuttgart Telex: 0722875
Despatch Off: Schockenriedstr 46, D-7000 Stuttgart 80
Branch Off: A-6971 Hard-Bei-Bregenz, Ankergasse 18a, Austria
Subjects: General Fiction, History, How-to, Reference, Dictionaries, Low-priced Paperbacks
Book Club: Fackel-Buchklub
Founded: 1919
ISBN Publisher's Prefix: 3-87220

Falk- Verlag für Landkarten & Stadtpläne Gerhard Falk GmbH, Burchardstr 8, Postfach 102122, D-2000 Hamburg 1 Tel: (040) 331981 Cable Add: falkverlag Telex: 02162175
Man Dir: Dr Helge Lintzhöft, Handelsregister AG Hamburg HRB 23204
Subjects: Maps, Guidebooks, Phrasebooks
1978: 12 titles *1979:* 10 titles *Founded:* 1945
ISBN Publisher's Prefixes: 3-920317, 3-88445

Falken-Verlag GmbH, Schöne Aussicht 21, Postfach 1120, D-6272 Niedernhausen Tel: (06127) 3011/3015 Telex: 4186585
Man Dir: Frank Sicker; *Deputy Dir:* Dietrich John; *Publishing Manager:* Ulrich Watschounek; *Sales:* Manfred Abrahamsberg; *Production:* Horst Gemmerich; *Rights & Permissions:* Jo Klein
Subjects: Health, Hobbies, Further Education, Family Life, Gardening, Cooking, Games, Sports
1980: 480 titles *Founded:* 1923
ISBN Publisher's Prefix: 3-8068

Dr Martin **Faltermaier**, see Juventa Verlag

Favorit-Verlag Huntemann & Co*, Stettiner Str 16, Postfach 1549, D-7550 Rastatt Tel: (07222) 22254/5 Cable Add: favoritverlag Telex: 0786630
Subjects: Juveniles, Calendars

Willy F P **Fehling** GmbH, Spichernstr 22-26, Postfach 1960, D-3000 Hanover Tel: (0511) 33921 Cable Add: Fehlingwerk Hannover Telex: 0922758
Publisher: Werner von Holtzendorff-Fehling; *Man Dir, Editorial:* Günther Ostermeier; *Production:* Gerd Gehrold
Orders to: B L V, Lothstr 29, D-8000 Munich 40
Subject: Horticulture
1978: 3 titles *1979:* 2 titles *Founded:* 1912
ISBN Publisher's Prefix: 3-921144

Dr Karl **Feistle**, see Dustri-Verlag

Feuervogel-Verlag GmbH, Gerh-Hauptmann Ring 107-109, Postfach 550122, D-6000 Frankfurt am Main Tel: (0611) 574257
Man Dir: Georg Treguboff
Subjects: Historical novels and documentation concerning post-1917 Russia
1980: 8 titles *Founded:* 1971
ISBN Publisher's Prefix: 3-921148

Wolfgang **Fietkau** Verlag, Potsdamer Chaussee 16, D-1000 Berlin 37 Tel: (030) 7743492
Publisher: Wolfgang Fietkau
Founded: 1959
Subject: Poetry, Belles Lettres
ISBN Publisher's Prefix: 3-87352

Fikentscher und Co, see Technik Tabellen Verlag

Emil **Fink** Verlag, Heidehofstr 15, D-7000 Stuttgart 1 Tel: (0711) 465330
Publisher: Richard Scheibel
Subjects: Arts, Maps
ISBN Publisher's Prefix: 3-7717

J **Fink-Kümmerly und Frey** Verlag GmbH, Zeppelinstr 29, D-7302 Ostfildern 4 Tel: (0711) 643091 Cable Add: Buch-Fink Telex: 723737 fkfd
Dir: Harry Neubauer; *Public Relations:* Brigitte Geyer
Subjects: Touring and walking guides to regions of Germany and Europe and related Non-fiction
1978: 180 current titles
Miscellaneous: Firm has developed from an association between the German company J Fink (founded 1894) and the Swiss cartographic company Kümmerly und Frey (founded 1852). The latter firm also continues as an independent company in Switzerland (qv)
ISBN Publisher's Prefix: 3-7718

Wilhelm **Fink** Verlag KG, Nikolaistr 2, D-8000 Munich 40 Tel: (089) 348017/348018 Cable Add: Fink München
Subjects: History, Literature, Law Study, Art, Criticism, Philosophy, Linguistics, Languages, Music, Classical Archaeology, Sociology, Psychology
1978: 98 titles
ISBN Publisher's Prefix: 3-7705

Finken-Verlag, Zimmersmühlenweg 40, Postfach 1420, D-6370 Oberursel/Ts Tel: 53073 Cable Add: Finkenverlag Oberursel
Dir: Manfred Krick
Subjects: Juveniles, Textbooks, Education, Games
1978: 10 titles
ISBN Publisher's Prefix: 3-8084

Gustav **Fischer** Verlag, Wollgrasweg 49, Postfach 720143, D-7000 Stuttgart 72 (Hohenheim) Tel: (0711) 455038 Cable Add: Fischerbuch
Man Dirs: Bernd von Breitenbuch, Dr W D von Lucius; *Sales, Advertising & Publicity Dir:* Gerhard Weber; *Rights & Permissions:* Dr W D von Lucius
Subjects: Medicine, Biology, Anthropology, Psychology, Social Sciences, Economics, Paperbacks, University Textbooks, Scientific Journals
1979: 120 titles *Founded:* 1878
ISBN Publisher's Prefix: 3-437

Rita G **Fischer** Verlag*, Alt Fechenheim 75, D-6000 Frankfurt 61 Tel: (0611) 422069/412048
Man Dir: Rita G Fischer
Subjects: Medicine, Politics, Psychology, Engineering, General and Social Science, How-to, University Textbooks, High-priced Paperbacks
1978: 50 titles *1979:* 100 titles *Founded:* 1977
ISBN Publisher's Prefix: 3-88323

S **Fischer** Verlag GmbH, Geleitsstr 25, Postfach 700480, D-6000 Frankfurt am Main 70 Tel: (0611) 60621 Cable Add: Buchfischer Telex: 0412410
Publisher: Monika Schoeller; *Editorial Dir:* Ivo Frenzel; *Financial and Admin Dir:* Karl-Michael Mehnert; *Sales:* Ulrich Fritz; *Production:* Wilfried Meiner; *Publicity:* Frank Scheffter; *Rights and Permissions:* Cornelia Wohlfarth
Subsidiary Companies: Fischer Taschenbuch Verlag GmbH (qv); Wolfgang Krüger Verlag GmbH (qv); Goverts im S Fischer Verlag
Subjects: General Fiction and Non-fiction, Belles Lettres, Poetry, Biography, History, Philosophy, Low- & High-priced Paperbacks, Psychology, Social Science, Music, Art, Reference Books for the layman
1980: 62 titles *Founded:* 1886
ISBN Publisher's Prefix: 3-10

W **Fischer** Verlag*, Stresemannstr 30, Postfach 621, D-3400 Göttingen Tel: (0551) 62038/9 Telex: 96746
Dir: Wilhelm Fischer; *Sales Manager:* Hans-Walter Planke
Subject: Juvenile Fiction and Nonfiction
Founded: 1948
ISBN Publisher's Prefix: 3-439

Fischer Taschenbuch Verlag GmbH*, Geleitstr 25, Postfach 700480, D-6000 Frankfurt am Main 70 Tel: (0611) 60621 Cable Add: Buchfischer Telex: 0412410
Man Dir: Monika Schoeller; *Editorial:* Iwo Frenzel; *Sales, Publicity:* Ulrich Meier; *Production:* Wilfried Meiner; *Rights & Permissions:* Cornelia Wohlfarth
Parent Company: S Fischer Verlag GmbH (qv)
Subjects: General Fiction & Nonfiction, Paperbacks
Founded: 1952
ISBN Publisher's Prefix: 3-596

Verlag Johannes **Fix***, Sonnenscheinstr 4, Postfach 1221, D-7060 Schorndorf Tel: (07181) 3236 Cable Add: Fix-Verlag Schorndorf
Man Dir: Johannes Fix
Subjects: Religion, Juveniles
ISBN Publisher's Prefix: 3-87228

Fleischhauer und Spohn Verlag, Maybachstr 18, Postfach 301160, D-7000 Stuttgart 30 Tel: (0711) 89241 Telex: 723113 umco d
Owned by: Dr Max Bez, Thomas Bez, Ursula Roth; *Man Dir:* Wolfgang Stammler
Associate Company: Barsortiment G Umbreit GmbH und Co, Maybachstr 18, D-7000 Stuttgart 30
Subjects: Belles Lettres, Travel Literature, Regional Literature
Founded: 1830
ISBN Publisher's Prefix: 3-87230

Focus-Verlag, Grünbergerstr 16, Postfach 110328, D-6300 Giessen Tel: (0641) 34760
Man Dirs: Mr Mende, Mr Schmidt; *Sales Dir, Rights & Permissions:* Mr Linke; *Publicity & Advertising Dir:* Mr Schmidt
Subjects: History, Reference, High-priced Paperbacks, Psychology, Social Science, University Textbooks
1980: 72 titles *Founded:* 1970
ISBN Publisher's Prefix: 3-920352

Alfred **Förg** GmbH & Co KG, see Rosenheimer Verlagshaus

Forkel-Verlag GmbH*, Königsträssle 2, Postfach 104, D-7000 Stuttgart 70 Tel: (0711) 764032 Cable Add: Forkelverlag Stuttgart; also Felsenstr 23, Postfach 2120, D-6200 Wiesbaden-Dotzheim Tel: (06121) 42785
Man Dir: Dr Herbert Braun; *Sales & Advertising Dir, Publicity, Rights & Permissions:* Friedrich Vohl
Branch Off: Felsenstr 23, Postfach 2120, D-6200 Wiesbaden 1
Subjects: Business Administration, Business Law, Promotion & Sales
Bookshop: Forkel-Kundendienst, Felsenstr 23, Postfach 2120, D-6200 Wiesbaden 1

1978: 16 titles
ISBN Publisher's Prefix: 3-7719

Rat für **Formgebung**, Eugen-Bracht-Weg 6, D-6100 Darmstadt Tel: (06151) 44051
Council of Design Publishing House
Editorial: Georg Buchner, Eckhard Neumann; *Publicity:* Eckhard Neumann
Subjects: Industrial Design, Graphic Design, Architecture

Fortschritt für alle-Verlag, Schlossweg 2, D-8501 Feucht Tel: (09128) 3126 Cable Add: Fortschrit
Man Dir: Erika Herbst
Orders to: Auslieferung-Lebenskunde Vertrieb, Jägerstr 4, D-4000 Düsseldorf 1
Subjects: Popular Explanation of Scientific Advances
1978: 1 title *Founded:* 1974
ISBN Publisher's Prefix: 3-920304

Fox produktionen traude Aubeck*, Postfach 1106, D-7550 Rastatt Tel: (07245) 5536
Subjects: Lyrical Poetry (individual vols and anthologies), Nonfiction by new authors

A **Francke** GmbH, Dachauer Str 42, Postfach 200909, D-8000 Munich Tel: (089) 594713 Cable Add: Franckeverlag Munich
Dir: C L Lang
Branch Off: Francke Verlag, Berne, Switzerland (qv)
Subjects: Linguistics, Literature, Sociology, Politics, History, Philosophy, Music, Periodicals
Founded: 1959

Verlag der **Francke** Buchhandlung GmbH*, Am Schwanhof 19, Postfach 640, D-3550 Marburg/Lahn Tel: (06421) 25036/37
Man Dir, Editorial, Production, Publicity: Gerhard Kuhlmann; *Sales:* Liselotte Kerste
Subjects: Evangelical Theology, Biblical Studies, Christian Books for Children
Bookshops: in Marburg, Hebronberg, Gunzenhausen, Velbert, Lemförde, Oberursel
1978: 51 titles *1979:* 54 titles *Founded:* 1950
Miscellaneous: Firm is contributor to the Telos series of evangelical paperbacks (qv)
ISBN Publisher's Prefix: 3-88224

Franckh'sche Verlagshandlung W Keller & Co, Pfizerstr 5-7, Postfach 640, D-7000 Stuttgart 1 Tel: (0711) 21911 Cable Add: Kosmosverlag Stuttgart Telex: 0721669 kosm d
Dirs: R Keller, C Keller, E Nehmann; *Sales Dir:* D Naveau; *Production:* H J Staelin; *Publicity Dir:* W Wollmann; *Rights & Permissions:* Mrs Ehrler
Subsidiary Companies: Franz Mittelbach-Verlag, Verlag Der Neue Schulmann (both at Pfizerstr 5-7, D-7000 Stuttgart 1); W Spemann Verlag (qv)
Subjects: Popular Science, Juveniles, General Reference, Technology, Railway Literature, Hobbies, Care of Pets/Animals, Nature Study, Aquarium; Periodicals and Records
Book Club: Kosmos-Gesellschaft der Naturfreunde
Bookshop: Richard Bucholz, Alexanderstr 27, D-7000 Stuttgart 1
1978: 100 titles *1979:* 120 titles *Founded:* 1822
ISBN Publisher's Prefix: 3-440

Verlag **Frankfurter Bücher**, part of Societäts-Verlag (qv)

Frankfurter Fachverlag Michael Kohl GmbH & Co KG, Emil Sulzbach Str 12, Postfach 970115, D-6000 Frankfurt am Main 97 Tel: (0611) 778410 and 776513
Associate Company: Kohl's Technischer Verlag Erwin Kohl GmbH & Co KG (qv)
Subjects: Electrical Engineering, Electronics, Industries, Crafts, Textbooks
ISBN Publisher's Prefix: 3-87234

Verlag **Frankfurter Kinderbücher** GmbH, Forsthausstrasse 9, D-6246 Glashuetten 1 Tel: (06174) 61116
Publisher: Gerhard Hirschfeld
Parent Company: Verlag Gerhard Hirschfeld GmbH
Imprint: Verlag Frankfurter Kinderbücher, Glashuetten/Taunus
Subjects: Picture Books and Textbooks for Children
Founded: 1976
ISBN Publisher's Prefix: 3-88162

Fränkische Gesellschafts-Druckerei Würzburg/Echter Verlag, Juliuspromenade 64, D-8700 Würzburg, Postfach 5560 Tel: (0931) 50258 Telex:068862 Cable Add: Echterverlag
Dirs: Elmar Wegner, Hans Kufner
Subjects: Religion, Art, Fiction, Youth, Periodicals
Founded: 1900
ISBN Publisher's Prefix: 3-429

Frankonius Verlag GmbH, Wiesbadener Str 1, Postfach 140, D-6250 Limburg 1 Tel: (06431) 401211 Telex: 0484764 palan d
Man Dir: Engelbert Tauscher; *Publicity:* Klemens Holdener; *Editorial:* Ursula Mock
Subjects: Textbooks for modern teaching methods, covering: History, Languages, Social Sciences, Physical Sciences, Pedagogy and Training, Sports
1978: 20 titles *Founded:* 1976
ISBN Publisher's Prefix: 3-87962

Verlag Ernst **Franz** und Sternberg-Verlag, Max Planck Str 25, Postfach 1262, D-7430 Metzingen/Württemberg Tel: (07123) 6237 Telex: 07245334
Publisher: Gerhard Heinzelmann
Subjects: Christian comment and exegesis; Swabian devotions
1978: 6 titles
ISBN Publisher's Prefix: 3-7722

Franzis-Verlag*, Karlstr 37, Postfach 370120, D-8000 Munich 2 Tel: (089) 5117/1 Telex: 522301
Dir: Peter Mayer; *Sales & Publicity Manager:* Georg Geschke; *Rights & Permissions:* Siegfried Pruskil
1978: 21 titles *Founded:* 1924
ISBN Publisher's Prefix: 3-7723

Frauen-Selbstverlag, Gustav-Müller-Platz 4, D-1000 Berlin 62 Tel: (030) 7849129
Subjects: Literature by and about Women (pedagogy, psychology, medicine, history, poetry)

Frauenbuchverlag*, Kreittmayrstr 26, D-8000 Munich 2 Tel: (089) 192970
Parent Company: Weismann Verlag - Frauenbuchverlag GmbH (qv)
Subjects: Political Texts on Women's Emancipation, Reportage, Novels, Cartoons, Illustrated Books

Frauenkalender Selbstverlag*, Breitenbachplatz 17, D-1000 Berlin 33 Tel: (0611) 654151
Subjects: Literature by and about Women, Calendars

Verlag **Frauenoffensive***, Kellerstr 39, D-8000 Munich 80 Tel: (089) 485102
Dirs: U Bauer, R Guckert, S Kahn-Ackermann, S Kohlstadt, G Kowitzke, G Meixner; *Editorial:* S K-Ackermann, G Kowitzke; *Sales:* S Kohlstadt; *Production:* R Guckert; *Publicity:* G Meixner
Subjects: Feminist publications, Posters and Records on Feminist Themes
1978: 13 titles *Founded:* 1976
ISBN Publisher's Prefix: 3-12045

Verlag **Frauenpolitik**, see VFP GmbH

Frech-Verlag GmbH und Co Druck KG, Turbinenstr 7, Postfach 310902, D-7000 Stuttgart 31 (Wellimdorf)
Man & Sales Dir: E A Krauss; *Publicity Dir, Rights & Permissions:* Mrs I Euler; *Advertising Dir:* W Krauss
Subjects: Topp series of books on crafts, hobbies and popular electronics
1978: 240 titles *1979:* 320 titles *Founded:* 1954
ISBN Publisher's Prefix: 3-7724

Verlag **freies Geistesleben***, Haussmann Str 76, D-7000 Stuttgart Tel: (0711) 283255
Man Dir: Dr W Niehaus; *Sales:* Heinrich Didwiszus
Subjects: Belles Lettres, Poetry, Biography, History, How-to, Music, Art, Philosophy, Juveniles, High-priced Paperbacks, Medicine, Psychology, General & Social Science, Educational Materials
Founded: 1947
Bookshop: Buchhandlung freies Geistesleben, D-7000 Stuttgart, Alexanderstr 11

Verlag Dieter **Fricke** GmbH, Gr Bockenheimer Str 32, D-6000 Frankfurt 1 Tel: (0611) 285139
Man Dir: Dieter Fricke
Subjects: Photography, Fine Arts, Architecture
1979: 12 titles *1980:* 22 titles *Founded:* 1976
ISBN Publisher's Prefix: 3-88184

Friedenauer Presse*, Jenaer Str 6, D-1000 Berlin 31 Tel: (030) 2115060
Subjects: Bibliophilia

Erhard **Friedrich** Verlag, Im Brande 15, D-3016 Seelze 6 Tel: (0511) 483051-54 Cable Add: Friedrich Telex: 0922923
Subjects: Theatre, Opera, Education, Arts
Founded: 1960
ISBN Publisher's Prefix: 3-7727

Frisia-Verlag GmbH, Mainzlarer Str 11, D-6301 Staufenberg 1 Tel: (06406) 3319
General Manager: Werner Struep; *Partner:* Gisela Struep
1979: 15 titles *Founded:* 1975
Subjects: North Sea Literature, Island Guides, Travel Guides
Miscellaneous: Agency for Posters and other publicity material
ISBN Publisher's Prefix: 3-88111

Edition der 2 Gerald **Fritsch** und Stephan Fritsch, see der 2

Verlag A **Fromm** GmbH & Co, Postfach 1948, D-4500 Osnabrück (Located at: Breiter Gang 11-14) Tel: (0541) 3101 Telex:-; 94916 fromm d
Publisher: Leo V Fromm; *Vice-President:* Annette Harms-Hunold; *Sales Manager:* Annegret Busch; *Public Relations:* Ursula Malzahn
Associate Companies: Edition Interfrom AG, Zurich, Switzerland (qv); Fromm International Publishing Corp, 1212 Ave of the Americas, New York, NY 10036
Subjects: Authoritative texts by German-Speaking Authors on Politics, Economics, Society, Culture and Education, Nature, the Environment
ISBN Publisher's Prefix: 3-7729

Frommann-Holzboog (Friedrich Frommann Verlag, Günther Holzboog GmbH & Co)*, König-Karl-Str 27, Postfach 500460, D-7000 Stuttgart 50 Tel: (0711) 569039
Man Dir & Editorial: Günther Holzboog, Eva-Maria Holzboog; *Sales Dir:* H Gündert; *Publicity & Advertising Dir:* U Vogel; *Rights and Permissions:* H Kruschwitz
Subjects: History, Philosophy, Political Science, Reference, Religion, Psychology, Social Science, Pedagogy, History of Science, University Textbooks,

FEDERAL REPUBLIC OF GERMANY 135

Philosophical Journal
Founded: 1727
ISBN Publisher's Prefix: 3-7728

Verlag Franz-Joachim **Gaber**, see megapress

Betriebswirtschaftlicher Verlag Dr Theodor
Gabler, Taunusstr 54, Postfach 1546, D-6200
Wiesbaden 1 Tel: (06121) 5341 Cable Add:
Gablerverlag Telex: 04186567
Parent Company: Verlagsgruppe
Bertelsmann GmbH (qv)
Subjects: Business Administration,
Personnel Management, Accounting,
Insurance, Banking, Periodicals
1978: 85 titles *1979:* 87 titles
ISBN Publisher's Prefix: 3-409

Verlag **Gaehme***, Henke, Kartäusergasse 24,
D-5000 Cologne Tel: (0221) 321562
Publisher: Rolf Henke
Subjects: Politics, Literature of the Working
Class

Verlag Werner **Gebühr***, Rosenwiesstr 7,
D-7000 Stuttgart 80 Tel: (0711) 716630
Dir: Erika Gebühr
Subjects: General Fiction, Belles Lettres
Founded: 1972
ISBN Publisher's Prefix: 3-920014

Dr Max **Gehlen** Verlagsbuch-handlung*,
Daimlerstr 12, Postfach 2247, D-6380 Bad
Homburg vor der Höhe 1 Tel: (06172)
23056 Cable Add: Taunusbote Badhomburg
Man Dir: Dr Alexander Krebs-Gehlen
Subjects: Reference, Social Science,
Commercial & Technical Textbooks,
Periodicals
Founded: 1913

Geo Center Internationales Landkartenhaus
GmbH, Honigwiesenstr 25, Postfach 800830,
D-7000 Stuttgart 80 Tel: (0711) 735031
Cable Add: Geocentre Telex: 7255405 geo d
Dir: Alexander Ettling; *Sales Manager:*
Wolfgang Völcker
Branch Offs: Liebherrstr 5, D-8000
Munich 22; Lützowstr 105-106, D-1000
Berlin 30
Subject: Maps, Travel Literature
Miscellaneous: The company also acts as
supplier and distributor on behalf of some 30
other German and foreign publishing
companies connected with Touring,
Geography and Cartography
ISBN Publisher's Prefix: 3-920137

Geographische Verlagsgesellschaft Velhagen
und Klasing und Hermann Schroedel GmbH
& Co KG, Lützowstr 105, Postfach 3144,
D-1000 Berlin 30 Tel: (030) 2616019
Man Dirs: Otto Berger, Götz Manth
Parent Companies: Velhagen und Klasing
(qv), Berlin, Hermann Schroedel Verlag KG
(qv), Stuttgart
Subjects: Secondary & Primary Textbooks
on Geography, Atlases
1978: 4 titles *1979:* 3 titles *Founded:* 1963
ISBN Publisher's Prefix: 3-7680

Verlag Dr Rudolf **Georgi**, Theaterstr 77,
Postfach 407, D-5100 Aachen Tel: (0241)
26141 Telex: 832337
Man Dirs: Werner and Manfred Georgi
Subjects: History, How-to, Music, Art,
Calendars, General Science
Founded: 1928
Bookshops: Fachbuchhandlung Dr Rudolf
Georgi, Theaterstr 77, Aachen
ISBN Publisher's Prefix: 3-87248

Carl **Gerber** Verlag, see Schwaneberger
Verlag GmbH

Gerhardt Verlag, Jenaer Str 7, D-1000
Berlin 31 Tel: (030) 8543009
Man Dir: Renate Gerhardt
Subjects: Belles Lettres, Poetry, Art, High-
priced Paperbacks, Educational Materials
Founded: 1962
ISBN Publisher's Prefix: 3-920372

Gerstenberg Verlag, Postfach 390, D-3200
Hildesheim (Located at: Rathausstr 20) Tel:
(05121) 37031 Telex: 0927108 gberg
Man Dir, Editorial: Martin Oesch; *Sales,
Publicity:* W J Dietrich; *Production:*
Reinhard Fabian; *Rights & Permissions:*
Elisabeth Franke
Subjects: Bibliographies, History, Politics,
Philosophy, Art, Music, Mathematics,
Physics, Psychology, Religion, Linguistics,
Literature, English, German, Roman
Historical, Historical Reprints
1978: about 100 titles *1979:* about 100 titles
Founded: 1969
ISBN Publisher's Prefix: 3-8067

Musikverlag Klaus **Gerth**, see Schulte und
Gerth

Verlag Ernst und Werner **Gieseking***,
Deckertstr 30, Postfach 130120, D-4800
Bielefeld 13 Tel: (0521) 14674
Telex: 932240
Publisher: Werner Gieseking
Subjects: Law, Music
ISBN Publisher's Prefix: 3-7694

Giesserei-Verlag GmbH (Foundry Press),
Breitestr 27, Postfach 3503, D-4000
Düsseldorf 1 Tel: (0211) 88941
Telex: 8587086
Man Dir: Dietrich Schnell; *Sales Manager:*
Günter Hecker
Associate Company: Verlag Stahleisen mbH
(Iron and Steel Press), (qv)
Subjects: Scientific and Technical (relating
to foundries)
1978: 4 titles *1979:* 5 titles *Founded:* 1927
ISBN Publisher's Prefix: 3-87260

Gilles und Francke Verlag, Blumenstr 67-69,
Postfach 100764, D-4100 Duisberg 1
Publisher, Proprietor: Werner Francke;
Editorial: Wolfgang Strähler, Dr K Körper;
Sales: Barbara Francke; *Production:*
Wolfgang Strähler; *Publicity:* Rolf Gruna
Subsidiary Company: G & F Book and
Periodical Sales
Subjects: Leisure Activities, Poetry,
Anthologies, Music, Fiction, Essays,
Periodicals
Bookshop: G & F Buch und
Zeitschriftenhandlung
1979: 15 titles *Founded:* 1900
ISBN Publisher's Prefix: 3-12251

Verlag W **Girardet**, Girardetstr 2-38,
Postfach 101365, D-4300 Essen 1 Tel:
(0201) 79961 Cable Add: Girardet Essen
Telex: 0857888
Publisher: Dr Paul Girardet; *Editorial:*
Ulrich Melzer
Subjects: Texts and Teachers' Texts for
Technical Training Colleges, Universities
and Institutions: Electro-Technology,
Engineering, Basic Sciences, Business
Administration, Languages etc
1979: 25 titles *Founded:* 1865
ISBN Publisher's Prefix: 3-7736

Globetrotter-Verlag see Friedemann von
Engel Verlag

Glock und Lutz Verlag Heroldsberg*, Hans-
Sachs-Str no 2, D-8501 Heroldsberg bei
Nürnberg Tel: (0911) 560738
Subjects: Religion, Regional Guides,
Biography, History, Art, Periodicals
Founded: 1923
ISBN Prefix: 3-7738

PR Verlag Kurt **Glombig**, see Pinx-Verlag

Verlagsgesellschaft R **Glöss** und Co*,
Mörkenstr 7, Postfach 500344, D-2000
Hamburg 50 Tel: (040) 388573
Telex: 0215667
Publisher: Wolfgang Glöss
Subjects: Periodicals, Politics, Biography
ISBN Publisher's Prefix: 3-87261

Wilhelm **Goldmann** Verlag GmbH,
Neumarkter Str 18, Postfach 800709, D-8000
Munich 80 Tel: (089) 41740 Cable Add:
Goldmannverlag Munich
Man Dir: Gert Friederking; *Editorial:* Hans-
Ulrich Göhler; *Sales:* Volker Neumann;
Publicity: Josef Schaaf
Subjects: General Fiction, Crime, Science
Fiction, Juvenile, Poetry, Biography,
History, How-to, Art, Classics, Religion,
Law, Medicine, Psychology & Education,
General & Social Science, Cinema,
Astrology
ISBN Publisher's Prefix: 3-442

Goldstadtverlag, see Karl A Schäfer Buch-
und Offsetdruckerei Goldstadtverlag

Gondrom Verlag GmbH & Co Kg,
Bahnhofstr 15, Postfach 2606, D-8580
Bayreuth Tel: (0921) 21031 Telex: 642771
Man Dir: Volker Gondrom; *Editorial,
Production, Rights & Permissions:* Eugen
Böck; *Sales:* Gert Schwabe
Subjects: Art, History, Juveniles, Literature
1978: 80 titles *1979:* 80 titles *Founded:* 1974
ISBN Publisher's Prefix: 3-8112

V **Gorachek** KG, see Possev-Verlag

Grabert-Verlag, Am Apfelberg 18-20,
Postfach 1629, D-7400 Tübingen
Tel: (07071) 61206 Cable Add: Grabert-
Tübingen Telex: 7262863 grav d
Man Dir and Owner: Wigbert Grabert
Subjects: Belles Lettres, Biography, History
(also pre-History and Contemporary
History), High-priced Paperbacks, Annual
Publication *Ihr Buchberater*
1979: 5 titles *1980:* 6 titles *Founded:* 1953
Book Club: Deutscher Buchkreis (qv)
ISBN Publisher's Prefix: 3-87847

Gräfe und Unzer GmbH, Isabellastr 32,
Postfach 400709, D-8000 Munich 40 Tel:
(089) 373791 Telex: 5216929 gu d
Man Dir: Kurt Prelinger; *Editorial:* Hans
Scherz; *Sales:* Fritz Petermuller; *Marketing:*
Dieter Banzhaf; *Rights & Permissions:*
Ursula Feuerbacher
Orders to: Verlegerdienst München,
Gutenbergstrasse, 8031 Gilching
Subjects: Cookery, Health, How-to, Nature,
Animals, Reference
1978: 32 titles *1979:* 35 titles *Founded:* 1722
ISBN Publisher's Prefix: 3-7742

Verlag der Stiftung **Gralsbotschaft** GmbH*,
Lenzhalde 15, D-7000 Stuttgart 1
Tel: (0711) 294355
Grail Message Foundation Publishing Co
Associate Company: Verlag Alexander
Bernhardt, Austria (qv)
Subjects: Philosophy, Religion

Greven Verlag Köln GmbH & Co, Neue
Weyerstr 1-3, D-5000 Cologne 1 Tel: (0221)
233333 Cable Add: Grevenverlag Köln
Telex: 8882249
Man Dir: Sigurd Greven
Subjects: Cologne and Region (Fine Art
editions)
1979: 12 titles *1980:* 13 titles *Founded:* 1827
ISBN Publisher's Prefix: 3-7743

Ukvary **Griff** Verlag Kiado*, Titurelstr 2/II,
D-8000 Munich 81 Tel: (089)
989423/989552
Publisher: Ursula von Ujváry; *Man Dir:* Dr
Sandor A Ujváry
Associate Company: Irodalmi Uj Ság, Paris,
France
Subsidiary Company: Griff Literary Agency
Subjects: Books in Hungarian
Founded: 1938

Julius **Groos** Verlag KG, Hertzstr 6,
Postfach 102423, D-6900 Heidelberg 1
Tel: (06221) 33621 Cable Add: Groos
Heidelberg

Man Dir: Dieter Wolff; *Sales Dir:* Renate Wolff
Subjects: Linguistics, Textbooks on Modern Languages, Educational Materials
1979: 20 titles *1980:* 24 titles *Founded:* 1804
ISBN *Publisher's Prefix:* 3-87276

Verlag und Landkartenhaus W **Grösschen** KG*, Suedwall 15, Postfach 170, D-4600 Dortmund 1 Tel: (0231) 528119 Telex: 822243 wigrod
Subjects: Maps, History, Schoolbooks

Grote'sche Verlagsbuch-handlung KG*, Luxemburger Str 72, D-5000 Cologne Tel: (0221) 426761 Cable Add: Groteverlag Telex: dgv Köln 08882662
Dir: Friedrich Plagge
Parent Company: Unternehmensgruppe Verlag W Kohlhammer GmbH (qv)
Branch Off: Luxemburger Str 72, Postfach 100448, D-5000 Cologne 1
Subjects: History, Law, Literature, Economics, Administration, Social & Political Science, Periodicals
Founded: 1661
ISBN *Publisher's Prefix:* 3-7745

F G Neuer Verlag **Gruenwald** GmbH, Neumarkter Str 22 Tel: (089) 41730 Telex: 523259
Dirs: Dr Andreas Ferenczy, Wolfgang Mertz
Parent Company: Verlagsgruppe Bertelsmann GmbH (qv)
Associate Companies: other subsidiaries of Verlagsgruppe Bertelsmann (qv)
Subjects: General Non-fiction, Belles Lettres
Founded: 1979

Verlag **Grundlagen** und Praxis GmbH & Co*, Wissenschaftlicher Autorenverlag KG, Bergmannstr 40, Postfach 507, D-2950 Leer Tel: (0491) 61886
Man Dir: Mrs M Harms
Subjects: Homoeopathy, Graphology, Philology
1978: 2 titles *Founded:* 1972

Matthias-**Grünewald**-Verlag, Bischofsplatz 6, Postfach 3080, D-6500 Mainz Tel: (06131) 26341
Publisher: Dr Jakob Laubach; *Editorial:* Mr Böttcher, Dr Geyer; *Sales Dir:* Ludwig Hahn; *Production:* Mr Wagner; *Publicity:* Christa Beiling
Subjects: Religion, Biography, History, Juveniles
1978: 58 titles *1979:* 60 titles *Founded:* 1918
ISBN *Publisher's Prefix:* 3-7867

Walter de **Gruyter** & Co, Mouton Publishers, Genthiner Str 13, D-1000 Berlin 30 Tel: (030) 2611341 Cable Add: Wissenschaft Berlin 0184027
Man Dirs: Dr Kurt-Georg Cram, Dr Kurt Lubasch; *Sales:* Dietrich Rackow; *Publicity:* Joachim Oest
Associate Company: J Schweitzer Verlag (qv)
Subsidiary Companies: Aldine Publishing Company, Moulton Publishers, Walter de Gruyter Inc, all at 200 Saw Mill River Road, Hawthorne, NY 10532, USA; Mouton Publishers, The Hague (qv) and Paris
Subjects: Liberal Arts, especially Law, History, Linguistics, Philosophy, Theology, Anthropology, Natural Sciences, Literary Criticism; also Commerce, Technology, Social Sciences, Medicine; Works in German, English, French
1979: approx 300 titles
ISBN *Publisher's Prefix:* 3-11

Gryphius-Verlag*, Harretstr 6, Postfach 754, D-7410 Reutlingen Tel: (07121) 8471 Cable Add: Buchhaus Reutlingen Telex: 0729733
Subjects: Special Editions and Reprints

Verlag Klaus **Guhl***, Königin-Elizabethstr 8, D-1000 Berlin 19 Tel: 3017482, 3011612
Man Dir: Klaus-Dieter Guhl; *Editorial:* H j von Hülst; *Sales:* Forian Guhl; *Production:* Robert Guhl; *Rights & Permissions:* Hans Paul Guhl
Branch Off: Oranienstr 188, D-1000 Berlin 36
Subjects: Politics, Literature, Textbooks on Jurisprudence, Literary Criticism
1978: 35 titles *1979:* 29 titles *Founded:* 1976
ISBN *Publisher's Prefix:* 3-88220

D **Gundert** Verlag*, Ostfeldstr 46, Postfach 710140, D-3000 Hannover-Kirchrode Tel: (0511) 522535
Publisher: Guy d'Hoedt
Subjects: Juveniles, Young Adult
Founded: 1878
ISBN *Publisher's Prefix:* 3-87279

Verlag August **Güse**, Hauptstr 103, D-6367 Karben 3 Tel: (06039) 2990/2991 Telex: 415505 Guese
Subjects: Calendars, Horticulture, Floriculture
1978: 3 titles *Founded:* 1954
ISBN *Publisher's Prefix:* 3-87278

Büchergilde **Gutenberg** Verlagsgesellschaft mbH*, Untermainkai 66, Postfach 16220, D-6000 Frankfurt am Main 16 Tel: (0611) 230131 Telex: 412063 buegi d
Subjects: Fiction, Reference, History, Politics, Biography, Art, Juveniles, 69 prizewinning 'Books of the Year' Records, Games

Gutenberg-Gesellschaft, Liebfrauenpl 5, D-6500 Mainz Tel: 06131/26420
Man Dir, President: J Fuchs; *Manager:* Heinz H Schmiedt; *Editorial:* Prof Koppitz
Subjects: Library Science, the Gutenberg Yearbook
Founded: 1901

Gütersloher Verlagshaus Gerd Mohn, Königstr 23, Postfach 2368, D-4830 Gütersloh 1 Tel: (05241) 1831 Cable Add: Gütersloher Verlagshaus Telex: 0933868
Man Dir: Gerd Mohn; *Sales Dir, Publicity:* Otfrid Seippel; *Rights & Permissions:* Dr Heinz Kühne
Subjects: Religion, Philosophy, Politics, Juveniles, Paperbacks
Imprints: Gütersloher Taschenbücher Siebenstern (paperback series)
1978: 120 titles *1980:* 120 titles *Founded:* 1959
Miscellaneous: Affiliated with Verlagsgruppe Bertelsmann
ISBN *Publisher's Prefix:* 3-579

H A D U – Hagemann Lehrmittel- und Verlagsgesellschaft mbH*, Karlstr 20, Postfach 5129, D-4000 Düsseldorf Tel: (211) 353811 Cable Add: Hagemannverlag Telex: 8587623 hage d
Man Dir: Maria Schütte-Hagemann; *Editorial, Production:* Hans Peisker, Heinz W Schmidt; *Sales, Export, Finance:* W Kils-Hütten; *Publicity:* H W Schmidt; *Rights & Permissions:* W Kils-Hütten, Hans Peisker, H W Schmidt
Parent Company: Lehrmittelverlag Wilhelm Hagemann (qv)
Associate Company: Verlagsgesellschaft Schulfernsehen mbH, D-5000 Cologne
Subjects: Teaching Aids and Pedadogy
1978: 130 titles *1979:* 151 titles (also numerous teaching aids) *Founded:* 1929
ISBN *Publisher's Prefix:* 3-544

Haag und Herchen Verlag, Fichardstr 30, D-6000 Frankfurt am Main 1 Tel: (0611) 550911
Man Dir: Hans-Alfred Herchen
Subjects: How-to, High-priced Paperbacks, Medicine, Politics, Psychology, Engineering, General & Social Science, University Textbooks
1978: 80 titles *1979:* 87 titles *Founded:* 1975
ISBN *Publisher's Prefix:* 3-88129

Verlag Josef **Habbel***, Gutenbergstr 8, Postfach 339, D-8400 Regensburg 11 Tel: (0941) 96044 Cable Add: Pustet Telex: 65672
Man Dir: Dr Friedrich Pustet; *Sales and Advertising:* Dr Reinhold Röttger
Parent Company: Verlag Friedrich Pustet (qv)
Subjects: Christian Juvenile; Leisure reading for the Christian home
Founded: 1870
ISBN *Publisher's Prefix:* 3-7748

Rudolf **Habelt** Verlag GmbH, Am Buchenhang 1, Postfach 150104, D-5300 Bonn 1 Tel: (0228) 232015 Cable Add: Buchhabelt Bonn
Man Dirs: Dr Rudolf Habelt, Wolfgang Habelt; *Editorial, Production:* Renate Schreiber
Subjects: Pre-History, Archaeology, Ancient History, Regional, Folklore, etc

Walter **Hädecke** Verlag, Postfach 1203, D-7252 Weil der Stadt Tel: (07033) 2264
Man Dir: Hilde Graff-Hädecke; *Sales & Advertising Dir, Rights & Permissions:* Joachim Graff
Subjects: Reference, High-priced Paperbacks, Cook Books, Public Health, Natural Medicine
Founded: 1919
ISBN *Publisher's Prefix:* 3-7750

Lehrmittelverlag Wilhelm **Hagemann**, Karlstr 20, Postfach 5129, D-4000 Düsseldorf Tel: (0211) 353811 Cable Add: Hagemannverlag Telex: 8587623 hage d
Sales: Walter Kils-Hütten; *Production, Rights & Permissions:* Hans Peisker, Heinz W Schmidt
Subsidiary Company: HADÜ – Hagemann Lehrmittel- und Verlagsgesellschaft mbH (qv)
Subjects: Textbooks, especially on Biology, Chemistry, Electrical Engineering, Electronics, Public Health, Mathematics, Education, Physics, Politics; also Teaching Transparencies, Biological Wall Charts
ISBN *Publisher's Prefix:* 3-544

Buchvertrieb **Hager** GmbH, Mainzer Landstr 147, Postfach 119151, D-6000 Frankfurt Am Main 2 Tel: (0611) 730234 Telex: 04-13080 kuehl d
Managing & Sales Dir: Hermann Figge
Subjects: History, Literature, Politics, Philosophy, Juveniles, Low-priced Paperbacks, Books from the People's Republic of China, Social Science
Founded: 1974
ISBN *Publisher's Prefix:* 3-88145

Mary **Hahn's** Kochbuchverlag*, Hubertusstr 4, D-8000 Munich 19 Tel: (089) 177041 Telex: 05215045
Subjects: Cookery, Home Economics
Miscellaneous: Firm is a member of Verlagsgruppe Langen-Müller/Herbig (qv)
ISBN *Publisher's Prefix:* 3-8004

Verlag Anton **Hain** KG, Adelheidstr 2, Postfach 1220, D-6240 Königstein/Ts Tel: 06174/3026 Cable Add: Hain Telex: 042507
Man Dir: Dieter Hain; *Sales:* Rudolf Klein; *Editorial:* Beate Pinkernel; *Publicity:* J E Schmidt-Braul
Associate Companies: Peter Hanstein Verlag GmbH; Athenaum Verlag GmbH; Scriptor Verlag GmbH & Co KG (qqv)
Subjects: Philosophy, Reference, Religion, Psychology, Social Science, University Textbooks

Founded: 1946
ISBN Publisher's Prefix: 3-445

Hallwag Verlagsgesellschaft mbH, Marco-Polo-Str 1, D-7302 Ostfildern 4 bei Stuttgart Tel: (0711) 4502266 Cable Add: Hallwagverlag Telex: 721796
Dir: Ulrich Mailänder; *Publicity Manager:* Brigitte Buschmann
Subjects: Maps, Town Plans, Travel and Touring Guides and Books; Pocket Information series on General Knowledge; Reference, Music
Head Office: Hallwag Verlag AG, Berne, Switzerland (qv)
ISBN Publisher's Prefix: 3-444

Hamburger Fremdenblatt Broschek und Co, see Broschek Druck GmbH & Co KG

Hamburger Lesehefte Verlag Iselt und Co Nfl mbH, Nordbahnhofstr 2, Postfach 1480, D-2250 Husum Tel: (04841) 6081/3
Man Dir, Editorial, Rights & Permissions: Ingwert Paulsen Jr; *Sales:* Alfred Lorenzen; *Production:* Bruno Czarski; *Publicity:* Hans-Heinrich Lüth
Parent Company: Husum Druck- und Verlagsgesellschaft mbH u Co KG (qv)
Associated Company: Matthiesen Verlag Ingwert Paulsen Jr (qv)
Subjects: Textbooks
Founded: 1953
ISBN Publisher's Prefix: 3-87291

Peter **Hammer** Verlag GmbH, Foehrenstr 33-35, Postfach 200415, D-5600 Wuppertal 2 Tel: (0202) 505066
Dir: Hermann Schulz
Associate Company: Jugenddienst Verlag (qv)
Subjects: Latin America, The Third World, Literature, Current Affairs, Meditation, Christian Action
1979: 16 titles *1980:* 18 titles
ISBN Publisher's Prefix: 3-87294

Hansa Verlag Heinz W Hass*, Feldstrasse Hochhaus 1, D-2000 Hamburg 4 Tel: (040) 4300862
Subjects: Belles Lettres, Literary Criticism
ISBN Publisher's Prefix: 3-920421

Carl **Hanser** Verlag, Kolbergerstr 22, Postfach 860420, D-8000 Munich 86 Tel: (089) 982511 Telex: 05/22837
Managing Partners: Joachim Spencker, Christoph Schlotterer, Franz-Joachim Klock; *Editorial:* Fritz Arnold, Burkhart Kroeber, Michael Krüger, Hans Joachim Simm, Günther Fetzer; *Sales Dirs:* Felicitas Feilhauer, Christoph Sickel; *Advertising Dir:* Günther Steidl; *Publicity Manager:* Fritz Arnold
Subsidiary Companies: Part-owner of Deutscher Taschenbuch Verlag, Friedrichstr 1, D-8000 Munich 40 (qv) and of Verlegerdienst München, Gutenbergstr, Gilching
Subjects: General Fiction, Belles Lettres, Poetry, Biography, History, Philosophy, High-priced Paperbacks, Engineering, General Science, Macromolecular Chemistry, Plastics, Business & Management, Dentistry, Periodicals
1979: 180 titles *Founded:* 1928
ISBN Publisher's Prefix: 3-446

Hänssler-Verlag, Friedrich Hänssler KG, Bismarckstr 4, Postfach 1220, D-7303 Neuhausen-Stuttgart Tel: (07158) 5001
Man Dir: Friedrich Hänssler; *Rights & Permissions:* Reinhold Lechler
Subjects: Music, Art, Religion, Low-priced Paperbacks
Founded: 1920
Bookshop: Laudate GmbH, Versandbuchhandlung Friedrich Hänssler, Bismarckstr 4, D-7303 Neuhausen-Stuttgart

Miscellanous: Firm is a member of the Telos (qv) series publishing group; it also publishes publications of the American Institute of Musicology
ISBN Publisher's Prefix: 3-7751

Peter **Hanstein** Verlag GmbH, Adelheidstr 2, Postfach 1220, D-6240 Königstein/Ts Tel: 06174/3026
Publisher: Dietrich Pinkerneil; *Editorial:* Hans-Georg Beer; *Sales:* Rudolf Klein; *Publicity:* J E Schmidt-Braul; *Rights & Permissions:* Hildegard Willhöft
Associate Companies: Athenaeum Verlag GmbH; Scriptor Verlag GmbH & Co KG; Hain Verlag GmbH (qqv)
Subjects: Law, Economic Sciences, Theology
Founded: 1878
ISBN Publisher's Prefix: 3-7756

Harlekin-Presse, see Hertenstein

Harrach und Sabrow, Wöllsteiner Str 8, Postfach 745, D-6550 Bad Kreuznach Tel: (0671) 67073 Telex: 042815
Associate Company: Inter-Kunst und Buch GmbH (qv)
Subjects: Children's Books, Poetry

Verlag Otto **Harrassowitz**, Taunusstr 6, Postfach 2929, D-6200 Wiesbaden 1 Tel: (06121) 521046 Cable Add: Otto Harrassowitz Wiesbaden Telex: 04186135
Man Dir: Dr Helmut Petzolt; *Sales & Publicity Dir:* Albrecht Weddigen
Subjects: History, Book Trade and Library Science, Bibliographies, Orientalia and associated Eastern linguistic and religious studies, East European History and associated Slavic Language and Educational Studies, Classical Philology, Ethnology, Middle East studies, Publication *ZDB — Zeitschriften-Datenbank* (Periodicals' Data Bank) in association with das Deutsche Bibliotheksinstitut and the Staatsbibliothek Preussischer Kulturbesitz (qv)
Bookshop: Otto Harrassowitz, D-6200 Wiesbaden, Taunusstr 5
1978: 67 titles *Founded:* 1872
ISBN Publisher's Prefix: 3-447

Verlag Karlheinz **Hartmann**, Rodheimer Str 17, D-6382 Friedrichsdorf im Taunus Tel: (06007) 622
Man Dir: Karlheinz Hartmann MA; *Editorial:* Roland Hunger, Monica Herber
Subjects: Contemporary Literature, Reprints, Literary Criticism, Scenarios and Film Scripts, Modern Poetry, Horror
Founded: 1976
ISBN Publisher's Prefix: 3-87293

Verlag **Harwalik** KG*, Hohbuchstr 5, Postfach 714, D-7410 Reutlingen Tel: (07121) 22041 Cable Add: Harwalik
Subjects: Woodcut Prints, Graphics etc, Books illustrated by Woodcuts

Verlag Gerd **Hatje**, Wildunger Str 83, Postfach 468, D-7000 Stuttgart 50 Tel: (0711) 561109 Cable Add: Hatjeverlag Stuttgart
Man Dir: Gerd Hatje
Subjects: Architecture, Interior Decoration, Art (especially Modern Art)
1979: 10 titles *Founded:* 1945
ISBN Publisher's Prefix: 3-7757

Haude und Spener Verlag, Postfach 147, D-1000 Berlin 62 (Located at: Grossgörschenstr 6) Tel: 030/7813514
General Manager: Volker Spiess
Associate Company: Verlag Volker Spiess
Subjects: Literary History, Bibliographies, Collected Works, History, Cultural History, Reminiscences of Berlin, Radio and TV
1980: 20 titles *Founded:* 1614
ISBN Publisher's Prefix: 3-7759

Rudolf **Haufe** Verlag, Hindenburgstr 64, Postfach 740, D-7800 Freiburg im Breisgau Tel: (0761) 31560 Cable Add: Haufeverlag
Man Dirs: Dr G Friedrich, Dr M Jahrmarkt, G Osswald, F J Ruebsam; *Editorial:* Dr G Friedrich, Dr M Jahrmarkt; *Sales, Production:* F J Ruebsam
Subsidiary Company: WRS-Verlag (Wirtschaft, Recht, Steuern) (qv)
Subjects: Business and Law, Financial, Management, Social Science, University Textbooks
1978: 35 titles *Founded:* 1934
ISBN Publisher's Prefix: 3-448

Karl F **Haug** Verlag GmbH & Co KG, Postfach 102840, D-6900 Heidelberg 1 (Located at: Fritz-Frey Str 21) Tel: (06221) 49974-7 Cable Add: haugverlag
Man Dir: Dr E Fischer; *Production:* Dietmar Sieber
Associate Companies: Arkana Verlag (qv); Verlag für Medizin Dr Ewald Fischer GmbH (qv); Fischer & Pflaum Verlag GmbH
Branch Off: Bergheimer Str 102, D-6900 Heidelberg
Subjects: Naturopathic, Homeopathic, fringe and auxiliary Medical, Acupuncture, Health and Preventive Medicine, Periodicals
Bookshop: Haug & Cie Nachf GmbH, Med wiss Buchhandlung und Antiquariat (Medical science books, new and second-hand/antiquarian)
Founded: 1903
ISBN Publisher's Prefix: 3-7760

Verlag H M **Hauschild** GmbH, Rigaer Str 3, D-2800 Bremen Tel: (0421) 385508 Telex: 244333 hwb d
Dir: Dr Hans-Dieter Fiedler; *Sales:* Ernst-August Echtermann
Parent Company: Werbedruck Bremen Grafischer Betrieb GmbH, HAG AG
Subjects: Art Books, Information Books, Bremen Regional
1978-79: 5 titles *Founded:* 1855
ISBN Publisher's Prefix: 3-920699

Dr Ernst **Hauswedell** und Co Verlag, Magdalenen Str 8, D-2000 Hamburg 13 Tel: (040) 448798
Man Dir: Dr Ernst L Hauswedell; *all other offices:* Reinhold Busch
Subjects: Reference Works for Book and Print Collectors, Bibliographies, Illustrated Books
1978: 10 titles *1979:* 11 titles *Founded:* 1927
ISBN Publisher's Prefix: 3-7762

Heckners Verlag*, Postfach 1260, D-3340 Wolfenbüttel Tel: (05331) 5166
Subjects: Vocational (Business), Economics
Founded: 1895

H **Heenemann** Verlagsgesellschaft mbH, Bessemerstr 83, Postfach 420320, D-1000 Berlin 42 Tel: (030) 7537051 Telex: 183 796 hekg d
Associate Company: Wilhelm Pansegrau Verlag (qv)
Subjects: Fishery and Fishing, Sociology and Popular Science, Enamels and Coatings
ISBN Publisher's Prefix: 3-87903

Heering-Verlag GmbH*, Ortlerstr 8, Postfach 700840, D-8000 Munich 70 Tel: (089) 7609023-27 Telex: 0522720
Man Dir: Gerfried Urban
Subjects: Photography, Cinematography, Mountaineering
Founded: 1932
ISBN Publisher's Prefix: 3-7763

Heidmük-Verlag Günther U Müller, C Fr Gauss-Str 59, D-2800 Bremen 33 Tel: (0421) 256454
Man Dir: Günther U Müller
Subjects: Juveniles, Games

138 FEDERAL REPUBLIC OF GERMANY

Ernst **Heimeran** Verlag*, Dietlindenstr 14, Postfach 400824, D-8000 Munich 40 Tel: (089) 399017/18
Man Dirs: Till Heimeran, Margrit Heimeran, Tillman Roeder; *Editorial:* Else Sommer; *Sales & Publicity, Rights & Permissions:* Thomas Kniffler
Associate Company: Kochbuchverlag Heimeran KG
Subjects: Latin and Greek Classics (bilingual), Philology, Modern Text Editions, Music, Cultural Histories, Poetry, Humour, Bavarica
1978: 16 titles *Founded:* 1922
ISBN Publisher's Prefix: 3-7765

Verlag Egon **Heinemann**, Kösliner Weg 16, D-2000 Norderstedt 3 Tel: (040) 5232368/5239023/5239024
Publisher: Egon Heinemann
Subjects: Sailing, Sailing Ships, Nautical Literature
1978: 6 titles
ISBN Publisher's Prefix: 3-87321

Heinrichshofen's Verlag, Liebigstr 16, Postfach 620, D-2940 Wilhelmshaven Tel: (04421) 26555/202004 Cable Add: Heinrichshofen Wilhelmshaven
Man Dir: Otto Heinrich Noetzel; *Editorial:* Dr Viktor Kreiner, Florian Noetzel; *Production:* Johann Reiners
Associate Companies: Otto Heinrich Noetzel Verlag; Arthur Türk KG
Subjects: Music & Musicology, Ballet, Opera, Song Books, Paperbacks
1978: 30 titles *Founded:* 1797
ISBN Publisher's Prefix: 3-7959

Verlag Georg **Heintz**, Wasserturmstr 7, D-6520 Worms Cable Add: Heintz
Subjects: Bibliography, Exile Literature, History and Documentation of Anti-Semitism, Fiction and Drama on related themes

G **Henle** Verlag, Postfach 710466, D-8000 Munich 71 (Located at: Forstenrieder Allee 122) Tel: (089) 754096/7/8
Subject: Music, Original and Facsimile Editions, Reference Books (Music)
ISBN Publisher's Prefix: 3-87328

Henssel Verlag, Glienicker Str 12, D-1000 Berlin 39 Tel: (030) 8051493 Cable Add: Hensselverlag Berlin
Man Dir: Karl-Heinz Henssel; *Editorial:* Asta-Maria Henssel
Subjects: General Fiction, Humour, Travel, Literary Theory, Theatre, Poetry, Biography, Art, High-priced Paperbacks
1979: 7 titles *Founded:* 1938
ISBN Publisher's Prefix: 3-87329

F A **Herbig** Verlagsbuchhandlung, Hubertusstr 4, D-8000 Munich 19 Tel: (089) 177041 Cable Add: Langenmüller Telex: 05215045
Man Dir: Dr Herbert Fleissner; *Editorial:* Dr Berhnard Strückmeyér; *Sales Manager:* Gisela Weichert; *Publicity Manager:* Dr Brigitte Sinhuber-Erbacher; *Rights & Permissions:* Renate Werner
Orders to: Vereinigte Verlagsauslieferung Reinhard Mohn, Carl-Bertelsmann-Str 161, D-4830 Gütersloh
Subjects: Novels, Belles Lettres, Poetry, History, Art, Hobbies, Gift Books
Founded: 1821
Miscellaneous: Firm is a member of Verlagsgruppe Langen-Müller/Herbig (qv)
ISBN Publisher's Prefix: 3-7766

Verlag **Herder** GmbH & Co, KG, Hermann-Herder-Str 4, Postfach, D-7800 Freiburg im Breisgau Tel: (0761) 27171 Cable Add: Herder Freiburgbreisgau Telex: 07721440 vhd
Man Dir: Fritz Knoch; *Sales Dir:* Franz Grossmann; *Publicity Manager:* Dr Ludwig Muth; *Rights & Permissions:* Alfred Zimmermann
Associate Companies: Verlag Herder & Co, Vienna, Austria (qv); Verlag Herder AG, Basel, Switzerland (qv); A G Ploetz KG, Wurzburg, Federal Republic of Germany
Subsidiary Companies: Verlag Karl Alber, Christophorus-Verlag Herder GmbH, Verlag F H Kerle, Ploetz GmbH & Co KG (qqv)
Book Club: Herder Buchgemeinde
Bookshops: Located in major cities throughout German Federal Republic
Subjects: General Fiction, Belles Lettres, Poetry, Biography, History, Art, Philosophy, Reference, Religion, Juveniles, Low- and High-priced Paperbacks, Psychology, Social Science, University, Secondary & Primary Textbooks, Educational Materials, Atlases, Encyclopaedias
Founded: 1801
ISBN Publisher's Prefix: 3-451

Herder und Herder GmbH*, Verlag für Wirtschaft und Gesellschaft, Rathenauplatz 14, D-6000 Frankfurt 1
Associate Companies: Verlag Herder KG, Ploetz KG, Federal Republic of Germany (qqv); Herder AG, Switzerland (qv)
Subjects: Politics, Social Sciences, Economics
ISBN Publisher's Prefix: 3-585

Herold Neue Verlagsgesellschaft GmbH*, Waldgarten Str 66, D-8000 Munich 70, Postfach 700849 Tel: (089) 7147550 Cable Add: Heroldverlag Munich
Dir: Dr Joseph S Herold; *Sales Dir:* Inge Angelletti
Associate Company: Vereinigte Herold Verlag GmbH (qv)
Subjects: Culture Guides, Culture and Art History, Pharmacy, Business Management, University Textbooks
Founded: 1883 (Leipzig)
ISBN Publisher's Prefix: 3-920451

Herold Verlag Brück KG, Alexanderstr 51, Postfach 507, D-7000 Stuttgart Tel: (0711) 240996
Dirs: Claus Runge, Hanna Bautze; *Editorial:* Hanna Bautze
Subjects: Juveniles
Founded: 1871
ISBN Publisher's Prefix: 3-7767

Vereinigte **Herold** Verlage GmbH*, Waldgarten Str 66, Postfach 700849, D-8000 Munich 70 Tel: (089) 7148146 Cable Add: Heroldverlag Munich
General Manager & Editor: Dr Joseph S Herold; *Man Dir:* Fritz Walter
Associate Company: Herold Neue Verlagsgesellschaft GmbH, D-8000 Munich 70, Waldgarten Str 66
Subjects: Encyclopaedias (Herold Deutschland Bibliothek)
Book Club: Herold Buch-club
Founded: 1970

Hertenstein-Presse, Mathystr 36, D-7530 Pforzheim Tel: (07231) 27084
Publicity Manager: Ulrike Strauss
Subject: Verse and other texts, with original illustrations
Miscellaneous: formerly known as Harlekin-Presse

Bruno **Hessling** Verlag*, Grossgörrschenstr 6, Postfach 147, D-1000 Berlin 62 Tel: 030/7813514
General Manager: Volker Spiess
Subjects: Art and History of Berlin, Art, Medical History, Political Periodicals
Founded: 1883
ISBN Publisher's Prefix: 3-7769

Hestia-Verlag GmbH, Eduard-Bayerlein-Str 1, D-858 Bayreuth Tel: (0921) 21007 Telex: 642103
Dirs: Heinz G Konsalik, Dagmar Stecher
Subjects: General Fiction, History, Biography
1978-79: 36 titles *Founded:* 1954
ISBN Publisher's Prefix: 3-7770

B **Heymann** Verlag*, Edition Ethnos, Bertramstr 21, Postfach 3065, D-6200 Wiesbaden Tel: (06121) 302861
Publisher: Bernd Heymann; *Press Chief & Sales Manager:* Klaus Baumann; *Publicity, Rights & Permissions:* Peter Heiligenthal
Subjects: Anthropology, Ethnology, Social Science, Philosophy, Reprints

Carl **Heymanns** Verlag KG, Gereonstr 18-32, D-5000 Cologne 1 Tel: (0221) 134022; Bonn (901) 234550; Berlin (030) 3913111/3913635/3917090; Munich (089) 224811 Cable Add: Köln Rechtsverlag; also Bonn/Munich/Berlin Rechtsverlag; Telex: Cologne 8881888; Munich 0524058; Berlin 0181811
Man Dir: Hans-Jörg Gallus; *Editorial:* K W Frohn, K Pompe, H E Wohlfarth; *Production:* C Free; *Publicity:* K. Brachvogel; *Sales:* N Becker
Subsidiary Companies: Gallus Druckerei KG, Berlin; Albert Nauck & Co, Cologne and Berlin; Gallus Verlag, Hans O Gallus KG, Munich; Euroliber Verlags- und Vertriebs-GmbH, Cologne; Gallus Verlag KG, Vienna, Austria; Scientia AG, Zug, Switzerland
Branch Off: Adalbert-Stifter-Str 15, D-5300 Bonn; Steinsdorfstr 10, D-8000 Munich 22; Gutenbergstr 3-4, D-1000 Berlin 10
Subject: Law
Founded: 1815
ISBN Publisher's Prefix: 3-452

Wilhelm **Heyne** Verlag, Türkenstr 5-7, Postfach 201204, D-8000 Munich 2 Tel: (089) 288211/16 Cable Add: Heyneverlag München Telex: 0524218
Publisher: Rolf Heyne; *Editorial Dir:* Reinhold G Stecher; *Editorial:* Roswitha Heyne, Manfred Kluge, Renate Matuschka, Wolfgang Jeschke, Bernhard Matt; *Sales Manager:* Friedhelm Koch; *Advertising Manager:* Horst Mikkat; *Rights & Permissions:* Traudel Eckardt
Subjects: Paperbacks only: General Fiction, Belles Lettres, Poetry, Biography, History, Religion, How-to, Music, Art, Juveniles, Psychology, Science Fiction and Westerns, Cartoons
1978: 500 titles *1979:* 600 titles *Founded:* 1934
ISBN Publisher's Prefix: 3-453

Anton **Hiersemann** Verlag, Rosenbergstr 113, Postfach 723, D-7000 Stuttgart 1 Tel: (0711) 638264/5
Man Dir: Karl G Hiersemann; *Editorial:* Dr R W Fuchs; *Rights & Permissions:* K G Hiersemann
Subjects: History, Art, Reference, Bibliography, Books about Books, Classical Studies, Germanic Literature, Theatre
1979: 35 titles *Founded:* 1884
ISBN Publisher's Prefix: 3-7772

Verlag **Hinder und Deelmann**, Postfach 1206, D-3554 Gladenbach (Hessen) Tel: (06462) 1301
Publishers: Johannes Deelmann, Rolf Hinder
Subjects: Philosophy, Religion, Social Science
1978: 4 titles
ISBN Publisher's Prefix: 3-87348

Gruppe **Hinterhaus**, now Elke Betzel Verlag (qv)

Hippokrates Verlag GmbH, Neckarstr 121, Postfach 593, D-7000 Stuttgart 1 Tel: (0711) 21511 Telex: 0722503 Cable Add: Hippokratesverlag
Dirs: Ehrenfried Klotz, P Eich; *Publicity:* H-G Zimnik; *Sales:* A Steiss
Associate Company: Paracelsus Verlag GmbH, Stuttgart
Subjects: Medicine, Psychology, University and Secondary Textbooks
1978: approx 45 titles *1979:* 50 titles
Founded: 1925
ISBN Publisher's Prefix: 3-7773

Hirmer Verlag, Gesellschaft für Wissenschaftliches Lichtbild GmbH, Maréesstrasse 15, D-8000 Munich 19 Tel: (089) 1781011
Man Dirs: Dr Max Hirmer, Aenne Hirmer, Albert Hirmer; *Editorial:* Heinz Friedrich Blaesing
Subjects: Archaeology, History of Art from earliest civilizations, German Art and Picture Galleries
1979: 8 titles *Founded:* 1948
Miscellaneous: Firm specialize in high quality photographic reproduction (especially in colour)
ISBN Publisher's Prefix: 3-7774

Ferdinand **Hirt**, Schauenburgerstr 36, Postfach 2580, D-2300 Kiel 1 Tel: (0431) 561066 Telex: 299873
Subjects: Science, Education, Academic, Geographical, Teacher Training
Founded: 1832
ISBN Publisher's Prefix: 3-554

S **Hirzel** Verlag GmbH und Co, Birkenwaldstr 44, Postfach 347, D-7000 Stuttgart 1 Tel: (0711) 294482 Cable Add: Hirzelverlag, Stuttgart Telex: 0723636 daz d
Man Dirs: Hans Rotta, Dr Hanskarl Hornung; *Sales Manager:* Karl Hübler; *Publicity Manager:* Barbara Schreck
Associate Companies: Wissenschaftliche Verlagsgesellschaft mbH (qv); Deutscher Apotheker Verlag Dr Roland Schmiedel (qv); Franz Steiner Verlag GmbH (qv)
Subjects: Philosophy, Medicine, Psychology, Engineering, General Science
Founded: 1853
ISBN Publisher's Prefix: 3-7776

Hobbit Presse, an imprint of Klett-Cotta Verlag (qv)

Hoch-Verlag, Kronprinzenstr 27, D-4000 Düsseldorf 1 Tel: (0211) 307001 Cable Add: Hochverlag
Man Dirs: Aenne Hafemann, Joachim Hoch, Eric Zinth de Kentzingen; *Sales, Publicity and Advertising Dir:* Joachim Hoch; *Rights & Permissions:* Eric Zinth de Kenzingen
Subject: Juveniles
Founded: 1949
ISBN Publisher's Prefix: 3-7779

Hofacker Ing W GmbH Verlag*, Tegernseerstr 18, D-8150 Holzkirchen/Obb Tel: 08024/7331
Man Dir, Rights & Permissions: Winfried Hofacker; *Editorial, Publicity:* J Maier; *Sales:* Evi Linkogel; *Production:* Th Kirschenhofer
Orders to: Ing W Hofacker GmbH, Tegernseer Str 18, D-8150 Holzkirchen
Subjects: Electronics, Micro-Computers, Micro-Processing
Founded: 1968
ISBN Publisher's Prefix: 3-921682

Dieter **Hoffmann** Verlag*, Senefelderstr 25, D-6500 Mainz 41 Tel: (06136) 416 Telex: 4187213
Dir: Dieter Hoffman
Subjects: History of German Aviation (in German and English texts), Aircraft Modelling, Hunting and Shooting Handbooks
Founded: 1960
ISBN Publisher's Prefix: 3-87341

Julius **Hoffmann** Verlag, Pfizerstr 5-7, Postfach 788, D-7000 Stuttgart 1 Tel: (0711) 2191320
Man Dir: Kurt Hoffmann
Subjects: Building and Architecture, History of Art
1978: 4 titles *Founded:* 1827
Miscellaneous: Many texts are in English and French
ISBN Publisher's Prefix: 3-87346

Hoffmann und Campe Verlag, Harvestehuder Weg 45, D-2000 Hamburg 13 Tel: (040) 441881 Cable Add: Hoca Telex: 02214259
Man Dirs: Thomas Ganske, Eberhard Boeckel, Hans Helmut Roehring; *Editorial:* Hermann Josef Barth, Dr Ingeborg Hillmann, Dr Renate Jürgens, Ulrike Rickert, Dr Hans-Jürgen Schmitt, Dr Anneliese Schumacher-Heiss, Dr Helmut Wiemken; *Sales Dir:* Bruno Laudien; *Publicity Dir:* Baerbel Naporowski; *Advertising Dir:* Rudolf Sommer; *Rights & Permissions:* Helga Eberhard, Ulla Thomsen
Subsidiary Company: Reich Verlag, Switzerland (qv)
Subjects: General Fiction, Belles Lettres, Poetry, Biography, History, How-to, Music, Art, Psychology, General & Social Science
1978: 72 titles *Founded:* 1781
ISBN Publisher's Prefix: 3-455

Verlag Karl **Hofmann**, Steinwasenstr 6-8, Postfach 1360, D-7060 Schorndorf bei Stuttgart Tel: (07181) 7811 Cable Add: Hofmannverlag Schorndorf
Man Dir: Ottmar Hecht; *Sales, Publicity:* Mr Pastorek
Subjects: Sports, Technical Literature on glass utilization; Periodicals
1980: 30 titles
ISBN Publisher's Prefix: 3-7780

Hohenloher Druck- und Verlagshaus, Verlag Hohenloher Tagblatt, Blaufelderstr 44, Postfach 80, D-7182 Gerabronn Tel: (07952) 5126 Cable Add: HDV-Gerabronn Telex: 74334
Publisher: Rolf Wankmüller
Subjects: Fiction, Poetry, Biography, Juveniles
ISBN Publisher's Prefix: 3-87354

Hohenstaufen Verlag Schumann KG, im Gries 17, Postfach 29, D-7762 Bodman/Bodensee Tel: (07773) 5616 Cable Add: Hohenstaufen
Dir: Gerhard Schumann; *Sales:* Erika Schumann
Subjects: Belles Lettres, Memoirs, Contemporary History

Verlag Wolfgang **Hölker**, Martinistr 2, Postfach 3820, D-4400 Munster Tel: (0251) 42225 Cable Add: Martinistrasse 2 Telex: 892112 msfro d
Man Dir: Wolfgang Hölker; *Sales:* Manfred Goldschmidt; *Production:* Martina Walter; *Publicity:* Wolfgang Förster
Parent Company: F Coppenrath Verlag (qv)
Subject: Cookery Books of all types
1978: 10 titles *1979:* 12 titles *Founded:* 1973
ISBN Publisher's Prefix: 3-88117

Holle Verlag GmbH*, Markgrafenstr 4, Postfach 320, D-7570 Baden-Baden Tel: (07221) 23591 Telex: 0781108
Man Dir: G Du Ry van Beest Holle; *Sales & Advertising Dir:* F Litten
Subjects: History, Art, Encyclopaedias
Founded: 1933
ISBN Publisher's Prefix: 3-87355

Holsten Verlag Wolf Schenke KG, Geschwister-Scholl-str 142, D-2000 Hamburg 20 Tel: (040) 470934
Man Dir: Wolf E Schenke
Subjects: History, Political Science
Founded: 1955

Verlag Gebr **Holzapfel**, Kienhorststr 61-63, D-1000 Berlin 51 Tel: (030) 4133098
Publisher: Klaus-J Holzapfel
Subject: Politics
ISBN Publisher's Prefix: 3-921226

Gunther **Holzboog** GmbH & Co, see Frommann-Holzboog

Hans **Holzmann** Verlag GmbH und Co KG, Gewerbestr 2, Postfach 460 & 480, D-8939 Bad Wörishofen Tel: (08247) 1031/8 Cable Add: Holzmann Verlag Telex: 0539331
Man Dir: Peter Holzmann; *Sales Dir:* Alfred Stempfle
Subjects: Management, Handicraft
Founded: 1936
Bookshop: Versandbuchhandlung Hans Holzmann, D-8939 Bad Wörishofen, Postfach 460
ISBN Publisher's Prefix: 3-7783

Horatio-verlag und Agentur*, Dirnitzweg 5, D-8491 Zandt Tel: (09944) 815
Dir: Genoveva Seydlitz; *Marketing Manager, Rights & Permissions:* Kurt Seydlitz; *Publicity:* Genoveva Seydlitz, Kurt Seydlitz
Subject: Humour; Jokes and Games

Werner **Hörnemann** Verlag, In der Wehrhecke 17, Postfach 130109, D-5300 Bonn 1 Tel: (02221) 251376
Subjects: Hobbies, Cookery, Pottery and Ceramics
1978: 15 titles
ISBN Publisher's Prefix: 3-87384

Horst-Werner Dumjahn Verlag, see Dumjahn

Edition Volker **Huber***, Berliner Str 218, Postfach 933, D-6050 Offenbach Tel: (0611) 814523
Publisher: Volker Huber; *Sales Managers:* Rosemarie Grenz, Helga Schwinn
Subject: Art

Max **Hueber** Verlag*, Krausstr 30, D-8045 Ismaning bei Munich Tel: (089) 96021 Telex: 05-23613 Cable Add: Hubook
Dirs: Dr Ingomar Hauchler, Heinrich Schrand, Gernot Keuchen; *Sales Dirs:* Bert Rech, Ekkehard Ziegler, Ulrich Heinerz
Subsidiary Companies: Hueber-Holzmann, Pädagogischer Verlag (qv)
Subjects: Textbooks, Reference, Bilingual Dictionaries, German for Foreigners, Linguistics
Founded: 1921
Bookshop: Universitätsbuchhandlung Max Hueber, Amalienstr 77-79, D-8000 Munich 40
ISBN Publisher's Prefix: 3-19

Hueber-Holzmann Pädagogischer Verlag, Max-Hueber-Str 4, D-8045 Ismaning/Munich Tel: (089) 96021 Cable Add: Hubook Telex: 0523613
Dir: Dr Harald Karja
Parent Company: Max Hueber Verlag (qv)
Subjects: Electrical Engineering, Electronics, Informatics, Data Processing, Textbooks, Mathematics, Music, Periodicals, Social Sciences, Arts
ISBN Publisher's Prefix: 3-8096

Hulsmanns & Reske GmbH, see Verlag Eremiten-Presse

Humboldt-Taschenbuchverlag Jacobi KG, Neusser Str 3, Postfach 401120, D-8000 Munich 40 Tel: (089) 38301 Cable Add:

Langenscheidt Munich Telex: 5215379 lkgm d
Man Dir: Karl-Ernst Tielebier-Langenscheidt; Editorial: Ursula Kopp; Sales Dir: Peter Haering; Advertising Dir: Dieter Krause; Sales, Promotion: through Langenscheidt KG (qv); Rights & Permissions: Manfred Überall
Subjects: Nonfiction Paperbacks
1979: 24 titles 1980: 24 titles Founded: 1970
Miscellaneous: Company is a member of the Langenscheidt Group (qv)
ISBN Publisher's Prefix: 3-581

Edition **Hundertmark**, Reinoldstr 6, D-5000 Cologne 1 Tel: (0221) 231603
Man Dir: Armin Hundertmark
Subjects: Contemporary Art Books, Literature; Periodicals
Founded: 1970

Husum Druck- und Verlagsgesellschaft mbH und Co KG, Nordbahnhofstr 2, Postfach 1480, D-2250 Husum Tel: (04841) 6081/3
Man Dir, Editorial, Rights & Permissions: Ingwert Paulsen Jr; Sales: Alfred Lorenzen; Production: Bruno Czarski; Publicity: Hans-Heinrich Lüth
Subsidiary Company: Hamburger Lesehefte Verlag Iselt & Co Nfl mbH (qv)
Associate Company: Matthiesen Verlag Ingwert Paulsen Jr (qv)
Subjects: Belles Lettres, Regional Interest
Founded: 1973
ISBN Publisher's Prefix: 3-88042

Dr Alfred **Hüthig** Verlag GmbH, Postfach 102869, D-6900 Heidelberg (Located at: Im Weiher 10) Tel: (06221) 4891 Cable Add: Hüthigverlag Heidelberg Telex: 0461727
Production: Willi Mayer; Publicity: Ulrich Stiehl
Subjects: Chemistry, Chemical Engineering, Medicine, Dentistry, Cosmetics, Electronics, Periodicals
1978: 15 titles Founded: 1925
ISBN Publisher's Prefix: 3-7785

Hüthig und Pflaum Verlag GmbH & Co KG, Postfach 201920, D-8000 Munich 2 (Located at: Lazarettstr 4, D-8000 Munich 19) Tel: (089) 186051
Telex: 0529408
Branch Off: Im Weiher 10, D-6900 Heidelberg 1
Subjects: Electrical Engineering, Electronics
Associate Companies: Richard Pflaum Verlag KG (qv), Dr Alfred Hüthig Verlag (qv)
ISBN Publisher's Prefix: 3-8101

I d W-Verlag GmbH, Cecilienallee 36, Postfach 320580, D-4000 Düsseldorf 30 Tel: (0211) 434391 Cable Add: ideweverlag
Telex: 8584270
Subject: Business Administration, Tax Law, Finance, Auditing
1980: 15 titles
ISBN Publisher's Prefix: 3-8021

I L S (Institut für Lernsysteme) GmbH, member of Verlagsgruppe Bertelsmann GmbH (qv)

I M S F, see Institut für Marxistische Studien und Forschungen eV

I S P-Verlag (Internationale Sozialistische Publikationen)*, Speicherstr 5, D-6000 Frankfurt am Main 2 Tel: (0611) 233012
Subject: Politics

I V A Verlag Bernd Polke GmbH*, Am Lastnauer Tor 4, D-7400 Tübingen 1 Tel: (07071) 212314
Man Dir, Rights & Permissions: Bernd Polke; Sales: Herbert Grohmann; Publicity: Cornelia Voester
Orders to: VVA, D-4830 Gütersloh

Ibnassus Presse*, Postfach 930, D-3400 Göttingen Tel: (0551) 72659
Man & Sales Dirs: Bert Schlender, Detlev Pawlik
Subjects: Belles Lettres, Poetry, Art
Bookshop: Versandbuchhandlung Bert Schlender, Postfach 930, D-3400 Göttingen
Founded: 1972

Idion Verlag*, Nussbaumstrasse 10, D-8000, Munich Tel: 593504 Telex: 8579460 vam D
Dirs: Hans-Lothar Merten, Manfred Stölting; Sales: Manfred Mayer; Production: Johannes Rüger
Subjects: Popular Facsimiles

Index eV*, Überlinger Str 13, Postfach 410511, D-5000 Cologne 41 Tel: (0221) 436939/372043
Publisher: Adolf Müller
Subjects: Belles Lettres, Poetry, Politics, Czech and Slovak Literature

Inform-Verlag, see Dreisam-Verlag

Insel Verlag, Postfach 3325, D-6000 Frankfurt am Main (Located at: Suhrkamp House, Lindenstr 29-35) Tel: (0611) 740231
Cable Add: Inselverlag Telex: 413972
Publisher: Dr Siegfried Unseld; Man Dir: Dr Heribert Marré; Sales: Dr Gottfried Honnefelder; Publicity: Claus Carlé; Rights & Permissions: Helene Ritzerfeld
Associate Companies: Suhrkamp Publishers Boston, Inc, 380 Green St, Cambridge, Mass 02139, USA; Suhrkamp Verlag AG, Zeltweg 25, CH-8032, Zurich, Switzerland; Suhrkamp Verlag KG, Federal Republic of Germany (qv)
Subjects: Classic German Literature (especially Goethe), Classic foreign authors in translation, Modern Classics, Cultural History, Bibliophilia, Books on Great Artists
Founded: 1899
ISBN Publisher's Prefix: 3-458

Institut für Lernsysteme (ILS), member of Verlagsgruppe Bertelsmann GmbH (qv)

Institut für Marxistische Studien und Forschungen eV (IMSF) Frankfurt am Main, Liebigstr 6, D-6000 Frankfurt am Main Tel: 724914
Man Dir: Prof Dr Schleifstein; All other offices: Dr Schmidt
The Institute for Marxist Studies and Research
Subjects: Publication of results of studies, research etc, commentary on current political and social questions; Periodicals
Founded: 1968
Miscellaneous: Member of Arbeitsgemeinschaft sozialistischer und demokratischer Verleger und Buchhändler (qv for other members)

Inter-Kunst und Buch GmbH, Wöllsteinerstr 8, D-6550 Bad Kreuznach Tel: (0671) 67073 Telex: 042815
Associate Company: Harrach und Sabrow (qv)
Subjects: Art Books, Graphics, Bibliophile Editions

Verlag **Internationale Solidarität** Verlagsgesellschaft mbH*, Zugweg 10, D-5000 Cologne Tel: (0221) 327817 Cable Add: Zugweg 10
Sales, Production: Ole Callsen
Subject: Politics

Irisiana Druck und Verlag, Wengenerstr 8, D-8961 Haldenwang Tel: (08374) 1574
1978: 3 titles
Subjects: Eastern Religion, Feminine Interest

Iselt und Co Nfl mbH, see Hamburger Lesehefte Verlag

Edition **Isis**, an imprint of Reinhard Becker Verlag (qv)

Verlag der **Islam***, Babenhäuserlandstr 25, D-6000 Frankfurt am Main 70 Tel: (0611) 653122 Cable Add: Islam
Man Dir: F I Anweri; Publicity Dir: Hadayatullah Hübsch
Subject: Religion

J R O-Kartografische Verlagsgesellschaft mbH*, Leopoldstrasse 175, Postfach 400940, D-8000 München 40 Tel: (089) 381031
Cable Add: hochbild Telex: 5215802
General Managers: Dr Bernd Koberg, Karl E Keck; Marketing and Publicity: Frieder Neher; Sales: Ingo Kruck; Production: Max Hann
Parent Company: Süddeutscher Verlag GmbH, Sendlonger Str 80, Postfach 202220, D-8000 Munich 2
Subjects: Road Maps, Town Maps, Walking Maps and Guides, School Wall Maps, Organisational Charts, Atlases, Globes
Founded: 1922
ISBN Publisher's Prefix: 3-87378

Jacobi Verlag GmbH*, Mühlenweg 67, D-2822 Schwanewede 1 — Leuchtenberg Tel: (0421) 631413
Man Dir, Editorial: Friedrich Röver; Sales: Heyke Weinbecker
Subjects: World Literature of the late 19th/early 20th century
Founded: 1974
ISBN Publisher's Prefix: 13198

Jaeger und Waldmann, see Telex-Verlag

Jahreszeitenverlag, Poßmoorweg 1, Postfach 601220, D-2000 Hamburg 60 Tel: (040) 27171 Cable Add: Jalag Telex: 0213214
Subject: Belles Lettres

Verlag Eduard **Jakobsohn**, Glogauer str 22, D-1000 Berlin 36 Tel: 6181258
Orders to: PRO MEDIA Literaturvertrieb GmbH, Werner Voss Damm 54, D-1000 Berlin 42
Subjects: Alternative Living, Communes, Spanish Civil War, Witch-hunting, Red Indians, Literature
1979: 10 titles 1980: 13 titles

Jal-Verlag/Jal-Reprint Arnulf Liebing, Werner-von-Siemens-Str 5, Postfach 5840, D-8700 Würzburg 1 Tel: (0931) 21120/22821 Cable Add: Journalfranz
Publishers: Arnulf Liebing, Hildgund Holler
Imprints: Slavica, History of Pharmacy
Subjects: Slavistics, History of Pharmacy
1978: 11 titles 1979: 3 titles
ISBN Publisher's Prefix: 3-7778

Stern-Verlag **Janssen** und Co, see Stern-Verlag

Reinhard **Jaspert**, see Safari-Verlag

Jugend und Volk Verlag GmbH, Claude-Lorrainstr, D-8000 Munich 40 Tel: (089) 374560
Parent Company: Jugend und Volk Verlagsgesellschaft mbH, Austria (qv)
Subject: Juveniles
ISBN Publisher's Prefix: 3-8113

Jugenddienst-Verlag, Foehrenstr 33-35, Postfach 200415, D-5600 Wuppertal 2 Tel: (0202) 551888
Dir: Hermann Schulz
Associate Company: Peter Hammer Verlag (qv)
Subjects: Playgroups, Learning, Sexual Instruction, Meditation, Christian Action
1979: 10 titles 1980: 14 titles
ISBN Publisher's Prefix: 3-7795

Axel-**Juncker**-Verlag Jacobi KG, Neusserstr 3, D-8000 Munich 40 Tel: (089) 38301
Man Dir: Karl Ernst Tielebier-

FEDERAL REPUBLIC OF GERMANY 141

Langenscheidt; *Sales Dir:* Peter Haering; *Publicity & Advertising:* Dieter Krause; *Sales, Promotion:* through Langenscheidt KG (qv); *Rights & Permissions:* Manfred Überall; *Export Dir:* Uwe Cordts
Subjects: Reference, Educational Materials
Titles in print: 42 *Founded:* 1902
Miscellaneous: Company is a member of the Langenscheidt Group (qv)
ISBN Publisher's Prefix: 3-558

Junior International, Postfach 285, D-7300 Esslingen (Located at: Liebigstr 1-11, D-7301 Deizisau) Tel: (07153) 22011 Cable Add: Verlag Schreiber Telex: 7266880 jfs d
Associate Company: Verlag J F Schreiber GmbH (qv)

Juventa Verlag, Dr Martin Faltermaier, Tizianstr 115, D-8000 Munich 19 Tel: (089) 155420
Man Dir: Dr Martin Faltermaier; *Publicity:* Elke Gerdes
Subjects: Mainly connected with young people's training, education, psychology, etc
1978: 14 titles *1979:* 16 titles *Founded:* 1953
ISBN Publisher's Prefix: 3-7799

Verlag Gerhard **Kaffke***, Echzellerstr 1, Postfach 640125, D-6000 Frankfurt am Main 64 Tel: (06194) 21493
Man Dir: Gerhard Kaffke; *Manager:* Gisela Kaffke; *Sales:* Ursula Wieder
Subjects: Theology, Religion, Paperbacks
Founded: 1955
ISBN Publisher's Prefix: 3-87391

Chr **Kaiser** Verlag, Postfach 509, D-8000 Munich 43 (Located at: Isabellastr 20, D-8000 Munich 40) Tel: (089) 372097/378786
Dir: Manfred Weber; *Sales Dir:* Uwe Fleischle
Subjects: Christian apologetics and exegesis, Theology, Religion and Society, Christian-Jewish Encounter
1979: 84 titles *1980:* 65 titles *Founded:* 1845
ISBN Publisher's Prefix: 3-459

Verlag Ferdinand **Kamp** GmbH & Co KG, Widumestr 2-8, Postfach 101309, D-4630 Bochum Tel: (0234) 15071
Subjects: Textbooks, Reference, Encyclopaedias, Dictionaries, Education, Nonfiction, Paperbacks, Periodicals
ISBN Publisher's Prefix: 3-592

S **Karger** GmbH, Verlag für Medizin & Naturwissenschaften, Angerhofstr 9, Postfach 2, D-8034 Germering, Munich Tel: (089) 844021 Cable Add: Kargermedbooks Telex: 524865
Man Dir: W Kunz
Subjects: Medicine, Psychology, Natural Science
Bookshop: Karger-Buchhandlung Ausstellung & Vertrieb internationaler medizinischer Fachliteratur, Angerhofstr 9, Postfach 2, D-8034 Germering, Munich

Karo-Bücher, an imprint of Neuer Jugendschriften-Verlag (qv)

Kartographisches Institut Bertelsmann, Carl-Bertelsmannstr 161, D-4380 Gütersloh 1 Tel: (05241) 801 Telex: 933832
Dir: Karlheinz Thieme
Parent Company: Verlagsgruppe Bertelsmann GmbH (qv for associate companies)
Subjects: Atlases of all kinds

Verlag **Katholisches Bibelwerk** GmbH, Silberburgstr 121A, D-7000 Stuttgart Tel: (0711) 629003
Editorial: Werner Meyer
Dir: Dieter Hirsmüller
Subject: Religious literature on practical aspects of Catholic Bible work in Belgium, Federal Republic of Germany, Netherlands, Austria and Switzerland
Miscellaneous: Company is a member of AMB (qv)
ISBN Publisher's Prefix: 3-460

Katzmann-Verlag KG, Doblerstr 33, Postfach 1827, D-7400 Tübingen Tel: (07071) 23115 Cable Add: Katzmann Verlag
Man Dir: Dr Volker Katzmann; *Sales Dir:* Sibylle Katzmann; *Production:* Margarete Knöpfle; *Publicity, Rights & Permissions:* Dr V Katzmann
Subjects: Sociology, Youth Work, Adult Education, Marriage and Family Counselling, Theology, Art, Religion, Periodical
1978: 11 titles *Founded:* 1945
ISBN Publisher's Prefix: 3-7805

Verlag Ernst **Kaufmann**, Alleestr 2, Postfach 1780, D-7630 Lahr/Schwarzwald Tel: (07821) 26083 Cable Add: Ernstkauf Telex: 0754973
Man Dir: Heinz Kaufmann; *Chief Editor:* R Dessecker-Kaufmann; *Public Relations, Distribution:* Michael Jacob
Subjects: Religious Education (books, materials); Children's Books
1978: 31 titles *Founded:* 1816
Miscellaneous: Member of Verlagsring Religionsunterricht (VRU = Religious Instruction Publishing Ring)
ISBN Publisher's Prefix: 3-7806

Verlag und Buchvertrieb E **Keimer***, Postfach 22, D-8014 Munich-Neubiberg Tel: (089) 6014811
Dir: Wolfgang Reuter
Subject: Textbooks
ISBN Publisher's Prefix: 3-920536

Verlag **Keip** KG Antiquariat*, Hainer Weg 46-48, D-6000 Frankfurt am Main 70 Tel: (0611) 614011 Cable Add: Antikeip Frankfurtmain Telex: D 689857 Keip
Publisher: Ulrich Keip; *Manager and Office Chief:* Johann Holler
Subjects: Law, Economics, History, Sociology, Socialism
1978: 100 titles *Founded:* 1967

Franckh'sche Verlagshandlung, W **Keller** & Co, see Franckh'sche

Verlag F H **Kerle**, Tennenbacher Str 4, Postfach, D-7800 Freiburg Tel: (0761) 2717512 Telex: 07721440
Man Dir: Dr Hermann Herder; *Sales:* Dr Jürgen Bach; *Publicity:* Fritz Knoch, Harald Gläser
Parent Company: Verlag Herder GmbH & Co KG (qv)
Subjects: Belles Lettres (covering novels, memoirs, reportage)
ISBN Publisher's Prefix: 3-600

Keysersche Verlagsbuchhandlung GmbH*, Widenmayerstr 41, Postfach 243, D-8000 Munich 22 Tel: (089) 225055
Publishers: Christian Neumann, Hans Joachim Neumann; *Production:* Joachim W Schmidt; *Public Relations, Advertising:* Silke Schreiber
Subjects: Art, Reference, Geography, Juveniles
1979: 10 titles *Founded:* 1777
ISBN Publisher's Prefix: 3-87405

Kibu-Verlag GmbH, Bräuckerweg 120, Postfach 329, D-5750 Menden 1 Tel: 02373 63131 Telex: 8202855
Dirs: Kunibert Birnkraut, Erhard Tamm
Subjects: Children's, Juveniles, Special Editions

Johannes **Kiefel** Verlag, Linderhauser Str 60, D-5600 Wuppertal 2 Tel: (0202) 642084/5 Cable Add: Kiefel, Wuppertal-2
Dir: Ingeborg Kiefel
Subjects: Religion, Juveniles, Textbooks
Founded: 1920
ISBN Publisher's Prefix: 3-7811

Friedrich **Kiehl** Verlag GmbH, Pfaustr 13, Postfach 210747, D-6700 Ludwigshafen Tel: (0621) 695041/2 Telex: 0464810
Dir: Ernst-Otto Kleyboldt; *Sales Manager:* Regina König
Parent Company: Verlag Neue Wirtschafts-Briefe GmbH (qv)
Subjects: Law, Economics, Commerce, Banking
ISBN Publisher's Prefix: 3-470

Verlag **Kiepenheuer und Witsch**, Rondorfer Str 5, D-5000 Cologne-Marienburg Tel: (0221) 387038 Cable Add: Kiepenbücher Cologne
Man Dir: Dr Reinhold Neven Du Mont; *Editorial:* Bärbel Flad, Dieter Wellershoff, Erika Stegmann, Renate Matthaei, Alexandra von Miquel; *Sales:* Heinz Biehn; *Foreign Rights & Permissions:* Traudel Jansen
Associate Company: Verlag für Politik und Wirtschaft (qv)
Subjects: General Fiction, Belles Lettres, Poetry, Biography, History, Social Science
1980: approx 55 titles *Founded:* 1948
ISBN Publisher's Prefix: 3-462

Kilda Verlag*, Münsterstr 71, D-4402 Greven/Westfalen Tel: (0251) 36229 Cable Add: Kildagreven
Man Dir: Mr Pölking

Kindler Verlag GmbH, Leopoldstr 54, Postfach 401043, D-8000 Munich 40 Tel: (089) 394041 Cable Add: Kindlerverlag Telex: 05215678
Editorial and Publicity: Traut Felgentreff; *Sales:* Elke Gerhart
Orders to: Vereinigte Verlagsauslieferung GmbH, Postfach 7777, D-4830 Gütersloh
Associate Company: Lichtenberg Verlag GmbH (qv)
Subjects: General Fiction, Belles Lettres, Biography, History, How-to, Art, Reference, Religion, Low- & High-priced Paperbacks, Medicine, Psychology, General & Social Science, University Textbooks, Educational Materials
Founded: 1951
ISBN Publisher's Prefix: 3-463

Klasing und Co GmbH, Siekerwall 21, Postfach 4809, D-4800 Bielefeld 1 Tel: (0521) 67015 Cable Add: Buchklasing Bielefeld Telex: 932934 Dekla
Publishers: Konrad-Wilhelm Delius, Kurt Delius; *Sales & Publicity Manager:* Wilhelm Meyerhenke; *Rights & Permissions:* Ilsemarie Steinbrinker
Parent Company: Delius, Klasing & Co (qv)
Subjects: Yachting, Motor Boats
ISBN Publisher's Prefix: 3-87412

Kunstverlag Woldemar **Klein***, Dr Rudolf Georgi, Aureliusstr 42, Postfach 407, 51 Aachen Telex: 832337 geac d Tel: (0241) 26141
Subjects: Art Calendars, Art Books

Klens Verlag GmbH, Prinz-Georg-Str 44, Postfach 320620, D-4000 Düsseldorf 30 Tel: (0211) 480023
Publisher: Viktor Nolden
Subjects: Popular Christian Aids, Juveniles, and Youth Training
1979: 3 titles
ISBN Publisher's Prefix: 3-87309

Ernst **Klett**, Rotebühlstr 77, Postfach 809, D-7000 Stuttgart Tel: (0711) 66720
Publisher: Michael Klett; *Publicity Manager:* Egon Schramm; *Foreign Relations:* Martin Veit; *Rights and Export Sales:* Joachim Lange
Associate Companies: Klett-Cotta Verlag (qv), Stuttgarter Verlagskontor, both

in Federal Republic of Germany;
Klett und Balmer Verlag, Switzerland (qv);
Editorial Pedagogica é Universitaria, Brazil
Subjects: Biology, Chemistry, History, Industries, Crafts, Arts, Textbooks, Reference, Dictionaries, Mathematics, Multimedia, Education, Music, Physics, Games, Linguistics, Languages, Periodicals
ISBN Publisher's Prefix: 3-12

Klett-Cotta Verlag, Rotebühlstr 77, Postfach 809, D-7000 Stuttgart 1   Tel: (0711) 66720   Cable Add: Klettverlag   Telex: 721715 Klett d
Man Dir: Michael Klett; *Editorial:* Dr Arbogast, Dr Dieckmann, Friedrich Kür; *Foreign Relations:* Mr Veit; *Rights and Export Sales:* Joachim Lange
Imprints: Hobbit Presse, Konzepte der Humanwissenschaften
Subjects: Literature, Linguistics, Psychoanalysis, Psychotherapy, Psychology, Education, Philosophy, Theology, Mythology, Ecology, History, Politics, Sociology, the Arts
Founded: 1844
Associate Companies: Klett und Balmer, Switzerland (qv); Ernst Klett; Stuttgarter Verlags Kontor, Federal Republic of Germany
ISBN Publisher's Prefix: 3-12

Klinkhardt und Biermann Richard Carl Schmidt Co*, Helmstedter Str 151, D-3300 Brunswick   Tel: (0531) 73189
Owner: Ilse Gutsch
Subjects: Art, Antiques, Numismatics
Founded: 1907
ISBN Publisher's Prefix: 3-7814

Erika **Klopp** Verlag GmbH, Kurfürstendamm 126, Postfach 310829, D-1000 Berlin 31   Tel: (030) 8911008
Publisher: Horst Meyer; *Rights & Permissions:* Katharina Janike
Subject: Juveniles
1978: 25 titles   *1979:* 20 titles   *Founded:* 1925
ISBN Publisher's Prefix: 3-7817

Vittorio **Klostermann**, Frauenlobstr 22, Postfach 900601, D-6000 Frankfurt am Main 90   Tel: (0611) 774011
Man Dirs: Michael Klostermann, Eckard Klostermann
Subjects: Philosophy, Bibliography, Romanistics, University Textbooks, General Science, History, Art, High-priced Paperbacks
1978: 50 titles   *1979:* 50 titles   *Founded:* 1930
ISBN Publisher's Prefix: 3-465

Ehrenfried **Klotz** Verlag, Theaterstr 13, Postfach 77, D-3400 Göttingen   Tel: (0551) 54031/3
Man Dir: Dr Arndt Ruprecht; *Sales:* Robert-Bosch-Breite
Subject: Religion
Parent Company: Vandenhoeck & Ruprecht, Göttingen (qv)
1978: 2 titles   *Founded:* 1949
ISBN Publisher's Prefix: 3-525

Fritz **Knapp** Verlag GmbH*, Neue Mainzer Str 60, D-6000 Frankfurt am Main 1   Tel: (0611) 280151   Cable Add: Schauinsland   Telex: 411397
Man Dirs: Alfons Binz, Peter Muthesius; *Sales Dir:* Alexander Rausch von Traubenberg; *Publicity Manager:* Karlheinz Möller; *Production:* K M Tecklenburg; *Advertising Dir:* Dieter Belz; *Rights & Permissions:* Alfons Binz
Subjects: Money, Banking, Stock Exchange, Economics, Economic Science, Reference, High-priced Paperbacks, Specialist Dictionaries, German Law in English/French Translation
1978: 35 titles   *Founded:* 1935
ISBN Publisher's Prefix: 3-7819

Wilhelm **Knapp** Verlag*, Pressehaus am Martin-Luther-Platz, Postfach 1122, D-4000 Düsseldorf 1   Tel: (0211) 885608
Man Dirs: Dr Max Nitsche, Dr Joseph Schaffrath, Werner Gutzki; *Publishing Dir:* Dr Manfred Lotsch; *Production, Promotion:* Helmut Schwanen
Parent Company: Droste Verlag GmbH, Düsseldorf, (qv)
Subjects: Photography, Cinematography
1978: 15 titles   *1979:* 12 titles   *Founded:* 1838
ISBN Publisher's Prefix: 3-87420

Albrecht **Knaus** Verlag, Postfach 520455, D-2000 Hamburg 52 (Located at: Beselerstr 2)   Tel: (040) 897401   Cable Add: knausbooks Hamburg
Man Dir: Dr Albrecht Knaus; *Sales:* Lothar Nalbach; *Production:* Johannes Eikel
Orders to: Vereinigte Verlagsauslieferung, Postfach 7777, D-4830 Gütersloh 1
Subjects: Fiction and Non-fiction: Memoirs, History, Politics
1978: 10 titles   *1979:* 20 titles   *Founded:* 1978
ISBN Publisher's Prefix: 3-8135

Verlag Josef **Knecht**-Carolus Druckerei GmbH, Liebfrauenberg 37, D-6000 Frankfurt am Main 1   Tel: (0611) 281767
Dirs: Dr Josef Knecht, Dr H Herder-Dorneich, Fritz Knoch; *Editorial:* Dr Marianne Regnier
Subjects: General Fiction, Paperbacks, Religion, Social Science, Philosophy, Non-fiction
1978: 15 titles   *1979:* 20 titles   *Founded:* 1946
ISBN Publisher's Prefix: 3-7820

Knorr und Hirth Verlag GmbH, D-3167 Ahrbeck vor Hanover   Tel: (05136) 5501   Cable Add: Knorrhirth Ahrbeck
Man Dir: Berthold Fricke
Subjects: Art, Geography, Travel Guides, Almanacs; Editions also in English, French, Dutch, Italian, Spanish and Japanese; Several Bilingual Editions
Founded: 1894
ISBN Publisher's Prefix: 3-7821

Verlagsanstalt Alexander **Koch** GmbH, Postfach 3081, D-7000 Stuttgart 1 (Located at: Fasanenweg 18, D-7022 Leinfelden-Echterdingen 1)   Tel: (0711) 79891   Telex: 7-255609 drw d
Man Dirs: Karl-Heinz Weinbrenner, L Drabarczyk; *Manager, Rights & Permissions:* Dr Erwin Schmid; *Editorial:* Max Fengler, Eberhard Höhn
Parent Company: DRW-Verlag Weinbrenner KG (qv)
Subjects: Architecture, Interior Decoration, Building Technology; Periodicals
1978: 3 titles   *Founded:* 1890
ISBN Publisher's Prefix: 3-87422

Kochbuchverlag Heimeran KG*, Dietlindenstr 14, Postfach 400824, D-8000 Munich 40   Tel: (089) 399017
Man Dir: Till Heimeran; *Editorial Production:* Tillmann Roeder; *Sales, Publicity, Rights & Permissions:* Thomas Kniffler
Associate Company: Ernst Heimeran Verlag (qv)
Subject: Cookery
1978: 12 titles   *Founded:* 1969
ISBN Publisher's Prefix: 3-8063

C A **Koch's** Verlag Nachfolger, see Deutsche Buchgemeinschaft

K F **Koehler** Verlag, Postfach 210, D-7000 Stuttgart 80 (Located at: Schockenriedstr 37)   Tel: (0711) 78601   Telex: 7255373 knobs d
Dir: Till Grupp
Subjects: Humanities, History, Politics, Law, Social Science, Geography
Founded: 1789
ISBN Publisher's Prefix: 3-87425

Koehlers Verlagsgesellschaft, Steintorwall 17, Postfach 21352, D-4900 Herford   Tel: (05221) 50001   Cable Add: Koehlers Vlg Herford/Westf   Telex: 934801 maxvg d
Publishers: Dr Kurt Schober, Gerhard Bollmann, Hans-Focko Koehler; *Sales:* Hans-Focko Koehler; *Publicity:* Gerhard Mindt
Associate Companies: Maximilian-Verlag, E S Mittler und Sohn GmbH, Verlag Offene Worte (all members of Maximilian-Verlagsgruppe — qv)
Subjects: Fiction and Non-fiction, Shipping, Shipbuilding, Maritime and Offshore interest, Contemporary maritime history, Periodicals
ISBN Publisher's Prefix: 3-7822

Verlag Valentin **Koerner** GmbH, Hermann-Sielcken-Str 36, Postfach 304, D-7570 Baden-Baden   Tel: (07221) 22423
Publisher: Valentin Koerner
1980: 23 titles
ISBN Publisher's Prefix: 3-87320

Unternehmensgruppe Verlag W **Kohlhammer** GmbH, Hessbrühlstr 69, Postfach 800430, D-7000 Stuttgart 80   Tel: (0711) 78631   Cable Add: Kohlhammer Stuttgart   Telex: 07255820
Man Dirs: Dr Jürgen Gutbrod, Günter Haberland; *Sales Dir:* Gerd W Ludwig; *Rights & Permissions:* Dr Alexander Schweickert
Subsidiary Companies: Berliner Union GmbH (qv); Deutscher Gemeindeverlag (qv); G Grote'sche Verlagsbuchhandlung GmbH & Co KG (qv); Kohlhammer und Wallishauser GmbH, Hechingen
Branch Offs: Berlin, Cologne, Mainz
Subjects: History, Art, Orientalia, Philosophy, Humanities, Religion, Law, Public Administration, Linguistics, Literary History, Economics, Natural Sciences, Architecture, Travel
1978: 380 titles   *1979:* 430 titles   *Founded:* 1866
ISBN Publisher's Prefix: 3-17

Kohl's Technischer Verlag Erwin Kohl GmbH & Co KG, Emil-Sulzbach-Str 12, Postfach 970115, D-6000 Frankfurt am Main 97   Tel: (0611) 778410 and 776513
Associate Company: Frankfurter Fachverlag Michael Kohl KG (qv)
Subjects: Civil & Mechanical Engineering
ISBN Publisher's Prefix: 3-87430

Kolibri-Verlag, Else-Lasker-Schüler-Str 47-49, D-5600 Wuppertal 1   Tel: (0202) 443143
Dir: Maria Pfriem; *Sales:* Karin Bambek
Associate Company: Engelbert Pfrim Verlag (qv)
Subjects: Books for Children of all ages, on all subjects, Fiction and Nonfiction
1978: 26 titles   *Founded:* 1950
ISBN Publisher's Prefix: 3-87434

Komar*, Oberaustr 1, Postfach 1132, D-8200 Rosenheim   Tel: (08031) 1280/33477/33499   Telex: 0525793
Subjects: Juveniles, Psychology, Sports

Verlag **Kommentator** GmbH*, Zeppelinallee 43, Postfach 970148, D-6000 Frankfurt am Main   Tel: (0611) 774055
Man Dir: Dr Caspar van Kempen; *Editorial:* Gunter Herz, Ulrich Neuhaus; *Sales, Publicity:* Ernst F Grundl
Associate Company: Alfred Metzner GmbH (qv)
Subject: Law, Taxation
Miscellaneous: Firm is a member of the Kluwer Group, Deventer, Netherlands (qv)
ISBN Publisher's Prefix: 3-7824

Konkordia AG für Druck und Verlag*, Eisenbahnstr 31-33, Postfach 1240, D-7580 Bühl/Baden Tel: (07223) 22501/23631
Telex: 784533
Subject: Textbooks
ISBN Publisher's Prefix: 3-7826

Anton H **Konrad** Verlag*, Erlenweg 7, Postfach 3, D-7912 Weissenhorn
Tel: (07309) 2657
Subjects: Arts, History
ISBN Publisher's Prefix: 3-87437

Konzepte der Humanwissenschaften, an imprint of Klett-Cotta Verlag (qv)

Kösel-Verlag GmbH & Co*, Flüggenstr 2, D-8000 Munich 19 Tel: (089) 175077 Cable Add: Köselverlag Munich Telex: 5215492 kvmud
Man Dirs: Dieter Munz, Dr Christoph Wild; *Production:* Friedhelm Jochems; *Rights & Permissions:* Ingrid Fink; *Advertising:* Gudrun Loesel
Orders to: Flugplatzstr 1, D-8031 Gilching Tel: (08105) 9014 Telex: 524199 kvgid
Subjects: Pedagogy, Philosophy, Religion, Educational Materials, History, Textbooks, Social Science, Fiction
1978: 76 titles *Founded:* 1593
ISBN Publisher's Prefix: 3-466

G **Kowalski**, see Concert Verlag

Karin **Kramer** Verlag, Postfach 106, D-1000 Berlin-Neukölln 44 (Located at: Braunschweiger Str 22) Tel: (030) 6845055/6842598
Editorial and Publicity: Bernd Kramer
Subjects: Politics, Art, Literature, Education, Psychology, Anarchist Literature
1978: 12 titles *Founded:* 1970
ISBN Publisher's Prefix: 3-87956

Karl **Krämer** Verlag GmbH und Co, Schulze-Delitzsch-Str 15, Postfach 800650, D-7000 Stuttgart 80 Tel: (0711) 610700 Cable Add: Fachbuchkraemer Stuttgart
Man Dir, Rights & Permissions: Karl H Krämer; *Sales Dir:* Bernhard Prokop; *Production, Publicity:* Annemarie Bosch
Orders to: Rotebühlstr 40, Postfach 808, D-7000 Stuttgart 1
Associate Company: Verlag Karl Krämer & Co, Spiegelgasse 14, CH-8001 Zurich, Switzerland
Subjects: Town Planning, Architecture, Building Construction, Sociology
Bookshop: Fachbuchhandlung Karl Krämer, Rotebühlstr 40, Postfach 808, D-7000 Stuttgart 1
1979: 15 titles *Founded:* 1930
ISBN Publisher's Prefix: 3-7828

Dr Waldemar **Kramer**
Verlagsbuchhandlung, Bornheimer Landwehr 57a, Postfach 600445, D-6000 Frankfurt am Main Tel: (0611) 434325
Publishers: Waldemar Kramer, Henriette Kramer
Subjects: Science and Natural History, Biology, History, Art Education, Psychology, Geography, Nature Study, Environment; Publications of the Senckenberg Nature Study Association; Periodicals
1978: 18 titles *1979:* 19 titles *Founded:* 1939
ISBN Publisher's Prefix: 3-7829

Krausskopf Verlag GmbH, Lessingstr 12, Postfach 2760, D-6500 Mainz Tel: (06131) 674041 Cable Add: Krausskopfverlag
Dirs: Hans Hauck, Peter M Fock
Parent Company: Elsevier-NDU nv, Netherlands (qv)
Subjects: Technical Books & Periodicals
Founded: 1937
ISBN Publisher's Prefix: 3-7830

Buch- und Bildverlag W **Kremnitz**, see Lacus

Kreuz Verlag, Breitwiesenstr 30, Postfach 800669, D-7000 Stuttgart 80 Tel: (0711) 734281/733135
Man Dir: Dieter Breitsohl; *Editor:* Helmut Weigel, Hildegunde Wöller; *Publicity, Rights & Permissions:* Barbara Dressler; *Production:* Brigitte Gnieser
Subsidiary Company:
Feuerseebuchhandlung, Breitwiesenstr 30, D-7000 Stuttgart 80 Tel: (0711) 732387
Subjects: Reference, Religion, Education, Juveniles, Psychology, Social Science, Periodicals
1978: 35 titles *Founded:* 1945
ISBN Publisher's Prefix: 3-7831

Kriminalistik Verlag GmbH*, Postfach 102640, 6900 Heidelberg (Located at: im Weiher 10) Tel: 06621/498250
Telex: 04-61727 huedh
Associate Companies: R V Decker's Verlag G Schenck GmbH (qv); C F Müller Jüristischer Verlag GmbH (qv)
Subject: Criminology

Alfred **Kröner** Verlag, Reuchlinstr 4, Postfach 1109, D-7000 Stuttgart 1 Tel: (0711) 620221
Man Dirs: Arno Klemm, Walter Kohrs
Subjects: History, Music, Art, Philosophy, Reference, Psychology, Engineering, General and Social Science, Economics, Literature, Education
Founded: 1904
ISBN Publisher's Prefix: 3-520

Buch und Werburg-Helmut **Krüger** GmbH, Kurfurstendamm 65, D-1000 Berlin 15
Man Dir: Helmut Krüger
Subjects: Art, Photography
Founded: 1974

Wolfgang **Kruger** Verlag*, Geleitsstrasse 25, Postfach 700480, D-6000 Frankfurt am Main 70 Tel: 0611/60621 Cable Add: buchfischer Telex: 0412410
Man Dir: Monika Schoeller; *Editorial:* Ivo Frenzel; *Sales, Publicity:* Ulrich Meier; *Production:* Wilfried Meiner; *Rights & Permissions:* Cornelia Wohlfarth
Parent Company: S Fischer Verlag GmbH (qv)
Subjects: General Fiction and Nonfiction
ISBN Publisher's Prefix: 3-8105

Kübler Verlag KG, Postfach 242, D-6840 Lampertheim 1 (Located at: Gaußstr 21) Tel: (06206) 51055
Dir: Marie-Luise Kübler
Subjects: Social Studies, Economics, Politics, Education, Picture Books
1979: 6 titles *Founded:* 1972
ISBN Publisher's Prefix: 3-921265

Kubon und Sagner, see Verlag Otto Sagner

Kühl KG, Verlagsgesellschaft, Mainzer Landstr 147, Postfach 119151, D-6000 Frankfurt am Main 2 Tel: (0611) 730234 Cable Add: kuhl Telex: 0413080 kuehl d
Managed by: Communist Party of the Federal Republic of Germany (KBW)
Branch Offs: Hanover, Cologne and Munich
Subjects: Publications by the Central Committee of the Communist Party of the Federal Republic of Germany
1980: 40 titles *Founded:* 1973

Wilhelm **Kumm** Verlag*, Tulpenhofstr 45, D-6050 Offenbach am Main Tel: 884349 Cable Add: Kummverlag
Proprietor & Man Dir: Wilhelm Kumm
Subjects: Belles Lettres, Poetry
Founded: 1967
ISBN Publisher's Prefix: 3-7836

Kunst und Wissen Erich Bieber OHG, Wilhelmstr 4, Postfach 46, D-7000 Stuttgart 1, Tel: (0711) 241152 Cable Add: Kunstwissen Telex: 721929

Publishers: Erich, Jürgen and Wolfgang Bieber
Subjects: Technical Textbooks
ISBN Publisher's Prefix: 3-87953

Kunst und Wohnen Verlag, see Dr Wolfgang Schwarze Verlag

Florian **Kupferberg** Verlag, Postfach 2680, D-6500 Mainz Tel: (06131) 24977
Owner: Christian A Kupferberg
Subjects: Art, Architecture, Cultural & Literary History, Mass Media
Founded: 1797/1938
ISBN Publisher's Prefix: 3-7837

Kyrios-Verlag GmbH*, Luckengasse 8, Postfach 1740, D-8050 Freising Tel: (08161) 5527
Dir: Ursula Blum; *Sales Manager:* Eveline Kamm
Subjects: Religion, Social Work, Periodicals
1979: 12 titles *Founded:* 1916
ISBN Publisher's Prefix: 3-7838

L N-Verlag Lübeck, Lübecker Nachrichten GmbH, Königstr 53-57, Postfach 2238, D-2400 Lübeck 1 Tel: (0451) 1441
Telex: 026801
Man Dirs: Charles Coleman, Jürgen Coleman, Bernd Ehrlich, Dr Günter Semmerow, Jürgen Wessel; *Editorial:* Jürgen W Scheutzow; *Sales Dir:* Elmar Bruns
Subjects: Series of guidebooks and illustrated volumes on various countries world-wide, and areas of Germany
1978: 10 titles *1979:* 9 titles
ISBN Publisher's Prefix: 3-87498

Ambro **Lacus**, Buch- und Bildverlag W Kremnitz, Frieding-Hurtenstr 25, D-8131 Andechs Tel: (08152) 1332 Cable Add: Kremnitz-Frieding
Man Dir: Ing Walter Kremnitz
Subjects: Illustrated foreign travel books, Folk Stories and Legends, Legal and Historical Reference, Botany
1978: 5 titles *1979:* 8 titles *Founded:* 1974
ISBN Publisher's Prefix: 3-921445

Laetare, see Burckhardthaus-Laetare Verlag GmbH

Lahn-Verlag*, Wiesbadener Str 1, Postfach 140, D-6250 Limburg Lahn 1 Tel: (06431) 401211 Telex: 0484764 palan d
Publisher: Engelbert Tauscher; *Editorial:* Ursula Mock; *Publicity Manager:* Raimund Zoellner
Subjects: Religion, Philosophy, Education
1978: 22 titles *Founded:* 1900
ISBN Publisher's Prefix: 3-7840

Lambertus Verlag GmbH, Sternwaldstr 4, Postfach 1026, D-7800 Freiburg im Breisgau Tel: (0761) 70721/2
Man Dirs: Dr Lioba Knöbber, Gerhild Neugart
Subjects: Social Work (Community and Case Work etc, with youth, the old and disabled), Social Security
Bookshop: Freiburger Bücherdienst, Sternwaldstr 4, Postfach 1026, D-7800 Freiburg
1978: 18 titles *1979:* 16 titles *Founded:* 1898
ISBN Publisher's Prefix: 3-7841

Landbuch-Verlag GmbH*, Kabelkamp 6, Postfach 160, D-3000 Hanover Tel: (0511) 632006 Cable Add: Landbuch Hanover
Telex: 921169
Man Dir, Production, Rights & Permissions: Alice Gross; *Sales:* Willi Ludwig Kroeck; *Publicity:* Ulrich Knocke
Subjects: Arts, Agriculture, Animal Breeding, Forestry, Sports, Nature, Hunting, Wildlife; Periodicals
1979: 14 titles *Founded:* 1945
ISBN Publisher's Prefix: 3-7842

Landsberger Verlagsanstalt Martin Neumeyer*, Museumstr 14, Postfach 104, D-8910 Landsberg Tel: (08191) 4055
Subjects: History, Hobbies, Mass Media, the Art of Living, How-To, Regional Interest
ISBN Publisher's Prefix: 3-920216

Albert **Langen**-Georg Müller Verlag, Hubertusstr 4, D-8000 Munich 19 Tel: (089) 177041 Telex: 05215045
Man Dir: Dr Herbert Fleissner; *Editorial:* Dr Herbert Greuèl, Dr Bernhard Struckmeyer; *Sales:* Gisela Weichert; *Publicity:* Dr Brigette Sinhuber; *Rights & Permissions:* Renate Werner
Subjects: General Fiction, Theatre, Reportage, Humour, Current Controversy
Founded: 1897
Miscellaneous: Firm is a member of the Verlagsgruppe Langen-Müller/Herbig (qv)
ISBN Publisher's Prefix: 3-7844

Verlagsgruppe **Langen-Müller**/Herbig, Hubertusstr 4, D-8000 Munich 19 Tel: (089) 177041 Telex: 05215045
Man Dir: Dr Herbert Fleissner
Members of the Group: Bechtle Verlag (qv); Mary Hahn's Kochbuchverlag (qv); F A Herbig Verlagsbuchhandlung (qv); Albert Langen-George Müller Verlag (qv); Georg Lentz Verlag (qv); Limes Verlag (qv); Nymphenburger Verlagshandlung (qv); Universitas Verlag (qv); Wirtschaftsverlag (qv) (all in Federal Republic of Germany); Amalthea-Verlag, Austria (qv)

The **Langenscheidt Group**, Neusser Str 3, Postfach 401120, D-8000 Munich 40 Tel: (089) 38301
The Group consists of: Humboldt-Taschenbuchverlag Jacobi KG (qv); Axel-Juncker-Verlag Jacobi KG (qv); Langenscheidt KG (qv); Langenscheidt-Hachette GmbH (qv); Langenscheidt-Longman GmbH (qv); Mentor-Verlag Dr Ramdohr KG (qv); Polyglott-Verlag Dr Bolte KG (qv)

Langenscheidt KG, Neusser Str 3, Postfach 401120, D-8000 Munich 40 Tel: (089) 3830-1 Cable Add: Langenscheidt Munich Telex: Munich 5215379 Lkgm-d (also at An der Langenscheidtbrücke, D-1000 Berlin 62)
Man Dir: Karl-Ernst Tielebier-Langenscheidt; *Editorial:* Dr Walter Voigt, Dr Wolfgang Wieter, Dr Heinz F Wendt; *Production:* Helmut Wahl; *Sales Dir:* Peter Haering; *Advertising Dir:* Dieter Krause; *Export Dir:* Uwe Cordts; *Rights & Permissions:* Manfred Überall
Subsidiary Companies: Langenscheidt AG, Switzerland (qv); Langenscheidt-Verlag GmbH, Austria (qv)
Associate Companies: See entry for The Langenscheidt Group
Subjects: Foreign Languages, German for Foreigners; Dictionaries, Textbooks, Records, Tapes, Cassettes
1979: 45 titles *1980:* 50 titles *Founded:* 1856
ISBN Publisher's Prefix: 3-468

Langenscheidt-Hachette GmbH, Neusser Str 3, Postfach 401120, D-8000 Munich 40 Tel: (089) 38301 Cable Add: Langenscheidt Munich Telex: 5215379 lkgm d
Man Dirs: Karl-Ernst Tielebier-Langenscheidt, Gérard Lilamand; *Editorial:* Brigitte Peters; *Sales & Promotion:* Through Langenscheidt KG
Associate Companies: See entry for The Langenscheidt Group, also for Hachette SA, France
Subjects: French (Language Teaching) for German-speaking people
1979: 26 titles *1980:* 40 titles *Founded:* 1977
ISBN Publisher's Prefix: 3-595

Langenscheidt-Longman GmbH, Neusser Str 3, Postfach 401120, D-8000 Munich 40 Tel: (089) 38301 Cable Add: Langenscheidt Munich Telex: 5215379 lkg md
Man Dir: Karl-Ernst Tielebier-Langenscheidt, David Mortimer; *Publishing Executive:* Uwe Mäder; *Sales & Promotion:* through Langenscheidt KG
Associate Companies: See entry for The Langenscheidt Group, also for the Longman Group, UK
Subjects: English Language Teaching
1979: 50 titles *1980:* 50 titles *Founded:* 1972
ISBN Publisher's Prefix: 3-526

Karl Robert **Langewiesche** Nachfolger Hans Koester KG, Grüner Weg 6, Postfach 1327, D-6240 Königstein 1 Tel: (06174) 7333 Cable Add: Langewiesche Königsteintaunus
Man Dir, Production, Sales and Publicity, Rights & Permissions: Hans-Curt Koester; *Editorial:* Hans Koester, Hans-Curt Koester
Orders to: Koch, Neff & Oetinger & Co, Abt VA, Postfach 800620, D-7000 Stuttgart
Subjects: Art, Geography, Biography, History, How-to, Music, University Textbooks, Architecture, Landscape; Low- and High-priced Paperbacks
1979: 15 titles *Founded:* 1902
ISBN Publisher's Prefix: 03-7845

Langewiesche-Brandt KG, Abholfach (Poste Restante), D-8026 Ebenhausen bei München Tel: (08178) 4857
Man Dir: Kristof Wachinger
Subjects: Belles Lettres, Art Books, Autobiographical, Poetry; High-priced Paperbacks, Posters
1978: 5 titles *1979:* 5 titles *Founded:* 1906
ISBN Publisher's Prefix: 3-7846

Verlag **Laterna Magica** Joachim F Richter*, Stridbeckstr 48, D-8000 Munich 71 Tel: (089) 797091/4 Telex: 05-22425 color d
Publisher: Joachim F Richter; *Sales, Publicity:* Christian Klages; *Production:* E W Panckow
Orders to: Stridbeckstr 48, D-8000 Munich 71
Subjects: Photography, Periodicals
Founded: 1966
ISBN Publisher's Prefix: 3-87467

H **Laupp'sche** Buchhandlung, an imprint of J C B Mohr (Paul Siebeck) (qv)

August **Lax**, Postfach, Weinberg 56, D-3200 Hildesheim Tel: (05121) 81074/81075
Man Dir, Editorial, Rights & Permissions: Lorenz Lax; *Sales:* D Lax; *Production:* Th Ahrens
Associate Company: Filmsatz Gesellschaft at above address
Subjects: Archaeology, History, Pre-history, Folklore, Art History, Literature (Prose, Poetry, Dialect), Lower Saxony Historical
Bookshop: Buchhandlung August Lax, Bernwardstr 7, D-3200 Hildesheim
1978: 18 titles *1979:* 29 titles *Founded:* 1849
ISBN Publisher's Prefix: 3-7848

J F **Lehmanns** Verlag*, Agnes-Bernauer-Platz 8, Postfach 210140, D-8000 Munich 21 Tel: (089) 581031 Cable Add: Lehmannverlag
Dirs: Bernard Spatz, Otto Spatz, Volker Schwartz; *Sales Manager:* Günther Heck; *Publicity:* Rolf Wendeler
Parent Company: Springer-Verlag (qv)
Subjects: Medicine, Psychology, Arts, Aviation, Military
Founded: 1890
Bookshops: Buchhandlung Für Medizin Otto Spatz, Schillerstr 51; D-8000 Munich 15; D-8000 Munich 55, Sauerbruchstr 10; D-2000 Hamburg-Eppendorf, Breitenfelder Str 62 (all in German Federal Republic)
ISBN Publisher's Prefix: 3-469

Verlag Hermann **Leins***, see Rainer Wunderlich Verlag Hermann Leins

Leitfadenverlag Dieter Sudholt*, D-8131 Berg 3 (Assenhausen) Tel: (08151) 5342
Publisher: Volker Sudholt
Subjects: Tax Directories, Business, Law, Economics
1978: 22 titles
ISBN Publisher's Prefix: 3-543

Verlag Otto **Lembeck**, Leerbachstr 42, D-6000 Frankfurt am Main 1 Tel: (0611) 720379 Cable Add: Lembeckdruck Frankfurtmain
Publications Manager: Helmut Nörenberg
Subject: Religion, Ecumenical Studies, Africa
1978-79: 14 titles *Founded:* 1945
ISBN Publisher's Prefix: 3-87476

Verlag Lambert **Lensing** GmbH, Kampstr 42, Postfach 875, D-4600 Dortmund 1 Tel: (0231) 148367 Cable Add: Lensingbuch Telex: 0822106
Man Dir: F C Lorson; *Editorial:* Dr Werner Jaeger; *Sales and Publicity:* H G Doenne; *Production:* G Marx
Subjects: Modern Languages, Modern Language Teaching, Educational Materials
Bookshop: Westenhellweg 86-88, Postfach 875, D-4600 Dortmund 1
1979: 45 titles *Founded:* 1870
ISBN Publisher's Prefix: 3-559

Georg **Lentz** Verlag*, Romanstr 16, D-8000 Munich 19 Tel: (089) 162051
Subjects: Fiction and Nonfiction for Juveniles
Miscellaneous: Firm is a member of Verlagsgruppe Langen-Müller/Herbig Munich (qv)

Leske Verlag und Budrich GmbH, Fürstenbergstr 23, Postfach 300406, D-5090 Leverkusen 3 Tel: (02171) 45525
Man Dir: Edmund Budrich
Subjects: Social Science, Sexology, Middle East, University, Secondary and Primary Textbooks, Educational Materials
Founded: 1974
ISBN Publisher's Prefix: 3-8100

Leuchter-Verlag AG*, Industriestr 6-8, Postfach 60, D-6106 Erzhausen Tel: (06150) 7565
Man & Sales Dir: Karl-Heinz Neumann
Subjects: Religion, Low-priced Paperbacks
Founded: 1946

Leuchtturm-Verlag*, Kreuzlinger Str 54, D-775 Konstanz 1 Tel: (07531) 26675
Man Dir: H-J Zebisch; *Sales Dir:* Frau von Ulardt; *Publicity & Advertising Dir, Rights & Permissions:* H-J Zebisch
Subjects: Engineering, General & Social Science
Founded: 1974

Lexika-Verlag, Chris Hablitzel, Forchenrain 11, D-7252 Weil der Stadt 5 Tel: (07033) 41077 Cable Add: fhwd Telex: 7265883 fhw d
Publisher, Man Dir: Chris Hablitzel
Subjects: Choice of studies and careers, Further and Adult Education, New learning techniques, Bookselling Aids
ISBN Publisher's Prefix: 3-920353

Lexikothek Verlag GmbH, Carl-Bertelsmannstr 270, D-4830 Gütersloh 1 Tel: (05241) 801 Telex: 933646
Dir: Werner Lenz
Parent Company: Verlagsgruppe Bertelsmann GmbH (qv for associate companies)
Subjects: Encyclopedias, Lexicons, Dictionaries and other Reference Works

FEDERAL REPUBLIC OF GERMANY 145

Liber Verlag GmbH, Hegelstr 45, Postfach 2946, D-6500 Mainz 1
Man Dir, Editorial: Tomo Matasić; *Production, Publicity:* Renate Ammersbach
Subjects: Literature, Literary Criticism, Linguistics, Foreign Language Teaching, Theses on Slavistics, History, Politics
1979: 13 titles *1980:* 4 titles *Founded:* 1977
ISBN Publisher's Prefix: 3-83111

Lichtenberg Verlag GmbH*, Leopoldstr 54, Postfach 401043, D-8000 Munich 40 Tel: (089) 394041 Cable Add: Lichtenbergverlag Telex: 05215678
Dirs: Peter Nikel, Klano Jost
Orders to: Vereinigte Verlagsauslieferung GmbH, Postfach 7777, 483 Gütersloh
Associate Company: Kindler Verlag GmbH (qv)
Subjects: General Fiction and Nonfiction, Belles Lettres, Practical Guides, Humour
Founded: 1962
ISBN Publisher's Prefix: 3-7852

Lichtkreis Christi*, Feldwieser-Str 84, Postfach 2, D-8212 Ubersee am Chiemsee Tel: 08642/6744
Subject: Die Neue Bibel (The New Bible) in 12 vols, appearing in numerous languages

Verlag der **Liebenzeller** Mission, Liobastr 8, Postfach 1223, D-7263 Bad Liebenzell 1 Tel: (07052) 2031
Publisher: Arthur Klenk
Subjects: Mission Reports, Theology, Methodology, also Fiction, Biographies and Devotional
1979: 25 titles *1980:* 23 titles *Founded:* 1906
Miscellaneous: Member of the Telos (qv) paperback series publishing group
ISBN Publisher's Prefix: 3-88002

Arnulf **Liebing**, see Jal-Verlag/Jal-Reprint

Rudolf **Liebing**, see Physica-Verlag

Edition/Galerie **Lietzow**, Knesebeckstr 32, D-1000 Berlin 12 Tel: (030) 8812895
Man Dir: Horst Hartmann; *Editorial:* Godehard Lietzow; *Sales, Production, Publicity:* Godehard Lietzow, Horst Hartmann
Subjects: Biography, Art, Reference
1978: 4 titles *1979:* 3 titles *Founded:* 1970

Limes Verlag*, Romanstr 16, D-8000 Munich 19 Tel: (089) 162051
Man Dir: Marguerite Schlüter; *Sales:* Brigitte Nunner
Subjects: General Fiction, Belles Lettres, Poetry, History, Music, Art
1978: 14 titles *Founded:* 1945
Miscellaneous: Firm is a member of Verlagsgruppe Langen-Müller/Herbig (qv)
ISBN Publisher's Prefix: 3-8090

Limpert Verlag, Ferdinandstr 18, Postfach 1727, D-6380 Bad Homburg vdH 1 Tel: (06172) 6038 Telex: 0418135 limp
Man Dir: H Farnung; *Sales:* Christine Sojka; *Rights & Permissions:* Hermann Farnung
Subject: Sport and Recreation
1980: c. 185 titles *Founded:* 1921

Lingen Verlag, Marienburger Strasse 17, Postfach 510729, D-5000 Cologne Tel: (0221) 380066 Telex: 8882138
Man Dir: Helmut Lingen
Subjects: Atlases, Language, Cookery, Popular Non-fiction

Paul **List** Verlag KG, Goethestr 43, D-8000 Munich 2 Tel: (089) 530561 Telex: 0522405
Man Dir: Robert Schäfer; *Editorial:* Dr Horst Ferle; *Sales:* Rose Heckenlaible; *Publicity:* Ulrike Ramsauer; *Advertising:* Michael Schindler; *Rights & Permissions:* Gabriele Fentzke
Associate Companies: Südwest Verlag GmbH & Co KG (qv); Süddeutscher Verlag Buchverlag (qv)
Subjects: General Fiction, Belles Lettres, Poetry, Biography, History, Music, Art, Philosophy, Reference, Religion, Psychology, General & Social Science, Secondary & Primary Textbooks
1979: 30 titles *Founded:* 1894
ISBN Publisher's Prefix: 3-471

Literarischer Verlag Steinhausen, see Steinhausen

Literarisches Colloquium Berlin*, Am Sandwerder 5, D-1000 Berlin 39 Tel: (030) 8035681
Man Dir: Walter Höllerer; *Sales Dir:* Wilhelm Standke; *Publisher's Reader:* Gerald Bisinger
Subjects: Belles Lettres, Poetry
Founded: 1963
ISBN Publisher's Prefix: 3-920392

Henry **Litolff's** Verlag, an imprint of C F Peters Musikverlag GmbH und Co KG (qv)

Loewes Verlag KG, Bahnhofstr 15, Postfach 2606, D-8580 Bayreuth Tel: (0921) 21031 Cable Add: Loewesverlag Bayreuth Telex: 642771
Man Dir: Volker Gondrom; *Editorial:* Ingrid Hammerstädt; *Publicity, Sales Dir, Rights & Permissions:* Werner Skambraks
Subject: Juveniles
1978: 30 titles *1979:* 30 titles *Founded:* 1863
ISBN Publisher's Prefix: 3-7855

Lorber-Verlag*, Hindenburgstr 3, Postfach 229, D-7120 Bietigheim Tel: (07142) 44446 Cable Add: Lorber, Bietigheim
Subject: Religion
Miscellaneous: Associate Company: Turm-Verlag, 3 Hindenburgstr, D-7120 Bietigheim (qv)
ISBN Publisher's Prefix: 3-87495

Lorch-Verlag GmbH, Schumannstr 27, Postfach 2625, D-6000 Frankfurt am Main Tel: (0611) 7433448/9 Telex: 0411862
Man Dirs: Eva Lorch, Klaus Kottmeier; *Publishing Manager:* Frank Sellien
Associate Companies: Spohr-Verlag, Eder-Verlag, Verlag C W Niemeyer (qv), Sponholz-Verlag (qv)
Subjects: Handbooks, Textile Trade Books, Management
1979: 60 titles *Founded:* 1950
Miscellaneous: Formerly known as Deutscher Fachverlag
ISBN Publisher's Prefix: 3-87496

Gustav **Lübbe** Verlag GmbH, Scheidtbachstr 29-31, Postfach 200127, D-5060 Bergisch Gladbach 2 Tel: (02202) 1211 Telex: 887922
Man Dir: Dr G Deschner; *Manager, Rights & Permissions:* Dr J Köhler; *Editorial:* A Kleinlein; *Sales:* Hans-Jochen Mundt; *Publicity:* Irmgard Sellmann
Associate Company: Bastei-Verlag Gustav Lübbe (qv)
Subjects: General Fiction and Non-fiction, Biographies, Illustrated books on Archaeology, History, Current Affairs
1980: 24 titles *Founded:* 1964
ISBN Publisher's Prefix: 3-7857

Hermann **Luchterhand** Verlag GmbH & Co KG*, Heddesdorfer Str 31, Postfach 1780, D-5450 Neuwied 1 Tel: (02631) 8011 Telex: 0867853
Man Dir: Fritz Berger; *Dir:* Karl-Heinz Westphal; *Marketing:* Dr Lothar Johannes
Associate Company: Druck- und- Verlag-Gesellschaft mbH, Darmstadt
Branch Off: Donnersbergring 18a, Postfach 4250, D-6100 Darmstadt
Subjects: General Fiction and Nonfiction, Belles Lettres, Juveniles, Social Sciences, Law, Economics, Education
Founded: 1924
ISBN Publisher's Prefix: 3-472

Verlag W **Ludwig**, Türltorstr 14, Postfach 86, D-8068 Pfaffenhofen/Ilm 1 Tel: (08441) 5051/5052 Telex: 55540
Man Dir: Wilhelm Ludwig; *Editorial, Rights & Permissions:* Michael Ludwig; *Sales:* Elfriede Bauer; *Production:* Werner Behrens; *Publicity:* Angelika Ludwig
Subsidiary Company: Afrika Verlag
Subjects: Popular Science, Current Affairs, Belles Lettres, Poetry, History
1979: 25 titles *Founded:* 1950
ISBN Publisher's Prefix: 3-7787

Luther-Verlag GmbH*, Postfach 5660, D-4800 Bielefeld 1 Tel: (0521) 44861 Telex: 0937325 epdbid
Dir: Dr Gerhard E Stoll
Subject: Religion
Bookshop: Luther Buchhandlung, Cansteinstr 1, D-4800 Bielefeld 14
1978: 8 titles *Founded:* 1911
ISBN Publisher's Prefix: 3-7858

Lutherisches Verlagshaus, Mittelweg 111, D-2000 Hamburg 13 Tel: (040) 452131
Publisher and Man Dir: Sepp Schelz
Subjects: Theology, Liturgical works and Practical aids, the Church today, General Religious Literature

M F B (Phono- und Schriftenmission des Missionstrupps Frohe Botschaft eV), Nordstr 15, Postfach 1180, D-3432 Grossalmerode bei Kassel Tel: (05604) 361 and 5120
The Record and Text Mission of 'Glad Tidings' Mission Group
Man Dir, Rights & Permissions: W Heiner
Subjects: Christian Evangelical; covering also Juvenile Interest, How-to, Paperbacks, Texts in English, Periodicals
1978: 19 titles *1979:* 8 titles

McGraw-Hill Book Co GmbH, Lademannbogen 136, D-2000 Hamburg 63 Tel: (040) 5382081-6 Telex: 2164048
Man Dir: Jolanda L von Hagen; *Sales:* Harry Robinson
Imprint: Schaum
Subjects: Medicine, Psychology, Engineering, General & Social Science, University & Secondary Textbooks, Educational Materials
1978-79: 30 titles under Schaum imprint
Founded: 1969
Miscellaneous: Firm is an associate company of McGraw-Hill International Book Co New York (see UK entry for other Associate Companies). The Hamburg branch is the one from which all McGraw-Hill publications in English may be ordered from any point in Europe
ISBN Publisher's Prefix: 0-07

Magnus Verlag*, im Teelbruch 60-62, Postfach 185528, 4300 Essen 8 Tel: (02054) 7077/7078
Man Dir: Walter Stender
Subjects: Reference Books, Dictionaries

Otto **Maier** Verlag*, Marktstr 22-26 & Robert Bosch Str 1, Postfach 1860, D-7980 Ravensburg Tel: (0751) 861 Cable Add: Maierverlag Telex: 0732926/0732925
President: Otto J Maier, Dorothee Hess-Maier; *Man Dir:* Claus Runge; *Editorial:* Walter Diem, Peter Hille, Christian Stottele; *Rights & Permissions:* Frank Jacoby-Nelson
Subsidiary Companies: Ravensburger Spiele GmbH, Vienna, Austria; Editions Ravensburger SA, Attenschwiller, France; Fritz Löhmann GmbH, Ravensburger graph Betriebe Otto Maier GmbH (qv), Ravensburger Verlag GmbH (qv), Union Verlag mbH (qv); Otto Maier Benelux BV, Netherlands (qv); Carlit und Ravensburger

146 FEDERAL REPUBLIC OF GERMANY

AG, Switzerland
Subjects: Juvenile Fiction and Nonfiction, Adult Craft and Hobby, Art, Educational (Pedagogics, Art, Pre- and Elementary School Materials), Paperbacks
Founded: 1883
ISBN Publisher's Prefix: 3-473

Mairs Geographischer Verlag*, Marco-Polo-Str 1, D-7302 Ostfildern 4 (Kemnat) Tel: (0711) 454055 Cable Add: Mairverlag Telex: 721796
Man Dir: Dr Volkmar Mair; *Sales Dir:* Claus Benath
Subjects: Road Maps & Atlases
Founded: 1948
ISBN Publisher's Prefix: 3-87504

Mai's Reiseführer Verlag, Unterlindau 80, D-6000 Frankfurt am Main 1 Tel: (0611) 723783
Man & Sales Dir: Ingo and Marie-Luise Schmidt di Simoni
Subjects: Pocket Guides and Travel Guides to non-European countries
1978: 13 titles *Founded:* 1951
ISBN Publisher's Prefix: 3-87936

Gebr **Mann** Verlag GmbH & Co, Lindenstr 76, Postfach 110303, D-1000 Berlin 61 Tel: (030) 2512028/2591865 Cable Add: Kunstbrief Berlin Telex: 183723
Man Dir: Professor Dr Heinz Peters
Associate Company: Deutscher Verlag für Kunstwissenschaft (qv)
Subjects: Archaeology, History of Art
1978: 29 titles *1979:* 37 titles *Founded:* 1917
ISBN Publisher's Prefix: 3-7861

Manz Verlag*, Anzinger Str 1, D-8000 Munich 80 Tel: (089) 403031 Cable Add: Manzverlag Telex: 522504
Publisher: Eduard Niedernhuber; *Sales:* Erna Schmidt; *Publicity:* Siegbert Seitz
Subsidiary Company: Erich Wewel Verlag (qv)
Subjects: Educational Materials
Founded: 1830
ISBN Publisher's Prefix: 3-7863

Tibor **Marczell***, Nederlinger Str 93, D-8000 Munich 19 Tel: (089) 155985
Man Dir: Tibor Marczell
Subjects: Medical, including History, Herbal and Fringe
Founded: 1964
ISBN Publisher's Prefix: 3-88015

Carl **Marhold** Verlagsbuchhandlung, Hessenallee 12, Postfach 191409, D-1000 Berlin 19 Tel: 3043732/3049032 Cable Add: Marholdverlag Berlin
Man Dir: Wolfgang Jaeh; *other offices:* Thomas Jaeh
Subjects: Special healing pedagogy; caring/nursing technologies; teaching of handicapped children
1978-79: 50 titles *Founded:* 1891
ISBN Publisher's Prefix: 3-7864

Maria-Verlag*, Rudolf-Diesel-Str 5, D-6300 Giessen Tel: (0641) 41041-43 Telex: 4821733 wsl d

Edition **Maritim**, Schwanenwik 27, D-2000 Hamburg 76 Tel: (040) 2296656
Dirs: Frank Grube, Gerhard Richter
Subjects: Yachting, Nautical
ISBN Publisher's Prefix: 3-922117

Maro Verlag*, Bismarckstr 7 1/2, D-8900 Augsburg Tel: (0821) 577131
Dir: B Kaesmayr
Subjects: Modern Poetry and Fiction
Founded: 1969
ISBN Publisher's Prefix: 3-87512

Verlag **Marxistische Blätter** GmbH*, Heddernheimer Landstr 78a, D-6000 Frankfurt am Main 50 Tel: (0611) 571051
Publisher: Albert Maag; *Dir:* Max Schafer
Subjects: Politics, Marxist Literature; Marxistische Blätter
1978: 55 titles *Founded:* 1969
Miscellaneous: Member of Arbeitsgemeinschaft sozialistischer und demokratischer Verleger und Buchhändler (qv for other members)
ISBN Publisher's Prefix: 3-88012

Hugo **Matthaes** Druckerei und Verlag GmbH & Co KG, Olgastr 87, Postfach 622, D-7000 Stuttgart 1 Tel: (0711) 21331 Cable Add: Matthaesverlag Telex: 721802
Subjects: Food Trade, Gastronomy

Matthes und Seitz Verlag GmbH*, Postfach 401324, D-8000 Munich 40 (Located at: Dietlindenstr 14) Tel: (089) 333170
Editorial, Rights & Permissions: Axel Matthes; *Sales, Production, Publicity:* Claus Seitz
Subjects: Literature, Art and the Arts generally, Fiction, Memoirs
1978: 12 titles *1979:* 14 titles *Founded:* 1977
ISBN Publisher's Prefix: 3-88221

Matthias-Grünewald-Verlag, see Grünewald

Matthiesen Verlag Ingwert Paulsen Jr, Nordbahnhofstr 2, Postfach 1480, D-2250 Husum Tel: (04841) 6081/3
Man Dir, Editorial, Rights & Permissions: Ingwert Paulsen Jr; *Sales:* Alfred Lorenzen; *Production:* Bruno Czarski; *Publicity:* Hans-Heinrich Lüth
Associate Companies: Husum Druck- und Verlagsgesellschaft (qv); Hamburger Lesehefte Verlag Iselt & Co Nfl mbH (qv)
Subjects: Textbooks, Science, Reference
Founded: 1892
ISBN Publisher's Prefix: 3-7868

Maximilian-Verlag, Steintorwall 17, Postfach 21352, D-4900 Herford Tel: (05221) 50001 Cable Add: Maximilian, Herford/Westf Telex: 934801 maxvg d
Publishers: Dr Kurt Schober, Gerhard Bollmann; *Sales:* Hans-Focko Koehler; *Publicity:* Gerhard Mindt
Associate Companies: Koehlers Verlagsgesellschaft, E S Mittler und Sohn GmbH, Verlag Offene Worte; all members of Maximilian-Verlagsgruppe (qv)
Subjects: Philosophy, Law, Administration, History, Social Sciences; Periodicals
ISBN Publisher's Prefix: 3-7869

Maximilian-Verlagsgruppe, Postfach 371, D-4900 Herford (Located at: Steintorwall 17) Tel: (05221) 3147 Telex: 0934801 maxgv d
Publishing Group comprising: Verlag E S Mittler und Sohn GmbH (qv), Maximilian-Verlag (qv), Koehlers Verlagsgesellschaft mbH (qv), Verlag Offene Worte (qv)
Branch Off (for all members of group): Bonngasse 3, Postfach 2009, D-5300 Bonn Tel: (0221) 630763
See individual Company entries for details of staff, publications etc

Karl-**May**-Verlag, Joachim Schmid & Co*, Karl-May-Str 8, D-8600 Bamberg Tel: (0951) 58451
Main Publicity Dir: Joachim Schmid; *Sales Dir:* Lothar Schmid; *Production Dir:* Roland Schmid; *Rights & Permissions:* Joachim, Lothar and Roland Schmid
Subject: Children's Fiction
Founded: 1913
ISBN Publisher's Prefix: 3-7802

Edition Hansjörg **Mayer**, Engelhornweg 11, D-7000 Stuttgart 1 Tel: (0711) 282036
Man Dir: Hj Mayer
Branch Offs: London, Reykjavik
Subjects: Belles Lettres, Poetry, Music, Art, High-priced Paperbacks
Founded: 1964

J A **Mayer'sche** Buchhandlung*, Ursulinerstr 17-19, Postfach 467, D-5100 Aachen Tel: (0241) 48142 Cable Add: Mayer Aachen Telex: 832768
Man Dir, Publicity: Helmut Falter
Branch Off: Templergraben 44, D-5100 Aachen
Bookshops: at company and branch office addresses
Founded: 1817
ISBN Publisher's Prefix: 3-87519

Verlag für **Medizin** Dr Ewald Fischer GmbH, Fritz-Frey-Str 21, Postfach 105767, D-6900 Heidelberg 1 Tel: (06221) 499747 Cable Add: verlagfürMedizin
Man Dir: Dr E Fischer; *Production:* Dietmar Sieber
Associate Companies: Arkana Verlag (qv); Karl F Haug Verlag GmbH & Co (qv); Fischer und Pflaum Verlag
Branch Off: Bergheimer Str 102, D-6900 Heidelberg
Subjects: Specializes in neglected/little-recognized Medical fields, Chinese diagnosis, Periodicals
Bookshop: as for Karl F Haug Verlag & Co KG (qv)
Founded: 1967
ISBN Publisher's Prefixes: 3-921003, 3-88463

Medizinisch-Literarische Verlagsgesellschaft mbH*, Ringstr 9, Postfach 120/140, D-3110 Uelzen Tel: (0581) 19091 Cable Add: ML-Verlag 3110 Uelzen 1 Telex: 091326
Man Dir, Rights & Permissions: Jens Buettler; *Editorial:* Dr med Dipl ing H Schuldt; *Sales:* B Pianka; *Production:* S Horstmann, G Grätz; *Publicity:* U Rath, M Jess
Parent Company: C Beckers Buchdruckerei, 3110 Uelzen 1
Subjects: Medical, Acupuncture, Orthopaedics, Electro-Acupuncture texts in English; Periodicals
1978: 13 titles *Founded:* 1957
ISBN Publisher's Prefix: 3-88136

megapress-Verlag Franz-Joachim Gaber KG*, Beethovenstr 64, PO Box 402, D-6078 Neu Isenburg-bei-Frankfurt am Main Tel: 06103/23817
Publisher: F J Gabert
Subjects: Politics, Socialist Magazine Monthly Review (German Edition)
ISBN Publisher's Prefix: 3-87979

Felix **Meiner** Verlag, Richardstr 47, D-2000 Hamburg 76 Tel: (040) 294870 Telex: 212120 hihe
Founded: 1911
Subjects: Philosophy, Critical editions of Hegel, de Cusa, Works of Nelson, Plotin, Spinoza, Periodicals
1978: 28 titles *1979:* 34 titles
ISBN Publisher's Prefix: 3-7873

Verlag Anton **Meisenheim** GmbH*, Adelheidstr 2, Postfach 1220, D-6240 Königstein/TS Tel: (06174) 3026 Telex: 410664
Man Dir, Rights & Permissions: Dietrich Pinkerneil, Dieter Hain; *Editorial:* Beate Pinkerneil; *Sales:* Rudolf Klein; *Production:* Mr Langer; *Publicity:* Mrs Hirschfeld
Parent Company: Publishing Group Athenäum/Hain/Scriptor/Hanstein
Subjects: Academic, Science
1978: 41 titles *Founded:* 1946
ISBN Publisher's Prefix: 3-445

Otto **Meissner** Verlag*, Schloss Str 10, Postfach 106, D-2122 Bleckede/Elbe Tel: (05852) 319
Dir: Reinhard Sonntag
Subjects: General Nonfiction, Hobbies, Humanities, Periodicals
Founded: 1848
ISBN Publisher's Prefix: 3-87527

Melanchthon Verlag, Postfach 1180, D-2915 Saterland 2 Tel: (04498) 1629
Subjects: Supply of Museum Catalogues etc

J CH **Mellinger** Verlag GmbH; Wolfgang Militz und Co KG, 55 Büssenstr, Postfach 131164, D-7000 Stuttgart 1 Tel: (0711) 463565/246401
Proprietors & Man Dirs: Wolfgang Militz, Elisabeth Militz
Orders to: Koch, Neff, Oettinger & Co, Abt Verlagsauslieferung, Am Wallgraben 110, D-7000 Stuttgart 80
Subjects: Religions, Biography, Aesthetics, Literature, Juveniles, Games
Founded: 1926
ISBN Publisher's Prefix: 3-88069

Verlag Abi **Melzer** GmbH*, Wildscheuerweg 1, Postfach 301117, D-6072 Dreieich-Buchschlag Tel: (06103) 63061/63062 Telex: 4185381 amp
General Manager: Abraham Melzer
Orders to: VVA, Gütersloh
Subjects: Picture Strips, Graphics, Comics, Children's Books, General Literature
1978: 20 titles *Founded:* 1975
ISBN Publisher's Prefix: 3-8201

Melzer Verlag KG, Gutenbergstr, D-6101 Weiterstadt Tel: (06151) 86056 Telex: 419249
Man Dir: Horst Göhde; *Sales Dir:* Horst Beitlich
Subjects: Comics, Art, Juveniles
Founded: 1972
ISBN Publisher's Prefix: 3-7874

Verlag **Mensch und Arbeit** Robert Pfützner GmbH, Sandstr 3, D-8000 Munich 2 Tel: (089) 55486 Cable Add: Pronto Munich
Man Dir: Robert Pfützner; *Rights & Permissions:* Gerhart Kindl
Subjects: How-to, Art, Social Science, Professional, Technical
Founded: 1957

Mentor-Verlag Dr Ramdohr KG, Neusser Str 3, Postfach 401120, D-8000 Munich 40 Tel: 38301 Cable Add: Langenscheidt Munich Telex: 5215379 lkgm d
Man Dir: Karl-Ernst Tielebier-Langenscheidt; *Editorial:* Katharina Baudach; *Sales Dir:* Peter Haering; *Advertising Dir:* Dieter Krause; *Sales, Promotion:* Through Langenscheidt KG (qv); *Rights & Permissions:* Manfred Überall
Subjects: Reference, Low-priced Paperbacks, Textbooks
1979: 4 titles *1980:* 7 titles *Founded:* 1904
Miscellaneous: Company is a member of the Langenscheidt Group (qv)
ISBN Publisher's Prefix: 3-580

Mergus Verlag Hans A Baensch, Postfach 86, D-4520 Melle 1 (Located at: Bergstr 3) Tel: (05422) 3636 Cable Add: Mergus Melle Telex: 941550 megus d
Man Dir: Hans A Baensch
Subjects: Natural History, Care of Pets
1978: 2 titles *1979:* 4 titles *Founded:* 1977
ISBN Publisher's Prefix: 3-88244

Merlin Verlag Andreas Meyer Verlags GmbH und Co KG, Sierichstr 54, D-2000 Hamburg 60 Tel: (040) 2791140
Publisher: Andreas J Meyer; *Sales Manager:* Ilse Meyer
Subjects: History, Arts, Literature
ISBN Publisher's Prefix: 3-87536

Merve Verlag, Crelle Str 22, D-1000 Berlin 62 Tel: (030) 7848433
Man Dir: Hans-Peter Gente
1978: 9 titles *1979:* 9 titles

Verlag für **Messepublikationen**, see Thomas Neureuter KG

Methodik-Verlag Manfred Helfrecht*, Markgrafenstr 27, D-8591 Alexandersbad Tel: (09232) 2655 Telex: 641180 thelf d
Dir: Josef Schmidt
Subject: Individual and Company planning methods
1978: 1 title *1979:* 1 title
ISBN Publisher's Prefix: 3-920986

J B **Metzlersche Verlagsbuchhandlung**, Kernerstr 43, Postfach 529, D-7000 Stuttgart 1 Tel: (0711) 225074/75/76 Cable Add: Metzlerverlag Stuttgart
Man Dir: Günther Schweizer; *Sales Dir:* Horst Cziszinsky; *Advertising Dir:* Ulrich Gensicke; *Rights & Permissions:* Dr Bernd Lutz
Orders to: (Book Trade): Goethestrasse 6, D-7400 Tübingen; (in Berlin) A Muschal & Sohn, Lützowstr 105-6, D-1000 Berlin 30
Associate Company: C E Poeschel Verlag (qv)
Subjects: Philology, Human Sciences, American Studies, Geodesy, Pedagogics, School Books
Founded: 1682
ISBN Publisher's Prefix: 3-476

Alfred **Metzner** Verlag GmbH, Zeppelinallee 43, Postfach 970148, D-6000 Frankfurt am Main Tel: (0611) 774055 Telex: 4189621 kome d
Dir: Dr Caspar van Kempen; *Editorial:* Dr Günther Köpcke; *Publicity and Sales:* Ernst F Grundl
Associate Company: Verlag Kommentator GmbH (qv)
Subjects: Law, University Textbooks
Founded: 1909
Miscellaneous: Alfred Metzner Verlag is a member of the Kluwer Group, Deventer, Netherlands (qv)
ISBN Publisher's Prefix: 3-7875

Meyster Verlag, Nymphenburger Str 139, D-8000 Munich 19 Tel: (089) 187069/187060 Telex: 522569 meyst d
Man Dir, Sales: Hermann Meyer; *Editorial:* Dieter Cürths; *Rights & Permissions:* Isolde Rieger
Parent Company: Verlag C Überreuter, Alser Str 24, A-1095 Vienna, Austria (qv)
Associate Company: Annette Betz Verlag, Austria (qv)
Subjects: Popular Science Works, Gift Books, the Family, Cookery, Illustrated Vols
1978: 11 titles *1979:* 31 titles *Founded:* 1978
ISBN Publisher's Prefix: 3-7057

Gertraud **Middelhauve** Verlag, Wiener Platz 2, D-5000 Cologne 80 (Mülheim) Tel: (0221) 614982
Man Dir, Editorial, Rights & Permissions: Gertraud Middelhauve; *Publicity:* Annemarie Balkenhol
Orders to: Vereinigte Verlagsauslieferung, Carl-Bertelsmann Str 161, D-4830 Gütersloh 1
Subjects: General Fiction, Juveniles
1979: 11 titles *Founded:* 1947
ISBN Publisher's Prefix: 3-7678

Wolfgang **Militz** und Co KG, see J Ch Mellinger Verlag

Missionstruppe Frohe Botschaft, see M F B

E S **Mittler** und Sohn GmbH, Steintorwall 17, Postfach 21352, D-4900 Herford Tel: (05221) 50001 Cable Add: Mittler & Sohn, Herford/Westf Telex: 934801 maxvg d
Publishers: Dr Kurt Schober, Gerhard Bollmann; *Sales:* Hans-Focko Koehler; *Publicity:* Gerhard Mindt; *Production:* Heinz Kameier
Associate Companies: Koehlers Verlagsgesellschaft, Maximilian-Verlag, Verlag Offene Worte (all members of Maximilian-Verlagsgruppe, qv)
Subjects: Military, Aviation, Political, NATO Affairs, Periodicals
Founded: 1789
ISBN Publisher's Prefixes: 3-87547, 3-8132

Verlag **Moderne Industrie** Wolfgang Dummer und Co, Ehrenbreitsteiner Str 36, D-8000 Munich 50 Tel: 14851 Telex: 05215566
Man Dir: Dr Reinhard Moestl; *Publicity:* Ulrich Eder; *Rights & Permissions:* Rita Ploetz
Associate Company: Economed (publishing medical books)
Subjects: Management (Personnel Management, Sales Management, Accountancy, Advertising, Data Processing), Investment, Textbooks, Technical
1978: 150 titles *Founded:* 1952
ISBN Publisher's Prefix: 3-478

Moderne Verlags GmbH (MVG), Ehrenbreitsteiner Str 36, D-8000 Munich 50 Tel: (089) 1485-1 Cable Add: Moderne Verlags GmbH Telex: 05215566
Man Dir: Dr Reinhard Moestl; *Publicity:* Ulrich Eder; *Rights & Permissions:* Rita Ploetz
Subjects: Hobbies, Arts, Popular Sciences, Careers
ISBN Publisher's Prefix: 3-478

Gütersloher Verlagshaus Gerd **Mohn**, see Gütersloher

J C B **Mohr** (Paul Siebeck), Wilhelmstr 18, Postfach 2040, D-7400 Tübingen Tel: (07071) 26064 Cable Add: Siebeck Tübingen Telex: 7262872 mohr d
Proprietor: Dr hc Hans Georg Siebeck; *Man Dir:* Georg Siebeck Jun; *Sales:* Johannes Krämer; *Production:* Rudolf Pflug; *Publicity:* Dr Arnulf Krais; *Rights & Permissions:* Maria Branse
Subsidiary Company: H Laupp'sche Buchhandlung (books on Tübingen and Suevia)
Subjects: History, Philosophy, Religion, General & Social Science, Economics, Law, University Textbooks
1978: 97 titles *1979:* 95 titles *Founded:* 1801
ISBN Publisher's Prefix: 3-16

Verlag Fritz **Molden**, Stievestr 9, D-8000 Munich 19 Tel: (089) 176071 Telex: 5-29993
Publisher: Fritz P Molden; *Man Dir:* Klaus-Peter Frank; *Publicity:* Marianne Menzel; *Sales:* Liane Kolf
Parent Company: Verlag Fritz Molden, Vienna, Austria (qv)

Mönch-Verlag GmbH & Co, Heilsbachstr 26, D-5300 Bonn 1 Tel: (02221) 643066-68 Telex: 8869429 mvkb d
Man Dir: Manfred Sadlowski; *Sales Dir:* Joachim Latka; *Publicity Dir:* Heinz-Jürgen Witzke; *Advertising Dir:* Peter Konietschke; *Rights & Permissions:* Herr Latka
Branch Off: Mönch-Verlag, D-5401 Waldesch, Hübingerweg 33
Subjects: History, How-to, Engineering, General Science, High-priced Paperbacks

Edizioni del **Mondo***, Hollerborn 77, Postfach 2380, D-6200 Wiesbaden Tel: (06121) 420186
Publisher: Comm. Olaf Hein
Subjects: First world-edition of the complete works of Athanasius Kircher (Opera Omnia Athanasii Kircheri) in 66 vols, Arts, Reprints, Sciences, Books on Rome
Founded: 1971
ISBN Publisher's Prefix: 3-920228

Monitor Verlag, see Arbeitsgemeinschaft sozialistischer und demokratischer Verleger und Buchhändler

Du **Mont** Buchverlag GmbH und Co KG, Apostelnkloster 21-25, Postfach 100468, D-5000 Cologne 1 Tel: (0221) 20531 Telex: 8882 975 dbe b d
Publisher: Rudolf Sommer; *Dir:* Ernst Brücher
Subjects: Archaeology, Art History, Art, Art Calendars
Founded: 1976
ISBN Publisher's Prefix: 3-7701

Heinz **Moos** Verlag Munich, Rottenbucher Str 30, D-8032 Gräfelfing Tel: (089) 851311 Cable Add: Moosverlag
Man Dir: Heinz Moos
Subjects: Town Planning, History of Architecture, Preservation of Monuments, Fringe Areas of Science and Art, Book Production and Printing, Monographs, Current Affairs, German-American Dual Language (International Relations) Texts
Founded: 1959
ISBN Publisher's Prefix: 3-7879

Morsak Verlag, Kröllstr 5, Postfach 5, D-8352 Grafenau Tel: (08552) 1015/6 Telex: 57431
Man Dir, Production, Rights & Permissions: Erich Stecher; *Sales:* Rosa Zarham
Subjects: Bavaria, School books, Textbooks
1978: 10 titles *Founded:* 1884
ISBN Publisher's Prefix: 3-87553

Morus-Verlag, Grünewaldstr 24, D-1000 Berlin 41 Tel: (030) 8210101/8213443
Dir: Erich Klausener; *Publicity Manager:* Elisabeth Jagdt
Subject: Religion
Founded: 1945
ISBN Publisher's Prefix: 3-87554

Mosaik Verlag, Neumarkter Str 18, Postfach 800360, D-8000 Munich 80 Tel: (089) 41730 Cable Add: Bertelsmann München Telex: 523259
Dir: Gerhard Zorn; *Advertising:* Lionel von dem Knesebeck; *Sales and Publicity:* Lothar Nalbach; *Rights & Permissions:* Udo Knispel, Peter Gutmann
Parent Company: Verlagsgruppe Bertelsmann GmbH (qv for associate companies)
Subjects: Family and Household Interest books, especially How-to, Cookery, Health & Medicine, Gardening, Furnishing, Crafts, Hobbies, Reference, General Literature
ISBN Publisher's Prefix: 3-570

Motorbuch-Verlag*, Böblinger Str 18, Postfach 1370, D-7000 Stuttgart 1 Tel: (0711) 642031 Cable Add: pico d Telex: 0722662
Man Dir: Wolfgang Schilling; *Sales:* Thomas Günther, Kurt Wölfle; *Rights & Permissions:* Brigitte Weller
Subjects: How-to, Reference, Engineering
1978: 112 titles *Founded:* 1962
Miscellaneous: Firm is a division of Buch- & Verlagshaus Paul Pietsch GmbH & Co KG
ISBN Publisher's Prefix: 3-87943

Verlag C F **Müller**, Rheinstr 122, Postfach 210949, D-7500 Karlsruhe 21 Tel: (0721) 555955 Telex: 7825909
Man Dir: Dr Christof Müller-Wirth; *Sales, Publicity:* Winfried Ammon; *Production, Rights & Permissions:* Jochen Schmitt
Subjects: Technical Specialist Books on Cold, Heat, Climate, Air, Environment, Energy and Solar Technology
1978: 8 titles *Founded:* 1797
ISBN Publisher's Prefix: 3-7880

C F **Müller** Jüristischer Verlag GmbH*, Postfach 102640, D-6900 Heidelberg (Located at: im Weiher 10) Tel: (06221) 489250 Telex: 0461727 huehd
Associate Companies: Kriminalistik Verlag GmbH (qv); R v Decker's Verlag G Schenck GmbH (qv)
Subjects: Jurisprudence Textbooks; Commentaries and Law Practice; Academic Series

Verlag Josef **Müller**, Friedrichstr 9, Postfach 360, D-8000 Munich 43 Tel: (089) 393045 Cable Add: Arssacra München
Subjects: Hummel Pictures, Hummel Books, Advent Calendars, Picture Books, Bohatta Books and Puzzles
Founded: 1896
ISBN Publisher's Prefix: 3-7607

Verlagsgesellschaft Rudolf **Müller** GmbH, Stolberger Str 84, Postfach 410949, D-5000 Cologne 41 Tel: (0221) 54971 Telex: 08881256
Publisher: Walther Müller; *Dir:* Helmut Evers; *Sales Manager:* Peter von Klaudy; *Publicity Manager:* Peter Groth
Branch Off: Johnsallee 53, D-2000 Hamburg 13
Subjects: Architecture, Electrical Engineering, Electronics, Textbooks, Education, Pets
ISBN Publisher's Prefix: 3-481

Verlag **Müller** und Kiepenheuer*, Frankfurter Landstr 32, Postfach 500, D-6450 Hanau am Main Tel: (06181) 22316/82353
Publisher: Werner Dausien
Parent Company: Werner Dausien (qv)
Subjects: General Fiction, Arts, Maps
ISBN Publisher's Prefix: 3-7833

Verlag **Müller** und Schindler, Sonnenbergstr 55, D-7000 Stuttgart Tel: (0711) 233204
Proprietor: Dr Rolf Müller
Subject: Facsimiles of manuscripts and historical prints relating to Art, Civilization and the Natural Sciences
Founded: 1965

Rudolf **Müller** und Steinicke Verlag*, Lindwurmstr 21, D-8000 Munich 2 Tel: (089) 265881
Publisher: Werner Gissler; *Sales:* Volker Keller
Subjects: Medicine and associated fields

Munin Verlag GmbH, Postfach 3023, D-4500 Osnabrück Tel: (0541) 572278
Subject: War History of the Waffen SS
1978: 3 titles *1979:* 3 titles *Founded:* 1955
ISBN Publisher's Prefix: 3-921242

Münster Verlag*, Hildastr 25, D-7800 Freiburg-im-Breisgau Tel: (0761) 35190
Subjects: Reference Works, Popular Fact-Books, Religious

Muster-Schmidt Verlag, Brauweg 36a, Postfach 421, D-3400 Göttingen Tel: (0551) 72011 Cable Add: Musterschmidt Telex: 096720
Dirs: Hans Hansen-Schmidt, Eva Maria Gerhardy-Löcken
Branch Off: Waldmannstr 10a, Zurich, Switzerland
Subjects: Biography, History, Anthropology
Founded: 1905
ISBN Publisher's Prefix: 3-7881

N D V (Neue Darmstädter Verlagsanstalt), Hauptstr 72, D-5342 Rheinbreitbach Tel: (02224) 3232
Publisher: Klaus-J Holzapfel
Subject: Politics
ISBN Publisher's Prefix: 3-87576

Nachrichten-Verlags-GmbH*, Glauburgstr 66, Postfach 180372, D-6000 Frankfurt am Main Tel: (0611) 599791
Man Dir: Dr Werner Petschick; *Sales Dir:* Elfriede Krüger; *Publicity & Advertising Dirs:* Renate Bastian, Gisela Mayer; *Rights & Permissions:* Ruth Malkomes
Subjects: How-to, Social Science

Founded: 1969
Miscellaneous: Member of Arbeitsgemeinschaft sozialistischer und demokratischer Verleger und Buchhändler (qv for other members)

Gunter **Narr** Verlag, Postfach 2567, D-7400 Tübingen 1 (Located at: Stauffenbergstr 42) Tel: (07071) 24156
Manager and Sales Dir: Gunter Narr; *Publicity Dir:* Brigitte Narr; *Advertising Dir:* Horst Schmid; *Rights & Permissions:* Gunter Narr
Subjects: Linguistic studies (especially German, English and French); Literary Criticism; Romanesque Studies
1978: 46 titles *Founded:* 1969
ISBN Publisher's Prefix: 3-87808

Paul **Neff** Verlag KG*, Herwarthstr 3, D-1000 Berlin 45 Tel: (030) 7725246
Man Dir: Fritz Pfenningstorff
Associate Company: Paul Neff Verlag KG, Austria (qv)
Subjects: Novels, Belles Lettres, Poetry, Music, Art, Biography, History, Textbooks, Geography
Founded: 1829

Nerva-Verlag*, Romanstr 7-9, D-8000 Munich 19 Tel: (089) 132051 Cable Add: Nerva-Verlag Telex: 5215959
Man Dir: Johann Milleder; *Sales & Advertising Dir:* Ernst K Jost
Subject: Reference

Verlag Günther **Neske**, Kloster, Postfach 7240, D-7417 Pfullingen Tel: (07121) 71339 Cable Add: Neske-Verlag Pfullingen Telex: nefen D 0729790
Publisher: Günther Neske; *Editorial, Publicity:* Brigitte Neske
Subjects: General Fiction, Humanities, Literary Criticism, Philosophy, Politics, Poetry, Psychiatry, Theology, Swiridoff Picture Books
1978: 10 titles *1979:* 10 titles *Founded:* 1951
ISBN Publisher's Prefix: 3-7885

Neue Darmstädter Verlagsanstalt, see N D V

Verlag **Neue Gesellschaft** GmbH, Godesberger Allee 143, D-5300 Bonn 2 Tel: (0228) 378021
Dir: Dr Heiner Lindner; *Editorial:* Dr Klaus Kamberger, Charles Schüddekopf; *Sales:* Peter Marold
Orders to: Verlagsauslieferung Georg Lingenbrink, Postfach 3584, D-6000 Frankfurt am Main 1; or (Berlin): Zirk & Ellenrieder, Lützowstr 15 (bbz), D-1000 Berlin 30
Associate Company: Verlag J H W Dietz Nachf GmbH (qv)
Subjects: Politics, Legal, History, Sociology, Economics, Periodicals
ISBN Publisher's Prefix: 3-87831

Neue Kommentare, see Arbeitsgemeinschaft sozialistischer und demokratischer Verleger und Buchhändler

Verlag **Neue Kritik** KG, Myliusstr 58, D-6000 Frankfurt am Main Tel: (0611) 727576
Orders to: Sozialistische Verlagsauslieferung, GmbH, Franziusstr 44, D-6000 Frankfurt am Main
Subjects: Mainly Socialist-orientated
1978: 8 titles *1979:* 8 titles *Founded:* 1965
ISBN Publisher's Prefix: 3-8015

Verlag Der **Neue Schulmann***, Pfizerstr 5-7, D-7000 Stuttgart 1, see Franckh'sche Verlagshandlung

Verlag **Neue Stadt** GmbH, Gleissner Str 87, D-8000 Munich 83 Tel: (089) 405081 Cable Add: Neue Stadt
Man Dir: Wolfgang Bader; *Sales Dirs:* Hans R Jurt, Enrico Giuliani; *Publicity and

FEDERAL REPUBLIC OF GERMANY 149

Advertising: Hans R Jurt; *Rights:* Wolfgang Bader
Parent Company: Città Nuova Editrice Italy (qv)
Associate Companies: Cidade Nova, Rua Pio Xii, 274 Paraiso São Paulo, Brazil; Citta Nuova, Italy (qv); Ciudad Nueva, Spain (qv); New City, UK (qv); Niewe Stad, St Stephanusstraat 11, Nijmegen, Netherlands; Nouvelle Cité, France (qv); Living City, New York, USA; Ciudad Nueva, Buenos Aires, Argentina
Branch Offs: Trostr 116, A-1100 Vienna, Austria; Hammerstr 9, Postfach 218, CH-8032 Zurich, Switzerland
Subjects: Music, Art, Religion, Juveniles, Periodicals
1978: 15 titles *1979:* 15 titles *Founded:* 1965
ISBN Publisher's Prefix: 3-87996

Verlag Neue Wirtschafts-Briefe GmbH*, Eschstr 22, D-4690 Herne 1 Tel: (02323) 54071 Telex: 08229870 Cable Add: Steuerbriefe Herne
Man Dir: E-O Kleyboldt; *Sales Dir:* J Müller-Grote; *Advertising Dir:* H Werner
Subsidiary Company: Friedrich Kiehl Verlag GmbH (qv)
Subjects: Trade Journals and books on Tax and Company Law, Accountancy, Industrial Management, Political Economics, Vocational Training
Founded: 1947
ISBN Publisher's Prefix: 3-482

Neuer Jugendschriften-Verlag, Tiestestr 14, D-3000 Hanover 1 Tel: (0511) 813068 Cable Add: Buchweichert Telex: 0923872 awv d
Man Dir: Alfred Trippo; *Sales:* Hans Droste
Imprint: Karo-Bücher
Man Dir: Alfred Trippo
Associate Company: A Weichert-Verlag (qv)
Branch Off: Hans Feulner, Lindenallee 25, D-1000 Berlin 19
Subject: Juveniles
1978: 23 titles *1979:* 17 titles
ISBN Publisher's Prefix: 3-483

Verlag Neuer Weg*, Heusteigstr 88a, D-7000 Stuttgart 1, Postfach 3080 Tel: (0711) 645894
Subjects: Marxist Politics, Communism, Novels, Song Books
Founded: 1971
ISBN Publisher's Prefix: 3-88021

Neukirchener Verlag des Erziehungvereins GmbH, Andreas-Braem-Str 18-20, Postfach 216, D-4133 Neukirchen-Vluyn 2 Tel: (02845) 39222 Cable Add: Verlagshaus neukirchenvluyn
Man Dirs: Werner Braselmann, Hans-Martin Dahlmann; *Editors:* Dr Chr Bartsch; *Sales Dir:* Thomas von Puskas; *Publicity & Advertising Dir:* Reinhard Lieber; *Rights & Permissions:* Werner Braselmann
Subsidiary Company: Kalendar-Verlag des Erziehungs-Vereins, D-4133 Neukirchen-Vluyn 2, Andreas-Braem Str 18-20 (Calendars)
Branch Off: Evangelische Schriften-Zentrale (esz), Barsortiment, Postfach 216, D-4133 Neukirchen-Vluyn 2
Subjects: Evangelical Christianity, Catholic and Reformed; Biblical Studies, Bible Archaeology, Belles Lettres
1978: 31 titles *Founded:* 1888
Bookshop: Neukirchener Buchhandlung, A-Braem-Str 20, D-4133 Neukirchen-Vluyn 2
ISBN Publisher's Prefix: 3-7887

Verlag J Neumann-Neudamm KG, Muhlenstr 9, Postfach 320, D-3508 Melsungen Tel: (05661) 2374/6374
Dirs: Günther Neumann, Friedrich Stange
Subjects: Agriculture, Horticulture, Forestry, Hunting, Fishing, Natural Science, Aquarian Science
ISBN Publisher's Prefix: 3-7888

Verlag für Messepublikationen Thomas Neureuter KG, Pettenkoferstr 7, Postfach 482, D-8000 Munich 2 Tel: (089) 597186
Publishers: Thomas Neureuter
Founded: 1948

Nicolaische Verlagsbuchhandlung GmbH und Co KG, Wilhelmsaue 11, D-1000 Berlin 31 Tel: 870497/98
General Manager: Dieter Beuermann
Subjects: All aspects of Berlin; Politics, European Art and Photography, Poetry
1978: 12 titles *1979:* 12 titles

Verlag C W Niemeyer, Osterstr 19, Postfach 447, D-3250 Hameln 1 Tel: (05151) 200326 Cable Add: Dewezet Telex: 92859
Dir: Erich Schoeneberg; *Sales:* Gerda Pfab
Orders to: Hamburger Kommissionsbuchhandlung GmbH, Libri-Haus, 2 Hamburg 36
Associate Company: Adolf Sponholtz Verlag (qv)
Subjects: Scenic Picture Books (Germany), Quality Illustrated Books, Humour
Founded: 1797
ISBN Publisher's Prefix: 3-87585

Max Niemeyer Verlag, Pfrondorfer Str 4, Postfach 2140, D-7400 Tübingen Tel: (07071) 81104 Cable Add: Niemeyer Tübingen
Man Dir: Robert Harsch-Niemeyer; *Rights & Permissions:* Cornelia Linz; *Publicity and Marketing:* Manfred Korn
Subjects: General Literary Criticism; German, English & Romance Philology; Linguistics, Philosophy, History
1979: 91 titles *Founded:* 1870
ISBN Publisher's Prefix: 3-484

Verlag Friedrich Nolte*, Postfach 475, D-1000 Berlin 61 Tel: (030) 6933080
Publisher: Friedrich Nolte; *Editorial:* Dr Franz Büchler, Dieter Straub
Subjects: Belles Lettres, Poetry, Modern Literature, Periodicals, Psychology
ISBN Publisher's Prefix: 3-921177

Nomos Verlagsgesellschaft mbH und Co KG, Waldseestr 3-5, Postfach 610, D-7570 Baden-Baden Tel: (07221) 3441 Telex: 0781201
Man Dir: Volker Schwarz; *Sales, Publicity:* Renatus Bräutigam
Associate Companies: Suhrkamp Verlag (qv); Insel Verlag (qv)
Subjects: Jurisprudence, Economics, European Economy, Admin Sciences, International Co-operation, Periodicals
1978: 104 titles *Founded:* 1936
ISBN Publisher's Prefix: 3-7890

Verlag Wissenschaft und Politik, Berend von Nottbeck*, Salierring 14-16, D-5000 Cologne 1 Tel: (0221) 312878/315787
Cable Add: Politikbuch 5 Köln 1
Man Dir: Berend von Nottbeck; *Sales & Advertising Dir:* Siegmund Mindt; *Publicity Dir:* C P von Nottbeck
Branch Off: Redaktion 'Deutschland Archiv', D-5000 Cologne 51, Goltsteinstr 185
Subjects: Political Science, especially in context of East-West relations; International Law and Problems, Dialogue with the German Democratic Republic etc
1978: 24 titles *Founded:* 1960
ISBN Publisher's Prefix: 3-8046

NovaPart Verlag GmbH*, Ismaningerstr 21, D-8000 Munich 80 Tel: (089) 281038 Telex: 529891 nopa d
Dir: Willi Hauck; *Editorial:* Rudolf Radler; *Sales, Publicity:* Werner Theidemann; *Production:* Anton Siesegger; *Rights & Permissions:* Barbara Hartl
Subsidiary Company: NovaBuch GmbH, Ismaningerstr 21, D-8000 Munich 80
Branch Off: Novapart BV, Amsterdam, Netherlands
Subject: Part-works
Founded: 1976

Verlag Monika Nüchtern, Breisacherstr 14, D-8000 Munich 80 Tel: (089) 481230
Man Dir: Monika Nüchtern
Subject: Films
1978: 4 titles *1979:* 2 titles *Founded:* 1976

Numismatischer Verlag P N Schulten, Bornwiesenweg 34, D-6000 Frankfurt am Main 1 Tel: (0611) 550286 Telex: 4189154
Publisher: Peter N Schulten
Subjects: Coins, Medals, Reprints
Founded: 1974
ISBN Publisher's Prefix: 3-921302

Nusser Verlag, Kaufbeurerstr 3, Postfach 500411, D-8000 Munich 50 Tel: (089) 146788
Man Dir: Dr Horst Nusser; *Sales:* Katharina Mühlberger; *Rights & Permissions:* Horst Hodemacher, Axel Poldner GmbH Co KG, Munich (qv under Literary Agents)
Subjects: History, Geography, Popular Science, Art, Culture, Asiatic Topics
1978: 1 title *1979:* 3 titles *Founded:* 1972
ISBN Publisher's Prefix: 3-88091

Nymphenburger Verlagshandlung GmbH*, Romanstr 16, D-8000 Munich 19 Tel: (089) 162051 Cable Add: Nymphenbuch Munich
Man Dir: Hans Adolf Neunzig; *Editorial:* Peter Bramböck; *Sales:* Peter Karg, Brigitte Nunner; *Advertising and Rights and Permissions:* Gisela Günther
Subjects: General Fiction, Belles Lettres, Poetry, Biography, History, How-to, Music, Art, Philosophy, Sports, Hobbies, Mountaineering, General and Social Science, High-priced Paperbacks
1978: 34 titles *Founded:* 1946
Miscellaneous: Firm is a member of Verlagsgruppe Langen-Müller/Herbig (qv)
ISBN Publisher's Prefix: 3-485

Oberbaumverlag*, Postfach 127, D-1000 Berlin 21 Tel: (030) 3953099
Man Dir: G Petermann; *Publicity & Advertising Dir:* Walter Knoblich
Subjects: Political (Left Wing, Revolutionary), Proletarian-Revolutionary Fiction, Materialism generally, pro-Mao, anti-Soviet Literature
Founded: 1966

Odörfer-Verlags GmbH*, Mohrengasse 10, D-8500 Nuremberg Tel: (0911) 203611
Dir: Kurt Odörfer
Subjects: Sexual Literature, Pornography
1978: 24 titles

Oekumenischer Verlag Dr R-F Edel*, D-355 Marburg an der Lahn, Cappelerstr 8, Postfach 1211 Tel: (02351) 83255
Publicity Manager: Dr Reiner-Friedemann Edel
Orders to: Annabergstr 46, D-5880 Lüdenscheid
Subject: Christian Evangelical and Devotional; Cultural, Philosophical, Art

Paul Oestergaard GmbH, see Columbus Verlag

Verlag Friedrich Oetinger, Poppenbutteler Chaussee 55, Postfach 220, D-2000 Hamburg 65 Tel: (040) 6070055 Cable Add: Oetingerbuch Telex: 02174230
Editorial: Else Marie Bonnet; *Sales:* Thomas Huggle; *Publicity:* Anke Lüdtke; *Rights & Permissions:* Uwe Weitendorf
Associate Company: Cecilie Dressler Verlag (qv)
Subjects: Juveniles, Illustrated Books
ISBN Publisher's Prefix: 3-7891

August **Oetker**, see Ceres-Verlag

Verlag **Offene Worte**, Steintorwall 17, Postfach 21352, D-4900 Herford Tel: (05221) 50001 Cable Add: Vlg Offene Worte, Herford/W Telex: 934801 maxvg d
Publishers: Dr Kurt Schober, Gerhard Bollmann; *Sales:* Hans-Focko Koehler; *Publicity:* Gerhard Mindt
Associate Companies: Koehlers Verlagsgesellschaft, Maximilian-Verlag, ES Mittler und Sohn GmbH (all members of Maximilian-Verlagsgruppe, qv)
Subjects: Military, Politics, Periodicals
ISBN Publisher's Prefix: 3-87599

Karl **Ohm** Verlag, Hauptstr 101, D-1000 Berlin 62 Tel: (030) 784001
Publisher: Kurt Meurer
Associate Company: Elwert und Meurer GmbH (qv)
Subject: Law
ISBN Publisher's Prefix: 3-87600

R **Oldenbourg** Verlag GmbH, Rosenheimer Str 145, Postfach 801360, D-8000 Munich 80 Tel: (089) 41121 Cable Add: Rograph München Telex: 0523789
Man Dirs: Walter Oldenbourg, Dr Thomas von Cornides, Götz Ohmeyer
Orders to: Verlegerdienst München, Auslieferung R Oldenbourg Verlag, Gutenbergstr 1, Postfach 1280, D-8031 Gilching Tel: (08105) 9031/32/33
Branch Off: Verlag Oldenbourg, Austria (qv)
Subjects: Modern Science and Technology (Data Processing, Statistics etc); History and the Liberal Arts (Politics, Current Affairs, Philosophy, Art History, and especially Austrian and European History); Social Sciences, Psychology, Pedagogics and School Text Books, Reference Works and Library Editions, Periodicals
1978: 186 titles *Founded:* 1858
ISBN Publisher's Prefix: 3-486 (Munich), 3-7029 (Vienna)

Verlag **Olle und Wolter**, Postfach 4310, D-1000 Berlin 30 (Located at: Paul Lincke Ufer 44a, D-1000 Berlin 36) Tel: (030) 6121973
General Manager: Günter Thielmeier; *Editorial:* Ulf Wolter; *Sales and Publicity:* Heide Schröder; *Production:* Dietmar Silber; *Rights & Permissions:* Karin Weingart
Subjects: History of the Workers' Movement, Politics, Economics, Philosophy, Literature, Scientific and Science Fiction, Ecology, Biography, Crime Fiction; Periodical *Kritik* (Socialist Discussion)
1979: 49 titles *Founded:* 1972
ISBN Publisher's Prefix: 3-921241, 3-88395

Georg **Olms** Verlag, Hagentorwall 7, D-3200 Hildesheim Tel: (05121) 37007 Cable Add: Bookolms Hildesheim
Publisher: W Georg Olms, Dr E Mertens; *Sales:* Edith Olms; *Production:* J-P Pracht; *Publicity:* Johannes Koeltzsch; *Rights & Permissions:* Mrs G Reichelt
Subsidiary Company: Editions Olms AG, Switzerland (qv)
Branch Off: Georg Olms Verlag, c/o Mrs Patricia Feeley, 1501 Broadway, Suite 2004, New York, NY 10036, USA
Bookshop: Georg Olms, Verlagsbuchhandlung, Hagentorwall 7, D-3200 Hildesheim
Subjects: Languages and Language History (especially Slavic, Germanic, Romance), Books in foreign languages (especially English, French), History (Classical, Renaissance etc), Geography and Travel, Literature and the Arts (Music, Theatre etc), Judaica, Science and Technology, Orientalia, Folklore, Theology, Law, Politics, Economics, Sociology, Psychology, Pedagogy, Philosophy, Paperbacks
1978: 452 titles *Founded:* 1945
Miscellaneous: The firm commenced production in 1976 of The *Bibliothek der Deutschen Sprache*, a complete library of significant writing in German from the earliest times till c.1900 in microfiche form (Olms Microform)
ISBN Publisher's Prefix: 3-487

Verlag **Ölschläger** GmbH, Amalienstr 81, D-8000 Munich 40
Man Dirs: Claus Ölschläger, Christina Ölschläger
Parent Company: Dipl-Kfm C Ölschläger GmbH
Associate Company: Verlag für Wirtschaftsskripten (qv)
Subjects: Communications, Journalism, Economics, Business and Management, Sociology, Psycho-analysis
1978: 12 titles *1979:* 30 titles *Founded:* 1977
ISBN Publisher's Prefix: 3-88295

Verlag für Wirtschaftsskripten, Dipl Kfm C **Ölschläger** GmbH, see Wirtschaftsskripten

Günter **Olzog** Verlag GmbH, Thierschstr 11, D-8000 Munich 22 Tel: (089) 293272
Man Dir: Dr Günter Olzog; *Sales, Publicity & Advertising Dir:* Johann Hacker; *Rights & Permissions:* Dr Günter Olzog
Subjects: History, Social Science, Educational Materials, Politics, East European Economics
1979: 25 titles *1980:* 30 titles *Founded:* 1949
ISBN Publisher's Prefix: 3-7892

Oncken Verlag KG, Postfach 110197, D-5600 Wuppertal 11 Tel: (02104) 6311/3
Subjects: Popular Religion: Biography, Devotional, Song Books etc
ISBN Publisher's Prefix: 3-7893

Orangerie Galerie und Verlag, Gerhard F Reinz, Helenenstr 2, D-5000 Cologne 1 Tel: (0221) 234684 Cable Add: Orangerie Telex: 8882939
Subject: Art

Orion-Heimreiter Verlag GmbH, Friedrich-Ebert-Str 5-7, Postfach 1324, D-6056 Heusenstamm Tel: (06104) 5013 Cable Add: Orionheimreiter
Publisher: Erich W Rüskamp; *Editorial:* Ernst Frank; *Sales, Production, Publicity:* Heidemarie Schaffer; *Rights & Permissions:* through Hodemacher-Poldner, 8 Munich 19
Subjects: Biography, Documentary, Local History, Art, History, Fiction
1978: 9 titles *1979:* 8 titles *Founded:* 1961
ISBN Publisher's Prefix: 3-87588

Verlag **Osterrieth**, part of Societäts-Verlag (qv)

P I A G, see Verlag Presse Information Agentur GmbH

P R Verlag Wiesbaden, H G Schwieger*, Glückstr 12, D-6200 Wiesbaden Tel: (06121) 520030 Cable Add: PR Verlag, Wiesbaden
Man Dir: H G Schwieger
Subjects: Belles Lettres, Poetry, Educational Materials
Founded: 1974
ISBN Publisher's Prefix: 3-921261

Päd extra buchverlag in der Pädex Verlags GmbH, Postfach 295, D-6140 Bensheim (Located at: Bahnhofstr 5) Tel: (06251) 6054/6055
Man Dir, Editorial, Sales: Jörg Jonas; *Production:* Christiane Bohm; *Publicity:* Hans Jürgen Blank
Parent Company: Pädex Verlags GmbH (at above address)
Subjects: Pedagogy, Social Sciences
1978: 14 titles *Founded:* 1976
ISBN Publisher's Prefix: 3-921450

Pädagogischer Verlag Schwann GmbH, Am Wehrhahn 100, Postfach 7640, D-4000 Düsseldorf 1 Tel: (0211) 360301 Cable Add: Schwannverlag Düsseldorf Telex: paed d 858 1345
Dirs: Dr Paul Böhringer, Wilhelm Biswanger; *Production:* Dr Hans Weymar; *Publicity Manager:* Albrecht Wages
Subjects: University, Secondary and Primary Textbooks, Educational Materials, History, Arts, Linguistics, Children's Books, Records
1978: 74 titles *Founded:* 1821
ISBN Publisher's Prefix: 3-508

Pahl-Rugenstein Verlag, Gottesweg 54, D-5000 Cologne 51 Tel: (0221) 364051
Dir: Paul Neuhöffer; *Editorial:* Jürgen Hartmann, Dr Jürgen Harrer; *Sales Manager:* Hajo Leib
Subjects: History, Literary Criticism, Education, Philosophy, Politics, Psychology, Social Science, Paperbacks, Economics, Periodicals, Sports
Miscellaneous: Member of Arbeitsgemeinschaft sozialistischer und demokratischer Verleger und Buchhandler (qv for other members)
ISBN Publisher's Prefix: 3-7609

Wilhelm **Pansegrau** Verlag, Bessemerstr 83, Postfach 420320, D-1000 Berlin 42 Tel: 7537051
Associate Company: H Heenemann Verlagsgesellschaft mbH (qv)
Subjects: Corrosion Protection, Plastics, Lacquer and Coatings

Parabel Verlag GmbH und Co KG, Bauerstr 20, Postfach 401024, D-8000 Munich Tel: (089) 374494 Telex: 055215697
Publisher: Nadine Lange-Siemens; *Sales:* Franz Eheberg; *Rights & Permissions:* Barbel Kistner
Subjects: Picture Books, Modern Literature
1978: 8 titles *1979:* 15 titles
ISBN Publisher's Prefix: 3-7898

Paracelsus Verlag GmbH, see Hippokrates Verlag GmbH

Verlag Paul **Parey**, Spitalerstr 12, Postfach 106304, D-2000 Hamburg 1; Lindenstr 44-47, D-1000 Berlin 61 Tel: (040) 321511 (Hamburg); (030) 2516011 (Berlin) Cable Add: Pareyverlag Hamburg or Berlin Telex: Hamburg 2161391; Berlin 184777
Man Dirs: Dr Friedrich Georgi, Dr Rudolf Georgi (Berlin); *Editorial Dir (Hamburg):* Gerhard Schwennesen; *Publicity:* Karlheinz Römer; *Rights & Permissions:* Gerhard Reichwald
Subjects: Biology, Veterinary Medicine, Foodstuffs, Agriculture, Starch Research and Application, Brewery and Distillery, Forestry, Horticulture, Plant Medicine and Protection; Environment Protection, Hydro- and Cultural Technologies, Hunting, Sporting and Professional Fishing, Riding and Horses, Technical and Scientific Journals
1978: 92 titles *Founded:* 1848
ISBN Publisher's Prefixes: 3-490 (Hamburg), 3-489 (Berlin)

Parkland Verlag GmbH und Co Verlags- & Vertriebs-KG, Schwabstr 189, D-7000 Stuttgart 1 Tel: (0711) 298805 Telex: 721907
Man Dirs: Gerd Seibert, Dr Erhard Wendelberger; *Sales Dir:* Martina Deissner
Subjects: Non-fiction, especially Belles Lettres, Art etc
Founded: 1974

Verlag **Passavia**, Postfach 2147, D-8390 Passau 2 Tel: (0851) 51081/82/83 and 56947 Cable Add: Passavia Telex: 57837
Publishing Dir and Rights & Permissions: M

FEDERAL REPUBLIC OF GERMANY 151

Teschendorff; *Sales:* Katharina Moritz
Subjects: Bavarian Topics, Folklore, Humour, Homecare, Belles Lettres, Fiction
1979: 6 titles *1980:* 12 titles *Founded:* 1888
ISBN Publisher's Prefix: 3-87616

Galerie **Patio** Verlag, Laubestr 24H, D-6000 Frankfurt am Main 70
Man Dir: Walter Zimbrich; *Editorial:* Volker Müller; *Sales:* Franz Gaber, Renate Kafitz-Pfeuffer; *Production:* David Albrecht, Manfred Linke; *Publicity:* Klaus Münschschwander; *Rights & Permissions:* Günter Scherer, David Ward
Subjects: New Editions of Rare Texts, Hand-Printed Texts, the *Parabü* series of new, experimental texts (Patio's Book Rarity Library)
1979: 7 titles *1980:* 8 titles *Founded:* 1964

Patmos Verlag GmbH, Am Wehrhahn 100, Postfach 6213, D-4000 Düsseldorf 1
Tel: (0211) 360301 Cable Add: Patmos Verlag Telex: paed d 8581345
Dir: Dr P Böhringer; *Sales:* Wilhelm Biswanger; *Publicity:* Albrecht Wages
Subjects: Roman Catholic Theology, Religion, Education, Juveniles, Textbooks
Founded: 1910
ISBN Publisher's Prefix: 3-491

Paul **Pattloch** Buchhandlung und Verlag GmbH & Co KG, Goldbacherstr IX, D-8750 Aschaffenburg Tel: (06021) 21277 Cable Add: Pattloch Aschaffenburg
Telex: 4188517
Man & Sales Dir: Clemens Pattloch; *Editorial:* Dr Bernd Pattloch
Subjects: Religion, Bibles
1978: 30 titles *1979:* 27 titles *Founded:* 1827
Bookshops: Buchhandlung Paul Pattloch, Herstallstr 17, D-8750 Aschaffenburg; City Galerie, Goldbacherstr 2, D-8750 Aschaffenburg
ISBN Publisher's Prefix: 3-557

Paulinus Verlag, Fleischstr 61, Postfach 3040, D-5500 Trier Tel: (0651) 46171 Telex: 04-727315
Dir: Erika Schwarzenberg
Parent Company: Paulinus Druckerei GmbH (at above address)
Associate Company: Spee Buchverlag GmbH (qv)
Subjects: Religion, Theology
ISBN Publisher's Prefix: 3-7902

Pawel Pan Presse, Kennedystr 25, D-6072 Dreieich Tel: 06103/81347
Man Dir, Production: Sascha Juritz; *Editorial:* Hanne F Juritz
Subjects: Contemporary Literature, Educative Art, Poetry, First Publications in Bibliophile Editions
1978: 3 titles *1979:* 8 titles *Founded:* 1972
ISBN Publisher's Prefix: 3-921454

Manfred **Pawlak** Grossantiquariat und Verlagsgesellschaft mbH*, Postfach 1149, D-8036 Herrsching (Located at: Gachenau Str 13) Tel: (08152) 1067-69 Telex: 0527724 mph d
Proprietor, Man Dir: Manfred Pawlak
Subjects: Biography, History, Music, Art
1979: about 600 titles *Founded:* 1949
Miscellaneous: The Company is a wholesale antiquarian and second-hand book dealer as well as a Publishing House

Pestalozzi-Verlag graphische Gesellschaft mbH*, Am Pestalozziring 14, Postfach 2829, D-8520 Erlangen Tel: 09131/6116 Cable Add: Pestalozzi Erlangen Telex: 629766 Pevau
Man Dirs: Dr Reinhold Weigand, Norbert Franke; *Editorial:* Wolfgang Kaiser
Subjects: Children's Books
1978: 105 titles *Founded:* 1844
ISBN Publisher's Prefix: 3-87624

Verlag J P **Peter**, Gebr Holstein*, Herrngasse 1, Postfach 19, D-8803 Rothenburg Tel: (09861) 3001 Cable Add: Peterverlag
Man Dir: Bernhard Doerdelmann; *Sales Dir:* Rainer Holstein; *Publicity Dir:* Bernhard Doerdelmann
Subjects: Belles Lettres, Poetry, History, Religion, Travel, Educational Materials, Fiction; Periodicals
Founded: 1825
ISBN Publisher's Prefix: 3-87625

C F **Peters** Musikverlag GmbH und Co KG, Kennedyallee 101, Postfach 700906, D-6000 Frankfurt-am-Main 70 Tel: (0611) 633066 Cable Add: Petersedit
Managing Partner: Dr Johannes Petschull
Associate Companies: Hinrichsen Edition Ltd, London, UK; C F Peters Corporation, New York, USA
Imprints: Edition Peters, Henry Litolff's Verlag, Edition Schwann, MP Belaieff
Subjects: Musical scores, Books on Music (all areas of Classical and Contemporary Music)
Founded: 1800
ISBN Publisher's Prefix: 3-87626

Dr Hans **Peters** Verlag, Salisweg 56, Postfach 2012, D-6450 Hanau 1 Tel: (06181) 21632 *Man Dir:* Wolfgang A Nagel; *Editorial:* Rainer G Tripp; *Sales:* Christa Buschbeck; *Production:* Barbara Nagel
Subjects: Art Books, Pictorial Books, Picture Books for Children
1978: 12 titles *1979:* 12 titles *Founded:* 1952
ISBN Publisher's Prefix: 87627

Fachbuchverlag Dr **Pfanneberg** & Co, Postfach 110910, D-6300 Giessen 11 (Located at: Schanzenstr 18) Tel: (0641) 74034
Man Dirs, Rights & Permissions: Dr Günther Pfanneberg, Gero Pfanneberg; *Editorial:* Gero Pfanneberg; *Sales:* Christa Horn; *Production:* Gerhard Duske
Subjects: Hotels and Catering Trade Textbooks, Technologies (automobile, electrical etc), Commerce, Botany, Textbooks for Trade Schools
Founded: 1949
ISBN Publisher's Prefix: 3-8057

Verlag J **Pfeiffer**, Herzogspitalstr 5, D-8000 Munich 2 Tel: (089) 2603036
Man Dir: Günter Müller; *Editorial:* A Arnold; *Sales, Publicity:* M Reile; *Production:* G Bitterauf; *Rights & Permissions:* Günter Müller
Associate Company: Claudius Verlag GmbH (qv)
Subjects: How-to, Philosophy, Psychology, Religion, Juveniles, High-priced Paperbacks, Social Science, Educational Materials
1978: 22 titles *Founded:* 1882
Bookshop: Buchhandlung J Pfeiffer, Herzogspitalstr 5, D-8000 Munich 2
ISBN Publisher's Prefix: 3-7904

E **Pfister** GmbH*, Postfach 6485, Hussenstr 6, D-7750 Constance Tel: (07531) 23598
Associate Companies: Verlag der Arche, Switzerland (qv); Dr Franz Hain, Austria (qv); Sanssouci Verlag AG, Switzerland (qv)

Richard **Pflaum** Verlag KG, Postfach 201920, D-8000 Munich 2 (Located at: Lazarettstr 4, D-8000 Munich 19) Tel: (089) 186051 Cable Add: Pflaumverlag Telex: 529408
Sales & Publicity Manager: Hans-Georg Scheideler
Subjects: Electrical Engineering, Electronics, Hobbies, Medicine, Periodicals
Associate Companies: Hüthig und Pflaum Verlag (qv), Dr Alfred Hüthig Verlag (qv)
ISBN Publisher's Prefix: 3-7905

Engelbert **Pfriem** Verlag, Else-Lasker-Schüler-Str 47-49, D-5600 Wuppertal 1 Tel: (0202) 447878
General Manager: Engelbert Pfriem
Associate Company: Kolibri Verlag (qv)
Subjects: Books and magazines for aquarium enthusiasts

Udo **Pfriemer** Verlag GmbH, Landwehrstr 68, Postfach 201940, D-8000 Munich 2 Tel: 531604 Telex: 0523398
Subjects: Energy, Alternative Energies, Maintenance Technology in Water, Gas, Helio systems; Sanitary, Health, Heating, Sewage Technology, History of Science and Technology

Robert **Pfützner** GmbH, see Verlag Mensch und Arbeit

Philips GmbH, Fachbuch-Verlag*, Mönckebergstr 7, Postfach 101420, D-2000 Hamburg 1 Tel: (040) 32971 Cable Add: Phihag Telex: 2161587 a dpu d
Man Dir: Wilfried von Hacht
Subjects: Electronics, Electrical Engineering, Radio & Television
1979: approx 100 titles
ISBN Publisher's Prefix: 3-87145

Physica-Verlag Rudolf Liebing GmbH und Co, Werner-von-Siemens-Str 5, Postfach 5840, D-8700 Würzburg 1 Tel: (0931) 22821
Man Dir: Arnulf Liebing
Branch Off: A-1010 Vienna, Seilerstätte 18, Austria
Subjects: University Textbooks (Management Science, Computing Science, Economics, Statistics)
1979: 15 titles *1980:* 20 titles *Founded:* 1952
ISBN Publisher's Prefix: 3-7908

Physik Verlag GmbH, Pappelallee 3, Postfach 1260-80, D-6940 Weinheim/Bergstr Tel: (06201) 14031 Telex: 465516
Man Dirs: Jürgen Kreuzhage, Hans Schermer; *Editorial:* Dr Hans-Friedrich Ebel, Dr Gerd Giesler; *Sales, Publicity and Advertising Dir:* Helmut Schmitzer; *Production:* Maximilian Montkowski; *Rights & Permissions:* Kornelia Herbig
Parent Company: Verlag Chemie, GmbH (qv)
Subjects: Science & Technology (especially Physics), University Textbooks
1978: 7 titles *1979:* 5 titles *Founded:* 1947
ISBN Publisher's Prefix: 3-87664

Buch- & Verlagshaus Paul **Pietsch** GmbH & Co KG*, Postfach 1370, D-7000 Stuttgart 1 (Located at: Boblinger Str 18)
Subsidiary Division: Motorbuch-Verlag (qv)

Pinx-Verlag Kurt Glombig*, Hartmann-Ibach-Str 68, D-6000 Frankfurt am Main 60 Tel: (0611) 461211, 454807
Publisher: Kurt Glombig
Subjects: Public Relations Texts in Popular editions; Pharmaceuticals; Travel Sketches; PR Paperbacks; Series of Primers; Animals

R **Piper** und Co Verlag, Georgenstr 4, Postfach 430120, D-8000 Munich 40
Tel: (089) 397071 Cable Add: Piperverlag Munich Telex: 5215385
Shipping Add: Koch, Neff & Oetinger & Co, Am Wallgraben 110, D-7000 Stuttgart 80
Co-owner & President: Klaus Piper; *Man Dir:* Matthias Pflieger; *Editorial:* Dr Rainer Weiss, Dr Klaus Stadler, Jochen Rahe; *Sales Dir:* Peter Wagner; *Rights & Permissions:* Dorothee Grisebach
Branch Off: R Piper & Co Verlag GmbH, Switzerland (qv)
Subjects: Novels, Poetry, Biography, General and Social Science, Several series of Quality Paperbacks, Philosophy, Psychology, Arts, Education, Biology, Children's Books

152 FEDERAL REPUBLIC OF GERMANY

1978: 88 titles   *1979:* 83 titles   *Founded:* 1904
ISBN Publisher's Prefix: 3-492

Plambeck & Co, Druck und Verlag GmbH, Xantener Str 7, Postfach 920, D-4040 Neuss   Tel: 57081/88   Telex: 8517506 and 8517530
Subjects: Paperbacks, Pocket Books; Periodicals
Miscellaneous: Member of Arbeitsgemeinschaft sozialistischer und demokratischer Verleger und Buchhändler (qv for other members)

Ploetz GmbH und Co KG, Habsburgstr 116, D-7800 Freiburg-im-Breisgau   Tel: (0761) 2717387
Man Dir: Harald Glaeser
Orders to: Verlag Herder, address as above
Parent Company: Verlag Herder GmbH & Co KG (qv)
Associate Companies: Herder AG, Switzerland (qv); Verlag Herder & Co, Austria (qv); Herder und Herder GmbH (qv)
1980: 150 titles   *Founded:* 1880
Subjects: Illustrated Popular Reference Works on Historical, Biographical, Geographical Themes; School Books, Sociology, Linguistics
ISBN Publisher's Prefix: 3-87640

Podzun-Pallas Verlag GmbH*, Markt 9, Postfach 14, D-6360 Friedberg 3-Dorheim   Tel: (06031) 3131   Cable Add: Podzun, Friedberg   Telex: 415961
Man Dir, Production, Rights & Permissions: Rainer Ahnert; *Editorial:* Mrs Neisel; *Sales:* Mrs Hergesell
Subjects: Modern History, Illustrated Books, Periodicals
1978: 12 titles
ISBN Publisher's Prefix: 3-7909

C E **Poeschel** Verlag, Kernerstr 43, Postfach 529, D-7000 Stuttgart 1   Tel: (0711) 225074-6
Man Dir: Mr Schweizer; *Sales Dir:* Mr Cziszinsky; *Advertising Dir:* Mr Kegler; *Rights & Permissions:* Mrs Kästing
Orders to: (Federal Republic of Germany): Goethestrasse 6, D-7400 Tübingen; (in Berlin) A Muschal & Sohn, Lützowerstr 105-6, D-1000 Berlin 30
Associate Company: J B Metzlersche Verlagsbuchhandlung (qv)
Subjects: Economics, 'The Encyclopaedia of Industrial Management Theory'
1978: 25 titles   *1979:* 26 titles   *Founded:* 1902
ISBN Publisher's Prefix: 3-7910

Pohl Druckerei und Verlagsanstalt Otto Pohl, Herzog-Ernst-Ring 1, Postfach 103, D-3100 Celle   Tel: (05141) 27081   Cable Add: Pohl, Celle
Dir: Manfred Senftleben
Subjects: Physical Education, Games, Sports, Gymnastics, Keep Fit
1978: 7 titles
ISBN Publisher's Prefix: 3-7911

Verlag für **polizeiliches Fachschrifttum**, see Georg Schmidt-Rämhild

Bernd **Polke** GmbH, see I V A Verlag

Polyglott-Verlag Dr Bolte KG, Neusser Str 3, Postfach 401120, D-8000 Munich 40   Tel: (089) 38301   Cable Add: Langenscheidt Munich   Telex: 5215379 lkgm d
Man Dir: Karl-Ernst Tielebier-Langenscheidt; *Editor:* Dr Wilhelm Trappl; *Sales Dir:* Peter Haering; *Export Dir:* Uwe Cordts; *Advertising Dir:* Dieter Krause; *Rights & Permissions:* Manfred Überall
Subjects: Travel Guides & Phrasebooks
1979: 12 titles   *1980:* 13 titles   *Founded:* 1902
Miscellaneous: Company is a member of the Langenscheidt Group (qv)
ISBN Publisher's Prefix: 3-493

Polyglotte Buch- und Schallplatten-Verlag und Vertrieb, Postfach 230147, D-4000 Düsseldorf   Tel: 683191
Man Dir: F W Kreft
Subject: Educational Materials
ISBN Publisher's Prefix: 3-920754

Polygraph Verlag GmbH, Schaumainkai 85, Postfach 700940, D-6000 Frankfurt am Main   Tel: 639066   Cable Add: Polygraphverlag Frankfurt am Main   Telex: 0413562
Man Dir: H J Teichmann; *Sales Dir:* W Kissel; *Publicity Dir:* R Kreis; *Rights & Permissions:* Ulrike Schulz, H Sidoruk
Subjects: Textbooks and Reference Works for the Printing Industry and Allied Trades
1978: 24 titles   *Founded:* 1947

Edition Georg **Popp***, Talavera 7-11, Postfach 5169, D-8700 Würzburg 1   Tel: (0931) 43061   Cable Add: Edition Popp   Telex: 068833
Publisher, Editorial, Rights & Permissions: Georg Popp; *Sales:* Günter Reich
Associate Company: Arena-Verlag Georg Popp, Wurzburg (qv)
Subjects: Art Books, Books for the Bibliophile
Founded: 1975
ISBN Publisher's Prefix: 3-881

Possev-Verlag V Gorachek KG, Flurscheideweg 15, D-6230 Frankfurt am Main 80   Tel: (0611) 341265
Publisher, Editorial, Production, Rights & Permissions: Lev Rahr; *Sales, Publicity:* N Jdanoff
Subjects: Contemporary Russian authors in the original Russian and in German translation; Periodicals in Russian
1978: 10 titles   *Founded:* 1945

Praesentverlag Heinz Peter*, Kleiststr 15, Postfach 2720, D-4830 Gütersloh   Tel: (05241) 3188/9   Telex: 0933831
Publisher: Heinz Peter
Subjects: General Fiction, Hobbies, Reference Books, Travel, Cookery
ISBN Publisher's Prefix: 3-87644

Präsenz-Verlag der Jesus Bruderschaft, Gnadenthal, D-6257 Hünfelden   Tel: (06438) 2003
Dir: Brother Samuel Ulmer
Subject: Religion
ISBN Publisher's Prefix: 3-87630

Verlag **Presse** Informations Agentur GmbH (PIAG), Stefanienstr 4, D-7570 Baden-Baden   Tel: (07221) 28994/25348   Cable Add: PIAG Baden-Baden   Telex: 781217 piag-d
Man Dir: Dieter Brinzer; *Publicity & Advertising Dir:* Thea Gutzeit; *Sales Dir:* Klaus Pittner
Subject: Photography
1978: 24 titles   *Founded:* 1963

Guido **Pressler** Verlag, Auf dem Strifft, D-5165 Hürtgenwald   Tel: (0249) 1385
Subjects: Art, History, Literature, Bibliographies, History of Sciences
ISBN Publisher's Prefix: 3-87646

Prestel Verlag, Mandlstr 26, D-8000 Munich 40   Tel: (089) 333055   Cable Add: Prestelverlag   Telex: 5216366
Man Dir, Sales Dir: Jürgen Tesch; *Advertising & Publicity Dir:* Eva von Reibnitz; *Rights & Permissions:* Miss Aasta Fischer
Subjects: General Nonfiction, Art, Reference, History
1978-79: 30 titles   *Founded:* 1924
ISBN Publisher's Prefix: 3-7913

Helmut **Preussler** Verlag, Rothenburger Str 25, D-8500 Nuremberg   Tel: (0911) 262323   Cable Add: Preussler-Verlag

Man Dir: Helmut Preussler; *Editorial:* Manfred Hessdorfe; *Sales, Publicity:* Annemarie Seeberger; *Production:* Rolf Marienfeldt, Werner Eckstein
Bookshop: Ernst Gebhard, Rothenburger Str 23-25, D-8500 Nuremberg
Founded: 1973
ISBN Publisher's Prefix: 3-921332

Prisma Verlag GmbH, Carl-Bertelsmannstr 270, D-4830 Gütersloh   Tel: (05241) 801   Telex: 933646
Dirs: Aloys Hellmold
Parent Company: Verlagsgruppe Bertelsmann GmbH (qv for associate companies)
Subjects: Reprints, Special Editions

Pro Schule Verlag GmbH, Corneliusstr 9-11, D-4000 Düsseldorf   Tel: (0211) 370266
Dir: Benno Hasselsweiler
Parent Company: Verlagsgruppe Bertelsmann GmbH (qv for associate companies)
Subjects: Instructional Works in German Language, Evangelical Religion, Mathematics, Natural Sciences

Albert **Pröpster**, Schillerstr 46, Postfach 2149, D-8960 Kempten   Tel: 22797
Subjects: Cookery Books, Specialist Gastronomy Books, Picture Books, Roman Catholic Interest Books

Propyläen Verlag, Lindenstr 76, D-1000 Berlin 61   Tel: (030) 25911   Cable Add: Ullsteinbuch Berlin   Telex: vlgul d 183723
Dirs: W Joachim Freyburg, Hans F Erb, Viktor Niemann, Wolfgang Richter; *Publicity:* Margrit Osterwold; *Press:* Wolfgang Mönninghof
Parent Company: Verlag Ullstein GmbH (qv)
Subjects: Arts, History, Literature
ISBN Publisher's Prefix: 3-549

Verlag für **Psychologie**, Dr C J Hogrefe*, Rohnsweg 25, Postfach 414, D-3400 Göttingen   Tel: (0551) 54044
Proprietor: Dr C J Hogrefe; *Man Dir:* Dr H Lundberg; *Sales & Publicity Dir:* O Kohl; *Advertising, Production, Rights & Permissions Dir:* B Otto
Branch Offs: C J Hogrefe Inc, 525 Eglinton Ave East, Toronto, Ontario M4P 1N5; Verlag fur Psychologie, Dr C J Hogrefe, Zürich, Switzerland (qv)
Subjects: Psychology, Textbooks, Handbooks, Conference Reports, Yearbooks
1978: 200 titles   *1979:* 230 titles   *Founded:* 1949
ISBN Publisher's Prefix: 3-8017

Anton **Pustet**, Postfach 498, D-8228 Freilassing
Man Dir: Dr F G Kuhn
Associate Company: Universitätsverlag Anton Pustet, Postfach, D-8228 Freilassing
Subjects: Philosophy, Religion, Psychology, Social Science, Music
Founded: 1958
ISBN Publisher's Prefix: 3-7025

Verlag Friedrich **Pustet***, Gutenbergstr 8, Postfach 339, D-8400 Regensburg 11   Tel: (0941) 96044   Cable Add: Pustet   Telex: 55672
Man Dir: Dr Friedrich Pustet; *Editorial:* Monika Bock, Dr Gerd J Maurer; *Sales & Advertising Dir, Rights & Permissions:* Reinhold Röttger; *Production:* Karl Wittman
Subsidiary Company: Verlag Josef Habbel (qv)
Subjects: Christian Religion, Art, Monographs, Biography, Folklore, Bavaria
1978: 68 titles   *Founded:* 1826
Bookshops: Buchhandlung Friedrich Pustet, Regensburg, Gesandtenstr 6; Kleiner

Exerzierplatz 4, Passau; Grottenau 4, Augsburg
ISBN Publisher's Prefix: 3-7917

Quell-Verlag, Furtbachstr 12A, Postfach 897, D-7000 Stuttgart 1 Tel: (0711) 605746/8
Dir: Dr Helmut Riethmüller; *Editorial, Rights & Permissions:* Helmut Zechner
Subjects: General Fiction, Biography, History, Philosophy, Religion
Bookshop: Buchhandlung der Evangelischen Gesellschaft, Stuttgart
1980: 20 titles *Founded:* 1830
ISBN Publisher's Prefix: 3-7918

Quelle und Meyer Verlag, Schloss-Wolfsbrunnen-Weg 29, Postfach 104480, D-6900 Heidelberg 1 Tel: (06221) 22443 Cable Add: Quellmeyer Heidelberg
Man Dir: Dr Walter Kissling; *Sales Dir:* Edith Teich; *Advertising & Publicity Dir:* Hermann Klippel; *Foreign Rights Dir:* Hildegard Müller
Orders to: KNOe, Stuttgart
Subjects: Philosophy, Religion, Psychology, Chemistry and Biology, General & Social Science, Education, Language and Literature, History and Geography, University, Secondary & Primary Textbooks
1979: 50 titles *Founded:* 1906
ISBN Publisher's Prefix: 3-494

R V, see Reise- und Verkehrsverlag

Radius-Verlag GmbH, Kniebisstr 29, D-7000 Stuttgart 1 Tel: (0711) 283091/2
Man Dir: Wolfgang Erk; *Sales, Publicity & Advertising Dir:* Gerhard Schroeder
Subjects: General Fiction, Philosophy, Religion, Paperbacks, Psychology, *Radius*
1979: 17 titles *1980:* 19 titles *Founded:* 1963
ISBN Publisher's Prefix: 3-87173

Rainer Verlag, Körtestr 10, D-1000 Berlin 61 Tel: (030) 6916536
Man Dir: Rainer Pretzell; *Sales Dir:* Agnes Pretzell; *Advertising Dir:* Rainer Pretzell
Subjects: Belles Lettres, Poetry, Art, High-priced Paperbacks
Founded: 1966

Dokument und Analyse Verlag Bogislaw von **Randow**, Barerstr 43, D-8000 Munich 40 Tel: (089) 283001
Publisher: Bogislaw von Randow; *General Manager:* Gerhard Fassmann; *Marketing Manager:* Renate Lotte; *Marketing Publicity:* Thomas Lingenthal
Orders to: above address
Subjects: Politics, Economics, Law, Sociology, Periodical *Dokument & Analyse* (monthly Current Affairs magazine)
Founded: 1972

Rathgeber Verlag*, Pettenkoferstr 10a, D-8000 Munich 2 Tel: (089) 597797
Publishers: Walter Rathgeber, Johanna Rathgeber-Knan
Subjects: Medicine, Social Science, Humanities
ISBN Publisher's Prefix: 3-921298

Rationalisierungs-Kuratorium der Deutschen Wirtschaft eV (RKW), Düsseldorfer Str 40, Postfach 5867, D-6236 Eschborn Tel: (06196) 4951 Telex: 0418362 rkw d
Branch Offs: in all areas of the Federal Republic of Germany
Subjects: Architecture, Electrical Engineering, Civil & Mechanical Engineering, Education, Economics, Industrial and Human Relations, Management Consultancy, Packaging, Innovation, Technology
1979: 722 titles *Founded:* 1921

Walter **Rau** Verlag, Benderstr 168a, Postfach 6508, D-4000 Düsseldorf Tel: (0211) 283095 Telex: 08586682
Dir: Gisela Rau
Subjects: Arts, Education, Nonfiction, Social Science, Literature, Translations, Chess
ISBN Publisher's Prefix: 3-7919

Karl **Rauch** Verlag KG, Am Wehrhahn 100, Postfach 6520, D-4000 Düsseldorf 1
Man Dir: Harald Ebner
Subjects: Documentation, History, Fiction, Book Industry, Translations
Founded: 1923
ISBN Publisher's Prefix: 3-7920

Agentur des **Rauhen Hauses** GmbH, Papenhuder Str 2, D-2000 Hamburg 76 Tel: (040) 2201291
Dirs: Max Lenz, Dieter Gätjens
Subjects: Religion, Belles Lettres, Fiction, Juveniles, Art, Paperbacks
Founded: 1842
ISBN Publisher's Prefix: 3-7600

Gerhard **Rautenberg** Druckerei und Verlag GmbH & Co KG, Blinke 8, Postfach 1909, D-2950 Leer/Ostfriesland Tel: (0491) 4288 Cable Add: Rautenberg Leer
Dirs: Gerhard Rautenberg Senior, Carl-Ludwig Rautenberg, Gerhard Rautenberg Junior; *Editorial:* Gerhard Rautenberg Junior
Branch Off: Druckerei und Verlag Gerhard Rautenberg GmbH & Co KG, Königstr 41, D-2208 Glückstadt
Subjects: Regional Guides within Germany, Humour, Popular Historical, General Fiction, Show Business, Pictorial Calendars
Bookshop: Rautenbergsche Buchhandlung, Postfach 1909, D-2950 Leer
1978: 12 titles *Founded:* 1825
ISBN Publisher's Prefix: 3-7921

Ravensburger Graphische Betriebe Otto Maier GmbH, see Otto Maier Verlag

Ravensburger Verlag GmbH, see Otto Maier Verlag

Ravenstein Verlag GmbH, Wielandstr 31-35, D-6000 Frankfurt am Main Tel: (0611) 590722/23/24 Cable Add: Ravensteinverlag
Man Dirs: Helga Ravenstein, Rüdiger Bosse; *Sales Dir:* R Dürr
Subjects: Country and Regional Touring and Walking Maps; Town Maps and Guides; Pictorial Guides
Founded: 1830
ISBN Publisher's Prefix: 3-87660

Verlagsgesellschaft **Recht und Wirtschaft** mbH, Häusserstr 14, Postfach 105960, D-6900 Heidelberg 1 Tel: (06221) 25661 Cable Add: Rechtwirtschaft Heidelberg Telex: 461665
Associate Company: I H Sauer Verlag, Heidelberg (qv)
Subjects: Specialist Literature in fields of Law and Economics, Tax, Social and Industrial Questions; Tax Guide and other periodicals

Philipp **Reclam** Jun, Postfach 466, D-7000 Stuttgart 1 (Located at:Siemensstr 32, D-7257 Ditzingen bei Stuttgart) Tel: (07156) 502125 Cable Add: Reclam Ditzingen Telex: 7266704 recl d
Publisher: Dr Heinrich Reclam; *Publicity Dir:* Christoph Wilhelmi; *Rights & Permissions:* Marianne Diehl
Subjects: General Fiction, Belles Lettres, Poetry, Music, Art, Philosophy, Reference, Religion, Low-priced Paperbacks; University, Secondary & Primary Textbooks
1980: approx 100 titles *Founded:* 1828
ISBN Publisher's Prefix: 3-15

Dr Ludwig **Reichert** Verlag, Reisstr 10, D-6200 Wiesbaden-Dotzheim Tel: (06121) 465686
Publisher: Ludwig Reichert
Subjects: Facsimile Reprints, Art, Books and Libraries, Orientalia, Linguistics
1978: 40 titles *1979:* 40 titles *Founded:* 1970
ISBN Publisher's Prefixes: 3-920153, 3-88226

Otto **Reichl** Verlag, 'Der Leuchter', Haus Herresberg, D-5480 Remagen Tel: 02642/22271
Man Dir: Herwart von Guilleaume
Subjects: Philosophy, Religion, Parapsychology, Mysticism, Supernatural
1979: 2 titles *1980:* 1 title *Founded:* 1957
ISBN Publisher's Prefix: 3-87667

Verlag Knut **Reim***, Kleine Theaterstr 11, Postfach 302824, D-2000 Hamburg 36 Tel: (040) 342641
General Managers: Jens Christians, Knut Reim
Subjects: Juvenilia, Jurisprudence, Economics
Founded: 1958

Ernst **Reinhardt** GmbH & Co Verlag, Kemnatenstr 46, D-8000 Munich 19 Tel: (089) 170266
Man Dir, Production: Karl Münster
Orders to: Postfach 380280, D-8000 Munich 38
Subjects: Psychology, Psychotherapy, Philosophy, Pedagogy
1978: 33 titles *Founded:* 1899
ISBN Publisher's Prefix: 3-497

Verlag Wilhelm G **Reinheimer**, see Edition Venceremos

Reise- und Verkehrsverlag GmbH (RV), Schockenriedstr 40a, Postfach 800863, D-7000 Stuttgart 80 Tel: (0711) 736379 Cable Add: Verkehrsverlag
Man Dirs: Peter Gutmann, Olaf Paeschke; *Editorial:* Helmut Schaub; *Sales Manager, Publicity:* Wolfgang Kunth
Parent Company: Verlagsgruppe Bertelsmann GmbH (qv for associate companies)
Subjects: Maps, Atlases, Guides
Founded: 1927

Relief-Verlag-Eilers, Martin Greif Str 3, D-8000 Munich 2 Tel: (089) 537213
Man Dir: Wolfgang Eilers
Subjects: General Fiction, Belles Lettres, Poetry, Biography, Juveniles
Founded: 1961

Rembrandt Verlag GmbH, Schaperstr 35, D-1000 Berlin 15 Tel: (030) 2115503
Man Dir: Dr Klaus J Lemmer
Subjects: Biography, History, Music, Art, Educational Materials
1978: 10 titles *1979:* 12 titles *Founded:* 1923
ISBN Publisher's Prefix: 3-7925

Verlag Klaus G **Renner**, Oesterreicher Str 15, D-8520 Erlangen Tel: (09131) 32177
Man Dir: Klaus Renner; *Editorial:* Thomas Milch
Subjects: Belles Lettres, Poetry, Limited Editions
Founded: 1973
ISBN Publisher's Prefix: 3-921499

Rheingauer Verlagsgesellschaft mbH, Postfach 90, D-6228 Eltville am Rhein (Located at: Walluferstr 5a) Tel: (06123) 2312 Telex: 04182921 rvg d
Man Dir, Rights & Permissions: Bernd Ley, Peter Halfar; *Sales:* Mr Mätzel, Mr Hülzer, Mr Stärk; *Production:* Bernd Ley; *Publicity:* Monika Ley, Ingrid Bader
Orders to: Above address or Vereinigte Verlagsauslieferung Reinhard Mohn OHG, Postfach 7777, D-4830 Gütersloh
Subjects: Quality Illustrated Works, Low-

priced Foreign Classics in Translation, Saga and Legend, Juvenile, General Non-fiction
1978: 25 titles *1979:* 14 titles *Founded:* 1975
ISBN Publisher's Prefix: 3-17319

Rheinland-Verlag GmbH*, Landeshaus, Kennedy-Ufer 2, Postfach 210720, D-5000 Cologne 21 Tel: 82832687
Orders to: Rudolf Habelt Verlag GmbH, Bonn (qv)
Branch Off: Postfach 150104, D-5300 Bonn
Subjects: Rhineland excavations, Regional Knowledge, Folklore, Care of Art and Monuments
1978: 54 titles

Dr **Riederer** Verlag GmbH, Johannesstr 60, Postfach 447, D-7000 Stuttgart 1
Tel: (0711) 613000
Man Dir: M Groitzsch; *Sales Dir:* H Schneider
Subjects: Science, Engineering, Metallography
Founded: 1945
1978: 3 titles
ISBN Publisher's Prefix: 3-87675

Ritter Verlag GmbH*, Sonnenwinkel 1, Postfach 1221, D-8031 Wörthsee/Steinebach Tel: (08152) 1525
Man Dir: Reinhold Schröder
Subjects: Natural Healing, Practical Psychotherapy and Fringe Medicine

Ritzau KG Verlag Zeit und Eisenbahn*, Landsberger Str 24, D-8911 Pürgen
Tel: (08196) 252
Subjects: History of German Railways; old Timetables and General History of Transport in Germany from late 19th Century
1978: 6 titles *1979:* 9 titles *Founded:* 1968
ISBN Publisher's Prefix: 3-921304

Rochus-Verlag, Düsseldorf, see Arbeitsgemeinschaft sozialistischer und demokratischer Verleger und Buchhändler

Röderberg-Verlag GmbH*, Schumannstr 56, Postfach 4129, D-6000 Frankfurt am Main 1 Tel: (0611) 751046 Telex: 414721
Editorial, Production: Peter Altmann; *Sales:* Hoerst Foerster
Subject: Politics
Miscellaneous: Member of Arbeitsgemeinschaft sozialistischer und demokratischer Verleger und Buchhändler (qv for other members)
ISBN Publisher's Prefix: 3-87682

Rogner und Bernhard GmbH & Co Verlags KG, König-Marke-Str 5, D-8000 Munich 40 Tel: (089) 363024 Telex: 05215482 buch d
Dirs: Antje Ellermann, Thomas Landshoff, W H Schünemann, Ulrich Meier
Subjects: General Fiction, Belles Lettres, Art, Photography
1978: 18 titles *1979:* 19 titles
ISBN Publisher's Prefix: 3-8077

Rudolf **Rolfs**, see Die Schmiere

Rombach und Co GmbH, Verlag & Buchdruckerei, Lörracher Str 3, Postfach 1349, D-7800 Freiburg im Breisgau
Tel: (0761) 42323 Telex: 772820
Man Dir: Dr Hodeige
Subjects: History, Art, Philosophy, Religion, Psychology, Economics, Social & Political Science, University Textbooks
Bookshop: Rombach-Center, Bertoldstr 10, D-7800 Freiburg
Founded: 1936
ISBN Publisher's Prefix: 3-7930

Rose-Verlag und Edition Rose-Verlag, Seestr 12, D-8221 Seebruck Chiemsee Tel: (08667) 420 Cable Add: Rose-Verlag 8221 Seebruck Telex: 0526144 M Piepenstock
Man Dir, Rights and Permissions: Marianne Piepenstock; *Editorial, Sales, Production:* Michael Piepenstock
Subjects: Education and Upbringing, Health, Food, Religion
Founded: 1955
ISBN Publisher's Prefix: 3-920803

Rosenheimer Verlagshaus Alfred Förg GmbH & Co KG, Am Stocket 12, D-8200 Rosenheim 2 Tel: (08031) 86332 Cable Add: Rosenheimer Verlagshaus Rosenheim Telex: 525732 rosen d
Man Dir: Alfred Förg; *Sales:* Hansjörg Decker; *Rights & Permissions:* Thea Roscher
Subjects: General Fiction, Belles Lettres, Poetry, Biography, History, Music, Art Needlecraft, Bavarica
1978: 91 titles *1979:* 108 titles *Founded:* 1968
ISBN Publisher's Prefix: 3-475

Rösler und Zimmer Verlag, see Verlag Wolfgang Zimmer

Rotbuch Verlag GmbH, Potsdamer Str 98, D-1000 Berlin 30 Tel: (030) 2611196
Man Dirs: Eberhard Delius, Manfred Naber; *Editorial:* Gabriele Dietze, Niels Kadritzke; *Sales, Advertising:* Dirk Nishen, Sigrid Ruschmeier, Angelika Spiekermann; *Rights & Permissions:* Uta Ruge, Ingrid Karsunke
Subjects: Belles Lettres, Poetry, History, Social Science
ISBN Publisher's Prefix: 3-88022

Verlag **Roter Morgen**, Wellinghoferstr 103, Postfach 300526, D-4600 Dortmund-Hörde (30) Tel: (0231) 433691/92
Subjects: Speeches and Writings of Stalin and Enver Hoxha; Communism; Publications of the Communist Party of Germany (Marxist-Leninist); Periodical *Roter Morgen*
1980: 75 titles *Founded:* 1977
ISBN Publisher's Prefix: 3-88196

Verlag **Roter Stern***, Postfach 180147, D-6000 Frankfurt am Main Tel: (0611) 599999
Publishers: K D Wolff, Angelika Schwarz
Subjects: Textbooks, Periodicals
ISBN Publisher's Prefix: 3-87877

Erich **Röth**-Verlag, Kassel, Korbacher Str 235, D-3500 Kassel-Nordshausen
Tel: (0561) 401206 Cable Add: Röthverlag
Subjects: Folk tales and Folklore, Music, Art
Founded: 1921
ISBN Publisher's Prefix: 3-87680

Bergverlag Rudolf **Rother**, see Bergverlag

Rowohlt Taschenbuch Verlag GmbH*, Hamburger Str 17, Postfach 1349, D-2057 Reinbek bei Hamburg Tel: (040) 72721 Cable Add: Rowohltverlag Reinbek Telex: 0217854
Man Dirs: Heinrich Maria Ledig-Rowohlt, Kurt Busch, Horst Varrelmann, Dr Matthias Wegner; *Editorial:* Freimut Duve, Richard K Flesch, Dr Uwe Wandrey, Dr Jürgen Manthey; *Rights & Permissions:* Eda Brigitta von Seebach
Subjects: Wide range of mainly low-priced, mainly Nonfiction Paperbacks; especially popular works on Life Sciences, History and Archaeology, Art, Politics, Psychology, Education, Philosophy, Religion, Social Sciences, Sports and Games
Founded: 1953
ISBN Publisher's Prefix: 3-499

Rowohlt Taschenbuch Verlag GmbH, Hamburger Str 17, Postfach 1349, D-2057 Reinbek bei Hamburg Tel: (040) 72721 Cable Add: Rowohltverlag Reinbek Telex: 0217854
Man Dirs: Heinrich Maria Ledig-Rowohlt, Kurt Busch, Horst Varrelmann (Sales), Dr Matthias Wegner; *Editorial:* Freimut Duve, Richard Flesch, Dr Uwe Wandrey, Dr Jurgen Manthey; *Publicity:* Klaus F von Sobbe; *Rights & Permissions:* Eda B von Seebach
Subjects: Paperbacks — covering General Fiction, Belles Lettres, Poetry, Biography, How-to, Philosophy, Reference, Psychology, General and Social Science, Education, History, Juveniles, Politics, Translations of International Literature
1979: 378 titles *Founded:* 1953
ISBN Publisher's Prefix: 3-499

Ruhland Verlag, Goethestr 27, D-6000 Frankfurt am Main 1 Tel: (0611) 285604
Publisher: Erich Ruhland; *Publicity, Rights & Permissions:* Habdank Philipp
Subject: Instruction courses and texts on Secretarial Work, Commerce etc

W **Runge** Verlag, see Arbeitsgemeinschaft sozialistischer und demokratischer Verleger und Buchhändler

VWK **Ryborsch** GmbH, see VWK

S A S S-Verlagsgesellschaft mbH und Co KG*, Postfach 249, D-6440 Bebra (Located at: Nürnberger Str) Tel: 06622/2005 Telex: 493412

s t v, see Stolfuss Verlag

Safari Verlag (Reinhard Jaspert)*, Welserstr 10, Postfach 1443, D-1000 Berlin 30 Tel: 2131049
Man Dir: Hans-Heinrich Kuemmel
Subjects: Travel and Geography, Ancient History, Mythology, Popular Science and Nature Study, Religion, Art, Philosophy
Founded: 1921
Miscellaneous: Firm is a member of Verlagsgruppe Langen-Müller/Herbig (qv)
ISBN Publisher's Prefix: 3-7934

Verlag Otto **Sagner**, Heßstr 39-41, Postfach 68, D-8000 Munich 34 Tel: (0811) 522027 Cable Add: buchsagner München
Publisher: Otto Sagner; *Editorial:* Dr Peter Rehder
Orders to: Kubon und Sagner (at above address)
Parent Company: Kubon und Sagner (at above address)
Subject: Slavistics (Language and History)
Founded: 1959
ISBN Publisher's Prefix: 3-87690

Otto **Salle** Verlag, see Verlag Moritz Diesterweg/Otto Salle Verlag

Salvator Verlag GmbH, Hermann-Josef-Str 4, Postfach 220, D-5370 Kall
Tel: (02441) 5047
Dir: Andreas Münck
Subject: Religion

Eugen **Salzer** Verlag, Titotstr 5, Postfach 3048, D-7100 Heilbronn 1 Tel: (07131) 68294 Cable Add: Salzerverlag
Man Dir: Hartmut Salzer; *Sales Dir:* J Glage
Subjects: Fiction, Belles Lettres, How-to, Reference, Juveniles
1978: 12 titles *Founded:* 1891
ISBN Publisher's Prefix: 3-7936

Dr Martin **Sändig** GmbH, Postfach 5120, D-6200 Wiesbaden 1 (Located at: Kaiser Friedrich Ring 70)
Dirs: Ulfa von den Steinen, Günther W Sprunkel
Orders to: Kraus-Thomson Organization Ltd, FL-9491 Nendeln, Liechtenstein (qv)
Parent Company: Kraus-Thomson Organization Ltd, Liechtenstein (qv)
Subjects: Natural Sciences, Linguistics, Fiction, Folklore, Music
ISBN Publisher's Prefix: 3-500

Verlag der **Sankt-Johannis-Druckerei**
C Schweickhardt*, Heiligenstr 24,
Postfach 5, D-7630 Lahr 12 Tel: (07821)
43014 Cable Add: Veritas Lahrschwarzwäld
Man Dir: Walter Guthmann; *Editorial,
Publicity, Rights & Permissions:* Karl-Heinz
Kern; *Sales:* Johannes Walter; *Production:*
Helmut Schlegel
Subjects: Christian Devotional: stories,
commentaries, travel books for young people
and adults
1978: 20 titles *Founded:* 1896
Miscellaneous: Member of the Telos (qv)
group publishing evangelical paperbacks
ISBN Publisher's Prefix: 3-501

Sankt Otto Verlag GmbH, Lange Str 22-24,
Abholfach, D-8600 Bamberg Tel: (0951)
25252 Telex: 0662860 etvl
Man Dir: Kurt Kiening; *Other Offices:*
Norbert Göbel
Parent Company: Bayerische Verlagsanstalt
Bamberg (qv)
Associate Companies: Morawa und Co,
Austria (qv); Adolf Zwimpfer, Switzerland
(qv)
Subjects: Roman Catholic Religious
Literature; Guides for Pilgrims, Bamberg
Diocesan interest, Hymn Books, Devotional
Bookshop: Goerres Buchhandlung at above
address
1978: 5 titles
ISBN Publisher's Prefix: 3-87693

Sassafras Verlag, Bismarckplatz 43, D-4150
Krefeld Tel: (02151) 599555
Subject: Contemporary Writing

Satire Verlag GmbH*, Auerstr 1, D-5000
Cologne 60 Tel: (0221) 735929
Man Dir: Saskia E Wollschon; *Editorial:*
Reinhard Hippen, Gerd Wollschon
Subject: Satire
1978: 4 titles *1979:* 6 titles *Founded:* 1977
ISBN Publisher's Prefix: 3-88268

I H **Sauer** Verlag GmbH, Häusserstr 14,
Postfach 105960, D-6900 Heidelberg
Tel: (06221) 25661 Cable Add:
Rechtwirtschaft Heidelberg Telex: 461665
Associate Company: Verlagsgesellschaft
Recht und Wirtschaft (qv)
Subjects: Industrial Management,
Economics, Organisation; Data Processing,
Personnel Questions, Works Psychology,
Leadership, Staff Training, Rhetoric,
Publicity; Series of Paperbacks for Industry

H R **Sauerländer** und Co, Finkenhofstr 21,
D-6000 Frankfurt am Main 1 Tel: (0611)
555217
Partners: Helmut Baetz, Hans C Sauerländer
Parent Company: Sauerländer AG,
Switzerland (qv)
Subjects: Juveniles, Fiction, Sciences
Founded: 1964
ISBN Publisher's Prefix: 3-7941

J D **Sauerländer's** Verlag, Finkenhofstr 21,
D-6000 Frankfurt am Main 1 Tel: (0611)
555217
Publisher: Helmut A Baetz
Subjects: Forestry and Agricultural Sciences
1978: 11 titles *1979:* 11 titles *Founded:* 1816
ISBN Publisher's Prefix: 3-7939

K G **Saur** Verlag KG, Pössenbacherstr 2b,
Postfach 711009, D-8000 Munich 70 Tel:
(089) 798901/2/3 Cable Add: saur Telex:
5212067
Man Dirs: Klaus G Saur, Rudiger
Hildebrandt; *Editorial:* Willi Gorzny, Dr
Helga Lengenfelder; *Sales:* Paul Ferti;
Production: Horst Ahaus; *Rights &
Permissions:* Dr Helga Lengenfelder
Subsidiary Companies: Minerva-Publikation
Saur GmbH (100%), Verlag Dokumentation
Saur GmbH (100%) (both at above address);
TR-Verlagsunion GmbH (qv); Uni-
Taschenbücher GmbH (qv); K G Saur
Publishing Inc, 175 5th Ave, New York
NY 10010 (100%); K G Saur Editeur Sàrl,
France (qv) (100%); Clive Bingley Ltd, UK
(qv) (100%)
Branch Off: Hallgartenstr 49, D-6000
Frankfurt am Main 60
Subjects: Reference, Social Science, Library
Management, Documentation and
Information Science, Data Processing
1979: 160 titles *Founded:* 1948
Miscellaneous: Formerly known as Verlag
Dokumentation Saur KG, Munich
ISBN Publisher's Prefixes: 3-7940, 3-598

Karl A **Schäfer** Buch-und Offsetdruckerei-
Goldstadtverlag*, Finkensteinstr 6, D-7530
Pforzheim Tel: (07231) 42095 Cable Add:
Goldstadtverlag
Publisher: Günter Schäfer
Orders to: Geo-Center, Honigwiesenstr 25,
D-7000 Stuttgart 80
Subject: Travel Guides
Founded: 1956
ISBN Publisher's Prefix: 3-87269

Schäfer und Brandt, see Sonnenweg-Verlag

Hermann **Schaffstein** Verlag, Postfach 1283,
D-4600 Dortmund 1 Tel: (0231) 527496
Sales: Paul Lazar; *Rights & Permissions:*
Gerd Bösenberg, Gerd F Rumbler
Parent Company: Hermann Schroedel
Verlag KG (qv)
Orders to: Schroedel-Verlagsauslieferung,
Postfach 810620, D-3000 Hanover
Subjects: Juveniles, High-priced Paperbacks
ISBN Publisher's Prefix: 3-7942

F K **Schattauer** Verlag GmbH*,
Lenzhalde 3, Postfach 2945, D-7000
Stuttgart 1 Tel: (0711) 221733-7
Telex: 721886
Publisher: Philipp Reeg; *Sales Manager:*
Jochen Hintermeier
Subject: All aspects of Medicine, including
hygiene, biochemistry, psychology etc, and
related sciences
ISBN Publisher's Prefix: 3-7945

Moritz **Schauenburg** Verlag GmbH und Co
KG, Schillerstr 13, Postfach 2120, D-7630
Lahr 1 Tel: (07821) 23091 Cable Add:
Schauenburg Lahrschwarzwald
Telex: 0754943
Dir: Jörg Schauenburg
Subjects: General Fiction, Dialect texts,
Music, Linguistics, Philosophy, Literature
1978: 10 titles *Founded:* 1794
ISBN Publisher's Prefix: 3-7946

Schaum, an imprint of McGraw-Hill Book
Co GmbH

Verlag Heinrich **Scheffler**, part of Societäts-
Verlag (qv)

Scherpe Verlag*, Glockenspitz 140, Postfach
2630, D-4150 Krefeld Tel: (02151) 59211
Telex: 0853892
Subjects: General Fiction, Juveniles, Arts,
Education, Illustrated Books, Belles Lettres,
Politics
ISBN Publisher's Prefix: 3-7948

Scherz Verlag GmbH, Stievestr 9, D-8000
Munich 19 Tel: (089) 172237/38
Telex: 5215282 sherz d
President: Rudolf Streit-Scherz; *Editorial
Dir:* Gert Woerner; *Sales Dir:* Wolfgang
Radaj; *Crime/Suspense Fiction:* Ingeborg
Efel; *For O W Barth-Verlag Affairs:*
Stephan Schuhmacher
Subsidiary Company: Otto Wilhelm Barth-
Verlag KG (qv)
Subjects: General Fiction, History, Politics,
Belles Lettres, Documentary Works
1978: 114 titles *Founded:* 1957
Miscellaneous: Company is a Branch Office
of Scherz Verlag, Switzerland (qv)
ISBN Publisher's Prefix: 3-502

FEDERAL REPUBLIC OF GERMANY 155

Gertrud E **Scheuerer** Verlag, Miesbacher
Str 16a, D-8201 Raubling Tel: (08035) 2586
Man Dir: Gertrud Scheuerer; *Production:*
Otto Scheuerer
Subject: Art
Founded: 1975

Fachverlag **Schiele und Schön** GmbH*,
Markgrafenstr 11, D-1000 Berlin 61
Tel: (030) 2516029 Cable Add: schieleschön
Berlin
Man Dir: Peter Schön
Subjects: Medicine, Engineering, Electronics,
Industry, Reference, Mathematics, Hobbies;
Periodicals
Founded: 1946

Kurt **Schilling**, see Scientia Verlag

G **Schindele** Verlag GmbH, Rheinstr 5,
D-7512 Rheinstetten-Neu 3 Tel: (07242)
4786
Man Dir: Gerlinde Schindele
Subjects: Pedagogy, Psychology, Sociology,
Rehabilitation, Special Teaching, Social
Instruction
1978: 24 titles *1979:* 26 titles *Founded:* 1969

Schirmer/Mosel Verlag GmbH,
Nikolaistr 15, D-8000 Munich 40 Tel: (089)
393037/8
Man Dirs: L Schirmer, E Mosel; *Sales Dir:*
L Schirmer; *Publicity & Advertising Dir:*
Erik Mosel
Subjects: Photography, Art

Verlag Bert **Schlender***, Postfach 930,
D-3400 Göttingen Tel: (0551) 72659
Man Dirs: Bert Schlender, Detlev Pawlik
Associate Company: Edgar Wüpper,
Wilhelm Weber Str 37, D-3400 Göttingen
Subjects: General Fiction, Belles Lettres,
Poetry, Art, Low- & High-priced
Paperbacks
Bookshop: Versandbuchhandlung Bert
Schlender, Auf der Vessel 531, Postfach 930,
D-3400 Göttingen
Founded: 1973

Joachim **Schmid** und Co (Karl-May Verlag),
see Karl-May Verlag

Erich **Schmidt** Verlag, Genthiner Str 30G,
D-1000 Berlin 30 Tel: (030) 2611741 Telex:
183 671 esbve d Cable Add: ESVerlag
Berlin
Publicity: Mr Florian Gehrke
Branch Offs: Viktoriastr 44a, Postfach 7330,
D-4800 Bielefeld Tel: (0521) 66061 Telex:
938064 esvbi d Cable Add: esv Bielefeld;
Paosostr 7, D-8000 Munich 60
Subjects: History, How-to, Reference, High-
priced Paperbacks, Engineering, Economics,
Social Science, Law, University & Secondary
Textbooks, Educational Materials,
Philology, Languages and Linguistics,
Folklore
1978: 130 titles *1979:* 130 titles *Founded:*
1924
ISBN Publisher's Prefix: 3-503

Verlag Dr Otto **Schmidt** KG, Ulmenallee
96-98, D-5000 Cologne 51 Tel: (0221)
373021 Telex: 8883381
Man Dir: Dr H M Schmidt; *Editorial:*
Lopau Mechthild, Dr Katherine Knauth;
Sales Dir, Publicity & Advertising Dir:
Edmund Arand
Subjects: University Textbooks,
Jurisprudence, Tax Law
Bookshops: Buchhandlung Hermann Sack,
Bahnstr 61, D-4000 Düsseldorf 1; Merlostr
4, D-5000 Cologne 1; Buchhandlung
Hermann Sack, Mercatorstr 27, D-6000
Frankfurt am Main
1978: 36 titles *1979:* 35 titles *Founded:* 1905
ISBN Publisher's Prefix: 3-504

156 FEDERAL REPUBLIC OF GERMANY

Richard Carl **Schmidt** und Co*, Helmstedter Str 151, D-3300 Braunschweig Tel: (0531) 73189 Cable Add: Schmidtverlag
Man Dir: Ernst Raschka
Subjects: Engineering, Technical, Maps, Aviation, Transport
Founded: 1897
ISBN Publisher's Prefix: 3-87708

Verlag für polizeiliches Fachschrifttum Georg **Schmidt-Römhild**, Mengstr 16, Postfach 2051, D-2400 Lübeck 1 Tel: 75001
Publisher: Norbert Beleke
Associate Company: Max Schmidt-Römhild Verlag (qv)
Subjects: Psychology, Criminology, Reference books for police officials, lawyers, public authorities
1978: 25 titles *Founded:* 1892
ISBN Publisher's Prefix: 3-8016

Max **Schmidt-Römhild**, Verlag, Mengstr 16, Postfach 2051, D-2400 Lübeck 1 Tel: 75001
Publisher: Norbert Beleke
Associate Company: Verlag für polizeiliches Fachschrifttum Georg Schmidt-Römhild (qv)
Subjects: History, Medicine, General & Social Science; Reference books in criminology, forensic medicine and for lawyers, public authorities and medical and chemical laboratories
1978: 30 titles *Founded:* 1579
ISBN Publisher's Prefix: 3-7950

Dr Roland **Schmiedel**, see Deutscher Apotheker-Verlag

Die **Schmiere** — Rudolf Rolfs*, Karmeliterkloster, D-6000 Frankfurt am Main Tel: (0611) 28066, 06074/90979
Subjects: Works of Rudolf Rolfs, Author and Manager of unsubsidised satirical Theatre Die Schmiere

Wilhelm **Schmitz** Verlag, Kattenbachstr 5, D-6300 Lahn-Wissmar Tel: (06406) 2324
Dir: S Schmitz
Subjects: Art, Languages, German Studies, Slav Studies, East European Studies, Folklore
1978-79: 24 titles *Founded:* 1847

Galerie **Schmücking** Verlag, Lessingplatz 12, D-3300 Braunschweig Tel: (0531) 44960
Branch Offs: D-2286 Archsum/Sylt, Bobtäärp, Federal Republic of Germany; Galerie Schmücking, Sattelgasse 2, CH-4000 Basel, Switzerland
Subject: Art

Franz **Schneekluth** Verlag, Postfach 466, D-8000 Munich 22 (Located at: Widenmayer Str 34) Tel: (089) 221391 Telex: 529070
Owned by: Ulrich Staudinger; *Editorial:* Dr Michael Schmidt; *Sales and Publicity:* Alf Jungermann; *Rights & Permissions:* Ellen Reuter, Dr Michael Schmidt; *Public Relations:* Sybille Maier
Subject: General Fiction
1980: 56 titles *Founded:* 1949
ISBN Publisher's Prefix: 3-7951

Franz **Schneider** Verlag GmbH und Co KG, Frankfurter Ring 150, D-8000 Munich 46 Tel: (089) 381911 Telex: 05215804
Publisher: Franz Schneider; *Editorial:* Gisela Schneider, Michael Kohlhammer; *Sales:* Kurt Gerber; *Production:* Josef Loher; *Publicity:* Dr Schäfer; *Foreign Rights:* Gisela Essig
Subject: Juveniles
1978: 135 titles *1980:* 600 titles *Founded:* 1913
ISBN Publisher's Prefix: 3-505

Verlag Lambert **Schneider** GmbH, Hausackerweg 15, Postfach 105802, D-6900 Heidelberg 1 Tel: (06221) 21354
Publisher: Lothar Stiehm

Associate Company: Lothar Stiehm Verlag (qv)
Subjects: Belles Lettres, Poetry, Biography, Literature, Humanities, History, Music, Art, Judaica, Philosophy, Reference, Religion, University & Secondary Textbooks
1979: 30 titles *Founded:* 1925
ISBN Publisher's Prefix: 3-7953

Verlag **Schnell und Steiner** GmbH und Co, Paganinistr 92, D-8000 Munich 60 Tel: (089) 8112015/8112016 Cable Add: Schnellsteiner München
Man Dir, Rights and Permissions: Karl A Stich; *Editorial:* Dr H Schnell, Dr P Mai; *Sales:* N Dinkel; *Production:* J A Fink, N Dinkel
Orders to: Schnell und Steiner, Postfach 112, D-8000 Munich 65
Branch Off: Schnell und Steiner, CH-8260 Stein am Rhein, Switzerland
Subjects: Biography, History, History of Art, Art Guides, Philosophy, Religion, Juveniles, High-priced Paperbacks, University and Secondary Textbooks, Travel Literature
Bookshop: Pötzlstr 2, Postfach 1109, D-8595 Waldsassen
1978: 80 titles *Founded:* 1934
ISBN Publisher's Prefix: 3-7954

Verlag Die **Schönen Bücher** Dr Wolf Strache KG*, Friedhofstr 11, Postfach 1124, D-7000 Stuttgart Tel: (0711) 297116 Cable Add: Schönbücher
Subjects: Arts, Mass Media, Education
ISBN Publisher's Prefix: 3-7956

Ferdinand **Schöningh** Verlag, Jühenplatz am Rathaus, Postfach 2540, D-4790 Paderborn Tel: (05251) 21322 Cable Add: Schönbuch Paderborn
Subjects: Educational Publishers for Schools and Colleges, Earth Sciences, History, Literary Criticism, Mathematics, Education, Philosophy, Physics, Politics, Psychology, Law, Religion, Social Science, Linguistics, Languages, Paperbacks; UTB Library of mini-paperbacks
1979: 184 titles
ISBN Publisher's Prefix: 3-506

B **Schott's** Söhne, Musikverlag*, Weihergarten, Postfach 3640, D-6500 Mainz 1 Tel: (06131) 10741 Cable Add: Scotson Mainz Telex: 4187821 scot d
Man Dirs: Ludolf Frhr von Canstein, Günther Schneider-Schott, Dr Peter Hanser-Strecker; *Sales & Export Dir:* Günther Schneider-Schott; *Editorial:* Friedrich Zehn, Friedrich Wanek; *Sales:* Hellmut Fischer; *Production, Publicity:* Dr Hanser-Strecker; *Rights & Permissions:* Heinz Wolf, Erhard Keller
Orders to: Carl-Zeiss Str 1, PO Box 3640, D-6500 Mainz-Hechtsheim Tel: (06131) 59035
Associate Companies: Wega Verlag GmbH, Mainz; Ars-Viva-Verlag GmbH, Mainz; Music Factory GmbH, Mainz; MGS Zimmerhansl, Munich; Schott & Co Ltd, 48 Great Marlborough St, London W1
Branch Offs: Schott Music Corp, New York, USA; Schott Japan Co Ltd, Tokyo, Japan
Subjects: Music and Music Reference, High-priced Paperbacks, Journals, University, Secondary & Primary Textbooks, Educational Materials
1978: 10 books, 160 sheet music *Founded:* 1770
ISBN Publisher's Prefix: 3-7957

Verlag J F **Schreiber** GmbH, Postfach 285, D-7300 Esslingen (Located at: Liebigstr 1-11, D-7301 Deizisau) Tel: (07153) 22011/3 Telex: 7266880 jfs d
Man Dirs: Gerhard Schreiber; *Sales:* H K Vahlbruch *Rights & Permissions:* Jutta Hinkelbein
Associate Company: Junior International (qv)
Branch Offs: Möhlstr 34, D-8000 Munich 80
Subjects: Juveniles, Educational Materials, Textbooks, Biology, Nonfiction
Founded: 1831
ISBN Publisher's Prefix: 3-480

Verlag und **Schriftenmission** der Ev Ges für Deutschland GmbH, see Evangelischer Gesellschaft

Schriftenmissions-Verlag*, Goethestr 79-81, Postfach 548, D-4390 Gladbeck Tel: (02143) 22654
Dir: Hans Steinacker; *Sales Manager:* Hermann Conrad; *Rights & Permissions:* Liesel Rennscheidt
Subjects: Periodicals, Religion
ISBN Publisher's Prefix: 3-7958

Hermann **Schroedel** Verlag KG, Hildesheimerstr 202 and Zeisstr 10, Postfach 810620, D-3000 Hanover 81 Tel: (0511) 83881; *(Despatch Dept)* (05066) 2081 Telex: 923527 HSV HA
Manager: Hermann von Schroedel; *Man Dirs:* Joachim Günther, Dr Ilse Ebeler, H A Koeppel; *Sales, Publicity:* Hans Freiwald; *Production:* Peter Brück; *Advertising:* Rudolf Wegner; *Rights & Permissions:* Gudrun Ruiner
Associate Company: Hermann Schroedel Verlag AG, Switzerland (qv)
Subsidiary Company: Hermann Schaffstein Verlag (qv)
Branch Offs: Lützowstr 105-106, D-1000 Berlin 30; Am Kavalleriesand 47, Postfach 1026, D-6100 Darmstadt; Marsstr 4, D-8000 Munich 2
Subjects: University, Secondary & Primary Textbooks; Art, Religion, Languages, Social Sciences, Pure Science, Philosophy, Psychology, Pedagogy, Technical Instruction, Sport
1979: 350 titles *Founded:* 1792
ISBN Publisher's Prefix: 3-507

Kurt **Schroeder** Verlag, Am weissen Stein 48, D-5653 Leichlingen 1 Tel: (02175) 3355
Man Dir: Hannsgeorg Schroeder
Subject: Travel Guides to foreign countries world-wide; Plant Guides
1979: 2 titles *1980:* 3 titles *Founded:* 1919
ISBN Publisher's Prefix: 3-87722

Marion von **Schroeder** Verlag GmbH, Postfach 9229, D-4000 Düsseldorf (Located at: Grupellostr 28) Tel: (0211) 360516 Telex: 8587327
Publisher: Erwin Barth von Wehrenalp; *Sales Manager:* Herbert Borgartz; *Publicity Manager:* Michael Tochtermann
Subjects: Belles Lettres, Fiction, Foreign Literature, Biography, Fantastica
Founded: 1935
Miscellaneous: Firm is part of Econ Verlagsgruppe (qv)
ISBN Publisher's Prefix: 3-547

Anton **Schroll** und Co GmbH, Boosstr 15, D-8000 Munich 95 Tel: (089) 653590
Man Dirs: Friedrich Geyer, Dieter Reisser
Branch Off: Anton Schroll & Co, Austria (qv)
Subjects: Art, Travel
Founded: 1953

Verlag **Schule und Elternhaus***, Wilhelmshöher Allee 254-256, Postfach 410160, D-3500 Kassel Tel: (0561) 30076 Cable Add: Schule und Elternhaus Kassel-Wilhelmshöhe Telex: 0992450
Editorial: Claus Reineke
Associate Company: Druck- und Verlagshaus Thiele und Schwarz, Kassel (qv)
Subjects: Education, Vocabularies, Series by

Young Writers
ISBN Publisher's Prefix: 3-88056

Schuler Verlagsgesellschaft mbH, Gachenaustr 13, D-8036 Herrsching Tel: (08152) 1087 Telex: 526493
Man Dir, Rights & Permissions: Anton Bolza; *Production:* Herstellungsbüro Rudolf Gorbach
Subjects: Art, Juveniles, Reference
Founded: 1946
ISBN Publisher's Prefix: 3-7796

Verlagsgesellschaft **Schulfernsehen** mbH & Co KG, Breite Str 118-20, D-5000 Cologne 1
School Television Publishing Company
Associate Companies: Verlag Eugen Ulmer GmbH & Co (qv), Uni-Taschenbücher GmbH (qv)

Verlag **Schulte** und Gerth GmbH & Co KG, Postfach 1148, D-6334 Asslar Tel: (06441) 8461 Telex: 483794
Publisher: Klaus Gerth
Subsidiary Company: Turmberg Verlag (Musikverlag Klaus Gerth) (qv)
Subjects: Music, Religion, Biography, Juveniles

P N **Schulten**, see Numismatischer Verlag

Ludwig **Schultheis**, Verlag Haus und Heim*, Heilwigstr 64, D-2000 Hamburg 20
Tel: (040) 4602644
Subject: Art

Schulverlag Vieweg GmbH, Corneliussstr 9-11, D-4000 Düsseldorf Tel: (0211) 370266
Dir: Benno Hasselsweiler
Parent Company: Verlagsgruppe Bertelsmann GmbH (qv for associate companies)
Subjects: Instructional Works in German Language, Evangelical Religion, Mathematics, Natural Sciences

Verlag R S **Schulz***, Berger Str 8-10, Seehang 4, D-8136 Percha-Kempfenhausen Tel: (08151) 13041 Telex: 0526427
Publisher: Rolf Simon Schulz
Subjects: Architecture, Fiction, Public Health, Law, Nonfiction, Social Science, Veterinary Science; Periodicals
ISBN Publisher's Prefix: 3-7962

Carl Ed **Schünemann** KG, Zweite Schlachtpforte 7, Postfach 106067, D-2800 Bremen 1 Tel: (0421) 36351 Cable Add: Schünemanns Bremen
Man Dir: Klaus Kirchner; *Sales & Publicity Dir:* Herbert Kuhangel
Subjects: Belles Lettres, Art
Founded: 1810
ISBN Publisher's Prefix: 3-7961

Verlag K W **Schütz** KG, Am Osttor 12, Postfach 1180, D-4994 Preußisch Oldendorf Tel: (05742) 2073/4
Man Dir: Erwin Höke
Subjects: History, Juveniles
Bookshop: Versandbuchdienst Göttingen, Postfach 1180, D-4994 Preussisch Oldendorf
Founded: 1948
ISBN Publisher's Prefix: 3-87725

Schwabe und Co GmbH Verlag*, Postfach 758, D-7000 Stuttgart 1
Subjects: History, Medicine, Philosophy, Psychology
ISBN Publisher's Prefix: 3-7965

Schwabenverlag AG, Senefelderstr 12, Postfach 4280, D-7302 Ostfildern 1 Tel: (0711) 412908 Telex: 0723556
Man Dir: Paul Löcher
Subsidiary Company: Süddeutsche Verlagsgesellschaft mbH (qv)
Subjects: Popular Christian Devotional; Juvenile Fiction and Nonfiction, Swabian Regional Interest, Large Print Books
Bookshops: Schwabenverlag Buchhandlung, Bahnhofstr 21, D-7080 Aalen; Spitalstr 17, D-7030 Ellwangen
1978: 14 titles *Founded:* 1848
ISBN Publisher's Prefix: 3-7966

Verlag Haus **Schwalbach***, Bethelstr 35, D-6200 Wiesbaden Tel: (06121) 429288
Subjects: Textbooks, Education, Periodicals
ISBN Publisher's Prefix: 3-920427

Schwaneberger Verlag GmbH*, Muthmannstr 4, D-8000 Munich 45
Tel: 381931 Cable Add: Schwanverlag München Telex: 5215342 gerb d
Man Dir: Hans Hohenester; *Editorial:* Gerhard Webersinke; *Sales:* Gerhard Recht; *Publicity:* Horst Rogg; *Rights & Permissions:* Hans Hohenester
Associate Company: Carl Gerber Verlag GmbH
Subject: Philately
Founded: 1910
ISBN Publisher's Prefix: 3-87858

Edition **Schwann**, an imprint of C F Peters Musikverlag GmbH und Co KG (qv)

Pädagogischer Verlag **Schwann** GmbH, se Pädagogischer

Verlag Otto **Schwartz** und Co, Annastr 7, D-3400 Göttingen Tel: (0551) 31051/2
Man Dir: Dr Herbert Weisser, Konrad Weisser
Subjects: Social Science, University Textbooks, Educational Materials
1978: 62 titles *1979:* 66 titles *Founded:* 1871
Bookshop: Fachbuchhandlung Otto Schwartz & Co, Annastr 7, D-3400 Göttingen
ISBN Publisher's Prefix: 3-509

Verlag **Schwarz** GmbH, Ooser Luisenstr 23, D-7570 Baden-Baden Tel: (07223) 52936
Man Dir: Elke Schwarz-Fritz; *Editorial:* Dieter Schwarz
Subjects: Belles Lettres, Poetry
Founded: 1980 (as GmbH)
ISBN Publisher's Prefix: 3-15859

Schwarz Bildbücher, an imprint of Verlag Wolfgang Zimmer (qv)

Dr Wolfgang **Schwarze** Verlag, Heckinghauser Str 65-67, Postfach 202015, D-5600 Wuppertal 2 Tel: (0202) 622005/6
Man Dir, Rights & Permissions: Dr Wolfgang Schwarze; *Sales, Office Chief:* Ursula Rumker-Schulze
Subsidiary Company: Kunst und Wohnen Verlag GmbH
Subjects: Art books on Antiquities, Illustrated books on the Home and Interior Architecture, Facsimile Engravings
Founded: 1968
ISBN Publisher's Prefix: 3-87741

Verlag der Sankt-Johannis-Druckerei G **Schweickhardt**, see Sankt-Johannis

J **Schweitzer** Verlag, Genthiner Str 13, D-1000 Berlin 30 Tel: (030) 2611341 Cable Add: Wissenschaft Berlin Telex: 0184027
Man Dirs: Dr Kurt-Georg Cram, Dr Arthur Sellier
Branch Off: Geibelstr 8/0, D-8000 Munich 80
Subjects: Jurisprudence, Legal Information

E **Schweizerbart'sche Verlagsbuchhandlung**, Johannesstr 3A, D-7000 Stuttgart 1 Tel: (0711) 623541/3
Man Dirs: Dr Erhard Naegele (Production), Klaus Obermiller (Sales)
Associate Company: Gebrüder Borntraeger Verlagsbuchhandlung (qv)
Subjects: Geology, Palaeontology, Mineralogy, Limnology, Botany, Fishery, Hydrobiology, Zoology, Anthropology; Periodicals (29 scientific journals)
Founded: 1826
ISBN Publisher's Prefix: 3-510

H G **Schwieger**, see P R Verlag

Verlag Junge Gemeinde E **Schwinghammer** KG, Fangelsbachstr 11, Postfach 979, D-7000 Stuttgart 1 Tel: (0711) 643015/16
Cable Add: Jungegemeindeverlag
Dir: Siegfried Krumrey
Subjects: Religion, Juveniles, Educational Materials, Periodicals
1980: 7 titles *Founded:* 1928
ISBN Publisher's Prefix: 3-7797

Scientia Verlag und Antiquariat Kurt Schilling*, Adlerstr 65, Postfach 1660, D-7080 Aalen 1 Tel: (07361) 41700 Cable Add: Scientia Aalenwuertt
Man Dir: Kurt Schilling; *Other Offices:* Günter Schilling
Subjects: Reprints in History, Education, Philosophy, Law, Social Science, Economics
Founded: 1953
ISBN Publisher's Prefix: 3-511

Scriptor Verlag, Adelheidstr 2, Postfach 1220, D-6240 Königstein/TS Tel: (06174) 3026
Publisher: Dietrich Pinkerneil; *Editorial:* Dr Beate Pinkerneil; *Sales:* Rudolf Klein; *Publicity:* J C Schmidt-Braul; *Rights & Permissions:* Hildegard Willhöft
Associate Companies: Athenäum Verlag GmbH (qv); Verlag Anton Hain GmbH (qv); Peter Hanstein Verlag GmbH (qv)
Subjects: Linguistics, Communications, Literature, Sociology, Education, Reprints
1978: 64 titles *Founded:* 1973
ISBN Publisher's Prefix: 3-589

E A **Seemann** Verlag, Nassestr 14, D-5000 Cologne 41 Tel: (0221) 461915
Man Dir: Elert A Seemann
Subjects: Artbooks and Colour Reproductions, 43-volume Thieme-Becker Artistlexicon
Founded: 1858

Seewald Verlag GmbH & Co, Obere Weinsteige 44, Postfach 6, D-7000 Stuttgart 70 Tel: (0711) 765085 Telex: 7255361
Man Dirs: Dr Heinrich Seewald, Sixt A Seewald; *Sales, Publicity:* York Seewald; *Rights & Permissions:* Heide Radkowitz
Subjects: History, Politics, Economics, Social Science, High-priced Paperbacks, Books on Wine, Biographies and Memoirs, Education, Philosophy
1978: 30 titles *1979:* 35 titles *Founded:* 1956
ISBN Publisher's Prefix: 3-512

Sellier Verlag GmbH, Bahnhofstr 14, D-8050 Freising Tel: (08161) 4046147 Telex: (05) 26511
Man Dir: Kurt Sellier; *Editorial:* Johanna Vogel; *Sales Dir:* Friedrich Otto
Subsidiary Company: Sellier Verlag GmbH, Erfurter Str 4, D-8051 Eching
Subjects: Juveniles, Secondary & Primary Textbooks, Educational Materials
Founded: 1702
ISBN Publisher's Prefix: 3-87137

Siebdruck Süd GmbH, Druck und Verlagshaus*, Hindenburgstr 30, D-7250 Leonberg-Eltringen Tel: (07152) 48053154
General Manager: Rolf Marxen and Lothar Mittelbach
Subjects: Art Calendars, Original Graphics, Art Books by Peter K Schaav and Elke Sommer
Founded: 1973

Siebert Verlag GmbH, see Siebert und Engelbert Dessart Verlag GmbH

Siebert und Engelbert Dessart Verlag GmbH*, Wildstr 7, Postfach 1240, D-8202 Bad Aibling Tel: (08061) 4045 Telex: 525957
Subjects: Children's Books, Puzzles and

158 FEDERAL REPUBLIC OF GERMANY

Games
Founded: 1967
ISBN Publisher's Prefixes: 3-8089 (Siebert), 3-920215 (Dessart)

Siemens AG — ZVW 5 Verlag, Postfach 3240, D-8520 Erlangen Tel: (09131) 76800 Cable Add: Siemens Telex: 62921-226
Subject: Electronics
1978: 47 titles *1979:* 48 titles *Founded:* 1963
ISBN Publisher's Prefix: 3-8009

Signal-Verlag Hans Frevert, Balger Hauptstr 8, Postfach 813, D-7570 Baden-Baden Tel: (07221) 61817 Cable Add: Signal-Verlag Baden-Baden
Publisher: Hans-Jürgen Frevert
Subjects: Juveniles, Reference, Encyclopaedias, Dictionaries, Politics
ISBN Publisher's Prefix: 3-7971

S **Simmat**, Twiskenweg 35, D-2900 Oldenburg im Oldenburg Cable Add: Oldenburg i. O., Twiskenweg 35
Publisher: Sigfried Simmat
Subjects: Philosophy, Politics, Scientific Theory

Verlag Ludwig **Simon**, Mozartstr 15, Postfach 247, D-8023 Munich-Pullach Tel: (089) 7930332
Subject: Illustrated Works
ISBN Publisher's Prefix: 3-7972

Skypress International, D-1000 Berlin 41, Grillparzerstr 10-11 Tel: (030) 3238089 Telex: 185275 SCA D

Slavika, see Jal-Verlag

Societäts-Verlag, Frankenallee 71-81, Postfach 2929, D-6000 Frankfurt am Main 1 Tel: (0611) 75011 Cable Add: Zeitung Frankfurtmain Telex: 0411655
Publisher: Marianne Menzel; *Sales Manager:* Jörg Emich
Imprints: Verlag Frankfurter Bücher, Verlag Heinrich Scheffler, Verlag Osterrieth
Subjects: History, Business, Non-fiction, Literature, Art, Economics
Founded: 1921
ISBN Publisher's Prefix: 3-7973

Sonnenweg-Verlag Schäfer und Brandt, Bahnhofstr 4, Postfach 48, D-7442 Neuffen-Württemberg Tel: (07025) 2230/4128
Publisher: Friedrich Schäfer
Subject: Religion
1978: 15 titles
ISBN Publisher's Prefix: 3-7975

Spangenberg, an imprint of Verlag Heinrich Ellermann (qv)

Spectrum Verlag Stuttgart GmbH*, Friedrichstr 16-18, Postfach 1940, D-7012 Fellbach 4 Tel: (0711) 513004 Cable Add: Spectrumverlag Telex: 07254675
Man Dir: Karl O Tritt; *Sales, Publicity, Advertising Dir, Rights & Permissions:* Ulrich Höfker
Subjects: How-to, Reference, Juveniles, Natural Science, Textbooks
Founded: 1963
ISBN Publisher's Prefix: 3-7976

Spee — Buchverlag GmbH, Fleischstr 61-65, Postfach 3040, D-5500 Trier Tel: (0651) 46171 Telex: 04-72735
Dir: Erika Schwarzenberg
Parent Company: Paulinus Druckerei GmbH (at above address)
Associate Company: Paulinus Verlag (qv)
Subjects: Pedagogy, History, Politics, Religion, Picture books
ISBN Publisher's Prefix: 3-87760

W **Spemann** Verlag, Pfizerstr 5-7, Postfach 640, D-7000 Stuttgart 1 Tel: (0711) 21911 Cable Add: Kosmosverlag Stuttgart Telex: 721669 kosm d
Dirs: Claus Keller, R Keller, E Nehmann
Parent Company: Franckh'sche Verlagshandlung W Keller & Co (qv)
Subjects: History, Culture, Art
1978: 25 titles *Founded:* 1873
ISBN Publisher's Prefix: 3-810305

Verlag Volker **Spiess**, Grossgörschenstr 6, Postfach 147, D-1000 Berlin 62 Tel: (030) 7813514
Publisher, Editorial: Volker Spiess; *Production:* Brigitte Mietz, Yvonne Goetz
Associate Company: Haude & Spener (qv)
Subjects: Library Science, Publishing, Literary Criticism, Mass Media, Education, Social Science, Linguistics, Languages
1980: 30 titles *Founded:* 1967
ISBN Publisher's Prefix: 3-920889

Adolf **Sponholtz** Verlag, Osterstr 19, Postfach 447, D-3250 Hameln 1 Tel: (05151) 200326 Cable Add: Dewezet Telex: 92859
Dir: Erich Schoeneberg
Associate Companies: Eder Verlag, Lorch Verlag (qv), Verlag C W Niemeyer (qv), Spohr Verlag
Orders to: Hamburger Kommissionsbuchhandlung GmbH, Libri-Haus, 2 Hamburg 36,
Subjects: General Fiction and Non-fiction, Juveniles, Literature, Animal stories, Hunting, Poetry
Founded: 1894
ISBN Publisher's Prefix: 3-87766

Verlag für **Sprachmethodik**, Kantering 51-55, D-5330 Königswinter am Rhein Tel: 22771
Man Dir: H Willi Wolter
Subjects: University, Secondary & Primary Textbooks, Educational Materials
Founded: 1953
ISBN Publisher's Prefix: 3-8018

Springer-Verlag Berlin-Heidelberg-New York, Neuenheimer Landstr 28-30, D-6900 Heidelberg Tel: (06221) 4871 Telex: 461723 (telefacs 06221 43982), and D-1000 Berlin 33, Heidelberger Platz 3 Tel: (030) 82071 Telex: 183319 (telefacs 030821 4091) Cable Add: Springerbuch
Managing Partners: Dr Heinz Götze, Dr Konrad Springer, Claus Michaletz; *Editorial Dir:* Karl Hauck; *Production Dir:* Heinz Sarkowski; *Sales Dir:* Gunther Holtz; *Advertising Dir:* Edgar Seidler
Parent Company: Springer Verwaltungs GmbH, Berlin
Associate Companies: Springer-Verlag New York – Heidelberg – Berlin, 175 Fifth Ave, New York, NY 10010, United States; Springer-Verlag KG, Vienna, Austria (qv); J F Bergmann, Federal Republic of Germany (qv); Eastern Book Service Inc, Tokyo
Branch Off: Heidelberger Pl 3, D-1000 Berlin 33; Neuenheimer Landstr 28-30, D-6900 Heidelberg 1; Mölkerbastei 5, A-1011 Vienna, Austria
Subjects: Scientific and Technical: especially Medicine, Psychology, Biology; Earth Sciences, Maths, Physics, Chemistry, Computers; Engineering, Economics, Philosophy, Law; Reference Books, Paperbacks, Technical Journals, Technical Journals in English (especially Medical)
Bookshops: Bookselling group comprises: Lange und Springer Antiquariat, Berlin; Lange und Springer Wissenschaftliche Buchhandlung, Berlin; Freihofer AG, Zürich, Switzerland; Minerva Wissenschaftliche Buchhandlung GmbH, Vienna, Austria
Founded: 1842
ISBN Publisher's Prefix: 3-540

L **Staackmann** Verlag KG, Leopoldstr 116, D-8000 Munich 40 Tel: (08027) 337 and (089) 342248
Man Dir: Dr Friedrich Vogel
Subjects: General Fiction, Historical Novels, Folk Stories, Illustrated Primers on Curiosities and Folklore Objects
1979: 8 titles *1980:* 8 titles *Founded:* 1869

Städte-Verlag, E v Wagner und J Mitterhuber, Daimlerstr 60, Postfach 501169, D-7000 Stuttgart-Bad Cannstatt (Printing works in Fellbach) Tel: (0711) 561496 Cable Add: staedteverlag
Shipping Add: Postfach 501169, D-7000 Stuttgart 50
Man Dir: J Mitterhuber; *Publicity Dir:* U H Moeller
Subject: Maps, District and Town plans (especially for touring and sightseeing); West German Town Directories
Annually 400 new titles
Founded: 1951

Stähle und Friedel Verlagsgesellschaft mbH und Co, Neue Weinsteige 36, Postfach 492, D-7000 Stuttgart 1 Tel: (0711) 604464/5 Cable Add: Stählefriedel
Man Dir: Willy Klahm
Subject: Travel
ISBN Publisher's Prefix: 3-8116

Verlag **Stahleisen** mbH, Breitestr 27, D-4000 Düsseldorf 1 Tel: (0211) 88941 Cable Add: Stahleisen Düsseldorf Telex: 8587086
Man Dir: Dietrich Schnell; *Sales Manager:* Günter Hecker
Associate Company: Giesserei-Verlag GmbH (Foundry Press) (qv)
Subjects: Scientific and Technical (title denotes 'Iron and Steel Publishing Co')
1978: 11 titles *1979:* 9 titles *Founded:* 1908
ISBN Publisher's Prefix: 3-514

Stalling Verlag GmbH, Druck und Verlagshaus*, Ammergaustr 72-78, Postfach 2580, D-2900 Oldenburg Tel: (0441) 34011 Cable Add: Stallingdruck Oldenburgoldb
Man Dir: Joachim Wisotzki; *Editorial:* Hans Jürgen Hansen, Christa Cordes, Rene Rilz; *Sales Dir:* Harry Sticklorat; *Rights & Permissions:* Barbara Zollickhofer
Editorial Offices: Boschstr 8, D-8031 Puchheim-Bahnhof
Subjects: General Nonfiction, Contemporary History, Art, Marine History, Humour, Juveniles
Founded: 1789
ISBN Publisher's Prefix: 3-7979

Stapp Verlag Wolfgang Stapp, Ehrenbergstr 29, D-1000 Berlin 33 Tel: (030) 8313445
Publishers: Wolfgang Stapp
Subjects: Illustrated Books, Books on Mark Brandenburg, Saxony and other areas of the German Democratic Republic, on Berlin and other Cities and Rural Areas, Monographs on Artists
ISBN Publisher's Prefix: 3-87776

Hanns-Joachim **Starczewski** Verlag/Künstlerhof-Galerie*, Kirchstr 15, Postfach 137, D-5410 Hohr-Grenzhausen Tel: (02624) 2052
Man Dir, Editorial: H-J Starczewski; *Sales:* Birgit Weyers
Subjects: Painting, Sculpture
Founded: 1964
ISBN Publisher's Prefix: 3-7981

Johannes **Stauda** Verlag*, Heinrich-Schütz-Allee 33, D-3500 Kassel Tel: 30013 Cable Add: Stauda Kassel Telex: 992376
Subjects: Theology, Religious Instruction, Wall Charts for Religious Instruction

Franz **Steiner** Verlag GmbH, Friedrichstr 24, Postfach 5529, D-6200 Wiesbaden Tel: (06121) 372011 Cable Add: Steinerverlag Wiesbaden
Man Dirs: Hans Rotta, Vincent Sieveking; *Production:* Gregor Hoppen; *Publicity:* Käte Schmidt

FEDERAL REPUBLIC OF GERMANY 159

Orders to: Birkenwaldstr 44, Postfach 347, D-7000 Stuttgart 1 Tel: (0711) 294482 Telex: 0723636 daz d
Associate Companies: Wissenschaftliche Verlagsgesellschaft mbH (qv); S Hirzel Verlag GmbH & Co (qv); Deutscher Apotheker-Verlag Dr Roland Schmiedel GmbH & Co (qv)
Subjects: Literary Criticism, Archaeology, Art, Music, History, Religion, Classical and Modern Philology, Oriental Studies, Ethnology, Philosophy, Geography, History of Medicine and Science, Sciences; Periodicals
1978: approx 200 titles *1979:* approx 200 titles *Founded:* 1949
ISBN Publisher's Prefix: 3-515

Literarischer Verlag **Steinhausen** GmbH, Neumarkterstr 18, D-8000 Munich 80 Tel: (089) 41730 Telex: 524631
Dir: Gerhard Beckmann
Parent Company: Verlagsgruppe Bertelsmann GmbH (qv for associate companies)
Subject: Contemporary International Literature
Founded: 1978

J F **Steinkopf** Verlag GmbH, Hermannstr 5, Postfach 849, D-7000 Stuttgart 1 Tel: (0711) 626303 Cable Add: Steinkopf Stuttgart
Man Dir: Ulrich Weitbrecht; *Sales:* Lieselotte Haering
Subjects: General Fiction & Nonfiction, Paperbacks, How-to, Religion, Social Science, Secondary & Primary Textbooks
1979: 15 titles *1980:* 25 titles *Founded:* 1792
ISBN Publisher's Prefix: 3-7984

Dr Dietrich **Steinkopff** Verlag, Saalbaustr 12, Postfach 111008, D-6100 Darmstadt 11 Tel: 26538/9 Cable Add: Steinkopff Telex: 419627 stvda d
Man Dir: Jürgen Steinkopff; *Sales Dir:* Luise Eckhardt; *Publicity, Rights & Permissions:* Jürgen Steinkopff; *Advertising Dir:* H Niedermeyer
Subsidiary Company: Uni-Taschenbücher GmbH (qv)
Subjects: Reference, Low- & High-priced Paperbacks, Medicine, Psychology, General & Social Science, University & Secondary Textbooks
1978: 50 titles *Founded:* 1948
ISBN Publisher's Prefix: 3-7985

Steintor Verlag, Rudolf Jüdes, Postfach 41, D-3167 Burgdorf (Located at: Markstr 36) Tel: (05136) 2110
Subject: Art
Bookshops: Gallerie Steintor Verlag, D-3167 Burgdorf; Gallerie Meiborssen, D-3451 Meiborssen
1978: 42 titles *Founded:* 1969

Stephanus Edition Verlags GmbH, Tüfinger Str 3-5, Postfach 1160, D-7772 Uhldingen 1 Tel: (07556) 6508
Dir: Hans-Martin Braun
Orders to: Stephanus Edition Verlags AG Seewis, Nationalstr 28, Postfach 721, D-8280 Kreuzlingen
Subjects: Religion, Periodicals
ISBN Publisher's Prefix: 3-921213

Carl **Stephenson** Verlag, Gutenbergstr 12, Postfach 291, D-2390 Flensburg Tel: (0461) 28041/7 Telex: 022710
Sales Manager: Klaus Uhse
Subjects: Popular and Erotic Literature, Belles Lettres

Stern-Verlag Janssen und Co, Friedrichstr 24-26, Postfach 7820, D-4000 Düsseldorf 1 Tel: (0211) 373033
Managing Partners: Horst and Klaus Janssen; *Production and Sales:* Oswald Sckaer
Bookshop: Friedrichstr 24-26, D-4000 Düsseldorf 1
Founded: 1900
Subjects: Philosophy, Philology (especially of English)
ISBN Publisher's Prefix: 3-87784

Sternberg-Verlag, see Verlag Ernst Franz

Steyler Verlag, Arnold-Janssen-Str 20-22, D-5205 St Augustin 1 Tel: (02241) 197304
Associate Company: Verlag Sankt Gabriel, Vienna, Austria (qv)
Subjects: Roman Catholic Theology, Novels, Juvenile, Meditations, Scientific Series, Hierarchicus Atlas and Bible

Lothar **Stiehm** Verlag GmbH, Hausackerweg 16, Postfach 105802, D-6900 Heidelberg 1 Tel: (06221) 21354
Publisher: Lothar Stiehm
Associate Company: Lambert Schneider Verlag GmbH (qv)
Subjects: Classical Philology, German Language & Literature, Bibliography, Literary Criticism
ISBN Publisher's Prefix: 3-7988

Stimme-Verlag GmbH, Mainz, see Arbeitsgemeinschaft sozialistischer und demokratischer Verleger und Buchhändler

Stollfuss Verlag Bonn GmbH & Co KG, Dechenstr 7-11, Postfach 2428, D-5300 Bonn 1 Tel: (0228) 631171-76 Cable Add: Stollfussverlag
Man Dir: Wolfgang Stollfuss; *Editorial:* Dr Joachim Lieser; *Sales:* Herbert Rolfsmeyer; *Production:* Werner Hartmann; *Publicity:* Ernst-Wolfgang Bucken
Subjects: Official Publications of German Finance Ministry, Reference Works, Fiscal Law, Administration, Economics, Investment, Taxes, Legal Studies etc.
1978: 25 titles *1979:* 25 titles
ISBN Publisher's Prefix: 3-08

Verlag für das **Studium** der Arbeiterbewegung, see VSA

Stürtz Verlag, Beethovenstr 5, D-8700 Würzburg Tel: (0931) 385235 Telex: 068798
Publisher: Rudolf Weiger; *Sales Manager:* Rosemarie Meisner
Subjects: Art, Wine, History of Travel, Guidebooks, Scenic photo books, Hobbies, Sports

Südbuch Vertriebsgesellschaft mbH, Mannheim, subsidiary of Bibliographisches Institut AG (qv)

Süddeutsche Verlagsgesellschaft Ulm, Sedelhofgasse 19-21, D-7900 Ulm Tel: (0731) 62447
Man Dir: Robert Abt
Parent Company: Schwabenverlag AG, German Federal Republic (qv)
Subjects: Christian Devotion and Meditation, Theology, Preparation for Sacraments, Juvenile, Religious, Liturgical, Pedagogy, Psychology, Social Problems, Current Affairs
1978: 14 titles *Founded:* 1898
ISBN Publisher's Prefix: 3-920921

Süddeutscher Verlag Buchverlag*, 43 Goethestrasse, Postfach 780, D-8000 Munich Tel: (089) 530561 Telex: 05/22405
Man Dir: Robert Schäfer; *Editorial:* Dr H-P Rasp; *Sales:* Volker Neumann; *Publicity:* Dr Rolf Cyriax; *Advertising:* Michael Schindler; *Rights & Permissions:* Gabriele Fentzke
Associate Companies: Paul List Verlag KG (qv); Sudwest Verlag GmbH & Co KG (qv)
Subjects: History, How-to, Music, Art, Fiction, Reference, Religion, Nonfiction
Founded: 1945
ISBN Publisher's Prefix: 3-7991

Südwest Verlag GmbH und Co KG, Goethestr 43, D-8000 Munich 2 Tel: (089) 530561 Telex: 05/22405
Man Dir: Robert Schäfer; *Editorial:* Dr Rolf Cyriax; *Sales:* Rose Heckenlaible; *Production:* Roger Seitz; *Publicity:* Ulrike Ramsauer; *Advertising:* Michael Schindler; *Rights & Permissions:* Gabriele Fentzke
Associate Companies: Paul List Verlag KG (qv); Süddeutscher Verlag Buchverlag (qv)
Subjects: History, How-to, Music, Art
1978: 38 titles *1979:* 40 titles *Founded:* 1950
ISBN Publisher's Prefix: 3-517

Suhrkamp Verlag KG, Lindenstr 29-35, Postfach 4229, D-6000 Frankfurt am Main Tel: (0611) 740231 Cable Add: Suhrkampverlag Telex: 413972
Publisher: Dr Siegfried Unseld; *Man Dir:* Dr Heribert Marré; *Sales:* Dr Gottfried Honnefelder; *Publicity:* Claus Carlé; *Rights & Permissions:* Helene Ritzerfeld
Associate Company: Insel Verlag (qv)
Imprints: Suhrkamp Taschenbuchverlag, Suhrkamp Verlag Wissenschaft
Subjects: General Fiction, Belles Lettres, Poetry, Biography, Philosophy, German-Jewish Writing in general,, General Science, High- & Low-priced Paperbacks, Juveniles, Education, Psychology
Founded: 1950
ISBN Publisher's Prefix: 3-518

Symposion-Verlag GmbH, Neckarstr 86, Postfach 33, D-7300 Esslingen/N Tel: (0711) 311141 Cable Add: Symposion, Esslingen
General Manager: H A Siegler
Associate Company: ER-Verlags GmbH, Postfach 8, D-7300 Esslingen N Tel: (0711) 317070/79 (Men's Magazine Publisher)
Subjects: Motor Sports, Equestrian Interest, International Model Railways Guide; Periodicals
Founded: 1964 in Stuttgart
ISBN Publisher's Prefix: 3-920877

Syndikat Autoren- und Verlagsgesellschaft, see Autoren- und Verlagsgesellschaft

T B L (Tübinger Beiträge zur Linguistik) Verlag, see Gunter Narr Verlag

T R-Verlagsunion GmbH*, Thierschstr 11, Postfach 5, D-8000 Munich 26
Parent Company: K G Saur Verlag KG (qv)
ISBN Publisher's Prefix: 3-8058

Taylorix Fachverlag Stiegler und Co, Rotebühlstr 72, Postfach 829, D-7000 Stuttgart 1 Tel: (0711) 611773 Telex: 0723810
Dir: Dr Werner Kresse; *Sales Managers:* Dip-Volkswirt Walter Alt, Dieter Salat
Subjects: Economics, Business, Law
ISBN Publisher's Prefix: 3-7992

Technik Tabellen Verlag Fikentscher und Co, Eschollbrücker Str 39, Postfach 4135, D-6100 Darmstadt Tel: (06151) 61025 Cable Add: Fikentscher Telex: 419460
Publisher: Christoph Kässner; *Editorial:* Dr Thomas Krist
Subjects: Civil & Mechanical Engineering, Textbooks
ISBN Publisher's Prefix: 3-87807

Telex-Verlag Jaeger Waldmann, Holzhofallee 38, Postfach 111060, D-6100 Darmstadt 11 Tel: (06151) 84036 Cable Add: Telexverlag Telex: (Home) 419389 tlx d; (Foreign) 419253 telex d
Man Dir: Heinz Waldmann; *Sales Dir:* Wolfgang Lich; *Advertising Dir:* Ludwig Nicolay
Subjects: International Telex Directories
Founded: 1953
ISBN Publisher's Prefix: 3-87810

160 FEDERAL REPUBLIC OF GERMANY

Alf **Teloeken** Verlag KG, see Alba Publikation

Telos series of Paperbacks. This is a series of Bible-based evangelical paperbacks (including works for children), each contributed by one of the following publishers:
Blaukreuz-Verlag Wuppertal (qv), Brendow-Verlag (qv), Verlag der Evangelischer Gesellschaft (qv), Verlag der Francke-Buchhandlung (qv), Hänssler-Verlag (qv), Verlag der Liebenzeller Mission (qv), Verlag der Sankt-Johannis-Druckerei G Schweickhardt (all in Federal Republic of Germany); Verlag der Schweizerischen Schallplattenmission (Swiss gramophone record mission), Evangelischer Schriften-Verlag Schwengeler (qv), Trachsel-Verlag (all in Switzerland)

Ernst **Tessloff** Verlag*, Bernadottestr 209, D-2000 Hamburg 52 Tel: (040) 8804753, 8801517 Cable Add: Tessloff Hamburg Telex: 0215167
Sales: Moika Leicher, Ursula Seike
Miscellaneous: Associate Company: Neuer Tessloff Verlag (same address)

B G **Teubner** GmbH, Industriestr 15, Postfach 801069, D-7000 Stuttgart 80 Tel: (0711) 733076
Man Dir: Heinrich Krämer; *Sales, Publicity & Advertising Dir:* Walter Hirtz; *Rights & Permissions:* Sophie Penner
Subjects: History, Classical Philology, Reference, High-priced Paperbacks, Mathematics, Physics, Biology, Geography, Engineering, General & Social Science, Secondary & University Textbooks
1979: 80 titles *Founded:* 1811
ISBN Publisher's Prefix: 3-519

Edition **Text und Kritik** GmbH, Levelingstr 6a, Postfach 800529, D-8000 Munich 80 Tel: (089) 432929
Man Dir: Dr Berndt Oesterhelt
Subjects: Contemporary Literature and Criticism, Reference Works, Musical Studies
ISBN Publisher's Prefixes: 3-921402, 3-88377

Konrad **Theiss** Verlag GmbH, Villastr 11, Postfach 730, D-7000 Stuttgart 1 Tel: (0711) 432981 Cable Add: Theissverlag Stuttgart
Dir: Hans Schleuning; *Publicity, Sales:* Bernhard Driehaus; *Production:* Rolf Biesterfeld
Subjects: History, Arts, Non-fiction
1978: 20 titles *1979:* 22 titles
ISBN Publisher's Prefix: 3-8062

Theologischer Verlag R Brockhaus, Postfach 110197, D-5600 Wuppertal 11 (Located at: Champagne 7, D-5657 Haan 2) Tel: (02104) 6311/12/13
Associate Company: R Brockhaus Verlag (qv)
Subjects: Christian Theological Studies and Reference Works, Judeo-Christian Encounter
ISBN Publisher's Prefix: 3-417

Thesen Verlag Vowinckel und Co, Kittlerstr 34, D-6100 Darmstadt Tel: (06151) 713326
Man Dir: Heinrich Schirmer, Dr Ilse Vowinckel
Subjects: Literary Criticism, Linguistics, Social Science, University Textbooks, Educational Materials, Book Review *Kritikon Litterarum*
1978: 6 titles *1979:* 6 titles *Founded:* 1970
ISBN Publisher's Prefix: 3-7677

Druck- und Verlagshaus **Thiele und Schwarz**, Wilhelmshöher Allee 254-256, Postfach 410160, D-3500 Kassel Tel: (0561) 30076 Cable Add: Thiele & Schwarz Kassel-Wilhelmshöhe Telex: 0992450
Proprietor: Rolf Schwarz; *Editorial:* Claus Reineke
Associate Company: Verlag Schule und Elternhaus, Kassel (qv)
Subjects: General Fiction, Juveniles, Reprints
ISBN Publisher's Prefix: 3-87816

Georg **Thieme** Verlag KG, Herdweg 63, Postfach 732, D-7000 Stuttgart 1 Tel: (0711) 2148/1 Cable Add: Thiemebuch Telex: 07/21942
Man Dirs: Dr G Hauff, Dr A Greuner; *Sales Manager, Publicity:* Joachim Hillig; *Rights & Permissions:* Achim Menge
Subjects: Medicine, Dentistry, Bio-Science, Chemistry, Pharmacy, Textbooks, Reference, Paperbacks
1978: 219 titles *1979:* 178 titles *Founded:* 1886
ISBN Publisher's Prefix: 3-13

Verlag Karl **Thiemig** AG, Pilgersheimerstr 38, Postfach 900740, D-8000 Munich 90 Tel: (089) 662493 Cable Add: Thiemigdruck
Man Dir: Peter Keskari; *Sales & Publicity Dir:* Werner Eyerich; *Advertising Dir:* Peter Schlaüss
Subjects: Art, Travel, Natural Science, Technical
1978: 28 titles *Founded:* 1950
ISBN Publisher's Prefix: 3-521

K **Thienemanns** Verlag, Blumenstr 36, D-7000 Stuttgart 1 Tel: 240641 Telex: 723933 thie d
Dirs: Hansjoerg Weitbrecht, Richard Weitbrecht, Gunter Ehni
Subjects: Juveniles, Children's Picture Books, Dietetics
1980: 30 titles *Founded:* 1849
ISBN Publisher's Prefix: 3-522

Jan **Thorbecke** Verlag KG*, Karlstr 10, Postfach 546, D-7480 Sigmaringen Tel: (07571) 3016 Cable Add: Thorbecke Telex: 732534
Dir, Rights & Permissions: Georg Bensch; *Editorial:* Erna Bensch; *Production, Publicity:* Ulrich Ulrichs; *Sales Dir:* Josef Müller
Subjects: Historical, Geographical, Cultural Accounts of various European Regions, especially in Germany and Switzerland; Art History, European History
1978: 52 titles *Founded:* 1946
ISBN Publisher's Prefix: 3-7995

Tips für Trips, see Friedemann von Engel Verlag

Titania-Verlag, Oberer Hoppenlauweg 26, Postfach 1352, D-7000 Stuttgart 1 Tel: (0711) 293551 Cable Add: Titaniaverlag Stuttgart
Publishers: Wolfgang Schroll, Gerdi Schroll
Subjects: General Fiction; Children's Story Books for all ages
ISBN Publisher's Prefix: 3-7996

S **Toeche-Mittler** Verlag*, Hindenburg Str 33, D-6100 Darmstadt Tel: (06151) 81551
Subjects: Nonfiction, Law, Sports, Economics
Miscellaneous: Firm was formerly Mittler & Sohn, Berlin
Founded: 1789
ISBN Publisher's Prefix: 3-87820

Tomus Verlag GmbH, Prinzenstr 7, D-8000 Munich 19 Tel: (089) 132001 Telex: 5215528
General Manager: Claus-Jürgen Frank; *Dir:* Klaus Britting; *Rights & Permissions:* Ursula Spörle
Associate Companies: Telelit Verlag AG
Branch Off: Dr Wernerstr 5, D-8031 Gröbenzell
Subjects: Nature, Science, Animals, Hobbies, Travel, Cookery; Exclusive Art Editions; Sale of Co-Publishing Rights
Founded: 1962
ISBN Publisher's Prefix: 3-920954

P J **Tonger** Musikverlag GmbH & Co, Auf dem Brand 3, D-5000 Cologne 50 Tel: (0221) 392998
Man Dir: P J Tonger; *Sales Dir:* Hans Paul Zimmer; *Publicity Dir:* Hildegard Schneider; *Advertising Dir:* Peter Tonger
Subsidiary Company: Carl Engels Musikverlag
Subjects: Music, Art
Founded: 1822

Touropa-Urlaubsberater*, Prinzregentenstr 18, Postfach 408, D-8000 Munich 22 Tel: (089) 21011 Cable Add: Touropa Telex: 22857
Subject: Travel

Tradis Verlag und Vertrieb GmbH*, Raderthalerstr 29-31, Postfach 520380, D-5000 Cologne 51 Tel: (0221) 383034 Cable Add: Tradisbuch Telex: 8883203
Man Dir: Klaus Kupfer
Subject: Low-priced Paperbacks
Founded: 1949; 1975 (merger with Distropa)
ISBN Publisher's Prefix: 3-87824

Transatlantik Verlags- und Vertriebsgesellschaft mbH, now known as Tradis Verlag & Vertrieb (qv)

Trautvetter und Fischer Nachf, Gladenbacher Weg 57, Postfach 546, D-3550 Marburg Tel: (06421) 23309
Owned by: Dr Wilhelm A Eckhardt
Subjects: Local History and Guidebooks; History of Hess and Marburg Districts and their peoples, Church Histories (Protestant), Lyrical Poetry
1978: 2 titles *1979:* 8 titles *Founded:* 1941
ISBN Publisher's Prefix: 3-87822

éditions **trèves***, Postfach 1401, D-5500 Trier 1 Tel: (0651) 78687
Man Dirs: Rainer Breuer, Uschi Dahm; *Chief Reader:* Bernhard Hoffmann
Branch Off: editione trèves Mainz, Postfach 1843, D-6500 Mainz
Subjects: Belles Lettres, Young Literature, Lyrical Poetry, Theatre, Art, Literary Periodicals
1978: 12 titles *Founded:* 1974 (as graphics publishers); in present form, 1976
Miscellaneous: Publishing company for a society for the promotion of artistic activities run by its own (largely young) authors from throughout Europe
ISBN Publisher's Prefix: 3-88081

Trikont Verlag GmbH, Kistlerstr 1, D-8000 Munich 90 Tel: (089) 6917821
Publisher, Rights & Permissions: Herbert Röttgen; *Editorial:* Achim Bergmann; *Production:* Michael Keller
Subjects: General Fiction, History, Public Health, Medicine, Politics, Nonfiction, Social Science, Economics, Biography
ISBN Publisher's Prefix: 3-920385

Editions **Trobisch** KG, Postfach 2048, D-7640 Kehl-am-Rhein 1 Tel: (07851) 4551
Man Dir: Volker Gscheidle
Subjects: Christian practice and devotions, sex and marriage counselling etc, in German, French and English
1978: 9 titles *1979:* 9 titles *Founded:* 1972
ISBN Publisher's Prefix: 3-87827

Tübinger Vereinigung für Volkskunde eV, Schloss, D-7400 Tübingen Tel: (07071) 292374
Man Dir: Karin Teufel; *Editorial, Production, Sales:* Prof H Bausinger, U Jeggle, M Scharfe, B F Warneken
Orders to: Chr Krämer, Postfach 1851,

D-7400 Tübingen 1
Subjects: Low- and High-priced Paperbacks, Reference (Humanities), History, Social Science, University Textbooks
1978: 3 titles *1979:* 3 titles *Founded:* 1963

tuduv Verlagsgesellschaft mbH, Gabelsbergstr 15, D-8000 Munich 2 Tel: (089) 2809095
Subjects: Political Texts, Textbooks, Series connected with Political Science, Economics, Sociology, Jurisprudence, Philology, Literary Criticism, Cultural Arts
1979: 60 titles

Turm-Verlag*, Hindenburgstr 3, Postfach 229, D-7120 Bietigheim Tel: (07142) 44446 Cable Add: Turm, Bietigheim
Associate Company: Lorber-Verlag (qv)
Subjects: Health, Religion
ISBN Publisher's Prefix: 3-7999

Turmberg-Verlag (Musikverlag Klaus Gerth), Emmeliusstr 31, Postfach 1148, D-6334 Asslar Tel: (06441) 8461 Telex: 483794
Parent Company: Verlag Schulte und Gerth (qv)
Subjects: Music

U P N-Volksverlag*, D-8531 Linden Tel: (09846) 397
Subjects: Underground Literature — newspapers, periodicals, comics; Picture-Books; Sub-Culture and Life-Reformation
Miscellaneous: The Publishing Company's workers live as a country commune

U T B, see Uni-Taschenbücher GmbH

Verlag Dr Alfons **Uhl***, Tannhäuser Str 33, D-7094 Unterschneidheim Tel: (07966) 486
Subjects: Architectural and Art History; Graphics and Book Illustration; Art Portfolios

Verlag **Ullstein** GmbH, PO Box 110303, D-1000 Berlin 11 (Located at: Lindenstr 76, D-1000 Berlin 61) Tel: (030) 25911 Cable Add: Ullsteinbuch berlin Telex: vlgul d 183723
Man Dir: W J Freyburg; *Editorial Dirs:* Hans F Erb, Wolfgang Richter; *Marketing and Sales Dir:* Viktor Niemann; *Publicity:* Wolfgang Mönninghoff
Subsidiary Companies: Propyläen Verlag (qv), Ullstein Taschenbuchverlag
Subjects: Belles Lettres, Poetry, Biography, History, How-to, Music, Art, Travel, Geography, Ethnology, Popular Science, Social Sciences, Low- & High-priced Paperbacks, Educational Materials, Fiction, Military, Politics
1978: 60 main titles, 300 paperbacks
Founded: 1877
ISBN Publisher's Prefix: 3-550

Verlag Eugen **Ulmer** GmbH & Co, Gerokstr 19, Postfach 1032, D-7000 Stuttgart 1 Tel: (0711) 246346 Telex: 721774
Man Dir: Roland Ulmer; *Deputy Dir:* Alexander Hunn; *Production:* Dieter Kleinschrot; *Reader:* Dr Steffen Volk; *Sales Dir:* Gerhard Rentschler; *Publicity Dir:* Siegfried Hauptfleisch
Associate Companies: Uni-Taschenbücher GmbH (qv), Verlagsgesellschaft Schulfernsehen mbH & Co KG (qv)
Subjects: How-to, Reference, General Science, University Textbooks, Agriculture, Horticulture, Veterinary Science, Gardening, Animals; Periodicals, Paperbacks
1978-79: 30 titles *Founded:* 1868
ISBN Publisher's Prefix: 3-8001

Umschau Verlag Breidenstein GmbH, Stuttgarter Str 18-24, D-6000 Frankfurt am Main 1 Tel: (0611) 26001 Cable Add: Umschau Frankfurtmain Telex: 0411964

Man Dir: Hans Jürgen Breidenstein; *Sales:* Peter Schumacher
Associate Companies: Brönner Verlag Breidenstein GmbH (qv), Brönnersdruckerei Breidenstein GmbH, Sigma Studio Klaus Schlotte GmbH, Dateam Vertriebsgesellschaft mbH & Co KG; all at Stuttgarter Str 18-24, D-6000 Frankfurt am Main 1; also Andres Verlag GmbH, Lenaustr 2, Hamburg (qv)
Subjects: Nonfiction; especially Photographic Travel Books, Art, General Science, Low- & High-priced Paperbacks, Periodicals
Founded: 1850
ISBN Publisher's Prefix: 3-524

Ungarischer Kultureller und Sozialer Fonds eV in der B R D*, Zweibrückenstr 2/IV, D-8000 Munich 2 Tel: (089) 294376
Hungarian Social and Cultural Foundation in the Federal Republic of Germany
Man Dir: András Piffkó; *Editorial:* János Röczey; *Rights & Permissions:* János Popovits
Parent Company: Zentralverband Ungarischer Organisationen in der B D R eV, at above address (Central Association of Hungarian Organisations in the Federal Republic of Germany)
Subjects: Works by Hungarian authors
Bookshops: Ungarischer Kultureller und Sozialer Fond in der BRD eV at above address
1978: 35 titles *1979:* 35 titles *Founded:* 1971

Uni-Taschenbücher (UTB) GmbH, Am Wallgraben 129, Postfach 801124, D-7000 Stuttgart 80 Tel: (0711) 734826
Dir: Volkmar Kalki
Orders to: Brockhaus Commission, Am Wallgraben 127-129, Postfach 800205, D-7000 Stuttgart 80
Subjects: Library Science, Biology, Chemistry, Electrical Engineering, Electronics, Humanities, History, Public Health, Business, Informatics, Data Processing, Engineering, Agriculture, Literary Criticism, Mathematics, Medicine, Education, Philosophy, Physics, Politics, Psychology, Religion, Social Science, Linguistics, Languages, Veterinary Science, Economics; all texts in paperback
Miscellaneous: The company represents a group of 17 publishers producing paperbacks of a general academic/technical/scientific nature

Union Verlag Stuttgart*, Alexanderstr 51, Postfach 326, D-7000 Stuttgart 1 Tel: (0711) 240996 Cable Add: Unionverlag
Man Dirs: Dr Heinz Winners, Ulrich Commerell
Parent Company: Otto Maier Verlag (qv)
Subject: Juveniles
Founded: 1890
ISBN Publisher's Prefix: 3-8002

Universitas Verlag*, Hubertusstr 4, D-8000 Munich Tel: (089) 177041
Man Dir: Dr Klaus Schweitzer
Subjects: General Fiction, Biography, History, Low-priced Paperbacks, Cookbooks, Juveniles, Nonfiction
Founded: 1922
Miscellaneous: Firm is a member of Verlagsgruppe Langen-Müller/Herbig (qv)
ISBN Publisher's Prefix: 3-8004

Verlag **Urachhaus** Johannes M Mayer GmbH und Co KG, Urachstr 41, Postfach 131053, D-7000 Stuttgart 1 Tel: (0711) 260589/265939
Dir: Johannes Mayer; *Reader:* Inge Thöns; *Publicity & Marketing:* Winfried Altmann
Orders to: Koch, Neff & Oetinger & Co, Verlagsauslieferung, Am Wallgraben 110, D-7000 Stuttgart 80

FEDERAL REPUBLIC OF GERMANY 161

Subjects: History, Literary Criticism, Philosophy, Religion, Anthroposophy, Occultism, Children's Books, Art Books, History of Art
1978: 27 titles *1979:* 18 titles *Founded:* 1924
ISBN Publisher's Prefix: 3-87838

Verlag **Urban und Schwarzenberg** (Medical Publishers), Pettenkoferstr 18, Postfach 202440, D-8000 Munich 2 Tel: (089) 530181 Cable Add: Urbanverlag Munich Telex: 0523864
Man Dir: Michael Urban; *Marketing Dir, Rights & Permissions:* Armin Jetter; *Sales:* Lieselotte Meyer; *Promotion:* Gerhard Leibssle
Associate Company: Urban & Schwarzenberg Inc, 7 East Redwood St, Baltimore, Md 21202, USA
Branch Offs: Frankgasse 4, Vienna, A-1096 Austria; Hardenbergstr 11, D-1000 Berlin 12, Federal Republic of Germany
Subjects: Medicine, Psychology, Pedagogics, University Textbooks; also Slides and Journals
Bookshops: Oscar Rothacker Buchhandlung, Pettenkoferstr 18, D-8000 Munich 2; Oscar Rothacker, Hardenbergstr 11, D-1000 Berlin 12; Oscar Rothacker, Universitätsstr 11, D-8400 Regensburg; Oscar Rothacker, Kerpenerstr 75, D-5000 Cologne 41
1978: 160 titles *1979:* 180 titles *Founded:* 1866
ISBN Publisher's Prefix: 3-541

V A P Verlag*, Rösslerstr 10, Postfach 5764, D-6200 Wiesbaden Tel: 06121/302323
Subject: Political Texts

V D E-Verlag GmbH, Bismarckstr 33, D-1000 Berlin 12 Tel: (030) 3413041 Telex: 0181683 vde d
Sales: Klaus Hitzschke
Orders to: D-6050 Offenbach, Merianstrasse 29
Miscellaneous: This is the publishing company of the Verband Deutscher Elektrotechniker (VDE — Association of German Electro-Technikers). Many specifications may be bought in English
Subjects: Electrical Engineering, Electronics, Technical Specifications
ISBN Publisher's Prefix: 3-8007

V D I-Verlag GmbH (Verlag des Vereins Deutscher Ingenieure), Graf-Recke-Str 84, Postfach 1139, D-4000 Düsseldorf 1 Tel: (0211) 62141 Cable Add: Ingenieurverlag Düsseldorf Telex: 08586525
Man Dir: J Larink; *Publishing Manager (books):* Klaus D Baldus; *Editorial:* Dr Gerhard Scheuch; *Rights & Permissions:* Marianne Diensthuber; *Sales:* Gunther Bicker; *Exports:* Inge Haury
Associate Company: Beuth Verlag GmbH (qv), D-1000 Berlin 30 and D-5000 Cologne 1
Subjects: Engineering, Chemistry, Technology, Scientific Reports, Reports of Proceedings, Series of VDI Guidelines, Paperbacks
1978: 43 titles *Founded:* 1923
Miscellaneous: V D I is German Engineers' Association Publishing Company
ISBN Publisher's Prefix: 3-18

V-Dia-Verlag GmbH*, Heinrich-Fuchs-Str 95-97, Postfach 105980, D-6900 Heidelberg Tel: (06221) 37041 Cable Add: Vaudia Heidelberg
Subjects: Science-Technology, Geography, Astronomy, Biology, Medicine, History, Economics
Founded: 1953

V F P (Verlag Frauenpolitik) GmbH, Hafenweg 2-4, D-4400 Munster Tel: (0251) 60363

Dir: Anne Mussenbrock; *Production:* Angelika Müller; *Publicity:* Petra Walter; *Rights & Permissions:* Erika Leuteritz
Subjects: History of Women's Movement, Historical Texts, Women in Fascism, Sexual and Social Topics, Belles Lettres
1978: 10 titles *1979:* 1 title *Founded:* 1976
ISBN Publisher's Prefix: 3-88175

V M B, see Verlag Marxistische Blätter

V S A (Verlag für das Studium der Arbeiterbewegung GmbH), Stresemannstr 384a, D-2000 Hamburg 50 Tel: (040) 8992561
Publishing House for the Study of the Workers' Movement
Manager: Gerd Siebecke; *Sales:* Bernhard Müller; *Rights & Permissions:* Brigitte Dudek
Orders to: VVA (Vereinigte Verlagsauslieferung GmbH), Gütersloh
Subjects: Political and Social Science, Political and Social Movements
ISBN Publisher's Prefix: 3-87975

V W K (Verlag für Wirtschafts-und-Kartographie Publikationen) Ryborsch GmbH*, Laubenstr 3, Postfach 2105, D-6053 Obertshausen 2 Tel: (06104) 7839
Dirs: Mrs H Ryborsch-Tschinkel, Reinhard Ryborsch
Subjects: Economics, Aviation, Geography, Travel, City and Road Maps, Aeronautical Charts and Maps
1978: 6 titles *1979:* 9 titles *Founded:* 1975
ISBN Publisher's Prefix: 3-920339

Franz **Vahlen** GmbH*, Wilhelmstr 9, D-8000 Munich 40 Tel: (089) 381891
Sales Dir: Günter Elze; *Publicity Dir:* Erhard Hoppe
Associate Companies: Verlag C H Beck (qv), Q Biederstein Verlag (qv)
Subjects: Law, Social Science, University Textbooks
Founded: 1870
ISBN Publisher's Prefix: 3-8006

Vandenhoeck und Ruprecht, Theaterstr 13, Postfach 77, D-3400 Göttingen Tel: (0551) 54031/3 Cable Add: Vandenhoeck
Dirs: Dr Arndt Ruprecht, Dr Dietrich Ruprecht; *Editorial:* Dr Winfried Hellmann; *Sales and Publicity:* Ursula Nahrgang
Subsidiary Companies: Druckerei Hubert & Co, Robert-Bosch-Breite 6, D-3400 Göttingen (Printers); Ehrenfried Klotz Verlag (qv)
Branch Off: Vandenhoeck & Ruprecht, Badener Str 69, CH-8026 Zürich, Switzerland
Subjects: University Textbooks, Research Monographs and Handbooks, Religion, Philology, History, Economics, Mathematics, Medical Psychology, Periodicals
Bookshop: Deuerlich'sche Buchhandlung, D-3400 Göttingen, Weender Str 33
1978: 240 titles *1979:* 260 titles *Founded:* 1735
ISBN Publisher's Prefix: 3-525

Velber Verlag GmbH*, Im Brande 15, D-3016 Seelze 6 Tel: (0511) 482091 Cable Add: Friedrich/Velber Telex: 0922923
Man Dir: Erhard Friedrich
Subjects: Juveniles, Games
Founded: 1972
ISBN Publisher's Prefix: 3-921187

Velhagen und Klasing, Lützowstr 105-106, D-1000 Berlin 30 Tel: (030) 2621071
Man Dir: Franz Cornelsen
Subsidiary Companies: Geographische Verlagsgesellschaft Velhagen & Klasing und Hermann Schroedel GmbH & Co KG (qv); Velhagen & Klasing und Schroedel Geographisch-Kartographische Anstalt GmbH, Düppelstr 21, D-4800 Bielefeld
Subjects: Cartography, Textbooks, Educational
Founded: 1835

Edition **Venceremos**, Verlag W G Reinheimer, Postfach 1212, D-6090 Rüsselsheim (Located at: Heinrichstr 15) Tel: (06142) 65280/42855
Man Dir, Sales, Production, Publicity: Wilhelm G Reinheimer; *Editorial, Rights & Permissions:* Heinz Mees
Subjects: German and International Folklore, Songs, Cabaret, Periodical *FOLKmagazin*
1978: 20 titles *1979:* 14 titles *Founded:* 1974
ISBN Publisher's Prefix: 3-88541

Klaus Dieter **Vervuert** Buchhandel und Verlag, Rheinstr 21, D-6000 Frankfurt am Main 1 Tel: (0611) 752256
Combined Bookshop and Publishing House
Subjects: Specialist in books about Latin America, Spain and Portugal
1979: 4 titles
ISBN Publisher's Prefix: 3-921600

Friedr **Vieweg** und Sohn Verlagsgesellschaft mbH, Faulbrunnenstr 13, Postfach 5829, D-6200 Wiesbaden 1 Tel: (06121) 5341 Telex: 4186928 vw v d
Orders to: VVA (Vereinigte Verlagsauslieferung), Postfach 7777, D-4830 Gütersloh 1
Man Dir: Dr Frank Lube; *Editorial:* Michael Langfeld; *Sales:* Heinz Detering; *Rights & Permissions:* Angelika Bolisega
Parent Company: Verlagsgruppe Bertelsmann GmbH (qv for associate companies)
Subsidiary Company: Deutscher Eichverlag, Büchnerstr 10, Postfach 3367, D-3300 Braunschweig
Subjects: Textbooks in Mathematics, Natural Sciences, Technology, Monographs, School Books, Teaching Programmes, Periodicals
1978: 125 titles *1979:* 75 titles *Founded:* 1786
ISBN Publisher's Prefix: 3-528

Schulverlag **Vieweg**, see Schulverlag

Curt R **Vincentz** Verlag, Schiffgraben 41-43, Postfach 6247, D-3000 Hanover 1
Tel: (0511) 1944944 Telex: 923846
Man Dir: Dr L Vincentz; *Sales:* Dr F Vincentz
Subjects: General Science, Commerce
1978: 13 titles *Founded:* 1893
ISBN Publisher's Prefix: 3-87870

Vogel-Verlag KG, Max-Planck-Str 7-9, Postfach 6740, D-8700 Würzburg 1
Tel: (0931) 41021 Cable Add: Vogelverlag Würzburg Telex: 068883
Man Dirs: Dr Kurt Eckernkamp, Wolfgang Lüdicke
Subjects: Agricultural, Automotive, Consulting, Electrical, Mechanical and Textile Engineering, Electronics, Metalworking, Management, Scientific and Technical Text Books, Foreign Language Publications (in 14 languages), Periodicals
1978: 220 titles, 25 technical journals
Founded: 1891
ISBN Publisher's Prefix: 3-8023

Emil **Vollmer** Verlag, see Vollmer/Löwit Verlagsgruppe

Vollmer/Löwit Verlagsgruppe, Gustav-Stresemann-Ring 12-16, Postfach 4060, D-6200 Wiesbaden Tel: (06121) 39331 Telex: 4186294
Dir: Sylvia Vollmer
Subjects: Art and Artists, Collectors' Books, Mythology, Natural History, Religions, History, Fiction, Belles Lettres, Juveniles, Popular Editions of Classics

Hartfrid **Voss** Verlag*, Lechner Str 27, Postfach 16, D-8026 Ebenhausen bei Munich Tel: (08178) 4857
Subjects: General Fiction, Music
ISBN Publisher's Prefix: 3-87878

Kurt **Vowinckel** Verlag, Assenbucherstrasse 28, 8131 Berg am See Tel: 08151, 51675
Dir: Dr Gert Sudholt
Subjects: Current Affairs, Politics
ISBN Publisher's Prefix: 3-87879

W R S — Verlag (Wirtschaft, Recht und Steuern), Irmgardstr 1, Postfach 711069, D-8000 Munich 71 Tel: 792077
Dirs: Dr Guenther Friedrich, Dr Manfred Jahrmarkt
Parent Company: Rudolf Haufe Verlag (qv)
Subjects: Economics, Law, Taxation

Karl **Wachholtz** Verlag, Gänsemarkt 1-3, Postfach 2769, D-2350 Neumünster
Tel: (04321) 46161 Cable Add: courier
Telex: 299618
Dir: Walter Kardel; *Sales & Publicity Manager:* Hans-Hermann Lipsius
Subjects: Humanities, History, Calendars, Arts, Reference, Encyclopaedias, Dictionaries, Literature, Music, Reprints, Linguistics, Languages, Periodicals
1978: 32 titles
ISBN Publisher's Prefix: 3-529

Verlag Klaus **Wagenbach**, Bamberger Str 6, Postfach 1409, D-1000 Berlin 30 Tel: (030) 2115060/69
Man Dir, Editorial: Dr Klaus Wagenbach; *Sales:* Galina Rave; *Production:* Gabriele Kronenberg; *Publicity, Rights & Permissions:* Barbara Herzbruch
Subjects: General Fiction, Belles Lettres, Poetry, Low- and High-priced Paperbacks, Political and Social Science, Periodical *Freibeuter*
Founded: 1964
ISBN Publisher's Prefix: 3-8031

Walter-Verlag GmbH, Erwinstr 58-60, D-7800 Freiburg-im-Breisgau Tel: (0761) 71050 Telex: 0772676
Dir: Burkhard Dähnert; *Sales:* Richard Urbahn; *Publicity:* Roland Wolfstädter
Parent Company: Walter Verlag AG, Switzerland (qv)
Subjects: Religion, Psychology, Travel Guides, Literature, Cultural History
Founded: 1924
ISBN Publisher's Prefix: 3-530

Ernst **Wasmuth** Verlagsbuchhandlung KG, Fürststr 133, Postfach 2728, D-7400 Tübingen Tel: (07071) 33658
Man Dir: Sibylle von Bockelberg; *Sales Dir:* Karl H Schattner; *Production:* Manfred Heinrich
Subjects: Architecture, Archaeology, History of Art, Applied Art
Bookshop: Wasmuth Buchhandlung & Antiquariat, D-1000 Berlin 12, Hardenbergstr 9A
Founded: 1872
ISBN Publisher's Prefix: 3-8030

Wehr und Wissen Verlagsgesellschaft mbH, Heilsbachstr 26, D-5300 Bonn 1 (Duisdorf)
Tel: (02221) 643066-68 Telex: 8869429 mvkb d
Man Dir: Manfred Sadlowski; *Sales Dir:* Joachim Latka; *Publicity Dir:* Heinz-Jürgen Witzke; *Advertising Dir:* Peter Konietschke; *Rights & Permissions:* J Latka
Subjects: History, How-to, High-priced Paperbacks, Military Manuals, Yearbooks

A **Weichert** Verlag, Tiestestr 14, D-3000 Hanover Tel: (0511) 813068 Cable Add: Buchweichert Telex: 0923872 awv
Man Dir: Alfred Trippo; *Sales:* Hans H Droste
Associate Company: Neuer Jugendschriften-

Verlag (qv)
Branch Off: Hans Feulner, Lindenallee 25, D-1000 Berlin 19
Subject: Juveniles (Story Books for all ages)
1978: 11 titles *1979:* 17 titles *Founded:* 1872
ISBN Publisher's Prefix: 3-483

Wolfgang **Weidlich** Verlag*, Savignystr 61, D-6000 Frankfurt am Main Tel: (0611) 746215
Publisher: Wolfgang H Weidlich; *Editorial:* Brigitte Weidlich; *Sales:* Doris Böhler; *Production:* Wilfred Sindt; *Publicity:* Ulrike Karmeier
Subjects: Architecture, General Fiction, History, Maps, Nonfiction
ISBN Publisher's Prefix: 3-8035

Verlag **Weinmann***, Beckerstr 7, D-1000 Berlin 41 Tel: (030) 8554895
Man Dir: Dr Weinmann
Subject: Sport, (especially the martial arts), Instruction books for all ages, Yoga
1978: 10 titles *Founded:* 1961
ISBN Publisher's Prefix: 3-87892

Weismann Verlag-Frauenbuchverlag GmbH*, Kreittmayrstr 26, D-8000 Munich 2 Tel: (089) 192970
Man Dir: Peter Weismann; *Editorial:* Frank Göhre, Antje Kunstmann
Orders to: AVS-Verlagsauslieferung Joachim Schäfer, Taunusstr 82, D-6237 Liederbach
Subsidiary Company: Frauenbuchverlag (qv)
Subjects: Literature and Nonfiction for young people; theatrical texts for Juveniles; Politics
Founded: 1970
ISBN Publisher's Prefix: 3-921040

Gebrüder **Weiss** Verlag, Hewaldstr 9, D-1000 Berlin 62 Tel: (030) 7817725
Owner: Richard Weiss
Subjects: General Fiction, Juveniles, Popular Science, Nonfiction, Paperbacks
Founded: 1945
ISBN Publisher's Prefix: 3-8036

Weitbrecht GmbH*, Blumenstr 36, D-7000 Stuttgart

Verlag **Welsermühl**, Kufsteiner Str 8, D-8000 Munich 80 Tel: (089) 982031 Cable Add: welsermuhldruck Telex: 5216349
Dir, Editorial, Rights & Permissions: Karl Prämendorfer; *Sales:* Friederike Weiss-Füreder; *Production:* Friedrich Spendou; *Publicity:* K Füreder
Orders to: Kufsteinerstr 8, D-8000 Munich 80
Subsidiary Company: Zweimühlen Verlag GmbH, Kufsteinerstr 8, Munich 80
Branch Off: Verlag 'Welsermühl' Fritsch & Dusl KG, Austria (qv)
Subjects: General Non-fiction, Travel, Illustrated Books, Current Events
1978: 18 titles *Founded:* 1928
ISBN Publisher's Prefix: 3-85339

Weltforum Verlags GmbH, Tintorettostr 1, D-8000 Munich 19
And Marienburgerstr 22, D-5000 Cologne 51
Dir: Sales, Rights & Permissions: Peter John von Freyend; *Editorial, Production:* Rena Hillebrand; *Publicity:* Karl Ludwig Ostermann
Subjects: Political, Economic and Technological aspects of the Developing Nations
1978: 13 titles *1979:* 9 titles
ISBN Publisher's Prefix: 3-8039

Weltkreis-Verlags-GmbH, Brüderweg 16, D-4600 Dortmund 1 Tel: (0231) 528581 Telex: 8227284 wkv el
Man Dir: H W v Oppenkowski; *Editorial:* Dr Rutger Booss; *Publicity & Advertising Dir:* Friedhelm Kuelpmann; *Rights & Permissions:* Helmuth Maidl
Orders to: (Federal Republic of Germany): Brücken Verlag, Postfach 1928, D-4000 Düsseldorf; (West Berlin): Zirk & Ellenrieder, Postfach 3147, D-1000 Berlin 30
Subjects: Belles Lettres, Poetry, Biography, How-to, Juveniles, Low-priced Paperbacks
1978: 21 titles *1979:* 29 titles *Founded:* 1958
Miscellaneous: Member of Arbeitsgemeinschaft sozialistischer und demokratischer Verleger und Buchhändler (qv for other members)
ISBN Publisher's Prefix: 3-88142

Karl **Wenschow** GmbH, Munich, see JRO – Verlagsgesellschaft, the subsidiary company which now handles all marketing and distribution

Werner Verlag GmbH, Berliner Allee 11a, D-4000 Düsseldorf 1 Tel: (0211) 320988 Cable Add: Wernerverlag Telex: 8587828
Man Dir: Klaus Werner; *Publicity Dir:* E Dickert
Subjects: University Textbooks, Reference, Engineering, Educational Materials, Law, Social Science, Economics
1978: 65 titles *Founded:* 1945
ISBN Publisher's Prefix: 3-8041

Westdeutscher Verlag GmbH, Faulbrunnenstr 13, Postfach 5829, D-6200 Wiesbaden Tel: (06121) 5341 Telex: 4186928 vwvd
Man Dir: Dr Frank Lube; *Editorial:* Manfred Müller; *Sales, Publicity:* Heinz Detering; *Rights & Permissions:* Angelika Bolisega
Orders to: VVA (Vereinigte Verlagsauslieferung), Postfach 7777, D-4830 Gütersloh 1
Parent Company: Verlagsgruppe Bertelsmann GmbH (qv for associate companies)
Branch Off: Reuschenberger Str 55, D-5090 Leverkusen 3
Subjects: History, Literature, Social Science, University Textbooks
1978: 55 titles *1979:* 30 titles *Founded:* 1947
ISBN Publisher's Prefix: 3-531

Georg **Westermann** Verlag, Druckerei & Kartographische Anstalt GmbH & Co, Georg-Westermann-Allee 66, D-3300 Brunswick Tel: (0531) 7081 Cable Add: Gewebuch Telex: 0952841
Man Dirs: Dr Jürgen Mackensen, Dirck Tebbenjohanns, Gerd Mackensen; *Marketing Dir:* Wolfgang Dick; *Exports:* Wolfgang Mann; *Publicity Dir:* Karl-Heinz Grothe; *Rights & Permissions:* Dr Carl-August Schröder
Subsidiary Companies: Lehrmittelanstalt Richard Herold, Bonn-Bad Godesberg; Lehrmittelhandlung Heinz Vogel, Wilhelmshaven and Bremen; Lehrmittelanstalt Köster, Munich
Subjects: History, Education, Paperbacks, University, Secondary & Primary Textbooks, Educational Materials, Periodicals
1978: 270 titles *Founded:* 1838
ISBN Publisher's Prefix: 3-14

Erich **Wewel** Verlag*, Anzinger Str 1, D-8000 Munich 80 Tel: (089) 403031 Telex: 522504
Sales: Erna Schmidt; *Publicity:* Siegbert Seitz
Parent Company: Manz Verlag (qv)
Subjects: Philosophy, Religion
ISBN Publisher's Prefix: 3-87904

Who's Who — Book & Publishing Company, Hauptstr 1, Postfach 1150, D-8031 Wörthsee/Steinebach Tel: (08153) 8033/8034
General Manager: Georg Otto
Subjects: Encyclopedias; Bibliographical, Arts, Literature, Medicine, Technology, Fashion, especially an international biographical Encyclopedia series
1978: 2 titles *1979:* 3 titles
ISBN Publisher's Prefix: 3-921220

Herbert **Wichmann** Verlag GmbH, Rheinstr 122, Postfach 210949, D-7500 Karlsruhe 21 Tel: (0721) 555955 Telex: 7825909
Man Dir: Dr Christof Müller-Wirth; *Sales, Publicity:* Winfried Ammon; *Production, Rights & Permissions:* Jochen Schmitt
Subjects: Geodesy, Photogrammetry, Land Registration, Cartography, Estate Evaluation
1978: 2 titles *Founded:* 1889
ISBN Publisher's Prefix: 3-87907

Rosa **Winkel** Verlags-und-Versand GmbH, Postfach 620304, D-1000 Berlin 62 (Located at: Bülowstr 17, D-1000 Berlin 30) Tel: (030) 2153742
Man Dirs: Egmont Fassbinder, Hans Huett
Subjects: Heterosexual-Homosexual 'Social Norms' Debate, Homosexual Emancipation, Gay Novels and Lyrics
1978: 3 titles *1979:* 8 titles *Founded:* 1975
ISBN Publisher's Prefix: 3-921495

Winkler-Verlag, Martiusstr 8, Postfach 26, D-8000 Munich 44 Tel: (089) 348074 Telex: 5215517
Man Dir: Dr Dieter Lutz; *Publicity:* Anita Donat
Parent Company: Artemis Verlag, see Artemis und Winkler
Subjects: Belles Lettres, Reference, General Science, University Textbooks, Reprints
Founded: 1945
ISBN Publisher's Prefix: 3-538

Carl **Winter** Universitätsverlag GmbH, Lutherstr 59, Postfach 106140, D-6900 Heidelberg 1 Tel: (06221) 49111 Telex: 0461660
Publisher: Dr Carl Winter; *Sales:* Ruth Wutke
Subject: University Books
1978: 75 titles *1979:* 85 titles
Founded: 1822
ISBN Publisher's Prefix: 3-533

Wirtschaft, Recht, Steuern, see WRS-Verlag

Verlag für **Wirtschafts-** und Kartographie-Publikationen, Ryborsch, see V W K

Verlag für **Wirtschaftsskripten**, Dipl-Kfm C Ölschläger GmbH, Amalienstr 81, D-8000 Munich 40 Tel: (089) 284942
Man Dirs: Claus Ölschläger, Christina Ölschläger
Associate Company: Verlag Ölschläger GmbH (qv)
Subjects: Economics, Business, Management, Law
1978: 35 titles *Founded:* 1974
ISBN Publisher's Prefix: 3-921636

Wirtschaftsverlag, Hubertusstr 4, D-8000 Munich 19 Tel: (089) 177041 Telex: 215045
Subjects: Business Economics, Work Study and Allied Subjects
Miscellaneous: Firm is a member of Verlagsgruppe Langen-Müller/Herbig (qv)

Wison Verlag GmbH, Weyertal 59, Postfach 410948, D-5000 Cologne 41 Tel: 443031
Subjects: Economic Sciences; Data Processing; Research Reports

Wissen Verlag GmbH, Gachenaustr 11-13, D-8036 Herrsching Tel: (08152) 1087 Telex: 526493
Dir: Anton Bolza; *Sales Manager:* Andreas Göess
Subjects: Reference, Encyclopaedias, Dictionaries
ISBN Publisher's Prefix: 3-8075

Verlag **Wissenschaft und Politik**, see von Nottbeck

Verlag für **Wissenschaft, Wirtschaft und Technik** GmbH und Co KG, An den Weiden 15, D-3388 Bad Harzburg Tel: (05322) 81385 Telex: 957623 DVG
Man Dir: Brigitte Barvencik; *Dirs:* Gisela Böhme, Reinhard Höhn
Subjects: Management, Sociology, Social Science, Primary and Secondary Textbooks, Economics, Rhetoric
Founded: 1960
ISBN Publisher's Prefix: 3-8020

Wissenschaftliche Buchgesellschaft, Hindenburgstr 40, Postfach 111129, D-6100 Darmstadt 11 Tel: (06151) 82141
Man Dir: Ernst Knauer; *Chief Reader:* Jürgen Bauer; *Rights & Permissions:* Uwe Lessing
Subjects: History, Music, Art, Philosophy, Reference, Religion, Medicine, Psychology, General & Social Science, Low-priced Paperbacks, Education, Mathematics, Theology, Archaeology, Jurisprudence, Economics
Book Club: Wissenschaftliche Buchgesellschaft
1980: 95 titles *Founded:* 1949
ISBN Publisher's Prefix: 3-534

Wissenschaftliche Verlagsgesellschaft mbH, Birkenwald Str 44, Postfach 40, D-7000 Stuttgart 1 Tel: (0711) 292559 Telex: 0723636 daz d
Man Dirs: Hans Rotta, Dr Hanskarl Hornung; *Sales Manager:* Karl Hübler; *Publicity Manager:* Barbara Schreck
Associate Companies: Deutscher Apotheker Verlag Dr Roland Schmiedel GmbH & Co (qv); S Hirzel Verlag GmbH & Co (qv); Franz Steiner Verlag GmbH (qv)
Subjects: Medicine, Pharmacy, Biology, Chemistry, Physics
Founded: 1921
ISBN Publisher's Prefix: 3-8047

Friedrich **Wittig** Verlag, Papenhuder Str 2, D-2000 Hamburg 76 Tel: (040) 221059 Cable Add: Wittigverlag
Man Dir: Friedrich Wittig; *Editorial:* Friedrich Wittig,, Henning Wendland; *Sales:* Friedrich B Holst; *Production:* Henning Wendland
Subjects: Religion, Arts, History, Bibliophily
1979: 9 titles *1980:* 6 titles *Founded:* 1946
ISBN Publisher's Prefix: 3-8048

Verlag Konrad **Wittwer** KG, Nordbahnhofstr 16, Postfach 147, D-7000 Stuttgart 1 Tel: 250211 Telex: 723751
Man Dir: Konrad Wittwer; *Editorial, Sales, Publicity:* Mr Hasler
Subjects: Mathematics (School Textbooks), Geodesy, Building Technology, General Literature
Bookshop: Königstr 30, D-7000 Stuttgart 1
1978: 4 titles *Founded:* 1867
ISBN Publisher's Prefix: 3-87919

Gerhard **Witzstrock** GmbH, Bismarckstr 9, Postfach 509, D-7570 Baden-Baden Tel: (07221) 2047 Telex: 781162 gewi d
Man Dir: Gerhard Witzstrock; *General Manager:* Lotte Witzstrock
Subsidiary Company: Gerhard Witzstrock Publishing House Inc, New York, 30 East 40th St, Suite 703, New York, NY 10016 USA
Subjects: Medicine, Electron Scanning Microscopy
1979: 21 titles *Founded:* 1969
ISBN Publisher's Prefix: 3-87921

Womm-Press*, Mittelstr 51, D-4934 Horn-Bad Meinberg 1 Tel: (05234) 3780
Man Dir: Burkhart Weecke; *Publicity:* Horst Knauf; *Editorial:* Uli Becker; *Production:* W Linnemann
Subjects: General Fiction, Belles Lettres, Poetry, Music, Art, University Textbooks

Founded: 1974
ISBN Publisher's Prefix: 3-88080

Rainer **Wunderlich** Verlag Hermann Leins*, Goethestr 6, Postfach 2740, D-7400 Tübingen Tel: (07071) 24354 Cable Add: Wunderlichverlag Telex: 7262891 mepo d
Man Dir: Günther Schweizer; *Sales & Publicity Manager:* Albrecht Karnbach; *Rights & Permissions:* Monika Mölle
Subjects: Belles Lettres, Poetry, Biography, History, Music, Art, Politics
1978: 19 titles *Founded:* 1926
ISBN Publisher's Prefix: 3-8052

Xenos Verlagsgesellschaft mbH & Co, Lottbekheide 17, D-2000 Hamburg 65 Tel: 6049140 Telex: 2174727
Man Dir: Erwin Heimberger; *Sales and Publicity:* Hans Klingenberg; *Sales:* Rene Kellmer; *Production:* Frau Rohardt; *Rights & Permissions:* Inge Heimberger
Subjects: Juveniles, Nonfiction, Belles Lettres; Paperbacks
1978: 134 titles *1979:* 109 titles *Founded:* 1975

Dr **Zambon**, Leipziger Str 24, D-6000 Frankfurt am Main 90 Tel: (0611) 779223
Publisher: Giuseppe Zambon; *Sales:* Arturo Campos
Subjects: Juveniles, Foreign-language Teaching, Reprints

Zechner und Hüthig Verlag GmbH*, Daimlerstr 9, Postfach 2080, D-6720 Speyer-am-Rhein Tel: (06232) 33076 Cable Add: Zechner Verlag Speyer Telex: 465167
Publisher: Rudolf Zechner
Subject: General Science
ISBN Publisher's Prefix: 3-87927

Verlag Andreas **Zettner** KG*, Hofweg 12, Postfach 13, D-8702 Würzburg-Veitshöchheim Tel: (0931) 91970 Cable Add: Zettner Würzburg
Man Dir: Andreas Zettner
Subject: General Fiction
Book Club: Buchclub 69
Bookshops: Dr Müllers Buchboutique, D-8000 Munich 13, Citta 2000 & D-8500 Nuremberg, Breite Gasse 62; D-8100 Augsburg, Neuburger Str 67; D-854 Schwabach, Neutorstr 1
Founded: 1955

Verlag Wolfgang **Zimmer**, Haunstetter Str 18, D-8900 Augsburg 1 Tel: (0821) 554135
Publisher: Wolfgang Zimmer
Imprint: Schwarz Bildbücher
Subjects: Hobbies, Maps, Transport, Commerce
Miscellaneous: Formerly Rösler und Zimmer Verlag
ISBN Publisher's Prefix: 3-87987

Zimmermann KG, see Engelbert Verlag

Verlagsgemeinschaft Friedrich **Zluhan***, Hindenburgstr 3, Postfach 229, D-7120 Bietigheim Tel: (07142) 44446
Subjects: Belles Lettres; Homeopathy; Works of Alice Bailey; Astrosophy

Paul **Zsolnay** Verlag GmbH, Hohe Bleichen 7/Libri Haus, D-2000 Hamburg Tel: (040) 345156 Cable Add: Hakobuch Hamburg Telex: 214900
Dirs: Kurt Lingenbrink, Hans Polak
Parent Company: Heinemann & Zsolnay Ltd, UK (qv)
Associate Company: Paul Zsolnay Verlag GmbH, Austria (qv)
Subjects: General Fiction, Poetry, Nonfiction
Founded: 1948
ISBN Publisher's Prefix: 3-552

Zweipunkt Verlag KG*, Wilhelm-Leuschner-Str 1, D-6078 Neu Isenburg Tel: (06102) 7247
Subjects: Picture Books, Activity Books, Puzzles

Zweitausendeins Versand*, Hahnstr 54-56, Postfach 710249, D-6000 Frankfurt/AM 71 Tel: (0611) 663386
Subjects: New German and International Books; Reprints; Co-operative Works

Literary Agents

Babylon Übersetzungen*, Düsseldorferstr 38, D-1000 Berlin 15 Tel: (03) 8838296
Man Dir: Walter Bengs
Literary, Copyright and Translation Agency

Balkan-Press*, D-8000 Munich 70, Schmied-Kochel-Str 20 Tel: 3204450
Specialization: General books, Novels, Short Stories; Theatrical and TV scripts; Education, Psychology, Sociology, Politics; copyright and novel serialisation for newspapers and magazines

Winfried **Bluth** Literary Agency*, D-5630 Remscheid, Augustinusstr 43

Buchagentur München*, D-8032 Gräfelfing, Maria-Eich-Str 54b
Contact: Dr Hanns Martin Elster

Dr rer pol Dr Julius **Démuth***, Krautgartenweg 22, D-6000 Frankfurt am Main 50 Tel: (0611) 571970

Fralit-F K Albrecht*, Brahmsallee 29/1, D-2000 Hamburg 13 Tel: (040) 456073 Cable Add: Fralitagentur

Geisenheyner und Crone, Gymnasiumstr 31B, D-7000 Stuttgart 1 Tel: (0711) 293738 Cable Add: Gecelit Telex: 722664
Proprietor: Ernst W Geisenheyner

Gustav **Greve***, D-1000 Berlin 12, Fasanenstr 15

Hans Hermann **Hagedorn**, Erikastr 142, D-2000 Hamburg 20 Tel: (040) 4603232

Dagmar **Henne***, D-8000 Munich 40, Seestr 6

Münchner Verlagsbüro Horst **Hodemacher**-Axel Poldner GmbH & Co KG*, D-8000 Munich 19, Barellistr 7 Tel: (089) 171789

Agence **Hoffman**, D-8000 Munich 40, Seestr 6 Tel: (089) 396402 Cable Add: Aghoff München
Contact: Frau Dagmar Henne

Gerhard **Kowalski**, Ringstr 105, Postfach 450328, D-1000 Berlin 45 Tel: (030) 8331265 Telex: 0184560
Specialization: Memoirs, Biographies, Reference, Fiction, Theatre
See also: Publishing Company Concert Verlag G Kowalski

Karl Ludwig **Leonhardt**, Mittelweg 22, D-2000 Hamburg 13

Rose M **Meerwein**, Literary Scout, Reuterpfad 6-8, D-1000 Berlin 33, Grünewald Tel: (030) 8262039

Münchner Verlagsbüro, Horst Hodemacher-Axel Poldner*, Barellistr 7, D-8000 Munich 19 Tel: (089) 171789

Gerd **Plessl** Agency, Seidlstr 18, D-8000 Munich 2 Tel: (089) 554084
Specialization: Selling rights to South and East European publishers

Axel **Poldner***, D-8000 Munich 21, Rauheckstr 11 Tel: (089) 574824

Quelle Press*, Postfach 1314, D-7800 Freiburg im Breisgau Tel: (0761) 7016 Cable Add: Quellepress Freiburg

Thomas **Schlueck**, Hinter der Worth 12, D-3008 Garbsen 9 Tel: (05131)93053 Telex: 923419 litag d
Specialization: Full representation to Anglo-American authors, agents and publishers in German language areas

Wilfried Th **Sieber***, D-4973 Viotho 2, Im Königsfeld 5 Tel: (05228) 336
Specialization: Science Fiction

BP **Singer** Features Inc*, Postfach 1314, D-7800 Freiburg im Breisgau Tel: (0761) 7016
US Office: 3164 West Tyler Ave, Anaheim, CA 92801, USA

Skandinavia Verlag, Knesebeckstr 100, D-1000 Berlin 12 Tel: (030) 8137006/8616074
Contact: Marianne Weno, Michael Günther
Specialization: Scandinavian Stage, Radio and TV plays

Herta **Weber-Stumfohl**, D-8035 Gauting, Waldpromenade 32 Tel: (089) 8501241
Specialization: Translations from Swedish; Reviews

Book Clubs

Bertelsmann Lesering, Carl-Bertelsmannstr 270, Postfach 555, D-4830 Gütersloh
Members: 3 million
Founded: 1950
Owned by: Verlagsgruppe Bertelsmann GmbH (qv)

Verlag **Bibliotheca** Christiana, D-5300 Bonn, Endenicher Str 125, Postfach 1246

Bonner Buchgemeinde (BBG), Endenicherstr 125, Postfach 1246, D-5300 Bonn

Buchclub 69 GmbH*, Hofweg 12, Postfach 13, D-8702 Würzburg-Veitshöchheim
Owned by: Verlag Andreas Zettner KG (qv)

Christlicher Bildungskreis Verlags GmbH*, D-7000 Stuttgart 1, Lindenspürstr 32, Postfach 285

Deutsche Buch-Gemeinschaft C A Koch's Verlag Nachfolger*, Berliner Allee 6, Postfach 4131, D-6100 Darmstadt
Owned by: Deutsche Buch-Gemeinschaft C A Koch's Verlag Nachfolger (qv)

Deutsche Hausbücherei GmbH*, D-2000 Hamburg 36, Gr Theaterstr 32

Deutscher Bücherbund GmbH*, Libanonstr 3-5, D-7000 Stuttgart 1
Owned by: Georg von Holtzbrinck (at above address)

Deutscher Buchkreis, D-7400 Tübingen, Postfach 1629
Owned by: Grabert-Verlag (Tübingen) (qv)
Tel: (07071) 61206 Telex: 7262863 grav-d

Freundeskreis des **Euphorion** Verlags*, D-6000 Frankfurt am Main 50, Neumannstr 13
Members: 28
Founded: 1976
Owned by: Euphorion Verlag (Frankfurt am Main)

Europäische Bildungsgemeinschaft Verlags GmbH, Lindenspürstr 32, Postfach 1069, D-7000 Stuttgart 1
Owned by: Verlagsgruppe Bertelsmann GmbH (qv)
Founded: 1950

Europarings der Buch- und Schallplattenfreunde, D-4830 Gütersloh, Carl-Bertelsmann-Str 270
Owned by: Verlagsgruppe Bertelsmann GmbH (qv)

Evangelische Buchgemeinde GmbH, Libanonstr 3-5, D-7000 Stuttgart 1
Owned by: Georg von Holtzbrinck (at above address)

Fackel-Buchklub, Verlags- und Vertriebs GmbH*, D-7000 Stuttgart 1, Herdweg 29-31, Postfach 442
Owned by: Fackelverlag G Bowitz GmbH (qv)

Herder Buchgemeinde, Hermann-Herder-Str 4, D-7800 Freiburg im Breisgau
Owned by: Verlag Herder

Herold Buch-Club*, D-8000 Munich 70, Waldgarten Str 66
Owned by: Vereinigte Herold Verlage (qv)

Kosmos Gesellschaft, D-7000 Stuttgart 1, Pfizerstr 5-7, Postfach 640
Owned by: Franckh'sche Verlagshandlung W Keller & Co (qv)

Kunstkreis für Bibliophile Mappen*, D-665 Homburg-Schwarzenacker/Saar
Owned by: Edition Monika Beck (qv)

Verlag für **Lehr- und Lernmittel***, D-7800 Freiburg im Breisgau, Richard-Strauss-Str 11

Verlag Das Beste GmbH **Reader's Digest***, Augustenstr 1, D-7000 Stuttgart 1 Tel: (0711) 66021 Telex: 0723539

Verlag Wilhelm **Rubsamen**, D-7000 Stuttgart 1, Reinsburgstr 102

Volksverband der Bücherfreunde Verlag GmbH, Heidberg 7, D-2000 Hamburg 60

Wissenschaftliche Buchgesellschaft, Hindenburgstr 40, Postfach 111129, D-6100 Darmstadt 11
Owned by: Wissenschaftliche Buchgesellschaft (Publisher) (qv)

Major Booksellers

Artibus et Literis, Friedrichstr 26, D-4000 Düsseldorf 1
Worldwide export and import of books and journals
Parent Company: The bookseller Stern-Verlag Janssen & Co (qv)

Buchhandlung G D **Baedeker***, D-4300 Essen 1, Kettwiger Str 33-35, Postfach 128 Tel: (02141) 221381

Blazek und Bergmann*, Inhaber Dr Hans Bergmann, Universitätsbuchhandlung, D-6000 Frankfurt am Main 1, Goethestr 1 Tel: (0611) 288648

Universitätsbuchhandlung **Bouvier** GmbH*, D-5300 Bonn 1, Am Hof 32 Tel: (02221) 654445

Buchhandlung **Elwert und Meurer** GmbH*, D-1000 Berlin 62, Hauptstr 101 Tel: (030) 784001

F B V Frauenbuchvertrieb GmbH, Mehringdamm 32-34, D-1000 Berlin 61 Tel: (030) 2511666
Books written by women for women and published by women; subjects relating to women's movements
Managers: M Emmerich, R Krause, S Spiesmacher

Buchhandlung Heinrich **Gonski***, D-5000 Cologne 1, Neumarkt 24 Tel: (0221) 210528

FEDERAL REPUBLIC OF GERMANY 165

Grossohaus Wegner und Co, Postfach 102540, D-2000 Hamburg 1 (Located at: Conventstr 14, D-2000 Hamburg 76) Tel: (040) 25761 Telex: (02) 15096 Cable Add: Grossohaus Hamburg
Wholesaler and Exporter of German books, including those in the English language published in German-speaking countries

Hamburger Kommissionsbuchhandlung GmbH*, D-2000 Hamburg 36, Postfach 303430 Tel: (040) 341061
Wholesaler; branch of Georg Lingenbrink (qv)

Otto **Harrassowitz***, Taunusstr 5, Postfach 2929, D-6200 Wiesbaden Tel: (06121) 521046

Buchhandlung H **Hugendubel**, D-8000 Munich 1, Salvatorpl 2 Tel: (089) 23891

Internationale Presse, Import- und Export GmbH, Borsigallee 17, D-6000 Frankfurt am Main 60 Tel: (0611) 419198 Cable Add: Airedition Frankfurt Telex: 4189645 ip d
Book and Periodical Wholesaler representing companies in France, Italy, Portugal, Spain, United Kingdom, United States
Managing Director and Associate: Gustav Stückrath
Founded: 1949

Buchhandlung Christian **Kaiser**, Marienplatz 8, D-8000 Munich 2 Tel: (089) 223441
Owned by: Fritz Lempp
Branch Off: Theologie und französische Literatur, Schellingstr 3, D-8000 Munich 40 Tel: (089) 2809078
Specialization: Theology and French Literature

Koch, Neff und Oetinger und Co*, Am Wallgraben 110, Postfach 800620, D-7000 Stuttgart 80 Tel: (0711) 78603325/78603352 Telex: 07255684 knov d stgt
Wholesaler

Barsortiment Georg **Lingenbrink** (Wholesale Bookseller)*, D-2000 Hamburg 36, Amelungstr 3-5, Postfach 303430 Tel: (040) 341061 Tel: 0214900 and 0214673 also at D-6000 Frankfurt-Preungesheim; D-5000 Cologne; D-8047 Munich-Karlsfeld; Nüremberg, Stuttgart, Berlin

J A **Mayer'sche** Buchhandlung*, D-5100 Aachen, Ursulinerstr 17-19 Tel: (0241) 22441/5 Cable Add: Mayer Aachen Telex: 832768

Vereinigte Verlagsauslieferung R **Mohn** oHG*, Carl-Bertelsmann Str 161, D-4830 Gütersloh, Postfach 7777 Tel: (05241) 853202 Telex: 0933827
Miscellaneous: Associate Company: Art Reference Reinhard Mohn oHG, Gütersloh

Hans Heinrich **Petersen** Buchimport GmbH, Rugenbarg 250, Postfach 530230, D-2000 Hamburg 53 Tel: (040) 831171-75 Cable Add: buchpetersen hamburg Telex: 211401 hhp d
Manager: Egon Schormann
Importer of books, journals, audiovisual material from throughout world (but especially UK, USA, Netherlands)

Pro Media Literaturvertrieb GmbH, Werner Voss Damm 54, D-1000 Berlin 42 Tel: (030) 7855971
This is a wholesale marketing organisation representing small Publishing Houses dealing with the Alternative Society

Martin **Sandkühler**, Verlagsauslieferungen, Paracelsusstr 26, Postfach 720308, D-7000 Stuttgart 72 Tel: (0711) 454723

Stern-Verlag Janssen und Co, Friedrichstr 24-26, D-4000 Düsseldorf 1, Postfach 7820 Tel: (0211) 373033
Bookseller dealing with New and Antiquarian/Second-hand books
Managing Partners: Horst and Klaus Janssen
Subsidiary Company: The bookseller Artibus et Literis (qv)
Worldwide export and import of books and journals

V V A (Vereinigte Verlagsauslieferung) Reinhard Mohn*, (United Publishers Deliveries), Carl-Bertelsmann Str 161, D-4830 Gütersloh Tel: (05241) 85 Telex: 0933827
Wholesale Book Supplier

Buchhandlung **Wendelin** Niedlich KG, D-7000 Stuttgart 1, Schmale Str 9 Tel: (0711) 223287

Buchhandlung Konrad **Wittwer** KG*, D-7000 Stuttgart 1, Königstr 30 Tel: (0711) 250211 Telex: 723751

Major Libraries

Bayerische Staatsbibliothek, Ludwigstr 16, Postfach 150, D-8000 Munich 34 Tel: (089) 21981
Librarian: Dr F G Kaltwasser

Bibliothek für Zeitgeschichte, Konrad-Adenauer-Strasse 8, D-7000 Stuttgart 1, Postfach 769 Tel: (0711) 244117
Library for Contemporary History
Director: Professor Dr Jürgen Rohwer
Publications: Jahresbibliographie, Schriften der Bibliothek für Zeitgeschichte, Dokumentationen der BfZ, Wehrtechnik im Bild
Miscellaneous: Special Subjects: International Literature on history of wars, revolutions and military sciences; international 20th-century politics. Library is housed in same building as the Württembergische Landesbibliothek (qv) but has separate administration

Bundesarchiv (National Archives), D-5400 Koblenz, Am Wöllershof 12

Deutsche Bibliothek (National Library), Zeppelinallee 4-8, D-6000 Frankfurt am Main 1 Tel: (0611) 75661 Telex: 416643 deubi

Herzog August Bibliothek, D-3340 Wolfenbüttel, Lessingplatz 1, Postfach 1227 Tel: (05331) 5081

Hessische Landes- und Hoch-schulbibliothek Darmstadt, D-6100 Darmstadt, Schloss Tel: (06151) 125420

Ibero-Amerikanisches Institut, Preussischer Kulturbesitz, Potsdamer Str 37, D-1000 Berlin 30 Tel: (030) 2662500

Bibliothek des **Instituts für Weltwirtschaft** — Zentralbibliothek der Wirtschaftswissenschaften, Postfach 4309, D-2300 Kiel 1 (Located at: Dusternbrooker Weg 120-122, D-2300 Kiel 1) Tel: (0431) 8841 Telex: 0292479
Library of the Institute for World Economics — National Library of Economics

Niedersächsische Staats- und Universitätsbibliothek*, D-3400 Göttingen, Prinzenstr 1, Postfach 318 Tel: (0551) 395212 (Secretariat)
Librarian: Dir Helmut Vogt

Staats- und Universitätsbibliothek*, D-2000 Hamburg 13, Moorweidenstr 40 Tel: (040) 41232213

Staatsbibliothek Bamberg, D-8600 Bamberg, Neue Residenz, Domplatz 8 Tel: (0951) 53014

Staatsbibliothek Preussischer Kulturbesitz, Potsdamer Str 33, Postfach 1407, D-1000 Berlin 30 Tel: (030) 2661 Telex 183160 staab d
State Library of the Prussian Cultural Foundation
Director: Dr Ekkehart Vesper
Publications: Jahresbericht (irregular); *Mitteilungen* (quarterly); *Zeitschriften-Datenbank* (Periodicals' Data Bank), semi-annual, produced in association with das Deutsche Bibliotheksinstitut and Publisher Otto Harrassowitz (qv)
ISBN Publisher's Prefix: 3-88053

Stadt- und Universitätsbibliothek, Bockenheimer Landstr 134-138, D-6000 Frankfurt am Main 1 Tel: (0611) 79071 Telex: 414024 stub d
Director: Mr Lehmann

Universitäts- und Stadtbibliothek*, Universitätsstr 33, D-5000 Cologne 41 Tel: (0221) 4702260/4702214

Universitätsbibliothek, Werthmannpl 2, Postfach 1629, D-7800 Freiburg im Breisgau Tel: (0761) 2033901 (management); 2034000 (enquiries); 2033940 (main reading room)

Universitätsbibliothek der Eberhard-Karls-Universität, D-7400 Tübingen 1, Wilhelmstr 32, Postfach 2620 Tel: (07071) 292577

Universitätsbibliothek Erlangen-Nürnberg, Universitätsstr 4/Schuhstr 1a, D-8520 Erlangen Tel: (09131) 852151

Universitätsbibliothek Heidelberg, Plöck 107-109, Postfach 105749, D-6900 Heidelberg 1 Tel: (06221) 542380
Library Dir: Dr E Mittler
Publications: Bibliothek und Wissenschaft, Neuerwerbungslisten der Sondersammelgebiete Ägyptologie, Klassische Archäologie, Mittlere und neuere Kunstgeschichte, Heidelberger Zeitschriftenverzeichnis

Württembergische Landesbibliothek, Konrad-Adenauer-Str 8, Postfach 769, D-7000 Stuttgart 1 Tel: (0711) 2125424
Württemberg State Library
Director: Dr Hans-Peter Geh
Miscellaneous: The Bibliothek für Zeitgeschichte (Library for Contemporary History) — qv — is housed in same building, but has separate administration

Library Associations

a s p b, see Arbeitsgemeinschaft der Spezialbibliotheken e V

Arbeitsgemeinschaft der Hochschulbibliotheken*, c/o Universitätsbibliothek, Olshausenstr 29, D-2300 Kiel
Joint Association of Academic Libraries
Chairman: Dr G Wiegand

Arbeitsgemeinschaft der kirchlichen Büchereiverbände Deutschlands, D-5300 Bonn, Wittelsbacherring 9
Joint Association of Library Associations of the Churches in Germany
Executive Secretary: Erich Hodick

Arbeitsgemeinschaft der Kunstbibliotheken, c/o Kunst-und-Museumsbibliothek Verwaltung, Kattenbug 18-24, D-5000 Cologne 1
Joint Association of Art Libraries

Arbeitsgemeinschaft der Parlaments- und Behördenbibliotheken, Bibliothek des Deutschen Bundestages, Bundeshaus, D-5300 Bonn
Joint Association of Parliamentary and Administration Libraries
Chairman: Wolfgang Dietz; *Executive Secretary:* Heinz-Ottmar Schmidt
Publications: Arbeitshefte (Work Programmes) and *Mitteilungen* (News Sheets)

Arbeitsgemeinschaft der Regionalbibliotheken, Staats- und Stadtbibliothek, Schaezlerstr 25, D-8900 Augsburg
Joint Association of Regional Libraries
President: Josef Bellot

Arbeitsgemeinschaft der Spezialbibliotheken e V, Universitätsbibliothek der Technischen Universität Berlin, Str des 17 Juni 135, D-1000 Berlin 12 (Charlottenburg) Tel: (030) 3143671 Telex: 0183872 ubtu d
Association of Special Libraries
Chairman: Prof Dr Paul Kaegbein; *Executive Secretary/Treasurer:* Dipl-Ing Ingeborg-Pohle
Publication: Bericht über die Tagung (Conference Report; every 2 years)

Arbeitsgemeinschaft der Archive und Bibliotheken in der evangelischen Kirche, Veilhofstr 28, D-8500 Nuremberg
Joint Association of Archives and Libraries in the Evangelical Church
President: Dr Helmut Baier
Publications: Mitteilungen der AABevK (AABevK News Bulletin); *Veröffentlichungen der AABevK* (Publications of the AABevK)

Arbeitsgemeinschaft für juristische Bibliotheks- und Dokumentationswesen, c/o Renate Bellmann, Bibliothek des Juristischen Seminars der Universität, D-7400 Tübingen
Joint Association for Law Libraries and Legal Documentation
Chairperson: Renate Bellmann
Publications: Mitteilungen der Arbeitsgemeinschaft für juristisches Bibliotheks- und Dokumentationswesen (3 times yearly) and *Arbeitshefte* (irregularly)

Arbeitsgemeinschaft für medizinisches Bibliothekswesen*, c/o Joseph-Stelzmann-Str 9, D-5000 Cologne-Lindenthal
Joint Association for Medical Libraries

Arbeitsgemeinschaft katholischtheologischer Bibliotheken, c/o Bibliothek des Priesterseminars, Postfach 1330, D-5500 Trier
Joint Association of Catholic Theological Libraries
Dir: Dr Franz Rudolf Reichert
Publications: Mitteilungsblatt (News Letter), *Veröffentlichungen der Arbeitsgemeinschaft katholisch-theologischer Bibliotheken Nr 1 ff* (Publications of the Association)

Arbeitsstelle für das Bibliothekswesen, see Deutscher Bibliotheksverband

Bundesarbeitsgemeinschaft der katholisch-kirchlichen Büchereiarbeit, Wittelsbacherring 9, D-5300 Bonn
National Joint Association of Library work in the Catholic Church
Executive Secretary: Erich Hodick

Deutsche Gesellschaft für Dokumentation e V, Westendstr 19, D-6000 Frankfurt am Main 1
German Society for Documentation
President: Prof Dip Ing P Canisius
Publications: Nachrichten für Dokumentation (Documentation News — 5 per year); *DGD Schriftenreihe* (Series of texts of above Society)

FEDERAL REPUBLIC OF GERMANY 167

Deutsches Bibliotheksinstitut, Bundesallee 184/185, D-1000 Berlin 31 Tel: (030) 85050 Telex: 184166 dbi d
German Library Institute
Publications: Bibliotheksdienst (monthly), *Forum Musikbibliothek* (quarterly), *Schulbibliothek Aktuel* (quarterly), also several reference books, monographs, bibliographical and statistical services

Deutscher Leihbuchhändler-Verband eV*
Martener Str 317, D-4600 Dortmund-Marten Tel: 614089
German Circulating Libraries Federation

Deutscher Verband evangelischer Büchereien eV, Bürgerstr 2, D-3400 Göttingen
German Association of Evangelical (Protestant) Libraries

Gesellschaft für Bibliothekswesen und Dokumentation des Landbaues (GBDL), Paracelsusstr 2, D-7000 Stuttgart 70 Tel: (0711) 4501-2111
Society for Librarianship and Documentation in Agriculture
Publication: Mitteilungen der Gesellschaft für Bibliothekswesen und Dokumentation des Landbaues

Gesellschaft für Information und Dokumentation mbH (GID), GID-Informationszentrum, Lyoner Str 44-48, Postfach 710370, D-6000 Frankfurt am Main 71 Tel: (0611) 66871 Telex: 414351
This organization continues work previously done by the Zentralstelle für maschinelle Dokumentation and also replaces the Institut für Dokumentations-Wesen
Dir: Dr Peter Budinger

Institut für Jugendbuchforschung der J W Goethe-Universität*, Georg Voigt-Str 10, D-6000 Frankfurt am Main
Institute for Research into Books for the Young

Internationale Vereinigung der Musikbibliotheken, Deutsche Gruppe BRD, pa Universität Bremen Bibliothek, Postfach 330160, D-2800 Bremen 33
German Section of the International Association of Music Libraries
Secretary-General: Dr Wolfgang Krueger

V D D, see Verein Deutscher Dokumentare eV

Verband der Bibliotheken des Landes Nordrhein-Westfalen, c/o Frau Renate Baumhoff, Maischützenstr 57, D-4630 Bochum 1
Association of Libraries of North Rhine-Westphalia
Secretariat: at above address; *Editorial:* Universitätsbibliothek, D-5300 Bonn
Publication: Mitteilungsblatt (News Sheet)

Verband deutscher Werkbibliotheken eV*, c/o BASF Aktiengesellschaft, Werkbücherei, Carl-Bosch Str, D-6700 Ludwigshafen Tel: (0621) 603689
Association of Industrial Libraries of the Federal Republic of Germany
President: Christiane Lüderssen

Verein Angehörige des mittleren und nichtdiplomierten Bibliotheksdienstes eV (Association of Nonprofessional Librarians)*, Bremen, Klattenweg 59
Secretary: Melitta Thomas

Verein der Bibliothekare an öffentlichen Büchereien eV, Roonstr 9, D-2800 Bremen
Association of Public Librarians
President: Dip-Bibl Karl-Heinz Pröve
Publication: Buch und Bibliothek

Verein der Diplom-Bibliothekare an Wissenschaftlichen Bibliotheken eV*, Universitätsbibliothek, D-4630 Bochum 1, Postfach 102148 Tel: (0234) 7005200

Association of Certified Librarians at Academic Libraries
Chairman: Ingeborg Sobottke
Publication: Rundschreiben

Verein Deutscher Archivare (VdA), Hessisches Staatsarchiv, Schloss, D-6100 Darmstadt
Association of German Archivists
Chairman: Dr Eckhart G Franz
Publication: Verzeichnis der Archivare (Register of Archivists) — at irregular intervals of several years

Verein Deutscher Bibliothekare eV, Universitätsbibliothek Stuttgart, Holzgartenstr 16, D-7000 Stuttgart 1 Tel: (0711) 2073/2222 Telex: 0722450
Secretary: Dr Eberhard Zwink
Association of German Librarians
President: Juergen Hering
Publications: Zeitschrift für Bibliothekswesen und Bibliographie; Jahrbuch der deutschen Bibliotheken

Verein Deutscher Dokumentare eV (VDD), Postfach 2509, D-5300 Bonn
Association of German Documentalists
Publication: Nachrichten für Dokumentation, D-6000 Frankfurt am Main 1, Westendstr 19

Württembergische Bibliotheksgesellschaft*, Postfach 769, D-7000 Stuttgart (Located at: Konrad-Adenauer Str 8)
Society of Friends of the Württemberg State Library
Secretary: Dr Gerhard Römer

Zentralstelle für maschinelle Dokumentation, see Gesellschaft für Information und Dokumentation

Library Reference Books and Journals

Books

Bibliothekswesen in Deutschland (Library Science in Germany), German Publishers' and Booksellers' Association, D-6000 Frankfurt 1, Großer Hirschgraben 17-21

Handbuch des Büchereiwesens (Handbook of Library Science), Verlag Otto Harrassowitz, D-6200 Wiesbaden, Taunusstr 6, Postfach 2929

Jahrbuch der Deutschen Bibliotheken (Yearbook of German Libraries), Verlag Otto Harrassowitz, D-6300 Wiesbaden 1, Taunusstr 6, Postfach 2929

Libraries in the Federal Republic of Germany, Verlag Otto Harrassowitz, D-6200 Wiesbaden 1, Taunusstr 6, Postfach 2929

Sigelverzeichnis für die Bibliotheken der Bundesrepublik Deutschland und West-Berlins (Classification List for the Libraries of the BRD and West Berlin), State Library of Prussian Cultural Foundation, D-1000 Berlin 30, Potsdamer Str 33, Postfach 1407

Verzeichnis der Archivare (Register of Archivists), Verein deutscher Archivare, Hessisches Staatsarchiv, Schloss, D-6100 Darmstadt

Verzeichnis der Spezialbibliotheken in der Bundesrepublik Deutschland einschl West Berlin (List of Special Libraries in the BRD including West Berlin), Friedr Vieweg & Sohn Verlagsgesellschaft mbH, D-6200 Wiesbaden, Gustav-Stresemann-Ring 12-16, Postfach 5829

Journals

Bibliotheksdienst (Library Service), German Library Association — Publications Dept, Fehrbelliner Platz 3, D-1000 Berlin 31

Buch und Bibliothek (Book and Library), K G Saur KG, D-8000 Munich 71, Pössenbacherstr 2

Dokumentation, Fachbibliothek, Werkbücherei (DFW) Zeitschrift für Allgemein- und Spezial-bibliotheken, Büchereien und Dokumentationsstellen (Documentation. Technical Libraries. Works Libraries. Journal for General and Special Libraries and Documentation Centres), Nordwestverlag Stephanie Schräpel, D-3000 Hanover-Waldhausen, Güntherstr 21

INSPEL, German Library Association — Publications Dept, Fehrbelliner Platz 3, D-1000 Berlin 31

Musikbibliothek aktuell (Music Library Today), German Library Association — Publications Dept, Fehrbelliner Platz 3, D-1000 Berlin 31

Nachrichten für Dokumentation (News for Documentation), German Society for Documentation, D-6000 Frankfurt am Main 1, Westendplatz 29

das neue buch; book profile for Catholic library work, Borromäusverein, Wittelsbacherring 9, D-5300 Bonn; St Michaelsbund, Herzog-Wilhelmstr 5, D-8000 Munich 2

schulbibliothek aktuell (School Library Today), German Library Association — Publications Dept, Fehrbelliner Platz 31, D-1000 Berlin 3

Zeitschrift für Bibliothekswesen und Bibliographie (Journal of Library Science and Bibliography), Association of German Librarians, Universitätsbibliothek der technischen Universität Braunschweig, Pockelstr 13, D-3300 Braunschweig, Strasse des 17 Juni 135, D-1000 Berlin 12

Zentralblatt für Bibliothekswesen (Central Journal for Library Science), Verlag Otto Harrassowitz, D-6200 Wiesbaden, Taunusstr 6, Postfach 2929

Literary Associations and Societies

Akademie der Wissenschaften und der Literatur (Academy of Sciences, Arts and Literature), D-6500 Mainz, Geschwister-Schollstr 2
President: Professor Dr Heinrich Offen; *Secretary-General:* Dr G Brenner
Publications: Jahrbuch, Abhandlungen, Forschungsreihen
Large number of learned studies in fields of Literature, Mathematics, History, and the Sciences and Arts generally; Periodicals

Deutsche Akademie für Sprache und Dichtung, Glückert-Haus, Alexandraweg 23, D-6100 Darmstadt Tel: 44823
German Academy of Language and Poetry. It is responsible for the administration of a number of literary prizes
President: Peter de Mendelssohn; *Secretary:* Dr Gerhard Dette

Deutsche Shakespeare-Gesellschaft West eV, D-4630 Bochum, Rathaus
West German Shakespeare Society
President: Professor Dr Habicht
Publications: Shakespeare Jahrbuch

Gutenberg-Gesellschaft (Gutenberg Society)*, D-6500 Mainz, Liebfrauenplatz 5
Chairman: Professor Dr H Widmann
Publications: Gutenberg-Jahrbuch, Kleine Drucke, Veröffentlichungen

Literarischer Verein in Stuttgart eV, Rosenbergstr 113, Postfach 723, D-7000, Stuttgart 1 Tel: (0711) 638265
Stuttgart Literary Society
Founded: 1839
Publication: Bibliothek des Literarischen Vereins in Stuttgart Vol 1 (1842) — Vol 300 (1978)
Published by Anton Hiersemann Verlag (qv) at above address
The aim of the Society is to publish the texts of valuable unpublished manuscripts and old printed texts in a new form — especially with regard to old German literature

P E N Zentrum Bundesrepublik Deutschland, Sandstr 10, D-6100 Darmstadt
Secretary-General: Martin Gregor-Dellin

Literary Periodicals

Akzente (Accents); journal for literature, Carl Hanser Verlag, D-8000 Munich 80, Kolberger Str 22, Postfach 860420

Bücherkommentare (Book Commentaries); journal for book criticism, Verlag Rombach, D-7800 Freiburg im Breisgau, Lörracher Str 3, Postfach 1349

Bücherschiff (Book Galley); the German book journal, Verlag Bücherschiff Walter Reutin, D-7500 Karlsruhe 21, Rheinstr 122, Postfach 210947

Bulletin Jugend + Literatur (Youth and Literature Bulletin), Lesen Verlag GmbH, Eulenhof, D-2351 Hardebek

Deutschheft (German Copy), Verlag Pohl und Mayer, Postfach 24, Kaufbeuren

Epitaph; young journal for literature, D-8000 Munich 40, Belgradstr 24

Formation, Zur Halle 5, D-6751 Sulybachtal 1, Kaiserlauten-Land

Imprint; the literary journal for German-language literature, Lesen Verlag GmbH, Eulenhof, D-2351 Hardebek

Lektüre (Reading), Lektüre Verlagsgesellschaft mbH, Friedrichstr 13, D-8000 Munich 40

Literarische Hefte (Literary Notes), Raith Verlag, D-8000 Munich 2, Herzog Heinrich Str 21

Literarische Umschau (Literary Review), Verlag Marie Hemmerle 1, D-8000 Munich 70, Pullacherstr

Literat (Man of Letters); journal for literature and art, Verband deutscher Schriftsteller Hessen, D-6000 Frankfurt am Main, Goethestr 29

Literature, Music, Fine Arts; a review of German-language research contributions on literature, music, and fine arts (text in English), Institut für Wissentschaftliche Zusammenarbeit (Institute for Scientific Co-operation), D-7400 Tübingen, Landhusstr 18

Litfass, Berlin journal for literature, Ostpreussendamm 159, D-1000 Berlin 45 Tel: (030) 7728339

Neue Rundschau (New Review), Fischer Verlag, D-6000 Frankfurt am Main, Mainzer Landstr 10-12

Text und Kritik (Text and Criticism); journal for literature, Edition Text un Kritik, D-8000 Munich 80, Levelingstr 6a

Universitas; journal for science, art and literature (editions in German, English and Spanish), Wissenschaftliche Verlagsgesellschaft mbH, Birkenwald Str 44, Postfach 40, D-7000 Stuttgart 1

Viergroschenbogen ('Four Groschen Sheets'); journal for contemporary literature and art), Relief-Verlag-Eilers, D-8000 Munich 2, Martin Greif Str 3

Wissenschaft-Literaturanzeiger (Scientific Literature Advertiser), Verlag Rombach, Lörracher Str 3, Postfach 1349, D-7800 Freiburg im Breisgau

Wolfenbütteler Notizen zur Buchgeschichte (Wolfenbütteler Notes on the History of the Book), Pöseldorfer Weg 1, D-2000 Hamburg 13

Literary Prizes

Georg **Büchner** Prize
Founded in 1923 by Volksstaat Hessen, it has been given since 1951 by the Academy to writers who have been especially noteworthy through their work and have contributed to the current cultural scene in Germany. 20,000 DM. Awarded annually. Enquiries to Deutsche Akademie für Sprache und Dichtung, Glückert-Haus, Alexandraweg 23, D-6100 Darmstadt

Konrad **Duden** Prize
For special achievement in the German language; co-sponsored by the Bibliographical Institute. 10,000 DM. Awarded every two years. Applications are not invited. Enquiries to Stadt Mannheim, Hauptamt, Rathaus E5, D-6800 Mannheim 1

Theodor **Fontane** Prize
Founded in 1948 and given for a single work or a body of work. 30,000 DM. Awarded every six years. Enquiries to Akademie der Künste, Hanseatenweg 10, D-1000 Berlin 21

Sigmund **Freud** Prize*
For a scientific presentation in prose. 10,000 DM. Awarded annually. Enquiries to Deutsche Akademie für Sprache und Dichtung, Glückert-Haus, Alexandraweg 23, D-6100 Darmstadt

Goethe Prize
Founded in 1927 for work showing the value of, or respect for Goethe's ideals and thoughts. 50,000 DM awarded every three years. Enquiries to Amt für Wissenschaft und Kunst, Brückenstr 3-7, D-6000 Frankfurt am Main 70

Friedrich **Gundolf** Prize for Germanistics abroad*
For essays in German. 6,000 DM. Awarded annually. Enquiries to Deutsche Akademie für Sprache und Dichtung, Glückert-Haus, Alexandraweg 23, D-6100 Darmstadt

The Alfred **Kerr** Prize for Literary Criticism
Founded in 1976/77 by the Börsenblatt für den deutschen Buchhandel (German Book Trade Gazette). 5,000 DM plus a Certificate and the reimbursement of expenses incurred by the Presentation Ceremony. Awarded annually. For outstanding continuing literary criticism in a German newspaper, magazine, or TV or radio programme. Won in 1979 by the Third Programme of Suedwest TV. Enquiries to Redaktion Börsenblatt, Chefredakteur Hanns Lothar Schütz, Grosser Hirschgraben 17-21, D-6000 Frankfurt am Main

Lessing Prize der Freien und Hansestadt Hamburg
To poets, writers, scholars in German cultural fields who are able to meet the challenge represented by the name of Lessing. 30,000 DM (less 10,000 for foundation fees). Awarded every four years. Enquiries to Kulturbehörde der Freien und Hansestadt Hamburg, Hamburgerstr 45, D-2000 Hamburg 76

Literature Prize
To a poet or writer for his whole work. A monetary prize awarded annually (no award in 1979). Enquiries to Bayerische Akademie der Schönen Künste, Max Joseph Platz 3, D-8000 Munich 22

Thomas **Mann** Prize
Founded in 1975 in honour of Thomas Mann, to celebrate the 100th anniversary of his birth. The prize will be awarded to personalities who have, through their literary work, shown the humanitarian spirit set out in the work of Thomas Mann. 10,000 DM. Awarded every three years. Enquiries to Der Senat der Hansestadt Lübeck, Amt für Kultur, Rathaushof, Postfach, D-2400 Lübeck 1

Johann Heinrich **Merck** Prize
For literary criticism. 10,000 DM. Awarded annually. Enquiries to Deutsche Akademie für Sprache und Dichtung, Glückert-Haus, Alexandraweg 23, D-6100 Darmstadt

Rheinland-Palatinate Prize
Founded in 1956 for a single work or body of work in literature (as well as fine art and music). Winner should be closely related to the area. 10,000 DM. Awarded in 1979 to Nino Erné, Peter Jokostra. Enquiries to Rheinland-Palatinate Ministry of Culture, Mittlere Bleiche 61, D-6500 Mainz 1

Nelly **Sachs** Prize
The cultural prize of Dortmund City, instituted by the Dortmund City Council in 1961. Awarded every 2 years: current value 20,000 DM. 1979 winner: Erich Fromm. Enquiries to Kulturamt der Stadt Dortmund, Karl-Marx-Strasse 24, D-4600 Dortmund 1

Schiller Prize
For outstanding achievements in the cultural field. 25,000 DM. Awarded every four years; applications are not invited. Enquiries to Stadt Mannheim, Hauptamt, Rathaus E5, D-6800 Mannheim 1

Johann Heinrich **Voss** Translation Prize*
For a single work or life's work in translation. 6,000 DM. Awarded annually. Enquiries to Deutsche Akademie für Sprache und Dichtung, Glückert-Haus, Alexandraweg 23, D-6100 Darmstadt

Carl **Zuckmayer** Medal
Instituted 1978 by the Minister President of Rheinland-Pfalz (Rhineland Palatinate). First award was made in 1979 to Günther Fleckenstein. The award is for those whose services to the German language make them worthy of honour in memory of Carl Zuckmayer, the noted German dramatist and poet. Enquiries to Rheinland-Pfalz Kulturministerium, Mittlere Bleiche 61, D-6500 Mainz 1

Translation Agencies and Associations

Babylon Übersetzungen*, Texts, Copyrights, Düsseldorfer Str 38, D-1000 Berlin 15 Tel: (030) 8838296
Man Dir: Walter Bengs

Bundesverband der Dolmetscher und Übersetzer eV (BDÜ), Schlossallee 9, D-5300 Bonn 2 Tel: (02221) 345000
Federal German Association of Interpreters and Translators
Secretary: Georg Frantz
Publication: Mitteilungsblatt für Dolmetscher und Übersetzer (Interpreters' and Translators' News Sheet), six times per year

Verband deutschsprachiger Übersetzer literarischer und wissenschaftlicher Werke eV (VDU)*, Fürststr 17, D-7400 Tübingen Tel: (07071) 32493
Association of German-speaking translators of Literary and Scientific Works
Dir: Ursula Brackmann
Publication: Der Übersetzer (The Translator — monthly)

Ghana

General Information

Language: English
Religion: About 40 per cent Christian, remainder follow traditional beliefs
Population: 11 million
Literacy rate (1970): 30.2%
Bank Hours: 0830-1400 Monday-Thursday; 0830-1500 Friday
Shop Hours: 0800-1200, 1400-1730 Monday-Friday
Currency: 100 pesawas = 1 cedi
Export/Import Information: No tariffs on books; advertising matter over 1 kg gross weight 50%. Import licence required, but single copies of books under Open General Licence. Levy of 10% charged on import licences required. Credit terms not permitted
Copyright: UCC, Florence (see International section)

Book Trade Organizations

Ghana Association of Writers*, PO Box 4414, Accra
Holds an annual writers' congress
Publications: Okyeame, Takra

Ghana Booksellers' Association, PO Box 7869, Accra Tel: 21551

Ghana National Book Development Council, Education Loop, PO Box M430, Accra Tel: 29178 Cable Add: Ghanabook Accra
Publications: Ghana Book World (annual)

Standard Book Numbering Agency, Ghana Library Board, Research Library on African Affairs, PO Box 2970, Accra
Administrator: A N de Heer

Book Trade Reference Journals

Ghana Book World (annual), Ghana National Book Development Council, Education Loop, PO Box M430, Accra

Ghana National Bibliography, c/o Research Library on African Affairs, PO Box 2970, Accra

Publishers

Advance Publishing Co Ltd*, New Town Rd, PO Box 2317, Accra New Town Tel: 21577
Man Dir: A O Mills
Subjects: General Nonfiction, Paperbacks

Afram Publications (Ghana) Ltd, 29 Ring Road East, PO Box M18, Accra Tel: 74248 Cable Add: Aframbooks Telex: 2171 SIC Accra
Man Dir, Rights & Permissions: Kwesi Sam-Woode; *Marketing Officer:* Emman A Manful; *Production:* Kofi A Duker
Subjects: General Fiction, Belles Lettres, Poetry, Biography, History, Africana, How-to Study Guides, Religion, General and Social Science, Paperbacks, Secondary and Primary Schools Text Books
1978: 38 titles *Founded:* 1974
Miscellaneous: The Company is partly owned by the State Insurance Corporation of Ghana

Africa Christian Press, PO Box 30, Achimota Tel: 77553
General Secretary: Donald Banks; *Sales Manager:* P Addo
Subjects: Christian Fiction & Nonfiction, Biography, Paperbacks and Booklets. No Tracts. Priority is given to African writers
1978-9: 12 titles *Founded:* 1964
ISBN Publisher's Prefix: 0-9964

Anowuo Educational Publications, 2R McCarthy Hill, PO Box 3918, Accra Tel: 24910
Publisher: S A Konadu; *Sales Manager:* Samuel Tetteh
Subjects: Africana, How-to, Study Guides, Reference, Juveniles, Books in Ghanaian Languages, Paperbacks, General Science, Secondary Textbooks, General Fiction, Belles Lettres, Poetry, History
Miscellaneous: Also Booksellers and Sales Representatives of Overseas Publishing Houses
Founded: 1966

Benibengor Book Agency*, PO Box 40, Aboso
Man Dir: J Benibengor Blay
Subjects: General Fiction, Belles Lettres, Poetry, Biography, Juveniles, Paperbacks

Bureau of Ghana Languages, PO Box 1851, Accra Tel: 64130/65194/65461 ext 513 Cable Add: Velbo, Accra, Ghana
Dir, Rights & Permissions: F S Konu; *Sales Manager:* A A Amartey
Branch Off: PO Box 177, Tamale, Northern Region, Ghana
Subjects: Fiction, Drama, Poetry, Biography, Science, School Text Books, Dictionaries, Bibliographies, Material for New Literates. Books are published in 11 Ghanaian languages
Founded: 1951
Miscellaneous: Also acts as a Translation Agency/Association

Editorial and Publishing Services*, PO Box 5743, Accra
Man Dir: M Danquah
Subjects: General, Reference

Encyclopaedia Africana Project*, PO Box 2797, Accra Tel: 77651 Cable Add: Enafsec
Man Dir: L H Ofosu-Appiah
Subject: Reference

Frank Publishing Ltd, PO Box M414, Ministry Branch Post Office, Accra Tel: 29510 Cable Add: Knowledge
Man Dir, Editorial, Production: Francis K Dzokoto; *Sales, Public Relations:* Moses K Dzokoto
Subjects: Secondary School Textbooks
Founded: 1976

Ghana Publishing Corporation*, Publishing Division, PMB, Tema Tel: 4166/2521 (Tema); 66349 (Accra) Cable Add/Telex: Publishing Tema
Man Dir: M W Ofori; *General Manager (Publishing Division):* K B Arkorful; *Chief Editor/Rights & Permissions:* Isaac Dankyi-Mensah; *Sales Manager:* M H K Attah; *Production:* K B Arkaful; *Publicity:* Fidelis D Adzakey
Parent Company: Ghana Publishing Corporation, Head Office, PO Box 4348, Accra
Printing Division: see Government Printer
Sales & Distribution Division: PO Box 3632 Accra
Branch Off: at Accra, Cape Coast, Ho, Tamale, Koforidua, Hohoe, Sunyani, Bolgatanga, Kumasi, Wa, Swedru
Subjects: General Fiction & Nonfiction; Belles Lettres, Poetry, Biography, History, Africana, Languages, Reference, Juveniles, Books in Various Ghanaian languages, Paperbacks, Science & Technology, General & Social Science; University, Secondary and Primary Textbooks
Bookshops: throughout Ghana
1978: 215 titles *1979:* 228 titles *Founded:* 1965

Ghana Universities Press, PO Box 4219, Accra Tel: 25032 Cable Add/Telex: Univpress Accra
Dir: A S K Atsu
Subjects: General Nonfiction, Belles Lettres, Poetry, Biography, History, Africana, Philosophy, Religion, Law, Paperbacks, Medicine, Psychology, Science & Technology, General & Social Science, University Textbooks
1978: 7 titles *Founded:* 1962
ISBN Publisher's Prefix: 9964-3

The **Government Printer** (Ghana Publishing Corporation, Printing Division)*, PO Box 124, Accra

Moxon Paperbacks Ltd*, Barnes Rd, PO Box M 160, Accra Tel: 66640
Man Dir: Chief James Moxon
Subjects: General Fiction & Nonfiction, Belles Lettres, Poetry, History, Africana, Reference, Juveniles, Guidebooks, Paperbacks
Bookshop: The Atlas Bookshop, Ambassador Hotel Gardens, PO Box M 160, Accra
Founded: 1967

Presbyterian Book Depot Ltd, PO Box 195, Accra, see main entry under Major Booksellers and range of publications under Waterville Publishing House below

Waterville Publishing House, PO Box 195, Accra Tel: 63124/62415 Cable Add: Books Accra
Man Dir: C A Aboagye; *Publications Manager:* E K Asante
Parent Company: Presbyterian Book Depot Ltd (qv under Major Booksellers)
Subjects: General Fiction & Nonfiction, Belles Lettres, Poetry, Biography, History, Africana, Religion, Juveniles, Paperbacks, General & Social Science, Secondary & Primary Textbooks
1978: 9 titles *1979:* 11 titles *Founded:* 1963

Major Booksellers

Astab Books Ltd*, Osu R E, PO Box 346, Accra Tel: 76766

The **Atlas** Bookshop Ltd*, Ambassador Hotel Gdns, PO Box M 160, Accra Tel: 66640

Cape Coast University Bookshop*, PMB, Cape Coast Tel: 24409

E P Book Depot*, PO Box 42, Ho

Ghana Publishing Corporation, Distribution and Sales Division*, PO Box 124, Accra

Kingsway Stores, Books and Periodicals Department*, PO Box 1638, Accra

Methodist Book Depot Ltd*, Head Off: Atlantis House, Commercial St, PO Box 100, Cape Coast Tel: 2133/4 Branches at Accra, Berekum, Kumasi, Swedru, Takoradi, Tarkwa, Tema

Presbyterian Book Depot Ltd*, Thorpe Rd, PO Box 195, Accra Tel: 63124/62415
Cable Add: Books Accra
Chairman: E H Booheme; *Man Dir:* A Ott
Branches at: Accra, Tudu, Koforidua, Kumasi, Nkawkaw, Tamale, Akim Oda, Odumase, Ada
Founded: 1910
Miscellaneous: The organization comprises bookselling, stationery supply, printing and publishing activities (see Waterville Publishing House)

Queensway Bookshop and Stores*, Bank Lane, PO Box 4276, Accra Tel: 62707 (Accra) Cable Add: Success Accra
Suppliers of Educational, Library and HMSO Publications

University Bookshop, University of Science and Technology, University Post Office, Kumasi Tel: 5351
Manager: J A Clifford-Wirrom

University Bookshop, University of Ghana, PO Box 1, Legon, Accra Tel: 75381 extensions 8227, 8827
Manager: S O Cofie

Major Librairies

Advanced Teacher Training College Library*, PO Box 129, Winneba Tel: 139 ext 18

American Center Library*, PO Box 2288, Accra Tel: 29179

Armed Forces Library Service, Ministry of Defence, Burma Camp, Accra Tel: 76111 ext 628
Librarian: Ebenezer Ekuban
Publication: Armed Forces Library Bulletin

British Council Library, Liberia Road, PO Box 771, Accra Tel: 21766

Central **Bureau of Statistics***, Economic Library, PO Box 1098, Accra Tel: 66512

C S I R Central Reference and Research Library, PO Box M 32, Accra Tel: 77651, extensions 32, 58
Librarian: J A Villars
Publications: Ghana Science Abstracts; Directory of Special and Research Libraries in Ghana; List of Publications by CSIR Staff, 1958-1971; Medical Research Centres in Ghana; Current Research Projects, 1973; Union List of Scientific Serials in Ghanaian Libraries (1976); C S I R Recorder; Directory of Research Projects (Science & Technology) in Ghana (1978)

Ghana Institute of Management and Public Administration, Library and Documentation Centre*, Greenhill, PO Box 50, Achimota Tel: 77625

Research Library on African Affairs, PO Box 2970, Accra Tel: 23526, 28402
Librarian: A N deHeer
Publications: Ghana National Bibliography (annual), Current Ghana Bibliography

University of Cape Coast Library*, PMB, Cape Coast Tel: 24409 ext 370
Publication: Bulletin

University of Ghana Library, PO Box 24, Legon Tel: 75381 ext 410
Librarian: J Michael Walpole
Publications: Annual Report, Bulletin

University of Science and Technology Library*, Private Bag, Kumasi Tel: 5351 ext 235

Library Associations

Ghana Library Association*, PO Box 4105, Accra
Secretary: Francis K Dzokoto
Publication: Ghana Library Journal (bi-annual)

Ghana Library Board*, Thorpe Rd, PO Box 663, Accra Tel: 62795, 65083, 66337
Publications: Ghana National Bibliography, Annual Reports

Library Reference Books and Journals

Books

Directory of Libraries in Ghana, Department of Library and Archival Studies, University of Ghana, Legon

Directory of Special and Research Libraries in Ghana, CSIR Library, PO Box M 32, Accra

Journals

Ghana Library Journal, Ghana Library Association, PO Box 4105, Accra

Literary Periodicals

Asemka, c/o French Department, University of Cape Coast, Cape Coast (A new biennial literary magazine published since 1974)

Okyeame, Ghana Association of Writers, PO Box 4414, Accra (This journal has been defunct for some time now, but there are plans to recommence publication shortly. The Association also publishes a newsletter entitled *Takra*)

Pleisure, Moxon Paperbacks, PO Box M 160, Accra (A popular magazine with many literary contributions in each number)

Transition, PO Box 9063, Accra (Most important bi-monthly magazine serving as a forum for free and outspoken intellectual discussion in the areas of art, politics, literature, sociology and economics. Originally published in Uganda, and edited by Rajat Neogy, it is now published from Ghana and edited by the Nigerian writer Wole Soyinka)

Translation Agencies and Associations

Bureau of Ghana Languages, PO Box 1851, Accra
See entry under Publishers

Gibraltar

General Information

Language: English (both English and Spanish used commercially)
Religion: Christian (mainly Catholic) and Jewish predominantly
Population: 30,000
Bank Hours: 0900-1530 Monday-Friday, plus 1630-1800 Friday
Shop Hours: 0900-1300, 1500-2000 Monday-Friday; 0900-1300 Saturday (Jewish shops closed Saturday)
Currency: 100 pence = 1 Gibraltar pound = £1 sterling. British coins are legal tender and Bank of England notes are widely used
Export/Import Information: No tariff on books or advertising matter. No import licence. Exchange controls except for transactions with the UK
Copyright: Berne, UCC see International section

Major Booksellers

The **Book Centre***, Church Lane
Junior fiction and non-fiction

Francis **Caruana***, 249 Main St

Gibraltar Bookshop, 300 Main St Tel: 71894
Manager: A Benady

Gibraltar Junior Bookshop*, Governor's Parade
Junior literature

Imperial News Agency and Bookshop*, 291/293 Main St Tel: 4823
Children and adult literature, especially paperbacks

Major Libraries

Gibraltar Garrison Library, Library Gardens, Governor's Parade Tel: 2418
Librarian: Mrs L M Huart
Local and military history. Lending service for subscribing members

Gibraltar Library Service*, 310 Main St Tel: 71564
Opened as public library in 1979

John **Mackintosh Hall** Library*, John Mackintosh Hall, Main St Tel: 4000
Free lending library set up under will of late John Mackintosh. Mainly adult fiction

Greece

General Information

Language: Greek
Religion: Greek Orthodox
Population: 9.4 million
Literacy Rate (1971): 84.4%
Bank Hours: 0800-1300, 1730-1930 Monday-Saturday. Some open 0800-2200 daily
Shop Hours: Vary. Generally 0800-1500 Monday, Wednesday, Saturday; 0800-1330 Tuesday, Thursday, Friday; 1630-2000 Monday-Saturday
Currency: 100 lepta = 1 drachma
Export/Import Information: Becomes a member of the European Economic Community in 1981. No tariff on non-Greek books except children's picture books: free from EEC, 13% from other. Foreign-language advertising catalogues free from EEC, 4.2% from other; other advertising matter free from EEC, 9% from other. Children's picture books and advertising matter subject to 3% stamp duty, and books and advertising subject to small additional taxes, 0.50% University Tax and 0.15% Bank Fee, 1% Contribution for Farmer's Social Assistance. Only books printed in Greek need import licence; all advertising matter other than price lists require licence. No special exchange controls
Copyright: UCC, Berne, Florence (see International section)

GREECE 171

Book Trade Organizations

The **Circle** of Greek Children's Books*, Zalongou 7, Athens 142 Tel: 3602990 Greek National Section of the International Board on Books for Young People (IBBY)
Founded: 1969

Etairia Ellinon Logotechnon, Mitropoleos 38, Athens 126
Society of Greek Writers
Secretary: Phaedra Lambatha-Pagoulatou

Federation of Printing and Bookbinding Enterprises*, Psaromilingoi 22, Athens

Fédération panhellénique des Editeurs et Libraires, 39 Hippokratous, Athens 144 Tel: 3625458
Director: T Kastaniotis

Silogos Ecdoton Bibliopolon (Greek Publishers' Association)*, 22-24 Har. Trikoupi St, Athens
President: D Papademas

Book Trade Reference Books and Journals

Books

Greek Bibliography, Ministry to the Prime Minister's Office, General Direction of Press, Research and Cultural Relations Division, Athens

Journals

Bulletin analytique de Bibliographie hellénique (Analytical Bulletin of Hellenic Bibliography), Institut Français d'Athènes, 29-31 Odos Sina, Athens 144

New Books, bibliographic quarterly bulletin, I D Kollaros & Co Corporation, 38 Stadiou St, Athens 132

O Kosmos Tou Vivliou (Book World), 43 Stadiou, Athens 141

Publishers

Alkaios-Tropaiatis*, Aristidou 5, Athens
Subjects: Literature, Children's Books

Anglo-Hellenic Publishing, D Harvey & Co, Anapiron Polemou 16, Athens 140 Tel: 7012240/726687 Telex: 6850 ADKK
Man Dir: Denise Harvey; *General Manager:* Mary Frangaki; *Editorial:* Phillip Sherrard
Subjects: In English; all aspects of Greek Life and Culture, Creative Writing, General Interest. In Greek: Original Works and Translations. Specialist in production of books with Greek texts, Classical or Modern, for other publishers

Angyra Ekdotikos Oikos*, Pireaus 18, Athens 101 Tel: (021) 5223694
Man Dir: D Papadimitriou; *Publicity, Advertising, Rights & Permissions:* Nestor Hounos
Subjects: General Fiction, Belles Lettres, Poetry, History, Religion, Juveniles, Low-priced Paperbacks, Psychology
Bookshops: Bookstore Angyra, Pireaus 18, Athens 101
1977: 56 titles *Founded:* 1932

John Arsenides Ekdotis*, Akadimias 57, Athens 143 Tel: (021) 618707/629538
Man Dir: John Arsenides
Subjects: Biography, History, Philosophy, Social Science

Aspioti-Elka SA*, 276 Vouliagmenis St, Athens 459 Tel: (021) 9711021/2/3 Cable Add: Elkasp Telex: 215519 GON GR
Subjects: History, Archaeology, Folklore

Assimakopouli*, 45 Harilaou Trikoupi St, Athens Tel: 611720

Astir*, Papadimitriou, Alexandros, Lycourgou 10, Athens
Subjects: Religion, especially referring to Greek Orthodox Church; Children's and Juveniles

Ekdotike **Athenon** SA, Vissarionos 1, Athens 135 Tel: (01) 3608911
Man Dirs: George A Christopoulos, John C Bastias
Associate Company: Ekdotike Hellados SA, 8 Philadelphias Street, Athens (Printer)
Subjects: History, Archaeology, Art, High-priced Paperbacks
Bookshop: Ekdotike Athenon, Omirou 11, Athens 135
1978: 60 titles *1979:* 64 titles *Founded:* 1961

Atlantis M Pechlivanides & Co SA*, 8 Korai St, Athens 132 Tel: 3222846/3231624
Subjects: General Fiction, Nonfiction, Education, Art, Children's

Atlas-Diagoras*, Ch Trikoupi 13, Athens 142 Tel: (021) 627342

Bergadi Editions, Michel Bergadis, 4 rue Mauromichali, Athens TT 143 Tel: 3614263
Also Doryleou 22, Athens 602 Tel: 3614263
Subjects: History, Sociology, Belles Lettres, Juveniles
1978: 1 title

Boukoumanis' Editions*, Ilias Boukoumanis, Mavromichali 1, Athens 143 Tel: 3606313 Cable Add: 214422 RC GR
Man Dir: Elias Boukoumanis; *Rights & Permissions:* Mrs Roee Scaras
Subjects: History, Sociology, Belles Lettres, Children's, Psychology, Education, Politics
Founded: 1968

Chrissi Penna — Les Editions de la Plume d'Or, 6 Argentinis Dimokratias Sq, Athens 708 Tel: (01) 3618711-2/3618503/8071150/8071704-5
Man Dir: Dip Eng K Papachrysanthou
Associate Company: Papachrysanthou Chryss SA (qv)
Subjects: Juvenile, Educational, Nonfiction, Political (for adult readers)
1978: 17 titles *1979:* 11 titles *Founded:* 1964

Chryssos Typos*, 28 Harilaou Trikoupi St, Athens Tel: 637945

G **Dardanos** — H Karakatsanis and Co Ltd — Gutenberg, 103 Solonos St, Athens Tel: 3600127/3626684/3624606
Also 55-57 Didotou St, Athens
Man Dir, Editorial, Publicity, Rights & Permissions: George Dardanos; *Sales:* Christos Dardanos; *Production:* Haralambos Karakatsonis
Orders to: 55-57 Didotou St, Athens
Subjects: Art, Chemistry, Physics, Mathematics, Politics, Economics
Bookshop: 103 Solonos St, Athens
1978: 70 titles *1979:* 80 titles *Founded:* 1968

Difros*, Giannis Goudelis, Akademias 57, Athens
Subjects: Modern Greek Literature

Dodoni*, Asklipiou 3, Athens 143
Subjects: Fiction, Nonfiction, Juveniles, Encyclopaedias, History, Maps

Ekdoseis **Domi** AE*, Navarinou 20, Athens 144
Subjects: History, Encyclopaedias

Dorikos Makridis*, Z Pigis 4, Athens
Subjects: General Literary

Educational Company, 34 Panepistimiou St, Athens Tel: 3618130/3636817
Associate Company: Papaioannou (qv)

P **Efstathiadis** & Sons SA*, Valtetsiou St 14, Athens TT 144 Tel: 3600495/615011 Cable Add: Efbook Athens Telex: 216176
Branch Off: 34 Olympou-Diikitiriou Str, Thessalonica Tel: 511781
Subjects: English language teaching books and courses for Greek students; miscellaneous books connected with English (and some other languages)

G C **Eleftheroudakis** SA, Constitution Square, Nikis 4, Athens 126 Tel: (00301) 3222255 Cable Add: Elefbooks Telex: 0219410 Elef GR
Man Dir: Mrs V Eleftheroudakis-Gregos
Branch Off: 2 Sinopis Str, Tower of Athens
Subjects: Greece, Dictionaries, Fiction, Juvenile, Texts in Greek, English
Bookshop: G C Eleftheroudakis SA, Nikis 4, Athens 126 (qv)
1979: 23 titles *Founded:* 1915

Ermis*, Ippokratous 20, Athens
Subjects: Paperbacks, Literary

Eteria Ellinikon Ekdoseon*, Akadimias 84, Athens 142 Tel: 3630282/3631724/3607343
Man Dir: Stavros Tavoularis; *Editorial:* by Committee; *Sales:* Dr Caounis; *Production:* Rodakis Pericles; *Publicity:* Karayannis Nicolaos
Subjects: General Fiction, Belles Lettres, Poetry, History, Philosophy, Primary Textbooks, Educational Materials
Bookshop: Etairia Ellinikon Ekdoseon, Ermou 44, Salonika
Founded: 1958

Ekdoseis **Filon***, Panepistimiou 10, Athens 135 Tel: (021) 311714
Subjects: Literature, Philosophy, Juveniles

Chr **Fytrakis***, Stadiou 33, Athens
Subjects: Art, Biography

Giovanis*, Zoodochou Pigis 7, Athens 142 Tel: (021) 638572
Subjects: General Science, Reference, Maps, Miscellaneous

Grafia Galaxias*, Sokratous 59, Benaki Library, Odos Anthimou Gazi, Athens

Kassandra M **Grigoris***, Solonos 73, Athens 143
Subjects: Greek History and Archaeology, Literature, Translations
Associate Companies: Imha; Athanassios Karavias; Nikolaos Karavias (qqv) all at above Athens address

Dardanos **Gutenberg**, see Dardanos

Ikaros Ekdotiki*, Voulis 4, Athens
Subjects: Literature

Imha*, Solonos 73, Athens 143 Tel: 629684
Subjects: Scientific Texts on Medieval and Modern Greek History
Associate Companies: see Kassandra M Grigoris

Athanassios **Karavias***, Solonos 73, Athens 143 Tel: 629684
Subjects: Science, History
Associate Companies: see Kassandra M Grigoris

Nikolaos **Karavias***, Solonos 73, Athens 143 Tel: 629684
Subjects: Catalogues, Bibliographies, Memoirs, Modern and Medieval Greek History
Associate Companies: see Kassandra M Grigoris

Kedros*, El Venizelou 44, Athens Tel: (01) 3615783/3603572
Subjects: Literature, Philosophy, Juveniles
1978: 140 titles

Kentavros Ekdoseis OE*, Ag Konstantinou 14, Athens 101 Tel: (021) 536553
Subjects: Poetry, Juveniles, Maps

I D Kollaros & Co Corporation, 60 Solonos St, Athens 135 Tel: (021) 3635970
Publicity Manager: Evangelos Daskalou
Subjects: Fiction, History, Geography, Juveniles, Literature
Bookshop: Hestia Bookstore, 60 Solonos St, Athens
1978: 70 titles

Koymantereas*, 83 Mavromihali St, Athens Tel: 3246188

Melissa Publishing House, Nayarinou 10, Athens 144 Tel: (01) 3611692
Man Dir: George Rayas; *Sales Dir:* Chrys Rayas
Branch Off: Tsimiski 41, Salonika
Subjects: History, Art
Book Club: Athens Union
1978: 1 title *1979:* 19 titles *Founded:* 1954

Minoas*, Stadiou 43, Athens 121 Tel: (021) 3217545
Man Dir: Elias Konstantazopoulos
Subjects: General Fiction, Belles Lettres, Poetry, Biography, History, Music, Art, Reference, Juveniles, High-priced Paperbacks
Bookshop: Patission 126, Athens
Founded: 1948

Nikas*, 102 Solonos and 16 Mavromihali St, Athens Tel: 634686

Papachrysanthou Chryss SA, Graphic Arts and 'Golden Pen' Editions, 5 Mantzarou St, Athens 135 Tel: 3618711-2/8071704-5/8071150
Man Dir: K Papachrysanthou
Associate Companies: Chrissi Penna (qv), Oscar Press
Subjects: General Books, Juveniles, Tourist Guides, Comic Magazines, Paperbacks
1979-80: 24 titles *Founded:* 1888

Papaioannou, 34 Venizelou St Athens Tel: 618139
Associate Company: Educational Company (qv)

Papazissis Publishers SA*, Nikitara 2, Athens TT 142, Greece
Tel: 3622496/3609150/3638020; Telex: 219139 HAPSGR
Man Dir: Victor Papazissis; *Sales, Advertising:* Marios Haritopoulos; *Rights & Permissions:* Costas Sophoulis
Orders to: Papazissis Publishers SA
Parent Company: Corais Ltd, Nikitara 2, Athens TT 142
Subjects: Economics, Sociology, Philosophy, Politics, Law, Education, Environment, Greek Recent History, University Handbooks (especially on economics), School Books
Bookshop: Papazissis Bookshop, Nikitara 2, Athens TT 142
Founded: 1929

Papyros Press*, 17 Voulis St, Athens Tel: 3220013

Grigorios **Parissianos** 'Epistemonikai Ekdoseis'*, Solonos 69, Athens 701 Tel: (021) 610519
Subjects: Science, Medicine

G **Rayas**, 10 Nayarinou Str, Athens Tel: 3611692
1978: 1 title *1979:* 19 titles

Siamandas*, Akadimias 61, Athens Tel: (021) 615777/627164
Subjects: General Fiction & Nonfiction, History, Juveniles

J **Sideris** OE Ekdoseis, Stadiou 44, Athens Tel: (021) 3229638
Subjects: Literature, Science, Linguistics, Juveniles

Costas **Spanos**, Mavromihali 7, Athens 143 Tel: 3614332
Man Dir, Editorial: C Spanos; *Sales:* John Papadakis; *Publicity:* Katerina Spiropoulou
Subsidiary Companies: 'Leon' editions, 'Pergamini' editions
Subjects: Rare Books, Limited Editions, Byzantine and Post-Byzantine
Bookshop: 7 Maupomichali Str, Athens 143

Syropoulos Adelfoi OE Ekdotikos Oikos*, Akadimias 64, Athens Tel: (021) 614146
Subjects: Reference, History

Technical Chamber of Greece*, 4 Kar Servias, Athens 125 Tel: (021) 3222466
General Director: Ath Iatrou
Subjects: Science, Technology, Periodicals
1978: 10 titles *Founded:* 1923
Miscellaneous: The Technical Chamber of Greece (TEE) is a corporate body, under public law, supervised by the Ministry of Public Works

Tegopoulos*, 57 Panepistimiou St, Athens

Typos* 8 Londou St, Athens Tel: 619084

J **Vasiliou** Bibliopoleion*, Ippocratous 15, Athens Tel: (021) 623382
Subjects: Fiction, History, Philosophy

M **Vergadis**, see Bergadi Editions

Frères **Vlasis***, Londou 2, Athens Tel: (021) 639128
Subjects: History, Reference, General Science

Word and Vision Ltd*, 42 Trivonianou, Mets, Athens Tel: (021) 9216590 Telex: 215910
Subjects: English Language General and Travel Books, English and Greek Language Teaching Books

Z O E*, Karytsih 14, Athens 124 Tel: (021) 3223560
Man Dir: G Karadzas
Subject: Religion
Bookshops: at Karytsih 14, Athens 124; St Sophia 41, Salonika; and in three other Greek cities
Founded: 1907

Har **Zolindakis***, Panepistimiou 65, Athens Tel: (021) 314546/316504
Subject: History

Literary Agents

Anglo-Hellenic Agency*, Koumpari 5, Kolonaki Sq, Athens 138
Tel: 3606808/3606807
Specializations: Translations, Medical

Book Clubs

Athens Union, Nayarinou 10, Athens 144 Tel: (01) 3611692
Owned by: Melissa Publishing House

Vivliofilia, Mavromihali 7, Athens 114

Major Booksellers

American Bookstore, Amerikis 23, Athens Tel: (021) 3624151
See also A Samouhos Bookstore

Librairie **Cacoulides** (T Cacoulides & Co), Blvd Panepistimiou 25-29 Athens 133 Tel: 3231703/3229560
Manager: Thomas Cacoulides

P **Efstathiadis** & Sons SA*, Valtetsiou Str 14, Athens TT 144 Tel: (021) 615011/3600495
Importers and exporters

G C **Eleftheroudakis** Co Ltd, International Bookstore, Constitution Sq, Nikis 4, Athens 126 Tel: (021) 229388

Kass M **Grigoris***, Solonos 71, Athens 143

Hestia Bookstore, 60 Solonos St, Athens 135 Tel: (021) 3635970
Owned by: I D Kollaros & Co Corporation (qv under Publishers)

C **Kakoulides**, now Librairie Cacoulides

Gr **Kaloudis***, Filonos 31, Piraeus Tel: (021) 479027

Kaufmann*, Stadiou 28, Athens Tel: (021) 3222160

John **Mihalopoulos** & Son, Booksellers, Hermou 75, Salonica Tel: 279695/263786 Telex: 418562

Minoas*, Patission 126, Athens Tel: (021) 815664

Solomon **Molcho***, International Bookshop, M Alexandrou 10, Salonica Tel: 275271

Pantelides*, Amerikis 11, Athens Tel: (01) 3623673

A **Samouhos** Bookstore, Aghias Sofias 28, Thessalonica Tel: 229936
And Kassaveti 4, Kifisia, Athens
Both under same management as American Bookstore (qv)

Major Libraries

Athens Academy Library*, Odos Venizelou, Athens

Athens College Library*, Athens College, PO Box 5, Psychico, Athens Tel: 6714621

British Council Library, PO Box 488, Athens 138 Tel: 3633211/5
Librarian: Hilary Lazard

Gennadius Library, American School of Classical Studies at Athens, Souidias 61, Athens 140 Tel: (021) 710536
Acting Librarian: S Papageorgiou

National Library of Greece*, Panepistimiou, Athens Tel: (021) 614413/606495/608597

Library of the **National Technological University** of Athens*, Odos 28, Octovriou 42, Athens

Pan Library ('Circle of the Friends of Progress')*, Odos Giorgios 43, Tripolis, Arcadia

Parliament Library*, Palaia Anactora, Athens Tel: (021) 3235030

Library of the **Technical Chamber** of Greece*, Odos Karageorgi Servias 4, Athens Tel: (021) 3226001

Library of the **Three Hierarchs***, Odos Demetriados-Ogl, Volos

Library of the **University of Salonika***, Salonika Tel: 9912218

Library Associations

Enossis Ellenon Bibliothakarion*, Skouleniou 4, PO Box 2118, Athens TT 124 Tel: 322625
Greek Library Association
Secretary: Sofia Palamiotou
Publication: Bulletin

GREECE — GUINEA 173

Library Reference Books and Journals

Books

Guide to Greek Libraries and Cultural Organizations, National Printing Office, Athens

Journals

Greek Library Association Bulletin, Amerikis 11, Athens 134

Literary Associations and Societies

Association of Arts and Letters*, c/o 38 Mitropoleos St, Athens Tel: (021) 3233033
General Secretary: S Xefloudas

Kentron Ekdoseos Ellinon Syngrafeon*, Academy of Athens, Panepistimiou, Athens
Centre for the Publication of Ancient Greek Authors
Dir: Ch Floratos

P E N Centre*, 60a rue Skoufa, Athens 144
Secretary: Yannis Manglis

Vivliografiki Etaireia tis Ellados (Bibliographical Society of Greece)*, Skoufa 60, Athens 144
General Secretary: J A Thomopoulos

Women's Literary Society*, Evrou 4, Athens 611

Literary Periodicals

Aiolika Grammatia (Aeolian Letters), Hodos Nircos 41, Palaion Phaliron, Athens

Diaghonios (Diagonal), Dinos Christianopoulous, Franklin Roosevelt, Salonika 4

Nea Hestia (text in Greek), G C Eleftheroudakis AE, Nikis 4, Athens 126

Literary Prizes

Circle of Greek Children's Books Prizes*
The Circle awards prizes for the following works: Greek tales for children submitted in manuscript; stories taken from nature; poems taken from nature; plays for children; illustration of Children's Books. Enquiries to the Circle of Greek Children's Books, Zalongou 7, Athens 142

King Paul National Foundation Prize*
For an essay on community development written by an adolescent. Awarded annually. Enquiries to King Paul National Foundation, Philellinon 9, Athens 118

Tsakalos Prize*
For prose work, poetry and criticism, published by the members of the Society. 50,000 drachmas. Awarded annually. Enquiries to Society of Greek Writers, Mitropoleos 38, Athens 126

Women's Literary Society Prizes*
Each year the Society awards prizes for the following works for children: historical novel on a subject from Greek history; poems for very young children; poems for older children; a book of short stories; a theatrical play for older children; journeys and excursions within Greece. Enquiries to Women's Literary Society, Evrou 4, Athens 611

Guatemala

General Information

Language: Spanish
Religion: Roman Catholic
Population: 6.6 million
Literacy Rate: (1973): 46.1% (71.8% of urban population, 31.4% rural)
Bank Hours: 0900-1500 Monday-Friday
Shop Hours: 0800-1200, 1400-1800 Monday-Friday; 0800-1200 Saturday
Currency: 100 centavos = 1 quetzal
Export/Import Information: Member of the Central American Common Market. Duty on catalogues is $0.03 per gross kilo. No import licences, no exchange control
Copyright: UCC, Buenos Aires, Florence (see International section)

Book Trade Organizations

Gremial de Libreros de Guatemala, Avenida Reforma 13-70, Zona 9, Edificio Real Reforma Interior 13N, Guatemala City Tel: 313326/27505/26478
Association of Booksellers of Guatemala
President: Victor Hugo Granados Gonzalez

Publishers

Editorial del **Ministerio de Educacion** 'Jose de Pineda Ibarra'*, 15° Ave 3-22, zona 1, Guatemala City

Piedra Santa, 7a Ave 4-45, zona 1, Guatemala City Tel: 21867, 23051
Man Dir: Oralia Díaz de Piedra Santa;
Sales: José Muñez; *Production:* Irene Piedra Santa
Subjects: Pre-Primary, Primary & Secondary Schoolbooks, University Textbooks, Further Education, Literature, Science & Technology, Social Sciences, Tourism, Pedagogy, Psychology, Philosophy, Belles Lettres, Accountancy, Engineering, Sports, Health
Bookshops: At above address and 6a Calle 9-68, zona 1; 11 Calle 6-50, zona 1; 9a Calle 3-64, zona 4; 1a Calle 6-20, zona 9; Ave Las Américas 15-89, zona 13 (Edificio Obelisco) (all Guatemala City)

Seminario de Integración Social Guatemalteca, 11 Calle No 4-31, zona 1, Guatemala City Tel: 29754
Subjects: Sociological, Ecological, Educational, Anthropological texts connected with Guatemala
Founded: 1956

Universidad de San Carlos*, Departmento de Publicaciones, Ciudad Universitaria, Guatemala City
Printing House: 10 Calle 9-59, Guatemala City 1

Book Clubs

Libroclub de Guatemala*, Ave Elena "B" 2-25 Zona 2, El Sauce, Guatemala City Tel: 313326
Man Dir: Victor Hugo G Gonzalez
See also Libreria Cervantes (Bookseller)

Major Booksellers

Librería **'13 Calle'**, 13 Calle 8-61, zona 1, Guatemala City Tel: 81055
Manager: Mrs Consuelo Martínez

Librería **Acrópolis***, 9 Ave 13-20, zona 1, Guatemala City Tel: 80819

Librería **C E E S***, Apdo postal 652, Guatemala City

Libreria **Cervantes** — Libroclub de Guatemala*, Ave Reforma 13-70, Zona 9, Edificio Real Reforma Interior 13N, Guatemala City Tel: 313326
Direct Importers and Distributors of books in Spanish, English, German and French

Distribuidora de Libros*, Rodrigo Galindo, 11 Calle 4-15, zona 1, Guatemala City Tel: 28746

Edelcid Libros Científicos*, 11 Calle 8-66, zona 1, Guatemala City Tel: 20934

Librería **Feria** del Libro*, 6 Ave 15-65, zona 1, Guatemala City

Ediciones **Hispanas***, 13 Calle, 6-77, zona 1, of 408, Guatemala City

Distribuidora Cultural **I G A***, Ruta 1 Via 4, zona 4, Guatemala City

Librería **Universal***, 13 Calle, 4-16, zona 1, Guatemala City

Piedra Santa, 7a Ave 4-45 zona 1, Guatemala City Tel: 510231, 21867, 23051
Owned by: Piedra Santa, Publisher (qv for full list of all bookshops under this proprietorship)

Librería **Tuncho** Granados G*, 10 Calle 6-56, zona 1, Apartado Postal 13, Guatemala City, CA Tel: 24736 and 27269 also at La Plaza del Sol, Calle Montúfar y 2 Ave, zona 9, Guatemala City CA

Major Libraries

Archivo General de Centro*, América, 4a Ave, 7a-8a Calles, zona 1, Guatemala City

Biblioteca Nacional de Guatemala (National Library), 5a Ave 7-26, zona 1, Guatemala City
Librarian: Eva Evans

Biblioteca Central de la **Universidad de San Carlos**, Ciudad Universitaria, zona 12, Guatemala City
Publications: Boletín Bibliográfico, Boletín Contenidos

Library Associations

Asociación Bibliotecologica Guatemalteca (Library Association of Guatemala)*, c/o The Director, Biblioteca Nacional de Guatemala, 5a Avenida 7-26, zona 1, Guatemala, CA

Literary Periodicals

Alero (Eaves), Universidad de San Carlos, Confederacions Universitaria Centroamericana, Guatemala City

Guinea

General Information

Language: French
Religion: Muslim predominantly
Population: 4.8 million
Bank Hours: 0800-1130 Monday-Saturday
Shop Hours: 0730-1230, 1430-1830 Monday-Saturday

Currency: 100 cauris = 1 sily
Copyright: No copyright conventions signed
Export/Import Information: Books imported by State Trading Corporation: LIBRAPORT BP 270, Conakry. Tariffs listed as free for books except children's picture books 15% revenue, 10% customs. 1% ad valorem Statistical Tax; 6% cost price stamp tax. Import licences

Major Booksellers

Libraport*, BP 270, Conakry

Major Libraries

Bibliothèque nationale (National Library)*, Conakry

Institut polytechnique de Conakry*, Bibliothèque, BP 1147, Conakry

International Communication Agency Library*, c/o American Embassy, BP 711, Conakry

Library Associations

Institut national de Recherches et Documentation (National Research and Documentation Institute)*, BP 561, Conakry
Dir: S Bounama Sy

Guyana

General Information

Language: English
Religion: Hindu, Muslim, Christian
Population: 820,000
Bank Hours: 0800-1200 Monday-Friday; 0800-1100 Saturday
Shop Hours: 0800-1130, 1300-1600 Monday-Friday; 0800-1130 Saturday
Currency: 100 cents = 1 Guyana dollar
Export/Import Information: No tariff on books. Only advertising of commercial value, subject to 45% duty. Guyana National Trading Corporation, Camp and South Rd, Georgetown is sole importer of books. Import licence required. Nominal exchange controls

Publishers

Guyana Printers Ltd*, 18-20 Industrial Estate, Ruimveldt

Peter **Taylor** & Co Ltd*, La Penitence, East Bank, Demerara
Subjects: Literature, Fiction

Major Booksellers

Guyana National Trading Corporation (GNTC), 45-47 Water St, Georgetown Tel: 66191/72051
Manager: L F Austin
Sole importer of books

Major Libraries

Guyana Medical Science Library*, Georgetown Hospital Compound, Georgetown

Guyana Society Library*, Georgetown

National Library*, PO Box 110, Georgetown
Chief Librarian: Joan L Christiani

Library Associations

Guyana Library Association, 76-77 Main St, PO Box 110, Georgetown Tel: 62690/62699
Secretary: P Dos Ramos
Publication: Bulletin

Library Journals

Bulletin, Guyana Library Association, 76-77 Main St, PO Box 110, Georgetown

Literary Periodicals

University of Guyana Language Forum; review of literary, linguistic and educational studies (text in English), University of Guyana, PO Box 841, Georgetown

Haiti

General Information

Language: French and Creole
Religion: Roman Catholic
Population: 4.8 million
Literacy Rate (1971): 23.3%
Bank Hours: 0900-1300 Monday-Friday
Business Hours: Winter: 0800-1700; Summer: 0700-1500
Currency: 100 centimes = 1 gourde = $US0.20. US currency is widely used
Export/Import Information: Books charged 4% ad valorem, children's picture books 0.20 gourdes per kilo net + 4%. Advertising matter under 1 kilo gross weight duty-free. No import licences or exchange controls, other than occasional exchange rationing, leading to delays
Copyright: UCC (see International section)

Publishers

Deschamps*, Imprimerie, Grand' Rue, PO Box 164, Port-au-Prince
Subjects: History, Religion, Literature, Education, Fiction

F **Joseph***, Editions Caraibes, Lalve, Port-au-Prince

Theodor*, Imprimerie, rue Dantes Destouches, Port-au-Prince
Subjects: History, Literature, Fiction

Major Libraries

Bibliothèque du petit Séminaire*, Port-au-Prince

Bibliothèque nationale d'Haiti (National Library)*, rue Hammerton Killick, Port-au-Prince

Centre de Documentation*, Port-au-Prince

Bibliothèque Saint Louis de Gonzague*, Port-au-Prince

Literary Associations and Societies

Le **Bibliophile** (The Book Lover)*, Cap Haïtien
Secretary: Louis Toussaint
Publications: La Citadelle (weekly), *Stella* (monthly)

Literary Periodicals

La Citadelle, Le Bibliophile, Cap Haïtien

Stella, Le Bibliophile, Cap Haïtien

Honduras

General Information

Language: Spanish (English on northern coast)
Religion: Roman Catholic
Population: 3.4 million
Literacy Rate (1974): 56.9% (78.9% of urban population, 45.6% rural)
Bank Hours: 0830-1200, 1400-1630 Monday-Friday
Shop Hours: Tegucigalpa: 0800-1200, 1330-1800 Monday-Friday; 0800-1200 Saturday; San Pedro Sula: 0730-1100, 1330-1800 Monday-Friday; 0800-1200 Saturday
Currency: 100 centavos = 1 lempira = $US0.50
Export/Import Information: Member of the Central American Common Market but has applied tariffs to imports from other CACM countries since December 1970. No tariff on books. Duty on catalogues is $0.03 per kilogram. No import licences. No exchange controls
Copyright: Buenos Aires (see International section)

Book Trade Reference Journal

Bibliografía hondureña (Honduras Bibliography), Banco Central de Honduras, PO Box C-58, 1A Calle, Tegucigalpa

Publishers

Editorial Universitaria*, Universidad de Honduras, Tegucigalpa

Editorial **Nuevo** Continente*, Ave Cervantes, Tegucigalpa Tel: 225073

Major Booksellers

Librería (The Bookstore)*, Edificio Midence Soto local 108, Apdo Postal 167 C, Tegucigalpa Tel: 226824

Ney's Libros and Revistas*, Apdo 609, Tegucigalpa Tel: 23865

Librería Universitaria Jose T **Reyes***, Universidad Nacional Autónoma de Honduras, Tegucigaipa DC

University Library, see Reyes

Major Libraries

Biblioteca Nacional de Honduras*, 6a Ave Salvador Mendieta, Tegucigalpa

Sistema Bibliotecario (Librarians' System)*, Ciudad Universitaria, Carretera Suyapa, Tegucigalpa Tel: 229101/229107 ext 212/122/124
Dir: Lic Liliana S Cañadas Mejia

Library Associations

Asociación de Bibliotecarios y Archiveros de Honduras (Association of Librarians and Archivists of Honduras)*, 3 Avenidas, 4 y 5 Calles, No 416 Comayagüela, DC, Tegucigalpa
Secretary-General: Juan Angel Ayes R

Library Journals

Catálogo de Préstamo, Association of Librarians and Archivists of Honduras, 3 Avenidas, 4 y 5 Calles, No 416, Comayagüela, DC, Tegucigalpa

Hong Kong

General Information

Language: English and Cantonese
Religion: Traditional Chinese beliefs, especially Buddhism
Population: 4.6 million
Literacy Rate (1971): 77.3%
Bank Hours: Many open 7 days until 2100. Department stores: 0900-1830 Monday-Friday; 0900-1730 Saturday
Currency: 100 cents = 1 Hong Kong dollar
Export/Import Information: No tariffs on books and advertising. No import licences required. No exchange controls
Copyright: Berne, UCC (see International Section)

Book Trade Organizations

Anglo-Chinese Textbook Publishers Organization Ltd*, c/o Heinemann Educational Books (Asia) Ltd, Yik Yin Bldg 1st Floor, 321-323 To Kwa Wan Rd, Kowloon Tel: 3649221/4
Chairman: L Comber

Books Registration Unit, City Hall Library 6/F, Edinburgh Pl, Hong Kong
ISBN Administrator: Timothy A Chow

Hong Kong Booksellers' & Stationers' Association*, Man Wah House, Kowloon Tel: 3882356

Hong Kong Educational Publishers Association Ltd*, 1105 Yau Yue Bldg, 127-131 Des Voeux Rd, C
President: Au Bak Ling

Hong Kong Publishers' & Distributors' Association*, National Bldg, 4th Floor, 240-246 Nathan Rd, Kowloon

Standard Book Numbering Agency, see Books Registration Unit

Publishers

A D I S Press International Ltd*, Unit 5B, Gardena Court, Kennedy Terrace, Kennedy Rd, Hong Kong
Associate Company: ADIS Press Australasia Ltd (qv)

The **Art** Publisher*, 166 Java Rd, 2/F, North Point
Subjects: Art, Textbooks

Asia Press Ltd*, 88 Yee Wo St, PO Box 20919, Causeway Bay
President: Chang Kuo-Sin
Subjects: General Fiction, Belles Lettres, General Science, Periodicals
Founded: 1952

Book Marketing Ltd, North Point Industrial Building, Flat A, 17F, 499 King's Rd Tel: 5620121 Cable Add: Marketbook Telex: eking 85987 hx
Man Dir: Bernard Chiu King Sum
Associate Companies: Swindon Book Co, Hong Kong Book Centre Ltd, Kelly and Walsh Ltd
Subjects: Educational books and periodicals
1980: 10 titles *Founded:* 1973
ISBN Publisher's Prefix: 0-962211

Books for Asia*, 30 Tat Chee St, Yau Yat Chuen, Kowloon
Subsidiary Companies: Books for Asia (M) Sdn Bhd, Malaysia (qv); Books for Asia, Philippines; Books for Asia (S) Pte Ltd, Singapore (qv Booksellers); Books for Asia, Thailand
Subject: Textbooks

The **Chinese University Press**, The Chinese University of Hong Kong, Shatin, New Territories, Hong Kong Tel: (12) 633111 ext 461 Cable Add: sinoversity
Man Dir: Richard M Lai; *Editorial:* William C Ho; *Sales:* Patrick Kwong; *Production:* Pansy Wong
Subjects: Chinese and South-East Asian Studies, Books on Hong Kong, Dictionaries, Books in Chinese and English, Humanities, Sciences, Reprints of Rare Books, Periodicals
1978: 14 titles *1979:* 25 titles *Founded:* 1977
ISBN Publisher's Prefix: 962-201

Chopsticks Cooking Centre (CCC)*, Kowloon Central PO Box 3515 (Located at: 122 Waterloo Rd, 3rd Floor, Kowloon) Tel: (3) 015989/015911
Dir, Rights & Permissions: Cecilia J Au-Yeung; *Editor:* Virginia Au-Yeung; *Sales, Production, Publicity:* Wilson Au-Yeung
Subject: Chinese Cuisine
1978: 2 titles *1979:* 1 title *Founded:* 1975
ISBN Publisher's Prefix: 962-7018

The **Educational Publishing** House Ltd, 196-8 Tsat Tse Mui Rd, 10th Floor, North Point
Subject: Textbooks

F E P International (HK) Ltd*, 1204 Odell Ho, 32 Laichikok Rd, Mongkok, Kowloon
Subject: Textbooks

Federal Publications (HK), Unit D, 2nd Floor, Freder Centre, 68 Sung Wong Toi Rd, Kowloon
Assistant Manager: Tom Ng
Subjects: Textbooks, General Subjects, Periodicals

Good Earth Publishing Co*, c/o Everyman Book Co Ltd, 71A Prince Edward Rd, Chit King Industrial Bldg, 10th Floor, San Po Kong, Kowloon
Subject: Textbooks

Greenwood Press, 47 Pokfulam Road, G/F
Subject: Textbooks

H K Health Knowledge Publication*, Flat A, 1st floor, 7 Gough St
Subject: Textbooks

Heinemann Educational Books (Asia) Ltd, Yik Yin Bldg, 1st Floor, 321-323 To Kwa Wan Rd, Kowloon Tel: 3649221-4 Cable Add: Heinebooks Hong Kong Telex: HK 84463 (answerback — 84463 hebhk hx)
Shipping Add: KPO Box 96086, Tsimshatsui PO, Kowloon
Man Dir: Leon Comber
Branch Offs: 41 Jalan Pemimpin, Singapore 20; 2 Jalan 20/16A, Paramount Garden, Petaling Jaya, Selangor, Malaysia
Subjects: Belles Lettres, Poetry, Biography, History, Music, Art, Philosophy, Reference, Religion, Medicine, Engineering, General & Social Science, University & Secondary Textbooks, Educational Materials, Asiatic Studies, Management, Accountancy, English as Second Language
1979: 39 titles *Founded:* 1962

Hong Kong Cultural Press Ltd*, 8/F Lee Sum Factory Bldg, 23 Sze Mei St, San Po Kong, Kowloon
Subject: Textbooks

Hong Kong University Press, University of Hong Kong, 139 Pokfulam Rd Tel: (05) 502703
Dir: Geoffrey W Bonsall; *Editor:* Y K Fung
Subjects: Archaeology, History, Life Sciences, Physical Sciences, Social Sciences, Economics, Languages (especially Chinese), Literature, Economics, Fine Arts, Geography, Law, Medicine, Philosophy, Seamanship, Paperbacks, Micro-prints
1978: 4 titles *1979:* 3 titles *Founded:* 1956
ISBN Publisher's Prefix: 962-209

Hong Kong Witman Publishing Co*, 72 Kai Yuen St, G/F, North Point
Subject: Textbooks

Hung Fung Book Co*, 18 Tsat Tse Mui Rd, G/F
Subject: Textbooks

Jing Kung Educational Press*, 53 Hollywood Rd
Subject: Textbooks

King Shing Publishing Co*, 89 Sai Yee St, G/F, Kowloon
Subject: Textbooks

T H Lee & Co Ltd*, 1-15 Electric St, Upper Ground Floor, Wanchai
Subject: Textbooks

Ling Kee Publishing Co, Zung Fu Industrial bldg, 1067 King's Rd Tel: (5) 616151/2 Cable Add: Bookland
Man Dir: B L Au; *Sales Dir:* Albert Au
Subjects: Reference, University, Secondary & Primary Textbooks, Educational Materials
Bookshops: Ling Kee Book Store, Yau Yue Building, 127-131 Des Voeux Rd Central Hong Kong, and 678 Nathan Rd, Kowloon
Founded: 1949
Miscellaneous: Firm is a division of Ling Kee Group Ltd

Longman Group (Far East) Ltd*, Longman House, Tong Chong St, Quarry Bay, PO Box 223 Tel: (05) 618171/5
Man Dir: W S V Shen
Subjects: General Fiction, Belles Lettres, Art, History, General Science, Textbooks, Educational Materials, Juveniles, Languages
Miscellaneous: Firm is a member of the Longman Group Ltd, UK (qv)

Macmillan Publishers (HK) Ltd, 19/F Warwick Ho, Taikoo Trading Estate, 28 Tong Chong St, Quarry Bay Tel: (05) 636206/9, 620101/2, 643115 Cable Add: Macpublish, Hong Kong Telex: 85969 Penhk Hx

Man Dir: Nigel Carr
Parent Company: Macmillan Publishers, UK (qv)
Subject: Secondary Textbooks
1978: 27 titles *1979:* 111 titles *Founded:* 1969

Oxford University Press, 18th Floor, Warwick House, Taikoo Trading Estate, 28 Tong Chong St, Quarry Bay Tel: (05) 610221/4, 610138/9 Cable Add: Oxonian Telex: HX 65522
Man Dir: A F D Scott; *Editorial, Rights & Permissions:* C G Riches; *Marketing:* P Tam; *Production:* P Ling; *Publicity:* Mrs R Mak
Parent Company: Oxford University Press, UK (qv)
Subjects: Textbooks and Readers, Reference Works, Hong Kong Studies
1978-79: 55 titles *Founded:* 1961
ISBN Publisher's Prefix: 0-19 (OUP UK)

Perfecting Press*, 233 Lockhart Rd, 20th Floor, Flat A
Publicity Manager: Fung Pui Ming
Subject: Textbooks
1978: 8 titles

Shanghai Book Co Ltd*, 179 Connaught Rd West, 6th Floor, Flat A
Subject: Textbooks

Times Educational Co Ltd, A 7/F Melbourne Industrial Bldg, 16 Westlands Road, Quarry Bay
Subjects: Educational, General Works, Trade Books

Tin Fung Book Co*, 533 Hennessy Rd, 1st Floor
Subject: Textbooks

Union Press Ltd*, 9 College Road, Kowloon
Subject: Textbooks

Major Booksellers

Asia Press Bookstore Ltd*, 88 Yee Wo St, Causeway Bay, PO Box 2919

East Asia Book Co*, 39 Shu Kuk St, North Point

Eastern Book Service Ltd*, 11-C Majestic Bldg, 80 Nathan Rd, Kowloon Tel: 3685645
Publishers' Agents and Stockists

Far East Publications Ltd, Times Book Centre, 67-71 Chatham Rd South, Oriental Centre, Tsimshatsui Tel: (3) 689276/673194
Subject: Running series of books
Miscellaneous: Also major distributor of books, from Mok Chong St, Kowloon City Rd

Hoi Ming Book Store*, 385A Nathan Rd, Alhambra Bldg, Kowloon

Hong Kong Book Centre*, On Lok Yuen Bldg, 25 Des Voeux Rd, C

Howard Book Co*, 74 Argyle St, Kowloon

Jing Kung Book Store*, 53 Hollywood Rd

Kwong Hin Bookstore*, 75 Hollywood Rd

Ling Kee Bookstore*, 100-102 Percival St, Causeway Bay

Swindon Book Co, 13-15 Lock Rd, Kowloon Cable Add: Swindon
Manager: Rupert Li
Branch Offs: Hong Kong Book Centre Ltd, 25 Des Vouex Rd, Central Hong Kong; Kelly and Walsh Ltd, GPO Box T6, Hong Kong

Tai Kuen Book Co*, 323 Queen's Rd West

Times Book Centre*, 67-71 Chatham Rd South, Tsimshatsui
Also G31 Hutchison Ho, 10 Harcourt Rd, Hong Kong

University Book Store*, University of Hong Kong, Pokfulam Rd

World Book Co*, 74A Hollywood Rd

Major Libraries

British Council Library*, Easey Commercial Bldg 1/F, 255 Hennessy Rd, Wanchai Tel: 5-756501

Chinese University of Hong Kong Library System, Shatin, New Territories
University Librarian: Dr Lai-bing Kan
Publications include: University Library Bibliographical Series: no 1 — Union Catalogue of Serial; no 2 — Union Catalogue of Audio-Visual Materials; no 3 — An Annotated Guide to Serial Publications of Hong Kong Government

Hong Kong Junior Chamber of Commerce Libraries*, 24 Ice House St, 4th Floor

Hong Kong Polytechnic Library, Hung Hom, Kowloon Tel: (3) 638344

Sun Yat-Sen Library, 172-174 Boundary St, Kowloon

University of Hong Kong Main Library, University of Hong Kong, Pokfulam Rd Tel: (5) 468161 ext 219

Urban Council Libraries*, City Hall, Edinburgh Pl, Hong Kong Tel: (5) 233688
Acting Librarian: Alexander Ng Wai-tak

Library Associations

Hong Kong Library Association, c/o University Library, University of Hong Kong Libraries, Pokfulam Rd, Hong Kong Tel: (5) 468161
Chairman: Susanna Ko; *Honorary Secretary:* Mary Leong
Publication: Journal of the Hong Kong Library Association (irregular)

Library Journals

Journal of the Hong Kong Library Association (text in English and Chinese), Hong Kong Library Association, The University of Hong Kong Library, Pokfulam Rd

Literary Associations and Societies

Chinese Language and Literature Association*, Block A1, Fa Po Villa, 1st Floor, Fa Po St, Yau Yat Chuen, Kowloon
Secretary: Leung Nga Mei

Hong Kong Chinese P E N Centre*, Victoria Park Mansion, 15th Floor, Flat A, Paterson St
Secretary: William Hsu
Publication: PEN News (weekly in Chinese)

Hong Kong English P E N Centre, Box 1528, Kowloon Central Post Office
Chairman: Professor Hsu Yu

Literary Periodicals

Eastern Horizon (text in English), Lee Tsung-ying, 472 Hennessy Rd, 3rd Floor

PEN News (text in Chinese), Hong Kong Chinese PEN Centre, Victoria Park Mansion, 15th Floor, Flat A, Paterson St

Shui Hsing Cha Chi (Mercury Magazine) (text in Chinese, title in Chinese and English), Louise Bao, GPO Box 13154

Wu Hsia Shih Chieh, 7-13 Hsin Chieh, 2nd Floor

Hungary

General Information

Language: Hungarian (German widely known)
Religion: Predominantly Roman Catholic
Population: 10.7 million
Literacy Rate (1971): 98%
Bank Hours: 0800-1300 Monday-Friday; 0900-1100 Saturday
Shop Hours: 0900-1800 Monday-Friday; 0900-1500 Saturday
Currency: 100 fillér = 1 forint
Export/Import Information: Importation is a state monopoly so licences and tariff not of concern to exporter. Exchange controls. Book importing done through Kultura, H-1389 Budapest, Postafiók 149; atlases through Cartographia, H-1443 Budapest, Postafiók 132. Exporting is through the Hungarian Foreign Trade Organization, H-1389 Budapest 62, Postfiók 149. Magyar Hirdeto, Budapest, is a full service advertising agency
Copyright: UCC, Berne (see International section)

Book Trade Organizations

Magyar Írók Szövetsége, Budapest VI, Bajza u 18
Association of Hungarian Writers
General Secretary: Imre Dobozy

Magyar Könyvkiadók és Könyvterjesztők Egyesülése, H-1051 Budapest V, Vörösmarty tér 1 X, Postafiók 130 Tel: 184758
Association of Hungarian Publishers and Booksellers
President: György Bernát; *Secretary General:* Ferenc Zöld
Founded: 1969
Publication: Könyvvilag; also 3 quarterly journals published in German, English and French on Hungarian books

Országos Széchényi Könyvtár Magyar ISBN Iroda, Pollack Mihálytér 10, H-1827 Budapest
ISBN Administrator: Dr Susánszky Zoltánné

Standard Book Numbering Agency, see Országos Széchényi Könyvtar Magyar ISBN Iroda

Book Trade Journals

Hungarian Book Review (text in English, French and German), Kultura, H-1389 Budapest, Postafiok 149

A Könyv (The Book), Association of Hungarian Publishers and Booksellers, Budapest V, Vörösmarty tér 1, Postafiók 130

Könyv és nevelés (Book and Education), Orszagos pedagógiai könyvtár és múzeum, Budapest V, Honvéd u 19, Postafiók 49

Könyvtäjèkoztató (Information on Books), Association of Hungarian Publishers and Booksellers, Budapest V, Vörösmarty tér 1, Postafiók 130

Könyvvilag (Book World), Association of Hungarian Publishers and Booksellers, Budapest V, Vörösmarty tér 1, Postafiók 130

Magyar könyvszemle (Hungarian Bibliographical Journal); review of Book history, Bibliography and Documentation (summaries in English, French, German or Russian), Akadémiai Kiadó, Publishing House of the Hungarian Academy of Sciences, H-1054 Budapest V, Alkotmány u 21

Magyar nemzeti bibliográfia (Hungarian National Bibliography), National Széchényi Library, H-1827 Budapest, Múzeum körút 14-x6

Uj könyvek (New Books), Centre for Library Science and Methodology, H-1827 Budapest, Múzeum u 3

Publishers

Akadémiai Kiadó (Publishing House of the Hungarian Academy of Sciences), Postafiók 24 H-1363 Budapest Tel: 111010 Cable Add: Akadémaiai Kiadó Budapest Telex: 226228 AK NYO H
Man Dir: György Bernát; *Sales & Advertising Dir:* Gyula Kiss; *Publicity Dir:* György Kürti; *Rights & Permissions:* Géza Takács
Subjects: Belles Lettres, General & Social Science, Medicine, Biology, Earth Sciences, Engineering, University Textbooks, Archaeology, Book Industry, History, Arts, Reference, Literature, Music, Philosophy, Psychology, Politics, Law, Languages, Veterinary Science, Economics
Bookshop: Akadémiai Könyvesbolt, H-1052, Budapest V, Váci u 22
1978: 646 titles *1979:* 668 titles *Founded:* 1828
ISBN Publisher's Prefix: 963-05

Cärtögraphia, H-1443 Budapest XIV, Bósnyák tér 5, Postfiók 132 Tel: 634639 Cable Add: Cartographia Telex: 226218
Subjects: Maps and Atlases (compiling, drawing, printing)

Corvina Press, H-1364 Budapest 4, Vörösmarty tér 1, Postafiók 108 Tel: 176222 Cable Add: Corvina Budapest
Dir: József Szabó; *Asst Dir:* Dr Miklós Tóth; *Production Manager:* István Murányi; *Sales, Advertising & Publicity Dir:* Gábor Ila; *Editorial Dir:* Karoly Uéber
Orders to: Kultura, H 1389 Budapest 62, Postafiók 149
Subjects: Books in Hungarian & foreign languages, Art, Music, Fiction, Juveniles, Tourist Guides, General Information, Cookery Books, Sport
1978: 208 titles *Founded:* 1955
ISBN Publisher's Prefix: 963-13

Európa Könyvkiadó (Europa Publishing House), H-1363 Budapest V, Kossuth Lajos tér 13-15, Postafiók 65 Tel: 312700 Cable Add: Euroliber Telex: 225645
Man Dir: János Domokos; *Editorial:* L Antal; *Sales, Rights & Permissions:* Dr L Sármány; *Production:* K Szegleth; *Publicity:* L Horváth
Branch Off: Magyar Helikon Department, Bibliophile Section, Budapest V, Eötvös Lóránd u 8
Subjects: General Fiction, Belles Lettres, Poetry, Biography, Philosophy, Bibliophile interest
1978: 214 titles *1979:* 223 titles *Founded:* 1945
ISBN Publisher's Prefix: 963-07, 963-207

Gondolat Könyvkiadó*, H-1088 Budapest, Bródy Sándor u 16 Tel: 134840/335560
Man Dir: Dr Margit Siklós
Subjects: Reference, Art, General & Social Science
Founded: 1957
ISBN Publisher's Prefix: 963-280

Képzömüveszeti Alap Kidaóvállalata*, H-1051 Budapest V, Vörösmarty tér 1, Postafiók 110 Tel: 176222
Manager: László Takács; *Editorial:* M Pásztói; *Sales:* Dr L Csajka; *Production:* G Szedlák; *Publicity:* T Geröly
Subject: Fine Art
Bookshop: Képesbolt, Budapest VI, Deák tér 6
1978: 21 titles *Founded:* 1954

Kossuth Könyvkiadó, Steindl u 6, Postafiók 127, 1366 Budapest Tel: 117440
Publishing House of Political Literature
Manager: Gyula Rapai; *Editorial:* György Nonn; *Production:* Sándor Méth; *Rights & Permissions:* Artisjus, Vörösmarty tér 1
Subjects: History, Philosophy, Belles Lettres, Social and Political Science, Psychology, Business; Periodicals
1978: 251 titles *1979:* 254 titles *Founded:* 1944
ISBN Publisher's Prefix: 963-09

Közgazdasági és Jogi Könyvkiadó (Publishing House for Economics & Law), Nagy Sándor u 6, Postafiók 578, 1374 Budapest V Tel: 126430/312327 Telex: 226511
Man Dir: V Dalos; *Editorial, Publicity:* Dr K Cotel; *Sales:* Mrs Tamás, Alfréd Büchler; *Rights & Permissions:* Artisjus, Budapest
Subsidiary Company: Editor Minerva
Distribution: Artisjus, Budapest
Subjects: Economics, Law, Sociology, Education, Children's Literature
Founded: 1955
ISBN Publisher's Prefix: 963-220, 963-223 (Minerva)

Magvetö Könyvkiadó (Publishing House of Belles Lettres), H-1806 Budapest V, Vörösmarty tér 1 Tel: 185109
Man Dir: G Kardos; *Sales, Publicity:* I Matolcsy; *Managing Editors:* M Hegedös, A Bor; *Rights & Permissions:* via Artisjus (qv under Literary Agents)
Subjects: General Fiction, Belles Lettres, Poetry, History, Music, Art, Aesthetics, Philosophy, Low-priced Paperbacks
1978: 200 titles *Founded:* 1955
ISBN Publisher's Prefix: 963-270

Medicina Könyvkiadó, H-1361 Budapest, Póstafiók 9 (Located at: H-1054 Budapest, Beloiannisz u 8)
Publishing House of Medical Literature
Man Dir: Dr István Árky; *Editors:* Dr János Brencsán, Dr Mihály Berend; *Production:* Ferenc Fraunhoffer; *Publicity:* Dr Bulcsu Buda; *Sales & Permissions:* Artisjus (qv under Literary Agents)
Orders to: H-1361 Budapest, Póstafiók 9

HUNGARY 177

Subjects: Medicine, Travel, Sports
Founded: 1957
ISBN Publisher's Prefix: 963-240 (Medical), 963-243 (Travel), 963-253 (Sports)

Mezögazdasági Könyvkiadó Vállalat*, Budapest V, Báthory u 10 Tel: 116650/318397
Agricultural Publishing House
Manager: Dr Pál Sárkány
Subjects: Agriculture, Reference, General Science, Textbooks
Book Club: Club for Bibliophiles
Bookshop: Agricultural Bookstore, Budapest V, Vécsei u 5
1978: 102 titles *Founded:* 1950

Editor **Minerva**, subsidiary of Közgazdasági és Jogi Könyvkiadó (qv)

Móra Ferenc Ifjúsagi Könyvkiadó, H-1146 Budapest XIV, Majus 1 út 57-59 Tel: 212390
Man Dir: György Szilvásy
Subject: Juveniles
1978: 166 titles *Founded:* 1950
ISBN Publisher's Prefix: 963-11

Editio **Musica**, see Zenemükiadó

Müszaki Könyvkiadó, H-1374 Budapest V, Bajcsy-Zsilinszky u 22 Tel: 113450 Cable Add: Editechn Telex: 226490 mkh
Publishing House of Technical Literature
Man Dir: Herbert Fischer; *Editorial:* András Kelen
Orders to: Müszaki Könyvkiadó, Postafiók 581, H-1374 Budapest 5
Subjects: Science, Technical, Textbooks, Yearbooks, Catalogues
Book Club: Müszaki Könyvklub
Bookshops: 100 in Budapest, 154 elsewhere throughout country
1978: 163 scientific/technical, 380 textbooks
Founded: 1949
ISBN Publisher's Prefix: 963-10

Statisztikai Kiadó Vállalat*, H-1300 Budapest, Póstafiók 99 (Located at: Kaszás-utca 10-12, H-1033 Budapest) Tel: 688460 Telex: 224308 statiH
Statistical Publishing House
Despatch Add: Budapest III, Kaszás u 10-12
Man Dir: József Kecskés; *Sales Dir:* András Tasnádi; *Publicity and Advertising Dir:* Gyula Timár; *Rights & Permissions:* Artisjus, Budapest (qv under Literary Agents)
Subjects: Engineering, General & Social Science
Bookshop: Statistical and Computing Bookshop, Budapest II, Keleti Károly u 10 Tel: 158018
Founded: 1954

Szépirodalmi Kiadó (Publishing House of Belles Lettres), H-1073 Budapest, Lenin Körút 9-11, Postfiók 58 Tel: 221285
Man Dir: Endre Illés; *Rights & Permissions:* Ministry of Culture
Subjects: General Fiction, Belles Lettres, Poetry, Low- & High-priced Paperbacks, Educational Materials
Founded: 1950
ISBN Publisher's Prefix: 963-15

Táncsics Szakszervezeti Kiadó (Publishing House of the Trade Union Movement)*, H-1139 Budapest, Váci u 69-79 Tel: 141479/335790
Manager: István Kádár
Subjects: Technical, Nonfiction, Reference, Periodicals

Tankönyvkiadó Vállalat*, H-1055 Budapest V, Szalay u 10-14, Póstafiók 20 Tel: 324915
Textbook Publishing House
Man Dir: András Petró; *Editorial:* Sándor Hinora; *Sales:* Hugó Dobos; *Production:*

178 HUNGARY

Lajos Lojd; *Rights & Permissions:* Artisjus, H-1051 Budapest V, Vörösmarty tér 1
Subjects: Textbooks; Educational Literature, Language Books; Periodicals
1978: 791 titles *Founded:* 1949
ISBN Publisher's Prefix: 96317

Editio Musica Budapest **Zeneműkiadö***, H-1370 Budapest, Póstafiók 322 (Located at: Budapest V, Vörösmarty tér 1) Tel: 176222/184228 Cable Add: Editiomusica
Man Dir: László Sarlós
Exports: via Kultura (qv under Major Booksellers)
Subject: Sheet Music, Books on Music
1978: 46 book, 994 sheet music titles
Founded: 1950

Zrinyi Katonai Kiadó (Publishing House of the Hungarian Army)*, H-1440 Budapest Kerepesi u 29
Manager: László Bedó
Subjects: Military & Popular Science

Literary Agents

Artisjus, Vörösmarty tér 1, Postafiók 67, H-1364 Budapest Tel: 184704 Cable Add: Artisjus Telex: 226527 Arjus H
Agency for Literature, Theatre and Music of the Hungarian Bureau for Copyright Protection
Contact: Vera Acs

Book Clubs

Club for Bibliophiles*, Budapest V, Báthory u 10
Owned by: Mezögazdasagi Könyvkiadó Vállalat (Agricultural Publishing House) (Budapest)

Muskaki Könyvklub*, Bajczy-Zs ut 22, H-1051 Budapest V
Owned by: Müszaki Könyvkiadó (qv)

Major Booksellers

Állami könyvterjesztö vállalat, Budapest V, Deák Ferenc u 15
Hungarian State Book-Distributing Enterprise. It distributes books to its 112 bookshops

Állami könyvterjesztö vállalat orzágos antikvár*, Budapest V, Múzeum körút 21
Hungarian State Book-Distributing Enterprise, Department for Antiquarian Books

Hungarian Foreign Trade Organizado*, H-1389 Budapest 62, Postafiók 149
The state exporting organization

Könyvértékesitö Vállalat, H-1052 Budapest, Petöfi Sandor u 3
Hungarian Wholesale Book Trading Enterprise
This organization stockpiles and despatches all editions from Hungarian publishers, and also imported books for the retail trade. It also sells books directly for bookshops owned by co-operatives, and has a Library Service Dept which supplies the entire Hungarian Library network

Kultura, H-1389 Budapest 62, Postafiók 149 Tel: 159450 Cable Add: Kulturpress
Man Dir: A Goenyei
This company is the Hungarian export-import organization

Müvelt nép könyvterjesztö vállalat (Hungarian Educated People Book-Distributing Enterprise)*, Budapest V, Népköztársaság u 21
Distributes books through all outlets throughout the country

Major Libraries

Budapesti Müszaki Egyetem Központi Könyvtára*, Budapest XI, Budafoki u 4-6
Budapest Technical University Central Library

Eötvös Loránd Tudományegyetem Egyetemi Könyvtár*, H-1364 Budapest V, Pesti Barnabás u 1 Tel: 180960
Central Library of Loránd Eötvös University

Föszékesegyházi könyvtár, H-2500 Esztergom, Bajcsy Zsilinszky u 28 Tel: Esztergom 527
Cathedral Library
Dir: Canon Dr Zoltán Kovách

József Attila Tudományegyetem Központi Könyvtára, H-6701 Szeged, Dugonics tér 13
Central Library of the Attila József University
Librarian: Dr Béla Karácsonyi
Publications: Dissertationes ex Bibliotheca Universitatis de Attila József Nominatae; Series Bibliographica Universitatis de Attila József Nominatae; Acta Universitatis Szegediensis de Attila József Nominatae: Acta Bibliothecaria (all irregular)

Kossuth Lajos Tudományegyetem Egyetemi Könyvtár*, H-4010 Debrecen
Lajos Kossuth University Library

Könyvtártudományi és módszertani központ, H-1827 Budapest, Múzeum u 3
Centre for Library Science and Methodology
Dir: István Papp
Publications: Uj könyvek, Könyvtári figyelö, Magyar könyvtári szakirodalom bibliográfiája, Hungarian Library and Information Science Abstracts; Könyvtári és Dokumentációs Szakirodalom, Referálo Lap

Központi statisztikai hivatal könyvtár és dokumentációs szolgálat, H-1525 Budapest II, Keleti Károly u 5, Postafiók 10
Library and Documentation Service of the Central Statistical Office
Librarian: Dr Deszö Dányi
Publications: Statisztikai módszerek (Statistical Methods Surveys); Történeti statisztikai kötetek (Historical Statistics); Történeti statisztikai füzetek (Papers in Historical Statistics).

Uj **Magyar Központi Levéltár** (New Central Archives of Hungary)*, H-1014 Budapest, Hess András tér 4

Magyar országos levéltár, H-1250 Budapest I, Bécsikapu tér 4 Pf 3 Tel: 160656
National Archives of Hungary

Magyar Tudományos Akadémia Könyvtára*, H-1361 Budapest V, Akadémia u 2, Póstafiók 7 Tel: 126779/113400
Library of the Hungarian Academy of Sciences

Országos Széchényi Könyvtár, H-1827 Budapest, Póstafiók 486 (Located at: Budapest VIII, Múzeum körút 14/16) Tel: 131019 Telex: biblnathung 224226 (Information Dept: Tel: 341684)
National Széchényi Library
Dir: Dr Magda Jóború
Publications: Magyar Nemzeti Bibliográfia; Konyvek bibliográfiája; Zenemüvek bibliográfiája; Idöszaki kiadványok repertóriuma; Az Országos Széchényi Könyvtár Evkönyue; Magyar Irodalomtudományi Bibliográfia
Also a National Centre for Library Science and Methodology

Fövárosi Szabó Ervin Könyvtár*, H-1371 Budapest, Szabó Ervin tér 1, Postafiók 487 Tel: 330580; Information Service, 141005
Ervin Szabó Municipal Library

Szent benedekrend*, Közp Fökönyvtára, H-9090 Pannonhalma Tel: Pannonhalma 5/Vár
Library of the Benedictine Abbey

Tiszáninneni Református Egyházkerület Nagykönyvtára, H-3950 Sárospatak, Rákóczy út 1 Tel: Sárospatak 29
Library of the Cistibiscan Reformed Church District

University of Loránd Eötvös Central Library, see Loránd Eötvös

Library Associations

Kulturális Minisztévium **Levéltári Osztaly***, H-1014 Budapest, Uri u 54-56
National Board of Archives

Magyar Könyvtárosok Egyesülete, H-1827 Budapest, Postafiók 486 (Located at: H-1088 Budapest VIII, Muzeum u 3)
Association of Hungarian Librarians
Secretary: Dezsö Kovács

Országos Müszaki Könyvtár és Dokumentációs Központ, H-1428 Budapest, Reviczky u 6, Postafiók 12 Tel: 340151/139851 Telex: OMKDKH 224944
Hungarian Central Technical Library and Documentation Centre
Director: Dr Mihály Ágoston

Tájékoztatási tudományos társaság*, Budapest VI, Anker köz 1
Information Science Society
Deputy General Secretary: Miklós Philip

Library Journals

Hungarian Library and Information Science Abstracts (text in English and Russian), Centre for Library Science and Methodology, H-1827 Budapest, Múzeum u 3

Könyvtári figyelo (Library Review); (summaries in English, German and Russian), Centre for Library Science and Methodology, H-1827 Budapest, Múzeum u 3

Magyar könyvtári szakirodalom bibliográfiája (Hungarian Library Literature), (text in Hungarian, titles and summaries in English), Centre for Library Science and Methodology, H-1827 Budapest, Múzeum u 3

Literary Associations and Societies

Magyar Bibliofil társaság*, Budapest VIII, Brody Sándor u 16
Hungarian Society of Bibliophiles

Magyar Irodalomtörténeti Társaság, Budapest V, Pesti Barnabás u 1
Society of Hungarian Literary History
President: Gabor Tolnai; *Editor-in-Chief:* Peter Nagy
Publications: Irodalomtörténet

Magyar Tudományos Akadémia Irodalomtudományi Intézete, H-1118 Budapest XI, Menesi u 11-13
Institute of Literary Studies of the Hungarian Academy of Sciences
Dir: Professor István Sötér
Publications: Irodalomtörténeti Közlemények (quarterly); Helikon (quarterly), Literatura (quarterly), Irodalomtörténeti Könyvtár (monographs), Irodalomtörténeti Füzetek (papers); Neo-Helikon (quarterly)

Magyar P E N Club, Budapest V,
Vörösmarty tér 1
General Secretary: László Kéry
Publications: The Hungarian PEN, Le PEN hongrois (yearly bulletin)

Literary Periodicals

Kortárs (Contemporary), Kultura, H-1389 Budapest, Postafiók 149

Kritica (Critic) (summaries in French, German and Russian), Kultura, H-1389 Budapest, Postafiók 149

Literatura, Institute of Literary Studies of the Hungarian Academy of Sciences, H-1118 Budapest XI, Menesi u 11-13

Magyar muhely (Hungarian Workshop); literary and artistic review (text in Hungarian), Paul Nagy, 139 ave Jean-Jaurès, F-92120 Montrouge, France

New Hungarian Quarterly (text in English), H-1088 Budapest 8, Rákóczi u 17

Literary Prizes

Jozsef **Attila** Prize
For highly significant work in prose or poetry. Given to writers, poets and critics. Awarded annually. Enquiries to Ministry of Culture of the Hungarian People's Republic, Budapest

Szot Literary Prizes*
For meritorious literary works. Awarded annually. Enquiries to Hungarian Trade Unions Council, Budapest VI, Dozsa György u 84 B

Translation Agencies and Associations

Magyar Írok Szövetsége (Association of Hungarian Writers), Budapest VI, Bajza u 18
Has a section of Literary Translators

Iceland

General Information

Language: Icelandic (widespread knowledge of Danish and English)
Religion: Lutheran
Population: 224,000
Bank Hours: 0930-1330 Monday-Friday
Shop Hours: 0900-1800 Monday-Friday; open until 2200 Thursday or Friday, open until noon Saturday
Currency: 100 aurar (singular: eyrir) = 1 króna (plural: krónur)
Export/Import Information: No tariff on books. Sales Tax of 20% or 22%. No import licences required. No exchange controls for books but they may not be imported on credit
Copyright: UCC, Berne, Florence (see International section)

Book Trade Organizations

Félag Islenskra Bókaútgefenda, Laufasvegi 12, 101 Reykjavik Tel: 9127820
Icelandic Publishers' Association
Chairman: Oliver Steinn Jóhannesson; *General Manager:* G Ólafsson
Publications: Íslensk Bókatídindi

Félag Islenzkra Bókaverzlana*, Skólavödustig 2, Reykjavik
Icelandic Booksellers' Association
Publications: Bóksalafélag Islands Sjöttu Og Fimm Ára

Innkaupasamband Boksala (Booksellers' Import Union Ltd)*, Skipholti 7, 105 Reykjavik

Rithöfundasamband Íslands, PO Box 949, 121 Reykjavik
Writers' Union of Iceland
Chairman: Njördur P Njardvík

Book Trade Reference Books and Journals

Books

Bóksalafélag Islands Sjötíu og Fimm Ára (75 years of the Icelandic Booksellers' Association), Skólavördustig 2, Reykjavik; contains addresses of publishers and booksellers

Journals

Arbók (Year Book), National Library of Iceland, Reykjavik; contains an annual list of Icelandic publications

Bókalisti (Booklist), City Library of Reykjavik, Thingholtsstr 29A, Reykjavik

Bokaskara Boksalafelags Islands, Icelandic Publishers' Association, Laufasvegi 12, 101 Reykjavik

Bókatídindi, Icelandic Publishers' Association, Laufasvegi 12, 101 Reykjavik (annual list of books published in Iceland)

Islensic Bó Kaskrá (The Icelandic National Bibliography), National Library of Iceland, Reykjavik (appears in *Íslensk Bókatídindi*)

Íslensk Bókatídindi (Icelandic Book News), Icelandic Publishers' Association, Laufasvegi 12, 101 Reykjavik

Publishers

Bókaútgáfa **Æskunnar***, Laugavegi 56, 101 Reykjavik

Almenna Bókafélagid, Austurstr 18, PO Box 9, 101 Reykjavik Tel: 19707 Cable Add: Bókafélagid Telex: 2046
Man Dir: Brynjólfur Bjarnason; *Editorial:* Eirikur H Finnbogason; *Sales Dir:* Anton Örn Kaernested; *Production:* Kristinn Dagsson; *Rights & Permissions:* Stefania Pétursdóttir
Subjects: General Fiction, Belles Lettres, Poetry, Biography, History, Secondary Textbooks, Juveniles
Bookshop: Bókaverzlun Sigfúsar Eymundssonar (BSE), Reykjavik
Book Club: The AB Book Club (BAB) PO Box 9
1978: 51 titles *1979:* 34 titles *Founded:* 1955

Atlantica, PO Box 1238, Reykjavik
Subjects: Books on Iceland in English: Travel, Geology, Folklore, Literature, Culture

Bókaútgáfa Thórhalls **Bjarnarsonar**, Skemmuvegi 4, 200 Kopavogi

Bókaútgáfan **Björk***, Háholti 7, 300 Akranes

Bokaforlag Odds **Björnssonar**, Tryggvabraut 18-20, PO Box 558, 600 Akureyri Tel: 22500 Cable Add: Prentverk
Man Dir: Geir S Björnsson; *Advertising Dir:* Kirstjan Kristjansson
Subjects: General Fiction, Belles Lettres, Poetry, Biography, History, How-to, Music, Art, Philosophy, Reference, Religion, Juveniles, Educational Materials
Book Club: Heima er Bezt Book Club
1978: 14 titles *1979:* 14 titles *Founded:* 1897

Bokas hf*, Adalstr 35, 400 Isafirdi

Bókaútgáfan **Bragi***, Austurstr 17, 101 Reykjavik

Bókaverslun Sigfusar **Eymundssonar***, Austurstr 18, 101 Reykjavik
Subject: Educational Books
Bookshop: Address as above

Bókaútgáfa Gudjóns Ó **Gudjónssonar***, Langholtsvegi 111, Reykjavik Tel: 85433

Haraldur J **Hamar**, PO Box 93, Reykjavik Tel: 81590 Telex: 2121
Associate Company: Saga Publishing Co (qv)
Subjects: Iceland
1978: 5 titles

Heimskringla, Laugavegi 18, Reykjavik Tel: 15199
Publications Editor: Thorleifur Hauksson; *General Manager:* Thröstur Ólafsson

Bókaútgáfan **Helgafell***, Veghúsastíg 7, Reykjavik Tel: 16837

Bókaútgáfan **Hildur***, Fögrubrekku 47, 200 Kópavogi Tel: 44400

Hladbúd hf, subsidiary of Idunn (qv)

Bókaútgáfan **Hlidskjálf***, Ingólfsstr 22, 101 Reykjavik Tel: 17520

Iceland Review, PO Box 93, 121 Reykjavik (Located at: Hverfisgötu 54) Tel: 27622 Telex: 2121
Man Dir: Haraldur J Hamar
Associate Company: Saga Publishing Co (qv)
Subjects: The *Iceland Review Series* (all in English) gives an overall picture of the country of Iceland, its culture and developing society; also History, Folklore, Industrial (in English); Icelandic Literature in Foreign Translation
1978: 5 titles *1979:* 4 titles *Founded:* 1962

Iceland Travel Books, subsidiary of Orn og Orlygur (qv)

Idunn*, Braedraborgarstíg 16, PO Box 294, 121 Reykjavik Tel: 19156 Cable Add: 2308 publis is
Owner: Valdimar Jóhannsson; *Man Dir:* J P Valdimarsson; *Rights & Permissions, Production:* S Ragnarsson
Subsidiary Companies: Hladbud (University Textbooks); Skalholt (Icelandic Literature)
Subjects: General Fiction, Juveniles, Educational, Poetry, Law, Psychology, Philology, History, Natural Sciences, Philosophy, Management, Social Sciences, Art
1978: 90 titles *Founded:* 1945

Ísafoldarprentsmidja hf*, Tningholtsstr 5, 101 Reykjavik Tel: 17165

Hid **Íslenzka Bókmenntafélag**, Thingholtstraeti 3, Reykjavik Tel: 21960
President: Sigurdur Lindar; *Chief Executive:* Sverrir Kristinsson
Subjects: Law, Linguistics, Literature, Philosophy, Politics, Psychology, Social Science, Natural Science
1979: 55 titles *Founded:* 1816

ICELAND

Snaebjörn **Jonsson** & Co HF (The English Bookshop), Hafnarstr 4 & 9, PO Box 1131, 101 Reykjavik Tel: 11936/13133 Cable Add: Books Reykjavik
Man Dir: Benedikt Kristjánsson
Subjects: All Subjects
Bookshops: The English Bookshop, Hafnarstr 9, Reykjavik; Bókaverzlun Snaebjarnar, Hafnarstr 4, Reykjavik
Founded: 1927

Bókaútgáfa Thorsteins M **Jónssonar***, Eskihlíd 21, 105 Reykjavik

Kynning Ltd,, PO Box 1238, Reykjavik Tel: 38456, 74153
Subjects: Books on Iceland in general and on special subjects such as volcanoes, geology, geography, history, literature etc

Leiftur hf*, Höfdatúní 12, 105 Reykjavik Tel: 17554

Bókagerdin **Lilja***, Amtmannsstíg 2b, 101 Reykjavik

Mál og menning, Laugavegi 18, Reykjavik Tel: 15199
Publications Editor: Thorleifur Hauksson; *General Manager:* Thröstur Ólafsson
Bookshop/Book Club: address as above

Bókaútgáfa **Menningarsjóds** og Thjód vinafélagsins*, Skálholtsstíg 7, 101 Reykjavik Tel: 13652/10282

Örn og Örlygur HF, Sídumúli 11, 105 Reykjavik Tel: 84866 Cable Add: Örn og Örlygur Telex: 2197
Owner and Man Dir: Örlygur Hálfdanarson
Subsidiary Companies: Iceland Travel Books, Vesturgötu 42, Reykjavik
Subjects: General Fiction, Belles Lettres, Poetry, Biography, History, How-to, Reference, Religion, Juveniles, Low- & High-priced Paperbacks, Social Science
Book Club: Hraundragni
1978: 60 titles *1979:* 60 titles *Founded:* 1965

Ríkisútgáfa Námsbóka, Tjarnagötu 10, Reykjavik 101, PO Box 1274 Tel: 10436/20830
State Educational Publishing Department
Dir: Bragi Gudjonsson; *Sales:* Vidar Gunnarsson; *Production/Publicity:* Bogi Indridason; *Rights & Permissions:* Eirikur Grimsson
Subjects: School Textbooks and Supplies
Bookshop: Skólavörubúdin, Tjarnargata 10, Reykjavik
1978: 48 titles *1979:* 98 titles *Founded:* 1937

Rökkur, bókaútgáfan*, Flókagötu 15, Reykjavik Tel: 18768

Saga Publishing Co, PO Box 93, 121 Reykjavik (Located at: Hverfisgotu 54) Tel: 27622 Telex: 2121
Man Dir: Haraldur J Hamar
Associate Company: Iceland Review (qv)
Subjects: General (Adults and Juveniles)
1978: 5 titles *1979:* 4 titles *Founded:* 1971

Setberg, Freyjugötu 14, 101 Reykjavik Tel: 17667 *Cable Add:* Setbergpublish
Subjects: History, Juveniles, General Non-fiction, Fiction, Illustrated Juvenile

Skalholt, subsidiary of Idunn (qv)

Bókaútgáfan **Skjaldborg** sf*, Hafnarstr 67, 600 Akureyri Tel: 11024

Skuggsja bókaforlag*, Strandgötu 31, 220 Hafnarfirdi Tel: 50045
Subject: General Fiction

Bókaútgáfan **Snaefell***, Alfaskeidi 58, 220 Hafnarfirdi

Bókaútgáfan **Sudri***, PO Box 1214, Kleppsvegi 2, 105 Reykjavik Tel: 36384

Bókaútgáfan **Thjódsaga***, Thingholtsstr 27, 101 Reykjavik Tel: 13510
Subjects: General Fiction, Travel, General Science, Juveniles

Bókaútgáfan **Valafell***, Thykkvabae 16, 110 Reykjavik Tel: 84179
Subject: General Fiction

Literary Agents

Sveinbjörn **Jonsson**, Gardastr 21, PO Box 438, Reykjavik Tel: (91) 28110/13206
Specialization: General Fiction and nonfiction, books, magazines, plays, TV scripts

Book Clubs

The **A B** Book Club, Austurstr 18, PO Box 9, Reykjavik
Owned by: Almenna Bókafélagid

Heima er Bezt Book Club, Tryggvabraut 18-20, PO Box 558, 600 Akureyri
Owned by: Bokaforlag Odds Björnssonar

Hraundragni Book Club, Sídumúli 11, 105 Reykjavik
Owned by: Örn og Örlygur

The **Icelandic Libertarians'** Book Club, PO Box 1334, 121 Reykjavik (Located at: Hafnarhvoll v/Tryggvagoetu, 101 Reykjavik) Tel: (91) 21850
Members: 320
Owned by: The Freedom Association
Specialization: Economics, History, Philosophy, Political Science, Libertarianism
Founded: 1979

Mal Og Menning, Laugavegi 18, Reykjavik Tel: 15199
Bookshop: Bókabúd Máls og Menningar, at same address

Major Booksellers

The **English Bookshop**, Hafnarstr 4 and 9, PO Box 1131, Reykjavik Tel: (91) 13133, 14281, 11936 Cable Add: Books Reyjavik
Owned by: Snaebjörn Jónsson & Co HF (qv)
Manager: Benedikt Kristjansson

Bókábudin **Helgafell***, Laugavegur 100, Reykjavik
also Njalsgata 64, Reykjavik

The **Icelandic Libertarians'** Bookshop, PO Box 1334, 121 Reykjavik (Located at: Hafnarhvoli v/Tryggvagoetu, 101 Reykjavik) Tel: (91) 21850 Telex: 2074 europa is
Specializing in History, Politics, Economics, Philosophy, with special emphasis on the ideology of Libertarianism
Manager: Skafti Hardarson
Owned by: The Freedom Association

The **International Bookshop***, Bókaverzlun Sigfúsar Eymundssonar, Austurstr 18, Reykjavik Tel: 19707/16997/32620

Bókaverzlun **Ísafoldar***, Austurstr 10, Reykjavik

Bókabúd **Máls og Menningar**, Laugavegi 18, Reykjavik Tel: 24242

Major Libraries

Borgarbókasafn*, Thingholtsstr 29A, Reykjavik
City Library of Reykjavik

Háskólabókasafn, 101 Reykjavik Tel: 25088 Telex: 2307 isinfo
University Library
Head Librarian: Einar Sigurdsson
Publication: Annual Report

Landsbókasafn Islands*, Reykjavik Tel: 13375 (Director); 16864 (Staff)
National Library of Iceland

Thjodskjalasafn (National Archives)*, Safnahús, Reykjavik

University Library, see Háskólabókasafn

Library Associations

Bókavardafélag Islands, Box 7050, 127 Reykjavik
Icelandic Library Association
President: Thórdís Thorvaldsdóttir
Secretary: Kristín Björgvinsdottir
Publication: Fréttabréf (Newsletter) and Bókasafnid

Deild bokavarda i islenskum rannsoknarbokasofnum, Landsbokasafn Islands, Reykjavik Tel: 13080
Division of Librarians in Icelandic Research Libraries
Executive Secretary: Helgi Magnússon

Library Journals

Fréttabréf (Newsletter), Icelandic Library Association, Box 7050 Reykjavik

Skírnir, Icelandic Literary Society, Reykjavik

Literary Associations and Societies

Íslenzka bókmenntafélag, Thingholtstraeti 3, Reykjavik
Icelandic Literary Society
President: Sigurdur Lindal
Publication: Annual Journal, Skírnir

International **P E N** Centre*, Fifuhvammsvegi 19, Reykjavik
Secretary: Gisli Astthorsson

India

General Information

Language: Hindi and English are used for official purposes. Fourteen other languages are accorded recognition by the constitution, including Sanskrit which is not now spoken. Generally each administrative state includes speakers of a particular major language. In all, over 1500 languages and dialects are spoken in India
Religion: Predominantly Hindu
Population: 638 million
Literacy Rate (1971): 33.4% (59.9% of urban population, 26.4% rural)
Bank Hours: 1000-1400 (1030-1430 Bombay) Monday-Friday; 1000-1200 Saturday (1030-1230 Bombay)
Shop Hours: Delhi: 0930-1930; Calcutta and Bombay: 1000-1830 Madras: 0900-1930. All effective Monday-Saturday, some open Sunday. Many close 2 hours for lunch
Currency: 100 paise = 1 rupee

Export/Import Information: No tariff on books but advertising matter subject to 100%. Import licences required. Educational books may be imported by booksellers under open general licence. Exchange transactions restricted.
Copyright: UCC, Berne, Buenos Aires (see International section)

Book Trade Organizations

Ahmedabad Publishers' & Booksellers' Association, 47 Gandhi Rd, Ahmedabad 380001 Tel: 366917
President: C C Vora

Akhil Bhartiya Hindi Prakashak Sangh*, Hindi Book Centre, 4/5-B Asaf Ali Rd, New Delhi 110001
President: K C Berry

All India Booksellers' & Publishers' Association*, 17-L Connaught Circus, PO Box 328, New Delhi 110001 Tel: 42166
President: A N Varma

Assam Publishers' & Booksellers' Association*, Lawyers Book Stall, Gauhati

Authors' Guild of India*, C-44 Gulmohar Park, New Delhi 110049
Secretary: D R Mankekar
Publication: The Indian Author

Bihar Pustak Vyayasayi Sangh, Bharat Bhawan, Govind Mitra Rd, Patna 4
Secretary: A Pandey

Bombay Booksellers' and Publishers' Association, 25 6th Floor Building No 3, Navjivan Co-op Housing Society Ltd, Dr Bhadkamkar Marg, Bombay 400008 Tel: 398691
Honorary Secretary: C P Gupta; *Executive Secretary:* U S Manikeri

Booksellers' and Publishers' Association of South India*, c/o Higginbothams Ltd, Mount Rd, Madras-600002

Chandigarh Booksellers' Association*, SCO No 3 Sector 17-E, Chandigarh Tel: 23594
President: V S Puri

Delhi State Booksellers' and Publishers' Association, c/o The Students' Stores, Kashmere Gate, PO Box 1511, Delhi 110006 Tel: 227088/225716
President: Devendra Sharma; *Hon Secretary:* Bhupinder Chowdhri

Educational Publishers' Association*, 2607 Amir Chand Marg, New Delhi 110006

Federation of Indian Publishers*, M-138 Aggarwal Bldg, Connaught Circus, New Delhi 110001 Tel: 350811
Executive Secretary: M C Minocha

Federation of Booksellers and Publishers Association in Gujarat*, Post Box 334 GPO, Ahmedabad 380001
Honorary Secretary: P D Shevade

Federation of Publishers and Booksellers Associations in India, 1st Floor, 4833/24 Govind Lane, Ansari Rd, New Delhi 110002 Tel: 272845
President: C M Chawla; *Honorary Secretary:* Vinod Kumar; *Executive Secretary:* J N Kapoor
Publications: Directory of Indian Publishers, Recent Indian Publications

Gujarat State English Language Booksellers' Association, Academic Book Centre*, 10 Walkeshwar, Ambawadi, Ahmedabad 380015 Tel: 837883
Honorary Secretary: R N Shah

The **Gujarat Textbook** Publishers' Association*, Balgovind Kuberdas & Co, Gandhi Rd, Ahmedabad

Himachal Publishers' & Booksellers' Association*, Goel Book Depot, Palampur Tel: 43151
President: H K S Goel

The **Hyderabad** & Secunderabad Publishers' & Booksellers' Association*, c/o Sri Satyanarayana Book House, Gowligudachaman, Hyderabad (AP)
Secretary: K Satya Narayana

Karnataka Publishers' and Booksellers' Association*, 504 Avenue Rd, Bangalore 560002

Kerala Publishers & Booksellers Association*, Paico Buildings, Jew Street, Ernakulam, Cochin 682011 Tel: 34068
Cable Add: Paico
President: D C Kezhakemuri

Lanka Booksellers' Association*, Kohinoor Bldgs, University Rd, Varanasi Tel: 62771
President: Lalchand Mankhand

Meerut Publishers' Association*, c/o Rastogi Publications, Shivaji Rd, Meerut 250002, Uttar Pradesh

Poona Booksellers' & Publishers' Association*, Hindustan Sahitya, 309 Shaniwar Peth, Poona 30

Publishers' & Booksellers' Association of Andhra Pradesh, Sree Venkateswara Book Depot, Main Rd, Guntur 522003
Secretary: P Narasimha Rao

Publishers' and Booksellers' Association of Bengal*, 93 Mahatma Gandhi Rd, Calcutta 700007
Publication: Granthajagat

Publishers' and Booksellers' Guild, 5A Bhawani Dutta Lane, PO Box 12341/700073, Calcutta 700073
President: S Sarkar; *Secretary:* B K Dhur

Publishers' Association of South India*, 1 Sunkurama Chetty St, Madras 600001 Tel: 29402
President: T V S Mani

Punjabi Publishers' Association*, 354 Purani Kutchery, Jullundur City

Rajasthan Pustak Vyavasayee Sangh*, SMS Highway, Jaipur 3
President: J L Jasoria

Standard Book Numbering Agency, Ministry of Education & Social Welfare (Department of Education), Raja Rammohun Roy National Educational Resources Centre, 1 W-3 C R Barracks, Kasturba Gandhi Marg, New Delhi 110001
ISBN Administrator: Mrs Nilima Devi

Book Trade Reference Books and Journals

Books

American Book Trade in India; a directory of wholesale and retail booksellers, Asian Bookmarket Information Service, 73-47-255th St, Glen Oaks, New York 11004, USA

Bookdealers in India; a directory of antiquarian booksellers in Bangladesh, Bhutan, India, Nepal, Pakistan and Sri Lanka, Sheppard Press Ltd, 15 James St, PO Box 42, London WC2E 8BX, UK

Directory of Book Trade in India, National Guide Books Syndicate, 5c/54 Rohtak Rd, New Delhi 110005

Directory of Foreign Book Trade in India, Lord International, 19 Netaji Subhash Marg, Daryaganj, New Delhi 110002

Directory of Indian Publishers, Federation of Publishers and Booksellers Associations in India, 1st Floor, 4833/24 Govind Lane, Ansari Rd, New Delhi 110002

Indian Books, Indian Bibliographic Centre, 236 Kot Kishan Chand, Jullundur 4, Punjab (books in English only) (annual)

Indian Books; an annual bibliography, Researchco Publications, 1865 Trinagar, Delhi 35 (books in English only) (annual)

Indian Books in Print, Indian Bibliographies Bureau, 2153/2 Fountain, Delhi 6

Indian Publishers' Directory, Mukherjee & Co Pvt Ltd, 2 Bankim Chatterjee St, Calcutta 700012

Journals

American and British Book News, Kunnuparampil P Punnoose, 6/77 WEA Karol Bagh, New Delhi 110005

BEPI; an annual bibliography of English publications in India, DKF Trust, 74-D Anand Nagar, Delhi 110035

Book Reviews in Public Administration, Indian Institute of Public Administration, Indraprastha Estate, Ring Rd, New Delhi 110001

Granthajagat, Publishers' and Booksellers' Association of Bengal, 93 Mahatma Gandhi Rd, Calcutta 700007

Indian Book Chronicle, Vivek Trust, G-11 Hauz Khas Market, New Delhi 110016. Book news and reviews (fortnightly)

Indian Book Industry, Sterling Publishers Pvt Ltd, AB/9 Safdarjang Enclave, New Delhi 110029

Indian Book Review Supplement, Delhi Library Association, PO Box 1270, c/o Hardinge Public Library, Queen's Garden, Delhi 6

Indian Books; an information leaflet, Mukherjee Library, 1 Gopi Mohan Dutta Lane, Calcutta 700003

Indian National Bibliography, Central Reference Library, c/o National Library, Belvedere, Calcutta 27

Indian Publisher and Bookseller, Popular Book Depot, Dr Bhadkamkar Rd, Bombay 400007

Literary Market Review, 6/77 WEA Karol Bagh, New Delhi 110005 (quarterly)

Paperbound Books, 6/77 WEA Karol Bagh, New Delhi 110005 (quarterly)

Publishing News, D K Agencies, 74-D Inderlok, Old Rohtak Rd, Delhi 110035

Pustak Parichaya (text in Hindi), 2/35 Ansari Rd, Daryaganj, Delhi 6

Recent Indian Publications, Federation of Publishers and Booksellers Associations in India, 1st Floor, 4833/24 Govind Lane, Ansari Rd, New Delhi 110002

Publishers

A U Press & Publications, Andhra University, Visakhapatnam 530003 Tel: 4871
Dir, Rights & Permissions: A U Waltiar
Subjects: Languages, Literature, Humanities, Sciences
1978-79: 27 titles 1979-80: 13 titles
Founded: 1926

Aadiesh Book Depot, 7A/29 WEA Karol Bagh, New Delhi 110005 Tel: 564103/221204
Chief Executive: Aadiesh Kumar Jain
Imprint: Nalanda Books
Subject: Dictionaries
Bookshop: 4123 Nai Sarak, Delhi 110006

Abhinav Publications, E-37 Hauz Khas, New Delhi 110016
Dir: Shakti Malik
Subjects: Indian Art & Archaeology, Indology, Humanities, Literature, Social Sciences, Criminology, Politics
1978: 17 titles *1979:* 29 titles *Founded:* 1970

Abhishek Publications, 3625 Sector 23-D, Chandigarh 160023
Chief Executive, Production, Publicity: S L M Prachand; *Editorial:* Sunil Kumar Chandna; *Sales, Rights & Permissions:* Bharat Bhushan
Associate Company: Nirjhar Prakashan (at above address)
Subjects: History, Politics, Philosophy, General
1978: 4 titles *1979:* 2 titles *Founded:* 1977

The **Academic Press**, Old Subzi Mandi, Gurgaon, Haryana 122001 Tel: 2205
Subjects: Social Sciences, Humanities
1978: 2 titles *1979:* 2 titles *Founded:* 1968

Academic Publishers, 5A Bhawani Dutta Lane, PO Box 12341/700073, Calcutta 7000073 Tel: 340936 Cable Add: Acabooks
Man Dir: Bimal Kumar Dhur; *Sales Dir:* Biren Dutta; *Publicity Dir:* S Das; *Rights & Permissions:* L K Ghosh
Branch Off: Shanti Mohun House, I-1/16 Ansari Rd, Delhi 110002
Subjects: Accountancy, Commerce, History, Indology, Literature, Management, Medicine, Philosophy, Research
1978: 4 titles *1979:* 4 titles *Founded:* 1958

Academy of Comparative Philosophy & Religion, Guruder Mandir, Hindwadi, Belgaum 590011 Tel: 22231
Chief Executive, Production, Publicity: J V Parulekar; *Editorial:* K D Tangol; *Sales:* G V Dharwadkar
Subjects: Philosophy, Religion, Mysticism, Morals
1978: 1 title *1979:* 5 titles *Founded:* 1966

Academy of Islamic Research and Publications, PO Box 119, Lucknow 226001 (Located at: Tagou Marg, Nadwa, Lucknow) Tel: 42948 Cable Add: Nadwa
President, Rights & Permissions: S Abdul Hasan Ali Nadwi; *Chief Executive:* Mohammad Ralicy; *Manager, Production:* Mohammad Ghiyathuddin; *Editorial:* S G Mohiwddin; *Sales:* Mohammad Zaki; *Publicity:* S M Ghujran
Branch Off: Karachi, Pakistan
Subjects: Islamic Literature, History, Current Affairs, Hadith and Quran
1978: 6 titles *1979:* 9 titles *Founded:* 1959

Directorate of **Adult** Education, 34 Community Centre, Basant Lok, Vasant Vihar, New Delhi 110057 Tel: 671890/674860 Cable Add: Adultedu
Chief Executive: A K Jalaluddin
Subject: Adult Education
Founded: 1978

Advaita Ashrama, 5 Dehi Entally Rd, Calcutta 700014 Tel: 44-2898 Cable Add: Vedanta
Subjects: Religion, Philosophy, Yoga, Vedanta, Indian Culture, Education
1978: 22 titles *1979:* 29 titles

Affiliated East-West Press Pvt Ltd, 92 Montieth Rd, Madras 600008 Tel: 812258 Cable Add: Knowledge
Man Dir: K S Padmanabhan; *Editorial Dir:* Kamal Malik
Subjects: Science, Engineering, Technology, Humanities, Social Sciences, Low-priced Reprints of US and British Textbooks
Founded: 1962

Agam Kala Prakashan, 34 Community Centre, Ashok Vihar, Delhi 110052 Tel: 713395
Editorial, Sales, Publicity, Rights & Permissions: Agam Prasad; *Production:* A K Bhargava
Associate Company: Agam Prakashan
Subjects: Indian Art, Archaeology, Culture
1978: 15 titles *1979:* 15 titles *Founded:* 1977

Ahlvwalia Book Depot, PO Box 2507, New Delhi 110005 (Located at: 9953-4 New Rohtak Rd, New Delhi)
Partners: J N Ahlvwalia, R K Ahlvwalia
Subject: Urdu Literature (Fiction and Non-fiction)
1978: 12 titles *1979:* 15 titles *Founded:* 1954

Ajanta Books International, PO Box 2194, Delhi 110007 (Located at: 1-UB Jawaharnagar, Bungalow Rd, Delhi) Tel: 227425
Chief Executive, Production, Publicity, Rights & Permissions: S Balwant; *Editorial:* Dr S S Noor; *Sales:* Ramesh Kumar
Associate Company: Ajanta Publications (India) (at above address)
Subjects: All Social Sciences, Indology
1978: 18 titles *1979:* 18 titles *Founded:* 1975

Akhila Bharaliya Sanskrit Parishad, Mahatma Gandhi Marg, Hazratganj, Lucknow 226001 Tel: 43962
Subjects: Sanskrit and Indology, based on Sanskrit, Pali and Psakrita
1978: 2 titles *1979:* 2 titles *Founded:* 1951

Alekh Prakashan, V-8 Navin Shahdara, Delhi 110032 Tel: 204331
Chief Executive: Umesh Chand
Subjects: Literature, Journalism, Linguistics (all in Hindi & English)
1978: 28 titles *1979:* 26 titles *Founded:* 1976

Allied Publishers Private Ltd, 16 J N Heredia Marg, Ballard Estate, Bombay 400038 Tel: 261959 Cable Add: Folio
Man Dir: R N Sachdev
Branch Offs: 13-14 Asaf Ali Rd, New Delhi 110002; 17 Chittaranjan Ave, Calcutta 700072; 150/B/6 Mount Rd, Madras 600002; Jayadeva Hostel Bldg, 5th Main Rd, Gandhinagar, Bangalore 560009
Subjects: General Fiction, Belles Lettres, Art, History, Philosophy, Education, How-to, Psychology, Law, Social, Political & General Science & Technology
1978: 45 titles *1979:* 57 titles *Founded:* 1934

Alpha-Beta Publications Ltd*, 55-1 College St, 2nd Floor, Calcutta 700012

Amar Prakashan, Al/139B Lawrence Rd, Delhi 110035 Tel: 713182 Cable Add: Amarpra
Chief Executive, Publicity, Rights & Permissions: H S Juneja; *Editorial:* Surjeet Anand; *Sales:* Hardeep Singh; *Production:* Pardee P Kumar
Subjects: Sociology, History, Political Science
1978: 9 titles *1979:* 10 titles *Founded:* 1977

Amarko Book Agency*, B-42 Amar Colony, Lajpat Nagar, New Delhi 110024
Man Dir, Production, Publicity, Rights & Permissions: V N Bhardwaj; *Sales:* Ashok Bhardwaj
Subjects: History, Philosophy, Religion
Founded: 1973

Ambika Publications, B-1/598 Janak Puri, New Delhi 110058 Tel: 591072 Cable Add: Ambika
Man Dir, Editorial, Rights & Permissions: P P Anand; *Sales:* Ms Manmeet Maini; *Production:* Suhas Nimbalkar; *Publicity:* Ms Nirdosh Anand
Associate Companies: Arpan International (at above address); Tagore Trading Co, ED 54 Tagore Gardens, New Delhi 110027
Subjects: Sociology, Politics, Anthropology, Ancient and Medieval History, Art, Religion, Buddhism, Tibetan Studies, Management
1978-79: 40 titles *Founded:* 1977

Amerind Publishing Co (P) Ltd, subsidiary of Oxford & IBH Publishing Co (qv)

Amina Book Stall, Post Office Rd, Trichur 680001 Tel: 23387/23254
Chief Executive: Haji K B Aboobacker
Associate Company: Amina Printers (at above address)
Subjects: Humanities, Social Science, Fiction
Founded: 1948

Amudha Nilayam Ltd, PO Box 674, Madras 600014 (Located at: 46 Royapettah High Rd, Madras) Tel: 841343
Man Dir: K V Jagannathan
Subjects: Tamil Classics, Literature, Fiction, Criticism
1978: 7 titles *1979:* 4 titles *Founded:* 1949

Anand Paperbacks, an imprint of Orient Paperbacks (qv)

Ankur Publishing House*, Uphaar Cinema Building, Green Park Extension, New Delhi 110016 Tel: 664611
Man Dir: Mrs Seema Mukerjee
Associate Company: Sanjay Composers and Printers (at above address)
Subjects: Politics, Science, Literature
1978: 5 titles *1979:* 3 titles *Founded:* 1976

Archaeological Survey of India, Janpath, New Delhi 110001 Tel: 382121 Cable Add: Archaeology
Editorial: H Sarkar; *Sales:* S R Varma
Subjects: Archaeology, Epigraphy, etc

Arnold-Heinemann Publishers (India) Pvt Ltd, AB/9 Safdarjang Enclave, New Delhi 110029 Tel: 667886 Cable Add: Heinemann
Man Dir: G A Vazirani; *Editorial:* Ms Kaushiki Sen Varma; *Accounts:* Bhagwan Singh; *Production:* Mukesh Vazirani; *Publicity:* Ms Rani Roy; *Rights & Permissions:* Ms Kaushiki Sen Varma; *Sales:* Maninder Singh
Associated Companies: Edward Arnold, UK (qv); Heinemann Educational Books, UK (qv)
Imprints: Mayfair Paperbacks, Sanskriti, Zebra Books for Children
Subjects: Art, General Fiction, Belles Lettres, Poetry, Philosophy, Religion, Reference, Literary Criticism, Medicine, Engineering, Social Science, Political Science, University, Secondary & Primary Textbooks, Low-priced Paperbacks
1978: 110 titles *1979:* 120 titles *Founded:* 1969

Ashish Publishing House, H-12 Rajouri Garden, New Delhi 110027 Tel: 587316/564319
Editorial: S B Nangia; *Sales:* Gopal Sharma
Subjects: History, Political Science, Economics, Education, Biography, Public Administration

Asia Publishing Co, A/132 College St Market, Calcutta 700007 Tel: 342386
Editorial: Gita Dutta; *Sales:* Ashim Mukherjee
Subject: Fiction
Founded: 1954

Asia Publishing House (P) Ltd*, Calicut St, Ballard Estate, Bombay 400038
Tel: 262631/3 Cable Add: Booklore
Chairman, Man Dir: Ananda Jaisingh;
Editorial Consultant: Homi Vakeel
Branch Offs in India: 67 Ganesh Chandra Ave, Calcutta 700013; Indra Palace, Connaught Circus, New Delhi 110001; 199 Mount Rd, Madras 600002; 18 Purana Quilla, Lucknow 226001
Branch Off outside India: 141 East 44th St, New York, NY 10017, USA
Subjects: General Fiction, Belles Lettres, Poetry, Biography, History, Music, Art, Philosophy, Reference, Religion, Low- & High-priced Paperbacks, Medicine, Psychology, Engineering, General & Social Science, University Textbooks, Educational Materials, Business Studies
Founded: 1961

Asian Educational Services, C-2/15 SDA, PO Box 4534, New Delhi 110016
Tel: 633325 Cable Add: Asia-Books New Delhi 110016
Chief Executive: Jagdish Jetley; *Production:* Mrs S Jetley; *Editorial, Rights & Permissions, Publicity:* A N Arora
Subjects: Ancient Indian History and Culture, Religion, Philosophy, Sociology, Literature, Linguistics
1978: 25 titles *Founded:* 1973

Asian Publishers, an imprint of Sterling Publishers Pvt Ltd (qv)

Asian Publishers, PO Box 205, 85-C New Mandi, Muzaffarnagar, Uttar Pradesh 251001 Tel: 3775
Man Dir and Publicity: Mittal Ved Prakash; *Sales:* Mittal Satya Prakash; *Production:* Mittal Dinesh Prakash
Subsidiary Company: Kalanidhi Printing Press (at above address)
Subjects: Technical, Scientific, Agricultural
Bookshop: Mittal & Company (at above address)
1978: 18 titles *1979:* 6 titles *Founded:* 1971

Asian Trading Corporation, PO Box 2587, Bangalore 560025 (Located at: St Thomas Building, 150-156 Brigade Rd, Bangalore)
Tel: 51807 Cable Add: Paspin
Chief Executive: F M Pais; *Sales:* P Travers
Associate Company: Jyothi Book House, 156 Brigade Rd, Bangalore
Subjects: Religion, Philosophy, Counselling & Sociology
1978: 7 titles *1979:* 5 titles *Founded:* 1946

Associated Publishing House, New Market, Karol Bagh, New Delhi 110005 Tel: 563069
Man Dir, Sales: Ravinder K Paul; *Editorial, Production Dir:* Ashok K Paul; *Publicity Dir, Rights & Permissions:* Sharda Paul
Subjects: General, Fiction, Belles Lettres, Poetry, History, Art, Reference, Social Science, Business, Reprints
1978: 18 titles *1979:* 11 titles *Founded:* 1966

Atma Ram & Sons, Kashmere Gate, PO Box 1429, Delhi 110006
Tel: 223092/228159 Cable Add: Books Delhi 6
Man Dir, Publicity, Rights & Permissions: Ish Kumar Puri; *Editorial, Production:* Sushil Kumar Puri; *Sales:* Ashutosh Pury
Branch Off: 17 Ashok Marg, Lucknow
Subjects: Belles Lettres, Art, History, Philosophy, Religion, Education, Reference, How-to, Juveniles, Medicine, Engineering, Social Science, Science & Technology, Paperbacks, Textbooks
Bookshop: At above address
1979: 31 titles *1980:* 36 titles *Founded:* 1909

Sri Aurobindo Books Distribution Agency (SABDA), Sri Aurobindo Ashram, Pondicherry 605002 Tel: 980 Cable Add: Sabda c/o Aurobindo
Man Dir: B Poddar; *Sales:* Sri Parasnath; *Rights & Permissions:* Sri Harikant Patel
Branch Off: 'Sahakar' B Rd, Bombay 400020
Subjects: Yoga, Philosophy, Religion, Education, History, Social & Political Science (English, French, German, Sanskrit etc)
Bookshops: 9B rue de la Marine; 2 rue de la Caserne (both in Pondicherry)
1979: 52 titles *1980:* 50 titles *Founded:* 1952

B R Publishing Corporation*, 461 Vivekananda Nagar, Delhi 110035
Tel: 274819 Cable Add: Dikay Book Telex: 31-3616-DK-IN
Chief Executive, Editorial, Production: I C Mitral; *Sales, Rights & Permissions:* S K Bhatia; *Publicity:* Praveen Mitaal
Orders to: D K Publishers' Distributors, 1 Ansari Rd, New Delhi 110002
Parent Company: D K Publishers' Distributors
Associate Company: D K Publications (qv for other associate companies)
Subjects: Art, Archaeology, History, Social Sciences, Anthropology
1978: 20 titles *Founded:* 1974

K P Bagchi & Co, 286 B B Ganguli St, Calcutta 700012, West Bengal Tel: 267474
Editorial, Chief Executive, Publicity, Rights & Permissions: P K Bagchi; *Editorial, Sales, Production:* K K Bagchi
Branch Off: I-1698 C R Park, New Delhi 110019
Subjects: Anthropology, History, Economics, Political Science, Indology, Sociology, Language and Literature
1978: 10 titles *1979:* 31 titles *Founded:* 1972

Baha'i Publishing Trust, PO Box 19, New Delhi 110001 (Located at: Baha'i House, 6 Canning Rd, New Delhi 110001) Tel: 389326/387004 Cable Add: Bahaifaith Telex: 0314881 Nsa In
Man Dir, Production, Rights & Permissions: D Vahedi; *Editorial, Publicity:* Surinder Mehta; *Sales:* N K Budhiraia
Parent Company: National Spiritual Assembly of the Baha'is of India (at the above address)
Subject: The Baha'i Religion
1978: 39 titles *1979:* 37 titles *Founded:* 1955

The **Bangalore** Printing & Publishing Co Ltd, 88 Mysore Rd, PO Box 1807, Bangalore 560018, Karnataka Tel: 601638/601027 Cable Add: Mudrashala
Man Dir: H C Ramanna
Branch Off: The Bangalore Press, Statue Sq, Mysore
Subjects: Biography, Philosophy, Religion, Psychology, Social Science, University, Secondary & Primary Textbooks, Agriculture, Fiction (in English and Kannada languages), Calendars, Diaries
Bookshop: Bangalore Press Agencies, Avenue Rd, Bangalore 2
1978: 20 titles *1979:* 21 titles *Founded:* 1916

Bani Mandir, New Market, Dibrugarh, Assam 786001 Tel: 1255 Cable Add: Bani Mandir
Chief Executive: Sri Chandra Kanta Hazarika; *Editorial, Production:* Surjya Kanta Hazarika; *Sales:* Ujjal Kumar Hazarika; *Publicity:* Utpal Hazarika
Subjects: Fiction, Criticism, School and College Textbooks, Reference Books
1978: 8 titles *1979:* 12 titles *Founded:* 1949

Bani Publications, 30 Pataldanga St, Calcutta 700009
Chief Executive: Sakti Sadan Bhattacharyya; *Editorial:* Sivasadhan Bhattacharjee; *Sales:* S R Mukherjee
Subject: Oriental & Indological Studies

Bansal and Co, K-16 Naveen Shahdara, Delhi 110032 Tel: 212292
Chief Executive: R S Bansal; *Editorial, Sales, Production, Publicity, Rights & Permissions:* Hari Gupta
Subjects: Bibliography, Indology, Hindi Literature in English (Series of 12 volumes, *Contours and Landmarks in Hindi Literature*)
Founded: 1959

Better Yourself Books, 28-B Chatham Lines, Allahabad 211002, Uttar Pradesh Tel: 53728
Man Dir: Mathew Veehoor; *Publicity:* Fr Mark Fonseca
Parent Company: Saint Paul Publications (qv)
Subjects: Home Life, Self-improvement, Biography, Moral Science, Indology, Fiction, Practical Psychology, Sex Education, Media Education
1978: 50 titles *1979:* 50 titles *Founded:* 1954

Bhaimi Prakashan, 537 Lajpat Rai Market, Delhi 110006 Tel: 269032
Editorial: P K Bhatia; *Sales:* Bhimsen Shastri
Subject: Sanskrit Literature

Bhaktivedanta Book Trust, Hare Krishna Land, Juhu, Bombay 400049 Tel: 566860 Cable Add: Iskcon Telex: 114964 Iskn In
Chief Executive: Poornabrahma Das; *Editorial:* Gopal Krishna Das; *Sales:* N Narayan
Subject: Religion

Bharat-Bharati*, B-28/15 Durgakund, Varanasi 5
Owner: Suresh Pandey; *Man Dir:* Ganga Nath Pandey
Subjects: Poetry, History, Music, Art, Philosophy, Religion, Oriental & Indian Studies
Founded: 1968

Bharat Law House, 15 Mahatma Gandhi Marg, Allahabad 211001 Tel: 3797
Chief Executive, Production: D C Puliani; *Sales:* Ashok Puliani; *Publicity:* Ravi Puliani
Subject: Law
1978: 5 titles *1979:* 3 titles *Founded:* 1957

Bharati Sahitya Sadan Sales, 30-90 Connaught Circus, New Delhi 110001 Tel: 343557
Editorial: Padmesh Datt; *Sales:* Yogendra Datt
Subject: Hindi Literature
Founded: 1946

Bharatiya Jnanpith, B/45-47, Connaught Pl, New Delhi 110001 Tel: 322294 Cable Add: Jnanpith
Dir and Rights & Permissions: Lakshmi Chandra Jain; *Sales, Production, Publicity:* Dr Gulab Chandra Jain
Branch Off: Durgakunda, Varanasi 221001
Subjects: Rare and unpublished texts of Indology (in Sanskrit, Pali, Prakrit, Apbhramsha, Kannada and Tamil, with their translations), Hindi Literature (in original, as well as translations from Indian languages)
1978: 15 titles *1979:* 18 titles *Founded:* 1944

Bharatiya Publishing House, 42-43 UB Jawaharnagar, Delhi 110007 Tel: 220274
Chief Executive, Production, Publicity: Gajendra Singh; *Sales:* Digvijay Singh
Subsidiary Company: Indological Book House, 7 Malka Ganj, Delhi
Branch Off: B/9-45, Pilkhana, Sonarpura, Varanasi
Subjects: Ancient Indian History, Art, Architecture, Archaeology, Religion, Philosophy, Jainism, Yoga, Sanskrit, etc
1978: 250 titles *1979:* 280 titles *Founded:* 1960

Bharatiya Vidya Bhavan, PO Box 4057, Munshi Sadan, Kulapati K M Munshi Marg, Bombay 400007 Tel: 351461 Cable Add: Bhavidya
Man Dir, Editorial, Rights & Permissions: S Ramakrishnan; *Sales:* V A Madhavan; *Production:* C K Venkataraman
Branch Off: Ahmedabad, Bangalore, Baroda, Bhopal, Bhubaneswar, Calcutta, Chandigarh, Coimbatore, Dakor, Delhi, Ernakulam, Guntur, Hyderabad, Jammu, Jamnagar, Kakinada, Kanpur, Kashmir, Madras, Madurai, Mangalore, Mukundgarh, Nagpur, Shillong, Trichur, Visakhapatnam (all in India); 4a Castle Town Rd, London W14, UK
Subjects: History, Philosophy, Religion, Art, Literature, Culture, Biography, Gita, Vedas, Upanishads, Gandhiana, Mythology, Fiction, Sociology
1978: 56 titles *Founded:* 1938

Bihar Hindi Granth Akademi, Sammelan Bhawan, Kadamkuan, Patna 800003 Tel: 50390
Chairman: Prof Devendra Nath Sharma; *Dir, Rights & Permissions:* Prof Damodar Thakur; *Editorial:* Dr Ramdeo Tripathy; *Sales, Production, Publicity:* Thakur Y N Singh
Subjects: Science and Humanities at University level (in Hindi)
1978: 22 titles *1979:* 10 titles *Founded:* 1970

The **Bihar State** Textbook Publishing Corporation Ltd, Budh Marg, Patna 800001 Tel: 21975
Chief Executive: D P Chaudhary; *Editorial:* D N Jha; *Production:* Devabrat Sarkar
Subject: Academic
Founded: 1966

Booklinks Corporation, 3-4-423/5 & 6 Narayanaguda, Hyderabad 500029 Tel: 65021/45830 Cable Add: Booklinks
Chief Executive, Editorial: K B Satyanarayana; *Sales, Production, Publicity:* T Jagannatham
Subject: Social Sciences
Bookshop: At above address
1978: 2 titles *1979:* 2 titles *Founded:* 1965

Book Field Centre, an imprint of Era Book Enterprises (qv)

Bookventure*, 14 Thaninabhalam Chetty Rd, Madras 600017 Tel: 441970
Proprietor: Lakshmi Krushnamurti
Subjects: General Fiction, Belles Lettres, Poetry, Biography, History, Music, Art, Philosophy, General Science
Founded: 1965

Bright Careers Institute, 1525 Nai Sarak, Delhi 110006 Tel: 262827
Chief Executive, Sales: S P S Phull; *Editorial:* D Sarna; *Production, Publicity:* P S Bright
Associate Company: Bright Careers Publications (at above address)
Branch Off: Bright Careers Publications, 17 Thambu Chetty St, Madras
Subjects: General Knowledge, English, Essays, Competition Books, History, Science, Mathematics
1978: 35 titles *1979:* 47 titles *Founded:* 1968

Business Promotion Bureau, 376 Old Lajpat Rai Market, Delhi 110006 Tel: 224666/237147/229355
President: G C Jain
Subsidiary Company: Radio & Crafts Publications, 4794 Bharat Ram Rd, 23 Daryaganj, New Delhi 110002
Subjects: Radio, Electronics (in English)
1980: 100 titles *Founded:* 1958

Central Book Depot (Publishers), 44 Johnstonganj, Allahabad Tel: 2408/2130/53727
Man Dirs: K L Bhargava, M L Bhargava; *Sales Dir:* H S Banerji
Subsidiary Company: Indian University Press, 18/C Queens Rd, Allahabad
Branch Off: 13 University Rd, Allahabad
Subjects: History, Philosophy, Medicine, Psychology, Engineering, General & Social Science, University & Secondary Textbooks
Founded: 1880

Central Hindi Directorate, West Block VII, R.K. Puram, New Delhi 110022 Tel: 699511 Cable Add: Rajbhasa
Chief Executive: A K Sukul; *Editorial:* R P Malviya; *Sales:* O P Bhardwaj; *Production:* H L Sharma
Subject: Hindi
Founded: 1968

Central Institute of Indian Languages, Manasagangotri, Mysore 570006 Tel: 24862/23558 Cable Add: Bharati
Chief Executive: D P Pattanayak
Subjects: Linguistics, Language Teaching
Founded: 1969

S **Chand** & Co Ltd, Ravindra Mansion, PO Box 5733, Ram Nagar, New Delhi 110055 Tel: 517531 Cable Add: Eschand, New Delhi Telex: 0312185
Man Dir: S L Gupta; *Editorial, Publicity:* R C Kumar; *Rights & Permissions:* R K Gupta
Associated Companies: Eurasia Publishing House Pvt Ltd (qv); Rajendra Ravindra Printers Ltd, New Delhi
Branch Offs: in Bombay, Calcutta, Patna, Lucknow, Jullundur, Hyderabad, Madras, Bangalore, Nagpur, Cochin
Subjects: Art, Philosophy, Economics, Social & Political Science, Science and Technology
Bookshop: 4/16-B Asaf Ali Rd, New Delhi 110002
1978: 125 titles *1979:* 90 titles *Founded:* 1917

Charotar Book Stall, Tulsi Sadan, Station Rd, Anand 388001 Tel: 182/358
Chief Executive, Editorial, Production, Publicity, Rights & Permissions: Ramanbhai C Patel; *Sales:* Bhavin R Patel
Branch Offs: Near Post Office, Vallabh Vidyanagar, Via Anand; Amul Dairy Rd, Anand
Subject: Engineering Textbooks
1978: 35 titles *1979:* 38 titles *Founded:* 1944

Chaukhambha Orientalia, Gokul Bhawan K 37/109, Gopal Mandir Lane, PO Box 32, Varanasi 221001 (UP) Tel: 63022 Cable Add: Gokulotsav
Managing Partner: Braj Bhavan Das Gupta
Branch Off: Delhi
Subjects: Indian Classical Literature, Oriental Art, Science (in Sanskrit, Hindi, English)

Chetana Publishers Pvt Ltd*, 34 Rampart Row, Bombay 400023
Man Dir: Chetana Kohli; *Sales & Publicity Dir, Rights & Permissions:* Suresh Kohli
Subjects: General Fiction, Biography, History, How-to, Philosophy, Religion, Low-priced Paperbacks, Social Science
Founded: 1974
Subsidiary: India Paperbacks, 11052 East Park Rd, New Delhi 110005

Children Book House, South Extension Part I, New Delhi 110049 Tel: 692003/4
Sales: Zakarias Joseph; *Production:* R S Gupta
Subject: Children's Books

Children's Book Trust, 4 Bahadur Shah Zafar Marg, New Delhi 110002 Tel: 2719215 Cable Add: Child Trust
Chief Executive: K Shankar Pillai; *General Manager, Rights & Permissions:* S P Chatterjea; *Editorial:* G Govindan; *Sales:* M S Kohli; *Production:* M L Gupta; *Publicity:* K Ramakrishnan
Subject: Children's Books
1978: 18 titles *1979:* 20 titles *Founded:* 1957

Chinmaya Mission, E-27 Defence Colony, Ring Road, New Delhi 110024 Tel: 617257
Chief Executive, Sales: Brahmachari Radhakrishnan; *Production:* Swami Chinmayananda
Subject: Vedantic Literature

The **Chowkhamba** Sanskrit Series Office, K37/99, Gopal Mandir Lane, PO Chowkhamba, PO Box 8, Varanasi-221001 Tel: 63145 Cable Add: Chowkhamba Series, Varanasi
Man Dir, Publicity, Rights & Permissions: Bithal Das Gupta; *Editorial:* Pandit Ramchandra Jha; *Sales, Production:* Brij Mohan Das Gupta
Associate Company: Chaukhamba Amarbharati Prakashan, K37/118, Gopal Mandir Lane, PO Box 138, Varanasi 221001
Subjects: Juveniles, Educational Materials, Primary, Secondary & University Textbooks, Poetry, Biography, History, Music, Art, Philosophy, Reference, Religion, Oriental, Indology
Bookshop: At above address
1978: 3 titles *Founded:* 1892

The **Christian** Literature Society, PO Box 501, Park Town, Madras 600003 Tel: 39296/7 Cable Add: Vedic
General Secretary, Editorial, Rights & Permissions: Dr T Dayanandan Francis; *Sales, Publicity:* D Paul Rajaratnam; *Production:* D Packiamuthu
Branch Offs: The Diocesan Press, PO Box 455, Madras 600007; The Wesley Press, PO Box 37, Mysore City 570001; The C.L.S. Press, PO Box 4234, 1 Dickenson Rd, Bangalore 560042
Subjects: Religion, Textbooks, General, Children's Books
Bookshops: CLS in Hyderabad, Madras, Bangalore, Mysore City, Cochin, Tiruvalla, Coimbatore, Madurai District, Madurai, Vellore
1978: 40 titles *1979:* 29 titles *Founded:* 1857

College Book House, PO Box 103, Trivandrum 695001 (Located at: 28/1549 Sudarsan, Overbridge, Trivandrum) Tel: 2214
Man Dir, Editorial, Production, Rights & Permissions: M Easwaran; *Sales:* M Girija; *Publicity:* R Radhakrishnan
Subjects: Indian Studies, Religion, Philosophy, Education, Economics, Sociology, History, Kerala (South India)
Bookshop: College Book House, Library Division (at above address)
1979: 20 titles *1980:* 12 titles *Founded:* 1973

Concept Publishing Co, H 13 Bali Nagar, New Delhi 110015 Tel: 503967
Chief Executive: Naurang Rai; *Editorial:* Suhasini Ramaswamy; *Sales, Publicity:* Ashok Kumar
Parent Company: D K Agencies, Delhi 110035
Associate Companies: D K Publishers' Distributors (qv); DKF Trust; University Publishers (qv)
Subjects: Indology, Anthropology, Art, Sociology, Philosophy, Economics, Public Administration, Geography, Bibliography, History, Political Science
1978: 30 titles *1979:* 45 titles *Founded:* 1975

Crescent Publishing Co, 4 Abdul Qadir Market, Jail Rd, Aligarh 202001 Tel: 3711 Cable Add: Milestone
Man Dir, Publicity, Rights & Permissions: Firoz Ahmad; *Editorial:* M Rafat; *Sales:* Anwar Hussain; *Production:* N R Farooqui
Subjects: Religion, Academic
1978: 2 titles *1979:* 3 titles *Founded:* 1976

Current Books, PO Box 212, Kottayam 686001 (Located at: VIII/493 Railway Station Rd, Kottayam) Tel: 2942 Cable Add: Current Books
Chief Executive: D C Kizhakemuri; *Editorial:* M S Chandrasekhara Warrier; *Sales:* P K Jayapalan; *Production, Publicity:* V R Radhakrishnan Nair; *Rights & Permissions:* Ponnamma Deecee
Branch Offs and Bookshops: Trivandrum, Alleppey, Kottayam, Ernakulam, Trichur, Calicut, Tellicherry
Subjects: Fiction, Non-fiction
Founded: 1952

D C Books, PO Box 214, Kottayam 686001 (Located at: Good Shepherd St, Kottayam) Tel: 3114/3226/8214 Cable Add: Deecibooks
Chief Executive, Rights & Permissions: D C Kizhakemuri; *Editorial:* M S Chandrasekhara Warrier; *Sales:* E T Abraham; *Production, Publicity:* Muttambalam Sathyan
Subjects: Fiction, Poetry, Literature, Children's Books, Reference Books
Book Club: D C Book Club
1978: 75 titles *1979:* 122 titles *Founded:* 1974

D K Publications, 1 Ansari Rd, New Delhi 110002 Tel: 247819 Cable Add: Dekaypub Telex: Dikay ND 3616
Partners: I C Mittal, Praveen Mittal, Pramil Mittal; *Editorial:* I C Mittal; *Sales, Production, Publicity, Rights & Permissions:* S K Bhatia
Parent Company: DK Agencies, 74D Inderlok, Old Rohtak Rd, Delhi 110035
Associate Companies: DK Book Organization, 74/D Anand Nagar, Delhi 110035; BR Publishing Corp, India (qv); Concept Publishing Co, India (qv); Inter-India Publications, India (qv)
Branch Off: No 4 Gurayoor Appan Mansions, No 28/30 Khana Bagh 3rd Lane, Triplicane, Madras 600005; T C 789 Devivilas Compound, Chenthittal, Trivanorum 23
Subjects: Humanities and Social Sciences
1978: 30 titles *Founded:* 1974

D K F Trust, 74-D Anandnagar, Delhi 110035 Tel: 504418 Cable Add: Dikaybook Telex: 313616 Dk
Chief Executive: Sh Khazan Chand; *Editorial, Sales, Production, Publicity, Rights & Permissions:* Naurang Rai
Associate Company: Concept Publishing Co
Subject: Directories
1978: 1 title *1979:* 1 title *Founded:* 1977

Dastane Ramchandra and Co*, 456 Raviwar Peth, Phadke Houd, PO Box 535, Poona 411002 Tel: 48193
Man Dir: R D Dastane; *Editorial, Production:* S R Dastane; *Sales, Publicity, Rights & Permissions:* V R Dastane
Associated Company: Abhang Stores, Printers & Stationers (address as above)
Subjects: Chemistry, Geology, Geography, Botany, Sociology, Economics, Literature, Archaeology
Founded: 1960

Daystar Publications, 23/2 Punjabi Bagh Extension, New Delhi 110026 Tel: 590747
Chief Executive: Indu Lekha; *Editorial, Sales, Production, Publicity, Rights & Permissions:* Dr G R Garg
Subject: Book Trade
Founded: 1978

Debooks, 9 Creek Row, Calcutta 700014
Publicity, Rights & Permissions: Mrs R De; *Marketing, Sales:* Ajoy De; *Accounts:* Asok De
1978: 4 titles *1979:* 4 titles *Founded:* 1975

Deep & Deep Publications, D-1/24 Rajouri Garden, New Delhi 110027 Tel: 504498
Chief Executive, Rights & Permissions: K D Singh; *General Manager, Sales, Publicity:* G D Singh; *Editorial:* H S Bhatia; *Production:* G S Bhatia
Subjects: Politics, Military Affairs, Law
1979: 8 titles *1980:* 16 titles *Founded:* 1974
Miscellaneous: Also booksellers and exporters

Dey Sahitya Kutir (P) Ltd, 21 Jhamapukur Lane, Calcutta 700009 Tel: 354294/5
Editorial: S C Mazumdar; *Sales:* Barun Chandra Mazumdar; *Production:* R Chatterjee
Subject: Children's Books

Dhanpat Rai & Sons, 1683 Nai Sarak, Delhi 110006 Tel: 265367
Partners: O P Kapur, J C Kapur, K K Kapur
Branch Offs: Delhi, Jullundur
Subjects: Engineering, Education, Commerce
1978: Over 100 titles *1979:* Over 100 titles
Founded: 1929

Diamond Comics*, 2715 Daryaganj, New Delhi 110002
Associate Companies: Diamond Books International, Diamond Pocket Books (both at above address); Punjabi Pustak Bhandar (qv)
Subject: Juveniles (in Hindi and English)

Dini Book Depot*, 4160 Urdu Bazar, Jamamasjid, Delhi 110006 Tel: 268632/274855 Cable Add: Dini Book
Man Partner, Sales, Production: Arshad Saeed; *Editorial:* Rashid Saeed; *Publicity:* Shahid Saeed
Subsidiary Company: Saeed International (Regd), 2112 Nahar Khan St, Daryaganj, New Delhi 2
Subjects: Islamic Studies, Textbooks
1978: approx 65 titles *1979:* approx 65 titles
Founded: 1945
Miscellaneous: Also importers, exporters and suppliers

Doaba House, 1688 Nai Sarak, Delhi 110006 Tel: 274669
Chief Executive, Editorial, Sales, Rights & Permissions: S N Malhotra; *Production, Publicity:* A C Seth
Subjects: Books in English, Literature, Education
1978: 15 titles *1979:* 20 titles *Founded:* 1924

Eastern Book Co, 34 Lalbagh, Lucknow 226001 Tel: 43171 Cable Add: Law Book
Chief Executive: C L Malik; *Editorial:* Surendra Malik; *Sales, Rights & Permissions:* P L Malik; *Production:* Kamal Malik; *Publicity:* Vijay Malik
Associate Companies: Current Legal Publications, Lucknow; Law Times Press, Lucknow; Manav Law House, Allahabad; Eastern Book Co (Sales), Delhi; SCC Reprinting & Binding Co, Lucknow
Subject: Law
1979: 89 titles *Founded:* 1947

Eastern Law House Pvt Ltd, 54 Ganesh Chunder Ave, Calcutta 700013 Tel: 274989 Cable Add: Lauriports, Calcutta
Man Dir: B C De; *Sales Executive:* Asok De; *Marketing Executive:* Ajoy De; *Editorial, Production, Publicity, Rights & Permissions:* A K De
Editorial Off: 11 Raja Subodh Mullick Sq, Calcutta 700013
Branch Off: 36 Netaji Subhas Marg, Daryaganj, New Delhi 110002
Subjects: Law, Accounting, Political & Social Science
Bookshops: 54 Ganesh Chunder Ave, Calcutta 700013; 36 Netaji Subhas Marg, Daryaganj, New Delhi 110002
1978: 22 titles *1979:* 31 titles *Founded:* 1918

Educational Enterprises, 5/1 Ramnath Mazumdar St, Calcutta 700009 Tel: 340101/424880
Chief Executive: S Ghosh; *Editorial:* Arun Ghosh
Subjects: Education, Psychology

Era Book Enterprises, 14 Mohan Nivas, Chandavarkar Rd, Bombay 400019 Tel: 473993 Cable Add: Goldenhill
Chief Executive, Rights & Permissions: Eranna R Jinde; *Editorial:* C V Bhimasankaram; *Sales:* V R Jinde; *Production:* B Ramakumar; *Publicity:* J E Rao
Subsidiary Company: Book Field Centre, PO Box 7228, Bombay and 316/3 Sir Balchandra Rd, Bombay
Imprint: Book Field Centre
Subjects: Mathematics, Education
Founded: 1979

Ess Ess Publications, 4837/24 Daryaganj, Ansari Rd, New Delhi 110002 Tel: 743401 Cable Add: Ess Ess Publications
Man Dir, Publicity, Rights & Permissions: Mrs Sheel Sethi; *Editorial, Sales, Production:* S K Sethi
Orders to: Ess Ess Publishers' Distributors, KD/6A Ashok Vihar, Delhi 110052
Parent Company: Ess Ess Publishers' Distributors, KD/6A Ashok Vihar, Delhi 110052
Subsidiary Company: Sumit Publications, KD/6A Ashok Vihar, Delhi 110052
Subjects: Humanities, Social Sciences
1978: 13 titles *1979:* 20 titles *Founded:* 1974

Eurasia Publishing House Pvt Ltd, Ravindra Mansion, Ram Nagar, New Delhi 110055 Tel: 266912 Cable Add: Eschand Telex: 0312185
Man Dir: S L Gupta; *Sales Dir:* R K Gupta
Associated Company: S Chand & Co Ltd (qv)
Subjects: Low-priced Paperbacks, Psychology, Engineering, General & Social Science, University, Secondary & Primary Textbooks, Educational Materials
Founded: 1960

Firma KLM Private Ltd (Incorporating Firma KL Mukhopadhyay), 257B BB Ganguly St, Calcutta 700012 Tel: 274391 Cable Add: Indology (Calcutta)
Man Dir, Rights & Permissions: K L Mukhopadhyay; *Editorial, Production:* S P Ghosh; *Sales, Publicity:* R N Mukherji
Associate Company: Firma Mukhopadhyay, 2/1 Dr Aksay Pal Rd, Calcutta 700034
Subjects: Humanities, Social Sciences
Founded: 1950

Frank Bros & Co, 4675-A Ansari Rd, 21 Daryaganj, New Delhi 110002 Tel: 263393
Man Dir: Suresh C Govil

G D K Publications, 3623 Chawri Bazar, Delhi 110006 Tel: 266901/2
Subjects: Indology, Social Sciences, History, Philosophy, Politics
1978-79: 10 titles *Founded:* 1978

Galgotia Publications, 3B/12 Uttri Marg, Rajinder Nagar, New Delhi 110060 Tel: 589334
Chief Executive, Editorial: Suneel Galgotia; *Sales:* Raj Kumar; *Production:* P D Galgotia; *Publicity:* Rajinder Singh Bisht
Associate Company: E D Galgotia & Sons, 17-B Connaught Place, PO Box 688, New Delhi
Subjects: Scientific, Technical, Humanities
Bookshop: E D Galgotia & Sons, 17-B Connaught Place, New Delhi
1979: 2 titles *Founded:* 1973

Ganesh & Co, 41 Pondy Bazar, Madras 600017 Tel: 444938
Partners: S Ganesh Prasad, S Ranganathan
Subjects: Philosophy, Religion, Nutrition
1978: 3 titles *1979:* 3 titles *Founded:* 1910

Geetha Book House*, New Statue Circle, Mysore 570001 Tel: 21589 Cable Add: Books
General Manager: M Gopalakrishna; *Sales Manager:* M Gururaja Rao; *Rights & Permissions:* M Sathyanarayana Rao
Subjects: Belles Lettres, Poetry, Biography, History, Philosophy, Reference, Religion, Low- & High-priced Paperbacks, General & Social Science, University Textbooks
Bookshop: At above address

Geological Survey of India, 29 Jawaharlal Nehru Rd, Calcutta 700016 Tel: 232314 Cable Add: Geosurvey
Dir-Gen: V S Krishnaswamy
Subject: Geology

Gitanjali Prakashan*, Lajpat Nagar 4, New Delhi 110024 Tel: 621991
Subjects: Economics, Social Science, History, Politics, Humanities
Bookshop: Indian Book Service, Lajpat Nagar 4, New Delhi 110024
1978: 4 titles *Founded:* 1974

Goel Publishing House, Subhash Bazar, Meerut 250002 Tel: 72843/76189
Man Dir, Editorial: B D Rastogi; *Sales:* Atul Krishna; *Production:* K Krishna *Publicity & Advertising Dir:* Kamalni Rastogi
Subsidiary Company: Krishna Prakashan Mandir, 119 Krishna Vihar, Shivaji Road, Meerut 250001
Bookshop: Goel publishing, Krishna Prakashan Mandir, Subhash Bazar, Meerut 250002 UP
Subjects: Mathematics, Chemistry, History, Art, Political Science, Economics, University & College textbooks
Founded: 1948

Gyan Bharati, 4-14 Roop Nagar, Delhi 7
An imprint of National Publishing House (qv)

Good Companions, Ushakirai Building, Raopura, Baroda Tel: 55433
Chief Executive: N K Kate; *Editorial, Sales, Production, Publicity:* Girish N Kate
Subjects: Economics, Social Science, Technical, General
1978: 6 titles *1979:* 2 titles *Founded:* 1945

Directorate of **Government** Publications, Netaji Subhash Marg, Bombay 400004 Tel: 355181 Cable Add: Diprintery
Chief Executive: V K Vispute
Subject: General

Hans Prakashan, 18 Nyaya Marg, Allahabad Tel: 3077
Chief Executive: Mahendra Pal Jha; *Production:* Amrit Rai
Subject: Fiction
Founded: 1949

Hans Publishers, Kamani Chambers, Ballard Estate, Bombay 400038 Tel: 263516 Cable Add: Bukmel
Chief Executive: Miss M Pereira
Parent Company: Myna Press (qv)
Subjects: Great works of the present century and reprints of outstanding books
Founded: 1963

Harjeet & Co, PO Box 5752, New Delhi 110055 (Located at: 1920, Street 10th, Chuna Mandi, New Delhi) Tel: 518445 Cable Add: Bookcentre ND
Chief Executive, Production: Dr P N Jain; *Editorial, Publicity, Rights & Permissions:* Ashok Jain; *Sales:* Pradeep Jain
Associate Companies: B Jain Publishers; Jain Publishing Co; World Homoeopathic Links (qqv)
Subjects: Homoeopathy, Biochemistry, Magnetotherapy, Acupuncture, Allied Medical Topics
1978: 12 titles *1979:* 15 titles *Founded:* 1972

Hemkunt Publishers Pvt Ltd*, 1-E/15 Patel Rd, New Delhi 110008 Tel: 584174 Cable Add: Hembooks
Man Dir: Bhagat Singh; *Sales, Publicity, Advertising, Rights & Permissions:* G P Singh
Subjects: Religion, Juveniles, Low-priced Paperbacks, University, Secondary & Primary Textbooks
Founded: 1948

Heritage Publishers, M-116 Connaught Circus, New Delhi 110001 Tel: 351156/310275
Man Dir: B R Chawla
Subsidiary Companies: Intellectuals' Rendezvous, M-116, Con Circus, New Delhi 110001
Subjects: Biography, History, Bibliography, Literature, Reference, Religion, Economics, Language, Social Science, Philosophy
1978-9: 20 titles *Founded:* 1973

Himalaya Prakashan*, 16 Resthouse Crescent, Bangalore 560001 Tel: 65207
Man Dir: Anand Kundaji
Associated Company: Artha Niti Publications, D390 Defence Colony, New Delhi 110024
Subjects: History, Philosophy, Religion, Mysticism
Founded: 1973

Himalaya Publishing House, 4A-16 Sangeeta, 71 Juhu Rd, Santa Cruz West, Bombay 400054 Tel: 351186, 355798
Chief Executive, Editorial, Sales, Publicity: D P Pandey; *Production:* Kooverjibhai; *Rights & Permissions:* Mrs Meena Pandey
Show Room: 'Ramdoot', Dr Bhalerao Marg (Kelewadi), Girgaum, Bombay 400004 Tel: 360170/355798
Subjects: Arts, Commerce, Science, Management, Law
1978: 100 titles *1979:* 110 titles *Founded:* 1976

Hind Pocket Books Private Ltd, GT Rd, Shahdara, Delhi 110032 Tel: 202046/202332 Cable Add: Pocketbook Delhi
Man Dir: Dina N Malhotra; *Marketing, Rights & Permissions:* Shekhar Malhotra
Associate Companies: Indian Book Company, Clarion Books, Saraswati Vihar (all at above address)
Subjects: General, Fiction, Non-Fiction, Self Improvement, Do-It-Yourself, Biography
Book Clubs: Gharelu Library Yojna, Clarion Book Club
1978: 100 titles *1979:* 50 titles *Founded:* 1958

Hindi Book Centre, 4/5-B Asaf Ali Rd, New Delhi 110002 Tel: 274874
Associate Company: Star Publications (P) Ltd (qv)
Subject: General books in Hindi

Hindi Pracharak Sansthan, PO Box 106, Pishachmochan, Varanasi 221001 Tel: 62867/62114 Cable Add: Prakashak
Editorial: K C Beri; *Sales:* M K Sharma
Subject: Hindi Literature
Founded: 1968

Hindustan Publishing Corporation (India)*, 6-U B Jawahar Nagar, Delhi 110007 Tel: 220201
Man Dir: S K Jain; *Editorial, Production, Rights & Permissions:* J K Jain; *Sales:* P C Kumar; *Production:* B B Jain
Subsidiary Company: Hindustan Book Agency, 17 U B, Jawahar Nagar, Delhi 110007
Subjects: Mathematics, Statistics, Physics, Chemistry, Earth Sciences, Life Sciences, Social Sciences
Founded: 1960

I B I, an imprint of Sterling Publishers Pvt Ltd (qv)

Idarah-I-Adabiyat-I-Delli, 2009 Qasimjan St, Delhi 110006 Tel: 513550
Editorial: Muhammad Ahmed; *Sales:* Lachhman Das
Subjects: Islamic Studies
Founded: 1972

Inba Nilayam, 95 Kutchery Rd, Mylapore, Madras 600004 Tel: 72547
Chief Executive: Soma Swaminathan; *All other offices:* Ramanathan S
Associate Company: Vellayan Pathippagam (at above address)
Subjects: Politics, Philosophy, History, Novels, Juveniles
1978: 15 titles *1979:* 20 titles *Founded:* 1947

India Book House, Mahalaxmi Chambers, 22 Bhulabhai Desai Rd, Bombay 400026 Tel: 365651, 365652, 365653 Cable Add: Indbook Bombay Telex: 0114060
Man Dir: G L Mirchandani; *Publisher:* H G Mirchandani; *Sales Dir:* Harkin Chatlani
Subjects: Fiction, General Nonfiction, Poetry, Humour, Cookery, Biography, Astrology, Sports, Self-improvement, Children's books
Bookshop: 3-a Rashtrapathi Rd, Secunderabad 500003

India Book House Education Trust, 29 Nathalal Parekh Marg, Bombay 400039 Tel: 233530/242586 Cable Add: Indbook
Managing Trustee: G L Mirchandani; *Trustee:* H G Mirchandani
Subjects: Juveniles, Low-priced Paperbacks, Illustrated Classics, Education
1978: 400 titles *Founded:* 1971

India Book House (P) Ltd, 412 Tulsiani Chambers, 212 Backbay Reclamation, Nariman Point, Bombay 400021 Tel: 240626/240678
Dir: H G Mirchandani; *Managing Editor:* P C Manaktala; *Exports:* Mohan Shahani, India Book House Export Division, PO Box 6301, Bombay 400013; *Imports:* H D Chatlani (Hardcover), Deepak Mirchandani (Paperback)
Subjects: Juveniles, Low-priced Paperbacks, Illustrated Classics, Children's Educational, Health, Management, Foreign Reprints
Founded: 1974

Indian Council for Cultural Relations*, Azad Bhawan, Indraprastha Estate, New Delhi 1 Tel: 272114
Subjects: Literature, Culture, International Relations, Performing and Fine Arts

Indian Council of Agricultural Research*, 26 Rajendra Prasada Rd, New Delhi 1
Man Dir: M G Kamath; *Sales Dir:* M Prasad; *Publicity & Advertising:* K E Sankaran
Subjects: How-to, Agriculture, University Textbooks

Indian Council of Medical Research, PO Box 4508, New Delhi 110016 Tel: 660707/667136 Cable Add: Scientific Telex: 031-3807
Editorial, Sales: G V Satyavati; *Production:* V Ramalingaswami
Subject: Medical Sciences

Indian Council of Social Science Research, 35 Ferozshah Rd, New Delhi 110001 Tel: 385959 Cable Add: Icsores
Chief Executive, Editorial, Production, Rights & Permissions: T N Madan; *Sales, Publicity:* S P Agrawal

Subject: Social Sciences
1978: 9 titles *1979:* 11 titles *Founded:* 1969

Indian Documentation Service, Gurgaon, Haryana 122001 Tel: 2205
Editorial, Production, Rights & Permissions: Satyaprakash; *Sales:* Pankaj Kumar, Sanjeev Kumar; *Publicity:* Pankaj Kumar
Subject: Bibliography
1978: 4 titles *1979:* 4 titles *Founded:* 1970

Indian Institute of Advanced Study, Rashtrapathi Nivas, Simla 171005 Tel: 2227 Cable Add: Institute
Publication Officer: S K Sharma; *Sales:* B B Lal
Subject: Scholarly

Indian Institute of World Culture, PO Box 402, Basavangudi, Bangalore 560004 (Located at: 6 Shri B P Wadia Rd, Basavangudi, Bangalore) Tel: 602581
Honorary Secretary: Anand R Kundaji
Subject: East-West Culture

Indian Museum, 27 Jawaharlal Nehru Rd, Calcutta 700016, West Bengal Tel: 239855, 234584, 230742 Cable Add: Imbot
Dir: Dr S C Ray
Subjects: Arts, Archaeology, Anthropology, Botany, Geology, Zoology
Founded: 1814

Indian Press (Publications) Pvt Ltd, 36 Pannalal Rd, Allahabad, Uttar Pradesh Tel: 53190 Cable Add: Publikason
Man Dir: D P Ghosh; *Editorial:* N K Roy; *Sales, Production, Publicity, Rights & Permissions:* N G Bagchi
Branch Off: Indian Publishing House, 22/1 Bidhan Sarani, Calcutta 6
Agencies: Indian Publishing House, 23 Daryaganj, Delhi; Indian Press (Pubs) P Ltd, Wright Town, Jabalpur; Indian Press (Pubs) P Ltd, Nicholson Rd, Ambala; Indian Press (Pubs) P Ltd, Jagatganj, Varanasi; Indian Book Depot, Jhandawala Park, Lucknow; Sahitya Ratnalaya, Shradhanand Park, Kanpur; Pustaksthan, Buxipur, Gorakhpur; Agarwal Bros, Katra, Azamgarh
Subject: Textbooks in Hindi, Bengali & English
1978: 8 titles *1979:* 10 titles *Founded:* 1884
Miscellaneous: Also publishes in Gurmukhi, Urdu, Marathi & Nepali languages

Indian Publications, 3 Abdul Hamid (British Indian) St, Calcutta 700069 Tel: 236334/344733
Man Dir: C R Sen; *Editorial, Production, Rights & Permissions:* Sankar Sen Gupta; *Sales:* D Bhownick; *Publicity:* Miss Putul Das
Subsidiary Company: Kalyani Prakashani (at above address)
Subjects: Social Science, Humanities, with special reference to Folklore, Anthropology, Archaeology, Ancient History, Bengali Literature, Mass Communication and Traditional Culture (in English and Bengali only)
Founded: 1957

Indian Publishing House, 22/1 Bidhan Saranee, Calcutta 700006 Tel: 347398
Manager, Sales: D K Bose; *Editorial:* S P Ghosh; *Production:* D P Ghosh
Subjects: Political Science, Philosophy, History, Economics, Science, Engineering
Founded: 1908

Indian Society for Promoting Christian Knowledge (I S P C K), PO Box 1585, Kashmere Gate, New Delhi 110006 Tel: 227363 Cable Add: Lithouse Delhi
General Secretary: V H Devadas; *Publications Secretary:* Rev James Massey; *Editor:* Motilal Pandit
Bookshops: 51 Chowringhee Rd, Calcutta 700016; opp Liberty Cinema, Residency Rd, Nagpur 440001
1978: 35 titles *1979:* 42 titles *Founded:* 1711 (as autonomous body 1958)

Intellectual Publishing House, 23 Daryaganj, Pratap Gali, New Delhi 2 Tel: 279911
Associate Company: Intellectual Book Corner
Subjects: History, Politics, Sociology
1978: 4 titles *1979:* 2 titles *Founded:* 1974

Inter-India Publications, 105 Anandnagar, Delhi 110035 Tel: 504418
Chief Executive, Editorial, Rights & Permissions: M C Mittal; *Sales:* Praveen Mittal
Parent Company: DK Publishers' Distributors, India (qv)
Subjects: Indology, Geography, Art, Anthropology, Sociology, Archaeology, Philosophy, Religion
1978: 5 titles *1979:* 4 titles *Founded:* 1977

Interprint, Mehta House, 16 A Naraina II, New Delhi 110028 Tel: 589760, 588305, 584387 Cable Add: Calmakers Telex: 2157 ND
Man Dir, Rights & Permissions: S N Mehta; *Production:* Dalip Tuli; *Publicity:* U Krishna Raj
Parent Company: Calendar Makers Corporation (at above address)
Branch Off: Calendar Makers Corporation, 27 Parsee Bazar St, Victoria Building, Bombay 400001
Subjects: Environmental Biology, Pediatrics, Himalayan Buddhist Art, Indian Art
1978: 6 titles *1979:* 4 titles *Founded:* 1976

Intertrade Publications (India) Pvt Ltd, subsidiary of Roy (Pvt) Ltd (KK) (qv)

Jaffe Books, Aymanathuparampil House, Kurichy PO, Kottayam, Kerala State
Man Dir: Santhamma Punnoose; *Editorial:* Augustine Veliath; *Publicity:* Thomas Cherian
Subjects: Social Science, History
1979: 2 titles *Founded:* 1979

Jaico Publishing House*, 125 Mahatma Gandhi Rd, Bombay 400023 Tel: 270621, 270746, 270760 Cable Add: Jaicobooks
Man Dir: Jaman H Shah; *Editorial, Production, Sales, Publicity, Rights & Permissions:* Ashwin J Shah
Subsidiary Company: Jaico Press Pvt Ltd
Branch Offs: Jaico Book House, 14-1 1st Main Rd, 6th Cross, Gandhi Nagar, Bangalore 560009; Jaico Book Distributors, G-2, 16 Ansari Rd, Daryaganj, New Delhi 110002
Subjects: Oriental and Western Classics, Indian and Western Fiction, Palmistry, Astrology, Philosophy, Religion, Biography, Autobiography, Reference, Language, Sex, Marriage, Love, Health, Yoga, Management, Economics, Humour, History, Politics, Cookery, Law, Crime, Psychology, Self-improvement
Bookshop: Jaico's Book Shop, 125 Mahatma Gandhi Rd, Bombay 400023
1978: 48 titles *Founded:* 1947

B Jain Publishers, 55/I Arjun Nagar, New Delhi 110029 Tel: 660391
Chief Executive, Sales, Production, Publicity: Kuldeep Jain; *Editorial, Rights & Permissions:* Ashok Jain
Orders to: PO Box 5752, New Delhi 110055
Associate Company: Harjeet & Co (qv)
Subjects: Homoeopathy, Magnetotherapy, Acupuncture, Nature Cure
1978: 40 titles *1979:* 30 titles *Founded:* 1967

Jain Publishing Co, 2798 Rajguru Rd, New Delhi 110055 Tel: 518445
Chief Executive, Production: Dr P N Jain; *Editorial, Sales, Publicity, Rights & Permissions:* Ashok Jain
Orders to: PO Box 5752, New Delhi 110055
Associate Company: Harjeet & Co (qv)
Subjects: Homoeopathy, Allied Medical Books
1978: 35 titles *1979:* 28 titles *Founded:* 1972

Jaipur Publishing House, Chaura Rasta, Jaipur 302003 Tel: 62257
Manager: Rajesh Agarwal; *Production:* R C Agarwal; *Sales:* Dhoop Chand Jain
Subject: Academic
Founded: 1960

Jaypee Brothers, 85-A Kamala Nagar, New Delhi 110007
Editorial: Jitendar Vij; *Sales:* P Paul
Subject: Medical Sciences

Jhanada Prakashan, Govind Mitra Rd, Patna 800004 Tel: 50331
Editorial: T Chowdhary; *Sales:* R Chowdhary
Subject: Academic
Founded: 1949

Kairali Mudralayam, Moolepparambil Buildings, opp R M S Office, Kottayam 686001
Managing Partner: D C Kizhakemuri; *Editorial:* M S Chandrasekhara Warrier; *Sales:* Mani Thomas; *Production, Publicity, Rights & Permissions:* Mary John
Subjects: Fiction, Biography, Humour
1978: 7 titles *1979:* 8 titles *Founded:* 1978

Kalyani Publishers*, 1/1 Rajinder Nagar, Ludhiana (Punjab)
Bookshop: Lyall Book Depot, Chaura Bazar, Ludhiana

Kapur Publications*, 2601 Nai Sarak, Delhi 110006
Subject: Educational

Karnataka Cooperative Publishing House Ltd*, 164 1st Main Rd, Chamarajpet, Bangalore 560018

B D Kataria & Sons, opp Clock Tower, Ludhiana Tel: 21107
Chief Executive: Verinder Kataria
Subjects: Engineering, Technology

Kendriya Hindi Sansthan, Agra 282005 Tel: 76758/72352 Cable Add: Shikshan Agra
Chief Executive, Editorial, Rights & Permissions: Prof Dr Bal Govind Mishra; *Sales, Production, Publicity:* Dr Devendra Kumar Sharma
Branch Offs: Delhi, Gauhati, Hyderabad
Subjects: Linguistics, Language, Language Teaching
1978: 4 titles *1979:* 5 titles *Founded:* 1961
Miscellaneous: Autonomous body fully financed by Ministry of Education, Government of India

Kerala Sahitya Akademi, PO Box 6, Trichur 680001 Tel: 23535/23569
Secretary: Pavanan; *Publications Officer:* C K Anandan Pillai
Subject: Literary
1978: 20 titles *1979:* 20 titles

Kerala University, Department of Publications, Trivandrum 695001 Tel: 60692
Chief Executive, Editorial: Chemmanom Chacko; *Production:* M A Karim; *Sales:* S Krishna Iyer
Subject: Scholarly
Founded: 1939

Khanna Publishers*, 2-B Nath Market, Nai Sarak, Delhi 110006
Subject: Engineering

Kitab Ghar, Main Bazar, Gandhi Nagar, New Delhi 110031 Tel: 213206
Chief Executive, Rights & Permissions: Satya Brat Sharma; *Editorial, Production:* Jagat Ram Sharma; *Sales, Publicity:* Dev Datt

Subjects: Social and General Sciences, Novels, Poetry, Drama, Biography (in Hindi)
1978: 15 titles *1979:* 12 titles *Founded:* 1970

Kitab Mahal (W D) Pvt Ltd*, 56 A Zero Rd, Allahabad, Uttar Pradesh Tel: 50540/2927 Cable Add: Kitab Mahal Allahabad
Man Dir: I K Agarwal; *Sales, Publicity & Advertising Dir:* Naresh Agarwal
Branch Offs: Kitab Mahal (W D) Pvt Ltd, Ashokrajpath, Patna 4 (Bihar); Kitab Mahal Distributors, 28 Netaji Subhash Marg, Daryaganj, Delhi 6
Founded: 1936

Kitabastan, 30 Chak, Allahabad 211003 Tel: 51885 Cable Add: Kitabastan
Chief Executive: Anwar Ullah Khan
Subject: General (in English, Urdu, Persian, Arabic)
1978: 3 titles *1979:* 2 titles *Founded:* 1932

Konkani Bhasha Mandal, 49/B Erasmo Carvalho St, Margao, Goa 403601 Tel: 2331
Editorial: M R Borkar; *Sales:* Udai L Bhembro
Subject: Konkani Literature

Kosi Books, an imprint of Vidyarthi Mithram Press & Book Depot (qv)

Kothari Publications, Jute House, 12 India Exchange Pl, Calcutta 700001
Tel: 229563/226572 Cable Add: Zeitgeist
Man Dir: H Kothari
Parent Company: Kothari Organisation (at above address)
Associate Company: India-International News Service (at above address)
Subjects: Technical, Reference
Founded: 1961
Miscellaneous: Publisher of *Who's Who* series in India

Krishna Brothers, Mahatma Gandhi Marg, Ajmer 305001 Tel: 20935
Editorial: J K Agarwal; *Sales:* C K Agarwal
Subject: Hindi literature
Founded: 1939

Krishna Prakasman Mandir, subsidiary of Goel Publishing House (qv)

Kunnuparampil Books, 14 Station Rd, Dewas
Chief Executive: K A Abraham; *Sales:* K A Raju
Subjects: General, Scientific, Technical
Founded: 1980

Kundalini Research and Publication Trust, B-98 Sarvodaya Enclave, New Delhi Tel: 653864 Cable Add: Innerlight
Subjects: Yoga, Philosophy, Religion
1978: 5 titles *1979:* 4 titles *Founded:* 1977

Kutub Khana Ishayat-ul-Islam, 3755 Churiwalan, Delhi 110006 Tel: 263567 Cable Add: Kutubiespo
Editorial: M L Sachdeva; *Sales:* V K Sachdeva
Subject: Islam

Lakshmi Narain Agarwal*, Hospital Rd, Agra 3 Tel: 73160
Man Dir: P N Agarwal
Subjects: Education, Textbooks
1978-79: 41 titles *Founded:* 1916

Lalit Kala Akademi (National Academy of Art)*, Rabindra Bhavan, Ferozeshah Rd, New Delhi 1 Tel: 387241 Cable Add: Arta-Kademie
Chairman: Aram Niwas Mirdha; *Secretary:* A K Dutta
Subject: Art (Monographs, Brochures, Portfolios and Multicolour Reproductions)
Publications: Lalit Kala (Ancient Art), *Lalit Kala Contemporary*

Lalvani Brothers*, PO Box 545, Taj Bldg, 210 Dr Dadabhai Naoroji Rd, Bombay 400001 Tel: 266811/2 Cable Add: Lalbrother Bombay Telex: 0115278
Man Dir: C P Karnire; *Editorial, Sales, Production, Publicity, Rights & Permissions:* S P Lalvani
Associated Company: Indian Lead, Rampart Ho, Rampart Row, Bombay
Branch Offs: 4 Daryaganj, Ansari Rd, Delhi 110006; 8 State Bank Lane, Mount Rd, Madras 2; Globe Bldg, 7-E Lindsey St, Calcutta 16
Subjects: Juvenile, Art, Technical
Founded: 1924
ISBN Publisher's Prefix: 112

Law Books in Hindi Publishers, Vidhi Sahitya Prakashan, Ministry of Law, Justice and Company Affairs, Indian Law Institute Building, Bhagwan Das Rd, New Delhi 110001 Tel: 389001 Cable Add: Patrika
Sales Man: C B Deogam
Subjects: Law, publications include *Uchchatama Nyayalaya Nirnaya Patrika* and *Uchcha Nyayalaya Nirnaya Patrika*
1978: 1 title *1979:* 2 titles

Law Publishers, PO Box 77, Allahabad 1 (Located at: Sardar Patel Marg, Allahabad) Tel: 2835/3716 Cable Add: Publishers Allahabad
Chief Executive: V Sagar
Associate Company: Delhi Law House, 13 Rajpur Rd, Delhi 54
Subject: Law
1978: 12 titles *1979:* 15 titles *Founded:* 1961

Light & Life Publishers, 2428 Tilak St, Paharganj, New Delhi 110055 Tel: 522455
Managing Partner: N Gopinath; *Sales & Publicity:* P N Nair; *Rights & Permissions:* Kartar Singh
Branch Offs: Residency Rd, Jammu Tawi (J & K); Delhi Rd, Model Town, Rohtak (Haryana)
Subjects: Philosophy, Political Science, Indology, Low-priced student editions of textbooks, Religion, History, Geography
1979: 65 titles *1980:* 104 titles *Founded:* 1971

Lipi Prakashan, 1 Ansari Rd, Daryaganj, New Delhi 110002 Tel: 273729
Editorial, Production, Publicity, Rights & Permissions: J S Vyas; *Sales:* M L Sharma
Subjects: Novels, Short Stories, Biographies, Literary Criticism, Linguistics, Philology, Education, Politics, Political Science, Dictionaries, Children's Literature (in Hindi)
1978: 40 titles *1979:* 39 titles *Founded:* 1970

Literary Market Review, 6/77 WEA Karol Bagh, New Delhi 110005 Tel: 56245
Man Dir, Rights & Permissions: K P Andrews; *Editorial, Sales, Production:* K P Punnoose; *Publicity:* Thomas Cherian
Parent Company: Literary Market Review, 73-47-255th St, Glen Oaks, New York 11004, USA
Subsidiary Company: Asian Bookmarket Information Service
Subject: Book Trade
1980: 3 titles *Founded:* 1980

The **Little Flower** Co*, 43 Ranganathan St, T Nagar, Madras 600017 Tel: 441538 Cable Add: Lifco
Senior Partner: T N C Varadan
Branch Off: Lifco Sales Dept, 17/1 Nandi Koil St, Teppakulam, Tiruchirapalli 620002
Subjects: General Fiction, History, How-to, Music, Art, Philosophy, Reference, Religion, Low-priced Paperbacks, Medicine, General Science, University, Secondary & Primary Textbooks
Founded: 1929

Little Swan, an imprint of Orient Longman Ltd (qv)

Lok Vangmaya Griha (Pvt) Ltd, 190-B Khetwadi Main Rd, Bombay 400004 Tel: 351324 Cable Add: Loksahitya
Man Dir: B D Gujarathi; *Sales:* S K Kulkarni
Parent Company: People's Publishing House Pvt Ltd (qv)
Branch Offs: Red Flag Building, Bindu Chowk, Kolhpur; 5-22-32 Tilak Path, Aurangabad; 562 Sadashive Peth, Pune 400030
Subjects: General, Humanities
Bookshops: PPH Book Stall, S V P Rd, Bombay 400004; People's Book House, Fort, Bombay 400001
Founded: 1973

Lord International, 19 Netaji Subhash Marg, Daryaganj, New Delhi 110002 Tel: 275863
Chief Executive, Rights & Permissions: Kamall Dev; *Editorial:* S P Gulati; *Sales:* Shiv Chaudhry; *Production:* Ramesh Chaudhry; *Publicity:* Rajesh Chaudhry
Subjects: Book Trade, Mailing Lists
Founded: 1971
Miscellaneous: Also Distributors and Publishers' Representatives

M P Text Book Corporation, M S Mandal Campus, Bhopal Tel: 62135/63059
Publisher: Raghunath Prasad
Subject: Academic
Founded: 1968

The **Macmillan** Co of India Ltd, 4 Community Centre, Naraina Industrial Area Phase I, New Delhi 110028 Tel: 393384/393799 Cable Add: Macind Telex: Nd 3741
Shipping Add: 6 Patullo Rd, Madras 600002
Man Dir: S G Wasani; *Rights & Permissions:* Nirupam Chatterjee; *Marketing Manager:* R S Anandan
Branch Offs: 12-A Mahatma Gandhi Rd, Bangalore 560001; Mercantile House, Magazine St, Reay Rd (East), Bombay 400010; 294 Bepin Behari Ganguly St, Calcutta 700012; 3-4-424 Narayanaguda, Hyderabad 500029; Kala Bhawan, 6 Naval Kishore Rd, Hazratganj, Lucknow 226001; 6 Patullo Rd, Madras 600002; 2/10 Ansari Rd, New Delhi 110002; Gandhari Bldg, Gandhari Amman Koil St, Trivandrum 695001
Subjects: Biography, History, Philosophy, Reference, Religion, Medicine, Psychology, Engineering, General & Social Science, University, Secondary & Primary Textbooks, Economics, Management, Political Science, Reference, Fiction
1978: 56 titles *1979:* 39 titles *Founded:* 1903
Miscellaneous: Firm is 40 per cent owned by Macmillan Publishers Ltd, UK (qv)
ISBN Publisher's Prefix: 3390

Madhyo Pradesh Hindi Granth Academy, Shirajj Nagar, Bhopal 462011 Tel: 62084 Cable Add: Academy
Director: Dr Bamila Kumar; *Editorial:* Narin Sagar; *Sales:* Ram Prakash Tripathi; *Production, Publicity:* Dr Shiv Kumar Awasthy
Subjects: University Textbooks, Humanities, Science, Agriculture, Engineering, Medical Sciences
1978: 236 titles *1979:* 251 titles

Mahajan Brothers, Super Market Basement, Ashram Rd, nr Natraj Cinema, Ahmedabad 380009 Tel: 78547 Cable Add: Periodical
Man Dir: Dinker Mahajan
Subject: Textiles
1978: 1 title *1979:* 4 titles *Founded:* 1953

Manohar Publications*, 2 Ansari Rd, Daryaganj, New Delhi 110002 Tel: 277162
Man Dir, Rights & Permissions: Ramesh C Jain; *Editorial:* N K Jain; *Sales, Production, Publicity:* M Saeed
Subjects: History, Sociology, Politics, Indology
1978: 25 titles *Founded:* 1969

Manosabdam Books, an imprint of Vidyarthi Mithram Press & Book Depot (qv)

Marg Publications, 3rd floor, Army and Navy Building, 148 Mahatma Gandhi Rd, Bombay 400023 Tel: 242520
Chief Executive: J J Bhabha; *Editorial:* Mulk Raj Anand; *Sales, Publicity:* A D Katrak; *Production:* Dolly Sahiar; *Rights & Permissions:* Mrs R S Sabavala
Parent Company: Tata Sons Ltd
Subject: Art
Founded: 1947

Markazi Maktaba Islami, 1353 Chitli Qabar, Delhi 110006 Tel: 269862
Sales: Mutiur Rehman
Subject: Islamic Literature

Marwah Publications, H-39 Green Park Extension, New Delhi 110016 Tel: 664296
Proprietor: Jaspal Singh; *Editorial:* Anees Chishti; *Sales:* Sudarshan Singh
Subjects: Humanities, Social Sciences
Founded: 1975

Mayfair Paperbacks, an imprint of Arnold-Heinemann Publishers (India) Pvt Ltd (qv)

Mayoor Paperbacks, an imprint of National Publishing House (qv)

Meenakshi Prakashan*, Begum Bridge, Meerut 250002 Tel: 74133, 75062, 72001
Chief Executive: Shri Chandra Prakash; *Editorial:* Ashok Gupta; *Sales:* V N Bajpal; *Production:* Ashok Kumar; *Publicity:* S N Sharma; *Rights & Permissions:* T C Sharma
Branch Off: 4 Ansari Rd, Daryaganj, New Delhi 110002
Subjects: Economics, Education, Commerce, Psychology, Hindi Literature, Physical and Biological Sciences, History, Management, Political Science, Sociology
Founded: 1964

Minerva Associates (Publications) Pvt Ltd, 7-B Lake Pl, Calcutta 700029 Tel: 42-3783
Chairman, Man Dir, Production, Publicity, Rights & Permissions: Sushil Mukherjea; *Editorial Director:* O K Ghosh; *Sales:* T K Mukherjee
Associate Company: Minerva Sales and Distribution (at above address)
Subjects: Political Science, History, Social Science, Economics, Psychology, Education, Belles Lettres, Philosophy
1979: 10 titles *Founded:* 1973

The **Minerva Publishing** House*, 32 Halls Rd, Egmore, Madras 8

Ministry of Information & Broadcasting, Publications Division, Government of India, Patiala House, New Delhi 110001
Dirs: S C Bhatt, G C Chukervartty; *Business Managers:* S L Jaiswal, R N Tyagi, O P Makar, N Mishra, Ishwar Chandra
Branch Offs: Super Bazar (2nd Floor), Connaught Circus, New Delhi; Commerce House, Ballard Pier, Karimbhai Rd, Bombay; 8 Esplanade East, Calcutta; Shastri Bhawan, 35 Haddows Rd, Madras
Subjects: Art & Culture, History, Speeches & Writings, Land & People, Flora & Fauna, Biographies, Reference, Juveniles, General & Social Science

Modern Book Agency Private Ltd, 10 Bankim Chatterjee St, Calcutta 700073 Tel: 34-6888/34-6889 Cable Add: Bibliophil
Man Dir, Rights & Permissions: Rabindranarayan Bhattacharya; *Sales:* Nisith Kumar Bose; *Production, Publicity:* Debnarayan Bhattacharya
Associate Company: B B Brothers & Co, 16/1 Shyarnacharandy St, Calcutta 700073
Subjects: School and College Textbooks, Reference, Children's Literature (in English and Bengali)
Bookshop: At above address
1978: 105 titles *1979:* 152 titles *Founded:* 1928

Motilal Banarsidass, 41 U A Bungalow Rd, Jawahar Nagar, Delhi 110007
Tel: 228355/221985 Cable Add: Gloryindia
Man Dir: Shantilal Jain; *Publication Dir:* Narendra Prakash Jain; *Sales Dir:* R P Jain; *Advertising Dir:* Jainendra Prakash
Branch Offs: Ashok Rajpath, Opp Patna College, Patna 800004 (Bihar) Tel: 51442; PO Box 75, Chowk, Varanasi 221001 (UP) Tel: 62898
Subjects: Religion, Philosophy, History, Linguistics, Sanskrit, Arts, Literature, Medicine
Bookshop: 41 U A Bungalow Rd, Jawahar Nagar, Delhi 110007
1978: 38 titles *1979:* 48 titles *Founded:* 1903

Mouj Prakashan Griha*, Khatau Wadi Girgaum, Bombay 400004, Maharashtra

A **Mukherjee** & Co Pvt Ltd*, 2 Bankim Chatterjee St, Calcutta 700012
Tel: 341606/341499
Dir: B K Chatterjee
Subject: Educational Materials
Founded: 1940

Mukherji Book House*, 1 Gopi Mohan Dutta Lane, Calcutta 700003
Subjects: Reference, Bibliography
Founded: 1963

Munshiram **Manoharlal** Publishers Pvt Ltd, PO Box 5715, New Delhi 110055 (Located at: 54 Rani Jhansi Rd, New Delhi) Tel: 513841/513600/512745 Cable Add: Literature New Delhi
Chief Executive: Manoharlal Jain; *Editorial:* Devendra Jain; *Sales:* Ashok Kumar Jain
Associate Companies: Indian Book Import Co, 11-B Court Rd, Delhi 110054; Oriental Books Reprint Corporation, PO Box 5715, 54 Rani Jhansi Rd, New Delhi 110055
Subjects: Art, Architecture, Religion, Philosophy, History, Politics, Linguistics, Languages, Encyclopaedias, Music, Dance, Drama, Theatre, Anthropology, Sociology
Bookshop: 4416 Nai Sarak (Amir Chand Marg), Delhi 110006
1978: 48 titles *1979:* 62 titles *Founded:* 1952

Mitra & Ghosh Publishers Pvt Ltd, 10 Shyama Charan De St, Calcutta 73 Tel: 343492/348791 Cable Add: Mitra & Ghosh, Calcutta
Chief Executive, Production: Sabitendra Nath Roy; *Editorial:* G K Mitra, S N Ghosh; *Sales:* M C Chakravarty; *Publicity:* P K Bose; *Rights & Permissions:* P K Pal
Branch Off: 86/1 Mahatma Gandhi Rd, Calcutta 700009
Subjects: Novels, Fiction, Travel, Essays, Juvenile
Bookshops: At both above addresses
1978: 75 titles *1979:* 80 titles *Founded:* 1934

Myna Press, PO Box 1526, Bombay 400038 (Located at: 32 R Kamani Marg, Bombay) Tel: 261347 Cable Add: Bukmel
Chief Executive: Mohan Panjabi
Subsidiary Company: Hans Publishers (qv)
Subject: Juveniles
1978: 14 titles *Founded:* 1970

S **Nagin** & Co*, Pratap Rd, Opp Sitla Mandir, Jullundur City 144008 (Punjab)

Nalanda Books, an imprint of Aadiesh Book Depot (qv)

Narosa Publishing House, 2/35 Ansari Rd, Daryaganj, New Delhi 110002 Tel: 260327 Cable Add: Narosa New Delhi
Man Dir: N K Mehra
Associate Company: Narosa Book Distributors (at above address)
Subjects: Pure and Applied Science, Medicine
1978: 13 titles *1979:* 19 titles *Founded:* 1977

National Book Agency (P) Ltd, 12 Bankim Chatterjee St, Calcutta 700073 Tel: 341677/348506 Cable Add: Marxislit
Man Dir: Sunil Kumar Basu
Subject: Marxist-Leninist Literature
Founded: 1939

National Book Trust*, A-5 Green Park, New Delhi 110016 Tel: 664020, 664667, 664540 Cable Add: Nabotrust
Dir: G Venkataramau; *Editorial Dir:* Lokenath Bhattacharya; *Sales Executive:* M A Krishnamachary; *Information & Publicity Executive:* D Das Gupta
Branch Off: Book Centre, City Central Library, Ashok Nagar, Hyderabad 500020
Subjects: Covering all aspects of human endeavour with particular reference to India; meant for a general readership
Bookshops: Book Centre, National Book Trust, City Central Library, Ashok Nagar, Hyderabad 500020; National Book Trust Book Shop, A-4 Green Park, New Delhi 110016
Founded: 1957

National Council of Applied Economic Research, Publications Division, Parisila Bhawan 11, Indraprastha Estate, New Delhi 110002 Tel: 273791/273798 Cable Add: Arthsandan Telex: 313380 Ncar In
Subject: Economics and allied subjects
1979-80: 10 titles

National Council of Educational Research & Training, Publication Department*, Sri Aurobindo Marg, New Delhi 110016 Tel: 678591/678425/678431 Cable Add: Eduprint
Secretary: V K Pandit; *Business Manager:* U N Jha; *Chief Editor:* Jaipal Nangia; *Chief Production Officer:* C N Rao; *Rights & Permissions:* Head, Publication Department
Subjects: Secondary & Primary Textbooks, Educational Materials
1978: 124 titles *Founded:* 1962

National Museum, Janpath, New Delhi 110011 Tel: 383459/389368
Editorial: C B Pandey; *Sales:* V P Dwivedi; *Production:* N R Banerjee
Subjects: Indian Art and Museology

National Publishing House, 23 Daryaganj, New Delhi 110006 Tel: 274161/275267
Man Dir: K L Malik; *Editorial, Production, Rights & Permissions:* S K Malik; *Sales:* M K Malik
Parent Company: K L Malik & Sons Pvt Ltd (at above address)
Imprints: Mayoor Paperbacks, Gyan Bharati
Branch Offs: K L Malik & Sons Pvt Ltd, 34 Netaji Subhash Marg, Allahabad 3; Malik & Co, Chaura Rasta, Jaipur 302003
Subjects: Humanities, Social Science, Hindi Literature

Bookshops: At company and branch office addresses
1978: 60 (Hindi), 24 (English) titles *1979:* 65 (Hindi), 24 (English) titles *Founded:* 1950

Navajivan Trust, Post Navajivan, Ahmedabad 380014 Tel: 447634/5
Man Dir, Rights & Permissions: Jitendra T Desai; *Editorial:* Balmukund Dave; *Sales, Publicity:* Ratilal Naik; *Production:* Ramanbhai Patel
Branch Off: 130 Princess St, Bombay 2
Subjects: Biography, History, Philosophy, Reference, Religion, Books on and by Mahatma Gandhi
1978: 3 titles *1979:* 3 titles *Founded:* 1919

Navyug Publishers, 9B Pleasure Garden Market, Chandni Chowk, Delhi 110006 Tel: 278370
Editorial: Pritam Singh; *Sales:* Gurbachan Singh
Subject: Bengali Literature
1978: 45 titles *Founded:* 1949

Naya Prokash, 206 Bidhan Sarani, Calcutta 700006 Tel: 349566
Man Dir, Production, Rights & Permissions: B Mitra; *Editorial:* Krisha Neyogi; *Sales:* P S Basu; *Publicity:* S Banik
Subsidiary Companies: Darbari Udjog; India Book Exchange
Subjects: Indology, Social Science, Management, History, Economics, Politics, Military Studies, Linguistics, Botany
Bookshop: 206 Bidhan Sarani, Calcutta 700006
1978: 12 titles *1979:* 12 titles *Founded:* 1962

Nem Chand & Brothers*, Civil Lines, Roorkee 247667 Tel: 258/752 Cable Add: Nemchand Bros
Warehouse: Opp Dy S P Office, Roorkee 247667
Man Dir, Rights & Permissions: N C Jain; *Sales Dir:* P K Jain; *Publicity & Advertising Dir:* T K Jain
Subsidiary Company: Roorkee Press, Roorkee
Subject: Engineering
Founded: 1951

New Book Centre, PO Box 10815, Calcutta 700009 (Located at: 14 Ramanath Majumdar St, Calcutta)
Manager, Sales: A K Das; *Editorial:* K Sen; *Production:* Suren Dutt
Subject: Reference

New Light Publishers, 202 Rattan Jyoti, 18 Rajendra Pl, New Delhi 110008 Tel: 582037
Managing Partner: A S Chowdhry; *Editorial:* Prof R P Chopra; *Publicity & Advertising:* R D Chowdhry
Subjects: Self-Improvement, General Knowledge, Books for Competitive Examinations
1978: 11 titles *1979:* 12 titles *Founded:* 1964

New Order Book Co, Ellis Bridge, Ahmedabad 6 Tel: 79065/445409 Cable Add: Nyuorder
Proprietor: D V Trivedi
Subjects: Humanities, Indology, Antiquarian, Art
Founded: 1939

Nirmal Book Agency, 89 Mahatma Gandhi Rd, Calcutta 700007 Tel: 348405
Editorial: Biswanath De; *Sales:* Nirmal Kumar Saha
Subject: Children's Books

Orient Longman Ltd, 3/5 Asaf Ali Rd, New Delhi 110002 Tel: 279256/7/8 Cable Add: Orlong New Delhi
Chairman: J Rameshwar Rao; *Editorial:* Sujit Mukherjee; *Sales:* E Raghavan; *Rights & Permissions:* N R Arur
Imprints: Sangam Books, Swan, Little Swan
Branch Offs: Kamani Marg, Ballard Estate, Bombay 400038; 17 Chittaranjan Ave, Calcutta 700072; 160 Anna Salai, Madras 600002; 1/24 Asaf Ali Rd, New Delhi 110002; 3-5-820 Hyderguda, Hyderabad 500001; 80/1 Mahatma Gandhi Rd, Bangalore 560001; SP Verma Rd, Patna 800001
Subjects: General Nonfiction, Biography, History, Philosophy, Reference, Juveniles, Low- & High-priced Paperbacks, Medicine, Psychology, Engineering, General & Social Science, Technology, University, Secondary & Primary Textbooks, Educational Materials
Bookshops: The Bookpoint, Kamari Marg, Ballard Estate, Bombay 700038
Founded: 1948

Orient Paperbacks (Division of Vision Books), 36-C Connaught Place, New Delhi 110001 Tel: 352081/312978 Cable Add: Visionbook
Man Dir: Vishwanath; *Editorial, Production:* Kapil Malhotra; *Publicity, Rights & Permissions:* Sudhir Malhotra; *Sales:* Rajendra Malhotra
Orders to: Sales Office, Madrassa Rd, Kashmere Gate, Delhi 110006 Tel: 227011/252267
Parent Company: Vision Books Pvt Ltd (qv)
Associate Companies: Raipal & Sons, Publishers, Madrassa Rd, Kashmere Gate, Delhi 6; Shiksha Bharati (qv); Shiksha Bharati Press, G T Rd, Shadara, Delhi 32
Imprints: Anand Paperbacks, Vision Books
Branch Off: Vasant, Ground Floor, 3-B Pedder Rd, Bombay 400026
Book Clubs: Orient Book Club
Subjects: International Bestseller Reprints, General Nonfiction, Self-Tuition Series, Indo Anglian Fiction, Indian Culture and Thought, Poetry, Drama, Occult, Palmistry, Astrology, Sports, Adventure, Yoga
1978: 129 titles *Founded:* 1967

Oriental Books Reprint Corporation, subsidiary of Munshiram Manoharlal Publishers Pvt Ltd (qv)

Oxford & I B H Publishing Co, 66 Janpath, New Delhi 110001 Tel: 321035/320518 Cable Add: Indamer
Dirs: Gulab Primlani, Mohan Primlani; *Editorial:* Mrs I V Ramchandani; *Sales, Publicity:* G C Sahajwalla; *Production Manager:* M L Gidwani
Subsidiary Companies: Amerind Publishing Co (P) Ltd, 66 Janpath, New Delhi 110001; Oxonian Press (P) Ltd (qv)
Branch Off: 17 Park St, Calcutta 700016
Subjects: Reference, Medicine, Psychology, Engineering, University Textbooks
Bookshops: Oxford Book & Stationery Co, Scindia House, New Delhi 110001; 17 Park St, Calcutta 700016
1978: 60 titles *1979:* 60 titles *Founded:* 1962

Oxford University Press, 2/11 Ansari Rd, PO Box 7035, Daryaganj, New Delhi 110002 Tel: 273841/2, 277812 Cable Add: Oxonian Delhi
General Manager: R Dayal; *Publicity:* Mrs A F Dhalla
Branch Offs: Faraday House, P17 Mission Row Extension, GPO Box 530, Calcutta 700013; Oxford House, Mount Rd, PO Box 1079, Madras 600006; Oxford House, Apollo Bunder, PO Box 31, Bombay 400039
Subjects: Academic & General books for all levels (school, college, University and research), Languages (Arabic, Assamese, Bengali, English, French, Garo, Gujarati, Hindi, Kannada, Khasi, Malayalam, Marathi, Oriya, Punjabi, Sanskrit, Tamil, Telugu, Urdu)
1978: 81 titles *1979:* 85 titles *Founded:* 1912
ISBN Publisher's Prefix: 19

Oxonian Press (P) Ltd, N-56 Connaught Circus, New Delhi 110001 Tel: 44957 Cable Add: Indamer
Dir, Rights & Permissions: Gulab Primlani; *Sales Dir:* Dr A M Primlani; *Publicity Dir:* M L Gidwani
Parent Company: Oxford & IBH Publishing Co (qv)
Branch Offs: 17 Park St, Calcutta 700016; 29 Wodehouse Rd, Bombay
Subjects: Reference, Medicine, Engineering, General Science, University Textbooks
Bookshops: See Oxford & IBH Publishing Co
1978: 30 titles

Paico Publishing House, M G Rd, Ernakulam, Cochin 11 Tel: 35835 Cable Add: Paico
Man Dir: Kenchana V Pai
Subjects: General Fiction, History, General Science, University, Secondary & Primary Textbooks, Childrens Books
Bookshop: Paico Books & Arts, M G Road, Cochin 682011
1978: 42 titles *Founded:* 1955

Panchasheel Prakashan, Film Colony, Chaura Rasta, Jaipur 302003 Tel: 65072
Editorial: M C Gupta; *Sales:* M P Gupta
Subjects: Academic, Fiction
Founded: 1968

Panjab University Publication Bureau, Chandigarh Tel: 22782
Secretary: R K Malhotra
Subjects: Belles Lettres, Poetry, Biography, History, Philosophy, Reference, Religion, Social Science, University Textbooks
Bookshop: Panjab University Publication Bureau, Chandigarh 160014
1978: 5 titles *1979:* 5 titles *Founded:* 1948

Parag Prakashan, 3/114 Karan Gali, Vishwas Nagar, Delhi 110032 Tel: 203850
Partner: Krishan
Subjects: Fiction, Poetry
Founded: 1972

Parimal Prakashan, 'Parimal', Khadkeshwar, Aurangabad 431001 Tel: 4556
Man Dir & Production: A B Dashrathe; *Sales:* K D Danekar
Branch Offs: 1397 Shukrawar Peth, Bajirao Rd, Pune; 31-A Saifee Manzil, Kennedy Bridge, Bombay
Subjects: Social Sciences, Humanities, Marathi Literature, Archaeology, Medical Science, English Literature
Bookshops: Marathwada Book Distributors at Tilak Rd, Aurangabad and Marathwada University Campus, Aurangabad
1978: 8 titles *1979:* 6 titles *Founded:* 1974

Parkash Brothers, 546 Books Market, Ludhiana 8 Tel: 32211 Cable Add: Parkash Books
Chief Executive, Editorial: R P Tondon; *Sales, Production, Publicity:* K L Tondon; *Rights & Permissions:* R P Tondon, K L Tondon
Subject: Educational
Bookshop: At above address
1978: 8 titles *1979:* 10 titles *Founded:* 1948/9

Path Publishers, 305A Hans Bhavan, Bahadur Shah Zafar Marg, New Delhi 110002 Tel: 272539/622120
Chief Executive, Editorial, Publicity, Rights & Permissions: P J Koshy; *Sales:* Mohan Eapen; *Production:* S K Bhatnagar
Subjects: Law, Commerce
1979: 3 titles *Founded:* 1979

Pearl Publishers, 206 Bidhan Saranee, Calcutta 700006
Proprietor: M Bhattacharjee; *Editorial:* S Roy; *Sales:* T Roy

Subjects: Political Science, Economics
Founded: 1977

People's Publishing House (P) Ltd, 5 Rani Jhansi Rd, New Delhi 110055
Tel: 529365/523349/521041 Cable Add: Quamikitab
Chairman: Dr G Adhikari; *General Manager:* Shri Jiten Sen; *Sales Manager:* Shri P N Gopinadhan
Subsidiary Company: Lok Vangmaya Griha (Pvt) Ltd (qv)
Subjects: Belles Lettres, Poetry, Biography, History, Philosophy, Juveniles, Low- & High-priced Paperbacks, Engineering, Social Science, University Textbooks
Bookshops: 2 Marina Arcade, Connaught Pl, New Delhi 110001
Founded: 1942

Pilgrim Publishers*, 56 Jatin Das Rd, Calcutta 700029, West Bengal Tel: 464323
Man Dir: S De; *Editorial:* Mrs R Mukherjee; *Sales:* F C Dutta; *Production, Publicity:* T K Mukherjee
Parent Company: Traco, India
Subjects: Literature, History, Art, Archaeology
Bookshop: 18B/1B Tamer Lane, Calcutta 700009
Founded: 1966

Pitambar Publishing Co, 888 East Park Rd, Karol Bagh, New Delhi 110005
Tel: 519433/562919/512041/561321/526933 Cable Add: Pitambar New Delhi
Man Dirs: Ved Bhushan, Anand Bhushan, Sushil Bhushan; *Sales:* P C Bhandari; *Publicity:* Anand Bhushan; *Editorial:* Dr Vijay B Aggarwal; *Production, Rights & Permissions:* Sushil Bhushan
Parent Company: Pitambar Book Depot (at above address)
Associate Companies: Bharat Enterprises, Delhi; Ambar Prakashan; Pitambar Industries; Pitambar Printing Press
Subjects: General Fiction, Reference, University, Secondary & Primary Textbooks
Bookshop: Pitambar Book Depot (at above address)
1978: 47 titles *1979:* 53 titles *Founded:* 1947

Popular Prakashan Pvt Ltd*, 35-C Tardco Rd, Bombay 400034 WB Tel: 376294/376295/370656
Man Dir: Ramdas Ganesh Bhatkal; *Dir:* Sadanand Ganesh Bhatkal
Subjects: Anthropology, Sociology, Arts, Crafts, Music, Biography, Economics, Education, History, Literature, Law, Philosophy, Religion, Politics, Administration, Physics, Mathematics, Chemistry
1978: 60 titles

Prabhat Prakashan, 205 Chawri Bazar, Delhi 110006 Tel: 264676
Chief Executive: Shyam Sunder; *Editorial:* Shyam Bahadur Verma; *Sales:* Raghuvir Verma; *Production:* Dharam Vir
Branch Off: Mathura
Subjects: Miscellaneous
1978: 48 titles *1979:* 65 titles *Founded:* 1952

Prachi Prakashan, PO Box 3537, New Delhi 110024 (Located at: L-3 Lajpatnagar III, New Delhi) Tel: 693331
Proprietor: A K Dash
Subject: Anthropology
Founded: 1976

Pragati Prakashan, Begum Bridge, PO Box 62, Meerut 250001 Tel: Meerut 73022
Man & Sales Dir: K K Mittal; *Publicity & Advertising Dir:* A K Mittal
Subjects: Physics, Chemistry, Mathematics, General & Social Sciences, University Textbooks, Commerce, Management
Bookshop: Pragati Prashan, Lajpat Rai Market, Begum Bridge, Meerut
1978: 20 titles *1979:* 29 titles *Founded:* 1955

Prakash Prakashan*, 8 Ram Nagar Colony, Agra 2, Uttar Pradesh

Prakasham Publications, Alleppey 688003, Kerala State Tel: 2771/2181
Chief Executive: Vithuvattickal Lucas; *Editorial:* Hormice C Perumali; *Sales:* J Chirayail
Subjects: General, Fiction
Founded: 1967

Prayer Books, 43/B Nandaram Sen St, Calcutta 700005 Tel: 54-2306
Chief Executive, Sales, Production: Subrata Saha; *Editorial:* Subhas Saha; *Publicity, Rights & Permissions:* Mrs Papiya Saha
Subject: Literature (in Bengali and English)
1978: 7 titles *1979:* 8 titles *Founded:* 1978

Prentice-Hall of India Pvt Ltd*, M-97 Connaught Circus, New Delhi 110001 Tel: 44769/43750 Cable Add: Prenhall New Delhi
Dirs: Asoke K Ghosh, Mrs Shanti Laroia
Subject: Textbooks
Founded: 1963
Miscellaneous: Firm is an associate company of Prentice-Hall Inc, Englewood Cliffs, NJ07632, USA

Printox, J-12 Jangpura Extension, New Delhi 110014 Tel: 693097
Proprietor: S G Nene
Branch Off: 1557 Sadashiv Peth, Pune 411030 Tel: 442960; K-15/7 Bibihatia, Varanasi 211001
Subjects: Politics, Social Science, Literary Criticism, Philosophy, Ancient Indian Literature, Art
1978/9: 3 titles

Progressive Corporation Pvt Ltd, 3rd floor, Jehangir Wadia Building, 51 Mahatma Gandhi Rd, Flora Fountain, Fort Bombay 400023 Tel: 251634/254813 Cable Add: Progcorp
Man Dir: Dr K D P Madon; *Sales Dirs:* Dr Rustom S Davar, Nanabhoy S Davar
Branch Off: 1 Velders St, Mount Rd, Madras 600002
Subjects: Management & Commerce, Accountancy, Business Law, Banking, Economics, Statistics, Marketing, Salesmanship, Advertising
1978: 4 titles *Founded:* 1932

Publication Board*, Assam, Bamunimaidan, Gauhati 781021

Publications & Information Directorate, Hillside Rd, New Delhi 110012 Tel: 586301 Cable Add: Publiform
Editorial: Y R Chadha; *Sales:* Kishan Singh
Subject: Scientific

Punjab State University Textbook Board, S C O 2935-36, Sector 22-C, Chandigarh 160022 Tel: 28983
Editorial: Prithipal Singh Kapur; *Production, Sales:* M Singh Rattan
Subject: Academic

Punjabi Pustak Bhandar*, Dariba, Delhi 110006
Associate Companies: Diamond Books International, Diamond Pocket Books, Diamond Comics (all at 2715 Daryaganj, New Delhi 11002)
1978: 34 titles

Radha Krishna Prakashan*, 2 Ansari Rd, Daryaganj, New Delhi 110002 Tel: 275851 Cable Add: Lokpriya Delhi
Man Dir: Om Prakash
Subjects: General Fiction, Belles Lettres, Poetry, Biography, Juveniles, High-priced Paperbacks, University Textbooks
Founded: 1965

Radha Soami Satsang Beas, PO Dera Baba Jaimal Singh, Distt Amritsar 143204 Tel: Rayya 50, Dhilwan 40 Cable Add: Radhasoami Satsang Beas
Man Dir, Production, Publicity: K S Narang; *Secretary, Rights & Permissions:* S L Sondhi; *Sales (Home):* J C Moorgai; *Sales (Abroad):* Krishin Babani
Parent Company: Charitable & Religious Society, Radhasoami Satsang Beas
Subjects: Religion, Philosophy
1978: 107 titles *1979:* 110 titles *Founded:* 1957

Radiant Publishers, E-155, State Bank of India Building, Kalkaji, New Delhi 110019
Man Dir, Sales, Rights & Permissions, Production, Publicity: V K Jain; *Editorial:* R Jain
Subjects: Politics, International Affairs, Economics, Sociology, History, Philosophy
1978: 6 titles *1979:* 7 titles *Founded:* 1973

Rajasthan Hindi Granth Academy, A 26/2 Vidyalaya Marg, Tilak Nagar, Jaipur 302004 Tel: 61410
Chief Executive: Dr Ram Bali Upadhyaya; *Editorial:* Dr M P Dadhich; *Sales, Publicity:* S N Sharma; *Production:* Y D Shalaya
Subjects: Social Science, Science, Humanities
1978: 17 titles *1979:* 4 titles *Founded:* 1969

Rajesh Publications, 1 Ansari Rd, Daryaganj, New Delhi 110002 Tel: 274550
Man Dir: Gupta Mohan Lal
Branch Off: 38 SC Basu Rd, Allahabad 211003
Subjects: History, Geography, Religion, Philosophy, Economics, General
1979: 10 titles *1980:* 10 titles *Founded:* 1970

Rajhans Prakashan Mandir*, Dharma Alok, Ram Nagar, Meerut, Uttar Pradesh

Rajkamal Prakashan Pvt Ltd*, 8 Netaji Subhash Marg, New Delhi 110002
Subjects: Juveniles, Education, Paperbacks

Rajneesh Foundation, Shree Rajneesh Ashram, 17 Koregaon Park, Poona 411001 Tel: 28127/20981/20982 Cable Add: Tathata Telex: 0145421 Tao
Man Dir, Sales, Rights & Permissions: Ma Yoga Laxmi; *Publicity:* Swami Krishna Prem
Subjects: Religion, Philosophy, Psychology; the teachings of Bhagwan Shree Rajneesh (English and Hindi)
Bookshop: At above address
1978: 54 titles *1979:* 52 titles *Founded:* 1969

Rajpal & Sons, Kashmere Gate, PO Box 1064, Delhi 110006 Tel: 229174, 223904 Cable Add: Rajpalsons Delhi
Man Dir: Mr Vishwanath; *Sales:* Ishwar Chandra; *Editorial:* Mahendra Kulshreshtna; *Production:* Roshan Lal; *Publicity, Rights & Permissions:* Kapil Malhotra
Associate Companies: Shiksha Bharati (qv); Vision Books Pvt Ltd (qv)
Subjects: General Fiction, Literary Criticism, Humanities, Science, Juveniles
Bookshop: At above address
1978: 125 titles *Founded:* 1891

Ram Prasad & Sons*, Hospital Rd, Agra 282003 Tel: 72935 Cable Add: Modern
Man Dir: H N Agarwala; *Sales Dir:* R N Agarwala; *Publicity & Advertising:* B N Agarwala
Subsidiary Companies: Modern Printers, 1153 Bagh Muzaffar Khan, Agra 2; Sanchi Prakashan, Bhopal 1
Subjects: Agriculture & Veterinary Science, Commerce & Economics, Education & Psychology, Engineering & Technology, Geography, Mathematics & Statistics, Physics, Political Science, Sociology, Social Work, Criminology, University, Secondary

& Primary Textbooks
Bookshops: Modern Book Depot, Hospital Rd, Agra 3; Bal Vihar, Hamidia Rd, Bhopal 1
Founded: 1905

Sri Ramakrishna Math, PO Box 635, Mylapore, Madras 600004 Tel: 71231
President: Sri Ramakrishna Math
Subjects: Religion, Culture, Philosophy
Bookshops: 16 Ramakrishna Math Rd, Mylapore, Madras 4; South Mada St, Mylapore Madras 4
1978: 12 titles *1979:* 34 titles *Founded:* 1897

Rastogi Publications*, Shivaji Rd, Meerut 250002 Tel: 73698, 73132 Cable Add: Rastogico
Editorial: Mrs Prakash Wati; *Sales, Publicity:* H K Rastogi; *Production, Rights & Permissions:* R K Rastogi
Associate Company: Rastogi Associates at above address
Subsidiary Companies: Pioneer Printers, Rastogi & Co, both at above address
Subjects: University Textbooks in Botany, Political Science, Zoology and Education
Founded: 1966

Ratnabharati, Ilaco House, Sir Pherozeshah Mehta Rd, PO Box 486, Bombay 400001 Tel: 297739 Cable Add: Pustaken
Editorial, Production: Punit Batra; *Sales, Publicity, Rights & Permissions:* Ranjit Batra
Subject: Illustrated children's books on Indian subjects
1978: 2 titles *Founded:* 1965

Rekha Prakashan, 16 Daryaganj, New Delhi 110002 Tel: 279907
Chief Executive, Rights & Permissions: K C Aryan; *Editorial:* S Aryan; *Sales:* B N Aryan; *Production, Publicity:* G D Aryan
Subjects: Art, Indology
1978: 3 titles *1979:* 2 titles *Founded:* 1973

Roli Books International, 4378/4 Ansari Rd, Daryaganj, New Delhi 110002 Tel: 268020 Cable Add: Rolipub
Chief Executive, Rights & Permissions: Pramod Kapoor; *Editorial:* Mrs Monisha Mukundan; *Sales:* Anand Khullar; *Publicity:* B S Kapoor
Associate Company: F E P International Pte Ltd, Singapore (qv)
Subjects: Illustrated Books of General Interest
1979: 15 titles *Founded:* 1979

Roorkee Press, see Nem Chand & Brothers (qv)

K K Roy (Pvt) Ltd, 55 Gariahat Rd, PO Box 10210, Calcutta 700019 Tel: 474872 Cable Add: Helbell
Man Dir: Dr K K Roy; *Sales Dir:* S Paul; *Publicity Dir:* Renu Roy; *Advertising Dir:* Abdul Salam; *Rights & Permissions:* Dr K K Roy
Subsidiary Company: Intertrade Publications (India) Pvt Ltd, 55 Gariahat Rd, PO Box 10210, Calcutta 700019
Subjects: Belles Lettres, Poetry, Biography, History, Philosophy, Reference, Religion, Medicine, University Textbooks
1978: 80 titles *1979:* 60 titles *Founded:* 1954

Rupa & Co, 15 Bankim Chatterjee St, PO Box 12333, Calcutta 700073 Tel: 344821/346305 Cable Add: Rupanco
Man Dir, Editorial, Rights & Permissions: D Mehra; *Sales:* R N Barman; *Production:* N D Mehra; *Publicity:* S K Mehra, C K Mehra
Branch Offs: 94 South Malaka, Allahabad 211001; 102 Prasad Chambers, Swadeshi Mills Compound, Opera House, Bombay 400004; 3831 Pataudi House Rd, Daryaganj, New Delhi 110002
Subjects: Art, Education, History, Literature, Fiction, Philosophy, Religion, Sport, Pastimes
1979-80: 29 titles *Founded:* 1936

Sahitya Bhawan Pvt Ltd, 93 KP Kakkar Rd, Allahabad 211003 Tel: 51077
Man Dir, Rights & Permissions: Girish Tandon; *Editorial:* Onkar Sharad; *Sales:* Ram Chandra Sharma; *Production:* P K Singh; *Publicity:* Ram Nath
Associate Company: Vivek Prakishthan (at above address)
Subjects: Hindi Literature and University Textbooks
Bookshop: At above address
1978: 23 titles *1979:* 27 titles *Founded:* 1917

Sahitya Pravarthaka Co-operative Society Ltd, PO Box 94, Kottayam 686001, Kerala Tel: 4111/4112/4114 Cable Add: Sahithyam
Secretary: M K Madhavan Nayar; *Sales:* P M George; *Production:* P Gopinath
Orders to: Sales Manager, National Book Stall, Kottayam
Subjects: Literature, Art, Science
Bookshops: National Book Stall, PO Box 40, Kottayam 686001 (and branches throughout Kerala)
1978: 365 titles *1979:* 400 titles *Founded:* 1945

Sahitya Samsad, an imprint of Shishu Sahitya Samsad Pte Ltd (qv)

Saint Paul Publications, 28-B Chatham Lines, Allahabad 211002 Tel: 53728
Chief Executive: Fr Anselm Poovathami Kummel; *Editorial, Rights & Permissions:* Joseph Maurus Ferrero; *Sales:* Thomas Poovathikal; *Production:* Amaldass Chacko; *Publicity:* Rockey Attokaram
Imprint: Better Yourself Books (qv)
Branch Offs: Bangalore 73; Bombay 50; Cochin 17; Delhi 24; Madras 1
Subjects: Practical Psychology, Self-improvement, Fiction, Spiritual
Bookshops: Examiner Press Bookshop, 35 Dalal St, Bombay 400023; Good Pastor International Book Centre, 63 Armenian St, Madras 600001
1978: 52 titles *1979:* 28 titles *Founded:* 1952

Sanchi Prakashan, subsidiary of Ram Prasad & Sons (qv)

Sangam Books, an imprint of Orient Longman Ltd (qv)

Sanskrit Pustak Bhandar, 38 Bidhan Sarani, Calcutta 700006 Tel: 34-1208
Chief Executive: Shyama Pada Bhattacharya
Subject: Indology
1978: 10 titles *1979:* 6 titles *Founded:* 1932

Sanskriti, an imprint of Arnold-Heinemann Publishers (India) Pvt Ltd (qv)

Saraswat Library*, 206 Bidhan Sarani, Calcutta 700006 Tel: 345492
Managing Partner: B Bhattacharyya
Subjects: Poetry, History, Music, Art, Philosophy, Reference, Religion, Juveniles, General & Social Science, University, Secondary Textbooks
Bookshop: At above address
Founded: 1914

Sarita Prakashan*, 175 Nauchandi Grounds, Meerut City Tel: 73515/75075 Cable Add: Prabhatpress Telex: 0594-215
Man Dir, Publicity, Rights & Permissions: K A Rastogi; *Editorial:* Rahul Rastogi; *Sales:* Atul Rastogi; *Production:* Abhay Rastogi
Subsidiary Companies: Prabhat Offset Printers Pvt Ltd; Prabhat Press
Branch Off: E-1 Jhandewalan Extn, Rani Jhansi Rd, New Delhi 110055
Subjects: Engineering, Botany, Literature, Reference
Founded: 1963

M C **Sarkar** & Sons (P) Ltd*, 14 Bankim Chatterjee St, Calcutta 700073

Sasta Sahitya Mandal*, N-77 Connaught Circus, New Delhi 110001 Tel: 40505 Cable Add: Satsahitya
Secretary: Shri Yashpal Jain
Branch Off: Zero Rd, Allahabad
Subjects: History, Agriculture, Textbooks, Literature, Education, Philosophy, Psychology, Languages, Paperbacks, Economics
1978: 13 titles *Founded:* 1925

Satya Press, c/o Ananda Ashram Thattanchavady, Pondicherry 605009 Tel: 2403 Cable Add: Yoga Life
Chief Executive: Dr Swami Gitananda; *Editorial:* Meenakshi Devi
Imprint: Yoga Life
Subjects: Yoga, Indian Philosophy (in English only)
Bookshop: Ananda Book Shop (at above address)
1978: 10 titles *1979:* 11 titles *Founded:* 1969

Sawan Kirpal Publications, 2 Canal Rd, Vijay Nagar, Delhi 110009 Tel: 718707
Editorial: H C Chadda; *Sales:* Jamieson Smith
Subject: Religion

Scientific Book Agency, 22 Raja Woodmunt St, PO Box 239, Calcutta 700001 Tel: 221500 Cable Add: Argosy Telex: Leo In/0212846
Man Dir: J Sinha; *Editorial:* P Sinha; *Sales Dir:* S P Sinha; *Production:* S Sinha; *Publicity & Advertising:* Snehamoy Sinha; *Rights & Permissions:* Swapan Mitra
Branch Off: 79/2 Mahatma Ghandi Rd, Calcutta 700009; 56-D Mirza Ghalib St, Calcutta 700016
Subjects: History, Medicine, Economics, Politics, Physics, Chemistry, Biological Sciences, Veterinary, Engineering
1978: 9 titles *1979:* 6 titles *Founded:* 1954

Seemant Prakashan, 922 Kucha Rohella Khan, Daryaganj, New Delhi 110002
Chief Executive: Narinder Nath Soz; *Sales:* Rajesh Didden; *Production:* Ajay Didden
Subject: General
1978: 5 titles *1979:* 5 titles *Founded:* 1976

Selina Publishers*, 4725/21A Dayanand Marg, Daryaganj, New Delhi 110002 Tel: 262359/273292
Man Dir, Editorial, Production: H L Gupta; *Sales:* P C Gupta; *Publicity, Rights & Permissions:* S S Dwivedi
Subsidiary Company: Sanket Paperbacks
Associate Company: Granth Bharati (Printing Press)
Branch Off: 113 Chhatta Bhawani Shanker, Fatehpuri, Delhi 110006
Subjects: Primary textbooks, Juveniles
Book Club: Sanket Library Yojna
Founded: 1975

Sharda Prakashan, Mehrauli, New Delhi 110030 Tel: 653982
Chief Executive, Production, Rights & Permissions: Vijay Dev Jhari; *Editorial:* Ravinder Jhari; *Sales:* R D Jhari
Subsidiary Company: Nalanda Prakashan, 33/1 Mehrauli, New Delhi 110030
Associate Company: Itihas Shodh Sansthan, 33/1 Mehrauli, New Delhi 110030
Subjects: Literary Criticism, Fiction, Drama, Memoirs, Children's Literature, General
Bookshop: 16/F3 Ansari Rd, Daryaganj, New Delhi 110002
1978: 35 titles *1979:* 40 titles *Founded:* 1971

R R **Sheth** and Co, PO Box 2517, Bombay 400002 (Located at: 110/112 S Gandhi Marg, Bombay) Tel: 313441 Cable Add: Literature Bombay 2
Man Dir: Bhagatbhai Bhuralal Sheth; *Other*

Offices: Dhirajlal Chunilal Mody
Associate Company: Lokpriya Prakashan, 110 S Gandhi Marg, Bombay 400002
Branch Off: Opp Phuvara, Gandhi Rd, Ahmedabad 380001 Tel: 380573
Subjects: Gujarati books on all subjects for all ages and tastes
Bookshops: PO Box 2517, 110-112 S Gandhi Marg, Bombay 400002; opp Phuvara, Gandhi Marg, Ahmedabad 380001
1978: 92 titles *Founded:* 1926
Miscellaneous: Largest wholesaler of Gujarati and Hindi books

Shiksha Bharati*, Madarsa Rd, Kashmere Gate, Delhi 110006 Tel: 223904
Man Dir, Rights & Permissions: D P Sehgal; *Editorial:* Miss Meera Malhotra; *Sales, Publicity:* Mrs Parveen Malhotra; *Production:* Indu Malhotra
Associate Companies: Orient Paperbacks (qv); Rajpal & Sons (qv); Vision Books Pvt Ltd (qv)
Subsidiary Company: Shiksha Bharati Press, 18 G T Rd, Shahdara, Delhi 110032
Subjects: Juveniles, Educational
1978: 60 titles *Founded:* 1959

Shishu Sahitya Samsad Pvt Ltd, 32A Acharya Prafulla Chandra Rd, Calcutta 700009 Tel: 35-7669
Man Dir: Mohendranath Dutt; *Editorial Manager, Publicity Manager:* Golokendu Ghosh; *Sales, Production, Rights & Permissions Dir:* Debajyoti Dutt
Imprint: Sahitya Samsad
Subjects: Juvenile Literature, Lexicons, Classics, Art
1978: 20 titles *1979:* 25 titles *Founded:* 1951

Shree Mahavir Book Depot (Publishers), 2603 Nai Sarak, Delhi 110006 Tel: 262993/710823
Chief Executive: Ram Kanwar; *Editorial:* Prem Chandra; *Sales, Rights & Permissions:* Hem Chandra; *Production:* Ram Chandra; *Publicity:* Harish Chandra
Subjects: Commerce, Accountancy, Economics, Political Science, History, Geography, Physics, Chemistry, Music, Domestic Science
1978: 18 titles *1979:* 24 titles *Founded:* 1948

Shree Saraswati Sadan, A-1/32 Safdarjang Enclave, New Delhi 110029 Tel: 661539
Chief Executive, Sales, Production, Rights & Permissions: Amitabh Ranjan; *Editorial, Publicity:* Mrs Abha Ranjan
Branch Off: Mussoorie (UP)
Subjects: History, Politics, Sociology, Historical Fiction (in English and Hindi)
1978: 8 titles *1979:* 9 titles *Founded:* 1972

Shri Ram Centre for Industrial Relations and Human Resources*, 5 Sadhu Vaswani Marg, New Delhi 110005 Tel: 568261
Cable Add: Sricir
Man Dir, Editorial, Rights & Permissions: Arun Joshi; *Sales, Production, Publicity:* K K Bhargava
Subject: Indian Journal of Industrial Relations
Founded: 1963

Skyline Publishing House, 28/2 St No 3, Friends Colony, Shahdara, Delhi 110032 Tel: 203346
Chief Executive: Surjeet Gupta; *Editorial, Rights & Permissions:* S N Sarkar; *Sales:* Nawab Singh; *Production, Publicity:* Chandrasekhar
Subjects: Current Affairs, Economics, Self-improvement, Yoga, Cookery, Beauty Culture
1979: 3 titles *Founded:* 1979

Smriti Prakashan, 124 Shah Rara Bagh, Allahabad 211003 Tel: 54589
Chief Executive, Editorial, Production: Bal Krishna Tripathi; *Sales:* Niraj Kumar Tripathi; *Publicity:* Deepak
Subjects: General
Bookshop: At above address
1978: 12 titles *1979:* 10 titles *Founded:* 1969

Somaiya Publications Pvt Ltd, 172 Mumbai Marathi Grantha Sangrahalaya Marg, Dadar, Bombay 400014 Tel: 440030 Cable Add: Bookmark, Bombay
Man Dir, Editorial, Rights & Permissions: Dr G S Koshe; *Education Manager:* P S Warty; *Production:* B H Pujar
Parent Company: The Godavari Sugar Mills Ltd, Fazalbhoy Building, Mahatma Ghandi Road, Bombay 400001
Associate Companies: The Book Centre Ltd (Book Sales Division), Ranade Rd, Dadar, Bombay 400028; The Book Centre Ltd (Printing Press Division), Plot No 103, 6th Rd, Sion, Bombay 400022
Branch Office: F-6 Bank of Baroda Bldg, Parliament St, New Delhi 110001
Subjects: Economics, Sociology, Education, Engineering, History, Politics, Civics, Language and Literature, Management, Mathematics, Physics, Chemistry, Psychology, Religion, Philosophy, Logic
1978: 19 titles *Founded:* 1967

South Asian Publishers Pvt Ltd, 36 Netaji Subhash Marg, Daryaganj, New Delhi 110002 Tel: 272425
Chief Executive, Editorial, Rights & Permissions: Vinod Kumar; *Sales:* K Srinivasa Murthy; *Production, Publicity:* K A Rastogi
Branch Off: 177 Avvai Shanmucham Salai, Madras 600086
Subjects: Academic Works in Science, Technology, Social Sciences
Founded: 1979

Spectrum Publications*, PO Box 45, Pan Bazar, Gauhati 781001, Assam Tel: 24791 Cable Add: Spectrum, Gauhati
Publisher: Krishan Kumar; *Editorial:* Alex P Joseph; *Sales:* R K Das; *Publicity:* Miss Rama Brahma
Subjects: Tourism, Reference, Anthropology, Sociology, Annual Yearbooks and Directories, Children's Books, Journals
1978: 5 titles *Founded:* 1976

Sree Rama Publishers*, 4000 Market St, Secunderabad 500025 Tel: 73128 Cable Add: Books, Secunderabad
Man Dir: Shiva Ramaiah Pabba; *Editorial:* Sreenivas Prabhu Pabba; *Sales:* Subash Chandra Sekhar Pabba; *Production:* Shivaramaiah Pabba; *Publicity & Rights & Permissions:* Shivarajaiah Pabba
Orders to: 113 Sarojini Devi Rd, Secunderabad 500003
Parent Company: Sree Rama Book Depot, Market St, Secunderabad
Associate Companies: Popular Book House, Pan Bazaar, Secunderabad; Sree Sita Rama Book Depot, Siddiamber Bazar, Hyderabad
Subjects: Primary & Secondary Textbooks, Theology in local language and English
Bookshops: Sree Rama Book Depot, Gunfoundry, Hyderabad 500001; Sree Rama Book Depot, Siddiamber Bazar, Hyderabad
Founded: 1916

The Standard Book Depot, Avenue Rd, Bangalore 560002 Tel: 26535/72625 Cable Add: Stanbook
Man Dir, Rights & Permissions: B Rajashekar; *Editorial:* B Gurunath; *Sales:* B Ananth; *Production:* R L Narasimhiah; *Publicity:* S Sudhindra
Subjects: Fiction, General Literature, Popular Science, Juveniles
Bookshop: At above address
1978: 12 titles *1979:* 15 titles *Founded:* 1935

Star Publications (P) Ltd, 4/5B Asaf Ali Rd, New Delhi 110002 Tel: 273335/274874
Man Dir, Sales, Production, Publicity: Amar Nath
Associate Companies: Hindi Book Centre (qv); Star Book Centre, Delhi 110006
Subsidiary Company: Publications India, New Delhi 110001, also London W1, UK
Subjects: Paperbacks in Urdu and Hindi
Book Club: Star Book Bank, Asaf Ali Rd, New Delhi
Founded: 1969
Miscellaneous: One of the largest exporters of Indian books to world libraries

State Institute of Languages, Kerala, 'Nalanda', Trivandrum 695003 Tel: 61306
Dir, Production, Publicity, Rights & Permissions: Dr A N P Ummerkutty; *Editorial:* Dr K Velayudhan Nair (Social Sciences), Dr C E Kartha (Physical Sciences), K N Sreenivasan (Natural Sciences), K K Krishna Kumar (Technical Sciences), N Ramesan (Languages); *Sales:* N Velappan Nair
Subjects: University Level Textbooks in Regional Languages, Malayalam
1978: 50 titles *1979:* 50 titles *Founded:* 1968

Sterling Publishers Pvt Ltd, AB/9 Safdarjang Enclave, New Delhi 110016 Tel: 669560 Cable Add: Paperbacks
Man Dir: O P Ghai; *Editorial:* T K Ghosh; *Publicity:* P K Kad; *Sales, Production, Rights & Permissions:* S K Ghai
Subsidiary Companies: Indian Book Industry, AB/9 Safdarjang Enclave, New Delhi 110016; Asian Publishers; Sterling Printers (both at L-11 Green Park Ext, New Delhi 110016)
Imprints: Asian Publishers; IBI; Sterling Paperbacks; Sterling Publishers
Subjects: History, Philosophy, Economics, Reference, Low-priced Paperbacks, Social Science, University Textbooks, Political Science, Agriculture, Art, Autobiography, Education, Fiction, International Relations, Library Science, Management and Administration, Religion, Sociology
Book Club: Sterling Book Club
Bookshop: At above address
1978: 120 titles *1979:* 115 titles *Founded:* 1965

The Students' Book Co*, SMS Highway, Jaipur 302003 Tel: 72455 (shop), 74087 (res)
Proprietor, Rights & Permissions: Tara Chand Verma; *Man Dir:* J D Verma; *Editorial, Sales, Production:* Subhash Chandra Verma; *Publicity:* Satish Chandra Verma
Subsidiary Company: United Printers, Radha Damoderji Ki Gali, Chaura Rasta, Jaipur 302003
Subjects: Science, Commerce, Arts, Sanskrit, Hindi, English, Rajasthani
Bookshops: Chinmaya Prakashan, Chaura Rasta, Jaipur 302003; Vaner Prakashan, Chaura Rasta, Jaipur 302003
Founded: 1939

Subodh Pocket Books, 2/4240A Ansari Rd, New Delhi 110002 Tel: 274513/278858
Chief Executive, Rights & Permissions: Vijay Kumar; *Sales, Production:* Anil Kumar Anjer
Subsidiary Company: Govindram Hasanand, 4408 Nai Sarak, Delhi
Subjects: Fiction, Non-fiction
1978: 50 titles *1979:* 45 titles *Founded:* 1965

Sudha Publications Pvt Ltd*, 604 Prabhat Kiran, Rajendra Pl, New Delhi 110008 Tel: 582898
Man Dir: S K Sachdeva; *Sales Dir:* Amar Nath; *Publicity & Advertising Dir:* Vijay Lakshmi; *Rights & Permissions:* C G Advani
Founded: 1960

Sultan Chand and Sons, 4792-23 Daryaganj, New Delhi 110002 Tel: 278659, 277843
Man Dir: Prakash Chand; *Editorial, Production:* Pratap Chand; *Sales, Publicity, Rights & Permissions:* Prabhat Chand
Associate Company: SCS Publishers' Distributors (at above address)
Subjects: Management, Business, Accounting, Commerce, Economics, Chemistry, Physics, Maths, Statistics, Public Administration
Bookshop: Premier Book Co, 4792-23 Daryaganj, New Delhi 110002
1978: 140 titles (including reprints) *1979:* 150 titles (including reprints) *Founded:* 1950

Suman Prakashan (P) Ltd*, 16/1022 Arya Samaj Rd, 18 Hari Singh Nalwa, New Delhi 110005

Surjeet Book Depot, 4074-75 Nai Sarak, PO Box 1425, Delhi 110006 Tel: 263080
1980: 150 titles
Miscellaneous: Also Booksellers and Distributors

Swan, an imprint of Orient Longman Ltd (qv)

Tamil Puthakalayam, 58 T P Koil St, Triplicane, Madras 600005 Tel: 843226
Chief Executive: K N Muthiah; *All offices:* K N Muthiah, A Kannan
Subjects: Fiction, Drama, Literary Criticism, Religion, Medicine, General
1978: 20 titles *1979:* 16 titles *Founded:* 1946

Taraporevala Publishing Industries Pvt Ltd*, 'Woodlands', 67 Dr D Deshmukh Marg, Bombay 400026 Tel: 393361 Cable Add: Tarabook, Bombay
Subjects: Management, Computer Technology, Social Science, Chemical Engineering, Natural Sciences, Technology, Reprints

Taraporevala Sons & Co Pvt Ltd, 210 Dr Dadabhai Naoroji Rd, Bombay 400001 Tel: 261433/269782 Cable Add: Bookshop, Bombay
Chief Executive: Professor Russi J Taraporevala; *Dirs:* Mrs Manekbai J Taraporevala, Miss Sooni J Taraporevala
Subjects: Indian Art, Culture, History, Sociology, Secondary & University Textbooks, Reprints of scientific and technical titles
Founded: 1864

Tata McGraw-Hill Publishing Co Ltd, 12/4 Asaf Ali Rd (3rd Floor), New Delhi 110002 Tel: 273105/271303/278711 Cable Add: Corinthian Telex: ND-2257
Dir: Balan Subramanian; *General Manager:* Ish C Dawar; *Editorial, Production:* Suresh Gopal; *Sales:* Hari Ganesh; *Publicity:* N S Nagan
Parent Company: McGraw-Hill International Book Co, 1221 Ave of the Americas, New York, NY 10020, USA
Subjects: Philosophy, Low- & High-priced Paperbacks, Medicine, Psychology, Engineering, General & Social Science, University Textbooks, Educational Materials, Agriculture, Biological Sciences, Management and Economics, Mathematics, Technology
1978: 42 titles *1979:* 60 titles *Founded:* 1970

Thacker & Co Ltd, 18-20 Kaikhushroo Dubash Marg, Bombay 400023 Tel: 242745/242683/242667 Cable Add: Booknotes
Dir: J M Chudasama; *Chief Executive:* Mrs D Puri
Subjects: History, Political & Social Science, Law, Business, University Textbooks
1978: 3 titles

The **Theosophical Publishing** House, Adyar, Madras 600020 Tel: 412904 Cable Add: Theotheca
Chairman of Council: Surendra Narayan; *Sales, Operations Manager:* C Seshadri; *Publicity & Advertising Manager, Rights & Permissions:* K N Ramanathan
Subjects: Philosophy, Religion, Universal Brotherhood, Occultism, Theosophy
1978: 26 titles *1979:* 29 titles *Founded:* 1910

Joseph **Thomasons** & Co, 7 Anand Bazar, Ernakulam, Kerala State Tel: 35235 Cable Add: Jetco
Chief Executive: Andrew Nettikadam
Subjects: General
Founded: 1958

Thomson Press (India) Ltd*, 9 K Block, Connaught Circus, New Delhi 110001 Tel: 40246/43818/45723/45995/43416 Cable Add: Thompress Telex: ND 2651
Man Dir: Aroon Purie; *Sales:* S Srinivasan
Branch Off: 49 Jolly Maker Chambers II, Nariman Point, Bombay 400021
Subject: Children's Books
Miscellaneous: Associate company of Living Media India Ltd, at same address

Central **Tibetan** Secretariat, Information Office, Dharamsala 176215, Himachal Pradesh Tel: 457
General Secretary: Sonam Topgyal; *Sales Manager:* Pasang Tsering
Subjects: Religion, Tibetan affairs generally, Tibetan Culture
1978: 3 titles *1979:* 3 titles *Founded:* 1961

Travancore Law House, M G Rd, Cochin 682001 Tel: 33766
Chief Executive: S Joseph
Subjects: Law, Commerce, Management
Founded: 1934

Trimurti Publications Pvt Ltd*, W-152 Greater Kailash-I, New Delhi 10048 Tel: 42015
Man Dir, Sales, Rights & Permissions: S P Kumria; *Publicity Dir:* Sudarshan Kumria
Branch Off: D-24, Odeon Bldg, Connaught Pl, New Delhi 11001
Subjects: History, Political Science, Economics, Religion, Philosophy, Reference, Social Science, University Textbooks
Founded: 1972

N M **Tripathi** Pvt Ltd, 164 Shamaldas Gandhi Marg, Bombay 400002
Man Dir: Arvind S Pandya; *Executive Manager:* Virendra Majmudar
Subjects: Law, Commerce, Gujarati
1978: 25 titles *1979:* 27 titles *Founded:* 1888

University Publishers*, Railway Rd, Jullundur City 144001 Tel: 2645 Cable Add: Best Books
Dirs: A N Chopra, R K Chopra; *Sales Dir:* O P Sharma; *Publicity Dir:* Rajinder Pal; *Advertising Dir:* Budhi Ram
Associate Company: Concept Publishing Co, India (qv)
Subjects: Fiction, History, Political Science, Technology, Educational Materials
Founded: 1947

Upkar Prakashan, 2/11A Swadeshi Bima Nagar, Agra 282002 Tel: 65110/66796 Cable Add: Competion
Chief Executive, Publicity, Rights & Permissions: M S Jain; *Sales, Production:* N S Jain
Associate Company: Pratiyogita Darpan (at above address)
Subjects: General Knowledge, Competition Books, General
Bookshop: Vijaysing Jain, Bookseller, Hospital Rd, Agra
1978: 50 titles *1979:* 75 titles *Founded:* 1973

The **Upper India** Publishing House Pvt Ltd*, Aminabad, Lucknow UP 226001 Tel: 42711 Cable Add: Balance
Man Dir: S Bhargava
Subjects: History, Reference, General & Social Science, Secondary & University Textbooks. (In Hindi & English)
Founded: 1921

Vakils Feffer & Simons Ltd, 9 Sprott Rd, Ballard Est, Bombay 38 Tel: 261221 Cable Add: Fleetbooks
Man Dir: G U Mehta
Subjects: Educational, College Textbooks, Cookery, Art

Vani Prakashan, 61/F Kamla Nagar, Delhi 110007 Tel: 225151
Chief Executive: Smt Shiramani Devi; *Editorial, Production, Publicity:* Ashok Kumar Maheshwari; *Sales:* Sushil Chandra Mahesh
Associate Company: Konarka Prakashan (at above address)
Subjects: Hindi Fiction, Poetry, Criticism
1978: 19 titles *1979:* 26 titles *Founded:* 1968

Venus Press & Book Depot, Konni, Kerala Tel: 16
Editorial: E K Sekhar; *Sales:* P Maheswaran Pillay
Subjects: Novels, Short Stories, Humour
Bookshop: Venus Book Depot (at above address)
1978: 24 titles *1979:* 18 titles *Founded:* 1946

Vidhi Sahitya Prakashan, see Law Books in Hindi Publishers

Vidyapuri, Balubazar, Cuttack 753002, Orissa Tel: 23637 Cable Add: Vidyapuri
Chief Executive, Editorial, Production, Publicity, Rights & Permissions: Pitamber Mishra; *Sales:* S K Sarangi
Associate Companies: Goswami Press, Cuttack 753002; Graftek Pvt Ltd, Bhubaneswar 751002
Subjects: College Textbooks, General Literature, Children's Literature
Bookshop: At above address
1978: 25 titles *1979:* 19 titles *Founded:* 1961

Vidyarthi Mithram Press & Book Depot, PO Box 81, Baker Rd, Kottayam 686001, Kerala State Tel: 2313/2316/4713 (after office hours 2616) Cable Add: Vidyarthi
Man Dir: Koshy P John
Associate Companies: Auroville Publishers, Kottayam; John Samuel Bros, Main Rd, Trivandrum
Imprints: Kosi Books, Manosabdam Books
Subjects: Fiction, Textbooks, Children's Books
Book Club: Vidyarthi Mithram Novel Club
Bookshop: Vidyarthi Mithram Book Depot (at above address, and ten other branches)
1978: 200 titles *1979:* 214 titles *Founded:* 1928

Vikas Publishing House Pvt Ltd, 20/4 Industrial Area, Sahibabad, Dist Ghaziabad (UP) Tel: 205290
Man Dir: Narendra Kumar
Subjects: Adventure, Mountaineering, Agriculture, Animal Husbandry, Art, Architecture, Travel, Biography, Memoirs, Botany, Chemistry, Cookery, Demography, Economics, Education, Engineering, Fiction, Futurology, Geography, Geology, History, Culture, Library Science, Literature, Management, Commerce, Mass Media, Mathematics, Medicine, Military Affairs, Philosophy, Religion, Physics, Politics, Current Affairs, Psychology, Public Administration, Science, Sociology, Anthropology, Sports, Games, Zoology, Children's Books
Founded: 1969

Vishal Publications*, Adda Hoshiarpur, Jullundur City 144001 Tel: 5177/5388
Man Dir: Pardeep Jain; *Sales Dir:* Rajinder K Jain; *Publicity & Advertising:* Sunil Jain
Branch Offs: Vishal Publications, 6 U B Bungalow Rd, Delhi 110007
Founded: 1973

Vision Books Pvt Ltd, Madarsa Rd, Kashmere Gate, Delhi 110004 Tel: 227011/252267/352081/312978 Cable Add: Vision Book
Chairman: Vishwa Nath; *Man Dir, Rights & Permissions, Publicity:* Sudhir Malhotra; *Publishing Dir:* Kapil Malhotra; *Editor:* Krishna Kumar; *Sales:* Rajendra Malhotra
Subsidiary Company: Anand Paperbacks; Orient Paperbacks (qv)
Associate Companies: Rajpal & Sons (qv); Shiksha Bharati, Delhi (qv)
Branch Off: 3-B Peddar Road, 'Vasant' Ground Floor, Bombay
Subjects: General Fiction, Military Science and History, Sciences, Current Affairs, Indology, Management, Religion, Anthropology, Education, International Relations, Medicine, Mountaineering, Travel
Book Clubs: Anand Book Club, Madrasa Rd, Kashmere Gate, Delhi 110006; Orient Book Club, Madrasa Rd, Kashmere Gate, Delhi 110006
1978: 18 titles *1979:* 27 titles *Founded:* 1975

Voluntary Health Association of India, C-14 Community Centre, Safdarjung Development Area, New Delhi 110016 Tel: 652007/652008 Cable Add: Volhealth
Editorial, Rights & Permissions: Dr James S Tong, SJ; *Sales, Production, Publicity:* Augustine J Veliath
Subjects: Health, Nutrition
1978: 10 titles *1979:* 12 titles *Founded:* 1974

Vora & Co Publishers Pvt Ltd, 3 Round Bldg, Kalbadevi Rd, Bombay 400002
Man Dir: Manherlal K Vora; *Publicity:* K K Vora
Subjects: Education, Textbooks, Law, Economics, Banking, Literature, History, Science

Wheeler-Pitman Publishing Co Pvt Ltd*, 15 Lal Bahadur Shastri Rd, Allahabad 211001

Wilco Publishing House*, 33 Ropewalk Lane, Rampart Row, Fort Bombay 400023 Tel: 242574
Man Dir: Jaisukh H Shah
Subjects: Fiction, Reference, Philosophy, Psychology, Business, Management, Inspirational, Self-help
1978: 10 titles *Founded:* 1958

Wiley Eastern Ltd, 4835/24 Ansari Rd, New Delhi 110002 Tel: 276802/277462 Cable Add: Wileyeast
Dir & Consultant: Anand R Kundaji; *Chief Executive:* Asanga Machwe; *Sales Manager:* K K Gulati; *Editorial:* Ravi Acharya; *Production:* M S Sejwal
Associate Company: John Wiley & Sons Ltd, UK (qv for other associates)
Subjects: Psychology, Engineering, Social Science, University Textbooks, Indian Art, Science
Bookshop: The Wiley Eastern Book Shop, 4654/21 Daryaganj, New Delhi 110002; The Wiley Bookshop, 16 Resthouse Crescent, Bangalore 560001; Abid House, Dr Bhadkamkar Marg, Bombay 400007; Wiley Eastern Bookshop, 40/8 Ballygunjo Circular Rd, Calcutta 700019; The Wiley Bookshop, No 6 Shri BP Wadia Rd, Basavanagudi, Bangalore 560004
1979: 49 titles *Founded:* 1966

World Homoeopathic Links, PO Box 5775, New Delhi 110055 (Located at: 1910 St 11, Chuna Mandi, New Delhi) Tel: 518445
Chief Executive: Dr P N Jain; *Editorial, Publicity, Rights & Permissions:* Ashok Jain; *Sales, Production:* Pradeep Jain
Associate Company: Harjeet & Co (qv)
Subjects: Homoeopathy, Medical Reference
1979: 2 titles *Founded:* 1979

The **World Press** Pvt Ltd*, 37A College St, Calcutta 700073 Tel: 341444/343591/342426 Cable Add: Takshasila
Chairman: J Sinha; *Man Dir, Production:* P C Bhattacharji; *Sales, Editorial:* S Bhattacharyya; *Publicity & Advertising, Rights & Permissions:* L Bhattacharjee
Subjects: Economics, History, Political & Social Science, Business, Law, Mathematics, Geology, Botany, Statistics, Library Science, Reference
Bookshop: 37A College St (First floor), Calcutta 73
Founded: 1947

Writers Workshop*, 162/92 Lake Gardens, Calcutta 700045 Tel: 468325
Man Dir: P Lal
Subjects: General Fiction, Belles Lettres, Poetry, Philosophy, Reference, Religion, Low- & High-priced Paperbacks
Founded: 1958

Yoga Life, an imprint of Satya Press (qv)

Zebra Books for Children, an imprint of Arnold-Heinemann Publishers (India) Pvt Ltd (qv)

Remainder Dealers

Gangaram Book Bureau, 72 Mahatma Gandhi Rd, Bangalore 560001 Tel: 50277
Manager: N Gangaram
All subjects

Jaffe Books, Aymanathuparampil House, Kurichy 686549, Kerala State
Proprietor: Santhamma Punnoose
Academic, scientific and technical

Koshal Book Depot, 3611/5 Nowrang Colony, Trinagar, Delhi 110035
Partner: Rishi Pal Sharma
All subjects

Literary Agents

Kunnuparampil P **Punnoose**, 6/77 WEA Karol Bagh, New Delhi 110005 Tel: 562495
Also at 73-47-255th St, Glen Oaks, New York 11004, USA Tel: (212) 3437285
Man Dir: K P Punnoose
Specialization: Original and reprint rights in academic books and general adult trade books. Sheet deals

Book Clubs

Anand Book Club, Madrasa Rd, Kashmere Gate, Delhi 110006
Owned by: Vision Books Pvt Ltd

B A L Milap, Court Rd, Bhavnagar 264001
Owned by: Lok Milap Trust

Clarion Book Club, G T Rd, Shahdara, Delhi 110032
Owned by: Hind Pocket Books Private Ltd

D C Book Club, Kottayam 1, Kerala State
Members: 2,500
Owned by: D C Books
Founded: 1975

E M E S C O Book Club, 3237 R P Rd, Secunderabad 500003
Members: 3,400
Founded: 1977

Gharelu Library Yojna, G T Rd, Shahdara, Delhi 110032
Owned by: Hind Pocket Books Private Ltd

Home Library Plan, 3237 R P Rd, Secunderabad 500003
Members: 1,000
Founded: 1960

Orient Book Club, Madarsa Rd, Kashmere Gate, Delhi 110006
Members: 35,000
Owned by: Vision Books Pvt Ltd

Pracharak Book Club, PO Box 106, C-21/30 Pishachochan, Varanasi 221001
Members: 3,978
Owned by: Hindi Pracharak Sansthan
Founded: 1976

Radical Book Club*, 6 Bankim Chatterjee St, Calcutta 12

Sanket Library Yojna*, 4725/21A Dayanand Marg, Daryaganj, New Delhi 110002
Owned by: Selina Publishers

Star Book Bank, 4/5B Asaf Ali Rd, New Delhi
Members: 5,000
Owned by: Star Publications (P) Ltd
Subject: Books in Hindi

Star Book Club, 4/5B Asaf Ali Rd, New Delhi 110002
Owned by: Star Publications (Pvt) Ltd
Founded: 1980

Sterling Book Club, AB/9 Safdarjang Enclave, New Delhi 110016
Owned by: Sterling Publishers Pvt Ltd

Vidyarthi Mithram Novel Club, PO Box 81, Baker Rd, Kottayam 686001, Kerala State
Owned by: Vidyarthi Mithram Press & Book Depot

Major Booksellers

Al Book Co (Pvt) Ltd, 210 D N Rd, Bombay 400001 Tel: 266812 Cable: Arabian
Man Dir: J K Kapur
Importers of children's books

Atma Ram & Sons, Kashmere Gate, Delhi 110006 Tel: 223092 Cable: Books
Manager: Ish Kumar Puri
Importers — all subjects

Bangalore Book Bureau, PO Box 9928, Subedar Chatraram Rd, Bangalore 560009 Tel: 77433
Manager: G D Prasad
Importers — all subjects

Current Technical Literature Co (Pvt) Ltd, India House, PO Box 1374, Bombay 400001 Tel: 261045 Cable: Cutelico
Man Dir: R K Murti
Scientific, technical and medical books

D K Publishers' Distributors, 1 Ansari Rd, Daryaganj, New Delhi 110002 Tel: 274819 Cable Add: Dekaypub Telex: Dikay ND-3616
Partners: I C Mittal, Praveen Mittal, Pramil Mittal; *Sales:* S K Bhatia
The largest wholesale house for Indian books, stockists of the publications of more than 600 Indian publishers

Daystar Publications, 23/2 Punjabi Bagh Extension, New Delhi 110026
Manager: Indu Lekha Garg
Importers & Exporters

English Book Store, 17/L Connaught Circus, New Delhi Tel: 352126/351731
Partners: S D Chowdhri, Bhupinder Chowdhri
Importers: Military Science and Aviation

196 INDIA

E D **Galgotia** & Sons, PO Box 688, New Delhi 110001 (Located at: 17-B Connaught Pl, New Delhi) Tel: 321844; I I T Hauz Khas, New Delhi 110029
Manager: R S Bisht
Largest retail bookstore of technical & scientific books, also importer

Higginbothams Ltd, 814 Anna Salai, Madras 600002 Tel: 86556 Cable Add: Booklover
Man Dir: V Balaraman
Importers — all subjects

India Book House, 3-a Rashtrapathi Rd, Secunderabad 500003

International Book House (Pvt) Ltd, Indian Mercantile Mansion (Extn), Madame Cama Rd, Bombay 400039 Tel: 231634 Cable Add: Interbook
Manager: R Gopalan
Importers — adult trade books

International Book Traders, G3/46 Model Town, Delhi 110009 Tel: 741817
Manager: D S Chaudhary
Importers: scientific and technical books

J K Export House, 3983/2 Jitendra Paper Market, Chawri Bazar, Delhi 110006
Proprietor: K Jitendra
Exporters of any books published in India

Jaffe Books, Kurichy 686549, Kerala State
Proprietor: Santhamma Punnoose
Importers — all subjects

Jaico Book Shop*, 121 Mahatma Gandhi Rd, Bombay 400023 Tel: 270261 Cable Add: Jaicobooks
Importers

Motilal Banarsidass, 41 U A Bungalow Rd, Jawahar Nagar, Delhi 110007 Tel: 221985/228355 Cable Add: Gloryindia
Importers and exporters of Indological books

Oxford Book and Stationery Co, Scindia House, New Delhi 110001; 17 Park St, Calcutta 700016 Tel: 44957 Cable Add: Indamer
Manager: Gulab Primlani
Importers

Popular Book Depot*, Dr Bhackamkar Rd, Bombay 400007 Tel: 359401 Cable Add: Quixote
Importers

Rupa & Co, 15 Bankim Chatterjee St, Calcutta 700073 Tel: 344821
Dir: D Mehra
Importers — all subjects

R R Sheth & Co, Princess St, Keshavbag, Bombay 400002 Tel: 313441

Star Publications (P) Ltd, 4/5B Asaf Ali Rd, New Delhi 110002 Tel: 273335/274874
Exporter of Indian books to world libraries

N M Tripathi Pvt Ltd, 164 Shamaldas Gandhi Marg, Bombay 400002 Tel: 313651/294048
Manager: A S Pandya
Importers of law books

U B S Publisher's Distributors Ltd*, 5 Ansari Rd, PO Box 7015, New Delhi 110002 Tel: 273601 Cable Add: Allbooks Telex: ND 3916
Importers

United Publishers*, PO Box 82, Pan Bazar Main Rd, Gauhati 781001 Assam Tel: 26381 Cable Add: Unipub Gauhati
Manager: Krishan Kumar
Wholesaler and exporter

Universal Book Distributors, 117/H-1/294-B Model Town, Pandu Nagar, Kanpur 208025 Tel: 81300

Manager: A K Chawla
Importers and subscription agents

Vidyarthi Mithram Book Depot, Baker Rd, Kottayam 686001, Kerala Tel: 2313/2316/2616 Cable Add: Vidyarthi
Branches at Calicut, Palghat, Ernakulam, Round North Trichur, Kottayam

Major Libraries

American Center Library, 24 Kastuba Gandhi Marg, New Delhi 110003
Also at 4 New Marine Lines, Bombay 400020; 7 Jawaharlal Nehru Marg, Calcutta 700013; 1 Bidhan Sarani, Calcutta 700073; Gemini Circle, Madras 600006

Asiatic Society Library, Town Hall, Bombay 400001

Bombay University Library*, Bombay University, Fort, Bombay 32BR Tel: 254372

British Council Library*, AIFACS Bldg, Rafi Marg, New Delhi 110001
South India: 150A Anna Salai, Madras 600002; *East India:* 5 Shakespeare Sarani, Calcutta 700016; *Western and Central India:* 178 Backbay Reclamation, Bombay 400020

The **British Library**, Lal Darwaja, Ahmedabad 380001
Also at 29 St Mark's Rd, Bangalore 560001; New Shopping Centre, Roshanpura Naka, Bhopal 462003; 5-9-20/A Secretariat Rd, Hyderabad 500004; Mayfair Building, Hazratganj, Lucknow 226001; Bank Rd, Patna 800001; 917/1 Ferugusson College Rd, Shivaji Nagar, Pune 411004; Club Rd, Ranchi; YMCA Bldg, Trivandrum 695001

Central Library*, Nr Mandvi Bank Rd, PO Box 15, Baroda Tel: 2932
Librarian: P V Mehta

Central Library, Town Hall, Bombay 400001

Central Secretariat Library, G Block, Shastri Bhavan, New Delhi 110001

Connemara (State Central) Public Library*, Egmore, Madras 600008

Delhi Public Library, S P Mukerji Marg, Delhi 110006 Tel: 252682 (Director)
Director: J C Mehta

Delhi University Library*, University of Delhi, Delhi 110007 Tel: 229888

Gujarat Vidyapith Granthalaya, Ahmedabad 380014 Tel: 446148
(Combined university, state central and public library)
Librarian: K L Shah
Publications: Tapas Nibandh Suchi (Gujarati) (Bibliography of Dissertations); Indexing of articles from *Gujarati Journals* (1975), published 1979

Indian Council of Social Science Research Library, 35 Ferozeshah Rd, New Delhi 110001

Indian Council of World Affairs Library*, Sapru House, Barakhamba Rd, New Delhi 110001
Librarian: Ashok Jambhekar
Publication: Documentation on Asia (annually)

Indian Institute of Technology Central Library, Madras 600036 Tel: 415342 ext 207 Telex: 417362 Iitm In

Madras Literary Society Library, College Rd, Madras 600006

National Archives of India*, Janpath, New Delhi 110001
Librarian: J C Srivastava

The **National Library**, Government of India, Belvedere, Calcutta 700027 Tel: 455381 Cable Add: Librarian Telex: Ca 7935
Director: Prof R K Dasgupta

National Museum Library, Janpath, New Delhi 110001

Nehru Memorial Museum Library, Tin Murti, New Delhi 110001

Sahitya Akademi Library, 35 Ferozeshah Rd, New Delhi 110001

State Central Library*, Hyderabad 12, Andhra Pradesh

Library Associations

Delhi Library Association*, PO Box 1270, c/o Hardinge Public Library, Queen's Garden, Delhi 110006
Publication: Indian Book Review Supplement (quarterly), *Library Herald* (quarterly), *Indian Press Index* (monthly)

Documentation Research and Training Centre, Indian Statistical Institute, 31 Church St, Bangalore 560001 Tel: 579741 Cable Add: Statistica
Head: G Bhattacharyya
Publications: Annual Seminar, DRTC (annual), *Refresher Seminar, DRTC* (annual), *Library Science with a slant to documentation* (quarterly)

Federation of Indian Library Associations*, Misri Bazar, Patiala, Punjab
President: Professor P N Kaula

Government of India Librarians Association, c/o Central Secretariat Library, Shastri Bhavan, New Delhi 110001
Secretary: Dhani Ram

Indian Association of Academic Librarians, c/o JNU Library, New Mehrauli Rd, New Delhi 110067 Tel: 651733
Secretary: S Ansari

Indian Association of Special Libraries and Information Centres, P 291 CIT Scheme No 6M, PO Kankurgachi, Calcutta 700054 Tel: 359651
General Secretary: S M Ganguly
Publications: Bulletin (4 a year), *Newsletter*

Indian Library Association, Delhi Public Library, S P Mukerji Marg, Delhi 110006 Tel: 254431
President: B L Bharadwaja; *Secretary:* O P Trikha
Publication: Bulletin

Library Reference Books and Journals

Books

University Libraries in India: A guide for direct mail promotion, Asian Bookmarket Information Service, 73-47-255th St, Glen Oaks, New York 11004, USA

Journals

Annals of Library Science and Documentation, Indian National Scientific Documentation Centre, Hillside Rd, New Delhi 110012

Bulletin, Indian Association of Special Libraries and Information Centres, P 291 CIT Scheme No 6M, PO Kankurgachi, Calcutta 700054

Bulletin, Indian Library Association, Delhi Public Library, S P Mukerji Marg, Delhi 110006

Herald of Library Science, Banaras Hindu University, c/o Editor P N Kaula, C-1, Varanasi 221005

Indian Librarian, 233 Model Town, Jullundur 3, Punjab

Indian Library Movement, 148 Allenby Lines, Ambala Cantt

Indian Library Science Abstracts, Indian Association of Special Libraries and Information Centres, Albert Hall, 15 Bankim Chatterjee St, Calcutta, (W Bengal)

Journal of Indexing and Reference Work, Mukherjee Library, 1 Gopi Mohan Dutta Lane, Calcutta 3

Journal of Library and Information Science, Department of Library Science, University of Delhi, Delhi 110007

Journal of Library Science, Nagpur University, Nagpur, Maharashtra

Journal of Library Service, Ravikrupa Trust, 1760 Gandhi Rd, Ahmedabad 1

Karnatak Granthalaya (text in Kannada, contents page in English and Kannada), S R Gunjal, Granthalaya Vijnana Prakashana, Saptapur, Dharwar, Karnatak State

Liblit, Library Literacy Circle, Kurukshetra, Haryana

Library Herald, Delhi Library Association, Queen's Garden, Delhi

Library Science with a Slant to Documentation (text in English), Documentation Research and Training Centre, 112 Cross Rd, Malleswaram, Bangalore 560001

Pustakalaya (text in Gujurati), Gujarat Pustakalaya Sahayak Sahkari Mandal Ltd, PO Box 10, Raopura, Baroda

Literary Associations and Societies

Madras Literary Society and Auxiliary of the Royal Asiatic Society, College Rd, Madras 600006
Honorary Secretary: U Ramesh Rao

National Academy of Letters (Sahitya Akademi) Rabindra Bhavan*, 35 Ferozeshah Rd, New Delhi 110001
Secretary: Dr R S Kelkar
Publications: Indian Literature (bi-monthly), Samskrita Pratibha (twice yearly)

P E N All—India Centre, Theosophy Hall, 40 New Marine Lines, Bombay 400020 Tel: 292175 Cable Add: Aryasangha, Bombay
Founder-Organizer: Sophia Wadia;
Secretary-Treasurer: Nissim Ezekiel
Publications: The Indian PEN (bimonthly), PEN series on Indian literatures, PEN Conference Proceedings

Literary Periodicals

Art & Poetry Today, Samkaleen Prakashan, 2762 Rajguru Marg, New Delhi 110055

Bengali Literature, 53 Bidhan Palli, Jadavpur, Calcutta 32

Contemporary Indian Literature (text in English), H 328 Narayana, New Delhi 28

Cultural News from India, Indian Council for Cultural Relations, I P Estate, New Delhi 110002

Dhara; a monthly review of Indian literature, Dhara Publications, 37 D Gupta Colony, Delhi 110009

Indian Author, C-44 Gulmohar Park, New Delhi 110049

Indian Horizons, Indian Council for Cultural Relations, Azad Bhavan, I P Estate, New Delhi 110002

Indian Literary Review, Chetna Publications, 4837/24 Ansari Rd, New Delhi 110002

Indian Literature, National Academy of Letters, Rabindra Bhavan, 35 Ferozeshah Rd, New Delhi 110001

Indian PEN (text in English), PEN All-India Centre, Theosophy Hall, 40 New Marine Lines, Bombay 400020

Indian Writing Today, Nirmala-Sadanand Publishers, 35c Tardeo Rd, Bombay 400034

Lalit Kala, Lalit Kala Akademi, 35 Ferozeshah Rd, New Delhi 110001

Language Forum, Bahri Publications (Pvt) Ltd, 57 Sant Nagar, New Delhi 110065

Literary Criterion, Popular Prakashan, 35-C Tardeo Rd, Bombay 400034 WB

Literary Half-Yearly, Literary Press, H H A Gowda, Mysore 9

Literary Studies; a quarterly review of literature and criticism from the Panjab, Razdan House, Sirhindi Darwaza, Patiala, Panjab

Marg, Army & Navy Bldg, M G Rd, Bombay 400001

Miscellany, Writers Workshop, 162-92 Lake Gardens, Calcutta 700045

Opinion Literary Quarterly, 40-C Ridge Rd, Bombay 400006

Poet, 3 Venkatesan St, Madras 600017

Samskrita Pratibha; a six-monthly journal in Sanskrit devoted to contemporary writing of creative quality in Sanskrit, National Academy of Letters, Rabindra Bhavan, 35 Ferozeshah Rd, New Delhi 1

Triveni, Machilipatnam 521001

Vagartha; critical quarterly of Indian literature, Joshi Foundation, N-3 Panchsheel Park, New Delhi 110017

Literary Prizes

Andhra Pradesh Sahitya Akademi Awards
For best literary works in Telugu. Two prizes of 3,500 Indian rupees each and seven prizes of 1,116 Indian rupees each. Awarded annually. Enquiries to The Secretary, A P Sahitya Akademi, Saifabad, Hyderabad 500004

Bhai Santokh Singh Prize
Awarded annually for substantial contribution towards Punjabi literature. 2,100 Indian rupees. Enquiries to The Director, Haryana Sahitya Akademi, Chandigarh 160018

Books for Neoliterates Prizes*
For books and manuscripts in Indian languages by Indian nationals. 1,000 Indian rupees for each book. Awarded annually. Enquiries to Ministry of Education and Social Welfare, Government of India, New Delhi

Certificate of Honour*
To Arabic, Persian and Sanskrit scholars who have made outstanding contributions to Arabic, Persian and Sanskrit study. 3,000 Indian rupees. Awarded annually by the President. Enquiries to Office of the President, Government of India, New Delhi

Commission for Scientific and Technical Terminology Prizes*
For fiction, drama, memoirs, travelogues and poetry in Indian languages except Hindi, Sanskrit, tribal languages and authors' mother tongue. 65 prizes of 1,000 Indian rupees each. Awarded annually. Enquiries to Commission for Scientific and Technical Terminology, Ministry of Education and Social Welfare, West Block VII R K Puram, New Delhi 22

Escorts Book Award
For books on management principles and practices in India by Indian nationals. 3,000 and 1,000 Indian rupees each. Awarded annually. Enquiries to Secretary, Delhi Management Association, 1/21 Asaf Ali Rd, New Delhi 2

Geetha Prize
Awarded annually for substantial contribution towards Hindi literature. 2,100 Indian rupees. Enquiries to The Director, Haryana Sahitya Akademi, Chandigarh 160018

Hali Prize
Awarded annually for substantial contribution towards Urdu literature. 2,100 Indian rupees. Enquiries to The Director, Haryana Sahitya Akademi, Chandigarh 160018

Haryana Sahitya Prize
Awarded annually to an Indian writer for outstanding work on literature, art, history and culture of Haryana, 2,100 Indian rupees. Enquiries to The Director, Haryana Sahitya Akademi, Chandigarh 160018

Indian National Academy of Letters (Sahitya Akademi) Awards*
For the most literary works written in each of the 22 regional languages of India recognized by the Academy (Sahitya Akademi). 5,000 Indian rupees each. Awarded annually to Indian nationals only, by the Executive Board of the Academy. Enquiries to The Secretary, Indian National Academy of Letters, Rabindra Bhavan, 35 Ferozeshah Rd, New Delhi 110001

Jnanpith Literary Award
For the best literary work in any Indian language by an Indian national. 100,000 Indian rupees awarded annually. Enquiries to Bharatiya Jnanpith, B/45-47 2nd Floor, Connaught Pl, New Delhi 110001

Kerala Sahitya Akademi Awards
For literary works in Malayalam. Six prizes of 2,000 Indian rupees each awarded annually. Enquiries to The Secretary, Kerala Sahitya Akademi, Trichur 680001, Kerala State

Kesari Award
Best unpublished novel in Malayalam, 2,500 Indian rupees. Awarded annually. Enquiries to The Manager, D C Books, Kottayam 1, Kerala State

C B Kumar Prize
For best collection of essays in Malayalam. 1,500 Indian rupees awarded annually. Enquiries to The Secretary, Kerala Sahitya Akademi, Trichur 680001, Kerala State

Kumkuman Award
For best unpublished novel in Malayalam. 5,000 Indian rupees awarded annually. Enquiries to The Editor, Kumkuman Weekly, Quilon, Kerala State

Law Books in Hindi Prize*
Awarded annually for law books/manuscripts in Hindi. 10,000 Indian

rupees. Enquiries to Vidhi Sahitya Prakashan, Ministry of Law, Justice and Company Affairs, Govt of India, Indian Law Institute Bldgs, Bhagwandas Rd, New Delhi 110001

Meera Memorial Award
For best literary work in Hindi. 9,000 Indian rupees awarded annually. Enquiries to The Secretary, Rajasthan Sahitya Akademi, Udaipur, Rajasthan

K R Namboodiri Award
For best work on Vedic literature. 1,000 Indian rupees awarded annually. Enquiries to The Secretary, Kerala Sahitya Akademi, Trichur 680001, Kerala State

Orissa Sahitya Akademi Award
Founded in 1960 for best literary works in regional language published during a particular period of three years in five different categories of books: (1) novel and short stories; (2) poetry and Kavya; (3) drama; (4) essay, literary criticism, travelogue, biography, scientific literature; (5) children's literature. 1,000 Indian rupees awarded annually. Enquiries to Orissa Sahitya Akademi, Museum Buildings, Bhubaneswar 751014, Orissa

M P Paul Award
For best unpublished fiction in Malayalam. 2,500 Indian rupees awarded annually. Enquiries to The Manager, D C Books, Kottayam 1, Kerala State

M P Paul Prize
For best published fiction in Malayalam. 1,000 Indian rupees awarded annually. Enquiries to The Secretary, Sahitya Pravarthaka Cooperative Society Ltd, PO Box No 94, Kottayam 1, Kerala State

Prithviraj Memorial Award
For the best literary work in Rajasthani. 7,000 Indian rupees awarded annually. Enquiries to The Secretary, Rajasthan Sahitya Akademi, Udaipur, Rajasthan

Prize for Non-Hindi Speaking Area Writers
For authors whose mother-tongue is an Indian language other than Hindi. Sixteen prizes of 1,500 Indian rupees each, awarded annually. Enquiries to The Director, Central Hindi Directorate, West Block No VII, R K Puram, New Delhi 110022

Rajasthan Sahitya Akademi Awards
For the best literary works in Hindi, Rajasthani and Sanskrit. Eight prizes of 2,000 Indian rupees each awarded annually. Enquiries to The Secretary, Rajasthan Sahitya Akademi, Udaipur, Rajasthan

Sahitya Akademi Award, see Indian National Academy of Letters (Sahitya Akademi) Awards

Sahitya Pravarthaka Benefit Fund Awards
For best works in Malayalam. Five prizes of 2,000 Indian rupees each awarded annually. Enquiries to The Secretary, Sahitya Pravarthaka Co-operative Society Ltd, PO Box 94, Kottayam 1, Kerala State

Soviet Land Nehru Awards
For Indian nationals. For literary works, journalistic works in Indian languages and in English and meritorious work done in creative, cultural and public fields for promoting Indo-Soviet friendship, world peace and international amity.
Three prizes of 10,000 Indian rupees with a fortnight's trip to USSR and three prizes of 5,000 Indian rupees with a fortnight's trip to USSR. Ten prizes of 1,500 Indian rupees each. Five awards for children 10–13 age group for painting competition — a month's holiday at the Artek Young Pioneers Camp, Black Sea Coast, Crimea. Awarded annually. Enquiries to Soviet Land, Embassy of the USSR in India, 25 Barakhamba Rd, New Delhi 1

Sur Prize*
Awarded annually to Indian nationals for outstanding contribution towards Hindi literature. 2,000 Indian rupees. Enquiries to Director, Haryana Sahitya Akademi, Chandigarh 160018

Tagore Award
For the best unpublished novel in Malayalam, 5,005 Indian rupees awarded annually. Enquiries to The Manager, D C Books, Kottayam 686001, Kerala State

Urdu Akademy Awards*
Awarded annually to Indian nationals for Urdu literature. Enquiries to U P Urdu Akademy, 11 Hazratganj, Lucknow

Major Tek Singh **Virdi** Literary Prizes*
Awarded annually to children under 15 years for short stories, essays and dramas in Punjabi. Three prizes of 100, 75 and 50 Indian rupees. Enquiries to Modern Sahit Academy, 'Gulfashan', East Mohan Nagar, Link Rd, Amritsar

Translation Agencies and Associations

Amerind Publishing Co (P) Ltd, N-56 Connaught Circus, New Delhi 110001 Tel: 44957 Cable: Indamer
Dir: Gulab Primlani
Translating Russian, German, Japanese, Hindi

Indian National Scientific Documentation Centre*, Hillside Rd, New Delhi 110012
Translating European languages into English

Indonesia

General Information

Language: Bahasa Indonesia (a form of Malay) is official language. English is common second language. About 250 other languages are spoken in Indonesia
Religion: About 85% Muslim, 5% Hindu (principally on Bali), 5% Christian
Population: 145 million
Literacy Rate (1971): 59.6% (79.1% Urban, 55.3% Rural)
Bank Hours: Generally 0800-1400 Monday-Thursday; 0800-1100 Friday; 0800-1300 Saturday
Currency: Rupiah
Export/Import Information: Books subject to 40% tariff and 10% import sales tax, but on recommendation of Minister of Basic Education and Culture, partial or total exemption may be granted. Advertising: 50% Duty, 10% tax. All imports subject to margin of Profit Tax (5% with Letter of Credit, 10% without). Exchange control. Books and printed matter using Indonesian languages prohibited. Imports require no licence but are categorized into four groups for credit arrangement controls
Copyright: No copyright conventions signed

Book Trade Organizations

Ikatan Penerbit Indonesia (IKAPI), Jalan Pengarengan (Kalipasir) 32, Jakarta Pusat III/4 Tel: 351907
Association of Indonesian Book Publishers
President: Ismid Hadad
Publication: Bulletin

Book Trade Reference Journals

Berita Bibliografi; Indonesian book news (text in Indonesian), Yayasan Idayu, Jl Dr Abdulrachman Salch 26, Jakarta

Bibliografi Nasional Indonesia Kumulasi (Cumulative Bibliography of Indonesia), National Scientific Documentation Centre, Jalan Jendral Gatot-Subroto, PO Box 3065/JKT, Jakarta

Bulletin, Association of Indonesian Book Publishers, Jl Pengarengan 32, Jakarta Pusat III/4

Publishers

Akadoma*, Jl Proklamasi No 61, Jakarta Tel: 882328

B P Alda*, Jl Tambak No 12-A, Jakarta

Alma'Arif*, Jl Tamblong No 48-50, Bandung Tel: 50708

Alumni Press, Jl Geusanulun 17, PO Box 272, Bandung Tel: (022) 50675/58290
Man Dir & Rights & Permissions: Eddy Damian; *Editorial:* I Wayan Parthiana, Yayat Ruchiyat; *Sales:* Philipus; *Production Manager:* Punomo Sadriman
Branch Off: Wisma Sawah Besar, 8th Floor, Jl S Su-Karjo Wiryopranoto 30, Jakarta Tel: 372730
Subjects: Law, Economics, Social Sciences
Founded: 1966

Angkasa*, Jl Merdeka No 6, Bandung Tel: 58330

Pustaka **Antara**, Jl Majaphit No 28, Jakarta Tel: 341321
Man Dir: H M Joesoef Ahmad
Founded: 1952
Subjects: School Textbooks, Children's books, Politics, Religion, General

Aries Lima, see PT New Aqua Press

Asia Afrika*, Jl Panggung X No 11, Surabaya Tel: 278175

PN **Balai** Pustaka, Jl Dokter Wahidin No 1, Jakarta Tel: 361701/365994/341714/374711/362981
Cable Add: PN Balai Pustaka
Chief Executive, Sales, Publicity, Rights & Permissions: Drs Soetojo Gondo; *Editorial, Production:* Mrs Dra Astuti Hendrato
Subjects: Literature, Juveniles, Science, Journals, Architecture, History, Engineering, Arts, Music, Education
Founded: 1917

Bale Bandung — Sumur Bandung*, Jl Asia Afrika 82, Bandung Tel: 59137/52156
Manager: H Moh Koerdi
Subject: Textbooks

P T **Bhakti** Centra Baru, Jl Jend Akhmad Yani No 15, Ujung Pandang Tel: 5192
Cable Add: Bhakti Baru Telex: 7156 Hakalla UP
Man Dir: Drs H M Jusuf Kalla; *Publicity Manager:* Alwi Hamu
Branch Off: Jl Lembang 9, Jakarta Tel: 356374
Subjects: Religion, General, Textbooks
Founded: 1972

Bhratara Karya Aksara*, Jl Oto Iskandardinata 111/29, Jakarta Tel: 811858
Subjects: History, Public Health, Industry, Maps, Agriculture, Textbooks, Reference, Education, Philosophy, Politics, Law, Social Sciences, Economics

Bina Ilmu*, Jl Genteng Kali 9 (Utara Siola), Surabaya Tel: 472214

Binacipta*, Jl Ganesya 4, Bandung Tel: 84319
1978: 15 titles

Bulan Bintang, Penerbit & Pustake NV*, Jl Kramat Kwitang I/8, Jakarta Tel: 342883
Manager: Mr Amelz
Subjects: Art, Sociology, Science, Religion
Founded: 1954

Bumi Restu*, Jl Letjen Haryono M T Persil 23, PO Box 404, Jakarta Tel: 882746

Cemerlang*, Jl Kesatrian VIII No 30, Jakarta Tel: 591431

Cerdas*, Jl Palasari No 125, Bandung

Dian Rakyat*, Jl Rawa Gelam I No 4, PO Box 51, Jakarta Tel: 481809/584845

C V Diponegoro*, Publisher, 44 Mohd Toha Bandung Tel: 50395 Cable Add: C V Diponegoro Bandung
Man Dir: A A Dahlan; *Editorial, Sales, Production, Publicity:* M D Dahlan
Subjects: Religion
1978: 45 titles *1979:* 13 titles *Founded:* 1962

P T Djambatan Penerbit NV*, Tromolpos 116, Jakarta Tel: 345131/341678
Manager: Roswitha Pamoentjak
Subjects: Art, Literature, Juveniles, Textbooks, Religion, Philosophy, Sociology, Maps
Founded: 1958

P T Dunia Pustaka Jaya, Jalan Kramat II/31A, Jakarta Pusat Tel: 336245, 367479 Cable Add: Depeje
Man Dir, Editorial, Rights & Permissions: Ajip Rosidi; *Sales Dir, Publicity:* Rachmat M A S; *Production:* Yus Rusamsi
Branch Off: Jalan Banteng 37, Bandung Tel: 59597
Subjects: General Fiction, Poetry, Art, Essays, Drama, Culture, Islam, Children's Books
1978: 77 titles *Founded:* 1971

Eresco, Jl Hasanudin No 9, Bandung Tel: (022) 82311 Cable Add: Erescopete Bandung
Man Dir: Mrs P Rochmat Soemitro; *Editorial:* Prof Dr Rochmat Soemitro; *Sales:* Mr Amun, Mr Harsono
Branch Off: Jl Perapatan 22 Pav Jakarta Tel: (021) 361782
Subjects: Law, Economics
Book Club: Himpunan Masyarakat Penainta Buku (HMPB)
Bookshops: Jl Hasanudin 9 Bandung; Jl Perapatan 22 Pav Jakarta Tel: (021) 361782
1978: 4 titles *1979:* 7 titles *Founded:* 1956

Erlangga, Jl Kramat IV (Kernolong) No 11, Jakarta Tel: 356593
Dir: M Hutauruk S H

P T Gaya Favorit Press, Book Division, Jalan Proklamasi 71, Jakarta Pusat Tel: 882148 Telex: 45734 Fega IA
Man Dir: Sofjan Alisjahbana; *Editorial:* Mrs Ediati Kamil, Soekanto SA; *Sales:* Irwan SLT; *Production, Publicity, Rights & Permissions:* Mrs Ediati Kamil
Parent Company: P T Gaya Favorit Press, Jalan Kebon Kacang Raya 1, Flat 3, tingkat 3, Jakarta Pusat
Subjects: Juvenile Fiction, Adult Fiction, Homecraft, other Non-fiction
1978: 28 titles *1979:* 54 titles *Founded:* 1975

PT Gramedia, PO Box 615, Dak Jakarta Pusat (Located at: Palmerah Selatan 22 lantai 4) Tel: 543008 Cable Add: Kompas Jakarta Telex: Kompas JKT 46327
General Manager: J Adisubrata; *Editorial:* A Haryono (Fiction), G Sugijanto (General, Non-fiction); *Sales:* A M Sutartono; *Production:* A Harijadi; *Publicity:* G Aris Buntarman; *Rights & Permissions:* Nora Sutadi
Subjects: Children's, General, Fiction and Non-fiction
Bookshops: Jalan Merdeka 43, Bandung; Jalan Gajah Mada 109, Jakarta; Jalan Pintu Air 72, Jakarta; Jalan Melawai IV/13, Jakarta; Jalan Basuki Rachmat 95, Surabaya; Jalan Jendral Sudirman 56, Yogyakarta
1978: 187 titles *1979:* 171 titles *Founded:* 1973

PT Grip*, Jl Kawung No 2, PO Box 129, Surabaya Tel: 22564
Man Dir, Editorial: Suripto; *Sales:* F D Praseno; *Production:* S Sawitri; *Publicity:* Satriyo Purwanto
Branch Off: Jl Kembung 22, Jakarta
Subjects: Textbooks, Politics, Social Science
Founded: 1957

Gunung Agung, PT, Jl Kwitang 6, PO Box 145, Jakarta Tel: 362909 Cable Add: Gunungagung Telex: 01144359 Jkt
President: Mr Masagung; *Manager:* Ali Amran
Branch Off: Gunung Agung (S) Pte Ltd, Suite 3808, OCBC Centre, Chulia St, Singapore 0104
Subjects: Librarianship, Juveniles, Textbooks, Science, Biography, Language, Literature
Founded: 1953

B P K Gunung Mulia*, Jalan Kwitang 22, Jakarta Tel: 343476
Dir: A Simandjuntak

Firma Harris*, Jl Veteran Gedung Olahraga No 6, Medan Tel: 22272

Hidakarya Agung*, Jl Kebon Kosong F-74, Jakarta Tel: 351074

Ichtiar Baru*, Jl Mojopahit 6, Jakarta Tel: 341226/41551
Subjects: Textbooks, Reference, Law, Social Sciences, Economics

PD & I Ikhwan*, Jl Bujana Dalam No 10, Blok G, Kebayoran Baru, Jakarta Tel: 772679

P T Indira, Jl Borobudur No 20, Jakarta Pusat Tel: 882754 Cable Add: Indira Jakarta
Man Dir: Wahyudi D
Bookshops: Jl Braga No 10, Bandung; Jl Kornel Simanjuntak No 76A, Jogjakarta; Jl Sam Ratulangi 37, Jakarta Pusat; Jl Gajah Mada 3-5, Duta Merlin Shopping Arcade, Jakarta Pusat; Jl Melawai V No 6, Jakarta Selatan; Jl Braga 111, Bandung; Jl Tunjungan 71, Surabaya; Jl Veteran 3394A, Palembang; Jl Sumatra 37, Den Pasar, Bali
Subjects: Education, Technical, General
Founded: 1950

Indrajaya*, Jl Jatibaru No 20, Jakarta Tel: 364372

Institut Dagang Muchtar*, Jl Embong Wungu 8, Surabaya Tel: 42973

Islamiyah*, Jl Sutomo P 328-329, Kotakpos 11, Medan Tel: 25421

Yayasan Jaya Baya, Jl Panghela 2 atas, Surabaya Tel: 41169

Jaya Murni*, Jl Ir H Juanda 34 Pav, Jakarta Tel: 359200
Manager: Tadjib Ermadi

Subject: Textbooks
Founded: 1945

Yayasan Kanisius*, Jl Pangeran Senopati 24, Jogjakarta Tel: 2309
Subjects: Textbooks, Religion, Engineering, Juveniles, Arts, Education, Economics

Karunia*, Jl Paneleh 18-A, Surabaya Tel: 44120

Yayasan Kawanku*, Jl Setia Budi Raya, Gg Sumbangsih 11/3A, Jakarta Tel: 583100

Kinta*, Jl Chik Di Tiro No 54-A, Jakarta Tel: 351394

Kurnia Esa*, Jl Kramat Raya 7-9, PO Box 3181, Jakarta Tel: 350043/5/6 Telex: 44328

L P3 E S (Lembaga Penelitian Pendidikan Dan Penerangan Ekonomi Dan Social)*, Jl Letjen S Parman 81, Slipi, PO Box 493, Jakarta Tel: 591528/594270
The Institute for Economics and Social Research Education and Information
Manager: Ismid Hadad
Subjects: Academic, Popular Science
Founded: 1971

Madju*, Jl Sutomo No P 341-342, Medan Tel: 25428

Marfiah*, Jl Kalibutuh No 131, Surabaya

Masa Baru*, Jl Gereja 3, Bandung Tel: 52045

Mutiara*, Jl Salemba Tengah No 36, Jakarta Tel: 882441
Subjects: Juveniles, Maps, Mathematics, Music, Education, Physics, Religion, Economics

P T New Aqua Press/Aries Lima*, Jl Rawa Gelam II/4, Jakarta Timur Tel: 482163

Nusa Indah*, Jl Katedral 5, Ende, Flores Tel: 198

Pelajar*, Jl Palasari 83-85, Bandung Tel: 57559

Pelita Masa*, Jl Lodaya No 25, Bandung Tel: 50823

Pembangunan*, Jl Raden Saleh No 2, Jakarta Tel: 342469
Managers: Mr Sumantri, Mr Soewando
Branch Offs: in Bandung, Jogjakarta, Madiun and Surabaya
Subjects: Textbooks, Juveniles, Sciences
Founded: 1953

Pembimbing Masa, Pusat Perdagangan Senen, Blok I, Lantai IV/2, PO Box 3281, Jakarta Tel: 367645

Pradnya Paramita, PO Box 146/Jkt, Jl Kebon Sirih 46, Jakarta Pusat Tel: (021) 360411 Cable Add: Pradnya/Jkt
Man Dir, Rights & Permissions: Sadono Dibyowiroyo SH *Editorial, Publicity:* Thaufik Arifin; *Sales:* A F Julianto; *Production:* Waslan Suriapranata
Subjects: General, Primary, Secondary & University Textbooks
Bookshops: Jl Kebon Sirih 46 pav, Jakarta Pusat; Jl Kiai Maja 2A, Kebayoran Baru, Jakarta Selatan
Founded: 1963

Remaja Karya*, Jl Ciateul No 34-36, kotakpos 284, Bandung Tel: 58226

Rosda*, Jl Raya Cimahi, Padalarang Km 12.5 No 858, Bandung Tel: 56627; Jl Kramat Kwitang II No 4, Jakarta Tel: 354920

Saiful*, Jl Pelangka Raya Baru 28, Medan Tel: 22384

Sastra Hudaya*, Jl Proklamasi No 61, Jakarta Tel: 882328

200 INDONESIA — IRAN

A B **Sitti** Syamsiyah*, Jl Secoyudan No 28, Sala/Surakarta Tel: 4721

Soeroengan*, Jl Pecenongan No 58, Jakarta Tel: 344460

Pustaka **Star***, Jl Moh Toha No 58, Bandung Tel: 58710

Sumatera*, Jl R Dewi Sartika I No 1, Bandung

Sumur Bandung*, Jl Asia Afrika 82, Bandung Tel: 59137

Tarate*, Jl Sumatera No 26-30, kotakpos 243, Bandung Tel: 51067
1978: 4 titles

Tintamas Indonesia PT*, Jl Kramat Raya 60, Jakarta Pusat Tel: 346186
Dir: Ali Audah
Subjects: Biography, History, Philosophy, Reference, Religion, Law, High-priced Paperbacks
Founded: 1947
Bookshop: Jl Kramat Raya 60, Jakarta Pusat

Toko Messir*, Jl Gudang No 135, Cirebon Tel: 57151

U P Indonesia*, Jl Jend A Yani No 19, Jogjakarta

Warga*, Jl Karangmenjangan 61, Surabaya Tel: 472160/472872

Widjaja*, Jl Pecenongan No 48-C, Jakarta Tel: 363446

C V **Yasaguna***, Gg Batik 7, Bendungan Hilir, Jakarta Tel: 581850
Manager: Hilman Madewa
Subjects: Textbooks, Agriculture, Juveniles

Book Clubs

Himpunan Masyarakat Penainta Buku, Jl Hasanudin No 9, Bandung
Owned by: Eresco

Major Booksellers

Effendi Harahap Bookstore*, Jl Abimanyu Raya 17, Semarang

Toko Buku **Gramedia**, 109 Jl Gajahmada, Jakarta Tel: 627809
Manager: Indra Gunawan

P T **Gunung Agung**, Jl Irian 5, Jayapura
Also: Kwitang 6, Jakarta

Toko Buku BPK **Gunung Mulia***, Jl Kwitang 22, Jakarta Tel: 41768

P T **Indira**, Jl Braga No 10, Bandung
For other addresses see entry under Publishers
Miscellaneous: Importers of General/Trade books and Educational/Scientific/Technical books and textbooks. Library suppliers to foreign libraries of Indonesian printed books

Toko Buku **Malabar***, 347 Oto Iskandardinata Bandung

Toko Buku **Melawai***, Jakarta

Toko Buku **Merbabu***, Semarang

Toko Buku Pustaka **Mimbar***, Medan

P T **Pembimbing** Masa, Pusat Perdagangan Senen, Blok I, Lantai IV No 2, PO Box 3281 Jkt, Jakarta Pusat Tel: 367645
Importer, bookshop, subscription agency

Pradnya Paramita, Jl Kebon Sirih 46, Jakarta Pusat Tel: (021) 360411
Man: Sadano Dibyowiroyo

Toko Buku **Sari Agung**, Tunjungan 5, Surabaya

CV Toko Buku **Tropen**, Tromolpos 3604/JKT, 113 Jl Pasar Baru, Jakarta Pusat Tel: 362695 Cable Add: Tokobuku Tropen
Manager: James Adam

Major Libraries

Arsip Nasional Republik Indonesia*, Jl Gajah Mada III, Jakarta
National Archives

Bibliotheca Bogoriensis*, Jl Ir Haji Juanda 20, Bogor
Central Library for Biology and Agriculture

Bidang Bibliografi dan Deposit, Pusat Pembinaan Perpustakaan*, Departemen P dan K, Jl Medan Merdeka Selatan 11, Jakarta Tel: 360136
National Bibliographic and Deposit Centre, Centre for Library Development
Librarian: Paul Permadi
Publication: Bibliografi Nasional Indonesia (quarterly)

Perpustakaan **Biro** Pusat Statistik*, Jl Dr Sutomo 7, Jakarta
Library of Central Bureau of Statistics

Perpustakaan **Dewan** Perwakilan Rakjat Gotong Rojong*, Senajan Pintu 8, Jakarta
Library of Indonesian Parliament

Pusat **Dokumentasi Ilmiah Nasional**, Jl Jenderal Gatot Subroto, PO Box 3065/JKT, Jakarta Selatan Tel: 583465/7, 510719, 511063 Telex: 45875 IA
National Scientific Documentation Centre
Publications: Directory of Special Libraries in Indonesia (irregular); *Index of Indonesian Learned Periodicals* (semi-annual); *Baca* (Read) (bi-monthly); *Bibliografi Khusus* (Special Bibliography) (irregular); *Indeks Laporan Penelitian dan Survai* (Index of Research and Survey Report) (annual); and lists of acquisitions

Library of **Hasanuddin University***, Jl Sunu, Makassar

Perpustakaan Jajasan **Hatta***, Malioboro 85, Jogjakarta
Hatta Foundation Library

Perpustakaan Pusat **Institut** Teknologi Bandung*, Jl Ganesya 10, Bandung
Central Library, Bandung Institute of Technology

Perpustakaan **Islam***, Jl P Mangkubumi 38, Jogjakarta
Islamic Library

Perpustakaan **Museum** Nasional, Departemen Pendidikan dan Kebudayaan, Merdeka Barat 12, Jakarta Tel: 360551
Library of the National Museum, Ministry of Education and Culture
Librarian: Miss M H Prakoso
Publications: Library Guide, Newspaper catalogue and other subject catalogues

Perpustakaan **Negara***, Malioboro 175, Jogjakarta
State Library

Pusat **Pembinaan** Perpustakaan, Departemen P dan K Bidang. Bibliografi dan Deposit*, Medan Merdeka Selatan 11, Tromolpos 274 Jakarta-Pusat Tel: 360136
Centre for Library Development, Department of Education and Culture, Deposit Library
Publication: Berita Bulanan, checklist of *Serials in the Libraries of Indonesia*

Library of **Political and Social History***, Medan Merdeka Selatan 11, Jakarta Tel: 360136
Librarian: Mrs Sayangbati-Dengah, WW

Publications: Press index; Index Artikel Tentang Negara (Index of Official Publications); *Index Pemilu* (Index of General Elections)

Tman Batjaan dan Perpustakaan Umum*, J Budi Keuliaan 3, Jakarta
Public Library Jakarta

Library Associations

Ikatan Pustakawan Indonesia*, c/o Centre for Library Development, Medan Merdeka Selatan 11, Belakang, Jakarta Tel: 360136
Indonesian Library Association
President: Sukarman Kartosedono
Secretary-General: J P Rompas
Publication: Majalah Ikatan Pustakawan Indonesia

Library Reference Books and Journals

Books

Directory of Special Libraries in Indonesia, National Scientific Documentation Centre, Jalan Jendral Gatot-Subroto, PO Box 3065/JKT, Jakarta

Journals

Baca (Read) (quarterly), PO Box 3065, Jakarta

Berita Bulanan (Bulletin), Centre for Library Development, Department of Education and Culture, Deposit Library, Medan Merdeka Selatan 11, Jakarta

Berita Idayu (Idayu News), Yayasan Idayu, Jl Dr Abdulrachman Saleh 26, Jakarta

Checklist of Serials in the Libraries of Indonesia, Centre for Library Development, Department of Education and Culture, Deposit Library, Medan Merdeka, Selatan 11, Jakarta

Diurnal Perpustakaan (Library Journal) (text in Indonesian or English), Perpustakaan Umum Makassar, Jl Kajaolalidjo 16, PO Box 16, Ujung Pandang

Index Artikel Tentang Negara (Index of Official Publications), Library of Political and Social History, Medan Merdeka Selatan 11, Jakarta

Majalah Ikatan Pustakawan Indonesia (Indonesian Library Association Journal), Indonesian Library Association, c/o Centre for Library Development, Medan Merdeka Selatan 11, Jakarta

Iran

General Information

Language: Persian (Farsi), Turkish and Armenian in Northwest, Arabic in Southwest, Kurdish in Kurdistan (English or French also)
Religion: Muslim (Shi'a sect)
Population: 35.2 million
Literacy Rate (1971): 36.9% of population aged 6 or over (58.6% of urban population, 20.4% rural)
Bank Hours: Generally Winter: 0800-1300 Saturday-Thursday; 1600-1800 Saturday-Wednesday; Summer: 0730-1300, 1700-1900

Saturday-Wednesday, 0730-1130 Thursday
Shop Hours: Generally Winter: 0800-2000 Saturday-Thursday; 0800-1200 Friday; Summer: 0800-1300, 1700-2100 Saturday-Thursday, 0800-1200 Friday
Currency: rial
Export/Import Information: No tariff on books and advertising but catalogues subject to 6% VAT. Import licences; publications offending public order, official religion or morality prohibited. Exchange controls, with new regulations issued each March
Copyright: No copyright conventions signed

Book Trade Organizations

Iranian Publishers' Association*, PO Box 1030, Tehran

Tehran Book Processing Centre (TEBROC), PO Box 51-1126, Tehran (Located at: 1188 Enqelab Ave, Tehran) Tel: 662940
Dir: Miss Z Shadman
Publications include: Books Catalogued by TEBROC; *Iranian National Union Catalogue; School Libraries; Directory of Iranian Periodicals; Directory of National and International Organizations of Library and Documentation*

Book Trade Reference Journals

Bibliography of Persia; National Bibliography, Book Society of Persia, PO Box 1936, Tehran (annual)

Books Catalogued by Tehran Book Processing Centre, Tehran Book Processing Centre, 46 Shahreza Ave, PO Box 11-1126, Tehran

Iranian National Union Catalogue, Tehran Book Processing Centre, 46 Shahreza Ave, PO Box 11-1126, Tehran

National Bibliography, Iranian Publications, National Library, Ghavamossaltań St, Tehran

Publishers

Amir Kabir Publishing & Distributing Corporation*, Shahabd St, Tehran
Dir: Abdulrahim Ja'fari
Parent company: Amir Kabir, 28 Vessal Shirazi St
Subjects: Textbooks, General
Founded: 1950

Boroukhim*, Ave Ferdowski, Tehran
Subjects: Dictionaries, Reference

Eghbal Co*, Shahabad Ave, Tehran
Dir: Djavad Eghbal
Subject: Juveniles, Fiction

Franklin Book Programs Inc*, 2 Alborz Ave, Tehran
Dir: Farhad Massoudi
Subjects: Encyclopaedias, Textbooks, Fiction, Biology, Chemistry, History, Engineering, Juveniles, Arts, Maps, Mathematics, Medicine, Education, Philosophy, Psychology, Politics, Physics, Social Sciences, Economics
Founded: 1952
Miscellaneous: A non-profit-making organization for International Book Publishing Development. Main office in New York

Ibn-Sina Publishers*, Shah Abad St, Tehran
Subjects: Textbooks, Directories, Multilingual Dictionaries, Fiction, Juveniles, Law, Economics

Majlis Press*, Ave Baharistan, Tehran
Subjects: Juveniles, Fiction

Shahrokh **Sabzerou**, PO Box 51/1318 Tehran 15 (Located at: 549 Mosadegh Ave, Tehran 15) Tel: 662692 Cable Add: Sabzerou Telex: 215574 Sbru
Man Dir: Shahrokh Sabzerou
Subjects: Children's Books, Painting and Colouring Books
1978: 43 titles *1979:* 20 titles *Founded:* 1972

Tehran Economist*, 99 Sevom Esfand, Tehran 11 Tel: 374181/5 Cable Add: Economist
Man Dir: Dr Bagher Shariat; *Editorial:* Mohammad Mehdi Fakhrizadeh; *Sales:* Mr Khadem; *Production:* Mr Hosseinpoor; *Publicity:* Mr Tavakoli
Subjects: Mining, Commerce, Agriculture, Food Science, Economics, Industry, Transport, Tourism
1978: 51 (Persian) 51 (English) *Founded:* 1953

Tehran University Press*, Amirabad Shomali, Tehran Tel: 632062/3, 630060/9
Man Dir: Dr B Farahrashi; *Editorial:* Dr H Erfani; *Editorial, Production:* Dr H Karimi; *Sales, Publicity:* K Esfahanian; *Rights & Permissions:* J Qajarieh
Subjects: University Textbooks
Bookshops: Ave 21 Azar, Tehran; Ave Shahreza (next to Royal Cinema House), Tehran; Amirabad Shomali, Tehran
Founded: 1944

Major Booksellers

Y **Beroukhim** & Sons, Booksellers*, 331 Ferdowsi Ave, Tehran Tel: 34526

Daneshdjou Bookstore*, 222 Shah Reza St, Tehran Tel: 48365

Mebso Bookshop*, 466 Naderi St, Tehran Tel: 46822/64091

Major Libraries

Astaneh Razavy Library*, Meshed

British Council Libraries*, 38 Ave Ferdowsi, PO Box 1589, Tehran Tel: 303346, 392571 Telex: 215361
Branches: PO Box 28, Isfahan; PO Box 13, Meshed; PO Box 65, Shiraz; PO Box 5, Tabriz; PO Box 896, Ahwaz

Imperial Library*, Tehran

Iranian Documentation Centre (IRANDOC), Ad 46, Enghelab Ave, Tehran Tel: 662223/662140 Cable Add: Asnad Telex: 2889 TN
Dir: Dr S A Mirzadeh

National Library, Si-Ye Tir St (Ghavamossaltane), Tehran
Librarian: Fereydoun Bodre'i
Publication: Kétab-Shinasi-Yé Méli-Yé Iran (Iran National Bibliography)

Pahlavi Library*, 9 Bisotoun Avenue, Aryamehr Sq, Tehran, Iran Tel: 623386/88 Telex: 212323
Managing Director: Shojaeddin Shafa
Publication: Acta Iranica

Pahlavi University Libraries*, Shiraz

Parliament Library*, Ketabkhaneh Majiles Showraie Melli, Tehran

Senate Library (Ketabkhaneh Majles Sena)*, Tehran

T E B R O C (Tehran Book Processing Centre), PO Box 51-1126 Tehran (Located at: 1188 Enqelab, Tehran) Tel: 662940 Telex: 212889 irdc ir

Central Library and Documentation Centre of **Tehran** University*, Shahreza Ave, Tehran

University of Ferdowsi Library*, PO Box 331, Mashhad Tel: 33075
Librarian: Dr A A M Safa

University of Isfahan Library*, Isfahan

Central Library, **University of Tabriz***, Tabriz
Dir: Asgar Delbaripour

Library Associations

Anjoman-e Ketabdaren-e Iran*, PO Box 11-1391, Tehran Tel: 622768
Iranian Library Association
Secretary: M Nikham Vazifeh
Publications: Nameh, Monthly News

Association of Registered Archivists of Iran Secretariat, Avenue Lalezar, Passage Afrashteh, 1st floor, Tehran

Library Reference Books and Journals

Books

Directory of National and International Organizations of Library and Documentation, Tebroc, PO Box 51-1126, Tehran

Journals

Monthly News, Iranian Library Association, PO Box 11-1391, Tehran

Nameh (Bulletin) (text in Persian, summaries in English), Iranian Library Association, PO Box 11-1391, Tehran

Literary Associations and Societies

Book Society of Persia*, PO Box 1936, Tehran
Publication: Bibliography of Persia

P E N Club of Iran*, Ave Pahlavi, 34th St No 9, Tehran 16
Founder and General Secretary: Z Rahnama

Iraq

General Information

Language: Arabic (English is the principal foreign language in Baghdad)
Religion: Muslim
Population: 12.3 million
Literacy Rate (1957): 11%
Bank Hours: Winter: 0900-1300 Saturday-Wednesday; 0900-1200 Thursday; Summer: 0800-1200 Saturday-Wednesday, 0800-1100 Thursday
Shop Hours: Winter: 0830-1430, 1700-1900 Saturday-Wednesday, 0830-1330 Thursday; Summer: 0800-1400, 1700-1900 Saturday-Wednesday, 0800-1300 Thursday
Currency: 1,000 fils = 1 Iraqi dinar
Export/Import Information: No tariffs on books and advertising. Import licences required. Exchange control, influenced by annual foreign exchange budget. Importation by state trading company or

established importer. The state trading company is the National House for Publishing, Distributing and Advertising, Aljamhuria St, PO Box 624, Baghdad
Copyright: No copyright conventions signed

Book Trade Journal

Iraqi Bulletin for Publications, National Library, Baghdad

Publishers

Al **Ma'arif** Ltd*, Mutanabi St, Baghdad
Subjects: Books in several Middle-Eastern languages, French and English, Fiction, Politics
Founded: 1929

National House for Distributing and Advertising*, Aljamhuria St, PO Box 624, Baghdad Tel: 68391 Cable Add: Donta Telex: 2392
Subjects: Politics, Economics, Education, Agriculture, Sociology, Commerce, General Science, Books in Arabic and other Middle-Eastern languages (also distributor)
Founded: 1972
Miscellaneous: Firm is attached to the Ministry of Information and is the sole importer and distributor of newspapers, magazines, periodicals and books

Major Booksellers

The export of Iraqi books is handled by the National House for Publishing, Distributing and Advertising (qv under Publishers)

Major Libraries

Al-Awqaf*, PO Box 14146, Baghdad Tel: 66104/65860
Library of Waqfs
Librarian: Jassim Al-Juboori
Branches at: Al-Qazzaza Library, Baghdad; Munier Al-Qadhi Library, Baghdad; Adhamiya, Mosul; Main Mosque, Anbar; Amarah; Nasiriyah; Sulaymaniyah; Kerkuk; Diala

College of Agriculture Library, University of Baghdad*, Abu Ghraib

The **Diwan** Library, Ministry of Education*, Baghdad

Library of the **Iraq Museum**, Baghdad

Library of the **Iraq Natural History** Research Centre and Museum, University of Baghdad, Bab Al-Muadham, Baghdad

Library of the **Mosul Museum***, Mosul

Mosul Public Library*, Mosul

National Centre of Archives, Waziriah, Amr bin Kalthoom St 15/10/9, Baghdad Cable Add: Centarchiv
Director-General: Salim Al-Alousi

National Library, al-Jumhuriya St, Baghdad
Dir: Fouad Y M Qazanchi
Publications: Iraqi National Bibliography (3 times yearly); *Accumulation List* (annual); *al-Maktaba al-Arabia Journal*

Scientific Documentation Centre*, Aqabba Bin Nafie Sq, Al-Masbah, PO Box 2441, Baghdad

Central Library of the **University of Baghdad***, Safi El-Din Ali-Hilli St, PO Box 12, Baghdad Tel: 64742

Library Associations

Arab Archivists Institute, c/o National Centre of Archives, Waziriah, Amr bin Kalthoom St 15/10/9, Baghdad

Iraq Library Association*, PO Box 4081, Baghdad-Adhamya Tel: 27077
Secretary: N Kamalal-Deen

Library Journals

Arab Archives Journal, National Centre of Archives, Waziriah, Amr bin Kalthoom St 15/10/9, Baghdad

Deposit Bulletin, National Library, Baghdad

The Library, Al-Muthanna Library, Al-Mutanabbi St, Baghdad

Republic of Ireland

General Information

Language: English and Irish
Religion: Roman Catholic
Population: 3.3 million
Bank Hours; 1000-1230, 1330-1500 Monday-Friday. Most open until 1700 one evening
Shop Hours: 0900 or 0930-1730 Monday-Saturday
Currency: 100 pence = 1 Irish pound
Export/Import Information: Member of the European Economic Community. No tariff on books except 4.8% on prayer and similar books from non-UK, 10.4% on children's picture books from non-EEC. Pamphlets dutied 8% from non-EEC. VAT is 10% on books, 20% on other printed matter. No import licences. Exchange controls
Copyright: UCC, Berne (see International section)

Book Trade Organizations

Book Association of Ireland, 21 Shaw St Dublin 2
Honorary Secretary: Eoin O'Keeffe
Association is inactive at present time

Booksellers Association of Great Britain & Ireland, 154 Buckingham Palace Rd, London SW1W 9TZ

Cumann Leabharfhoilsitheoirí Éireann (CLÉ), 55 Dame St, Dublin 2 Tel: (01) 775138
Irish Book Publishers' Association
Contact: Hilary Kennedy

Irish Book Publishers' Association, see Cumann Leabharfhoilsitheoirí Éireann

Irish Educational Publishers' Association*, C J Fallon Ltd, Lucan Rd, Palmerston, Dublin 20 Tel: (01) 365777
Honorary Secretary: M A Ledwidge

National Federation of Retail Newsagents*, Republic of Ireland District Council, 63 Middle Abbey St, Dublin 1 Tel: (01) 745347

Book Trade Journals

Books Ireland, Goslingstown, Kilkenny Tel: (0409) 5964 Telex: 8727 Kdw Ei (Attn Addis)
The trade journal and review medium of the Irish publishing industry. Published 10 times a year

Irish Publishing Record, School of Librarianship, University College, Belfield, Dublin 4

Leabharagan An Aosa Oig (Primary Bookshelf) (text in English and Gaelic), Nessa Ni Mhurchu, 45 St Brendan's Ave, Malahide Rd, Dublin 5

Publishers

A P C K*, Dawson St, Dublin 2

The **Academy** Press, 124 Ranelagh, Dublin 6 Tel: (01) 961133
Publisher: Sean I Browne; *Editorial:* Olwyn Callaghan
Associate Company: Irish Microforms Ltd (at above address)
Subjects: History, Biography, Scholarly Monographs, Literature, Literary Criticism
1978: 5 titles *1979:* 10 titles *Founded:* 1976
ISBN Publisher's Prefix: 0-906187

Anvil Books Ltd, 90 Lower Baggot St, Dublin 2 Tel: (01) 762359 Cable Add: Anvil, Dublin
Man Dir Sales, Production, Publicity, Rights & Permissions: Rena Dardis;
Editorial: Dan Nolan
Imprint: The Geraldine Press
Subjects: Biography, Irish History, Folklore, Sociology, Children
1978: 1 title *1979:* 2 titles *Founded:* 1964
ISBN Publisher's Prefix: 0-900068

Arlen House Ltd, 2 Strand Rd, Baldoyle, Dublin 13 Tel: (01) 392520
Chief Executive, Editorial, Production, Rights & Permissions: Catherine Rose;
Sales, Publicity: Mike Roberts
Imprints: Turoe Press, The Women's Press
Subjects: Women's Studies, Feminism, Child Care, Poetry, Fiction
1978: 3 titles *1979:* 8 titles *Founded:* 1975
ISBN Publisher's Prefix: 0-905223

The **Blackwater** Press, c/o Folens & Co Ltd, Airton Rd, Tallaght, Co Dublin Tel: 515311
Publisher: T F Turley
Associate Company: Folens & Co Ltd (qv)
Subjects: Non-fiction books of Irish interest, Local History, History
1978: 5 titles
ISBN Publisher's Prefix: 0-905471

An **Clócomhar** TTA*, 13 Gleann Carraig, Dublin 13 Tel: (01) 324906
1979: 9 titles

Clódhanna Teo*, c/o 6 Harcourt St, Dublin 2 Tel: (01) 757401

Co-op Books (Publishing) Ltd, 50 Merrion Sq, Dublin 2
Dirs: Steve MacDonogh, Ronan Sheehan
Subjects: Fiction, Drama
1978: 6 titles *1979:* 6 titles *Founded:* 1976
ISBN Publisher's Prefix: 0-905441

Cork University Press, University College, Cork Tel: (021) 26871 ext 2348
Sales Dir & Executive Secretary: D J Counihan
Subjects: Biography, History, Music, Art, Philosophy, Literature, Reference, Religion, Medicine, Psychology, Engineering, General & Social Science, University Textbooks
Bookshop: Cork University Press (Retail

REPUBLIC OF IRELAND 203

Sales), University College, Cork
1978: 3 titles *1979:* 1 title *Founded:* 1925
ISBN Publisher's Prefix: 0-902561

Cuala Press, Avalon, Leslie Ave, Dalkey, County Dublin Tel: Dublin 808221
Directors: M B Yeats, Anne Yeats, Thomas Kinsella, Liam Miller, Patrick O'Carroll
Subjects: Books formerly selected by W B Yeats. The press continues the tradition of Irish hand-printing & publishing, and issues first editions of Irish writers, booklets, ballad sheets & hand-coloured prints
Founded: 1908

Gilbert **Dalton** Ltd, 4 Dublin Rd, Stillorgan, Blackrock, Co Dublin Tel: (01) 889231
Chief Executive, Production, Publicity, Rights & Permissions: Séan O'Boyle;
Editorial: Monica O'Boyle; *Sales:* Jim McGowan
Subjects: Irish Tradition, Folklore, Folk Music, Science Fiction, Gaelic Books
Bookshop: McGowan's Bookshop (at above address)
1978: 6 titles *1979:* 10 titles *Founded:* 1975
ISBN Publisher's Prefix: 0-86233

The **Dolmen** Press Ltd, The Lodge, Mountrath, Portlaoise Tel: Abbeyleix (0502) 32213
Man Dir: Liam Miller; *Sales, Publicity & Advertising Dir:* William C Browne
Orders to: Irish Bookhandling, North Richmond Industrial Estate, Dublin 1 Tel: (01) 740325
Subsidiary Company: The Five Lamps Press (at above address)
Subjects: Belles Lettres, Poetry, Biography, High-priced Paperbacks
1978: 13 titles *1979:* 14 titles *Founded:* 1951
ISBN Publisher's Prefix: 0-85105

Dominican Publications, Saint Saviour's, Granby Lane, Dublin 1 Tel: (01) 744144
Chief Executive, Editorial: Austin Flannery; *Sales, Production:* Bernard Treacy
Subject: Religion
Bookshop: At above address
ISBN Publisher's Prefix: 0-9504797

Dublin Institute for Advanced Studies, 10 Burlington Rd, Dublin 4 Tel: Dublin 680748
Subjects: Celtic Studies, Physics

Eason & Son Ltd, 65 Middle Abbey St, Dublin 1 Tel: (01) 741161 Telex: 4286
Man Dir: S D Carpenter; *Editorial, Sales, Production, Publicity, Rights & Permissions:* W H Clarke
Associate Companies: Eason & Son (NI) Ltd, 17 Donegall St, Belfast
Imprint: Irish Heritage Series
Subject: Irish interest
Bookshops: Antrim, Belfast, Cork, Craigavon, Dublin, Dun Laoghaire, Limerick, Newtownards
1978: 14 titles *1979:* 7 titles *Founded:* 1886
ISBN Publisher's Prefix: 0-900346

Ecclesia Press, an imprint of Irish Academic Press (qv)

Educational Company of Ireland, PO Box 43A, Ballymount Rd, Walkinstown, Dublin 12 Tel: (01) 500611 Telex: 5864
Man Dir: W J Connolly; *Dir:* F Maguire
Branch Offs: 2 Cook St, Cork; 20-1 Talbot St, Dublin 1
Subjects: History, Religion, Irish, English, Geography, French, Technical, Domestic Science
Subsidiary Company: Talbot Press Ltd (qv)
Founded: 1877
ISBN Publisher's Prefix: 0-901802

C J **Fallon** Ltd*, 77 Marlboro St, Dublin 1 Tel: (01) 46191
Shipping Add: Lucan Rd, Palmerstown, Dublin 20
Sales Dir: Edward J White; *Advertising, Publicity, Rights & Permissions:* Maurice A Ledwidge
Branch Off: 36 Marlboro St, Cork
Subjects: Secondary & Primary Textbooks, Business
Bookshops: Fallon's Book Shops, 77 Marlboro St, Dublin 1; 36 Marlboro St, Cork
Founded: 1927
ISBN Publisher's Prefix: 0-7144

Allen **Figgis** & Co Ltd, The Mall, Donnybrook, Dublin 4 Tel: (01) 760461
Man Dir: Allen Figgis
Subjects: General Fiction & Nonfiction
1978: 2 titles
ISBN Publisher's Prefix: 0-900372

The **Five Lamps** Press, subsidiary of The Dolmen Press Ltd (qv)

Foilseacháin Náisiúnta Tta*, 29 Sraid Ui Chonaill Iocht, Ath Cliath 1 Tel: Ath Cliath 745314

Folens and Co Ltd, Airton Rd, Tallaght, Co Dublin Tel: 515311
Man Dir: A Folens; *General Manager:* T F Turley
Associate Company: The Blackwater Press (qv)
Subject: Educational
1978: 65 titles
ISBN Publisher's Prefix: 0-86121

An **Foras** Forbartha*, St Martin's House, Waterloo Rd, Ballsbridge, Dublin 4 Tel: (01) 764211 Cable Add: Foras, Dublin Telex: 30846
National Institute for Physical Planning and Construction Research
Chief Executive Officer: George O'Hara; *Rights & Permissions:* C S Curran
Subject: Environmental Research
Founded: 1964
ISBN Publisher's Prefix: 0-906120

Four Courts Press, 3 Serpentine Ave, Dublin 4 Tel: (01) 688033/688236
Man Dir: Michael Adams; *Publicity Manager:* J G O'Connor
Associate Company: Irish Academic Press Ltd (qv)
Subjects: Irish Studies, Philosophy, Theology
1978: 3 titles *1979:* 5 titles *Founded:* 1977
ISBN Publisher's Prefix: 0-906127

The **Gallery** Press, 19 Oakdown Rd, Dublin 14 Tel: (01) 985161
Chief Executive, Editorial: Peter Fallon
Associate Company: The Deerfield Press, Deerfield, Mass 01342, USA
Subjects: Poetry, Plays, Prose, Drawings
1978: 15 titles *1979:* 14 titles *Founded:* 1970
ISBN Publisher's Prefix: 0-902996

The **Geraldine** Press, an imprint of Anvil Books Ltd (qv)

Gifford & **Craven***, 50 Merrion Square, Dublin 2 Tel: (01) 767882

Gill & **Macmillan** Ltd, 15-17 Eden Quay, Dublin 1 Tel: (01) 788455 Cable Add: Gillmac Dublin Telex: 4142
Man Dir: M H Gill; *Editorial Director:* H Mahoney; *Sales Dir:* Peter Thew; *Publicity Manager:* Eveleen Coyle; *Production Manager:* Eamonn O'Rouke
Associate Company: Macmillan Publishers Ltd, UK (qv)
Subjects: Belles Lettres, Biography, History, Philosophy, Religion, Paperbacks, University, Secondary & Primary Textbooks
1978: 40 titles *1979:* 45 titles *Founded:* 1968 (formerly Gill & Son)
ISBN Publisher's Prefix: 0-7171

Golden Eagle Books Ltd, subsidiary of the Mercier Press Ltd (qv)

The **Goldsmith** Press, Martinstown Rd, The Curragh
Publicity Manager: M McGlinchey
Subjects: Literature, Fiction, Poetry, Art, Children's, Cookery
1978: 8 titles *1979:* 8 titles
ISBN Publisher's Prefix: 0-904984

Institute of Public Administration, 59 Lansdowne Rd, Dublin 4 Tel: (01) 686233 Cable Add: Admin Dublin
Dir (Publications): James D O'Donnell; *Manager:* Tony Farmar; *Sales:* James Moraghan
Subjects: Irish Government, Economics, Law, Social Policy and Administrative History, Administration Yearbook & Diary, Administration (journal), Young Citizen
1978: 8 titles *1979:* 6 titles *Founded:* 1957
ISBN Publisher's Prefixes: 0-902173, 0-906980

Irish Academic Press, 3 Serpentine Ave, Dublin 4 Tel: (01) 688236/688033
Shipping Add: Bay 92, Shannon
Man Dir: Michael Adams
Associate Company: Four Courts Press (qv)
Imprints: Irish University Press, Ecclesia Press
Subjects: History, Government Documents, Irish Studies
Founded: 1974
ISBN Publisher's Prefix: 0-7165

Irish Heritage Series, an imprint of Eason & Son Ltd (qv)

Irish Humanities Centre and Keohanes, 23 Westland Row, Dublin 2 Tel: (01) 603565
Editorial: Grattan Freyer, Michael Keohane
Subjects: Irish Literary, Political, Historical
1979: 1 title *Founded:* 1979
ISBN Publisher's Prefix: 0-906462

Irish Management Institute*, Sandyford Rd, Dublin 14 Tel: (01) 983911 Telex: 30325
Chief Executive: Ivor E Kenny; *Editorial, Rights & Permissions:* Alex Miller; *Sales, Publicity & Advertising Dir:* Diarmuid O'Broin; *Production:* Eric Carroll
Subjects: Management Training and Education Textbooks, Research Reports
1978: 3 titles *Founded:* 1952

Irish Microforms, see The Academy Press

The **Irish Times** Ltd*, General Services, 11-15 D'Olier St, Dublin 2 Tel: (01) 722022 Telex: 5167
Subjects: Reprints, Microfilm
1978: 3 titles

Irish University Press, an imprint of Irish Academic Press (qv)

Albertine **Kennedy** Publishing, 5 Henrietta St, Dublin 1 Tel: (01) 740983/280236
Man Dir: Thomas Kennedy
Subjects: Irish Interest, Travel, Literature, Photography
Bookshop: Source Gallery (at above address)
1978: 2 titles *1979:* 3 titles *Founded:* 1975
ISBN Publisher's Prefix: 906002

The **Mercier** Press Ltd, 4 Bridge St, Cork Tel: 504022
Man Dir: Captain J M Feehan; *Editorial:* M Feehan, C Ó Marcaigh; *Sales Manager:* F Corcoran; *Rights & Permissions:* J F Spillane
Subsidiary Companies: Mercier Distributors Ltd; Golden Eagle Books Ltd (both at above address)
Branch Off: 25 Lower Abbey St, Dublin Tel: (01) 744141
Subjects: Irish Literature, History, Biography, Folklore, Travel, Humour, Theology, Philosophy, Religion, Music, Art,

Reference, High-priced Paperbacks, Educational Materials
Bookshops: The Mercier Bookshop Ltd, 4 Bridge St, Cork; The University Bookshop, University College, Cork; Mercier Library Supplies, 24 Lower Abbey St, Dublin 1
1979: 48 titles *1980:* approx 45 titles
Founded: 1946
ISBN Publisher's Prefix: 0-85342

The **National Press***, 2 Wellington Rd, Ballsbridge, Dublin 4 Tel: (01) 681905
Dir: P Cannon
Subjects: Belles Lettres, Religion, Education, Paperbacks

New Writers' Press*, 61 Clarence Mangan Rd, Dublin 8
Man Dir: Michael Smith
Subjects: Poetry, Criticism, Hardbacks and Paperbacks
Founded: 1967

O'Brien Educational, 11 Clare St, Dublin 2 Tel: (01) 979598
Editorial, Rights & Permissions: Seamus Cashman; *Sales, Production:* Michael O'Brien
Associate Companies: The O'Brien Press (qv); Wolfhound Press (qv)
Subjects: Science, Humanities, English, History, Celtic Studies, Contrast Studies, Teachers Handbooks
1978: 8 titles
Miscellaneous: Publishers to the Curriculum Development Unit, Trinity College, Dublin 2
ISBN Publisher's Prefix: 0-905140

The **O'Brien** Press, 11 Clare St, Dublin 2 Tel: (01) 979598
Man Dir, Rights & Permissions: Michael O'Brien; *Production, Publicity:* Catheine Boland
Orders to: Irish Bookhandling Ltd, Nth Richmond Industrial Est, Dublin 1 Tel: (01) 740324
Associate Companies: O'Brien Educational (qv); Wolfhound Press (qv)
Subjects: General Fiction, Belles Lettres, Poetry, Biography, History, Architecture/Planning, Anthropology, Quality Paperbacks, Ornithology, Natural History, Illustrated Books, Folklore, Children's Books
1978: 12 titles *Founded:* 1974
ISBN Publisher's Prefix: 0-905140

Poolbeg Press Ltd*, Knocksedan House, Forrest Great, Swords, Co Dublin Tel: (01) 401133/401675/402681/401957 Telex: 4639
Man Dirs: Philip Mac Dermott, David Marcus; *Editorial:* D Marcus; *Sales:* P Mac Dermott; *Production, Publicity, Rights & Permissions:* Adrienne Fleming
Imprint: Ward River
Subjects: Fiction
1978: 7 titles *1979:* 10 titles *Founded:* 1976

Runa Press, 2 Belgrave Terrace, Monkstown, Dublin Tel: (01) 801869
Subjects: Poetry, Philosophy, Sociology, Fiction, Psychology

Stationery Office (Oifig an tSolathair), St Martin's House, Waterloo Rd, Dublin 4

Talbot Press Ltd, PO Box 43A, Ballymount Rd, Walkinstown, Dublin 12 Tel: (01) 500611
Dirs: W J Connolly, F Maguire
Parent Company: Educational Co of Ireland (qv)
Subjects: General Fiction, History, Music, Religion, Juveniles, Political Science, Folklore, Religious & Liturgical
Founded: 1913
ISBN Publisher's Prefix: 0-85452

Tansy Books*, Glaskenny, Enniskerry, Co Wicklow Tel: 868514
Dir: John Feeney
Subjects: Fiction, Psychology, Essays, History
Founded: 1976

Turoe Press, an imprint of Arlen House Ltd (qv)

Veritas Publications*, Veritas House, 7-8 Lower Abbey St, Dublin 1 Tel: (01) 788177
Dir: Sean O'Boyle
Parent Company: The Catholic Communications Institute of Ireland
Subjects: Religion, Low- & High-priced Paperbacks, University, Secondary & Primary Textbooks, Educational Materials
1978: 18 titles *Founded:* 1900
Bookshop: Veritas, 7-8 Lower Abbey St, Dublin 1
Miscellaneous: Veritas Publications is the publishing division of the Catholic Communications Institute of Ireland Inc
ISBN Publisher's Prefix: 0-905092

Villa Books Ltd, 55 Dame St, Dublin 2 Tel: (01) 775138
Man Dir: Anthony Dwyer; *Editorial:* Susan Dwyer
Subjects: General Non-fiction, Religion
1978: 4 titles *1979:* 8 titles *Founded:* 1978
ISBN Publisher's Prefix: 0-906408

Ward River, an imprint of Poolbeg Press Ltd (qv)

Wolfhound Press, 98 Ardilaun, Portmarnock, County Dublin Tel: (01) 462162
Publisher: Seamus Cashman
Orders to: Irish Bookhandling Ltd, North Richmond Industrial Estate, North Richmond St, Dublin 1 Tel: (01) 740324
Associate Companies: O'Brien Educational (qv); The O'Brien Press (qv)
Subjects: Belles Lettres, Poetry, Biography, History, Juveniles, Fiction, Literary Studies, Law
1978: 6 titles *1979:* 10 titles *Founded:* 1974
ISBN Publisher's Prefixes: 0-9503454, 0-905473

The **Women's** Press, an imprint of Arlen House Ltd (qv)

Major Booksellers

Eason & Son Ltd, Patrick St, Cork; 40 Lower O'Connel St, Dublin 1 Tel: (01) 803005; Middle Abbey St, Dublin 1 Tel: (01) 741161

The **Eblana** Bookshop*, 46 Grafton St, Dublin 2 Tel: (01) 770178

Wm **Egan** & Sons*, Patrick St, Cork, Co Cork

Greene & Co, 16 Clare St, Dublin 2 Tel: (01) 762554

Fred **Hanna** Ltd, 27-29 Nassau St, Dublin 2 Tel: (01) 771255/720797

Hodges Figgis & Co Ltd, Stephen Court, St Stephen's Green, Dublin 2 Tel: (01) 760461; The Mall, Donnybrook, Dublin 4 Tel: (01) 760461; Shopping Centre, Dun Laoire Tel: 809917; 56 Dawson St, Dublin 2 Tel: (01) 774754; High St, Kilkenny Tel: (056) 22974; Queen's Old Castle Centre, Cork Tel: (021) 962322

The **Kilkenny** Bookshop Ltd*, High St, Kilkenny Tel: (056) 22974 (New retail books); Kieran St, Kilkenny Tel: (056) 22974 (Secondhand and antiquarian books)
Proprietors: Don and Mary Roberts

The **Library** Shop, Trinity College, College St, Dublin 2 Tel: (01) 772941
Manager: J G Duffy

The **Mercier** Bookshop Ltd, 4 Bridge St, Cork Tel: (021) 54022

O'Mahony & Co Ltd, 120 O'Connell St, Limerick Tel: (061) 48155
School Booksellers Department at 40 Thomas St, Limerick
Manager: Arthur O'Leary

Paperback Centre*, 20 Suffolk St, Dublin 2 Tel: (01) 774210; Stillorgan Shopping Centre, Co Dublin Tel: (01) 886341

Willis Bookshops, 31 South Anne St, Dublin 2 Tel: (01) 719273
Manager: Miss G Wratt
Also 37 Cook St, Cork Tel: (021) 20937
Manager: Miss B Russell

Major Libraries

The Chester **Beatty** Library and Gallery of Oriental Art*, 20 Shrewsbury Rd, Dublin 4 Tel: (01) 692386
This library, bequeathed to the Irish nation by Sir Chester Beatty, includes manuscripts and works of art which illustrate the history of mankind from 2700 BC (the Babylonian clay tablets) to the present century
Librarian: P Henchy

Central **Catholic** Library, 74-75 Merrion Sq, Dublin 2

Dublin Public Libraries, Pearse St, Dublin Tel: (01) 777662
City and County Librarian: Mairin O'Byrne

National Library of Ireland, Kildare St, Dublin 2 Tel: (01) 765521

Oireachtas Library*, Leinster House, Dublin 2
(Selective works of parliamentary interest)

Public Record Office of Ireland, Four Courts, Dublin 7 Tel: (01) 725275

Representative Church Body Library, Braemor Park, Rathgar, Dublin 14 Tel: (01) 979979
Librarian: Miss G Willis

Royal College of Surgeons in Ireland Library, St Stephen's Green, Dublin 2 Tel: (01) 780200 Ex 248
Librarian: Professor J B Lyons FRCPI; *Executive Librarian:* Mrs K M Bishop

Royal Dublin Society Library, Ballsbridge, Dublin 4 Tel: (01) 680645 Cable Add: Society, Dublin Telex: 4409 Alrt Ei

Trinity College Library, College St, Dublin 2 Tel: (01) 772941 Telex: 25442
Librarian: Peter Brown

University College Cork Library, University College, Cork

University College Dublin Library, Belfield, Dublin 4 Tel: (01) 693244 Telex: 4114
Librarian: S Phillips
Publications: Annual Report, *Irish Publishing Record*

University College Galway Library, Galway
Librarian: Christopher Townley

Library Associations

Central **Catholic** Library Association Inc, 74 Merrion Sq, Dublin 2
Honorary Secretary: Anthony J Litton

Cumann Leabharlann na h-Éireann*, Thomas Prior House, Merrion Rd, Dublin 4
Library Association of Ireland

Honorary Secretary: Nodlaig P Hardiman
Publication: An Leabharlann (The Irish Library) (published jointly with the Northern Ireland Branch, The Library Association) (4 per year)

Cumann Leabharlannaithe Scoile (CLS) *
Executive Secretary: Sister Monaghan, Irish Schools Library Association, Loreto College, Foxrock, Co Dublin
Irish Association of School Librarians

Irish Association for Documentation and Information Services (IADIS), The National Library of Ireland, Kildare St, Dublin 2
Inactive at present time

Irish Society for Archives, 82 Saint Stephen's Green, Dublin 2
Publication: Irish Archives Bulletin

National Library of Ireland Society, Kildare St, Dublin 2

Library Journals

An Leabharlann (The Irish Library), Library Association of Ireland, 46 Grafton St, Dublin 2 (published jointly with Northern Ireland Branch)

Long Room, Trinity College, Friends of the Library, College St, Dublin 2

Literary Associations and Societies

Irish Academy of Letters*, 4 Ailesbury Grove, Dundrum, Dublin 14
Secretary: Evan Boland

Irish P E N*, 52 Silchester Park, Glenageary, Dun Laoghaire, Co Dublin
Secretary: Alun Llewellyn

Literary Periodicals

Comhar (Cooperation) (text in Irish), 37 Sraid na Bhfinini, Dublin

Dublin Magazine, Irish Academy of Letters, 4 Ailesbury Grove, Dundrum, Dublin 14

Journal of Irish Literature, Proscenium Press, PO Box 361, Newark, DE 19711, USA

Studies; an Irish quarterly review of letters, philosophy and science, Talbot Press Ltd, PO Box 43A, Ballymount Rd, Walkinstown Rd, Dublin 12

Literary Prizes

Allied Irish Banks' Awards for Literature
For excellence in creative writing. Awards are nominated by the Irish Academy of Letters. One for £2,000 and one for £1,000 to a new writer. Enquiries to Allied Irish Banks Ltd, Development Division, Bankcentre, Ballsbridge, Dublin 4

Denis **Devlin** Memorial Award for Poetry
For the best book of poetry in the English language written by an Irish citizen. £600. Awarded every three years, next awarded 1982. Enquiries to Irish Arts Council, 70 Merrion Sq, Dublin 2

Gregory Medal*
For distinction in letters or outstanding literary work in Irish. Awarded periodically, Enquiries to Irish Academy of Letters, 4 Ailesbury Grove, Dundrum, Dublin 14

Macaulay Fellowships
Awarded in literature every three years to young Irish writers. Value £2,500. Next awarded 1981. Enquiries to Irish Arts Council, 70 Merrion Sq, Dublin 2

Novel Prize*
For the best novel written in Irish. Awarded annually. Enquiries to Irish Academy of Letters, 4 Ailesbury Grove, Dundrum, Dublin 14

George **Russell** (AE) Memorial Award
Awards are made approximately every five years from the Fund on recognition of published or unpublished work, creative or scholarly, which, in the opinion of the Advisory Committee is of a high standard of merit. Awards may also be made for similar work planned, although not yet completed. The Award consists of a cash payment of £100. Candidates must be of Irish birth and ordinarily resident in any part of Ireland, and must not have attained 35 years of age on the 1st day of January of the year in which the Award is made. Enquiries to George Russell (AE) Memorial Fund, Bank of Ireland, Lower Baggot St, Dublin 2

Marten **Toonder** Award
Awarded in literature every three years. Value £2,500. Next award in 1980. Enquiries to Irish Arts Council, 70 Merrion Sq, Dublin 2

Israel

General Information

Language: Hebrew and Arabic (English and German widely known)
Religion: Predominantly Jewish
Population: 3.7 million
Literacy Rate (1971): 87.9% (89.4% of urban population, 78.6% rural)
Bank Hours: 0830-1230 Sunday-Friday
Shop Hours: Usually Sunday 0800-1300, 1600-1800; weekdays 0800-1300, 1600-1900
Currency: 100 agorot (singular: agora) = 1 Israel shekel
Export/Import Information: Books (except for 27.5% on children's picture books) and advertising duty-free. Books exempt from most additional taxes. No import licence required for books but must apply for importing number; exchange granted automatically
Copyright: UCC, Berne, Florence (see International section)

Book Trade Organizations

Acum Ltd (Society of Authors, Composers and Music Publishers in Israel), 118-120 Rothschild Blvd, PO Box 11201, Tel Aviv Tel: (03) 240115
Dir-General: M Avidom

Association of Hebrew Writers, PO Box 7111, Tel Aviv
Secretary General: Mordechy Ot-Yakar
Publication: Moznayim (monthly)

Book and Printing Center — Israel Export Institute, 29 Hamered St, PO Box 29732, Tel Aviv Cable Add: Memex Telex: 35613
Dir: Shlomo Erel
Division of the Israel Export Institute.
Publications: Jerusalem Post Literary Supplement (incorporating *Israel Book World*) (monthly); *Typeface Catalogue* of the printing industry in Israel; *Israel Book Trade Directory* (biennially); *Books from Israel* (biennially); *Science Books Published in Israel* (in languages other than Hebrew); Catalogue of books on the Holyland, Israel, Bible and Religion, *Books from Israel Export Catalog* (annual); *Children's Books from Israel*; *Israeli Publishers and Authors and Their Books on the World Scene*

Book Publishers' Association of Israel, 29 Carlebach St, PO Box 20123, Tel Aviv 67132 Tel: (03) 284191
Executive Dir: Benjamin Sella
Publication: Katalog Sefarim Kelali

Economic Council for Israel Printing & Publishing Committee, Michael Ho, Baker St, London W1, UK Tel: (01) 935 4422
Executive Secretary: Cyril Jacobs

The **Institute** for the Translation of Hebrew Literature Ltd, 66 Shlomo Hamelech St, Tel Aviv Tel: (03) 244879
Man Dir: Mrs Nilli Cohen
Publications: Modern Hebrew Literature (quarterly, incorporating Hebrew Book Review); *Bibliography of Modern Hebrew Literature in Translation* (bi-annual)
Activities of the Institute include promotion of modern Hebrew literature in translation and co-publishing projects, subsidies to authors and publishers for translations of Hebrew literary works and their publication abroad

Israel Book Importers' Association*, c/o Emanuel Brown, 35 Allenby Rd, Tel Aviv

Israel ISBN Group Agency*, c/o Centre for Public Libraries, PO Box 242, Jerusalem

Standard Book Numbering Agency, see Israel ISBN Group Agency

Book Trade Reference Books and Journals

Books

Children's Books from Israel, Book & Printing Center—Israel Export Institute, 29 Hamered St, PO Box 29732, Tel Aviv

Israeli Publishers and Authors and Their Books on the World Scene, Book and Printing Center — Israel Export Institute, 29 Hamered St, PO Box 29732, Tel Aviv

Publishers & Printers of Israel, Book & Printing Center—Israel Export Institute, 29 Hamered St, PO Box 29732, Tel Aviv

Science Books Published in Israel in languages other than Hebrew, Book and Printing Center—Israel Export Institute, 29 Hamered St, PO Box 29732, Tel Aviv

Journals

Books from Israel Export Catalog (biennially), Book & Printing Center—Israel Export Institute, 29 Hamered St, PO Box 29732, Tel Aviv

Hadashot al Pirsuma Ha-memshala (News about Government Publications), Israel Government Printer, Jerusalem

Israel Book Trade Directory (biennially), Book & Printing Center—Israel Export Institute, 29 Hamered St, PO Box 29732, Tel Aviv

Katalog Sefarim Kelali (Israel Books In Print), Book Publishers' Association of Israel, 29 Carlebach St, PO Box 20123, Tel Aviv 67132

Kirjath Sepher (City of the Book); bibliographical quarterly (text in Hebrew), Jewish National and University Library, PO Box 503, Jerusalem

Publishers

'A' Publishing Institute*, PO Box 894, Jersualem
Manager: A Chitov
Subjects: Orthodox Textbooks, Religion

Academon (The Hebrew University Students' Printing and Publishing House), The Hebrew University Campus, PO Box 41, Jerusalem Tel: (02) 636253
Man Dir: Yitzhal Tzur; *Sales Manager:* Haim Hazan
Bookshop: Academon, The Hebrew University Campus, Jerusalem
Manager: Richard Sherman
Subjects: Academic
Founded: 1952

Academy of the Hebrew Language, The Hebrew University, PO Box 3449, Jerusalem
Subjects: Hebrew: Linguistics, Dictionaries, Terminology, Periodicals

Achiasaf Publishing House Ltd, 13 Yosef Hanassi St, PO Box 4810, Tel Aviv
Tel: (03) 283339
Man Dir: Schachna Achiasaf
Founded: 1933
Subjects: General Nonfiction, Reference, Juveniles, Popular Science, Textbooks, Fiction, Dictionaries
1978: 12 titles

Achiever*, 22 Hahistadrut St, Jerusalem
Tel: (02) 225740
Managers: H Rolnik, D Kessler, S Atzmon
Subject: Maps

Adam Publishers, PO Box 3329, Jerusalem (Located at: 18 Yehoshua Ben-Nun, Jerusalem) Tel: (02) 664893
Man Dirs: Yehuda Melzer, Aryeh Mor; *Editorial:* Muli Melzer; *Sales, Rights & Permissions:* Janee Hahn
Associate Company: The Dvir Publishing Co Ltd (qv)
Subjects: Belles Lettres, Juveniles, University Textbooks, Biography, Politics, Philosophy, General
1978: 5 titles *1979:* 10 titles *Founded:* 1978

Agudat Harashash*, 7 Bezalei St, Jerusalem
Tel: (02) 226904
Manager: I Hasid
Subjects: Orthodox Textbooks, Religion

Aleph Publishers Ltd*, 49 Nachmani St, Tel Aviv Tel: (03) 612003
Manager: B Feldenkreis
Subjects: Art, Science, History of Israel, Textbooks, Belles Lettres, Poetry, Juveniles, Reference
Founded: 1962

Am Hasefer*, 9 Bialik St, PO Box 4055, Tel Aviv Tel: (03) 53040
Man Dir: D Lipetz
Subjects: Belles Lettres, Biography, History, Art, Political Science, Periodicals, Numismatics
Founded: 1955

Am Oved Publishers Ltd, 22 Mazeh St, PO Box 470, Tel Aviv Tel: (03) 291526 Cable Add: Amoved, Telaviv
Man Dir: Dov Garfung
Orders to: Distributor's Centre for Israeli Books Ltd, 22 Nachmani St, PO Box 2811, Tel Aviv
Subjects: General Fiction, Belles Lettres, Poetry, Biography, History, Philosophy, Reference, Juveniles, Low-priced Paperbacks, Psychology, Social Science, University, Secondary & Primary Textbooks, Educational Materials
Founded: 1942

American-Israel Publishing Co Ltd*, 15 Carlebach St, PO Box 20181, Tel Aviv
Tel: (03) 280251 Telex: 605 paper il
Man Dir: Joseph Vardi; *Editorial:* Myrna Pollack
Branch Off: 11 West 42 St, New York
Subjects: Art Books, Archaeology, Heavily Illustrated Nonfiction, General Fiction, Juveniles
Founded: 1968

Amichai Publishing House Ltd*, 5 Josef Ha-Nassi St, Tel Aviv Tel: (03) 284990
Man Dir: Yehuda Orlinsky
Subjects: Reference, General Fiction, Juveniles, Popular Science, Textbooks, Languages
Founded: 1948

Amikam*, 33 Frishman St, Tel Aviv

Amir Publishing-Japheth Press Ltd, 5 Engel St, Tel Aviv Tel: (03) 615943
Man Dir: Avraham Amir; *Editorial:* Immanuel Blauschild
Subjects: Cartography, Guide Books, Historical and Biblical Subjects, Judaica
Founded: 1965

Ariel Publishing House, PO Box 3328, Jerusalem (Located at: 23 Hechalutz St, Jerusalem) Tel: (02) 524414
Chief Executive: Schiller Ely
Subjects: History, Travel, Photography, Art, concerning Jerusalem and the Holy Land
1978: 6 titles *1979:* 8 titles *Founded:* 1976

Armon Publishing House Ltd*, 36 Beit Vegan St, Jerusalem Tel: (02) 533991
Subjects: General Fiction, Languages
Founded: 1965

Arrow Co*, 6 Wedgwood St, PO Box 8022, Jerusalem

Bar Ilan University, Book Publishing Committee, Bar Ilan University, Ramat Gan Tel: 718111
Chairman: Professor Daniel Sperber
Subjects: Judaica, Philosophy, Psychology, Law, Literature, Linguistics, Education
Founded: 1958

Bar Urian Publishing House*, Bar Ilan University, Ramat Gan Tel: 756012
Man Dir: Jac J L Engelsman
Founded: 1965
Bookshop: Bar Ilan University
Subject: University Textbooks

Barlevi*, 57 Allenby St, Tel Aviv
Tel: (03) 283691
Manager: Mr Barlevi
Subjects: Juveniles, Hobbies, Games, Sports

Beit Lochamei Hagetha'ot*, Kibbutz Lochamei Hagetha'ot Tel: (04) 920412
Manager: B Anulik
Branch Off: 102 Arlogoroff St, Tel Aviv
Subjects: Holocaust, World War II, Jewish Resistance against Nazism
1978: 7 titles *Founded:* 1950

Ben-Zvi Institute, Abarbanel St, Jerusalem
Tel: (02) 639204; Yad Ben-Zvi Tel: 39201/2
Dir: Professor Amnon Cohen
Subject: History of Jewish Communities

The **Bialik** Institute, 3 Ibn Gabirol St, PO Box 92, Jerusalem Tel: (02) 639261
Man Dir: Chaim Milkov
Subjects: Philosophy, Hebrew and Yiddish Literature, Belles Lettres, Palestinology, Archaeology, Jewish Studies, History, Arts
Founded: 1935

Biblos*, 54 Sokolov St, Holon
Miscellaneous: Also an exporter to Latin America

Bitan, 8 Mordechai St, Ramat-Hasharon
Tel: 484565
Manager: A Bitan
Associate Company: Zmora, Bitan, Modan-Publishers (qv)
Subjects: General

Boostan Publishing House*, 22 Nachmani St, Tel Aviv Tel: (03) 298883/5 Cable Add: Boostanmod Telaviv
Man Dir: Mordechai Sheingarten; *Sales Dir:* Roni Birkenfield; *Publicity Dir:* Riva Almagor; *Advertising Dir:* Sara Wohlfeiler; *Rights & Permissions:* Dalia Sheingarten
Subsidiary Company: Distributors' Centre for Israeli Books Ltd (address as above)
Subjects: General Fiction, Belles Lettres, Poetry, Biography, History, How-to, Juveniles, High-priced Paperbacks, Medicine, Psychology, Educational Materials
Founded: 1969

Bronfman's Agency Ltd, 2 Tchelnov St, PO Box 1109, Tel Aviv Tel: (03) 611243
Manager: I Bronfman; *Publicity:* C Aronson
Subject: Textbooks
Bookshop: 2 Chelnov St, Tel Aviv

Carta, The Israel Map and Publishing Co Ltd, Yad Harutzim St, PO Box 2500, Jerusalem Tel: (02) 713536/7 Cable Add: Carmap
Man Dir: Emanuel Hausman; *Editorial:* Lorraine Kessel, Eviatar Nur; *Sales:* Shay Hausman
Subjects: Cartography, Juveniles, Educational Materials, General, History, Reference (publishes in Hebrew and English)
1978: 18 titles *1979:* 12 titles *Founded:* 1958
ISBN Publisher's Prefix: 965-220

Chatam Sofer Institute*, PO Box 836, Jerusalem Tel: (02) 38175
Manager: Mr Leible
Subject: Religion

Gaalyah Cornfeld*, 185 Hayarkon St, Tel Aviv 63453 Tel: (03) 221737 Cable Add: Cornfeld Hayarkon 185
Chief Executive, Editorial: G Cornfeld
Subjects: Bibles, Archaeology, Palestine
1978: 2 titles *Founded:* 1957

Davar*, 45 Sheinkin St, Tel Aviv
Tel: (03) 286141
Manager: I Shoham

The **Dvir** Publishing Co Ltd*, 58 Mazeh St, PO Box 149, Tel Aviv Tel: (03) 622991
Man Dir: Alexander Broido
Associate Company: Adam Publishers (qv)
Subsidiary Companies: Amud Ltd; Karni Publishers Ltd; Megiddo Publishing Co Ltd
Subjects: Belles Lettres, Poetry, Biography, History, Art, Philosophy, Reference, Juveniles, Low & High-priced Paperbacks, Psychology, General & Social Science, University, Secondary & Primary Textbooks, Educational Materials
1978: 10 titles *Founded:* 1924

E S H (English for Speakers of Hebrew), an imprint of Universal Publishing Projects (qv)

Edanim Publishers, 24 Agron St, PO Box 7705, Jerusalem Tel: (02) 224486 Cable Add: Weilpub Jerusalem
Man Dir: Asher Weill
Parent Companies: Weill Publishers Ltd (qv) and Yediot Aharonot Newspaper
Subjects: Contemporary Events, Fiction, Biography, History, Reference
1979-80: 25 titles *Founded:* 1975

Eked Publishing House*, 29 Bar-Kochba St, Tel Aviv Tel: (03) 283648
Man Dir: Maritza Rosman
Subjects: Belles Lettres, Poetry, Fiction
Founded: 1959

ISRAEL 207

El-Am Publishing (Israel) Ltd*, PO Box 16495, Tel Aviv Tel: (03) 228964/442918
Cable Add: Elampub, Telaviv
Man Dirs: Eliyahu Amiqam, Moshe Segalovitz; *Editorial:* Rabbi Dr A Zvi Ehrman
Subject: Judaica
Founded: 1966

Encyclopaedia Judaica*, Givat Shaul B, PO Box 7145, Jerusalem Tel: (02) 523261/521201 Telex: 25-275
Man Dir: Eliav Cohen; *Sales Dir:* Nissan Balaban
Parent Company: Keter Publishing House Ltd, Givat Shaul, Industrial Area, Jerusalem
Subject: Reference

Eshkol-Haifa, 25 Herzl St, Haifa Tel: (04) 532206
Manager: I Fish
Subject: General Fiction

Eshkol-Jerusalem, PO Box 5202, Jerusalem Tel: (02) 285351
Manager: Mr Weinfeld
Subject: Judaica

Feldheim Publishers Ltd*, PO Box 6525, Jerusalem Tel: (02) 533947/8/9
Man Dir: Yaakov Feldheim; *Sales Dir:* Yossie Katzberg
Branch Off: P Feldheim, 96 East Broadway, New York, NY
Subjects: Biography, History, Philosophy, Reference, Religion, Juveniles
1978: 13 titles *1979:* 12 titles *Founded:* 1939
ISBN Publisher's Prefix: 0-87306

H Fisher, PO Box 1951, Tel Aviv Tel: (03) 744892
Manager: H Fisher
Subject: Juveniles

Franciscan Printing Press, PO Box 14064, Jerusalem Tel: (02) 286594 Cable Add: Terrasanta Jerusalem
Man Dir: Costantino Baratto (Father Claudio)
Subjects: Religion, Theology, Archaeology, Guide Books, Periodicals
1978: 4 titles *1979:* 8 titles *Founded:* 1847

Freund Publishing House Ltd, 61 Nachmani St, PO Box 35010, Tel Aviv Tel: (03) 615335
Man Dir: Chaim Freund
Subjects: Scientific, Juveniles, Educational Games

S Friedman, 27 Gruzenberg St, Tel Aviv Tel: (03) 656091/659756
General Manager: Sara Friedman
Subjects: General
1978: 12 titles

Gazit, 8 Zvi Brook St, Tel Aviv Tel: (03) 53730
Manager: G Talpir
Subject: Art

Ghetto Fighters' House Publishers, see Beit Lochamei Hagetha'ot

Hadar, PO Box 17061, Tel Aviv (Located at: 50 Reiness Street, Tel Aviv) Tel: (03) 237082/417971
Manager: I Amrami
Subjects: General

Hakibbutz Hameuchad Publishing House Ltd*, PO Box 16040, Tel Aviv Tel: (03) 220402
Man Dir: A Avishai; *Sales Manager:* Moshe Ne'eman
Subjects: General Fiction, Belles Lettres, Poetry, Biography, History, How-to, Music, Art, Philosophy, Reference, Religion, General & Social Science, University, Secondary & Primary Textbooks, Educational Materials, Agriculture, Psychology
Founded: 1940

Hamenorah Publishers Ltd*, 24 Zangwill St, PO Box 6012, Tel Aviv Tel: (03) 230670
Man Dir: Mordechai Sonschein
Subjects: General Fiction, Poetry, Biography, History, Literature (Books in Hebrew, Yiddish and English)
Founded: 1958

Heritage, 2 Kfar Yona St, Ramat Aviv

Holy Land Map Co Ltd, now Terra Sancta Arts (qv)

Institute for the Talmudic Encyclopaedia and Complete Israeli Talmud*, Bait-Vagan, PO Box 16066, Jerusalem Tel: (02) 423242
Manager: Rabi Y Hotner

International Science Service*, PO Box 4059, Jerusalem Tel: (02) 34405; and Boston University, Center for Philosophy and History of Science, Boston, Ma 02115 USA Tel: 617-353 2604
Man Dir: Miriam Balaban
Subjects: Science, Technology, Medicine, Social Science, Philosophy, Communications
Founded: 1968

The **Israel Academy** of Sciences & Humanities, 43 Jabotinsky Rd, PO Box 4040, Jerusalem 91040 Tel: (02) 636211
Man Dir: Dr Yehezkel Cohen
Bookshop: Direct sales at the Academy
Subjects: Archaeology, History, Philosophy, Religion, Scholarly Publications in Sciences, Humanities, Judaica

Israel Exploration Society, 3 Shmuel Hanagid St, PO Box 7041, Jerusalem Tel: (02) 227991
Man Dir: J Aviram
Subjects: Archaeology, Ancient History, Geography
1978: 3 titles *Founded:* 1913

Israel Program for Scientific Translations, subsidiary of Keter Publishing House Ltd (qv)

Israel Universities Press*, Givat Shaul B, PO Box 7145, Jerusalem Tel: (02) 523261/521201 Telex: 25-275
Man Dir: Eliav Cohen
Parent Company: Keter Publishing House Ltd, Givat Shaul, Industrial Area, Jerusalem
Subjects: General & Social Science, Reference, Middle East Studies, University Textbooks, Politics

Israel Yearbook Publications*, 21 Hasharon St, PO Box 1199, Tel Aviv

Israeli Music Publications Ltd*, 105 Ben Yehuda St, PO Box 6011, Tel Aviv 61060 Tel: (03) 23078 Cable Add: Ismusica Tel Aviv
Man Dir: Dr P E Gradenwitz
Subjects: Music
Founded: 1949

Izrael Publishing House Ltd*, 76 Dizengoff St, Tel Aviv Tel: (03) 285350
Man Dir: Alexander Izrael
Subjects: General Fiction, Belles Lettres, Poetry, Biography, History, Reference, Psychology, Juveniles, University, Secondary & Primary Textbooks, Educational Materials
Founded: 1933

Jerusalem Publishing House Ltd, 39 Tchernechovski St, PO Box 7147, Jerusalem Tel: (02) 667744/636511 Cable Add: Pubjer Telex: 26144 ext 7065
Man Dir: Shlomo S Gafni; *Editorial:* Rachel Gilon; *Production:* Ofra Kamar
Subjects: Encyclopaedias, History, Archaeology, Reference, Literature, Politics, Art
1978: 17 titles *1979:* 15 titles *Founded:* 1967

The **Jewish Agency**, Publishing Department, 27 Hillel St, PO Box 7044, Jerusalem Tel: (02) 233271
Man Dir: Asher Bukshpan
Founded: 1945
Subjects: Hebrew & Zionist political thought and education

Karni Publishers Ltd*, 58 Mazeh St, PO Box 149, Tel Aviv Tel: (03) 622991
Man Dir: Alexander Broido; *Sales:* Nili Sadeh
Subsidiary Company: Megiddo Publishing Co (at above address)
Subjects: General Fiction, Belles Lettres, Poetry, Biography, How-to, Juveniles, Secondary & Primary Textbooks, Reference
1978: 3 titles *Founded:* 1951

Keter-Li, an imprint of Keter Publishing House Ltd (qv)

Keter Publishing House Ltd*, Giv'at Shaul Industrial Area, PO Box 7145, Jerusalem Tel: (02) 521201 Cable Add: Matam Telex: 25275
Man Dir: M Shani; *Sales Dir:* Nissan Balaban
Subsidiary Companies: Israel Program for Scientific Translations, Israel Universities Press (qv), Keter Press Ltd, Keter Publishing Ltd UK, Keter Inc, New York, Encyclopaedia Judaica (qv)
Imprints: Keter-Li, Kitri
Subjects: Philosophy, Reference, Religion, Juveniles, Medicine, Psychology, Engineering, Social Science
Founded: 1959

Kiryat Sefer Ltd, 15 Arlosorof St, PO Box 370, Jerusalem Tel: (02) 521141
Man Dir: Avraham Sivan
Subjects: Poetry, Juveniles, Atlases, Dictionaries, Secondary & Primary Textbooks, Fiction, Religion
Founded: 1933

Kitri, an imprint of Keter Publishing House Ltd (qv)

Koren Publishers*, 33 Herzog St, PO Box 4044, Jerusalem Tel: (02) 660188
Man Dirs: Eliahu Koren, Eli Kahn
Subjects: Bibles, Religion
1978: 5 titles *Founded:* 1962

Ledori, 19 Geula St, Tel Aviv Tel: (03) 58662
Manager: B Gefner
Subjects: General Books

The **Van Leer** Jerusalem Foundation*, 43 Jabotinsky St, PO Box 4070, Jerusalem Tel: (02) 667141
Executive Editor: Esther Shashar
1978: 2 titles

Lewin-Epstein Ltd, Rechov Harikma 7, PO Box 1020, Jerusalem Tel: (02) 531929
Dirs: J Gerlitz, M Weksler, A Friedman
Subjects: Judaica

A Lewin-Epstein-Modan Ltd*, 17 Mossinson St, PO Box 33316, Tel Aviv
Cable Add: Offset
Man Dir: C Modan; *Sales Dir:* Eliezer Ben-Ami
Associate Company: Zmora, Bitan, Modan Publishers (qv)
Subjects: General Fiction, Belles Lettres, Poetry, History, How-to, Music, Art, Reference, Juveniles, High-priced Paperbacks, Education, Science
Founded: 1930

Ma'alot, 29 Carlebach St, Tel Aviv Tel: (03) 284191
Dir: Elazar Goor
Subjects: Secondary & Primary Textbooks
1978: 50 titles *Founded:* 1969
Miscellaneous: Established by the Book

Publishers' Association of Israel as a jointly owned publishing house in which most of the members of the Association are shareholders

Ma'arachot, imprint of Ministry of Defence Publishing House (qv)

Ma'ariv Book Guild (Sifriat Ma'ariv)*, 72A Dereh Petah Tikra Rd, PO Box 20208, Tel Aviv Tel: (03) 287211 Cable Add: Ma'ariv Telaviv Telex: 033735
Publisher: Naftali Arbel
Branch Off: Room 162, 7 Park Ave, New York, NY, USA
Subjects: Biography, Reference, Education, History, Juveniles, Travel, Politics, Religion, Popular Science, Geography, Children, Encyclopaedias
Founded: 1954

Machbarot lesifrut, PO Box 22383, Tel Aviv (Located at: 88 Usishkin St, Tel Aviv)
Manager: Ohad Zmora
Associate Company: Zmora, Bitan, Modan-Publishers (qv)
Subjects: Fiction, History, Juveniles, Literature (especially of Middle Ages), Politics, Linguistics

The **Magnes** Press*, Hebrew University, Jerusalem Tel: (02) 660341
Man Dir: B Yehoshua
Subjects: Biography, History, Music, Art, Philosophy, Psychology, Archaeology, Oriental Studies, Law, Sciences, Bibliography, University Textbooks
Founded: 1929

Makor Publishing Ltd*, 14 Nili St, Jerusalem Tel: (02) 717257
Man Dir: I Ravitzki; *Sales Manager:* E Fisher
Subjects: Judaica, Reprints
Founded: 1969

S J Mansour*, 1 Meyouhas St, Mahane Yehuda, Jerusalem Tel: (02) 221650
Manager: S J Mansour
Subject: Judaica

Y Marcus & Co Ltd, PO Box 10354, Jerusalem (Located at: 59 Beth-Lehem Rd, Jerusalem) Tel: (02) 228281
Manager: Y Marcus
Subjects: General
Bookshop: 6 Ben Yehuda St, Jerusalem Tel: (02) 228281

Masout*, 2 Shonzino St, Tel Aviv Tel: (03) 36898
Manager: Z Lewin
Subject: Textbooks

Rubin **Mass**, 11 David Marcus St, PO Box 990, Jerusalem Tel: (02) 632565 Cable Add: Rubin Mass Jerusalem
Man Dir: Oren Mass; *Sales:* Aharon Bier
Subjects: Religion, Medicine, Secondary Textbooks, Jewish Studies, Educational Materials, Politics, Philosophy, Psychology, Meteorology, Science
1978: 1,020 titles *Founded:* 1927

Massada Press Ltd, 46 Beth Lehem Rd, Jerusalem Tel: (02) 719441/719444 Cable Add: Encyclomas Telex: 26144 Bxjm Il Ext 7067
Board Chairman, Chief Executive: Alexander Peli; *Sales, Production:* Nathan Regev; *Rights & Permissions:* David Peli; *Projects Manager:* I Hess; *Production Manager:* Eli Shimoni
Branch Off: 21 Jabotinsky Rd, Ramat Gan 52511 Tel: (03) 734202/3
Subjects: Belles Lettres, Poetry, Biography, History, How-to, Cookery, Music, Art, Philosophy, Encyclopaedias, Judaica, Reference, Religion, Juveniles, High-priced Paperbacks, Psychology, General and Social Science, Educational Materials
Book Club: Massada Press Ltd, 46 Beth Lehem Rd, Jerusalem
Bookshops: Ruth Ltd, 2 Herzl Street, Tel Aviv
1979: 62 titles *Founded:* 1932

Massada Publishing Ltd, Pelmas, 11 Alouf Sadeh St, PO Box 842, Givatayim Tel: (03) 740811 Cable Add: Peliprint Givatayim Telex: (03) 35770/1 Coin Il/Att Pelmas Printing
Man Dir: Yoav Barash; *Sales Dir:* Joel Bendel; *Production Dir:* Jaap Leuvenberg
Parent Company: Massada Publishing Ltd, 11-15 Tfutzot Israel St, Givatayim
Subsidiary Companies: Pelmas (the Export Division of Massada Publishing Ltd) (qv); Peli Printing Works Ltd (both at 11 Alouf Sadeh St, Givatayim)
Associate Company: Reprocolour Ltd
Subjects: History, Art, Juveniles, Educational, Cookery, General Fiction, Reference, Travel
1978: 328 titles *1979:* 305 titles *Founded:* 1932
ISBN Publisher's Prefix: 965-10

Megiddo Publishing Co, subsidiary of Karni Publishers Ltd (qv)

Merkaz Le-Chinuch Torani, PO Box 18, Zichron Yaakov Tel: (063) 99540 Telex: 35770 Coin Il
Man Dir: Rabbi Shalom Meir Jungerman
Subject: Orthodox Textbooks

Michaelmark Books Ltd, PO Box 45089, Tel Aviv (Located at: 12 Stand St, Tel Aviv) Tel: (03) 234144 Telex: 341667 Att MIC
Publisher: Myrna Pollak
Subjects: Fiction, Popular Nonfiction
Founded: 1976

Microshur Ltd, PO Box 2493, Jerusalem (Located at: 8 Rabbi Akiva St) Tel: (02) 232713 Telex: 26244 Raveh Il Microshur
Manager: Menachem Shalev; *Editorial:* Dr Gabriella Shalev
Subjects: Legal
1978: 3 titles *1979:* 11 titles *Founded:* 1978
ISBN Publisher's Prefix: 965-215

Mifalei Tarbut Vehinuch*, 53 Weizmann St, Tel Aviv Tel: (03) 254867
Manager: Y Silver
Subjects: Music, Textbooks, Pedagogy

Ministry of Defence Publishing House*, 29 Bet St, Hakiriya, Tel Aviv Tel: (03) 259165/212605
Dir: Shalom Seri; *Sales:* Jacob Bloch; *Production:* Izack Kempler
Subjects: Military Science & History, Israeli Geography & History
1978: 40 titles *Founded:* 1939
Miscellaneous: Firm also publishes under Ma'arachot imprint

M Mizrachi Publishers*, 67 Lewinsky St, Tel Aviv Tel: (03) 625652 Cable Add: Mizedition, Telaviv
Man Dir: Meir Mizrachi
Subjects: Engineering, History, Medicine, Science, Juveniles, Encyclopaedias, Fiction
Founded: 1960

M C Mor-Carmi Ltd, 13 Tiomkin St, Tel Aviv Tel: (03) 623266/7/8
Man Dir, Sales, Rights & Permissions: Ram Carmi; *Editorial, Production, Publicity:* Uri Mor
Subsidiary Companies: Elrad Engineering Planning Ltd; M C Electronics Ltd
Subjects: Technical, Scientific
Founded: 1968

Moreshet*, 166 Ibn Gavirol St, Tel Aviv

Mossad Harav Kook, PO Box 642, Jerusalem 91000 Tel: (02) 526231
Man Dir: Dr Yitzchak Raphael; *Editorial:* Rabbi M Katznelbogen
Subject: Judaica
1979: 20 titles *Founded:* 1937

Nateev-Printing and Publishing Enterprises Ltd, by Reading Bridge, PO Box 6048, Tel Aviv Tel: (03) 454135 Cable Add: Nateevpub, Telaviv Telex: 03-2470 Att Nateev
Man Dir: Mordecai Ra'anan
Subjects: Religion, Juveniles, General
Miscellaneous: Associated imprints include Otpaz
1978: 9 titles *Founded:* 1971

Netzach*, PO Box 164, Bnei Brak Tel: 796413
Manager: Mr Rootenberg
Subject: Judaica

M **Newman***, 12 Hasharon St, Tel Aviv Tel: (03) 30621
Manager: M Newman
Subjects: Judaica, Bible Studies, Fiction, Juveniles, Education

Nitzaninn, an imprint of Zur & Zur Ltd (qv)

Ofer Publishing House*, 7 Tabenkin St, Petach Tikva Tel: 625483
Manager: S Aluf
Subject: Juveniles

Olamenu*, 7 Frishman St, Tel Aviv

Olive Books of Israel*, Reka-Or Production and Publishing Ltd, 22 Shlom-Zion Hamalka St, PO Box 22305, Tel Aviv Tel: (03) 448676/455199
Publishers: Yoad Avissar, Yosseph Zetouni
Associate Company: Omanei Offset, Printing House, Tel Aviv
Subsidiary Companies: Madim, Limud both publishing and distribution
Subjects: Israeli history, Judaica, Educational
Founded: 1974
Miscellaneous: Publishers of *Who's Who in World Jewry*

Otpaz, an imprint of Nateev-Printing and Publishing Enterprises Ltd (qv)

Otzar Hamoreh, Israel Teachers' Union, 8 Ben Saruk St, PO Box 303, Tel Aviv Tel: (03) 260211
Man Dir: Menachem Levanon; *Production:* Rachel Uri
Subjects: Education, Pedagogy, Textbooks, Mathematics, Psychology, Didactic Games
1978: 4 titles *1979:* 5 titles *Founded:* 1951

Pe'er Hatora*, 7 Mea Shearim, Jerusalem Tel: (02) 285997
Manager: Rabbi Weingarten
Subject: Bible

Alexander **Peli** Ltd*, 46 Beth Lehem Rd, Jerusalem
Subsidiary Companies: Alumoth Company Ltd; Encyclopedia Publishing Company; Jewish History Publications 1961 Ltd; Ruth Ltd
Subjects: General, Judaica, Encyclopaedias, Belle Lettres, Poetry, Biography, History, How-to, Music, Art, Philosophy, Reference, Religion, Juveniles, High-priced Paperbacks, Psychology, General and Social Science, Secondary and Primary Textbooks, Educational Materials

Pelmas*, 11 Alouf Sadeh St, PO Box 842, Givatayim Tel: (03) 740811 Cable Add: Peliprint Telex: 03/35770 Coin Il/Att: Massada/Peli
The Export Division of Massada Publishing Ltd and Peli Printing Works Ltd
Man Dir: Yoav Barash; *Sales Dir:* Joel Bendel; *Director: (production):* Jaap Leuvenberg; *Coordinator:* Bridget Lahat
Parent Company: Massada Publishing Ltd (qv)
Associate Companies: Peli Printing Works Ltd; Reprocolor Ltd
Subjects: History, Art, Juveniles, Cookery, General Fiction, Reference, Travel
Founded: 1975

Y L **Peretz** Publishing Co*, 31 Allenby St, Tel Aviv Tel: (03) 595927
Man Dir: Moshe Gershonowitz
Subjects: Books (Poetry, Essays, History, Judaica, Belles Lettres, Philosophy, Sociology, Art) in Yiddish, also some in Hebrew
Founded: 1956

Ramdor Publishing Co Ltd*, 23 Levanda St, Tel Aviv Tel: (03) 32332
Man Dir: Uri Shalgi
Founded: 1960
Subject: Mass-market paperbacks

Rav Kook Institute, PO Box 642, Jerusalem Tel: (02) 526231
Dir: Rabbi M Katzenelenbogen
Subjects: Jewish Studies, History, Philosophy, Midrashic & Halachic Law, Theology
Founded: 1937
Miscellaneous: A non-profit-making public corporation supported by the Jewish Agency, Ministry of Education & Culture and Ministry of Religious Affairs. Also provides financial support for works in above subjects

Reka-Or Production and Publishing Ltd, see Olive Books of Israel

E **Rubinstein***, 1 King David St, Jerusalem Tel: (02) 225785
Manager: E Rubinstein
Subject: Textbooks

Sadan Publishing House Ltd, 1 David Hamelech Blvd, PO Box 16096, Tel Aviv 64-953 Tel: (03) 267543 Cable Add: Sadanbooks Telex: 35770 Coin Il Sadan
Man Dir: David Sadan; *Editorial:* Ronny Stein
Subjects: History, Archaeology, Guides, Folklore, How-to, Orientalia, Judaica, Art, Religion, Law, Business-management
1978: 20 titles *1979:* 48 titles *Founded:* 1962
Miscellaneous: Firm is also an international co-publisher and packager
ISBN Publisher's Prefix: 965-234

Schocken Publishing House Ltd*, 8 Rothschild Blvd, PO Box 2316, Tel Aviv Tel: (03) 50961
Man Dir: Racheli Eidelman
Subjects: General Fiction, Belles Lettres, Religion, Literature, Poetry, Philosophy, General Science, Politics, Law
Founded: 1938

Shikmona Publishing Co Ltd*, 33 Herzog St, PO Box 4044, Jerusalem Tel: (02) 660188
Man Dirs: Eli Kahn, Eliyahu Korén
Subjects: History, Art, Politics, Textbooks
1978: 7 titles *Founded:* 1965

Joseph **Shimoni***, 13 Rambam St, Tel Aviv Tel: (03) 611732
Manager: J Shimoni
Subjects: General

Shmulik*, 18 Shivtei Yisrael St, Ramat Hasharon

Sifriat Poalim Ltd, 66 Ahad Ha'am St, PO Box 37068, Tel Aviv Tel: (03) 291535
Dir: Ya'acov Dror; *Editorial:* Nathan Yonathan; *Sales:* Hsak Yagen; *Production:* Efraim Ben-Dor; *Rights & Permissions:* Levavi Bracha
Subjects: General Fiction, Belles Lettres, Art, Juveniles, History, Philosophy, Social Science, Paperbacks
Founded: 1939
Bookshop: 73 Allenby St, Tel Aviv
Miscellaneous: Publishing House of the Labour Zionist Movement

Samuel **Simson** Ltd*, 100 Yehuda Halevi St, PO Box 14227, Tel Aviv Tel: (03) 280456
Man Dir: Samuel Simson
Subject: Juveniles

Siman Krai, an imprint of University Publishing Projectr (qv)

Sinai Publishing Co*, 72 Allenby St, Tel Aviv Tel: (03) 623622
Man Dir: Akiva Schlesinger; *Editorial, Rights & Permissions:* Moshe Schlesinger
Subsidiary Company: Sinai Export Co Ltd, 15 Balfour St, Tel Aviv
Subject: Judaica
Bookshop: Sinai Bookstore, 72 Allenby St, Tel Aviv
Founded: 1853

Spotlight Publications*, 88 Hachashmonaim St, Tel Aviv

J **Sreberk**, 16 Balfour St, Tel Aviv Tel: (03) 293343
Manager: Z Namir
Subjects: Textbooks, Juveniles, Literature

Steimatzky's Agency Ltd, Citrus House, PO Box 628, Tel Aviv Tel: (03) 622536/7 Cable Add: Steimatzky Beithadar Telaviv Telex: 341118 Bxtv Il ext 6409
Man Dirs: Ezekiel Steimatzky, Eri M Steimatzky
Subjects: General Fiction, Music, Art, Juveniles, Reference, Social Science, University, Secondary & Primary Textbooks, Low-priced Paperbacks
Bookshops: 30 bookshops and outlets throughout Israel
1978: 20 titles *Founded:* 1925

Talmudic Encyclopaedia Publications*, Yad Harav Herzog, Beit Vegan, Jerusalem

Tarbut Vehinuch*, 53 Weizmann St, Tel Aviv

Tarshish Books*, 14 Hanassi St, PO Box 4130, Jerusalem Tel: (02) 636332
Man Dir: Dr M Spitzer
Subjects: General Fiction, Belles Lettres, History, Art, Philosophy, Religion
Founded: 1940

Tcherikover Publishers Ltd, 12 Hasharon St, Tel Aviv 66185 Tel: (03) 330621
Manager: B Tcherikover; *Editorial:* S Tcherikover
Subjects: Textbooks, Pedagogy, Education, Children's Books, Handbooks, Psychology, Economics, Literature, History, Art, Languages, Geography, Criminology, Management, Bibles
1978: 30 titles *1979:* 25 titles

Teachers' Union, see Otzar Hamoreh

Tel Aviv University, Publications Sales Division*, Admin Hill, Bldg H, rooms 22-23, Tel Aviv Tel: (03) 426262 ext 897
Manager: Ya'akov Yariv

Terra Sancta Arts, PO Box 10009, Zahala, Tel Aviv (Located at: 31 Ehud St) Tel: (03) 473597 Telex: 35770 Coin Il
Man Dir: Nachman Ran
Subjects: Maps, Books on the Holy Land
Founded: 1972
Miscellaneous: Formerly Holy Land Map Co Ltd

Tor, an imprint of Turtledove Publishing Ltd (qv)

Turtledove Publishing Ltd, PO Box 1337, Ramat Gan (Located at: 15 Kinneret St, Bnei Brak) Tel: (03) 707125
Man Dir: Louis Williams
Orders to: Europan, 3 Henrietta St, London WC2E 8LY, UK or ISBS, PO Box 555, Forest Grove, Oregon 97116, USA
Imprints include: Tor
Subjects: Academic-Interdisciplinary: Political Science, Middle East Affairs, International Law, Medicine & Law, Federal Studies
1978: 3 titles *1979:* 13 titles *Founded:* 1978
ISBN Publisher's Prefix: 965-20

University Publishing Co*, 28 Hanatziv St, Tel Aviv Tel: (03) 259057
Dirs: Mordechai Mass, Natan Tzipkis
Imprints: ESH (English for Speakers of Hebrew), Siman Kria
Subjects: School Texts, Belles Lettres, Academic

Vaad Hayeshivot Be'eretz Israel*, 4 Havatzelet St, Jerusalem Tel: (02) 225042
Man Dir: A Halevi Sher
Subject: Judaica

Weill Publishers Ltd, 24 Agron St, PO Box 7705, Jerusalem Tel: (02) 224486 Cable Add: Weilpub Jerusalem
Man Dir: Asher Weill
Subsidiary Company: Edanim Publishers (qv)
Subjects: Children's Books, Educational, Illustrated Books in English and Hebrew
Founded: 1975
Miscellaneous: Firm also offers publishers' editorial and production services

The **Weizmann** Science Press of Israel, Horkania 8a, PO Box 801, Jerusalem 91000 Tel: (02) 663203
Man Dir: Rami Michaeli; *Publicity Manager:* Mrs Hava Aspler
Subjects: General Science, General Technology
Founded: 1951
Miscellaneous: Publish nine scientific journals

Yachdav, United Publishers Co Ltd, 29 Carlebach St, PO Box 20123, Tel Aviv Tel: (03) 284191
Chairman: Mordechai Bernstein; *Man Dir:* Benjamin Sella
Subjects: Philosophy, Psychology, Social Science, Administration
1979-80: 10 titles *Founded:* 1960

Yad Eliahu Chitov*, PO Box 894, Jerusalem Tel: (02) 285617
Man Dir: H Ben-Arza
Subject: Orthodox Textbooks

Yad Vashem — Martyrs' and Heroes' Remembrance Authority, PO Box 3477, Jerusalem Tel: (02) 531202 Cable Add: YadVashem Jerusalem
Chairman: Dr Yitzhak Arad; *Editorial:* Dr Livia Rothkirchen, Dr Yisrael Gutman; *Sales:* Emmanuel Man; *Production:* Y Gutman; *Secretary General:* Shimshon Eden
Branch Off: Heychal Wolyn, 10 Korazin St, PO Box 803, Givatayim, near Tel Aviv
Subject: Nazi Holocaust
1978: 5 titles *1979:* 5 titles *Founded:* 1953

Yavneh Ltd, 4 Mazeh St, Tel Aviv Tel: (03) 297856
Man Dir: Avshalom Orenstein
Subjects: General Fiction, Reference, Music, Religion, General Science, Juveniles, Textbooks, Atlases
Founded: 1932

Yedioth Ahronoth Enterprises (Book Dept), 12 Mikveh Yisrael St, PO Box 37744, Tel Aviv Tel: (03) 621065 Telex: 33847
Manager: Moshe Babmerger
Parent Company: Yedioth Ahronoth (The Evening Newspaper of Israel)
Subjects: Nonfiction, Judaica, Childrens Books
1978: 18 titles *1979:* 24 titles *Founded:* 1952

Yeshurun, Merkaz Le-Sifrut Chareidit, PO Box 511, Jerusalem Tel: (02) 534211
Dir: Mr Pardes
Subject: Orthodox Textbooks

Yesod*, 16 Mazeh St, Tel Aviv Tel: (03) 291180
Manager: Y Wachtel
Subject: Textbooks

210 ISRAEL

Yuval*, 13a Yeffe Nof St, Haifa
Tel: (04) 521564
Manager: I Blachman
Subject: Textbooks

S Zak & Co*, 2 King George St, Jerusalem
Tel: (02) 227819
Man Dirs: D Zak, M Zak
Subjects: Science, Fiction, Philosophy, Reference, Religion, Juveniles, University, Secondary & Primary Textbooks, Educational Materials
Founded: 1930
Bookshop: 2 King George St, Jerusalem

Zelkowitz*, 6 Mazeh St, Tel Aviv Tel: (03) 296648
Manager: A Zelkowitz
Subject: Juveniles

Zmora, Bitan, Modan-Publishers, 88 Usishkin St, PO Box 22383, Tel Aviv
Tel: (03) 450750/457165
Editorial, Rights & Permissions: Ohad Zmora; *Editorial, Production:* Asher Bitan; *Sales:* Oded Modan
Associate Companies: Bitan (qv); A Lewin-Epstein-Modan Publishers (qv); Machbarot lesifrut (qv)
Subsidiary Companies: Bayt-Va'gan, 12 Bei-Dan St, Tel Aviv; Erez Books (at above address); Adar Distribution, 13 Shefa-Tal St, Tel Aviv; Metziuth Books (at above address); Levanda Press, 30 Levanda St, Tel Aviv
Subjects: Fiction, Politics, Middle East Studies, Juveniles, Military, History, Textbooks, Cookery, Nature
1978: 90 titles *Founded:* 1973

Zur & Zur Ltd*, 103 Shlomo Hamelech St, Tel Aviv 64586 Tel: (03) 223764 Cable Add: Zunil Telaviv
Man Dir: Shmuel Zur
Imprint: Nitzanim
Subjects: Pocket guides on Cookery, How-to, Children's Books
1978: 12 titles *Founded:* 1972

Literary Agents

Bar-David Literary Agency, 1 Hashahar St, PO Box 1104, Tel Aviv Tel: (03) 656814/5/6 Cable Add: Davidbarco Telex: 33721 Brvid Il
Contact: Mrs Varda Mor

The **Book** Publishers' Association of Israel, International Promotion and Literary Rights Department, 29 Carlebach St, PO Box 20123, Tel Aviv 67132 Tel: (03) 284191
Contact: Lorna Soifer

Peter **Halban** Literary Agency*, 21 Ibn Shaprut St, PO Box 7474, Jerusalem Tel: (02) 639658
Contact: Peter Halban

Moadim, 144 Hayarkon St, 63451 Tel Aviv
Tel: (03) 228449
Play Publishers and Literary Agents
Contact: Maya Tavi

Barbara **Rogan** Literary Agency, PO Box 4006, 12 George Eliot St, Tel Aviv Tel: (03) 285589 Cable Add: Overworked Tel Aviv
Dir: Barbara Rogan

Shalom **Sella**, PO Box 1154, 9 Heleni Hamalka St, Jerusalem Tel: (02) 242881/242882/243962 Cable Add: Scitrans Telex: 26140

Book Clubs

Massada Press Ltd, 46 Beth Lehem Rd, Jerusalem

Major Booksellers

A B C Bookstore Ltd, 71 Allenby Rd, PO Box 1283, Tel Aviv Tel: (03) 296058

Librarie **Alcheh***, 55 Nachlat Benyamin St, Tel Aviv Tel: (03) 614173 (Largest Importer of French books in Israel)

Bronfman's Agency Ltd, 2 Chlenov St, PO Box 1109, Tel Aviv Tel: (03) 611243 (Also exporter)

Emanuel **Brown***, 35 Allenby Rd, PO Box 4101, Tel Aviv Tel: (03) 51049 (Specializes in academic books and is sole distributor for books published by the United Nations and its associated agencies)

Distributors' Centre for Israeli Books Ltd*, 22 Nachmani St, PO Box 2811, Tel Aviv

Educational Book Centre (The Modern Library)*, PO Box 202, Ramallah
Tel: 952122

Israbook*, 13 Blum St, Ramat Aviv
Tel: 416881
Suppliers of books and journals in all languages originating with all publishers and learned institutions in Israel

Lonnie **Kahn** and Co Ltd*, 5 Bachlat Benyamin St, Tel Aviv Tel: (03) 623693 (Also importer)

Ludwig **Mayer** Ltd, 4 Shlomzion Hamalka St, PO Box 1174, Jerusalem 91000
Tel: (02) 222628

J **Robinson** & Co, 31 Nachlat Benjamin St, PO Box 4308, 61040 Tel Aviv
Tel: (03) 615461
(also exporter and antiquarian bookseller)

Sharbain's Bookshop, Salah Eddin St, Jerusalem Tel: (02) 286775

Sifriat Poalim Ltd*, 66 Ahad Haam St, PO Box 37068, Tel Aviv Tel: (03) 291535

Steimatzky's Agency Ltd, Citrus House, PO Box 628, Tel Aviv Tel: (03) 622536/7 Cable Add: Steimatzky Beithadar Tel Aviv Telex: 341118 Bxtv Il Ext 6409
Owns the largest chain of bookshops in Israel

Universal Library*, Salah-e-Din St, East Jerusalem Tel: (02) 82624 (Specializes in books on the Middle East and religious books)

Major Libraries

Central Library of **Agricultural Science***, PO Box 12, Rehovot 76100

The Central **Archives** for the History of the Jewish People (formerly Jewish Historical General Archives), Jerusalem University Campus, Sprinzak Bldg, PO Box 1149, Jerusalem Tel: (02) 635716
Director: Dr Daniel J Cohen

Bar-Ilan University Library*, Ramat Gan

Ben-Gurion University of the Negev Library, PO Box 653, Beersheva 84120 Tel: (057) 64422

'**Dvir Bialik**' Municipal Central Public Library, Hibat-Zion St 14, Ramat Gan
Librarian: Ora Nebenzahl

Elisas Sourasky Central Library, Tel Aviv University, PO Box 39038, Ramat Aviv, Tel Aviv Tel: (03) 420745/420883

Israel State Archives, Prime Minister's Office, Jerusalem Tel: (02) 639231
Publication: Israel Government Publications (annual)

Jerusalem City (Public) Library*, Betzalel St 11, PO Box 1409, Jerusalem Tel: (02) 226785

Jewish National and University Library, PO Box 503, Jerusalem Tel: (02) 585039
Dir: Prof M Beit-Arié

Knesset Library*, Hakirya, Jerusalem 91999
Tel: (02) 61211

Municipal Library*, 25 King Saul Blvd, PO Box 32, Tel Aviv

Pevsner Public Library, 54 Pevsner St, PO Box 5345, Haifa 31051 Tel: (04) 667766

Tel Aviv University Library*, PO Box 39038, Ramat Aviv, Tel Aviv

University of Haifa Library, Mount Carmel, Haifa 31999 Tel: (04) 240289 Telex: 04660
Dir: Dr Shmuel Sever
Publication: Annual Index to Hebrew Periodicals

Weizmann Institute of Science Libraries, Rehovot Tel: (054) 83298 (Central Library)/(054) 82111 (Weizmann Institute)
Cable Add: Weizinst Telex: 31934
Chief Librarian: Alma Rosenheck

Library Associations

Centre for Public Libraries*, PO Box 242, Jerusalem 91000
Publications: Leket (reviews of books); *Yad-la-Koré* (The Reader's Aid) (library quarterly), and library monographs

Information Processing Association of Israel*, PO Box 13009, Jerusalem
Secretary: Tuvia Saks
Publication: Ma'ase Cho-shev (6 a year)

Israel Library Association*, PO Box 7067, Jerusalem
Executive Secretary: Ruth Porath

Israel Society of Special Libraries and Information Centres (ISLIC)*, PO Box 20125, Tel Aviv 61200 Tel: (03) 297781
Executive Secretary: Susane Weil
Publications: Bulletin (3 times a year), *Contributions to Information Science* (irregular)

Library Journals

Annual Index to Hebrew Periodicals, University of Haifa Library, Mount Carmel, Haifa 31999

Bibliography of Modern Hebrew Literature in Translation (bi-annually), The Institute for the Translation of Hebrew Literature Ltd, 66 Shlomo Hamelech St, Tel Aviv

Bulletin, Israel Society of Special Libraries and Information Centres PO Box 20125, Tel Aviv 61200

Kethavim Benossey Med'a (Contributions to Information Science), Israel Society of Special Libraries and Information Centres, PO Box 20125, Tel Aviv 61200

Leket (Gleaning), Centre for Public Libraries, PO Box 242, Jerusalem 91000

Ma'ase Cho-shev (Action and Thought), Information Processing Association of Israel, PO Box 13009, Jerusalem

Yad-la-Koré (The Reader's Aid), Centre for Public Libraries, PO Box 242, Jerusalem 91000

Literary Associations and Societies

Mekise Nirdamin Society*, 22 Hatibonim St, Jerusalem
Secretary: Professor E E Urbach
Publishes Hebrew works of the older classical Jewish literature

Israeli **P E N** Centre*, 19 Shmaryahu Lewine St, Jerusalem
Secretary: Haim Toren

Literary Periodicals

Caiet Pentru Literatura Si Istoriografie (Journal of Literature and Historiography) (text in Hebrew, Romanian and Yiddish), Cenaclul Literar 'Menora', PO Box 763, Jerusalem

HSL (Hebrew University Studies in Literature) (text in English and French), The Hebrew University of Jerusalem, Institute of Languages and Literatures, Jerusalem

Ha-Sifrut (Literature); theory, poetics, Hebrew and comparative literature (text in Hebrew, summaries in English), Tel Aviv University, Ramat Aviv, Tel Aviv

Image; English literary magazine, The Hebrew University of Jerusalem, Jerusalem

Jerusalem Post Literary Supplement (incorporating *Israel Book World*) (monthly), Book and Printing Center — Israel Export Institute, 29 Hamered St, PO Box 29732, Tel Aviv

Modern Hebrew Literature (quarterly, incorporating Hebrew Book Review), Institute for the Translation of Hebrew Literature, 8 Modigliani St, Tel Aviv 64687

Siidemot (English Edition); literary digest of the kibbutz movement, Ichud Hakvutzot and Hakibbutzim, Youth Division, 10 Dubnov St, Tel Aviv

Literary Prizes

Bialik Prize for Literature
The highest literary award of the Tel-Aviv-Yafo Municipality, awarded in two categories: belles-lettres and Jewish studies. 40,000 Israeli pounds. Awarded annually. Enquiries to Tel-Aviv-Yafo Municipality, Tel Aviv

Brenner Prize
In recognition of outstanding literary works. 20,000 Israeli pounds. Awarded annually. Enquiries to Hebrew Writers' Association, PO Box 7111, Tel Aviv

Holon Literary Prize*
To encourage literary talent in Israel. 5,000 Israeli pounds. Awarded every year. Enquiries to Holon Municipality, Holon

Israeli Prize in Jewish Studies, Hebrew Literature and Education, see Israeli Prize in Humanities and Social Sciences

Israeli Prize in the Arts, see Israeli Prize in Humanities and Social Sciences

Israeli Prize in Humanities and Social Sciences
For outstanding contribution to the humanities and social sciences. 50,000 Israeli pounds. Awarded annually in each one of the following areas: (1) Judaica, Modern Hebrew Literature and Education; (2) the Humanities and the Social Sciences; (3) the Arts; (4) Science and Technology; (5) outstanding life-long service to the welfare of Israeli society. Enquiries to Israeli Ministry of Education and Culture, 15 Keren Hayesod St, Jerusalem

Shazar Prize*
For outstanding works by immigrant writers. 5,000 Israeli pounds divided between two authors. Awarded annually. Enquiries to Israeli Ministry of Education and Culture, Jerusalem

Tchernichowsky Prize
For outstanding translations into Hebrew. 20,000 Israeli pounds divided between two translators: one of belles-lettres and one of scientific material. Awarded biennially. Enquiries to Tel-Aviv-Yafo Municipality, Tel Aviv

Translation Agencies and Associations

The **Institute** for the Translation of Hebrew Literature Ltd, 66 Shlomo Hamelech St, Tel Aviv Tel: (03) 244879

Scientific Translations International Ltd, 9 Heleni Hamalka St, PO Box 1154, Jerusalem Tel: (02) 242881/242882/243962 Cable Add: Scitrans Telex: 26140

Italy

General Information

Language: Italian. German and Ladin are officially recognized in Trentino-Alto Adige; Slovene in Trieste
Religion: Roman Catholic
Population: 56.7 million
Literacy Rate (1971): 93.9%
Bank Hours: 0830-1330 Monday-Friday
Shop Hours: Vary locally. Winter: 0900-1300, 1330-1930 Monday-Saturday; Summer: 0900-1300, 1430-2000 Monday-Saturday. Often closed Monday morning
Currency: Lira
Export/Import Information: Member of the European Economic Community. No tariff on books except children's picture books 13% from non-EEC; advertising matter not single copies 13%. VAT 6% on books, 12% on advertising matter. No import licence required.
Copyright: UCC, Berne, Florence (see International section)

Book Trade Organizations

Agenzia per l'Area di Lingua Italiana ISBN*, Associazione Italiana Editori, Via delle Erbe 2, I-20121 Milan Tel: (02) 8059244
ISBN Administrator: Gianni Merlini

Associazione Italiana Editori*, Via delle Erbe 2, I-20121 Milan Tel: (02) 8059244
Rome office: Via Pietro della Valle 13, I-00193 Rome Tel: (06) 6540298
Italian Publishers' Association
Secretary-General: A Ormezzano
Publications: Catalogo dei Libri Italiani in Commèrcio; Editori, Librai, Cartolibrai e Biblioteche d'Italia; Giornale della Libreria

Associazione Librai Antiquari d'Italia, Via Jacopo Nardi 6, I-50132 Florence
Antiquarian Booksellers' Association of Italy
President: Dr Renzo Rizzi, Via Cernaia 4, I-20121 Milan

Associazione Librai Italiani*, Piazza G G Belli 2, I-00153 Rome Tel: 5803844
Italian Booksellers' Association
Publication: Libreria

Associazione Italiana degli **Editori** di Musica (AIDEM), Piazza del Liberty 2, I-20121 Milan Tel: 796473
Italian Association of Music Publishers

I P L (Istituto Propaganda Libraria)*, Via Mercalli 23, Milan
Institute of Bookshop Advertising

Standard Book Numbering Agency, see Agenzia per l'Area di Lingua Italiana ISBN

Unione Editori di Musica Italiani (UNEMI)*, Via F Sforza 1, I-20122 Milan
Publishing Union of Italian Music

Book Trade Reference Books and Journals

Books

Editori, Librai, Cartolibrai e Biblioteche d'Italia (Publishers, Booksellers, Stationers and Libraries of Italy), Italian Publishers' Association, Foro Buonaparte 24, I-20121 Milan

Gli Editori Italiani (over 2,000 Italian publishers listed), Editrice Bibliografica SRL, Viale Veneto 24, I-20124 Milan

Le Librerie Italiane (Italian Booksellers), Editrice Bibliografica SRL, Viale Veneto 24, I-20124 Milan

Journals

Bibliografia Nazionale Italiana (Italian National Bibliography), Central Institute of the Union Catalogue of Italian Libraries and Bibliographical Information, Viale del Castro Pretorio, Rome

Bollettino (Bulletin), Ufficio della Proprietà Letteraria, Artistica e Scientifica, Rome (monthly)

Bollettino bibliografico, Libreria Seeber, Via dei Tornabuoni 70 r, I-50123 Florence

Catalogo dei Libri Italiani in Commèrcio (Italian Books in Print), Italian Publishers' Association, Foro Buonaparte 24, I-20121 Milan

Il Compratore (The Buyer), Editoriale A-Z, Via P Kolbe 8, I-20317 Milan

Gazzettino Librario (Book Trade Gazette), Piazza Lotario 6, Rome (advertises book wants and offers)

Giornale della Libreria (Book Trade Journal), Italian Publishers' Association, Foro Buonaparte 24, I-20121 Milan

Libreria (The Book Trade), Italian Booksellers' Association, Piazza G G Belli 2, I-00153 Rome

Libri e Riviste d'Italia (Italian Books and Periodicals) (available in Italian edition and international edition in English, French, German and Spanish), Via Boncompagni 15, I-00187 Rome

Libro Cattòlico (The Catholic Book), Union of Italian Catholic Publishers, Via Domenico Silveri 9, I-00165 Rome

Mundus, CP 2236, Rome

Ragguaglio Librario (Book Report), Institute of Bookshop Advertising, Via Mercalli 23, Milan

Publishers

A M Z Editrice sas di Mario Abriani e C, Corso di Porta Romana 63, I-20122 Milan Tel: (02) 581071 Cable Add: Editamz Telex: 310607 Amzed I
Publisher: Mario Abriani; *Editorial:* Gioacchino Forte, Elena Fasanella; *Rights & Permissions:* Lucia Calza
Branch Off: Lungotevere della Vittoria 5, I-00195 Roma Tel: (06) 3600839
Subjects: Books and Albums for Children and Young People, How-to, Non-fiction
Bookshop: Quartiere Albanova, I-20083 Gaggiano (Milan)
Founded: 1955

Edizioni **A R E S**, Via Stradivari 7, I-20131 Milan Tel: (02) 209202
Dir: Dr Cesare Cavalleri
Subjects: Philosophy, Theology, Architecture, Psychology
1978: 24 titles *Founded:* 1957

Adelphi Edizioni SpA, Via G Brentano 2, I-20121 Milan Tel: (02) 871266/866177
Man Dir: Luciano Foà; *Editorial Dir:* Roberto Calasso; *Publicity, Production:* Piero Bertolucci
Orders to: Edizioni Adelphi, Servizio Vendita Libri, c/o Fratelli Fabbri Editori, Via Mecenate 91, I-20138 Tel: 5095
Subjects: General Fiction, Belles Lettres, Biography, Music, Art, Philosophy, Religion, Psychology, General Science
1978: 34 titles *Founded:* 1962

Giacomo **Agnelli** Editore, see Giunti Publishing Group

Alfa Edizioni e Rappresentanze Editoriali, Via Santo Stefano 13, I-40125 Bologna Tel: (051) 262805
Man Dir: Elio Castagnetti
Subjects: Belles Lettres, Poetry, History, Music, Art, Philosophy
1978: 10 titles *Founded:* 1954

Alfieri Edizioni d'Arte*, Via Goldoni 1, I-20124 Milan Tel: (02) 704023
Dirs: Giorgio Fantoni, Massimo Vitta Zelman; *Editorial:* Carlo Pirovano; *Rights & Permissions:* Mirella V Tenderini
Parent Company: Gruppo Editoriale Electa SpA
Associate Company: Electa Editrice (qv)
Subjects: Modern Art, Venetian Art, Architecture, Periodicals, Numbered Editions
Founded: 1939

Alinari Fratelli SpA Istituto di Edizioni Artistiche, Via Nazionale 6, I-50123 Florence Tel: (055) 212105 Cable Add: Idea
Man Dir: Nicola Gandini
Bookshops: Fratelli Alinari, Via Strozzi 19r, Florence; Fratelli Alinari, Via del Babuino 98, Rome
Subjects: Art, Educational Materials
Founded: 1854

Editrice **Ancora** Milano*, Via Niccolini 8, I-20154 Milan Tel: (02) 3189941
Man Dir: Medici Severino; *Editorial Dir:* Zini Vigilio; *Sales Dir:* Giordani Saverio
Subjects: Religion, Juveniles, Social Science
1978: 25 titles *Founded:* 1937

Franco **Angeli** Editore*, Viale Monza 106, CP 4294, I-20127 Milan Tel: 2827651/2/3/4/5
Man Dir: Dr Franco Angeli; *Editorial:* L Gambi, E Becchi, M Cesa-Bianchi; *Sales:* Livio Casati; *Production:* Marilena Aliata; *Publicity:* Ugo Carutli
Subjects: Anthropology, Architecture, Law of Employment and Labour Relations, Economics, Teaching and Education, Geography, History, Politics, Psychology, Finance, Sociology, Urban and Regional Studies, Physics, Electrical Engineering, Electronics, Data Processing, Mathematics, Science, Management, Marketing, Publicity, Public Relations, Essays
1978: 292 titles *Founded:* 1955

Ruggero **Aprile**, Via San Quintino 43, I-10121 Turin Tel: (011) 538665/546289
Man Dir: Ruggero Aprile; *Editorial:* Ottaviano Ottaviani; *Sales:* Valerio Aprile
Subjects: Fiction, History, Juveniles, Art
1978: 50 titles *Founded:* 1973

Arcana Editrice Srl, Via Giulia 167, I-00186, Rome Tel: (06) 6542409
Publicity: Raimondo Biffi
Subjects: Youth Questions, Pop Music, Oriental Thought
1978: 25 titles *1979:* 25 titles

Editore Armando **Armando**, Via della Gensola 60-61, I-00153 Rome Tel: (06) 588441/5894525
Man Dir: Prof Armando Armando
Subjects: Psychology, Philosophy, Social Sciences, Politics, Textbooks, Education, Linguistics, Languages, Children's books, Sociology
1978: 90 titles *Founded:* 1963

Arti Grafiche della Venezie SpA*, Viale S Agostino 152, I-36100 Vicenza Tel: (02) 563011
Parent Company: Arnoldo Mondadori Editore (qv)
Subject: Arts

Edizioni Dell'**Ateneo** e Bizzarri SRL, Via Giovanni Amendola 7, CP 7216, I-00185 Rome Tel: (06) 7578853/7593456
Man Dir: Franco Volta; *Sales:* G Santo Geraci; *Production:* Sergio Petrelli
Orders to: Via Ruggero Bonghi 11/B, I-00184 Rome
Subjects: Belles Lettres, Poetry, Biography, History, Music, Art, Philosophy, Classical Philology, Cinema, Reference, Religion, High-priced Paperbacks, Psychology, Engineering, General & Social Science, Secondary and University Textbooks, Economics, Medicine, Aeronautics, Navy, Army
Founded: 1946

Verlagsanstalt **Athesia**, Lauben 41, Postfach 417, I-39100 Bolzano-Bozen Tel: (0471) 41444 Cable Add: Athesia, Verlag, Bozen Telex: 400161
Man Dir: Dr Toni Ebner; *Production:* Peter Plattner; *Sales Manager:* Richard Fieg; *Publicity Manager:* Gustav Theiner
Subjects: Art, Travel, Periodicals, History, Maps, Textbooks, Poetry, Mountaineering
Bookshops: in Bozen, Meran, Brixen, Bruneck, Sterzing, Schlanders
1978: 28 titles *1979:* 50 titles *Founded:* 1907

M d'**Auria**, Editore, Calata Trinità Maggiore 52, I-80134 Naples Tel: (081) 328963
Dir: Ugo d'Auria
Subject: Religion
1978: 2 titles *1979:* 3 titles *Founded:* 1887

Baldini e Castoldi, Viale Majno 23, I-20122 Milan Tel: (02) 782568
Dir: Dr Enrico Castoldi
Subjects: General Fiction, Juveniles, Memoirs
Founded: 1896

Giunti **Barbera** Editore, see Giunti Publishing Group

Edizioni Oreste **Barjes**, see Giunti Publishing Group

Edizioni d'Arte Carlo **Bestetti***, Via di San Giacomo 18, I-00187 Rome Tel: (06) 6790174
Man Dir: Carlo Bestetti
Subjects: Art, Architecture, Industry
1978: 1 title *Founded:* 1947

Del **Bianco** Editore, Via S Daniele 11, CP 40, I-33100 Udine Tel: (0432) 22134 Cable Add: Del Bianco Udine
Subjects: Engineering, General Science, University & Secondary Textbooks, Art, History

Biblical Institute Press (Pontificio Istituto Biblico)*, Piazza della Pilotta 35, I-00187 Rome Tel: (06) 6781567
Subjects: Scientific Studies, Biblical Studies, Ancient languages, Archaeology
Founded: 1909

Bibliopolis—Edizioni di Filosofia e Scienze SpA*, Via Arangio Ruiz 83, I-80122 Naples Tel: (081) 664606
Man Dir: Dr Francesco del Franco
Subjects: Science and Philosophy
1978: 6 titles *1979:* 10 titles *Founded:* 1976

Bietti SpA*, Via Crescenzio 58, I-00193 Rome Tel: (06) 6545501
Subjects: Fiction, Foreign Languages, Humanities, History, Hobbies, Juveniles, Literature Criticism, Education, Philosophy, Games, Sports, Theatre

B **Boggero** Editore, see Giunti Publishing Group

Casa Editrice Valentino **Bompiani** & C SpA, Via Mecenate 87/6, I-20138 Milan Tel: (02) 5095 Cable Add: Bompiani Milano Telex: 311321
President: Valentino Bompiani; *Man Dir:* Vittorio Di Giuro; *Editorial:* Franco Occhetto; *Rights & Permissions:* Nicoletta Grill
Subjects: General Fiction, Belles Lettres, History, General & Social Science, Low & High-priced Paperbacks, Biography, Philosophy, Reference
1978: 116 titles *1979:* 128 titles *Founded:* 1929

Bonacci-Libreria Editrice, Via Paolo Mercuri 23, I-00193 Rome Tel: (06) 6565995
Man Dir: Giorgio Bonacci
Subjects: Belles Lettres, History, Secondary Textbooks
Bookshop: Bonacci — Libreria Editrice, Via Paolo Mercuri 23, I-00193 Rome
1978: 2 titles *1979:* 10 titles *Founded:* 1942

Casa Editrice **Bonechi***, Via dei Cairoli 18b, I-50131 Florence Tel: (055) 576841/2 Telex: 571323 CEB
Man Dir: Giampaolo Bonechi; *Editorial:* Giovanna Magi
Subjects: Art, Travel, Reference
1978: 15 titles

Editore **Boringhieri** SpA, Corso Vittorio Emanuele 86, I-10121 Turin Tel: (011) 541371 Cable Add: Edibor
Man Dir: Paolo Boringhieri; *Editorial Manager:* Ernesto Ferreto
Subjects: Philosophy, Science, Psychology, Economics, Low- & High-priced Paperbacks, University Textbooks
1978: 55 titles *Founded:* 1957

SIL Srl Edizioni **Borla***, Via delle Fornaci 50, I-00165 Rome Tel: (06) 6382998
Man Dir: Dr Vincenzo D'Agostino
Subjects: Philosophy, Psychology, Sociology, Anthropology, Education, History, Religion, Politics, Juveniles, Periodicals
1978: 40 titles

Bottega d'Erasmo, Via G Ferrari 9, I-10124 Turin Tel: (011) 830331/831264 Cable Add: Erasmus Turin
Subjects: Religion, Philosophy, Medieval, Art, Literature, Philology, History

Ugo **Bozzi** Editore*, Via Polonia 2, I-00198 Rome Tel: (06) 862179 Cable Add: Uberart
Man Dir: Dr Ugo Bozzi
Subject: History of Art (in Italian and English)
1978: 2 titles *Founded:* 1965

Bracciodieta Editore, Corso Sonnino 8, I-70121 Bari Tel: (080) 540267
Man Dir: Dr Giuseppe Bracciodieta; *Editorial:* Domenico Bracciodieta; *Sales:* Rete Concessionari; *Publicity:* Dr Francesco Miccoli
Subsidiary Company: Editorialebari (qv)
Subjects: Fiction, Culture, Scholarly
1980: 7 titles *Founded:* 1979

Bramante Editrice SpA, Via G Biancardi 1 bis, I-21052 Busto Arsizio Tel: (0331) 620324
Man Dir: Dr Guido Ceriotti
Subjects: History, Music, Art, General Science, Military, Architecture
1979: 12 titles *Founded:* 1958

L'Erma di **Bretschneider** SpA*, Via Cassiodoro 19, CP 6192, I-00193 Rome Tel: (06) 353259/350765
Man Dir: Erminia Bretschneider Marcucci; *Publisher:* Dr Roberto Marcucci; *Bookstore:* Maria Silvia Marcucci
Subjects: Archaeology, Classical Art, Classical Philology, Ancient History, Roman Law

Dr Giorgio **Bretschneider**, Publisher & Bookseller, Via Crescenzio 43, I-00193 Rome Tel: (06) 659361 Cable Add: Giobrerom
Man Dir: Dr Giorgio Bretschneider
Subjects: Classical Antiquity-Archaeology, Philology, Ancient History
1978: 25 titles

Bulzoni Editore SRL, Via Dei Liburni 14, I-00185 Rome Tel: (06) 4955207
Man Dir, Editorial: Mario Bulzoni; *Sales:* Ivana Capitani; *Production:* Paola Bulzoni; *Publicity:* Anna Catarinozzi
Subjects: Medicine, Law, Sociology, Science, Fiction, Engineering, Arts, Literature, Philosophy, Linguistics, University Textbooks, Theatre, Cinema, Essays
Bookshop: Libreria Ricerche, Via Liburni 10/12, I-00185 Rome
Founded: 1969

C E D A M (Casa Editrice Dr A Milani), Via Jappelli 5, I-35100 Padua Tel: (049) 23234/23442
Dirs: Antonio Milani, Carlo Porta
Subjects: Belles Lettres, Philosophy, General & Social Science, Textbooks, Book Industry, Engineering, Arts, Literature, Languages, Fiction, Economics, Politics, Medicine

C E L I (Edizioni)*, Via Gandino, I-40137 Bologna Tel: (051) 391755/309922
Subjects: Medicine, Civil Engineering, Electronics, Radio, Television

Edizioni **C E P I M**, Via Buonarroti 38, I-20145 Milan Tel: (02) 4982129/4694778
Man Dir: Sergio Bonelli; *Editorial:* Decio Canzio; *Sales:* Liliana Gentini; *Production:* Luigi Corteggi
Subsidiary Companies: Altamira; Araldo; Edizioni Daim Press; all in Milan
Subjects: Comic Strip Books, Far West Stories, Adventure Tales, Stories of Exploration and Travel
1978: 150 titles *1979:* 150 titles *Founded:* 1968

Edizioni **Calderini**, Emilia Lev 31, I-40139 Bologna Tel: (051) 492211 Cable Add: Calderini Telex: 510336 I Edagri
Man Dir: S Perdisa; *Rights & Permissions:* Luisa Manzoni B; *Publicity:* C Corsini
Parent Company: Calderini SRL (at above address)
Associate Companies: Edagricole (qv); Gruppo Giornalistico Edagricole Srl (at above address); Officine Grafiche Calderini, 14 Emilia, I-40126 Ozzano
Branch Offs: Via Bronzino 14, Milan; Via Puglie 3, Rome
Subjects: Art, Sport, Electronics, Mechanics, Electrical Engineering, University & Secondary Textbooks, Nursing, Veterinary Science, Architecture, Natural Sciences, Travel Guides
1978: 85 titles *1979:* 88 titles *Founded:* 1952
ISBN Publisher's Prefix: 88-7019

Capitol Editrice Dischi CEB*, CP 441, I-40100 Bologna (Located at: Via Minghetti 17/19, I-40057 Cadriano di Granarolo Emilia (Bologna)) Tel: (051) 766612/766421/2 Cable Add: Edicapitol Bologna Telex: 511039 Edcapi I
Man Dir: Maurizio Malipiero; *Rights & Permissions:* Raffaele Malipiero; *Production Manager:* Guiseppe Parini
Subjects: General Fiction, Art, Biography, Reference, Medicine, Juveniles, Secondary & Primary Textbooks, Educational Materials, Audiovisual
Founded: 1956

Nuova Casa Editrice Licinio **Cappelli** SpA*, Via Marsili 9, CP 385, I-40124 Bologna Tel: (051) 330411 Cable Add: Cappelli Editore Bologna Telex: 510198 pp bo i per cappelli
Man Dir: Giuseppe Milano; *Editorial:* Dr Cesare Sughi; *Textbooks:* Dr Umberto Magrini; *Publicity, Advertising, Rights & Permissions:* Augusto Magagnoli
Subjects: General Fiction, Belles Lettres, Poetry, Biography, History, Art, Philosophy, Reference, Religion, Juveniles, Low-priced Paperbacks, Medicine, Psychology, General & Social Science, Primary, Secondary and University Textbooks, Filmscripts, Drama, Music, Politics
1978: 107 titles *Founded:* 1851

Casalini Libri*, Via B da Maiano 3, I-50014 Fiesole (Florence) Tel: (055) 599941 Cable Add: Casalini Fiesole
Man Dirs: Mario Casalini, Gerda Casalini von Grebmer
Subjects: History, Philosophy, Sociology, Musicology
1978: 6 titles *Founded:* 1968
Miscellaneous: Also a book exporter (address as above)

Celuc Libri, Via Santa Valeria 5, I-20123 Milan Tel: (02) 806976/800113
Man Dir: Giovanni Barbatiello
Subjects: History, Philosophy, Religion, Low-priced Paperbacks, Psychology, Engineering, General & Social Science, University Textbooks
Bookshop: At above address
1978: 8 titles *1979:* 11 titles *Founded:* 1969 (as CELVC, 1974 as Celuc)

Centro Di, Piazza de'Mozzi 1 r, CP 1500, I-50125 Florence Tel: (055) 23222/282729 Cable Add: Centrodi Florence
Man Dir: Dr F Marchi; *Sales Dir:* P Riccetti
Subjects: Art, Reference
Bookshop: Centro Di, Piazza d'Mozzi 1 r, I-50125, Florence; 18 via di San Giacomo, I-00187 Rome Tel: 6786963
1978: 25 titles *1979:* 26 titles *Founded:* 1968

Centro Internazionale del Libro, see Giunti Publishing Group

Verlag **Chiessi-Morra***, Via Calabrillo 20, I-8021 Naples Tel: (081) 402025
Dirs: Rosanna Chiessi, Guiseppe Morra

Ciarrapico Editore, Via Parioli 3, I-00197 Rome Tel: (06) 4741151/2/3
Publisher: Giuseppe Ciarrapico; *Dir:* Gianni Pirrone; *Publicity Manager:* Stefania Sinapi
Subjects: Politics, History, Science, Law, Philology Philosophy

Città Armoniosa, CP 243, I-42100 Reggio Emilia (Located at: Via Lungocrostalo 1/A, I-42100 Reggio Emilia) Tel: (0522) 25973
Man Dir: Mario Ghinoi; *Editorial:* Giovanni Riva; *Sales:* Riccardo Mammi; *Production:* Massimo Rocchi; *Publicity:* Gino Ruozzi; *Rights & Permissions:* Paola Leoni
Parent Company: Novastampa di Masini Mauro SNC
Subsidiary Company: Novalito di Persona Francesco E C SNC, Via Cecati 15/A, I-42100 Reggio Emilia
Subjects: Fiction, Poetry, Theatre, Juveniles, Cartoons
1979: 42 titles *1980:* 42 titles *Founded:* 1976

Città Nuova Editrice, Via degli Scipioni 265, I-00192 Rome Tel: (06) 3595212/310955
Man Dir: Dr Giambattista Dadda
Branch Off: Via Degli Scipioni 265, I-00192 Rome
Subsidiary Companies: Argentina: Ciudad Nueva, Ave da Rivadavia 4939, Buenos Aires 24; Austria: Verlag Neue Stadt GmbH, A-6263 Fügen 73 (Zillertal); Brazil: Cidade Nova, Rua Pio XII 274, Paraiso, São Paulo; France: Nouvelle Cité (qv); Federal Republic of Germany: Neue Stadt (qv); Italy: Via Bonvicini 2, Florence; Netherlands: Nieuwe Stad, St Stephanusstr 11, Nijmegen; Philippines: New City, 363 Ycaza St, San Miguel, Manila; Spain: Ciudad Nueva, Luis Cabrera 12, III Dcha, Madrid 2; Switzerland: Verlag Neue Stadt, CH-8032 Zürich, Postfach 218; UK: New City (qv); USA: Living City, 360 East 65th St, 16G, New York, NY 10021
Subjects: Religion, Philosophy, Psychology, Social Science, Reference, Juveniles
1979: 75 titles

Cittadella Editrice, Via Ancajani 3, CP 46, I-06081 Assisi Tel: (075) 813595 Cable Add: Cittadella Editrice
All offices: Nello Giostra, Gabriella Persico, Giuseppina Pompei, Virginia Pagani
Subjects: Biography, Religion, Psychology, Social Science, Social Problems, Theology
1978: 40 titles

Coines Edizioni*, Corso Vittorio Emanuele 337, I-00186 Rome Tel: (06) 657948/6543840
Man Dir: Roberto Miotti; *Editorial:* Pierpaolo Benedetti; *Rights & Permissions:* Roma Eulama
Subjects: History, Education, Politics, Psychology, Religion, Social Science, Economics, Periodicals
Founded: 1970

Edizioni di **Comunità** SpA, Via Manzoni 12, I-20121 Milan Tel: 790957
Man & Sales Dir: Dr S Gallo; *Publicity Dir:* Dr A Scoccimarro; *Advertising & Rights & Permissions:* R Cambiaghi
Subjects: Philosophy, Psychology, Social Science, Architecture, Town Planning
1978: 25 titles *Founded:* 1946

Controinformazione*, Corso di Porta Ticinese 87, I-20123 Milan
Subjects: Anti-Fascism, International Anti-Capitalist Movement; Alternative Information

Edizioni **Cremonese** SpA, Via Della Croce 77, I-00187 Rome Tel: (06) 6793995 Cable Add: Edizioni Cremonese

214 ITALY

Man Dir: Alberto Stianti
Subjects: History, Reference, Engineering, General Science, University & Secondary Textbooks, Architecture, Mathematics, Aviation
1978: 35 titles *1979:* 40 titles *Founded:* 1930

Edizioni **Curci** SRL, Galleria del Corso 4, I-20122 Milan Tel: (02) 794746 Cable Add: Curcimusic Telex: 332683 Curci I
Subjects: Music, Arts, Textbooks
1978: 28 titles *1979:* 44 titles *Founded:* 1860

Armando **Curcio** Editore SpA, Via Arno 64, I-00198 Rome Tel: (06) 84871 Cable Add: Curcioroma Telex: 614666 Curcio I
Chairman: Dr Alfredo Curcio; *Man Dir:* Dr Luciano Delmirani; *General Manager:* Massimo Petrangeli
Subjects: Art, Reference, Geography, History, Travel, Encyclopaedias
Founded: 1928

Editoriale **Dado***, Via Mameli 31, I-20100 Milan

Dall'Oglio Editore SpA, Via Santa Croce 20-2, I-20122 Milan Tel: (02) 8351575
President: Andrea dall'Oglio; *Man Dir:* Bruno Romano
Subjects: General Fiction, Belles Lettres, Poetry, Biography, History, Low-priced Paperbacks
Founded: 1925

Piero **Dami** Editore SpA*, Piazza Velasca 5, I-20122 Milan Tel: (02) 802731/866514 Cable Add: Eurostudio Milan Telex: 311499
Subjects: Fiction, Illustrated Children's Books, Animals
1978: 15 titles

De Donato Editore, Lungomare Nazario Sauro 25, I-70121 Bari Tel: 331574/334159
Man Dir, Sales: Diego De Donato; *Editorial:* Giancarlo Aresta; *Production:* Cesare Caleno; *Publicity:* Lalla Martellotti; *Rights & Permissions:* Isidoro Mortellaro
Associate Company: Consorzio del Libro srl, Corso Re Umberto 12, I-10121 Torino (Promotion company for Boringhieri, Dedalo, De Donato and Stampatori, publishers)
Subjects: Politics, Economics, Sociology, Literature, Fiction, Psychology, Archaeology, Philosophy
1978: 41 titles *1979:* 48 titles *Founded:* 1970

Giovanni **De Vecchi** Editore SpA*, Via Vittor Pisani 16, I-20124 Milan Tel: 664851/2/3 Telex: 37081 devedit
Associate Companies: Éditions De Vecchi SA, France (qv); Editorial De Vecchi SA, Spain (qv)
Subjects: Archaeology, Astronomy, Psychology, Sports, Hunting and Fishing, Domestic Animals, Humour, Occult Sciences, Gardening and Agriculture, Medicinal Herbs, Medical, Yoga, Legal

Edizioni **Dedalo***, CP 362, I-70100 Bari (Located at: Traversa de Blasio, Zona Industriale, I-70123 Bari) Tel: 371555/371025/371008
Man Dir: Raimondo Coga
Subjects: Politics, History, Architecture, Urban Studies, Science
1978: 45 titles *1979:* 20 titles *Founded:* 1965

Edizioni **Dehoniane** Bologna (EDB), Via Nosadella 6, I-40123 Bologna Tel: (051) 330301/306812
Shipping Add: Via Dal Ferro 4, I-40138 Bologna
Man Dir: Andrea Tessarolo; *Sales Dir, Rights & Permissions:* Giuseppe Albiero; *Publicity Dir:* Sancini Vittorio
Subjects: Philosophy, Religion, Juveniles, Secondary & Primary Textbooks, Educational Materials
Bookshop: Libreria Presbyterium, Padua
Founded: 1965

Delta Editrice SpA*, Piazza dei Martiri 1, I-40121 Bologna Tel: (051) 228219
Telex: 51524
Subjects: History, Travel, Natural History, Astrology

Diki-Books Srl*, Via Della Spiga 1, I-20121 Milan Tel: 784129
Man Dir: Massimo Baletti
Subjects: Children's books, Foreign language texts for infants & primary schools
1978: 9 titles *Founded:* 1975

Domus Editoriale, Via Achille Grandi 5/7, I-20089 Rozzano (Milan) Tel: (02) 82472
Telex: 313589 Edidom I
Subjects: Art, Motorcars, Cooking, Tourism, Architecture, Periodicals

E D B, see Edizioniehoniane Bologna

E D I 3*, Corso di Porta Nuova 34, I-20121 Milan Tel: (02) 638873
Man Dir: Paolo Colombo
Subjects: Juveniles, Educational Materials

E R I — Edizioni R A I Radiotelevisione Italiana SpA*, Via Arsenale 41, I-10121 Turin Tel: (011) 57101 Cable Add: Edrad Turin
Man Dir: Dr Alberto Luna
Orders to: Via del Babuino 51, I-00187 Rome
Parent Company: RAI Radiotelevisione It, Viale Mazzini 14, Rome
Associate Companies: Sacis, Via del Babuino 9, Rome; Sipra, Via Bertola 34, Turin; Fonit Cetra, Via Meda 45, Milan; Telespazio, Corso d'Italia 42-43, Rome
Subjects: Art and Collector's editions, Literature and Civilization, Essays, General Culture, Sociology, Classics in Translation, Home and Garden, Children's books, Language courses, Communications, Public opinion polls, Music
Bookshops: Via Arsenale 41, I-10121 Turin; Via del Babuino 51, I-00187 Rome
1979: 9 titles *Founded:* 1949

Edagricole (Edizioni Agricole), Emilia Lev 31, CP 2202 I-40139 Bologna Tel: (051) 492211 Cable Add: Edagri Telex: 510336
Man Dir: Sergio Perdisa; *Editorial:* Luisa Manzoni; *Sales:* Cesare Perdisa; *Production:* Guido Giorgi; *Publicity:* Giuliano Avoni
Associate Companies: Calderini Industrie Grafiche ed Editoriali; Edizioni Calderini (qv); Gruppo Giornalistico Edagricole
Branch Offs and Bookshops: Via Bronzino 14, Milan; Via Boncompagni 73, Rome; Via Zamboni 13, Bologna
Subjects: Agriculture, Veterinary Science, Gardening, Biology, Directories
1978: 160 titles *1979:* 125 titles *Founded:* 1936
ISBN Publisher's Prefix: 88-206

Edibimbi SRL, Via Speroni 14, I-21100 Varese Tel: (0332) 287766
Subject: Juveniles

Edipem SpA*, Corso Della Vittoria 91, CP 157, I-28100 Novara Tel: (032) 28694
Subjects: Juridical; Medical; Scientific and Technical; Encyclopaedias; Classical Literature; School Books

Editalia (Edizioni d'Italia), Via di Pallacorda 7, I-00186 Rome Tel: (06) 6569537/6541592
Man Dir: Lidio Bozzini; *Rights & Permissions:* Arrigo Pecchioli
Subjects: History, Art, Customs
Founded: 1952

Editnemo*, Via Telesio 15, I-20145 Milan Tel: (02) 4983375
Man Dir: Sandro Nardini; *Sales Dir:* Alberto Nardini; *Rights & Permissions:* S A Nardini
Subject: Juveniles
Founded: 1972

Editorialebari, Corso Sonnino 8, I-70121 Bari Tel: (080) 540267
Parent Company: Bracciodieta Editore (qv)
Subjects: Fiction, Philosophy, Education
Founded: 1965

Editrice Bibliografica, Viale Vittorio Veneto 24, I-20124 Milan Tel: (02) 6597950/6597246
Subjects: Bibliographies and Reference Publications for the Book Trade
1978: 10 titles *1979:* 10 titles
ISBN Publisher's Prefix: 88-7075

Giulio **Einaudi** Editore SpA, Via Umberto Biancamano, CP 245, I-10121 Turin
Tel: (011) 533653/545384 Telex: 220344
Subjects: General Fiction, Belles Lettres, Poetry, History, Music, Art, Philosophy, Juveniles, Low- & High-priced Paperbacks, Psychology, Social Science, University Textbooks
1978: 178 titles *1979:* 183 titles *Founded:* 1933

Eldec SpA Edizioni Pregiate*, Viale Tiziano 25, I-00196 Rome Tel: (06) 3960041/4
Publisher: Giulio de Cicco; *Dir:* Milko Skofic
Subjects: Art, Encyclopaedias, Facsimile Editions, Bibliophilic Editions

Electa Editrice, Via Goldoni 1, I-20124 Milan Tel: (02) 704023
Dirs: Giorgio Fantoni, Massimo Vitta Zelman; *Editorial:* Carlo Pirovano; *Rights & Permissions:* Mirella V Tenderini
Parent Company: Gruppo Editoriale Electa SpA
Associate Company: Alfieri Edizioni d'Arte (qv)
Subsidiary Company: Electa France, Paris; Electa Mailing, Milan
Subjects: Art, History of Art, Architecture, High-priced Paperbacks, Numbered Editions, Catalogues of major exhibitions, Periodicals
1978: 100 titles *Founded:* 1945

Emme Edizioni, Via San Maurilio 13, I-20123 Milan Tel: (02) 865459/865951
Man Dir, Editorial: Rosellina Archinto Marconi; *Rights & Permissions:* Renata Discacciati
Subjects: How-to, Juveniles, High-priced Paperbacks, Educational Materials
1978: 64 titles *1979:* 63 titles

Eulama SA*, Via Torino 135, I-00184 Rome Tel: (06) 460636
Man Dir: Harald Kahnemann
Subjects: Fiction, Sociology, Law
Also Literary Agent (qv)

Fabbri Editori SpA*, Via Mecenate 91, I-20138 Milan Tel: (02) 5095 Cable Add: Librifabbri Milan Telex: 311321
Man Dir: Giorgio Manina; *Editorial:* Giorgio Savorelli; *Sales:* Giorgio Paolo Tabacchi
Subjects: General Fiction, History, Music, Art, Philosophy, Juveniles, Reference, Low- & High-priced Paperbacks, Medicine, General Science, Secondary & Primary Textbooks, Educational Materials, Hobbies, Sports, Encyclopaedias
Founded: 1945

Faenza Editrice SpA*, Via Firenze 60, CP 68, I-48018 Faenza Tel: (0546) 43120
Cable Add: Editfaenza
Man Dir: Prof Goffredo Gaeta; *Editorial, Sales, Publicity:* Franco Rossi
Subjects: Architecture, Science, Technology,

Industries, Crafts, Arts
Founded: 1965

Giangiacomo Feltrinelli SpA*, Via Andegari 6, I-20121 Milan Tel: (02) 808346/7 Cable Add: Fedit Milan
Subjects: General Fiction, Belles Lettres, Poetry, Art, Music, History, General Science, Reference, Paperbacks, University Textbooks, Philosophy, Juveniles
1978-79: 350 titles *Founded:* 1954

Edizioni **Ferro** SpA*, Via Cusani 5, I-20121 Milan Tel: (02) 866272
Man Dir: Pia Ferro
Subjects: Geography, Ethnology, Medicine, Religion, Pedagogy, Fiction, Sociology
1978: 3 titles *Founded:* 1963

Libreria Editrice **Fiorentina** di Vittorio e Valerio Zani snc, Via Ricasoli 105-107r, I-50122 Florence Tel: (055) 216533
Editorial: Vittorio Zani; *Sales:* Valerio Zani
Subjects: Religion, Social Problems, Education, Local Interest, Architecture
Bookshop: At above address
1978: 43 titles *1979:* 48 titles *Founded:* 1901

S F **Flaccovio** Editore, Via Ruggiero Settimo 37, I-90139 Palermo Tel: 589442/334249/584268
Subjects: General Science, History
Bookshops: Via R Settimo 37, Palermo; Piazza Orlando 15, Palermo; Via E Basile 136, Palermo; Piazza Don Bosco 3, Palermo; Libreria Dante, Quattro Canti Citta, Palermo
1978: 22 titles

Il **Formichiere**, Via del Lauro 3, I-20121 Milan Tel: (02) 86693
Subjects: Theatre, Cinema, Music, Fiction, Psychology

Editrice **Gammalibri**, Via Poma 4, I-20129 Milan Tel: (02) 718315
Man Dir: Domenico Nodari; *Publicity:* Felice Bassi
Subjects: Music, Sport, Politics, Cinema, Theatre
1978: 12 titles *1979:* 15 titles *Founded:* 1976

Garzanti Editore*, Via Senato 25, I-20121 Milan Tel: (02) 705721/705741 Cable Add: Garzantieditore Telex: Garzal 31461
Publisher: Dr Livio Garzanti; *Editorial:* Piero Gelli; *Sales Manager:* Francesco Rampini; *Rights & Permissions:* Paola Dala
Subjects: General & Crime Fiction, Literature, Poetry, Art, Politics, Biography, History, Reference, Juveniles, Low- & High-priced Paperbacks, Secondary & Primary Textbooks, Encyclopaedias, Dictionaries
Founded: 1861
Bookshops: Libreria Garzanti, Galleria Vittorio Emanuele 66-68, I-20121 Milan; Libreria Garzanti, Palazzo Dell' Università, Pavia
Subsidiaries: Antonio Vallardi Editore, Via Senato 25, (qv); Centri Garzanti, Via Senato 15; Enciclopedia Europea SaS, Via Senato 25 (all in Milan)

Creazioni **Gensy**, see Giunti Publishing Group

Giorgio **Giappichelli***, Via Po 21, I-10124 Turin Tel: (011) 553140/513346
Subjects: University Publications, Humanities (Economics, Law, Philosophy, Politics, Sociology, Classical and Modern Philology)
Bookshops: Libreria Editrice Scientifica di G Giappichelli, Via Vasco 2, I-10124 Turin; Libreria della Facolta' Umanistiche, Via Verdi 39 bis, I-10124 Turin
1978: 71 titles *Founded:* 1921

A **Giuffré** Editore SpA*, Via Statuto 2, I-20121 Milan Tel: (02) 652341/2/3
Publicity Manager: Roberto Musicco
Branch Off: Via V Colonna 40, I-00193 Rome
Subjects: History, Law, Social & Political Science, Economics
1979: approx 300 titles *Founded:* 1931

Giunti Publishing Group, Via V Gioberti 34, I-50121 Florence Tel: (055) 670451/5 Cable Add: Marzolib Florence Telex: 571438 Giunti
Dirs: Dr Renato Giunti, Dr Sergio Giunti
Subjects: Art Books, Essays, Fiction, Psychology, Pedagogy, Mathematics, Chemistry, National Edition of Works of Leonardo da Vinci, Galileo Galilei, Italian publishers of National Geographic Society books, Linguistics, Dictionaries, School Textbooks, Juveniles, Popular Science, History, Guidebooks, Handbooks, Periodicals
Miscellaneous: Group comprises: Editrice Giunti Marzocco, Giunti Barbera Editore, Editrice Universitaria, Edizioni Ofiria, Giunti Nardini Editore, Centro Internazionale del Libro, Giacomo Agnelli Editore, Giunti Martello Editore, Creazioni Gensy, Edizioni Oreste Barjes, ME/DI Sviluppo, Organizzazioni Speciali (qv), B Boggero Editore, Lisciani e Giunti Editori

Gregorian University Press (Universitá Gregoriana Editrice), Piazza della Pilotta 4, I-00187 Rome Tel: (06) 6701
Man Dir: Angelo Damboriena
Subjects: Theology, Philosophy, Canon Law, Sociology, Psychology
1978: 12 titles *1979:* 13 titles *Founded:* 1914

Libreria Editrice **Gregoriana***, Via Roma 37, I-35100 Padua Tel: 36133/38869
Man Dir: Clodio Fasolo
Subjects: Religion, Philosophy, Sociology, Psychology
Bookshop: Via Roma 37, I-35100 Padua; Via Vescovado 33, I-35100 Padua
Founded: 1922

Piero **Gribaudi** Editore, Corso Galileo Ferraris 67, I-10128 Turin Tel: (011) 500360
Publishers: Piero Gribaudi, Maria Luisa Gribaudi Monferrini
Subjects: Philosophy, Religion, Social Science
1978: 30 titles *1979:* 34 titles

L'Editrice Scientifica SaS di L G **Guadagni**, Via Ariberto 20, I-20123 Milan Tel: (02) 8390274
Dir: Dr Leonarda Guadagni
Subjects: Pharmaceuticals, Chemistry, University Textbooks
1978: 2 titles *Founded:* 1940

Guanda Editore SRL, Via Daniele Manin 13, I-20121 Milan Tel: (02) 654628, 650973
Man Dir: Dr Giancarlo Paolini; *Rights & Permissions:* Dr Carlo Alberto Corsi
Subjects: Poetry, General Fiction, Essays
1978: 45 titles *1979:* 50 titles *Founded:* 1933

Guaraldi Editore SpA*, Via Masaccio 268, I-50100 Florence Tel: (055) 573968/573978
Man Dir: Mario Guaraldi; *Editorial:* Sandro Savorelli; *Sales:* Rosiano Sensini; *Production:* Vittorio Giudici; *Publicity:* Andrea Rauch; *Rights & Permissions:* Eulama SA
Subjects: Sociology, Pedagogy, Psychoanalytics
Founded: 1970

Guida Editori SRL*, Via Port'Alba 19, I-80134 Naples Tel: (081) 457111
Publisher: Mario Guida
Subjects: History, Philosophy, Ideology, Sociology, Anthropology, Political Science, Literary Criticism, Linguistics, Periodical *Sigma* (Art Criticism)
1978: 48 titles

Herder Editrice e Libreria, Piazza Montecitorio 117-120, I-00186 Rome Tel: (06) 6794628
Man Dir: Oriol Schaedel
Subjects: Religion, History, Philosophy, Archaeology, Oriental Studies, Philology and Linguistics, Periodicals, Occasional titles
Founded: 1955

Casa Editrice Libraria Ulrico **Hoepli** SpA, Via Hoepli 5, I-20121 Milan Tel: (02) 865446 Cable Add: Hoepli Milan
Shipping Add: Via Mameli 13, I-20129 Milan
Man Dirs: Dr Ulrico Hoepli, Dr Gianni Hoepli; *Sales Dir:* Lodovico Colombo; *Rights & Permissions:* Dr Ulrico Carlo Hoepli, Dr Susanna Schwarz Bellotti
Branch Off: Via Mameli 13, I-20129 Milan
Subjects: How-to, Music, Art, Philosophy, Reference, Religion, Juveniles, Low- & High-priced Paperbacks, Psychology, Engineering, General & Social Science, University & Secondary Textbooks, Technology
Bookshop: Ulrico Hoepli Libreria Internazionale, Via Hoepli 5, I-20121 Milan
1978: 103 titles *1979:* 89 titles *Founded:* 1870

Idea Editions, Via Cappuccio 21, I-20123 Milan Tel: (02) 807997 Cable Add: Ideabooks Milano
Dirs: Alvise Passigli, Filippo Passigli; *Editorial:* Andrea Cestelli-Guidi, Andrea Branzi
Associate Companies: Idea Books, Ideart (both at above address); Ideeboek BV, Netherlands (qv)
Subjects: Visual Arts, Photography, Architecture, Design
Bookshop: Museum Bookshop, Padiglione d'Arte Moderna, Milan
1979: 25 titles *Founded:* 1976

Istituto Centrale di Statistica*, Via C Balbo 16, I-00184 Rome Tel: (06) 471666
Subject: Political Economy

Istituto della Enciclopedia Italiana*, Piazza Paganica 4, CP 717, I-00186 Rome Tel: (06) 6544337 Cable Add: Enciclopedia
Subjects: Encyclopaedias, Dictionaries, Reference, Art

Istituto Editoriale Italiano SpA*, Via Priv Passo Pordoi 21, I-20139 Milan
Subjects: Fine & Applied Arts, Illustrated Books, Encyclopaedias & Dictionaries

Istituto Geografico de Agostini SpA*, Via Giovanni da Verrazzano 15, I-28100 Novara Tel: (0321) 471201 Cable Add: Geografico Novara Telex: 20020 Igda No
Subjects: Belles Lettres, Art, Reference, History, Religion, Juveniles, Textbooks, Geography, Literature

Istituto Italiano D'Arti Grafiche*, Via Zanica 92, I-24100 Bergamo Tel: (035) 246292/243645/249675 Cable Add: Grafiche Bergamo Telex: 30114
Man Dir: Comm Remo Montanari
Subjects: Art, Juveniles, Reference, Textbooks, Religion
Founded: 1873

Istituto Poligrafico e Zecca dello Stato, Piazza Verdi 10, I-00100 Rome
Subjects: Law, Politics, Linguistics, Literature, Fiction, Arts, Stamps, Metal Coins
Founded: 1928
Miscellaneous: State Publishing House and Italian State Stationery Office, Mint and School of Medal's Art

Jaca Book Edizioni, Via Aurelio Saffi 19, I-20123 Milan Tel: (02) 8052132/8057055 Telex: 331393
Man Dir: Dr Sante Bagnoli; *Editorial Dir:*

Dr Maretta Campi; *Editors:* Dr Elio Guerriero (Theology), Dr Massimo Guidetti (History); *Production:* Dr Guido Orsi; *Rights & Permissions:* Laura Geronazzo
Subjects: History, Philosophy, Religion, Psychology, Social & Political Science, Economics, Juveniles, Fiction, Literature, Art
1978: 60 titles *1979:* 65 titles *Founded:* 1966

L U **Japadre** Editore, CP 170, I-67100 L'Aquila (Located at: Corso Federico II 49, L'Aquila) Tel: 25587/26025/26488 Cable Add: Japadre L'Aquila
Man Dir and other offices: Leandro Ugo Japadre
Branch Off: Via Catalani 50, Rome
Subjects: Art, Literature, History, Philosophy, Science, Technology, Economics, Religion, Psychology, Sociology, Folklore, Fiction, Poetry, Linguistics
Bookshops: 2 Corso Federico II 49, L'Aquila; Piazza dell'Annunziata 6, L'Aquila; Uff Import-esport, Via Catalani 50/9, Rome
1978: 15 titles *1979:* 22 titles *Founded:* 1968
ISBN Publisher's Prefix: 88-7006

Casa Editrice Dr Eugenio **Jovene** SpA, Via Mezzocannone 109, I-80134 Naples Tel: 206518/206575 Cable Add: Jovene
Man Dir: Dr Alessandro Rossi
Subjects: Law, Economics
1978: 50 titles *1979:* 30 titles *Founded:* 1854

Kina Italia SpA*, Piazza Aspromonte 13, Milan Cable Add: 296263, 293284
Subjects: Art, Tourist Publications

Etas **Kompass***, Via Mantegna 6, I-20154 Milan Tel: (02) 347051/314007/341137 Telex: 33152
Man Dir: Aldo Lanza
Subjects: Reference, Law, Medicine, General & Socal Science, Technical, Periodicals

Editrice **Lanterna***, Via Robino 71 a/r, I-16142 Genoa Tel: 881441
Dirs: Lino De Benetti, Dino Galiazzo
Subjects: Religion, Theology, Sociology, Politics, Feminism, Non-violence
Founded: 1969

Giuseppe **Laterza** e Figli SpA, Via di Villa Sacchetti 17, I-00197 Rome Tel: (06) 803693/878053
Shipping Add: Via F Zippitelli 3, Zona Industriale, I-70123 Bari
Editorial Dir: Vito Laterza (Rome); *Vice Editorial Dir:* Enrico Mistretta (Rome); *Sales Dir:* Domenico Scoppio (Bari); *Press, Publicity & Advertising:* Nico Perrone (Bari); *Rights & Permissions:* Eulama Agency, Via Torino 135, Rome
Other Office: Via D Alighieri 51, I-70121 Bari Tel: (081) 213413/214024/219452
Subjects: Belles Lettres, Biography, Art, Reference, Religion, Architecture, Classics, History, Economics, Philosophy, Low- & High-priced Paperbacks, Psychology, Social Science, University & Secondary Textbooks
Bookshop: Via Sparano 134, I-70121 Bari
1979: 130 titles *Founded:* 1889

Casa Editrice Felice **Le Monnier***, Via Scipione Ammirato 100, CP 202, I-50136 Florence Tel: (055) 676201
Subjects: Belles Lettres, Poetry, Biography, History, How-to, Music, Art, Philosophy, Religion, Juveniles, Multilingual Dictionaries,Languages

Leschiera Valerio*, Via Perugino 21,I-21 Cologno Monzese (Milan)
Tel: 2546545/2543986

Edizioni **Librex***, Via Bellezza 15, I-20136 Milan Tel: (02) 544407/584523 Cable Add: Librex Milan Telex: 34208
General Manager: Antonio Mancia; *Export Manager:* Anna Vanzo; *Production:* Fabiola Ferrario
Subjects: Reference, Juveniles, International Co-productions, Encyclopedias

Etas **Libri** SpA*, Via Mecenate 87/6, I-20138 Milan Tel: (02) 5065249/5065223/501101 Telex: Fabbri 32321
Man Dir: Romano Trabucchi
Subjects: General & Social Science, Economics, Technical, Mathematics, Management
1978: 44 titles

Licosa SpA, Via Lamarmora 45, CP 552, I-50121 Florence Tel: 579751/3, 571809 Cable Add: Licosa Firenze Telex: 570466 Licosa I
Man Dir, Sales, Rights & Permissions: Mirko Zanello; *Editorial:* Barbara Adamska; *Publicity:* Capo Servizio, Barbara Adamska
Branch Off: Via Bartolini 29, I-20155 Milan
Subjects: Philology, Linguistics, Archaeology
Bookshops: Via Lamarmora 45, Florence; Libreria Desi, Via Bartolini 29, Milan
1978: 18 titles *Founded:* 1954

Liguori Editore SRL, Via Mezzocannone 19, I-80134 Naples Tel: (081) 203606/206077 Cable Add: Liguori Napoli
Man Dir: Dr Rolando Liguori; *Editorial and Rights & Permissions:* Guido Liguori; *Sales:* Franco Liguori
Subjects: Linguistics, Lit Criticism, Philosophy, History, Sociology, Anthropology, Law, Economics, Mathematics, Astronomy,Natural Sciences, Medicine, Technology, Periodical — *Lo Statuto dei Lavoratori*
1978: 85 titles

Loescher Editore SpA, Via Vittorio Amedeo 18, I-10121 Turin Tel: (011) 549333
Dir: Maurizio Pavia
Subjects: University & Secondary Textbooks
Founded: 1867

Longanesi e C, Via Salvini 3, I-20122 Milan Tel: (02) 782551/5 Cable Add: Editlong Milan
President: Stefano Passigli; *Man Dir:* Mario Spagnol; *Editorial:* Ferruccio Viviani; *Sales:* Guglielmo Tognetti; *Production:* Lorenzo Pellizzari; *Publicity:* Mario Biondi; *Rights & Permissions:* Olivia Olivieri, Carla Tanzi
Subjects: General Fiction, Belles Lettres, Biography, History, How-to, Music, Art, Philosophy, Religion, Low-priced Paperbacks, Medicine, Psychology, General & Social Science
1978: 148 titles *1979:* 87 titles *Founded:* 1946

Longman Italia SRL, Via Giovanni Pascoli 55, I-20133 Milan
Associate company of Longman Group Ltd, UK (qv)

Longo Editore, Via Rocca ai Fossi 6, CP 431, I-48100 Ravenna Tel: (0544) 27026
Editorial, Production: Alfio Longo; *Sales:* Angelo Longo
Subjects: Art, Archeology, Bibliography, Philology, Italian Classics, Philosophy, Linguistics, Pedagogy, Critical Literature, Sociology, History, History of Art, Poetry, Fiction, Theatre, History of Masonry
Bookshop: Libreria Longo, Via Diaz 39, I-48100 Ravenna
1978: 60 titles *1979:* 64 titles *Founded:* 1962

M E/D I Sviluppo, see Giunti Publishing Group

Malipiero SpA*, Viale Liguria 12-14, CP 788, I-40064 Ozzana Emilia (Bologna) Tel: (051) 799264 Cable Add: TLX 51260 Matex, Ozzanoemilia Telex: 51260
Dirs: Dr Pierpaolo Malipiero, Comm Giuseppe Malipiero; *Editorial Dir:* Donato Malipiero
Subjects: Juveniles, Hobbies, Education
Founded: 1969

Marietti Editori SpA, Via Adam 15, I-15033 Casale Monferrato Tel: (0142) 55181/2 Cable Add: Marietti Editori Telex: 212458 Edicem I
Man Dir: Ing Pietro Marietti
Branch Offs: Largo Card, A Galamini 7, I-00165 Rome; Via Legnano 23, I-10128 Turin
Subjects: Religion, Secondary & Primary Textbooks, History

Alberto **Marotta** Editore SpA*, Via Francesco Giordani 21,I-80122 Naples Tel: (081) 685144 (PBX)
Man Dir: Alberto Marotta; *Editorial:* Dott Giuseppe Maggi; *Sales:* Pasquale Marotta
Branch Offs: Via Monte di Pieta 1/A, I-20121 Milan; Via Nizza 45,I-00198 Rome
Subjects: General Fiction, Belles Lettres, Poetry, Biography, Music, Art, Social Science, Dictionaries, Encyclopaedias, History, Neapolitan Studies, Medicine, Science
Bookshops: Via dei Mille 78-80-82; Via Francesco Giordani 46; Via Giuseppe Verdi 46 (all in Naples)
Founded: 1959

Marsilio Editori, Fondamenta S Chiara, S Croce 518a, I-30125 Venice Tel: (041) 707188
Man Dirs: Prof Paolo Legreuz, Dr Paolo Lenardo
Subjects: General Fiction, Architecture, Social & Political Science, Economics, Psychology, Literature, Languages

Giunti **Martello** Editore, see Giunti Publishing Group

Editrice Giunti **Marzocco**, see Giunti Publishing Group

Marzorati Editore SRL*, Via Piero Martinetti 6, I-20147 Milan Tel: (02) 405050
Man Dir: Antonio Marzorati; *Editorial:* Romain Rainero; *Sales:* Franco Faglioni; *Production:* Fiorenza Vittori; *Publicity:* Patrizia Fatigati; *Rights & Permissions:* Elena Maglia
Subjects: Literature, History, Philosophy
1978: 15 titles *Founded:* 1942

Editrice **Massimo**, Corso di Porta Romana 122, I-20122 Milan Tel: (02) 544104
Man Dir: Dr Cesare Crespi
Subjects: General Fiction, Biography, History, Religion, Juveniles, Low- & High-priced Paperbacks, Psychology, General & Social Science, Secondary Textbooks, Philosophy
Bookshops: Via dei Pellegrini 1, I-20122 Milan; Agenzia Mescat, Corso di Porta Romana 122, I-20122 Milan
1978: 27 titles *1979:* 26 titles *Founded:* 1951
ISBN Publisher's Prefix: 88-7030

Franca **May** Edizioni SRL, Via Giacinta Pezzana 50, I-00185 Rome Tel: (06) 805738
Man Dir: Franca Frattini Gatto
Subject: Art
1978: 1 title *Founded:* 1974

Gabriele **Mazzotta** Editore SpA*, Foro Buonaparte 52, I-20121 Milan Tel: (02) 895803
Shipping Add: Via Col di Lana 6/a
Man Dir: Gabriele Mazzotta; *Sales Dir:* Alberto Bini; *Publicity Dir:* Nadine Bortolotti; *Rights & Permissions:* Pierrette Coppa
Subjects: Biography, History, Architecture, Art, Low- & High-priced Paperbacks,

Psychology, Social Science
1978: 65 titles *Founded:* 1966

Organizzazione Editoriale Medico Farmaceutica SRL, Via Edolo 42, CP 10434, I-20125 Milan Tel: (02) 600376
Dir: Lucio Marini
Subjects: Medicine, Pharmacy

Edizioni Mediterranee SRL, Via Flaminia 158, I-00196 Rome Tel: (06) 3601656
General Manager: Giovanni Canonico; *Editorial:* Romualdo d'Alessandro; *Sales:* Graziella Torre; *Publicity:* Nadia Bocchini; *Rights & Permissions:* Luigi Coppe
Subjects: ESP, Parapsychology, Occult, Magic, Yoga, Zen, Meditation, UFOs, Philosophy, Psychology, Art, Archaeology, Sport
1978: 50 titles *1979:* 45 titles *Founded:* 1953

Milano Libri Edizioni*, Corso Garibaldi 86, I-20121 Milan Tel: (02) 650518/651597
Subjects: Fiction, Juveniles, Essays, Manuals

Minerva Italica SpA, Via Maglio del Rame 6, I-24100 Bergamo, CP 216 Tel: (035) 237331/232688
Man Dir: Arnoldi Gianni
Branch Offs: Via Alfani 68, I-50121 Florence; Via S Sebastiano is 247a, I-98100 Messina; Via Petrella 6, I-20124 Milan; Via A Emo 162-168, I-00136 Rome; via Lattanzio 90-94, I-70126 Bari (all in Italy)
Subjects: General Fiction, Juveniles, University, Secondary & Primary Textbooks, Educational Materials
1978: 574 titles *Founded:* 1951

Moizzi, Via Fiori Chiari 12, I-20121 Milan Tel: (02) 886169/873453
Subjects: Anthropology, Feminism

Monas Hierogliphica Inc Cooperativa Editrice*, Via Borghetto 5, I-20122, Milan Telex: 32108 Martemon
Editorial: Nicolas Monti; *Publicity:* Carla Manenti
Subjects: Erotica, Art, Architecture
Founded: 1978

Arnoldo **Mondadori** Editore*, CP 1772, I-20100 Milan (Located at: Via Marconi 27, I-20090 Segrate) Tel: (02) 75421 Cable Add: Mondadori Segrate (MI) Telex: 34457
Man Dir: Sergio Polillo; *Editorial:* Dr Franco Migiarra, Dr Sergio Morando; *Sales:* Gian Paolo Slaviero; *Marketing:* Dr Leonardo Mondadori; *Production:* Bruno Borghini; *Publicity:* Dr Romano Billet; *Rights & Permissions:* Donatella Ciapessoni, Dr Marco Polillo
Associate Companies: Auguri di Mondadori, Sommacampagna, I-37066 Verona; Arti Grafiche della Venezie (qv); Cartiera di Ascoli, Mariono del Tronto, I-63046 Ascoli Piceno; Arti Grafiche della Lombardia, San Donato, I-20097 Milan; Nuova Stampa Mondadori, I-38023 Trento (all in Italy)
Branch Offs: Mondadori EPEE, France; Arnoldo Mondadori Deutschland GmbH, German Federal Republic; Arnoldo Mondadori Editore, Via Belvedere N1, I-37100 Verona, Italy; Arnoldo Mondadori Scandinavia AB, Scandinavia; Arnoldo Mondadori Co Ltd, UK; Mondadori Publishing Co, USA
Subjects: General Fiction, Belles Lettres, Poetry, Biography, History, How-to, Music, Art, Philosophy, Reference, Religion, Juveniles, Low- & High-priced Paperbacks, Medicine, Psychology, General Science, Secondary Textbooks, Educational Materials
Book Club: Club Degli Editori (with Giulio Einaudi Editore)
Bookshops: Branches throughout Italy
Founded: 1907

Edizioni Scolastiche Bruno **Mondadori**, Via Archimede 23, CP 1772, I-20129 Milan Tel: (02) 5456036 Telex: 34457
Man Dir: Roberta Mondadori; *Dirs:* Roberto Gulli, Mario Candiani
Subject: Textbooks
1979: 20 titles

Mondadori Ragazzi*, Via Zeviani 2, I-37100 Verona Tel: 75421 (Segrate) Telex: 34457 Mondedit

Mondoperaio edizioni Avanti SpA*, Via Tomacelli 146, I-00186 Rome
Editorial: Settimio Cavalli
Subjects: Political and Social Science, Philosophy, History of Labour and the Trade Unions, Workers' Movements in Italy and World-Wide, Periodicals — *Mondoperaio, Economia e territorio, Economia e politica*

Editrice **Morcelliana** SpA*, Via Gabriele Rosa 71, I-25100 Brescia Tel: (030) 46451
Man Dir: Stephano Minelli
Associate Company: Editrice La Scuola SpA (qv)
Subjects: History, Philosophy, Religion, Social Science
1978: 18 titles *Founded:* 1925

Verlag **Morra**, Via Calabritto 20, I-80121 Naples Tel: 402025
Man Dir: Giuseppe Morra; *Sales:* Giuseppe Orabona
Subject: Art
1978: 3 titles *Founded:* 1974

Federico **Motta** Editore*, Via Branda Castiglioni 7, I-20156 Milan Tel: (02) 390404/367708
Subjects: Encyclopaedias, Dictionaries

Società Editrice Il **Mulino**, Via Santo Stefano 6, I-40125 Bologna Tel: (051) 233415/6
Man Dir: Giovanni Evangelisti; *Sales Dir:* Marcello Bolognini; *Publicity Dir:* Giuseppe Lovato; *Rights & Permissions:* Luisa Pece
Subjects: History, Philosophy, Linguistics & Literary Criticism, Political Science, Law, Economics, Reference, Low-priced Paperbacks, Psychology, Social Science, University Textbooks, Journals
1978: 112 titles *1979:* 136 titles *Founded:* 1954

Ugo **Mursia** Editore SpA, Via Tadino 29, I-20124 Milan Tel: (02) 209341 Cable Add: Umedizioni Milan
Subsidiary Company: Edizioni Scolastiche APE SpA (qv)
Man Dir: Dr Ugo Mursia; *Editorial:* Dr Piero Bajetta; *Publicity:* Floriana De Martino; *Production:* Dario Maggi; *Rights & Permissions:* Dr Flavio Fagnani
Subjects: General Fiction, Belles Lettres, Poetry, Biography, History, Music, Art, Philosophy, Reference, Religion, Juveniles, Low- & High-priced Paperbacks, General & Social Science
1978: 175 titles *1979:* 160 titles *Founded:* 1922

Società Editrice **Napoletana** SRL*, Corso Umberto I 34, I-80138 Naples Tel: (02) 206602
Man Dir: Avv A De Dominicis
Subjects: Belles Lettres, Poetry, History, Art

Nardini Editore — Centro Internazionale del Libro SpA*, Via Gioberti 34, I-50121 Florence Tel: (055) 670451
Subjects: Juveniles, History, Biography, Art, Essays, Classics, Science, Educational
Founded: 1970
Miscellaneous: Part of Giunti Publishing Group (qv)

New Interlitho SpA*, Via Curiel, I-20090 Trezzano S/N Tel: 4451926/4452753 Telex: 32140
Dir & Sales Manager: Renzo Aimini
Subjects: Juveniles, Encyclopaedias

Newton Compton Editori SRL*, Via Germanico 197, I-00192 Rome Tel: 3580205/3580201
Subjects: Paperbacks on General Fiction, Belles Lettres, Poetry, History, Philosophy, Social & General Science, Anthropology, Mathematics, Psychology, Political Science, Reference, How-to, Archaeology

Editrice **Nord** Sdf, Via Rubens 25, I-20148 Milan Tel: 405708/4042207
Man Dir: Gianfranco Viviani; *Editorial:* Sandro Pergameno, Inisero Cremaschi
1978: approx 200 titles
Subjects: Fantasy and Science Fiction

Edizioni di **Novissima***, Via Civitavecchia 102, I-20132 Milan Tel: (02) 2563141/2563151
Subjects: General Fiction, Belles Lettres, Paperbacks

La **Nuova Foglio** SpA*, Piane di Chienti 12, I-62010 Pollenza (MC) Tel: (0733) 517145 Cable Add: La Nuova Foglio Pollenza
Subject: Art

La **Nuova Italia** Editrice*, Via Antonio Giacomini 8, I-50132 Florence Tel: (055) 2798
Man Dirs: Tristano Codignola, Mario Casalini
Branch Offs: Via Dieta di Bari 38/c, I-70121 Bari; Via Brugnoli 7, I-40122 Bologna; Via D Cimarosa 14, I-09100 Cagliari; Via Etnea 688, I-95128 Catania; Corso Italia 158/D, I-87100 Cosenza; Via G Fattori 7-9, I-50132 Florence; Corso Europa 454/A, I-16132 Genoa; Via Boncompagni 51/2, I-20139 Milan; Via G Carducci 15, I-80121 Naples; Via M Buonarroti 4, I-35100 Padua; Via F Cordova 95, I-90143 Palermo; Via P Maroncelli 25, I-65100 Pescara; Viale Carso 44-46, I-00195 Rome; Via Colli 24 (angolo Corso Montevecchio), I-10129 Turin; Via Adigetto 39, I-37100 Verona
Subjects: Biography, History, Art, Philosophy, Reference, Young Adult, Low- & High-priced Paperbacks, Psychology, Social Science, University & Secondary Textbooks
1978: 75 titles *Founded:* 1926

Nuova Vallecchi Editore SpA, Via Gino Capponi 26, CP 409, I-50121 Florence Tel: (055) 587141/2/3 Cable Add: Nuova Vallecchi Editore, Firenze
Man Dir: Lodovico Bevilacqua
Subjects: Art, Fiction, Classics
1978: 80 titles *1979:* 70 titles *Founded:* 1975

O S (Organizzazioni Speciali SRL), CP 1442, I-50136 Florence (Located at: Via S Ammirato 37, Florence) Tel: 672997/675446
Subjects: Psychology, Economics, Education
Miscellaneous: Member of Giunti Publishing Group

Edizioni **Ofiria**, see Giunti Publishing Group

Leo S **Olschki**, CP 66, I-50100 Florence Tel: (055) 687444/5
Shipping Add: Viuzzo del Pozzetto (Viale Europa), I-50126 Florence
Man Dir: Alessandro Olschki
Subjects: Biography, History, Music, Art, Reference, Bibliography, Religion, Paperbacks, Medicine, Social Science, University Textbooks, General Humanities
1978: 102 titles *Founded:* 1886

Olympia Press Italia*, Corso Concordia 9, I-20129 Milan Tel: (02) 780164
Man Dir: Mario Carrillo
Subjects: General Fiction, General Science, Erotica

Edizioni **Omnia** Medica*, Via San Michele degli Schlazi 63, I-56100 Pisa Tel: (050) 570016
Subjects: Science, Medicine

Nuove Edizioni **Operaie** SRL, Via Crescenzio 58, I-00193 Rome Tel: (06) 6545506
Man Dirs: Angelo Ruggieri; Pietro Brugnoli
Subjects: Politics, Sociology, Religion, Culture
1978: 27 titles *1979:* 21 titles *Founded:* 1976

Organizzazioni Speciali SRL, see O S

Edizioni **Orientalia** Christiana*, Piazza Santa Maria Maggiore 7, I-00185 Rome Tel: (06) 7312254/55
General Dir: Ignacio Ortiz de Urbina
Subjects: Eastern Christianity (History, Theology, Liturgy, Canon Law etc), *Periodicals: Orientalia Christiana Analecta, Concilium Florentinum, Documenta et Scriptores, Anaphorae Syriacae*
Founded: 1923

Edizioni **Ottaviano***, Via S Croce 2, I-20122 Milan Tel: 8350832
Subjects: Politics, Law
1978: 25 titles *Founded:* 1974

Paideia Editrice, Via Corsica 58m, I-25100 Brescia Tel: (030) 342523
Man Dir: Prof Dr Giuseppe Scarpat
Subjects: Belles Lettres, Poetry, Music, Art, Philosophy, Religion, University Textbooks
1978: 33 titles *1979:* 35 titles

G B **Palumbo** e C Editore SpA, Via B Ricasoli 59, 90139 Palermo Tel: (091) 588850/334961
Manager: Giovan Battista Palumbo
1978: 27 titles

Panda Press SRL*, Via Curiel 19, I-20090 Trezzano S/N (MI) Tel: 4451926/4452753 Telex: 32140
Man Dir: Renzo Aimini; *Rights & Permissions:* Louise Kissane
Subject: Juveniles
Founded: 1971

Edizioni **Panini** SpA, Viale Emilio Po 380, I-41100 Modena Tel: (059) 331133 Cable Add: Edipan Modena Italia Telex: 510650
Publisher: Franco Panini
Subjects: Educational, Sport, Card albums for children

Edizioni **Paoline**, Corso Regina Margherita 1/2, CP 1333 I-10100 Turin Tel: (011) 836744/5/6/7 Cable Add: Edipaoline
Man Dir, Sales: Gino Pizzeghello; *Editorial:* Valentino Gambi; *Production:* Francesco Chessa; *Publicity:* Lamberto Schiatti
Parent Company: Società San Paolo
Associated Companies: Edizioni Paoline Dischi — Audiovision; Editrice SAIE (qv); Publi EPI-Gruppo Periodici EP, Milan
Subjects: General Fiction, Belles Lettres, Biography, History, How-to, Music, Art, Philosophy, Reference, Religion, Juveniles, Low- & High-priced Paperbacks, Medicine, Psychology
Bookshops: 98 bookshops throughout Italy
1979: 282 titles *Founded:* 1914

Casa Editrice **Pàtron** SAS, Quarto Inferiore, Via Badini 12-14, I-40127 Bologna Tel: 767003
Executive Dir: Bruno Pasquetto; *Production Dir:* Massimo Manzoni
Subjects: Literature, Linguistics, History, Philosophy, Psychology, Sociology, Art, Medicine, Engineering
Bookshops: Libreria Editrice Universitaria Pàtron, Via Marzolo 28, I-35100 Padua; Libreria Internazionale Pàtron, Via Zamboni 24, I-40126 Bologna
1978: 82 titles *1979:* 135 titles

'**Pensiero Scientifico**' SRL*, Via Panama 48, I-00198 Rome Tel: 863633/859506
Subject: Medicine
1978: 34 titles

Piccin Editore sas, Via Brunacci 12, I-35100 Padua Tel: (049) 38955/24841/23350
Man Dir, Editorial, Production, Rights & Permissions: Dr Massimo Piccin; *Sales:* Dr Raffello Steccanella
Subjects: Medicine, Chemistry, General Science
Bookshops: Via Festa del Perdono 14, Milan; Via Porciglia 10, Padua; Via Lancisi 37, Rome
1978: 78 titles *1979:* 75 titles *Founded:* 1954
ISBN Publisher's Prefix: 88-212

Editrice **Piccoli** SpA, Via Rosellini 12, I-20124 Milan Tel: (02) 606341 Cable Add: Lapiccoli Milano
Man Dir, Editorial: Oliviero Dolci; *Sales:* Giuliano Barisone; *Marketing:* Leonardo Vasco
Subject: Children's Books
1978: 50 titles *1979:* 52 titles *Founded:* 1943

La **Pietra**, Via Fulvio Testi 75, I-20126 Milan Tel: (02) 6428440
Man Dir: Enzo Nizza
Subjects: Politics, Anti-Fascism and Resistance, History, Art
1979: 15 titles *1980:* 30 titles *Founded:* 1962

Amilcare **Pizzi** SpA*, Via M de Vizzi 86, Cinisello Balsamo, Milan Tel: (02) 6188821 Telex: 330006
Chairman: Rodolfo Pizzi; *Man Dir:* Fulvio G Nembrini; *Sales:* Gilberto Leuci
Parent Company: Silvana Editoriale SRL (qv)
Subjects: Art, Illustrated Books, Encyclopaedias, Paperbacks, Calendars, Catalogues
Founded: 1920

Neri **Pozza**, CP 513, I-36100 Vicenza (Located at: Via Gazzolle 6, I-36100 Vicenza) Tel: (0444) 27228/36585 Cable Add: Edipozza
Man Dir: Neri Pozza
Subjects: Ancient and Modern Art, Literary Criticism and History, Politics, Local Interest
1978: 14 titles *Founded:* 1946

Priuli e **Verlucca**, Editori*, Via Soana 6, I-10015 Ivrea Tel: (0125) 48364 Cable Add: Priuli Verlucca Ivrea
Chairman: Cesare Verlucca; *Production Dir:* Gherardo Priuli
Subjects: Life and Traditions of the Alpine Region, Mountains and Mountaineering, Photographic Studies of Regional Costume and Culture, Graphic Arts
Founded: 1971

Quadragono Libri, Viale Diaz 8, I-31015 Conegliano (TV) Tel: (0438) 21240/31840
Man Dir: Vigiak Bugara Mario
Subjects: Illustrated books for children and adults
1978: 6 titles *1979:* 6 titles *Founded:* 1974

Editrice **Queriniana**, Via Piamarta 6, I-25100 Brescia Tel: (030) 294653
Man Dir: Gianfranco Ransenigo; *Sales:* Ettore Pelati; *Advertising:* Mario de Risio; *Rights & Permissions:* Rosino Gibellini
Branch Offs: Rome, Milan, Turin, Verona
Subjects: Philosophy, Religion, Theology
Founded: 1965

R Editore*, Via Larga 9, Ortonovo (LS)
Associate Company: Editions R, France (qv)

Edizioni **R A I** Radiotelevisione Italiana (ERI) SpA, see ERI

Franco Maria **Ricci** Editore, Via Cino Del Duca 4/8, I-20122 Milan Tel: (02) 798804/793117/780275 Telex: 313514 Fmri
Man Dir: Franco Maria Ricci
Associate Companies: Fine Books, 160 East, 92 St, New York, USA; Galerie 12, 12 rue des Beaux Arts, Paris 6, France
Subsidiary Company: Deco Press
Subjects: Art, Graphic Design, Reference
Bookshop: Franco Maria Ricci, 12 rue des Beaux-Arts, Paris 6, France
Book Clubs: Club dei Bibliofili; Collectors Club of Franco Maria Ricci
1978: 70 titles *1979:* 11 titles *Founded:* 1965
Miscellaneous: Publish limited editions, including Bodoni editions & *Encyclopédie* of Diderot & D'Alembert

Riccardo **Ricciardi** Editore SRL, Via G Morone 3, I-20121 Milan Tel: (02) 875155/804248
Man Dir: Dr Maurizio Mattioli
Subjects: Italian Classics, History, Philosophy
1978: 6 titles *1979:* 8 titles

Rico SpA*, I-50029 Florence-Certosa Tel: 2020141/2/3 Telex: 57407
Subjects: Art, Scientific, Geography, Posters

Arti Grafiche **Ricordi** SpA, Via Cortina d'Ampezzo 10, I-20139 Milan Tel: (02) 536355 Telex: 31177 Idrocir Cable Add: Graficordi
Man Dir: Giulio Sala
Parent Company: G e C Ricordi SpA (qv)
Subject: Fine Art Prints

G e C **Ricordi** SpA, Via Berchet 2, I-20121 Milan Tel: (02) 8881 Telex: 310177 Ricor I
President: N H Carlo Origoni; *Vice-President:* Eugenio Clausetti; *Man Dir:* Dr Guido Rignano
Subjects: Scholarly, Music, Art
Subsidiary Companies: Ricordi Dischi SpA (at above address); Arti Grafiche Ricordi SpA (qv); Gruppo Editoriale Musica Leggera Ricordi (at above address)
1978: 76 titles

Editori **Riunti**, Via Serchio 9-11, Rome Tel: (06) 866383
Man Dir: Roberto Bonchio; *Sales Dir:* Giuseppe Paschetto; *Publicity & Advertising:* Giovanna Carlo; *Rights & Permissions:* Cecilia Fasano
Subjects: General Fiction, Textbooks, Reference, Paperbacks, History, Art, General & Social Science, Religion, Juveniles
Founded: 1953

Rizzoli Editore SpA*, Via Rizzoli 2, I-20132 Milan Tel: (02) 2588 Cable Add: Rizzoli Editore, Milan Telex: Rizzoli 33119
Chairman: Andrea Rizzoli; *Man Dir:* Angelo Rizzoli; *Editorial:* Dr Sergio Pautasso; *Marketing:* Dr Romano Zago; *Rights & Permissions:* Anita Calabi, Vera Salvago
Subsidiary Companies: Rizzoli Film SpA; Cineriz SpA
Subjects: General Fiction, Belles Lettres, Poetry, Biography, History, Music, Hobbies, Medicine, Art, Religion, Juveniles, Low- & High-priced Paperbacks, Social Science, Reference, Textbooks

Rosenberg e **Sellier** Editori in Torino, Via Andrea Doria 14, I-10123 Turin Tel: (011) 532150 Cable Add: Rosenberg Sellier
Man Dir: Ugo Gianni Rosenberg; *Editorial, Rights & Permissions:* Katie Roggero, Cristina Savio; *Production, Publicity:* Katie Roggero
Subjects: Philology, Social Sciences, Philosophy
Bookshop: Via Andrea Doria, I-10123 Turin
1978: 15 titles *1979:* 24 titles *Founded:* 1883
Miscellaneous: Firm is International import-export bookseller and subscription agent

Rusconi Editore*, Via Oldofredi 23, I-20124 Milan Tel: (02) 6964 Cable Add: Rusconi Editore Milan
Editor: Alfredo Cattabiani; *Sales Dir:* Giuseppe Zanetti; *Publicity Dir:* Carlo Arditi de Castelvetere; *Advertising Dir:* Domenico Cattaneo; *Rights & Permissions:* Maura Bastiglia
Branch Off: Via Leonida Bissolati 76, I-00100 Rome
Subjects: General Fiction, Belles Lettres, Poetry, History, Philosophy, Religion, Low- and High-priced Paperbacks
Bookshops: Libreria Internaz Rusconi, Via Vitruvio 43, I-20124 Milan & Via Carlo Porta 1, Milan
Founded: 1957

S A G E P, Piazza Merani 1, I-16145 Genoa Tel: (010) 313453 Telex: 211343 SAGEP I
Publisher: Eugenio de Andreis; *Sales Manager:* Carla Bisacchi; *Press Chief:* Carla Costa
Subjects: Architecture, Art, Economy, Ethnography, History, Natural Sciences, Travel and Tourism
1978: 46 titles *1979:* 42 titles *Founded:* 1965

S A I E Editrice*, Corso Regina Margherita 2, I-10153 Turin Tel: (011) 870887
Associate Company: Edizioni Paoline (qv)
Subjects: Reference, Encyclopaedias, Dictionaries, Literature Criticism, Multimedia, Philosophy, Linguistics, Languages, Economics, Religion, Medicine, History, Earth Sciences, Philosophy, Education, Art, Juveniles

S C O D E, Via Ampère 28/a, I-20131 Milan Tel: (02) 2360244/5 Cable Add: SCODE Milano
President: Carlo Gandini
Subjects: Architecture, History, Hobbies, Arts, Maps, Literary Criticism, Religion, Encyclopaedias, Linguistics, Educational

S E I (Società Editrice Internazionale), Corso Regina Margherita 176, I-10152 Turin Tel: (011) 481604/5/6/7/8 Cable Add: SEI Turin Telex: 221114 CSIND I 114 SEI
Man Dir: Gian Nicola Pivano; *Editorial:* Francesco Meotto; *Sales:* Paolo Bottazzi; *Production:* Enrico Paolucci Delle Rowcole
Branch Off: at Bari, Bologna, Florence, Genoa, Milan, Naples, Palermo, Padua, Rome, Turin, Pescara, Catania
Subjects: General Fiction, Belles Lettres, Biography, History, Art, Philosophy, Religion, Juveniles, Psychology, General & Social Science, Educational Materials, Textbooks, Paperbacks
1978: 110 titles *Founded:* 1910

S I S A R Edizioni (Società italiana stampati affini reclame) SpA, Via Marco d'Agrate 35, I-20139 Milan Tel: (02) 5393846/5397441/2
Man Dir: Occhipinti Mazio
Subjects: Art, Architecture
1978: 30 titles *Founded:* 1953

S T E M-Mucchi (Società Tipografica Editrice Modenese)*, Via Tabboni 4, I-41100 Modena Tel: (059) 222162/214152
Subjects: History, Philosophy, Science, Technical, Textbooks, Hobbies, Literature, Education, Law, Languages
1978: 6 titles

Saar SRL, Viale di Porta Vercellina 14, I-20123 Milan Tel: (02) 4696251 Cable Add: Saar Milano
Man Dir: Walter Gurtler; *Sales:* Sergio Balloni
Subject: Juveniles

Il **Saggiatore** SpA, Via San Senatore 10, I-20122 Milan Tel: (02) 875119/875892
Man Dir: Maria Laura Boselli; *Rights & Permissions:* Elena Panizza
Subjects: History, Philosophy, Economics, Architecture, Mathematics, Social Sciences, Geography, Linguistics, Art, Music, Belles Lettres, Afro-Asian Studies, Latin American Studies, Juveniles
1978: 40 titles *Founded:* 1958

La **Salamandra**, Via Fabio Filzi 27, I-20124 Milan Tel: (02) 667097
Man Dir, Editorial, all other offices: Giovanni Barbatiello
Subjects: Feminism, Critiques of society, Libertarian thought, Critical Marxism, Sexual freedom, Psychoanalysis, Biography, Autobiography
Bookshop: Celuc Libri SRL, Via Santa Valeria 5, I-20123 Milan
1978: 16 titles *1979:* 12 titles *Founded:* 1975

Salamon e Agustoni Editori, Via Montenapoleone 3, I-20121 Milan Tel: (02) 700832
Man Dir: H Salamon
Subject: Art, Il Conoscitore di stampe — Print Collector
Founded: 1970

Adriano **Salani** SpA, Via Cittadella 7, I-50144 Florence Tel: (055) 472968/9 Cable Add: Salani Editore Florence
Man Dir: Mauro Finardi
Subjects: Art, Classics, History, Juveniles, Fiction
Founded: 1862

Casa Editrice G C **Sansoni** SpA*, Via Varchi 47, I-50132 Florence Tel: (055) 571334 Cable Add: Sansedi Telex: 57466 Sansint
Man Dir: Federico Gentile; *General Manager:* Giovanni Gentile; *Publicity & Advertising:* Mario Biondi
Associate Companies: USES-Utet/Sansoni Edizioni Scientifiche, Via J Nardi 37, I-50132 Florence; SADEA SpA, Viale Mazzini 46, I-50132 Florence
Subsidiary Companies: Licosa-Libreria Commissionaria Sansoni SpA, Via Lamarmora 45, I-50132 Florence; Industria Grafica L'Impronta SpA, Via di Scandicci Alto 28, I-50018 Scandicci (Florence)
Subjects: Belles Lettres, Poetry, Biography, History, How-to, Music, Art, Philosophy, Reference, Religion, Low- & High-priced Paperbacks, Medicine, Psychology, General & Social Science, Secondary & Primary Textbooks, Educational Materials, Juveniles, Law
Founded: 1873
Miscellaneous: Coproduction with Sansoni International

Scala Istituto Fotografico Editoriale*, Via Chiantigiana 56, I-50011 Antella-Florence Tel: (055) 641541 Cable Add: Scalafoto Telex: Scalapub 58428
Subjects: Textbooks, Multimedia, Illustrated Art Books, Photography, Slides

Salvatore **Sciascia**, Corso Umberto 111, I-93100 Caltanissetta Tel: 21946
Subjects: Fiction, History, Business, Industry, Arts, Maps, Agriculture, Literature, Mass Media, Medicine, Music, Education, Philosophy, Politics, Psychology, Religion, Social Sciences, Linguistics
Bookshops: Corso Umberto 111, Caltanissetta; Via Liberta 86, Caltanissetta
Founded: 1946

Libreria **Scientifica Editrice***, Corso Umberto I 38-40, I-80138 Naples Tel: (02) 206247
Dir: Dr A De Dominicis
Associate Company: Società Editrice Napoletana SRL (qv)
Subjects: Belles Lettres, Poetry, History, Philosophy, Low-priced Paperbacks, University & Secondary Textbooks
Bookshop: Corso Umberto I-38-40, I-80138 Naples
Founded: 1944

Edizioni **Scientifiche Italiane***, Via Chiatamone 7, I-80121 Naples Tel: (081) 393346/391921/230021
Subjects: General & Social Science, Architecture, History, Arts, Maps, Agriculture, Literature, Medicine, Music, Philosophy, Law, Religion, Languages

Edizioni **Scolastiche** APE SpA, Via Abbondio Sangiorgio 12, I-20145 Milan Tel: (02) 315118/341807
Man Dir: Dr Franco Turri
Subjects: Textbooks
1979: 35 titles *Founded:* 1974
Miscellaneous: Firm is a subsidiary of Ugo Mursia Editore SpA (qv)

Editrice La **Scuola** SpA, Via Cadorna 11, Brescia Tel: (030) 47461 Cable Add: Lascuola Brescia Telex: 300836 Scuola
President: Dr Ing Paolo Peroni; *Man Dir:* Dr Ing Adolfo Lombardi; *General Manager:* Dr Prof Giusto Marchese
Associate Companies: E Co S Didattica SpA, I-10799 Rome, Italy; Morcelliana Editrice (qv); Edizione Studium (Vita Nova SpA) (qv)
Branch Offs: Bari, Bologna, Milan, Naples, Rome
Subjects: Philosophy, Religion, Juveniles, Psychology, Secondary & Primary Textbooks, Educational Materials
1978: 200 titles *1979:* 150 titles *Founded:* 1904

Sellerio Editore, Via Siracusa 50, I-90141 Palermo Tel: (091) 250390/250587
Subjects: Literature, Popular Art, Anthropology, Archaeology, History, Photography, Semiotics, Sociology
1978: 21 titles *1979:* 19 titles *Founded:* 1969

Silvana Editoriale Srl, Via M de Vizzi 86, I-20092 Cinisello Balsamo, Milan Tel: (02) 6172464
Chairman: Rodolfo Pizzi; *Foreign Rights:* Fulvio G Nembrini
Parent Company: Amilcare Pizzi SpA, Italy (qv)
Subjects: Art, Facsimile books, Photographs, Architecture, Illustrated books
1978: 13 titles

Sonzogno SpA*, Via Mecenate 87/6, I-20138 Milan Tel: (02) 501101/2/3 Telex: 32321
Dir: Vittorio Di Giuro
Subjects: Fiction, Crafts, Nonfiction, Games, Sports, Hobbies, Languages
Founded: 1861

La **Sorgente** Srl, Via Garofalo 44, I-20133 Milan Tel: (02) 230025 and 230720
Man Dir, Rights & Permissions: Dr Giorgio Vignati
Subject: Juveniles
1979: 80 titles *Founded:* 1936

Sperling e Kupfer Editori SpA, Via Monte di Pietà 24, I-20121 Milan Tel: 861980/867358/8056407 Cable Add: Kupferedit, Milan
General Manager: Tiziano M Barbieri; *Editor-in-Chief:* Nino Mandato; *Rights & Permissions:* Marica Fioroni
Subjects: General Fiction & Nonfiction, Biography, Health, Travel, Sports, How-to
1979: 80 titles *1980:* 80 titles *Founded:* 1889

Le **Stelle** SpA, Via G Vasari 15, I-20135 Milan Tel: (02) 5455641
Subjects: General Fiction, Belles Lettres, Poetry, Biography, History, Religion, Juveniles, Secondary & Primary Textbooks, Educational Materials
1978: 26 titles *1979:* 17 titles *Founded:* 1954

Studio Editoriale*, Via Spiga 1, I-20121 Milan Tel: (02) 784129
Subjects: Textbooks, Juveniles, Flowers, Herbalism, Graphics

Edizioni **Studium** (Vita Nova SpA), Via Crescenzio 63, I-00193 Rome Tel: (06) 6565846/655456 Cable Add: Studium Rome
Associate Company: Editrice La Scuola SpA (qv)
Subjects: Literature, Pedagogy, Psychology, History, Philosophy, Religion, General & Social Science, University Textbooks, Periodical—*Studium*
1978: 33 titles *Founded:* 1973

Sugarco Edizioni SRL*, Viale Tunisia 41, I-20154 Milan Tel: (02) 652192/6570569
Man Dir: Dr Massimo Pini; *Editorial:* Massimo Rondinelli; *Sales:* Vincenzo Nagari; *Production:* Gianni Bagetto
Subjects: General Fiction, Belles Lettres, Biography, History, Philosophy, Guides
Founded: 1956

Tamburini Editore SpA*, Via Pascoli 55, I-20133 Milan Tel: (02) 292320/296662/235740/235772 Cable Add: Tambeditor Milan
Man Dir: Gianni Tamburini; *Sales Dir:* Laura Piatti; *Publicity & Advertising, Rights & Permissions:* Sergio Guida
Subjects: Medicine, Psychology, Engineering, General Science, University & Secondary Textbooks
Bookshop: Via Pascole 55, I-20133 Milan
Founded: 1868

Nicola **Teti** e C Editore SRL*, Via Enrico Nöe 23, I-20133 Milan Tel: (02) 2043597/2043539
Man Dir: Nicola Teti; *Editorial:* Piero Lavatelli; *Sales:* Vincenzo Fracchiolla; *Production:* Rita Vaccari, Vanna Guzzi; *Publicity:* Nino Oppo; *Rights & Permissions:* Rita Vaccari
Subjects: Textbooks, Encyclopaedias, Politics, Marxism, Social Science, Juveniles, Reprints of Socialist documents, Natural History, History, Pedagogy
Founded: 1971

Trec Edizioni Pregiate, Via Cassia Antica 132, I-00191 Rome Tel: 3288361
Sole Administrator: Antonino Pecora
Subjects: Old Artistic Treasures, Graphics, Reproduction of Antique Manuscripts, Illuminated Miniatures
Founded: 1971

Edizioni Il **Tripode** SRL, Viale Gramsci 12, I-80122 Naples Tel: (081) 683086
Man Dir: Dott Giuseppe Martano

U T E T (Unione Tipografico-Editrice Torinese)*, Corso Raffaello 28, CP 1166 Ferrovia, I-10125 Turin Tel: (011) 688666
Cable Add: UTET Turin
President: Dr Gianni Merlini
Subjects: Belles Lettres, History, Art, Architecture, Music, Religion, Philosophy, Reference, Psychology, Law, Veterinary Science, General & Social Science, Juveniles, University Textbooks
Founded: 1795

Unites SRL, Annuario Politecnico Italiano, Via Silvio Pellico 12, I-20121 Milan Tel: (02) 874566/874658 Telex: 334647 Techs I
Publicity: Gianola Carlo
Subjects: Year-books, Reference

Editrice **Universitaria**, see Giunti Publishing Group

Società Editrice **Universo***, Via G Battista Morgagni 1, I-00161 Rome Tel: (06) 859063/8445243
Subjects: Medicine, Physics, Chemistry, Engineering, Mathematics

Antonio **Vallardi** Editore*, Via Senato 25, I-20121 Milan Tel: (02) 705741/4
Telex: Garzal 31461
Dir: Luciano Schinetti
Subjects: Art, How-to, Reference, Industries, Maps, Juveniles, Textbooks, Literature, Travel, Architecture
Founded: 1822

Vallardi Industrie Grafiche, Via Trieste 20, I-20020 Lainate (Milan) Tel: (02) 9370284/5 Cable Add: Valgraf, Lainate
Publisher: Giuseppe Vallardi; *Dir:* Victor Hayow; *Editorial:* Elisabetta Vallardi
Subjects: Atlases, Juveniles

Augusto **Vallerini** Editore di Alberto Vallerini*, Via Consoli del Mare 15, Pisa Tel: 40604
Orders to: Andrea Vallerini (Libri Esteri e Abbonamenti), Via dei Mille 13, I-56100 Pisa Tel: 40393
Subjects: Pisa — past and present, Italian Scientific and Medical books, Reprints

Società Editrice **Vannini***, Viale d'Italia 8b, CP 68, I-25100 Brescia Tel: (030) 56272/57089 Cable Add: Vannini Brescia
Subjects: Scholastic, Reference, Law
1978: 13 titles

Giovanni de **Vecchi** Editore SpA, see De Vecchi

Z I R A L (Zajednica Izdanja Ranjeni Labud)*, Via Merulana 124b, Rome
Dirs: Dr Lucijan Kordic, Professor Dr D Vinko Lasic
Head Off: 4851 Drexel Blvd, Chicago Il, 60515 USA
Subjects: Religion, History, Literature

Nicola **Zanichelli** SpA*, Via Irnerio 34, I-40126 Bologna Tel: (051) 293111
Chairman: Giovanni Enriques
Subjects: History, Philosophy, Reference, Mathematics, Chemistry, Biology, Engineering, General Science, University & Secondary Textbooks, Law, Psychology, Visual Design, Architecture, Juveniles, Physics, Electronics, Linguistics, Literature, Geography, Earth Sciences, Paperbacks
Bookshop: Libreria Zanichelli, Portici del Pavaglione, CP 227, I-40124 Bologna
Founded: 1859

Casa Editrice La **Zattera***, Largo C Felice 76, I-09100 Cagliari
Bookshop: Libreria Internazionale Fratelli Cocco, Largo C Felice 76, Cagliari
Subjects: Books on Sardinia

Literary Agents

Agenzia Letteraria Internazionale*, Via Manzoni 41, I-20121 Milan Tel: (02) 6572465/6572594/6572596

Maria-Pia **D'Arborio***, Viale Tiziano 5, Rome

Ursula **Caputo***, Via Pisacane 25, I-20129 Milan

Dais Literary Agency, Via di Santa Maria in Monticelli 67, 00186 Rome Tel: (06) 655356

Eulama SA*, Via Torino 135, I-00184 Rome Tel: (06) 460636
President: Harald Kahnemann
Specializes in social sciences, politics, psychology, education, philosophy, religion, linguistics and literature, mass-media, architecture, urban studies, Latin-American literature and books for young readers

I L A (International Literary Agency), I-18015 Terzorio — IM Tel: San Remo (0184) 484048 Cable Add: Friedmann Terzorio (IM)
Specializes in handling of foreign language translation rights to multi-volume book and magazine projects, Children's books, Encyclopedias, Best Sellers (in all European languages)

Living Literary Agency Elfriede Pexa, Via E Q Visconti 103, I-00193 Rome Tel: (06) 381720 Cables: Living Roma

William **Morris** Organization SpA*, Via Nomentana 60, I-00161 Rome

Natoli and Stefan Literary Agency*, Galleria Buenos Aires 14, I-20124 Milan

Christa **Pucci***, Largo Generale Gonzaga del Vodicez, I-00195 Rome Tel: (06) 317996

Rizzoli Editore SpA*, Via Rizzoli 2, I-20132 Milan

Transafrica*, Via Trieste 34, I-25100 Brescia Tel: (03) 55080/54844
Specialization: African Subjects

Book Clubs

Club Degli Editori*, Viale Majno 10, I-20129 Milan
Owned by: Arnoldo Mondadori Editore (Milan)

Club dei Bibliofili, Via Cino del Duca 4-8, I-20122 Milan
Owned by: Franco Maria Ricci Editore (Milan)

Collectors Club of Franco Maria Ricci, Via Santa Sofia 8, I-20122 Milan
Owned by: Franco Maria Ricci Editore (Milan)

Major Booksellers

Casalini Libri*, Via B da Maiano 3, I-50014 Fiesole (Florence) Tel: (055) 599941 Cable Add: Casalini Fiesole
Man Dirs: Mario Casalini, Gerda Casalini von Grebmer
General Book Exporter

Libreria Internazionale Fratelli **Cocco***, Largo C Felice 76, I-09100 Cagliari, Sardinia
Also at Via Manno 9, I-09100 Cagliari, Sardinia

Libreria **Feltrinelli***, Via del Babuino 41, Rome Tel: (06) 6793360; Via Carlo Alberto 2 and Piazza Castello 9, Turin; Piazza Porta Ravegnana 1, Bologna; Via Cavour 12-20, I-50129 Florence Tel: (055) 292196

Libreria SF **Flaccovio**, Via Ruggiero Settimo 37, I-90139 Palermo

Libreria **Gregoriana***, Via Roma 37, I-35100 Padua
Also at Via Vescovado 33, I-35100 Padua

Ulrico **Hoepli** Libreria Internazionale, Via Hoepli 5, I-20121 Milan Tel: (02) 865446
Managers: Dr Ulrico Carlo Hoepli, Roberto Taneggi

Libreria **Liberma**, Via di Saponara 20A, I-00125 Acilia-Roma, CP 492 (San Silvestro) Roma

Libreria A **Longo**, Via A Diaz 39, I-48100 Ravenna Tel: (0544) 33500

Libreria G **Luna***, I-06034 Foligno

Libreria Editrice **Minerva***, Via Castiglione 13-15, Bologna

Libreria Commissionaria Internazionale di Raffaele **Pancaldi**, Via S Petronio Vecchio 3, I-40125 Bologna Tel: (051) 229466
Manager: Raffaele Pancaldi

Libreria Internazionale **Pàtron**, Via Zamboni 24, I-40126 Bologna Tel: (051) 275735

Libreria all' Accademia SNC di **Randi** Pietro*, Via S Lucia 1, I-35100 Padua
(The above is the head office address only)
Shops: Libreria Draghi-Randi, Via Cavour 17-19; Libreria Universitaria, Via 8 Febbraio 10; Libraria Accademia,Via Accademia 2-4; Libreria Nuova Moderna, Via Paolotti 5 (all CP 1003, I-35100 Padua Tel: (049) 20425/35976/26676/24525/26648

Libreria **Rizzoli***, Galleria Colonna, Largo Chigi, Rome
Manager: Enrico Di Nappo
Galleria Vittorio Emanuele II 79, I-20121 Milan
Manager: Attilio Pupella

Rosenberg e Sellier SRL, Via Andrea Doria 14, I-10123 Turin
Proprietors: Ugo Gianni Rosenberg, Elvi Rosenberg
International import-export booksellers and subscription agents

Libreria **Rosmini** di R Maly*, Corso Rosmini 30, I-38068 Rovereto

Libreria **Seeber***, Via dei Tornabuoni 70 r, I-50123 Florence

Libreria **Sperling & Kupfer**, Piazza San Babila 1, I-20122 Milan Tel: 701495/790712/791912
Manager: Onorato Ciriotti

Major Libraries

Biblioteca **Ambrosiana**, Piazza Pio XI, 2, I-20123 Milan Tel: (02) 800146
Librarian: Angelo Paredi

Biblioteca **Angelica**, Piazza S Agostino 8, I-00186 Rome Tel: (06) 655874

Biblioteca Comunale dell' **Archiginnasio***, Portici del Pavaglione, Piazza Galvani 1, I-40124 Bologna Tel: 225509/279565

Biblioteca dell' **Archivio Storico** Civico e Biblioteca Trivulziana, Castello Sforzesco, I-20121 Milan Tel: 6236, int 3946/3960/3967
Librarian: Prof Dr Giulia Bologna

Archivio Centrale dello Stato, Piazzale degli Archivi, EUR, I-00144 Rome Tel: (06) 596555
General Dir: Prof Dr Renato Grispo
National Archives

Biblioteca **Universitaria**, Largo Porta S Agostino 309, I-41100 Modena Tel: Central (059) 222248; Director 230195

Biblioteca **Nazionale Braidense**, Palazzo di Brera, Via Brera 28, I-20121 Milan Tel: (02) 872376/808345
Dir: Dr Letizia Pecorella Vergnano

Biblioteca **Nazionale Centrale***, Piazza Cavalleggeri 1, Florence Tel: 287052; Director 294423

Biblioteca **Nazionale Centrale**, Vittorio Emanuele II, Viale Castro Pretorio, I-00185 Rome Tel: (06) 4989
Dir: Dr Luciana Mancusi

Biblioteca **Nazionale Marciana**, Palazzi della Libreria Vecchia e della Zecca, San Marco 7, I-30124 Venice Tel: (041) 708788
Dir: Dr Gian Albino Ravalli Modoni

Biblioteca **Nazionale Vittorio Emanuele III***, I-80132 Naples (Palazzo Reale) Tel: (081) 407921/40282/425093/416212
Dir: Dr Maria Cecaro

Biblioteca Musicale Governativa del **Conservatorio di Musica** S Cecilia*, Via dei Greci 18, Rome Tel: (06) 6784552/12

Biblioteca **Estense**, Largo Porta San Agostino 309, I-41100 Modena Tel: Central (059) 222248; Director 230195

European University Institute Library, Badia Fiesolana, Via dei Roccettini 5, I-50016 San Domenico di Fiesole, Florence Tel: (055) 477931 Telex: 58528 ive

Biblioteca Medicea **Laurenziana**, Piazza S Lorenzo 9, I-50123 Florence Tel: (055) 210760/214443
Chief Librarian: Dr Antonietta Morandini

Biblioteca Comunale **Malatestiana**, Piazza Bufalini 1, I-47023 Cesena (Forlì) Tel: 21297
Librarian: Dr Antonio Brasini

Biblioteca **Palatina***, Palazzo della Pilotta, Parma Tel: (0521) 22217

Biblioteca **Riccardiana**, Via dei Ginori 10, I-50129 Florence Tel: (055) 212586, 211379
Dir: Dr Maria Jole Minicucci

Università degli Studi di Firenze, Biblioteca della Facolta di Lettere e Filosofia, Piazza Brunelleschi, I-50121 Florence Tel: (55) 264081
Dir: Dr Tomaso Urso

Library Associations

Associazione Italiana Biblioteche, c/o Istituto di Patologia del Libro, Via Milano 76, I-00184 Rome
Italian Library Association
Chairman: Dr Angela Vinay; *Secretary:* Dr Attilio Mauro Caproni
Publications: Bollettino d'Informazioni; Quaderni del Bollettino d'Informazione

Associazione Italiana per la Documentazione e Informazione*, Piazza Indipendenza 11 B, I-00185 Rome
Italian Association of Documentation and Information
Secretary: Rag Bruno Fratter
Publications: Documentazione e Informazione (yearly)

Associazione Nazionale Archivistica Italiana*, Viale Trastevere 215, I-00153 Rome
National Association of Italian Archivists
Secretary: Antonio Dentoni-Litta
Publication: Archivi e Cultúra (2 a year)

Ente Nazionale per le Biblioteche Popolari e Scolastiche*, Via Michele Mercati 4, I-00197 Rome
National Organization for Public and Academic Libraries
Publication: La Parola e il Libro (monthly)

Federazione Italiana delle Biblioteche Popolari*, c/o La 'Società Umanitaria', Via Daverio 7, I-20122 Milan
Federation of Italian Public Libraries
General Dir: Marco Cavallotti
Publication: La Cultura Popolare (6 a year)

Istituto Centrale per il Catalogo Unico delle Biblioteche Italiane e per le Informazioni Bibliografiche*, Viale del Castro Pretorio, Rome
Central Institute of the Union Catalogue of Italian Libraries and Bibliographical Information
Publications: Bibliografia Nazionale Italiana; Manuale del Catalogatore; Soggettario per i Cataloghi delle Biblioteche Italiane

Istituto Centrale per la Patologia del Libro, Via Milano 76, I-00184 Rome
Central Institute of Book Pathology
Dir: Dr Maria Di Franco

Library Reference Books and Journals

Books

Almanàcco dei Bibliotecari Italiani (Almanac of Italian Libraries), Fratelli Palombi Editori, Via del Gracchi 181-185, I-00192 Rome

Annuario Bibliografico per Le Biblioteche (Bibliographical Annual for Libraries), Federation of Italian Public Libraries, c/o La 'Società Umanitaria', Via Daverio 7, I-20122 Milan

Annuario delle Biblioteche Italiane (Italian Library Annual), Fratelli Palombi Editore, Via del Gracchi 181-185, I-00192 Rome

Guida delle Biblioteche Italiane (Guide to Italian Libraries), National Organization for Public and Academic Libraries, Via Michele Mercati 4, I-00197 Rome

Journals

Accademie e Biblioteche d'Italia (Academies and Libraries of Italy), Fratelli Palombi Editori, Via del Gracchi 181-185, I-00192 Rome

Archivi e Cultura (Archives and Culture), National Association of Italian Archivists, Viale Trastevere 215, I-00153 Rome

Bollettino d'Informazioni (Information Bulletin), Italian Library Association, c/o Istituto di Patologia del Libro, Via Milano 76, I-00184 Rome

La Cultura Popolare (Popular Culture), Federation of Italian Public Libraries, c/o La 'Società Umanitaria', Via Daverio 7, I-20122 Milan

Manuale del Catalogatore (Cataloguing Manual), Central Institute of the Union Catalogue of Italian Libraries and Bibliographical Information, Viale del Castro Pretorio, Rome

La Parola e il Libro (The Word and the Book), National Organization for Public and Academic Libraries, Via Michele Mercati 4, I-00197 Rome

Soggettario per i Cataloghi delle Biblioteche Italiane (Subject Collections in Italian Libraries), Central Institute of the Union Catalogue of Italian Libraries and Bibliographical Information, Viale del Castro Pretorio, Rome

Literary Associations and Societies

Accademia di Scienze, Lettere ed Arti*, Piazza Indipendenza 17, Palermo
Secretary: Professor Romualdo Giuffrida

Accademia Ligure di Scienze e Lettere*, Via Balbi 10, I-16126 Genoa
Secretary-General: P Scotti

Accademia Nazionale di Scienze, Lettere ed Arti*, Palazzo Coccapani, Corso Vittorio Emanuele II 59, Modena
President: Professor Antonio Pignedoli
Publications: Atti e Memorie

Accademia Petrarca di Lettere, Arti e Scienze*, Via dell'Orto Arezzo
Secretary: Dr Guido Goti
Publication: Atti e *Memorie della Accademia, Studi Petrarcheschi*

Accademia Toscana di Scienze e Lettere la Colombaria*, Via S Egidio 21-23, Florence

Accademia Virgiliana di Scienze, Lettere ed Arti di Mantova, Via Accademia 47, I-46100 Mantua Tel: (0376) 320314
Secretary: Comm G Amadei
Periodical Publication: Atti e Memorie NS (annual)

Istituto Lombardo Accademia di Scienze e Lettere*, Via Brera 28, I-20121 Milan
President: Prof A Giordano
Publications: Rendiconti della Sezione di Scienze Matematiche e Naturali, Rendiconti della Sezione di Scienze Biologiche e Mediche, Rendiconti della Classe di Scienze Morali, Rendiconti-Parte Generale e Atti Ufficiali, Memorie della Classe di Scienze Matematiche e Naturali, Memorie della Classe di Scienze Morali, Proceedings and Symposiums

Keats-Shelley Memorial Association, Piazza di Spagna 26, Rome
Dir: Sir Joseph Cheyne
Publications: Bulletin, Journal, A Room in Rome by Vera Cacciatore

P E N International Centre*, Via Fratelli Ruspoli 2, Rome
President: Maria Bellonci

Società Dante Alighieri*, Palazzo di Firenze, Piazza Firenze 27, I-00186 Rome
Secretary-General: G Cota
For the teaching and diffusion of Italian language and culture throughout the world

Società Dantesca Italiana, Via dell'Arte della Lana 1, I-50123 Florence
President: Prof Dr Francesco Mazzoni
Publications: Studi Danteschi, Quaderni degli Studi Danteschi, Edizione Nazionale delle Opere di Dante Alighieri (Library open to public)

Società Letteraria*, Piazzetta Scalette Rubiani 1, Verona
Dir: Alfonso Balis Crema
Publication: Bollettino (annually)

Literary Periodicals

Belfagor, Leo S Olschki, CP 66, I-50100 Florence

Bibliofilia (Bibliophily) (text in English, French, German and Italian), Leo S Olschki, CP 66, I-50100 Florence

Il giornale storico della letteratura italiana (Historical Journal of Italian Literature), Loescher Editore, Via Vittorio Amedeo 18, I-10121 Turin

Italia Che Scrive (The Italy That Writes), Via dei Banchi Vecchi 61, Rome

Lettere Italiane (Italian Letters), Viuzzo del Pozzetto (Viale Europa), I-50126 Florence

Libri Paese Sera (*Paese Sera* book supplement), Società Editrice 'Il Rinnovamento', Via dei Taurini 19, I-00185 Rome

Nuòva Corrènte (New Current) (text in several languages), Via Lattuada 26, Milan

Paideia; literary review with bibliographical information (text in English, French, German and Italian), Via Corsica 58m, I-25100 Brescia

Penarete-Letture d'Italia (Readings from Italy), Via Beruto 7, I-20131 Milan

Pròve di Letteratura (Examinations of Literature), Nino Palumbo, Via Ai Castagneti 4, San Michele di Pagana, Rapallo

Rassegna della Letteratura Italiana (Review of Italian Literature), Casa Editrice GC Sansoni SpA, Viale Mazzini 46, I-50132 Florence

Revue des Etudes italiennes, Librairie Marcel Didier SA, 15 rue Cujas, F-75005 Paris

Rivista di Letteratura Moderne e Comparate (Review of Modern and Comparative Literature) (text in English, French and Italian), Casa Editrice G C Sansoni SpA, Viale Mazzini 46, I-50132 Florence

Uomini e libri (Men and Books), Emme Edizioni, Via San Maurilio 13, I-20123 Milan

Literary Prizes

Andersen Prize*
For a fairy tale for children. 300,000 lire. Awarded annually. Enquiries to Comune di Sestri Levante, CP 60, Genoa

Bagutta Prize
For the best book of the year, given for several literary forms including the novel and poetry. Awarded annually. Enquiries to Bagutta Restaurant, Via Bagutta 14, Milan

Bancarella Prize
Founded in 1953 for books of high quality and great popular appeal. A golden album is awarded annually. The 1979 winner was Massimo Grillandi for *La Contessa di Castiglione* (Rusconi). Enquiries to Unione Librai Pontremolesi, Via Ricci Armani 8, Pontremoli, Massa Carrara

Bancarellino Prize
Founded in 1958 for children's books of high quality and great popular appeal, preferably written by an Italian author. A golden album is awarded annually. The 1979 winner was Santesso of Padoa for *La Carica della Patate* (AMZ Editore). Enquiries to Unione Librai Pontremolesi, Via Ricci Armani 8, Pontremoli, Massa Carrara

Campiello Prize
For the best Italian prose works. 10,000,000 lire. Awarded annually. Enquiries to Ca' Mocenigo Gambara, Secretariat of the Campiello Prize, Accademia 1056, Venice

Castello-Sanguinetto Prize
For a novel for young readers between 11 and 14. 1,500,000 lire and 750,000 lire. Awarded annually. Enquiries to Castello-Sanguinetto Prize, Community of Sanguinetto, Verona

Golden Book Prize
To the publisher who has most influenced the public culturally. Awarded annually. Enquiries to Italian Council of Ministers, Via Bancopagni 15, Rome

Golden Pen Prize*
To an author who has made an important contribution to Italian culture. 5,000,000 lire. Awarded annually. Enquiries to Italian Council of Ministers, Via Bancopagni 15, Rome

Laura Orvieto Prize*
For the manuscript of a book of fiction or poetry for children. 1,000,000 lire for a novel and 500,000 lire for poetry. Awarded every other year. Enquiries to Orvieto Prize, Piazza Indipendenza 23, Florence

Strega Prize*
Founded in 1947 by the Strega liquor producer Alberti for the best novel of the year. 1,000,000 lire. Awarded annually. Enquiries to Strega Prize, Via Fratelli Ruspoli 2, Rome

Tormargana Prize*
To outstanding writers, publishers, artists, architects, actors and film makers. Awarded every few months. Enquiries to Angelino Restaurant (Hosteria Angelino a Tormargana), Piazza Margana 37, I-00186 Rome

Viareggio Prizes
For the best novel, poetry, essay, best first work, occasionally for drama and journalism. Sometimes given to foreign writers and poets. 3,000,000 lire. Awarded annually. Enquiries to Viareggio Prize, Via Lima 28, Rome

Villa Benia Prize*
For the best storybook for young readers. Enquiries to International Institute for the Elimination of Speech Deficiencies, Villa Benia, Rapallo

Olga Visentini Prize*
For the best book for young people. 500,000 lire. Awarded biennially. Enquiries to Olga Visentini Foundation, Cerea, Verona

Translation Agencies and Associations

Associazione Italiana Traduttori e Interpreti (AITI)*, Via Arrigo Boito 126, 00199 Rome Tel: 8393457
Italian Association of Translators and Interpreters
Secretary: Anna Bonanome-Via

Eulama*, Via Torino 135, I-00184 Rome Tel: (06) 460636 (also Publisher and Literary Agent)

Transafrica, Via Trieste 34, I-25100 Brescia Tel: (030) 55080
Specialization: African texts

Ivory Coast

General Information

Language: French
Religion: Animism, Muslim and some Christian
Population: 7.6 million
Bank Hours: 0800-1130, 1430-1630 Monday-Friday
Shop Hours: 0800-1200, 1430-1830 or 1900 Monday-Friday; 0800-1200, 1430-1730 Saturday
Currency: CFA franc
Export/Import Information: Member of West African Economic Community. No tariff on books; single copies free but most advertising subject to 5% customs duty, 20% fiscal duty and 20.5% VAT. No import licences required for imports from EEC or Franc Zone.
Copyright: Berne, Florence (see International section)

Book Trade Reference Journal

Bibliographie de la Côte-d'Ivoire, Bibliothèque universitaire, BP 8859, Abidjan (the national bibliography, published annually in two volumes since 1969)

IVORY COAST — JAMAICA 223

Publishers

Centre d'Edition et de Diffusion africaines*, BP 4541, Abidjan Plateau Tel: 222055/228137 Telex: Ediceda 2451
Man Dir: Venance Kacou; *Editorial Dir:* Christian Lescure
Subjects: General Nonfiction, Biography, History, Africana, Philosophy, Reference, Religion, Juveniles, Law, Paperbacks, General & Social Science, Secondary & Primary Textbooks
Bookshop: At above address
1977-78: 21 titles
Miscellaneous: Distributors on behalf of INADES, the National University of the Ivory Coast, and the bibliotheque nationale

Centre de Publications Evangeliques, 08 BP 900, Abidjan 08 Tel: 444805
Dir: Marjorie Shelley; *Administrator:* E T Emmett
Subjects: General Nonfiction, Religion, Christian Tracts, Paperbacks, Periodicals for adults and children
1978: 22 titles *1979:* 25 titles *Founded:* 1970

Government Printer, Imprimerie nationale, BP V87, Abidjan

I N A D E S — Edition (Institut africain pour le developpement économique et social)*, 08 BP 8, Abidjan 08 Tel: 441594
Man Dir, Editorial: Raymond Deniel; *Sales:* Albert Hanrion
Subjects: African studies, Philosophy, Religion, Economics, Agriculture, Sociology, Essays
1978: 2 titles *1979:* 2 titles *Founded:* 1975

Les Nouvelles Editions Africaines*, 01 BP 3525, Abidjan 01 (Located at: 15 ave Noguès, Résidence Noguès, 2e etage, Abidjan 01) Tel: 32924/324907
Parent Company: Les Nouvelles Editions Africaines Dakar, Senegal (qv)
Associate Company: NEA, BP 4862, Lormé, Togo
Subjects: Bibliography, Fiction, Poetry, Religion, Art, Juveniles, History, Textbooks
1978: 34 titles

Université Nationale de Côte d'Ivoire, BP V34, Abidjan 01 Tel: 439000 Cable Add: Rectuniv Abidjan Telex: 469
Secretary General in Charge of Publications: Mme Dehail-Michèle
Subjects: General Nonfiction, History, Africana, Reference, Law, Medicine, General & Social Science, Economics, Geography, Linguistics, Sociology, Journals
1980: 11 titles *Founded:* 1964
ISBN Publisher's Prefix: 2-7166

Major Booksellers

Librairie **Carrefour***, 09 BP 326, Abidjan 09 Tel: 442370

Centre d'Edition et de Diffusion africaines*, BP 4541, Abidjan Tel: 222055/228137
Manager: Kakou Venance

Librairie de **France***, ave Chardy, BP 228, Abidjan Tel: 322655

Maison des Livres*, 23 blvd de la République, BP 4645, Abidjan Tel: 322887

Librarie **Villepastour***, 01 BP 2461, Abidjan 01 Tel: 353352/355117 Telex: 2454 Pastour
Manager: J Villepastour

Major Libraries

Bibliothèque centrale de la Côte d'Ivoire*, BP 6243, Abidjan-Treichville Tel: 227536

Bibliothèque municipale*, Plateau, Abidjan

Bibliothèque nationale*, BP V180, Abidjan Tel: 323872
National Library

Bibliothèque de l'Université nationale de Côte d'Ivoire, 08 BP 859, Abidjan 08 Tel: 439000 Telex: 467 Rectunis
Librarian: Mme N'goran; *Publications enquiries:* Mme Dehail-Leoni
Publications include: Annales de l'Université d'Abidjan; Bibliographie de la Côte d'Ivoire

Centre culturel américain*, Bibliothèque, BP 1866, Abidjan

Centre culturel français*, Bibliothèque, ave Noguès, Abidjan

I N A D E S (Institut africain pour le Développement économique et social) Documentation, 08 BP 8, Abidjan 08 Tel: 441594
Librarian: Nicole Vial
Publication: Le Fichier-Afrique (bi-monthly), Suggestions de Lectures (biannually)

Library Associations

Association pour le Développement de la Documentation, des Bibliothèques et Archives de la Côte d'Ivoire (ADBACI)*, c/o Bibliothèque Nationale, BP V180, Abidjan
Secretary General: Cangah Guy

Literary Associations and Societies

P E N Club International Centre de Côte d'Ivoire*, BP 1718, Abidjan
Secretary: Jean Dodo

Jamaica

General Information

Language: English
Religion: Predominantly Protestant
Population: 2 million
Literacy Rate (1960): 80.5%
Bank Hours: 0900-1400 Monday-Thursday; 0900-1200, 1430-1700 Friday
Shop Hours: Downtown Kingston: 0900-1600 Monday and Tuesday, Thursday-Saturday; 0900-1200 Wednesday. Other areas: 0900-1700, with early closing Thursday
Currency: 100 cents = 1 Jamaican dollar
Export/Import Information: No tariff on books, 45% on advertising matter. No import licence required for books; no obscene literature permitted. Exchange restrictions
Copyright: No copyright conventions signed

Book Trade Organizations

Booksellers' Association of Jamaica, c/o Sangster's Book Stores Ltd, 101 Water Lane, Kingston Tel: 9223640
Secretary: B A Sangster

Book Trade Reference Books and Journals

Books

Book Production in Jamaica: A Select List of Jamaican Publications, Jamaica Library Service, PO Box 58, Kingston 5

Journals

Jamaican National Bibliography, Institute of Jamaica, 12-16 East St, Kingston

Publishers

Caribbean Universities Press Ltd, PO Box 83, Kingston 7 Tel: (92) 62628
Man Dir: Carmen Latty
Parent Company: Ginn & Co, UK (qv)
Subjects: Academic, Education (Spanish and English)

William **Collins** & Sangster (Jamaica) Ltd*, PO Box 881, Kingston (Located at: Barclays Building, 54 King St, Kingston) Tel: 9224783
Man Dir: Jan Collins; *Editorial & Production:* G R Luff; *Sales & Publicity:* T D Menzies; *Rights & Permissions:* P M Clark
Parent Company: William Collins Sons & Co Ltd, UK (qv)

Government Printing Office*, 77 Duke St, Kingston
Subject: Law

Jamaica Publishing House Ltd, 97 Church St, Kingston Tel: (0922) 2038 Cable Add: Japub
Chairman: Fay E Saunders; *Manager:* Thelma E L Pyne
Parent Company: Jamaica Teachers' Association
Subject: Educational
1978: 1 title *1979:* 2 titles *Founded:* 1969

Kingston Publishers Ltd, 1A Norwood Ave, Kingston 5 Tel: 9265506/9265714 Cable Add: Kingbooks
Warehouse: 40 East St, Kingston Tel: 9225649
Chairman: L M J Henry
Founded: 1972

Major Booksellers

Bolivar Bookshop, 1D Grove Rd, Kingston 10 Tel: 9268799
Owner: Hugh Dunphy

Henderson's Book Store*, 27 St James St, Montego Bay

Kingston Bookshop*, 70b King St, Kingston

Literary Supplies*, 38 Mandeville Plaza, Mandeville

Novelty Trading Co*, 53 Hanover St, Kingston

Readers' Book Shop*, Liguanea Plaza, 134 Old Hope Rd, Kingston 6

Sangster's Book Stores Ltd*, PO Box 366, 101 Water Lane, Kingston Tel: 9223640

Shadeed's Educational & General Supplies*, 14 French St, Spanish Town

Stationery & Educational Book Centre*, Silver Slipper Plaza, Kingston 5

Teachers' Book Centre Ltd*, 95 Church St, Kingston Tel: (09) 26295/24716/27921

Times Stores Ltd*, 8 King St, Kingston

Major Libraries

Jamaica Archives*, Spanish Town

Jamaica Library Service, PO Box 58, 2 Tom Redcam Dr, Kingston 5 Tel: 936 3310
Dir: Leila T Thomas
Publications include: Book production in Jamaica: a select list of Jamaican publications

National Library of Jamaica, Institute of Jamaica*, 12-16 East St, Kingston

University of the West Indies Library*, Mona, Kingston 7 Tel: Librarian 9276661 ext 294; Reference Desk 9276661 ext 296 or 9270923
Librarian: K E Ingram
Publication: Annual Report

Library Associations

Jamaica Library Association*, PO Box 58, Kingston 5
Honorary Secretary: Ms A Chambers
Publication: Bulletin (annual)

Library Journals

Bulletin, Jamaica Library Association, PO Box 58, Kingston 5

Literary Associations and Societies

P E N Club, 1 Norbrook Rd, Apt 4, Kingston 8
Secretary: George Clough

Japan

General Information

Language: Japanese
Religion: Buddhism and Shinto
Population: 115 million
Literacy Rate (1960): 96.6%
Bank Hours: 0900-1500 Monday-Friday; 0900-1200 Saturday
Shop Hours: No fixed weekly holiday; department stores usually close Wednesday or Thursday, others Sunday. Generally department store hours are 1000-1800
Currency: yen
Export/Import Information: No tariff on books and advertising matter. Only declaration by importer to a foreign exchange bank is required
Copyright: UCC, Berne, Florence (see International section)

Book Trade Organizations

Antiquarian Booksellers' Association of Japan, 29 San-Ei-Cho, Shinjuku-ku, Tokyo 160 Tel: (03) 3595519 Cable Add: Yushodo Tokyo Telex: 0232-4136
President: Ukichi Sakai

Japan Book Importers' Association*, Room 302, Aizawa Bldg, 20-3 Nihonbashi 1-chome, Chuo-ku, Tokyo 103
Secretary: Kazushige Terakubo

Japan Book Publishers' Association*, 6 Fukuro-machi, Shinjuku-ku, Tokyo 162 Tel: (03) 2681301 Cable Add: Shosekiyo Tokyo
Secretary General: Shigeshi Sasaki; *Dir:* Masaaki Shigehisa
Publication: Publishing in Japan, Japanese Books in Print, The Catalogue of Books in the Near Future

Nihon Shoten Kumiai Rengokai*, 1-2 Kanda Surugadai, Chiyoda-ku, Tokyo 101 Tel: (03) 2940388
Japan Booksellers' Federation
Publications: Zenkoku Shoten Meibo (Address Book of Japan Booksellers); *Zenkoku Shoten Shinbun*

Publishers' Association for Cultural Exchange, 1-2-1, Sarugaku Cho, Chiyoda-ku, Tokyo 101 Tel: (03) 2915685
Cable Add: Publishersasso
President: Mr Shoichi Noma; *Man Dir:* Shoichi Nakajima
European Rep: c/o Euro-Japanische Gesellschaft eV, Bonifaciusplatz 3, D-6500 Mainz, Federal Republic of Germany
Publications: Guide to Publishers and Related Industries in Japan, Guide to Foreign Publishers, Annotated Catalogue of Books Published in Japan

Standard Book Numbering Agency, c/o Japan Book Publishers Association, 6 Fukoro-machi, Shinjuku-ku, Tokyo 162 Tel: (03) 2681301
Administrator: Shigeshi Sasaki

Textbook Publishers' Association of Japan (Kyokasho Kyokai), 20-2 Honshiocho Shinjuku-ku, Tokyo 160
Secretary: Masae Kusaka

Women Writers' Association*, 17 Yanaka-Shinizucho, Daito-ku, Tokyo

Book Trade Reference Books and Journals

Books

Annotated Catalogue of Books Published in Japan, Publishers' Association for Cultural Exchange, 1-2-1, Sarugaku Cho, Chiyoda-ku, Tokyo 101

Directory of Japanese Publishing and Bookselling, British Book and Educational Display Centre, Iwanami Jimbo-Cho Bldg, 1 Jimbo 2 2-chome, Kanda, Chiyoda-ku, Tokyo 101

Guide to Foreign Publishers, Publishers' Association for Cultural Exchange, 1-2-1, Sarugaku Cho, Chiyoda-ku, Tokyo 101

Publishing in Japan, Japan Book Publishers' Association, 6 Fukuro-machi, Shinjuku-ku, Tokyo 162

Journals

Biblia (text in Japanese), Tenri University Press, Tenri Central Library, Tenri City, Nara

The Catalogue of Books in the Near Future, Japan Book Publishers' Association, 6 Fukuro-machi, Shinjuku-ku, Tokyo 162

Guide to Publishers and Related Industries in Japan, Publishers' Association for Cultural Exchange, 1-2-1, Sarugaku Cho, Chiyoda-ku, Tokyo 101

Japan Book News, Publishing Research Associates, c/o Kyowa Book Co, Kanda, PO Box 173, Tokyo

Japanese Books in Print, Japan Book Publishers' Association, 6 Fukuro-machi, Shinjuku-ku, Tokyo 162

Japanese Publications News and Reviews, 3-2-4 Misaki-cho, Chiyoda-ku, Tokyo

Newsletter, Tokyo Book Development Centre, 6 Fukuro-machi, Shinjuku-ku, Tokyo

Seihon Kai (text in Japanese), Tokyodo Co Ltd, 3-5 Kanda-Nishiki-cho, Chiyoda-ku, Tokyo

Shinkan Nyusu (News of New Books), Tokyo Shuppan Hanbai Co Ltd, 53 Higashigoken-cho, Shinjuku-ku, Tokyo

Shuppan Nenkan; information on publishing for the previous year, Shuppan Nyusu-sha, Tokyo (annual)

Suppan Nyusu (Publishers' News), Shuppan Nyusu-sha, 2-4 Misaki-cho 3-chome, Chiyoda-ku, Tokyo 101 (3 times a month)

Zen Nihon Shuppanbutsu Somokuroku (Japanese National Bibliography), National Diet Library, 10-1, 1-chome, Nagata-cho, Chiyoda-ku, Tokyo

Zenkoku Shoten Meibo (address book of Japanese booksellers), Japan Booksellers' Federation, 1-2 Kanda Surugadai, Chiyoda-ku, Tokyo 101

Publishers

A D A Edita Tokyo Co Ltd, 3-12-14 Sendagaya, Shibuya-ku, Tokyo 151 Tel: (03) 4031581
Director: Yukio Futagawa; *Sales Manager:* Takato Kawahara
Subject: Architecture
1978: 5 titles *1979:* 3 titles *Founded:* 1972

Akane Shobo Co Ltd*, 3-2-1 Nishikanda, Chiyoda-ku, Tokyo Tel: (03) 2630641
President: Mutsuto Okamoto; *Editor-in-Chief:* Yoshiaki Ushiro
Subjects: Juveniles, Science, Literature, Picture Books

Akita Shoten Publishing Co Ltd*, 2-10-8 Iidabashi, Chiyoda-ku, Tokyo 102 Tel: (03) 2647011
Man Dir: Sadami Akita; *Editorial:* Nobumichi Akutsu; *Sales:* Toshimichi Okubo
Subjects: General Subjects, Juveniles, History, Social Science, Literature, Magazines
Founded: 1948

Aoki Shoten Co Ltd*, 60 Kanda Jimbo-cho 1-chome, Chiyoda-ku, Tokyo 101 Tel: (03) 2920481
President: Noboru Yamane; *Foreign Trade:* Kiyoshi Furukawa; *Foreign Rights:* Toyoichi Eguchi
Subject: Social Science
Founded: 1947

Asakura Publishing Co Ltd*, 2-10 Shinogawama-chi, Shinjuku-ku, Tokyo 162 Tel: (03) 2600141
President: Kozo Asakura; *Foreign Trade:* Nobuji Okada; *Foreign Rights:* Akira Hata

Subjects: Medicine, Natural Science, Engineering, Industry, History, Geography, Pedagogy, Sociology
Founded: 1929

Baifukan Co Ltd, 3-12 Kudan-Minami 4-chome, Chiyoda-ku, Tokyo 102 Tel: (03) 2625256
President: Kenji Yamamoto; *Editorial:* Kunihiko Watanabe, Tsuyoshi Nohara; *Sales, Publicity:* Itaru Yamamoto; *Production:* Fumio Shigematu; *Rights & Permissions:* Tsuyoshi Nohara
Subjects: Mathematics, Statistics, Computer Science, Physics, Chemistry, Biology, Engineering, Psychology, Sociology
1978: 46 titles *1979:* 54 titles *Founded:* 1924
ISBN Publisher's Prefix: 4-563

Baseball Magazine Sha, 3-3 Kanda-Nishiki-cho, Chiyoda-ku, Tokyo Tel: (03) 2917901/2917909
President: Tsuneo Ikeda; *Chief Executive:* Ikuo Ikeda
Branch Off: Tokuma Building, 6-16 Nozaki-cho, Kita-ku, Osaka-shi, Osaka Tel: (06) 3156141/3156144
Subjects: Sports, Physical Education, Psychology, History, Fitness
1978-9: 150 titles *Founded:* 1946
ISBN Publisher's Prefix: 4-583

Bijutsu Shuppan-Sha, 15 Ichigaya Honmura-cho, Shinjuku, Tokyo 162 Tel: (03) 2602151 Cable Add: Fineart Book Tokyo
President: Atsushi Oshita; *Sales Manager:* Koichi Matsumura
Subsidiary Company: Bijutsu Shuppan Design Centre, Yamato Bldg, 1-7-4 Yaesu Chuo-ku, Tokyo 103
Subjects: Art, Architecture, Design
1978: 65 titles *Founded:* 1905

Bungeishunju Ltd, 3 Kioi-cho, Chiyoda-ku, Tokyo Tel: (03) 2651211
President: Genzo Chiba; *Foreign Trade:* Yoneki Kobayashi; *Foreign Rights:* Itaro Abe
Subjects: General Fiction and Nonfiction, Philosophy, Religion, History, Geography, Social Science, Art, Economics, Politics, Natural Science, Industry, Language, Literature, High- and Low-priced Paperbacks
Founded: 1923

Centre for Academic Publications Japan, 4-16 Yayoi 2-chome, Bunkyo-ku, Tokyo 113 Tel: (03) 8150416
Man Dir: T Yamada; *Editorial, Sales, Production, Publicity, Rights & Permissions:* K Oshida
Orders to: Business Centre for Academic Societies Japan at above address
Associate Company: Japan Scientific Societies Press, 2-10 Hongo, 6-chome, Bunkyo-ku, Tokyo 113
1978: 8 titles *1979:* 9 titles *Founded:* 1972

Chikuma Shobo Publishing Co Ltd, 8, 2-chome, Kanda Ogawamachi, Chiyoda-ku, Tokyo 101-91 Tel: (03) 2917651
Administrator: Kakuzaemon Nunokawa; *Editorial, Rights & Permissions:* Mineo Nakajima; *Sales:* Tetsuo Mukaiyama; *Production:* Kazuyoshi Tsunoda; *Publicity:* Toshihiko Ebisawa
Subjects: General Fiction, Belles Lettres, Poetry, Biography, History, Religion, Music, Art, Philosophy, Juveniles, High-priced Paperbacks, Medicine, Psychology, General & Social Science, Secondary Textbooks
1978: 429 titles *Founded:* 1930

Child-Honsha Co Ltd, 24-21 Koishikawa 5-chome, Bunkyo-ku, Tokyo 112 Tel: (03) 8133781
President: Shinko Miyata; *Editorial:* Yasuyuki Ouchi; *Sales:* Hirosato Okada; *Production:* Kotaro Ohashi; *Rights & Permissions:* Ikuzo Shibasaki
Associate Company: Kyodo Printing Co Ltd
Subsidiary Company: Basic Inc
Imprints: Kyodo Printing Co Ltd
Subjects: Juveniles, Education
1978: 30 titles *Founded:* 1930

Chuo-Tosho Shuppan-Sha, Aburanokoji-dori, Motoseiganji-sagaru, Kamigyo-ku, Kyoto 602 Tel: 4412174
President: Toshihiko Hirokou; *Foreign Trade:* Keizou Hirotsu; *Foreign Rights:* Takanori Ikeda
Subjects: Language, Literature, Reference Books
1979: 25 titles *Founded:* 1946

Chuokoron-Sha Inc*, 2-8-7 Kyobashi, Chuo-ku, Tokyo 104 Tel: (03) 5615921 Cable Add: Chuokoron Tokyo
President: Hoji Shimanaka; *Man Dir:* Shigeru Takanashi; *International Section Manager:* Yukio Shimanaka
Subjects: General Fiction, Belles Lettres, History, Art, Philosophy, Low-priced Paperbacks, Politics, Economics, Natural Science, Social Science, Religion, Periodicals
Founded: 1887

Consolidated Labor Institute (Japan)*, 38 Yoyogi 1-chome, Shibuya-ku, Tokyo 151 Tel: (03) 3792281 Cable Add: Sogoroken Tokyo
President: Mrs Fujiko Hongo; *Foreign Trade Executive:* Kenji Hongo; *Foreign Rights Executive:* Chiyoshi Otuka
Subjects: Social Science, Law, Educational, History, Journals
Founded: 1950

Corona Publishing Co Ltd*, 4-46-10 Sengoku, Bunkyo-ku, Tokyo 112 Tel: (03) 9413131
Executive Director and Foreign Rights: Tatsuo Fujita; *Foreign Trade:* Tatsumi Gorai
Subjects: Natural Science, Technology
1978: 70 titles *Founded:* 1927

Daiichi Shuppan Co Ltd*, 1-39 Kanda Jimbo-cho, Chiyoda-ku, Tokyo 101 Tel: (03) 2914576
President: Gen Kurita; *Foreign Trade Executive:* Yoshiya Takamatsu; *Foreign Rights Executive:* Yoshiya Takamatsu
Subjects: Medicine, Natural Science, Nutrition, Magazines
1978: 15 titles *Founded:* 1945

Diamond Inc*, 1-4-2 Kasumigaseki, Chiyoda-ku, Tokyo Tel: (03) 5046381 Cable Add: Keizaidia Tokyo
President: Yoshio Tsubouchi; *Editorial:* Hideki Fujishima; *Sales:* Minami Takahashi; *Production:* Kiyoji Ogo; *Publicity:* Kenichiro Iwasaki; *Rights & Permissions:* Katsuyoshi Saito
Associate Company: President KK
Subsidiary Companies: Diamond (weekly economics Journal); Diamond Agency; Diamond Big; Diamond Fund; Diamond Graphics; Diamond Service
Branch Off: Osaka
Subjects: Non-fiction, Business, Economics, Management, Finance, Politics
Founded: 1913

Froebel-Kan Co Ltd*, 3-1 Kanda Ogawa-machi, Chiyoda-ku, Tokyo 101 Tel: (03) 2927781/9 Cable Add: Froebelkan Tokyo Telex: J24907
General Manager (International Division): Harry H Idichi; *Assistant Manager, International Division:* Tony S Endo
Subjects: Juveniles, Educational Materials
Founded: 1907

Fukuinkan Shoten Publishers, 1-9 Misakicho 1-chome, Chiyoda-ku, Tokyo 101 Tel: (03) 2923401/2303821 Cable Add: Fukuinkanshoten Tokyo
Man Dir: Tadashi Matsui; *Editorial:* Ken Minakuchi; *Sales:* Katsumi Sato, Kishiro Kikuma; *Publicity:* Hiroshi Ishikawa; *Rights & Permissions:* Minoru Tamura, Tamotsu Hozumi
Subjects: Children's books
Book Club: Ehon Library (Picture Book Library)
1978: 26 titles *1979:* 30 titles *Founded:* 1951

Fuzambo Publishing Co*, 1-3 Kanda Jimbo-cho, Chiyoda-ku, Tokyo 101 Tel: (03) 2912171
President: Kiichi Sakamoto
Subjects: General Works, Philosophy & Religion, History, Geography, Law, Literature, Language, Art, Juveniles, Dictionaries
Founded: 1886

Gakken Co Ltd, 4-40-5 Kami-ikedai, Ohta-ku, Tokyo 145 Tel: (03) 7201111 Cable Add: Gakkencol Tokyo Telex: Gakkenco J26389
Man Dir: Hiroshi Furuoka; *Foreign Affairs Executive:* Ryu Tanaka; *Foreign Rights:* Kazuo Chuma
Subjects: General Fiction, Fine Arts, Encyclopaedias, Dictionaries, Juveniles, Children's Picture Books, Illustrated Books, History, Natural and Social Science, Japanese, Languages, Music, Textbooks, Reference, Education, Educational Materials, Audio-visual Aids, Magazines, Sports, Hobbies
1979: 206 titles *Founded:* 1946

Gakuseisha Publishing Co Ltd*, 2-2-4 Kudan-Minami, Chiyoda-ku, Tokyo 102 Tel: (03) 2632611
President: Masami Tsuruoka; *Foreign Rights Executive:* Atsuo Miki
Subjects: Ancient History, Archaeology, Reference
1978: 55 titles *Founded:* 1952

Hakusui-Sha, 3-24 Kanda-Ogawamachi, Chiyoda-ku, Tokyo 101 Tel: (03) 2917811
President: Sueo Nakamori; *Foreign Trade Executive:* Souichi Kobayashi; *Foreign Rights Executive:* Tsutomu Izumikawa
Subjects: Science, Languages, Fiction, Literature, Education, Art, Philosophy
Founded: 1915

Hakuyu-Sha*, 9 Ageba-cho, Shinjuku-ku, Tokyo 162 Tel: (03) 2688271
Man Dir: Eiji Takamori; *Foreign Trade Executive:* Montaro Ono; *Publicity & Advertising:* Kazuya Baba; *Foreign Rights:* Eiji Takamori
Subjects: Dictionaries, Natural Science, Industry
Founded: 1948

Hayakawa Publishing Inc, 2-2 Kanda-Tacho, Chiyoda-ku, Tokyo 101 Tel: (03) 2541551 Cable Add: Hayakawashobo Tokyo
Executive Vice-President, Foreign Trade & Rights Executive: Hiroshi Hayakawa
Subjects: Foreign Fiction, Nonfiction, History, Philosophy & Religion, Art, Juveniles, Natural, Social & Political Sciences, Literature, Magazines, Plays, Mysteries, Science Fiction, Fantasy

Heibonsha Ltd, Publishers, 4 Yonbancho, Chiyoda-ku, Tokyo 102 Tel: (03) 2650451 Cable Add: Booksheibonsha
President: Kunihiko Shimonaka; *Dirs:* Masakiyo Nakajima, Tadashi Uemura
Subjects: Encyclopedias, Japanese & Chinese studies, General nonfiction, Art, Reference, Education, History, Philosophy, Social

Science, Graphic monthly magazine, *The Sun*
1978: 225 titles *Founded:* 1914

Hikarinokuni Co Ltd*, 3-2 Uehon-machi, Tennoji-ku, Osaka 543 Tel: 7681151
Man Dir: Yotaro Matsumoto; *Editorial & Export Dir:* Masaaki Tsuchiya
Subjects: Juveniles, Education
Founded: 1945

Hirokawa Publishing Co*, PO Box 38 Hongo, Bunkyo-ku, Tokyo 113-91 (Located at: 27-14 Hongo 3-chome, Bunkyo-ku, Tokyo 113) Tel: (03) 8153651 Cable Add: Higesehi Tokyo
President: Genji Hirokawa; *Man Dir (Editor):* Setsuo Hirokawa; *Sales Dir:* Hideo Hirokawa
Subjects: Medicine, Pharmacy, Natural Sciences, Engineering
Founded: 1926

Hoikusha Publishing Co Ltd*, 17-13, 1-Chome Uemachi, Higashi-ku, Osaka 540 Tel: (06) 7621731 Cable Add: Hoikusha
President: Tatsuo Imai; *Man Dir:* Ryoji Nakanishi; *Editorial:* Masao Ikeyama
Branch Off: 1-1 Minami-Otsuka, Toshima-ku, Tokyo 170
Subjects: Natural History, Poetry, Biography, History, How-to, Music, Art, High-priced Hard cover books, General Science, Illustrated Nature & Craft Books in English & Japanese
1978: 46 titles *Founded:* 1947

Hokuryukan Co Ltd, Bunkyo Trading Bldg, 2-12-7 Iidabashi, Chiyoda-ku, Tokyo 102 Tel: (03) 2919511
President & Editorial: Kisaburo Fukuda
Subjects: Juveniles, General Science, Reference, Engineering
Founded: 1919

The **Hokuseido** Press, 12 Nishikicho 3-chome, Kanda, Chiyoda-ku, Tokyo Tel: (03) 2943301 Cable Add: Hokusedpres Tokyo
Dir: Jumpei Nakatsuchi; *Sales, Advertising, Rights & Permissions:* Katsuo Wakiyama
Subjects: Belles Lettres, Poetry, Biography, Philosophy, Religion, University Textbooks
1978: 35 titles *1979:* 24 titles *Founded:* 1914

Holp Book Co Ltd, 2-19-13 Shinjuku, Shinjuku-ku, Tokyo 160 Tel: (03) 3566211 Cable Add: Holpbook Tokyo Telex: 2322421
President: Makito Nakamori; *Editorial:* Hiroyoshi Shimizu; *Rights & Permissions:* Minoru Shibuya; *International Trade:* Masumi Misaki
Branch Offs: 180 throughout Japan
Subsidiary Companies: Holp Shuppan, Publishers Ltd; Shumi-to-Seikatsu Co Ltd
1979: 68 titles *Founded:* 1964
Subjects: Art, Education, Geography, Juveniles, Literature, Mathematics, Reproductions, Science

Hyoronsha Publishing Co Ltd*, 2-16 Kanda Jimbo-cho, Chiyoda-ku, Tokyo 101 Tel: (03) 2651961
President: Mrs Mina Takeshita; *Chief Editor:* Saburo Tsuyama; *Sales Manager:* Zenzo Uchida
Subjects: Philosophy & Religion, Education, History, Social Science, Industry, Language, Juveniles, Reference
Founded: 1948

Ie-No-Hikari Association*, 11 Funakawara-cho, Ichigaya, Shinjuku-ku, Tokyo 162 Tel: (03) 2603151 Cable Add: IeNoHikari Tokyo Telex: 2322367
Man Dir: Yoshiro Takahashi; *Editorial, Sales:* Mareki Kuruba; *Book Publication Department:* Naomichi Muratani; *Production:* Shinichi Saito; *Publicity:* Yoshiro Takahashi
Subjects: General, Social Science, Industry, Periodicals
Founded: 1925

Igaku-Shoin Ltd, PO Box 5063, Tokyo International (Located at: 5-24-3 Hongo, Bunkyo-ku, Tokyo 11391) Tel: (03) 8111101 Cable Add: Igakushoin Telex: 2723334 (Head Office and Publishing Departments)/2722738 (Foreign Book Department)
President, Editor-in-Chief: Izumi Hasegawa; *Executive Vice-President (Sales, Foreign Books):* Takao Tsubaki; *Vice-Presidents:* Naobumi Ando (Medical Publications), Noboru Nakajima (Nursing Publications), Yu Kanehara (Foreign Operations, International Publishing); *Senior Editor (International Publishing):* Hideo Okada; *Managers:* Makoto Yamamoto (Reprint, Export), Ikuro Noda (Book Imports), Yasuo Sakaguchi (Journal Imports)
Subsidiary Companies: Igaku-Shoin Medical Publishers Inc, 50 Rockefeller Plaza, New York, NY 10020, USA; Medical Sciences International Ltd, Kida Bldg, 1-2-13 Yushima, Bunkyo-ku, Tokyo 113, Japan
Subjects: Medical and Dental Sciences, Nursing
1978: 129 titles *1979:* 112 titles *Founded:* 1944
ISBN Publisher's Prefixes: 4-260, 0-89640

The **International Nursing** Foundation of Japan, 1-32 4-chome Kudan Kita, Chiyoda-ku, Tokyo 102 Tel: (03) 2646667 Cable Add: Infurse Tokyo
Man Dir: Kazuharu Ogura, Mrs Sada Nagano; *Editorial, Rights & Permissions:* Tetsuro Nishizaki; *Publicity & Advertising:* Miss Fujiko Masame
Subjects: Nursing Science (National & International)
1978: 7 titles *1979:* 6 titles *Founded:* 1971

International Society for Educational Information Inc, Kikuei Bldg 7-8, Shintomi 2-chome, Chuo-ku, Tokyo Tel: (03) 5529481/2
Executive Director: Michiko Kaya
Subject: Japan

Ishiyaku Publishers Inc, PO Box 8, Hongo, Tokyo 113-91 (Located at: 7-10 Honkomagome 1-chome, Bunkyo-ku, Tokyo 113) Tel: (03) 9443131 Cable Add: Mepharma Tokyo Telex: 2723298 Mdp J
President: Dr Takashi Imada; *Dir:* Hiroshi Miura; *Publishers:* Yukio Hata (Medical Division), Yutaka Shimizu (Dental Division), Haruo Kitano (Nutrition & Pharmaceutical Division); *Editor-in-Chief:* Takao Suda (Dental Division); *Marketing Dir:* Akira Iwase
Orders to: Tokyo Mail Service Co Ltd, PO Box 101, Hongo, Tokyo 113-91
Branch Off: 4-11-23 Manden Bldg, Nishintenma, Kitaku, Osaka
Bookshop: Shiensha Ltd, c/o Nakayama Bldg, 8-6 Misakicho 2-chome, Chiyoda-ku, Tokyo 101
Subjects: Medicine, Dentistry, Pharmacology, Nutrition, Veterinary Medicine, University textbooks, Educational materials
1978: 88 titles *1979:* 120 titles *Founded:* 1921

Iwanami Shoten, Publishers, 2-5-5 Hitotsubashi, Chiyoda-ku, Tokyo Tel: (03) 2654111 Cable Add: Iwanamipress Tokyo
Chairman: Yujiro Iwanami; *President:* Toru Midorikawa; *Executive Dir, Publicity & Advertising:* Akira Kigoshi; *Dir, Chief Editor:* Yoshikatsu Nakajima; *Foreign Rights:* Mitsuko Takiguchi, Takao Hori, Takeko Tomita
Subjects: Biography, Economics, History, Reference, Philosophy, Psychology, Art, Juveniles, Social & Natural Science, Paperbacks, University Textbooks, Dictionaries, Periodicals
1978: 329 titles *1979:* 418 titles *Founded:* 1913

Iwasaki Shoten Co Ltd*, 1-9-2 Suido, Bunkyo-ku, Tokyo 112 Tel: (03) 8129131
Man Dir: Koyu Moriyama; *Sales Manager:* Matsutoshi Ohkawa; *Editorial:* Masayasu Konishi
Subjects: Juveniles, Art
Founded: 1934

Japan Broadcast Publishing Co Ltd*, 41-1 Udagawa-cho, Shibuya-ku, Tokyo 150 Tel: (03) 4647311 Cable Add: Nhpublishco Tokyo
President: Kazuo Fujinei; *Foreign Trade Executive:* Tsuguo Mizutani; *Foreign Rights Executive:* Yoshio Nemoto
Subjects: Radio, Television, Philosophy, Religion, History, Geography, Social & Natural Sciences, Politics, Law, Economics, Engineering, Medicine, Technology, Industry, Art, Language, Juveniles, Literature, Reference, Textbooks
Founded: 1931

Japan Publications Inc*, PO Box 5030 Tokyo International, Tokyo 101-31 (Located at: 1-2-1 Sarugaku-cho 1-chome, Chiyoda-ku, Tokyo 101) Tel: (03) 2958411 Cable Add: Shutsubo Tokyo Telex: J 27161
President: Iwao Yoshizaki; *Executive Dir:* Soshichi Toyoshima; *Editor-in-Chief:* Richard L Gage; *Sales Manager:* Akio Takeuchi; *Rights & Permissions:* Masatoshi Sato
Subsidiary Companies: Japan Publications Trading Co Ltd, PO Box 5030, Tokyo International, Tokyo 101-31; Japan Publications Trading Co (USA) Inc, 1174 Howard St, San Francisco, CA 94103, USA
Subjects: History, How-to, Reference, Juveniles, Health, High-priced Paperbacks
1978: 36 titles *Founded:* 1942

Japan Times, Publishing Department, 5-4 Shibaura 4-chome, Minato-ku, Tokyo
Man Dir: Toshio Tojo
Subjects: Nonfiction, Reference, Textbooks

Japan Travel Bureau Inc, Publishing Division, 8th Floor, OKI Bldg, 3 Kanda Kaji-Cho 3-chome, Chiyoda-ku, Tokyo 101 Tel: (03) 2578320 Cable Add: Jtbbook Tokyo J24418 Telex: 2228020
Man Dir: Shigeo Miyakoshi; *Editorial:* Akito Hiroki; *Foreign Trade, Foreign Rights:* Kunihiko Shibuya
Subsidiary Companies: Densan Process Co; Kotsu Print Co; Kotsu Seihon Co; Toyo Books Co
Branch Offs: The International Bldg, 45 Rockefeller Plaza, New York, NY 10020, USA; 510 West Sixth St, Los Angeles, Calif, 90014, USA; 402 Qantas Bldg, Union Sq, 360 Post St, San Francisco, Calif 94108, USA; The Royal Exchange Bldg, 56 Pitt St, Sydney, Australia; Waikiki Business Plaza, 2270 Kalakaua Avenue, Honolulu, Hawaii 96815; 20 rue Quentin Bauchart, Paris 75008, France; Room 2123, Hotel Miramar, Nathan Rd, Kawloon, Hong Kong; 5 Rue Chantepoulet, Geneva, Switzerland; 32 Old Burlington St, London W1X 1LB, UK; c/o Guam Hilton Hotel, Ipao Beach, Guam; Via Emilia 47, Rome, Italy
Subjects: General, Travel Guides, Maps, History, Geography, Language
Founded: 1945
ISBN Publisher's Prefix: 0-87040

Kadokawa Shoten*, 2-13-3 Fujimi-cho, Chiyoda-ku, Tokyo Tel: (03) 2657111
Man Dir: Haruki Kadokawa; *Editorial:* Sadaharu Mouri; *Sales:* Tsuguhiko Kadokawa; *Production:* Shigeo Nakai; *Publicity:* Akio Baba; *Rights & Permissions:* Hiroshi Tagami
Subjects: General Fiction, Fine Arts, History, Religion, Literature, Dictionaries
1978: 350 titles *Founded:* 1945

Kaibundo Publishing Co Ltd, 2-5-4 Suido, Bunkyo-ku, Tokyo 112 Tel: Tokyo 815 3291
President: Yoshihiro Okada; *Editorial Dir:* Yuji Tamura; *Foreign Trade, Foreign Rights:* Shin-ichi Arihara
Subjects: Engineering, Industry, Natural Science
Founded: 1914

Kairyudo Publishing Co Ltd*, 3-18 Kanda Nishiki-cho Chiyoda-ku, Tokyo 101 Tel: (03) 2931811-9
Man Dir: Takahiro Nakamura; *Editorial:* Masatoshi Yoshinari; *Foreign Trade, Foreign Rights:* Shoju Yoshinari; *Sales:* Shoichi Akane; *Production:* Kenji Nakamura; *Publicity:* Mistunobu Okawa
Associated Company: Kairyukan Publishing Co Ltd
Branch Offs: at Fukuoka, Nagoya, Osaka, Sapporo
Subjects: Textbooks, Natural Science, Art, Language, Reference, Teaching Aids
Founded: 1926

Kaisei-Sha, 3-5 Ichigaya, Sadohara-cho, Shinjuku-ku, Tokyo 162 Tel: (03) 2603221 Cable Add: Kaiseisha
President: Hiroshi Imamura; *Editorial Dir:* Mitsuo Takamori; *Sales Dir:* Rokuroh Isohata; *Editor & Foreign Rights:* Hiroshi Konno
Subject: Juveniles
1979: 120 titles *Founded:* 1936

Kaitaku-Sha, 2-5 Kanda Jinbo-cho, Chiyoda-ku, Tokyo 101 Tel: (03) 2657641
President: Kunio Naganuma; *Foreign Trade:* Takehito Yamaguchi; *Foreign Rights:* Yasuhiko Yamamoto
Subjects: Reference, Education, Language, Literature
Founded: 1927

Kajima Institute Publishing Co Ltd, 6-5-13 Akasaka, Minato-ku, Tokyo 107 Tel: (03) 5822251
President: Zenjiro Kawai; *Foreign Trade:* Tsunesuke Utsumi; *Foreign Rights:* Hiroshi Yamamoto
Subjects: Architecture, Urban Engineering, Civil Engineering
Bookshops: Kasumigaseki Bookstore, 3-2-5 Kasumigaseki, Chiyoda-ku, Tokyo; Shinjuku Mitsui Building Bookstore, 2-1 Nishishinjuku, Shinjuku-ku, Tokyo; Shibuya Tohoseimei Building Bookstore, 2-15 Shibuya, Shibuya-ku, Tokyo
1978: 765 titles *Founded:* 1963

Kanehara & Co Ltd, 31-14, 2-chome, Yushima, Bunkyo-ku, Tokyo 113, Tel: (03) 8117161 Cable Add: Kaneharaco Tokyo
President and General Manager: Hideo Kanehara; *Director (Foreign Business):* Hiroshi Kohno
Subjects: Medicine, Technology, Industry
Founded: 1875
Miscellaneous: Publish Ishihara's Tests for Colour-blindness

Kawade Shobo Shinsha*, 95 Sumiyoshi-cho, Shinjuku-ku, Tokyo 162 Tel: (03) 3555311
President: Kozo Sato
Subjects: General Fiction, Natural & Social Science, Art, History, Philosophy
Founded: 1957

Kenkyusha Ltd, 1-2 Kagurazaka, Shinjuku-ku, Tokyo 162 Tel: (03) 2694521
President: Torao Uyeda; *Foreign Trade Executive:* Shiro Nagai; *Foreign Rights Executive:* Yukio Kohno
Subjects: Reference, Languages, Dictionaries
1979: 20 titles *Founded:* 1907

Kinokuniya Bookstore Co Ltd (Publishing Department)*, 12 Gobancho, Chiyoda-ku, Tokyo 102 Tel: (03) 2634914/5 & 2639006 Cable Add: Kinokuni
General Manager: Toshio Kaneko; *Sales:* Shigeru Yagi
Associate Companies: Kinokuniya Book-Stores of America Co Ltd, 1581 Webster St, San Francisco, CA 94115, USA, 110 S Los Angeles St, Los Angeles, CA 90012, USA; Kinokuniya Publications Service of New York Co Ltd, 633 Third Ave, Suite 1925, New York, NY 10017, USA; Kinokuniya Publications Service of London Co, Radnor House, 93-97 Regent St, London W1, UK
Subjects: Biography, History, Music, Art, Philosophy, Politics, Medicine, Psychology, Engineering, General Science, Social Science, University Textbooks
Bookshops: 17-7 Shinjuku 3-chome, Shinjuku-ku, Tokyo 160, (23 branches throughout Japan)
1978: 45 titles *Founded:* 1926

Kodansha Ltd, 2-12-21 Otowa, Bunkyo-ku, Tokyo 112 Tel: (03) 9451111 Cable Add: Kodanshapublish Tokyo Telex: 2722570 Kodanc J
President: Shoichi Noma; *Foreign Trade:* Shoji Nadaya; *Editorial:* Koremitsu Noma; *Sales:* Kanzo Yamaguchi; *Production:* Teikichi Tarusawa; *Publicity:* Tsutomu Matsubayashi; *Rights & Permissions:* Samio Degawa
Subsidiary Companies: Kodansha International, Japan (qv); Kodansha Scientific, Japan (qv)
Branch Off: in Fukuoka, Hiroshima, Nagoya, Osaka, Sapporo, Sendai, Takamatsu
Subjects: General Non-fiction, Religion, Philosophy, History, Geography, Art, Politics, Economics, Pedagogy, Sociology, Natural Science, Medicine, Social Science, Engineering, Language, Literature, Juveniles, Reference Books
Book Clubs: Kodansha Disney Children's Book Club
Founded: 1909

Kodansha International Ltd, 12-21 Otowa 2-chome, Bunkyo-ku, Tokyo Tel: (03) 9446491 Cable Add: Kodanshaint Tokyo
Man Dir: Saburo Nobuki; *Editorial:* Kim Schuefftan; *Sales & Rights & Permissions:* Yukimori Akanoma; *Publicity:* Drew Stroud
Parent Company: Kodansha Ltd (qv)
Branch Offs: Kodansha International/USA Ltd, 10 East 53rd St, New York, NY 10022, USA; 44 Montgomery St, San Francisco, Calif 94104, USA
Subjects: Specializing in Japan and Asia: General Fiction, Belles Lettres, Art, How-to, History, Philosophy, Reference, Traditional Crafts, Martial Arts, Cooking
1978: 26 titles *1979:* 37 titles *Founded:* 1963
ISBN Publisher's Prefix: 0-87011

Kodansha Scientific Ltd*, 2-12-21 Otowa, Bunkyo-ku, 112 Tokyo Tel: 9434541
Parent Company: Kodansha Ltd (qv)
Subjects: Scientific Texts
Founded: 1970

Komine Shoten Publishing Co Ltd*, 6 Yotsuya Funa-machi, Shinjuku-ku, Tokyo
Man Dir: Hiroe Komine
Subjects: Education, Juveniles
Founded: 1946

Kosei Publishing Co Ltd, 2-7-1, Wada, Suginami-ku, Tokyo 166 Tel: (03) 3833151 Cable Add: Koseishuppansha Tokyo
President: Tadashi Furukawa; *Foreign Trade Executive:* Hiroshi Nomura; *Foreign Rights Executive:* Masuo Nezu
Subjects: Religion, Juveniles, English Translations, Literature, Magazines
1978: 26 titles *Founded:* 1950

Koseisha-Koseikaku Co Ltd*, 8 San-ei-cho, Shinjuku-ku, Tokyo 160 Tel: (03) 3597371
President: Hisao Satake; *Editorial:* Fukase Simao; *Publishing:* Hajime Torizuka
Subjects: Philosophy, Sociology, Natural Sciences, Technology, Industry, Astronomy
Founded: 1922

Kyo Bun Kwan Inc*, 4-5-1 Ginza, Chuo-ku, Tokyo 104 Tel: (03) 5618446 Cable Add: Kyobunkwan Tokyo
Subject: Religion
Founded: 1885
Bookshop: 4-5-1 Ginza, Chuo-ku, Tokyo 104

Kyoritsu Shuppan Co Ltd, 6-19 Kobinata, 4-chome, Bunkyo-ku, Tokyo 112 Tel: (03) 9472511
Chief Man Dir: Masataka Takeuchi
Subjects: Natural Science & Technology, Medicine, Industry, Textbooks
1978: 119 titles *Founded:* 1926

Maruzen Co Ltd, PO Box 5050, Tokyo International 10031 (Located at: 3-10 Nihonbashi 2-chome, Chuo-ku, Tokyo 103) Tel: (03) 2727211 Cable Add: Maruya Tokyo Telex: J26517
President: Shingo Iizumi; *Man Dir:* Kumao Ebihara; *Dir (Export and Import):* Yasuo Kanazawa; *General Manager (Publishing Division):* Junji Sekine; *Dir (Import):* Tadashi Fukuda
Subsidiary Companies: Maruzen Asia (Pte) Ltd, Singapore (qv); Maruzen International Co Ltd, New York, USA
Subjects: Linguistics, Medicine, Pure & Applied Chemistry, Technical, Architecture, Mathematics, Engineering, Economics, Management, Dictionaries
Bookshops: 3-10 Nihonbashi 2-chome, Chuo-ku, Tokyo 103; also at Fukuoka, Hiroshima, Kobe, Kyoto, Nagoya, Okayama, Osaka, Sapporo, Sendai, Tsukuba
1978: 63 titles *1979:* 62 titles *Founded:* 1869

Medical Friend Co Ltd, 1-32 4-chome Kudan Kita, Chiyoda-ku, Tokyo 102 Tel: (03) 264 6611
President: Kazuharu Ogura; *Editorial, Publicity & Advertising, Sales, Rights & Permissions:* Yoshihiro Ogura
Branch Off: 2-2-1200 1-chome Umeda, Kita-ku, Osaka 530
Subjects: Medical, Paramedical, Nursing Science & Arts, Expert Publications, Textbooks and Periodicals
1978: 45 titles *1979:* 60 titles *Founded:* 1947

Minerva Shobo Co Ltd, 1 Tsutsumidani-cho, Hinooka Yamashina, Yamashina-ku, Kyoto 607 Tel: Kyoto 5815191
President: Nobuo Sugita; *Editorial Dir:* Keiji Nakanishi; *Foreign Trade:* Keizo Sugita; *Foreign Rights:* Takeo Isozaki
Subjects: Philosophy & Religion, History, Social Welfare, Gerontology, Social Science, Literature, Reference
1978: 262 titles *1979:* 260 titles *Founded:* 1948

Misuzu Shobo Publishing Co Ltd, 17-15 Hongo 3-chome, Bunkyo-ku, Tokyo 113 Tel: (03) 8159181
Foreign Trade, Foreign Rights: Toshito Obi; *Sales Dir:* Yoshio Aida

Subjects: General, History, Art, Literature, Philosophy, Religion, High-priced Paperbacks, Psychiatry, Mathematics, Natural Science, General Science, Social Science
Founded: 1946

Morikita Shuppan Co Ltd, 4-11 Fujimi 1-chome, Chiyoda-ku, Tokyo 102 Tel: (03) 2658341
President: Hajime Morikita; *Foreign Trade Executive:* Kazuo Mori; *Foreign Rights Executive:* Mohachi Yanagisawa
Subjects: Natural Science, Technology, Secondary Textbooks
1980: 50 titles *Founded:* 1940 (as Morikita Shoten)

Nagai Shoten Co Ltd, 21-15, Fukushima 8-chome, Fukushima-ku, Osaka 553 Tel: (06) 4521881
President: Hideichi Nagai; *Man Dir, Editorial:* Tadao Nagai
Subject: Medicine
1978: 18 titles *1979:* 27 titles *Founded:* 1946

Nankodo Co Ltd*, PO Box 5272, Tokyo International, Tokyo 100-31 (Located at: 42-6 Hongo, 3-chome, Bunkyo-ku, Tokyo 113) Tel: (03) 8117234 Cable Add: Booknankodo
President: Takehiko Kodachi; *Dir (Publications):* Kaguhiko Ootomo; *Dir (Foreign Division):* Shoji Sano; *Manager of Planning, Publicity:* Takayuki Izumi; *Sales Dir:* Takashi Ito; *Manager, Imports:* Masao Takahashi
Branch Off: Oike-minami Teramachi dori, Nakakyo-ku, Kyoto 604
Subjects: Medicine, Language, Natural Science, Technology
1978: 45 titles *Founded:* 1879

Nanzando Co Ltd, 4-1-11 Yushima, Bunkyo-ku, Tokyo 113 Tel: (03) 8143681
Man Dir: Kimio Suzuki
Subjects: Reference, High-priced Paperbacks, Medicine, University Textbooks, Pharmacology
Founded: 1901

Nihon Bunka Kagakusha Co Ltd, 15-17 Honkomagome 6-chome, Bunkyo-ku, Tokyo 113 Tel: (03) 9463131 Cable Add: Nihonbunkamm Tokyo
President: Mohachi Motegi; *Foreign Trade Executive:* Haruo Kurihara; *Foreign Rights Executive:* Yagoro Kojima
Subjects: Education, Social Science, Medicine, Reference Books
1979: 30 titles *Founded:* 1948

Nihon Vogue (Publishing) Co Ltd, 34 Ichigaya-Honmuracho, Shinjuku-ku, Tokyo 162 Tel: (03) 2698711 Cable Add: Spinningwheel
Editorial Manager: S Noguchi; *Foreign Trade:* N Seto
Subjects: Knitting, Crocheting, Embroidery, Handicrafts (in Paperback)
Founded: 1954

Obunsha Co Ltd*, 55 Yokodera-cho, Shinjuku-ku, Tokyo 162 Tel: (03) 2666100
President: Yoshio Akao
Subjects: General Fiction, Biography, How-to, Reference, General Science, Secondary & Primary Textbooks, Educational Materials, Cassettes
1978: 300 titles *Founded:* 1931
Affiliates: The Japan Society of English Study; The Society for Testing English Proficiency (both at 55 Yokodera-cho, Shinjuku-ku, Tokyo 162); The Japan LL Education Center, 3-14-16 Shimo-ochiai, Shinjuku-ku, Tokyo 161; Asahi National Broadcasting Co Ltd, 6-4-10 Roppongi, Minato-ku, Tokyo 106

Ohmsha Ltd, 1-3 Kanda Nishiki-cho, Chiyoda-ku, Tokyo 101 Tel: (03) 2330641 Cable Add: Ohmsha
President: S Mitsui; *Man Dir:* K Tobe; *Foreign Rights Executive:* Seiji Sato
Subjects: Science and Engineering, Periodicals
1978: 130 titles *1979:* 150 titles *Founded:* 1914

Ondori Sha Publishers Co Ltd, 32 Nishi Goken-cho, Shinjuku-ku, Tokyo 162 Tel: (03) 2681501
President: Toshizo Takeuchi; *Editor:* Takeo Sanada; *Sales:* Shigeo Yamamoto
Subjects: Knitting, Lacework, Embroidery, Handicrafts
1978: 52 titles *1979:* 55 titles *Founded:* 1945

Ongaku No Tomo Sha Corporation, 6-30 Kagurazaka, Shinju-ku, Tokyo Tel: (03) 2606271/8 Cable Add: Ongakuno Tomo Tokyo
President: Sunao Asaka; *Rights & Permissions:* Teruaki Kurata
Subsidiary Companies: Toa Music International Co, 6-32 Kagurazaka, Shinju-ku, Tokyo; Suiseisha Music Publishers, 3-3 Sanban-cho, Chiyoda-ku, Tokyo; Musica Nova, 6-30 Kagurazaka, Shinjuku-ku, Tokyo
Subjects: Classical and Popular Music, Educational, Periodicals
1978: 1048 titles *1979:* 1332 titles *Founded:* 1941

Oriental Economist Ltd (K K Toyo Keizai Shimposha), 4 Hongoku-cho 1-chome, Nihonbashi, Chuo-ku, Tokyo Tel: (03) 2704111
Man Dir: Iko Furukawa
Subjects: Scholastic, Economics, General Nonfiction, Directories

Otsuki Shoten Publishers, 11-9 Hongo 2-chome, Bunkyo-ku, Tokyo 113 Tel: (03) 8134651 (Sales)/8142931 (Editorial)
President, Production: Tomotaka Taira; *Editorial:* Isao Saho; *Sales:* Hiroshi Suzuki
Subjects: Economics, Philosophy, History, Socialism, General Arts
1978: 43 titles *1979:* 41 titles *Founded:* 1946

Pacifica Ltd*, Time-Life Books, PO Box 88, Tokyo 100-91 Tel: (03) 2706611 Cable Add: Publiftim Tokyo Telex: J 22276
Publisher: Mitsuo Honda; *Editor-in-chief:* Masatoshi Takeuchi; *Rights & Permissions:* Chiz Nakao
Parent Company: Time Inc
Subjects: General Fiction and Nonfiction
Founded: 1977

Poplar Publishing Co Ltd, 5 Suga-cho, Shinjuku-ku, Tokyo 160 Tel: (03) 3572211 Cable Add: Poplarpub
President: Tadao Kubota; *Foreign Trade Executive:* Haruo Tanaka; *Foreign Rights Executive:* Hideo Tanaka; *Foreign Rights Editor:* Tetsuo Kubota
Subjects: Juveniles, Fiction, Biography, History, Geography, Natural Sciences, Picture Books
1978: 180 titles *1979:* 180 titles *Founded:* 1947

Prentice-Hall of Japan Inc, Akasaka Mansion Room 405, 12-23 Akasaka 2-chome, Minato-ku, Tokyo 107 Tel: 5832591
Manager (Books & Rights Sales): Tetsuo Fujiyama
Subjects: Engineering, Technology, Sciences, Social Sciences, Business, Economics, Humanities, Medicine, Nursing, ESL, Children's, Audio-visual materials
Miscellaneous: Firm is a affiliate of Prentice-Hall International, Englewood Cliffs NJ 07632, USA (see Prentice-Hall UK for Associated Companies)
Founded: 1961

The **Reader's Digest** of Japan Limited, 1-1 Hitotsubashi 1-chome, Chiyoda-ku, Tokyo 100 Tel: (03) 2844111 Cable Add: Readigest Tokyo Telex: J23941 Rdtyo
President: Kaoru Ogimi; *Editor-in-Chief* (Magazine): Ko Shioya; *Editor* (Condensed Books): Yoshihiro Hiwano; *Marketing Dir:* Katoatsu Nakamura; *Production Dir:* Shugi Fujimori
Subjects: Geography, Education, Natural Science, Art, Language, Literature, Juveniles
1978: 2 titles *1979:* 2 titles *Founded:* 1946 (in Japan)

Risosha Ltd*, 46 Akagishita-machi, Shinjuku-ku, Tokyo 162 Tel: (03) 2681306
President: Tetsuo Shimomura; *Foreign Trade:* Tsugumoto Ishii; *Foreign Rights:* Kazumasa Doi
Subjects: Philosophy, Religion, Literature
1978: 11 titles *Founded:* 1927

Ryosho-Fukyu-Kai Co Ltd*, 8-2 Kasuga 1-chome, Bunkyo-ku, Tokyo 112 Tel: (03) 8131251
President & Editor: Ichigaku Kawanaka; *Foreign Trade Executive:* Isao Hiramatsu; *Foreign Rights Executive:* Shigeru Fukuhara; *Man Dir:* Kiyoshi Funakoshi
Subjects: Law, Social & Political Sciences, Public and Local Administration
Founded: 1914

Saera Shobo (Librairie Çà et Là), 1 Ichigaya-Sadoharacho, 3 chome, Shinjuku-ku, Tokyo 162 Tel: (03) 2684261
Chief Executive: Mitsusato Uraki
Imprint: Mitsusato Uraki
Subject: Children's
1978: 16 titles *1979:* 26 titles *Founded:* 1948
ISBN Publisher's Prefix: 378

Sangyo Tosho Publishing Co Ltd, 1-4-21 Soto-Kanda, Chiyoda-ku, Tokyo 101 Tel: (03) 2537821
Man Dir: Katsuhisa Morita; *Editorial:* Takehiko Ezura; *Sales:* Eiji Horino
Subjects: Natural Science, Engineering, Technology, Industry
1979: 23 titles *Founded:* 1925

The **Sankei** Shimbun Shuppankyoku Co*, 3-15 Kanda Nishiki-cho, Chiyoda-ku, Tokyo 101 Tel: (03) 2950911 Telex: J2-2235
Man Dir: Masashi Onoda; *Editorial:* Katsumi Shirai; *Sales:* Hiroshi Ohsato; *Rights & Permissions:* Nobaru Enomoto
Parent Companies: The Sankei Shimbun (Newspaper), Fuji Television Co, Nippon Broadcasting Co
Subjects: History, Social & Political Sciences, Industry, Art, Literature, Juveniles, Journals
1977: approx 100 titles *Founded:* 1950

Sanseido Co Ltd, 2-22-14 Misaki-cho, Chiyoda-ku, Tokyo 101 Tel: (03) 2309411
President: Hisanori Ueno; *Man Dir:* Masaaki Moriya; *Editorial:* Kiyohide Kato; *Sales:* Toshio Gomi; *Production:* Takaaki Hisashi; *Publicity:* Yasuo Nomura; *Rights & Permissions:* Kohji Suzuki
Subjects: Law, History, Reference, High-priced Paperbacks, General & Social Science, Natural Science, University & Secondary Textbooks, Educational Materials, Dictionaries, Literature, Languages
Bookshop: Sanseido Bookstore Ltd, 1-1 Kanda-Jimbocho, Chiyoda-ku, Tokyo
Founded: 1881

Sansyusya Publishing Co Ltd, 1-5-34 Shitaya, Taito-ku, Tokyo 110 Tel: (03) 8421711 Cable Add: Sansyusyapubl Tokyo
Man Dir: Kanji Maeda; *Sales, Publicity, Advertising, Rights & Permissions Dir:*

Shohei Ohara
Subjects: Language Textbooks, Educational Materials, Scientific Linguistic Reprints
1978: 79 titles *1979:* 109 titles *Founded:* 1938

Sanyo Shuppan Boeki Co Inc, PO Box 5037, Tokyo International 100-31 Tel: (03) 6693761 Cable Add: Sanyobook Tokyo Telex: 02524435 Sanyob
President: Tsuneo Suzuki; *Editorial:* Toshiaki Ibe; *Foreign Trade:* Masahiro Takeda; *Rights & Permissions:* Makoto Ito
Associate Company: Shinryo Bunko K K (medical bookstore)
Branch Offs: at Kyoto, Machida, Niihama, Osaka, Tsukuba
Subjects: Food and Cookery, Science, Chemistry
Founded: 1956
Miscellaneous: Also importers

Seibundo Shinkosha Publishing Co Ltd, 5 Nishikicho 1-chome, Kanda, Chiyoda-ku, Tokyo 101 Tel: (03) 2921211 Cable Add: Varipubco Tokyo
Man Dir, Sales: Shigeo Ogawa; *Editorial:* Teruaki Shimada; *Publicity:* Kazuhiko Furuya
Subjects: Commerce, Agriculture, Horticulture & Landscaping, Natural Science, Technology, Industry, Audio Electronics, Hobbies, Games, Juvenile
1979: 440 titles *Founded:* 1912

Seiwa Shoten Co Ltd, 2-5 Kamitakaido, 1-chome, Suginamiku, Tokyo 168 Tel: 3290031 Cable Add: Seiwapublishers
President: Youji Ishizawa; *Editor-in-Chief:* Yoshinori Asanuma; *Sales Manager:* Masaharu Fujiwara; *System Manager:* Yukio Shimura; *Foreign Books Manager:* Yumi Matsuzawa
Subjects: Medicine, Psychiatry, Psychology, Language
Book Club: Bookclub Psyche
Bookshops: 1-11 Kamitakaido, 1-chome, Suginamiku, Tokyo 168; 2-5 Kamitakaido, 1-chome, Suginamiku, Tokyo 168; 1-48 Sengawacho, Chofushi, Tokyo 182
1978: 12 titles *1979:* 14 titles *Founded:* 1976

Seizando-Shoten Publishing Co Ltd, 4-51 Minami-motomachi, Shinjuku-ku, Tokyo 160 Tel: (03) 3575861
President: Minoru Ogawa; *Editorial:* Yoshihiro Munekata; *Sales:* Jitsuo Moriyama; *Production:* Yuhei Shibuya, Nobuyuki Tanaka; *Publicity:* Yoshio Kimura; *Rights & Permissions:* Kokichi Shioji
Subjects: Maritime, Technology, Transport
1978: 110 titles *1979:* 120 titles *Founded:* 1953
ISBN Publisher's Prefix: 7911

Sekai Bunka Publishing Inc*, 4-2-29 Kudan Kita, Chiyoda-ku, Tokyo 102 Tel: (03) 2625111 Cable Add: Sebunpub
President: Tsutomu Suzuki; *Foreign Trade & Rights:* Kazumi Haga
Branch Off: 501 Fifth Ave, Suite 2102, New York, NY 10017, USA
Subjects: Art, History, Geography, Juveniles, Educational Materials, Audiovisual
Founded: 1946

Shakai Shiso-Sha*, 25-21 Hongo 1-chome, Bunkyo-ku, Tokyo 113 Tel: (03) 8138101
President: Kazuki Komorida; *Editorial:* Hitoshi Tanaka; *Sales:* Tadashi Kamatsuka
Subjects: General Fiction, Fine Arts, Architecture, Poetry, Music, History, Travel, Social Science, Theatre
Founded: 1947

Shiko-Sha Co Ltd, 10-12 Hiroo 2-chome, Shibuya-ku, Tokyo 150 Tel: (03) 4007151/4 Cable Add: Lmdecw Tokyo Telex: J24903
Man Dir: Yasoo Takeichi
Subject: Juveniles
Founded: 1950

Shinchosha Co, 71 Yarai-cho, Shinjuku-ku, Tokyo 162 Tel: (03) 2665101 Cable Add: Shinchosha
President: Ryoichi Sato; *Sales:* Shunichi Sato; *Publishing Department:* Hiroshi Nitta
Subjects: General Fiction, Fine Arts, History, Philosophy, Social Science, Reference, Literature
Founded: 1896

Shindan to Chiryo Co Ltd*, Room 406, Marunouchi Bldg, Marunouchi 2-4-1, Tokyo 100 Tel: (03) 2144957
President: Hiroshi Fujizane; *Editorial:* Takeshi Hisatsugi
Subject: Medicine
1978: 30 titles *Founded:* 1914

Shinkenchiku-Sha Co Ltd, 31-2 Yushima 2-chome, Bunkyo-ku, Tokyo 113 Tel: (03) 8117101 Cable Add: Japanarch Tokyo
President: Yoshio Yoshida; *General Manager:* Masao Nakamura; *Foreign Rights Executive:* Masao Nakamura
Subsidiary Company: The Japan Architect Co Ltd, 31-2, Yushima 2-chome, Bunkyo-ku, Tokyo 113
Subjects: Architecture, Periodicals
1978: 16 titles *Founded:* 1925

Shogakukan Publishing Co Ltd, 2-3 Hitotsubashi, Chiyoda-ku, Tokyo 101 Tel: (03) 2305655 Cable Add: Tokyo Shogakukan Telex: 2322191 (Shogak-J)
President: Tetsuo Ohga; *Man Dir:* Shuichi Nozaki; *Editorial:* Kiichi Toyoda; *Sales:* Tokio Ueno; *Production:* Mitsuo Kokubo
Associated Company: Shueisha Publishing Co (qv)
Subjects: Art, How-to, Juveniles, Dictionaries, Geography, History, Encyclopaedias, Travel
1978: 531 titles *1979:* 495 titles *Founded:* 1922

Shokabo Publishing Co Ltd*, 8-1 Yonban-cho, Chiyoda-ku, Tokyo 102 Tel: (03) 2629166
Man Dir: Tatsuji Yoshino
Subjects: Mathematics, Natural Science, Technology
1977: 11 titles *Founded:* 1897

Shokoku-Sha Publishing Co Ltd*, 25 Saka-machi, Shinjuku-ku, J-160 Tokyo Tel: (03) 3593231
President: Genshichi Shimoide; *Sales Dir:* Hideo Shimizu; *Editorial Dir:* Taishiro Yamamoto
Subjects: Fine Arts, Technical, Architecture, Engineering, General Science, University Textbooks, Educational Materials
Founded: 1932

Shueisha Publishing Co Ltd*, 2-5-10 Hitotsubashi, Chiyoda-ku, Tokyo 101 Tel: (03) 2306111
President: Sueo Horiuchi; *Editorial:* Shusei Suzuki; *Sales:* Hisao Suzuki; *Foreign Trade:* Takeo Hasegawa; *Foreign Rights:* Hajime Kanazawa
Associate Company: Shogakukan Publishing Co Ltd (qv)
Subjects: General Fiction, Nonfiction, Art, Language, Literature, Juveniles, Periodicals
Founded: 1926

Shufu-to-Seikatsu Sha Ltd*, 5-3-chome, Kyobashi, Chuo-ku, Tokyo 104 Tel: (03) 5625951
Man Dir: Tokumitsu Higuchi; *Editor-in-Chief:* Miss Miyako Kiyohara; *Publishing Department, Foreign Rights:* Shujiro Murakawa
Subjects: Philosophy & Religion, History, Medicine, Technology, Art, Literature, Juveniles
Founded: 1935

Shufunotomo Co Ltd, 6, 1-chome Surugadai, Kanda, Chiyoda-ku, Tokyo 101 Tel: 2941111 Cable Add: Shufunotomo Tokyo Telex: 26925
President: Haruhiko Ishikawa; *Manager of International Department:* Kazuhiko Nagai
Subjects: Cookery, Flower Arrangement, Bonsai, Gardening, How-to, General Fiction
1978: 180 titles *Founded:* 1916

The **Simul** Press Inc, Kowa Bldg No 9, 1-8-10, Akasaka, Minato-ku, Tokyo 107 Tel: (03) 5824221 Cable Add: Simulshuppan Tokyo
President and Editor-in-Chief: Katsuo Tamura; *Senior Man Dir:* Eiko Ikuta; *Man Dir:* Yutaka Suzuki; *Dir (overseas affairs):* Masumi Muramatsu; *Secretary (foreign relations):* Masako Miyoshi; *Senior Editor:* Daitaro Suwabe; *Marketing:* Motoo Miyashita; *Publicity:* Koichiro Watanabe
Associate Company: Simul International, Inc
Subjects: General, Philosophy and Religion, Social Sciences, History, Education, Business and Economics, Current Affairs, Language, Literature, English-language books on Japan and Asia
1978: 40 titles *1979:* 44 titles *Founded:* 1967

Sogensha Publishing Co Ltd*, 4-2 1-chome, Nishitenma, Kita-ku, Osaka 530 Tel: (06) 3632531
President: Bunji Yabe
Associate Company: Tokyo Sogensha Co Ltd, Japan (qv)
Subjects: Art, History, Philosophy, Religion, Low-priced Paperbacks, Medicine, University Textbooks, Educational Materials
Founded: 1925

Syokabo Publishing Co Ltd*, 8-1 Yomban-cho, Chiyoda-ku, Tokyo 102 Tel: (03) 2629166
President: Tatsuji Yoshino; *Foreign Trade:* Tatsuji Yoshino; *Foreign Rights:* Kyohei Endo
Subjects: Natural Science and Engineering
1978: 15 titles *Founded:* 1895

Taishukan Publishing Co Ltd (Taishukan Shoten), 3-24 Kanda-Nishiki-cho, Chiyoda-ku, Tokyo 101 Tel: (03) 2942221
Man Dir: Toshio Suzuki; *Sales, Publicity & Advertising:* Shigeo Suzuki; *Rights & Permissions:* Toshio Saeki
Subjects: Reference, High-priced Paperbacks, Language & Linguistics, Sports, Social Science, University & Secondary Textbooks, Educational Materials, Dictionaries, Periodicals
1978: 65 titles *1979:* 64 titles *Founded:* 1918

Takahashi Shoten Co Ltd*, 22-13 Otowa 1-chome, Bunkyo-ku, Tokyo 112 Tel: (03) 9434525
President: Kyushiro Takahashi; *Foreign Trade Executive:* Yukihiko Takahashi
Subjects: Technology, Law Education, Medicine, Language, Juveniles
Founded: 1939 (as Kowado Co Ltd)

Tanko-Sha Publishing Co Ltd*, Tanko Bldg, Horikawa Kuramaguchi-agaru, Kita-ku, Kyoto 603 Tel: Kyoto 4325151
Man Dir: Saburo Iguchi; *Editorial Dir:* Shiro Usui
Subjects: Philosophy & Religion, History, Art, Japanese Culture
Founded: 1945

Teikoku-Shoin Co Ltd, 3-29 Kanda Jinbo-cho, Chiyoda-ku, Tokyo 101 Tel: (03) 2611584 Cable Add: Books Teikoku Telex: 2324921 Tekoku J
President: Takashi Goto; *Foreign Trade:* Takashi Saito; *Foreign Rights:* Yukio Eguchi
Subjects: History, Geography, Maps, Textbooks
1978: 150 titles *Founded:* 1926

Tokai University Press, Shinjuku Tokai Bldg, 3-27-4 Shinjuku, Shinjuku-ku, Tokyo 160 Tel: (03) 3561541
Man Dir: Tatsuro Matsumae; *Editorial:* Yasunosuke Yamamoto; *Sales:* Eizaburo Okada; *Production:* Chimaju Kato; *Publicity:* Wataru Yamada
Orders to: Orion Books, Export Dept of Orion Service & Trading Co Inc, PO Box 5216, Tokyo International
Subjects: Philosophy, Religion, History, Social & Natural Science, Technology, Art, Language, Literature
1978: 49 titles *Founded:* 1962
Miscellaneous: Tokai University European Center is at Strandvej 476, DK-2950, Vedbæk, Denmark

Tokuma-Shoten, 4-10-1 Shinbashi, Minato-ku, Tokyo 105 Tel: (03) 4336231
President: Yasuyoshi Tokuma; *Editor:* Minoru Hagiwara; *Foreign Trade:* Osamu Okamura
Subjects: General Fiction, Nonfiction, Belles Lettres, How-to, Social Science, Art, Games, Sports
Founded: 1954

Tokyo Kagaku Dozin Co Ltd*, 36-7 Sengoku 3-chome, Bunkyo-ku, Tokyo 112 Tel: (03) 9465311
President: Atsushi Ueki; *Editorial:* Minako Ozawa
Subjects: Natural Science, Medical Science, Chemistry
1978: 63 titles *Founded:* 1961

Tokyo News Service Ltd, 8-10 Ginza-Nishi, Chuo-ku, Tokyo
President: T Okuyama
Subjects: Social Science, Economics, Business, General Nonfiction, Periodicals
Founded: 1947

Tokyo Sogensha Co Ltd*, 1-16 Shin Ogawa-machi, Shinjuku-ku, Tokyo 162 Tel: (03) 2688201
President: Takao Akiyama; *Editorial:* Jun Atsuki; *Sales:* Ichiro Hiramatsu; *Production:* Haruo Hashimoto; *Publicity:* Nobuko Okubo; *Rights & Permissions:* Yasunobu Togawa
Subjects: Detective Stories, Science Fiction, Social Science, Literature
Founded: 1925

Tokyo Tosho Co Ltd*, 2-5 Suido, Bunkyo-ku, Tokyo 112 Tel: (03) 8147818
President: Susumu Otake; *Foreign Trade Executive:* Hiroyasu Katayama; *Foreign Rights:* Shigeaki Matsumoto
Subjects: Natural Science, Popular Science, Engineering, Biographies
Founded: 1955

Toppan Co Ltd, Shufunotomo Bldg, 1-6 Kanda Surugadai, Chiyoda-ku, Tokyo 101 Tel: 2953461 Cable Add: Toppan Book Tokyo Telex: J27317
Chief Executive: Kazuo Suzuki; *Man Dir:* Hiroyuki Watanabe; *General Managers:* Moto Sekino, William A Feuillan
Associate Company: Toppan Co (S) Pte Ltd, Singapore (qv)
Subjects: Medicine, Psychology, Engineering, Social Science, Agriculture, Economics, Mathematics, Statistics, Zoology, Chemistry, Physics, Languages and Linguistics in authorized International Student Edition reprints for university students
1978-9: 37 titles *Founded:* 1963

Toyo Keizai Shinposha Ltd*, 4 Hongokucho 1-chome, Nihonbashi, Chuo-ku, Tokyo 103 Tel: (03) 2704111
President: Yoshiyuki Nakai; *Foreign Trade:* Sasuke Takahashi; *Foreign Rights:* Ikuo Inada
Subjects: Economic Science, Industry, Social Science, General
1978: 100 titles *Founded:* 1895

Tsuru-Shobo Co Ltd*, 12-2 Fujimi 2-chome, Chiyoda-ku, Tokyo 102 Tel: (03) 2654781 Cable Add: Bookstsuru Tokyo
Man Dir: Mitsusaburo Sadahira; *Foreign Rights & Permissions:* Hiro Nagano
Subjects: How-to, Juveniles, Art, Reference
Founded: 1926

Charles E **Tuttle** Co Inc, 2-6 Suido 1-chome, Bunkyo-ku, Tokyo 112 Tel: (03) 8117106/9 Cable Add: Tuttbooks Telex: 0272-3170
President, Editorial, Sales, Publicity: Keiko Iwamoto; *Production:* Satoru Iwamoto; *Rights & Permissions:* Keiko Iwamoto
Branch Offs: 402 Seki, Tama-ku, Kawasaki-shi 214; 2-7 Showa-cho, Suita-shi, Osaka 564; CPO Box 302, Naha-shi, Okinawa 900-91
Subjects: Japanese & Asian Studies, Art, Domestic & Handicrafts, Fiction, Martial Arts, Poetry, Belles Lettres, Political & Social Science, Juveniles, Languages
Bookshops: Kanda Book Shop, 1-3 Jimbo-cho, Kanda, Chiyoda-ku, Tokyo 101; American Club Book Shop, 4 Mamiana-cho, Azabu, Monato-ku, Tokyo 106
1978: 52 titles *Founded:* 1948
ISBN Publisher's Prefix: 0-8048

U N A C Tokyo*, 1-4-7 Azabu-da, Minato-ku, Tokyo 106 Tel: (03) 5857069/5853069 Cable Add: Unacprod
Publisher: Masaomi Unagami

University of Tokyo Press, 7-3-1 Hongo, Bunkyo-ku, Tokyo 113-91 Tel: (03) 8110964 Cable Add: Universitypress
Man Dir: Kazuo Ishii; *Associate Dirs:* Senzaburo Nakahira, Hitoshi Tada; *Sales:* Kazuhiko Kurata; *Publicity, Rights & Permissions:* Masami Yamaguchi
Subsidiary Companies: Centre for Academic Publications Japan; Business Centre for Academic Societies Japan (both at 2-14-16 Yayoi, Bunkyo-ku, Tokyo 113)
Subjects: History, Philosophy, Reference, Religion, Medicine, Psychology, Engineering, Natural & Social Sciences, University Textbooks
Bookshop: Yurinsha Ltd, PO Box 63, Hongo Post Office, Tokyo
1978: 163 titles *1979:* 153 titles *Founded:* 1951

Mitsusato **Uraki**, an imprint of Saera Shobo (Librarie Ça et Là) (qv)

John **Weatherhill** Inc*, 7-6-13 Roppongi, Minato-ku, Tokyo Tel: 4048871 Cable Add: Weatherhill Tokyo Telex: 23424004
Man Dir: Meredith Weatherby; *Sales & Advertising:* Jun'ichiro Minagawa; *Rights & Permissions:* Emile Dubrule, 149 Madison Ave, New York, NY 10016, USA
Subjects: Belles Lettres, Poetry, Biography, History, How-to, Music, Art, Reference, Religion, Juveniles, High-priced Paperbacks — all on Asia
Founded: 1962

Yama-Kei (Publishers) Co Ltd*, 1-1-33 Shiba-Daimon, Minato-ku, Tokyo 105 Tel: (03) 4364021
President: Yoshimitsu Kawasaki; *Foreign Trade:* Susumu Harada; *Foreign Rights:* Naotake Murakami
Branch Off: Riverside Bldg, 4-11-12 Kamiji, Higashinari-ku, Osaka
Subjects: Mountaineering, Skiing, Geography, Natural Science
Founded: 1930

Yamada Shoin (Yamada Publishing Co)*, 26 Saka-machi, Shinjuku-ku, Tokyo 160 Tel: (03) 3534331
Chairman: Yonekichi Yamada; *President:* Minoru Yamada; *Sales:* Akira Shimizu
Subjects: Fine Arts, History, Juveniles, Travel, Textbooks
Founded: 1919

Yohan Publications Inc, 14-9 Okubo 3-chome, Shinjuku-ku, Tokyo 160 Tel: (03) 2080181
President: Masahiro Watanabe

Yokendo Ltd, 5-30-15 Hongo, Bunkyo-ku, Tokyo 113 Tel: (03) 8140911
President: Toshio Oikawa
Subjects: Natural Science, Engineering, Industry
1979: 16 titles *Founded:* 1914

Yuhikaku Publishing Co Ltd*, 17 2-chome, Kanda Jinbo-cho, Chiyoda-ku, Tokyo 101 Tel: (03) 2641311 Cable Add: Yuhikakubook
Dirs: Shiro Egusa, Tadaatsu Egusa
Subjects: Law, Economics, Sociology, Psychology, History, Education
1978: 230 titles *Founded:* 1877

Yushodo Booksellers Ltd, 29 San-ei-cho, Shinjuku-ku, Tokyo 160 Tel: (03) 3571411 Cable Add: Yushodo Tokyo Telex: 0232-4136
President: Mitsuo Nitta; *Editorial:* Yoshito Yamada
Subsidiary Companies: Publishers International Corp, Yushodo Film Publications Ltd
Branch Off: Kansai, Kyoto
Subjects: Political Economics, Japanese Classical Literature
1978: 24 titles *1979:* 21 titles
Miscellaneous: Company are also Booksellers

The **Zauho** Press, Sogo Daiichi Bldg, 3-2 Kojimachi, Chiyoda-ku, Tokyo 102 Tel: (03) 2623661 Cable Add: Zauhopress
President: Shigeki Gotoh; *Foreign Trade Executive:* Yoshiki Gotoh; *Foreign Rights Executive:* Masao Nishida
Subjects: Art, History, Co-editions
1978: 1 title *Founded:* 1925

Zoshindo Juken-Kenkyusha, 19-15 2-chome Shinmachi, Nishi-ku Osaka 550
President: Shigetoshi Okamoto
Subjects: Education, Juveniles
1978: 442 titles *1979:* 406 titles *Founded:* 1890

Literary Agents

The **English Agency**, 705 Azabu Empire Mansion, 4-11-28 Nishi Azabu, Minato-ku, Tokyo Tel: (03) 4065385 Cable Add: Enagent
Dirs: Anthony Blond, Desmond Briggs, William Miller, Peter Thompson
Specialization: English books

Japan Uni Agency Inc, Naigai Bldg, 1-1 Kanda Jimbocho, Chiyoda-ku, Tokyo 101 Tel: (03) 2950301 Cable Add: Uniliterary Telex: J27260
President: Noboru Miyata; *Man Dir:* Kozaburo Yano; *Dirs:* Hideo Aoki (Co-Production); Yoshio Taketomi (Copyrights); *Foreign Rights:* Akiko Kurita

Kern Associates, 5-18 Sakae-cho, Sagamihara-shi Kanagawa-ken 228 Tel: 0427461829/31/32 Cable Add: Kern Machida
Chairman: Lawrence E Kern; *Dirs:* D Kern, N Kern
Specialization: Fiction, Nonfiction, Academic, Juvenile

Orion Press, 55, 1-chome, Kanda-Jimbocho, Chiyoda-ku, Tokyo 101 Tel: (03) 2951405/2951406 Cable Add: Orionserv Tokyo Telex: J24447 Orionprs
Contact: G G Pompilio, T Sakai

Toppan Co Ltd, Rights Agency Section, Shufunotomo Building, 1-6 Kanda Surugadai, Chiyoda-ku, Tokyo 101 Tel: (03) 295 3461 Cable Add: Toppanbook Tokyo Telex: J27317
Contact: William A Feuillan

Tuttle-Mori Agency Inc, Fuji Bldg 8F, 2-15 Kanda-Jimbocho, Chiyoda-ku, Tokyo Tel: (03) 230 4081 Cable Add: Tuttmori Tokyo Telex: 2324915 Tutmor J
President: Tom Mori; *Editorial Dir:* Kiyoshi Asano; *Editorial Manager:* Yoshikazu Iwasaki
Also offices at:
Sandford J Greenburger Associates Inc, 825 Third Ave, New York, NY 10022, USA Tel: (212) 7538581 Cable Add: Inlitbur Telex: 420633
Contact: Ms Nikki Smith
61 Blenheim Terrace, London NW8 0EJ Tel: 624 9601 Telex: 28905 Monref G
Contact: Anne Martyn
Dealing in Book Rights, Serial Rights, Co-Production, Motion Picture Rights, TV Rights, Radio Rights, Stage Rights, Merchandising Rights

United Publishers Services Ltd*, Shimura Building, 4-1, Kojimachi, Chiyoda-ku, Tokyo 102 Tel: (03) 2625278 Cable Add: Unitedbooks Tokyo
General Manager: Sumio Saito

Book Clubs

Books-on-Japan-in-English Club*, Shin Nichibo Bldg, 2-1 Sarugaku-cho 1-chome, Chiyoda-ku, Tokyo 101
President: Katsuji Yabuki; *Secretary General:* Akio Takeuchi
Founded: 1955
Miscellaneous: Club consists of 36 leading publishers, bookstores, exporters, and printers of English-language books and periodicals dealing with Japan and Orient

Ehon Library, 1-9 Misaki-cho 1-chome, Chiyoda-ku, Tokyo 101
Owned by: Fukuinkan Shoten Publishers (Tokyo)
Subject: Picture Books

Kodansha Disney Children's Book Club, 2-12-21 Otowa, Bunkyo-ku, Tokyo
Owned by: Kodansha (Tokyo)
Subject: Children's Books

Bookclub **Psyche**, Seiwa Shoten Co Ltd, 2-5 Kamitakaido, 1-chome, Suginamiku, Tokyo 168
Owned by: Seiwa Shoten Co Ltd
Subject: Psychiatry

Major Booksellers

Asahiya Shoten Ltd (Booksellers), Osaka-Fukoku-Seimei Bldg 3F, 2-4 Komatsubara-cho Kita-ku, Osaka 530 Tel: (06) 3150971
Foreign Books Department: c/o Asahi Building, 17-9 Toyosaki 3-chome, Ohyodo-ku, Osaka 531 Tel: (06) 3727251
16 bookstores throughout the country

Goethe Book Dealers Inc*, Room 560, Marunouchi Bldg, Chiyoda-ku, Tokyo 100 Tel: (03) 2117839

Ikubundo Publishers Co*, 30-21 Hongo 5-chome, Bunkyo-ku, Tokyo 113 Tel: (03) 8145571/5

Japan Publications Trading Co Ltd (Import and Export), 2-1, 1-chome, Sarugaku-cho, Chiyoda-ku, Tokyo 101 Tel: (03) 2923751 Telex: J27161

Kinokuniya Bookstore Co Ltd*, 17-7 Shinjuku 3-chome, Shinjuku-ku, Tokyo 160-91 Tel: (03) 3540131 (and 37 branches throughout Japan)

Kurita Shuppan Hanbai Co Ltd*, 3-1 Higashisakashita 1-chome, Itabashi-ku, Tokyo 174 Tel: (03) 9652111
Distributor

Maruzen Co Ltd, 3-10 Nihonbashi 2-chome, Chuo-ku, Tokyo 103 Tel: (03) 2727211
Branches: Sapporo, Sendai, Tsukuba, Nagoya, Kyoto, Osaka, Kobe, Okayama, Hiroshima, Fukuoka
Importer/Exporter

Nippon Shuppan Hanbai KK*, 3 4-chome, Kanda Surugadai, Chiyoda-ku, Tokyo 101 Tel: (03) 2932111 Cable Add: Honnippan Tokyo Telex: J 25627 Nippan
Distributors

Tokyo Shuppan Hanbai Co Ltd (Distributors)*, 53 Higashigoken-cho, Shinjuku-ku, Tokyo 162 Tel: (03) 2696111 Cable Add: Hontohan Tokyo Telex: 2322141

Charles E **Tuttle** Co Inc, 2-6 Suido 1-chome, Bunkyo-ku, Tokyo 112 Tel: 8117106

United Publishers Services Ltd, Shimura Bldg, 4-1, Kojimachi, Chiyoda-ku, Tokyo 102 Tel: (03) 2625278 Cable Add: Unitedbooks Tokyo
The largest stock holding agent of overseas publishers in the Japanese foreign book market

Yohan (Western Publications Distribution Agency), 14-9 Okubo 3-chome, Shinjuku-ku, Tokyo 160 Tel: (03) 2080181 Cable Add: Bookyohan Tokyo
President: Masahiro Watanabe

Major Libraries

Hokkaido University Library, Kita-8, Nishi-5, Sapporo 060 Tel: (011) 711-2111
Librarian: Yutaka Shioya
Publication: Yuin (The Hokkaido University Library Bulletin, only in Japanese, quarterly)

Kokuritsu Kobunshokan*, 3-2 Kitanomaru Park, Chiyoda-ku, Tokyo
National Archives

Kyoto Sangyo University Library*, Kamigamo, Kita-ku, Kyoto Tel: (075) 7012151

Kyushu University Library*, 3576 Hakozaki-machi, Fukuoka City, Fukuoka Prefecture

School of **Library** and Information Science*, Keio University, Mita Minato-ku, Tokyo 108 Tel: (03) 4533920

Nagoya University Library*, Furo-cho, Chikusa-ku, Nagoya

National Diet Library, 10-1, 1-chome, Nagata-cho, Chiyoda-ku, Tokyo100 Tel: (03) 5812331
Librarian: Minoru Kishida

Osaka Prefectural Nakanoshima Library, 1-2-10 Nakanoshima, Kita-ku, Osaka Tel: (06) 2030474

Osaka Gakuin University Library*, Kishibe, Suita City, Osaka

Tenri Central Library, Tenri University, Somanouchi-cho 1050, Tenri City, Nara 632 Tel: (07436) 31511 ext 6750
Chief Librarian: Hidetsugu Ueda

Tohoku University Library*, Kawauchi, Sendai City 980

Tokyo Metropolitan Central Library*, 5-7-13 Minami-Azabu, Minato-ku, Tokyo 106

The **Toyo** Bunko, Honkomagome 2-chome, 28-21, Bunkyo-ku, Tokyo 113 Tel: (03) 9420121
Publications: Memoirs of the Research Department of the Toyo Bunko
Also Centre of East Asian Cultural Studies for UNESCO, for which publications include various directories, bibliographies, textbooks, etc

University Libraries, see also under town names

University of Tokyo Library*, 3-1 Hongo 7-chome, Bunkyo-ku, Tokyo 113 Tel: (03) 8122111

Waseda University Library, 6-1 Nishiwaseda 1-chome, Shinjuku-ku, Tokyo 160

Library Associations

Gakujutsu Bunken Fukyu-Kai*, c/o Tokyo Institute of Technology, 2-15-1 O-okayama, Meguro-ku, Tokyo
Association for Science Documents Information
President: Taku Uemura
Publications: Union Catalog of Books on Japan in Western Languages (English), Reports on Progress in Polymer Physics in Japan (English), Directory of Japanese Scientific Periodicals (English), Aseismic Design and Testing of Nuclear Facilities (English), Union Index of Books in the Field of Documentation (English)

Joho Shori Gakkai*, Kikai Shinko-Kai Building No 3-5-8, Shiba-Koen, Minato-ku, Tokyo
Information Processing Society of Japan
President: K Kobayashi
Publications: Journal of Information Processing (English, quarterly), Joho-shori (Journal of IPSJ, Japanese, monthly), Transactions of IPSJ (Japanese, bi-monthly)

Nippon Dokumentesyon Kyokai*, Sasaki Bldg, 5-7 Koisikawa 2, Bunkyo-ku, Tokyo 112 Tel: (03) 8133791
Japan Documentation Society
President: S Hamada
Publication: Documentation Study

Nippon Igaku Toshokan Kyokai*, c/o Business Centre for Academic Societies, 4-16 Yayoi 2-chome, Bunkyo-ku, Tokyo 113
The Japan Medical Library Association

Nippon Nogaku Toshokan Kyogikai (JAALD), Taiyo Seimei Building, 2-17-2, Shibuya, Shibuya-ku, Tokyo 150 Tel: (03) 4090722
Japan Association of Agricultural Librarians and Documentalists
Secretary: Masatada Oyama
Publications: Quarterly Bulletin of JAALD, Japanese Agricultural Sciences Index (monthly with semi-annual indexes)

Nippon Toshokan Gakkai*, c/o National College of Library Science, 1-1 Simouma 4-chome, Setagaya-ku, Tokyo
Japan Society of Library Science
Executive Secretary: Takaaki Kuriwa
Publication: Toshokangakki Nempo (Annals) (2-4 a year)

Nippon Toshokan Kyokai, 1-10, 1-chome, Taishido, Setagaya-ku, Tokyo 154
Japan Library Association
Secretary-General: Hitoshi Kurihara
Publications: Toshokan Zasshi (monthly), *Gendai no Toshokan* (quarterly), *Nippon no Sankotosho Shikiban* (quarterly), *Nippon no Toshokan* (annually)

Nippon Yakugaku Toshokan Kyogikai*, c/o Library, Faculty of Pharmaceutical Sciences, Hongo 7-3-1, Bunkyo-ku, Tokyo 113
Japan Pharmaceutical Library Association
Publication: Yakugaku Toshokan (Pharmaceutical Library Bulletin)

Senmon Toshokan Kyogikai (SENTOKYO), c/o National Diet Library, 1-10-1, Nagata-cho, Chiyoda-ku, Tokyo 100
Tel: (03) 5811364
Japan Special Libraries Association
President: Shigeo Nagano
Publications: Bulletin (quarterly), *Directory of Special Libraries*, 1979 (in Japanese); *Directory of Information Sources in Japan*, 1980 (in English)

Library Reference Books and Journals

Books

Directory of Information Sources in Japan (in English), Japan Special Libraries Association, c/o National Diet Library, 1-10-1 Nagata-cho, Chiyoda-ku, Tokyo

Directory of Special Libraries, Japan Special Libraries Association, c/o National Diet Library, 1-10-1 Nagata-cho, Chiyoda-ku, Tokyo

Nippon no Toshokan (Library of Japan), Japan Library Association, 1-10, 1-chome, Taishido Setagaya-ku, Tokyo

Union Index of Books in the Field of Documentation, Association for Science Documents Information, c/o Tokyo Institute of Technology, 2-15-1 O-okayama, Meguro-ku, Tokyo

Journals

Biburosu Biblos, National Diet Library, 10-1, 1-chome, Nagata-cho, Chiyoda-ku, Tokyo

Bulletin, Special Libraries Association, c/o National Diet Library, 10-1, 1-chome, Nagata-cho, Chiyoda-ku, Tokyo

Dokumentesyon Kenkyu (Documentation Study), Japan Documentation Society, Sasaki Bldg, 5-7 Koisikawa 2, Bunkyo-ku, Tokyo 112

Handbook, Special Libraries Association, c/o National Diet Library, 10-1, 1-chome, Nagata-cho, Chiyoda-ku, Tokyo

Library System (text in Japanese), Medical Library and Information Centre, Keio Unveristy, 35, Shinanomachi, Shinjuku-ku, Tokyo

Nippon no Sakotosho Shikiban (Reference Library Quarterly of Japan), Japan Library Association, 1-10, 1-chome, Taishido Setagaya-ku, Tokyo

Reference, National Diet Library, 10-1, 1-chome, Nagata-cho, Chiyoda-ku, Tokyo

Toshokan-Kai (Library World) (text in Japanese, table of contents in English), Japan Institution for Library Science, Tenri University, Tenri, Nara

Toshokan Zasshi (Library Journal), Japan Library Association, 1-10, 1-chome, Taishido Setagaya-ku, Tokyo

Sendai no Toshokan (Library of Today), Japan Library Association, 1-10, 1-chome, Taishido Setagaya-ku, Tokyo

Literary Associations and Societies

The **Dickens** Fellowship*, Bungei-Gakuba, Seijo University 6-1-20, Seijo Setagaya, Tokyo
Honorary Secretary: Prof Koichi Miyazaki

Japan Contemporary Poets' Society, c/o Hideki Isomura, 1-14-6 Kamata, Setagaya-ku, Tokyo

Japan Essayists' Club*, c/o Yujiro Chiba, 1-1-1 Shimbashi, Minato-ku, Tokyo

Japan Poet Club*, c/o Showa Joshi University, 1-7 Taishido, Setagaya-ku, Tokyo

Nihon Eibungakkai, 18 Nakamachi, Shinjuku-ku, Tokyo 162
English Literary Society of Japan
President: Yoshiaki Fuhara
Publication: Studies in English Literature (three times yearly)

Nippon Bungaku Kyokai, 2-17-10 Minami-otsuka, Toshima-ku, Tokyo Tel: (03) 9412740
Japanese Literature Association
President: Tamotsu Hirosue
Publication: Japanese Literature (monthly)

Nippon Dokubungakkai*, c/o Ikubundo, Hongo 5-30-21, Bunkyo-ku, Tokyo 113
Japanese Society of German Literature
President: Professor Sakae Hamakawa
Publication: Doitsu Bungaku (German Literature) (twice yearly)

Nippon Furansu-go Furansu-bungaku Kai*, c/o La Maison franco-japonaise, 2-3, Kanda-Surugadai Chiyoda-ku, Tokyo
Japanese Society of French Language and Literature
President: Takeo Kuwabara
Publication: Etudes de Langue et Littérature françaises (half-yearly)

Nippon Hikaku Bungakukai*, Aoyamagakuim University, Shibuya-ku, Tokyo
Comparative Literature Society of Japan
General-Secretary: Saburo Ota
Publications: Journal (annually), *Bulletin* (quarterly)

Nippon Romazikai*, Yosida Honmati 27, Kyoto
Japanese Society of Roman Letters
President: Akabori Siro
Publication: Romazi Sekai (The World of Roman Letters)

Nippon Rosiya Bungakkai*, Faculty of Literature Waseda University, Toyama-cho, Shinjuku-ku, Tokyo
Russian Literary Society of Japan
Secretary-General: General K Nakano
Publication: Bulletin

Japan P E N Club, Room 265, Syuwa Residential Hotel, 9-1-7 Akasaka, Minato-ku, Tokyo 107
Secretary: Yuzo Toki
Publications include: Japanese Literature Today (1976-80) (annual); *Japan PEN News* (twice yearly)

Society for the Promotion of Japanese Literature, c/o Bungei Shunju Publishing Co Ltd, 3 Kioi-cho, Chiyoda-ku, Tokyo

Literary Periodicals

Doitsu Bungaku (German Literature), Japanese Society of German Literature, Hongo 5-30-21, Bunkyo-ku, Tokyo 113

Doshisha Literature; a journal of English literature and philology (text in English), Doshisha University, English Literature Society, Kyoto

Doshisha Studies in Foreign Literature (text in Japanese, English, French or German), Doshisha University, Foreign Literature Society, Kyoto

East-West Review; essays on literature and translations of literary works, Doshisha University, Department of English, Kyoto

Etudes de Langue et Littérature françaises (Studies in French Language and Literature), Japanese Society of French Language and Literature, c/o La Maison franco-japonaise, 2-3, Kanda-Surugadai Chiyoda-ku, Tokyo

Hon: a Book-bin for Scholars, Yushodo Booksellers Ltd, 29 Saneicho, Shinjuku-ku, Tokyo 160

Japan Quarterly, Asahi Shimbun-Sha, Tokyo

Japanese Literature, Japanese Literature Association, 2-17-20 Minami-otsuka, Toshima-ku, Tokyo

Japanese Literature Today (1976-80) (annual), Japan P E N Club, Room 265, Syuwa Residential Hotel, 9-1-7 Akasaka, Minato-ku, Tokyo 107

Mototachi no Kagaribi (The Little Sister's Watchfire), Kodansha International Ltd, 2-12-21 Otowa, Bunkyo-ku, Tokyo

Outlook (Japan), Yoshidahon-machi, Sakyo-Ka, Kioto

The Sea, Chuokoron-Sha Inc, 2-8-7 Kyobashi, Chuo-ku, Tokyo 104

Studies in English Literature, English Literary Society of Japan, 18 Nakamachi, Shinjuku-ku, Tokyo 162

Literary Prizes

Akutagawa Prize
In memory of Ryunosuke Akutagawa for works written by unknown authors. One of the most important literary prizes in Japan. 500,000 yen. Awarded twice a year. Enquiries to The Society for the Promotion of Japanese Literature, c/o Bungei Shunju Publishing Co Ltd, 3 Kioi-cho, Chiyoda-ku, Tokyo

Culture Prize*
For outstanding achievement in the following areas: illustrations, photographs, book designs, juvenile cartoons and picture books. 300,000 yen. Awarded annually to publishers in Japan. Enquiries to Kodansha International Ltd, 2-12-21 Otowa, Bunkyo-ku, Tokyo

Japan Essayists' Club Prize*
For the best essays and criticism including those in book form, especially the work of new authors. 100,000 yen. Awarded annually. Enquiries to Japan Essayists' Club, c/o Yujiro Chiba, 1-1-1 Shimbashi, Minato-ku, Tokyo

Japan Poet Club Prize*
For an author who has contributed significantly to poetry. 50,000 yen. Awarded annually. Enquiries to Japan Poet Club, c/o Showa Joshi University, 1-7 Taishido, Setagaya-ku, Tokyo

Japan Translation Prize for Publisher*
For outstanding translations. Awarded annually. Enquiries to Japan Society of Translators, Rm 208, Shiba Mansion, 5-11-6 Toranomon, Minato-ku, Tokyo

Japan Woman Writer Prize*
For the best novel. 500,000 yen. Awarded annually. Enquiries to Chuokoron-Sha Inc, 2-8-7 Kyobashi, Chuo-ku, Tokyo

Japan Women Writers' Literary Prizes*
To encourage women novelists. Awarded annually. Enquiries to Women Writers' Association, 17 Yanaka-Shimizucho, Daito-ku, Tokyo

Kikuchi Prize
In memory of Hiroshi Kan Kikuchi. Awarded annually. This prize is given for significant achievement in Japanese literature, drama, cinema, newspaper, broadcasting, book or magazine publication. It can otherwise be given to the individual or group who showed the most creative achievement in the year in the introduction of Japanese literature to foreign countries. Enquiries to The Society for the Promotion of Japanese Literature, c/o Bungei Shunju Publishing Co Ltd, 3 Kioi-cho, Chiyoda-ku, Tokyo

Kishida Prize for Drama*
In commemoration of the playwright Kunio Kishida for an outstanding contribution to theatre. 100,000 yen. Awarded annually. Enquiries to Shin-cho-Sha, 71 Yarai-cho, Shinjuku-ku, Tokyo 162

Mainichi Publishing Culture Prize*
To the authors and publishers of works contributing to human culture. 100,000 yen. Awarded annually. Enquiries to Mainichi Newspapers Publishing Co, 1-1, 1-chome, Hitotsubashi, Chiyoda-ku, Tokyo

Mr H's Prize
For works by a new poet. 100,000 yen and a table clock. Awarded annually. Enquiries to Japan Contemporary Poets' Society, c/o Mr Hideki Isomura, 1-14-6 Kamata, Setagaya-ku, Tokyo

Nakamori Prize
Founded 1975 for imported or translated children's books. To be awarded to one work annually. In addition there is a Readers' Prize for the most popular book selected by readers (authors, artists and publishers are eligible for this prize). Enquiries to Holp Book Co Ltd, 2-19-13 Shinjuku, Shinjuku-ku Tokyo 160

Naoki Prize
Im memory of Sanjugo Naoki, for the most promising writer of popular literature. 500,000 yen. Awarded twice a year. Enquiries to The Society for the Promotion of Japanese Literature, c/o Bungei Shunju Publishing Co Ltd, 3 Kioi-cho, Chiyoda-ku, Tokyo

Noma Prize for Juvenile Novel
For the best juvenile novel. 500,000 yen. Awarded annually. Enquiries to Kodansha Ltd, 2-12-21 Otowa, Bunkyo-ku, Tokyo

Noma Prize for Literature
For the best Japanese novel of the Year. 2,000,000 yen. Awarded annually. Enquiries to Kodansha Ltd, 2-12-21 Otowa, Bunkyo-ku, Tokyo

Oya Soichi Nonfiction Prize
To encourage new non-fiction writers. 300,000 yen, plus Round-the-World air ticket, contributed by JAL Co Ltd. Awarded annually. Enquiries to Bungei Shunju Co Ltd, 3 Kioi-cho, Chiyoda-ku, Tokyo

Sankei Juvenile Literature Prize*
For authors of outstanding works published for children. First prize of 500,000 yen and five prizes of 50,000 yen. Publishers of the works are also recognized. Awarded annually. Enquiries to Sankei Newspaper Co, 1-7-2 Otemachi, Chiyoda-ku, Tokyo

Shincho Prizes*
For the best work published during the preceding year, including stories for children and dramatic works. Jury of authors and editorial staff of the monthly magazine 'Shincho' (New Friends). 500,000 yen. Awarded annually. Enquiries to Shincho-Sha, 71 Yarai-cho, Shinjuku-ku, Tokyo 162

Shogakukan Literary Prize
For the best novel, poem, drama and non-fiction for children published during the preceding year. 500,000 yen. Awarded annually. Enquiries to Shogakukan, 2-3-1 Kanda-Hitotsubashi, Chiyoda-ku, Tokyo 101

Tanizaki Junichiro Prize*
To recall the works by Tanizaki and to celebrate the publisher's birthday. 500,000 yen. Enquiries to Chuokoron-Sha Inc, 2-8-7 Kyobashi, Chuo-ku, Tokyo 104

Yomiuri Literature Prize*
For the best work in six categories: novel, essay and travels, drama, literary study and translation, poetry and haiku, critique and biography. 500,000 yen each. Awarded annually. Enquiries to Yomiuri Newspapers Publishing Co, 1-7-1 Otemachi, Chiyoda-ku, Tokyo

Yoshikawa Prize for Popular Novel*
For the most popular novel. 1,000,000 yen. Awarded annually. Enquiries to Kodansha International Ltd, 2-12-21 Otowa, Bunkyo-ku, Tokyo

Translation Agencies and Associations

Japan Society of Translators*, Room 208, Shiba Mansion, 5-11-6 Toranomon, Minato-ku, Tokyo

Jordan

General Information

Language: Arabic (and English)
Religion: Muslim (and large Christian minority)
Population: 3 million
Literacy Rate (1961): 39%
Bank Hours: 0800-1330 Saturday-Thursday; cashiers close at 1230
Shop Hours: 0800-1300, 1500-1800 Saturday-Thursday
Currency: 1000 fils = 1 dinar
Export/Import Information: No tariffs on books and advertising matter, but 2% tax applies. Import licences required but granted freely. Air freight must be by Jordanian national airline. Transportation insurance must be arranged in Jordan
Copyright: No copyright conventions signed

Publishers

Jordan Distribution Agency, PO Box 375, Amman Tel: 30191/2 Cable Add: Jodistag Amman Telex: 1497 JO ALRAI
Man Dir: Raja Elissa; *Manager:* Mrs Nadia Elissa
Subjects: Jordanian Tourism and History
1978: 2 titles *Founded:* 1951

Jordan Press and Publishing Co Ltd*, Amman
Publishes daily newspaper, *al-Destour*
Founded: 1967
Miscellaneous: 25% of capital held by government

National Press Library*, Amman
Subjects: Education, Politics, Law, Textbooks

Major Booksellers

Gibralter Book Store*, Corner Faisal St, Amman

Al Istiklal Library*, PO Box 156, Amman

George Y Koro*, Petra Library, PO Box 1061, Amman

Al Ma'aref Library*, PO Box 650, Amman

Yarmouk University Bookshop, PO Box 566, Irbid Tel: 71100-15 Cable Add: Yarmouk Jordan Telex: 51533 Jo

Youth's Library Mohamad Ahmed Sharareh*, PO Box 180, Amman

Major Libraries

American Library*, Kabarday St, Amman

Amman Public Library, c/o City Librarian, PO Box 132, Amman Tel: 24174 Telex: 21969 Amcitygo
Librarian: Farouk Móaz

British Council Library, Amman Centre, Jebel Amman, PO Box 634, Amman Tel: 36147/38194/24686 Telex: 21823 Bcjor Jo

Public Library*, PO Box 348, Irbid

Public Library*, Nablus

University of Jordan Library, University of Jordan, Amman Tel: 843555-74/843666-80 Telex: 1629 unuj jo
Director: Dr Kamel Asali
Publications include: Al-Maktaba (monthly newsletter), *The Library Guide* (in English and Arabic), *The Students' Guide* (in Arabic), various bibliographies

Yarmouk University Library, PO Box 566, Irbid Tel: 71100-15 Cable Add: Yarmouk Jordan Telex: 51533 Jo
Director: Dr T Akasheh

Library Associations

Jordan Library Association, PO Box 6289, Amman
President: Anwar Akroush; *Executive Secretary:* Medhat Mar'ei
Publications: Rissalat al-Maktaba (The Message of the Library) (quarterly); *Palestinian-Jordanian Bibliography 1900-1970*, 1972; *1971-1975*, 1976; *Directory of Libraries in Jordan 1976*, 1976; *Jordanian National Bibliography 1979*

Library Journals

Rissalat al-Maktaba (Message of the Library) (text in Arabic, summaries in English), Jordan Library Association, PO Box 6289, Amman

Kampuchea

General Information

It has not been possible to obtain information on publishing and bookselling in Kampuchea for several years. In view of the changed circumstances of the country, information obtained in the past has been omitted from this edition of *International Literary Market Place*
Language: Khmer, French
Religion: Theravada Buddhist
Population: 8.6 million
Literacy Rate (1962): 36.1%
Business Hours: 0700-1400 Monday-Saturday
Currency: riel
Export/Import Information: Little current information available; free foreign exchange market arrangements not operating
Copyright: UCC, Florence (see International section)

Kenya

General Information

Language: Swahili (also English)
Religion: About 30% Christian, 6% Muslim; rest follow traditional beliefs
Population: 14.9 million
Bank Hours: 0900-1300 Monday-Friday; 0900-1100 Saturday (except on coast, where banks open and close half an hour earlier)
Shop Hours: 0830-1230, 1400-1630 Monday-Friday; 0830-1200 or 1230 Saturday
Currency: 100 cents = 1 Kenya shilling
Export/Import Information: No tariff on books or advertising matter. Import licences and exchange controls
Copyright: UCC (see International section)

Book Trade Organizations

Kenya Booksellers' and Stationers' Association, PO Box 49597, Nairobi Tel: 335205
Secretary: C D Shah

Kenya Publishers' Association, c/o PO Box 14681, Nairobi Tel: 60960
Secretary: K W Martin

Book Trade Reference Books and Journals

Books

Catalogue of Government Publications, Government Printing Press, PO Box 30128, Nairobi

Journals

Bookshop Bulletin, Kijabe St, PO Box 47540, Nairobi

Publishers

Comb Books*, PO Box 20019, Nairobi Tel: 332270
(Distributed by the Text Book Centre Ltd, PO Box 47540, Nairobi)
Man Dir: David Maillu
Subjects: General Fiction, Social & Sexual Problems, Paperbacks
Founded: 1972

East African Directory Co*, PO Box 41237, Nairobi Tel: 24151
Man Dir: T A Bhatt
Parent Company: United Africa Press Ltd (qv)
Subject: Reference
Founded: 1947

East African Literature Bureau, see Kenya Literature Bureau

East African Publishing House, Lusaka Close, PO Box 30571, Nairobi Tel: 557417 Cable Add: Afrobooks Nairobi
Man Dir: E N Wainaina; *Chief Editor, Rights & Permissions:* Richard C Ntiru; *Editorial:* P Njoroge; *Senior Editor:* D N Waiyaki; *Marketing, Publicity, Sales, Distribution:* J J Atunga; *Production:* John Mwazo; *Design:* Alex T Echaria
Parent Company: E A Cultural Trust
Associate Company: Afropress Ltd, PO Box 30502, Nairobi
Branch Off: PO Box 3209, Dar es Salaam, Tanzania
Subjects: General Fiction & Nonfiction, Belles Lettres, Poetry, Biography, History, Africana, How-to, Study Guides, Reference, Religion, Juveniles, Books in Kiswahili and other East African languages, Paperbacks, General & Social Science, University, Secondary & Primary Textbooks
1978: 30 titles *Founded:* 1965

Evangel Publishing House, PO Box 28963, Nairobi Tel: 802033 Cable Add: Evangelit Nairobi
Man Dir, Editorial, Rights and Permissions: Rev R J Skinner; *Sales, Publicity:* Rev Elkanah S Ayiga; *Production:* Bruce Brandt
Subjects: General Nonfiction, Reference, Religion, Christian Tracts, Paperbacks, Children's Books
Bookshop: PO Box 28963, Nairobi

Foundation Books, NCM House, Tom Mboya St, PO Box 73435, Nairobi Tel: 333118
Sub-regional co-ordinator, Regional Centre for Book Promotion in Africa; Co-publishing office Eastern Africa Region
Man Dir: F O Okwanya; *Editorial:* C R Ojienda; *Sales Manager:* J K Musyoki; *Production:* Sophia Wanjiku Ojienda
Subjects: Belles Lettres, Poetry, Biography, History, Africana, Juveniles, Books in Kiswahili, Paperbacks, Social Science, Secondary & Primary Textbooks, Adult Education Primers, Mathematics
Founded: 1974

Gaba Publications (AFER), AMECEA Pastoral Institute, PO Box 908, Eldoret (Formerly at PO Box 4165, Kampala, Uganda)
Manager: Peter Dougherty; *Editor:* Brian Hearne
Subjects: Religion, Anthropology, Scripture, Third World Theology, Religious Education
1978: 11 titles *1979:* 11 titles

Government Printer*, Government Printing Press, PO Box 30128, Nairobi

Heinemann Educational Books (East Africa) Ltd, International House, Mama Ngina St, PO Box 45314, Nairobi Tel: 22057/338642 Cable Add: Hebooks Nairobi
Man Dir, Rights and Permissions: Henry Chakava; *Editorial:* Laban O Erapu, Ben Ole Mollel; *Sales:* Johnson K Mugweru
Parent Company: Heinemann Educational Books (International) Ltd, UK (qv)
Subjects: General Fiction & Nonfiction, Belles Lettres, Poetry, Biography, History, Africana, Study Guides, Juveniles, Swahili Language & Literature, Paperbacks, General & Social Science, University, Secondary & Primary Textbooks
1978: 20 titles *1979:* 23 titles *Founded:* 1967

Kenya Literature Bureau*, PO Box 30022, Nairobi Tel: 26411 Cable Add: Literature Nairobi
Man Dir: N G Ngulukulu; *Managing Editor:* Rose Mwangi; *Sales:* A R Minja
Branch Offs: Branches in Dar es Salaam and Kampala
Subjects: General Fiction & Nonfiction, Belles Lettres, Poetry, Biography, History, Africana, Reference, Religion, Juveniles, Books in numerous East African Languages, Paperbacks, Medicine, Psychology, Science & Technology, General & Social Science, University, Secondary and Primary Textbooks
Founded: 1947

The Jomo **Kenyatta** Foundation, PO Box 30533, Nairobi Tel: 20704 Cable Add: Foundation
Man Dir: S C Lang'at; *Production Manager:* Len M Fernandes
Subjects: Secondary & Primary Textbooks

Longman Kenya Ltd, 6th Floor, Kenya Commercial Bank, PO Box 18033, Nairobi Tel: 555477/555530
Man Dir: T J Openda; *Publishing Manager:* Charlotte Rolfe; *Sales Manager:* T Kamuyu; *Rights & Permissions:* Longman Group Ltd, UK (qv)
Associate Company: Longman Group Ltd, UK (qv)
Subjects: General Fiction & Nonfiction, Belles Lettres, Poetry, Biography, History, Africana, Reference, Juveniles, Books in 14 Kenyan languages, Paperbacks, General & Social Science, Secondary & Primary Textbooks
Founded: 1965

Newspread International, PO Box 46854, Nairobi Tel: 331402 Cable Add: Newspread
Man Dir: Kul Bhushan; *Publishing Manager:* Ashok Kumar; *Production Manager:* Benedict Nzomo
Subjects: Reference
Founded: 1971

Njogu Gitene Publications*, PO Box 72989, Nairobi
Subjects: Belles Lettres, Poetry, Juveniles, Books in Kiswahili, Secondary & Primary Textbooks
Founded: 1970

Oxford University Press, Eastern Africa Branch, PO Box 72532, Nairobi (Located at: First Floor, Science House, Monrovia St, Nairobi) Tel: 336377 Cable Add: Oxonian Nairobi
General Manager: Abdilahi Nassir; *Senior Editor:* Jonathan Kariara; *Production:* Godfrey Nyerwanire; *Publicity:* Sam Mbure; *Rights & Permissions:* Abdilahi Nassir; *Sales:* A K Ismaily; *Administration:* E M Nyang'aya
Branch Off: Dar es Salaam, Tanzania (qv)
Subjects: General Fiction & Nonfiction, Belles Lettres, Poetry, Biography, History, Africana, Reference, Juveniles, Books in 12 East African languages, Paperbacks, General

& Social Science, Secondary & Primary Textbooks
Founded: 1963
Miscellaneous: Firm is a branch of Oxford University Press, UK (qv)
ISBN Publisher's Prefix: 0-19

Salama Publications Ltd*, PO Box 48009, Nairobi
Subjects: How-to, Study Guides, Secondary Textbooks

Success Publications*, PO Box 10893, Nairobi
Subjects: How-to, Study Guides

Text Book Centre Ltd, Kijabe St, PO Box 47540, Nairobi Tel: 337337/8
Man Dir: M J Rughani; *General Manager:* C D Shah
Subjects: Belles Lettres, Poetry, Juveniles, Books in Kiswahili, Paperbacks, Secondary & Primary Textbooks
Bookshop: Kijabe St, PO Box 47540, Nairobi

Transafrica Book Distributors*, Kenwood House, Kimathi St, PO Box 49421, Nairobi Tel: 861253
Man Dir: John Nottingham
Subjects: General Fiction & Nonfiction, Belles Lettres, Poetry, Biography, History, Africana, How-to, Study Guides, Reference, Religion, Juveniles, Books in Kiswahili, Paperbacks, Social Science, Secondary & Primary Textbooks

United Africa Press Ltd*, Victoria Ho, Victoria St, PO Box 41237, Nairobi Tel: 24151
Man Dir: T A Bhatt
Subsidiary Company: East African Directory Co (qv)
Subjects: General, Educational, Reference, Animals
Founded: 1952

University Press of Africa Ltd*, Bank Ho, Government Rd, PO Box 3981, Nairobi Tel: 26060
Man Dir: R R Ryan
Subjects: Reference, Travel Guides, Medicine, Science & Technology, General & Social Science

Uzima Press Ltd*, PO Box 48127, Nairobi Tel: 20239
Man Dir: Rev Horace Etemesi
Subjects: Religion, Fiction
1978: 60 titles *Founded:* 1974

Vipopremo Agencies*, Koinange St, PO Box 47717, Nairobi Tel: 27189
Subjects: How-to, Study Guides

Literary Agents

Africa Educational Representatives*, PO Box 20521, Nairobi Cable Add: Afragency Tel: 26543
Head Office: Africa Educational Reps, 639 Massachusetts Ave, Suite 335, Cambridge, Mass, 02139, USA

Major Booksellers

The **Bookshop** Ltd*, Esso Ho, Kaunda St, PO Box 30247, Nairobi Tel: 23364

The **Catholic** Bookshop Ltd, Kaunda St, PO Box 30249, Nairobi Tel: 25172

Dhanani's Ltd*, Kimasi St, Corner Ho, PO Box 72399, Nairobi Tel: 27049

E S A Bookshop*, Church Ho, Government Rd, PO Box 30167, Nairobi Tel: 20158

Keswick Book Society, Portal Ho, Banda St, PO Box 10242, Nairobi Tel: 26047

Macdonald's*, Kimathi St, PO Box 49240, Nairobi Tel: 21979

S J Moore Ltd, Moi Ave, PO Box 30162, Nairobi Tel: 22213
Manager: Marjorie Oludhe Macgoye

Mount Kenya Bookshop Ltd, PO Box 281, Nyeri Tel: 2513; PO Box 47772, Nairobi Tel: 337883; PO Box 659, Nakuru Tel: 2806; PO Box 10, Kakamega Tel: 63; PO Box 29, Meru Tel: 36
Man Dir: David M Mwangi

Patwa (Embakasi) Ltd, PO Box 19200, Nairobi Airport, Embakasi, Nairobi

Prestige Booksellers, Prudential Assurance Bldg PO Box 45425, Nairobi Tel: 23515

The **Textbook** Centre Ltd*, Kijabe St, PO Box 47540, Nairobi
Tel: 337337/335205/24672/24308 Cable Add: Text books

University of Nairobi Bookshop, PO Box 30197, Nairobi Tel: 334244 ext 2111 Cable Add: Varsity
Manager: N J Patel

Wanyee Bookshop Ltd, Aga Khan Walk, PO Box 46815, Nairobi Tel: 331769

Major Libraries

East African Statistical Department Library*, PO Box 30462, Nairobi Tel: 26411 ext 425

Egerton College Library*, PO Njoro Tel: 27/44/47

Kabete Library*, University of Nairobi, PO Box 29053, Kabete

Kenya National Archives*, Jogoo House 'A', PO Box 30520, Nairobi

Kenya National Library Service*, Ngong Rd, PO Box 30573, Nairobi Tel: 27871/29186
Librarian: Apollo R Oluoch
Publications: Annual Audit Report; Quarterly Accession; List of Adult Books

Kenya Polytechnic Library, PO Box 52428, Nairobi Tel: 338231
Librarian: Stanley K Nganga

Kenya Technical Teachers' College Library, PO Box 44600, Nairobi Tel: 520211
Librarian: William G Kinyarrjui
Publications include: Secondary School Library Facilities in Central Province, Kenya; The Problems of Providing Library Services to School Children in Developing Countries; Serials Literature, Exploitation and Use in Libraries

Kenyatta University College Library, PO Box 43844, Nairobi Tel: Kahawa 356/7/8/9; 247/249/346/421/442/459
Librarian: James Mwangi Nganga
Publications: Directory of Research in the College; Annual Report; Directory of Libraries in Kenya; Occasional Bibliographies; Seminar Papers; Accession List

McMillan Memorial Library, Banda St, PO Box 40791, Nairobi Tel: 21844
Chief Librarian: R G Opondo

Mombasa Polytechnic Library*, Tom Mboya Ave, PO Box 90420, Mombasa

University of Nairobi Library*, PO Box 30197, Nairobi Tel: 334244

Library Associations

Kenya Library Association*, PO Box 46031 Nairobi
Secretary: Rosemary Kiathe
Publication: Maktaba

Library Reference Books and Journals

Books

Directory of Libraries in Kenya, Kenyatta University College Library, PO Box 43844, Nairobi

Journals

Maktaba, Kenya Literature Bureau, PO Box 30022, Nairobi (The official, biannual, journal of the Kenya Library Association)

Literary Periodicals

Busara, Kenya Literature Bureau, PO Box 30022, Nairobi (biannual literary magazine published under the auspices of the Department of Literature, University of Nairobi)

Dhana, Kenya Literature Bureau, PO Box 30022, Nairobi (The Makerere University, Department of Literature, journal of creative writing; twice yearly)

Joe; Africa's entertainment monthly, Joe Publications Ltd, PO Box 30362, Nairobi (a popular magazine with regular literary contributions, review of new books and plays, etc)

Joliso (East African Journal of Literature and Society), Kenya Literature Bureau, PO Box 30022, Nairobi (new literary and cultural magazine edited by Chris Wanjala and published twice yearly since 1973)

Umma, Kenya Literature Bureau, PO Box 30022, Nairobi (The University of Dar es Salaam, Department of Literature, journal of creative writing; twice yearly)

Translation Agencies and Associations

Kenya Literature Bureau*, PO Box 30022, Nairobi

Democratic People's Republic of Korea

General Information

Language: Korean
Religion: Confucian, Buddhist
Population: 17 million
Currency: 100 jun = 1 won
Export/Import Information: No tariff information; all importation must go through Korea Publications Export and Import Corporation, Pyongyang

Publishers

Academy of Sciences Publishing House*, Central District Nammundong, Pyongyang
Subjects: Science, Chemistry, Geology, Metallurgy, Physics, Biology, History, Maps, Mathematics, Meteorology, Education, Economics
Founded: 1953

Academy of Social Sciences Publishing House*, Pyongyang
Subject: Social Sciences

Agricultural Books Publishing House*, Pyongyang
President: Li Hyun U
Subjects: Agriculture, Industry

Economic Publishing House*, Pyongyang
Subject: Economics

Educational Books Publishing House*, Pyongyang
Subject: Education, Textbooks

Foreign Languages Publishing House*, Pyongyang
President: L Ryang Hun
Subject: Books on Korea, Periodicals (English language)

Publishing House of the **General Federation of Literary and Art Unions***, Pyongyang
Subjects: Fiction, Arts

Higher Educational Books Publishing House*, Pyongyang
Acting President: Shin Jong Sung
Subjects: Education, Academic, Mathematics, Physics

Industry Publishing House*, Pyongyang
Subjects: Trade, Industry

Korean Workers' Party Publishing House*, Pyongyang
Subjects: Fiction, Politics

Mass Culture Publishing House*, Pyongyang

Medical Science Publishing House*, Pyongyang
Subject: Medicine, Psychology, Veterinary Science

Transportation Publishing House*, Pyongyang
Acting Editor: Paek Jong Han
Subject: Transport
Founded: 1952

Major Booksellers

Korea Publications Export and Import Corporation*, Pyongyang
The sole importing organization

Major Libraries

State Central Library*, Pyongyang

Library Associations

Library Association of the Democratic People's Republic of Korea*, State Central Library, Pyongyang Tel: 3-8741
Executive Secretary: Li Geug

Republic of Korea

General Information

Language: Korean (English also spoken in business)
Religion: Confucian, Buddhist
Population: 37 million
Literacy Rate (1970): 87.6% (94.3% Urban, 82.2% Rural)
Bank Hours: 0930-1600 Monday-Friday; 0930-1300 Saturday
Shop Hours: 0930-1200, 1300-1700 Monday-Friday; 0930-1300 Saturday
Currency: won
Export/Import Information: No tariffs on books and advertising matter. 2.5% Defence Tax. No import licences required. Exchange controls; prior deposits required at present
Copyright: No copyright conventions signed

Book Trade Organizations

Korean Publishers Association*, 105-2 Sagan-dong, Chongno-ku, Seoul 110 Tel: (72) 5904 Cable Add: Bookhouse Seoul
Secretary: Kyung-hoon Lee
Publications: Korean Books Journal (monthly); *Korean Publication Yearbook* (annual); *Books from Korea* (biennial)

Book Trade Reference Books and Journals

Books

Books from Korea, Korean Publishers Association, 105-2 Sagan-dong, Chongno-ku, Seoul 110

Catalogue of Government Publications (including University publications), National Assembly Library, Taepyong-ko, Chung-ku, Seoul

Korean Publication Yearbook, Korean Publishers Association, 105-2 Sagan-dong, Chongno-ku, Seoul 110

Journals

Ch'ulp'an Munhwa (Korean Books Journal) (text in Korean), Korean Publishers' Association, 105-2 Sagan-dong, Chongno-ku, Seoul 110

Han-gug Chulpanyungam (Korean Publication Yearbook) (text in Korean), Korean Publishers' Association, 105-2 Sagan-dong, Chongno-ku, Seoul 110

Korean National Bibliography (text in Korean), Central National Library, 6 Sokong-dong, Chung-ku, Seoul

Publishers

Bak Yung Sa*, 184 Kwanchul-dong, Chongno-ku, Seoul 110
President: Won Ok Ahn
Subjects: Philosophy, Literature, Social Science
Founded: 1952

Beupmun Sa Publishing Co, 1-48 Cheung-dong, Chung-Ku, Seoul 100 Tel: (75) 6317/6318/6319
President: Sung Soo Kim; *Man Dir:* Byeong Cheol Park; *Sales:* Hyo Seon Bae; *Editorial:* Bok Hyun Chok; *Publicity:* Myeong Hwan Kim
Subsidiary Company: Minjungseokim Publishing Co (qv)
Subjects: Law, Economics, Management, Politics, Public Administration, Education, Psychology
1978: 58 titles *1979:* 54 titles *Founded:* 1952

Changjak Kwa Pipyung Sa*, 3 Kongpyong-dong, Chongno-ku, Seoul 110
President: Yom Hong-gyong
Subjects: Literature and other subjects of general interest
Founded: 1974

Changjo Sa*, 92 Sinmun-ro 2-ka, Chongno-ku, Seoul 110
President: Deok Kyu Choi
Subjects: Literature, Linguistics, History
Founded: 1963

The **Christian Literature** Society of Korea*, 84-8 Chongno, 2-ka, Chongno-ku, Seoul 110 Tel: 74-3092, 1792, 5981 Cable Add: Chlisoofko
General Secretary: Rev Sun Chool Chough
Subjects: Religion, Theology, Sociology

Dongwha Publishing Co*, 130-4 Wonhyo-ro, Yongsan-ku, Seoul 100
President: In Kyu Lim
Subjects: Literature, Fine Arts, Philosophy
Founded: 1968

Eulyoo Publishing Co Ltd, PO Box 362 Gwanghwa-Mun, 46-1 Susong-dong, Jongro-gu, Seoul 110 Tel: (73) 8150, (74) 3515 Cable Add: Eulyoo
President: Chin Sook Choung; *Man Dir:* Pil Young Choung; *Editorial, Production:* Il Joon Park; *Sales:* Byung Gi Choung
Subjects: General
1978: 300 titles *Founded:* 1945

Ewha Woman's University Press*, 11-1 Daehyun-dong, Seodaemun-ku, Seoul 120
President: Ok Kil Kim
Subjects: General, Literature, History, Linguistics
Founded: 1954

Hak Won Sa*, 147 Chongno-3-ka, Chongno-ku, Seoul 110
President: Ik Tal Kim
Subjects: General, Juveniles, Educational Materials, Encyclopaedias
Founded: 1945

Hollym Corporation, 14-5 Kwanchol-dong, Chongno-ku, Seoul 110 Tel: (75) 7551/4
President: In Soo Rhimm; *Man Dir:* Yong Won Kim; *Sales Dir:* Yong Kwon Kim; *Publicity Dir:* Shin Won Zoo; *Advertising Dir:* Tae Hong Jeong
Subjects: General Fiction, Belles Lettres, Poetry, Biography, History, Juveniles, High-priced Paperbacks
Book Club: Korea Book Club
Founded: 1963

Hwimoon Publishing Co*, 30 Kyunji-dong, Chongno-ku, Seoul 110 Tel: (72) 4897
Man Dir: Myong Hui Yi
Subjects: General Fiction, Belles Lettres, Poetry, Biography, History, Philosophy, Religion, Juveniles
Founded: 1961

Hyangmun Sa*, 39-16 Kyunji-dong, Chongno-ku, Seoul 110
President: Mal Sun Na
Subjects: Agriculture, Science
Founded: 1957

Hyun Am Sa*, 1 Chongno 5-ka, Chongno-ku, Seoul 110 Tel: (75) 5421
Man Dir: Sang Won Cho
Subjects: History, Philosophy, Literature, Religion
Founded: 1951

Il Cho Kak*, 9 Gongpyung-dong, Chongno-ku, Seoul 110 Tel: (73) 5430/1 Cable Add: Ichopublico Seoul
Man Dir: Man-Nyun Han; *Sales Dir:* L J

Kim; *Publicity Dir:* J Y Choi
Subjects: History, High-priced Paperbacks, Medicine, Psychology, Engineering, General & Social Science, Secondary & University Textbooks, Educational Materials, Law, Philosophy
Founded: 1953

Il Ji Sa*, 46-1 Chunghak-dong, Chongno-ku, Seoul 110
Man Dir: Sung Jae Kim; *Publicity Dirs:* Byungki Yoo, Donhong Cho
Subjects: General Fiction, Belles Lettres, Criminology, Poetry, History, Reference, Low- & High-priced Paperbacks, University & Secondary Textbooks, Educational Materials
Founded: 1956

Il Shinsa*, 22-1 Samkak-dong, Chung-ku, Seoul 100 Tel: 749005/736948/736980
Man Dir: Kwang-mo Yun; *Editorial:* Ryun So; *Sales:* Jong-sun Ahn; *Production:* Sang-kap La
Subjects: Philosophy, Law, Politics, Economics, Literature, Natural Science
Founded: 1959

Jeongeumsa Publishing Co*, PO Box 7, 22-5 Chungmu-ro 5-ka, Chung-ku, Seoul 100 Tel: (27) 9580/3 & (25) 5681/2 Cable Add: Jeongeumsa
President: Yong Hae Choi; *Sales Dir:* Young-tek Yoon; *Publicity & Advertising:* Dae-hee Park
Subjects: General Fiction, Belles Lettres, Philosophy, Social Science
Bookshop: 22-5, 5-ka, Chungmu-Ro, Jung-Gu, Seoul
Founded: 1928

Jisik Sanup Sa*, 18-8 Kwanchul-dong, Chongno-ku, Seoul 110
President: Kyung Hee Kim
Subjects: Fine Arts, Social Sciences, History, Literature, Technical and Scientific
Founded: 1969

Junpa Kwahak Sa*, 156-10 Dongkyo-dong, Mapo-ku, Seoul 121
President: Yung Soo Shon
Subjects: Sciences, Engineering
Founded: 1956

Korea Britannica Corp, CPO Box 690, Seoul (Located at: 58-14 Sinmun-ro 1 ka, Chongno-ku, Seoul)
President: Changgi Hahn
Associate Company: Encyclopaedia Britannica International Ltd, UK (qv)
Subjects: Reference Books, Periodicals

Korea Directory Co*, 12-20 Chungmuro 2-ka, Chung-ku, Seoul
President: Saeung Tae Kim
Subject: Directories

Korea University Press*, 1 Anam-dong 5-ka, Sungbuk-ku, Seoul 132
President: Sang Hyop Kim
Subjects: Philosophy, History, Literature, Sociology, Language, Education Psychology, Social Science, Natural Science, Engineering, Agriculture
Founded: 1956

Kwan Dong Publishing Co*, 195-11 Yeongun-dong, Chongno-ku, Seoul 110 Tel: 29-6517, 99-4638
President: Seung Woo Kim; *Editorial:* Hyo Ja Kim; *Sales:* Heung Jo Choi; *Production:* Ki Dong Park; *Publicity:* Ill Kyoun Oh; *Rights & Permissions:* Hyong Sook Park
Subjects: Literature, Textbooks, Monthly magazines
Founded: 1964

Kwangmyong Printing & Publishing Co Ltd*, CPO Box 3785, Seoul (Located at: 62 Manri-dong 1-ka, Chung-ku, Seoul) Tel: (23) 0671/9, 6584 Cable Add: Kwangmyong, Seoul
President: Kim Hak-Jin; *Dirs:* Hwang Tong-Kyu, Yoon Yun-Bai
Subsidiary Companies: Korea Textbook Co; Kwangmyong Toppan Moore Printing Co; Kwangmyong Toppan Printing Co
Subject: Korean Art (ancient and contemporary)
1978: 15 titles *Founded:* 1951

Kyemong-sa*, 128-1 Kwanchul-dong, Chongno-ku, Seoul
President: Chun Sik Kim
Subjects: Children's Books

Kyohak Sa*, 92 Sunhwa-dong, Seodaemun-ku, Seoul
Man Dir: Cheol U Yang
Subjects: Educational Materials, Industry, Nonfiction

Kyung In Munwha Sa*, 86-2 Yunhee-dong, Seodaemun-ku, Seoul 120
President: Sang Ha Han
Subjects: General, History, Philosophy
Founded: 1969

Min Eum Sa*, 44-1 Kwanchul-dong, Chongno-ku, Seoul 110
President: Maeng Ho Pak
Subjects: Literature, Philosophy, Engineering, Social Science
Founded: 1966

Minjungseogwan*, 35 Tongeu-dong, Chongno-ku, Seoul 110
President: Byung Jun Lee
Subjects: General Fiction, Belles Lettres, Music, Reference, Medicine, Agriculture, Business, Law, Political Science, Science & Technology, Textbooks
Bookshop: 35 Tongeui-dong, Chongno-ku, Seoul
Founded: 1946

Minjungseokim Publishing Co, 1-48 Cheung-dong, Chung-Ku, Seoul 100 Tel: (075) 6473
President: Myong Hwan Kim; *Editorial:* Han Seong Yu
Parent Company: Beupmun Sa Publishing Co (qv)
Subjects: Dictionaries
Founded: 1979

Moonye Publishing Co*, 115 Doryum-dong, Chongno-ku, Seoul
President: Byung Suk Jun
Subjects: Literature, Fine Arts, Philosophy, Social Science, Psychology
Founded: 1966

Mun Woon Dang*, 45-3 Myongryun-dong, Chongno-ku, Seoul
President: Sung Bum Lee
Subjects: Engineering, Science
Founded: 1962

Omun Kak*, 39-1 Ankuk-dong, Chongno-ku, Seoul 110
President: Yung Whan Kim
Subjects: Literature, Korean Language, Social Science, Children's Books
Founded: 1960

Panmun Book Co Ltd*, PO Box 1016, 40 Chongno 1-ka, Seoul 110 Tel: (73) 8688, (72) 5131/3 Cable Add: Panmuse Seoul
Man Dir: I H Liu; *Sales Dir:* H B Choi
Subjects: Medicine, General & Social Science, University Textbooks
Bookshops: 40 Chongro 1-ka, Seoul; 16 Kwangbok-dong 1-ka, Pusan
Founded: 1956

Pochinjae*, 8 Dangsan-dong 5-ka, Yungdeungpo-ku, Seoul
President: Jun Ki Kim

Pomso Publishers*, 3-2 Kwansu-dong, Chongno-ku, Seoul
President: So Yong Yi

Sam Joong Dang Publishing Co*, 244-5 Huam-dong, Yongsan-ku, Seoul 140
President: Kun Suk Seo
Subjects: Literature, History, Philosophy, Social Science
Founded: 1946

Sam-sung Publishing Co*, 43-7 Kwanchul-dong, Chongno-ku, Seoul 110
President: Bong Kyu Kim
Subjects: Literature, Dictionaries, History, Children's Books
Founded: 1952

Samwha Publishing Co*, 15 Ulchiro 2-ka, Chung-ku, Seoul 100
President: Kon Su Yu
Subjects: Children's Books, Social Science, Linguistics, Fine Arts
Founded: 1962

Se Kwang Musical Publication Co*, 232-32 Sogye-dong, Yongsan-ku, Seoul Tel: (25) 3616/8
President: Jin Joon Pak; *Sales Dir:* Chun Chae Ho; *Publicity Dir:* Ban Kwang Sik
Subject: Music
Founded: 1953

Sejong Daewang Kinyom Saophoe*, 1-57 Chongryangli-dong, San, Dondaemun-ku, Seoul
President: Gwan Ku Yi
Subjects: Religion, Classical Literature, Modern History

Seomun Dang*, 94-97 Yongdeungpo, 3-dong, Yongdeungpo-ku, Seoul
President: Suk Ro Choi
Subjects: Philosophy, Ancient History, Literature, Fine Arts
Founded: 1973

Seonjin Publishing Co*, 35-5 Supyo-dong, Chung-ku, Seoul
President: Gon Haeng Yi
Subject: Literature

Si-Sa-Yong-O-Sa, 5-3 Kwanchul-dong, Chongno-ku, Seoul 110 Tel: 26966212 Cable Add: English books, Seoul, Korea
President: Yung Bin Min; *Vice-President:* J S Min; *Editorial Dir:* Myungki Kim; *Publicity Manager:* Chongman Choi; *Sales Manager:* Kapchin Cho
Subject: Linguistics
1978: 45 titles *1979:* 42 titles *Founded:* 1961

Singu Munwha Sa*, 68-2 Susong-dong, Chongno-ku, Seoul
President: Yong Ik Yi
Subjects: Literature, History, Linguistics, Children's Books
Founded: 1952

Taeguk Publishing Co*, 47-11 Cho-dong, 2-ka, Chung-ku, Seoul 110
President: Yoon Hee Hong
Subjects: Dictionaries, Literature, History, Science, Fine Arts
Founded: 1969

Tamgu Dang Book Centre*, 101-1 Kyungwoon-dong, Chongno-ku, Seoul 110 Tel: (72) 2004/5
Shipping Add: PO Box 240, Kwang-hwa-mun, Seoul
President: Suk Woo Hong; *Sales Dir:* Jean Byong-hun; *Publicity Dir:* Kim Chang-su; *Advertising Dir:* Lee Chung-rim
Subjects: History, Classics, Art, Reference, Low- & High-priced Paperbacks, University & Secondary Textbooks
Founded: 1950

Universal Publications Agency Ltd*, UPA Building, 54 Kyonjindong, Chongno, Seoul
Man: C Y Park
Miscellaneous: Also booksellers and distributors

Yonsei University Press*, 134 Shinchon-dong, Seodaemun-ku, Seoul 120
President: Pong-Kook Lee
Subjects: General, Philosophy, Religion, Social Science, Natural Science, Literature, Art, Technical Science
Founded: 1955

Yulwha Dang*, 3-3 Chungjin-dong, Chongno-ku, Seoul 110
President: Ki Woong Lee
Subjects: Fine Arts, History, Literature
Founded: 1971

Book Clubs

Korea Book Club, 14-5 Kwanchol-dong, Chongno-ku, Seoul
Owned by: Hollym Corporation Publishers (Seoul) (qv)

Major Booksellers

Airport Bookshop*, Civil International Airport, Seoul

Hyun Dae Mun Hak, 136-46 Yunji-dong, Chongro-ku, Seoul Tel: (763) 7319
Wholesaler

Panmun Book Co Ltd*, CPO Box 1016, Seoul
Also 16 Kwangbok-dong 1-ka, Pusan Tel: (73) 8688

Science Publications Centre*, 21 1-ka, Chongno, Chongno-ku, Seoul

Seungmun-gak*, 155-12 Kwanhun-dong, Chongno-gu, Seoul Tel: (73) 6148
Specialize in second-hand and antiquarian books

Universal Publications Agency Ltd*, UPA Building, 54 Kyonjindong, Chongno, Seoul
Manager: C Y Park
Also distributors

Major Libraries

Dongguk University Library*, 263-ka, Pil-dong, Seoul

Ewha Woman's University Library*, 11-1 Daehyon-dong, Sudaemun-ku, Seoul 120

International Communication Agency Library*, 63 1-ka, Ulchiro, Choung-ku, Seoul

Korea University Library*, 1 Anam-dong, Sungbuk-ku, Seoul

Kyungpook National University Central Library, 1370 Sankyuck-dong, Pukku, Taegu Tel: 920268

National Assembly Library*, Yoi-dong 1, Yeongdeungpo-gu, Seoul
Publication: Review

Central National Library*, 100-171 1-ga, Hoe-hyeon-dong, Jung-gu, Seoul

Seoul National University Library*, San 56-1 Sinlim-Dong, Gwanag-gu, Seoul 151

Transport Library*, Seoul

United Nations Depository Library, Korea University, 1 An-Am-Dong, Sungbuk-ku, Seoul
Librarian: Park Hu-Yong

Yonsei University Library, Yonsei University, 134 Sinchon-dong, Sudaemoon-ku, Seoul 120

Library Associations

Hanguk Seoji Hakhoe*, c/o National Assembly Library, 1-ka Taepyung, Chung-ku, Seoul
Korean Bibliographical Society

Hanguk Tosogwan Hakhoe, c/o Department of Library Science, Sung Kyun Kwan University, 53, 3-ka, Myonglyun-dong, Chongno-ku, Seoul 110
Korean Library Science Society
Publication: Tosogwan Hak (Journal of the Korean Library Science Society, Korean with English abstracts)

Korean Library Association*, 100-177, 1-ka, Hoehyun-dong, Choong-Ku, Seoul
Executive Director: Dae Kwon Park
Publication: KLA Bulletin (monthly)

Korean Micro-Library Association*, Central National Library Bldg, 6 Sokong-dong, Chung-ku, Seoul
Publication: Micro-Library Bulletin

Library Reference Books and Journals

Books

Bibliography of Korean Bibliographies, Kyong'in Munwha Sa, 86-2 Yonhi-dong, Seodaemun-ku, Seoul

Journals

KLA Bulletin, Korean Library Association, 100-177, 1-Ka, Hoehyun-Dong, Choong-Ku, Seoul (monthly)

Micro-Library Bulletin, Korean Micro-Library Association, Central National Library Bldg, 6 Sokong-dong, Choong-Ku, Seoul

National Assembly Library Review (test in Korean), National Assembly Library, Processing and Reference Bureau, Yoi-dong 1, Yeongdeungpo-gu, Seoul

Tosogwan Hak (Journal of the Korean Library Science Society) (text in Korean with English abstracts), c/o Ewha Woman's University Library, 11-1 Daehyon-dong, Seodaemun-Ku, Seoul 120

Literary Associations and Societies

Korean P E N Centre*, 163 Ankuk-dong, Jongno-ku, Seoul 110
Secretary-General: Dr Jung-kee Lee
Publications: The Korean PEN, Asian Literature

Literary Prizes

Hyun Dae Mun Hak Prize
Established 1955. Awarded annually for poetry, fiction, drama, or criticism.
Enquiries to Hyun Dae Mun Hak, 136-46 Yunji-dong, Chongro-ku, Seoul

Literary Prize*
In recognition of an outstanding literary work. $US5,000. Awarded annually.
Enquiries to Korean National Academy of Arts, 1 Seajong Ro, Chongro-gu, Seoul

Kuwait

General Information

Language: Arabic (English used also)
Religion: Muslim
Population: 1.2 million
Literacy Rate (1975): 59.6%
Bank Hours: Winter: 0730-1330 Saturday-Wednesday; 0730-1130 Thursday. Summer: 0700-1300 Saturday-Wednesday; 0700-1030 Thursday
Shop Hours: 0800-1300, 1600-2000 Saturday-Thursday; 0800-1200 Friday (markets and shopping centres open 1600-2000)
Currency: 1000 fils = 1 Kuwaiti dinar
Export/Import Information: No tariffs on books or advertising in reasonable quantity; all immoral and seditious publications prohibited. Import licence required. No exchange permit required
Copyright: No copyright conventions signed

Publishers

Kuwait Publishing House*, PO Box 5209 Tel: 510188

Ministry of Information, PO Box 193, Kuwait
Subjects: Art, Geography, History, Physics, Sociology, Textbooks, Maps, Literature, Mathematics, Education, Linguistics

Press Agency*, PO Box 1019, Kuwait Tel: 432269/411495 Cable Add: Matboat
Man Dir: Abdullah M N Harami; *Editorial:* K A Harami
Subjects: General (in Arabic and English)
Bookshops: in Kuwait and Salmiayit
Founded: 1954

Wkallat Matbouat*, PO Box 1019
Subject: Travel, Maps

Major Booksellers

Tahseen S Khaya, Gulf Union Co, Qubla Bldg, Al Soor St, Apt No 10, PO Box 2911, Safat Tel: 411688/411880 Cable Add: Florya Kuwait Telex: 3491 Florya Kt

Major Libraries

Kuwait Central Library*, Kuwait City

Kuwait University Central Library, Kuwait University, Libraries Department, PO Box 17140, Khaldiya, Kuwait Tel: 813182 Telex: Kuniver 2616 KT

Library Association

Kuwait University Libraries Department*, Chief Librarian's Office, PO Box 5969

Library Journals

The Library Bulletin, Kuwait University Central Library, Kuwait City

The University Library, Kuwait University Libraries Department, PO Box 5969, Kuwait

Laos

General Information

Language: Lao
Religion: Theravada Buddhist
Population: 3.5 million
Bank Hours: 0800-1200, 1400-1700 Monday-Friday
Shop Hours: 0800-2200 Monday-Friday
Currency: kip
Export/Import Information: No tariff on books (except children's picture books, 15%), none on most advertising matter. No import licences required for books. Exchange controls
Copyright: UCC (see International section)

Publishers

Lao-phanit*, Vientiane Ministère de l'Education nationale, Comité littéraire, Bureau des Manuels scolaires, Vientiane
Subjects: Education, Physics, Sociology, Economics, History, Cookery, Arts, Geography, Music, Fiction

Pakpassak Kanphin*, 9-11 quai Fa-Hguun, Vientiane

Vieng Krung*, Khoualuang Rd, Vientiane

Major Booksellers

M **Jumsai***, Manich Bookshop, BP 28, Vientiane

Kaye Ando Technical Services*, 3-8 Villa Khamsouk, Sethathirath St, Vientiane Tel: 2760 Cable Add: Kaye Ando

M **Nicolai***, Casa Lao, Vientiane

Major Libraries

Direction des **Archives** nationales*, Présidence du Conseil des Ministres, BP 59, Vientiane

Bibliothèque nationale*, BP 704, Vientiane

Centre national de Documentation*, Vientiane

Bibliothèque de l'**Ecole** royale de Médecine*, BP 131, Vientiane

Library Associations

Association des Bibliothécaires Laotiens*, c/o Direction de la Bibliothèque nationale, Ministry of Education, BP 704, Vientiane Association of Laos Librarians

Library Journals

Journal officiel (Official Journal), Centre national de Documentation, Vientiane

Lebanon

General Information

Language: Arabic (French and English also used)
Religion: Half Christian, with Maronites predominant, half Muslim
Population: 3.1 million
Bank Hours: 0830-1230 Monday-Friday; 0830-1200 Saturday
Shop Hours: Vary. Generally 0900-1900 in winter, 0800-1500 in summer
Currency: 100 Lebanese piastres = 1 Lebanese pound
Copyright: UCC, Berne (see International section)

Publishers

Dar al **Adab***, Beirut
Subject: Fiction

Arab Institute for Research and Publishing*, Syria St and Samadi Bldg, 5th Floor, PO Box 5460, Beirut
Subjects: Works in Arabic and English

Dar **Assayad***, BP 1038, Beirut
Man Dir: Bassam Freiha
Subjects: Politics, Periodicals and Newspapers
Founded: 1943

Geoprojects Sàrl*, PO Box 113, 5294 Beirut Tel: 344346 Telex: 22661 Khayat le
Man Dirs: Mac Purcell, Tahseen Khayat
Associate Companies: Gulf Union Co, PO Box 2911 Safat, Kuwait; All Prints Bookshop, PO Box 857, Abu Dhabi, UAE; Uncle Sam's Bookshop, PO Box 8375, Beirut
Subjects: Tourist Maps & Guides Series, Arabic books
1978: 2 titles *1979:* 8 titles *Founded:* 1978

Dar el-**Ilm** Lilmalayin*, PO Box 1085, Beirut (Located at: rue de Syrie, Beirut) Tel: 224502/291027 Cable Add: Malayin
Owners: Munir Ba'albaky, Bahij Osman
Subjects: Textbooks, Islamic Studies, Dictionaries, History, Mathematics, Physics, Law, Children, Health, Languages, Literature, Philosophy, Education, Psychology, Biographies
Founded: 1945

Institute for Palestine Studies, Publishing and Research Organization*, Institute Bldg, Anis Nsouli St, PO Box 11-7164, Beirut Tel: 319627/301599/ 301941/301089 Cable Add: Dirasat
Executive Secretary: Prof Walid Khalidi; *Editorial:* Miss Ghada Malki; *Sales:* Ghazi Khorshid
Subjects: Palestine and the Arab-Israeli conflict
1978: 21 titles *Founded:* 1963

The **International** Documentary Centre of Arab Manuscripts*, Darwish Bldg, rue de Syrie, BP 2668, Beirut
Proprietor: Zouhair Baalbaki
Subjects: Reprints, Facsimiles
Founded: 1965

Dar al **Kash'shaf***, Assad Malhamee St, PO Box 112091, Beirut Tel: 296805 Cable Add: Dakashaf Beirut
Proprietor: M Fathallah
Subjects: Scouting, Atlases, Maps
Founded: 1930

Khayat Book and Publishing Co SAL*, 90-94 rue Bliss, Beirut
Man Dir: Paul Khayat
Subjects: Fiction, History, Juveniles, Arts, Maps, Medicine, Education, Law, Religion, Social Sciences, Games, Sports, Economics, Books on the Middle East, Islam, Arabic, Reprints

Dar Al-**Kitab** Allubnani, PO Box 3176, Beirut Telex: 22865
Man Dir: El-Zein Hassan
Subsidiary Company: Dar Al-Kitab Al-Masri, Egypt (qv)
Branch Offs: Paris, Geneva, Madrid, Casablanca
Subjects: Islamic, Turath, Textbooks (in Arabic, English, French)
Bookshop: Librairie de l'Ecole, PO Box 3176, Beirut
1978: 197 titles *1979:* 237 titles *Founded:* 1929

Librairie du Liban*, Riad Al-Solh Sq, PO Box 945 Beirut Tel: 258259/295735 Cable Add: Librarie du Liban, Beirut Telex: 21037
Man Dirs: Khalil and George Sayegh; *Editorial:* Ahmad Khatib; *Sales:* Suhail Berjawi; *Production:* Albert Mutlag; *Publicity:* George Sayegh; *Rights and Permissions:* Khalil Sayegh
Subjects: Textbooks, Fiction, Linguistics, Travel, Islam, Dictionaries, Children's Books
Bookshops: Lebanon Bookshop, Bliss St, Beirut; Librairie du Liban, Hamra St, Beirut; Librairie sayegh, Damascus, Syria; Sphinx Bookshop, Cairo, Egypt
Founded: 1944

Longman Arab World Centre*, PO Box 945, Beirut
Associate Company: Longman Group Ltd, UK (qv)

Dar Al-**Maaref** Liban SAL*, Esseily Bldg, sq Riad Al-Solh, PO Box 11-2320, Beirut Tel: 223574/294064/383621 Cable Add: Damaref Beirut
Man Dir: Dr Fouad Ibrahim; *General Manager:* Joseph Nachou; *Sales:* Joseph Ibrahim
Parent Company: Dar Al Maaref, Egypt (qv)
Subjects: Juveniles, Textbooks in Arabic
Founded: 1959

Mac Purcell*, PO Box 1135294, Beirut

Dar-el **Mashreq***, c/o Librairie orientale, BP 1986, Beirut Tel: 234942/326469 Cable Add: Cathopress
Man Dir: Paul Brouwers; *Rights & Permissions:* Paul Brouwers
Orders to: Librairie orientale, BP 1986, Beirut
Subjects: Archaeology, Geography, Educational, History, Dictionaries, Religion, Art, Literature, Languages, Science, Philosophy, Periodicals
1978: 30 titles *Founded:* 1853
ISBN Publisher's Prefix: 2-7214

Middle East Publishing Co*, rue G Picot, Imm El Kaissi, Beirut
Man Editor: Elie Sawaf
Subjects: Medicine, Periodicals
Founded: 1954

Major Booksellers

Librairies **Antoine***, Rue Patriarche Hoyek, Beirut Tel: 229745

Esquire*, Rue Sidani, Beirut Tel: 348074

Help Bookshop*, Rue Jeanne d'Arc, Im Saghiri, Beirut Tel: 341679

Tahseen S **Khayat***, Uncle Sam's Bookshop, PO Box 8375 Beirut Tel: 344346

Lebanon Bookshop*, Bliss St, Beirut

Librairie du **Liban***, Hamra St, Beirut

Georges **Murr***, Rue Ahmed Chawki, Beirut Tel: 233810

Major Libraries

Library of **American University** of Beirut*, Beirut Tel: 340740 Telex: amunob 20801 le

Library of **Beirut Arab University***, PO Box 5020, Beirut

Bibliothèque nationale du Liban*, à la pl de l'Etoile, Imm du Parlement, Beirut Tel: 256160/256161

Bibliothèque orientale*, rue de l'Université St Joseph, BP 293, Beirut

Bibliothèque de l'**Ecole** supérieure des Lettres*, rue de Damas, Beirut

Library of the **Faculty of Engineering**, Université St Joseph, BP 1514, Beirut

Library of the **Faculty of Law***, Université St Joseph, BP 293, Beirut

Library of the **French Faculty of Medicine***, Pharmacy and Dentistry, Université St Joseph, BP 5076, Beirut

Bibliothèque de l'**Institut** français d'Archéologie*, rue Omar Daouk, BP 11-1424, Beirut

Nami C **Jafet** Memorial Library*, American University of Beirut, Beirut Tel: 340740 ext 2205

Librairie du Liban*, Imm Esseily, pl Riad Solh, BP 945, Beirut

Library of the **Monastery of St-Saviour** (Basilian Missionary Order of St-Saviour)*, Saïda

Library of the **Near East School** of Theology*, PO Box 7424, Beirut

Library of the **Syrian Patriarchal Seminary***, Seminary of Charfet, Daroon-Harissa

Library Associations

The **Lebanese Library** Association*, c/o National Library, pl de l'Etoile, Beirut Tel: 256160
Executive Secretary: Linda Sadaga
Publication: Newsletter

Library Journals

Bulletin bibliographique (Bibliographic Bulletin), Bibliothèque nationale du Liban, à la pl de l'Etoile, Imm du Parlement, Beirut

Newsletter, The Lebanese Library Association, c/o National Library, pl de l'Etoile, Beirut

Literary Associations and Societies

Lebanese **P E N** Club*, c/o M Camille Aboussouan, 12 ave Marie Curie, Beirut
Secretary: Zakaria Nsouli

Lesotho

General Information

Language: English, Sesotho (a Bantu language)
Religion: Roman Catholic and Protestant
Population: 1.3 million
Literacy Rate (1966): 58.6%
Bank Hours: 0830-1300 Monday-Friday; 0830-1100 Saturday
Shop Hours: Winter: 0830-1630 Monday-Friday; 0830-1300 Saturday; Summer: 0800-1630 Monday-Friday; 0800-1300 Saturday. Usually closed weekdays 1300-1400
Currency: 100 lisente = 1 loti (plural: maloti)
Export/Import Information: No tariffs on books or advertising matter. No import licence required; no obscene literature permitted. Exchange controls being relaxed

Publishers

Government Printer*, Mazenod Printing Press, PO Mazenod, Maseru

Mazenod Institute*, PO Box 18, Mazenod 160 (Railhead: Maseru Station) Tel: 0502224
Manager: Father B Mohlalisi
Subjects: History, Africana, Religion, Sotho Language & Literature, Secondary & Primary Textbooks
Founded: 1933

Morija Sesuto Book Depot, PO Box 4, Morija
Subjects: Belles Lettres, Poetry, History, Africana, Religion, Juveniles, Southern Sotho Language, Paperbacks, General Science, Secondary & Primary Textbooks
Founded: 1862

Saint Michael's Mission*, The Social Centre, PO Box 25, Roma
Man Dir: Rev Father M Ferrange; *Production:* Peter Ntsaoana
Subjects: Biography, History, Africana, Religion, Social Science, Secondary & Primary Textbooks, Anthropology
1978: 5 titles *Founded:* 1968

Major Booksellers

Catholic Book Depot*, PO Box MS 78, Maseru Tel: 2634

Lesotho Book Centre*, PO Box MS 608, Maseru Tel: 3783

Mazenod Book Centre, PO Box 39, Mazenod (Located at: Mazenod. Railhead: Maseru Station) Tel: 0502224 Cable Add: Books Mazenod Lesotho

Morija Sesuto Book Depot*, PO Box MJ 4, Morija Tel: 204

Major Libraries

British Council Educational Resource Centre, PO Box 429, Maseru 100 Tel: 22609

Lesotho National Library Service, PO Box 985, Maseru 100 Tel: 22592

National University of Lesotho Library*, PO Roma Tel: 201

Liberia

General Information

Language: English and a number of African languages
Religion: Muslim, Protestant; traditional beliefs followed by many
Population: 1.7 million
Literacy Rate (1962): 8.6%
Bank Hours: 0800-1200 Monday-Thursday; 0800-1400 Friday
Shop Hours: 0730-1200, 1400-1600 or longer
Currency: 100 cents = 1 Liberian dollar
Export/Import Information: No tariff on books and advertising matter. 5% f.o.b. Public Fund Levy. No import licence or exchange control
Copyright: UCC (see International section)

Publishers

Cole & Yancy*, PO Box 286, Monrovia
Man Dir: Henry B Cole
Subjects: General, Reference, Annuals, Paperbacks
Bookshop: PO Box 286, Monrovia

Government Printer*, Government Printing Office, Department of State, Monrovia

Liberian Literary & Educational Publications*, PO Box 2387, Monrovia
Man Dir: S Henry Cordor
Subjects: General, Educational, Belles Lettres, Poetry

Major Booksellers

Wadih M Captan Bookstores*, Randall St, PO Box 414, Monrovia Tel: 21393

Cole and Yancy Bookshop Ltd*, PO Box 286, Monrovia

Liberian Educational Materials Supply Corporation*, New Port St, PO Box 2088, Monrovia Tel: 22356
Manager: N Chandru

University Bookstore*, University of Liberia, Monrovia Tel: 22515 ext 225

Major Libraries

College of Our Lady of Fatima Library*, Harper

Cuttington College and Divinity School Library*, PO Box 277, Monrovia Tel: 21065

Government Public Library*, Ashmun St, Monrovia

International Communication Agency Library*, Broad St, Monrovia

University of Liberia Libraries*, PO Box 9020, Monrovia Tel: 22537
Dir: Dr C Wesley Armstrong
Publication: Newsletter

Literary Associations and Societies

Literary Club of Monrovia*, Monrovia

Literary Prizes

Edward Wilmot **Blyden** Prize*
For literary achievement. Awarded annually. Enquiries to Literary Club of Monrovia, Monrovia

Libya

General Information

Language: Arabic
Religion: Muslim
Population: 2.7 million
Literacy Rate (1964): 21.7%
Bank Hours: Generally Winter: 0900-1300; Summer: 0800-1230 Saturday-Thursday
Shop Hours: Vary greatly. Friday is weekly holiday but some Christian shops closed Sunday. Many are open 0830-1230, 1500-1730 Saturday-Thursday (slightly earlier hours in summer months)
Currency: 1,000 dirhams = 1 Libyan dinar
Export/Import Information: No tariff on books; advertising dutied 15%. Charity Tax of 5% and Municipal Tax of 5% levied on dutiable goods. Open General Licence for books. Exchange permit, liberally granted, required. Import and export of books is handled by the General Company for Publishing, Advertising and Distribution, Tripoli
Copyright: Berne (see International section)

Publishers

Dar Libya Publishing House*, PO Box 2487, Benghazi
Subject: Literature

General Press Corporation*, General Publication and Advertising Co, PO Box 959, Tripoli Tel: 45773/77/45537
Publicity: Moustafa A Elmasri
Subjects: General Books; Educational and Academic Books

Government Printer*, Agency for Development of Publication and Distribution, PO Box 34/35, Tripoli

Major Booksellers

General Company for Publishing, Advertising and Distribution*, Suf el Mahmudi, PO Box 959, Tripoli Tel: 457736777 Telex: 20235

Major Libraries

American Cultural Center Library*, Al Qayrawaan St, Tripoli

Arts and Crafts School Library*, Shar'a 24 December, Tripoli

al-Fateh University, The Central Library, PO Box 13104, Tripoli Tel: 604000 ext 2466

Government Library*, 14 Shar'a al-Jazair, Tripoli

Institut Culturel Français Bibliothèque*, 15-17 Sciara Karachi, PO Box 683, Tripoli Tel: 35567
Librarian: Mme Bianciotto
Publication: Bulletin (monthly)

National Archives*, Castello, Tripoli

National Library*, Secretariat of Information and Culture, PO Box 9127, Benghazi Tel: 90509, 96379, 96380
Librarian: Mohammed O Fannoush

Public Library*, Shar'a 'Umar al-Mukhtar, Benghazi

Qurinna Library*, Mukhtar St, Benghazi

University of Garyounis Library*, Central Library Benghazi Tel: 87633
Librarian: Ahmed M Gallal

University of Libya*, Library, Benghazi

Literary Associations and Societies

Intellectual Society of Libya*, 136 Shar'a Baladia, PO Box 1017, Tripoli

Liechtenstein

General Information

Language: German
Religion: Roman Catholic
Population: 25,000
Bank Hours: 0800-1200, 1330-1600 Monday-Friday
Shop Hours: 0800-1200, 1330-1830 Monday-Friday; 0800-1600 Saturday
Currency: Swiss
Export/Import Information: No tariff on books. Most books exempt from Turnover Tax. Advertising matter usually dutiable, some exempt from Turnover Tax. No import licences required. No exchange controls
Copyright: UCC, Berne, Florence (see International section)

Publishers

Buch und Verlagsdruckerei AG*, FL-9490 Vaduz, Im Städtle 32

A R Gantner Verlag KG*, FL-9490 Vaduz, Postfach 225 (Located at: Beckagässle 4)
Subjects: Art, Literature, Botany

Kraus Reprint, FL-9491 Nendeln Tel: (075) 71155 Cable Add: Kraus Nendeln Telex: 77800
Dir: Günther W Sprunkel; *Manager:* Frank P van Eck
Associate Companies: Kraus International Publications, Kraus Periodicals
Branch Offs: Rückertstrasse 1, D-8000 Munich 2, Federal Republic of Germany; Route 100, Millwood, New York, NY 10546, USA
Subjects: Scholarly publications and reference works in all subjects and languages
Founded: 1956
Miscellaneous: A division of Kraus-Thomson Organization Ltd (qv under Major Booksellers)
ISBN Publisher's Prefix: 3-262

Liechtenstein Verlag AG, FL-9490 Vaduz, Schwefelstr 33 Tel: (075) 23925 Telex: 77826
Man Dir: Albart Piet Schiks
Subjects: Belles Lettres, Poetry, History, Educational Materials
Founded: 1945
Miscellaneous: Firm is also a literary agency

Literarische Agentur und Verlagsgesellschaft*, Litag Etablissement, FL-9490 Vaduz, Beckägassle 4
Dir: Dr Anton Gantner

Park & Roche Establishment*, 256 Kirchenstrasse, FL-9494 Schaan
Subjects: Music, Art, Architecture, History

Quarto Press, Postfach 143, Beckägässli 8, FL-9490 Vaduz Tel: (075) 24855 Telex: 77030
Man Dir: Elmar Bissig
Subjects: Art, Architecture, Orientalia

Founded: 1976
ISBN Publisher's Prefix: 3-85851

Topos Verlag AG, Aeulestrasse 74, Postfach 668, FL-9490 Vaduz Tel: (075) 21711 Cable Add: Topos Vaduz Telex: 77817
Man Dir: Graham A P Smith
Subjects: Law, Economics, Social Science, Periodicals
1979: 60 titles *Founded:* 1977
ISBN Publisher's Prefix: 3-289

Literary Agents

Liechtenstein Verlag AG, FL-9490 Vaduz, Schwefelstr 33 Tel: (075) 23925 Telex: 77826
Firm is also a publisher (qv)

Major Booksellers

Buchhandlung im Stadtle*, FL-9490 Vaduz

Kraus-Thomson Organization Ltd, FL-9491 Nendeln Tel: (075) 71155

Major Libraries

Liechtensteinische Landesbibliothek, Offentliche Stiftung, Postfach 385, FL-9490 Vaduz Tel: (075) 66111
National Library
Director: Dr Alois Ospelt

Literary Associations and Societies

P E N Centre, Postfach 416, FL-9490 Vaduz
Secretary: Manfred Schlapp

Luxembourg

General Information

Language: Mainly French, but also German. Also Luxembourg dialect, Letzeburgesch
Religion: Roman Catholic
Population: 356,000
Bank Hours: 0900-1200, 1400-1430 Monday-Friday
Shop Hours: 0800-1200, 1400-1800 Monday-Saturday
Currency: 100 centimes = 1 Luxembourg franc
Export/Import Information: Member of the European Economic Community. In customs union with Belgium and Netherlands. No tariff on books except children's picture books, 13% from non-EEC; advertising other than single copies 9%. VAT 5% on books and advertising. No import licence required. No exchange controls
Copyright: UCC, Berne, Florence (see International Section)

Book Trade Organizations

Fédération des Commerçants, Groupement Papetiers-Libraires, Journaux, Editeurs et Galeries d'Art*, 21 allée Scheffer, Luxembourg Tel: 473125
Federation of Retailers Group for Stationers and Booksellers, Journals, Publishers and

LUXEMBOURG

Art Galleries
Dir: Victor Delcourt

Fédération luxembourgeoise des Travailleurs du Livre, 38 rue Goethe, Luxembourg
Luxembourg Federation of Workers in the Book Trade
President: Mathias Warny
Secretary: Nicolas Weber

Book Trade Reference Journal

Bibliographie luxembourgeoise (Luxembourg Bibliography), National Library, 37 blvd F D Roosevelt, Luxembourg

Publishers

Christian **Butterbach***, BP 516, Luxembourg Tel: 26926/26927/22022
Cable Add: Interferences
Owner and Manager: Christian Butterbach
Subjects: Literature, Periodical
1978: 1 title *Founded:* 1959
ISBN Publisher's Prefix: 3-921400

Hasso **Ebeling** Verlag*, 4 rue Pierre de Coubertin, Luxembourg Tel: 488348
Telex: 1354
Man Dir: Hasso Ebeling
Subsidiary company: Ebeling Publishing Ltd, 63 Kings Rd, Windsor, Berkshire, UK
Tel: 56 966 Telex: 848516
Subjects: Art, Architecture
Founded: 1974

Publisher **Krippler-Muller**, 52 bld G-D Charlotte, Luxembourg Tel: 470339
Man Dir: J-P Krippler
Subjects: Belles Lettres, History, Maps, Regional Literature, Law, Languages
Bookshop: address as above
1978: 3 titles *1979:* 5 titles *Founded:* 1949

Edouard **Kutter**, 17 rue des Bains, Luxembourg
Subjects: Art, Photography, Facsimile editions on Luxembourg
1978: 4 titles *1979:* 2 titles

Imprimerie **Saint-Paul** SA, 2 rue Christophe-Plantin, Luxembourg
Man Dir: André Heiderscheid; *Production:* Paul Thill; *Publicity:* Charles Jourdain
Subject: Literature
1979: 30 titles
Miscellaneous: Publishes newspaper *Luxemburger Wort*

Verlag-Buchhandlung Joseph **Thielen***, 222 route de Thionville, Luxembourg
Owner and Manager: Joseph Thielen
Founded: 1950

Literary Agents

Hasso **Ebeling***, 4 rue Pierre de Coubertin, Luxembourg Tel: 488348 Telex: 1354

Major Booksellers

Librairie De **Bourcy** Lucien, 49 blvd Royal, Luxembourg

Librairie Paul **Bruck***, 22 Grand-rue, Luxembourg

Librairie du **Centre**, 49 blvd Royal, Luxembourg Tel: 26613/27999
Proprietor: L de Bourcy

Librairie R **Daman**, 4 rue de Brabant, Diekirch

Librairie **Diderich** Sàrl, 2 rue Victor-Hugo, PO Box 70, Esch/Alzette Tel: 52695, 554083
Manager: J-Cl Diderich

Librairie Pierre **Ernster***, 27 rue du Fossé, Luxembourg

Librairie **Française***, 1 pl d'Armes, Luxembourg

Librairie des Messageries Paul **Kraus***, 5 rue de Hollerich, Luxembourg

Librairie **Muller-Groff***, 4a ave Pasteur, Luxembourg

Librairie Armand **Peiffer***, ave Monterey, Luxembourg

Librairie **Promoculture**, BP 1142, 14 rue Duchscher, Luxembourg Tel: 480691
Manager: Albert P Daming

Major Libraries

Archives de l'Etat, Plateau du St-Esprit, BP 6, Luxembourg 2
National Archives

Bibliothèque de la Ville, 26 rue Emile Mayrisch, Esch-sur-Alzette
Librarian: Fernand Roeltgen

Bibliothèque de Gouvernement, 37 blvd F D Roosevelt, Luxembourg

Bibliothèque nationale du Grand-Duché de Luxembourg, 37 blvd F D Roosevelt, Luxembourg Tel: 26255

Macau

General Information

Language: Portuguese, Cantonese (English used in business)
Religion: Chinese, the majority of population are Buddhist and Catholic is religion of Europeans
Population: 276,000
Literacy Rate (1970): 79.4%
Bank Hours: 1000-1500 Monday-Friday; 0930-1200 Saturday
Shop Hours: 0900-1730 Monday-Saturday
Currency: 100 avos = 1 pataca. Hong Kong currency is also widely used but there is no fixed exchange rate
Export/Import Information: Macau is a free port
Copyright: Berne, UCC (see International section)

Major Booksellers

The **World** Book Company, PO Box 201, 68 Rua Dos Mercadores Tel: 3591 Cable Add: Libiblioteca
Manager: V M Lam

Major Libraries

Biblioteca Nacional de Macau*, Edificio do Leal Senado, Macau

Biblioteca **Sir Robert Ho Tung***, Largo do Sto Agostinho, Macau

Democratic Republic of Madagascar

General Information

Language: French and Malagasy
Religion: About 40% Christian, 5% Muslim; rest follow traditional beliefs
Population: 8.3 million
Bank Hours: 0815-1100, 1400-1600 Monday-Friday. Closed afternoon preceding a holiday
Shop Hours: 0800-1200, 1400-1800 Monday-Saturday
Currency: Malagasy franc
Export/Import Information: For books, 5% customs duty, 22% import duty, 10% unique tax. For advertising matter, 5%, (31%) and 10%. Import licence required
Copyright: Berne, Florence (see International Section)

Book Trade Organization

Office du Livre Malagasy (OLM),* BP 257, Tananarive Tel: 25872
Secretary-General: Juliette Ratsimandrava

Book Trade Reference Journal

Bibliographie annuelle de Madagascar, Bibliothèque universitaire de Madagascar, BP 908, Tananarive (The national bibliography, published annually since 1964)

Publishers

Maison d'Edition Protestante '**Antso'***, Imarivolanitra, BP 660, Tananarive Tel: 20886 Cable Add: Fijekrima Tfbpi
Man Dir: Hans Andriamampianina;
Editorial: Charles Ramaniraka
Subjects: Religion, Sociology, Politics, Economics, Journals
Bookshop: Bookshop Antso, Lot IIB 18, Totohabato Ranavalona 1, Tananarive
1978-79: 18 titles *Founded:* 1966

Government Printer*, Imprimerie nationale, BP 38, Tananarive

Société de Presse et d'Edition de Madagascar*, BP 1570, Tananarive
Man Dir: Mme Rajaofera-Andriambelo
Subjects: General Nonfiction, Reference, General Science, University Textbooks

Société Malgache d'Edition*, BP 659, Ankorondrano, Tananarive Tel: 22635
Man Dir: Rahaga Ramaholimihaso;
Publicity: Daniel Ramanandraibe
Subjects: University & Secondary Textbooks
Bookshop: address as above
Founded: 1959

Société Nouvelle de l'Imprimerie Centrale*, BP 1414, Tananarive
Man Dir: M Hantzberg
Subjects: Paperbacks, General Science, University, Secondary & Primary Textbooks
Founded: 1959

Imprimerie **Takariva***, 4 rue Radley, BP 1029, Antanimena, Tananarive
Tel: 22128
Man Dir: Paul Rapatsalahy
Subjects: General Fiction, Malagasy Languages, Paperbacks, Secondary

Textbooks
Founded: 1933

Trano Printy Loterana-Trano Printy Fiangonana Loterana Malagasy (TPFLM)-(Imprimerie Luthérienne)*, 9 ave Grandidier, BP 538, Antsahamanitra, Tananarive Tel: 24569
Man Dir: Abel Arnesa; *Editorial:* Pastor Rasolofomanana; *Production:* Razafindramanitra Georges
Subjects: General Fiction, Religion, Paperbacks, Secondary & Primary Textbooks
Bookshop: address as above
Founded: 1875

Major Booksellers

Bibliomad*, 11 rue de Nice, BP 602, Tananarive Tel: 23280
Manager: Ramaromandray Amedée

Librairie de Madagascar*, 38 ave de l'Indépendance, BP 402, Tananarive Tel: 22454

Librairie lutherienne*, ave Grandidier, BP 538, Tananarive Tel: 23340

Librairie mixte Sàrl*, 37 bis Ave du 26 Juin 1960, Analakely, BP 3204, Tananarive Tel: 25130
Manager: Jean Razakasoa

Librairie universitaire*, 26 rue Amiral Pierre, Tananarive

Sociéte Malgache d'Edition*, BP 659, Ankorondrano, Tananarive

Librairie **'Tout pour l'Ecole'***, Immeuble Vitasoa, rue de Nice, BP 1099, Tananarive Tel: 23521

Trano Printy Loterana*, 9 ave Grandidier, BP 538, Antsahamanitra, Tananarive Tel: 24569

Major Libraries

Archives de Madagascar*, BP 3384, Tananarive
Dir: Mrs Razoharinoro-Randriam-Boavonjy

Bibliotheque municipale*, ave 18 Juin, BP 729, Tananarive Tel: 21176

Bibliotheque nationale*, BP 257, Antaninarenina, Tananarive Tel: 20511
Publications include: Ny Boky loharanom-pandrosoana (Le Livre Source de Progrès)

Bibliothèque universitaire*, Campus universitaire, BP 908, Tananarive Tel: 26000
Librarian: Miss de Nuce
Publication: Bibliographie annuelle

Bibliothèque du Centre culturel 'Albert **Camus'***, 11 ave Grandidier, Isoraka, Tananarive

Collège rural d'Ambatobe*, Bibliothèque, BP 1629, Tananarive

International Communication Agency Library*, 26 rue Paul Dussac, Tananarive Tel: 20238

Library Journals

Ny Boky loharanom-pandrosoana (Le Livre Source du Progrès) (The Book, Source of Progress) National Library, Antaninarenina, BP 257, Tananarive

Literary Periodicals

Fanasina, BP 1574, Analakely-Tananarive (literary and current affairs weekly edited by Paul Rakotovololona)

Literary Prizes

Literature Prize*
For an outstanding novel. 130,000 Malagasy francs. Awarded every two years. Enquiries to Malagasy Ministry of Cultural Affairs, Anosy-Tananarive

Malawi

General Information

Language: English, Cinyanja and Citumbuku (Bantu languages) are official languages
Religion: About 35% Christian (Roman Catholic and Presbyterian); 10% Muslim; rest follow traditional beliefs
Population: 5.7 million
Literacy Rate (1966; African Population): 22.1%
Bank Hours: 0800-1230 Monday, Tuesday, Thursday, Friday; 0800-1130 Wednesday; 0800-1030 Saturday
Shop Hours: 0730 or 0800-1600 or 1700 Monday-Friday (with some closing for lunch); until midday Saturday
Currency: 100 tambala = 1 Malawi kwacha
Export/Import Information: No tariff on books; some advertising matter subject to 30%. No import licence required. Exchange controls
Copyright: UCC (see International section)

Book Trade Reference Journal

Malawi National Bibliography, c/o National Archives of Malawi, PO Box 62, Zomba

Publishers

Christian Literature Association in Malawi*, PO Box 503, Blantyre Tel: 635046
Subjects: General Fiction, Poetry, Biography, History, Africana, Religion, Juveniles, Christian Tracts, Paperbacks
Bookshop: CLAIM, at above address
Founded: 1968

Government Printer (Imprimerie National)*, Government Printing Department, Office of the President and Cabinet, PO Box 37, Zomba

Popular Publications, PO Box 5592, Limbe Tel: 651139/651833 Telex: 4130
General Manager: John Kleinpenning; *Editorial, Production, Rights & Permissions:* Allan E Ulanga; *Sales, Publicity:* Zachary D Mullewa
Subsidiary Company: Montfort Press, PO Box 5592, Limbe
Subjects: Belles Lettres, Poetry, Paperbacks, Biography, Plays, Religion, Malawian Writers Series
Bookshop: Moni Bookshop, PO Box 5592, Limbe
1978: 1 title *1979:* 1 title *Founded:* 1975

Major Booksellers

C L A I M Bookshop*, PO Box 503, Blantyre Tel: 635046

Central Bookshop Ltd, PO Box 264, Blantyre Tel: 635447
Manager: A Hamid Sacranie
School suppliers

Malawi Book Service*, PO Box 30044, Chichiri, Blantyre 3
Branches in Zomba, Lilongwe, Kasungu, Mzuzu

Times Bookshop Ltd, Victoria Ave, Private Bag 39, Blantyre Tel: 636355
Manager: Shaibu Itimu
Parent Company: Blantyre Printing and Publishing Co

Major Libraries

British Council Library*, Victoria Rd, PO Box 456, Blantyre Tel: 636500
Also Taurus House, PO Box 30222 Area 40/4, Capital City, Lilongwe 3 Tel: 30484/30266

Malawi National Library Service, PO Box 30314, Lilongwe 3
Dir: R S Mabomba

The **Malawi Polytechnic** Library, PMB 303, Chichiri, Blantyre 3 Tel: Blantyre 32144 Telex: Polytechnic 632144 Blantyre
Acting Librarians: Paul Kanthambi and R Masnjika
Publications: Accessions List, Annual Report

National Archives of Malawi, PO Box 62, Zomba Tel: 2478/9
Librarian: H W Ndau
Publication: Malawi National Bibliography

University of Malawi Library, PO Box 280, Zomba Tel: 2791
Librarian: S A Patchett

Library Associations

The **Malawi Library Association**, c/o National Archives of Malawi, PO Box 62, Zomba Tel: 2478/9
Secretary: D D Najira
Publication: MALA Bulletin

Literary Associations and Societies

The **Writers'** Group, PO Box 280, Zomba
Secretary: K D Lipenga
Publications: Odi, The Muse

Literary Periodicals

Odi, The Writers' Group, PO Box 280, Zomba

The Muse, The Writers' Group, PO Box 280, Zomba

Malaysia

General Information

Language: Bahasa Malaysia (Malay) is official language; English widely used; Chinese, Tamil and several local languages
Religion: Predominantly Muslim (Islam is the official religion) and large Buddhist group
Population: 12.6 million
Literacy Rate (1970): Sabah 44.3% total (69.1% Urban, 38.9% Rural); Sarawak 38.3% (64.1% Urban, 32.6% Rural); West Malaysia 60.8% (68.2% Urban, 57.6% Rural)
Bank Hours: (some states observe Muslim weekly holiday) Peninsula: 1000-1500 Monday-Friday; 0930-1130 Saturday. Sabah: 0800-1200, 1400-1500 Monday-Friday; 0900-1100 Saturday. Sarawak: 1000-1500 Monday-Friday; 0930-1130 Saturday
Shop Hours: Peninsula varies; average 0830-1830 Monday-Saturday. Sabah: 0830-1830 Monday-Saturday. Sarawak: 0900-1800 Monday-Friday; 0900-1300 Saturday
Currency: 100 cents = 1 Malaysian dollar (or ringgit)
Export/Import Information: No tariff on books. Advertising matter dutied at 25 cents per lb, subject to 5% c.i.f. surtax. No obscene literature allowed. Import licences required only in Sabah, for books not having on first or last printed page the name and address of printer and publisher. No exchange controls
Copyright: Florence (see International section)

Book Trade Organizations

Malaysian Book Publishers' Association, PO Box 335, Kuala Lumpur Tel: 941344
Honorary Secretary: J B Ho

Book Trade Reference Journals

Berita Oxford (text in English and Malay), Oxford University Press, East Asian Branch, Bangunan Loke Yew, Jalan Belanda, Kuala Lumpur

Bibliografi Negara Malaysia (Malaysian National Bibliography), National Library of Malaysia, 1st Floor, Wisma Thakurdas, Jalan Raja Laut, Kuala Lumpur

Publishers

Academia Publications P Ltd*, 10 Jalan 217, Petaling Jaya, Selangor

Pustaka **Aman** Press Sdn Bhd*, 4200-A Simpang Tiga-Telipot, Jalan Pasir Puteh, Kota Bharu, Kelantan

Pustaka **Antara***, 399A Jalan Tuanku Abdul Rahman, Kuala Lumpur 02-01 Tel: 24622
Bookshop: 399A Jalan Tuanku Abdul Rahman, Kuala Lumpur 02-01

Anthonian Stores Sdn Bhd, 235 Jalan Brickfields, Kuala Lumpur 09-08 Tel: 441711
Man Dir, Publicity: Soh Boon Chuan; *Editorial, Production, Rights & Permissions:* Francis C K Lee; *Sales:* Y S Tan
Associate Company: Anthonian Store Sdn Bhd, Ipoh
Subsidiary Company: Anthonian (Pte) Ltd, Singapore
Subjects: Educational, General

Bookshops: in 108 schools
1978: 21 titles *1979:* 12 titles *Founded:* 1953

Book Distributors Sdn Bhd*, 8-1/8-2 Jalan Batai, PO Box 944, Kuala Lumpur 01-02

The **Cultural Supplies** Co*, 8-1 Pater Bldg, Jalan Brunei off Jalan Pudu, Kuala Lumpur

Dewan Bahasa dan Pustaka*, PO Box 803, Kuala Lumpur 08-08 Tel: 481169 Cable Add: Bahasa
Director General: Datuk Hj Hassan Ahmad; *Editorial:* Baha Zain, Noor Azam; *Sales:* Mokhtar Mohamad; *Production:* Rahmat Ramly; *Publicity:* A Rahim Esa; *Rights & Permissions:* Ariffin Siri
Branch Off: Kota Kinabalu, Sabah; Kuching, Sarawak
Subjects: Textbooks in Malay Language, Literature, General Books, Children's Books
Bookshop: address as above
1978: 200 titles *Founded:* 1956

Eastern Cultural Organizations Sdn Bhd*, 27-9 Jalan Loke Yew, Kuala Lumpur

Eastern Universities Press, No 134 Jalan Kasah, Damansara Heights, Kuala Lumpur Tel: 944062
Manager: Ong Kim Chuan
Parent Company: (Majority shareholder) Hodder & Stoughton, Sevenoaks, Kent, UK (qv)
Subjects: Primary and Secondary Schoolbooks, Art, Archaeology, Architecture, Biography, Botany, Customs and Usage, Economics and Politics, Languages, Sociology, Religion, Travel, Topography
1978: 50 titles

F E P International Sdn Bhd (Far Eastern Publishers), 8246 Jalan 225, PO Box 1091, Petaling Jaya, Selangor Tel: 560877/560381 Cable Add: Bookmark
Man Dir: Lim Mok Hai
Subjects: Reference, General Nonfiction, Secondary & Primary Textbooks
1980: 150 titles

Penerbit **Fajar** Bakti Sdn Bhd, 3 Jalan 13/3, PO Box 1050, Jalan Semangat, Petaling Jaya, Selangor Tel: 563111 Cable Add: Oxonian Petaling Jaya Telex: 37578
Regional Manager: J A Nicholson; *General Manager:* M Sockalingam; *Publishing Manager:* Mohd Yusoff Shamsuddin; *Sales:* Koh Seng Hwi; *Production:* Yap Kok Hoong; *Publicity:* Thor Gim Lock
Parent Company: Oxford University Press (qv)
Imprint: PFB
Subjects: Malay Language Teaching, Dictionaries, Reference, Secondary Textbooks, General
Bookshop: at same address
1978: 92 titles *1979:* 45 titles *Founded:* 1969
ISBN Publisher's Prefix: 019

Federal Publications Sdn Bhd, Lot 8238, Jalan 222, Petaling Jaya, Selangor
General Manager: H H Chiam
Subject: Education

M S Geetha Publishers*, 13A Jalan Kovil Hilir, Batu 2½, Jalan Ipoh, Sentul, Kuala Lumpur 13-05
Man Dir: Mr Sethu
Subjects: History, Education, How-to, Reference, Textbooks, Bibliography, Book Industry

Heinemann Educational Books (Asia) Ltd, No 2, Jalan 20/16A, Paramount Garden, Petaling Jaya, Selangor
Parent Company: Heinemann Educational Books (International) Ltd, UK (qv)

Penerbit **Jaya**, PO Box 6103, Pudu PO, Kuala Lumpur
Subjects: Dictionary (*English—Bahasa Malaysia Idiomatic Phrases*)
1978: 1 title

Longman Malaysia Sdn Bhd, PO Box 63, Kuala Lumpur Tel: 941344/941461 Cable Add: Freegrove Kualalumpur
Man Dir: J E Ho
Parent Company: Longman Group Ltd, UK (qv)
Subjects: Educational Materials, Textbooks
1978: 35 titles *1979:* 43 titles

Macmillan Malaysia*, Rm 805, 8th Floor, Selangor Complex, Jalan Sultan, Kuala Lumpur 01-26 Tel: 299194/5

Pustaka **Mahligai** Press*, 4591 Jalan Pasir Puteh, Kota Bharu, Kelantan

Malaya Books Suppliers Co*, 183 Lebuh Carnarvon, Pulau Pinang

Malaya Educational Supplies Sdn Bhd*, 48 Jalan Raja Laut, Kuala Lumpur
Subject: Education

The **Malaya Press** Sdn Bhd*, 24B Jalan Bukit Bintang, Kuala Lumpur Tel: (03) 428831/425764
Man Dir: Yu Nan Shen; *Editorial:* Yiu Hong; *Sales:* Chong Tek Seng
Parent Company: Union Cultural Organization Sdn Bhd, 10 Jalan 217, Petaling Jaya, Malaysia
Associated Companies: Hong Kong Cultural Press Ltd, 9 College Rd, Kowloon, Hong Kong; Singapore Press (Pte) Ltd, 303 North Bridge Rd, Singapore 7
Subject: School Textbooks
Bookshops: Ipoh Book Co, 75 Market St, Ipoh, Perak; Malaya Book Co, 22-24 Jalan Bukit Bintang, Kuala Lumpur
Founded: 1958

Pustaka **Melayu** Baru*, 1015 Selangor Mansion, Jalan Masjid India, Kuala Lumpur

Oxford University Press, 3 Jalan 13/3, PO Box 1050, Jalan Semangat, Petaling Jaya, Selangor Tel: 563111 Cable Add: Oxonian Petaling Jaya Telex: 37578
Regional Manager: J A Nicholson; *General Manager:* M Sockalingham; *Sales:* Koh Seng Hwi; *Production:* Yap Kok Hoong; *Publicity:* Thor Gim Lock
Parent Company: Oxford University Press, UK (qv)
Subsidiary Company: Penerbit Fajar Bakti Sdn Bhd (qv)
Branch Off: 4th Floor, Tong Lee Bldg, 35 Kallang Pudding Rd, Singapore 1334
Subjects: Educational, English Language Teaching, General, Dictionaries, Reference, Malaysiana
Bookshop: address as above
Book Club: Triple Crown Club
1978: 40 titles *1979:* 48 titles *Founded:* 1957
ISBN Publisher's Prefix: 0-19

P F B, an imprint of Penerbit Fajar Bakti Sdn Bhd (qv)

Pan Malayan Publishing Co Sdn Bhd*, 211 Jalan Bandar, Kuala Lumpur 01-30

Penerbitan Buku **Panther** (Panther Books Malaysia), 135A Jalan Abdul Samad, Brickfields, Kuala Lumpur 09-02 Tel: 442364/442841
Chief Executive, Publicity: R Vijesurier; *Editorial, Production:* Bella Mary Peters; *Sales:* Irene Khoo
Branch Off: 8 Cambridge Rd, Singapore 10
Subjects: School Textbooks, Revision Guides, Travel Books, Street Guides
Founded: 1972

Pustaka **Pendidekan** Sdn Bhd*, 19 Jalan Ismail, Kluang, Johore

Preston Corporation Ltd*, 18 Jalan 19/3, Petaling Jaya, Selangor Tel: 563734/5 Telex: Prest MA 37433
Associate Companies: Preston Publications Ltd, and Vista Productions Ltd, 1 & 6, 7th Floor Block E, Sunway Gardens, 989 King's Rd, North Point, Hong Kong; Preston Corporation (Pte) Ltd, 9 Irving Place, Singapore 13

Preston-Times Printing & Publishing*, Lots 2, 4 & 6 Kawasan MIEL, Phase 3, Shal Alam Industrial Estate, Selangor, Malaysia
Associate Company: Preston Corporation (Pte) Ltd, 9 Irving Place, Singapore 13
Subjects: General Non-fiction, Reference Books, Primary and Secondary Textbooks, Library Books

Sino-Malay Publishing Co*, 183 Lebuh Carnarvon, Pulau Pinang

Pustaka **Sistem** Palajaran*, 77 & 79 Jalan Jejaka Dua, Batu 3, Cheras, Kuala Lumpur
Subjects: School Textbooks, Children's Books

Pustaka **Sri Jaya** Sdn Bhd, 14 Jalan Kancil, off Jalan Pudu, Kuala Lumpur 06-13
Subjects: Juveniles, Textbooks

Syarikat Cultural Supplies Sdn Bhd*, 8-1 Pater Bldg, Jalan Brunei, Off Jalan Pudu, Kuala Lumpur 06-18

Syarikat Dian Sdn Bhd*, 97A Jalan Raja Abdullah, Kampung Baru, Kuala Lumpur

Syarikat United Book Sdn Bhd*, 187-189 Lebuh Carnarvon, Pulau Pinang

Text Books Malaysia Sdn Bhd*, Peti Surat 30, Segamat, Johore (Located at: 39 Jalan Buloh Kasap, Segamat, Johore)

Times Educational Co Ltd*, 22 Jalan 19/3, Petaling Jaya, Selangor Tel: 51194 Cable Add: Timesbooks Telex: Prest MA 37433
Orders to: Preston Corporation Ltd, 18 Jalan 19/3, Petaling Jaya Selangor
Parent Company: Times Educational Co Ltd, 1 & 6, 7th Floor, Block E, Sunway Gardens, 989 King's Road, North Point, Hong Kong
Associate Companies: Preston Corporation Ltd, Petaling Jaya Selangor, Malaysia; Preston-Times Printing & Publishing, Selangor, Malaysia; Preston Corporation (Private) Ltd, Singapore
Subjects: Textbooks (Primary & Secondary), Library books, General & Reference books
1978: 198 titles

Uni-Text Book Company, 50 Jalan SS2/61, Petaling Jaya, Selangor Tel: 764128/764084
Man Dir: Bob E S Lim; *Editorial:* Munir Ali; *Production:* E H Lim; *Sales:* Theresa Chung
Associate Company: Uni-Text Distributors Private Ltd, at above address
Subjects: Malay History, Religion, Literature
Bookshop: address as above
1978-79: 265 titles

United Publishers Services (M) Sdn Bhd, 134 Jalan Kasah, Damansara Heights, Kuala Lumpur Tel: 942604
Man Dir, Editorial, Production, Rights & Permissions: Goh Kee Seah; *Sales, Publicity:* Johnny K C Ong
Associate Companies: United Publishers Service Hong Kong Ltd; United Publishers Services Tokyo Ltd, Japan (qv)
Branch Off: No 8, 1st Floor, Leboh Naning, Penang; 112F Boon Keng Rd, Block 5, Singapore 12
Subjects: Educational, General, Paperbacks
Founded: 1968

United Publishing House and Stationers Sdn Bhd*, 21-23 Jalan Taiping, Off Jalan Pahang, Kuala Lumpur 02-14, Kuala Lumpur

Universal Publications Sdn Bhd*, 6 Jalan 13/6, Petaling Jaya, Selangor Tel: 773630
Subjects: School textbooks

University of Malaya Press Ltd*, University of Malaya, Pantai Valley, Kuala Lumpur 22-11 Tel: (03) 774361 Cable Add: Vasitipres Kuala Lumpur
Man Dir, Publicity, Rights & Permissions: Harun Haji Abdullah; *Editorial:* Syed Zulflida Shahabuddin; *Sales:* Yang Sharifah Baharuddin; *Production:* Kamar Bidin
Subjects: General Fiction, Belles Lettres, Poetry, History, Politics, Economics, General & Social Science, Medicine, Bahasa Malaysia
Founded: 1954

Utusan Publications and Distributions Sdn Bhd, PO Box 2235, Lot 1-29, Tingkat Satu, Pertama Kompleks, Jalan Tuanku Abdul Rahman, Kuala Lumpur 01-08 Tel: 920170 Cable Add: Utusan Kualalumpur

Yayasan Buku*, 143 C Jalan Sungai Besi, Kuala Lumpur
Subjects: How-to, Reference, Juveniles, Nonfiction, Bibliography, Book Industry

Book Clubs

Triple Crown Club, 3 Jalan 13/3, PO Box 1050, Jalan Semangat, Petaling Jaya, Selangor Cable Add: Oxonian Petaling Jaya Telex: 37578
Members: 300
Owned by: Oxford University Press (Selangor) (qv)
Founded: 1963

Major Booksellers

Anthonian Store Sdn Bhd, 235 Jalan Brickfields, Kuala Lumpur 09-08 Tel: 441711

Cosdel (Singapore) Pte Ltd, PO Box 6073, Pudu, Kuala Lumpur 06-10 (Located at: 23-25 Jalan Jejaka 7, Taman Maluri; Batu 3, Jln Cheras, Kuala Lumpur)
Distributors

Eastern Book Service Sdn Bhd (wholesalers)*, 10-A Jalan Telawi 4, Bangsar Baru, Kuala Lumpur Tel: 80445

Johore Central Store Sdn Bhd, 55-56 Jalan Ibrahim, Johor Bahru Tel: 23637

Kwang Hwa Bookstore Pte Ltd*, 26 Carpenter St, PO Box 326, Kuching, Sarawak Tel: 22968
Manager: Francis Hsu Cheng Loo

M P H Distributors Sdn Bhd, Peti Surat 1076, Jalan Semangat, Petaling Jaya

Marican & Sons (M) Sdn Bhd*, 321 Jalan Tuanku Abdul Rahman, Kuala Lumpur 02-01 Tel: 981133/981218
Branch Offs: 211 Ampang Park Shopping Centre, Jalan Ampang, Kuala Lumpur Tel: 485172; Weld Supermarket (First Floor), Jalan Raja Chulan, Kuala Lumpur Tel: 27994

Nabco Pendidekan Sdn Bhd, 24 Market St, Ipoh, Perak Tel: (05) 78456/518439
Branch Off: 44 Jln Persiaran Ipoh Satu, Ipoh Garden, Ipoh, Perak (formerly New Asia Book Co) Tel: (05) 556655

Parry's Book Center (Sri Abdul Wahab Sdn Bhd), KL Hilton Hotel, PO Box 960, Kuala Lumpur Tel: 422631 (showroom), 922329, 924985 (office)
Dir: Abdul Wahab
University and Library suppliers. Also foreign publishers' representatives

Rex Book Store*, 40-2 K L Arcade, Jalan Masjid India, Kuala Lumpur

Times Distributors Sdn Bhd, NZI Building, 2 Jalan 52/10, Petaling Jaya, Selangor
Also 1 New Industrial Rd, Singapore 1953
General Manager: Michael Toh

University of Malaya Co-operative Bookshop Ltd, PO Box 1127, Jalan Pantai Baru, Kuala Lumpur Tel: 565000/565425 Telex: MA 37453

Major Libraries

British Council Library, PO Box 539, Jalan Bukit Aman, Kuala Lumpur 01-02 Tel: (03) 22601 Telex: MA 31052
Branches: Penang (PO Box 595); Kota Kinabalu (PO Box 746)

Kuala Lumpur Public Library*, Sam Mansion, Jalan Tuba, Kuala Lumpur

Lincoln Cultural Center, 181 Jalan Ampang, Kuala Lumpur 04-07 Tel: 420291/425478/484865
Chief Librarian: Ch'ng Kim See

Ministry of Agriculture Library, Swettenham Rd, Kuala Lumpur 10-02
Librarian: Beatrice Lip

National Archives of Malaysia*, Federal Government Building, Jalan Sultan, Petaling Jaya
Publications: Annual Report of the National Archives, Siri Ucapan Perdan Menteri Tun Abdul Razak (Speeches of Tun Abdul Razat, Prime Minister of Malaysia), inventories and lists of archives groups

National Library of Malaysia, 1st Floor, Wisma Thakurdas, Jalan Raja Laut, Kuala Lumpur 02-07
Deputy Director General: D E K Wijasuriya
Publications: Malaysian National Bibliography (quarterly, annually); *Malaysian Periodicals Index* (semi-annually); *Malaysian Newspaper Index* (semi-annually)

National University of Malaysia Library, Bangi, Selangor Tel: 331500/331099
Chief Librarian: (acting) Zainal Azman Rajuddin

Rubber Research Institute of Malaysia Library, PO Box 150, Kuala Lumpur 16-03 Tel: 467033
Librarian: J S Soosai

Sabah State Library, PO Box 1136, Kota Kinabalu, Sabah Tel: 54333
Director: Mrs Adeline Leong

Sarawak State Library*, Jalan Jawa, Kuching

Selangor Public Library*, 21 Jalan Raja, Kuala Lumpur 01-02 Tel: (03) 85370
Librarian: Mrs Shahaneem Mustafa
Publication: Annual Report; Accession List (quarterly)

Tun Razak Library, Jalan Club, Ipoh, Perak Tel: (05) 514979/514808
Librarian: Chang Sinn Nean
Publications: Malaysiana Collection (plus supplement), *Accession Lists* (in English, Malay, Chinese and Tamil)

University of Agriculture Malaysia Library, Serdang, Selangor Tel: 356101
Chief Librarian: Tuan Syed Salim Agha

University of Malaya Library, Pantai Valley, Kuala Lumpur 22-11

246 MALAYSIA — MALTA

University of Science Malaysia Library, Minden, Penang Tel: 883822
Chief Librarian: Lim Huck Tee

University of Technology Malaysia Library, Jalan Gurney, Kuala Lumpur Tel: 202233
Chief Librarian: Che Sham Hj Mohd Darus

Library Associations

Persatuan Perpustakaan Malaysia, PO Box 2545, Kuala Lumpur
Library Association of Malaysia
Honorary Secretary: Chew Wing Foong
Publications: Majallah Perpustakaan Malaysia (twice yearly); *Sumber Pustaka* (bi-monthly)

Library Reference Books and Journals

Books
Directory of Libraries in Malaysia, National Library of Malaysia, Jalan Raja Laut, Kuala Lumpur

Journals
Majallah Perpustakaan Malaysia (Official Journal) (text in English and Malay), Library Association of Malaysia, PO Box 2545, Kuala Lumpur

Sumber Pustaka, Library Association of Malaysia, PO Box 2545, Kuala Lumpur
Official Newsletter, text in English and Malay

Literary Associations and Societies

Dewan Bahasa dan Pustaka*, PO Box 803 Jalan Lapangan Terbang, Kuala Lumpur 08-08
Language and Literary Agency of the Ministry of Education
Dir General: Datuk Haji Hassan bin Ahmad
Publications: Dewan Bahasa, Dewan Masyarakat, Dewan Pelajar, Dewan Sastera (monthly); *Dewan Budaya, Dewan Siswa* (monthly); *Tenggara* (half-yearly)

Literary Periodicals

Tenggara (half-yearly — text in English and Malay), Dewan Behasa dan Pustaka, PO Box 803 Jl Lapangan Terbang, Kuala Lumpur 08-08

Literary Prizes

National Literary Awards*
Panel established in 1971 by the late Tun Abdul Razak to award prizes. Enquiries to Dewan Bahasa dan Pustaka, PO Box 803, Kuala Lumpur 08-08

Mali

General Information

Language: French
Religion: Muslim
Population: 6 million
Literacy Rate (1960): 2.2%
Working Hours: normally 0800 or 0900-1200, 1500-1800 Monday-Friday; 0800 or 0900-1200 Saturday
Currency: Malian franc
Export/Import Information: Member of the West African Economic Community. No tariff on books but subject to 10% VAT; children's picture books 20% VAT; atlases 10% VAT. Advertising matter (more than single copy): 5% tariff, 25% import tax, 20% VAT. All goods subject to local tax of 3% customs value. Import licence required. Importation is either by private importers or state enterprises. Exchange controls for non-franc zone
Copyright: Berne (see International section)

Publishers

Government Printer (Imprimerie Nationale)*, ave Kasse Keita, BP 21, Bamako

Editions Imprimeries du **Mali***, ave Kasse Keita, BP 21, Bamako Tel: 22041
Man Dir: Barthélémy Koné
Subsidiary Companies: Editions populaires; Imprimerie Kasse Keita; Imprimerie nationale
Subjects: General Fiction & Nonfiction, Belles Lettres, Poetry, Biography, History, Africana, Religion, Paperbacks, Social Science, University, Secondary & Primary Textbooks
Founded: 1972

Major Booksellers

Librairie **Deves et Chaumet***, BP 64, Bamako

Librairie populaire de Mali*, ave Kasse Keita, BP 28, Bamako Tel: 23403

Major Libraries

Archives nationales du Mali*, Institut des Sciences Humaines, BP 159, Koulouba, Bamako
Dir: A Gamby N'Diaye

Bibliothèque municipale*, Bamako

Bibliothèque nationale*, Institut de Sciences humaines, BP 159, Koulouba, Bamako

Centre français de Documentation*, Ambassade de France, BP 1547, Bamako Tel: 24019

Ecole normale supérieure*, Bibliothèque, BP 241, Bamako

Library Associations

Inspection des **Archives**, Musées et Bibliothèques du Mali*, BP 241, Bamako
Inspectorate of Archives, Museums and Libraries of Mali

Malta

General Information

Language: Maltese (English second language)
Religion: Roman Catholic
Population: 340,000
Literacy Rate (1948): 56%
Bank Hours: 0830-1230 Monday-Friday; 0830-1200 Saturday
Shop Hours: 0900-1300, 1500-1800 Monday-Friday; most shops open Saturday at least half day
Currency: 100 cents (1,000 mils) = 1 Maltese pound
Export/Import Information: No tariff on books or advertising. No import licence required. Exchange control by Central Bank
Copyright: Berne, UCC (see International section)

Publishers

A C **Aquilina** & Co*, 58D Republic St, Valletta
Subjects: Literature, History
Bookshop: At above address

Lux Press, St Joseph St, Hamrun
Subject: Literature

Progress Press*, PO Box 328, Valetta (Located at: Strickland Ho, 341 St Paul St, Valletta) Tel: 24031 Cable Add: Progress Telex: MW341
Man Dir: W B Asciak
Subjects: Literature, Malta
1978: 4 titles *Founded:* 1957

A **Vassallo** and Sons Ltd*, 49 Main Gate St, Victoria, Gozo Tel: 76609
Subjects: School Textbooks, Maps, Guides
Bookshop: The Ideal Bookshop

Major Booksellers

A C **Aquilina** & Co*, 58D Republic St, Valletta Tel: 624774

Hamrun Library*, The, 673 St Joseph Rd, Hamrun Tel: 28542

The **Ideal** Bookshop*, 49 Main Gate St, Victoria, Gozo Tel: 76609
Owned by: A Vassallo and Sons Ltd

Merlin Library Ltd, Mountbatten St, Blata I-Bajda Tel: 625838 Telex: MW 558
Also Wholesalers and Remainder Dealers
Director: A J Gruppetta

Giov **Muscat** & Co Ltd, 213 St Ursola St, Valletta Tel: 27668/625729/605923 Telex: 727 MW; 48 Merchants St, PO Box 348, Valletta
Man Dir: A de Domenico

Sapienza's Library*, 26 Republic St, Valletta Tel: 625621

Major Libraries

Gozo Public Library, Vajringa St, Victoria, Gozo Tel: 556200

National Library of Malta*, 36 Old Treasury St, Valletta Tel: Central 26585
Librarian: Dr Vincent A Depasquale
Publication: Annual Report

University of Malta Library, Msida Tel: 36451
Librarian: Paul Xuereb
Publications include: Malta, Official Statistical Publications 1975; Il-Poezija bil-Malti 1964-74; Liberty to Print: Catalogue of

an exhibition of Street Literature 1976; A Bibliography of Maltese Bibliographies 1978

Library Associations

Ghaqda Bibljotekarji/Library Association (Valletta), c/o Din l-Art Helwa, 133 Britannia St, Valletta
Secretary: Margaret R Psaila
Publications: GhB/LA Newsletter; GhB/LA Yearbook; Bibliography of Children's Literature in Malta; Handlist of Writings on Art in Malta

Library Reference Books and Journals

Books

A Bibliography of Maltese Bibliographies, University of Malta Library, Msida

GhB/LA Yearbook, Ghaqda Bibljotekarji/Library Association (Valletta), c/o Din l-Art Helwa, 133 Britannia St, Valletta

Journals

GhB/LA Newsletter, Ghaqda Bibljotekarji/Library Association (Valletta), c/o Din l-Art Helwa, 133 Britannia St, Valletta

Isle of Man

General Information

Language: English. Manx is spoken as a second language by about 500 people
Religion: Predominantly Protestant
Population: 63,000
Bank Hours: 0930-1530 Monday to Friday
Shop hours: 0900-1730
Currency: 100 pence = 1 Isle of Man pound = £1 sterling. British coins and banknotes are legal tender
Export/Import Information: In customs union with UK. No tariff or VAT on books
Copyright: Berne, UCC (see International section)

Publisher

Shearwater Press Limited*, Welch Ho, Church Rd, Onchan, Isle of Man Tel: Douglas 3598 (STD code 0624)
Man Dir: Ian Faulds; *Editorial:* Clare Faulds; *Sales:* Susan Quayle
Imprint: Manxman Publications
Subjects: History, Local History, Topography, Fine Art, Fiction, Isle of Man
Bookshop: Glebe Books, Welch Ho, Church Rd, Onchan
1978: 5 titles *Founded:* 1973
ISBN Publisher's Prefix: 0-904980

Literary Association

Romantic Novelists' Association, Hillfoot, Brookfield Crescent, Ramsey
Treasurer: Beatrice Taylor

Literary Prizes

Netta **Muskett** Award
Established 1960. For an unpublished romantic novel by an author who has not previously had a romantic novel published. A trophy is awarded annually and the winning novel is guaranteed publication. Enquiries to Beatrice Taylor, Romantic Novelists' Association, Hillfoot, Brookfield Crescent, Ramsey

R N A Major Award
Established 1960. For the best romantic novel (modern or historical) published during the year. Trophy awarded annually, open to non-members. The 1979 award was to Mary Howard for *Mr Rodriguez*. Enquiries to Beatrice Taylor, Romantic Novelists' Association, Hillfoot, Brookfield Crescent, Ramsey

Martinique

General Information

Language: French
Population: 325,000
Literacy Rate (1967): 87.8%
Currency: French Guiana, Guadeloupe and Martinique franc
Export/Import Information: Tariff same as France. 7% overseas tax and reduced VAT on books, 3.5%. Small quantity of advertising free. No import licences required. Exchange restrictions as in France
Copyright: Berne, UCC (see International section)

Major Booksellers

A **Jean-Charles***, 32 & 47 rue Schoelcher, Fort de France Tel: 4155
Branches: 4

Major Libraries

Direction des Services d'**Archives** de la Martinique, Tartenson, Route de la Clairière, BP 649, 97262 Fort de France
Director: Miss Chauleau
Publication: Guide des Archives de la Martinique

Bibliothèque Victor **Schoelcher**, Rue de la Liberté, 97200-Fort de France, Martinique
Librarian: Jacqueline Leger

Mauritania

General Information

Language: Arabic and French
Religion: Muslim
Population: 1.5 million
Literacy Rate (1977): 17.4% of population aged 6 or over (36.9% of urban population, 11.5% rural)
Bank Hours: 0800-1115, 1430-1630 Monday-Saturday

Shop Hours: Vary. Generally 0800-1200, 1430-1800 Monday-Saturday. Some closed Monday morning, some open Sunday morning
Currency: 1 ouguiya = 5 khoums
Export/Import Information: Member of the West African Economic Community. No tariff on books. Advertising matter (other than single copies) 10% fiscal, 5% customs duty and added tax of 12%. Import licences and exchange controls apply to imports outside of EEC and franc zone
Copyright: Berne (see International section)

Publishers

Government Printer (Imprimerie Nationale)*, BP 618, Nouakchott

Imprimerie Commerciale et Administrative de Mauritanie*, BP 164, Nouakchott
Subjects: Education, Textbooks

Major Booksellers

Librairie-Papeterie **Mauritanie** Nouvelle*, BP 61, Nouakchott

Major Libraries

Arab Library*, Chinguetti

Bibliothèque nationale*, BP 20, Nouakchott Tel: 24-35 or 278

Bibliothèque publique centrale*, BP 77, Nouakchott

Mauritius

General Information

Language: English and French
Population: 924,000
Bank Hours: Banks close 1130 on Saturday
Currency: 100 cents = 1 Mauritius rupee
Export/Import Information: No tariff on books and advertising but 25% special levy. No import licence required
Copyright: UCC (see International section)

Book Trade Journals

Mauritius Archives, Memorandum of Books Printed in Mauritius, Mauritius Archives, Sir William Newton St, Port Louis

Publishers

Editions **Croix** de Sud*, 1 Barracks St, Port Louis
Subjects: General, Educational

Government Printer (Imprimerie National)*, Government Printing Office, Elizabeth II Ave, Port Louis

Editions **Nassau***, rue Barclay, Rose Hill
Man Dir: R A Y Vilmont
Subjects: General Fiction, Paperbacks

Major Booksellers

Librairie **Allot**, Botanical Gardens St, Curepipe Tel: 61253 Cable Add: Allot Mtius
Manager: M F Jean Allot

Librairie **Bonanza***, Corner of Virgile Naz and Monsignor Gonin Sts, Port Louis Tel: 5179

Librairie **Bourbon***, 28 Bourbon St, Port Louis Tel: 21467
Manager: Mrs M Allagapen

Librairie Le **Colibri***, St Jean Rd, Quatre Bornes Tel: 2445; Arcades Atchia, Royal Rd, Rose Hill Tel: 1126

Librairie Le **Cygne***, Royal Rd, Rose Hill Tel: 2444

Librairie **Nationale***, 25 Bourbon St, Port Louis Tel: 0748

Librairie des **Mascareignes**, 5 Queen St, Rose Hill Tel: 42748 Cable Add: Manjoo Rose Hill

Nalanda Co Ltd*, 30 Bourbon St, Port Louis Tel: 0160

Librairie du **Trèfle***, Royal St, Port Louis Tel: 1106; Les Arcades, Curepipe Tel: 25

Major Libraries

British Council Library*, PO Box 111, Royal Rd, Rose Hill Tel: 42034/5

Carnegie Library, Queen Elizabeth II Terrace, Curepipe Tel: 86-4041/44
Librarian: Madeleine Philippe

City Library, City Hall, Municipality of Port Louis, PO Box 422, Port Louis Tel: (2) 0831 Cable Add: Cerne/Port Louis
Librarian: Gaetan Benoit
Publication: Annual Report, Newspapers Index: Mauritius

Mauritius Archives, Sunray Hotel, Coromandel
Dir: Dr P H Sooprayen
Publication: Annual Report of the Archives Department (including a bibliographical supplement), *Quarterly Memorandum of Books Printed in Mauritius and Registered in the Archives*

Mauritius Institute Public Library, PO Box 54, Port Louis Tel: 20639
Librarian: S Jean-Francois

University of Mauritius Library*, Reduit Tel: 41041
Librarian: Jean de Chantal
Publication: Vice-Chancellor's Annual Report

Library Associations

Mauritius Library Association*, c/o The British Council, Rose Hill
Secretary: Ms M C Benoit
Publication: Mauritius Library Association Bulletin

Literary Associations and Societies

Académie mauricienne de Langue et de Littérature*, Curepipe
Secretary: C de Rauville
Publication: Oeuvres et Chroniques de l'Océan indien

Mexico

General Information

Language: Spanish
Religion: Roman Catholic
Population: 66.9 million
Literacy Rate (1970): 74.2%
Bank Hours: 0900-1330 Monday-Friday
Shop Hours: 1000-1900 Monday, Tuesday, Thursday, Friday; 1100-2000 Wednesday and Saturday
Currency: 100 centavos = 1 peso
Export/Import Information: Member of the Latin American Free Trade Association. Foreign language books and textbooks generally dutied at 38 pesos per kg legal weight, children's picture books 65% ad valorem or 14 pesos per kg, whichever greater and require import licence. Three copies of non-Spanish advertising catalogues free but all others require licence and dutied 35% ad valorem. Customs request from Bank of Mexico all necessary information to decide cases of tariff
Copyright: UCC, Berne, Buenos Aires (see International section)

Book Trade Organizations

Cámara Nacional de Comercio, Sección de Librerías*, Paseo de la Reforma 42, México 1, DF
National Trade Association, Booksellers' Section

Cámara Nacional de la Industria Editorial*, Calle Vallarta 21, 3° piso, México 4, DF Tel: 5669333
Mexican Publishers' Association
Secretary General: R Servin Arroyo

Centro Mexicano de Escritores AC*, San Francisco No 12, Col del Valle, México 12, DF
Mexican Authors' Centre
Secretary of Executive Committee: Felipe García Beraza
Publication: Recent Books in Mexico

Instituto Mexicano del Libro, AC, Paseo de la Reforma 95, Depto 1024, México 4, DF
Mexican Book Institute
Secretary-General: Isabel Ruiz González

Standard Book Numbering Agency, Direccion General de Autor Centro Nacional de Informacion, Mariano Escobedo 438 5°, Col Anzures, Mexico 5, DF

Book Trade Reference Journals

Anuario Bibliográfico (Bibliographical Yearbook), National Library, República de El Salvador 70, México 1, DF

Bibliografía Mexicana (Mexican Bibliography), National Library, República de El Salvador 70, México 1, DF

Boletín Bibliográfico Mexicano (Mexican Bibliographical Bulletin), Editorial Porrúa SA, Argentina 15, 5° piso, México 1, DF

Recent Books in Mexico, Mexican Authors' Centre, San Francisco 12, Col Del Valle, México 12, DF

Publishers

Aconcagua Edic y Pub SA, Blvd Adolfo López Mateos 235, Periferico, Col Mixcoac, México 19, DF Tel: 5635480
Man Dir: Julio Sanz Crespo; *Sales Dir:* Hector Delgado Narvaez
Subjects: Literature, History, How-to, Religion, Technology, Juveniles, Low-priced Paperbacks, University Textbooks, Educational Materials

M **Aguilar** Editor SA, Ave Universidad 757, México Tel: 5755511 Cable Add: Guilarditor
Man Dir: Antonio Ruano Fernández
Parent Company: Aguilar SA de Ediciones, Spain (qv)
Subject: General Literature
Founded: 1965

Alianza Editorial Mexicana*, José Morán 93-1A, México 18, DF
Associate Companies: See under Alianza Editorial SA, Spain

Ariel-Seix Barral SA, Morelos 98, 304 Mezanine, Mexico 1, DF
Parent Company: Ariel-Seix Barral Editoriales, Spain (qv)

Editorial **Azteca** SA*, Calle La Luna 225-227, México 3, DF Tel: 5261157 Cable Add: Edasa
Man Dir: Alfonso Alemón Jalomo; *Sales Dir:* Juan Alemón Jalomo
Subjects: General Literature, Technical, Popular Science
1978: 15 titles *Founded:* 1956

Editorial **Banca y Comercio** SA, Reforma 202, México 6, DF Tel: 5353587
Man Dir: Luis Ruiz de Velasco; *Assistant Manager:* Antonio Zellek Guaida
Subjects: Business & Administration, Mathematics, Law
1978: 80 titles *Founded:* 1934

Libreria y Ediciones **Botas** SA*, Justo Sierra 52, Apdo 941, México 1, DF Tel: 5223896/5224717
Man Dir: Andres Botas Arredondo; *Sales Dir:* Everado Jiménez Martínez
Subjects: Art, History, Economics, General Fiction, Philosophy, Law, General Science, Medicine, Reference
Founded: 1910

Editorial **Bruguera** Mexicana SA*, Ave Popacatapetl, 421 Colonia General Amaya, México B
Parent Company: Editorial Bruguera SA, Spain (qv)

Buena Prensa AC*, Orozco y Berra 180, Apdo 2181, México 1, DF Tel: 5357304
Man Dir: Wilfredo Guinea
Subjects: Religion, Education
Founded: 1936

Editorial **Cajica***, 19 Sur 2501, Apdo 336, Puebla, Pue
Manager: José M Cajica
Subject: Law

Centro de Estudios Monetarios Latinoamericanos (CEMLA), Durango 54, México 7, DF Tel: 5330300 Cable Add: Cemla, Mexico Telex: 1771229
Man Dir: Jorge González del Valle; *Editorial, Rights & Permissions:* Juan Manuel Rodriguez; *Sales:* Genoveva de Mária y Campos de Gil; *Production, Publicity:* Cristina Conde
Subjects: Economics, Finance
Founded: 1952

El **Colegio** de México, Depto de Publicaciones, Apdo 20-671, México 20, DF (Located at: Camino al Ajusco 20, México 20, DF) Tel: 5840585/5848663 Cable Add:

Colmex
Man Dir: Alberto Dallal
Subjects: Literature, Social Science, History, International Relations, Demography, Economy
Bookshop: Librería de El Colegio de México, Camino al Ajusco 20, México 20, DF
1978: 150 titles *Founded:* 1940

Compañía General de Ediciones SA*, Schiller 227D, México 5, DF Tel: 5437016
Man Dir: Santiago Sanz
Subjects: Textbooks, Fiction

Editorial **Concepto** SA, Av Cuauhtémoc 1434, México 13, DF Tel: 5594631
Man Dir, Rights & Permissions: Gerardo Gally; *Editorial:* Francisco Javier Fonseca; *Production:* Margara Clavé
Subjects: Architecture, Psychology, Pedagogy, Children's books, Alternative Technology, How-to
1979: 78 titles *Founded:* 1977
ISBN Publisher's Prefix: 968-405

Ediciones **Contables y Administrativas**, SA, H Frías 1451-101, México 12, DF Tel: 5590443
Man Dir: Pedro Gasca Rocha; *Sales Dir:* Gustavo Gasca Bretón
Branch Off: Zaragoza 39-106, Guadalajara, Jalisco, Mexico
Subjects: Technical, Accounting & Management
1978: 11 titles *Founded:* 1967

Cía Editorial **Continental** SA (CESCA)*, Calzada de Tlalpan 4620, Apdo 22022, México 22, DF Tel: 5732300 Cable Add: Ediconti
Man Dir: Elena Ocampo de Lanz; *Sales Manager:* Eduardo A Tappan
Subjects: Science & Technology, Textbooks
Founded: 1954

Publicaciones **Cosmos**, España 396, México 13, DF Tel: 5829928
Man Dir: Catalina Ramirez de Arellano; *Editorial:* Cesar Macazaga; *Sales, Publicity:* Raul Macazaga; *Production:* Carlos Macazaga
Subjects: Technical dictionaries (Spanish-English)
1978: 6 titles *1979:* 5 titles *Founded:* 1963
ISBN Publisher's Prefixes: 968-7095, 968-440

B **Costa Amic***, Editor, Mesones 14, Apdo 29-188, Mexico 1, DF Tel: 5124810
Man Dir: Bartolome Costa Amic; *Editorial, Production:* Bartomeu Costa L; *Sales, Publicity:* Jordi Costa L; *Rights & Permissions:* Bartolome Costa Amic, Bartomeu Costa L
Subjects: Fiction, Literature, Biography, History, Psychology, Social Science, Low-priced Paperbacks, University & Secondary Textbooks
Bookshop: Bolivar 55, México 1, DF
Founded: 1941

Editorial **Diana**, SA Roberto Gayol 1219, Apdo 44-986, México 12, DF Tel: 5750711 Cable Add: EDISA Telex: 1777618 DIME
Man Dir: José Luis Ramírez Junior; *Assistant General Manager:* Homero Gayosso Animas; *Sales:* Iván García; *Production:* Manuel Landaverde
Subjects: Fiction, Juveniles, General Nonfiction
Bookshop: address as above
Founded: 1946

Editorial **Diogenes**, SA*, Apdo 82-016, Contadero Cuajimalpa, México 18, DF (Located at: Arteaga y Salazar 21, Lonbolero Lusjimalpa, México 18, DF) Tel: 9158120046
Subjects: Belles Lettres, History, Social & Political Science, Medicine

E D A M E X, see Editores Asociados Mexicanos SA

Editora Nacional*, Dr Erazo 42, México 7, DF Tel: 5782353
Subject: General Literature

Editores Asociados Mexicanos SA (EDAMEX), Angel Urraza 1322, México 12, DF Tel: 5757035/5591499/5591566
Man Dir: Manuel Colmenares G; *Editorial, Rights & Permissions:* Mrs Ella de Gedovius; *Sales:* Hector Gonzalez; *Production, Publicity:* Mauro Alvarado
Associate Company: Editorial Meridiano SA
Subjects: Social Sciences, Economics, Politics, Literature, Communications, Recreation, Humour
Founded: 1973
ISBN Publisher's Prefix: 968-409

Empresas Editoriales SA*, Río Nazas 55, Dto 1 & 2, Apdo 5-188, México 5, DF Tel: 5144303
President: Martín Luis Guzmán; *Technical Dir:* Rafael Giménez Siles
Subject: General Fiction
Founded: 1944

Editorial **Epoca** SA, Emperadores 185, Apdo 69-647, México 13, DF Tel: 5328163 Cable Add: Epocasa
Director-General: Rubén Rendón Vargas
Subject: General Literature

Ediciones **Era** SA, Avena 102, Col Granjas Esmeralda, Apdo 74-092, México 13, DF Tel: 5817744 Cable Add: Liberamex
Man Dir: Mrs Nieves Espresate Xirau
Subjects: General Fiction, Art, Belles Lettres, Social & Political Science, Economics, Quarterly Political Reviews
1978: 28 titles *Founded:* 1960

Editorial **Esfinge** SA*, Colima 220-503, México 7, DF Tel: 5112771/5142823
Man Dir: Agustín Mateos Muñoz; *Sales Dir:* Eduardo Mateos Gay
Subjects: Literature, Law, Science, University, Secondary & Primary Textbooks
1978: 60 titles *Founded:* 1957

Ediciones **Euroamericanas**, Perugino 35-1, México 19, DF Tel: 5632063
Man Dir: Klaus Thiele; *Sales:* Ma del Rocío Sánchez Vega
Subjects: History and Anthropology of the Americas, Practical Technology, Languages
1978: 2 titles *1979:* 7 titles *Founded:* 1971
ISBN Publisher's Prefix: 968-414

Editorial **Extemporaneos** SA*, Poniente 126-A, No 400 Col Residencial Vallejo, Apdo 78-048, México 14, DF Tel: 5875424/5878785 Cable Add: Ediextempo México
Director General, Editorial: Lautaro Gondalez Porcel; *Sales, Publicity:* Humberto Reyes Ordoñez; *Production:* Eduardo Peña Alfaro; *Rights & Permissions:* Eva Somlo
Associate Company: Librerias Extemporaneos SA
Subjects: Anthropology, Architecture, Art, Economics, Philosophy, Humour, Literature, Pedagogy, Politics, Sociology, Theatre
Book Club: Club de Lectores Extemporaneos
Bookshops: Condesa, Tamaulipas 203-A, México 11, DF; Del Valle, Ave Coyoacán 512-A, México 12, DF; Santa Maria, Amado Nervo 47-B, México 4, DF; Jaurez, Hamburgo 260, México 6, DF
Founded: 1970
ISBN Publisher's Prefix: 968-415

Fernández Editores SA, Eje 1 Pte México Coyoacán 321, Col General Anaya, México 13, DF Tel: 5244600
Man Dir: Luis Fernández González; *Assistant Man Dir, Sales Manager:* Luis Gerardo Fernández; *Production Manager:* Luis Ramón Fernandez
Subjects: Textbooks, Education, Technical Subjects, Children's Books
Founded: 1943

Fondo de Cultura Económica, Ave Universidad 975, Apdo 44975 México 12, DF Tel: 5244376 Cable Add: Doraca
Man Dir: José Luis Martínez; *Assistant Dir, Editorial:* Jaime García Terrés; *Senior Editor:* Alí Chumacero; *Business Manager:* Jorge Farías Negrete; *Production:* Felipe Garrido; *Sales:* Hero Rodríguez Toro; *Publicity:* Alba Rojo; *Rights & Permissions:* Alicia Hammer
Branch Offs: Argentina: Suipacha 617, Buenos Aires; Chile: Tarapacá 1224, Santiago de Chile; Colombia: Av Jiménes 8-39, Bogotá; Peru: Berlín 238, Miraflores, Lima; Spain: Vía de los Poblados s/n, Edif Indulbuilding Goico 4-15, Hortaleza, Madrid 33; Venezuela: Edif Polar, planta baja, Plaza Venezuela, Caracas
Subjects: Social Sciences, Humanities, Literature, University Textbooks, Periodicals
Bookshop: Ave Universidad 975
Founded: 1934

Fondo Educativo Interamericano, Apdo 19188, México 19, DF
Parent Company: Addison-Wesley Publishing Co Inc, Reading Mass 01867, USA (see Addison-Wesley UK for associate companies)
Subjects: School and University Textbooks in Spanish

Librería **Font**, SA*, López Cotilla 440, Guadalajara, Jalisco Tel: 140820 Telex: 0682715
Man Dir: Leopoldo Font Hernández; *Sales Dir:* Leopoldo Font Solana
Subjects: Literature, History, Art, Philosophy, University & Secondary Textbooks
Bookshop: López Cotilla 440, Guadalajara, Jalisco
Founded: 1908

Editorial Gustavo **Gili** de Mexico Sa*, Tácatas 218, México 12, DF
Parent Company: Editorial Gustavo Gili SA, Spain (qv)

Editorial **Grijalbo** SA, Apdo 17-568, México 17, DF (Located at: Ave Granjas 82, México 16, DF) Tel: 3520688 Cable Add: Grijalmex
Editorial: Andrés Léon Quintanar; *Sales:* Juan Orraca; *Production:* Rogelio Carvajal; *Publicity:* Rocio Escalona
Parent Company: Ediciones Grijalbo SA, Spain (qv)
Associate Companies: Grijalbo SA, Argentina (qv); Grijalbo Bolivia Ltda, Bolivia (qv); Editorial Grijalbo Ltda, Brazil (qv); Distribuidora exclusivo Grijalbo, Colombia; Grijalbo y Cía Ltda, Chile (qv); Distribuidora exclusiva Grijalbo SA, Perú (qv); Grijalbo SA, Venezuela (qv); Grijalbo Centroamerica y Panamá SA, Costa Rica (qv); Editorial Grijalbo Ecuatoriana Ltda, Ecuador
Subjects: General Fiction & Nonfiction
Founded: 1954

Harla, SA de CV, see Harper & Row Latinoamericana

Harper & Row Latinoamericana-Harla, SA de CV, Antonio Caso 142, Apdo 30-546, México 4, DF Tel: 5924277 Cable Add: Harpemex Telex: 1777235
Dir General: Jaime Arvizu; *Sales:* Juan Granados

Parent Company: Harper & Row Publishers Inc, 10 East 53rd St, New York, NY 10022, USA
Associate Companies: Harper & Row (Australasia) Ltd, Australia; Harper & Row Ltd (UK) (qqv)
Subsidiary Companies: Editora Harper & Row do Brasil Ltda, Brasil (qv)
Subjects: University & Secondary Textbooks, Science & Technology, Medicine, Psychology, Engineering
1980: 80 titles *Founded:* 1970
ISBN Publisher's Prefix: 968-006

Editorial **Hermes** SA, Castilla 229-A, México 13, DF Tel: 5790468 Cable Add: Editermes
Man Dir: Antonio López Rivero
Subjects: General Fiction, Belles Lettres, History, Art
Founded: 1945

Editorial **Herrero** SA*, Río Amazonas 44, Apdo 2404, México 5, DF Tel: 5664900
General Dir: Donato Elías Herrero; *Manager:* Ricardo Arancón L
Subjects: Art, Technical, Textbooks
Founded: 1945

Herrero Hermanos Sucesores SA*, Comonfort 44, Apdo 671, México 2, DF Tel: 5299235
Man Dir: Jorge Rodríguez Fernandez
Subjects: Belles Lettres, Psychology, Economics, Social Science, Business
Founded: 1883

Impulso*, Tehuantepec 170, Apdo 27-718, México 7, DF Tel: 5644100 Cable Add: IEELM, México Telex: 01776359
Director General, Editorial: Rafael Giménez Navarro; *Sales:* Gerardo Sánchez; *Production:* Marta Carpio
Parent Company: Libreros Mexicanos SA de CV, Mexico
Subjects: Children's Books, Literature, Technical and Scientific
Founded: 1976
ISBN Publisher's Prefix: 968-17

Editorial **Innovacion** SA, Calz México Tulyehualco 2612 Km 21.2, Col Nopalena, México 23, DF Tel: 6703485
Man Dir: Catalina Ramirez de Arellano; *Editorial:* Cesar Macazaga; *Sales, Publicity:* Raul Macazaga; *Production:* Carlos Macazaga
Subjects: Camping, Touring, Pre-Hispanic and Mexican History, Novels
1978: 18 titles *1979:* 23 titles *Founded:* 1971

Instituto de Investigaciones Sociales — Universidad Nacional Autonoma de Mexico*, Torre de Humanidades 5° piso, Ciudad Universitaria, México 20, DF Tel: 5486500 ext 196
Man Dir: Raúl Benítez Zenteno; *Sales Dir:* Armida Vazquez A
Subjects: Social Science
Founded: 1939

Instituto Indigenista Interamericano, Av Insurgentes Sur No 1690, Col Florida, Mexico 20, DF Tel: 5786101/5786210 Cable Add: Indigeni
Man Dir, Rights & Permissions: Oscar Arze Quintanilla; *Sales:* Raquel Mendez de Hoyle
Subjects: Social Studies, Anthropology, Periodicals
Founded: 1940

Instituto Nacional de Antropologia e Historia*, Córdoba 45, Mexico 7, DF Tel: 5144222
Subjects: Mexican Archaeology & Anthropology, History
Founded: 1822

Instituto Nacional de Bellas Artes*, Oficina de ventas de publicaciones, Palacio de Bellas Artes, México 1, DF Tel: 5123811
Subjects: Art, Biography, Literature, Philosophy, Reference, Educational Materials

Instituto Panamericano de Geografía e Historia, Ex-Arzobispado 29, México 18, DF Tel: 2775888
Secretary General: José A Sáenz G; *Editorial Dir:* Lea Salinas
Subjects: Geography, Cartography, History, Anthropology, Geophysics, Folklore, Periodicals
1978: 9 titles

Editorial **Iztaccihuatl** SA*, Miguel Schultz No 21, Apdo 2343, México 4, DF Tel: 5352321 Cable Add: Eiztamexa
President: Orlando Vieyra Legorreta
Subject: General Literature
Founded: 1946

Editorial **Jus** SA*, Plaza de Abasolo 14, Col Guerrero, México 3, DF Tel: 5629959/5260616/ 5260540/5260538
Man Dir: Armando Avila Sotomayor; *Sales Manager:* Dalila Farias Godinez
Subjects: General Fiction, Law, Textbooks, History, Political & Social Sciences
Founded: 1941

Lasser Press Mexicana, SA*, Praga 56, Apdo 6-791, México 6, DF Tel: 5142215 Cable Add: Laspresa
Subjects: General Fiction & Nonfiction
Founded: 1972

Editora **Latino Americana** SA*, Guatemala 10-220, México 1, DF Tel: 5211909
Dir: Roger Orellana Gallardo
Subject: Popular Literature

Editorial **Limusa** SA, Balderas 95, 1er Piso, México 1, DF Tel: 5853500 Cable Add: Elimusa Telex: 5125610
Man Dir: Carlos Noriega Milera; *Executive Vice-President:* Francisco Trillas Mercader; *Assistant Executive Manager:* Juan Antonio Hernández Zamudio
Associate Company: John Wiley & Sons Ltd, UK (qv for other associates)
Subjects: Science & Technology, Social Science, History, Psychology, University & Secondary Textbooks
Founded: 1962

Logos Consorcio Editorial, SA*, General Molinos del Campo 64, Col San Miguel Chapultepec, México 18, DF Tel: 5151633
Man Dir: Fernando Rodriguez Diaz
Subject: General

Libros **McGraw-Hill** de Mexico SA de CV, Atlacomulco 499-501, San Andrés Atoto, Naucalpan, Edo de México, Apdo 5-237, México 5, DF Tel: 5769044 Cable Add: Limcoramex Telex: 01774284
Director General: Raymundo Cruzado; *Publishers:* Guillermo Hernández, Moisés Pérez Zavala, Enrique Pereda; *Production:* Oscar Alvarez; *Rights & Permissions:* Ernesto Bañuelos
Parent Company: McGraw-Hill Inc, 1221 Ave of the Americas, New York, NY 10020, USA
Associate Companies: See McGraw-Hill Book Co (UK) Ltd
Branch Offs: Monterrey, N L; Guadalajara, Jal
Subjects: Natural Sciences, Technology, Textbooks, Education, Business, General
1978: 34 titles *1979:* 49 titles *Founded:* 1967

El **Manual** Moderno, SA*, Ave Sonora 206, México 11, DF Tel: 5740333/5746646
Man Dir: Gustavo Setzer; *Editorial:* Armando Soto; *Sales:* Juan Sánchez Villarreal; *Production:* Felipe Vaquez; *Rights & Permissions:* Lourdes Reyes
Parent Company: Elsevier-NDU nv, Netherlands (qv)
Subjects: Medicine, Psychology, Nursing, Veterinary Science, Chemistry, Economics
Founded: 1958
ISBN Publisher's Prefix: 968-426

Masson Editores, Dakota 383, Colonia Napoles, México 18, DF Tel: 6870933 Telex: 77604
President: Pierre Lahaye; *Man Dir:* Andre Cohen
Parent Company: Masson Editeur, France (qv)
Associate Companies: Masson do Brasil, Rua da Quitanda 20, Sala 301, 20011 Rio de Janeiro, Brazil; Toray-Masson, Spain (qv); Masson Publishing USA Inc, 111 West 57th St, New York, NY, USA
Founded: 1978

Editorial **Mexicana***, S de RL, Orizaba 115 y 119, Apdo 7-852, México
Parent Company: Editorial Labor, Spain (qv)

Editores **Mexicanos Unidos** (Edimex), L González Obregón 5-B, Apdo 45-671, México 1, DF Tel: 5217596/5125552/ 5210925
Man Dir & Editorial: Fidel Miro Solanes; *Sales:* Roque Laclau; *Production, Publicity and Rights & Permissions:* Sonia Miro de Laclau
Subjects: General Fiction & Nonfiction
Bookshops: Libro-Mex Editores SRL, Argentina 23, Mexico 1, DF
Founded: 1954
ISBN Publisher's Prefix: 968-15

Galeria de Arte **Misrachi** SA, Génova 20, Mexico 6, DF Tel: 5334551
Manager: Alberto J Misrachi; *Editorial, Sales, Production, Rights & Permissions:* Enrique Beraha; *Publicity:* Amelie Beraha de Esquenazi
Subject: Art
Bookshops: Génova 20, Mexico 6, DF; Central de Publicaciones SA, Juárez 4, Mexico 1, DF
Founded: 1961
ISBN Publisher's Prefix: 968-7047

Editorial Joaquín **Mortiz** SA, Tabasco 106, Apdo 7-832 México 7, DF Tel: 5331250 Cable Add: Morditor
Man Dir, Editorial: Joaquín Diez-Canedo; *Sales, Rights & Permissions:* Magdalena Blanco; *Production, Publicity:* Bernardo Giner de Los Ríos
Subjects: General Fiction & Nonfiction, History, Psychology, Social Science
1978: 72 titles *Founded:* 1962
ISBN Publisher's Prefix: 968-27

Organización Editorial **Novaro** SA, Apdo 10500, México 1, DF Tel: 5760155 Cable Add: Novaromex Telex: 01774419 Novame
Director General: John S Wiseman; *Commercial Director:* Miguel Sánchez Navarro
Subjects: Juveniles, Popular Paperbacks
Founded: 1950

Nueva Editorial Interamericana SA de CV, Cedro 512, Apdo 26370, México 4, DF Tel: 5413155 Cable Add: Tusmexa
President: Luis Castañeda M; *Commercial Director:* Rafael Sáinz
Associate Company: CBS Publishing Group (see Holt-Saunders UK for other associates)
Subjects: Medicine and Health Sciences, General Science and Technology, Textbooks
1980: 450 titles *Founded:* 1944

Editorial **Nueva Imagen** SA, PO Box 600, México 1, DF (Located at: Sacramento 109, México 12, DF) Tel: 5361015/5361055/ 5237373 Telex: 1771427 Eni Me

Administrative Dir: Enrique Sealtiel Alatriste L; *Editorial Dir:* Guillermo J Schavelzon; *Sales Manager:* Roberto Espinoza Rocco
Subjects: General Fiction, History, Psychology, Economics, Art, Science, Social Science, Anthropology, Sociology, Humour, Linguistics, Mass Communication, Latin American problems
1979: 120 titles *1980:* 120 titles *Founded:* 1976
ISBN Publisher's Prefix: 968-429

Ediciones **Oasis** SA*, Oaxaca 28, Apdo 24-416, México 7, DF Tel: 5259171/2
Man Dir: Ruben Rizo Lopez *Sales Dir:* Ricardo Rizzo Lavarino
Subjects: General Fiction, Belles Lettres, History, Education
Founded: 1954

Editorial **Orion**, Sierra Mojada 325, Lomas de Chapultepec, México 10, DF Tel: 5200224
Man Dir: Silvia Hernandez Vda de Cárdenas; *Sales Dir, Rights & Permissions:* Laura Hernandez Baltazar; *Publicity Dir:* Silvia Hernandez Baltazar; *Advertising:* Mariaelena Molina
Subsidiary Companies: Edit Vila; Edit Cuzamil
Subjects: Literature, Philosophy, Religion, Mysticism, Yoga, Astrology, Theosophy, Psychology, & Parapsychology
1978: 20 titles *1979:* 10 titles *Founded:* 1942
ISBN Publisher's Prefix: 968-6053

Editorial **Patria**, SA, Uruguay 25, 2° piso, Apdo 784, México 1, DF Tel: 5127651/5184509
Man Dir: Isabel Lasa de la Mora; *Deputy Manager & Administrator:* Rafael Guerrero; *Sales Dir:* Eduardo Robles Boza; *Publicity Dir:* Santiago Hernandez; *Rights & Permissions:* Isabel Lasa
Subjects: Literature, Biography, History, Philosophy, How-to, Secondary & Primary Textbooks, Pre-School Teaching Aids
1978: 10 titles *1979:* 20 titles *Founded:* 1933
ISBN Publisher's Prefix: 968-6054, 968-39

Libreria **Patria** SA*, 5 de Mayo No 43, Apdo 2055, México 1, DF Tel: 5852099
Man Dir: Florian Trillas Rafols; *Sales:* Francisco Majewski M.
Orders to: Belisario Dominguez 53, México 1, DF
Subsidiary Company: Samara, Cia Papelera SA, Av. 5 de Mayo 29-C, México 1, DF
Subjects: Textbooks, Literature, General
Bookshop: Av 5 de Mayo 43, Belisario Dominguez 53
Founded: 1940

Ediciones **Paulinas** SA, Ave Taxqueña 1792, México 21, DF Tel: 5491454
General Manager: Ricardo Rojas Sarmiento
Subjects: Religion, Education
Bookshop: Librería San Pablo, Ave Madero 61-A, México 1, DF
1978: 40 titles *Founded:* 1948

Editorial **Pax** México*, Rep Argentina 9, Apdo 45-009, México 1, DF Tel: 5425890
Man Dir: Humberto Gally Grivé
Subjects: Technical, Psychology, Education
Bookshop: Librería Carlos Cesarman SA, Rep Argentina 9, México 1, DF
Founded: 1920

Editorial **Pomaire** SA, Apdo 20-569, Manuel M Ponce 143, México 20, DF Tel: 6512853 Telex: 1771979 Pomame
Man Dir: Iván Mozó Lira
Parent Company: Editorial Pomaire SA, Spain (qv for list of other branches)
Subjects: Fiction, Belles Lettres, Juveniles
Founded: 1962

Editorial **Porrúa** SA, Argentina 15, 5° piso, México 1, DF Tel: 5224866 Cable Add: Porruas Mexico
Man Dir: José Antonio Pérez Porrúa; *Sales Dir:* Francisco Pérez Porrúa
Subject: General Literature
Bookshop: Librería de Porrúa Hnos y Cía, Argentina 15, México 1, DF
Founded: 1944

Librería de Manuel **Porrúa***, 5 de Mayo 49, Apdo 45-590, México 1, DF Tel: 5102634
Manager: Manuel Porrúa
Subject: University Textbooks

La **Prensa** Editora de Periodicos SCL*, Basilio Vadillo 40, Apdo 947, México 4, DF Tel: 5120851
Subjects: Popular Literature, Juveniles

La **Prensa Médica** Mexicana, Paseo de Las Facultades 26, Fraccionamiento Copilco-Universidad, Apdo 20-413, México 20, DF Tel: 5504500 Cable Add: Laprememex
Man Dir: Carolina Amor de Fournier; *Assistant Manager:* Guadalupe Arias de Gutiérrez; *Medical Editor:* Dr Jorge Avendaño Inestrillas; *Sales Dir:* Juan de Dios Díaz Salgado
Subjects: Medicine, Social Science
Founded: 1947

Editorial **Progreso** SA*, Naranjo 248, Apdo 26-372, México 4, DF Tel: 5477304
Subjects: Secondary & Primary Textbooks

Publicaciones Cultural SA, Lago Mayor 186, Colonia Anáhuac, México 17, DF Tel: 5456860/1/2
President: Gustavo González Lewis; *Man Dir:* Carlos Frigolet Lerma; *Assistant Manager:* Pedro de Andres Romero; *Sales:* Javier Saavedra; *Rights & Permissions:* Abelardo Fabrega Esteba
Subjects: University, Secondary and Primary Textbooks, Educational Materials
Founded: 1965
ISBN Publisher's Prefix: 968-6058

Queromón Editores SA*, Bucareli 59-A, Apdo M-7914, México 6, DF Tel: 5356040 Cable Add: Queromón
Man Dir: Manuel Mallén Sangüesa
Subject: Juveniles
Founded: 1951

Editorial **Renacimiento** SA*, Blvd Xola 1408, Apdo 1506, México 12, DF Tel: 5309404/5 Cable Add: Edirensa
Man Dir: Juan Sapiña Camaro
Subjects: General Fiction, Belles Lettres
Founded: 1958

Representaciones y Servicios de Ingeniería SA, Apdo 61-195, México 6, DF (Located at: Roma 37 12-A Col Juqrez, Mexico 6) Tel: 5634740/5635721/0
Man Dir, Editorial: Enrique Reyes Morfin; *Production, Publicity:* Gonzalo Ferreyra Cortes; *Rights & Permissions:* Baltazar Feregrino Paredes
Subjects: Engineering, Management
1978: 6 titles *1979:* 1 title *Founded:* 1965
ISBN Publisher's Prefix: 968-6062

Editorial **Reverté** Mexicana SA*, Río Pánuco 141-A, México 5, DF Tel: 5335658
Man Dir: Pedro Reverté Planells
Associate Companies: See under Editorial Reverté SA, Spain
Subjects: Science, Technical
Founded: 1955

Riomar Editores y Distribuidores S de CV, see Emecé Editores SA, Argentina

Ediciones **Rusbet***, Apdo 12-621, Pitagoras 25-101, Mexico 12, DF Tel: 5233655
Man Dir: Frederick A Clark
Subject: Self-improvement
Founded: 1977
ISBN Publisher's Prefix: 968-7190

Siglo XXI Editores SA, Ave Cerro del Agua 248, Apdo 20626, Mexico 20 DF Tel: 5503011 Cable Add: Sigloedit
Man Dir, Editorial: Arnaldo Orfila R; *Sales:* María Dolores de la Peña; *Production:* Mart Soler V; *Publicity:* Bertha Inés Concha; *Rights & Permissions:* Guadalupe Ortíz
Parent Company: Siglo XXI de España Editores SA, Spain (qv)
Associate Company: Siglo XXI de Colombia Ltda, Colombia (qv)
Subjects: General Fiction, History, Psychology, Economics, Arts, Literature, Health Science & Technology, Education, Criminology & Law, Social Science, Anthropology, Architecture, Planning, Philosophy, Languages, Latin-American Politics, Marxism
1978: 80 titles *1979:* 82 titles *Founded:* 1966
ISBN Publisher's Prefix: 968-23

Editorial V **Siglos**, SA, Calle Oculistas 43, Col Sifón, Mexico 13 DF Tel: 6700698/5811958/6703837
Man Dir: Guillermo Garavito Escobar; *Editorial, Production, Publicity, Rights & Permissions:* Amapola Garavito López; *Sales:* Daniel Márquez C
Subjects: General Fiction & Non-fiction, How-to
Bookshop: At above address
1978: 69 titles *1979:* 83 titles *Founded:* 1973

Editorial **Sopena** Colombiana SA*, Ave Chapultepec 153, Mexico City 6
Parent Company: Ramón Sopena SA, Spain (qv)

Time — Life International de México, SA*, Paseo de la Reforma 195, Apdo 5-592, México 5, DF Tel: 5469000 Cable Add: Tlimsa Telex: (017) 71358
General Manager: Koos H Siewers
Subject: Nonfiction
Founded: 1962

Editorial **Trillas** SA, Ave Río Churubusco 385 Pte, México 13, DF Tel: 5244480 Cable Add: Etrillasa
Man Dir: Francisco Trillas Mercader; *Editorial, Rights & Permissions:* Gonzalo Godínez; *Sales:* Jesús Galera; *Production:* Alfonso Durán; *Publicity:* Jorge Mario Blostein
Associate Companies: Cía Editorial Carmex SA, Argentina; Cía Editorial Comex SA, Colombia; Alamex SA, Spain
Subjects: Psychology, Education, Mathematics, General & Social Science, Technical, University & Secondary Textbooks, Business
1978: 92 titles *1979:* 80 titles *Founded:* 1954

Universidad Nacional Autónoma de México, Distribuidora de Libros de la Unam, Porto Alegre 260, México 13, DF Tel: 6742552
Subjects: University Textbooks, Scholarly
Founded: 1935

Book Clubs

Bertelsmann de Mexico SA, Div Circulo de Lectores, Av la Paz No 26, México 20, DF, Col San Angel
Members: 200,000
Owned by: Bertelsmann AG, Federal Republic of Germany (qv)

Círculo Mexicano de Lectores, see Bertelsmann de Mexico SA

Club de Lectores Extemporaneos*, Poniente 126-A, No 400 Col Residencial Vallejo, Apdo 78-048, México 14
Owned by: Editorial Extemporaneos SA (México)

Major Booksellers

American Book Store SA, Ave Madero No 25, Apdo 79 Bis, México 1, DF Tel: 5127279/5127284/5120306/5852576/5126350
Branches: Circuito Médicos No 3, Ciudad Satélite, Edo de México Tel: 3930682/3930843; Ave Revolución No 1570-A, México 20, DF Tel: 5500162

Librería **Bellas Artes***, Ave Juárez No 18, México 1, DF Tel: 5182917
Manager: Carlos Noriega M

Central de Publicaciones, Ave Juárez 4, Apdo 2430, México 1, DF Tel: 5104331

Cia Internacional de Publicaciones SA de CV, (Libreria Anglo Americana), Serapio Rendon 125, Apdo Postal 30-528, Mexico 4, DF Tel: 5666400 Cable Add: Mexbri Telex: Cxpme 01771743 Mex

Librería **Cosmos***, Ave Padre Mier 474 Oriente, Monterrey Tel: 431074

Librerías de **Cristal***, Calle del Rio 10, México, DF Tel: 5762530 (Centre for reception and distribution). Many branches in Mexico City and other cities

Librería **Font***, López Cotilla 440, Guadalajara, Jalisco Tel: 140820

Librerías **Gonvill** de Guadalajara*, Ave Chapultepec Sur No 146, Guadalajara Tel: 163060

Librería **Hamburgo** Antonio Navarrete, Insurgentes Sur No 58, México 6, DF Tel: 5287316/5145086
Also: Ribera de San Cosme 133, México 4, DF Tel: 5464736; Insurgentes Sur 317, México 11, DF Tel: 5744015; Tiber 87, México 5, DF Tel: 5285415

Librerías **Iztaccihuatl***, Miguel Schultz No 21, México 4, DF Tel: 5352321 (and several provincial addresses)

Librería **Letrán***, Ave San Juan de Letrán 5-C, México, DF Tel: 5123232

Librería **Intercontinental** SA*, Actopan No 3, Esq Monterrey, Col Roma Sur, México 7, DF Tel:5641718

Librería **Internacional** SA*, Ave Sonora 206, México 11, DF Tel: 5330905
Owned by: Elsevier-NDU nv, Netherlands (qv)

Librería **Tecnológico** SA, Ave E Garza Sada 2440, Col Tecnológico, Monterrey, Nuevo León Tel: 583812
Manager: Carlos Amero Diaz

Librería **Universitaria***, Insurgentes Sur No 299, México, DF Tel: 5646637 (and several branches)

Librolandia del Centro SA*, Matamoros 83, Hermosillo, Sonora Tel: 37491/37492 Telex: Liceme 058788
Dir: Gerardo Cantú
60 bookshops located in 33 cities throughout México

Librería Editorial Gerardo **Mayela***, Emiliano Zapata 60-B, México 1, DF Tel: 5225556

Editores **Mexicanos** Unidos, Luis González Obregón 5-B, México, DF Tel: 5217596

Librería **Patria***, Ave 5 de Mayo 43, México 1, DF Tel: 5852099

Librería de **Porrúa** Hnos y Cía, Argentina 15, México 1, DF Apdo M-7990 Tel: 5228800

Librería del **Sotano***, Ave Juárez 64, México, DF Tel: 5217044

Librería **Studio**, Benjamin Franklin 44, México, DF Tel: 5167486

Major Libraries

Archivo General de la Nación*, Tacuba 8-20 Piso, Apdo 1999, México 1, DF Tel: 5851833
Librarian: Alejandra Moreno Toscano

Archivos Históricos y Bibliotecas*, Instituto Nacional de Antropologia e Historia, Calzada M Gandi y Paseo de la Reforma, México 5, DF Apdo Postal M20-29 Tel: 5536342/5536231

Biblioteca Central, Ciudad Universitaria, Villa Obregón, AP 70-219 México 20, DF Tel: 5489780
Librarian: Q F B Margarita Almada de Ascencio
Publications: Informe de actividades; Directorio de Bibliotecas UNAM; Informes Técnicos, Catálogo de Públicaciones Periódicas

Biblioteca de México, Plaza de la Ciudadela 6, México 1, DF Tel: 5104945/5104644
Librarian: Carmen E de García Moreno

Biblioteca Nacional de Agricultura*, Biblioteca Central, Escuela Nacional de Agricultura, Universidad Autónoma de Chapingo, Chapingo, Texcoco, Est de México

Biblioteca Nacional de Antropología e Historia, Paseo de la Reforma y Calzada Gandhi, México 5, DF Tel: 5536231/5536342
Director: Yolanda Mercader Martinez

Biblioteca Nacional de México*, República de El Salvador 70, México 1, DF Tel: 5129316/5103161/5121771

Biblioteca del **Congresso de la Unión***, Tacuba 29, México, DF

Biblioteca 'Benjamin **Franklin**' (USICA)*, Calle Londres 16, México 6, DF Tel: 5910244

Hemeroteca Nacional de México*, Calle del Carmen 31, México 1, DF
National Periodicals Library
Publication: Hemerografia Literaria (monthly)

Biblioteca del **Instituto Anglo-Mexicano de Cultura***, Calle M Antonio Caso 127, México 4, DF
British Council Library

Biblioteca del **Instituto Panamericano de Geografía** e Historia, Ex-Arzobispado 29, México 18, DF
Pan American Institute of Geography and History

Biblioteca del **Instituto Tecnológico** y de Estudios Superiores de Monterrey, Sucursal de Corres 'J', Monterrey, NL, México

Biblioteca de la **Universidad Iberoamericana**, Centro de Informacion Academica, Ave Cerro de las Torres 395, México 21, DF Tel: 5448755 ext 34 Cable Add: Uniberomex
Director: Juan Anaya Duarte

Library Associations

Asociación de Bibliotecarios de Instituciones de Enseñanza Superior e Investigación (ABIESI), Apdo Postal 5-611, México 5, DF
Association of Librarians of Higher Education and Research Institutions

Asociación Mexicana de Bibliotecarios AC (AMBAC)*, Apdo 27-132, México 7, DF Tel: 5489780
Mexican Association of Librarians
Secretary: N Pérez Paz
Publication: Noticiero (Bulletin); *Memorias de Congreso*

Departamento de Bibliotecas y Publicaciones, Dr Velasco 181, Col de los Doctores, México 7, DF Tel: 5788564/7614981

Escuela Nacional de Biblioteconomía y Archivonomía*, Viaducto Miguel Alemán 155, México 13, DF
National School of Librarianship and Archives
Dir: Professor Eduardo Salas Estrada
Publication: Bibliotecas y Archivos

Instituto de Investigaciones Bibliográficas*, c/o Biblioteca Nacional de México, República de El Salvador 70, México 1, DF and Hemeroteca Nacional de México, Calle del Carmen 31, México 1, DF
Institute of Bibliographical Research
Dir: María del Carmen Ruiz Castañeda
Publications: Boletin; Bibliografía Mexicana; Anuario Bibliográfico

Library Reference Books and Journals

Books

Anuario Bibliográfico, Instituto de Investigaciones Bibliograficas, c/o Biblioteca Nacional de Mexico, Republica de El Salvador 70, México 1, DF

Anuario de Bibliotecología Archivología Informática (Annual of Library Science, Archives, and Information Science), Universidad Nacional Autónoma de México, Ciudad Universitaria, Villa Obregón, México 20, DF

Bibliografía Mexicana, Instituto de Investigaciones Bibliograficas, c/o Biblioteca Nacional de Mexico, Republica de El Salvador 70, México 1, DF

Directorio de Bibliotecas de la Ciudad México (Directory of Libraries of the City of Mexico), Universidad de las Américas, Biblioteca, 16 Carretera Mexico-Toluca, México 10, DF

Journals

Bibliotecas y Archivos (Libraries and Archives), Escuela Nacional de Biblioteconomía y Archivonomía, Viaducto Miguel Alemán 155, México 13, DF

Boletín (Bulletin), Institute of Bibliographical Researchs, c/o National Library, República de El Salvador 70, México 1, DF

Boletín (Bulletin), National Archives, Palacio Nacional, México, DF

Boletín (Bulletin), National Library, República de El Salvador 70, México 1, DF

Noticiero (News), Mexican Association of Librarians, Apdo 27-132, México 7, DF

Literary Associations and Societies

Mexican **P E N** Club*, Filomeno Mata 8, Mexico City 1, DF
Secretary: Marco Antonio Montes de Oca

Sociedad Mexicana de Bibliografía*, Hemeroteca Nacional, Carmen 31, México 1, DF

Mexican Bibliographical Society
Dir: Dr Agustín Millares Carlo
Publication: Boletin (quarterly)

Literary Periodicals

Comunidad (Community), Universidad Iberoamericano, Cerro de las Torres 395, México 21, DF

Cuadernos Americanos (American Notebooks), Ave Coyocán 1035, Apdo Postal 965, México, DF

El Cuento (The Story); magazine of imagination, Ave División del Norte 521-101, México 12, DF

Lectura (Readings), Apdo 545, Bolivar 23-4, México, DF

Letras (Letters); literary and bibliographical publication, Libreria y Ediciones Botas SA, Justo Sierra 52, Apdo 941, Mexico 1, DF

Mexico Quarterly Review (text in English and Spanish), University of the Americas, 15 Sta Catavina Martir, via Puebla, Ruebla México

Plural, Cía Editorial Excelsior, SCL, Reforma 18, México, DF

Salamandra (Salamander), Editorial Alfonso Reyes, Adolfo Prieto 2407 Oriente, Monterrey, NL

Literary Prizes

Miguel Lanz **Duret** Prize*
Founded in 1941 for the best novel written by a young author. Awarded annually. Enquiries to El Universal, Bucareli 8, México, DF

National Prize for Literature*
For the best literary works in the fields of the novel, poetry, essay, biography, drama and motion picture scriptwriting. 100,000 Mexican pesos. Awarded annually. Enquiries to Mexican Ministry of Public Education, Brazil 21, México 1, DF

Villaurrutia Prize*
For poetry, prose, drama or essays by a new author. Awarded annually. Enquiries to Society of Friends of Xavier Villaurrutia, Paseo de la Reforma 18, Galeria Excelsior, México 1, DF

Monaco

General Information

Language: French
Religion: Roman Catholic
Population: 26,000
Bank Hours: 0830-1730 Monday-Friday
Shop Hours: 0830-1300, 1600-1930 Monday-Friday
Currency: French franc
Copyright: Berne, UCC (see International section)

Publishers

Académie Internationale de Tourisme, 4 rue des Iris, Monte-Carlo Tel: 309768
President: Georges Daskalakis
Subjects: Travel Literature, Dictionary of Tourism
Founded: 1951

Editions de l'**Oiseau-Lyre**, Les Remparts Tel: (93) 300944
Man Dir: Margarita M Hanson
Subject: Music

Editions **Regain***, Palais Miami, 10 blvd d'Italie, Monte-Carlo
Subjects: Poetry, Literature

Les Editions du **Rocher***, 28 Rue du Comte Félix Castaldi, Monaco
Subject: General Literature

Editions du Livre André **Sauret***, SA, 8 quai Antoine Ier, BP 48, Monte-Carlo Tel: 306884
Subjects: Art, Fiction
ISBN Publisher's Prefix: 2-85051

Union Continentale d'Editions SA*, 17 rue de Millo, Monte-Carlo
Subject: Literature

Major Booksellers

Les **Beaux Livres***, 4 rue des Iris, Monte Carlo Tel: 307390

Quartier-Latin*, 26 blvd Princess-Charlotte, Monte Carlo Tel: 302621

Sainte-Devote*, 19 blvd Princess-Charlotte, Monte Carlo Tel: 302279

Major Libraries

Bibliothèque de Monaco, 8 rue de la Poste Tel: 309509
Director: Pierre Fénart

Literary Associations and Societies

P E N Club, Musée d'Anthropologie Préhistorique, blvd du Jardin Exotique
Secretary: Louis Barral

Mongolian People's Republic

General Information

Language: Mongolian
Religion: None (Tibetan Buddhist Lamaism suppressed in 1930's)
Population: 1.6 million
Bank Hours: Vary. 0800-1700 or 1800 with lunch closing
Shop Hours: Generally 0900-1500
Currency: 100 mongo = 1 tugrik

Publishers

Mongolgosknigotorg*, Ulan-Bator
Function: Distributor

State Press*, Ulan-Bator
Subjects: Geography, Politics, Law

Major Booksellers

State Book Trading Office*, Leniny gudamch 41, Ulan-Bator Tel: 22312 Cable Add: Mongolbook

Major Libraries

State Archives*, Ulan-Bator State Public Library of the Mongolian People's Republic, Lenin Prospekt, Ulan-Bator Tel: 22396
Dir: M Bayaizul

Montserrat

General Information

Language: English
Religion: Anglican and other Protestant denominations and Catholic
Population: 11,000
Bank Hours: 0800-1200 Monday-Thursday; 0800-1200, 1500-1700 Friday
Shop Hours: 0800-1200, 1300-1600 Monday-Thursday; 0800-1200, 1300-1700 Friday; 0800-1300 Saturday
Currency: 100 cents = 1 East Caribbean dollar
Export/Import Information: No tariffs on books and advertising catalogues. Parcel Tax of 15 cents on each postal parcel. No import licences required
Copyright: Berne, UCC (see International section)

Major Bookseller

Empire Shop, George St, Plymouth Tel: Montserrat 2400
Manager: Ernst S Herman

Major Libraries

Montserrat Public Library, Plymouth, Montserrat
Librarian: V J Grell

Morocco

General Information

Language: Arabic, French, Spanish
Religion: Muslim
Population: 18.9 million
Literacy Rate (1971): 21.4% (49.5% Urban, 11.5% Rural)
Bank Hours: Winter: 0815-1130, 1415-1630 Monday-Friday; Summer: 0830-1130, 1500-1700 Monday-Friday
Shop Hours: Tangiers: 0900-1200, 1600-

2000; rest: 0900-1200, 1500-1800 or 1900
Currency: 100 centimes = 1 Dirham
Export/Import Information: No tariff on books; most advertising dutiable. 5% Special Tax and Stamp Duty of 2% of amount of import duty. No import licences required. Exchange controls but permission liberally granted
Copyright: UCC, Berne (see International section)

Book Trade Organizations

Syndicat des Editeurs du Maroc*, rue de Vesoul, Casablanca
Federation of Moroccan Publishers

Syndicat des Librairies du Moroc*, 10 ave Dar el Maghzen, Rabat

Book Trade Journals

Bibliographie nationale marocaine, Bibliothèque générale et Archives du Maroc, ave Moulay Chérif, Rabat (national bibliography published monthly)

Publishers

Government Printer (Imprimerie Officielle), ave Jean Mermoz, Rabat-Chellah, Chellah

Dar El **Kitab***, pl de la Mosqueé, Quartier des Habous, BP 4018, Casablanca Tel: 23381 Telex: 22620 Darki
Foreign Department: 18 rue Marechal, Casablanca Tel: 241168/246326
Dir: Boutaleb Abdou Abdelhay; *Manager:* Mme Soad Kadiri; *Publicity Manager:* Mounjedine Abdel-Ghani
Subjects: History, Africana, Philosophy, General & Social Science
Founded: 1948

Editions La **Porte**, 281 Ave Mohammed-V, Rabat Tel: 24977
Man Dir: Paul Souchon; *Sales:* Mohamed Rafii
Subsidiary Companies: Librairie aux Belles Images (Bookshop)
Subjects: Law — Constitutional, Social, Labour etc; Economics, Ministry of Justice Publications (in French and Arabic), Morocco Tourist Guides, Arab and French Language Teaching, Religion — the Koran, Islam
Bookshops: Librairie aux Belles Images (qv), address as above

Les Editions **Maghrebines***, 5-13 rue Soldat Roch, Casablanca Tel: 245148 Telex: Edima 22994 M
Subjects: General Nonfiction, History, Africana, Reference, Law, Science & Technology, General Science, Medicine
Founded: 1962

Major Booksellers

Librairie '**Aux Belles Images**', 281 ave Mohammed V, Rabat Tel: 24977
Parent Company: Editions La Porte (Publisher — qv)

Librairie des **Colonnes**, 54 Ave Pasteur, BP 352, Tangier Tel: 36955
Director: Mrs R Muyal
Parent Company: Sté Atlantique d'Edition

Cultura-Maroc*, 10 rue Bendahan, Casablanca Tel: 275990

Librairie des **Ecoles***, 12 ave Hassan II, Casablanca Tel: 66741

Librairie des **Etudes***, rue Allal B Abdallah, Rabat

Librairie **Farairre***, 43 rue de Foucauld, Casablanca Tel: 220388

Librairie de **France***, 4 rue Chenier, Casablanca Tel: 26534

Librairie **nationale***, 2 ave Mers Sultan, Casablanca Tel: 23678

Maghreb Livres*, 57 rue Oved Ziz, BP 725, Rabat Tel: 70340

Major Libraries

Bibliothèque générale et Archives*, BP 41, Tetuan

Bibliothèque générale et Archives du Maroc*, ave Moulay Chérif, Rabat Tel: 71890/72152
Publication: Bibliographie nationale marocaine

Bibliothèque municipale*, 142 ave de l'Armeé Royales, Casablanca Tel: 274170/223798
Dir: Haj Mohamed Bouzid

British Council Library*, 22 Ave Moulay Youssef, BP 427, Rabat Tel: 20314

Centre Africain de Formation et de Recherche administrative pour le Développement, Centre de Documentation, BP 310, Tangier Cable Add: Cafrad Tangier Telex: 33664 M
Librarian: Lelo Mamosi

Centre national de Documentation, Charil Maa El Ainain, BP 826, Rabat Tel: 74944 Telex: 31052M

Ecole Mohammedia d'Ingénieurs*, Bibliothèque, BP 765, Rabat Tel: 72647

Institut scientifique chérifien*, Bibliothèque, ave Moulay Chérif, Rabat
Publication: Travaux

Bibliothèque de l'**Université Al Quarawiyin***, 27 rue St Pierre et Miquelon, Rabat

Bibliothèque de l'**Université Mohammed V***, ave Moulay Chérif, Rabat

Mozambique

General Information

Language: Portuguese in and near large towns; Bantu languages; English widely spoken in business circles
Religion: About 1 million Christian (mostly Roman Catholic), 800,000 Muslim (in north); rest follow traditional beliefs
Population: 9.9 million
Literacy Rate: Civilized Population, 1955, 87.5%; Noncivilized, 1950, 1.3%
Bank Hours: 0800-1100 Monday, Tuesday, Thursday, Friday; 0800-1000 Wednesday and Saturday
Shop Hours: 0800-1130, 1400-1700 Monday-Friday; 0800-1200 Saturday
Currency: 100 centavos = 1 Mozambique escudo
Export/Import Information: Children's picture books dutied at 20 escudos per kg net weight, otherwise books and advertising matter duty-free. No additional taxes apply. Import licences and strict exchange controls; authorities have classified books and advertising as List 3 in priorities

Book Trade Organization

Instituto Nacional do Livro e do Disco, CP 4030, Avda 24 de Julho 1921, Maputo Tel: 20839/20870 Telex: 6-288 Inld Mo
Director: João Correia

Publishers

Empresa Moderna Lda*, 13 Ave da Republica, CP 473, Maputo
Man Dir: Louis Galloti
Subjects: General Fiction & Nonfiction, History, Africana, University & Secondary Textbooks
Founded: 1937

Government Printer (Impressa Nacional de Moçambique)*, CP 275, Maputo

Editora **Minerva** Central*, 84 Rua Consigliere Pedroso, CP 272, Maputo
Man Dir: J A Carvalho
Subsidiary Company: J A Carvalho & Co Ltd
Subjects: Medicine, General Science, University & Secondary Textbooks
Founded: 1908

Major Booksellers

Academica Lda*, 47 rua Joaquim Lapa, Maputo Tel: 3576

Armazens Distribuidores Lta*, CP 1215, Maputo

A W **Bayly** & Co Lda*, CP 185, Maputo

Cooperative das Casas*, 32 rua Major Araujo, Maputo

Minerva Central*, J A Carvalho & Co Lda, CP 212, Maputo

Major Libraries

Arquivo Historico de Moçambique, CP 2033, Maputo
Director: Maria Inês Nogueira da Costa

Biblioteca Municipal*, Maputo

Biblioteca Nacional de Moçambique*, CP 141, Maputo

Universidade Eduardo Mondlane, Centro Coordenador da Documentação, CP 1169, Maputo Tel: 743828

Namibia

General Information

Language: Afrikaans, German and English
Religion: About half of population Christian; rest follow traditional beliefs
Population: Estimates vary between 852,000 and 1.2 million (for 1974)
Literacy Rate: 35%
Currency: South African
Copyright: Berne (see International section)

Book Trade Reference Book

Namibische National Bibliographie 1971-75, contact Nordiska Afrikaininstitutets Bibliotek, BP 2126, S-750 02 Uppsala, Sweden

Publishers

Gamsberg Publishers, PO Box 22830, Windhoek 9100 (Located at: 21 Post St, Windhoek) Tel: 28714/35296
Man Dir, Editorial: J J Hans Viljden; *Sales:* Anne Buys; *Production:* Herman van Wyk; *Publicity:* Cecelia Blom; *Rights & Permissions:* Petrus Amakali
Subjects: School Textbooks (in eight indigenous languages of Namibia, English and Afrikaans), Fiction, Poetry, Non-fiction
Bookshop: Gamsberg Bookshop, at above address
1978: 22 titles *1979:* 45 titles *Founded:* 1977
ISBN Publisher's Prefix: 86848

Native Language Bureau*, Department of Bantu Education, PMB 13236, Windhoek 9100 Tel: 24601 Cable Add: Imfundo Windhoek Telex: 3178
Head: W Zimmermann; *Rights & Permissions:* Department of Bantu Education, Pretoria, South Africa
Subjects: Primary and Secondary School Textbooks in indigenous languages, Nama, Ndonga, Kwanyama, Kwangali, Mbukushu, Herero
Founded: 1964
ISBN Publisher's Prefix: 0-621

Major Booksellers

Bible Society of South Africa, 428 Kaiser St, Windhoek 9000
Regional office of Bible Society of South Africa, Republic of South Africa (qv)

The **Bookshop**, PO Box 119, Keetmanshoop Tel: (0631) 2309
Owner and Manager: Th Prahl-Andresen

Central News Agency*, PO Box 2104, Windhoek

Educmeds Pty Ltd*, PO Box 2961, Windhoek 9100

Nasionale Boekhandel (SWA) (Pty) Ltd*, PO Box 1099, Windhoek 9100 Tel: 22711
Parent Company: Nasionale Boekhandel Ltd, South Africa (qv)

Major Libraries

Government Archives, Department of National Education, PB 13250, Windhoek Tel: 38841

Library Services for South West Africa, Huegel St, PB 13186, Windhoek Tel: 24528 Cable Add: Swasec Telex: 56665
Librarian: Mrs I Klüsener

Technical High School Library*, PMB 12014, Windhoek 9111

Windhoek Public Library, PO Box 3180, Windhoek 9000 Tel: 30295

Translation Agencies and Associations

Native Language Bureau*, PMB 13236, Windhoek 9100

Nepal

General Information

Language: Nepali
Religion: Hindu, Tibetan Buddhist
Population: 13.4 million
Literacy Rate (1975): 19.2%
Bank Hours: 1000-1700 Sunday-Friday
Shop Hours: 1000-1700 Sunday-Friday
Currency: 100 paise = 1 Nepalese rupee
Export/Import Information: No tariff on books and advertising. Import licences required. Exchange controls

Publishers

Department of Publicity*, Ministry of Communications, Katmandu

Educational Enterprise*, Mahankalsthan, Katmandu Tel: 13749
Subject: Education

Lakoul Press*, Palpa-Tanben
Subjects: Education, Physical Sciences

Mahabir Singh Chiniya Main*, Makhan Tola, Katmandu

Mandas Sugatdas*, Kamabachi, Katmandu

Nepal Academy*, Ganabahal Dharhara, Katmandu
Subjects: Science, Literature, History, Art, Social Science

Ratna Pustak Bhandar*, Bhotahity, Katmandu

Sajha Prakashan, Co-operative Publishing Organization*, Pulchowk lalitpur, Katmandu Tel: 21023/21118 Cable Add: Sajha Prakashan Katmandu
Chairman: Shri Kshetra Pratap Adhikary; *General Manager:* Mr K C S Pradhan
Branch Offs: 40 branches and sub-offices throughout Nepal
Subjects: Literary, Educational Textbooks, General (published in English and Nepali)
Founded: 1966

Major Booksellers

Educational Enterprises (Pvt) Ltd, Kingsway, Kantipath, Katmandu Tel: 12508/13749

International Progressive Books and Periodicals Store*, Centre for General Selling, Distribution and Publication, PO Box 2131, Katmandu
General Manager: Sugat Dass Tuladhar

Januka Pustak Bhandar*, Budhhat Chowk, Biratnagar (Morang) Tel: 226 Cable Add: Januka Biratnagar

Nepal Booksellers*, 6/78 Dharmapath, Katmandu Tel: 14603

Ratna Pustak Bhandar*, Bhotahity, Katmandu

Sahayogi Prakashan*, Tripureshwar, Katmandu

Major Libraries

American Library*, Katmandu

Bir Library*, Ranipolhari, Katmandu

British Council Library*, PO Box 640, Kanthi Path, Katmandu Tel: 11305/13796

National Library*, Katmandu

Nepal-Bharat Sanskritik Kendra Pustakalay*, Ganga Path, Katmandu

Tribhuvan University Library*, Kirtipur, Katmandu
Plays the leading role in library development

Library Associations

Nepal Library Association*, PO Box 207 GPO, Asan Tole, Katmandu

Netherlands

General Information

Language: Dutch; Frisian in Friesland (though all speakers of Frisian also speak Dutch). English is common second language
Religion: Roman Catholic and Protestant
Population: 14 million
Bank Hours: 0900-1500 Monday-Friday
Shop Hours: 0830-1800 Monday-Saturday. Half day one day a week
Currency: 100 cents = 1 Netherlands gulden
Export/Import Information: Member of the European Economic Community. No tariff on books except children's picture books, 13% from non-EEC; advertising other than single copies 9%; VAT, 18% on books except children's picture books, 4%; 18% on advertising matter. Import licences required for certain countries (not US or UK)
Copyright: UCC, Berne, Florence (see International section)

Book Trade Organizations

Centraal Boekhuis BV, Erasmusweg 10, Postbus 125, 4100 AC Culemborg Tel: (03450) 4841/4208

Collectieve Propaganda van het Nederlandse Boek (CPNB), Langestr 61, Postbus 10576, Amsterdam C Tel: (020) 264971
Committee for the Collective Promotion of Dutch Books
Dirs: Dick Ouwehand, Wim Berbers
Publications: Boekenmolen (quarterly); *Premium Bookweek* (booklet); *Children's Bookweek* (booklet); *Books of the Month*

Bureau I S B N, Centraal Bookhuis, Postbus 125, Culemborg (Located at: Erasmusweg 10)
ISBN Administrator: J van Leeuwen

Koninklijke Nederlandse Uitgeversbond*, Keizersgracht 391, 1016 EJ Amsterdam Tel: (020) 267736
Royal Dutch Publishers' Association
Secretary: R M Vrij
Founded: 1880

Nederlandsche Vereniging van Antiquaren, Nieuwe Spiegelstraat 40, 1017 DG Amsterdam
Netherlands Association of Antiquarian Booksellers

Nederlandsche Vereeniging voor Druk- en Boekkunst, Bestevaerstr 10, Haarlem
Netherlands Society for the Art of Printing and Book Production
Secretary: F Mayer
Publications: Mededelingen (irregular) and books

Nederlandse Boekverkopersbond, Waalsdorperwegg 119, 2597 HS The Hague Tel: (070) 244395
Dutch Booksellers' Association
President: H Nelissen
Publication: De Boekverkoper (quarterly)

NETHERLANDS

Standard Book Numbering Agency, see under ISBN

Stichting Speurwerk betreffende het Boek*, Keizersgracht 144, 1015 CX Amsterdam Tel: (020) 264974
Book Research Foundation
Secretary: A A Herpers

Vereeniging ter bevordering van de belangen des Boekhandels, Lassusstr 9, Postbus 5475, 1007 AL Amsterdam
Association for the Promotion of the Interests of Booksellers and Publishers
Secretary: Mrs M van Vollenhoven
Publications: Nieuwsblad voor de Boekhandel (weekly); *Lijstenboek* (annual)

Vereniging van Uitgeversvertegenwoordigers*, Westerstr 62, Wormerveer
Association of Publishers' Representatives
Publication: Vertegenwoordiger

Book Trade Reference Books and Journals

Books

Bibliografie van in Nederland verschenen Officiële en Semi-officiële Uitgaven (Bibliography of Official and Semi-official Publications), Royal Library, Lange Voorhout 34, The Hague

Lystenboek (List of Dutch Booksellers), Nieuwsblad voor de Boekhandel, Postbus 5475, Amsterdam Z

Journals

Boeken-kijkboek (Book Review), Commission for the Collective Promotion of the Netherlands Book, N Z Voorburgwal 44, Amsterdam C

Boekenband (The Bond of Books), Christelijke Blindenbibliotheek (Evangelical Library for the Blind), Putterweg 140, Ermelo

De Boekverkoper (The Bookseller), Dutch Booksellers' Association, Waalsdorperweg 119, NL-2019 The Hague

Book Mill, Netherlands Graphic Export Centre, Prinsengracht 668, Amsterdam Tel: (020) 234283

Brinkman's Cumulatieve Catalogus (Brinkman's Cumulative Book Catalogue), A W Sijthoff International Publishing Co BV, Schuttersveld 9, Postbus 9, Leiden

Buitenlandse Boek (The Foreign Book), Prinsengracht 1083, Amsterdam

Duitse Boek (The German Book), (text in Dutch and German), Editions Rodopi NV, Keizersgracht 302-304, Amsterdam

Gouden Uren (Golden Hours), Netherlands Book Club, Prinsevinkenpark 2, The Hague

Nieuwe Pockets en Paperbacks (New Pocket-books and Paperbacks), Nederlandse Boek, Prinsengracht 1083, Amsterdam

Nieuwsblad voor de Boekhandel (News-sheet for the Book Trade), Vereniging ter Bevordering van de Belangen des Boekhandels, Lassusstr 9, Postbus 5475, Amsterdam Z

Nijhoff Information; books and periodicals from the Netherlands in foreign languages, Martinus Nijhoff FB, Lange Voorhout 9-11, Postbus 269, The Hague

Prisma; book reviews for public libraries, Protestant Foundation for the Promotion of Librarianship and Reading Information in the Netherlands, Parkweg 20a, Voorburg

Spectrum Boekengids, Uitgeverij Het Spectrum BV, Park Voorn 4, De Meern

De Uitgever (The Publisher), Royal Dutch Publishers' Association, N Z Voorburgwal 44, Amsterdam C

Vertegenwoordiger (The Representative), Association of Publishers' Representatives, Westerstr 62, Wormer

Publishers

A P A (Academic Publishers Associated), Postbus 1850, NL-1000 BW Amsterdam
Man Dir: G van Heusden
Orders to: Postbus 122, NL-3600 AC Maarssen Tel: (030) 445700, (020) 240536
Subsidiary Companies: Fontes Pers (qv); Holland University Press BV (qv); Oriental Press BV (qv); Philo Press/Van Heusden/Hissink & Co CV (qv); University Press Amsterdam BV (qv)
Subjects: Academic Books in the Arts, Humanities and Sciences
1979: 35 titles *Founded:* 1967
ISBN Publisher's Prefixes: 90-302, 90-6022, 90-6023, 90-6024, 90-6025, 90-6037, 90-6039, 90-6042
Miscellaneous: Formerly Associated Publishers Amsterdam

Academic Publishers Associated, see APA

Addison-Wesley Publishing Group, Postbus 5598, 1007 AN Amsterdam (Located at: de Lairessestr 90, 1071 PJ Amsterdam)
Tel: (020) 764044/45 Cable Add: Adiwes Amsterdam Telex: 14046 wss nl
Marketing Manager: Frans Gianotten;
Rights & Permissions: S B Warren, Addison-Wesley, USA; *Operations:* Jan Fleere
Parent Company: Addison-Wesley Publishing Co Inc, Reading, Mass 01867, USA
Subsidiary Companies: Addison-Wesley Publishers BV; Inter-European Editions
Associate Companies: Addison-Wesley Publishers Ltd, UK (qv for other associates)
Subjects: Humanities, Reference, Juveniles, General & Social Science, Technology, Economics, University, Secondary & Primary Textbooks, Educational Materials, General, EFL, Business, Management
Founded: 1942
ISBN Publisher's Prefixes: 0-201 (Addison-Wesley), 0-8053 (Benjamin), 0-8465 (Cummings)

Agathon, see Uniebook NV

Uitgeverij **Ambo** BV, Parkstraat 47, PO Box 308, 3740 AH Baarn Tel: (02154) 18441 Telex: 43272
Publisher: H Pijfers
Imprints: Basis
Subjects: Religion, Philosophy, Psychiatry, Sociology, Psychology
Miscellaneous: Firm is a member of the Combo Group, Netherlands (qv)
1979: 50 titles
ISBN Publisher's Prefix: 90-263

Amsterdam Boek BV, now incorporated in Uitgeverij Het Spectrum BV (qv)

Ankh-Hermes BV, Smyrnastr 5, Postbus 125, Deventer Tel: (05700) 33355
Man Dir, Rights & Permissions: Paul Kluwer
Subjects: History, Philosophy, Religion, Juveniles, Psychology, Archaeology, Astrology, Occult, Yoga, Sport
Founded: 1949
ISBN Publisher's Prefix: 90-202

BV Uitgeverij de **Arbeiderspers**, Singel 262, Postbus 3879, 1016 AC Amsterdam
Tel: (020) 239326 Telex: 11556 Apqwu

Man Dir: Theo A Sontrop; *Editorial:* Martin Ros; *Publicity:* Gert Jan Hemmink
Associate Companies: Em Querido's Uitgeverij BV (qv); Wetenschappelijke Uitgeverij BV (qv)
Subjects: General Fiction & Non-fiction, Paperbacks
1979: 120 titles *1980:* approx 140 titles
ISBN Publisher's Prefix: 90-295

Uitgeverij **Archipel**, an imprint of Succes BV (qv)

Argus Elsevier BV*, Rivierstaete, Amsteldijk 166, Amsterdam
Parent Company: Elsevier NDU nv (qv)

A **Asher** & Co, BV*, Keizersgracht 526, Amsterdam Tel: (020) 222255 Cable Add: Asherbooks Telex: 14070 ashni-nl
Man Dir: Nico Israel; *Sales Dir:* Julius W Steiner
Associate Companies: Nico Israel (qv), Theatrum Orbis Terrarum (qv)
Subjects: General & Natural Science, Reference
1978-79: 10 titles *Founded:* 1830

Associated Publishers Amsterdam, renamed APA (Academic Publishers Associated) (qv)

B R E S*, Madoerastr 10, 2585 VB The Hague Tel: (070) 656592
Editorial: A Gabrielli, J Klautz
Subjects: Comparative Religion, Parapsychology, Metaphysics, Philosophy, Alternative Medicine, Fantastic Art, Archaeology

Baedeker voor de Vrouw, an imprint of Succes BV (qv)

Bert **Bakker** BV, Herengracht 406, Amsterdam C Tel: (020) 241934
Man Dir: Bert Bakker; *Editorial:* Harko Keijzer, Marijke Bartels, Mai Spijkers;
Rights & Permissions: Jenny de Vries
Subjects: Dutch and Foreign Literature, Psychology, Social Science, Handicrafts, Cookery, Family Interest
Founded: 1893
Miscellaneous: Firm is member of the Kluwer Group (qv)
ISBN Publisher's Prefix: 90-6019

A A **Balkema**, PO Box 1675, 3000 BR Rotterdam Tel: (010) 666861 Telex: 27070 promx nl
Man Dir: A T Balkema; *Rights & Permissions:* G Balkema-Pieterse
Branch Offs: Lisplein 11, 3037 AR Rotterdam; PO Box 3117, Cape Town, South Africa; 99 Main St, Salem, NH 03097, USA
Subjects: History (especially South African), Art, African Studies, Palaeontology, Biology, Ecology, Botany, Zoology, Soil and Rock Mechanics
1979: 15 titles *1980:* 20 titles *Founded:* 1932
ISBN Publisher's Prefix: 90-6191

Basis, an imprint of Uitgeverij Ambo BV (qv)

H J W **Becht's** Uitgeversmij bv/Uitgeverij H J de Bussy BV, Keizersgracht 810, PO Box 162, NL-1000 AD Amsterdam Tel: 242449 Telex: 18069 bebus nl
Dirs: J J F Aleva, M de Metz, J Schilt
Subjects: General Fiction and Non-fiction, Juveniles, Hobbies, Leisure Activities, History, Arts and Crafts, Health, General and Social Science, Textbooks

John **Benjamins** BV, Postbus 52519, 1007 HA Amsterdam (Located at: Amsteldijk 44, Amsterdam) Tel: (020) 738156 Cable Add: Benper, Amsterdam Telex: 15798 jbds
Man Dir: John L Benjamins
Subjects: Linguistics, Literature, Philosophy,

Reference, Social Science, Educational Materials, Reprints of Backfile-Periodicals
1978: 30 titles *Founded:* 1964
ISBN Publisher's Prefix: 90-272

De **Bezige** Bij, Van Miereveldstr 1, Postbus 5184, Amsterdam Z Tel: (020) 735731
Cable Add: Beebook
Man Dirs: G Lubberhuizen, J L Witteman, A J R Hamming
Subjects: General Fiction, Belles Lettres, Poetry, Children's Books, Low-priced Paperbacks
1978: 120 titles *1979:* 120 titles *Founded:* 1945
ISBN Publisher's Prefix: 90-234

Bigot en Van Rossum BV*, Bloemlandseweg 6, Postbus 10, 1260 AA Blaricum Tel: (02153) 82548
Dir: Mrs M H van Rossum-Berg; *Sales Dir:* E L Westra-Sillevis
Subsidiary Company: Mulder en Co, Bloemlandsweg 6, Blaricum
Subjects: General Fiction, Paperbacks
1978: 14 titles *Founded:* 1934
ISBN Publisher's Prefix: 90-6134

Erven J **Bijleveld**, Janskerkhof 7, Utrecht Tel: (030) 317008
Man Dir: J B Bommeljé Jr
Subjects: Philosophy, Religion, Medicine, Psychology, Social Science, History
1979: approx 10 titles *Founded:* 1864

Andries **Blitz** BV*, Oud Blaricummerweg 31, Postbus 3, Laren Tel: (02153) 2401
Subjects: General Fiction, Belles Lettres, Poetry, Biography, History, Music, Art
Founded: 1929
ISBN Publisher's Prefix: 90-6081

H W **Blok** Uitgeverij BV*, Schiedamsevest 51, 3012 BD Rotterdam Tel: (010) 137997
Subjects: Medical Year Books, Dutch for Spanish-speaking and Portuguese for Dutch-speaking persons, *Handbook gymnastics*
ISBN Publisher's Prefix: 90-70008

Boek Promotions bv, Neuhuijsweg 8, 1251 LW Laren NH Tel: (02153) 10154
Owner: Peter J Houbolt
Act mainly as packagers

Boekencentrum BV, Scheveningseweg 72, Postbus 84176, 2508 AD The Hague Tel: (070) 512111
Subjects: Education, Theology, Religion

De **Boekerij**, an imprint of BV Uitgeversmaatschappij Elsevier Boekerij (qv)

de **Boer** Maritiem, see Uniebook NV

Bohn, Scheltema & Holkema, Wetenschappelijke Uitgeverij, Emmalaan 27, Utrecht Tel: (030) 511274
Man Dirs: Fons Drabbe, Jan van Geelen
Subjects: University Textbooks (Medicine, Biology, Linguistics)
Founded: 1752
Miscellaneous: Firm is a member of the Kluwer Group (qv)
ISBN Publisher's Prefix: 90-313

Boom-Pers Boeken- en Tijdschriftenuitg BV, Kromme Elleboog 2, Postbus 58, 7940 AB Meppel Tel: (05220) 54306 Editorial & Directors' Off: Sarphatistr 9, 1017 WS Amsterdam Tel: (020) 226107 Cable Add: Boompers
Man Dirs: H L Bouman, J H Boom
Subjects: Philosophy, Philosophy of Science, Psychology, General, Social & Political Science, Periodicals
1979: 48 titles *Founded:* 1842
Bookshops: Kamper Boekhandel, Oude Str 82, Kampen; Elburger Boekhandel, Beekstr 26, Elburg; De Brunte, Snijderstr 11, Lelystad; Boekhandel Boom, Winkelcentrum Gordinan, Lelystad; Boekhandel v/h G Taconis, Hoofdstraat West 10, Wolvega (all in Netherlands)
ISBN Publisher's Prefix: 90-6009

Born NV Uitgeversmaatschappij*, Esstr 10, Postbus 22, Assen
Man Dir: H Born
Subjects: General Fiction, How-to, Philosophy, Textbooks, Reference, Juveniles, Medicine, Engineering, Social Science, Low- & High-priced Paperbacks
Founded: 1885
Miscellaneous: Firm is a member of the Kluwer Group (qv)
ISBN Publisher's Prefix: 90-283

Bosch en Keuning NV*, Bremstr, Postbus 1, Baarn Tel: (02154) 8241 Telex: beka-43272
Man Dir: Aize de Visser
Subjects: Biography, History, Music, Art, Religion, Low- & High-priced Paperbacks, Medicine, Primary Textbooks, Educational Materials, Popular Science (Sesam Pocketbooks)
Founded: 1925
Miscellaneous: Firm is a member of the Combo Group, Netherlands (qv)
ISBN Publisher's Prefix: 90-246

Redactie **Bres***, Madoerastraat 10, 2585 VB The Hague Tel: 070-656592
Subjects: Fantastic Art, Metaphysics, Religion, Natural Medicine, Psychology

Bresboek, an imprint of Zuidgroep BV (qv)

NV Boekhandel & Drukkerij voorheen E J **Brill**, Oude Rijn 33a, Leiden Tel: (071) 146646 Cable Add: Brill Leiden Telex: 39296
Manager: T A Edridge
Branch Offs: Orient Buchhandlung am Friesenplatz, E J Brill GmbH, D-5000 Cologne 1, Antwerpener Str 6-12, German Federal Republic; E J Brill London Ltd, 41 Museum St, London WC1A 1LX, UK
Subjects: Classical, Mediaeval and Renaissance Studies, Religion, Oriental & Islamic Studies, University Textbooks
Founded: 1683
ISBN Publisher's Prefix: 90-04

Educatieve Uitgeverij Ten **Brink** BV, Stationsweg 44, Postbus 56, 7940 AB Meppel Tel: (05220) 50622 Telex: c/o Drukkerij Ten Brink BV: 42469 Brink NL
Man Dir: B W Weerdmeester
Subject: Educational books for 6-18 year olds
Founded: 1848
ISBN Publisher's Prefix: 90-248

A W **Bruna** & Zoon's Uitgeversmaatschappij BV, Postbus 8181, 3503 RD Utrecht (Located at: Hollantlaan 2, 3526 AM Utrecht) Tel: 884233 Cable Add: Brunazoon Telex: 47518
Dirs: H Bruna, H M Bruna; *Man Dir:* J Buis; *Assistant Man Dir:* J C Bloemsma; *Sales:* K Eksteen; *Rights & Permissions:* Ellen-C van der Ploeg
Branch Off: Antwerpen Steenweg 29A, B-2630 Aartselaar, Belgium
Subjects: General Fiction, Belles Lettres, History, Philosophy, Children's Picturebooks, Juveniles, Low- & High-priced Paperbacks, Psychology, General & Social Science
1978: 180 titles *Founded:* 1868
ISBN Publisher's Prefix: 90-229

Buijten en Schipperheijn BV Drukkerij en Uitg Mij v/h, Valkenburgerstr 106, NL-1001 Amsterdam Tel: (020) 236612
Subject: Philosophy, Religion, History, Literature
1978: 20 titles *Founded:* 1902
ISBN Publisher's Prefix: 90-6064

Uitgeverij G F **Callenbach** BV, Hoogstr 24, Postbus 86, Nijkerk Tel: (03494) 51241 Telex: beka-43722
Man Dir: G F Callenbach; *Rights & Permissions:* Mrs P van Elven-Scholtes
Subjects: General Fiction, Belles Lettres, Poetry, Religion, Juveniles, Low- & High-priced Paperbacks, Psychology, Psychiatry, Medicine, Sociology, Hobbies
1979: 500 titles *Founded:* 1854
Miscellaneous: Firm is a member of the Combo Group, Netherlands (qv)
ISBN Publisher's Prefix: 90-266

Uitgeverij **Cantecleer** BV, PO Box 24, 3730 AA De Bilt (Located at: Dorpsstraat 74, De Bilt) Tel: (030) 764014
Man Dir: K J Bekkers; *Publisher:* J A J Jungerhans; *Editors:* H Stenfert Kroese, G G J van Schaik
Subjects: Art, Juveniles, Handicrafts, Travel Guides, Paperbacks
Founded: 1947
Miscellaneous: Firm is a member of the Combo Group, Netherlands (qv)
ISBN Publisher's Prefix: 90-213

Castrum Peregrini Presse, Herengracht 401, Postbus 645, 1000 AP Amsterdam Tel: (020) 235287
Man Dir: M R Goldschmidt; *Editorial:* Th Karlauf
Subjects: History of Literature, History of Art, Belles Lettres, Poetry, Biography, History, Archaeology, Philology, History of Ideas, Reference
1978-79: 6 titles *Founded:* 1950
ISBN Publisher's Prefix: 90-6034

De **Centaur**, an imprint of Omega Boek BV (qv)

Combo Uitgeversgroep*, Bremstr 11, Baarn Tel: (02154) 18241
Miscellaneous: Members of the Combo Group in the Netherlands include: Uitgeverij Ambo BV (qv), Uitgeverij Bekadidact, Bosch & Keuning NV (qv), Uitgeverij Callenbach BV (qv), Uitgeverij Cantecleer BV (qv), Uitgeverij De Fontein BV (qv), Uitgeverij ten Have (qv), Uitgeverij Market Books BV, Uitgeverij 'In den Toren' (qv), Uitgeverij Van Walraven (qv)
ISBN Publishers' Prefixes: 90-263 (Ambo), 90-321 (Bekadidact), 90-246 (Bosch & Keuning), 90-266 (Callenbach), 90-213 (Cantecleer), 90-261 (De Fontein), 90-259 (ten Have), 90-6049 (Van Walraven)

Uitgeverij **Contact** BV, now fully integrated in Bert Bakker BV (qv)

Federatie **D J O** (de jonge onderzoekers), Groesbeekseweg 70, Nijmegen Tel: (080) 229549
Publicity Manager: Drs L P v Loon

Dekker en Van de Vegt, Fransestr 30, 6524 JC Nijmegen Tel: (080) 232765 Cable Add: Dekkervegt Nijmegen
Man Dir: K W J van Rossum
Parent Company: Van Gorcum BV (qv)
Subjects: High-priced Paperbacks, Medicine, Social Sciences, Psychology, Secondary Textbooks
1978: 23 titles *1979:* 22 titles *Founded:* 1856
ISBN Publisher's Prefix: 90-255

Delft University Press, Mijnbouwplein 11, 2628 RT Delft, PO Box 5 Tel: (015) 783254
Dir: Ir P A M Maas; *Editorial:* Lydia tes Horst-ten Wolde; *Sales:* J J Bruystens
1978: 15 titles *1979:* 10 titles *Founded:* 1972
ISBN Publisher's Prefix: 90-6275

Jacob **Dijkstra**'s Uitg Mij BV*, Helperoostsingel 20, Postbus 284, Groningen Tel: (050) 262866

258 NETHERLANDS

Dijkstra's Uitgeverij Zeist BV*, Dijnselburgerlaan 9, Postbus 48, 3700 AA Zeist Tel: (03404) 21021

Diligentia BV*, Tesselschadestr 18-22, NL-1013 Amsterdam Tel: (020) 211911 Cable Add: Publipress Amsterdam Telex: 14407
Dir: C van der Sluys
Subjects: Directories, Trade Journals

van **Dishoeck**, see Unieboek NV

Djambatan BV*, Postbus 43110, 2504 AC The Hague Tel: (070) 299180 Cable Add: Djambatan Den Haag
Man Dir: E G Niessen
Parent Company: NV Falkplan/CIB (qv)
Subjects: History, Reference, Geography, Cartography, Educational Materials (Atlases, Wall Maps)
Founded: 1949

Uitgeversmaatschappij Ad **Donker** BV, Koningin Emmaplein 1, 3016 AA Rotterdam Tel: (010) 362851
Dir: W A Donker
Subjects: General Fiction, Belles Lettres, Poetry, Biography, History, Music, Art, Juveniles, High-priced Paperbacks
Founded: 1938
ISBN Publisher's Prefix: 90-6100

Dragon's Dream, Postbus 212, AE 3340 Hendrik Ido Ambacht Tel: (01858) 7070 Telex: 28856
Editorial: Roger Dean; *Sales:* Evert Chevalier; *Production:* Ellen Pardede
Subjects: Speculative art in the fields of science fiction, fantasy, prophecy, past, future and other worlds
1980: 20 titles *Founded:* 1975
ISBN Publisher's Prefix: 90-6332

De **Driehoek** BV, Keizersgracht 756, 1017 EZ Amsterdam Tel: (020) 246426
Director: H J Heule
Subjects: Medicine, Health, Yoga, Herbs, Nutrition, Vegetarianism, Mysticism, Buddhism etc, Astrology

East-West Publications Fonds BV, Anna Paulownastraat 78, POB 85617, 2508 CH-The Hague Tel: (070) 461594 Telex: 16384
Subjects: Books on Sufism, Religions, Mysticism, Symbolism, Middle East Culture, Medieval Art & Iconography
1978: 6 titles

Edicom NV*, Rivierstaete, Amsteldijk 166, Amsterdam
Presidents: Dr P A F van Veen, J H Docter Edicom; *Rights & Permissions:* Henk Drijvers; *Contracts & Subsidiary Rights Dept:* 27 Torenlaan, Postbus 44, Laren, Noord Holland Tel: (02153) 87075
Subjects: General Fiction, Belles Lettres, Poetry, Biography, History, How-to, Philosophy, Reference, Religion, Juveniles, High-priced Paperbacks, Medicine, Psychology, General & Social Science, Secondary & Primary Textbooks, Educational Materials
Foreign Group Members: A Manteau NV, Belgium (qv); Ikhtiar, Indonesia (qv)
Bookshop: Co-libri BV (wholesaler), Frankenslag 173, Postbus 290, The Hague
Miscellaneous: Firm is a member of the Kluwer Group (qv)
ISBN Publisher's Prefixes: 90-6006 (Paris), 90-224 (Meulenhoff)

Educaboek BV, Industrieweg 1, Postbus 48, 4100 AA Culemborg Tel: (03450) 3143 Telex: 47306
Chairman: P D Zuiderveld; *Dirs:* B Balder; J Th Timmer
Subjects: Textbooks, Secondary, General and Vocational Education, Technical

Founded: 1970
Miscellaneous: Firm is a member of the Kluwer Group (qv for associate companies), and production and selling company for Stam Technische Boeken, Stam/Robijns, Tjeenk Willink-Noorduijn and Schoolpers (qqv)

Eindhovensche Drukkerij BV, Cederlaan 2, Postbus 382, Eindhoven Tel: (040) 513620 Telex: 51476
Dir: Peter Smeets; *Export Manager:* Willem Ambaum
Subjects: Illustrated Children's Paperbacks, Activity Books, Board Books

Elmar BV, Delftweg 147, 2289 BD Rijswijk (2.H) Tel: (015) 123623
Man Dir: A C Roodnat
Subjects: Biography, History, How-to, Reference, Medicine & General Science, Sci-Fic, Sport
1978: 41 titles *1979:* 50 titles *Founded:* 1961

Elsevier-NDU nv, Jan van Galenstr 335, 1061A2 Amsterdam Tel: (020) 5159111 (Internal and External Relations Tel: (020) 5152350) Cable Add: Elsevier Telex: 16479 epc nl
Presidents: W Pluygers, Prof P J Vinken; *Other members of Executive Board:* H N Appel, D P van de Merwe, J H Verleur
Dutch Subsidiaries: BV Uitgeversmaatschappij Elsevier, Elsevier International Projects BV/Tirion, W van Hoeve BV, Elsevier Nederland BV, BV Uitgeversmaatschappij Elsevier Argus (qv), BV Uitgeversmaatschappij Elsevier Boekerij (qv), BV Uitgeversmaatschappij Elsevier Focus, Edicom BV (qv) (all at Rivierstaete, Amsteldijk 166, Amsterdam); Multiboek BV, Pruimendijk 104, Ridderkerk; Nederlandse Dagbladunie BV, NRC BV (both at Westblaak 180, Rotterdam); De Courant Het Vaderland BV, Parkstr 25-27, The Hague; Dagblad van Rijn en Gouwe BV, P Doelmanstr 8, Alphen a/d Rijn; BV De Dordtenaar, Johann de Wittstr 17-19, Dordrecht; Necomin BV, Molenstr 7, Roosendaal; Elsevier-NDU Grafische Groep BV, Van Boekhoven-Bosch BV (both at Europalaan 12, Utrecht); Boom-Ruygrok BV, Hulswitweg 15, Haarlem; Henkes-Senefelder BV, Van IJsendijkstraat 150, Purmerend; Krips Repro BV, Industrieweg 5, Meppel; Misset Grafische Bedrijven BV, Uitgeversmaatschappij C Misset BV (both at IJsselkade 32, Doetinchem); Periodieken Service Holland BV, Keppelseweg 15, Doetinchem; Vlasveld & Co's Drukkerij BV, Parmentierplein 31, Rotterdam; Zetterij Holland BV, Nw Zijds Voorburgwal 303, Amsterdam; Elsblad BV, Prof J H Bavincklaan 5, Amstelveen; BV Uitgevermaatschappij Bonaventura, Spuistr 110-112, Amsterdam; BV Uitgeversmaatschappij Annoventura, Kloveniersburgwal 51, Amsterdam; Folio Groep BV, Welboom Bladen BV, Herengracht 362, Amsterdam; Fonorama BV, Kon Wilhelminalaan 12, Amersfoort; Jongerenmedia BV, IJselstraat 20-24, Amsterdam; Koninklijke PBNA NV, Velperbuitensingel 6, Arnhem; Elsevier Detailhandel BV, Kring van Boekspecialisten BV (both at Vredenburg 139, Utrecht); Dekker & Nordemann's Wetenschappelijke Boekhandel BV, Meulenhoffbruna BV (both at Beulingstr 2, Amsterdam); Elsevier Science Publishers BV, Overschiestr 55-57, Amsterdam; Elsevier's Wetenschappelijke Uitgeverij BV (qv), BV Noord-Hollandsche Uitgeversmaatschappij (qv), Elsevier/North-Holland Biomedical Press BV (qv) (all at Jan van Galenstraat 335, Amsterdam); Northprint BV, Industrieweg 1b, Meppel; Excerpta Medica International BV, Excerpta Medica BV (both at Keizersgracht 305-311, Amsterdam); Het Vrije Volk BV (50%), W de Withstraat 25, Rotterdam
Foreign Subsidiaries: American Elsevier Publishers Inc, Elsevier-Dutton Publishing Co Inc, Education & Economic Systems Inc, Congressional Information Service Inc, D & N Library Services (USA) Inc, Elsevier North-Holland Inc, Excerpta Medica Inc, Medical Examination Publishing Company Inc (all in USA); Elsevier Publishing Projects SA, Elsevier Sequoia SA (qv), Excerpta Medica SA (all in Switzerland); Elsevier Oxford Ltd (qv), Phaidon Publishers Ltd, Phaidon Press Ltd (qv), Applied Science Publishers Ltd (qv), Elsevier Editorial Services Ltd, Elsevier-IRCS Ltd (all in UK); Elsevier Sequoia SA (qv), Elsevier Sequoia NV, Librico NV, A Manteau NV (qv), Elsevier Business Press NV, International Equipment News Europe NV (50%), Computer Product News Europe NV (50%) (all in Belgium); Editions Elsevier Sequoia SARL, France (qv); Selecciones Editoriales SA, Spain (qv); Elsevier Zeitschriften-Verlag GmbH, Krausskopf Verlag GmbH (qv), Ingenieur Digest Verlag GmbH (all in Federal Republic of Germany); Dekker en Nordemann Ireland Ltd, Elsevier/North-Holland Scientific Publishers Ltd, Irish Elsevier Printers Ltd (all in Republic of Ireland); Librería Internacional SA (qv), El Manual Moderno SA (qv) (both in Mexico); Editora Campus Ltda, Brazil (qv)
Subjects: Archaeology, Art, Agricultural/Environmental Sciences, Biochemistry, Biology, Chemistry, Computer and Information Sciences, Dictionaries, Earth Sciences, Economics, History, Law, Linguistics, Literature, Medicine, Neurology, Philosophy, Physics (Atomic, General & History), Psychology, Religion, Management Sciences, Mathematics, Social Sciences, Space Sciences, Metallurgy, Engineering, Reference Works, Handbooks, Paperbacks, Juveniles, Textbooks, Illustrated Books, Atlases, Newspapers, Periodicals, Audiovisual and Educational Materials
Bookshops: Elsevier Retailers Group; Dekker en Nordemann BV, Sims; Scholtens en Zoon BV
1979: 1969 titles *Founded:* 1979 (NV Uitgeversmaatschappij Elsevier 1880)
Miscellaneous: Elsevier-NDU nv is holding company which was formed in 1979 by a merger of NV Uitgeversmaatschappij Elsevier and Nederlandse Dagbladunie NV. BV Uitgeversmaatschappij, Elsevier Nederlandse Dagbladunie BV, Elsevier-NDU Grafische Groep BV, Elsblad BV, Elsevier Detailhandel BV, Elsevier Science Publishers BV and American Elsevier Publishers Inc are subholdings

BV Uitgeversmaatschappij **Elsevier Boekerij**, Riverstaete, Amsteldijk 166, Postbus 70707, Amsterdam Tel: (020) 5412333 Cable Add: Elsbook Telex: 14481
Publishers: Tj Dijkstra, Wim Hazeu, T G Verweij; *Man Dirs:* J C de Graaff, C van der Sluys; *Sales:* H Betzema
Parent Company: Elsevier-NDU nv (qv)
Imprints: Zuid-Hollandsche UM, De Boekerij, Manteau, Van Goor Jeugdboeken
Subjects: Fiction (adult and children's)

Elsevier/North Holland Biomedical Press, PO Box 1527 Amsterdam Tel: (515) 9222 Cable Add: Elspubco Telex: 16479
Publisher: Dr J Hillier; *Production:* H Ostendorf; *Publicity:* D Sar
Orders to: PO Box 211, Amsterdam
Parent Company: Elsevier-NDU nv (qv)
Subjects: Life Sciences, Medicine
1978: 80 titles *1979:* 90 titles *Founded:* 1974
ISBN Publisher's Prefix: 0-444, 0-7204

NETHERLANDS 259

Elsevier's Wetenschappelijke Uitgeverij (Elsevier Scientific Publishing Co) BV, Jan van Galenstr 335, Postbus 330, 1000 AH Amsterdam Tel: (020) 5159222 Telex: 16479 epc nl
Dir: Dr V M Atkins
Parent Company: Elsevier-NDU nv (qv)
Subjects: Social Science, Technology, Chemistry, Earth Sciences, Agricultural Sciences, Multilingual Dictionaries
1978: 85 titles *1979:* 86 titles

Enschede en Zonen Grafische Inrichting BV, Klokhuisplein 5, Postbus 114, 2000 AC Haarlem Tel: (023) 319240 Telex: 41049

Eska*, Lijnmarkt 41-43, Utrecht Tel: (030) 328411 Telex: 47188
Publisher: Cees Smaling
Subjects: Periodicals, Hobbies
Miscellaneous: Firm is a member of the Kluwer Group (qv)

Europese Bibliotheek Uitgeverij Boekhandel Antiquariaat*, Gasthuisstr 12, Zaltbommel Tel: (04180) 3144
Man Dir: J C Lissenberg; *Assistant Dir:* M Uijthaven
Orders to: Korte Steigerstr 12-14, Zaltbommel
Subjects: History, Topography
Bookshop: Europese Bibliotheek, Gasthuisstr 12, Zaltbommel
Founded: 1963
ISBN Publisher's Prefix: 90-288

Uitgeverij **F E D** BV, part of the Kluwer Group (qv)

Facsimile Uitgaven Nederland BV (FUN), subsidiary of Theatrum Orbis Terrarum (qv)

NV **Falkplan/CIB***, Zichtenburglaan 52, Postbus 43107, 2504 AC The Hague Tel: (070) 299180 Cable Add: falkplan den haag Telex: 33290
Publisher: Edmond Gerrit Niessen; *Sales Manager:* Aad Kistemaker; *Editorial:* Martinus de Smit
Subsidiary Company: Djambatan BV (qv)
Subject: Maps

Frank **Fehmers** Productions, Herengracht 487, Amsterdam Tel: (020) 238766 Cable Add: Intpubcon Telex: 16740 fepro nl
Man Dir: Frank Fehmers; *Rights & Permissions:* Nancy Patricia Lund
Associate Companies: FFP Licensing North America, FFV Licensing Latin America, Frank Fehmer Productions Inc
Subjects: Juveniles, Television, Merchandising, Licensing, International Book and Film Co-productions
1978: 25 titles *1979:* 80 titles
ISBN Publisher's Prefix: 90-6151

Fibula van Dishoek, see Unieboek NV

Focus Elsevier BV*, Rivierstaete, Amsteldijk 166, Amsterdam, Postbus 70707 Tel: (020) 5413413 Cable Add: Elsbook Telex: 14481
Man Dir: J Schilt
Parent Company: Elsevier-NDU nv (qv)

Uitgeverij De **Fontein** BV, Parkstr 47, Postbus 308, 3740 AH Baarn Tel: (02154) 18441 Telex: beka-43272
Man Dir: H Pijfers
Subjects: General Fiction & Nonfiction, Juveniles, High-priced Paperbacks
Founded: 1946
Miscellaneous: Firm is a member of the Combo Group, Netherlands (qv)
ISBN Publisher's Prefix: 90-261

Fontes Pers (APA), Postbus 1850, NL-1000 BW Amsterdam
Parent Company: APA (Academic Publishers Associated) (qv)
Subjects: Maritime History, History of Law
ISBN Publisher's Prefix: 90-302; 90-6039

Foris Publications*, Postbus 509, 3300 AM Dordrecht (Located at: Nijverheidsweg 65, HI Ambacht) Tel: (01858) 2622 Cable Add: Intergraph Dordrecht Telex: 29337 icg nl
Man Dir: Henk J La Porte; *Sales:* Mrs E C Ijsselsijn-Oosterling
Parent Company: Intercontinental Graphics Holland BV
Subsidiary Companies: Interset Holland, ICG Printing BV
1978: 2 titles *1979:* 10 titles *Founded:* 1978
ISBN Publisher's Prefix: 90-701

W **Gaade** BV, Postbus 10, 3958 ZT Amerongen Tel: (03434) 1044
Man Dir: Marinus Beck
Subjects: Art, Biology, Cultural History, General Science, Nature, Illustrated books, Co-productions
1978: 15 titles *Founded:* 1954
ISBN Publisher's Prefix: 90-6017

Van **Gennep** Ltd, Nes 128, Amsterdam C Tel: (020) 247033
Man Dirs: R O van Gennep, J H Jansen; *Foreign Rights:* Ms Annelies de Korver
Bookshops: Van Gennep Nieuwezijds, Nieuwe Zijds Voorburgwal 330, Amsterdam C; Boekhandel Van Gennep, Nes 128, Amsterdam C; Boekhandel Van Gennep, Grimburgwal 1-5, Amsterdam C; Boekhandel Van Gennep, Oude Binnenweg 131b, Rotterdam
Subjects: Belles Lettres, Poetry, History, Philosophy, Political Science, Economics, Marxist Publications, Architecture
1978: 35 titles *Founded:* 1969
ISBN Publisher's Prefix: 90-6012

BV Uitgeversbedryf Het **Goede Boek**, Koningin Wilhelminastr 8, Postbus 122, 1270 AC Huizen Tel: (02152) 53508
Dir: W E J Rikmans; *Advertising Dir:* F Rikmans
Subject: Children's Books
1978: 29 titles *1979:* 31 titles *Founded:* 1932
ISBN Publisher's Prefix: 90-240

de **Gooise**, see Unieboek NV

van **Goor Jeugdboeken**, an imprint of BV Uitgeversmaatschappij Elsevier Boekerij (qv)

Van **Gorcum** BV, Industrieweg 38, 9403 AB Assen Tel: (05920) 15647 Cable Add: Vangorcum Telex: 77101
Man Dirs: H M G Prakke, G Vlieghuis; *Dirs:* J W Meijer (General & Academic Books), K W J van Rossum (Dekker & Van de Vegt, Nijmegen); *Sales:* A W J Rousseau; *Rights & Permissions:* D Bakkes
Orders to: Van Gorcum, PO Box 43, 9400 Assen AA
Subsidiary Company: Dekker en Van de Vegt (qv)
Subjects: Social Science, Anthropology, Medicine, History, Language & Literature, Law, Philosophy, Psychology, Economics, Religion, Geography, Education, University Textbooks, Educational Materials
1978: 100 titles *Founded:* 1800
ISBN Publisher's Prefixes: 90-232 (Van Gorcum BV), 90-255 (Dekker en Van de Vegt)

J H **Gottmer Publishers**, Postbus 555, Haarlem, NL-1542 (Located at: Prof van Vlotenweg la, Bloemendaal) Tel: (023) 257150 Telex: 41856
Dir: Mrs H V M Gottmer; *Editorial:* J F Schoolenaar; *Publicity:* M P Gottmer
Subjects: General Fiction, Religion, Juveniles, Educational, General Nonfiction
Founded: 1937
ISBN Publisher's Prefix: 90-257

BV v/hB **Gottmer's** Uitgeversbedrijf, Sint Annastraat 167, Postbus 103, 6500 AC Nijmegen Tel: (080) 231098
Man Dir: B Gottmer

Subjects: Religion, Humour, Cartoons, Scientific Works, Mysticism
1979: 18 titles *Founded:* 1950
ISBN Publisher's Prefix: 90-6075

S **Gouda** Quint, Postbus 1148, 6801 MK Arnhem (Located at: Willemsplein 2, Arnhem) Tel: (085) 454762
Man Dir: K H Mulder
Parent Company: Kluwer Group (qv)
Subjects: Textbooks, Law, Taxation, Periodicals
1978: 15 titles *1979:* 20 titles *Founded:* 1739
ISBN Publisher's Prefix: 90-6000

De **Graaf** Publishers, Zuideinde 40, Postbus 6, NL-2420 AA Nieuwkoop Tel: (01725) 1461 Cable Add: Degraaf Nieuwkoop
Man Dir: Bob de Graaf
Subsidiary Company: Miland Publishers (qv)
Subjects: Reference, Religion, University Textbooks
1978: 350 titles *Founded:* 1959
ISBN Publisher's Prefix: 90-6004

B R **Grüner** BV, Nieuwe Herengracht 31, 1011 RM Amsterdam Tel: (020) 264371 Cable Add: Veriditas
Publisher: Bruno Roland Grüner
Subjects: Philosophy, Religion, Social Science, Periodicals, Poetry, Politics, Classical history
1978: 18 titles

de **Haan**, see Unieboek NV

Ten **Hagen** BV*, Carnegiepl 5, Postbus 34, The Hague Tel: (070) 924311
Subjects: Fiction, Periodicals
Miscellaneous: Firm is a member of the Kluwer Group, Netherlands (qv)

De **Harmonie**, Postbus 3547, 1001 AH Amsterdam (Located at: Singel 390, Amsterdam) Tel: (20) 245181
Man Dir: Jaco Groot; *Rights & Permissions:* Dieneke Corvers
Associate Company: Gaberbocchus Press
Subjects: Modern Dutch and International Literature, Illustrated Books, Juveniles, Humour
1978: 15 titles *1979:* 15 titles *Founded:* 1972
ISBN Publisher's Prefix: 90-6169

Uitgeverij ten **Have** NV*, Bremstr 11, Postbus 1, Baarn Tel: (02154) 18241 Telex: beka-43272
Man Dir: Ton van der Worp
Subjects: History, Religion, Paperbacks, Maps
Founded: 1831
Miscellaneous: Firm is a member of the Combo Group, Netherlands (qv)
ISBN Publisher's Prefix: 90-259

Helmond*, Churchil-laan 107, Postbus 23, Helmond Tel: (04920) 39802 Telex: 51337
Man Dir: Dr M H J Hendriks Jr
Subjects: How-to, Juveniles, Low- & High-priced Paperbacks, Primary Textbooks, Reference
1978: 200 titles *Founded:* 1913
ISBN Publisher's Prefix: 90-252

Alexander **Herzen** Foundation*, 268 Amstel, Amsterdam Tel: (020) 225343
Subject: Russian Fiction & Nonfiction
Founded: 1969

Uitgeverij **Heuff**, Postbus 40, 2420 AA Nieuwkoop (Located at: Bachstr 24, 2421 TS Nieuwkoop) Tel: (01725) 1649 Cable Add: Heuff/Nieuwkoop
Man Dir: H Heuff
Subjects: Music, Art, History, Illustrated Books, Juveniles, Fiction
1979: 16 titles *1980:* 28 titles *Founded:* 1970
ISBN Publisher's Prefix: 90-6141

260 NETHERLANDS

Uitgeverij **Heureka**, Postbus 5347, 1380 GH Weesp (Located at: Hoogstr 20, 1381 VS Weesp) Tel: (02940) 17912
Man Dir: F H B Cladder
Subjects: History (Political, Social & Cultural)
1978: 6 titles *Founded:* 1976
ISBN Publisher's Prefix: 90-6262

Gérard Th van **Heusden** (APA), Postbus 1850, NL-1000 BW Amsterdam
Parent Company: APA (Academic Publishers Associated) (qv)
Subjects: Bibliography, Typography, History of Printing
ISBN Publisher's Prefix: 90-6024

Hippoboek/Studio de Zuid, see Zuidgroep BV

G W **Hissink** & Co (APA), Postbus 1850, NL-1000 BW Amsterdam
Parent Company: APA (Academic Publishers Associated) (qv)
Subjects: History of the Fine and Graphic Arts
ISBN Publisher's Prefix: 90-6025

Van **Holkema** en Warendorf, see Unieboek NV

Holland, Spaarne 110, 2011 CM Haarlem Tel: (023) 323061
Man Dir: Rolf van Ulzen; *Sales Dir:* Mike de Wijs; *Permissions:* Rolf van Ulzen
Subjects: General Fiction, Belles Lettres, Poetry, Reference, Religion, Juveniles, High-priced Paperbacks, General Science
Founded: 1922
ISBN Publisher's Prefix: 90-251

Holland University Press BV (APA), Postbus 1850, NL-1000 BW Amsterdam
Parent Company: APA (Academic Publishers Associated) (qv)
Subjects: Academic Books on the Humanities, European Studies
ISBN Publisher's Prefix: 90-302

Hollandia BV, Beukenlaan 16-20, Postbus 70, 3741 BP Baarn Tel: (02154) 18941 Cable Add: Hollandia, Baarn Telex: 43776 incom attn Hollandia
Man Dir: J Muntinga
Subjects: General (by Dutch and translated foreign authors), Nautical, Water Sports, Gymnastics, Popular Medical, Gardening, Children's Books
1978: 68 titles *Founded:* 1899
Book Club: (part-owner) Nederlandse Lezerskring
ISBN Publisher's Prefix: 90-6045

NV **I C U** (Informatie en Communicatie Unie NV), Burg Van Royensingel 19, Postbus 1115, Zwolle Tel: (05200) 15910
Miscellaneous: Members of the ICU Group: Samsom Uitgeverij BV (qv), Sijthoff en Noorhoff International Publishers Co BV (qv), A W Sijthoff's Uitg Mij BV (qv), Staflen's Wetenschappelijke Uitgeverij (qv), H D Tjeenk Willink BV (qv), Wolters Noordhoff BV (qv) (all Netherlands); Croner Publications Ltd, UK (qv); Aspen Systems Corporation, USA
ISBN Publisher's Prefixes: 90-14 (Samsom), 90-6092 (Tjeenk Willink), 90-01 (Wolters Noordhoff)

Stichting **I V I O***, Maerlanthuis, Maerlant 2, Postbus 37, 8200 AA Lelystad Tel: (03200) 26514
Subject: Educational
1978: 10 titles

Icob cv Uitgeverij, Postbus 392, 2400 AJ Alphen aan den Rijn (Located at: Ondernemingsweg 60, Alphen aan den Rijn) Tel: (01720) 23202 Telex: 39700 icob nl
Man Dir: Hans Meijer; *Editorial:* Peter Albarda
Subjects: Art, Natural History, Reference, Illustrated
1978: 25 titles *1979:* 27 titles *Founded:* 1969
ISBN Publisher's Prefix: 90-6113

Ideeboek BV, Koningslaan 19, 1075 AA Amsterdam
Parent Company: Meijer Pers BV (qv)

Uitgeverij **In den Toren***, Bremstr 11, Postbus 1, Baarn Tel: (02154) 8241 Telex: 43272
Man Dir: Aize de Visser
Subjects: History, Social Sciences, Politics
Miscellaneous: Firm is a member of the Combo Group (qv)

Inter-European Editions, De Lairessestr 90, 1071 PJ Amsterdam Tel: 764044/45 Cable Add: Adiwes Amsterdam Telex: 1406 wssnl
Operations: Jan Fleere; *Marketing:* Frans Gianotten
Parent Company: Addison-Wesley BV (qv)
Subsidiary Company: Inter-Editions, France (qv)
Subjects: General Science, University Textbooks, General Reading
ISBN Publisher's Prefix: 0-201

B M **Israel** BV, NZ Voorburgwal 264, 1012 RS Amsterdam Tel: 247040 Cable Add: Isrealbook
Subjects: Reference, History of Medicine, Sciences, Arts

Nico **Israel***, Keizersgracht 526, 1017 EK Amsterdam Tel: (020) 222255 Cable Add: Ennibook Telex: 14070 ashni nl
Man Dir: Nico Israel
Associate Companies: A Asher en Co BV (qv), Theatrum Orbis Terrarum (qv)
Subjects: History, Reference, University Textbooks, Geography, Cartography, Bibliography, Travel, Periodicals
Founded: 1950
ISBN Publisher's Prefix: 90-6072

Stichting De **Jonge** Onderzoekers, see Stichting DJO

Dr W **Junk** BV, Publishers, Lange Voorhout 9, Postbus 13713, 2501 ES-The Hague Tel: (070) 463256
Publisher: Wil R Peters
Subjects: Biology, Ophthalmology
1978: 40 titles *Founded:* 1899
Miscellaneous: Firm is a member of the Kluwer Group (qv)
ISBN Publisher's Prefix: 90-6193

K B S, see Katholieke Bijbelstichting

Uitgeverij Van **Kampen** BV*, Nassaulaan 10, Postbus 4, Baarn Tel: (02154) 13480/16646 Cable Add: Stanu nl Telex: 43580
Parent Company: Standaard Uitgeverij en Distributie BV (qv)

PN Van **Kampen** & **Zoon** BV, Nieuwe 's-Gravelandseweg 17, Postbus 17, 1400 AA Bussum Tel: (02159) 34241 Telex: 43064 Unieboek
Subjects: Belles Lettres, How-to, Art, History, Literature, Popular Science, Fiction, Architecture, Maps, Games, Sports
Founded: 1841

Katholieke Bijbelstichting, Baroniestraat 43, PB 27, 5280 AA Boxtel Tel: 04116 73537
Subjects: Religious literature on practical aspects of Catholic Bible work in Belgium and the Netherlands
1978: 15 titles *1979:* 16 titles

Uitgeverij **Kluitman** Alkmaar BV*, Postbus 123, 1800 AC Alkmaar (Located at: Kelvinstraat 20, Heerhugowaard) Tel: (02207) 17326
Dirs: P Kluitman, W Gerla
Subject: Juveniles
Founded: 1864
ISBN Publisher's Prefix: 90-206

Kluwer Algemene Boeken BV, Postbus 235, 6710 BE Ede (Located at: Kernhemseweg 7, Ede) Tel: (08380) 19031 Cable Add: Zkede Telex: 45836 Zkede
Man Dir, Permissions: Hans Mons; *Deputy Dir:* Floris Eijffinger; *Editorial:* Martin van Huijstee, Benno von Lochem, Rien Meyer, Piet Terlouw
Subjects: How-to, General Science, Atlases, Domestic, Countryside, Needlework, Novels, Human Relations, Religion
Founded: 1970
Miscellaneous: Firm is a member of the Kluwer Group (qv)
ISBN Publisher's Prefix: 90-6117

Kluwer Fiscale en Juridische Boeken en Tijdschriften, Staverenstr 15, Postbus 23, 7400 GA Deventer Tel: (05700) 91911 Telex: 49295
Man Dir: J H Brouwer; *Sales, Publicity:* M Nieuwenhuis; *Production:* G J Hupse
Subsidiary Companies: Alfred Metzner, Kommentator Verlag — both in Federal Republic of Germany
Branch Offs: Antwerp, Belgium; Boston, USA
Subjects: Law, Taxation, Labour Law and Industrial Relations, Social Security; Periodicals
Bookshops: 10 associated bookshops
1979: 200 titles
Miscellaneous: Firm is a member of the Kluwer Group (qv)
ISBN Publisher's Prefixes: 90-268, 90-200, 90-312

Kluwer Group, Postbus 23, 7400 GA Deventer (Located at: Stromarkt 8, Deventer) Tel: (05700) 91911 Telex: 49660
Man Dirs: B Zevenbergen, J J C Alberdingk, A M W Resius, J Somerwil
Members of the Kluwer Group in the Netherlands: Publishing Houses: Bert Bakker (qv); Bohn, Scheltema & Holkema (qv); Uitgeversmij Born (qv); Born Periodieken; van Dale Projektontwikkeling; Educaboek (qv); Educa International; Eska Tijdschriften (qv); S Gouda Quint (qv); Ten Hagen (qv); ID Tijdschriften; Dr W Junk (qv); Kluwer Algemene Boeken (qv); Kluwers Couranten Bedrijf (qv); Kluwer Fiscaal en Juridische Boeken (qv); Kluwer Publiekstijdschriften; Kluwer Sociaal-Wetenschappelijke Boeken (qv); Kluwer Technische Boeken (qv); Kluwer Technische Tijdschriften (qv); Kluwerpers; Kosmos (qv); Libresso; Van Loghum Slaterus (qv); Luitingh (qv); Nederlandse Bouw-Dokumentatie; Novapres; Martinus Nijhoff (qv); Noorduijn (qv); Oosthoek (qv); Reidel Publishing (qv); Scheltens & Giltay; Schoolpers (qv); Skarabee; van Soeren; Stam/Robijns (qv); Stam Technische Boeken (qv); Stam Tijdschriften (qv); Stenfert Kroese; Tjeenk Willink/Noorduijn (qv); W E J Tjeenk Willink (qv); L J Veen (qv); Zomer & Keuning Boeken (qv); Z & K Tijdschriften
Members outside the Netherlands: Eskabel; Heideland-Orbis; Uitgeverij Kluwer (qv) (all in Belgium); Educalivre (France); Hulton Educational Publications (qv); Kluwer Publishing Ltd (qv); Van Leer; MTP Press (qv); Stanley Thornes/Stam Press (qv) (all in UK); Information und Kontakt Kluwer Seminar; Kommentator (qv); Metzner (qv); Verlag Schubert; Verlag H Stam; Thalhammer Verlags GmbH (all in Federal Republic of Germany); Delta, Spès SA, Switzerland (qqv); Kluwer Boston Inc; Nijhoff Boston (both in USA)
Affiliate Company: Succes (qv)
Subjects: Law and Taxation, Academic Publications in various fields, Educational, Technical, Encyclopaedias, Trade Books and

Magazines, Graphic Industries, Newspapers and Periodicals
Bookshops: Broese Kemink, Utrecht; Dekker Van de Vegt, Nijmegen; De Gelderse Boekhandel, Arnhem; Boekhandel Gianotten, Tilburg — Breda; International Journals Group, Amsterdam; Praamstra, Deventer; Scheltema Holkema Vermeulen, Amsterdam — Haarlem; Stamboekhandel, Eindhoven — Venlo; Studieboekencentrale, Ede/Zoetermeer Verwijs & Stam, The Hague; Wetenschappelijke Boekhandel Rotterdam, Rotterdam
Founded: 1889
ISBN Publisher's Prefixes: 90-6117 (Kluwer NV), 90-313 (Bohn, Scheltema & Holkema), 90-283 (Born), 90-11 (Educaboek), 90-267 (Kluwer Soc-Wet), 90-201 (Kluwer Tec), 90-6001 (Van Loghum Slaterus), 90-245 (Luitingh), 90-247 (Martinus Nijhoff), 90-6318 (Novapres), 90-207 (Stenfert-Kroese), 90-6117 (Kluwer Algemene Boeken), 90-200 (Kluwer Fiscale en Juridische Boeken), 90-6019 (Bert Bakker), 90-254 (Uitgeverij Contact),90-6071 (Skarabee), 90-204 (Veen), 90-210 (Zomer & Keuning)

Kluwer Sociaal-Wetenschappelijke Boeken en Tijdschriften, Postbus 23, 7400 GA Deventer Tel: (05700) 20577 Telex: 49774
Publisher: Wouter van Zeytveld
Subjects: Business, Economics, Periodicals
Miscellaneous: Firm is a member of the Kluwer Group (qv)
1978: 60 titles *1979:* 170 titles
ISBN Publisher's Prefix: 90-267

Kluwer Technische Boeken BV, Brink 25, Postbus 23, 7400 GA Deventer Tel: (05700) 91911 Telex: 49560 klutb nl
Man Dir: Noud H L van Herk; *Editorial:* Wim van Oosten-John Smal; *Foreign Rights:* Oeble Hoekstra; *Sales:* Jan Willems; *Production:* Dick Laus
Subsidiary Companies: Kluwer Technische Boeken; Santvoortbeeklaan, Deurne (both Belgium)
Subjects: Electronics, Motor Engineering, Hobbies, Do-it-yourself, Engineering, Building, Dictionaries
1979: 81 titles
Miscellaneous: Firm is a member of the Kluwer Group (qv)
ISBN Publisher's Prefix: 90-2010

Kluwers Couranten Bedrijf, Assenstr 8-14, Deventer
Dir: H J van den Beld
Miscellaneous: Firm is a member of the Kluwer Group (qv)

F **Knuf** Publishers, Postbus 720, 4116 ZJ Buren Tel: 034471691
Subjects: Musicology and Musical Theory, Biography and Musical History, Periodicals
1979: 18 titles *1980:* 22 titles

Uitgeversmaatschappij J H **Kok** BV, Gildestraat 5, 8263 AH Kampen Tel: (05202) 13545 Cable Add: Kok Kampen Telex: 42721 jh kok nl
Man Dir: W E Steunenberg; *Assistant Man Dir:* A C Van Dam; *Editorial, Rights & Permissions:* Gerrit Brinkman, Rien Ipenburg
Subsidiary Companies: J N Voorhoeve, The Hague (Religion, Educational Materials, Juveniles); Uitgeverij Omniboek, The Hague (Juveniles, Belles Lettres, General Non-fiction)
Subjects: General Fiction, Belles Lettres, Poetry, Biography, History, How-to, Art Philosophy, Religion, Textbooks, Educational Materials, Reference, Juveniles, Psychology, General & Social Science, Low- & High-priced Paperbacks
Founded: 1894
Book Club: VCL (series of novels)
ISBN Publisher's Prefix: 90-242

Kooyker Scientific Publications BV, Postbus 23096, 3016 AA Rotterdam (Located at: Koningin Emmaplein 1, Rotterdam) Tel: (010) 363009
Man Dir: W A Donker; *Sales and Publicity:* W A Donker
Subjects: Medicine, Psychology, Sociology, Education
1978: 18 titles *1979:* 20 titles *Founded:* 1975
ISBN Publisher's Prefix: 90-6212

Kosmos BV, Keizersgracht 133, 1015 CJ Amsterdam Tel: (020) 240897
Publisher: S P Bakker; *Editorial:* Willem G Benthem, P Smulders, J Vonk, M Both
Subjects: Children, Juveniles, Crafts and Hobbies, Natural History, Plants and Gardening, Dogs, Travelling, Psychology
Miscellaneous: Firm is a member of the Kluwer Group (qv)

Kugler Publications BV, PO Box 516, 1180 AM Amstelveen (Located at: Prinsengracht 573, Amsterdam) nl Tel: (3120) 278070 Telex: 18180 kukos nl
Man Dir: Simon Kugler
Subjects: Medical, Criminology

Allert de **Lange** BV, Damrak 62, 1012 LM Amsterdam Tel: (020) 246744

Uitgeverij **Lannoo**, Lichttorenhoofd 28-30, Postbus 1009, 4870 BA, Etten-Leur (N-Br) Tel: (01608) 13750 Telex: 54202 stadi NL
Parent Company: Standaard Uitgeverij en Distributie BV (qv)
Subjects: General Nonfiction covering Travel, Philosophy, Genetics, Reference, Children's, Religious
1978: 48 titles *1979:* 50 titles
ISBN Publisher's Prefix: 90-209

Leiden University Press, c/o Martinus Nijhoff, PO Box 566, Lange Voorhout 9, 2501 CN The Hague Tel: (070) 469460 Telex: 34164 Cable Add: Books Hague
Subjects: History, Languages, Law, Social Sciences, Biology, Medicine
1980: 18 titles
ISBN Publisher's Prefix: 90-6021

Lemniscaat, Vijverlaan 48, Postbus 4066, Rotterdam Tel: 141744 Cable Add: Lemniscaat Rotterdam
Man Dir: J L Boele van Hensbroek; *Editorial:* Dr Marijke Boele van Hensbroek-Ressink; *Rights & Permissions:* Els Pikaar
Subjects: Juveniles, Picture Books, Psychology, Social Science
1979: 30 titles *Founded:* 1963
ISBN Publisher's Prefix: 90-6069

Uitgeverij **Leopold** BV, Badhuisweg 232, The Hague Tel: (070) 549604
Man Dir: Liesbeth ten Houten; *Permissions:* Jacolien Kingmans
Parent Company: BV Uitgeverij Nijgh en Van Ditmar (qv)
Subjects: General Fiction, Juveniles, History, Philosophy, High-priced Paperbacks
1978: 40 titles *Founded:* 1923
ISBN Publisher's Prefix: 90-258

Littera Scripta Manet, Joppelaan 60, PO Box 20, 7213 ZG- Gorssel Tel: (05759) 1950
Man Dir: A Rutgers; *Editorial:* Mrs R L Rutgers-Schiff; *Other Offices:* A Rutgers
Subjects: General Science, Ornithology
Bookshop: International Hobby-Bookshop, Gorssel
1978: 6 titles *1979:* 6 titles *Founded:* 1947
ISBN Publisher's Prefix: 90-6036

Uitg Mij van der **Loeff** BV*, Getfertsingel 41, Postbus 28, Enschede Tel: (053) 320420
Subjects: Newspapers, Free Sheets

Van **Loghum** Slaterus, Geert Grootestr 4, Postbus 23, NL-6600 Deventer Tel: (05700) 10811 Telex: 49295
Publisher: Fons Drabbe
Subjects: Humanities, Public Health, Education, Psychology, Social Science, Linguistics, Languages, Periodicals
Miscellaneous: Firm is a member of the Kluwer Group (qv)
1978: 46 titles
ISBN Publisher's Prefix: 90-6001

Luctor Publishing — Stadler & Sauerbier BV, Weegbreestr 11, Postbus 33017, NL-3012 Rotterdam Tel: (010) 180081 Cable Add: Sensoffset Telex: 23411
Subjects: Juveniles, Educational, Calendars

Uitgeverij **Luitingh** BV, Hilversumseweg 16, 1251 EX-Laren, Noord Holland Tel: (02153) 87214/86567 Cable Add: Luitingh Laren Telex: 730 96 luiti nl
Man Dir: Peter J Houbolt
Subsidiary Companies: Uitgeverij Skarabee BV; Boek Promotions BV; Novapres BV
Subjects: General Fiction and Nonfiction, Science Fiction, Games and Pastimes, History, How-to, Reference, Religion, Juveniles, Low- & High-priced Paperbacks, General Science, Educational Materials; Sponsored Books, Homecrafts (cookery, gardening etc)
1978: 150 titles *Founded:* 1946
Miscellaneous: Firm is a member of the Kluwer Group (qv)
ISBN Publisher's Prefix: 90-245

Otto **Maier** Benelux BV*, Heliumweg 16, Amersfoort Tel: (03490) 11445 Telex: 47991
Parent Company: Otto Maier Verlag, Federal Republic of Germany (qv)
Subjects: Architecture, Hobbies, Juveniles, Nonfiction

Malmberg BV, Leeghwaterlaan 16, Postbus 233, 's-Hertogenbosch Tel: (073) 215565 Cable Add: Malmberg 's-Hertogenbosch Telex: 50058
Man Dir: Dr O O Gorter; *Publishers:* F Geurts (Primary Education), Dr M J van Dalen (Secondary Education), G Struyk (Educational Magazines)
Subjects: Pre-school, Primary & Secondary Textbooks, Educational Materials, Educational Juveniles, Teaching Equipment for Physics, Chemistry and Biology
1978: 100 titles *Founded:* 1885
Miscellaneous: Firm is a member of VNU Verenigde Nederlandse Uitgeversbedrijven BV Group (qv)
ISBN Publisher's Prefix: 90-208

Manteau, an imprint of BV Uitgeversmaatschappij Elsevier Boekerij (qv)

Meijer Pers BV, PO Box 7897, 1008-AB Amsterdam (Located at: Koningslaan 19, 1075 AA-Amsterdam) Tel: (020) 644131
Man Dir: G Michon
Parent Company: Meijer Wormerveer NV, Wormerveer
Subsidiary Company: Ideeboek BV (qv)
Subjects: Do-it-yourself Books, Cookery and Sponsored Books Generally
Book Club: Librah
1978: 45 titles *Founded:* 1966

Meinema/Waltman, Hippolytusbuurt 4, Postbus 3150, Delft Tel: (015) 125915
Subject: Textbooks

Meulenhoff Educatief BV, Postbus 100, 1000 AC Amsterdam (Located at: Herengracht 507, 1017 BV Amsterdam) Tel: (020) 235707 Cable Add: Manuscript Telex: 16234
Man Dirs: D van Foeken, Cl W Suermondt, AC van Hoek, M A Nouwen;
Editorial: T A vd Veen, W ten Oever, T Scheffer, M Sombogaart

NETHERLANDS

Parent Company: Meulenhoff en Co BV (at above address)
Associate Companies: Meulenhoff Informatief BV, Meulenhoff International BV, Meulenhoff Nederland BV (qqv)
Subjects: Educational Materials, Textbooks
1979: 106 titles
ISBN Publisher's Prefix: 90-280

Meulenhoff Informatief BV, Postbus 100, 1000 AC Amsterdam (Located at: Herengracht 507, 1017 BV Amsterdam) Tel: (020) 235707 Cable Add: Manuscript Telex: 16234
Editorial Dir: Mrs E van Unen
Parent Company: Meulenhoff en Co BV (at above address)
Associate Companies: Meulenhoff Educatief BV, Meulenhoff International BV, Meulenhoff Nederland BV (qqv)
Subjects: Informative Non-fiction, Reference
1979: 25 titles
ISBN Publisher's Prefix: 90-290

Meulenhoff International BV, Postbus 100, 1000 AC Amsterdam (Located at: Herengracht 507, 1017 BV Amsterdam) Tel: (020) 235707/241611 Cable Add: Intart Telex: 16234
Man Dir: W J van Hoorn; *Editorial Dir:* B van Dobbenburgh
Parent Company: Meulenhoff en Co BV (at above address)
Associate Companies: Meulenhoff Educatief BV, Meulenhoff Informatief BV, Meulenhoff Nederland BV (qqv)
Subjects: Coproductions, General Nonfiction, Art
Miscellaneous: Firm's main activity is selling foreign rights internationally

Meulenhoff Nederland BV, Postbus 100, 1000 AC Amsterdam (Located at: Herengracht 507, 1017 BV Amsterdam) Tel: (020) 235707 Cable Add: Manuscript Telex: 16234
Man Dir: Laurens van Krevelen; *Financial Dir:* Wim van der Wilk; *Editorial:* Wouter Donath Tieges; *Rights & Permissions:* Sarely Bourdrez
Parent Company: Meulenhoff en Co BV (at above address)
Associate Companies: Meulenhoff Educatief BV, Meulenhoff International BV, Meulenhoff Informatief BV (qqv), Meulenhoff/Landshoff
Subjects: Dutch and translated foreign literature, Science Fiction, Detective Stories, Nonfiction
1979: 100 titles *Founded:* 1895
ISBN Publisher's Prefix: 90-290

Miland Publishers, Zuideinde 40, Postbus 6, NL-2420 AA Nieuwkoop
Parent Company: De Graaf Publishers (qv)
ISBN Publisher's Prefix: 90-6003

Mirananda Publishers BV, Zijdeweg 5A, Wassenaar 2270 Tel: (01751) 78471
Man Dir: Carolus Vehulst;
General Manager: Manda Plettenburg
Orders to: Centraal Boekhuis, Erasmusweg 10, Culemborg
Subjects: Art (Western and Oriental), Religion, Mysticism, Yoga, Theosophy, Astrology, Popular Science, Psychology, Philosophy, Quality Paperbacks, Linguistics, Education, Literature, Outstanding Children's Books
1978: 22 titles *1979:* 20 titles *Founded:* 1976
ISBN Publisher's Prefix: 90-6271

Moussault's Uitgeverij BV, Nieuwe 's-Gravelandseweg 17, Postbus 17, 1400 AA Bussum Tel: (02159) 34241 Cable Add: Stanu NL Telex: 43064 Unieboek
Dir/Editorial/Permissions: I Gay;
Production: G Priem
Parent Company: Standaard Uitgeverij en Distributie BV (qv)
Orders to: Standaard Uitgeverij en Distributie bv, Postbus 1009, 4870 BA-Etten-Leur
Subjects: Primary Textbooks, Horticulture, Hobbies, Illustrated Nature Guides, Antiques and Collecting
1979: 115 titles *Founded:* 1941
ISBN Publisher's Prefix: 90-226

Mouton Publishers*, Noordeinde 41, 2514 GC The Hague Tel: (070) 649910/11/12/13 Telex: 33630 mopub nl
Man Dir: A Bornkamp
Parent Company: (since 1977) Walter de Gruyter und Co, Federal Republic of Germany (qv)
Branch Offs: Editions Mouton & Cie, 7 rue Dupuytren, F-75006 Paris, France; Mouton Publishers, Walter de Gruyter Inc, 200 Saw Mill River Rd, Hawthorne, NY 10532, USA
Subjects: Anthropology, Art, Economics, Education, Geography, History, Law, Linguistics, Belles Lettres, Mathematics, Philosophy, Psychology, Religion, Social Science
Founded: 1954
ISBN Publisher's Prefix: 90-279

De Muiderkring BV, Nijverheidswerf 17-21, Postfach 10, NL 1400 AA Bussum Tel: 02159-31851 Telex: 15171
Man Dir: R Bayards; *Sales Dept:* P Oosterlaak
Subjects: Specialist Literature connected with Electronics, Hobbies

Mulder en Co, subsidiary of Bigot & Van Rossum NV (qv)

Mulder Holland BV, Transformatorweg 35, Postbus 8064, Amsterdam Tel: (020) 824805 Cable Add: Emzet Amsterdam Telex: 14627
Subject: Juveniles
1980: 58 titles

J Muusses BV*, Kerkstr 20-33, Postbus 13, 1440 AA Purmerend Tel: (02990) 23746
Man Dir: D Struving
Subjects: History, Education, Music, How-to, General Science, Textbooks
1978: 18 titles *Founded:* 1873
ISBN Publisher's Prefix: 90-231

Uitgeverij **N I B**, Postbus 144, 3700 AC Zeist (Located at: Wilhelminalaan 7, Zeist) Tel: (03404) 21624
Man Dir: Dr H C van Hummel; *Editorial:* A J W Boks
Bookseller: Netherlands Importing Booksellers, PO Box 144, 3700 AC Zeist
Subjects: Textbooks for Secondary Education on: Chemistry, Biology, Modern Languages, History
1978: 25 titles *1979:* 26 titles
ISBN Publisher's Prefix: 0075-4

Nederland's Boekhuis BV, Erasmusweg 10, Culemborg Tel: (03450) 4841
Subjects: General Fiction, Belles Lettres, Religion, Juveniles
Founded: 1919
ISBN Publisher's Prefix: 90-6070

Nederlandsche Zondagsschool Vereeniging, Bloemgracht 65, NL-1016 KG Amsterdam Tel: (020) 239121
Subjects: Religion, Juveniles
1978: 24 titles

Nederlandse Lezerskring Boek en Plaat BV*, Postbus 2201, 1000 EK Amsterdam (Located at: Wildenborch 2, 1112 XB Diemen) Tel: (020) 906911 Telex: 16188

Uitgeverij **H Nelissen** BV, Duinlustweg 36, 2051 AB Overveen Tel: (023) 245481
Man Dir, Editorial, Permissions: R M M Nelissen; *Sales, Publicity:* Dick Boer;
Production: Net Ekering
Subjects: General Fiction, Religion, Sociology, Politics, Education, Philosophy, High-priced Paperbacks
1978: 14 titles *1979:* 20 titles *Founded:* 1922
ISBN Publisher's Prefix: 90-244

Nieuwe Wieken, an imprint of Omega Boek BV (qv)

BV Uitgeverij **Nijgh en Van Ditmar***, Badhuisweg 232, 2597 JS The Hague Tel: (070) 512711
Man Dir: A J J Siebelink; *Editorial:* N D Dekker, A E Blatter, J D M Mulder, Miss J Waereabeek; *Permissions:* Miss J Waereabeek
Subsidiary Companies: Uigeverij Leopold BV, Rotterdam University Press (qqv)
Subjects: General Fiction, Belles Lettres, Poetry, Biography, History, Juveniles, High-priced Paperbacks, Engineering, Secondary Textbooks, Home Economics
Founded: 1837
ISBN Publisher's Prefix: 90-236

Martinus **Nijhoff** Publishers*, Postbus 566, 2501 CN The Hague (Located at: Lange Voorhout 9-11, The Hague) Tel: (070) 469460 Cable Add: Books Hague
Dir: F H van Eysinga; *Production:* Mrs S Oostenrijk
Subjects: Biography, History, Music, Art, Philosophy, Religion, Textbooks, Reference, Psychology, Social Science, Medicine, Applied Sciences, Veterinary Sciences, Agriculture
Bookshop: Postbus 269, The Hague
Founded: 1853
Miscellaneous: Firm is a member of the Kluwer Group (qv)
ISBN Publisher's Prefix: 90-247

BV **Noord-Hollandsche Uitgeversmaatschappij** (North Holland Publishing Company), Jan van Galenstraat 335, Postbus 103, 1000 AC Amsterdam Tel: (020) 5159222 Cable Add: nohum amsterdam Telex: 16479 epc nl
Dir: Drs W H Wimmers; *Deputy Dir:* Dr E H Fredriksson
Parent Company: Elsevier-NDU nv (qv)
Subjects: Mathematics, Mechanics, Information Processing, Telecommunications, Management Science & Operations, Research, Physics, Chemical Physics, Economics, Accountancy, Law, Linguistics, History, Humanities, Psychology
1979: 121 titles

Noordhoff International Publishing, see Sijthoff en Noordhoff

Noorduijn BV, Postbus 1148, 6801 MK Arnhem (Located at: Willemsplein 2, Arnhem) Tel: (085) 454762
Man Dir: K H Mulder
Parent Company: Firm is a member of the Kluwer Group (qv)
Subjects: Law and Taxation
1978: 3 titles *1979:* 4 titles *Founded:* 1819
ISBN Publisher's Prefix: 90-203

Oisterwijk, an imprint of Omega Boek BV (qv)

Omega Boek BV, Postbus 20072, 1000 HB Amsterdam (Located at: Sarphatistraat 13, 1017 WS Amsterdam) Tel: (020) 231969/245284
Orders to: Centraal Depot Culemborg
Imprints: De Centaur, Nieuwe Wieken, Triton Pers, Omega Jeugdboekerij, Oisterwijk
Subjects: General Fiction and Nonfiction, War Stories, Thrillers, Art, Children's Books, Gift Books
1978: 60 titles *Founded:* 1968
ISBN Publisher's Prefixes: 90-6057, 90-6142, 90-70015

NETHERLANDS 263

Uitgeverij **Omniboek**, subsidiary of Uitgeversmaatschappij J H Kok BV (qv)

Oosthoek*, Domstraat 5-13, Utrecht Tel: (030) 334464
Man Dirs: H Smit, K Booden
Subject: Encyclopedia Publishers
Miscellaneous: Firm is a member of the Kluwer Group (qv)
ISBN Publisher's Prefix: 90-6046

Orbit NV, Keisersgracht 526, Amsterdam, subsidiary of Theatrum Orbis Terrarum (qv)

Oriental Press BV (APA), Postbus 1850, NL-1000 BW Amsterdam
Parent Company: APA (Academic Publishers Associated) (qv)
Subjects: Oriental Studies, Text editions
ISBN Publisher's Prefix: 90-6023

Overseas Publishers Association Amsterdam BV, Postbus 19178, 100 GD Amsterdam (Located at: Rokin 84, 1012 KX Amsterdam
Man Dir: W C Stevens
Parent Company: Overseas Publishers Association Antilles NV
Associate Company: Central Data Services Ltd
Subjects: Scientific, Trade (also Licenses and Packages)
Founded: 1978

Philo Press-van Heusden-Hissink & Co CV (APA), Postbus 1850, NL-1000 BW Amsterdam
Parent Company: APA (Academic Publishers Associated) (qv)
Subjects: Academic Books on the Arts and Humanities, History of Sciences, Oriental Studies
ISBN Publisher's Prefixes: 90-6022, 90-6024, 90-6025

Uitgeverij **Ploegsma**, Postbus 19857, 1000 GW Amsterdam (Located at: Keizersgracht 616, 1017 ER Amsterdam) Tel: (020) 262907
Man Dir: Paul Brinkman
Subjects: Children's books, Juveniles, How-to, Natural Science, Handicraft, Leisure
ISBN Publisher's Prefix: 90-216

Polak en Van Gennep Uitg Mij BV*, Keizersgracht 608, 1017 EP-Amsterdam Tel: (020) 226288
Man Dir: B M Hosman
Subjects: Scientific Literature, General Literature
1978: 235 titles *Founded:* 1964
ISBN Publisher's Prefix: 90-253

Pudoc, Centre for Agricultural Publishing and Documentation, Marijkeweg 17, Postbus 4, 6700 AA Wageningen Tel: (08370) 19146 Telex: 45015
Man Dir: A Rutgers; *Sales Dir:* J Vermeulen
Subjects: Natural Science, Agriculture
1978: 30 titles *1979:* 30 titles *Founded:* 1957
ISBN Publisher's Prefix: 90-220

Putsj Publications Antwerpen*, 86 Alice Hahonlei, NL-2120 Shoten Tel: (031) 589272 Telex: 32432
Subjects: Original-style colouring and reading books for infants (3-7 yrs)

Em **Querido's** Uitgeverij BV, Singel 262, 1016 AC Amsterdam Tel: (020) 237195
Man Dir: Ary T Langbroek
Associate Companies: Uitgeverij De Arbeiderspers BV, Wetenschappelijke Uitgeverij BV (qqv)
Imprint: Salamander Paperbacks
Subjects: General Fiction, Belles Lettres, Poetry, Biography, History, Music, Art, Juveniles, Low-priced Paperbacks
1978: 124 titles *Founded:* 1915
ISBN Publisher's Prefix: 90-214

van **Reemst**, see Unieboek NV

D **Reidel** Publishing Co, Postbus 17, Dordrecht (Located at: Voorstraat 479-483, Dordrecht) Tel: (078) 135388 Cable Add: Reipubco Telex: 29245
Publisher: B Vance; *Sales and Promotion Manager:* J F Hattink; *Production:* R Doornebal; *Permissions:* J F Hattink
Parent Company: Kluwer Group (qv)
Subsidiary Companies: D Reidel, 160 Old Derby St, Hingham, Mass 02034, USA
Subjects: Philosophy, Humanities, Linguistics, Mathematics, Astronomy, Chemistry, Environmental Sciences, Earth Sciences, Periodicals
1979: 80 titles *1980:* 95 titles
ISBN Publisher's Prefix: 90-277

Rekreaboek, an imprint of Zuidgroep BV (qv)

Peter de **Ridder** Press BV*, Postbus 168, 2160 AD-Lisse (Located at: 8 Johan Vermeerstr, 2162 BJ Lisse) Tel: 15239
Dir: Peter de Ridder
Subjects: Semiotics, Linguistics, Literary Theory, Anthropology
1978: 32 titles *Founded:* 1974
ISBN Publisher's Prefix: 90-316

Editions **Rodopi** NV, Keizersgracht 302-304, Amsterdam Tel: (020) 227507
Dir: Fred van der Zee
Subjects: History, Philosophy, Religion, University Textbooks, Languages and Literature, Classical Antiquity, Communications
Founded: 1966
ISBN Publisher's Prefix: 90-6203

Romen, see Unieboek NV

Rotterdam University Press, Badhuisweg 232, 2597 JS The Hague Tel: (070) 512711
Man Dir: J Dijkema
Parent Company: BV Uitgeverij Nijgh en Van Ditmar (qv)
Subjects: Economics, Development Planning, Social Science, University Textbooks
Founded: 1964
ISBN Publisher's Prefix: 0-90237

Uitgeverij **S M D** BV (Spruyt, Van Mantgem en De Does), Postbus 63, 2300 AB Leiden (Located at: Langebrug 87, 2311 TJ Leiden) Tel: (071) 146541
Subjects: Medical, Educational, Technical
1978: 36 titles *1979:* 29 titles

S U N socialistische Uitgeverij Nijmegen, Bijleveldsingel 9, 6521 AM Nijmegen Tel: (080) 221700
Publicity, Permissions: Wilfried Uitterhoere
Subjects: Marxism, Culture, Philosophy, History of the Workers' Movements, Architecture, Periodicals
1978: 25 titles *Founded:* 1969
ISBN Publisher's Prefix: 90-6168

Salamander Paperbacks, an imprint of Em Querido's Uitgeverij BV (qv)

Samsom Uitgeverij BV*, Postbus 4, Alphen aan den Rijn Tel: (01720) 66633 Cable Add: Samsom Alphenrijn Telex: 39682
Dirs: Dr W P N Schrijver, C Verweij; *Editorial:* H J Demoet, F Gorter; *Rights & Permissions:* José van der Meer
Associate Company: Sijthoff en Noordhoff International Publishers (qv)
Imprint: H D Tjeenk Willink BV
Subjects: Business, Fiscal Law, Management, Textbooks, Social Science, Computer Science, Administration, Public Health
1978: 120 titles *Founded:* 1882
Miscellaneous: Firm is a member of NV ICU (Informatie en Communicatie Unie NV) (qv)
ISBN Publisher's Prefix: 90-14

Schipper*, Printers/Publishers BV, Klaaskampen 36, Postbus 141, Laren, Noord-Holland Tel: (02153) 15754 Cable Add: Printhouse Laren Telex: 43776 Inco nl att spp
Dir: C C Schipper
Subjects: Juveniles, Calendars

Schoolpers, PO Box 48, 4100 AA Culemborg Tel: (03450) 3143
Chairman: P D Zuiderveld; *Man Dir:* J Th Timmer; *Production & Sales:* Educaboek BV (qv)
Subject: Textbooks
Miscellaneous: Firm is a member of the Kluwer Group (qv)

Schuyt en Co CV, Postbus 563, 2003 RN Haarlem (Located at: Gedempte Oude Gracht 35, 2011 GL Haarlem) Tel: (023) 325440 Telex: 41532 sco nl
General Manager: K C Schuyt; *Sales:* W G Kok
Subsidiary Company: Schuyt en Co nv, Hansahuis, Suikerrui 5, 2000 Antwerp, Belgium
Subjects: Juveniles, Art, History, Railways
1980: 78 titles *Founded:* 1953
ISBN Publisher's Prefix: 90-6097

Uitgeverij Gary **Schwartz**, Herengracht 22, Postbus 162, 3600 AD Maarssen Tel: (03465) 62778 Telex: 39556 habla
Dir & Other Offices: Gary Schwartz
Subjects: Fine Art Books
1978: 3 titles *Founded:* 1972
ISBN Publisher's Prefix: 90-6179

Semic Press*, Brouwersgracht 97-99, Amsterdam Tel: 226341 Telex: 15558 semic nl
Man Dir: Hierro Guillermo
Subjects: Comic Magazines, Colouring Books, Albums, Pocket Books

Uitgeverij **Semper** Agendo BV*, Prins Willem Alexanderlaan 601, Postbus 327, Apeldoorn Tel: (055) 773232

Septuaginta BV Uitgeverij, now known as Icob cv (qv)

Servire BV Uitgevers, Secr Varkevisserstr 52, 2225 LE Katwijk aan Zee Tel: (01718) 16741
Chief Executive: Fazal Inayat-Khan; *Other Executives:* Isha Francis (Hunter House), Malik Lechelt (Qalandar); *Editorial:* Felix Erkelens; *Production:* Anwar Martin; *Rights:* Ide Wiener
Associate Companies: Momenta Publishing Ltd, UK (qv); Qalandar Verlag GmbH, Sauerbruchstr 8, D-708 Aalen 9, Federal Republic of Germany
Subsidiary Companies: Hunter House Inc, Publishers, 748 East Bonita Ave, Suite 105, Pomona, CA 91767, USA; Omnibus Book Service, UK (qv)
Subjects: Books in Dutch, German, English on Human Endeavour and Creativity, Mysticism, Alternative Living, Education, Psychology
1978: 30 titles *1979:* 40 titles *Founded:* 1932
ISBN Publisher's Prefixes: 90-6077, 90-6325

Sijthoff en Noordhoff International Publishers*, Postbus 4, 2400 MA Alphen aan den Rijn (Located at: Stadhoudersplein 1, 2400 MA Alphen aan den Rijn) Tel: (1720) 62270 Telex: 39682
Man Dir/Editorial: Arne Visser; *Sales:* Rafael Grasso
Parent Company: Firm is a member of NV ICU (Informatie en Communicatie Unie NV) (qv)
Associate Companies: Samsom Uitgeverij, Wolters-Noordhoff (qqv)
Branch Off: 20010 Century Boulevard, Germantown, Md 20767, USA
Subjects: International Law, International Political and Economic Relations, Pure and

Applied Mechanics and Mathematics, Applied Science
1978: 90 titles *Founded:* 1839
Miscellaneous: The company combines two firms which formerly operated separately as A W Sijthoff International Publishing Co and Noordhoff International Publishing
ISBN Publisher's Prefix: 90-286

A W **Sijthoff's Uitg** Mij BV*, Postbus 4, 2400 MA- Alphen aan den Rijn Tel: (01720) 62465 Cable Add: Sijthoff Alphen aan den Rijn Telex: 39682
Dir: Frans Pruyt; *Editorial:* Willemien Hoogendijk
Parent Company: Firm is a member of NV ICU (Informatie en Communicatie Unie NV) (qv)
Subjects: How-to, Fiction (Detective), Nonfiction, History, Illustrated books
1978: 55 titles *Founded:* 1851
ISBN Publisher's Prefix: 90-218

Uitgeverij **Skarabee** BV, subsidiary of Uitgeverij Luitingh BV (qv)

Smeets Illustrated Projects, Molenveldstr 90, Postbus 17, 6001 HL Weert Tel: (04950) 38055 Telex: 51101
Manager: A de Jong
Subject: Art

Uitgeverij Het **Spectrum** BV*, Park Voorn 4, 3454 JR De Meern Tel: (03406) 3737 Cable Add: Het Spectrum BV, De Meern Telex: 4677
Dir: R A J Huyzer
Orders to: Postbus 2073, 3500 GB Utrecht
Amsterdam Boek Division: Wibautstr 129, Amsterdam Tel: (020) 934933 Telex: 15033 (Orders to: Postbus 543, Amsterdam)
Branch Off: Bijkhoevelaan 12, B-2110 Wijnegem, Belgium
Subjects: General Fiction, Encyclopaedias, Religion, Science & Technical, Textbooks, Paperbacks, Juveniles, Partworks
1978: 450 titles *Founded:* 1935
Miscellaneous: Firm is a member of the VNU Verenigde Nederlandse Uitgeversbedrijven BV Group (qv)
ISBN Publisher's Prefix: 90-274

Spruyt, van Mantgem en de Does BV, see SMD

Staatsdrukkerij en Uitgeverijbedrijf, Chr Plantijnstr 1, The Hague Tel: 814511
Man Dir: H J A M van Haaren
Subjects: Government Publications
ISBN Publisher's Prefix: 90-9012

Stafleu's Wetenschappelijke Uitgeversmaatschappij BV en Stafleu en Tholen BV*, Postbus 4, 2400 MA Alphen aan den Rijn (Located at: Stadhouderspleis 1, 2404 MA Alphen aan den Rijn) Tel: (01720) 62371 Cable Add: Stafleu Publishers Alphen aan der Rijn
Man Dirs: C L Stafleu, J B Oonk
Parent Company: Firm is a member of NV ICU (Informatie en Communicatie Unie NV) (qv)
Subjects: Medicine, Psychology, General Science, Nursing, Dental Science
1978: 32 titles *Founded:* 1947
ISBN Publisher's Prefixes: 90-6016, 90-6065

Stam/Robijns, Industrieweg 1, Postbus 48, 4100 AA Culemborg Tel: (03450) 3143 Telex: 47306
Chairman: P D Zuiderveld; *Man Dir:* B Balder; *Production & Sales:* Educaboek BV (qv)
Subjects: Commercial and Business Education
Miscellaneous: Firm is a member of the Kluwer Group (qv)

Stam Technische Boeken, Industrieweg 1, Postbus 48, 4100 AA Culemborg Tel: (03450) 3143 Telex: 47306
Chairman: P D Zuiderveld; *Man Dir:* B Balder; *Production & Sales:* Educaboek BV (qv)
Subjects: Architecture, Chemistry, Electrical Engineering, Electronics, Earth Sciences, Industries, Crafts, Civil & Mechanical Engineering, Agriculture, Literary Criticism, Aviation, Mathematics, Physics, Law, Linguistics, Languages, Transport, Economics
Miscellaneous: Firm is a member of the Kluwer Group (qv)

Stam Tijdschriften BV, PO Box 235, 2280 AE Rÿswÿk Tel: (070) 991516
Subjects: Engineering, Chemistry, Economics, Computers, Periodicals
Miscellaneous: Firm is a member of the Kluwer Group (qv)
1978: 18 titles

Standaard Uitgeverij en Distributie BV, Lichttorenhoofd 28-30, 4870 BA Etten-Leur (N-Br) Tel: (01608) 13750
Subjects: Juveniles, Religion, Paperbacks
Subsidiary Companies: Editions Erasme (NV Scriptoria), D A P-Reinaert Uitgaven, De Nederlandse Boekhandel, Standaard Uitgeverij (all in Belgium) (qqv); Uitgeverij Van Kampen NV, Uitgeverij Lannoo, Moussault's Uitgeverij BV, Het Wereldvenster BV Internationale Uitg Mij (all in The Netherlands) (qqv)
ISBN Publisher's Prefixes: 90-02 (Standaard), 90-266 (Moussault), 90-293 (Wereldvenster), 90-6091 (Van Kampen), 90-209 (Lanoo), 90-310 (Dap-Reinaert), 90-289, 90-292, 90-616 (Nederlandse Boekhandel)

Uitgeverij M **Stenvert** en Zoon BV*, Postbus 70, 7300 AB Apeldoorn (Located at: Sutton 10, Apeldoorn) Tel: (055) 414644

Uitgeverij W P Van **Stockum** en Zoon NV*, Noorderbeekdwarsstr 45-47, Postbus 6032, The Hague Tel: (070) 180721
Dir: H Sloterdijk
Subjects: General Fiction, Belles Lettres, Philosophy, Juveniles, General Science, Chemistry, History
Founded: 1833
ISBN Publisher's Prefix: 90-6059

A J G **Strengholt's** Boeken Anno 1928 BV*, Hofstede 'Oud Bussem', Flevolaan 41, Naarden Tel: (02159) 46266 Telex: 43191 (Shipping Add: Postbus 338, Bussum)
Man Dir: F E Breitenstein; *Rights & Permissions:* Céline Gockinga
Subjects: General Fiction, Belles Lettres, Biography, History, How-to, Music, Art, Textbooks, Reference, High-priced Paperbacks
1978-79: 75 titles *Founded:* 1928
ISBN Publisher's Prefix: 90-6010

Succes BV*, Uitgeversmaatschappij, Prinsevinkenpark 2, PO Box 16, The Hague Tel: 514351 Cable Add: Success Denhaag
Man Dir/Sales: P Schreuder; *Editorial/Permissions:* J Kasander; *Production:* J Verhoef; *Publicity:* R Wentholt
Parent Comapny: Kluwer (50%); Buhrmann-Tetterode (50%)
Subsidiary Companies: Succes NV, Belgium, Success Verlag GmbH, Federal Republic of Germany
Imprints: Baedeker voor de Vrouw, Uitgeverij Archipel, Universiteit voor Zelfstudie
Subjects: General
Book Club: Nederlandse Boekenclub
Founded: 1928

Swets en Zeitlinger BV, Heereweg 347B, 2161 CA-Lisse Tel: (02521) 19113 Cable Add: Swezeit-Lisse Telex: 41325 slzis nl
Dirs: A Swets, C Schuurman;
Editorial, Permissions: K J Plasterk; *Sales, Production, Publicity:* J Lammerts
Subsidiary Companies: Swets North America Inc, PO Box 517, Berwyn, Pa 19312, USA; Europeriodiques SA, 31 ave de Versailles, F-78170 La Celle St Cloud, France; Swets-Servicos para Bibliotecas Ltda, Rua Olimpio Machado 58, Ilha do Governador, 21911 Rio de Janeiro, RJ, Brazil
Subjects: Music, Medicine, Child Psychology, Engineering, Life Sciences, Education, English Language, Psychological Tests
1978: 38 titles *Founded:* 1901
ISBN Publisher's Prefix: 90-265

Theatrum Orbis Terrarum, Keizersgracht 526, 1017 EK Amsterdam Tel: (020) 222255 Cable Add: Toterra Telex: 14070 ashni nl
Publisher: Nico Israel
Subsidiary Companies: Orbit BV, Keizersgracht 526, Amsterdam; Facsimile Uitgaven Nederland NV (FUN) Amsterdam (both in Netherlands)
Associate Companies: A Asher & Co, Nico Israel (qqv)
Subjects: Biography, Bibliography, History, Cartography, Music, Art, Philosophy, Reference, Religion, High-priced Paperbacks, Medicine, General Science
1979-80: 75 titles *Founded:* 1963
ISBN Publisher's Prefix: 90-221

BV Uitgeverij en Boekhandel W J **Thieme** & Cie, Industrieweg 85, Postbus 7, 7200 AA Zutphen Tel: (05750) 10566 Cable Add: Thieme Zutphen
Dirs: L Groenendijk, K Schillemans
Subjects: General Science, Biology, Schoolbooks
1978: 210 titles *Founded:* 1863
ISBN Publisher's Prefix: 90-03

Uitgeversmaatschappij de **Tijdstroom** BV, Postbus 14, Noorderwal 38, Lochem Tel: (05730) 3651 Telex: 49642
Man Dir: B Mathis
Subsidiary Company: Tijdstroom-Amsterdam
Subjects: Art, Antiques, Medicine, Nursing, Hospital Sciences, Physiotherapy
1978: 50 titles *1979:* 40 titles *Founded:* 1924
ISBN Publisher's Prefix: 90-6087

Time-Life Books, Ottho Heldringstr 5, NL-1066 AZ Amsterdam Tel: (020) 157551 Cable Add: Time-Life Amsterdam Telex: 14288
Editorial: Kit van Tulleken (London); *Production:* T Maloney (Amsterdam); *Rights & Permissions:* Christian Strasser (Munich, for Eastern Europe and Scandinavia), Richard Stollenwerck (Paris, for Southern Europe)
Branch Offs: Time & Life Bldg, New Bond St, London W1Y 0AA, UK; 21-23 rue d'Astorg, F-75008 Paris, France; Akademiestrasse 7, 8 Munich 40, Federal Republic of Germany
Subjects: Art, Cookery, Gardening, General, Social & Political Science, History, How-to, Photography
ISBN Publisher's Prefix: 90-6182

H D **Tjeenk Willink** BV, an imprint of Samson Uitgeverij BV (qv)

W E J **Tjeenk Willink** BV, Koestr 8, Postbus 25, 8000 AA Zwolle
Man Dir: R J Kasteleijn; *Publicity:* M Nieuwenhuis
Subjects: Textbooks and Periodicals on Law
Miscellaneous: Firm is a member of the

Kluwer Group (qv)
ISBN Publisher's Prefix: 90-271

Tjeenk Willink-Noorduijn BV,
Industrieweg 1, Postbus 48, 4100 AA
Culemborg Tel: (03450) 3143 Telex: 47306
Chairman: P D Zuiderveld; *Man Dir:* J Th
Timmer; *Production & Sales:* Educaboek BV
(qv)
Subjects: Secondary & Primary Textbooks,
Educational Materials
Miscellaneous: Firm is a member of the
Kluwer Group (qv)

Uitgeverij De **Toorts**, Nijverheidsweg 1,
Postbus 576, 2003 RN Haarlem Tel: (023)
319360 Cable Add: Gradus Haarlem Telex:
41494
Man Dir: J Hesseling; *Editorial:* Mrs M
Klis, Mrs W Gaus; *Sales:* C Klemann;
Production: R Leideritz; *Publicity:*
C Klemann, Mrs M Klis, R Leideritz;
Permissions: Jan de Vries
Subjects: Humanities, Religion, Medicine,
Music, Psychology
1978: 24 titles *1979:* 29 titles *Founded:* 1936
ISBN Publisher's Prefix: 90-6020

Triton Pers, an imprint of Omega Boek BV
(qv)

Unieboek NV, Nieuwe S'Gravenlandseweg
17-19, Postbus 17, Bussum Tel: (02159)
34241 Cable Add: Unieboek Telex: 43064
Dirs: C A J van Dishoeck, J J Weggemans,
N H Witteman; *Permissions:* Jane Baird
Subjects: General Fiction, History,
Reference, Maritime, Juveniles, Music, Art,
Archaeology, Cookery, Politics, Books for
Pre-School Children, General Non-fiction,
Geography
Founded: 1890
Miscellaneous: The Unieboek group
comprises de Boer Maritiem, van Dishoeck,
Fibula van Dishoeck, de Haan, van
Holkema en Warendorf, Agathon, de
Gooise, Romen, van Reemst
ISBN Publisher's Prefixes: 90-228, 90-269
(Unieboek) 90-616 (De Gooise Uitgeverij)

Universitarie Pers Leiden, see Leiden
University Press

Universiteit voor Zelfstudie, an imprint of
Succes BV (qv)

University Press Amsterdam BV (APA),
Postbus 1850, NL-1000 BW Amsterdam
Parent Company: APA (Academic
Publishers Associated) (qv)
Subjects: History of Law, Political Studies
ISBN Publisher's Prefix: 90-6042

Stichting **V A M***, Papelaan 85,
Voorschoten Tel: (01717) 4141

V N U Verenigde Nederlandse
Uitgeversbedrijven BV, Postbus 4079,
Ceylonpoort 5-25, Haarlem Schalkwijk Tel:
(023) 339000/339040
Subsidiary Company: VNU Business Press
Group (qv)
Miscellaneous: Members in the Netherlands
include Malmberg BV (qv), Uitgeverij Het
Spectrum BV (qv)
ISBN Publisher's Prefixes: 90-208
(Malmberg), 90-274 (Het Spectrum)

V N U Business Press Group*, NZ
Voorburgwal 225, 1012 RL Amsterdam Tel:
(020) 249465 Telex: 14407 Publi NL
Man Dir: F X I Koot
Parent Company: VNU Verenigde
Nederlandse Uitgeversbedrijven BV (qv)
Subsidiary Companies: Intermediar and
Diligentia; in Amsterdam and Brussels,
Belgium
1978: 25 titles

De **Vaar** bv Dordrecht*, Voorstraat 149,
POB 427, Dordrecht Tel: 44567, 44066
Subjects: Sexual Education, Multilingual
Sexual Periodicals

Uitgeverij L J **Veen** BV, Postbus 2004,
Mariaplaats 3, 3500 GA Utrecht Tel: (030)
331484
Man Dir: Bert de Groot; *Editorial:* Bert
Onninck (Fiction), Christian van Gelderen
(Non-fiction); *Sales, Publicity Manager:*
Chris de Graaf
Subjects: General Fiction, Thrillers, Dutch
and International Literature, General Non-
fiction, History, Health
1978: 38 titles *Founded:* 1887
Miscellaneous: Firm is a member of the
Kluwer Group (qv)
ISBN Publisher's Prefix: 90-204

W **Versluys'** Uitg Mij BV, Postbus 4037,
1009 AA-Amsterdam (Located at: 2e
Oosterparkstr 221-223, 1092
BL-Amsterdam) Tel: (020) 650817/947588
Man Dir: H M A Bakker; *Sales Manager:*
J H Goedheer; *Editor:* W L Miner
Subject: Textbooks
1978: 139 titles *1979:* 139 titles *Founded:*
1875
ISBN Publisher's Prefix: 90-249

J N **Voorhoeve**, The Hague, subsidiary of
Uitgeversmaatschappij J H Kok BV (qv)

De **Walburg** Pers, PO Box 222, Zaadmarkt
84a-86, Zutphen Tel: 05750/10522
Man Dir, Publicity, Rights & Permissions:
C F J Schriks; *Editorial Dir:* Dr W R
Wybrands Marcussen; *Sales:* J Rietbergen;
Production: J van 't Leven
Subjects: History, Culture, Monuments,
Architecture, Theatre
1979: 40 titles *1980:* 40 titles *Founded:* 1961
ISBN Publisher's Prefix: 90-6011

Uitgeverij Van **Walraven** BV, Emmalaan 1,
Apeldoorn Tel: (055) 218959
Miscellaneous: Firm is a member of the
Combo Group (qv)
ISBN Publisher's Prefix: 90-6049

Wereldbibliotheek BV, Keizersgracht 810,
PO Box 162, 1000 AD
Amsterdam Tel: 242449 Telex: 18069
bebus nl
Man Dirs: J J F Aleva, J Schilt
Subjects: High quality Fiction and Non-
fiction, Belles Lettres, Juveniles

Het **Wereldvenster** BV Internationale Uitg
Mij, Nieuwe 's-Gravelandseweg 17, Postbus
17, 1400 AA Bussum Tel: (02159) 34241
Cable Add: Stanu nl Telex: 43064 Unieboek
Dir, Editorial, Permissions: J Gay;
Production: G Priem
Orders to: Standaard Uitgeverij, Postbus
1009, 470 BA-Etten-Leur
Parent Company: Standaard Uitgeverij en
Distributie BV, Etten-Leur (qv)
Subjects: Philosophy, Religion, Natural
History, Travel, Paperbacks, Social Science,
Political Science, Environment, Biography
etc
1979: 240 titles *Founded:* 1947
ISBN Publisher's Prefix: 90-293

Uit-Mij **'West-Friesland'**, Kleine Noord 7-9,
Postbox 45, 1620 AA- Hoorn Tel: (02290)
18941 Cable Add: Westfriesland
Man Dir: Mevr J C Jonkers-Butter;
Editorial: A M J C Ripken
Subjects: General Fiction, Juveniles, General
Science, Low- & High-priced Paperbacks
1978: 77 titles *1979:* 110 titles *Founded:*
1918
ISBN Publisher's Prefix: 90-205

Uitgeverij **Westers**, Hammarskjöldhof 7,
3527 HC Utrecht Tel: (030) 931043/932859
Cable Add: Westers Utrecht

Man Dir and other offices: R J N M
Westers Sr
Subjects: Children's Books, Novels
Bookshop: at above address
1978: 12 titles *1979:* 14 titles *Founded:* 1967
ISBN Publisher's Prefix: 90-6107

Wetenschappelijke Uitgeverij, Singel 262,
1016 AC Amsterdam Tel: (020) 247674
Cable Add: Scientpublish
Man Dir: Th A Sontrop; *Publicity:* Gert Jan
Hemmink
Associate Companies: Uitgeverij De
Arbeiderspers BV, Em Querido's Uitgeverij
BV (qqv)
Subjects: Biography, History, Music, Art,
Philosophy, Religion, High-priced
Paperbacks, Medicine, Psychology, General
& Social Science, Secondary & University
Textbooks
1979: 20 titles *1980:* 20 titles *Founded:* 1948
ISBN Publisher's Prefix: 90-6287

Uitgeverij **Wever** BV, Zilverstr 12-16,
Franeker Tel: (05170) 3147
Subjects: History, Philosophy, Politics

Wolters-Noordhoff BV, Oude Boteringestr
22, Postbus 58, 9700 MB Groningen
Tel: (050) 162911 Telex: 53443
Man Dir: J de Groot, J Buiring; *Rights &
Permissions:* P G A Geenen
Orders to: PO Box 567, 9700 A N Groningen
Parent Company: Firm is a member of NV
ICU (Informatie en Communicatie Unie NV)
(qv)
Associate Companies: Wolters-Noordhoff
Longman BV (qv); Sijthoff en Noordhoff
International Publishers (qv)
Subjects: Secondary, Primary & Tertiary
Textbooks, Educational Materials, *Easy
Readers*, Maps, Atlases
1978: 261 titles *Founded:* 1836, 1858
ISBN Publisher's Prefix: 90-01

Wolters Noordhoff Longman BV, Postbus
58, 9700 MB Groningen (Located at: Oude
Boteringestraat 22, 9700 MB Groningen)
Tel: (050) 162236 Telex: 53443/53529
General Executive: Aloys Doodkorte
Associate Companies: Wolters-Noordhoff
BV (qv); the Longman Group Ltd, UK (qv)
Subjects: Texts connected with English
Language Teaching

Zomer en Keuning Boeken BV, Postbus 235,
6710 BE Ede (Located at: Kernhemseweg 7,
6718 ZB Ede) Tel: (08380) 19031 Cable
Add: Zkede Telex: 45836 Zkede
Man Dir: Hans Mons; *Deputy Dir:* Floris
Eijffinger; *Editors:* Benno van Lochem,
Martin van Huijstee, Piet Terlouw, Rien
Meyer; *Permissions:* Hans Mons
Subjects: General Fiction, How-to,
Reference, Religion (Protestant), Bibles,
High-priced Paperbacks, Nature, Gardening,
Cookery, Handicrafts
1978: 80 titles *1979:* 95 titles *Founded:* 1919
Book Club: Spiegelserie
Miscellaneous: Firm is a member of the
Kluwer Group (qv)
ISBN Publisher's Prefix: 90-210

Zuid-Hollandsche UM, an imprint of BV
Uitgeversmaatschappij Elsevier Boekerij (qv)

Zuidgroep BV (formerly Hippobook/Studio
de Zuid)*, Postbus 245, 2501 CE The Hague
(Located at: Koninginnegracht 49 2514 AE
The Hague) Tel: (070) 637950
General Dirs: A L van Ingen Schenau,
J H Bartels; *Publisher, Sales, Foreign
Rights:* D J Rog
Imprints: Zuidboek, Hippoboek, Bresboek,
Rekreaboek
Subjects: Pets, Equestrian, Nature Study,
Gardening, Plants and Flowers, Sports,
Crafts, Hobbies, Travel, Cookery, Games,
Photography, Film

1978: 68 titles *Founded:* 1975
ISBN Publisher's Prefix: 90-6248

Uitgeverij **Zwijsen** BV, Gasthuisring 58, Postbus 805, Tilburg Tel: (013) 353635
Man Dirs: J N A Verwielen, G M Janssen
Subjects: Juveniles, Primary Textbooks
Founded: 1846
ISBN Publisher's Prefix: 90-276

Remainder Dealers

Icob cv, Postbus 392, 2400 AJ Alphen aan den Rijn (Located at: Ondernemingsweg 60, Alphen aan den Rijn) Tel: (01720) 23202 Telex: 39700 icob nl
Man Dir: Hans Meijer

Literary Agents

Auteursbureau Greta **Baars-Jelgersma**, Den Heuvel 73, NL-6881 VD-Velp Tel: (85) 635017 Telex: Incom 43776/11000
Specialization: International co-printing of illustrated books; mediation of copyrights; translations from Scandinavian and German languages into Dutch

Gans en Rombach Auteursagenten, Postbus 144, 2060 AC Bloemendaal Tel: (023) 262907
Contact: Coen J Rombach

International Bureau voor Auteursrecht BV*, Goudestein 1, 2352 JX Leiderdorp Tel: (071) 891056
Contact: Hans Keuls

International Literatuur Bureau BV, Koninginneweg 2A, 1217 KW Hilversum Tel: (035) 13500 Cable Add: ILB Telex: 73201 ILB
Contact: Menno Kohn

Prins en Prins, De Lairessestr 6, Postbus 5400, 1007 AK Amsterdam Tel: (020) 761001 Cable Add: prinsrights

Servire BV Uitgevers, Secr Varkerisserstr 52, Katwijk aan Zee Tel: (01718) 16741
Chief Executive: Fazal Inayat-Khan
Also Publishers (qv)

Book Clubs

E C I voor Boeken en Grammofoonplaten BV*, Gebouw Cranenborch, Jaarbeursplein 17, 3521 AN Utrecht Tel: (030) 910911 Telex: 47449

English Book Club*, Leidestr 52, 1017 PC, Amsterdam
The above address is for Netherlands enquiries. Head office is Book Club Associates, UK (qv under UK Book Clubs)
Owned by: W H Smith & Son Ltd (London) and Doubleday & Co Inc (New York)

Librah, Postbus 123, 1520 AC Wormerveer
Owned by: Meijer Wormerveer NV (Wormerveer)

Nederlandse Boekenclub (Netherlands Book Club), Prinsevinkenpark 2, The Hague
Manager: P Schreuder
Subject: General
Members: 350,000
Owned by: Succes BV (The Hague)

Nederlandse Lezerskring, c/o Hollandia BV, Beukenlaan 16-20, Postbus 70, Baarn
Owned by: Hollandia BV (part-owner)

Uitgeversmaatschappij, **Reader's Digest** NV*, Postbus 7300, Amsterdam

Spiegelserie Boekenclub, Postbus 235, 6710 BE Ede (Located at: Huis Kernhem, Kernhemseweg 7, 6718 ZB Ede)
Owned by: Zomer en Keuning Boeken BV (Ede)

V C L, Gildestraat 5, 8263 AH Kampen
Owned by: Uitgeversmaatschappij J H Kok BV (Kampen)

Major Booksellers

Athenaeum Boekhandel, Spui 14-16, Amsterdam Tel: (020) 233933
Manager: G Schut

Broese-Kemink BV, Stadhuisbrug 5, Postbus 38, 3511 KP Utrecht Tel: (030) 313804

H **Coebergh***, Gedempte Oude Gracht 74, Postbus 98, Haarlem Tel: (023) 319198
Manager: J B I M Kat

Dekker en Nordemann BV/Meulenhoff-bruna, Postbus 19084, 1000 GB Amsterdam (Located at: Beulingstr 2-4, Amsterdam Tel: (020) 240885
The above is the address of the new book and subscription department. The antiquarian department is located at Lippijnstr 4, Amsterdam Tel: (020) 861541
Managers: J Mendels (Subscriptions), E Richter (Books), A Gerits (Antiquarian)
International booksellers and subscription agency. Branches in Republic of Ireland and USA
A Division of Elsevier

Dekker en Van de Vegt*, Plein 1944 129-131, Nijmegen Tel: (080) 221010

Boekhandel **Gianotten** BV, Heuvel 43, Tilburg
Orders to: Jac Oppenheimstr 15, 5042 NM-Tilburg Tel: (013) 682991 (two branches in Tilburg and one in Breda)

Ginsberg Univ Boekhandel, Schuttersveld 9, Postbus 9003, 2300 PA Leiden Tel: (071) 124642, 141773
Manager: Mrs C Bos-Vink

C **Kooyker** BV, Nieuwe Rijn 15-16, Postbus 24, 2300 AA Leiden Tel: (071) 144146 Telex: 39434
Man Dir: Fj Arkenau

Meulenhoff Bruna BV, see Dekker en Nordemann BV/Meulenhoff-bruna

Rudolf **Müller** International Booksellers BV, Overtoom 487, Postbus 9016, 1006 AA Amsterdam Tel: (020) 165955
Managers: R Muller, Mrs C M Griffioen

Martinus **Nijhoff** BV, Postbus 269, 2501 AX The Hague Tel: (070) 469460 Cable Add: books hague Telex: 34164 nijbu nl

Boekhandel **Scheltema**, Holkema Vermeulen BV, Spui 10, 1012 WZ Amsterdam Tel: (020) 267212 Telex: 17193

Scholtens en Zoon BV, Grote Markt 43-44, Postbus 1, 9700 AA-Groningen Tel: (050) 139788
Manager: R A Koops
Owned by: Elsevier-NDU

Universitaire Boekhandel Nederland, Oosterstr 11, 9711 NN Groningen
Branches at Damsterdiep 1, 9711 SG Groningen; Haringvliet 100, 3011 TH Rotterdam

Major Libraries

Bibliotheek van het **Centraal Bureau** voor de Statistiek*, Prinses Beatrixlaan 428, Postbus 959, 2270 AZ Voorburg
Library of the Netherlands Central Bureau of Statistics

Bibliotheek- en Documentatie-centrum van de **Economische Voorlichtingsdienst***, Bezuidenhoutseweg 151, The Hague
Library and Documentation Centre of the Economic Information Service

Gemeentebibliotheek Rotterdam, Nieuwe Markt 1, 3011 HP Rotterdam Tel: (010) 135040
Rotterdam Municipal Library
Librarian: P J Th Schoots

Bibliotheek van het **Internationaal Instituut** voor Sociale Geschiedenis, Herengracht 262-266, Amsterdam C Tel: (020) 246671
Library of the International Institute of Social History
Dir: Rein van der Leeuw
Librarian: Gerhard J A Riesthuis

Koninklijke Bibliotheek*, Lange Voorhout 34, The Hague Tel: (070) 644920
Royal (National) Library
Publication: (in co-operation with others) Dutch Bibliography — Brinkman's Cumulatieve Catalogus; Centrale Catalogus voor Periodieken (Union Catalogue of Periodicals, in book form)

Bibliotheek der **Koninklijke Nederlandse Akademie** van Wetenschappen, Kloveniersburgwal 29, 1011 JV Amsterdam
Library of Royal Netherlands Academy of Arts and Sciences
Librarian: Drs J A W Brak

Bibliotheek der **Landbouwhogeschool**, Postbus 9100, 6700 HA Wageningen Tel: (08370) 82006 Telex: 45015
Library of the Agricultural University

Openbare Bibliotheek*, Bilderdijkstr 1-3, 2513 CM The Hague Tel: (070) 469235
Public Library

Rijksmuseum Meermanno-Westreenianum/Museum van het Boek, Prinsessegracht 30, 2514 AP The Hague Tel: (070) 462700
Book Museum
Keeper: R E O Ekkart

Bibliotheek der **Rijksuniversiteit**, Wittevrouwenstr 9-11, PB 16007 Utrecht Tel: (030) 333116 Telex: NL 47103
Librarian: Drs J van Heijst

Bibliotheek der **Rijksuniversiteit te Groningen**, Oude Kijk in't Jatstr 5, Postbus 559, 9700 AN Groningen

Bibliotheek der **Rijksuniversiteit te Leiden***, Rapenburg 70-74, 2311 EZ-Leiden
And Postbus 9501, 2300 RA-Leiden Tel: (071) 148333 ext 7501 Telex: 31513

Universiteitsbibliotheek van Amsterdam*, Singel 425, Amsterdam Tel: (020) 5252333

Library Associations

Algemene Nederlandse Bond van Leesbibliotheekhouders*, Litslaan 14, Santpoort-Zuid Tel: 7566
Netherlands Association of Reference Librarians

Centrum voor Literatuuronderzoekers*, Debijeweg 82, Rotterdam
Centre for Literary Research — a section of the Dutch Librarians' Association

Convent van Universiteitsbibliothekarissen in Nederland (Association of University Librarians in the Netherlands), see UKB

Federatie van Organisaties van Bibliotheek-, Informatie-, Dokumentatiewezen (FOBID), Taco Scheltemastr 5, The Hague Tel: (070) 264351
Federation of Library Information and Documentation Organizations
Co-ordinating Officer: C J M Bruin

NETHERLANDS

Nederlands Bibliotheek en Lektuurcentrum (NBLC), Taco Scheltemastr 5, Postbus 93054, 2509 AB The Hague Tel: (070) 264351 Telex: 32102 nblc nl
Netherlands Centre for Public Libraries and Literature
Executive Dir: D Reumer
Publication: Bibliotheek en Samenleving; Open (published jointly with 2 other associations: Nederlandse Vereniging van Bedrijfsarchivarissen and Nederlandse Vereniging van Bibliothekarissen)

Nederlandse Vereniging van Bedrijfsarchivarissen, Aalsburg 2526, 6602 WD Wijchen
Netherlands Association of Business Archivists
Publication: Open (published jointly with 2 other associations: Nederlands Bibliotheek en Lektuurcentrum and Nederlandse Vereniging van Bibliothekarissen)

Nederlandse Vereniging van Bibliothecarissen, Documentalisten en literatuuronderzoekers (NVB), pa Mw H J Krikke-Scholten, Nolweg 13, 4209 AW Schelluinen Tel: (01030) 23306
Netherlands Librarians' Society
Secretary: D R F van Bremen
Publication: Open (published jointly with 2 other associations: Nederlands Bibliotheek en Lektuurcentrum and Nederlandse Vereniging van Bedrijfsarchivarissen)

Protestantse Stichting tot Bevordering van het Bibliotheekwezen en de Lectuurvoorlichting in Nederland*, Parkweg 20a, Voorburg
Protestant Foundation for the Promotion of Librarianship and Reading Information in the Netherlands
Publication: Prisma

Stichting Bibliotheek en Documentatieacademies, Keizersgracht 225, Postbus 10895, 1001 EW Amsterdam 2 Tel: (020) 265155
Foundation for Library and Documentation Academies
Secretary: P den Hoed

U K B (Samenwerkingsverband van de Universiteits- en Hogeschoolbibliotheken en de Koninklijke Bibliotheek), c/o J L M van Dijk, Librarian, State University Limburg, Postbus 616, 6200 MD Maastricht Tel: (043) 888888 Telex: 56726
President: W R H Koops
Secretary: Dr J L M van Dijk

Vereniging van Archivarissen in Nederland*, Ter Pelkwykpark 21, Zwolle
Association of Archivists in the Netherlands
Executive Secretary: Casper van Heel
Publication: Archievenblad

Vereniging voor het Theologisch Bibliothecariaat, Postbus 289, 6500 AG Nijmegen
Association for Theological Librarianship (the above is the address of the Secretariat)
Executive Secretary: R van Dijk
Publications: Mededelingen van de VTB; Bibliografie Doctorale Scripties Theologie

Library Reference Books and Journals

Books

Bibliotheek-en Documentatiegids (Library and Documentation Guide), NOBIN, Van Karnebeeklaan 19, The Hague

Brinkman's Cumulatieve Catalogus (Dutch Bibliography), Koninklijke Bibliotheek, Lange Voorhout 34, The Hague

Journals

Archievenblad (Archive News), Association of Archivists in the Netherlands, Ter Pelkwykpark 21, Zwolle

Bibliotheek en Samenleving (Library and Social Life), Netherlands Centre for Public Libraries and Literature, Central Bureau, Taco Schetemastr 5, Postbus 2054, The Hague

Mededelingen (Communications), Association for Theological Librarianship, Doddendaal 20, Nijmegen

Open, professional journal for librarians, researchers, archivists and documentalists, Netherlands Librarians' Society, Abel Tasmankade 9, Haarlem (published jointly with Netherlands Centre for Public Libraries and Literature and Netherlands Association of Business Archivists)

Literary Associations and Societies

The **Dickens** Fellowship*, Banstr 60, Amsterdam Z
Honorary Secretary: Frank H Keene

Foundation for the Promotion of the Translation of Dutch Literature, Singel 450, 1017 AV Amsterdam Tel: (020) 231056/257189
Dir: Joost de Wit
Publication: Writing in Holland and Flanders

Maatschappij der Nederlandse Letterkunde, R Breugelmans, c/o Universiteitsbibliotheek, Rapenburg 70-74, 2311 EZ Leiden
Society of Netherlands Literature (the above is the address of the Secretariat)
Publications: Tijdschrift voor Nederlandse Taal- en Letterkunde (quarterly), *Jaarboek der Maatschappij* (annually)

Netherlands Centre of the International **P E N**, Wevelaan 39, 3571 XS Utrecht Tel: (030) 714179
Secretary: (internal business) Dirk Kroon; (foreign business) Dr Mineke Schipper

Literary Periodicals

Amsterdamer Publikationen zur Sprache und Literatur (Amsterdam Publication on Language and Literature), Editions Rodopi NV, Keizersgracht 302-304, Amsterdam

Boeken-Zoekblad (Hard-to-Find Books), 'Stabo/All-Round' BV, Oosterweg 68, Groningen

Castrum Peregrini; journal for literature and art (text in German), Castrum Peregrini Presse, Herengracht 401, Postbus 645, Amsterdam

Forum der Letteren (Forum of Letters), Smits NV, Westeinde 135, 15 The Hague

Gids (Guide), Meulenhoff Nederland NV, Prinsengracht 468, Amsterdam

Hemelspleet (Poles Apart), Bilderdijksstr 45a, Rotterdam

Hollands Maandblad (Holland Monthly), Drukkeij Trio, Nobelstr 27, The Hague

Kentering (The Turning-point) literary review, Nijgh & Van Ditmas, Badhuisweg 232, The Hague

Lezen om te Leven (Reading as a Life Style), 'Stabo/All-Round' BV, Oosterweg 68, Groningen

Quaerendo; a quarterly journal from the Low Countries devoted to manuscripts and printed books (text mainly in English, occasionally in French and German), Theatrum Orbis Terrarum, Keizersgracht 526, Amsterdam

Revisor (The Inspector), Keizersgracht 608, Amsterdam

Trotwaer (The Pavement), (text in Frisian), Miedema Pers, Nieuweburen 97-103, Postbus 45, Leeuwarden

Writing in Holland and Flanders (text in English), Foundation for the Promotion of Dutch Literary Works, Singel 450, Amsterdam C

Literary Prizes

Amsterdam Prizes*
For the best drama, novel, poetry, essay, novella and short story. Awarded annually. Enquiries to Amsterdam City Government, Town Hall, O Z Voorburgwal 197, Amsterdam

F **Bordewijk** Prize
For the best Dutch novel. 4,000 Dutch florins. Awarded annually. Enquiries to Jan Campertstichting, Burg de Monchyplein 9, The Hague

Jan **Campert** Prize
For outstanding Dutch poetry. 4,000 Dutch florins. Awarded annually. Enquiries to Jan Campertstichting, Burg De Monchyplein 9, The Hague

Dutch (Flemish) Literature Grand Prizes, see International Literary Prizes

Dutch Prize for the Best Children's Book
For the best Dutch children's books (maximum 3). 3,000 Dutch florins. For foreign, translated books (maximum 9, minimum 7), silver slate pencils. Awarded annually. Enquiries to the Commission for the Collective Promotion of the Netherlands Book, Langestr 61, Amsterdam C

The G H **'s-Gravensande** Prize
For special services to literature. 4,000 Dutch florins. Awarded irregularly. Enquiries to Jan Campertstichting, Burg De Monchyplein 9, The Hague

J **Greshoff** Prize
For the best Dutch essay. 4,000 Dutch florins. Awarded every two years. Enquiries to Jan Campertstichting, Burg de Monchyplein 9, The Hague

Nienke van **Hichtum** Prize
For the best Dutch children's book. 4,000 Dutch florins. Awarded every two years. Enquiries to Jan Campertstichting, Burg de Monchyplein 9, The Hague

Lucy B en C W van der **Hoogt** Prize
To an outstanding Dutch writer. 1,000 Dutch florins and a medal. Awarded annually. Enquiries to Maatschappij der Nederlandse Letterkunde (Society of Netherlands Literature), Rapenburg 70-74, 2311 EZ Leiden

Constantijn **Huygens** Prize
To a distinguished Dutch author for all his works. 8,000 Dutch florins. Awarded annually. Enquiries to Jan Campertstichting, Burg De Monchyplein 9, The Hague

Reina **Prinsen-Geerlings** Prize*
Established by the parents of Reina Prinsen-Geerlings to commemorate her execution by the Germans and awarded to a young Dutch author. 200 Dutch florins. Awarded annually. Enquiries to Reina Prinsen-Geerlings Foundation, Koninginneweg 141, Amsterdam

State Prize for Children's and Youth Literature*
For the best author's work for children and young people. 6,500 Dutch florins. Awarded triennially. Enquiries to Netherlands Ministry of Culture, Recreation and Social Welfare (CRS), Postbus 5406, 2280 HK Rijswijk

State Prize for Literature, the P C Hooft Prize
For important and original literary works in Dutch. 10,000 Dutch florins. Awarded annually where possible: one year for poetry, the next year for prose, the next year for literary essay. Enquiries to Netherlands Ministry of Culture, Recreation and Social Welfare (CRS), Postbus 5406, 2280 HK Rijswijk

Vijverberg Prize, replaced by The G H 's-Gravensande Prize (qv)

Netherlands Antilles

General Information

Language: Dutch (and English)
Religion: Roman Catholic
Population: 246,000
Literacy rate (1971): 92.5%
Bank Hours: 0830-1130, 1400-1600 Monday-Friday. St Maarten: 0800-1300 Monday-Friday (also 1600-1700 on Friday)
Shop Hours: 0800-1200, 1400-1800 Monday-Saturday
Currency: 100 cents = 1 Netherlands Antilles florin or guilder
Export/Import Information: No tariff on books or advertising. No import licences. No exchange controls
Copyright: Berne, UCC (see International section)

Publishers

Curaçaosche Drukkerij en Uitgevers Maatschappij*, Pietermaaiweg, Willemstad, Curaçao
Subjects: Geography, Travel

Van **Dorp** Aruba NV*, Nassaustr 77, PO Box 596, Oranjestad, Aruba

Van **Dorp** Eddine NV, Book Department, PO Box 200, Willemstad, Curaçao

Drukkerij de Stad NV*, Compagniestr 41, Willemstad, Curaçao
Dir: Ronald Yrausquin
Subject: Law

Ediciones Populares*, Compagniestr 41, Willemstad, Curaçao
Dir: Ronald Yrausquin
Subjects: Popular Sciences, Literature
Founded: 1929

Tipografia Nacional*, Bitterstr 3, Curaçao
Subject: Law

De Wit Stores NV*, VAD Bldg, L G Smith Blvd 110, Oranjestad, Aruba
Man Dir: F Olmtak

Major Booksellers

Casa **America***, Madurostraat 3, Curaçao

Aruba Boekhandel*, Nassaustraat 94, Oranjestad, Aruba

Curaçao Plaza Hotel, Plaza Piar, Curaçao
Tel: 12500 Cable Add: Curplahot Telex: 1237 Plaza NA/3324 CPH NA
General Manager: Robert M Souers

Hollandsche Boekhandel*, Breedestraat (P) 22 Curaçao

Major Libraries

Openbare Leeszaal en Bibliotheek*, Johan van Walbeeckplein 6-13, Willemstad, Curaçao
Public Reading Room and Library

Openbare Leeszaal en Boekerij, Eilandgebied, Aruba
Public Reading Room and Library
Librarian: Alice van Romondt

Universiteits-Bibliotheek, Universiteit van de Nederlandse Antillen, PO Box 682, Jan Noorduynweg z/n, Willemstad, Curaçao
Tel: 84422 Telex: 110111
Librarian: Maritza F Eustatia

Library Associations

Asociation di Biblioteka i Archivo di Korsow (Carbidor)*, Drukkerijstr 4, Willemstad, Curaçao Tel: 23434
Association of Libraries and Archives
President: Maritza F Eustatia

New Caledonia

General Information

Language: French
Population: 138,000
Literacy Rate (1976): 91.3%
Currency: CFP franc
Export/Import Information: No tariff on books except luxury bindings, 15%, and children's picture books, 10%. Advertising matter generally dutiable at 10%. Special Tax of 0.5% on all. No import licences required

Major Booksellers

Barrau*, 16 et 18 rue Anatole-France, Nouméa Tel: 3093

J-P Layraud*, rue de la République, Nouméa Tel: 2197

Modernix*, 7 ave du Maréchal-Foch, BP 129 Tel: 2001 Nouméa

Montaigne*, 24 rue de Sébastopol, BP 267 Tel: 3488 Nouméa

Pentecost*, 24 rue de l'Alma, Nouméa
Tel: 2114
Importer/Exporter

Major Libraries

Bibliothèque **Bernheim**, Bibliothèque territoriale de la Nouvelle-Caledonie*, Route 13, BP G 1, Nouméa
Librarian: Hélène Colombani

South Pacific Commission Library, South Pacific Commission, PO Box D5, Nouméa Cedex

New Zealand

General Information

Language: English
Religion: Predominantly Protestant
Population: 3.1 million
Bank Hours: 1000-1600 Monday-Friday
Shop Hours: 0900-1730 Monday-Friday (open until 2100 either Thursday or Friday). Some local shops open Saturday
Currency: 100 cents = 1 New Zealand dollar
Export/Import Information: No tariffs on books and advertising. No import licences, but literature 'indecent' or 'advocating violence, lawlessness, disorder or seditiousness' prohibited. No special exchange controls
Copyright: UCC, Berne, Florence (see International section)

Book Trade Organizations

Book Publishers Association of New Zealand, Box 78071, Grey Lynn, Auckland 2 (Located at: 180 Surrey Cres, Grey Lynn, Auckland 2) Tel: 767251
President: D J Heap; *Dir:* Gerard Reid
Publication: Publishing News (members only)

Booksellers Association of New Zealand (Inc), PO Box 11-377, Wellington Tel: (04) 728678
Dir: Kate R Fortune

Christian Booksellers' Association (NZ Chapter), PO Box 34-015, Auckland 10
Secretary: R A Woodhams

The **New Zealand Authors** Fund, Department of Internal Affairs, Private Bag, Wellington
Secretary: Ms M McKee

New Zealand Book Council, PO Box 11377, Wellington
Secretary: Margaret McLeod

New Zealand Book Trade Organization, PO Box 78071, Auckland 2 (Located at: 180 Surrey Cres, Auckland 2) Tel: (01) 767251
Chairman: R Goddard; *Secretary:* G E Reid

Standard Book Numbering Agency, c/o D M McIntosh, National Library of New Zealand, Private Bag, Wellington 1

Book Trade Journals

Book Trade Monthly, PO Box 46, Albany

New Zealand Book World; journal of the New Zealand book trade, PO Box 9405, Courtenay Pl, Wellington

New Zealand Books in Print, c/o D W Thorpe Pty Ltd, 384 Spencer St, Melbourne, Victoria 3003, Australia

New Zealand National Bibliography, National Library of New Zealand, PMB, Wellington 1

Spotlight; on the book, stationery, magazine, greeting cards, and toys trades in New Zealand, PO Box 3911, Auckland

Publishers

A B P (NZ) Ltd, see Associated Book Publishers (NZ) Ltd

Action Publications, PO Box 5160, Christchurch (Located at: 49 Hudson St, Christchurch) Tel: 516460
Man Dir: Desmond Sewell; *Sales:* Pamela Sewell
Subjects: Secondary Textbooks, Geography, Social Studies
1979: 5 titles *1980:* 7 titles *Founded:* 1971
ISBN Publisher's Prefix: 0-908586

H J **Ashton** Co Ltd*, PO Box 12328, Auckland (Located at: 9-11 Fairfax Ave, Penrose, Auckland 6) Tel: 596089 Cable Add: Ashco Telex: 21203
Branch Off: 290 Clyde Rd, PO Box 29031, Fendalton, Christchurch 5 Tel: 518614
1978: 1 title
ISBN Publisher's Prefix: 0-86896

Asia Pacific Research Unit Ltd, PO Box 3978, Wellington Tel: (04) 850237 Cable Add: Haaspress
Man Dir: Anthony Haas; *Editorial:* Pam Brown; *Sales:* Michael Hart; *Production:* Neil Evans
Associate Companies: Oriental Press Service, Central Postbox 1226, Tokyo 100-91, Japan; Read Thompson, 6th Floor, World House, 29 Reiby Pl, Sydney, New South Wales, Australia
Branch Offs: Auckland, New Zealand; Bangkok, Thailand; Palmerston, New Zealand; Suva, Fiji; Sydney, Australia; Tokyo, Japan
Subjects: Economics, Geography, Politics, Social Change
Founded: 1970
ISBN Publisher's Prefix: 0-908583

Associated Book Publishers (NZ) Ltd, Private Bag Auckland (Located at: 61 Beach Rd, Auckland) Tel: 796369 Cable Add: Methlisps Telex: NZ 21944
Man Dir: A David Mackie; *Publishing Manager:* Rosamund M Henry; *Sales Manager:* Kenneth W Shearman
Parent Company: Associated Book Publishers Ltd, London, UK (qv)
Subsidiary Companies: Methuen New Zealand, Sweet and Maxwell (NZ) Ltd (both at above address)
Associate Company: Associated Book Publishers (Aust) Ltd, Australia (qv)
Subjects: General, Educational (School), Tertiary (Social Sciences, Management), Legal
Book Shop: Sweet and Maxwell (NZ) Ltd, 54 The Terrace, Wellington
1979: 30 titles *1980:* 25 titles
ISBN Publisher's Prefix: 0-456/0457

Auckland University Press, University of Auckland, PMB, Auckland Tel: (09) 792300
Managing Editor: R D McEldowney
Orders to: Oxford University Press, PO Box 27-344, Wellington
Subjects: Education, History, Literature, Social Sciences, Textbooks
1978: 4 titles *1979:* 7 titles *Founded:* 1966
ISBN Publisher's Prefix: 0-19

Thomas **Avery** & Sons Ltd*, PO Box 442, New Plymouth, North Island Tel: (067) 78122 Cable Add: Avery New Plymouth
Man Dir: D V Avery
Subjects: History, Secondary & Primary Textbooks
Founded: 1882
Bookshop: Thomas Avery & Sons Ltd, 79 Devon St, New Plymouth, North Island

David **Bateman** Ltd, PO Box 65062, Mairangi Bay, Auckland 10 Tel: 4444680 Telex: NZ 2244
Shipping Add: Golden Heights, 30-34 View Rd, Glenfield, Auckland 10
Man Dir, Editorial: David L Bateman; *Sales:* David Presland Tack; *Publicity, Rights & Permissions:* Janet Bateman
Branch Off: c/o Mr Tony Tizzard, Fiesta Products, PO Box 4176, Christchurch
Founded: 1979
ISBN Publisher's Prefix: 0-908610

Beaux Arts Ltd*, PO Box 1459, Seiko House, 20 Fanshawe St, Auckland 1 Tel: 771774 Cable Add: Beauxarts
Editorial Off: 395 Remuera Rd, PO Box 28017, Auckland 5
Man Dir: R Innes; *Sales:* Mrs M Dunkley
Subjects: Arts, Crafts, History
Bookshop: N W Wheeler Ltd
1978: 2 titles *Founded:* 1975

Black Apple, PO Box 23, Port Chalmers, Dunedin Tel: 739885
Man Dir and all offices: H Scott
Orders to: More than 10 copies: to above address; less than 10 copies: Macmillan Publishers Ltd, PO Box 33570, Takapuna, Auckland
Subjects: Children's Books, Dual Language Books (Japanese and English, Arabic and English, etc)
1978: 2 titles *Founded:* 1977
ISBN Publisher's Prefix: 0-908589

Brick Row Publishing Co Ltd, 1st Floor, CMC Bldg, 89 Courtenay Pl, PO Box 190, Wellington 1 Tel: 736708 Cable Add: Brickrow Wellington
Man Dir, Editorial: Oswald L Kraus; *Sales, Publicity:* Ruth Kraus
Associate Company: Graphic and Allied Systems, PO Box 1267, Wellington 1
Subjects: Poetry, Fiction, Crafts, General Non-fiction
1979: 6 titles *Founded:* 1978
ISBN Publisher's Prefix: 0-908595

Bush Press Communications Ltd, PO Box 32-037, Devonport, Auckland 9 (Located at: 20a Coronation St, Takapuna, Auckland 9) Tel: 492667
Man Dir: Gordon Ell
Orders to: Leonard Fullerton Ltd, 5-7 Shaddock St, Eden Terrace, Auckland
Imprint: Gordon Ell
Subjects: Wildlife and Outdoor, Guide Books, Applied Arts, Hobbies, General New Zealand Non-fiction
1979: 3 titles *1980:* 8 titles *Founded:* 1979
ISBN Publisher's Prefix: 0-908608

Butterworths of New Zealand Ltd, PO Box 472, T & W Young Building, 77-85 Custom House Quay, Wellington 6001 Tel: 722021 Cable Add: Butterwort Wellington Telex: 31306
Man Dir: D A Day
Parent Company: Butterworth & Co (Publishers) Ltd, UK (qv)
Subjects: Legal, Medical, Scientific, Technical
1979: 11 titles *Founded:* 1914
ISBN Publisher's Prefix: 0-409

Cambridge University Press, PO Box 33055, Takapuna, Auckland 9 Tel: 451609
Man Dir: R M Ross
Parent Company: Cambridge University Press, UK (qv)

Cape Catley Ltd*, PO Box 199, Picton Tel: 1086 W, Picton
Man Dir: Christine C Catley
Subject: Fiction
1978: 2 titles
ISBN Publisher's Prefix: 0-908561

Capper Press Ltd*, PO Box 1388, Christchurch Tel: 67170 Cable Add: Avonprint Christchurch
Associate Company: Avon Fine Prints Ltd
Subjects: Reprints of rare and out-of-print New Zealand, Australian and Pacific books
Bookshops: The Bookshop in Campbell Grant, 196 Hereford St, Christchurch
1978: 12 titles

Cassell Ltd, 46 Lake Rd, PO Box 36013, Northcote Central, Auckland 9 Tel: 484055/371 Cable Add: Caspeg Auckland Telex: NZ 2244
Manager: Margaret Gibson
1978: 3 titles *1979:* 5 titles
Miscellaneous: Firm is a registered branch in New Zealand of Cassell Ltd UK (qv) and Collier Macmillan International Inc, USA
ISBN Publisher's Prefix: 0-908572

Caveman Publications Ltd, PO Box 1458, Dunedin (Located at: 2nd Floor, OSB Building, 106 George St, Dunedin) Tel: 772326
Publisher: Trevor Reeves; *Distribution:* Richard Layton
Subsidiary Companies: Mediaprint Services Ltd, Kirlian Books
Subjects: Literature, Non-fiction, Health, Welfare, Medical, Social, Politics, Humour, Women's Books, Science Speculation
1979: 5 titles *1980:* 8 titles *Founded:* 1971
ISBN Publisher's Prefix: 0-908562

The **Caxton** Press, 113 Victoria St, PO Box 25088, Christchurch Tel: 68516 Cable Add: Imprint
Man Dir: E B Bascand
Subjects: General Fiction, Belles Lettres, Poetry, Biography, History, Music, Art, High-priced Paperbacks, Juveniles, Education
Miscellaneous: Publishers of literary periodical, *Landfall*
ISBN Publisher's Prefix: 0-908563

William **Collins** Publishers Ltd, PO Box 1, Auckland (Located at: 31 View Rd, Glenfield) Tel: 4443740 Cable Add: Folio Telex: 21685
Man Dir: B D Phillips; *Marketing Dir:* B J Davies
Branch Offs: 44 Webb St, PO Box 3737, Wellington; 234 Barbadoes St, PO Box 2162, Christchurch
Subjects: Fiction, History, Juveniles, Arts, Maps, Reference, Natural Science, Paperbacks, Educational, New Zealand titles
Founded: 1870
Miscellaneous: Firm is a branch of William Collins Sons & Co Ltd, UK (qv)

Cranwell Publishing Co Ltd, 419a Queen St, Auckland Tel: 774139 Cable Add: Crancat
Man Dir: R G Riddell; *Editorial & Sales:* G A Tait; *Production:* D Reddaway
Branch Off: 32 Burton St, Milsons Point, New South Wales, Australia
Subjects: Building, Architecture, Reference, New Zealand Export, Commercial Fishing
1978: 3 titles *Founded:* 1947

Doubleday New Zealand Ltd, 8 Taylors Rd, Morningside, Auckland 3
Manager: Keith Paterson
Parent Company: Doubleday Australia Pty Ltd, Australia (qv)
Book Club: See Doubleday New Zealand Ltd, Book Club Associates Division in Book Club section for individual clubs.

Dunmore Press Ltd, PO Box 5115, Palmerston North (Located at: 661 Main St, Palmerston North) Tel and Cable Add: 79242 Telex: NZ 3960
Man Dir: John Dunmore; *Sales:* Joyce Dunmore; *Editorial, Publicity, Rights & Permissions:* Patricia Chapman
Subjects: History, Fiction, General, Academic, Political
1978: 10 titles *1979:* 16 titles *Founded:* 1975
ISBN Publisher's Prefix: 0-908564

Forum, an imprint of Sevenseas Publishing Pty Ltd (qv)

Fourth Estate Books Ltd, PO Box 9344, Wellington Tel: 736876 Cable Add: Natbus
General Manager: Ian F Grant
Parent Company: Fourth Estate Holdings
Subjects: Business, History, Law, Politics, Sociology
1978: 3 titles *1979:* 4 titles *Founded:* 1976

Leonard Fullerton Ltd, PO Box 316, Auckland (Located at: 5-7 Shaddock St, Auckland) Tel: 371674
Man Dir, Sales: D L Hart
Founded: 1967
ISBN Publisher's Prefix: 0-903680

Golden Press Pty Ltd*, PO Box 71036, Rosebank, Auckland 7 Tel: 8845889 Cable Add: Gold Press Auckland
Imprints: Golden Press, Whitman
Branch Off: 35 Osborne St, Christchurch
1978: 22 titles

Heinemann Publishers (New Zealand) Ltd, PO Box 36064, Northcote Central, Auckland 9 Tel: (09) 487193 Cable Add: Hebooks Telex: NZ 21902 Hebooks Shipping Add: Corner College Rd and Kilham Ave, Northcote, Auckland 9
Joint Man Dirs: M G Dowthwaite, D J Heap; *Rights & Permissions:* D J Heap; *Publicity:* T Schwarcz; *Sales:* Peter Redgrove; *Editorial, Production:* David Ling
Parent Company: Heinemann Group of Publishers Ltd, UK (qv)
Subjects: University & Secondary Textbooks, Fiction, Hobbies, Technical, Children's, General, Medical, Religious
1978: 21 titles *1979:* 19 titles *Founded:* 1980
ISBN Publisher's Prefix: 0-86863

Hodder & Stoughton Ltd*, PO Box 3858, Auckland 1 (Located at: 44-46 View Rd, Glenfield, Auckland 10) Tel: 4443640 Cable Add: Expositor Auckland Telex: NZ 21422
Editorial Dir: N C Robinson
Parent Company: Hodder & Stoughton Ltd, UK (qv)
Subjects: Fiction, Non-fiction, Education, Children's books
1978: 15 titles

Holt-Saunders Pty Ltd, 10 Moa Street, PO Box 22-245, Otahuhu, Auckland 6 Tel: 2762087 Cable Add: Aytcholt, Auckland
Manager: Ian C Swallow
Associate Company: Holt-Saunders Ltd, UK (qv)

Hutchinson Group (NZ) Ltd, 32-34 View Rd, Glenfield, PO Box 40086, Auckland 10 Tel: 4447197/524
Man Dir: K C Pounder; *General Manager:* N G Sturt
Associate Company: Hutchinson Publishing Group Ltd, UK (qv)
Subjects: General & Academic
1979: 6 titles *Founded:* 1977
ISBN Publisher's Prefix: 0-09

Jacaranda Wiley Ltd, PO Box 2259, Auckland (Located at: 4 Kirk St, Grey Lynn, Auckland) Tel: 764620 Cable Add: Japress
Miscellaneous: Firm is a branch of Jacaranda Wiley, Australia (qv)

Jason Publishing Co Ltd, PO Box 9390, Newmarket, Auckland (Located at: Kingdon House, Kingdon St, Newmarket, Auckland 1) Tel: 546-091 Cable Add: Jasonpub Telex: NZ 21157 Jasonpub
Man Dir, Editorial, Rights & Permissions: John Sandford; *Sales:* Doug Vance; *Production:* Johan Newby; *Publicity:* Johan Newby
Subjects: Sports, Agriculture, Tourism, Travel, Periodicals
1978: 3 titles *1979:* 4 titles *Founded:* 1969

Lancaster Publishing, PO Box 6134, Auckland
Man Dir: Sir Bruce Henderson; *Editorial:* Olive L Rance; *Sales:* Michael Sinclair; *Rights & Permissions:* Red Parsons
Orders to: PO Box 6134, Auckland, New Zealand
Subsidiary Company: Dharma Press
Branch Off: PO Box 1706, Palmerston North
Subjects: Art, Radical Politics, Children's, General
Founded: 1976
ISBN Publisher's Prefix: 0-908576

Longman Paul Ltd, CPO Box 4019, Auckland 1 (Located at: 182-190 Wairau Rd, Takapuna, Auckland 10) Tel: (09) 4444968 Cable Add: Freegrove Telex: NZ 21041
Publisher: Rosemary Stagg; *Editors:* John Barnett, David Pointon, Anne Else
Associate Company: Longman Group Ltd, UK (qv)
Subjects: General Fiction, Primary, Secondary & Tertiary Textbooks
1978: 12 titles *Founded:* 1968
ISBN Publisher's Prefix: 0-582

Thomas C Lothian Pty Ltd*, 88 Nelson St, PO Box 68247, Auckland Tel: 373692 Cable Add: Lothwell
Manager: D H Forrester
Head Office: Thomas C Lothian Pty Ltd, 4-12 Tattersalls Lane, Melbourne, Victoria, Australia
Subjects: General Nonfiction, Educational, Children's
Founded: 1954
ISBN Publisher's Prefix: 0-85091

McGraw-Hill Book Co, New Zealand Ltd*, 28 Airedale St, CPO Box 85, Auckland 1 Tel: 779368
Man Dir: Richard J A Bird; *Promotion:* Margaret Railton
Associate Company: McGraw-Hill Book Co (UK) Ltd, UK (qv)
Subjects: Educational
1978: 1 title *Founded:* 1974
ISBN Publisher's Prefix: 0-07

John McIndoe Ltd, PO Box 694, Dunedin Tel: 70355
Shipping Add: 51 Crawford St, Dunedin
Man Dir: J H McIndoe; *Advertising, Publicity, Rights & Permissions:* B L Turner
Subjects: General Fiction, Belles Lettres, Poetry, Biography, History, How-to, Music, Art, Reference, High-priced Paperbacks, Medicine, General Science, University Textbooks
1979: 18 titles *Founded:* 1893
ISBN Publisher's Prefixes: 0-908565, 0-86868

Mallinson Rendel Publishers Ltd, 5A Grass St, Oriental Bay, PO Box 9409, Wellington Tel: 857340
Joint Man Dirs: E A Malinson, D Rendel
Associate Company: David Rendel Associates Ltd, PO Box 10058, Wellington
Subjects: Historical, Social, Philosophical
Founded: 1980
ISBN Publisher's Prefix: 0-908606

Methuen New Zealand, a subsidiary of Associated Book Publishers (New Zealand) Ltd (qv)

Millwood Press Ltd, 19 Ottawa Rd, Ngaio, Wellington 4 Cable Add: Siersprod
Dirs: Jim and Judy Siers
Subjects: New Zealand and Pacific
ISBN Publisher's Prefix: 0-908582

Minerva Bookshop Ltd*, 13 Commerce St, PO Box 2597, Auckland 1 Tel: (09) 30863 Cable Add: Minerva
Man Dir: Esther Porsolt; *Dir:* Nigel Faigan
Subjects: General Nonfiction, Textbooks, Education
Founded: 1946

Moa Publications*, 23 Orakau Ave, PO Box 26092, Auckland Tel: 655306 Cable Add: Moabooks
Man Dir: John G Blackwell
Subjects: Sport
1978: 8 titles *1979:* 8 titles *Founded:* 1971
ISBN Publisher's Prefix: 0-908570

G W Moore Ltd, PO Box 26-222, Epsom, Auckland (Located at: 69 Great South Rd, Remuera, Auckland) Tel: 548283
Man Dir: G W Moore; *Marketing Manager:* Graham O Walker

N Z E I, see New Zealand Educational Institute

New Zealand Council for Educational Research, PO Box 3237, Wellington Tel: 847939 Cable Add: Edsearch
Dir: John E Watson; *Sales Dir:* Llewelyn M Richards; *Publicity Dir, Rights & Permissions:* Alistair T A Campbell
Subject: Educational Materials
Founded: 1934
ISBN Publisher's Prefix: 0-908567

New Zealand Educational Institute (NZEI), West Block, Education House, 178 Willis St, PO Box 466, Wellington Tel: 849689 Cable Add: Edistute
National Secretary: J E Smith
Orders to: Education House Ltd, Publications Division, PO Box 466, Wellington
Subsidiary Company: Price, Milburn & Co Ltd (qv)
Subject: Educational
1978: 4 titles *1979:* 3 titles *Founded:* 1883
ISBN Publisher's Prefix: 0-908579

New Zealand Government Printing Office, Private Bag, Wellington
Book Shops: Hannaford Bldgs, Rutland St, Auckland; 130 Oxford Terrace, Christchurch; Alexandra St, Hamilton; T and G Bldg, Princes St, Dunedin
ISBN Publisher's Prefix: 0-477

Newrick Associates Ltd, PO Box 820, Wellington Tel: 728231/843676 Cable Add: Backgam Telex: 3353 AH Newrick
Man Dir: Henry P Newrick
Associated Companies: Medici Galleries Ltd, Professional Publications (qv)
Subjects: Art, Antiques, Reference
1978: 2 titles *Founded:* 1967

Nexus Books, PO Box 67-008, Mount Eden, Auckland 3
Manager: A J C Begg
Subject: Mathematics
1978: 1 title *Founded:* 1973
ISBN Publisher's Prefix: 0-85912

Outrigger Publishers, PO Box 13049, Hamilton Tel: 85602
Man Dir, Editorial: Norman Sims; *Sales:* Robin Haughey; *Publicity:* Martha Simms; *Production:* Jack Parker; *Circulation Manager:* L E Scott
Subjects: Literature, Criticism, Folklore, Periodicals
ISBN Publisher's Prefix: 0-908571

Oxford University Press*, 2nd Floor, McKenzies Bldg, 222-236 Willis St, Wellington, C1 Tel: (04) 843723 Cable Add: Oxonian, Wellington
Shipping Add: PO Box 27344, Wellington, C1
Manager: J W B Griffin
Subjects: Belles Lettres, Poetry, History, Social Science, University & Primary Textbooks, New Zealand
1978: 8 titles *1979:* 14 titles *Founded:* 1947
Miscellaneous: Branch of Oxford University Press, UK (qv)
ISBN Publisher's Prefix: 0-19

Pegasus Press Ltd, 14 Oxford Terrace, PO Box 2244, Christchurch 1 Tel: 64509
Chairman: Albion Wright; *Man Dir:* Don Wallace; *Editor:* Robin Muir; *Rights & Permissions:* Pamela Rogers
Subjects: General Fiction, Poetry, Biography, History, Sports, Library and Paperback editions
1978: 13 titles *1979:* 14 titles *Founded:* 1948
ISBN Publisher's Prefix: 0-908568

Penguin Books (NZ) Ltd*, PO Box 4019, Auckland 1 (Located at: 183-190 Wairau Rd, Auckland 10) Tel: 448396 Cable Add: Penguinook Auckland Telex: 21041
Man Dir: Graham Beattie; *Sales & Publicity:* Margaret Greer
Parent Company: Penguin Books Ltd, UK (qv)
Founded: 1973
ISBN Publisher's Prefix: 0-14

N M Peryer Ltd*, 93-97 Cambridge Terrace, PO Box 833, Christchurch 1 Tel: 64733
Cable Add: Medico
Branch Offs: Cnr John St & Adelaide Rd, PO Box 7389, Wellington; PO Box 8542, Symonds St, Auckland; 8 Park Ave, Grafton, Auckland
Subjects: Medical, Educational
Founded: 1932
ISBN Publisher's Prefix: 0-85185

Pitman Publishing NZ Ltd*, PO Box 38688, Petone, Wellington
Associate Company: Pitman Publishing Ltd, UK (qv)
1978: 2 titles
ISBN Publisher's Prefix: 0-85896

Price Milburn & Co Ltd, Suite 4, Book House, Boulcott St, PO Box 2919, Wellington Tel: 727533/758838/285254
Cable Add: Mice Wellington
Man Dir: Hugh Price; *Secretary:* Sidney Heppleston; *Sales Manager:* Barbara Milburn; *Editor, Permissions:* Beverley Price
Parent Company: New Zealand Educational Institute (NZEI) (qv)
Subjects: Juveniles, Social Science, University, Secondary & Primary Textbooks, particularly Junior Readers
Bookshop: Bilbo's Book Centre, 2 Whiteman Rd, Silverstream
1980: 60 titles *Founded:* 1957
Miscellaneous: Publishes for New Zealand Institute of International Affairs, New Zealand University Press, Victoria University Press, New Zealand Council for Civil Liberties and Kea Press imprints
ISBN Publisher's Prefix: 0-7055

Professional Publications, PO Box 820, Wellington Tel: 728231 Cable Add: Backgam Telex: 3353 AH Newrick
Man Dir: Henry P Newrick
Associate Companies: Medici Galleries Ltd, Newrick Associates Ltd (qv)
Subjects: Business, Economics, Taxation
1979: 2 titles *Founded:* 1979

A H & A W Reed Ltd Publishers, 68-74 Kingsford Smith St, Wellington Tel: (04) 873045 Cable Add: Reedkiwi Telex: NZ 31489
Chairman: J M Reed; *Man Dir:* P M Bradwell; *Executive Dir (Overseas):* Murray McL Humphries
Subsidiary Company: A H & A W Reed Pty Ltd (Australia) (qv)
Branch Offs: 16 Beresford St, Auckland; 85 Thackeray St, Christchurch (both in New Zealand); 11 Southampton Row, London WC1B 5HA, UK
Bookshop: Reed Books Ltd, Wellington
Subjects: General Fiction, Belles Lettres, Poetry, Biography, History, How-to, Music, Art, Reference, Juveniles, High-priced Paperbacks, Social Science, Agriculture
1979: 143 titles *Founded:* 1907
ISBN Publisher's Prefix: 0-589

Richards Publishing, PO Box 31285, Milford, Auckland 9 (Located at: 49 Aberdeen Rd, Castor Bay, Auckland 9) Tel: 469681
Man Dir: Ray Richards; *Editorial:* Barbara Richards; *Production:* Don Sinclair
Associate Company: Richards Publishing Consultants (Literary Agents, qv)
Branch Off: 54 Ranui Terrace, Linden, Wellington
Subject: New Zealand Biography, History, Art, Adventure
1979: 3 titles *1980:* 4 titles *Founded:* 1978
ISBN Publisher's Prefix: 0-908596

Sevenseas Publishing Pty Ltd, 5-7 Tory St, PO Box 1431, Wellington 1 Tel: 859759
Cable Add: Vikseven
Man Dir, Editorial, Production, Rights & Permissions: Murdoch Riley; *Sales, Publicity Dir:* K Southern
Associate Companies: Viking Record Co Ltd, Delta Trading Co Ltd
Imprints: Forum, Viking Sevenseas
Branch Off: ANZ Bank Bldg, 68 Pitt St, Sydney, Australia
Subjects: How-to, Music, Art, South Pacific, Health, Nutrition, General
1978: 6 titles *1979:* 3 titles *Founded:* 1963
ISBN Publisher's Prefix: 0-85467

Shortland Educational Publications, PO Box 56113, Auckland Tel: 689959
Cable Add: Newspress
Managing Editor: Wendy Pye
Parent Company: NZ Newspapers Ltd, PO Box 1409, Auckland
Branch Offs: Newspaper House, Wellington; Christchurch Star, Christchurch
Subjects: Gardening, Cookery, Sports, Children's Activities, General
Founded: 1977
ISBN Publisher's Prefix: 0-86867

Stockton House*, Box 46, Albany Tel: GNH 528
Man Dir: R S Witter
Subjects: Educational, General
Founded: 1974

Sweet and Maxwell (NZ) Ltd, a subsidiary of Associated Book Publishers (New Zealand) Ltd (qv)

Alister **Taylor** Publishers, The Old Post Office, Martinborough Tel: Featherston 69847 Cable Add: Taylor, Martinborough
Subjects: Limited Editions, Fiction, Poetry, New Zealand, Art, Photography, General
1980: 20 titles *Founded:* 1971
ISBN Publisher's Prefix: 0-908578

University of Canterbury Publications, PB, Christchurch Tel: 482009 Cable Add: Canterbury University
Secretary: The Registrar
Subjects: Fine Art, History, Literature, Physics, Chemistry, Social Sciences
1978: 2 titles *1979:* 1 title *Founded:* 1960
ISBN Publisher's Prefix: 0-900392

University of Otago Press, PO Box 56, Dunedin Tel: 40109
Orders to: John McIndoe Ltd, PO Box 694, Dunedin
Subjects: Scholarly Monographs, Biography, Music, Poetry, Literature, History, Medicine
1980: 3 titles *Founded:* 1959
ISBN Publisher's Prefix: 0-908569

Victoria University Press, Victoria University of Wellington, Private Bag, Wellington Tel: 721000
Editorial: Pamela Tomlinson; *Sales, Production:* Hugh Price
Orders to: Price Milburn & Co Ltd, PO Box 2919, Wellington
Associate Company: Price Milburn & Co Ltd (qv)
Imprint: Price Milburn
Subjects: General Academic, New Zealand Drama, Short Stories, History, Politics, Sociology, Anthropology, Language and Communications, Law, Religion, Psychology, Zoology
1978: 4 titles *1979:* 5 titles
ISBN Publisher's Prefix: 0-7055

Viking Sevenseas Ltd, an imprint of Sevenseas Publishing Pty Ltd (qv)

Whitcoulls Publishers, Private Bag, Christchurch Tel: 794580 Telex: NZ 4205
Publishing Manager, Editorial, Sales: Max Rogers; *Assistant Publishing Manager, Production, Promotion, Rights & Permissions:* Edward C Day; *Senior Editor:* R S Gormack
Parent Company: Whitcoulls Ltd, Private Bag, Christchurch
Subsidiary Company: Whitcombe & Tombs Pty Ltd, Australia
Subjects: General, Fiction, Non-fiction, New Zealand, Educational
Bookshops: Throughout New Zealand (Whitcoulls Ltd)
1978: 19 titles *1979:* 16 titles *Founded:* 1882
ISBN Publisher's Prefix: 0-7233

Whitman, an imprint of Golden Press Pty Ltd (qv)

Wilson & Horton Ltd*, PO Box 32, Auckland Tel: 795050 Cable Add: Herald Telex: 2325
1978: 14 titles
ISBN Publisher's Prefix: 0-86864

Literary Agents

Butler Richards Agency, PO Box 31285, Milford, Auckland (Located at: 172 Sunnybrae Rd, Auckland 9 and 49 Aberdeen Rd, Auckland 9) Tel: 488359/469681
Contacts: Dorothy Butler, Ray Richards
Specialization: Books for Children and Young People

Richards Publishing Consultants, PO Box 31285, Milford, Auckland (Located at: 49 Aberdeen Rd, Castor Bay, Auckland 9 and 54 Ranui Terrace, Linden, Wellington) Tel: 469681
Contacts: Ray Richards, Barbara Richards
Specialization: General, Educational and Academic (not juvenile)

Book Clubs

20th Century Classics, see Doubleday New Zealand Ltd, Book Club Associates Division

Doubleday Book Club, see Doubleday New Zealand Ltd, Book Club Associates Division

Doubleday History Book Club, see Doubleday New Zealand Ltd, Book Club Associates Division

Doubleday New Zealand Ltd, Book Club Associates Division, 8 Taylors Rd, Morningside, Auckland 3
Includes: Doubleday Book Club, Doubleday History Book Club, The Literary Guild, 20th Century Classics

The **Literary Guild**, see Doubleday New Zealand Ltd, Book Club Associates Division

Major Booksellers

A B C Bookshop*, 284 Trafalgar St, Nelson

G H **Bennett** & Co Ltd, 38-42 Broadway, PO Box 138, Palmerston North

Dorothy **Butler** Ltd*, 172 Sunnybrae Rd, Auckland 9
Children's Book Specialists

Goddard's Bookshop Ltd, 21 Devonport Rd, PO Box 41, Tauranga
Man Dir: Ray Goddard

Horizon Bookshop Ltd, T & G Bldg, Queens Drive, Lower Hutt, Wellington Tel: (04) 698406/663256
Manager: Steven Sedley

London Bookshops Ltd, 106 Cuba St, PO Box 6143, Wellington 1
Branches: St Luke's Shopping Centre, Mount Albert, Auckland; Shore City, Takapuna, Auckland; Downtown Mall, Queen St, Auckland; 99 Cashels St, Christchurch; 239 George St, Dunedin; Hartham Pl, Porirua; Maidstone Mall, Upper Hutt; 326 Lambton Quay, Wellington; Manners Plaza, Wellington (Educational Division); Kirkcaldies, Brandon St, Wellington

Roy **Parsons**, Massey House, 126 Lambton Quay, Wellington 1

Pauls University Bookshop Ltd, 211 Victoria St, PO Box 928, Hamilton Tel: 80379
Manager: A N Kerby

School Supplies Ltd, 6 Gordon Rd, Morningside, PO Box 41-163, Auckland 3
Branches: 5 Wall Pl, Linden, Wellington 1; PO Box 50-384 Porirua; Rathbone St, PO Box 224, Whangarei; PO Box 22-512, 363 Tuam St, Christchurch

Unity Books Ltd, 42 Willis St, PO Box 3676, Wellington
Manager: A H Preston

University Book Shop (Auckland) Ltd, Student Union Bldg, 34 Princes St, Auckland 1
Manager: Kitty Wishart

University Book Shop (Canterbury) Ltd*, University Drive, University of Canterbury, Christchurch Tel: 488579 Cable Add: Unibooks
Also The Book Shop in the Arts Centre, Arts Centre, Christchurch Tel: 60568

University Book Shop (Otago) Ltd, 378 Great King St, PO Box 6060, Dunedin North Tel: 776976 Cable Add: Unibooks
Manager: Bill Noble

Whitcoulls Ltd, 111 Cashel St, PMB, Christchurch 1
and 50 branches throughout New Zealand

Wholesale Book Distributors, Box 4149, New Plymouth Telex: DCS NZ 3939
Publishers Representatives; Paperback Specialists
Also Novalit Books, PO Box 40047, Glenfield, Auckland
Publishers Representatives: Hardcover Specialists
Both are divisions of Marketing Services (1974) Ltd, a subsidiary of BPC, UK (qv)

Major Libraries

Auckland Public Library, Lorne St, PO Box 4138, Auckland 1 Tel: 770209
Telex: NZ2750
Librarian: Robert Duthie

Canterbury Public Library, PO Box 1466, 109 Cambridge Terrace, Christchurch Tel: (03) 796914 Telex: NZ 4620
Librarian: J E D Stringleman
Publication: Canterbury Public Library Journal (monthly)

Canterbury University Library, Private Bag, Christchurch
Librarian: R W Hlavac

Dunedin Public Library, PO Box 906, Moray Place, Dunedin
City Librarian: Michael Wooliscroft

General Assembly Library*, Parliament House, Wellington 1 Tel: 738288

National Archives, 129-141 Vivian St, Box 6162, Te Aro, Wellington Tel: 738699
Chief Archivist: Miss J S Hornabrook
Publication: A Summary of Work (annually)

National Library of New Zealand, Private Bag, Wellington 1 Tel: 722101 Telex: nz 3076

Otago University Library, PO Box 56, Dunedin
Librarian: W J McEldowney
Publication: Annual Report

Palmerston North Public Library, PO Box 1948, Palmerston North
Librarian: I W Malcolm

Alexander **Turnbull** Library, 44 The Terrace, PO Box 12349, Wellington Tel: 722107

University of Auckland Library, PB, Auckland Tel: Auckland 792-300 Telex: NZ 21480
Librarian: P B Durey

Wellington Public Library, PO Box 1992, Wellington
Librarian: B K McKeon

Library Associations

Bibliographical Society of Australia and New Zealand, see Australia

International Association of Music Libraries, Australia/New Zealand Branch, see Australia

New Zealand Library Association, 10 Park St, PO Box 12212, Wellington 1 Tel: 735834
Executive Officer: H Stephen-Smith
Publications: Library Life (11 a year), *New Zealand Libraries* (4 a year)

New Zealand Library Committee, PO Box 37-030, Parnell, Auckland

Library Reference Books and Journals

Books

Special Libraries and Collections: A New Zealand Directory, New Zealand Library Association, 10 Park St, PO Box 12212, Wellington 1

Who's Who in New Zealand Libraries, New Zealand Library Association, 10 Park St, PO Box 12212, Wellington 1

Journals

Library Life (11 times yearly), New Zealand Library Association, 10 Park St, PO Box 12212, Wellington 1

New Zealand Libraries (quarterly), New Zealand Library Association, 10 Park St, PO Box 12212, Wellington 1

Literary Associations and Societies

Bibliographical Society of Australia and New Zealand, 117 Georges Rd, North Fitzroy, Victoria 3068, Australia
Secretary: Trevor Mills
Publications: Bulletin, Broadsheet

The **Dickens** Fellowship, 18 Spencer St, Christchurch 2
Honorary Secretary: G J H Fox
Branches: Dunedin, Wellington

International Writers Workshop New Zealand Inc, 13 Valkyria Pl, Auckland 10

New Zealand Maori Artists & Writers Society Inc, 8/87 Beresford St, Freemans Bay, Auckland 1

New Zealand Playwrights Association, c/o The Play Bureau (NZ) Ltd, PO Box 3611, Wellington

New Zealand Women Writers' Society, 75 Hall Crescent, Lower Hutt
Secretary: Eleanor Stahl

New Zealand Writers Guild, c/o 4 Shirley St, Karori, Wellington

P E N International New Zealand Centre*, 30 Verviers St, Karori, Wellington
Secretary: Gillian Shadbolt
Publication: PEN Gazette (quarterly)

Literary Periodicals

Arena; a literary magazine, Noel Farr Hoggard, PO Box 6188, Te Aro, Wellington

Islands; a New Zealand quarterly of arts and letters, Robin Dudding, 4 Scaly Rd, Torbay, Auckland 10

Landfall, Caxton Press, 113 Victoria St, PO Box 25088, Christchurch

Mate; a magazine of New Zealand writing, Wellesley St, PO Box 5670, Auckland

New Quarterly Cave; an international magazine of arts and ideas, Outrigger Publishers Ltd, 1 Von Tempsky St, Hamilton

Northland, Northland Magazine Inc, PO Box 694, Whangarei

Literary Prizes

A H I Literary Research Award
An award of $7,000 (New Zealand) to enable an established writer to undertake research towards the publication of literary, historical or critical works. Enquiries to Secretary, New Zealand Literary Fund Advisory Committee, c/o Department of Internal Affairs, Private Bag, Wellington

Award for Achievement
For a contribution to literature. $500 (New Zealand). Awarded annually. Enquiries to Secretary, New Zealand Literary Fund Advisory Committee, c/o Department of Internal Affairs, Private Bag, Wellington

Bank of New Zealand Young Writers' Awards
For unpublished short stories written by young people in two age groups: Senior

(under 25 years); and Junior (school age). $250 and $150 (New Zealand). A grant of $150 is given to the library of the secondary school attended by the Junior awardee. Awarded every other year. Enquiries to New Zealand Women Writers' Society, 75 Hall Crescent, Lower Hutt

Best First Book of Poetry Award (incorporating the Jessie Mackay Award)*
For the best first book of published poetry. $600 (New Zealand). Awarded annually. Enquiries to PEN International New Zealand Centre, PO Box 2283, Wellington

Best First Book of Prose Award (Incorporating the Hubert Church Award)*
For the best first book of prose. $600 (New Zealand). Awarded annually. Enquiries to PEN International New Zealand Centre, PO Box 2283, Wellington

Buckland Literary Award*
Founded in 1966 by the late Freda M Buckland for the work of the highest literary merit by a New Zealand writer. Awarded annually. Enquiries to Buckland Literary Award, Trustees Executors and Agency Company of New Zealand Ltd, 24 Water St, PO Box 760, Dunedin

Choysa Bursary for Children's Writers
A bursary of $5,000 (New Zealand) to enable an author of imaginative work for children to work full-time for a period of up to one year on an approved project(s) which will reach book form. Enquiries to Secretary, New Zealand Literary Fund Advisory Committee, c/o Department of Internal Affairs, Private Bag, Wellington

Russell Clark Award
For the most distinguished illustrations for a children's book. Illustrator must be a citizen or resident of New Zealand. Bronze medal and $50 (New Zealand). Awarded annually. Enquiries to New Zealand Library Association, 10 Park Street, Wellington 1

Esther Glen Award
For the best children's book by an author who is a citizen of, or resident in, New Zealand. $50 (New Zealand). Awarded annually. Enquiries to New Zealand Library Association, 10 Park St, Wellington 1

I C I Writing Bursary
An annual award of $5,000 is made to one or more writers (not necessarily of repute) with potential to work full-time for one year on an approved project. Enquiries to The Secretary, New Zealand Literary Fund, Advisory Committee, c/o Department of Internal Affairs, Private Bag, Wellington

Katherine Mansfield Memorial Award
For an unpublished short story. Sponsored by the Bank of New Zealand. $500 (New Zealand) awarded in 1979. Awarded biennially. Enquiries to New Zealand Women Writers' Society, 75 Hall Crescent, Lower Hutt

New Zealand Book Awards
Annual awards of $2,000 (New Zealand) for the best book published each year in the categories of poetry, fiction, non-fiction and book production. Enquiries to The Secretary, New Zealand Literary Fund, Advisory Committee, c/o Department of Internal Affairs, Private Bag, Wellington

New Zealand Literary Fund
In addition to awards specifically mentioned, various grants are made from time to time by the above Fund to writers, publishers of creative literature and literary magazines. Enquiries to The Secretary, New Zealand Literary Fund, Advisory Committee, c/o Department of Internal Affairs, Private Bag, Wellington

The **Scholarship** in Letters
An award of $9,000 (New Zealand) to enable an established writer to work full-time for one year on an approved project. Enquiries to The Secretary, New Zealand Literary Fund, Advisory Committee, c/o Department of Internal Affairs, Private Bag, Wellington

Sir James **Wattie** Book of the Year Award
Established 1967. For the book of the year based on: (1) quality of writing and illustrations; (2) quality of editing, design and production; (3) impact on the community. Open only to members of the Publishers Association of New Zealand. First prize $4,000 (New Zealand), second $2,500 (New Zealand), third $1,000 (New Zealand). The 1979 winner was *Plumb* by Maurice Gee (Oxford University Press). Enquiries to Book Publishers Association of New Zealand, PO Box 78071, Grey Lynn, Auckland 2

Young Writers' Incentive Awards
For prose and poetry by New Zealanders under 20. $100 and $50 (New Zealand). Enquiries to PEN International New Zealand Centre, PO Box 2283, Wellington

Nicaragua

General Information

Language: Spanish
Religion: Roman Catholic
Population: 2.4 million
Literacy Rate (1971): 57.5% (80.5% of urban population, 34.6% rural)
Bank Hours: 0900-1500 Monday-Friday; 0900-1130 Saturday
Shop Hours: 0800-1200, 1430-1730 or longer Monday-Saturday
Currency: 100 centavos = 1 córdoba
Export/Import Information: Catalogues dutied at $0.03 per gross kilo. 10% Compensatory Tax on advertising. No import licences or exchange controls
Copyright: UCC, Buenos Aires, Florence (see International section)

Publishers

Academia Nicaragüense de la Lengua*, Biblioteca Nacional, Managua
Subject: Languages

Editorial **Alemana***, 2A Calle SO 108, Managua

Editorial **Chile***, 8 Ave, Calle SE 604, Managua

Editorial **Nicaragüense***, Calle del Triunfo, Managua
Dir: Mario Cajina Vega

Editorial **Lacayo***, 2A Avda SE 507, Managua
Subject: Religion

Editorial **Nuevos Horizontes***, Calle de Candelaria, Managua
Dir: María Teresa Sánchez

Editorial **San José***, Calle Central Este 607, Managua

Club del Libro Nicaragüense, Librería y Editorial **Siglo XX***, Apdo 2173, Managua
Dir: Dr Fernando Centeno Zapata
Subject: Law

Editorial **Unión***, Avda Central Norte, Managua
Subject: Travel

Librería y Editorial, **Universidad Nacional** de Nicaragua*, León
Subjects: Education, History, Mathematics, Law, Philology, Economics, Sciences, Politics, Literature

Major Booksellers

Librería **América***, Bosques de Altamira, Managua Tel: 80895

Centro Cultural **Bautista**, Apdo 5776, Cuidad Jardin No E5, Managua Tel: 24714
Manager: Stanley D Stamps

Librería **Blandon***, Apdo 2206, Managua

Librería **Club** de Lectores*, Centro Comercial Módulo 9, Managua Tel: 82240

Librería Recinto 'Ruben **Dario**'*, Universidad Nacional Autonoma de Nicaragua, Apdo 663, Managua

Librería **Cultural Nicaraguense***, Apdo 807, Managua Tel: 6663

Librería **Tecnológica Universitaria***, Universidad Centroamericana, Apdo 69, Managua Tel: 80351

Librería **Universitaria**, Universidad Nacional Autónoma de Nicaragua, León Tel: 2612

Librería **Recalde***, Apdo 666, Managua Tel: 81156/61239

Major Libraries

Archivo General de la Nación*, 6a Calle 402, Managua

Biblioteca Nacional*, Calle del Triunfo 302, Managua

Biblioteca Central del **Universidad Nacional** de Nicaragua*, León

Library Associations

Asociación de Bibliotecas Universitarias y Especializadas de Nicaragua*, Apdo 68, León
Association of University and Special Libraries of Nicaragua
Publication: Boletín

Asociación Nicaraguense de Bibliotecarios (ASNIBI)*, Biblioteca Nacional, Ministerio de Educacion Publica, Barrio 'La Fuente', Managua
Nicaraguan Association of Librarians
Executive Secretary: Susana Morales Hernández

Library Journals

Boletín (Bulletin), Association of University and Special Libraries of Nicaragua, Apdo 68, León

Niger

General Information

Language: French
Religion: 85% Muslim; rest follow traditional beliefs
Population: 5 million
Currency: CFA franc
Export/Import Information: Member of West African Economic Community. No tariff on books; advertising matter subject to 10% Fiscal and 5% Customs Duty (EEC members pay 50% of Customs Duty). 2.5% Statistical Tax.
Copyright: Berne (see International section)

Publishers

Church World Service*, BP 624, Niamey Tel: 2449   Cable Add: Le Sahel
Telex: 5232NI
Man Dir: Jon Otto
Subjects: Reference, Religion, Paperbacks

Government Printer (Imprimerie Générale du Niger)*, BP 61, Niamey

Major Booksellers

Librairie **Fellicelli & Poli***, BP 331, Niamey

Librairie **Mauclert***, BP 868, Niamey
Tel: 722778

Major Libraries

Archives nationales*, Présidence de la République, Niamey

Centre d'Enseignement supérieur de Niamey*, Bibliothèque, BP 237, Niamey
University Education Centre

Centre de Documentation*, Commission du Fleuve Niger, BP 933, Niamey   Tel: 723101/723102   Cable Add: Comfleuniger Niamey
Dir: Dr I Insa
Parent organization: Commission du fleuve Niger
Publications: Concerning development of the natural resources of the River Niger Basin
Founded: 1971

Bibliothèque de l'**Université de Niamey***, BP 237, Niamey   Tel: 732713

Library Associations

River Niger Commission, Documentation and Analysis Centre*, PO Box 729, Niamey
Publication: Bulletin of Bibliographic Descriptions and Abstracts

Library Journals

Bulletin of Bibliographic Descriptions and Abstracts, River Niger Commission, Documentation and Analysis Centre, PO Box 729, Niamey

Nigeria

General Information

Language: English, Hausa
Religion: 45% Muslim (mainly in north), 35% Christian; rest follow traditional beliefs
Population: 72.2 million
Bank Hours: 0800-1500 Monday; 0800-1300 Tuesday-Friday
Shop Hours: Vary locally. 0800-1230, 1400-1630 Monday-Friday; 0800-1230 Saturday
Currency: 100 kobo = 1 naira
Export/Import Information: No tariffs on books or advertising matter. Open general licence. Obscene literature prohibited. Exchange controls
Copyright: UCC, Florence (see International section)

Book Trade Organizations

Nigerian Booksellers' Association, PO Box 3168, Ibadan
President: 'Wunmi Adegbonmire; *Secretary:* Sam Olaniyan

Nigerian Publishers' Association, c/o PMB 5164, Ibadan   Tel: 462972   Telex: 31104
President: Bankole Olayiwola Bolodeoku
Publication: Book Publishing Process

Standard Book Numbering Agency, c/o Mrs O Omolayole, National Library of Nigeria, 4 Wesley St, PMB 12626, Lagos

Book Trade Reference Books and Journals

Books

Publishing in Nigeria, Ethiope Publishing Corporation, PMB 1192, Benin City (Contains several informative articles on the publishing scene in Nigeria)

Serials in Print in Nigeria, National Library of Nigeria, 4 Wesley St, PMB 12626, Lagos

Journals

National Bibliography of Nigeria, National Library of Nigeria, 4 Wesley St, PMB 12626, Lagos (Published annually since 1950. Cumulations before 1971 published by the Ibadan University Press. Also available as a weekly service)

New Nigeriana, University of Ife Bookshop Ltd, Ile-Ife (Bi-annual checklist, available free of charge from the Ife bookshop)

Nigerian Books in Print, National Library of Nigeria, 4 Wesley St, PMB 12626, Lagos

Northern Nigerian Publications, Ahmadu Bello University Library, Zaria (annual)

Publishers

A B I C Publishers*, PMB 1161, Oshodi, Lagos
Branch Off: 6 Old Cemetry Rd, Onitsha
Subjects: Reference, Dictionaries
ISBN Publisher's Prefix: 978-2269

Academy Press Ltd, subsidiary of West African Book Publishers Ltd (qv)

African Resources Publishing Co*, PMB 5398, Ibadan
Subjects: General Fiction & Nonfiction, Belles Lettres, Poetry, Biography, History, Africana, How-to, Study Guides, Secondary Textbooks

African Universities Press, Pilgrim Books Ltd, PMB 5617, Ibadan (Located at: 9 First Rd, Oluyole Estate, Ring Rd, Ibadan)   Cable Add: Pilgrim Ibadan
Man Dir: John E Leigh; *General Manager:* N P Legg; *Sales Manager:* J A Kilanko
Parent Company: Pilgrim Books Ltd (at above address)
Subjects: Primary, Secondary and Tertiary Textbooks
Miscellaneous: Depots at 21 Ikorodu Rd, Obanikoro; PO Box 3560, Lagos; 74 Oguta Rd, PO Box 21, Onitsha; 17 Ciroma St, Gellesu, Tundun Wada, PMB 1146, Zaria. Main warehouse at New Oluyole Industrial Estate (Phase 2), Ibadan Expressway, PMB 5617, Ibadan

Africana Educational Publishers (Nig) Ltd, PMB 1639, Onitsha (Located at: 79 Awka Rd, Onitsha)
Man Dir: P N C Omabu; *Editorial:* K B C Onwubiko; *Marketing:* Ralph O Ekpeh
Branch Off: 49 Zik's Ave, Uwani, Enugu
Subjects: How-to, Study Guides, General Science, Secondary & Primary Textbooks, *At a Glance* and *Made Easy* series
Founded: 1971

Africani Agency*, 98 Emir's Rd, PO Box 38, Ilorin
Subjects: General Nonfiction, History, Africana, How-to, Study Guides, Paperbacks, Secondary Textbooks

Ahmadu Bello University Press Ltd*, PMB 1094, Zaria   Tel: 2054   Cable Add: Unibello Press Zaria   Telex: 75241 Zarabu Ng
Man Dir: Mrs Modupe Adeogun
Subjects: Biography, History, Africana, Reference, Social Science, University Textbooks
1978: 5 titles   *Founded:* 1974
ISBN Publisher's Prefix: 978-125

Alliance West African Publishers & Co*, Orindingbin Estate, New Aketan Layout, PMB 1039, Oyo   Tel: Oyo 124
Manager: Chief M O Ogunmola BA; *Editorial:* Poju Amori BA; *Sales:* L Oyeniji; *Publicity, Permissions:* Kehinde Ogunmola
Subjects: Biography, History, Africana, How-to, Study Guides, Nigerian Languages, General Science, Secondary & Primary School Textbooks
1978: 1 title   *Founded:* 1971

Aowa Press & Publications*, PO Box 3090, Ibadan
Subjects: How-to, Study Guides, Primary & Secondary Textbooks

Aromolaran Publishing Co Ltd, PO Box 1800, Ibadan   Tel: 410529   Telex: 31158 Arbook Nigeria
Man Dir: Adekunle Aromolaran; *Sales:* Mrs V M Aromolaran
Subjects: Belles Lettres, Poetry, Biography, How-to, Study Guides, Religion, Juveniles; Arts, Science and General Books for Primary and Secondary Schools and Universities
1980: 300 titles   *Founded:* 1970

Black Academy Press*, PO Box 255, Owerri, Imo State   Cable Add: Bapress
Man Dir: Dr S Okechukwu Mezu
Subjects: General Nonfiction, Belles Lettres, Poetry, Biography, History, Africana
Miscellaneous: Publishers of *Black Academy Review* (quarterly of the Black World)

C S S Bookshops, Agency and Publishing Division*, 50 Broad St, PO Box 174, Lagos
Tel: 25517/9   Cable Add: Bookshops
Man Dir: Akin O Shenbanjo; *Publicity:* 'Dele Oladuiyuye
Subsidiary Company: CSS Bookshops, PO Box 174, Lagos (and regional offices at

Ibadan, Zaria, Port Harcourt)
Subjects: General Nonfiction, Biography, History, Africana, Religion, General Science, Law, Medicine, Secondary & Primary Textbooks

Conch Magazine Ltd*, Publishers, 113 Douglas Rd, Owerri
Man Dir: Sunday Anozie
Subsidiary Company: Conch Magazine Ltd, 65 Jenkenstown Rd, New Paltz, NY 12561, USA
Subjects: General Nonfiction, Belles Lettres, Poetry, History, Africana, Paperbacks, Social Science

Cross Continent Press Ltd, 226 Murtala Muhammed Way, PO Box 282, Yaba, Lagos Tel: (01) 961894 Cable Add: Croconpres Lagos
Man Dir: T C Nwosu; *Editorial, Publicity:* O A Achonu; *Marketing:* N S Wokocha; *Financial:* L O Oshin
Subsidiary Companies: Editorial Consultancy & Agency Services (Authors' and Publishers' Agents and Consultants) GPO Box 4573, Lagos; Toscana Printers Ltd, PO Box 282, Yaba, Lagos
Subjects: General Fiction & Non-fiction, Belles Lettres, Poetry, Biography, How-to, Study Guides, Juveniles, Paperbacks, Primary, Secondary & Tertiary Textbooks
Founded: 1974
ISBN Publisher's Prefix: 978-134

Daily Times of Nigeria Ltd*, Book Sales Division, 3-7 Kakawa St, PO Box 139, Lagos Tel: 26611 Telex: 21333
Chief Executive: Dr P D Cole; *Editorial:* Peter Osugo; *Sales:* J Tan Olu; *Production:* E A Cole
Subsidiary Company: Times Press Ltd
Subjects: Reference, Nigerian Who's Who
Book Club: Times Book Club
Founded: 1925

Daystar Press (Publishers), Daystar Ho, PO Box 1261, Ibadan Tel: 23230
Man Dir, Editorial, Permissions: Modupe Oduyoye; *Production:* Gabriel Ojo; *Trade:* James Akimboye; *Publicity:* A Osuji
Subjects: Christian Religions, Health, Home & Family Life, Nigerian Culture
1978: 7 titles *1979:* 6 titles *Founded:* 1962
ISBN Publisher's Prefix: 978-122

E C W A Productions Ltd, PMB 10, Jos
Man Dir: G D H Stanley; *Publishing Dir:* Rev J K Bolarin
Subjects: General, Educational, Religion
Bookshops: Challenge Bookshops (qv)
1978: 124 titles

Educational Research Institute*, PO Box 277, Ibadan
Man Dir: Areoye Oyebola
Subjects: General Nonfiction, Biography, History, Africana, How-to, Study Guides, Religion, General & Social Science, Secondary & Primary Textbooks
Founded: 1970

Elizabethan Publishing House*, 41 Ogunlena Drive, Surulere, Lagos Tel: 45305
Man Dir: C A Kogbe
Subjects: Academic, Geology

Emotan Publishing Co (Nigeria) Ltd*, 152nd Ire St, Benin City
Man Dir: P O Onaghise
Subjects: General Fiction, Belles Lettres, Poetry, Paperbacks

Ethiope Publishing Corporation, Ring Road, PMB 1332, Benin City Tel: 243036 Cable Add: Ethiope Telex: 41110
Man Dir: Clement Okosun; *Publishing Manager, Rights & Permissions:* Sunday Olaye
Subjects: General Fiction, & Nonfiction, Belles Lettres, Poetry, Biography, History, Africana, How-to, Study Guides, Philosophy, Reference, Juveniles, Paperbacks, Science & Technology, General & Social Science, Law, University & Secondary Textbooks
Founded: 1970

Evans Brothers (Nigeria Publishers) Ltd, Jericho Rd, PMB 5164, Ibadan Tel: 462970/71/72 Cable Add: Edbooks Ibadan Telex: 31104 Edbook
Man Dir: B O Bolodeoku; *Publishing Dir:* C T McGregor; *Trade Dir:* R A Oyewole; *Publishing Manager:* Valentine Olayemi; *Sales Dir:* S A Oke
Associate Company: Evans Brothers Ltd, UK (qv)
Branch Offs: Kaduna, Onitsha and Osogbo
Subjects: Educational generally: General Non-fiction, Belles Lettres, Poetry, Biography, History, Africana, Reference, Juveniles, Paperbacks, Science & Technology, General & Social Science, Secondary & Primary Textbooks
Founded: 1966
ISBN Publisher's Prefix: 978-167

Olaiya **Fagbamigbe** Ltd (Publishers), 11 Methodist Church Rd, PO Box 14, Akure Tel: 2075 Cable Add: Fagbamigbe Akure
Man Dir: O Fagbamigbe; *General Manager:* Oyewumi Oladeji; *Publicity:* Gbolagade Adesina; *Rights & Permissions:* E Fagbamigbe
Branch Offs: Old Ife Rd, PO Box 1176, Agodi, Ibadan
Subjects: Educational and General
1979: 35 titles *1980:* 50 titles *Founded:* 1976
ISBN Publisher's Prefix: 978-164

Grassroots Books, an imprint of Third World First Publications

Heinemann Educational Books (Nigeria) Limited, Ighodaro Road, Jericho, PMB 5205, Ibadan Tel: 462060/462061/410267 Cable Add: Hebooks Ibadan Telex: 31113 Hebook NG
Dep Chairman & Man Dir: Aigboje Higo; *Publishing Dir and Rights & Permissions:* Akin Thomas; *Sales & Publicity Dir:* Joe Osadolor
Parent Company: Heinemann Educational Books (International) UK Ltd (qv for associate companies)
Branch Offs: 17 Sherikin Ruwa St, Gyelesu, Via Institute of Administration, PMB 1112, Zaria, Kaduna State; PO Box 2722, Jos, Plateau State; PMB 5648, Port Harcourt, Rivers State; PO Box 675, Benin City, Bendel State; PO Box 129, Kano, Kano State; PO Box 661, Ilorin, Kwara State; PO Box 1727, Enugu, Anambra State; PO Box 378, Gusau, Sokoto State; PO Box 46, Bida, Niger State; PO Box 95, Maiduguri, Borno State; PO Box 1165, Owerri, Imo State; PO Box 692, Yola, Gongola State; PO Box 197, Uyo, Cross River State
Subjects: Educational (Primary, Post-Primary and Tertiary), Law, Medicine and General
1978: 27 titles *1979:* 33 titles *Founded:* 1960
ISBN Publisher's Prefix: 978-129

I C I C (Directory Publishers) Ltd, PMB 3204, Surulere, Lagos (Located at: Directory House, 28 Taoridi St, opp Census Office, Surulere, Lagos) Tel: 831909 Cable Add: ICIC
Subjects: General, Reference, Telephone and Business Directories
Founded: 1965

Ibadan University Press*, Ibadan Tel: 462550 ext 1244 Cable Add: Univpress Ibadan
Subjects: Biography, History, Africana, Philosophy, Reference, Paperbacks, Medicine, Psychology, Science & Technology, General & Social Science, Law, University & Secondary Textbooks
Founded: 1952
ISBN Publisher's Prefix: 978-121

Ilesanmi Press & Sons (N) Ltd*, B61, Okesha St, PO Box 204, Ilesha Tel: 2062/2017 Cable Add: Ilesanmi Press Ilesha
Man Dir/Rights & Permissions: G E Ilesanmi; *Editorial:* A Omowaiye; *Sales:* D Ayeni; *Production:* M Adedipe; *Publicity:* Mrs M Ilesanmi
Branch Offs: Uyo, Kano, Ibadan, Lagos, Akure, Jos, Calabar, Enugu
Subjects: Educational Books generally; Biography, History, Africana, How-to, Study Guides, Books in Yoruba Language, Teacher Training Manuals, General & Social Science
Bookshop: Faji, Ilesha
Founded: 1956
ISBN Publisher's Prefix: 978-157

Islamic Publications Bureau*, 39 Payne Crescent, PO Box 3881, Apapa, Lagos Tel: 48097 Cable Add: Islambureu
Man Dir: Ahmad Patel
Subjects: Islamic and Arabic Language and Literature
Founded: 1969

Kolasanya Publishing Enterprise*, PO Box 252, Ijebu-Ode
Man Dir: Kola Osunsanya
Subjects: General Nonfiction, How-to, Study Guides, General Science, Secondary & Primary Textbooks

Longman Nigeria Ltd*, 52 Oba Akran Ave, PMB 1036, Ikeja, Lagos Tel: 33007/33176 Cable Add: Longman Ikeja
Man Dir: Felix A Iwerebon; *Marketing Manager:* O Bankole; *Publishing Manager:* D Royle; *Production:* A W Amaeshi
Associate Company: Longman Group Ltd, UK (qv)
Subjects: General Fiction & Nonfiction, Belles Lettres, Poetry, Biography, History, Africana, Reference, Religion, Juveniles, Books in Nigerian Languages (various), Paperbacks, Psychology, Science & Technology, General & Social Science, University, Secondary & Primary Textbooks
Founded: 1961

Macmillan Nigeria Publishers Ltd*, Lagos-Ibadan Expressway Link, PO Box 1463, Ibadan Tel: 413917 Cable Add: Macbooks Ibadan Telex: Mabook 31141
Man Dir: Olu Anulopo; *Publishing:* A Amori; *Marketing:* S Asere, E Ohuka, I Ademokun; *Production:* K Adekogbe; *Publicity:* D Obisesan
Orders to: PO Box 264, Yaba
Associate Companies: Macmillan Education Ltd, UK (qv); Northern Nigerian Publishing Co Ltd (qv)
Branch Offs: Onitsha; Benin City; PO Box 264, Yaba
Subjects: Educational and General Fiction & Non-fiction: Biography, History, Africana, Religion, Juveniles, Books in various Nigerian Languages, Paperbacks, General & Social Science, University, Secondary, Primary and Nursery Textbooks
Founded: 1965
ISBN Publisher's Prefix: 978-132

Thomas **Nelson** (Nigeria) Ltd, Nelson House, 8 Ilupeju By-Pass, PMB 21303, Ikeja, Lagos Tel: 931452 Cable Add: Thonelson Ikeja
Administrative Dir: Gervase E Muller; *Publishing Manager:* S Mabogunje; *Marketing Dir:* Ezekiel Iyekolo
Parent Company: Thomas Nelson & Sons Ltd, UK (qv)
Associate Company: University Publishing Co (qv)

Subjects: General Nonfiction, History, Africana, Books in various Nigerian Languages, General & Social Science, Secondary & Primary Textbooks
1979-80: 32 titles

New Horn Press Ltd*, PO Box 4138, Ibadan
Man Dir: Dr Abiola Irele; *Senior Editor, Rights & Permissions:* Kole Omotoso
Subjects: General Fiction & Nonfiction, Belles Lettres, Poetry, How-to, Study Guides, Paperbacks
Founded: 1974

Nigerian Trade Review, PO Box 603, Lagos
Man Dir: Chief P A Dawodu
Subjects: General, Business Directories
Founded: 1958
Miscellaneous: Publish *General Trade Directory of Nigeria*

Northern Nigerian Publishing Co Ltd, Gaskiya Bldg, PO Box 412, Zaria Tel: 2087 Cable Add: Gasmac Telex: 75243 Gasmac Nig
General Manager: Alhaji Husaini Hayat; *Publishing Executive:* John Watson
Associate Companies: Macmillan Education Ltd, UK (qv); Macmillan Nigeria Publishers Ltd (qv)
Subjects: General Nonfiction, Belles Lettres, Poetry, Biography, History, Africana, Religion, Juveniles, Books in Hausa and other Nigerian Languages, Paperbacks, Secondary & Primary Textbooks

Nwamife Publishers Ltd, 10 Ibiam St, Uwani, PO Box 430, Enugu Tel: (042) 254566 Cable Add: Nwamife Enugu
Chairman: Dr Felix C Adi; *Sales, Production, Publicity:* Samuel Umesike; *Editorial, Rights & Permissions:* Dr Nina Mba
Subjects: General Fiction & Non-fiction; Belles Lettres, Poetry, Biography, History, Africana, How-to, Study Guides, Juveniles, Igbo Language & Literature, General Science, Law; University, Secondary & Primary Textbooks; Paperbacks
1979: 50 titles *Founded:* 1970
ISBN Publisher's Prefix: 978-124

Ogunsanya Press, Publishers and Bookstores Ltd*, PO Box 95, Ibadan (Located at: SW9/1133 Orita Challenge, Ibadan) Tel: Ibadan 410619 Cable Add: Pombapress
Man Dir, Editorial, Rights & Permissions: Lucas Justus Popo-Ola Ogunsanya; *Sales, Publicity:* J P F Adeyoju; *Production:* S B O Folayan
Branch Off: Popo-Ola Jubilee Lodge, Oke Imoru, PO Box 155, Ijebu Ode, Ogun State
Subjects: History, Geography, Mathematics, English, Science, Social Studies, Arabic
Bookshop: 64 Agbeni St (opp Foko Junction), Ibadan
1978: 27 titles *Founded:* 1970

Onibonoje Press & Book Industries (Nigeria) Ltd, Felele Layout, PO Box 3109, Ibadan Tel: 413956
Chairman: Gabriel Onibonoje; *Man Dir:* J Olu Onibonoje; *Editorial Dir, Rights & Permissions:* E A Onibonoje
Subjects: General Fiction & Non-fiction, Belles Lettres, Poetry, Biography, History, Africana, How-to, Study Guides, Religion, Juveniles, Yoruba Language & Literature, Paperbacks, General & Social Science, Primary, Secondary & Teacher Training College Textbooks
Book Club: Onibonoje Book Club
Bookshop and Showroom: SW8/77 Oke-Ado, Ibadan
Founded: 1958

Orisun Editions*, PO Box 3079, Ibadan
Man Dir: Bola Ige
Subjects: General, Belles Lettres, Poetry

Paico Ltd*, 46 Commercial Ave, PO Box 3944, Yaba, Lagos
Man Dir: A S Ette
Subjects: General Non-fiction, How-to, Study Guides, General Science, Secondary & Primary Textbooks
Founded: 1971

People's Publishing Co Ltd*, PO Box 3121, Lagos
Subjects: General Non-fiction, Socialism

Pilgrim Books Ltd, see African Universities Press

Publications International (Nigeria) Ltd*, PMB 5097, Ibadan
Man Dir: 'Bisi Talwo
Subjects: General, Secondary & Primary Textbooks
Founded: 1971

Scholar Publications International (Nigeria) Ltd*, PO Box 5097, Ibadan
Subjects: Government, Economics, English, Religion, Chemistry
Founded: 1972
ISBN Publisher's Prefix: 978-138

Sketch Publishing Co Ltd*, Sketch Bldgs, New Court Rd, PMB 5067, Ibadan Tel: 25191/93 Cable Add: Sketch
Man Dir: Felix A Adenaike; *Editorial:* 'Tola Adeniyi
Subjects: General Books, Reference Books
Founded: 1964

Third World First Publications, 10-14 Calcutta Crescent, PO Box 610, Apapa, Lagos
Man Dir: Naiwu Osahon; *Senior Editor, Rights & Permissions:* Bakin Kunama; *Advertising:* L Williams
Imprints: Grassroots Books
Subjects: General Fiction and Non-fiction, Belles Lettres, Poetry, Black Power, Paperbacks (quarterly publication, *Third World First*)
Founded: 1971

Town & Gown Press*, 4 Kajew St, Akoka, PMB 5073, Yaba, Lagos
Man Dir: J E Adetoro
Subjects: General Non-fiction, Belles Lettres, Poetry, Biography, History, Africana, Paperbacks, Secondary Textbooks

University of Ife Press*, Ile-Ife Tel: 2291 ext 308 Cable Add: Press Ifevarsity
Acting Executive Editor: 'Gbemi Sodipo
Subjects: Biography, History, Africana, Philosophy, Reference, Religion, Law, Social Science, University Textbooks
Founded: 1968

University of Lagos Press*, Yaba, Lagos
Secretary: E Bejide Bankole
Orders to: Evans Brothers (Nigeria Publishers) Ltd, PMB 5164, Ibadan
Subjects: Biography, History, Africana, Law, Social Science, University Textbooks

University of London Press*, PO Box 62, Ibadan

University Press Ltd*, Oxford House, Iddo Gate, PMB 5095, Ibadan Tel: 23066/7 & Warehouse, PMB 5142 Jericho, Ibadan Tel: 24117 Cable Add: Oxonian Ibadan Telex: Ibadan 31121
Man Dir: Michael O Akinleye; *Publishing Services Manager:* T J Benbow; *Editorial:* B O Adeleke; *Production Manager:* G O Abegunde; *Sales Manager:* M A Akpan
Associate Company: Oxford University Press, UK (qv)
Founded: 1949
Subjects: General Fiction & Nonfiction, Poetry, Biography, History, Africana, Reference, Religion, Juveniles, Books in various Nigerian Languages, Paperbacks, Medicine, Science & Technology, General & Social Science, University, Secondary & Primary Textbooks

University Publishing Co*, 11 Central School Rd, PO Box 386, Onitsha Tel: 223 Onitsha Cable Add: Varsity Box 386 Onitsha
Dirs: F C Ogbalu, W C Ifezue; *Editorial:* J U Eburne; *Sales:* D O Orakwue; *Production:* I Nweke; *Publicity:* Christian Ogbalu; *Permissions:* Cecilia Ogbalu
Orders to: Varsity Bookshop, 64 New Market Rd, Onitsha
Associate Companies: Cynako International Press, Aba; Thomas Nelson (Nigeria) (qv); African Literature Bureau, Aba
Branch Offs: Varsity Bookshop/Press, Eke-Oyibo, Abagana, Njikoka, LGA; 64 New Market Rd, Onitsha
Subjects: General Non-fiction, Belles Lettres, Poetry, Biography, History, Africana, Philosophy, Religion, Juveniles, Igbo Language & Literature, Quality Paperbacks, Primary & Secondary Textbooks, Periodicals, Books in Vernacular and Dialect
Bookshops: Varsity Bookshop/Press at: Oye-Agu, Abagana, Njikoka LGA; Eke-Amawbia, Amawbia, Awka LGA; Abiriba, Ohafia LGA
Founded: 1959
ISBN Publisher's Prefix: 978-160

Varsity Industrial Press, 11 Central School Rd, PO Box 386, Onitsha
Man Dir: Walter Ifezue
Subjects: Igbo Language & English, Primary & Secondary Textbooks

John West Publications Ltd, John West House, Plot A Block 2, Acme Rd, Ogba, PMB 2100, Ikeja — Lagos Tel: 24388/20558 Cable Add: Jakpress
Executive Dir: Bayo Fadoju
Subjects: General Non-fiction, Biography, How-to, Study Guides, Reference, Annuals, Paperbacks
Founded: 1962

West African Book Publishers Ltd*, PO Box 3445, Ilupeju Industrial Estate, Lagos Tel: 34555/6 Cable Add: Acadpress
Man Dir: B A Idris Animashaun; *Sales Manager:* J O A Onifade; *Editorial:* Laoye Egunjobi
Subjects: Reference, Guide Books, Paperbacks, Health, General Science
Founded: 1967
Subsidiary: Academy Press Ltd, PO Box 3445, Lagos

Literary Agents

Africa Agency*, PO Box 3810, Lagos

Editorial Consultancy & Agency Services, PO Box 4573, Lagos (Located at: 226 Murtala Muhammed Way) Tel: (01) 961894 Cable Add: Edicanses Lagos
Authors' & Publishers' Agents & Consultants
Editorial Director: T C Nwosu
Special Interests: Africana/Nigeriana, Fiction, Plays, Educational Books at all levels
Parent Company: Cross Continent Press Limited, Lagos, Nigeria (qv)

F C **Ogbalu**, PO Box 386, Onitsha

NIGERIA

Book Clubs

Onibonoje Book Club, PO Box 3109, Ibadan
Owned by: Onibonoje Press & Book Industries (Nigeria) Ltd (Ibadan)
Subjects: Fiction, Drama

Times Book Club*, 3-7 Kakawa St, PO Box 139, Lagos
Owned by: Daily Times of Nigeria

Varsity Book Club, 11 Central School Rd, Onitsha
Organized by: Varsity Industrial Press (Publisher, qv)

Major Booksellers

Ahmadu Bello University Bookshop, Zaria
Manager: Sam A Oyabambi

Benin University Bookshop, University of Benin, PMB 1154, Benin City Tel: 240115 ext 271
Manager: S O Ethiede

The **Bestseller**, Universal Distributors Ltd, PO Box 7036, Falomo Shopping Centre, SW Ikoyi, Lagos Tel: 22407 (subsidiary of Nigerian Book Suppliers Ltd)
Manager: O Makate
Also at Durbar Hotel, Kaduna

Book Representation Co Ltd*, PMB 5349, E9/806B Ife Rd, Agodi Area, Ibadan

C S S (Nigeria) Bookshops Ltd*, 50 Broad St, PO Box 174, Lagos Tel: 25517 (branches throughout the country)

Challenge Bookshops*, Agege Motor Rd, PMB 12256, Lagos Tel: 847690 30 branches throughout the country, and several wholesale outlets

Edekes Bookshop Stores Ltd*, 2 Falolu Rd, PO Box 974, Surulere, Lagos

Hart Mossman & Co Ltd*, PMB 2283, Lagos

Kingsway Stores*, PO Box 652, Lagos
Major department store with book department — branches throughout the country

Kwaratech Bookshop*, Kwana State College of Technology, PMB 1375, Ilorin Tel: 2440 ext 14

Mabrochi International Co, PO Box 1572, Lagos
Specializes in mail order services. Academic jobbers for overseas universities

Morison Arnold Ltd*, 63 Hadejia Rd, PO Box 251, Kano

Niger (Acada) Bookshop Ltd*, 35 Ishaga Rd, Surulere, Lagos Tel: 834016

Nigerian Baptist Book Stores*, Lagos By-Pass, PMB 5070, Ibadan

Nigerian Book Suppliers Ltd, PO Box 4440, 20 Akinremi St, Ikeja, Lagos Tel: 22407
General Manager: Mrs O Williams
Library Suppliers specializing in Legal and Academic Books
 (*Retail Shops:* The Bestseller (Lagos and Kaduna) (qv))

Odusote Bookstores Ltd, 68 Lagos Bye-Pass, Oke-Ado, PO Box 244, Ibadan Tel: 414419 Cable Add: Odbook, Ibadan Telex: 31215 (Odbook NG)
Also at 177 Herbert Macaulay St, Yaba, Lagos State Tel: 844015
Man Dir: Ola Odusote

Rational Bookshops (Nigeria)*, Rational Bldgs, Oke-Bola, PO Box 3162, Ibadan

University Bookshop (Nigeria) Ltd*, University of Ibadan, Ibadan Tel: 62550 ext 1208 (branches in Ilorin, Port Harcourt, Calabar, and Maiduguri)
General Manager: Simon Walton

University of Ife Bookshop Ltd, University of Ife, Ile-Ife Tel: Ife 2291 ext 2145 and 2146 Cable Add: Bookshop Ifevarsity
Branch at Ondo

University of Lagos Bookshop, Yaba, Lagos Tel: 841361/9
Also at: College of Medicine, University of Lagos, Idi-Araba, Surulere, Lagos

University of Nigeria Bookshop Ltd, Nsukka Tel: 6251 ext 7
Manager: K K Oyeoku

Major Libraries

Agricultural Library*, PMB 1044, Samaru, Zaria Tel: 2091
Librarian: Malam R Salami
Publications include: Library Accession List (monthly), List of Current Serials in the Library (annually), KWIC Index to the Abstracting & Indexing Publications currently being received by the IAR Library, 2nd edition 1976

Ahmadu Bello University Library*, Samaru-Zaria Tel: 06322553
Publication: Northern Nigerian Publications

Bendel State Library, PMB 1127, Benin City, Bendel State Tel: 243380 Cable Add: Library Benin
Dir: Mrs W Onyeonwu
Bendel Book Depot, a division of Bendel State Library, is also at the above address

Benin University Library*, PMB 1191, Benin City Tel: 240115
University Librarian: O O Ogundipe;
Publications: Annual Report, Library News, List of Serials, Current Awareness Bulletin of the Medical Sub-library

Ibadan University Library*, Ibadan Tel: 462550 ext 1424-26
Librarian: T Olabisi Odeinde
Publications: Library Record (m); Annual Report, 1976/77; Humanities: A Guide to Reference Sources in the Library (1976) (Library Guide No 3); Biological Sciences: A Guide to Reference Sources in the Library (1976) (Library Guide No 4); Education: A Guide to Reference Sources in the Library (1978) (Library Guide No 5)

International Institute of Tropical Agriculture Library*, PMB 5320, Ibadan Tel: 413440 Cable Add: Tropfound Ikeja Telex: 31417 Tropic NG

Library Board of **Kaduna** State*, PMB 2061, Bida Rd, Kaduna Tel: 242590/210322
Dir: Inuwa Diko
Publications: Annual Report, New Additions to Stock (monthly)

Kano State Library*, PMB 3094, Kano

Lagos City Council Libraries*, 48 Broad St, PMB 2025, Lagos Tel: 50246

National Archives of Nigeria Library*, PMB 4, University of Ibadan Post Office, Ibadan
Library Officer: O A Momoh
Publications: Catalogues; Bibliographies; Handlists; Guides

National Library of Nigeria*, 4 Wesley St, PMB 12626, Lagos Tel: 56547 Cable Add: Biblios
Publication: National Bibliography of Nigeria

Nnamdi Azikiwe Library*, University of Nigeria, Nsukka Tel: 6251 ext 59
Librarian: S C Nwoye
Publication: Nsukka Library Notes

University of Ife Library*, Ile-Ife Tel: 2290

University of Lagos Library*, Akoka, Yaba, Lagos Tel: 41361/2

Library Associations

Anambra/Imo States School Libraries Association, c/o Enugu Campus Library, University of Nigeria, Enugu Tel: 252080 Cable Add: Nigersity Enugu
Hon Sec: Dr Dorothy S Obi
Publications include: School Libraries Bulletin (3 times a year); Manual for School Libraries on Small Budgets

Nigerian Library Association*, PMB 12655, Lagos Tel: 56590
Secretary: Inuwa Diko
Publications: Nigerian Libraries (3 a year), NLA Newsletter
(There are also regional associations in the various states under the umbrella of the Nigerian Library Association)

Library Reference Books and Journals

Books

Directory of Lagos Libraries, Oceana Publications Inc, Dobbs Ferry, NY 10522, USA

Libraries in Nigeria. A Directory, National Library of Nigeria, 4 Wesley St, PMB 12626, Lagos

Nominal List of Practising Librarians in Nigeria, National Library of Nigeria, 4 Wesley St, PMB 12626, Lagos (Useful listing providing names and addresses of practising librarians at 59 libraries in Nigeria. To be published annually in the future)

Journals

ECS School Libraries Bulletin, East Central State School Libraries Association, c/o Enugu Campus Library, University of Nigeria, Enugu

Library Record, Ibadan University Library, Ibadan

NLA Newsletter, Nigerian Library Association, PMB 12655, Lagos

Nigerian Libraries, Nigerian Library Association, PMB 12655, Lagos (the official publication of the Nigerian Library Association; the Association also publishes a mimeographed newsletter)

Literary Associations and Societies

There is no national literary association or professional body of writers, but small literary societies and writers' circles, etc are attached to the English departments at the various universities

Literary Periodicals

Afriscope, Pan Afriscope (Nigeria) Ltd, 45 Saibu St, PMB 1119, Yaba, Lagos (An influential and widely circulated monthly current affairs, political, economic, and cultural magazine. Contains a regular 'Literary Scene' column edited by the

Nigerian writer Kole Omotoso, which features book reviews and gives extensive coverage to cultural and literary events throughout Africa)

The Benin Review, Ethiope Publishing Corporation, PMB 1192, Benin City. (The journal covers all the arts in Africa, both traditional and modern, and is also concerned with cultural life in the Black World generally)

The Muse; literary journal of the English Association at Nsukka, University of Nigeria, Nsukka (An irregularly published literary magazine. Another literary magazine, *Okike*, originally published from Nsukka and edited by Chinua Achebe, is now published in the USA)

Nigeria Magazine, Cultural Division, Federal Ministry of Information, PMB 12524, Lagos (Bi-monthly cultural and literary magazine published since 1932)

Oduma, Rivers State Council for Arts and Culture, 74-76 Bonny St, PMB 5049, Port Harcourt (Covers a wide spectrum of the arts, history, languages and philosophy)

Note: There are several more 'little magazines', largely in mimeographed form, published by English departments and writers' groups at the various universities

Literary Prizes

Ife Book Fair Prizes
For children's books in the age groups up to 6, and 7 to 12. Awarded annually. Enquiries to Ife Book Fair Director, University of Ife Bookshop Ltd, Ile-Ife

Nigerian Broadcasting Corporation*
Various literary and drama competitions are sponsored by the Nigerian Broadcasting Corporation, Lagos, from time to time. Enquiries to Nigerian Broadcastng Corporation, Broadcasting Ho, Ikoyi, Lagos

Translation Agencies and Associations

Igbo Language Translation Agency, c/o University Publishing Co Ltd, 11 Central School Rd, PO Box 386, Onitsha

The **Nigeria** Educational Research Council, PO Box 8058, Lagos (Located at: 3 Jibowu St, Yaba, Lagos) Tel: 862272/862269 Cable Add: Edusearch, Lagos
The Research Council has a Translation Bureau attached to it

Norway

General Information

Language: Norwegian. There are two distinct forms: Bokmål (sometimes called Riksmål) and Nynorsk (formerly called Landsmål) whose relative importance has changed in recent years. About 90% of Norwegian books are now published in Bokmål and it is the medium of instruction in most schools. Danish and Swedish are usually intelligible to speakers of Norwegian
Religion: Lutheran
Population: 4 million
Bank Hours: 0845-1615 Monday-Wednesday and Friday; 0845-1800 Thursday
Shop Hours: 0830-1700 Monday-Friday; 0830-1400 Saturday
Currency: 100 øre = 1 Norwegian krone (plural: kroner)
Export/Import Information: Member of the European Free Trade Association. No tariff on books except children's picture books, normally 12% but EFTA free, EEC 4.8% and preferential to long list of 'developing countries'. Books exempt from VAT. No duty on advertising. No import licence required. Nominal exchange controls
Copyright: UCC, Berne, Florence (see International section)

Book Trade Organizations

Norsk Antikvarbokhandlerforening, Ullevålsveien 1, Oslo 1
Norwegian Antiquarian Booksellers' Association

Norsk Bokhandler Medhjelper Forening*, Ovre Vollgate 15, Oslo 1
Norwegian Book Trade Employees' Association
Publications: Norsk Bokhandler Matrikel, Krebsen, Norsk Boknøkkel

Norsk Bokhandlersamband, Kirkegt 32, Oslo 1
Norwegian Christians Booksellers' Union
Chairman: Odd Løver

Norsk Bokimport A/S, Postboks 784, Ovre Vollgate 15, Oslo 1 Tel: (02) 417050

Norsk Boknummerkontor, Universitetsbiblioteket i Oslo, Drammensvegen 42, Oslo 2
ISBN Agency
Administrator: May Ruth Novakowski

Norsk Forleggersamband, Kirkegt 32, Oslo 1
Norwegian Christians Publishers' Union
Secretary: Per Johnsen

Norsk Musikkforleggerforening*, c/o Musikk-Huset, Karl Johansgate 45, Oslo 1 Tel: 334897
Norwegian Music Publishers' Association

Norske Bokhandlerforening*, Ovre Vollgate 15, Oslo 1 Tel: (02) 410760
Norwegian Booksellers' Association
Publications: Bokcentralens Fortegnelse Over Bokhandlers, Norsk Bokfortegnelse, Norsk Bokhandlertidende

Norske Forfatterforening, Rådhusgata 7, Oslo 1
Norwegian Authors' Association
Secretary: Tordis Olsen

Den **Norske Forleggerforening**, Ovre Vollgate 15, Oslo 1 Tel: (02) 422285/411858
Norwegian Publishers' Association
Dir: T Solumsmoen

Norwegian Association of Children's and Young People's Authors, Rådhusgata 7, Oslo 1

Sentral Bokhandel A/S, Gml Drammensvei 48, Postboks 170, N-1321 Stabekk Tel: (02) 532376
Dir: Cathrine Holst

Standard Book Numbering Agency, see Norsk Boknummerkontor

Book Trade Reference Books and Journals

Books

Bibliografi over Norges Offentlige Publikasjoner (Bibliography of Norwegian Government Publications), The Royal University Library, Drammenesveien 42, N-1302, Oslo

Bokcentralens Fortegnelse over Bokhandlere (The Book Centre's List of Booksellers), Norwegian Booksellers' Association, Ovre Vollgate 15, Oslo 1

Norsk Bokhandler Matrikel (Norwegian Booksellers Membership List), Norwegian Book Trade Employees' Association, Ovre Vollgate 15, Oslo 1

Journals

Krebsen (The Crab); Norwegian journal for booksellers, Norwegian Book Trade Employees' Association, Övre Vollgate 15, Oslo 1

Norsk Bokfortegnelse (Norwegian National Bibliography), Norwegian Booksellers' Association, Ovre Vollgate 15, Oslo 1

Norsk Bokhandlertidende (Norwegian Booksellers' News), Norwegian Booksellers' Association, Ovre Vollgate 15, Oslo 1

Publishers

Ansgar Forlag A/S*, Møllergate 26, Oslo 1 Tel: (02) 208518
Manager: Edvin Tinnesand
Subjects: Fiction, General, Religion
ISBN Publishers' Prefix: 82-503

H Aschehoug & Co (W Nygaard) A/S, Sehestedsgate 3, Oslo 1 Tel: (02) 337990 Cable Add: Aco Oslo
Man Dir: William Nygaard; *Editorial:* Oivind Blom, Harald Horjen, Irja Thorenfeldt, Ivar Havnevik; *Rights & Permissions:* Harald Horjen
Subsidiary Company: Kunnskapsforlaget (jointly owned with Gyldendal Norsk Forlag) (qv)
Book Club: Den Norske Bokklubben A/S, Bokklubben Nye Bøker (with three other Norwegian publishers)
Subjects: General Fiction and Nonfiction, Reference, Juveniles, Quality Paperbacks, General & Social Science, Secondary & Primary Textbooks
1978: 600 titles *1979:* 532 titles *Founded:* 1872
ISBN Publisher's Prefix: 82-03

Bladkompaniet A/S, Stålfjæra 5, Oslo 9 Tel: (02) 257190
Man Dir: Claus Huitfeldt; *Sales Dir:* Reidar Myhre; *Advertising:* Ole Wågenes; *Rights & Permissions, Editor-in-Chief:* Finn Arnesen
Subjects: General Fiction, Paperbacks, Magazines
1979: 105 titles *Founded:* 1915
ISBN Publisher's Prefix: 82-509

F Bruns Bokhandels Forlag A/S*, Kongensgate 10, Postboks 476, N-7001 Trondheim Tel: (075) 20625
Dir: Finn Brun
Subjects: Science, Technology
Founded: 1873
Bookshop: Kongensgate 10, Postboks 476, N-7000 Trondheim
ISBN Publisher's Prefix: 82-7028

J W Cappelens Forlag A/S*, Kirkegaten 15, Oslo 1 Tel: (02) 336280 Cable Add: Cappelen
Man Dirs: Sigmund Strømme, Jan Wiese; *Editorial:* Per Glad, Aase Gjerdrum, Egil A. Kristoffersen, Ola Haugen; *Sales:* Per Pedersen; *Production:* Erik Pettersen; *Rights & Permissions:* Marie L Holm
Subjects: General Fiction, Nonfiction, Textbooks, Reference, Maps, Religion, Juveniles, Low- & High-priced Paperbacks, Encyclopaedias
Founded: 1829

Book Club: Den Norske Bokklubben A/S (with three other Norwegian publishers)
Antiquarian Booksellers: J W Cappelens Antikvariat, Kirkegaten 15, Oslo 1
Subsidiaries: Wennergren-Cappelen A/S, Nedre Vollgate 4, Oslo 1; Cappelen Musikk, Kirkegaten 15, Oslo 1
ISBN Publisher's Prefix: 82-02

N W **Damm** og Søn A/S, Tvetenveien 32, Postboks 6140 Etterstad, Oslo 6 Tel: (02) 687406 Cable Add: Damson
Dirs: Arne Damm, Niels Wilhelm Damm, Per Støkken
Subjects: How-to, Children's Books, Textbooks, Dictionaries, Guidebooks
1978: 85 titles *Founded:* 1843
ISBN Publisher's Prefix: 82-517

Dreyers Forlag, (B A Butenschøn A/S & Co), Arbiensgate 7, Oslo 2 Tel: (02) 443810 Cable Add: Dreyerbok
Man Dir: Halfdan Kielland; *Editorial:* Anton Fr Andresen, Oistein Parmann; *Sales & Publicity:* Per Erik Thorsfeinsen; *Production:* Bjørn Pedersen
Imprint: Perspektiv
Subjects: General Fiction, Non-fiction, Belles Lettres, Music, Art, Low- & High-priced Paperbacks
1978: 56 titles *Founded:* 1942
ISBN Publisher's Prefix: 82-09

J W **Eide** Forlag A/S, Fosswinckelsgate 8, Postboks 146, N-5001 Bergen Tel: (05) 215801 Cable Add: Eidebok
Man Dir: Sigvald Flataker
Subjects: General Fiction, History, Music, Art, University, Secondary & Primary Textbooks, Educational Materials, Juveniles
ISBN Publisher's Prefix: 82-514

Elingaard Forlag A/S, now Nå Forlag (qv)

Fabritius Forlagshus, Postboks 1156, Sentrum, Oslo 1 Tel: (02) 220354
Man Dir: Öyvind Skarlund; *Sales:* Laila Jensen
Subjects: General Nonfiction, Technical, Textbooks, Educational Materials
Founded: 1844
ISBN Publisher's Prefix: 82-07

Fonna Forlag L/L, St Olavs Plass 3, Boks 6912 Oslo 1 Tel: (02) 201303/201201
Chief Executive: Arne Lauvhjell; *Chief Editor:* Boerge Hofset
Subjects: General Fiction, Poetry, Biography, Magazines, Juveniles
1978: 7 titles *1979:* 7 titles *Founded:* 1940
ISBN Publisher's Prefix: 82-513

E **Greens** Forlag*, Sverdrupsgaten 8, Oslo 5 Tel: (02) 376602
Subjects: General Fiction, Belles Lettres, Juveniles
ISBN Publisher's Prefix: 82-01

John **Griegs** Forlag, Vaskerelven 8, Postboks 248, N-5001 Bergen Tel: (05) 233900 Cable Add: Bokgrieg
Man Dir: Rolf Moe Nilssen
Subjects: Non-fiction, Fiction for Children, Co-editions
1978: 17 titles *Founded:* 1721
ISBN Publisher's Prefix: 82-533

Grøndahl og Søn Forlag A/S*, Munkedamsveien 35, Oslo 2 Tel: (02) 419740 Cable Add: Bokgrøndahl
Man Dir: Finn P Nyquist; *Editor:* Sølvi Foseide
Subjects: General Nonfiction, Reference, Crime, Textbooks, Illustrated Books, Fiction
Founded: 1812
Bookshop: Grøndahl & Søn Bokhandel A/S, Slottsgate 12, Oslo 1
ISBN Publisher's Prefix: 82-504

Gyldendal Norsk Forlag, Universitetsgaten 16, Postboks 6860 St Olavs Plass, Oslo 1 Tel: (02) 200710 Cable Add: Gyldendal
Man Dir: Andreas Skartveit
Subsidiary Company: Kunnskapsforlaget (jointly owned with H Aschehoug og Co A/S) (qv)
Subjects: General Fiction, Science Fiction, Belles Lettres, Poetry, Art, Music, Biography, History, How-to, Politics, Philosophy, Psychology, Reference, Religion, Juveniles, Low-priced Paperbacks, Social Science, Secondary & Primary Textbooks, *Easy Readers*, Encyclopaedias, Periodicals
1978: approx 730 titles *1979:* approx 690 titles *Founded:* 1925
Book Club: Den Norske Bokklubben A/S and Bokklubben Nye Bøker (with three other Norwegian publishers)
ISBN Publisher's Prefix: 82-05

Henny's Forlag, Hagalivegen 1, Postboks 1894 Uika, Oslo 1
Man Dir: M Andenäs; *Dirs:* P Christiansen, J Jansen
Subjects: General Fiction, Biography, History, How-to, Philosophy, Religion
Founded: 1962

Hjemmenes Forlag A/S*, Postboks 1739, Vika, Oslo 1 Tel: (02) 143151
Publisher: Yngve Woxholth
Subject: Cultural and Historical Books (mainly in colour)

Hjemmet A/S, Kristian den 4des Gate 13, Oslo 1 Tel: (02) 332880 Telex: 17074 Novel N
Parent Company: Gutenberghus Group, Denmark
Associate Companies: Ehapa-Verlag GmbH, Federal Republic of Germany; Gutenberghus Publishing Service, Denmark; Hemmets Journal AB, Sweden (qqv)
Subjects: Juveniles, Business, Periodicals
Founded: 1969

Kunnskapsforlaget, Postboks 6736, Sehestedsgt 4, Sankt Olavs Plass, Oslo 1 Tel: (02) 205215
Man Dir: Lars Bucher Johannessen; *Chief Editor:* Egil Tveterås; *Marketing Dir:* Reidar Bøe; *Production:* Rolf Andersson; *Sales Manager:* Tom Thorsteinsen
Parent Companies: H Aschehoug og Co A/S, Gyldendal Norsk Forlag (qqv)
Subjects: Encyclopaedias, Dictionaries
1979: 10 titles *Founded:* 1975
ISBN Publisher's Prefix: 573

Lunde Forlag og Bokhandel A/S, Grensen 19, Oslo 1 Tel: (02) 332525 Cable Add: Norskluth
Editor: Torstein Lindhjem; *Production:* Paul Odland; *Rights & Permissions:* Jan Bøe
Subjects: General Fiction, Belles Lettres, Poetry, Biography, Music, Art, Religion, Juveniles, High-priced Paperbacks, Secondary & Primary Textbooks, Educational Materials
1978: 78 titles *1979:* 76 titles *Founded:* 1905
Bookshop: Lunde Forlag og Bokhandel A/S, C Sundtsgate 2, N-5000 Bergen, Norway
ISBN Publisher's Prefix: 82-520

Luther Forlag A/S, Kirkegaten 32, Oslo 1 Tel: (02) 332180
Man Dir: Nils Tore Andersen
Subjects: General Fiction, Biography, History, Religion, Juveniles, Low- & High-priced Paperbacks, Dictionaries
1978: approx 140 titles
Miscellaneous: Firm is a merger of Nomi Forlag & Luther Forlag A/S, Kirkegate 32, Oslo 1
ISBN Publisher's Prefix: 82-531

Harald **Lyche** og Co A/S*, N Storgaten 2, Postboks 1102, N-3000 Drammen Tel: (02) 837970
Subjects: General Fiction & Nonfiction, Textbooks
ISBN Publisher's Prefix: 82-7008

Ernst G **Mortensens** Forlag, Sørkedalsveien 10A, Oslo 3 Tel: (02) 603090 Cable Add: Pressmort Telex: 17626
Man Dir: Arne Bonde; *Editorial:* Asbjørn Andresen, Rigmor Foss, Solveig Høysaeten, Reidar Martinsen; *Sales:* O E Grønaker; *Administration:* E Werner Hansen; *Information:* Knut-Jørgen Erichsen; *Advertising:* R Marthinsen; *Rights & Permissions:* Per R Mortensen, Jr
Parent Company: Ernst G Mortensen & Co A/S
Subsidiary Companies: NPs/AssP (Norsk Presseservice/Associated Press A/s, Oslo; Forenede Trykkerier A/s, Oslo; Centralfilm A/s, Oslo
Subjects: General, Magazines
Founded: 1933
ISBN Publisher's Prefix: 82-527

N K I-forlaget, Løxavn 15, Postboks 113, N-1351 Rud Tel: (02) 135790
Publisher: Jan Lien; *Editorial:* Sverre Harald Amündsen, Solvar Hofsøy; *Sales:* Bjørn Ribsskog; *Publicity:* Anne L Foûgli
Subsidiary Company: NKI Educational Services Ltd, UK (qv)
Subjects: Primary & Secondary Textbooks, Technical Textbooks, General Non-fiction
1978: 65 titles *1979:* 76 titles *Founded:* 1967
ISBN Publisher's Prefix: 82-562

Nå Forlag A/S (formerly Elingaard Forlag), Postboks 7058 H, Oslo 3 (Located at Oscarsgate 55, Oslo 2) Tel: (02) 565070
Parent Company: Libertas, Oscarsgate 55, Oslo 2
Subjects: Politics, Marketing, Economy, Crime
1978: 8 titles
ISBN Publisher's Prefix: 82-505

Noregs Boklag, Kr Augustsgate 14, Oslo 1 Tel: (02) 202823
Manager: Per Roar Öian
Subjects: Plays, Poetry, Biography, Music, Juveniles
Founded: 1925
ISBN Publisher's Prefix: 82-522

Olaf **Norlis** Forlag A/S, see Tanum-Norli

Norsk Kunstforlag A/S*, Arbiensgate 13, Oslo 2 Tel: (02) 566180
Man Dir: Arne Dahl; *Sales Dir:* Simon Gundhus
Subjects: General, Art, Atlases
ISBN Publisher's Prefix: 82-90069

Det **Norske Samlaget**, Postboks 4672 Sofienberg, Oslo 5 (Located at: Trondheimsvegen 15, Oslo 5) Tel: (02) 687600
Man Dir: Olav Vesaas; *Editorial:* Olav Hr Rue; *Sales:* Roar Hauge
Subjects: General Fiction, Belles Lettres, Poetry, Biography, History, Philosophy, Religion, Textbooks, Reference, Juveniles, High-priced Paperbacks
1978: 138 titles *1979:* 128 titles *Founded:* 1868
Miscellaneous: Publish periodicals *Syn og Segn, Vår Samtid,* & *Maal og Minne*
ISBN Publisher's Prefix: 82-521

Novus Forlag A/S, Postboks 748, Sentrum, Oslo 1 Tel: (02) 353314
Man Dir: Olav Røsset
Subjects: Education, General
1978: 3 titles *1979:* 8 titles *Founded:* 1972
ISBN Publisher's Prefix: 82-7099

Pax Forlag A/S, Gøteborggt 8, Oslo 5
Tel: (02) 379082
Man Dir: John-Willy Rudolph; *Editorial:* Paul Hedlund; *Sales:* Wiggo Frantzen; *Production:* Aage-H Hansen; *Publicity:* Toralf Sandåker; *Rights & Permissions:* John-Willy Rudolph, Paul Hedlund
Imprint: Unipax
Subjects: Radical and Alternative Publications on Politics, History, Philosophy, Social science, Women in society, Education, Children's books, Modern Classics, General literature, Quality paperbacks
1978: 50 titles *1979:* 52 titles *Founded:* 1964
ISBN Publisher's Prefix: 82-530

Pedagogisk Forlag A/S*, Dronningensgaten 23, Oslo 1 Tel: (02) 414927
Subjects: Textbooks, Educational Materials

Perspektiv, an imprint of Dreyers Forlag (qv)

Rune Forlag*, Postboks 1202, N-7001 Trondheim Tel: (075) 32362
Publisher: Erling Skjølberg
Subject: General
ISBN Publisher's Prefix: 82-523

Chr **Schibsteds** Forlag, Kristian IV's Gate 1, Postboks 1178, Sentrum, Oslo 1 Tel: (02) 205060 Telex: 11230 aft w
General Manager: Ola Veigaard; *Editorial:* Kirsti Schei; *Sales Dir:* Arne Andreassen; *Rights & Permissions:* Ola Veigaard
Orders to: Forlagssentralen, Postboks 6005, Etterstad, Oslo 6
Parent Company: Schibsted-gruppen, Postboks 1178, Sentrum, Oslo 1
Subjects: How-to, Reference, Juveniles, Nature
1978: 49 titles *1979:* 45 titles *Founded:* 1839
ISBN Publisher's Prefix: 82-516

Snøfugl Forlag, Postboks 95, N-7084 Melhus Tel: (074) 70743
Chief Executive, Editorial: Åsmund Snøfugl; *Sales:* Johan Snøfugl
Associate Company: A/s Bygdetrykk, 7084 Melhus
Subjects: General
1978: 12 titles *Founded:* 1972
ISBN Publisher's Prefix: 82-7083

Solum Forlag A/S*, Asveien 5, 1324 Lysaker Tel: 534692
Subject: General
ISBN Publisher's Prefix: 82-560

Stabenfeldt Forlag, Tanke Svilandsgate 55, Postboks 189, N-4001 Stavanger Tel: (045) 21553 Cable Add: Bokorm
Man Dir: Hugo Stabenfeldt; *Publishing Dir:* Tor Tjeldflåt
Subsidiary Companies: SE-bladene, Stabenfeldthūs (Divisions)
Subjects: General Fiction & Nonfiction, Biography
1978: 14 titles *1979:* 27 titles *Founded:* 1920
ISBN Publisher's Prefix: 82-532

P F **Steensballes** Boghandels Eftg*, Postboks 130, N-2261 Kirkenaer Tel: (066) 47588
Publisher: Bjarne H Reenskaug
Subjects: General, Schoolbooks
ISBN Publisher's Prefix: 82-7004

Tanum-Norli (Johan Grundt Tanum Forlag og Olaf Norlis Forlag A/S)*, Kr Augustsgate 7A, Oslo 1 Tel: (02) 110260 Cable Add: Tanumlag
Man Dir: Ingar Tanum; *Editorial:* Birger Huse, Helge G Simonsen
Subjects: General Nonfiction, Reference, Textbooks, Education
Bookshops: Tanum/Cammermeyer, Karl Johansgate 41-43, Oslo 1; Tanum bøker Bekkestua, Ringeriksvei 31, N-1340 Bekkestua; Tanum bøker Oppegård, Kolbotnveien 5, N-1410 Kolbotn; Tanum bøker Oppsal, Haakon Tveters Vei 96, Oslo 6; Karl P Thorstensen A/S, Storgt 19, N-2000 Lillestrøm; Alida Waaler Bok- og Papirhandel, Bogstadvn 43, Oslo 6
ISBN Publisher's Prefix: 82-518

Teknologisk Forlag, Enebakkveien 117, Oslo 6 Tel: (02) 679690
Man Dir, Rights & Permissions: Rudolf Jenssen; *Assistant Dir:* Tom Harald Jenssen; *Editorial Dir:* Tore Egeberg; *Sales Dir:* Karl H Ormen
Subjects: How-to, Philosophy, Textbooks, Reference, Engineering, General Science
1978: 25 titles *Founded:* 1958
ISBN Publisher's Prefix: 82-512

Tiden Norsk Forlag, Postboks 8326, Hammersborg (Located at: Youngstorget 2, Oslo 1) Tel: (02) 335380 Cable Add: Tiden
Man Dir: Trygve Johansen; *Sales, Publicity:* Hans Raastad; *Editorial and Rights & Permissions:* Miss Signe Bakken; *Production:* Jakob Rask Arnesen
Subsidiary Companies: Tiden Finans A/S, Aktuell Kunst, Læremiddelhuset
Subjects: General Fiction & Nonfiction, Textbooks, Reference, Paperbacks, Juveniles
Book Clubs: Den Norske Bokklubben A/S; Bokklubben Nye Bøker (with three other Norwegian publishers)
Bookshop: Arbeidernes Bok- og Papirhandel, Youngstorget 4, Oslo 1
Founded: 1933
ISBN Publisher's Prefix: 82-10

Unipax, an imprint of Pax Forlag A/S (qv)

Universitetsforlaget, Postboks 2959, Tøyen, Oslo 6 Tel: (02) 276060 Cable Add: Universitypress, Oslo Telex: 11896 Ufor N
Man Dir: Tor Bjerkmann; *Editorial:* Fredrik Lund; *Sales Manager:* Jon Oestboe; *Rights & Permissions:* Vibeke Siegwarth
Orders to: Postboks 2977, Tøyen, Oslo 6
Subjects: Technical, Reference, Science, Paperbacks, Textbooks, Educational Materials
1979: 500 titles *Founded:* 1950
Miscellaneous: Publishers for the University of Oslo, The University of Bergen, the University of Tromsø, and other institutions of higher learning
ISBN Publisher's Prefix: 82-00

Literary Agents

E M B L A, see Pat Shaw Associates

Carlota **Frahm** Literary Agency, Valkyriegaten 17, Postboks 5385, Majorstua, Oslo 3 Tel: (02) 463002 Cable Add: Frahmbook
Dirs: Carlota Frahm, Suzanne Palme

Edith **Kiilerich***, Fiolstr 12, DK-1171 Copenhagen K, Denmark
Miscellaneous: This Danish literary agency also acts in Finland, Iceland, Norway and Sweden for foreign authors

Hanna-Kirsti **Koch***, Postboks 3043, Oslo 2
Contact: Eilif Koch

Pat **Shaw** Associates (formerly EMBLA)*, Fredbosvei 61, N-1370 Asker Tel: (02) 782829

Book Clubs

Bokklubbens **Barn**, see Den Norske Bokklubben A/S
Subject: Juveniles

Det **Beste** A/S*, Postboks 726-Sentrum, Oslo 1

Bokklubbens **Lyrikkvaennene***, see Den Norske Bokklubben
Subject: Poetry

Den **Norske Bokklubben** A/S, Postboks 150, Vollsveieu 13, Lysaker, N-1321 Stabekk
Includes: Bokklubbens Lyrikkvenner, Bokklubbens Barn, Bokklubben Nye Bøker
Members: 366,000
Owned by: H Aschehoug & Co (W Nygaard) A/S (Oslo), J W Cappelens Forlag A/S (Oslo), Gyldendal Norsk Forlag (Oslo), Tiden Norsk Forlag (Oslo)
Subjects of Den Norske Bokklubben: Fiction, Biography, Travel

Bokklubben **Nye Bøker** (New Book Club), see Den Norske Bokklubben

Major Booksellers

F **Beyer** Bok-Og Papirhandel A/S, Strandgate 4, N-5000 Bergen Tel: (05) 215020 Cable Add: Bokbeyer, Bergen
Manager: Birger Knudsen

F **Bruns** Bokhandel*, Kongensgate 10, Postboks 476, N-7000 Trondheim

Gardum, Søregate 22, 4001 Stavanger Tel: (045) 20200/20400

Ed B **Giertsen** A/S*, Småstrandgate, Postboks 217, N-5001 Bergen Tel: (05) 219680

Johan **Grundt** Tanun A/S, Postboks 1177, Sentrum, Oslo 1 Tel: (02) 801260 Cable Add: Tanumbok
Import, export, wholesalers

Lyngs Bokhandel A/S, Postboks 328, N-7001 Trondheim (Located at: Olav Trygvasonsgate 26, N-7000 Trondheim) Tel: (075) 28616
Manager: Ragnvald C Knudsen

Olaf **Norlis** Bokhandel A/S, Universitetsgaten 24, Oslo 1 Tel: (02) 336190
Shipping Add: 1850 Mysen
Specialists in school books, medical and maritime literature, antiquarian books. Also exporters.

Norsk Bokimport A/S, Ovre Vollgate 15, Postboks 784, Oslo 1 Tel: (02) 417050
Manager: Einar Bruvik

Erik **Qvist** Bokhandel A/S, Drammensveien 16, Oslo 2 Tel: (02) 445269
Manager: Erik Chr Qvist

Sellevolds Bokhandel A/S, Nedre Slottsgate 8, Oslo 1 Tel: 425258/414150/421529

Sentral Bokhandel a/s, Gml Drammensvei 48, Postboks 170, N-1321 Stabekk Tel: (02) 532376

H **Sundems** Bokhandel A/S, Storgate 12, N-8000 Bodø Tel: (081) 20154
Manager: Carl August Veigård

Tapir, Universitet i Trondheim, N-7034 Trondheim NTH

Universitetsbokhandeln, PO Box 307, Blindern, Oslo 3
Manager: Tom Vister

Major Libraries

Bergen offentlige Bibliotek Horda land Fylkesbibliotek, Bergen
Municipal and County Library

Deichmanske Bibliotek, Henrik Ibsens gate 1, Oslo 1 Tel: (02) 204335 Telex: 18337 deich n
City Library of Oslo
Chief Librarian: Hans Fløgstad

Drammen Folkebibliotek, Gamle Kirkeplass 7, Postboks 1136, N-3001 Drammen
Public Library of Drammen

Styret for det **Industrielle Rettsvern** Bibliotek, Middelthunsgate 15b, Postboks 8160 Dep, Oslo 1 Tel: (02) 461900 Telex: 19152 nopat n
Library of the Norwegian Patent Office
Librarian: Kjell A Hansen

Kristiansand Folkebibliotek, Kristiansand S
Municipal Library

Norges Landbrukshøgskoles Bibliotek*, N-1432 Ås-NLH
Library of the Agricultural University of Norway

Riksarkivet*, Folke Bernadottes veg 21, Oslo 8
National Archives of Norway

Statistisk Sentralbyras Bibliotek, Postboks 8131 Dep, Oslo 1
Library of the Central Bureau of Statistics

Stavanger Bibliotek, Postboks 310-320, 4001 Stavanger Tel: (04) 528020 Telex: 33181 fb sta n

Universitetsbiblioteket i Bergen, Möhlenprisbakken 1, N-5000 Bergen

Universitetsbiblioteket i Oslo, Drammensveien 42, N Oslo 2 Tel: (02) 564980
The Royal University Library (National Library)

Universitetsbiblioteket i Trondheim, Avd B(Kongelige Norske Videnskabers Selskab Biblioteket)*, Erling Skakkes Gt 47C, N-7000 Trondheim Tel: 92204
University of Trondheim, Library of the Royal Norwegian Society of Sciences and Letters

The **University of Trondheim**, The Norwegian Institute of Technology, University Library, Division A, Høgskoleringen 1, N-7034 Trondheim-NTH Tel: (075) 95110 Cable Add: NTHB Telex: 55186 nthhb n

Library Associations

Arkivforeningen, Postboks 10, Kringsjå, Oslo 8
The Association of Archivists

Kommunale Bibliotekarbeiderers Forening*, c/o Kari Hjelde, Oppegårdbibliotekene, N-1410 Kolbotn
Municipal Librarians' Association
Publication: Kontakten (6 a year)

Norsk Bibliotekarlag*, Notodden Bibliotek, N-3670 Notodden
Norwegian Librarians' Association
Executive Secretary: Helge Laerum
Publications: Meldinger (12 a year)

Norsk Bibliotekforening*, Malerhaugveien 20, Oslo 6 Tel: (02) 688576
Norwegian Library Association
Secretary-Treasurer: Gro Langeland

Norsk Dokumentasjonsgruppe, Postboks 350, Blindern, Oslo 3
Norwegian Documentation Society

Norske Deitidsbibliotekarers Yrkeslag*, c/o Norsk Bibliotekforening, Malerhaugveien 20, Oslo 6
Norwegian Association for Part-Time Librarians

Norske Forskningsbibliotekarers Forening*, Malerhaugveien 20, Oslo 6 Tel: (02) 688576
Norwegian Research Librarians' Association
Executive Secretary: Gro Langeland

Riksbibliotektjenesten, Postboks 2439, Solli, Oslo 2 (Located at: Drammensveien 42, Oslo 2) Tel: (02) 550880
National Office for Research and Special Libraries
Director: Gerhard Munthe
Publications: Handbook of Research and Special Libraries (irregular), *Synopsis* (6 per year), *Annual Report*

Library Reference Books and Journals

Books

Bibliothek og Forskning (Library and Research), The University Library of Bergen, Fastings Minde, N-5000 Bergen

Journals

Bok og Bibliotek (Book and Library), Statens Bibliotektilsyn, Munkesdamsveien 62, N-1301 Oslo

Meldinger (Announcements), Norwegian Librarians' Association, Notodden Bibliotek, N-3670 Notodden

Literary Associations and Societies

Norske Akademi for Sprog og Litteratur, Oslo
Norwegian Academy for Language and Literature
Secretary: L R Langslet

Det **Norske Videnskaps-Akademi**, Drammensveien 78, Oslo 2 Tel: (02) 444296
Cable Add: Norakad
The Norwegian Academy of Science and Letters
Secretary-General: Professor Dr A Semb-Johansson; *Executive Secretary:* Kjell Herlofsen
Publications: Skrifter, Avhandlinger, Årbok

Den Norske **P E N-Klubb**, c/o Professor Johan Vogt, Postboks 1095, Blindern, Oslo 3
Norwegian Centre of International PEN
President: Professor Johan Vogt

Literary Periodicals

Edda (Scandinavian); literary research, Universitetsforlaget, Postboks 307, Blindern, Oslo 3

Norseman, Nordmanns-Forbundet, Raadusgate 23b, Oslo

Samtiden (The Age); journal for politics, literature and social questions, H Ascheoug (W Nygaard), Sehestedgate 3, Oslo 1

Syn og Segn (Vision and Tradition), Norske Samlaget, Trondheimsveien 15, Oslo 5

Vinduet (The Window), Gyldendale Norsk Forlag, Universitetsgate 16, Oslo 1

Literary Prizes

Bastian Prize*
Awarded annually for an outstanding translation by one of the members of the Norwegian Association of Translators. Enquiries to Norwegian Association of Translators, Rådhugata 7, Oslo 1

Children's Book Prize
For the best books for children by Norwegian authors, for illustrations by Norwegian artists in books for children, for picture-books, and for comic strips. Awarded annually. Enquiries to Royal Norwegian Ministry of Education and Ecclesiastical Affairs, Oslo 1

Rolf **Stenersen** Prize
For the best drama by a young playwright. Awarded every two years. Enquiries to Norwegian Authors' Association, Rådhusgata 7, Oslo 1

Translation Prize
Established 1968. For translations from foreign literature. 15,000 Norwegian kroner. Awarded annually. The winner in 1979 was Carl Hambro. Enquiries to Norwegian Cultural Council, Rosenkrantzgate 11, Oslo 1

Tarjei **Vesaas** Debutant Prize*
To a writer under 30 for the best first book of prose or poetry. 3,000 Norwegian kroner. Awarded annually. Enquiries to Norwegian Authors' Association, Rådhusgata 7, Oslo 1

Translation Agencies and Associations

Norwegian Association of Translators*, Rådhusgata 7, Oslo 1

Pakistan

General Information

Language: Urdu is national language but English is used commercially
Religion: Muslim
Population: 76.8 million
Literacy Rate (1960): 21.8%
Bank Hours: 0900-1300 Saturday-Thursday
Shop Hours: 0930-1300, 1500-2000 Monday-Saturday
Currency: 100 paisa = 1 Pakistan rupee
Export/Import Information: No tariff on books, magazines and advertising matter. Import licence issued freely if required. Anti-Islamic and obscene literature prohibited. Exchange controls
Copyright: UCC, Berne, Buenos Aires, Florence (see International section)

Book Trade Organizations

National Book Council of Pakistan*, Theosophical Hall, MA Jinnah Rd, Karachi
Dir General: Mr S H R Rizvi
Publications: Kitab (Urdu, monthly), trade directories, manuals, bibliographies

Pakistan Publishers' and Booksellers' Association*, YMCA Bldg, Shahra-e-Quaid-e-Azami, Lahore

Pakistan Writers' Guild*, B-16 Sindhi Muslim Housing Society, Karachi
Secretary-General: Mahbub Jamal Zahedi
Publication: Ham Qalam (monthly)

Book Trade Reference Books and Journals

Books

Books from Pakistan, National Book Council of Pakistan, Theosophical Hall, Bunder Rd, Karachi

Karachi Book Trade Directory, National Book Council of Pakistan, Theosophical Hall, Bunder Rd, Karachi

Journals

Kitab (text in Urdu), National Book Council of Pakistan, 126 Riwaz Garden, Lahore

Pakistan National Bibliography, Directorate of Libraries, National Bibliographical Unit, c/o Liaquat Library, Stadium Rd, Karachi (annual)

Publishers

Aane-Adab, Anarkali, Lahore Tel: 67504
Proprietor: Sh Abdul Salam

Ahsan Brothers*, Chowk Anarkali, Lahore
Proprietor: Mohammad Ahsan
Subjects: Literature, Education

Shaikh Muhammad **Ashraf***, Kashmiri Bazar, Lahore 8 Tel: 53171 Cable Add: Islamiclit Lahore
Chief Literary Adviser: M Ashraf Darr
Subjects: Books about Islam, Islamic history, biography, in English
Bookshop: address as above
1978: 6 titles *Founded:* 1923

Azim Publishing House, Khyber Bazar, Peshawar Tel: 73313
Subjects: History, Literature, Islamiat

Barque & Co*, Barque Chambers, Barque Sq, 87 Shahrah-e-Liaquat Ali Khan, PO Box 201, Lahore
Man Dir: A M Barque
Branch Off: Karachi
Subjects: Trade Directories, Journals, Who's Who
Founded: 1930

Bisat-e-Adab*, Circular Rd, Lahore Tel: 65621
Proprietor: Sana-Ullah Bhutta
Subjects: Politics, Islamic Studies

The **Book** House*, PO Box 734, Lahore 2 (Located at: 8 Trust Building, Urdu Bazar, Lahore 2) Tel: 61212 Cable Add: Bookhouse
Proprietor: Muhammad Saeed; *General Manager:* Muhammad Hamid Saeed
Subjects: Religion, Library, Textbooks
Founded: 1951
Miscellaneous: Exporters of English and Urdu books

Carvan Book House, Kutchery Rd, Lahore Tel: 52296
Proprietor: Ch Abdul Hameed
Subjects: General, Textbooks

Classic*, 42 Shahrah-e-Quaid-e-Azam, Lahore Tel: 61830 Cable Add: Classic 42 Mall Lahore
Man Dir, Editorial, Production, Permissions: Agha A Hussain; *Sales, Publicity:* S Akbar Zaidi
Orders to: Classic, 42 The Mall Lahore
Subsidiary Companies: Shish Mahal Kitab Ghar, Classic Bookshop (both in Lahore)
Associate Company: Menarva Publications, Lahore
Subjects: The Arts, National Topics, Fiction
Bookshop: 42 The Mall, Lahore
Founded: 1956

Crescent Publications*, Urdu Bazar, Lahore

East and West Publishing Co*, 22 Corner Chambers, Chundrigar Rd, Karachi-0102 Tel: 212036 Cable Add: Goodbooks
Publisher: Rafique Akhtar
Subjects: Pakistan, Research Material
Founded: 1971

Economic and Industrial Publications, Al-Masiha, 47 Abdullah Haroon Rd, PO Box 7843, Karachi 3
Subjects: Economics, Industrial Development, Finance; Periodical journals and reports on economics and investment
Founded: 1965

Ferozsons Ltd, 60 Shahrah-e-Quaid-e-Azam, Lahore Tel: 65196/65197/65198 Cable Add: Ferozsons
Man Dir, Publicity: A Salam; *Editorial, Sales:* Zaheer Salam
Branch Offs: 150 outlets throughout Pakistan
Subjects: Islamic, Regional, Juveniles, Dictionaries (native and foreign languages)
Bookshops: At above address, and 277 Peshawar Rd, Rawalpindi
Founded: 1894

Frontier Publishing Co*, Urdu Bazar, Lahore

Sh **Ghulam** Ali & Sons, Chowk Anarkali, Urdu Bazar, Lahore
Proprietor: Sh Niaz Ahmed
Branch Offs: Jinnah Rd, Karachi; Chotki Ghiti, Hyderabad
Subjects: Islamic Studies, General Books

Government Publications*, Manager of Publications, Central Publications Branch, Government of Pakistan, Stationery and Forms Building, University Rd, Karachi

Hamdard National Foundation*, Nazimabad, Karachi 18
President: Hakim Mohammed Said
Subjects: Health, Medicine (Traditional), Islam
1978: 6 titles

Idara-e-Faroghe-Undu*, Aibak Rd, Lahore
Proprietor: Mohammad Tufail
Subjects: Literature, Education

Idara Siqafat-e-Islamia*, Club Rd, Lahore

Ilmi Kitab Khana*, Urdu Bazar, Lahore Tel: 62833
Proprietor: Ch Sardar Mohammad
Subjects: Textbooks, Educational

Islami Kitab Khana*, Sadar Bazar, Mianwali, Punjab
Subject: Law

Islamic Book Centre*, 25B Masson Rd, PO Box 1625, Lahore 3 Tel: 66272 Cable Add: Islamibook
Man Dir: Rozina Saeed; *Sales Dir:* Muhammad Bashir; *Publicity Dir:* Muhammad Sajid Saeed; *Advertising Dir:* Muhammad Hamid Saeed
Branch Off: J M Malik, 35 Cawdor Rd, Fallowsfields, Manchester M14 6LS, UK
Subjects: Religion, University, Secondary & Primary Textbooks, Reference
1978: 24 titles

Institute of **Islamic Culture***, Club Rd, Lahore Tel: 53908 Cable Add: ICULT
Subject: Islamic ideology
Founded: 1950

Islamic Publications Ltd*, 13-E Shahalam Market, Lahore 7 Tel: 68341 Cable Add: Alilm
Man Dir: Ashfaque Mirza; *Manager:* Abdul W Khan
Subjects: Standard Islamic literature on current topics
Founded: 1960

Islamic Research Institute, PO Box 1035, Islamabad Tel: 27156/27295/21705/20952 Cable Add: Islamserch
Dir: Dr A J Abdul Wahid Halepota; *Sales:* Mumtaz Liaqat
Subjects: History, Law, Religion, Periodicals (in English, Arabic and Urdu)
1978: 5 titles *Founded:* 1962
Miscellaneous: The Institute is a semi Government research organization

Kitabi Dunya*, Mcleod Rd, Lahore
Proprietor: Ch Sultan Ahmed
Subject: Detective Fiction

Maktaba Jadeed*, PO Box 456, Lahore
Proprietor: Ch Rasheed Ahmed
Subject: Fiction

Maktaba Meri Library*, Chowk Urdu Bazar, Lahore
Proprietor: Basheer Ahmed
Subject: Paperbacks

Maktaba Shahkar*, Chowk Urdu Bazar, Lahore Tel: 354103
Proprietor: S Qasim Mahmud
Subjects: Encyclopedias, Paperbacks

Malik Din Mohammad & Sons*, Bull Rd, Lahore Tel: 54315, 52621
Proprietor: Malik Mohammad Arif
Branch Off: Chundrigar Rd, Karachi
Subject: Islamic Studies

Malik Sirajuddin & Sons, Kashmiri Bazar, Lahore 8 Tel: 52169/311498/65539/67832 Cable Add: Serajsons Tele 52169
Man Dir: A R Malik; *Editorial:* S A Malik; *Sales:* A A Malik; *Production, Publicity & Permissions:* S A Malik
Subsidiary Companies: Siraj Mohammadi Press, 73 Circular Rd, Outside Akbari Gate, Lahore; Ayaz Book Binding Works, Bazar Tezabian, Kashmiri Bazar, Lahore 8
Branch Off: Chowk Urdu Bazar, Lahore 2
Subject: Religion
Book Club: Malik Sirajuddin & Sons (Sales & Depot), Kashmiri Bazar, Lahore 8
1978: 10 titles *1979:* 32 titles *Founded:* 1934

Maqbool Academy*, Adabi Market, Chowk Anarkali, Lahore Tel: 64740
Proprietor: Maqbool Ahmed Malik
Subject: Fiction

Mercantile Guardian Press and Publishers*, 81-83 Shahra-e-Quaid-e-Azami, Lahore
Subject: Trade Directories
Founded: 1949

Nafees Academy, PO Box 91, Karachi (Located at: Stratchan Rd) Tel: 213303
Proprietor: Saleem Gahandri
Subject: History, Educational, General

Nairoshni*, Nicol Rd, Karachi 2

The **Oriental & Religious** Publishing Corp Ltd, Rabwah
Subjects: The Holy Qur'an in Arabic and English; Commentaries on the Qur'an; Books on Islam

Orientalia Publishers, PO Box 1338, Lahore (Located at: 6 Habib Bank Bldg, Chowk Urdu Bazar
Subjects: Islamic literature, Rare Oriental Books

Oxford University Press*, GPO Box 442, Karachi 1 (Located at: 2nd floor, Haroon House, Dr Ziauddin Ahmed Rd, Karachi)
Manager: C H Lewis
Subjects: Textbooks, Reference Books, Educational, Economics, History, Islamic Studies

Bookshop: address as above
1978: 5 titles

Pak Publishers*, Urdu Bazar, Lahore

Pakistan Law Times Publications*, Kabir St, Urdu Bazar, Lahore

Pakistan Publications*, Shahrah Iraq, PO Box 183, Karachi 1
Subjects: Books about Pakistan in Urdu, Arabic and English

Pakistan Publishing Co Ltd*, 56-N Gulberg Industrial Colony, Lahore
Man Dir: S M Shah
Subject: Textbooks
Founded: 1932
Miscellaneous: Government Printers

Pakistan Publishing House, Victoria Chambers 2, A Haroon Rd, Sadar, Karachi 3 Tel: 511457 Cable Add: Prilect
Dir: M Noorani; *Editorial Dir:* Kamran Noorani; *Sales Manager:* Matin M Khan; *Production Manager:* Mohammad Yusuf; *Publicity Manager:* Ghulam Husain; *Rights & Permissions:* Mohammad Iqbal
Subsidiary Company: Maktaba-i-Danial, at above address
Associate Company: Pakistan Law House, Pakistan Chowk, PO Box 90, Karachi 1
Imprints: PPH, Maktaba-i-Danial
Subjects: History, Law, Literature
1978: 5 titles *1979:* 3 titles *Founded:* 1966

People's Publishing House*, PO Box 862, Lahore (Located at: 26 Shahrah-e-Quaid-e-Azam, Lahore) Tel: 54512
Man Dir, Publication: Abdur Rauf Malik; *Sales:* G Mustafa; *Publicity:* M Siddique
Subject: Social Science
1978: 20 titles *Founded:* 1947

Premier Book House, PO Box 1888, Lahore (Located at: Room 2, Shahin Market, Anarkali, Lahore) Tel: 56294
Proprietor: Mohammad Khalil
Subject: Islamic Literature
Bookshop: at above address
1978: 10 titles *1979:* 15 titles *Founded:* 1950

Publishers International*, Bandukwala Bldg, 4 McLeod Rd, Karachi
Man Dir: Kamaluddin Ahmad
Subjects: Advertising, Reference, Science, Technical, Textbooks
Founded: 1948

Publishers United Ltd*, PO Box 1689, Lahore (Located at: 176 Anarkali, Lahore) Tel: 52238 Cable Add: Pubun (Warehouse: 9 Rattigan Rd, Lahore Tel: 53423)
Man Dir: Mohammad Amin
Subjects: Religion, Economics, Technical, Reference
1978: 7 titles *Founded:* 1942

Qaumi Kutab Khana*, Railway Rd, Lahore Tel: 53810
Proprietor: Mohammad Ahsan & Bros

'Rast Gufter' Press*, Bhawana Bazar, Lyallpur
Manager & Proprietor: Shamshar Ali Baskhshi
Founded: 1889

Royal Book Co, PO Box 7737, Karachi 3 (Located at: 232 Saddar Cooperative Market, Abdullah Haroon Rd, Karachi 3) Tel: 514244
Proprietor: Jamshed Mirza
Subjects: Politics, Economics, Banking, General History, Asian Historical Reprints
Bookshop: At above address
1978: 7 titles *1979:* 6 titles *Founded:* 1963

H M Saeed Co*, Dr Ziauddin Ahmad Rd, Pakistan Chowk, Karachi
Proprietor: Mohammad Zaki
Subject: Islamic Studies, Literature (in Arabic, Urdu, Persian)

Sang-e-Meel Publications, Chowk Urdu Bazar, Lahore
Proprietor: Niaz Ahmed
Subjects: History and Islamic Studies

Taj Co Ltd*, Manghopir Rd, PO Box 530, Karachi Tel: Karachi 292021/292648 Cable Add: Kalampak
Man Dir: Sheikh Enayat Ullah
Branch Offs: Rawalpindi, Lahore
Subject: Religion
Founded: 1929
Bookshop: Agency Taj Co, M A Jinnah Rd, Karachi

Taxation*, 6 Liaquat Rd, Lahore 6

University Book Agency, Khyber Bazar, Peshawar Tel: 62534
Branch Off: University Campus, Peshawar
Subjects: General, Textbooks

Urdu Academy Sind*, Jinnah Rd, Karachi Tel: 73730
Proprietor: Ala-ud-Din Khalid
Branch Offs: Lahore, Hyderabad
Subjects: General, Textbooks

West Pakistan Publishing Co Ltd*, PO Box 374, Lahore 2 Tel: 80409
Proprietor: Mohammad Shah
Subject: Textbooks

Writers' Guild Publishing House*, Strachan Rd, Karachi
Subject: Literature

Book Club

Malik Sirajuddin & Sons, Kashmiri Bazar, Lahore 8
Owned by: Malik Sirajuddin & Sons (Publisher, qv)

Major Booksellers

Bookcentre*, Lakshmi Mansion, Shahrah-e-Quaid-e-Azam, Lahore

Ferozsons Ltd, 60 Shahrah-e-Quaid-e-Azam, Lahore
Also 277 Peshawar Rd, Rawalpindi

S I Gillani*, 65 Shahrah-e-Quaid-e-Azam, Lahore 3

Liberty Bookstall, PO Box 7427, Karachi 03 Tel: 513026/510798 Cable Add: Bookazine
Managing Partner: A Hussein

Maktaba Ishaat-e-Adab*, Anarkali, Lahore

S M Mir*, 40 Chartered Bank Chambers, Talpur Rd, Karachi 2
Also Publishers' Agent

Mirza Book Agency*, 65 Shahrah-e-Quaid-e-Azam, PO Box 729, Lahore 3 Tel: 66839 Cable Add: Knowledge

Oxford University Press, 2nd floor, Haroon House, Dr Ziauddin Ahmed Rd, GPO Box 442, Karachi 1
Manager: C H Lewis

Pak American Commercial Inc*, Zaibunnisa St, Karachi 3

Pak Book Corporation, 37 Commercial Bldg, Shahrah-e-Quaid-e-Azam (The Mall), Lahore Tel: 55166 Cable Add: Magbookco
Dir: M Iqbal Cheema; *Man Dir:* M A Khan Akter
Also I & T Centre, G-6/1/1, Islamabad

Paradise Book Stall, Shambhu Nath Rd, Saddar, Karachi 3

Paramount Book Stall*, Preedy St, Saddar, Karachi 3
Branches at Lahore, Peshawar
Also wholesaler

Petiwala Corporation, Ismail Mansion, Strechen Rd, Pakistan Chowk, Karachi 1 Tel: 218643

Royal Book Co, 232 Saddar Cooperative Market, Abdullah Haroon Rd, Karachi 3

Major Libraries

Agriculture University Library*, Lyallpur
Head Department of Library: Najif Ali Khan

British Council Libraries*, 32 Mozang Rd, PO Box 88, Lahore Tel: 52755/6
Also Tilak Incline, Jacob Rd, PO Box 126 Hyderabad; 14 Civic Centre, Ramna 6, PO Box 1135, Islamabad; 20 Bleak House Rd, PO Box 146, Karachi 4; 35 The Mall, PO Box 49, Peshawar; Lansdowne Gardens, The Mall, PO Box 1135, Rawalpindi; Chartered Bank Building, Shahrah-e-Quaid-e-Azam, PO Box 88, Lahore

Central Secretariat Library*, Government of Pakistan, Islamabad

Ewing Memorial Library*, Forman Christian College, Lahore 11

Government College Library*, Lahore

Dr Mahmud Husain Library, University of Karachi, Karachi 32 Tel: 418227
Librarian: Akhter Hanif
Publications include: Guide to Bibliographical Sources; Catalogue of rare books

Islamabad University Library*, PO Box 1190, Islamabad

Islamic Research Institute Library, PO Box 1035, Islamabad

Liaquat Memorial Library*, Stadium Rd, Karachi 5

National Archives of Pakistan, Commercial Area F/8, Nr Zafar Chowk, Islamabad
Branches: Quaid-e-Azam Papers Unit, Secretariat Block-D, Islamabad; SK Centre Bldg, 2nd Floor, Nr Frere Market Rd, AM2, Karachi

National Library*, Islamabad

Pakistan Forest Institute, Central Forest Library*, PO Forest Institute, Peshawar

Pakistan Institute of Nuclear Science & Technology Library*, PO Nilore, Rawalpindi

Pakistan Scientific and Technological Information Centre (PASTIC)*, 435 F-6/3 Islamabad

Planning Commission Library, Government of Pakistan, 'P' Block, Pakistan Secretariat, Islamabad

Punjab Public Library*, Lahore

Punjab University Library*, 1 Kutchery Rd, Lahore 2/12 Tel: 52262

Sind University Central Library*, University of Sind, New Campus, Jamshoro, Sind
Librarian: Moinuddin Khan

University of Baluchistan Library*, Quetta, Baluchistan

University of Engineering and Technology, Lahore Tel: 339243 Cable Add: Univengtech
Acting Librarian: Mohammad Ramzan

University of Karachi Library, see Dr Mahmud Husain Library

University of Peshawar Library*, Peshawar
Librarian: I U Khan

Library Associations

Directorate of Libraries*, National Bibliographical Unit, Karachi
Director: Hafiz Akhtar
Publication: Pakistan National Bibliography

Federal Library Association*, Pakistan National Centre, 169 Sawar Rd, Rawalpindi
Publication: Federal Librarian

Karachi University Library Science Alumni Association*, c/o Dept of Library Science, University of Karachi, Karachi 32
Publication: Newsletter

Library Promotion Bureau*, Old Students' Lodge, Karachi University, Karachi 32
Tel: 418227
Executive Secretary: M Adil Usmani
Publications: Pakistan Library Bulletin (quarterly); *Pakistan Book Trade Directory; Who's Who in Librarianship in Pakistan*

Library Science Society*, c/o Department of Library Science, Karachi University, Karachi 32

Mehran Library Association*, PO Box 126, Hyderabad
Secretary: I A S Bokhari MA
Publication: Newsletter

Pakistan Library Association*, c/o University of Peshawar, Peshawar
Publications: PLA Newsletter, Proceedings

Society for the Promotion and Improvement of Libraries*, 54 M A Jinah Rd, Hameed Manzil, Karachi 5
Publications: Karachi Public Library: A Scheme; Report of the School Library Workshop; School Library Handbook; Newsletter and others

Library Journals

Federal Librarian, Federal Library Association, Pakistan National Centre, 169 Sawar Rd, Rawalpindi

Newsletter, Karachi University Library Science Alumni Association, Karachi 32

Newsletter, Pakistan Library Association, c/o University of Peshawar, Peshawar

Pakistan Library Bulletin (international edition in English, domestic edition in English and Urdu), Library Promotion Bureau, Old Students' Lodge, University Campus, Karachi 32

Literary Associations and Societies

Anjuman Taraqqi-e-Urdu Pakistan*, Baba-e-Urdu Rd, Karachi 1
For the promotion of the Urdu language and literature
President: Akhter Husain; *Secretary:* Jamiluddin A'Ali
Publications: Urdu (quarterly), *Qaumi Zaban* (monthly); various books

Pakistan Board for Advancement of Literature*, Narsing Das Garden, Club Rd, Lahore

Pakistan Writers' Guild*, B-16 Sindhi Muslim Housing Society, Karachi
Secretary-General: Mahbub Jamal Zahedi
Publication: Ham Qalam (monthly)

Punjab Text Board*, 21/E-11, Gulberg 111, Lahore
Similar Text Boards exist in Sind at Karachi, Baluchistan at Quetta, NWFP at Peshawar

Sindhi Adabi Board*, Sind University Campus, Jamshoro, Hyderabad, Sind
To promote the language, literature and culture of the Sind region

Literary Periodicals

Ham Qalam, Pakistan Writers' Guild, B-16 Sindhi Muslim Housing Society, Karachi 3

Perspective, Pakistan Publications, Shahrah Iraq, PO Box 183, Karachi

Literary Prizes

Adamjee Prize*
Founded in 1960 for the best book of creative and progressive poetry, novel, short story, drama, travelogue or biography. 20,000 rupees. Awarded annually. Administered by the Pakistan Writers' Guild in Karachi. Enquiries to Pakistan Writers' Guild, B-16 Sindhi Muslim Housing Society, Karachi 3

Dawood Prize for Literature*
Founded in 1963 for the best books on literary research, literary history, literary criticism; for research works on the Pakistan movement; and for the best translation. 25,000 rupees. Sponsored by the Dawood Foundation. Awarded annually. Enquiries to the Pakistan Writers' Guild, B-16 Sindhi Muslim Housing Society, Karachi 3

Habib Bank Prize for Literature*
Founded in 1968 for the best translation or adaptation of the year (into English or a Pakistani language) of a modern or classical work in any Pakistani language, 25,000 rupees. Awarded annually. Enquiries to Pakistan Writers' Guild, B-16 Sindhi Muslim Housing Society, Karachi 3

National Bank of Pakistan Prize for Literature*
Founded in 1964 for the best books on economics and scientific, technical and professional subjects. 25,000 rupees. Awarded annually. Enquiries to Pakistan Writers' Guild, B-16 Sindhi Muslim Housing Society, Karachi 3

Pakistan Board for Advancement of Literature Awards*
For academic works in Urdu, and for articles and poems published in Pakistan journals. Awarded annually. Enquiries to Pakistan Board for Advancement of Literature, Narsing Das Garden, Club Rd, Lahore

President's Award for Pride of Performance*
For notable achievements in literature. Awarded annually. Enquiries to Pakistan Ministry of Education, Islamabad

Prizes for Manuscripts for Juveniles*
Six prizes for creative writing in the field of children's literature in the Urdu language. Awarded annually. Enquiries to Pakistan Writers' Guild, B-16 Sindhi Muslim Housing Society, Karachi 3

Punjab Advisory Board for Books Prizes*
For books of high educational and literary value in the Urdu language. Awarded annually. Enquiries to the Secretary, Punjab Advisory Board for Books, Lahore

Regional Literature Awards*
For the best literary works, including the novel, short story, drama, poetry, biography, travel, literary criticism or research work, in each of the four regional languages of Punjabi, Pushto, Sindhi and Gujrati. Awarded annually. Enquiries to Pakistan Writers' Guild, c/o Regional Secretary, Princess Hotel, Montgomery Rd, Lahore

United Bank Prize for Literature*
Founded in 1967 for books in Urdu and Bengali in the following categories: for children up to 15 years of age; and poetry or prose, fiction or nonfiction, for young children. 20,000 rupees. Awarded annually. Enquiries to Pakistan Writers' Guild, B-16 Sindhi Muslim Housing Society, Karachi 3

Panama

General Information

Language: Spanish (English widely used)
Religion: Roman Catholic
Population: 1.8 million
Literacy Rate (1970): 78.3%
Bank Hours: 0800-1300 or 1330 Monday-Friday
Shop Hours: 0700 or 0800-1800 or 1900 Monday-Saturday, with 2-hour lunch closing
Currency: 100 centesimos = 1 balboa = $US1. US currency is used
Export/Import Information: No tariffs on books and advertising matter. No import licences or exchange controls
Copyright: UCC, Buenos Aires (see International section)

Publishers

Dirección de Estadística y Censo, Contraloría General de la República, Apdo 5213, Panama 5 Tel: 640777 Cable Add: Estadicen-Contraloría Panama
Man Dir: D Castillo; *Editorial:* J M Caballero; *Sales, Production, Publicity:* R Tapia
Subject: Panamanian Statistics
1978: 30 titles *1979:* 28 titles *Founded:* 1941

Ediciones Instituto Nacional de Cultura, Apdo 662, Panamá 1 Tel: 220880/84 Cable Add: Inac
President: Aristides Martínez Ortega; *Editorial, Sales:* Arysteides Turpana; *Production:* Pedro Montañez; *Publicity:* Norma de la Espada
Subjects: Literature in general, History, Anthropology, Archaeology, Folklore, Sociology
Founded: 1976

Ediciones **Librería Cultural Panameña** SA, Apdo de Correos 2018, Panamá 1 Tel: 235628/236267 Cable Add: Culpasa
Man Dir, Editorial: A J Fraguela R; *Sales:* F M Fraguela Ruiz
Subjects: University, Secondary & Primary Textbooks, Antiquaria, Reference Works
Bookshop: Vía España 16, Apdo 2018, Panama 1 (and two other branches)
1978: 32 titles *Founded:* 1955

Editorial Universitariá*, Estafeta Universitariá, Universidad de Panamá Tel: 23-0210 ext 11 Cable Add: Cuidad Universitariá
Man Dir, Editorial: Dr Carlos M Gasteazoro; *Sales:* Carlos Castro Jr; *Production:* Prof C A Araúz; *Publicity:* H Muñoz
Subjects: History, Philosophy, Geography, Sciences, Law, Literature, Art, Architecture, Social Sciences, Technical, Education
Bookshops: University Bookshop
Founded: 1969

Editorial **McGraw-Hill** Latino-Americana SA, Apdo 2036, Colón Tel: 474900 Cable Add: Books-Panama
Man Dir, Editorial, Permissions: Dubier Alvarez; *Sales, Promotion:* Hermencia Morales
Parent Company: McGraw-Hill Inc, USA
Associate Companies: see McGraw-Hill Book Co (UK) Ltd
Subsidiary Companies: McGraw-Hill Latino-Americana (Puerto Rico); Editorial McGraw-Hill Latino-Americana (Colombia) (qqv)
Subjects: Scholarly, Reference, University, Secondary & Primary Textbooks
Founded: 1966

Major Booksellers

Librería **Argosy***, Vía Argentina, Edificio Pancho Verde, and Vía España, Apdo 6620, Panamá 5 Tel: 235344

Librería Cultural Panameña, SA, Apdo de Correos 2018, Panamá 1 Tel: 235628 (and 2 other branches) Cable Add: Culpasa

Librería **Menéndez***, Galerías Obarrio, Via Brasil, Panamá
Branches: Ave Justo Arosemena y Calle 36, Panamá; Aeropuerto Tocumen, Panamá; Librería Santa Ana, Plaza Santa Ana, Panamá; Librería La Escolar SA, Plaza Cervantes, David

Servicio Continental de Publicaciones*, Calle 29 Este 5-70, Apdo 1379, Panamá Tel: 250614 (and 2 other branches)

Servicio de Lewis*, Calle 26 y Ave Balboa, Apdo 1634, Panamá 1 Tel: 627000

Major Libraries

Biblioteca Nacional*, Apdo 3435, Panamá

Biblioteca Bio-Médica del Laboratorio Conmemorativo **Gorgas**, Apdo 6991, Panamá 5 (Located at: Ave Justo Arosemena, No 35-30, Panamá 5) Tel: 274111/256550/620864/525533/525544 Cable Add: Gomela Telex: Gml pa 3480333
Also at Box 935, APO Miami, Florida 34002, USA
Gorgas Memorial Laboratory, Bio-medical Research Library
Dir: Dr Abram Benenson
Medical librarian: Professor M Víctor De Las Casas
Publications include: Annual Report, Bibliography of Papers Emanating from the Gorgas Memorial Laboratory; El Laboratorio Conmemorativo Gorgas; su Historia y su Labor; 40 Years of Tropical Medicine Research: a History of the Gorgas Memorial Institute of Tropical and Preventive Medicine, Inc and the Gorgas Memorial Laboratory

Universidad de Panama, Biblioteca Interamericana Simón Bolívar, Estafeta Universitaría, Panamá
Librarian: Nuria F de González

Library Associations

Associación de Bibliotecarios Graduados del Istmo de Panamá, c/o Director, Biblioteca Bio-Médica del Laboratorio Commemorativo Gorgas, Apdo 6991, Panamá 5, Panama Tel: 274111
Association of Graduate Librarians of the Isthmus of Panama
President: Professor Manuel Víctor de las Casas; *Secretary:* Iris de Espinosa

Asociación Panameña de Bibliotecarios*, Apdo 3435, Panamá
Panama Library Association
President: Nuria F De Gonzalez
Publication: Boletín

Universidad de Panama, Escuela de Bibliotecologia*, Estafeta Universitaría, Panamá 3
University of Panama, School of Library Science
Publication: Boletín

Library Journals

Boletín (Bulletin), Panama Library Association, c/o Inés Maria Herrera, President, Apdo 3435, Panamá

Boletín (Bulletin), University of Panama, School of Library Science, Apdo 3277, Panamá 3

Literary Prizes

Literary Prize
Founded in 1946 by Ricardo Miró to pay tribute to those who furthered the cause of learning, arts and sciences. Awarded annually. A prize of $2,000 is given in each of five sections: poetry, short story, fiction, theatre, essay. The 1979 winners in each section were, respectively, Matilde Real de González and José Franco, no award, Acracia Sarasqueta de Smith, Jarl Babot, no award. Enquiries to 'Revista Nacional de Cultura', Instituto Nacional de Cultura, Apdo 662, Panama 1

Papua New Guinea

General Information

Language: English is one of official languages, as is pidjin English or neo-Melanesian, and 700 distinct languages are in use
Religion: Majority follow traditional beliefs. Sizeable Anglican, Roman Catholic and Ecumenist congregations
Population: 3 million
Literacy Rate (1971): 32.1% of population aged 10 or over
Currency: 100 toea = 1 kina
Export/Import Information: No tariff on books and advertising but 5% import tax on non-educational books. No import licence for books, but no obscene literature permitted. No exchange controls

Publishers

The **Christian Book** Centre, PO Box 222, Madang
Subjects: Literature, Religion

Gordon and Gotch (PNG) Pty Ltd, PO Box 3395, Port Moresby Tel: 254551/254855 Cable Add: Gotchbooks Port Moresby Telex: Pngotch NE 22263
General Manager: Rex P Lingard
Parent Company: Gordon and Gotch (Australia) Pty Ltd
Subsidiary Companies: Waigani Enterprises, New Guinea Book Depot, Taurama Newsagency, Gerehu Newsagency
Subjects: Travel, Natural History, Languages, Cookery, New Guinea History, Art and Folklore
1978: 7 titles *Founded:* 1970
ISBN Publisher's Prefix: 0-909093

Isopang Publishing Pty Ltd*, Cnr Wards Rd and Mango St, Hohola, Port Moresby

Major Booksellers

Burns Philp (NG) Ltd*, Kieta, Bougainville (and other branches)

Papua New Guinea Book Depot, PO Box 5495, Boroko Tel: 254267 Cable Add: Gotchbooks Telex: Pngotch NE 22263
Manager: Don Smith
Owned by: Gordon and Gotch (PNG) Pty Ltd

Rabaul Newsagency, c/o Bali Merchants Pty Ltd, PO Box 390, Rabaul

Steamships Trading Co, PO Box 30, Goroka

University Book Shop*, PO Box 4614, University PO

Major Libraries

University of Papua New Guinea Library*, PO Box 4819, University Post Office, Waigani Tel: 53900 Port Moresby

Library Associations

Papua New Guinea Library Association*, PO Box 5368, Boroko Tel: 424999, ext 270
Executive Secretary: Ms W Avosa

School Library Association of Papua New Guinea*, c/o School Library Officer, Department of Education, Konedobu Tel: 56358
Executive Secretary: S Rauka

Literary Periodicals

Kovave; journal of New Guinea literature, Jacaranda Press Pty Ltd, 65 Park Rd, Milton, Queensland 40664, Australia

Papua New Guinea Writing, Literature Bureau, Office of Information, PO Box 2312, Konedobu

Paraguay

General Information

Language: Spanish (Guarani, an aboriginal Indian tongue, is universally spoken)
Religion: Roman Catholic
Population: 2.9 million
Literacy Rate (1972): 80.1% (88.6% of urban population, 74.1% rural)
Bank Hours: 0730-1100 Monday-Friday
Shop Hours: 0700 or 0730-1200, 1500-1800 Monday-Friday; open until noon Saturday
Currency: guarani
Export/Import Information: Member of Latin American Free Trade Association. Children's picture books: 10% ad valorem, 7.5% added tax, 12% compensatory tax, Atlases: 11% ad valorem, 15% added tax,

24% compensatory tax. Advertising catalogues subject to 15% added tax and compensatory tax of 24%. Additional taxes on all goods totalling 6½% VAT C & I + 20%; also Consular Fee 5% VAT FOB. No import licences required. Exchange controls; foreign exchange surcharge is 36%, VAT C & I + 20%
Copyright: UCC, Buenos Aires (see International section)

Book Trade Organizations

Cámara Paraguaya del Liibro*, Librería Internacional, Estrella 380, Asunción
Paraguayan Publishers' Association

Publishers

La **Colmena**, SA*, Presidente Franco 328, Casilla 302, Asunción
Dir: Daumas Ladouce

Editorial **Comuneros***, Presidente Franco 480, CC980, Asunción Tel: 46176
Subjects: Social History, Poetry

Ediciones **Diálogo***, Calle Brasil 1391, Asunción
Manager: Miguel Angel Fernández
Subjects: Fine Arts, Literature, Poetry, Criticism, History, Science
Founded: 1957

Ediciones **Nizza**, Tacuari 144, Asunción Tel: 47160
President: Dr Jose Ferreira Martinez
Subject: Medicine
Bookshop: Agencia de Librerías Nizza (at above address)

Major Booksellers

Librería El **Ateneo***, General Diaz 347, Asunción Tel: 43668

El **Colegio** SA*, Estrella 372, Asunción
Importer/Exporter, Wholesaler

Librería **Comuneros***, Presidente Franco 480, CC980 Asunción Tel: 46176

Librería La **Cultura***, Palma esq Montevideo, Asunción Tel: 45093

Librería Internacional*, Estrella 380, Casilla de Correo 991, Asunción Tel: 41423

Librería Universal, Palma 519, Casilla de Correo 432, Asunción

Agencia de Librerías **Nizza**, Tacuari 144, Asunción Tel: 47160

Selecciones SA Comercial*, Iturbe 436, Asunción Tel: 41588

Major Libraries

Biblioteca y Archivo Nacionales*, Mariscal Estigarriba 95, Asunción
National Library and Archives

Biblioteca de la **Sociedad Científica** del Paraguay*, Ave España 505, Asunción
Library of the Paraguayan Scientific Society

Library Associations

Asociación de Bibliotecarios del Paraguay*, Calle Casilla de Correo 1505, Asunción
Association of Paraguayan Librarians
Secretary: Mafalda Cabrerar
Publication: Revista de Bibliotecologia y Documentación Paraguaya

Asociación de Bibliotecarios Universitarios del Paraguay, c/o Professor Yoshiko M de Freundorfer, Head, Escuela de Bibliotecologia, Universidad Nacional de Asunción, Asunción
Paraguayan Association of University Librarians
President: Profesora Gloria Ondina Ortiz C;
Secretary: Celia Villamayor de Díaz

Comisión Paraguaya Documentación e Información*, c/o Instituto de Ciencias, Universidad Nacional, Ave España 1098, Asunción
Paraguayan Committee of Documentation and Information
Executive Secretary: Luis Fernando Meyer

Library Journals

Revista de Bibliotecologia y Documentación Paraguaya (Review of Paraguay Library Science and Documentation), Association of Paraguay Librarians, Calle Casilla de Correo 1505, Asunción

Peru

General Information

Language: Spanish
Religion: Roman Catholic
Population: 16.8 million
Literacy Rate (1972): 72.5% (87.4% of urban population, 49.1% rural)
Bank Hours: January-March: 0830-1130 Monday-Friday; April-December: 0830-1200 Monday-Friday
Shop Hours: January-March: 0930-1245, 1615-1900 Monday-Saturday; April-December: 0900-1245, 1515-1900 Monday-Saturday (some close Saturday afternoon)
Currency: 100 centavos = 1 sol
Export/Import Information: Member of Andean Group within the Latin American Free Trade Association. Children's picture books 6 soles kg + 82% VAT. Advertising matter 5 soles kg + 82% VAT, 5% sales tax applies. No freight tax on books but there is 1% wholesalers' tax. Import licences required. Exchange controls
Copyright: UCC, Buenos Aires (see International section)

Book Trade Organizations

Asociación Nacional de Escritores y Artistas (ANEA)*, Jirón de la Unión Belén 1054, Lima
National Association of Writers and Artists
President: Dr Pedro Ugarteche

Cámara Peruana del Libro*, Calle Washington 1206, Of 508 Apdo 3744, Lima 1 Tel: 325694
Peruvian Publishers' Association
Secretary: A Carbone

Book Trade Reference Journal

Anuario Bibliográfico Peruano (Peruvian National Bibliography), National Library, Ave Abancay, Apdo 2335, Lima 1

Publishers

Librerías **A B C** SA, Las Magnolias 841, Of 201, San Isidro, Apdo 5595, Lima Tel: 413712 Cable Add: Molagent
Man Dir: H H Moll; *Editorial:* Eduardo Nugent V
Associate Companies: Florida 725, Cordoba 685, Martinez, Argentina; Librerias Galax, Pl las Americas, Loc 59, Caracas, Venezuela; Centro Iñaquito, Quito, Ecuador
Subjects: History, Peruvian Art & Archaeology
Bookshops: Colmena 725; Hotel Bolivar, Lima; Centro Comercial Todos, San Isidro; Centro Comercial Galax, Chacarilla del Estanque; Edificio El Pacífico, Miraflores; Aeropuerto Jorge Chavez, Callao
Founded: 1956

Aguilar Peruana de Ediciones SA*, Ave Inca Garcilaso de la Vega 1156, Lima
Parent Company: Aguilar SA de Ediciones, Spain (qv)

Editorial **Arica**, SA*, Casilla 3537, Lima 1 Tel: 401670
Man Dir: Boris Romero Accinelli; *Sales Manager:* Angélica Li; *Editorial Dir:* Benjamin Romero Accinelli
Subjects: Literature, Technical, Textbooks, Educational Materials, Law, History
Founded: 1958

Asociación Editorial **Bruño**, Ave Arica 751, Breña, Apdo 1759, Lima Tel: 244134
Man Dir: Hno Francisco Alvarez Penelas
Subjects: University, Secondary & Primary Textbooks and Educational Materials
Founded: 1950

Editorial **Desarrollo**, SA, Lampa 921, 2° piso, Apdo 3824, Lima Tel: 285380 Cable Add: Edidesa
Man Dir: Luis Sosa Núñez; *Assistant Manager:* Bertha de Berrospi
Bookshop: Librería de Editorial Desarrollo, Lampa 921, 2° piso, Lima
Subjects: Business, Accounting, General Reference, Industrial Engineering
1978: 29 titles *1979:* 39 titles *Founded:* 1965

Editorial **Ecoma** SA*, Ave Arequipa 4168 'B', Miraflores 18, Lima Tel: 473017 Cable Add: Ecoma
Man Dir: Eduardo Congrains Martin; *Sales Dir:* Ramón Lalupu Lazaro
Subjects: Paperbacks, Literature, Biography, History, Philosophy, Juveniles
Founded: 1970

Distribuidora exclusivo **Grijalbo** SA*, Apdo 4978, Lima
Parent Company: Editorial Grijalbo SA, Spain (qv)

Editorial **Horizonte***, Jirón Camaná 878, Lima Tel: 279364
Man Dir: Humberto Damonte Larraín
Subject: Literature in general
Bookshop: Jirón Camaná 878, Lima

Promotion Editorial **Inca** SA, now Ediciones Peisa (qv)

Instituto de Estudios Peruanos*, Horacio Urteaga 694, Jesus Maria, Lima 11 Tel: 323070/244658 Cable Add: Ieperu
Man Dir: José Matos Mar; *Sales Manager:* Ursula Lizarraga
Subjects: Peruvian studies in Agriculture, Archaeology, Economics, History, Anthropology
1978: 12 titles *Founded:* 1964

Librería-Editorial Juan **Mejía** Baca, Jirón Azángaro 722, Lima Tel: 274067
Man Dir: Juan Mejía Baca
Subjects: Peruvian Literature and History
Founded: 1945

Mosca Azul Editores SRL, PO Box 11020, Sta Beatriz, Lima 18 Tel: 470655
Dirs: Mirko Lauer, Abelardo Oquendo
Subjects: Fiction & Non-fiction, Social Science, University Textbooks
1978: 9 titles *1979:* 10 titles *Founded:* 1972

Ediciones **Peisa** (Promoción Editorial Inca SA), Emilio Althaus 460, Oficina 202, Lima 14 Tel: 718884
Man Dir: Martha Muñoz de Coronado;
Sales Dir: Nora Muñoz de Degregori
Subjects: Peruvian Literature and History, Juvenile, Children's Books

Editorial **Plata** SA, Casilla 5595, Lima Tel: 413712
Man Dir: Herbert H Moll
Subjects: South America — History, Art, Guidebooks, Juveniles, Maps
Founded: 1971 (in Venezuela)

Librería **Studium** SA*, Pl Francia 1164, Apdo 2139, Lima Tel: 326278 Cable Add: Studium
Man Dir: Andrés Carbone O; *Assistant Manager:* Andrés Carbone Montes;
Exports: José Córdova C
Subjects: Textbooks and General Culture
Founded: 1936
Bookshops: At above address and Jiron de la Union 560, Lima; Colmena 626, Lima; Ave Larco 720, Miraflores; Saenz Peña 625, Callao; Francisco Pizarro 533, Trujillo; General Morán 123, Arequipa; Calle Moral 107A-107B, Arequipa; Elías Aguirre 251, Chiclayo; Calle Real 377, Huancayo; Calle Arequipa 110, Ayacucho; Tacna 216, Piura; Mesón de la Estrella 144, Cuzco (all in Peru)

Fondo Editorial de la **Universidad Católica**, Apdo 12514, Lima 21 (Located at: Fundo Pando, Pueblo Libre, Lima 21) Tel: 622540 ext 128
Man Dir: Dr F Pease G Y
Subjects: Humanities, Social Sciences, Mathematics, Engineering, Law, Education, Periodicals, Journals
1979: 3 titles *1980:* 6 titles

Universidad Nacional Mayor de San Marcos*, Apdo 454, Lima (Located at: Direccion Universitaria de Biblioteca y Publicaciones, Ave República de Chile 295, of 508) Apdo 454, Lima Tel: 319689
Man Dir: Juan de Dios Guevara, Rector de la Universidad
Subjects: Medicine, Law, Science, General Literature, Engineering, Textbooks
Founded: 1952

Editorial **Universo** SA*, Ave Nicolás Arriola 2285, La Victoria, Apdo 241, Lima 30 Tel: 241639/233190
Man Dir: Augusto Sandoval Valcárcel;
Executive Manager: Paulino Advíncula Rios
Subjects: Social Science, Textbooks
Founded: 1967

Major Booksellers

Librerías **A B C** SA, Las Magnolias 841, Of 201, San Isidro, Apdo 5595, Lima
Branches: Colmena 725; Hotel Bolivar, Lima; Centro Comercial Todos, San Isidro; Centro Comercial Galax, Chacarilla del Estanque; Edificio El Pacifico, Miraflores; Aeropuerto Jorge Chavez, Callao

Librería **Arica***, Paseo de la República 3285, San Isidro, Lima, Casilla 3537, Lima 1 Tel: 401670

Editorial **Interamericana** SA*, Apdo 76, Lima 1 (Located at: Av 28 de Julio 787, Lima 1) Tel: 233471/241944/241845
General Manager: Dr José de la Riva-Agüero

Librería **Epoca***, Jirón Unión 1042, Apdo 4703, Lima Tel: 249545

Librerías La **Familia**, Ave Nicolás de Pierola 346, Lima Tel: 243544/248031

Librería **Galería** Castro Soto*, Miguel Dasso 200, San Isidro, Lima Tel: 401343

Editorial **Horizonte***, Jirón Camaná 878, Lima Tel: 279364

Librería **Internacional** del Perú*, Casilla 1417, Boza 892, 2° piso, Lima Tel: 288611

Librería Juan **Mejía** Baca, Jirón Azángaro 722, Lima Tel: 274067

Nicolas **Ojeda** Fierro e Hijos, see Librería 'La Universidad'

Librería **Studium** SA*, Pl Francia 1164, Apdo 2139, Lima Tel: 326278 (for branches see Publisher entry)

Librería de la **Universidad Nacional Mayor de San Marcos***, Jirón Unión (Belén) 1098, Lima 1 Tel: 2894255

Librería '**La Universidad**', Nicolas Ojeda Fierro e Hijos SRL Ltda, Ave Nicolás de Piérola 639, Lima Tel: 282461/282036
Branch Off: Ave Nicolás de Piérola 677, Lima Tel: 282036

Major Libraries

Archivo General de la Nación, Calle Manuel Cuadros, s/n, Palacio de Justicia, Apdo 3124, Lima Tel: 275930

Biblioteca Nacional, Ave Abancay, Apdo 2335, Lima 1 Tel: 277331/287690
Dir: María C Bonilla de Gaviría
Publications: Anuario Bibliográfico Peruano (Bibliographical Annual of Peru); *Boletín de la Biblioteca Nacional* (Bulletin of the National Library); *Revista Fénix* (Phoenix Magazine); *Gaceta Bibliotecaria* (Library Gazette)

Biblioteca Central de la **Pontificia Universidad Nacional** Católica del Perú, Final de la Ave Bolivar s/n, Apdos 1761-5729, Lima

Biblioteca Central de la **Universidad Nacional de Cuzeco***, Apdo 167, Cuzco

Biblioteca Central de la **Universidad Nacional de San Agustín***, Apdo 23, Arequipa

Biblioteca Central de la **Universidad Nacional Mayor de San Marcos***, Apdo 454, Lima

Library Associations

Agrupación de Bibliotecas para la Integración de la Información Socio-Económica (ABIISE)*, Apdo 2874, Lima 100 Tel: 351760
Library Group for the Integration of Socio-economic Information
Dir: Isabel Olivera Rivarola
Publications: Directorio de Bibliotecas Especializadas del Perú

Asociación de Bibliotecas Agricolas*, c/o Library, Universidad Nacional Agraria, La Molina, Lima
Association of Agricultural Librarians

Asociación Peruana de Archiveros*, Archivo General de la Nación, Calle Manuel Cuadros s/n, Palacio de Justicia, Apdo 1802, Lima
Peruvian Association of Archivists

Asociación Peruana de Bibliotecarios*, General La Fuente 592, Lima 27
Peruvian Association of Librarians

Publication: Carta Informativa (Newsletter)
Executive Secretary: Amparo Geraldino de Orban

Library Reference Books and Journals

Books

Directorio de Bibliotecas Especializadas del Perú (Directory of Special Libraries of Peru), Library Group for the Integration of Socio-economic Information, Apdo 2874, Lima 100

Journals

Boletín (Bulletin), National Library, Ave Abancay, Apdo 2335, Lima 1

Boletín Bibliografico (Bibliographical Bulletin), Universidad Nacional Mayor de San Marcos, Ave República de Chile 295, Apdo 454, Lima

Fénix (Phoenix): review of Peruvian libraries, National Library, Ave Abancay, Apdo 2335, Lima 1

Gaceta Bibliotecaria del Peru (Peruvian Library Gazette), National Library, Ave Abancay, Apdo 2335, Lima 1

Literary Associations and Societies

Centro del **P E N** Internacional*, Santa Teresita 327, San Isidor, Lima
Secretary: Blanca Varela

Literary Periodicals

Después (Afterwards), Roca y Boloña 633, Lima 18

Revista Peruana de Cultura (Peruvian Review of Culture), Institute Nacional de Cultura, Ancash 390, Lima 1

Textual, Instituto Nacional de Cultura, Ancash 390, Lima 1

Literary Prizes

Premio José María **Arguedas***
For the best novel, under auspices of the Goodyear del Perú. Awarded every other year. Enquiries to Goodyear del Perú, Casio de la Republic 959, La Victoria, Apdo 1690, Lima

Premio **Universo***
For the best novel. Awarded every other year. Enquiries to Editorial Universo SA, Ave Nicolás Arriola 2285, San Luis, Apdo 241, Lima 30

Philippines

General Information

Language: Pilipino (also called Tagalog) is official language. English widely used. Nine other major languages of the Malayo-Polynesian group, and about 60 other languages, are also spoken
Religion: Predominantly Roman Catholic; Muslim on Mindanao and the Sulu

PHILIPPINES

Archipelago
Population: 46 million
Literacy Rate (1970): 83.3%
Bank Hours: 0800-2000 Monday-Friday; some open Saturday
Shop Hours: Vary. Many open 0900-1200, 1400-1930 Monday-Saturday (some close 1730; some open Sunday)
Currency: 100 centavos =1 peso
Export/Import Information: 10% duty on books except those which are philosophical, historical, economic, scientific, technical or vocational, approved by Department of Education for use of certain institutions (not exceeding 10 copies for an institution, or 2 for an individual) or for encouragement of sciences or fine arts; no tariffs on Bibles and similar religious books. No duty on advertising matter. No import licences, but no obscene or immoral literature permitted. Release certificate issued on behalf of Central Bank required to clear goods. Imports subject to 7% sales tax. No formal exchange controls but most imports need Letter of Credit (over $100 in any month, for example)
Copyright: Berne, UCC, Buenos Aires, Florence (see International section)

Book Trade Organizations

Philippine Book Dealers' Association, MCC PO Box 1103, Makati Commercial Centre, Makati, Metro Manila
President: Jose Benedicto

Philippine Educational Publishers' Association*, 315 Quezon Blvd Extension, Quezon City Tel: 993897
President: Jesus Ernesto Sibal

Standard Book Numbering Agency, The National Library of the Philippines, T M Kalaw St, Manila
ISBN Administrator: Lily Orbase

Publishers

Abiva Publishing House Inc, 851-881 G Araneta Blvd, Quezon City Tel: 615403/4
Man Dir: Luis Q Abiva Jr; *Sales Dir:* Alfredo de Guzman; *Publicity Dir:* Mila S Precioso; *Advertising Dir:* Felicito Q Abiva; *Rights & Permissions:* Milagros R Arceo
Subsidiary Company: Hiyas Press Inc
Subjects: History, Reference, Religion, General Science, Primary Textbooks, Educational Materials
1978: 10 titles *Founded:* 1963

Addison-Wesley Publishing Co Inc*, PO Box 1802, Manila Cable Add: Adiwes Manila
General Manager: Ricardo M Hizon
Miscellaneous: Firm is a branch of Addison-Wesley Publishing Co Inc, USA. See Addison-Wesley Publishers Ltd, UK for associated companies and ISBNs

Alemar-Phoenix Publishing House Inc*, 927 Quezon Ave, Quezon City 3008 Tel: 991682/993897/997647
President: Jesus Ernesto R Sibal; *Advertising, Marketing Dir:* Pilar R Sibal; *Editor-in-Chief:* Dr Máximo D Ramos; *Associate Editor:* Avelina J Gil
Orders to: Alemar's, 769 Rizal Ave, Manila
Subjects: Educational and Non-Fiction Books
Bookshops: Alemar's, 769 Rizal Ave, Metro Manila; 526-8 United Nations Ave, Ermita, Metro Manila; 927 Quezon Ave, Quezon City; Makati Arcade, Makati; Commercial Center, Makati, Metro Manila; Corner General Roxas Ave, Times Sq St, Araneta Center, Cubao, Quezon City; Harrison Plaza Commercial Center, Malete, Metro Manila; Corner CM Recto and Nicanor Reyes Sts, Metro Manila

Alip & Sons Publishing Inc*, 1306 Dos Castillas St, Manila
Man Dir: Dr E M Alip; *Sales Dir:* Ella B Ortega; *Publicity Dir:* Miss Bellen A Alip; *Advertising Dir:* Rita A Aramil
Subjects: Textbooks, Reference
Founded: 1946

Associated Publishers Inc*, 63 Quezon Blvd Extension, Quezon City, PO Box 449, Manila
President: J V Roxas
Subjects: Medicine, Education, Law
Founded: 1952

Bookman Publishing House, PO Box 709, Manila (Located at: 373 Quezon Ave, Quezon City) Tel: 614631/621706/62187 Cable Add: Bookman
President: Ceferino M Picache; *Sales Dir:* Soriano Seda; *Editorial Dir:* Mrs Patrocinio S Picache
Subsidiary Companies: Bookman Printing House, Mission Publishing Co (both at 373 Quezon Ave, Quezon City)
Subjects: Textbooks & Reference for Elementary, Secondary & Collegiate Schools, Educational Materials
1978: 183 titles *Founded:* 1945

Bustamente Press Inc*, 155 Panay Ave, Quezon City
President: Pablo N Bustamente Jr
Subjects: Textbooks on English, Sciences, Mathematics
Founded: 1949

Capitol Publishing House Inc*, 54 Don Alejandro A Roces Ave, Quezon City

Communication Foundation for Asia*, PO Box SM-434, Manila 2806 Tel: 602689/607659 Cable Add: Socomter Manila Telex: 7527854 SCC PH
Man Dir: G V Ong Jr; *Editorial:* Fr P Diaz, J Ballesteros; *Publicity:* Rosario D Nolasco
Subjects: Pastoral and Human Interests/Educational Materials
Book Clubs: Foundation Book Club
Founded: 1968

Erehwon Publishing House*, 569 Padre Faura, Ermita, Manila
Subjects: General Fiction, Belles Lettres, How-to
Bookshop: 569 Padre Faura, Ermita, Manila

Fotomatic Philippines Inc, PO Box 295, Cebu City (Located at: F Ramos St, Cebu City) Tel: 92287/93702/71236
President, General Manager & Sales: Leonardo V Laconico; *Editorial:* Corsina L Sugarol; *Production:* Rosalinda A Laconico; *Rights & Permissions:* Andy Flores
Subjects: Primary, Secondary & University Textbooks
1978: 8 titles *1979:* 8 titles *Founded:* 1966

R M Garcia Publishing House, 903 Quezon Ave, Quezon City Tel: 999847/993286 Cable Add: Romgar
Orders to: PO Box 1860, Manila
Man Dir: Rolando M Garcia; *Editorial:* Ms J Cruz; *Sales:* R M Garcia Jr; *Publicity:* R G Garcia; *Permissions:* Ms B Gutierrez
Parent Company: R P Garcia Publishing & Printing Co
Subjects: College Textbooks for Philippine Schools; Elementary and Secondary Textbooks
Founded: 1951

Industry & Trade Publishers*, 5 Martelino St, Quezon City
Subjects: Business, Industry

Jonef Publications*, 1137 Looban, Paco, Manila Tel: 598910/502702/597647
Man Dir: J N Francisco
Subjects: Reference, Primary & Intermediate Textbooks
Founded: 1950

Lawyers' Co-operative Publishing Co (Philippines) Inc, Quezon Blvd Extension 63, PO Box 449, Quezon City, Manila
President: Magdangal B Elma
Subjects: Law, Medicine, Dental, Nursing, Technical
Founded: 1913
Miscellaneous: Firm is an affiliate of Lawyers' Co-operative Publishing Co, New York, NY 14603

M C S Enterprises Inc*, 1835-B Recto Ave, PO Box 3667, Manila
President: Mar C Sanchez Sr; *Man Dir:* Constancia P Puno
Subjects: Art, Anthropology, History, Political Science
Bookshop: 1835-B Recto Ave, Manila

Macaraig Publishing Co*, 1144 Vermont St, Manila
President: Serafin E Macaraig
Subjects: Social Science, Textbooks
Founded: 1926

Manor Press*, 715 Evangelista Sq, Quiapo, Manila

Modern Book Company Inc*, 926 Rizal Ave, PO Box 632, Manila Tel: 274318 Cable Add: Moboco
Man Dir: Exequiel Villacorta
Subjects: History, Social Science, Secondary & Primary Textbooks
1978: 1 title *Founded:* 1945
Bookshop: 926 Rizal Ave, Manila

Mutual Books Inc, 425 Shaw Blvd, Mandaluyong, Metro Manila Tel: 797538/796050 Cable Add: Mubinc
Shipping Add: PO Box 245, Greenhills, San Juan, Metro Manila
President: Alfredo S Nicdao Jr; *Vice-President:* F F Gonzalez IV
Associate Company: Alfredo S Nicdao Jr Inc
Subjects: Business, Economics, Management, Accounting, Mathematics, Secretarial
1978: 36 titles *Founded:* 1959

National Book Store*, 701 Rizal Ave, Manila Tel: 494306/07/08/09 Cable Add: Nabost Manila Telex: 7890 NBS-PH
Man Dir: Benjamin C Ramos; *Sales Dir:* Mitto Licauco; *Publicity & Advertising:* Mrs Socorro C Ramos; *Rights & Permissions:* Alfredo C Ramos
Subjects: General Fiction & Non-fiction, How-to, Music, Art, Juveniles, Low-priced Paperbacks, University, Secondary & Primary Textbooks
Founded: 1945
Bookshops: 701 Rizal Ave, Manila; C M Recto Ave, near Morayta, Manila; Araneta Coliseum Bldg, Cubao, Quezon City; The Quad, Makati; Harrizon Plaza, Mabini
Miscellaneous: Firm reprints over 300 titles annually for foreign publishers
New City, 363 Ycaza St, San Miguel, Manila, subsidiary of Città Nuova Editrice, Rome (qv)

Philippine Arts and Architecture*, 1346 UN Ave, Ermita, Manila
Subjects: Art, Architecture

Philippine Book Co*, 851 Orouieta St, Sta Cruz, Manila Tel: 274337
Subjects: General Fiction, Belles Lettres, School texts
Bookshop: Address as above

Philippine Education Co Inc, PO Box 706, Makati Commercial Center, Manila (Located at: Banawe St, corner Quezon Ave, Quezon City) Tel: 604666, 603041/42/43 Cable Add: Pecoi Manila Telex: 7222321
General Manager: Antero L Soriano
Subjects: General Fiction, Belles Lettres, Art, Social Science, Textbooks, Educational Materials
Bookshops: Araneta Center, Cubao, Quezon City; Makati Commercial Center, West Drive Arcade, Makati; Broadway Centrum, Doña Juana Rodriguez and Aurora Blvd, Quezon City; Banawe St, corner Quezon Ave, Quezon City

Philippine International Publishing Co*, 1789 A Mabini St, Ermita, Manila

Regal Publishing Co, 1729 J P Laurel St, San Miguel, Manila 2804 Tel: 479981 Cable Add: Repress Manila
Man Dir, Editorial, Publicity: Corinna B Mojica; *Sales:* Ms C B Benipayo; Production: L B Benipayo; *Permissions:* A B Benipayo
Associate Companies: Benipayo Press Inc, 1131 Quezon Ave, Heroes Hills, Quezon City 3008
Subjects: Philippine Writings, Philippine and English Translations of German Books
1978: 2 titles *Founded:* 1958

Sinag-Tala Publishers Inc, Greenhills, PO Box 536, Manila 3113 (Located at: 2506 Taft Ave, Manila 2801) Tel: 582966/581524/505215 Cable Add: Sinapub Manila
Man Dir, Rights & Permissions: E Q Laureola; *Editorial:* M R B Bulao; *Sales:* L A Uson; *Production:* B S Perez
Subjects: Business, Economics, Educational Textbooks, Home and Family, Religion
1978: 15 titles *1979:* 16 titles *Founded:* 1969

Solidaridad Publishing House*, 531 Padre Faura, Ermita, Manila Tel: 586581/591241 Cable Add: Soldad
Man Dir: F Sionil Jose
Subjects: Biography, Fiction, History, Reference
Founded: 1965
Bookshop: Solidaridad Bookshop, 531 Padre Faura, Ermita, Manila
Miscellaneous: Publish monthly journal, Solidarity

Tamaraw Publishing Co*, Cebu Ave, Quezon City

University of the Philippines Press*, Gonzalez Hall, Diliman, Quezon City 3004
Acting Dir, Rights & Permissions: Luis D Beltran; *Editorial:* Renato Correa; *Sales, Publicity:* Pilar E Tongson; *Production:* Francisco Felix
Subjects: General Fiction, Belles Lettres, Art, Music, Religion, Philosophy, How-to, Medicine, Business, Law, Psychology, Political & Social Science, Science & Technology, Educational Materials

University Publishing Co*, Central Office, 1128 Washington, Sampaloc, Manila
Dirs: Dr José M Aruego and Constancia E Aruego
Subjects: Business, Law, Educational Materials
Founded: 1936

Vera-Reyes Inc, 40 Valencia St, Quezon City 3008 Tel: 783976 Cable Add: Verareyes Manila Telex: Verareyes c/o 63199 Etpimo pn
Man Dir: L O Reyes
Subjects: Arts & Culture
1979: 12 titles *Founded:* 1964

Vision Publishing Corporation*, Room 305, B Jalandoni Bldg, Mabini, Cor. Romero Salas Sts, Ermita, Manila Tel: 571234/571225
Man Dir: Anacleto del Rosario; *Advertising Dir:* Betty B Tipon
Branch Off: L & S Bldg, 1414 Roxas Blvd, Manila
Founded: 1962

Book Club

Foundation Book Club, PO Box 5M-434, Manila 2806
Owned by: Communication Foundation for Asia (Manila)

Major Booksellers

Alemar's, PO Box 2119, Manila (Located at: 769 Rizal Ave, Manila) Tel: 475502 Telex: 27634 ALE PH
Branches: see Alemar-Phoenix Publishing House (under Publishers)

Bookmark Inc*, 357 T Pinpin, Escolta, Manila Tel: 497939; Ayala Arcade, Makati Commercial Center, Makati, Rizal

Eastern Book Service Corp, UPPO Box 10, Diliman, Quezon City 3004 (Located at: 3 Malamig St, UP Village, Quezon City 3004) Tel: 994388 Cable Add: Eastbook Manila
Manager: Fiorello Rifareal
Publishers' Agents and Stockists

Goodwill Trading Co Inc, (Goodwill Book Store), 711-715 Rizal Ave, Manila Tel: 402427/402627/403368/403612 Cable Add: Gotrade Manila Telex: 27302 Gtc Ph
President and General Manager: Manuel Cancio

G Miranda & Sons, 1887 C M Recto Ave, Manila Tel: 274867/274862

Modern Book Co Inc*, 926 Rizal Ave, PO Box 632, Manila 2800

National Book Store, 701 Rizal Ave, Manila Tel: 494306/07/08/09
Branches: see entry under Publishers

Philippine Book Co*, 851 Oroquieta St, Sta Cruz, Manila Tel: 274337

Philippine Education Co Inc, PO Box 620, Manila (Located at: 245 Banawe St, cnr Quezon Blvd, Quezon City) Tel: 604666, 603041/42/43 Cable Add: Pecoi Manila Telex: 7222321
General Manager: Antero L Soriano

Popular Book Store, 1572 Doroteo Jose, PO Box 2855, Manila Tel: 274762
General Manager: Joaquin Po
Owned by: Popular Trading Corporation

Major Libraries

Ateneo de Manila University Libraries, PO Box 154, Loyola Heights, Quezon City, Manila

Far Eastern University Library, PO Box 609, Manila 2806

Manila City Library, Kamaynilaan Bldg, Arroceros St, Manila 10401

The **National Library** of the Philippines*, T M Kalaw St, PO Box 2926 Ermita, Manila Tel: Filipiniana 485519; Reference 485588; Public Documents 491114

Silliman University Library*, Dumaguete City 6501
Librarian: Professor Gorgonio D Siega

Publications: Selected Philippine Periodical Index; Student's Library Manual (revised annually); *Occasional Library Bulletin*

Ramona S **Tirona** Memorial Library*, The Philippine Women's University, Taft Ave, Manila 2801 Tel: 503277
Librarian: Esperanza A Sta Cruz
Publications: Philippine Educational Forum, Administrative Bulletin, The Philwomenian, Research Abstracts

University of Manila Central Library*, 546 Dr M V de los Santos, Sampaloc, Manila

University of San Carlos Library*, P del Rosario St, Cebu City 6401
Dir: Mrs Marilou P Tadlip

University of Santo Tomas Library*, España, Manila 2806 Tel: 210081 local 234

University of the East Library*, Claro M Recto Ave, Manila ZC 2806

University of the Philippines Library*, Gonzalez Hall, Diliman, Quezon City 3004 Tel: 976061/8, local 284

Library Associations

Association of Special Libraries of the Philippines (ASLP)*, PO Box 4118, Manila
President: Potenciana D David
Publications: ASLP Bulletin (quarterly), *Directory of Special Library Resources in the Philippines*

Bibliographical Society of the Philippines*, c/o National Archives, National Library Bldg, T M Kalaw, Ermita, Manila
Secretary-Treasurer: Leticia R Maloles
Publications: Newsletter

Division of Documentation, **National Institute** of Science and Technology, see Scientific Library and Documentation Division

Philippine Library Association*, c/o National Library, T M Kalaw St, Manila 2801 Tel: 590177
Secretary: Ms H Ll Carpio
Publication: PLAI Bulletin (irregular); *PLAI Newsletter* (bi-monthly)

Scientific Library and Documentation Division, National Science Development Board, Bicutan, Taguig, PO Box 3596, Manila
Chief: Dr Irene D Amores

University of the Philippines*, Institute of Library Science, Diliman, Quezon City 3004 Tel: 976061 ext 249
Dir: Ursula Picache (Dean)
Publications: Journal of Philippine Librarianship, Newsletter

Library Reference Books and Journals

Books

Bibliography of Philippine Bibliographies, Ateneo de Manila University Press, PO Box 154, Manila

Directory of Special Library Resources in the Philippines Association of Special Libraries of the Philippines, PO Box 4118, Manila

Philippine Bibliography, University of the Philippines Library, Gonzalez Hall, Diliman, Quezon City 3004

290 PHILIPPINES — POLAND

Journals

Bulletin, Association of Special Libraries of the Philippines (ASLP), PO Box 4118, Manila

Bulletin, Philippine Library Association, c/o National Library, T M Kalaw, Ermita, Manila

Journal of Philippine Librarianship (text in English), University of the Philippines, Institute of Library Science, Diliman, Quezon City

Newsletter, Bibliographical Society of the Philippines, c/o National Archives, National Library Bldg, T M Kalaw, Ermita, Manila

Newsletter, University of the Philippines, Institute of Library Science, Diliman, Quezon City

Literary Associations and Societies

Kawika*, 1655 Soler, Santa Cruz
Society of Tagalog Writers
Secretary: Gemiliane Pinade
Publication: Liwayway (weekly)

International **P E N** Centre*, Solidaridad Publishing Ho, 531 Padre Favra, Ermita, Manila
Secretary: F Sionil José

Literary Periodicals

Balthazar, Balthazar Publishing House, 1782 M Adriatico, Malate, Manila

Diliman Review, University of the Philippines, College of Arts and Sciences, Diliman, Quezon City D-505

Far Eastern University Journal, Far Eastern University, PO Box 609, Manila 2806

Manila Review (text in English); Philippines journal of literature and the arts, Bureau of National and Foreign Information, Department of Public Information, PO Box 3396, Manila

Philippine Studies, Ateneo de Manila University Press, PO Box 154, Manila

Literary Prizes

Cultural Centre of the Philippines Literary Awards
For the best volume of verse and best play written in English and in Pilipino languages, including fiction (novel), epic poetry, criticism and biography once every five years marking the special inaugurations of the Centre, with correspondingly bigger prizes. Open to Filipino citizens, resident or non-resident. Prizes 5,000 Philippine pesos for best verse volume, 7,000 Philippine pesos for best play. Prizes also for 2nd and 3rd places. Awarded annually and published in the series *Gantimpala*. Enquiries to Cultural Centre of the Philippines, Roxas Blvd, Manila

Carlos **Palanca** Memorial Awards for Literature*
For short stories, poems and plays written in English and in Pilipino languages. 10,000 Philippine pesos for the best work in three-act plays both in English and in Pilipino; 5,000 pesos for the best work in short stories, poems and one-act plays also in English and in Pilipino. Awarded annually. Enquiries to Carlos Palanca Senior Memorial Foundation, 453 C Palanca St, Quiapo, Manila

Poland

General Information

Language: Polish (German and Russian used, English especially among young people)
Religion: Roman Catholic
Population: 35 million
Literacy Rate (1970): 97.8% (98.8% Urban, 96.5% Rural)
Bank Hours: 0900-1300 Monday-Friday; 0800-1300 Saturday
Shop Hours: 1100-1900 Monday-Saturday
Currency: 100 groszy = 1 zloty
Export/Import Information: Book importation done by the Foreign Trade Enterprise Ars Polona, ul Krakowskie Przedmieście 7, PO Box 1001, 00-068 Warsaw, which pays any duties applicable. Advertising may be placed through AGPOL Foreign Trade Advertising agency, Kierbedzia 4, PO Box 7, 00-957 Warsaw, or through its London agent, Albert Milhado & Co Ltd. No import licences as such required. All overseas trade is conducted in foreign currency. Small quantities of advertising materials duty free
Copyright: Berne, UCC (see International section)

Book Trade Organizations

A G P O L (Przedsiebiorstwo Reklamy i Wydawnictw Handlu Zagranicznego), ul Kierbedzia 4, PO Box 7, 00-957 Warsaw Tel: 416061 Telex: 813364 agpol pl Cable Add: Agpol Warszawa
Foreign Trade Publicity and Publishing Enterprise
Dir: Tadeusz Polanowski
Offers Publicity services abroad for Polish foreign trade and in Poland for foreign companies
Founded: 1956

Foreign Trade Enterprise **Ars Polona**, see RSW (below) and Major Booksellers

Bioru Miedzynarodowego Numeru Ksiazki, ul Jasna 26, 00-950 Warsaw

Editorial Office for **Polish Bibliography** (formerly Karol Estreicher Republication Centre of Polish 19th Century Bibliography)*, ul Jagiellońska 15, Cracow
Dir: Professor Dr Karol Estreicher

Polskie Towarzystwo Wydawców Ksiazek*, ul Mazowiecka 2-4, 00-048 Warsaw Tel: 260735
Polish Publishers' Association
Publication: Przeglad Ksiegarski i Wydawniczy (jointly with Zjednoczenie Ksiegarstwa (United Booksellers, qv under Major Booksellers)

R S W (Robotnicza Spóldzielnia Wydawnicza)*, 'Prasa-Ksiazka-Ruch', ul Bagatela 14, 00-950 Warsaw Tel: 28851
Workers' Publishing Cooperative
Includes 'Ksiazka i Wiedza' (qv), Interpress (qv), Krajowa Agencja Wydawnicza (qv), Agencja Wydawnicza (qv) and Wydawnictwo Artystyczno-Graficzne; also the Foreign Trade Enterprise Ars Polona (qv under Booksellers)

Standard Book Numbering Agency, see Bioru Miedzynarodowego Numeru Ksiazki

Stowarzyszenie Autorow Zaiks, 2 rue Hipoteczna, 00-902 Warsaw Tel: 277577 Telex: 812470 zaikz pl
Polish Society of Authors
President: Karol Malcużyński; *General Manager:* Witold Kolodziejski; *Foreign Dept Manager:* Wlodzimierz Lalak

Stowarzyszenie Ksiegarzy Polskich*, ul Mokotowska 4-6, 00-641 Warsaw Tel: 252874
Association of Polish Booksellers
President: Tadeusz Hussak
Social organization for State book trade employees
Publication: Ksiegarz

Zjednoczenie Przedsiebiorstw Wydawniczych Naczelny Zarzad Wydawnictw (United Publishers — Central Publishing Board)*, ul Krakowskie Przedmieście 15-17, 00-071 Warsaw Tel: 268830

Zwiazek Literatów Poliskich (Union of Polish Writers), Krakowskie Przedmieście 87-89, Warsaw

Book Trade Reference Books and Journals

Books

Bibliografia Bibliografii i Nauki o Ksiazce. Bibliografia Poloniae Bibliographica (Bibliography of Bibliographies and Library Science), National Library, ul Hankiewicza 1, 00-973 Warsaw

Polish Publishers and Booksellers (text in English), Państwowy Instytut Wydawniczy, ul Foksal 17, 00-372 Warsaw

Journals

Biuletyn (Bulletin), Bibliographical Institute, National Library, ul Hankiewicza 1, 00-973 Warsaw

Books in Polish or Relating to Poland, Polish Library, 9 Princes Gardens, London SW7, UK

Ksiegarz (The Bookseller), Association of Polish Booksellers, ul Mokotowska 4-6, 00-641 Warsaw

New Books (editions in English and Polish), Ossolineum, Rynek 9, PO Box 70, 50-106 Wroclaw

New Polish Publications; a monthly review of Polish books (editions in English, German and Russian), Ars Polona-Ruch, ul Krakowskie Przedmieście 7, 00-068 Warsaw

Przeglad Ksiegarski i Wydawniczy (Publishing and Bookselling Review), United Booksellers, ul Jasna 26, 00-950 Warsaw (published jointly with the Polish Publishers' Association)

Przewodnik Bibliograficzny. Urzedowy wykaz druków wydanych w Polskiej Rzeczypospolitej Ludowej (Bibliographical Guide. Official List of Publications Issued in Poland), National Library, ul Hankiewicza 1, 00-973 Warsaw

Rocznik Literacki (The Literary Yearbook), Państwowy Instytut Wydawniczy, ul Foksal 17, 00-372 Warsaw

Soon to Appear (French, German and Russian editions), Foreign Trade Publicity and Publishing Enterprise, ul Kierbedzia 4, PO Box 7, 00-957 Warsaw

Zapowiedzi Wydawnicze (Publishing Announcements), United Booksellers, ul Jasna 26, 00-950 Warsaw

Publishers

Agencja Autorska, ul Hipoteczna 2, 00-092 Warsaw Tel: 278396
Authors' Agency
Subjects: Contemporary Polish writers; Periodicals
Also Literary Agency (qv)

Arkady Publishing House, ul Sienkiewicza 14, PO Box 169, 00-950 Warsaw Tel: 269316
Man Dir: Eugeniusz Piliszek; *Rights & Permissions:* Andrzej Karpowicz
Subjects: Art, Architecture, Building
1978: 100 titles *Founded:* 1957
ISBN Publisher's Prefix: 83-213

Ars Christiana*, ul Ogrodowa 37, PO Box 471, 00-873 Warsaw Tel: 204738
Subjects: Religion Problems, Periodicals
Founded: 1951

Wydawnictwa **Artystyczne i Filmowe**, ul Pulawska 61, 02-595 Warsaw Tel: 455301/455584
Man Dir: Jerzy Wittlin; *Editorial:* Edward Rylukowski; *Editorial, Publicity:* Barbara Olszańska; *Production:* Jerzy Mika
Orders to: Ars Polona (see Major Booksellers)
Subjects: Art, Film, Theatre, Reprints of old books and engravings
1978: 52 titles *Founded:* 1959

Instytut Wydawniczy **Centralnej Rady Związków Zawodowych** (Publishing House of the Central Council of Trade Unions)*, ul W Spasowskiego 1-3, 00-389 Warsaw Tel: 279011
Dir: Tadeusz Lipski
Subjects: Health and Safety at Work, Workers' Education, Sociology
Bookshop: Księgarnia Skladowa, Mariensztat 8, 00-302 Warsaw
Founded: 1950

Spóldzielnia Wydawnicza **'Czytelnik'***, ul Wiejska 12a, Warsaw Tel: 281441 Cable Add: Czytelnik Warsaw
Man Dir: Stanislaw Bebenek; *Publicity & Advertising:* Zenon Skuza
Subjects: General Fiction, Belles Lettres, Poetry, Juveniles, Low-priced Paperbacks, Social Science, Memoirs, Journalism
Founded: 1944

Drukarnia Narodowa, an imprint of Polskie Wydawnictwo Muzyczne (qv)

Państwowe Wydawnictwo **Ekonomiczne** (State Economic Publishers), ul Niecala 4a, 00-098 Warsaw Tel: 278001 Cable Add: Pewue
Man Dir: Zbigniew Gajczyk
Imprint: PWE
Subjects: Scholarly, Reference, Economics, Social Science, Business
Bookshop: address as above
1978: 122 titles *1979:* 104 titles *Founded:* 1949

Wydawnictwo **'Epoka'***, ul W Hibnera 11, PO Box 393, 00-018 Warsaw Tel: 278081 Cable Add: Wydawnictwo Epoka Warszawa
Subjects: Publications of the Central Committee of the Democratic Party, Periodicals
Founded: 1957

Wydawnictwa **Geologiczne**, ul Rakowiecka 4, PO Box 72, 00-975 Warsaw Tel: 495081
Dir: Franciszek Szejgis
Subjects: Academic and professional books on Geology, Surveying
1979: 72 titles *1980:* 77 titles *Founded:* 1953
ISBN Publisher's Prefix: 83-220

Zarzad Wydawnictw **Głównego Urzedu Statystycznego** (Publishers of the Central Statistical Office)*, ul Wawelska 1-3, 02-034 Warsaw Tel: 253454
Subject: Statistics
Founded: 1966

Wydawnictwo Harcerskie **'Horyzonty'***, incorporated in new organization Mlodziezowa Agencja Wydawnicza (qv)

Państwowy **Instytut** Wydawniczy, ul Foksal 17, PO Box 377, 00-950 Warsaw Tel: 260201 Cable Add: Piw
Polish State Publishing House
Man Dir: Andrzej Wasilewski; *Editor-in-Chief:* Jerzy Skórnicki
Subjects: General Fiction, Belles Lettres, Poetry, Biography, History, History of Culture, Essays, Memoirs
1978: 263 *1979:* 235 titles *Founded:* 1946
ISBN Publisher's Prefix: 83-06

Wydawnictwo **'Interpress'**, ul Bagatela 12, PO Box 388, 00-585 Warsaw Tel: 219325 Cable Add: Interpress Warszawa Telex: 814481/814775 pai pl
Editor-in-Chief: Lubomir Mackiewicz; *Editorial:* Janusz Podoski; *Production, Sales:* Witold Bójski; *Publicity, Rights & Permissions:* Jerzy Guz
Branch Offs: Dechant Heimbachstr 19, Bad Godesberg, D-5300 Bonn 2, Federal Republic of Germany (Tel: 353808); Hagalundsgatan 101, 151, S-171 50 Solna, Stockholm, Sweden (Tel: 821065); Atzgerdorferstr 48, A-1238 Vienna XXIII, Austria (Tel: 8833722)
Subjects: Contemporary and Historical Poland, Popular Science, Tourist Guides
1978: 87 titles *1979:* 116 titles *Founded:* 1967
Miscellaneous: Member of RSW (see under Book Trade Organizations)
ISBN Publisher's Prefix: 83-223

Państwowe Wydawnictwo **'Iskry'**, ul Smolna 11-13, PO Box 897, 00-375 Warsaw Tel: 276001/3 (Central) 279415 (Director) Cable Add: Iskry
Man Dir: Lukasz Szymański
Subjects: General Fiction, Belles Lettres, Poetry, Biography, Travel-Adventure books, How-to, Religion, Juveniles, Low- & High-priced Paperbacks, Social Science
1978: 95 titles *1979:* 97 titles *Founded:* 1952
ISBN Publisher's Prefix: 83-207

Państwowe Przedsiebiorstwo Wydawnictw **Kartograficznych***, ul Solec 18, 00-410 Warsaw Tel: 283251 Cable Add: Pepewuka, Warszawa
Dir: Jan Rzedowski (Tel: 280236)
Subjects: Geographical, Historical, Maps and Atlases; Geodetic, Cartographic books
1979: 122 titles *Founded:* 1951

Wydawnictwo **Katalogów i Cenników** (Catalogue and Price List Publishers)*, ul Wiejska 12a, 00-490 Warsaw Tel: 291396 Cable Add: Wukace Warszawa
Subject: Catalogues, Price Lists, Handbooks, Guidebooks
Founded: 1962

Wydawnictwa **Komunikacji i Laczności**, ul Kazimierzowska 52, PO Box 71, 02-546 Warsaw Tel: 492751
Transport and Communications Publishers
Dir: Czeslaw Kulesza
Subjects: Mechanical Engineering, Aeronautics, Electronics, Radio, Communications, Transport
1978: 212 titles *1979:* 190 titles *Founded:* 1949

Krajowa Agencja Wydawnicza (KAW), ul Wilcza 46, PO Box 179, 00-679 Warsaw Tel: 286481/286485 (5 lines) Telex: 813487 KAW PL
Man Dir, Editor-in-Chief: Dobroslaw Kobielski
Subjects: Culture, Science, Educational material, Juveniles, Politics, Guides, Belles Lettres, Sport, Science and Detective Fiction
Founded: 1974
Miscellaneous: Member of RSW 'Prasa-Ksiazka-Ruch' (qv under Book Trade Organizations)

Wydawnictwo **'Ksiazka i Wiedza'***, ul Smolna 13, PO Box 476, 00-375 Warsaw Tel: 275401 Cable Add: KiW Warszawa
Subjects: History, Politics, Sociology, Philosophy
Founded: 1948
Miscellaneous: Member of RSW (see under Book Trade Organizations)

Państwowy Zaklad Wydawnictw **Lekarskich**, Dluga 38-40, PO Box 379, 00-238 Warsaw Tel: 314281 Cable Add: Wydlek Warszawa
Dir: Benedykt Nowakowski; *Chief Editor:* Andrzej Wiczynski; *Editorial Secretary:* Ewa Cierniak
Polish State Medical Publishers
Subjects: Medicine, Biology, Biochemistry, Pharmacy, Psychology, Textbooks, Monographs, Dictionaries, Periodicals, Audio-Visual Materials
1979: approx 200 titles *Founded:* 1945

Wydawnictwo **Literackie**, ul Dluga 1, 31-147 Cracow Tel: 25423/24644/24761
Dir: Andrzej Kurz; *Editorial:* Katarzyna Krzemuska, Jan Pieszczachowicz, Ireneusz Maślarz
Subjects: Classical and Contemporary Belles Lettres, Memoirs, History, Literature, Theatre, Film, Art, Translations
1979: 189 titles *1980:* 236 titles *Founded:* 1953

Wydawnictwo **Lodzkie** (Lodz Publishing House)*, ul Piotrkowska 171-173, PO Box 372, 90-447 Lodz Tel: 60331
Editorial Dir: Jacek Zaorski; *Sales & Publicity:* Janina Sobczak; *Production:* Pawel Marchewka; *Rights & Permissions:* Jerzy Badowski
Subjects: Socio-Political Literature, Belles Lettres, Memoirs, Translations of modern Yugoslav and Soviet Union Literature
Founded: 1957

Wydawnictwo **Lubelskie** (Lublin Publishers), ul Okopowa 7, 20-022 Lublin Tel: 27344
Dir and Editor-in-Chief: Ireneusz Caban
Subjects: Social & Political Sciences, Humanities, Belles-Lettres, Juveniles, Poetry, Translations from Ukrainian
1979: 65 titles *Founded:* 1957

Ludowa Spóldzielnia Wydawnicza*, ul Grzybowska 4, 00-131 Warsaw Tel: 200251 Cable Add: LSW, Warszawa
People's Publishing Cooperative
Chairman, Editor-in-Chief: Leon Janczak
Subjects: Polish Literature, History, The Peasant Movement, Agricultural Problems
1978: 150 titles *Founded:* 1946

Wydawnictwo **Ministerstwa Obrony Narodowej**, ul Grzybowska 77, 00-844 Warsaw Tel: 201261
Publishing House of the Ministry of National Defence
Dir: Lech Szymański
Subject: Military (History, Memoirs, Technical Literature)
Founded: 1947

Mlodziezowa Agencja Wydawnicza, ul Koszykowa 6A, PO Box 188, 01-564 Warsaw
Youth Publishing Agency and Publishing Co-operative
Agency Editor-in-Chief: Zygmunt Konopka (Tel: 280973); *Books Editor-in-Chief:* Irena Kuźniewska (Tel: 211757); *Publicity Manager:* Beata Wójcikiewicz (Tel: 289030); *Production Dir:* Waldemar Piasecki (Tel: 219848); *Rights & Permissions:* Ludwik

Zukowski (Tel: 289030)
Subjects: Literature for young people; Instructions and Programmes of Activity of Polish Socialist Youth Organizations; Belles Lettres, Sociology, Politics, Popular Science; Handbooks
1978: 137 titles *Founded:* 1974
Miscellaneous: This organization replaces the former Wydawnictwo Harcerskie 'Horyzonty'. It is also a Workers' Publishing Co-operative, allied to R S W (see under Book Trade Organizations). Mlodziezowa acts as both Agency and Publisher for Polish youth

Wydawnictwo **Morskie***, ul Szeroka 38-40, 80-835 Gdansk Tel: 311031
Man Dir: Edward Mazurkiewicz; *Editorial:* Stanislaw Ludwig; *Sales, Publicity:* Jerzy Szulczewski; *Production:* Wladyslaw Kawecki; *Rights & Permissions:* Magdalena Tomsio
Subjects: Maritime, Technical, Economics, Popular Science, Belles Lettres, History
Book Club: Publisher's Club, address as above
Bookshop: Publisher's Bookshop, address as above
1978: 86 titles *Founded:* 1951
ISBN Publisher's Prefix: 83-215

Polskie Wydawnictwo **Muzyczne**, Al Krasińskiego 11a, PO Box 115, 31-111 Cracow Tel: 27044 Cable Add: PWM
Polish Music Publishers
Man Dir: Mieczyslaw Tomaszewski; *Editorial:* Stanislaw Haraschin; *Sales:* Wladyslaw Duda; *Production:* Stanislaw Blawacki; *Publicity:* Halina Czubińska; *Rights & Permissions:* Jan Paździora
Orders to: Biuro Handlu Zagranicznego, ul Krak Przedmieście 7, Warszawa
Associate Company: Agencja Autorska, ul Hipoteczna 2, Warszawa (qv)
Subsidiary Company: Centralna Biblioteka Muzyczna-Nutowa, ul Senatorska 13/15, Warsaw
Imprint: Drukarnia Narodowa
Branch Off: 'Synkopa', ul Senatorska 13/13 Warsaw
Subject: Music
Book Clubs: Skladnica Ksiegarska, ul Smoleńsk 33, Cracow; Dom Ksiazki, ul Smoleńsk, Cracow
Bookshop: Skladnica Ksiegarska, ul Smoleńsk, Cracow
1978: 359 titles *1979:* 377 titles *Founded:* 1945

Instytut Wydawniczy '**Nasza Ksiegarnia**', ul W Spasowskiego 4, PO Box 380, 00-389 Warsaw Tel: 262431 Cable Add: Nasza Ksiegarnia
Man Dir: Czeslaw Wiśniewski
Subjects: Juveniles, General Science, Education, Translations into Polish, Periodicals
1978: 205 (including 56 translations) *1979:* 176 (including 46 translations) *Founded:* 1921

Państwowe Wydawnictwo **Naukowe**, ul Miodowa 10, PO Box 391, 00-251 Warsaw Tel: 262291 Cable Add: Pewuen Warszawa
Polish State Academic and Scientific Publishing House. Publishes books in foreign languages and co-operates with foreign publishers
Man Dir: Stanislaw Puchala; *Sales Dir:* Jerzy Kozlowski; *Rights & Permissions:* Zygmunt Gebethner; *Editorial:* Work is divided among large number of teams which themselves are sub-divisions of four major groups dealing with the Humanities, Science & Technology, Popular Science and Language & Reference
Branch Offs: ul Wieckowskiego 13, 90-721 Lódź; ul Smoleńsk 14, 31-112 Cracow; ul Ratajczaka 35, 61-816 Poznań; ul Wierzbowa 15, 50-056 Wroclaw
Orders to: Ars Polona, Importers & Exporters, Krakowskie Przedmieście 7, PO Box 1001, 00-950 Warsaw Cable Add: Arspolona Warsaw; or to Orpan Export, Palac Kultury, 00-901 Warsaw
Subjects: History, Philosophy, Sociology, Psychology, Pedagogics, Economy, Law, Linguistics, Literary Studies, Geography, the Arts, Biology, Mathematics, Physics, Chemistry, Engineering, Agricultural Sciences, Political Science, Information on Warsaw, University Textbooks, Popular Scientific Works, Encyclopaedias, Polish Dictionaries, Scientific Periodicals (in Polish and foreign languages)
1979-80: approx 1,100 titles *Founded:* 1951

Wydawnictwa **Naukowo-Techniczne***, ul Mazowiecka 2-4, PO Box 359, 00-950 Warsaw Tel: 267271 Cable Add: Ente Warszawa
Man Dir: Ryszard Pogonowski; *Foreign Dept, Rights & Permissions:* Zofia Kochanowicz
Subjects: Applied Mathematics & Physics, Computer Science, Electrical & Electronic Engineering, Chemistry, Automation, Machine Design and Technology, Foodstuffs Industry, Light Industry, Technical & Scientific Encyclopedias, Dictionaries & Vocabularies at all levels
1979: 124 titles *Founded:* 1949

Wydawnictwa **Normalizacyjne***, ul Nowogrodzka 22, PO Box 206, 00-375 Warsaw Tel: 287261 Cable Add: Wuen Warszawa
Standardization Publishers
Subject: Standardization
Founded: 1956

Zaklad Narodowy im **Ossolińskich**
Wydawnictwo Polskiej Akademii Nauk, Rynek 9, PO Box 911, 50-106 Wroclaw Tel: 38625 Cable Add: Ossolineum Wroclaw Telex: 0712771
Ossolineum-Publishing House of the Polish Academy of Sciences
Man Dir: Eugeniusz Adamczak
Orders to: Foreign Trade Enterprise, Ars Polona, Krakowskie Przedmieście 7, PO Box 1001, 00-950 Warsaw
Branch Offs: ul Dluga 26, 00-238 Warsaw; Manifestu Lipcowego 19a, 31-110 Cracow; ul Lagiewniki 56, 80-855 Gdansk
Subjects: Bibliographies, History, Art, Philosophy, Psychology, Physical Sciences, Life Sciences, Earth Sciences, Law, Politics, Literature, Pedagogy/Education, Sociology, Technology, Geography, Economics, Languages, Ethnology; University Textbooks, Educational Materials
1979: 520 titles *Founded:* 1817
ISBN Publisher's Prefix: 83-04

P W N (Panstwowe Wydawnictwo Naukowe), see Naukowe

'**Pallottinum**' Wydawnictwo Stowarzyszenia Apolstolstwa Katolickiego, PO Box 1095, 60-959 Poznan (Located at: Al S Przybyszewskiego 30, Poznan) Tel: 47212
Publishers of the Catholic Apostolate Association
Manager: Stefan Dusza
Subjects: Catholic Philosophy and Theology
Founded: 1948

Instytut Wydawniczy **Pax**, ul Chocimska 8-10, 00-791 Warsaw Tel: 499517
Dir: Józef Wójcik; *Chief Editor:* Antoni Kapliński
Subjects: Contemporary trends in Christian Theology, Philosophy and Literature
Founded: 1949

Wydawnictwo Stowarzyszenia Społeczno-Kulturalnego '**Pojezierze**'*, ul Zwyciestwa 32, 10-578 Olsztyn Tel: 22352/22285
Subjects: Belles Lettres, Popular Science, Art

Wydawnictwo **Poznańskie** (Poznań Publishers)*, ul A Fredry 8, PO Box 63, 60-967 Poznań Tel: 58534
Man Dir: Dr Jerzy Ziolek; *Publicity Dir:* Miss Mag Krystyna Woźniak
Subjects: History of Great Poland and Polish culture, Modern Polish and Foreign Fiction, Science Fiction
Founded: 1956
Miscellaneous: Specializes in translations from the literature of Scandinavian and German-speaking countries

Wydawnictwo **Prawnicze**, ul Wiśniowa 50, 02-520 Warsaw Tel: 496151-53
Man Dir: Dr Stanislaw Ziembinski (Tel: 494705)
Law Publishers
Subjects: All aspects of Law and Criminology
1978: 57 titles *1979:* 79 titles *Founded:* 1952
ISBN Publisher's Prefix: 83-219

Wydawnictwo **Radia i Telewizji***, ul Chelmska 9, 00-724 Warsaw Tel: 412264
Radio and Television Publishers
Subjects: Radio and Television
Founded: 1968

Państwowe Wydawnictwo **Rolnicze i Leśne***, Al Jerozolimskie 28, PO Box 374, 00-024 Warsaw Cable Add: Pewril Warszawa Tel: 266451
State Agricultural and Forestry Publishers
Man Dir: Mr Marian Bajorek
Subjects: Textbooks, Reference, Agriculture, Forestry, Food Science, Veterinary Science
Founded: 1947

Zaklad Wydawnictw CRS '**Samopomoc Chlopska**'*, ul Jasna 1, PO Box 38, 00-013 Warsaw Tel: 271529 Cable Add: Zetwuceres Warszawa Telex: 81622
Publishing Institute of the 'Samopomoc Chlopska' — Peasant Cooperative
Subjects: Books and Periodicals for the Peasant Cooperative
Founded: 1957

Wydawnictwo '**Slask**', ul Armii Czerwonej 51, PO Box 67, 40-161 Katowice Tel: 583220
'Silesia' Publishing House
Dir and Editor-in-Chief: Jeremi Gliszczynski
Subjects: Mining and Metallurgy, Polish Literature, Translations from Czech and Slovak, Social and Political Literature
1978: 70 titles *1979:* 72 titles *Founded:* 1954

Slaska kjiegarnia Techniczna*, ul Zwirki i Wigury 33, 40-063 Katowice
Subjects: Metallurgy, Technical
Book Club: Klub Czytelników Literatury Hutniczej

Wydawnictwo **Sport i Turystyka***, ul H Rutkowskiego 7-9, 00-021 Warsaw Tel: 262451 Cable Add: Sportur Warszawa
Sport and Tourism Publishers
Dir: Alfred Górny; *Editor-in-Chief:* Engeniusz Skrzypek
Subjects: Sport, Travel
Book Club: Klub Czytelników Literatury Gorniczej
Founded: 1953

Statistical Publications and Printing Board of the Central Statistical Office*, al Niepodleglosci 208, 00-925 Warsaw Tel: 259545/254886 Cable Add: GUS Telex: 814581
Man Dir: Jerzy Sufin-Suliga; *Editorial:* Jozef Gluzinski

Subject: State statistics
1978: 24 titles *Founded:* 1966

Ksiegarnia Św Wojciecha, pl Wolności 1, PO Box 288, 60-967 Poznań Tel: 59186/7
Cable Add: Albertinum Poznan
Man Dir: Ludwik Bielerzewski
St Adalbert's Bookshop
Branch Off: ul Królewska 15, Lublin; ul Freta 48, Warsaw
Subjects: Biblical Texts, Theology; Periodicals
Bookshops: Plac Wolności 1, Poznań; ul Królewska 15, Lublin; ul Freta 48, Warsaw
1978: 16 titles *Founded:* 1895

Wydawnictwa Szkolne i Pedagogiczne (The Publishing House for School and Pedagogical Books), pl H Dabrowskiego 8, 00-950 Warsaw, PO Box 480 Tel: 265451/55 Cable Add: Wuesipe Warszawa
Man Dir: Jerzy Loziński; *Rights & Permissions:* Andrzej Syta; *Advertising and Head of Foreign Department:* Marek Szopski
Orders to: Ars Polona-Ruch, ul Krakowskie Przedmieście 7, Warsaw (qv under Book Trade Organizations)
Branch Off: Delegatura WSiP, Basztowa 15, 31-143 Cracow
Subjects: Primary, Secondary and Vocational Textbooks, Education, Pedagogics, Psychology, Pedagogical Periodicals
1978: 255 titles *1979:* 280 titles *Founded:* 1945

Towarzystwo Przyjaciól Ksiazki (TPK)*, ul Hipoteczna 2 ZAIKS, 00-092 Warsaw Tel: 277304
Society of Friends of Books
Man Dir: Alexandre Bochenski
Br Off: Rynek Gl 35, 31-011 Kraków; Plac Wolnosci 12, 40-078 Katowice; uk św Jadwigi 3/4, 50-266 Wroclaw; ul Slowackiego 9, Rzeszów
Subject: Book Collecting
Founded: 1957

Wydawnictwa Kultura Zycia Codziennego 'Watra'*, PO Box 17, 02-001 Warsaw (Located at: Aleje Jerozdimskie 87) Tel: 212241-8
Subjects: Health, Domestic Science, Food, Family Life, Periodicals
Founded: 1954

Wydawnictwa Przemyslu Maszynowego 'Wema', ul Danitowiczowska 18, PO Box 90, 00-950 Warsaw Tel: 275456
Chief Executive: Czeslaw Borski; *Editorial Dir:* Maria Hoffmann
Subjects: Mechanical Engineering
1978: 1,295 titles *1979:* 1,600 titles
Founded: 1967

'Wiedza Powszechna' Państwowe Wydawnictwo, ul Jasna 26, PO Box 162, 00-054 Warsaw Tel: 277651
Orders to: Ars Polona (see Major Booksellers)
Man Dir & Editor-in-Chief: Tadeusz Kosmala
Subjects: Encyclopaedias, Dictionaries, General Reference, Language Handbooks, Popular Science
1978: 85 titles *Founded:* 1952

Wydawniczo Oświatowa Spóldzielnia Inwalidów 'Wspólna Sprawa' (Educational Publishing Cooperative of the Disabled)*, ul Zelazna 40, 00-838 Warsaw Tel: 209071
Subjects: Graphic art textbooks for primary and nursery schools; Periodicals for foreign language sessions; Games
Founded: 1956

Spoleczny Instytut Wydawniczy 'Znak' (Social Publishing Institute), ul Wiślna 12, 31-007 Cracow Tel: 24548
Man Dir: Jacek Wozniakowski
Subjects: Religious Subjects, Philosophy, History, Belles Lettres
Founded: 1959

Literary Agents

Agencja Autorska, ul Hipoteczna 2, 00-950 Warsaw Tel: 278396
Contact: Wladyslaw Jakubowski, Andrzej Mierzejewski
Also Publisher (qv)

Mlodziezowa Agencja Wydawnicza — Polish Youth Publishing Agency, see main entry under Publishers

Book Clubs

Club of Mining Books, Wydawnictwo 'Slask', ul Armii Czerwonej 51, PO Box 67, 40-161 Katowice

Club of Twentieth Century Poetry*, Horizons of Technology Club of Popular Science Books, ul Nowolipie 4, 00-950 Warsaw

Dom Ksiazki*, ul Smoleńsk, Cracow
Owned by: Polskie Wydawnictwo Muzyczne (Cracow)

Klub Czytelnikow Literatury Gorniczej, ul Armii Czerwonej 51, 40-161 Katowice
Owned by: Wydawnictwo Slask (qv)

Klub Czytelnikow Literatury Hutniczej*, ul Zwirki i Wigury 33, 40-063 Katowice
Owned by: Slaska Ksiegarnin Techniczna (qv)

New Countryside Book Club*, ul Nowolipie 4, 00-950 Warsaw

Publisher's Club, ul Szeroka 38/40, 80-835, Gdańsk
Owned by: Wydawnictwo Morskie (Gdansk)

Sktachnica Ksiegarska*, ul Smoleńsk 33, Cracow
Owned by: Polskie Wydawnictwo Muzyczne (Cracow)

Major Booksellers

Ars Polona*, ul Krakowskie Przedmieście 7, PO Box 1001, 00-068 Warsaw Tel: 261201
Cable Add: Ars Polona Warszawa Telex: 813498
Foreign Trade Enterprise
Miscellaneous: Member of RSW (see under Book Trade Organizations)

Dom Ksiazki, ul Jasna 26, 00-950 Warsaw Tel: 277651 Telex: 812448
Collective name for the State-owned Polish book-retailing enterprises. There are 18, each controlling 50-250 bookshops throughout Poland, subordinate to Zjednoczenie Ksiegarstwa (qv)

Orpan Export*, Palac Kultury, 00-901 Warsaw

Publisher's Bookshop, ul Szeroka 38/40, 80-835, Gdańsk

Powszechna Ksiegarnia Wysylkowa*, ul Nowolipie 4, 00-950 Warsaw Tel: 310021
Organization for mail order, subordinate to Zjednoczenie Ksiegarstwa (qv)

Państwowe, Przedsiebiorstwo 'Skladnica Ksiegarska', ul Mazowiecka 9, 00-950 Warsaw
Organization for wholesale book trade, subordinate to Zjednoczenie Ksiegarstwa (qv)

Zjednoczenie Ksiegarstwa, PO Box 48, 00-950 Warsaw (Located at: ul Jasna 26) Tel: (General) 277651; (Dir) 268393 Telex: 81-2448 deka pl
Dir: Kazimierz Majerowicz Tel: 268393 (Dir) or 277651
National organization for the sale of books; subordinate to the Minister of Culture and Art and controlling Skladnica Ksiegarska (wholesale), Dom Ksiazki (retail), and Powszechna Ksiegarnia Wysylkowa (mail order) (qqv under 'Major Booksellers')
Publication: Przeglad Ksiegarski i Wydawniczy (jointly with the Polish Publishers' Association)

Major Libraries

Naczelna Dyrekcja **Archiwów Państwowych** (Main Directorate of the Polish State Archives)*, Dluga St 6, Warsaw

Archiwum Akt Nowych (Centre for Recent Documents)*, Al Niepodleglości 162, 02-554 Warsaw

Archiwum Glówne Akt Dawnych (Central Archives for Historical Documents), Dluga 7, 00-263 Warsaw
Dir: Dr Mieczyslaw Motas

Biblioteka Jagiellońska*, Aleja Mickiewicza 22, 30-059 Cracow Tel: 33505/33500/36377; Secretary 30903; Director 31971 Telex 0325682 bj pl
Dir: Professor Dr Stanislaw Grzeszczuk
Publication: Biuletyn Biblioteki Jagiellońskiej (Biannual)

Biblioteka Narodowa, ul Hankiewicza 1, 00-973 Warsaw Tel: Main Bldg 224621; Special Collections: 313241 Telex: 813702 bn pl
This is the National Library, Warsaw. See also Instytut Bibliograficzny
Dir: Professor Witold Stankiewicz

Biblioteka Publiczna m st Warszawy*, ul Koszykowa 26, 00-503 Warsaw Tel: 283147
Public Library of Warsaw
Librarian: Stefan Durmaj
Publication: Prace Biblioteki Publicznej m st Warszawy

Biblioteka Śląska, ul Francuska 12, 40-015 Katowice Tel: (General) 516441-44 Telex: 0312534 bsk pl
Silesian Library
Dir: Doc dr Andrzej Szefer
Miscellaneous: A major Polish library. Specializes in scientific publications, but has many special collections covering Literature, History, Law and Religion and especially Silesian Interest

Centrum Informacji Naukowej, Technicznej i Ekonomicznej (National Centre for Scientific, Technical and Economic Information)*, al Neipodleglości 186, 00-931 Warsaw
Publication: Aktualne Problemy Informacji i Dokumentacji

Glówna Biblioteka Lekarska, Chocimska 22, 00-791 Warsaw
Central Medical Library

Biblioteka Glówna Politchniki Warszawskiej, plac Jedności Robotniczej 1, 00-662 Warsaw Telex: 816467 bgpw pl
Library of the Technical University of Warsaw

Biblioteka Glówna Uniwersytetu im Adama Mickiewicza (Library of Adam Mickiewicz University)*, ul Ratajczaka 38-40, Poznan

Instytut Bibliograficzny, National Library, ul Hankiewicza 1, 00-973 Warsaw
Bibliographical Institute. The Institute is a

Division of the National Library (see Biblioteka Narodowa above)

Zaklad Narodowy im **Ossolińskich Biblioteka** Polska Akademia Nauk (Library of the Ossoliński National Institute of the Polish Academy of Science)*, ul Szewska 37, Wroclaw Tel: 44471/44472; Director 34304

Biblioteka **Uniwersytecka w Toruniu**, Gagarina 13, 87-100 Toruń Tel: 13-408, 233-52 Telex: 055382 butor pl
Library of the University of Toruń
Librarian: Dr Bohdan Ryszewski

Biblioteka **Uniwersytecka w Warszawie***, Krakowskie Przedmieście 26-28 and 32, 00-927 Warsaw Tel: Chief Librarian 264155; Department of Scientific Information 264047
Library of the University of Warsaw
Chief Librarian: Jan Baculewski
Publications: Prace Biblioteki Uniwersyteckiej w Warszawie (Irregular); *Uniwersytet Warszawski Materialy bibliograficzne* (annually) in *Roczniki Uniwersytetu Warszawskiego*

Biblioteka **Uniwersytecka w Wroclawiu** (Library of the University of Wroclaw), ul Karola Szajnochy 10, 50-076 Wroclaw Tel: 443432 Telex: 0712477 buw PL
Librarian: Dr Bartlomiej Kuzak

Library Associations

Polish Academy of Sciences*, Documentation and Scientific Information Centre, ul Nowy Swiat 72, 00-330 Warsaw

Stowarzyszenie Bibliotekarzy Polskich, ul Konopczyńskiego 5/7, 00-953 Warsaw Tel: 275296/270847
Polish Librarians' Association
Chairman: Witold Stankiewicz; *Secretary-General:* Leon Los
Publications: Przegląd Biblioteczny, Bibliotekarz, Poradnik Bibliotekarza, Informator Bibliotekarza i Ksiegarza

Library Reference Books and Journals

Books

Informator Bibliotekarza i Ksiegarza (Guide for the Librarian and Bookseller), Polish Librarians Association, ul Konopczyńskiego 5-7, 00-953 Warsaw

National Library Yearbook (covers scientific library science) (text in Polish with English summaries), National Library, ul Hankiewicza 1, 00-973 Warsaw

Journals

Aktualne Problemy Informacji i Dokumentacji (Current Problems in Information and Documentation) (summaries in English, French, Polish and Russian), National Centre for Scientific, Technical and Economic Information, ul Niepodległości 186, 00-931 Warsaw

Bibliotekarz (The Librarian) (text in Polish, summaries in English and Russian), Polish Librarians Association, ul Konopczyńskiego 5-7, 00-953 Warsaw

Poradnik Bibliotekarza (The Librarian's Handbook), Polish Librarians Association, ul Konopczyńskiego 5-7, 00-953 Warsaw

Przegląd Biblioteczny (Library Review) (summaries in English), Polish Librarians Association, ul Konopczyńskiego 5-7, 00-953 Warsaw

Studia o Ksiazce (Studies on the Book), Ossolineum, Rynek 9, PO Box 70, 50-106 Wroclaw

Literary Associations and Societies

Instytut Badań Literackich, Nowy Świat 72, Palac Staszica, 00-330 Warsaw Tel: 265231/269945
Institute of Literary Research
Acting Dirs: Prof Mieczyslaw Klimowicz, Doc Stefan Treugutt, Ryszard Górski
Publications: Pamietnik Literacki (Literary Journal quarterly); *Biuletyn Polonistyczny* (Bulletin of Polish Literary Scholarship, quarterly); *Teksty* (Texts, fortnightly); *Kwartalnik Historii Prasy Polskiej* (Quarterly of the History of Polish Journalism); and other Literary Study series
Founded: 1948

Polish **P E N** Club, Palac Kultury i Nauki, 00-901 Warsaw Tel: 263948
Secretary: Wladyslaw Bartoszewski

Towarzystwo Literackie im Mickiewicza (The Mickiewicz Literary Society)*, Nowy Świat 72, Warsaw
President: Julian Krzyzanowski
Publication: Rocznik (Yearbook)

Towarzystwo Przyjaciól Ksiazki (Society of Friends of Books)*, ul Hipoteczna 2, 00-092 Warsaw

Towarzystwo Przyjaciól Nauk w Przemyślu, ul Orzechowskiego 2, 37-700 Przemyśl
Society of Science and Letters of Przemyśl
Chairman: M Mazurek; *Secretary:* Mgr Z Felczyński
Publications: include *Rocznik Przemyski* (21 vols), *Biblioteka Przemyska* (7 vol), *Sprawozdania z dzialalności towarzystw naukowych miasta Przemyśla* (5 vol); *Bocznik Nauk Medycznych* (2 vols)

Literary Periodicals

Literatura (Literature), RSW, ul Bagatela 14, 00-950 Warsaw

Literatura na świecie (World Literature), Ars Polona, ul Krakowskie Przedmieście 7, PO Box 1001, 00-068 Warsaw

MKL (Miesiecznik Kulturalny Litery) (Monthly Journal of Literary Culture), Targ Drzewny 3-7, 80-886 Gdansk

Miesiecznik Literacki (Monthly Review of Literature), Ars Polona, ul Krakowskie Przedmieście 7, PO Box 1001, 00-068 Warsaw

Nowy Wyraz (New Expression), Ars Polona, ul Krakowskie Przedmieście 7, PO Box 1001, 00-068 Warsaw

Pamietnik Literacki (Literary Diary) (contents page in English, Polish and Russian), Institute of Literary Research, Nowy Świat 72, Palac Staszica, 00-330 Warsaw

Poezja (Poetry), Ars Polona, ul Krakowskie Przedmieście 7, PO Box 1001, 00-068 Warsaw

Polish Literature (text in English and French), Agencja Autorska, ul Hipoteczna 2, 00-092 Warsaw

Ruch Literacki (The Literary Movement), Polish Academy of Sciences, Historico-Literary Commission, ul Slawkowska 17, Cracow

Teksty (Texts), Institute of Literary Research, Nowy Świat 72, Palac Staszica, 00-330 Warsaw

Teksty (Texts), RSW, ul Bagatela 14, 00-950 Warsaw

Twórczość (Literary monthly), Ars Polona, ul Krakowskie Przedmieście 7, PO Box 1001, 00-068 Warsaw

Zycie Literackie (Literary Life), ul Wislna 2, Cracow

Literary Prizes

Cracow City Literary Prize*
For the entire work of an author whose life and writings were connected with Cracow. Awarded annually. Enquiries to Cracow City Council and Cracow Section of the Union of Polish Writers, ul Krupnicza 22, Cracow

Polish Ministry of National Defence Prize
For the best book dealing with the history of the Polish Armed Forces and with the defence of the country. Awarded annually. Enquiries to Polish Ministry of National Defence Publishing House, ul Grzybowska 77, Warsaw

Polish Prime Minister Award for Literature for Children and Youth
For the entire work of an author of books for children and young people. Awarded annually. Enquiries to Polish Prime Minister's Office, ul Ujazdowskie 113, Warsaw

Polish Union of Socialist Youth Prose Award*
For the best novel by an author under 30. Awarded annually. Enquiries to Polish Union of Socialist Youth and the Daily Paper 'Sztandar Mlodych', ul Wspolna 61, Warsaw

Poznan Poetical November Prize*
For the book judged the best first work of the year by a young poet. Awarded annually. Enquiries to Poznan City Council, ul Stalingradska 18, Poznan

Warsaw City Prize*
For the entire work of a distinguished author writing for children and young people. Awarded annually. Enquiries to Warsaw Municipal Council, Department of Culture, pl Dzierzynskiego 3-5, Warsaw

Warsaw City Prize for Young Poets*
For best poetry written by a young author. Co-sponsored by the Warsaw Creative Youth Club of the Polish Union of Writers and the Students' Club 'Hybrydy'. Awarded annually. Enquiries to Warsaw Municipal Council, Department of Culture, pl Dzierzynskiego 3-5, Warsaw

Mariusz **Zaruski** Literary Prize*
For the authors of best books about the sea. Awarded annually. Enquiries to Marine Club of the League of the Friends of Soldiers, ul Chocimska 14, Warsaw

'Zycie Literackie' Prize*
For literary criticism, journalism and essays. Awarded annually. Enquiries to Zycie Literackie, ul Wislna 2, Cracow

Portugal

General Information

Language: Portuguese
Religion: Roman Catholic
Population: 9.8 million
Literacy rate (1970): 71%
Bank Hours: 0900-1200, 1400-1530 Monday-Friday
Shop Hours: 0900-1300, 1500-1900 Monday-Friday (some open continuously); 0900-1300 Saturday. Generally closed Monday morning October-November
Currency: 100 centavos = 1 Portuguese escudo
Export/Import Information: Foreign language books from most countries dutied at 0.08 escudos per kg (free from UK and reduced from EEC); atlases and children's picture books have higher tariff rate and children's picture books have 30% import surcharge. Small quantity of advertising duty-free. No import licence required for goods not exceeding 5,000 escudos, otherwise licence including permission to transfer foreign exchange required. Deposit scheme: importer must deposit 50% value in non-interest bearing account for 180 days
Copyright: UCC, Berne (see International section)

Book Trade Organizations

Associação Portuguesa dos Editores e Livreiros, Largo de Andaluz, 16-1° Esq°, 1000 Lisbon Tel: 546182 Cable Add: Apel
Portuguese Association of Publishers and Booksellers
President: Alvaro de Moura Bessa; *Secretary-General:* Dr Jorge de Carvalho Sá Borges

Book Trade Reference Books and Journals

Books

O Mundo do Edição Luso-Brasileira (The World of Publishing, Portugal and Brazil), Publicações Europa-Americana, Apdo 8, Mem Martins

Journals

Boletim de Bibliografia Portuguesa (Portuguese Bibliographical Bulletin), National Library, Rua Ocidental do Campo Grande 83, Lisbon 5

Livros de Portugal (Portuguese Books), Portuguese Association of Publishers and Booksellers, Largo de Andaluz, 16-1°, Esq°, Lisbon 1

Publishers

Edições **70** Lda, Ave Duque d'Ávila 69 R/C Esq, 1000 Lisbon 1 Tel: 556898/572001/578322
Man Dir: J J Soares da Costa; *Editorial, Rights & Permissions:* Carlos Araújo; *Copy Editor:* João R Nunes; *Production Dir:* Rui Oliveira; *Sales:* Alfredo Sarmento
Subjects: General Fiction, Literature, Biography, History, Philosophy, Psychology, Social Science, Politics, Economics, Educational, Occult, Leisure Pursuits; University Textbooks
1979: 233 titles *Founded:* 1970

A E I International*, Rua Sampaio e Pina, 7-1° Fte, Lisbon 1 Tel: 654664/680628
Telex: 16423 aei p
Firm is also a Literary Agency

Edições **A O V***, Rua Formosa, 189 Oporto Tel: 28756/22058 Cable Add: Olival-Porto
Man Dir and other offices: Dr José Rebelo
Subjects: History of World War II, Reportage, Politics, Fiction
Founded: 1925

Edições **Acrópole***, Rua Alberto Aldim, Alfragide, Damaia, Lisbon Tel: 971379/972302/972433
Man Dir: Neves Ramos
Subjects: General Fiction, Belles Lettres, Poetry, Biography, History, Philosophy, Juveniles, Low- & High-priced Paperbacks, Psychology, General & Social Science
Founded: 1974
Bookshop: Edições Acrópole, Rua Alberto Aldim, Alfragide, Damaia, Lisbon

Ediçoes **Afrontamento**, Rua Costa Cabral 859, Apartado 1309, Oporto Tel: 489271
Man Dir, Editorial, Production: Jose Sousa Ribeiro; *Sales, Publicity:* Marcela Figueiredo Torres; *Rights & Permissions:* Arnaldo Fleming
Subjects: General Literature, Social Sciences, Urbanism, Politics, Cinema
1978: 14 titles *Founded:* 1965

Arménio **Amado** Editor Suc, Ceira, Coimbra
Man Dir: Simões Pereira
Subjects: Philosophy, Religion, Psychology, Social Science, Law, Architecture, History, Politics, Languages
Founded: 1929

Livraria **Apostolado** da Imprensa, Rua da Boavista 591, Oporto Tel: 27875
Man Dir, Editorial: José Maria de Azeredo Pinto, Luiz Archer; *Publicity:* A Nunes da Rocha
Branch Off: Rua da Lapa 111, 1200 Lisbon Tel: 660214
Subjects: General Fiction, Belles Lettres, Poetry, Biography, Philosophy, Religion, Juveniles, Secondary Textbooks
Bookshop: address as above
1978: 6 titles *1979:* 7 titles *Founded:* 1922

Editora **Arcádia** Sarl*, Campo de Santa Clara 160, Lisbon 2 Tel: 863151/3 Cable Add: Arcádia
Shipping Add: Ave Camilo Castelo Branco, 9-A, Buraca-Damaia
Dirs: Ricardo F Martins, Dr João Rodrigues Martins, Dr Alberto dos Santos Antonio; *Sales Dir:* Alvaro A F Ferreira
Subjects: General Fiction, Belles Lettres, Biography, History, How-to, Music, Art, Philosophy, Religion, Juveniles, Paperbacks, Medicine, Psychology, Engineering, General & Social Science
Founded: 1957

Livraria **Arnado** Lda, Rua Joao Machado 9-11, Coimbra Tel: 27573
Man Dir: José Fernandes de Almeida
Parent Company: Porto Editora Lda (qv)
Subsidiary Company: Empresa Literária Fluminense Lda
Subjects: Scholarly, Scientific, Legal, Literary
1978: 45 titles *1979:* 35 titles *Founded:* 1966

Editorial **Aster**, Largo D Estefânia 8-1° Esq°, Lisbon 1 Tel: 534611/532973
Man Dir, Sales, Publicity, Rights & Permissions: Fernando de Souza; *Editorial:* Dr H Barrilaro Ruas; *Production:* João Alves
Branch Offs: Praça Guilherme Gomes Fernandes 24-2° Esq°, Oporto; Rua de Santo André 7, 4700 Braga
Subjects: General Fiction, Belles Lettres, Poetry, Biography, History, Music, Art, Philosophy, Religion, Psychology, How-to, Juveniles, Paperbacks, Secondary and University Textbooks
1978: 86 titles *Founded:* 1954

Livraria Editora **Atlântida** Ltda*, Rua Ferreira Borges 103, Coimbra
Dir: Afonso Queiró
Subject: Law

Editorial **'Avante!'**, Ave Santos Dumont 57, 3° 1000 Lisbon Tel: 76972/3/4/5
Man Dir: Francisco Melo
Orders to: C D L (Central Distribuidora Livreira) SARL, Ave Santos Dumont 57, 4° 1000 Lisbon
Subjects: Politics, Economics, Philosophy, General Fiction
1978: 39 titles *1979:* 18 titles *Founded:* 1974

Livraria **Bertrand** SARL, Rua João de Deus, Venda Nova, Amadora Tel: 974571
Cable Add: Libertran Telex: 12709
Man Dirs: Manuel Boullosa, Eduardo Martins Soares; *Editorial, Rights & Permissions:* Piedade Ferreira, Pina Mendes; *Sales:* Carlos Grade; *Production:* Antero Branco; *Publicity:* Ferreira da Cruz
Subjects: General Portuguese and Foreign Literature, Social Sciences, Juveniles (all ages), Dictionaries, School Books, Cartoon Strips
Bookshops: (Lisbon) Rua Garrett 73/75, Ave Roma 13-B, Rua Dr J Soares 4-A, Rua D Estefânea 46-C/D, Rua Latino Coelho 12A-12B; (Coimbra) Largo da Portagem 9; (Oporto) Rua de Santo António 43, 45, 65, Shopping Center, Brasilia; (Aveiro) Ave Dr L Peixinho 87-B; (Vian do Castelo) Rua Sacadura Cabral 32; (Faro) Rua D Francisco Gomes 27
1978: 187 titles *1979:* 193 titles *Founded:* 1732

Brasília Editôra (J Carvalho Branco & Cia Lda)*, Rua José Falcão 173, CP 101 Oporto Tel: 315854 Cable Add: Brasiliaeditora
Man Dir: J Carvalho Branco; *Editorial, Rights & Permissions:* Dr Zulmira C Branco; *Sales, Publicity:* Dr Isabel C Branco; *Production:* J Silvo Couto
Associate Company: Livraria Leitura — Fernandes & Branco Lda, Rua de Ceuta 88, Oporto
Subsidiary Company: Livraria Boa Leitura, Av Almirante Reis 256, Lisbon
Subjects: Portuguese and Foreign Literature; Belles Lettres, Fiction, Poetry, Biography, How-to, Philosophy, Religion, Psychology, Social Science, Politics, Yoga, Sex, Occult
Bookshops: Livraria Leitura, Ave Almirante Reis 256B, Lisbon; Livraria Leitura, Rua de Ceuta 88, Oporto
1978: 26 titles *Founded:* 1961

Editorial **Caminho** SARL, Rua João de Deus, 24 Venda Nova, 2700 Amadora Tel: 766402
Man Dir: Zeferino Antas de Sousa Coelho
Orders to: C D L — see 'Major Booksellers'
Subjects: General Fiction, Socio-Political, Juveniles
1978: 32 titles *1979:* 42 titles *Founded:* 1977

Centro do Livro Brasileiro, Rua Almirante Barroso 13-2°, Lisbon 1000 Tel: 560165/6/7/8 Cable Add: Celbrasil
Man Dir, Editorial: Alvaro Conçalves Pereira
Branch Off: Rua De Ceuta 79, Oporto
Subjects: Philosophy, Religion, Social Science, Philology, Pure and Applied Science, Art, History, Geography, General
Bookshops: Rodrigues Sampaio 30B, Lisbon; Rua de Sao Antonio 146, Oporto; Rua de Ceuta 79, Oporto
1978: 49 titles *Founded:* 1963

Livraria **Civilização** (Américo Fraga
Lamares 8 Ca Lda), Rua Alberto Aires de
Gouveia 27, Oporto 1 Tel: 22286, 22287,
32382 Cable Add: Alamares
Man Dir: Arquitecto Moura Bessa; *Rights &
Permissions:* Maria Alice Moura Bessa
Branch Off: Ave Almirante Reis 102 r/c-
Dtº, Lisbon 1 (Tel: 823389)
Subjects: Social and Political Science,
Economics, History, Art, Fiction, Juveniles
1979: 8 titles *Founded:* 1921

Edições **Cosmos**, Rua da Emenda 111-2º,
1200 Lisbon 2 Tel: 322050 Cable Add:
Cosmos-Lisboa
Man Dir: Manuel R de Oliveira
Subjects: Music, Sociology, History
1978: 10 titles *1979:* 9 titles *Founded:* 1938

Sá da **Costa** Editora, Praça Luís de Camões
22 4, Lisbon 1294 codex Tel: 360721 Cable
Add: Livrosacosta Telex: Sacost 15574-P
Man Dir, Editorial: João Sá da Costa; *Sales,
Publicity:* Manuel Sá da Costa; *Production:*
Idalina Sá da Costa
Subjects: Textbooks, History, Philosophy,
Literature, Classics, Essays
Bookshop: Rua Garrett 100-102,
Lisbon 1294 codex
Founded: 1913

Publicações **Dom Quixote***, Rua Luciano
Cordeiro 119, 1098 Lisbon codex Tel:
40250/538079/538088 Cable Add: Quixote
Telex: 14331 Quixot P
Man Dir: Snu Abecassis; *Sales:* Fernando
Silva; *Production:* Virginia Caldeira; *Rights
& Permissions:* Cristina Potier
Subjects: General Fiction, Belles Lettres,
Poetry, History, Education, Philosophy,
Social Science, Reference
1978: 56 titles *Founded:* 1965

Editorial **Enciclopédia** Lda*, Rua António
Maria Cardoso 33, Lisbon 2 Tel:
326452/33330
Subjects: Encyclopaedias, Fiction, History,
Art, Technical
Founded: 1934

Livraria **Escolar** Infante*, Manuel Ferreira
& Gomes Lda, Rua de Santa Teresa 20-22,
Oporto Tel: 26281/37098
Subjects: History, Religion, Juveniles,
Paperbacks, General & Social Science,
Secondary & Primary Textbooks,
Educational Materials, Law
Founded: 1962
Bookshop: Livraria Escolar Infante, Rua de
Santa Teresa 22, Oporto

Editorial **Estúdios** Cor Sarl*, Rua João
Pereira da Rosa 20-A, Lisbon 2 Tel:
328889/362146
Subjects: Belles Lettres, Biography, History,
Music, Art, Philosophy, Politics, Juveniles,
General Science, Translations; General
Fiction; Paperbacks
Founded: 1949

Publicações **Europa-America** Lda, Apdo 8,
Estrada Lisbon-Sintra Km 14, Mem
Martins Tel: 2911461/2/3 Cable Add:
Europamérica
Man Dir: Francisco Lyon de Castro; *Sales
Dir:* Tito Lyon de Castro
Subsidiary Companies: Publicações Forum,
Publicações Trevo
Branch Offs: Delegação de Lisbon, Rua da
Flores, 45-2º, Lisbon; Delegação do Pôrto,
Rua 31 de Janeiro, 221 Oporto
Subjects: General Fiction, Biography,
History, How-to, Music, Art, Philosophy,
Reference, Medicine, Psychology, General &
Social Science, Nursery books, Juveniles,
Low- & High-priced Paperbacks, University
Textbooks, Educational Materials, Belles
Lettres, Poetry, Engineering, Technical
Bookshops: Lojas Europa-America, Ave

Marquês de Tomar 1-B, Rua das Flores 45,
1º, Lisbon; Ave António Enes 14-B, Ave
Elias Garcia 104-B, Queluz; Ave 1 de Maio
61, Castelo Branco; Ave 31 de Janeiro 221,
Alameda Eça de Queirós 32, Oporto; Pr
Ferreira de Almeida 21-22, Faro; Av 25 de
Abril 48, Almada; Rua José Relvas, 15 B-C,
Parede
1978: 104 titles *1979:* 132 titles *Founded:*
1945

Familia 2000*, Rua 5 de Outubro, 484-488,
Porto
Man Dir: Adriano Correia Pinho

Livraria **Ferin** Lda, Rua Nova do Almada
70-74, Lisbon 1200 Tel: 324422
Man Dir: Margarida dias Pinheiro; *Sales:*
Isabel Carvalho
Subjects: Law, Geological Maps, Soil Maps
Bookshop: Rua Nova do Almada 70-74,
Lisbon
1978: 3 titles *1979:* 5 titles *Founded:* 1840

Livraria Editora **Figueirinhas** Lda, Praça da
Liberdade 67, 4000 Oporto Tel:
24985/25751/317698
Man Dir: João Pimenta; *Editorial, Sales,
Production, Publicity, Rights & Permissions:*
Mario Figueirinhas
Subjects: General Literature
Founded: 1944

Forja Editora SARL*, Rua da Emenda 30
3º C, Lisbon 2 Tel: 322334 Cable Add:
Ediforja
*Man Dir, Editorial, Production, Rights &
Permissions:* Anibal Telo; *Sales:* João Sá;
Publicity: Aida Soeiro
Subjects: Fiction, Juveniles, Theatre,
Cinema
Founded: 1974

Editorial **Franciscana***, Montariol,
Apartado 17, Braga 4701 codex Tel: 22490
Man Dir: António Pedro da Anunciação
Branch Off: Apartado 17, Braga 4701 codex
Subjects: Biography, History, Music, Art,
Philosophy, Religion, Juveniles, Theology
Bookshop: Livraria Editorial Franciscana,
Rua de Cedofeita 350, Oporto; Montariol,
Braga
1978: 29 titles *Founded:* 1922

Editorial **Futura**, Ave 5 de Outubro 317-1º,
Lisbon 1600 Tel: 779114
Man Dir: José Chaves Ferreira
Subjects: General Literature
Founded: 1970

G E C T I (Gabinete de Especialização e
Cooperação Tecnica Internacional L), Ave
Republica 47-6D, PO Box 1918, 1004 codex
Lisbon 1000 Tel: 768877/771940/772154/
763465
Man Dir, Editorial: A Almeida Teixeira;
Sales: Ester Malafaia
Subjects: Business, Administration,
Marketing, Professional Training,
Programmed Learning
Founded: 1963

Gabinete de Especialização e Cooperação
Tecnica Internacional, see G E C T I

Livros **Horizonte** Lda, Rua das Chagas 17-
1º Dt, Apdo 2818, 1200 Lisbon Tel:
366917/368505 Cable Add: Livroshorizonte
Man Dir, Rights & Permissions: Rog
Mendes de Moura; *Sales:* Francisco Ramos
Vasquez; *Production:* Henrique Grácio;
Publicity: M C Ribeiro da Silva; *Foreign
Rights:* M H Fernandes
Subjects: Pedagogy, Philosophy, Sociology,
Art
Founded: 1953

Edições **I T A U** (Instituto Tecnico de
Alimentação Humana) Lda, Ave da
República 46-A r/c Esq, Lisbon 1 Tel:
733307/733482/733245/733019/733265

Man Dir: Júlio Roberto; *Editorial, Sales,
Production, Publicity:* José Maria Paula
Orders to: Ave Elias Garcia 87-A, Lisbon 1
Parent Company: Instituto Tecnico de
Alimentação Humana Lda
Subjects: Human Nutrition, Pedagogy,
Poetry, Literature, Sociology, Juvenile
Literature
Bookshop: Galerias Itau, Rua de
Entrecampos 66-A
1978: 7 titles *1979:* 10 titles *Founded:* 1969

Imprensa Nacional-Casa da Moeda, Rua D
Francisco Manuel de Melo No 5, Lisbon 1
Tel: 685684 Cable Add: INCM
Man Dir, Editorial, Sales & Publicity: Dr
Américo Farinha de Carvalho
Branch Offs: 4 in Lisbon, 1 each in Oporto
and Coimbra
Subjects: Political and Civil Administration,
Archeology, Arts, Economics, Ethnography,
Ethnology, Pharmacy, Philology,
Philosophy, History, Memoirs, Religion
Bookshops: Livraria Camões, Rua
Bittencourt da Silva 12C, Rio de Janeiro,
Brazil; Gabinete Portugues de Lectura, Rua
do Imperador 290, Recife, Brazil
Founded: 1768

Editorial **Inquérito** Lda*, Travessa da
Queimada 23, 1º D, Lisbon 2 Tel: 328659
Subjects: General Fiction, Belles Lettres,
History, Philosophy, Juveniles, Social
Science, Law
Founded: 1938

Instituto Tecnico de Alimentação Humana,
see I T A U

Americo Fraga **Lamares** & Ca Lda, see
Livraria Civilizacao

Lello e Cia Lda*, Rua Conde de Vizela 12,
Oporto 1 Tel: 23209
Dir: J Pinto Mesquita Lello
Subjects: Fine Arts, Education, Textbooks

Lello e Irmão, Rua das Carmelitas 144,
Oporto 4000 Tel: 22037/318170 Cable
Add: Jolello
Man Dir: Edgar Pinto Da Silva Lello
Subjects: General Literature, Juveniles,
History, Dictionaries
Founded: 1868

Editora **Livros** do Brasil Sarl, Rua dos
Caetanos 22, PO Box 2953, Lisbon 2 Tel:
362621/323170/326113 Cable Add: Librasil
Man Dir, Rights & Permissions: Antonio de
Souza-Pinto; *Editorial, Publicity:*
Mascarenhas Barreto; *Sales:* José Manuel
Lopes Filipe
Associate Company: Editores Associados
Lda
Branch Off: Rua de Ceuta 80, Oporto
Subjects: General and Science Fiction,
Politics, History, Biography, Philosophy,
Scientific Research
Founded: 1944

Livraria **Lopes Da Silva**-Editôra de M
Moreira Soares Rocha Lda, Rua Chã
101-103, 4000 Oporto Tel: 21678/26017
Man Dir: Mário Moreira Soares Da Rocha
Subjects: Medicine, Science, Technical
1980: 130 titles *Founded:* 1870

Livraria **Luso-Espanhola** Lda*, Rua Nova
do Almada 86-90, Lisbon 2 Tel:
324917/367667 Cable Add: Livraluso
Man Dir: Inocencio Casimiro Araujo
Branch Off: Livraria-Médica do Porto,
Rua do Carmo 14, Oporto; Livraria Luso-
Espahola, Rua da Sofia 121-1º, Coimbra
Subjects: Medicine, Technical, Textbooks,
Law, Economics
Founded: 1941
Bookshops: Livraria Luso-Espanhola e
Brasileira Lda, Ave 13 Maio 23-4º, Rio de
Janeiro, Brasil; Livraria Científico Médico
do Porto, Rua do Carmo 14, Oporto

Fernando **Machado** e Co Ltd, Rua das Carmelitas 15, Oporto Tel: 25718
Man Dir: Manuel Correia Vieira
Branch Off: Rua dos Clérigos 23, Oporto
Founded: 1922
Bookshop: Livraria Fernando Machado, Rua das Carmelitas 15, Oporto

Livraria Tavares **Martins**, Rua dos Clérigos 14, Oporto Tel: 23459
Man Dir: Américo Tavares Martins
Subjects: Drama, Poetry, Biography, History, Art, Philosophy, Religion, Juveniles
Founded: 1934

Meribérica — Editorial e Comercialização de Direitos Lda*, Rua Dona Filipa de Vilhena 8-3° Dt°, Lisbon 1 Tel: 58433/578485/577947/576085
Man Dirs: Adriano Eliseu, Telmo Protásio; *Editorial:* Adriano Eliseu; *Production:* Branca Protásio
Subjects: Children's Books
Book Club: Clube Walt Disney

Editorial **Minerva**, Rua Luz Soriano 31-33, 1200 Lisbon Tel: 322535
Dir: Artur Augusto Campos
Subjects: General Fiction, Juveniles, Paperbacks, Reference
Founded: 1927

Moraes Editores*, Rua do Século 34-2°, Lisbon 2 Tel: 325391/327717/320636
Man Dir, Editorial, Rights & Permissions: Nelson De Matos; *Sales:* Carlos Mendonça
Subjects: General Fiction, Belles Lettres, Poetry, Biography, Philosophy, Reference, Juveniles, High-priced Paperbacks, Psychology, History, Religion, Law, General & Social Science
Bookshop: Livraria Moraes, Largo do Picadeiro 11, Lisbon 2
1978: 56 titles *Founded:* 1955

Livraria Editora **Pax** Lda, Rua do Souto 73-77, Braga 4700 Tel: 22604 Cable Add: pax
Man Dir and other offices: José Moreira
Subjects: Fiction, Belles Lettres, Poetry, History, Ethnography, Travel, Spiritual Life, Theatre, Education
1978: 25 titles *Founded:* 1928

Parceria A M **Pereira** Lda*, Rua Augusta 44-54, Lisbon 2 Tel: 361730/361710 Cable Add: Parcepereira
Subjects: General Fiction, Belles Lettres, Biography, History, How-to, Juveniles, Social Science, Technical, Primary Textbooks
Founded: 1848

Editorial **Perpétuo** Socorro*, Rua Dr Alves da Veiga 207, Oporto Tel: 564251
Subject: Religion, Education
Founded: 1946

Platano Editora SARL, Ave de Berna, 31-2° Esq, Lisbon 1 Tel: 774250/779278 Telex: 13659 platan p
Editorial: Francisco Prata Ginja
Subsidiary Companies: Alicerce Editora Lda, Oporto; Paralelo Editora Lda, Lisbon
Associate Companies: Alicerce Editora SARL, Rio de Janeiro, Brazil
Subjects: Primary, Secondary and Technical School Books, Theatre, Poetry, Juveniles
Bookshop: Alicerce Editora Lda, Rua Guerra Junqueiro 456, Oporto

Editorial **Portico***, Rua Dr Julio Dantas 4, Lisbon 1

Porto Editôra Lda, Rua da Restauração 365, Oporto Tel: 25813
Dir: Vasco Teixeira
Man Dir: Mario Trindade
Associated Companies: Empresa Literaria Fluminense Lda, Rua de S João Nepomuceno 8-A, Lisbon; Livraria Arnado Lda, Rua João Machado 9, Coimbra
Subjects: University, Secondary & Primary Textbooks, Educational Materials, Foreign Language Teaching and Dictionaries, Law; General Nonfiction
Bookshops: Rua da Fabrica 90, Oporto; Praça D Filipa de Lencastre 42, Oporto
Founded: 1944

Portugalia Editôra Lda*, Rua Luciano Cordeiro 81-C, Lisbon 2 Tel: 535741
Man Dir: Diniz Gandon da Nazareth Fernandes
Branch Off: Rua da Condessa 74-78, Lisbon
Subjects: General Fiction, Belles Lettres, Poetry, Biography, History, Philosophy, Juveniles, Low- & High-priced Paperbacks, Psychology
Bookshop: Rua Luciano Cordeiro 81C, Lisbon 1100
1978: 18 titles *Founded:* 1942

Prelo Editora Sarl*, Alameda de Sto Antonio dos Capuchos 6B, Lisbon 1 Tel: 572224
Man Dir: Viriato Camilo
Subjects: Portuguese Fiction, Theatre, Belles Lettres, History, Social Science, Political Science, Economics
Bookshop: at above address
Founded: 1960

Editorial **Presença**, Rua Augusto Gil 35-A, Lisbon 1 Tel: 766912/763060 Cable Add: Editorial Presença Lisboa
Man Dir, Editorial: Francisco Espadinha; *Sales:* Francisco Santos; *Production:* Manuel Aquino; *Publicity:* Wanda Ramos; *Rights & Permissions:* Carlos Grifo
Subjects: Sociology, Politics, Philosophy, History, Children's Books, Hobbies, School Textbooks
1979: 120 titles *Founded:* 1960

Edicões António **Ramos***, Rua Padre Luis Aparício 9-1° F, Lisbon 1 Tel: 577205
Man Dir, Editorial: António Ramos; *Sales:* Jorge Peralta; *Production:* Margarida Fonseca; *Publicity:* Nuno Vasco
Orders to: C L B, Rua Almirante Barroso, 13-2° Lisbon 1
Subjects: General Fiction and Nonfiction
1978: 45 titles *Founded:* 1977

Realizações Artis Lda*, Rua das Taipas 12, r/c Esq, Lisbon 2 Tel: 363796
Man Dirs: Rogério de Freitas, Leão Penedo
Subjects: Belles Lettres, Poetry, Biography, Music, Art
Founded: 1950

A **Regra** do Jogo, Rua Sousa Martins 5, 2° Dto, Lisbon Tel: 571631
Man Dir: Jose Leal de Loureiro; *Rights & Permissions:* Fernando P Marques
Subjects: Fiction, Poetry, Music, History, Juveniles; Anthropology, Philosophy, Economy
1980: 68 titles *Founded:* 1974

M Moreira Soares **Rocha** Lda, see Livraria Lopes da Silva

Edições **Rotep***, Rua de São Bento 39, Lisbon 2 Tel: 601501
Man Dir: João Camacho Pereira
Subjects: Iconography, Reproductions of Ancient Engravings, Ideographic Maps of Portugal
Founded: 1944

Editorial **Ruiz** Romero, see A E I International

Edições **Salesianas**, Rua Dr Alves da Veiga 128, Oporto Tel: 565750
Man Dir: João António Machado; *Editorial, Sales, Production, Publicity:* Elías de Jesus
Branch Off: Rua Saraiva de Carvalho 275, Lisbon
Subjects: Biography, Religion, Juveniles, Paperbacks, Psychology, Technical, Educational Materials
Bookshops: Livraria Salesiana, Largo Luis de Camões 6-9, Evora; Livraria Salesiana, Rua Sanaiva de Carvalho 275, Lisbon
1978: 20 titles *1979:* 16 titles *Founded:* 1947

Empresa de Publicidade **Seara** Nova SARL*, R Bernardo Lima, 42-r/c 1199 Lisbon codex Tel: 530869/571302
Man Dir, Editorial, Sales: Dr Ulpiano Nascimento; *Production, Publicity, Rights & Permissions:* Costa Marques
Subjects: Fiction, Sociology, Politics, Economics, History, Pedagogics, Juveniles, Belles Lettres
Bookshop: Livraria Seara Nova, R Conde Redondo 38-A, 1100 Lisbon
Founded: 1921

A M **Teixeira** e Cia (Filhos) Lda (Livraria Classica Editora), Praça dos Restauradores 17, 1298 Lisbon codex Tel: 321229/321391/321286 Cable Add: Classica
Editorial, Rights & Permissions: Antonio B Teixeira; *Production, Publicity:* Jose F Teixeira
Subjects: General Fiction, Belles Lettres, Poetry, History, Reference, Religion, Juveniles, General and Social Science, Psychology, University and Primary Textbooks, Agriculture, Philology, Electronics, Economics, Management
1978: 37 titles *1979:* 38 titles *Founded:* 1903

João Romano **Torres** & Cia Lda, Livraria Romano Torres, Largo de Sao Mamede 3-A, 1200 Lisbon Tel: 601244
Man Dir: Amelia Lucas Torres Farinha; *Editorial, Publicity, Rights & Permissions:* Francisco de Noronha e Andrade; *Sales, Production:* Osorio Marques Martins
Subjects: Historical Works, World Classics, Romantic Fiction, Juvenile Adventure Stories
Founded: 1885

União Gráfica Sarl*, Rua de Santa Marta 48, Lisbon 2 Tel: 44191/2, 46174/5 Cable Add: Novidades
Dir: Carlos M Castelo Gonçalves
Subjects: General Fiction, Belles Lettres, Poetry, Biography, History, Philosophy, Religion, Juveniles, Low- & High-priced Paperbacks, Psychology, Social Science
Founded: 1923

Verbo Sarl, Rua Carlos Testa 1, Lisbon Tel: 562131 Cable Add: Verbo
Man Dir: Fernando Guedes; *Sales Dir:* David Duarte
Subjects: History, Juveniles, General Science, Secondary and Primary Textbooks, Educational Materials
1978-79: 193 titles *Founded:* 1959
Book Club: Companhia Editora de Livros e Discos Sarl
Miscellaneous: Door-to-door sales by EDC-Empresa de Divulgaçao Cultural Sarl, Ar Duque de Avila, 193 Lisbon

Livraria **Verdade e Vida** Editora*, Cava da Tria, Fatima Tel: 97417
Subjects: Biography, History, Philosophy, Religion, Juveniles, Fiction, Education
Founded: 1945
Bookshop: Livraria Verdade & Vida, Cava da Tria, Fátima

Literary Agents

A E I International*, Rua Sampaio e Pina, 7-1° Fte, Lisbon 1 Tel: 654664/680628 Telex: 16423 aei p
Firm is also a Publisher

Ilidio da Fonseca Matos, Rua de S
Bernardo, 68-3 Lisbon 2 Tel: 669780 Cable
Add: Ilphoto
Man Dir: Ilidio Matos

Book Clubs

Amigos do Livro, Rua Fernão Mendes Pinto
42, 1400 Lisbon

Círculo de Leitores, Rua Eng° Paulo de
Barros, 22-1599 Lisbon codex Tel:
709215/709221/709224 Telex: 18343 cilecl p
Man Dir: Manfred Grebe; *Editorial Dir:*
Manuel Dias de Carvalho
Subjects: Fiction, Biography, Juvenile,
Encyclopedias, Scientific, Historical, General
Non-fiction, Special Editions
Owned by: Verlagsgruppe Bertelsmann
GmbH, Federal Republic of Germany (qv)
Founded: 1971

Clube **Walt Disney***, Rua Filipa de Vilhena,
8-3° Dt° Lisbon 1
Owned by: Meribérica-Editorial e
Comercializaçao de Directos Lda (Lisbon)

Major Booksellers

Livraria **Bertrand***, Rua Garrett 73-75,
Apdo 2078, Lisbon 2

Biblarte Lda, Rua de Sao Pedro de
Alcantara 71, Lisbon 1200
Manager: Ernesto Martins

Livraria **Bucholz***, Rua Duque de
Palmela 4, Lisbon

C D L (Central Distribuidora Livreira)
SARL, Ave Santos Dumont 57-2°, 1000
Lisbon Tel: 731752, 769744, 779825
Dir: Mario Lino
Company also has 5 other Bookshops in
Lisbon, and others in 12 other cities in
Portugal

Livraria **Castro e Silva**, Rua da Rosa 31,
1200 Lisbon

Livraria Sá da **Costa**, Rua Garrett 100-102,
1294 Lisbon codex
Manager: Manuel F da Costa

D I G Ldá (Distribuidora Geral de
Informação)*, Rua Vitor Cordon 45 (Páteo
Bragança, porta B), Lisbon 2

Expresso*, Sarl, Apdo 21, Buraca/Damaia,
Lisbon

Livraria **Nunes***, Rua de S Domingos de
Benfica 5-A, Lisbon 4

Livraria **Portugal**, Dias e Andrade Lda,
Apdo 2681, Rua do Carmo 70-74, 1200
Lisbon codex

Regimprensa*, Sarl, Ave D José I, lote 12,
Reboleira (Amadora), Lisbon

Livraria **Sam Carlos***, Largo de S Carlos 11,
Lisbon

Editorial o **Século***, Rua do Século 73,
Lisbon 2

Livraria **Sousa e Almeida***, Rua da
Fabrica 42, Oporto

Major Libraries

Biblioteca da **Academia** das Ciências de
Lisboa*, Rua da Academia das Ciências 19,
Lisbon 2
Library of the Academy of Sciences

Biblioteca da **Ajuda**, Palacio da Ajuda, 1300
Lisbon Tel: 638592

Arquivo Nacional da Torre do Tombo,
Palácio de S Bento, Lisbon 1200
National Archives of Torre do Tombo
Dir: José Pereira da Costa

Biblioteca Municipal Central*, Palácio
Galveias, Largo do Campo Pequeno, Lisbon

Biblioteca Nacional de Lisboa, Rua
Ocidental do Campo Grande 83, 1751
Lisbon codex Tel: 767786/7/8/9/0

Biblioteca Popular de Lisboa*, Rua Ivens 35
and Rua de Academia das Ciências 19,
Lisbon

Biblioteca Pública de Ponta Delgada*, The
Azores

**Biblioteca Pública e Arquivo Distrital de
Braga***, Braga
Public Library and District Archives

**Biblioteca Pública e Arquivo Distrital de
Évora***, Évora
Public Library and District Archives

Biblioteca Pública Municipal do Porto,
Oporto
Dir: M F de Brito
Municipal Library of Oporto

Centro de Documentacão Científica e
Técnica, Ave Prof Gama Pinto 2, 1699
Lisbon codex Tel: 772886/762891/765622/
731300/731350 Telex: 18428 educa p
Centre of Scientific and Technical
Information. The Library is a branch of the
Instituto Nacional de Investigação Científica
(National Scientific Research Institute)
Dir: Eng Carlos Pulido

Biblioteca do **Palácio** Nacional de Mafra*,
Terreiro de João V, Mafra Tel: 52398

Biblioteca Geral da **Universidade de
Coimbra***, Coimbra Tel: 23015/25541

Library Associations

Associação Portuguesa de Bibliotecários
Arquivistas e Documentalistas, Edificio da
Biblioteca Nacional, Campo Grande 83,
1700 Lisbon Tel: 767786
Portuguese Association of Librarians,
Archivists and Documentalists
President: Dr L F Abreu Nunes

Library Reference Books and Journals

Books

Lista das Bibliotecas Portuguesas (List of
Portuguese Libraries), Centre of Scientific
Documentation, Campo dos Mártires da
Pátria 130, Lisbon

Journals

Boletim de Bibliografia Portuguesa
(Portuguese Bibliographical Bulletin),
National Library, Rua Ocidental do Campo
Grande 83, Lisbon 5

*Cadernos de Biblioteconomia, Arquivistica e
Documentacao* (Library Management,
Archives and Documentation) (summaries in
English), Apdo 103, Coimbra

Literary Associations and Societies

Instituto Português da Sociedade Científica
de Goerres (Portuguese Institute of the
Goerres Research Society)*, Rua Visconde
de Seabra 2-3, Lisbon 5
Researches into the language and literature
of the 16th and 17th centuries
Secretary: Dr Helga Bauer
Publication: Portugiesische Forschungen
(Researches in Portuguese)

Portuguese **P E N** Centre*, Rua Tomas da
Anunciaçao 58-5° Esq, Lisbon 3
Secretary: Ana Hatherly

Literary Periodicals

Coloquio-Letras (Dialogue-Literature),
Empresa Nacional de Publicidade, Ave da
Liberdade 266, Lisbon 2

Jornal de Letras e Artes (Journal of Letters
and Arts), Rua Vitor Bastos 14A, Lisbon 1

Ocidente (The West); Portuguese review of
culture, Antonio H de Azevedo Pinto and
Amelia de Azevedo Pinto, Rua de S Felix
41D

Peninsula, Agencia Internacional de Livraria
e Publicações Lda, R S Pedro de Alcantara,
63-1 D, Lisbon

Seara Nova (New Harvest), Empresa de
Publicidade 'Seara Nova' Sarl, R Bernardo
Lima, 23-1 Esq, Lisbon

Literary Prizes

Children's and Juvenile Literature Prize*
For the best book written for readers
between four and sixteen. 15,000 escudos.
Awarded annually. Enquiries to Portugal
State Secretariat for Information and
Tourism, Palacio Foz, Lisbon 2

National Award for Poetry and the Novel*
Two prizes, one for the best book of poetry
and the other for the best novel or book of
short stories. 50,000 escudos each. Awarded
annually. Enquiries to Portugal State
Secretariat for Information and Tourism,
Palacio Foz, Lisbon 2

National Essay Award*
For the best essay written by a Portuguese
author and printed in Portuguese. 50,000
escudos. Awarded every other year.
Enquiries to Portugal State Secretariat for
Information and Tourism, Palacio Foz,
Lisbon 2

Revelation Awards (Poetry and Prose)*
Four prizes, two given for the best
unpublished manuscript of poetry and two
for prose. 5,000 escudos. Awarded annually.
Enquiries to Portugal State Secretariat for
Information and Tourism, Palacio Foz,
Lisbon 2

Puerto Rico

General Information

Language: English and Spanish
Religion: Roman Catholic
Population: 3.3 million
Literacy Rate (1970): 89.2%
Currency: US currency
Export/Import Information: No tariff on
books and advertising matter. No import
licences required
Copyright: UCC (see International section)

Book Trade Organizations

Sociedad Puertorriqueña de Escritores, Apdo 4962, San Juan
Puerto Rican Society of Writers
President: Ernesto Juan Fonfrías

Book Trade Reference Journal

Anuario bibliográfico puertorriqueño (Puerto Rican Annual Bibliography), Estado Libre Asociado de Puerto Rico, Dept de Instrucción Pública, Río Piedras

Publishers

Distribuidora **Cima** Inc*, PO Box G-2172, San Juan, PR 00936 (Located at: Calle O'Neill 177, Hato Rey, PR 00919) Tel: 7676188/7647635 Cable Add: CIMA
President: Héctor E Serrano; *Vice-President:* Miguel A Serrano
Subjects: General Literature, Textbooks, Technical Books
Founded: 1969

Editorial **Club** de la Prensa*, Apdo 4692, San Juan, PR 00903
Subjects: Fiction, Maps, Folklore

Editorial **Cordillera** Inc, Calle O'Neill 177, Hato Rey, PR 00918 Tel: 7676188/7647635 Cable Add: Cordillera
Man Dir, Editorial, Production: Héctor E Serrano; *Sales, Publicity:* Isaac Serrano
Subjects: General Literature, Social Studies, Spanish
1977: 10 titles *Founded:* 1962
ISBN Publisher's Prefix: 0-88495

Editorial **Edil** Inc, Apdo 23088, Universidad de Puerto Rico, Río Piedras, PR 00931 (Located at: Calle Julian Blanco, Esquina Ramírez Pabón, Rio Pedras 00925) Tel: (809) 7632958/7643740 Cable Add: Edil
Man Dir: Norberto Lugo Ramírez; *Sales Dir:* Eunice Lugo Frank; *Publicity Dir:* Consuelo Andino
Subjects: General Literature (especially major Puerto Rican and South American authors), Social & Political Sciences, Economics, Law, Education, Life Sciences, History, Language, Poetry, Drama, Belles Lettres
1978: 200 titles *Founded:* 1967

Editorial Cultural, Apdo 21056, Rio Piedras Station, PR 00928 Tel: 7663234
Man Dir: Francisco Vázques; *Sales Dir:* Aida Vázquez; *Publicity Dir:* F V Alumo
Imprint: Editorial Antillana
Branch Off: Editorial Antillana, Roble 51, Río Piedras, PR 00925
Subjects: Literature, Biography, History, University and Secondary Textbooks
Bookshop: Librería Cultural, Roble 51, Río Piedras, PR 00925
1979: 36 titles *Founded:* 1949

Instituto de Cultura Puertorriqueña, Apdo 4184, San Juan, PR 00905 Tel: 7232115/7251988/7240910 Telex: 3453096
Man Dir, Editorial, Rights & Permissions: Luis M Rodríguez Morales; *Sales:* Ileana Colon de Barreto
Orders to: San Francisco 305, San Juan, PR 00901
Subjects: General Literature, History, Music, Poetry, Anthropology
Bookshop: Librería del Instituto de Cultura Puertorriqueña, San Francisco 305, San Juan, PR 00901
Founded: 1955

Editorial **McGraw-Hill** Latinoamerica SA*, Apdo 20712, Rio Piedras, Puerto Rico 00928
Subjects: Primary, Secondary & University Textbooks, Reference
Miscellaneous: Branch office of Editorial McGraw-Hill Latino-Americana SA, Panama (qv)

Editorial y Librería La **Reforma***, Calle El Roble 54, Río Piedras, PR 00925 Tel: 7651635
Man Dir: Germán Stevenson
Parent Company: Fortress Church Supply Stores
Subject: Religion
1978: 5 titles *Founded:* 1954

University of Puerto Rico Press (UPRED)*, Apdo X, Estacion UPR, Río Piedras, PR-00931 Tel: 7651924/7643670/7643770 Cable Add: UPRED
Dir: Carmelo Delgado-Cintrón; *Subdirector:* Pablo Vincenty; *Chief Editor:* Juan Martínez-Capó; *Publicity:* María Teresa Flórez
Subjects: General Fiction, Belles Lettres, Poetry, History, Art, Philosophy, Reference, Low- & High-priced Paperbacks, Medicine, Psychology, Engineering, General & Social Science, University Textbooks, Educational Materials
Founded: 1932
ISBN Publisher's Prefix: 0-8477

Major Booksellers

Librería **Alma Mater** Inc, 867 Cabrera St, Santa Rita, Río Piedras, PR 00925 Tel: 7646752/7646276
Manager: Elías Cruz

Distribuidora de Libros Inc*, Calle Norte 52, Apdo 1669, Río Piedras

Librería **Escorial***, Recinto Sur 313, San Juan, PR 00901 Tel: 7250972

Librería **Hispanoamericana***, Ave Ponce de León 1013, Apdo 20830, Río Piedras, PR 00928 Tel: 7633415

Librería **Contemporanea***, Ave González 1054, Río Piedras, PR 00925

Librería **Cultural**, Roble 51, Río Piedras, PR 00925 Tel: 7659767

Librería **Cultural Puertorriqueña** Inc*, Ave Fernandez Junco 1406 — Parada 20, Apdo 8863, Santurce, PR 00910

Librería **Universitaria** de Puerto Rico*, Apdo B J Estación UPR, Río Piedras

Librería La **Tertulia**, Amalia Marin esq Ave González, Río Piedras, PR 00925 Tel: 7651148

Librería **Thekes***, Plaza las Américas, San Juan Tel: 7651539

Major Libraries

Agricultural Experiment Station Library*, Box H, Río Piedras

Archivo General de Puerto Rico, Instituto de Cultura Puertorriqueña, Apdo 4184, San Juan 00905 Tel: 7220331/7222113
National Archives of Puerto Rico
Dir: Miguel Angel Nieves

Biblioteca General de Puerto Rico (General Library)*, Instituto de Cultura Puertorriqueña, Apdo 4184, San Juan PR 00905 Tel: 7242680
Dir: Roberto Beascoechea Lota

Caribbean Regional Library, University Station, Apdo 21927, San Juan 00931 Tel: 7640000 ext 3319
Librarian: Ramon Arroyo-Carrión
Publications: Current Caribbean Bibliography

Inter American University of Puerto Rico Library*, San Germán

University of Puerto Rico, General Library, Mayaguez Campus*, Mayaguez

University of Puerto Rico, General Library, Río Piedras Campus, Box C, UPR Station 00931 Tel: (809) 7640000
Dir: Rafael R Delgado
Specialist collections in all fields of knowledge, Book and Newspaper Library on Puerto Rican subjects

University of Puerto Rico, Medical Sciences Campus Library*, Apdo 5067, San Juan 00936

Library Associations

Sociedad de Bibliotecarios de Puerto Rico, Apdo 22898, Universidad de Puerto Rico, Rio Piedras, PR 00931 Tel: 7640000 ext 2211
Society of Librarians of Puerto Rico
President: Carmencita León; *Executive Secretary:* Belsie I C de Pinero
Publications: Boletín, Informa (News Letter), Cuadernos Bibliotecologicos, Cuadernos Bibliograficos

Library Journals

Boletín (Bulletin) (text in English and Spanish), Society of Librarians of Puerto Rico, Apdo 22898, Universidad de Puerto Rico, Río Piedras, PR 00931

Informa (Newsletter), Society of Librarians of Puerto Rico, Apdo 22898, Universidad de Puerto Rico, Rio Piedras, PR 00931

Literary Associations and Societies

Congreso de Poesia de Puerto Rico (Puerto Rican Congress of Poetry)*, c/o Colegio de Agricultura y Artes Mecánicas, Mayaguez
President: Francisco Lluch Mora

P E N Club de Puerto Rico*, Cordero 55 Santurce, San Juan, PR 00911
President: Nilita Vientes Gaston

Literary Periodicals

Asomante, Asociación de Graduadas de la Universidad de Puerto Rico, Apdo 1142, San Juan, PR 00902

Atenea (text in Spanish, English, French and Italian), University of Puerto Rico at Mayaguez, College of Arts and Sciences, Mayaguez, PR 00708

Sin Nombre (Nameless), Sin Nombre Inc, 55 Cordero St, Santurce, Pr 00911

Zona Carga y Descarga (Loading and Unloading Area), Apdo 3871, San Juan, PR 00903

Qatar

General Information

Language: Arabic (English used commercially)
Religion: Wahabi Muslim, officially
Population: 201,000
Bank Hours: 0730-1130 Saturday-Thursday
Shop Hours: 0730-1200, 1430-1800 Saturday-Thursday (some open few hours Friday morning)
Currency: 100 dirhams = 1 Qatar riyal
Export/Import Information: No tariff on books or advertising matter. No import licence; no obscenity permitted

Major Booksellers

Abdulla **Abdulghani** & Sons Co*, PO Box 111, Doha

Codco Est*, PO Box 1990, Doha Tel: 26573/25867

Family Bookshop, PO Box 5769, Doha Tel: 24148

Major Libraries

National Library, PO Box 205, Doha Tel: 22842/321390/321391/321392
Dir: Mohammed Hamad Al-Nassr

Réunion

General Information

Language: French
Religion: Predominantly Roman Catholic
Population: 496,000
Literacy Rate (1967): 62.9%
Business Hours: Generally 0800-1200, 1400-1800
Currency: 100 centimes = 1 Réunion franc
Export/Import Information: No tariff on books and advertising. Books have reduced VAT of 3.5%. No import licence. Nominal exchange control over 1,500 franc value
Copyright: Berne, UCC (see International section)

Major Booksellers

Librairie **Daude***, 97400 St-Denis

Firmin **Pause***, 2 rue Sadi-Carnot, Le Port

Librairie Universitaire de la Réunion*, 13 ave de la Victoire Tel: 210758

Major Libraries

Archives départementales de la Réunion, Le Chaudron 97490 Sainte-Clotilde Tel: 280244

Bibliothèque centrale de Prêt*, pl Joffre, 97400 St-Denis Tel: 210324
Librarian: Yves Drouchet

Bibliothèque départementale*, rue Roland Garros, 97400 St-Denis

Bibliothèque municipale*, rue Rodier, 97410 St-Pierre

Bibliothèque universitaire, Campus universitaire du Chaudron, 97400 Sainte-Clotilde Tel: 281873

Rhodesia

See **Zimbabwe**

Romania

General Information

Language: Romanian, French, German and English
Religion: Romanian Orthodox
Population: 21.9 million
Literacy Rate (1956): 85.8%
Bank Hours: 0900-1200, 1300-1500 Monday-Friday; 0900-1200 Saturday
Shop Hours: 0900-1900 Monday-Friday; early closing Saturday
Currency: 100 bani = 1 leu
Export/Import Information: Book import and export co-ordinated by the Publishing Centre, Piata Scînteii 1, R-71350 Bucharest, 1. The commercial operations are carried out by the Foreign Trade Enterprise ILEXIM, Str 13 Decembrie 3, PO Box 136-137, Bucharest. Import licences required. Exchange controls: terms of payment established in the sales contract made with the Romanian enterprise
Copyright: Berne (see International section)

Book Trade Organizations

Centrala Cartii (Book Centre)*, Str Biserica Amzei 5-7, Bucharest

Centrala Editoriala (Publishing Centre)*, Piata Scînteii 1, R-71341 Bucharest Tel: 183520
The state body which co-ordinates the whole book publishing and selling activity
General Dir: Gheorghe Trandafir

Uniunea Scriitorilor din Republica Socialista România, Calea Victoriei 115, 71102 Bucharest
Writers' Union of the Socialist Republic of Romania
President: George Macovescu
Publications: România Literara, Luceafarul, Viata Românesca, Secolul XX, Steaua, Orizont, Vatra, Convorbiri literare, Utunk, Igaz Szó, Neue Literatur, Knijevni Jivot

Book Trade Reference Journals

Bibliografia Republicii Populare Romîne (Romanian National Bibliography), Central State Library, Str Ion Ghica 4, Bucharest

Carti Noi (New Books), Book Centre, Str Biserica Amzei 5-7, Bucharest

Romanian Books; a quarterly bulletin (text in English or French), Publishing Centre, Foreign Relations Department, Piata Scînteii 1, R-71341 Bucharest

Romanian Books in Foreign Languages, Book Centre, Str Biserica Amzei 5-7, Bucharest

Publishers

Editura **Academiei** Republicii Socialiste România, Calea Victoriei 125, Bucharest R-71021 Tel: 507680 Cable Add: Edacad
Publishing House of the Academy of the Socialist Republic of Romania
Man Dir: C Busuioceanu; *Editorial:* D Trifu; *Production:* F Stoenescu
Orders to: ILEXIM, PO Box 136-137, R-70116 Bucharest (see Major Booksellers)
Subjects: Scientific Works, Monographs, Documents, General Science, Social Science, Mathematics, Technical, Economics, Philology, Physics, Chemistry, Biology, Medicine, Periodicals (67 in Romanian and foreign languages)
1978: 90 titles *1979:* 110 titles *Founded:* 1948

Editura **Albatros**, Piata Scînteii 1, R-71341 Bucharest Tel: 180448
Man Dir: Mircea Sântimbreanu
Subject: Juveniles
1978: 119 titles *1979:* 137 titles *Founded:* 1969

Editura **'Cartea Românesca'** (Publishing House of 'The Romanian Book')*, Str Nuferilor 41, R-70749 Bucharest Tel: 149352
Dir: Marin Preda
Subject: Romanian Contemporary Literature
Founded: 1969

Editura **Ceres***, Piata Scînteii 1, R-71341 Bucharest Tel: 180174
Man Dir: Gabriel Manoliu
Subjects: Agriculture, Veterinary Medicine, Textbooks
Founded: 1953

Editure Ion **Creanga**, Piata Scînteii 1, R-71341 Bucharest Tel: 182525/182566/176010/176020
Man Dir: Tiberiu Utan; *Editor-in-Chief:* Alexandru Georgescu; *Sales, Production, Publicity:* Jenica Panaitescu
Subjects: Poetry, Biography, History, Music, Art, Belles Lettres, Literature, Fiction — all for Juvenile appeal only
1978: 163 titles *Founded:* 1969

Editura **Dacia**, Str 1 Mai 23, R-3400, Cluj-Napoca Tel: (951) 145-48 and 11665
Dir: Alexandru Capraru; *Chief Executive:* Constantin Cublesan; *Production Dir:* Vasile Vancea; *Publicity, Public Relations:* Dana Prelipceanu; *Rights & Permissions:* Aurel Câmpeanu
Subjects: Literature, Art, Science (in Romanian, Hungarian, German, Serbo-Croatian)
1978: 129 titles *1979:* 126 titles *Founded:* 1969

Editura **Didactica si Pedagogica***, Str Spiru Haret 12, R-70738, Sectorul 7, Bucharest Tel: 152455 Telex: 011352
Man Dir: Dr Ion Stanciu; *Editorial:* Roman Mihai; *Sales, Publicity, Rights & Permissions:* Stelian Galos; *Production:* Trifan Onoriu
Subjects: History, Philosophy, Juveniles, Medicine, Psychology, Engineering, General & Social Science, University, Secondary & Primary Textbooks (in various languages), Educational Materials
Founded: 1951

Editura **Eminescu***, Piata Scînteii 1, R-71341 Bucharest Tel: 177380
Man Dir: Valeriu Rîpeanu

Subjects: Romanian Classical & Contemporary Literature, Poetry, History (all in various languages)

Editura **Facla**, J-H Pestalozzi Str 14, R-1900 Timisoara Tel: 36880
Dir: Simion Dima
Subjects: Socio-Political, Poetry, Fiction, Humour, Art and Music, Literary Criticism, Medicine, Scientific; Publications in Romanian, Hungarian, German, Serbo-Croat
1978: 55 titles *Founded:* 1972

Editura **Junimea***, 1 rue Gh Dimitroff, R-6600 Iassy Tel: 17290
Dir: Mircea Radu Iacoban
Subjects: Original and Translated Works in Literary and Technical fields, Literary Theory and Criticism
Founded: 1969

Editura **Kriterion***, Piata Scînteii 1, R-71341 Bucharest Tel: 176010/174060
Dir: Géza Domokos
Subjects: General Fiction, Classical & Contemporary Literature, How-to, Poetry, Music, Art, General Science, Education, Translations
Founded: 1969

Editura **Medicala** (Medical Publishing House), Str Smîrdan 5, R-70006 Bucharest Tel: 142152
Man Dir: Dr Ghoerghe Panaitescu
Subjects: Medical & Pharmaceutical Literature, Textbooks
Founded: 1954
Miscellaneous: Specialize in reviews in Romanian and foreign languages

Editura **Meridiane**, Piata Scînteii 1, R-71341 Bucharest Tel: 181087
Man Dir: George Sorin Movileanu; *Editor-in-Chief:* Modest Morariu
Subjects: Fine Arts, Folk Art, Theatre, Cinema, Architecture, Economic, Social, Political and Cultural Information on Romania
1979: approx 110 titles *Founded:* 1952

Editura **Militara**, Str Izvor 137, R-76111 Bucharest Tel: 310852
Man Dir: Tudor Tamas
Subjects: Belles Lettres, Poetry, Biography, History, Medicine, Psychology, Engineering, Social Science, Military, Fiction
Founded: 1950

Editura **Minerva**, Piata Scînteii 1, 71341 Bucharest Tel: 176010/176020
Subjects: Literary (especially Classical and Foreign), Bilingual Editions, Poetry, Folklore, Various Series
Founded: 1969

Editura **Muzicala***, Str Poiana Narciselor 6 sector 7, R-70732 Bucharest Tel: 164099
Man Dir: Aurel Popa
Subjects: Scores, Musicology
Founded: 1958

Editura **Politica***, Piata Scînteii 1, R-71341 Bucharest Tel: 176010/172987
Man Dir: Valter Roman
Subjects: Biography, History, Philosophy, Reference, Political & Social Science, Economics, International Relations, University Textbooks
1978: 240 titles *Founded:* 1944

Editura **'Scrisul Românesc'** ('Romanian Writing' Publishing House), Str Al I Cuza 7, R-1100 Craiova Tel: 30253
Dir: Ilarie Hinoveanu
Subjects: Social & Political Science, Literature, Technical
Founded: 1972

Editura **Stadion**, Str Vasile Conta 16, R-70139 Bucharest Tel: 121480
Sports and Tourism Publishing House
Editor: Ionel Simion
Subjects: Sports, Travel Guides
Founded: 1950

Editura **Stiintifică si Enciclopedică**, Piata Scînteii 1, R-71341 Bucharest Tel: 175168
Man Dir: Dr Mircea Mâciu; *Production Manager, Sales Dir:* Alexandru Banciu
Subjects: Encyclopaedias, Dictionaries, Reference, Physical & Social Sciences, World Literature, Romanian Language Studies, Philology, Foreign Language Reference, Biography, History, How-to, Music, Art, Philosophy, High- & Low-priced Paperbacks, Medicine, Psychology, Engineering
1978: 135 titles *1979:* 120 titles *Founded:* 1975 (by amalgamation of Romanian Encyclopaedic Publishing House and Scientific Publishing House)

Editura **Tehnica**, Piata Scînteii 1, R-71341 Bucharest Tel: 180630
Man Dir: Mihai Condruc
Subjects: Engineering, General Science, Dictionaries, Reference
1979: 140 titles *Founded:* 1950

Editura **Univers**, Piata Scînteii 1, R-71341 Bucharest Tel: 181762
Man Dir: Professor Dr Romul Munteanu; *Sales Dir:* Emil Idriceanu; *Publicity, Advertising:* N Alexe
Subjects: Translations of Fiction, Poetry, Drama, Biography, Literary Criticism, Low-priced Paperbacks
Founded: 1961

Major Booksellers

I L E X I M — Foreign Trade Enterprise*, Str 13 Decembrie 3, PO Box 136-137, R-70116 Bucharest Tel: 504095 Telex: 226
Carries out all the commercial operations connected with book import and export

Major Libraries

Biblioteca Centrala, **Academia de Studii Economice**, Piata Romana 6, sector 1, R-70167 Bucharest

Biblioteca **Academiei Republicii Socialiste România***, Calea Victoriei 125, Bucharest Tel: 503043

Biblioteca Filialei Cluj a **Academiei Republicii Socialiste România** (The Library of the Cluj Branch of the Academy of the RSR)*, Blvd Lenin 9, Cluj

Archivele Statului (National Archives), Bul Gheorge, Gheorghiu-Dej 29, Bucharest

Biblioteca Centrala de Stat a Republicii Socialiste România (Central State Library)*, Str Ion Ghica 4, R-70018 Bucharest Tel: 161260/507063/140746

Biblioteca Centrala Universitara*, Str Onesti 1, Sectorul 1, Bucharest 1 Tel: 132557

Biblioteca Centrala Universitara*, Str Clinicilor 2, 3400 Cluj-Napoca Tel: 21092

Biblioteca Centrala Universitara 'Mihail Eminescu'*, Str Pacurari 4, Jassy Tel: 40709

Biblioteca Judeteana Mures*, Str Enescu 2, Tîrgu-Mures

Biblioteca Judeteana Timis*, Piata Libertatii 3, Timisoara

Biblioteca **Facultatii** de Medicina din Bucuresti, renamed Institutul de medicina si farmacie din Bucuresti (qv)

Biblioteca Institutului Politehnic **'Gheorge Gheorghiu-Dej'** Bucuresti, Calea Grivitei 132, Bucharest

I N I D, see Institutul National de Informare si Documentare

Institutul National de **Informare si Documentare** (INID), Str Cosmonautilor 27-29, 70141 Bucharest 1 Tel: 134010 Telex: 11247
National Institute for Information and Documentation
Dir: eng Gheorghe Anghel
Publications: Reviste de sumare ale periodicelor intrate in biblioteca INID (Current Contents Reviews of Periodicals in INID Library); *Abstracts of Romanian Scientific and Technical Literature* (in English, French, Russian and Romanian); *Information and Documentation Problems* (in English and Romanian)

Institutul de **medicina si farmacie** din Bucuresti Biblioteca Centrala, Blvd Dr Petru Grosza no 8, Sector 5, R-76241 Bucharest
Central Library of the Institute of Medicine and Pharmacy (formerly Biblioteca Facultati de Medicina)
Dir: Silvica Petre

Oficiul de Informare Documentara in Stiintele Sociale si Politice (Office of Information and Documentation in Social and Political Sciences)*, Str Mihail Moxa 3-5, Bucharest
Dir: M Ioanid
Publication: Romanian Scientific Abstracts (2 a year)

Biblioteca Municipala **'Mihail Sadoveanu'***, Str Nikos Beloiannis 4, Bucharest

University Libraries, see Biblioteca

Library Associations

Asociatia Bibliotecarilor din RSR (Librarians' Association of Romania)*, Biblioteca Centrala de Stat, Str Ion Ghica 4, 70018 Bucharest Tel: 503765
Executive Secretary: St Gruia
Publication: Revista Bibliotecilor (Library Review) (monthly)

Library Reference Books and Journals

Books

Ghidul Bibliotecilor din România (Guide to Libraries in Romania), Editura Enciclopedica Româna, Calea Victoriei 126, Bucharest

Journals

Buletinul de Informare în Bibliologie (Librarianship Information Bulletin), Central State Library, Str Ion Ghica 4, Bucharest

Fise Signaletice ale Articolelor din Domeniul Bibliologiei (Indicative Cards for Articles in the Field of Librarianship), Central State Library, Str Ion Ghica 4, Bucharest

Information and Documentation Problems (text in English and Romanian), National Institute for Information and Documentation, Str Cosmonautilor 27-29, Bucharest 1

Revista Bibliotecilor (Library Review), Librarians' Association of Romania, Biblioteca Centrala de Stat, Str Ion Ghica 4, 70018 Bucharest

Revista de Referate in Bibliologie (Librarianship Abstracts Review), Central State Library, Str Ion Ghica 4, Bucharest

Revista de Titluri: Informare Documentare (Review of Titles: Information and Documentation), National Institute for Information and Documentation, Str Cosmonautilor 27-29, Bucharest 1

Literary Associations and Societies

Institutul de Istorie si Teorie Literara 'George **Calinescu**'*, Bul Republicii 73, Bucharest
Dir: Professor Dr Zoe Dumitrescu-Busulenga
Publication: Revista de Istorie si Teorie Literara (quarterly)

Centrul de Lingvistica Istorie Literara si Folclor*, Aleea Mihail Sadoveanu 12, Jassy
Dir: A Teodorescu
Publication: Anuar de Linguisticasi Istorie Literará

Comitetul National pentru Literatura Comparata (National Committee for Comparative Literature)*, Str Onesti 2, Bucharest
Secretary: Dr Alexandru Dutu
Publication: Synthesis (annual)

P E N Club, Casa Scriitorilor Mihail Sadoveanu, Calea Victoriei 115, Bucharest
Vice-Presidents: Eugen Jebeleanu, Horia Lovinescu; *Secretary:* Geo Dumitrescu

Literary Periodicals

Cahiers roumains d'Etudes Littéraires (Romanian Literary Studies) (text in French and English, occasionally German, Russian, Spanish, Italian), Editura Univers, Piata Scînteii 1, R-71341 Bucharest

Convorbiri Literare (Literary Conversations), Writers' Union of the Socialist Republic of Romania (Jassy branch), Palatul Culturii, Jassy

Manuscriptum (Manuscripts), Muzeul Literaturii Romane, Central State Library, Str Ion Ghica 4, Bucharest

Orizont (Horizon), Writers' Union of the Socialist Republic of Romania (Timisoara branch), Pta Vasile Roaita 3, Timisoara

Revista de Istorie si Teorie Literara (Review of Literary History and Theory) (summaries in French and Russian), Publishing House of the Academy of the Socialist Republic of Romania, Str Gutenberg 3 bis, Bucharest

Romania Literara (Literary Romania), Writers' Union of the Socialist Republic of Romania, Sos Kiseleff 10, Bucharest

Romanian Review (texts in English, French, German and Russian), Foreign Languages Press, Str Ion Ghica 5, Bucharest

Secolul XX (Twentieth Century) Writers' Union of the Socialist Republic of Romania, Sos Kiseleff 10, Bucharest

Steaua (The Star), Writers' Union of the Socialist Republic of Romania, Sos Kiseleff 10, Bucharest

Viata Romineasca (Romanian Life) Writers' Union of the Socialist Republic of Romania, Sos Kiseleff 10, Bucharest

Literary Prizes

Literary Award*
For literary works reflecting humanistic and democratic ideals. Awarded annually. Enquiries to Romanian Union of Communist Youth, Bucharest

Writers' Union Prize
For an outstanding contribution to Romanian literature in poetry, prose, drama, literary criticism, history of literature, literary reportage, literature for children and youth, translations from world literature, and for a promising new literary work by a young writer. Awarded annually. Enquiries to Writers' Union of the Socialist Republic of Romania, Calea Victoriei 115, Bucharest. (Separate prizes are awarded by Bucharest, Cluj, Jassy, Timisoara, Craiova, Sibiu, Brasov and Tirgu-Mures Writers' Associations. Awarded annually. For further information contact the appropriate Associations of the Writers' Union of the Socialist Republic of Romania)

Rwanda

General Information

Language: Kinyarwanda (a Bantu tongue) and French
Religion: About half of population follow traditional beliefs, most of the rest are Roman Catholic, some Muslim
Population: 4.5 million
Bank Hours: 0830-1130 Monday-Friday for cash transactions; other business 1400-1700 Monday-Friday
Shop Hours: Dawn to dusk
Currency: Rwanda franc
Export/Import Information: No tariff on books and advertising, but Statistical Tax of 3%. Import licence, for statistical purposes, and Foreign Exchange Licence required. Application to National Bank, through authorized bank

Publishers

Government Printer (Imprimerie de Kabgayi)*, BP 9, Gitarama

Government Printer (Imprimerie National du Rwanda)*, BP 114, Kigali

Editions **Rwandaises***, Caritas Rwanda, BP 124, Kigali Tel: 5786
Man Dir: Abbé Cyriaque Munyansanga;
Editorial: Albert Nambaje
Subsidiary Company: Caritas Rwanda (at above address)
Subjects: Religion, Kinyarwanda language, General, Educational, Children's Paperbacks
Bookshop: address as above

Major Booksellers

Librairie **Caritas**, BP 1078, Kigali Tel: 6503

Somec-Rwanda*, BP 628, Kigali Tel: 5378/5497

Major Libraries

Ecole Technique officielle **Don Bosco** Bibliothèque*, BP 80, Kigali
There are Don Bosco Publishers/Bookshops in Bolivia, Spain and Federal Republic of Germany (qqv)

Bibliothèque de l'**Université Nationale du Rwanda***, BP 54, Butare Tel: 3071
Librarian: Emmanuel Serugendo

Saudi Arabia

General Information

Language: Arabic (English widely understood)
Religion: Muslim (officially)
Population: 7.9 million
Bank Hours: 0830-1200 Saturday-Thursday. Varies during month of Ramadan
Shop Hours: Vary greatly. Generally (except during Ramadan): Jedda: 0900-1330, 1630-2000. Riyadh: 0830-1200, 1630-1930. Eastern Province: 0730-1200, 1430-1700 Saturday-Thursday
Currency: 5 halala = 1 qursh; 20 qursh = 1 Saudi riyal
Export/Import Information: No tariffs on books; advertising matter subject to 3% ad valorem but if total duty on one consignment is less than 50 riyals, matter can enter free. Catalogues distributed gratis, usually admitted free. All printed matter except textbooks subject to censorship. No import licences required
Copyright: No copyright conventions signed

Publishers

Al **Jazirah** Organization for Press, Printing, Publishing*, Ap 88, Municipality Bldg, Safat, PO Box 354, Riyadh
Dir-Gen: Saleh Al-Ajroush; *Editor-in-Chief:* Khalid el Malek
Subject: Politics, Law
Founded: 1964

Saudi Publishing and Distributing House*, Al-Jauhara Bldg, Flats 7 and 12, PO Box 2043, Baghdadia
Man Dir: Muhammed Salahuddin; *General Manager:* Adnan K Salah
Subjects: Arabic and English publications

Major Booksellers

Al-**Adab** Bookshop*, Riyadh Tel: 27865

Dabbous Stores*, King St, Jeddah

Abdullah **Dawood***, El-Jilani, El-Ashaf Bldg, King St, Jeddah

Dar al-**Ilm** Bookshop*, Riyadh Tel: 29947

Mohamed Noor Salah **Jamjoom & Bros***, PO Box 12, Jeddah

Al-**Maktaba***, King St, Jeddah

Riyadh Modern Bookshop*, Riyadh Tel: 27993

Al-**Sha'b** Bookshop*, Riyadh Tel: 22635

Ali **Wahbah** Bookshop*, Riyadh Tel: 67654

Major Libraries

Educational Library*, General Directorate of Broadcasting, Press and Publications, Jeddah

Institute of Public Administration Library, PO Box 205, Riyadh Tel: 61600 Cable Add: Ipadmin Telex: 201160 SJ

Islamic University Library*, Medina Munawarah

King Abdulaziz University Library, Deanship of Library Affairs, King Abdulaziz University, PO Box 3711, Jeddah Tel: 79033/79130/79202 (extensions 1170-76) Telex: 40141 Azizuni SJ
A Central Library with 8 branches in various faculties
Dean: Dr Abbas S Tashkandy
Publications: Annual Index of Ummu'l-Qura; Catalogue of MSS in the Central Library

Dar al **Kutub** al-Wataniya*, King Faisal St, Riyadh

National Library*, King Faisal St, Riyadh
Publication: Bulletin

Saudi Library*, Riyadh

University Libraries*, University of Riyadh, PO Box 2454, Riyadh Tel: 21722
Dean: Dr A M Al-Dhubaib
Publications: Riyadh University Periodicals (Bulletins published by the Arts, Science, Agricultural Research and Education Depts; Journals of the Agricultural College, Engineering Science and Commerce Depts); Abstracts of and Indexes to Riyadh University Periodicals; Abstracts and Proceedings of Conferences held by or in collaboration with Riyadh University; Manuals, Textbooks, Directories and other Reference Works connected with Riyadh University; Information Bulletin; Union Lists; Accession List; Bibliographies; Riyadh University Council Resolution Indexes

Library Journals

Bulletin, National Library, King Faisal St, Riyadh

Senegal

General Information

Language: French
Religion: About 80% Muslim, 10% Christian (mostly Roman Catholic)
Population: 5 million
Literacy Rate (1961): 5.2%
Bank Hours: Generally 0800-1115, 1430-1630 Monday-Saturday
Shop Hours: Vary, and some open Sunday morning, some close Monday morning. Generally are 0800-1200, 1430-1800 Monday-Saturday
Currency: CFA franc
Export/Import Information: Member of West African Economic Community. No tariff on books except atlases. Added taxes apply to atlases. Advertising matter (more than one copy) subject to 10% fiscal and 5% customs duty plus added taxes of 4% + 22% + 13.5%. Import licences and exchange controls apply for imports from outside EEC, Franc Zone, USA and Canada

Copyright: Berne, UCC (see International section)

Book Trade Journals

Bibliographie du Sénégal, Archives du Sénégal, Immeuble administratif, ave Roume, Dakar

Publishers

Africa Editions*, 12 rue Bourgi Dr Theze, BP 1926, Dakar Tel: 22222
Man Dir: Joel Decuper
Subjects: General Literature, Reference Works, Annuals, Telephone Directory, Periodicals
Founded: 1958

Edition **Afrique-Levant***, 50 rue de Grammont, Dakar Tel: 36372
Man Dir: Mroueh Brahum
Subjects: General, Religion, Islam
Founded: 1974

Agence de Distribution de Presse*, BP 374, Dakar Tel: 23522
Man Dir: Michel Bedoux
Subjects: General, Reference
Miscellaneous: Affiliated to Librairie Hachette, Paris

Centre Sénégalaise d'Editions et de Diffusion*, 31 rue Wagane Diouf, BP 1745, Dakar Tel: 26994
Man Dir: Jacques Coudon Jaefus
Subjects: General Fiction, Law, Medicine, Paperbacks, Secondary Textbooks
Founded: 1974

Government Printer (Imprimerie du Gouvernement)*, rue Fisque, BP 1, Dakar

Les **Nouvelles Editions** Africaines, 10 rue A Assane Ndoye, BP 260, Dakar Tel: 211381, 221580
General Manager: Mamadou Seck; *Editorial:* Roger Dorsinville; *Commercial Manager:* Ojibril Faye; *Publicity:* Jacques de Longeville; *Production:* Sathewar Diop
Subsidiary Companies: NEA, ave Noguès, 01 BP 3525 01 Abidjan, Ivory Coast; NEA, BP 4862, Lomé, Togo
Subjects: General Fiction & Non-fiction, Belles Lettres, Poetry, Biography, History, Africana, Philosophy, Religion, Juveniles, Paperbacks, Psychology, General & Social Science, University & Secondary Textbooks
Founded: 1972

Société Africaine d'Edition, 16 bis rue de Thiong, BP 1877, Dakar Tel: 217977, 220284
Man Dir: Pierre Biarnes
Branch Off: 32 rue de l'Echiquier F-75010 Paris, France Tel: 5230233
Subjects: African Political and Economic mainly
1978: 20 titles *Founded:* 1961

Société d'Edition d'Afrique Nouvelle, 9 rue Paul Holle, BP 283, Dakar Tel: 223825
Man Dir: Paul Fondeur; *Senior Editor/Rights & Permissions:* Alcino Louis da Costa
Subjects: Information, statistics and analyses of African affairs, Religion, Magazines

Editions des **Trois Fleuves**, 57 ave du Pdt Lamine Gueye, BP 123, Dakar Tel: 222077
Man Dir: Roland de Boistel, Bertrand de Boistel
Subjects: General Nonfiction, Luxury Editions
Founded: 1972

Major Booksellers

Afrique-Levant*, 60 rue de Grammont, Dakar Tel: 36372

Agence de Distribution de Presse*, 4 rue Carnot, BP 374, Dakar

Librairie afrique*, 58 ave William Ponty, BP 1240, Dakar Tel: 23618

Librairie clairafrique*, pl de l'Indépendance, BP 2005, Dakar

Librairie nouvelle de l'Ouest Africain (LINOA)*, Bldg Maginot, 43 ave Maginot, BP 2039, Dakar Tel: 26450

Librairie universitaire et technique*, BP 396, Dakar

La **Maison** du Livre*, 13 ave Roume, BP 2060, Dakar

Mamadou Traoré Ray Autra*, BP 2380, Dakar

Librairie du **Point d'Interrogation***, BP 437, Dakar

Librairie **Sankore***, 25 ave William Ponty, BP 7040, Dakar Tel: 22105

Major Libraries

L'Alliance française*, Bibliothèque, 10 rue Colbert, BP 1777, Dakar Tel: 20105

Archives de Sénégal, Immeuble administratif, ave Roume, Dakar Tel: 215072
National Archives of Senegal
Dir: Saliou Mbaye
Publication: Bibliographie du Sénégal

Centre culturel américain, Bibliothèque, pl de l'Indépendance, BP 49, Dakar Tel: 225928/220124

Centre culturel français, Bibliothèque, 96 rue Blanchot, BP 4003, Dakar Tel: 211821/216427

Centre de Recherches et de Documentation du Sénégal (CRDS)*, rue Neuville, Pointe Sud, BP 382, St-Louis Tel: 71050
Dir: Mohamed Fadel DIA

Lycée technique Maurice **Delafosse***, Bibliothèque, BP 4004, Dakar Tel: 33897

Lycée Blaise **Diagne***, Bibliothèque, Canal IV, BP 12003, Dakar-Colobane Tel: 33535

Lycée de Jeunes Filles Ameth **Fall***, Bibliothèque, BP 1, St-Louis Tel: 71000

I D E P, see Institut Africain

Institut africain de Développement Économique et de Planification (IDEP), Bibliothèque, rue de 18 Juin, BP 3186, Dakar Tel: 214831 Telex: 579 Dakar

Institut fondamental d'Afrique noire*, Bibliothèque, Université de Dakar, BP 206, Dakar-Fann Tel: 34002

Université de Dakar, Bibliothèque*, BP 2006, Dakar-Fann Tel: 32918/19/20

Library Associations

A N B A D S*, see Association nationale des Bibliothécaires, Archivistes et Documentalistes sénégalais

Association nationale des Bibliothécaires, Archivistes et Documentalistes sénégalais*, Ecole de Bibliothécaires, Archivistes et Documentalistes de Dakar (EBAD), PO Box 3252, Dakar Tel: 24039
Executive Secretary: Theodore Ndiaye

Commission des Bibliothèques de l'ASDBAM (Association Senegalaise pour le Développement de la Documentation, des Bibliothèques, des Archives et des Musées)*, BP 375, Dakar Tel: 34139
Commission of the Libraries of the Senegal Association for the Development of Documentation, Libraries, Archives and Museums

Library Reference Books

Répertoire des Bibliothèques et Organismes de Documentation au Sénégal (Catalogue of the Libraries and Documentation Centres of Senegal), Ecole de Bibliothécaires, Archivistes, et Documentalistes, BP 3252, Dakar-Fann (Information on 124 libraries, archives and documentation centres throughout Senegal)

Literary Associations and Societies

Senegal **P E N** Centre*, Presidential Residence, Dakar
President: HE Leopold Senghor

Seychelles

General Information

Language: English and French
Religion: Roman Catholic
Population: 62,000
Literacy Rate (1971): 57.7%
Currency: 100 cents = 1 Seychelles rupee
Export/Import Information: No tariffs on books and advertising. Books on Open General Licence

Major Booksellers

Chez Nanon*, Royal St, Victoria

Newservice Ltd*, Seychelles News Service, PO Box 131, Kingsgate House, Mahe Tel: 22309 Cable Add: Legal Seychelles
Man Dir: Paul B Chow

Sierra Leone

General Information

Language: English
Religion: Majority follow traditional beliefs; significant numbers of Muslims and Christians
Population: 3.47 million
Literacy Rate (1963): 6.7%
Bank Hours: 0800-1300 Monday-Friday; 0800-1100 Saturday
Shop Hours: 0800-1200 or 1230, 1400-1630 or 1700 Monday-Friday; 0800-1230 Saturday
Currency: 100 cents = 1 leone
Export/Import Information: No tariff on books except children's picture books 40%. Advertising matter 40%. Open general licence. Exchange controls

Book Trade Reference Journal

Sierra Leone Publications, Sierra Leone Library Board, PO Box 326, Freetown (the national bibliography, published annually since 1962)

Publishers

Government Printer, Government Printing Department, New England, Freetown

Njala University Publishing Centre*, Njala University, PMB, Freetown
Subjects: Science & Technology, University Textbooks
Miscellaneous: UNESCO sponsored

Sierra Leone University Press, Fourah Bay College, PO Box 87, Freetown Tel: 27300/23494/27399/27323 Cable Add: Fourahbay
Chairman, Honorary Editor: Professor Eldred Jones; *Honorary Secretary, Rights & Permissions:* Dr W S Marcus Jones
Subjects: General Nonfiction, History, Africana, Religion, Social Science, University Textbooks
1979: 2 titles *Founded:* 1968

United Christian Council Literature Bureau*, Bunumbu Press, Bo
Subjects: Books in Mende, Temne, Susu

Major Booksellers

Fourah Bay College Bookshop Ltd*, University of Sierra Leone, Freetown Tel: 27351/25307

Njala University College Bookshop, PMB, Freetown Tel: Njala exchange: ext 26, 71
Manager: Prof D R G Gwynne-Jones

The **Sierra Leone** Diocesan Bookshops Ltd, PO Box 104, Freetown Tel: 22302 Cable Add: Bookshop Freetown

Major Libraries

Public **Archives** of Sierra Leone*, c/o Fourah Bay College Library, PO Box 87, Freetown

British Council Library*, PO Box 124, Freetown Tel: 22223

Fourah Bay College Library, University of Sierra Leone, Freetown Tel: 27337
Librarian: Gladys M Jusu-Sheriff
Publications include: Annual Report; List of New Accessions to the Sierra Leone Collection; Printed Catalogue of the Sierra Leone Collection; Report on Visit to Francophone University Libraries in West Africa

International Communication Agency Library*, American Embassy, Walpole St, Freetown

Milton **Margai** Teachers' College Library, Goderich, PMB, Freetown Tel: 024305

Njala University College Library (University of Sierra Leone), Private Mail Bag, Freetown Tel: 00412
Librarian: Mrs M O Akinsulure
Publications: Library Bulletin; Annual Report; Occasional papers

Sierra Leone Library Board*, PO Box 326, Freetown Tel: 23848
Acting Chief Librarian: Mrs G E Dillsworth
Publications: Annual Report; *Sierra Leone Publications* (annual)

University of Sierra Leone, see Njala

Library Associations

Sierra Leone Library Association*, c/o Sierra Leone Library Board, PO Box 326, Freetown Tel: 23848
Secretary: Ms M A Roberts
Publications: Sierra Leone Library Journal (biannual), *Directory of Libraries and Information Services*

Library Reference Books and Journals

Books

Directory of Libraries and Information Services, Sierra Leone Library Association, c/o The Secretary, High Court Library, Siaka Stevens St, Freetown

Journals

Sierra Leone Library Journal, Sierra Leone Library Association, c/o The Secretary, High Court Library, Siaka Stevens St, Freetown

Republic of Singapore

General Information

Language: English
Religion: All major religions, especially Confucianism, Muslim, Buddhism, Taoism
Population: 2.3 million
Literacy rate (1970): 68.9%
Bank Hours: 1000-1500 Monday-Friday; 0930-1130 Saturday
Shop Hours: 0900-1800 Monday-Saturday
Currency: 100 cents = 1 Singapore dollar
Export/Import Information: No tariffs on books and advertising. Import licences; no seditious publications permitted. Nominal exchange control
Copyright: Florence (see International section)

Book Trade Organizations

Book Publishers' Association*, M/S Eastern Universities Press Sdn Bhd, 112F, Block 5, 6th Floor Boon Keng Rd, Singapore 12 Tel: 2582077
Secretary-General: C Nair

National Book Development Council of Singapore*, c/o National Library, Stamford Rd, Singapore 0617
Publication: Singapore Book World

Singapore Booksellers' Association*, 428-429 Katong Shopping Centre, Singapore 15 Tel: 401495
President: N T S Chopra

Singapore Chinese Booksellers' Association*, 19b Carpenter St, Singapore 1

Standard Book Numbering Agency, National Library, Stamford Rd, Singapore 0617
ISBN Administrator: Mrs Kee Yew Siew

Book Trade Reference Books and Journals

Books

Books in Singapore; a survey of publishing, printing, bookselling and library activity in the Republic of Singapore, Chopmen Enterprises, 428-429 Katong Shopping Centre (4th Floor), Singapore 15

Singapore Periodicals Index; published biennially by the National Library, Stamford Rd, Singapore 0617

Journals

The Memoranda of Books Registered in the 'Catalogue of Books Printed at Singapore under the Provisions of the Printer's and Publisher's Ordinance', National Library, Stamford Rd, Singapore 6

Singapore Book World, National Book Development Council of Singapore, c/o National Library, Stamford Rd, Singapore 6

Singapore National Bibliography (SNB), National Library, Stamford Rd, Singapore 6

Publishers

Addison-Wesley Singapore (Pte) Ltd, Room 456 4th Floor, Peoples Park Centre, 101 Upper Cross St, Singapore 1 Cable Add: Adiwes Singapore
Manager: Benjamin Kong Tan Ho
Associate Company: Addison-Wesley Publishers Ltd, UK (qv)

Angus & Robertson (South-East Asia) Ltd, 159 Boon Keng Rd, Block 2, Ground Floor, Singapore 12 Tel: 2582663/2582889 Cable Add: Austbook Singapore Telex: RS 24297
Man Dir, Editorial, Rights & Permissions: Richard Walsh; *Sales:* Patrick Tan; *Publicity:* Bessie Tay, Ng Kheng Chuan
Parent Company: Angus & Robertson Publishers, Australia (qv)
Associate Company: Angus & Robertson (UK) Ltd, UK (qv)
Branch Offs: Angus & Robertson (Publishers) Pty Ltd, Philippines; PO Box 1072, MCC Makati, Metro Manila, Philippines (Miss M Mariano)
Subjects: Educational, Business Management, Academic, Library Science, General, Medical, Children's Books
Founded: 1968

Apa Productions (Pte) Ltd, 349 Pasir Panjang Rd, Singapore 0511 Tel: 7767606/7767006 Cable Add: Apaproduct Telex: rs 23660 delite
Publisher: Hans Hoefer; *Marketing Dir, Rights & Permissions:* Leo Haks; *Production:* Raymond Boey; *Publicity:* Qirone Haddock
Associate Companies: Apa Productions (HK) Ltd, 1505 Prince's Bldg, Hong Kong; Apa Productions Hawaii Inc, 339 Saratoga Rd, Suite 21, Honolulu, Hawaii 96815
Subjects: Travel Guides, Culture, History, Religion, Photography
1980: 2 titles *Founded:* 1971
ISBN Publisher's Prefix: 941

Graham **Brash** Pte Ltd, see Literary Agents

Chopmen Enterprises, 428-429 Katong Shopping Centre (4th Floor), Singapore 1543 Tel: 3441495 Cable Add: Nirmalji Singapore
Man Dir: N T S Chopra
Subjects: Reference, Social & General Science, Fiction, General, Religion, Poetry, Asiatic Studies, University & Secondary Textbooks, Paperbacks, Educational Materials
1979: 15 titles *Founded:* 1966
ISBN Publisher's Prefix: 9971-68

Eastern Universities Press Sdn Bhd, 112F, Block 5, Boon Keng Rd, PO Box 1742, Singapore 12 Tel: 2582077 Cable Add: Eastup
Man Dir: Goh Kee Seah; *Editorial:* Anne Marie Nalpon; *Production, Rights & Permissions:* Violet Phoon
Orders to: United Publishers Services Pte Ltd, 112-F Boon Keng Rd, Block 5, 6th Floor, Singapore 12
Subsidiary Company: Eastern Universities Press (Malaysia) Sdn Bhd (qv)
Subjects: Biography, History, English Language, Cookery, Juvenile Fiction, Economics; Primary, Secondary and University Textbooks
1978: 54 titles *1979:* 90 titles *Founded:* 1958

F E P International Private Ltd*, Jalan Boon Lay, Jurong, Singapore 22 Cable Add: bookmark Telex: rs 2560
Man Dir: David Chew; *Executive Dir:* Cho Jock Min
Br Offs: Accra, Hong Kong, Karachi, Kingston, Lagos, London, Manila, Maseru, Mbabana, Nairobi, Petaling Jaya, Port-of-Spain, Singapore, Sydney

Federal Publications (S) Pte Ltd, No 1 New Industrial Road, Singapore 1953 Tel: 2848844 Cable Add: Fedpubs, Singapore Telex: RS 25713
General Manager: H H Chiam; *Sales Manager:* L H Teo *Publishing Manager:* Y H Mew
Parent Company: Times Publishing Berhad, 1 New Industrial Rd, Singapore 1953
Associate Companies: Federal Publications (HK) Ltd, Unit D, 2nd Floor, Freder Centre, 68 Sung Wong Toi Rd, Tokwawan, Kowloon; Federal Publications Sdn Bhd, 8238 Jalan 222, Petaling Jaya, Selangor; Times Periodicals Pte Ltd, 422 Thomson Rd, Singapore 1129; The Straits Times Press (1975) Ltd, 390 Kim Seng Rd, Singapore 0923
Subjects: Secondary and Primary Textbooks, Teaching and Study Aids, Reference Works, Juvenile Story Books; also *Asia Pacific* series (socio-political on SE Asia), *Tangent* series (popular knowledge about current topics)
1978: 74 titles *1979:* 70 titles *Founded:* 1957

Institute of Southeast Asian Studies, Heng Mui Keng Terrace, Pasir Panjang, Singapore 0511 Tel: 7758111 Cable Add: ISEAS
Man Dir: Kernial S Sandhu; *Editorial, Sales, Production, Publicity, Rights & Permissions:* Christine Tan; *Librarian:* Mrs Lim Pui Huen
Subjects: Modernization in Southeast Asia, Social and Political Change
1979: 12 titles *1980:* 5 titles *Founded:* 1968

Longman Malaysia Sdn Bhd*, 25 First Lokyang Rd, Jurong Town, Singapore 2262 Tel: 2682666
Man Dir: James B Ho
Associate Company: Longman Group Ltd, UK (qv)
Subjects: Textbooks, Medical, Science and Technology
1977: 73 titles *1978:* 14 titles

McGraw-Hill International Book Co, 348 Jalan Boon Lay, Jurong, Singapore 2261 Tel: 654633/654156 Cable Add: McGrawbook Singapore
Man Dir: Harry B Engelander; *Marketing Manager, Asia:* R Radhakrishnan
Parent Company: McGraw-Hill Inc, New York, USA
Subject: Educational Materials
Founded: 1969

Macmillan Southeast Asia Pte Ltd, 41 Jalan Pemimpin, Singapore 2057 Tel: 2521337 Cable Add: Publish Singapore Telex: RS 23196
Executive Dir: Loh Mun Wai
Parent Company: Macmillan Publishers Ltd, UK (qv)

Malayan Law Journal (Pte) Ltd, 1302-1305 (13th Floor), Shenton Ho, 3 Shenton Way, Singapore 0106 Tel: 2203684 Cable Add: Malool
Man Dir, Editorial, Production, Rights & Permissions: Al-Mansor Adabi; *Sales, Publicity:* Amir Mallal
Branch Off: 4th Floor Bangunan Ming, Jalan Bukit Nanas, Kuala Lumpur 04-01, Malaysia (Tel: (03) 21219)
Subjects: Law, Accountancy, Tax
Bookshops: 1302-1305 (13th Floor) Shenton Ho, Shenton Way, Singapore 0106; 4th Floor Bangunan Ming, Jalan Bukit Nanas, Kuala Lumpur 04-01, Malaysia
1978: 8 titles *1979:* 8 titles *Founded:* 1932

Malaysia Press Sdn Bhd, 745-747 North Bridge Rd, Singapore 0719 Tel: 2933454
Man Dir: Omar Bin Ally; *Sales Dir:* Abu Talib Bin Ally; *Publicity and Advertising:* Abdullah Bin Ally
Subsidiary Company: Pustaka Melayu, 745-747 North Bridge Rd, Singapore 0719
Subjects: School Textbooks, Educational Books etc, in the Malay language
Founded: 1950

Maruzen Asia (Pte) Ltd*, 6th Floor, Block 7, Ayer Rajah Industrial Estate, Singapore 0513 Tel: 7759844-6 Telex: Mapore RS26521 Cable Add: Maruzen Singapore
Man Dir: Minoru Taguchi
Associate Company: Maruzen Co Ltd, Japan (qv)
Subjects: Technical, Social and Medical Sciences
1978: 5 titles *Founded:* 1978

Medical World Book Co Pte Ltd*, Newton PO Box 96, Singapore 11
Man Dir: Andrew Lee
Associate Company: University Education Press, Singapore (qv)
Subjects: Medical, Scientific and Technical books

Pustaka **Nasional** Pte Ltd, Suite 1211, Shaw Towers Beach Rd, Singapore 0718 Tel: 2941917/8
Subjects: Malay books
Bookshop: 40 Kandahar St (also Distributors)

Oxford University Press, Unit 4-2 Block A, 4th Floor, Tong Lee Bldg, 35 Kallang Pudding Rd, Singapore 13
Tel: 2840566/2840567 Cable Add: Oxonian Singapore
Regional Manager: J A Nicholson
Subjects: Education, History, Low- and High-priced Paperbacks, General and Social Sciences, Secondary Textbooks, Educational Materials
Miscellaneous: Firm is a branch of Oxford University Press, UK (qv)

P G Medical Books, 441 Tanglin Shopping Centre, 19 Tanglin Rd, Singapore 10 Tel: 2350006
Man Dir: Chan Poh Geok; *Editorial:* A S M Lim
Parent Company: P G Lim (Pte) Ltd
Subsidiary Company: P G Books (Pte) Ltd
Branch Off: 227 Tanglin Shopping Centre, 19 Tanglin Rd, Singapore 10
Subject: Medical
1978: 1 title *1979:* 1 title *Founded:* 1974

Pan Pacific Book Distributors (S) Pte Ltd, 597 Havelock Rd (Teck Huat Chambers), Singapore 0316 Tel: 436411/981526 Cable Add: Pacolmac Telex: RS 25210
Man Dir: Seow Kui Lim; *Publishing Manager:* Loh Peng Yim
Editorial Off: Rooms 1011 & 1013, 10th Floor, Manhattan Ho, 151 Chin Swee Rd, Singapore 0316 Tel: 915530/431961
Subjects: Secondary and Primary Textbooks, Reference, General Literature
Bookshop: Pacific Book Centre, 597 Havelock Rd (Teck Huat Chambers), Singapore 0316
1978: 65 titles *1979:* 80 titles *Founded:* 1971

Prentice-Hall of Southeast Asia Pte Ltd, 4, 4B, Block 1, Ayer Rajah Industrial Estate, Singapore 0513 Tel: 7759085 Cable Add: Prenhall Singapore
General Manager: K C Ang
Parent Company: Prentice-Hall International Inc, Englewood Cliffs, NJ 07632, USA
Associate Companies: See Prentice-Hall, UK
Subjects: Belles Lettres, Poetry, History, How-to, Music, Art, Philosophy, Reference, Religion, Medicine, Psychology, Engineering, Computer Textbooks, General and Social Science, University Textbooks, Educational and Audio-Visual Materials

Singapore University Press Pte Ltd, University of Singapore, Kent Ridge, Singapore 0511 Tel: 7761148/775666 ext 323 Cable Add: Singpress
Manager, Editor: Marian Pan
Subjects: Scholarly studies relating to all aspects of life in SE Asia and/or Singapore; Sociology, Law, the Arts and Sciences, Medicine, Politics, Pedagogy, Bibliographies; *Journals: Journal of SE Asian Studies, SE Asia Ethnicity & Development Newsletter, Contemporary SE Asia*
Founded: 1971

Southeast Asian Ministers of Education Organization (SEAMEO)*, Regional Language Centre (RELC), 30 Orange Grove Rd, Singapore 1025 Tel: 7379044 Cable Add: Relcentre
Subjects: Language Teaching and Research, Linguistics, English for Special Purposes
1979: 27 titles *Founded:* 1968

Stamford College Publishers, 218 Queen St, Singapore 0718 Tel: 3373144/8
Man Dir, Publicity: L P Nicol; *Editorial:* L Thomas; *Sales:* J Dennis; *Production:* Mr Arangasamy
Branch Off: Stamford Executive Bookshop, Petaling Jaya, Malaysia
Subjects: Educational Books
Bookshop: 218 Queen St, Singapore 0718
1978: 9 titles *1979:* 11 titles *Founded:* 1970

Toppan Co (Singapore) Private Ltd, PO Box 22, Jurong Town Post Office, Singapore 2262 (Located at: 38 Liu Fang Rd, Jurong, Singapore 2262) Tel: 656666/656105 Cable Add: Toppan Singapore Telex: RS 21596
Man Dir: Naomi Yoshikawa; *General Manager:* Chu Bong; *Production:* Y Yamamoto
Parent Company: Toppan Co Ltd, Japan (qv)
Associate Company: Froebel-Kan Ltd, Tokyo, Japan

Subjects: Agriculture, Biochemistry, Biology, Botany, Chemistry, Civil, Electrical and Industrial Engineering, Earth Sciences, Economics, Mathematics, Mechanics, Medicine, Physiology, Physics, Statistics, Zoology

University Education Press*, Newton, PO Box 96, Singapore 11
Manager: Yeo Teo Kong
Associate Company: Medical World Book Co, Singapore (qv)
Subjects: East and South-East Asia, Humanities, Social Sciences, History of Singapore

Literary Agents

Graham **Brash** Pte Ltd*, Prinsep House, 36-C Prinsep St, Singapore 0718 Tel: 332497/333705 Cable Add: Bookscout Singapore
Manager: K C Campbell
This Company acts mainly as an Agency, but also engages in occasional minor publishing

Chopmen Enterprises, 428-429 Katong Shopping Centre (4th Floor), Singapore 1543
Contact: Mr N T S Chopra

Major Booksellers

Asia Book Co, 71B, (2nd Floor) Block 52, Chin Swee Rd, Singapore 0316 Tel: 983186/983188/983420

Books for Asia (Singapore) Pte Ltd, c/o 65 Crescent Rd, Singapore 1543 Tel: 4462903/4462377 Cable Add: Asiabooks (Wholesalers)

Chopmen Bookshop*, B-72 Katong Shopping Centre (Lower Ground Floor), Singapore 15 Tel: 401606

East and West Centre Pte Ltd, 124 First Floor, Bt Timah Plaza, Jalan Anak Bukit, Singapore 2158

Eastern Book Service Pte Ltd*, 11 Irving Place, Singapore 13 Tel: 801077 Cable Add: Eastbook, Singapore Telex: RS 23163
Group Dir: Jack Sherman; *Executive Dir:* Brian Lim
Publishers' Agents and Stockists

Educational Aids Production Co Pte Ltd*, 33 Beo Crescent, Singapore 3

Educational Book Centre*, 69 Stamford Rd, Singapore 6 Tel: 327731

Far East Book Co, now known as East and West Centre Pte Ltd (qv)

Haji Hashim bin Haji Abdullah*, 134 Arab St, Singapore 7

M P H Pte Ltd*, 71-77 Stamford Rd, GPO Box 347, Singapore 6 Tel: 363633

Michael's Bookshop*, 22 Orchard Rd, Singapore 9 Tel: 361327

Modern Book Store*, 34 Bras Basah Rd, Singapore 7

Pustaka **Nasional** Pte Ltd, Suite 1211 (12th Floor) Shaw Towers, Beach Rd, Singapore 7 Tel: 2937791
Booksellers and Distributors
Miscellaneous: Firm has taken over the activities of the former Pustaka Nasional of 40 Kandahar St, Singapore 7

National Book Store*, 72 Bras Basah Rd, Singapore 7 Tel: 321165

Pacific Book Centre, 597 Havelock Rd, (Teck Huat Chambers) Singapore 0316 Tel: 436411, 981526 Cable Add: Pacolmac
Managing Partner: Low Tai Ee

S T P Distributors Sdn Bhd*, B4 International Bldg, Orchard Rd, Singapore 9 Tel: 379522

Shanghai Book Co Pte Ltd, 81 Victoria St, Singapore 0718 Tel: 360144 Cable Add: Shoobook

Singapore Book Store*, 66 Bras Basah Rd, Singapore 7

University Bookstore*, 13 Orchard Rd, Singapore 9 Tel: 32631!

The **World** Book Company Pte Ltd, 708-710 Tan Boon Hai Bldg, 315 Outram Rd, Singapore 0316

Major Libraries

American Library Resource Center, American Embassy, 30 Hill St, Singapore 0617

Nanyang University Library, Upper Jurong Rd, Singapore 2263
Since July 1980, the Nanyang University has been merged with the former University of Singapore to form the National University of Singapore Library (see below)

National Archives and Records Centre*, 16-18 Lewin Terrace, Singapore 7

National Library, Stamford Rd, Singapore 0617 Tel: 327355/8 Cable Add: Natlib Singapore Telex: RS 26620
Dir: Mrs Hedwig Anuar
Major Publications: Annual Report; Books about Singapore (biennial); *Checklist of Current Serials; Singapore National Bibliography* (quarterly, with annual supplement); *Singapore Periodicals Index* (biennial); *Union Catalogue of Scientific and Technical Serials*

National University of Singapore Library, Bukit Timah Rd, Singapore 1025 Tel: 2560451, 2560454
Librarian: Peggy W C Hochstadt
Publications: Catalogue of Singapore/Malaysia Collection and Supplements; Checklist of Current Serials; Accessions List (monthly); *Dissertations, Theses and Academic Exercises, 1947-1976, 1977; Annual Report;* handbooks and guides to the various libraries of the National University

Library Associations

Library Association of Singapore, c/o National Library, Stamford Rd, Singapore 0617

Honorary Secretary: Sylvia Yap
Publications: Singapore Libraries (annual), *Directory of Libraries in Singapore*, 2nd edition, *Who's Who in Singapore Librarianship, LAS newsletter* (irregular)

Library Reference Books and Journals

Books

Directory of Libraries in Singapore, Library Association of Singapore, c/o National Library, Stamford Rd, Singapore 6

Singapore Libraries, Library Association of Singapore, c/o National Library, Stamford Rd, Singapore 6

Journals

Newsletter, Library Association of Singapore, Stamford Rd, Singapore 6

Literary Associations and Societies

Chinese Language and Literary Society*, Jurong Rd, Singapore 22
Publication: Hsin Sheng

Literary Periodicals

Hsin Sheng (New Life), Chinese Language and Literary Society, Jurong Rd, Singapore 22

Literary Prizes

National Book Development Council of Singapore Book Awards*
For outstanding works of creative and non-creative writing by local authors in any of the four official languages (Malay, English, Chinese, and Tamil). The awards are for fiction, poetry, drama, non-fiction, and children's and young people's books. Up to fifteen prizes of 500 to 1,000 Singapore dollars. Awarded every three years (or annually if there are sufficient works of merit). Enquiries to National Book Development Council of Singapore, c/o National Library, Stamford Rd, Singapore 0617

Somalia

General Information

Language: Somali is the national language; Arabic, Italian and English are official languages and widely spoken
Religion: Muslim
Population: 3.4 million
Bank Hours: 0800-1130 Saturday-Thursday
Currency: 100 cents = 1 Somali or Samli shilling
Export/Import Information: No tariff on books; advertising matter distributed gratis is free, otherwise 40% Revenue and 10% Customs Duty. Administration Tax, 10%; Wharfage Tax, 1.5%. Exchange controls

Publishers

Government Printer*, Ministry of Information, Mogadishu

Somalia d'Oggi*, Piazzale della Garesa, PO Box 315, Mogadishu
Subjects: Law, Economics

Major Booksellers

New Africa Booksellers*, PO Box 897, Mogadishu Tel: 30087

Major Libraries

National Library of Higher Education and Culture*, Ministry of Higher Education and Culture, Mogadishu

Biblioteca dell' Universita Nazionale della Somalia*, PO Box 15, Mogadishu Tel: 2535

Republic of South Africa

General Information

Language: English and Afrikaans
Religion: Predominantly Protestant. Politically most important is the Dutch Reformed Church (about 3 million adherents). About 1.8 million Methodists, 1.5 million Anglicans, 1.2 million Roman Catholics. Most Blacks belong to separatist churches practising a mixture of ancient pagan and Christian rites
Population: 27.7 million
Literacy Rate (1960): 57% Total (50% Bantu, 98% White, 74% Asiatic, 69% Coloured)
Bank Hours: 0900-1530 Monday-Tuesday, Thursday, Friday; 0900-1300 Wednesday; 0830-1100 Saturday
Shop Hours: Vary province to province. Often 0830-1700 Monday-Friday; 0830-1230 Saturday
Currency: 100 cents = 1 rand
Export/Import Information: No tariffs on books or advertising matter. No import licence required. No obscene literature permitted. Exchange controls being relaxed
Copyright: Berne (see International section)

Book Trade Organizations

Associated Booksellers of Southern Africa Ltd, 1 Meerendal, Nightingale Way, Pinelands 7405 Tel: 533952
Secretary: P G van Rooyen

Book Trade Association of South Africa, (President's Office) PO Box 337, Bergvlei, 2012 Transvaal Tel: (786) 2983

Directorate of Publications, Private Bag 9069, Cape Town 8000 Tel: 211000 Telex: 570165
Dir: D Vosloo
See also Publications Appeal Board below

Overseas Publishers' Representatives Association of Southern Africa, PO Box 61342, Marshalltown 2107 Tel: (011) 215247
Secretary: P Hardingham

Publications Appeal Board, Private Bag X114, Pretoria 001 Tel: 36353 Telex: 53668
Subsidiary to the Directorate of Publications (qv)

South African Publishers' Association, PO Box 123, Kenwyn 7790
Secretary: P G van Rooyen

Standard Book Numbering Agency, State Library, PO Box 397, Pretoria 0001
ISBN Administrator: Dr H J Aschenborn

Book Trade Reference Books and Journals

Books

Catalogue of Books (English) Published in Southern Africa, Still in Print (1970), C Struik, Corner Wale and Loop Sts, PO Box 1144, Cape Town (useful compilation produced by the prominent firm of booksellers)

Journals

Central News, Central News Agency Ltd, PO Box 9, Cape Town 8000 (trade organ published by CNA, the large bookselling chain with branches throughout the country)

South African National Bibliography (text in Afrikaans, Bantu languages and English), The State Library, Vermeulen St, PO Box 397, Pretoria (published since 1933; annual volume and quarterly cumulations; also available as a weekly card service)

Publishers

Africana Book Society (Pty) Ltd, PO Box 1071, Johannesburg
Man Dir: L W Bolze
Parent Company: Books of Zimbabwe Publishing Co (Pvt) Ltd, Zimbabwe (qv)
Subjects: General Academic, Biography, History, Africana, Hunting, Wildlife, Illustrated & Fine Editions, Reprints
Founded: 1975
ISBN Publisher's Prefix: 0-994971

B L A C Publishing House*, PO Box 17, Athlone, Cape Town
Man Dir: James Matthews
Subjects: General Fiction, Belles Lettres, Poetry, Paperbacks
Founded: 1974

A A **Balkema** Publishers, 93 Keerom St, PO Box 3117, Cape Town Tel: (021) 229009/431935 Cable Add: Balkema Cape Town
Man Dir: A A Balkema
Head Office: A A Balkema, Postbus 1675, 3000 BR Rotterdam, Netherlands (qv)
Orders to: A A Balkema, 99 Main St, Salem, NH 03079
Subjects: Texts of scientific nature covering Anthropology, African and Oriental Studies, Palaeontology, Archaeology, Botany, Zoology, Ecology, Agriculture, Soil Engineering
1979: 15 titles *1980:* 15 titles *Founded:* 1930
ISBN Publisher's Prefix: 0-86961

Jonathan **Ball** Publishers (Pty) Ltd, PO Box 32213, Braamfontein, Johannesburg 2017 (Located at: 19th Floor Braamfontein Centre, Jan Smuts Ave, Braamfontein) Tel: 391911/2/3/4 Telex: 42-4235 SA
Man Dir, Rights & Permissions: Jonathan Augustus Ball; *Editorial:* Alison Lowry; *Sales:* Nicholas Britt
Orders to: Hodder & Stoughton Southern Africa, PO Box 32213, Braamfontein, Johannesburg 2017
Subsidiary Company: Jonathan Ball Paperbacks
Imprints include: The Fountain Press
Branch Off: PO Box 94, Cape Town (Located at: The Link, Cavendish Sq, Claremont)
Subjects: South African History & Politics, African Interest, Fiction
1978: 10 titles *1979:* 14 titles *Founded:* 1977
ISBN Publisher's Prefix: 0-86850

Bateleur Press, PO Box 31910, Braamfontein 2193 (Located at: 416-419 Dunwell, 35 Jorissen St, Braamfontein) Tel: 397832/5, 7252094/6 and 375960/1; also at PO Box 6690, Johannesburg 2000 and Sana Petersen House, 62 Davies St, Doornfontein, Johannesburg 2094
Subjects: General Fiction and Non-fiction, Poetry
Founded: 1974

Bible Society of South Africa, PO Box 6215, Roggebaai 8012 Cape Town Tel: 212040 Cable Add: Testaments Cape Town Telex: 577964
Chief Executive, General Secretary, Rights & Permissions: Rev G E van der Merwe; *Editorial Dir:* Rev P L Olivier; *Sales, Production:* Rev A Stranex; *Publicity:* N Turley
Imprints: Bible Society, Bybelgenootskap
Branch Offs: Kempton Park, Bloemfontein, Durban, Port Elizabeth, Cape Town; also BSSA Regional Office, 428 Kaiser St, Windhoek 9000 SWA/Namibia
Subjects: Bibles, Scriptural Selections, Bible Society historical research material, Bible translation and research aids
Bookshops: 15 Anton Anreith Arcade, Roggebaai, CT 8001; 97 Russel St, Durban 4001; Brister Ho, 187 Main St, Port Elizabeth 6001; Sonop Bldg, 3rd Floor, 65 Maitland St, Bloemfontein 9301; Bible Ho, 18 Central Ave, Kempton Park 1620; 219 Bree St, Johannesburg 2001
1978: 45 titles *1979:* 35 titles *Founded:* 1820 (as auxiliary of British & Foreign Bible/Socy), 1965 as autonomous body
ISBN Publisher's Prefix: 0-7982

Black Community Programmes Ltd*, 86 Beatrice St, Durban Tel: 67558
Executive Dir: B A Khoapa; *Senior Editor:* Thoko Mbajwa
Branch Off: 15 Leopold St, King Williams Town
Subjects: General Nonfiction, Community Development, Reference, Annuals, Paperbacks
Founded: 1972

Books of Africa, now incorporated in T V Bulpin (qv)

The **Brenthurst** Press (Pty) Ltd, Suite 19, Hyde Sq, Jan Smuts Ave, Hyde Park, Sandton 2196 Tel: (011) 427607
Chief Executive: Mr N J Diemont; *Editorial and other Offices:* Mrs C Kemp
Subjects: Fine editions of hitherto unpublished Africana from the private library of H F Oppenheimer of Johannesburg
1978: 2 titles *1979:* 1 title *Founded:* 1974
ISBN Publisher's Prefix: 0-909079

T V **Bulpin** (Pty) Ltd, 1004 Cape of Good Hope Bldg, 117 George St, PO Box 1516, Cape Town 8000 Tel: 227921
Man Dir, Rights & Permissions: T V Bulpin; *Sales:* M Bulpin, Ray Howell; *Production, Publicity:* A N Monro, H Rennie
Subsidiary Company: Books of Africa (Pty) Ltd
Subjects: Biography, History, Africana, Art
1979: 7 titles *Founded:* 1947
ISBN Publisher's Prefix: 0-949956

Butterworth & Co (SA) (Pty) Ltd, PO Box 792, Durban 4000 (Located at: 152/154 Gale St, Durban 4001) Tel: (031) 66516/68070 Cable Add: Butterlaw Durban
Man Dir, Rights & Permissions: A McAdam; *Editorial, Production:* K Prinsloo, A Bricker; *Sales:* J Destombes; *Publicity:* Mrs B Chedzey
Parent Company: Butterworth & Co (Publishers) Ltd, UK (qv)
Branch Off: PO Box 27711, Sunnyside 0132
Subjects: Law, Medicine, Science & Technology, General Science, University Textbooks
1978: 41 titles *1979:* 130 titles *Founded:* 1935
ISBN Publisher's Prefix: 0-409

C N A, see Central News Agency Ltd

C P S A, an imprint of The Ecumenical Literature Distribution Trust (qv)

C U M, an imprint of Christian Publishing, Co — Newman Art (qv)

Calvyn Jubileum Boekefonds, PO Box 2004, Noordbrug 2522

Killie **Campbell** Africana Library, see University of Natal Press

Central News Agency Ltd*, Laub St, New Centre, PO Box 10799, Johannesburg 2000 Tel: (011) 8361711
Subjects: Children's Books, Paperbacks
Bookshops: Retail outlets throughout the country (see under Booksellers)

Christian Publishing Co — Newman Art, PO Box 132, Roodepoort 1725 (Located at: Baanbreker Avenue 2, Helderkruin, Roodepoort 1725) Tel: (011) 7642466 Cable Add: Chrispub Telex: 84667
Chairmen: Timo Crous (CUM Communications), Pat Lubbe; *Editorial:* Jan du Plessis, B Kloppers; *Production, Publicity, Rights & Permissions:* Pat Lubbe
Imprint: C U M Communications (Pty) Ltd
Subjects: Religion, Juveniles, Paperbacks, Educational
1978: 60 titles *1979:* 67 titles *Founded:* 1939

Church Publishing Trust, see Interkerklike Uitgewerstrust

College of Careers (Pty) Ltd*, PO Box 2081, Cape Town 8000 (Located at: 4th Floor, Garmar Ho, 121-127 Plein St, Cape Town 8001) Tel: 452041 Cable Add: Colcareers
Man Dir: Cyril Kemp; *Production:* Ivor Furman
Subjects: Educational
Founded: 1946

Collier-Macmillan South Africa (Pty) Ltd, PO Box 17, Kempton Park 1620, Transvaal (Located at: 51 Forge Rd, Spartan Industrial Township, Kempton Park)
Tel: 9701827/8/9 Cable Add: Pachamac
Man Dir: L James Armstrong
Parent Company: Macmillan Inc, New York, USA
Allied and Subsidiary Companies: Cassell Australia (qv); Cassell & Co, New Zealand (qv); Cassell Ltd, Collier Macmillan Ltd, UK (qqv); Collier Macmillan Australia (qv); Collier Macmillan Canada Ltd; Collier Macmillan International, Philippines; Collier Macmillan International, USA

Ad Donker (Pty) Ltd*, PO Box 41021, Craighall 2064 (Located at: Hyde Park Corner, Jan Smuts Ave, Hyde Park, Johannesburg 2196) Tel: 7885030 Cable Add: Reppub
Man Dir, Rights & Permissions: Adriaan Donker; *Sales:* Karen Lubisch; *Editorial:* Christine Susman; *Publicity:* Gillian Sellers
Subsidiary Company: Ad Donker Ltd, UK (qv)
Associate Company: International Publishers' Representatives (SA) (Pty) Ltd
Subjects: General Fiction & Nonfiction, Poetry, Africana, Academic
1978: 14 titles *1979:* 14 titles *Founded:* 1973
ISBN Publisher's Prefix: 0-949937

Dutch Reformed Church Publishers, PO Box 4539, Cape Town 8000 Tel: 221376 Cable Add: D R C Publishers Telex: 76922
Man Dir: W J van Zijl; *Editorial, Rights and Permissions:* Mrs B Smit; *Sales:* A Peens; *Production:* W Theron; *Publicity:* Mrs M Volschenk
Parent Company: N G Kerk-Uitgewers en Boekhandel (qv)
Associate Company: Verenigde Protestantse Uitgewers (qv)
Branch Off: PO Box 2309, Kempton Park, South Africa
Subjects: Christian Literature (Educational and General)
Bookshops: 20 Bookshops throughout South Africa
1978: 52 titles *1979:* 29+ titles *Founded:* 1818
ISBN Publisher's Prefix: 0-86991

E L D Trust, an imprint of The Ecumenical Literature Distribution Trust (qv)

The **Ecumenical Literature** Distribution Trust, PO Box 2115, Johannesburg 2000 (Located at: 38 Melle St, Braamfontein, Johannesburg 2001) Tel: 396675
General Manager: W Westenborg; *Sales:* Ms K L Coupar
Imprints: CPSA, ELD Trust, Pula Press
Subjects: Religious, Liturgical
Bookshops: ELD Bookshops at 75 de Korte St, Braamfontein, Johannesburg 2001; 11 Grace At, Port Elizabeth 6001; 18b Rissik St, Pietersburg 0700 (all in Republic of South Africa); and Botswana Book Centre, The Mall Gaborone, Botswana
1978: 11 titles *1979:* 26 titles *Founded:* 1973 (as ELD Trust; 1970 CPSA, pre-1970 SPCK)
ISBN Publisher's Prefix: 0-86881

Educum Uitgewers Beperk*, Posbus 87, King Williams Town 5600

Erudita Publications (Pty) Ltd*, PO Box 25111, Ferrairas Town 2048, Transvaal
Subjects: Reference, Directories

Flesch Financial Publications (Pty) Ltd, 58 Burg St, PO Box 3473, Cape Town Tel: (021) 436625 Cable Add: Fairlead Telex: 577826
Man Dir: W J Flesch; *Editorial:* C G Thompson; *Sales Manager:* Derek Wood
Branch Off: SARB Ho, 80 Commissioner St, PO Box 3473, Johannesburg
Subjects: Reference, Finance
1980: 2 titles *Founded:* 1966
ISBN Publisher's Prefix: 0-949989

Da Gama Publishers (Pty) Ltd*,
311 Locarno Ho, Loveday St, Johannesburg
Man Dir: Daphne de Freitas
Subjects: General Nonfiction, Educational, Reference, Travel Books

Government Printer*, Bosman St, Pretoria

T W Griggs & Co (Pty) Ltd*, PO Box 466, Durban 4000 (Located at: 341 West St, Durban, 4001) Tel: 328571/2 Cable Add: Adamsco
Dir, Editorial, Sales, Production, Publicity: E G Rabjohn; *Rights & Permissions:* P B Harvey
Parent Company: Adams & Company Ltd, 341 West St, Durban, 4001 (qv)
Subsidiary Companies: Adams & Griggs Educational Suppliers; Thirty Three Victory Street (Pty) Ltd; both at 33 Victoria St, Durban 4001
Subjects: Africana

H & R Academica, subsidiary of Human & Rousseau Publishers (Pty) Ltd (qv)

H A U M (Hollandsch Afrikaansche Uitgevers Maatschappij), 58 Long St, PO Box 1371, Cape Town 8000 Tel: (021) 435008 Cable Add: Haum
Manager, Publisher: C J Hage; *Editorial:* Elsa Naudé
Associate Companies: De Jager/HAUM, Publishers, Pretoria; P J de Villiers, Publishers, Bloemfontein
Subjects: General Fiction & Nonfiction, Belles Lettres, Poetry, Biography, History, Juveniles, Books in Afrikaans, Science and Technology, General Science, University Textbooks
Bookshops: 480 Paul Kruger St, PO Box 460, Pretoria 001; HAUM Akademiese Boekhandel, Trust Bank Centre, Stellenbosch 7600
1978: 45 titles *1979:* 49 titles *Founded:* 1894
ISBN Publisher's Prefix: 0-7986

Human & Rousseau Publishers (Pty) Ltd, State House, 3-9 Rose St, PO Box 5050, Cape Town Tel: (021) 410625 Cable Add: Persdiens Telex: 570294
General Manager: J J Human; *Publicity:* D Saayman
Parent Company: Nasionale Boekhandel Ltd (qv)
Subsidiary Company: H & R Academica, PO Box 558, Pretoria 0001
Branch Offs: 607 Southern Life Building, 239 Pretorius St, Pretoria Tel: (012) 37588 Cable Add: Hurou
Subjects: General Fiction & Nonfiction, Belles Lettres, Poetry, Biography, History, Africana, Philosophy, Reference, Religion, Juveniles, Books in Afrikaans, General Science, University and Secondary Textbooks
1978: 138 titles *1979:* 111 titles

Hutchinson Group (SA) (Pty) Ltd, PO Box 337, Bergvlei 2012 Tel: (786) 2983 Cable Add: Hutchbooks
Man Dir: John F Banks
Associate Company: Hutchinson Publishing Group Ltd, UK (qv)
Subjects: General Fiction & Nonfiction, Belles Lettres, Poetry, University & Secondary Textbooks, Paperbacks, Juvenile
Founded: 1966

Interkerklike Uitgewerstrust, PO Box 2744, Pretoria 0001 Tel: (012) 215132
Inter-Church Publishing Trust
Chief Executive: I B Kasselman; *Editorial Manager:* Rev H J Kleinschmidt
Associate Companies: HAUM (qv); Calvyn Jubileum Boekefonds (qv); N G Kerkboekhandel Transvaal (qv); N G Kerk-Uitgewers en Boekhandel (qv)
Subjects: Religious handbooks for Schools, Universities, Colleges and Churches; also Visual Aids
1978-79: 10 titles
ISBN Publisher's Prefix: 0-620

Juta & Co Ltd, PO Box 123, Kenwyn 7790 (Located at: Mercury Cres, Hillstar Industrial Township, Wetton) Tel: (021) 711181 Cable Add: Juta
Man Dir: J D Duncan; *Sales Manager:* L Massella; *Senior Editor, Rights & Permissions:* J Potgieter, J D Duncan
Branch Off: PO Box 403, Umtata, Transkei
Subjects: Reference, Law, Medicine, Science and Technology; General School, University & Educational Textbooks
Bookshops: Church St, PO Box 30, Cape Town 8000; Cnr Pritchard & Loveday Sts, PO Box 1010, Johannesburg 2000; Suite 5b, Mangrove Beach Centre, 91 Somtseu Rd, Durban 4001
1978: 101 titles *1979:* 70 titles *Founded:* 1853
ISBN Publisher's Prefix: 0-7021

Die Kinderpers Van SA, PO Box 2652, Cape Town 8000
Subject: Children's Books
1978: 29 titles

Kosmo Uitgewery Beperk*, Posbus 178, Stellenbosch 7600

Longman Penguin Southern Africa (Pty) Ltd, Marine Drive, Paarden Eiland, PO Box 1616, Cape Town 8000 Tel: (021) 517324/5 and 515758 Cable Add: Freegrove Capetown Telex: 570841
Man Dir: M A Peacock; *Publishers:* N D van der Horst, I R Scott; *Marketing Manager (Education):* G F Visser; *Sales, Marketing (General), Publicity, Advertising Manager:* J H Allen; *Production Manager:* E L Visser; *Rights & Permissions:* N D van der Horst
Parent Company: Longman Group Ltd, Harlow, Essex, England
Branch Off: PO Box 559, Johannesburg 2000 Tel: (011) 8344439
Subjects: Primary, Secondary and Tertiary Textbooks, General Non-fiction, History and Africana, Juveniles, Books in Zulu, Xhosa, Tswana & other Southern African languages
1979: 13 titles *Founded:* 1960

Lovedale Press, Private Bag X 1346, Alice 5700, Cape Province Tel: Alice 167/278
Man Dir: R B Raven
Subjects: General Fiction and Nonfiction, Belles Lettres, Poetry, Biography, History, Africana, Books in various Southern African languages, Educational Books
Bookshop: 26 Fuller St, Butterworth, Transkei; Bookshop, Main St, Alice 5700
Founded: 1841

M S A, an imprint of Purnell & Sons (SA) (Pty) Ltd (qv)

McGraw-Hill Book Co (South Africa) (Pty) Ltd, Hulley Rd, PO Box 371, Isando 1600 Tel: (011) 361181 Cable Add: McGraw-Hill Isando Telex: 89272
Man Dir, Rights & Permissions: Rolf Pakendorf; *Editorial:* Basil van Rooyen; *Sales:* Charles Grobler; *Publicity:* Monica Nelson
Parent Company: McGraw-Hill International Book Co, New York
Subjects: General Nonfiction, Medicine, Science and Technology, General Science, University Textbooks
1978: 24 titles *1979:* 15 titles *Founded:* 1966
ISBN Publisher's Prefix: 0-007

Macmillan South Africa Publishers (Pty) Ltd, Braamfontein Centre, PO Box 31487, Braamfontein 2017 Tel: 396761 Cable Add: Macbooks Telex: 87280
Man Dir: David Mitchell
Parent Company: Macmillan Publishers Ltd, UK (qv)
Subjects: General Non-fiction, Biography, History, Africana, Reference, Social Science; University, Secondary and Primary Textbooks; Paperbacks
Founded: 1966
ISBN Publisher's Prefix: 0-86954

John Malherbe (Pty) Ltd, Sanso Centre, 8 Adderley St, PO Box 1207, Cape Town 8001 Tel: (021) 431485 Telex: 570261
Man Dir: John Malherbe, A Ashworth (Brit)
Subjects: General Fiction & Nonfiction, Belles Lettres, Poetry, Biography, History, Africana, Philosophy, Juveniles, Paperbacks
Book Club: Pluim Book Club
Founded: 1963
ISBN Publisher's Prefix: 0-86966

Maskew Miller Ltd, PO Box 396, Cape Town 8000 (Located at: 50 Glynn St, Cape Town 80001) Tel: (021) 457731 Cable Add: Maskewmiller Capetown Telex: 576053
Man Dir: T Myburgh; *Publishing Dir:* F C H Rumbal
Branch Offs: Trust Bank Centre, George St, Kimberley; 11 Grace St, Port Elizabeth; PO Box 11430, Johannesburg; Morningside Centre, 197 Globe Rd, Morningside, Durban; Oxford Shopping Centre, 256 Oxford St, East London; 27 Smith St, King William's Town; PO Box 9251, Eros; PO Box 781, Umtata; Sunday School Building, Room No 2, First Floor, 154B Maitland St, Bloemfontein
Subjects: General Fiction & Non-fiction, Juveniles, Books in Afrikaans and in the African languages, Paperbacks, General Science, Secondary Textbooks
Bookshops: As listed under Branch Offices above and under Major Booksellers
ISBN Publisher's Prefix: 0-623

The Methodist Publishing House and Book Depot*, 52 Burg St, PO Box 708, Cape Town 8000 Tel: (021) 220527 Cable Add: Methodist
Book Steward: M Fearns
Subjects: Religion, Books in Xhosa and Zulu
1978: 8 titles
ISBN Publisher's Prefix: 0-949942

N G Kerk Jeugboekhandel, PO Box 396, Bloemfontein 9300
Formerly Sondagskool Boekhandel
Bookshop: at above address

N G Kerkboekhandel Transvaal (DRC Publishers), Schoemanstr 260, PO Box 245, Pretoria 0001 Tel: 38401
General Manager: J Olivier; *Publication Manager:* Dr F A H van Staden MPC
Branch Offs: 15 branches in Transvaal and Natal
Subjects: Religion
Bookshop: Schoemanstr 260, Pretoria
1979: 58 titles *1980:* 42 titles

Nasionale Boekhandel Ltd, 386 Voortrekker Rd, PO Box 122, Parow 7500 Tel: 591131 Cable Add: Nasboek
Group Man Dir: H G Jaekel
Subsidiary and Associate Companies: Cape Booksellers Ltd; Drakensberg Boekhandel; Human & Rousseau (qv); Nasionale Boekhandel (SWA) (Pty) Ltd, Namibia (qv); Nasionale Boekwinkels Ltd (qv under Booksellers); Nasou Ltd (qv); Natal Booksellers Ltd, Durban; Oudiovisio Productions (Pty) Ltd (qv); Tafelberg Publishers Ltd (qv); Via Afrika Ltd (qv); Via Afrika (Botswana) Ltd, PO Box 332, Gaborone; Via Afrika (Ciskei) Ltd, King Williamstown; Via Afrika (Transkei) Ltd, Umtata; Via Afrika (Kwazulu) Ltd, Umlazi, Durban; Via Afrika (Lebowa) Ltd,

Pietersburg; Rygill's Educational Suppliers, Pinetown; Heer Printers (Pty) Ltd, Pretoria
Subjects: General, Educational, Academic, Medicine
Founded: 1950

Nasou Ltd, 386 Voortrekker Rd, PO Box 105, Goodwood, Parow 7500 Tel: (021) 987021 Cable Add: Nasou Cape Town Telex: 7751
Man Dir: H G Jaekel; *General Manager, Rights & Permissions:* W R van der Vyer; *Publicity & Advertising:* F D Maree
Parent Company: Nasionale Boekhandel Ltd (qv for Associated Companies)
Branch Offs: PO Box 361, Pietermaritzburg 3200; PO Box 9898, Johannesburg 2000; PO Box 1058, Bloemfontein 9300
Subjects: Reference, University, Secondary & Primary Textbooks
1979: 35 titles *Founded:* 1963
ISBN Publisher's Prefix: 0-625

Newman Art, see Christian Publishing Company

Rebecca **Ostrowiak** School of Reading, PO Box 4106, Germiston South 1411 Tel: 514262
Principals: Rebecca Ostrowiak, Edna Freinkel
Subjects: Remedial reading teaching for children (Series *Teach Any Child to Read*)
Founded: 1965

Oudiovista Productions (Pty) Ltd, PO Box 122, Parow 7500 Tel: 591131 Cable Add: Oudiovista
Man Dir: H G Jaekel; *Manager:* G J Bezuidenhout
Parent Company: Nasionale Boekhandel Ltd (qv)
Subjects: Educational, Audio-Visual Aids
Founded: 1969

Oxford University Press Southern Africa, PO Box 1141, Cape Town 8000 (Located at: Top Floor, Harrington Ho, 37 Barrack St, Cape Town 8001) Tel: (021) 457266/7/8/9 Cable Add: Oxonian Capetown
General Manager: N C Gracie; *Editorial:* P Branford; *Sales Manager:* Peter Hyde
Parent Company: Oxford University Press, UK (qv)
Branch Offs: PO Box 41390 Craighall 2024; PO Box 37166, Overport 4067; PO Box 3892, Salisbury, Zimbabwe
Subjects: General Fiction and Non-fiction, Belles Lettres, Poetry, Biography, History, Africana, Juveniles; Books in Xhosa, Zulu, Sotho, Tswana, Shona and Afrikaans; General & Social Science, Educational, Textbooks, Music, Prayer Books; Paperbacks
1978: 18 titles *1979:* 20 titles *Founded:* 1915
ISBN Publisher's Prefix: 0-19

P S A, an imprint of Purnell & Sons (SA) (Pty) Ltd (qv)

Perskor Books (Pty) Ltd*, 28 Height St, Doornfontein, PO Box 845, Johannesburg 2000 Tel: 285460 Cable Add: Vaderland Telex: 83561, 87483/4
Man Dir: D S van der Merwe; *Editorial, Rights & Permissions:* P V Heerden; *Sales:* N P Fourie; *Production:* A Bothma; *Publicity:* S J Fourie
Orders to: Perskor-Boekwinkel, 4 Banfield Rd, Industria North (Postal Add: PO Box, Maraisburg, 1700)
Subsidiary Company: Perskor Publishers (at above address)
Subjects: Education, Law, General
Bookclubs: Klub 707; Dagbreek-Boekkring; Voortrekker-Boekklub; all at PO Box 4892, Johannesburg 2000
Bookshops: PO Box 102, Maraisburg 1700; PO Box 309, Kroonstad 9500; PO Box 133, Bellville 7530; PO Box 15531 Lynn East 0039; Johannesburgse Boekwinkel, PO Box 91119, Aucklandpark 2006
Founded: 1940
ISBN Publisher's Prefix: 0-628

David-**Philip** Publisher (Pty) Ltd, PO Box 408, Claremont, Cape 7735 (Located at: 217 Werdmuller Centre, Claremont, Cape Province Tel: Cape Town 654968/653046 Cable Add: Philipub, Cape Town Telex: 5727566 Philipub
Man Dir: David Philip; *Marketing Dir:* Murray Coombes; *Rights and Permissions Dir:* Marie Philip
Subjects: General Fiction- & Nonfiction, Belles Lettres, Poetry, Biography, History, Africana, Philosophy, Juveniles, Social Science, Politics, University Textbooks, Reference Books, Paperbacks
1978: 15 titles *1979:* 18 titles *Founded:* 1971
ISBN Publisher's Prefix: 0-908396

Pitman Publishing Co SA (Pty) Ltd*, PO Box 41021 Craighall 2024 (Located at: Hyde Park Corner, Jan Smuts Ave, Hyde Park, Johannesburg 2196) Tel: 7885030 Cable Add: Reppub
Man Dir: Adriaan Donker
Associate Company: Pitman Ltd, UK (qv)
Subjects: Reference, Commercial and Business Studies, Secondary Textbooks, Shorthand
1978: 6 titles *1979:* 4 titles
ISBN Publisher's Prefix: 0-273

President Publishers*, PO Box 488, Krugersdorp 1740
Subjects: General Fiction, Books in Afrikaans

Pretoria Boekhandel Ltd, PO Box 23334, Innesdal 0031

Pride, an imprint of Purnell & Sons (SA) (Pty) Ltd (qv)

Pro Rege Press Ltd*, PO Box 343, Potchefstroom 2520
Associate Companies: N G Kerkboekhandel Transvaal (qv); HAUM (qv); Interkerklike Uitgewerstrust (qv); N G Kerk-Uitgewers en Boekhandel (qv)
Subjects: General Fiction & Non-fiction, Religion, Secondary Textbooks
ISBN Publisher's Prefix: 0-949988

Pula Press, an imprint of The Ecumenical Literature Distribution Trust (qv)

Purnell & Sons (SA) (Pty) Ltd, 9 Sloane Centre, PO Box 98508, Sloane Park 2152 Tel: (011) 7066026 Cable Add: Purprint Johannesburg Telex: 8-3630 SA
Man Dir: J St Clair Whittall; *Sales Manager:* N Hargreaves
Parent Company: BPC Ltd, UK (qv)
Associate Companies: Futura Publications Ltd, UK (qv); Macdonald & Jane's Publishers Ltd, UK (qv); Macdonald Educational Ltd, UK (qv); Macdonald Raintree Inc, USA; Phoebus Publishing Co, UK (qv); Purnell Books, UK (qv)
Imprints: MSA, PSA, Pride
Subjects: Non-fiction (South African interest), Botany, Natural History
Founded: 1948
ISBN Publisher's Prefix: 0-86843

Ravan Press (Pty) Ltd, PO Box 31134, Johannesburg (Located at: 409-416 Dunwell, 35 Jorissen St, Braamfontein 2017 Johannesburg) Tel: 397832/5
Man Dir: Mike Kirkwood
Subjects: Specializes in Socio-Political problems of Southern Africa; also General Fiction & Non-fiction, Poetry, Biography, History, Africana, Philosophy, Reference, Religion, Juveniles, Paperbacks, Periodicals
1978: 11 titles *Founded:* 1973
ISBN Publisher's Prefix: 0-86975

S A Cultural Holdings (Pty) Ltd, PO Box 9019, Johannesburg 2000 Tel: 219211 Telex: J83031 Cable Add: Knowingly
Man Dir: Jeffrey A Miller
Parent Company: Calan Ltd
Subsidiary Companies: Die Kinderkultuurvereniging (Edms) Bpk; Encyclopaedia Britannica (SA) (Pty) Ltd; Ensiklopedie Afrikana (Edms) Bpk; Systems for Education (SA) (Pty) Ltd

S A Kultuurbeleggings, see S A Cultural Holdings Ltd

J L van **Schaik** (Pty) Ltd, Libri Bldg, Church St, PO Box 724, Pretoria Tel: (012) 212441 Cable Add: Bookschaik Pretoria
Man Dir: J van Schaik
Subjects: General Fiction- & Nonfiction, Belles Lettres, Poetry, Biography, History, Africana, How-to, Study Guides, Reference, Religion, Juveniles, Books in Afrikaans and Southern African languages, Psychology, General & Social Science, University & Secondary Textbooks
Bookshop: Libri Bldg, Church St, Pretoria
1979: 30 titles *Founded:* 1914
ISBN Publisher's Prefix: 0-627

Shuter & Shooter (Pty) Ltd, 230 Church St, PO Box 109, Pietermaritzburg 3200, Natal Tel: (0331) 28121 Cable Add: Shushoo Telex: 563771 SA
Man Dir: M N Prozesky; *Editorial:* L van Heerden; *Sales, Publicity:* J A Wilken; *Production:* J Sharpe; *Rights & Permissions:* Mary Monteith
Parent Company: The Natal Witness (Pty) Ltd
Associate Company: Kwa-Zulu Booksellers (Pty) Ltd, PO Box 100, Imbali
Subsidiary Company: Shuter & Shooter (Transkei) (Pty) Ltd, PO Box 648, Umtata, Transkei
Branch Offs: E G Castle, 5th floor, Plein Centre, 100 Plein St, Johannesburg; M Bonga, PO Box 723, King William's Town
Subjects: General Non-fiction, Biography, History, Africana, Books in Zulu and Xhosa, Science and Technology, General and Social Sciences, Primary and Secondary Textbooks
Bookshop: 230 Church St, Pietermaritzburg
1978: 40 titles *1979:* 41 titles *Founded:* 1925
ISBN Publisher's Prefix: 0-86985

Simondium Publishers (Pty) Ltd*, Old Mill Rd, PO Box 3737, Cape Town Tel: (021) 532011 Cable Add: Labels Capetown
Man Dir: W P Loubser
Subjects: General Fiction & Nonfiction

Sondagskool Boekhandel, now known as N G Kerk Jeugboekhandel (qv)

South African Natural History Publications Co, c/o Bitou Craft, Thesen House, 6 Long Street, Knysafa 6570 Tel: (04452) 1012
Man Dir, Editorial, Rights & Permissions: A V Bird; *Sales, Production, Publicity:* H Lutzeyer
Subjects: Flowers, Birds
Founded: 1957
ISBN Publisher's Prefix: 0-620

Ernest **Stanton** Publishers (Pty) Ltd, PO Box 25803, Denver 2027, Transvaal (Located at: Keartland Press Bldg, Nicholson St, Denver, Transvaal) Tel: 6162100/16 Cable Add: Lithocraft Johannesburg Telex: 80309 Johannesburg
Man Dir: Ernest Stanton; *Sales:* Norman Barber; *Marketing:* Tim Lister; *Publicity:* Vyn Stanton; *Rights and Permissions:* M V Stanton
Subsidiary Company: (Associated) Professional Book Services (Pty) Ltd

Subjects: South African interest, Biography, Wild Life and Nature Conservation, Gardening, General Literature
1979: 6 titles *Founded:* 1964
ISBN Publisher's Prefix: 0-949997

Struik (Pty) Ltd, Struik House, Oswald Pirow St, Foreshore, PO Box 1144, Cape Town 8000 Tel: (021) 216740 Cable Add: Dekena Capetown
Man Dir, Sales, Publicity, Promotion and Advertising Manager: G Struik; *Production:* Pieter Struik
Bookshop: Bookwise (Pty) Ltd, Heerengracht Branch, Trust Bank Centre, PO Box 6294, Roggebaai 8012
Subjects: Biography, History, Africana, Reprints, Travel
Founded: 1957
ISBN Publisher's Prefix: 0-86977

Tafelberg Publishers Ltd, 28 Wale St, PO Box 879, Cape Town 8000 Tel: (021) 410127 Cable Add: Boeknuus Cape Town
Man Dir: H G Jaekel; *General Manager, Rights & Permissions:* D J van Niekerk; *Publicity/Promotion/Advertising Manager:* D Saayman
Parent Company: Nasionale Boekhandel Ltd, Parow (qv)
Subjects: General Fiction & Nonfiction Belles Lettres, Poetry, Biography, History, Africana, How-to, Study Guides, Reference, Religion, Juveniles, Books in Afrikaans, Paperbacks
1979: 102 titles *Founded:* 1950
ISBN Publisher's Prefix: 0-624

Target Publishers (Edms) Bpk*, PO Box 910, Klerksdorp 2570

Technitrain (Pty) Ltd*, 117 Everite Ho, 20 de Korte St, PO Box 31648, Braamfontein Tel: 7242465
Man Dir: W M Smith
Subjects: Vocational Guidance, Science & Technology, University & Secondary Textbooks
Founded: 1974
Miscellaneous: Affiliated with the Argus Group of Newspapers; Eastern Province Herald; SABC

Thomson Publications South Africa (Pty) Ltd*, Marcuson Centre, Park & Menton Rds, PO Box 8308 Richmond, Johannesburg 2000 Tel: (011) 7263100
Man Dir: W Corry
Subjects: Reference, Daily/Monthly Bulletins and Journals, Annual/Biennial Buyers' Guides
1978: 1 title
Miscellaneous: Affiliated to Thomson Newspaper Group

Howard B **Timmins** (Pty) Ltd, PO Box 94, Cape Town 8000 (Located at: Sanso Centre, 8 Adderley St, Cape Town 8001) Tel: (021) 411228, 431485 Telex: 570261
Chairman: Howard B Timmins; *Man Dir:* John Malherbe; *Dirs:* A Ashworth, P Jooste
Subjects: General South African Nonfiction, Biography, History, Books in Afrikaans, Travel, Medicine, Gardening, Cookery
Founded: 1937

Torpis Publishing Co*, PO Box 1275, Bloemfontein Tel: (051) 71506
Man Dir: D Pistor

Treffer Uitgewers (Edms) Ltd*, Posbus 3599, Pretoria 0001

United Protestant Publishers (Pty) Ltd, see Verenigde Protestantse Uitgewers

University of Natal Press, PO Box 375, Pietermaritzburg 3200 Tel: (0331) 63320
Man Dir: Ms M P Moberly
Imprints: Killie Campbell Africana Library (Durban)
Subjects: South African History, Politics, Botany; Natal and Zulu Studies, Africana; General Literature, Reprints
1978: 4 titles *1979:* 3 titles *Founded:* 1947
ISBN Publisher's Prefix: 0-86980

University of South Africa, Department of Publishing Services, PO Box 392, Pretoria 0001 Tel: (012) 4402202 Cable Add: Unisa Telex: 3777
Publications Management: by Publications Committee
Subjects: General Non-fiction, Belles Lettres, Anthropology, Accountancy, Botany, Chemistry, Communications, Criminology, Economics, Education, Fine Arts, Poetry, Biography, History, Africana, Philosophy, Reference, Religion, Theology, Psychology, Science & Technology, Social Science, Geography, Geology, Academic Journals, Library Science, Linguistics, Literature, Law, Mathematics, Music, Physics, Politics, Statistics, University Textbooks
1978: 16 titles *1979:* 24 titles (also large number of textbooks, not for sale to booksellers)
Founded: 1873
ISBN Publisher's Prefix: 0-86981

University Publishers & Booksellers (Pty) Ltd, PO Box 29, Stellenbosch 7600 Tel: (02231) 70337/70397 Cable Add: Biblio Stellenbosch
Man Dir: B B Liebenberg
Subjects: General Non-fiction, Juveniles, University & Secondary Textbooks

Valiant Publishers (Pty) Ltd*, Sandton City, PO Box 78236, Sandton 2146 Tel: 7835012/5 Telex: 83023
Man Dir: F R Metrowich; *General Manager, Rights & Permissions:* A N Keevy
Subjects: General Non-fiction, History, Africana, Reference, Religion, TFH Pet Books
1978: 9 titles *Founded:* 1975

Verenigde Protestantse Uitgewers (Edms) Bpk, Posbus 1822, Cape Town 8000 Tel: 437618
Man Dir: W J van Zijl
Parent Company: N G Kerk-Uitgewers en Boekhandel (qv)
Associate Company: Dutch Reformed Church Publishers (qv)
Subject: Christian Literature
1978: 4 titles *Founded:* 1956
ISBN Publisher's Prefix: 0-86997

Via Afrika Ltd, PO Box 114, Parow 7500 Tel: (021) 987021 Cable Add: Via Afrika
Publisher: E R Arnold; *General Manager:* G J J Rousseau; *Production Manager:* W Struik; *Marketing Manager:* T Priem
Parent Company: Nasionale Boekhandel Ltd (qv)
Subjects: General Fiction, Belles Lettres, Poetry, Books in Zulu, Xhosa and other Southern African Languages, Science and Technology, General & Social Science, Secondary & Primary Textbooks
Bookshops: Several retail outlets (see under Booksellers)
Founded: 1970
ISBN Publisher's Prefix: 0-7994

J P van der **Walt** & Seun (Pty) Ltd, 80 Bosman St, PO Box 123, Pretoria 0001 Tel: (012) 32341
Man Dir: D H van der Walt; *Sales Manager:* A Christie; *Editorial:* R J J van Rensburg
Subjects: General Fiction & Nonfiction, Philosophy, Reference, Religion, Law, Juveniles, Books in Afrikaans, Paperbacks, University Textbooks
Founded: 1947
Book Clubs: Eike-Boekklub, Keurblioteek, Treffer-Boekklub
ISBN Publisher's Prefix: 0-7993

Who's Who of Southern Africa, 47 Sauer St, PO Box 8620, Johannesburg Tel: 8363388
Managing Editor: T Binns
Parent Company: Argus Group, Johannesburg
Associate Companies: Argus South African Newspapers Ltd, 85 Fleet St, London EC4Y 1ED, UK and 1500 Broadway, New York 10036, USA
Subjects: Reference, Annuals

Witwatersrand University Press, 1 Jan Smuts Ave, Johannesburg 2001 Tel: (011) 394011 ext 794
Chairman of Publications Committee: Professor Desmond T Cole; *Publications Officer:* Mrs N H Wilson
Subjects: General Non-fiction, Belles Lettres, Poetry, Biography, History, Philosophy, Reference, Religion, Medicine, Psychology, Science & Technology, Social Science, University Textbooks, Africana, Books in Zulu, Xhosa and other Southern African Languages
1978: 3 titles *1979:* 6 titles *Founded:* 1923
ISBN Publisher's Prefix: 0-85494

Literary Agents

The **International Press** Agency (Pty) Ltd, PO Box 682, Cape Town 8000 (Located at: 44 Howard Centre, Pinelands 7405, Cape Province) Tel: (021) 531926 Cable Add: Inpra Howard Place South Africa
Man Dir: Dr Ursula A Barnett

Book Clubs

Africana Book Society Ltd, PO Box 1071, Johannesburg
Owned by: Books of Zimbabwe Publishing Co (Pvt) Ltd, Zimbabwe (qv)
Subjects: Africana, Hunting, Wildlife, Historical Reprints

Associated Book Clubs*, PO Box 9909, Johannesburg
Managers: D B Mackenzie, R L Nathan
Subjects: General Books & Records
Members: 130,000

Klub Dagbreek, PO Box 4892, Johannesburg 2000
Owned by: Perskor Books (Pty) Ltd, Johannesburg (qv)
Subject: Fiction

Eike-Boekklub, 80 Bosman St, PO Box 123, Pretoria
Owned by: J P van der Walt en Seun (Pty) Ltd, Publisher, Pretoria (qv)
Subject: Children's Books

Keurbiblioteek, 80 Bosman St, PO Box 123, Pretoria
Owned by: J P van der Walt en Seun (Pty) Ltd, Publisher, Pretoria (qv)
Subject: Fiction

Klub 707, PO Box 4892, Johannesburg 2000 Tel: 285460
Owned by: Perskor Books (Pty) Ltd, Johannesburg (qv)
Subjects: Fiction: especially Suspense, Espionage, Whodunnits, Thrillers (in Afrikaans)
1979: 12 titles *1980:* 12 titles

Pluim Book Club, PO Box 1207, Cape Town 8000 (Located at: Sanso Centre, 8 Adderley St, Cape Town 8001)
Owned by: John Malherbe (Pty) Ltd (Cape Town)
Subject: Adult Fiction

Klub Saffier, PO Box 4892, Johannesburg 2000
Owned by: Perskor Books (Pty) Ltd,

Johannesburg (qv)
Subject: Fiction

Treffer-Boekklub, 80 Bosman St, PO Box 123, Pretoria
Owned by: J P van der Walt en Seun (Pty) Ltd, Publisher, Pretoria (qv)
Subject: Fiction

Major Booksellers

Adams & Co Ltd*, 341 West St, PO Box 466, Durban 4000 Tel: (031) 69381/328571/2

Central News Agency Ltd, PO Box 10799, Johannesburg 2000 Tel: (011) 8361711; PO Box 9, Cape Town 8000 Tel: (021) 413281; PO Box 938, Durban 4000 Tel: (031) 451875 (and further 220 branches throughout the country)

Exclusive Books (Pty) Ltd*, 48 Pretoria St, PO Box 17554, Hillbrow 2038, Transvaal Tel: (011) 6425068 Telex: 8-6579 SA; PO Box 4628, Cape Town 8000 (Located at: Southern Life Arcade, 101 St Georges St, Cape Town 8000) Tel: (021) 226860 Telex: 57-6078 SA

Fogarty's Bookshop*, Main St at Market Sq, Port Elizabeth Tel: (041) 21035

H A U M Academic Bookshop*, PO Box 343, Stellenbosch 7600 (Located at: Trust Bank Centre, Andringa Street) Tel: 70385/70315

H A U M Booksellers, 480 Paul Kruger St, PO Box 460, Pretoria 0001 Tel: 36417, 34931 Telex: 30962 SA

Johanesburgse Boekwinkel, PO Box 91119, Aucklandpark 2006

Juta & Co Ltd, PO Box 30, Cape Town 8000 (Located at: Regis Ho, Church St, Cape Town 8001) Tel: (021) 224571; Cnr Pritchard/Loveday Sts, PO Box 1010, Johannesburg 2000 Tel: (011) 8336113; Suite 5b, Mangrove Beach Centre, 91 Somtseu Rd, Durban 4001; PO Box 123, Kenwyn 7790 Tel: 711181

Literary Services (Pty) Ltd, PO Box 31361, Braamfontein 2017 Tel: 391711

Logans University Bookshop (Pty) Ltd, 227-229 Francois Rd, Durban
Office & Warehouse: 622 Umbilo Rd, Durban 4001; also Nedbank Plaza, Pietermaritzburg Tel: 354111

Maskew Miller Ltd, 50 Glynn St, Cape Town 8001 Tel: (021) 457731
Branches: Trust Bank Centre, George St, Kimberley 8301; PO Box 11430, Johannesburg; 20 Simmonds St South, Selby, Johannesburg; Room 236, Transkei Hotel, Cnr Elliot & Madeira Sts, Umtata; and at Branch Offices listed under Publisher entry

N G Kerkboekhandel Transvaal, Schoemanstr 260, PO Box 245, Pretoria 0001 Tel: 38401
Owned by: N G Kerkboekhandel, Publisher (qv)
Subjects: Religion, Books in Afrikaans and English

Nasionale Boekwinkels Bpk, PO Box 122, Parow 7500 Tel: 591131
General Manager: C J Coetzee
Owned by: Nasionale Boekhandel Beperk, Publisher (qv)
Branches: PO Box 119, Parow 7500 Tel: 987021; PO Box 912, Kimberley 8300; PO Box 2063, Cape Town 8000; PO Box 9898, Johannesburg 2000; PO Box 95, Port Elizabeth 6000; PO Box 1715, Port Elizabeth; PO Box 1058, Bloemfontein 9300; PO Box 1047, Bloemfontein 9300; 78

Maitland St, Bloemfontein 9301; PO Box 279, East London 5200

Ulrich **Naumann***, Park Gerou 303, Durban Rd/Weg 49, Bellville 7530
Academic and Scientific Booksellers

Perskor Bookshop*, PO Box 102, Maraisburg
Branches: PO Box 309, Kroonstad 9500; PO Box 133, Bellville 7530; Burnettstraat 1072, Hattfield, Pretoria 0083

Pilgrims Booksellers (Pty)*, Old Mutual Centre and Cavendish Sq, PO Box 3559, Cape Town

Van Schaik's Bookstore (Pty) Ltd*, Church St, PO Box 724, Pretoria 0001

Shuter and Shooter (Pty), Church St, PO Box 109, Pietermaritzburg Tel: (0331) 28121 Telex: 563771 SA
Owned by: Shuter and Shooter (Pty) Ltd, Publishers (qv)

C Struik (Pty) Ltd, see Bookwise (Pty) Ltd

United Book Distributors (Pty) Ltd, PO Box 17294, Hillbrow 2038 (Located at: 1st Floor, Permad House, 28 Betty St, Jeppestown) Tel: (614) 6431/2/3 Cable Add: Unibooks Telex: 424094 SA
Wholesalers and Distributors

Universitas Books (Pty) Ltd, PO Box 1557, 0001 Pretoria

Via Afrika Book Store, PO Box 9898, Johannesburg
Also PO Box 248, Pietersburg; PO Box 380, Pietermaritzburg; PO Box 107, King William's Town; PO Box 259, Umtata

Major Libraries

Cape Town City Libraries, 30 Chiappini St, Cape Town Tel: 2102036

Central Agricultural Library, Department of Agriculture & Fisheries, Private Bag X116, Pretoria 0001 Tel: 413111

Centre for Scientific and Technical Information, PO Box 395, Pretoria 0001 Tel: (74) 9111 Telex: 3630 Cable Add: Navorslig
Publicity Dir: J F Herbst
A department of the Council for Scientific and Industrial Research (CSIR), at the same address. Library stock covers Science and Technology

Department of National Education Library, Oranje-Nassau Bldg, Schoeman St, PB X122, Pretoria Tel: 29971
Librarian: Miss J Burrows
Publication: Library News

Durban Municipal Library, PO Box 917, Durban 4000 Tel: 320111
Publications: Annual Report; Accessions Lists; Booklists; Bookworm (Staff Quarterly Magazine)

Government Archives, Cape Archives Depot, Library*, Queen Victoria St, PB X9025, Cape Town 8000 Tel: 411888 (Branch of Department of National Education)
Archivist: F S van Rensburg

Government Archives, Natal Archives Depot, Library, 231 Pietermaritz St, PB X9012, Pietermaritzburg 3200 Tel: 24712
Chief Archivist: F Nel

Government Archives, Orange Free State Archives Depot, Library, 37 Elizabeth St, PB X20504, Bloemfontein 9300 Tel: 72840
Archivist: J W Cronje

Government Archives, Transvaal Archives Depot, Library*, Union Bldgs, Church St, PB X236, Pretoria 0001 Tel: 24971
Archivist: Dr M H Buys

Johannesburg Public Library, Market Sq, Johannesburg 2001 Tel: 8363787
City Librarian: Miss L Kennedy
Publications: Annual Report; Municipal Reference Library Bulletin (monthly); *Index to South African Periodicals* (annual)

Library of Parliament, PO Box 15, Cape Town 8000 Tel: 458165
Chief Librarian: J C Quinton

Royal Society of South Africa Library, University of Cape Town Libraries, Rondebosch 7700 Tel: (021) 698531
Publications: Transactions of the Royal Society of South Africa (irregular)

South African Library, Queen Victoria St, Cape Town 8001
Tel: 431132/433829/432486
Dir: Dr A M Lewin Robinson
Publications: Quarterly Bulletin; Grey Bibliographies; Reprint series

State Library, Vermeulen St, PO Box 397, Pretoria 0001 Tel: (012) 218931 Telex: SA 3778
Publications: South African National Bibliography; Reprint series; Micrographic series; Contribution to Library Science; Bibliographic series

University of Cape Town Libraries, Private Bag, Rondebosch 7700 Tel: (021) 698531
Librarian: A S C Hooper
Publications: Bibliographical series (irregular); *Varia series* (irregular)

University of Natal Library, King George V Ave, Durban 4001 Tel: (031) 352461 Telex: 60177 SA

University of Pretoria, Merensky Library, Brooklyn, Pretoria Tel: (012) 746051
Dir: Prof E D Gerryts
Publication: Bibliotekdiens Verslagreeks (series of reports, published only in Afrikaans)

University of South Africa Library, PO Box 392, Pretoria 0001 Tel: (012) 4401902 Cable Add: Unisarand Telex: 3777
Librarian: J Willemse

University of the Witwatersrand Library, Private Bag 31550, Braamfontein, 2007 Tel: (011) 394011 Telex: SA 87330
Librarian: Prof R Musiker
Publications include: *Historical and Literary Papers*, Inventories of Collections, Bibliographical Series (Occasional Publications Series); *Africana, Annual Report*

Library Associations

African Library Association of South Africa*, c/o Library, University of the North, Private Bag X5090, Pietersburg
Secretary-Treasurer: Mrs A N Kambule
Publication: Newsletter (quarterly)

South African Library Association, c/o Ferdinand Postma Library, Potchefstroom University, Potchefstroom 2520
Publications: South African Libraries, Newsletter

Library Reference Books and Journals

Books
Handbook of South African Libraries, The State Library, Vermeulen St, PO Box 397, Pretoria

Journals
Bookworm, Durban Municipal Library, PO Box 917, Durban 4000

The Cape Librarian (text in Afrikaans and English), Cape Provincial Library Service, Hospital and Chiappini Sts, PO Box 2108, Cape Town

Free State Libraries, Orange Free State Provincial Library, PO Box X0606, Bloemfontein

Library News, Department of National Education Library, Oranje-Nassau Bldg, Schoeman St, PB X122, Pretoria 0001

Mousaion II, Department of Library Science, University of South Africa, PO Box 392, Pretoria

Newsletter, South African Library Association, c/o Ferdinand Postma Library, Potchefstroom University, Potchefstroom

Quarterly Bulletin of the South African Library, South African Library, Queen Victoria St, Cape Town 8001

South African Libraries, South African Library Association, c/o Ferdinand Postma Library, Potchefstroom University, Potchefstroom (the official publication of the South African Library Association, published quarterly)

Literary Associations and Societies

Afrikaans Literature Society (ALV)*, ATKV Bldg 706, Cnr Eloff & Wolmarans Sts, Johannesburg 2001 Tel: 7251996

Artists' and Writers' Guild of South Africa*, 37-17th St, Parkhurst, Johannesburg 2001

South African **P E N** Centre (Cape)*, Apartment C, 2 Scott Rd, Claremont 7700 Cape Province
Secretary: Adele Naudé

Literary Periodicals

Contrast; South African literary journal (text in English and Afrikaans), South African Literary Journal Ltd, 3 Scott Rd, PO Box 3841, Claremont, Cape Town

Dialogue; a literary annual for young writers, PO Box 102, Wynberg 7824

New Classic, Ravan Press (Pty) Ltd, 508 Diakonia Ho, 80 Jorissen St, PO Box 31134, Braamfontein 2017 (important quarterly literary and cultural magazine, originally published as *The Classic*, edited by Sydney Sipho Sepamla)

Ophir, Ravan Press (Pty) Ltd, 508 Diakonia Ho, 80 Jorissen St, PO Box 31134, Braamfontein (biannual poetry magazine)

Literary Prizes

Afrikaans Literature Society Prize*
To encourage Afrikaans authors, artists and research workers. 300 pounds sterling. Awarded annually. Enquiries to Afrikaans Literature Society (ALV), ATKV Bldg 706, Cnr Eloff & Wolmarans Sts, Johannesburg 2001

Stephen **Black** Prize for Drama, see Department of National Education Literary Prizes

Jochem van **Bruggen** prys vir Prosa, see Department of National Education Literary Prizes

C N A Literary Award*
Established in 1961 for the best original works, one in English and one in Afrikaans, published for the first time during the calendar year of the competition. 3,500 rand each plus a bronze plaque. Awarded annually.
Books must be in one of following categories: Novels, Short Stories, Poetry, Biography, Drama, History, Travel. Authors must be South African citizens or registered permanent residents of South Africa. Winners in 1979 were: (English) Nadine Yordimer for novel *Burger's Daughter* (Cape); (Afrikaans) Prof D Opperman for poetry volume *Komas Uit 'n Bamboesstok* (Human & Rousseau). Enquiries to Central News Agency Literary Award, PO Box 9380, Johannesburg

Roy **Campbell** Prize for Poetry, see Department of National Education Literary Prizes

Department of National Education Literary Prizes
Established 1957 and awarded in 3-year cycles. In the English Section, the names of the prizes awarded are as follows: Stephen Black Prize for Drama (awarded in 1977 to Mrs J Fletcher for *Mr Stone and the Architect*); Roy Campbell Prize for Poetry; Pauline Smith Prize for Prose.
In the Afrikaans Section, the names of the prizes are as follows: J W F Grosskopf Prys vir Drama; Louis Leipoldt Prys vir Poesie; Jochem van Bruggen Prys vir Prosa.
Prizes of 750 and 500 rand are awarded to the authors of the two best entries in each of the two sections. Enquiries to Director-General for National Education, Private Bag X122, Pretoria 0001

English Association (South African Branch) Literary Prize*
For an original unpublished manuscript by a South African citizen or permanent resident of South Africa. Subject, literary form and amount of award vary from year to year. Usually awarded annually. Enquiries to English Association, PO Box 81, Rondebosch 7700

Percy **Fitzpatrick** Medal
For outstanding books for children written in English. Awarded annually. Enquiries to South African Institute for Library and Information Science, c/o Ferdinand Postma Library, Potchefstroom University, Potchefstroom 2520

J W F **Grosskopf** prys vir Drama, see Department of National Education Literary Prizes

Katrine **Harris** Award
For outstanding illustrations in South African children's books, regardless of language. Awarded annually. Enquiries to South African Institute for Library and Information Science, c/o Ferdinand Postma Library, Potchefstroom University, Potchefstroom 2520

Hertzog Prize
A Prestige Prize for Afrikaans Literature. Prizes are awarded in rotation for Poetry, Drama and Prose. 1,500 rand. Awarded annually. Enquiries to South African Academy of Science and Arts, PO Box 538, Pretoria 0001

W A **Hofmeyr** Prize
Awarded annually for the best book of a belletristic nature published by Tafelberg, Human & Rousseau, Nasou and Via Afrika; 1000 rand and a Gold Medallion. Enquiries to Nasionale Boekhandel, Voortrekker Rd, PO Box 122, Parow 7500

C P **Hoogenhout** Award
To encourage the production of outstanding Afrikaans children's books. Awarded annually. Enquiries to South African Institute for Library and Information Science, c/o Ferdinand Postma Library, Potchefstroom University, 2520

Ingrid **Jonker** Prize*
For the best first volume of poetry in English or Afrikaans written during the two previous years. Awarded alternately for English and Afrikaans poetry. 50 rand. Awarded annually by the panel of critics appointed by the Funds Board of Trustees. Enquiries to Funds Board of Trustees, Pretoria

C J **Langenhoven** Prize
For outstanding work in field of Afrikaans linguistics. 250 rand. Awarded every three years. Enquiries to South African Academy of Science and Arts, PO Box 538, Pretoria 0001

Louis **Leipholdt** prys vir Poesie, see Department of National Education Literary Prizes

H R **Malan** Prize
Awarded annually for the best non-fiction book published by Tafelberg, Human & Rousseau, Nasou and Via Afrika, 1000 rand and a Gold Medallion. Enquiries to Nasionale Boekhandel, Voortrekker Rd, PO Box 122, Parow 7500

Eugène **Marais** Prize
For a first, or early, work of belles lettres in Afrikaans. 250 rand. Awarded annually. Enquiries to South African Academy of Science and Arts, PO Box 538, Pretoria 0001

Mofolo-Plomer Prize*
Initiated by Nadine Gordimer for a South African writer resident in Southern Africa or elsewhere. For a novel or a collection of short stories in English. Enquiries to Mofolo-Plomer Prize Committee, c/o Ravan Press (Pty) Ltd, 409/416 Dunwell, 35 Jorissen St, Braamfontein 2017, Johannesburg

Perskor Prize for Literature*
For the best literary work published in Afrikaans by Perskor. 3,000 rand awarded biennially. Enquiries to Perskor Publishers, PO Box 845, Johannesburg 2000

Perskor Prize for Youth Literature*
For the best youth work published in Afrikaans by Perskor Press. 3,000 rand. Awarded every second year. Enquiries to Perskor Publishers, PO Box 845, Johannesburg 2000

Gustav **Preller** Prize
For literary science and literary criticism in Afrikaans. Awarded every 3 years. Enquiries to South African Academy of Science and Arts, PO Box 538 Pretoria 0001

Reina **Prinsen**-Geerlings Prize for South Africa*
For an outstanding new literary contribution by an Afrikaans author between 20 and 30. 350 Netherlands guilder Awarded every three years. Enquiries to Algemeen Nederlands Verbond, PO Box 4543, Cape Town

Scheepers Prize
For the best books written for children. 250 rand. Awarded every three years. Enquiries to South African Academy of Science and Arts, PO Box 538, Pretoria 0001

Olive **Schreiner** Prize for English Literature
For original literary work in English by a promising South African writer and published in South Africa. 250 rand. Awarded annually in one of the following categories: Prose, Poetry, Drama. Enquiries to English Academy of Southern Africa, Ballater House, 35 Melle Str, Braamfontein, Johannesburg 2001

Pauline **Smith** Prize for Prose, see Department of National Education Literary Prizes

South African Academy of Science and Arts Prizes
The Academy awards a number of prizes for works in Afrikaans; the following are noted in this section: Hertzog Prize; C J Langenhoven Prize; Eugène Marais Prize; Gustav Preller Prize; Scheepers Prize; Translation Prize. See individual entries for details. Enquiries to South African Academy of Science and Arts, PO Box 538, Pretoria 0001

Translation Prize
For translation of Belles Lettres from any language into Afrikaans. 250 rand awarded annually. Enquiries to South African Academy of Science and Arts, PO Box 538, Pretoria 0001

Spain

General Information

Language: Castilian (the most widely used) is what foreigners know as Spanish; Basque in the north, Catalan in the east, Galician in the north-west. Most speakers of Basque, Catalan and Galician also speak Castilian
Religion: Roman Catholic
Population: 37.1 million
Literacy Rate (1970): 90.1%
Bank Hours: Vary. Generally 0900-1300 or 0900-1600 Monday-Friday; half day Saturday
Shop Hours: Generally 0900-1300, 1700-2000 Monday-Saturday
Currency: 100 céntimos = 1 peseta
Export/Import Information: Varying tariffs on books, related to type, binding, language, etc; children's picture books 13% duty, 11% tax; 10% compensatory tax on books in general.
Most advertising matter free of tariff but have 11% tax. Import licence required; foreign books subject to censorship.
Exchange controls
Copyright: UCC, Berne, Florence (see International section)

Book Trade Organizations

Asociación de Escritores y Artistas Españoles*, Calle de Leganitos 10, Madrid 13
Spanish Writers' and Artists' Association
Secretary: José G Manrique de Lava

Asociacion Española de Editores de Musica (AEDEM), Carrera de San Jeronimo, No 29-1°C Madrid 14
Spanish Association of Music Publishers

Federación de Gremios de Editores de España, Calle General Pardinas 29 6° Izqda, Madrid Tel: 4454462
Federation of Spanish Publishers' Associations
Secretary: I Buell Fontsené

Gremio Sindical de Libreros de Barcelona (Association of Barcelona Booksellers)*, Calle Mallorca 272-276, Barcelona 9
Publication: Librería

Instituto Nacional del Libro Español, Calle Santiago Rusiñol 8, Madrid 3 Tel: (01) 2330802/2330902/2334502
Spanish Publishers' and Booksellers' Association
Secretary: Eduardo Nolla López
Publications: El Libro Español (monthly); *Libros Españoles ISBN* (annual); *Libros y Material de de Enseñanza* (annual); *Libros Infantiles y Juveniles* (biannual); *Llibres en Català* (annual)

Instituto Nacional del Libro Español, Delegación de Barcelona, Calle Mallorca 272-276, Barcelona 3 Tel: (03) 2155650
Barcelona Section of the Spanish Publishers' and Booksellers' Association
Executive Delegate: S Olives Canals
Publications: Guía de Editores de España, Catálogo ISBN, Catalogo de Libros de Ensenanze, Llibres en Català, Quién es quién

Sociedad General de Autores de España, Fernando VI 4, Apdo 484, Madrid 4
General Society of Spanish Authors
Secretary-General Carlos Galiano de Prados

Sociedad General Española de Librería, Evaristo san Miguel 9, Madrid 8
Spanish Association for Bookshops

Spanish Book Center, Milanesado 21-23, Barcelona 17 Tel: (93) 2039916 Telex: 54675 contb-e
Man Dir: Jürgen Bernardi
Export organization for all books published in Spain
Publication: New Books from Spain

Standard Book Numbering Agency, Instituto Nacional del Libro Español, Calle Santiago Rusiñol 8, Madrid 3 Tel: (01) 2330802
ISBN Administrator: José M Garcia Diéguez

Book Trade Reference Books and Journals

Books

Guía de Editores de España (Guide to the Publishers of Spain), Spanish Publishers' and Booksellers' Association, Calle Santiago Rusiñol 8, Madrid 3

Guía de Libreros y Distribuidores de España (Guide to the Booksellers and Distributors of Spain), Spanish Publishers' and Booksellers' Association, Calle Santiago Rusiñol 8, Madrid 3

Indice Cultural Español (Spanish Cultural Index), Dirección General de Relaciones Culturales, Ministerio de Asuntos Exteriores, Plaza de la Provincia 1, Madrid 12

Indice de la Producción Editorial Española (Index of Spanish Book Production), Spanish Publishers' and Booksellers' Association, Calle Santiago Rusiñol 8, Madrid 3 (four-year cumulation of *El Libro Español*)

Libros en Venta (Books for Sale); annual supplements including Spanish language book production of the year from all countries, Turner Ediciones Chile 1441, 1° piso, of 3, Buenos Aires

Libros Españoles ISBN (Spanish Books assigned ISBNs), Spanish Publishers' and Booksellers' Association, Calle Santiago Rusiñol 8, Madrid 3

Llibres en Català (Books in Catalan), Spanish Publishers' and Booksellers' Association, Calle Santiago Rusiñol 8, Madrid 3

Quién es Quién (Who's Who), Spanish Publishers' and Booksellers' Association, Calle Mallorca 272-276, Barcelona 3

Journals

Bibliografía Española (Spanish Bibliography), Hispanic Bibliographical Institute, Calle de Atocha 106, Madrid 12

Cuadernos de Bibliografía Española (Notebook of Spanish Bibliography), Hispanic Bibliographical Institute, Calle de Atocha 106, Madrid 12

Librería (Bookselling), Association of Barcelona Booksellers, Calle Mallorca 272-276, Barcelona 9

El Libro Español (The Spanish Book), Spanish Publishers' and Booksellers' Association, Calle Santiago Rusiñol 8, Madrid 3

New Books from Spain, Spanish Book Center, Milanesado 21-23, Barcelona 17

Publishers

Ediciones **29***, Mandri 41, Barcelona 22 Tel: (93) 2123836
Man Dir: Alfredo Lloreme Diez
Subjects: Fiction, Literature, General Nonfiction
1978: 22 titles *Founded:* 1968
ISBN Publisher's Prefix: 84-7175

Edicions **62** SA, Provenza 278 1°-1a, Barcelona 8 Tel: (93) 2160062
Dir: Romà Cuyàs Sol; *Editorial:* Josep M Castellet; *Production:* Ramon Bastardes; *Publicity:* Eliseu Gil
Associate Company: Ediciones Peninsula (qv)
Subsidiary Company: Distribuciones de Enlace SA (Distributors)
Subjects: General (in Catalan)
1978: 101 titles *1979:* 186 titles *Founded:* 1963
ISBN Publisher's Prefix: 84-297

Ediciones **99** SA*, Calle General Martínez Campos 42-Bajo, Madrid 10
Part of Grupo Editorial Guadiana (qv)

Editorial **A E D O S**, Consejo de Ciento 391, Barcelona 9 Tel: (03) 3170141/3012845 Cable Add: Aedos
Man Dir: Juan Badosa
Subjects: Agriculture, Veterinary Science, Sports, How-to, Biography
1979: 13 titles *Founded:* 1939
ISBN Publisher's Prefix: 84-7003

Publicacions de l'**Abadia** de Montserrat, Abadia de Montserrat, Barcelona Tel: 2450303
Shipping Add: Ausias March, 92-98, Barcelona 13
Man Dir: Josep Massot Muntaner; *Sales, Advertising & Publicity:* Jordi Ubeda; *Rights & Permissions:* Bernabé Dalmau
Subjects: Religion, History, Geography, Biography, Literature, Juveniles, Travel (mostly in Catalán)
1978: 62 titles *1979:* 66 titles *Founded:* 1915
ISBN Publisher's Prefix: 84-7202

Ediciones **Acervo**, Julio Verne 5-7, Apdo 5319, Barcelona 6 Tel: (93) 212264/2474425

Man Dir: José A Llorens
Subsidiary Company: Ediciones Acervo de Argentina SRL, Argentina (qv)
Subject: General Literature
1978: 23 titles *Founded:* 1954
ISBN Publisher's Prefix: 84-70002

Editorial **Acribia**, C Royo 23, Apdo 466, Saragossa Tel: 232089
Man Dir: Pascual López Lorenzo; *Sales, Publicity & Advertising:* Mercedes Marcen
Subjects: Veterinary Science, Agriculture, General Science, Medicine, Oceanography, Marine Biology
1978: 36 titles *1979:* 20 titles *Founded:* 1957
ISBN Publisher's Prefix: 84-200

Afha Internacional SA, Aribau 200-210, Apdo 75, Barcelona 36 Tel: 2091800 Cable Add: Afhinter Telex: 52743
Man Dir: José Ma Llovet; *Editorial:* Diego de Herrera; *Sales:* Ramón Bertrand; *Production, Rights & Permissions:* Ulisses Farreras; *Publicity:* Pedro Richard
Parent Company: Ediciones Afha
Subsidiary Company: Editorial Columna
Imprint: Emograph
Subjects: Juveniles, Education
Founded: 1951
ISBN Publisher's Prefix: 84-201

Aguilar SA de Ediciones*, Juan Bravo 38, Madrid 6 Tel: (91) 2763800 Cable Add: Guilarditor
Man Dir: Carlos Aguilar; *Sales Dir:* Jaime Lejarraga; *Rights & Permissions:* Manuel Aguilar
*Branch Offs:*Argentina (qv); Aguilar Chilena de Ediciones, Santiago, Chile; Colombia (qv); Mexico (qv); Peru (qv); Venezuela (qv)
Subjects: General Fiction, Belles Lettres, Poetry, Biography, History, Music, Art, Philosophy, Reference, Religion, Juveniles, Paperbacks, Medicine, Psychology, Engineering, General & Social Science, Law, Technical, Educational Materials
Bookshops: M Aguilar, Librería General, Serrano 24; Goya 18; Ave Generalísimo 44-46 (all in Madrid)
ISBN Publisher's Prefix: 84-03

Editorial **'Alas'**, Valencia 234, Apdo 707, Barcelona 7 Tel: (93) 2537506
Subjects: Sports, How-to, Para-psychology, Crosswords, Martial Arts, Periodicals
1978: 31 titles
ISBN Publisher's Prefix: 84-203

Ediciones **Alfaguara** SA, Ave de América 37, Madrid 2 Tel: (91) 4160850/4160860 Cable Add: Guara Madrid Telex: 27575
Man Dir: Jaime Salinas; *Rights & Permissions:* Rosa Benavides
Subjects: General Fiction, Literature, Children's Books, Universal Classics
1978: 60 titles *1979:* 130 titles *Founded:* 1964
ISBN Publisher's Prefix: 84-204

Editorial **Alhambra** SA, Claudio Coello 76, Madrid 1 Tel: (91) 2764209 Cable Add: Edimbrasa
President: Erich Ruiz Albrecht; *Sales:* Angeles Z Huerta; *Production:* Santiago Diáz-Hellín María Teresa Esteban Fernández; *Rights & Permissions:* Ana Ma Sampedro
Branch Offs: Enrique Granados 61, Barcelona 8; Doctor Albiñana 12, Bilbao 14; Pasadizo de Pernas 13, La Coruña; La Regente 5, Málaga 9; Avda del Cristo 9, Oviedo; Reina Mercedes 35 (entrada por Marqués de Luca de Tena), Sevilla 12; General Porlier, 14, Santa Cruz de Tenerife; Cabillers 5, Valencia 3; Concepcion Arenal, 25 Zaragoza 5
Subjects: Medicine, General Science, Literature, History, Philology, Philosophy, Reference, University, Secondary and Primary Textbooks, Audiovisual Aids, Languages
1978: 39 titles *1979:* 38 titles *Founded:* 1952
ISBN Publisher's Prefix: 84-205

Alianza Editorial SA, Milán 38, Apdo 9107, Madrid 33 Tel: (91) 2000045
President: Jose Vergara Doncel; *Editorial:* Javier Pradera; *Sales & Marketing:* Faustino Linares; *Production:* Ascension Vazquez; *Publicity:* Antonio Paton; *Rights & Permissions:* Monica Acheroff
Associate Companies: Alianza Editorial Mexicana, Mexico (qv); Distasa, Argentina (qv); Revista de Occidente SA, Madrid (qv)
Subjects: General Fiction, Belles Lettres, Poetry, History, Music, Art, Philosophy, Political and Social Science, High-priced Paperbacks, Mathematics, General Science
1978: 81 titles *1979:* 88 titles *Founded:* 1959
ISBN Publisher's Prefix: 84-206

Ediciones **Altea** SA, General Mola 84, Madrid 6 Tel: (91) 2625300 Cable Add: Edialtea Telex: 43879
Man Dir: Miguel Azaola; *Sales:* Carlos Martínez; *Publicity:* Arturo Gonzalez; *Co-productions:* Juan Ramón Azaola
Subjects: Activity books, Children's Books, Picture Books
1978: 16 titles *1979:* 29 titles *Founded:* 1973
ISBN Publisher's Prefix: 84-372

Editorial **Anagrama**, Calle La Cruz 44, Barcelona 17 Tel: (93) 2037652
Man Dir: Jorge de Herralde Grau
Subjects: Literature, Philosophy, Psychology, Social Science, Anthropology
1980: 400 titles *Founded:* 1968
ISBN Publisher's Prefix: 84-339

Ediciones **Anaya** SA*, Calle Iriarte 4, Madrid 28 Tel: (91) 2468604/5/6 Cable Add: Edinaya Telex: 26825 Edaya E
President: Germán Sánchez Ruiperez; *Man Dir:* Ambrosio María Ochoa Vázquez; *Editorial:* Ramiro Sánchez Sanz; *Rights & Permissions:* José M Delgado de Luque
Branch Off: Iriarte 3-4, Madrid 28
Subjects: University, Secondary & Primary Textbooks, Educational Materials
Founded: 1959
ISBN Publisher's Prefix: 84-207

Editorial **Aranzadi***, Carlos III, 34, Pamplona Tel: 243112/249950
Man Dir: Estanislao de Aranzadi; *Sales Dir:* Javier de Epalza y Aranzadi
Subject: Law
1978: 18 titles *Founded:* 1929
ISBN Publisher's Prefix: 84-7018

Editorial **Argos** Vergara SA*, Aragón 390, Barcelona 13 Tel: (03) 2457600 Cable Add: Leargos
President: Enrique Moyá; *Man Dir:* Mario Lacruz; *Editor-in-Chief:* Anne-Marie Comert
Subjects: Fiction, Nonfiction, Reference, Art Books
Bookshop: Librería Editorial Argos, Paseo de Gracia 30, Barcelona 7
ISBN Publisher's Prefix: 84-7017

Editorial **Ariel** SA, Tambor del Bruch s/n, Sant Joan Despi, Barcelona Tel: (93) 3731409
Man Dir: Antonio Comas Baldellou; *Editorial, Rights & Permissions:* Alejandro Argullós Marimón; *Sales:* Luis Carlos Sanchez Montoya; *Production & Publicity:* Angel Jasanada París
Associate Company: Editorial Seix Barral SA (qv for subsidiary companies). The two Companies constitute the organization Ariel/Seix Barral Editoriales
Subjects: General and Social Sciences, Psychology, Philosophy, Religion, Economics, History, Literature, Texts in Catalan, Geography, Biography, University Textbooks
1978: 45 titles *1979:* 52 titles *Founded:* 1941
ISBN Publisher's Prefix: 84-344

Asesoría Técnica de Ediciones SA, Ronda General Mitre 90, Barcelona 21 Tel: (93) 2479133/2477066
Man Dir, Editorial: José Dalmau Salvia; *Sales:* Antonio Dalmau Salvia; *Production:* José Luis Arribas; *Rights & Permissions:* Carmen de Eulate Echagüe
Subsidiary Company: Libroexpress
Subjects: Fiction, Communications, Science Fiction, Classics, Microbiology
1979: 250 titles
ISBN Publisher's Prefix: 84-7442

Asociación para el Progresso de la Dirección (APD)*, Montalban 3, Madrid 14 Tel: (91) 2325487
Dir of Publications: Vidal Pérez Herrero
Subject: Business Administration
ISBN Publisher's Prefix: 84-7019

Sociedad de Educación **Atenas** SA, Mayor 81, Apdo 1096, Madrid 13 Tel: (91) 2480127
Parent Company: Ediciones Sigueme SA (qv)
Subjects: Religion, Education, Psychology, Biography
ISBN Publisher's Prefix: 84-7020

Atika SA*, Fuencarral 138, Madrid 10 Tel: (91) 4485361
Man Dir: Mr Thermolle
Subjects: Technical, How-to, Automobile Manuals
Founded: 1964
ISBN Publisher's Prefix: 84-7022

Biblioteca de **Autores** Cristianos*, Mateo Inurria 15, Madrid 16 Tel: 2592800
Editorial: José L García; *Sales:* Eduardo M de Sequera; *Publicity:* Bartolomé P Galmes
Subjects: Theology, Philosophy, History, the Scriptures, Liturgical
ISBN Publisher's Prefix: 84-220

Aymá SA Editora (& Edicions Proa), Tuset 3 3°, Barcelona 22 Tel: (93) 2000933/200576 Cable Add: Aymol
President: Joan B Cendrós Carbonell
Subjects: General Fiction, Belles Lettres, Poetry, Biography, History, How-to, Music, Art, Philosophy, Religion, Low- and High-priced Paperbacks, Juveniles. In both Castilian and Catalan
1978: 46 titles *1979:* 87 titles *Founded:* 1952
ISBN Publisher's Prefix: 84-209

Editorial **Ayuso***, San Bernardo 34, Madrid 8
Subject: Social Sciences
ISBN Publisher's Prefix: 84-336

Barral Editores SA*, Calabria 235, Barcelona 29 Tel: (93) 3220551
Subjects: General Fiction, Belles Lettres, Poetry, Art, Theatre, Paperbacks
Founded: 1970
ISBN Publisher's Prefix: 84-211

Ediciones **Bellaterra** SA*, Felipe de Paz 12, Barcelona 28 Tel: (93) 3390511
Man Dir: Felio Riera Domenech; *Editorial:* Jeannine Rochefort; *Sales:* Angeles Galán Gallego
Subjects: Science & Technology, Social Sciences
Founded: 1972
ISBN Publisher's Prefix: 84-7290

Ediciones **Betis***, Calle Bot 4 bis, Barcelona 2 Tel: (93) 3175844
Man Dir, Editorial, Rights & Permissions: Santiago Subirana; *Sales:* Eugenio Subirana
Subjects: Juveniles, Popular Science,

316 SPAIN

History, Philosophy, Infants
1978: 28 titles *Founded:* 1939
ISBN Publisher's Prefix: 84-7160

Editorial **Biblioteca** Nueva SL, Almagro 38, Madrid 4 Tel: (91) 4100436
Man Dir: Miguel Ruiz-Castillo; *Sales Dir:* José Ruiz-Castillo
Subjects: Belles Lettres, Poetry, Biography, History, Psychology
Founded: 1920
ISBN Publisher's Prefix: 84-7030

Editorial **Biblograf** SA*, Calle de Bruch 151, Barcelona 9 Tel: (93) 2571304/2573158
Cable Add: Biblograf
Man Dir: Antonio Mercadé Oliu
Subjects: Dictionaires, Philology
Founded: 1952
ISBN Publisher's Prefix: 84-7153

Editorial **Blume**, Calle Milanesado 21-23, Barcelona 17 Tel: (93) 2042300/04/08
Cable Add: Ediblume Telex: 54675 Contbe; also H Blume Ediciones, Rosario 17, Madrid 5 Tel: (91) 2659200
Man Dir: Siegfried Blume; *Editorial:* José Maria Riaño; *Rights and Permissions:* Rita Blume
Imprints: Ed R Torres, Floraprint, Galaxis SA
Founded: 1965
Subjects: Architecture and Building Construction, Art, History, Politics, Technology, Ecology, Nature Study, Physical and Life Sciences, books in English and Catalan
ISBN Publisher's Prefix: 84-7031

Al-**Borak** SA*, Calle General Martínez Campos, 42-Bajo, Madrid 10
Part of Grupo Editorial Guadiana (qv)

Bosch Casa Editorial SA, Calle Urgel 51 bis, Barcelona 11 Tel: (93) 2548437
Man Dir: Agustín Bosch Domenech
Subjects: Law, Economics, Science & Technology, Philology, General Literature
1978: 40 titles *1979:* 35 titles
ISBN Publisher's Prefix: 84-7162

Editorial **Bruguera** SA, Camps y Fabrés 5, Barcelona 6 Tel: (93) 2282107 Cable Add: Brugueditor Telex: 52551
Man Dirs: Guillermo Molinas Bruguera, Joaquin Miñano, Consuelo Bruguera; *Editorial:* Jorge Gubern, Ricardo Rodrigo, Miguel Pellicer; *Sales:* Emilio Martinez; *Production:* Guillermo Molinas Carreño; *Rights & Permissions:* Ute Körner de Moya
Associate Company: Nueva Linea
Subsidiary Companies: Argentina; Colombia; Mexico; Venezuela (qqv)
Branch Offs: Ave del Mediterráneo 7, Madrid 7; Canarias 2-A, Bilbao 14; Luis Oliag 71-73, Valencia 6; Elda 44, Alicante; Juan M Rodríguez Correas 3-9, Seville; Durán y Borrell 24-26, Barcelona 6
Subjects: General Fiction, Belles Lettres, Biography, History, How-to, Juveniles; Paperbacks
Bookshop: Librería Proa SL, Rambla Cataluña 72, Barcelona
1978: 380 titles *Founded:* 1954
ISBN Publisher's Prefix: 84-02

Editorial **Bruño**, Marqués de Mondéjar 32, Madrid 28 Tel: (91) 2460607/06/05
Man Dir: Juan Santaeulalia
Subjects: Secondary & Primary Textbooks, Education, Communication
1980: 426 titles *Founded:* 1882
ISBN Publisher's Prefix: 84-216

Burulan, SA de Ediciones*, Avenida de Francia 4, POB 754, San Sebastian
Tel: (93) 426220, (93) 416829 Cable Add: Burulan Telex: 36228 Camino-E Ref Burulan
Subjects: Encyclopedias, Various Publications for Children and Juveniles

Editorial **C E D E L** (Centro de Difusión del Libro), Mallorca 257, Barcelona 8 Tel: (93) 2156039
Man Dir: Jose O Avila Monteso
Subjects: Hygiene, Health and Body Culture, Psychology, Magic and the Occult, Radio, Television, Electronics, Electroplating; General Technical; General Literature
Bookclub: Club de Amigos del Libro (qv)
1978: 500 titles *Founded:* 1959
ISBN Publisher's Prefix: 84-352

Editorial **Cantabrica** SA*, Plaza Conde de Aresti 51°, Bilbao Tel: (044) 217197
Man Dir: Rosario Fernandez Urcelay
Branch Offs: Calle Marqués de Sentemenat 55-57, Barcelona; Calle O'Connell, 43 bajo, Madrid
Subject: Juveniles
Founded: 1960
ISBN Publisher's Prefix: 84-221

Luis de **Caralt** Editor SA, Rosellón 246, Barcelona 8 Tel: (93) 2156516 Cable Add: Edinoguer Barcelona Telex: 52534
Man Dir, Editorial: Emilio Ardévol; *Sales:* Jorge Figueras; *Production:* Manuel Tort; *Rights & Permissions:* Luis N Lattore
Orders to: Luis de Caralt Editor SA
Associate Companies: Editorial Noguer (qv); NRL-Norildis (qv)
Subjects: General Fiction and Non-fiction, History, Art, Medicine, Geography, Paperbacks
1978: 70 titles *Founded:* 1942
ISBN Publisher's Prefix: 84-217

Editorial **Castalia**, Zurbano 39, Madrid 10
Tel: (91) 4198940/4195857
Man Dir: Amparo Soler; *Sales Dir:* Federico Ibáñez
Subjects: Literature, Criticism, Classics, Philology
Founded: 1941
Miscellaneous: Specializes in editions of the classics
ISBN Publisher's Prefix: 84-7039

Ediciones **Cátedra** SA*, Don Ramón de la Cruz, Apdo 50512, Madrid Tel: (91) 4011200 Cable Add: Grupedi
Man Dir: José Luis Torres; *Rights & Permissions:* Gustavo Dominguez
Orders to: Grupo Editorial SA, Don Ramón de la Cruz 67, Madrid 1
Subjects: Literature, Criticism, Humanities, Linguistics, Art
Founded: 1974
ISBN Publisher's Prefix: 84-376

La Editorial **Católica** SA*, Mateo Inurria 15, Madrid 16 Tel: (91) 2592800 Cable Add: Edica
Dirs: Mariana de Rioja, Fernández de Mesa; *Sales Manager:* Eduardo Masip; *Advertising & Publicity:* Vicente Lasheras
Subjects: Philosophy, Religion, Theology
Founded: 1912
ISBN Publisher's Prefix: 84-720

Ediciones **Ceac** SA, Via Layetana 17, Barcelona 3 Tel: (93) 3197400 Cable Add: Ediceac
Man Dirs: Juan Martí, José Menal; *Advertising & Publicity Dir:* J M Quesade; *Foreign Sales:* G Menal
Subjects: Technical, Arts & Crafts, Homecrafts & Domestic Science
Founded: 1954
ISBN Publisher's Prefix: 84-329

El **Cid** Editor SAE, Cardenal Vives y Tutó 43 2° 3a, Barcelona 34 Tel: 2045067
Man Dir, Rights & Permissions: Dr Eduardo Varela-Cid; *Editorial:* Jorge Sanchez; *Sales:* Adriana Buguña; *Production:* José Ignacio Domench; *Publicity:* Marcial Dominguez
Parent Company: El Cid Editor SRL, Argentina (qv)
Subsidiary Company: El Cid Editor CA, Apdo 60010, Caracas 1060, Venezuela
Associate Companies (all in Argentina): Ciudad Educativa SAIC, Alsina 500, 1087 Buenos Aires; La Casa de los Papeles, Bolivar 218, 1066 Buenos Aires; El Cid Distribuidor SA, Guise 1637, 1425 Buenos Aires
Subjects: Fiction, Sociology and Social Work, Juvenile, Economics, Geo-politics, Research Technology, History
Bookshops: Librería del Colegio, Ciudad Educativa SA, Buenos Aires
1978: 102 titles *1979:* 74 titles *Founded:* 1970

Editorial **Científico Médica**, Vía Layetana 53, Barcelona 3 Tel: (93) 3186832
Man Dir: Eugeniano Barrera San Martín; *Chief Editor:* Dr Enrique Sierra Ruiz
Distributor: Científico Médica Dossat SA, Plaza de Santa Ana 9, 1°, Madrid 12
Subjects: Medicine, Psychology, Veterinary Science, Engineering, Architecture, Technical Subjects
Founded: 1915
ISBN Publisher's Prefix: 84-224

Compañía Bibliográfica Española SA*, Sánchez Pacheco 52-54, Madrid 2 Tel: (91) 4155300
Man Dir: Rafael Agulló
Subjects: Biography, History, Music, Art, Philosophy, Religion, Reference, Linguistics, Juveniles, Social Science, Textbooks, Educational Materials
Founded: 1951
ISBN Publisher's Prefix: 84-326

Alberto **Corazón** Editor, Roble 22, Madrid 15 Tel: (91) 2704378
Man Dir: Alberto Corazón; *Sales Dir:* José Miguel García
Subjects: Literature, History, Philosophy, Poetry, Social Sciences, University Textbooks
Founded: 1969
ISBN Publisher's Prefix: 84-7053

Ediciones **Cristiandad***, Huesca 30, Madrid 20 Tel: (91) 2701636
Subjects: Religion, History
ISBN Publisher's Prefix: 84-7057

Editorial **Crítica** SA, Calle de la Cruz 58 1° 1a, Barcelona 34 Tel: 2049311
Man Dir: Xavier Folch y Gonzalo Pontón
Orders to: Deu y Mata 98, Barcelona
Parent Company: Ediciones Grijalbo (qv)
Subjects: Social Sciences, Politics, Current Affairs, Marxism, Philosophy
1978: 40 titles *1979:* 30 titles *Founded:* 1976
ISBN Publisher's Prefix: 84-7423

Ediciones **Cultura** Hispánica*, Ave de los Reyes Católicos 4, Madrid 3 Tel: (91) 2440600 (287, 285)
Subjects: Literature, Biography, History, Art, Economics, Law, Philology, Social Science
ISBN Publisher's Prefix: 84-7232

Editorial **D O P E S A** (Documentacion Periodistica SA)*, Cardenal Reig s/n, Edificio Grupo Mundo, Barcelona 28 Tel: (93) 334200
Man Dir: Juan Agut; *Editorial:* Mauricio Waquez; *Sales, Publicity:* Pablo Bordona BA; *Production:* Manuel Gallego; *Rights & Permissions:* José Planas
Subjects: General
Bookshop: Libreria Grop, Ave infanta Carlota 37, Barcelona 15
1978: 180 titles *Founded:* 1969
ISBN Publisher's Prefix: 84-7235

Ediciones **Daimon** — Manuel Tamayo*, Provenza 284, Barcelona 8
Subjects: Art, History, How-to, Reference,

Medicine, Cinematography, Photography, Sexology, Astrology, Philosophy, Science
ISBN Publisher's Prefix: 84-231

Ediciones **Danae** SA, Paseo de Gracia 24-26, Barcelona 7 Tel: 3174508/3010182
Sales: Luis López Cabañas; *Production, Rights & Permissions:* Isabel Gortazar
Subjects: Belles Lettres, History, Geography, Social Science, Art, Religion, Technical, Encyclopaedias, Juveniles, General Culture
Founded: 1963
ISBN Publisher's Prefix: 84-7060

Editorial **De Vecchi** SA, Balmes 247, Barcelona 6 Tel: (93) 2171854/217858 Cable Add: Deveditor Telex: 51042 Deve E
Man Dir: Giovanni de Vecchi
Subjects: How-to and Practical Books generally, Animals, UFO investigation
Founded: 1967
ISBN Publisher's Prefix: 84-315

Editorial de **Derecho Financiero**, see EDERSA

Editorial Revista de **Derecho Privado**, see EDERSA

Ediciones **Destino** SL, Consejo de Ciento 425, Barcelona 9 Tel: (93) 2462305
Man Dir: José Vergés
Subjects: General Fiction, Art Books, History
Bookshop: Librería Ancora y Delfín, Ave Generalísimo Franco 564, Barcelona 11
Founded: 1942
ISBN Publisher's Prefix: 84-233

Diafora SA*, Lauria 118, Barcelona Tel: (93) 2577889
Subjects: Cartographic Studies; Audio-Visual aids; Geography

Centro de **Difusión** del Libro, see Editorial CEDEL

Dilagro SA, Editorial-Librería, Comercio 40, Apdo 114, Lérida Tel: 233480
Man Dir: Jorge Marimón; *Sales Dir:* Antonio Miñano
Subjects: Agriculture, History and Customs of the region of Lérida
Bookshops: Librería Ténica, Gral Brito 1; Librería Universitaria, Ave Cataluña 7
1978: 3 titles *1979:* 6 titles
ISBN Publisher's Prefix: 84-7234

Grupo Editorial **Distein**-CEAC-Timun Mas, see Timun

Ediciones **Don Bosco***, Paseo San Juan Bosco 62, Barcelona 17 Tel: (93) 2037408
Associate Companies: Don Bosco Verlag, Federal Republic of Germany (qv), and Publishers and/or Booksellers of same name in Bolivia and Rwanda (qqv), all under the parentage of the Religious Order of the Salesians, Rome, Italy
Subjects: Technical works on Printing, Graphics, Typography, Technical Drawing, Computers and Electronics
ISBN Publisher's Prefix: 84-236

Doncel*, Perez Ayuso 20, Madrid 2 Tel: (91) 4257400 Cable Add: Edidoncel
Man Dir: Juan Van Halen Acedo
Subjects: Juveniles, Secondary & Primary Textbooks
Founded: 1959
Bookshops: Librería Doncel, Ave Calvo Sotelo 7, Zaragoza and José Ortega y Gasset 71, Madrid 6
ISBN Publisher's Prefix: 84-325

Editorial **Dossat** SA, Plaza de Santa Ana 9°, Madrid 12 Tel: (91) 4334000 Telex: 42572 Doate
Man Dir, Sales and Other Offices: Eugeniano Barrera San Martín
Branch Off: Via Layetana 53, Barcelona 3
Subjects: Medicine, Engineering, General Scientific, University Textbooks
ISBN Publisher's Prefix: 84-237

Durvan SA de Ediciones, Colón de Larreátegui 13, Bilbao
Associate Company: Editorial Marin SA (qv)

E D E R S A (Editoriales de Derecho Reunidas SA), Caracas 21, Apdo 4032, Madrid 4 Tel: (91) 4101862/4199623 Cable Add: Revipriv
Man Dir: Antonio Alvarez de Morales
Imprints: Ediciones Pegaso, Editorial de Derecho Financiero, Editorial Revista de Derecho Privado
Subjects: Biography, History, Philosophy, Social Science, Law, Technical, University Textbooks
Founded: 1900
ISBN Publisher's Prefix: 84-7130

E D H A S A (Editora y Distribuidora Hispano-Americana SA)*, Diagonal 521, 2°, Barcelona 29 Tel: (93) 2395104
Man Dir: Jaime Rodrigué
Subjects: Literature, History, Essays
1978: 50 titles
ISBN Publisher's Prefix: 84-350

E U N S A (Ediciones Universidad de Navarra SA), POB 396, Pamplona (Located at: Plaza de los Sauces, 1 & 2 Barañain, Pamplona) Tel: (948) 256850 Cable Add: EUNSA Pamplona
Man Dir: Francisco Salvadó; *Sales:* Robert Kimball; *Production:* Luis Ma Echeverría; *Publicity:* Tomás C Lizarrondo; *Rights & Permissions:* Eugenia Puyales
Imprint: Biblioteca 'nt' (number of paperback series covering the Arts and Sciences, Current Affairs, Religion and Philosophy etc)
Subjects: Architecture, Business Administration, Economics, Education, History, Journalism, Law, Language and Literature, Medicine, Sciences and Engineering, Nursing, Philosophy, Religion, Theology, Bibliography, Librarianship, Encyclopedias, Periodicals
1979: 95 titles *Founded:* 1967
ISBN Publisher's Prefix: 84-313

Edaf Ediciones y Distribuciones SA, Jorge Juan 30, Madrid 1 Tel: (91) 2263500
Bookshop: Librería Edaf, Jorge Juan 30, Madrid 1
Subjects: History, Philosophy, Juveniles, Reference, Textbooks
ISBN Publisher's Prefix: 84-7166

Edica SA*, Calle Mateo Inurria 15, Apdo 466, Madrid 16 Tel: (91) 2592800 Cable Add: Edica Telex: 27727
Dir: Dr José Luis Gutierrez Garcia; *Sales:* Dr Eduardo Masip de Sequera
Subjects: Theology, Asceticism, Mysticism, History, Philosophy, Hagiography, Pocket Editions
1978: 46 titles

Ediciones **Iberoamericanas** SA (EISA)*, Oñate 15, Madrid 20 Tel: (91) 2795804 Cable Add: Asepe
Dir: Rafael Ordoñez Miranda
Subjects: Social Sciences, Medicine, Biography, Religion, Psychology, Law, others
Founded: 1949
ISBN Publisher's Prefix: 84-7084

Edigraf, Editorial Vilcar y Gráficas Hamburg SA, Tamarit 130, Barcelona 15 Tel: (05) 3255550
Man Dir: Francisco Vilar
Subject: Juveniles
ISBN Publisher's Prefix: 84-7066

Editora Nacional, Calle Torregalindo 10, Madrid 16 Tel: (91) 2508600
President: José Luis Castillo-Puche; *Dir:* Alberto de la Puente O'Connor
Subjects: Poetry, History, Art, Essays, Literature, Law
1978: 53 titles *Founded:* 1937
ISBN Publisher's Prefix: 84-276

Emograph, an imprint of Afha Internacional SA (qv)

Editorial **Espasa-Calpe** SA, Apdo 547, Madrid 34 (Located at: Carretera de Irún, km 12,200 (variante de Fuencarral))
Tel: (91) 7343800 Cable Add: Espacalpe
Man Dir: Fermín Vargas Lázaro
Branch Offs: Espasa-Calpe SA, Diputación 251, Barcelona 7; Espasa-Calpe SA, General Salazar 1, Bilbao 12 (both in Spain); Espasa-Calpe Argentina SA, Tacuarí 328, Buenos Aires, Argentina; Espasa-Calpe Mexicana SA, Pitágoras 1139, Mexico City 12, Mexico; Espasa Calpe Ecuatoriana CA, Manuel Larrea y Asunción 239, Quito, Ecuador; Espasa-Calpe Ecuatoriana CA, José Luis Inés Juan Severino, 391 y Eloy Alfaro, Quito (Ecuador)
Subjects: General Fiction, Belles Lettres, Biography, History, How-to, Music, Art, Philosophy, Reference, Religion, Juveniles, Paperbacks, Medicine, Psychology, Law, Technical, University Textbooks
Founded: 1925
Bookshops: Casa del Libro, Ave José Antonio 29, Madrid 13; Material de Enseñanza, Barquillo 23, Madrid 4
ISBN Publisher's Prefix: 84-233

Editorial **Espaxs** SA*, Calle Rosellón 132, Barcelona 36 Tel: (93) 2530706 Cable Add: Editespaxs
Subject: Medicine
Bookshops: Librería Espaxs, Calle Rosellón 132, Barcelona 36; Librería Espaxs, Calle Fernando el Católico 57, Zaragoza; Libreria Espaxs, Calle Zaragoza 5, Cadiz
ISBN Publisher's Prefix: 84-7179

Editorial **Everest** SA, Apdo 339, León (Located at: Carretera León-Coruña, Km 5 León) Tel: (987) 235904 Cable Add: Everest León Telex: 89916
Man Dir: José Antonio López Martínez; *Administrative Dir:* Rafael Siguienza Benaquero
Subsidiary: Everest Libros SA, Apdo 339, León-España
Subjects: Belles Lettres, History, How-to, Juveniles, Engineering, Technical, Secondary & Primary Textbooks, Tourist Guides, Paperbacks, Educational Materials
Founded: 1958
ISBN Publisher's Prefix: 84-241

Editorial **Fher** SA*, Gordoniz 44, 6a planta, Apdo 362, Bilbao 2 Tel: (044) 4318000/4325090 Cable Add: Gerfu Telex: 32195
Man Dir: Juan José Fuentes; *Editorial:* José Luis Ayarzagüena
Subject: Juveniles
Founded: 1941
ISBN Publisher's Prefix: 84-243

Editorial **Fontanella** SA, Escorial 50, Barcelona 24 Tel: (93) 2131731
Man Dir: F Fortuny Comaposada; *Permissions:* C Lopez
Subjects: Social and Political Science, Education, Psychology, Sexology, Religion, Philosophy, History, Economy, Biography
1978: 32 titles *1979:* 31 titles *Founded:* 1962
ISBN Publisher's Prefix: 84-244

Heraclio **Fournier** SA, Heraclio Fournier 19, POB 94, Vitoria Tel: 251100 Cable Add: Fournier Telex: 35510
Subjects: High Quality Illustrated Books in

Fields of Art, History, Science, General Knowledge etc

Fragua Editorial, Gaztambide 77 & Andres Mellado 64, Madrid 15 Tel: (91) 2442430/4497315/2431595
Man Dir: Mariano Muñoz Alonso
Subjects: Linguistics, Philosophy, Communications, Political Science
Bookshop: Librería Augustinus
Founded: 1971
ISBN Publisher's Prefix: 84-7074

Editorial **Fundamentos**, Caracas 15, Madrid 4 Tel: (91) 4199619/4195584
Man Dir: Juan Serraller Ibañez;
Permissions: Cristina Vizcaino
Subjects: Social Sciences, Philosophy, Psychology, Psychiatry, Sexology, History, Theatre, Literature, Cinema, Low-priced Paperbacks
1978: 30 titles
ISBN Publisher's Prefix: 84-245

Ediciones **Gaisa** SL*, Gran Via Marques del Turia 64, Valencia Tel: (96) 3339321/3333976 Cable Add: Gaisa
Man Dir: Manuel Mas Santacreu
Subjects: Juveniles, Encyclopaedias, Multi-volume Collections
Founded: 1960
ISBN Publisher's Prefix: 84-7077

La **Galera** SA Editorial, Ronda del Guinardó 38, Barcelona 25 Tel: (93) 2557991/2360203
Man Dir: Roman Doria Forcada
Subjects: Pre-School and Infant Teaching texts, Children's Books, Education
1978: 51 titles *1979:* 82 titles *Founded:* 1965
ISBN Publisher's Prefix: 84-246

Ediciones **Garriga** SA*, París 143, Barcelona 36 Tel: (93) 2306825/2393547
Man Dir: Xavier Garriga Jové
Subjects: Art, Archaeology, Ancient History, Religion, Technical (Nautical)
Founded: 1957
ISBN Publisher's Prefix: 84-7079

Geocolor SA*, Travesera de Gracia 15 3°-2°, Barcelona 21 Tel: 2009489
Man Dir, Editorial: Enric Gras P; *Sales:* Matt Areny; *Production:* Lidia Beltran; *Publicity:* Xavier Gras S
Subjects: Tourism, Art, Archaeology, Biography, Cookery, Magic
1978: 21 titles *1979:* 20 titles *Founded:* 1977
ISBN Publisher's Prefix: 84-7424

Editorial Gustavo **Gili** SA, Rosellón 87-89, Barcelona 29 Tel: (93) 2591400 Cable Add: Gusto Barcelona
Man Dir: Gustavo Gili; *Sales:* Ramón Pascual; *Production:* Andres Martinez
Associate Companies: Ediciones G Gili SA Argentina (qv); Editorial Gustavo Gili Ltda, Chile (qv); Editorial Gustavo Gili Ltda, Calle 22, No 6-28, Bogotá, Colombia; Editorial Gustavo Gili de Mexico SA, Mexico (qv)
Branch Offs: Alcántara 21, Madrid 6; Marqués de Valladares 47, 1, Vigo; Colón de Larreátegui 14, 2, Bilbao 1; Madre Rafols 17, Seville 11 (all in Spain)
Subjects: Architecture, Art, Communication and Technology in general
Founded: 1902
ISBN Publisher's Prefix: 84-252

Editorial **Gredos** SA, Sánchez Pacheco 81, Apdo 2076, Madrid 2 Tel: (91) 4157408/4156836
Man Dirs: Mr Calonge, Mr Escolar, Mr Yebra, Mr Oliveira
Subjects: Philology, Criticism, Classical Literature, Literary History, Dictionaries
ISBN Publisher's Prefix: 84-249

Ediciones **Grijalbo** SA, Deu y Mata 98, Barcelona 29 Tel: 3223753 Cable Add: Edigrijalbo Telex: 53940 egri e
President: Juan Grijalbo; *General Manager:* José M Vives; *Editorial:* Ana Dexeus
Subsidiary Companies and Branch Offs: Ediciones Junior, Editorial Critica — both in Barcelona; Editorial Grijalbo, Mexico (qv); Distrib Exclusiva Grijalbo, Peru (qv); Juan Grijalbo, Editor, Uruguay; Grijalbo SA, Venezuela (qv); Grijalbo SA, Argentina (qv); Grijalbo Boliviana Ltda, Bolivia (qv); Distrib Exclusiva Grijalbo, Colombia (qv); Grijalbo Centroamericana y Panama, Costa Rica (qv); Grijalbo & Cia Ltda, Chile (qv); Editorial Grijalbo Ecuatoriana Ltda, Ecuador; Ediciones Grijalbo de Guatemala SA, Guatemala; Grijalbo Pto Rico Inc., Puerto Rico
Subjects: General Fiction & Non-fiction, Biography, Philosophy, History, Politics, Religion, Psychology, Technology, Art, Social Science, Reference Works
1978: 96 titles *1979:* 80 titles *Founded:* 1962
ISBN Publisher's Prefix: 84-253

Artes Gráficas **Grijelmo** SA*, Uribitarte 4, Bilbao 1 Tel: (344) 4239628 Telex: 31209 aggc e
Man Dir, Rights & Permissions: Federico Guillermo Grijelmo Ribechini; *Editorial:* Amancio Gerardo Grijelmo Ribechini; *Sales:* Juan Santiago Grijelmo Ribechini
Subsidiary Companies: Ediciones Deusto SA (qv); Urmo SA de Ediciones (qv); Ediciones Moreton (qv)
Branch Off: Barcelona, Madrid
Subjects: Art Books, Appointment Diaries

Ediciones **Guadarrama***, Alcalá 144, Madrid 9 Tel: (91) 4021642 Cable Add: Edirrama
Man Dir: Francisco Gracia Guillen; *Advertising Dir:* Silverio Ruiz Daimiel
Associate Company: Editorial Labor SA (qv)
Subjects: General Fiction, Nonfiction, Belles Lettres, Music, Art, Philosophy, Paperbacks
1978: 14 titles *Founded:* 1955
ISBN Publisher's Prefix: 84-250

Grupo Editorial **Guadiana** SA*, Calle General Martínez Campos 42-Bajo, Madrid 10 Cable Add: Guadisa
Man Dir: Gabriel Camuñas
Subjects: Social Science, History, Business Administration
Founded: 1967
Miscellaneous: Firm is a holding company of Guadiana de Publicaciones SA, Al-Borak SA & Ediciones 99 SA
ISBN Publisher's Prefix: 84-251

Editorial **Herder** SA, Provenza 388, Barcelona 25 Tel: (93) 2577700 Cable Add: Herder
Man Dir: Antonio Valtl Friedl
Branch Offs: Editorial y Librería Herder, Ave Callao 565, Buenos Aires, Argentina; Herder Editorial y Librería, Calle 12, No 6/89, Apdo Aereo 6855, Bogotá, Colombia
Subjects: Philosophy, Theology, Religion, Medicine, Psychology, Social Science, Reference Works, Economics, Languages, University & Secondary Textbooks, Atlases
Bookshop: Librería Herder, Balmes 26, Barcelona 7
1979: 938 titles *Founded:* 1943
ISBN Publisher's Prefix: 84-254

Editorial **Hispano Europea**, Bori y Fontestá 6, Barcelona 21 Tel: (93) 2397023
Man Dir, Editorial, Publicity: J Prat Ballester; *Sales:* J Carrió Sarrato; *Production:* J Madueño Machado
Subjects: Business Management, Sports, Social Science, Industrial Processes, General Technology, Photography
Founded: 1956
ISBN Publisher's Prefix: 84-255

Hogar del Libro — Nova Terra, Riera Blanca 78, Barcelona 28
Bookshops: Vergara 3, Barcelona 2; Via Layetana 85, Barcelona 10; Via Augusta 64, Barcelona 6; Primo de Rivera 12, Sabadell (Barcelona); Primo de Rivera 34, Sabadell (Barcelona); Carretera Barcelona/Sabadell (Barcelona)
Miscellaneous: Group of companies comprising one publisher, one major distributor and six bookshops
ISBN Publisher's Prefix: 84-7279

Hrvatska Revija, San Juan Bosco 62, Apartado Correos 14030, Barcelona 17 Tel: 2037408
Man Dir, Editorial: Vinko Nikolić
Subjects: Politics, History, Literature, Sociology, Memoirs; Periodical — *Hrvatska Revija* (in Croatian)
1978: 4 titles *1979:* 4 titles *Founded:* 1951
ISBN Publisher's Prefix: 84-399

Publicaciones **I C C E**, Calle Eraso 3, Madrid 28 Tel: (91) 2557200
Man Dir: E Olcina
Subjects: Education, Psychology Tests, History, Religion, Social Sciences
1979: 14 titles *Founded:* 1970
ISBN Publisher's Prefix: 84-7278

Ibérico Europea de Ediciones SA*, Serrano 44-3°, Madrid 1 Tel: (91) 2253527/2261578/2754492
Subjects: Biography, How-to, Music, Art, Social Science, Business Management
Founded: 1966
ISBN Publisher's Prefix: 84-256

Iberlibros — Unidad de Exportación*, Magallanes 25, Madrid 15 Tel: (91) 2764391
Publisher: Angel Orbegozo
Subjects: Human Sciences, Religion, Technical, School Texts, Dictionaries

Editorial **Incafo** SA, Castello 59, Apdo 202, Madrid 1 Tel: (226) 5450-5459 Telex: 42459 icf e
Man Dir: Luis Blas Aritio; *Editorial:* Santiago Saavedra; *Production:* Javier Echevarri; *Rights & Permissions:* Alicia Losada
Subjects: Natural History, Art, Ecology and Exploration in Spain and South America, including some books in English, Periodical *Periplo*
Book Club: Club del Libro de la Naturaleza (qv)
1978: 12 titles *1979:* 16 titles *Founded:* 1973
ISBN Publisher's Prefix: 84-85389

Editorial **Index** (Tormes, SL), Comandate Zorita 13-6°, Madrid 20 Tel: 2349150/2544980
Man Dir: R L Ortueta
Orders to: Hernani 17/19, Madrid 20 Tel: 2343761
Subjects: Science & Technology
1980: 100 titles *Founded:* 1965
ISBN Publisher's Prefix: 84-7087

Instituto de Estudios de Administración Local, Publicaciones*, Joaquín García Morato 7, Madrid 10
Dir: Gregorio Burgueño Alvarez
Subjects: Public Administration, Urbanism, City Planning, Periodicals
ISBN Publisher's Prefix: 84-7088

Instituto de Estudios Politicos*, Plaza Marina Española 8, Madrid 13 Tel: (91) 2415000, 2418300/09
Distributor: LESPO, Calle Arriza 16
Subjects: Law, Politics, History, Social Science, Philosophy
Founded: 1939
ISBN Publisher's Prefix: 84-259

Ediciones **Instituto Pontificio** San Pío X*, Ave Cardenal Herrera Oria 242, Apdo 54027, Madrid 35 Tel: (91) 7399151
Man Dir: Eduardo Malvido Miguel; *Editorial:* Serafín Tapia Nevado; *Sales:* José Luis Peralta García; *Production:* Rafael Pascual
Subjects: Theology, Pedagogy, Psychology, Religion
Bookshop: Librería La Salle, Bocángel 15, Madrid 28
Founded: 1964
ISBN Publisher's Prefix: 84-7221

Ediciones y Publicaciones de **Insula**, Benito Gutiérrez 26, Madrid 8 Tel: (91) 2435415
Man Dir: Enrique Canito Barrera; *Publicity:* A Muñoz Canito
Subjects: Fiction, Poetry, Literary Studies, Criticism, Essays
Bookshop: Insula, Librería de Ciencias y Letras, Benito Gutiérrez 26, Madrid 8
1978: 20 titles *1979:* 18 titles *Founded:* 1944
ISBN Publisher's Prefix: 84-7185

Ediciones **Istmo***, General Pardiñas 26, Madrid 1 Tel: (91) 2263127
Man Dir: José Antonio Llardent Viciana; *Sales Dir:* Deogracias González; *Publicity Dir:* Leoncio Martín
Subjects: History, Reference, Social Science, Philosophy, Literature, University Texts
1978: 6 titles *Founded:* 1969
ISBN Publishers Prefix: 84-7090

Taller Ediciones **J B**, see Taller

Editorial **Jims** SA, Calle Regás 7-9, Barcelona 6 Tel: (93) 2188800 Cable Add: EDITOJIMS
Man Dir, Editorial, Publicity: Antonio Jimenez Sánchez; *Sales:* Teresa Jimenez Sayo; *Production:* Luis Jimenez Sayo
Subject: Medicine
1978: 17 titles *1979:* 19 titles *Founded:* 1956
ISBN Publisher's Prefix: 84-7092

Editorial **Jover** SA, San Pedro Matir 18, Barcelona 12 Tel: (93) 2185662/2185408/2185216 Cable Add: Edijover
Subjects: Educational Materials
ISBN Publisher's Prefix: 84-7093

Editorial **Juventud** SA, Provenza 101, Apdo 3, Barcelona 29 Tel: (93) 2392000/3212100/2398383 Cable Add: Juventud
Man Dirs: Pablo Zendrera, José María Zendrera
Associated Company: Distr del Pacifico, Jiron Camaná 953, Lima, Peru
Subsidiary Companies: Editorial Juventud Argentina (qv); Editorial Juventud Ltda, Colombia (qv)
Subjects: General Fiction, Biography, History, How-to, Music, Art, Nautical, Travel, Pocketbooks, Textbooks, Reference, Juveniles, Paperbacks
1978: 119 titles *Founded:* 1923
ISBN Publisher's Prefix: 84-261

Editorial **Kairos** SA*, Numancia 110, Barcelona 29 Tel: (93) 2303746/2505166
Man Dir: Salvador Pániker; *Editorial, Rights & Permissions:* Carmen Tord; *Sales:* José Miralles; *Production, Publicity:* Pilar Tomás
Subjects: Philosophy, Religion, Psychology, Reference, General and Social Science
1977: 12 titles *Founded:* 1966
ISBN Publisher's Prefix: 84-7245

L E D A (Las Ediciones de Arte), Riera San Miguel 37, Barcelona 6 Tel: (93) 2284029
Man Dir: Daniel Basilio Bonet
Subjects: Art and Craft techniques, Technical drawing
1978: 2 titles *1979:* 5 titles *Founded:* 1942
ISBN Publisher's Prefix: 84-7095

Editorial **Labor** SA, Calabria 235-239, Barcelona 29 Tel: (93) 3220551 Cable Add: Edilabor Telex: (51130) 1600091
Man Dir: Francisco Gracia Guillen
Associate Company: Ediciones Guadarrama (qv)
Branch Offs: Argentina; Brazil; Colombia; Ecuador; Mexico; Venezuela (qqv)
Subjects: Science and Technology, Medicine, Engineering, Encyclopedias, Dictionaries, Humanities, History, Art, Business Management, Juveniles, University Textbooks
Founded: 1915
ISBN Publisher's Prefixes: 84-335 (Labor), 84-250 (Ediciones Guadarrama)

Editorial **Laia**, Calle Constitucion 18-20, Barcelona 14 Tel: (93) 3328408
Man Dir: Josep Verdura Tenas; *Editorial:* Alfonso Carlos Comin Ros; *Sales:* Frederic Pagès; *Production:* Montserrat Corral; *Publicity:* Àngels Jové; *Rights & Permissions:* Pilar Esteve
Orders to: Itaca, SA Distribuciones Editoriales, Lopez de Hoyos 141, 5°, Madrid 2
Subjects: General Nonfiction, Social Sciences, Politics, Literature, Essays, Psychology, Pedagogy
1978: 77 titles *1979:* 120 titles *Founded:* 1972
ISBN Publisher's Prefix: 84-7222

Editorial **Linosa-Linomonograph** SA*, Calle Riera de San Miguel 9, Barcelona 6 Tel: (93) 2285504/03/02
Man Dir: José Chimenos Reig; *Sales Dir:* José Antonio Chimenos Calderon; *Publicity Dir:* Ma Mercedes Chimenos Calderon; *Advertising Dir:* Elena Isabel Gil Fornas
Subjects: Fiction, Literature, History, How-to, Reference, Social Science, Juveniles
Founded: 1968
ISBN Publisher's Prefix: 84-7097

Editorial **Lumen**, Ramón Miquel y Planas 10, Barcelona 34 Tel: (93) 2043496/2042139
Man Dir: Esther Tusquets
Subjects: General Fiction, Belles Lettres, Biography, History, Music, Art, Juveniles, Social Science, Paperbacks
Founded: 1939
ISBN Publisher's Prefix: 84-264

Editorial **Magisterio** Español SA, Calle de Quevedo 1, Madrid 14 Tel: (91) 2287900 Cable Add: Magisterio Telex: 44259 EM E
Man Dir: Manuel Méndez Encina; *Rights & Permissions:* Ma del Carmen Núñez Amador
Subjects: Education, Fiction, Essays, Philosophy, Pedagogy
Bookshop: Calle Cervantes 18, Madrid 14; Calle Ecuador 3, Barcelona 29
Founded: 1866
ISBN Publisher's Prefix: 84-265

Editorial **Marbán***, Hilarión Eslava 55, Madrid 15 Tel: (91) 2433767/2444673
Man Dir, Editorial: Jose Marban Gonzalez; *Sales, Production, Publicity:* Jose M Marban Corral
Subjects: Medicine, Physiology
Founded: 1949
ISBN Publisher's Prefix: 84-7101

Marcombo SA de Boixareu Editores, Gran Via de les Corts Catalanes 594, Barcelona 7 Tel: (93) 3180079
Dir: Josep Ma Boixareu Vilaplana; *Editorial:* José Ma Boixareu Ginesta; *Sales:* Juan Plans Comas; *Production:* José Costa Ardiaca; *Publicity:* José Romero González; *Rights & Permissions:* José Deckler Martí
Subsidiary Company: Boixareu Editores SA (at above address)
Branch Off: Marcombo-Boixareu Editores, Plaza de la Villa 1, Madrid 12
Subjects: Technology, Science, Automation, Economics, Accounting, How-to, University and Secondary Textbooks, Electronics, Mathematics
Bookshop: Librería Hispano Americana (at above address)
1978: 56 titles *1979:* 49 titles *Founded:* 1949
ISBN Publisher's Prefix: 84-267

Editorial **Marfil** SA*, Plaza de Emilio Sala 3, Alcoy Tel: 541746/540233 Cable Add: Marfil
Sales: Rafael Ortiz Botí
Parent Company: Papeleras Reunidas SA
Subjects: Secondary & Primary Textbooks
Founded: 1947
ISBN Publisher's Prefix: 84-268

Editorial **Marin** SA, Calle Nicaragua 85-95, Barcelona 29 Tel: (93) 3216800 Cable Add: Marinedi
Man Dirs: Manuel Marin Correa, Luis Marin Correa; *Editorial, Rights & Permissions:* Manuel Marin Correa; *Sales:* Luis Marin Correa; *Production:* Manuel Marin Bruna
Associate Company: Durvan SA de Ediciones (qv)
Branch Offs: Ave Belgrano 3715, 1210 Buenos Aires, Argentina; Carrera 15 no 32-41, Bogota DE, Colombia; Anaxágoras 1400, Mexico 13 DF, Mexico; San Rafael 1400, Santurce, PR 00909, Puerto Rico
Subjects: Art Books, Reference, Medicine, Non-fiction, Encyclopedias, Children's Books
Founded: 1900
ISBN Publisher's Prefix: 84-7102

Ediciones **Marova** SL, Viriato 55, Madrid 10 Tel: (91) 4486856/4487355
Man Dir: Germán Alonso Fernández; *Publicity & Advertising Manager:* Mariano Moreno
Subjects: Religion, Psychology, Education
Founded: 1956
ISBN Publisher's Prefix: 84-269

Editorial **Marsiega** SA, E Jardiel Poncela 4, Madrid 16 Tel: (91) 2598364
Parent Company: Promoción Popular Cristiana (qv under PPC)
1978: 10 titles

Ediciones **Martínez** Roca SA, Ave José Antonio 774, 7a planta, Barcelona 13 Tel: (93) 2251576 Telex: 97278 mrrm e
Man Dirs: Francisco Martínez Roca, Manuel Martínez Roca; *Sales:* Fernando Calvo; *Production:* Sergio Puyol; *Permissions:* Manuel Martínez Alsinet
Branch Off: Ediciones Roca SA, General Francisco Murguía 7, Col Escandón, Mexico 18 DF
Subjects: General Fiction & Non-fiction, Science & Technology, Human & Social Sciences, Chess, Occult Sciences, Science Fiction
1978: 98 titles *1979:* 51 titles *Founded:* 1965
ISBN Publisher's Prefix: 84-270

Ediciones **Mensajero**, Ave de las Universidades 13, Apdo 73, Bilbao 7 Tel: (94) 4457750 Cable Add: Mensajero
Man Dir: José Velasco; *Editorial, Production:* Jesús Leguina; *Sales:* Juan Aguirre; *Publicity:* Alvaro Sánchez
Branch Offs: Templarios 12, Barcelona 2; EAPSA, Velázquez 28, Madrid 1
Subjects: Social Science, Religion, Philosophy, Education, How-to, Psychology, Juveniles
1978: 62 titles *1979:* 65 titles *Founded:* 1915
ISBN Publisher's Prefix: 84-271

Editorial Luis **Miracle** SA*, Calle Sicilia 402, Barcelona 25 Tel: (93) 2581800/9 Cable Add: Micle
Editorial: Josefina Vera Vera

320 SPAIN

Subjects: Anthropology, Philosophy, Education, Economics, Social Science, Business, Psychology, History, Religion, Encyclopedia
Founded: 1929
ISBN Publisher's Prefix: 84-7109

Editorial **Molino**, Calabria 166, Barcelona 15 Tel: (343) 2434769 Cable Add: Molino Barcelona
Man Dir: Luis del Molino Mateus; *Sales & Advertising Dir:* Pablo del Molino Sterna; *Permissions:* L A del Molino
Subjects: Juveniles, Popular Paperbacks, Cookery, Children's books, Education
1978: 64 titles *Founded:* 1933
ISBN Publisher's Prefix: 84-272

Editorial **Moll**, Torre del Amor 4, Apdo 142, Palma de Mallorca Tel: (071) 971224176/971224472
Man Dir: Francisco Moll
Subjects: Fiction, Literature, Biography, History, Art, Reference, Works, Dictionaries, Linguistics, Social Sciences, Secondary & Primary Textbooks, Natural Science
Bookshop: Libros Mallorca, Fortuny 5, Palma de Mallorca
1978: 56 titles *1979:* 44 titles *Founded:* 1934
ISBN Publisher's Prefix: 84-273

Montaner y Simon SA*, Aragón 255, Apdo 322, Barcelona 7
Subjects: General Literature, History, Belles Lettres, Reference, Dictionaries, Encyclopedias, Geography, Scientific and Technical
ISBN Publisher's Prefix: 84-274

José **Montesó** — Editor*, Vía Augusta 251-253, Barcelona 17 Tel: (93) 2301739
Man Dir: José M Montesó
Branch Off: Calle Paraná 480, Buenos Aires, Argentina
Subjects: How-to, Engineering, Technical, University Textbooks
Founded: 1928
ISBN Publisher's Prefix: 84-7186

Ediciones **Morata** SA, Mejía Lequerica 12, Madrid 4 Tel: (91) 4480926 Cable Add: Moratedi
Man Dir: Flora Morata
Subjects: Psychology, Medicine, Pedagogy, Philosophy, Psychiatry, Sexology, Sociology, Politics, Mathematics, University Textbooks
1978: 16 titles *Founded:* 1920
ISBN Publisher's Prefix: 84-7112

Ediciones **Moreton** SA*, Espartero 10, Bilbao 9 Tel: (094) 4239169
Man Dir: C Moretón; *Sales:* Victoria Peña; *Publicity & Advertising:* Maria Saturnina Abón
Subjects: Literature, Biography, History, Music, Art, Reference (in luxury and multi-volume editions)
Founded: 1964
ISBN Publisher's Prefix: 84-7113

Mundi-Prensa Libros SA, Castelló 37, Apdo 1223, Madrid 1 Tel: (91) 2754655/2760253 Cable Add: Mundipren
Man Dir: Pedro Hernández; *Editorial, Publicity:* José Ma Hernández; *Sales:* Alfonso Hernández
Subjects: Agriculture, Technology, Ecology, Livestock, University & Secondary Textbooks
Bookshops: Librería Mundi-Prensa, Castelló 37, Apdo 1223, Madrid 1; Librería Agrícola, Fernando VI, 2, Madrid 4
1978: 10 titles *1979:* 20 titles *Founded:* 1948
ISBN Publisher's Prefix: 84-7114

Editorial La **Muralla**, Constancia 33, Madrid 2 Tel: (91) 4161371/4153687/4159148
Man Dir: Lidio Nieto; *Sales Dir:* Pilar Jiménez; *Publicity, Permissions:* Ma Antonia Casanova
Subjects: Art, Literature, Geography, History, Religion, Technology, Life and Culture, Biology, all in books with slides for visual education, Primary and University Textbooks
1979: 286 titles *1980:* 483 titles *Founded:* 1968
ISBN Publisher's Prefix: 84-7133

Editorial **Musica** Moderna*, Antonio Carmona Reverte, Calle Marqués de Cubas 6, Madrid 14 Tel: (91) 2215593
Editor and Dir: Antonio Carmona Reverte
Subject: Music
1978: 2,000 titles *Founded:* 1935

Ediciones **Naranco** SA, Asturias 27, Apdo 542, Oviedo Tel: 236537
President: Santiago Rubio Sáinido; *Man Dir:* Graciano García; *Production:* José Antxon F Lupiáñez; *Sales, Publicity:* Emilio García; *Rights & Permissions:* José Antonio A Rodríguez
Subjects: Photo-strip Editions of Don Quixote, Juveniles, Part-Works, weekly parts editions of major collections

Narcea SA de Ediciones, Dr Federico Rubio 89 & 91, Madrid 20 Tel: (91) 2546484
Subjects: Education, Psychology, Pedagogy, Religion, Juveniles, Textbooks
1978: 66 titles *1979:* 89 titles
ISBN Publisher's Prefix: 84-277

Ediciones **Nauta** SA, Loreto 16, Barcelona 29 Tel: (343) 2392204 Cable Add: Edinauta Telex: 54495 sele e
Man Dir: José Luis Ruiz de Villa Macho
Subjects: General Fiction and Nonfiction, Classics, Art Books, Reference
1978: 15 titles *Founded:* 1962
ISBN Publisher's Prefix: 84-278

Neguri Editorial SA, Juan Ajuriaguerra 10-1°, Bilbao 9 Tel: (94) 4233070/4245307
President: José Ignacio Zarza Stuyk; *Manager:* Augustin Gairiza
Subjects: Atlases, Agendas, Plans of Spanish Cities, Road Maps
Bookshop: Librería Deusto, Calle O'Donnell 43, Madrid 9
1979: 17 titles *1980:* 13 titles *Founded:* 1960
ISBN Publisher's Prefix: 84-85085

Editorial **Noguer** SA, Paseo de Gracia 96, Barcelona 8 Tel: (93) 2156516 Cable Add: Edinoguer Barcelona Telex: 52534
Man Dir, Editorial: Emilio Ardevo; *Sales:* Jorge Figueras; *Rights & Permissions:* Luis N Latorre; *Production:* Manuel Tort
Associate Company: Luis de Caralt Editor SA (qv)
Subjects: General Fiction and Non-fiction, Belles Lettres, Biography, History, Encyclopaedias, Art, Juveniles, Paperbacks
1978: 50 titles *Founded:* 1949
ISBN Publisher's Prefix: 84-279

Nova Terra, Rivera Blanca 78, Barcelona 28, see Hogar del Libro

Oikos-Tau SA Ediciones, Montserrat 12-14, Vilassar de Mar, Apdo 5347, Barcelona Tel: (93) 7590791
Man Dir, Editorial: Jordi Garcia-Bosch; *Sales:* Climent Garcia-Bosch; *Production, Rights & Permissions:* Jordi Garcia-Jacas
Subjects: Scientific and Technical, Economics, Marketing and Management, Agriculture, Geography, Education, History, Politics, Psychology, Architecture, Town Planning
1978: 25 titles *Founded:* 1963
ISBN Publisher's Prefix: 84-281

Ediciones **Omega** SA, Casanova 220, Barcelona 36 Tel: (93) 2392328
Man Dir: Gabriel Paricio, Antonio Paricio
Subjects: Science & Technology, Photography, Cinema, Agriculture, University textbooks on Biology, Biochemistry, Geology
ISBN Publisher's Prefix: 84-282

Alfredo **Ortells** Ferriz*, Sagunto 5, Valencia 9 Tel: (06) 3651549/3650786
Man Dir: Alfredo Ortells Ferriz
Subjects: Infants and Juvenile, Children's Classics, Popular Knowledge series
1978: 14 titles *Founded:* 1952
ISBN Publisher's Prefix: 84-7189

P P C (Promoción Popular Cristiana), E Jardiel Poncela 4, Apdo 19049, Madrid 16 Tel: (91) 2592300 Cable Add: Pepece
Man Dir: José Ma Burgos; *General Manager:* Manuel Sobrado; *Sales Dir:* Catalina Jaume; *Publicity & Advertising:* Pedro G Candanedo
Subsidiary Company: Editorial Marsiega SA (qv)
Subjects: Religion, Philosophy, Textbooks
Founded: 1955
Bookshops: Retail outlets throughout Spain (see under Booksellers)
ISBN Publisher's Prefix: 84-288

Pala SA, now Sadko SA (qv)

Editorial **Paraninfo** SA, Magallanes 25, Madrid 15 Tel: (91) 4463350
Man Dir: Alfonso Mangada Sanz; *Sales Dir:* Manuel Montalbán Beltrán
Subjects: Science & Technology, Data Processing & Computation, Business Administration, How-to, Secondary & University Textbooks
Bookshops: Librería Paraninfo, Magallanes 25; Meléndez Valdés 65, Madrid 15
1978: 93 titles *Founded:* 1948
ISBN Publisher's Prefix: 84-283

Instituto **Parramon** Ediciones SA, Calle Lepanto 264, Apdo 2001, Barcelona 13 Tel: (93) 2457002/3
Man Dir: José Ma Parramón; *Sales:* José Mira del Rio
Subjects: Art, Photography, Drawing (Instruction), Languages, Botanical Interest, Reference
1978: 30 titles *1979:* 47 titles *Founded:* 1958
ISBN Publisher's Prefix: 84-342

Ediciones **Partenon**, Paseo de la Habana 56, Madrid 16 Tel: (91) 2505498 Cable Add: Partenón Madrid
Man Dir: Rafael Torres Gorriz
Subjects: Literature, Language and Philology, Social Science, University Textbooks
Founded: 1969
ISBN Publisher's Prefix: 84-7119

Ediciones **Paulinas**, Carretera de La Coruña, Km 16 800, Las Rozas, Madrid Tel: (91) 6371000
Subjects: Biography, Philosophy, Psychology, Education, Religion
ISBN Publisher's Prefix: 84-285

Editorial **Paz** Montalvo, Jorge Juan 127, Madrid 9 Tel: (91) 4019722
Man Dir: José Fernando de Paz; *Advertising:* José Luis Fernández
Subject: Technical literature on all aspects of medicine, ophthalmology, psychiatry, pediatrics, biochemistry and associated fields
1978: 6 titles *1979:* 4 titles *Founded:* 1947
ISBN Publisher's Prefix: 84-7121

Editorial **Pediátrica**, Mayor de Gracia 102, Barcelona 12 Tel: (93) 2174996
Man Dir: Anselmo Garrido
Subject: Medicine
1978: 8 titles *Founded:* 1969
ISBN Publisher's Prefix: 84-7193

Ediciones **Pegaso**, see EDERSA

Ediciones **Peninsula***, Provenza 278 1°-1a, Barcelona 8 Tel: (93) 2160062
Dir: Romà Cuyàs Sol; *Editorial:* Josep M Castellet; *Production:* Ramon Bastardes; *Publicity:* Eliseu Gil
Associate Company: Edicions 62 SA (qv)
Subsidiary Company: Distribuciones de Enlace SA
Subjects: General (in Castilian)
1978: 34 titles *Founded:* 1963
ISBN Publisher's Prefix: 84-297

Ediciones **Pirámide** SA, Don Ramón de la Cruz 67, Apdo 50512, Madrid 1 Tel: (91) 4011200 Cable Add: Grupedi
Man Dir: Jose Ma Esteban; *Rights & Permissions:* Esther Rincón Quemada, Guillermo de Toca
Orders to: Grupo Editorial SA, Don Ramón de la Cruz 67, Madrid 1
Subjects: Economics, Business, Science and Technology, Law
1979: 126 titles *Founded:* 1974
ISBN Publisher's Prefix: 84-368

Editorial **Planeta** SA*, Córcega 273, Barcelona 8 Tel: (93) 217550 Cable Add: Ediplan
Man Dir, Editorial: José Manuel Lara Hernández; *Sales:* José Miguel García Piriz; *Production:* José Grasa; *Publicity:* Rafael Abella
Branch Offs: Editorial Planeta Argentina SAIC, Viamonte 1451, Buenos Aires, Argentina; Planeta Colombiana, Editorial, Carrera 7-A, No 13-41 Mezzanine, Bogotá, Colombia; Editorial Planeta Chilena, Bombero Augusto Salas 1361-5, Santiago, Chile; Editorial Planeta Mexicana SA, Vallarta 21, 1er piso, Mexico City 4, Mexico; Planeta Venezolana, Edif Pigalle, Ave Leonardo da Vinci, Colinas de B Monte, Apdo 51285, Caracas, Venezuela
Subjects: General Fiction & Nonfiction
Founded: 1958
ISBN Publisher's Prefix: 84-320

Playor, Santa Polonia 7, Madrid 14 Tel: (91) 2306097 Telex: 42252 IVSAE
Man Dir: Carlos A Montaner; *Sales:* Ramón Rodriguez; *Production:* Pio E Serrano
Subjects: Art, Linguistics, Literature, Spanish and Latin-American Studies, Cuban Studies, Illustrated Juvenile
1978: 48 titles
ISBN Publisher's Prefix: 84-359

Plaza y Janés SA, Editores, Virgen de Guadalupe 21-33, Esplugas de Llobregat, Barcelona Tel: (93) 3710200
Executive President: Carlos Plaza de Diego; *Man Dir:* Julio Jordán Seguí; *Editor-in-Chief:* José Moya
Subjects: General Fiction & Non-fiction, Classics, Paperbacks
ISBN Publisher's Prefix: 84-01

Ediciones **Poligrafa** SA, Balmes 54, Barcelona 7 Tel: (93) 3019100
Sales: Juan de Muga
Subject: Art Books, mainly of the works of Spanish artists, with texts in several languages
ISBN Publisher's Prefix: 84-313

Editorial **Pomaire** SA*, Ave Infanta Carlota 114, Barcelona 29 Tel: (93) 2501363
Man Dir: José Manuel Vergara
Br Offs: Argentina; Chile; Colombia; Mexico; Uruguay; Venezuela (qqv)
Subjects: General Fiction & Nonfiction
Founded: 1957
ISBN Publisher's Prefix: 84-286

Ediciones José **Porrúa** Turanzas SA, Cea Bermúdez 10, Madrid 3 Tel: (91) 2542344/2541466
Man Dir, Editorial: José Porrúa Venero; *Sales:* Mauricio Maroto Maroto; *Production, Publicity:* Constantino García Garvía; *Rights & Permissions:* Enrique Porrúa Venero
Subsidiary Company: North American Division, 1383 Kersey Lane, Potomac, MD 20854, USA
Subjects: History of Mexico and Latin America, Humanistic Literature and Commentary
Bookshop: Cea Bermúdez 10, Madrid 3
1978: 16 titles *Founded:* 1958
ISBN Publisher's Prefixes: 84-7317, 0-935568

Editorial **Pòrtic**, Ave Marqués de Argentera 17, Barcelona 3 Tel: 3196684
Man Dir: Núria Fornas; *Administration and Sales:* Salvador Llimona
Subjects: Religion, Politics, Essays, Poetry & Prose-poetry, Novels, Memoirs (in Catalan)
Bookshops: Llibreria Claris, Vía Layetana 82, Barcelona 10
1978: 23 titles *1979:* 9 titles
ISBN Publisher's Prefix: 84-7306

Editorial **Prensa** Española*, Serrano 61, Apdo 43 and 6004, Madrid 6 Tel: (91) 2758148
Dir: Rogelio González-Ubeda
Subjects: General Fiction & Non-fiction
Founded: 1905
ISBN Publisher's Prefix: 84-287

Edicions **Proa**, see Ayma SA Editora

Editorial **Prometeo**, Pl Cánovas del Castillo 9-6a, Valencia 5 Tel: (96) 3344107
Man Dir: Juan de Dios Leal Castellote; *Sales Dir:* Ma Luisa Sagreras
Subjects: Fiction, Literature, Geography & Travel, Philosophy
Founded: 1966
ISBN Publisher's Prefix: 84-7199

Ediciones de **Promoción** Cultural SA*, Rocafort 256-258, Barcelona 15 Tel: (93) 2590140 Cable Add: Edsprocusa
Man Dir: J Ma Mas Solench
Subjects: Social Sciences, Education, General Science & Technology, University Textbooks
Founded: 1972

Promocion Popular Cristiana, see PPC

Selecciones del **Reader's Digest** (Iberia) SA*, Calle Telémaco 3, Madrid 27 Tel: (91) 7420011 Cable Add: Readigest Telex: 27407
Director General: Mario A Freude; *Editorial, Rights & Permissions:* Joaquín Amado; *Sales:* Ivo Duchacek; *Production:* Alfredo Latour; *Publicity:* Xavier Muntañola
Parent Company: The Reader's Digest Association Inc, 750 Third Ave, New York, NY 10017, USA
Branch Off: Barcelona
Subjects: Education, Pocket editions, General Interest, Atlases
Book Club: Biblioteca de Selecciones
Founded: 1952
ISBN Publisher's Prefix: 84-7142

Editorial **Reus** SA, Preciados 23, Madrid Tel: (91) 2213619/2223054
Man Dir: Rafael Martinez Reus
Subjects: Law and General Culture
Bookshop: Librería Reus, Calle de Preciados 6, Madrid
Founded: 1852
ISBN Publisher's Prefix: 84-290

Editorial **Reverté** SA*, Calle Encarnación 86-88, Apdo 1237, Barcelona 24 Tel: (93) 2194353 Cable Add: Edirever
Dirs: Pedro Reverté Gil, Felipe Reverté Planells; *Editorial:* Juan Sala Inglabaga; *Sales:* Magin Hortal Samsó; *Rights & Permissions:* Andres Doria Dexeus
Associate Companies: Editora Reverté Ltda, Brazil (qv); Editorial Reverté Colombiana SA, Calle 22, No 6-16, of 202 Bogotá, Colombia; Editorial Reverté Mexicana SA, Mexico (qv); Editorial Reverté Venezolana SA, Venezuela (qv)
Branch Offs: Ave Angel Gallardo 613, Buenos Aires 5, Argentina
Subjects: Engineering, General Science, University & Secondary Textbooks
Founded: 1947
ISBN Publisher's Prefix: 84-291

Revista de Occidente SA, Milán 38, Madrid 33 Tel: (91) 2000045
Man Dir: José Vergara Doncel
Associate Company: Alianza Editorial SA, Madrid (qv)
Subjects: History, Philosophy, Political & Social Science
Founded: 1923
ISBN Publisher's Prefix: 84-292

Ediciones **Rialp** SA, Preciados 34, Madrid 13 Tel: (91) 2311004
Subjects: Belles Lettres, Poetry, History, Music, Art, Philosophy, Religion, Textbooks, Engineering, General & Social Science, High-priced Paperbacks
Founded: 1945
ISBN Publisher's Prefix: 84-321

Ediciones **Rodas** SA*, Donoso Cortés 39, Madrid 15 Tel: (91) 2548641 Telex: 42710
Man Dir: José Manuel Zañartu; *Literary Agent:* International Editors' Co, Rambla Cataluña 39, Barcelona
Subjects: General Fiction, Essays, Juveniles, How-to
Founded: 1972
ISBN Publisher's Prefix: 84-347

Litografia A **Romero** SA*, Ave Angel Romero s/n, Apdo 324, Santa Cruz de Tenerife Tel: 221540-2 Cable Add: Larsa, Tenerife Telex: 92159 Larsa E
Dir: Edgardo Romero
Subjects: Textbooks, Juveniles

Sadko SA, Paso de los Olmos 5 (Parque Bidebieta), San Sebastian Tel: 398780/395345
President: Luis Gasco Burges; *Dir:* Miguel Arrieto Losorte
Subjects: Juveniles, Reference Works, Cinema, Parapsychology, Astronautics
Miscellaneous: Formerly known as Pala SA (at same address)

Victor **Sagi** Servicios Editoriales*, Av Generalisimo 614, Barcelona 29 Tel: (93) 3220053 Telex: 54254
Man Dir: C H Knapp; *Sales:* Eva Alsina
Parent Company: Victor Sagi Communications Group
Subjects: Cinema, Art, Photography, Health, General Interest
1978: 2 titles *Founded:* 1977
ISBN Publisher's Prefix: 84-85186

Editorial **Sal Terrae***, Geuvara 20, Apdo 77, Santander Tel: 212617
Man Dir: Manuel Gutiérrez
Subjects: Religion, Philosophy, Parapsychology, Essays, Biography, History, Juveniles, Textbooks
1978: 24 titles *Founded:* 1919
ISBN Publisher's Prefix: 84-293

Salvat Editores SA*, Mallorca 41-49, Barcelona 15 Tel: (93) 2303607 Telex: 53132
Man Dir: Manuel Salvat; *Sales Dir:* Juan José Deiros García; *Permissions:* Julián Viñuales Solé
Branch Offs: Salvat Editores Argentina SA; Salvat Editores Mexicana SA; Salvat Editores Venezolana SA, Edif Arauca, Gran Avenida, Apdo 51106-105, Caracas, Venezuela

SPAIN

Subjects: Reference, History, Art, Music, Literature, Medicine, Veterinary Science, Agriculture, Science, Technology, Geography, Paperbacks
Founded: 1869
ISBN Publisher's Prefix: 84-345

Salvat SA de Ediciones, Arrieta 25, Pamplona Tel: 248600 Telex: 37739 saaae e
Subjects: Encyclopedias, Dictionaries, Art, History
ISBN Publisher's Prefix: 84-7137

Editorial Miguel A **Salvatella**, Santo Domingo 5, Barcelona 12 Tel: (93) 2189026
Subjects: Primary Textbooks, Educational Materials
Founded: 1922
ISBN Publisher's Prefix: 84-7210

Editorial **San Martin***, Puerta de Sol 6, Apdo 97, Madrid 14 Tel: (91) 2214292/2216897
Man Dir: Jorge Tarazona
Subjects: History, Aviation, Military
Bookshop: Librería San Martin, Puerta del Sol 6, Madrid 14
Founded: 1854
ISBN Publisher's Prefix: 84-7140

Santillana SA de Ediciones*, Calle Elfo 32, Madrid 27 Tel: (91) 4034000 Cable Add: Santillana Telex: 43879
President: Jesús de Polanco Gutérrez; *Vice-Presidents:* Francisco Pérez González, Ricardo Díez Hochleitner; *Man Dir:* Emiliano Martinez Rodriguez; *Editorial:* Antonio Ramos Perez; *Sales:* Jose Muñoz Juan; *Production:* Francisco Jerez Vazquez; *Publicity:* Jose Manuel Lopez Bottiglieri; *Rights & Permissions:* Gloria Roldan Perez
Associate Companies: Editorial Santillana, Argentina; Edyca SA, Dominican Republic; Nutesa, Mexico; Santillana del Pacifico SA, Chile; Santillana Publishing Co, USA; Teduca, Venezuela (qv)
Branch Offs: Capitán Segarra 41, Alicante; Rambla de Cataluña 81, Barcelona 7; Ave del Ejército 3, Deusto (Vizcaya); Julián Romero Brionez 4, Las Palmas; Placentines 2, Sevilla; Jacinto Benavente 19, Valencia 5; Almirante Carrero Blanco 91 (bloque 3), Granada; Av del Mar 7, Oviedo; Polígono Industrial Portazgo, Bloque B, Nave 105, Cra de Logroño Km 6,600, Zaragoza; Polígono BENS parcela S-1-B, La Coruña; Conde de Ribadeo 4, 2°-C, Valladolid (all in Spain)
Subjects: Textbooks, Educational Materials for Kindergarten, Primary and Secondary, Teachers and Educational Specialists
Founded: 1960
ISBN Publisher's Prefix: 84-294

Sedmay Ediciones SA*, Dr Fleming 51, Madrid Tel: 4161200 Telex: 43239
Man Dir: José Mayá Rius; *Export Manager:* Dr Sabine Kleinhaus
Subjects: Novels, Biography, Essays, Politics, Cinema, Juveniles

Editorial **Seix** Barral SA, Apdo de Correos 31, Tambor del Bruch s/n, Sant Joan Despi, Barcelona Tel: 3731409/3731652/3731208 Cable Add: Seibarh Telex: 53066 seix e
Man Dir: Antonio Comas Baldellou; *Editorial:* Alejandro Argullos Marimón; *Sales:* Luis Carlos S Montoya; *Production, Publicity, Rights & Permissions:* Angel Jasanada Paris
Associate Company: Editorial Ariel SA (qv). The two companies constitute the organization Ariel/Seix Barral Editoriales
Subsidiary Companies: Formentor Argentina, Argentina (qv); Formentor Ltda, Chile; Ariel Seix Barral Ltda, Ecuador; Ed Ariel-Seix Barral, Colombia; Ariel-Seix Barral, Mexico; Ediciones Andinas SA, Peru; Ediciones Formentor SRL, Venezuela; Ariel Seix Barral, Costa Rica
Subjects: Stories from Spanish, Latin-American, German, French, English, Italian, Soviet Russian, North American, Oriental and other literatures; Poetry, Drama, the Classics, Literary Criticism, Linguistics, Economics, Philosophy, Science, Politics, History, Psychology, Sociology, the Arts, Memoirs, Travel
1978: 41 titles *1979:* 21 titles *Founded:* 1945
ISBN Publisher's Prefix: 84-332

Selecciones Editoriales SA, Rita Bonnat 9, Barcelona Telex: 54495 Sele e Barcelona 29
Parent Company: Elsevier-NDU nv, Netherlands (qv)

Siglo XXI Editores de España SA, Plaza 5, Apdo 48023, Madrid 33 Tel: (93) 7594809 Cable Add: Sigloedit
Man Dir: Faustino Lastra; *Sales:* Eduardo Rivas; *Production, Publicity:* Javier Abasolo
Subsidiary Companies: Siglo XXI de Colombia Ltda (qv); Siglo XXI Editores SA, Mexico (qv)
Subjects: Anthropology, Psychology, Sociology, History, Philosophy, Politics, Literature and Criticism
Bookshop: address as above
1978: 44 titles *1979:* 31 titles *Founded:* 1967
ISBN Publisher's Prefix: 84-323

Ediciones **Sigueme** SA, García Tejado 3, Apdo 332, Salamanca Tel: 218203 Cable Add: Sigueme Salamanca
Man Dir, Editorial: Germán González; *Sales:* Primitivo Fernández; *Production:* Francisco Lansac; *Publicity:* Leandro Cuadrado
Associate Company: Editorial Patria Grande, Argentina
Subsidiary Company: Sociedad de Educación Atenas SA (qv)
Subjects: Philosophy, Religion, Juveniles, Psychology, Social Science, University Textbooks, Cinema, Education
Bookshop: Librería Sigueme, García Tejado 3, Salamanca
1978: 49 titles *Founded:* 1958
ISBN Publisher's Prefix: 84-301

Silex*, Cid 4, Of 502, Madrid 1 Tel: (91) 2255534
Man Dir: E Domínguez; *Sales Dirs:* Mrs de Cruz (Spain), Rose Mayer (Foreign); *Publicity, Advertising, Permissions:* P S Parrent
Subjects: Art, Reproductions of Prado and other Museum Paintings
Founded: 1972
ISBN Publisher's Prefix: 84-85041

Ediciones **Sima***, Apdo 1317, Bilbao Tel: (044) 4312135
Man Dir: Victoria Inunciaga
Subject: Juveniles
Founded: 1975

Editorial **Sintes** SA, Apdo 1078, Barcelona Tel: (93) 3182838
Man Dirs, Editorial: Luis Sintes Pros, Jorge Sintes Pros
Orders to: Ronda Universidad 4, Barcelona 7
Subjects: Sports, Technical, Health
Bookshop: Librería Sintes, Ronda Universidad 4, Barcelona
1978: 45 titles *1979:* 43 titles *Founded:* 1968
ISBN Publisher's Prefix: 84-302

Ramón **Sopena** SA, Provenza 93-95, Barcelona 15 Tel: (93) 2303809 Cable Add: Sopenar Telex: 52195 Sopec E
Man Dir: Dr Ramón Sopena Rimblas; *Sales:* Javier Egusquiza Trabudua; *Permissions:* Domingo Castellar Andreu; *Production:* Antonio Bometon Garcés
Subjects: History, How-to, Art, Reference, Juveniles, Paperbacks, General Science, Languages, Dictionaries, Children's books
Founded: 1894
Subsidiary Companies: Editorial Ramon Sopena del Río de la Plata SA y C, Argentina (qv); Editorial Sopena Colombiana SA, Colombia (qv); Editorial Sopena Mexicana SA, Mexico (qv); Editorial Ramón Sopena Venezolana SA, Venezuela (qv)
ISBN Publisher's Prefix: 84-303

Studium Ediciones*, Bailén 19, Madrid 13 Tel: (91) 2485921
Distribution: Difusora del Libro, Bailén 19, Apdo 5018, Madrid 13
Man Dir: José Guerrero Carrasco
Subjects: Religion, Philosophy, Psychology, Education, Juveniles
Founded: 1949
ISBN Publisher's Prefix: 84-304

Ediciones **Susaeta** SA, Km 11 Carretera de Barcelona, Madrid 22 Tel: (91) 2051642/4 Telex: 22148 Ssta e
Sales Dir: José Luis Mejias Cubero
Subject: Juveniles
ISBN Publisher's Prefix: 84-305

Taller Ediciones JB*, Ambrós 8, Apdo 9129, Madrid 28 Tel: (91) 2551266
Man Dir: J Betancor; *Sales Dir:* I Izquierdo; *Publicity Dir:* M Padorno; *Permissions:* J Betancor
Subjects: General Literature, Fiction, Philosophy, Psychology, Social Sciences, Art, Cinema
Founded: 1972

Taurus Ediciones SA, Apdo de Correos 10.161, General Mola, 81, Madrid 6
Man Dir: José Ignacio C Abaitua; *Editorial:* José Maria F Guelbenzu
Subjects: Philosophy, Political Science, Linguistics and Philology, Literature, History, Biography, Aesthetics, Art History, Music, Cultural Anthropology
1978: 23 titles *1979:* 45 titles *Founded:* 1956
ISBN Publisher's Prefix: 84-306

Editores **Técnicos Asociados** SA, Maignón 26, Barcelona 24 Tel: (93) 2144178/2144266
Man Dir: Carlos Palomar Llovet; *Sales, Publicity & Advertising:* Juan Cuenca Martínez
Subjects: Engineering, Technical, Construction, Computers, Organization, How-to, University Textbooks
Founded: 1963
ISBN Publisher's Prefix: 84-7146

Editorial **Tecnos** SA*, O'Donnell 27, Apdo 18, Madrid 9 Tel: (91) 2262923
Man Dir, Editorial: Gabriel Tortella; *Sales:* Pilar Lagarma; *Production:* Julio Sanchez; *Publicity, Rights & Permissions:* Fernando Valesco
Branch Off: Brusi 46, Barcelona 6
Subjects: Social Sciences, History, Art, Philology, Science and Technology, Psychology, Philosophy, Literature
1978: 34 titles *Founded:* 1947
ISBN Publisher's Prefix: 84-309

Editorial **Teide** SA, Calle Viladomat 291, Barcelona 29 Tel: (93) 2504507 Cable Add: Editeide
Man Dir, Rights & Permissions: Federico Rahola de Espona; *Editorial, Sales:* Federico Rahola Aguade; *Production:* Christian Rahola Aguade; *Publicity:* Francisco Queraltó
Subsidiary Companies: Editorial Varazen, Monterrey 70-101, Mexico 7, DF; Teide Ltda, Apdo 53694, Bogota 2, Colombia
Subjects: University, Secondary & Primary Textbooks, Pedagogy, Art, Educational Materials, Navigation, Dictionaries, Languages, Mathematics, Literature, Geography, History, Philosophy

Founded: 1940
ISBN Publisher's Prefix: 84-307

Ediciones **Telstar**, Consejo de Ciento 257-1°
1a, Barcelona 11 Tel: (93) 2534670
Man Dirs: Miguel Boladeras Cucurella, José
Nin Catalá; *Sales:* José Nin Catalá;
Production: Boladeras Cucurella
Subjects: Tourist Guidebooks & Maps
Founded: 1967
ISBN Publisher's Prefix: 84-7237

Editorial **Timun** Mas SA, Via Layetana 17-3
3a, Barcelona Tel: (93) 3103714
Dirs: Juan Antonio Martí Castro, Guillermo
Menal Alonso
Subjects: Children's, Juveniles, Teaching
Manuals
1978: 51 titles

Ediciones **Toray** SA, Duero 6, Barcelona 31
Tel: (93) 3577550 Cable Add: Toray
Dirs: Mariano Torrecilla, Miguel Vilanova
Branch Off: Cea Bermúdez, 44, Madrid 3;
Junín 925, 1113 Buenos Aires, Argentina
Subjects: General Fiction, Art, Juveniles,
Medicine, Psychology, University Textbooks
1978: 217 titles *1979:* 288 titles *Founded:*
1945
ISBN Publisher's Prefix: 84-310

Toray-Masson SA, Balmes 151, Barcelona 8
Tel: (93) 2179954 Cable Add: Massonsa
Telex: 54327 tmbn
Man Dir: Patrick Martin
Associate Company: Masson SA, France
(qv)
Subjects: Medicine, Science
ISBN Publisher's Prefix: 84-311

G del **Toro** Editor, Hortaleza 81, Madrid 4
Tel: (91) 4190486/4199518/4190139/4190184
Subjects: Fiction & Nonfiction, Juveniles,
Secondary Textbooks
ISBN Publisher's Prefix: 84-312

Instituto Eduardo **Torroja***, Costillares,
Chamartín, Apdo 19002, Madrid 33
Tel: (91) 2020440
Subjects: Construction, Engineering
ISBN Publisher's Prefix: 84-7292

Tusquets Editores, Calle Iradier 24 bajos,
Barcelona 17 Tel: (93) 2474170
Man Dirs: Beatriz de Moura, Antonio López
Lamadrid; *Sales:* Josefa Valero; *Production,
Rights & Permissions:* Lía Nouguès;
Publicity: Pep Albanell
Subjects: Fiction, Literature in general,
Biography, History, Philosophy, Art, Social
Science, Erotism, Gastronomy
1978: 23 titles *1979:* 32 titles *Founded:* 1969
ISBN Publisher's Prefix: 84-7223

Editorial **Txertoa**, Plaza de las Armerías 4,
Apdo 767, San Sebastian Tel: 459757/
460941
Man Dir: Luis Aberasturi
Subjects: Literature, Biography, History and
Art of the Basque Region
1978: 49 titles *Founded:* 1968
ISBN Publisher's Prefix: 84-7148

Ultramar Editores SA, Mallorca 49,
Barcelona 29 Tel: 3212400
Above is address for all matters relevant to
sales and administration
Man Dirs: José Sedó, Emilio Teixidor
Head Office: Hermosillo 63, Madrid 1
Subjects: General Literature, Fiction,
Science Fiction, Paperbacks, Juveniles
Founded: 1973

Universidad de Granada, Secretariado de
Publicaciones, Hospital Real, Granada Tel:
(958) 234397
Subjects: Literature, History, Law, Art,
Sciences, Philosophy, Social Sciences,
Philology, Biology, Geology, Botany,
Anthropology, Archaeology, Medicine,
Geography, Music, General Interest
1978: 52 titles

Universidad de Malaga*, Avda del
Generalísimo 23, Malaga Tel: (952) 213314
Subjects: Sociology, Philosophy

Ediciones **Universidad** de Navarra SA, see
EUNSA

Urmo SA de Ediciones, Juan de
Ajuriaguerra 10, Apdo 1506, Bilbao 9 Tel:
(94) 4245307
Chairman: José Angel Grijelmo Ribechini;
Man Dir: J Ignacio Zarza
Branch Offs: Librería Deusto, Madrid;
Urmo SA de Ediciones, Barcelona
Subjects: Engineering, General Science,
University Textbooks
1978: 9 titles *1979:* 9 titles *Founded:* 1963
ISBN Publisher's Prefix: 84-314

Editorial **Vasco** Americana SA (EVA)*, Ave
de Castilla 79, Apdo 731, Bilbao Tel: (044)
4333700
Subject: Juveniles and Children's books
ISBN Publisher's Prefix: 84-319

Editorial De **Vecchi**, see De Vecchi

Editorial **Verbo** Divino, Carretera de
Pamplona 41, Estella, Navarra Tel: 550449
Cable Add: Verbodivino
Man Dir: Father Miguel Angel Gimeno;
Sales Dir: Angel Egurza; *Advertising,
Permissions:* Angel Beltran
Subjects: Religion, Biography, Social
Science, Educational Materials
Founded: 1957
ISBN Publisher's Prefix: 84-7151

Veron Editor*, Ronda del General Mitre
163, Barcelona 22 Tel: (93) 2121599/(93)
2119300
Man Dir, Sales: Climent Luis Veron;
Editorial, Publicity: Jane Luis Veron;
Production, Rights & Permissions: Rafael
Zendrera Pijoan
Subjects: Escapist Literature, Juvenile,
Ancient & Modern Classics
Bookshops: Libreria Scriba at above
address Tel: (93) 2477124
1978: 6 titles *1979:* 8 titles *Founded:* 1965
ISBN Publisher's Prefix: 84-7255

Editorial **Vicens**-Vives, Ave de Sarriá
132-136, Barcelona 17 Tel: (93) 2034400
Man Dirs: Roser Rahola, Pere Vicens
Subjects: General Literature, Belles Lettres,
Art, History, Biography, Geography,
General Science, Mathematics, Secondary
Textbooks, Education
ISBN Publisher's Prefix: 84-316

Editorial Luis **Vives** (Edelvives), Carretera
de Madrid, Km 315 7, Apdo 387, Saragossa
Tel: 344100 Cable Add: Edelvives
Man Dir: David Sebastián; *Sales Dir:* Luis
Fernández
Branch Offs: Barcelona, Bilbao, Madrid,
Seville, Valencia, Valladolid, Vigo,
Saragossa
Subjects: University, Secondary & Primary
Textbooks, Educational Materials
1978: 40 titles *1979:* 38 titles *Founded:* 1932
ISBN Publisher's Prefix: 84-263

Xarait Ediciones, Juan Vigón 3, Madrid 3
Proprietor, Dir: Miguel Ortiz Martinez
Subjects: Architecture, Art
Bookshop: Xarait Libros (qv)
1978-79: 6 titles *Founded:* 1978
ISBN Publisher's Prefix: 84-85434

Zero SA, now Zero-Zyx SA (qv)

Editorial **Zero**-Zyx SA*, Lérida 80, Madrid
20 Tel: (91) 2796591
Man Dir: Jesús Carrascosa; *Sales:* Jose
Lozano; *Publicity & Advertising:* Manuel
Irusta; *Rights & Permissions:* Teresa Garcia-
Abad
Subjects: Belles Lettres, Poetry, Biography,
History, Philosophy, Religion, Juveniles,
Paperbacks, Psychology, Social Science
1978: 48 titles *Founded:* 1963

Literary Agents

A C E R, Calle Bolenia 5, Madrid 28 Tel:
2559943/2461776 Cable Add: Teleacer
Manager: Marcel Laignoux

Carmen **Balcells** Agencia Literaria,
Diagonal 580, Barcelona 21 Tel: (93)
2008565/2008933 Cable Add: Copyright
Barcelona Telex: 50459 copy E (Barcelona)
Manager: Carmen Balcells
Branch Off: Rio de Janeiro, Brazil (qv)

Cecilio **Cardeñoso***, Juan Güell 74-76,
Barcelona 28 Tel: (93) 3303416
Specializations: Philosophy, Psychology,
Politics, Sociology, General Interest, General
Spanish and Latin-American language
Fiction

International Editors' Co SA, Rambla de
Cataluña 39, Barcelona 7 Tel: (93) 3188980
Cable Add: Lifeplay
Manager: Isabel Monteagudo
Branch Off: Buenos Aires, Argentina (qv)

Andrés de **Kramer**, Castello 30, Madrid 1

José **Moya** und Ute Körner de Moya, Ronda
Guinardo 32 5° 5a, Barcelona 25

Saga Literaria SL, Calle Recoletos 11 3° B,
Madrid 1 Tel: 2756252
Manager: Frédérique Porretta
Specializations: How-To, Juvenile, Co-
Editions, Spanish and South American
authors

J F **Yañez**, Agencia Literaria (Universitas),
Marco Aurelio 5 5° 3a, Barcelona 6
Tel: 2479360 Cable Add: Agenliter
Dirs: Julio F Yañez and Mrs Mayte Yañez

Book Clubs

Círculo de Amigos de la Historia*, Conrado
del Campo 9 & 11, Madrid 27

Círculo de Lectores SA, Valencia 344,
Barcelona 9

Club de Amigos del Libro, Mallorca 257,
Barcelona 8 Tel: (93) 2156088
Secretary: Amparo Antiga
Owned by: Editorial CEDEL (qv)
Subjects: Radio, Television, Metallurgy,
Yoga, Naturism, Chemistry, Industrial
Studies

Club del **Libro** de la Naturaleza, Castello 59,
Madrid 1
Owned by: Editorial Incafo, Publisher (qv).
The Club is open only to subscribers to the
proprietors' periodical *Periplo*
Subjects: (Books published by Incafo at a
20% discount) Natural History, Geography,
Ethnology, especially with regard to Spain
and Spanish America

Biblioteca de **Selecciones** (Selections from
the Reader's Digest) (Iberia) SA, Calle
Telémaco 3, Madrid 27 Tel: (91) 7420011

Major Booksellers

M **Aguilar***, Goya 18, Madrid
also: Serrano 24, Madrid; Ave Generalísimo
44-46, Madrid

Librería **Ancora** y Delfín*, Diagonal 564,
Barcelona 21 Tel: (93) 2000746

Librería Editorial **Argos** SA*, Paseo de
Gracia 30, Barcelona 7 Tel: (93) 3014558

Librería **Augustinus**, Gaztambide 75,
Madrid 15 Tel: (91) 2442430

324 SPAIN

Librería **Bastinos***, Pelayo 52, Barcelona 1
Tel: (93) 3018474

Librería **Bosch**, Ronda de la Universidad 11,
Barcelona 7 Tel: (93) 3175308

Casa del Libro SA*, Ronda de San Pedro 3,
Barcelona 10 Tel: (93) 3182640

Cinc d'Oros — Jaime Farrás Solé*,
Diagonal 462, Barcelona 8

Delsa, Importadora de Publicaciones SA,
Serrano 80, Madrid 6 Tel: 2268880

Librería **Díaz** de Santos*, Lagasca 95,
Madrid 6 Tel: (91) 2255697

Casa del Libro **Espasa-Calpe** SA*, Ave José
Antonio 29, Madrid 13 Tel: (91) 2216657

Librería **Francesa**, Paseo de Gracia 91,
Barcelona 8 Tel: (93) 2151417/
2151426/2156618
Manager: Mr Joan Tur Palerm

Librería **Herder**, Balmes 26, Barcelona 7
Tel: (93) 3170578
Manager: Hermann Nahm

Librería **Hispano Americana***, Ave de José
Antonio 594, Barcelona 7 Tel: (93)
3175337/3180079
Manager: José M B Ginesta

Hogar del Libro SA, Vergara 3,
Barcelona 2 Tel: (343) 3182700 Telex:
50066 ogar
Manager: Sebastià Fàbregues
Also Publisher (qv), and Major Distributor,
with five other Bookshops in Barcelona area

Insula, Librería de Ciencias y Letras, Benito
Gutiérrez 26, Madrid 8 Tel: (91) 2435415

H F **Martínez** de Murguía*, Valverde 30,
Madrid 13 Tel: (91) 2226634
Universal supplier and distributor of books
published in Spain

Librería **Mediterranea***, Ave Generalísimo
Franco 403, Barcelona 9

Miessner Libreros, José Ortega y Gasset 14,
Madrid 6 Tel: (91) 2250978/2250998
Subjects: General Literature, Classical
Studies, Language, Philosophy,
Archaeology, Art, Hebraic and Islamic
Studies

Librería **Mundi-Prensa**, Castelló 37, Apdo
1223, Madrid 1 Tel: (91) 2754655
Man Dir: Pedro Hernández
Subsidiary Company: Libreria Agricola,
Fernando VI, no 2, Madrid
Specializations: Economics, Life Sciences,
Agriculture, Engineering, Technology
Founded: 1948

Librerías **P P C** (Promoción Popular
Cristiana)*, San Mateo 30, Madrid Tel: (91)
4190034/4190906; E Jardiel Poncela 4,
Madrid 16 Tel: (91) 4582335; Librería PPC,
Canuda 9, Barcelona Tel: (93) 3172939;
Librería Remel, Carrer Badal 144,
Barcelona Tel: (93) 2578652 (and 13 other
branches of PPC throughout Spain)

Librería **Passim**, Bailén 134, Barcelona 9
Tel: (93) 2574757 Cable Add: Passim
Publishes catalogues of new and out of print
books about Spain and Latin America
published in Spain. Specializes in export
sales to foreign Universities and Libraries

Librería José **Porrúa** Turanzas SA, Cea
Bermúdez 10, Madrid 3 Tel: (91)
2542344/2541466
Manager: José Porrúa Venero

Porter-Libros, Ave Puerta del Angel 9,
Barcelona 2 Tel: (93) 2226437

Praxis Libros, now Xarait Libros (qv)

Librería Pedro **Pueyo***, Arenal 16, Madrid
13 Tel: (91) 2213344

Xarait Libros, San Francisco de Sales 32,
Madrid 3

Major Libraries

Archivo General de la **Administracion** Civil
del Estado*, Ronda Fiscal 1, Alcalá de
Henares, Madrid
General Archives of the Civil Administration
of the State
Documents on administration no longer of
current relevance

Archivo General de Indias*, Queipo de
Llano 3, Seville
Archives of the Indies

Archivo Historico Nacional, Calle Serrano
115, Madrid
National Historical Archives
Director: Dr Sanchez Belda

Archivo y Biblioteca Capitulares*, Cathedral
of Toledo, Toledo
Archives and Library of the Cathedral
Chapter
Dir: Ramón Gonzálvez

Biblioteca del **Ateneo de Barcelona***, Calle
Canude, Barcelona
Library of the Athenaeum of Barcelona

Biblioteca del **Ateneo de Madrid***, Prado 21,
Madrid
Library of the Madrid Athenaeum

Biblioteca del **Ateneo Mercantil**
Valenciano*, Plaza del Generalísimo,
Valencia
Library of the Mercantile Athenaeum of
Valencia

Biblioteca Nacional, Paseo de Calvo Sotelo
20, Madrid 1 Tel: (91) 2756800
Dir: D Hipolito Escolar Sobrino

Biblioteca del **Consejo** Superior de
Investigaciones Científicas*, Medinaceli 4,
Madrid
Library of the Council for Scientific
Research

Archivo de la **Corona** de Aragon, Conde de
Barcelona 2, Barcelona
Royal Archives of Aragon
Dir: Dr Federico Udina Martorell
*Publications: Colección de Documentos
Inéditos del Archivo de la Corona de
Aragón (from 1847)*

Biblioteca de **Catalunya** Diputación de
Barcelona, Calle del Carmen 47, Apdo 1077,
Barcelona 1 Tel: (Director) 3178990;
(General) 3170778
Library of Cataluña

Hemeroteca Municipal de Madrid, Plaza de
la Villa 3, Madrid
Madrid Periodical Library

Biblioteca del **Instituto de Cultura**
Hispánica*, Madrid
Library of the Institute of Hispanic Culture

Biblioteca del **Instituto Nacional** del Libro
Español*, Calle Mallorca 272-276,
Barcelona 37
Library of the Spanish Publishers' and
Booksellers' Association

Biblioteca de **Menéndez Pelayo**, Rubio 6,
Santander Tel: 234534
Librarian: Manuel R Sañudo
*Publication: Boletín de la Biblioteca de
Menéndez Pelayo* (annual)

Biblioteca del **Ministerio de Información y
Turismo***, Ave Generalísimo 39, Planta 2,
Madrid 16
Library of the Ministry of Information and
Tourism

Biblioteca del **Palacio** Real, Plaza de Oriente
Madrid 13
Library of the Royal Palace

Real Biblioteca de San Lorenzo de El
Escorial*, El Escorial
Escorial Library

Biblioteca General, **Universidad Autónoma**
de Barcelona, Campus Universitario,
Bellaterra (Barcelona) Tel: 6920200,
6921166 Telex: 52040
Dir: M Mundó Marcet

Biblioteca de la **Universidad Complutense** de
Madrid*, Ciudad Universitaria, Madrid 3

Biblioteca Universitaria, **Universidad
Pontificia** de Salamanca*, Calle de Libros,
Salamanca Tel: 213964

Biblioteca **Universitaria de Barcelona***, Gran
Vía de las Cortes Catalanas 585, Barcelona 7
Librarian: Rosalia Guilleumas Brosa

Library Associations

Associació de Bibliotecàrios*, Via Augusta
120, Pl Baixa Local G, Barcelona 6 Tel:
2181997
Association of Librarians
Secretary: N Ventura

**Asociación Nacional de Bibliotecarios,
Archiveros y Arqueólogos**, (National
Association of Librarians, Archivists and
Archaeologists)*, Paseo Calvo Sotelo 22,
Madrid 1 Tel: (91) 2756800
Chief Executive: Dr Justo García Morales
Secretary: Celina Iñiguez Galíndez
Section for Catalonia and the Balearics:
Apdo 1868, Barcelona
President: Mercé Rossell
Publications: Include *Boletín* (which has
bibliography section), *Inspección General de
Archivos*

Instituto Bibliográfico Hispánico, Calle de
Atocha 106, Madrid 12 Tel: (91) 2283878
Dir: Vicente Sánchez Muñoz
Hispanic Bibliographical Institute
Publications: Bibliografía Española
(monthly), *Indices de Revistas de
Bibliotecologia* (3 a year)

Servicio de Bibliotecas Populares de la
Diputación Provincial de Barcelona, Carmen
47, Barcelona 1 Tel: 3185996

Library Reference Books and Journals

Books

Bibliotheca Hispana (Spanish Library),
Consejo Superior de Investigaciones
Cientificas, Serrano 117, Madrid

Inspección General de Archivos (Report on
Spanish Archives), General Directorate of
Archives and Libraries, Paseo Calvo Sotelo
22, Madrid 1

Journals

Boletín (Bulletin), General Directorate of
Archives and Libraries, Paseo Calvo Sotelo
22, Madrid 1

Boletín (Bulletin), National Association of
Librarians, Arichivists and Archaeologists,
Paseo Calvo Sotelo 22, Madrid 1

Indices de Revistas de Bibliotecologia (Indexes to Library Science Periodicals), Spanish Bibliographical Institute, Paseo Calvo Sotelo 22, Madrid 1

Informacion Librera (Library Information), Javier Romani Sopena, Pelayo 11, 4, Barcelona

Revista de Archivos, Bibliotecas y Museos (Review of Archives, Libraries and Museums), Ministerio de Educación y Ciencia, Servicio de Publicaciónes, Ciudad Universitaria, Madrid 3

Literary Associations and Societies

Academia de Buenas Letras de Barcelona*, Calle Obispo Cassador 3, Barcelona 22
Barcelona Academy of Belles Lettres
Secretary: José Alsina Clota
Publications: Boletín, Memorias

Ateneo Cientifico, Literario y Artistico*, Calle del Prado 21, Apdo 272, Madrid
Scientific, Literary and Artistic Athenaeum
President: José Maria de Cossío
Publication: Hoja del Ateneo

Ateneo Cientifico, Literario y Artistico*, Calle Cifuentes 25, Mahón, Minorca, Balearic Islands
Scientific Literary and Artistic Athenaeum
Secretaries: Calixto Martín Neé, María Esther Sebastian Sandino
Publication: Revista de Menorca (quarterly)

Mutualidad Laboral de Escritores de Libros*, General Mola 34, 2° izqda, Madrid 1 Tel: 2756192
Book Writers' Friendly Society

Spanish **P E N** Club*, Libréria Turner, Génova 3, Madrid
Secretary: José Antonio Gabriel y Galan

Spanish **P E N** Club (Cataluña)*, Apdo 2502, Central de Correos, Barcelona
Secretary: A Artis-Gener, c/o Josep Paulau i Fabre at above address

Real Academia de Ciencias, Bellas Letras y Nobles Artes*, Madrid
Royal Academy of Science, Literature and Fine Arts
Secretary: Juan Gómez Crespo
Publications: Boletín (half-yearly), scientific, historical and literary works

Real Academia Sevillana de Buenas Letras*, Plaza del Museo 8, Selville
Seville Royal Academy of Belles Lettres
Secretary: Dr Ildefonso Camacho Baños
Publication: Boletín de Buenas Letras (quarterly)

Sociedad de Ciencias, Letras y Artes*, Dr Chil 33, Las Palmas, Canary Islands
Scientific, Literary and Art Society
Secretary: Juan Rodríguez Doreste
Publication: El Museo Canario (quarterly)

Literary Periodicals

Camp de l'Arpa, Valencia 72, Entlo 4a, Barcelona 15

Destino (Destiny), Ediciones Destino SL, Consejo de Ciento 425, 5, Barcelona 9

La Estafeta Literaria (The Literary Courier), Editora Nacional, Ave del Generalísimo 29, Madrid 16

Insula (Island); bibliographical review of sciences and letters, Ediciones y Publicaciones de Insula, Benito Gutiérrez 26, Madrid 8

Litoral; monthly poetry review, Visor-Libros, Calle del Roble 22, Madrid 20

Nuestro Tiempo (Our Time), Ediciones Universidad de Navarra SA, Plaza de los Sauces, 1 & 2 Barañain, Pamplona

Razon y Fe; Spanish-American review, Pablo Aranda 3, Madrid 6

Revista de Literatura (Review of Literature), Libreria Cientifico Medinaceli del CSIC, Madrid

Revista de Occidente (Review of the West), Revista de Occidente SA, General Mola 11, Madrid 1

Revista Literaria Azor (The Goshawk — a Literary Review), C Borell 128, 1 2A Barcelona 15

Serra d'Or, Publicaciones de l'Abadia de Montserrat, Abadia de Montserrat, Barcelona

El Urogallo (The Capercailzie), Matias Montero 24, Madrid 6

Literary Prizes

Adonais Prize*
For the best poetry. Awarded annually, Enquiries to Ediciones Rialp SA, Preciados 34, Madrid 13

Miguel de **Cervantes** Prize*
For the best novel published during the year. 200,000 pesetas. Awarded annually. Enquiries to Ministry of Information and Tourism, Ave Generalísimo 39, Madrid 16

Duke of Alba Prize*
Established 1905 for original, unpublished works in Spanish. 48,000 pesetas. Awarded once every nine years. Enquiries to Royal Spanish Academy, Felipe IV, 4, Madrid 14

Manuel **Espinosa** y Cortina Prize*
Established 1891 for the best dramatic work performed for the first time. 4,000 pesetas. Awarded once every five years. Enquiries to Royal Spanish Academy, Felipe IV, 4, Madrid 14

Fastenrath Prize*
Established 1909 for works of excellence written in the Spanish language. 6,000 pesetas. Awarded annually in rotation for the following categories of writing: poetry; essays, criticism; novel or story; history, biography; drama. Enquiries to Royal Spanish Academy, Felipe IV, 4, Madrid 14

Marques of Cerralbo XVII Prize*
Established 1922 for the best original, unpublished work related to Spanish language and literature. 40,000 pesetas. Awarded once every four years. Enquiries to Royal Spanish Academy, Felipe IV, 4, Madrid 14

Eugenio **Nadal** Prize*
For the best novel, preferably by a young writer. 200,000 pesetas. Awarded annually. Enquiries to Ediciones Destino SL, Consejo de Ciento 425, 5, Barcelona 9

Alvarez **Quintero** Prize*
Established 1949 for the best work in two categories alternately: novel or story collection and theatrical works. 5,000 pesetas. Awarded biennially. Enquiries to Royal Spanish Academy, Felipe IV, 4, Madrid 14

Rivadeneyra Prizes*
Established 1940 for the best work on Spanish literature and linguistics. Two prizes, of 30,000 pesetas and 20,000 pesetas. Awarded annually. Enquiries to Royal Spanish Academy, Felipe IV, 4, Madrid 14

Sri Lanka

General Information

Language: Sinhalese and Tamil (also English)
Religion: Buddhist
Population: 14 million
Literacy Rate (1971): 77.6% (85.9% of urban population, 75% rural)
Bank Hours: 0900-1330 Monday-Friday
Shop Hours: 0900-1700 Monday-Friday
Currency: 100 cents = 1 Sri Lanka/Ceylon rupee
Export/Import Information: No tariff on books or advertising. Import licence required for most book importation. Exchange controls.
Copyright: Berne, Florence (see International section)

Book Trade Organizations

Booksellers' Association of **Sri Lanka***, PO Box 25, Colombo 1 Tel: 22675/7
Secretary: R J Faber

Sri Lanka Publishers' Association*, 61 Sangaraja Mawatha, Colombo 10
Secretary-General: Eamon Kariyakarawana

Book Trade Journals

Ceylon National Bibliography (text in English, Sinhalese and Tamail), Sri Lanka National Library Services Board, 72 Bauddhaloka Mawatha, Colombo 4

Publishers

Architecture & Arts Publications Co*, 75 Ward Pl, Colombo 7
Subjects: Art, Architecture

W E **Bastian** & Co*, 23 Canal Row, Fort, PO Box 10, Colombo 1
Man Proprietor: W D E Bastian
Subjects: Literary, Technical
Founded: 1904

H W **Cave** & Co, 81 Sir Baron Jayatilaka Mawatha, PO Box 25, Colombo 1 Tel: 22675/6/7 Cable Add: Cave Telex: 1241
Man Dir: B J L Fernando; *Dirs:* K Prabachandran, C J S Fernando; *Dir/General Manager:* J R W Rerera
Subjects: History, Archaeology, Juveniles, Literature, Law, Management, Medicine, Engineering, Economics, Education, Psychology, Environmental Studies
Founded: 1876

Ceylon Printers Ltd, No 20 Sir Chittampalam Gardiner Mawatha, Colombo
Subject: Belles Lettres

Colombo Catholic Press*, 956 Gnanartha Pradipaya Mawatha, Colombo 8 Tel: 95984
Dir and Manager: Rev Father Benedict Joseph
Founded: 1865

Cultural Council of Sri Lanka*, 135 Dharmabala Mawatha, PO Box 307, Colombo 7 Tel: 27505/26125 Cable Add: Sanskriti
Dir: R L Wimaladharma; *Editorial:* Prof D E Hettiaratchi, Prof J D Dheerasekera, D P Ponnamperuma
Subjects: Literature, Religion, Art, Culture
Book Club: Book Club of the Cultural Council of Sri Lanka
Bookshop: Jayanti Bookshop, 135

Dharmapala Mawatha, Colombo 7
1978: 15 titles *Founded:* 1971

M D **Gunasena** & Co Ltd, 217 Olcott Mawatha, PO Box 246, Colombo 11 Tel: 23981/4 Cable Add: emdeegee Colombo Telex: 1306 a/b Davasa Colombo
Subjects: University & School Books on all subjects
Founded: 1915
Miscellaneous: Associated imprints include Ananda Books, Sirisara Vidyalaya

Hansa Publishers Ltd*, Hansa Ho, Clifford Ave, Colombo 3
Subjects: General and Children's Fiction, Biographical, Politics, Law, Economics, Children's Science

J K G **Jayawardena** & Co*, BTS Bldg, 203, 1/13 Olcott Mawatha, Colombo 11

Karunaratne & Co*, 145 Olcott Mawatha, Colombo 11

Lake House Investments Ltd*, 41 WAD Ramanayake Mawatha, PO Box 1453, Colombo 2 Tel: 33271/2/3
Chairman: R S Wijewardene; *Dir:* G B S Gomes; *Editorial, Production, Publicity, Rights & Permissions:* H Amarasinghe (Tel: 35175); *Sales:* V L C Walatara (Tel: 27316)
Orders to and Bookshop: The Manager, Lake House Bookshop, 100 Sir Chittampalam Gardiner Mawatha, PO Box 244, Colombo 2
Subjects: Education, Law, General Fiction, Children's Books, Dictionaries, Medicine (in English and Sinhala)
Founded: 1965

Department of **National Museums**, PO Box 854, Sir Marcus Fernando Mawata, Colombo 7 Tel: 94767
Subjects: Publications relating to Sri Lanka's Antiquities, Anthropology, Natural History, *Spolia Zeylanica* (Journal of the National Museums of Sri Lanka)
See also: National Museum Library (under Major Libraries)

Ratnakara Press Ltd*, 74 Dam St, Colombo 12

Saman Publishers Ltd*, 49/16 Iceland Bldgs, Colombo 3

Sandesa Ltd*, 44A Alfred House Gardens, Colombo 3
Branch Off: 185 Grandpass Rd, Colombo 14

K V G De **Silva** & Sons (Kandy), 44/9 YMBA Bldg, Fort, Colombo Tel: 083254/26831 Cable Add: Silco
Man Dir: K V N De Silva; *Sales Dir:* Miss D De Silva; *Publicity & Advertising Dir:* Mrs K V N De Silva; *Permissions:* K V N De Silva
Shipping Add: 86 D S Senanayake Veediya, Kandy
Subjects: History, Religion
Bookshops: 86 D S Senanayake Veediya, Kandy; 44/9 YMBA Bldg, Fort, Colombo
Founded: 1898

Sri Lanka Publishing Co*, 209 Norris Rd, Colombo 11

The **Union** Press*, 169 Union Pl, PO Box 362, Colombo 2 Tel: 20485/35912 Cable Add: Unionpress
Managing Proprietor: A H Dhas
Founded: 1942

Book Club

Book Club of the **Cultural Council** of Sri Lanka*, 135 Dharmabala Mawatha, PO Box 307, Colombo 7
Owned by: Cultural Council of Sri Lanka (Colombo)

Major Libraries

British Council Libraries, PO Box 753, 154 Galle Rd, Colombo 3
Branch Library: Dalada Vidiya, Kandy

Ceylon Institute of Scientific and Industrial Research Library, 363 Bauddhaloka Mawatha, Colombo 7
Librarian: Clodagh Nethsingha
Publications: Current Technical Literature (quarterly; bibliographical series; state-of-the-art surveys of spices, essential oils

Colombo Public Library System*, 18 Sir Marcus Fernando Mawatha, Colombo 7 Tel: 95156/96530/91968
Librarian: Mrs Ishvari Corea
Publications: Libraries and People; A Manual for Public Libraries in Sri Lanka

National Archives, 7 Reid Ave, Colombo 7 Tel: 94523/96917 Cable Add: Archives

National Museum Library, Department of National Museums PO Box 854, Sir Marcus Fernando Mawatha, Colombo 7 Tel: 93314
Librarian: C I Karunanayake
Publications: Sri Lanka Periodicals Index; Ceylon Periodicals Directory (Annual Supplements)
See also Department of National Museums (Publisher)

University of Peradeniya Library*, University Park, Peradeniya
Acting Librarian: S Murugaverl
Publications (on exchange): *Modern Ceylon Studies, A Journal of the Social Sciences, Sri Lanka Journal of Humanities, Ceylon Journal of Science* (Biological Sciences)

Library Associations

Sri Lanka Library Association*, University of Sri Lanka, Colombo Campus, PO Box 1698, Colombo 3 (Located at: Reid Avenue, Colombo 7)
Secretary: Jayasiri Lankage
Publication: Sri Lanka Library Review (biannual)

Sri Lanka National Library Services Board, 3rd Floor, New Secretariat, Maligawatte, Colombo 10 Tel: 31332
Director/Secretary: N Amarasinghe

Library Journals

Library News, Sri Lanka National Library Services Board, 72 Bauddhaloka Mawatha, Colombo 4

Sri Lanka Library Review, Sri Lanka Library Association, University of Sri Lanka, Colombo Campus, PO Box 1698, Colombo 3

Literary Associations and Societies

Afro-Asian Writers' Bureau*, 73 Castle St, Colombo 8
Publication: Call

The **Dickens** Fellowship, University of Ceylon, Thurston Rd, Colombo
Honorary Secretary: M M Aryrtane

Literary Periodicals

Call (Editions in English and French), Afro-Asian Writers' Bureau, 73 Castle St, Colombo 8

New Ceylon Writing; creative and critical writing of Sri Lanka, Macquarie University, School of English and Linguistics, North Ryde, NSW 2113, Australia

Vidyodaya; journal of arts, science and letters (text in English, Sinhalese and Tamil), University of Sri Lanka, Vidyodaya Campus Library, Nugegoda

Literary Prizes

Literary Prizes for Sinhala Literature*
For the best books published in the previous year in the Sinhala language in the following categories: novels, short stories, poetry, translations, children's literature, scientific literature, drama; also three awards in miscellaneous literary areas and awards for original works in Pali, Sanskrit and Arabic. 1,000 Sri Lanka rupees each. Awarded annually. Enquiries to Sri Lanka Cultural Council and the Department of Cultural Affairs, 135 Dharmapala Mawatha, Colombo 7

Literary Prizes for Tamil Literature*
For the best books of the year in Tamil in the following categories: novels, short stories, poetry (plus three prizes in miscellaneous literary areas). 1,000 Sri Lanka rupees. Awarded annually. Enquiries to Sri Lanka Cultural Council and the Department of Cultural Affairs, 135 Dharmapala Mawatha, Colombo 7

Don **Pedrick** Memorial Literary Award*
For the best original literary work in Sinhala. 1,000 Sri Lanka rupees. Awarded annually. Enquiries to Don Pedrick Memorial Literary Award Committee, 79 Dharmapala Mawata, Colombo 7

Sudan

General Information

Language: Arabic (English also used)
Religion: Muslim (Sunni sect) in north, pagan in south
Population: 17 million
Literacy Rate (1956): 9.6%
Bank Hours: 0830-1200 Saturday-Thursday
Shop Hours: 0800-1300, 1700-2000 Saturday-Thursday
Currency: 100 piastres (1,000 milliemes) = 1 Sudanese pound
Export/Import Information: No tariff on books; some advertising matter may be dutied at 40% and 5% ad valorem. Import licences required. Exchange controls; annual foreign exchange budget

Publishers

Al-**Ayam** Press Co Ltd*, Aboul Ela Bldgs, United Nations Sq, PO Box 363, Khartoum
Man Dir: Beshir Muhammad Said
Subjects: General Fiction & Nonfiction, Belles Lettres, Poetry, Reference, Magazines, Books in Arabic, Paperbacks
Founded: 1953

Government Printer*, Government Printing Press, PO Box 38, Khartoum

Khartoum University Press*, PO Box 321, Khartoum Tel: 80558/81806/81869/73222
Man Dir: El-Fatih Mahgoub; *Sales Manager:* Abdel Raham Ibrahim; *Editorial, Rights & Permissions:* Ali El-Mak
Subjects: General Fiction and Nonfiction, Belles Lettres, Poetry, Biography, History, Africana, Philosophy, Reference, Religion, Books in Arabic, Paperbacks, Science & Technology, General & Social Science, University & Secondary Textbooks
Bookshop: PO Box 321, Khartoum
Founded: 1968

Major Booksellers

The **Apaya** Bookshop, PO Box 110, Juba
The Bookshop of the Episcopal Church of Sudan (formerly The Church Bookshop)

Al **Bashir** Bookshop*, PO Box 1118, Khartoum

The **Church** Bookshop, now The Apaya Bookshop (qv)

The **Khartoum** Bookshop*, PO Box 968, Khartoum Tel: 77594/74425

The **Sudan** Bookshop Ltd, PO Box 1610, Khartoum Tel: 74123/76781 Cable Add: Bookshop Khartoum Telex: 480 sisco km

University of Khartoum Bookshop*, PO Box 321, Khartoum Tel: 72271

Major Libraries

American Cultural Center Library*, Qasr Ave, Khartoum

British Council Library*, 45 Sharia Gama'a, PO Box 1253, Khartoum Tel: 70159/70308/73454/76607/80269
Houses both books and periodicals

Higher Teachers' Training Institute Library*, PO Box 406, Omdurman

Khartoum Polytechnic Library*, PO Box 407, Khartoum Tel: 78922

University of Cairo*, Khartoum Branch Library, PO Box 1055, Khartoum

University of Khartoum Library*, PO Box 321, Khartoum Tel: 72271

Library Associations

Sudan Library Association*, PO Box 32, Khartoum North Tel: 33804
Secretary: Mohd Abashar
Publication: Sudan Library Journal

Library Journals

Sudan Library Journal (Text in Arabic and English), Sudan Library Association, PO Box 32, Khartoum North

Suriname

General Information

Language: Dutch (and English)
Religion: Hindu, Roman Catholic, Muslim, Protestant
Population: 374,000
Literacy Rate (1964): 83.6%
Bank Hours: 0800-1230 Monday-Friday; 0800-1100 or 1200 Saturday
Shop Hours: Generally 0700-1300, 1600-1800 Monday-Friday; 0700-1300, 1600-1900 Saturday
Currency: 100 cents = 1 Suriname gulden
Export/Import Information: No tariff on books except children's picture books, 20% ad valorem; none on small quantities of advertising matter. Added taxes of $1\frac{1}{2}$ + $\frac{1}{2}$%. Import licences liberally granted. Exchange controls
Copyright: Berne

Book Trade Organization

Standard Book Numbering Agency*, Suriname Publishers Association, Domineestr 26, Paramaribo
ISBN Administrator: Dr Ellen Kensmil

Suriname Publishers' Association*, Domineestr 26, PO Box 1841, Paramaribo Tel: 72545

Publishers

Lionarons Drukkerij NV*, Dr J F Nassylaan 107-109, Paramaribo

Vaco NV*, PO Box 1841, Paramaribo Tel: 72545 Cable Add: Vaco Telex: 123 Inco sme (Located at: Domineestraat 26, Paramaribo)
Man Dir: E Hogenboom
Subjects: History, Low-priced Paperbacks, Primary and Secondary Textbooks, Maps
1978: 5 titles *Founded:* 1952
Bookshop: Vaco NV, Domineestr 26, Paramaribo

Leo **Victor***, Gemenlandsweg 4, Paramaribo

Major Booksellers

Vaco NV*, Domineestr 26, Paramaribo

Major Libraries

Bibliotheek CCS, see Cultural Centre

Library of the **Cultural Centre** Surinam (Bibliotheek CCS), Gravenstr 112-114, PO Box 1241, Paramaribo
Librarian: Mrs C Carrilho-Fazal Alikhan

Swaziland

General Information

Language: English and Afrikaans
Religion: Tribal religions, some Christianity
Population: 544,000
Banks close 1100 Saturday
Currency: 100 cents = 1 lilangeni (plural: emalangeni)
Export/Import Information: Same as South Africa

Major Booksellers

Swaziland News Agency*, PO Box 171, Manzini

Major Libraries

Swaziland National Library Service*, PO Box 652, Manzini Tel: Manzini 2433
Acting Dir: D Simelane

University College of Swaziland Library*, PB Kwaluseni Tel: 52111 (Manzini)
Librarian: A W Z Kuzwayo

Sweden

General Information

Language: Swedish. Danish and Norwegian are usually intelligible to speakers of Swedish. German is common second language
Religion: Protestant
Population: 8.28 million
Bank Hours: 0930-1500 Monday-Friday
Shop Hours: 0900-1800 (later Friday) Monday-Friday; early closing Saturday
Currency: 100 öre = 1 Swedish krona (plural: kronor)
Export/Import Information: No tariff on books, Advertising Tax is 10%. 17.65% VAT on most imported goods. No import licences. No exchange controls
Copyright: UCC, Berne, Florence (see International section)

Book Trade Organizations

Bok-, Pappers- och Kontorsvaruförbundet, Skeppargatan 27, S-114 52 Stockholm Tel: Växel (08) 630205
Swedish Federation of Book, Stationery and Office Supplies Dealers
Publications: Bok och Papper: Svensk Bokhandel (jointly with Swedish Publishers' Association)

Bokbranschens Finansierings-institut AB (Book Trade Finance Institute)*, Klara Norra Kyrkogata 34, S-111 22 Stockholm

Bokbranschens Marknadsinstitut AB, Sveavägen 52, S-111 34 Stockholm
Book Trade Marketing Institute

Bokhandelsrådet, c/o Svenska Bokförläggareföreningen, Sveavägen 52, S-111 34, Stockholm
Book Trade Council

Kristna Bokförläggareföreningen, Tegnérgatan 34, S-113 59 Stockholm Tel: (08) 340290
Christian Publishers' Association
Secretariat: Tony Guldbrandzén

Standard Book Numbering Agency, see Swedish National ISBN Centre

Svenska Antikvariatföreningen, Birger Jarlsgatan 32, S-114 29 Stockholm
Swedish Antiquarian Booksellers' Association

SWEDEN

Svenska Bokförläggareföreningen, Sveavägen 52, S-111 34 Stockholm Tel: (08) 231800
Swedish Publishers' Association
Secretary: Jonas Modig
Publication: Svensk Bokhandel (jointly with the Swedish Booksellers' Association)

Svenska Bokhandels-Medhjälpare-Föreningen, Luntmakargatan 15, S-111 37 Stockholm Tel: 109698
Swedish Booksellers' Assistants' Association

Svenska Bokhandlareföreningen, Skeppargatan 27, S-114 52 Stockholm Tel: (08) 630205
Secretary: Per Nordenson
Swedish Booksellers' Association

Svenska Musikförläggareföreningen UPA (Swedish Music Publishers' Association), c/o Svensk Musik, Birger Jarlsgatan 6B, Box 5091, S 102 42 Stockholm

Sveriges B-Bokhandlareförbund (Swedish Association of Smaller Booksellers)*, S-280 10 Sösdala Tel: (0451) 60096

Sveriges Författarförbund, Linnégatan 10, Box 5252, S-102 45 Stockholm
Swedish Authors' Alliance
Secretary: Sonja Thunborg
Publication: Författaren

Swedish National ISBN Centre, Bibliographical Institute, Royal Library, PO Box 5039, S-10241 Stockholm 5
ISBN Administrator: Folke Hermanson-Snickars

Book Trade Reference Books and Journals

Books

Boksverige, Författare, Förlag, Bokhandel, Bibliotek (The Book in Sweden: Author, Publisher, Bookshop, Library), Albert Bonniers Förlag AB, Sveavägen 56, S-111 34 Stockholm

Svenska Bokförläggareföreningens. Matrikel över dess Medlemmar och Kommissionärer samt Bokhandelns Föreningar och Organisationer (Swedish Publishers' Association. List of Members and Agents, together with Book Trade Associates and Organizations), Swedish Publishers' Association, Sveavägen 52, S-111 34 Stockholm

Journals

Bok och Papper (Book or Paper), Swedish Federation of Book, Stationery and Office Supplies Dealers, Skeppargatan 27, S-114 52 Stockholm

Bokrevy (Book Review), Bibliotekstjänst AB, Tornvägen 9, Fack, S-221 01 Lund

Bokvännen (The Bibliophile), Sällskapet Bokvännera, Ulvsatervagen 18, S-191 43 Sollentuna 3

Svensk Bokförteckning (Swedish National Bibliography), Royal Library, Bibliographical Institute, Box 5039, S-102 41 Stockholm 5. Cumulates into the *Svensk Bokkatalog*

Svensk Bokhandel (Swedish Book Trade), Swedish Publishers' Association, Sveavägen 52, S-111 34 Stockholm (jointly with Swedish Federation of Book, Stationery and Office Supplies Dealers)

Svensk Bokkatalog, see *Svensk Bokförteckning*

Text; Swedish bibliographical journal (text in English and Swedish), Centre for Bibliographical Studies, Uppsala

Publishers

Acta Universitatis Gothoburgensis, PO Box 5096, S-402 22 Göteborg 5 Tel: (031) 810400 Telex: 20896 (UBGBG S)
Man Dir: Paul Hallberg
Parent Company: Göteborgs Universitetsbibliotek (qv)
Subjects: Scholarly works in the humanities and the social sciences (monograph series)
1978: 17 titles *1979:* 13 titles
ISBN Publisher's Prefix: 91-7346

Akademiförlaget, PO Box 3075, S-400 10 Göteborg 3 Tel: 031/179600
Manager: Gunnar Jedenius
Order Department: Esselte Studium AB, S-112 85 Stockholm Tel: (08) 520660
Subjects: Languages, Medicine, Technical Economics, Textbooks
1978: 30 titles *1979:* 30 titles *Founded:* 1835
Miscellaneous: Firm is a part of Esselte Studium AB (qv)

Akademilitteratur Förlaget AB, PO Box 50016, S-104 05 Stockholm Tel: (08) 152182 Cable Add: stockacademic Telex: 13115 Akademi S
Man Dir: Hanserik Tönnheim
Parent Company: Förlagsbokhandelsaktiebolaget Akademibokhandeln AB, PO Box 50016, S-104 05 Stockholm (a student-owned, non-profit-making chain of bookshops)
Subjects: Economics, Aesthetics, Philosophy, Law, Cultural History, Social Sciences, Linguistics, General
1978: 41 titles *1979:* 50 titles *Founded:* 1976
ISBN Publisher's Prefixes: 91-7410, 91-7200

Alba AB, Karlavägen 86, Box 10041, S-100 55 Stockholm Tel: (08) 600050 Telex: 11620 Bonbook
Man Dir & Editorial: Dr Daniel Hjorth; *Rights & Permissions:* Ann-Mari Torstensson
Parent Company: Albert Bonniers Förlag AB (qv)
Associate Companies: Bokforlaget Forum, Bonniers Juniorförlag (qqv)
Subjects: General Fiction and Nonfiction
1978: 54 titles *Founded:* 1977
ISBN Publisher's Prefix: 91-7458

Allhems Förlag AB*, Norra Bulltoftavägen 65, S-212 20 Malmö Tel: (040) 934060 Cable Add: Allhem
Man Dir: Einar Hansen; *Editorial:* S Arthur Svensson
Subjects: Classics, Biography, Natural History, Art, Reference, Guide Books, Marine, Naval and Aviation Interest, Swedish/Scandinavian Culture, Illustrated works
1978: 16 titles *Founded:* 1932
ISBN Publisher's Prefix: 91-7004

AB **Allmänna** Förlaget, see LiberFörlag

Almqvist och Wiksell Förlag AB, Brunnsgränd 4, POB 2120, S-103 13 Stockholm Tel: (08) 245290 Cable Add: AWE/Gebers
Man Dir: Göran Ahlberg; *Editorial Dir:* Karl-Åke Kärnell
Subjects: General Fiction, Biography, Medicine, Reference, Juveniles, Low- and High-priced Paperbacks, Psychology, Engineering, General and Social Science, University Textbooks
Founded: 1878
Miscellaneous: Firm is one of the companies comprising Esselte Förlag AB (qv)
ISBN Publisher's Prefix: 91-20

Almqvist och Wiksell International, Gamla Brogatan 15-17, PO Box 62, S-101 20 Stockholm Tel: (08) 237990 Cable Add: Almqvistbook Telex: 12430 Almqwik S
Dir: F Davids Thomsen; *Sales Manager:* Bengt Sjöström
1978: 232 titles *1979:* 174 titles
Subjects: Scientific & Technical books and periodicals
Miscellaneous: Publishers to the universities of Stockholm, Uppsala and Lund
ISBN Publisher's Prefix: 91-22

Almqvist och Wiksell Läromedel AB, Gamla Brogatan 26, Box 159, S-10122 Stockholm 1 Tel: (08) 229180 Cable Add: AWEDUC
Man Dir: Lars-G Ståhl; *Marketing Dir:* E Edman; *International Sales:* Claes Witthoff
Subjects: Schoolbooks and Educational Aids (all levels), Foreign Languages, Music, Preschool Material
1978: 81 titles *1979:* 75 titles

Apoteksbolaget AB*, Humlegårdsgatan 20, S-105 14 Stockholm Tel: (08) 240800 Telex: 11553 apobol s
Man Dir: Åke Nohrlander
Subject: Special Pharmaceutical Textbooks

Förlagsaktiebolaget **Arbetarkultur***, Kungsgatan 84, S-112 27 Stockholm Tel: (08) 543882
Man Dir: Claes-Göran Jönsson
Subjects: Fiction, Political Science, Social Sciences
ISBN Publisher's Prefix: 91-7014

AB **Arcanum**, Box 14116, S-400 12 Gothenburg Tel: (031) 871516
Man Dir: Bo Ramme
Subjects: Homoeopathy, Natural Medicine, Osteopathy and other techniques (mainly as translations from other languages)

Askild och Kärnekull Förlag AB, Banérgatan 37, Box 10148, S-100 55 Stockholm Tel: (08) 140880 Cable Add: Timjan Telex: 12475
Man Dir: Timo Kärnekull; *Sales:* Jerker Wennhag; *Production:* Stella Åkerstedt; *Publicity:* Susanne Wigforss; *Rights & Permissions:* Bertil Almgren
Subjects: Fiction & Nonfiction, Science Fiction Memoirs, Guidebooks
1980: 100 titles *Founded:* 1969
ISBN Publisher's Prefix: 91-7008

Bokförlaget **Atlantis** AB, Västra Trädgårdsgatan 11 B, S-111 53 Stockholm Tel: (08) 200350 Cable Add: Atlantisbooks
Man Dir: Kjell Peterson; *Dir:* Lars Falk, Ove Pihl; *Production:* Lennart Rolf; *Rights & Permissions:* Maj-Britt Jonsson
Subjects: Quality Non-fiction, Illustrated Books, Swedish and Foreign Fiction, including Classics, Art Books
1979: 40 titles *Founded:* 1977
ISBN Publisher's Prefix: 91-7486

Förlaget **Barrikaden** AB, Bjurholmsplan 22, S-116 63 Stockholm Tel: (08) 7149353
Man Dir, Editorial, Publicity, Rights & Permissions: Dag Hernried; *Sales, Production:* Eva Spångberg
Subjects: Fiction, Non-fiction
1978: 15 titles *1979:* 20 titles *Founded:* 1976
ISBN Publisher's Prefix: 91-85328

Beckmans Bokförlag AB, see Liber Grafiska AB

Berghs Förlag AB, Box 17049, S-200 10 Malmö 17 Tel: (040) 231333 Cable Add: Sebergh Malmö
Chairman: Sven-Erik Bergh; *Man Dir:* Karin Bergh; *Production Manager:* Ingrid Bergh; *Executive Editor:* Liselotte Weiss
Orders to: Seelig och Co, Stockholm (qv

under Booksellers)
Subsidiary Companies: Edition Sven Erik Bergh, Federal Republic of Germany (qv); Edition Sven Erik Bergh in Europabuch AG, Switzerland (qv)
Subjects: General Fiction, Belles Lettres, Poetry, History, Music, Art, Juveniles, Religion, Low- and High-priced Paperbacks, Medicine, Psychology, General Science, Educational Materials, Mysteries, Thrillers, Books in German
Book Club: Berghs Bokklubb
1979: 72 titles *1980:* 64 titles *Founded:* 1954

Bernces Förlag AB, Södergatan 20, S-211 37 Malmö Tel: (040) 77265 Cable Add: Beobolag
Man Dir: Arvid Bernce; *Editorial:* Margaret Bernce
Subjects: General Fiction and Non-fiction, Biography, Cookery, History, Reference, Art, Large Illustrated Books
ISBN Publishers Prefix: 91-500

Biblioteksförlaget AB, PO Box 14143, S-104 41 Stockholm (Located at: Skolgatan 25, Stockholm) Tel: (08) 143460 Telex: 11785 Unpress S
Man Dir: Sven Hartman
Subjects: Reference, University and Secondary and Primary Textbooks, Maps and Atlases, Physics, Chemistry, Mathematics, Social Sciences, Children's Books
1978: 50 titles *1979:* 40 titles *Founded:* 1923
ISBN Publisher's Prefix: 91-542

Bibliotekstjänst AB, Tornavägen 9, Box 1706, S-221 01 Lund Tel: (046) 140480 Telex: 32200 btjlund s
Subjects: Library Science, Reference
Founded: 1951
ISBN Publisher's Prefix: 91-7018

Albert **Bonniers** Förlag AB, Sveavägen 56, Box 3159, S-103 63 Stockholm Tel: (08) 229120 Cable Add: Bonniers Telex: 11620 Bonbook S
Chairman: Gerard Bonnier; *Man Dir:* Olle Måberg; *Editorial Dirs:* Karl O Bonnier, Åke Runnquist, Bo Streiffert; *Sales:* Arne Berggren; *Rights & Permissions:* Monica Norberg
Subsidiary Companies: Bokförlaget Alba (qv); Bokförlaget Forum (qv); Bonniers Juniorförlag (qv)
Associate Company: Ahlén & Åkerlund (Periodicals)
Subjects: General Fiction and Non-fiction, Medical and Technical, Reference Works, Juvenile, Young Adult, Paperbacks, Periodical
Book Clubs: Bokklubben Svalan, Bonniers Bokklubb, Underhållningsbokklubben, Stora Romanklubben, part-owner of Månadens Bok (qv); also Nationwide Book Services, 21-22 The Old Steine, Brighton, Sussex BN1 1DV, UK (owned jointly with William Collins Sons & Co Ltd, William Heinemann (International) Ltd, Martin Secker & Warburg Ltd (all UK) (qqv)
Bookshops: Bokman (chain, with 15 shops)
1978: 300 titles *1979:* 300 titles *Founded:* 1837
ISBN Publisher's Prefix: 91-0

Bonniers Juniorförlag AB, Kammakargatan 9A, Box 3159, S-103 63 Stockholm Tel: (08) 229120
Parent Company: Albert Bonniers Förlag (qv)
Subject: Children's Books

Bokförlaget **Bra** Böcker AB*, Södra vägen, S-263 00 Höganäs Tel: (042) 39000 Cable Add: Bebebooks Telex: 72643 S BBBOOKS
Man Dir: Bengt Revin; *Publicity:* Rolf G Jansing; *Editorial, Rights & Permissions:* Sven Gunnar Särman; *Production:* Lars Danielsson
Subjects: General Fiction, History, Geography, Classics, Crime novels, Illustrated Books, Encyclopaedia, Art Reproductions
1978: 68 titles *Founded:* 1965
Book Clubs: Bokklubben Bra Böcker, Bra Deckare (detective novels); Bra Klassiker (classics); Bra Konst (Art Reproduction Club)

Brombergs Bokförlag Scientia, östra Ågatan 39, Box 23052, S-750 23 Uppsala Tel: (018) 121880
Man Dir, Editorial, Sales & Publicity: Dorotea Bromberg, MA; *Production, Rights & Permissions:* Dr Adam Bromberg
Subjects: General Fiction and Non-fiction, Political Science, Popular Science, Medicine
1978: 25 titles *1979:* 31 titles *Founded:* 1975
ISBN Publisher's Prefix: 91-7608

Förlaget **By & Bygd**, Box 22087, S-104 22 Stockholm Tel: (08) 520955
Man Dir: Lars-Olof Johansson
Subjects: Politics, Social Questions

Carlsen/if AB, Bredgatan 2, S-111 30 Stockholm Tel: (08) 246880
Man Dir: Arne Mossberg; *Sales:* Bengt Stagman
Parent Company: Carlsen/if A/S, Copenhagen, Denmark
Associate Company: Carlsen Verlag GmbH, Hamburg, Federal Republic of Germany
Subjects: Children's Picture-books
1979: 125 titles *Founded:* 1968
ISBN Publisher's Prefix: 91-510

Bokförlaget **Carmina**, Box 26016, S-100 41 Stockholm Tel: (08) 105785
Man Dir: Jörn Johanson
Subjects: General Fiction, History, Art, Sciences, Classics, Textbooks

Bo **Cavefors** Klassiker och Förlag AB, Box 1047, S-221 04 Lund Tel: (046) 151504/140764
Man Dir: Bo Cavefors
Subjects: General Fiction, Belles Lettres, Poetry, Biography, History, Music, Art, Philosophy, Psychology, Low- & High-priced Paperbacks, General & Social Science, University Textbooks
1979: 20 titles *Founded:* 1959
ISBN Publisher's Prefix: 91-584

René **Coeckelberghs** Bokförlag AB, Saltmätargatan 3B, Box 45059, S-104 30 Stockholm Tel: (08) 248245 Telex: 14277 reco S
Man Dir: René Coeckelberghs
Subjects: Fiction, Nonfiction, Poetry, Political Science, Social Sciences, High-priced Paperbacks
1978: 32 titles
ISBN Publisher's Prefix: 91-7250

Combi International AB, Box 5315, S-102 46 Stockholm Tel: (08) 432860
Man Dir: Tord Pramberg
Subjects: Reference, Knowledge Books, Educational Materials
Subsidiary Company: Förlagshuset Norden AB
Founded: 1963
ISBN Publisher's Prefix: 91-548

Edition **Corniche** AB, a subsidiary of Bengt Forsbergs Förlag AB (qv)

Bokforlaget **Corona** AB, Nobelvägen 135, Box 5, 201 20 Malmö Tel: (040) 189480
Publisher: Nils-Åke Janséus; *Dir:* Lars Welinder
Subjects: Juveniles, Textbooks, Education, Fiction, Non-fiction

Tidnings AB **Dagen**, S-105 36 Stockholm (Located at: Gammelgårdsvägen 38, Stora Essingen) Tel: (08) 130340 Cable Add: Dagen Telex: 10888 dagen
Man Dir, Production, Rights & Permissions: Sverre Larsson; *Editorial:* Olof Djurfeldt; *Sales:* David Edström; *Publicity Dir:* Rune Flygg; *Advertising Dir:* Gunnar Forsberg
Subsidiary Companies: Förlaget Filadelfia AB (qv), Normans Förlag AB (qv)
Subjects: Biography, History, Music, Art, Religion, Juveniles, Low-priced Paperbacks, Educational Materials
Book Club: Den Kristna Bokringen, Dagenhuset, S-105 36 Stockholm
Bookshop: Gospel Center, Kungsgatan 62, S-111 22 Stockholm
1978: about 40 titles *1979:* 30-35 titles
Founded: 1945

Dahlia Books, International Publishers and Booksellers, Box 23037, S-75023 Uppsala 23 Tel: (018) 100525 Cable Add: Dahlia, Uppsala
Man Dir: Gun-Britt Du Rietz
Subjects: Botany, Zoology, Australiana, Bibliography, Publications of the Royal Swedish Academy of Science
Founded: 1973
Miscellaneous: Major function of this company is Bookselling (antiquarian and new) at above address

Delta Förlags AB*, Box 15123, S-161 15 Bromma Tel: (08) 254781
Man Dir: Sam J Lundwall
Subjects: General Fiction and Non-fiction, Science fiction, High-priced Paperbacks
Founded: 1973
Book Club: Delta Science Fiction Bok Klubb
ISBN Publisher's Prefix: 91-7228

E C P Förlags AB, Långängen 5, S-417 05 Gothenburg Tel: (031) 513430
Man Dir: Carlos Alvear
Subjects: Science and Technology, Handbooks

E F S-förlaget, see Evangeliska Fosterlands-Stiftelsen

Ehrlingförlagen AB, PO Box 5268, S-102 45 Stockholm (Located at: Linnégatan 9-11, Stockholm) Tel: (08) 630760 Cable Add: Ehrlingmusik
Man Dir: Staffan Ehrling
Associate Company: Belwin-Mills Nordiska AB
Subsidiary Companies: Thore Ehrling Musik AB, Nils-Georgs Musikförlags AB, Edition Sylvain AB; all at above address
Subject: Music
1978: 22 titles *1979:* 10 titles *Founded:* 1952

Elkan och Schildknecht, Emil Carelius, Västmannagatan 95, S-113 43 Stockholm Tel: (08) 338463/338464
Man Dir: Bengt Carelius
Subject: Music

Esselte Förlag AB, Tryckerigatan 2, S-103 12 Stockholm 2 Tel: (08) 228040 Telex: 17155 esprint s
Man Dir: Göran Ahlberg
Book Clubs: Vår Bok
1979: 350 titles
Miscellaneous: Esselte Förlag is the name of the Publishing Divison within the Esselte Group. It consists of five independent houses, namely Almqvist och Wiksell Förlag AB (qv), Focus Uppslagsböcker AB (qv), Gebers Förlag (AWE/Gebers), P A Norstedt och Söners Förlag (qv), Esselte Video AB

Esselte Herzogs AB*, Box 155, S-131 06 Nacka Tel: (08) 7162680 Cable Add: Herzogs Telex: 12297
Man Dir: Rune Sirvell
Parent Company: Esselte AB, Sturegatan 11, Stockholm
Subjects: Bibles, Hymnals, Religion
Founded: 1862

Esselte Map Service, Garvargatan 9, POB 22069, S-104 22 Stockholm Tel: (08) 541920 Cable Add: Esseltemap Telex: 120 84 EMS S
General Manager: Lars Brenner; *Cartographic Manager:* Rune Hermansson; *Marketing Manager:* Bo Gramfors
Subsidiary Company: Generalstabens Litografiska Anstalts Förlag, at above address
Subjects: Atlases, Maps
Founded: 1872

Esselte Studium AB, Scheelegatan 24, S-112 85 Stockholm Tel: (08) 520660 Cable Add: Esseltestudium Telex: 11681 Studium S
Man Dir: Olle Emilsson; *Editorial:* Kjell S Johansson; *Sales:* Sven-Erik Westerlund; *International Development:* Bo Petersen
Subsidiary Company: Akademiförlaget (qv)
Subjects: Educational, Primary and Secondary Textbooks, Languages, Arts, Social Sciences, Natural Sciences, Mathematics, Technical and Scientific, Economics, Medical and Nursing, Dictionaries, Scandinavian University Books, Educational Aids
ISBN Publisher's Prefix: 91-24

Evangeliska Fosterlands-Stiftelsens Förlag, Tegnérgatan 34, S-113 59 Stockholm Tel: (08) 340290 Cable Add: Stiftelsen
Man Dir: Tony Guldbranzén
Subjects: Theology and Religion, General Fiction and Non-fiction, Poetry, Reference, Juveniles, Young Adult, High-priced Paperbacks
1978: 27 titles *Founded:* 1856
ISBN Publisher's Prefix: 91-7080

Fib's Lyrikklub, an imprint of Bokforlags AB Tiden (qv)

Förlaget Filadelfia AB, Dagen-huset, S-105 36 Stockholm Tel: (08) 130340 Cable Add: Dagen Telex: 10888 dagen
Man Dir, Editorial, Production, Rights & Permissions: Sverre Larsson; *Sales:* David Edström; *Publicity:* Rune Flygg
Parent Company: Tidnings AB Dagen (qv)
Associate Companies: Den Kristna Bokringen (Book Club), Normans Förlag (qv)
Subjects: Christian religious
1978: 40 titles *1979:* 33 titles *Founded:* 1915
ISBN Publisher's Prefix: 91-536

Focus Uppslagsböcker AB (Focus International Book Production AB), Brunnsgränd 4, Stockholm Tel: (08) 245290
Man Dir: Göran Ahlberg
Subject: Reference (Encyclopaedias)
Miscellaneous: Firm is one of the companies comprising Esselte Förlag AB (qv)

Författares Bokmaskin, Svarvargatan 14, S-112 49 Stockholm Tel: (08) 535880
Associate Company: Bokmaskinen i Göteborg, Kungshojdsgatan 11, S-411 20 Göteborg Tel: (031) 133562
Subjects: General Fiction and Non-fiction, Poetry, Juvenile, Current Controversies

Bengt **Forsbergs** Förlag AB, Södra Tullgatan 4, S-211 40 Malmö Tel: (040) 76320 Cable Add: Godbok
Man Dir: Bengt Forsberg; *Sales Dirs:* Jörgen Forsberg, Claës Forsberg, Matts Forsberg
Subsidiary Company: Edition Corniche AB (qv)
Subjects: History, Medicine, Photography, Yearbooks
Founded: 1943
ISBN Publisher's Prefix: 91-7046

Bokförlaget **Forum** AB, Tegnérgatan 40, Box 45134, S-104 30 Stockholm Tel: (08) 311064 Cable Add: Bokforum
Man Dir: Bertil Käll; *Editorial:* Sven Olof Sundborg; *Sales Dir:* Jan-Olof Westrell; *Production Dir:* Majbritt Hagdahl; *Rights & Permissions:* Monica Heyum
Parent Company: Albert Bonniers Förlag AB (qv)
Associate Companies: Bokförlaget Alba, Bonniers Junior verlag (qqv)
Shipping Add: Malmvägen 80-82, S-191 47 Sollentuna
Subjects: General Fiction and Non-fiction, Biography, Popular History, How-to, Music, Art, Science, High- & Low-priced Paperbacks
1979: 103 titles *Founded:* 1944
ISBN Publisher's Prefix: 91-37

AB Carl **Gehrmans** Musikförlag, Apelbergsgatan 58, Box 505, S-101 26 Stockholm 1 Tel: (08) 103004 Cable Add: Musikgehrman
Man Dir: Kettil Skarby
Subject: Music
1978: 50 titles *Founded:* 1893

Generalstabens Litografiska Anstalts Förlag a subsidiary of Esselte Map Service (qv)

Gidlunds Förlag, PO Box 120 16, 10221 Stockholm (Located at: Karlsviksgatan 16, S-112 41 Stockholm) Tel: (08) 549985/540180
Man Dir: Krister Gidlund; *Sales Dir:* Gertrud Gidlund; *Editorial:* Ylva Holm, Ayperi Karabuda; *Literary Agent:* Lennart Sane Agency
Subjects: General Fiction, Belles Lettres, Poetry, Biography, History, Music, Art, Philosophy, Juveniles, High-priced Paperbacks, Psychology, Social Science
1978: 60 titles *Founded:* 1968
ISBN Publisher's Prefix: 91-7021

AB C W K **Gleerup** Bokförlag, see Liber Grafiska AB

Gullers International AB*, Kungsgatan 30xv, S-111 35 Stockholm Tel: (08) 230585 Telex: 13437 Cable Add: Gullersfoto
Publisher: Karl Werner Gullers; *Man Dir:* Claes Jugård
Subjects: Health, Industrial, Crafts

Gummessons Bokförlag, Tegnérgatan 8, Box 6302, S-113 81 Stockholm Tel: (08) 151830 Cable Add: Förbundet Telex: 14275 smfsmu s
General Manager, Rights & Permissions: Ulf Heimdahl; *Editorial:* Olof Melander; *Sales:* Ingemar Eriksson
Subjects: General Fiction, Theology, Social Controversy, Juvenile, Biography, Travel
1978: 30 titles *1979:* 30 titles *Founded:* 1895
ISBN Publisher's Prefix: 91-7070

Hälsaböcker/Allt om Hälsa AB, Box 1, Torsviksvängen 26, S-181 21 Lidingö Tel: (08) 7652760
Man Dir: Eskil Svensson
Subject: Health

Hamrelius & Stenvall Förlag AB, Malmgatan 3, S-211 32 Tel: (040) 127703
Publishers: Gudmund Hamrelius, Frank Stenvall; *Sales:* Gudmund Hamrelius; *Production:* Frank Stenvall
Associate Company: Frank Stenvalls Förlag (qv)
Subjects: Popular Management, Travel
1980: 5 titles projected *Founded:* 1980
ISBN Publisher's Prefix: 91-7658

Hanse Production AB, Hamra 620 10 Burgsvik Tel: (0498) 98034 and 99008
Chief Executive: Torsten Gislestam
Subject: History, especially local history of the island of Gotland
1978: 1 title *1979:* 7 titles *Founded:* 1978
ISBN Publisher's Prefix: 91-85716

Harriers Bokförlag AB, PO Box 143, S-162 12 Vällingby Tel: (08) 380335
Man Dir, Rights & Permissions: Kjell-Erik Sellin; *Editorial, Production:* Bertil Almebäck; *Sales:* Daniel Lindberg, Göran Soöström; *Publicity:* Birgitta Bengtzon
Subjects: General Fiction and Non-fiction, Biography, Documentaries, Juvenile, Religious
Book Club: Önskeboken
1979: 25 titles *1980:* 30 titles *Founded:* 1932
ISBN Publisher's Prefix: 91-7068

Hemmets Journal AB, Fack, S-212 05 Malmö
Parent Company: Gutenberghus Group, Denmark
Associate Companies: Ehapa-Verlag GmbH, Federal Republic of Germany; Gutenberghus Publishing Service, Denmark (qv), Hjemmenes Forlag A/S, Norway (qv)
Subjects: Juveniles, Fiction, Human Interest
Founded: 1927

Hermods Publishing House, see Liber Grafiska AB

Hillelförlaget, Nybrogatan 19, S-114 39 Stockholm Tel: (08) 621078
Man Dir: Bo Sallmander
Subjects: Judaica, Jewish History, Hebrew Fiction

Lars **Hökerbergs** Bokförlag, Box 8071, S-104 20 Stockholm (Located at: Fleminggatan 21) Tel: (08) 244360
Man Dir: Rolf Hökerberg
Subsidiary Company: I T K-skolan
Subjects: General Fiction and Non-fiction, Technical, Textbooks, Educational Materials, Vocational Training by Correspondence
1978: 50 titles *1979:* 35 titles *Founded:* 1882
ISBN Publisher's Prefix: 91-7084

I C A-Förlaget AB, Stora Gatan 41, S-721 85 Västerås Tel: (021) 144000 Telex: 40486 ica s Cable Add: Icaförlaget
Man Dir: Erik Rydholm; *Publisher:* Birgitta O'Nils; *Sales:* Ulf Åberg; *Production:* Stig Österlund
Branch Off: Grev Turegatan 19, S-114 38 Stockholm Telex: 19435 Ica-s
Subjects: Cookery, Handicrafts, Hobbies, Gardening, Health, Domestic Animals, Antiques, Periodicals
1979: 34 titles *1980:* 41 titles *Founded:* 1947
ISBN Publisher's Prefix: 91-534

Ingenjörsvetenskapsakademien (I V A)*, Grev Turegatan 14, Box 5073, S-102 42 Stockholm 5 Tel: (08) 220760 Cable Add: Ivacademi
Royal Swedish Academy of Engineering Sciences
Man Dir: Gunnar Hambraeus; *Editorial:* Peter Wilhelm
Subjects: Science, Technology
ISBN Publisher's Prefix: 91-7082

Interpublishing AB Rahm and Stenström, Taptogatan 4, S-115 28 Stockholm Tel: (08) 637601/02 Cable Add: Interpublishing
Managers: Anders Rahm, Bengt Stenström
Subjects: Biography, History, Hobby, Engineering, General Science, Reference
Miscellaneous: Previously Interbook Publishing AB

Interskrift Publishing House*, PO Box 135, S-527 00 Herrljunga Tel: (0513) 11930 Telex: Startex S 42109
Man Dir: Per-Ove Lannerö; *Editorial, Production:* Nils Erik Karlsson; *Rights & Permissions:* Rigmor Andersson
Parent Company: Tyndale House Publisher, 336 Gondersen Drive, Wheaton, Illinois 60187 USA
Associate Company: Living Bibles International, PO Box 155, S-52700 Herrljunga, Sweden
Subjects: Bibles, General Religious
Book Clubs: Info Book

1978: 30 titles *1979:* 35 titles *Founded:* 1974
ISBN Publisher's Prefix: 91-7336

Jannersten Förlag AB, Myrgatan 52, Box 45, S-77401 Avesta Tel: (0226) 52045
Man Dir: Eric Jannersten
Subject: Books on Bridge

Kometförlaget AB, subsidiary of B Wahlströms Bokförlag AB (qv)

Kursverksamhetens Förlag, Magle Lilla Kyrkogata 4, S-223 51 Lund Tel: (046) 148720 and 148722
Man Dir: Hjördis Lundgren; *Editorial, Production, Rights & Permissions:* Daqmar Hallstam; *Sales, Publicity, Assistant Editor:* Annalisa Mikaelsson
Subjects: Educational material for Adults, especially Swedish as a foreign language
1978: 7 titles *1979:* 6 titles *Founded:* 1971
ISBN Publisher's Prefix: 91-7434

L I C—Förlag, S-171 83 Solna Tel: (08) 981060 Cable Add: Licentral, Stockholm Telex: 10528 lic s
Chief Executive: Björn Bergman; *Publishing Manager:* Olle Sundling; *Editorial, Production:* Bernt Sahlberg, Ulf Broberg; *Sales, Publicity, Rights & Permissions:* Olle Sundling
This is the Publishing Department of L I C (Landstingets Inköpscentral = County Council Central Purchasing), which deals with the supply of hospital and health care equipment
Parent Company: L I C, at above address. The parent company has numerous subsidiaries
Subjects: Educational books and pamphlets relating to health care
1978: 27 titles *1979:* 31 titles *Founded:* 1977
ISBN Publisher's Prefix: 91-7584

L Ts Förlag AB (Lantbrukarnas Riksförbund och Studieförbundet Vuxenskolan)*, Vasagatan 12, S-105 33 Stockholm Tel: (08) 141620 Cable Add: Lantförbundet Telex: 12396 land s
Man Dir, Editorial: Uno Larsson; *Sales Dir:* Bo Norberg; *Production Manager:* Harry Krieg; *Permissions:* Elly Widell
Subjects: Specialize in books used in the agricultural schools of Sweden; also Household Economy, Ecology, Ethnology, Politics, Adult Education, General Fiction, Biography, History, How-to, Economics, General Science, Handicrafts
Founded: 1935
ISBN Publisher's Prefix: 96-36

Bokförlaget Robert **Larson** AB, Box 3063, S-183 03 Täby Tel: (08) 7565640 Cable Add: Larson books
Dirs: Birgitta and Robert Larson
Subjects: New-wave Literature and Non-fiction, especially Psychology, Philosophy, Current Events, Animals and Nature, Astrology, Ecology, Alternative Medicine
1978: 8 titles *1979:* 8 titles *Founded:* 1971
ISBN Publisher's Prefix: 91-514

Liber Grafiska AB, Sorterargatan 23, S-162 89 Vällingby Tel: (08) 890200 Cable Add: Libergraph
Man Dir: Karl-Axel Swedérus; *Dirs:* Anders Jurell (general publishing), Erna Prior (tele-education), Olle Hedbom (maps), Nils Zetterberg (educational publishing)
Divisions: LiberFörlag, (qv) (formed by amalgamation of AB Allmänna Förlaget and Beckmans Bokförlag AB); LiberHermods (formed by Hermods Skola);
LiberLäromedel (qv) (formed by amalgamation of AB C W K Gleerup Bokförlag, Svenska Utbildningsförlaget Liber AB and Hermods Läromedel);
LiberKartor (Svensk Karttjänst AB, Swedish Map Service) (qv)
Orders to: Liber Distribution, 162 89 Vällingby
Imprint: Publica
Bookshops: AB C E Fritzes Kungl Hovbokhandel, Regeringsgatan 12, Stockholm (qv)
Miscellaneous: Liber Grafiska is the name of the publishing and printing company of Statsföretag, the group of Swedish state-owned industries. The Educational Publishing Division (LiberLäromedel, qv) assists the Swedish educational authorities with their publishing
ISBN Publisher's Prefix: 91-23, 91-38, 91-40, 91-47

Liber Tryck, an imprint of LiberLäromedel (qv)

LiberFörlag, PO Box, S-162 89 Vällingby Tel: (08) 7399000 Cable Add: Libergraph Telex: 12801
Divisional Man Dir: Anders Jurell; *Publishing:* Trygve Carlsson; *Sales:* Bärt Berggren; *Marketing:* Per Lidberg; *Production:* Ingemar Johansson; *Rights & Permissions:* Alva Jansson
Orders to: Liber distribution, Förlagsorder, S-162 89 Vällingby
Parent Company: Liber Grafiska AB (qv) of which LiberFörlag is General Publishing Division
Associate Company: Allmänna Förlaget
Subjects: Government Publications, High-priced Paperbacks, General Fiction, Environment, Social Sciences, University Textbooks
Bookshops: AB C E Fritzes Kungl Hovbokhandel, Regeringsgatan 12, Box 16356, S-103 27 Stockholm
Miscellaneous: LiberFörlag is official publisher for the Government authorities
1979: 500 Government, 130 other titles
Founded: 1969
ISBN Publisher's Prefix: 91-38

LiberHermods, Slottsgatan 24, S-205 10 Malmö Tel: (040) 76900 Cable Add: Libergraph
Rights & Permissions: Alva Jansson
Subjects: Educational Materials for School and Adult Education
1979: 50 titles
Miscellaneous: Division of Liber Grafiska AB (qv)
ISBN Publisher's Prefix: 91-23

LiberKartor (Svensk Karttjänst AB, Swedish Map Service), Sorterargatan 23, S-16289 Vällingby Tel: (08) 890200 Cable Add: Libergraph
Division for Map Services of Liber Grafiska AB (qv)
Subjects: Maps and charts of all kinds for Sweden (especially) and world

LiberLäromedel, Sorterargatan 23, S-162 89 Vällingby Tel: (08) 890200 Cable Add: Libergraph
Divisional Man Dir: Nils Zetterberg; *Sales Dir, Publicity:* Karl Glansborg; *Rights & Permissions:* Alva Jansson (Malmö office)
Parent Company: Liber Grafiska AB (qv), of which LiberLäromedel constitutes the Educational Publishing Division
Associated Companies: See Liber Grafiska AB
Imprint: Liber Tryck
Branch Offs: Slottsgatan 24, S-205 10 Malmö, Öresundsvägen 1, S-221 05 Lund
Subjects: Official Swedish Educational Publisher: Textbooks and Educational Aids for all levels from Kindergarten to University. The Division also publishes scientific literature and assists the Swedish Educational Authorities with their publishing
1978: 500 titles *Founded:* 1969

Book Clubs: Bättre Ledarskap, Lärarbokklubben
Bookshop: Fritzes Kungl Hovbokhandel, Regeringsgatan 12, Box 16356, S-103 27 Stockholm
ISBN Publisher's Prefixes: 91-23, 91-40, 91-47

Libris Publishing House, PO Box 1623, Skolgatan 11, S-701 16 Örebro Tel: (019) 119360 Cable Add: Örebromission
Man Dir: Björn-Ingvar Olsson; *Editorial:* Gunnar Jonsson; *Production:* Arnold Segerlund; *Sales, Publicity:* Kenneth Pettersson; *Rights & Permissions:* Erik Österlund
Subjects: General Interest, Theological, Juveniles, Fiction
Book Club: Libris Bookclub
Bookshops: Libris Bookshop, Storgatan 23, Box 1623, S-701 16 Örebro
1979: 27 titles *1980:* 35 titles *Founded:* 1916
ISBN Publisher's Prefix: 91-7194

Lidman Production AB, Karlavägen 71, Box 5098, S-102 42 Stockholm Tel: (08) 232805
Publisher: Sven Lidman
Subjects: Educational, Encyclopaedias

J A **Lindblads** Bokförlag AB, Warfvinges väg 30, S-112 51 Stockholm Tel: (08) 534640 Cable Add: Bookjal Telex: 17174 (Wahlströms)
Man Dir: Bo Wahlstöm; *Production:* Tord Pramberg; *Permissions:* Eva Melin
Shipping Add: c/o B Wahlströms Bokindustri AB, Lövåsvägen 24, S-791 00 Falun
Parent Company: B Wahlströms Bokförlag AB (qv)
Subjects: General Fiction and Non-fiction, Juveniles
1979: 18 titles *Founded:* 1894
ISBN Publisher's Prefix: 91-32

Linguaphone Institutet AB, Skolsektionen, Drottninggatan 1, S-733 00 Sala Tel: (0224) 15774
Man Dir: Nils Boethius; *Manager:* Ebbe Lindblom
Subject: Language Instruction

Abr **Lundqvists** Musikförlag AB, Katarina Bangatan 17, S-116 25 Stockholm Tel: (08) 436767
Man Dir: Helge Roundqvist; *Editorial:* Anders Roundqvist
Subject: Music
Founded: 1838

Bokförlaget **Medium** AB, Box 511, S-162 15 Vällingby Tel: (08) 380340
Man Dir: Bo Pederby
Subject: School Textbooks
ISBN Publisher's Prefix: 91-512

Gustav **Melins** AB*, Box 5057, S-402 22 Gothenburg Tel: (031) 400140 Cable Add: Wezätamelins Telex: 20872
Man Dir: N Jonas Forssman
Subjects: Bibles, Hymn Books, Juvenile
Founded: 1898

Metodistkyrkans Förlag, see Sanctus

Bokförlaget **Natur och Kultur***, Torsgatan 31, Box 6408, S-113 82 Stockholm Tel: (08) 340660 Cable Add: Naturkultur
Man Dir: Lars Almgren; *Deputy Man Dir:* Per Ivarsson; *Editorial:* Harriet Alfons; *Publicity and Sales Manager:* Ini Ljung (General Books), P G Mohss (Educational); *Rights and Permissions:* Britta Svensson
Orders to: Gårdsvägen 6, S-171 52 Solna
Subjects: General Non-fiction: Biography, History, Medicine, Psychology, General Science, University, Secondary & Primary Textbooks, Audiovisual Materials
1978: 150 titles *Founded:* 1922
ISBN Publisher's Prefix: 91-27

332 SWEDEN

AB Nautic*, Skeppsbron 3, S-411 21 Gothenburg Tel: (031) 111200/111500 Cable Add: Nautic Telex: 21785 nautic s
Man Dir: Björn Traung
Subjects: Nautical Literature, Sea Charts
Miscellaneous: Agent for International Hydrographic publications
Founded: 1953

Nautiska Förlaget Sjökortshallen AB*, Box 19059, S-104 32 Stockholm Tel: (08) 345493/345682 Cable Add: Namco
The Nautical Publishing Co Ltd
Manager: S Hiljding
Subjects: Shipping Publications, Sea Charts, Navigational Literature

Bokforlaget **Niloe** AB, Box 45, S-451 15 Uddevalla (Located at: N Drottninggatan 15-17) Tel: (0522) 10708
Man Dir: Olof Ericson; *Editorial:* Harry Lundin; *Sales:* Sture Marcusson
Subjects: Classical Literature, Reference
1978: 7 titles *1979:* 12 titles *Founded:* 1953
ISBN Publisher's Prefix: 91-7102

AB Nordbok, PO Box 7095, S-40232 Gothenburg (Located at: Pusterviksgatan 13, Gothenburg) Tel: (031) 171085 Cable Add: Nordbokab Telex: 21782
Publishers: Gunnar Stenmar, Turlough Johnston
Subjects: History, Reference, Educational Materials, How-to, Sports, Hobbies, Outdoor Interest
1979: 3 titles *1980:* 2 titles *Founded:* 1974

Förlagshuset **Norden** AB, subsidiary of Combi International AB (qv)

AB Nordiska Bokhandeln, Box 7, S-101 20 Stockholm Tel: (08) 227380 Cable Add: Nordbok
Man Dir: Hans Molander
Parent Company: Esselte Group
Subjects: Medicine mainly, also covering Psychology, Social Science, University Textbooks
Founded: 1851
Bookshop: Kungsgatan 4, Box 7, S-101 20 Stockholm
ISBN Publisher's Prefix: 91-516

AB Nordiska Musikförlaget (Edition Wilhelm Hansen Stockholm), Warfvinges vag 32, Box 745, S-101 30 Stockholm Tel: (08) 132480 Cable Add: Musicalia Telex: 11859
Man Dir: Bengt Edwardsson
Parent Company: Edition Wilhelm Hansen, Denmark (qv)
Associate Companies: J & W Chester Ltd, Eagle Court, London EC1M 5 QD, UK; Norsk Musikforlag, Postboks 1499, Vika, N-Oslo 1, Norway; Edition Wilhelm Hansen, Postfach 2684, D-6000 Frankfurt am Main, Federal Republic of Germany
Bookshop: Drottninggatan 37, S-101 30 Stockholm

AB P A Norstedt och Söners Förlag, Tryckerigatan 2, Box 2052, S-103 12 Stockholm 2 Tel: (08) 228040 Cable Add: Norstedts Telex: 17155 esprint
Man Dir: Göran Ahlberg; *Editorial Dir:* Lasse Bergström; *Rights & Permissions:* Agneta Markas
Subjects: General Fiction, Belles Lettres, Poetry, Biography, History, How-to, Music, Art, Philosophy, Reference, Religion, High-priced Paperbacks, Medicine, Psychology, Engineering, General and Social Science, Law
Book Club: part-owner of Månadens Bok
1978: 200 titles *1979:* 200 titles *Founded:* 1823
Miscellaneous: Firm is one of the companies comprising Esselte Förlag AB (qv)
ISBN Publisher's Prefix: 91-1

Normans Förlag AB, Gammelgårdsvägen 38-42, Dagenhuset, S-105 36 Stockholm Tel: (08) 130340 Cable Add: Normanbok
Man Dir: Sverre Larsson
Parent Company: Tidnings AB Dagen (qv)
Subject: Religion
ISBN Publisher's Prefix: 91-536

Nybloms Förlag, Lästmakargatan 1E, Box 154, S-751 04 Uppsala 1 Tel: (018) 257350 Cable Add: Nybloms
Man Dir: Carl-G Swanström
Subjects: Archaeology, Popular Science, Hobbies, Technology, Biography, General Non-fiction
Founded: 1939
ISBN Publisher's Prefix: 91-85040

AB Håkan **Ohlssons** Förlag, see S K E A B Forlag

Oktoberförlaget AB, PO Box 5398, S-102 46 Stockholm (Located at: Nybrogatan 25) Tel: (08) 600043 Cable Add: Oktpublish Telex: 110832 telsbjs
Man Dir: Karl Hägglund
Orders to: Oktober Centrallager, PO Box 3144, S-103 62 Stockholm
Subjects: General Fiction and Non-fiction, Journalism, Juveniles, Social Science, Politics
Bookshops: Bokhandeln Oktober, Holländargatan 9A, S-111 36 Stockholm; also fifty further bookshops throughout Sweden
1978: 25 titles *1979:* 40 titles *Founded:* 1966
ISBN Publisher's Prefix: 91-7242

Bokförlaget **Opal** AB*, Tegelbergsvägen 31, Box 20113, S-161 20 Bromma Tel: (08) 282179
Joint Publishers: Bengt Christell, Valborg Segerhjelm
Subject: Juveniles
1978: 50 titles *Founded:* 1973
ISBN Publisher's Prefix: 91-7270

Ordfront tryckeri & förlag AB, Box 19504, S-104 32 Stockholm (Located at: Dobelnsgatan 52, Stockholm) Tel: (08) 341925/160335
Man Dir: Leif Eriksson; *Editorial, Rights and Permissions:* Dan Israel
Subjects: Fiction, Home and International Politics, Social Science, History, Juveniles; Quality Paperbacks
1978: 27 titles *1979:* 23 titles *Founded:* 1969
ISBN Publisher's Prefix: 91-7324

Bokförlaget **Plus** AB*, Skt Eriksgatan 48, S-11234 Stockholm Tel: (08) 547408
Man Dir: Bengt Svensson
Subjects: General Fiction and Non-fiction, Juvenile
Founded: 1976

Press' Förlag AB, PO Box 78, S-651 03 Karlstad (Located at: Östra Kyrkogatan 4, Karlstad) Tel: (054) 185250
Man Dir, Editorial: Barry Press; *Publicity, Rights & Permissions:* Lena Lagerkvist
Branch Off: Press' Förlag AB, Svartbrödragatan 3, S-621 00 Visby
Subjects: Science, General Subjects
1978: 16 titles *1979:* 20 titles *Founded:* 1970
ISBN Publisher's Prefix: 91-7400

Bokförlaget **Prisma** AB*, Apelbergsgatan 56, Box 3192, S-103 63 Stockholm Tel: (08) 237280 Cable Add: Prismabok
Man Dir: Stig Edling
Subjects: General Fiction, Quality Paperbacks, Politics, Social Science, Dictionaries, Handbooks, Reference, University Textbooks, General Science
1978: 60 titles *Founded:* 1963
ISBN Publisher's Prefix: 91-518

Production AB, Hamra, S-620 10 Burgsrik Tel: (0498) 98034, 99008
Man Dir: Torsten Gislestam
Formerly Hanse Production AB
Subject: General

Psykologiförlaget AB, Störtloppsvägen 40, Box 461, S-12604 Hägersten Tel: (08) 970395
Man Dir: Lars Lindquist
Subjects: Psychology, Education
1978: 6 titles *1979:* 8 titles *Founded:* 1957

Publica, an imprint of Liber Grafiska AB

AB **Rabén** och Sjögren Bokförlag, Tegnérgatan 28, Box 45022, S-104 30 Stockholm 45 Tel: (08) 349960 Cable Add: Rosbook Stockholm
Man Dir: Per A Sjögren; *Rights & Permissions:* Kerstin Kvint
Subjects: Speciality: Juveniles; also General Fiction, Belles Lettres, Poetry, Biography, History, How-to, Music, Art, Philosophy, Reference, Paperbacks, Psychology, Social Science, University Textbooks; Book Club
1978: approx 300 titles *Founded:* 1942
ISBN Publisher's Prefix: 91-29

Bokförlaget **Rediviva**, Facsimileförlaget*, Box 19511, S-104 32 Stockholm 19 Tel: (08) 157271
Man Dir: Greta Helms
Subjects: Speciality: Reprints generally; also Bibliography, Topography, Facsimile Reprints of old Swedish books of travel, Dictionary of Anonymous and Pseudonymous Swedish Literature
Founded: 1968
ISBN Publisher's Prefix: 91-7120

S A M-förlaget*, PO Box 615, S-551 02 Jönköping Tel: (46036) 119130 Cable Add: SAM
Man Dir and other offices: Ragnwald Ahlnér
Subjects: Religious
1978: 8 titles *1979:* 9 titles
ISBN Publisher's Prefix: 91-7484

S E M I C Förlags AB*, PO Box 74, Landsvägen 57, S-172 22 Sundbyberg Tel: (46-8) 981140 Cable Add: semicpress, Stockholm Telex: 173 70 semic s
Man Dir: Kurt Björkman; *Editorial:* Agneta Hyllén (books), Ebbe Zetterstad (magazines); *Rights & Permissions:* Leif Kronbladh
Parent Company: Bonnier Magazine Group
Associate Company: Interpresse A/S, Bagsvaerd, Denmark
Subsidiary Companies: Kustannus Oy SEMIC, Tampere, Finland; SEMIC/Norge, Oslo, Norway
Subjects: Comic Magazines, Comic Albums, Comic Books, Knitting, Sports, Children's Books, Christmas Publications
Book Club: Serie-pocket-klubben
1978: about 160 titles *Founded:* 1950
ISBN Publisher's Prefix: 91-552

S K E A B Förlag AB, Älvsjö Ängsväg 6, PO Box 1504, S-125 25 Älvsjö Tel: (08) 860340 Cable Add: Skeab Publishing
Man Dir: Lars Kamlin; *Editorial:* John F Ivarsson; *Sales:* Åke Hybbinette; *Production:* Bertil Bergström; *Publicity:* Kari Aarnivaara; *Rights & Permissions:* Elisabeth Jörgensen
Orders to: PO Box 1501, S-125 25 Älvsjö
Subsidiary Company: Berlings Tryckeri, Företagsvägen 28, S-232 00 Arlöv
Branch Off: Box 1025, Sankta Annegatan 4, S-221 04 Lund Tel: (046) 124240
Subjects: Religion, Juveniles, Educational books for all levels, Textbooks and Audio-Visuals
1979: approx 90 titles *Founded:* 1910
Miscellaneous: This company results from

the merger of the two former independent publishing companies Verbum and Håkan Ohlssons
ISBN Publisher's Prefix: 91-526

Förlaget Sanctus*, (Metodistkyrkans Förlag), Sibyllegatan 18, Box 5020, S-102 41 Stockholm Tel: (08) 670155
The Publishing House of the United Methodist Church in Sweden
Man Dir: Karin Hellberg
Orders to: Sibyllegatan 18, S-114 42 Stockholm
Subjects: Theology and Christian Devotional

Bokförlaget **Settern**, Drakabygget, S-286 00 Örkelljunga Tel: (0435) 80050/80070
Man Dir: Magdalena Rönneholm; *Sales, Publicity & Advertising Dir:* Tomas Wahlén
Orders to: Seeling & Co, Stockholm (qv under Booksellers)
Subjects: General Fiction and Non-fiction, High-priced Paperbacks
1978: 26 titles *1979:* 39 titles *Founded:* 1974
ISBN Publisher's Prefix: 7586

Sjöstrands Förlag, Hässelby Strandväg 22, S-162 39 Vällingby Tel: (08) 383856
Man Dir: Ulla-Britt Sjöstrand
Subjects: General Fiction and Non-fiction, Juveniles, Handbooks

Skolförlaget Gävle AB, Box 646, S-801 27 Gävle 1 (Located at: Rälsgatan 2, Gävle) Tel: (026) 115335 Cable Add: Skolförlaget
Man Dir: Barbro Larsson; *Editorial:* Jan-Olov Molin, Eva Winkler
Subjects: School Textbooks (especially Languages & Mathematics), Educational Materials
ISBN Publisher's Prefix: 91-42

Smålänningens Forlag AB*, Sveavägen 98, S-113 50 Stockholm Tel: (08) 344296
Man Dir: Bengt-Ola Söder
Founded: 1964
Subjects: Hunting, Fishing, Hobbies
ISBN Publisher's Prefix: 91-7132

Sober Förlags AB, Bolidenvägen 14, S-121 63 Johanneshov Tel: (08) 810620
Man Dir: Stig Kroon
Subjects: Alcohol, Narcotics and Tobacco addiction

Sohlmans Förlag AB, Tegnérgatan 4, Box 45054, S-10430 Stockholm Tel: (08) 349890 Telex: 13434
Dir: Hans Hedström
Subjects: Music, Encyclopaedias, Sport
Founded: 1975

Sparfrämjandet, Förlagsaktiebolag, Box 16425 Drottninggatan 29, S-103 27 Stockholm Tel: (08) 141020 Telex: 11834 saveorg s
Man Dir: Torbjörn Hessling
Subjects: School Textbooks, Handbooks
Founded: 1925
ISBN Publisher's Prefix: 91-7208

Bokförlaget **Spektra** AB, Box 7024, S-300 07 Halmstad 7 Tel: (035) 36030 Cable Add: Comprint
Man Dirs: Åke Hallberg, Solveig Hallberg; *Literary Agent:* Lennart Sane Agency
Subjects: General Fiction, How-to, Music, Arts & Crafts, Reference, General Science
ISBN Publisher's Prefix: 91-7136

Språkförlaget Skriptor AB*, Södermalmstorg 8, Box 15055, S-10465 Stockholm Tel: (08) 7430555 Telex: 10393 Kval S
Man Dir: Jan Olsson
Founded: 1976

Leif **Stegeland** Förlag AB, Box 446, Södra Hamngatan 45, S-40126 Gothenburg Tel: (031) 192540 Cable Add: Stegeland Telex: 27172 Stebook S

Man Dir: Leif Stegeland; *Sales Dir:* Gunnar Gärdhagen; *Rights & Permissions:* Agnita R-Börjesson
Subjects: Educational Materials, General Fiction and Non-fiction, Juveniles
Founded: 1967

Frank **Stenvalls** Förlag, Malmgatan 3, S-211 32 Malmö Tel: (040) 127703
Man Dir: Frank Stenvall
Subsidiary Company: Distrirail, Ave J B Sluysmans 135, B-4030, Liège, Belgium (Distributors)
Associate Company: Hamrelius & Stenvall Förlag AB (qv)
Subjects: Railway, Maritime, Motoring Interest
1978: 8 titles *1979:* 8 titles *Founded:* 1966
ISBN Publisher's Prefix: 91-7266

Stiftelsen Kursverksamhetens Förlag, see Kursverksamhetens

Studentlitteratur AB, PO Box 1719, S-221 01 Lund 1 Tel: (046) 307070 Cable Add: Studlitt Telex: 33345 educate s
Man Dir: Bertil Bratt; *Publicity and Advertising:* Elisabeth Karlsson; *Rights and Permissions:* Inge Helander
Orders to: PO Box 1719, S-221 01 Lund 1
Subjects: School and University Textbooks, covering Data Processing, Technology, Medicine, Social Sciences, Economics, Humanities
Founded: 1963
ISBN Publisher's Prefix: 91-44

Svensk Kartjänst AB, Swedish Map Service, see Liber Grafiska AB

Svenska Utbildningsförlaget Liber AB, see Liber Grafiska AB

Sveriges Exportrads Förlag, Storgatan 19, PO Box 5513, S-11485 Stockholm Tel: (08) 630580 Cable Add: Export Stockholm Telex: 19620 export a
Publishing Department of the Swedish Export Council
Man Dir: Anders Ring
Subjects: International Marketing, Customs, Shipping & Export Regulations, Market Reports
Bookshop: at above address
1978: 72 (incl 64 Marketing Reports) *1979:* approx 65 titles (incl 55 Marketing Reports)
Founded: 1887
ISBN Publisher's Prefix: 91-7548

Sveriges Radios Förlag, S-105 10 Stockholm Tel: (08) 7840000 Cable Add: Broadcast Telex: 100 00 srcent s
Man Dir: Karl-Vilhelm Holne
Subjects: Juveniles, Paperbacks
Founded: 1947
ISBN Publisher's Prefix: 91-522

Teknografiska Institutet AB, Industrivägen 5, Box 1013, S-17121 Solna Tel: (08) 834285
Man Dir: Bertil Silwer
Subject: Technical books
Founded: 1946
ISBN Publisher's Prefix: 91-7172

Bokförlags AB **Tiden**, Torsgatan 2, Box 130, S-101 21 Stockholm 30 Tel: (08) 237640 Cable Add: Tidenbok
Man Dir: Anders Ferm; *Editorial:* Ebbe Carlsson, Ulla Freidh, Eva Maria Westberg
Imprint: Fib's Lyrikklubb
Subjects: General Fiction and Non-fiction; Juveniles, Politics, History, Social Science, Psychology, Memoirs, Poetry, Illustrated Books, High-priced Paperbacks
Founded: 1912
ISBN Publisher's Prefix: 91-550

Tidnings AB Dagen, see Dagen

AB **Timbro**, Valhallvägen 66, S-114 27 Stockholm Tel: (08) 243775
President: Sture Eskilsson; *Deputy:* Claes Löfgren
Associate Companies: Bokförlaget Ratio, Opinion för marknadsekonomi
Subjects: General Non-fiction, Science

Tomas Förlag AB, Mälarlunden 4, S-152 00 Strängnäs Tel: (0152) 109 31
Man Dir: Alrik Hummel-Gumælius
Subject: Fiction
ISBN Publisher's Prefix: 91-85070

Bokförlaget **Trevi** AB, Barnhusgatan 3, S-111 23 Stockholm Tel: (08) 101850/101590 Cable Add: Bok Trevi
Owners: Adam Helms, Solveig Nellinge
Subjects: General Fiction & Non-fiction, Biography, How-to, Illustrated Books, Feminism
Founded: 1971
ISBN Publisher's Prefix: 91-7160

Unicart Kartografisk Produktion AB, Kungsgatan 24, S-111 35 Stockholm Tel: (08) 208838/118168 Cable Add: Universitypress Telex: 11785 Unpress S
Man Dir: Lars E Frieberg; *Dir:* Wilhelm Tham
Subjects: Atlases, Wall Maps, Special Maps for Reference Works, Textbooks
Founded: 1973

Utbildningsbolaget M M AB*, Box 4092, S-171 04 Solna Tel: (08) 7302848
Man Dir: Mats Myrén
Subject: Teaching Aids

Vår Skola Förlag AB*, Grev Magnigatan 11, S-114 55 Stockholm Tel: (08) 623351
Man Dir: Gunnel Rådahl
Subjects: School Textbooks, Magazines for teachers and pupils

Förlagsaktiebolaget **Västra** Sverige*, Box 10238, S-434 01 Kungsbacka Tel: (0300) 11570 Cable Add: Printer Telex: 21234 eba s
Man Dir: Per Elander; *Sales Dir, Permissions:* Otto Elander; *Advertising Dir:* Lars Henriksson
Subsidiary Company: Elanders Boktryckeri AB
Subjects: General Non-fiction, especially How-to, Hobbies, Hunting and Fishing, Paperbacks
Book Club: Jaktjournalens Bokklubb
Founded: 1912

Verbum, see S K E A B

AB **Wahlström och Widstrand**, Tysta Gatan 10, S-115 24 Stockholm Tel: (08) 679815 Cable Add: Wahlwid s Telex: 12757
Man Dir: Per I Gedin; *Sales Dir:* Sigvard Olsson; *Rights & Permissions:* Ulla Asplund
Subjects: General Fiction & Non-fiction, Handbooks, University & Quality Paperbacks
1979: 110 titles *Founded:* 1884
ISBN Publisher's Prefix: 91-46

B **Wahlströms** Bokförlag AB, Warfvinges väg 30, S-112 51 Stockholm Tel: (08) 244600 Cable Add: Wahlbook, Stockholm Telex: 17174
Man Dir: Bo Wahlström; *Production:* Tord Pramberg; *Permissions:* Eva Melin
Subsidiary Companies: J A Lindblads Bokförlag AB (qv); Kometförlaget AB (both at the above address)
Subjects: General Fiction, Juveniles, Low-priced Paperbacks
1979: 425 titles *Founded:* 1911
ISBN Publisher's Prefix: 91-32

AB **Waldia** Förlag*, Brogatan 41, Box 35, 57100 Nässjö Tel: (038) 016200
Man Dir: Ernst Wallin

334 SWEDEN

Ernst **Westerbergs** Förlags AB,
Norrtullsgatan 10, Box 6911, S-102 39
Stockholm Tel: (08) 241650 Cable Add:
Baptistförlaget
Man Dir: Bengt Sjöblom
Subjects: Education, Juveniles, Music,
Religion, Philosophy
Founded: 1897

Wezäta Förlag, Grafiska Vägen, Box 5057,
S-402 22 Gothenburg Tel: (031) 400140
Cable Add: Wezätamelins Telex: 20872
Man Dir: Claes Lundgren; *Publicity
Manager:* Arne Arvidsson
Subject: How-to
Founded: 1886
ISBN Publisher's Prefix: 91-85074

Zindermans Förlag*, Götgatan 13, Box 310,
S-401 25 Gothenburg 1 Tel: (031)
136890/137832 Cable Add: Zindermans
Man Dir: Sune Stigsjöö
Subjects: General Fiction and Non-fiction,
Biography, History, How-to, Psychology,
Social & Political Science
1978: 50 titles *Founded:* 1960
ISBN Publisher's Prefix: 91-528

Literary Agents

Arlecchino Teaterförlag, Gränsvägen 14,
S-131 41 Nacka Tel: (08) 7181717/8

D Richard **Bowen**, Box 30037, S-200 61
Malmö 30
Contact: D Richard Bowen Tel: (040)
161200/30

Gösta **Dahl** och Son AB*, Aladdinsvägen
14, S-161 38 Bromma/Stockholm Tel: (08)
256235 Cable Add: Literarius

Teaterförlag Arvid **Englind** AB,
Karlavägen 56, Box 5124, S-102 43
Stockholm 5
Contact: Christer Englind

Mrs Lena I **Gedin**, Linnégatan 38, S-114 47
Stockholm Tel: 606067

Folmer **Hansen** Teaterförlag, Lundagatan 4,
S-171 63 Solna Tel: (08) 279838 Cable
Add: Folmerhansen Stockholm
Dir: Gerd Widestedt-Ericsson; *Dramaturgist:*
Peter Böök; *Public Relations:* Annika
Ånnerud
Specialization: Foreign Plays in
Scandinavia, Scandinavian Plays in
Scandinavia and Abroad, Children's Plays

Edith **Kiilerich**, Fiolstr 12, DK-1171
Copenhagen K, Denmark
This Danish literary agency also acts in
Sweden, Finland, Iceland and Norway for
foreign authors

Nordiska Teaterförlaget/Edition Wilhelm
Hansen*, Norrlandsgatan 16, S-111 43
Stockholm Tel: (08) 104613 Cable Add:
Hammersmidt
Head Office: Gothersgade 9-11, DK-1123
Copenhagen, Denmark

Lennart **Sane** Agency, Holländereplan 9,
S-292 00 Karlshamn Tel: (0454) 12356
Cable Add: Saneagency Karlshamn
Dir: Lennart Sane; *Assistant Dir:* Elisabeth
Cederholm
Branch Off: Norra Vallgatan 98, S-211 22
Malmö Tel: (040) 123440
Founded: 1968

Book Clubs

Bättre Ledarskap, S-205 10 Malmö Tel:
(00946) 4070650
Owned by: LiberLäromedel, Publisher (qv);
Contact: Ingemar Ternbo
Subjects: Management, Business

Administration, Economics
Founded: 1977

Berghs Bokklub, Box 17049, S-200 10
Malmö 17
Owned by: Berghs Forlag AB (Malmö)

Bonniers Bokklubb, Sveavägen 56, S-111 34
Stockholm
Owned by: Albert Bonniers Förlag AB (qv)

Bokklubben **Bra** Böcker, Södra Vägen,
S-263 00 Höganäs
Owned by: Bokförlaget Bra Böcker AB
(Höganäs)

Delta Science Fiction Bok Klubb*, Fack,
S-161 16 Bromma 16
Owned by: Delta Förlags AB (Bromma)

Info Book*, PO Box 135, S-527 00
Herrljunga
Owned by: Interskrift Publishing House
Subject: Religion

Jaktjournalens Bokklubb*, Box 10238,
S-434 01 Kungsbacka Tel: 0300/11570
Cable Add: Printer, Kungsbacka
Telex: 21234
Owned by: Elanders Boktryckeri AB, Box
10238, S-434 01 Kungsbacka (a printing
company and a subsidiary of
Förlagsaktiebolaget Västra Sverige, qv)

Den **Kristna** Bokringen, Dagenhuset,
S-105 36 Stockholm
Owned by: Tidnings AB Dagen (Stockholm)

Lärarbokklubben, LiberLäromedel, S-205 10
Malmö Tel: 00946 4070650
Owned by: LiberLäromedel, Publisher (qv)
Subject: Education (Book Club for
Teachers)
Founded: 1975

Libris Bookclub, PO Box 1623, S-701 16
Örebro
Owned by: Libris Publishing House,
Publisher (qv)

Månadens Bok, Box 2255, S-103 16
Stockholm (Located at: Skeppsbron 20)
Tel: (08) 232310
Man Dir: Erik Hyllner
Owned by: Albert Bonniers Förlag AB and
AB P A Nordstedt och Söners Förlag (both
Stockholm)

Önskeboken, PO Box 143, S-162 12
Vällingby
Owned by: Harriers Bokforlag AB,
Publisher (qv)

Readers' Digest AB, Box 6064, S-102 31
Stockholm 6 Tel: (08) 340780 Telex: 11689

Stora Romanbokklubben, Sveavägen 56, S-
111 34 Stockholm
Owned by: Albert Bonniers Förlag AB,
Publisher (qv)

Bokklubben **Svalan**, Sveavägen 56, S-111 34
Stockholm
Owned by: Albert Bonniers Förlag AB,
Publisher (qv)

Underhållnings-bokklubben, Sveavägen 56,
S-111 34 Stockholm
Owned by: Albert Bonniers Förlag AB,
Publisher (qv)

Vår Bok AB, Tryckerigatan 2, Box 2052,
S-103 12 Stockholm 2
Subjects: Classics, Current Affairs,
Dictionaries, Encyclopedias, Detective
fiction, Periodicals
Owned by: Esselte Forlag AB (Stockholm)

Major Booksellers

Johan **Åkerbloms** Universitetsbokhandel*,
Östra Rådhusgatan 6, Box 83, S-901 03
Umeå Tel: (090) 125770
Manager: Bengt Gyllengahm

Almqvist och Wiksell Bokhandel AB, Gamla
Brogatan 26, Box 62, S-101 20 Stockholm
Tel: (08) 237990

Eckersteins Universitetsbokhandel AB,
Grönsakstorget, Box 3050, S-400 10
Gothenburg 3 Tel: (031) 171100

AB C E **Fritzes** Kungl Hovbokhandel,
Regeringsgatan 12, Box 16356, S-103 27
Stockholm Tel: (08) 238900 Cable Add:
Bokfritze Telex: 123 87 S Fritzes
Man Dir: Eide Segerbäck
Parent Company: Liber Grafiska AB (qv)
Founded: 1837

AB **Gleerupska** Universitetsbokhandeln*,
Fack, S-221 01 Lund Tel: (046) 117260

Gumperts Universitetsbokhandel AB, Norra
Hamngatan 26, Box 346, S-401 25
Gothenburg Tel: (031) 235480 Telex: 21178
Manager: John Tengberg

Söderbokhandeln **Hansson och Bruce** AB*,
Götgatan 37, S-116 21 Stockholm Tel: (08)
405432
Manager: T Fredriksson

AB **Lundequistska** Bokhandeln, Östra
Ågatan 31, Box 610, S-751 25 Uppsala 1
Tel: (018) 139830
Manager: Börje Zettervall
Owned by: Esselte Bokhandel, Box 62, S-101
20 Stockholm Tel: (08) 237990

AB Edvin **Lundgrens** Bokhandel,
Södergatan 3, S-211 34 Malmo Tel: (040)
76660

AB **Nordiska Bokhandeln**, Kungsgatan 4,
Fack, S-101 10 Stockholm Tel: (08) 227380
Forms part of Esselte Group of Booksellers

AB **Sandbergs** Bokhandel*,
Humlegårdsgatan 12, Box 5518, S-114 85
Stockholm Tel: (08) 236480
Manager: Ann-Mari Ericson

AB **Seelig** och Co*, Karlsrogatan 2, S-17120
Solna Tel: 08850300 Telex: 12081 Cable
Add: Seelig
(Book Importers)

Wettergrens Bokhandel AB, Västra
Hamngatan 22, S-41117, Gothenburg
Tel: (031) 170090

Major Libraries

Göteborgs Stadsbibliotek (City Library and
County Library), Götaplatsen, Gothenburg

Göteborgs Universitetsbibliotek,
Centralbiblioteket, Renströmsgatan 4, Box
5096, S-402 22 Gothenburg 5 Tel: (031)
810400 Telex: 20896 Ubg bg s
Librarian: Paul Hallberg
Publications: Årsberättelse (Annual Report);
*Acta Bibliothecae Universitatis
Gothoburgensis* (irregular)

Kungliga Biblioteket, Box 5039, S-102 41
Stockholm 5 Tel: (08) 241040
Royal Library of Stockholm Telex: 19640
kbs s
Secretary: Eva Andersson

Kungliga Svenska Vetenskapsakademiens
Bibliotek, Box 50001, S-104 05 Stockholm
Library of the Royal Swedish Academy of
Sciences. It constitutes the Mathematics and
Natural Sciences division of Stockholm
University Library (Stockholm
Universitetsbibliotek, qv)
Librarian: Erica Ljungdahl

SWEDEN 335

Lund Universitetsbibliotek, Box 1010,
S-221 03 Lund Tel: (046) 124620 Telex:
322 08 LUB LUND
Librarian: Björn Tell

Malmö Stadsbibliotek, Regementsgatan 3,
S-21142 Malmö Tel: (040) 77810
Telex: 32577
City Library, County Library and Loan
Centre for Southern and Western Sweden
Librarian: Bengt Holmström
Publications: Annual Report; Catalogue of Annual Acquisition; Bibliographies

Riksarkivet (National Record Office),
Fyrverkarbacken 13-17, Box 34104, S-100 26
Stockholm 34

Statistiska Centralbyråns Bibliotek, S-115 81
Stockholm
Library of the National Central Bureau of Statistics

Stiftelsen Svenska Barnboksinstitutet,
Tjärhovsgatan 36, S-116 21 Stockholm Tel:
446355
Swedish Institute for Children's Books

Stockholm Universitets Bibliotek
(Stockholm University Library)*, S-106 91
Stockholm
This Library now also incorporates the
Library of the Royal Swedish Academy of
Sciences (Kungliga Svenska
Vetenskapsakademiens) (qv) covering
Humanities, Law, Social Sciences,
Mathematics and Science

Stockholms Stadsbibliotek*, Box 6502,
S-113 83 Stockholm
City Library of Stockholm

Sveriges Lantbruksuniversitets Bibliotek,
Central Library Ultunabiblioteket, S-750 07
Uppsala Tel: (18) 102000
Libraries of the Swedish University of
Agricultural Sciences
Dir: Lars-Erik Sanner

University Libraries, see under town names

Uppsala Universitetsbibliotek, Box 510,
S-751 20 Uppsala Tel: (018) 139440 Telex:
76076 ubupps s
Librarian: Thomas Tottie

Library Associations

Svenska Arkivsamfundet*, c/o Riksarkivet,
Fack S-100 26 Stockholm
Swedish Association of Archivists

Svenska Bibliotekariesamfundet, Sveriges
Lantbruksuniversitets Bibliotek,
Ultunabiblioteket, S-750 07 Uppsala Tel:
018-102000
Swedish Association of University and
Research Librarians
Executive Secretary: Birgit Nilsson
Publication: Bibliotekariesamfundet Meddelar

Svenska Folkbibliotekarieförbundet*,
Secretarial Office: Box 36, S-13106 Nacka
Union of Swedish Public Librarians
President: Barbro Forsberg

Sveriges Allmänna Biblioteksförening,
Tornavägen 9, Box 1706, S-221 01 Lund
Swedish Library Association
Acting Secretary: Jan Nyberg
Publication: Biblioteksbladet

Sveriges Vetenskapliga Specialbiblioteks
Förening*, c/o Statens Psykologisk-
Pedagogiska Bibliothek, Box 23099, S-104
35 Stockholm 23
Association of Special Research Libraries
Tel: (08) 228160/232
Secretary: I Bjorkman

Tekniska Litteratursällskapet*, Box 5073, S-
102 42 Stockholm 5
Swedish Society for Technical
Documentation
Secretary: Birgitta Levin
Publications: Tidskrift för Dokumentation
(6 a year)

Vetenskapliga Bibliotekens
Tjänstemannaförening VBT*, c/o
D I K-förbundet, Box 36, S-131 06 Nacka
Association of Research and University
Librarians
President: Bo Stenström, Library of
Parliament, S-100 12 Stockholm

Library Journals

Bibliotekariesamfundet Meddelar (Reports
of the Librarians' Association), Swedish
Association of University and Research
Librarians, c/o Linköping University
Library, Fack, S-581 83 Linköping

Biblioteket Presenterar Nya Boecker (The
Library Presents News Books),
Bibliotekstjänst AB, Tornavägen 9, Fack,
S-221 01 Lund

Biblioteksbladet (Library Journal) (text in
Scandinavian languages, summaries in
English), Swedish Library Association,
Tornavägen 9, Fack, S-221 01 Lund

Tidskrift för Dokumentation (Scandinavian
Documentation Journal) (text in Swedish,
occasionally in English, summaries in
English), Tekniska Litteratursällskapet, Grev
Turgatan, S-114 35 Stockholm

Literary Associations and Societies

Kungl Vitterhets Historie och Antikvitets
Akademien, Villagatan 3, S-114, 32
Stockholm
Royal Academy of Letters, History and
Antiquities
Secretary: Örjan Lindberger
Publications: Fornvännen (journal),
Handlingar (memoirs), *Arkiv* (archives),
Årsbok (Yearbook), monographs, Library
and Archives

Litteraturfrämjandet, Bellmansgatan 30,
S-116 47 Stockholm Tel: (08) 449175
Foundation for Promotion of Literature

Svenska Pennklubben (Swedish Centre of
International P E N), AB P A Nordstedt &
Söners Förlag, Tryckerigatan 2, Box 2052,
S-103 12 Stockholm 2
President: Thomas von Vegesack; *Secretary:*
Kerstin M Lundberg
International Secretary: Britt Arenander

Samfundet de Nio, c/o Anders Öhman,
Smålandsgatan 14, S-111 46 Stockholm
Nine Swedish Authors' Society ('The Society
of Nine')
Secretary: Anders R Öhman (lawyer)
Publication: Svensk Litteraturtidskrift
(quarterly)

Svenska Österbottens Litteraturförening, c/o
Olof Haegerstrand, Fasanvaegen 4, S-775 00
Krylbo
Swedish Österbottens Literary Association
Publication: Horisont

Literary Periodicals

BLM (Bonniers Litteraera Magasin)
(Bonniers Literary Magazine), Albert
Bonniers Förlag AB, Sveavägen 56, S-111 34
Stockholm

Horisont (Horizon), Svenska Österbottens
Litteraturförening, c/o Harry Jarv,
Fyreerkarbacken 32, S-112 60 Stockholm

Ord och Bild (Word and Picture), Stiftelsen
Ord och Bild, Box 15116, S-104, 65
Stockholm

Svensk Litteraturtidskrift (Swedish Journal
of Literature), Almqvist och Wiksell Förlag
AB, Gamla Brogatan 26, S-101 20
Stockholm

Swedish Books (The Translator's Review of
Work Produced in Swedish), Box 2387, S-
403 16 Göteborg
Quarterly review, in English, of works
written in Swedish, originating from Sweden
or Swedish writers in Finland

Tulimuld (Scorched Earth); literary and
cultural magazine of Estonian exiles (text in
Estonian), Bernard Kangro, Skördevägen 1,
S-222 38 Lund

Literary Prizes

Ida **Bäckman** Prize, see Swedish Academy
Prizes

Bellmans Prize
For poetry. 50,000 Swedish crowns.
Awarded annually. Enquiries to Swedish
Academy, Börshuset, Källargränd 4,
S-111 29 Stockholm

Beskow Prize, see Swedish Academy Prizes

Blom Prize, see Swedish Academy Prizes

The **Dalén-Engqvists** Prize
Annual award for Swedish Literature and
Cultural Journalism. 15,000 Swedish crowns.
This prize cannot be applied for. Enquiries
to Swedish Academy, Börshuset,
Källargränd 4, S-111 29 Stockholm

Dobloug Prize, see Swedish Academy Prizes

Signe **Ekblad-Eldhs** Prize
To a famous Swedish writer. 25,000 Swedish
crowns. Enquiries to Swedish Academy,
Börshuset, Källargränd 4, S-111 29
Stockholm

The Lydia and Herman **Erikssons** Prize
Annual award to a Swedish writer for a
work of prose or poetry. 15,000 Swedish
crowns. This prize cannot be applied for.
Enquiries to Swedish Academy, Börshuset,
Källargränd 4, S-111 29 Stockholm

Karin **Gierows** Prizes, see Swedish Academy
Prizes

Grand Prize
For outstanding literary work. 50,000
Swedish crowns. Awarded annually.
Enquiries to The Foundation for Promotion
of Literature, Bellmansgatan 30, S-116 47
Stockholm

Grand Prize for a Book of Poetry
For the best original collection of new poems
by a single author. 25,000 Swedish crowns.
Awarded annually. Enquiries to Foundation
for the Promotion of Literature,
Bellmansgatan 30, S-116 47 Stockholm

Grand Prize for a Novel
For the best novel. 25,000 Swedish crowns.
Awarded annually. Enquiries to The
Foundation for Promotion of Literature,
Bellmansgatan 30, S-116 47 Stockholm

Kalleberger Foundation — The Tekla **Hanssons** and Gösta Ronnströms Prize
Annual award in memory of Tekla Hansson to a Swedish writer for a work of prose or poetry. 4,000 Swedish crowns. This prize cannot be applied for. Enquiries to Swedish Academy, Börshuset, Källargränd 4, S-111 29 Stockholm

Axel **Hirsch** Prize, see Swedish Academy Prizes

Nils **Holgersson** Plaque
The highest award for children's literature in Sweden. Awarded annually. Enquiries to Swedish Library Association, Tornavägen 9, Box 1706, S-22101 Lund

Kalleberger Foundation, see Hanssons

Ilona **Kohrtz** Prize, see Swedish Academy Prizes

The **'Nine'** Prize
For an author of outstanding literary merit, whether established or not. 25,000 Swedish crowns. Awarded annually. This prize cannot be applied for. Enquiries to Nine Swedish Authors' Society, Smålandsgatan 14, S-111 46 Stockholm

Royal Prize, see Swedish Academy Prizes

Birger **Schöldström** Prize, see Swedish Academy Prizes

Henrik **Schück** Prize, see Swedish Academy Prizes

Swedish Academy Prizes
In addition to those fully listed individually, the Swedish Academy awards the following prizes — all of a literary nature:
Royal Prize (Cultural/Literary: annual); *Beskow Prize* (Literary: biennial); *Blom Prize* (Swedish Language: annual); *Ida Bäckman Prize* (Literature/Journalism: biennial); *Dobloug Prize* (Swedish Literature: annual); *Karin Gierows Prizes* for (1) Cultural Information: annual; (2) Promotion of Knowledge: annual); *Axel Hirsch Prize* (Biographic/Historic: biennial); *Ilona Kohrtz Prize* (Prose/Poetry: annual); *Henrik Schück Prize* (Literary History: annual); *Birger Schöldström Prize* (Literary History/Biography: every 4 years); *Swedish Linguistics Prize* (annual); *Swedish into Foreign Language Translation Prize* (annual); *Translation into Swedish Prize* (annual); *Zibet Prize* (Literary/Historic referring to reign of Gustav III: irregular); miscellaneous prizes for work in literary or linguistic fields.
Enquiries to The Swedish Academy, Börshuset, Källargränd 4, S-111 29 Stockholm

Swedish into Foreign Language Translation Prize, see Swedish Academy Prizes

Swedish Linguistics Prize, see Swedish Academy Prizes

Translation into Swedish Prize, see Swedish Academy Prizes

Zibet Prize, see Swedish Academy Prizes

Zorn Prize
For outstanding literary work. 20,000 Swedish crowns. Awarded annually. Enquiries to Swedish Academy, Börshuset, Källargränd 4, S-111 29 Stockholm

Translation Agencies and Associations

Språktjänst*, PO Box 5513, S-114 85 Stockholm (Located at: Storgatan 19)
Translating and Interpreting Service of the Swedish Export Council (see Sveriges Exportråds Förlag under Publishers)

Switzerland

General Information

Language: 65% German (dialect known as Swiss German or Schwyzerdütsch), 18% French (in southwest), 12% Italian (in Ticino), 1% Romansh (in Graubünden)
Religion: Protestant and Catholic
Population: 6.34 million
Bank Hours: Vary. Often 0800-1230, 1330-1630 Monday-Friday
Shop Hours: 0800-1200, 1330-1830 Monday-Friday; in most cities, closed Monday morning; 0800-1200, 1330-1600 or 1700 Saturday
Currency: 100 centimes = 1 Swiss franc
Export/Import Information: No tariff on books. Most books exempt from Turnover Tax. Advertising matter usually dutiable, some exempt from Turnover Tax. No import licences required. No exchange controls
Copyright: UCC, Berne, Florence (see International Section)

Book Trade Organizations

A R P L E (Association romande du Personnel de la Librairie et de l'Edition), see Syndicat Romand des Employés du Livre

Association suisse des Editeurs de Langue française*, 2 ave Agassiz, CH-1001 Lausanne Tel: (021) 202811
Swiss Publishers' Association (French Language)
Secretary General: Robert Junod

Association suisse des Libraires de Langue française*, 2 ave Agassiz, CH-1001 Lausanne Tel: (021) 202811
Association of Swiss French-language Bookshops

Association suisse romande des Diffuseurs de Livres*, 2 ave Agassiz, CH-1001 Lausanne Tel: (021) 202811
Association of Book Distributors of French-speaking Switzerland

Associazione dei Librai della Svizzera Italiana (ALSI), CH-6948 Porza Tel: (091) 519688
Association of Italian-speaking Swiss Booksellers
Secretary: Luigi Rusconi

S B I, see Schweizer Buchwerbung und Information

Schweizer Buchwerbung und -Information (S B I), CH-8245 Feuerthalen Tel: (053) 44877
Swiss Book Publicity and Information Service
Dir: Gottfried Bürgin
Publications: Bucherkatalog des Schweizer Buchhandels, Schweizer Buchspiegel; also Wir Lesen — Sie auch? (a twice-yearly publication distributed to every household in German-speaking Switzerland)

Schweizer Buchzentrum*, Hägendorf, POB 522, CH-4600 Olten 1
Swiss Book Centre

Schweizer Verband der Musikalienhändler und Verleger*, Secretariat: Dr A Huber, Buchhaltungs und Revisions AG, Treuhandgesellschaft, CH-6301 Zug, Neugasse 29, Postfach
Swiss Association of Music Sellers and Publishers

Schweizerischer Adressbuchverleger-Verband*, c/o Verlag für Wirtschaftsliteratur GmbH, Birmendorferstr 421, Postfach 271, CH-8055 Zurich Tel: (01) 335030/36
Swiss Association of Directory Publishers
President: Chr Laemmel

Schweizerischer Buchhändler- und Verleger-Verband (SBVV), Postfach 408, CH-8034 Zurich (Located at: Bellerivestr 3, CH-8008 Zürich) Tel: (01) 2513345
Swiss Booksellers' and Publishers' Association (German language)
Secretary: Peter Oprecht
Publications: Der Schweizer Buchhandel (bi-monthly) (official organ of this association, also its French equivalent SLESR, and its Italian equivalents SESI and ALSI; also publishes *Das Schweizer Buch, Adressbuch des Schweizer Buchhandels, Schweizer Bücherverzeichnis*; see also similar publications by the SBI (above)

Schweizerischer Bühnenverleger-Verband, c/o Edition Eulenburg GmbH, Grütstr 28, CH-8134 Adliswil
Association of Swiss Publishers for the Stage
President: Albert Kunzelmann

Schweizerischer Schriftsteller-Verband, Kirchgasse 25, CH-8001 Zürich 1
Society of Swiss Writers
Secretary: Otto Böni

Societa Editori della Svizzera Italiana (SESI), Viale Portone 4, POB 282, CH-6501 Bellinzona Tel: (092) 258555/56 Telex: 79018 ASEG
Association of Publishers for Italian-speaking Switzerland
Dir: Romano Montalbetti

Société des Librairies et Editeurs de la Suisse romande (SLESR)*, 2 ave Agassiz, CH-1001 Lausanne Tel: (021) 202811
Booksellers' and Publishers' Association of French-speaking Switzerland
Secretary General: Robert Junod
Publications: La Librairie suisse (bi-monthly) official organ of this association, its German equivalent (SBVV), its Italian equivalent (SESI)

Standard Book Numbering Agency (French-language), see Agence francophone pour la Numérotation internationale du Livre, France

Standard Book Numbering Agency, Schweizerischer Buchhändler und Verleger-Verband, Bellerivstr 3, CH-8008 Zurich
This is the agency for German-language ISBNs
ISBN Administrator: Peter Oprecht

Syndicat de la Librairie ancienne et du Commerce de l'Estampe en Suisse (Vereinigung der Buchantiquare und Kupferstichhändler in der Schweiz), Bälliz 64, CH-3601 Thun
Association of Antiquarian Book and Print Sellers in Switzerland

Syndicat Romand des employés du Livre, 45 Quai Charles-Page, CH-1205 Geneva
Union of French-speaking Swiss Book Employees
President: Christian Ciocca; *Secretary:* Jean-Marie Racine

Verband evangelischer Buchhandlungen und Verlage der Schweiz*, Badenerstr 69, CH-8026 Zurich Tel: (01) 2428155
Association of Swiss Protestant Booksellers and Publishers
Dir: Mr Voemel

Verband schweizerischer Antiquare und Kunsthändler*, CH-3011 Bern, Gerechtigkeitsgasse 30 Tel: (031) 221104
Association of Swiss Antiquarian Booksellers and Art Dealers

Verband schweizerischer Zeitungsagenturen und Büchergrossisten (Union d'Agences suisses de Journaux et Livres en Gros)*, CH-4002 Basle, St Jakobsstr 25 Tel: (061) 225500
Association of Swiss Newspaper Distributors and Book Wholesalers

Vereinigung der Schweizerischen Buchgemeinschaften*, CH-8048 Zurich, Hermetschloostr 77 Tel: 625100
Association of Swiss Book Clubs

Vereinigung katholischer Buchhändler und Verleger der Schweiz, c/o Leobuchhandlung, Gallusstr 20, CH-9001 St Gallen Tel: 222917
Association of Swiss Catholic Booksellers and Publishers

Book Trade Reference Books and Journals

Books

Adressbuch des schweizer Buchhandels, Schweizerischer Buchhändler- und Verleger-Verband, CH-8008 Zurich, Bellerivestr 3
Directory of the Swiss Book Trade, containing Lists of Publishers, Booksellers, Distributors, Trade Organizations and Cross-Reference Indices.

Adressbuch für den deutschsprachigen Buchhandel. This Directory of the German-speaking Book Trade lists all Swiss, Austrian and German publishers. See Book Trade Reference Books, Federal Republic of Germany.

Schweizer Buchspiegel (Swiss Book Mirror), Swiss Booksellers' and Publishers' Association, CH-8008 Zurich, Bellerivestr 3

Wir Lesen — Sie Auch? (We are Readers — You, too?), Swiss Book Publicity and Information Service, CH-8245 Feuerthalen

Journals

Bibliographie analytique des Bibliographies suisses courantes (Analytical Bibliography of Current Swiss Bibliographies), Swiss National Library, CH-3003 Berne, Hallwylstr 15

Bibliographie des Publications officielles suisses (Bibliography of Swiss Official Publications), Swiss National Library, CH-3003 Berne, Hallwylstr 15

Der Buchhändler (The Bookseller), Association of Swiss Book Trade Employees, CH-3110 Münsingen, Aeschistr 5, Postfach 144

Edition, Stauffacher Verlag AG, CH-8055 Zürich 3, Birmensdorfer Str 318 (book advertiser)

Guilde du Livre (Book Guild), 5 rue de l'Ecole Supérieure, CH-1005 Lausanne

Librarium (text in German and French), Schweizerische Bibliophilen-Gesellschaft, CH-8001 Zurich, Zwingliplatz 3

Das schweizer Buch (The Swiss Book); bibliographical bulletin, Swiss Booksellers' and Publishers' Association, CH-8008 Zurich, Bellerivestr 3

Schweizer Bücherverzeichnis (Swiss Book Catalogue), Swiss Booksellers' and Publishers' Association, CH-8008 Zurich, Bellerivestr 3

Der Schweizer Buchhandel (La Librairie suisse) (The Swiss Bookseller), Swiss Booksellers' and Publishers' Association, CH-8008 Zurich, Bellerivestr 3

Publishers

Editions **24 Heures**, 33 ave de la Gare, CH-1001 Lausanne Tel: (021) 203111 Telex: CH 24495
Man Dir: P Ruckstuhl; *Advertising, Permissions:* L R Pisler
Subjects: Belles Lettres, History, Music, Art, Juveniles, Educational Materials
1978: 10 titles *1979:* 14 titles *Founded:* 1969
Miscellaneous: Associated imprints include Imprimeries Réunies SA (qv)

A B C Verlag, Rüdigerstr 12, Postfach, CH-8021 Zurich Tel: (01) 2077291 Cable Add: ABC Verlag Zurich
Man & Sales Dir: Konrad Baumann
Subjects: Graphic Design, Art
1979: 5 titles *1980:* 6 titles *Founded:* 1936
ISBN Publisher's Prefix: 3-85504

A L A Verlag*, Klosbachstr 46, CH-8032 Zurich Tel: (01) 320890
Man Dir and other offices: Berta Rahm
Subjects: Human Rights (and especially Women's Emancipation); Social Science, Biography, History
1978: 1 title *1979:* 1 title *Founded:* 1968
ISBN Publisher's Prefix: 3-85509

Aare-Verlag, see Schweizer Jugend-Verlag

Aargauer Tagblatt (AT) Verlag AG, Bahnhofstr 39-43, CH-5001 Aarau Tel: (064) 251133
Dir: A Häfeli
Subjects: Technical, Reference
Founded: 1847
ISBN Publisher's Prefix: 3-85502

Editions **Adversaires**, now known as Francois Grounauer (qv)

Aesopus Verlag GmbH, Grellingerstr 95, CH-4058 Basel Tel: (061) 423373
Man Dir: Nicolaus M Fisch
Branch Off: Munich
Subjects: Health, Sports, Accident Prevention
Miscellaneous: Publish in 9 languages

Editions **L'Age d'Homme** — La Cité*, 10 Métropole, PO Box 263, CH-1003 Lausanne Tel: (021) 220095
Man Dir: Vladimir Dimitrijevic
Parent Company: Alfred Eibel, Editeur, France (qv)
Subjects: General Fiction, Belles Lettres, Poetry, Biography, Music, Art, Philosophy, Religion, Psychology, Social Science, Futurism and Esoterica, Slavica, Sci-Fic, Cinema, Literary Criticism, Reprints
Bookshops: Librairie la Proue, Escaliers du Marché 17, CH-1000 Lausanne
1978: approx 60 titles *Founded:* 1966
ISBN Publisher's Prefix: 2-8251

Albanus Verlag*, J H Göhre, Hulfteggstr 10, Postfach, CH-8401 Winterthur 1 Tel: (052) 293503
ISBN Publisher's Prefix: 3-85510

Albatros Verlag AG*, Lenzenwiesstr 2, CH-8702 Zollikon Tel: (01) 340866
Subjects: Illustrated Reference Books, Animals and Plants, Technical, Culture
1978: 9 titles

Ansata-Verlag*, Paul A Zemp, 'Helfenstein', CH-3150 Schwarzenburg Tel: (031) 931586
Cable Add: Ansata, Schwarzenburg Tel: (031) 931586
Subjects: Occultism, Astrology, Folklore, History of Culture and Science

Editions **Anthroposophiques Romandes**, 13 rue Verdaine, CH-1204 Geneva Tel: (022) 285150
Subjects: Anthroposophical/Rosicrucian Literature in French
1979: 25 titles

Antonius-Verlag*, CH-4500 Solothurn, Gärtnerstr 7 Tel: (065) 223912
Subjects: Psychology, Therapeutics, Pedagogy
ISBN Publisher's Prefix: 3-85520

Verlag der **Arche** Peter Schifferli AG, Rosenbühlstr 37, CH-8044 Zurich Tel: (01) 2522154 Cable Add: Archeverlag
Owner: Peter Schifferli
Orders to: Erikastr 11, CH-8003 Zurich
Branch Offs: Zurich (2), Konstanz (1), Vienna (2)
Associate Companies: Sanssouci Verlag AG, Zürich (qv); Dr Franz Hain, Austria (qv); E Pfister GmbH, Federal Republic of Germany (qv)
Subjects: General Fiction, Belles Lettres, Scholastic
Founded: 1944
ISBN Publisher's Prefix: 3-7160

Archimedes Verlag, Rolf Christiani, Marktweg 7, Postfach 180, CH-8280 Kreuzlingen Tel: (072) 722672
Subjects: Mathematics, Electronics, Mechanical Engineering; Periodical *Technik heute*
ISBN Publisher's Prefix: 3-85525

Verlag für **Architektur**, Limmatquai 18, CH-8024 Zurich Tel: (00411) 2521100/2522102/2527771 Telex: 0045/59477
Parent Company: Verlag für Architektur, Federal Republic of Germany (qv)
Associate Companies: Artemis und Winkler Verlag, Druckenmüller Verlag, Winkler Verlag (qqv in Federal Republic of Germany); Artemis Verlag (qv)

Ariston Verlag (formerly Ramòn F Keller), 39 rue Peillonnex, PO Box 82, CH-1225 Chêne-Bourg, Geneva Tel: (022) 481262/3
Cable Add: Ariston CH-1225 Chêne-Bourg
Man Dir/Editorial: Dr Heinz Bundschuh; *Sales/Rights & Permissions:* Mrs A Bundschuh; *Production:* U Lerf; *Publicity:* C Chenevard
Imprints: Ariston Verlag Genf
Subjects: How-to, Psychology, Nature Medicine, Parapsychology, Hypnosis, Yoga, Self-Help, General Fiction
1979: 99 titles *Founded:* 1964
ISBN Publisher's Prefix: 3-7205

Artemis Verlags AG, CH-8024 Zurich, Limmatquai 18 Tel: (01) 2521100 Cable Add: Artemis Zurich Telex: 59477
Man Dir: Dr Bruno Mariacher; *Rights & Permissions:* Rosmarie Roth
Branch Off: Verlag für Architektur Artemis, Federal Republic of Germany (qv)
Subjects: General Fiction, Philosophy, Art, Architecture, Encyclopaedias, Ancient/Medieval History, Literary History, Classics, Textbooks, Juvenile, Travel Guides
1978: 54 titles *1979:* 49 titles *Founded:* 1943
ISBN Publishers Prefix: 3-7608

SWITZERLAND

Athenaeum Verlag AG, Via Miravalle 23, CH-6900 Lugano-Massagno Tel: (091) 571536 Cable Add: athenag
Man Dir: J-E Nussbaumer; *Administration:* I Wolfensberger; *Editorial:* Dr von Zschinski, J Steiner
Branch Off: Buchauslieferung, Schweizer Buchzentrum, Olten
Subjects: General Nonfiction: Art, History, Science, Literature, Biography, Politics
1978: 1 title *Founded:* 1972
ISBN Publisher's Prefix: 3-85532

Atlantis Verlag AG, Zürichbergstr 66, Postfach 200, CH-8044 Zürich Tel: (0411) 2515343
Man Dir: Dr Max Mittler
Branch Off: Atlantis Verlag KG, Federal Republic of Germany (qv)
Subjects: Pictorial Geography and Travel, Art, Literature, History, Colonialism, Music and Theatre, Juveniles
1979: 20 titles *1980:* 32 titles *Founded:* 1930
ISBN Publisher's Prefix: 3-7611

Atrium Verlag AG*, Rütistr 4, CH-8030 Zürich Tel: (01) 479006
Subjects: Fine & Applied Arts, Illustrated Books, Juveniles, Belles Lettres, Fiction
Founded: 1936
ISBN Publisher's Prefix: 3-85535

Augustin-Verlag*, Schlatterweg 11, CH-8240 Thayngen Tel: (053) 67131
Subjects: Geography, History, Textbooks — especially series of anatomical booklets for schoolchildren (*Unser Korper* = Our Body)
ISBN Publisher's Prefix: 3-85540

Editions de la **Baconnière** SA, 7 ave du Collège, BP 185, CH-2017 Boudry-Neuchâtel Tel: (038) 421004 Cable Add: Baconnière Boudry
Man Dir, Editorial, Production, Sales: Dr Hermann Hauser; *Publicity, Rights & Permissions:* Miss Marie-Christine Hauser
Orders to: Diffusion Payot (Booksellers), 30 rue des Côtes de Montbenon, CH-1002 Lausanne
Subjects: Belles Lettres, Poetry, Biography, History, Music, Art, Philosophy, Reference, Psychology, Social Science, University Textbooks
1978: 26 titles *1979:* 23 titles *Founded:* 1927
Miscellaneous: Publish the international periodical *Cultures*
ISBN Publisher's Prefix: 2-8252

H R Balmer AG Verlag, Neugasse 12, Ch-6301 Zug Tel: (042) 214141 Telex: 78812
Man Dir: Christoph Balmer
Associate Company: Verlag Klett und Balmer (qv)
Subjects: Local History, Literature, Psychology, Pedagogics
Bookshop: Neugasse 12, CH-6301 Zug
ISBN Publisher's Prefix: 3-85548

U **Bär** Verlag, CH-8008 Zurich, Hufgasse 17 Tel: (01) 472377
Man Dir: Dr Ulrich Bär; *Permissions:* Marianne Widmer
Subjects: How-to, Art, Reference

Librairie **Barblan et Saladin***, 10 rue de Romont, CH-1701 Fribourg Tel: (037) 226065
Bookshop: Address as above
Founded: 1954

Bargezzi-Verlag AG*, Wasserwerkgasse 17-19, Postfach 1199, CH-3001 Berne Tel: (031) 221380 Cable Add: Bargezzi Bern
Man Dir, Editorial, Sales, Publicity, Rights & Permissions: Josef Grübel; *Production:* Hugo Tanner
Subjects: Novels, Religious Literature
1978: 3 titles *Founded:* 1948

Basileia Verlag, CH-4003 Basel, Missionsstr 21 Tel: (061) 251766
Man Dir: Rudolf Kellenberger
Subject: Religion
ISBN Publisher's Prefix: 3-85555

Basilius Presse, Güterstr 86, Postfach 153, CH-4002 Basle Tel: (061) 228000 Cable Add: Basiliuspresse Telex: 62553
Man Dir: F S Kern
Orders to: Basilius Presse 176, Güterstr 86, CH-4002 Basle
Subjects: General Fiction, Non-fiction, Juveniles, Music, Art (Paintings), High-priced Paperbacks, General Science
Founded: 1957
ISBN Publisher's Prefix: 3-85560

Baufachverlag AG, Schöneggstr 102, Postfach 6721, CH-8953 Dietikon Tel: (01) 7407677 Telex: 52702 impagch
Dir: Wolfgang R Felzmann
Subject: Building Trade and Architecture (Technical and Specialist Books)
1979: 4 titles *Founded:* 1970
ISBN Publisher's Prefix: 3-85565

Beltz, Rittergasse 20, Postfach 227, CH-4051 Basle Tel: (061) 239470
Owner: Dr Manfred Beltz Rübelmann
Subjects: Textbooks, Psychology, Juveniles, Social Science, Primary and University Textbooks
ISBN Publisher's Prefix: 3-407

Benteli Verlag, Gerechtigkeitsgasse 6, Postfach 102, CH-3000 Berne 8 Tel: (031) 228866 Cable Add: Bag 3000 Berne 8
Man Dir: Ted Schaap (Scapa)
Subjects: General Fiction, Belles Lettres, Poetry, History, Art, Textbooks, Reference,
1979: 35 titles *Founded:* 1899
ISBN Publisher's Prefix: 3-7165

Benziger AG, Bellerivestr 3, CH-8008 Zurich Tel: (01) 2527050 Cable Add: Benzigerverlag Zurich Telex: 004554545
Man Dir: Dr Oscar Bettschart; *Editorial:* Dr Renate Nagel, Willy Walker, Anton Scherer; *Sales and Rights & Permissions Dir:* Robert F Oehler; *Production:* Walter Eberle; *Advertising Dir:* Heinrich Flüeler
Branch Off: Benziger Verlag, Federal Republic of Germany (qv)
Subjects: General Fiction, Belles Lettres, Poetry, Religion, Juveniles, Educational Materials
1978: 85 titles *1979:* 95 titles *Founded:* 1792
Bookshops: Buchhandlung Benziger, Martinstr 16, D-5000 Cologne; Carolus, Kunst- und Bücherstube, Neue Kräme 21, D-6000 Frankfurt am Main (both in the German Federal Republic)
ISBN Publisher's Prefix: 3-545

Berchtold-Haller-Verlag, Nägeligasse 9, Postfach 15, CH-3000 Berne 7 Tel: (031) 222583 Cable Add: BEG Berne
Manager and Sales Dir: Peter Schranz
Branch Offs: Buchhandlung der Evangelischen Gesellschaft, Nägeligasse 9, CH-3000 Berne; Evangelische Buchhandlung, Schmiedengasse 26, CH-3400 Burgdorf; BEG-buechlade, Maiktgasse 27, CH-4900 Langenthal
Subjects: Religion, Juveniles
1978: 4 titles *1979:* 4 titles *Founded:* 1848
ISBN Publisher's Prefix: 3-85570

Edition Sven Erik **Bergh** im Europabuch AG, Erlenweg 6, CH-6314 Unterägeri, Zug Tel: (042) 723077/721010 Cable Add: Sebergh CH-6314 Unterägeri Telex: 862112
Man Dir: Dr S E Bergh; *Editorial:* Liselotte Bergh; *Rights & Permissions:* Karin Bergh
Orders to: Vereinigte Verlagsauslieferung, Postfach 7777, D-4830 Gütersloh 1, Federal Republic of Germany
Parent Company: Berghs Förlag AG, Sweden (qv)
Associate Company: Edition Sven Erik Bergh, Federal Republic of Germany (qv)
Branch Off: c/o H Bettschart, Bellariarain 10, CH-8038 Zurich Tel: (01) 436670
Subjects: General Fiction, Belles Lettres, Mystery Novels, Picture Books, Juveniles
1978: 16 titles *1979:* 15 titles *Founded:* 1976

Berichthaus Verlag, Dr Conrad Ulrich, Voltast, 43, CH-8044 Zurich Tel: (01) 2526349
Subject: History
Founded: 1730
ISBN Publisher's Prefix: 3-85572

Editions **Berlitz**, an imprint of Macmillan SA (qv)

Beyeler Editions Basel, Bäumleingasse 9, CH-4001 Basel Tel: (061) 235412
Owner: Ernst Beyeler
Subject: Art
Founded: 1967
ISBN Publisher's Prefix: 3-85575

The **Bhaktivedanta** Book Trust*, 94 rue de Lausanne, CH-1202 Geneva Tel: (022) 326368
Subjects: Indian Philosophy, Religion & Culture
Miscellaneous: Firm is also a distributor

Bibliographisches Institut AG, Hardturmstr 76, Postfach 130, CH-8021 Zurich Tel: (01) 446642 Telex: 58480 bilag
Man Dir: Rudolf Hans Fürrer; *Production:* B Mannheim
Parent Company: Bibliographisches Institut AG, Mannheim
Subjects: Philosophy, Linguistics, General Science, Reference Works
Founded: 1967
ISBN Publisher's Prefix: 3-411

Verlag **Bibliophile Drucke** von Josef Stocker AG*, Hasenbergstr 7, CH-8953 Dietikon-Zurich Tel: (01) 7404444
Man Dir: Mr Stocker
Parent Company: Verlag Stocker-Schmid AG (qv)
Associate Company: Urs Graf-Verlag GmbH (qv)
Subjects: Belles Lettres, Poetry, Reference, Historical Manuscript facsimiles
Bookshop: Buchhandlung Stocker-Schmid, CH-8953 Dietikon, Hasenbergstr 7
ISBN Publisher's Prefix: 3-85577

Bibliothèque cantonale et universitaire de Lausanne, 6 pl de la Riponne, CH-1005 Lausanne Tel: (021) 228831 Telex: 24014 lauc ch
ISBN Publisher's Prefix: 2-88888

Birkhäuser Verlag, Elisabethenstr 19, Postfach 34, CH-4010 Basle Tel: (061) 231810 Cable Add: Edita Telex: 63475
Man Dir: Carl Einsele; *Sales Dir:* H Jo Pfeiffer
Subsidiary Companies: 'Interavia' SA, Switzerland (qv); Birkhäuser Verlag GmbH, Federal Republic of Germany (qv); Birkhaeuser Boston Inc, 380 Green St, PO Box 2007, Cambridge, MA 02139, USA
Subjects: Art, Architecture, Engineering, Mathematics, Natural Science, Pharmacy, Railway Interest, General & Social Science, University Textbooks, Paperbacks, 22 scientific journals
1978: 78 titles *1979:* 80 titles *Founded:* 1879
ISBN Publisher's Prefix: 3-7643

Blaukreuz-Verlag Bern, Postfach 1196, Lindenrain 5a, CH-3001 Berne Tel: (031) 235866 Cable Add: Blaukreuzverlag
Man Dir: Eduard Müller
Parent Company: Blaues Kreuz der deutschen Schweiz
Subjects: Belles Lettres, Poetry, Biography,

Religion, Juveniles; Addiction Problems (Alcohol, Drugs, Tobacco)
1979: 8 titles *1980:* 10 titles *Founded:* 1884
ISBN Publisher's Prefix: 3-85580

Les Editions de la Fondation Martin **Bodmer**, CP 7, CH-1223 Cologny-Geneva Tel: (022) 362370
Subjects: Philology, Papyrus Editions
ISBN Publisher's Prefix: 3-85682

Boersig Verlag AG, Drusbergstr 1, CH-8703 Erlenbach ZH
Subject: Art

Bohem Press Kinderbuchverlag, Asylstr 67, CH-8007 Zürich Tel: (01) 2527714
Dir: O Bozejovsky v Rawennoff; *Art Dir:* S Zavrel
ISBN Publisher's Prefix: 3-85581

Brain Anatomy Institute, Untere Zollgasse 71, CH-3072 Ostermundigen/BE Tel: (031) 512411
Dir, Rights & Permissions: Prof G Pilleri
Subjects: Biology of Marine Animals, Comparative Anatomy, Investigations on Cetacea
1980: 10 titles *Founded:* 1969

Brunnen-Verlag, Spalenberg 20, CH-4001 Basle Tel: (061) 254406
Man Dir: Hans-Peter Züblin
Subject: Religion
Bookshops: Buchhandlung Pilgermission, CH-4001 Basel, Spalenberg 20; CH-9500 Wil/SG, Untere Bahnhofstr 20
Miscellaneous: Firm is branch office of Brunnen-Verlag GmbH, Pestalozzistr 1, D-6300 Giessen, Federal Republic of Germany (qv)
Founded: 1921
ISBN Publisher's Prefix: 3-7655

Bubenberg Verlag AG*, Postfach 2736, CH-3007 Berne (Located at: Monbijoustr 61) Tel: (031) 455941
Subjects: Belles Lettres, Poetry, How-to, Reference
Founded: 1951
ISBN Publisher's Prefix: 3-85585

Verlag der **Buchdruckerei** Ostschweiz AG*, CH-9001 St Gallen, Hintere Poststr 2 Tel: (071) 208585 Telex: 77393
Man & Sales Dir: Dr Hans Schmid
Subjects: Belles Lettres, Poetry, History, Music, Art, Social Science
Bookshop: Thorbecke Verlag KG, Sigmaringen, Federal Republic of Germany
Founded: 1892
ISBN Publisher's Prefix: 3-85837

Verlag Alfred **Bucheli***, CH-6301 Zug, Baarerstr 61, Postfach 281 Tel: 211247 Telex: 78737
Subjects: Car and Motor Cycle Engineering, Flying

Verlag C J **Bücher** AG, Zürichstr 3, CH-6002 Lucerne Tel: (041) 391111 Cable Add: Cibag Luzern Telex: 65245 edbuch
Publishing Dir: Hans Peter Renner; *Editorial:* Axel Schenck; *Sales, Publicity:* Eduard Gogel; *Rights & Permissions:* Maryam Sauer; *Production:* Hans Blender
Subsidiary Company: C J Bücher GmbH, Federal Republic of Germany (qv)
Subjects: Natural History, Animals, Cities and Countries, Art, Cultural History, Photography, Reference, Film Book Series, General Non-fiction
1979: 27 titles *1980:* 26 titles *Founded:* 1870
ISBN Publisher's Prefix: 3-7658

Buchhaus AG, see Office du Livre SA

Büchler-Verlag, Seftigenstr 310, CH-3084 Wabern-Berne Tel: (031) 541111 Telex: 32697
Man Dir, Rights & Permissions: Richard Wieser; *Advertising:* Bücherpick-Werbung AG
Parent Company: Büchler & Co AG, Printers and Publishers, CH-3084 Wabern-Bern
Subjects: How-to, Reference, Guidebooks, Art, Educational Materials
1980: 6 titles *Founded:* 1886
ISBN Publisher's Prefix: 3-7170

Hugo **Buchser** SA*, 4 Tour de l'Ile, CH-1211 Geneva Tel: (022) 288155 Telex: 289469 HB8A CH
Subjects: Management, Directories, Periodicals
Founded: 1927

Bundesamt für Landestopographie, see Landestopographie

C E E L (Centre Expérimental pour l'Enseignement des Langues)*, Palais Wilson, 52 rue des Pâquis, 1211 Geneva 14 Tel: (022) 325893/325612
Centre for Experimentation and Evaluation of Language Learning Techniques
Man Dir: Nicolas Ferguson
Orders to: Sistemas Educativos SA, Mexico DF (for Mexico); CEEL Finland, Albertinkatu 6B 30, SF-00150 Helsinki, Finland (for Finland, Norway, Sweden); Geneva address above for rest of world
Subjects: Applied Linguistics, English, French, German, Spanish, Italian, Russian, Greek and Finnish as Foreign Languages
1978: 6 titles *Founded:* 1972
ISBN Publisher's Prefix: 2-88047

C V B Buch und Druck, CH-8026 Zurich, Badenerstr 69 Tel: (01) 2428155
Man Dir: Max Hirt; *Sales Dir:* Paul Hauser
Associate Company: Gotthelf Verlag (qv)
Bookshop: Company owns 6 bookshops in Switzerland
Founded: 1892
ISBN Publisher's Prefix: 3-85628

Cahiers de la Renaissance Vaudoise*, 18 rue du Petit-Chêne, CH-1003 Lausanne Tel: (021) 221914
President: Marcel Regamey; *Dir:* Olivier Delacrétaz
Subjects: Belles Lettres, History, Secondary Textbooks, Politics, Militaria
ISBN Publisher's Prefix: 2-88017

Camera-Verlag, CH-6002 Lucerne, Zürichstr 3-7 Tel: (041) 391111 Cable Add: Cibag Telex: Innch 78122
Editor-in-Chief: Allan Porter
Subject: Photography (in separate editions in English, French, German)
ISBN Publisher's Prefix: 3-0008

Edizioni del Prof Mario Agliati **Cantonetto***, CH-6900 Lugano, Via Greina 2

Caritas-Verlag, Löwenstr 3, Postfach 902, CH-6002 Lucerne Tel: (041) 232295
Subject: Religion
ISBN Publisher's Prefix: 3-85592

Carta, Lüthi und Ramseier*, Haslerstr, CH-3000 Bern Tel: (031) 259548 Cable Add: Zeilerag Telex: 32391 (Zeiler AG)
Man Dir, Rights & Permissions: Lüthi Heinz; *Sales:* Volders Viktor; *Production:* Ramseier Ulrich
Orders to: Zeiler AG, Gartenstadstr 5, Postfach 32, Dept Geo-Carta, CH-3098 Köniz-Bern
Subjects: Maps of Europe and World in various scales and layouts, Atlases, Street Maps, Local Area Maps
Founded: 1964

Edizioni **Casagrande** SA, Via del Bramantino, Postfach 489, CH-6501 Bellinzona Tel: (092) 256622 Telex: 73131
Man Dirs: Giampiero Casagrande, Libero Casagrande; *Editorial:* Gianni Grassi, Giampiero Casagrande
Subsidiary Company: Istituto Grafico Casagrande-Veladini-Grassi
Associate Company: Istituto Editoriale Ticinese (IET)
Subjects: Literature, Art, Academic, History, Art History, Scholarly
1978: 25 titles *1979:* 20 titles *Founded:* 1950
ISBN Publisher's Prefix: 3-85897

Caux Verlag-, Theater- & Film-AG, Postfach 218, CH-6002 Lucerne Tel: (041) 422213
Subsidiary Company: Editions de Caux (qv)
Subjects: Social Science, Biography, Religion
ISBN Publisher's Prefix: 3-85601

Editions de **Caux**, CH-1824 Caux Tel: (021) 614241 Telex: 24278
Man Dir, Editorial, Production, Publicity: Chas Piguet; *Sales, Rights and Permissions:* B Utzinger
Parent Company: Caux Verlag AG (qv)
Subjects: Moral Rearmament, Social Sciences, Religion, Theatre, Biographies
Bookshop: Librairie de Caux, CH-1824 Caux
1978: 1 title *1979:* 1 title
ISBN Publisher's Prefix: 2-88037

Cedilivre SA, subsidiary of Editions Foma SA (qv)

Centre Expérimental pour l'Enseignement des Langues (Centre for the Experimentation and Evaluation of Language Learning Techniques), see C E E L

VC Verlag **Chemie** AG, Elisabethenstr 19, CH-4010 Basle
Parent Company: Verlag Chemie GmbH, Federal Republic of Germany (qv)

Christiana-Verlag*, CH-8260 Stein am Rhein Tel: (054) 86820/86847
Man Dir: Arnold Guillet
Subject: Religion
Founded: 1948
ISBN Publisher's Prefix: 3-7171

Werner **Classen** Verlag*, Splügenstr 10, Postfach 683, CH-8027 Zurich Tel: (01) 2015606 Cable Add: Classenverlag Zurich
Dir: Werner Classen
Subjects: Belles Lettres, Poetry, Music, Juveniles, Psychology, Humour, Technical Paperbacks
1978: 12 titles *Founded:* 1945
ISBN Publisher's Prefix: 3-7172

De **Clivo** Press*, Dr Walter Amstutz, Usterstr 126, PO Box, CH-8600 Duebendorf, Zurich Tel: (01) 8201224/8201216 Cable Add: declivopress Duebendorf Telex: CH 55256 Serco
Proprietor: Dr Walter Amstutz
ISBN Publisher's Prefix: 3-85634

Imprimerie La **Concorde***, PO Box 330, CH-1010 Lausanne (Located at: 6 ch des Croisettes CH-1066 Epalinges) Tel: (021) 33141
Dir: Paul Perrin
Subjects: Religion, Science, Art
Founded: 1910
ISBN Publisher's Prefix: 2-88000

Manesse-Verlag, **Conzett und Huber**, Morgenstr 29, CH-8004 Zurich Tel: (01) 2424455
Man Dir: Dr Hans Conzett
Subsidiary Company: Manesse und Morgarten Verlag (qv)
Subjects: Belles Lettres, Art, World Classics translated from original languages into German (Manesse-Bibliothek der Weltliteratur)
Founded: 1886
ISBN Publisher's Prefix: 3-7175

Cosmos-Verlag AG, Postfach 2637, CH-3001 Berne (Located at: Oberer Wehrliweg 5, CH-3074 Muri bei Bern) Tel: (031) 526611
Man Dir: H R Aeberli
Subjects: Tax and Finance Laws, Politics, High-priced Paperbacks, including publications on behalf of the Swiss Institute of Business Management (Schweizerisches Institut für Unternehmungs-führung im Gewerbe)
1978: 8 titles *1979:* 9 titles *Founded:* 1923
ISBN Publisher's Prefixes: 3-85621, 2-8296

Cratander AG, Druckerei, Petersgasse 34, CH-4001 Basle Tel: (061) 258166
Subject: Civil Engineering
ISBN Publisher's Prefix: 3-85622

Edizioni Armando **Dadò**, Tipografia Stazione*, CP 229, CH-6601 Locarno (Located at: Via Bramantino 6) Tel: (093) 314802
Man Dir: Armando Dado
Subjects: Books in Italian on Art, History, Literature, Photography, Swiss Italian Costume

Daphins-Verlag*, J Fischlin, Rainweg 2, CH-8704 Herrliberg Tel: (01) 9153639
Man Dir: J Fischlin
Subjects: Belles Lettres, Poetry, Limited Editions
Founded: 1959
ISBN Publisher's Prefix: 3-85631

Editions **Delachaux et Niestlé** SA, CH-1099 Corcelles-le-Joras Tel: (021) 93166 Telex: 25822
Man Dir: David Perret; *Sales, Advertising Dir:* Pierre de Heaulme; *Permissions:* Yvette Perret
Subsidiary Company: Delachaux et Niestlé, 32 rue de Grenelle, F-75007 Paris
Subjects: Biography, How-to, Philosophy, Reference, Religion, Juveniles, Medicine, Pedagogy, Psychology, General & Social Science, Natural Sciences, Educational Materials
Founded: 1860
Bookshops: Librairie Delachaux et Niestlé, 1 rue Fausses-Brayes, CH-2000 Neuchâtel
ISBN Publisher's Prefix: 2-603

Delphin Verlag*, Postfach 157, CH-8031 Zurich (Located at: Limmatstr 111) Tel: 440733/6 Cable Add: Delphinverlag Zürich Telex: 53815
Man Dir: Oswald Boxer
Subject: Juveniles, Non-fiction, Paperbacks
Founded: 1962
ISBN Publisher's Prefix: 3-7735

Delta SA, 2 rue du Château, BP 20, CH-1800 Vevey 2 Tel: (021) 510526 Telex: 451165 dlta
Publisher: André Delcourt; *Man Dir:* René Galimont
Subjects: History, Sociology, Art, Engineering, General Science, University, Secondary & Primary Textbooks, Educational Materials
1979: 30 titles *Founded:* 1963
Miscellaneous: Firm is a member of the Kluwer Group, Netherlands (qv)

Desertina Verlag, CH-7180 Disentis Tel: (086) 7544142 Cable Add: Desertina Disentis
Man Dir, Rights & Permissions, Editorial, Production, Publicity: P Condrau; *Sales:* D Candinas
Subjects: Belles Lettres of Romance Literature, Art Reproductions
Bookshop: Condrau, Disentis
Founded: 1953

Verlag Harri **Deutsch***, Riedstr 2, CH-3600 Thun Tel: (033) 223975
Man Dir: Harri Deutsch
Parent Company: Verlag Harri Deutsch, Federal Republic of Germany (qv)
Subjects: Maths, Physics, Chemistry, Other Natural Sciences, Technology, Economics
ISBN Publisher's Prefix: 3-87144

Diana-Verlag AG*, Hadlaubstr 131, CH-8006 Zurich Tel: (01) 264850 Cable Add: Dianaverlag
Dir: Dr S Menzel
Subjects: Belles Lettres, Psychology, Religion, Law
Founded: 1946
ISBN Publisher's Prefix: 3-87158

Didax, an imprint of Editions Foma SA (qv)

Diogenes Verlag AG, CH-8032 Zurich, Sprecherstr 8 Tel: (01) 478947 Cable Add: Diogenesverlag Zurich Telex: 52810
Man Dirs & Owners: Daniel Keel (Publisher), Rudolf C Bettschart (Administration & Finance); *Editorial Dir:* Gerd Haffmans; *Sales Dir:* Hartmut Radel; *Rights & Permissions:* Anne Elisabeth Suter
Subjects: Fiction, Art, Paperbacks, Pocket Books, Children's Books
Founded: 1953
ISBN Publisher's Prefix: 3-257

Drei Eichen Verlag AG*, Mühlematt 11, CH-6390 Engelberg Tel: (041) 941129 Cable Add: Dreieichen Engelberg
Dirs: Hermann Kissener, Hans Rudi Marti, Josef Waser
Subjects: Comparative Religion, Popular Medicine, Education, Philosophy, Yoga Instruction
1978: 8 titles *Founded:* 1931
ISBN Publisher's Prefix: 3-7699

Drei Eidgenossen Verlag*, Rottmannsbodenstr 77, CH-4102 Binningen Tel: (061) 475166
Man Dir: Mr Hosch
Subject: Juveniles
Founded: 1936
ISBN Publisher's Prefix: 3-85643

Droemersche Verlagsanstalt AG*, CH-8021 Zurich, Stauffacherquai 46, Postfach 670 Tel: (00411) 394214
Subjects: Fiction, Non-fiction, Natural Sciences

Librairie **Droz** SA, 11 rue Massot, CP 389, CH-1211 Geneva 12 Tel: (022) 466666
Man Dir, Rights & Permissions: A Dufour; *Sales Dir:* Miss Gueguen
Subjects: French language publisher of Belles Lettres, Poetry, History, Literature Reference, Religion, Social Science, University Textbooks
1979: 80 titles *Founded:* 1924
ISBN Publisher's Prefix: 2-600

Henry-Robert **Dufour**, 7 ave du Théâtre, CH-1005 Lausanne (021) 233062/233070 Telex: HRD 26186
Subjects: French language publisher of General Non-fiction, Fine Arts, Technical, Industrial, Belles Lettres, Education

Gottlieb **Duttweiler** Institute for Economic & Social Studies*, CH-8803 Rueschlikon-Zurich Tel: (01) 7240020 Cable Add: Green Meadow Telex: 55699
Subjects: Reference, Social Science, Economics
Bookshop: Verlagsbuchhandlung GDI, CH-8803 Rueschlikon-Zurich
Founded: 1963
Miscellaneous: Specialists in distributive trades, management education, economic growth and new forms of organization

Dynamis Verlag, Brückenstr 22, Postfach 256, CH-8280 Kreuzlingen Tel: (072) 727781 Cable Add: Dynamis
Man Dir: David Tschudi
Subject: Religion
1978: 4 titles *1979:* 4 titles *Founded:* 1973

Bookshop: Christliche Buchhandlung, Hauptstr 7, CH-8280 Kreuzlingen Tel: (072) 727781

Ecart Publications, 6 rue Plantamour, PO Box 253, CH-1211 Geneva 1 Tel: 457395/288803/313473
Man Dirs: John M Armleder, Patrick Lucchini; *Editorial:* John Armleder
Subsidiary Companies: Leathern Wing Scribble Press, The Geneva Pond Bubbles
Associate Companies: Centre d'Art Contemporain, 16 rue d'Italie, CH-1204 Geneva, Marika Malacorda Editions, 1 rue de l'Evêché, CH-1204 Geneva
Subjects: Art (especially New Trends), Photography, Video, Cinema
Bookshops: Ecart Books, Librairie, 14 rue d'Italie, PO Box 253, CH-1211 Geneva 1
1978: 10 titles *1979:* 10 titles *Founded:* 1969

Edita SA, 3 rue de la Vigie, CP 121, CH-1000 Lausanne 9 Tel: (021) 205631 Telex: 26296 Cable Add: Editasa Lausanne
Man Dir: Ami Guichard; *Editorial:* Joseph Jobé, Tim Chilvers; *Production:* Charles Riesen
Subjects: Art, Social and Military Popular Historical, Transport Popular Historical (especially Automobile), How-to, General Science
Founded: 1952
ISBN Publisher's Prefix: 2-88001

Editeurs Associes SA, 5 rue César-Soulié, PO Box 84, CH-1260 Nyon Tel: (022) 612676 Telex: Buco 22886 Nyon
Man Dir: F Gendreau
Subjects: Fiction, History
Founded: 1966
ISBN Publisher's Prefix: 2-8291

Editions Universitaires (Universitätsverlag), 40 Pérolles, CH-1700 Fribourg Tel: (037) 246812
Man Dir, Publicity: Dr Martin Nicoulin
Subjects: Literature, History, Music, Art, Philosophy, Reference, Religions, Theology, Psychology, Economic and Political Sciences, Secondary and University Textbooks, Medicine, Ethnology, Law
Bookshops: Librairie et Edition de la Suisse Romande
1978: 33 titles *1979:* 50 titles
ISBN Publisher's Prefixes: 3-7278 (German books), 2-8271 (French books)

Edito-Service SA, 9 ter chemin de Roches, BP 307, CH-1211 Geneva 6 Tel: (022) 357233 Cable Add: Editoservice Geneva
Man Dir: Gaston Burnand; *Publisher:* Yvonne Rosso; *Marketing Manager:* Julian Trunkfield; *Permissions:* Anne Hauser
Subjects: General Fiction, Belles Lettres, Poetry, Biography, Reference, History, How-to, Music, Art, Religion, Juveniles, Medicine, Psychology, General Science, Educational Materials, Co-editions in all languages
1979: 220 titles

Alfred **Eibel** Editeur*, 7 rue de Genève, CH-1002 Lausanne
Subsidiary Company: Alfred Eibel Editeur, Montparnasse Diffusion, France (qv for full list of Associate Companies etc)

André **Eiselé***, Editeur, 17 route de Cossonay, BP 19, CH-1008 Prilly/Lausanne Tel: (021) 256324
Subjects: Arts, Education, Popular Science, Juveniles, Belles Lettres, Textbooks
ISBN Publisher's Prefix: 2-88002

Verlag **Eisenbahn**, R Jeanmaire & Co, Gut Vorhard, CH-5234 Villigen AG Tel: (056) 982595 Cable Add: Verlageisenbahn Villigen
Dirs: Rose Jeanmaire, Jeannine Claudine J dit-Quartier

Subjects: Railway, Tramcar and Model Rail Literature, Model Railways, Toys of the Past
Bookshops: Company acts as Distribution Centre for rail publications of every country
1980: 6 titles *Founded:* 1961
ISBN Publisher's Prefix: 3-85649

Elektrowirtschaft, Schweizerische Gesellschaft für Elektrizitätsverwertung, CH-8023 Zurich, Bahnhofplatz 9, Postfach 2272 Tel: (01) 2110355
Swiss Electricity Marketing Association
Subject: Electrical Engineering
ISBN Publisher's Prefix: 3-85651

Elsevier Sequoia SA, 50 ave de la Gare, BP 851, CH-1001 Lausanne 1 Tel: (021) 207381 Cable Add: Elsevier Lausanne Telex: 26620 elsa ch
Man Dir, Rights & Permissions: Louk Bergmans; *Editorial:* E Vogelezang, I Holmes; *Sales, Publicity:* P Schafer; *Production:* E Vogelezang
Parent Company: Elsevier-NDU nv, Netherlands (qv)
Associate Companies: Thomond Books, Republic of Ireland; Elsevier's Wetenschappelijke Uitgeverij, Noord-Hollandsche Uitgeversmaatschappij, Elsevier/North Holland Biomedical Press (all in Netherlands, qqv); Applied Science Publishers, UK (qv); Elsevier North Holland Inc, USA
Subjects: Chemistry, Technology, Energy; Biological, Medical, Environmental and Social Sciences, Psychology, Periodicals (39)
1978: 5 titles *Founded:* 1967

'**Elvetica**' Edizioni SA, CP 694, CH-6830 Chiasso Tel: (091) 435056
Subjects: Works of Piero Scanziani (in Italian), Swiss Financial Year Book
1978: 2 titles *Founded:* 1967

Emmentaler Druck AG, Postfach 2502, Dorfstr 5, CH-3550 Langnau Tel: (035) 21911 Cable Add: Emmentalerdruck Langnau Telex: 915100
Man Dir: P Gerber; *Editorial:* N Stuber; *Sales:* H R Bodenmann; *Production:* L Martin; *Publicity:* P Blaser
Subjects: Novels and Art Books
1978: 5 titles *1979:* 4 titles *Founded:* 1845
ISBN Publisher's Prefix: 3-85654

Erker-Galerie AG*, Franz Larese und Jürg Janett, Gallustr 32, CH-9000 St Gallen Tel: (071) 227979/233607
Subject: Modern Art, Literature
Founded: 1964

Edition **Etcetera***, Postfach 572, CH-4001, Basel Tel: (061) 380570
Subjects: Theory of Socialism, Third World, Near East, Switzerland, The Media and Mass Communications
Miscellaneous: Company has common interests with the Z-Verlag (qv) and Lenos Press (qv)

Eulenburg Edition GmbH, Grütstr 28 CH-8134 Adliswil-Zürich Tel: (01) 7103681
Subjects: Instrumental Sheet Music; Books on Music and Musicians
Founded: 1945
ISBN Publisher's Prefix: 3-85662

Europa-Verlag AG, CH-8001 Zurich, Rämistr 5 Tel: (01) 471629 Cable Add: Europaverlag Zurich Telex: 55210 feren ch
Man Dir: Emmie Oprecht
Associate Company: Verlag Oprecht, Zurich (Theatrical)
Subjects: History, Politics, Philosophy, Art, Belles Lettres
Founded: 1933
Miscellaneous: Distributor for UNESCO, Paris
ISBN Publisher's Prefix: 3-85665

Europabuch AG, see Edition Sven Erik Bergh im Europabuch AG

Evangelischer Schriften Verlag Schwengler, see Schwengler (Switzerland) and Telos (Federal Republic of Germany)

Ex Libris*, Hermetschloostr 77, CH-8023 Zürich
Subjects: Belles Lettres, Children's Books, Reference Books
Book Clubs: Ex Libris (qv), Edition Kunstkreis (qv)

Pierre Marcel **Favre***, rue de Bourg 29, PO Box 3569, CH-1002 Lausanne Tel: (021) 221717 Cable Add: Favrepublisa Lausanne
Man Dir: P M Favre
Subjects: Current Affairs, Politics, Sport, Ecology, Illustrated Editions, Fiction
1978: 9 titles *1979:* 11 titles *Founded:* 1975
ISBN Publisher's Prefix: 2-8289

Fehr'sche Buchhandlung AG*, Schmiedgasse 16, CH-9001 St Gallen Tel: (071) 221152/231381 Telex: 77588
Subjects: History, Law, Political Economy, Textbooks
Founded: 1780
Bookshop: Address as above
ISBN Publisher's Prefix: 3-85674

François **Feij**, pl de l'Eglise, CH-1166 Perroy Tel: (021) 752777

Ferenczy Verlag AG, CH-8024 Zurich, Rämistr 5 Tel: 2516054 Cable Add: Ferenczyverlag Zürich Telex: 55210

Maurice et Pierre **Foetisch** SA*, CP 2793, CH-1002 Lausanne (Located at: 6 rue de Bourg, CH-1002 Lausanne) Tel: (021) 239444/5 Telex: 24227
Man Dir and other offices: Jean-Claude Foetisch
Associate Company: Disco SA
Subjects: Music, Records, Pianos, TV, Educational, Textbooks (especially ASSIMIL Language Teaching Courses)
Founded: 1947

Editions **Foma** SA, Ave de Longemalle 5, CP 226, CH-1020 Renens-Lausanne Tel: (021) 351361 Telex: CH-Cedil 25416
Man Dir, Editorial: J-L Peverelli; *Sales:* M Sculati; *Publicity:* Ann-Mari Mingard; *Rights & Permissions:* F Buhler
Subsidiary Companies: 5 Continents, Cedilivre SA
Imprints: foma, didax, cedilivre
Subjects: Cinema, Photography, Psychology, Secondary and Primary Textbooks, Yoga, General Literature
Bookshop: Didax
1980: 8 titles *Founded:* 1948
ISBN Publisher's Prefix: 2-88003

Editions de **Fontainemore**, 5 chemin du Port, CH-1094 Paudex Tel: (021) 392716
Man Dir: René Creux
Subjects: Biography, History, Sailing, Art and Folk Art
1978: 1 title *1979:* 1 title *Founded:* 1962
ISBN Publisher's Prefix: 2-88004

Fortuna-Verlag W Heidelberger, Postfach, CH-8172 Niederglatt/ZH Tel: (01) 8503586
Man Dir: W Heidelberger
Imprints: Fortuna Finanz Verlag, W Heidelberger AG
Subject: Financial Publications
1978: 2 titles *1979:* 3 titles *Founded:* 1953
ISBN Publisher's Prefix: 3-85684

Foto und Schmalfilm-Verlag, subsidiary of Gemsberg-Verlag (qv)

Francke Verlag, Hochfeldstr 113, CH-3000 Berne 26 Tel: (031) 237469 Cable Add: Frankeverlag Bern
Man Dir: Dr Carl L Lang; *Production:* K Gschwend; *Publicity:* Mrs B Bieri
Parent Company: Francke Verlag GmbH, Federal Republic of Germany (qv)
Subjects: Germanic, Romanic and Anglian Language Studies, History, Philology, Philosophy, Psychology, Textbooks, Reference; Paperbacks, Periodicals
Bookshop: Buchhandlung A Francke AG, CH-3001 Berne, Neuengasse 43
1978: 58 titles *Founded:* 1831
ISBN Publisher's Prefix: 3-7720

Freihofer AG, Weinbergstr 109, Postfach, CH-8033 Zurich Tel: (01) 3634282 Telex: 57305 frbk
Man Dir: R Gösken; *Sales:* E K Jansen; *Publicity:* A Fröhlich
Parent Company: Springer-Verlag (qv), Berlin-Heidelberg-New York
Subsidiary Company: Freihofer AG Inc, 175 Fifth Ave, New York NY 10010
Subjects: Medicine, Natural Sciences
Bookshops: Universitätsstr 11, Rämistr 37 (Medicine/Psychology), Sonneggstr 21 (all in Zürich)
Founded: 1957

Verlag Gebrüder **Fretz** AG, Mühlebachstr 54, Postfach, CH-8032 Zurich Tel: (01) 2521444 Telex: 58897 frez
Subjects: Fine and Applied Arts, Illustrated Books, Belles Lettres, Fiction
Founded: 1860
ISBN Publisher's Prefix: 3-85692

Fretz und Wasmuth Verlag AG*, Bellerivestr 5, CH-8008 Zurich Tel: (01) 323585
Subjects: Archaeology, Architecture, Civil Engineering, Fine & Applied Arts, Illustrated Books
Founded: 1927
ISBN Publisher's Prefix: 3-7180

Frobenius AG, Spalenring 31, CH-4012 Basle Tel: (061) 437610
Subjects: History, Law, Literature (especially local)
ISBN Publisher's Prefix: 3-85695

G S Verlag Basle*, Postfach 55, CH-4003 Basle (Located at: Petersgraben 29, CH-4003 Basle) Tel: (061) 253514
Man Dir: Hugo Weibel
Branch Offs: Falkenplatz 22, CH-3012 Berne Tel: (031) 235651; Wiesenstr 48, BP 47, CH-8703 Erlenbach Tel: (01) 9105313
Subjects: General Fiction, Belles Lettres, Biography, History, Music, Art, Juveniles, Low-Priced Paperbacks
Founded: 1889
ISBN Publisher's Prefix: 3-7185

Editions Bertil **Galland**, 29 rue du Lac, CH-1800 Vevey Tel: (021) 511732
Proprietor: Bertil Galland
Subject: Modern Literature
Founded: 1972
ISBN Publisher's Prefix: 2-88015

Rudolf **Geering** Verlag, see Philosophisch-Anthroposophischer/Rudolf Geering Verlag

Gemsberg-Verlag, Foto+Schmalfilm-Verlag, Garnmarkt 10, Postfach 778, CH-8401 Winterthür Tel: (052) 857171 Cable Add: Gemsberg-Verlag Telex: 76417
Sales: Hans Egli; *Production:* Hans Ziegler
Parent Company: Ziegler Druck- und Verlags-AG (Proprietors)
Subsidiary Company: Foto Schmalfilm-Verlag (Winterthur)
Subjects: Amateur Photography and Film-making
1978: 9 titles *Founded:* 1838
ISBN Publisher's Prefix: 3-85701

Genfer Bibelgesellschaft, Das Haus der Bibel, 11 rue de Rive, CH-1211 Geneva 3
German title of the Société biblique de Genève (qv under Maison de la Bible)

SWITZERLAND

Pierre Genillard, Editeur, 9 ch de Primerose, CH-1007 Lausanne Tel: (021) 264632
Subjects: Religion, Philosophy, Psychology, Naturism, Esotericism, Rosicrucian Thought
Founded: 1949
ISBN Publisher's Prefix: 2-88005

Georg et Cie SA*, Libraries-Editeurs, 5 rue de la Corraterie, CH-1211 Geneva 11 Tel: (022) 216633 Telex: 23985
Man Dir: Henri Longchamp
Subjects: Medical Science, Administration, Law, Secondary & Primary Textbooks, Religion, Philosophy, Psychology, Economics, Statistics, Social & Natural Sciences, Politics, Military Subjects, Languages, Literature, Geography, Ethnology, Travel, History
Bookshop: 5 rue de la Corraterie, CH-1211 Geneva 11
Founded: 1857

Georgi Publishing Company/Editions Georgi, CH-1813 Saint-Saphorin Tel: (021) 529508 Cable Add: Georgedi S Saphorin Lavaux
Owner/President: Heinz Georgi
Associate Company: Editions du Couchant, CH-1260 Nyon
Imprints: Georgi, Presses Polytechniques Romandes
Subjects: Scientific and technical books and journals in Computer Science, Engineering, Electrical Engineering and Electronics, Metallurgy, Human Ecology, Environment, Social and Political Sciences (publications may be in English, French or German, or a combination of 2 or 3 languages)
1978-79: 20 titles *Founded:* 1975
ISBN Publisher's Prefix: 2-604

Gesellschaft für Volkskunde, associated imprint of G Krebs Buchdruckerei AG (qv)

Gesellschäftsstelle der Schweiz, associated imprint of G Krebs Buchdruckerei AG (qv)

Globi Verlag AG, Eichstr 27, CH-8045 Zurich Tel: (01) 354135 Cable Add: Globiverlag Zürich Telex: 52791
Man Dir: Emil M Herzog
Subject: Juveniles, especially Illustrated Books
Founded: 1935
ISBN Publisher's Prefix: 3-85703

Viktor Goldschmidt Verlagsbuchhandlung, Mostackerstr 17, CH-4051 Basel Tel: (061) 236565
Subjects: German-Judaica, Hebraica
Founded: 1902
ISBN Publisher's Prefix: 3-85705

André et Pierre **Gonin**, Editions d'Art, 2 rue Etraz, CH-1003 Lausanne Tel: (021) 226492/229996
Subject: Art
Founded: 1902
ISBN Publisher's Prefix: 2-88016

Gotthelf-Verlag, CH-8026 Zurich, Badenerstr 69 Tel: (01) 2428155
Man Dir: Max Hirt
Associate Company: CVB Buch & Druck (qv) at same address
Subjects: Religion, Juveniles
1979: 7 titles *Founded:* 1928
ISBN Publisher's Prefix: 3-85706

Editions du **Grand-Pont***, Jean-Pierre Laubscher, 2 pl Bel-Air, CH-1003 Lausanne Tel: (021) 223222

Editions du **Griffon***, 17 Faubourg du Lac, BP 545, CH-2001 Neuchâtel Tel: (038) 252204
Chairman: Dr Marcel Joray
Subject: Modern Art (especially sculpture and the plastic arts generally)
Founded: 1944
ISBN Publisher's Prefix: 2-88006

Editions François **Grounauer**, 1 rue du Belvédère, CH-1203 Geneva 1 Tel: (022) 447948
Subjects: History, Politics, Social Sciences
1978: 3 titles *Founded:* 1972

Th **Gut** & Co Verlag, Seestr, CH-8712 Stäfa Tel: (01) 9281101 Telex: 875668
Subjects: Politics, Swiss and Regional History and Culture
ISBN Publisher's Prefix: 3-85717

Gute Schriften Verein, Basel, see GS Verlag

Verlag **Habegger** AG, Gutenbergstr 1, CH-4552 Derendingen-Solothurn Tel: (065) 411151 Telex: 34744
Dir: Gerda Raschendorfer; *Production Manager:* Josef Baumgartner
Subjects: Sports, Photography and Films, Texts in Dialect, Juvenile, Medical, Archaeology
1978: 14 titles *1979:* 16 titles *Founded:* 1900
ISBN Publisher's Prefix: 3-85723

F **Haeschel-Dufey**, Comptoir du Livre — now Editions Novos SA (qv)

Berchtold **Haller** Verlag, see Berchtold-Haller

Hallwag Verlag AG, CH-3000 Berne, Nordring 4 Tel: (031) 423131 Cable Add: Hallwag Berne Telex: 32460
President: Otto Erich Wagner; *Dir:* Dr U P Thoenen; *Editorial, Permissions:* Dr K Weibel; *Sales:* Jürg Burri, Klaus Wolfgramm
Branch Off: Hallwag Verlagsgesellschaft GmbH, D-7301 Kemnat bei Stuttgart, Marco-Polo-Str 1, Federal Republic of Germany
Subjects: General Non-fiction, Travel, History, How-to, Music, Art, Culinary Arts, Horses, General Science
Founded: 1912
ISBN Publisher's Prefix: 3-444

Harwood Academic Publishers GmbH*, Poststr 22, CH-7000 Chur
Man Dir: A Theus; *Editorial:* M B Gordon; *Sales:* Patricia Bardi; *Production:* Bernard J Yates; *Publicity:* Lila Henry; *Rights & Permissions:* Françoise Chantrel-Riols
Branch Off: Harwood Academic Publishers, 7-9 rue Emile Dubois, F-75014 Paris, France
Subjects: Astronomy and Astrophysics, Chemical & Nuclear Engineering, Chemical & Chemical Technology, Civil Engineering, Computers, Systems & Control Engineering, Earth & Extraterrestrial Sciences, Economics, Electronics & Electrical Engineering, Life Sciences & Medicine, Management Science & Business, Mathematics & Statistics, Mechanical Engineering, Metallurgy & Materials Science, Physics, Social Sciences, Space Science & Technology, Learned Journals
1978: 1 title *1979:* 10 titles *Founded:* 1978
ISBN Publisher's Prefix: 3-786

Paul **Haupt** Bern, CH-3001 Berne, Falkenplatz 14 Tel: (031) 232425 Cable Add: Hauptbern Telex: 33561 haupt ch
Man Dir: Dr Max Haupt; *Production:* Kurt Thönnes; *Sales, Publicity, Advertising Dir:* Ulrich Dodel; *Permissions:* Wilhelm Jost
Subjects: Business Economics, General and Social Science, University, Secondary and Primary Textbooks, Pedagogy, Handicrafts, How-to, Music, Art, Educational Materials
Bookshops: Falkenpl 14 and Triangel, Länggass Str 8 (both Berne); Höheweg 11, Interlaken
1979: 107 titles *Founded:* 1906
ISBN Publisher's Prefix: 3-258

Haus der Bibel, see Maison de la Bible

W **Heidelberger**, see Fortuna-Verlag

Helbing und Lichtenhahn Verlag AG, Steinenvorstadt 73, CH-4051 Basle Tel: (061) 231116
Dir: H Helbing; *Procuring Editor:* Beat A Jenny
Subjects: History, Law, Textbooks
Founded: 1822
ISBN Publisher's Prefix: 3-7190

Arts Graphiques **Héliographia** SA*, 2 ave de Tivoli, BP 1060, CH-1001 Lausanne Tel: (021) 204151 Telex: 24060
Man Dir: Philippe Luquiens

Helvetica Chimica Acta-Verlag, CH-4002 Basle, Postfach Tel: (061) 376652
President: Prof E Heilbronner; *Editor:* Prof E Giovannini
Parent Company: Schweizerische chemische Gesellschaft, Postfach, CH-4002 Basle
Subject: Chemistry
ISBN Publisher's Prefix: 3-85727

Walter **Herdeg**: The Graphis Press, see Graphis Press

Herder AG, Malzgasse 18, 4002 Basle 21 Tel: 230818 Telex: 64358
Associate Companies: Verlag Herder GmbH & Co KG, A G Ploetz KG, Herder und Herder GmbH (all in Federal Republic of Germany, qqv); Verlag Herder & Co, Austria (qv)

Rolf **Heyne** Verlag*, CH-8832 Woolerau/SZ, Bächerstr Tel: (01) 7841722 Telex: 75113
Man Dir: Rolf Heyne
Subjects: Reference, Pocket Books

Verlag für Psychologie Dr C J **Hogrefe***, Zeltweg 6, CH-8032 Zurich
Parent Company: Verlag für Psychologie, Göttingen, Federal Republic of Germany (qv)
Subjects: All aspects of general and applied Psychology; Handbooks, Conference Reports, Directories

Van **Hoorick** Verlag*, Postfach, CH-8805 Richterswil Tel: (01) 764272
Subjects: Books and Cards for Meditation Practice, Christmas Cards etc; Colour Slide Library

Verlag **Huber** & Co AG, Promenadenstr 16, Postfach 83, CH-8500 Frauenfeld Tel: (054) 73739/73737 Telex: 76383
Man Dir, Publisher: Dr Peter Keckeis; *Sales, Publicity:* Hansrudolf Frey; *Production:* Clemens Harling; *Rights & Permissions:* Silvia Fust
Subjects: Belles Lettres, Biography, History, Politics, Folklore, Linguistics, Art, Juveniles, Social Science, Forestry, Agriculture, Thurgau Canton Interest, Educational Books and Materials
Bookshop: Buchhandlung Huber & Co AG, CH-8500 Frauenfeld, Freiestr 8
1979: 40 titles *1980:* 45 titles *Founded:* 1809
ISBN Publisher's Prefix: 3-7193

Hans **Huber** AG, Medical Publisher and Bookseller, Länggassstr 76 & Marktgasse 9, Postfach, CH-3000 Berne 9 Tel: (031) 242533 Cable Add: Huberverlag Telex: 32516
Man Dir: Dr Walter Jäger; *Editorial Dir:* Heinz Weder; *Sales Dir:* Max Pauli; *Publicity & Advertising:* Peter Köhli
Branch Off: Verlag Hans Huber, Am Wallgraben 127-131, D-7000 Stuttgart-Vaihingen, Federal Republic of Germany
Subjects: Medicine, Psychology, Pedagogy, Sociology
1979: 110 titles *Founded:* 1927
Bookshops: Länggassstr 76 & Marktgasse 9, CH-3000 Berne 9 (for books on Medicine and Psychology); Marktgasse 9, CH-3000 Berne 9 (for General Literature)
ISBN Publisher's Prefix: 3-456

Humata Verlag Harold S Blume*, CH-3000 Berne 6, Dufourstr 7 Tel: (031) 444600
Man Dir: Harold S Blume
Shipping Add: CH-3000 Berne, BP 74
Subjects: How-to, Philosophy, Medicine, Psychology
Founded: 1951
ISBN Publisher's Prefix: 3-85120

Hüthig und Wepf Verlag, Eisengasse 5, CH-4001 Basle Tel: (061) 256379 Cable Add: Wepfco Telex: 0045-62027
Associate Companies: Verlag Wepf, Basel (qv); Dr A Hüthig Verlag, Heidelberg, Federal Republic of Germany (qv)
Subsidiary Company: Hüthig & Wepf Verlag, 13 East 16th St, New York, NY 10003, USA
Branch Off: Hüthig und Wepf, im Weiher 10, D-6900 Heidelberg, Federal Republic of Germany
Subjects: Macromolecular Chemistry and Related Subjects
Miscellaneous: Publishes two Scientific Journals
ISBN Publisher's Prefix: 3-85739

Idéa Editions*, BP 424, CH-2300 La Chaux-de-Fonds Tel: (039) 236725
Sales Dir: Claude Garino
Subjects: General Fiction, Music, Art, Juveniles, University Textbooks
Founded: 1974

Ides et Calendes SA, 19 Evole, CH-2001 Neuchâtel Tel: (038) 253861 Cable Add: Idecal
Man Dir: André Rosselet; *Administration Chief:* Fred Uhler; *Editorial:* Joan Rosselet
Subjects: Art, Belles Lettres, Law, University Textbooks
1978: 7 titles *1979:* 4 titles *Founded:* 1941
ISBN Publisher's Prefix: 2-8258

Imba Verlag, 4 ave de Beauregard, BP 1052, CH-1701 Friburg Tel: (037) 241341 Cable Add: Kanisiuswerk Friburg
Man Dir: Martin Stieger; *Production Manager:* Rudolf Studer
Associate Company: Kanisius Verlag (qv)
Subjects: Social Science, Religion
ISBN Publisher's Prefix: 3-85740

Impressum Verlag AG*, CH-8953 Dietikon, Schöneggstr 102 Tel: (01) 7407673
ISBN Publisher's Prefix: 3-7200

Editions **Imprimerie** Fédérative SA Berne, see Verbandsdruckerei

Verlag **Industrielle Organisation**, CH-8028 Zurich, Zürichbergstr 18 Tel: (01) 470802
Man & Publicity Dir: Dr Roland Scheuchzer; *Sales, Advertising Dir:* Fritz Dedial
Subjects: Management and Organisation, Personnel Studies, Problem-Solving Activities, Product Planning, Marketing, EDP
Publication: Management-Zeitschrift Industrielle Organisation (Industrial Organisation Management Magazine)
1978: 6 titles *1979:* 6 titles
ISBN Publisher's Prefix: 3-85743

Institut für Heilpädagogik Verlag*, CH-6000 Lucerne, Löwenstr 5
Therapeutic Pedagogy Institute Publishing House
Subjects: Education, Diagnostic Therapy Publications

Institut Universitaire de Hautes Etudes Internationales*, 132 rue de Lausanne, CH-1211 Geneva 21 Tel: (022) 311730
Subject: Politics

Inter Documentation Co AG, Poststr 14, Zug Tel: (42) 214974 Cable Add: INDOCO ZUG Telex: 78819 Zugal
President: Dr L Vieli

Subsidiary Companies: Inter Documentation Co BV, Uiterste Gracht 45, Leiden, Netherlands
Subjects: Microfiche/microfilm editions of rare scholarly publications, especially in connection with Slavic and Oriental studies, African, Latin American, Middle Eastern and Jewish Studies, Development Plans, History, Musicology, Anthropology, Natural Sciences, Art, Social Sciences, Religion, Language
Founded: 1957
ISBN Publisher's Prefix: 38575

'Interavia' SA (Société anonyme d'Editions aéronautiques internationales), 86 Ave Louis Casaï, CH-1216 Cointrin, Geneva Tel: (022) 980505 Telex: 22122 itav ch
Dirs: K Regelin, P Russak, R H Gasser
Parent Company: Birkhäuser Verlag (qv)
Subjects: World Directory of Aviation and Astronautics (Interavia ABC-Annual); Periodicals
Founded: 1933
ISBN Publisher's Prefix: 3-85749

Edition **Interfrom**, Postfach 5005, CH-8022 Zürich (Located at: Scheideggstr 76-78) Tel: (01) 2020900
Publisher: Leo V Fromm; *Executive Vice-President:* Annette Harms-Hunold; *Sales Manager:* Annegret Busch; *Public Relations:* Ursula Malzahn
Associate Companies: Verlag A Fromm GmbH & Co, Federal Republic of Germany (qv); Fromm International Publishing Corp, 1212 Ave of the Americas, New York, NY 10036, USA (German into English Literary Translation)
Subjects: Authoritative Texts by celebrated German-speaking Authors on Politics, Economics, Culture/Education, Society, Nature and the Environment, also Periodicals, Newspapers
ISBN Publisher's Prefix: 3-7201

Iris Verlag AG*, CH-3177 Laupen Tel: (031) 947744
ISBN Publisher's Prefix: 3-85751

J H Jeheber SA*, 3 chemin du Vallon, CH-1224 Chênes-Bougeries Tel: (022) 493543
Manager: Jean H Jeheber
Subjects: History, Religion, Juveniles, Sports and Games
Founded: 1797

Johannesverlag Einsiedeln, Arnold Böcklinstr 42, CH-4051 Basle
Chairman: Dr Hans Urs von Balthasar
Orders to: Bücherdienst, Kornhausstr 23, CH-8840 Einsiedeln
Shipping Add: Benziger Buchzentrum, CH-8840 Einsiedeln
Subjects: Philosophy, Religion, Spirituality
1979: 13 titles *1980:* 17 titles *Founded:* 1947
ISBN Publisher's Prefix: 3-265

Juris Druck & Verlag AG, Basteiplatz 5, Postfach, CH-8039 Zurich Tel: (01) 2117727
Man Dir: Dr H Christen
Subjects: History, Music, Art, Philosophy, Religion, Medicine, Psychology, Engineering, General & Social Science
Bookshop: Juris Druck & Verlag AG, Buchhandlung, Postfach, CH-8039 Zurich
1979: 170 titles *Founded:* 1945
ISBN Publisher's Prefix: 3-260

Kanisius Verlag, 4 ave du Beauregard, CH-1701 Fribourg Tel: (037) 241341 Cable Add: Kanisiuswerk Freiburg
Man Dir: Martin Stieger; *Production Manager:* Rudolf Studer
Associate Company: Imba Verlag (qv)
Subjects: Religion
Founded: 1898
ISBN Publisher's Prefix: 3-85764

S **Karger** AG, Medical and Scientific Publishers, Allschwilerstr 10, PO Box, CH-4009 Basle Tel: (061) 390880 Cable Add: Kargermed Basle Telex: CH 62652
Man Dir: Dr Thomas Karger
Subsidiary Company: Karger Libri AG (Bookshop and Subscriptions), Petersgraben 31, CH-4011 Basle
Imprints: S Karger (Basle, Munich, Paris, London, New York, Sydney)
Subjects: Medical and Scientific Publications (Series and Journals); Reference Works, Medicine, Psychology, University Textbooks
1979: about 150 titles *Founded:* 1890
Bookshop: Karger Libri AG, Petersgraben 31, CH-4011 Basle
Miscellaneous: S Karger Literary Agencies in North America are: S Karger, Publishers Ltd, Suite 319, 4141 Sherbrooke St West, Montreal, Quebec, Canada H3Z 1BB; S Karger Publishers Inc, 150 Fifth Ave, Suite 1103, New York, NY 10011, USA
ISBN Publisher's Prefix: 3-8055

Verlag Ramon F **Keller**, now known as Ariston Verlag (qv)

Kinderbuchverlag Reich Luzern AG, see Reich

Kindler Verlag AG, Nelkenstr 20, CH-8006 Zurich Tel: (00411) 3633007 Cable Add: Kindlerverlag Zurich Telex: 0045 57608
Publishers: Helmut Kindler, Nina Kindler
Subjects: Encyclopedias (modern Psychology)

Editions **Kister** SA*, 33 quai Wilson, CH-1211 Geneva 1 Tel: (022) 315000
Subjects: General Non-fiction, Mathematics, Physics, Music, Games and Sports, Reference Books
ISBN Publisher's Prefix: 3-463

Verlag **Klett und Balmer** & Co, Chamerstr 12a, Postfach 287, CH-6300 Zug Tel: (042) 214131/32
Man Dir: Chr Balmer, Dr Thomas Klett; *Editorial, Sales, Publicity, Production, Rights & Permissions:* H Egli
Parent Company: Ernst Klett Verlag, Federal Republic of Germany
Associate Company: H R Balmer AG, Zug, Switzerland (qv)
Subjects: School Textbooks, Teachers' Training, Educational Politics in Switzerland, Adult Education, fringe areas of Science, Philosophy, Theology
1978: 5 titles *Founded:* 1967
ISBN Publisher's Prefix: 3-264

Kober'sche Verlagsbuchhandlung AG*, Maulbeerstr 10, Postfach 2481, CH-3001 Berne Tel: (031) 251648
Man & Publicity Dir: Harald F Blum; *Sales Dir:* Roland Triet
Subject: Religious/Philosophical, especially the teaching texts of Bô Yin Râ
1978: 4 titles by Bô Yin Râ *Founded:* 1926
ISBN Publisher's Prefix: 3-85767

Kolumbus-Verlag, Muhlebuhl 248, CH-5737 Menziken Tel: (064) 711370 Cable Add: Vdb Menziken
Man Dir: Dr G van den Bergh
Subjects: Schoolbooks (ref languages)

Kornfeld & Co, Laupenstr 41, CH-3008 Berne Tel: (031) 254673 Cable Add: Artus
Proprietor: Eberhard W Kornfeld
Subjects: Fine Arts, 19th-20th Century Illustrated Books
Founded: 1864
ISBN Publisher's Prefix: 3-85773

Kossodo Verlag AG, 27a chemin des Hutins, CH-1247 Anières/Geneva Tel: (022) 512247/511156
Dir: Martha Düssel
Subjects: Art Books, De Luxe Limited

SWITZERLAND

Editions
Founded: 1956
ISBN Publisher's Prefix: 3-7208

Verlag Karl **Krämer** & Co, Spiegelgasse 14, CH-8001 Zurich
Associate Company: Karl Krämer Verlag GmbH und Co, Federal Republic of Germany (qv)
ISBN Publisher's Prefix: 3-85774

Verlag René **Kramer** AG*, Strada di Gandria 48, PO Box 90, CH-6976 Lugano-Castagnola Tel: (091) 518941 Cable Add: Edikramer
Man Dir, Publicity: René Kramer
Subjects: Gastronomy and the Culinary Arts, Pastry-Cookery

Verlag G **Krebs** AG, CH-4006 Basle, St Alban-Vorstadt 56 Tel: (061) 239723
Orders to: Gesellschaft für Volkskunde, CH-4006 Basel, Postfach
Dirs: Franz Käser, Willy Kohler
Subjects: Folklore Studies, Swiss Handicrafts, Song Books; Periodicals
1978: 8 titles *Founded:* 1897
Miscellaneous: Associated imprints include Geschäftsstelle der Schweiz, Schweizerische Gesellschaft für Volkskunde (Swiss Folklore Society)
ISBN Publisher's Prefix: 3-85775

Kümmerly und Frey (Geographischer Verlag), Hallerstr 6-10, CH-3001 Berne Tel: (031) 235111 Cable Add: Kümmerlyfrey Telex: 32860
Man Dir: W Frey; *Dirs:* P Etzweiler, Toni Kaufmann
Associate Company: J Fink-Kümmerly und Frey Verlag GmbH, Federal Republic of Germany (qv), Kummerly und Frey Verlags-Gesellschaft mbH, Nikolsdorferstr 8, A-1050 Vienna, Austria
Subjects: Geography, Maps, Topography, Photobooks
Founded: 1852
ISBN Publisher's Prefix: 3-259

Imprimerie Albert **Kündig** SA*, 10 rue Vieux-Collège, CH-1204 Geneva Tel: (022) 285188
Manager: André Kundig
Founded: 1828

Verlag **Kunstkreis**, Buch- und Kunstversand bei Ex Libris, Postfach, CH-8023 Zurich
Subject: Art
Book Club: address as above

Labor et Fides, 1 rue Beauregard, CH-1204 Geneva Tel: (022) 291134
Man Dir, Sales, Production, Rights & Permissions, Editorial, Publicity: Pierre Gisel
Subjects: Religion, Theology and General Subjects
Bookshops: Librairie Labor et Fides SA, 1 rue Beauregard, CH-1204 Geneva
1978: 8 titles *Founded:* 1924
ISBN Publisher's Prefix: 2-8259

Bundesamt für **Landestopographie**, Seftigenstr 264, CH-3084 Wabern
Federal Office of Topography
Subject: Maps (Switzerland)

Herbert **Lang** & Cie AG, Münzgraben 2, PO Box 82, CH-3000 Berne 7 Tel: (031) 228871 Cable Add: Librilang Telex: 33173
President: Christoph H Lang
Subject: Science
Bookshop: Münzgraben 2, CH-3011 Berne
Founded: 1813 (re-formed 1921)
Miscellaneous: Agents for libraries throughout the world
ISBN Publisher's Prefix: 3-261

Verlag Peter **Lang** AG, Jupiterstr 15, Postfach, CH-3015 Berne Tel: (031) 321122 Cable Add: Pelag Bern Telex: 32420 verl ch
Subjects: Liberal Arts, Sciences

Langenscheidt AG, CH-8021 Zurich, Hardturmstr 76
Parent Company: Langenscheidt KG, Federal Republic of Germany (qv)
Subjects: Linguistics, Languages
ISBN Publisher's Prefix: 3-269

Franz **Larese** und Jürg Janett, see Erker-Galerie AG

Larousse (Suisse) SA, BP 120, 1211 Geneva 6 Tel: (022) 369140
Man Dir: Jean-Claude Viatte
Subjects: Reference Works, Dictionaries, School Books
ISBN Publisher's Prefix: 28276

Lector-Verlag GmbH, Höhgaden, CH-8852 Altendorf Tel: (055) 633729 Cable Add: lectorverlag altendorfschwyz Telex: 875257 lecv ch
Man Dir and Other Offices: Walter E Krüttner
Subjects: Belles Lettres, Nonfiction, Art
1979: 26 titles *Founded:* 1978
ISBN Publisher's Prefix: 3-272

Leemann AG, Buchdruckerei und Verlag*, CH-8034 Zurich, Arbenzstr 20 Tel: (01) 346650/1
Dir: Emil Kappeler
Subjects: Metallurgy, Physics
Founded: 1853
ISBN Publisher's Prefix: 3-85786

Lenos Verlag, Postfach 794, CH-4002 Basle
Subjects: Belles Lettres, Pedagogics, Politics, Literary Periodical — *drehpunkt*
Miscellaneous: Company has common interests with the Z-Verlag (qv) and Edition Etcetera (qv)

Leobuchhandlung, Verlag der Quellenbändchen*, Gallusstr 20, CH-9001 St Gallen Tel: (071) 222917/228475 Telex: 77452
Man Dir: Walter Gnägi
Associate: Vereinigung Katholischer Buchhändler (qv under Book Trade Organizations)
Founded: 1918
Bookshop: Leobuchhandlung, at above address
ISBN Publisher's Prefix: 3-85788

Leonis Verlag, Villa Meridiana, Titlisstr 14, CH-8032 Zurich
Sales and distribution: PO Box 952, CH-8034 Zurich (Located at: Klausstr 49) Tel: (01) 2517560/475565 Cable Add: Leonisverlag Zurich
Owner & Man Dir: Dr Wolfgang M Metz
Subjects: Biography, Politics, Social Science; Paperbacks, Travel Books
1978: 3 titles *Founded:* 1976
ISBN Publisher's Prefix: 3-721

Edition **Leu**, Verlag für nichtkommerzielle Kunst und Literatur, Asylstr 110a, CH-8032 Zurich Tel: (01) 692894
Man Dir, Production, Publicity: Al' Leu;
Editorial: Brigit Hotz, Gerti Leitner
Publishing House for non-commercial Art and Literature
Associate Companies: L und L Publikationen, Zurich
Subjects: Literature (Prose and Poetry), Mythology, Social Criticism, Experimental Literature, Graphics
Book Club: AGAV, Stuttgart, Federal Republic of Germany
1978: 3 titles *1979:* 3 titles *Founded:* 1977

Lia Rumantscha (Ligia Romontscha), Via Plessur 47, CH-7000 Cuoira/Cuera Tel: (081) 224422/224448
Subjects: Publishers of books in the Romantsch language of Switzerland; dictionaries, grammar, linguistics, background and history of Romantsch; Biography, Belles Lettres, Poetry, Music and Songs, Religion, Periodicals
1979: 20 titles
Miscellaneous: Company also gives financial support to other publications in Romantsch

Limmat Verlag Genossenschaft, Wildbachstr 48, Postfach, CH-8034 Zürich Tel: (01) 556300
Subjects: Academic and Popular Texts on the Worker's Movement and Associated Socialist-orientated Organizations, Socialism in Switzerland, Socio-Political Studies, Feminist Juvenile

Logos-Verlag*, CH-8021 Zurich, Witikonerstr 368 Tel: (01) 530340
Subject: Textbooks
Founded: 1932
ISBN Publisher's Prefix: 3-85790

E **Löpfe-Benz** AG Rorschacht, Graphische Anstalt und Verlag, Signalstr 7, CH-9400 Rorschach Tel: (071) 414341
Graphical Institute and Publisher
Dirs: Emil Enderle, Dieter Mildenberger;
Editorial: Franz Mächler; *Sales:* Peter Kruijsen; *Advertising:* Theo Walser, Hans Schöbi, Peter Bick
Subsidiary Company: Nebelspalter Verlag (qv)
Subjects: Topical Works, Humour, Satire, Juvenile, Poetry, History; Periodical *Der Nebelspalter* (qv under Nebelspalter Verlag)
1978: 4 titles *1979:* 4 titles *Founded:* 1875
ISBN Publisher's Prefix: 3-85819

Hans-Rudolf **Lutz**, Lessingstr 11, CH-8001 Zurich Tel: 2017672
Man Dir and other offices: H-R Lutz
Subjects: Biography, Art, Architecture, Revolutionary Art
1978: 2 titles *1979:* 1 title *Founded:* 1966

McGraw-Hill Book Co, Museggstr 7, CH-6004 Lucerne Tel: (041) 230030 Telex: 72386
General Manager: Alfred van der Marck;
Managing Editor, Sales: Francine Peeters;
Editorial: David Baker; *Production Manager:* Franz Gisler
Subjects: Illustrated General Literature, Reference Works, History, Pictorial Biographies
Miscellaneous: Firm is a Co-Publishing Office of the McGraw-Hill Book Co, 1221 Ave of the Americas, New York, NY 10020
See McGraw-Hill (UK) for Associate Companies etc

Macmillan SA, 1 ave des Jordils, CH-1000 Lausanne 6 Tel: (021) 277561 Cable Add: Berledit Lausanne Telex: 25492 CH
Man Dir: Marshall D Mascott; *Editorial:* Konrad Fuchs, Henning Madsen;
Production Manager: Jean-Paul Minder
Parent Company: Macmillan Inc, 866 Third Ave, New York, NY 10022, USA
Imprint: Editions Berlitz
Subjects: Travel, Tourism, Language Teaching, Dictionaries, Leisure
1978: approx 100 titles *1979:* approx 100 titles *Founded:* 1970
ISBN Publisher's Prefix: According to distributor

La **Maison** de la Bible, Société Biblique de Genève, 11 rue de Rive, CH-1211 Geneva 3 Tel: (022) 285259
Subjects: Religion, Juveniles, Educational
Bookshop: La Maison de la Bible, at above address
1978: 4 titles *1979:* 7 titles *Founded:* 1917
Miscellaneous: Also known as Das Haus der Bibel (Genfer Bibelgesellschaft)
ISBN Publisher's Prefix: 2-8260

Marika **Malacorda** Editions, 1 rue de l'Évêché, CH-1204 Geneva
Associate Company: Ecart Publications (qv)

Manesse-Verlag, see Conzett und Hubert

Manesse und Morgarten Verlag, Morgartenstr 29, Postfach, CH-8004 Zurich Tel: (01) 2424455 Cable Add: Cozetthuber
Man Dir: Dr Hans Conzett; *Editorial, Rights & Permissions:* Dr F Hindemann; *Sales, Publicity:* Alex Aepli; *Production:* Kurt Oggier
Parent Company: Manesse-Verlag, Conzett und Huber; see Conzett und Huber
Subjects: Literary Works in German and from other worldwide languages in translation; the Classics, Fables and Legends; Religion, Music; Presentation Editions
Founded: 1886
ISBN Publisher's Prefix: 3-7175

Librairie-Editions J **Marguerat**, 2 pl St François, CH-1003 Lausanne 2 Tel: (021) 237717
Dir: Jean Marguerat
Subjects: Belles Lettres, History, Travel, Music, Geography, Ethnology
Founded: 1940
ISBN Publisher's Prefix: 2-88008

Marva*, route des Acacias, BP 254, CH-1211 Geneva 26 Tel: 925671 Cable Add: Marva Geneva 26
Publisher: Hennecke Kardel and Dietrich Bronder
Subject: Modern History (especially European and Nazi-related)
1978: 2 titles

Editions la **Matze**, Guy Gessler, Case Postale, CH-1950 Sion (Located at: Bellevue B, CH-1964 Chateauneuf-Conthey) Tel: 363232
Man Dir: Guy Gessler; *Sales Dir:* Nelly Tanner
Subjects: General Fiction, Military and General History, Archaeology, Swiss Painters series
Founded: 1975

Verlag A & G de **May***, 6 chemin des Sorbiers, BP 52, CH-1012 Lausanne Tel: (021) 289608
Subjects: History, Arts, Archaeology

Médecine & Hygiène, BP 229, 78 Ave de la Roseraie, CH-1211 Geneva 4 Tel: (022) 469355/56
Man & Sales Dir: J P Balavoine; *Publicity and Advertising Dir:* P Y Balavoine
Subjects: Medicine, Psychology, General Science, University Textbooks, Specialized Medical and other Periodicals
Founded: 1943

Peter **Meili** & Co, CH-8200 Schaffhausen, Fronwagpl 13 Tel: (053) 54144/5
Subjects: History, Literature about the Schaffhausen area, Dialect Stories
Bookshop: Buchhandlung Meili & Co (at above address)
Founded: 1838
ISBN Publisher's Prefix: 3-85805

Christoph **Merian** Verlag*, St Alban-Vorstadt 5, CH-4052 Basle Tel: (061) 221288
Subjects: Basle and Area
ISBN Publisher's Prefix: 3-85616

Henri **Messeiller***, 11 rue St Nicolas, CH-2000 Neuchâtel Tel: (038) 251296
Subjects: Textbooks, Education, Art, Belles Lettres, Religion, Psychology, Law, Administration
Founded: 1887
ISBN Publisher's Prefix: 2-8261

Max S **Metz** Verlag AG*, CH-8022 Zurich, Limmatquai 36 Tel: (01) 325357
Man Dir: Max S Metz
Subjects: Culture, Politics, Economics, Technical, History, Maps

Founded: 1946
ISBN Publisher's Prefix: 3-85807

Editions **Minkoff** Reprint, 46 chemin de la Mousse, CH-1225 Chêne-Bourg, Geneva Tel: (022) 485568
Dir and all offices: Youval Minkoff, Sylvie Minkoff
Subjects: Music and Musicology, Musical Iconography, Theatre, Fine Arts, Japanese Art, General History of Socialism
1978: 25 titles *1979:* 30 titles *Founded:* 1972
ISBN Publisher's Prefix: 2-8266

Moderne Industrie AG*, Dörflistrasse 73, 8050 Zürich Tel: (01) 468140 Telex: 57547
Subjects: Technical, Data Processing, Personnel, Marketing, Sales
ISBN Publisher's Prefix: 3-478

Alfred **Mohler** Verlag*, CH-8800 Thalwil, Seestr 1 Tel: (01) 7207691
Founded: 1970
ISBN Publisher's Prefix: 3-85808

Editions **Mon Village** SA, CH-1099 Vulliens, Vaud Tel: (021) 931363
Man Dir, Sales, Production, Publicity, Rights & Permissions: Albert-Louis Chappuis; *Editorial:* André Plomb
Subjects: Novels of rural life
Book Club: Club Mon Village SA
1978: 4 titles *1979:* 4 titles *Founded:* 1955

Mondo SA, 18 ave Reller, 1800 Vevey Tel: (021) 528021 Telex: 24207a spnv ch
Man Dir: P Mayor

Les Editions du **Mont-Blanc** SA, 26 rue du Mont Blanc, CH-1201 Geneva Tel: (022) 315650
Man Dir: Chantal Buxo
Subjects: Philosophy, Religion, Medicine, Psychology, Social Science
1980: 40 titles *Founded:* 1942

Morgarten-Verlag, see Manesse und Morgarten Verlag

Verlag **Mosse-Ars** Medici, Limmatquai 94, CH-8023 Zurich
Man Dir: Franz Ebner
Subject: Medical
Founded: 1933
Miscellaneous: formerly Lüdin AG
ISBN Publisher's Prefix: 3-85792

Verlag Rudolf **Mühlemann***, Haus Z Wolfau, CH-8570 Weinfelden Tel: (072) 50888
Founded: 1949
ISBN Publisher's Prefix: 3-85809

Jacques **Muhlethaler***, 5 rue du Simplon, CH-1211 Geneva 6 Tel: (022) 364451/2
Subjects: Fine & Applied Arts, Illustrated Books, Belles Lettres, Dietary, Handicrafts
Founded: 1945

Albert **Müller** Verlag AG, CH-8803 Rüschlikon/Zürich, Bahnhofstr 69, Postfach 150 Tel: (01) 7241760 Cable Add: Müllerverlag Rüschlikon Telex: 56320 AMV CH
Man Dir: Adolf Recher-Vogel; *Editorial:* Dr Marta Jacober-Züllig; *Sales, Rights & Permissions:* Dr Bernhard Recher; *Publicity:* Paul Freitag; *Production:* R Kleinschnittger
Subjects: Books on a variety of domestic and pet animals, especially horses, dogs, cats; also Juvenile Animal Stories and Science Fiction, How-to, Music, Reference, Sports, Recreation, Cookery, Self-Help, Health, Yoga, Homecrafts
1978: 80 titles *1979:* 80 titles *Founded:* 1938
ISBN Publisher's Prefix: 3-275

Multiling Verlag AG, subsidiary of U Bär AG (qv)

N Z N-Buchverlag AG, Zeltweg 71, Postfach A25, CH-8032 Zurich Tel: (01) 474951
Man Dir: Trottmann Alphons
Subjects: Art, Religion, Architecture, History
1978: 5 titles *1979:* 7 titles *Founded:* 1972
ISBN Publisher's Prefix: 3-85827

Les Editions **Nagel** SA*, 5-5 bis rue de l'Orangerie, CH-1211 Geneva 7 Tel: (022) 341730/9 Cable Add: Nageledit Geneva
Man Dir: Louis Nagel
Subjects: Philosophy, Politics, Archaeology, Art, Travel Guides
Founded: 1952
Miscellaneous: Publishes 'Who's Who in Switzerland'
ISBN Publisher's Prefix: 2-8263

Natura-Verlag*, Pfeffingerweg 1, CH-4144 Arlesheim Tel: (061) 721011
Subjects: Nature Cure, Philosophy, Therapeutic Pedagogy texts
1978: 2 titles *1979:* 2 titles
ISBN Publisher's Prefix: 3-85817

Naville & Cie SA, 5-7 rue Lévrier, CH-1201 Geneva Tel: (022) 322400 Telex: navico 28469
President: Marc Payot; *General Manager:* Gilles Martin
Founded: 1877

Nebelspalter Verlag, CH-9400 Rorschach Tel: (071) 414341
Parent Company: E Löpfe-Benz AG, CH-9400 Rorschach (qv)
Subjects: Humour, Satire, Cartoons
Publication: Periodical: Der Nebelspalter
1978: 4 titles
ISBN Publisher's Prefix: 3-85819

Neptun-Verlag*, Ing H Frei, CH-8280 Kreuzlingen 1, Postfach 307 Tel: (072) 727262 Telex: Nept ch 77414
Manager: H Frei-Gmür
Subjects: Contemporary History, Art Reproductions, Travel
Founded: 1946
ISBN Publisher's Prefix: 3-85820

Neue Diana Press AG, Splügenstr 10, CH-8002 Zurich Tel: (01) 2027441 and 2016370
Man Dirs: Dr Rolf Zollikofer, Dr Richard Bechtle
Subjects: General Fiction, Biography, History
Founded: 1973
ISBN Publisher's Prefix: 3-87158

Verlag **Neue Stadt**, Postfach 435, CH-8038 Zürich (Located at: Seestr 426, CH-8038 Zurich)
Parent Company: Verlag Neue Stadt, Federal Republic of Germany (qv)
Associate Company: Verlag Neue Stadt, Austria (qv)

Neue Zürcher Zeitung, Buchverlag, CH-8021 Zürich, Postfach Tel: (01) 2581111 Telex: 52137 nzz ch
Publicity Manager: Walter Köpfli
Subject: Textbooks
ISBN Publisher's Prefix: 3-85823

Neufeld Verlag und Galerie, PO Box, CH-9434 Au/SG Tel: (071) 712977 Cable Add: neufeld
Man Dir: K G Löpfe; *Editorial and other offices:* Kurt Prantl
Orders to: Lustenau, A-6890 Austria
Parent Company: Löpfe KG, Lustenau, A-6890 Austria
Branch Off: Levehus, Löwenstr, Zurich
Subject: Art
1978: 2 titles *Founded:* 1962

Verlag Arthur **Niggli** AG, CH-9052 Niederteufen Tel: (071) 331772 Cable Add: Niggliverlag, Niederteufen Appenzell

Man Dir: Arthur Niggli
Shipping Add: c/o Danzas und Co,
St Gallen
Subsidiary Company: Gallery Ida Niggli
Ltd, CH-9052 Niederteufen
Subjects: Visual Arts, Architecture, Fine
Arts, Periodical: *Archithese*
Bookshop: Buchhandlung Niggli, CH-9052
Niederteufen
1980: 20 titles *Founded:* 1950
ISBN Publisher's Prefix: 3-7212

Nord-Süd Verlag, CH-8617 Mönchaltorf
Tel: (01) 9351335 Cable Add: nordsued
Telex: 875759 Schi ch
Dir, Editorial: Brigitte Sidjanski-Hanhart;
*Sales, Production, Publicity, Rights &
Permissions:* Davy Sidjanski
Orders to: Sauerländer AG, Postfach,
CH-5001 Aarau Tel: (064) 221264 Telex:
68736 (for Switzerland)
Subjects: Children's Picture Books, Picture
Calendars, Posters
Book Club: Punktum (qv)
1980: 14 titles *Founded:* 1961
ISBN Publisher's Prefix: 3-85825

Nova-Press International Publishers Ltd*,
Hallwylstr 71, Postfach 275, CH-8036
Zurich Tel: (01) 2418117 Telex: 53094 npz
Man Dir, Rights & Permissions: Marcel H
Huber; *Editorial:* H P Elermann; *Sales:*
Hans Wiederkehr; *Production:* D Weimar;
Publicity: J W Geisen
Imprints: Nova-Press International, Zurich,
Munich, Vienna, Paris, London
Subjects: Popular texts on Economics,
Politics, History, Factual Reportage, Art
and Picture Books, 30-vol Musical
Encyclopaedia with records
Book Club: International Classical Music
Ltd: Zurich, Munich, Vienna, Paris, London
Founded: 1976
ISBN Publisher's Prefix: 3-85826

Novalis Verlag AG*, 8200 Schaffhausen,
Vordergasse 58 Tel: (053) 88111
Subjects: Arts, Social Sciences, Educational
ISBN Publisher's Prefix: 3-7214

Editions **Novos** SA*, 4 ave Ruchonnet,
CH-1001 Lausanne Tel: (021) 226372
Dir: Gabrielle Philippin
Subjects: Fiction, Calendars, Desk
Calendars, Art

Emil **Oesch** Verlag AG, CH-8800 Thalwil,
Zürich, Seestr 3 Tel: 7201333 Cable Add:
Oesch
Subjects: General Fiction, How-to,
Philosophy, Religion, Psychology, General
& Social Science, Educational Materials
Founded: 1935
ISBN Publisher's Prefix: 3-85833

L'Oeuvre Gravée*, Münstergasse 36,
Postfach 205 (CH-3000 Berne 8), CH-3011
Berne Tel: (031) 225071 Cable Add:
Schindlerart
Editorial, Publicity: Werner Schindler

Office du Livre SA (Buchhaus AG), 101
route de Villars, CP 1061, CH-1701
Fribourg Tel: (037) 240744 Cable Add:
LIVREOFFICE Telex: 36227
Man Dir: Jean Hirschen; *Editorial:* Didier
Coigny; *Sales Manager:* Pierre Engel
Subjects: Art, Architecture, Arts and Crafts,
Golf
1979: 80 titles *1980:* 90 titles *Founded:* 1947
ISBN Publisher's Prefix: 37215

Edition **Olms** AG, Postfach 159, CH-8033
Zurich (Located at: Haldenbachstr 17) Tel:
(01) 691160
Man Dir and Other Offices: Manfred Olms
Subjects: First Editions, Facsimile Reprints
(especially of illustrated Travel Works),
Bibliophile, Myth and Legend, Magic,
Helvetica, Humour, Chess, Toy Catalogues,
Rock Literature
1978: 10 titles *1979:* 14 titles *Founded:* 1977
ISBN Publisher's Prefix: 3-283

Inigo von **Oppersdorff** Verlag,
Waldschulweg 5, CH-8032 Zurich Tel: (01)
551140
Man Dir: B Lennier
Subjects: Belles Lettres, Poetry, History,
Music, Art, Religion
1978: 5 titles *1979:* 1 title *Founded:* 1966
ISBN Publisher's Prefix: 3-85834

Orell Füssli Verlag, CH-8022 Zurich,
Nüschelerstr 22 Tel: (01) 2113630 Cable
Add: Orellverlag Zurich Telex: 54021
orlag ch
Man Dir: Gian Laube; *Editorial:* Ernst
Halter, Armin Ochs, Jutta Redel; *Sales &
Advertising Dir:* Martin Brugger; *Publicity:*
Michael Lang; *Rights & Permissions:* Armin
Ochs
Parent Company: Orell Füssli Graphische
Betriebe AG, Dietzingerstr 3, CH-8036
Zürich
Subjects: Belles Lettres, Biography, History,
How-to, Music, Art, Juveniles, Educational
Materials, Railways and Aircraft,
Photographic Picture Books
Bookshops: Pelikanstr 10, CH-8022 Zurich
Founded: 1519
ISBN Publisher's Prefix: 3-280

Verlag **Organisator** AG, Löwenstr 16,
CH-8021 Zurich Tel: (01) 2118155 Cable
Add: orga/ch Telex: 813834
Man Dir, Editorial: Dr V Bataillard; *Sales,
Publicity:* V A Bataillard; *Production:*
K Raggenbach
Subjects: Swiss Law and Taxes,
International Taxes, Industrial Management;
Monthly Management Periodical *Der
Organisator*
Bookshops: In Basle, Lucerne, St Gallen,
Schaffhausen, Winterthur, Zurich and many
other Swiss towns
1978: 12 titles *Founded:* 1919
ISBN Publisher's Prefix: 3-7220

Origo-Verlag, Rathausgasse 30, CH-3011
Berne Tel: (031) 224480 Cable Add:
Wildbuch
Man Dir: Alexander Wild (owner)
Associate Company: Verlag Alexander Wild,
at same address
Subjects: Philosophy and Religion of East
and West
1978: 8 titles *Founded:* 1947
ISBN Publisher's Prefix: 3-282

Orte-Verlag, Postfach 2028, CH-8006 Zurich
(Located at: Ekkehardstr 14) Tel: (01)
3630234
Man Dir: Werner Bucher
Subjects: Poetry, Belles Lettres

Ott Verlag AG Thun, CH-3600 Thun 7,
Länggasse 57 Tel: (033) 221622 Cable Add:
Ottpubl Thun Telex: 33991
Man Dir: Walter Knecht; *Publicity &
Advertising:* Hans M Ott; *Sales Manager:*
Nino D'Andrea
Subsidiary Company: Verlags und
Versandbuchhandlung Thun AG, Thun
Subjects: General Non-fiction, Lexicons,
Earth Sciences, Military, Sports,
Industry/Commerce
1978: 5 titles *Founded:* 1923
ISBN Publisher's Prefix: 3-7225

Editions du **Panorama**, CP 38 CH-2500
Bienne 3 Tel: (032) 224240
Man Dir: Paul Thierrin
Subjects: General Fiction, Commerce,
Secondary, Textbooks, Languages, Belles
Lettres
1978: 6 titles *Founded:* 1951

Edizioni **Pantarei***, CH-6900 Lugano, Via
Sempione 2
Subjects: Music, Belles Lettres

Park and Roche Establishment*, 11 rue
Général Dufour, CH-1211 Geneva 11 Tel:
282744
Editorial, Permissions: Peter Bellew, Canto
Lou Vent, Route de la Colle, 06570 St Paul
de Vence, France Tel: (93) 329338
Subjects: Illustrated books on Art,
Architecture, Cookery, Cultural History,
Music, General Knowledge: published in
international co-editions

Paulusverlag, 36 Pérolles, CH-1700
Fribourg Tel: (037) 246812
Dir: Martin Nicoulin
Subjects: Religion, Philosophy, History,
Anthropology, Theology, Periodicals

Librairie **Payot** SA*, Case Postale 3212,
CH-1002 Lausanne (Located at:
4 pl Pépinet, CH-1003 Lausanne) Tel: (021)
203331 Cable Add: Payotco Telex: 24961
Manager: Jean Hutter
Associate Company: Editions Payot,
France (qv)
Branch Offs: 107 Freiestr, CH-4051 Basle;
16 Bundegasse, CH-3011 Berne; 2 rue Vallin,
PO Box 381, CH-1211 Geneva 11; 14 Grand-
Rue, CH-1820 Montreux; 8a rue du Bassin,
CH-2000 Neuchâtel; 51 rue d'Italie, CH-1800
Vevey; 9 Bahnhofstr, CH-8001 Zurich
Subjects: Belles Lettres, Poetry, History,
Music, Art, General and Natural Sciences,
Philosophy, Psychology, Law, Commerce,
Regional, University, Secondary & Primary
Textbooks, Transport, Agriculture,
Domestic, Sport
Bookshops: Librairie Payot SA, 1 rue de
Bourg, CH-1003 Lausanne; 4 pl Pépinet,
CH-1003 Lausanne; Tel: (021) 203331
Telex: 24961 for both shops
See also list of Branch Offices above
Founded: 1835
ISBN Publisher's Prefix: 2-601

Pedrazzini Tipografia, Via B Varenna 7, CH-
6600 Locarno Tel: (093) 317734-35
Man Dir and other offices: Carlo Pedrazzini
Subjects: Scholastic, Historical, Church
Historical, Literary, Printing and Book
Production
1980: 35 titles *Founded:* 1880

Pendo-Verlag, Wolfbachstr 9, CH-8032
Zürich Tel: (01) 693737
Dirs: Gladys Weigner, Bernhard
Moosbrugger
Subjects: Travel, Religion, Literature and
Poetry, International Co-operation
ISBN Publisher's Prefix: 3-85842

Pharos-Verlag*, Hansrudolf Schwabe AG,
CH-4002 Basel, Postfach 917 Tel: (061)
395671
Man Dir: Hansrudolf Schwabe; *Advertising
Dir:* Heiner Hartmann
Subjects: Belles Lettres, Poetry, Juveniles
Bookshop: Buchhandlung Münsterberg,
CH-4000 Basel, Münsterberg 13
Founded: 1958
ISBN Publisher's Prefix: 3-7230

Philosophisch-Anthroposophischer Verlag,
Goetheanum, Hügelweg 63, Postfach,
CH-4143 Dornach Tel: (061) 721116
Orders to: Koch, Neff und Oetinger & Co,
Schockenriederstr 37, D-7000 Stuttgart 80,
Federal Republic of Germany
Subsidiary Company: Rudolf Geering-
Verlag, at above address
Subjects: Philosophy, Anthroposophy,
Nature Study, Eurhythmics, Music,
Literature, Medicine etc; all subjects
especially in connection with the thought of
Rudolf Steiner
Bookshop: at above address
ISBN Publisher's Prefix: 3-7235

Phoebus-Verlag GmbH*, CH-4052 Basle, Malzgasse 7
Subject: Arts
ISBN Publisher's Prefix: 3-85841

Phoenix Verlag AG, see Scherz Verlag AG

Editions **Pierrot** SA, 51 ave de Rumine, CH-1005 Lausanne Tel: (021) 220779
Dir: Ghislaine Vautier
Orders to: Éditions Pierrot, Case Postale 3513, CH-1002 Lausanne
Subjects: Literature, Juveniles, Periodical (Children's)
1978-79: 6 titles *Founded:* 1966

R **Piper** & Co Verlag GmbH*, Alte Landstr 67, CH-8700 Küsnacht Tel: (062) 482181
Parent Company: R Piper & Co Verlag, Federal Republic of Germany (qv)
Subjects: Belles Lettres, Juveniles, Politics, Social Science, Psychology, Education, Natural Sciences
ISBN Publisher's Prefix: 3-7236

Polana AG*, Postfach 1173 CH-8036 Zürich
Subjects: Belles Lettres, Poetry, Politics

Populaires*, Ave Tivoli 2, Lausanne
Tel: (022) 332600
Man Dir: Philippe Luquiens

Presses Centrales Lausanne SA*, 7 rue de Genève, CH-1003 Lausanne Tel: (021) 205901
Dir: Gilbert Rohrer
Subject: Art

Les **Presses de la Connaissance***, c/o Weber SA d'Editions, 13 rue de Monthoux, BP 385, CH-1211 Geneva 2 Tel: 326450 Cable Add: Livrart
Parent Company: Les Presses de la Connaissance, Paris, France
Subjects: Mythology; Witnesses and Testimonies

Presses Polytechniques Romandes, an imprint of Georgi Publishing Co (qv)

Pro Juventute Verlag, Seefeldstr 8, Postfach, CH-8022 Zurich Tel: (01) 2517244
Subjects: Children's Education and Welfare generally; covers Family, Playgroups, Playgrounds, Pedagogy, Teaching Media etc: Texts in German, French, Italian and English
1978-79: 5 titles

Editions **Pro Schola**, 29 rue des Terreaux, CH-1003 Lausanne Tel: (021) 236655 Cable Add: Dirbenedict
Man Dir: Dr Jean J Bénédict
Orders to: BP 298, CH-1000 Lausanne 9
Subjects: Language: Textbooks, Reference; especially, language teaching by the "Bénédict Direct Progressive Method"
Founded: 1928
ISBN Publisher's Prefix: 2-88009

Problem-Verlag*, CH-6000 Lucerne, Hirschmattstr 1, Postfach 834
Subject: Hobbies

Verlag fur **Psychologie** Dr C J Hogrefe, see Hogrefe

Psychosophische Gesellschaft*, CH-8021 Zurich, Postfach 204
Subjects: Psychology, Philosophy, Theology, Pedagogy, Mysticism and Magic, the Works of Aleister Crowley

R A Verlag, CH-8640 Rapperswil, Postfach 120
Subjects: Art, Education, Games

Rabe Verlag Zurich, Oberdorfstr 23, CH-8001 Zurich Tel: (01) 478540; Depot at: CH-8608 Bubikon Zurich Tel: (055) 382383; Cable Add: rabeverlag Zurich
Man Dir, Sales: Dr J Kanitz; *Editorial, Rights & Permissions:* Dr Elsa Kanitz;
Production, Publicity: Dr P Portmann
Subjects: Art Books, Cards; Large-format graphics on old/modern art; Art Prints
Bookshop: rabe verlag, at above address
Founded: 1962
ISBN Publisher's Prefix: 3-85852

Raeber AG Luzern, CH-6002 Lucerne, Frankenstr 7-9 Tel: (041) 227422/3/4 Telex: 72381
Man Dir: B L Raeber
Imprint: Edition Raeber
Subjects: General Fiction, Belles Lettres, Poetry, History, Music, Art, Juveniles, Secondary Textbooks, Religion
Bookshops: Raeber Buchhandlung, CH-6002 Lucerne, Frankenstr; Taschenbuchladen Kornmärt, Lucerne, Kornmarktgasse 7
1978: 8 titles *Founded:* 1825
ISBN Publisher's Prefix: 3-7239

Verlag für **Recht und Gesellschaft** AG*, Postfach 1004, CH-4002 Basel (Located at: 15 Bundesstr, CH-4054 Basel) Tel: (061) 396600 Cable Add: Regesverlag
Man Dir: Berta Hess
Subject: Law, Taxation
Founded: 1933
ISBN Publisher's Prefix: 3-7242

Regenbogen-Verlag, Postfach 240, CH-8025 Zurich Tel: (01) 475860
General Manager: Theo Ruff
Orders to: Neue Bücher AG, Gotthardstr 49, CH-8027 Zürich Tel: (01) 2027474
Subjects: Travel Guides, Art Books, Swiss Literature, Objets d'Art in the 'Edition Regenbogen'
ISBN Publisher's Prefix: 3-85862

Kinderbuchverlag **Reich** Luzern AG, Zinggentorstr 4, CH-6000 Lucerne 6 Tel: (041) 228871 Telex: 72508 reic ch
Man Dir: Jürgen Braunschweiger; *Editorial:* Heidrun Diltz; *Sales, Admin, Publicity:* Verlag Sauerländer, CH-5001 Aarau (qv)
Subjects: Juvenile Fiction and Non-fiction with photographic illustrations
1979: 10 titles *Founded:* 1979
ISBN Publisher's Prefix: 3-7941

Reich Verlag AG, Zinggentorstr 4, CH-6000 Lucerne 6 Tel: (041) 220721 Cable Add: Reich Luzern Telex: 72508 reic ch
Man Dir: Jürgen Braunschweiger; *Sales & Administration:* Alfons Wüest; *Editorial and Publicity:* Heidrun Diltz
Parent Company: Hoffmann und Campe Verlag, Federal Republic of Germany (qv)
Subjects: Photographic Picture Books (terra magica), Hippology Books (terra hippologica), Belles Lettres (Edition Reich)
1979: 15 titles *Founded:* 1974
ISBN Publisher's Prefix: 3-7243

Verlag Friedrich **Reinhardt** AG, Missionstr 36, CH-4000 Basle 12 Tel: (061) 253390 Cable Add: Freinhardt Basel
Man Dir, Rights & Permissions: Dr Ernst Reinhardt
Subjects: General Fiction, Belles Lettres, Biography, History, How-to, Religion, Juveniles, General Science, University Textbooks, Educational Materials
1980: 19 titles
ISBN Publisher's Prefix: 3-7245

Editions **Rencontre** SA*, 29 chemin d'Entre-Bois, CH-1018 Lausanne Tel: (021) 323841 Cable Add: Rencontre Lausanne Telex: 24876
Subjects: General Fiction, Belles Lettres, Poetry, Biography, History, Music, Art, Philosophy, Reference, Religion, Juveniles, Medicine, General Science, Educational Materials
Founded: 1950

Eugen **Rentsch** Verlag AG, Wiesenstr 48, Postfach 47, CH-8703 Erlenbach-Zurich Tel: (01) 9100133 Telex: CH 59784 Revag
Man Dir, Rights & Permissions: Dr Eugen Rentsch; *Publicity Dir:* Dr Leonore Rentsch
Subjects: Biography, History, Biology, Psychology, Economy, Social Science, Environmental, Political, Educational Books and Materials, Children's Books
1978: 20 titles *Founded:* 1910
ISBN Publisher's Prefix: 3-7249

Imprimeries **Réunies** SA*, ave de la Gare, CH-1003 Lausanne Tel: (021) 203111 Telex: 24495
Subjects: Art, Belles Lettres, Natural Sciences, Geography, Travel
Miscellaneous: Associated imprints include Editions 24 Heures (qv)

Rex-Verlag, St Karliquai 12, Postfach 161, CH-6000 Lucerne 5 Tel: (041) 514914
Man Dir: Dr Zeno Inderbitzin
Subjects: Belles Lettres, Education, Guides to Conduct, Juveniles, Religion (Catholicism)
Bookshop: Rex Buchladen, St-Karliquai 12, CH-6000 Lucerne 5
Founded: 1931
ISBN Publisher's Prefix: 3-7252

Edizioni Raimondo **Rezzonico***, CH-6600 Locarno, Via Luini

Ringier & Co AG*, Graphisches Institut und Verlagsanstalt, CH-4800 Zofingen, Florastr Tel: (062) 510101
President: Hans Ringier; *Executive President:* Dr Hch Oswald
Subjects: Fashion, Directories
Founded: 1833
ISBN Publisher's Prefix: 3-85859

Editiones **'Roche'**, F Hoffmann – La Roche & Co, Aktiengesellschaft, Postfach CH-4002 Basle Tel: 273611 Cable Add: Roche Basle Telex: 62922 a roch ch
Man Dir, Sales, Production, Publicity: Martin Schneider; *Editorial:* Dr W Kolditz
Orders to: H Huber, Länggassstrasse 76, CH-3000 Berne 9 (for Editiones 'Roche'); F Hoffmann – La Roche & Co, Aktiengesellschaft, Rocom, Postfach, CH-4002 Basle (for Rocom Publications)
Imprints: Editiones Roche, Rocom
Subject: Medical
Founded: 1971

Rocom, imprint of Editiones 'Roche' (qv)

Rodana Verlag, see Schweizer Spiegel Verlag AG

Hans **Rohr***, Oberdorfstr 5, CH-8024 Zurich 1 Tel: (01) 2513636 Telex: 56385
Man Dir: H Rohr
Subjects: Tourist Interest, Swiss History, Swiss Dialect, Classical Antiquity, Books on Films and the Cinema
Bookshops: Buchhandlung Hans Rohr, Oberdorfstr 5, CH-8024 Zurich; Filmbuchhandlung Hans Rohr, Oberdorfstr 3, CH-8024 Zurich (Films and Cinema)
1978: 6 titles *Founded:* 1921
ISBN Publisher's Prefix: 3-85865

Rosepierre SA, Chemin Chateau-l'Évêque 11, CH-1254 Jussy Tel: (022) 591452
Man Dir: Pierre Bouffard

Rotapfel-Verlag AG, Frankengasse 6, CH-8024 Zurich Tel: (01) 470388
Dir: Dr Paul Toggenburger
Subjects: Textbooks, Juveniles, Beaux-arts, Belles Lettres
Founded: 1919
ISBN Publisher's Prefix: 3-85867

SWITZERLAND

Roth et Sauter SA*, à l'Enseigne du Verseau, La Pâle, CH-1026 Denges/Lausanne Tel: (021) 717561
Man Dirs: Michel Logoz, Pierre Sauter
Imprints: Include Editions du Verseau
Subjects: Art, Belles Lettres, General
Founded: 1890

Rotten-Verlags AG, Terbinerstr 2, CH-3930 Visp Tel: (028) 462252

Editions **Roulet** & Cie*, 2 bis blvd des Promenades, CH-1227 Carouge Tel: (022) 425560
ISBN Publisher's Prefix: 2-88010

Rütten und Loening Verlag GmbH, see Scherz Verlag AG

Verlag **S O I** (Schweizerisches Ost-Institut), CH-3000 Berne 6, Jubiläumsstr 41 Tel: (031) 431212 Cable Add: Schweizost Telex: 32728
Man Dir: Peter Sager; *Sales Manager:* Bea Sager; *Production Manager:* Peter Dolder
Subjects: History, Politics, Social Science, especially with respect to the Eastern Bloc countries
Bookshop: Buchhandlung SOI, CH-3000 Berne 6, Jubiläumsstr 41
1978: 5 titles *Founded:* 1958
ISBN Publisher's Prefix: 3-85913

Société de l'Oeuvre **Saint-Augustin**, 1890 St-Maurice Tel: (025) 651022
Man Dir: R Donnet-Descartes

Saint-Paul, Imprimerie et Librairie, Pérolles 38-42, CH-1700 Fribourg Tel: (037) 823121
Dir: Dr Hugo Baeriswyl
Subjects: Philosophy, Religion, Educational
Founded: 1873

Salvioni & Co*, CH-6500 Bellinzona, Via Franscini

Sanssouci Verlag, Rosenbühlstr 37, CH-8044 Zurich Tel: (01) 2522154 Cable Add: Archeverlag
Owner: Peter Schifferli
Orders to: Erikastr 11, CH-8003 Zurich
Associate Companies: Verlag der Arche Peter Schifferli (qv); E Pfister GmbH, Federal Republic of Germany (qv); Dr Franz Hain, Austria (qv)
Subjects: General Fiction, Humour, Cookery
1978-79: 30 titles
ISBN Publisher's Prefix: 3-7254

Säntis Verlag*, CH-9107 Urnäsch

Sauerländer AG*, Laurenzenvorstadt 89, Postfach 570, CH-5001 Aarau Tel: (064) 221264 Telex: 68726
Man Dir: Hans Christof Sauerländer;
Editorial: Rolf Inhauser, Jitka Bodlakova, Dörthe Binkert; *Sales and Publicity:* Peter Streit; *Production:* Albert Steinmann, Fritz Gebhard; *Rights & Permissions:* Renate Fischer
Subsidiary Companies: H R Sauerländer & Co, Frankfurt-am-Main, German Federal Republic; Verlag Sauerländer, Salzburg, Austria
Associate Companies: SABE-Verlag für Lehrmittel, CH-8001 Zurich
Subjects: Belles Lettres, Poetry, Biography, History, Reference, Juveniles, Medicine, General & Social Science, University, Secondary & Primary Textbooks, Educational Materials
Founded: 1807
ISBN Publisher's Prefix: 3-7941

Scherz Verlag AG, Marktgasse 25, CH-3011 Berne Tel: (031) 226831 Cable Add: Scherzedit Telex: 32552 sherz d
President, Man Dir: Rudolf Streit-Scherz;
Sales Dirs: Wolfgang Radaj, Elmar Send;
Editorial Department: Ursula Ibler, Jürgen Lütge; *Subsidiary Rights & Permissions:* Ursula Griessel
Subsidiary Companies: Otto Wilhelm Barth-Verlag KG, Federal Republic of Germany (qv); Phoenix, Rütten & Loening; Spectrum
Branch Off: Scherz Verlag GmbH, Federal Republic of Germany
Subjects: General Fiction & Nonfiction, Biography, History, Psychology, Parapsychology, Philosophy; Paperback series of Crime Thrillers
Bookshop: Marktgasse 25, CH-3011 Berne
1978: 114 titles *1979:* 116 titles *Founded:* 1939
ISBN Publisher's Prefix: 3-502

Verlag der Arche Peter **Schifferli**, see Arche

Otto **Schlaefli** Verlag*, CH-3800 Interlaken, Bahnhofstr 15 Tel: (036) 221312/3
Subjects: Belles Lettres, Fiction
Founded: 1930
ISBN Publisher's Prefix: 3-85884

Schläpfer & Co AG, CH-9100 Herisan 1 Tel: (071) 513131 Telex: 77147
Man Dir: P Schläpfer
Branch Off: Schläpfer & Co AG, CH-9043 Trogen
Subjects: Books on the Home
1978: 3 titles *Founded:* 1974

Verlag fur **Schöne Wissenschaften** (Belles Lettres Publishing Co — Albert Steffen Foundation), Unterer Zielweg 36, CH-4143 Dornach
Subjects: Poetry, Art, Anthroposophic Literature, Cultural History, Philosophy, Pedagogy, Therapeutics, Literary Criticism; specialises in Editions of the Works of the Swiss poet Albert Steffen (1884-1963), covering novels, stories, memoirs, verse, drama, essays, paintings and sketches
Publication: Therapeutische Dichtung (Therapeutic Poetry)
1978: 2 titles *1979:* 5 titles
ISBN Publisher's Prefix: 3-85889

Hermann **Schroedel** Verlag AG, Hardstr 95, CH-4020 Basel Tel: (061) 423330
Associate Company: Hermann Schroedel Verlag KG, Federal Republic of Germany (qv)
Subjects: Artistic Picture Books for Nursery Children and Adults, Bibliophile Volumes, Facsimiles and Graphics
ISBN Publisher's Prefix: 3-285

Schubiger Verlag AG*, Mattenbachstrasse 2, CH-8400 Winterthur Tel: (052) 297221
Man Dir: E R Benz; *Sales, Publicity:* A Jaermann; *Production:* A Keller
Subject: Educational

F **Schuler***, CH-7002 Chur, Postplatz Tel: (081) 221160
Bookshop: As above
ISBN Publisher's Prefix: 3-85894

Schulthess Polygraphischer Verlag AG, Zwingliplatz 2, CH-8022 Zurich Tel: (0!) 349336 Telex: 56736 Cable Add: Buchschulthess
Man Dir, Advertising, Permissions: Dr Charlotte Mark-Hürlimann; *Sales Dir:* Bruno Waldburger
Subjects: Law, Commerce, Social Science, University Textbooks, Schoolbooks, Law Periodical
1978: 73 titles *Founded:* 1791
ISBN Publisher's Prefix: 3-7255

Schwabe & Co AG, Steinentorstr 13, Postfach 190, CH-4000 Basle 10 Tel: (061) 235523 Cable Add: Schwabeco Basel
Man Dir: Dr Christian Overstolz, Hans Reimann, Josef A Niederberger, Marc Götz
Subjects: History, Art, Philosophy, Medicine, Psychology, University and Secondary Textbooks
1978: 20 titles *Founded:* 1494
ISBN Publisher's Prefix: 3-7965

Schweiz Verlag Arbeitsgemeinschaft für die Bergbevölkerung (SAB)*, CH-5200 Brugg, Laur-Str 10, Postfach 174

Aare-Verlag/**Schweizer Jugend**-Verlag*, Kapuzinerstr 6, CH-4502 Solothurn Tel: (065) 229458
Publishing Manager: Felix Furrer
Subsidiary Company: Eulen-Verlag, Postfach 1164, D-7000 Stuttgart 1, Federal Republic of Germany
Subjects: Reference, Juveniles, Primary Textbooks, Educational Materials
Miscellaneous: Aare-Verlag and Schweizer Jugend-Verlag are divisions of the one company, and are under the same management
ISBN Publisher's Prefix: 3-7260

Schweizer Spiegel Verlag AG & Rodana Verlag, Rämistr 18, Postfach 5837, CH-8024 Zurich 1 Tel: (01) 472195
Dir: Dr P Huggler
Subjects: Belles Lettres, Poetry, Music, Art, Philosophy, Juveniles, Psychology, Social Science
Founded: 1925
ISBN Publisher's Prefixes: 3-85900 (Schweizer Spiegel), 3-85863 (Rodana)

Schweizer Verlagshaus AG, CH-8008 Zurich, Klausstr 10 Tel: (01) 2519134 Cable Add: svzuerich Telex: 53514
Dirs: Dr Armin Meyer, Walter Meyer;
Editorial, Rights & Permissions: Dr A Meyer
Subjects: General Fiction, Biography, Art, Music, How-to, History, Travel, Juveniles, General Science, Textbooks, Medicine, Entertainment, Reference etc
1978: 19 titles *Founded:* 1907
ISBN Publisher's Prefix: 3-7263

Schweizerische Stiftung für Alpine Forschungen, Binzstr 17, CH-8045 Zurich Tel: (01) 660147
Swiss Foundation for Alpine Research
Subjects: Alpine Research Publications

Schweizerische Zentralstelle für Stahlbau*, CH-8034 Zurich, Seefeldstr 25 Tel: (01) 478980
Man Dir: Urs Wyss
1979: 6 titles

Verlag der **Schweizerischen Schallplattenmission**, member of the Telos group (qv in Federal Republic of Germany), publishing evangelical paperbacks

Schweizerisches Jugendschriftenwerk, CH-8008 Zürich, Seehofstr 15, Postfach 8022 Tel: (01) 2517244
Subjects: Literature for Juveniles in the four Swiss languages — German, French, Italian and Romantsch
Founded: 1931
ISBN Publisher's Prefix: 3-7269

Verlag **Schweizerisches katholisches Bibelwerk***, Institut Biblique de l'Université, CH-1700 Freiburg Tel: (037) 219385
Subjects: Religious Literature (Roman Catholic) on biblical subjects
Miscellaneous: Company is a member of AMB (qv under Federal Republic of Germany)

Schweizerisches Ost-Institut, see Verlag SOI

Schwengeler-Verlag, Rosenberg, CH-9442 Berneck Tel: (071) 725666 and (071) 721232
Subjects: Christian Literature
Founded: 1969
Miscellaneous: Member of the Telos group (qv in German Federal Republic), publishing evangelical paperbacks
ISBN Publisher's Prefix: 3-85666

SWITZERLAND 349

Schwitter Edition GmbH, Allschwilerstr 90, Postfach 312, CH-4000 Basle 9
Tel: 061381230 Telex: 62934
Subjects: Art Books, Calendars, Art Reproductions, Facsimiles

F P **Schwitter** Holding Inc, PO Box 636, CH-8065 Zurich Tel: (01) 8101166 Telex: 58178 swint (Publishing Division located at: Talackerstr 9, Glattbrugg)
Editorial offices: Tel (057) 52555
Man Dir: Fridolin Schwitter; *Editorial Dir:* Norma Schwitter
Subjects: Reference Works and Encyclopedias, Science and Technology, Medicine, Countries and Peoples, Natural History, Art, Juveniles
Founded: 1972
ISBN Publisher's Prefix: 3-284

Editions **Scriptar** SA, 23 ave de la Gare, CH-1003 Lausanne Tel: (021) 202351 Cable Add: Orlog Telex: Green 25587
Subjects: Watches and Jewellery, Gemmology; Art productions connected with these interests
1978: 3 titles *Founded:* 1946
ISBN Publisher's Prefix: 2-88012

Edition **Seefeld**, Minervastr 33, CH-8032 Zurich Tel: (01) 2524717
Man Dirs: T P A Flueler, Claudio de Polo
Subjects: Facsimile Reprints of Old MS; Art Books with Original Prints
Bookshop: Galerie Edition Seefeld, at address above
1978: 5 titles *Founded:* 1976

Sinwel-Buchhandlung Verlag*, Lorrainestr 10, CH-3000 Bern 22
Subjects: Belles Lettres, Current Affairs
1978: 6 titles
ISBN Publisher's Prefix: 3-85911

Editions D'Art Albert **Skira** SA, 89 route de Chêne, CH-1208 Geneva Tel: (022) 495533 Cable Add: Edart Geneva
Man Dir, Editorial: Mrs R Skira; *Sales, Production, Publicity:* J Skira
Parent Company: Flammarion et Cie, France (qv)
Subjects: Art, Art History, Art Reference, Low- & High-priced Paperbacks, Educational Materials
1978: 7 titles *1979:* 8 titles *Founded:* 1928
ISBN Publisher's Prefix: 2-605

Slatkine Reprints*, 5 rue des Chaudronniers, CH-1211 Geneva 3 Tel: (022) 200476/762551

Scherz Taschenbuch Verlag **Spectrum**, see Scherz Verlag AG

Speer-Verlag, R Römer, CH-8044 Zurich, Hofstr 134 Tel: (01) 2511203 Cable Add: Sperverlag
Man Dir: R Römer
Subjects: General Fiction, Belles Lettres, Philosophy, Juveniles, Poetry
Founded: 1944
ISBN Publisher's Prefix: 3-85916

Spes SA, BP 20, CH-1800 Vevey (Located at: 2 rue du Château) Tel: (021) 510527 Telex: 451165 dlta
Man Dir: René F Galimont; *Publisher:* André Delcourt
Associate Company: Editions Delachaux et Niestlé SA (qv)
Subjects: Scientific and Technical textbooks, Primary and Secondary textbooks, Mathematics, Physics, Chemistry, Mechanics, Automobile, Electronic technology, Civil Engineering, Horticulture
Founded: 1917
ISBN Publisher's Prefix: 2-602
Miscellaneous: Firm is part of Educagroep, a member of the Kluwer Group, Netherlands (qv)

Sphinx Verlag, Spalenberg 37, CH-4003 Basle Tel: (061) 258583
Dir: D A Hagenbach
Orders to: Neue Bücher AG, Zürich
Subjects: Fantasy, Magic, Philosophy, Religion, Art, Picture Books, General Fiction
Bookshops: Sphinx, D A Hagenbach, Nadelberg 47 and Spalenberg 38, CH-4051 Basle Tel: 259292
1978: 6 titles *Founded:* 1975
ISBN Publisher's Prefix: 3-85914

Sport Verlags AG*, Zweierstrasse 138, 8003 Zürich Tel: (01) 355683
Dirs: J Stemmie, Max Frey, H Brunner, G Furrer
Subject: Sport
ISBN Publisher's Prefix: 3-85917

Verlag **Stämpfli** & Cie AG, Haller-Str 7-9, Postfach 2728, CH-3001 Berne Tel: (031) 232323 Cable Add: Buchstaempfli Bern Telex: 32950
Man Dir, Rights & Permissions: Dr Jakob Stämpfli; *Sales & Advertising Dir:* K Zeller
Subjects: Jurisprudence, Political Science, Economics, History, Social Science, University Textbooks, Swiss Law
1978: 30 titles *1979:* 38 titles *Founded:* 1799
ISBN Publisher's Prefix: 3-7272

Rudolf **Steiner** Verlag, Haus Duldeck, Postfach 135, CH-4143 Dornach Tel: (061) 722240
Man Dir, Editorial, Sales: Benedikt Marzahn; *Publicity:* Peter J-Möller; *Production:* B Marzahn, C Frigori; *Rights & Permissions:* Administrators of the Rudolf Steiner Literary Estate
Subjects: All branches of the Arts and Sciences in the context of anthroposophical (Rudolf Steiner) world conception
Bookshops: Duldeck, CH-4143 Dornach
1978: 30 titles *Founded:* 1956
ISBN Publisher's Prefix: 3-7274

Josef **Stocker** AG*, CH-6002 Lucerne, Kapellgasse 5 Tel: (041) 224948
Subjects: Fiction, Law, Politics, Philosophy, Religion
Bookshop: As above
ISBN Publisher's Prefix: 3-85922

Verlag **Stocker**-Schmid AG*, CH-8953 Dietikon-Zurich, Hasenbergstr 7 Postfach 66 Tel: (01) 7404444
Man Dir: Mr Stocker
Subsidiary Companies: Verlag Bibliophile Drucke von Josef Stocker AG, Dietikon (qv); Urs Graf-Verlag GmbH (qv)
Bookshop: Buchhandlung Stocker-Schmid, CH-8953 Dietikon, Hasenbergstr 7
Subjects: Modern and Historical Weapons and Equipment of the Swiss Army, subjects of Swiss Interest, especially Bibliophile Editions, Facsimiles of Incunabula, Old Maps, MSS
ISBN Publisher's Prefix: 3-7276

Strom-Verlag*, E Kobelt-Schultze, Staffelhof 21, CH-8055 Zurich 3 Tel: (01) 357415
Man Dir: Ernst Kobelt
Subjects: General Fiction, Art, Philosophy, High-priced Paperbacks, Psychology, Social Science, Poetry
ISBN Publisher's Prefix: 3-85921

Sumus Verlag Jutta Gütermann, Höschstr 19, Postfach 2, CH-8706 Feldmeilen Tel: (01) 9230259 Cable Add: Sumus
Editorial: Jutta Gütermann
Subject: Belles Lettres in Large Print, Swiss Literature
Titles: 1 per year *Founded:* 1976
ISBN Publisher's Prefix: 385926

Swedenborg Institut, c/o Dr P Stamm, Lautengartenstr 12, CH-4052 Basle
President: Björn Holmström (resident at PO Box 99 MC, Principality of Monaco)
Subject: Religion
Founded: 1952
ISBN Publisher's Prefix: 3-85925

T V F, an imprint of Trachsel Verlag (qv)

Tages-Nachrichten*, 3110 Münsingen
Founded: 1884
Subjects: Belles Lettres, Juveniles

Theologischer Verlag AG, Postfach, CH-8026 Zurich
Dir, Editorial: Werner Blum; *Rights & Permissions:* R von Siebenthal; *Sales:* C Salden; *Publicity:* E Gutmann
Consignment Add: Brauerstr 60, CH-8004 Zurich Tel: (01) 2413938
Orders to: Auwiesenstr 1, Postfach CH-8406 Winterthür
Subjects: Religion; Theology, emphasising Scriptural Knowledge and Reformation History; Works of Barth and Brunner; Popular Religious Works
Bookshops: Nova Buchhandlung — Sihlstr 33, Zurich; Nansenstr 4, Zurich; Freiestr 5, Uster; Bahnhofstr 12, Wetzikon
1978: 14 titles *Founded:* 1934
ISBN Publisher's Prefix: 3-290

Theseus Verlag AG, Freudwilerweg 7, CH-8044 Zürich
Subject: Eastern Religions

Thomas-Verlag*, CH-8000 Zurich, Rennweg 14
Subjects: Belles Lettres, Religion
ISBN Publisher's Prefix: 3-85938

Verlags und Versandbuchhandlung **Thun** AG, subsidiary of Ott Verlag AG Thun (qv)

Tipografia Stazionne SA, see under Edizioni Armando Dado

Edizioni Giulio **Topi***, CH-6900 Lugano, Cso Elvezia 9

Editions **Townson**, Townson Publishing Co Ltd, PO Box 859, CH-1211 Geneva 3
Branch Off: PO Box 1414, Gibsons, BC VON 1VO, Canada
Subjects: Books in French and English languages
ISBN Publisher's Prefix: 0-920822

Trachsel Verlag, CH-3714 Frutigen Tel: (033) 711407
Man Dir: Ernst Trachsel-Pauli; *Editorial, Production, Rights & Permissions, Sales, Publicity:* Ernst Trachsel
Imprints: TVF, Trachsel Verlag
Subjects: Christian Religious
Bookshop: At CH-3714 Frutigen
1978: 4 titles *1979:* 8 titles *Founded:* 1946
ISBN Publisher's Prefix: 3-7271

Tradexim SA*, 10 rue du Prince, CH-1204 Geneva Tel: (022) 213444 Telex: 23947 Dexim ch

Trans Tech Publications SA, CH-4711 Aedermannsdorf Tel: (062) 741379
Subjects: Materials Science, Physics, Technology for Heavy Industry, Mining Engineering, Geology

Edizioni **Trelingue**, Luigi Rusconi, CH-6948 Porza-Lugano
Subjects: Philosophy, Geography, Economics, Law

Tribune Editions, PO Box 434, CH-1211 Geneva 11 Tel: (022) 212121 Telex: 23381 trib ch
Man Dir, Rights & Permissions: Drago Arsenijevic; *Literary Dir:* Jean Vuilleumier; *Sales:* Christiane Lançon
Parent Company: La Tribune de Genève SA

350 SWITZERLAND

Subjects: Current Affairs, History, Documentaries, Series on Health, also on Television, Illustrated Books, Juveniles
1978: 16 titles *1979:* 19 titles *Founded:* 1977

Editions du **Tricorne***, 5 route des Jeunes, CH-1211 Geneva 26, PO Box 228 Tel: (022) 431600 Cable Add: Studerprint Geneve Telex: 22406 Press ch
Man Dir: Serge Kaplun
Subjects: Art (Tapestry); Pedagogy (Maths); Poetry, Local Interest
Founded: 1976

Editions des **Trois Collines***, 1 rue de la Cité, BP 470, CH-1211 Geneva Tel: (022) 561309
Dir: François Lachenal
Subjects: Art, Politics, Belles Lettres, Philosophy, Psychology
Founded: 1936

Editions des **Trois Continents**, 3 rue de la Vigie, CP 121, CH-1000 Lausanne 9 Tel: (021) 205631 Cable Add: editasa Telex: 26296 edita ch
Chairman: Ami Guichard; *Man Dir:* Stéphane Hobeika
Subjects: History, Ethnology, Politics, Religion, Philosophy, General and Social Science, Art, Photography, Biography, Guide Books, Facsimile Editions; Co-Editions in all languages (including Mid- and Far-Eastern), especially books on Arab and Moslem world
Founded: 1976
ISBN Publisher's Prefix: 288042

U **Bar** Verlag, see Bar

Union dals Grischs*, CH-7505 Celerina

Union Helvetia Fachbuchverlag, Adligenswilerstr 22, Postfach 1115, CH-6002 Lucerne Tel: (041) 235454
Orders to: Postfach 1115, CH-6002 Lucerne
Subjects: Hotel-keeping and Catering (including Foreign Language Instruction), Gastronomy, Bar-tending
Bookshops: Adligenswilerstr 22, Lucerne; Freigutstr 10, Zurich; 16 ave des Acacias, Lausanne
Miscellaneous: Publishing branch of the Schweizerischer Zentralverband der Hotel- und Restaurant-Angestellten (Swiss Industrial Union of Hotel and Restaurant Employees)

Unionsverlag, Postfach 3348, CH-8048 Zurich Tel: (01) 644886
Man Dir: Josef Wandeler; *Editorial:* Lucien Leitess; *Publicity:* Alex Wick
Subjects: International and Swiss Literature
1978: 2 titles *1979:* 5 titles *Founded:* 1976
ISBN Publisher's Prefix: 3-293

Universitätsverlag, see Editions Universitaires

Uranium Verlag, Postfach 42, CH-6317 Oberwil Tel: (042) 217744 Telex: Topaz 58280
Man Dir, Sales: L Young; *Editorial:* Mrs Young
Branch Off: Atzlbergstr 22, D-6000 Frankfurt-am-Main
Subjects: Children's Books (Picture Story Books and Nonfiction)
1980: 70 titles *Founded:* 1976
ISBN Publisher's Prefix: 294

Urs Graf-Verlag GmbH*, CH-8953 Dietikon, Hasenbergstr 7 Tel: (01) 7404444
Man Dir: Mr Stocker
Parent Company: Verlag Stocker-Schmid AG (qv)
Associate Company: Verlag Bibliophile Drucke Von Josef Stocker AG (qv)
Subjects: University Textbooks, Facsimile Editions of Old Maps and MSS
ISBN Publisher's Prefix: 3-85951

Verband schweizerischer Schreinermeister und Möbelfabrikanten Verlag und Fachbüchervertrieb, Postfach 134, CH-8044 Zurich (Located at: Schmelzbergstr 56, CH-8044 Zurich) Tel: (01) 473540 Cable Add: VSSM
General Secretary and all offices: Dr Josef Kaufmann
Subjects: Specialist Literature for the Joinery Trade
1978: 1 title *1979:* 1 title *Founded:* 1889

Buchverlag der **Verbandsdruckerei**/Editions Imprimerie Fédérative SA Berne*, Maulbeerstr 10, Postfach 2741, CH-3001 Berne Tel: (031) 252911 Cable Add: verbandsdruck bern Telex: 32255
Man Dir: Roland Triet
Parent Company: Verbandsdruckerei AG, Berne
Subjects: Specialist Agricultural Texts, Belles Lettres, Travel, Swiss and Berne Regional Interest, General Nonfiction
Founded: 1919
Miscellaneous: Book publishing branch of Verbandsdruckerei/Imprimerie Fédérative (Printers' Federation)
ISBN Publisher's Prefix: 3-7280

Verkehrshaus der Schweiz*, Lidostr 3-7, CH-6006 Lucerne
Subjects: Transport, Traffic, Communications, Tourism, Planetarium, Cosmorama
ISBN Publisher's Prefix: 3-85954

Verlagsgenossenschaft*, Lessingstr 11, Postf 157 8059 Zürich, CH-8002 Zürich Tel: 367672
Subjects: Socially-orientated Literature on Current Problems, especially connected with Switzerland

Editions du **Verseau**, an imprint of Roth et Sauter SA (qv)

Verlag Alfred F **Vetter**, Schifflande 22, CH-8001 Zürich
ISBN Publisher's Prefix: 3-85956

Viktoria Verlag, CH-3072 Ostermundigen, Obere Zollgasse 69e Tel: (031) 514283
Subjects: Belles Lettres, Books on Berne, Dialect Texts, Humour
ISBN Publisher's Prefix: 3-85958

Vogt-Schild AG Druck & Verlag, CH-4501 Solothurn Tel: (065) 214131 Telex: 349146
Subjects: Vehicles (Utility), Chemistry, Pharmacy, Plastics, Environment, Hospital, Nursing, Horology
Founded: 1906
ISBN Publisher's Prefix: 3-85962

Verlag Die **Waage**, Zurich, Dorfstr 90, CH-8802 Kilchberg, Zurich Tel: (01) 7155569
Publisher and all offices: Felix M Wiesner
Subjects: Old Chinese Fiction and Folktales in their original translations into German; also other Non-fiction and Belles Lettres, Poetry etc from other countries; Paperback series
Founded: 1951
ISBN Publisher's Prefix: 3-85966

Gebrüder **Wagner** & Co Verlag*, CH-4024 Basle, Meyer-str 14
Subject: Textbooks
ISBN Publisher's Prefix: 3-85969

Walter Verlag AG, CH-4600 Olten, Amthausquai 21 Tel: (062) 217621 Cable Add: Walterverlag Olten Telex: 68226
Man Dir: Guido Elber; *Editorial:* Dr F J Metzinger, B Jentzsch, K Baumann; *Sales:* C Götz; *Production:* T Frey; *Publicity:* B Dähnert, R Wolfstäder; *Rights & Permissions:* Niedieck Linder AG
Subsidiary Company: Walter-Verlag GmbH D-7800 Freiburg im Breisgau, Erwinstr 58-60, Federal Republic of Germany

Subjects: Literature, Cultural History, Travel Guides, Psychology, Religion, Picture Books, Children's Fiction
1978: 45 titles *1979:* 40 titles *Founded:* 1916
ISBN Publisher's Prefix: 3-530

Weber SA d'Editions, 13 rue de Monthoux, CP 385, CH-1211 Geneva 2 Tel: (022) 326450/59 Cable Add: Livrart, Geneva
Man Dir: Marcel Weber; *All other offices:* Marcel and Hilde Weber
Subjects: Books on Art and Architecture; Photographic, Bibliophile, Practical Living
Founded: 1951
ISBN Publisher's Prefix: 3-295

v **Wehrenalp** & Co*, Sevogelstr 34, CH-4002 Basel Tel: (061) 421290

Weltrundschau Verlag AG, Obernreuhofstr 1, PO Box 427, CH-6340 Baar Tel: (042) 315431 Telex: 865309 Tel: (091) 27801 Cable Add: Worldreview Telex: 79682
Man Dir: G Braun; *Editorial:* E Gysling; *Rights & Permissions:* Jeunesse Verlagsanstalt, Kirchstr 1, FL-9490 Vaduz, Liechtenstein
Founded: 1962

Verlag **Wepf** & Co, Eisengasse 5, CH-4001 Basle Tel: 256377 Cable Add: Wepfco Basle Telex: 62027
Dir: Robert Wepf
Associate Company: Huthig & Wepf Verlag (qv)
Subsidiary Companies: Wepf GmbH, Obere Schanzstr 18, Postfach 1610, D-7858 Weil am Rhein; Wepf & Co, Booksellers, 13 East 16th St, New York, NY 10003, USA
Subjects: Geology, Mineralogy, Natural Sciences, Helvetica
Bookshops: Eisengasse 5, CH-4000 Basle; Marktgasse 42, CH-4310 Rheinfelden
1978: 2 titles *1979:* 5 titles *Founded:* 1902
ISBN Publisher's Prefix: 3-85977

Werner & Bischoff AG*, CH-4001 Basle, Kanonengasse 32, Postfach Tel: (061) 220690
President & Co-Dir: Karlmartin Werner; *Co-Dir:* Ch Bischoff
Subjects: Fine & Applied Arts, Illustrated Books
Founded: 1862
ISBN Publisher's Prefix: 3-85979

Buchverlag der Druckerei **Wetzikon** AG*, CH-8620 Wetzikon
Subjects: Nature Protection, Belles Lettres
ISBN Publisher's Prefix: 3-85981

Richard Rudolf **Wieland**, Postfach 24, CH-8136 Gattikon Tel: (01) 7201666 Cable Add: rrwieland Zurich
Man Dir: R R Wieland
Imprints: R R Wieland Autor & Selbst Verlag
Subjects: Books by Hans B Wieland: Drawings, Letters, Memoirs etc
Founded: 1977
ISBN Publisher's Prefix: 3-85984

Verlag Alexander **Wild**, Rathausgasse 30, CH-3011 Berne Tel: (031) 224480 Cable Add: Wildbuch
Man Dir/Owner: Alexander Wild
Associate Company: Origo-Verlag (qv)
Subjects: Academic Publications
ISBN Publisher's Prefix: 3-7284

Verlag der **Wolfsbergdrucke**, J E Wolfensberger AG, CH-8059 Zurich, Bederstr 109 Tel: (01) 2012777
Dir: Ulla Wolfensberger
Subjects: Fine & Applied Arts, Illustrated Books, Juveniles
Founded: 1905
ISBN Publisher's Prefix: 3-85987

K J **Wyss** Erben AG, CH-3001 Berne, Effingerstr 17 Tel: (031) 253715
Dir: Christoph Wyss, Markus Traber

Subjects: History, Jurisprudence, Art, Agriculture, Food Science
1978: 5 titles *1979:* 8 titles *Founded:* 1849
ISBN Publisher's Prefix: 3-7285

Genossenschaft **Z-Verlag***, Postfach 6, CH-4020 Basle
Subjects: Problems connected with the Workers' Movement and Politics generally; socio-political literature and current affairs commentary
Miscellaneous: Has common interests with Edition Etcetera (qv) and Lenos Press (qv)

Zbinden Druck und Verlag AG, St Albanvorstadt 16, CH-4006 Basle Tel: (061) 232105
Man Dir: Kurt Krause
Subjects: Belles Lettres, Poetry, Biography, Educational, Anthroposophical Literature
1978: 5 titles *1979:* 8 titles
ISBN Publisher's Prefix: 3-85989

Zodiaque, La Pierre-qui-Vire*, c/o Weber SA d'Éditions, 13 Rue de Monthoux, Postf 385, CH-1211 Geneva 2 Tel: 326450 Cable Add: Livrart
Subjects: Collected Editions (various)

Zollikofer Fachverlag AG*, Fürstenlandstr 122, Postfach 805, CH-9001 St Gallen Tel: (071) 292222 Telex: 77537
Man Dir, Rights & Permissions: Peter Kleiner; *Marketing Dir:* P Kleiner; *Marketing Assistant, Production, Publicity:* Roger Albert
Subjects: Travel Guides, Miscellaneous
1978: 8 titles *Founded:* 1977
ISBN Publisher's Prefix: 3-85993

Zumstein & Cie, Zeughausgasse 24, CH-3001 Berne
Owned by: Hertsch & Co
Subject: Philately (specialist catalogues and texts)
1978: 4 titles *1979:* 3 titles
ISBN Publisher's Prefix: 3-85994

Zwei-Bären Verlag der VDB*, CH-3001 Berne, Maulbeerstr 10, Postfach 2741
Man Dir: Hans Erpf
Parent Company: Buchverlag der Verbandsdruckerei (qv)
Subjects: Fiction, Juveniles, Mass Media

Adolf **Zwimpfer**, CH-8954 Geroldswil ZH
Associate Companies: Bayerische Verlagsanstalt Bamberg (BVB), Sankt Otto Verlag GmbH, both Federal Republic of Germany (qqv); Morawa und Co, Austria (qv)

Zytglogge Verlag, Eigerweg 20, Postfach 118, CH-3073 Gümligen Tel: (031) 522030
Programme Dir: Beat Brechbühl; *Sales Dir:* Rolf Attenhofer; *Reader:* Willi Schmid; *Publicity:* Thomas Baer
Subjects: Belles Lettres, Pedagogy, Theatre, Art
1978: 15 titles *1979:* 17 titles *Founded:* 1964
ISBN Publisher's Prefix: 3-7296

Literary Agents

Boxerbooks Inc, Limmatstr 111, POB 157, CH-8031, Zürich Tel: 440733 Cable Add: Boxerbooks Zurich Telex: 53815
Representatives of British, American and Japanese publishing companies

Gesellschaft für **Verlagswerte** GmbH, CH-8280 Kreuzlingen, Hafenstr 38

Dr Ruth **Liepman**, CH-8044 Zurich, Maienburgweg 23 Tel: (01) 477660 Cable Add: Litagent Telex: Litag 56739

Linder AG Literary Agency, Postfach, CH-8032 Zurich (Located at: Jupiterstr 1, CH-8032 Zurich) Tel: (01) 534140 Cable Add: Linderag Zürich Telex: 55123 Linag
Man Dirs: Paul Fritz, Peter S Fritz
Founded: 1962
Specialization: Representation of American and English authors/agents/publishers in German-language areas

Litpress, Rudolf Streit & Co, Amtshausgässchen 3, CH-3011 Berne Tel: (031) 226831
Associated with the Scherz Verlag Publishing Co (qv)

Mohrbooks Literary Agency*, CH-8030 Zurich, Klosbachstr 110 Tel: (01) 321610
Contact: Rainer Heumann

Neue Presse Agentur (NPA), Haldenstr 5, Haus am Herterberg, CH-8500 Frauenfeld-Herten Tel: (054) 74374
Contact: René Marti
Specialization: Edits Women's Interest and Education Interest Correspondence; markets fiction, features, exclusive articles

Niedieck Linder AG*, Holzgasse 6, CH-8039 Zurich Tel: (01) 2021450 Cable Add: Linderag Zürich Telex: 55123 Linag ch
General Manager: Gerda Niedieck
Founded: 1975
Specialization: Representation of German language authors on a world-wide basis

rabe verlag zürich*, Oberdorf str 23, CH-8001 Zürich Tel: (01) 478540

Book Clubs

Europaring der Buch- & Schallplattenfreunde*, Worblentalstr 33, 3063 Papiermühle-Bern

Ex Libris*, Hermetschlossstrasse 77, CH-8048 Zürich

Büchergilde **Gutenberg***, Kasernenstr 25, CH-8004 Zürich
Owned by: Büchergilde Gutenberg (Frankfurt am Main, Federal Republic of Germany)

Edition **Kunstkreis** im Ex Libris Verlag, Postfach, CH-8023 Zurich
Subject: Art

Club **Mon Village** SA, CH-1099 Vulliens, Vaud
Owned by: Editions Mon Village SA (qv)
Subjects: Novels on rural life

Neue Schweizer Bibliothek*, Schweizer Verlagshaus AG, Klausstr 10, CH-8008 Zürich

Punktum, CH-8617 Mönchaltorf Tel: (01) 93513135
Owned by: Nord-Süd Verlag (Mönchaltorf)
This club deals exclusively with children's books, intended as gifts

Schweizer Volksbuchgemeinde AG*, Habsburgerstr 44, CH-6003 Lucerne

Major Booksellers

Athena-Verlag AG*, Langmattweg 36, CH-4123 Allschwil 3 Tel: (061) 380343
Wholesaler

Librairie **Barblan et Saladin***, 10 Rue de Romont, CH-1701 Fribourg
See also entry under Publishers

Buchhandlung zum **Elsässer** AG, Postfach, CH-8022 Zurich (Located at: Limmatquai 18, CH-8001 Zurich) Tel: (01) 470847 Telex: 57268

Fehr'sche Buchhandlung AG*, CH-9001 St Gallen, Schmiedgasse 16 Tel: (071) 221152

Film buchhandlung Hans Rohr*, Oberdorfstr 3, CH-8024 Zurich Tel: (01) 2513636

Buchhandlung A **Francke** AG, Neuengasse 43, Von Werdt-Passage, CH-3001 Berne Tel: (031) 221715 Cable Add: Frankebuch Bern Telex: 32326
Manager: Christian Lang

Georg et Cie SA, Librairie de l'Université, 5 rue de la Corraterie, CH-1211 Geneva 11 Tel: (022) 216633

Hans **Huber***, Zeltweg 6, CH-8032 Zurich Tel: (01) 343426/343360
Specializes in books on Medicine and Psychology

Buchhandlung **Jäggi** AG, CH-4001 Basle, Freiestr 32 Tel: (061) 255200

Leobuchhandlung*, Gallusstr 20, CH-9001 St Gallen Tel: 222917

Buchhandlung **Meili** & Co, Fronwagpl 13, CH-8200 Schaffhausen Telex: 76777 meibu ch
Owned by: Peter Meili & Co, Publisher (qv)
International Bookseller and Publisher

Orell Füssli, Pelikanstr 10, CH-8022 Zurich 1 Tel: (01) 2118011

Librairie **Payot** SA, 1 rue de Bourg, CH-1003 Lausanne Tel: (021) 203331 Telex: 24961 (See entry for Librairie Payot under Publishers for other addresses)
Wholesale Supplier: Diffusion Payot SA, 30 rue des Côtes de Montbenon, CH-1003 Lausanne Tel: (021) 205221 Telex: 24953

Buchhandlung Hans **Rohr***, Oberdorfstr 5, CH-8024 Zurich Tel: (01) 25136 36 Telex: 56385

Dr A **Scheidegger***, Kaltackerstr 32, Postfach 4, CH-8908 Hedingen Tel: (01) 995234/993188
Wholesaler

Buchhandlung **Scherz** AG, CH-3000 Berne, Marktgasse 25 Tel: (031) 226837

Buchhandlung Kurt **Stäheli** & Co, Bahnhofstr 70, CH-8021 Zurich Tel: (01) 2117362 Telex: 813771

Theologischer Verlag (wholesaler)*, Auwiesenstr 1, Postfach, CH-8406 Winterthur Tel: (052) 221138

Buchhandlung W **Vogel***, CH-8400 Winterthur, Marktgasse 41-43 Tel: (052) 226588 Telex: 74622 vogel ch

Wepf & Co Buchhandlung und Antiquariat, Eisengasse 5, Postfach, CH-4000 Basle Tel: (061) 256377 Cable Add: Wepfco Basel Telex: 62027
Dir: H U Herrmann
Owned by: Verlag Wepf & Co (qv)

Major Libraries

Archives fédérales, 24 rue des Archives, CH-3003 Berne Tel: (031) 618989
Swiss Federal Archives

Bibliothèque cantonale et universitaire (Kantons- und Universitätsbibliothek)*, 16 rue St-Michel, CH-1701 Fribourg

Bibliothèque cantonale et universitaire de Lausanne, 6 Pl de la Riponne, CH-1005 Lausanne Tel: (021) 228831 Telex: 24014 lauc-ch

Bibliothèque de la Ville, 3 Place Numa-Droz, CH-2000 Neuchâtel Tel: (038) 251358
Librarian: Jacques Rychner
Publications: Ville de Neuchâtel: Bibliothèques et Musées (annual); *Bulletin de la Société neuchâteloise des sciences*

naturelles (annual); *Memoires de la Société neuchâteloise des sciences naturelles* (irregular); *Bulletin de la Société neuchâteloise de géographie*

Bibliothèque Nationale Suisse*, CH-303 Berne Tel: (031) 618911 Telex: 32526 slbbe ch

Bibliothèque publique et universitaire de Genève, Promenade des Bastions, CH-1211 Geneva 4 Tel: (022) 208266
Director: Paul Chaix
Publication: Compte rendu (annual)

Fondation Martin **Bodmer**, Bibliotheca Bodmeriana, BP 7, CH-1223 Cologny/Geneva Tel: (022) 362370
Dir: Dr Hans E Braun

Bureau International du Travail, see International Labour Office Library

E T H Bibliothek (Eidgenossische Technische Hochschule Bibliothek)*, Rämistr 101, CH-8092 Zürich Tel: (01) 326211 Telex: 53178 (ethbich)
Library of the Swiss Federal Institute of Technology

International Labour Office Library (ILO)*, 4 rte des Morillons, CH-1211 Geneva 22
Librarian: Geo K Thompson
Publication: International Labour Documentation (bi-monthly)

Schweizerische Landesbibliothek (Bibliothèque nationale suisse), CH-3003 Berne, Hallwylstr 15 Tel: Secretary (031) 618921; Lending Department (031) 618931
Swiss National Library

Schweizerisches Wirtschaftsarchiv (Archives économiques suisses), Kollegienhaus der Universität, Basel, Petersgraben
Swiss Economic Archives
Founded: 1910

Stadt- und Universitätsbibliothek, CH-3000 Berne 7, Münstergasse 61

Stiftsbibliothek*, CH-9000 St Gallen, Klosterhof 6 Tel: (071) 225719 (library of former Benedictine abbey of St Gall)

United Nations Library*, Palais des Nations, Geneva

Öffentliche Bibliothek der **Universität Basel***, CH-4056 Basel, Schönbeinstr 18-20 Tel: (061) 252250

Zentralbibliothek Zürich, Kantons- Stadt- und Universitätsbibliothek, CH-8025 Zurich, Zähringerplatz 6, Postfach Tel: (01) 477272 Telex: 54669 zbzh ch
Librarian: Hans Baer

Library Associations

Association des Bibliothécaires Suisses (Vereinigung Schweizerischer Bibliothekare), Bibliothèque nationale suisse, Hallwylstr 15, CH-3003 Berne Tel: (031) 618911
Association of Swiss Librarians
Secretary: W Treichler
Publication: Nouvelles (jointly with Swiss Association for Documentation) (6 times a year)

Association suisse des Bibliothèques d'Hôpitaux*, c/o Mme J Schmid-Schädelin, Executive Director, Hirschengraben 22, CH-8001 Zurich
Association of Swiss Hospital Libraries

Kantonale Kommission für Jugend- und Volksbibliotheken, Zurich, Postfach 474, CH-8610 Uster Tel: (01) 9413725
Cantonal Commission for Juvenile and Public Libraries
President: Prof Dr Egon Wilhelm

Publications: Numerous handbooks, catalogues etc relating to library procedures and practice

Vereinigung Schweizerischer Archivare (Association of Swiss Archivists), Bundesarchiv, Archivstr 24, CH-3003 Berne Tel: (031) 618988
Secretary: Dr Christoph Graf
Publication: Mitteilungen (News Sheet)
Founded: 1922

Library Journals

Mitteilungen (News), Association of Swiss Archivists, Bundesarchiv, Archivstr 24, CH-3003 Berne

Nouvelles (News), Association of Swiss Librarians, Swiss National Library, CH-3003 Berne (jointly with Swiss Association for Documentation)

Literary Associations and Societies

Gesellschaft für deutsche Sprache und Literatur in Zürich, Deutsches Seminar der Universität Zürich, Postfach 147, CH-8028 Zürich
Society for German Language and Literature in Zurich
Secretary: J Etzensperger

P E N Club de Suisse romande, 4 rue Mont de Sion, CH-1206 Geneva
Secretary: Juliette Monnin-Hornung

P E N Club di Italian Romansch*, Via Signore in Croce 12, CH-6612 Ascona
Secretary: Maddalena Kerenyi

Schweizerische Bibliophilen-Gesellschaft*, c/o Herrn K Kahl, Wolfbachstr 17, CH-8032 Zurich
Swiss Society of Bibliophiles
President: Dr Conrad Ulrich
Publications: Stultifera Navis, published 1944–1957; *Librarium,* published 3 times a year since 1958

Literary Periodicals

Cenobio (text in French and Italian), Dr Pier-Riccardo Frigeri, CP 6655, CH-6901 Lugano

drehpunkt, CH-4002 Basel, Postfach 794

Ecriture (Writing), Editions Bertil Galland, 29 rue du Lac, CH-1800 Vevey

Etudes de Lettres (Literary Studies), Université de Lausanne, Faculté des Lettres, Lausanne

Niemo Press; topical press and literature references with commentary (text in German), Emil Rahm, CH-8215 Hallau

Revue de Belles-Lettres (Review of Belles Lettres) (text in French), Société de Belles-Lettres de Lausanne, 4 Plainpalais, BP 216, CH-1211 Geneva

Schweizer Monatshefte (Swiss Monthly Magazine), Gesellschaft Schweizer Monatshefte, CH-8034 Zurich, Postfach 86

Syria

General Information

Language: Arabic. French and English are widely spoken in business and official circles
Religion: Sunni Muslim
Population: 8 million
Literacy Rate (1970): 40%
Bank Hours: 0800-1400 Saturday-Thursday
Shop Hours: Vary greatly. Closed Friday. Generally long lunch closing
Currency: 100 piastre = 1 Syrian Pound
Export/Import Information: No tariffs on books except children's picture books 15%, with additional taxes of 26.80%; most advertising matter dutied at 15%. State organization for control and execution of publicity and advertising within Syria is Arab Advertising Organization, Damascus. The General Advertising Institute, PO Box 2842, must get samples of commercial advertising and promotional materials before distribution permitted. Import licence must be submitted to Commercial Bank of Syria in order to obtain exchange licence
Copyright: No copyright conventions signed

Publishers

Arab Advertising Organization*, 28 Moutanabbi St, PO Box 2842 & 3034, Damascus Tel: 225219/225220/1 Cable Add: Arador Damascus Telex: Arador 77923 SY
Dir-General: George Khoury; *Publicity:* Haitham Basheer
Imprint: Arador
Branch Off: Aleppo, Hama, Homs, Lattakia
Subject: Directories
Founded: 1963

Arador, an imprint of Arab Advertising Organization (qv)

Bureau des Documentations Syriennes et Arabes, an associated imprint of Office Arabe de Presse et de Documentation (qv)

Damascus University Press*, Damascus
Subjects: Education, History, Geography, Engineering, Medicine, Law, Sociology, School Textbooks

Office Arabe de Presse et de Documentation, 67 pl Chahbandar, PO Box 3550, Damascus Tel: 559166/559892
President: Samir A Darwich
Subjects: Periodical and non-periodical publications about Economics, Politics, Syria and the Arab World
Founded: 1964
Miscellaneous: Associated imprints include Bureau des Documentations Syriennes et Arabes, PO Box 3550, Damascus

Syrian Documentation Papers*, PO Box 2712, Damascus
Dir-General: Louis Farés
Subjects: Reference, Directories, Politics, Economics, Sociology, Law
Founded: 1968

al-**Tawjih** Press*, Palestine St, PO Box 3320, Damascus
Subject: Literature

Major Booksellers

Dar **Dimashk** (Adib Tunbakji) Bookshop*, Port Said St Tel: 111048

Dummar & Mowakadeh & Co*, Tajhiz St, PO Box 2456 Tel: 112911

Dar Al-**Fikr** (Salem & Zu'bi) Bookshop*, Saadallah Al-Jabiri St, PO Box 962 Tel: 111041

Kutubi Moh'd Nihad Hashem*, Souk Al-Asrounieh Tel: 110512

Dakr Abdul **Wahab***, Port Said St Tel: 115486

Major Libraries

Damascus University Library*, Damascus

Dar al-Kutub al-Wataniah (National Library)*, Homs

Al **Maktabah** Al Wataniah (National Library)*, Bab El-Faradj, Aleppo

National Library of Latakia*, Latakia

Al **Zahiriah** (National Library)*, Bab el Barid, Damascus

Library Journals

Damascus University Library Review, Damascus University Library, Damascus

Literary Periodicals

Al-Mawgif Al-Adabi, Ittihad al-Kuttab al-Arab, Shari Murshid Khatir, Damascus

Tanzania

General Information

Language: Swahili is official language. English is widely used
Religion: About 30% Muslim, 25% Christian (mostly Roman Catholic); rest follow traditional beliefs
Population: 16.6 million
Bank Hours: Mainland Tanzania: 0900-1200 Monday-Friday; 0900-1100 Saturday. Zanzibar: 0830-1130 Monday-Friday; 0830-1000 Saturday
Shop Hours: 0800-1200, 1400-1715 or 1800 Monday-Saturday
Currency: 100 cents = 1 Tanzania shilling
Export/Import Information: No tariff on books or advertising matter. Import licence and exchange controls
Copyright: Florence (see International section)

Book Trade Reference Journals

Government and Tanu Publications List, Government Publications Agency, PO Box 1801, Dar es Salaam

Tanzania National Bibliography, Tanzania Library Service, PO Box 9283, Dar es Salaam (the national bibliography, published annually since 1969)

Publishers

Central Tanganyika Press, PO Box 15, Dodoma
Manager: Alexander Chibehe
Subject: Religion
1978: 2 titles *1979:* 11 titles *Founded:* 1954

Dar es Salaam University*, PO Box 35091, Dar es Salaam Tel: 53611 Cable Add: University Dar es Salaam
University Publications Officer: Z K Rigby
Subjects: History, Africana, Reference, Religion, Medicine, Psychology, Science & Technology, Social Science, University Textbooks
1978-79: 90 titles

East African Literature Bureau*, PO Box 1408, Dar es Salaam
(see under Kenya for full information)

Government Printer*, Government Publications Agency, PO Box 1801, Dar es Salaam

Inland Publishers, Africa Inland Church Literature Department, PO Box 125, Mwanza Tel: 40064
Dir: S M Magesa
Subjects: General Nonfiction, Religion, Books in Kiswahili, Paperbacks

Longman Tanzania Ltd, Independence Ave, PO Box 3164, Dar es Salaam Tel: 29748 Cable Add: Longman Dar es Salaam
Man Dir: A B Moshi
Associate Company: Longman Group Ltd, UK (qv)
Subjects: General Nonfiction, Belles Lettres, Poetry, Biography, History, Africana, Juveniles, Books in Kiswahili, General Science, Secondary & Primary Textbooks, Science & Technology
Founded: 1965

Ndanda Mission Press*, Ndanda PO Box 1004, Ndanda via Lindi
Subject: Religion
1978: 7 titles

Oxford University Press, Maktaba Rd, PO Box 5299, Dar es Salaam Tel: 29209 Cable Add: Oxionian
Sales: Anthony Theobald
Subjects: General Nonfiction, Literature, Poetry, Biography, History, Africana, Reference, Books in Kiswahili, General & Social Science, Secondary & Primary Textbooks
Founded: 1969
Miscellaneous: Firm is a branch of Oxford University Press, Eastern Africa, Nairobi, Kenya (qv)

T M P Book Department*, PO Box 550, Tabora
Subject: Religion

Tanzania Library Service, PO Box 9283, Dar es Salaam Tel: 26121
Parent Company: The Ministry of National Education, Dar es Salaam
Associate Company: Transafrica (1976)
Founded: 1963

Tanzania Mission Press, see T M P Book Department

Tanzania Publishing House*, 47 Independence Ave, PO Box 2138, Dar es Salaam Tel: 32164 Cable Add: Publish Dar es Salaam
General Manager: Walter Bgoya; *Sales Manager:* S Nkini
Subjects: General Fiction & Nonfiction, Belles Lettres, Poetry, Biography, History, Africana, Philosophy, Juveniles, Paperbacks, Social Science, University & Secondary Textbooks (in Kiswahili and English)
Founded: 1966

Major Booksellers

The **Cathedral** Bookshop*, Mansfield St, PO Box 2381, Dar es Salaam Tel: 22873

The **Dar es Salaam Bookshop**, Makunganya St, PO Box 9030, Dar es Salaam Tel: 23416
Manager: E Charokiwa

Dar es Salaam University Bookshop*, PO Box 35091, Dar es Salaam Tel: 53137

International Bookshop, PO Box 21341, Dar es Salaam Tel: 21930/27458 Cable Add: Safina, Dar es Salaam
Dir: Murtaza Alidina
Wholesale, Distribution: International Publishers Agencies (at above address)
Retail Outlet: International Bookshop (at above address)

The **Standard** Bookshop*, Independence Ave, PO Box 9402, Dar es Salaam Tel: 23126

T M P Book Department*, PO Box 550, Tabora

Tanzania Elimu Supplies*, Book Division, IPS Bldg, PO Box 20873, Dar es Salaam

Tanzania Mission Press, see T M P Book Department

Major Libraries

Arusha Public Library*, PO Box 1273, Arusha

British Council Library, Independence Ave, Ohio St, PO Box 9100, Dar es Salaam Tel: 22726

Dar es Salaam Technical College Library*, Morogoro Rd, PO Box 20571, Dar es Salaam Tel: 23231

Faculty of Agriculture, Forestry and Veterinary Science, University of Dar es Salaam, PO Box 704, Morogoro Tel: 2511
Librarian: S S Mbwana
Publications include: Library Accessions List (quarterly)

Faculty of Medicine Library*, University of Dar es Salaam, PO Box 20693, Dar es Salaam Tel: 27081 ext 266

International Communication Agency Library, PO Box 9170, Dar es Salaam Tel: 26611

Kibaha Public Library*, PO Box Kibaha, Kibaha Tel: 258

Marangu College of National Education Library*, PO Box 3080, Moshi Tel: 16 Himo

National Archives of Tanzania*, India St, PO Box 2006, Dar es Salaam Tel: 23954

Tanzania Library Service, PO Box 9283, Dar es Salaam Tel: 26121
Publication: Tanzania National Bibliography

University of Dar es Salaam Library, PO Box 35092, Dar es Salaam Tel: 53162

Zanzibar Government Archives*, PO Box 116, Zanzibar

Library Associations

Tanzania Library Association*, PO Box 2645, Dar es Salaam Tel: 26121
Secretary: T E Mlaki
Publications: Someni (journal); *Matukio* (newsletter)

Tanzania Library Service, PO Box 9283, Dar es Salaam
Publication: Printed in Tanzania, Directory of Libraries in Tanzania

Library Reference Books and Journals

Books

Directory of Libraries in Tanzania, Tanzania Library Service, PO Box 9283, Dar es Salaam (comprehensive annotated listing)

Journals

Matukio, Tanzania Library Association, PO Box 2645, Dar es Salaam

Someni (text in English), Tanzania Library Association, PO Box 2645, Dar es Salaam

Literary Periodicals

Umma, East African Literature Bureau, PO Box 1408, Dar es Salaam (or PO Box 30022, Nairobi, Kenya) (a biannual literary magazine published under the auspices of the Department of Literature, University of Dar es Salaam)

Translation Agencies and Associations

East African Literature Bureau*, PO Box 1408, Dar es Salaam

Thailand

General Information

Language: Thai is official language. English is widely used in government and commercial circles. There are sizeable populations of Chinese, Malay and Khmer speakers
Religion: Theravada Buddhist
Population: 45 million
Literacy Rate (1970): 78.6% (87.7% Urban, 77.1% Rural)
Bank Hours: 0830-1530 Monday-Friday
Shop Hours: Vary. Those catering for tourists generally open 0830-1800 or later
Currency: 100 stangs = 1 baht
Export/Import Information: No tariff on books but 5% Standard Profit Tax and 1.5% Business Tax apply (also a Municipal Tax of 10% of Business Tax). Advertising subject to same taxes and 3% ad val import duty. No import licences for books, but special permit required by importer for orders over 3,000 bahts (approx $150). Certificate of payment (from Exchange Control Authority) required
Copyright: Berne, Florence (see International section)

Book Trade Organizations

Publishers' and Booksellers' Association of Thailand, 25 Sukhumvit Soi 56, Bangkok Tel: 3112447
Secretary: W Tantinirandr
President: M L M Jumsai, Chalermnit Press, 1-2 Erawan Arcade, Bangkok Tel: 528759

Standard Book Numbering Agency, The National Library of Thailand, Samsen Rd, Bangkok 3 Tel: 2815449
ISBN Administrator: Mrs Suwakhon Phadung-Ath

Publishers

Aksorn Charerntat*, 142 Praengsanpasart, Tanao Rd, Bangkok Tel: 214587
Subjects: Textbooks, Industry, Arts, Maps, Literature, Mathematics, Education, Physics, Linguistics

Aksorn Charoen Tasna Ltd*, 195 Bamrung Muang Rd, Bangkok
Subject: Textbooks

Bandarnsarn*, 136-138 Nakorn Sawan Rd, Bangkok Tel: 82551
Subject: Thai books

Banmai*, 1 Soi Prasanmit, Sukhumvit, Bangkok

Barnakarn*, 236 Nakern Kashem, Bangkok Tel: 227796
Subject: Thai books

Barnakieh Trading*, 34 Nakorn Sawan Rd, Bangkok Tel: 825520
Subject: Thai books

Barnasilpa*, 1 Soi Praengsanpasart, Asdang Rd, Bangkok Tel: 220060
Subject: Thai books

Chalermnit Press*, 108 Sukhumvit Soi 53, Bangkok Tel: 2528759
Managers: M L M Jumsai, Mrs Jumsai
Subjects: Books on Thailand, Pocket books and Children's books in English, French & German, Magazines, Dictionaries
Founded: 1957
Bookshop: 1-2 Erawan Arcade, Bangkok

Chiangmai Book Centre*, 2 Kochasam Rd, Suriya Cinema, Chiangmai
Bookshop: Address as above

Office of **Christian** Education and Literature, an imprint of Suriyaban Publishers (qv)

Dhammabucha*, 5/1-2 Asdang Rd, Bangkok Tel: 223549/850010
Subject: Thai books on Buddhism

Duang Kamol*, 244-246 Siam Sq Soi 2, Patumwan, Bangkok Tel: 2516335/6
Subjects: English, French and Thai books

Hor Samut Klang *, 5 Soi Praeng Sanpasart, Asdang Rd, Bangkok Tel: 219751
Subject: Thai books

Klang Vidhya*, 742 Wang Burapa, Bangkok Tel: 224546
Subject: Thai books
Bookshops: 742 Wang Burapa, Bangkok; 3931/26-29 Chumpol Rd, Nakorn Rajsima; 197/2 Srichan Rd, Tambon Wat Mai, Chantaburi

Languages School*, Wat Phra Singha, Chiangmai

Narongsarn*, 647/14 Charernrat Rd, (Big Circle), Dhonburi, Bangkok

Nibondh*, 40-42 New Rd, Bangkok Tel: 212611
Subjects: English and Thai books
Bookshop: 40-42 New Rd, Bangkok; 975/4 Gaysorn Rd, Bangkok

Niyom Vidhya*, 192 Bamrungmuang Rd, Bangkok Tel: 217661
Subject: Thai Technical Textbooks

Norn*, 1/1 Boonsiri, Sukhumvit Rd, Paknam Tel: 90130
Subject: Thai books

Odeon Store LP*, 862 Wang Burapa, Bangkok Tel: 2210742/2216567 Cable Add: Odeonstore
Man Dir: Vichai Praepanich
Branch Off: Siain Sq soi 1, Bangkok
Subjects: Textbooks, Nonfiction, Paperbacks
Founded: 1947

Parnfah Pittaya*, 440-2 Nakornsawan Rd, Bangkok
Subjects: Thai books, Comics

Pikkhanet*, 99 Praeng Sanpasart, Tanao Rd, Bangkok Tel: 222850
Subject: Thai pocket books

Pittayakarn*, 226 Nakorn Kashem, Bangkok Tel: 221501
Subject: Thai books

Pra Cha Chang & Co Ltd*, 816/3 Talad Noi, New Rd, Bangkok
Subject: Academic

Prae Pittaya Ltd*, 716-718 Burapa Palace, PO Box 914, Bangkok Tel: 2214283/221286
Manager: Chitt Praepanich
Subjects: Fiction, Juveniles
Bookshop: as above

Pramuansarn Publishing House*, 703/15-16 Petchaburi Rd, Bangkok
Manager: Lime Taechatada
Subjects: Guidebooks, Popular Sciences, Juveniles
Founded: 1955

Praphansarn Book Centre*, 236/6-7 Beside Lido Theatre, Siam Square Soi 2, Rama 1 Rd, Bangkok Tel: 2512342/3
Man Dir: Suphol Taechatada

Prasarnmitr*, 3382 New Petchaburi Rd, Bangkok Tel: 915387/925230
Subject: Textbooks

Progress*, 882 Wang Burapa, Bangkok Tel: 226541
Subject: Thai books, English occasionally

Religious Revival Organization*, 176 Sukhumvit, Santikam Soi 1, T Samrong North, Samutprakarn

Ruamsarn (1977) Co Ltd*, Part, 864 Burapa Palace, Bangkok 2 Tel: 2216483
Man Dir: Bumrung Tawewatanasarn; *Sales Dir:* Nongyao Tawewatanasarn; *Publicity Dir:* Piya Tawewatanasarn; *Advertising Dir:* Piti Tawewatanasarn
Subsidiary Company: Bumrungsarn Ltd, Part, 864 Burapa Palace, Bangkok 2
Subjects: General Fiction, Belles Lettres, Poetry, Biography, History, How-to, Music, Art, Philosophy, Reference, Religion, Low-priced Paperbacks, General Science, University & Secondary Textbooks
Bookshops: Ruamsarn (1977) Co Ltd, 864 Burapa Palace, Bangkok 2; Dheerasarn Ltd, Part, 326-8 Siam Sq 4, Bangkok 5; Tawesarn, 89/51 Near President Theatre, Bangkok 5
Founded: 1951

Rungvit Sawarn-Apichon*, Chiengmai Book Centre, 2 Kochasarn Rd, opposite Suriya Cinema, Chiengmai

Sangna Vuddhichai Saranonda*, Prabhasarn, 130 Nakornsauran Rd, Bangkok

Sayam Paritat*, 14-6 Nakorn Lane, Taprachand, Maharat Rd, Bangkok Tel: 219108
Subject: Thai books

Sermwit Barnakarn*, 222 Nakorn Kashem, Bangkok Tel: 214541
Subject: Thai books

Siam Directory*, 2 Mansion, 96 Rajdamnern Ave, Bangkok
Subjects: History, Politics, Technical

Sinpattana*, 74 Pra Atit Rd, Bangkok Tel: 824357/816917
Subject: Thai books

Social Science Association Press*, 2 Chula Soi, Phya Thai Rd, Bangkok
Manager & Editor: Sulak Sivaraksa
Subject: Textbooks
Founded: 1961

Sommai Press*, 90-18 Ekkachai Rd, Bangkok Tel: 30037
Subject: Thai books

Suksapan Panich (Business Organization of Teachers' Institute)*, 9 Mansion, Rajdamnern Ave, Bangkok Tel: 816543
Manager: Kamthon Sathirakul
Subjects: Juveniles, Textbooks, Dictionaries
Founded: 1950

Suksit Siam Co Ltd, 1715 Rama IV Rd, Samyan, Bangkok 5 Tel: 511630
Publicity: Mrs Nilchawee Sivaraksa
Subjects: Mainly Thai books on Social Science & Politics
Bookshop: 1715 Rama IV Rd, Bangkok

Suriyaban Publishers, 14 Pramuan Rd, Bangkok Tel: 2347991 Cable Add: CCT Office
Man Dir, Editorial, Publicity, Rights & Permissions: Mrs Bampen Krishnakan;
Sales: Philip Tsang; *Production:* Thanom Pinta
Parent Company: Department of Christian Education and Literature, Church of Christ in Thailand, at above address
Imprint: Office of Christian Education and Literature
Subjects: Religion, Children's Books, Buddhism, Thai Culture
Bookshops: The Christian Bookstore, 14 Pramuan Rd, Bangkok; Suriyaban Bookstore, 124/1 Silom Rd, Bangkok 5; Suriyaban Bookstore, 1 Charoen Muang Rd, Chiang Mai
1978: 20 titles *Founded:* 1953

Sutpaisarn*, 638 Somdet Chaopaya Rd, Bangkok Tel: 664392
Subject: Thai books on Law

Thai Commercial Printing Press*, Bangkok
Subjects: Law, Management

Thai Inc*, 96 Mansion, 2 Rajdamnern Ave, Bangkok
Subjects: Politics, History, Religion

Thai Watana Panich*, 599 Maitrijit Rd, Bangkok Tel: 210111
Subject: School books in Thai (occasionally English)

Tong-In Sunsawat*, Wat Prasing, Chiengmai
Subject: English books

Vadhana Panich*, 216-220 Bumrungmuang Rd, Bangkok
Subject: School Textbooks

Vajarindra*, 364 Sumeru Rd, Bangkok Tel: 816207

Viratham*, 141 St Louis Soi 2, Sathorn Tai Rd, Bangkok Tel: 866848
Subjects: English, French and English-Thai books

Wattana Panich*, 216-220 Bumrungmuang Rd, Bangkok
Subjects: Textbooks, Fiction, Maps

Major Booksellers

Asia Books Co Ltd, 6/1 Soi Childlom, Ploenchit Rd, Bangkok Tel: 2526400/2520064/2516008 Cable Add: Asiabooks Telex: TH81043 Asiabooks
Showroom: 221 Sukhumvit Rd, between Soi 15 and 17, Bangkok Tel: 2527277
Man Dir: Vinai Suttharoj; *General Manager:* Miss Somporn Suttharoj
Also publishers' agent, distributor and retailer of English books

Bangkok Central Book Depot*, Sikak Phya Sri, Bangkok

Central Department Store, 306 Silom Rd, Bangkok Tel: 23369309 Telex: Cetrac TH2768
Manager: Mrs Ratana Norabhanlobh
Largest distributor, wholesaler and retailer of magazines, paperbacks, trade books, textbooks, school books and children's books

Chalermnit Bookshop*, 1-2 Erawan Arcade, Bangkok Tel: 528759
Also importers

Christian Bookstore, 14 Pramuan Rd, Bangkok
Acting Manager: Philip Tsang

Dheerasarn Ltd*, Part, 326-8 Siam Sq, Bangkok 5
Also at: Tawesarn 89/51 Near President Theatre, Bangkok 5

International Book Distributors Co Ltd*, 1035-4 Pleonchit Shopping Centre, Pleonchit Rd, PO Box 5-59, Bangkok

Klang Vidhya*, 742 Wang Burapa, Bangkok
Also at: 3931/26-29 Chumpol Rd, Nakorn Rajsima; 197/2 Srichan Rd, Tambon Wat Mai, Chantaburi

Nibondh (Gaysorn)*, 975/4 Gaysorn Rd, Bangkok
English books at the above address
English, Thai books and magazines at Nibondh (Sikak), 40-42 New Rd, Bangkok

Praepittaya Ltd*, 716-718 Burapa Palace, PO Box 914, Bangkok
Also importers and wholesaler

Pramual Sarn Book Centre Ltd*, Partnership, 678 Chalerm Khetr Bldg, Bangkok

Ruamsarn (1977) Co Ltd*, 864 Burapa Palace, Bangkok 2 Tel: 2216483
Manager: Nongyao Tawewatanasarn

Siam Book House*, 11 Silom Rd, Corner Saladeng, Bangkok

Suksit Siam Co Ltd*, 1715 Rama IV Rd, Samyan, Bangkok 5 Tel: 2511630
Also importers and library suppliers

Suriwongs Book Centre, Suriyong Cinema Arcade, Chiengmai Tel: 236299/235889
Manager: Miss J Jittidecharaks

Suriyaban Bookstore, 124/1 Silom Rd, Bangkok Tel: 2356200
Acting Manager: Philip Tsang

Major Libraries

British Council Library, 428 Rama I Rd, 2 Siam Sq, Bangkok 5 Tel: 2526136

Chulalongkorn University Library, Academic Resource Center, Phya Thai Rd, Bangkok 5
Director: Mrs Knid Tantavirat
Includes Central Library, Thailand Information Center and Audio-Visual Center
Publications: Academic Resources, Union Catalog of Chulalongkorn University Libraries

Department of Science Library*, Rama VI St, Bangkok 4

Main Library, Kasetsart University, Bangkok 9 Tel: 5792539
Librarian: Miss Daruna Somboonkun

National Archives Division*, Fine Arts Department, Samsen Rd, Bangkok 3

The **National Library of Thailand**, Samsen Rd, Bangkok 3 Tel: 2815449/2810263 Telex: 84189
Librarian: Mrs Kullasap Gesmankit

Siriraj Medical Library, Mahidol University, Bangkok 7
Director: Miss Uthai Dhutiyabhodhi

Sri Nakharinwirot University Library*, Sukhumvit 23, Bangkok 11

Thai National Documentation Centre (TNDC)*, 196 Phahonyothin Rd, Bang Khen, Bangkok 9

Thammasat University Library*, Bangkok

United Nations, Economic and Social Commission for Asia and the Pacific Library*, United Nations Bldg, Rajadamnern Ave, Bangkok 2
Librarian: Mrs Zerrin Polite

Library Associations

Thai Library Association*, c/o The National Library of Thailand, Samsen Rd, Bangkok 3 Tel: 2815449
Secretary: N Puakpong
Publication: Bulletin (6 a year)

Library Reference Books and Journals

Books

An Annotated Bibliography of Librarianship in Thailand, Department of Library Science, Chulalongkorn University, Faculty of Arts, Phya Thai Rd, Bangkok 5

List of Scientific Libraries in Thailand, Thai National Documentation Centre, 196 Phahonyothin Rd, Bangkhen, Bangkok 9

Journals

Bulletin. Thai Library Association, Samsen Rd, Bangkok 3

Literary Associations and Societies

P E N International-Thailand Centre*, 56/21-22 Rama I Rd, Bangkok 5
Secretary: K Direk

The **Siam** Society, PO Box 65, Bangkok (Located at: 131 Soi Asoke, Sukhumvit 21, Bangkok) Tel: 3914401
President: HSH Prince Subhadradis Diskul; *Honorary Secretary:* Mrs Nongyao Narumit; *Rights & Permissions:* F W C Martin
Publications: Journal of the Siam Society (twice yearly), *Natural History Bulletin of the Siam Society* (annual)
Miscellaneous: Formerly The Thailand Society. Founded 1904. Under Royal Patronage. For promotion of Thai and South East Asian art, science and literature

Literary Prizes

Bangkok Bank Foundation Prize
For prose or poetry in Thai concerning history, art, culture, religion, social affairs, philosophy or new creative ideas. 50,000 baht each for prose and poetry. Awarded annually. Enquiries to Secretary, Bangkok Bank Foundation, Suapa Rd, PO Box 95, Bangkok

Kennedy Prize*
For promoting understanding of Thailand, the Thai people or Thai culture, using the Thai language. 30,000 baht each for prose and poetry. Awarded annually. Enquiries to John F Kennedy Foundation of Thailand, Ministry of Foreign Affairs, Bangkok 2

Togo

General Information

Language: French is official language
Religion: About 25% Christian (mostly Roman Catholic), 8% Muslim; rest follow traditional beliefs
Population: 2.4 million
Bank Hours: 0730-1130, 1430-1530 Monday-Friday
Shop Hours: 0800-1200, 1430 or 1500-1730 or 1800 Monday-Friday; 0730-1230 Saturday
Currency: CFA franc
Export/Import Information: No tariff on books; advertising catalogues 10%. Additional taxes: 18% Tax Forfaitaire, 2% Statistical Tax, and Customs Stamp Tax of 4% of duties and added taxes. Small Wharfage Tax. Import licence required for goods from non-franc zones (except under 12,500 CFA francs); from franc zone, need authorization of Togolese Government Office. Exchange controls on non-franc zone.
Copyright: Berne (see International section)

Publishers

Ecole Professionelle de la Mission Catholique*, BP 341, Lomé
Subjects: Religion, Secondary & Primary Textbooks

Editogo*, BP 891, Lomé
Subjects: General and Educational
Founded: 1962

Les **Nouvelles** Editions Africaines (NEA), BP 4862, Lomé
Parent Company: Les Nouvelles Editions Africaines, Senegal (qv)
Associate Company: NEA, ave Noguès, 01 BP 3525, 01 Abidjan, Ivory Coast

Major Booksellers

Librairie du **Bon Pasteur***, rue du Commerce, BP 1164, Lomé Tel: 213279

Librairie **Evangélique***, 1 rue du Commerce, BP 378, Lomé Tel: 2967

Nouvelle Librairie **Togolaise***, BP 2096, Lomé

Major Libraries

American Cultural Center Library*, BP 852, Lomé

Bibliothèque de l'Université du Benin*, BP 1515, Lomé Tel: 2748

Bibliothèque nationale*, BP 1002, Lomé Tel: 6367
Dir: Kanaoua Bekoutare

Centre culturel français, Bibliothèque*, BP 2090, Lomé Tel: 7232/3442
Librarian: Mme Lacrampe

Library Associations

Association togolaise pour le Développement de la Documentation, des Bibliothèques, Archives et Musées*, c/o Bibliothèque de l'Université du Bénin, BP 1515, Lomé Tel: 4843
Secretary: E E Amah

Trinidad and Tobago

General Information

Language: English
Religion: Roman Catholic and Anglican
Population: 1 million
Literacy Rate (1970): 92.2%
Bank Hours: 0800-1230 Monday-Thursday; 0800-1200, 1500-1700 Friday
Shop Hours: 0800-1630 Monday-Friday; 0800-1200 Saturday
Currency: 100 cents = 1 Trinidad and Tobago dollar
Export/Import Information: No tariff on books; 45% duty and 25 cents postal fee on advertising matter. No import licence required for books; no obscene literature permitted. Exchange controls

Book Trade Organizations

Booksellers' Association of Trinidad and Tobago, Metropolitan Book Suppliers, Time Plaza, Henry St, Port of Spain
Secretary: Terry Cassim

Standard Book Numbering Agency, c/o S B Maharaj, The Caribbean Book Centre, 64a Independence Sq, Port of Spain

Book Trade Journals

Trinidad and Tobago and West Indian Bibliography, Central Library of Trinidad and Tobago, West Indian Reference Section, 20 Queens Park East, Port of Spain

Publishers

Charran Educational Publishers, 58 Western Main Rd, St James
Dirs: Reginald Charran, Betty Charran;
Sales: David Deonarine
Subjects: Textbooks, Children's Books
Bookshop: Charran's Bookshop (1978) Ltd (at above address)

Columbus Publishers Ltd, 64 Independence Sq, PO Box 140, Port of Spain Tel: (62) 53695
Dir: P A Hoadley
Subjects: General, Books for Students
1980: 18 titles *Founded:* 1969
ISBN Publisher's Prefix: 0-85643

Longman Caribbean Ltd*, 79 Belmont Circular Rd, Port of Spain
Dir: Percy Cezair
Associate Company: Longman Group Ltd, UK (qv)
Subject: General

Trinidad Publishing Co*, 22-26 St Vincent St, Port of Spain
Subjects: Law, Political Economy

Major Booksellers

Abercromby Bookshop*, 22 Abercromby St, Port of Spain Tel: 6237752

Asgar Ali Book Centre*, 90 Duke St, Port of Spain

Campus Corner Ltd*, 72 Pembroke St, Port of Spain

Cassia House Bookshop, Corner Pembroke and Oxford Sts, Port of Spain Tel: 6235156

Charran's Bookshop (1978), 58 Western Main Rd, St James
Manager: David Deonarine
Caribbean educational distributors, wholesale and retail

F W M Books Ltd, PO Box 6, Port of Spain Tel: (62) 54780
Manager: Teresa Pierre-Davis

Hobby Centre*, 86 Frederick St, Port of Spain

The **Ideal Leather** Store Ltd*, Jermingham St, Scarborough, Tobago

Jeffers Bookstore*, 28 Independence Square, Port of Spain

Victor **Manhin** Ltd, 49 High St, San Fernando

Muir **Marshall** Ltd*, 64a Independence Square, Port of Spain

Metropolitan Book Suppliers Ltd, 17 Time Plaza, 26-28 Henry St, Port of Spain
Manager: Terry Cassiiy

J C **Sealy**, The Book Shop, 22 Queen's Park West, Port of Spain

Stephens Book Department*, 8/10 Frederick St, Port of Spain

Major Libraries

Carnegie Free Library, 19-21 St James St, San Fernando Tel: (652) 3228

National Archives*, The Government Archivist, Whitehall, 29 Maraval Rd, Port of Spain

Central Library of **Trinidad and Tobago** (County Library Department of the Government)*, PO Box 547, Port of Spain

Trinidad Public Library, Knox St, Port of Spain

University of the West Indies Library, St Augustine

Library Associations

Library Association of **Trinidad and Tobago**, c/o PO Box 1177, Port of Spain
Secretary: Ann Beckles
Publication: Blatt (Bulletin of the Library Association of Trinidad and Tobago) (annual)

Library Journals

Blatt (Bulletin of the Library Association of Trinidad and Tobago), Library Association of Trinidad and Tobago, c/o PO Box 1177, Port of Spain

Tunisia

General Information

Language: Arabic (also French)
Religion: Muslim (Sunni)
Population: 6.08 million
Literary Rate (1975): 38% (50.5% of urban population, 24.6% rural)
Bank Hours: Winter: 0800-1100, 1400-1600 Monday-Friday; Summer: 0730-1130 Monday-Friday
Shop Hours: Generally 0800-1200, 1500-1800 Monday-Saturday
Currency: 1,000 millimes = 1 Tunisian dinar
Export/Import Information: Tunisia has preferential tariffs and EEC agreement but most books are dutied 26%, children's picture books 6%, and advertising free. Customs Formalities Tax of 40 millimes per 1,000 kg or less gross weight, with minimum rate of 2.5%. Consumption Tax on duty and tax paid for books: 46% if importer is merchant, 36.5% if importer is manufacturer; for advertising matter, 28.5% or 23%. Advertising matter subject to Production Tax of 26% of duty and tax paid if importer merchant, 20.5% if importer a manufacturer. Imports liberalized but in practice licences granted dependent on foreign exchange position
Copyright: UCC, Berne (see International section)

Book Trade Organizations

Syndicat des Librairies de Tunisie*, 10 ave de France, Tunis
Tunisian Booksellers' Association

Book Trade Journals

Bibliographie nationale de la Tunisie (Tunisian National Bibliography), National Library, 20 Souk-el-Attarine, Tunis

Publishers

Ceres Productions, BP 56 Tunis Belvedere, Tunis Tel: 282033 LG Cable Add: Cerepro Telex: Ceresp 12363 TN
Man Dir: Mohamed Ben Smail; *Editorial:* Moncef Guellaty
Orders to: Demeter, 2 rue de la Coté d'Ivoire, Tunis Tel: 283579
Subsidiary Company: Demeter (address as above)
Associate Company: Sud Editions, 9 bis rue de la Nouvelle Delhi, Tunis

Dar Arabia Lil Kitab, 43 bis, avenue Jugurtha, BP 1104, Tunis Tel: 288688
Man Dir: Mohamed Ahmed En Neifer
Subjects: General Literature, Biography, Bibliography, Linguistics, Pedagogy, Religion, History, Economics, Children's Books
1978: 104 titles *Founded:* 1975

En-Najah*, Editions Hedi Ben Abdelgheni, 11 ave de France, Tunis
Bookshop: Address as above

Faculté des Lettres et Sciences Humaines de Tunis*, Service des Publications et Echanges, 94 blvd du 9 Avril 1938, BP 1128, Tunis Tel: 260858
Secretary: O Bchini
Subjects: History, Africana, Philosophy, Paperbacks, Social Science, University Textbooks

Government Printer (Imprimerie Officielle de la République Tunisienne)*, Route de Rades Km2, Chouchet Rades, Tunis Tel: 295 124/014
Publication: Journal Officiel de la République Tunisienne

Maison Tunisienne d'Edition, Rue de l'Oasis, El Menzah V, Tunis Tel: 235600/235873/235878 Cable Add: Matédition
Man Dir: Azouz Rebai
Subsidiary Company: Imprimerie de la MTE, Rue du 2 Mars 34, Tunis
Subjects: General Fiction & Nonfiction, Belles Lettres, Poetry, Biography, History, Africana, Philosophy, Reference, Religion, Juveniles, Paperbacks, Social Science, University & Secondary Textbooks, Law, Medicine, Literature, Sciences
1978: 122 titles *1979:* 147 titles *Founded:* 1966

Imprimerie/Librairie Al **Manar***, BP 121, Tunis Tel: 243224 Cable Add: Manar
Man Dir: T El M'Hamdi
Subsidiary Company: Librairie Al Manar, 60 ave Bab Djedid, Tunis
Subjects: History, Africana, Religion, Arabic Language, Islam

Société nationale d'Edition et de Diffusion*, 5 ave de Carthage, BP 440, Tunis Tel: 255000 Cable Add: Studiffusion
Bookshop: address as above

Sud Editions*, 9 bis rue de la Nouvelle Delhi, Tunis Tel: 280400/281994 Telex: 12363 TN
Man Dir: Mohamed Masmoudi; *Editorial:* Abderrazak Khadraoui; *Sales:* Moncef Guellaty
Orders to: Demeter, 2 rue de la Coté d'Ivoire, Tunis
Associate Company: Ceres Productions, 6-8 avenue Montplaisir, Tunis
Subjects: Art, Art History
1979: 2 titles *Founded:* 1976
ISBN Publisher's Prefix: 2-86444

Major Booksellers

La **Caravelle** Librairie*, 8 ave H Bourguiba, Sfex

Librairie **En-Najah***, 11 ave de France, Tunis

Librairie Al **Manar***, 60 ave Bab Djedid, PO Box 121, Tunis Tel: 243224

Société Librairie nouvelle*, 15 ave de France, Bizerte

Société nationale d'Edition et de Diffusion*, 5 ave de Carthage, BP 440, Tunis Tel: 255000

Major Libraries

Archives nationales*, Présidence de la République, Pl du Gouvernement, Tunis

Bibliothéque nationale, 20 Souk-el-Attarine, BP 42, Tunis Tel: 245338
Librarian: M A Guellouz
Publications: Bibliographie nationale; Informations bibliographiques; le catalogue des manuscrits

British Council Library, c/o British Embassy, 5 pl de la Victoire, Tunis Tel: 245100/259053

Ecole nationale d'Administration Bibliothèque, 24 ave Docteur Calmette, Mutuelleville, Tunis 1060 Tel: 288300/288167/288435
Librarian: Fatma Chaman
Publications: Servir (semi-annual)

Direction de la **Lecture Publique**, 10 rue de Russie, Tunis (branches throughout the country)

Bibliothèque de l'**Université de Tunis***, 94 blvd du 9 Avril 1938, Tunis Tel: 260858

Library Associations

Association tunisienne de Documentalistes, Bibliothécaires et Archivistes, 43 Rue de la Liberté, le Bardo
President: M Abdeljaoued
Tunisian Association of Record-Keepers, Librarians and Archivists
Publication: Bulletin ATD (4 a year)

Library Journals

Bulletin, Association tunisienne des Documentalistes, Bibliothécaires et Archivistes, BP 575, Tunis

Literary Associations and Societies

Institut des Belles Lettres arabes, 12 rue Jamâa el Haoua, 1008 Tunis Bab Menara Tel: 260133
Institute of Arab Belles Lettres
Publication: Revue IBLA (biannual study of cultural problems in the Arab-Moslem world)

Union tunisienne des Ecrivains*, rue dar Jeld, Tunis
Tunisian Writers' Union

Turkey

General Information

Language: Turkish (English spoken by many)
Religion: Predominantly Muslim
Population: 43.2 million
Literacy Rate (1975): 60.3%
Bank Hours: 0900-1200, 1400-1730 Monday-Friday
Shop Hours: 0900-1200, 1330-1900 Monday-Saturday
Currency: 100 kurus = 1 Turkish lira (or pound)
Export/Import Information: No tariffs on books and advertising matter. Advertising

matter subject to 15% Expenditure Tax. Books on liberalized list, so import licences are granted freely, but textbooks must be imported with permission of Ministry of Education. Exchange controls
Copyright: Berne, Florence (see International section)

Book Trade Organizations

Türk Editörler Derneği, Ankara Cad 60, Istanbul
Turkish Publishers' Association

Book Trade Reference Books and Journals

Books

T C Devlet Yayinlarl Bibliyografyasi (Bibliography of Turkish Government Publications), National Library, Yenisehir, Ankara

Journals

Turkiye Bibliyografyasi (Turkish National Bibliography), National Library, Bibliographical Institute, Yenisehir, Ankara

Publishers

A B C Yayinevi, PO Box 539, Karakoy, Istanbul (Located at: Erkânı Harp Sokak, Seferoğlu Han, D-3, Tünel, Beyoğlu, Istanbul) Tel: 444242/442581 Cable Add: Abckit, Istanbul
Chief Executive, Editorial: Artun Altıparmak; *Sales:* Necip Inselel; *Production:* Kadri Karakus; *Publicity:* Seyitali Gürsu; *Rights & Permissions:* Ismail Tunçludemir
Orders to: Tünel Meydani 1, Beyoğlu, Istanbul
Subjects: Languages, Dictionaries
Bookshop: ABC Kitabevi (at above address)
1979: 2 titles *Founded:* 1979

Arkın Kitabevi, Ankara Cad 60, Istanbul Tel: 750734/750600/1 Cable Add: Birarkinlar Istanbul
Man Dir, Rights & Permissions: Ramazan Gökalp Arkın;
Branch Offs: Arkın Dagitim Ltd, Sti, Ankara Cad 60, Istanbul; Arkın Ofset Basimevi, Merter Sitesi Buberoğlu Sokak No 5, Bayrampasa, Istanbul
Subjects: Juveniles, Maps, Educational Materials, Reference, General Science, Secondary & Primary Textbooks
Bookshop: Arkın Kitabevi, Ankara Cad 60, Istanbul
Founded: 1957

Artel Publishing & Commercial Organization Co Ltd, Halaskârgazi Cad 214/4, Osmanbey, Istanbul Tel: 486040
Man Dir: Engin Serozan
Subjects: Reference, High-priced Paperbacks, Educational Materials
1978: 1 title

Aydinlik Yayinlari*, Nuruosmaniye Caddesi 34/204, Cagaloglu, Istanbul
Man Dir, Rights & Permissions: Mrs Leyla Yurdakul; *Editorial:* Dogan Yurdakul; *Sales:* Hüseyin Göçer; *Production:* Alp Hamuroglu; *Publicity:* Leyla and Dogan Yurdakul
Parent Company: Aydınlık Dergisi
Subjects: Marxism, Turkey and World Affairs
Founded: 1974

Dergâh Yayinlari AS, see Kara

Dogan Kardes Matbaacilik SAS*, Türbedar Sok 22, Istanbul
Subjects: Juveniles, Educational Materials, Weekly Magazines

Elif Kitabevi, Sahaflar Çarsisi 4, Beyazit, Istanbul Tel: 222096
Man Dir: Arslan Kaynardag; *Sales Dir:* Gani Yener
Subjects: Belles Lettres, Poetry, History, Music, Art, Philosophy, Social Science
Founded: 1957
Bookshop: Sahaflar Çarsisi 4, Beyazit, Istanbul
Miscellaneous: Firm distributes Turkish publications. Associated imprints include Elif Yayinlari

Gelisim Publishing, Safak sokak No 2, Nisantasi, Istanbul Tel: 486182/486183/475445 Cable Add: Gelbay
Chairman and Man Dir: Ercan Arikli
Associate Company: Süreli Yayinlar AS (Periodical Press, Inc), Dr Sevkibey sokak No 6, Divanyolu, Istanbul Tel: 286478/276817
Subjects: Encyclopaedias, Reference, Nonfiction

Hürriyet Yayinlari (Hür Yayin)*, Cemal Nadir Sokak 7-Cagaloglu, 1183 Istanbul Tel: 222038, 271502 Telex: 22276 HA TR, 22277 HA TR
Dir: Ali Z Oraloglu
Parent Company: Hürriyet Holding
Subjects: Fiction, History, Classics, Poetry, TV Series, Yearbooks, General Reference

Inkilâp Ve Aka Kitabevleri, Ankara Cad 95, Istanbul Tel: 222851
Man Dir: Nazar Fikri; *Sales Manager:* Aka Eren
Subjects: General Fiction & Nonfiction, Cartography, Politics, Religion, Literature, History, Juveniles, Technical, Domestic, Maps, Atlases

Ismail **Kara**/Dergâh Yayinlari AS Müessese Müdürü*, PO Box 1240 Sirkeci, Istanbul (Located at: Nuruosmaniye Cad 3/1 Cagaloglu, Istanbul) Tel: 265370
Man Dir: Ezel Erverdi; *Editorial:* Mustafa Kutlu; *Sales:* Fatih Gokdag; *Production:* Ahmet Debbagoglu; *Publicity:* Mustafa Modanlioglu
Subsidiary Companies: Dergâh kitapcilk AS, Ankara Cad 85 Cagaloglu, Istanbul; Emek matbaacilik ve ilancilik Ltd sti; Derya Dagitim AS, Babiali Cad 52 Cagaloglu, Istanbul
Subjects: Encyclopedias, Islamic Classics, History, Books of 'Hareket', Modern Turkish Philosophy, Modern Turkish Policy, Culture, Islamic Thought, Western Thought, Education, Turkish Literature
Book Clubs: Dergâh kitabevi, Istanbul; Dergâh kitabevi, Erzurum
Bookshops: Dergâh kitabevi, Istanbul; Dergâh kitabevi, Erzurum
1978: 11 titles *Founded:* 1977

Altin Kitaplar Publishing Co*, Altin Kitaplar, Cagaloglu, Istanbul Tel: 224045/268012 Telex: 23382 mudo TR
Man Dir: Mr Fethi Ul; *Editorial:* Dr Turhan Bozkurt; *Sales:* Mr Mursit Ul; *Production:* Mr Ugur Gergin; *Publicity:* Mr Ferhan Filiztekin
Associate Companies: Ders Kitaplari SA, Babiali Cad 39, Istanbul; Bozkurt Publishing Co, Ticarethane Sokak Sultanahmet, Istanbul
Subjects: Fiction, Non-fiction, Memoirs, Textbooks, Children's Books, Classics, History, Crime, Holy Koran
Bookshop: Altin Kitaplar, Cagaloglu, Istanbul
1978: 119 titles *1979:* 70 titles *Founded:* 1959

Milliyet Yayinlari AS*, Basın Sarayı Cagaloglu, Istanbul Tel: 270034 Cable Add: Mlliyet-Yayn Telex: 22251
Man Dir: Ülkü Tamer; *Editorial:* Gul Onet; *Production:* Ulvi Okar; *Publicity:* Ismet Istinyeli
Parent Company: Milliyet Holding AS
Subjects: General Fiction, Literature, History, Reference, Philosophy, Dictionaries, Encyclopaedias, Children's Books, Magazines
Bookshop: Basın Sarayı Cagaloglu, Istanbul
1978: 98 titles *Founded:* 1970

Redhouse Press*, PK 142, Istanbul
Editor: Robert Avery
Subjects: Turkish-English Dictionaries, Guidebooks in English, Cookery (in English and Turkish), General
Bookshop: Redhouse Kitabevi, Rizapasa Yokusu 48, Sultanhaman, Istanbul
1978: 15 titles

Remzi Kitabevi, Selvilimescit Sokak No 8, Cagaloglu, Istanbul Tel: 220583/227248 Cable Add: Remzi Kitabevi Istanbul
Man Dir, Sales, Rights & Permissions: Erol Erduran; *Publicity & Advertising:* Nejat Ebcioglu
Subsidiary Company: Evrim Matbaacılık Ltd, Sirketi Cagaloglu, Istanbul
Subjects: General Fiction, Biography, History, Philosophy, Reference, Low-priced Paperbacks, Medicine, Psychology, General & Social Science, Secondary & Primary Textbooks, Educational Materials
Bookshop: Ankara Cad 93, Istanbul
1978: 22 titles *1979:* 24 titles *Founded:* 1931

Sander Yayinlari, Kiragi Sok 78, Osmanbey, Istanbul Tel: 408475/483209
Man Dir, Production, Rights & Permissions: Necdet Sander; *Editorial:* Nuran Ücok; *Sales:* Ali Unver Tatlici; *Publicity:* Allegra Mitrani
Parent Company: Sander Kitabevi
Subjects: Literature, Fiction, Poetry, Essays, Political History, Sport, Education, Tourist Guides (of Turkey)
Bookshops: Sander Kitabevi, Halaskargazi Cad 275-277, Osmanbey, Istanbul; Istiklal Cad 178, Beyogiu, Istanbul

Literary Agents

Hür Yayin ve Ticaret*, Cemai Nadir Sokak 7, Cagaloglu, Istanbul Tel: 222038/262000 Cable Add: PK 1183 Istanbul

Nurcihan **Kesim**, Basinkoy Ahmet Ihsan No 6, Istanbul Telex: 22418 nek Tr
Branch Off: Nuruosmaniye Caddesi No 8, Cagaloglu, Istanbul Tel: 790222/285800/285394 Cable Add: Nurcihan Kesim, Basinkoy, Istanbul
Man Dir: Nurcihan Kesim; *Sales:* Ertugrul Kesim; *Rights & Permissions:* Oya Alpar
Specialization: Fiction, Nonfiction, Art Works, Serials, Encyclopaedias

O N K Copyright Agency, Ankara Cad 40, PO Box 983, Istanbul Tel: 267074/275345 Cable Add: Copyright Istanbul
Dir: Osman N Karaca
Specialization: Books, Serials, Plays, TV Programmes

Book Clubs

Dergâh kitabevi*, Istanbul
Owned by: Ismail Kara (qv)

Dergâh kitabevi*, Erzurum
Owned by: Ismail Kara (qv)

TURKEY — UGANDA 359

Major Booksellers

A B C Kitabevi, Tünel Meydanı 1, Beyoğlu, Istanbul
Owned by: ABC Yayinevi

Bilgi Yayinevi*, Tuna Cad, Kizilay, Ankara

Gençlik Kitabevi*, Muvakkithane Cad, 35 Kadiköy, Istanbul Tel: 363017

Hakki Bigeç*, Baskeny Yayinevi, Izmir Cad 55/22, Ankara

Haset Kitabevi AS, Istiklal cad 469, Beyoğlu, Istanbul Tel: 449470/1 Telex: 24446 Hsttr
Manager: Kenan Eren
Branches at Cumhuriyet Bulvari 143/G, Izmir; Ziya Gökalp cad 14/E, Yenisehir, Ankara
Formerly Hachette Kitabevi (Librairie Hachette-Succursale de la Turquie)

Nejat Yalki Kitabevi*, Valikonagi Cad, Nisantasi, Istanbul

Orhan Özsisman*, Datiç AS, 452 Sokak, No 5, Konak, Izmir

Redhouse Kitabevi*, Rizapasa Yokusu 48, Sultanhamam, Istanbul Tel: 223905

Sander Kitabevi*, Halaskârgazi Cad 275-277, Osmanbey, Istanbul Tel: 483209; Istiklal Cad 178, Beyoglu, Istanbul Tel: 440134

Major Libraries

Ankara University Library*, Ankara

The Beyazit State Library, Imaret Sokak No 18, Beyazit, Istanbul Tel: 223167
Librarian: Hasan Duman

Bogaziçi University Library (formerly Robert College Library), Bebek, PK 2, Istanbul Tel: 653400
Acting Librarian: Nurten Gakir

Library of the Grand National Assembly*, Palais de la Grande Assemblée Nationale, Ankara Tel: 251352

Il Halk Kütüphanesi*, Balikesir
Provincial Public Library, formerly the Vatan Library

Istanbul Üniversitesi Merkez Kütüphanesi, Besim Ömer Pasa Cad 15, Beyazit, Istanbul Tel: 222180
Istanbul University Central Library

Izmir General Library*, Millî Kütuphane Cad 39, Izmir

Middle East Technical University Library*, Ankara

Millet Library*, Fatih, Istanbul

Millî Kütüphane, Yenisehir, Ankara Tel: 253498
National Library
Dir: Nejat Sefercioğlu

Library of the Mineral Research and Exploration Institute*, Ismet Inönü Bulvari, Ankara Tel: 234255
Librarian: Sevim Özertan;
Publication: Selected list of New Publications in *MTA News* (Monthly)

Selimiye Library*, Edirne

Süleymaniye Kütüphanesi Müdürlüğü, Suleymaniye Mahallesi, Ayse Kadin Sokak 30; 35, Beyazit-Istanbul Tel: 206460
Library of the Süleymaniye

Technical University Library*, Istanbul Teknik Üniversitesi, Merkez Kütüphane Mudürlöğü, Gümüssuyu Cad 87, Beyoglu

Vatan Library, see Il Halk Kütüphanesi

Library Associations

Türk Kütuphaneciler Dernegi, Necatibey Cad 19/22, PK 175, Yenisehir, Ankara Tel: 301325
Turkish Librarians' Association
Secretary: M N Sefercioğlu
Publication: Bülten (4 a year)

Library Journals

Bülteni (Bulletin), Turkish Librarians' Association, Necatibey Cad 19/22, PK 175, Yenisehir, Ankara

Literary Associations and Societies

P E N Yazarlar Dernegi*, Cagoglu Yokusu 40, Istanbul
President: Yasar Nabi Nayir
PEN-Turkish Centre

Literary Periodicals

Orta Dogu (Middle East), Celal Tevfik Karasapan, Tunali Hilmi Cad 121-5, Kavaklidere, Ankara

Varlik (Existence), Varlik Yayinevi, Cagaloglu Yokusu, Ankara Cad, Istanbul

Literary Prizes

Award for Literature and Scientific Publications*
To encourage the use of the Turkish language. Five prizes of 5,000 Turkish liras each for literature and one prize of 5,000 liras for scientific publication. Awarded annually. Enquiries to Turkish Language Society, Kavaklidere, Ankara

Sait Faik Prize*
For the best short story. 5,000 Turkish liras. Awarded annually. Enquiries to Darussafaka Association, Halaskargazl Cad 231, Istanbul

Orhan Kemal Award*
To encourage publication of novels which reflect the views of Orhan Kemal. Awarded annually. Enquiries to Orhan Kemal Family and Associates, c/o Turkish Language and History Society, Kavaklidere, Ankara

Fikret Madarali Prize*
For the best novel. Three prizes of 10,000, 5,000 and 3,000 Turkish liras. Awarded annually. Enquiries to Fikret Madarali Family and Associates, c/o Turkish Language and History Society, Kavaklidere, Ankara

Uganda

General Information

Language: English is official language. Swahili is widely spoken in commercial centres
Religion: About 30% Christian, 5% Muslim; rest follow traditional beliefs
Population: 12.8 million
Literacy Rate (1959 African Population): 20%
Bank Hours: 0830-1230 Monday-Friday; 0800-1100 Saturday
Shop Hours: 0800-1230, 1400-1630 or longer Monday-Friday; 0800-1230 Saturday
Currency: 100 cents = 1 Uganda shilling
Export/Import Information: No tariff on books or advertising matter but subject to 10% sales tax. Import licence and exchange controls (granted automatically with import license)

Book Trade Journals

The Uganda Journal, PO Box 4980, Mapala (published by the Uganda Society and includes an annual bibliography of books published in or about Uganda)

Publishers

East African Literature Bureau*, Uganda Branch, PO Box 1317, Kampala
For full information see under Kenya

Government Printer*, PO Box 33, Entebbe

Longman Uganda Ltd, PO Box 3409, Kampala Tel: 42940 Cable Add: Longman Kampala
Manager: M K L Mutyaba
Associate Company: Longman Group Ltd, UK (qv)
Subjects: Biography, History, Africana, Juveniles, Books in Luganda & other Ugandan Languages, General Science, Secondary & Primary Textbooks
Founded: 1965

Uganda Publishing House*, UTA Ho, Bombo Rd, PO Box 2923, Kampala Tel: 59601/42362
Man Dir: G Rugege; *Sales Manager:* John B Bugembe
Subjects: General Fiction & Nonfiction, Belles Lettres, Poetry, Biography, History, Africana, Reference, Juveniles, General & Social Science, Secondary & Primary Textbooks
Founded: 1966

Major Booksellers

E S A Bookshop*, PO Box 2515, Kampala

Makerere University Bookshop*, PO Box 7062, Kampala

Saint Paul Book Centre, PO Box 4392, Kampala Tel: 56346

Uganda Bookshop*, Colville St, PO Box 7145, Kampala Tel: 43756

Major Libraries

Albert Cook Library, Makerere University, Makarere Medical School, PO Box 7072, Kampala Tel: 58731
Medical Librarian: Leonard Ssennyonjo
Publications: East African Medical Bibliography (bi-monthly); *Bulletin and Accession List* (monthly) *Annual Report*

International Communication Agency Library*, PO Box 7186, Kampala Tel: 54351

Kabarole Public Library*, PO Box 28, Fort Portal Tel: 2255

Makerere Institute of Social Research Library, PO Box 16022, Kampala Tel: 54582
Librarian: Nsamba Boaz

Makerere University Library*, PO Box 16002, Kampala Tel: 31041/2
Librarian: T K Lwanga
Publication: Library Bulletin (quarterly)

National Institute of Education Library*, Makerere University, PO Box 7062, Kampala
Publication: Journal

Public Libraries Board, Buganda Rd, PO Box 4262, Kampala Tel: 54661 Cable Add: Library, Kampala
Dir: P K Birungi
Publications: Annual Report, Accessions List (quarterly) and occasional publications

Uganda Technical College Library, PO Box 1991, Kampala Tel: 65211 ext 37 Cable Add: Technical
Senior Librarian: R Nganwa

Library Associations

Uganda Library Association*, PO Box 5894, Kampala Tel: 54661
Executive Secretary: I M N Kigongo-Bukenya
Publication: Ugandan Libraries

Uganda Schools Library Association*, PO Box 7014, Kampala
Executive Secretary: J W Nabembezi
Publication: Newsletter (quarterly)

Uganda Special Library Association*, c/o PO Box 9, Entebbe
Secretary: M D'Mello

Library Journals

Newsletter, Uganda Schools Library Association, PO Box 7014, Kampala

Ugandan Libraries, Uganda Library Association, PO Box 5894, Kampala

Literary Periodicals

Dhana, East African Literature Bureau, PO Box 1317, Kampala (or PO Box 30022, Nairobi) (biannual literary magazine published on behalf of the Department of Literature at Makerere University)

Translation Agencies and Associations

East African Literature Bureau*, PO Box 1317, Kampala

Union of Soviet Socialist Republics

General Information

Language: Russian is the official language. Large number of other languages spoken including Ukrainian, Byelorussian, several Turkic languages, Armenian, Georgian, Lithuanian and Moldavian. English is the commonest foreign language known
Religion: About 25% Christian (mainly Russian Orthodox), 12% Muslim (in the southwest), 2 million Jewish, ½ million Buddhist; rest atheist
Population: 262 million
Literacy Rate (1970): 99.7% of population aged 9 to 49
Bank Hours: 0900-1600 Monday-Friday
Shop Hours: 0830-1800 Monday-Saturday
Currency: 100 kopeks = 1 rouble
Export/Import Information: Foreign trade is state monopoly and duties and licences only the concern of the corporation Mezhdunarodnaya Kniga, Smolenskaya Sennaya 32-34, Moscow G-200. The State Bank of USSR or its subsidiary, USSR Bank for Foreign Trade, is only organization handling foreign currency matters
Copyright: UCC (see International section)

Book Trade Organizations

Komitet po pechati pri Sovete Ministrov SSSR*, Petrovka 26, Moscow K-51
Committee for Publishing and the Press under the Council of Ministers of the USSR
Foreign Trade Dir: I V Shamraev

Publishing Council of the Academy of Sciences of the USSR*, Leninsky prospekt 13, Moscow

Standard Book Numbering Agency, Bibliografičeskij Institut SSSR, Kremlevskaja nab 1-9, 119816 Moscow G-19
ISBN Administrator: Ju I Fartunin

U S S R Union of Writers*, Vorovskogo ul 52, Moscow
First Secretary of the Board: Professor K A Fedin
Publications: Voprosy Literatury (jointly with the Institute of World Literature of the USSR Academy of Sciences); *Soviet Literature, Literaturnaya Gazeta, Literaturnaya Rossiya, Neva, Novyi Mir*

Vsesoyuznaya Knichnaya Palata*, Kremlevskaya naberezhnaya 1-9, Moscow
All-Soviet Book Chamber
Publications: Knizhnaya Letopis'
All books and publications are registered and described

Book Trade Reference Books and Journals

Books

Knizhnaya Moskva: Putevoditel'-Spravochnik (Books in Moscow: A Guide and Handbook), 'Reklama', Moscow

Spravochnik Normativnykh Materialov dlya Rabotnikov Knizhnoi Torgovli (Handbook of Rules and Precedents for Book Trade Workers), Izdatelstvo 'Kniga', Nezhdanovoi pereulok 8-10, Moscow K-9

Journals

Ezhegodnik Knigi SSSR (USSR National Bibliography), Izdatelstvo 'Kniga', Nezhdanovoi pereulok 8-10, Moscow K-9

Index to Forthcoming Russian Books; English translation of bibliographic entries from *Novye Knigi*, Scientific Information Consultants Ltd, 661 Finchley Rd, London W2 2HN, UK

Knizhnaya Letopis' (Book Chronicle) (weekly bulletin), All-Soviet Book Chamber, Kremlevskaya naberezhnaya 1-9, Moscow

Knizhnaya Letopis' — Dopolnitel'nyi Vypusk; monthly supplement to *Knizhnaya Letopis'*, quoting 'restricted' publications, small imprints, 'not-for-sale' or institutional items etc, All-Soviet Book Chamber, Kremlevskaya naberezhnaya 1-9, Moscow

Knizhnaya Torgovlya (Book Trade), Mezhdunarodnaya Kniga, Smolenskaya Sennaya pl 32-34, Moscow G-200

Knizhnoe Obozrenie (Book Reviews), USSR Library Council, The Lenin State Library of the USSR, Prospect Kalinina 3, Moscow 101 000

Letopis' Pechati BSSR (Byelorussian National Bibliography), Godudarstvennaya Biblioteka BSSR im V I Lenina, Knizhnaya Palata BSSR, Minsk

Letopis' Periodicheskikh i Prodolzhaiushchikhsya Izdanii (Periodicals and Continuations), Mezhdunarodnaya Kniga, Smolenskaya Sennaya pl 32-34, Moscow G-200

Novye Knigi (New Books); announcements of forthcoming books, Mezhdunarodnaya Kniga, Smolenskaya Sennaya pl 32-34, Moscow G-200

Sovetskaya Bibliografia (Soviet Bibliography), USSR Library Council, The Lenin State Library of the USSR, Prospect Kalinina 3, Moscow 101 000

Ukrainska Knyha (Ukrainian Book) (text in Ukrainian), Association of Book Lovers, Kyiw Publishing, 4800 North 12th St, Philadelphia, PA 19141, USA

Publishers

Atomizdat*, ul Zhdanova 5, 103031 Moscow K-31 Tel: 2942228/2959993
Publishing House for Atomic Literature
Dir: V A Kulyamin
Subjects: Nuclear Science and Technology (peaceful use of nuclear energy)

Aurora Art Publishers*, 7-9 Nevsky prospekt, 191065 Leningrad Tel: 2151924 Cable Add: Exportizdat Aurora Leningrad Telex: 81562
President, Rights & Permissions: Boris Pidemsky; *Editor-in-Chief:* Alla Slizhevskaya; *Production:* Anatoly Peshkov
Subject: Art
Founded: 1969
Miscellaneous: Publishes in foreign languages

Detskaya Entsiklopediya*, Khokhlovskii pereulok 16, Moscow
Children's Encyclopaedia

Izdatelstvo **Detskaya Literatura***, Malyi Cherkaskii pereulok 1, Moscow
Children's Literature Publishing House
Dir: G K Peshekhodova
Subject: Juveniles

Znak Pochyota Order **Dosaaf** Publishing House*, Novo-Ryazanskaya 26, Moscow 107066
Voluntary Society for the Promotion of the Army, Air Force and Navy
Subject: Military

Izdatelstvo **'Ekonomika'***, Berezhovskaya naberezhnaya 6, Moscow
Economics Publishing House
Dir: K V Grechishnikov
Subjects: Economics, Industry, Agriculture, Textbooks
Founded: 1963

Izdatelstvo '**Energiya**', Shluzovaya
naberezhnaya 10, Moscow 113114
Energy Publishing House
Dir: S P Rozanov; *Editor-in-Chief:*
V Sidorov
Subjects: Scientific and technical literature
on Power Engineering, Radio Engineering,
Thermal, Hydro and Electrical Engineering,
Popular Radio Library, Automatic and
Computer Science
Founded: 1931

Izdatelstvo '**Finansy**', Chernyshevskogo ul 7,
Moscow K-142
Finances Publishing House
Dir: V I Vinogradov
Subjects: Banking, Taxation, Accounts

Izdatelstvo '**Fizkultura i Sport**'*,
Kalyaevskaya ul 27, Moscow 103006
Physical Culture & Sport Publishing House
Man Dir: Yurii Metaev
Subjects: Sport Games

Gidrometeorizdat*, Moskovskoe Otdelenie,
Gor'kovo ul 18a, Moscow
Hydrometeorology

Izdatelstvo **Iskusstvo***, Tsvetnov bul'var' 25,
Moscow K-51
Publishing House for Art Literature
Dir: E Y Savostianov
Subjects: Fine Arts, Music, Theatre

Izvestiya Publishing House*, Pushkinskaya
pl 5, Moscow K-6
Dir: L P Grachev
Subjects: Izvestiya, Official Publications of
USSR and RSFSR Supreme Soviets

Izdatelstvo '**Khimiya**'*, Strominka ul 23,
Moscow B-76
Publishing House for Chemistry
Dir: Ya S Mashkevich
Subject: Chemistry

Izdatelstvo '**Khudozhestvennaya
Literatura**'*, Novo-Basmannaya ul 19,
Moscow B-66
Publishing House for Fiction & Poetry
Dir: V S Somov
Subjects: Fiction, Literature

Khudozhnik RSFSR Publishers*,
Bolsheokhtinsky Pereulok 6, Block 2,
Leningrad 195027
Subjects: General, Catalogues

Izdatelstvo '**Kniga**'*, Nezhdanovoi ul 8-10,
Moscow K-9
Dir: V F Kravchenko
Subjects: Bibliography, Printing, Publishing,
Bibliology, Bibliophilism, Miniature and
Facsimile Editions

Izdatelstvo '**Kolos**'*, Sadovaya-Spasskaya ul
18, Moscow I-139
Dir: I P Khramkov
Subjects: Agriculture, Veterinary Science

Izdatelstvo '**Legkaya Industriya**'*, Kuznetskii
most 22, Moscow K-31
Light Industry Publishing House
Dir: T G Gromova; *Publicity:* Y Y
Gosenpoud
Subject: Light Industry

Izdatelstvo '**Lenizdat**'*, Fontanka 59,
Leningrad D-23
Leningrad Publishing House
Subjects: Politics, Technical, Agriculture,
Fiction, Juveniles, Art, Popular Science,
Folklore

Izdatelstvo '**Lesnaya Promyshlennost**'*,
Kirova ul 40a, Moscow
Forest Industry Publishing House
Dir: B S Oreshkin
Subjects: Forestry, Wood & Paper Products,
Logging, Woodworking, Dendrochemistry,
Nature Conservation
1978: 130 titles

Izdatelstvo '**Malysh**'*, Butyrskii val 68,
Moscow A-55
Children's World Publishing House
Dir: I N Boronetsky
Subject: Pre-school Publications

Izdatelstvo '**Mashinostroenie**'*, Pervyi
Basmannyi pereulok 3, Moscow
Publishing House for Mechanical
Engineering
Dir: A V Astakhov
Subject: Mechanical Engineering

Izdatelstvo '**Meditsina**'*, Petroverigskii
pereulok 6-8, Moscow K-142
Publishing House for Medicine
Dir: V I Maevsky
Subjects: Medicine, Health
Founded: 1918

Izdatelstvo '**Metallurgiya**'*, 2-oi Obydenskii
pereulok 14, Moscow G-34, 119034
Publishing House for Metallurgy
Dir: M A Kovalevskiy
Subject: Metallurgy
1978: 246 titles

Izdatelstvo '**Mezhdunarodnye
Otnosheniya**'*, Kuznetskii most 24, 103031
Moscow K-31
International Relations Publishing House
Dir: S P Emelyanikov
Subjects: International Information,
Translations for UN Textbooks

Leidykla '**Mintis**'*, Sierakausko 15, Vilnius
Tel: 632943
Dir: Algimantas Garliauskas
Subjects: Politics, Law, Philosophy,
Tourism, Sport Directories, Economics,
History, Hobbies, Social Sciences,
Textbooks, Juveniles, Periodicals, Calendars
1978: 148 titles *Founded:* 1949

Izdatelstvo **Mir***, 129820, 2 Pervyi Rizhskii
pereulok, Moscow I-110, GSP Telex:
411466 MIR SU
Dir: S G Sosnovsky; *Editor-in-Chief:* Dr
G B Kurganov
Orders to: Mezhdunarodnaya Kniga,
Moscow
Subject: Translations from and into Russian
of technical and scientific works
1978: 431 titles *Founded:* 1946

Izdatelstvo **Molodaya Gvardiya***,
Sushchevskaya ul 21, Moscow K-30 Tel:
2511145
Young Guard Publishing House of All-
Union Leninist Young Communist League
Dir: Vladimir Desyaterik
Subjects: Political Science, Social Science,
History, Biography, Art, Science Fiction,
Juveniles
1978: 340 titles *Founded:* 1922

Izdatelstvo '**Moskovskii Rabochiy**'*,
Kuibysheva ul 21, Moscow
Moscow Worker Publishing House
Dir: N H Eselyek
Subjects: General Fiction & Nonfiction

Izdatelstvo **Moskovskogo Universiteta***,
Gertzena ul 5-7, Moscow K-9
Moscow University Press
Dir: Dr A K Avelitchev; *Rights &
Permissions:* VAAP, Bolshaya Bronnaya 6a,
Moscow
Subject: Science
Founded: 1926

Izdatelstvo '**Muzyka**', Neglinnaja ul 14,
Moscow 103045
Music Publishing House
Subject: Music
1978: 615 titles

Izdatelstvo **Mysl***, Leninsky prospekt 15,
Moscow V-71
Thought Publishing House
Dir: A P Porivaev

Subjects: Science, Economics, Geography,
Philosophy, History

Izdatelstvo '**Nauka**'*, Podsosenskii pereulok
21, Moscow K-62
Science Publishing House
Dir: G D Komkov
Subjects: General & Social Science,
Mathematics, University Textbooks,
Educational Materials
Founded: 1964

Izdatelstvo '**Nedra**'*, Tret'yakovskii pereulok
1-19, Moscow K-12
Natural Resources Publishing House
Dir: M S Lvov
Subjects: Meteorology, Geology, Energy

Agentstvo Pechati '**Novosti**' (Apn)*, 13/5
Podkolokolny pereulok, Moscow 109028
Tel: 2971953 Telex: 7581, 7582
Novosti Press Agency Publishing House
Dir: N I Efimov; *Editorial:* Yu S Fantalov;
Sales, Publicity: S G Mishchenko;
Production: R S Vakhitova; *Rights &
Permissions:* M B Krupkin
Subjects: History, Philosophy, Social
Science, Politics, Economics, International
Affairs, General Informative Books, Low- &
High-priced Paperbacks
1978: 760 titles *Founded:* 1964

Pedagogika*, Pogodinskaya 8, Moscow
Dir: Mr Razumny
Subject: Pedagogics

Izdatelstvo '**Pishchevaya Promyshlennost**'*, 1
Kadashevskii pereulok 12, Moscow
Publishing House for the Food Industry
Dir: N A Zarin
Subjects: Food Science & Technology

Planeta Publishers*, Petrovka 8/11,
Moscow 103031
Subjects: Guidebooks, Illustrated books

Politizdat*, Myusskaya pl 7, Moscow D-47
Publishing House for Political Literature
Dir: H B Tropkin
Subjects: Political Literature, History
1978: 381 titles

Pravda Publishing House*, Pravdy ul 24,
Moscow
Dir: B A Feldman

Profizdat, Kirova ul 13, Moscow
Publishers for Trade-union Literature
Dir: Vladimir A Boldyrev
Subjects: Economics, Sociology, Psychology
of Work, Trade Union Movement,
Literature, Fiction, Prose
Miscellaneous: Publishers for the All-Union
Central Council of Trade Unions

Progress Publishers*, Zubovsky
Boulevard 17, Moscow 119021 Tel: 2469032
Dir: Volf Nikolayevich Sedykh; *Editor-in-
Chief:* Viktor Ivanovich Neznanov;
Production: Mikhail Pavlovich Kryakovkin
Subjects: Scientific Socialism, Marxism-
Leninism, Philosophy, Political Economy,
International Relations, International
Communist and Workers Movement,
History, Sociology, Law, Russian Classics
and Modern Soviet Literature, Russian
Translations of Fiction, Social and Political
Literature, Art, Children's Books
1978: 1161 titles *Founded:* 1931

Izdatelstvo '**Prosveshchenie**'*, 3-ii proezd
Marinoi Roshchi 41, Moscow 129846
Dir: D D Zuev
Subjects: Education, Textbooks

Russky Yazyk*, Luchnikov Pereulok 5,
Moscow 101000
Russian Language Publishing House
Subjects: Textbooks, Reference, Dictionaries

362 UNION OF SOVIET SOCIALIST REPUBLICS

Izdatelstvo **'Sovetskaya Entsiklopediya'***, Pokrovskii bul'var' 8, Moscow 109817 Tel: 2973562/2977483
Soviet Encyclopaedia Publishing House
Chairman of Editorial Council:
A Prokhorov
Founded: 1925

Izdatelstvo **'Sovetskaya Rossiya'***, Suapnova Proezd 13-15, Moscow K-12
Soviet Russia Publishing House
Dir: E A Petrov

Izdatelstvo **'Sovetskii Khudozhnik'***, Chernyahovskogo ul 4a, Moscow 125319
Soviet Artist Publishing House
Dir: V Goryainov
Subject: Art, Reference
1978: 1583 titles

Izdatelstvo **'Sovetskii Kompozitor'***, 14-12 Sadovaya-Triumfalnaya St, Moscow 103006 Tel: 2092384
Soviet Composer Publishing House
Dir: M Y Kunin
Subject: Music
Founded: 1957
Bookshop: Magazin-Salon Sovetskaya Muzika (at above address)

Izdatelstvo **Sovietskii Pisatel***, 121069 Moscow 69, ul Vorovskovo 11
USSR Writer's Union Publishing House
Dir: V N Eramenko
Subjects: Belles Lettres, Art History, Literary History, Poetry, Literary Criticism, Literary Translations
Founded: 1935
Miscellaneous: Publishes monthly magazine *Soviet Motherland* in Yiddish

Izdatelstvo **'Sovetskoe Radio'** Glavnyi Pochtamt p/ya693*, Moscow
Dir: N G Zabolotsky
Subjects: Radio, TV

Sovremennik Publishers*, Yartsevskaya 4, Moscow 121351
Subjects: Fiction, Literary Criticism, Drama

Znak Pochyota Order Izdatelstvo **Standartov***, Novopresnensky Pereulok 3, Moscow 123022
Subject: Official Standards

Statistika, Kirova ul 39, Moscow
Dir: E I Kobzar
Subjects: Statistics on economics, on demography and on computers in the national economy
1978: 113 titles

Stroyizdat Publishing House*, Kalyayevskaya 23a, Moscow 102006
Subjects: Building Sciences, Machinery, Urban Development, Architecture, Geology, Hydrogeology

Izdatelstvo **'Sudostroenie'**, 8 Gogolya St, Leningrad 191065 Tel: 2153048
Publishing House for Shipbuilding
Man Dir: V Iv Lapin; *Editor-in-Chief:* A L Mitrofanov; *Production:* V Iv Pashko; *Rights & Permissions:* Iv G Russetsky
Subjects: Shipbuilding, Ship Repairing, Ship Installations Equipment and Devices, Navigation, Underwater Exploration, University and Secondary Textbooks on these subjects
Bookshop: Shipbuilding, 40 Sadovuja St, Leningrad
1978/9: 86 titles *Founded:* 1940

Izdatelstvo **'Svyaz'***, Chistoprudnyi bul'var' 2, Moscow
Communications Publishing House
Dir: G Rodin
Subject: Communications (postal, telegraphic and wireless, television, Hi-Fi equipment), Philately

Izdatelstvo **'Transport'**, Basmannyi Tupik 6a, Moscow 107174
Dir: V P Titov
Subjects: Railway, Automobile, Air, Sea and Naval Transport

Vsesoyuznoe Obyedineniye **'Vneshtorgizdat'**, 1 Fadyeev St, Moscow 107207 Tel: 411238 Telex: 7238 VTI SU
Foreign Trade Publishing House
President: Sergey P Emelyanikov; *Editorial:* Boris V Lensky; *Sales:* Leonid G Koftov; *Production:* Anatoly D Sorokin
Subject: Foreign Trade
Founded: 1925
Miscellaneous: Publish Catalogues, Prospectuses and Advertising Material in Russian and Foreign Languages on Soviet exports. Execute orders of foreign organizations for translation and publishing in Russian of maintenance and other documents

Voyenizdat*, Upravleniye Voyennogo Izdateltsva, Moscow K-160
Chief: A I Kopytin
Subject: Military

Izdatelstvo **'Vysshaya Shkola'***, Neglinnaya ul d29/14, Moscow
Higher School Publishing House
Dir: V G Panov
Subject: Textbooks (Secondary Education)

Izdatelstvo **'Yuridicheskaya Literatura'***, Chkalova 38-40, Moscow
Law Literature Publishing House
Dir: V G Yuzbashev
Subject: Law

Znanie*, Novaya ploshchad 3-4, Moscow K-12
Knowledge Publishing House
Dir: V Belyakov
Subjects: General Science, Education, Culture

Literary Agents

V A A P, see entry below

Vsesoyuznoe agenstvo po avtorkskim pravam (VAAP)*, Bolshaya Bronnaya ul 6a, Moscow K-104 Tel: 2034599 Cable Add: Moscow Avtor Telex: 7627Avtor SU
Copyright Agency of the USSR
Contact: B Pankin, Chairman; or M Shisigin, Vice-Chairman

Major Booksellers

Mezhdunarodnaya Kniga*, Smolenskaya sennaya pl 32-34, Moscow G-200 Tel: 2441022 Cable Add: Mezhkniga Moscow
(The sole organization in the USSR through which foreign purchasers can obtain books)

The leading agent for distribution of USSR books and periodicals abroad is Les Livres Etrangers SA, 10 rue Armand-Moisant, F-75737 Paris cedex 15 Tel: (01) 7342727/5665680; retail bookshop Maison du Livre Etranger ('Dom Knigi'), 9 rue de l'Eperon, F-75006 Paris Tel: (01) 3261060

Major Libraries

Fundamental Library of the **Academy** of Medical Sciences*, Baltiyskaya ul 8, Moscow

Biblioteka **Akademii Nauk SSSR***, Birzhevaya liniya 1, Leningrad V-164 Tel: Director's Office 183592 and 184091; Information and Bibliographical Department 183991
Library of the Academy of Sciences of the USSR

Gosudarstvennaya publichnaya nauchno-tekhnicheskaya biblioteka Sibirskogo otdeleniya **Akademii Nauk SSSR***, Voskhod ul 15, 630200 Novosibirsk Tel: Director 661860; Reference and Bibliography Department 661991; Reader Registration 668071
State Public Scientific and Technical Library of the Siberian Department of the Academy of Sciences of the USSR

Institut nauchnoy informatsii po obschestvennym naukam **Akademii Nauk SSSR***, Krasikova ul 28/45, 117418 Moscow V-418 Tel: 1288930
Institute of Scientific Information in the Social Sciences of the Academy of Sciences of the USSR

Tsentral'naya nauchnaya biblioteka **Akademii Nauk USSR***, Vladimirskaya ul 62, 252601 Kiev 601 Tel: Director 243126; Reference/Bibliography Section 213231
Central Scientific Library of the Academy of Sciences of the Ukrainian SSR

All-Union Patent and Technical Library*, Berezhkovskaya naberezhnaya 24, Moscow

Central State **Archives of Early Russian Historical Records***, Bolshaya Pirogovskaya ul 17, Moscow

Central State **Archives of the October Revolution** and Higher State Bodies*, Bolshaya Pirogovskaya ul 17, Moscow

Central State **Archives of the RSFSR***, Berezhkovskaya naberezhnaya 26, Moscow

Central State Historical **Archives of the USSR***, Naberezhnaya Krasnogo Flota 4, Leningrad

Central State Literature and Art **Archives of the USSR***, Leningradskoe chausee 50, Moscow
Dir: N B Volkova

Azerbaidzhanskaya gosudarstvennaya respublikanskaya biblioteka im. M F Akhundova*, Tsentr ul Khagani 29, 37061 Baku Tel: 936801; Reference and Bibliography Department 936004
M F Akhundov State Republic Library of Azerbaizhan

Nauchnaya biblioteka im A M **Gor'kovo Leningradskovo** gosudarstvennovo universiteta im A A Zhdanova*, Universitetskaya naberezhnaya 7-9, Leningrad 199164 Tel: Director 2-182741; Reference and Information Department 2-189555
A M Gor'kii Scientific Library of the A A Zhdanov State University of Leningrad
Dir: Mrs K M Romanovskaya

Nauchnaya biblioteka im A M **Gor'kogo Moskovskogo** gos universiteta im M V Lomonosova*, Marx prospekt 20, Moscow K-9 Tel: Director's Office 2036525; Service Department 2033751
Gor'kii Scientific Library of The Lomonosov State University of Moscow

Vsesoyuznaya **gosudarstvennaya ordena Trudovogo Krasnogo Znameni biblioteka** inostrannoi literatury*, Ulyanovskaya 1, Moscow 109240 Tel: 2972839
All-Union State Library of Foreign Literature

Gosudarstvennaya publichnaya istoricheskaya biblioteka RSFSR*, 101839 Moscow, Bogdana Khmel'nitskogo ul, Starosadskii per d 9 Tel: Director 2956514; Information 2280582
State Public Historical Library of the RSFSR

Gosudarstvennaya publichnaya nauchno-tekhnicheskaya biblioteka SSSR*, Kuznetskii most 12, Moscow K-31 Tel: Director K59288; Reference-Bibliography B87379
State Public Scientific and Technical Library of the USSR

Gosudarstvennaya ordena Lenina biblioteka SSSR imeni V I Lenina*, Prospect Kalinina 3, Moscow 101000 Tel: 2024056 Telex: 7167 wgbibl su
V I Lenin State Library of the USSR
Secretary: G A Semenova

Gosudarstvennaya Respublikanskaya biblioteka Gruzinskoi SSR im K Marksa*, Ketskhoveli ul 5, Tbilisi 380007 Tel: Director's Office 931233/999286
State Republican Karl Marx Library of the Georgian SSR

Gosudarstvennaya biblioteka UzSSR im Alishera Navoi*, Alleya paradov 5, Tashkent 700000 Tel: 398658/394341/394440/394450
Alisher Navoi State Public Library of the Uzbek SSR

Gosudarstvennaya publichnaya biblioteka im M E Saltykova-Schedrina*, Sadovaya ul 18, Leningrad D-69 Tel: 152856
M E Saltykov-Shchedrina State Public Library

Tartu Riikliku Ulikooli Teaduslik Raamatükogu*, Toomemägi, 202400 Tartu, Estonian SSR Tel: Tartu 34121/286 Telex: 208010 Nauka
Scientific Library of Tartu State University
Librarian: Laine Peep
Publication: Publicationes bibliothecae universitatis litterarum Tartuensis: Raamat-aeg-restaureer imine; Tedusliku Raamatukogu töid (serials); *Eksliibris TRÜ Teaduslikus Raamatukogus*

The Scientific Library of the **Vilnius** Vincas Kapsukas State University*, Universiteto gatve 3, 232633 Vilnius Tel: 26787/26389

Library Associations

Council on Libraries of the **Academy** of Sciences of the USSR*, Prospect Leninsky 14, Moscow
Academy Chairman: P N Fedoseev

U S S R Library Council*, The Lenin State Library of the USSR, Prospect Kalinina 3, Moscow 101000 Telex: 7167 wgbibl su Tel: 2024656/2228551
President: Professor N M Sikorsky;
Executive Secretary: G A Semenova
Publications: Bibliotekar (Librarian); *Sovetskoje bibliotekovedonie* (Former: Biblioteki SSSR) (Soviet Library Science); *Nauchnye i tekhnicheskie biblioteki SSSR* (Scientific and Technical Libraries of the USSR); *Nauchnaya i tekhnicheskaya informatsiya* (Scientific and Technical Information) *Seriya I:* Organizatsiya i metodika informatsionnoi raboty (Organisation and Methodology of Information Work) *Seriya 2:* Informatsionnye processy i systemy (Information Processes and Systems); *Sovetskaya Bibliografia* (Soviet Bibliography); *Bibliotekovedenie i bibliografiya za rubezhom* (Librarianship and Bibliography Abroad); *Kniga Issledovaniya i materialy* (Book Studies and Materials); *V mire knig* (In the World of Books); *Knizhnoe obozrenie* (Book Reviews); *Informatika* (Information Science) *Bibliotekovedenie i Bibliografovedenie* Bibliograficheskaya informatsiya
(a) Sovetskaya literatura (b) Inostrannaya literatura (Library Science and Theory of Bibliography, Bibliographic Information
(a) Soviet Literature (b) Foreign Literature;Bibliotekovedenie i Bibliografovedenie (Library Science and Theory of Bibliography) (a) Nauchnyi Referativnyi Sbornik (Abstracts Collection) (b) Obzornaya informatsiya (Survey Information) (c) Express-informatsiya (Express-Information)

Library Reference Books and Journals

Books

Bibliotekovedenie i bibliografiya za rubezhom (Librarianship and Bibliography Abroad), USSR Library Council, The Lenin State Library of the USSR, Prospect Kalinina 3, Moscow 101 000

Bibliotekovedenie i Bibliografovedenie, Bibliograficheskaya informatsiya (Library Science and Theory of Bibliography, Bibliographie Information), USSR Library Council, The Lenin State Library of the USSR, Prospect Kalinina 3, Moscow 101 000

Libraries in the USSR, Clive Bingley Ltd, 16 Pembridge Rd, London W11, UK

Nauchnye i tekhnicheskie biblioteki SSSR (Scientific and Technical Libraries of the USSR), USSR Library Council, The Lenin State Library of the USSR, Prospect Kalinina 3, Moscow 101 000

Journals

Bibliotekar (The Librarian), USSR Library Council, The Lenin State Library of the USSR, Prospect Kalinina 3, Moscow 101 000

Sovetskoje bibliotekovedenie (Soviet Library Science), USSR Library Council, The Lenin State Library of the USSR, Prospect Kalinina 3, Moscow 101 000

Literary Periodicals

Culture and Life (text in English, French, German, Russian and Spanish), Union of Soviet Societies for Friendship and Cultural Relations with Foreign Countries, proezd Sapunova 13-15, Moscow-Centre

Litaratura i Mastatstva (Literature and Art), Ministerstva Kul'tury i Sayuz Pismennikaw BSSR, Zakharava ul 19, Minsk

Literaturnaya Gazeta (Literary Newspaper), USSR Union of Writers, Vorovskogo ul 52, Moscow

Literaturnaya Rossiya (Literary Russia), USSR Union of Writers, Vorovskogo ul 52, Moscow

Molodaya Gvardiya (The Young Guards), Vsesoyuznyi Leninskii Kommunisticheskii Soyuz Molodozhi, Tsentral'nyi Komitet, Sushchevskaya ul 21, Moscow A-55

Moskva; literary magazine, Arbart 20, Moscow

Neva, USSR Union of Writers, Vorovskogo ul 52, Moscow

Novyi Mir (New World); literary, artistic and socio-political journal, USSR Union of Writers, Vorovskogo ul 52, Moscow

Radyans'ke Literaturoznavstvo (Soviet Literary Studies), Akademiya Nauk Ukrayinskoyi SSR, Instytut Literatury im T H Shevchenka ta Spilka Pys'mennykiv Ukrayiny, Kirova 4, Kiev

Russian Literature, North-Holland Publishing Co, PO Box 211, Amsterdam, Netherlands

Russian Literature Triquarterly, Ardis Publishers, 2901 Heatherway, Ann Arbor, Mich 48104, USA

Russkaya Literatura (Russian Literature), Nauka (Science Publishing House), Podsosenskii pereulok 21, Moscow K-62 (journal of the Institute of Russian Literature of the USSR)

Soviet Literature (editions in English, German, Polish, Spanish, Japanese and Czech), USSR Union of Writers, Vorovskogo ul 52, Moscow

V Mire Knig (In the World of Books), USSR Library Council, The Lenin State Library of the USSR, Prospect Kalinina 3, Moscow 101 000

Voprosy Literatury (Questions of Literature), USSR Union of Writers, Vorovskogo ul 52, Moscow

United Arab Emirates

General Information

Language: Arabic (English used in business)
Religion: Muslim
Population: 711,000
Bank Hours: Abu Dhabi: 0800-1200 Saturday-Wednesday; 0800-1100 Thursday. Northern Emirates: 0800-1200 Saturday-Thursday
Shop Hours: Abu Dhabi: Summer: 0800-1300, 1600-dusk Saturday-Thursday; Winter: 0800-1300, 1530-1900 Saturday-Thursday. Northern Emirates: Summer: 0900-1300, 1630-2000 or 2100 Saturday-Thursday; Winter: 0900-1300, 1600-2000 or 2100 Saturday-Thursday
Currency: 100 fils = 1 UAE dirham
Export/Import Information: No tariff on books or advertising matter, except 3% duty on imports by sea, 2% by air in Dubai; 1% ad valorem in Ras al Khaimah and 2% ad valorem in Sharjah. No import licence required except for obscene publications in Dubai

Major Booksellers

Family Bookshop, PO Box 956 Abu Dhabi Tel: 45702 Cable Add: Fambooks

Tahseen S **Khayat***, PO Box 857, Abu Dhabi Tel: 41853

Major Libraries

Centre for Documentation and Research*, Old Palace, PO Box 2380, Abu Dhabi
Dir: Mohammad Morsi Abdullah PhD
Publication: Arabian Gulf Research Review (quarterly)

United Kingdom

General Information

Language: English; Welsh in most of Wales (where it is used alongside English for official purposes). About 80,000 speak Scots Gaelic (in Highlands and Islands of Scotland). Irish is used in parts of Northern Ireland
Religion: Protestant officially. Numerous other religions have significant numbers of adherents
Population: 56 million
Bank Hours: 0930-1530 Monday-Friday
Shop Hours: Generally 0900-1730 Monday-Saturday. Early closing one day week usually.
Currency: 100 pence = 1 pound sterling
Export/Import Information: No tariffs on books; advertising matter dutiable over $2^1/_4$ lb gross weight. No import licences required; nominal exchange controls. Advertising in UK is regulated by statutes and voluntary codes; for information contact Advertising Standards Authority Ltd, 15 Ridgmount St, London WC1
Copyright: UCC, Berne, Florence (see International section)

Book Trade Organizations

Advisory Committee on the Selection of Low-Priced Books for Overseas, c/o The British Council, 10 Spring Gardens, London SW1A 2BN Tel: (01) 930 8466
Secretary: A M Clark

Antiquarian Booksellers' Association, 154 Buckingham Palace Rd, London SW1 Tel: (01) 730 9273
Secretary: Cynthia Bonham-Carter

Association of Authors' Agents, 10 Buckingham Street, London WC2N 6BU Tel: (01) 839 2556
President: Michael Sissons
Secretary: Deborah Rogers

Association of British Directory Publishers, Windsor Court, East Grinstead Ho, East Grinstead, West Sussex RH19 1XA
Chairman: John Dawson *Hon Secretary:* R Duncombe

Association of British Science Writers, c/o 21 Albermarle St, London W1X 4BS
Secretary: Peter Cooper

Association of Learned & Professional Society Publishers, R J Millson, c/o Institution of Mechanical Engineers, 1 Birdcage Walk, London SW1H 9JJ Tel: (01) 222 7899

Association of Mail Order Publishers, 1 New Burlington St, London W1X 1FD Tel: (01) 437 0706
Dir: D R Vickers

Association of Publishers' Educational Representatives
Secretary: John Sayer, 7 Westbury Rd, St Ives, Cambs Tel: St Ives 68364 (STD code 0480)

Authors' Lending & Copyright Society, 20 Garrick St, London WC2E 9BJ Tel: (01) 240 3144
Secretary-General: Elizabeth Thomas

B A Service House Ltd (BASH), 154 Buckingham Palace Rd, London SW1W 9TZ Tel: (01) 730 8214
Company Secretary: Miss P Jewell
Administration Manager: Ms Chris Larkin
Publications: List of Members, Lists of Specialist Booksellers, Directory of British Publishers, Trade Reference Book, Charter Group Economic Survey, Machine Readable Codes, Opening a Bookshop, and other publications relating to the bookselling trade

B A S H, see B A Service House Ltd

B O D, see Booksellers' Orders Distribution

Book Centre Ltd, Southport PR9 9YF Tel: Southport 26881/24331 (STD code 0704) Telex: 67457

The **Book Development** Council, 19 Bedford Sq, London WC1B 3HJ Tel: (01) 580 6321
Chairman: Timothy Rix
International Division of the Publishers Association

The **Book Marketing** Council, 19 Bedford Sq, London WC1B 3HJ Tel: (01) 580 6321/5
Chairman: Charles Clark
Dir: Nigel Sisson
A new home trade division of the Publishers Association, working to promote and expand sales of books in the home market

Book Publishers' Representatives' Association
Honorary Secretary: David Oliphant, 74a Grosvenor Rd, Caversham, Reading RG4 0ES Tel: Reading 475254 (STD code 0734)

Book Tokens Ltd*, 152 Buckingham Palace Rd, London SW1W 9TZ Tel: (01) 730 9258
Secretary: J S Crowe

The **Book Trade** Benevolent Society, Dillon Lodge, The Booksellers Retreat, Kings Langley, Herts WD4 8LT Tel: Kings Langley 63128
Secretary: Ann Brown

Booksellers Association of Great Britain and Ireland, 154 Buckingham Palace Rd, London SW1W 9TZ Tel: (01) 730 8214
Executive Secretary: Tim Godfray
Membership Secretary: M J Bedford
Publications: see B A Service House Ltd

Booksellers Clearing House, 152 Buckingham Palace Rd, London SW1W 9TZ Tel: (01) 730 9258
Man Dir: W A Barnes

Booksellers' Order Distribution Ltd (BOD), 4 Grosvenor Rd, Aldershot, Hants GU11 1DS Tel: Aldershot 20697 (STD Code 0252)
Man Dir and Secretary: Robin Young

Children's Writers' Group, The Society of Authors, 84 Drayton Gardens, London SW10 9SD
Secretary: Diana Shine

Crime Writers' Association, c/o National Book League, Book House, East Hill, Wandsworth, London SW18
Secretary: Marian Babson

Cyngor Llyfrau Cymraeg, see Welsh Books Council

Educational Publishers' Council, 19 Bedford Sq, London WC1B 3HJ Tel: (01) 580 6321/5
Dir: John R M Davies
Schools Division of The Publishers Association

Educational Writers' Group*, 84 Drayton Gardens, London SW10 9SD
Secretary: Philippa MacLiesh

Federation of Children's Book Groups, 30 Sennelys Park Rd, Northfields, Birmingham B31 1AL Tel: (021) 427 4860
Chairman: David Blanch
Publication: ABC (annual, available from Martin Kromer, Secretary, 22 Beacon Row, Bradford 6

Guild of Travel Writers*, 20 Great Chapel St, London W1V 3AQ
Honorary Secretary: Gerry Brenes

I B I S, see International Book Information Services

Independent Publishers Guild
Secretary: Rosemary Pettit,
52 Chepstow Rd, London W2 Tel: (01) 727 0919

International Book Information Services, Waterside, Lowbell Lane, London Colney, St Albans, Herts AL2 1DX Tel: St Albans 25209 (STD code 0727) Telex: 261721
Operates a questionnaired computerized mailing list of academics, schools, libraries, booksellers, worldwide

Lancashire Authors' Association, 8 Whitefield Rd East, Penwortham, Preston PR1 0XJ
General Secretary: Celia Harvey
Publication: The Record (quarterly)

National Federation of Retail Newsagents, 2 Bridewell Pl, London EC4 6AR Tel: (01) 353 6816

Orders Clearing, Waterside, Lowbell Lane, London Colney, St Albans, Herts AL2 1DX Tel: St Albans 25209 (STD code 0727) Telex: 261721

P B D S, see Publishers/Booksellers Delivery Service

P I C S, see Publishers' Information Card Services

Printing and Publishing Industry Training Board, Merit Ho, Edgware Rd, London NW9 5AG Tel: (01) 205 0162
Secretary: George Reid

Publishers Association, 19 Bedford Sq, London WC1B 3HJ Tel: (01) 580 6321/5 Cable Add: Publasoc London WC1 Telex: 21792
Chief Executive: C Bradley

Publishers/Booksellers Delivery Service (PBDS)*, PO Box 30, North Circular Rd, London NW10 0JE Tel: (01) 459 1222

Publishers' Information Card Services, IBIS Ltd, Waterside, Lowbell Lane, London Colney, St Albans, Herts AL2 1DX Tel: St Albans 25209 (STD code 0727) Telex: 261721
Man Dir: Philip J Sturrock
Direct mail promotion for publishers

Publishers' Overseas Circle
Chairman: Nicholas Boon, Mills & Boon Ltd, 17-19 Foley St, London W1A 1DR Tel: (01) 580 9074

Publishers Publicity Circle, c/o J M Dent & Sons Ltd, Aldine Ho, 33 Welbeck St, London W1M 8LX
Publications: Directory of members

Retail Book, Stationery and Allied Trades Employees' Association, 7 Grape St, London WC2 Tel: (01) 836 4897

Retail Bookselling and Stationery Wages Council (Great Britain)*, 12 St James's Square, London SW1Y 4LL Tel: (01) 214 6573

School Bookshop Association, 1 Effingham Rd, Lee, London SE12 Tel: (01) 352 4953
Director: Richard Hill
Publication: Books for Keeps

Scottish Publishers' Association, 25a South West Thistle St La, Edinburgh EH2 1EW Tel: (031) 225 5795
Administrative Executive: Janis G Fox
Chairman: Norman Wilson; *Secretary:* Bill Campbell
Publications: New Books from Scottish Publishers (twice a year)

Society of Authors, 84 Drayton Gardens, London SW10 9SD Tel: (01) 373 6642
General Secretary: David Machin
Publication: The Author (quarterly)

The Society of Indexers
Secretary: Mrs C Robertson, 7A Parker St, Cambridge CB1 1JL Tel: Cambridge 311913 (STD code 0223)
Publication: The Indexer

Society of Young Publishers, c/o Fiona Fullerton, The Bookseller, 12 Dyott St, London WC1A 1DF
Chairman: John Doyle, ITV Books Ltd, 247 Tottenham Court Rd, London W1P 0AU Tel: (01) 636 3666
Publication: Inprint (monthly)

Standard Book Numbering Agency Ltd, 12 Dyott St, London WC1A 1DF Tel: (01) 836 8911
Secretary: Miss E F Budworth
Parent Company: J Whitaker & Sons Ltd, UK (qv)
Publication: International Standard Book Numbering

U K National Serials Data Centre, British Library, Store St, London WC1 Tel: (01) 636 1544
Allocates ISSNs in UK

Union of Welsh Publishers and Booksellers, c/o Welsh Books Council, Queen's Sq, Aberystwyth, Dyfed, Wales

Welsh Books Council (Cyngor Llyfrau Cymraeg), Queen's Sq, Aberystwyth, Dyfed, Wales Tel: Aberystwyth 4151/3 (STD code 0970)
Director: Alun Creunant Davies

Writers' Guild of Great Britain, 430 Edgware Rd, London W2 1EH
General Secretary: Ian Rowland-Hill

Book Trade Reference Books and Journals

Books

The British Book Trade, a Bibliographical Guide, André Deutsch Ltd, 105 Great Russell St, London WC1B 3LJ

The British Library General Catalogue of Printed Books to 1975 (first volumes of total estimated 360 published 1979, completion due 1984); Clive Bingley Ltd, 1-19 New Oxford St, London WC1A 1NE

British Official Publications, Pergamon Press Ltd, Headington Hill Hall, Oxford OX3 0BW

Cassell's Directory of Publishing in Great Britain, the Commonwealth, Ireland and South Africa, Cassell & Co Ltd, 35 Red Lion Sq, London WC1R 4SG

Current British Directories; a guide to the directories published in Great Britain, Ireland, the British Commonwealth and South Africa, CBD Research Ltd, 154 High St, Beckenham BR3 1EA

Dealers in Books: a Directory of Dealers in Secondhand and Antiquarian Books in the British Isles, Sheppard Press Ltd, 15 James St, London WC2E 8BX

Directory of Book Wholesalers, Booksellers Association of Great Britain and Ireland, 154 Buckingham Palace Rd, London SW1W 9TZ

Paperbacks in Print, J Whitaker & Sons Ltd, 12 Dyott St, London WC1A 1DF

Picture Research Handbook, Samuel Smiles Ho, 11 Granville Park, London SE13 7DY

Publishing and Bookselling, Jonathan Cape Ltd, 30 Bedford Sq, London WC1B 3EL

Trade Reference Book, Booksellers Association of Great Britain and Ireland, 154 Buckingham Palace Rd, London SW1W 9TZ

UK Book Readership 1979, Euromonitor Publications Ltd, PO Box 115, 41 Russell Sq, London WC1B 5DL

Writer's and Artist's Yearbook, A & C Black Ltd, 35 Bedford Row, London WC1R 4JH

Journals

Antiquarian Book Monthly Review, 3 Brayfield Ho, Cold Brayfield, Nr Olney, Bucks

The Author, Society of Authors, 84 Drayton Gardens, London SW10 9SD

Book Exchange, Fudge & Co Ltd, Sardinia Ho, 52 Lincolns Inn Fields, London WC2A 3NW

Book Market; for antiquarian and out-of-print books, Clique Ltd, 75 World's End Rd, Handsworth Wood, Birmingham B20 2NS

Bookdealer, Fudge & Co Ltd, Sardinia Ho, 52 Lincolns Inn Fields, London WC2A 3NW

Books from Scotland, Scottish General Publishers' Association, 25 London St, Edinburgh EH3 6LY

Books of the Month and Books To Come, J Whitaker & Sons Ltd, 12 Dyott St, London WC1A 1DF

Bookseller, J Whitaker & Sons Ltd, 12 Dyott St, London WC1A 1DF

Bookselling News, Booksellers' Association of Great Britain and Ireland, 154 Buckingham Palace Rd, London SW1W 9TZ

British Book News, British Council, 65 Davies St, London W1Y 2AA

British Book Production, NBL, Book House, East Hill, London SW18

British Books in Print, J Whitaker & Sons Ltd, 12 Dyott St, London WC1A 1DF (also in microfiche)

British National Bibliography, British Library, Bibliographic Services Division, 7 Rathbone St, London WC1E 7DG

Children's Books of the Year, NBL, Book House, East Hill, London SW18

Clique; the antiquarian booksellers' medium, Clique Ltd, 75 World's End Rd, Handsworth Wood, Birmingham B20 2NS Tel: (021) 554 7308
Editor: Margaret Pamphilon

Directory of British Publishers and their Terms, Booksellers Association of Great Britain and Ireland, 154 Buckingham Palace Rd, London SW1W 9TZ

Gee Report, 15 Hanover Sq, 3rd Floor, London W1

Good Book Guide (quarterly), Braithwaite & Taylor Ltd, PO Box 28, London SW11 4BT

The Indexer, Journal of British, Australian and American Societies of Indexers
Honorary Editor: Hazel K Bell, 139 The Ryde, Hatfield, Herts AL9 5DP Tel: Hatfield 65201 (STD code 070 72)

List of Members, Booksellers Association of Great Britain and Ireland, 154 Buckingham Palace Rd, London SW1W 9TZ

Llais Llyfrau, Cyngor Llyfrau Cymraeg, Queen's Sq, Aberystwyth, Wales (list of all books published in Welsh during previous 6 months and list of books to be published)

National Newsagent, Bookseller, Stationer (weekly), National Newsagent Ltd, Lennox Ho, Norfolk St, London WC2

Publishers in the United Kingdom and their Addresses, J Whitaker & Sons Ltd, 12 Dyott St, London WC1A 1DF

Publishing News, 37-49 Brick St, London W1A 1AN

The Radical Bookseller, Unit 265, 27 Clerkenwell Close, London E1

School Book Review, (half-yearly) Europa Publications Ltd, 18 Bedford Sq, London WC1B 3JN

School Bookshop News, School Bookshop Association, 7 Albermarle St, London W1X 4BB

Smith's Trade News, W H Smith & Son Ltd, Strand Ho, Portugal St, London WC2A 2HS

Whitaker's Books of the Month and Books to Come, J Whitaker & Sons Ltd, 12 Dyott St, London WC1A 1DF

Whitaker's Cumulative Book List, J Whitaker & Sons Ltd, 12 Dyott St, London WC1A 1DF

Publishers

A B C D Group*, 18 Brewer St, London W1R 4AS Tel: (01) 734 1985/6900
Sales: Michael Hayes
This is the marketing organization for Allison & Busby, Marion Boyars, John Calder, Davis Poynter (see individual entries for further details)

Abacus, an imprint of Sphere Books Ltd (qv)

Abacus Press, Abacus House, Speldhurst Rd, Tunbridge Wells, Kent TN4 0HU Tel: Tunbridge Wells 29783/27237 (STD code 0892) Cable Add: Abacus Tunbridgewells Telex: 95652
Man Dir, Publisher: N A Jaysekera; *Editorial:* C T Rivington; *Sales, Rights & Permissions:* Mrs J M White; *Publicity:* Mrs A Terry
Associate Company: Abacus-Kent Ltd
Subjects: Medicine, Science, Technology, Engineering, Mathematics, Computer Sciences, Architecture, Design, Travel Guides, Agriculture, Environmental Sciences, Health Books for Lay Readers, Crafts
1978: 14 titles *Founded:* 1971
ISBN Publisher's Prefix: 0-85626

Abbeville Press, see André Deutsch Ltd

Abbey, an imprint of Murrays Remainder Books (qv)

Abelard-Schuman Ltd, Furnival Ho, 14/18 High Holborn, London WC1 Tel: (01) 242 5832
Man Dir: R Michael Miller; *Editorial:* Rosemary Lanning, Olga Norris, A D Mitchell; *Sales Manager:* Geoff Meakin; *Publicity:* HPR Publicity, 9 Fitzroy Sq, London W1 (Tel: (01) 388 2613); *Rights & Permissions:* Roseanne Holme
Parent Company: Blackie & Son Ltd (qv)

Imprints: include Grasshopper Books
Subjects: Children's Books
1978: 31 titles *1979:* 39 titles *Founded:* 1958
ISBN Publisher's Prefix: 0-200

Aberdeen University Press Ltd, see Pergamon Press Ltd

Abson Books, Abson, Wick, Bristol BS15 5TT Tel: Abson 2446 (STD code 027582)
Partners: Anthea Bickerton, Pat McCormack
Subjects: Language Glossaries, Cookery, Regional Eating Out Guides, Sports, Humour, Gardening, Local Bristol & Bath books
ISBN Publisher's Prefix: 0-902920

Academic Press Inc (London) Ltd*, 24-28 Oval Rd, London NW1 7DX Tel: (01) 267 4466 Cable Add: Acadinc London NW1 Telex: 25775
Shipping Add: High St, Footscray, Sidcup, Kent
Man Dir & Editorial: R A Farrand; *Marketing Dir:* A J Cornwall; *Promotions Manager:* D C Sanderson; *Advertising Manager, Rights & Permissions:* P A Spencer
Parent Company: Academic Press Inc, 111 Fifth Ave, New York, NY10003, USA
Subsidiary Companies: Johnson Reprint Co Ltd; Harcourt Brace Jovanovich Ltd (qv)
Associate Companies: Harcourt Brace Jovanovich Group (Australia) Pty Ltd, Australia (qv); Grune & Stratton Inc and Johnson Reprint Corporation (both at 111 Fifth Ave, New York, NY 10003)
Subjects: Reference, Scientific, Technical, Medicine, Psychology, Social Science, University Textbooks, Educational Materials
1978: 565 titles
ISBN Publisher's Prefixes: 0-12 (Academic Press), 0-15 (Harcourt Brace Jovanovich), 0-8089 (Grune & Stratton), 0-384 (Johnson Reprint)

Academic Publications*, Highfield, Dane Hill, Haywards Heath, West Sussex RH17 7EX Tel: Dane Hill 214 (STD code 082573) Cable Add: Copen Telex: 95246 (Copen-G)
Subjects: University Textbooks, Technical & Scientific, Medical, Philosophy, General Literature
Founded: 1974
ISBN Publisher's Prefix: 0-900307

Academy Editions, 42 Leinster Gardens, London W2 Tel: (01) 402 2141 Telex: 896928
Man Dir: Dr Andreas C Papadakis; *Sales Manager:* John Rule; *Rights & Permissions, Publicity:* Solveig Williams; *Production:* Richard Kelly
Orders to: Academy Editions, 7/8 Holland St, London W8 Tel: (01) 937 6996
Parent Company: Academy Art Books Ltd (at above address)
Subsidiary Companies: Academy Editions, France (qv); Architectural Design, 42 Leinster Gardens, London W2
Imprint: Alec Tiranti (firm also publishes *Architectural Design* and *Architectural Monographs*)
Subjects: Architecture, Fine and Applied Arts, Photography
Bookshops: Academy Bookshop & London Art Bookshop, 7/8 Holland St, London W8 Tel: (01) 937 6996
Founded: 1967
ISBN Publisher's Prefixes: 0-85670, 0-85458, 0-902620

Actinic Press Ltd, 129 St John's Hill, London SW11 1TD Tel: (01) 228 8091
Man Dir: J G F Miller
Subjects: Technical & Scientific, Medical
Founded: 1926
ISBN Publisher's Prefix: 0-900024

Addison-Wesley Publishers Ltd, 53 Bedford Sq, London WC1B 3D2 Tel: (01) 631 1636 Cable Add: Adiwes London WC1 Telex: 8811948
Man Dir: Paul R Chapman; *Sales Dir:* Stanley B Malcolm; *Rights & Permissions:* Tim Davison
Parent Company: Addison-Wesley Publishing Co Inc, Mass 01867, USA
Associate Companies: Addison-Wesley Publishing Co, Australia (qv); Addison-Wesley (Canada) Ltd, 36 Prince Andrew Pl, Don Mills, Ontario, Canada; Addison-Wesley Publishing Group, Netherlands (qv); Intereditions, 87 Ave du Maine, 75014 Paris, France; Addison-Wesley (Singapore) Private Ltd, Singapore (qv); Addison-Wesley Publishing Co Inc, Philippines (qv); Benjamin/Cummings Inc, UK (qv); Benjamin/Cummings Publishing Co Inc, 2727 Sand Hill Rd, Menlo Park, Calif 94025; Fondo Educativo Interamericano CA, Venezuela (qv); Fondo Educativo Interamericano de Mexico SA, Mexico (qv)
Subjects: Reference, Business, Juveniles, Humanities, General & Social Sciences, Textbooks, Educational Materials, Medicine
Founded: 1942
ISBN Publisher's Prefixes: 0-201 (Addison-Wesley), 0-8053 (Benjamin/Cummings), 0-8465 (Cummings)

Adkinson Parrish Ltd, 49 Great Marlborough St, London W1V 1DB Tel: (01) 434 2617 Cable Add: Macjan Telex: 23168
Chairman: Ronald Whiting; *Man Dir:* Robert Adkinson; *Managing Editor:* Clare Howell
Parent Company: BPC Ltd (qv)
Associate Company: Macdonald/Futura Publishers Ltd (qv)
Subjects: General Nonfiction, Biography, History, How-to, Music, Art, Reference, Religion
Miscellaneous: Editorial and production organization producing books for international co-editions

Adlard Coles Ltd, see Granada Publishing

Alex **Aiken**, 48 Merrycrest Ave, Glasgow G46 6BJ Tel: (041) 637 2438
Principal: Alex Aiken
Subjects: Military and Naval History, Biography, Natural Sciences
Founded: 1971
ISBN Publisher's Prefix: 0-9502134

Airlife Publications (Shrewsbury) Ltd*, 7 St John's Hill, Shrewsbury, Salop SY1 1JE Tel: Shrewsbury 3651 (STD code 0743)
Man Dir, Rights & Permissions: A D R Simpson; *Editorial, Sales:* C A Nelson
Associate Company: Anthony Nelson Ltd (address as above)

Akros Publications, 25 Johns Rd, Radcliffe-on-Trent, Nottingham NG12 2GW Tel: Radcliffe-on-Trent 4802 (STD code 06073)
Man Dir, Editorial, Production, Publicity, Rights & Permissions: Duncan Glen; *Sales:* Margaret Glen
Subjects: Scottish Poetry and Literary Criticism
1978: 6 titles *Founded:* 1965

Aladdin Books Ltd, 70 Old Compton St, London W1V 5PA Tel: (01) 734 5186 Telex: 21115
Man Dir: Charles Nicholas; *Art, Editorial Dir:* Charles Matheson; *Sales Dir:* Lynn Lockett
Subjects: Juveniles, Co-editions
Founded: 1980

Albyn Press Ltd, 2 & 3 Abbeymount, Edinburgh EH8 8JH Tel: (031) 661 9339
Man Dir: Charles Skilton
Parent Company: Charles Skilton Ltd (qv)
Subjects: Scottish, General, Prints
ISBN Publisher's Prefix: 0-284

Alden & Mowbray Ltd, see A R Mowbray & Co Ltd

Aldine Paperbacks, an imprint of J M Dent & Sons Ltd (qv)

Aldus Books Ltd*, Aldus House, 17 Conway St, London W1P 6BS Tel: (01) 387 2811
Cable Add: Alday London W1
Telex: 261675
Chairman: John T Sargent; *Man Dir:* Wolfgang Foges; *Dirs:* Nelson Doubleday, Miss Frame-Smith, D H Bekhor; *Editorial:* John Mason; *European Sales Manager:* Florence Robbins
Subject: General Nonfiction
ISBN Publisher's Prefix: 0-490

Aldwych Press, 3 Henrietta St, London WC2E 8LU Tel: (01) 240 0856
Man Dir, Rights & Permissions: Danny Maher; *Editorial:* Robert Hagelstein; *Sales, Publicity:* Jessica Kingsley
Subjects: Academic, Library Science, Sociology, Economics, Politics, European Studies, Reference
1979: 4 titles *1980:* 10 titles *Founded:* 1979
ISBN Publisher's Prefix: 0-86172

Alison Press, an associate of Secker & Warburg (qv)

Ian **Allan** Ltd, Terminal Ho, Shepperton, Middx TW17 8AS Tel: Walton-on-Thames 28950 (STD Code 09322) Cable Add: Ianallanshepp Telex: 929806
Chairman & Man Dir: Ian Allan; *Editorial:* A Hollingsworth; *Sales:* Richard Fagge; *Production:* R Dymott; *Rights & Permissions:* R Dymott
Parent Company: Ian Allan (Group) Ltd
Associate Companies: A Lewis (Masonic Publishers) Ltd; Locomotive Publishing Co Ltd; Modern Transport Publishing Co Ltd; Railway Publications Ltd; Railway World Ltd
Imprints: Ian Allan, A Lewis, Modern Transport
Subjects: Transport, Travel, Aviation, Militaria, Naval
1978: 98 titles *Founded:* 1945
ISBN Publisher's Prefix: 0-7110

Philip **Allan** Publishers Ltd, Market Pl, Deddington, Oxford OX5 4SE Tel: Deddington 38652 (STD code 0869)
Man Dir, Editorial, Sales: Philip Allan; *Production, Publicity, Rights:* Ann Hirst
Subjects: University & College Textbooks in Economics, Accounting and Business Studies
1978: 6 titles *1979:* 4 titles *Founded:* 1973
ISBN Publisher's Prefix: 0-86003

J A **Allen** & Co Ltd, 1 Lower Grosvenor Pl, London SW1W 0EL Tel: (01) 834 5606/7
Cable Add: Allenbooks London
Sales Dir: C Kendall; *Publicity & Advertising:* Mrs E Martyn; *Rights & Permissions:* J A Allen
Subsidiary Companies: The Caduceus Press, Sporting Book Services (both at above address)
Associate Company: Sporting Book Centre Inc, Canaan, New York 12029, USA
Branch Off: D M S Bldg, Sheldon Way, New Hythe Lane, Larkfield, Maidstone, Kent
Subject: Horsemanship, Horses & Horse Sports
Book Club: Horseman's Bookclub
Bookshop: The Horseman's Bookshop, 1 Lower Grosvenor Pl, London SW1

UNITED KINGDOM 367

1978: 15 titles *1979:* 25 titles *Founded:* 1926
ISBN Publisher's Prefix: 0-85131

W H Allen & Co Ltd, 44 Hill St, London W1X 8LB Tel: (01) 493 6777 Cable Add: Wyndhoward London Telex: 28117
Man Dir: Bob Tanner; *Marketing Dir, Publicity & Advertising:* Henry Kitchen; *Sales Managers:* Ray Mudie, Lester Heath; *Editorial:* Mike Bailey, Amanda Girling, Hilary Muray; *Production Manager:* Mark Pickard; *Rights & Permissions:* Lesley Toll
Orders to: Tiptree Book Services Ltd, Tiptree, Colchester, Essex CO5 0SR
Parent Company: Howard & Wyndham Ltd (qv)
Subsidiary Company: Allan Wingate (Publishers) Ltd (qv)
Associate Companies: Brown Watson Ltd (qv); Murrays Remainder Books (qv); The Grant Educational Co Ltd
Imprints: W H Allen, Longbow, Made Simple Books, Star, Tandem, Target
Branch Offs: W H Allen & Co Ltd, 20 Upper Merrion St, Dublin
Subjects: Belles Lettres, Poetry, Biography, History, How-to, Reference, Juveniles, Paperbacks, Social Science, Primary & Secondary Textbooks
1978: 350 titles *Founded:* 1780
ISBN Publisher's Prefixes: 0-352 (Star), 0-491 (W H Allen), 0-85523 (Allan Wingate), 0-426 (Target)

George Allen & Unwin (Publishers) Ltd, 40 Museum St, London WC1A 1LU Tel: (01) 405 8577 Cable Add: Deucalion London WC1 Telex: 826261
Shipping Add: United Cargo Containers, Thameside Industrial Estate, Silvertown, London E16
Chairman: Rayner Unwin; *Publicity Manager:* Victoria Carew Hunt; *Sales Development Manager:* Martin Blackman; *Production:* Laurie Pine; *Foreign Rights Manager:* Alina Dadlez; *Paperbacks Manager:* David Fielder
Sales, Distribution, Accounts & Publicity Off: PO Box 18, Park Lane, Hemel Hempstead, Herts Tel: Hemel Hempstead 3244 (STD Code 0442) Telex: 826261
Subsidiary Companies: George Allen & Unwin (Australia) Ltd; Allen & Unwin Inc, USA; Thomas Murby Ltd (qv)
Imprint: Unwin Paperbacks
Subjects: Biography, History, Outdoor and Indoor Sports, Animals, Music, Architecture, Railways, Carpets, Costume, Religions, Health, Nutrition, Child Care, Humour, Fantasy, Social Sciences, Humanities, Education, Life and Earth Sciences, Civil Engineering
1978: 150 titles *Founded:* 1914
ISBN Publisher's Prefix: 0-04

Allison & Busby Ltd, 6a Noel St, London W1V 3RB Tel: (01) 734 1498
Dirs: Clive Allison, Margaret Busby
Imprints: Alternative Editions, Motive
Subjects: General Fiction, Belles Lettres, Music, Art, Biography, History, Political & Social Science, Economics, Juveniles
1978: approx 40 titles *1979:* approx 50 titles *Founded:* 1968
ISBN Publisher's Prefix: 0-85031

Allman & Son (Publishers) Ltd, see Mills & Boon Ltd

Alphabet & Image Ltd, Sherborne, Dorset Tel: Bishop's Caundle 588 (STD Code 096323) Cable Add: Alphabook Sherborne Telex: 46534 Alphab G
Man Dir, Production: A E Birks-Hay; *Editorial:* M L Birks-Hay; *Sales:* C Morrison
Imprint: Alphabooks
Branch Off: 63a Lancaster Grove, London NW3
Subjects: Illustrated Books on Crafts, Fine Arts, Architecture, Horticulture, Archaeology, History, Bee-keeping
1978: 10 titles *1979:* 10 titles *Founded:* 1972
ISBN Publisher's Prefixes: 0-906670, 0-9506171

Alphabooks, an imprint of Alphabet & Image Ltd (qv)

Alpine Books, an imprint of Everest Books Ltd (qv)

Alternative Editions, an imprint of Allison & Busby Ltd (qv)

Althea's Pet Series, an imprint of Dinosaur Publications Ltd (qv)

American University Publishers Group Ltd, 1 Gower St, London WC1 E6HA Tel: (01) 580 3994 Cable Add: Amunpress
Man Dir: John Dawson; *Sales Manager:* P Chapman; *Publicity:* J Browning
Orders to: International Book Distributors Ltd, 66 Wood Lane End, Hemel Hempstead, Herts
Subjects: Belles Lettres, Poetry, Biography, History, Music, Art, Philosophy, Reference, Religion, High-priced Paperbacks, Medicine, Psychology, General & Social Science
Founded: 1965
Miscellaneous: Group includes University of Alabama Press, University of Illinois Press, Indiana University Press, University of Missouri Press, University of Nebraska Press, University of Notre Dame Press, Ohio University Press, Pennsylvania State University Press, University of Texas Press, University of Washington Press, University of Wisconsin Press

Anchor, an imprint of Doubleday & Co Inc (qv)

Andersen Press Ltd, 3 Fitzroy Sq, London W1P 6JD Tel: (01) 387 2888, (01) 637 1694 Cable Add: Literarius London W1 Telex: 261212
Man Dir, Editorial: Klaus Flugge; *Sales:* (export) Clyde Hunter; *Publicity, Rights & Permissions:* Audrey Adams
Associate Company: Hutchinson Publishing Group Ltd (qv)
Subjects: Children's Books
1978: 24 titles *1979:* 25 titles *Founded:* 1975
ISBN Publisher's Prefix: 0-905478

Angus & Robertson (UK) Ltd, 10 Earlham St, London WC2H 9LP Tel: (01) 240 2935 Cable Add: Ausboko Telex: 897284 arpubg
Man Dir: David Harris; *Sales Manager:* Bob Siwecki; *Publicity and Promotions Manager:* Susan Oudôt; *Rights & Permissions:* Jane Gregory
Orders to: Tiptree Book Services Ltd, Tiptree, Colchester, Essex CO5 0SR
Parent Company: Angus & Robertson Publishers, Australia (qv)
Subjects: General Fiction & Non-fiction, Biography, Beauty & Health, Autobiography, Cookery, Craft, Natural History, Poetry, Sports & Outdoor Games, Children's Books
1978: 50 titles *Founded:* 1884
ISBN Publisher's Prefix: 0-207

The **Appletree** Press Ltd, 7 James St South, Belfast BT2 8DL Tel: Belfast 43074/46756 (STD code 0232)
Man Dir, Sales, Publicity: J D Murphy; *Editorial:* D Marshall, Peter Carr; *Rights & Permissions:* D Webster; *Production:* P Moss
Associate Company: Appletree Press (Printers) Ltd (at above address)
Subjects: Belles Lettres, Poetry, History, Music, Art, Juveniles, Low- & High-priced Paperbacks, Educational Materials, Photography, Fishing, Guide Books
1978: 8 titles *Founded:* 1974
ISBN Publisher's Prefix: 0-904651

Applied Science Publishers Ltd, Rippleside Commercial Estate, Barking, Essex Tel: (01) 595 2121 Cable Add: Elsbark Barking
Man Dir, Overseas Sales: Leslie E Rayner; *Editorial, Rights & Permissions:* George Olley; *Production:* Alan Chesterton; *UK Sales:* Clive Rayner; *Promotions Manager:* Robert Young
Parent Company: Elsevier-NDU nv, Netherlands (qv)
Imprints: Institute of Petroleum
Subjects: Agriculture, Architectural Science, Building, Civil Engineering, Bakery, Materials Science, Chemistry, Chemical Engineering, Mechanical Engineering, Environmental Science, Food Technology, Petroleum Technology, Plastics & Rubber, Dictionaries
1978: 50 titles *1979:* 50 titles *Founded:* 1936
Miscellaneous: Publish journals covering agriculture, food technology, applied energy, conservation, pollution, plastics, acoustics, material science associates, mechanical engineering
ISBN Publisher's Prefix: 0-85334

Aquarian Press Ltd, Denington Estate, Wellingborough, Northamptonshire NN8 2RQ Tel: Wellingborough 76031 (STD code 0933) Cable Add: Thorgroup Wellingborough Telex: 311072 Thopub G
Chairman: J A Young; *Man Dir:* D J Young; *Rights & Permissions:* J A Winslow; *Editor:* M A Cox
Parent Company: Thorsons Publishers Ltd (qv)
Subjects: Astrology, Comparative Religion, Magic & Occultism, Occult History, Paranormal & Psychical Phenomena, Philosophy, Qabalah, Tarot
1980: 27 titles *Founded:* 1953
ISBN Publisher's Prefix: 0-85500

Aquila Publishing, PO Box 1, Portree, Isle of Skye IV51 9BT Tel: Sligachan 257 (STD code 047 852)
Chairman, Man Dir, Editorial, Production: James Green; *Sales:* A Johnston; *Publicity, Rights & Permissions:* A Green
Associate companies: Johnston Green & Co (Publishers) Ltd, 27 Hamilton Dr, Glasgow G12; Wayzgoose Press
Subsidiary Company: The Phaethon Press; Prospice
Imprints: Aquila, Aquila/The Phaethon Press, Prospice, Aquila/The Wayzgoose Press
Subjects: Literature, Cookery, Ecology, Poetry, Critical Studies
Bookshop: address as above
1978: 12 titles *Founded:* 1968
ISBN Publisher's Prefixes: 0-903226, 0-7275

Architectural Press Ltd, 9 Queen Anne's Gate, London SW1H 9BY Tel: (01) 222 4333 Cable Add: Buildable London SW1 Telex: 8953505
Book Publishing Dir: Godfrey Golzen; *Man Dir:* Michael Regan; *Technical Editor:* Maritz Vandenberg; *Trade Sales Manager:* Alan Mason; *Marketing & Business Manager:* William Hiller; *Publicity Manager:* Sally Evans; *Production:* Keith Kneebone; *Rights & Permissions:* Jenny Towndrow
Subsidiary Company and Imprint: Astragal Books
Subjects: Architecture, High-priced Paperbacks, Urban Planning, Reference, University Textbooks, Energy Conservation, Design
1979: 35 titles *1980:* 65 titles *Founded:* 1895
ISBN Publisher's Prefix: 0-85139 (Architectural Press), 0-906525 (Astragal Books)

UNITED KINGDOM

The **Archon** Press Ltd*, c/o Pandemic Ltd, 24 Red Lion St, London WC1R 4PX Cable Add: Archon London Telex: 21115
Man Dir: Charles V Nicholas; *Production Manager:* Sue Glover; *Foreign Rights:* Lynn Lockett
Parent Company: Grampian Holdings Ltd
Subjects: Juveniles, Co-editions
1978: 23 titles *Founded:* 1973

Arena, an imprint of Inter-Varsity Press (qv)

Argus Books Ltd*, Argus House, 14 St James Rd, Watford, Herts Tel: Watford 47281/2 (STD code 0923)
Man & Sales Dir: H Ricketts
Parent Company: Argus Press Ltd
Associate Company: Wayland Publishers Ltd (qv)
Imprints: Fountain Press, Model & Allied Publications (qv), Harleyford Publications, Bellona Publications
Subjects: Hobbies, Photography, Technical
ISBN Publisher's Prefixes: 0-85242, 0-85344

Argus Communications (UK Division), Edinburgh Way, Harlow, Essex CM20 2HL Tel: Harlow 39441/4 (STD code 0279) Telex: 817086
General Manager: Richard De Rosa; *Marketing Manager:* James Forman
Parent Company: DLM Inc, 7440 Natchez Ave, Niles, Illinois 60648, USA
Subjects: Religion, Popular Psychology, Education
1978-79: 26 titles *Founded:* (UK) 1975
ISBN Publisher's Prefix: 0-913592

Aris & Phillips Ltd, Teddington Ho, Warminster, Wilts BA12 8PQ Tel: Warminster 213409 (STD code 0985)
Orders to: La Haule Books Ltd, West Lodge, La Haule, Jersey, Channel Islands
Man Dir: Adrian Phillips; *Editorial:* John Aris; *Sales, Publicity, Rights & Permissions:* Lucinda Phillips; *Production:* Michael Coultas
Associate Companies: La Haule Books Ltd, West Lodge, La Haule, Jersey, Channel Islands; Serindia Publications, 10 Parkfields, Putney, London SW15
Subjects: Ancient History, Oriental, Classical, Middle East, Archaeology
1978: 15 titles *1979:* 15 titles *Founded:* 1972
ISBN Publisher's Prefix: 0-85668

Ark, an imprint of Scripture Union (qv)

Arlington Books (Publishers) Ltd, 3 Clifford St, Mayfair, London W1X 1RA Tel: (01) 439 1688
Chairman, Man Dir: Desmond Elliott; *Rights & Permissions Dir:* Christine Lunness; *Sales Dir:* Dallas Manderson; *Production and Editorial:* Angela Dahms
Trade Dept: Biblios Ltd, Glenside Industrial Estate, Partridge Green, Horsham, West Sussex Tel: Horsham 710971 (STD Code 0403)
Subjects: General Fiction and Non-fiction, Health, Biography
1978: 20 titles *Founded:* 1960
ISBN Publisher's Prefix: 0-85140

Armada Books, see William Collins Sons & Co Ltd

Arms & Armour Press, an imprint of Lionel Leventhal Ltd (qv)

E J **Arnold** & Son Ltd, Butterley St, Leeds LS10 1AX Tel: Leeds 442944 (STD Code 0532) Cable Add: Arnold Leeds Telex: 556347
Publishing Dir: M E Wayte; *Editorial:* S D L Keating; *Sales, Rights & Permissions:* Brian Green; *Production:* D R Shenton; *Publicity:* Mrs P Jackson
Imprint: Pepper Press (Children's Books)
Subjects: Primary & Secondary Educational Books, Language kits, Audio Visual Material, Educational Supplies
Book Club: Bookworm Club (owned jointly with W Heffer & Sons Ltd, Cambridge)
1978: 59 titles *1979:* 28 titles *Founded:* 1863
ISBN Publisher's Prefix: 0-560

Edward **Arnold** (Publishers) Ltd, 41 Bedford Sq, London WC1B 3DQ Tel: (01) 637 7161 Cable Add: Scholarly London W1 Telex: 847918
Chairman & Man Dir: Anthony Hamilton; *Sales:* George Davies, John Russell; *Production:* Robin Smeeton; *Publicity:* Jane Oakley; *Rights & Permissions:* Arlene Seaton
Subsidiary Company: Edward Arnold (Australia) Pty Ltd, Australia (qv)
Branch Off: Woodlands Park Ave, Woodlands Park, Maidenhead, Berks (Trade)
Subjects: Humanities, General & Science, Medicine, University & Secondary Textbooks, Technical, Education, English Language Teaching
1978: 195 titles *1979:* 228 titles *Founded:* 1890
ISBN Publisher's Prefix: 0-7131

Arrow Books Ltd, 3 Fitzroy Sq, London W1P 6JD Tel: (01) 388 7601
Chairman: R A A Holt; *Man Dir:* Roger Lloyd-Taylor; *Sales:* Richard Tucker; *Editorial:* Terence Blacker
Orders to: Tiptree Book Services, Church Rd, Tiptree, Nr Colchester, Essex
Subjects: General Fiction & Nonfiction, Paperbacks
Founded: 1948
Miscellaneous: Arrow Books is a Division of The Hutchinson Publishing Group Ltd (qv)
ISBN Publisher's Prefix: 0-09

Art Heritage, an imprint of Scorpion Publications Ltd (qv)

Artemis Press Ltd, Sedgwick Park, Horsham, West Sussex Tel: Lower Beeding 369 (STD code 040376) Cable Add: Artemis Horsham
Man Dir: M T Bizony; *Sales Manager:* A B Simmons
Subsidiary Companies: Riband Books, Sedgwick Park, Horsham, Sussex; New Educational Press (imprint)
Subjects: General Fiction, Belles Lettres, Poetry, History, Music, Art, Philosophy, Reference, High-priced Paperbacks, General Science, Technical, University, Secondary & Primary Textbooks, Educational Materials, Large-type Reprints
Founded: 1955
ISBN Publisher's Prefix: 0-85141

Artists House, an imprint of Mitchell Beazley London Ltd (qv)

Ascent Books Ltd, 49-51 Bedford Row, London WC1V 6RL Tel: (01) 242 7866 Telex: 28413
Man Dir, Editorial, Sales, Production, Rights & Permissions: Christopher Foster; *Publicity:* Ingela Claxton
Orders to: George Philip & Son, PO Box 1, Littlehampton, Sussex BN17 7EN
Subject: European History
ISBN Publisher's Prefix: 0-906407

Ashmolean Museum Publications, Ashmolean Museum, Beaumont St, Oxford OX1 2PH Tel: Oxford 511281/57522 (STD code 0865)
Publications Officer: R I H Charlton
Subjects: European & Oriental Art & Archaeology, Numismatics, Classical Studies, Egyptology
1978: 10 titles *1979:* 9 titles
ISBN Publisher's Prefix: 0-900090

Aslan Publishing Services Ltd, see Lion Publishing

Associated Book Publishers Ltd, 11 New Fetter Lane, London EC4P 4EE Tel: (01) 583 9855 Cable Add: Elegiacs London EC4P 4EE Telex: 263398
Shipping Add: North Way, Andover, Hants
Chairman: P H B Allsop; *Sales Dir:* C H Shirley
See subsidiary company individual entries for further details
Subsidiary Companies: Associated Book Publishers (Aust) Ltd, Australia (qv); Associated Book Publishers (New Zealand) Ltd, New Zealand (qv); Associated Book Publishers (UK) Ltd; Associated Book Publishers (Services) Ltd; Chapman & Hall Ltd (qv); Current Law Publishers Ltd; Eyre & Spottiswoode (Publishers) Ltd (qv); W Green & Son Ltd (qv); Magnum Books (imprint only) (qv); Methuen & Co Ltd (qv); Methuen Children's Books Ltd (qv); Eyre Methuen Ltd (qv); Methuen Educational Ltd; Methuen Paperbacks Ltd; Momentum Licensing Ltd; New Cavendish Books Ltd; Police Review Publishing Co Ltd; E & F N Spon Ltd (qv); Stevens & Sons Ltd (qv); Sweet & Maxwell Ltd (qv); Sweet & Maxwell Spon (Booksellers) Ltd; Tavistock Publications Ltd (qv)
Subjects: Legal, Periodicals, Academic & Scientific, Children's, General
Bookshops: Hammicks Bookshops Ltd at Alton, Farnham, Basingstoke, Horsham, London, Southampton, Windsor
1978: 597 titles *1979:* 661 titles *Founded:* 1958

Associated Business Press, Ludgate Ho, 107-111 Fleet St, London EC4A 2AB Tel: (01) 353 3851 Telex: 917036
Publishing Director: Arthur Johnson
Subject: Management

Associated University Presses, associate company of Thomas Yoseloff Ltd (qv)

Astragal Books, see Architectural Press Ltd

Antony **Atha** Publishers Ltd, Hillmorton Rd, Rugby, Warwickshire CV22 5AN Tel: Rugby 72755 (STD code 0788)
Man Dir: C A Atha
Subjects: Sporting Books, Limited Editions, Educational Materials
1978: 5 titles *1979:* 1 title *Founded:* 1975
ISBN Publisher's Prefix: 0-904475

Athene Publishing Co, an imprint of Thorsons Publishers Ltd (qv)

The **Athlone** Press*, 90-91 Great Russell St, London WC1B 3PY Tel: (01) 631 4141
Shipping Add: Tiptree Book Services Ltd, Tiptree, Colchester, Essex
Sales Manager: P N Marks; *Rights & Permissions:* Miss S Fairbairn
Parent Company: Bemrose UK Ltd (qv for associate companies)
UK Trade Representation: Constable & Co Ltd, 10 Orange St, London WC2
Subjects: Architecture, Archaeology, Bibliography, Biological Sciences, Chemistry, Ecology, Physics, Astronomy, Computer Science, Economics, Modern & Classical Languages, Belles Lettres, Poetry, Biography, History, Music, Art, Philosophy, Religion, High-priced Paperbacks, Medicine, Engineering, General & Social Science, University & Secondary Textbooks, Law
1978: 20 titles *Founded:* 1949
ISBN Publisher's Prefix: 0-485

Atlantic, an imprint of Ramboro Enterprises Ltd (qv)

Atlantic Communications Ltd*, 19 Coalecroft Rd, London SW15 Tel: (01) 7892740

Subjects: Contemporary History, Current Affairs, Ecology & the Environment
Augener, an imprint of Stainer & Bell Ltd (qv)

Aurum Press Ltd, 11 Garrick St, London WC2E 9AR Tel: (01) 240 2826/3072 Telex: 299557 Carlar
Joint Man Dirs: Timothy Chadwick, Michael Haggiag; *Publishing Dir:* Michael Haggiag; *Managing Editor:* Ray Martin; *Sales Dir:* Timothy Chadwick; *Art Dir:* Neil Clitheroe; *Publicity:* HPR Publicity, 9 Fitzroy Sq, London W1 (Tel: (01) 388 2613)
Orders to: J M Dent & Sons (Distribution) Ltd, Dunhams Lane, Letchworth, Herts SG6 1LF
Subjects: Large Format, Illustrated, General
1978: 4 titles *1979:* 1 title *Founded:* 1977
ISBN Publisher's Prefix: 0-906053

Autobooks Ltd, Golden Lane, Brighton, East Sussex BN1 2QJ Tel: Brighton 721721 (STD code 0273)
Man Dir: Michael A McKirdy; *Sales Dir:* Stuart C Forbes
Parent Company: Siemssen Hunter Ltd
Subjects: Do-it-Yourself, Car Workshop Manuals
1978: 18 titles *1979:* 24 titles *Founded:* 1958
ISBN Publisher's Prefixes: 0-85146, 0-85147

Automobile Association, Fanum Ho, Basingstoke RG21 2EA Tel: Basingstoke 62929 (STD Code 0256) Telex: 858538
Editorial: T E G Davies; *Sales:* Victor Press
Subjects: Tourist Guides, Guidebooks, Maps, Atlases, Leisure, Travel
1978: 12 titles *1979:* 16 titles
ISBN Publisher's Prefix: 0-861450

Avebury Publishing Co Ltd, Olympic Ho, 63 Woodside Rd, Amersham, Bucks HP6 6AA Tel: Amersham 22121 (STD code 02403)
Man Dir: J M Dening
Orders to: The Distribution Centre, Blackhorse Rd, Letchworth, Herts SG6 1HN
Imprints: Avebury, Gregg International
Subjects: Scholarly Monographs and Reprints in Humanities, Languages, Philosophy, Landscape Studies; Business/Professional (publishes some titles in microfiche)
Founded: 1977
ISBN Publisher's Prefixes: 0-86127 (Avebury), 0-576 (Gregg)

B B C Publications, 35 Marylebone High St, London W1M 4AA Tel: (01) 580 5577
Cable Add: Broadcasts London
Telex: 265781
General Manager: J G Holmes; *Head of Exports, Rights:* John Hore; *Circulation Manager:* P G Shaw; *Production Manager:* P Birch; *Publicity:* K J Bristow
Orders to: 144/152 Bermondsey St, London SE1 3TH
Subjects: General Fiction, History, How-to, Music, Art, Reference, Religion, Juveniles, Low- & High-priced Paperbacks, Medicine, Engineering, General & Social Science, Secondary Textbooks, Adult Education
Bookshops: 35 Marylebone High St, London W1M 4AA; Broadcasting House, Portland Pl, London W1A 1AA; BBC Television Centre, Wood Lane, London W12 7RJ
Founded: 1925
ISBN Publisher's Prefix: 0-563

B C W, an imprint of LSP Books Ltd (qv)

B H R A Fluid Engineering*, Cranfield, Bedford MK43 0AJ Tel: Bedford 750422 (STD code 0234) Telex: 825059
Subjects: Reviews, Bibliographies, Conference Proceedings and Abstracts Journals on Fluid Engineering
1978: 10 titles *1979:* 8 titles
ISBN Publisher's Prefix: 0-906085

B P C Ltd (formerly British Printing Corporation Ltd), 44 Great Queen St, London WC2B 5AS Tel: (01) 240 3411
Cable Add: Britprint Telex: 262725
Supervising Dir: (Publishing Division) A M Alfred
Subjects: General Fiction, Belles Lettres, Poetry, Biography, History, How-to, Music, Art, Philosophy, Reference, Low-priced Paperbacks & Part-works, Primary & Secondary Textbooks
Miscellaneous: BPC is a holding company which controls Adkinson Parrish Ltd (qv); Arben Publishing Co Ltd; The Caxton Publishing Co Ltd (qv); Latimer House Ltd (qv); Macdonald/Futura Publishers Ltd (qv); Macdonald Educational (qv); New Caxton Library Service Ltd (qv); Phoebus Publishing Co (qv); Waterlow (London) Ltd (qv)
Overseas Subsidiaries: Novalit (ANZ) Pty Ltd, Australia; IPA Produktion AS, Denmark; International Learning Systems (Japan) Ltd, Tokyo, Japan; Purnell & Sons (SA) Pty Ltd, South Africa (qv); Novalit (Books) Ltd, New Zealand; IPA Distributusjon Als, Norway; KG Bertmarks Förlag AB, Sweden; Delphin Verlag GmbH, Switzerland (qv); Macdonald Middle East Sarl, Lebanon; Macdonald & Janes (Australia) Pty Ltd

B S C Books Ltd, 33 Maiden Lane, London WC2 Tel: (01) 836 3341
Man Dir: Bill Smith
Imprint: The Booksmith
Bookshops: Booksmith chain
1980: 10 titles
Miscellaneous: Firm is also a wholesaler and remainder dealer
ISBN Publisher's Prefix: 0-900123

Bernard **Babani** (Publishing) Ltd, The Grampians, Shepherds Bush Rd, London W6 7NF Tel: (01) 603 2581/7296 Cable Add: Radiobooks London W6
(Formerly Babani Press and Bernards (Publishers) Ltd)
Man Dir, Editorial: M H Babani; *Sales, Rights & Permissions:* S Babani; *Production, Publicity:* P Pragnell
Associate Companies: Babani Press; Bernards (Publishers) Ltd
Subjects: Low-priced Paperbacks, Radio & Electronics
1978: 11 titles *Founded:* 1977 (Babani Press 1974, Bernards Publishers 1942)
ISBN Publisher's Prefixes: 0-85934, 0-900162

Bachman & Turner Ltd*, The Old Hop Exchange, 1/3 Central Bldgs, 24 Southwark St, London SE1 1TY Tel: (01) 403 3366
Man Dir: Simon Bott; *Chairman:* Cecil Turner; *Director:* Marta Bachman
Subjects: General Fiction, Biography, History, Music, Art, Philosophy
1978: 9 titles *Founded:* 1972
ISBN Publisher's Prefix: 0-85974

Backpacker's Guides Series, an imprint of Bradt Enterprises (qv)

Samuel **Bagster** & Sons Ltd*, 1 Bath St, London EC1V 9LB Tel: (01) 251 2925
Parent Company: Marshall, Morgan & Scott Publications Ltd (qv)
Subjects: Religious, Reference, Bibles, Prayer and Hymn Books
Founded: 1794
ISBN Publisher's Prefix: 0-85150

Bailey Brothers & Swinfen Ltd, Warner Ho, Folkestone, Kent Tel: Folkestone 56501 (STD code 0303) Cable Add: Forenbuks Telex: 96328
Man Dir: J R Bailey; *Publicity, Advertising, Rights & Permissions:* Malcolm Maclean
Subsidiary Companies: Bailey Bros & Swinfen Exports Ltd; Bailey Subscription Agents Ltd
Imprints: Fantasy Library, Ghost Hunters' Library, Hour-Glass Press
Subjects: General Fiction, History, How-to, Reference, Engineering
Book Clubs: Bailey's German, French, Italian & Spanish Book Clubs
Founded: 1929
ISBN Publisher's Prefix: 0-561

Baillière Tindall, 35 Red Lion Sq, London WC1R 4SG Tel: (01) 831 6100 Telex: 28648 CASMAC-G
Divisional Dirs: S A Reynolds, N J Mendelson, D H Tindall; *Rights & Permissions:* N J Mendelson
Subjects: Medical, Veterinary, Nursing, Pharmaceutical
Founded: 1826
Miscellaneous: Division of Cassell Ltd (qv)
ISBN Publisher's Prefix: 0-7020

John **Baker** (Publishers) Ltd, 35 Bedford Row, London WC1R 4JH Tel: (01) 242 0946 Cable Add: Biblos, London WC1 Telex: 21792 ref 2546
Dirs: C A A Black, D E Gadsby
Parent Company: A & C Black Ltd (qv)
Subjects: Art, Archaeology, History
1978: 3 titles
ISBN Publisher's Prefix: 0-212

Balding & Mansell, Park Works, Wisbech, Cambs PE13 2AX Tel: Wisbech 2011 (STD code 0945) Cable Add: Mansell Wisbech Telex: 32162
Dir: Alan Dickenson; *Sales Managers:* Guy Dawson, Robert Hatch
Subject: Primary Education, Art books for young people, Museum Guides

Ballantine, an imprint of Macdonald/Futura Publishers Ltd (qv)

Arthur **Barker** Ltd, 91 Clapham High St, London SW4 7TA Tel: (01) 622 9933 Cable Add: Nicobar London SW4 7TA Telex: 918066
Sales Dir: D Livermore; *Publicity & Advertising:* Rosalind Lewis; *Rights & Permissions:* Miss B J Maclennan
Parent Company: George Weidenfeld & Nicolson Ltd (qv)
Subjects: Biography, How-to, Reference, Military History, Crime, Sport
Founded: 1946
ISBN Publisher's Prefix: 0-213

Barnes & Noble, see Harper & Row Ltd

Barracuda Books Ltd, Meadows House, Well St, Buckingham, Buckinghamshire Tel: Buckingham 4441 (STD code 02802)
Editorial Offices: Radclive Hall, Radclive, Buckingham, Buckinghamshire
Chief Executive and Publisher: Clive Birch
Imprint: Sporting and Leisure Press
Subjects: Local History and Countryside
1978: 15 titles *1979:* 17 titles *Founded:* 1974
ISBN Publisher's Prefix: 0-86023

Barrie & Jenkins, an imprint of Hutchinson General Books Ltd (qv)

John **Bartholomew** & Son Ltd, 12 Duncan St, Edinburgh EH9 1TA Tel: (031) 667 9341 Cable Add: Bartholomew Edinburgh Telex: Chacom 72465
Man Dir: D A Ross Stewart; *Editorial:* J C Bartholomew; *Marketing:* M J Chittleburgh; *Production:* R G Bartholomew; *Rights & Permissions:* I Jackson (Maps), C B Kirkwood (Books); *Publicity:* I Jackson
Subsidiary Company: T & T Clark Ltd (qv)
Subjects: Maps, Atlases, Leisure Books
1978: 50 titles *1979:* 50 titles *Founded:* 1826
ISBN Publisher's Prefix: 0-7028

Bartholomew Books*, 216 High St, Bromley, Kent BR1 1PW Tel: (01) 460 3239 Cable Add: Bartholomew Bromley

Telex: 896521
Head Off: 12 Duncan St, Edinburgh EH9 1TA
Man Dir: David Ross Stewart; *Editorial:* Christopher Wheeler; *Sales Dir:* Michael J Chittleburgh; *Production:* John M Shillingford; *Rights & Permissions:* Christine Pott
Parent Company: John Bartholomew & Son Ltd (qv)
Subjects: Biography, History, How-to, Reference, Educational Materials, Guidebooks, Architecture, History of Art, Cooking, Hobbies, Natural History, Atlases
1978: 15 titles *Founded:* 1972
ISBN Publisher's Prefixes: 0-7028, 0-85152

Basic Books, see Harper & Row Ltd

The **Basilisk** Press Ltd, 32 England's Lane, London NW3 1YB Tel: (01) 722 2142
Man Dir: Charlene B Garry
Subjects: Literature, Botany, Architecture, Landscape Gardening
Bookshop: address as above
1978: 1 title *1979:* 1 title *Founded:* 1973

B T **Batsford** Ltd, 4 Fitzhardinge St, London W1H 0AH Tel: (01) 486 8484 Cable Add: Batsfordia London
Shipping Add: PO Box 4, Braintree, Essex CM7 7QY
Man Dir: Peter Kemmis Betty; *Editorial Dir, Rights & Permissions:* William Waller; *Editorial:* Samuel Carr, Thelma M Nye, Paula Shea, Tim Auger; *Sales Manager:* Robert Beard; *Publicity Manager:* Richard Coltart
Subjects: History, How-to, Music, Art & Craft, Juveniles, Psychology, Engineering, Social Science, Educational Materials, Topography, Needlecraft, Sports, Hobbies, Cookery, Costumes
1978: 150 titles *1979:* 160 titles *Founded:* 1843
ISBN Publisher's Prefix: 0-7134

Beaver Books, an imprint of The Hamlyn Publishing Group Ltd (qv)

Bedford Square Press of the National Council for Voluntary Organizations, 26 Bedford Sq, London WC1B 3HU Tel: (01) 636 4066
Subjects: Social Policy and Planning, services and training; Counselling; Voluntary Community Action
1978: 20 titles *1979:* 12 titles
Miscellaneous: Bedford Square Press also publishes for or in association with other organizations
ISBN Publisher's Prefix: 0-7199

Bell & Hyman Ltd, Denmark Ho, 37-39 Queen Elizabeth St, London SE1 2QB Tel: (01) 407 0709/5237 Cable Add: Bellhyman London SE1 Telex: 886245
Chairman, Man Dir: R P Hyman; *Marketing Dir:* N C Britten; *Production:* Norman Turpin; *Publicity:* Elizabeth Sich; *Rights:* Mary Butler
Subjects: Secondary Textbooks, Collecting and Crafts, Chess, Pepys
1978: 40 titles *1979:* 40 titles *Founded:* 1838
ISBN Publisher's Prefix: 0-7135

Bellew & Higton Publishers Ltd, 19-21 Conway St, London W1P 5HL Tel: (01) 388 7601 Telex: 261212
Man Dir: Ib Bellow; *Editorial Dir:* Gill Rowley; *Production Dir:* Graham Saunders; *Design Dir:* Bernard Higton
Parent Company: The Hutchinson Publishing Group Ltd (qv)
Subject: International co-editions
Founded: 1979

Bellona Publications, an imprint of Argus Books Ltd (qv)

Belton Books, an imprint of Stainer & Bell Ltd (qv)

Bemrose UK Ltd, Publishing Division, 90-91 Great Russell St, London WC1B 3PY Tel: (01) 631 4141 Telex: 262284 Ref 3747
Firm is not itself a publishing company, but parent company of The Athlone Press (qv), Grant McIntyre Ltd (qv), Mansell Publishing (qv), Jill Norman Ltd (qv), Scolar Press Ltd (qv)

Benjamin/Cummings Inc, 53 Bedford Sq, London WC1B 3DZ Tel: (01) 631 1636 Cable Add: Adiwes London WC1 Telex: 8811948
Manager: Paul R Chapman; *Rights & Permissions:* Tim Davison
Subjects: Reference, Science, Technology, University Textbooks
Founded: 1960
Miscellaneous: Firm is a member of the Addison-Wesley Publishing Group (qv)
ISBN Publisher's Prefix: 0-8053

Ernest **Benn** Ltd, 25 New Street Sq, London EC4A 3JA Tel: (01) 353 3212 Telex: 27844
Chairman & Man Dir: Timothy Benn; *Deputy Man Dir:* John Beer; *Sales Dir:* Anthony Llewellyn; *Publicity & Advertising:* Sarah Groom; *Editors:* John Collis (Academic), Michael Gale (Fishing & Technical), Paul Langridge (Juveniles and Blue Guides)
Orders to: Sovereign Way, Tonbridge, Kent TN9 1RW Tel: Tonbridge 364422 (STD Code 0732)
Parent Company: Benn Brothers Ltd
Associate Company: Benn Publications Ltd
Subsidiary Company: Charles Knight Publications, 25 New Street Sq, London EC4A 3JA
Imprints include: Tolley Publishing Co, Charles Knight Ltd, Williams & Norgate
Subjects: History, Music, Literature, Archaeology, Current Affairs, Guide Books, Fishing, Technology, Juvenile, Picture Books, Fiction
1978: 58 titles *1979:* 58 titles *Founded:* 1925
ISBN Publisher's Prefixes: 0-510 (Ernest Benn), 0-85314 (Charles Knight)

Bergström & Boyle Books Ltd*, 31 Foubert's Place, London W1 Tel: (01) 437 4825 Cable Add: Berbo London
Dir: Alexandra Boyle; *Editorial:* Veronica Pratt
Subjects: Art, Architecture, Design (photographic and graphic)
1978: 2 titles *Founded:* 1973
ISBN Publisher's Prefix: 0-903767

Bernards (Publishers) Ltd, see Bernard Babani (Publishing) Ltd

Better Books, 11 Springfield Pl, Lansdown Rd, Bath BA1 5RA Tel: Bath 28010 (STD code 0225)
Proprietor: H Welchman; *Publicity Manager:* Pip Mason
Subject: Remedial Education
1978: 8 titles *Founded:* 1974
ISBN Publisher's Prefix: 0-904700

Big O Publishing Ltd*, 228 Fulham Rd, London SW10 9NB
Man Dir: Peter Ledeboer; *Sales Manager:* Paul Henderson; *Marketing:* Ron Ford; *Production:* Alice Lindsay
Parent Company: Big O Posters Ltd
Associate Companies: Big O Inc, Charlottesville Va, USA; Big O Verlag GmbH, Munich, Federal Republic of Germany
Subjects: Illustrated Books, Art
1978: 11 titles *Founded:* 1975
ISBN Publisher's Prefix: 0-905664

Clive **Bingley** Ltd, 1-19 New Oxford St, London WC1A 1NE Tel: (01) 404 4818 Telex: 24902 bingle g
Warehouse: Wentworth Book Co, Pindar Rd, Hoddesdon, Herts
Man Dir: Jim Emmett; *Sales Dir:* Brian K Tomes; *Publicity Dir:* Hazel Hill
Parent Company: K G Saur Verlag KG, Federal Republic of Germany (qv)
Associate Companies: K G Saur Ltd, UK; K G Saur Publishing Inc, 45 North St, Ridgewood, New Jersey, USA; K G Saur Editeurs, France (qv)
Subjects: Library Science, Textbooks, Technical, Science, Reference, Music, Hotels, Catering, Directories, Bibliographies
1979: 20 titles
ISBN Publisher's Prefixes: 0-85157 (Bingley), 0-907150 (K G Saur)

Birmingham Museums and Art Gallery, Publications Unit, Chamberlain Sq, Birmingham B3 3DH Tel: (021) 235 4051
Publications Manager: Trevor Jones
Subjects: Fine & Applied Arts, Archaeology, Natural History
1978: 7 titles
ISBN Publisher's Prefix: 0-903504

Bison Books Ltd, 4 Cromwell Pl, London SW7 Tel: (01) 584 9597/8 Telex: 888014 Bison G
Director: Sydney L Mayer
Subjects: Military and Modern History, Animals, Cookery, Transport, Sport, Modelling
1980: 27 titles *Founded:* 1975

A & C **Black** (Publishers) Ltd, 35 Bedford Row, London WC1R 4JH Tel: (01) 242 0946 Cable Add: Biblos London WC1 Telex: 21792 ref 2546
Shipping Add: Howard Rd, Eaton Socon, Huntingdon, Cambs PE19 3EZ Tel: Huntingdon 212666 (STD code 0480)
Man Dirs: Charles Black, David Gadsby; *Editorial:* Paul White (Children's Books)
Subsidiary Companies: John Baker (Publishers) Ltd (qv); F Lewis (Publishers) Ltd (qv)
Subjects: History, Music, Art, Sports, Reference, Religion, Juveniles, Primary Textbooks
Book Club: Fishing Book Club
1978: 75 titles *1979:* 77 titles *Founded:* 1807
ISBN Publisher's Prefixes: 0-7136 (Black), 0-212 (Baker), 0-85317 (Lewis)

Black Pig Press*, Garreg Fawr, Porthyrhyd, Aanwrda, Dyfed
Man Dir, Rights & Permissions: R F Plewes; *Editorial:* John Anthony West; *Sales:* O Caldicott; *Production:* R Clarke
Subjects: Autobiography, Fiction, Alternative Society
1978: 3 titles *Founded:* 1977
ISBN Publisher's Prefix: 0-906180

Blacker Calmann Cooper Ltd, see Calmann & Cooper Ltd

Blackie & Son Ltd, Bishopbriggs, Glasgow G64 2NZ Tel: (041) 772 2311 Cable Add: Blackie Glasgow
Man Dir: R Michael Miller; *Editorial:* A D Mitchell, Rosemary Lanning, Olga Norris (Children's); Dr A G MacKintosh (Academic); *Sales Managers:* Geoff Meakin (Children's), John Drummond (Educational), Bill Baird (Academic); *Publicity:* HPR Publicity, 9 Fitzroy Sq, London W1 (Tel: (01) 388 2613) (Children's), John Drummond (Educational), Bill Baird (Academic); *Rights & Permissions:* Roseanne Holme
Subsidiary Companies: Abelard-Schuman Ltd (qv); International Textbook Co Ltd (qv); Leonard Hill; Surrey University Press (qv)

UNITED KINGDOM 371

Branch Off: Furnival House, 14-18 High Holborn, London Tel: (01) 242 5832
Subjects: School Textbooks, Reference, Children's, Scientific & Engineering, General & Social Science, Quality Paperbacks
1978: 177 titles *Founded:* 1809
ISBN Publisher's Prefix: 0-216

Blacklock Farries & Sons, 18-26 Church Crescent, Dumfries DG1 1DQ Tel: Dumfries 4288 (STD code 0387) Telex: 777530
Man Dir, Rights & Permissions: T C Farries; *Editorial & Production Manager:* Mary Nettlefold; *Sales Manager:* Craig Watson; *Export Manager:* Peter J Allen
Parent Company: Holmes McDougall Ltd (qv)
Miscellaneous: Also export booksellers
ISBN Publisher's Prefix: 0-900173

Blackstaff Press Ltd, 3 Galway Park, Dundonald, Belfast BT16 0AN Tel: Dundonald 7161 (STD code 02318)
Man & Sales Dir: Jim Gracey; *Publicity & Advertising Dir, Rights & Permissions:* Anne Tannahill; *Sales:* Sally Kelso; *Production:* Wendy Dunbar
Subjects: General Fiction, Poetry, Biography, History, Reference, Paperbacks, General & Social Science, Art, Music, Photography, Children's Books, Natural History, Folklore, Sport, Philosophy, Politics, Archaeology, Humour, Education
1978: 21 titles *1979:* 27 titles *Founded:* 1971
ISBN Publisher's Prefix: 0-85640

Basil Blackwell Publisher Ltd, 5 Alfred St, Oxford OX1 4HB Tel: Oxford 722146 (STD Code 0865) Cable Add: Books Oxford
Shipping Add: 108 Cowley Rd, Oxford OX4 1JF
Man Dir: David Martin; *Editorial Dir:* John Davey; *Sales Dir:* Norman Drake; *Publicity:* Ludo Craddock; *Production:* Ray Addicott; *Rights & Permissions:* Stella Welford
Allied Company: Blackwell Scientific Publications Ltd (qv)
Subsidiary Companies: Blackwell Press Ltd, Osney Mead, Oxford; Marston Book Services Ltd, Oxford; Martin Robertson & Co Ltd (qv)
Imprints: Basil Blackwell, Shakespeare Head Press
Subjects: Economics and Industrial Relations, History, Philosophy, Politics, Languages, Linguistics, History, Geography, Children's Books, Reference, Religion, Academic Paperbacks, Social Sciences, Primary and Secondary Textbooks, Journals
1978-79: 123 titles *Founded:* 1921
Miscellaneous: Member of the Blackwell Group (qv B H Blackwell Ltd under Major Booksellers)
ISBN Publisher's Prefix: 0-631

Blackwell Scientific Publications Ltd, Osney Mead, Oxford OX2 0EL Tel: Oxford 40201 (STD code 0865) Cable Add: Research Oxford Telex: 83118
Man, Editorial Dir and Rights & Permissions: Per Saugman; *Sales Dir:* Keith Bowker; *Production:* John Robson; *Publicity:* Andrew Bax
Allied Company: Basil Blackwell Publisher Ltd (qv)
Branch Offs: 9 Forrest Rd, Edinburgh EH1 2QH; 8 John St, London WC1N 2ES; 214 Berkeley St, Carlton, Victoria 3053, Australia; 52 Beacon St, Boston, Massachusetts 02108, USA
Subjects: Medicine, Dentistry, Veterinary Medicine, Botany, Biology, Ecology, Earth Sciences, Zoology, University Textbooks
1978: 53 titles *1979:* 68 titles *Founded:* 1939
ISBN Publisher's Prefix: 0-632

William **Blackwood** & Sons Ltd, 32 Thistle St, Edinburgh EH2 1HA Tel: (031) 225 3411/3
Man Dir, Publishing, Rights & Permissions: J M D Blackwood
Subjects: Monographs of Scottish Subjects, General Non-fiction
1979: 4 titles *Founded:* 1804
ISBN Publisher's Prefix: 0-85158

Blandford Books Ltd, Robert Rogers Ho, New Orchard, Poole, Dorset BH15 1LU Tel: Poole 71171 (STD code 02013) Cable Add: Blandpress Poole Telex: 418304
Chairman: R G Dingwall; *Man Dir:* R B Erven; *Publishing Dir, Rights & Permissions:* T Goldsmith; *Managing Editor:* Stuart Booth; *Sales & Marketing Manager:* Christopher Lloyd; *Production Manager:* Alan Howell; *Publicity:* Pauline Jaffray
Parent Company: Link House Publications Ltd, Robert Rogers Ho, New Orchard, Poole BH15 1LU
Subjects: History, Religion, Music, Art, Archaeology, Biology, Crafts, Education, Geography, Horticulture, Militaria, Natural History, Riding, Space, Astronomy, Transport, Educational, Academic
Founded: 1919
ISBN Publisher's Prefix: 0-7137

Geoffrey **Bles**, an imprint of Garnstone Press Ltd (qv)

Blond & Briggs Ltd, an imprint and subsidiary company of Frederick Muller Ltd (qv)

The **Bodley Head** Ltd, 9 Bow St, London WC2E 7AL Tel: (01) 836 9081 Cable Add: Bodleian London WC2 Telex: 299080
Man Dir: Max Reinhardt; *Home Sales:* Norman Askew; *Overseas Sales:* Quentin Hockliffe; *Publicity Dir:* Euan Cameron; *Rights & Permissions:* Ms Reet Nelis, Guido Waldman
Subsidiary Companies: Max Reinhardt Ltd (qv); Hollis & Carter; T Werner Laurie; The Nonesuch Library; Putnam & Co Ltd (qv); (all at 9 Bow St, London WC2E 7AL)
Subjects: General Fiction, Belles Lettres, Poetry, Biography, History, Juveniles
1978: 73 titles *Founded:* 1887
Miscellaneous: Firm is a member of the Chatto, Bodley Head & Jonathan Cape Ltd Group (qv)
ISBN Publisher's Prefix: 0-370

Bonfini, an imprint of Clematis Press Ltd (qv)

Book Sales Ltd, 78 Newman St, London W1P 3LA Tel: (01) 636 9033 Telex: 21892 Musicsales
A division of Music Sales Ltd
Man Dir: Robert Wise; *Sales:* Ken Denham
Subjects: Music (Learning and Biography), General Books
ISBN Publisher's Prefix: 0-86001

The **Booksmith**, an imprint of BSC Books Ltd (qv)

Boosey & Hawkes Music Publishers Ltd, 295 Regent St, London W1R 8JH Tel: (01) 580 2060 Cable Add: Sonorous London W1 Telex: 895461 Boosey G
Man Dir: R Antony Fell
Subjects: Music, Secondary & Primary Music Textbooks
ISBN Publisher's Prefix: 0-85162

Bowker and Bertram Ltd (Marine Publishers), Whitewalls, Harbour Way, Old Bosham, Sussex PO18 8QH
Subjects: Marine (Literary and Technical)
1979: 6 titles *1980:* 7 titles

Bowker Publishing Co, Xerox Publishing Group Ltd, PO Box 5, Epping, Essex CM16 4BU (Located at: Erasmus Ho, 58-62 High St, Epping) Tel: Epping 77333 (STD Code 0378) Telex: 81410
Warehouse: H Kent Ltd, 135 South St, Bishop's Stortford, Herts
Man Dir and Rights & Permissions: David Collischon; *Marketing Manager:* Patrick Wynne-Jones
Parent Company: R R Bowker Co, 1180 Ave of the Americas, New York, NY 10036, USA. Ultimate holding company Xerox Corporation
Subjects: Works of Bibliography, Reference, and Library Science handbooks for Libraries and the Book Trade
1978: 2 titles *1979:* 3 titles
ISBN Publisher's Prefixes: 0-8352, 0-85935

Marion **Boyars** Publishers Ltd, 18 Brewer St, London W1R 4AS Tel: (01) 439 7827/8 Cable Add: Bookdom
Man Dir, Editorial, Rights & Permissions: Marion Boyars; *Editorial:* Arthur Boyars; *Sales:* Michael Hayes; *Publicity:* Ken Hollings
Associate Company: Marion Boyars Inc, 99 Main St, Salem, New Hampshire 03079, USA
Subjects: General Fiction, Belles Lettres, Poetry, Literary Criticism, Plays, Music, Philosophy, Sociology, Psychology
Series: Open Forum, Ideas in Progress, Signature, Critical Appraisals
1978: 35 titles *Founded:* 1975
ISBN Publisher's Prefix: 0-7145

Boydell & Brewer Ltd, PO Box 9, Woodbridge, Suffolk IP12 3DF Tel: Woodbridge 411320 (STD code 0394)
Chairman: R W Barber
Imprints: Boydell Press, D S Brewer
Distributors for: Suffolk Record Society, Royal Historical Society, Folklore Society, Horn Book Inc, Royal Society of Literature
Subjects: Medieval and Renaissance Literature and History, General Non-fiction, Sport
1978: 25 titles *1979:* 28 titles
ISBN Publisher's Prefix: 0-85115 (Boydell), 0-85991 (Brewer)

Bradt Enterprises, Overmead, Monument Lane, Chalfont St Peter, Bucks SL9 0HY Tel: Chalfont St Giles 3865 (STD Code 02407)
Man Dir: Mrs Hilary Bradt; *Editorial:* George Bradt, Hilary Bradt; *Manager:* Janet Mears
Orders to: Hannafore, 41 Nortoft Rd, Chalfont St Peter, Bucks SL9 0LA Tel: Chalfont St Giles 3478 (STD code 02407)
Imprint: Backpacker's Guides Series
Branch Offs: Yugilbar, Rankine's Rd, St Andrews, Victoria 3761, Australia; 409 Beacon St, Boston, Mass 02115, USA
Subjects: Trekking and Backpacking
1978: 1 title *1979:* 2 titles *Founded:* 1975
ISBN Publisher's Prefix: 0-9505797

Branch Line, an imprint of The Harvester Press Ltd (qv)

Brassey's Publishers Ltd*, 10 Upper Berkeley St, London W1H 7PE Tel: (01) 262 7448
Publisher: A H Begg
Orders to: Croom Helm Ltd, 2-10 St John's Rd, London SW11
Subjects: Defence & Military Books
1978-9: 15 titles *Founded:* 1886
ISBN Publisher's Prefix: 0-904609

D S **Brewer** Ltd, see Boydell & Brewer Ltd

Brimax Books, 347U Cherry Hinton Rd, Cambridge CB1 4DH Tel: Cambridge 44914/5 (STD code 0223) Cable Add:

UNITED KINGDOM

Brimax Cambridge Telex: 817625
Man Dir: A G Rogers; *Editorial:* Marjorie Rogers; *Rights & Permissions:* Brimax Rights Ltd, Long Ace, Newmarket Rd, Moulton, Newmarket, Suffolk
Subjects: General Children's Books, Toy Books
ISBN Publisher's Prefixes: 0-900195, 0-904494, 0-86112

British & Foreign Bible Society, 146 Queen Victoria St, London EC4V 4VX Tel: (01) 248 4751 Cable Add: Testaments, London EC4V 4BX
Gen Dir: N B Cryer; *Publishing Dir:* R Worthing-Davies; *Sales:* C Mungeum; *Production:* J Ball
Subjects: Bibles, Testaments, Bible Books, Bible Study and Educational Materials (in English and many foreign languages)
Bookshop: Bible House Booklounge (at above address)
1978: 45 titles *1979:* 50 titles *Founded:* 1803
ISBN Publisher's Prefix: 0-564

The **British Council**, Printing and Publishing Department, 65 Davies St, London W1Y 2AA Tel: (01) 499 8011
HQ: 10 Spring Gardens, London SW1A 2BN Tel: (01) 930 8466
Director: B Humphreys
Subjects: Those related to the promotion of a wider knowledge of Britain and the English language abroad and developing closer cultural relations with other countries.
Co-publishers for some titles including: *Writers & their Work* Series: Longman Group Ltd (qv)
Journals; British Book News, British Medical Bulletin, Educational Broadcasting International (published by Peter Peregrinus), *English Language Teaching Journal* (published by OUP), *ELT Documents, English Teaching & Linguistic Abstracts* (published by CUP)
ISBN Publisher's Prefix: 0-900229

The **British Horse** Society, The British Equestrian Centre, Kenilworth, Warwickshire CV8 2LR Tel: Coventry 52241 (STD code 0203) Cable Add: Brithorse, Kenilworth
Subjects: Equestrian Reference Books
ISBN Publisher's Prefix: 0-900226

British Library, Bibliographic Services Division, Store St, London WC1E 7DG Tel: (01) 636 1544 Telex: 21462
Subjects: Bibliographies, Indexes, *British National Bibliography, British Education Index, British Catalogue of Music, Books in English, British Catalogue of Audiovisual Materials* (experimental)
Founded: 1973
ISBN Publisher's Prefix: 0-900220

British Museum (Natural History), Cromwell Rd, London SW7 5BD Tel: (01) 589 6323
Head of Publications: Robert Cross; *Editorial:* Chris Owen, Myra Givans; *Sales, Publicity:* J Abraham; *Production:* M Gilmartin, Eric Dent; *Rights & Permissions:* V Campbell
Subjects: Natural History, Scientific, Popular, Periodicals
Bookshops: Museum Bookshop (address as above); Museum Bookshop at Zoological Museum, Tring, Herts
1978: 9 titles *1979:* 11 titles *Founded:* 1963
ISBN Publisher's Prefix: 0-0565

British Museum Publications Ltd, 6 Bedford Sq, London WC1B 3RA Tel: (01) 323 1234
Man Dir, Rights & Permissions: M J Hoare; *Editorial:* Celia Clear; *Sales, Publicity:* Heather Dean; *Production:* Nicholas Russell
Orders to: Thames & Hudson Ltd, 44 Clockhouse Rd, Farnborough, Hampshire
Imprints: British Museum Publications, Colonnade
Subjects: Reference Books, Art & Architecture, Archaeology, Oriental, General Guides to British Museum
Bookshop: Bernard Shaw Bookshop, British Museum, Great Russell St, London WC1
1978: 49 titles *1979:* 24 titles *Founded:* 1973
ISBN Publisher's Prefix: 0-7141

British Printing Corporation Ltd, see B P C

James **Brodie** Ltd*, 15 Queen Sq, Bath, Avon BA1 2HW Tel: Bath 22110 (STD code 0225)
Subjects: Primary & Secondary Education, *Notes on Chosen Texts* series (which are produced by Brodie and published by Pan Books Ltd (qv))
ISBN Publisher's Prefix: 0-7142

Brodies Notes, an imprint of Pan Books Ltd (qv)

Broomsleigh Press, an imprint of Fudge & Co Ltd (qv)

Brown Watson Ltd & Brown Watson Juvenile*, 135-41 Wardour St, London W1V 4QA Tel: (01) 734 3493 Cable Add: Bookstocks London Telex: 21996
Man Dirs: Brian D Babani, Peter Babani; *Sales, Rights & Permissions:* Bernhardt Marcus
Parent Company: Howard & Wyndham Ltd (qv)
Subsidiary Company: Murrays Childrens Books, at above address
Associate Company: Murrays Remainder Books (qv)
Imprint: Rainbow Books
Subject: Juveniles
ISBN Publisher's Prefixes: 0-7027, 0-85175 (Brown Watson), 0-7239 (Juvenile)

Bunch Books*, 14 Rathbone Place, London W1P 1DE Tel: (01) 637 7991/2/3 Cable Add: Bunch Books, London Telex: 943763
Man Dir: Felix Dennis; *Editorial, Rights & Permissions:* Andrew Fisher; *Production:* Richard Pountain
Parent Company: H Bunch Associates Ltd
Subsidiary Company: Sportscene Publishers Ltd
Subjects: Sport, Martial Arts, Film, TV, Biography, Leisure, General Interest
Founded: 1974

Burke Publishing Co Ltd, Pegasus Ho, 116-120 Golden Lane, London EC1Y 0TL Tel: (01) 253 2145/6 Cable Add: Burkebooks London EC1 Telex: c/o 27931
Chairman, Export Sales: H Starke; *Man Dir, Editorial, Rights & Permissions:* Miss N Galinski; *Production:* C Tuthill; *Publicity:* Miss Pat Mitchell
Orders to: The Barn, Northgate, Beccles, Suffolk
Subsidiary Company: Harold Starke Ltd (qv)
Branch Offs: Burke Publishing (Canada) Ltd, 91 Station St, Ajax, Ontario, Canada L1S 3H2; Burke Publishing Co Inc, 1 Emerald St, Norwalk, Connecticut 06850, USA
Subjects: Juveniles, Secondary & Primary Textbooks, Educational Materials
1978: 21 titles *Founded:* 1934
ISBN Publisher's Prefix: 0-222

Burke's Peerage Ltd, 56 Walton St, London SW3 1RB Tel: (01) 584 1106 Telex: 916851
Man Dir: Jeremy G Norman; *General Manager:* Felicity Mortimer
Subjects: Genealogy, Heraldry, Architectural, Biographical, and Social History
1978: 1 title *Founded:* 1826
ISBN Publisher's Prefix: 0-85011

Burnett Books, see André Deutsch Ltd

Burns & Oates Ltd, 2-10 Jerdan Pl, London SW6 5PT Tel: 385 6261 Telex: 935841
Man Dir, Sales: Charlotte de la Bedovere; *Editorial, Rights & Permissions:* John Cumming; *Production:* Bobby Maier
Associate Companies: Search Press Ltd (qv); Search for Leisure Ltd (at above address)
Subjects: Philosophy, History, Religion, Moral Education
Founded: 1847
ISBN Publisher's Prefix: 0-86012

Business Books Ltd, 24 Highbury Crescent, London N5 1RX Tel: (01) 359 3711 Cable Add: Hutchbiz Telex: 21373
Man Dir: Mark Cohen; *Sales Dir:* John Fulford; *Editorial:* Vivien James
Orders to: Tiptree Book Services, Church Rd, Tiptree, Nr Colchester, Essex
Subjects: Management, Advertising, Marketing, Finance, Personnel, Computers, Business Law, Small Business
1978: 23 titles *1979:* 18 titles
Miscellaneous: Business Books Ltd is an imprint of Hutchinson Educational (qv)
ISBN Publisher's Prefixes: 0-220 (for pre-1979 publications), 0-09 (for 1979 onwards)

Butterworth & Co (Publishers) Ltd, Borough Green, Sevenoaks, Kent TN15 8PH Tel: Borough Green 884567 (STD code 0732) Cable Add: Butterwort Sevenoaks Kent TN15 8PH Telex: 95678
Chairman and Chief Executive: W Gordon Graham; *Dirs:* Simon Partridge (Law), David Summer (Scientific, Technical and Medical), Don Saville (Financial), George Norton (Administrative), Colin Whurr (Marketing); *International Sales Manager:* Phillip Woods; *Marketing Administrative Manager:* Geoff Hill; *Production:* P E Cheeseman (Law), J Carruthers (Scientific, Technical and Medical); *Publicity:* Sue Henderson; *Rights & Permissions:* R J Hedley-Jones (UK), Betty Cottrell (Foreign Rights)
London Off: 88 Kingsway, London WC2 6AB Tel: (01) 405 6900 Cable Add: Butterwort London WC2
Parent Company: International Publishing Corporation Ltd (qv)
Subsidiary Companies: Butterworths Pty Ltd, Australia (qv); Butterworth & Co (Canada) Ltd, 2265 Midland Ave, Scarborough, Ontario M1P 4S1, Canada; Butterworths of New Zealand Ltd, New Zealand (qv); Butterworth & Co (South Africa) (Pty) Ltd, South Africa (qv); Butterworth (Publishers) Inc, 10 Tower Office Park, Woburn, Mass 01801, USA
Imprints: Newnes-Butterworths, Newnes Technical
Bookshop: 9-12 Bell Yard, Temple Bar, London WC2
Subjects: Law, Medicine, Engineering, Technology, Science, Social Science, Business Studies
1978: approx 180 titles *1979:* approx 220 titles *Founded:* before 1905
ISBN Publisher's Prefixes: 0-0406/7/8/9, 0-0592, 0-06004

Buzby Books Ltd, an imprint of Severn House Publishers Ltd (qv)

Bwrdd Croeso Cymru, see Wales Tourist Board

C B D Research Ltd, 154 High St, Beckenham, Kent BR3 1EA Tel: (01) 650 7745
Man Dir: G P Henderson
Subject: Reference
1978: 4 titles *1979:* 3 titles *Founded:* 1961
ISBN Publisher's Prefix: 0-900246

UNITED KINGDOM 373

C C J Ltd, 2-4 Brook St, London W1Y 1AA Tel: (01) 493 5061/499 4688 Cable Add: Unibooks London W1 Telex: 24224 ref 3545
Warehouse: International Book Distributors, 66 Wood End Lane, Hemel Hempstead, Hertfordshire
Dirs: James Clark, Roger Howley, J E Goellner; *Man Dir:* Trevor Brown; *Sales Manager (Exports):* Anna Simpson-Muellner; *Promotion Manager:* Andrew Nolan
Miscellaneous: Firm is the London office of University of California Press (qv), Cornell University Press (qv) and the Johns Hopkins University Press (qv)
ISBN Publisher's Prefixes: 0-520 (California), 0-8014 (Cornell), 0-8018 (Johns Hopkins)

Caffrey, Smith Publishing Co, Station House, Darkes Lane, Potters Bar, Herts EN6 1AT Tel: Potters Bar 50055 (STD code 0707) Cable Add: Cafsaun Potters Bar Telex: 25264
Subject: Educational (Primary & Secondary)
1978: 7 titles
ISBN Publisher's Prefix: 0-7024

John **Calder** (Publishers) Ltd, 18 Brewer St, London W1R 4AS Tel: (01) 734 3786 Cable Add: Bookdom London
Man, Publishing Dir: John Calder; *Sales:* Michael Hayes, Alice Watson; *Production:* Chris Davidson; *Promotion, Rights & Permissions:* Alice Watson
Subjects: Modern Literature, Classics, Belles Lettres, Poetry, Biography, History, Music, Art, Philosophy, Reference, High-priced Paperbacks, Psychology, Social Science, University Textbooks
1978: 41 titles *1979:* 23 titles *Founded:* 1950
ISBN Publisher's Prefix: 0-7145

John **Calmann & Cooper** Ltd, 71 Great Russell St, London WC1B 3BN Tel: (01) 831 6351 Telex: 298246 Owls G
Man Dir, Sales, Rights & Permissions: John Calmann; *Editorial:* Elisabeth Ingles; *Production:* Colin Cohen
Founded: 1976
Miscellaneous: Designers and producers of high quality illustrated books, and specialists in international co-editions

Cambridge Information and Research Services Ltd, School House, Heydon, Royston, Herts SG8 8PW Tel: Royston 83615 (STD code 0763)
Dir: A R Buckley
Subsidiary Company: The Clavering Press Ltd
Subjects: Reference, Energy Management, Regional Locations, Social Science
1980: 6 titles *Founded:* 1975
ISBN Publisher's Prefix: 0-905332

Cambridge University Press, PO Box 110, Cambridge CB2 3RL Cable Add: Unipress, Cambridge Tel: Cambridge 312393 (STD code 0223) Telex: 817342
Chief Executive: G A Cass; *Man Dir (Publishing Division):* P E V Allin; *Publisher:* M H Black; *Marketing:* D A Knight; *Sales Dirs:* John Adamson, Dennis Stanton; *Publicity:* Paul Clifford; *Rights & Permissions:* Sarah Chapman, Irena Jeziorska
Branch Offs: Cambridge University Press (Australia) Pty Ltd, Australia (qv); Cambridge University Press (American Branch), 32 East 57th St, New York, NY 10022, USA, and 510 North Ave, New Rochelle, NY 10801, USA; Cambridge University Press, New Zealand (qv)
Subjects: Anthropology, Archaeology, Architecture, Area Studies, Art, Bibliography, Biological Sciences, Classical Studies, Drama, Economics, Education (primary, secondary, tertiary and further education, trade, juvenile information books), Engineering, English Language Teaching, Environmental Sciences, Geography, History, Languages, Law, Linguistics, Literature, Mathematics, Medicine, Music, Philosophy, Physical Sciences, Politics, Psychology, Sociology, Theology, Bibles and Prayer Books, Examination Papers
1978: 460 titles *1979:* 590 titles *Founded:* 1534
ISBN Publisher's Prefix: 0-521

Cameron & Tayleur (Books) Ltd, 25 Lloyd Baker St, London WC1X 9AT Tel: (01) 837 7126/7 Cable Add: Garamond London WC1
Dirs: Ian A Cameron, Bettina Tayleur
Associate Company: Carter Nash Cameron Ltd (qv)
Subjects: Nonfiction, Illustrated Reference Books, Encyclopedias, Cinema, Cookery, Decorative Arts, Collecting
1980: 2 titles
ISBN Publisher's Prefix: 0-7153

Canongate Publishing Ltd, 17 Jeffrey St, Edinburgh EH1 1DR Tel: (031) 556 0023/1954
Man Dir: Stephanie Wolfe Murray; *Executive Dirs:* Peter Chiene, Stewart Anderson; *Sales Manager:* Dave Morgan; *Publicity:* Robin Hodge
Subsidiary Companies: Southside (Publishers) Ltd, Q Press Ltd
Subjects: General Fiction, Poetry, Biography, History, Art, Current Affairs, Juveniles
1979: 13 titles *Founded:* 1973
ISBN Publisher's Prefix: 0-86241

Jonathan **Cape** Ltd, 30 Bedford Sq, London WC1B 3EL Tel: (01) 636 5764 Cable Add: Capajon London WC1
Shipping Add: 9 Bow St, London WC2
Man Dir: Graham C Greene; *Sales:* Quentin Hockliffe (Export), Norman Askew (Home); Gaye Poulton (Continental), Jean Mossop (American)
Subsidiary Companies: Cape Goliard Press Ltd; Jackdaw Publications Ltd
Subjects: General Fiction, Belles Lettres, Poetry, Biography, History, Music, Art, Philosophy, Juveniles, High-priced Paperbacks, Social Science, Educational Materials
Founded: 1921
Miscellaneous: Firm is a member of the Chatto, Bodley Head & Cape Ltd Group (qv)

Carcanet Press Ltd, 330 Corn Exchange Bldgs, Manchester M4 3BG Tel: (061) 834 8730
Shipping Add: Noonan Hurst Ltd, 131 Trafalgar Rd, London SE10 9TX
Man Dir: Peter Jones; *Editorial Dir:* Michael Schmidt; *Sales Dir:* Helen Lefroy
Subjects: Belles Lettres, Poetry, Religion, Low-priced Paperbacks
1978: 40 titles *1979:* 20 titles *Founded:* 1969
ISBN Publisher's Prefixes: 0-85635, 0-902145

Carousel Books Ltd, a subsidiary of Transworld Publishers Ltd (qv)

Carter Nash Cameron Ltd, 25 Lloyd Baker St, London WC1X 9AT Tel: (01) 837 7126/7 Cable Add: Garamond London WC1
Directors: Ian A Cameron, Bettina Tayleur
Associate Company: Cameron & Tayleur (Books) Ltd (qv)
Subjects: Nonfiction, Reference, Encyclopaedias, Decorative Arts, Crafts, Collecting

Frank **Cass** & Co Ltd, Gainsborough Ho, 11 Gainsborough Rd, London E11 1HT Tel: (01) 530 4226 Cable Add: Simfay London Telex: 897719
Shipping Add: Macdonald & Evans Ltd, Purdeys Way, Sutton Rd, Rochford, Essex SS4 1LX
Man Dir: Frank Cass; *Editorial:* Margaret Goodare; *Production:* Kenneth Cowell; *Publicity:* Jacqui Beryl; *Trade Manager:* Richard Norris
Subsidiary Companies: The Woburn Press (qv); Vallentine Mitchell & Co Ltd (qv)
Subjects: Third World Studies, Economics, Economic History, Social History, Politics, History, Africana, Middle East Studies
Bookshop: Frank Cass (Books) Ltd, 10 Woburn Walk, London WC1
1978: 20 titles *Founded:* 1957
ISBN Publisher's Prefixes: 0-7146 (Frank Cass), 0-7130 (Woburn Press), 0-85303 (Vallentine Mitchell)

Cassell Ltd, 35 Red Lion Sq, London WC1R 4SG Tel: (01) 831 6100 Cable Add: Caspeg, London WC1 Telex: 28648 Casmac-G
Man Dir: Marshall D Mascott
Trade Division: Editorial: J J Greenwood; *Sales:* H Kesselman; *Production:* G S Mitchell; *Publicity:* B Holmes; *Rights & Permissions:* June Badcock, Patsy Wilson
Ballière Tindall Division: S A Reynolds
Educational Division: D Napier
International Division: F Kobrak
Orders to: 8 Trident Way, Brent Rd, Southall, Middlesex
Parent Company: Cassell & Collier Macmillan Ltd, London
Subsidiary Company: Cassell Australia Ltd, Australia (qv)
Divisions: Studio Vista, Geoffrey Chapman, Ballière Tindall, Johnston & Bacon (qqv)
Imprints: As under Divisions
Branch Offs: Cassell Ltd, New Zealand (qv)
Subjects: General, Biography, Fiction, Music, Nonfiction, Medical, Educational, Technical
Founded: 1848
ISBN Publisher's Prefix: 0-304

Castle, an imprint of Murrays Remainder Books (qv)

Castle House Publications Ltd, Castle House, 27 London Rd, Tunbridge Wells, Kent TN1 1BX Tel: Tunbridge Wells 39606 (STD code 0892)
Man Dir: Donald Reinders; *Editorial:* Stephen L Jackson; *Sales:* Andrew Durnell; *Production:* Ray Green; *Publicity:* Marilyn Dunkelman; *Rights & Permissions:* Wendy Hunter
Associate Company: Weald Publishing Company (Europe), at above adress
Subjects: Scientific, Academic, Medical
1978: 3 titles *1979:* 34 titles *Founded:* 1978
ISBN Publisher's Prefix: 0-7194

Cathay, an imprint of Octopus Books Ltd (qv)

Caxton Publications Ltd, Holywell Ho, 72-90 Worship St, London EC2A 2EN Tel: (01) 247 8492 Cable Add: Interknow London EC2 Telex: 886048
Shipping Add: Unit 19, Mowlem Trading Estate, Leeside Rd, London N17 0QL
Man Dir: D Rodrigues; *Editorial Dir, Rights & Permissions:* Graham Clarke; *Marketing Manager:* E La Frenais
Subjects: Encyclopaedias, Education, Yearbooks, History, Reference, Dictionaries, *The New Caxton Encyclopedia, Chamber's Encyclopedia*
Miscellaneous: Firm is part of the Caxton Publishing Group, and a member company of B P C Ltd (qv)

Founded: 1966
ISBN Publisher's Prefix: 0-7014

Cedar Books, an imprint of World's Work Ltd (qv)

Celtic Educational Ltd, Celtic House, St James's Gardens, Swansea SA1 6EA Tel: Swansea 56205 (STD code 0792)
Subjects: Education, Science, Commerce, Management, Law, Wales, Scotland

Cement & Concrete Association, Wexham Springs, Slough, Bucks SL3 6PL Tel: Fulmer 2727 (STD code 02816) Telex: 848352
Subjects: Engineering, Concrete, Cement
Miscellaneous: Associated imprints include Viewpoint
ISBN Publisher's Prefix: 0-7210

Centaur Press Ltd, Fontwell, Arundel, Sussex Tel: Eastergate 3302 (STD code 024368)
Shipping Add: 11-14 Stanhope Mews West, London SW7
Man Dir: T J L Wynne-Tyson
Subsidiary Company: The Linden Press (at above address)
Subjects: General, Fiction, Biography, Philosophy, Social Science, Textbooks, Reference
Bookshop: Keele's, 9 St Pancras, Chichester, Sussex
1978: 2 titles *1979:* 5 titles *Founded:* 1954
ISBN Publisher's Prefixes: 0-900000 (Centaur), 0-900001 (Linden Press)

Centre for Investment Studies, an imprint of Teakfield Ltd (qv)

Chadwyck-Healey Ltd, 20 Newmarket Rd, Cambridge CB5 8DT Tel: Cambridge 311479 (STD code 0223)
Dirs: Charles E Chadwyck-Healey, A M Chadwyck-Healey, H Fellner
Subjects: Reference, Nonfiction, Art, Economics, History, Literary History, Bibliography, Radio and TV

W & R Chambers Ltd, 11 Thistle St, Edinburgh EH2 1DG Tel: (031) 225 4463
Cable Add: Chambers Edinburgh Telex: 727967 G
Chairman: A S Chambers; *Man Dir, Chief Executive, Rights & Permissions:* I Gould; *Sales Manager:* David Mill; *Publicity Manager:* Liz Austin
Subjects: General Textbooks, Reference, Juveniles, Educational Materials, Mathematical Tables, Low-priced Paperbacks
1978: 28 titles *1979:* 29 titles *Founded:* 1820
ISBN Publisher's Prefix: 0-550

Chancerel Publishers Ltd, 40 Tavistock St, London WC2E 7PB Tel: (01) 240 2811
Vice-President: J M Idé; *General Manager:* D Prowse
Associate Company: Chancerel Editions SA, France (qv)
Subjects: Leisure Activities (Sports, Hobbies, Homecraft), Co-editions, Illustrated How-to, Educational, Paperbacks, Picture Strips
1979-80: 20 titles *Founded:* 1976
ISBN Publisher's Prefix: 0-905703

Geoffrey Chapman, 35 Red Lion Sq, London WC1R 4SG Tel: (01) 831 6100
Telex: 28648 CASMAC-G
Editorial: John Ainslie; *Publicity:* Piers Newton
Subjects: Religion, Religious Educational, Liturgy, Specialized African Publishing
1978: 10 titles *1979:* 15 titles *Founded:* 1957
Miscellaneous: Division of Cassell Ltd (qv)
ISBN Publisher's Prefix: 0-225

Chapman & Hall Ltd, 11 New Fetter Lane, London EC4P 4EE Tel: (01) 583 9855
Cable Add: Elegiacs London EC4P 4EE
Telex: 263398
Man Dir: R Stileman; *Marketing:* Peter F Shepherd; *Production:* B West; *Publicity:* L Williams; *Rights & Permissions:* J V Anderson
Orders to: North Way, Andover, Hants SP10 5BE
Parent Company: Associated Book Publishers Ltd (qv)
Subjects: Science, Technology, Medicine
1978: 61 titles *Founded:* 1830
ISBN Publisher's Prefix: 0-412

Chatto & Windus Ltd, 40-42 William IV St, London WC2 Tel: (01) 836 0127 Cable Add: Bookstore London WC2 Telex: 299080
Chairman: Nora Smallwood; *Man Dir:* Hugo Brunner; *Deputy Man Dir:* John Charlton; *Sales:* Norman Askew (Home), Quentin Hockliffe (Export); *Publicity & Advertising:* Rosalind Bell; *Rights & Permissions:* Jill Rose
Subsidiary and Associate Company: The Hogarth Press Ltd (qv)
Subjects: General Fiction, Belles Lettres, Poetry, Art, Biography, History, Philosophy, Juveniles, Psychology, Travel, High-priced Paperbacks
Founded: 1855
Miscellaneous: Firm is a member of Chatto, Bodley Head & Jonathan Cape Ltd Group (qv)
ISBN Publisher's Prefix: 0-7011

Chatto, Bodley Head & Jonathan Cape Ltd, 35 Bow St, London WC2E 7AN Tel: (01) 379 6831 Telex: 299080
Parent Company of Chatto & Windus, Jonathan Cape, The Bodley Head

The Chemical Society*, Burlington House, London W1V 0BN Tel: (01) 734 9864
Telex: 268001
Dir, Information Services: Dr A K Kent; *Sales & Marketing Manager:* Dr A Kabi; *Advertising Manager:* Jill Gunsell
Orders to: The Chemical Society, Distribution Centre, Blackhorse Rd, Letchworth, Herts SG6 1HN
Subjects: General Science, University Textbooks
Founded: 1841
ISBN Publisher's Prefixes: 0-85186, 0-85404, 0-85990

Child's Play (International) Ltd, Restrop Manor, Purton, Swindon, Wilts
Tel: Swindon 770389/850901 (STD code 0793) Telex: 449391
Man Dir: Michael Twinn; *Sales, Publicity:* Neil Burden
Subsidiary Companies: D A Finnigan Ltd, Aylesbury, UK; Child's Play Inc, Chicago, USA
Associate Company: F X Schmid (UK) Ltd, Swindon
Subject: Juveniles (pre- and Primary School ages)
1979: 5 titles *1980:* 16 titles *Founded:* 1972
ISBN Publisher's Prefix: 0-85953

Chivers Press Publishers, 93-100 Locksbrook Rd, Bath BA1 3HB Tel: Bath 331945 (STD code 0225) Telex: 449897
Man Dir: C A Coles (to whom all correspondence)
Associate Companies: Chivers Book Sales Ltd; Firecrest Publishing Ltd (qv); Lythway Press (qv)
Imprints: New Portway Large Print, New Portway Facsimile Editions
Subjects: General Fiction and Nonfiction
ISBN Publisher's Prefixes: 0-85594 (Chivers), 0-85997 (Portway)

The **Christian Community** Press, see Floris Books

Christian Journals Ltd, 2 Bristow Park, Upper Malone Rd, Belfast BT9 6TH
Tel: Belfast 668268 (STD code 0232)
Man Dir: W G Forker; *Rights & Permissions:* Miss P Lovegrove
Subject: Religion
1978: 16 titles *Founded:* 1974
ISBN Publisher's Prefix: 0-904302

Church Book Room Press, now Vine Books Ltd (qv)

Church Pastoral Aid Society, an imprint of Kingsway Publications Ltd (qv)

Churchill Livingstone, Robert Stevenson Ho, 1-3 Baxter's Pl, Leith Walk, Edinburgh EH1 3AF Tel: (031) 556 2424
Cable Add: Churchliv Telex: 727511 Longman G (Edin)
Shipping Add: Longman Group Ltd, Pinnacles, Harlow, Essex
Man Dir: R G B Duncan; *Sales, Publicity & Advertising:* A J Smith; *Production:* A D Lewis; *Rights & Permissions:* Sheena Gibb
Branch Off: 5 Bentinck St, London W1M 5RN Tel: (01) 935 0121
Subjects: Medicine, Dentistry, Nursing
1978: 97 titles *Founded:* 1863
Miscellaneous: Firm is a division of Longman Group Ltd (qv)
ISBN Publisher's Prefix: 0-443

Citadel, an imprint of L S P Books Ltd (qv)

Clarendon Press, see Oxford University Press

Robin Clark Ltd, 27-29 Goodge St, London W1P 1FD Tel: (01) 636 3992-5 Telex: 919034
Chairman: Naim Attallah; *Man Dir:* D Elliott; *Production Dir:* R J Reilly; *Editorial:* Janet Law; *Publicity:* Sheila Turnbull
Associate Company: Quartet Books Ltd (qv)
Subjects: Non-fiction Paperbacks: Reprints; Biography, Social History, Humour, County Guides, Animal Books, Practical Handbooks including Cookery and Gardening
1978: 8 titles *Founded:* 1976
Miscellaneous: Firm is a member of the Namara Group, Namara Ho, 45-46 Poland St, London W1
ISBN Publisher's Prefix: 0-86072

T & T Clark Ltd, 36 George St, Edinburgh EH2 2LQ Tel: (031) 225 4703 Cable Add: Dictionary Edinburgh
Man Dir: T G Ramsay D Clark; *Editorial, Sales, Production, Publicity, Rights & Permissions:* Geoffrey F Green
Parent Company: John Bartholomew & Son Ltd (qv)
Subjects: Philosophy, Theology, History, Law
1978: 10 titles *1979:* 75 titles *Founded:* 1821
ISBN Publisher's Prefix: 0-567

Anthony Clarke Books, 16 Garden Court, Wheathampstead, Herts AL4 8RF
Tel: Wheathampstead 2460 (STD code 058283) Cable Add: Clarkbook St Albans
Shipping Add: 27 Brewhouse Hill, Wheathampstead, Herts AL4 8RE
Proprietor: Anthony Clarke
Subject: Religion
Bookshop: All Saints Bookshop, All Saints, London Colney, Herts
1978: 4 titles *1979:* 4 titles *Founded:* 1970
ISBN Publisher's Prefix: 0-85650

James Clarke & Co Ltd, 7 All Saints' Passage, Cambridge CB2 3LS
Tel: Cambridge 350865 (STD code: 0223)
Telex: 817570
Man Dir: A C Brink
Subsidiary Company: Allenson & Co Ltd,

7 All Saints' Passage, Cambridge
Subjects: Librarianship, Religion, Textbooks, Reference, Technical
1979: 9 titles *1980:* 12 titles *Founded:* 1859
ISBN Publisher's Prefix: 0-227

E W **Classey**, Park Rd, Faringdon, Oxfordshire SN7 7DR Tel: Faringdon 20911 (STD code 0367)
Publisher: E W Classey
Subject: Entomology
ISBN Publisher's Prefix: 0-900848

Clematis Press Ltd, 18 Old Church St, London SW3 5DQ Tel: (01) 352 8755 Cable Add: Clematis London
Man Dir: Mrs Clara Waters
Trade Counter: Wentworth Book Co Ltd, Pindar Rd, Hoddesdon, Herts EN11 0HF
Imprints: Bonfini, Corvina, Uffici
Subjects: Art, Architecture, Sport, Cookery
Founded: 1950
ISBN Publisher's Prefix: 0-568

William **Clowes** (Publishers) Ltd*, 31 Newgate, Beccles, Suffolk NR35 9QP Tel: Beccles 712884 (STD code 0502)
Manager: Gordon Knights
Subjects: General, Religion, Hymn Books
ISBN Publisher's Prefix: 0-85194

Club Leabhar, 91 Cromwell St, Stornoway, Isle of Lewis Tel: Stornoway 3812 (STD code 0851)
Subjects: Books in Gaelic, Juveniles, Fiction in English
1978: 1 title
ISBN Publisher's Prefix: 0-902796

Co-chuideachd Leabhneachean Gaidhlig, an imprint of Volturna Press (qv)

Collet's Holdings Ltd, Denington Estate, Wellingborough, Northants NN8 2QT Tel: Wellingborough 224351 (STD code 0933) Cable Add: Colholdin Wellingborough
Man Dir: Joan Birch; *Advertising:* Philip Taylor
Subjects: Music, Art (History), Textbooks, Reference (Modern Language, Audiovisual), Engineering, General & Social Science, Low- & High-priced Paperbacks
Bookshops: Collet's Chinese Bookshop, 40 Great Russell St, London WC1; Collet's London Bookshop, 66 Charing Cross Rd, London WC2; Collet's International Bookshop, 129/131 Charing Cross Rd, London WC2; Collet's Penguin Bookshop, 52 Charing Cross Rd, London WC2; Collet's Record Shop, 180 Shaftesbury Ave, London WC2
Founded: 1934
Miscellaneous: Specialists in Russian language teaching materials
ISBN Publisher's Prefix: 0-569

Collier Macmillan Ltd, Stockley Close, Stockley Rd, West Drayton, Middx UB7 9BE Tel: West Drayton 40651 (STD code 089 54) Cable Add: Pachamac West Drayton Telex: 28648 Casmac-G
Man Dir: Brian J Collins; *Sales, Marketing Manager:* Alastair Gordon; *Publicity, Promotion:* R Bower
Parent Company: Cassell & Collier Macmillan Ltd, London
Subjects: Academic, Primary and Secondary Textbooks, Trade, Professional Reference, English as a second Language
1978: 192 titles *1979:* 184 titles *Founded:* 1964
ISBN Publisher's Prefix: 0-02

Collingridge, an imprint of The Hamlyn Publishing Group Ltd (qv)

Rex **Collings** Ltd, 6 Paddington St, London W1M 3LA Tel: (01) 487 4201
Man Dir: Rex Collings

Orders to: Noonan Hurst Ltd, 131 Trafalgar Rd, London SE10
Subjects: General, Poetry, Juveniles, Africana, Biography, Drama, Reference
1978: 30 titles
ISBN Publisher's Prefix: 0-86036, 0-901720

William **Collins** Sons & Co Ltd, 14 St James's Pl, London SW1A 1PS Tel: (01) 493 7070 Cable Add: Herakles London SW1 Telex: 25611 and PO Box, Glasgow G4 0NB Tel: (041) 772 3200 Telex: 778107
Chairman: W J Collins; *Vice-Chairman & Group Man Dir:* D W Nickson; *Publishing:* S A M Collins (General), C E Allen (Children's, Biblical, Reference); *Production:* G Craig
Subsidiary Companies: Harvill Press Ltd (qv); Hatchards Ltd (qv under Major Booksellers); Wm Collins Pty Ltd, Australia (qv); Wm Collins Sons & Co (Canada) Ltd, 100 Lesmil Rd, Don Mills, Ontario, Canada; Wm Collins Ltd, New Zealand Publishers (qv); Wm Collins (Africa) (Pty) Ltd, PO Box 8879, Johannesburg, South Africa
Imprints include: Armada Books, Fontana Books
Subjects: General Fiction & Nonfiction, Belles Lettres, Biography, History, How-to, Art, Archaeology, Philosophy, Reference, Religion, Bibles, Low- & High-priced Paperbacks, General & Natural Sciences, University, Secondary & Primary Textbooks, Educational Materials, Juveniles, Military, Sports, Travel
Bookshops: Hatchards Ltd, 187 Piccadilly, London W1; Hatchards at Harvey Nichols, Knightsbridge, London SW1; The Ancient House, Ipswich, Suffolk; Hanningtons, 53 Market St, Brighton, Sussex; The Deben Bookshop, Woodbridge, Suffolk
Book Club: Nationwide Book Services (owned jointly with William Heinemann (International) Ltd, UK, Martin Secker & Warburg Ltd, UK and Albert Bonniers Förlag AB, Sweden)
Founded: 1819
Miscellaneous: Collins-Longman Atlases, Westerhill Rd, Bishopbriggs, Glasgow G64 2PW distributes atlases for Wm Collins and the Longman Group
ISBN Publisher's Prefixes: 0-00 (Collins), 0-01 (Armada, Fontana, Harvill)

Colonnade, an imprint of British Museum Publications (qv)

Colour Library International Ltd, CLI House, 80-82 Coombe Rd, New Malden, Surrey KT3 4QZ Tel: (01) 942 7781/949 6071 Cable Add: Colorfile New Malden Telex: 928505
Man Dir: Barry Austin; *Editorial:* David Gibbon; *Sales:* Barry Austin, George Sprankling; *Production, Publicity:* Ted Smart; *Rights & Permissions:* Barry Austin, George Sprankling, Ted Smart
Subsidiary Company: Colour Library International (USA) Ltd, 163 East 64th St, New York, NY 10021, USA
Subjects: Travel, Nature, Art, Animals, Inspirational, Religion
1978: 51 titles *1979:* 101 titles *Founded:* 1959
ISBN Publisher's Prefix: 0-906558

Columbia University Press, see University Presses of Columbia and Princeton

Common Ground, an imprint of Longman Group Ltd (qv)

Concertina Publications Ltd, 11-13 Broad Court, Covent Garden, London WC2B 5QJ Tel: (01) 836 1758/2929
Subjects: Illustrated Nonfiction, Reference

Condor Books, an imprint of Souvenir Press Ltd (qv)

The **Connoisseur**, an imprint of National Magazine Co Ltd (qv)

Connoisseur Carbooks, see Motor Racing Publications Ltd

Conservative Political Centre, 32 Smith Sq, London SW1P 3HH Tel: (01) 222 9000 Cable Add: Constitute, London, SW1P 3HH
Director: David Knapp
Subjects: Reference Books, Politics, Political Economy, Sociology, Questions of the Day
1978: 20 titles *1979:* 14 titles
ISBN Publisher's Prefix: 0-85070

Constable & Co Ltd, 10 Orange St, London WC2H 7EG Tel: (01) 930 0801 Cable Add: Dhagoba London WC2H 7EG
Man Dir: B K Glazebrook; *Editorial:* Elfreda Powell; *Sales:* Paul Marks; *Publicity & Editorial:* Miles Huddleston; *Rights & Permissions:* Christine Senior
Orders to: Tiptree Book Services Ltd, Tiptree, Colchester, Essex Tel: (0621) 816362 Cable Add: Literarius Tiptree Telex: 99487
Subjects: General Fiction, Literature, Biography, Memoirs, History, Politics, Current Affairs, Food, Travel & Guidebooks, Social Sciences, Psychology & Psychiatry, Counselling, Social Work, Sociology, Mass Communications
1978: 47 titles *Founded:* 1896
ISBN Publisher's Prefix: 0-09

Construction Press Ltd, Lunesdale Ho, Hornby, Lancaster LA2 8NB Tel: Hornby 21888 (STD code 0468) Telex: 81259
Man Dir & Publicity: P J Horrobin; *Editorial:* Shirley Crabtree; *Sales:* Michael Wymer; *Production:* Terry Mann; *Rights & Permissions:* Lynette Owen
Orders to: Longman Group Ltd, Fourth Ave, Harlow, Essex
Parent Company: Longman Group Ltd (qv)
Subjects: Architecture, Building, Civil Engineering
1978: 24 titles *Founded:* 1974
ISBN Publisher's Prefixes: 0-904406, 0-86095

Continua Productions Ltd, see Macdonald & Evans Ltd

Conway Maritime Press Ltd, 2 Nelson Rd, Greenwich, London SE10 9JB Tel: (01) 858 7211
Man Dir: W R Blackmore; *Editorial Dir:* Robert Gardiner; *Sales Manager:* Alexandra Lenton
Orders to: Marston Book Services Ltd, PO Box 87, Marston St, Oxford OX4 1LB
Associate Company: Paul Popper Ltd, 24 Bride Lane, Fleet St, London EC4Y 8DR
Subjects: Naval, Maritime
Bookshop: Meridian Books, 2 Nelson Rd, Greenwich, London SE10 9JB
1978: 20 titles *1979:* 20 titles *Founded:* 1968
ISBN Publisher's Prefix: 0-85177

Leo **Cooper** Ltd, see Frederick Warne (Publishers) Ltd

Trewin **Copplestone** Publishing Ltd*, Advance House, 101-109 Ladbroke Grove, London W11 1PG Tel: (01) 229 8861/3 Cable Add: Trewcop London W11 Telex: 25766
Man Dir: Trewin Copplestone
Subjects: History, Rock Music, Art, Reference, Regional Encyclopedias, Low- & High-priced Paperbacks, General Science
1978: 8 titles *Founded:* 1972
Miscellaneous: Firm originates, designs and produces books for co-edition publication
ISBN Publisher's Prefix: 0-85674

Corgi Books, a subsidiary of Transworld Publishers Ltd (qv)

Cornell University Press, 2-4 Brook St, London W1Y 1AA Tel: (01) 493 5061, (01) 499 4688 Cable Add: Unibooks London W1 Telex: 24224 ref 3545
Warehouse: International Book Distributors, 66 Wood Lane End, Hemel Hempstead, Herts
Man Dir: J Trevor Brown; *Promotion Manager:* Andrew Nolan; *Export Sales Manager:* Anna Simpson-Muellner
Parent Company: Cornell University Press, 124 Roberts Pl, Ithaca, NY 14850, USA
Subjects: Academic (all disciplines)
1978: 56 titles *1979:* 40 titles
ISBN Publisher's Prefix: 0-8014

Coronet, an imprint of Hodder & Stoughton Ltd (qv)

Corvina, an imprint of Clematis Press Ltd (qv)

David **Costello** Ltd, 43 High St, Tunbridge Wells, Kent TN1 1XU Tel: Tunbridge Wells 39386 (STD code 0892)
Man Dir: David Costello; *Editorial Dir:* Roland Elgey
Associate Companies: Weald Publishing Agency UK, EC Exports Ltd (both at above address)
Imprints: Costello Educational, Travelog
Subjects: Special Education, Archeology, Medicine, Foreign Travel
1979: 3 titles *Founded:* 1979
ISBN Publisher's Prefix: 0-7104

Cotman Colour and **Cotman House**, imprints of Jarrold Colour Publications (qv)

Country Life Books, an imprint of Hamlyn Group Ltd (qv)

Coventure Ltd, 1 Prince of Wales Passage, 117 Hamstead Rd, London NW1 3EE Tel: (01) 388 5389 Cable Add: Coventure
Man Dir, Editorial: Ian Fenton; *Sales:* Rathan Sippy; *Production:* Jim Hall; *Rights & Permissions:* Ian Fenton
Subjects: Juveniles, Psychology, Sociology, International Co-editions
1978: 10 titles *Founded:* 1973
ISBN Publisher's Prefix: 0-904576

Coverdale House Publishers Ltd, an imprint of Kingsway Publications Ltd (qv)

The **Crafts** Council, 12 Waterloo Pl, London SW1Y 4AU Tel: (01) 839 1917
Publications Officer: Marigold Coleman
Bookshop: Crafts Council Gallery, 12 Waterloo Pl, London SW1Y 4AU
Subject: Crafts
1978: 4 titles *1979:* 5 titles *Founded:* 1971
Miscellaneous: Government-financed body promoting Britain's artist craftsmen
ISBN Publisher's Prefix: 0-903798

Cressrelles Publishing Co Ltd, Kestrels House, Peppard Common, Henley-on-Thames, Oxon RG9 5EP Tel: Kidmore End 3165 (STD code 073525)
Man Dir: Leslie Smith
Subjects: Juveniles, Pre-school Education, Fiction, General
1978: 5 titles *1979:* 5 titles *Founded:* 1972
ISBN Publisher's Prefix: 0-85956

Paul H **Crompton** Ltd, 638 Fulham Rd, London SW6 Tel: (01) 736 2551
Publicity & Sales: Paul Crompton; *Subscription Enquiries:* B Crompton; *Shop Enquiries:* C Hanson
Subjects: Oriental Martial Arts and Survival
Miscellaneous: Publish magazine *Karate & Oriental Arts* (bi-monthly)

Croner Publications Ltd, Croner House, 173 Kingston Rd, New Malden, Surrey KT3 3SS Tel: (01) 942 9615
Man Dir: A S Brode; *Marketing Dir:* D E Sleat

Subject: Business Reference Books
1978: 1 title
Miscellaneous: Firm is member of NV I C U Group, Netherlands (qv)
ISBN Publisher's Prefix: 0-900319

Croom Helm Ltd, 2-10 St John's Rd, London SW11 Tel: (01) 228 9343/4
Man Dirs: Christopher Helm, David Croom; *Editorial:* Melanie Crook; *Sales:* Graham Harris; *Production:* Mike Conway; *Publicity:* Richard Stoneman
Subjects: Scientific, Legal & Parliamentary, Medical, Commercial & Professional, Military, Reference Books, Art & Architecture, Games & Pastimes, History, Archaeology, Biography & Memoirs, Politics, Political Economy, Sociology, Questions of the Day, Oriental, Directories & Guidebooks, Classical Studies, Economics
1979: 144 titles
ISBN Publisher's Prefixes: 0-85664, 0-7099

Curzon Press Ltd, 88 Gray's Inn Rd, London WC1 Tel: (01) 405 1865 and 9325
Shipping Add: Biblios Publishers Distribution Services Ltd, Glenside Industrial Estate, Partridge Green, Horsham, Sussex
Man Dir: J F Standish
Subjects: Oriental and African Studies
1978: 18 titles *1979:* 21 titles *Founded:* 1970
ISBN Publisher's Prefix: 0-7007

Cut & Colour Books, an imprint of Dinosaur Publications Ltd (qv)

D P Publications, 16 Bere Close, Winchester, Hants SO22 5HY Tel: Winchester 881806 (STD code 0962) or Watford 31754 (STD code 0923)
Subjects: Finance, Law, Accountancy, Quantitative Techniques, Management, Data Processing, Computer Science, Management Information Systems, Auditing
1979: 10 titles
ISBN Publisher's Prefix: 0-905435

The C W **Daniel** Co Ltd, 1 Church Path, Saffron Walden, Essex CB10 1JP Tel: Saffron Walden 21909 (STD code 0799)
Man Dir: Ian Miller; *Editorial:* Mrs Jana Garai; *Sales:* Tracy Stevens; *Production:* Barnaby Miller; *Publicity:* Ida Honorofe; *Rights & Permissions:* Jennie Miller
Associate Company: Health Science Press (qv)
Subjects: Natural Healing, Homoeopathy
ISBN Publisher's Prefix: 0-85207

Dark Star, an imprint of Scorpion Publications Ltd (qv)

Darton, Longman & Todd Ltd, 89 Lillie Rd, London SW6 1UD Tel: (01) 385 2341
Cable Add: Librabook London SW6 1UD
Dirs: Adrian Brink, J M Todd, Miss E A C Russell; *Publicity & Advertising:* Miss A Hornby
Subjects: History, Philosophy, Reference, Religion, Bibles, High-priced Paperbacks, Medicine, Psychology, Secondary Textbooks, Travel Guides, Gardening
1979: 35 titles *Founded:* 1959
ISBN Publisher's Prefix: 0-232

Darwen Finlayson Ltd, Shopwyke Hall, Chichester, West Sussex Tel: Chichester 787636 (STD code 0243)
Chairman & Man Dir: Philip Harris; *Editorial Director:* Noel H Osborne
Parent Company: Phillimore & Co Ltd (qv)
Subjects: History, Historical Biography, Company Histories, Family Histories
ISBN Publisher's Prefix: 0-85208

David & Charles, Brunel Ho, Forde Rd, Newton Abbot, Devon TQ12 2DW
Tel: Newton Abbot 61121 (STD code 0626)
Cable Add: Books Nabbot Telex: 42904

Chairman: David St John Thomas; *Man Dir:* J Angell; *Sales Dir:* Colin Macleod; *Publicity Dir:* Nicholas Loasby; *Rights & Permissions:* Dieter L Klein
Parent Company: David & Charles (Holdings) Ltd
Subsidiary Company: David & Charles Inc, North Pomfret, Vermont 05053, USA
Subjects: History, How-to, Architecture, Archaeology, Reference, Engineering, General Science, Marine & Railway Transport, Countryside, Natural History, Cookery, Sport
Bookshop: St John Thomas, The Baker St Book & Record Shop, 33 Baker St, London W1M 1AE
Book Club: Readers Union Ltd (qv)
Founded: 1960
ISBN Publisher's Prefix: 0-7153

Christopher **Davies** Publishers Ltd, 52 Mansel St, Swansea, West Glamorgan SA1 5EL Tel: Swansea 41933 (STD code 0792)
Joint Man Dirs: John M Phillips, Christopher Davies
Subjects: Literature, Belles Lettres, Poetry, History, Religion, Sport, Welsh Language Publications, General
1978: 17 English titles *Founded:* 1941
ISBN Publisher's Prefixes: 0-7154, 0-85339

Peter **Davies** Ltd, 10 Upper Grosvenor St, London W1X 9PA Tel: (01) 493 4141
Cable Add: Pedebooks London W1
Chairman: C S Pick; *Dir:* Nigel Hollis; *Rights:* Caroline Ball
Parent Company: Heinemann Group of Publishers Ltd (qv)
Branch Offs: The Windmill Press, Kingswood, Tadworth, Surrey; 11a Gower Mews, London WC1
Subjects: General Fiction, Biography, History, Religion, Travel, Seafaring, Theatre, Countryside, Cookery
1978: 20 titles *1979:* 16 titles *Founded:* 1925
ISBN Publisher's Prefix: 0-432

Davis-Poynter Ltd, 20 Garrick St, London WC2E 9BJ Tel: (01) 240 3144 Cable Add: Deepeebook, London WC2E 9BJ
Orders to: George Philip & Son Ltd, PO Box 1, Arndale Rd, Lineside Industrial Estate, Littlehampton, Sussex BN17 7EN
Man Dir Editorial, Publicity: R G Davis-Poynter; *Sales, Production, Rights & Permissions:* Susan Herbert
Subjects: Fiction, History, Politics, Naval & Military, Music, Poetry & Drama, Biography, Memoirs, Politics, Sociology, Travel, Gardening, Folklore
1978: 8 titles *1979:* 9 titles *Founded:* 1970
ISBN Publisher's Prefix: 0-7067

Davison Publishing Ltd, 109 Southampton Row, London WC1B 4HH Tel: (01) 637 2541
Dirs: Thomas Tessier, Phil Edwards
Imprint: Millington Books
Subjects: Science Fiction, Gothic/Romance Fiction, Biography, History, General Non-fiction, High-priced Paperbacks
1979: 21 titles *Founded:* 1973
ISBN Publisher's Prefix: 0-86000

Dawson Publishing, Cannon Ho, Folkestone, Kent CT19 5EE
Tel: Folkestone 57421 (STD code 0303)
Cable Add: Dawbooks Folkestone
Telex: 96392
Man Dir: D A Brewer; *Publishing Dir:* Ian Williams; *Rights & Permissions:* Linda Webb
Subjects: Music, Art, Geography, University Textbooks, Biography, History, Reference, Medicine, General & Social Science, Cartography
Bookshops: Dawson Book Service, 10-14 Macklin St, London WC2B 5NG;

Cannon Ho, Folkestone, Kent CT19 5EE; Dawson-France SA, BP 40, F-91121 Palaiseau, France (all three general sales); Dawson Rare Books, 16-17 Pall Mall, London SW1Y 5WB; Bow Windows Book Shop, 128 High St, Lewes, East Sussex BN7 1XL; Deighton, Bell & Co and Frank Hammond, both at 13 Trinity St, Cambridge CB2 1TD (all antiquarian sales); Stevens and Brown Ltd, Ardon House, Mill Lane, Godalming, Surrey GU7 1HA
1978: 48 titles *Founded:* 1809
ISBN Publisher's Prefix: 0-7129

Dean & Son, an imprint of The Hamlyn Publishing Group (qv)

Delightful Books, an imprint of Ramboro Enterprises Ltd (qv)

Delmar, an imprint of Van Nostrand Reinhold Co Ltd (qv)

Dempsey & Squires Publishers Ltd*, 4 West London Studios, 404 Fulham Rd, London SW10
Man Dir: Michael Dempsey; *Sales:* Martin Squires
Subjects: Fiction, Non-fiction illustrated books & large format paperbacks

Denholm House Press, see National Christian Education Council

J M **Dent** & Sons Ltd, Aldine House, 33 Welbeck St, London W1M 8LX Tel: (01) 486 7233 Cable Add: Malaby London W1 Telex: 8954130
Chairman: Piers Raymond; *Man Dir:* Peter Shellard; *Editorial:* Malcolm Gerratt, Peter Shellard (General), Vanessa Hamilton (Juvenile), Jocelyn Burton (Everyman); *Marketing Dir:* Peter Collins; *Production:* David Rye; *Publicity Manager:* Elizabeth Newlands; *Contracts & Permissions:* John Sundell; *Rights:* Maggie Hemingway (General); Clarissa Cridland (Juvenile)
Orders to: J M Dent (Distribution) Ltd, Dunhams Lane, Letchworth, Herts SG6 1LF
Parent Company: J M Dent & Sons (Holdings) Ltd
Subsidiary Companies: J M Dent Pty Ltd, PO Box 289, Ferntree Gully, Victoria 3156, Australia; J M Dent & Sons (Canada) Ltd, Don Mills, Ontario
Associate Companies: J M Dent (Distribution) Ltd; J M Dent (Sales) Ltd; J M Dent & Sons (Letchworth) Ltd (Bookbinders)
Imprints: Aldine Paperbacks, Dent Dolphins, Everyman's Library, Everyman's Reference Library, Everyman's University Library, Malaby Press
Subjects: Belles Lettres, Biography, History, Natural History, Music, Reference, Juveniles, Low- & High-priced Paperbacks, Social Science, University Textbooks, Regional, Topography, Archaeology, Cookery, Gardening, Popular Science
1978: 100 titles *Founded:* 1888
Miscellaneous: Publishers of *Everyman's Encyclopaedia*
ISBN Publisher's Prefix: 0-460

Design Council Books, The Design Centre, 28 Haymarket, London SW1Y 4SU Tel: (01) 839 8000 Telex: 8812963
Publications Manager: Terry Bishop; *Editorial:* Nicola Hamilton
Promotion, Sales & Rights: Pam Solomon
Orders on general trade books to: Macdonald/Futura Publishers Ltd, 8 Shepherdess Walk, London N1
Parent Company: Design Council, 28 Haymarket, London SW1Y 4SU
Imprints: Design Centre Books, Design Council
Bookshops: The Design Centre Bookshop and The Design Centre Bookshop Mail Order, 28 Haymarket, London SW1Y 4SU
Subjects: Design in the Home, Design Books for the General Public, Design Education and Design in General Education, Professional Design Books, Management Books, Educational Visual Aids, Design History Books
1978: 11 titles *Founded:* 1974
ISBN Publisher's Prefix: 0-85072

André **Deutsch** Ltd, 105 Great Russell St, London WC1B 3LJ Tel: (01) 580 2746 Cable Add: Adlib, London WC1 Telex: 21792
Man Dir: André Deutsch; *Editorial Dirs:* Piers Burnett, David Harsent; *Sales Dir:* Mike Beattie; *Production:* Jeff Sains; *Publicity & Advertising Dir:* Sheila Murphy; *Rights & Permissions:* Anne-Louise Fisher
Associate Companies: Abbeville Press; Burnett Books; Private Eye Books
Imprints: Grafton Books, The Language Library
Subjects: General Fiction, Belles Lettres, Poetry, Biography, History, Music, Art, Philosophy, Reference, Juveniles, High-priced Paperbacks, Psychology, General & Social Science, Humour, Politics, Travel, Cookery
1978: 72 titles *1979:* 88 titles *Founded:* 1951
ISBN Publisher's Prefix: 0-233

Diagram Visual Information Ltd, 22 Chenies St, London WC1E 7EX Tel: (01) 637 4646 Telex: 21120 ref 2978
Dirs: Bob Chapman, Bruce Robertson, Trevor Bounford
Subjects: Reference, Juveniles
Miscellaneous: Creators of *Diagram Group* books

Dinosaur Publications Ltd, Beechcroft Ho, Over, Cambridge CB4 5NE Tel: Swavesey 30324 (STD code 0954)
Man Dir: Bruce Graham-Cameron; *Managing Editor:* Althea Braithwaite; *Marketing Dir:* Mike Graham-Cameron; *Rights & Permissions:* Bruce Graham-Cameron, Sarah Allen; *Publicity:* HPR Publicity, 9 Fitzroy Sq, London W1 (Tel: (01) 388 2613)
Associate Companies: Polyhedron Printers Ltd; Graham Cameron & Braithwaite, Advertising Consultants
Imprints: Althea, Cut & Colour Books, Dinosaur's Althea Books, National Trust Children's Series, Dinosaur's Action Books, Althea's Pet Series, Wingate Series
Subjects: Juveniles, Educational Materials, Sponsored Books
1978: 31 titles *1979:* 30 titles *Founded:* 1968
ISBN Publisher's Prefix: 0-85122

'**Discovering**' Books, see Shire Publications Ltd

Dennis **Dobson** (Dobson Books Ltd), 80 Kensington Church St, London W8 4BZ Tel: (01) 229 0225/6022
Shipping Add: 186 Campden Hill Rd, London W8
Man Dir: Margaret Dobson; *Sales, Publicity:* Vicky Carne
Subjects: General Fiction, Belles Lettres, Poetry, Biography, History, Music, Art, Theatre, Juveniles, General & Social Science, Economics, Political Science
1979: 65 titles
ISBN Publisher's Prefix: 0-234

Dolphin, an imprint of Doubleday & Co Inc (qv)

Dolphin Books, see Blandford Books Ltd

John **Donald** Publishers Ltd, 138 Stephen St, Edinburgh EH3 5AA
Man Dir: D M Morrison; *Editorial, Rights & Permissions:* J B Tuckwell; *Sales, Production, Publicity:* J E Bruce
Subjects: Academic, Scottish
1979: 14 titles *1980:* 20 titles *Founded:* 1973
ISBN Publisher's Prefix: 0-85976

Ad **Donker** Ltd*, 1 Prince of Wales Passage, 117 Hampstead Rd, London NW1 3EE
Man Dir: David Harrison
Parent Company: Ad Donker (Pty) Ltd, South Africa (qv)
Subjects: General Fiction & Nonfiction, Belles Lettres, Poetry, Biography, Reference
Founded: 1976

Dorling Kindersley Ltd, 9 Henrietta St, Covent Garden, London WC2E 8PS Tel: (01) 240 5151 Telex: 8954527 Deekay G
Man Dirs: Christopher Dorling, Peter Kindersley; *Foreign Sales:* Caroline Oakes; *Editorial:* Christopher Davis; *Design:* Roger Bristow
Subjects: Illustrated Reference Books for the International Market on Photography, Gardening, Cookery, Crafts, Family Health, Child Care, History, Sport, DIY, Leisure
1980: 10 titles *Founded:* 1974

Doubleday & Co Inc, 100 Wigmore St, London W1H 9DR Tel: (01) 935 1269 Cable Add: Doubco Telex: 264676
Editorial: Margaret Pringle; *Sales, Rights & Permissions:* Gloria Ferris
Orders to: Transatlantic Book Service Ltd, 24 Red Lion St, London WC1R 4PX
Parent Company: Doubleday & Co, Inc, 245 Park Ave, New York, NY 10017, USA
Associate Companies: Doubleday Canada Ltd; Doubleday-France, Paris
Imprints: Anchor, Dolphin, Image
Subjects: General
Book Clubs: Book Club Associates (qv)
Founded: 1897
ISBN Publisher's Prefix: 0-385

Dragon Books, see Granada Publishing

Dragon's World Ltd, High St, Limpsfield, Surrey RH8 0DY Tel: Oxted 5044 (STD code 08833) Telex: 95631
Dir, Publisher, Sales, Rights & Permissions: H A Schaafsma; *Production:* 33 Portland Rd, London W11 4LH; *Publicity:* Irene Howells
Orders to: PHIN Distributors Ltd, Phin House, Bath Rd, Cheltenham, Glos
Imprint: Paper Tiger
Subjects: Illustrated Science Fiction, Art, Children's Books
1978: 14 titles *1979:* 12 titles *Founded:* 1976
ISBN Publisher's Prefix: 0-905895

Gerald **Duckworth** & Co Ltd, The Old Piano Factory, 43 Gloucester Crescent, London NW1 Tel: (01) 485 3484 Cable Add: Platypus
Man Dir: Colin Haycraft; *Sales Manager:* David Lines; *Publicity Advertising Manager, Rights & Permissions:* Isolde Simmonds
Subjects: Fiction, General, Academic
1979: 87 titles *Founded:* 1898
ISBN Publisher's Prefix: 0-7156

Martin **Dunitz** Ltd, Flat 5, 25 Cleveland Sq, London W2 6DD Tel: (01) 262 7491 Telex: 21120 ref 3686
Man Dir, Sales, Rights & Permissions: Martin Dunitz; *Editorial:* Elizabeth Brooke-Smith; *Production:* Alan Coombes; *Publicity:* Ruth Dunitz
Orders to: Macdonald/Futura Publishers Ltd, 8 Shepherdess Walk, London N1 7LW
Subjects: Popular Health, Sailing, Ski-ing, Livestock & Poultry Breeding
1979: 6 titles *Founded:* 1978
ISBN Publisher's Prefix: 0-906348

E P Publishing Ltd, Bradford Rd, East Ardsley, Wakefield, West Yorkshire WF3 2JN Tel: Wakefield 823971 (STD code 0924) Cable Add: Edpro, Wakefield Telex: 917963 Solomon, London
Man Dir, Rights & Permissions: Brian Lewis; *Editorial:* Frances Royle; *Sales:* Brian Lewis; *Production:* Keith Dobson; *Publicity:*

378 UNITED KINGDOM

Sharon Mitchell
Parent Company: Siemssen, Hunter Ltd
Subsidiary Companies: Educational Productions Ltd, Tabard Press Ltd
Subjects: Sport, History, Health, Reprints
1978: 30 titles *Founded:* 1946
ISBN Publisher's Prefixes: 0-7158 (Educational Productions), 0-85409 (SRP), 0-85948 (Tabard)

E S A Creative Learning Ltd*, PO Box 22, Pinnacles, Harlow, Essex CM19 5AY Tel: Harlow 21131 (STD code 0279)
Dir: Michael Bodman
Imprint: Good Reading
Subject: Primary Education
Miscellaneous: Publish reprints of GCE Examination Papers
ISBN Publisher's Prefix: 0-7159

E S C Publishing Ltd, 25 Beaumont St, Oxford OX1 2NP Tel: Oxford 512281 (STD code 0865) Telex: 83147
Editorial: Hugh Brett; *Sales, Production, Publicity, Rights & Permissions:* Nicholas G Ingell
Associate Company: European Study Conferences Ltd, Kirby House, High St East, Uppingham, Leicestershire
Subjects: Law, Industrial Relations, Periodicals
1979: 3 titles *1980:* 2 titles *Founded:* 1978
ISBN Publisher's Prefix: 0-906214

East-West Publications (UK) Ltd, 120 Charing Cross Rd, London WC2H 0JR Tel: (01) 379 6838
Man Dir: L W Carp
Associate Company: Words & Music Ltd, Words & Music (Wholesale) Ltd
Subjects: Far & Middle East Culture & Religion, Children's & Adults Reference Books, Children's Music, Music
1979: 10 titles
ISBN Publisher's Prefix: 0-85692

Ebury Press, an imprint of National Magazine Co Ltd (qv)

The **Economist** Newspaper Ltd*, 25 St James's St, London SW1A 1HG Tel: (01) 839 7000 Cable Add: Mistecon Ldn Telex: 919555
Man Dir: Ian Trafford; *Rights & Permissions:* David McGill
Subsidiary Companies: Economist Intelligence Unit Ltd (UK); The Economist Newspaper Inc, 75 Rockefeller Plaza, NY 10019, USA
Branch Off: 75 Rockefeller Plaza, New York, NY 10019, USA
Subjects: Economic Reference Books, Diaries, Educational Materials
Founded: 1843
ISBN Publisher's Prefix: 0-85058

Eddison Press Ltd, 58 North Hill, Colchester, Essex CO1 1PX Tel: Colchester 44526/7 (STD code 0206)
Dirs: R Rayner, Roger W G Curtis
Orders to: c/o Melrose Press Ltd, 17/21 Churchgate St, Soham, Ely, Cambs CB7 5DS
Imprints: Eddison Bluesbooks, Eddison Musicbooks
Subjects: Reference, Music
ISBN Publisher's Prefix: 0-85649

Edinburgh University Press, 22 George Sq, Edinburgh EH8 9LF Tel: (031) 667 1011 Cable Add: Edinpress Telex: 727872
Man Dir, Rights & Permissions: A R Turnbull; *Sales Manager:* J G Angus; *Assistant Secretary & Production Manager:* J McI Davidson
Subjects: Belles Lettres, Poetry, Biography, History, Music, Art, Philosophy, Religion, Textbooks, Reference, Medicine, Psychology, General & Social Science
1978: 4 titles *1979:* 16 titles *Founded:* 1948
ISBN Publisher's Prefix: 0-85224

Edinburgh University Student Publications Board*, 1 Buccleuch Pl, Edinburgh EH8 9LW Tel: (031) 667 1011/5718
Subjects: Politics, Sociology, Fiction, Poetry, History, all with special regard to Scotland
1978: 3 new titles *1979:* 8 new titles

Educational Book Promotions, see Macdonald & Evans Ltd

Educational Explorers Ltd, 40 Silver St, Reading, Berkshire RG1 2SU Tel: Reading 83103 (STD code 0734)
Man Dir: Dr Caleb Grattegno; *Editorial:* Rachel Bleackley; *Sales:* Jackie House
Parent Company: Educational Solutions (UK) Ltd of Reading
Associate Companies: Educational Solutions Inc, 80 Fifth Ave, New York, NY 10011; The Cuisenaire Co Ltd, and Educational Explorers Film Co Ltd, both of 40 Silver St, Reading, Berkshire RG1 2SU
Subjects: Primary & Secondary Textbooks and Teachers Guides, Mathematics, Reading, Foreign Languages, Educational Psychology, Career Biographies, Library Science, Humanities, Public Health, Social Science, Military History
ISBN Publisher's Prefix: 0-85225

Educational Productions Ltd, see E P Publishing Ltd

Educational Systems Ltd, Waverley Rd, Yate, Bristol BS17 5RB Tel: Chipping Sodbury 316774 (STD code 0454)
Man Dir: N Whalley; *Publications Manager:* R E Smith
Parent Company: ESL Bristol Ltd
Subjects: Secondary & Primary Textbooks, Nautical, Management and Industrial Training Manuals, Audio-visual Aids
1979: 10 titles *Founded:* 1964
ISBN Publisher's Prefix: 0-900737

Eel Pie Publishing, 43-45 Broadwick St, London W1V 1FS Tel: (01) 434 3953 Telex: 932577 Eel Pie
Man Dir: Roy Massey; *Publishing Manager:* Mathew Price; *Music Editor:* Peter Hogan; *Sales:* John Brown; *Publicity:* Jenny Marshall, HPR Publicity, 9 Fitzroy Sq, London W1 (Tel: (01) 388 2613) *Production:* Heather Cooper; *Rights & Permissions:* Penny Morris
Subjects: Music, Juveniles, Gift Books, Cookery, Fiction, General
Bookshop: Magic Bus, 10 King St, Richmond, Surrey
1979: 7 titles *Founded:* 1978
ISBN Publisher's Prefix: 0-906008

Paul **Elek** Ltd, see Granada Publishing Ltd

Elliot Right Way Books, Kingswood Bldgs, Lower Kingswood, Tadworth, Surrey KT20 6TD Tel: Mogador 2202 (STD code 073783)
Man Dir: Andrew G Elliot; *Sales Dir:* A Clive Elliot
Imprints: Paperfronts, Right Way Books
Subjects: How-to, Reference, Juveniles, Low-priced Paperbacks, Sport, Technical, Education
1978: 18 titles *1979:* 24 titles *Founded:* 1945
ISBN Publisher's Prefix: 0-7160

Aidan **Ellis** Publishing Ltd, Cobb Ho, Nuffield, Henley-on-Thames, Oxfordshire RG9 5RU Tel: Nettlebed 641496 (STD code 0491) Cable Add: Aidanellis Henley-on-Thames
Man Dir: Aidan Ellis
Orders to: J M Dent & Sons (Distribution) Ltd, Dunhams Lane, Letchworth SG6 1LF, Herts
Subjects: Fiction, General, Children's, Sport
1979: 12 titles *1980:* 11 titles *Founded:* 1971
ISBN Publisher's Prefix: 0-85628

Elm Tree Books Ltd, see Hamish Hamilton Ltd

Elmfield Press, see Severn House Publishers Ltd

Elron Press Ltd, 20 Garrick St, London WC2E 8BJ Tel: (01) 836 0670/0771
Dirs: Tim Jenns, Viv Whiteley, Alan Smith
Subjects: General Non-fiction, Illustrated Adult Reference, Children's Books
Miscellaneous: Provides editorial, design and production services for other publishers
ISBN Publisher's Prefix: 0-904499

Elsevier Oxford Ltd, Mayfield House, 256 Banbury Rd, Oxford OX2 7DH Tel: Oxford 511151 (STD code 0865) Telex: 837484
Man Dir: George Riches; *Editorial Dir:* Ben Lenthall; *Chief Editor:* Michael Desebrock
Parent Company: Elsevier-NDU nv, Netherlands (qv)
Associate Companies: E P Dutton & Co Inc, New York; Elsevier Sequoia, Paris and Brussels (qv); Phaidon Press, UK (qv); Selecciones Editoriales, Spain (qv)
Subjects: Reference, Illustrated Nonfiction
Founded: 1969 as Elsevier International Projects Ltd

Elsevier-Phaidon, see Phaidon Press Ltd

Emblem, an imprint of Mitchell Beazley London Ltd (qv)

Embryo, an imprint of William Maclellan (qv)

Encyclopaedia Britannica International Ltd, Mappin House, 156-162 Oxford St, London W1N 0HJ Tel: (01) 637 3371 Cable Add: Knowingly London W1 Telex: 23866
Man Dir: Joe D Adams; *National Sales Manager:* K Lee; *Advertising Manager:* A Tebbutt; *Publicity:* Leslie Smith; *Rights & Permissions:* Robin Sales
Parent Company: Encyclopaedia Britannica Inc, 425 North Michigan Ave, Chicago, Ill 60611, USA
Associate Companies: Encyclopaedia Britannica (Australia) Inc, Australia (qv); Encyclopaedia Britannica Publications Ltd, Two Bloor St West, Toronto 5, Ontario, Canada; Encyclopaedia Britannica, German Federal Republic (qv); Korea Britannica Corp, Korea (qv); G & C Merriam Co, 47 Federal St, Springfield, Mass 01101, USA
Subject: Reference
ISBN Publisher's Prefix: 0-85229

Epworth Press, an imprint of Methodist Publishing House (qv)

Ethnographica Ltd, 19 Westbourne Rd, London N7 8AN Tel: (01) 607 4074
Man Dir: Stuart Hamilton; *Sales, Publicity, Rights & Permissions:* Jane Hansom; *Production:* Roger Davies; *Publicity:* Stuart Hamilton
Subjects: Anthropology, Archaeology, Ethnography, Social Studies, Folk Arts and Crafts
1978: 4 titles *1979:* 2 titles *Founded:* 1976
ISBN Publisher's Prefix: 0-905788

Eurobook Ltd, 49 Uxbridge Rd, London W5 Tel: (01) 840 4411 Cable Add: Beurok London W5 Telex: 934610
Warehouse: PDAS Ltd, Unit B1, Bilton Fairway Estate, Long Drive, Greenford, Middlesex
Man Dir, Rights & Permissions: Peter S Lowe; *Editor:* Ruth Spriggs; *Sales, Publicity & Advertising:* Kim P Richardson; *Production:* Douglas Quiggan
Imprint: Peter Lowe

Subjects: Natural History, Illustrated Information Books, International Co-productions
Founded: 1968
ISBN Publisher's Prefix: 0-85654

Euromonitor Publications Ltd, PO Box 26, 18 Doughty St, London WC1N 2PN Tel: (01) 242 0042 Telex: 21120
Man Dir, Editorial: Robert N Senior; *Sales & Marketing Dir:* Trevor J Fenwick
Subjects: Statistical Yearbooks, Marketing, Reference
1978: 20 titles *1979:* 32 titles *Founded:* 1972
ISBN Publisher's Prefix: 0-903706

Europa Publications Ltd, 18 Bedford Sq, London WC1B 3JN Tel: (01) 580 8236
Cable Add: Europub London
Chairman: C H Martin; *Man Dir:* Walter Simon; *Editorial:* P A McGinley; *Business Manager:* H J Wombill; *Sales, Publicity & Advertising:* Peter G C Jackson
Associate Company: Gresham Books Ltd (qv)
Subjects: Reference, History, International Affairs
1978: 10 titles *1979:* 10 titles *Founded:* 1928
ISBN Publisher's Prefix: 0-905118

European Schoolbooks Ltd*, 122 Bath Rd, Cheltenham, Gloucestershire GL53 7LW Tel: Cheltenham 45252 (STD code 0242)
Cable Add: Eurobooks, Cheltenham
Telex: 43658
Man Dir: F A Preiss; *Sales Manager:* D Young
Imprint: European Schoolbooks Hatier Ltd
Subjects: Educational, Modern Languages
1978: 11 titles
ISBN Publisher's Prefix: 0-85048

Evangelical Press and Services Ltd, 16-18 High St, Welwyn, Herts AL6 9EQ Tel: Welwyn 7025 (STD code 043 871)
General Manager: J H Rubens
Orders to: Blossomgate, Ripon, North Yorkshire HG4 2AJ Tel: Ripon 2362 (STD code 0765)
Subsidiary Company: Welwyn Books Ltd
Imprint: Ediciones Perecrino
Subjects: Christian Books
1978: 12 titles *1979:* 12 titles *Founded:* 1967
ISBN Publisher's Prefix: 0-85234

Evans Brothers Ltd, Montague Ho, Russell Sq, London WC1B 5BX Tel: (01) 637 1466
Cable Add: Byronitic London WC1
Telex: 8811713
Chairman, Man Dir: L J Browning; *Dirs:* Miss A F White (Trade Books, Rights), F J Austin (Educational, Overseas), D S Dyerson (Periodicals), J Bentley (Production); *Rights & Permissions:* Miss L Shaughnessey
Associate Company: Evans Brothers (Nigeria Publishers) Ltd, Nigeria (qv)
Subsidiary Companies: Evans Brothers (Africa) Ltd; Evans Brothers (Periodicals) Ltd (both at Montague Ho, Russell Sq, London WC1B 5BX); Rivingtons (Publishers) Ltd, UK (qv)
Subjects: Craft, ELT, How-to, General Non-fiction, Juveniles, Pre-school, Primary & Secondary Textbooks, Educational Periodicals, Plays
1978: 120 titles *Founded:* 1905
ISBN Publisher's Prefix: 0-237

Hugh Evelyn Ltd,* 53 Charlbert St, St John's Wood, London NW8 6JN Tel: (01) 586 5108/9 Cable Add: Bookstreet
Man & Sales Dir: Hugh Street; *Rights & Permissions:* Barbara Mills
Subsidiary Company: Hugh Evelyn Prints Ltd
Subjects: Architecture, Transport History, Military, Nautical
Founded: 1958
ISBN Publisher's Prefix: 0-238

Everest Books Ltd, 4 Valentine Pl, London SE1 8QH Tel: (01) 261 1536
Man Dir: Robin McGibbon; *Sales Manager:* Gillian Schofield; *Publicity, Rights & Permissions:* Rita Fenn
Imprints: Alpine Books, Everest Books
Subjects: Biography
1978: 4 titles *Founded:* 1973
ISBN Publisher's Prefix: 0-905018

Everymans Library, Reference Library and University Library, see J M Dent & Sons Ltd

Exley Publications Ltd, 12 Ye Corner, Chalk Hill, Watford, Herts, WD1 4BS Tel: Watford 43892 (STD code 0923) Telex: 261234 Ref: H/5753L
Man Dir: Richard Exley; *Editorial Dir:* Helen Exley
Orders to: Noonan Hurst Ltd, 131 Trafalgar Rd, E Greenwich, London SE10
Subjects: Anthologies of Children's Work, Directories, Humour, Travel, General Trade Books, Old Age
1979: 4 titles *1980:* 3 titles *Founded:* 1976
ISBN Publisher's Prefix: 0-905521

Express Logic Ltd*, Foley Estate, Hereford HR1 2SJ Tel: Hereford 4516 (STD code 0432)
Man Dir: C B Tannatt Nash; *Dir:* Miss J L Craig
Parent Company: Business Management Promotions Ltd
Subjects: General Literature
Founded: 1970
ISBN Publisher's Prefix: 0-904464

Eyre & Spottiswoode (Publishers) Ltd, 11 New Fetter Lane, London EC4P 4EE Tel: (01) 583 9855 Cable Add: Exaltedly London EC4P 4EE Telex: 263398
Shipping Add: North Way, Andover, Hampshire
Chairman: Charles Shirley; *Man Dir:* Austin Holder; *Marketing Dir:* David Ross; *Dir:* Charles Friend
Parent Company: Associated Book Publishers Ltd (qv)
Subjects: Bibles, Book of Common Prayer, Summa Theologiae, Religion
1978: 11 titles *1979:* 10 titles *Founded:* 1769
ISBN Publisher's Prefix: 0-413

Eyre Methuen Ltd, 11 New Fetter Lane, London EC4P 4EE Tel: (01) 583 9855
Cable Add: Elegiacs London EC4
Telex: 263398
Shipping Add: North Way, Andover, Hampshire
Chairman: Christopher Falkus; *Man Dir:* Geoffrey Strachan; *Editorial:* Bob Woodings, Nicholas Hern; *Marketing Dir:* David Ross; *Publicity Dir:* Jan Hopcraft; *Rights & Permissions:* Ann Mansbridge
Parent Company: Associated Book Publishers Ltd (qv)
Subjects: General Fiction, Belles Lettres, Poetry, Biography, History, Low- & High-priced Paperbacks, Current & Social Affairs, Plays, Humour, Film
1978: 100 titles
ISBN Publisher's Prefix: 0-413

Faber & Faber Ltd, 3 Queen Sq, London WC1N 3AU Tel: (01) 278 6881 Cable Add: Fabbaf London WC1
Shipping Add: Elizabeth Way, Harlow, Essex
Man Dir: Matthew Evans; *Export Sales Manager:* Michael McLennan; *Publicity Manager:* John Bodley; *Rights & Permissions:* Judith Fiennes
Branch Off: Faber & Faber Inc, 99 Main St, Salem, New Hampshire 03079, USA
Subjects: General Fiction, Belles Lettres, Poetry, Biography, History, How-to, Music, Art, Philosophy, Religion, Juveniles,

Paperbacks, Medicine, Psychology, Social Science, University & Secondary Textbooks
1978: 207 titles *Founded:* 1929
ISBN Publisher's Prefix: 0-571

Fairmont Press, an imprint of Van Nostrand Reinhold Co Ltd (qv)

Falcon Books, an imprint of Kingsway Publications (qv)

Fantasy Library, an imprint of Bailey Brothers & Swinfen Ltd (qv)

The **Financial Times** Business Publishing Ltd, Greystroke Pl, Fetter Lane, London EC4A 1ND Tel: (01) 405 6969 Telex: 883694
Man Dir: John McLachlan; *Sales Manager:* Patricia Morris; *Diary Manager:* John Suffolk; *Circulation Development Manager:* Ken McAllister
Subjects: Investment and Financial Planning Guides, Directories, Specialized Banking Studies, Periodicals
ISBN Publisher's Prefix: 0-900671

Financial Training Publications Ltd, 136-142 Bramley Rd, London W10 6SR Tel: (01) 960 4486
Man Dir: John Gibbs; *Managing Editor:* Heather Saward
Parent Company: Park Place Investments Ltd
Subjects: Accountancy, Finance, Management, also publishes professional examination study manuals for students
1978: 20 titles *1979:* 28 titles *Founded:* 1976
ISBN Publisher's Prefix: 0-906322

Findhorn Publications, The Park, Forres IV36 0TZ Tel: Findhorn 2582 (STD code 030 93)
Man Dir: Stephen Clark; *Editorial:* Jeremy Slocombe; *Sales:* Ron Parker; *Rights & Permissions:* Polly Parker
Parent Company: Findhorn Foundation (address as above)
Subjects: Spiritual Philosophy, Metaphysics, Inspirational and Alternative Lifestyles, Ecology
Bookshop: Cluny Hill Bookshop, Cluny Hill College, Forres IV36 0RD
1978: 8 titles *1979:* 7 titles *Founded:* 1965
ISBN Publisher's Prefix: 0-905249

Firecrest Publishing Ltd, 93-100 Locksbrook Rd, Bath BA1 3HB Tel: Bath 331945 (STD code 0225) Telex: 449897
Man Dir: E Hudson (to whom all correspondence)
Associate Companies: Chivers Book Sales Ltd; Lythway Press Ltd (qv); Chivers Press Publishers (qv)
Imprint: Firecrest Large Print
Subjects: Contemporary Fiction and Nonfiction
1978: 16 titles *Founded:* 1977
ISBN Publisher's Prefix: 0-85119

Fishing News Books Ltd, 1 Long Garden Walk, Farnham, Surrey GU9 7HX Tel: Farnham 726868 (STD code 0252)
Editorial, Production: W E Redman; *Sales, Publicity, Rights & Permissions:* Vivien M Heighway
Subjects: Commercial Fisheries, Aquaculture, Marine Engineering, Scientific Angling
1978: 4 titles *1979:* 4 titles *Founded:* 1953
ISBN Publisher's Prefix: 0-85238

Fitzwilliam Museum, Trumpington St, Cambridge CB2 1RB Tel: Cambridge 69501 (STD code 0223)
Dir: Prof A M Jaffé; *Bookshop Manager:* R Maddicott
Subjects: Antiquities, Coins Medals & Gems, Applied Arts, Medieval Manuscripts, Early Printed Books, Music & Letters, Paintings,

Drawings & Miniatures, Prints
Bookshop: Fitzwilliam Museum Enterprises Ltd
1978: 6 titles *1979:* 2 titles *Founded:* 1816

Flare Books, an imprint of The Harvester Press Ltd (qv)

Floris Books, 21 Napier Rd, Edinburgh EH10 5AZ Tel: (031) 337 2372
Editorial: Michael Jones; *Sales, Production, Publicity, Rights & Permissions:* Christian Maclean
Subsidiary Company: The Christian Community Press
Subjects: Religion, Children's Books, General
1978: 7 titles *1979:* 9 titles *Founded:* 1976
ISBN Publisher's Prefixes: 0-903540 (Floris), 0-900285 (Christian Community Press)

Focal Press Ltd, 31 Fitzroy Sq, London W1P 6BH Tel: (01) 387 0711 Cable Add: Focalpres London W1
Chairman: Nicholas Thompson; *Man Dir:* Colin Ancliffe; *Deputy Man Dir:* R W Dear; *Production:* Finn Jensen; *Editorial:* Paul Petzold; *Marketing:* N Ross; *Rights:* V A Talbot
Orders to: Book Centre, Slaidburn Crescent, Fylde Rd, Southport, Merseyside PR9 9YF
Parent Company: Pitman Books Ltd (qv)
Associate Company: Focal Press Inc, 10 East 40th St, New York, NY 10016, USA
Subjects: Audiovisual Methods, Graphic Arts, Textbooks, Reference, Technical & Scientific Books on Photography, Cinematography, Television, Sound, Printing Technology, How-to, Low-priced Paperbacks, Secondary & Further Education
1978: 41 titles *Founded:* 1938
ISBN Publisher's Prefix: 0-240

The **Folio** Society Ltd, see Book Clubs

Fontana Books, see William Collins Sons & Co Ltd

Forbes Publications Ltd, Hartree House, 151a Queensway, London W2 4SH Tel: (01) 229 9322
Man Dirs: Rosemary Crellin, Joan Forbes
Subjects: Secondary, University, Commercial & Technical Education, Educational & Scientific, Reference Books
ISBN Publisher's Prefix: 0-901762

Foreign Affairs Publishing Co Ltd, 139 Petersham Rd, Richmond, Surrey TW10 7AA Tel: (01) 948 4833
Director: Geoffrey Stewart-Smith
Subjects: Politics, Communist Affairs, Defence, East-West Relations
ISBN Publisher's Prefix: 0-900380

Fortune Press, see Charles Skilton Ltd

Foulis Books, an imprint of The Haynes Publishing Group (qv)

Foulsham & Co Ltd*, Yeovil Rd, Slough, Berkshire SL1 4JH Tel: Slough 26769/30956 (STD code 0753) Cable Add: Bariebooks Slough Bucks
Man Dir: R S Belasco; *Editorial Dir:* B A R Belasco; *Editorial Controller:* Marion Harris; *Financial Dir:* G M Kitchen; *Sales & Marketing Manager:* Nigel Stovin-Bradford; *Production Manager:* Roy Mantel
Subsidiary Company: W Foulsham & Co (Canada) Ltd, 184 Front St E, Toronto, Canada
Subjects: General, Technical, Educational
Founded: 1819
ISBN Publisher's Prefix: 0-572 (W Foulsham)

The **Foundational** Book Co Ltd, 29 Pinfold Rd, Streatham, London SW16 2SL Tel: (01) 584 1053
Man Dir: Peggy M Brook

Subject: Religion
1978: 1 title *Founded:* 1946
ISBN Publisher's Prefix: 0-85241

Fountain Press, an imprint of Argus Books Ltd (qv)

Foxcub, an imprint of Foxwood Publishing Ltd (qv)

Foxwood Publishing Ltd*, 635 River Gardens, North Feltham Trading Estate, Feltham, Middlesex TW14 0RW Tel: (01) 890 2610 Telex: 21451
Chairman: J P Howitt; *Man Dir:* Brian Thompson; *Editorial:* Gillian Schwab; *Production:* Claudia Wondrausch
Parent Company: J Howitt & Son Ltd
Imprints: Foxcub, Foxwood
Subjects: Children's Books
1978: 22 titles *Founded:* 1977 (under new ownership)
ISBN Publisher's Prefixes: 0-861070, 0-904897

W & G **Foyle** Ltd & John Gifford Ltd, 119-125 Charing Cross Rd, London WC2H 0EB Tel: (01) 437 0216 Cable Add: Foylibra London WC2 Telex: 261107
Chairman & Man Dir: Christina Foyle; *Man Dir:* (John Gifford Ltd): C Batty; *Editorial, Sales, Publicity, Rights & Permissions:* Alistair MacQueen
Subjects: Crafts, Antiques, Reference, Gardening, Natural History
Book Clubs: The Book Club, Thriller Book Club, Romance Book Club, Western Book Club, Travel Book Club, Catholic Book Club, Children's Book Club, Quality Book Club, Garden Book Club, Scientific Book Club
Bookshop: W & G Foyle, 119-125 Charing Cross Rd, London WC2H 0EB
1978: 15 titles *Founded:* 1904
Miscellaneous: Firm is owned by W & G Foyle Ltd
ISBN Publisher's Prefixes: 0-7071 (Foyle), 0-7072 (Gifford)

Gordon **Fraser** Gallery Ltd, Fitzroy Rd, London NW1 8TT Tel: (01) 722 0077 Cable Add: Frasercard London NW1 Telex: 25848
Dirs: Gordon Fraser, Ian G Fraser; *General Manager:* Peter Guy; *Editorial, Rights & Permissions:* Simon Kingston; *Publicity:* Shelley Bourne; *Promotion, Sales:* Alison Browne
Orders to: Eastcotts Rd, Bedford MK42 0JX
Subsidiary Company: The Roundwood Press Ltd (qv)
Subjects: Photography, Art, Architecture, Graphic Arts, High-priced Paperbacks
1978: 17 titles *Founded:* 1936
ISBN Publisher's Prefixes: 0-900406, 0-86092

Freeland Press Ltd, see The Technical Press Ltd

W H **Freeman** & Co Ltd, 20 Beaumont St, Oxford OX1 2NQ Tel: Oxford 726975 (STD code 0865)
Dirs: Sir Jonathan Backhouse, S Schaefer; *Executive Editor:* Dr Michael Rogers; *Promotion Manager:* Julian Lynn-Evans; *Rights & Permissions:* Hilary Woodford
Parent Company: W H Freeman & Co, 660 Market St, San Francisco, Calif 94104, USA. Ultimate holding company Scientific American, 415 Madison Ave, New York, NY 10014, USA
Subjects: University Textbooks & Monographs in Pure & Applied Science
1978: 71 titles *1979:* 72 titles *Founded:* 1959
ISBN Publisher's Prefix: 0-7167

Samuel **French** Ltd, 26 Southampton St, Strand, London WC2E 7JE Tel: (01) 836 7513 Cable Add: Dramalogue London WC2
Chairman: Abbott van Nostrand; *Man Dir:*

John Laurence Hughes; *Editorial Dir:* Lionel Noel Woolf; *Dirs:* John Bedding, Harold Pumfrett
Associate Companies: Samuel French (Australia) Pty Ltd, Dominie Pty Ltd, 8 Cross St, Box 33 PO Brookvale, NSW 2100, Australia; Samuel French (Canada) Ltd, 80 Richmond St East, Toronto, Canada; Samuel French Inc, 25 West 45th St, New York, NY 10036 and 7623 Sunset Blvd, Hollywood, Calif 90046, USA
Subjects: Drama, Reference (Theatre)
Bookshop: French's Theatre Bookshop, 26 Southampton St, Strand, London, WC2E 7JE
Founded: 1830
ISBN Publisher's Prefix: 0-573

Julian **Friedmann** Publishers Ltd, 15 Catherine St, Covent Garden, London WC2 Tel: (01) 379 3248
Man Dir: Julian Friedmann; *Sales:* Jean Beith
Associate Companies: Julian Friedmann Books, Julian Friedmann Literary Agency Ltd (qv)
Subjects: Fiction, Politics, History, African Studies, Gardening and General Trade Books
1978: 8 titles *1979:* 10 titles *Founded:* 1974
ISBN Publisher's Prefix: 0-904014

Fudge & Co Ltd, Sardinia Ho, 52 Lincoln's Inn Fields, London WC2A 3NW Tel: (01) 242 8258
Man Dir: B K Shaw
Associate Company: Charles Skilton (qv)
Imprints: Research Publishing Co, Broomsleigh Press, Skilton & Shaw
Subjects: Fiction, Biography, History, Spirituality, Juvenile, General
ISBN Publisher's Prefix: 0-7050

Futura Publications Ltd, see Macdonald/Futura Publishers Ltd

Gaberbocchus Press Ltd, all correspondence (except orders from UK) to de Harmonie Publishers (Gaberbocchus Books), Singel 390, 1016 AJ Amsterdam, Netherlands. Orders from UK to Big O (Gaberbocchus Books), 228 Fulham Rd, London SW10 9NB

Gall & Inglis, 12 Newington Rd, Edinburgh EH9 1RB Tel: (031) 667 2791 Cable Add: Reckoners, Edinburgh
Man Dir: J Horsburgh
Subjects: Technical & Scientific, Commercial & Professional, Guidebooks
ISBN Publisher's Prefix: 0-85248

Galliard, an imprint of Stainer & Bell Ltd (qv)

Garnstone Press Ltd*, Barlavington Farm House, Barlavington, Nr Petworth, West Sussex Tel: Sutton, West Sussex 349 (STD code 07987)
Man & Sales Dir: Michael Balfour
Associated Imprint: Geoffrey Bles
Subjects: Nonfiction, Guides, Information, Hobbies, Prehistory, Ancient Science and Mysteries
1979: 10 titles *1980:* 12 titles *Founded:* 1966
ISBN Publisher's Prefixes: 0-900391, 0-85511 (Garnstone Press), 0-7138 (Geoffrey Bles)

Gemini Publishing, 8 Herrick Rd, London N5 2JX Tel: (01) 226 4747
Dir: Cliff Hopkinson
Subjects: Games, Educational Materials

Gentry Books Ltd, 15 Pont St, London SW1X 9EH Tel: (01) 235 3851
Chairman: Lord Montagu of Beaulieu; *Man Dir:* C F Burness; *Editorial Dir:* Lorna Gentry; *Production, Marketing Manager:* Paula Levey
Subjects: Motoring, Travel, Business History

1978: 6 titles *1979:* 9 titles *Founded:* 1971
ISBN Publisher's Prefix: 0-85614

Geographia Ltd, 93 St Peter's St, St Albans, Hertfordshire AL1 3EH Tel: St Albans 30121 (STD code 0727) Telex: 261212
Man Dir: Graham Lane; *Sales & Marketing Dir:* Colin Tagg
Associate Company: Hutchinson Publishing Group (qv)
Subsidiary Company: Robert Nicholson Publications Ltd (qv)
Subjects: Maps & Atlases, Directories & Guide Books
Bookshop: 63 Fleet St, London EC4Y 1PE Tel: (01) 353 2701
ISBN Publisher's Prefix: 0-09

Ghost Hunters' Library, an imprint of Bailey Brothers & Swinfen Ltd (qv)

Stanley **Gibbons** (Publications) Ltd, 391 Strand, London WC2R 0LX Tel: (01) 836 8444 Cable Add: Philatelic, London WC2R 0LX Telex: 28883
Trade Department: Stangib Ho, Sarehole Rd, Birmingham B28 8EE Tel: (021) 777 7255
Subject: Philately
ISBN Publisher's Prefix: 0-85259

John **Gifford** Ltd, see W & G Foyle Ltd

Ginn & Co Ltd, Elsinore Ho, Buckingham St, Aylesbury, Buckinghamshire HP20 2NQ Tel: Aylesbury 88411 (STD code 0296) Cable Add: Ginnbooks Aylesbury Telex: 83535
Warehouse: Unit 1 Block H, Long Eaton Industrial Estate, Acton Grove, Long Eaton, Nottingham NG10 1GG
Man Dir: D Blunt; *Marketing Dir:* E F Keartland; *Publishing Manager:* W Shepherd; *Production:* D Miller; *Art & Design Manager:* A Miller; *Publicity:* R T Tadman; *International Manager:* A G Pittam
Parent Company: Thomas Tilling Ltd (also parent company of Heinemann Group (qv))
Subsidiary Companies: Caribbean Universities Press, Barbados (qv); Caribbean Universities Press, Jamaica (qv)
Subjects: Primary & Secondary Textbooks
1978: 126 titles *1979:* 39 titles *Founded:* 1862 (USA), 1920 (London)
ISBN Publisher's Prefix: 0-602

Mary **Glasgow** Publications Ltd, 140 Kensington Church St, London W8 4BN Tel: (01) 229 9531 Telex: MGP KNT 31440
Man Dir: B J Clifton; *Editorial:* S Nugent, L K Upton; *Marketing:* C A Bayne; *Sales & Distribution:* D J Raggett; *Production:* A E J Bedale; *Publicity:* Miss D Horton
Orders to: Brookhampton Lane, Kineton, Warwicks CV35 0JB
Subsidiary Company: Sound Communication (Publishers) Ltd
Subjects: Educational Magazines and Audio Visual Materials in EFL, Modern Languages, English, Geography
Founded: 1956
ISBN Publisher's Prefixes: 0-900400, 0-905999, 0-86158

Glaven, an imprint of Jarrold Colour Publications (qv)

Gleniffer Press, 11 Low Rd, Castlehead, Paisley, PA2 6AQ Tel: (041) 889 9579
Man Dir: Ian Macdonald
Subjects: Poetry, History, Short Stories, Essays, Art, Specialists in Miniature Books
1978: 3 titles *Founded:* 1968
ISBN Publisher's Prefixes: 0-9502177, 0-906005

Global Book Resources Ltd, 109 Great Russell St, London WC1B 3NA Tel: (01) 580 4011 Cable Add: Globooks, London WC1
Man Dir: John Walter; *Publicity:* Jane Price
Subjects: Academic, Scientific

Felix **Gluck** Press Ltd, 72 Northcote Rd, Twickenham, Middx TW1 1PA Tel: (01) 892 3834 Telex: 21792/2886
Man Dir: Felix Gluck
Subjects: Nature, Classics, Juvenile, Reference, Children's Books, High quality Paperbacks
1978: 10 titles *1979:* 8 titles

George **Godwin** Ltd, Builder House, 1-3 Pemberton Row, Red Lion Court, Fleet St, London EC4P 4HL Tel: (01) 353 2300 Telex: 25212
Man Dir: John L Brooks; *Editorial:* Bridget Buckley; *Production:* Rosemary Burgin; *Sales, Publicity:* Paul Whitnall
Orders to: MacDonald & Evans, Estover Road, Plymouth, Devon PL6 7PZ
Parent Company: The Builder Ltd
Subjects: Architecture, Planning, Design Building, Technology & Crafts, Chemical & Process Engineering, Manufacturing Chemistry, Arts & Crafts, Educational
ISBN Publisher's Prefix: 0-7114

Golden Pleasure Books Ltd, Astronaut House, Hounslow Rd, Feltham, Middx TW14 9AR Tel: (01) 890 1480 Cable Add: Pleasbooks Feltham Telex: 25650
Dirs: Hugh Campbell, Douglas Dring
Subjects: Juveniles, Reference
Founded: 1961
Miscellaneous: Firm is a member of The Hamlyn Publishing Group Ltd (qv)
ISBN Publisher's Prefix: 0-601

Goldex, an imprint of Murrays Remainder Books (qv)

Victor **Gollancz** Ltd, 14 Henrietta St, Covent Garden, London WC2E 8QJ Tel: (01) 836 2006 Cable Add: Vigollan London WC2
Man Dirs: Livia Gollancz, John Bush; *Sales Dir:* Kenneth Kemp; *Rights & Permissions:* Jane Blackstock
Subjects: General Fiction, Belles Lettres, Biography, History, Music, Art, Architecture, Philosophy, Juveniles, Travel, Mountaineering, General & Social Science
1978: 130 titles *1979:* 128 titles *Founded:* 1928
ISBN Publisher's Prefix: 0-575

Gomer Press (J D Lewis & Sons Ltd), Llandysul, Dyfed SA44 4BQ Tel: Llandysul 2371 (STD code 055932) Cable Add: Gomerian Llandysul
Man Dir: J H Lewis; *Editorial, Rights & Permissions:* D Elis-Gruffydd; *Sales, Publicity:* John H Lewis; *Production:* J Huw Lewis
Parent Company: J D Lewis & Sons Ltd
Imprint: Gwasg Gomer
Subjects: Welsh Language Publications, Books on Wales
Bookshop: Gomerian Press, Llandysul, Dyfed
1978: 50 titles *Founded:* 1892
ISBN Publisher's Prefix: 0-85088

Good Reading an imprint of ESA Creative Learning Ltd (qv)

Gordon and Breach Science Publishers Ltd, 41-42 William IV St, London WC2N 4DE Tel: (01) 836 5125 Cable Add: Sciencepub, London WC2 Telex: 23258
Dirs: Martin B Gordon (USA), J A Levene; *Editorial:* Alison Lovejoy; *Rights:* Françoise Chantrel-Riols (7-9 rue Emile Dubois, Paris F-75014, France)
Orders to: Gordon and Breach Science Publishers Inc, 1 Park Ave, New York, NY 10016, USA
Parent Company: Gordon and Breach Science Publishers Inc (at US address)
Subjects: Astronomy and Astrophysics, Chemistry & Nuclear Engineering, Chemistry & Chemical Technology, Civil Engineering, Computers, Systems & Control Engineering, Earth & Planetary Sciences, Economics, Electronics & Electrical Engineering, Languages & Dictionaries, Life Sciences & Medicine, Management Science & Business, Mathematics & Statistics, Mechanical Engineering, Metallurgy & Materials Science, Physics, Social Sciences, Space Science & Technology, Learned Journals
1978: 35 titles *1979:* 35 titles
ISBN Publisher's Prefix: 0-677

Gordon & Cremonesi, New River House, 34 Seymour Rd, London N8 0BE Tel: (01) 348 7042 Cable Add: Cremones London N8
Man Dirs: Gilles Cremonesi, Heather Gordon
Orders to: Biblios, Glenside Industrial Estate, Partridge Green, Nr Horsham, W Sussex RH13 8LD
Subjects: Biography, History, High-priced Paperbacks, Social Science
1978: 17 titles *1979:* 17 titles *Founded:* 1975
ISBN Publisher's Prefix: 0-86033

Henry **Goulden** Ltd, 22 High St, East Grinstead, Sussex Tel: (0342) 22669
Man Dir: L H Goulden
Subjects: Rudolf Steiner
ISBN Publisher's Prefix: 0-904822

Gower Press, 1 Westmead, Farnborough, Hampshire GU14 7RU Tel: Farnborough 519221 (STD code 0252)
An imprint of Gower Publishing Co Ltd (qv), details as for Gower Publishing except as follows:
Editorial: Malcolm Stern
Subjects: Practical management and business information
1978: 15 titles *1979:* 20 titles
ISBN Publisher's Prefixes: 0-7161 (pre-1976 titles), 0-566

Gower Publishing Co Ltd, 1 Westmead, Farnborough, Hampshire GU14 7RU Tel: Farnborough 519221 (STD code 0252) Cable Add: Gower Farnbro Telex: 858623
Man Dir, Sales, Rights & Permissions: N Farrow; *Marketing Manager:* C Simpson; *Customer Service Manager:* M Sedgebeer; *Production Manager:* C Barber
Parent Company: Teakfield Ltd
Imprints: Gower Press (qv), Saxon House (qv), Wilton Publications (qv) and English-language programme of Rotterdam University Press
Subjects: See under individual imprint
1978: 60 titles *1979:* 100 titles *Founded:* 1967
ISBN Publisher's Prefix: 0-566

Grafton Books, an imprint of André Deutsch Ltd (qv)

Graham & Trotman Ltd, Bond St House, 14 Clifford St, London W1X 1RD Tel: (01) 493 6351 Telex: 21879/25247 (Grahamco)
Man Dir, Rights & Permissions: A Graham; *Editorial:* G Bricault, M Lawn; J Alban-Davies; *Sales:* D Costello, *Marketing Dir:* I Pulley; *Production:* D Blakeley; *Marketing:* G Steddy
Subjects: Business Reference, Business Management, Business Law, Applied Technology, Earth Sciences, Energy Resources, Pollution Control
1979: 36 titles *Founded:* 1974
ISBN Publisher's Prefix: 0-86010

Granada Publishing Ltd, PO Box 9, 29 Frogmore, St Albans, Herts AL2 2NF Tel: St Albans 72727 (STD code 0727) Cable Add: Granada St Albans Telex: 262802

Man Dir: A R H Birch; *Sales Dir:* T J Kitson; *Editorial:* Mark Barty-King (Paperback), Roger Schlesinger (Hardback); *Production Managers:* M Lee (Paperback), J Parsons (Hardback); *Publicity:* H Wesolowski (Paperback), K O'Connor (Hardback); *Rights & Permissions:* M Brozicevic; *Man Dirs:* D Fulton (Technical Div), K Hills (Education Div), Angela Sheehan (Children's Div)
Subsidiary Companies controlled by Granada Publishing: (Hardcover) Granada Trade Books Ltd; Hart-Davis Educational Ltd; Adlard Coles Ltd; Paul Elek Ltd; (Paperback) Panther Books Ltd; Mayflower Books Ltd; Dragon Books, Paladin Books
Branch Offs: 3 Upper James St, London W1R 4PB; Granada Publishing Ltd, 117 York St, Sydney, NSW 2000, Australia; Granada Publishing Canada Ltd, 100 Skyway Ave, Toronto, Ontario M9W 3A6, Canada; Granada Publishing Ltd, 110 Northpark Centre, Cnr 3rd & 7th Aves, Parktown North, 2193, Johannesburg, South Africa; Granada Books New Zealand Ltd, 61 Beach Road, Auckland, New Zealand; Granada Publishing Ltd, Suite 405, 4th Floor, 866 United Nations Plaza, New York, NY 10017, USA
Subjects: Agriculture, Architecture, Building, Fiction, Leisure & Hobbies, Nautical and Sailing, Biography, History, Mathematics, Nonfiction, Physics, Science, Technology, Music, Art, Philosophy, Reference, Juveniles, Low- & High-priced Paperbacks, Engineering, General & Social Science, University, Primary & Secondary Textbooks
1978: 400 titles
ISBN Publisher's Prefixes: 0-7053 (Granada), 0-229 (Adlard Coles), 0-286 (Granada Technical Books Ltd), 0-247 (Hart-Davis Educational), 0-246 (Granada Trade Books), 0-586 (Panther Books), 0-583 (Mayflower Books)

Grant McIntyre Ltd, see under McIntyre

Grasshopper Books, an imprint of Abelard-Schuman Ltd (qv)

W Green & Son Ltd, St Giles St, Edinburgh EH1 1PU Tel: (031) 225 4879 Cable Add: Viridis Edinburgh
Subject: Law
Parent Company: Associated Book Publishers Ltd (qv)
ISBN Publisher's Prefix: 0-414

Gregg International, an imprint of Avebury Publishing Co Ltd (qv)

John **Gresham**, an imprint of Robert Hale Ltd (qv)

Gresham Books Ltd, The Gresham Press, Old Woking, Surrey GU22 9LH Tel: Woking 61971 (STD code 04862)
Chief Executive: L H Green
Parent Company: Martins Publishing Group, Staples Printers Ltd, 94 Wigmore St, London W1H 0BR
Associate Companies: Europa Publications Ltd (qv); Gift Book Promotions, Market Entry Publications, both at 94 Wigmore St, London W1
Subjects: Music, Hobbies, Leisure, Biography, Careers, Facsimile Reproductions of Rare Books
1978: 10 titles *1979:* 11 titles *Founded:* 1977
ISBN Publisher's Prefix: 0-905418

Charles **Griffin** & Co Ltd, Charles Griffin House, Crendon St, High Wycombe, Buckinghamshire HP13 6LE Tel: High Wycombe 36341 (STD code 0494) Cable Add: Explanatus High Wycombe
Man Dir, Rights & Permissions: James R Griffin; *Sales, Publicity & Advertising Manager:* Kathleen Mansfield
Branch Off: Finance: 87 Chancery Lane, PO Box 63, London WC2A 1DW
Subjects: High-priced Paperbacks, Engineering, General & Social Science, University & Secondary Textbooks especially Statistics
1978: 7 titles *Founded:* 1820
ISBN Publisher's Prefix: 0-85264

Grisewood & Dempsey Ltd, Grosvenor Ho, 141-43 Drury Lane, London WC2B 5TG Tel: (01) 379 7333 Cable Add: Greatbooks, London Telex: 27725 Gridem
Man Dir: D Grisewood; *Editorial:* M Dempsey; *Sales:* D Risner
Subjects: Children's Colour Information Books, Adult Reference
1978: 70 titles *Founded:* 1973
Miscellaneous: Firm is an editorial and production organization producing books for other publishers

Grosvenor Books (The Good Road Ltd), 54 Lyford Rd, London SW18 3JJ Tel: (01) 870 2124
Man Dir, Rights & Permissions: J H V Nowell; *Sales Dir:* D A Hind; *Production Dir:* J P Faber
Subjects: Contemporary Philosophy, Biography, Children's Books
1978: 9 titles *1979:* 10 titles
ISBN Publisher's Prefix: 0-901269

The **Gubblecote** Press, see Shire Publications Ltd

Guild Publishing, 87 Newman St, London W1P 4EN Tel: (01) 637 0341 Cable Add: Booklub Telex: 24359 Bcalon
Publishing Manager: Jonathan Martin
Parent Company: Book Club Associates (qv under Book Clubs)
Subjects: Archaeology, Juveniles, Cookery, History, Humour, Leisure, Natural History
1979: 8 titles *1980:* 9 titles

Guinness Superlatives Ltd, 2 Cecil Court, London Rd, Enfield, Middx EN2 6DJ Tel: (01) 367 4567 Cable Add: Mostest Telex: 23573 Enfield
Man Dir: D F Hoy; *Marketing Manager:* M J Hodge (Home)
Parent Company: Arthur Guinness Son & Co (Park Royal) Ltd, Park Royal, London NW10
Subject: Reference
1979-80: 57 titles *Founded:* 1954
ISBN Publisher's Prefixes: 0-900424, 0-85112

Gwasg Gomer, imprint of Gomer Press (qv)

Gwasg Prifysgol Cymru, an imprint of University of Wales Press (qv)

Gwasg y Dref Wen, 28 Church Rd, Whitchurch, Cardiff CF4 2EA Tel: Cardiff 617860 (STD code 0222)
Man Dir, Production, Publicity, Rights & Permissions: Roger Boore; *Editorial:* Aled Islwyn; *Sales:* Anne Boore
Subjects: Welsh-language books for Children and Schools (Fiction & Non-fiction) including Welsh Children's Encyclopedia, Picture Dictionary
1978: 20 titles *1979:* 11 titles *Founded:* 1970

H F L (Publishers) Ltd, 9 Bow St, London WC2E 7AL Tel: (01) 836 9081 Cable Add: Fimexted, London WC2 Telex: 299080
Man Dir: J R Hews; *Sales Dir:* Quentin Hockliffe
Subjects: Commercial & Technical Education, Legal & Parliamentary, Commercial & Professional
ISBN Publisher's Prefix: 0-372

H M & M Publishers Ltd, Milton Rd, Aylesbury, Buckinghamshire Tel: Aylesbury 5781 (STD code 0296) Telex: 837216
Chairman: P G Medcalf; *General Manager:* Mary Sketch; *Editor:* Patrick West
Subjects: Medicine, Nursing
1978: 5 titles *1979:* 7 titles *Founded:* 1971
ISBN Publisher's Prefix: 0-85602

H M S O, see Her Majesty's Stationery Office

Peter **Haddock** Ltd*, Pinfold Lane, Bridlington, North Humberside YO16 5BT Tel: Bridlington 78121 (STD code 0262) Cable Add: Bridbooks Telex: 52180
Man Dir: Peter Haddock
Subjects: Low-priced Children's Painting, Activity and Story Books

Robert **Hale** Ltd, Clerkenwell Ho, 45-47 Clerkenwell Green, London EC1R 0HT Tel: (01) 251 2661 Cable Add: Barabbas London EC1
Shipping Add: 4 Vestry Rd, Vestry Estate, Sevenoaks, Kent
Man Dir: John Hale; *Editorial:* Gordon Chesterfield; *Marketing Dir:* Martin Kendall; *Production:* Eric Restall; *Advertising:* John Gittens; *Publicity:* Diana Colbert; *Rights & Permissions Dir:* Betty Weston
Imprints: Include John Gresham
Subjects: General Fiction, Belles Lettres, Poetry, Biography, History, How-to, Music, Art, Sport, Philosophy, Reference, Religion, Low- & High-priced Paperbacks
1978: 641 titles *Founded:* 1936
ISBN Publisher's Prefix: 0-7091

Hamish **Hamilton** Ltd, Garden Ho, 57-59 Long Acre, London WC2E 9JL Tel: (01) 836 7733 Cable Add: Hamisham Westcent London Telex: 298265
Chairman: Hamish Hamilton; *Man Dir, Editorial:* Christopher Sinclair-Stevenson; *Marketing Dir:* Andrew Connel; *Production Dir:* Peter Kilborn; *Publicity Dir:* Juliet Nicolson; *Rights & Permissions Dir:* Jane Turnbull
Subsidiary Companies: Hamish Hamilton Children's Books Ltd; Elm Tree Books Ltd
Subjects: General Fiction, Biography, History, Music, Art, Juveniles
Founded: 1931
Miscellaneous: Company is a member of the Thomson Books Ltd group, a part of International Thomson Organization Ltd (Canada)
ISBN Publisher's Prefix: 0-241

Hamlyn Paperbacks, Banda House, Cambridge Grove, Hammersmith, London W6 0LE Tel: (01) 741 4441
The paperback division of The Hamlyn Publishing Group Ltd (qv)

The **Hamlyn Publishing** Group Ltd, Astronaut House, Hounslow Rd, Feltham, Middlesex TW14 9AR Tel: (01) 890 1480 Cable Add: Pleasbooks Feltham
Shipping Add & Trade Office, Sanders Lodge Industrial Estate, Rushden, Northamptonshire
Chief Executive: Hugh Campbell; *Man Dir:* Barry Rowland; *Sales:* William Dancer, David Foster, David Burbage; *Distribution:* Ron Chopping; *Publicity:* Brough Girling; *Rights & Permissions:* Terence Cross, David Halford, Margaret Hutchinson
Parent Company: International Publishing Corporation (qv)
Imprints: Beaver Books, Collingridge, Country Life, Dean & Son, Golden Pleasure Books (qv), Paul Hamlyn, Newnes, Odhams, Optimum, Pearson, Spring Books, Temple Press
Subjects: General Non-fiction, Fiction, History, How-to, Music, Art, Reference, Juveniles, Paperbacks
Book Club: Companion Book Club
Founded: 1947

ISBN Publisher's Prefixes: 0-600 (Beaver Books, Collingridge, Country Life, Hamlyn, Newnes, Odhams, Optimum, Pearson, Spring, Temple), 0-601 (Golden Pleasure), 0-603 (Dean & Son)

Hampton House Productions Ltd*, 9 York Rd, Maidenhead, Berks SL6 15Q Tel: Maidenhead 70014 (STD code 0628) Telex: 847295
Subjects: Juveniles, General
ISBN Publisher's Prefix: 0-905015

Heinrich **Hanau** Publications Ltd, PO Box 2JG, London W1A 2JG Tel: (01) 734 4353 Telex: 28604 Ref 909
Man Dir: John Hanau
Associate Company: H H Publications Ltd, Suite 460, 230 Park Ave, New York, NY10017, USA
Subjects: International Co-publications
ISBN Publisher's Prefix: 0-902826

The **Handsel** Press, 33 Montgomery St, Edinburgh EH7 5JX Tel: (031) 556 2796
Man Dir, Editorial, Rights & Permissions: Douglas Grant
Subject: Theology
1980: 8 titles *Founded:* 1976
Miscellaneous: Associated with Sussex University Press and The Scottish Academic Press (qqv)
ISBN Publisher's Prefix: 0-905312

J **Hannon** & Co (Publishers) Oxford, 36 Great Clarendon St, Oxford OX2 6AT Tel: Oxford 57824 (STD code 0865)
Chief Executive, Editorial: Jim Hannon
Subsidiary Company: J Hannon & Co (Book Distributors), at above address
Branch Off: Twanagh, Boyle, Republic of Ireland
Subjects: Latin, Music, Poetry, Philosophy
Bookshop: J Hannon & Co, at above address
1978: 6 titles *1979:* 5 titles *Founded:* 1974
ISBN Publisher's Prefix: 0-904233

Hansen House (London) Ltd, 64 Dean St, London W1 Tel: (01) 439 7797
Publisher: Charles Hansen
Subject: Music

Harcourt Brace Jovanovich Ltd, 24-28 Oval Rd, London NW1 7DU Tel: (01) 485 7074/5 Cable Add: Harbrex London NW1 Telex: 25775
Man Dir: Stanley Malcolm; *Executive Dir:* N Godber; *Publicity Manager:* A Greenwood
Subjects: Fiction, Educational, Religious, Technical & Scientific, Medical, Commercial & Professional, Music, Art & Architecture, Children's Books, Sports, Games & Pastimes, Poetry & Drama, History, Biography & Memoirs, Sociology, Philosophy, Psychology, Economics, School Books
Miscellaneous: Firm is a subsidiary of Harcourt Brace Jovanovich Inc, 757 Third Ave, New York, NY 10017, and of Academic Press Inc (London) Ltd (qv)
ISBN Publisher's Prefix: 0-15

Harley & Jones, 24 Quentin Rd, London SE13 5DF Tel: (01) 852 1490
Partners: Rosemary Harley, Humphrey Jones
Subjects: General Non-fiction
Founded: 1978
Miscellaneous: Consultant editors, designers, publishers, printers. Co-publishers and packagers

Harleyford Publications, an imprint of Argus Books Ltd (qv)

Harper & Row Ltd, 28 Tavistock St, London WC2E 7PN Tel: (01) 836 4635 Cable Add: Harprow, London WC2E 7PN Telex: 267331
Publisher: Michael Forster; *Man Dir:* Ian Savage; *Sales, Promotion Manager:* John Beale; *Rights & Permissions:* New York Office
Parent Company: Harper & Row Inc, 10 East 53rd St, New York, NY 10022, USA
Subsidiary Companies: Barnes & Noble; Basic Books; Beacon Press; Russell Sage Foundation; Canfield Press; T Y Crowell; Quadrangle/New York Times Book Co; J B Lippincott Co
Associate Companies: Harper & Row Latinoamericana-Harla, SA de CV, Mexico (qv), Harper-Row (Australasia) Ltd, PO Box 226, Artamon, NSW 2067, Australia
Subjects: Education, Geography, Psychology, Nursing
ISBN Publisher's Prefix: 0-06

George G **Harrap** & Co Ltd, 182 High Holborn, London WC1V 7AX Tel: (01) 405 9935, 405 0941/2, 405 2853/5 Cable Add: Harrapbook London WC1 Telex: 28673 consol g
Hon President: R Olaf Anderson; *Chairman, Joint Man Dir & General Books Publisher:* G Paull M Harrap, CBE; *Joint Man Dir:* N W Berry; *Publicity Dir:* C R Butterworth; *Educational & Dictionary Publisher:* P H Collin; *UK Sales Dir:* M P Hills; *Home Sales Manager:* M B Armstrong; *Overseas Marketing Manager:* M Allen; *Rights & Permissions:* Martin Lee
Associate Company: Nautical Publishing Co Ltd (qv)
Subjects: Modern Language Dictionaries, General Fiction, Biography, History, Howto, Music, Art, Reference, Juveniles, Highpriced Paperbacks, Psychology, Engineering, Sports, General & Social Science, University, Secondary & Primary Textbooks, Educational Materials
1978: 95 titles *Founded:* 1901
ISBN Publisher's Prefix: 0-245

Paul **Harris** Publishing, 25 London St, Edinburgh EH3 6LY Tel: (031) 556 9696 Cable Add: Publisher, Edinburgh Telex: 727891 Harris G
Man Dir: Paul Harris; *Editorial:* Trevor Royle; *Production:* Robert Wishart; *Publicity:* J Geddes Wood
Parent Company: ARG Investments Ltd
Subjects: General Non-fiction, Maritime, Fine Arts, Limited Editions
1978: 20 titles *1979:* 32 titles *Founded:* 1974
ISBN Publisher's Prefix: 0-904505

Harrow House Editions Ltd, 7a Langley St, Covent Garden, London WC2H 9JA Tel: (01) 836 6072/6041/6031/6069 Telex: 8813235
Man Dirs: Graham D Sadd, Nicholas J Eddison; *Editorial:* Nicholas J Eddison; *Sales, Rights & Permissions:* Graham D Sadd, Ruth Sandys; *Production:* Kenneth D Cowan
Parent Company: Time Life International Ltd
Subjects: Music, Arts, Natural History, General Reference
1978: 4 titles *Founded:* 1976
ISBN Publisher's Prefix: 0-905663

Hart-Davis Educational Ltd, see Granada Publishing Ltd

Harvard Business Review Library, an imprint of William Heinemann (International) Ltd (qv)

Harvard University Press, see The MIT Press

The **Harvester** Press Ltd, 16 Ship St, Brighton, East Sussex Tel: Brighton 723031 (STD code 0273) Cable Add: Harvester Brighton
Chairman and Man Dir, Rights & Permissions: John Spiers; *Sales, Marketing:* Mark Holland; *Promotion, Advertising:* Richard Welsh
Imprints: Harvester Press, Flare Books, Branch Line
Subjects: History, Politics, Economics, Philosophy, Psychology, Reference, Literature, Fiction, also Microform Publications
1979: 90 titles *1980:* 100 titles *Founded:* 1969
ISBN Publisher's Prefixes: 0-901759, 0-85527

Harvill Press Ltd, 30a Pavilion Rd, London SW1X 0HJ Tel: (01) 589 1096/1631 Cable Add: Harvill Western Union Telex: 25611
Parent Company: William Collins Sons & Co Ltd (qv)
1978: 8 titles

Haynes Publishing Group, Sparkford, Yeovil, Somerset BA22 7JJ Tel: North Cadbury 0635 (STD code 0963), (Sales) Yeovil 840811 (STD code 0935), (Trade Orders) Yeovil 24258 Telex: 46212
Chairman: John H Haynes; *Chief Executive:* Frank Day; *Executive Sales Manager:* Andy Lynch; *Editorial Dir, Public Relations Officer and Rights & Permissions:* J R Clew
Associate Company: Haynes Publications Inc, California, USA
Imprint: Foulis Books
Subjects: Motoring History, Motorcar Tuning & Overhaul, Motor Sport, Touring, Aviation, Motorcycle Histories, Automobile Engineering
Founded: 1960
ISBN Publisher's Prefixes: 0-85696, 0-900550, 0-85429 (Foulis)

Health Science Press (Leslie J Speight Ltd)*, Hengiscote, Bradford, Holsworthy, Devon EX22 7AP Tel: Shebbear 469
Dirs: Leslie J Speight, Phyllis M Speight, Ian Miller
Orders to: The C W Daniel Co Ltd, 1 Church Path, Saffron Walden, Essex CB10 1JP
Associate Company: The C W Daniel Co Ltd (at above address)
Subjects: Homoeopathy, Acupuncture, Radionics, Radiesthesia, Nature Cure, Biochemistry, Diet and Health
ISBN Publisher's Prefix: 0-85032

Heatherbank Press, 163 Mugdock Rd, Milngavie, Glasgow G62 6BR Tel: (041) 956 2687
Editorial: Colin Harvey; *Sales, Marketing & Public Relations:* Rosemary Harvey
Subjects: History of Social Work & Social Welfare, Topography (Glasgow), Occupational Costume, Community Publishing (Also publish Film Strips & Slides)
1978: 6 titles *1979:* 4 titles *Founded:* 1974
ISBN Publisher's Prefix: 0-905192

William **Heinemann** (International) Ltd, 10 Upper Grosvenor St, London W1X 9PA Tel: (01) 493 4141 Cable Add: Sunlocks London W1 Telex: 8954961
Shipping Add: The Windmill Press, Kingswood, Tadworth, Surrey
Chairman: Charles Pick; *Publishing Dir:* Nigel Hollis; *Rights & Permissions:* Anne Garwood, Elizabeth Wright
Parent Company: The Heinemann Group of Publishers (qv)
Subsidiary Companies: William Heinemann Australia Pty Ltd, Australia (qv); William

384 UNITED KINGDOM

Heinemann South Africa (Pty) Ltd, South Africa (qv)
Imprints: Harvard Business Review Library, Loeb Classical Library
Subjects: General Fiction, Belles Lettres, Poetry, Biography, History, Music, Art, Philosophy, Juveniles, Psychology, Technical, Management, Finance
Book Club: Nationwide Book Services (owned jointly with William Collins Sons & Co Ltd, UK, Martin Secker & Warburg, UK and Albert Bonniers Förlag AB, Sweden)
Founded: 1890
ISBN Publisher's Prefix: 0-434

Heinemann Educational Books Ltd, 22 Bedford Sq, London WC1B 3HH Tel: (01) 637 3311 Cable Add: Hebooks London W1 Telex: 261888
Orders to: The Windmill Press, Lower Kingswood, Tadworth, Surrey Tel: Mogador 3511 (STD code 073783)
Chairman: A R Beal; *Man Dir:* H MacGibbon; *Publicity Manager:* Robert Creffield
Parent Company: Heinemann Educational Books (International) Ltd (qv)
Subjects: Belles Lettres, History, Music, Engineering, General & Social Science, Economics, Political Science, University, Secondary & Primary Textbooks, Education
1979: 230 titles *Founded:* 1961
ISBN Publisher's Prefix: 0-435

Heinemann Educational Books (International) Ltd, 22 Bedford Sq, London WC1B 3HH Tel: (01) 637 3311 Cable Add: Hebooks London W1 Telex: 261888
Chairman: A R Beal
Parent Company: The Heinemann Group of Publishers Ltd (qv)
Subsidiary Companies: Heinemann Educational Books Ltd (qv); Heinemann Educational Australia Pty Ltd, Australia (qv); Heinemann Educational Books (Asia) Ltd, Hong Kong (qv); Heinemann Educational Books (East Africa) Ltd, Kenya (qv); Heinemann Educational Books (Nigeria) Ltd, Nigeria (qv); Heinemann Educational Books (Caribbean) Ltd, Jamaica; Heinemann Educational Books Inc, USA

The **Heinemann Group** of Publishers Ltd, 10 Upper Grosvenor St, London W1X 9PA Tel: (01) 493 4141 Cable Add: Sunlocks London W1 Telex: 8954961
Shipping Add: Heinemann Publishers Ltd, Lower Kingswood, Tadworth, Surrey
Chairman: Michael Kettle; *Man Dir:* Charles Pick
Parent Company: Thomas Tilling Ltd
Subsidiary Companies: William Heinemann (International) Ltd (qv), Heinemann Educational Books (International) Ltd (qv), William Heinemann Medical Books Ltd (qv), Kaye and Ward Ltd (qv), Martin Secker & Warburg Ltd (qv), Peter Davies Ltd (qv), World's Work Ltd (qv); Heinemann & Zsolnay Ltd (see Paul Zsolnay Verlag GmbH, Austria and Federal Republic of Germany); Heinemann Publishers (New Zealand) Ltd, New Zealand (qv)

William **Heinemann Medical Books** Ltd, 23 Bedford Sq, London WC1B 3HH Tel: (01) 580 0641 Cable Add: Heinmed, London WC1B 3HH Telex: 261 888 (please quote 'medical') Answerback: Hebldn G
Man Dir: Richard S Emery; *Sales Manager:* Michael Pearman; *Production Manager:* Ninetta Martyn
Parent Company: The Heinemann Group of Publishers (qv)
Subjects: Medicine, Dentistry, Veterinary Medicine, General Science
1978: 44 titles *1979:* 28 titles *Founded:* 1913
ISBN Publisher's Prefix: 0-433

Heinemann/Octopus, an imprint of Octopus Books Ltd (qv)

Helicon Press, Knight St, Sawbridgeworth, Herts CM21 9AX Tel: Bishop's Stortford 722318 (STD code 0279)
Man Dir, Editorial: Candida Tobin; *Sales, Production, Publicity, Rights & Permissions:* Christopher Dell
Imprint: Tobin Music Books
1978: 4 titles *1979:* 2 titles *Founded:* 1973
ISBN Publisher's Prefix: 0-905684

Ian **Henry** Publications Ltd, 38 Parkstone Ave, Hornchurch, Essex RM11 3LW Tel: Hornchurch 42042 (STD code 04024)
Man Dir: Ian Wilkes; *Sales Dir:* William G S Oliver
Orders to: J M Dent & Sons Ltd, Dunhams Lane, Letchworth, Hertfordshire
Associate Company: Emerson Book Supplies Ltd, 38 Parkstone Ave, Hornchurch, Essex RM11 3LW
Subjects: Plays, Natural History, Travel, History, Fiction Reprints, Sport, Automobile Engineering, Medical
1978: 35 titles *1979:* 34 titles *Founded:* 1975
ISBN Publisher's Prefix: 0-86025

Her Majesty's Stationery Office, Sovereign House, Botolph St, Norwich NR3 1DN Tel: Norwich 22211 (STD code 0603) Telex: 97301 hemstonery
Publishing Group: Saint Crispin's House, Duke St, Norwich Tel: Norwich 22211 (STD code 0603)
Dir: B C E Lee
London Office: Atlantic House, Holborn Viaduct, London EC1P 1BN Tel: (01) 583 9876 ext 6386 Cable Add: Hemstonery London EC1 Telex: 22805
Subjects: General Nonfiction, Government Publications
1978: approx 8000 titles
Bookshops: 49 High Holborn, London WC1V 6HB (counter sales); Cornwall House, Stamford St, PO Box 569, London SE1 9NH (trade & mail orders); 13A Castle St, Edinburgh EH2 3AR; 258 Broad St, Birmingham B1 2HE; 41 The Hayes, Cardiff CF1 1JW; Southey House, Wine St, Bristol BS1 2BQ; 80 Chichester St, Belfast BT1 4JY; Brazennose St, Manchester M60 8AS
ISBN Publisher's Prefixes: 0-10, 0-11, 0-337

The **Herbert** Press Ltd, 65 Belsize Lane, London NW3 5AU Tel: (01) 794 5965
Man Dir: David Herbert
Orders to: Ernest Benn Ltd, Sovereign Way, Tonbridge, Kent TN9 1RW
Subjects: Art, Design, Crafts, Music, Literature, Biography, Ballet, Theatre
1979: 3 titles *1980:* 4 titles *Founded:* 1975
ISBN Publisher's Prefixes: 0-273, 0-906

Heyden & Son Ltd, Spectrum Ho, Hillview Gardens, London NW4 2JQ Tel: (01) 203 5171 Cable Add: Heyspectra London Telex: 28303
Man Dir: K G Heyden; *Editorial:* K G Heyden, P M Williams; *Production:* M Moran; *Publicity:* A Greene; *Rights & Permissions:* P M Williams
Subsidiary Companies: Heyden & Son GmbH, Münsterstrasse 22, 4440 Rheine, Federal Republic of Germany; Heyden & Son Inc, 247 South 41st St, Philadelphia, Pa 19104, USA
Subjects: Secondary, University, Commercial & Technical Education, Technical & Scientific, Medical
ISBN Publisher's Prefix: 0-85501

Adam **Hilger** Ltd, Techno Ho, Redcliffe Way, Bristol BS1 6NX Tel: Bristol 297481 (STD code 0272) Telex: 449149
Man Dir: Cecil I Pedersen; *Editorial, Production:* Ken J Hall; *Sales, Publicity,*
Rights & Permissions: Malcolm Clarke
Parent: Institute of Physics (qv)
Subjects: Mathematics, Computer Science, Electronics, Energy, Earth and Environmental Sciences, Astronomy, Physics, Technology, Optics/Colour Science, Analytical and Applied Chemistry, Plastics, Medical Physics, General Science, History of Science
1978: 27 titles *1979:* 15 titles *Founded:* 1967
ISBN Publisher's Prefix: 0-85274

Leonard **Hill**, a subsidiary of Blackie & Son (qv)

Hobsons Press (Cambridge) Ltd, Bateman St, Cambridge CB2 1LZ Tel: Cambridge 69811 (STD code 0223) Telex: 81546
Man Dir: Adrian Bridgewater; *Sales:* Alison Peasson
Subject: Education
ISBN Publisher's Prefix: 0-86021

Hodder & Stoughton Children's Books, see Hodder & Stoughton Ltd

Hodder & Stoughton Ltd, Mill Rd, PO Box 700, Dunton Green, Sevenoaks, Kent TN13 2YA Tel: Sevenoaks 50111 (STD code 0732) Cable Add: Expositor Sevenoaks Telex: 95122
London Off: 47 Bedford Sq, London WC1B 3DP Tel: (01) 636 9851
Company is organized in divisions with the following divisional managing directors: Hodder & Stoughton: Eric Major; Hodder & Stoughton Educational: L M H Timmermans; Hodder & Stoughton Paperbacks: Michael Attenborough
Rights & Permissions: Clare Bristow
Subsidiary Companies (UK): Hodder & Stoughton Dunton Green Ltd, Hodder & Stoughton Storage Ltd, Hodder & Stoughton Overseas Ltd, The Lancet Ltd
Subsidiary Companies (Outside UK): Hodder & Stoughton (Australia) Pty Ltd, Australia (qv); Hodder & Stoughton Ltd New Zealand (qv); Hodder & Stoughton (Pty) Ltd, 19th Floor, Braamfontein Centre, 23 Jorissen St, Braamfontein, Johannesburg, South Africa; Hodder & Stoughton Ltd, 30 Lesmill Rd, Don Mills, Ontario M3B 2T6, Canada
Associate Company: Hodder & Stoughton Paperbacks
Imprints: Include Coronet, Knight, Teach Yourself Books
Subjects: General Fiction, Religion and Theology, Educational, Children's (Fiction & Nonfiction), Medical, Dictionaries, Guidebooks, Travel, Sports & Games, Co-editors (Reader's Digest and Consumers' Association)
Founded: 1838
ISBN Publisher's Prefix: 0-340

Alison **Hodge**, 5 Chapel St, Penzance, Cornwall Tel: Penzance 5444 (STD code 0736)
Man Dir: Alison Hodge
Subjects: Social and Regional History, Traditional and Contemporary Crafts, Collections of Photographs
Bookshop: Alison Hodge, at above address
1979: 2 titles *Founded:* 1979
ISBN Publisher's Prefix: 0-906720

Francis **Hodgson**, a division of the Longman Group Ltd (qv)

The **Hogarth** Press Ltd, 40-42 William IV St, London WC2 Tel: (01) 836 0127 Cable Add: Hogarth London WC2 Telex: 299080
Chairman & Man Dir: Norah Smallwood; *Deputy Man Dir:* John Charlton; *Sales:* Norman Askew (Home), Quentin Hockliffe (Export); *Publicity & Advertising:* Rosalind Bell; *Rights & Permissions:* Jill Rose
Parent Company: Chatto & Windus Ltd (qv)

Subjects: General Fiction, Belles Lettres, Poetry, History, Art, Architecture, Philosophy, Juveniles, Travel, Psychology, Psychoanalysis, Social Science
Founded: 1917
ISBN Publisher's Prefix: 0-7012

The **Holland** Press, 37 Connaught St, London W2 2AZ Tel: (01) 262 6184, (01) 723 1623
Proprietor: R H Leech
Subjects: Reference, Music, Travel, Bibliography, Art, Cartography
1979: 30 titles *Founded:* 1956
ISBN Publisher's Prefix: 0-900470

Hollis & Carter, see The Bodley Head Ltd

Holmes McDougall Ltd, Allander Ho, 137-141 Leith Walk, Edinburgh EH6 8NS Tel: (031) 554 9444 Cable Add: Educational Telex: 727508
Man Dir: H G Bennett; *Editorial Dir:* I M Christie; *Export Manager, Rights & Permissions:* R B Shepherd
Subsidiary Companies: W & R Holmes; Harold Hill & Son; Blacklock, Farries & Sons (qv); Pace/Minerva Posters; Scottish Field; Climber and Rambler; Business Scotland; Scottish Farmer; The Great Outdoors
Subjects: Secondary & Primary Textbooks, Leisure, Outdoor Activities, Scottish Interest
Founded: 1870
ISBN Publisher's Prefix: 0-7157

Holt-Blond Ltd, now Holt-Saunders Ltd (qv)

Holt-Saunders Ltd, 1 St Anne's Rd, Eastbourne, East Sussex BN21 3UN Tel: Eastbourne 638221 (STD code 0323) Cable Add: Volumists Eastbourne Telex: 877503 Volmist
Shipping Add: Unit 5B, Edison Rd, Highfield Industrial Estate, Lottbridge Drove, Hampden Park, Eastbourne
Man Dir: Robert Kiernan; *Professional Division Dir:* David S B Inglis; *College Division Dir:* Stephen White; *Publicity Manager:* Eoin MacGillivray
Parent Company: CIP, (a division of Columbia Broadcasting System Inc), 385 Madison Ave, New York, NY 10017, USA
Associate Companies: Editorial Interamericana de Argentina SACel, Argentina (qv); Holt-Saunders Pty Ltd, Australia (qv); Holt, Rinehart & Winston of Canada Ltd, 55 Horner Ave, Toronto, Ontario, Canada; Holt, Rinehart et Winston Ltée, 8305 est, rue Jarry Anjou, Montreal, PQ, Canada; Editorial Interamericana de Colombia SA, Apdo Aéreo 6131, Bogotá, Colombia; Editorial Interamericana del Ecuador SA, Ecuador (qv); Nueva Editorial Interamericana SA de CV, Mexico (qv); Holt, Saunders (NZ) Pty Ltd, New Zealand (qv); Editorial Interamericana de Peru SA, Peru; Distribuidora Interamericana de España SA, Spain; Editorial Interamericana del Uruguay SA, Uruguay (qv); Editorial Interamericana de Venezuela CA, Venezuela (qv); Holt, Rinehart & Winston Inc, 383 Madison Ave, New York, NY 10017; W B Saunders Co, West Washington Sq, Philadelphia, Pa 19105, USA
Subsidiary Companies: Holt, Rinehart & Winston Ltd; W B Saunders Co Ltd
Subjects: Medicine, Nursing, Veterinary, Dentistry, Biology, Mathematics, Physics, Chemistry, University Textbooks, Education, Business Studies
Founded: 1900
ISBN Publisher's Prefixes: 0-03 (Holt, Rinehart & Winston), 0-7216 (Saunders)

Home Health Education Service, 653 St Albans Rd, Garston, Watford, Hertfordshire WD2 6JP Tel: Garston (Herts) 71635 (STD code 09273)
Man Dir: Roland Fidelia
Subjects: Secondary & Primary Education, Religion, Medical, Juveniles
ISBN Publisher's Prefix: 0-900703

Ellis **Horwood** Ltd, Coll Ho, Market Cross Ho, 1 Cooper St, Chichester, West Sussex PO19 1EB Tel: Chicester 789942 (STD code 0243) Cable Add: Horwood Chichester Telex: 86402 Horwood
Editorial: Ellis Horwood, Michael Horwood; *Sales, Production:* Clive Horwood; *Art & Design:* James Gillison; *Publicity:* Sue Gibson; *Marketing:* Felicity Horwood; *Rights & Permissions:* Christine Burbridge
Orders to: John Wiley & Sons Ltd, Baffins Lane, Chichester, West Sussex
Subjects: Advanced Scientific Technology, Environmental Science, Engineering, Geology
1981: 180 titles *Founded:* 1973
ISBN Publisher's Prefix: 0-85312

Hour-Glass Press, an imprint of Bailey Brothers & Swinfen Co Ltd (qv)

How & Why Books, imprint of Transworld Publishers Ltd (qv)

Howard & Wyndham Ltd, 44 Hill St, London W1X 8LB Tel: (01) 493 6777
Firm is not itself a publisher, but the parent company of: W H Allen & Co Ltd (qv), Brown Watson Ltd (qv), Grant Bookshops Ltd, Murrays Remainder Books Ltd (qv)

Hugo's Language Books Ltd, 104 Judd St, London WC1H 9NF Tel: (01) 278 6136
Dirs: Mrs V Lock, Mrs J Lock, Mrs M Kerr, R J Batchelor-Smith; *Sales, Publicity, Rights & Permissions:* R J Batchelor-Smith
Subjects: How-to, Reference, Secondary Textbooks, Courses on disc, tape & cassette
1980: 6 titles (books) 6 titles (cassettes)
Founded: 1875
ISBN Publisher's Prefix: 0-85285

Hulton Educational Publications Ltd, Raans Rd, Amersham, Buckinghamshire HP6 6JJ Tel: Amersham 4196 (STD code 02403) Cable Add: Hulted Amersham Bucks Telex: 837916
Dirs: L G Marsh, J van der Veen, Stanley Thornes; *Man Dir:* Herman Bruggink
Subjects: History, Religion, Juveniles, General & Social Science, University, Secondary & Primary Textbooks, Educational Materials
1978: 20 titles *1979:* 24 titles *Founded:* 1954
Miscellaneous: Firm is a member of the Kluwer Group, Netherlands (qv)
ISBN Publisher's Prefix: 0-7175

C **Hurst** & Co (Publisher's) Ltd, 1-2 Henrietta St, London WC2E 8PS Tel: (01) 240 2666
Shipping Add: J M Dent & Sons Ltd, Dunhams Lane, Letchworth, Herts SG6 1LF
Man Dir: Christopher Hurst; *Rights & Permissions:* Julia Hogg
Subjects: Area Studies (Politics, Economic Development, Anthropology)
Founded: 1968
ISBN Publisher's Prefixes: 0-838905, 0-903983

Hutchinson Educational, 24 Highbury Crescent, London N5 1RX Tel: (01) 359 3711
Man Dir: Mark Cohen; *Sales:* John Fulford; *Export:* Clyde Hunter
Orders to: Tiptree Book Services, Church Rd, Tiptree, Nr Colchester, Essex
Imprints: Hutchinson Technical Books, Hutchinson University Library, Business Books Ltd (qv)
Subjects: School Books, Technical & Academic
Miscellaneous: Hutchinson Educational is a Division of The Hutchinson Publishing Group Ltd (qv)

Hutchinson General Books Ltd, 3 Fitzroy Sq, London W1P 6JD Tel: (01) 387 2888
Man Dir: Brian Perman; *Editorial:* James Cochrane; *Sales:* David Roy; *Export:* Clyde Hunter; *Marketing:* Jeremy Cox
Orders to: Tiptree Book Services, Church Rd, Tiptree, Nr Colchester, Essex
Imprints: Barrie & Jenkins, Hutchinson Junior Books, Popular Dogs Publishing Co Ltd, Rider & Co, Stanley Paul & Co Ltd
Subjects: General Fiction, Crime & Nonfiction, Biography, Memoirs, Travel, Reference, Juvenile, Fine Arts & Collecting, Dog Breeds, Eastern Philosophy and Mysticism, Sports & Hobbies
Miscellaneous: Hutchinson General Books is a Division of The Hutchinson Publishing Group Ltd (qv)

Hutchinson Junior Books, an imprint of Hutchinson General Books Ltd (qv)

The **Hutchinson Publishing Group** Ltd, 3 Fitzroy Sq, London W1P 6JD Tel: (01) 387 2888 (Sales: (01) 388 7601) Cable Add: Literarius London W1 Telex: 261212
Man Dir: Charles Clark; *Rights & Permissions:* Susanna Yager
Orders to: Tiptree Book Services, Church Rd, Tiptree, Nr Colchester, Essex
The Hutchinson Publishing Group operates three publishing divisions:
Hutchinson General Books Ltd, Hutchinson Educational Books, Arrow Books Ltd (qqv for details)
Subsidiary Company: Bellew & Higton Publishers Ltd (qv)
Associate Companies: Andersen Press Ltd (qv), Hutchinson Group (Australia) Pty Ltd, Australia (qv), Hutchinson Group (NZ) Ltd, New Zealand (qv) and Hutchinson Group (SA) (Pty) Ltd, South Africa (qv), Geographia Ltd (qv)
Subjects: General Fiction & Nonfiction, Juveniles, Paperbacks, Science & Technical, Textbooks, Biography, Memoirs, Travel, Reference
Founded: 1887
ISBN Publisher's Prefix: 0-09

Hutchinson Technical Books, an imprint of Hutchinson Educational (qv)

Hutchinson University Library, an imprint of Hutchinson Educational (qv)

Hylton Lacy Publishers, an imprint of Profile Books Ltd (qv)

I C Magazines Ltd, 63 Long Acre, London WC2E 9JH Tel: (01) 836 8731 Cable Add: Machrak London WC2 Telex: 8811757 Araby G
Chairman: Afif Ben Yedder; *Editorial:* Hilda Igloi; *Sales:* Nejib Ben Yedder; *Production:* Jean Norton; *Publicity, Rights & Permissions:* Christian Digby-Firth
Subsidiary Companies: I C Publications Ltd, Room 1121, 122 East 42nd St, New York, NY 10017, USA; I C Expo Ltd, London
Subjects: Business, Economics, Political History, Regional Affairs, Yearbooks, Tourist Guides
1978: 5 titles *1979:* 5 titles *Founded:* 1974
ISBN Publisher's Prefix: 0-905268

I P C, see International Publishing Corporation Ltd

I T V Books, an imprint of Independent Television Books Ltd (qv)

Idea Editions Distribution*, 31 Oval Rd, London NW1
Man Dir, Rights & Permissions: Anthony Mathews; *Sales Dir:* Christopher Gates;

Publicity, Advertising Manager: Ian Shipley
Associate Companies: Idea Books, 104-108 Sussex St, Sydney, NSW 2000, Australia; Idea Books, France (qv); Idea Books, Italy (qv)
Subjects: Biography, Music, Art, High-priced Paperbacks
ISBN Publisher's Prefix: 0-85988

Image, an imprint of Doubleday & Co Inc (qv)

Imprint Academic, Imprint Apollo, Imprint Arts, Imprint Capablanca, Imprint Pitman, Imprint Shiva, Imprint Software, all imprints of Imprint Editions Ltd (qv)

Imprint Editions Ltd, 16 Milton Ave, Highgate, London N6 Tel: (01) 348 3998 Telex: 298801
Man Dir: John Graham; *Sales:* Tom Duffy; *Production:* Keith Sutherland; *Art & Publicity:* Roy Wyand; *Rights & Permissions:* Liz Yang
Parent Company: Newcomb International, 415 South Howes, Fort Collins, Colorado, USA
Subsidiary Companies: Imprint Pitman, 37 South Hill Park, London NW3; Imprint Software, 16 Milton Ave, London N6
Associate Company: Imprint (Print and Design) Ltd, Howell Rd, Exeter
Imprints: Imprint Academic, Imprint Apollo, Imprint Arts, Imprint Capablanca, Imprint Pitman, Imprint Shiva, Imprint Software
Branch Off: 420 South Howes St, Fort Collins, Colorado, USA
Subjects: Academic (particularly Mathematics & Computing), Political History, Art, Chess, Finance, Microcomputer Software, Co-editions
1979: 3 titles *Founded:* 1979
ISBN Publisher's Prefix: 0-907352

Independent Television Books Ltd, 247 Tottenham Court Rd, London W1P 0AU Tel: (01) 636 3666 Telex: 27813
Chairman: R W Phillis; *Editorial:* John Doyle; *Production:* Jerry Dixon
Parent Company: Independent Television Publications Ltd, at above address
Imprints: ITV Books, Look-In Books
Subjects: General, Adult Education, Humour, Reference, TV tie-ins, Children's Paperbacks

The **Initial Teaching** Alphabet Foundation, 9 Brindle Close, Bamber Bridge, Preston PR5 6ZN Tel: Preston 36963 (STD code 0772)
Executive Dir: J Bromley
Subject: Primary Education
ISBN Publisher's Prefix: 0-254

Ink Links Ltd, 271 Kentish Town Rd, London NW5 2JS Tel: (01) 267 0661
Staff: John Weal, Susan Trangmar, Malcolm Imrie
Orders to: Noonan Hurst Ltd, 131 Trafalgar Rd, London SE10
Subjects: History, Economics, Marxist Analysis, Labour Movement History, Experimental Fiction, Photography
1978: 4 titles *1979:* 10 titles *Founded:* 1977
ISBN Publisher's Prefix: 0-906133

Institute of Personnel Management*, Central House, Upper Woburn Pl, London WC1 0HX Tel: (01) 387 2844
Editorial, Rights & Permissions: Sally Herbert; *Sales & Publicity:* David Grieves; *Production:* Marcella Randall
Orders to: IPM Distribution Centre, The Technical Press Ltd, Freeland, Oxford OX7 2AP
Associate Company: The Technical Press Ltd (qv)
Subjects: Management, Personnel Management
1978: 12 titles
ISBN Publisher's Prefix: 0-85292

Institute of Petroleum, an imprint of Applied Science Publishers Ltd (qv)

The **Institute of Physics**, Techno House, Redcliffe Way, Bristol BS1 6NX Tel: Bristol 297481 (STD code 0292) Telex: 449149
Publishing Dir: C I Pedersen; *Editorial:* Ken J Hall; *Sales, Publicity, Rights & Permissions:* M D Clarke
Orders to: (Books) Adam Hilger Ltd, Techno House, Redcliffe Way, Bristol BS1 6NX; (Journals/Magazines) Physics Trust Publications, The Distribution Centre, Blackhorse Rd, Letchworth, Herts
Subsidiary Company: Adam Hilger Ltd (qv)
Subjects: Physics, General Science, Journals
1978: 12 titles *Founded:* 1874
ISBN Publisher's Prefix: 0-85498

Institute of Pyramidology, 31 Station Rd, Harpenden, Herts AL5 4XB Tel: Harpenden 64510 (STD code 05827) Telex: 826957 Institute of Pyramidology
Vice President: James Rutherford
Associate Company: Top Stone Books, 29 Station Rd, Harpenden, Herts AL5 4XB
Subject: Pyramidology
Founded: 1940
ISBN Publisher's Prefix: 0-903402

The **Institution of Civil Engineers** (Publications Division), see Thomas Telford Ltd

Institution of Electrical Engineers*, Publishing Dept, PO Box 8, Southgate House, Stevenage, Herts SG1 1HQ Tel: Stevenage 3311 (STD code 0438) Cable Add: Voltampere Stevenage Telex: 261176
Publishing Dir: D H Barlow; *Editor in Chief:* J D St Aubyn; *Marketing Manager:* O Ball
Orders to: Publication Sales Dept, Institution of Electrical Engineers, PO Box 26, Hitchin, Herts SG5 1SA Tel: Hitchin 53331 (STD code 0462) Telex: 825962
Branch Off & Bookshop: Savoy Pl, London WC2R 0BL
Subjects: (Periodicals) Electrical & Electronic Engineering, Power & Control & Science, Computer Technology, IEE Conference Publication, Colloquium Digests, Technical Regulations, Vacation Schools
1978: 100 titles *Founded:* 1871
Miscellaneous: Represented by Association of Learned & Professional Society Publishers (qv under Book Trade Organizations)
ISBN Publisher's Prefix: 0-85296

Inter-Varsity Press*, 38 De Montfort St, Leicester LE1 7GP Tel: Leicester 551700 (STD code 0533) Cable Add: Unifell
Man Dir: F R Entwistle; *Editorial:* D R W Wood; *Marketing, Publicity:* J S Hey; *Production:* M R Sims; *Rights & Permissions:* Miss M K Gladstone
Orders to: IVP, Norton St, Nottingham NG7 3HR
Parent Company: UCCF
Imprints: Arena; Tyndale Press
Subject: Religion
Bookshops: UCCF Bookcentre, Norton St, Nottingham
1978: 20 titles *Founded:* 1928
ISBN Publisher's Prefix: 0-85110

Intercontinental Book Productions Ltd, Berkshire House, Queen St, Maidenhead, Berkshire SL6 1NF Tel: Maidenhead 34433 (STD code 0628) Telex: 848036 Ibpmhdg
Man Dir: Michael J Morris; *Publishing Dir:* Desmond Marwood *Production Dir:* David Wescott; *Foreign Rights Manager:* Elisabeth Marks
Subjects: Full colour co-edition packages, General Nonfiction, How-to, Juveniles, Paperbacks, Educational Aids and Toys
1978: 60 titles *1979:* 36 titles *Founded:* 1972
ISBN Publisher's Prefix: 0-85047

International Bible Reading Association, see National Christian Education Council

International Biographical Centre, an imprint of Melrose Press, (qv)

International Communications, see I C Magazines Ltd

International Correspondence Schools Ltd, Intertext House, Stewart's Rd, London SW8 Tel: (01) 622 9911 Cable Add: Intertext, London SW8 Telex: 918658
Subjects: Commercial & Technical Education, Commercial & Professional, Art & Architecture, Leisure
ISBN Publisher's Prefix: 0-7002

International Publishing Corporation Ltd*, King's Reach Tower, Stamford St, London SE1 9LF Tel: (01) 261 5000
This firm is the holding company for Butterworth & Co (Publishers) Ltd (qv), and the Hamlyn Publishing Group Ltd (qv)

International Textbook Co Ltd, Bishopbriggs, Glasgow G64 2NZ Tel: (041) 772 2311
London office: Furnival House, 14-18 High Holborn, London Tel: (01) 242 5832
Shipping Add: J & M Dent (Distribution) Ltd, Dunhams Lane, Letchworth SG16 1LF
Dir: Dr G MacKintosh
Parent Company: Blackie & Son Ltd (qv)
Subjects: Chemistry, Physics, Mathematics, Computing, Engineering, Environmental Sciences, Business Studies, Hotel and Catering
Founded: 1902
ISBN Publisher's Prefix: 0-7002

The **Islamic Foundation**, 223 London Rd, Leicester LE2 1ZE Tel: Leicester 700725 (STD code 0533) Cable Add: Islamfound Leicester UK Telex: 341539
Director General, Editorial: K Murad; *Sales, Production, Publicity:* T A Dale
Subjects: Islamic Topics
1978: 12 titles *1979:* 11 titles *Founded:* 1973

Jackdaw Publications Ltd, see Jonathan Cape Ltd

Arthur **James** Ltd, The Drift, Greenhill Park Rd, Evesham, Worcs WR11 4NW Tel: Evesham 6566 (STD code 0386) Cable Add: James Evesham
Man Dir: F A Russell; *Editorial:* M MacQueen
Subjects: Religion, Psychology
1978: 5 titles *Founded:* 1935
ISBN Publisher's Prefix: 0-85305

Jane's Publishing Company Ltd, 238 City Rd, London EC1V 2PU Tel: (01) 251 9281 Telex: 23168
Man Dir: Sidney Jackson; *Editorial:* Christy Campbell; *Sales:* Jeremy Gambrill; *Production:* Ken Harris; *Publicity:* Andrea Pomroy; *Rights & Permissions:* Pat James
Parent Company: Thomson Books Ltd (qv for associate companies)
Subsidiary Company: Jane's Publishing Inc, 730 Fifth Ave, New York, NY 10019, USA
Subjects: Naval, Military, Aviation, Transport Reference
1979: 40 titles *Founded:* 1979
ISBN Publisher's Prefix: 0-7106

Jarrold Colour Publications, Barrack St, Norwich NR3 1TR Tel: Norwich 60211 (STD code 0603) Cable Add: Jarrolds Telex: 97497
Man Dir, Rights & Permissions: Antony Jarrold; *Sales Manager:* T A Thompson

Imprints: Cotman House, White Horse Books, Cotmancolour, Glaven, Walsingham
Subjects: Topography, Travel, Natural History, Gardening, Hobbies
Bookshop: Jarrold & Sons Ltd, Barrack St, Norwich
1978: 500 titles *Founded:* 1770
ISBN Publisher's Prefix: 0-85306

The **Johns Hopkins** University Press, 2-4 Brook St, London W1Y 1AA Tel: (01) 493 5061, (01) 499 4688 Cable Add: Unibooks London W1 Telex: 24224 ref 3545
Warehouse: International Book Distributors, 66 Wood Lane End, Hemel Hempstead, Herts
Man Dir: J Trevor Brown; *Publicity Manager:* Andrew Nolan; *Export Sales Manager:* Anna Simpson-Muellner
Parent Company: The Johns Hopkins University Press, Baltimore, Maryland 21218, USA
Subjects: Literature, Humanities, Social Sciences, Sciences
1978: 95 titles
ISBN Publisher's Prefix: 0-8018

Johnson Publications Ltd, 11-14 Stanhope Mews West, London SW7 Tel: (01) 373 8543
Subjects: Medicine, History, Archaeology, Biography, Memoirs, Politics, Political Economy, Sociology, Questions of the Day, Travel & Adventure, Directories & Guidebooks, General Literature
ISBN Publisher's Prefix: 0-85307

Johnston & Bacon Publishers, 35 Red Lion Sq, London WC1R 4SG Tel: (01) 831 6100
Editorial: A G Sanders
Subjects: Road & Tourist Maps, Atlases, Scottish Publications, Books of General Leisure Interest
1978: 12 titles *Founded:* 1825
Miscellaneous: Division of Cassell Ltd (qv)
ISBN Publisher's Prefix: 0-7179

Jordan & Sons Ltd, PO Box 260, 15 Pembroke Rd, Bristol BS99 7DX Tel: Bristol 32861 (STD code 0272) Telex: 449119
Man Dir: Dennis Lloyd; *Editorial, Sales Dir:* Patrick Lockstone; *Publishing Executive:* Angela Gibbs; *Marketing Dir:* Andrew Kampe
Subsidiary Company: Oswalds of Edinburgh Ltd, 24 Castle St, Edinburgh EH2 3HT Tel: (031) 2257308/9 Telex: 261010
Imprint: Rose-Jordan Ltd
London Off: Jordan House, 47 Brunswick Pl, London N1 6EE Tel: (01) 253 3030
Branch Offs: 3 Victoria St, Liverpool L2 5QF Tel: (051) 227 4064;
44 Whitchurch Rd, Cardiff CF4 3UQ Tel: Cardiff 371901 (STD code 0222)
Subjects: Secondary, University, Commercial & Technical Education, Legal & Parliamentary, Commercial & Professional
Bookshops: 20 Clothier Rd, Brislington, Bristol (Warehouse)
Founded: 1866
ISBN Publisher's Prefix: 0-85308

Michael **Joseph** Ltd, 44 Bedford Sq, London WC1 3EF Tel: (01) 323 3200 Cable Add: Emjaybuks London WC1 Telex: 21322
Shipping Add: TBL Book Service Ltd, 17-23 Nelson Way, Tuscam Trading Estate, Camberley, Surrey
Man Dir: Alan Brooke; *Marketing Dir:* Richard Douglas-Boyd; *Publicity & Advertising:* Karen Geary; *Rights & Permissions:* Diana Mackay
Associate Company: Pelham Books (qv)
Subjects: General, Fiction, Biography, History, How-to, Reference, Young Adult, High-priced Paperbacks, Music
1978: 200 titles *Founded:* 1936
Miscellaneous: Company is in the Thomson Books Ltd Group, a part of International Thomson Organization Ltd (Canada)
ISBN Publisher's Prefixes: 0-7181, 0-7207

The **Journeyman** Press, 97 Ferme Park Rd, Crouch End, London N8 9SA Tel: (01) 348 9261 Cable Add: Journeyrad, London N8 Telex: 25247 Journeyrad
Man Dir: Peter Sinclair
Orders to: Central Books Ltd, 14 The Leather Market, London SE1 3ER
Imprints: Journeyman Press, Radical Reprints
Subjects: Politics, Socialist and Marxist History, Fiction, Biography, Art, Poetry
1978: 8 titles *1979:* 8 titles *Founded:* 1975
ISBN Publisher's Prefix: 0-904526

Jupiter Books (London) Ltd*, 167 Hermitage Rd, London N4 1LZ Tel: (01) 800 6601
Man Dir, Rights & Permissions: S H Austen; *Editorial Dir:* Anthony Frewin
Subjects: History, Music, Art, Juveniles
Founded: 1973
ISBN Publisher's Prefix: 0-904041

K & R Books Ltd, Edlington Hall, Edlington, Horncastle, Lincolnshire LN9 5RJ Tel: Horncastle 6361 (STD code 065 82)
Editorial Dir: D Kelsey-Wood; *Dirs:* E Kelsey-Wood, W J Rowley; *Production Manager:* W Pryde; *Sales, Publicity Manager:* C J Fairhurst
Subjects: Natural History, Pets (including Colourmaster series)
1979: 15 titles *1980:* 17 titles
ISBN Publisher's Prefix: 0-93264

Kahn & Averill, 11-14 Stanhope Mews West, London SW7 Tel: (01) 743 3278
Man Dir: M Kahn
Subjects: General Non-fiction (with emphasis on music)
1978: 7 titles *1979:* 8 titles *Founded:* 1947
ISBN Publisher's Prefix: 0-900707

Kaye & Ward Ltd*, Century House, 82-84 Tanner St, London SE1 Tel: (01) 231 7433 Cable Add: Kayebooks London
Shipping Add: The Windmill Press, Kingswood, Tadworth, Surrey
Man Dir: S H Pickard; *Editorial:* Diane Burston, Rosemary Debham; *Sales & Publicity Dir:* Austen Smith; *Production:* Ian MacFarlen
Parent Company: The Heinemann Group of Publishers Ltd (qv)
Subjects: Novels, Belles Lettres, Biography, History, How-to, Juveniles, Sport, Hobbies, Handicrafts
1978: 35 titles *Founded:* 1942
ISBN Publisher's Prefix: 0-7182

Kelly's Directories Ltd, Windsor Court, East Grinstead House, East Grinstead, West Sussex RH19 1XB Tel: East Grinstead 26972 (STD code 0342)
Man Dir: R Haddrell; *Publishing Dir:* T J Ulrick; *Publicity Manager:* Philip Robinson
Parent Company: IPC Business Press Information Services Ltd
Subject: Directories
Founded: 1799
ISBN Publisher's Prefix: 0-610

Kemps Group (Printers & Publishers) Ltd, 1-5 Bath St, London EC1V 9QA Tel: (01) 253 4761 Cable Add: Kemptory London EC1
Branch Off: 2309 Coventry Rd, Sheldon, Birmingham B26 3PG
Subject: Reference and General
1980: 17 titles *Founded:* 1946
ISBN Publisher's Prefix: 0-905255

Kershaw Publishing Co Ltd, 109 Gt Russell St, London WC1B 3ND Tel: (01) 580 1862 Cable Add: Eurospan London WC2
Shipping Add: International Book Distributors Ltd, 66 Wood Lane End, Hemel Hempstead, Hertfordshire
Man Dir: Peter K Taylor; *Sales, Publicity, Advertising, Rights & Permissions:* Janet Buttery
Branch Off: Bolholt, Walshaw Rd, Bury, Lancs
Subjects: Mathematics, Business, Social Sciences, Scholarly Reprints
1978: 5 titles *Founded:* 1969
ISBN Publisher's Prefix: 0-901665

Kestrel Books, an imprint of Penguin Books Ltd (qv)

Keswick, an imprint of Marshall Morgan & Scott (Publications) Ltd (qv)

William **Kimber** & Co Ltd, Godolphin Ho, 22a Queen Anne's Gate, London SW1H 9AE Tel: (01) 222 7684/6
Man Dir: William Kimber; *Editorial, Rights & Permissions:* Amy Howlett; *Sales:* W L Vaughan; *Production:* O J Colman; *Publicity:* Lisa-Jane Kelly
Orders to: 72-74 Paul St, London EC2
Subjects: Biography, History, General, Fiction, Current Affairs, Travel, Memoirs, Naval, Military, Aviation
1978: 36 titles *1979:* 40 titles *Founded:* 1950
ISBN Publisher's Prefix: 0-7183

Henry **Kimpton** (Publishers) Ltd, 7 Leighton Pl, Leighton Rd, London NW5 2QL Tel: (01) 267 5483
Man Dir: Ronald Deed; *Editorial, Rights & Permissions:* Pat Pembroke; *Production:* G McMahon
Associate Companies: Henry Kimpton Ltd, Lepus Books (qv)
Subject: Medicine
Bookshops: Kimptons, 205 Great Portland St, London W1N 6LR; Kimptons, 49 Newman St, London W1P 4BB
1978: 1 title *1979:* 3 titles *Founded:* 1900
ISBN Publisher's Prefix: 0-85313

Kingfisher Books, an imprint of Scripture Union (qv)

Kingsmead Press, Rosewell Ho, Kingsmead Sq, Bath BA1 2AD Tel: Bath 64474 (STD code 0225)
Man Dir: Mrs S Dix
Imprints: Kingsmead Press, Kingsmead Reprints
Subjects: Art Reference, Illustrated Reference Books of Towns etc
Bookshops: Rosewell Ho, Kingsmead Sq, Bath; 18 Old St, Clevedon, Avon
1978: 14 titles *1979:* 6 titles *Founded:* 1969
ISBN Publisher's Prefixes: 0-901571, 0-906230

Kingsway Publications Ltd, Lottbridge Drove, Eastbourne, East Sussex BN23 6NT Tel: Eastbourne 27454/5 (STD code 0323) Telex: 877415
Chairman: Dr J Hywel-Davies; *Man Dir:* Hugh D Fuller; *Editorial Dir:* Charles Henshall; *Sales Manager:* Geoff Booker
Imprints: Church Pastoral Aid Society, Coverdale House, Falcon Books, Kingsway, Victory Press
Subjects: Religion, High- & Low-priced Paperbacks
Miscellaneous: Firm was formed in 1977 by the merger of Coverdale House Publishers Ltd and Victory Press
1978: 27 titles
ISBN Publisher's Prefixes: 0-86065 (Kingsway), 0-902088 (Coverdale), 0-85476 (Victory)

Kluwer Publishing Ltd, Harlequin Ave, Gt West Rd, Brentford, Middx TW8 9EW Tel: (01) 568 6441
Man Dir: W E Porter; *Marketing Dir:* J G Paul
Parent Company: Kluwer BV, Netherlands (qv)
Imprints: Kluwer Business Handbooks, Kluwer Medical Handbooks
Subjects: Business, Management, Law, Taxation, Insurance, Finance, Medicine, Farming (Mostly loose-leaf)
1978: 8 titles *1979:* 6 titles *Founded:* 1972
Miscellaneous: Firm was created by Kluwer BV, Netherlands (qv) and George G Harrap & Co (qv)

Knight, an imprint of Hodder & Stoughton Ltd (qv)

Charles **Knight**, see Ernest Benn Ltd

Kogan Page Ltd, 120 Pentonville Rd, London N1 9JN Tel: (01) 837 7851
Man Dir, Editorial, Rights & Permissions: Philip Kogan; *Marketing Dir:* Peter Newman; *Production:* Janson Woodall; *Publicity, Advertising Manager:* Jane Tatam
Associate Company: Nichols Publishing Co, PO Box 96, New York, NY 10024, USA
Subjects: Business Reference, General Management, Personnel Management, Industrial Relations, Training, Energy and Energy Exploration, Educational Technology and Innovation, Careers, Transport, Journals
1978: 35 titles *1979:* 60 titles *Founded:* 1967
ISBN Publisher's Prefix: 0-85038

L S P Books Ltd, 8 Farncombe St, Farncombe, Surrey GU7 3AY Tel: Godalming 28622 (STD code 04868) Cable Add: Litserve, Godalming Telex: 919101 Video-Teknik
Man Dir: C P de Laszlo; *Rights & Permissions:* B Jafrato
Imprints: BCW, Citadel, Lorrimer Books, Odeon
Subjects: Art, Cinema, Reference, Paperbacks, Travel
1978: 2 titles *1979:* 2 titles *Founded:* 1964
ISBN Publisher's Prefixes: 0-85321 (LSP), 0-8065 (Citadel), 0-8184 (Lorrimer)

Ladybird Books Ltd, Beeches Rd, PO Box 12, Loughborough, Leicestershire LE11 2NQ Tel: Loughborough 68021 (STD code 0509) Cable Add: Ladybird, Loughborough Telex: 341347
Man Dir: M P Kelley; *Editorial Dir:* V Mills; *Works Dir:* C W Hall; *Art Dir:* R Smith; *Sales Dir:* B Cotton; *Sales Managers:* G Duncan (UK), R Webster (Export)
Subjects: Children's Books, Educational (Infants, Primary, Secondary), Educational Materials
1978: 42 titles *Founded:* 1924
Miscellaneous: Formerly Wills & Hepworth Ltd. Associated companies include Longman Group (qv) and Penguin Books Ltd (qv)
ISBN Publisher's Prefix: 0-7214

Lakeland Paperbacks, an imprint of Marshall, Morgan & Scott (Publications) Ltd (qv)

Jay **Landesman** Ltd, 159 Wardour St, London W1V 3AT Tel: (01) 439 1644/734 3233 Telex: 935163
Man Dir, Publicity: Jay Landesman; *Editorial:* Cosmo Landesman; *Sales:* Stan Stunning; *Production, Rights & Permissions:* Pam Hardyment
Orders to: Kogan Page, 120 Pentonville Rd, London N1
Imprint: Polytantric Press
Subjects: Satire, Sociology, Poetry, Fiction
1978: 4 titles *1979:* 5 titles *Founded:* 1977
ISBN Publisher's Prefix: 0-905150

Allen **Lane**, 536 Kings Rd, London SW10 0UH Tel: (01) 351 2393 Cable Add: Penguinook West Drayton Telex: 263130 Penbok g
Chief Executive: Peter Mayer; *Joint Editors-in-Chief:* Peter Carson, Philippa Harrison; *Man Editor:* Eleo Gordon; *Sales:* Alan Wherry (UK), Mike Hogben (Export); *Production:* Richard Keller; *Marketing:* David Brown; *Publicity:* Lorraine Cooper; *Rights & Permissions:* Carol Heaton
Orders to: Penguin Books, Bath Road, Harmondsworth, Middx
Parent Company: Penguin Books Ltd (qv) (Allen Lane is hardcover imprint)
Associate Company: Longman Group (qv)
Branch Off: See Penguin Books Ltd
Subjects: Fiction, General Non-fiction, Biography, Travel, Cookery, History, Art, Social Science
1978: 60 titles *Founded:* 1969
ISBN Publisher's Prefix: 0-7139

The **Language** Library, an imprint of André Deutsch (qv)

Latimer House Ltd, 150 Southampton Row, London WC1 Tel: (01) 278 6668
Man Dir: P J Kinden
Parent Company: BPC Ltd (qv)
Subjects: Secondary, Middle and Primary Library Books, Atlases
ISBN Publisher's Prefix: 0-906704

T Werner **Laurie**, see The Bodley Head Ltd

Lawrence & Wishart, 39 Museum St, London WC2 Tel: (01) 405 0103 Cable Add: Interbook London WC1
Man Dir: J Skelley; *Sales Dir:* K Waddington
Subjects: Biography, History, Philosophy, Politics, Economics
Founded: 1936
ISBN Publisher's Prefix: 0-85315

Leicester University Press, Fielding Johnson Bldg, University of Leicester, University Rd, Leicester LE1 7RH Tel: Leicester 551860/555510 (STD code 0533)
Secretary to the Press: P L Boulton
Subjects: Archaeology, History, Literature, International Relations
1978: 13 titles *1979:* 15 titles *Founded:* 1951
ISBN Publisher's Prefix: 0-7185

Leisure Arts Ltd*, 18 St Ann's Crescent, London SW18 2LX Tel: (01) 874 0441 Cable Add: Cohallclub London Telex: 25881
Dirs: Leonard Joseph (USA), L Phillips, Lord Redesdale
Subsidiary Companies: International Art Club Editions, The Corsano Co (both at 18 St Ann's Crescent, London SW18 2LX)
Subjects: General Fiction, History, Art, Reference, Cooking, How-to, Philosophy, Poetry, Sport
Book Club: Heron Books
ISBN Publisher's Prefix: 0-900948

Leopard, an imprint of Scripture Union (qv)

Lepus Books, 7 Leighton Pl, Leighton Rd, London NW5 2QL Tel: (01) 267 5483
Man Dir: R G Deed; *Editorial:* Pat Pembroke
Associate Companies: Henry Kimpton Ltd, Henry Kimpton (Publishers) Ltd (qv)
Subjects: Philosophy, Psychology, Social Science, University Textbooks, Educational Materials, Sport
1978: 4 titles *1979:* 4 titles
ISBN Publisher's Prefix: 0-86019

Charles **Letts** & Co Ltd, Diary Ho, Borough Rd, London SE1 1DW Tel: (01) 407 8891 Cable Add: Diarists London Telex: 884498
Chairman: A A Letts; *Marketing Dir:* J A Kearns; *General Manager:* T M Green
Subjects: Guide Books, Travel, Education, General Non-fiction
1980: 65 titles *Founded:* 1796
ISBN Publisher's Prefix: 0-85097

Lionel **Leventhal** Ltd, 2-6 Hampstead High St, London NW3 1QQ Tel: (01) 794 0246 Cable Add: Armsbooks Ldn NW3 Telex: 896691
Man Dir: Lionel Leventhal
Imprint: Arms & Armour Press
Subjects: Military and Illustrated Reference
Bookshop: Ken Trotman Arms Books, 2-6 Hampstead High St, London NW3 1QQ
Founded: 1966
ISBN Publisher's Prefix: 0-85368

Leviathan House Ltd, 238 Temple Chambers, London EC4Y 0ER Tel: (01) 353 4802
Man Dir: George Gremin; *Rights & Permissions:* Mrs M Broderick
Parent Company: W Dummer Ltd, Zurich, Switzerland
Associate Company: Verlag Moderne Industrie, Munich, Federal Republic of Germany
Subjects: Management, Marketing
Founded: 1971
ISBN Publisher's Prefix: 0-900537

A **Lewis**, an imprint of Ian Allan Ltd (qv)

F **Lewis** (Publishers) Ltd, The Tithe House, 1461 London Rd, Leigh-on-Sea, Essex SS9 2SD Tel: Southend-on-Sea 78163 (STD code 0702)
Chairman: Charles A A Black; *Man Dir:* Frank Lewis
Parent Company: A & C Black (Publishers) Ltd (qv)
Subjects: Fine & Applied Art, Ceramics, Textiles
1978: 6 titles *Founded:* 1932
ISBN Publisher's Prefix: 0-85317

H K **Lewis** & Co Ltd, 136 Gower St, London WC1E 6BS Tel: (01) 387 4282 Cable Add: Publicavit, London WC1E 6BS
Subjects: Technical & Scientific, Medical, Foreign Languages, Dictionaries
ISBN Publisher's Prefix: 0-7186

J D **Lewis** & Sons Ltd, see Gomer Press

Frances **Lincoln** Publishers Ltd, 91 Clapham High St, London SW4 7TA Tel: (01) 622 9933 Telex: 918066
Man Dir: Frances Lincoln; *Sales (UK):* David Livermore; *Production:* Richard Hussey; *Publicity:* Rosalind Lewis
Orders to: Weidenfeld & Nicolson, Heinemann Group Services, Windmill Press, Kingswood, Tadworth, Surrey KT20 6TG
Associate Company: George Weidenfeld & Nicolson Ltd (qv)
Subjects: High quality illustrated books for international co-editions
1979: 4 titles *Founded:* 1978
ISBN Publisher's Prefix: 0-906459

Linden Press, see Centaur Press Ltd

Linguaphone Institute Ltd*, Linguaphone Ho, 207-209 Regent St, London W1R 8AU Tel: (01) 741 1655 Cable Add: Linguafone, London W6 Telex: 266181
Chairman: Lord Evans of Hungershall; *Editorial, Rights & Permissions:* K Rawson-Jones; *Sales, Publicity:* L J Goodwin; *Production:* S Evans
Parent Company: Westinghouse Learning Corporation, USA
Subsidiary Company: Language Tuition Centre Ltd
Subject: English and Foreign Language Courses
Founded: 1922
ISBN Publisher's Prefix: 0-85320

Lion Publishing, Aslan Publishing Services Ltd, Icknield Way, Tring, Herts Tel: Tring 5151 (STD code 044 282)
Man Dir: David S Alexander; *Editorial:* Pat Alexander; *Rights & Permissions:* Tony Wales; *Marketing Manager:* David Wavre
Subjects: Religion, Educational Materials
1978: 20 titles *1979:* 65 titles *Founded:* 1972
ISBN Publisher's Prefix: 0-85648

Litor Publishers, 45 Grand Parade, Brighton, East Sussex BN2 2QA Tel: Brighton 603254 (STD code 0273) Telex: 87369
Dir: Bengt Christiansen
Subjects: Encyclopaedias, Children's Books
ISBN Publisher's Prefix: 0-85322

Liverpool University Press, 123 Grove St, Liverpool L7 7AF Tel: (051) 709 3630/7303 Cable Add: Cormorant
Chairman of the Board: H R Parker; *Man Dir:* J G O'Kane; *Assistant Secretary, Sales & Promotion:* Mrs R P Campbell
Orders to: The Stonebridge Press, 823-25 Bath Road, Brislington, Bristol B54 5NU Tel: Bristol 775375 (STD code 0272)
Subjects: Architecture, Archaeology, Oriental Studies, Economics, Education, Philosophy, General & Social Science, Politics, History, Literature, Environmental Sciences, University Textbooks
Founded: 1899
ISBN Publisher's Prefix: 0-85323

Lloyd-Luke (Medical Books) Ltd, 49 Newman St, London W1P 4BX Tel: (01) 580 4255
Man Dir, Editorial, Production, Rights & Permissions: Douglas Luke; *Sales, Publicity:* Susan H Luke
Subject: Medical
1978: 5 titles *1979:* 8 titles *Founded:* 1951
ISBN Publisher's Prefix: 0-85324

Locomotive Publishing Co Ltd, an associate company of Ian Allan Ltd (qv)

Loeb Classical Library, an imprint of William Heinemann (International) Ltd (qv)

London Editions Ltd*, 9 Longacre, London WC2 Tel: (01) 379 6966 Cable Add: Lonedit London W12 Telex: 933855 Lonedi G
Chairman: David St John Thomas; *Man Dir:* Hugh Begg; *Sales Dir:* John Turner
Parent Company: David & Charles (Holdings) Ltd (qv)
Subjects: Art, Anthropology, Reference, Sports, History, Natural History
Founded: 1973
Miscellaneous: Firm designs and produces books for publication by other firms

London Magazine Editions, 30 Thurloe Pl, London SW7 Tel: (01) 589 0618/584 9682
Man Dir: Alan Ross; *Sales Dir, Rights & Permissions:* C Hawtrey
Subsidiary: 'London Magazine' (a monthly review of the contemporary arts)
Subjects: General Fiction, Belles Lettres, Poetry, Biography
Founded: 1965

Longbow, an imprint of W H Allen & Co Ltd (qv)

Longman Group Ltd, Longman House, Burnt Mill, Harlow, Essex Tel: Harlow 26721 (STD code 0279) Cable Add: Longman Harlow Telex: 81259
Shipping Add: Pinnacles, Harlow, Essex
Chairman: C R E Brooke; *Chief Exec:* T J Rix; *Sales Dir:* M G P Wymer; *Publicity:* Chris Kirby; *Foreign Rights:* Lynette Owen; *Permissions:* C Nelson
Branch Off: 5 Bentinck St, London W1M 5RN
Subsidiary Company: Construction Press Ltd (qv)
Associate Companies: Longman Cheshire Pty Ltd, Australia (qv); Armand Colin-Longman, France (qv); Langenscheidt-Longman GmbH, Federal Republic of Germany (qv); Longman Group (Far East) Ltd, Hong Kong (qv); Longman Italia Srl, Italy (qv); Longman Caribbean Ltd, Jamaica and Trinidad (qv); Longman Kenya Ltd, Kenya (qv); Longman Arab World Center, Lebanon (qv); Longman Malaysia Sdn Bhd, Malaysia (qv) and Singapore (qv); Wolters Noordhoff Longman BV, Netherlands (qv); Longman Paul Ltd, New Zealand (qv); Longman Nigeria Ltd, Nigeria (qv); Longman Publishers (Pvt) Ltd, Zimbabwe (qv); Longman Tanzania Ltd, Tanzania (qv); Longman Uganda Ltd, Uganda (qv); Allen Lane, UK (qv); Ladybird Books Ltd, UK (qv); Penguin Books Ltd, UK (qv); Longman Inc, 19 West 44th St, New York, NY 10036, USA
Francis Hodgson, Churchill Livingstone (qv) and Oliver & Boyd (qv), all UK, are Divisions of Longman Group Ltd; Collins-Longman Atlases, Glasgow, distributes atlases.
Imprint: Common Ground
Subjects: Biography, History, Children's Books, Dictionaries, Sociology, Education, Sciences, Geography, Travel, Educational Books
1978: 400 titles *Founded:* 1724
ISBN Publisher's Prefix: 0-582

Look-In Books, an imprint of Independent Television Books Ltd (qv)

Lorrimer Books, an imprint of L S P Books Ltd (qv)

Peter **Lowe**, an imprint of Eurobook Limited (qv)

Robson **Lowe** Ltd, 50 Pall Mall, London SW1Y 5JZ Tel: (01) 839 4034 Cable Add: Stamps London SW1 Telex: 915410
Man Dir: Alan Bosworth; *Publicity & Advertising:* Anne Lyon
Branch Offs: The Auction House, 39 Poole Hill, Bournemouth BH2 5PX, Dorset; Robson Lowe International, Via Dell'Orso 7a, 20121 Milan, Italy; Robson Lowe (Bermuda) Ltd, Harrington Sound, PO Box 88, Bermuda
Subjects: Philately, Postal History
1978: 4 titles *1979:* 8 titles *Founded:* 1920
ISBN Publisher's Prefix: 0-85397

Lucis Press Ltd, Suite 54, 3 Whitehall Court, London SW1A 2EF Tel: (01) 839 4512
Dirs: Mary Bailey, Jack Albert (both NY), J J G Bourne, Winifred H Brewin (both UK)
Subjects: Educational, Religious, Politics, Political Economy, Sociology, Questions of the Day, Philosophy
Associate Company: The Lucis Publishing Co, 866 United National Plaza, Suite 356-7, New York NY 10017, USA
ISBN Publisher's Prefix: 0-85330

Lund Humphries Publishers Ltd*, 26 Litchfield St, London WC2H 9NJ Tel: (01) 836 4243 Cable Add: Lundhumpub London WC2
Parent Company: A Zwemmer Ltd (qv) who also distribute for Lund Humphries
Subjects: Art, Architecture, Graphic Arts, Languages
1978: 12 titles
ISBN Publisher's Prefix: 0-85331

William **Luscombe**, an imprint of Mitchell Beazley London Ltd (qv)

Lutterworth Press, Luke House, Farnham Rd, Guildford, Surrey Tel: Guildford 77536/0 (STD code 0483) Cable Add: Lutteric Guildford Telex: 858623 Telburg
Man Dir: M E Foxell; *Sales Manager:* J R Sams; *Publicity Manager:* L J Folkes; *Rights & Permissions:* J Bunn
Subjects: Biography, History, How-to, Music, Philosophy, Reference, Religion, Juveniles, Paperbacks, General Science, Garden and Craft, Sport
1978: 35 titles *1979:* 47 titles *Founded:* 1932
ISBN Publisher's Prefix: 0-7188

Luxor Press, see Charles Skilton Ltd

Lyle Publications Ltd, Glenmayne, Galashiels, Selkirkshire TD1 3PT Tel: Galashiels 2005 (STD code 0896) Telex: 727195
Dirs: T Curtis, Annette Hogg
Subjects: How-to, Reference, Art, Directories, Antiques
ISBN Publisher's Prefix: 0-902921

Lythway Press Ltd, 93-100 Locksbrook Rd, Bath BA1 3HB Tel: Bath 331945 (STD code 0225) Telex: 449897
Man Dir: E Hudson (to whom all correspondence)
Associate Companies: Chivers Book Sales Ltd; Chivers Press Publishers (qv); Firecrest Publishing Ltd (qv)
Imprint: Lythway Large Print
Subjects: General Fiction, Mystery, Crime, Romance
1978: 52 titles *Founded:* 1972
ISBN Publisher's Prefix: 0-85046

The **M I T** Press*, 126 Buckingham Palace Rd, London SW1W 9SD Tel: (01) 730 9208/9 Cable Add: Chibooks Telex: 23933 Chibooks Ldn
Man Dir: Graham K Voaden; *Sales Dir:* Warren Bertram
Associate Companies: University of Chicago Press Ltd, Harvard University Press (both at above address)
Subjects: Biography, History, Music, Art, Philosophy, Reference, Paperbacks, Medicine, Psychology, Engineering, General & Social Science, Education
1978: 90 titles
Miscellaneous: Branch of MIT Press, Cambridge, Mass, USA
ISBN Publisher's Prefixes: 0-262 (MIT), 0-226 (University of Chicago), 0-674 (Harvard University Press)

M R P, see Motor Racing Publications Ltd

M T P Press Ltd, Falcon Ho, Cable St, Lancaster LA1 1PE Tel: Lancaster 68765 (STD code 0524) Telex: 65212
Man Dir: D G T Bloomer; *Managing Editor:* P M Lister; *Sales Dir:* C K Timms; *Production Manager:* M Clarke; *Rights & Permissions:* C K Timms
Parent Company: Kluwer Group, Netherlands (qv)
Subjects: Medicine, Psychology
1978: 35 titles *1979:* 47 titles *Founded:* 1969
ISBN Publisher's Prefix: 0-85200

M W H London Publishers*, 233 Seven Sisters Rd, London N4 2DA Tel: (01) 272 5170 Cable Add: Muslimdar London N4 Telex: 8812176 Muslim G
Man Dir: Ashur A Shamis
Associate Company: Muslim Information Services, UK
Subjects: Islamic and Arabic Studies
Bookshop: address as above
1978: 5 titles *1979:* 9 titles *Founded:* 1970
ISBN Publisher's Prefix: 0-906194

Macdonald, an imprint of Macdonald/Futura Publishers Ltd (qv)

Macdonald & Evans Ltd, Estover, Plymouth, Devon PL6 7PZ Tel: Plymouth 705251 (STD code 0752) Cable Add: MacEvans, Plymouth Telex: 45635
Man Dir: G B Davis, R B North; *Editorial:* D A F Sutherland; *Sales & Publicity:* G J Marshall
Subsidiary Companies: Continua

Productions Ltd; Macdonald & Evans (Publications) Ltd; Educational Book Promotions; Macdonald & Evans Distribution Services Ltd (all at Estover, Plymouth)
Subjects: Commercial, Professional & Business Studies, Dance & Movement, Geography, Language & Literature, Law, Science & Technology, Social Studies
1978: 85 titles *1979:* 76 titles *Founded:* 1907
ISBN Publisher's Prefix: 0-7121

Macdonald Educational Ltd, Holywell House, Worship St, London EC2A 2EN Tel: (01) 247 5499 Cable Add: Maced Ldn EC2 Telex: 885233
Man Dir: T V Boardman Jr; *Deputy Man Dir & Editorial Dir:* Stephen Pawley; *Sales Dir:* K E Pickett; *Rights & Permissions:* Jane Cholmeley; *Production Dir:* Philip Hughes; *Marketing Manager:* Derek Cross
Orders to: Macdonald Publishing Services (Paulton) Ltd, Paulton, Bristol, Avon BS18 5LQ
Parent Company: B P C Ltd (qv)
Associate Companies: Macdonald/Futura Publishers Ltd (qv for other UK associate companies); Macdonald (Middle East) Sarl, Holywell Ho, Worship St, London EC2; Macdonald Raintree Inc, 205 West Highland Ave, Milwaukee, Wisconsin 53203, USA; Macdonald Educational Australia Pty Ltd, 203 Drummond St, Carlton, Victoria 3053, Australia
Imprints: Macdonald, Macdonald Guidelines, Macdonald Starters, Macdonald 3/4/5
Subjects: Colour Information and Reference Books for pre-School, Primary, Middle and Secondary Schools; Adult Reference Books
1978: 107 titles *1979:* 129 titles *Founded:* 1971
ISBN Publisher's Prefix: 0-356

Macdonald/Futura Publishers Ltd, 8 Shepherdess Walk, London N1 7LW Tel: (01) 251 1666 Cable Add: Macjan Telex: 23168
Chairman: Ronald Whiting; *Man Dir:* Anthony Cheetham; *Marketing & Sales Dir:* David Rivers; *Editorial:* Carol O'Brien (Non-fiction), Rosemary Cheetham (Fiction), Nicholas Chapman (Paperback), Alan Smith (Queen Anne Press); *Production:* Victor Morrison; *Publicity:* Susan Lamb (Hardback), Judy Dobias (Paperback); *Rights & Permissions:* Pat James
Orders to: Macdonald Publishing Services (Paulton) Ltd, Nr Bristol, Avon BS18 5LQ; Futura Paperbacks: 110b Warner Rd, London SE5
Parent Company: B P C Ltd (qv)
Associate Companies: Adkinson Parrish Ltd (qv); Macdonald Educational Ltd (qv); Phoebus Publishing Co (qv); Purnell Books (qv)
Imprints: Ballantine, Futura, Macdonald, Orbit, Playfair, Queen Anne Press, Troubador (Hardback and Paperback)
Subjects: General Fiction and Non-fiction, Juveniles, Sport
1978: approx 160 titles *1979:* approx 180 titles *Founded:* 1980 (previously Macdonald & Jane's (founded 1973) and Futura Publications (founded 1973))
ISBN Publisher's Prefixes: 0-354 (Macdonald), 0-362 (Queen Anne Press), 0-7088 (Futura)

Macdonald Guidelines, Macdonald Starters, Macdonald 3/4/5, all imprints of Macdonald Educational Ltd (qv)

Macdonald Publishers (Edinburgh), Edgefield Rd, Loanhead, Midlothian EH20 9SY Tel: (031) 440 0246
Publishing Manager: Ian Burgham
Subjects: Biography, Criticism, Fiction, General Non-fiction, Children's Books, Poetry
ISBN Publisher's Prefix: 0-904265

McGraw-Hill Book Co (UK) Ltd, Shoppenhangers Rd, Maidenhead, Berkshire SL6 2QL Tel: Maidenhead 23431 (STD code 0628) Cable Add: McGrawHill Telex: 848484
Man Dir: Edward T Reilly; *Publishing Dir:* Margaret Tilling; *Rights & Permissions:* Lena Armstrong; *Marketing Dir:* Ian McIntyre
Parent Company: McGraw-Hill Inc, 1221 Ave of the Americas, New York, NY 10020, USA
Associate Companies: McGraw-Hill Book Co Australia Pty Ltd, Australia (qv); McGraw-Hill Ryerson Ltd, Canada; Editôra McGraw-Hill do Brasil Ltda, Brazil (qv); McGraw-Hill Inc, France (qv); McGraw-Hill Book Co GmbH, Federal Republic of Germany (qv); Tata McGraw-Hill Publishing Co Ltd, India (qv); McGraw-Hill Kogakusha Ltd, Japan; Libros McGraw-Hill de Mexico SA de CV, Mexico (qv); McGraw-Hill Book Co, New Zealand, Ltd, New Zealand (qv); Editorial McGraw-Hill Latinoamericana SA, Panama (qv); McGraw-Hill International Book Co, Singapore (qv); McGraw-Hill Book Co (SA) (Pty) Ltd, Republic of South Africa (qv); McGraw-Hill Book Co, Switzerland; McGraw-Hill de Espana SA, Spain; Editora McGraw-Hill, Portugal
Subjects: Reference, Medicine, Psychology, Engineering, General & Social Science, University, Secondary Textbooks, Educational Materials, Gregg Shorthand, Further Education
1979: 50 titles *1980:* approx 60 titles *Founded:* 1899
ISBN Publisher's Prefix: 0-07

Grant **McIntyre** Ltd, 31 Great Russell St, London WC1B 3PH Tel: (01) 631 4141, (01) 636 0648
Man Dir, Editorial: Grant McIntyre; *Sales Dir:* Henry Fryer; *Production, Publicity, Rights & Permissions:* Imogen Olsen
Orders to: Bemrose UK Ltd, Publishing Division, 90-91 Great Russell St, London WC1B 3PY
Parent Company: Bemrose UK Ltd, Wayzgoose Dr, Derby DE2 6XP
Associate Companies: See Bemrose UK Ltd entry
Subjects: Medical, Behavioural, Social Science
1980: 17 titles *Founded:* 1979
ISBN Publisher's Prefix: 0-86216

William **Maclellan***, 104 Hill St, Glasgow G3 6UA Tel: (041) 332 0727
Imprint: Embryo
Subjects: Art, Folklore, Poetry, Music, Travel, Philosophy, all with particular reference to Scotland
ISBN Publisher's Prefix: 0-85335

Macmillan Children's Books, 4 Little Essex St, London WC2R 3LF
Man Dir: Michael Wace
Miscellaneous: A Division of Macmillan Publishers Ltd (qv)

Macmillan Education Ltd, Houndmills, Basingstoke, Hampshire RG21 2XS Tel: Basingstoke 29242 (STD code 0256) Cable Add: Publish Basingstoke Telex: 858493
Chairman: N G Byam Shaw; *Man Dir:* S A Josephs; *Publishing Dirs:* R S Balkwill (Primary Schools & Educational Media); A S Feldmann (Secondary Schools); M J Thorrowgood (Overseas Schools); *Marketing Dir:* D Fothergill; *Dirs:* W S D Jollands (Special Education); C R Harrison (West Africa)
Parent Company: Macmillan Publishers Ltd (qv)
Subjects: Reference, Juveniles, Secondary & Primary Textbooks, Educational Materials
ISBN Publisher's Prefix: 0-333

Macmillan London Ltd, 4 Little Essex St, London WC2R 3LF Tel: (01) 836 6633
Cable Add: Publish London WC2
Telex: 262024
Shipping Add: Houndmills, Basingstoke, Hampshire RG21 2XS
Chairman: A D Maclean; *Man Dir:* Robert McKay; *Publishing Dirs:* Lord Hardinge (Crime & Suspense), Julian Ashby, Richard Garnett (Popular Illustrated and Production); *Rights & Permissions Dir:* Tess Sacco; *Marketing Dir:* Paul Richards; *Home Sales Manager:* Tim Hely-Hutchinson; *Publicity Manager:* Gillian Vincent
Parent Company: Macmillan Publishers Ltd (qv)
Subjects: General Fiction, Belles Lettres, Poetry, Biography, History, How-to, Reference, Juveniles, High-priced Paperbacks
ISBN Publisher's Prefix: 0-333

The **Macmillan Press** Ltd, 4 Little Essex St, London WC2R 3LF Tel: (01) 836 6633
Cable Add: Publish London WC2
Telex: 262024
Shipping Add: Houndmills, Basingstoke, Hampshire RG21 2XS
Man Dir: A Soar; *Sales:* Barry Turner; *Publicity Manager:* M Horsfield; *Publishing Dirs:* T M Farmiloe, T J Jackman; *European Sales:* J M Arnhard Aretz; *Rights Manager:* N Piggot
Parent Company: Macmillan Publishers Ltd (qv)
Subjects: College and University Textbooks, Monographs and Reference Books in Science, Technology, Medicine, Humanities, Social Sciences, English as a Foreign Language
1979: 533 titles
ISBN Publisher's Prefix: 0-333

Macmillan Publishers Ltd, 4 Little Essex St, London WC2R 3LF Tel: (01) 836 6633
Cable Add: Publish London WC2 Telex: 262024
Firm is a holding company
Man Dir: N G Byam Shaw
Orders to: Macmillan Distribution Ltd, Houndmills, Basingstoke, Hants
Parent Company: Macmillan Ltd
Associate Companies: The Macmillan Company of India Ltd India, (qv); Macmillan Nigeria Publishers Ltd, Nigeria (qv); The Northern Nigerian Publishing Co Ltd, Nigeria (qv)
Subsidiaries in the UK: Grove's Dictionaries of Music Ltd; Hospital and Social Service Publications Ltd; Macmillan Education Ltd (qv); Macmillan Journals Ltd; Macmillan London Ltd (qv); The Macmillan Press Ltd (qv)
Subsidiaries outside the UK: Gill & Macmillan Ltd, Republic of Ireland (qv); Grove's Dictionaries of Music Inc, USA; The Macmillan Co of Australia Pty Ltd, Australia (qv); Macmillan Publishers (HK) Ltd, Hong Kong (qv); Macmillan Shuppan, Japan; Macmillan Books for Africa, Kenya (only 40% owned); Macmillan South East Asia Private Ltd, Singapore (qv); Macmillan South Africa (Publishers) Pty Ltd, South Africa (qv); Peninsula Publishers Ltd, Hong Kong; St Martin's Press Inc, 175 Fifth Ave, New York, NY 10010, USA; The Macmillan

UNITED KINGDOM 391

Co of New Zealand Ltd, New Zealand
Branch Office outside the UK: PO Box 10722, Off Link Rd, Accra, Ghana

Julia **MacRae** Books, 8 Cork St, London W1X 2HA Tel: (01) 437 0713 Telex: 262655 Groluk
Man Dir: Julia MacRae; *Rights & Permissions:* Rosemary C Lister
Associate Company: Franklin Watts Ltd (qv)
Subjects: Juveniles, Picture Books
1980: 30 titles *Founded:* 1979
ISBN Publisher's Prefix: 0-86203

Made Simple Books, an imprint of W H Allen & Co Ltd (qv)

Magna Print Books, Skirden, Anna Lane, Bolton-by-Bowland, Clitheroe, Lancs BB7 4NZ Tel: Bolton-by-Bowland 243 (STD code 02007)
Man Dir, Production: Derek Cressey; *Sales:* Margaret Cressey
Parent Company: Library Magna Books Ltd
Imprint: Magna Large Print Series
Subjects: Fiction, Nonfiction, Handicrafts & Pastimes in Large Print
1978: 53 titles *Founded:* 1973
ISBN Publisher's Prefix: 0-86009

Magnum Books, 11 New Fetter Lane, London EC4P 4EE Tel: (01) 583 9855 Cable Add: Elegiacs London EC4 Telex: 263398
Chairman (Trade Division): Christopher Falkus; *Editorial Dir:* Ms Dot Houghton; *Marketing Dir:* Charles Shirley; *Production Dir:* Chris Holgate; *Art Dir:* Peter Bennet; *Publicity:* Nichola Wilson; *Rights & Permissions:* Ann Mansbridge
Miscellaneous: An imprint of Associated Book Publishers Ltd (qv)
ISBN Publisher's Prefix: 0-417

Mainstream Publishing Co (Edinburgh) Ltd, 28 Barony St, Edinburgh EH3 6NY Tel: (031) 556 9913
Dirs: Bill Campbell, Peter Mackenzie
Branch Off: 5 Glen St, Edinburgh EH3 9JD
Subjects: Literature, History, Current Affairs, Politics, General
1978: 3 titles *1979:* 4 titles *Founded:* 1978
ISBN Publisher's Prefix: 0-906391

Malaby Press, an imprint of J M Dent & Sons Ltd (qv)

Manchester University Press, Oxford Rd, Manchester M13 9PL Tel: (061) 273 5539
Publisher: J M N Spencer; *Editorial:* Ray Offord; *Marketing:* Clive Luhrs; *Rights & Permissions:* Miss S A Lawrence
Subjects: English Language and Literature, Modern Languages, History, Philosophy, Religion, Medicine, Psychology, Engineering, General & Social Science, Economics, Geography, University Textbooks
Founded: 1912
ISBN Publisher's Prefix: 0-7190

Mansell Publishing, 3 Bloomsbury Pl, London WC1A 2QA Tel: (01) 580 6784 Cable Add: Infoman London Telex: 28604 ref 1647
Man Dir: John E Duncan; *Editorial, Rights & Permissions:* Murray Mindlin; *Sales Manager:* June S Eaton; *Publicity & Advertising:* Catherine Johnston
Parent Company: Bemrose UK Ltd (qv for associate companies)
Subjects: Bibliographic Reference
1978: 26 titles *1979:* 37 titles *Founded:* 1966
ISBN Publisher's Prefix: 0-7201

Manxman Publications, an imprint of Shearwater Press Ltd, Isle of Man (qv)

Map Productions Ltd, see George Philip & Son Ltd

Marshall Cavendish Books Ltd, 58 Old Compton St, London W1V 5PA Tel: (01) 734 6710 Cable Add: Marcav London W1 Telex: 23880
Chairman: George Amy; *Man Dir:* Frank Marvin; *Publishing Dir:* Nicholas Evans; *Sales, Marketing Dir:* Tony Grabrovaz; *Production Dir:* Erik Pordes
Reference Set Rights: Jeremy Westwood; *Single Volume Book Rights:* Philip Costick
Parent Company: Marshall Cavendish Ltd (at above address)
Subsidary Company: Marshall Cavendish Corporation, 575 Lexington Ave, New York, NY 10022, USA
Associate Companies: Marshall Cavendish Partworks Ltd, Marshall Cavendish Children's Books Ltd, both at above address
Branch Off: Marshall Cavendish (Australia), Edgecliffe Centre, (5th Floor), 203-33 New South Head Rd, Edgecliffe, NSW 2027, Australia
Subjects: How-to, Reference, Partworks, General Science
1978: approx 80 titles *1979:* approx 90 titles
Founded: 1968
ISBN Publisher's Prefixes: 0-462, 0-85080, 0-85685

Marshall Editions Ltd, 71 Eccleston Sq, London SW1V 1PJ Tel: (01) 834 0785 Cable Add: Marsheds Telex: 22847 Marsh G
Man Dir & Editorial: Bruce Marshall; *Sales:* Barbara Anderson; *Production:* Hugh Stancliffe
Subjects: Highly-illustrated Non-fiction including Cookery, Travel, Wild Life, Photography, Interior Design, Homemaking, Medicine
1978: 3 titles *1979:* 5 titles

Marshall, Morgan & Scott Publications Ltd*, 1 Bath St, London EC1V 9LB Tel: (01) 251 2925
Warehouse: Unit 14, Trident Industrial Estate, Pindar Rd, Hoddesdon, Herts EN11 0LD
Chairman: Michael Raeburn; *Man Dir:* David A Payne; *Sales, Publicity & Advertising:* Noël Halsey; *Rights & Permissions:* Noël Halsey, David A Payne
Subsidiary Company: Samual Bagster & Sons Ltd (qv), Pilgrim Records
Imprints: include Keswick, Lakeland Paperbacks, Oliphants
Subjects: Religion, Hymns
1978: 32 titles *Founded:* 1859
Miscellaneous: Holding company is Pentos Ltd (qv)
ISBN Publisher's Prefix: 0-551

Marsland Press, an imprint of Volturna Press (qv)

Martin Books, an imprint of Woodhead-Faulkner (Publishers) Ltd (qv)

Martin Robertson & Co Ltd, 108 Cowley Rd, Oxford OX4 1JF Tel: Oxford 49109 (STD code 0865) Cable Add: Marcobooks Oxford
Production: Rowena Friedman; *Sales:* Norman Drake; *Editorial:* Michael Hay; *Promotion:* Sue Corbett
Orders to: Marston Book Services, PO Box 87, Oxford OX4 1LB
Parent Company: Basil Blackwell Publishers Ltd (qv)
Subjects: Social Sciences at Degree Level, Sociology, Politics, Public Administration, Economics, Social Policy, Criminology, Education, International Affairs
1978: 26 titles *1979:* 32 titles
ISBN Publisher's Prefix: 0-85520

Kenneth **Mason** Publications Ltd, Homewell, Havant, Hampshire PO9 1EE Tel: Havant 486262 (STD code 0705)
Man Dir: Kenneth Mason; *Dir:* Robert Anderson
Distributor: J M Dent & Sons Ltd
Subjects: Nautical, Leisure Activities, Licensing, Slimming Paperbacks
1978: 22 titles *1979:* 17 titles *Founded:* 1958
ISBN Publisher's Prefixes: 0-85937, 0-900534

Mayflower Books Ltd, see Granada Publishing Ltd

Kevin **Mayhew** Ltd, 55 Leigh Rd, Leigh-on-Sea, Essex SS9 1JP Tel: Southend-on-Sea 76425 (STD code 0702)
Man Dir, Production: Kevin Mayhew; *Editorial, Rights & Permissions:* Hugh McGinlay; *Sales, Publicity:* Anthony P Castle
Subjects: Popular Religious Liturgy, Music, Theology, Educational
1978: 20 titles *1979:* 25 titles *Founded:* 1976
ISBN Publisher's Prefix: 0-905725

Mayhew-McCrimmon Ltd, 10-12 High St, Great Wakering, Essex Tel: Southend-on-Sea 218956 (STD code 0702)
Man Dir: Joan McCrimmon; *Sales Manager:* Sylvia McDonald
Associate Companies: Celebration Records; Rainbow Books; House of McCrimmon
Subjects: Religion, Primary & Secondary Textbooks, Educational Materials, Music, Prayer Books, Liturgy, Hymn Books
1979: 200 titles *Founded:* 1968
ISBN Publisher's Prefix: 0-85597

Meadowfield Press Ltd, ISA Bldg, Dale Rd Industrial Estate, Shildon, Co Durham DL4 2QZ Tel: Morpeth 55860 (STD code 0670)
Man Dir: J Gordon Cook
Associate Company: Merrow Publishing Co Ltd (qv)
Subjects: Technical, Scientific, Academic

The **Medici** Society Ltd, 34-42 Pentonville Rd, London N1 9HG Tel: (01) 837 7099 Cable Add: Medici N1
Man Dir: J Gurney; *Rights & Permissions, Art Dir:* H B Jane
Subjects: Art, Juveniles
Bookshops: The Medici Galleries, 7 Grafton St, London W1 3LA; 26 Thurloe St, London SW7 2LT; 63 Bold St, Liverpool L1 4HP
1980: 5 titles *Founded:* 1908
ISBN Publisher's Prefix: 0-85503

Melbourne House (Publishers) Ltd, 24 Red Lion St, London WC1R 4PX Tel: (01) 405 6347 Telex: 28257 Octabs
Dir & Publisher: Alfred Milgrom; *Rights & Permissions:* Naomi Besen
Orders to: Pandemic Ltd (address as above)
Subjects: General Fiction and Non-fiction
1978: 2 titles *1979:* 20 titles *Founded:* 1978
ISBN Publisher's Prefix: 0-86161

Melrose Press Ltd, 17-21 Churchgate St, Soham, Ely, Cambs CB7 5DS Tel: Ely 721091 (STD code 0353) Cable Add: Melrosepres Ely Telex: 81584
Man Dir: Robert Rayner; *Editorial:* Patricia J McClatchie; *Sales:* Roger W G Curtis; *Production:* Nicholas S Law
Imprint: International Biographical Centre
Subject: Reference
1978: 6 titles *1979:* 5 titles *Founded:* 1969
ISBN Publisher's Prefix: 0-900332

Mentor, an imprint of New English Library Ltd (qv)

Mercat Press, 53-59 South Bridge, Edinburgh EH1 1YS Tel: (031) 556 6743 Cable Add: Bookman Edinburgh
Joint Man Dirs: James Thin, Ainslie Thin
Parent Company: James Thin Ltd (at above address)
Subsidiary Company: Melven Press (at above address)

Associate Company: Melven Bookshop Ltd, 60 Fountainhall Rd, Edinburgh EH9 2LP
Subjects: Scottish
Bookshops: Melven, 29 Union St, Inverness; Melven, 176 High St, Perth; Melven, The Centre, Aviemore
1978: 10 titles *1979:* 7 titles *Founded:* 1970
ISBN Publisher's Prefix: 0-901824

The **Merlin** Press Ltd, 3 Manchester Rd, London E14 Tel: (01) 987 7959
Man Dir: Martin Eve
Imprint: Seafarer Books
Subjects: History, Economics, Philosophy, Political & Social Science
Book Club: Merlin Book Club
Founded: 1956
ISBN Publisher's Prefix: 0-85036

Charles E **Merrill** Publishing Co, Alperton Ho, Bridgewater Rd, Wembley, Middlesex Tel: (01) 902 8812 Cable Add: Behow Wembley Telex: 261378
Sales, Advertising, Publicity, Rights & Permissions: Paul Poynton
Parent Company: Charles E Merrill Publishing Co, 1300 Alum Creek Drive, Columbus, Ohio, USA
Subjects: Education, Educational Psychology, Special Education, Technology, Social Sciences, Business & Economics, Science, Communication & Speech, Mathematics, Multi-media Programmes
1979: 80 titles *1980:* approx 80 titles
Founded: 1842
ISBN Publisher's Prefix: 0-675

The **Merrion** Press, 16 Groveway, London SW9 0AR Tel: (01) 735 7791 & 733 5173
Partners: Montague & Susan Shaw
Subjects: Finely produced books on English Literature, Printing, Calligraphy, Fine Arts
ISBN Publisher's Prefix: 0-903560

Merrow Publishing Co Ltd, ISA Bldg, Dale Rd Industrial Estate, Shildon, Co Durham DL4 2QZ Tel: Morpeth 55860 (STD code 0670)
Man Dir: J Gordon Cook
Associate Company: Meadowfield Press Ltd (qv)
Subjects: Technical, Scientific, Academic
ISBN Publisher's Prefixes: 0-900541, 0-904095

Metal Bulletin Books Ltd*, Park House, Park Terrace, Worcester Park, Surrey KT4 7HY Tel: (01) 330 4311 Cable Add: Metalbul Worcester Park Telex: 21383 Metbul-G
Man Dir: T J Tarring; *Sales & Advertising Dir:* B R Orbell; *Editorial Dir:* R P Cordero
Branch Offs: 45/46 Lower Marsh, London SE1 7RG; 708 Third Ave, New York, NY 10017, USA
Subjects: Steel and Metal Industries, Industrial Minerals
1978: 9 titles *Founded:* 1937

Methodist Publishing House, Wellington Rd, Wimbledon, London SW19 8EU Tel: (01) 947 5256/9 Cable Add: Metodico, London SW19 8EU
General Manager, Rights & Permissions: Albert M Jakeway; *Sales Manager:* Paul Mansbridge; *Publicity Manager:* David W Hirst
Imprint: Epworth Press
Subjects: Religion, History, Archaeology, Biography, Memoirs, Philosophy, Directories
1978: 16 titles *1979:* 26 titles *Founded:* 1733
ISBN Publisher's Prefixes: 0-7150, 0-7162, 0-7192, 0-901027

Methuen & Co Ltd, 11 New Fetter Lane, London EC4P 4EE Tel: (01) 583 9855 Cable Add: Elegiacs London EC4 Telex: 263398
Man Dir: John Naylor; *Editorial:* Janice Price; *Sales:* Peter Shepherd; *Production:* Carol Somerset; *Publicity:* Lyndsay Williams; *Rights & Permissions:* Vicki Anderson
Orders to: Associated Book Publishers Ltd, North Way, Andover, Hampshire SP10 5BE
Parent Company: Associated Book Publishers Ltd (qv)
Subjects: Academic
ISBN Publisher's Prefix: 0-416

Methuen Children's Books Ltd, 11 New Fetter Lane, London EC4P 4EE Tel: (01) 583 9855 Cable Add: Elegiacs, London EC4P 4EE Telex: 263398
Chairman: Christopher Falkus; *Man Dir:* Marilyn Malin; *Sales:* David Ross; *Production:* Christopher Holgate; *Publicity:* John Mason; *Rights & Permissions:* Rosalind Nell
Orders to: Associated Book Publishers Ltd, North Way, Andover, Hampshire SP10 5BE Tel: Andover 62141 (STD code 0264) Cable Add: APT Andover Telex: 47214
Parent Company: Associated Book Publishers Ltd (qv)
Subjects: Juveniles, Fiction & Nonfiction
1978: approx 98 titles *1979:* approx 105 titles
ISBN Publisher's Prefix: 0-416

Methuen/Walker Books, see Walker Books Ltd

Maurice **Michael**, Partridge Green, Horsham, West Sussex Tel: Horsham 710412 (STD code 0403) Cable Add: Bartolo Horsham Telex: 912881 Bartolo
Publisher: Maurice Michael
Subjects: Military, Gardening, Sport, Cookery, Co-editions, Illustrated History
1978: 4 titles

Michelin Tyre Co Ltd, Maps & Guides Dept, 81 Fulham Rd, London SW3 6RD Tel: (01) 589 1460 Cable Add: Pneumicilin London Telex: 919071
Sales Manager: E G Whiston
Associate Company: Michelin et Cie (Services de Tourisme), France (qv)
Subjects: Guides (Tourist, Hotel & Restaurant), Maps
ISBN Publisher's Prefixes: 0-206, 0-392

Midas Books, 12 Dene Way, Speldhurst, Tunbridge Wells, Kent TN3 0NX Tel: Langton 2860 (STD code 089286)
Man Dir: Ian Morley-Clarke; *Editorial:* Kathleen Morley-Clarke, William Eden, Robert Hardcastle; *Production:* Raymond Green, Eric Hardisty
Subsidiary Company: Buildtay Ltd, address as above
Subjects: Militaria, Leisure, Sport, Social History, Biography, Music, Guides, Collectors' Library Series, Art, Craft Library Series
1978: 24 titles *1979:* 22 titles *Founded:* 1973
ISBN Publisher's Prefix: 0-85936

J Garnet **Miller** Ltd, 129 St John's Hill, London SW11 1TD Tel: (01) 228 8091
Man Dir: J G F Miller
Subsidiary Company: Steele's Play Bureau
Subjects: Music, Drama, Juveniles, General Science
Founded: 1951
ISBN Publisher's Prefix: 0-85343

Harvey **Miller** Publishers, 20 Marryat Rd, London SW19 5BD Tel: (01) 946 4426
Publishers: Mrs Elly Miller, Harvey Miller
Orders to: Heyden & Son Ltd, Spectrum House, Hillview Gardens, London NW4 2JQ Tel: (01) 203 5171
Subject: History of Art
1978: 2 titles *1979:* 2 titles
Miscellaneous: Publishers of *Courtauld Institute Illustration Archives*
ISBN Publisher's Prefix: 0-905203

Millington Books, an imprint of Davison Publishing Ltd (qv)

Mills & Boon Ltd*, 17-19 Foley St, London W1A 1DR Tel: (01) 580 9074/0 Cable Add: Millsator London W1 Telex: 24420
Chairman: J T Boon; *Man Dir:* P J Scherer; *Editorial:* Alan Boon, Heather Jeeves, Michael Stephenson, Frances Whitehead; *Export:* N S Boon; *Publicity & Advertising:* G Britton; *Rights & Permissions:* Deborah Burgess
Subsidiary Companies: Allman & Son (Publishers) Ltd (at above address); Mills & Boon Pty Ltd, Suite 404, 282 Victoria Ave, Chatswood, NSW 2067, Australia
Imprints: include Owlet
Subjects: General Fiction, History, How-to, Music, Art, Reference, Religion, Low-priced Paperbacks, General Science, Secondary & Primary Textbooks
Founded: 1908
Miscellaneous: Distribution by Distribution & Management Services, Sheldon Way, Larkfield, Kent
ISBN Publisher's Prefix: 0-263

The **Minerva** Press Ltd, 44 Great Russell St, London WC1B 3PA Tel: (01) 580 7200
Subjects: Natural History, Art & Architecture, General Children's Books, Oriental, Travel & Adventure, General Literature
ISBN Publisher's Prefix: 0-85636

Mirror Books Ltd, Athene Ho, 66-73 Shoe Lane, London EC4P 4AB Tel: (01) 353 0246 Cable Add: Mirror London EC1 Telex: 27286
Man Dir: Peter K Robins; *Editorial, Rights & Permissions:* Michael Glover, Anthony Finn; *Sales:* Gerry Bolt; *Production:* Bernard Smith; *Publicity:* James Hole
Parent Company: Mirror Group Newspapers Ltd
Subjects: General
1978: 50 titles *1979:* 50 titles
ISBN Publisher's Prefix: 0-85939

Mitchell Beazley London Ltd, Artists House, 14-15 Manette St, London W1V 5LB Tel: (01) 434 3272 Telex: 24892
Man Dir, Rights & Permissions: Ken Banerji; *Marketing Dir:* David Hight; *Publicity:* Belinda Harley
Imprints: Emblem, William Luscombe, Artists House
Subjects: General Books, Encyclopaedias, Dictionaries, Atlases, Practical Books, High-priced Paperbacks
1978: 88 titles *1979:* approx 50 titles
Founded: 1969
ISBN Publisher's Prefixes: 0-85533 (Mitchell Beazley), 0-86002 (William Luscombe), 0-86134 (Artists House)

Model & Allied Publications Ltd, 13-35 Bridge St, Hemel Hempstead, Hertfordshire HP1 1EE Tel: Hemel Hempstead 41221 (STD code 0442)
Subjects: Modelling, Hobbies, Leisure Interests
Miscellaneous: An imprint of Argus Books Ltd (qv)
ISBN Publisher's Prefixes: 0-85076, 0-85242, 0-85344

Modern Transport, an imprint of Ian Allan Ltd (qv)

The **Molendinar** Press, 16 Laurel St, Glasgow G11 7QR Tel: (041) 334 8540 Cable Add: Greenleaf Glasgow
Rights & Trade Enquiries: Richard Drew
Subjects: Leisure, General Interest, Fiction, Humour, Sport
1980: 20 titles

Monthly Review Press, 47 Red Lion St, London WC1R 4PF Tel: (01) 242 3501
Publisher: Jules Geller
Subjects: University, Commercial & Technical Education, Politics, Social Science
1980: 25 titles
ISBN Publisher's Prefix: 0-85345

Moonlight Publishing, an imprint of Christine and Robin Baker, c/o Mitchell Beazley London Ltd (qv)

Moonraker Press, 26 St Margarets St, Bradford-on-Avon, Wiltshire Tel: Bradford-on-Avon 3469 (STD code 02216)
Man Dir, Sales, Publicity & Advertising, Rights & Permissions: Anthony Adams
Subjects: Biography, History, Reference
Founded: 1975
ISBN Publisher's Prefix: 0-239

Moorland Publishing Company Ltd, PO Box 2, Ashbourne, Derbyshire DE6 1DE Tel: Ashbourne 5086 (STD code 03355)
Editorial Dir, Production: Dr J A Robey; *Sales, Publicity, Rights & Permissions:* C L M Porter
Subjects: History, Geography, General Nonfiction, Railways, Natural History, Architecture
1978: 11 titles *1979:* 17 titles *Founded:* 1972
ISBN Publisher's Prefixes: 0-903485, 0-086190

Morgan-Grampian Book Publishing Co Ltd*, 30 Calderwood St, Woolwich, London SE18 6QH Tel: (01) 855 7777
Subjects: Reference, Directories
ISBN Publisher's Prefix: 0-900865

Motive, an imprint of Allison & Busby Ltd (qv)

Motor Racing Publications Ltd, 28 Devonshire Rd, Chiswick, London W4 2HD Tel: (01) 994 6783
Man Dir, Editorial, Publicity, Rights & Permissions: John Blunsden; *Sales:* Bryan Kennedy; *Production:* Jim Starr
Associate Company: Connoisseur Carbooks (address as above)
Imprint: MRP
Branch Offs: (Editorial and Promotion) 56 Fitzjames Ave, Croydon, Surrey CR0 5DD; (Production) 1530 London Rd, Norbury, London SW16 4EU Tel: (01) 679 7358
Subjects: Motor Racing and Rallying, Racing Car Design, Motoring History including Cars, Trucks and Motorcycles
1978: 3 titles *1979:* 5 titles *Founded:* 1948
ISBN Publisher's Prefix: 0-900549

A R **Mowbray** & Co Ltd, St Thomas Ho, Becket St, Oxford OX1 1SJ Tel: Oxford 42507 (STD code 0865)
Shipping Add: Dent Distribution Ltd, Dunhams Lane, Letchworth, Herts SG6 1LF
Man Dir: K B Baker; *Sales Dir:* Eva Jesse; *Rights & Permissions:* S Davidson
Subjects: History, Philosophy, Reference, Religion, Juveniles, Low- & High-priced Paperbacks, Social Science, University Textbooks
Bookshops: 28 Margaret St, Oxford Circus, London W1N 7LB; 8-10 Cambridge Terrace, Oxford; 14 King's Parade, Cambridge; St Martins, The Bull Ring, Birmingham
1978: 37 titles *1979:* 35 titles *Founded:* 1858
ISBN Publisher's Prefix: 0-264

Frederick **Muller** Ltd, Victoria Works, Edgware Rd, London NW2 6LE Tel: (01) 450 2566 Cable Add: Efmull London NW2
Man & Marketing Dir: Antony White; *Dir:* M A A Baig; *Editorial, Rights & Permissions Dir:* Andrew Mylett (*Foreign Rights* (Blond & Briggs): Rosemarie Buckman, Ryman's Cottage, Little Tew, Oxon); *Publicity:* Johanna Fawkes
Subsidiary Companies and Imprints: Muller Educational; Blond & Briggs Ltd
Subjects: Biography, History, How-to, Reference, Juveniles, Science & Technology, Secondary & Primary Schoolbooks, Fiction, Collectors, General, Natural History, Occult, Music, Horticulture
1979: 40 titles *1980:* 51 titles *Founded:* 1933
ISBN Publisher's Prefixes: 0-584 (Muller), 0-85634 (Blond & Briggs)

Munch Bunch, an imprint of Studio Publications (Ipswich) Ltd (qv)

Thomas **Murby** & Co, 40 Museum St, London WC1A 1LU Tel: (01) 405 8577
Cable Add: Deucalion, London WC1A 1LU
Orders to: Park Lane, Hemel Hempstead, Hertfordshire HP2 4TE Tel: Hemel Hempstead 3244 (STD code 0442)
Parent Company: George Allen & Unwin (Publishers) Ltd (qv)
Subjects: Technical & Scientific, Geology
ISBN Publisher's Prefix: 0-04

Donald **Murray** (Ramboro Books), 6 Highbury Corner, London N5 1RD Tel: (01) 609 3091/2
Subjects: Children's Books, Dictionaries, Art, Cookery
Miscellaneous: Also Remainder Dealers

John **Murray** (Publishers) Ltd, 50 Albemarle St, London W1X 4BD Tel: (01) 493 4361
Cable Add: Guidebook London W1 Telex: 21312 Murray G
Man Dir: Kenneth Foster; *Editorial:* John G Murray, Simon Young, Roger Hudson, Mrs Leeston; *Educational Marketing Dir:* Nick Perren; *Sales Dir:* John R Murray; *Sales Manager:* John Harbour; *Publicity & Advertising:* John Gammons; *Rights & Permissions:* Valerie Ripley
Subjects: General Fiction, Travel, Aviation, Nautical, Poetry, Biography, History, Architecture, Music, Art, Craft, Philosophy, Religion, Reference, Juveniles, Low- & High-priced Paperbacks, General Science, Textbooks, *Easy Readers*, *Success Study Books* series
1978: 93 titles *1979:* approx 90 titles
Founded: 1768
ISBN Publisher's Prefix: 0-7195

Murrays Childrens Books, a subsidiary of Brown Watson Ltd (qv)

Murrays Remainder Books Ltd*, 146-152 Holloway Rd, London N7 Tel: (01) 609 1234 Cable Add: Goldex London N7 Telex: 261670
Shipping Add: 11 Benwell Rd, London N7
Man Dir: Peter Kite
Parent Company: Howard & Wyndham Ltd (qv)
Associate Companies: W H Allen & Co Ltd (qv); Brown Watson Ltd (qv); Murrays Childrens Books
Imprints: Abbey, Castle, Goldex, Rex
Subjects: Belles Lettres, Poetry, Music, Art, Reference, Juveniles, *Treasure Hour* Books
Founded: 1954
Miscellaneous: Firm's main activity is as Remainder Dealer

Music Sales Ltd, see Book Sales Ltd

Muslim Welfare House, see M W H London Publishers

N A G Press, an imprint of Northwood Books (qv)

N C C Publications, The National Computing Centre Ltd, Oxford Rd, Manchester M1 7ED Tel: (061) 228 6333 Telex: 668962
Man Dir: G E Hall; *Publicity:* M Bridge
Orders to: J M Dent & Sons (Distribution) Ltd, Dunhams Lane, Letchworth, Herts SG6 1LF
Subjects: Secondary & University Textbooks, Educational Materials on Computing and allied subjects
1979: 90 titles *Founded:* 1971
ISBN Publisher's Prefix: 0-85012

N E L, an imprint of New English Library (qv)

N F E R Publishing Co Ltd*, Darville Ho, 2 Oxford Rd East, Windsor, Berkshire SL4 1DF Tel: Windsor 69345 (STD code 07535)
Man Dir: A Yates; *Manager, Publications Dept:* J K Sansom
Subjects: Education, Special Education, Social Sciences, Psychology, Educational Materials
1978: approx 22 titles *Founded:* 1970
ISBN Publisher's Prefixes: 0-85633, 0-901225

N K I Educational Services Ltd, 33 Market Place, Dereham, Norfolk NR19 2AP Tel: Dereham 5710 (STD code 0362)
Man Dir: Alan N Kershaw
Parent Company: NKI Foundation, Norway (qv)
Subjects: Engineering, Technology
Founded: 1980
ISBN Publisher's Prefix: 0-907244

National Christian Education Council, Robert Denholm Ho, Nutfield, Redhill, Surrey RH1 4HW Tel: Nutfield Ridge 2411 (STD code 073 782)
General Secretary: Rev G R Chapman; *Publicity:* Eric A Thorn
Subjects: Primary, Secondary, Education, Religion, Maps & Atlases, Music, Bible Reading Guides, Pictures
Subsidiary Companies: Denholm House Press, International Bible Reading Association
1978-79: 40 titles
ISBN Publisher's Prefixes: 0-7197 (National Christian Council), 0-85213 (Denholm House)

National Computing Centre, see NCC

National Council for Voluntary Organizations, see Bedford Square Press

National Foundation for Educational Research in England & Wales, see NFER

National Magazine Co Ltd, National Magazine Ho, 72 Broadwick St, London W1V 2BP Tel: (01) 439 7144 Cable Add: Shanmag, London W1 Telex: 263879
Man Dir: Marcus Morris; *Publisher:* Roger Barrett; *Editorial:* Robert Smith; *Advertising, Rights & Permissions:* Tim Whale
Orders to: Michael Joseph Limited, 44 Bedford Sq, London WC1 3DU
Subjects: General Non-fiction, How-to, Reference
1979: 20 titles
Miscellaneous: Books are published under the imprints of The Connoisseur and Ebury Press
ISBN Publisher's Prefixes: 0-85223 (Ebury Press), 0-900305 (The Connoisseur)

National Portrait Gallery (Publications Dept), 2 St Martins Place, London WC2H 0HE Tel: (01) 930 1552
Deputy Director, Head of Publications: Richard Ormond; *Editorial, Production:* Mary Pettman; *Publications Manager:* Roger Sheppard; *Publicity, Rights & Permissions:* Judith Prendergast
Subjects: Art (particularly portraits in the Gallery), Reference
1978: 4 titles *1979:* 5 titles *Founded:* 1976 (book publishing division)
ISBN Publisher's Prefix: 0-904017

394 UNITED KINGDOM

National Trust Children's Series, an imprint of Dinosaur Publications Ltd (qv)

Natural History Museum, see British Museum (National History)

Nautical Publishing Co Ltd, Nautical House, Lymington, Hampshire SO4 9BA Tel: Lymington 72578 (STD code 0590) Telex: 47674
Man & Sales Dir: Commander Erroll Bruce; *Publicity Dir:* Richard Creagh-Osborne; *Advertising Dir:* Sir Peter Johnson Bt
Associate Companies: United Nautical Publishers SA, Basle, Switzerland; George Harrap & Co Ltd (qv)
Subjects: Sailing, Nautical Subjects, Maritime History, Pilotage, Navigation, Design and Construction
1978: 12 titles *Founded:* 1967
ISBN Publisher's Prefix: 0-245

Thomas **Nelson** & Sons Ltd, Nelson House, Mayfield Rd, Walton-on-Thames, Surrey KT12 5PL Tel: Walton-on-Thames 46133 (STD code 09322, from London 96) Cable Add: Thonelson Walton-on-Thames Telex: 929365
Man Dir: John G Jermine; *Assistant Man Dirs:* David R Worlock (Publishing), Roger Pudney (Marketing); *Rights & Permissions:* Allan Ramsay
Subsidiary Companies: Thomas Nelson (Australia) Ltd, Australia (qv); Thomas Nelson & Sons (Canada) Ltd, 81 Curlew Dr, Don Mills, Ontario, Canada; Thomas Nelson (Nigeria) Ltd, Nigeria (qv)
Subjects: History, Reference, Religion, High-priced Paperbacks, Engineering, General & Social Science, Medicine, Psychology, University, Secondary & Primary Textbooks, Educational Materials, English Language Teaching
1978: 288 titles *1979:* 311 titles *Founded:* 1798
Miscellaneous: Company is part of Nelson International Inc, a member of the International Thomson Organization Ltd (Canada)
ISBN Publisher's Prefix: 0-17

New Cavendish Books, 50 Porchester Terrace, London W2 Tel: (01) 262 4905
Publisher: Allen Levy
Subjects: Toys (history & collection), Mechanical Antiquities, Models, 19th and 20th Century Art and Technology
Founded: 1973

New Caxton Library Service Ltd, Premier House, 150 Southampton Row, London WC1B 5AL Tel: (01) 837 4145
Man Dir: P J Kinden
Parent Company: BPC Ltd (qv)
Subjects: University, Secondary & Primary Textbooks, English Dictionaries, Reference Books, Maps & Atlases, Juveniles, History, Archaeology, Biography & Memoirs, Encyclopaedias
ISBN Publisher's Prefix: 0-903322

New City, London, 57 Twyford Ave, London W3 9PZ Tel: (01) 992 7666
Chairman, Editorial: D Bregant; *Sales, Production, Publicity, Rights & Permissions:* R van Geffen
Associate Company: Citta Nuova Editrice, Italy (qv for other Associates)
Subjects: Christian Concerns, Spirituality, Witness, Ecumenism
1978: 3 titles *1979:* 4 titles *Founded:* 1958
ISBN Publisher's Prefix: 0-904287

New Educational Press, an imprint of Artemis Press Ltd (qv)

The **New English Library** Ltd*, Barnard's Inn, Holborn, London EC1N 2JR Tel: (01) 242 0767 Cable Add: Nelpublish Telex: 21924
(Trade Counters: (Hardcover) The Airfield, Norwich Rd, Mendlesham, Suffolk; (Paperbacks) Fulham Wharf, Townmead Rd, London SW6)
Man Dir: T R D'Cruz; *Sales Dirs:* D F Morse, J B O'Leary; *Rights & Permissions:* M Pachnos
Parent Company: The Times Mirror Co, Times Mirror Sq, Los Angeles, Calif 90053, USA
Associate Companies: New American Library Inc; Harry N Abrams Inc (both New York, USA)
Imprints: NEL, Mentor, Plume
Subjects: General Fiction & Nonfiction, Art, Biography, Classics, Paperbacks
Founded: 1957
ISBN Publisher's Prefix: 0-450

New Leaf Books Ltd, 38 Camden Lock, Chalk Farm Rd, London NW1 8AF Tel: (01) 267 6183 Cable Add: Nuleaf London NW1 Telex: 261507 Ref 3228
Man Dir: Michael Wright
Subjects: Highly Illustrated Practical, Reference and General Books (International Co-editions)
Founded: 1973

New Left Books, 7 Carlisle St, London W1 Tel: (01) 437 3546
also Verso Editions
Orders to: IBD, 66 Wood Lane End, Hemel Hempstead, Herts HP2 4RG
Subjects: Philosophy, History, Economics, Politics, Aesthetics, Psychology, Sociology
1978: 16 titles *1979:* 9 titles
ISBN Publisher's Prefixes: 0-902308, 0-86091

New Portway, an imprint of Chivers Press Publishers (qv)

New University Education, an imprint of Clive Bingley Ltd (qv)

Newnes Books, an imprint of Hamlyn Publishing Group Ltd (qv)

Newnes-Butterworths, an imprint of Butterworth & Co (qv)

Newnes-Technical, an imprint of Butterworth & Co (qv)

Robert **Nicholson** Publications Ltd, 93 St Peter's St, St Albans, Hertfordshire AL1 3EH Tel: St Albans 30121 (STD code 0727) Telex: 261212
Man Dir: Graham Lane; *Sales & Marketing Dir:* Colin Tagg
Parent Company: Geographia Ltd (qv)
Subjects: Maps and Guides
ISBN Publisher's Prefix: 0-90

Nile & Mackenzie Ltd, 43 Dover St, London W1 Tel: (01) 493 0351 Cable Add: Nilemac Telex: 8954665 Gits G (Nilemac)
Man Dir: D S Sehbai; *Rights & Permissions:* Penelope Carreau
Subjects: Reference, Juveniles, Educational Materials
Founded: 1974

James **Nisbet** & Co Ltd, Digswell Pl, Welwyn, Hertfordshire AL8 7SX Tel: Welwyn Garden 25491/3 (STD code 096) Cable Add: Stebsin, Welwyn Garden City
Chairman: G H B McLean
Subjects: Dictionaries, Economics, University, Secondary & Primary Textbooks, Education
Founded: 1810
ISBN Publisher's Prefix: 0-7202

The **Nonesuch** Library, see The Bodley Head Ltd

Norfolk Press*, 52 Manchester St, London W1M 6DR Tel: (01) 935 3441/3481
Man Dir: Raymond Holdsworth
Subjects: Religion, Philosopy, History, Literature, Outdoor Life
Founded: 1969
ISBN Publisher's Prefix: 0-85211

Jill **Norman** Ltd, 90 Great Russell St, London WC1B 3PY Tel: (01) 631 4141 Telex: 262284 Ref 3747
Man Dir: Jill Norman; *Publicity:* HPR Publicity, 9 Fitzroy Sq, London W1 (Tel: (01) 388 2613)
Orders to: J M Dent & Sons Ltd, Dunhams Lane, Letchworth, Hertfordshire SG6 1LF
Parent Company: Bemrose UK Ltd (qv for associate companies)
Subjects: Politics, History, Social History, Medicine, Psychology, Travel, Cookery, Handbooks
Founded: 1979
ISBN Publisher's Prefix: 0-906908

North Light, an imprint of Van Nostrand Reinhold Co Ltd (qv)

Northwood Books, 93-99 Goswell Rd, London EC1V 7QA Tel: (01) 253 9355 Telex: 21746
Man Dir: William Heaps; *Publisher, Sales, Rights & Permissions:* Douglas Westland; *Editorial:* Diana Briscoe; *Production:* Helen McKay; *Publicity:* Susan Hunt
Parent Company: Thomson Organization Ltd, Elm Ho, Elm St, London WC1X 0BP
Associate Companies: Northwood Publications Ltd; N A G Press Ltd (at above address)
Imprint: N A G Press
Subjects: Horology, Gemmology, Precious Metals, Catering and Hotel Management, Brewing, Building and Construction, Electronics, Medicine, Printing and Graphic Arts, Meat Trades
1978: 18 titles *1979:* 25 titles *Founded:* 1954
ISBN Publisher's Prefix: 0-7198

Nova Hrvatska Ltd, 30 Fleet St, London EC4Y 1AJ Tel: (01) 947 0498 Telex: 896616 Sendit G Nova Hrvatska
Man Dir: J Kusan; *Sales Dir:* G Saganic
Subjects: Joint publishers with Hrvatska Revija of Munich and Barcelona of: Secondary Textbooks, Educational Materials, Memoirs. Also *Hrvatska Revija* (quarterly literary review), *Nova Hrvatska* (Fortnightly current affairs magazine)
1978: 15 titles *Founded:* 1959
Miscellaneous: Publishers of reprinted *Croatian Orthography* and *Croatian Grammar* (Zagreb editions)

Novello & Co Ltd, Borough Green, Sevenoaks, Kent TN15 8DT Tel: Borough Green 883261 (STD code 0732) Cable Add: Novellos Sevenoaks
Man Dir: G Rizza; *Sales Manager:* S W Freeman; *Publicity & Advertising Manager:* J Woodmason; *Rights & Permissions:* B Axcell
Subject: Music
1978: 4 titles

Oasis Books, 12 Stevenage Rd, London SW6 6ES Tel: (01) 736 5059
Man Dir: Ian Robinson
Subjects: General Fiction, Poetry, Literature, Translations, Periodical *Oasis*
1978: 10 titles *1979:* 7 titles *Founded:* 1969
ISBN Publisher's Prefix: 0-903375

The **Octagon** Press Ltd, 14 Baker St, London W1M 1DA Tel: (089 286) 2045 Cable Add: Octapress London W1
Man Dir: Sally Mallam
Subjects: General Fiction, Philosophy, Religion, Psychology
1978: 37 titles
ISBN Publisher's Prefix: 0-900860

Octopus Books Ltd, 59 Grosvenor St, London W1X 9DA Tel: (01) 493 5841 Cable Add: Octobooks

Chairman: Paul Hamlyn; *Man Dir:* Timothy Clode; *Marketing Dir:* Peggy Singleton; *Rights & Permissions:* Caroline Gueritz
Imprints: Cathay, Sundial, Heinemann/Octopus
Branch Offs: Octopus Pty Ltd, 7th Floor, 55 Lavender St, Milsons Point, NSW 2061, Australia; Octopus Books Inc, 747 Third Ave, New York, NY 10017, USA
Subjects: Children's Classics, Cookery, Handicrafts, Gardening, Natural History, Militaria, Transport, Entertainment, Art, Antiques, Adult and Children's Fiction
Founded: 1971
ISBN Publisher's Prefixes: 0-7064, 0-86178, 0-915712

Odeon, an imprint of LSP Books Ltd (qv)

Odhams Books an imprint of Hamlyn Publishing Group Ltd (qv)

The **Oleander** Press*, 17 Stansgate Ave, Cambridge CB2 2QZ Tel: Cambridge 44688 (STD code 0223)
Office for USA & Canada: 210 Fifth Ave, New York, NY 10010, USA
Subjects: Middle East & Far East, Cambridge, Arabic, Language & Literature, Libya, Poetry, Drama, Travel
1978: 15 titles *Founded:* 1960
ISBN Publisher's Prefixes: 0-900891, 0-902675

Oliphants, an imprint of Marshall, Morgan & Scott Publications Ltd (qv)

Oliver & Boyd, Robert Stevenson Ho, 1/3 Baxter's Pl, Edinburgh EH1 3BB Tel: (031) 556 2424 Cable Add: Almanac Edinburgh Telex: 727511
Shipping Add: Pinnacles, Harlow, Essex
Man Dir: Roger Watson; *General Manager:* A A Dunnett; *Man Editor:* A Paulin; *Sales Manager:* Rhys Edwards; *Publicity:* Rhys Edwards
Subjects: Secondary & Primary Textbooks, Educational Materials
1978: 78 titles *Founded:* 1778
Miscellaneous: Division of Longman Group Ltd, UK (qv)
ISBN Publisher's Prefix: 0-05

Open Books Publishing Ltd, West Compton Ho, Shepton Mallet, Somerset Tel: Pilton 548 (STD code 074 989)
Man Dir: Patrick Taylor
Subjects: Social Sciences & Humanities
1978: 10 titles *Founded:* 1974
ISBN Publisher's Prefix: 0-7291

The **Open University** Press (Open University Educational Enterprises Ltd), 12 Cofferidge Close, Stony Stratford, Milton Keynes MK11 1BY Tel: Milton Keynes 566744 (STD code 0908) Telex: 826147
Man Dir: J E Cox; *General Manager, Marketing and Product Development:* Donald M Hill
Subjects: Books, Films and Audiotapes in the fields of Arts, Education, Mathematics, Science, Social Science, Technology, Adult Education
1978: 133 titles *1979:* 120 titles
ISBN Publisher's Prefix: 0-335

Optimum, an imprint of The Hamlyn Publishing Group Ltd (qv)

Orbis Publishing Ltd, 20-22 Bedfordbury, London WC2N 4BT Tel: (01) 379 6711 Cable Add: Orbooks London WC2 Telex: 22725
Man Dir: Martin Heller; *Editorial:* Stephen Adamson; *Sales:* Geoffrey Howard; *Publicity:* Penny Pilch; *Rights & Permissions:* Charles Merullo
Subjects: Ancient History and Archaeology, Architecture, Aviation, Cookery, Educational, English Literature, Fine Arts, Gardening, General Nonfiction, Military History, Motoring, Nautical, Ornithology, Practical Crafts, Sociology, How-to, Music, Reference, Juveniles, Medicine, General Science, Natural History
1978: 39 titles *1979:* 48 titles
ISBN Publisher's Prefix: 0-85613

Orbit, an imprint of Macdonald/Futura Publishers Ltd (qv)

Ordnance Survey, British Government Map Publishers, Romsey Rd, Maybush, Southampton SO9 4DH Tel: Southampton 775555 (STD code 0703) ext 305 Cable Add: Ordsurvey, Southampton
Deputy Dir: Allan Marles; *Publishing Manager:* Peter C Hodge
Subject: Maps
1978-9: 21 titles

Oresko Books*, 167 Hermitage Rd, London N14 1LZ Tel: (01) 800 6601
Director & Editor: Robert Oresko
Subjects: Art, Pictorial Biographies

Oriel Press Ltd, Stocksfield Studio, Branch End, Stocksfield, Northumberland NE43 7NA Tel: Stocksfield 3065 (STD code 06615)
Man Dir: Bruce Allsopp; *Sales Manager:* David O'Connor
Orders to: Routledge & Kegan Paul Ltd (qv)
Parent Company: Routledge & Kegan Paul Ltd (qv)
Subjects: Religious, Technical & Scientific, Reference Books, Art & Architecture, History, Archaeology, Biography & Memoirs, Politics, Political Economy, Sociology, Questions of the Day, Philosophy, Oriental, Directories & Guidebooks
ISBN Publisher's Prefix: 0-85362

Osprey Publishing Ltd, 12-14 Long Acre, London WC2E 9LP Tel: (01) 836 7863 Cable Add: Philip London WC2 Telex: 21667
Man Dir: M A Bovill; *Export Sales Manager:* Rex Knott; *Rights & Permissions:* Tony Bovill
Associate Company: George Philip & Son Ltd (qv)
Subjects: History, Militaria, Motoring, Aviation, Reference
ISBN Publisher's Prefix: 0-85045

Overseas Publications Interchange Ltd*, 40 Elsham Rd, London W14 8HB Tel: (01) 994 4723
Subjects: Publish and distribute books in Russian and East European languages — especially Soviet and Polish dissident literature

Peter **Owen** Ltd, 73 Kenway Rd, London SW5 0RE Tel: (01) 373 5628
Man Dir, Sales & Advertising, Publicity, Rights & Permissions: Peter Owen
Subjects: General Fiction, Belles Lettres, Biography, Music, Art, Sociology
1979: 16 titles *Founded:* 1950
ISBN Publisher's Prefix: 0-7206

Owlet, an imprint of Mills & Boon Ltd (qv)

Oxford Illustrated Press Ltd, Shelley Close, Headington, Oxford OX3 8HB Tel: Oxford 63739 (STD code 0865)
Man Dir: John Webb; *Editorial Dir:* Jane Marshall
Parent Company: Oxford Illustrators Ltd
Subjects: Illustrated Leisure, Transport, Local History
1978: 8 titles
ISBN Publisher's Prefix: 0-902280

Oxford Microform Publications Ltd, 19A Paradise St, Oxford OX1 1LP Tel: Oxford 46252 (STD code 0865) Telex: 83147
Subjects: Out-of-print books, Scholarly & Scientific Journals, Collections, Serial Publications in Economics, Colour Microfiche in Art, Science, Humanities, Bibliography

Oxford Polytechnic Press, Oxford Polytechnic, Gipsy Lane, Headington, Oxford OX3 0BP Tel: Oxford 64777 (STD code 0865) Cable Add: Polypress Oxford
Chief Executive, Sales: Keith Vaughan; *Editorial, Rights & Permissions:* Laura Cohn; *Production:* S G Colverson
Subjects: General
1978: 4 titles *1979:* 3 titles *Founded:* 1972
ISBN Publisher's Prefix: 0-902692

The **Oxford Railway** Publishing Co Ltd, 8 The Roundway, Headington, Oxford OX3 8DH Tel: Oxford 66215 (STD code 0865)
Man Dir: C W Judge
Subsidiary Company: The Railway Book Centre, 8 The Roundway, Headington, Oxford OX3 8DH
Subject: Railways
1978: 64 titles *1979:* 74 titles
ISBN Publisher's Prefixes: 0-902888, 0-86093

Oxford University Press, Walton St, Oxford OX2 6DP Tel: Oxford 56767 (STD code 0865) Cable Add: Clarendon Press Oxford Telex: (Clarpress) 837330
Secretary to the Delegates and Chief Executive: G B Richardson; *Academic and General Publisher:* R A Denniston; *Educational Publisher:* R E Brammah; *Sales and Marketing:* S W H Wratten; *Rights & Permissions:* Judith Haworth
Orders to: Press Rd, Neasden, London NW10 0DD
London Off and Music Departments: Ely Ho, 37 Dover St, London W1X 4AH Tel: (01) 629 8494
Associate Companies: Cornelsen & Oxford University Press GmbH, Federal Republic of Germany (qv); University Press Ltd, Nigeria (qv)
Branch Offs: Oxford University Press, Australia (qv); Oxford University Press, 70 Wynford Dr, Don Mills 403, Toronto, Ontario, Canada; Oxford University Press, Hong Kong (qv); Oxford University Press, India (qv); Oxford University Press, P T Pustaka Ilmu, Jalan Kebon Kacang XII/23, Jakarta Pusat, Indonesia; Oxford University Press KK, Enshu Bldg, 3-3 Otsuka, 3-chome, Bunkyo-ku, Tokyo, Japan; Oxford University Press, Kenya (qv); Oxford University Press, Malaysia (qv); Oxford University Press, New Zealand (qv); Oxford University Press, Pakistan (qv); Oxford University Press Southern Africa, Zimbabwe (qv); Oxford University Press, Singapore (qv); Oxford University Press Southern Africa, South Africa (qv); Oxford University Press, Tanzania (qv); Oxford University Press, 2-3 Stafford St, Glasgow G4 0HA, UK; Oxford University Press, 200 Madison Ave, New York, NY 10016, USA, Oxford University Press, c/o Intersaf Co Ltd, 140 Wireless Rd, 11th Floor, Shell Ho, Bangkok, Thailand. Branches also in Beirut, Cairo, Argentina, Brazil, Uruguay and Mexico City
Subjects: Belles Lettres, Poetry, Biography, History, English Language Teaching, Music, Art, Classics, Language, Law, Philosophy, Reference, Bibles, Religion, Juveniles, Paperbacks, Medicine, Psychology, Engineering, General & Social Science, Atlases, University, Secondary & Primary Textbooks, Educational Materials, Journals
1979: 1048 titles *Founded:* 1478
ISBN Publisher's Prefix: 0-19

Oyez Publishing Ltd, Norwich House, 11-13 Norwich St, London EC4A 1AB Tel: (01) 404 5721/8 Telex: 8812079
Man Dir: Oliver Freeman; *Sales Publicity Manager:* A Hall
Orders to: Riverside Way, Northampton NN1 5AR
Parent Company: The Solicitors Law Stationery Society Ltd, UK
Subjects: Law, Tax, Commercial & Professional
1978: 38 titles *1979:* 37 titles
ISBN Publisher's Prefixes: 0-85120, 0-85121

Packard Publishing Ltd*, 16 Lynch Down, Funtington, Chichester, West Sussex PO18 9LR Tel: West Ashling 621 (STD code 024 358)
Man Dir: Michael Packard
Subjects: Biology, Environmental Studies, Applicable Mathematics

Paintaway, an imprint of Ramboro Enterprises Ltd (qv)

Paladin Books, see Granada Publishing Ltd

Pan Books Ltd, 18/21 Cavaye Pl, London SW10 9PG Tel: (01) 373 6070 Cable Add: Pandition London Telex: 917466
Warehouse: Brunel Rd, Basingstoke, Hampshire
Deputy Chairman: R Vernon-Hunt; *Man Dir:* S H Master; *Sales Dirs:* R J Williams (Home), N S Potts (Export); *Publicity Dir:* M Cheyne; *Editorial Dir:* A S Mehta
Imprints: Pan, Piccolo, Picador, Brodies Notes
Subjects: Low-priced Paperbacks, General Fiction & Non-fiction
Founded: 1947
ISBN Publisher's Prefix: 0-330 (Pan)

Panther, an imprint of Scripture Union (qv)

Panther Books Ltd, see Granada Publishing Ltd

Paper Tiger, an imprint of Dragon's World Ltd (qv)

Paperfronts, an imprint of Elliot Right Way Books (qv)

Walter **Parrish** Ltd, see Adkinson Parrish Ltd

The **Paternoster** Press Ltd, Paternoster House, 3 Mount Radford Crescent, Exeter, Devon, EX2 4JW Tel: Exeter 50631 (STD Code 0392)
Chairman and Man Dir: Jeremy H L Mudditt; *Editorial, Rights and Permissions:* P E Cousins; *Sales, Publicity, Advertising:* Jeremy H L Mudditt
Subjects: History, Philosophy, Religion, Paperbacks
Founded: 1934
ISBN Publisher's Prefix: 0-85364

Stanley **Paul** & Co Ltd, an imprint of Hutchinson General Books Ltd (qv)

Pearson, an imprint of The Hamlyn Publishing Group Ltd (qv)

Pelham Books Ltd, 44 Bedford Sq, London WC1B 3EF Tel: (01) 323 3200 Cable Add: Emjaybuks London WC1 Telex: 21322
Man Dir: Eric T L Marriott; *Sales Dir:* R Douglas-Boyd; *Publicity & Advertising:* Susan Palmer; *Rights & Permissions:* Sarah Fulford
Associate Company: Michael Joseph Ltd (qv)
Subjects: Biography, How-to, Reference, Juveniles, Sports, Crafts
1978: 80 titles
Miscellaneous: Company is a member of the Thomson Books Ltd group, a part of International Thomson Organization Ltd (Canada)
ISBN Publisher's Prefix: 0-7207

Pelican, an imprint of Penguin Books Ltd (qv)

Pemberton Publishing Co Ltd*, 88 Islington High St, London N1 8EN Tel: (01) 226 7251 Cable Add: Ratiopres London N1 4EN
Managing Editor, Rights & Permissions: Nicolas Walter
Parent Company: Rationalist Press Association (same address)
Subjects: Philosophy, Religion, Low-priced Paperbacks, Psychology, General & Social Science, University Textbooks
Founded: 1960
ISBN Publisher's Prefix: 0-301

Penguin Books Ltd, 536 King's Rd, London SW10 0UH Tel: (01) 351 2393 Cable Add: Penguinook SW10
Warehouse & Accounts: Bath Rd, Harmondsworth, West Drayton, Middlesex UB7 0DA Tel: (01) 759 1984 Cable Add: Penguinook West Drayton Telex: 263130
Chairman: E J B Rose; *Vice-Chairman:* R J E Blass; *Chief Executive:* P Mayer; *Editorial Dirs:* Peter Carson (Non-fiction), Philippa Harrison (Fiction); *Sales, Marketing:* Patrick Wright; *Rights & Permissions:* Carol Heaton; *Publicity Dir:* John Hitchin; *Press Officer:* Jenny Wilford
Parent Company: Pearson Longman Ltd, Millbank Tower, Millbank, London SW1P 4QZ
Associate Companies: Viking Penguin Inc, 625 Madison Ave, New York, NY 10022, USA; Longman Group (qv); Ladybird Books Ltd (qv)
Subsidiary Companies: Penguin Books Australia Ltd, Australia (qv); Penguin Books Canada Ltd, 41 Steelcase Rd West, Markham, Ontario L3R 1B4, Canada; Penguin Books New Zealand Ltd, New Zealand (qv)
Imprints: Allen Lane (qv), Kestrel Books (qv) (both hardcover); others include Pelican Books, Peregrine Books, Puffin Books
Book Clubs: Puffin Book Club; Junior Puffin Club
Subjects: Low- & High-priced Paperbacks (General Fiction, General Nonfiction, Juveniles, Technical, Educational)
Bookshop: Penguin Bookshop, Covent Garden, London WC2
1979: 4000 titles *1980:* 4000 titles *Founded:* 1936
ISBN Publisher's Prefixes: 0-14 (Penguin), 0-7139 (Allen Lane), 0-7226 (Kestrel)

Pentos Ltd, New Bond Street Ho, 1-5 New Bond St, London W1Y 0SB Tel: (01) 499 0386
Firm is (non-publishing) ultimate holding company of group of subsidiaries owned by (non-publishing) Pentos Publishing Group Ltd and Pentos Bookselling Group Ltd
General Publishing: Ward Lock Ltd (qv); Ward Lock Educational Ltd (qv); Marshall Morgan & Scott Publications Ltd (qv) Popular Publishing; Sandle Brothers Ltd; World International Publishing Ltd (qv)
The company owns Dillon's University Bookshop Ltd, Hudsons Bookshops Ltd and Hodges Figgis & Co Ltd, Dublin, Republic of Ireland (qqv under Major Booksellers), also Sisson & Parker Ltd, F F Allsopp & Co Ltd and Brown's of Hull (all UK)

Pepper Press, an imprint of E J Arnold & Son Ltd (qv)

Peregrine Books, an imprint of Penguin Books Ltd (qv)

Pergamon Press Ltd, Headington Hill Hall, Oxford OX3 0BW Tel: Oxford 64881 (STD code 0865) Cable Add: Pergapress Telex: 83177
Chairman & Publisher: I R Maxwell; *Joint Man Dirs:* C R Ellis and G F Richards; *Sales Manager:* J G Ennals; *Publicity Manager:* Graham Jones; *Rights & Permissions:* Anna Moon
Associate and Subsidiary Companies: The Aberdeen University Press Ltd, UK; Pergamon Press (Australia) Pty Ltd, Australia (qv); Pergamon Press Canada Ltd, Toronto, Canada; Pergamon Press Sàrl, Paris, France; Pergamon Press GmbH, Kronberg, Federal Republic of Germany; Bumpus, Haldane & Maxwell, UK; Religious Education Press, UK (qv); A Wheaton & Co, UK (qv); Pergamon Press Inc, Elmsford, New York, USA
Subjects: Philosophy, Religion, Music, Art, Biography, History, How-to, General Science, Life Sciences & Medicine, Veterinary Sciences, Physical Sciences, Engineering, Psychology, Social & Behavioural Sciences and Liberal Arts, Business Management, University, Secondary & Primary Textbooks, Educational Materials
1978: 350 titles *Founded:* 1949
ISBN Publisher's Prefix: 0-08

Permanent Press, 52 Cascade Ave, London N10 Tel: (01) 444 8591
Man Dir: Robert Vas Dias
Branch Off: !040 Park Ave, New York, NY 10028, USA
Subject: Poetry
1978: 2 titles *1979:* 2 titles *Founded:* 1972
ISBN Publisher's Prefix: 0-905258

The **Phaethon** Press, an imprint of The Aquila Publishing Co Ltd (qv)

Phaidon Press Ltd*, Littlegate Ho, St Ebbe's St, Oxford OX1 1SQ Tel: Oxford 46681 (STD code 0865) Cable Add: Phaidon Oxford Telex: 83308
Man Dir: George Riches; *Editorial Dirs:* Simon Haviland, Jean-Claude Piessel; *Marketing Dir:* Robert Sarsfield; *Rights & Permissions:* Alice Hammond
Orders to: Unit B, Ridgeway Trading Estate, Iver, Buckinghamshire
Parent Company: Elsevier-NDU nv, Netherlands (qv)
Associate Company: Elsevier Oxford Ltd (qv)
Imprints: Elsevier Phaidon, Phaidon
Subjects: Art, Art History, Music, Natural History, Illustrated Reference Books
1978: 70 titles *1979:* 80 titles *Founded:* 1925
ISBN Publisher's Prefixes: 0-7148 (Phaidon), 0-7290 (Elsevier Phaidon)

Pharos Books, an imprint of Rudolf Steiner Press (qv)

George **Philip** & Son Ltd, 12-14 Long Acre, London WC2E 9LP Tel: (01) 836 7863 Telex: 21667
Shipping Add: Lineside Industrial Estate, Littlehampton, Sussex
Man Dir: R J Shattock; *Export Sales Manager:* Rex Knott; *Rights & Permissions:* M A Bovill
Associate Companies: George Philip Printers; E Stanford Ltd; Stanford Maritime Ltd (qv); Map Productions Ltd; Osprey Publishing Ltd (qv)
Subjects: Atlases and Maps, Textbooks, Educational Materials, Maritime, Militaria, Motoring
Founded: 1834

Philip & Tacey Ltd, see Philograph Publications Ltd

Phillimore & Co Ltd, Shopwyke Hall, Chichester, West Sussex PO20 6BQ Tel: Chichester 787636 (STD code 0243) Cable Add: Phillimore Chichester
Honorary President: Lord Darwen; *Chairman & Man Dir:* Philip Harris;

Editorial Dir: Noel H Osborne
Subsidiary Company: Darwen Finlayson Ltd (qv)
Subjects: History, Historical Biography, Architectural History, Archaeology, Genealogy, Heraldry
Bookshop: The Phillimore Bookshop, Shopwyke Hall, Chichester
Founded: 1875 (incorporated: 1897)
ISBN Publisher's Prefixes: 0-900592, 0-85033

Philograph Publications Ltd, North Way, Andover, Hampshire SP10 5BA Tel: Andover 61171 (STD code 0264) Telex: 47496
Man Dir: Jon Tacey
Associate Company: Philip & Tacey Ltd, Andover
Subjects: Primary Education, Teaching Aids
ISBN Publisher's Prefix: 0-85370

Phoebus Publishing Co, 52 Poland St, London W1A 2JX Tel: (01) 734 9131 Cable Add: Phoebus Ldn Telex: 23451
Chief Executive: Peter Morrison; *Deputy Chief Executive:* Philip Nugus; *Editorial Dir:* Nicolas Wright; *Production Dir:* Mike Emery; *Sales Dir:* Richard Ganson; *Rights & Permissions:* Roberta Bailey
Parent Company: B P C Ltd (qv)
Associate Company: Macdonald/Futura Publishers Ltd (qv)
Subjects: Naval & Military, Aviation, Cookery, Social Science, Reference Books, Encyclopaedias
ISBN Publisher's Prefix: 0-7026

Piatkus Books, 17 Brook Rd, Loughton, Essex Tel: (01) 508 7362
Man Dir: Judy Piatkus
Orders to: George Philip & Son Ltd, PO Box 1, Littlehampton, West Sussex BN17 7EN
Parent Company: Judy Piatkus (Publishers) Ltd (address as above)
Subjects: Fiction, Cookery, Leisure, Arts, History, Biography
1979: 12 titles *Founded:* 1979
ISBN Publisher's Prefix: 0-86188

Picador, an imprint of Pan Books Ltd (qv)

Piccolo, an imprint of Pan Books Ltd (qv)

Pickering & Inglis Ltd, 26 Bothwell St, Glasgow G2 6PA Tel: (041) 552 5044
Man Dir: Andrew Gray; *Production Dir:* Andrew Kerr; *Marketing and Sales Dir:* Nicholas Gray
Subjects: Religion, Juveniles
Bookshops: 1 Creed Lane, London EC4V 5BR; 26 Bothwell St, Glasgow G2 6PA
1978: 21 titles *1979:* 43 titles *Founded:* 1870
ISBN Publisher's Prefix: 0-7208

Pied Piper, an imprint of World Book-Childcraft International Inc (qv)

Pierrot Publishing Ltd, 60 Greek St, Soho Sq, London W1V 5LR Tel: (01) 439 2596 Telex: 261416
Managing: Philip Dunn; *Editorial:* Jane Dunn, Karen Thesen; *Publicity:* Annie Hayman
Orders to trade distribution: New English Library, Barnard's Inn, Holborn, London EC1
Subjects: Large format Colour Paperbacks/Originals, Science Fiction, Non-fiction, General, Reference. Co-editions
Founded: 1975
ISBN Publisher's Prefix: 0-905310

James Pike Ltd (EJP Publications), Consols Ho, St Ives, Cornwall Tel: St Ives (Cornwall) 6363 (STD code 073670) Cable Add: Piktorial St Ives Cornwall
Man Dir: E J Pike
Subjects: Juveniles, Education, Games, Sports, Commercial & Technical Textbooks, Guidebooks
ISBN Publisher's Prefixes: 0-85932, 0-900850

Frances Pinter Ltd, 5 Dryden St, Covent Garden, London WC2E 9NW Tel: (01) 240 2430 Telex: 299533
Subjects: International Relations, Political Economy, Social Policy, Socio-legal Studies, Technology
1979: 15 titles
ISBN Publisher's Prefix: 0-903804

Pitkin Pictorials Ltd, 11 Wyfold Rd, London SW6 6SG Tel: (01) 385 4351/3 Cable Add: Pitkins London SW6
Subjects: Architectural History, and Guides for the Tourist Industry
ISBN Publisher's Prefix: 0-85372

Pitman Books Ltd, 39 Parker St, Kingsway, London WC2B 5PB Tel: (01) 242 1655 Cable Add: Ipandsons London WC2 Telex: 261367
Chairman, Man Dir: Nicholas Thompson; *Sales Dir:* Neill Ross; *Export Dir:* Ian Pringle; *Home Sales Dir:* Kenneth Welham; *Rights & Permissions:* Veronica Sahiby
Subsidiary Companies: Focal Press Ltd (qv); Pitman Education Ltd; Pitman House Ltd; Pitman Medical Ltd (qv); Pitman Publishing Ltd
Associate Companies & Branch Offs: Pitman Publishing Pty Ltd, Australia (qv); Copp Clark Pitman Publishing Co, 517 Wellington St West, Toronto 135, Ontario, Canada; Pitman Publishing New Zealand Ltd, New Zealand (qv); Pitman Publishing Co SA (Pty) Ltd, South Africa (qv); Fearon-Pitman Publishers Inc, 6 Davis Dr, Belmont, California 94002, USA; Pitman Publishing Inc, 1020 Plain St, Marshfield, Massachusetts 02050, USA
Subjects: Art, Craft, Cookery, Hobbies, How-to, Theatre, Technical, Business, University, Technical & Professional Textbooks, Advanced Monographs & Reference Works, Shorthand, Medical, Photography
Book Club: The Artists Book Club
ISBN Publisher's Prefix: 0-273

Pitman Medical Publishing Co Ltd*, PO Box 7, Tunbridge Wells TN1 1XH Tel: Tunbridge Wells 38488 (STD code 0892)
Parent Company: Pitman Books Ltd (qv)
Subjects: Medical Texts, Reference, Monographs, Symposia
1978: 40 titles

Playfair, an imprint of Macdonald/Futura Publishers Ltd (qv)

Plexus Publishing Ltd, 30 Craven St, London WC2N 5NT Tel: (01) 839 1315 Telex: 261234 Ref H5991C
Sales, Production: Terence Porter; *Editorial, Publicity, Rights & Permissions:* Sandra Wake, Nicola Hayden
Subjects: Illustrated Books on Films, Rock, Folk, Biography, Popular Culture and Art
1978: 3 titles *1979:* 3 titles *Founded:* 1973
ISBN Publisher's Prefix: 0-85965

Plough Publishing House, Darvell, Robertsbridge, East Sussex TN32 5DR Tel: Robertsbridge 880626 (STD code 0580)
Man Dir, Rights & Permissions: Peter P Cavanna; *Sales, Publicity & Advertising Dir:* Mrs Cavanna
Subjects: Biography, Reference, Religion, Juveniles
1978: 3 titles *1979:* 4 titles *Founded:* 1937
Miscellaneous: Firm is the publishing house of the Hutterian Society of Brothers
ISBN Publisher's Prefix: 0-87486

Plume, an imprint of New English Library Ltd (qv)

Pluto Press, Unit 10, Spencer Court, 7 Chalcot Rd, London NW1 8LH Tel: (01) 722 0141 Cable Add: Plutonic, London Telex: 21879/25247
Editorial: Michael Kidron, Richard Kuper; *Sales:* Ric Sissons; *Production:* Anne Benewick; *Publicity:* Kerry Hamilton; *Rights & Permissions:* Nina Kidron
Subjects: Biography, History, Workers' Handbooks, Politics, Social Sciences, Plays, Literature, Low- & High-priced Paperbacks, Popular Culture
1978: 42 titles *Founded:* 1970
ISBN Publisher's Prefixes: 0-902818, 0-904383

Policy Studies Institute, 1/2 Castle Lane, London SW1E 6DR Tel: (01) 828 7055
Dir: John Pinder; *Editor:* Thelma Liesner
Subjects: Politics, Economics, Education, Social Policy
1978: 6 titles *1979:* 10 titles
ISBN Publisher's Prefix: 0-85374

Polybooks Ltd, see Charles Skilton Ltd

Polytantric Press, an imprint of Jay Landesman Ltd (qv)

Pond Press*, 7 Beasleys Ait, Sunbury on Thames, Middlesex Tel: Sunbury on Thames 80091 (STD code 09327)
Subjects: University, Secondary & Primary Education, Reference Books, Poetry & Drama, Directories & Guidebooks
ISBN Publisher's Prefix: 0-85375

Popular Dogs Publishing Co Ltd, an imprint of Hutchinson General Books Ltd (qv)

H Pordes, 529b Finchley Rd, London NW3 7BH Tel: (01) 435 9878/9
Man Dir: H Pordes
Subjects: History, Reference
Founded: 1947
Book Club: The Jewish Book Club (R Pordes)
Miscellaneous: See also under Remainder Dealers
ISBN Publisher's Prefix: 0-85376

T & A D Poyser Ltd, Town Head House, Calton, Waterhouses, Staffordshire ST10 3JQ Tel: Waterhouses 366 (STD code 053 86)
Man Dir: Trevor Poyser; *Sales, Foreign Rights:* Dorothy Poyser
Subjects: Ornithology, Aviation
1978: 3 titles *Founded:* 1972
ISBN Publisher's Prefix: 0-85661

Pre-School Publishing Co, 116-120 Golden Lane, London EC1Y 0TL Tel: (01) 253 2145
Editorial, Rights & Permissions: Miss N Galinski; *Sales:* H Starke; *Production:* C Tuthill
Orders to: The Barn, Northgate, Beccles, Suffolk NR34 9AX
Subject: Pre-school books

Prentice-Hall International, 66 Wood Lane End, Hemel Hempstead, Hertfordshire HP2 4RG Tel: Hemel Hempstead 58531 (STD code 0442) Cable Add: Prenhall Hemel Telex: 82445
Vice President: Donald Deeks; *Sales Managers:* Haydn Jenkins (UK/Middle East, Africa excl south), Gary Utterson (Western Europe), Tony Murray (Eastern Europe), Roy Jones (UK Trade), Jeremy Dicks (UK Academic); *Rights & Permissions:* Tony Murray
Associate Companies: Prentice-Hall Inc, Englewood Cliffs, NJ 07632, USA; Prentice-Hall of Australia Pty Ltd, Australia (qv); Prentice-Hall of Canada Ltd, 1870 Birchmount Rd, Scarborough, Ontario, Canada; Prentice-Hall of India Pvt Ltd, India (qv); Prentice-Hall of Japan Inc, Japan

(qv); Goodyear Publishing Co Inc, 15113 Sunset Blvd, Pacific Palisades, Calif 90272, USA; Institute for Business Planning Inc, IBP Plaza, 320 Hudson Terrace, Englewood Cliffs, NJ 07632, USA; Parker Publishing Co, West Nyack, NY 10994, USA; Reston Publishing Co, Box 547, Reston, Va 22090, USA; Winthrop Publishers Inc, 17 Dunster St, Cambridge, Mass 02138, USA; International Book Distributors Ltd, UK Division: Appleton-Century-Crofts (US)
Subjects: History, Music, Art, Philosophy, Religion, Medicine, Psychology, University Textbooks and Postgraduate Material in Science and Technology, Sociology, Education, Business, Economics, English, English as a Second language, Political Science, Speech, Drama, Trade Books
1978: 748 titles Founded: 1913
Miscellaneous: Firm is a branch of Prentice-Hall International Inc, Englewood Cliffs, NJ 07632, USA
ISBN Publisher's Prefixes: 0-13 (Prentice-Hall and Parker), 0-87620 (Goodyear), 0-87624 (Institute for Business Planning), 0-87909 (Reston), 0-87626 (Winthrop), 0-8385 (Appleton-Century-Crofts)

Princeton University Press, see University Presses of Columbia and Princeton

George **Prior** Associated Publishers Ltd, 37-41 Bedford Row, London WC1R 4JH Tel: (01) 405 6603/6626
Shipping Add: Biblios, Glenside Industrial Estate, Partridge Green, Horsham, West Sussex RH13 8RA Tel: Horsham 710971 (STD code 0403)
Man Dir, Rights & Permissions: George Prior; Editorial: Stephen Dobell; Publicity & Advertising Dir: Brian O'Cathain
Subsidiary Companies: George Prior Publishers; Book Mail International; George Prior Co, PO Box 68363, Portland, Oregon 97268, USA
Subjects: General Fiction, History, Music, Art, Philosophy, Reference, High-priced Paperbacks, Social Science
1978: 42 titles 1979: 75 titles Founded: 1972
ISBN Publisher's Prefixes: 0-904000, 0-86043

Priory Press Ltd, see Wayland Publishers Ltd

Prism Press, Stable Court, Chalmington, Dorchester, Dorset DT2 0HB Tel: Maiden Newton 524 (STD code 03002)
Dirs: Julian King, Colin Spooner
Subjects: Alternative Technology, Self-Sufficiency, Philosophy, Politics, Literature
Miscellaneous: Distributed by George Philip & Co, PO Box 1, Littlehampton, Sussex
ISBN Publisher's Prefix: 0-904727

Profile Books Ltd*, Dial House, 6 Park St, Windsor, Berks SL4 1UU Tel: Windsor 69777
Dirs: P E Butler, H B Jones; Mail Order: P Bridgeman
Imprints: Profile Publications, Hylton Lacy Publishers
Subjects: Aircraft, Cars, AFVs, Warships, Small Arms, Locomotives

Prospice, an imprint of Aquila Publishing (qv)

Proteus (Publishing) Ltd, Bremar Ho, Sale Pl, London W2 1PT Tel: (01) 402 7360 Telex: 21969
Man Dir, Editorial: Michael Brecher; Marketing: George Loucaides; Production: Sharon Barnfield; Publicity: Fenella Greenfield; Rights & Permissions: Elisabeth Wilson
Subsidiary Company: Proteus Publishing Co, 14th Floor, 747 Fifth Avenue, New York, NY 10017, USA
Subjects: General Non-fiction, Fiction, Travel and Professional Guides, Leisure
1979: 12 titles 1980: 24 titles Founded: 1977
ISBN Publisher's Prefix: 0-906071

Psychic Press Ltd*, 23 Great Queen St, London WC2B 5BB Tel: (01) 405 2914/5
Cable Add: Psychic London WC2
Man Dir: Maurice Barbanell; Advertising Dir: Ronald Baker; Rights & Permissions: Gordon Adams
Subjects: Philosophy, Reference
Bookshops: Psychic News Bookshop, 23 Great Queen St, London WC2B 5BB
Founded: 1932
ISBN Publisher's Prefix: 0-85384

Puffin Books, an imprint of Penguin Books Ltd (qv)

Purnell Books, Berkshire House, Queen St, Maidenhead, Berkshire SL6 1NF
Tel: Maidenhead 37171 (STD code 0628)
Telex: 847747
General Manager: Charles Harvey; Publishing Manager: Michael Gabb; Editorial: Susan Hook; Sales: R T Wroe; Production: Martyn Lewis; Publicity: Fiona Lock; Rights & Permissions: Lesley Willcock
Orders to: Purnell Books, Paulton, Bristol BS18 5LQ
Parent Company: Purnell & Sons Ltd, Paulton, Bristol BS18 5LQ
Associate Company: Macdonald/Futura Publishers Ltd (qv)
Imprint: Sampson Low
Subjects: Reference, Juveniles, Leisure (under Sampson Low imprint)
ISBN Publisher's Prefixes: 0-361, 0-430, 0-562 (Sampson Low)

Putnam & Co Ltd, 9 Bow St, London WC2E 7AL Tel: (01) 836 9081 Cable Add: Bodleian London WC2 Telex: 299080
Parent Company: The Bodley Head (qv for further details)

Q Press Ltd, see Canongate Publishing Ltd

Q E D Publishing Ltd, 32 Kingly Court, London W1 Tel: (01) 734 4611 Telex: 298844
Man Dir: Laurence F Orbach; Art Dirs: Alastair Campbell, Edward Kinsey; Editorial Dir: Jeremy Harwood; Rights & Co-editions: Tamar Karet
Parent Company: Quarto Publishing Ltd (qv)
Subjects: International Co-editions, Illustration Techniques, Wine, Animals, Performing Arts

Quartet Books Ltd, 27-29 Goodge St, London W1P 1FD Tel: (01) 636 3992, (01) 636 0968 Telex: 919034
Chairman: Naim Attallah; Sales: David Elliott; Production: Gary Grant; Publicity: Sheila Turnbull; Rights & Permissions: Gloria Ferris
Associate Company: Robin Clark Ltd (qv)
Subsidiary Companies: Quartet Books Australia Pty Ltd, 10 Hyland St, South Yarra, Victoria 3141, Australia; Quartet Books Inc, 12 East 69th St, New York, NY 10021, USA; Namara Publications, Namara Ho, 45-46 Poland St, London W1
Subjects: Fiction, Biography, Music, History, Philosophy, Politics, Social Science, Trade Paperbacks, Psychology, The Arab World, Sexual Politics
1978: 74 titles Founded: 1972
Miscellaneous: Firm is a member of the Namara Group, Namara House, 45-46 Poland St, London W1
ISBN Publisher's Prefix: 0-7043

Quarto Publishing Ltd, 32 Kingly Court, London W1 Tel: (01) 734 4611 Telex: 298844
Man Dir: Laurence F Orbach; Editorial Dir: Jeremy Harwood; Art Dir: Robert J Morley; Rights & Co-editions: Tamar Karet
Parent Company: Quarto Ltd, 212 Fifth Ave, New York, NY 10010, USA
Subsidiary Companies: QED Publishing Ltd (qv); Quill Publishing Ltd (qv)
Subjects: International Co-editions, Illustrated books on Wine & Food, Transport, Travel, Photography, Music
1978: 12 titles 1979: 12 titles

Queen Anne Press Ltd, now part of Macdonald/Futura Publishers Ltd (qv)

Quentin Press Ltd, 11-12 West Stockwell St, Colchester, Essex CO1 1HN Tel: Colchester 65151 (STD code 0206) Cable Add: Paterson, Colchester Telex: 896616 MP Sendit G, Markit 987562 Cochac
Man Dir: Mark Paterson
Subjects: High-class Illustrated Books
Founded: 1978
Miscellaneous: Packagers of books for other publishers

Quill Publishing Ltd, 32 Kingly Court, London W1 Tel: (01) 734 4611 Cable Add: Quartopub Telex: 298844 Quarto
Man Dir: Laurence F Orbach; Editorial: James Marks; Production: Nigel Osborne; Publicity: Robert Morley; Rights & Permissions: Tamar Karet
Parent Company: Quarto Publishing Ltd (at above address)
Subjects: International Co-editions, Horse Racing, Popular Medicine
Founded: 1980

R I B A Publications Ltd*, Finsbury Mission, 35-37 Moreland St, London EC1 Tel: (01) 251 0791 Cable Add: Ribazo London
Man Dir: R H McKie; Production: M Stribbling
Parent Company: Royal Institute of British Architects
Associate Company: RIBA Services Ltd
Subjects: Architecture and Design
Bookshop: RIBA Bookshop, 66 Portland Place, London W1N 4AD
Founded: 1967
Miscellaneous: Represented by Association of Learned & Professional Society Publishers (qv under Book Trade Organisations)
ISBN Publisher's Prefix: 0-900630

Radical Reprints, an imprint of The Journeyman Press (qv)

Railway Publications Ltd, an associate company of Ian Allen Ltd (qv)

The **Rainbird** Publishing Group, 36 Park St, London W1Y 4DE Tel: (01) 491 4777
Cable Add: Rainmac London Telex: 261472
Man Dir: Michael Rainbird; Publishing Dir: Michael O'Mara; Production: Peter Phillips; Publicity: Annette Denniff; Rights & Permissions: Valerie Reuben
Subsidiary Companies: Albany Books; Park Lane Press; George Rainbird Ltd; Rainbird Reference Books Ltd
Subjects: Art, Archaeology, Architecture, History, Travel, Hobbies, Leisure, Sport, Natural History, Crafts, Medical
1978: 23 titles Founded: 1951
Miscellaneous: Company is a member of the Thomson Books Ltd group, a part of International Thomson Organization Ltd (Canada)
ISBN Publisher's Prefix: 0-902935

Rainbow Books, an imprint of Brown Watson Ltd (qv)

Ramboro Enterprises Ltd, 6 Highbury Corner, London N5 1RD Tel: (01) 609 3091/2 Cable Add: Dons Bar Telex: 24224 ref 1297
Man Dir, Sales: Donald Murray; Rights &

Permissions: E Lacher
Associate Company: Number One Publishing Co Ltd
Imprints: Atlantic, Delightful Books, Paintaway, Ramboro, University, Varsity
Subjects: Children's Books, Art, Cookery, Dictionaries
Founded: 1960
Miscellaneous: Also Remainder Dealers

The **Ramsay** Head Press, 36 North Castle St, Edinburgh EH2 3BN Tel: (031) 556 4534
Editorial Dir: Norman Wilson
Subjects: Biography, Literature, Poetry, Art, Architecture, History, Fiction, Reference, New Assessments series (critical studies of outstanding figures in literature and arts)
1978: 8 titles *1979:* 9 titles *Founded:* 1971
ISBN Publisher's Prefix: 0-902859

Ranelagh Editions*, 82 Hurlingham Court, Ranelagh Gardens, London SW6 3UR Tel: (01) 736 0189
Man Dir: Raymond Holdsworth
Subject: Limited Editions
Founded: 1975
ISBN Publisher's Prefix: 0-904862

Rationalist Press Association, see Pemberton Publishing Co Ltd

The **Reader's Digest** Association Ltd*, 25 Berkeley Sq, London W1X 6AB Tel: (01) 629 8144 Cable Add: Readigest London W1X 6AB Telex: 264631
Distributors: Hodder & Stoughton Ltd (qv)
Subjects: Fiction, English Dictionaries, References, Maps & Atlases, Travel, Encyclopaedias, Directories, Guidebooks
ISBN Publisher's Prefix: 0-276

Reference International Publishers Ltd, 21 Soho Sq, London W1V 5FD Tel: (01) 437 7624/5 Telex: 22635
Director: Martin Self
Subjects: Encyclopaedias, Dictionaries, General Reference

Max **Reinhardt** Ltd*, 9 Bow St, London WC2E 7AL Tel: (01) 836 9081 Cable Add: Bodleian London WC2 Telex: 299080
Parent Company: The Bodley Head (qv for further details)

Religious Education Press, Hennock Rd, Exeter, Devon EX2 8RP Tel: Exeter 74121 (STD code 0392) Telex: 42749
Publishing Dir: John Halsall; *Editorial:* William Pridie; *Marketing:* Don Bibey
Parent Company: Pergamon Press Ltd (qv)
Subjects: Religion, Juveniles, Secondary & Primary Textbooks, Educational Materials
Founded: 1921
ISBN Publisher's Prefix: 0-08

Reprographia, an imprint of Gordon Wright Publishing (qv)

Research Publishing Co, an imprint of Fudge & Co Ltd (qv)

Rex, an imprint of Murrays Remainder Books (qv)

Riband Books, see Artemis Press

The **Richmond** Publishing Co Ltd*, Orchard Rd, Richmond, Surrey Tel: (01) 876 1091
Subjects: Reprints, History, Social Sciences, Botany, Limited & De Luxe Editions
ISBN Publisher's Prefix: 0-85546

Rider & Co, an imprint of Hutchinson General Books Ltd (qv)

Right Way Books, an imprint of Elliot Right Way Books (qv)

Rivers Press, an imprint of Writers and Readers Publishing Co-operative (qv)

Rivingtons (Publishers) Ltd*, Montague Ho, Russell Sq, London WC1B 5BX Tel: (01) 637 1466 Cable Add: Byronitic, London WC1B 5BX
Parent Company: Evans Brothers Ltd (qv)
Subjects: Classics
ISBN Publisher's Prefix: 0-280

Martin **Robertson**, see Martin

Robinson & Watkins Books Ltd, see Watkins Publishing

Robson Books Ltd, 28 Poland St, London W1V 3DB Tel: (01) 734 1052 Cable Add: Robsobook London W1
Man Dir: Jeremy Robson; *Sales Manager:* Martin Hanks; *Editor:* Anna Selby; *Publicity:* Katie Walsh
Subjects: General, Literature, Children's Books, Biography, Music, Humour
1978: 40 titles *1979:* 48 titles *Founded:* 1973
ISBN Publisher's Prefix: 0-903895, 0-86051

George **Ronald**, 46 High St, Kidlington, Oxford OX5 2DN Tel: Oxford 5273 (STD code 08675) Cable Add: Talisman Oxford
General Manager: Russell Busey
Subjects: Religion, The Bahá'í Faith, High-priced Paperbacks
1978: 6 titles *Founded:* 1947
ISBN Publisher's Prefix: 0-85398

Barry **Rose** (Publishers) Ltd, Little London, Chichester, West Sussex PO19 1PG Tel: Chichester 783637 (STD code 0243)
Chairman and Man Dir: Barry Rose; *Sales & Publicity:* R S Childs
Parent Company: Justice of the Peace (Holdings) Ltd
Associate Companies: Professional Training Consultants Ltd; Countrywise Press Ltd
1978: 23 titles *1979:* 18 titles *Founded:* 1971
ISBN Publisher's Prefixes: 0-85992, 0-900500

Rose-Jordan Ltd, an imprint of Jordan & Sons Ltd (qv)

The **Roundwood** Press (1978) Ltd, Kineton, Warwick CV35 0HW Tel: Kineton 640400 (STD code 0926) Telex: 311610
Man Dir: P J Asprey; *Sales, Publicity, Rights & Permissions:* Neil Gordon
Parent Company: Gordon Fraser Gallery Ltd (qv)
Subjects: History, Social History, Biography, General
ISBN Publisher's Prefixes: 0-900093, 0-906418

Routledge & Kegan Paul Ltd, 39 Store St, London WC1E 7DD Tel: (01) 637 7651 Cable Add: Columnae London WC1
Shipping Add: Broadway Ho, Newtown Rd, Henley-on-Thames, Oxfordshire RG9 1EN Tel: Henley-on-Thames 78321 (STD code 04912)
Chairman: Norman Franklin; *Sales Dir:* Richard Bailey; *Publicity Dir:* Terence Lucas; *Advertising:* Heather Moss; *Foreign Rights:* Gela Jacobson
Subsidiary Company: Oriel Press Ltd (qv)
Branch Off: Routledge & Kegan Paul of America, 9 Park St, Boston, Mass 02108, USA
Subjects: General Fiction, Belles Lettres, Biography, History, Education, Occult, Art, Philosophy, Reference, Religion, High-priced Paperbacks, Psychology, Social Science, University & Secondary Textbooks
Bookshop: Kegan Paul, Trench, Trubner & Co, 39 Store St, London WC1E 7DD
1978: 243 titles *Founded:* 1834
ISBN Publisher's Prefix: 0-7100

Roxby Press Ltd, 98 Clapham Common North Side, London SW4 9SG Tel: (01) 228 2558
Man Dir: Hugh Elwes; *Rights & Permissions:* Grania Kearsley

Subjects: Illustrated Reference Books, Encyclopaedias
1979: 10 titles *Founded:* 1973

S A G E Publications Ltd, 28 Banner St, London EC1Y 8QE Tel: (01) 253 1516 Cable Add: SAGEPub London
Man Dir: David Brooks; *Editorial, Production, Rights & Permissions:* Michael Witchell; *Marketing Manager:* Philip Glover
Associate Company: SAGE Publications Inc, 275 South Beverly Dr, Beverly Hills, California 90212, USA
Subjects: Social Sciences (Sociology, Political Science, Methodology, International Relations, Human Services)
1978: 10 titles *1979:* 10 titles *Founded:* 1971
ISBN Publisher's Prefix: 0-8039

S C M Press Ltd, 56-58 Bloomsbury St, London WC1B 3QX Tel: (01) 636 3841/4 Cable Add: Torchpres London WC1
Man Dir: The Rev John Bowden; *Production:* Mark Hammer; *Rights & Permissions:* Margaret Lydamore
Subjects: Religion, Theology, Religious Education
Bookshop: SCM Bookroom, 58 Bloomsbury St, London WC1B 3QX
1979: 45 titles *1980:* 44 titles *Founded:* 1929
ISBN Publisher's Prefix: 0-334

S P C K (The Society for Promoting Christian Knowledge), Holy Trinity Church, Marylebone Rd, London NW1 4DU Tel: (01) 387 5282 Cable Add: Futurity London NW1
General Secretary: Patrick Gilbert; *Publishers:* Robin Brookes, Darley Anderson; *Sales Manager:* Alan Goodworth; *Promotion:* Sandie Byrne
Subjects: Philosophy, Religion, Specialist Paperbacks
1979: 70 titles *Founded:* 1698
Miscellaneous: A division of this Society is Sheldon Press (qv)
ISBN Publisher's Prefix: 0-281

S T L Books, PO Box 48, 9 London Rd, Bromley, Kent BR1 1BY Tel: (01) 464 1191 Cable Add: Mobiliser Bromley Telex: 896706 EBE G
Dir: G M Davey; *General Manager:* Dave Brown
Orders to: S T L Distributors, 1 Sherman Rd, Bromley, Kent BR1 3JH
Parent Company: Send the Light Trust, address as above
Subjects: Religion, Juveniles, Bibles
Bookshops: Bromley Christian Supply Centre, 9 London Rd, Bromley, Kent; Christian Bookshop, 17 Lordship Lane, London SE22; Bolton Christian Bookshop, 204 St Georges Rd, Bolton, Lancs; Coventry Christian Bookshop, 21 City Arcade, Coventry CV1 3HX
1978: 10 titles *Founded:* 1963
ISBN Publisher's Prefix: 0-903843

Saint Andrew Press, 121 George St, Edinburgh EH2 4YN Tel: (031) 225 5722 Cable Add: Free, Edinburgh
Secretary to Publications Committee: T B Honeyman; *Publisher:* Douglas Law; *Editorial:* Mary Kerr; *Production Manager:* John Leslie; *Publicity, Rights & Permissions:* Jo Currie
Subjects: Religion, Theology, Scottish Affairs, Current Issues, History
1978: 27 titles *1979:* 18 titles
Miscellaneous: Parent body is The Church of Scotland Committee on Publications
ISBN Publisher's Prefix: 0-7152

Saint James Press, 3 Percy St, London W1P 9FA Tel: (01) 580 4155
Man Dir: George Walsh
Subject: Reference
Founded: 1968
ISBN Publisher's Prefixes: 0-900997, 0-86066

400 UNITED KINGDOM

Saint Paul Publications, St Paul's House, Middlegreen, Slough SL3 6BT Tel: Slough 20621 (STD code 0753)
Associate Company: Saint Paul Publications, Ballykeeran, Athlone, Republic of Ireland
Subject: Christian Religion
Related Bookshops: Saint Paul Book Centres at 128 Notting Hill Gate, London W11 4BA; 133 Corporation St, Birmingham B4 6PH; 82 Bold St, Liverpool L1 4HR; 5A-7 Royal Exchange Sq, Glasgow G1 3AH
1978: 11 titles *1979:* 10 titles *Founded:* 1967
ISBN Publisher's Prefix: 0-85439

Salamander Books Ltd, 27 Old Gloucester St, London WC1N 3AF Tel: (01) 242 6693 Cable Add: Salamander London WC1 Telex: 261113
Chairman: J Proost; *Man Dir, Production:* Malcolm Little; *Editorial:* Ray Bonds; *Sales, Rights & Permissions:* Janet Pilch
Orders to: New English Library Ltd, Barnard's Inn, Holborn, London EC1N 2JR
Parent Company: Henri Proost & Cie, Belgium (qv)
Subjects: Illustrated Reference Books: Military, Natural History, Music
1978: 10 titles *1979:* 10 titles *Founded:* 1974
ISBN Publisher's Prefix: 0-86101

Salesian Publications & Don Bosco Film Strips, Blaisdon Hall, Longhope, Gloucestershire GL17 0AQ Tel: Longhope 830247 (STD code 0452)
Subject: Religion

The **Saltire** Society, Saltire Ho, 13 Atholl Crescent, Edinburgh EH3 8HA Tel: (031) 228 6621
Subsidiary Company: New Saltire Ltd (at above address)
Imprint: Saltire Classics
Subjects: Scottish Art, Literature, Law, Music
Founded: 1936
Miscellaneous: Associated with The Scottish Civic Trust, 24 George Sq, Glasgow, in publishing *The Scottish Review*
ISBN Publisher's Prefix: 0-85411

Salvationist Publishing & Supplies Ltd, 117-121 Judd St, King's Cross, London WC1H 9NN Tel: (01) 387 1656 Cable Add: Savingly, London WC1H 99
Rights & Permissions: Lt Col B Sylvester
Associate Company: Campfield Press, St Albans
Subjects: Religion, Music, Juveniles
1978: 5 titles
ISBN Publisher's Prefix: 0-85412

Sampson Low, a division of Purnell Books (qv)

Satellite Books Publishers, Kendall Ho, 9 Kendall Rd, Isleworth, Middlesex Tel: (01) 568 4506
Man Dir, Rights & Permissions: Charles Ejiofor; *Editorial:* Jeremy Hudson, Bernadette Deacon; *Publicity:* Audrey Holmwood
Subjects: General Fiction, Biography, Occult, Politics, Humour
1978: 6 titles *Founded:* 1976
ISBN Publisher's Prefix: 0-905186

W B **Saunders** Co Ltd, see Holt-Saunders Ltd

Saxon House, 1 Westmead, Farnborough, Hampshire GU14 7RU Tel: Farnborough 519221 (STD code 0252)
An imprint of Gower Publishing Co Ltd (qv), with details as for Gower Publishing except as follows:
Editorial: John Irwin
Subjects: Sociology, Economics, Politics, Law, Medicine, Psychology, Engineering, Public Administration, Environment

ISBN Publisher's Prefixes: 0-347 (pre-1976 titles), 0-566

Schofield & Sims Ltd, Dogley Mill, Fenay Bridge, Huddersfield HD8 0NQ Tel: Kirkburton 5643 (STD code 048483) Cable Add: Schosims Huddersfield
Deputy Chairman & Man Dir: John S Nesbitt; *Sales Dir:* Jack Brierley
Subjects: Secondary & Primary Textbooks, Educational Materials
1978: 30 titles *1979:* 38 titles *Founded:* 1901
ISBN Publisher's Prefix: 0-7217

Scholastic Publications*, 161 Fulham Rd, London SW3 6SW Tel: (01) 581 0241/3 Cable Add: Scholastic, London SW3 Telex: 22281
Man Dir: David Kidd; *Editorial Dir:* Dorothy Wood
Subjects: Primary Education, Juvenile Fiction and Non-fiction
Book Clubs: Lucky, See-saw, Chip, Scene, Criterion
1978: 10 titles
ISBN Publisher's Prefix: 0-590

School of Oriental & African Studies, Malet St, London WC1E 7HP Tel: (01) 637 2388 Cable Add: Soasul London WC1
Publications Officer: M J Daly
Subjects: Oriental and African Language, Literature, History, Religion, Bibliography, Art
1978: 10 titles *1979:* 8 titles *Founded:* 1917
ISBN Publisher's Prefix: 0-901877, 0-7286

Science Research Associates Ltd, Newtown Rd, Henley-on-Thames, Oxfordshire RG9 1EW Tel: Henley-on-Thames 5959 (STD code 04912) Cable Add: Sciresuk, Henley-on-Thames RG9 1EW Telex: 848454
Man Dir & Editorial: David M Neale; *Sales, Advertising, Publicity:* B Preston; *Rights & Permissions:* K L Turner
Parent Company: Science Research Associates Inc, 155 North Wacker Dr, Chicago, Ill 60606 (Science Research Associates Inc is a subsidiary of IBM)
Associate Companies: Science Research Associates Pty Ltd, Australia (qv); Science Research Associates (Canada) Ltd, 707 Gordon Baker Rd, Willowdale, Ontario, Canada; Société de Recherche Appliquée à l'Education, 92 blvd de Latour-Maubourg, F-75007 Paris, France
Subjects: University, Secondary & Primary Textbooks, Commercial & Technical Education, Academic & Vocational Guidance Publications, Educational & Industrial Tests
ISBN Publisher's Prefix: 0-574

Scientechnica (Publishers) Ltd, see John Wright & Sons Ltd

Scolar Press, 90 Great Russell St, London WC1 Tel: (01) 631 4141
Chairman: J E Commander: *Man Dir:* James Price; *Marketing Manager:* Ann Sexsmith
Parent Company: Bemrose UK Ltd (qv for associate companies)
Subjects: English Literature, History, Music, Art, Horticulture, Photographic, Children's Books, Social Sciences, Facsimile and Limited Editions
Bookshop: Scolar Book-room, 90 Great Russell St, London WC1
1980: 50 titles *Founded:* 1966
ISBN Publisher's Prefixes: 0-85417, 0-85967

Scorpion Publications Ltd, 377 High St, Stratford, London E15 4QZ Tel: (01) 555 3339 Telex: 261547
Editorial: L Harrow; *Sales:* A Grangelin; *Production, Publicity, Rights & Permissions:* Colin Larkin

Associate Company: Comrade Productions, 28 Clavering Rd, Wanstead, London E12 5EX
Imprints: Art Heritage, Dark Star
Subjects: Art, Architecture, Photography, Music, Juveniles, Oriental Carpets, General Non-fiction
1978: 8 titles *1979:* 8 titles *Founded:* 1976
ISBN Publisher's Prefix: 0-905906

Scottish Academic Press Ltd, 33 Montgomery St, Edinburgh EH7 5JX Tel: (031) 556 2796 Telex: 727872
Dirs: J Steven Watson, Douglas Grant, Christopher Blake, W N Everitt,, P Mc L D Duff, Ronald Crawford, David Dorward
Subjects: Scholarly, Scottish interest
1980: 232 titles *Founded:* 1969
Miscellaneous: Owned jointly by the Universities of St Andrews, Dundee and Strathclyde, and associated with Sussex University Press and The Handsel Press (qqv)
ISBN Publisher's Prefix: 0-7073

Scripture Union, 130 City Rd, London EC1V 2NJ Tel: (01) 250 1966
Publishing Dirs: Paul Marsh and Robert Hicks; *Rights & Permissions:* Paula Sandison, Gill Rennie
Subsidiary Companies: Frontier Youth Trust; Inter School Christian Fellowship; Ark Publishing
Imprints: Ark, Kingfisher, Leopard, Panther, Tiger
Subjects: Music, Religion, Juveniles, Educational Materials
Bookshops: 5 Wigmore St, London W1H 0AD; 77 Bridge St, Manchester M3 2RH; 16 Park St, Croydon CR0 1YE; 3 King Edward St, Leeds LS1 6AX; 3 Suffolk Rd, Cheltenham, Gloucestershire; 280 St Vincent St, Glasgow C2; 30 Cow Wynd, Falkirk, Stirlingshire; 21 Rutland Sq, Edinburgh; 8 Kings Rd, Brighton, Sussex BN1 1NE; 22 Fisher St, Carlisle, Cumbria CA3 8RH; 14 North Bridge St, Sunderland, Tyne and Wear SR5 1LD; 14 Eton St, Richmond, Surrey TW9 1EE; 29 Woodthrope Rd, Ashford, Middx; 22 Lower Hillgate, Stockport, Cheshire SK1 1JE; 18 Slater St, Liverpool L1 4BS; 12 Wellington Pl, Belfast BT1 6JB; 38 Ardconnel, Inverness; 68 Princes St, Perth; 4 Peterborough Rd, Harrow, Middx HA1 2BQ
Founded: 1867
ISBN Publisher's Prefixes: 0-85421, 0-86201

Seafarer Books, an imprint of The Merlin Press Ltd (qv)

Search Press Ltd, 2-10 Jerdan Pl, Fulham, London SW6 5PT Tel: (01) 385 6261
Man Dir, Sales, Publicity: Charlotte de la Bedoyere; *Editorial, Rights & Permissions:* John Cumming, David Lewis; *Production:* Roberta Maier
Associate Companies: Burns & Oates Ltd (qv); Search for Leisure Ltd (at above address)
Subjects: Philosophy, Theology, Literature and Literary Criticism, Poetry, History, Biography, Religion, General, Moral Education, Mysticism, Third World, Children's, Arts and Crafts
1978: 31 titles *Founded:* 1962
ISBN Publisher's Prefix: 0-85532

Martin **Secker & Warburg** Ltd, 54 Poland St, London W1V 3DF Tel: (01) 437 2075 Cable Add: Psophidian London W1
Man Dir: T G Rosenthal; *Editorial Dir:* A J Blackwell; *Sales Dir:* T R Manderson; *Production Dir:* P Ireland; *Publicity Manager:* Beth Macdougall; *Rights & Permissions:* Gillian Vale
Orders to: The Windmill Press, Kingswood,

UNITED KINGDOM 401

Tadworth, Surrey KT20 6TG Tel: Mogador 3511 (STD code 073783)
Parent Company: Heinemann Group of Publishers Ltd (qv)
Associate Company: Alison Press, 5 Harley Gardens, London SW10 9SW
Subjects: General Fiction, Belles Lettres, Poetry, Biography, History, Music, Cinema, Art, Philosophy, Reference, Psychology, Social Science, High-priced Paperbacks, Criticism, Photography, Judaica, Political Science
Book Club: Nationwide Book Services (owned jointly with William Collins Sons & Co Ltd, UK, William Heinemann (International) Ltd, UK, and Albert Bonniers Förlag AB, Sweden)
1978: 82 titles *1979:* 86 titles *Founded:* 1910
ISBN Publisher's Prefix: 0-436

Seeley, Service & Co Ltd, see Frederick Warne (Publishers) Ltd

Severn House Publishers Ltd, 144-46 New Bond St, London W1Y 9FD Tel: (01) 499 3784
Chairman: Edwin Buckhalter; *Commissioning Editor:* Ian Jackson; *Man Dir:* Philip Cotterell; *Production Manager:* Louisa Lazarus; *Rights & Permissions:* Barbara Levy
Orders to: Tiptree Book Services Ltd, St Luke's Chase, Tiptree, Colchester, Essex CO5 0SR
Parent Company: Severn House Publishers (Holdings) Ltd, 144-46 New Bond St, London W1Y 9FD
Subsidiary Companies: Severn House Paperbacks Ltd (address as above); Buzby Books Ltd (address as above)
Associate Companies: Elmfield Press Ltd, White Lion Publishers Ltd
Imprint: Buzby Books Ltd
Subjects: Fiction, Thrillers, Romance, War, Historical, Science Fiction, Westerns, Film and TV tie-ins, Juveniles, Natural History, Cookery, Biography
1978: 84 titles *1979:* 124 titles *Founded:* 1974
ISBN Publisher's Prefixes: 0-7278 (Severn House), 0-7284 (White Lion), 0-7057 (Elmfield Press)

Shakespeare Head Press, an imprint of Basil Blackwell Publisher Ltd (qv)

Sheed & Ward Ltd, 6 Blenheim St, London W1Y 0SA Tel: (01) 629 0306 Cable Add: Stanza London W1
Dirs: M T Redfern, K G Darke
Subjects: Biography, History, Philosophy, Reference, Religion
Founded: 1926
ISBN Publisher's Prefix: 0-7220

Sheldon Press, SPCK Bldg, Marylebone Rd, London NW1 4DU Tel: (01) 387 5282 Cable Add: Futurity London NW1
General Secretary: P N G Gilbert; *Editorial Dir:* Darley Anderson; *Sales Dir:* Alan Goodworth; *Advertising Dir:* Sandie Byrne
Subjects: Biography, Religion, Philosophy, High-priced Paperbacks, Social & Political Science, Psychology, Animals
1979: 25 titles
Miscellaneous: Division of SPCK (qv)
ISBN Publisher's Prefix: 0-85969

Shepheard-Walwyn (Publishers) Ltd, 51 Vineyard Hill Rd, London SW19 7JL Tel: (01) 946 0437 Cable Add: Shepwyn, London SW19
Man Dir: A R A Werner
Subjects: General Nonfiction
1978: 5 titles *Founded:* 1971
ISBN Publisher's Prefix: 0-85683

Sheppard Press Ltd, PO Box 42, Russell Chambers, Covent Garden, London WC2E 8AX Tel: (01) 240 0406 Cable Add: Iffcass London WC2
Man Dir: T Rendall Davies
Subjects: Book Trade Reference
1978: 3 titles *Founded:* 1944
ISBN Publisher's Prefix: 0-900661

Shire Publications Ltd, Cromwell House, Church St, Princes Risborough, Aylesbury, Buckinghamshire HP17 9AJ Tel: Princes Risborough 4301 (STD code 08444)
Man Dir: John W Rotheroe
Subsidiary Companies: The Gubblecote Press; Cadbury Lamb
Subjects: Paperbacks on Antiques, Collecting, Architecture, Social History, Military History, Transport, Archaeology, Hand Craft Industries. Publishers of *Discovering* Books, *Lifelines* and Shire Albums
1978: 45 titles *1979:* 55 titles *Founded:* 1966
ISBN Publisher's Prefix: 0-85263

Sidgwick & Jackson Ltd, 1 Tavistock Chambers, Bloomsbury Way, London WC1A 2SG Tel: (01) 242 6081 Cable Add: Watergate Westcent London
Chairman: The Earl of Longford; *Man Dir, Rights & Permissions:* William Armstrong; *Sales Dir:* Stephen du Sautoy; *Editorial:* Margaret Willes; *Publicity:* Victoria Stace; *Foreign Rights:* Katrina Chalmers
Subjects: General Fiction, Belles Lettres, Poetry, Biography, History, Music, Art, Philosophy, Religion, Juveniles, General & Social Science, High-priced Paperbacks, Science Fiction
1978: 70 titles *Founded:* 1908
ISBN Publisher's Prefix: 0-283

Charles **Skilton** Ltd, 2 & 3 Abbeymount, Edinburgh EH8 8JH Tel: (031) 661 9339
Man Dir: Charles Skilton; *Editorial:* Jean Desebrock
Associate Company: Fudge & Co Ltd (qv)
Subsidiary Companies: Albyn Press Ltd (qv), Luxor Press Ltd, Tallis Press Ltd, Fortune Press, Polybooks Ltd (all at 2 & 3 Abbeymount, Edinburgh 8)
Branch Off: 115 Old St, London EC1
Subjects: Art, Graphic Arts, Reference, Biography, Antiquarian, Cookery, Sexology, Scottish Fiction
Founded: 1943
ISBN Publisher's Prefixes: 0-284 (Skilton, Albyn, Luxor, Tallis), 0-85240 (Fortune), 0-7050 (Fudge)

Skilton & Shaw, an imprint of Fudge & Co Ltd (qv)

Thomas **Skinner** Directories, Windsor Court, East Grinstead House, East Grinstead, West Sussex RH1G 1XE Tel: East Grinstead 26972 (STD code 0342)
Man Dir: R Haddrell; *Publishing Dir:* R J E Dangerfield
Parent Company: IPC Business Press Information Services Ltd
Subject: Directories
ISBN Publisher's Prefixes: 0-611, 0-900808

Colin **Smythe** Ltd, PO Box 6, Gerrards Cross, Buckinghamshire SL9 7AE Tel: Gerrards Cross 86000 (STD code 02813) Cable Add: Smythebooks Gerrards Cross
Man Dir: Colin Smythe
Subjects: Belles Lettres, Poetry, Biography, History, Music, Art, Philosophy, Reference, Religion, Parapsychology, High-priced Paperbacks, English and Anglo-Irish Literature & Criticism
1978: 19 titles *1979:* 13 titles *Founded:* 1966
ISBN Publisher's Prefixes: 0-900675, 0-901072, 0-86140

The **Society** for Promoting Christian Knowledge, see SPCK

The **Solicitors' Law** Stationery Society Ltd, see Oyez Publishing Ltd

Soncino Press Ltd, Dutch House, 307-8 High Holborn, London WC1V 7LL Cable Add: Soncino London W1
Man Dir: P Bloch
Subsidiary Company: J Saville & Co Ltd (at above address)
Branch Off: 405 Lexington Ave, New York, NY 10017
Subject: Religion (Jewish)
Founded: 1929
ISBN Publisher's Prefix: 0-900689

Sotheby Parke Bernet Publications, an imprint of Philip Wilson Publishers (qv)

Southside, see Canongate Publishing Ltd

Souvenir Press Ltd, 43 Great Russell St, London WC1B 3PA Tel: (01) 580 9307/8 & 637 5711/2/3 Cable Add: Publisher London WC1 Telex: 24710
Shipping Add: Tiptree Book Services, Tiptree, Colchester, Essex
Man Dir & Rights & Permissions: Ernest Hecht; *Editorial:* Rosalynde de Lanerolle; *Production:* Rodney King; *Publicity & Advertising Manager:* Tessa Harrow
Associate Company: Souvenir Press (Australia) Pty Ltd
Subsidiary Companies: Souvenir Press (Educational & Academic) Ltd; Euro-Features Ltd; Pictorial Presentations Ltd; Pop-Universal Ltd; Condor Books
Imprints: Condor Books, Souvenir Press
Branch Off: 311 Singel, Amsterdam, Netherlands
Subjects: General Fiction, Belles Lettres, Poetry, Biography, History, How-to, Music, Art, Philosophy, Religion, Juveniles, Large-format Paperbacks, Medicine, Psychology, Social Science
Bookshop: Souvenir Press Bookshop, 43 Great Russell St, London WC1B 3PA
1979: 50 titles *1980:* 44 titles *Founded:* 1954
ISBN Publisher's Prefix: 0-285

Neville **Spearman***, The Priory Gate, 57 Friars St, Sudbury, Suffolk Tel: Sudbury 71818 (STD code 07873)
Dirs: Neville Armstrong, M J Armstrong
Subsidiary Company: Neville Spearman (Jersey) Ltd, Normandy House, PO Box 75, St Helier, Jersey, Channel Islands
Subjects: Specialists in the Occult, Metaphysical and Unorthodox
ISBN Publisher's Prefixes: 0-85435, 0-85978 (Jersey)

Sphere Books Ltd, 30-32 Gray's Inn Rd, London WC1X 8JL Tel: (01) 405 2087 Cable Add: Spherbooks London Telex: 299342
Warehouse: High St, Sandhurst, Camberley, Surrey
Imprints: include Abacus, Sphere
Subjects: General Fiction and Nonfiction, Biography, History, How-to, Music, Art, Philosophy, Reference, Low- & High-priced Paperbacks, Medicine, Psychology, General & Social Science
1978: 262 titles *Founded:* 1967
Miscellaneous: Company is a member of the Thomson Books Ltd group, a part of International Thomson Organization Ltd (Canada)
ISBN Publisher's Prefixes: 0-7221 (Sphere), 0-349 (Abacus)

E & F N **Spon** Ltd, 11 New Fetter Lane, London EC4P 4EE Tel: (01) 583 9855 Cable Add: Fenspon London EC4 Telex: 263398
Shipping Add: Associated Book Publishers Ltd, North Way, Andover, Hampshire

Editorial: Phillip Read; *Marketing:* Peter F Shepherd; *Production:* Brian West; *Rights & Permissions:* Vikki Anderson
Parent Company: Associated Book Publishers Ltd (qv)
Subjects: Reference, Engineering, Building, Applied Sciences
1978: 10 titles *1979:* 11 titles *Founded:* 1834
ISBN Publisher's Prefix: 0-419

Sporting and Leisure Press, an imprint of Barracuda Books Ltd (qv)

Sporting Handbooks Ltd, 12 Dyott St, London WC1A 1DF Tel: (01) 836 8911
Parent Company: J Whitaker & Sons Ltd (qv)
Subjects: Sports, Games & Pastimes
ISBN Publisher's Prefix: 0-85020

Spring Books, an imprint of The Hamlyn Publishing Group (qv)

Springwood Books Ltd, 49-51 Bedford Row, London WC1V 6RL Tel: (01) 242 7866/7
Telex: 28413
Man Dir, Editorial, Sales, Production, Rights & Permissions: Christopher Foster; *Publicity:* Ingela Claxton
Orders to: George Philip & Son, PO Box 1, Littlehampton, Sussex BN17 7EN
Subjects: Fiction, Poetry, Biography, Children's Books, History, Finance, Music, Archeology, Art, Cookery
1978: 20 titles *1979:* 40 titles *Founded:* 1976
ISBN Publisher's Prefix: 0-905947

Spurbooks Ltd, 6 Parade Court, Bourne End, Bucks SL8 5SF Tel: Bourne End 25350 (STD code 06285) Cables: Spurbooks Bourne End Bucks
Man Dir: Robin Neillands; *Editorial Dir:* Estelle Huxley; *Publicity:* Margaret Feldon
Subjects: Venture Sports, Outdoor Leisure, History
1979: 80 titles *Founded:* 1968
ISBN Publisher's Prefix: 0-902875, 0-904978

Stacey International, 128 Kensington Church St, London W8 4BH Tel: (01) 727 5627/221 6109 Cable Add: Staceybook London W8 Telex: 298768
Man Dir: T Stacey
Subjects: General, Middle East
1978: 11 titles *Founded:* 1974
ISBN Publisher's Prefix: 0-905743

Stage 1, 47 Red Lion St, London WC1R 4PF Tel: (01) 405 7780
Publisher: Richard Handyside
Subjects: University & Secondary Education, Politics, Economics, Social Sciences
1980: 5 titles
ISBN Publisher's Prefix: 0-85035

Stainer & Bell Ltd, 82 High Rd, London N2 9PW Tel: (01) 444 9135
Man Dir: Bernard A Braley; *Marketing Dir:* Keith Robinson; *Executive Chairman & Editorial Dir:* Allen Percival
Imprints: include Augener, Belton Books, Galliard, A Weekes, Joseph Williams
Subjects: Music, Education, Drama, History, Religion, Biography, Sociology
ISBN Publisher's Prefix: 0-85249

Stam Press Ltd, Educa House, Liddington Estate, Leckhampton Rd, Cheltenham, Glos GL53 0DN Tel: Cheltenham 42127/42451 (STD code 0242) Telex: 43592
Man Dir: Stanley Thornes; *Production Dir:* Roy Kendall; *Trade Manager:* Margot van de Weijer
Parent Company: The Kluwer Group, Netherlands (qv)
Associate Company: Stanley Thornes (Publishers) Ltd (qv)
Subjects: Technical & Scientific
1978: 5 titles *1979:* 3 titles

Stanford Maritime Ltd, 12-14 Long Acre, London WC2E 9LP Tel: (01) 836 7863
Cable Add: Philip London WC2
Telex: 21667
Man Dir: M A Bovill; *Export Sales Manager:* Rex W Knott; *Rights & Permissions:* Phoebe Mason
Orders to: George Philip & Son Ltd, Arndale Rd, Lineside Industrial Estate, Littlehampton, Sussex BN17 7EN
Associate Company: George Philip & Son Ltd (qv)
Subjects: Nautical books and charts for yachtsmen and professional seamen
ISBN Publisher's Prefix: 0-540

Star, an imprint of W H Allen & Co Ltd (qv)

Harold **Starke** Ltd, Pegasus House, 116-120 Golden Lane, London EC1Y 0TL Tel: (01) 253 2145/6
Editorial, Rights & Permissions: Miss N Galinski; *Sales:* H Starke; *Production:* C Tuthill; *Publicity:* Miss Pat Mitchell
Orders to: The Barn, Northgate, Beccles, Suffolk
Parent Company: Burke Publishing Co Ltd (qv)
Subjects: General Nonfiction, Reference, Medical
Founded: 1960
ISBN Publisher's Prefix: 0-287

Rudolf **Steiner** Press, 35 Park Rd, London NW1 6XT Tel: (01) 723 9514
Editorial, Rights & Permissions: J Collis; *Sales:* M McAlister; *Production, Publicity:* J Playfoot
Subjects: Art & Architecture, Philosophy, Education, Religion, Social Sciences, Natural Sciences, Agriculture
Imprint: Pharos Books (paperback)
Bookshops: 35 Park Rd, London NW1; 38 Museum St, London WC1
1979: 25 titles *Founded:* 1920
ISBN Publisher's Prefix: 0-85440

Patrick **Stephens** Ltd, Bar Hill, Cambridge CB3 8EL Tel: Crafts Hill 80010 (STD code 0954) Cable Add: Peeselpubs, Cambridge Telex: 817677
Man Dir: Patrick Stephens; *Deputy Man & Editorial Dir:* Darryl Reach; *Sales Manager:* Peter Townsend; *Production:* Ian Heath; *Managing Editor, Rights & Permissions:* Bruce Quarrie
Subjects: How-to, Maritime, Military, Modelling, Motoring, Motorcycling, Aviation, Art, Photography, Wargaming, Crafts, Railways, Angling, Boating & Sailing, Commercial Vehicles
1978: 39 titles *1979:* 46 titles *Founded:* 1967
ISBN Publisher's Prefix: 0-85059

Stevens & Sons Ltd, 11 New Fetter Lane, London EC4P 4EE Tel: (01) 583 9855
Cable Add: Subjicio London EC4
Shipping Add: North Way, Andover, Hampshire
Man Dir: C D O Evans
Parent Company: Associated Book Publishers Ltd (qv)
Subjects: Reference books for lawyers and solicitors, Textbooks for law students and law teachers
Founded: 1888
ISBN Publisher's Prefix: 0-420

Stillitron, 72 New Bond St, London W1Y 0QY Tel: (01) 493 1177 Cable Add: Stillitron, Ldn Telex: 23475
President: Gerald B Stillit
Subject: Modern Languages
1978: 11 titles *Founded:* 1964
ISBN Publisher's Prefix: 0-288

Stobart & Son Ltd, 67-73 Worship St, London EC2A 2EL Tel: (01) 247 0501
Publicity: B J Davies
Subjects: Woodwork, Timber, Forestry, Handicrafts
1979: 8 titles
ISBN Publisher's Prefix: 0-85442

Student Christian Movement Press, see S C M Press Ltd

Studio Publications (Ipswich) Ltd, 32 Princes St, Ipswich, Suffolk IP1 1RJ Tel: Ipswich 217127 (STD code 0473)
Man Dir: Barrie John Henderson; *Publicity:* Elizabeth Henderson
Orders to: (Sports Books) Ken Dickson (Marketing) Ltd, 14 Crossways, Silwood Rd, Sunninghill, Ascot, Berkshire SL5 0PY; (Children's Books) WHS Distributors, Freemans Common, Leicester
Imprints: Munch Bunch, Studio Publications
Subjects: Sports, Children's
1978: 8 titles *1979:* 18 titles *Founded:* 1975
ISBN Publisher's Prefixes: 0-904584, 0-86215

Studio Vista, 35 Red Lion Sq, London WC1R 4SG Tel: (01) 831 6100 Cable Add: Caspeg London WC1 Telex: 28648 Casmac G
Managing Editor, Rights & Permissions: John L Smith
Subjects: Art, Applied Art, Design, Crafts, Architecture, Interior Decoration, Theatre, Dance, Cinema
1979: 49 titles
Miscellaneous: Division of Cassell Ltd (qv)
ISBN Publisher's Prefix: 0-289

Sundial, an imprint of Octopus Books (qv)

Surrey University Press, Bishopbriggs, Glasgow G64 2NZ Tel: (041) 772 2311
London Off: Furnival Ho, 14-18 High Holborn, London Tel: (01) 242 5832
Dir: Dr G MacKintosh
Parent Company: Blackie & Son (qv)
Subjects: Engineering, Microbiology, Biomedicine, Chemistry, Physics, Hotel & Catering Studies
Founded: 1972
ISBN Publisher's Prefix: 0-903384

Sussex University Press, Sussex House, Falmer, Brighton, East Sussex BN1 9RH Tel: Brighton 606755 (STD code 0273)
Publications Committee: Professors G F A Best, R J Blin-Stoyle, D F Pocock, A K Thorlby
Subjects: Scholarly
1978: 3 titles *Founded:* 1971
Miscellaneous: Associated with The Scottish Academic Press and The Handsel Press (qqv)
ISBN Publisher's Prefix: 0-85621

Sussex Video Ltd, educational video tape-producing associate company of World Microfilms Publications Ltd (qv)

Sweet & Maxwell Ltd, 11 New Fetter Lane, London EC4P 4EE Tel: (01) 583 9855
Cable Add: Subjicio London EC4
Shipping Add: North Way, Andover, Hampshire
Man Dir: C D O Evans
Parent Company: Associated Book Publishers Ltd (qv)
Subjects: Law (Reference & University Textbooks), Business
Founded: 1799
ISBN Publisher's Prefix: 0-421

Systems Publications Ltd, now Caxton Publications Ltd (qv)

Tabard Press Ltd, see E P Publishing Ltd

Tabor Publications*, 3-5 Valentine Pl, London SE1 Tel: (01) 928 4468
Publisher: Colin Heard

Tallis Press Ltd, see Charles Skilton Ltd

Talmy, Franklin Ltd*, 29 Rupert House, Nevern Sq, London SW5 Tel: (01) 584 7545 Cable Add: Franklit, London
Man Dir: Mike Franklin; *Sales, Publicity, Advertising, Rights & Permissions:* Madeleine Morel
Branch Off: 170 Philip St, Sydney, Australia
Subjects: General Fiction, Belles Lettres, Biography, History, How-to, Philosophy
ISBN Publisher's Prefix: 0-900735

Tanden, an imprint of W H Allen & Co Ltd (qv)

Tantivy Press, associate company of Thomas Yoseloff (qv)

Target, an imprint of W H Allen & Co Ltd (qv)

Tate Gallery Publications, Millbank, London SW1P 4RG Tel: (01) 834 5651/2 Cable Add: Tategal London
Publications Manager: Iain Bain; *Sales Manager:* Brian Lawler; *Rights & Permissions:* Graham Langton; *Shop Manager:* Stanley Bennett
Retail Shop: Tate Gallery, Millbank, London SW1P 4RG
Subjects: Art books and catalogues
1979: 3 titles *Founded:* 1931
ISBN Publisher's Prefixes: 0-900874, 0-905005

Tavistock Publications Ltd*, 11 New Fetter Lane, London EC4P 4EE Tel: (01) 583 9855 Cable Add: Subjicio London
Shipping Add: Associated Book Publishers Ltd, North Way, Andover, Hampshire
Editorial Dir: Gill Davies; *Marketing Dir:* Peter Shepherd; *Advertising:* Lyndsay Williams; *Rights & Permissions:* V Anderson
Parent Company: Associated Book Publishers Ltd (qv)
Subjects: Sociology, Anthropology, Psychiatry, Psychology, Philosophy, Social Medicine, Paperbacks, Reference
Bookshop: Sweet & Maxwell Spon Booksellers, North Way, Andover, Hampshire
Founded: 1947
ISBN Publisher's Prefix: 0-422

Taylor & Francis Ltd, 4 John St, London WC1N 2ET Tel: (01) 405 2237 Telex: 858540
Man Dir: S A Lewis; *Publishing Dir:* M I Dawes; *Sales & Marketing Manager:* K R Courtney
Branch Off: Trade, Publicity, Warehouse
Orders to: Taylor & Francis Ltd, Rankine Rd, Basingstoke, Hampshire RG24 0PR
Subsidiary Companies: Wykeham Publications (London) Ltd; Taylor & Francis (Printers) Ltd; Taylor & Francis (Filmsetting) Ltd
Subjects: Physics, Medicine, Psychology, Engineering, General Science, University Textbooks, International Affairs
1978: 21 titles *1979:* 17 titles *Founded:* 1798
ISBN Publisher's Prefix: 0-85066

Teach Yourself Books, an imprint of Hodder & Stoughton Ltd (qv)

Teacher Publishing Co Ltd, Derbyshire House, Lower St, Kettering, Northamptonshire NN16 8BB Tel: Kettering 518407 (STD code 0536)
ISBN Publisher's Prefix: 0-900642

Teakfield Ltd, see Gower Publishing Co Ltd

The **Technical** Press Ltd, Freeland, Oxford OX7 2AP Tel: Freeland 881788 (STD code 0993) Cable Add: Tecpreslon Oxford Telex: 847777 Tecpreslon
Chairman, Editorial: Paul Stobart; *Man Dir, Production, Rights & Permissions:* Patrick Tickell; *Sales, Publicity:* David Wilson
Associate Company: Freeland Press Ltd (details as for The Technical Press); Institute of Personnel Management
Subjects: How-to, Reference, High-priced Paperbacks, Engineering, General Science, University & Secondary Textbooks
1978: 10 titles *1979:* 11 titles *Founded:* 1933
ISBN Publisher's Prefixes: 0-291 (Technical), 0-900363 (Freeland), 0-85292 (IPM)

Thomas **Telford** Ltd*, Telford House, PO Box 101, 26-34 Old St, London EC1P 1JH Tel: (01) 253 9999 Telex: 21792 ref 966
Parent Company: The Institution of Civil Engineers
Subjects: Engineering, Transportation, Hydraulics, Hydrology and Public Health, Soil Mechanics & Foundations, Structures and Buildings, Education & Training, Nuclear Engineering, Journals
Bookshop: 26-34 Old St, London EC1P 1JH
1978: 40 titles *Founded:* 1973
ISBN Publisher's Prefixes: 0-91948, 0-7277

Temple Press, an imprint of The Hamlyn Publishing Group (qv)

Maurice **Temple Smith** Ltd, 37 Great Russell St, London WC1B 3PP Tel: (01) 636 9810
Man Dir: Maurice Temple Smith
Subjects: Biography, History, Philosophy, Religion, High-priced Paperbacks, Psychology, Social Science
Founded: 1970
ISBN Publisher's Prefix: 0-85117

Teredo Books Ltd, 19 Waldegrave Rd, Brighton, East Sussex BN1 6GR Tel: (0273) 505432
Man Dir: Alex A Hurst; *Trade Manager:* R M Cookson
Orders to: PO Box 430, Brighton, East Sussex BN1 6BT
Subjects: High-quality Nautical, Marine Art
1978: 1 title
ISBN Publisher's Prefix: 0-903662

Tetrad Press*, 3 Limehouse Wharf, 148-150 Narrow St, London E14 8BP
Subject: Art

Thames & Hudson Ltd, 30-34 Bloomsbury St, London WC1B 3QP Tel: (01) 636 5488 Cable Add: Thameshuds London WC1 Telex: 25992/3
Shipping Add: 44 Clockhouse Rd, Farnborough, Hampshire
Dirs: Thomas Neurath, Eva Neurath; *Editorial:* Stanley Baron; *Sales:* Simon Huntley; *Production:* Werner Guttmann; *Rights & Permissions:* Ian Middleton
Associate Companies: Thames & Hudson (Australia) Pty Ltd, 86 Stanley St, West Melbourne, Victoria 3003, Australia; Thames & Hudson Inc, 500 Fifth Ave, New York, NY 10036, USA
Subjects: Art, Architecture, History, Archaeology, Biography, Photography, Topography, Music, Theatre
ISBN Publisher's Prefix: 0-500

A **Thomas**, imprint of Thorsons Publishers Ltd (qv)

Henry **Thompson** Ltd, London Rd, Sunningdale, Berks SL5 0EP Tel: Ascot 24615/22639 (STD code 0990)
Man Dir: G C Thompson; *Marketing Services Manager:* Mrs P M Cooper; *Sales:* E C M Brown, G E Scoffin

Thomson Books Ltd, 4 Bloomsbury Sq, London WC1A 2RL Tel: (01) 404 4300 Telex: 21746
Man Dir: B H Llewellyn
Parent Company: International Thomson Organization (Canada)
Group Companies' Imprints:
Paperback: Abacus; Sphere Books (qv)
General Trade: Elm Tree; Hamish Hamilton (qv); Hamish Hamilton Children's Books; Michael Joseph (qv); Pelham (qv); Rainbird (qv)
Educational: Thomas Nelson (qv)
Naval, Military, Aviation: Jane's Publishing Co Ltd (qv)
Overseas Companies: Nelson (Canada); Thomas Nelson (Nigeria-40 per cent holding) (qv); Thomas Nelson (Australia) (qv); Bowmar/Noble Publishers (USA)
Founded: 1977
Miscellaneous: See separate group company entries where marked (qv) for further information. T B L Book Service Ltd, 17-23 Nelson Way, Tuscan Trading Estate, Camberley, Surrey GU15 3EU, is the warehousing and distribution subsidiary of the company

Stanley **Thornes** (Publishers) Ltd, Educa Ho, Liddington Estate, Leckhampton Rd, Cheltenham, Glos GL53 0DN Tel: Cheltenham 42127/42451 (STD code 0242) Telex: 43592
Man Dir: Stanley Thornes; *Production Dir:* Roy Kendall; *Trade Manager:* Margot van de Weijer
Parent Company: The Kluwer Group, Netherlands (qv)
Associate Company: Stam Press Ltd (qv)
Subjects: Mathematics, Engineering, Chemistry, Biology, Business Studies, Modern Languages, Physics, English Language
1978: 22 titles *1979:* 19 titles
ISBN Publisher's Prefix: 0-85950

Thornhill Press Ltd, 24 Moorend Rd, Cheltenham, Glos GL53 0AU Tel: Cheltenham 519137 (STD code 0242)
Man Dir: D Badham-Thornhill
Subjects: Topographical Guides, also Poetry, Medical, Juveniles
1979: 6 titles *Founded:* 1972
ISBN Publisher's Prefix: 0-904110

Thornton Cox Ltd*, 45 Flood St, London SW3 Tel: (01) 589 2620
Man Dir: Richard Cox
Orders to: Geographia Ltd, 93 St Peter's St, St Albans, Herts
Subjects: Travel Guides
Founded: 1966
ISBN Publisher's Prefix: 0-902726

F A **Thorpe** (Publishing) Ltd, The Green, Bradgate Rd, Anstey, Leicester LE7 7FU Tel: Anstey 4325 (STD code 053721)
Man Dir: F A Thorpe
Subjects: Fiction, Travel & Adventure, Nonfiction
1978: 168 titles
Miscellaneous: Publishers of Ulverscroft Large Print Books
ISBN Publisher's Prefixes: 0-85456, 0-7089

Thorsons Publishers Ltd, Denington Estate, Wellingborough, Northamptonshire NN8 2RQ Tel: Wellingborough 76031/4 (STD code 0933) Cable Add: Thorgroup Wellingborough Telex: 311072 Thopub G
Chairman: J A Young; *Man Dir:* D J Young; *Rights & Permissions:* Janet Winslow; *Editorial Dir:* J R Hardaker; *Production Dir:* D C J Palmer; *Sales Manager:* C T M How
Associate Company: Turnstone Press Ltd (qv)
Imprints: Aquarian Press Ltd (qv), Athene

Publishing Co, A Thomas, Turnstone Press Ltd (qv)
Subjects: Health and healing embracing Nature cure and Diet Reform, Natural Foods & Cookery, Herbalism, Acupuncture, Homoeopathy, Yoga, Self-sufficiency and Gardening, Occultism, Self-improvement, Guides to Practical Management Techniques, Psychology
1980: 87 titles *Founded:* 1930
ISBN Publisher's Prefixes: 0-7225, 0-85030, 0-85454, 0-85385, 0-85500

The **Thule** Press, 63 Kenneth St, Stornoway, Isle of Lewis, Western Isles Tel: Stornoway 4404 (STD code 0851)
Editorial: John Button; *Sales:* Mary Anne Macdonald
Subjects: History, Topography and Literature of Scotland and Scandinavia
1978: 6 titles *1979:* 11 titles *Founded:* 1973

Thurman Publishing Ltd, 28 The Mill Trading Estate, Acton Lane, Harlesden, London NW10 7NP Tel: (01) 961 4477 Telex: 24339
Man Dirs: S J T Marshall, R C Williams; *Editorial:* Mrs S M Snow; *Sales:* S J T Marshall; *Production, Publicity:* Mrs C Piper; *Rights & Permissions:* Mrs C Piper, S J T Marshall
Parent Company: Atlantic & Western Ltd (at above address)
Associate Companies: Thurman Litho Ltd, Printers and W J Thurman Ltd, Binders (both at above address)
Subjects: Children's Books
1978: 19 titles *1979:* 18 titles *Founded:* 1974
ISBN Publisher's Prefix: 0-85985

Tiger, an imprint of Scripture Union (qv)

Times Books Ltd, 16 Golden Sq, London W1R 4BN Tel: (01) 434 3767 Telex: 264971
Chairman: Derek Jewell; *Man Dir:* B Winkleman; *Senior Editor:* P Middleton; *Assistant Editors:* A Hudson, Lawson Nagel, Pauline Batchelor; *Production Manager:* D Osler
Orders to: Hamish Hamilton, 57/59 Long Acre, London WC2E 9JL
Subjects: Atlases, General Nonfiction, Reference
ISBN Publisher's Prefix: 0-7230

Alec **Tiranti** Ltd, an imprint of Academy Editions (qv)

Tobin Music Books, an imprint of Helicon Press (qv)

Tolly Publishing Co, an imprint of Ernest Benn Ltd (qv)

Top Stone Books, 29 Station Rd, Harpenden, Herts AL5 4XB
Tel: Harpenden 64510 (STD code 05827) Telex: 826957 Top Stone
Manager: James Rutherford
Subjects: Esoteric, Religion
1978: 2 titles *1979:* 2 titles *Founded:* 1976
ISBN Publisher's Prefix: 0-906907

Topaz Publishing Ltd, 67 High St, Gt Missenden, Bucks Tel: Gt Missenden 4161/2/3/4 (STD code 02406) Cable Add: Rosco Gt Missenden Telex: Delray G 847777 Attn Topazco 431
Man Dir, Editorial & Sales: Colin Rose; *Rights & Permissions:* Diana Rose
Subjects: Nonfiction, Popular Science, Psychology, Humour
Founded: 1975
ISBN Publisher's Prefix: 0-905553

Tops'l Books, 9 Queen Victoria St, Reading RG1 1SY, Berkshire Tel: Reading 56061 (STD code 0734)
Chief Executive: Colin Elliott
Subject: Maritime History
1978: 1 title *1979:* 2 titles *Founded:* 1978
ISBN Publisher's Prefix: 0-906397

Transworld Publishers Ltd, Century House, 61-63 Uxbridge Rd, Ealing, London W5 5SA Tel: (01) 579 2652/9471 Cable Add: Transcable London W5 Telex: 267974 Shipping Add: Sanders Rd, Wellingborough, Northamptonshire
Chairman: Patrick Newman; *Man Dir:* Philip Flamank; *Editorial Dir:* Alan Earney; *Publicity Dir:* Wendy Tury; *Rights & Permissions:* Lavinia Trevor, Jane Smith
Parent Company: Bantam Books Inc, 666 Fifth Ave, New York, NY 10019, USA
Subsidiary Companies: Carousel Books Ltd; Corgi Books Ltd
Associate Companies: Transworld Publishers (Australia) Pty Ltd, Australia (qv); Bantam Books of Canada Inc, 888 Dupont St, Toronto, Ontario, Canada; Transworld Publishers (Pty) Ltd, South Africa
Branch Offs: Equity Life Bldg, 3 Bowen Crescent, Melbourne, Victoria 3004, Australia; PO Box 1872, Johannesburg, South Africa
Subjects: General Fiction, Low-priced Paperbacks, How and Why, Wonder Why, Storychair, Carousel Children's Books
1978: 450 titles *Founded:* 1950
ISBN Publisher's Prefix: 0-552

Travelaid Publishing, PO Box 369, London NW3 4ER Tel: (01) 794 2647
Man Dir: M Von Haag
Orders to: PO Box 28, Southwater Industrial Estate, Southwater, Sussex Tel: Southwater 731174 (STD code 0403) Telex: 87493
Subjects: Travel (Travelaid Publishing), General (Michael Haag Ltd)
1980: 4 titles (Travelaid), 3 titles (Michael Haag Ltd) *Founded:* 1969
ISBN Publisher's Prefix: 0-902743

Trigon Press, 117 Kent House Road, Beckenham, Kent BR3 1JJ Tel: (01) 778 0534
Man Dir, Sales: Roger Sheppard; *Editorial, Production:* Judith Sheppard; *Publicity:* Angela Roberts; *Rights & Permissions:* Pat Palmer
Subsidiary Company: Museum and Gallery Publishing (at above address)
Subjects: Bibliography, Business, Typography, Book Collecting, Publishing, Bookselling
1978: 2 titles *1979:* 3 titles *Founded:* 1974
ISBN Publisher's Prefix: 0-904929

Troubador, an imprint of Macdonald/Futura Publishers Ltd (qv)

Turnstone Press Ltd, Denington Estate, Wellingborough, Northamptonshire NN8 2RQ Tel: Wellingborough 76031 (STD code 0933) Cable Add: Thorgroup Wellingborough Telex: 311072 Thopub G
Man Dir: D J Young; *Editorial Dir:* Alick Bartholomew (at 37 Upper Addison Gardens, London W14 8AJ Tel: (01) 602 6885 Cable Add: Perception W14)
Associate Company: Thorsons Publishers Ltd
Subjects: Alternative Lifestyles and Philosophies, Radical Psychology, Holistic Medicine, Prehistory
1980: 15 titles *Founded:* 1971
ISBN Publisher's Prefix: 0-85500

Tyndale Press (qv), an imprint of Inter-Varsity Press

Uffici, an imprint of Clematis Press Ltd (qv)

Ulverscroft Large Print Books Ltd, see F A Thorpe (Publishing) Ltd

Uni Books, an imprint of Volturna Press (qv)

University, an imprint of Ramboro Enterprises Ltd (qv)

University Microfilms International, Xerox Publishing Group Ltd, 30-32 Mortimer St, London W1N 7RA Tel: (01) 631 5030 Telex: 8811363
International Marketing Dir: Timothy Smartt; *Sales Development Manager:* Kim Deshayes; *Publicity Manager:* Patricia Sheldon; *Area Manager, Europe:* Gavin Hilton-Jones
Parent Company: Ultimate holding company Xerox Corporation
Subjects: Multi-disciplinary materials in microfilm and hardcopy at tertiary & professional levels including dissertations and periodicals
1978: 35,000 Dissertations, 7000 serials in microform *Founded:* 1938 (USA); 1952 (UK)

University of California Press, 2-4 Brook St, London W1Y 1AA Tel: (01) 499 4688/493 5061 Cable Add: Unibooks London W1 Telex: 24224 Ref 3545
Shipping Add: International Book Distributors, 66 Wood Lane End, Hempstead, Herts
Man Dir: Trevor Brown; *Publicity Manager:* Andrew Nolan; *Sales Manager* (Exports): Anna Simpson-Muellner
Parent Company: University of California Press, 2223 Fulton St, Berkeley, California 94720, USA
Subjects: Academic (all disciplines)
1978: 219 titles *1979:* 193 titles
ISBN Publisher's Prefix: 0-520

University of Chicago Press Ltd, see The MIT Press

University of London Press Ltd (now Hodder & Stoughton Educational), see Hodder & Stoughton

University of Wales Press, 6 Gwennyth St, Cathays, Cardiff CF2 4YD Tel: Cardiff 31919 (STD code 0222)
Dir: John Rhys; *Sales:* Richard Houdmont
Imprint: Gwasg Prifysgol Cymru
Subjects: History, Music, Art, Reference, Religion, Science, Humanities, Social Sciences, University, Secondary Textbooks (Welsh & English), Journals
1978: 31 titles *1979:* 37 titles *Founded:* 1922
ISBN Publisher's Prefixes: 0-7083, 0-900768

University Presses of Columbia and Princeton, 15A Epsom Rd, Guildford, Surrey GU1 3JT Tel: Guildford 69800 (STD code 0483)
Manager: Wolfgang Wingerter
Parent Companies: Columbia University Press, New York, USA and Princeton University Press, Princeton, New Jersey, USA
Subjects: Academic Books and Paperbacks in the Humanities, Social and Natural Sciences
1978: 210 titles *1979:* 190 titles
ISBN Publisher's Prefixes: 0-231 (Columbia), 0-691 (Princeton)

University Tutorial Press Ltd, Bateman St, Cambridge CB2 1NG Tel: Cambridge 350949 (STD code 0223)
Man Dir: R R Briggs; *Trade Dir:* R E Everard
Orders to: 842 Yeovil Rd, Slough, Berkshire SL1 4JQ
Subjects: University & Secondary Textbooks
1979: 5 titles *Founded:* 1901
ISBN Publisher's Prefix: 0-7231

Unwin Paperbacks, an imprint of George Allen & Unwin (Publishers) Ltd

Update Books Ltd, 33-34 Alfred Pl, London WC1E 7DP Tel: (01) 637 4544 Cable Add: Updatepub London WC1
Executive Chairman: Dr Abraham Marcus; *Editorial, Rights & Permissions:* Mrs M E

Pettifer; *Sales, Promotion Manager:* Miss A Thorneywork; *Production:* Alan Savill
Parent Company: The Update Group Ltd
Associate Companies: Update Group Management Ltd; Update Publications Ltd; Update Hospital Publications Ltd; Update Publications (Dental) Ltd; Update Postgraduate Medical Publications Ltd; Update Nursing Publications Ltd
Branch Off: Update Publishing International Inc, 44 Engle St, Englewood, New Jersey 07631, USA
Subjects: Medical, Dental
1978: 5 titles *1979:* 1 title *Founded:* 1978
ISBN Publisher's Prefix: 0-906141

Laurence **Urdang** Associates Ltd, Market Ho, Market Sq, Aylesbury, Bucks HP20 1TN Tel: Aylesbury 84911 (STD code 0296) Telex: 83635
Chairman: A Issacs; *Dirs:* T H Long, J Daintith, L Urdang; *Production:* J Daintith
Associate Company: Laurence Urdang Inc, Essex, Conn 06426, USA
Founded: 1969
Miscellaneous: Firm compiles reference books (dictionaries, encyclopaedias, etc) and provides editorial services for publishers

Usborne Publishing Ltd, 20 Garrick St, London WC2E 9BJ Tel: (01) 379 3535 Cable Add: Uspub, London Telex: 8953598 Uspub G
Man Dir: Peter Usborne; *Production, Rights & Permissions:* David Lowe
Subjects: Children's Books (Nonfiction)
1978: 100 titles *Founded:* 1973
ISBN Publisher's Prefix: 0-86020

Vallentine, Mitchell & Co Ltd, Gainsborough House, 11 Gainsborough Rd, Leytonstone, London E11 1RS Tel: (01) 530 4226 Cable Add: Valmico London Telex: 897719
Warehouse: Macdonald & Evans Ltd, Estover Rd, Estover, Plymouth PL6 7PZ
Man Dir: Frank Cass; *Editorial:* Margaret Goodare; *Trade:* Richard Norris; *Production:* Kenneth Cowell; *Publicity:* Jacqui Beryl
Parent Company: Frank Cass & Co Ltd (qv)
Associate Company: The Woburn Press (qv)
Subjects: Jewish Studies, Literature, History, Politics
Founded: 1950
ISBN Publisher's Prefix: 0-85303

Van Nostrand Reinhold Co Ltd, Molly Millar's Lane, Wokingham, Berkshire RG11 2PY Tel: Wokingham 789456 (STD code 0734) Telex: 847798 BORDS-G
Man Dir: R S R Hutchinson; *Publisher:* David Winsor; *Sales Manager:* Roy Smith; *Promotion Sales Manager:* Roger Horton
Parent Company: Litton Educational Publishing Co Inc, 450 West 33rd St, New York, NY 10001, USA
Associate Company: Van Nostrand Reinhold, Australia (qv)
Imprints: Delmar, Fairmont Press, North Light
Subjects: Art, Reference, Professional, General & Social Science, University Textbooks, Educational Materials, High-priced Paperbacks, Medicine, Medical Economics, Psychology, Engineering, Practical, Crafts
ISBN Publisher's Prefix: 0-442

Variorum, 20 Pembridge Mews, London W11 3EQ Tel: (01) 727 5492
Proprietor: Mrs E Turner
Subjects: Architecture, History, Arts, Reference, Religion, University Textbooks, Archaeology, Economics, Oriental
1978: 17 titles *1979:* 19 titles *Founded:* 1969
ISBN Publisher's Prefixes: 0-902089, 0-86078

Varsity, an imprint of Ramboro Enterprises Ltd (qv)

Ventura Publishing Ltd, 44 Uxbridge St, London W8 7TG Tel: (01) 221 6395 Telex: 8953658 venpub G
Man Dir, Rights & Permissions: Robin Ellis
Subjects: Art, Graphics, Cookery, Practical Reference, How-to, Namesake Books (with Seymour Press)
1978: 24 titles (own imprint) *Founded:* 1977
Miscellaneous: Firm is mainly an editorial and production organization producing books for other publishers
ISBN Publisher's Prefix: 0-906284

Verso Editions, see New Left Books

Victory Press, an imprint of Kingsway Publications Ltd (qv)

Viewpoint, see Cement & Concrete Association

Vine Books Ltd*, Dean Wace House, 7 Wine Office Court, Fleet St, London EC4 Tel: (01) 583 1484
Subjects: Religious, Hymn Books, History
1978: 2 titles
ISBN Publisher's Prefix: 0-85190

Virago Ltd, Ely House, 37 Dover St, London W1X 4AH Tel: (old number—new number not available at time of going to press) (01) 734 4608/9 Cable: Caterwaul London W1
Man Dir, Rights & Permissions: Carmen Callil; *Editorial Dir:* Ursula Owen; *Production Dir:* Harriet Spicer; *Sales Manager:* Kate Griffin; *Publicity Manager:* Lennie Goodings
Orders to: (UK orders only) Routledge-Harrap Storage, Broadway House, Newtown Rd, Henley-on-Thames, Oxfordshire RG9 1EN Tel: Henley-on-Thames 78321 (STD code 04912) or from London 753 9435 Overseas orders to Virago
Subjects: Fiction, Biography, History, Philosophy, Education, Politics, Social Science & History, Women's Studies, Education, Health, Reference, Feminist Books
1979: 30 titles *1980:* 40 titles *Founded:* 1973
ISBN Publisher's Prefix: 0-86068

Virtue & Co Ltd, 25 Breakfield, Coulsdon, Surrey CR3 2UE Tel: (01) 668 4632 Cable Add: Virtutis Croydon Telex: 261507 Ref 3393
Man Dir: Michael Virtue; *Sales Dir:* R S Cook
Imprint: Harwin Press
Branch Offs: London, Bristol, Dublin
Subjects: Hotel and Catering, Reference, Religion, Educational Materials
1978: 3 titles *1979:* 4 titles *Founded:* 1819
ISBN Publisher's Prefix: 0-900778

Vision Press Ltd, 11-14 Stanhope Mews West, London SW7 5RD Tel: (01) 589 9773
Man Dir: Alan Moore
Subjects: Belles Lettres, Biography, History, Music, Art, Philosophy, Religion, Psychology
1978-79: 14 titles *Founded:* 1947
ISBN Publisher's Prefix: 0-85478

Voltaire Foundation, Taylor Institution, St Giles, Oxford OX1 3NA Tel: Oxford 512931 (STD code 0865) Telex: 83295 Nuclox G (mark for Voltaire Foundation)
Publications Manager: Andrew Brown
Subjects: Modern Languages, History, Philosophy
1978: 6 titles *1979:* 11 titles *Founded:* 1971
ISBN Publisher's Prefix: 0-7294

Volturna Press, 52 Ormonde Rd, Hythe, Kent Tel: Hythe (Kent) 69465 (STD code 0303)
Sole Partner: Dr D M C MacEwan

Imprints: Marsland Press, Uni Books, Co-chuideachd Leabhneachean Gaidhlig
Branch Off: Peterhead, Aberdeenshire
Subjects: Religion, Conservation, Biographies, Family Memoirs; All types of books in minor languages including Scottish Gaelic
1978: 3 titles *Founded:* 1968
ISBN Publisher's Prefix: 0-85606

Wales Tourist Board, Sales and Distribution Centre, Davis St, Cardiff CF1 2FU Tel: Cardiff 372685 (STD code 0222) Telex: 497269
Sales & Distribution Manager: Rhys Jones
Subjects: Maps, History, Archaeology, Accommodation & Travel Guides, Angling, Guides & Posters
ISBN Publisher's Prefix: 0-900784

Walker Books Ltd, 17-19 Hanway House, 7-12 Hanway Pl, London W1 Tel: (01) 636 0374 Telex: 299080
Man Dir: Sebastian Walker; *Editorial:* Wendy Boase; *Production:* Judy Burdsall
Orders to: Methuen Children's Books, 11 New Fetter Lane, London EC4
Subjects: Children's Books: Colour, Non-fiction, Picture Books, Novelty, Pop-up Books
1980: 17 titles *Founded:* 1978
ISBN Publisher's Prefix: 0-416

Walsingham, an imprint of Jarrold Colour Publications (qv)

Henry E **Walter** Ltd, 26 Grafton Rd, Worthing, West Sussex Tel: Worthing 204567 (STD code 0903)
Subjects: Religious, Children's Books (Rewards and Activity), Bibles, Prayer & Hymnbooks
ISBN Publisher's Prefix: 0-85479

The **Warburg** Institute (University of London), Woburn Sq, London WC1H 0AB Tel: (01) 580 9663
Assistant Secretary: Angela Barlow (to whom all enquiries about publications)
Subjects: Art, History
1979: 2 titles *Founded:* (The Institute) 1921
Miscellaneous: The Institute is a non-commercial organization
ISBN Publisher's Prefix: 0-85481

Ward Lock Educational Ltd, 116 Baker St, London W1 Tel: (01) 486 3271 Cable Add: Warlock London W1 Telex: 262364
Warehouse: Unit 14, Trident Industrial Estate, Pindar Rd, Hoddesdon, Hertfordshire EN11 0LD
Man Dir: Julian Rivers; *Editorial Dir, Production:* Christopher Kington; *Sales, Publicity, Rights & Permissions:* Judith Reinhold
Subjects: Educational
1978: 60 titles *1979:* 80 titles
Miscellaneous: Holding company is Pentos Ltd (qv for associated publishing companies)
ISBN Publisher's Prefix: 0-7062

Ward Lock Ltd, 116 Baker St, London W1 Tel: (01) 486 3271 Cable Add: Warlock London W1 Telex: 262364
Warehouse: Unit 14, Trident Industrial Estate, Pindar Rd, Hoddesdon, Herts EN11 0LD
Chairman: T A Maher; *Man Dir:* Peter Lock; *Rights & Permissions Dir:* Timothy Evans
Subjects: Equestrian, Sailing, Crafts, Yoga, Sports, Antiques, Specialist Colour Illustrated International Co-editions, How-to, Children's Information Books, Sport, Paperbacks, Reference, Cookery, Gardening
1978: 70 titles *1979:* 70 titles *Founded:* 1854
Miscellaneous: Holding company is Pentos Ltd (qv for associated publishing companies)
ISBN Publisher's Prefix: 0-7063

Frederick **Warne** (Publishers) Ltd,
40 Bedford Sq, London WC1B 3HE
Tel: (01) 580 9622 Cable Add: Warne
London WC1 Telex: 25963
Man Dir, Rights & Permissions: C W
Stephens; *Editorial Dir:* D W Bisacre; *Sales
Dir:* R D Traube
Orders to: Warne House, Vincent Lane,
Dorking, Surrey RH4 3FW Tel: Dorking
5081 (STD code 0306) Telex: 859635
Subsidiary Companies: Frederick Warne &
Co Inc, 2 Park Ave, New York NY 10016,
USA; Leo Cooper Ltd; Seeley, Service & Co
Ltd
Subjects: How-to, Music, Art, Reference,
Religion, Juveniles, Natural History,
University, Secondary & Primary
Textbooks, Educational Materials
1978: 66 titles *1979:* 64 titles *Founded:* 1865
ISBN Publisher's Prefix: 0-7232

Waterlow (London) Ltd, Holywell House,
Worship St, London EC2A 2EN Tel: (01)
247 5400 Telex: 888804
Man Dir: E Carter; *Publishing:*
V Williamson
Parent Company: BPC Ltd (qv)
Subjects: Banking, Legal, General Business
ISBN Publisher's Prefix: 0-900791

Watkins Publishing*, Bridge St, Dulverton,
Somerset Tel: Dulverton 23395 (STD code
0398)
Man Dir: Richard Robinson
Subsidiary Company: Robinson & Watkins
Books Ltd
Subjects: Religion, Technical, Science,
Medicine, Music, History, Archaeology,
Biography, Memoirs, Philosophy, Oriental,
Travel & Adventure, General Literature
Bookshop: Cecil Court, London
WC2N 4HB Tel: (01) 836 2182
ISBN Publisher's Prefix: 0-7724

W **Watson** & Co*, St Ann's Hill, Carlisle,
Cumbria
Subject: Religion

Franklin **Watts** Ltd, 8 Cork St, London W1
Tel: (01) 437 0713 Cable Add: Frawatts
London W1 Telex: 262655 Groluk
Shipping Add: J M Dent & Sons
(Distribution) Ltd, Dunhams Lane,
Letchworth, Hertfordshire SG6 1LF
Man Dir: David Howgrave-Graham;
Marketing Dir: G R Rae; *Editorial Director:*
Chester Fisher; *Rights & Permissions:*
Elizabeth Hamilton
Associate Company: Julia MacRae
Books (qv)
Subjects: Reference, Juveniles
Founded: 1969
ISBN Publisher's Prefix: 0-85166

Wayland Publishers Ltd*, 49 Lansdowne Pl,
Hove, East Sussex BN3 1HS Tel: Brighton
722561 (STD code 0273) Cable Add:
Bookwright Hove Telex: 23961
Shipping add: Book Centre Ltd, Rufford
Rd, Crossens, Southport, Merseyside
PR9 8LA
Man Dir, Editorial: Roger Ferneyhough;
Man Dir, Sales, Publicity & Advertising:
John Lewis; *Rights & Permissions:* Roger
Ferneyhough
Associate Company: Argus Books Ltd (qv)
Subsidiary Company: Priory Press
Subjects: Illustrated School library Books,
Biography, History, Natural History,
Science, Crafts, Careers, General, Socio-
medicine, Mass Market Tourist Guides
1978: 60 titles *Founded:* 1969
ISBN Publisher's Prefixes: 0-85340
(Wayland), 0-85078 (Priory Press)

The **Wayzgoose** Press, an imprint of Aquila
Publishing (qv)

Webb & Bower (Publishers) Ltd,
33 Southernhay East, Exeter, Devon
EX1 1NS Tel: 35362/3 (STD code 0392)
Cable Add: Webbower Exeter
Telex: Chamco 42603
Man Dir: Richard Webb; *Editorial Dir:*
Delian Bower; *Publishing Dir:* Nicholas
Facer; *Publicity:* HPR Publicity, 9 Fitzroy
Sq, London W1 (Tel: (01) 388 2613)
Subjects: General Non-fiction
1979: 12 titles *1980:* 17 titles *Founded:* 1975
Miscellaneous: Editorial, design and
production organization specializing in
producing illustrated books for the UK,
USA and the international co-edition market

A **Weekes**, an imprint of Stainer & Bell
Ltd (qv)

George **Weidenfeld & Nicolson** Ltd, 91
Clapham High St, London SW4 7TA Tel:
(01) 622 9933 Cable Add: Nicobar
SW4 7TA Telex: 918066
Shipping Add: The Windmill Press,
Kingswood, Tadworth, Surrey KT20 6TG
Chairman, Chief Executive and Man Dir:
Lord Weidenfeld; *Joint Deputy Man Dirs:*
Ray Compton, Richard Hussey; *Sales Dir:*
David Livermore; *Publicity & Advertising:*
Rosalind Lewis; *Rights & Permissions:* Miss
B J MacLennan
Subsidiary Company: Arthur Barker
Ltd (qv)
Associate Company: Frances Lincoln
Publishers Ltd (qv)
Imprints: Include World University Library
Subjects: General Fiction, Belles Lettres,
Poetry, Biography, History, Music, Art,
Philosophy, Reference, Religion, High-
priced Paperbacks, Psychology, General &
Social Science, University Textbooks
ISBN Publisher's Prefix: 0-297

A **Wheaton** & Co Ltd, Hennock Rd, Exeter,
Devon EX2 8RP Tel: Exeter 74121 (STD
code 0392) Telex: 42749
Man Dir: John Halsall; *Publicity:* Don
Bibey
Parent Company: Pergamon Press Ltd (qv)
Subjects: Juveniles, Secondary & Primary
Textbooks, Educational Materials
Founded: 1780
ISBN Publisher's Prefix: 0-08

J **Whitaker** & Sons Ltd, 12 Dyott St,
London WC1A 1DF Tel: (01) 836 8911
Cable Add: Whitmanack London WC1
Man Dir: Haddon Whitaker
Subsidiary Companies: Sporting Handbooks
Ltd (qv); The Standard Book Numbering
Agency Ltd; Whitaker's Book Listing
Services Ltd (all at 12 Dyott St, London)
Subjects: Textbooks, Reference
1978: 6 titles *Founded:* 1841
ISBN Publisher's Prefixes: 0-85021
(Whitaker), 0-949999 (Standard Book
Numbering Agency)

White Eagle Publishing Trust, New Lands,
Liss, Hampshire GU33 7HY Tel: Liss 3300
(STD code 073082)
Man Dir: Mrs Y G Hayward; *Sales, Rights
& Permissions:* G R H Dent; *Publicity &
Advertising:* Colum Hayward
Subjects: Religion, Astrology, Vegetarian
Cookery
1978: 2 titles *1979:* 2 titles *Founded:* 1953
Miscellaneous: Publishing house of the
White Eagle Lodge, an undenominational
Christian church
ISBN Publisher's Prefix: 0-85487

White Horse Books, an imprint of Jarrold
Colour Publications (qv)

White Lion Publishers Ltd, see Severn
House Publishers Ltd

Whittet Books Ltd, The Oil Mills,
Weybridge, Surrey KT13 8LD Tel:
Weybridge 42274 (STD code 0932) Telex:
929823 Pitman G
Chief Executive: Annabel Whittet
Parent Company: A Whittet & Co Ltd, at
above address
Subjects: Non-fiction, History, Illustrated,
Practical
1978: 4 titles *1979:* 3 titles *Founded:* 1976
ISBN Publisher's Prefix: 0-905483

Wildwood House Ltd, 1 Prince of Wales
Passage, 117 Hampstead Rd, London
NW1 3EE Tel: (01) 388 5389 Cable Add:
Wildwood London NW1
Shipping Add: Routledge-Harrap Storage
Ltd, Broadway House, Newton Rd, Henley-
on-Thames, Oxfordshire RG9 1EN
Chairman: L W Carp; *Dirs:* Oliver
Caldecott, Dieter Pevsner, Stuart Creggy,
Jack Stacey; *Sales Manager:* Rathan Sippy;
Rights & Permissions: Oliver Caldecott
Subjects: General Nonfiction, Biography,
History, How-to, Music, Art, Philosophy,
Reference, Religion, Medicine, Psychology,
General & Social Science, Occasional
Fiction
1978: 27 titles *1979:* 29 titles *Founded:* 1972
Miscellaneous: Firm is a member of the East-
West Group, 120 Charing Cross Rd,
London WC2
ISBN Publisher's Prefix: 0-7045

John **Wiley** & Sons Ltd, Baffins Lane,
Chichester, West Sussex PO19 1UD Tel:
Chichester 784531 (STD code 0243) Cable
Add: Wilebook Chichester Telex: 86290
Warehouse: John Wiley & Sons Ltd,
Distribution Centre, Southern Cross Trading
Estate, Shripney Rd, Bognor Regis, West
Sussex PO22 9SA
Man Dir: J A E Higham; *Marketing Dir:*
M B Foyle; *Sales Manager:* J Durrant;
Publicity: J D E Lea
Parent Company: John Wiley & Sons Inc,
605 Third Ave, New York, NY 10016, USA
Associate Companies: Jacaranda Wiley Ltd,
Australia (qv); Livros Técnicos e Científicôs
Editôra SA, Brazil (qv); John Wiley & Sons
Canada Ltd, 22 Worcester Rd, Rexdale,
Ontario, Canada; Wiley Eastern Ltd,
India (qv); Editorial Limusa SA,
Mexico (qv); Halsted Press, 605 Third Ave,
New York, NY 10016, USA; Hamilton
Publishing Co, 1129 State St, Santa
Barbara, Calif 93101, USA; The Ronald
Press Co, 79 Madison Ave, New York,
NY 10016, USA
Subjects: Chemistry, Physics, Life Sciences,
Earth Sciences, Mathematics, Medicine,
Psychology, Engineering, Reference, Social
Science, Business Science, University
Textbooks, Educational Material
1978: 1000 titles
ISBN Publisher's Prefixes: 0-471 (Wiley),
0-470 (Halsted)

Wilfion Books Publishers, 12 Townhead
Terrace, Paisley, Renfrewshire PA1 2AX
Tel: (041) 887 1241 Ext 264
Dirs: Konrad Hopkins. Ronald van Roekel
Subjects: Poetry, Psychic/Spiritual
Phemonema, Translations, Fiction,
Biography
1980: 10 titles *Founded:* 1975

Joseph **Williams**, an imprint of Stainer &
Bell Ltd (qv)

Williams & Norgate, an imprint of Ernest
Benn Ltd (qv)

Philip **Wilson** Publishers, Russell Chambers,
Covent Garden, London WC2E 8AA Tel:
(01) 240 1091/2 Telex: 22158
Man Dir: Philip Wilson; *Editorial Manager:*
Anne Jackson; *Sales Manager:* Juliana
Powney; *Production Manager:* Peter Ling;

UNITED KINGDOM 407

Publicity Manager: Stephen Trombley
Imprint: Sotheby Parke Bernet Publications
(*USA office:* 81 Adams Drive, Totowa, NJ 07512, USA)
Subjects: Art, Antiques, Reference
1978: 14 titles *1979:* 12 titles *Founded:* 1975
ISBN Publisher's Prefix: 0-85667

Wilton Publications, 1 Westmead, Farnborough, Hampshire GU14 7RU Tel: Farnborough 519221 (STD code 0252)
An imprint of Gower Publishing Co Ltd (qv), with details as for Gower Publishing except as follows:
Editorial: John Irwin
Subjects: Business, Finance, Economics
ISBN Publisher's Prefixes: 0-904655 (pre-1978 titles), 0-566

Wine & Spirit Publications Ltd, Harling Ho, 47-51 Gt Suffolk St, London SE1 Tel: (01) 261 1604
Man Dir: T J Straker
Subjects: General Nonfiction, Wine, Travel, Entertaining
Founded: 1958

Allan **Wingate** (Publishers) Ltd*, 44 Hill St, London W1X 8LB Tel: (01) 493 6777
For personnel see W H Allen & Co Ltd
Parent Company: W H Allen & Co Ltd (qv)
Subjects: General Fiction, Nonfiction, Juveniles
ISBN Publisher's Prefix: 0-85523

Wingate Series, an imprint of Dinosaur Publications Ltd (qv)

H F & G **Witherby** Ltd and Witherby & Co Ltd, 5 Plantain Pl, Crosby Row, London SE1 1YN Tel: (01) 407 1801
Man Dirs: Antony Witherby (H F & G Witherby), Alan Witherby (Witherby & Co Ltd)
Subjects: Biography, History, How-to, Secondary & University Textbooks, Reference, Natural Science, Insurance & Banking
ISBN Publisher's Prefixes: 0-85493 (H F & G Witherby), 0-900886 (Witherby & Co)

The **Woburn** Press, Gainsborough House, 11 Gainsborough Rd, Leytonstone, London E11 1RS Tel: (01) 530 4226 Cable Add: Simfay London Telex: 897719
Warehouse: Macdonald & Evans Ltd, Estover Rd, Estover, Plymouth PL6 7PZ
Man Dir: Frank Cass; *Editorial:* Margaret Goodare; *Trade:* Richard Norris;
Production: Kenneth Cowell; *Publicity:* Jacqui Beryl
Parent Company: Frank Cass & Co Ltd (qv)
Associate Company: Vallentine, Mitchell & Co Ltd (qv)
Subjects: Literature Criticism, Educational Studies, Social Science, General Literature
1978: 11 titles *1979:* 6 titles *Founded:* 1969
ISBN Publisher's Prefix: 0-7130

Wolfe Medical Publications Ltd, Wolfe House, 3 Conway St, London W1P 6HE Tel: (01) 636 4622 Cable Add: Wolfebooks London Telex: Wmpltd G 8814230
Chairman & Man Dir: Peter Wolfe; *Deputy Man Dir:* Peter Heilbrunn; *Editorial:* Patrick Daly; *Home Sales:* George Hayward; *Export Sales:* Stuart Binns; *Production:* Kenneth Briscoe; *Publicity:* Evanna Morris; *Rights & Permissions:* Fiona Aretz
Subjects: Medical, Dental, Veterinary, Scientific
1978: 8 titles *1979:* 8 titles *Founded:* 1969
ISBN Publisher's Prefix: 0-7234

Wolfe Publishing Ltd, see Wolfe Medical Publications Ltd

Oswald **Wolff** (Publishers) Ltd, 52 Manchester St, London W1M 6DR Tel: (01) 935 3441/3481 Cable Add: Bookwolff
Man & Sales Dir, Rights & Permissions: Mrs I R Wolff; *Editorial Dir:* R W Last
Subjects: Biography, History, Music, Art, Literary Criticism, German Studies, High-priced Paperbacks
1978: 6 titles *1979:* 4 titles *Founded:* 1958
ISBN Publisher's Prefix: 0-85496

The **Women's** Press Ltd, 124 Shoreditch High St, London E1 6JE Tel: (01) 729 5257 Cable Add: Namara London SW1 Telex: 919034
Man Dir: Stephanie Dowrick; *Editorial:* Stephanie Dowrick, Sue Gerry; *Publicity, Rights & Permissions:* Sarah LeFany; *Design:* Suzanne Perkins
Orders to: Quartet Books Ltd, 27 Goodge St, London W1
Parent Company: Namara Ltd, 18b Wellington Court, Knightsbridge, London SW1
Subjects: Fiction, Literature and Criticism, Art History, Politics, Physical and Mental Health (all women writers)
Book Club: The Women's Press Book Club
1978: 12 titles *Founded:* 1977
ISBN Publisher's Prefix: 0-7043

Woodhead-Faulkner (Publishers) Ltd, 8 Market Passage, Cambridge CB2 3PF Tel: Cambridge 66733 (STD code 0223)
Man Dir: Martin J Woodhead; *Editorial:* Ian C Faulkner; *Sales:* Gilmour Drummond
Imprint: Martin Books
Subjects: Business Investment and Finance, Social Welfare and Rehabilitation, Careers, Popular Nonfiction
1978: 18 titles *1979:* 25 titles *Founded:* 1972
ISBN Publisher's Prefix: 0-85941

Word Books (Word (UK) Ltd)*, Northbridge Rd, Berkhamsted, Hertfordshire HP4 1EH Tel: Berkhamsted 74711-5 (STD code 04427)
Man Dir: W T Hamilton
Parent Company: Word Inc, Waco, Texas, USA
Subjects: Religion, Music
ISBN Publisher's Prefix: 0-85009

Workshop Press Ltd*, 2 Culham Court, Granville Rd, London N4 4JB Tel: (01) 348 4054
Subjects: Poetry
1978: 2 titles
ISBN Publisher's Prefix: 0-902705

World Book—Childcraft International Inc, Canterbury House, Sydenham Rd, Croydon, Surrey CR9 2LR Tel: (01) 686 6421 Cable Add: World Book Int, Croydon Telex: 946314
Man Dir: J R Threlfall; *Editorial, Publicity:* Howard Timms
Parent Company: World Book—Childcraft International Inc, Merchandise Mart Plaza, Chicago, Illinois, USA
Imprint: Pied Piper
Subjects: Primary & Secondary Education, English Dictionaries, Reference Books, Juveniles, Encyclopaedias
1978: 10 titles *1979:* 6 titles
ISBN Publisher's Prefix: 0-7166

World International Publishing Ltd, PO Box 111, Manchester M60 1TS (Located at: Great Ducie St, Manchester M60 3BL) Tel: (061) 834 3110 Cable Add: Sydpem Manchester Telex: 668609
Chief Executive: Michael Raeburn; *Sales:* Eric Whitehouse; *Publisher:* Roger Lewis; *Production Manager:* David Sheldrake; *Publicity:* Julian Batson
Subjects: Children's Books and Annuals
Miscellaneous: Holding company is Pentos Ltd (qv)
ISBN Publisher's Prefix: 0-7235

World Microfilms Publications Ltd, 62 Queen's Grove, London NW8 6ER Tel: (01) 586 3092 Cable Add: Microworld
Man Dir: Stephen Albert; *Technical:* Michael J Gunn
Associate Company: Sussex Video Ltd
Subjects: Research Collections in Microform, Periodical Reprints in Microform
1978: 30 titles *1979:* 30 titles *Founded:* 1969

World of Information, 21 Gold St, Saffron Walden, Essex CB10 1EJ Tel: (0799) 21150 Cable Add: Jaxpress Telex: 817197 Jaxprs G
Man Dirs: David J C Jamieson, Anthony Axon; *Sales:* Michael G Morris; *Production:* Alan J Asbridge; *Publicity:* Sue Hewitt
Parent Company: Middle East Review Co Ltd (at above address)
Branch Off: World of Information, Box 58, 15 Central St, Woodstock, Vermont 05091, USA
Subject: Third World Countries (Commerce, Economics, Politics)
1978: 5 titles *1979:* 6 titles *Founded:* 1972
ISBN Publisher's Prefix: 0-904439

World of Islam Festival Trust*, 1 Adam Court, Gloucester Rd, London SW7 4SS Tel: (01) 370 6002/3/4 Cable Add: Islamtrust London SW7
Dir: Alistair Duncan
Orders to: Thorsons Publishers Ltd, Dennington Estate, Wellingborough, Northants
Subjects: Islamic Art, Culture and Civilisation
1978: 2 titles *Founded:* 1974
ISBN Publisher's Prefix: 0-905035

World University Library, an imprint of Weidenfeld & Nicolson Ltd (qv)

World's Work Ltd, The Windmill Press, Kingswood, Tadworth, Surrey Tel: Mogador 3511 STD code 073 783 Cable Add: Sunlocks Tadworth Telex: 947458 Press G
Man Dir: C Forster; *Deputy Man Dir:* D Elliot; *Production Dir:* Robert Aspinall; *Trade Manager:* Daphne Mallard; *Exhibition Manager:* Peggy Lince; *Promotion Manager:* Miriam Maxim
Parent Company: Heinemann Group of Publishers Ltd (qv)
Imprint: Cedar Books
Subjects: Business, How-to, Religion, Juveniles, Sport, Archaeology
1978: 79 titles *1979:* 73 titles
ISBN Publisher's Prefix: 0-437

Gordon **Wright Publishing**, 55 Marchmont Rd, Edinburgh EH9 1HT Tel: (031) 229 8566
Proprietor: Gordon Wright
Imprints: Reprographia
Subjects: General, Scottish Literature, Non-fiction and Fiction
1978: 6 titles *Founded:* 1969
ISBN Publisher's Prefix: 0-903065

John **Wright** & Sons Ltd, 42-44 Triangle West, Bristol BS8 1EX Tel: Bristol 23237 (STD code 0272) Cable Add: Wright Publishers Bristol Telex: 449752
Chairman: C N Clarke; *Publishing Dir:* D Kingham; *Editorial:* J Gillman; *Executive Sales Dir, Rights & Permissions:* Miss J M Eales; *Production:* R Lamb; *Publicity:* R Pitt
Orders to: 823-825 Bath Rd, Bristol BS4 5NU
Associate Company: Scientechnica (Publishers) Ltd
Subsidiary Company: Henry Ling Ltd, Dorchester, Dorset
Subjects: Medicine, Veterinary Medicine, Dentistry, Psychology, Science, University

Textbooks
Bookshop: John Wright & Sons Ltd,
44 Triangle West, Bristol BS8 1EX
1978: 35 titles *1979:* 37 titles *Founded:* 1825
ISBN Publisher's Prefixes: 0-7236 (Wright),
0-85608 (Wright-Scientechnica)

Writers and Readers Publishing Co-
operative, 9-19 Rupert St, London
W1V 7FS Tel: (01) 437 8942/8917
Man Dir: Glenn Thompson; *Editorial Dir:*
Richard Appignanesi; *Sales Dir:* Siân
Williams; *Publicity & Advertising Dir:* Gary
Pulsifer; *Rights & Permissions Dir:* Lisa
Appignanesi
Subsidiary Company: Rivers Press
Subjects: Education, Primary, Secondary &
University Textbooks, Feminism, General
Literature, Fiction, Poetry, Juveniles,
Politics, Sociology, Humour, Biography, Art
1978: 21 titles *Founded:* 1974
Miscellaneous: Firm is a collective
publishing model, member of Industrial
Common Ownership Movement
ISBN Publisher's Prefixes: 0-904613,
0-906386, 0-906495

Wykeham Publications (London) Ltd, see
Taylor & Francis Ltd

Xerox Publishing Group Ltd, see Bowker
Publishing Co and University Microfilms
International

Yale University Press Ltd, 13 Bedford Sq,
London WC1B 3JF Tel: (01) 580 2693
Cable Add: Yalepress London WC1
Manager: Stephanie Sutton; *Editorial,
Production:* John Nicoll; *Publicity:*
Christiane Logan; *Rights & Permissions:*
Kathleen Yorke
Orders to: International Book Distributors,
66 Wood Lane End, Hemel Hempstead,
Hertfordshire HP2 4RG Tel: Hemel
Hempstead 58531 (STD code 0442) Telex:
82445
Subject: Scholarly Books
1978: 85 titles *1979:* 90 titles
Miscellaneous: Firm is the British office of
Yale University Press, 302 Temple St, New
Haven, Conn 06511, USA
ISBN Publisher's Prefix: 0-300

Thomas **Yoseloff** Ltd, Magdalen Ho,
136-148 Tooley St, London SE1 2TT
Tel: (01) 407 7566 Cable Add: Tantivy
London SE1
Man Dir, Rights & Permissions: Peter
Cowie; *Editorial:* Allen Eyles; *Sales:*
Elisabeth Cowie; *Publicity:* Katherine Davies
Associate Companies: The Tantivy Press,
Associated University Presses
Subject: General Non-fiction
1979: 100 titles
ISBN Publisher's Prefix: 0-498

Zed Press, 57 Caledonian Rd, London
N1 9DN Tel: (01) 837 4014 Telex: 912881
Zed
Sales, Publicity, Rights & Permissions:
Roger van Zwanenberg; *Editorial:* Robert
Molteno
Branch Off: c/o Lawrence Hill Inc, 520
Riverside Ave, Westfort, Connecticut 06880,
USA
Subjects: Third World Social Science,
Africa, Middle East, Asia, Imperialism
1979: 12 titles *1980:* 22 titles *Founded:* 1976
ISBN Publisher's Prefix: 0-905762

Hans **Zell** (Publishers) Ltd, PO Box 56, 14A
St Giles, Oxford, OX1 3EL Tel: Oxford
512934 (STD code 0865)
Man Dir, Editorial, Rights & Permissions:
Hans M Zell; *Sales, Publicity:* Beryl
Schweder
Subjects: Reference, Africana, Periodicals
1979: 2 titles *Founded:* 1975
ISBN Publisher's Prefixes: 0-86070, 0-905450

Zeno Booksellers & Publishers,
6 Denmark St, London WC2H 8LP
Tel: (01) 836 2522 Cable Add: Zengreek
London WC2
Man Dir: M P Zographos
Subjects: Belles Lettres, Poetry, History,
Art, Travel
Bookshop: 6 Denmark St, London
WC2H 8LP (specializing in Greek books,
Books on Greece, The Balkans, Middle East,
Antiquarian and Modern)
Founded: 1944
ISBN Publisher's Prefixes: 0-900834, 0-7228

A **Zwemmer** Ltd, 26 Litchfield St, London
WC2H 9NJ Tel: (01) 836 1749 Cable Add:
Zwemmera Lesquare London WC2H 9NJ
Warehouse: Unit 27, Bermondsey Trading
Estate, Rotherhithe New Rd, London SE16
Man Dir: D Zwemmer
Subsidiary Company: Lund Humphries
Publishers Ltd (qv), for whom Zwemmer
Ltd is also distributor
Subjects: Art, Architecture
Bookshops: Zwemmers Bookshop,
76-80 Charing Cross Rd, London
WC2H 0BH; Zwemmers OUP Bookshop,
72 Charing Cross Rd, London WC2H 0BE

Remainder Dealers

B S C Books Ltd, 33 Maiden Lane,
London WC2 Tel: (01) 836 3341 (Owners
of the Booksmith chain of bookshops; also
publishers)
Sales: Bill Smith

Roy **Bloom** Ltd, 81 Goswell Rd, London
EC1 Tel: (01) 251 4345 Telex: 24224 Ref
2121
Sales: Paul White

Bridge Book Co Ltd*, Unit 4, Goldsworth
Park Trading Estate, Woking, Surrey
GU21 3BA Tel: Woking 20505 (STD code
04862) Cable Add: Pembridge Woking
Remainder paperback book merchants,
importers and exporters in bulk

Donald **Murray** (Ramboro Books),
6 Highbury Corner, London N5 1RD Tel:
(01) 609 3091/2
See also under Publishers

Murrays Remainder Books*, 146-152
Holloway Rd, London N7 Tel: (01) 609
1234
See also under Publishers

H **Pordes**, 529b Finchley Rd, London
NW3 7BH Tel: (01) 435 9878/9
See also under Publishers

Ramboro Enterprises Ltd, 6 Highbury
Corner, London N5 1RD Tel: (01) 609
3091/2 Telex: 24224
See also under Publishers

Literary Agents

Michael **Bakewell** & Associates Ltd, see
MBA Literary Agents Ltd

Bolt & Watson Ltd, 8-12 Old Queen St,
London SW1 Tel: (01) 222 5378 Cable
Add: Bandwag London SW1
Dirs: David Bolt, Sheila Watson

E J **Carnell** Literary Agency, Rowneybury
Bungalow, Nr Old Harlow, Essex
CM20 2EX Tel: Harlow 29408 (STD code
0279)
Contact: Leslie Flood
Specialization: Science Fiction, Fantasy

Curtis Brown Academic Ltd, 1 Craven Hill,
London W2 3EW Tel: (01) 262 1011
Man Dir: Andrew Best

Curtis Brown Group Ltd, 1 Craven Hill,
London W2 3EW Tel: (01) 262 1011
Chairman: Richard Odgen

John **Farquharson** Ltd, Bell House, 8 Bell
Yard, London WC2A 2JU Tel: (01) 242
2445 Cable Add: Jofachad London WC2
Contact: George Greenfield, Vanessa Holt or
Vivienne Schuster
Also office at 250 West 57th St, New York,
NY 10019 Tel: (0212) 245 1993 Cable Add:
Jofachad New York
Contact: Jane Gelfman

Julian **Friedmann** Literary Agency Ltd, 15
Catherine St, Covent Garden, London
WC2B 5JZ Tel: (01) 379 3248
Man Dir: Julian Friedmann
Specialization: Thrillers, Film and TV
development, also broad range of fiction and
non-fiction

Peter **Galliner** Associates Ltd*, 27 Queen's
Grove, London NW8 6HL Tel: (01) 722
0361

David **Grossman** Literary Agency Ltd*,
12-13 Henrietta St, London WC2

A M **Heath** & Co Ltd, 40-42 William IV St,
London WC2N 4DD Tel: (01) 836 4271
Cable Add: Script London WC2
Man Dir: Mark Hamilton

David **Higham** Associates Ltd*, 5-8 Lower
John St, Golden Sq, London W1R 4HA
Tel: (01) 437 7888 Cable Add: Highlit
London W1 Telex: 28910

Hope Leresche & Sayle*, 11 Jubilee Pl,
London SW3 3TE Tel: (01) 352 4311 Cable
Add: Bookishly London

Hughes Massie Ltd*, 31 Southampton Row,
London WC1B 5HL Tel: (01) 405 8137
Cable Add: Litaribus London Telex: 298391
Dirs: Edmund Cork, Patricia Cork, J E
Lunn, N E Cork, Brian Stone

Inpra International Press Agency, 411
London Press Centre, 76 Shoe Lane,
London EC4A 3JB Tel: (01) 353 0186
Cable Add: Barpress, Kingston on Thames

Intercontinental Literary Agency, foreign
rights company of A D Peters & Co Ltd (qv)

London Independent Books Ltd,
1a Montagu Mews North, London
W1H 1AJ Tel: (01) 935 8090 Cable Add:
Trifem London W1
Dirs: Carolyn Whitaker, Patrick Whitaker

London Syndication, Redhill, Nr
Buntingford, The Old Forge, Hertfordshire
SG9 0TH Tel: Broadfield 348 (STD code
076388)

M B A Literary Agents Ltd, 118 Tottenham
Court Rd, London W1P 9HL Tel: (01) 387
2076/4785
Dirs: Diana Tyler, Janet Freer

Andrew **Nurnberg** Associates Ltd,
Clerkenwell Ho, 45-47 Clerkenwell Green,
London EC1R 0HT Tel: (01) 251 0321
Cable Add: Nurnbooks London
Telex: 23353
Specialization: Translation Rights

Mark **Paterson** & Associates, 11-12 West
Stockwell St, Colchester, Essex CO1 1HN
Tel: Colchester 65151 (STD code 0206)
Cable Add: Paterson Colchester Telex:
896616MP Sendit G or markit 987562
Cochac
Specialization: Psychoanalysis, Psychiatry,
Sigmund Freud copyrights, but other
subjects also handled

Peterborough Literary Agency, The Daily
Telegraph, 135 Fleet St, London EC4P 4BL
Tel: (01) 353 4242 ext 529 Cable Add:
Telenews London EC4 Telex: 22874

UNITED KINGDOM 409

Telesyndic
Executive Managers: Ewan MacNaughton, Andrea Whittaker

A D **Peters** & Co Ltd, 10 Buckingham St, London WC2N 6BU Tel: (01) 839 2556
Man Dir: Michael Sissons

Laurence **Pollinger** Ltd, 18 Maddox St, London W1R 0EU Tel: (01) 629 9761 Cable Add: Laupoll London W1
Man Dir: Gerald J Pollinger; *Foreign Rights:* Yvonne Muller

Deborah **Rogers** Ltd, 5-11 Mortimer St, London W1H 7RH Tel: (01) 580 0604/5 Cable Add: Deborgers London W1

Sheri **Safran** Associates Ltd, 21 Ladbroke Gardens, London W11 Tel: (01) 229 7819
Also office at 866 United Nations Plaza, Suite 4030, New York, NY 10017, USA Tel: (0212) 355 3362
Representing agents in France, Federal Republic of Germany, Latin America, Scandinavia, Spain, and agents and publishers in USA with a general list, but specializing in women's books

Patrick **Seale** Books Ltd, 2 Motcomb St, Belgrave Sq, London SW1X 8JU Tel: (01) 235 0934 Cable Add: Obseale London SW1

Anthony **Sheil** Associates Ltd, 2-3 Morwell St, London WC1B 3AR Tel: (01) 636 2901 Cable Add: Novelist
Man Dir: Anthony Sheil

A P **Watt** Ltd, 26-28 Bedford Row, London WC1R 4HL Tel: (01) 405 1057 Cable Add: Longevity London WC1
Contact: Michael Horniman, Hilary Rubinstein, Maggie Noach or Caradoc King

Book Clubs

20th Century Classics, see Book Club Associates

Ancient History Book Club, see Book Club Associates

The **Artists'** Book Club, PO Box 244, London WC2B 5PB
Owned by: Pitman Books Ltd

Arts Book Society, see Readers Union Ltd

Arts Guild, see Book Club Associates

Biography Book Club, see Book Club Associates

The **Book Club**, see Foyles Book Clubs

Book Club Associates, 87-91 Newman St, London W1P 4EN Tel: (01) 637 0341 Cable Add: Booklub Telex: 24359
Chief Executive: S T Remington; *General Manager (Books):* M Lawson; *General Manager (Editorial and Creative):* J Goehr
Monthly Book Clubs: Ancient History Book Club; Biography Book Club; Book of the Month Club; Family Book Club; History Guild; Literary Guild; Master Storytellers; Military Book Society; Mystery Guild; Skylark Children's Book Club; World Books
Bi-monthly Book Club: Book Lovers
Quarterly Book Clubs: Arts Guild; British Heritage; Encounters; English Book Club (Netherlands and Federal Republic of Germany); Home & Garden Guild; Military Guild; The Railway Book Club; Readers Choice; World of Nature
Book Series: 20th Century Classics, Kings & Queens of England, Great English Classics
Subsidiary Company: Guild Publishing (qv under Publishers)
Owned by: W H Smith & Son Ltd (London) and Doubleday & Co Inc (New York)

Book Lovers, see Book Club Associates

Book of the Month Club, see Book Club Associates

The **Bookworm** Club, Napier Pl, Cumbernauld, Glasgow G69 0DN
Owned by: W Heffer & Sons Ltd (Cambridge) and E J Arnold & Son Ltd (Leeds)
Subject: Paperbacks for 5-12-year-olds

British Heritage, see Book Club Associates

Catholic Book Club, see Foyles Book Clubs

Children's Book Club, see Foyles Book Clubs

Chip Book Club*, 161 Fulham Rd, London SW3 6SW
(Junior and low senior school)
Owned by: Scholastic Publications

Collectors' Editions Book Club, see Heron Books

Companion Book Club, Hamlyn Group, Mail Order Division, Sanders Lodge Estate, Rushden, Northants
Members: 12,500
Owned by: The Hamlyn Group (Feltham)
Subjects: Fiction, Biographies, True Adventure

Country Book Club, see Readers Union Ltd

Country Book Society, see Readers Union Ltd

Craft Book Society, see Readers Union Ltd

Criterion: Teachers' Book Shelf Book Club*, 161 Fulham Rd, London SW3 6SW
Owned by: Scholastic Publications

Encounters, see Book Club Associates

Family Book Club, see Book Club Associates

Fishing Book Club, Howard Rd, Eaton Socon, Huntingdon, Cambs PE19 3EZ Tel: Huntingdon 212666 (STD code 0480)
Owned by: A & C Black (Publishers) Ltd

The **Folio** Society Ltd*, 202 Great Suffolk St, London SE1 1PR Tel: (01) 407 7411 Cable Add: Folios Telex: 8951460
Man Dir: H Lynner; *Sales, Publicity, Advertising, Rights & Permissions:* J Letts
Subsidiaries: Folio Press, UK; Folio Fine Editions, UK; Folio Books Ltd New York, at 575 Lexington Avenue, New York, NY 10022, USA
Subjects: General Fiction, Belles Lettres, Poetry, Biography, History
1979: 123 titles *Founded:* 1947
Bookshop: Folio Gallery, 5 Royal Arcade, 28 Old Bond St, London W1
Miscellaneous: Firm publishes finely produced editions of the classics and eye-witness accounts of historical events; for sale to members only

Foyles Book Clubs, 119-125 Charing Cross Rd, London WC2H 0EB Tel: (01) 437 0216 Cable Add: Foylibra Telex: 261107
Owned by: W & G Foyle & John Gifford Ltd (London)
Includes: The Book Club, Catholic Book Club, Children's Book Club, Garden Book Club, Quality Book Club, Romance Book Club, Scientific Book Club, Thriller Book Club, Travel Book Club, Western Book Club

French Book Club, Warner Ho, Folkestone, Kent
Owned by: Bailey Brothers & Swinfen Ltd (Folkestone)

Garden Book Club, see Foyles Book Clubs

Gardeners Book Society, see Readers Union Ltd

German Book Club, Warner Ho, Folkestone, Kent
Owned by: Bailey Brothers & Swinfen Ltd (Folkestone)

Great English Classics, see Book Club Associates

Heron Books, 2nd Floor, Lawrence House, St Andrew's Hill, Norwich, Norfolk Tel: (0603) 60111
Includes: Collectors' Editions Book Club, The Nobel Prize Library
Owned by: Leisure Arts Ltd
Miscellaneous: Also publishes finely bound, illustrated reprints, including Literary Heritage (English classics), Russian Classics, Women Who Made History, Books That Have Changed Man's Thinking, Explorer's Bookshelf, Immortal Moderns; and collected works of individual authors

History Guild, see Book Club Associates

Home and Garden Guild, see Book Club Associates

Horseman's Bookclub, 1 Lower Grosvenor Pl, London SW1
Owned by: J A Allen & Co Ltd (London)

Italian Book Club, Warner House, Folkestone, Kent
Owned by: Bailey Brothers & Swinfen Ltd (Folkestone)

The **Jewish** Book Club, 529b Finchley Rd, London NW3 7BH
Owned by: R Pordes

Junior Puffin Club, Penguin Books Ltd, Bath Rd, Harmondsworth, Middlesex UB7 0DA
Owned by: Penguin Books Ltd

Kings & Queens of England, see Book Club Associates

The **Leisure Circle** Ltd, York Ho, Empire Way, Wembley, Middlesex HA9 0PF Tel: (01) 902 8888 Telex: 8951315
Man Dir: Dr M Herriger; *Publishing:* C Goulden; *Sales:* D M Cripps; *Marketing:* H Bickon; *Member Service:* L Grothues
Owned by: Bertelsmann Group, (Federal Republic of Germany)
Subjects: General Fiction, Nonfiction, Biography, History, Children's Books

Literary Guild, see Book Club Associates

Lucky Book Club*, 161 Fulham Rd, London SW3 6SW
(Infants, low juniors)
Owned by: Scholastic Publications

Mainstream Book Club*, 108 Cowley Rd, Oxford Tel: Oxford 724041 (STD code 0865)
Owned by (majority share): B H Blackwell Ltd (qv under Major Booksellers)
Subject: Middle-of-the-road political books

Maritime Book Society, see Readers Union

Master Storytellers, see Book Club Associates

Merlin Book Club, 3 Manchester Rd, London E14
Owned by: Merlin Press Ltd

Military Book Society, see Book Club Associates

Military Guild, see Book Club Associates

Mystery Guild, see Book Club Associates

Nationwide Book Services, 21-22 The Old Steine, Brighton, East Sussex BN1 1DV
Owned by: William Collins Sons & Co Ltd, William Heinemann (International) Ltd, Martin Secker & Warburg Ltd (all UK) and Albert Bonniers Förlag AB (Sweden)

410 UNITED KINGDOM

The **New Fiction** Society*, Book House, East Hill, Wandsworth, London SE18 2HZ Tel: (01) 870 8259
Sponsored by the Arts Council and the National Book League

The **Nobel Prize** Library, see Heron Books

Phoenix Book Society, see Readers Union Ltd

Poetry Book Society, 9 Long Acre, London WC2E 9LH Tel: (01) 379 6597
Publications: Bulletin (quarterly); *Poetry Supplement 1979*

The **Puffin** Club, Penguin Books Ltd, Bath Rd, Harmondsworth, Middlesex UB7 0DA
Owned by: Penguin Books Ltd

Quality Book Club, see Foyles Book Clubs

The **Railway** Book Club, see Book Club Associates

Readers Choice, see Book Club Associates

Readers Union Book Club, see Readers Union Ltd

Readers Union Ltd, PO Box 6, Newton Abbot, Devon TQ12 2DW Tel: Newton Abbot 69881 (STD code 0626) Cable Add: Books Nabbot Telex: 42904
Man Dir: E A Howes; *Marketing Dir:* M Deane; *Product Dir:* S Margrett; *Sales Dir:* B Bailey; *Literary Dir:* R Allen; *Fulfilment Dir:* J R D Thomas
Includes: Arts Book Society, Country Book Club, Country Book Society, Craft Book Society, Gardeners Book Society, Maritime Book Society, Phoenix Book Society, Readers Union Book Club, Science Fiction Book Club, Sportsman's Book Club
Owned by: David & Charles (Holdings) Ltd (Devon)
Founded: 1937

Romance Book Club, see Foyles Book Clubs

Scene Book Club*, 161 Fulham Rd, London SW3 6SW
Owned by: Scholastic Publications
Subjects: Books for secondary school and top juniors

Science Fiction Book Club, see Readers Union Ltd

Scientific Book Club, see Foyles Book Clubs

See-saw Book Club*, 161 Fulham Rd, London SW3 6SW
Owned by: Scholastic Publications
Subjects: Books for nursery and infants

Skylark Children's Book Club, see Book Club Associates

Spanish Book Club, Warner Ho, Folkestone, Kent
Owned by: Bailey Brothers & Swinfen Ltd (Folkestone)

Sportsman's Book Club, see Readers Union Ltd

Thriller Book Club, see Foyles Book Clubs

Travel Book Club, see Foyles Book Clubs

Western Book Club, see Foyles Book Clubs

The **Wine** Book Club, Woodlands, Hazel Grove, Hindhead, Surrey GU26 6BJ

The **Women's** Press Book Club, 124 Shoreditch High St, London E1 6JE Tel: (01) 729 5257
Owned by: The Women's Press Ltd
Subjects: Books by or about women, with emphasis on fiction, art, politics, health

World Books, see Book Club Associates

World of Nature, see Book Club Associates

Major Booksellers

Austick's Headrow Bookshop*, 64 The Headrow, Leeds LS1 8EH Tel: Leeds 39607 (STD code 0532)

B H **Blackwell** Ltd*, 48-51 Broad St, Oxford Tel: Oxford 49111 (STD code 0865)
Book Club: Mainstream Book Club

Bookwise Service Ltd, Langham Trading Estate, Catteshall, Godalming, Surrey Tel: Godalming 4152 (STD code 04868)
Major wholesalers

Bowes & Bowes Books, 1 Trinity St, Cambridge CB2 1SX Tel: Cambridge 355488 (STD code 0223)

Dillon's University Bookshop Ltd, 1 Malet St, London WC1E 7JB Tel: (01) 636 1577
Owned by Pentos Ltd (qv)

W & G **Foyle** Ltd, 119-125 Charing Cross Rd, London WC2H 0EB Tel: (01) 437 5660

William **George's** Sons Ltd, 89 Park St, Bristol BS1 5PW Tel: Bristol 26602 (STD code 0272)

Grant Educational Co Ltd*, 91 Union St, Glasgow (Home and Export)

Haigh & Hochland Ltd*, 11 Whitworth St, Manchester 1 Tel: (061) 236 9950; The Precinct Centre, Oxford Rd, Manchester M13 9QZ Tel: (061) 273 4156

Hammicks Wholesale, 16 Newman Lane, Alton, Hants GU34 2PJ Tel: Alton 85822 (STD code 0420) (wholesalers)

Harrods Ltd, Knightsbridge, London SW1 Tel: (01) 730 1234 Cable Add: Harrods London Telex: 24319

Hatchards Ltd, 187 Piccadilly, London W1V 9DA Tel: (01) 439 9921 Telex: 8953970
Owned by William Collins Sons & Co Ltd (qv)

Heffers Booksellers, 20 Trinity St, Cambridge CB2 3NG Tel: Cambridge 358351 (STD code 0223) Telex 81298
Owned by W Heffer & Sons Ltd

Hudsons Bookshops Ltd, 116 New St, Birmingham B2 4JJ Tel: (021) 643 8311 Library and School Division, Priory House, 38 Colmore Circus, Queensway, Birmingham B4 6UR Tel: (021) 233 2670
Owned by Pentos Ltd (qv)

John **Menzies** (Holdings) Ltd, Villiers Ho, 40 Strand, London WC2 Tel: (01) 930 0033 (many branches throughout the United Kingdom)

Parker & Son Ltd*, 27 Broad St, Oxford OX2 6AQ Tel: Oxford 54156 (STD code 0865)

Sherratt & Hughes (Bowes & Bowes), 17 St Ann's Sq, Manchester M2 7PD Tel: (061) 834 7055

John **Smith** & Son (Glasgow) Ltd, 57-61 St Vincent St, Glasgow G2 5TB Tel: (041) 221 7472 Cable Add: Books: Glasgow Telex: 777967 Chacomb G-362

W H **Smith** & Son Ltd*, 11 Kingsway, London WC2B 6YA Tel: (01) 836 5951; W H Smith & Son Ltd (Wholesale), Strand Ho, 10 New Fetter Lane, London EC4A 1AD Tel: (01) 353 0277 (many branches throughout the United Kingdom)

James **Thin**, Bookseller, 53-59 South Bridge, Edinburgh Tel: (031) 556 6743

Major Libraries

Belfast Public Library, Central Library, Royal Ave, Belfast, Northern Ireland Tel: Belfast 43233 (STD code 0232) Telex: 747359
Chief Librarian: I A Crawley

Birmingham Public Libraries, Central Library, Paradise, Birmingham B3 3HQ Tel: (021) 235 4511 Telex: 337655
Librarian: B H Baumfield
Publication: Bibliography of National Socialist Literature

Bodleian Library, Oxford OX1 3BG Tel: Oxford 44675 (STD code 0865) Telex: 83656
Librarian: E R S Fifoot

British Library, Bibliographic Services Division, Store St, London WC1E 7DG
Publications: British National Bibliography; British Education Index; British Catalogue of Music; Books in English (ultrafiche); *Research in British Universities, Polytechnics and Colleges*

British Library Lending Division, Boston Spa, Wetherby, West Yorkshire LS23 7BQ Tel: Boston Spa 843434 (STD code 0937) Telex: 557381
Publications: Keyword Index to Serial Titles (on microfiche); Current Serials Received; Index of Conference Proceedings Received; Interlending Review; BLLD Announcement Bulletin
The Lending Division lends only to libraries and organizations, not to individual members of the public

British Library Reference Division, Great Russell St, London WC1B 3DG Tel: (01) 636 1544
Publications: British Library Journal (twice yearly); Catalogue of Additions to the Manuscripts in the British Museum; General Catalogue of Printed Books, supplements, 1971-5; Catalogue of the Newspaper Collections in the British Library; Subject Index of Modern Books; Guide to the Department of Oriental Manuscripts and Printed Books; numerous catalogues of special types of material and of books in different languages; exhibition catalogues; facsimiles, slides, postcards, etc. Full list obtainable from Reference Division, Publications British Library, Great Russell St, London WC1B 3DG

British Library, Science Reference Library, 25 Southampton Bldgs, Chancery Lane, London WC2A 1AW Tel: (01) 405 8721 Telex: 266959
and 10 Porchester Gardens, Queensway, London W2 4DE Tel: (01) 727 3022 Telex: 22717
Lists of publications available on request

British Library of Political and Economic Science*, 10 Portugal St, London WC2A 2AE Tel: (01) 405 7686

Cambridge University Library, West Rd, Cambridge CB3 9DR Tel: Cambridge 61441 (STD code 0223) Telex: 81395
Librarian: Dr F W Ratcliffe
List of publications available on request

The **Dean and Chapter** Library, The College, Durham DH1 3EH Tel: Durham 62489 (STD code 0385)
Deputy Librarian: R C Norris

Durham University Library, Palace Green, Durham DH1 3RN Tel: Durham 61262/3 (STD code 0385) Telex: 537351 Durlib
Librarian: A M McAulay

Edinburgh University Library, George Sq, Edinburgh EH8 9LJ Tel: (031) 667 1011 Telex: 727442 Unived G

Guildhall Library, Aldermanbury, London EC2P 2EJ Tel: (01) 606 3030
Librarian: Godfrey Thompson
Publications: Guildhall Studies in London History (twice a year), various handlists of Library material

India Office Library and Records, Orbit Ho, 197 Blackfriars Rd, London SE1 8NG Tel: (01) 928 9531
Director: B C Bloomfield
Publications include: Catalogue of Persian Manuscripts in the Library of India Office, 1980; *Catalogue of Burmese Printed Books,* 1969; *Catalogue of Panjabi Printed Books 1902-64,* 1975

Leeds University Library, Leeds LS2 9JT Tel: Leeds 31751 (STD code 0532)
Librarian: D Cox
Publications: Catalogue of the Romany Collection, 1962; *Catalogue of the Icelandic Collection,* 1978; *Catalogue of German Literature Printed in the 17th and 18th Centuries,* 1973, supplement 1976

Liverpool City Libraries, William Brown St, Liverpool L3 8EW Tel: (051) 207 2147 Telex: 62500

Llyfrgell Genedlaethol Cymru (National Library of Wales), Aberystwyth, Dyfed SY23 3BU Tel: Aberystwyth 3816/9 (STD code 0970) Telex: 35165
Librarian: R Geraint Gruffydd
Publications: The National Library of Wales Journal (semi-annual); *Handlist of Manuscripts in the National Library of Wales* (annual); *Bibliotheca Celtica* (annual)

The **Mitchell** Library (Glasgow District Libraries)*, North St, Glasgow G3 7DN Tel: (041) 248 7121 (12 lines) Telex: 778732
Librarian: R A Gillespie

National Library of Scotland, George IV Bridge, Edinburgh EH1 1EW Tel: (031) 226 4531 Telex: 72638 nlsedi g; Map Room, NLS Annexe, 137 Causewayside, Edinburgh EH9 1PH Tel: (031) 667 7848

Oxford University*, Taylor Institution Library, St Giles, Oxford OX1 3NA Tel: Oxford 57917 (STD code 0865)

P R O N I (Public Record Office of Northern Ireland), 66 Balmoral Ave, Belfast BT9 6NY

Public Record Office, Ruskin Ave, Kew, Richmond, Surrey TW9 4DU Tel: (01) 876 3444
and Chancery Lane, London WC2A 1LR Tel: (01) 405 0741 (national archives of the United Kingdom)

John **Rylands** University Library of Manchester, Oxford Rd, Manchester M13 9PP Tel: Main Library Bldg (061) 273 3333; Deansgate Bldg (061) 834 5343
Librarian: F W Ratcliffe
Publication: The Bulletin of the John Rylands University Library of Manchester

School of Oriental and African Studies Library, Malet St, London WC1E 7HP Tel: (01) 637 2388

Scottish Record Office, PO Box 36, HM General Register Ho, Edinburgh EH1 3YY Tel: (031) 556 6585

Trinity College Library, Cambridge CB2 1TQ Tel: Cambridge 358201 (STD code 0223)

University Libraries, see also under names of towns

University of London Library, Senate House, Malet St, London WC1E 7HU Tel: (01) 636 4514 Telex: 269400 senlib g
Director: D J Foskett

Wellcome Institute for the History of Medicine Library, 183 Euston Rd, London NW1 2BP Tel: (01) 387 4477

Westminster City Libraries, Central Administration, Marylebone Rd, London NW1 5PS Tel: (01) 828 8070 Telex: 263305
City Librarian: Melvyn Barnes

Library Associations

A R L I S (The Art Libraries Society), c/o The Library, Faculty of Architecture, Art and Design, Hull College of Higher Education, Queen's Gardens, Hull HU1 3DH Tel: Hull 224121 ext 268 (STD code 0482)
Secretary: G R Bullock
Publications: Art Libraries Journal (quarterly), *ARLIS News-sheet* (six a year), *Directory* (annually)

Aslib, 3 Belgrave Sq, London SW1X 8PL *Dir:* Basil Saunders
Incorporating the Association of Special Libraries and Information Bureaux and the British Society for International Bibliography
Publications: Index to Theses accepted for Higher Degrees in the Universities of Great Britain and Ireland (half-yearly), *Journal of Documentation* (quarterly), *Aslib Proceedings* (monthly), *Aslib Information* (monthly), *Aslib Book List* (monthly), *Program* (quarterly), *Forthcoming International Scientific and Technical Conferences* (quarterly), *Audiovisual Librarian* (quarterly), handbooks, reports, directories and membership list

Association of Assistant Librarians *Honorary Secretary:* K Crawshaw, Sheffield City Libraries, Central Library, Surrey Street, Sheffield S1 1XZ Tel: Sheffield 734711 (STD code 0742)

Association of British Library and Information Studies Schools (ABLISS), c/o A E Day, Chairman, ABLISS, Department of Library and Information Studies, Manchester Polytechnic, Ormond Bldg, Lower Ormond St, All Saints, Manchester M15 6BX
Chairman: A E Day

Association of British Theological and Philosophical Libraries*, King's College Library, Strand, London WC2R 2LS *Honorary Secretary:* Miss E M Elliott
Publication: Bulletin

Association of London Chief Librarians, *Honorary Secretary:* D F Parker, Wandsworth Public Library, Battersea District Library, Lavender Hill, London SW11 1JB
Publications: Directory of London Public Libraries

Association of Scottish Health Sciences Librarians*, Mrs E A Ferro, General Library, Royal Infirmary of Edinburgh, Edinburgh EH3 9YW

Bibliographical Society, British Academy, Burlington Ho, London W1V 0NS *Honorary Secretaries:* R J Roberts, Mrs Mirjam Foot
Publications: The Library (quarterly), various books on bibliographical subjects

British and Irish Association of Law Librarians, c/o Harding Law Library, University of Birmingham, PO Box 363, Birmingham B15 2TT
Honorary Secretary: Miss D M Blake
Publication: The Law Librarian

Cambridge Bibliographical Society, University Library, Cambridge CB3 9DR Tel: Cambridge 61441 (STD code 0223)
Honorary Secretary: F R Colliesson
Publications: Transactions (annually), *Monographs* (irregular)

Circle of State Librarians*,
Honorary Secretary: Mrs D C Scott, c/o Royal Botanic Gardens, Kew, Richmond, Surrey TW9 3AE Tel: (01) 940 1171 Ext 222
Publication: State Librarian (3 a year)

Classification Research Group*,
Honorary Secretary: D J Foskett, School of Library, Archive and Information Studies, University College, London WC1

Committee for Postgraduate Awards in Librarianship and Information Work, c/o Office of Arts and Libraries, Department of Education and Science, Elizabeth House, 39 York Rd, London SE1 7PH Tel: (01) 928 9222
Secretary: R H Shearman

Friends of the National Libraries, c/o The British Library, Great Russell St, London WC1B 3DG Tel: (01) 636 1544 ext 207 *Honorary Secretary:* Sir Edward Warner
Publication: Annual Report

Institute of Information Scientists, 62 London Rd, Reading, Berks RG1 5AS *Honorary Secretary:* Mrs S A Carter
Publications: Journal of Information Science; Inform

Institute of Reprographic Technology, PO Box 101, Witham, Essex CM8 1QS Tel: Witham 516297 (STD code 0376)
Secretary: Mrs J C Odell

International Association of Music Libraries (UK Branch), c/o Miss S M Clegg, Birmingham School of Music, Paradise Circus, Birmingham B3 3HG Tel: (021) 359 6851
General Secretary: Miss S M Clegg
Publication: Brio (twice yearly)

Library Advisory Council for England*, c/o Department of Education and Science, Elizabeth Ho, York Rd, London SE1 7PH Tel: (01) 928 9222
Secretary: K L R English

Library Advisory Council for Wales, General I Division, Welsh Office, Cathays Park, Cardiff Tel: Cardiff 825111 (STD code 0222) ext 5322
Secretary: Peter G Smith

The **Library Association**, 7 Ridgmount St, London WC1E 7AE Tel: (01) 636 7543 Telex: 21897
Secretary: K Lawrey
Publications: include *Library Association Record, British Technology Index* (both monthly), *British Humanities Index, Journal of Librarianship* (both quarterly), *Library and Information Science Abstracts* (bi-monthly), *Radials Bulletin* (2 a year), *Year Book* (annually), books and pamphlets on librarianship and bibliography, including *Guide to Reference Material, Libraries in the United Kingdom and the Republic of Ireland:* a complete list of public library services and a select list of academic and other library addresses; *A Librarian's Handbook:* documentary and statistical material; *British Librarianship and Information Science*

Microfilm Association of Great Britain, 8 High St, Guildford, Surrey GU2 5AJ Tel: Godalming 6653
Executive Secretary: Mrs P A Baker

Oxford Bibliographical Society*, Bodleian Library, Oxford
Secretary: Mrs G I Hampshire
Publications: First Series, Vols I-VII, 1923-46. *New Series,* Vol I, 1948-, *Occasional Publications,* No 1, 1967-

School Library Association, Victoria House, 29-31 George St, Oxford OX1 2AY
Tel: Oxford 722746 (STD code 0865)
Secretary: Miriam Curtis
Publication: The School Librarian (quarterly)

Scottish Library Association, c/o Secretary, M C Head, Department of Librarianship, Robert Gordon's Institute of Technology, St Andrew St, Aberdeen AB1 1HG
Tel: Aberdeen 574511 ext 564 (STD code 0224)
Publications: SLA News (every two months); Scottish Library Studies Series

Society of Archivists, South Yorkshire County Record Office, Ellin St, Sheffield S1 4PL, South Yorkshire
Secretary: Mrs C M Short
Publication: Journal of the Society of Archivists

Society of County Librarians, County Library Headquarters, Princes St, Huntingdon, Cambridgeshire Tel: Huntingdon 52181 (STD code 0480) ext 244
Telex: 32180
Secretary: R Brown

Society of Metropolitan & County Chief Librarians, c/o Central Library, Prince's Way, Bradford, West Yorkshire BD1 1NN

Standing Conference of National and University Libraries (SCONUL), 102 Euston St, London NW1 2HA Tel: (01) 387 0317
Executive Secretary: A J Loveday

Welsh Library Association, Gwynedd County Council, County Library Headquarters, Maesincla, Caernarvon LL55 1LH Tel: Caernarvon 4441 ext 87 (STD code 0286) Telex: 61565
Honorary Secretary: Geoffrey Thomas
Publications include: *A Bibliography of Anglo-Welsh Literature 1900-65,* 1970

Library Reference Books and Journals

Books

Address List of Public Library Authorities in the United Kingdom and the Republic of Ireland, The Library Association, 7 Ridgmount St, London WC1E 7AE

Aslib Directory, Association of Special Libraries and Information Bureaux, 3 Belgrave Sq, London SW1X 8PL

Aslib Membership List, Association of Special Libraries and Information Bureaux, 3 Belgrave Sq, London SW1X 8PL

British Librarianship and Information Science, The Library Association, 7 Ridgmount St, London WC1E 7AE

British Library General Catalogue, Clive Bingley Ltd, 1-19 New Oxford St, London WC1A

Guide to Reference Material, The Library Association, 7 Ridgmount St, London WC1E 7AE

A Librarians's Handbook; documentary and statistical material, The Library Association, 7 Ridgmount St, London WC1E 7AE

Libraries, Museums and Art Galleries Year Book, James Clarke & Co Ltd, 7 All Saints Passage, Cambridge CB2 3LS

Libraries in the United Kingdom and the Republic of Ireland: a complete list of public library services and a select list of academic and other library addresses, The Library Association, 7 Ridgmount St, London WC1E 7AE

Library Association Year Book, The Library Association, 7 Ridgmount St, London WC1E 7AE

Who's Who in Librarianship and Information Science, Abelard-Schuman Ltd, 450 Edgware Rd, London W2 1EG

Journals

Archives, British Records Association, Indian Office Records, 197 Blackfriars Rd, London SE1 8NG

Art Libraries Journal, ARLIS (The Art Libraries Society)
Secretary: Mrs G Varley, Kingston upon Thames Polytechnic Library, Knights Park, Kingston upon Thames, Surrey

Aslib Information, Aslib Journal of Documentation, Aslib Proceedings, Aslib Book List, Association of Special Libraries and Information Bureaux, 3 Belgrave Sq, London SW1X 8PL

Assistant Librarian, Association of Assistant Librarians, c/o Editor, Brian Arnold, Central Library, Southgate, Stevenage Hertfordshire SG1 1HD

BLL Review, British Library, Lending Division, Boston Spa, Wetherby, West Yorkshire LS23 7BQ

Bibliotheck; a Scottish journal of bibliography and allied topics, Library Association, Scottish Group, University College & Research Section, c/o Editor, Douglas S Mack, University Library, Stirling FK9 4LA

Brio, International Association of Music Libraries (UK Branch), Music Department, Town Hall, Green Lanes, Palmers Green, London N13 4XD

British Library Journal, British Library, Reference Division, Great Russell St, London WC1B 3DG

Information Scientist, Institute of Information Scientists, 657 High Rd, Tottenham, London N17

Journal of Documentation, Association of Special Libraries and Information Bureaux, 3 Belgrave Sq, London SW1X 8PL

Journal of Librarianship, The Library Association, 7 Ridgmount St, London WC1E 7AE

Journal of the Society of Archivists, Society of Archivists, c/o Editor, Mrs F Strong, South Cloister, Eton College, Windsor, Berkshire SL4 6DB

The Law Librarian, British and Irish Association of Law Librarians, c/o Harding Law Library, University of Birmingham, PO Box 363, Edgbaston, Birmingham B15 2TT

The Library, Bibliographical Society, British Academy, Burlington Ho, London W1V 0NS

Library and Information Science Abstracts, The Library Association, 7 Ridgmount St, London WC1E 7AE

Library Association Record, The Library Association, 7 Ridgmount St, London WC1E 7AE

Library Review, W & R Holmes (Book), 30 Clydeholm Rd, Glasgow G14 0BJ

New Library World, Clive Bingley (Journals) Ltd, 16 Pembridge Rd, London W11

Private Library, Private Libraries Association, Ravelston, South View Rd, Pinner, Middlesex

SLA News, Scottish Library Association, c/o M C Head, Department of Librarianship, Robert Gordon's Institute of Technology, St Andrew's St, Aberdeen AB1 1HG

State Librarian, c/o Editor, Mrs B Howard, Civil Service Department Library, Whitehall, London SW1A 2AZ

Literary Associations and Societies

Yr **Academi** Gymreig (The Welsh Academy), Swyddfa'r Academi Gymreig, 4 Llawr, Adeilad Cory, Heol Bute, Caerdydd/Cardiff CF1 6QP
Secretary: Ann Beynon
English Language Section Secretary: Mrs Sue Harries, 4th Floor, Cory Bldg, Bute St, Cardiff CF1 6QP

Association for Scottish Literary Studies, Department of English, University of Aberdeen, Aberdeen AB9 2UB
Secretary: K Buthay, Department of Scottish Literature, the University of Glasgow
Publications: Scottish Literary Journal (twice yearly plus survey of past year's work and review supplements); an edited work of Scottish literature (annually)

Association of Yorkshire Bookmen*, 28 Crawshaw Rd, Pudsey, West Yorkshire
Honorary General Secretary: Miss W M Heap Tel: Pudsey 567977 (STD code 0532)

Authors' Club, 40 Dover St, London W1
Honorary Secretary: Mrs Lesley Weissenborn

Francis **Bacon** Society Inc, Canonbury Tower, Islington, London N1
President: Commander Martin Pares
Publication: Baconiana (periodically), *Jottings* (periodically)

Books Across the Sea, The English-Speaking Union, Dartmouth Ho, 37 Charles St, London W1X 8AB Tel: (01) 408 0013
Librarian: Jean Huse
Publication: Ambassador Booklist (quarterly)

The **British Science Fiction** Association Ltd, 18 Gordon Terrace, Blantyre, Lanarkshire G72 9NA
Membership Secretary: Sandy Brown
Publications: Vector (quarterly critical journal); *Focus* (semi-annual SF writers' magazine); *Matrix* (bi-monthly newsletter)

The Incorporated **Brontë** Society, The Brontë Parsonage, Haworth, nr Keighley, West Yorkshire BD22 8DR Tel: Haworth 42323 (STD code 0535)
Honorary Secretary: A H Preston, 4 Mytholmes Lane, Haworth, Keighley, West Yorkshire BD22 8EZ
Publication: Brontë Society Transactions (annually)

Bulwer-Lytton Circle, 125 Markyate Rd, Dagenham, Essex RM8 2LB
Founder: E Ford
Publication: Bulwer-Lytton Chronicle

The **Dickens** Fellowship, Dickens Ho, 48 Doughty St, London WC1N 2LF
Tel: (01) 405 2127
Honorary Secretary: Alan Watts
Publication: The Dickensian (four-monthly)

UNITED KINGDOM 413

Early English Text Society, Lady Margaret Hall, Oxford
Honorary Dir: Professor Norman Davis; *Executive Secretary:* Dr Anne Hudson
Publications: texts (annually)

East Anglian Writers, Wood Cottage, Wattisfield, Suffolk
Honorary Secretary: P Somerset Fry

Edinburgh Bibliographical Society, c/o National Library of Scotland, George IV Bridge, Edinburgh EH1 1EW
Honorary Secretary: I C Cunningham
Publication: Transactions (irregular — for Members only)

Edwardian Studies Association, 125 Markyate Rd, Dagenham, Essex
Publication: Edwardian Studies

English Association, 1 Priory Gardens, London W4 1TT
Secretary: Lt-Col R T Brain
Publications: English (3 times yearly), *Essays and Studies, The Year's Work in English Studies, Guide to Degree Courses in English*

Thomas **Hardy** Society Ltd, 8 Brooklands Rd, Langport, Somerset TA10 9SZ
Secretary: John C Pentney
Publications: Thomas Hardy and the Modern World, 1974; *Budmouth Essays on Thomas Hardy,* 1976

The Sherlock **Holmes** Society of London*, 5 Manor Close, Warlingham, Surrey CR3 9SF
Honorary Secretary: Captain W R Michell

The **Hopkins** Society*, 162 Turkey St, Enfield, Middx EN1 4NW
Chief Executive: Dr A Thomas
Publications: Hopkins Research Bulletin, Annual lecture, Annual sermon

Johnson Society of London, c/o 15 St John's Mansions, Clapton Sq, London E5
Honorary Secretary: Miss S B S Pigrome
Publication: The New Rambler (annually)

Kipling Society*, 18 Northumberland Ave, London WC2N 5BJ
Honorary Secretary: John Shearman
Tel: (01) 930 6733
Publication: The Kipling Journal (quarterly)

Charles **Lamb** Society, 9 Baronsmead Rd, London SW13 9RR
Honorary Secretary: Mrs M R Huxstep
Publication: The Charles Lamb Bulletin (quarterly)

London Writer Circle, 308 Lewisham Rd, London SE13 7PA
Honorary Secretary: Miss M E Harris

The **National Book** League, Book House, East Hill, Wandsworth, London SW18 2HZ
Tel: (01) 870 9055
Dir: Martyn Goff
Libraries: Reference library of current British children's books; The Mark Longman Library on books and the book trade, with a book information service
Publications: Booknews, British Book Design and Production, Children's Books of the Year, annotated book lists on specialist topics

P E N English Centre, 7 Dilke St, Chelsea, London SW3 4JE Tel: (01) 352 6303
Secretary: Miss Josephine Pullein-Thompson
Publication: Broadsheet (biannually)

P E N Scottish Centre, 18 Crown Terrace, Glasgow G12 9ES Tel: (041) 332 0391 (day), (041) 357 0327 (eve)
Hon Secretary: Miss Mary Baxter

Poetry Society, 21 Earls Court Sq, London SW5 Tel: (01) 373 7861
General Secretary: Brian G Mitchell
Publication: The Poetry Review

Royal Literary Fund, 11 Ludgate Hill, London EC4M 7AE

Royal Society of Literature of the United Kingdom, 1 Hyde Park Gardens, London W2 2LT Tel: (01) 723 5104
Secretary: Mrs P M Schute
Publications: Transactions, Report, Special Editions

Shakespearean Authorship Society, 10 Uphill Grove, Mill Hill, London NW7 4NJ
Honorary Secretary: Dr D W Thomson Vessey
Publication: The Bard (semi-annual)

Bernard **Shaw** Centre, 125 Markyate Rd, Dagenham, Essex RM8 2LB
Director: E Ford
Publications: Shaw Centre Series

Bernard **Shaw** Society, 125 Markyate Rd, Dagenham, Essex RM8 2LB
Secretary: Eric Ford
Publications: The Shavian, etc

Society for the Study of Medieval Languages and Literature,
Treasurer: Dr D G Pattison, Magdalen College, Oxford
Publications: Medium Aevum, Medium Aevum Monographs (new series)

Society of Australian Writers*, Australia House, Strand, London UK
Secretary: Alessandra Miach

The **Tolkien** Society, 11 Regal Way, Harrow, Middlesex HA3 0RZ
Secretary: Mrs Helen Armstrong
Publications: Amon Hen (approx 6 issues a year), *Mallorn* (occasional magazine)

Jules **Verne** Circle, 125 Markyate Rd, Dagenham, Essex RM8 2LB
Founder: E Ford
Publication: Voyages

H G **Wells** Society, 24 Wellin Lane, Edwalton, Nottingham
Secretary: J R Hammond
Publications: Newsletter (quarterly), *The Wellsian* (annually)

Wellsiana—The World of Wells, 125 Markyate Rd, Dagenham, Essex RM8 2LB
Publication: Wellsiana

Literary Periodicals

Bananas (quarterly), 60 Elgin Crescent, London W11

Blackwood's, William Blackwood & Sons Ltd, 32 Thistle St, Edinburgh EH2 1HA

Book Collector, Collector Ltd, 58 Frith St, London W1V 6BY

Books, National Book League, Book Ho, East Hill, London SW18

Books and Bookmen, 2-4 Old Pye St, off Strutton Ground, Victoria St, London SW1

Books & Issues, Stephen Trombley, 40 Mildmay Grove, London N1

Critical Quarterly, Manchester University Press, Oxford Rd, Manchester M13 9PL

Encounter, Encounter Ltd, 59 St Martins Lane, London WC2N

The Literary Review, 7 Northumberland St, Edinburgh EH3 6L1

The London Review of Books, 1 Malet St, London WC1

New Statesman, Statesman & Nation Publishing Co, 10 Great Turnstile, London WC1V 7HJ

Notes and Queries; for readers and writers, collectors and librarians, Oxford University Press, Press Rd, Neasden, London NW10 0DD

Oasis Magazine, 12 Stevenage Rd, London SW6 6ES, 6 times a year, each issue devoted to work by one author

Phoenix; a magazine for writers, Phoenix Publications, 60 Abbey Ho, 2 Victoria St, London SW1

Poetry London, 24 Old Gloucester St, London W1

Poetry Review, Poetry Society, 21 Earls Court Sq, London SW5

Quarto, 20 Fitzroy Sq, London W1

Review of English Studies; a quarterly journal of English literature and the English language, The Clarendon Press, Walton St, Oxford OX2 6DP

Scottish Literary Journal, Association for Scottish Literary Studies, Department of English, University of Aberdeen, Aberdeen AB9 1FX

Spectator, Spectator Ltd, 99 Gower St, London WC1E GAE

Taliesin; the Welsh literary journal, Garth Martin, Ffordd Llysonnen, Carmarthen

Times Literary Supplement, Times Newspapers Ltd, Gray's Inn Rd, PO Box 7, London WC1X 8EZ

Transatlantic Review, 33 Ennismore Gardens, London SW7

Literary Prizes

Authors' Club First Novel Award
For the most promising first novel published in English in the UK in the preceding year. Award consists of a silver-plated quill presented to the author at a dinner. Awarded annually. Last award was to Martin Page for *The Pilate Plot* (Heinemann). Enquiries to the Honorary Secretary, Authors' Club, 40 Dover St, London W1X 3RB

Authors' Club Sir Banister Fletcher Prize Trust
For the most deserving book on architecture or the arts. Awarded annually. Enquiries to the Honorary Secretary, Authors' Club, 40 Dover St, London W1X 3RB

Benson Medal
Founded 1916 by Dr A C Benson. For meritorious work in poetry, fiction, history, biography and belles lettres. A silver medal given at the discretion of the Council of the Royal Society of Literature. Applications are not invited. Last awarded in 1975 to Philip Larkin. Enquiries to Royal Society of Literature, 1 Hyde Park Gardens, London W2 2LT

Besterman Medal
The Library Association awards this medal annually for an outstanding bibliography or guide to the literature first published in the United Kingdom during the preceding year. Recommendations for the award are invited from members of The Library Association. Among criteria for the award are the authority of the work, quality of articles and entries, accessibility of information, scope and coverage, up-to-dateness, and originality. Two awards were made in 1979, one to Grainne Morbey for *Knowhow: A Guide to Information Training and Campaigning Materials for Information and Advice Workers,* edited by Elaine Kempson (Library Association for The British Library, a Community Information project), and the

other to the South Asia Library Group, general editor J D Pearson, for *South Asian Bibliography: A Handbook and Guide* (Harvester Press). Enquiries to The Library Association, 7 Ridgmount St, London WC1E 7AE

James Tait **Black** Memorial Prizes
These literary prizes were founded by the late Mrs Janet Coats Black in memory of her husband, a partner in the publishing house of A & C Black Ltd, London. Mrs Black set aside £11,000 to be used for two prizes of whatever income the fund would produce after paying expenses. The prizes, supplemented by the Scottish Arts Council, now amount annually to approximately £1,000 each. One prize is given to the author of the best biography in the English language first published in the United Kingdom during the year and the other to the author of the best novel. The choice is made in the spring for books of the preceding year by the Regius Professor of English Literature at the University of Edinburgh, preferably, or the Professor of English at the University of Glasgow. Awarded in 1980 for 1979 to Brian Finney for his biography *Christopher Isherwood* and William Golding for his novel *Darkness Visible*. Enquiries to Department of English Literature, David Hume Tower, George Sq, Edinburgh EH8 9JX

Arnold Vincent **Bowen** Competition
Awarded annually for the best single lyric poem in English of up to thirty lines. Prize of £10. Enquiries to the General Secretary, The Poetry Society, 21 Earls Court Sq, London SW5

British Science Fiction Award
Awarded annually for the best science fiction book published in Britain for the first time in the previous year. The award for 1979 was to J G Ballard for *The Unlimited Dream Company* (Jonathan Cape). Enquiries to Alan Dorey (BSFA Chairman), 20 Hermitage Woods Crescent, St John's, Woking, Surrey GU21 1UE

Carnegie Medal
First awarded 1936. Instituted by The Library Association to commemorate the centenary of Andrew Carnegie's birth in 1835. Annual award for an outstanding book for children written in English and first published during the preceding year in the UK. Recommendations for the award are made by members of The Library Association. The 1979 Medal was awarded to Peter Dickinson for *Tulku* (Gollancz). Enquiries to The Library Association, 7 Ridgmount St, London WC1E 7AE

Sid **Chaplin** Literary Award
Established in 1977 to encourage the writing of short stories. £100 and a scroll to be awarded annually. The 1979 award was won by Doreen Dade from Taunton for *Woman of Taste*. A separate prize of £25 has been introduced for the best story by a writer aged eighteen or under. Enquiries to Public Relations Department, Aycliffe Development Corporation, Churchill Ho, Newton Aycliffe, Co Durham

John **Creasey** Memorial Award
Founded 1973. Magnifying glass with onyx handle and inscribed plate for best first crime-fiction novel. Awarded annually by a panel of reviewers. The 1979 award was made to David Serafin for *Saturday of Glory* (Collins). Enquiries to Crime Writers' Association, c/o The National Book League, Book House, East Hill, Wandsworth, London SW18

Eleanor **Farjeon** Award
The Eleanor Farjeon Award was established in 1965 to commemorate the work of the late children's author. The Children's Book Circle makes an annual award of £75 which may be given to a librarian, teacher, author, artist, publisher, reviewer, bookseller or television producer who, in the judgment of the Awards Committee, is considered to have done outstanding work for children's books. Awarded in 1980 to Dorothy Butler. Enquiries to Ms Linda Summers, Julia McRae Books, 8 Cork St, London W1

Prudence **Farmer** Poetry Prize
Founded 1974. Awarded annually for the best poem printed in the *New Statesman* during the previous year. In 1979 the prize was awarded to John Fuller. Enquiries to Literary Editor, 10 Great Turnstile, London WC1V 7HJ

Authors' Club Sir Bannister **Fletcher** Prize Trust, see under Authors' Club

John **Florio** Prize
Established in 1963 under the auspices of the Italian Institute and the British-Italian Society, and named after John Florio. For the best translation into English of a twentieth-century Italian work of literary merit and general interest, published by a British publisher during the preceding year. £500. The 1979 award was presented to Julian Mitchell for his translation of *Henry IV* by Pirandello (Eyre Methuen). Enquiries to Secretary, Translators' Association, 84 Drayton Gardens, London SW10 9SD

Glaxo Travelling Fellowships for Science Writers
Founded 1966. Three awards annually to anyone writing popular scientific material published in English, in national papers or magazines, regional papers or magazines, radio or TV, and trade, technical or house magazines. The major criterion in judging is that the entrants must have significantly improved the quality of science journalism. The 1979 winners were: Oliver Gillie, Medical Editor, *The Sunday Times*; David Paterson, Science Unit, BBC Radio, and Dr Ian Kennedy, King's College, London; and Stephanie Yanchinski, *New Scientist*. The awards are sponsored by Glaxo Holdings Ltd and administered by the Association of British Science Writers. Enquiries to Association of British Science Writers, c/o 21 Albemarle St, London W1X 4BS

Gold Dagger Award
Inaugurated 1956, revised 1970. A gilded dagger for the best crime-fiction novel of the year awarded annually by a panel of reviewers. The 1979 fiction award was made to Dick Francis for *Whip Hand* (Michael Joseph). The non-fiction Gold Dagger (inaugurated 1978) went to Shirley Green for *Rachman* (Michael Joseph). Enquiries to Crime Writers' Association, c/o The National Book League, Book House, East Hill, Wandsworth, London SW18

Kate **Greenaway** Medal
First awarded 1955. Offered annually by The Library Association for the most distinguished work in the illustration of children's books first published in the UK during the preceding year. Recommendations for the award are made by members of The Library Association. The 1979 medal was awarded to Jan Pienkrwski for illustrating *The Haunted House* (Heinemann). Enquiries to The Library Association, 7 Ridgmount St, London WC1E 7AE

Eric **Gregory** Trust Fund Awards
A number of awards are made each year to encourage young poets. Candidates for awards must be British subjects by birth, ordinarily resident in the UK and under the age of 30 on 31 March in the year of the award. Candidates must submit a published or unpublished volume of belles lettres, poetry or drama-poems. In 1980 awards were made to Michael Hulse, Medbh McGuckian, Robert Minhinnick and Blake Morrison. Enquiries to Society of Authors, 84 Drayton Gardens, London SW10 9SD

Hawthornden Prize
Founded in 1919 by Miss Alice Warrender and administered now by the Society of Authors. It is awarded annually in June to a British subject under 41 for the best work of imaginative literature. In 1978 it was increased to £500 through the generosity of the Arts Council of Great Britain. It is especially designed to encourage young authors, and the word 'imaginative' is given a broad interpretation. Biographies are not excluded. Books do not have to be submitted for the prize; it is awarded without competition. A panel of judges chooses the winner. In 1979 the prize was awarded to P N Rushforth for *Kindergarten* (Hamish Hamilton). Enquiries to Society of Authors, 84 Drayton Gardens, London SW10 9SD

Heinemann Award for Literature
A foundation was established in 1944 through a bequest in the will of the late William Heinemann, eminent British publisher. The Royal Society of Literature administers the annual foundation award which is 'primarily to reward those classes of literature which are less remunerative, namely, poetry, criticism, biography, history, etc' and 'to encourage the production of works of real merit'. The amount of the award is not definitely specified. Submitted works must have been written originally in English. A reading committee decides on the winner, whose name is announced in April or May; the prize is presented at a meeting of the Royal Society of Literature in June or July. The 1979 award was shared between Brian Fothergill for *Bexford of Fonthill* and Ted Hughes for *Moortown* (both published by Faber & Faber). Enquiries to Royal Society of Literature, 1 Hyde Park Gardens, London W2 2LT

Felicia **Hemans** Prize for Lyrical Poetry
For a lyrical poem by past and present members and students of the University of Liverpool. Books or cash awarded annually. Enquiries to Registrar, University of Liverpool, PO Box 147, Liverpool L69 3BX

Winifred **Holtby** Memorial Prize
Founded in 1966 by Vera Brittain in memory of Winifred Holtby. An annual award for the best regional novel of its year. Submissions by publishers, not by individual authors. No award was made for 1979. Enquiries to Secretary, Royal Society of Literature, 1 Hyde Park Gardens, London W2 2LT

Martin Luther **King** Memorial Prize
Inaugurated 1968. For a literary work reflecting the ideals to which Dr King devoted his life. It may be given for a novel, story, poem, play, television, radio or film script first published or performed in the UK during the preceding year. Prize of £100 awarded annually. 1979 prize awarded to André Brink for *A Dry White Season* (W H Allen). Enquiries to Martin Luther King Memorial Prize, c/o National Westminster Bank, 7 Fore St, Chard, Somerset TA20 1PJ.
No enquiries answered without stamped and addressed envelope

McColvin Medal
This annual award is given for an outstanding reference book first published in the United Kingdom. Encyclopaedias, dictionaries, biographical dictionaries, annuals, year-books and directories, handbooks and compendia of data, and atlases are eligible. Recommendations are invited from members of The Library Association who are asked to submit a preliminary list of not more than three titles. No award has been made since 1977. Enquiries to The Library Association, 7 Ridgmount St, London WC1E 7AE

Arthur **Markham** Memorial Prize
Instituted 1927. For a poem, short story, first chapter of a novel or a one-act play by a manual worker in coal-mining. There are specified themes and strict limits on length. Prize of £125 annually. Enquiries to Registrar and Secretary, The University, Sheffield S10 2TN

Somerset **Maugham** Award
Founded 1946 by Somerset Maugham to encourage young writers to travel abroad. Given to a promising author of a published work of poetry, fiction, criticism, biography, history, philosophy, belles lettres or travel. Candidates must be British subjects by birth and ordinarily resident in the UK and under 35. Awards of £1,000 must be used for foreign travel. The 1980 awards were to Max Hastings for *Bomber Command*, Christopher Reid for *Arcadia* and Humphrey Carpenter for *The Inklings*. Enquiries to Society of Authors, 84 Drayton Gardens, London SW10 9SD

Netta **Muskett** Award, see under Literary Prizes section, Isle of Man

Sir Roger **Newdigate** Prize for English Verse
The Newdigate Prize Foundation was established in 1806 by Sir Roger Newdigate who had been a member of Parliament for Oxford University from 1750 to 1780. This foundation was the first one founded solely to award a literary prize. The sum of £1,000 was bequeathed by Sir Roger with the stipulation that £21 of the income should be awarded each year to a member of Oxford University for 'a copy of English verse of fifty lines and no more, in recommendation of the study of the ancient Greek and Roman remains of architecture, sculpture, and painting'. Later, with the consent of the Newdigate heirs, these restrictions were modified. The award, increased to about £80, is now open to undergraduate members of the University of Oxford who have not exceeded four years from their matriculation. It is given for a poem of no more than 300 lines on a given subject. Three judges award the prize. Announcement is made by Oxford University annually in May or early June; the winner recites part of the poem at commemoration in June. The award was not given during the war, but was resumed again in 1947. Enquiries to Head Clerk, University of Oxford, University Offices, Wellington Sq, Oxford OX1 2JD

Frederick **Niven** Literary Award
Founded in 1950 by Pauline, widow of the Scottish novelist Frederick Niven. For the best novel by a Scotsman or Scotswoman published during the preceding three years. £100 awarded every three years. Enquiries to Honorary Secretary, PEN Scottish Centre, 18 Crown Terrace, Glasgow G12 9ES

George **Orwell** Memorial Prize*
Founded 1975. For an article, essay or a series of articles commenting on current cultural, social or political issues anywhere in the world and published in the UK. The judges will look for originality, literary merit and expressive power. £750 awarded annually. Submissions must be made by the editor of the publication in which articles appeared or the organization which commissioned a pamphlet. Enquiries to Penguin Books Ltd, 536 Kings Rd, London SW10 0UH

The **Other** Award
Commendation of a number of children's books a year as non-biased works of literary merit. In 1979 the chosen books were Dick Cate's *Old Dog, New Tricks*, Sue Wagstaff's *Two Victorian Families*, Roger Mills' *A Comprehensive Education* and Farrukh Dhondy's *Come to Mecca*. Enquiries to The Other Award, 4 Aldebert Terrace, London SW8 1BH

Provincial Booksellers Fairs Association Annual Book Awards*
Two awards of £250 each are made annually covering different types of books. Enquiries to Mrs Edna Whiteson Ltd, 343 Bowes Rd, London N11

The **Queen's** Gold Medal for Poetry
Instituted in 1933 by King George V, at the suggestion of the Poet Laureate, John Masefield, this Medal is given for a book of verse, on the recommendation of a committee of eminent men and women of letters headed by the Poet Laureate. The Medal is usually given for a book by a British subject writing in the English language, but an exceptional translation may also be considered. The Medal is not necessarily awarded every year. Awarded in 1977 to Norman Nicholson. Enquiries to the Press Secretary to the Queen, Buckingham Palace, London SW1

R N A Major Award, see under Literary Prizes section, Isle of Man

Schlegel-Tieck Prize
Established in 1964 under the auspices of the Translators Association, a subsidiary organization of the Society of Authors, to be awarded annually for the best translation published by a British publisher during the previous year. Only translations of German twentieth-century works of literary merit and general interest will be considered. The work should be entered by the publisher and not the individual translator. In 1979 a first prize of £1,000 was awarded to Janet Seligman for her translation of *The English House* by Hermann Mathesius (Granada). A runner-up prize of £600 was awarded to Hazel and David Harvey for their translation of *Sophocles* by Carl Reinhardt (Basil Blackwell). Enquiries to Secretary, The Translators Association, 84 Drayton Gardens, London SW10 9SD

Scott-Moncrieff Prize
Established in 1964 under the auspices of the Translators Association of the Society of Authors to be awarded annually for the best translation published by a British publisher during the previous year. Only translations of French twentieth-century works of literary merit and general interest will be considered. The work should be entered by the publisher and not the individual translator. The £1,000 prize for books published in 1979 was won by Brian Pearce for his translation of *The Institutions of France under the Absolute Monarchy 1598-1789* (University of Chicago Press). Enquiries to Secretary, Translators Association, 84 Drayton Gardens, London SW10 9SD

Scottish Arts Council Book Awards
A limited number of Awards, value £500 each, are made each year by the Scottish Arts Council to published books of literary merit written by Scots or writers resident in Scotland. The Awards fall into two categories: Scottish Arts Council New Writing Awards for first books, and Scottish Arts Council Book Awards for established authors. All types of books are eligible for consideration and the closing date is the 31 October of each year. Books are submitted by the author's publisher. Enquiries to Literature Department, The Scottish Arts Council, 19 Charlotte Sq, Edinburgh EH2 4DF

Silver Dagger Award
Inaugurated 1956, revised 1970. A silvered dagger for the runner-up crime-fiction novel of the year (see Gold Dagger Award). Awarded annually by a panel of reviewers. The 1979 fiction award was made to Colin Dexter for *Service of All the Dead* (Macmillan). The non-fiction Silver Dagger (inaugurated 1978) went to Jon Connell and Douglas Sutherland for *Fraud* (Hodder & Stoughton). Enquiries to Crime Writers' Association, c/o The National Book League, Book House, East Hill, Wandsworth, London SW18

W H **Smith** & Son Children's Literary Competition*
Established in 1958 and previously backed by the 'Daily Mirror', the competition aims to encourage expression in the written word. Open to all children up to the age of 16 years and of British nationality. Sixty-three awards totalling £2,150 are made and the award-winning work is published in book form. Enquiries to Public Relations Department, W H Smith & Son Ltd, Strand Ho, 10 New Fetter Lane, London EC4A 1AD

W H **Smith** & Son Literary Award
Established 1959 to encourage and bring international esteem to authors of the Commonwealth. Given to an author whose book, written in English and published in the UK, makes the most significant contribution to Literature. Award of £2,500 annually. The award for 1980 was made to Thom Gunn for *Selected Poems — 1950-1975* (Faber & Faber). Enquiries to W H Smith & Son Ltd, Strand House, 10 New Fetter Lane, London EC4A 1AD

Reginald **Taylor** Prize
Instituted 1932. For the best unpublished essay, not exceeding 7,500 words, on any subject of archaeological, art historical, or antiquarian interest within the period from the Roman era to AD 1830. Prize of £30 awarded annually. Enquiries to the Honorary Editor, British Archaeological Association, c/o County Planning Department, County Offices, Newland, Lincoln

Tom-Gallon Trust Award
Founded 1943. Given to short-story writers of limited means. Entrants must submit a list of already published fiction, one published or unpublished short story, and a brief statement of their financial position and willingness to devote substantial time to writing fiction as soon as they are financially able. It is awarded every other year. The award has been increased to £500 through the generosity of the Arts Council of Great Britain. Enquiries to Society of Authors, 84 Drayton Gardens, London SW10 9SD

Welsh Arts Council Awards to Writers
Since 1968, the Welsh Arts Council has given awards to authors whose books are of exceptional literary merit or which make an important contribution to the literature of Wales. The books must be written in English or Welsh. The prizes are awarded to recognize achievement, to draw attention to writers of promise and to encourage the

writing of creative literature in English and Welsh. Cash prizes of £300 to £500 awarded annually. Bursaries of up to £5,000 each are awarded to enable writers to devote themselves, for periods of up to one year, to their writing. Enquiries to Welsh Arts Council, Museum Pl, Cardiff CF1 3NX

Wheatley Medal
Instituted 1961. Presented by The Library Association, after consultation with The Society of Indexers, for a book published in the UK during the preceding three years which sets an outstandingly high standard in the quality of its index. The 1979 medal was awarded jointly to K G B Bakewell for *Index to Anglo-American Cataloguing Rules, 2nd ed* (The Library Association) and Mrs A Surrey for the index to *Circulation of the Blood* (Pitman Medical). Enquiries to The Library Association, 7 Ridgmount St, London WC1E 7AE

Whitbread Literary Awards
Instituted 1971. Annual awards of £2,500 each to acknowledge outstanding published books in each of three categories of literature: best novel; best biography or autobiography; best children's book. An additional award of £2,500 is given for the Whitbread Book of the Year, chosen from the winners of the three categories. Authors must be domiciled in the UK or the Republic of Ireland. 1979 awards were made to Jennifer Johnston for *The Old Jest* (Hamish Hamilton), Penelope Mortimer for *About Time* (Allen Lane) and Peter Dickinson for *Tulku* (Gollancz). Enquiries to the Booksellers Association of Great Britain and Ireland, 154 Buckingham Palace Rd, London SW1W 9TZ

Francis **Williams** Book Illustration Award*
This award is given every five years to practising book illustrators, professional or student, for books published in Great Britain in which illustration is a major element. Books privately printed or in limited editions are excluded. Books to be submitted by their publishers. Illustrations of a purely technical nature and photographs are excluded. The first Exhibition was held at the Victoria and Albert Museum in 1972 and the second in 1977. Enquiries to The Victoria and Albert Museum Library, South Kensington, London SW7 2RL
or The National Book League, Book House, East Hill, Wandsworth, London SW18

Griffith John **Williams** Memorial Prize
(Gwobr Goffa Griffith John Williams)
Awarded to non-members of the Welsh Academy for the best literary work in Welsh produced in the previous year. About £50 awarded annually. Enquiries to Yr Academi Gymreig, 4 Llawr, Adeilad Cory, Heol Bute, Cardiff CF1 6QP

Wolfson History Awards
Founded 1972. Two awards are made annually to authors of published works on history. A first prize is given for an author's published body of work culminating with the particular work for which the award is given. In 1979 £5,000 was awarded to Richard Cobb for *Death in Paris* and two second prizes of £3,500 each were awarded to Mary Soames for *Clementine Churchill* and Quentin Skinner for *The Foundations of Modern Political Thought*. Enquiries to Paisner & Co (Solicitors), Bouverie House, 154 Fleet St, London EC4A 2DQ

Yorkshire Arts Association Literary Awards
The Association offers a number of biennial awards, together worth £2,000 for published books of poetry, drama, novels or works of nonfiction, having strong literary connections with Yorkshire. Some of the awards are usually made to new writers (ie with only one work in print) whilst the others are for more established authors (with two or more books published). Enquiries to The Director, Yorkshire Arts Association, Glyde House, Glydegate, Bradford, West Yorkshire BD5 0BQ

Translation Agencies and Associations

Tek Translation & International Print Ltd, 11 Uxbridge Rd, London W12 8LH Tel: (01) 749 3211 Telex: 265658

Thames Translations, 65-67 Kingston Rd, New Malden, Surrey Tel: (01) 949 5711

Translators Association, 84 Drayton Gardens, London SW10 9SD Tel: (01) 373 6642

Translators' Guild Ltd, Mangold House, 24a Highbury Grove, London N5 2EA Tel: (01) 359 7445

Upper Volta

General Information

Language: French, officially
Religion: About 1 million Muslim, ¼ million Roman Catholic; rest follow traditional beliefs
Population: 6.6 million
Bank Hours: 0800-1200 Monday-Friday
Currency: CFA franc
Export/Import Information: Member of West African Economic Community. No tariff on books except children's picture books and atlases, 52%; single advertising catalogues sent as printed matter free but otherwise 64%. Statistical Tax 1%; Customs Stamp Tax 6%. No import licences required for imports from EEC or Franc Zone
Copyright: Berne (see International section)

Publishers

Government Printer, Imprimerie Nationale*, BP 7040, Ouagadougou

Les **Presses** Africaines*, BP 90, Ouagadougou
Man Dir: M Armand
Subjects: General Fiction, Religion, Secondary & Primary Textbooks
Bookshop: Librairie Jeunesse d'Afrique, BP 90, Ouagadougou
Book Club: Librairie 'Jeunesse et Afrique'

Book Club

Librairie **'Jeunesse et Afrique'***, BP 90, Ouagadougou
Owned by: Les Presses Africaines (Ouagadougou)

Major Booksellers

Librairie **Attié***, BP 64, Ouagadougou

Librairie **Evangélique***, BP 29, Ouagadougou

Librairie de **France***, BP 73, Ouagadougou

Librairie **Jeunesse d'Afrique***, BP 90, Ouagadougou

Major Libraries

American Cultural Center Library*, BP 539, Ouagadougou

Bibliothèque universitaire*, Université de Ouagadougou, BP 7021, Ouagadougou Tel: 3310/11

Library Associations

Association voltaique pour le Développement des Bibliothèques, des Archives et de la Documentation (AVDBAD)*, BP 1140, Ouagadougou
Voltan Association for the Development of Libraries, Archives and Documentation
Executive Secretary: Louis Aristide Rouamba

Uruguay

General Information

Language: Spanish
Religion: Roman Catholic
Population: 2.9 million
Literacy Rate (1975): 93.9%
Bank Hours: 1300-1700 Monday-Friday
Shop Hours: 0900-1200, 1400-1900 Monday-Friday; 0900-1230 Saturday
Currency: peso
Export/Import Information: Member of the Latin American Free Trade Association. No tariffs on books or single copies catalogues but 75% surcharge on advertising matter. 7% Additional Surcharge on all imports, plus 18% VAT CIF, plus Stamp Tax of 5% total invoice value. No Import licences. No exchange controls
Copyright: Berne, Buenos Aires (see International section)

Book Trade Organizations

Asociación de Libreros del Uruguay*, Ave Uruguay 1325, Montevideo
Uruguayan Booksellers' Association

Asociación Uruguaya de Escritores*, Bartolomé Mitre 1260, Montevideo
Uruguayan Writers' Association

Cámara Uruguaya del Libro*, Carlos Roxlo 1446 piso 1°, Apdo 2, Montevideo Tel: 411860
Uruguayan Publishers' Association
Secretary: Arnaldo Medone

Book Trade Reference Journals

Anuario bibliográfico uruguayo (Uruguayan Bibliographical Annual), National Library, Calle Guayabo 1793, Montevideo

Bibliografía uruguaya (Uruguayan Bibliography), Library of the Legislative Power, Palacio Legislativo, Ave Agradiada, Montevideo

URUGUAY 417

Publishers

Editorial **Alfa** SA*, Cuidadela 1393,
Montevideo Tel: 981244/80417
Man Dir: Leonardo Milla
Subjects: General Fiction, Poetry, Belles
Lettres, History, Social Science
Founded: 1960

Editorial **Arca** SRL, Andes 1118,
Montevideo
Man Dir: Alberto Oreggioni
Subjects: General Literature, History, Social
Science

Ediciones de la **Banda** Oriental SRL*, Yi
1364, Montevideo Tel: 982810
Man Dir: Heber Raviolo
Subjects: Literature, Fiction, History,
Education, Social Science
Founded: 1961

Barreiro y **Ramos** SA, Juan Carlos Gómez
1436, Casilla de Correo 15, Montevideo
Tel: 919202 Cable Add: Bareiramos
Man Dir: Gaston Barreiro Zorrilla; *Sales
Dir:* Raúl Catelli
Subjects: General Literature, Textbooks
Reference
Bookshops: Juan Carlos Gómez 1436 (For
branches see under Booksellers)
Founded: 1871

Editorial y Librería Juridica Amalio M
Fernández*, 25 de Mayo 477, planta baja,
Of 11, Montevideo Tel: 916384
Man Dir: Amalio M Fernández; *Editorial:*
Carlos W Deamestoy Perez; *Sales:* Andrés
Paz López
Subjects: Law, Sociology
1978: 7 titles *Founded:* 1951

Fundación de Cultura Universitaria*, 25 de
Mayo 537, Montevideo Tel: 913385
Man Dir: Román Delgado; *Sales Dir:*
Ignacio Sanz; *Editorial Dir:* José Moura
Branch Offs: Artigas 1251, Salto; Zorrilla
975, Paysandú
Subjects: Social Science, Law
Founded: 1946

Editorial **Interamericana** del Uruguay SA*,
Casilla de Correos 357, Montevideo
Manager: Mirta Gaidos
Associate Company: Holt-Saunders Ltd (qv
for other associates)

Editorial **Medina** SRL*, Gaboto 1521,
Montevideo Tel: 44100/45800
Man Dir: Marcos Medina Vidal
Subject: Low-priced Paperbacks
Founded: 1933

A **Monteverde** y Cia SA*, 25 de Mayo 577,
Casilla de Correo 371, Montevideo Tel:
902473
Man Dir: Héctor Mussini; *Sales Dir:* Néstor
Barón; *Production:* Leandro Mendaro
Subjects: Literature, Primary & Secondary
Textbooks, Educational Materials
Bookshop: Palacio del Libro, 25 de Mayo
577, Montevideo
Founded: 1879

Mosca Hnos SA*, Ave 18 de Julio 1578,
Montevideo Tel: 404131 Cable Add:
Moscaher
Man Dir: Miguel Angel Mosca; *Sales Dir:*
Raúl Mosca
Subjects: General Literature, Religion,
Textbooks
Bookshop: Ave 18 de Julio 1578,
Montevideo
Founded: 1888

Editorial **Nuestra Tierra***, Cerrito 566,
Montevideo Tel: 916217
Man Dir: Daniel Aljanati; *Editorial Dir:*
Jaime D Aljanati
Subject: General Literature
Founded: 1968

Ediciones **Papacito***, Andes 1346,
Montevideo Tel: 987250
Bookshop: Librerías Papacito, Andes 1340,
Montevideo
Subject: Essays

Editorial **Pomaire** Ltda, Somme 1612,
Montevideo Tel: 792125
Man Dir: Luis A Artioas G
Parent Company: Editorial Pomaire SA,
Spain (qv)

Major Booksellers

Albe Soc Com*, Cerrito 566, Montevideo
Tel: 85692

America Latina*, 18 de Julio 2089,
Montevideo Tel: 415127

Librería Los **Apuntes***, Eduardo Acevedo
1490, Montevideo Tel: 43651

Barreiro y **Ramos** SA, Juan Carlos Gómez
1430, Montevideo Tel: 986621
Branches at: Ave 18 de Julio 941 and 1777;
Ave General Flores 2426; Ave 8 de Octubre
3728; Ave Agraciada 3945; Ave Rivera 2684;
Calle 21 de Setiembre 2753 (all in
Montevideo); Ave General Artigas 714, Las
Piedras

Feria del Libro*, Ave 18 de Julio 1308,
Montevideo Tel: 902070

Librería Amalio M **Fernández***, 25 de Mayo
477 planta baja ofic 11, Montevideo Tel:
916384

Ibana, SA, Julio Herrera y Obes 1626,
Montevideo Tel: 94738
Manager: Tomás J Raphael

Librería **Inglesa***, Sarandi 530, Montevideo
Tel: 81955

Librería Adolfo **Linardi**, Linardi y Risso,
Juan Carlos Gomez 1435, Montevideo Tel:
912749/901506 Cable Add: Linbooks

Mosca Hnos, Ave 18 de Julio 1578,
Montevideo Tel: 404131

Palacio del Libro*, Casilla de Correo 371,
Montevideo Tel: 902473

Librerías **Papacito***, Andes 1340/46,
Montevideo Tel: 82872/987250

Major Libraries

Archivo General de la Nación*, Calle
Convención 1474, Montevideo

Biblioteca **Artigas-Washington** (ICA)*, Calle
Paraguay 1217 Tel: 917423

Biblioteca Central de **Educación** básica,
secundaria y superior*, Eduardo Acevedo
1419, Montevideo
Central Library of Primary, Secondary and
Higher Education
Dir: David Yudchak

Biblioteca **Nacional** del Uruguay*, 18 de
Julio 1790, Casilla de Correo 452,
Montevideo Tel: 45030/496011

Centro Nacional de Información y
Documentación*, Plaza de Cagancha 1175,
Montevideo
Dir: Mercedes Fitz-Patrick
*Publications: Anales, Enciclopedia de
educación, Legislación escolar*

Departamento de Documentación y
Biblioteca, Faculted de Humanidades y
Ciencias, Universidad de la República,
Tristán Narvaja 1674, Montevideo
Dir: Matilde Jaureguiberry Barbagelata

Biblioteca del **Instituto Cultural** Anglo-
Uruguayo*, San José 1426, Montevideo

Biblioteca del **Museo** Histórico Nacional*,
Casa Lavalleja, Zaballa 1469, Montevideo

Biblioteca del **Poder** Legislativo*, Palacio
Legislativo, Ave Agradiada, Montevideo
Library of the Legislative Power

Biblioteca Municipal 'Dr Joaquín de
Salterain'*, Palacio Municipal, Ave 18 de
Julio, Santiago de Chile

Library Associations

Agrupación Bibliotecológica del Uruguay,
Cerro Largo 1666, Montevideo Tel: 405740
Uruguayan Library and Archive Science
Association
President: Luis Alberto Musso
*Publications: Bibliografía uruguaya sobre
Brasil, Aportes para la historia de la
bibliotecología en el Uruguay, Bibliografía y
documentación en el Uruguay, La estrella
del sur-Indice, Bibliografía bibliográfica y
bibliotecologca, Uruguay-Brasil y sus
medallas, Bibliografía de numismática
uruguaya, Anales del Senado del Uruguay,
El Río de la Plata en el Archivo General de
Indias de Sevilla, Legislación uruguaya sobre
Brasil, Bibliografía de historia de la
República O del Uruguay hasta 1973,
primera parte*

Asociación de Bibliotecarios del Uruguay*,
N/D Ibicuy, 1276-Esc-No 3, Casilla de
Correo 1415, Montevideo
Uruguayan Library Association
President: Hortensia Braceras

Library Reference Books

*Bibliografía bibliográfica y bibliotecología
del Uruguay* (Bibliography of Bibliography
and Library Science in Uruguay),
Uruguayan Library and Archive Science
Association, Cerro Largo 1666, Montevideo

Bibliografía y documentación en el Uruguay
(Bibliography and Documentation in
Uruguay), Uruguayan Library and Archive
Science Association, Cerro Largo 1666,
Montevideo

Literary Associations and Societies

Academia Nacional de Letras, Calle Solís
1446, (Palacio Taranco), Montevideo
Secretary: Fernando García Esteban
*Publications: Boletín de la Academia
Nacional de Letras*

Literary Periodical

Revista de la Biblioteca Nacional (National
Library Review), National Library, Calle
Guayabo 1793, Montevideo

Literary Prizes

Concurso Literario Municipal (Municipal
Literary Competition)*
Three prizes are awarded in each of the
following four groups: prose, fiction, essay,
and biography and history. The most recent
first-prize awards in each group were to Sara
Bollo for *Mundo Secreto*, Julio Ricci for *El
Grongo*, Fernando Assunçao for *Pilchas
Criollas*, and Saúl D Cestau for *Historia del
Notariado Uruguayo desde la época
Colonial hasta la sanción de la Ley N° 1421*.
Enquiries to Intendencia Municipal de
Montevideo (Palacio Municipal), 18 de Julio
1360, Montevideo

418 URUGUAY — VENEZUELA

Gran Premio Nacional de Literatura*
For the total work of an author, Awarded every three years. Enquiries to Ministerio de Educación y Cultura, Sarandi 444, Montevideo

Premio de Remuneraciones Literarias*
Four prizes: poetry; fiction, juveniles or biography; essays; science and technology, sociology, history, education or philosophy. Awarded annually. Enquiries to Ministerio de Educación de Cultura, Sarandi 444, Montevideo

Premio Nacional de Literatura*
For a book in the field of culture. Awarded every two years. Enquiries to Ministerio de Educación y Cultura, Sarandi 444, Montevideo

Vatican City State

General Information

Language: Italian
Religion: Roman Catholic
Population: 728
Currency: Vatican lira = Italian lira. Italian currency is used
Copyright: Berne, UCC (see International section)

Publishers

Biblioteca **Apostolica** Vaticana, I-00120 Vatican City Tel: 6983302
Man Dir: Don Alphons M Stickler; *Sales:* Franz Werlen
Subjects: Philology, Classics, Medieval History, Manuscript Facsimiles, Exhibition Catalogues
1978: 10 titles *1979:* 10 titles

Tipografia Poliglotta Vaticana*, Vatican City
Dir: Very Rev Angelo Vedani
Subjects: Juveniles, Education, Natural & Social Science

Libreria Editrice **Vaticana**, I-00120 Vatican City Tel: 6983345/6984834
Dir: Rag Brenno Bucciarelli
Subjects: Religion, Philosophy, Literature, Art, Latin Philology, Theology, History, Works of Karol Wojtyla
Bookshop: I-00120 Vatican City
1978: 26 titles *1979:* 25 titles *Founded:* 1926

Major Libraries

Biblioteca **Apostolica Vaticana***, I-00120 Vatican City Tel: (06) 6983323
Vatican Apostolic Library

Venezuela

General Information

Language: Spanish
Religion: Roman Catholic
Population: 13.1 million
Literacy Rate (1971): 82.4%
Bank Hours: 0830-1130, 1400-1630 Monday-Friday
Shop Hours: 0900-1300, 1500-1900 Monday-Saturday
Currency: 100 centimos = 1 bolivar
Export/Import Information: Member of the Latin American Free Trade Association. Hardcover children's picture books and atlases pay 1% duty 200% duty on catalogues. 3½% VAT CIF Customs Service Tax (1% for parcel post) 2% VAT FOB Air Cargo Tax (excluding postal packets) No import licences or exchange controls
Copyright: UCC (see International section)

Book Trade Organizations

Asociación Nacional de Escritores Venezolanos*, Velázquez a Miseria 22, Apdo 429, Caracas
National Association of Venezuelan Writers
General Secretary: Angel Mancera Galetti
Publication: Cuadernos

Cámara de Editores*, Puente Yanes a Tracabordo 80-82, Edificio Belvel, Of 4-3, Apdo 14234, Caracas 101
Publishers' Association

Cámara Venezolana del Libro*, Torre Lincoln piso 10, Ave Lincoln con Ave las Acacias, Sabana Grande, Apdo 51858, Caracas 105 Tel: 7812809
Venezuelan Publishers' Association
Secretary: M Morales C

Book Trade Journals

Bibliografía venezolana (Venezuelan Bibliography), National Library, San Francisco a Bolsa, Apdo 6525, Caracas 101

Indice bibliográfico (Bibliographical Index), National Library, San Francisco a Bolsa, Apdo 6525, Caracas 101

Publishers

Aguilar Venezolana SA de Ediciones*, Ave San Juan Bosco, Qta Pasecita (entre 3a y 5a Altamira), Apdo 1768, Caracas Tel: 324177/78/327376
Man Dir: José Luis Inés
Parent Company: Aguilar SA de Ediciones, Spain (qv)

Ernesto **Armitano***, Editor, Cuarto Transversal de la Ave Principal de Boleita, Edificio Centro Industrial 2° piso, Apdo 50853, Sabana Grande, Caracas
Tel: 342565/68 Cable Add: Armitpress
Man Dir: P Salazar; *Sales Dir:* E Armitano
Subjects: Venezuelan Painters, Venezuelan Studies (some titles also in English, German, French and Italian)

Editorial **Ateneo** de Caracas, Apdo 662, Caracas (Located at: Plaza Morelos, Caracas) Tel: 5711354
Man Dir: Miguel Henrique Otero; *Editorial:* Carmen Ramia; *Sales:* Alicia de Santos; *Production:* Rafael Calcaño, María del Pilar Puig
Subjects: Psychology, Arts, Sciences, Politics, History, Literature, Poetry

Bookshops: Librería El Foro, Pasaje Humboldt, Gradillas a Sociedad, Caracas; Librería Ateneo de Caracas, Plaza Morelos, Caracas
1979: 20 titles *1980:* 41 titles *Founded:* 1978

Biblioteca **Ayacucho**, AP 14413, Caracas 101 (Located at: Edificio JA p/1° Ave Universidad, de Corazón de Jesús a Coliseo, Caracas) Tel: 454507/454411 Cable Add: Biayacucho Telex: 23420 WPSV
President of Editorial Commission: Dr José Ramón Medina; *Editorial, Rights & Permissions:* Prof Ángel Rama; *Sales, Publicity:* Dr Daniel Divinsky; *Production:* Andrés Eloy Romero
Subjects: Latin-America, Classic and Contemporary Literature, Belles Lettres, Politics, History, Art
1978: 25 titles *1979:* 28 titles *Founded:* 1975
ISBN Publisher's Prefix: 84-660

Editorial **Bruguera** Venezolana SA*, Ave Andrés Bello esq Ave de las Acacias, La Florida, Caracas
Parent Company: Editorial Bruguera SA, Spain (qv)

Colegial Bolivariana CA*, Ave Principal de Los Ruices, Edificio Co-Bo, Apdo del Corres 70324, Caracas 107 Tel: 364755 Cable Add: Colegial
Man Dir: José Juzgado C
Subjects: Primary & Secondary Textbooks, Juveniles
Founded: 1961

Ediciones y Distribuciones **E D I M E***, Apdo 51666, Caracas 105 (Located at: Prolong Ave Sur Las Acacias, Qta Provi, Urb San Antonio, Caracas) Tel: 7824510/7826943 Cable Add: Agedime
Man Dir: Nils Koehler; *Sales Dir:* Dietrich Sellhorn; *Publicity & Advertising:* E Mascaraque; *Permissions:* Juan Agero
Subjects: Literature, Biography, History & Art of Venezuela, Low-priced Paperbacks, Secondary & Primary Textbooks
Founded: 1948

Ediciones de la Biblioteca (EBCV)*, Servicio de Distribución de Publicaciones, Biblioteca, 1er piso, Universidad Central de Venezuela, Caracas Tel: 622811/619811 ext 2130
Editorial Dir: Marcio S Meléndez
Subjects: Belles Lettres, History, Philosophy, Paperbacks, Medicine, Psychology, Engineering, General & Social Science, Law, University Textbooks
Founded: 1961

Fondo Editorial Común SC*, Ave Abraham Lincoln, Apdo de Correos 50992, Caracas 105 Tel: 726705/723921/5 Cable Add: Editcomun
Man Dir: Rolando Grooscors; *Director:* Peter Neumann
Subjects: Social Science, Communication, Urban Planning, Law

Fondo Educativo Interamericano CA, Apdo del Este 62361, Caracas (Located at Calle Madariaga, Qta El Lago, Los Chaguaramos, Caracas) Tel: 6612356/6618407 Cable Add: Adiwes Caracas Telex: 21901 Fondo VC
Vice-President: Jorge José Giannetto; *Editorial:* in Bogotá, Colombia (qv)
Associate Company: Addison-Wesley Publishers Ltd, UK (qv)
Subjects: Mathematics, Biology, Engineering, Business, Textbooks

Ediciones **Formentor** SRL, 3a Transversal de Los Palos Grandes, Quinta Horizonte, entre 1a Ave y Luis Roche, Caracas 106
Parent Company: Ariel/Seix Barral Editoriales, Spain (qv)

Grijalbo SA, Apdo 62260, Caracas (Located at: Edificio Palmira, piso 1-D, Esq B Campo, Ave Fco Miranda, Caracas) Tel: 316746/316721
Man Dir: Manuel de los Reyes
Parent Company: Editorial Grijalbo SA, Mexico (qv)

Grolier de Venezuela*, Apdo 50930, Caracas (Located at: Edificio Continental, Esq Jabillos, S Grande) Tel: 762659/7828609
Man Dir: Gilberto Livay
Associate Companies: See under the Grolier Society of Australia

Editorial **Interamericana de Venezuela** CA*, Apdo 50785, Caracas Tel: 729492/723720
General Manager: Pedro Alvarez
Associate Company: Holt-Saunders Ltd, UK (qv for other associates)

Editorial **Kapelusz** Venezolana SA*, Apdo 14234, Caracas (Located at: Ave Urdaneta, Animas a Platanal, Edificio Camoruco, Caracas) Tel: 5629177/5629188 Cable Add: Kapelusz
Man Dir: Horacio Perotti Beraldo
Subject: Secondary & Primary Textbooks
Founded: 1963

Editorial **Labor** de Venezuela SA*, Apdo 14165, Caracas (Located at: Ave Andrés Bello, Edificio Garten, Caracas) Tel: 7811398/7815819
Man Dir: Lorenzo Nasarre
Parent Company: Editorial Labor, Spain (qv)

Editorial **Libertador**, Apdo 1331, Maracaibo Tel: 228804/228806
Man Dir, Rights & Permissions and Production: Jake Zondag; *Sales Dir:* John Cornell; *Publicity Dir:* Douglas Hillis
Subjects: History, Religion, How-to, Juveniles, Bible Textbooks
1979: 100 titles *Founded:* 1966

Monte Avila Editores CA, Apdo 70712, (zona 1070), Caracas (Located at: Ave Principal de la Castellana con 1a, Transversal-Qta Cristina, (zona 2003), Caracas) Tel: 326020/330760/332137
Man Dir: Juan Liscano; *Editorial, Rights & Permissions:* Oscar Rodriguez Ortiz; *Sales:* Ricardo Lozano; *Publicity:* Liliana Cheren; *Production:* Hugo García Robles
Subjects: Fiction, Literature, Biography, History, How-to, Art, Philosophy, Medicine, Psychology, General Science, Social Science, University Textbooks
1980: 1,200 titles *Founded:* 1968

Editorial **Natura** SRL*, Ave Boyaca (Cota Mil), Edificio Fundación La Salle, PB 3, Apdo 8150, Caracas 101 Tel: 727145/747467
Man Dir: Serafín Mazparrote
Orders to: Distribuciones Maytex SRL, Ave Norte-Sur 4, No 154 (Pilita a Mamey), Caracas
Subjects: Primary & Secondary Textbooks, Science

Editorial **Plata** SA, now in Peru (qv)

Pomaire Venezuela, Apdo 51960 Caracas 105 (Located at: Ave El Cafetal, Qta La Mora, Chuao, Caracas) Tel: 924658
Man Dir: José Cayuela
Parent Company: Editorial Pomaire SA, Spain (qv)

Editorial **Reverté** Venezolana SA*, Apdo 68685, Caracas (Located at: Peligro a Pele el Ojo, Edif Torre Carabobo, PB, Caracas 106) Tel: 5726670
Associate Companies: See under Editorial Reverté SA, Spain

Editorial Ramón **Sopena** Venezolana SA*, Apdo 14267, Caracas (Located at: Alcabala a Puente Anauco, Edificio AN-VI, 1er piso, Caracas) Tel: 5729709/5728368
Man Dir: A García Sánchez
Parent Company: Ramón Sopena SA, Spain (qv)

Teduca, Técnicas Educativas, CA, 4a Ave No 15, Qta Mari-Ana, Altamira, Caracas Tel: 338078/339185
Chairman: Hugo Manzanilla; *General Manager:* Carlos García Ortubia
Parent Company: Santillana SA de Ediciones, Spain (qv)
Subject: Education

Editorial **Tiempo** Nuevo SA*, Apdo 50304, Caracas (Located at: Calle San Antonio, Edificio Hotel Royal, Sabana Grande, Caracas) Tel: 729073
Man Dir: Benito Milla Navarro; *Sales Dir:* Ricardo Lozano
Subject: General Literature
Founded: 1970

Ediciones **Vega** SRL, Apdo 51662, Caracas 1404 (Located at: Calle Sorbona, Edificio Saturno, Colinas de Bello Monte, Caracas) Tel: 763068/762997 Cable Add: Edivega
Man Dir: Fernando Vega Alonso
Subjects: Secondary & University Textbooks
Bookshop: Librería Técnica Vega, Plaza Las Tres Gracias, Los Chaguaramos, Caracas
Founded: 1965

Major Booksellers

Librería Anibal **Alvárez***, Apdo 13462, Caracas

El **Amigo** de Todos*, Madrices a Ibarras, Loc 7, Edificio Bergantín, Caracas Tel: 815580

Librería del **Este**, Ave Miranda 52, Edificio Galipán, Apdo 60-337, Caracas 1060-A Tel: 332604/322301/315838
Manager: Juan Pericás

Librerías **Kuai-Mare**, Final Ave Abraham Lincoln, Edificio Fundacomun PB, Chacaito, Caracas 105 Tel: 716657
This is the distribution side of the Instituto Autónomo Bibioteca Nacional y de Servicios de Bibliotecas, specializing in publications by official, cultural and university organizations. There are five other branches

Librería **Lectura***, Centro Comercial Chacaito, local 129, Caracas Tel: 717861

Librería **Cultural***, Apdo 15156, Ave 5 de Julio 17-31, Maracaibo Tel: 517446/511009 Cable Add: Licultura

Librería **Cultural Venezolana***, Santa Capilla a Mijares 26, Caracas Tel: 813306

Librería **Medica** Paris, Gran Ave, Edif Medica Paris, Apdo 60681, Caracas 1060-A Tel: 7812709 Telex: 21420 Cable Add: Libmedica
Manager: Pierre Paneyko

Librería **Mundial***, Véroes a Jesuitas, 16, Caracas Tel: 820337

Organización Bienestar Estudiantes (OBE)*, Universitaria Central de Venezuela, Ciudad Universitaria, Caracas

El **Palacio** del Libro*, Bloque 3, loc 4, El Silencio, Caracas Tel: 452854

Librería **Politécnica Moulines**, Calle Villaflor, Apdo 50738, Sabana Grande, Caracas 105 Tel: 710692/729370

Publicaciones Españolas SA*, Pele el Ojo a Puente Brion, Ave Mexico, Caracas Tel: 5715943/5727302/5725224

Librería **Selecta***, Ave 3, 231-23, Apdo 111, Mérida Tel: 23609

Librería **Suma***, Real Sabana Grande 90, Apdo del Este 5346, Caracas Tel: 724449

Tecni Ciencia Libros*, Torre Phelps, Mezz, Central, Plaza Venezuela, Caracas Tel: 552091

Librería Técnica **Vega**, Plaza Tres Gracias, Edificio Odeón, Apdo 3093, Caracas 1041 Tel: 6622848
Manager: Lucia Ribas
Owned by: Fernando Vega, Ediciones Vega SRL (qv)

Major Libraries

Archivo General de la Nación*, Santa Capilla a Carmelitas 5, Caracas

Biblioteca de la Universidad Catolica 'Andres **Bello**'*, Urb Montalban, La Vega, Apdo 29068, Caracas

Biblioteca del Congreso*, Plaza del Capitolio, Caracas

Biblioteca Nacional, see Instituto Autónomo Biblioteca Nacional y de Servicios de Bibliotecas

Biblioteca Central 'Tulio **Febres Cordero**', Edificio Administrativo de la ULA 2° piso, Ave Tulio Febres Cordero, Mérida Tel: (074) 522011 ext 312/553 Telex: 74173 CDCHULA
Director: Dra Francisca Rodríguez C
Publications: Boletín Bibliográfico; Catálogo de Publicaciones Periódicas; Catálogo de Tesis de Grado; Catálogo de Obras Editadas en los Talleres Gráficos de la Universidad de los Andes

Instituto Autónomo Biblioteca Nacional y de Servicios de Bibliotecas, Apdo 6525, Caracas 101 (Located at: San Francisco a Bolsa, Caracas 101 and Calle París, Edificio Macanao, Urbanización Las Mercedes, Caracas 106) Tel: 42814/4832705/911444
National Library and Library Services
Publications include: Anuarios Bibliograficos, Catalogo de Publicaciones Oficiales, Directorio Musical Venezolano, Directorio Preliminar de Diseñadores
See also Librerías Kuia-Mare (Major Booksellers)

Biblioteca del **Instituto Venezolano** de Investigaciones Científicas*, Altos de Pipe, Km 11 Carretera Panamericana, Apdo 1827, Caracas
Library of the Venezuelan Institute for Scientific Research

Biblioteca Central de la **Universidad Central** de Venezuela*, Ciudad Universitaria, Caracas Tel: 619811

Biblioteca Central de la **Universidad de Zulia***, Grano de Oro Apdo 526, Maracaibo Tel: 515390
Librarian: Margarita Alvárez
Publication: Boletín (biennial)

Library Associations

Colegio de Bibliotecólogos y Archivólogos de Venezuela, Apdo 6283, Caracas Tel: 7816533
Venezuelan College of Librarians and Archivists
President: Florencia Fuentes

Library Journal

Codex, Boletin de la Escuela de Bibliotecomia y Archivos (Bulletin of the School of Librarianship and Archives), Universidad Central de Venezuela, Facultad de Humanidades y Educación, Escuela de Biblioteconomia y Archivos, Ciudad Universitaria, Caracas

Literary Associations and Societies

Galaxia*, Canje al Apdo 4023, Carmelitas 101, Caracas
Venezuelan Writers' Group
Director-Editor: Modesto Vargas Lopez
Publications: Galaxia 71:
Books by Venezuelan Authors

International P E N Centre*, Biblioteca Ayacuche, Apdo 14-413, Caracas (Located at: Edificio Banco Exterior, Of 322, Ave Urdaneta-Esq Urapal, Caracas)
President: José Ramon Medina

Literary Periodicals

Analítica para una Problemática del Sujeto, Editorial Ateneo de Caracas, Plaza Morelos, Apdo 662, Caracas

Cuadernos (Notebooks), National Association of Venezuelan Writers, Velázquez a Miseria 22, Apdo 429, Caracas

Galaxia 71, Venezuelan Writers' Group, Canje al Apdo 4023, Carmelitas 101, Caracas

Literary Prizes

Municipal Prize for Prose and Poetry*
For the best prose or poetry work published in the Federal District or an unpublished work from any part of Venezuela. 5,000 bolivares. Awarded annually. Enquiries to Caracas Municipal Council of Federal District, Caracas

El Nacional Annual Story Award*
For the best story by a Venezuelan or foreign resident in Venezuela. Awarded annually. Enquiries to Edificio El Nacional, Puente Nuevo a Puerto Escondido, Apdo 209, Caracas

National Prize for Literature*
Awarded annually to the best Venezuelan author. 30,000 bolivares. Also includes contestants in narrative prose and essays. Enquiries to Concejo Nacional de la Cultura (CONAC), Apdo 50995, Caracas 105

Socialist Republic of Viet Nam

General Information

Language: French and English as well as Vietnamese
Religion: Taoist predominantly
Population: 49.9 million
Currency: 10 xu = 1 hào; 10 hào = 1 dông
Export/Import Information: None available at present
Copyright: Florence (see International section)

Book Trade Organizations

Syndicat des Libraires*, 185 rue Catinat, Hô Chí Minh City
Union of Booksellers

Book Trade Journals

Thu-tich Quôc-gia Viet Nam (National Bibliography of Viet Nam), The Archives Service of the Prime Minister's Office of the Socialist Republic of Viet Nam, 72 Nguyên-Du, PO Box 15, Hô Chí Minh City

Publishers

Foreign Languages Publishing House*, Hanoi
Chief Editor: Nguyen Huu Ngoc
Subjects: Books and Periodicals from Viet Nam (English language)

Giao Duc Publishing House*, 81 Tran Hung Dao, Hanoi
Dir: Nguyen Si Ty
Subjects: Education, School Books
Founded: 1957

Khoa Hoc (Social Sciences) Publishing House*, Hanoi
Subject: Social Science

Lao Dong (Labour) Publishing House*, Hanoi

Nha Xuat Ban Van Hoc (Literature Publishing House)*, 49 Tran Hung Dao, Hanoi
Dir: Nhu Phong
Subject: Literature
1978: 46 titles

Pho Thong (Popularization) Publishing House*, Hanoi

Popular Army Publishing House*, Hanoi
Subject: Military

Sa Tu-Thu Dich-Thuat Va An-Loat*, Le Ván Duyèt, Hô Chí Minh City
(Service de Traduction et de Publication des Manuels scolaires)
Subjects: All Academic, Textbooks

Scientific Publishing House*, Hanoi
Subject: Scientific

Su Hoc (Historical) Publishing House*, Hanoi
Subjects: Politics, Philosophy, Marxist Classics

Su That (Truth) Publishing House*, Hanoi (Controlled by the Government)
Subjects: Marxist Classics, Politics, Philosophy, Social Science

Trung-Tam San Xuat Hoc-Lieu*, Tran-binh-Trong 240, Hô Chí Minh City 5
Subjects: Textbooks, Audiovisual, Instruction Materials

Vietnamese Publishing House*, Hanoi
Subjects: Politics, Law

Y Hoc Publishing House*, Hanoi
Subject: Medical

Major Booksellers

Xunhasoba*, 32 Hai Ba Trung, Hanoi
Distributor for foreign orders

Major Libraries

The Archives Service of the Prime Minister's Office of the Socialist Republic of Viet Nam*, South Viet Nam Branch, 72 Nguyên-Du, Hô Chí Minh City

Central Library of the **Department of Information***, Hô Chí Minh City

Municipal Library*, 22 Yersin St, Dalat

National Institute of Administration Library*, 10 Tran Quoc Toan, Hô Chí Minh City

Social Sciences Library*, 34 Ly tu Trong, Hô Chí Minh City

Thu Viên Quóc Gia Viet Nam*, 31 Tràng Thi, Hanoi Tel: 2643
National Library of the Socialist Republic of Viet Nam

Library Associations

Hôi Thu-Viên Viet Nam*, 8 Le Qui Don, Hô Chí Minh City
Vietnamese Library Association
Secretary: Nguyen Van Thu
Publication: Thu'-Viên Tâp-san (Library Bulletin)

Library Journals

Thu'-Viên Tâp-san (Library Bulletin), Vietnamese Library Association, 8 Le Qui Don, Hô Chi Minh City

Literary Periodicals

Van Hoc, c/o Phan Kim Thinh, 449 Bhai Ba Trung, Q3 Hô Chí Minh City

Western Samoa

General Information

Language: Samoan, English
Population: 154,000
Literacy Rate (1971): 97.8%
Currency: 100 sene = 1 tala
Export/Import Information: No tariff on most books, printed advertising generally free but some subject to 52%. No import licence or exchange controls

Major Libraries

Avele College Library*, Avele

Nelson Memorial Public Library*, PO Box 598, Apia

People's Democratic Republic of Yemen

General Information

Language: Arabic, English is common second language
Religion: Muslim
Population: 1.9 million
Literacy rate (1973): 27.1% of population aged 10 or over (40.9% of urban population, 22.6% rural, 5.8% nomads)
Bank Hours: 0745-1400 Saturday-Wednesday; 0745-1330 Thursday
Currency: 1,000 fils = 1 South Yemen dinar
Export/Import Information: 14th October Corporation has sole right to import and distribute books. Import licences required. Exchange controls

Major Booksellers

14th October Corporation, PO Box 4227, Crater, Aden
Sole importer and distributor of books

Major Libraries

Miswat Library*, Aden
(Previously called Lake Library. Administration by Aden Municipality)

Teachers' Club Library*, Aden

Yemen Arab Republic

General Information

Language: Arabic (English and Russian common foreign languages)
Religion: Muslim
Population: 5.6 million
Bank Hours: 0800-1200 (1130 Thursday) Saturday-Thursday
Shop Hours: 0800-1300, 1600-2100 Saturday-Thursday
Currency: 100 fils = 1 Yemeni riyal
Export/Import Information: No tariff on books except 10% on children's picture books. Advertising matter dutied at 20%. 5% Defence Tax, 2% Statistical Tax; Cooperation Tax is 15% CIF. Small Welfare Tax, Import licence required; no pornography permitted. Exchange control approval readily available, generally

Major Libraries

British Council Library*, PO Box 2157, Sana'a (Located at: Beit 41, Mottahar, Harat Handhal, Sana'a) Tel: 3179

Library of the **Great Mosque of Sana'a***, Sana'a

Yugoslavia

General Information

Language: Serbo-Croatian in most of the country; Slovene in Slovenia, Macedonian in Macedonia. English is commonest foreign language known
Religion: About 40% Eastern Orthodox, 30% Roman Catholic, 10% Muslim
Population: 21.9 million
Literacy Rate (1971): 83.5% (92.3% Urban, 77.7% Rural)
Bank Hours: 0730-1200 Monday-Friday
Shop Hours: 0800-1200, 1700-2000 Monday-Friday; 0800 or 0900-1400 Saturday. Some open weekdays continuously and early Sunday morning
Currency: 100 para = 1 new dinar
Export/Import Information: No tariffs on books except 28% on publications of Yugoslav publishers printed abroad. Advertising catalogues for such books dutied at 27%, otherwise free; non-Yugoslavian language advertising materials dutied at 18%. 5% special equalization tax, 1% Customs Clearance Charge and 10% import surcharge when goods are subject to duty. No import licences required. Exchange controls. The basic commercial unit is known as an enterprise but there are no state monopolies
Copyright: Berne, UCC (see International section)

Book Trade Organizations

Association of Yugoslav Publishers and Booksellers*, YU-11000 Belgrade, Kneza Milosa 25/I, Poštanski fah 883 Tel: (011) 642533/642248
Dir: Jelenko Bučevac
Publications: Knjiga i svet (The Book and the World); *Catalogue of Book Fair in Belgrade; Directory of Members of the Association of Yugoslav Publishers and Booksellers; Publishing Plans of the Publishing Houses in Yugoslavia* (annual); *Books Published by Yugoslav Publishers* (annual)

Standard Book Numbering Agency, YU-61001 Ljubljana, Kopitarjeva ul 2, Postni Predal 201-IV
ISBN Administrator: Martin Znidersic

Book Trade Reference Journals

Bibliografija domace i strane literature (Bibliography of Native and Foreign Literature) (text in Serbo-Croatian), Centralna Biblioteka JNA, Belgrade, Balkanska 53a

Bibliografija Jugoslavije (Yugoslavia Bibliography), Yugoslav Bibliographic Institute, YU-11000 Belgrade, Terazije 26

Books Published by Yugoslav Publishers. Association of Yugoslav Publishers and Booksellers, YU-11000 Belgrade, Kneza Milósa 25/I, Póstanski fah 883

Directory of Members, Association of Yugoslav Publishers and Booksellers, YU-11000 Belgrade, Kneza Milósa 25/I, Poštanski fah 883

Katalog Medunarodnog Sajma Knjige u Beogradu (Catalogue of the International Book Fair at Belgrade), Association of Yugoslav Publishers and Booksellers, YU-11000 Belgrade, Kneza Milósa, Póstanski fah 883

Knjiga i svet (The Book and the World), Association of Yugoslav Publishers and Booksellers, YU-11000 Belgrade, Kneza Miloša 25/I, Poštanski fah 883

Publishing Plans of the Publishing Houses in Yugoslavia, Association of Yugoslav Publishers and Booksellers, YU-11000 Belgrade, Kneza Milósa 25/I, Póstanski fah 883

Slovenska Bibliografija (Slovene Bibliography), Državna Založba Slovenije, YU-61000 Ljubljana, Mestni trg 26, Poštanski fah 50-I

Publishers

A L F A — Radna organizacija za izdavačku djelatnost, YU-41000 Zagreb, Čerinina 9a, Póstanski fah 32 Tel: (041) 217614
Manager: Stjepan Martinović
Subjects: War, History, Popular Science, Fiction

August Cesarec*, YU-41000 Zagreb, Braće Oreški 18 Tel: (041) 576615/576651
Dir: Mirko Andrić
Subjects: Belles Lettres, Politics, Science, Fiction

Beogradski Izdavačko-Grafički Zabod*, YU-11000 Belgrade, blvd vojode Mišića 17, Poštanski fah 340 Tel: 651666 Cable Add: BEOGRAF Telex: 11855 yu bigz
Man Dir: Dušan Popović; *Editorial Dir, Permissions:* Uglješa Krstić

YUGOSLAVIA

Branch Offs: BIGZ-OOUR, Zagreb, Ilica 132; BIGZ-OOUR, Sarajevo, Stjepana Radića 10a
Subjects: General Fiction, Belles Lettres, Poetry, How-to, Philosophy, Juveniles, Low-priced Paperbacks, Social Science, University Textbooks

Birografika*, YU-24000 Subotica, Put Moše Pjade 72 Tel: (024) 26215 Cable Add: YU BIGRAF 15111
Dir: Andrija inž Bukvić

Borba*, YU-11000 Belgrade, trg Marksa i Engelsa 7, Poštanski fah 629 Tel: (011) 334531/344201
Dir: Novica Dukić

Bratsvo-Jedinstvo, YU-21000 Novi Sad, Arse Teodorovića 11, Poštanski fah 274 Tel: 28032/28036
Dir: Srboslav Bojović
Subjects: Textbooks in Serbo-Croat, Belles Lettres

C D D (Centar društvenih djelatnosti Saveza socijalističke omladine Hrvatske), YU-41001 Zagreb, Opaticka 10, Poštanski fah 99 Tel: (041) 419026/443809/447055/415659/449817
General Manager: Josip Čondić; *Publishing Manager:* Petar Strpić; *Art Manager:* Ivan Dorogi
Subjects: Fiction, Marxism, Philosophy, Social Sciences, Political Journalism, Science Journalism; *Pitanja* (Scientific and Cultural Review); *Polet* (Youth Weekly)
1979: 29 titles

Cankarjeva Založba, YU-61001 Ljubljana, Kopitarjeva 2, Poštanski fah 201/IV
Tel: 323841
Man Dir: Miloš Mikeln
Subjects: Belles Lettres, Poetry, General Fiction, Biography, History, How-to, Philosophy, Reference, Social Science, Psychology
Bookshops: Kopitarjeva 2, Wolfova 5, Titova 15, Miklošičeva 16, Tržaška 59, Založka 35 (all in Ljubljana), Trbovlje, 1 junija 27
Founded: 1945
Miscellaneous: Also antiquarian booksellers

Dečje Novine*, YU-32300 Gornji Milanovac, Takovska 6 Tel: (032) 81527/81073/81195 Telex: 13731 YU DNGRM
Subjects: Juveniles, Picture-books, Albums

Delta Press*, YU-11000 Belgrade, Draže Pavlovića 14, Poštanski fah 467 Tel: (011) 333969
Dir: Jovan Janićijević
Subjects: Reference Material, Juveniles and Young People, Social Sciences
1978: 35 titles *Founded:* 1969

Državna Založba Slovenije, YU-61000 Ljubljana, Mestni trg 26, Poštanski fah 50-1 Tel: (061) 24695 Cable Add: DZS Ljubljana
Man Dir: Ivan Bratko
Subjects: General Fiction, Belles Lettres, Poetry, Biography, History, Music, Art, Philosophy, Reference, General & Social Science, University, Secondary & Primary Textbooks, Educational Materials
Bookshops: DZS at Bled, C Svobode 15; Brežice, C Prvih borcev 37; Celje, trg V Kongresa 3; Ljubljana, Mestni trg 26; Ljubljana, Šubičeva 1a; Foreign Dept, Ljubljana, Titova 25; Ljubljana, Čopova 3
Founded: 1945

NiP Edit*, YU-51000 Rijeka, bulevar Marxa i Engelsa 20, Poštanski fah 137-138
Tel: 22516/22443/22646 Telex: 24247
Director: Ennio Machia
Subjects: Books, Papers, Periodicals in Italian
Bookshop: YU-51000 Rijeka, Korzo Narodne Revolucije 37

Forum*, YU-21000 Novi Sad, vojvode Mišića 1, Poštanski fah 200 Tel: 57207 Telex: 14199
Director: Kálmán Petkovics
Subjects: Periodicals, Fiction, Politics in Hungarian and Serbo-Croatian

Glas*, YU-11000 Belgrade, Vlajkovićeva 8 Tel: (011) 335380
Director: Radojko Mrlješ
Provides complete printing services to other publishers

Globus, YU-41000 Zagreb, Ilica 12, Poštanski pretinac 232 Tel: (041) 447300/447500 Cable Add: Globus Zagreb
Editors: V Ogrizović, I Sor, B Zadro
Parent Company: ČGP Delo, YU-61000 Ljubljana, Titova Cesta 35
Subjects: Politics, History, Sociology, Philosophy, General Fiction, Handbooks
1978: 46 titles *1979:* 37 titles *Founded:* 1948

Izdavačka ustanova **Gradina***, YU-18000 Niš, ul Pobede br 38/I, Poštanski fah 242 Pobede 38/I Tel: 25864
Dir: Dobrivoje Jevtić
Subjects: Belles Lettres, Science, Art, Periodicals
Bookshops: (all at Niš) ul Pobede br 38; Pobede 113; Voždova 74; 12 februar 56a; Obilićev venac 50

Gradjevinska Knjiga*, YU-11000 Belgrade, trg Marksa i Engelsa 8, Poštanski fah 798 Tel: (011) 333565
Man Dir: Ljubica Jurela; *Sales Dir:* Radovan Vuković
Subjects: Technical, Engineering & University Textbooks
Bookshops: Gradjevinska Knjiga, Narodnog fronta 14 & bulevar Revolucije 84; Student, 27 marta 78 (all in Belgrade)

Grafički zavod Hrvatske, YU-41000 Zagreb, Frankopanska 26, Poštanski fah 227 Tel: (041) 418600/419005 Cable Add: GZH Zagreb Telex: 21606 YUGZH
Man Dir: Vladimir Štokalo; *Editors:* Vjeran Zuppa, Albert Goldstein, Nenad Popović
Subjects: Belles Lettres, Art, Tourism, Dictionaries
Bookshop: GZH, YU-41000 Zagreb, Frankopanska 26
Founded: 1874

Grafos*, YU-11000 Belgrade, Simina 9A, Poštanski fah 459 Tel: 623980 Cable Add: Grafos Belgrade
Dir: Vito Marković
Subjects: Lexicography, Rare Publications, Fiction, Science, Juveniles, Periodicals

I C S Izdavačko Informativni Centar Studenata*, YU-11000 Belgrade, Balkanska 4/III Tel: 325854
Dir: Aleksandar Urdarević
Bookshops: Novi Belgrade: Studentski grad, II Blok & Dom kultur Studenski grad, bulevar Avnoja 152a; Belgrade: Fakultet političkih nauka, Jove Ilića 165 & Arhitektonski fakultet, bulevar Revolucije 73

Informator*, Izdavački i Birotehnički Zavod, YU-41001 Zagreb, Masarykova ul 1, Poštanski fah 794 Tel: 442222 Cable Add: YU INF Telex: 21264
General Dir: Nikola Šaranović
Subjects: Dictionaries, Law

Jedinstvo*, YU-38000 Priština, Dom Štampe bb, Poštansk: pregradak 81 Tel: (038) 27549/29090 Cable Add: Jedinstvo Pristina
Director: Milan Śešlija
Subjects: Belles Lettres, Social & Political Science, History, Philosophy, Medicine

Jugoreklam*, YU-61000 Ljubljana, Moše Pijade 5, Poštanski fah 142 Tel: 316075
Dir: Hinko Urbanc
Branch Offs: YU-11000 Belgrade: Nebojšina 2 & Dure Dakovića 88; YU-41000 Zagreb, Petretičev trg 4; YU-63320 Velenje, Celjska 27
Subjects: Juveniles, Economics

Jugoslovenska Revija*, YU-11000 Belgrade, Terazije 31 Tel: 332625
Dir: Nebojša Tomašević
Subjects: Art, Tourism, Periodicals

Izdavački Zavod **Jugoslavenske Academije** Znanosti i Umjetnosti*, YU-41000 Zagreb, Gundulićeva 24, Poštanski fah 1017
Tel: 449099
Publishing House of the Yugoslav Academy of Sciences and Arts
Man Dir: Josip Hanževački
Subjects: History, Philosophy, Medicine, Technical, General & Political Science, Education
Founded: 1918

Jugoslavenski Leksikografski Zavod*, YU-41000 Zagreb, Strossmayerov trg 4, Poštanski fah 410 Tel: 36743/36871
Director: Miroslav Krieža
Subjects: Encyclopaedias, Bibliography
Bookshop: Poslovnica Zagreb Masarykova 26
Founded: 1951

Jugoslavija*, Izdavački Zavod, YU-11000 Belgrade, Nemanjina 34, Poštanski fah 52 Tel: 643870/643852 Cable Add: Pubzavod Belgrade Telex: 11265
Shipping Add: c/o Transjug-Split, YU-11000 Belgrade, Pop Lukina 12
Dir, Editor-in-Chief: Živislav-Žika Bogdanović
Subjects: Art, Travel Guides, Reference, How-to, General Non-fiction, Juveniles, Science Fiction & Epic Fantasy
Founded: 1948

Izdavački Centar **Komunist***, Belgrade, trg Marksa i Engelsa 11, Poštanski fah 233
Tel: 335061/334189
Dir: David Atlagić
Subjects: Communism, Marxism, Literary Criticism
Bookshop: Klub Citalaca 70, Belgrade, trg Marksa i Engelsa 9

Kršćanska sadašnjost*, YU-41000 Zagreb, Marulićev trg 14, Postf 02748 Tel: 444102
Subjects: Bible, Liturgy, Theology, Art History, Church History, Fine Arts, Periodicals
Miscellaneous: Company also acts as a press agency

Kultura (Izdavačko Pretprijatie)*, YU-91000 Skopje, bulevar JNA 68A, Poštanski fah 298 Tel: 35361/23437 Cable Add: Kultura
Man Dir: Dušan Crvenkovski
Subjects: Art, Philosophy, Political Science, Economics, Juveniles
Bookshops: 32 bookshops throughout Yugoslavia
Founded: 1945

Sveučilišna Naklada **Liber***, YU-41000 Zagreb, Savska cesta 16, Poštanski fah 493 Tel: (041) 415602
Dir: Slavko Goldstein
Subjects: Croatian culture and scientific heritage, Literature, *Povijesti, Temelji, Znanstven Radovi* and *Razlog* collections
Miscellaneous: Publishing service of Zagreb University

Libertatea*, YU-26000 Pančevo, Žarka Zrenjanina br 7, Poštanski fah 27 Tel: 3401/3351 Cable Add: Libertatea Pančevo
Dir: Todor Gilezan
Subjects: Textbooks, Periodicals, Rare

Publications, Reprints, Romanian Language publications

Makedonska Knjiga (Knigoizdatelstvo), YU-91000 Skopje, 11 Oktomvri bb, Poštanski fah 349 Tel: (091) 235524 Cable Add: Makedonska Kniga
Man Dir: Nikola Todorov
Subjects: General Fiction, Belles Lettres, Art, Juveniles
Bookshops: 26 bookshops

Medicinska Knjiga*, YU-11000 Belgrade, Mata Vidakovića 24, Poštanski fah 681 Tel: (011) 458135/458165
Dir: Jovan Duletić; *Editor-in-Chief:* Mile Medić; *Sales Dir:* Milojko Gajić
Subjects: Medicine, Pharmacy, Stomatology, Textbooks, Popular literature
1978: 23 titles *Founded:* 1946

Medicinska Naklada*, YU-41000 Zagreb, Šalata bb, Poštanski fah 517 Tel: (041) 33630
Dir: Mirko Madjor

'Minerva'*, YU-24000 Subotica, trg 29 novembra br 3, Poštanski fah 116 Tel: (024) 25701 Cable Add: Minerva Subotica
Dir: Josip Prčić
Subjects: Textbooks, Dictionaries, Scientific and Children's Literature
Bookshops: YU-24000 Subotica: ul oktobra 4; Maksima Gorkog 20; Put M Pijade 25

Misla*, YU-91000 Skopje, Gradski zid, Blok 2, Poštanski fah 460 Tel: 23336 Cable Add: Misla Skopje
Dir: Božin Pavlovski; *Head of Sales:* Vanćo Spasovski

Mladinska Knjiga*, YU-61000 Ljubljana, Titova 3, Poštanski fah 36/I Tel: (060) 24851 Telex: 31345 yu emka
Director General: Karel Trplan; *Publishing Dir:* Ivan Bizjak; *Editor-in-Chief:* Borut Ingolič; *Sales:* Joze Wagner; *Production:* Marjan Černe; *Co-production:* Ciril Treek; *Publicity:* Nace Borštnar
Branch Off: YU-11000 Belgrade, 27 Merte; YU-41000 Zagreb, Ilica 30
Subjects: Children's books, General Fiction, Art, Popular Science, Geography, How-to
Book Club: Svet Knjige, Ljubljana, Nazorjeva 6
Bookshops: 23 throughout Yugoslavia
Founded: 1945

Mladost*, YU-11000 Belgrade, Maršala Tita 2, Poštanski fah 252 Tel: (011) 323390
Dir: Borisav Džuverović
Subjects: Marxist literature, Philosophy, Fiction, Periodical *Mladost*
Founded: 1956

Mladost, Izdavačka i knjižarska radna organizacija, YU-41000 Zagreb, Ilica 30, Poštanski fah 1028 Tel: (041) 440211 Cable Add: Ikape Zagreb Telex: 21263
Man Dir: Branko Juričević; *Import-Export Dir:* Branko Vuković; *Publisher:* Josip Fruk; *Production Manager:* Stipan Medak; *Publicity & Advertising:* Lidija Grabúsnik
Subjects: Picture Books, Juveniles, General Fiction, Belles Lettres, Poetry, History, How-to, Music, Art, Philosophy, Reference, General & Social Science, Sports, Hobby Books, Dictionaries
Book Club: Mladost's Book Fans Club, Zagreb, Radićeva 37
Bookshops: 20 in Zagreb, 2 in Rijeka, 1 in Osijek, 1 in Belgrade, 1 in Zadar, 1 in Split, 1 in Pula, 1 in Banja Luka
1978: 83 titles *Founded:* 1948

Muzička Naklada*, Zagreb, Nikole Tesle 10/I, Poštanski fah 543
Dir: Albert Trinki
Subject: Music
Founded: 1952

Nakladni Zavod Matice Hrvatske*, YU-41000 Zagreb, ul Matice Hrvatske 2, Poštanski fah 515 Tel: (041) 33573/33359/33967/35325/6
Man Dir, Rights and Permissions: Pero Badak; *Editorial:* Zane Turtko; *Sales:* Jakov Ćurić; *Production:* Anton Galic; *Publicity:* Luka Roić
Branch Offs: YU-71000 Sarajevo, Maršala Tita 22; YU-11000 Belgrade, Tršćanska 5
Subjects: General Fiction, Reference, Art, Literature, Political & General Science, Biography, History, Dictionaries
Bookshops: 41000 Zagreb, Ilica 62 & Dure Salaja 3; YU-50000 Dubrovnik, Poljana Paska Miličevića bb; Dakova, ul Jna 15; YU-47000 Karlorac, Autobusni kolodvor; YU-54500 Našice, Radićeva 23; YU-51270 Senj, Obala Maršala Tita 2; YU-79000 Mostar, Braće Brkića 8; YU-51000 Rijeka, Dure Dakovića 20
Founded: 1960

Naprijed*, YU-41000 Zagreb, Palmotićeva 30, Poštanski fah 1029 Tel: 442001/442400/442283 Cable Add: Izdavacko Naprijed Telex: 21449 yu ikpnzg
Man Dir: Autun Žvan; *Sales:* Dragiša Marković
Subjects: General Fiction, History, Art, General Science, Psychology, Political & Social Science, Economics

Narodna Biblioteka Srbije*, YU-11000 Belgrade, Skerlićeva 1 Tel: 451242/9
Dir: Svetislav Durić
Subjects: Bibliography, Reference, History

Narodna Knjiga*, YU-11000 Belgrade, Safarikova 11, Poštanski fah 241 Tel: (011) 328610
Dir: Vidak Perić
Subjects: Politics, Encyclopaedias, Dictionaries, Textbooks, Science, Juveniles, Belles Lettres

Narodne Novine*, YU-41000 Zagreb, Ratkajev prolaz 4, Poštanski fah 557 Tel: 411611/411666
Dir: Ilija Dautović
Subjects: Science, Textbooks, Careers
Bookshops: 21 throughout Yugoslavia

Naša Djeca*, YU-41000 Zagreb, Gajeva 25, Poštanski fah 563 Tel: (041) 447077 Cable Add: Násadjeca
Dir: Petar Butković
Subject: Juveniles

Naša Kniga*, YU-91000 Skopje, Partizanski odred 17, Poštanski fah 132 Tel: (091) 228066/237014
Dir: Vlado Popovski
Subjects: Textbooks, Sociology, Politics, Agriculture, Literature

Naučna Knjiga*, YU-11000 Belgrade, Uzun Mirkova 5, Poštanski fah 690 Tel: 637230 Cable Add: Naučna Knjiga
Man Dir: Dragoslav Joković
Subjects: Reference, Medicine, Engineering, Science, University Textbooks, Educational Materials, Maps, Atlases
Bookshops: 'Znanje', Belgrade, Gračanička br 16; 'Naučna knjiga', Belgrade, Knez Mihailova br 19
Founded: 1947

Nolit Publishing House*, YU-11000 Belgrade, Terazije 27/II, Poštanski fah 369 Tel: 332357 Cable Add: Nolit BGD Telex: 11603 nolit bgd
Man Dir: Dragoljub Gavaric; *Editorial:* Miloš Stambolić; *Sales:* Milorad Mojsilović; *Production:* Nicola Kandić
Subjects: General Fiction, Philosophy, Psychology, Sociology, Agriculture, History, Art, Juveniles
Bookshops: 50 bookshops throughout Yugoslavia
Founded: 1928

Mip Nota*, YU-19350 Knjaževac, Karadordeva 15/I, Poštanski fah 63 Tel: 84375/84516 Cable Add: Nota-Knjaževac
Dir: Nenad Živković; *Editorial:* Stojanović Ljubomir; *Sales:* Jovanovic Negica; *Production:* Nikolić Alexsandar; *Rights & Permissions:* Simić Dura
Branch Off: YU-11000 Belgrade, Balkanska 9
Subject: Music
Founded: 1970

Nova Knjiga*, Obrenovac, Maršala Tita

Obod*, YU-81250 Cetinje, Njegoševa 3, Poštanski fah 59 Tel: 22020 Cable Add: Obod Cetinje
Dir: Slobodan Koljević
Branch Off: Belgrade, Dobračina 32
Subjects: Belles Lettres, Fiction, Textbooks, Dictionaries
Bookshop: Belgrade, Njegoševa 11

Obzor*, YU-21000 Novi Sad, bulevar 23, Oktobra 31/V, Poštanski fah 267 Tel: 21555 Cable Add: Obzor, Novi Sad
Dir: Anna Makanová
Bookshop: Bački Petrovac Bodviš Jan

NIP Oslobodenje*, YU-71000 Sarajevo, Maršala Tita 13, Poštanski fah 663 Tel: 35177/34233 Telex: 41148/41136
Dir: Ivica Lovrić

Otokar Keršovani-Rijeka, YU-51410 Opatija, Maršala Tita 65, Poštanski fah 13 Tel: 711099/711922 Cable Add: Otakar Kerošovani
Man Dir, Rights & Permissions: Drago Crnčević; *Sales:* Vladimir Bakotić
Branch Offs: Zagreb, Biankinijeva 11; Belgrade, Zrmanjska 2/a; Sarajevo, Mehmed paše Sokolovića 24; Skopje, Bulevar nar osl 9-Kula 25-Gradski zid
Subjects: Fiction, Horticulture, Picture Books
Bookshop: Pančevo 26000, Borisa Kidriča 6
Founded: 1954

'Petar Kočić'*, YU-11000 Belgrade, Nevesinjska 2 Tel: (011) 432477 Cable Add: 'Petar Kočić'

Pobjeda*, YU-81000 Titograd, Bulevar revolucije 11 Tel: 45955
Dir: Ljubo Burić
Branch Off: Zemun, Karadordev trg 7
Subjects: Belles Lettres, Popular Scientific Literature and Lexicography

Pomurska založba, YU-69000 Murska Sobota, Lendavska cl, Poštni p136 Tel: 6923491
Dir: Jože Ternar; *Editor-in-Chief:* Jože Hradil
Subjects: Literature, Fiction, Poetry, Essays (Original and Translations)
Bookshops: Dobra knjiga, 69000 Murska Sobota, Titova c; Knjigarna Ljutomer, YU-69240; Knjigarna Lendava, YU-69220; Knjigarna Gornja Radgona, YU-69250; Knjigarna Lenart, YU-62230
1978: 41 titles *1979:* 48 titles

Izdavačko Preduzeće Matice Srpske*, YU-21000 Novi Sad, trg Svetozara Markovića 2 Tel: (021) 29777/43040 (director)
Dir: Sava Josić
Subjects: Belles Lettres, Science, Politics, Juveniles, Textbooks, Encyclopaedias, Dictionaries
Bookshops: Belgrade, Studentski trg 5; Backa Palanka, Maršala Tita 40 and others

Izdavačko Preduzeće Sloboda*, YU-11000 Belgrade, Vojvode Stepe 315 Tel: 462131/461721/462341 Cable Add: Sloboda

Belgrade
Dir: Streten Hrkalović
Subjects: Belles Lettres, Juveniles, Reference

Primorski Tisk*, YU-66000 Koper, Muzejski trg 7, Poštanski fah 132 Tel: 23291
Dir: Črtomir Kolenc
Branch Off: Studenski servis, Ljubljana, Borstnikov trg 25
Subject: Fiction
Bookshops: 9 throughout Yugoslavia

Privredni Pregled*, YU-11000 Belgrade, Maršala Birjuzova 3, Poštanski fah 903 Tel: 623399/625662 Cable Add: Privredni Pregled Bgd Telex: 11509 yu pp
Dir: Toma Marković
Branch Offs: Zagreb, Moše Pijade 21; Ljubljana, Hala 'Tivoli'; Skopje, Orce Nikolova 79; Sarajevo, Maršala Tita 86
Subject: Production Reference Books

Prosveta, YU-11000 Belgrade, Dobračina 30 Tel: (011) 625234/625743/625766/625987
Dir: Božidar Perković
Subjects: General Fiction, History, Philosophy, Sociology, Law, Lexicography, Music, Art, Reference, Paperbacks, Juveniles, Textbooks

Prosvetno Delo*, YU-91000 Skopje, Ulica Ivo Lola Ribar, bb, Gradski zid, Blok IV, Poštanski fah 6 Tel: 33675/31398
Man Dir: Mihajlo Korveziroski
Subjects: Reference, Textbooks, Educational Materials, Juveniles
Bookshop: Br 1 Skopje, bulevar Kočo Racin, kula B-20

Prosvjeta*, YU-41000 Zagreb, Berislavićeva 10, Poštanski fah 634 Tel: 445450/444664 Cable Add: Prosvjeta Zagreb
Dir: Branislav Ćelap
Subjects: Journalism, Business Books
Bookshop: Zagreb, trg Bratstva i Jedinstva 5

Prosvjeta (Novinsko-izdavačko i Štamparsko)*, Bjelovar, Vladimira Nazora 25 Tel: 3150 Cable Add: Nišp Prosvjeta Bjelovar
Dir: Branimir Premužić; *Production:* Ivan Ninić
Branch Off: Zagreb, Moše Pijade 31

Prva Književna Komuna*, YU-79000 Mostar, trg 14 februar 3/III Tel: 25798 Cable Add: PKK Mostar
Man Dir: Ico Mutevelić
Subjects: Bibliophile Editions, Tourist Publications
Bookshop: Mostar, ul Stari most 3

Izdavačka Organizacija **Rad**, YU-11000, Belgrade, Moše Pijade 12, Poštanski fah 881 Tel: (011) 330923/339758/338994
Man Dir: Milenko Kovačević; *Sales Dir:* Milovan Vlahović
Subjects: Belles Lettres, Poetry, Biography, Philosophy, Low-priced Paperbacks, Engineering, Social Science, Politics, Economics, University Textbooks
Bookshops: Papirus, Belgrade, Terazije 26; Zagreb, Frankopanska 5, and 20 other bookshops throughout Yugoslavia
Miscellaneous: Publishes critical magazine *Književna kritika*

Radnička Štampa*, YU-11000 Belgrade, trg Marksa i Engelsa 5, Poštanski fah 995 Tel: (011) 330927 Cable Add: Radnička štampa Belgrade
Dir: Života Kamperelić; *Sales Manager:* Dragan Kreclović
Subjects: Social, Political and Economic Sciences, Textbooks, Encyclopedias, *Rad* newspaper

Republički Zavod za Unaprediivanje Školstva*, YU-81000 Titograd, Novaka Miloševa 36 Tel: (081) 24168, 24126 (Director)
Subjects: Primary and Secondary Textbooks, Education
Miscellaneous: This is the Republic Bureau for the Advancement of Education

Rilindja*, YU-38000 Priština, Dom Štampe, Poštanski fah 27 Tel: (038) 23868/28611/28411
Dir: Rexhep Zogaj
Subjects: Textbooks, Belles Lettres (in Albanian), Periodicals, *Rilindja* newspaper

Savez Inženjera i Tehničara Jugoslavije, 11000 Belgrade, Kneza Mološa 9, Poštanski fah 187 Tel: 343653/335816/332924
Secretary: Dr Petar Radičević
Founded: 1945
Miscellaneous: Union of Engineers and Technicians of Yugoslavia

Savremena Administracija*, YU-11001 Belgrade, Knez Mihajlova 6/V, Poštanski fah 479 Tel: 648567/647436/687913
Dir: Živorad Jevtić
Subjects: Literature, Law, Work Study, Economics, Reference
Founded: 1954

Škola za Strane Jezike*, YU-41000 Zagreb, Varšavska 14 Tel: (041) 419895
Subjects: Language textbooks and teaching materials

'Školska knjiga', YU-41000 Zagreb, Masarykova 28, Poštanski fah 1039 Tel: 449505/448111 Cable Add: Školska knjiga Zagreb
Man Dir: Professor Josip Malić; *Sales Manager:* Dr Ivo Bekić; *Production Dir:* Mira Krizmanić
Subjects: University, Secondary & Primary Textbooks, Educational Materials, History, Music, Art, Philosophy, Reference, Juveniles, Low- & High-priced Paperbacks, Medicine, Psychology, Engineering, General & Social Science, Belles Lettres, Poetry, Biography, How-to
Bookshop: Knjižara 'Školske knjige', YU-41000 Zagreb, Bogovićeva 1/a; Knjižara 'Studentski trg', YU-11000 Belgrade, Studentski trg 6
1979: 133 titles *Founded:* 1950

Sloboda*, YU-11040 Belgrade, Vojvode Stepe 315 Tel: (011) 462131/461721/462341 Cable Add: Sloboda Beograd
Dir: Miroslav Marković
Subjects: Historical Literature, Belles Lettres, Juveniles, Encyclopaedias

Slovo Ljubve, YU-11000 Belgrade, Mutapova 12 Tel: (011) 436360/454987
Dir: Ljubiša Pantić; *Editorial, Production:* Rade Vojvodić; *Sales:* Sreten Hrkalović; *Publicity:* Svetlana Milošević
Book Club: Klub čitalaca, Belgrade, Save Kovačevića 26
1978: 31 titles *1979:* 77 titles *Founded:* 1971

Službeni List*, YU-11000 Belgrade, Jovana Ristića 1, Poštanski fah 226 Tel: 650155 Telex: 11756 yu slist
Dir: Dušan Mašović
Subjects: Službeni List (Official Register) in languages of peoples and nationalities of Yugoslavia; collections of court decisions, university textbooks, federation regulations, handbooks for applying regulations, comments on codes, special and periodical publications
Bookshops: Belgrade: Prodavnica 1, Brankova 16; Prodavnica 2, 29 Novembra 1a

Sportska Knjiga*, YU-11000 Belgrade, Makedonska 19, Poštanski fah 720 Tel: 25361 Cable Add: Sportska Knjiga
Dir: Miloš Petronić; *Editor:* Dušan Cvetković
Subject: Sport
Bookshop: Belgrade, Makedonska 19
Founded: 1949

Srpska Književna Zadruga*, YU-11000 Belgrade, Maršala Tita 19 Tel: 330305/334977
President: Risto Tošović
Subjects: History, Belles Lettres
Bookshop: Belgrade, Maršala Tita 19
Founded: 1892

Stručna Štampa*, YU-11000 Belgrade, Francuska 24, Poštanski fah 618 Tel: 335483

Stvarnost*, YU-41000 Zagreb, Frankopanska 11, Poštanski fah 734 Tel: 413808
Man Dir: Petar Majstorović; *Editorial:* Marijan Sinković; *Sales:* Miroslav Mišković
Subjects: General Fiction, Biography, History, How-to, Music, Art, Philosophy, Reference, Juveniles, High-priced Paperbacks, Medicine, General & Social Science
Book Club: Klub 42, Zagreb, Leskovačka 18
Bookshop: Zagreb: Knjižara Stvarnost, Savska 1; Jlica 163b; Roooseveltov trg 4
Founded: 1952

Svjetlost*, YU-71000 Sarajevo, Petra Preradovića 3, Poštanski fah 129 Tel: (071) 512144/31100 Cable Add: Svjetlost Sarajevo Telex: 41326 yu Ikpres
Man Dir: Abdulah Jesenković; *Sales Dir:* Rizvanbegović Enver; *Editorial:* Miodrag Bogićević
Branch Offs: Belgrade, Obilićev venac 10; Zagreb, Šubičeva 65
Subjects: Belles Lettres, Reference, Science, Juveniles, Business, Textbooks, Business Directories, Encyclopaedias, Periodicals
Bookshops: At above address, and 42 branches throughout the country

Tehnička Knjiga*, YU-11000 Belgrade, ul 7 jula br 26/I, Poštanski fah 307 Tel: (011) 626046
Man Dir: Prvoslav Trajković
Subjects: General Science, Engineering, Secondary & Primary Textbooks

Tehnička Knjiga, YU-41000 Zagreb, Jurišićeva 10, Poštanski fah 816 Tel: 278172 Cable Add: Tehnoknjiga
Man Dir: Kuzman Ražnjević; *Dir, Chief Editor:* Zvonko Vistrićka
Subjects: Science, Technical Engineering, Periodicals
Bookshops: Knjižara Tehnička Knjiga, Zagreb Masarykova 19; Antikvarijat, Zagreb Masarykova 17
Founded: 1947

Tehnika, formerly publishing house of Savez Inženjera i Tehničara Jugoslavije (qv)

Tiskarna Ljudske Pravice*, Kopitarjeva 2, YU-61000 Ljubljana Tel: 323841 Telex: 31177 ljudne
Subjects: Children's and Juvenile Books; Periodicals and Newspapers

Turistička Štampa*, YU-11000 Belgrade, Knez Mihajlova 21/II, Poštanski fah 606 Tel: (011) 621080
Man Dir: Dragan Nikolić
Subjects: Art, Tourist Guides
Bookshop: Belgrade, Obilićev venac 26

Veselin Masleša*, YU-71000 Sarajevo, Sime Milutinovića 4, Poštanski fah 237 Tel: (071) 34633/24634 Cable Add: Vesmas Masleša Telex: 41154 ju vesmas
Man Dir, Editorial, Rights and Permissions: Ahmed Hromadžić
Branch Offs: in Zabreb, Belgrade, Skopje
Subjects: General Fiction, General & Political Science, Reference, Philosophy,

Juveniles
Bookshops: Sarajevo, Maksima Gorkog 2 & Pavla Goranina 2; Belgrade, Terazije 38. Also over 30 group bookshops throughout Yugoslavia
Founded: 1950

Vesti*, YU-31000 Titovo Užice, 4 jula br 14 Tel: 21262
Dir: Mihajlo Rebić

Vojnoizdavački Zavod*, YU-11002 Belgrade, Balkanska 53 Tel: (011) 641586
Subject: Military

Vuk Karadžic, YU-11000 Belgrade, Kraljevića Marka 9, Poštanski fah 762 Tel: (011) 628066/628043/620024 (Director) Cable Add: Vuk Karadžić Belgrade
Man Dir: Slobodan Durić
Branch Offs: Zagreb, Nikole Tesle 14/III; Sarajevo, Sime Milutinovića 10; Novi Sad, Laze Kostića 22; Svetozarevo, Slavke Durdević bb zgr B-3
Subjects: Encyclopedias and Reference, Art, Popular Science, History, Criticism, Psychology, Sociology, Philosophy, Children's books, Education, Periodicals
Founded: 1956

Založba Obzorja*, YU-62000 Maribor, Partizanska 5, Poštanski fah 135 Tel: 25681/21086
Dir: Drago Simončič
Subjects: Professional, Science, Journalism

Zavod za Izdavanje Udžbenika*, YU-71000 Sarajevo, Otokara Keršovanija 3, Poštanski fah 262 Tel: 33728
Man Dir: Dr Ljubomir Berberović
Subjects: Education, Textbooks

Zavod za obrazovanje kadrova za administrativne poslove SR Srbije*, Izdavačko-Stamparska OOUR Stručna Knjiga, YU-11000 Belgrade, ul Lole Ribara 48 Tel: 341332/342512/342514 Cable Add: Stručna knjiga
Dir: Mrs V Brgulan
Subjects: Textbooks, Business, Management

Zavod za udžbenike i nastavna sredstva, YU-11000 Belgrade, Obilićev Venac 5, Poštanski fah 312 Tel: 335337
Dir: Dr Tomislav Bogavac
Subjects: Textbooks, Educational Materials
Bookshop: YU-11000 Belgrade, Kosovska 45

Zavod za Udžbenike i Nastavna Sredstva Sap Kosovo*, YU-38000 Priština, Beogradska 29, Poštanski fah 112 Tel: (038) 24752
Dir: Ramuš Rama
Subjects: Textbooks, Educational Materials
Bookshop: Priština, Lenjinova 66
Founded: 1958

Nakladni Zavod **'Znanje'**, YU-41000 Zagreb, Socijalističke revolucije 17, Pretinac 955 Tel: (041) 411500/411483/411474 Cable Add: Znanje Zagreb
Man Dir: Dragutin Brenčun
Branch Offs: Sarajevo, A Šence 14; Belgrade, Bulevar Lenjina 119
Subjects: General Fiction, Popular Science, Agriculture
Bookshops: August Šenoa, Socijalističke revolucije 17; Trg Republike 17; 'Ivan Goran Kovačić', Martićeva 12; Antikvarijat, Tin Ujević, Zrinjevac 17 (all in Zagreb)
Founded: 1946

Literary Agents

Jugoslovenska Autorska Agencija*, Belgrade, Majke Jevrosime 38

V P A (Vjesnikova Press Agencija)*, YU-41000 Zagreb, Ave bratstva i jedinstva 4 Tel: (041) 515555 Telex: 21121

Book Clubs

Klub 42*, Zabreb, Leskovacka 18
Owned by: Stvarnost (Zagreb)

Klub čitalaca, Belgrade, Save Kovačevića 26
Owned by: Slovo Ljubve (Belgrade)

Mladost's Book Fans Club, YU-41000 Zagreb, Ilica 30, Poštanski fah 1028
Owned by: Mladost (Zagreb)

Svet Knjige, Ljubljana, Nazorjeva 6
Members: 160,000
Owned by: Mladinska Kujiga (Ljubljana)
Founded: 1971

Major Booksellers

Cankarjeva Zalozba, YU-61001 Ljubljana, Kopitarjeva 2, Poštni predal 201-IV Tel: (061) 323841
Importer/Exporter

Državna Založba Slovenije, YU-61000 Ljubljana, Mestni trg 26, Postanski fah 50/1 Tel: 24695/310736
Importer/Exporter

Export-Press*, YU-11000 Belgrade, Francuska 27, Poštanski fah 358 Tel: (011) 625363
Importer/Exporter (the latter particularly as supplier to various US libraries, and UK and US Slavic departments)

Forum*, YU-21000 Novi Sad, Vojvode Mišića 1, Poštanski fah 200 Tel: (021) 57207
Importer/Exporter

Jugoslavenska Knjiga, Trg Republike 5/VIII, Postf 36, YU-11000 Belgrade Tel: 621992 Cable Add: Jugoknjiga Beograd Telex: 12466 yu jkbdg
Import and Export of Books, Periodicals and Newspapers

Kultura*, YU-91000 Skopje, JNA 68a, Postanski fah 298 Tel: 35361
32 bookshops throughout Yugoslavia

Makedonska Knjiga, YU-91000 Skopje, 11 Oktomvri bb, Poštanski fah 349 Tel: (091) 33710
26 bookshops in Skopje and in all major towns in Macedonia

Mladinska Knjiga*, YU-61000 Ljubljana, Titova 3, Poštanski fah 36/1 Tel: (061) 24851/6
Importer/Exporter (Children's Books)

Mladost*, YU-41000 Zagreb, Ilica 30, Poštanski fah 1028 Tel: (041) 440211 Telex: 21263 YU MLADZG
Importer/Exporter

Nolit*, YU-11000 Belgrade, Terazije 27/II, Poštanski fah 369 Tel: (011) 332257/332258/333353
Importer/Exporter

Prosveta*, YU-11000 Belgrade, Terazije 16/I Tel: (011) 320566
Importer/Exporter

Svjetlost*, YU-71000 Sarajevo, Radojke Lakić 3 Tel: (071) 38678
Importer/Exporter

Tehnička Knjiga, YU-41000 Zagreb, Jurišićeva 10, Poštanski fah 816 Tel: (041) 271608
General Manager: Kuzman Raznjević
Importer/Exporter (Technical Books)

Veselin Masleša*, YU-71000 Sarajevo, Sime Milutinovića 4 i 2 Tel: (071) 24634
Importer/Exporter

Vuk Karadžic, YU-11000 Belgrade, Kraljevića Marka 9, Poštanski fah 762 Tel: (011) 628066/628043
Manager: Slobodan Durić
Importer/Exporter

Major Libraries

Arhiv Hrvatske, YU-41000 Zagreb, Marulićev trg 21
Archives of Croatia
Publications: Archival Review (annual); *Acts of Croatian Parliament*

Arhiv na SR Makedonija*, Skopje, Kej Dimitar Vlahov bb, Poštanski fah 496
Archives of Macedonia

Arhiv SR Slovenije, YU-61000 Ljubljana, Zvezdarska 1 Tel: 21436
Dir: Marija Oblak-Čarni

Arhiv Srbije, YU-11000 Belgrade, Karnedžijeva 2
Librarian: Mrs L Mirković
Archives of Serbia

Institute for Scientific and Technical Documentation and Information*, Belgrade, Kataniceva 15
Publication: Yugoslav Research Guide

Jugoslovenski centar za tehničku i naučnu dokumentaciju*, Belgrade, S Penezića-Krcuna 29, Poštanski fah 724
Dir: Aleksić Miodrag
Yugoslav Centre for Technical and Scientific Documentation
Publications: Bulletin of Documentation (24 series abstracts from technical literature), *Informatika* (periodical for theory and practice of documentation and information), *Bibliography on Automatic Data Processing, Scientific and Professional Meetings in Yugoslavia and Foreign Countries, MF-Technique* (journal on applying microfilm)

Univerzitetska biblioteka 'Svetozar **Markovič'**, YU-11000 Belgrade, Bulevar revolucije 71 Tel: (011) 342116/341446
University Library 'Svetozar Markovič'
1978-79: 7 titles

Nacionalna i Sveučilišna Biblioteka, YU-41001 Zagreb, Marulićev trg 21, Poštanski fah 550 Tel: Director 445440; Secretariat 446725; Information Office 446525
National and University Library

Narodna biblioteka NR Bosne i Hercegovine*, YU-71000 Sarajevo, Obala 42
National Library of Bosnia and Herzegovina

Centralna **narodna biblioteka** SR Crne Gore*, Cetinje, Njegoševa 100
Central National Library of Montenegro

Narodna biblioteka SR Srbije*, YU-11000 Belgrade, Skerlićeva 1 Tel: 451242/9
National Library of Serbia

Narodna in univerzitetna knjižnica (Ljubljana)*, YU-61001 Ljubljana pp 259, Turjaška 1 Tel: Central (061) 23197; Information (061) 22045
National and University Library

Naučna biblioteka, Rijeka, Dolac 1
Research Library

Narodna i univerzitetska biblioteka 'Kliment **Ohridski***, YU-91000 Skopje, ul 'Goce Delčev' bb Tel: 34360/50301/50303
'Kliment Ohridski' National and University Library

Biblioteka **Srpske** Akademije Nauka i Umetnosti, YU-11001 Belgrade, Knez Mihailova 35
Library of the Serbian Academy of Sciences and Arts
Librarian: Mile Žegarac

Library Associations

Crnogorska akademija nauka i umjetnosti*, YU-81000 Titograd, Rista Stijovića 5 Tel: (081) 24023
League of the Librarians' Associations of Yugoslavia: official titles rotate every two years among Zveza društev bibliotekarjev Jugoslavije (Slovene), Savez društava bibliotekara Jugoslavije (Serbo-Croatian) and Sojuz na društvata na bibliotekarite na Jugoslavija (Macedonian)
Secretary: Ms M Adžić

Društvo bibliotekara Bosne i Hercegovine*, YU-71000 Sarajevo, Obala 42 Tel: 36047
Library Association of Bosnia and Herzegovina
Executive Secretary: Kalender Fahrudin
Publication: Bibliotekarstvo (quarterly)

Društvo bibliotekarjev Slovenije*, YU-61000 Ljubljana, Turjaška 1 Tel: 23197/8
Library Association of Slovenia
Executive Secretary: Majda Armeni
Publications: Knjižnica (quarterly)

Društvo na arhivskite rabotnici i arhivite na SRM*, YU-91000 Skopje
Society of Archivists of Macedonia
Secretary: Zvonko Janevski
Publication: Makedonski arhivist

Društvo na bibliotekarite na Makedonija*, 'Kliment Ohridski' National and University Library, YU-91000 Skopje, ul 'Goce Delčev' bb
Librarians' Society of Macedonia
Secretary: Kiro Dojčinovski
Publication: Bibliotekarska iskra

Hrvatsko bibliotekarsko društvo*, YU-41000 Zagreb Marulićev trg 21
Croatian Library Association
Secretary: Nada Gomerčić
Publications: Vjesnik bibliotekara Hrvatske (quarterly), *Knjiga i čitaoci* (six per year)

Jugoslovenski bibliografski institut, YU-11000 Belgrade, Terazije 26, Poštanski fah 20 Tel: 328513
Yugoslav Bibliographic Institute
Dir: Dr Venceslav Glišić
Publishes the *Yugoslavia Bibliography*, which includes books, pamphlets, music scores and articles of literary, scientific interest, philology, art and sport

Savez bibliotečkih radnika Srbije, YU-11000 Belgrade, Skerlićeva 1 Tel: 451242
Union of Library Workers of Serbia
Executive Secretary: Branka Popović
Publication: Bibliotekar (bimonthly)

Savez društava bibliotekara Jugoslavije (Serbo-Croatian), see Crnogorska akademija nauka i umjetnosti

Sojuz na društvata na bibliotekarite na Jugoslavija (Macedonian), see Crnogorska akademija nauka i umjetnosti

Zveza društev bibliotekarjev Jugoslavije (Slovene), see Crnogorska akademija nauka i umjetnosti

Library Reference Books and Journals

Books

Biblioteke u Jugoslaviji (Libraries in Yugoslavia), Yugoslav Bibliographic Institute, YU-11000 Belgrade, Terazije 26

Biblioteke u SR Srbiji (Libraries in Serbia), National Library of Serbia, YU-11000 Belgrade, Skerlićeva 1

Journals

Bibliotekar (The Librarian), Union of Library Workers of Serbia, YU-11000 Belgrade, Skerlićeva 1

Bibliotekarska iskra (The Librarian's Spark), Librarians' Society of Macedonia, 'Kliment Ohridski' National and University Library, YU-91000 Skopje, ul 'Goce Delčev' bb

Bibliotekarstvo (Librarianship), Library Association of Bosnia and Herzegovina, YU-71000 Sarajevo, Obala 42

Knjiga i čitaoci (Book and Readers), Croatian Library Association, YU-41000 Zagreb, Marulićev trg 21

Knjižnica (The Library) (text in Slovenian, summaries in English) Library Association of Slovenia, YU-61000 Ljubljana, Turjaška 1

Makedonski arhivist (Macedonian Archivist) (text in Macedonian, summaries in French), Society of Archivists of Macedonia, YU-91000 Skopje

Viesnik bibliotekara hrvatske (Croatian Librarians' Bulletin), Croatian Library Association, YU-41000 Zagreb, Marulićev trg 21

Literary Associations and Societies

Društvo na pisatelite na SRM*, YU-91000 Skopje, Maksim Gorki 18
Society of Writers of Macedonia
Secretaries: Adem Gajtani, Eftim Manev

Društvo za srpski jezik i književnost*, Belgrade University, Belgrade
Society of Serbian Language and Literature
Secretary: D Pavlović
Publication: Pritozi za knjizevnost, jezik, istorija i folklor

Literary Club 'Oktobar'*, Kraljevo, Mire Cukulica 2
Publication: Oktobar

Yugoslav P E N Club*, Serbian Centre, YU-11000 Belgrade, 7 Francuska St
Publication: Literary Quarterly

Pedagoško-književni zbor, pedagoško društvo SR Hrvatske*, Zagreb
Pedagogical and Literary Union of Croatia

Sojuz na društvata za makedonski jazik i literatura*, Institute for the Macedonian Language 'Krste Misirkov', YU-91000 Skopje, Grigor Prlicev 5
Federation of Societies for Macedonian Language and Literature
Secretary: Olga Ivanova
Publication: Literaturen zbor (Literary Door)

Literary Periodicals

Bagdala; literature, art and culture (text in Serbo-Croatian), Knjizevni Klub, Krusevac, Obilićeva 20

Brazde (Furrows); journal for literature and culture, Narodni Univerzitet, Bijeljina, Vase Pelagica 1

Bridge; literary review, Zagreb, trg Republike 7

Delo (The Literary Work) (text in Serbo-Croatian), Nolit Publishing House, YU-11000 Belgrade, Terazije 27/II, Poštanski fah 369

Forum; journal of the Section for Contemporary Literature of the Yugoslav Academy of Sciences and Arts (Text in Serbo-Croatian), Zagreb 1, Zrinski trg 11

Izraz (Expression); journal of literary and artistic criticism, Sarajevo, Radojke Lakio Broj 3-1, Poštanski fah 322

Knjizevne novine (Literary News) (text in Serbo-Croatian), Novinsko Izdavačko Preduzeće 'Knjizevne Novine', Belgrade, Francuska 7

Literary Quarterly (text in English and French), Yugoslav PEN Club, Belgrade Centre, Jugoslavenska Knjiga, Belgrade, Poštanski fah 36

Literaturen zbor (Literary Door) (text in Macedonian); journal of the Federation of Societies for Macedonian Language and Literature, Institute for the Macedonian Language, 'Krste Misirkov', YU-91000 Skopje, Grigor Prličev 5

Lumina (Light); literary and cultural review, Panciova, Zarka Zrenjanina 7

Macedonian Review; history, culture, literature, arts, Cultural Life, Skopje, Poštanski fah 85

Oktobar (October); review of literature, art and culture, Literary Club 'Oktobar', Kraljevo, Mire Cukulica 2

Pregled naših i stranih knjiga i članaka (Review of Domestic and Foreign Books and Articles), Centralna biblioteka JNA, Belgrade, Balkanska 53a

Razgledi (Perspectives), review of literature, art and culture (text in Macedonian), Maršala Tita Iv Baraka, Skopje, Maršala Tita 4, Poštanski fah 345

Savremenik (Contemporary); literary monthly (text in Serbo-Croatian), Beogradski Izdavačko-Grafički Zavod, YU-11000 Belgrade, bulevar vojode Mišića 17, Poštanski fah 340

Stremez (Aspiration); journal for literature and culture (text in Macedonian), Prilep, Joska Jordanovski 2

Stremliena; literary review published every two months, Jedinstvo, YU-38000 Priština, Dom Štampe bb, Postanski, pregradak 81

Stvaranje (Creation); journal for literature and culture, Cedo Vukovic, Titograd, Marka Miljanova 11A

Translation Agencies and Associations

Društvo na literaturnite preveduvači na SRM*, YU-91000 Skopje
Society of Literary Translators of Macedonia
Secretary: Taško Širilov

Zaire

General Information

Language: Officially French; Swahili common in east, Lingala in west
Religion: About 25% Roman Catholic; rest follow traditional beliefs
Population: 27.7 million
Bank Hours: 0800-1130 Monday-Friday
Shop Hours: 0800-1200, 1500-1800 Monday-Saturday; generally early closing Wednesday
Currency: 100 makutu (singular likuta) = 1 zaïre; 100 sengi = 1 likuta

Export/Import Information: No tariff but for books not of educational, scientific or cultural use, revenue tax of 25%; children's picture books and atlases, 10% tax. Small quantities of advertising matter free. 3% Statistical Tax on all imports. Goods subject to duty also subject to Turnover Tax of 8³/₄% CIF value + customs + statistical tax. No import licences for books. Exchange controls
Copyright: Berne, Florence (see International section)

Book Trade Journal

Bibliographie nationale (National Bibliography), Bibliothèque nationale, 10 blvd Tshatshi, BP 3090, Kinshasa-Gombe

Publishers

Bureau d'Etudes et de Recherches pour la Promotion de la Sante, BP 1977, Kangu-Mayombe
Man Dir, Rights & Permissions: J Courtejoie
Subject: Health Education

C E E B A Publications, BP 19, Bandundu Cable Add: CEEBA Bandundu
Man Dir, Editorial: Dr Hermann Hochegger; *Sales:* P J Dufraing
Orders to: Steyler Verlag, D-5202 St Augustin, Federal Republic of Germany
Parent Company: Anthropos Institut
Subjects: Social Anthropology, Ethnology, Myths, Rituals, Sociology, Linguistics, Arts, Agriculture, History, Religion
1978: 6 titles *1979:* 6 titles *Founded:* 1965
ISBN Publisher's Prefix: 84-399

Centre International de Sémiologie*, Ave Pruniers 109, Zone de Kampemba, BP 1825, Campus de Lubumbashi
Secretary: Dr V Y Mudimbe
Publications: Bulletins on Medical Anthropology, Religious Syncretisms, Culture-contact, Africanisms

Centre Protestant d'Editions et de Diffusion (CEDI)*, 209 ave Kalemie, BP 11398, Kinshasa I Tel: 22202
Man Dir: Volker Gscheidle
Subjects: General Fiction, Belles Lettres, Poetry, Biography, Religion, Juveniles, Christian Tracts, Books in Kikongo, Lingala and other Zaïre languages, Paperbacks
Bookshops: CEDI Bookshop, 209 ave Kalemie, BP 11398, Kinshasa I
Founded: 1935

Commission de l'Education chrétienne*, BP 3258, Kinshasa-Gombe Tel: 30087 Telex: 203 DIA
Man Dir: Abbé Dibalu-Didi
Subjects: Educational, Academic, Religion

Government Printer (Imprimerie du Gouvernement Central)*, BP 3021, Kinshasa-Kalina

Editions Lokole, BP 5085 Kinshasa X (Located at: Ave Colonel Ebeya no 1082, Kinshasa/Gombe) Tel: 22559
Dir: Nzengo Popo
Miscellaneous: State organization charged with the promotion of literature in Zaïre

Editions du Mont Noir*, BP 1944, Lubumbashi
Man Dir: V Y Mudimbe; *Sales:* Pierre Detienne; *Secretary and Publicity:* Mukala Kadima Nzuji
Subjects: General Fiction, Belles Lettres, Poetry, Reference
Founded: 1971

Les **Presses Africaines***, pl du 27 Octobre, BP 12924, Kinshasa I
Man Dir: Mwamba-di-Mbuyi
Subjects: General Nonfiction, Belles Lettres, Poetry, Paperbacks

Presses universitaires du Zaïre et l'Office du Livre (PUZ)*, BP 1682 Kinshasa I Tel: 31380/30652/24786 Cable Add: PUZ Rectorat Unaza Telex: 331
Man Dir, Rights & Permissions: Makanda Mpinga Shambuyi; *Editorial:* Kabukala Mulowayi; *Sales:* Ngalahvlume Kanku; *Production:* Memvanga Kanza; *Publicity:* Wiluwilu Mabanza
Branch Off: Lubumbashi
Subjects: Belles Lettres, Poetry, Biography, History, Africana, Philosophy, Reference, Religion, Paperbacks, Psychology, Medicine, Science & Technology, Agronomy, Social Science, University Textbooks, Economics, Law, Literature, Education
Bookshop: Librairie des Presses universitaires, BP 1682, Kinshasa I
Founded: 1972

Editions **Saint Paul***, ave du Commerce 76, BP 8505, Kinshasa Tel: 25544
Dir: Sister Lucia d'Agosto
Subjects: General Fiction & Nonfiction, Belles Lettres, Poetry, Religion, Juveniles, Christian Tracts, Paperbacks
Bookshop: Firm has bookshop outlets in Kinshasa (BP 8505) and Lubumbashi (BP 2447)

Librairie Les **Volcans***, 22 ave Président Mobuto, BP 400, Goma (Kivu) Tel: 366
Man Dir: Ruhama Mukandoli; *Sales Manager:* Pierre Mangez
Subjects: Reference, Social Science
Bookshop: 22 ave President Mobuto, BP 400, Goma (Kivu)

Major Booksellers

C E D I Bookshop*, 209 ave Kalemie, BP 11398, Kinshasa I

Librairie **Declés***, BP 224, Kinshasa

Diffusion de la Presse*, BP 505, Kisangani

La **Générale des Carrières et des Mines** (GECAMINES)*, BP 450, Lubumbashi Telex: 234
and BP 8714, Kinshasa Telex: 21207

Librairie de l'**Institut** national d'Etudes politiques*, BP 2307, Kinshasa

Librairie évangélique*, BP 123, Kinshasa

Okapi Centre de Diffusion*, BP 908, Kinshasa

Librairie des **Presses** universitaires*, BP 1682, Kinshasa I Tel: 24786

Procure scolaire*, BP 70, Kanaga

Librairie **Saint Paul***, 76 ave du Commerce, BP 8505, Kinshasa
and BP 2447, Lubumbashi

Librairie **Salutiste***, 249 ave du Plateau, BP 8905, Kinshasa

Librairie **Sarma***, BP 7098, Kinshasa

Librairies **Sodimca***, BP 2700, Kinshasa

Librairie Les **Volcans***, 22 ave Président Mobutu, BP 400, Goma

Librairie du **Zaïre***, 12 ave des Aviateurs, BP 2100, Kinshasa I Tel: 26748

Major Libraries

Alliance française*, Bibliothèque, BP 5237, Kinshasa

Archives nationales du Zaïre*, 42 ave Valcke, BP 3428, Kinshasa

Bibliothèque nationale*, 10 blvd Tshatshi, BP 3090, Kinshasa-Gombe Tel: 30834
Publication: Bibliographie nationale

Bibliothèque publique*, 2 ave Bawaboli, BP 1741, Kisangani Tel: 2617

Centre culturel français, Bibliothèques, BP 5236, Kinshasa

Institut pédagogique national, Bibliothèque, BP 8815, Kinshasa I Tel: 80573

Bibliothèque centrale de l'**Université nationale du Zaïre**, Campus de Kinshasa, BP 125, Kinshasa XI Tel: 30123 ext 161
Librarian: Tubomeshi Milambo
Publication: Chronique des Bibliothèques

Bibliothèque centrale de l'**Université nationale, Campus de Kisangani***, BP 2102, Kisangani Tel: 2153
Chief Librarian: Lelo Mamosi

Bibliothèque centrale de l'**Université nationale, Campus de Lubumbashi***, BP 2896, Lubumbashi Tel: 4479

Library Associations

Association Zaïroise des Archivistes, Bibliothécaires et Documentalistes*, BP 805, Kinshasa XI Tel: 30123/4
Zaire Association of Archivists, Librarians and Documentalists
Executive Secretary: E Kabeba-Bangasa
Publication: Mukanda

Library Reference Books and Journals

Book

Liste des bibliothèques publiques (List of Public Libraries), Ministère de la culture et des arts, Bibliothèque centrale, Kinshasa-Kalina

Journal

Mukanda; archives, libraries and documentation bulletin, Zaire Association of Archivists, Librarians and Documentalists, BP 805, Kinshasa XI

Literary Periodicals

Cahiers de Littérature et de Linguistique appliqué (Journal of Literature and Applied Linguistics), Université nationale du Zaïre, Faculté des Lettres, BP 1825, Campus de Lubumbashi

Dombi; Congolese review of letters and the arts, BP 3498, Kinshasa-Kalina (bi-monthly 'little magazine' edited by Philippe Masegabio)

Zambia

General Information

Language: English is official language
Religion: About 50% Christian (25% Roman Catholic, 25% Protestant); rest follow traditional beliefs
Population: 5.5 million
Literacy Rate (1969): 47.3%
Bank Hours: 0815-1245 Monday, Tuesday, Wednesday, Friday; 0815-1200 Thursday; 0815-1100 Saturday
Shop Hours: Generally 0800-1700 Monday-Friday; 0800-1300 Saturday
Currency: 100 ngwee = 1 Zambia kwacha
Export/Import Information: No tariffs on books but all imports subject to sales tax (10% of duty value + 20%). Single copies of advertising free. Import licence required. Exchange controls
Copyright: UCC (see International section)

Book Trade Organizations

Booksellers' and Publishers' Association of Zambia, c/o PO Box 32664, Lusaka
Secretary: C H Chirwa

Publishers

Africa Literature Centre*, PO Box 1319, Kitwe Tel: 84712/3 Cable Add: Mincen
Man Dir: E C Makunike
Subjects: General, Educational, Religion, Books in Zambian Languages
Bookshop: address as above

Directory Publishers of Zambia Ltd*, PO Box 1659, Ndola (Located at: Rooms 101-103 First Floor, Security Ho, Buteko Ave, Ndola) Tel: 4882
Man Dir, Rights & Permissions: D E Smith; *Editorial & Publicity:* Mrs D E Bell; *Sales:* Mrs J M Maxwell
Subjects: Reference, Directories
Founded: 1958

Government Printer*, PO Box 136, Lusaka

Multimedia Zambia, PO Box 8199, Lusaka Tel: 53864
Man Dir: Mr Chimfwabwa
Parent Company: Christian Council of Zambia/Zambia Episcopal Conference
Subjects: Biography, Africana, Religion, Juveniles, Drama, Law, Physiotherapy
Founded: 1970

N E C Z A M Library, an imprint of National Educational Company of Zambia Ltd (qv)

National Educational Company of Zambia Ltd, Chishango Rd, PO Box 32664, Lusaka Tel: 75121/3 Cable Add: Neczam Lusaka
General Manager: Christopher Chirwa; *Editorial:* M J Phiri; *Production:* G K Simanwe; *Sales:* H Chisulo, D Sialyainda (Educational); *Publicity:* D Sialyainda; *Rights & Permissions:* Paulsen Himwiinga
Parent Company: Kenneth Kaunda Foundation, PO Box 2708, Lusaka
Associate Company: National Educational Distribution Company of Zambia Ltd, PO Box 2666, Lusaka
Imprint: NECZAM Library
Subjects: General, Poetry, Biography, History, Agriculture, Children's Books, Educational, Language, Literature, Fiction, Folklore, Drama, Politics, Sociology, Zambia Primary Course
Bookshop: Chishango Rd, PO Box 2664, Lusaka
1978: 125 titles *1979:* 10 titles *Founded:* 1967

Prometheus Publishing Co*, PO Box 1850, Lusaka
Subjects: General Nonfiction, Biography, History, Africana, Social Science

Temco Publishing Ltd, No 10 Kabelenga Rd, PO Box 30886, Lusaka Tel: 73746 Cable Add: Longman Telex: ZA 45250
Man Dir, Editorial, Production, Publicity, Rights & Permissions: S V Tembo; *Sales:* Sylvia Sakala
Subjects: Educational, General
Founded: 1977

Major Booksellers

The **Bookshelf***, Caravelle Ho, Buteko Ave, PO Box 977, Ndola Tel: 3438

Christian Bookshop*, PO Box 1206, Kitwe

Christian Council of Zambia*, Farmers Ho, PO Box 315, Lusaka Tel: 73287

Kingstons (Zambia) Ltd, PO Box 70139, Ndola
Department store with book department (12 other branches)

Malsa Book Service Ltd*, Cairo Rd, PO Box 1700, Lusaka Tel: 81155

Standard Books Ltd*, PO Box 94, Lusaka

University Bookshop, PO Box 32379, Lusaka Tel: 54755 Cable Add: UNZA Bookshop, Lusaka
Manager: A M Simbeya
Owned by: University of Zambia

Zambia Catholic Bookshop, PO Box 1581, Ndola

Major Libraries

Evelyn Hone College Library*, PO Box 29, Lusaka Tel: 72961

Kitwe Public Library, PO Box 20070, Kitwe Tel: 213685

Lusaka City Libraries*, PO Box 1304, Katondo Rd, Lusaka Tel: 81762
City Librarian: P C Kulleen
Publications: Annual Report; New Additions List (quarterly)

Mindolo Ecumenical Foundation, Hammarskjold Memorial Library, PO Box 1493, Kitwe Tel: 215198/214572 Cable Add: Mincen Kitwe
Librarian: Nyambe Namushi
Publications: Annual Report; Mindolo Newsletter (occasional); various reports of conferences and seminars

National Archives of Zambia*, PO Box RW 10, Ridgeway, Lusaka Tel: 51677

Natural Resources Development College Library*, PO Box CH 99, Lusaka Tel: 73046
Senior Librarian: Edward Tankersley

Ndola Public Library, PO Box 70388, Ndola Tel: 4049/2637/8
Librarian: K Mumba Chisaka

Nkrumah Teachers' College Library*, PO Box 404, Kabwe Tel: 3221

Northern Technical College Library, PO Box 71563, Ndola Tel: 86210 ext 18

University of Zambia Library, PO Box 32379, Lusaka Tel: 54755 Cable Add: UNZA-Library
Chief Librarian: E T K Lwanga

Zambia Institute of Technology Library, PO Box 21993, Kitwe
Librarian: M C Banda
Publications: ZIT Library Catalogue (quarterly); *Annual Report; ZIT Prospectus* (annual)

Zambia Library Service, Educational Services Centre, PO Box 30802, Lusaka Tel: 54655 Cable Add: Zamlibs
Chief Librarian: M Walubita

Library Associations

Zambia Library Association, PO Box 32839, Lusaka
Executive Secretary: Adrian Pamba
Publications: Journal (twice a year); *Newsletter* (6 times a year)

Library Reference Books and Journals

Book

Directory of Libraries in Zambia, Zambia Library Association, PO Box 32839, Lusaka (provides details on all the major libraries in the country)

Journal

Zambia Library Association Journal, PO Box 32839, Lusaka

Literary Associations and Societies

Mphala Creative Society*, c/o International House 5-13, University of Zambia, PO Box 2379, Lusaka
Publication: The Jewel of Africa

Literary Periodicals

The Jewel of Africa, Mphala Creative Society, c/o International House 5-13, University of Zambia, PO Box 2379, Lusaka (literary and cultural quarterly edited by Steven May and published since 1968)

Zimbabwe

General Information

Language: English and native dialects
Population: 6.9 million
Currency: 100 cents = 1 Zimbabwe dollar
Export/Import Information: No tariff on books. Advertising matter in bulk has 30% duty and VAT. No import licence required for books or advertising matter

Book Trade Organizations

Booksellers' Association of Zimbabwe, PO Box 1934, Salisbury (Located at: Equity House, Rezende St, Salisbury) Tel: 708611
Secretary: Mrs L Craven

Standard Book Numbering Agency, National Archives, Private Bag 7729, Causeway, Salisbury Tel: 792741
ISBN Administrator: E E Burke

Book Trade Reference Journal

Zimbabwe National Bibliography, National Archives, Causeway, Private Bag 7729, Salisbury

Publishers

B & T Directories (Pvt) Ltd, PO Box 2119, Bulawayo
Subject: Directories

Books of Zimbabwe Publishing Co (Pvt) Ltd, 137A Rhodes St, PO Box 1994, Bulawayo Tel: 61135
Man Dir & Editor: L W Bolze; *Rights & Permissions:* Joan Hopcroft
Orders to: Books of Zimbabwe Publishing Co, PO Box 1994, Bulawayo
Subsidiary Company: Africana Book Society (Pty) Ltd, PO Box 1071, Johannesburg 2000 Republic of South Africa (qv)
Subjects: Rhodesiana Reprints & New Works, Fine Prints, Antique Maps of Africa, General Fiction and Non-fiction, Biography, History, Colour-plate Fine editions, Education, Visual Aids
Book Clubs: Books of Zimbabwe Book Club, Africana Book Society, Republic of South Africa (qv)
1978-79: 22 titles *Founded:* 1968
ISBN Publisher's Prefix: 0-86920

A C **Braby** (Zimbabwe) (Pvt) Ltd*, PO Box 1027, Bulawayo
Subjects: Reference, Directories, Telephone Books

Burke Enterprises (Pvt) Ltd*, PO Box 550, Gatooma

M O **Collins** (Pvt) Ltd, PO Box 3094, Dublin House, Victoria St/Albion Rd, Salisbury Tel: 704719
Man Dir: Brig M O Collins
Subjects: Science & Technology, General Science, Textbooks, Biography, Atlases
1978: 3 titles *Founded:* 1965
ISBN Publisher's Prefix: 0-86919

Peter **Dearlove** Publishers, PO Box UA 106, Salisbury
Man Dir: Peter Dearlove
Subjects: General Nonfiction, Biography, History, Africana, Paperbacks, Social Science

Dominion Press (Pvt) Ltd*, PO Box 1160, Salisbury

Flame Lily, an imprint of The Literature Bureau (qv)

Galaxie Press (Pvt) Ltd, PO Box 3041, Salisbury

Government Printer, PO Box 8062, Causeway, Salisbury

The **Literature Bureau**, Ministry of Education and Culture, PO Box 8137, Causeway, Salisbury Tel: 26929 Cable Add: Rholitburo
Dir: E W Krog; *Assistant Dir:* David Hlazo; *Editorial:* B Chitsike (Shona); P Mpofu (Ndebele)
Imprint: Flame Lily
Branch Off: PO Box 555, Bulawayo
Subjects: General Fiction & Non-fiction, Belles Lettres, Poetry, Biography, History, Africana, How-to, Study Guides, Books in Shona, Ndebele and English
Book Club: Shona Readers' Book Club; Ndebele Readers' Book Club; both at Box 8137, Causeway, Salisbury
Bookshop: Electra House, Jameson Ave, Salisbury
1978: 36 titles *1979:* 19 titles *Founded:* 1954
ISBN Publisher's Prefix: 0-86926

Lomagundi Printing (Pvt) Ltd*, PO Box 110, Sinoia

Longman Publishers (Pvt) Ltd, PO Box ST125, Southerton, Salisbury Tel: 62711/2/3/4 Cable Add: Freegrove Salisbury
Man Dir: Ben Gingell; *General Manager:* D R Mackenzie; *Marketing Manager:* S G Mpofu; *Senior Editor, Rights & Permissions:* Marilyn Poole; *Publicity:* Mia Sullivan
Associate Company: Longman Group Ltd, UK (qv)
Subjects: General Fiction & Nonfiction, Belles Lettres, Poetry, Biography, History, Africana, Juveniles, Books in Shona and Ndebele, Paperbacks, General & Social Science, Secondary & Primary Textbooks
1979-80: 25 titles *Founded:* 1964
ISBN Publisher's Prefix: 0-582

Mambo Press*, PO Box 779, Gwelo Tel: 4016
Man Dir: Albert Plangger; *Sales Manager:* James Amrein
Branch Offs: 51 Stanley Ave, PB 6602, Kopje, Salisbury Tel: 705899; Fort Victoria, PB 9213, Gokomere Tel: 2519-12
Subjects: General Fiction & Non-fiction, Poetry, Religion, Books in Shona, Ndebele and English, Secondary & Primary Textbooks
Bookshop: Mambo Press Bookshop, 51 Stanley Ave, PB 6602, Kopje, Salisbury; PO Box 779, Gwelo
1978: 36 titles *Founded:* 1958
ISBN Publisher's Prefix: 0-86922

Oxford University Press Southern Africa, Rooms 317-20, Roslin House, Baker Ave, PO Box 3892, Salisbury Tel: 27848 Cable Add: Oxonian
General Manager: N C Gracie; *Publicity:* C Rambanepasi
Subjects: General Non-fiction, Belles Lettres, Poetry, Biography, History, Africana, Books in Shona & other Zimbabwean Languages, Secondary Textbooks, Music, Prayer Books
Founded: 1915
Miscellaneous: Firm is a branch office of Oxford University Press Southern Africa, Republic of South Africa (qv)
ISBN Publisher's Prefix: 0-19

Publications Central Africa*, PO Box 1027, Bulawayo
Subjects: Reference, Annuals

R C P (Private) Ltd*, Bulawayo
(formerly Rhodesian Christian Press)

Rhodesian Christian Press, see R C P (Private) Ltd

Zimbabwean Publications, PO Box 1210, Salisbury
Founded: 1969

University of Zimbabwe, Publications Officer, PO Box MP45, Mount Pleasant, Salisbury Tel: 303211 Cable Add: University Telex: 4152 RH
Subjects: Biography, History, Africana, Philosophy, Reference, Religion, Medicine, Science & Technology, General & Social Science, University Textbooks
1978: 5 titles *1979:* 4 titles

Book Clubs

Books of Zimbabwe Book club, 137A Rhodes St (14th, 15th Aves), PO Box 1994, Bulawayo
Founded: 1968
Owned by: Books of Zimbabwe Publishing Co (Pvt) Ltd, Bulawayo (qv)
Subjects: Reproductions of scarce early Rhodesiana/Africana

Ndebele Readers' Book Club, Box 8137, Causeway, Salisbury
Sponsored by: The Literature Bureau (qv)
Subject: Ndebele Literature

Shona Readers' Book Club, Box 8137, Causeway, Salisbury
Sponsored by: The Literature Bureau, Salisbury (qv)
Subject: Shona literature

Major Booksellers

Adventist Book Centre*, 114 Jameson St, PO Box 573, Bulawayo Tel: 61845

African Book Centre*, PO Box 2020, Bulawayo Tel: (19) 65919

Alpha Books, PO Box 1056, Salisbury Tel: 22553
Manager: L Craven

Archibald Brothers*, PO Box 280, Gwelo Tel: (154) 2871

Baptist Book Centre, PO Box 831, Gwelo (Located at: 5th Street, Mandis Bldg, Gwelo) Tel: (154) 4242
Manager: Shayne T Masimira

Belmont Press, PO Box 31, Fort Victoria Tel: 2633
Managers: D G Hill, C L A Chadder
Also printers, stationers, office suppliers

Book Centre, PO Box 3799, Salisbury (Located at: Gordon Ave and Union Ave, Salisbury) Tel: 704621 Cable Add: textbook
Miscellaneous: This bookshop is associated with Books of Africa (qv under Publishers, Republic of South Africa)

The **Book Exchange***, 57 Stanley Ave, Salisbury Tel: 22468

Evans Shepherd*, PO Box 36, Salisbury Tel: 702531

Kingstons Ltd*, PO Box 2374, Salisbury Tel: 700526
Wholesaler, also retailer with 7 branches

The **Literature Bureau**, PO Box 8137, Causeway, Salisbury (Located at: Electra House, Jameson Ave, Salisbury) Tel: 26929 Cable Add: Rholitburo
Wholesale and retail distributors

Mambo Press Bookshop, Gelfand House, PB 66002, Kopje, Salisbury Tel: 705899

Matopo Book Centre, PO Box 554, Bulawayo Tel: (19) 71152
Manager: Agrippa V Masiye

Philpott & Collins (1978) (Pvt) Ltd*, PO Box 1977, Salisbury Tel: 705441

Townsend & Co (Pvt) Ltd, PO Box 3281, Salisbury Tel: 24611/26679
Manager: D Evans

Major Libraries

Bulawayo Public Library, PO Box 586, Bulawayo Tel: Bulawayo 60966
Librarian: R W Doust
Publications: Triennial Report; Spectrum: Quarterly Guide to new books

National Archives, Pvt Bag 7729, Causeway Tel: 792741
Publication: Zimbabwe National Bibliography

National Free Library Service, Twelfth Ave, PO Box 1773, Bulawayo Tel: 62359 Telex: 3128
Librarian: N Johnson
Publication: Shelfmark

ZIMBABWE

Nyatsime College Library*, Seke

Queen Victoria Memorial Library, PO Box 1087, Salisbury Tel: 704921
Librarian: Mrs M Ross-Smith

Salisbury Polytechnic Library, Causeway, PO Box 8074, Salisbury Tel: 705951
Librarian: Mrs D M Thorpe

Turner Memorial Library, Queen's Way Civic Complex, PO Box 48, Umtali Tel: 63412

University of Zimbabwe Library, PO Box MP45, Mount Pleasant, Salisbury Tel: 303211 Cable Add: University Telex: 4152 rh

Library Associations

Zimbabwe Library Association, PO Box 3133, Salisbury
Honorary Secretary: B L B Mushonga
Publication: The Zimbabwean Librarian

Library Reference Books and Journals

Books

Directory of Zimbabwean Libraries, National Archives, Pvt Bag 7729, Causeway, Salisbury

Journals

The Zimbabwean Librarian, Zimbabwe Library Association, PO Box 3133, Salisbury

Literary Associations and Societies

P E N Centre of Zimbabwe*, PO Box 1900, Salisbury
Secretary: Nora S Kane, 4 Avonfriars, Oxford Rd, Avondale, Salisbury

Shona/Ndebele Writers' Association*, PO Box 7009, Mzilikazi
Secretary: Mrs J G Sibanda

Literary Periodicals

Moto, PO Box 779, Gwelo (A political, cultural and religious weekly published by Mambo Press since 1958, with contributions in English and Shona. It has however been banned in recent years)

Literary Prizes

Kingston's Literary Awards*
The awards are for outstanding published works in English, Shona and Sindebele. Three awards, each of 500 Zimbabwe dollars, one in respect of each language. Enquiries to P E N International, Zimbabwe Centre, PO Box 1900, Salisbury

The **Literature Bureau** Annual Literary Award
500 Zimbabwe dollars for the best works in Shona and Ndebele. Most genres, including translations, qualify for entry. Enquiries to The Literature Bureau, PO Box 8137, Causeway, Salisbury

Two Tone Poetry Awards*
'Two Tone' is published quarterly. A prize of fifteen Zimbabwe dollars is awarded for the best poem in each issue, with a further prize of fifty Zimbabwe dollars for the poet who has sent in the best contributions to be published throughout the year. Winners of the latter award will not be eligible to compete for awards in the following two years. Enquiries to PO Box MP 79, Mount Pleasant, Salisbury

International Section

Copyright Conventions

The Universal Copyright Convention was sponsored by UNESCO in 1952. It states that 'Each signatory country extends to foreign works covered by UCC the same protection which such country extends to works of its own nationals published within its own borders'.

The Berne Convention is a system of international copyright which is maintained among countries which have become signatories to the International Copyright Union for the Protection of Literary and Artistic Works. This Union plan, which was first agreed upon at Berne, Switzerland, in 1888, has been subject to revisions every 20 years. The basic principle of the agreement is that any work properly copyrighted in its country of origin has protection in every Union country. Any work originating in a non-Union country, if it is simultaneously published in a Union country has the same standing as it would if it had originated in a Union country. Since different countries have different relationships under one or more of the revisions (Paris, 1896; Berlin, 1908; Rome, 1928; Brussels, 1948; and Stockholm, 1968), persons interested in obtaining information, including application of the various provisions to territorial areas, should consult the Bureau de l'union internationale pour la protection des oeuvres littéraires et artistiques, 32 chemin des Colombettes, Geneva, Switzerland.

The Florence Agreement, also known as the 'free flow of books', is a UNESCO-sponsored international agreement aimed at easing the flow of books and other scientific, educational and cultural materials, through the elimination or reduction of tariffs and other barriers.

The Buenos Aires Convention: In most Latin-American countries, compliance with the copyright law of the country of first publication protects the work in other countries of the Buenos Aires Convention, 1910. To secure copyright, each work must carry a notice to the effect that any use of the book or article will not be permitted without the consent of the copyright owner, and that copyright is reserved in English or any other language; for complete safety it is advised to add 'All rights reserved'. A later revision of the Buenos Aires Convention was made at the Washington Conference (Pan-American Copyright Convention) of 1946 which goes into greater detail than the Buenos Aires Convention. This Convention has been ratified by Argentina, Bolivia, Brazil, Chile, Costa Rica, Cuba, Dominican Republic, Ecuador, Guatemala, Haiti, Honduras, Mexico, Nicaragua and Paraguay

International Organizations

International Book Trade, Literary and Library Organizations

ACURIL, Box S, University Station, San Juan, Puerto Rico 00931
Association of Caribbean University, Research and Institutional Libraries
General Secretary: Oneida R Ortiz;
President: (1980-81) Mariano Morales (Library Director, Cayey University College, University of Puerto Rico, Cayey, Puerto Rico
Publications: ACURIL Newsletter; Proceedings of Annual Conference; CARINDEX (Indexing Committee — English)

Afro-Asian Writers' Permanent Bureau*, 104 Kasr el-Aini St, Cairo, Egypt
Secretary-General: Youssef El-Sebai
Publications: Lotus (magazine of Afro-Asian writing in English, French and Arabic), *Afro-Asian Literature Series*

Arab Regional Branch of the International Council on Archives*, Dr E M El Sheneti, President, c/o The National Library, Midan Ahmed Maher (Post Office), Bab El-Khalq, Cairo, Egypt
Secretary General: M J Abdusalim (Sudan)

Arab University Library Association*, c/o Chief Librarian, Kuwait University, Kuwait

Asociación Interamericana de Bibliotecarios y Documentalistas Agrícolas, IICA-CIDIA*, Turrialba, Costa Rica
Inter-American Association of Agricultural Librarians and Documentalists
Secretary-Treasurer: Ana María Paz de Erickson
Publications: Bibliografía Agrícola Latinoamericana (up to 1975); *Boletín Informativo, Boletín Técnico* (up to 1979), *Boletín Especial* (these three bulletins sent free to members); *Informe RIBDA*; *Revista Aibda* (twice yearly, starting 1980)

Asociación Interamericana de Escritores*, Casilla de Correo 4852, Humberto I No 431, Buenos Aires, Argentina
Inter-American Association of Writers
Secretary: Maria E Pardo M de Gomis
Publications: Hoja Informativa; Biblioteca Interamericana

Asociación Latinoamericana de Escuelas de Bibliotecología y Ciencias de la Información (ALEBCI)*, Colegio de Bibliotecología, Universidad Nacional Autónoma de México, México 20 DF, Mexico
Latin American Association of Schools of Library and Information Science
President: Judith Licea de Arenas
Publications: ALEBCI; Boletín Informativo

Association des Bibliothèques Internationales*, c/o Library, United Nations, Palais des Nations, CH-1211 Geneva 10, Switzerland
Association of International Libraries
President: Th Dimitrov
Publication: Newsletter

Association européenne des Editeurs de Publications pour la Jeunesse (EUROPRESS-JUNIOR)*, 99 ave de la Brabançonne, B-1040 Brussels, Belgium
Tel: (02) 341276
European Association of Publishers of Publications for Young People

Association for the Promotion of the International Circulation of the Press, CH-8002 Zürich, Beethovenstrasse 20, Switzerland
Association pour la Promotion de la Diffusion Internationale de la Presse
Vereinigung zur Förderung des internationalen Pressevertriebes
This is Distripress

Association internationale de Bibliophilie, c/o Bibliothèque nationale, 58 rue de Richelieu, F-75084 Paris cedex 02, France
This is a book collectors' association
Secretary-General: Antoine Coron
Publication: Le Bulletin du Bibliophile (quarterly)

Association internationale des Documentalistes et Techniciens de l'Information AID, 74 rue des Saints-Pères, F-75007 Paris, France
International Association of Documentalists and Information Officers
General Secretary: Dr Jacques Samain

Association internationale pour le Développement de la Documentation, des Bibliothèques et des Archives en Afrique*, BP 375, Dakar, Senegal Tel: 34139
International Association for the Development of Documentation, Libraries and Archives in Africa
Secretary: E K W Dadzie

432 INTERNATIONAL ORGANIZATIONS

Association littéraire et artistique internationale (ALAI)*, Cercle de la Librairie, 117 blvd St-Germain, F-75279 Paris cedex 06, France
International Literary and Artistic Association
Permanent Secretary: André Françon, 55 rue des Mathurins, F-75008 Paris, France
Founded: 1878

Association of Libraries of Judaica and Hebraica in Europe, Bibliothèque de l'Alliance Israelite Universelle, 45 rue La Bruyère, F-75425 Paris, France
Chairman: Mr Georges Weill
Librarian Publications: Chairman issues an occasional newsletter

Association of South-East Asian Publishers (ASEAP)*, c/o University of Malaysia Press, Pantai Valley, Kuala Lumpur, Malaysia
President: Encik Ghazali Yunua; *Secretary-General:* R Narayana Menon

Bibliographical Society of Australia and New Zealand (BSANZ)*, 117 St George's Rd, North Fitzroy, Victoria 3068, Australia
Secretary: Trevor Mills
Publication: Bibliographical Society of Australia and New Zealand Bulletin; Broadsheet; Occasional Publications

Books in Progress, Literature Department, Arts Council of Great Britain, 9 Long Acre, London WC2, UK
Register of Literary and Technical Research Confidential (i.e. not open for inspection) register of works in progress. Writers planning to start work on a book or research project may contact the register to elicit whether subject already covered by another writer. There is no charge for writers registering works for inclusion or for enquiries

Bureau de l'union internationale pour la protection des oeuvres littéraires et artistiques, see International Copyright Union for the Protection of Literary and Artistic Works

Centre de Documentation économique et sociale africaine (CEDESA)*, 7 pl Royale, B-1000 Brussels, Belgium
Centre for African Economic and Social Documentation
Secretary-General: J-B Cuyvers
Publications: Bibliographical Enquiries, Documentary monographs

Centre régional de Promotion du Livre en Afrique*, BP 1646, Yaoundé, Cameroun
Regional Centre for Book Promotion in Africa
Secretary: William Moutchia
Publication: Bulletin

Centro Di (International Documentation Centre), see under Italian publishers

Centro Regional para el Fomento del Libro en América Latina y el Caribe (CERLAL), Calle 70 No 9-52, Apdo Aereo 17438, Bogotá, Colombia
Regional Centre for Encouragement of Books in Latin America and Caribbean
Director: Jaime Jaramillo Uribe; *Secretary-General:* Lucila de Jíménez
Publications: CERLAL; noticias sobre el Libro y Bibliografía (news on books and bibliographies); *Boletín Bibliográfico del CERLAL* (current Latin-American bibliography)

Commonwealth Library Association*, 2a Ruthven Rd, PO Box 534, Kingston 10 Jamaica Tel: 9264929
Secretary: Mrs C P Fray
Publication: COMLA Newsletter (quarterly)

Congress of South-East Asian Librarians IV (CONSAL IV)*, c/o The National Library of Thailand, Samsen Road, Bangkok 3, Thailand
Chairman: Mrs Maenmas Chavalit
Publications include: Proceedings of Congresses

Conseil International des Associations de Bibliothèques de Théologie, Gereonstr 2, Cologne 1, Federal Republic of Germany
International Council of Theological Library Associations
Secretary: J A Cervelló-Margalef

Distripress, see Association for the Promotion of the International Circulation of the Press

East and Central Africa Regional Branch of the International Council of Archives (ECARBICA)*, c/o Kenya National Archives, Jogoo House 'A', PO Box 30520, Nairobi, Kenya
Publication: ECARBICA Journal

European Association of Directory Publishers, rue Antoine Dansaert 42, B-1000 Brussels, Belgium Tel: 5124499
Association Européene des Editeurs d'Annuaires
Europäischer Adressbuchverleger — Verband
President: Konrad Bryde; *Secretary-General:* Jean Lerat

F I D, see International Federation for Documentation

Fédération Internationale des Libraires (FIL), see International Booksellers Federation

Fédération Internationale des Traducteurs (FIT)*, Heiveldstr 269, B-9110 Sint-Amandsberg, Belgium
International Federation of Translators
Secretary-General: Dr Rene Haeseryn

Groupe des Editeurs de Livres de la CEE, 111 ave du Parc, B-1060 Brussels, Belgium Tel: (02) 5382167
EEC Book Publishers Group

Intergovernmental Copyright Committee, Copyright Division, UNESCO, pl de Fontenoy, F-75700 Paris, France
Chairman: Ndéné Ndiaye

International Association for Mass Communication Research, c/o Professor J D Halloran, Centre for Mass Communication Research, University of Leicester, 104 Regent Road, Leicester LE1 7LT, UK Tel: (0533) 555557
Association internationale des etudes et recherches sur l'information
Secretary-General: Emil Dusiska; *Administrative Secretary:* Peggy Gray
Publications include: Mass Media and Socialization; Mass Media and Man's View of Society; Mass Media and National Cultures

International Association of Agricultural Librarians and Documentalists — IAALD*, Library, Ministry of Agriculture Fisheries and Food, Central Veterinary Laboratory, New Haw, Weybridge, Surrey KT15 3NB, UK
Association Internationale des Bibliothécaires et Documentalistes Agricoles
Secretary-Treasurer: D E Gray
Publications: Quarterly Bulletin; Current Agricultural Serials; Primer for Agricultural Libraries

International Association of Law Libraries (IALL)*, c/o Vanderbilt Law Library, Nashville, Tennessee 37203, USA
Association internationale des bibliothèques de droit
Secretary-Treasurer: Professor Arno Liivak; *President:* Professor Igor I Kavass
Publications: International Journal of Law Libraries; IALL Newsletter; Directory

International Association of Literary Critics, 38 rue du Faubourg-St-Jacques, F-75014 Paris, France
Association internationale des critiques littéraires
President: Robert André
Publication: Revue

International Association of Metropolitan City Libraries (INTAMEL), Hamburger Offentliche Bücherhallen, Gertrudenkirchhof 9, Hamburg, Federal Republic of Germany

International Association of Music Libraries, c/o Svenskt Musikhistoriskt Arkiv, Sibyllegatan 2, S-11451 Stockholm, Sweden
Association internationale des bibliothèques musicales
Internationale Vereinigung der Musikbibliotheken
President: Prof Barry S Brook (City University of New York); *Secretary-General:* Anders Lönn
Publication: Fontes artis musicae

International Association of Orientalist Librarians
Secretary-Treasurer: John E Leíde, c/o Asian Studies Program, University of Hawaii at Manoa, 315 Moore Hall, 1890 East-West Road, Honolulu, Hawaii 96822, USA
Publication: International Association of Orientalist Librarians Bulletin (half-yearly)

International Association of School Librarianship, School of Librarianship, Western Michigan University, Kalamazoo, Michigan 49008, USA
Publications: Newsletter of the International Association of School Librarianship (quarterly to members); *Annual Conference Proceedings; Directory of National School Library Associations; People to Contact for Visiting School Libraries/Media Centers*

International Association of Scholarly Publishers (IASP), Tickner & Fields, 383 Orange St, New Haven, Connecticut 06511, USA
Dir: C Kerr

International Association of Sound Archivesderkolon*, Imperial War Museum, Lambeth Road, London SE1 6HZ, UK
Publication: Phonographic Bulletin

International Association of Technological University Libraries (IATUL)*, c/o Bibliotheek Technische Hogeschool Twente, Campus Drienerlo, Postbus 217, Enschede, Netherlands
(Association internationale des bibliothèques d'universités polytechniques)
President: Dr G A Hamel; *Secretary:* Dr Sven Westberg, Chalmers Tekniska Høgskolas Bibliotek, Fack, Gothenburg, Sweden
Publications: IATUL Proceedings; IATUL Conference Proceedings

INTERNATIONAL ORGANIZATIONS 433

International Board on Books for Young People (IBBY), CH-4051 Basle, Leonhardsgraben 38a, Switzerland
Secretary: Mrs Leena Maissen
Publications: Bookbird (quarterly); *20 Years of IBBY; IBBY's International Guide to Sources of Information about Children's Literature; Congress Reports*

International Booksellers Federation (IBF), Grünangergasse 4, A-1010 Vienna, Austria
Fédération Internationale des Librairies (FIL)
Internationale Buchhändler-Vereinigung (IBV)
General Secretary: Dr Gerhard Prosser

International Comparative Literature Association*, Institut de littératures modernes comparées, 17 rue de la Sorbonne, Paris 5e, France
Association internationale de littérature comparée
Secretaries-General: Douwe W Fokkema, 31 Ramstr, Utrecht, Netherlands; Frederick Garber, State University of New York, Binghampton, NY 13901, USA
Founded: 1954

International Confederation of Societies of Authors and Composers, 11 rue Keppler, F-75116 Paris, France
Confédération internationale des sociétés d'auteurs et compositeurs
Secretary-General: Jean-Alexis Ziegler
Publication: Interauteurs

International Copyright Union for the Protection of Literary and Artistic Works, 32 chemin des Colombettes, Geneva, Switzerland
Administers the Berne Convention

International Council of Theological Library Associations, see Conseil International des Associations de Bibliothèques de Théologie

International Council on Archives*, 60 rue des Francs-Bourgeois, F-75003 Paris, France
Conseil international des archives
General Secretary: Dr Carlos Wyffels
Publications: Archivum; ADPA/Archives and Automation; Bulletin of the Microfilm Committee; Bulletin of the ICA

International Federation for Documentation (FID), PO Box 30115, 2500 GC, The Hague, Netherlands
Fédération internationale de documentation
Publications: FID News Bulletin; International Forum on Information and Documentation; R & D Projects in Documentation and Librarianship; FID Directory; Annual Report; Extensions and Corrections to the UDC (annual)
Proceedings of Congresses and Seminars, UDC editions in several languages, Studies on Information Science, Manuals, Bibliographies and Directories

International Federation of Film Archives, Coudenberg 70, B-1000 Brussels, Belgium Tel: (02) 5111390
Fédération internationale des archives du film
Executive Secretary: Brigitte van der Elst

International Federation of Library Associations and Institutions (IFLA), Netherlands Congress Building, Postbus 82128, 2508 EC, The Hague, Netherlands
Fédération internationale des associations de bibliothécaires et des bibliothèques
Secretary-General: Miss M Wijnstroom
Publications: IFLA Journal including *IFLA News, IFLA Annual, IFLA Directory, IFLA Publications* (series of monographs, published by K G Saur, Munich)

International Fiction Association, Department of German and Russian, University of New Brunswick, Frederiction, New Brunswick, Canada
Publication: The International Fiction Review (biannual)

International Group of Scientific, Technical and Medical Publishers (STM), Keizersgracht 462, 1016 GE Amsterdam, Netherlands Tel: (020) 225214
Secretary-General: P Nijhoff Asser

International Institute for Children's Literature and Reading Research, UNESCO category C, A-1040 Vienna, Mayerhofgasse 6, Austria Tel: 651754
Institut International de Littérature pour Enfants et de Recherches sur la Lecture
Director: Dr Lucia Binder
Publications include: Bookbird; Jugend und Buch; PA-Kontakte

International Institute of Iberoamerican Literature, 1312 CL, University of Pittsburgh, Pa 15260, USA
Secretary-Treasurer: Bruce Stiehm
Publications: Revista Iberoamericana; Memorias

International League of Antiquarian Booksellers*, 5 Bloomsbury St, London WC1B 3QE, UK Tel: (01) 580 3976
President: Stanley Crowe (at above address);
General Secretary: Dr Maria Conradt, Poststr 14-16, D-2000 Hamburg 36, Federal Republic of Germany Tel: (040) 343236

International Publishers Association, 3 ave de Miremont, CH-1206 Geneva, Switzerland
Secretary-General: J Alexis Koutchoumow
Publication: IPA Publishing News
Founded: 1896

International Reading Association, 800 Barksdale Rd, PO Box 8139, Newark, Delaware 19711, USA

International Scientific Film Library (ISFL)*, 31 rue Vautier, B-1040 Brussels, Belgium
Cinémathèque scientifique internationale
Director-Curator: P Bormans
Publications: Catalogue of Films Deposited; The Pioneers of the Scientific Cinema (series)
Founded: 1961

International Study Group of Restorers of Archives, Libraries and Graphic Reproductions, Geschäftsstelle der IADA, Postfach 540, 3550 Marburg, Federal Republic of Germany Tel: (06421) 25078
Internationale Arbeitsgemeinschaft der Archiv-, Bibliotheks-und Grafikrestauratoren
General Secretary: Ludwig Ritterpusch
Publications: IADA-Mitteilungen, in: Maltechnik

International Translations Centre, Doelenstr 101, 2611 NS Delft, Netherlands
The object of the Centre is to encourage, improve and facilitate the use of literature published in less accessible languages and of interest to science and industry, and also to promote international co-operation in this field
Director of Centre: D van Bergeijk
Publications: World Transindex; Journals in Translation

International Youth Library*, D-8000 Munich 22, Kaulbachstr 11a, Federal Republic of Germany
Internationale Jugendbibliothek
Director: Walter Scherf
Publications: Catalogues of various exhibitions; *Prize Book Catalogue; The Best of the Best; Bewältigung der Gegenwart? Das Porträt der Frau in der zeitgenössischen Jugendliteratur*

Internationale Buchhändler-Vereinigung (IBV), see International Booksellers Federation

Ligue des Bibliothèques Européenes de Recherche (LIBER), c/o The Library, European University Institute, Badia Fiesolana, 50016 San Domenico di Fiesole, Italy
League of European Research Libraries
President: Dr K W Humphreys
Publication: LIBER Bulletin

Middle East Librarians Association, Room 310, Main Library, Ohio State University, 1858 Neil Avenue Mall, Columbus, Ohio 43210, USA Tel: (614) 4223362
Secretary and Treasurer: Marsha McClintock
Publication: MELA Notes (three times a year)

Nordisk Musikforleggerunion, Gothersgade 9-11, DK-1123, Copenhagen, Denmark
Also: Postboks 1499, Vika, Oslo, Norway
Nordic Music Publishers Union

Nordiska Vetenskapliga Bibliotekariefõrbundet*, Aalborg University Library, Postboks 8200, DK-9220 Aalborg OEst, Denmark
Scandinavian Association of Research Librarians
Secretary-Treasurer: Lizzi Kirkegaard

P E N, International, 7 Dilke St, London SW3 4JE, UK Tel: (01) 352 9549
A World Association of Writers
General-Secretary: Peter Elstob
Publications: Broadsheet; New Poetry and *New Stories* (in collaboration with Arts Council) (English Centre); *Bulletin of Selected Books* (in English and French, with the assistance of UNESCO); various regional bulletins

The **Penman** Club, 175 Pall Mall, Leigh-on-Sea, Essex SS9 1RE, UK Tel: Southend-on-Sea 74438 (STD Code 0702)
Secretary: Leonard G Stubbs
Literary advice, criticism

Private Libraries Association (PLA), Ravelston, South View Rd, Pinner, Middlesex, UK
Executive Secretary: Frank Broomhead
Publications include: The Private Library (official journal); *Newsletter*

S T M, see International Group of Scientific, Technical and Medical Publishers

Seminar on the Acquisition of Latin American Library Materials (SALALM), SALALM Secretariat, Memorial Library, University of Wisconsin-Madison, Madison, Wisconsin 53706, USA Tel: (608) 2623240
Executive Secretary: Suzanne Hodgman
Publications: Newsletter; Final Report and Working Papers; Microfilming Projects Newsletter; Bibliography Series

Société africaine de Librairie-Papeterie (SALP)*, BP20, Libreville, Gabon
African Society of the Stationery and Book Trade

Société internationale de Bibliographie classique, 11 ave René Coty, F-75014 Paris, France
General Secretary: Juliette Ernst Tel: 3276790
Publication: L'Année philologique (Bibliographie de l'antiquité grécolatine 1923 ss)

Société internationale des Bibliothèques-Musées des Arts du Spectacle (SIBMAS), 1 rue de Sully, 75004 Paris, France Tel: 2774421
International Society of Libraries and Museums for the Performing Arts
Publications: L'Information du Spectacle; Bibliotheques et Musées des Arts du Spectacle dans le Monde (both France)

South East Asian Regional Branch of the International Council on Archives (SARBICA), c/o National Archives of Malaysia, Jalan Sultan, Petaling Jaya, Malaysia Tel: 569311/569815
Chairman: Zakiah Hanum Nor (Malaysia)
Publications: Southeast Asian Archives; Southeast Asian Microfilms Newsletter; Masterlist of Southeast Asian Microforms

Standing Conference of African Library Schools (SCALS)*, c/o School of Librarians, Archivists and Documentalists, University of Dakar, BP 3252 Dakar, Senegal
Publications: SCALS Newsletter

Standing Conference of African University Libraries (SCAUL)*, c/o E Bejide Bankole, University Librarian, University of Lagos, Yaba, Lagos, Nigeria
Publication: SCAUL Newsletter

Standing Conference on Library Materials on Africa (SCOLMA), c/o Institute of Commonwealth Studies, 27 Russell Sq, London WC1B 5DS, UK Tel: (01) 580 5876
Publication: African Research and Documentation (Subscriptions to Mrs P Naish, Centre for West African Studies, University of Birmingham, Birmingham B15 2SD, UK)

Union des Editeurs de Langue française*, 117 blvd St-Germain, F-75279 Paris cedex 06, France
Union of French-language Publishers

Union of Writers of the African Peoples*, c/o Ghana Association of Writers, PO Box 4414, Accra, Ghana
Union des Ecrivains Negro Africains
Among its objectives: to operate a writers' publishing co-operative; to encourage the use of Swahili as the common language of all black African peoples
Secretary-General: Wole Soyinka, Dept of Literature, University of Ife, Ife-Ife, Nigeria
Publication: African World Alternatives

West African Library Association (WALA)*, c/o Ghana Library Association, PO Box 4105, Accra, Ghana
Publications: West African Libraries Newsletter

United Nations Agencies with Publishing Activities

Food and Agriculture Organization of the United Nations (FAO)*, Via delle Terme di Caracalla, I-00100 Rome, Italy Tel: (06) 5797 Cable Add: Foodagri Rome
Director-General: E Saouma; *Chief Editor:* D J Grossman; *Sales, Advertising & Publicity Dir:* C Beauchamp
Subjects: Agriculture, World Food Situation, Economics & Statistics, Fisheries, Forestry & Forest Products, Nutrition, Legislation, Educational Materials
Founded: 1945
A specialized agency of the United Nations, the Food and Agriculture Organization was created in 1945. Since the purpose of FAO is to increase world agricultural production and raise the standard of living, all its publications are directed toward that goal. The FAO titles consist of monographs, periodicals, official records of the work of FAO, yearbooks and annuals — in sum, what the FAO describes as a 'world intelligence service on production, price and trade that covers almost every commodity used to feed, clothe and house people throughout the world'. Unsolicited manuscripts are automatically rejected. Technical articles of no more than 2,500 words on international aspects of the animal industry, forestry, and food and nutrition are occasionally accepted; no payment is made
ISBN Publisher's Prefixes: 92-5 (publications by Headquarters), 92-851 (African Regional Office), 92-852 (Regional Office for Asia and Far East), 92-853 (European Regional Office), 92-854 (Latin American Regional Office), 92-855 (Near East Regional Office)

Inter-Governmental Maritime Consultative Organization (IMCO)*, 101 Piccadilly, London W1, UK Tel: (01) 499 9040 Cable Add: Inmarcor Telex: 04423588
Subjects: Texts of International Maritime Treaties concluded under its auspices, Maritime Technical Publications
1978: 17 titles
ISBN Publisher's Prefix: 92-801

International Atomic Energy Agency (IAEA), Vienna International Centre, Wagramerstr 5, Postfach 100, A-1400 Vienna, Austria Tel: 2360 Cable Add: Inatom Vienna
Publications Dir: A K Brown; *Editorial:* L A Self; *Sales, Publicity:* K Fiala; *Production, Rights & Permissions:* W Dietl
Subjects: Life Sciences, Nuclear Safety and Environmental Protection, Physics, Chemistry, Geology and Raw Materials, Reactors and Nuclear Power, Industrial Applications, Miscellaneous
1978: 47 titles *1979:* 57 titles *Founded:* 1957
The International Atomic Energy Agency is an international organization within the United Nations family, having the general purpose of seeking 'to accelerate and enlarge the contribution of atomic energy to peace, health and prosperity throughout the world'. The Agency's publications result, almost exclusively, from its own activities; published material is of intense interest only to a relatively small group of scientists and technicians and, therefore, unlikely to be published commercially.
ISBN Publisher's Prefix: 92-0

International Bureau of Education, Palais Wilson, CH-1211 Geneva 14, Switzerland Tel: 313735 Cable Add: Intereduc Geneve Telex: 22644
Dir: James B Chandler; *Chief, Publications Unit:* Rodney Stock; *Editorial, Sales, Production, Publicity, Rights & Permissions:* See United Nations Educational, Scientific and Cultural Organization
Orders to: National distributors of Unesco publications, or Unesco, 7 pl de Fontenoy, F-75700 Paris, France
Subject: Comparative Education
Founded: 1925

International Institute for Educational Planning (IIEP)*, 7-9 rue Eugène-Delacroix, F-75016 Paris, France Tel: (01) 5042822 Cable Add: Eduplan Paris Telex: 620074
Dir: Michel Debeaurais
Publications Officer: John Hall
Subjects: Economics of education, costs and financing; administration and management of education (including statistics, methodologies, techniques and models); curriculum development and evaluation (including the qualitative aspects of education); manpower and employment; educational technology; etc
1979: 30 titles *Founded:* 1963
Established by UNESCO, IIEP is an international centre for advanced training and research in educational planning. The Institute's aim is to contribute to the development of education by expanding both knowledge and the supply of competent professionals in the field of educational planning. In this endeavour the Institute cooperates with interested training and research institutions throughout the world. IIEP is financed by UNESCO and by voluntary contributions from individual member states. The programme and budget of the Institute is approved by its own Governing Board.
ISBN Publisher's Prefix: 92-803

International Labour Organisation (ILO)*, International Labour Office, ILO Publications, 4 route des Morillons, CH-1211 Geneva 22, Switzerland Tel: (022) 996111 Cable Add: Interlab Geneva Telex: 22271
Director-General: Francis Blanchard; *Chief, Editorial Services:* R P Payró; *Chief, Sales, Marketing & Foreign Rights Services:* I M C S Elsmark
Branch Offs: 87-91 New Bond St, London W1Y 9LA, UK; 1750 New York Ave NW, Washington, DC 20006, USA
Subjects: Conditions of Work and Welfare, Cooperatives, Developing Countries & Technical Cooperation, Economics, Employment and Employment Creation, Holidays & Weekly Rest, Human Rights, Labour & Discrimination, Standards & Administration, Migration of Workers & Popular Questions, Productivity & Management Development & Training, Occupational Safety & Health, Statistics, Social Security, Trade Unions, Unemployment, Vocational Guidance & Training, Wages & Hours of Work, Worker's Education & Vocational Training, etc
Founded: 1919
Miscellaneous: Publishes periodicals: International Labour Revue, Official Bulletin, Legislative Series, Social and Labour Bulletin, Bulletin of Labour Statistics, Year Book of Labour Statistics, Documents & Proceedings of the International Labour Organisation & the International Labour Conference, Labour Management Relations Series, International Labour Documentation, Occupational Safety and Health Series, Management Development Series
From the creation of the ILO in 1919, publishing has formed an important part of its activities. The publishing work falls into six main categories: international exchange of factual information; analysis of trends in social affairs; issuing the results of ILO research, including comparative studies as a basis for international cooperation in

solving economic and social problems; issuing the required reports for the discussions of international labour conferences leading to the adoption of international labour standards; providing government officials, employers and workers with practical information and guidance; and issuing official records.
This substantial publishing programme has over 1,300 titles in print which cover not only studies, monographs, handbooks and periodicals, but also reports on conditions and practices in different countries prepared for the General Conference, regional conferences and meetings for special industries and subjects.
ISBN Publisher's Prefix: 92-2

International Telecommunication Union (ITU)*, pl des Nations, CH-1211 Geneva 20, Switzerland
Secretary-General: Mohamed Mili
The ITU was founded in 1865 as the International Telegraphic Union. It became the International Telecommunication Union in 1934 and a specialized agency of the UN in 1947. Structure: 4 permanent organs – General Secretariat, International Telegraph and Telephone Consultative Committee (CCITT), International Radio Consultative Committee (CCIR) and the International Frequency Registration Board (IFRB). It encourages world cooperation for the improvement and rational use of telecommunications.
ISBN Publisher's Prefixes: 92-61, 92-71

U N C T A D, see United Nations Conference on Trade and Development

U N E S C O, see United Nations Educational, Scientific and Cultural Organization

U N E S C O Institute for Education (UIE)*, Feldbrunnenstr 58, D-2000 Hamburg 13, Federal Republic of Germany
The UIE was created in 1951 with the financial support of UNESCO and a number of member states. It is funded by the Federal Republic of Germany, UNESCO and other donors, and housed in premises provided by the City of Hamburg. It is a research centre which has enabled more than 2,000 scholars to participate in international cooperative research projects and has developed a particular interest in lifelong education. Major areas of the current research programme include the relation of lifelong education to national systems of education, to school curriculum, to basic education, teacher training, evaluation and research. Publications include over 120 titles and the quarterly *International Review of Education.*
1978: 7 titles
ISBN Publisher's Prefix: 92-820

United Nations*, Sales Section, Publishing Service, 801 United Nations Plaza, New York, NY 10017, USA Tel: (212) 7541234
Chief of Section: Bjorn Hafgren
European Office: Palais des Nations, Geneva, Switzerland
Chief of Unit: Roland Furstenberg
Subjects: Reference, Economics, International Trade, International Law, Social Science
Founded: 1945
Since 1946, United Nations has published more than 2,000 reports, studies, annual surveys, yearbooks, and monthly and quarterly periodicals in addition to the United Nations official records.
Reflecting the varied work of the Organization, the subjects include international trade, world and regional economic questions, international law, social questions, atomic energy, public administration, and literature concerning the role and activities of the United Nations.
ISBN Publisher's Prefix: 92-1

United Nations Conference on Trade and Development (UNCTAD), Palais des Nations, CH-1211 Geneva 10, Switzerland Tel: (022) 346011 Cable Add: Unations Geneve Telex: 289696
Secretary-General: Gamani Corea
Subjects: Trade & Development
Founded: 1964

United Nations Educational, Scientific and Cultural Organization (UNESCO), 7 pl de Fontenoy, F-75700 Paris, France Tel: (01) 5771610 Cable Add: Unesco Paris Telex: 204461 Paris
Director-General: Amadou-Mahtar M'Bow; *Director, The Unesco Press:* Ramón Nieto; *Editorial:* Georges Provenchere; *Sales:* Bruce Clark (English), Eduardo Sainz (French and Spanish); *Production:* Jean-Louis Ferru; *Publicity:* Alison Clayson (English), Michiko Tanaka (French and Spanish); *Rights & Permissions:* Suzanne Adlung
Orders to: The Unesco Press, Commercial Services Division (at above address)
Subjects: Education, Science, Social Science, Culture, Communications
Bookshop: Unesco (at above address)
1978: 88 titles *1979:* 87 titles *Founded:* 1946
Miscellaneous: Co-publish with commercial publishers under joint imprint.
The work of UNESCO, a specialized agency of the United Nations, is primarily concerned with programs in the scientific, educational and cultural fields. It provides assistance to its member nations for programs which develop and improve educational facilities, stimulate scientific research, encourage the exchange of ideas and the free flow of information and bring about mutual understanding of cultures.
UNESCO now has more than 1,000 titles in print, intended for specialists in the fields of libraries, culture and art, international exchange, education, mass communications, museums and monuments, social sciences, and science and technology.
UNESCO publishes eight periodicals and three series (issued irregularly) in the fields of social science, of mass communications and statistics.
UNESCO acts as Standard Book Numbering Agency, administering ISBNs, for UN publications.
ISBN Publisher's Prefix: 92-3

United Nations Institute for Training and Research (UNITAR)*, 801 United Nations Plaza, New York, NY 10017, USA Tel: (212) 7541234 Cable Add: Uninstar
Subjects: Peaceful Settlement of Disputes, Transfer of Technology, Environment, Communications, Economic Development, UN Functions

United Nations Research Institute for Social Development (UNRISD), Palais des Nations, CH-1211 Geneva 10, Switzerland Tel: 988400 Cable Add: Unations Geneve Telex: 289696
Dir: Solon L Barraclough
Orders to: Reference Center (at above address)
Subjects: Social Development, Food systems, Participation
1978: 3 titles *1979:* 10 titles *Founded:* 1963

Universal Postal Union (UPU)*, CP, CH-3000 Berne 15, Switzerland Tel: (031) 432211
Director-General: Mohamed Ibrahim Sobhi
1978: 38 titles *Founded:* 1874
ISBN Publisher's Prefix: 92-62

World Health Organization (WHO)*, 20 ave Appia, CH-1211 Geneva 27, Switzerland Tel: (022) 346061 Cable Add: Unisante Geneva Telex: 27821
Chief, Distribution & Sales Section: E S Annaheim
Subjects: Reference, Medicine, Psychology, Social Science, Textbooks
The pattern of WHO publications derives, in part, from the work of earlier and similar organizations — the Office International d'Hygiène Publique, and the Health Organization of the League of Nations, from which WHO inherited certain functions.
The main purpose of WHO's publications programme is to convey information relating to the various aspects of medicine and public health.
ISBN Publisher's Prefix: 92-4

World Meteorological Organization (WMO)*, CP 5, CH-1211 Geneva 20, Switzerland
In early 1951, the WMO took over the work of the 73-year-old International Meteorological Organization; later that year, it became a specialized agency of the United Nations. It promotes world-wide cooperation in weather science by establishing a network of observation stations, helps to bring about the development of service centres, sets up systems of rapid exchange of information, standardizes statistics and observations, furthers the application of meteorology to aviation, shipping, water problems, agriculture and other human activities and encourages research and training
The publications of WMO include the records and reports of the World Meteorological Congresses; cloud atlases; manuals on nomenclature; weather reporting; and guides to regulations and instrumentation.
ISBN Publisher's Prefix: 92-63

Other International Organizations with Publishing Activities

Commonwealth Agricultural Bureaux, Farnham House, Farnham Royal, Slough, Berkshire SL2 3BN, UK Tel: Farnham Common 2281 (STD code 02814) Cable Add: Comag Slough Telex: 847964 Comagg G
Executive Director: N G Jones; *Editorial:* J R Metcalfe; *Sales, Publicity, Rights & Permissions:* J Newton; *Production:* P Healey
Subjects: Agriculture, Applied Biology, Forestry, Economics, Rural Sociology, Nutrition, Environmental Medicine
1978: 10 titles *1979:* 10 titles *Founded:* 1929
ISBN Publisher's Prefix: 0-85198

Conference of European Churches, 150 route de Ferney, PO Box 66, CH-1211 Geneva 20, Switzerland Tel: (022) 989400 Cable Add: Oikiymene Telex: 23423 Oik Ch
General Secretary: Dr Glen Garfield Williams

Orders to: (English) The Saint Andrew Press, 121 George St, Edinburgh EH2 4YN, UK; (French) Editions Labor et Fides, 1 rue Beauregard, CH-1204 Geneva, Switzerland; (German) Verlag Otto Lembeck, Leerbachstr 42, D-6000 Frankfurt am Main, Federal Republic of Germany
Subjects: Ecumenical Theology, International Relationships
1978: 2 titles *1979:* 2 titles *Founded:* 1959
ISBN Publisher's Prefixes: 0-99070 (English), 2-88070 (French), 3-88070 (German)

Council of Europe, Publications Section, Palais de l'Europe, F-67006 Strasbourg Cedex, France Tel: (88) 614961 Cable Add: Europa Strasbourg Telex: 870943
Head of Publications: P Michelet
Subjects: Human Rights, Law, Criminology, Public Health, Sociology, Nature, Consumer Protection, Education, Sport
1978: 36 titles *1979:* 43 titles *Founded:* 1949

International African Institute, 38 King Street, London WC2E 8JR, UK Tel: (01) 379 7636 Cable Add: Afrilac London WC2
Director: Dr David Dalby; *Editorial:* Dr Jocelyn Murray; *Rights & Permissions:* Bridget Itsueli
Branch Offs: Paris, Nigeria
Subjects: Academic books on Africa, including History, Ethnography, Environmental Studies, Bibliography
1978: 3 titles *1979:* 3 titles *Founded:* 1926
Miscellaneous: 2,500 institutions and individuals are subscribing members and the governing body includes representatives from 50 countries, 30 in Africa
ISBN Publisher's Prefix: 0-85302

International Union for Conservation of Nature and Natural Resources (IUCN), ave du Mont Blanc, CH-1196 Gland, Switzerland Tel: (022) 643254 Cable Add: Iucnature Gland Telex: 22618 Iucn Ch
Dir General: Dr D A Munro
Orders to: Bowker Publishing Co, PO Box 5, Epping, Essex CM16 4BU, UK (for all regions except North America); Unipub, Box 433, Murray Hill Station, New York, NY 10016, USA (for North America)
Subjects: Conservation and development, Land and freshwater animals, Marine and coastal ecology and management, National parks and other protected areas, regional conservation, Environmental policy and law papers
1978: 9 titles *1979:* 6 titles *Founded:* 1948
ISBN Publisher's Prefix: 2-88032

International Union of Geological Sciences (IUGS), Room 177, 601 Booth St, Ottawa, Canada K1A 0E8 Tel: (613) 9954927 Telex: 0533117 Emar Ott
Union internationale des Sciences Géologiques
Secretary-General, Rights & Permissions: Dr W W Hutchison; *Editorial:* Dr V Lafferty
Subjects: Earth Sciences, Quarterly *Episodes* (since 1978)
Founded: 1961

World Council of Churches (WCC), 150 route de Ferney, CP 66, CH-1211 Geneva 20, Switzerland Tel: (022) 989400 Cable Add: Oikoumene Geneva Telex: 23423 Oik Ch
General Secretary: Dr Philip A Potter; *Director, Publications:* Jan H Kok
Subjects: Ecumenism, Church Unity, Mission and Evangelism, Dialogue with people of other faiths and ideologies, Social Justice, Human Rights, Development, Racism, etc
1978: 35 titles *1979:* 30 titles *Founded:* 1948
ISBN Publisher's Prefix: 2-82544

World Intellectual Property Organization (WIPO), 34 chemin des Colombettes, CH-1211 Geneva 20, Switzerland Tel: (022) 999111 Cable Add: Ompi Telex: 22376
Organisation Mondiale de la Propriété Intellectuelle
Director General: Dr Arpad Bogsch
Subjects: Intellectual Property, Industrial Property, Copyright, Neighbouring Rights (all multilingual)
Publications: La Droit d'Auteur; La Propriété industrielle; Les Marques internationales

International Bibliography

Books

Adressbuch für den deutschsprachigen Buchhandel (Directory of the German-language Book Trade), Buchhändler-Vereinigung GmbH, Adressbuch-Redaktion, Postfach 2404, D-6000 Frankfurt 1, Federal Republic of Germany

The African Book World and Press: A Directory, Hans Zell Publishers Ltd, PO Box 56, Oxford OX1 3EL, UK. Information in English and French

African Books in Print, Mansell Information/Publishing Ltd, 3 Bloomsbury Pl, London WC1A 2QA, UK

Asian Book Trade Directory, Nirmala Sadanand Publishers, 35c Tardeo Rd, Bombay 34 WB

Australian and Pacific Book Prices Current, OP Books Pty Ltd, PO Box 591, Brookvale, NSW 2109, Australia

Author's and Writer's Who's Who, Burke's Peerage Ltd, 56 Walton St, London SW3 1BB, UK

Bibliographie nationale courante de l'Année ... des pays d'Afrique d'expression française (National Bibliography for the Year ... of Francophone African Countries), annual bibliography covering books and other materials, published in Francophone Africa since 1967, Ecole de Bibliothécaires, Archivistes, et Documentalistes, Université de Dakar, BP 2006, Dakar, Senegal

Bibliography of the Middle East; A complete and classified list of all the books published in about ten Middle Eastern countries, Damascus University Library, Damascus, Syria

Bibliothèques et Musées des Arts du Spectacle dans le Monde (Performing Arts Libraries and Museums of the World), Société internationale des Bibliothèques et Musées des arts du Spectacle, c/o President, 1 rue de Sully, F-75004 Paris, France

Book-Auction records, Dawsons of Pall Mall, Cannon House, Folkestone, Kent CT19 5EE, UK

Book Markets in The Americas, Asia, Africa, Australasia, Euromonitor Publications Ltd, PO Box 115, 41 Russell Sq, London WC1B 5DL, UK

Book Markets in Western Europe, Euromonitor Publications Ltd, PO Box 115, 41 Russell Sq, London WC1B 5DL, UK

The Book Revolution; a detailed examination and analysis of book production and distribution throughout the world, George G Harrap & Company Ltd, 182-184 High Holborn, London WC1V 7AX, UK

The Book Trade of the World, Verlag für Buchmarktforschung, D-2000 Hamburg 1, Beim Strohhause 34, Federal Republic of Germany. André Deutsch Ltd, 105 Great Russell St, London WC1B 3LJ; R R Bowker Co, 1180 Ave of the Americas, New York, NY 10036, USA

Bookdealers in India, Pakistan and Sri Lanka, Sheppard Press, PO Box 42, Russell Chambers, Covent Garden, London WC2E 8AX, UK

The Bowker Annual of Library and Book Trade Information, Bowker Publishing Company, Erasmus House, Epping, Essex, CM16 4BU, UK

British Library Catalogue of Printed Books to 1975 (first volumes, of estimated total of 360, published in 1979). Clive Bingley Ltd, 1-19 New Oxford St, London WC1A, UK

Cassell's Directory of Publishing, Cassell & Co Ltd, 35 Red Lion Sq, London WC1R 4SG, UK

Catalogue général des ouvrages parus en langue française (Catalogue of Books Published in the French Language), Cercle de la Librairie, 117 blvd St-Germain, F-75279 Paris cedex 06, France

Clegg's Directory of the World's Book Trade, James Clarke & Co Ltd, 7 All Saints Passage, Cambridge CB2 3LS, UK

Cumulative Book Index, H W Wilson Co, 950 University Ave, New York, NY 10452, USA (world index of English language books)

Current African Directories; incorporating *African Companies*, a guide to directories published in or concerned with Africa, and to sources of information on business enterprises in Africa. CBD Research Ltd, 154 High St, Beckenham, Kent BR3 1EA, UK

Current European Directories; annotated guide to international, national, city and specialised directories and similar reference works for all countries of Europe, CBD Research Ltd, 154 High St, Beckenham, Kent BR3 1EA, UK

Dictionarium bibliothecarii praticum (ad usum internationalem in XXII linguis). (The Librarian's practical dictionary in 22 languages), Akadémiai Kiadó, H-1054 Budapest V, Alkotmány u 21, Hungary; and K G Saur KG, D-8000 Munich 71, Postfach 711009, Federal Republic of Germany

Directory of East African Libraries, Makerere University Library, Kampala, Uganda

Directory of Government Printers and Prominent Bookshops in the African Region, UN Economic Commission for Africa, Africa Hall, PO Box 3001, Addis Ababa, Ethiopia

La Empresa del Libro en América Latina (Companies in the Book Trade in Latin America), R R Bowker Co, 1180 Ave of the Americas, New York, NY 10036, USA

Ensemble; international literary yearbook (Text in English, French, German) Verlagsgruppe Langen-Müller Herbig, D-8000 Munich 19, Hubertusstr 4, Federal Republic of Germany

European Bookdealers: A Directory of Dealers in Secondhand and Antiquarian Books on the Continent of Europe, Sheppard Press Ltd, PO Box 42, Russell Chambers, Covent Garden, London WC2E 8AX, UK

European Law Libraries Guide (Guide européen des bibliothèques de droit), Morgan-Grampian Book Publishing Co Ltd, 30 Calderwood St, Woolwich, London SE18 6QH, UK

European Library Directory, Geographical and Bibliographical Guide Leo S Olschki, Viuzzo del Possetto, I-50126 Florence, Italy

Guia de Bibliografía Especializada (Guide to Specialist Libraries), Brazilian Library Association, Rua Martins Torres 99, Santa Rosa, Niterói, 24000 Rio de Janeiro, Brazil (covers all Latin America)

Guide du Livre Ancien et du Livre d'occasion (Guide to Antiquarian and Second-Hand Books), Association of Antiquarian and Modern Booksellers, 117 Blvd St Germain, F-75279 Paris cedex 06, France

IFLA Directory (annual), International Federation of Library Associations, Netherlands Congress Bldg, Postbus 9128, 2508 EC The Hague, Netherlands

IFLA Standards for Public Libraries, International Federation of Library Associations, Netherlands Congress Bldg, Postbus 9128, 2508 EC The Hague, Netherlands

International Academic and Specialist Publishers' Directory, Bowker Publishing Co, Erasmus House, High St, Epping, Essex CM16 4BU, UK

International Authors and Writers Who's Who; information on 10,000 of world's leading writers, including index of pseudonyms and literary agents, Melrose Press Ltd, International Biographical Centre, Cambridge CB2 3QP, UK

International Bibliography of Reprints/Internationales Verzeichnis der Reprints: K G Saur KG, D-8000 Munich 71, Postfach 711009, Federal Republic of Germany

International Book Trade Directory, Bowker Publishing Co, Erasmus House, High St, Epping, Essex CM16 4BU, UK Listing details of booksellers world-wide

International Books in Print, K G Saur KG, D-8000 Munich 71, Postfach 711009, Federal Republic of Germany; Clive Bingley Ltd, 1-19 New Oxford St, London WC1A, UK Listing titles published in the English language outside the UK and USA

International Directory of Antiquarian Booksellers, International League of Antiquarian Booksellers, Poststr 14-16, D-2000 Hamburg 36, Federal Republic of Germany

International Directory of Booksellers, K G Saur KG, D-8000 Munich 71, Postfach 711009, Federal Republic of Germany

International Librarianship, UNESCO, pl de Fontenoy, F-75700 Paris, France

International Library Directory: A World Directory of Libraries, A P Wales Organization, 18 Charing Cross Rd, London WC2H 0HR, UK

International Literary Market Place, Bowker Publishing Co, Erasmus House, Epping, Essex CM16 4BU, UK (covers the world apart from the North American continent, which is covered by *Literary Market Place*)

International Maps and Atlases in Print, Bowker Publishing Co, Erasmus House, High St, Epping, Essex CM16 4BU, UK

International Who's Who in Poetry, International Biographical Centre, Cambridge CB2 3QP, UK

Irregular Serials and Annuals: An International Directory, Bowker Publishing Co, Erasmus House, High Street, Epping, Essex CM16 4BU, UK

Jahrbuch der Auktionspreise (Yearbook of Auction Prices), Hauswedell & Co, D-2000 Hamburg 13, Pöseldorfer Weg 1, Federal Republic of Germany (book auction prices in Germany, Austria, Switzerland and the Netherlands)

Libros en Venta (Books for Sale) annual supplements including Spanish language book production of the year from all countries, Turner Ediciones SRL, Alsina 1535, 8° piso, of 803, 1088 Buenos Aires, Argentina

Literary and Library Prizes, Bowker Publishing Co, Erasmus House, Epping, Essex CM16 4BU, UK

Literary Market Place, R R Bowker Co, 1180 Ave of the Americas, New York, NY 10036, USA (covers North American continent — rest of world covered by *International Literary Market Place*)

Major Libraries of the World: A Selective Guide, Bowker Publishing Co, Erasmus House, High St, Epping, Essex CM16 4BU, UK

A Manual of European Languages for Librarians, Bowker Publishing Co, Erasmus House, High St, Epping, Essex CM16 4BU, UK

Mason's Publishers, Kenneth Mason Publications Ltd, 13-14 Homewell, Havant, Hampshire PO9 1EF, UK

Private Press Books; an annual bibliography of the work of private presses throughout the world, Private Libraries Association, Ravelston, South View Rd, Pinner, Middlesex, UK

Publishers' International Directory/ Internationales Verlagsadressbuch, K G Saur KG, D-8000 Munich 71, Postfach 711009, Federal Republic of Germany

Publishing in Africa in the Seventies, University of Ife Press, Ile-Ife, Nigeria

Reference Resources on South Asia, Indian Librarian, 233 Model Town, Jullundur 3, India

Répertoire international des Editeurs et Diffuseurs de Langue française (International List of French-Language Publishers and Distributors), Syndicat national de l'Edition, 117 blvd St-Germain, F-75279 Paris cedex 06, France

Répertoire international des Libraires de Langue française (International List of French Language Bookshops), Cercle de la Librairie, 117 blvd Saint-Germain, F-75006 Paris, France

South Asian Bibliography: A Handbook and Guide, Harvester Press, 16 Ship St, Brighton, East Sussex, UK

Subject Collections in European Libraries, Bowker Publishing Co, Erasmus House, High St, Epping, Essex CM16 4BU, UK

Ulrich's International Periodicals Directory, Bowker Publishing Co, Erasmus House, High St, Epping, Essex CM16 4BU, UK

Who Distributes What and Where: An International Directory of Publishers, Imprints, Agents and Distributors, R R Bowker Co, 1180 Ave of the Americas, New York, NY 10036, USA

Who's Who at the Frankfurt Book Fair: An International Publishers' Guide, K G Saur KG, D-8000 Munich 71, Postfach 711009, Federal Republic of Germany

Who's Who in African Literature, Horst Erdmann Verlag für Internationalen Kulturaustausch, D-7400 Tübingen, Hartmeyerstr 117, Postfach 1380, Federal Republic of Germany

Willings Press Guide, Thomas Skinner Directories, 41-43 Perrymount Rd, Haywards Heath, West Sussex RH16 3BS, UK

World Guide to Libraries, K G Saur KG, D-8000 Munich 71, Postfach 711009, Federal Republic of Germany

World Guide to Library Schools and Training Courses in Documentation (Guide mondial des écoles de bibliothecaires et documentalists), Clive Bingley Ltd, 1-19 New Oxford St, London WC1A 1NE, UK

The Writers' & Artists' Year Book, Adam & Charles Black Ltd, 35 Bedford Row, London WC1R 4JH, UK

The Writers Directory, St James Press, 3 Percy St, London W1P 9FA, UK

Journals

African Book Publishing Record (text occasionally in French), Hans Zell Publishers Ltd, PO Box 56, Oxford OX1 3EL, UK

African Books Newsletter; a checklist of recent books published in English, arranged according to subject, K K Roy (Private) Ltd, 55 Gariahat Rd, PO Box 10210, Calcutta 700019, India

African Research and Documentation, Standing Conference on Library Materials on Africa, c/o Institute of Commonwealth Studies, 27 Russell Sq, London WC1B 5DS, UK

L'Afrique littéraire et artistique, Société Africaine d'Edition, 6 Passage Leblanc, BP 1877, Dakar, Senegal

Anales de Literatura Hispanoamericana (Annals of Spanish-American literature); Universidad Complutense de Madrid, Cátedra de Literatura Hispanoamericana, Ciudad Universitaria, 3, Madrid, Spain

Asian Book Development, Asian Cultural Centre for Unesco, 6 Fukuro-machi, Shinjuku-ku, Tokyo, Japan

Asian Books Newsletter; a checklist of recent books published in English, arranged according to subject, K K Roy (Private) Ltd, 55 Gariahat Rd, PO Box 10210, Calcutta 700019, India

Babel (International Journal of Translation), D-6000 Frankfurt am Main, Wolfsgangstr 148, Federal Republic of Germany

Bibliografia actual de Caribe (Current Caribbean Bibliography) Caribbean Regional Library, Ponce de León 452, Hato Rey, Puerto Rico 00919

Bibliographie Documentation, Terminologie (Bibliography, Documentation, Terminology) (Editions in English, French, Russian and Spanish), UNESCO, Département de la Documentation des Bibliothèques et des Archives, 7 pl de Fontenoy, F-75700 Paris, France

Bibliophilie (text in English, French and German), Association Internationale de Bibliophilie, 58 rue de Richelieu, F-75084, Paris cedex 02, France

Bibliotheca Orientalis; international bibliographical and reviewing bi-monthly for Near Eastern and Mediterranean Studies (text in English, French and German), Nederlands Instituut voor Het Nabije Oosten, Noordeindplein 4-6, Leiden, Netherlands

Boletim Internacional de Bibliografia Luso-Brasileira, Calouste Gulbenkian Foundation, 98 Portland Pl, London W1, UK

Boletín Bibliográfico del CERLAL (current Latin-American bibliography), CERLAL, Calle 70 No 9-52, Apdo Aereo 17438, Bogota, Colombia

Bookbird, literature for children and young people, news from all over the world, recommendations for translation, International Institute for Children's Literature and Reading Research, Karl Werner, A-1040 Vienna, Mayerhofgasse 6, Austria

Bulletin, Bibliographical Society of Australia and New Zealand, 117 St George's Road, North Fitzroy, Victoria 3068, Australia

Bulletin de l'Association internationale des Documentalistes et Techniciens de l'Information (Bulletin of the International Association of Documentalists and Information Officers), 74 rue des Saints-Pères, F-75007 Paris, France

CERLAL: noticias sobre el Libro y Bibliografía (news on books and bibliographies), CERLAL, Calle 70 No 9-52, Apdo Aereo 17438, Bogota, Colombia

Caribbean Quarterly, Department of Extra-Mural Studies, University of the West Indies, Mona, Kingston 7, Jamaica

Cumulative Book Index; a world list of books in the English language, H W Wilson Co, 950 University Ave, Bronx, NY 10452 USA

Current Contents Africa; current periodical literature dealing with Africa (quarterly), Hans Zell Publishers Ltd, PO Box 56, Oxford OX1 3EL, UK

Edition; international book advertiser (text in English, French and German), Stauffacher-Verlag AG, CH-8055 Zurich 3, Birmensdorfer Str 318, Switzerland

Fichero Bibliográfico Hispanoamericano; monthly review of librarians, booksellers, distributors and publishers, Turner Ediciones SRL, Alsina 1535, 8° piso, of 803, 1088 Buenos Aires, Argentina

Francophonie-Edition, France Expansion, 336-340 rue St-Honoré, F-75001 Paris, France (review of French-language publishing throughout the world)

Germanistik, Internationales Referatenorgan mit bibliographischen Hinweisen (German Language and Literature: International Review Journal with Bibliographical References), Max Niemeyer Verlag, D-74 Tübingen, Pfrondorfer Str 4, Federal Republic of Germany

Helikon Vilagirodalmi Figyelo. (Helikon Review of World Literature) (summaries in French and Russian), Akademiai Kiadó, H-1054 Budapest V, Alkotmány u 21, Hungary

Index translationum. International bibliography of translations, UNESCO, pl de Fontenoy, F-75700 Paris, France

International Association of Orientalist Librarians Bulletin (half-yearly), International Association of Oriental Librarians, c/o Asian Studies Program, University of Hawaii at Manoa, 315 Moore Hall, 1890 East-West Rd, Honolulu, Hawaii 96822, USA

International Cataloguing, IFLA Committee on Cataloguing, Longman Group Ltd, Journals Division, 43/45 Annandale St, Edinburgh EH7 4AT, UK

International Fiction Review, (bi-annually) Dr S Elkhadem, Dept of German and Russian, University of New Brunswick, Federicton, NB, Canada

International Library Review (quarterly), Academic Press Inc (London) Ltd, 24-28 Oval Rd, London NW1 7DX, UK

International PEN Bulletin of Selected Books (issued with the assistance of UNESCO) (text and title in English and French), International PEN, 7 Dilke St, London SW3 4JE, UK

Journal, East and Central Africa Regional Branch of the International Council on Archives, c/o Kenya National Archives, Jogoo House 'A', PO Box 30520, Nairobi, Kenya

Jugend und Buch (Youth and Books), International Institute for Children's Literature and Reading Research, Karl Werner, A-1040 Vienna, Mayerhofgasse 6, Austria (Co-Sponsor: Österreichischer Buchklub der Jugend)

LIBER Bulletin (text in English and French), Ligue des Bibliothèques européenes de Recherche, c/o The Library, European University Institute, Badia Fiesolana, Florence, Italy

Library & Information Science Abstracts (LISA), The Library Association, 7 Ridgmount St, London WC1E 7AE, UK

Newsletter, West African Library Association, c/o Ghana Library Association, PO Box 4105, Accra, Ghana

Nordisk Tidskrift för Bok- och Biblioteksväsen (Scandinavian Journal for Bibliography and Librarianship), Almqvist & Wiksell, Gebers Förlag AB, Gamla Brogatan 26, Box 159, S-10122 Stockholm 1, Sweden

Review; journal on contemporary Latin American literature in English translation, Center for Inter-American Relations, 680 Park Ave, New York, NY 10021, USA

Revista Interamericana de Bibliografía (Inter-American Review of Bibliography), Department of Cultural Affairs, Pan American Union, Washington, USA

SCALS Newsletter, c/o School of Librarians, Archivists and Documentalists, University of Dakar, BP 2006, Dakar, Senegal (official publication of the Standing Conference of African Library Schools)

SCAUL Newsletter, c/o E Bejide Bankole, University Librarian, University of Lagos, Yaba, Lagos, Nigeria (official publication of the Standing Conference of African University Libraries)

Scandinavian Public Library Quarterly, German Library Association — Publications Dept, Fehrbelliner Platz 3, D-1000 Berlin 31, Federal Republic of Germany

South Asia: Library Notes and Diaries, University of Chicago Library, 5801 Ellis Ave, Chicago, Illinois 60637, USA

South Asian Book News, Duke University, Program in Comparative Studies on Southern Asia, Durham, NC 27706, USA (Co-sponsor: Duke University Library)

South-East Asian Archives, South-East Regional Branch of the International Council on Archives, c/o National Archives and Library of Malaysia, Jalan Sultan, Petaling Jaya, Malaysia

Third World First (a bi-monthly journal of arts, culture and letters of Africa), 10-14 Calcutta Crescent, PO Box 610, Apapa, Lagos, Nigeria

UNESCO Book Promotion News (text in English and French), UNESCO, Bureau of Documents and Publications, 7 pl de Fontenoy, F-75700 Paris, France

International Literary Prizes

Jane Addams Children's Book Award
Established 1979. To the author of the book for children that is most outstanding in literary merit and contains themes on brotherhood and peace. Awarded biennially. Enquiries to Women's International League for Peace and Freedom, 1 rue de Varembé, CH-1211 Geneva 20, Switzerland

Afriscope/University of Ife Bookshop Ltd Prize*
For (1) the best piece of creative writing by an African author and published in Africa, (2) for an outstanding contribution in the field of African literature. Enquiries to Dr K Omotoso, Department of Arabic and Islamic Studies, University of Ibadan, Ibadan, Nigeria

Aleko International Competition Awards in Comic Short Story*
Gold and Silver medals. No more than six first and second prizes are awarded annually. Enquiries to 'Narodna Mladez' (National Youth) Newspaper, Lenin 47, Blvd Sofia, Bulgaria

Alexander Prize
For an essay in English on a historical subject; must be a genuine work of original research, not hitherto published, and not awarded any other prize. Silver medal, awarded annually. Enquiries to Secretary, Royal Historical Society, University College London, Gower St, London WC1E 6BT, UK

Amade Prize
The Amade Prize is awarded for a work judged capable of arousing readers' interest, with the aim of promoting the well-being and happiness of children and adolescents. The 1979 prize was awarded to Doctor Abdenahim Harrouchi, a Moroccan, for the whole of his work. Enquiries to Festival International du Livre de Nice, Rue Stanislas 5, F-75006 Paris, France

American-Scandinavian Foundation/PEN Translation Prizes
Initiated in 1980 by 'Scandinavian Review' (quarterly magazine of ASF) to bring best of contemporary Scandinavian literature to American readers. There are two prizes of $500, one each for poetry and fiction. To be awarded annually to the best translations of work by Danish, Finnish, Icelandic, Norwegian or Swedish authors born after 1880. Enquiries to American-Scandinavian Federation, 127 East 73rd St, New York, NY 10021, USA

Hans Christian Andersen Awards
The International Board on Books for Young People (IBBY) awards this prize every two years to a living author and a living illustrator who, through their life's work, have made a distinguished contribution to international children's and young adult literature. (Until 1966 the prize was awarded for a specific book and to an author only.)
A jury of ten members, appointed by the Executive Committee of IBBY, makes the decision from selections submitted from member countries all over the world. Awarded in 1980 to Bohumil Riha, Czechoslovakia (author) and Suekichi Akaba, Japan (illustrator). Enquiries to IBBY Secretariat, CH-4051 Basle, Leonhardsgraben 38a, Switzerland

Argentine Authors Society Medal of Honour*
For a contribution to literature. Honorary recognition. Awarded annually. Enquiries to Association of Argentine Writers, Uruguay 1371, 1016 Buenos Aires, Argentina

Arts Council Awards and Bursaries
Full details of the help given to playwrights is available on request. Enquiries to Drama Director, Arts Council of Great Britain, 105 Piccadilly, London W1V 0AU, UK

Austrian State Prize for European Literature*
A prize of 150,000 Austrian schillings and testimonial, established in 1964, are presented by the Austrian Minister of Education to a renowned European author for the sum of his work. Awarded annually. The 1978 winner was Simone de Beauvoir for her contribution to European literature. Enquiries to Bundesministerium für Unterricht, Postfach 65, A-1014, Vienna, Austria

Alice Hunt Bartlett Prize
To the poet the Society most wishes to honour. In the case of poems translated into English, the prize of £500 will be divided equally between the poet and translator. The original poet must be living. Awarded annually. Closing date for entries each year is 31st December. Enquiries to The Secretary, The Poetry Society, 21 Earls Court Sq, London SW5, UK

Charles Baudelaire Poetry Prize*
To discover and encourage a poet under 21 years of age. $500. Awarded irregularly. Enquiries to International Who's Who in Poetry, International Biographical Centre, Cambridge CB2 3QP, UK

Bennett Award
For a writer of substantial achievement whose work has not received full recognition, or who is at a critical stage. $12,500, biennially. No applications or nominations accepted. Enquiries to The Hudson Review, 65 East 55 St, New York, NY 10022, USA

Anton Bergmann Prize
For the author of a historical account or monograph, written in Dutch and relating to a Flemish town or community in Belgium. 50,000 francs. Awarded every five years for a work appearing in print or (provisionally) in manuscript form, during the period. Foreign authors may also compete, provided work is in Dutch and is published in Belgium or the Netherlands. Winner for 17th period (1975-1980), P Van Nieuwenhuysen. Enquiries to Académie Royale de Belgique, Palais des Académies, 1 rue Ducale, B-1000 Brussels, Belgium

David Berry Prize
For an essay in English on any subject dealing with Scottish history within the reigns of James I to James VI inclusive. Awarded every 3 years. Enquiries to Secretary, Royal Historical Society, University College London, Gower St, London WC1E 6BT, UK

Best Book of the Sea Award*
Established 1971. For a non-fiction book about the sea judged to have made the most valuable contribution to the knowledge and enjoyment of those interested in sailing. £250 and a gold medal. Awarded annually. Enquiries to John Coote, 47 Caversham St, London SW3, UK

Biennial International Art Book Prize*
To promote the publication of fine illustrated books on archaeology, fine arts, architecture and applied arts, including photography. Prize consists of silver medals, free hotel accommodation in Jerusalem during the Jerusalem International Book Fair for the publisher and designer of the winning entry. Three to four books will also be awarded silver medals. All entries to be exhibited as a special exhibit of the International Book Fair. Awarded every two years. Enquiries to The Public Affairs Department, The Israel Museum, Jerusalem, Israel

James Blish Award*
Awarded biennially for excellence in science fiction criticism which has been published in the English language. The prize is a bronze plaque and a small sum of money. First awarded in 1977. Enquiries to Science Fiction Foundation, North East London Polytechnic, Longbridge Road, Barking, Essex RM8 2AS, UK

Bologna Fair Budding Critics' Prize
Awarded by jury of children on the basis of geographic requisites, originality of presentation and impression made by the work on the child reader. 1980 award to *The Book of the Village* by Birke Bärwinkel and Wilfried Mose, published by Fabula Verlag (Federal Republic of Germany). Enquiries to Fiera del Libro per Ragazzi — Ente Autonomo per le Fiere di Bologna, Piazza della Costituzione 6, I-40128 Bologna, Italy

Bologna Fair Graphic Prize for Children and Youth
Awarded for typographical, artistic and technical merit or innovation at the Bologna Children's Book Fair, by a Committee of experts made up of the G B Bodoni Study Centre in Parma. The prizes, consisting of golden plates, are awarded to the publishers of the winning works. The graphic prize for children was awarded in 1980 to *Anno's Song Book* by Yasusi Akutagawa and Mitsumasa Anno, published by Kodansha (Japan). The graphic prize for youth was awarded in 1980 to *Vault of Heaven and Snail-shell* by Rita Mühlbauer and Hanno Rink, published by Verlag Sauerländer (Switzerland). Enquiries to Fiera del Libro per Ragazzi — Ente Autonomo per le Fiere di Bologna, Piazza della Costituzione 6, I-40128 Bologna, Italy

Booker McConnell Prize
Instituted in 1969. £10,000 donated by Booker McConnell Ltd and administered by The National Book League, for any full-length novel, written in English by a citizen of the British Commonwealth, Eire, Pakistan or South Africa. Any United Kingdom publisher who publishes works of fiction may enter not more than four full-length novels, with scheduled publication dates between 1 January and 30 November. Awarded in 1980 to William Golding for *Rites of Passage* (Faber & Faber). Enquiries to The National Book League, Book House, East Hill, London SW18 2HZ, UK

Books Abroad/English-Speaking Union of the United States Best Book of Belles Lettres*
Instituted 1973, to foster creative writing by African and Asian writers in the English language. $2,000. Awarded annually. Enquiries to Professor Charles R Larson, 3600 Underwood St, Chevy Chase, Md 20015, USA

Christo **Botev** International Prize for Revolutionary Poetry*
To distinguished authors. Gold medal and 2,000 leva. Awarded every five years. Enquiries to Bulgarian People's Republic State Council, Sofia, Bulgaria

Brasilia Prize for Poetry*
For poets writing in Italian, Spanish, French and Portuguese. Monetary prize and medal 'Amicia Italo-Braziliana'. Awarded annually. Enquiries to Brasilia City Government, Brasilia, Brazil

Brazil Theatre Prize*
For the best play written by a Latin American author. Enquiries to Brazilian Ministry of Foreign Affairs, Cultural Division, Brasilia, Brazil

Bremen Literature Encouragement Prize
5,000 DM awarded annually. Won in 1980 by Peter Paul Zahl for *Die Glücklichen*. Enquiries to Senator für Wissenschaft und Kunst, Freie Hansestadt Bremen, D-2800 Bremen 1, Federal Republic of Germany

Bremen Literature Prize
Given by Rudolf-Alexander-Schröder Foundation to German-speaking poets and writers in order to encourage literature. 10,000 DM awarded annually. Won in 1980 by Peter Rühmkorf for *Haltbar bis Ende 1999*. Enquiries to Senator für Wissenschaft und Kunst, Freie Hansestadt Bremen, D-2800 Bremen 1, Federal Republic of Germany

John W **Campbell** Memorial Award
Founded 1973 for the best science-fiction novel in any language. First prize according to funding of sponsoring institution. Enquiries to The Secretary, Prof T A Shippey, School of English, Leeds University, Leeds LS2 9JT, UK

Carducci Prize*
Established 1950. For poetry, monographs and essays on poetry and poets. 1,000,000 liras. Awarded annually. Enquiries to Bologna University, Bologna, Italy

Pierre **Chauveau** Medal
Established 1952. In recognition of an outstanding contribution to literature. Medal and $1,000. Awarded biennially. Enquiries to Royal Society of Canada, 344 Wellington St, Ottawa, Ontario, K1A 0N4 Canada

Cheltenham Festival of Literature Poetry Competition
An annual competition in association with the Cheltenham Festival of Literature which takes place between September and November. The closing date is in April or May. Enquiries to Festival Organizer, Cheltenham Festival of Literature, Town Hall, Imperial Sq, Cheltenham, Glos GL50 1QA, UK

Children's Book Award
Established 1974. For a new author who shows unusual promise. Awarded annually. Enquiries to International Reading Association, 800 Barksdale Rd, PO Box 8139, Newark, Delaware 19711, USA

Cholmondeley Award for Poets
Established by the Marchioness of Cholmondeley in 1965 for 'the benefit and encouragement of poets of any age, sex or nationality'. The non-competitive award is for work generally, *not* for a specific book and submissions are not required. Approximately £2,500 awarded annually. 1980 award to Roy Fuller, Terence Tiller and George Barker. Enquiries to Society of Authors, 84 Drayton Gardens, London SW10, UK

Collins Religious Book Award
Founded 1969 to commemorate the 150th anniversary of the publisher William Collins Sons & Co Ltd. For the book which has made the most distinguished contribution to the relevance of Christianity in the modern world on one of the following subjects: science, ethics, sociology, philosophy, psychology and other religions. Open to living citizens of the UK, the Commonwealth, the Republic of Ireland and South Africa. Prize of £1,000 awarded every two years. Awarded in 1979 to W H Vanstone for *Love's Endeavour, Love's Expense* (Darton, Longman & Todd). Enquiries to William Collins Sons & Co Ltd, 14 St James's Pl, London SW1A 1PS, UK

Commonwealth Poetry Prize
Instituted 1972. For a first published book of poetry (in English) by an author from a Commonwealth country other than Britain. £500 awarded annually. Awarded in 1979 to Brian Turner for *Ladders of Rain* (John McIndoe). Enquiries to Librarian, Commonwealth Institute, Kensington High Street, London W8 6NQ, UK

Albert **Counson** Prize
For a scholarly work on romance languages. Monetarry prize. Awarded every five years. Enquiries to Royal Academy of French Language and Literature, Palais de Académies, 1 rue Ducale, B-1000 Brussels, Belgium

Count of Cartagena Prizes
Established 1929. For unpublished works by Spaniards or Latin-Americans written in Spanish on a theme to be decided for each competition. 90,000 pesetas. Awarded annually. Enquiries to Royal Spanish Academy, Filipe IV 4, Madrid, Spain

The Rose Mary **Crawshay** Prizes
Founded 1888. Awarded by the Council of the British Academy to women writers of any nationality on an historical or critical work of value on any subject concerning English literature. Preference is given to works on Byron, Shelley or Keats. One or more prizes awarded annually. The 1980 winner was Dame Helen Gardner for *The Composition of Four Quartets* (Faber & Faber). Enquiries to The Secretary, British Academy, Burlington House, Piccadilly, London W1V 0NS, UK

Franz **Cumont** Prize
For a work by a Belgian or foreign author dealing with the history of religion or science in antiquity, i.e. in the Mediterranean area prior to the time of Mohammed. No application necessary. The prize cannot be divided, except where one or more authors have acted in collaboration. 90,000 Belgian francs. Awarded every three years. Winner for 3rd period (1976-1978) Mrs A Duhoux-Tihon. Enquiries to Académie Royale de Belgique, Palais des Académies, 1 rue Ducale, B-1000 Brussels, Belgium

Cyril and Methodius Prize*
For original research in the field of old Bulgarian literature, linguistics and art. 2,000 leva. Awarded annually. Enquiries to Bulgarian Academy of Sciences, 7th November 1, Sofia, Bulgaria

Isaac **Deutscher** Memorial Prize
Instituted 1968. For a work published or in typescript in any of the main European languages which contributes to the development of Marxist thought. £100 awarded annually. Enquiries to Isaac Deutscher Memorial Prize, c/o Lloyds Bank Ltd, 68 Warwick Sq, London SW1, UK

Ernest **Discailles** Prize
Alternates between the best work on the history of French literature and on contemporary history. Open to (1) Belgians, (2) Foreigners who are studying or have studied at the University of Ghent. 40,000 francs. Awarded every five years. Winner for 14th period (1972-1976) Francis Balace. Enquiries to Académie Royale de Belgique, Palais des Académies, 1 rue Ducale, B-1000 Brussels, Belgium

Dobloug Prize
For outstanding literary work by one Norwegian and one Swedish writer 25,000 Swedish crowns. Awarded annually. Enquiries to Swedish Academy, Börshuset 11129, Stockholm, Sweden

Duff Cooper Memorial Prize
First awarded 1956. For a nonfictional literary work published in English or French. The Prize is the interest from a Trust Fund. Awarded annually. The 1979 winner was Geoffrey Hill for his book of poems, *Tenebrae*. Enquiries to Lord Norwich, 24 Blomfield Rd, London W9, UK

Dutch Literature Prize
Established 1956. To the most outstanding prose writer or poet in the Netherlands and in Belgium writing in Dutch. 18,000 Dutch florins. Awarded triennially. Enquiries to Netherlands Government, c/o Ministry of Culture, Recreation and Social Welfare, Postbus 5406, 2280 HK Rijswijk Z-H, Netherlands
or Belgian Government, Ministry of Culture, Brussels, Belgium

The **Dutton** Animal Book Award
Inspired by the great success of Gavin Maxwell's *Ring of Bright Water*, the story of two otters, E P Dutton & Company, New York, in 1962 established an international literary prize of $7,500, to be given as an advance on publication to the author of the manuscript judged by the editors of Dutton to be the best book-length work of adult fiction or non-fiction relating to animals. In 1967 the award was raised to $10,000 and it has now been raised to $15,000. The contest is open to new authors and to previously published authors throughout the world, but manuscripts must be submitted in English. No manuscripts of fewer than 35,000 words are eligible. The contest is annual. The opening date is January 1, and the closing date is December 31. Enquiries to E P Dutton, 2 Park Avenue, New York, NY 10016, USA

Mary **Elgin** Prize
For the encouragement of gifted new writers of fiction published by Hodder & Stoughton. £50 awarded annually. Enquiries to Hodder & Stoughton Ltd, 47 Bedford Square, London WC1, UK

Camille Engelman Prize
For the outstanding literary work of the year (published or unpublished) written in French. Monetary prize. Awarded annually. Enquiries to Royal Academy of French Language and Literature, Palais des Académies, 1 rue Ducale, B-1000 Brussels, Belgium

English-Speaking Union Book Award
For the best non-technical work published in the English language by an author whose native language is not English. $2,000, annual. Enquiries to the English-Speaking Union, 16 East 69 St, New York, NY 10021, USA

Etna-Taormina International Poetry Prize
Established 1951. To one or more poets. Awarded irregularly. Enquiries to Ente Provinciale Turismo, Largo Paisiello 5, Catania, Italy

European Cortina-Ulisse Prize
Instituted 1949 for a work of popular science on a set subject, first published in Europe during the 5 years prior to the year of award. A work published in a language other than Italian, English, French, German or Spanish must be accompanied by a printed or typed translation into one of these languages. 1,000,000 lire. Awarded annually. Enquiries to the Editor, 'Rivista Ulisse', Sezione Premio Europeo Cortina-Ulisse, Via Po 11, I-00198, Rome, Italy

Christopher **Ewart-Biggs** Memorial Prize
Established in 1977 to commemorate Christopher Ewart-Biggs, the British Ambassador to Ireland, who was assassinated in Dublin in 1976. This award is to be made annually to the writer of any nationality whose published work contributes most to peace and understanding in Ireland, closer ties between the peoples of Britain and Ireland, or to cooperation between the partners of the European Community. Entries should be in English and the prize is £1,500. In 1979 the award was made to Stewart Parker for *I'm a Dreamer, Montreal*. Enquiries to The National Book League, Book House, East Hill, London SW18 2HZ, UK

The Geoffrey **Faber** Memorial Prize
Established in 1963 by Faber & Faber Ltd as a memorial to the founder and first Chairman of the firm, this prize of £500 is awarded annually, with the assistance of The Arts Council of Great Britain. It is given, in alternate years, for a volume of verse and for a volume of prose fiction. It is given to that volume of verse or prose fiction first published originally in the UK during the two years preceding the year in which the Award is given which is, in the opinion of the judges, of the greatest literary merit. To be eligible for the prize the volume of verse or prose fiction in question must be by a writer who is: (a) not more than forty years old at the date of publication, (b) a citizen of the United Kingdom and Colonies, of any other Commonwealth state, of the Republic of Ireland or of the Republic of South Africa. There are three judges, who are reviewers of poetry or fiction as the case may be, and they are nominated each year by the editors or literary editors of newspapers and magazines which regularly publish such reviews. Faber & Faber invite nominations from such editors and literary editors. No submissions for the prize are to be made. The 1980 prize was awarded jointly to George Szirtes for *Slant Door* (Secker & Warburg) and Hugo Williams for *Love Life* (Whizzard/André Deutsch). Enquiries to Faber & Faber Ltd, 3 Queen Sq, London WC1N 3AU, UK

Antonio **Feltrinelli** Prize*
Each year the Lincei Academy (the National Italian Academy of Sciences) awards Antonio Feltrinelli prizes for accomplishment in the various branches of sciences, humanities, and literature. These prizes were instituted by an Italian businessman who died in 1942 and bequeathed his fortune to the Academy for the purpose of 'rewarding toil, study, intelligence....those men who with greater success distinguished themselves with high achievements in art and science, since they are the true benefactors of their own country as well as of all humanity'. The literature award is granted every five years and the amount varies — the 1977 prize was approximately $30,000. Enquiries to Accademia Nazionale dei Lincei, Via della Lungara 10, I-00165 Rome, Italy

City of **Florence** International Poetry Prize*
Established 1955. For an outstanding book of poetry. 1,000,000 liras and Dante Alighieri Medal. The Medal of the Community of Florence (Comune di Firenze) to the publisher of the award-winning poetry. Awarded annually. Enquiries to Florence City Prize, c/o Nuovo Cenacolo Fiorentino, Piazza Pietro Leopoldo 11, Florence, Italy

Foreign Poetry Prize*
Monetary Prize. Enquiries to Recontres Poetiques du Mont-Saint-Michel, rue Saint Michel, Granville (Manche), France

Formentor Prize*
For fiction sponsored by publishers from 14 nations. Enquiries to Nuovo Cenacolo Fiorentino, Piazza Pietro Leopoldo II, Florence, Italy

Franco-German Friendship Prize*
For any work of literature, theatre, sociology, art or psychology that furthers good relations between France and Germany. Monetary prize. Awarded annually. Enquiries to Franco-German Association, 168 Quai de Javel, Paris 15, France

French Academy, Foreigner's Book Award*
For the best book written in French by an author of any nationality other than French. Medal. Enquiries to French Academy, Institut de France, 23 Quai de Conti, F-75006 Paris, France

French Language Prize*
Established 1914. For work done abroad in the best interests of the French language. 50 francs; two prizes of 20 francs and medals. Awarded annually. Enquiries to French Academy, Institut de France, 23 Quai de Conti, F-75006 Paris, France

Rómulo **Gallegos** International Novel Prize*
The prize was established in 1965 by the National Institute of Culture and Fine Arts of the Republic of Venezuela. Originally instituted to mark the 80th anniversary of the birth of the illustrious author Rómulo Gallegos, which was celebrated in August 1964, the first award was made in 1967, the 400th anniversary of the founding of Caracas — birthplace of the novelist. Competition is open to any writer from Latin America, Spain or the Philippines whose novel is written in Spanish and has been published originally in one of the countries of the above designated areas. The amount of the prize is approximately $22,223 and will be granted every five years — the next award to be in 1982. Enquiries to Consejo Nacional de la Cultura, Premio Internacional de Novela 'Rómulo Gallegos', Apdo de Correos 50995, Caracas 105, Venezuela
or from Centro de Estudios Latinoamericanos 'Rómulo Gallegos', Apdo 75667, Caracas 107, Venezuela

German Peace Prize
The Peace Prize of the German Book Trade (Friedenspreis des Deutschen Buchhandels) is awarded annually during the Frankfurt Book Fair. The prize is supported by the Boersenverein des Deutschen Buchhandels (organization of the German Book Trade) and is awarded without regard to nationality, race or creed. Prize of DM 25,000 since 1979. Enquiries to Börsenverein des Deutschen Buchhandels, Friedenspreisarchiv, Grosser Hirschgraben 17-21, D-6000 Frankfurt am Main, Federal Republic of Germany

The **German Youth** Book Award
The German Youth Book Award is given by the Federal Ministry for Youth, Family and Health. The selection of the books and the arrangements for granting the award are in the hands of the Arbeitskreis für Jugendliteratur eV, a body in which the organizations concerned with promoting good books for the young in Germany are represented. The selection is restricted to books published in the German language, primarily books from the Federal Republic of Germany, Austria and Switzerland (translations included). The rules for the award have been altered periodically. Since 1971 the award consists of a total of five prizes, each DM 7,500, which can be awarded for picture books, fiction, non-fiction and for appreciation of outstanding achievement. 1979 prizes to Janosch for *Oh, wie schön ist Panama* (Verlag Beltz und Gelberg), Tormod Haugen for *Die Nachtvögel* (Benziger Verlag), Virginia Allen Jensen and Dorcas Woodbury Haller for *Was ist das?* (Verlag Sauerländer), Peter Parks for *Das Leben unter Wasser* (Tessloff Verlag), Rosemarie Wildermuth for *Heute — und die 30 Jahre davor* (Ellermann Verlag). Enquiries to Arbeitskreis für Jugendliteratur eV, Elisabethstr 15, 8 Munich 40, Federal Republic of Germany

Golden Eagle Award of the Festival International du Livre
This festival, held in Nice, annually awards the Golden Eagle Prize, worth 30,000 francs, to an author of any nationality for his total literary work. The recipient of the award is selected by an international jury consisting of well-known authors and literary critics. Enquiries to Festival International du Livre, 5 rue Stanislas, 75006 Paris, France

Grand Prize for Children's Literature
For an unpublished children's book in the French language. Monetary prize. Awarded annually. Enquiries to Association 'Salon de l'Enfance', 11 rue Anatole de la Forge, Paris 17, France

Grand Prize for the Dissemination of the French Language*
For work contributing to the dissemination of the French language. Monetary prize. Enquiries to French Academy, Institut de France, 23 Quai de Conti, F-75006 Paris, France

The **Guardian** Award for Children's Fiction*
The Guardian's annual prize of £150 (subject to revision) for an outstanding work of fiction for children by a British or Commonwealth writer, instituted in 1967. Enquiries to Literary Editor, The Guardian, 119 Farringdon Rd, London EC1R 3ER, UK

The **Guardian Fiction** Prize*
Instituted in 1965 and awarded annually. The prize of £500 is given for a novel published by a British or Commonwealth writer and is intended to encourage ambitious and original work by British writers. The judges are the Literary Editor and fiction reviewers of *The Guardian*. Enquiries to Literary Editor, The Guardian, 119 Farringdon Rd, London EC1R 3ER, UK

Heredia Prize*
Given in alternate years to (1) a Latin American writer for a piece of prose or poetry written in French; (2) the author of a collection of sonnets (printed or typed). Monetary award. Awarded annually. Enquiries to French Academy, Institut de France, 23 Quai de Conti, F-75006 Paris, France

The Georgette **Heyer** Historical Novel Prize
Established in 1977 for previously unpublished outstanding historical novel written in English. Annual award of £1,500. Awarded in 1980 to Lynn Guest for *Children of Hachiman* (The Bodley Head). Enquiries to The Bodley Head, 9 Bow St, Covent Garden, London WC2E 7AL, UK or Transworld Publishers Ltd, Century House, 61-63 Uxbridge Rd, Ealing W5 5SA, UK

David **Higham** Prize for Fiction
Founded 1975. For the best first novel or book of short stories, in the opinion of the judges, written in English by a citizen of the Commonwealth, Republic of Ireland or Republic of South Africa. Prize of £500 awarded annually. Awarded in 1979 to David Harvey for *The Plate Shop* (Collins). Enquiries to The National Book League, Book House, East Hill, London SW18 2HZ, UK

The **Hugo** Awards*
Established 1953, for the best science fiction writing in several categories. Chrome-plated rocket ship. Awarded annually. Enquiries to c/o Howard DeVore, 4705 Weddel St, Dearborn Heights, Michigan 48125, USA

International Grand Prize for Poetry
For poetry by a living author. Monetary prize. Awarded every two years. Enquiries to International House of Poetry, 147 Chaussée de Maecht, Brussels, Belgium

International Literary Braille Competition Awards
Established 1940. To an individual who is legally blind. Cash prizes in the categories of fiction, nonfiction and poetry. Awarded every five years. Enquiries to Jewish Braille Institute of America Inc, 110 East 30th St, New York, NY 10016, USA

International Prize for the First Novel*
For a novel written in, or translated into French. Monetary prize and publication of the book by the Julliard Publishing House. Awarded annually. Enquiries to International Prize for the First Novel, Editions René Juilliard, 8 rue Garancière, F-75008, Paris, France

International Prize of French Friendship*
For poetry written in French by a foreigner. Awarded biennially. Last awarded in 1979. Enquiries to Society of French Poets, 38 rue du Faubourg St Jacques, F-75014 Paris, France

International Publication Cultural Award*
Awarded for the book published in Japan in English or with a summary in English which has made the most outstanding achievement in the presentation of Japanese culture to people abroad. Enquiries to Secretary, Publishers Association for Cultural Exchange, 2-1 Sarugaku-cho, 1-chome, Chiyoda-ku, Tokyo, Japan

International Publications Cultural Prize*
Established 1965. To stimulate the development of Japanese publications in foreign languages, and to promote cultural exchange between Japan and other countries. Awarded irregularly. Enquiries to Japanese Ministry of Foreign Affairs and Publishers Association for Cultural Exchange, Shin Nichi-Bo Building, 1-2-1 Sarugaku-cho, Kanda, Chiyoda-Ku, Tokyo, Japan

International Who's Who in Poetry Awards*
To discover new poets and to encourage existing poets. Prizes total $2,500; First prize: $1,000. Awarded irregularly. Enquiries to 'International Who's Who in Poetry', International Biographical Centre, Cambridge CB2 3QP, UK

Irish-American Cultural Institute Literary Awards
Established 1967. For writers in the Irish or English language. Two awards, each of $5,000, for each language in alternate years. Awarded in 1980 to poet Michael Hartnett; and towards the translation of The Bible into Irish. Enquiries to Irish-American Cultural Institute, 683 Osceola Ave, St Paul, Minnesota 55105, USA

Japan Translation Prize*
To encourage translation from and into Japanese language. Honorary recognition and trophy. Awarded annually. Enquiries to Japan Society of Translators, Room 208, Shiba Mansion, 5-11-6, Toranomon, Minato-Ku, Tokyo, Japan

The **Jerusalem** Prize
This international prize of $3,000 is awarded during the Jerusalem International Book Fair which is held every two years. The award is made to an author or philosopher whose life's work has been devoted to the ideal of man's freedom in society. In 1979 the winner was Sir Isaiah Berlin. Enquiries to Mr Gershon Polak, Executive Director, Book Fair, 22 Jaffa Rd, Jerusalem 91000, Israel

Jewish Chronicle — Harold H Wingate Book Awards
Instituted in 1977 by the 'Jewish Chronicle' and the Wingate Foundation, and administered by The National Book League. Awards of £1,000 each are made annually for a work of fiction and of non-fiction which stimulate an interest in Jewish themes. They are aimed equally at encouraging writers and scholars to handle Jewish themes and stimulating an awareness of these subjects among the reading public. Awarded in 1979 to Emanuel Litvinof for *The Face of Terror* (fiction) and Dr Nelly Wilson for *Bernard-Lazare* (non-fiction). Enquiries to The National Book League, Book House, East Hill, London SW18 2HZ, UK

Stanislas **Julien** Prize*
For the best work related to China. Monetary prize. Awarded annually. Enquiries to Academy of Inscriptions and Belles-Lettres, 23 Quai de Conti, F-75006 Paris, France

Kalinga Prize
This prize, awarded annually by UNESCO, was established in 1951 by the Kalinga Foundation Trust, for the dual purpose of recognizing outstanding interpretation of science to the general public and of strengthening scientific and cultural links between India and other nations. The recipient of the prize is selected by an international jury and may be anyone who has contributed to the promotion of the public understanding of science and technology. The winner receives a cash prize of £1,000 sterling. The award takes its name from an ancient empire of the Indian subcontinent, which was conquered in the third century BC by the Emperor Asoka, who was so appalled by the cost of his conquest in terms of human life and suffering that he swore never to wage war again. Enquiries to UNESCO SC/SER/SCW, 7 pl de Fontenoy, F-75700 Paris, France

Jomo **Kenyatta** Prize for Literature*
For the most outstanding work of literature in English or Swahili published in the preceding year (July-June) and written by a citizen of Kenya, Uganda or Tanzania. Prize of 10,000 Kenya shillings (half each for the best English and the best Swahili books). Awarded annually. Enquiries to Kenya Publishers' Association, PO Box 72532, Nairobi, Kenya

The **Lanchester** Prize
Since 1954, The Operations Research Society of America has awarded an annual prize (now $2,000) for the best paper in English on operations research. Occasionally, it is awarded to a book. The prize commemorates the work of Frederick W Lanchester (1868-1946), an automotive and aeronautical pioneer. Enquiries to Business Manager, Operations Research Society of America, 428 East Preston St, Baltimore, Md 21202, USA

Latin Friendship Prize*
Established 1958. For the work of a French, or Latin-American, writer which expresses solidarity of Latin countries and Latin culture of Europe or America. Monetary prize. Enquiries to Amitiés Latines, Impasse Truillot, Paris 9, France

Lazarillo Prize*
To Spanish and Latin-American candidates in the following categories: (1) to the author of the best book for children and teenagers; (2) for the best illustration of a book for children; (3) to a publishing house. Monetary prizes and honorary citations. Awarded annually. Enquiries to Spanish Ministry of Information and Tourism, Ave del Generalisimo 39, Madrid 16, Spain

Pierre **Lecomte** du Nouy Award*
Established 1954. For an outstanding essay, biography, autobiography, or other work concerning the spiritual life of our epoch, and the defence of human dignity. Silver medal and $2,000. Awarded annually alternately for works written in French or translated into French, and for similar literary works published in English. Enquiries to Lecomte du Nouy Association, United States Trust Co, 45 Wall St, New York, NY 10005, USA

Manchester Odd Fellows Social Concern Annual Book Awards
Established 1977. Two prizes of £500 each are awarded for the book, or pamphlet of not less than 10,000 words, that provides the most stimulating impetus for the improvement in living conditions within fields of social concern (to be specified each year). Entries must first have appeared in English and been written by citizens of the UK, Commonwealth, Republic of Ireland, Pakistan or South Africa. The 1980 winners were Christopher Evans for *The Mighty Micro* (Gollanz), and Corbett Woodall for *A Disjointed Life* (Heinemann). Enquiries to The National Book League, Book House, East Hill, London SW18 2HZ, UK

Mandat des Poètes Prize*
Founded in 1950 by Pierre Béarn, to aid a French-language poet of talent, young or old, in time of need. Awarded annually. Enquiries to Pierre Béarn, 60 rue Monsieur-le-Prince, F-75006 Paris, France

The **Man in His Environment** Book Award
In February 1969, E P Dutton & Company established The Man in His Environment Book Award. This prize is offered annually for an unpublished manuscript written in English dealing with the past, present or future of man in his environment, natural or manmade. Dutton guarantees a minimum of $10,000 advance on publication against all earnings. The contest is open to new authors and to authors whose work has already been published, to authors in the United States and abroad. Enquiries to Man in His Environment Book Award, E P Dutton, 2 Park Ave, New York, NY 10016, USA

Katherine **Mansfield** Menton Memorial Prize
Instituted 1959. Two prizes awarded for published short stories, one English and one French. Just over £100 each. Awarded triennially (next award 1981). Enquiries to The Secretary, English PEN Centre, 7 Dilke St, London SW3 4JE, UK
(Enquiries regarding the French short story to Monsieur Dimitri Stolypine, General Secretary, Maison Internationale des PEN Clubs, 6 rue François Miron, Paris IV, France - marked Prix Menton)

Medicis Foreign Prize*
For the best foreign novel appearing in French during the preceding year. Monetary prize. Awarded annually. Enquiries to Medicis Prize, c/o Francine Mallet, 25 rue Dombasle, Paris 15, France

Ramón **Menéndez** Pidal Prize
For an outstanding work in the fields of Spanish linguistics or Spanish literature. 30,000 pesetas. Awarded biennially. Enquiries to Royal Spanish Academy, Felipe IV No 4, Madrid, Spain

Neustadt International Prize for Literature
'World Literature Today', an international literary quarterly, established in 1969 an award for distinguished and continuing artistic achievement in the fields of poetry, drama or fiction. A new international jury of twelve is appointed for each successive award by the editor in consultation with the editorial board. Each juror presents one candidate for the prize. A majority (7) of the jury must be present for the deliberations and the final voting. Representative selections of a candidate's work must be available to the jury in either French or English translation.
Announcement of the winner is made in February, and the award is officially presented at The University of Oklahoma, Norman, Oklahoma, every other year. The prize is an award certificate, a replica of an eagle's feather in silver, and $10,000. 'World Literature Today' dedicates one issue to the recipient. The University of Oklahoma Press will seriously consider the publication of a book by or on the winner. In 1980 the prize was awarded to Josef Skvorecky (Czech novelist). Prize not open to application. Enquiries to 'World Literature Today', 630 Parrington Oval, Room 110, Norman, Oklahoma 73019, USA

Martinus **Nijhoff** Prize
Established 1953. For translation of literary work into and from Dutch. 7,500 Dutch florins. Awarded annually. Enquiries to Prince Bernhard Fund, Leidsegracht 3, Amsterdam, Netherlands

Nobel Prize for Literature*
Of all the literary prizes, the Nobel Prize for literature is the highest in value and in honour bestowed. It is one of the five prizes founded by Alfred Bernhard Nobel (1833-1896); the other four awards are for physics, chemistry, physiology or medicine, and peace. By the terms of Nobel's will, the prize for literature is to be given to the person 'who shall have produced in the field of literature the most distinguished work of an idealistic tendency'. It consists of a gold medal, a diploma and a sum of money; the amount in 1977 was about $147,000. The award is administered by the Swedish Academy in Stockholm and official presentation is made on December 10, the anniversary of Nobel's death. No one may apply for the Nobel Prize; there is no competition. It is awarded to an author usually for his total literary output and not for any single work. Awarded in 1979 to Odysseus Elytis. Enquiries to Nobel Foundation, Swedish Academy, Sturegatan 14, S-11436 Stockholm, Sweden

Nordic Council Literary Prize
Established 1962. To an individual author for a current work of literature in one of the Scandinavian Languages. 75,000 Danish crowns. Awarded annually. Enquiries to Nordic Council, Box 7765, 10396 Stockholm, Sweden

Leopoldo **Panero** Prize*
For poetry. 100,000 pesetas. Awarded annually. Enquiries to Madrid Institute of Hispanic Culture, Ave Reyes Catolicos, Ciudad Universitaria, Madrid, Spain

Yugoslav **P E N Club** Award*
For the translation of a book from and into languages spoken or used in Yugoslavia. Monetary prize. Enquiries to Yugoslav PEN Club, Serbian Centre, YU-11000 Belgrade, 7 Francuska St, Yugoslavia

Hungarian **P E N Club Medal***
For translation of Hungarian literary work into foreign languages. Awarded when merited. Enquiries to Hungarian PEN Club, Vörösmarty ter 1, Budapest V, Hungary

Polish **P E N Club Prizes***
For best translations of foreign poetry and prose into Polish, and of Polish literature into foreign languages. Three awards 20,000 zlotys each. Awarded annually. Enquiries to Polish PEN Club, Palac Kultury i Nauki, Warsaw, Poland

Lorne **Pierce** Medal
Established 1926. For achievement and conspicuous merit in the field of imaginative or critical literature, in English or French. Medal and $1,000. Awarded biennially. Enquiries to Royal Society of Canada, 344 Wellington St, Ottawa, Ontario K1A ON4, Canada

Pilgrim Award
Established 1970 and awarded annually by a committee of the Science Fiction Research Association for outstanding contributions made over a period of time to scholarship relating to the study of science fiction and modern fantasy. Enquiries to Science Fiction Research Association Inc, Box 3186, The College of Wooster, Wooster, Ohio 44691, USA

Planeta Prize*
Established 1952. For the best unpublished novel. Open to writers of Spanish speaking countries. 4,000,000 pesetas, and publication by Planeta Publishing House. Awarded annually. Enquiries to Planeta Publishing House, Corcega 273-277, Barcelona, Spain

Edgar **Poe** Prize*
To the best foreign poet writing in the French language. 100 francs. Awarded annually. Enquiries to Maison de Poèsie, 11 bis rue Ballu, F-75009 Paris, France

Poetry in Irish Award
Established 1962. To the author of best book of poetry in the Irish language. IR£600. Awarded triennially. Enquiries to Irish Arts Council, 70 Merrion Sq, Dublin 2, Republic of Ireland

Polish Authors' Society (Zaiks) Prizes
For best translations of Polish literature into foreign languages. Three prizes, 20,000 zlotys each. Awarded annually. Enquiries to Society of Authors Zaiks, ul Hipoteczna 2, Warsaw, Poland

Prince Pierre de Monaco Prize for Literature
Restricted to French-speaking writers. For the entirety of the literary work of one author. 30,000 French francs awarded annually. 1980 winner was Marcel Schneider. Enquiries to Fondation Prince Pierre de Monaco, Ministère d'Etat, Monaco

Prix des Sept, see Prix Internationale des Editeurs

Prix Internationale des Editeurs (Prix des Sept)*
Radical literature prize established in 1977 by the below-mentioned 8 publishers. $5,000 to be awarded for a work already accepted for publication by one of them (to be subsequently published by each in the appropriate language). The most recent (1977) award was to Erich Fried for *100 Poems Without a Country* and a special award was made to Breyten Breytenbach for *In Africa even the Flies are Happy*. The 8 publishers are: Christian Burgois (France), Verlag Klaus Wagenbach (Federal Republic of Germany), G Feltrinelli SpA (Italy), Van Gennep Ltd (Netherlands), Publições Dom Quixote (Portugal), Editorial Anagrama (Spain), John Calder (Publishers) Ltd (UK), Urizen Press (USA). Prize not open to application. Enquiries to John Calder (Publishers) Ltd, 18 Brewer Street, London W1R 4AS, UK

Putnam Awards*
Established 1960. For outstanding manuscripts in the English language already under contract to the house, fiction or non-fiction, not previously published by Putnam's. Advance of $7,500 against royalties and $7,500 for advertising and promotion. Not more than three awarded annually. Enquiries to G P Putnam's Sons, 200 Madison Ave, New York, NY 10016, USA

Regina Medal
Established 1959. For recognition of continued distinguished contributions to children's literature. Silver medal. Awarded annually. Won in 1980 by Beverly Cleary. Enquiries to Catholic Library Association, 461 West Lancaster Ave, Haverford, Pennsylvania 19041, USA

Remembrance Award*
Established 1964. To an author of a literary work of high merit that was inspired by the experience of the Nazi holocaust and which most effectively presents this experience for the benefit of the present and future generations. $2,500. Awarded annually. Enquiries to World Federation of the Bergen-Belsen Associations, PO Box 333, Lenox Hill Station, New York, NY 10021, USA

Felix **Restrepo** Prize*
For distinguished contributions to philology. 100,000 Colombian pesos and publication of the work. Awarded annually. Enquiries to Academia Colombiana, Bogotá, Colombia

John Llewelyn **Rhys** Memorial Prize
Established in 1941 by the widow of an airman killed on active service who was awarded the Hawthornden Prize posthumously. For a 'memorable work' by a Commonwealth citizen who was under 30 at the time of its publication. Prize of £500 awarded annually for a book published the previous year. Entries should be received by 30 April of the year of the award. 1980 prize awarded to Desmond Hogan for *Diamonds at the Bottom of the Sea* (Hamish Hamilton). Enquiries to The National Book League, Book House, East Hill, London SW18 2HZ, UK

Rose of French Poets Prize*
Established 1949. For a foreign poet who has celebrated France in his verse. Medal. Enquiries to Society of French Poets, 38 rue du Faubourg St Jacques, F-75014 Paris, France

'La **Sonrisa** Vertical' Prize
Founded in 1978 in homage to Lopez Barbadillo. Awarded annually to the best erotic novel written in Spanish or another language of the Spanish State. The 1979 winner was Ojélia Dracs (pen-name of a literary Catalan group) for *Deu pometes tè el pomer*. The prize is 500,000 pts advance on the work prior to publication, together with an artistic object designed by Francis Closas. Enquiries to 'La sonrisa vertical', Tusquets Editores, Calle Iradier 24 bajos, Barcelona 17, Spain

The **'Times Educational Supplement'** Information Book Awards
Instituted 1972. For outstandingly good information books originating in Britain or the Commonwealth. Two awards are offered for a book for children up to the age of 9 and for a book for those aged between 10 and 16, both awards for £150. The judges may award a further £150 to the illustrator of either or both books. Won in 1979 by George Bernard (Oxford Scientific Films) for a photographic study *The Common Frog* (G Whizzard/André Deutsch) (Junior Award) and by Jane Cousins for *Make It Happy* (Virago) (Senior Award). Enquiries to Literary Editor, Times Educational Supplement, Times Newspapers Ltd, New Printing House Square, Gray's Inn Rd, London WC1X 8EZ, UK

Translation Prize*
For the best translation of a literary, scientific or cultural work written by a Portuguese author which is published in the form of a book. 30,000 escudos. Awarded biennially. Enquiries to Portugal State Secretariat for Information and Tourism, Palacio Foz, Lisbon 2, Portugal

Triennial Prize for Bibliography
The International League of Antiquarian Booksellers (ILAB) awards a prize, every three years, of $1,000 to the author of the best work, published or unpublished, of learned bibliography, of research into the history of the book or typography, or a book of general interest on the subject. The competition is open, without restriction, but entries must be submitted in a language which is universally read. An already published work is eligible only if it has an imprint bearing a date within the three years preceding the closing date for submission. Enquiries to Dr Frieder Kocher-Benzing, Rathenaustr 21, D-7000 Stuttgart 1, Federal Republic of Germany

Walmap Prize*
Created by Waldomiro Magalhães Pinto for unpublished literary works in the Portuguese language. Prizes total $13,000. Awarded biennially. Enquiries to Antônio Olinto, 34 Landward Ct, Harowby St, London W1, UK

John Rowan **Wilson** Award
An annual award made by 'World Medicine' in memory of John Rowan Wilson — surgeon, novelist, journalist — to a doctor for a piece of writing of fiction or fact, or to a lay person writing on a medical subject. The prize is £500 and a silver goblet. Enquiries to The Editor, World Medicine, Clareville House, 26 Oxendon St, London SW1Y 4EL, UK

World Festival of Negro Arts Literary Prizes*
For the following works in English or French: a novel by a Negro author; a collection of poetry by a Negro author; an essay by a Negro writer; a work on the subject of Negro art, whoever the author; a scientific or historical essay by a Negro author; a piece of reporting on the Negro world, whoever the author; a play by a negro playwright. Monetary prizes. Awarded every 4 years (next 1981). Enquiries to Secretariat, World Black and African Festival of Arts and Culture, PMB 12568, Ikoyi, Lagos, Nigeria

Abraham **Woursell** Prize (University of Vienna)*
Instituted 1965. For young creative writers. 200,000 Austrian schillings annually for 5 years. Enquiries to Selection Committee Chairman, Faculty of Philosophy, University of Vienna, Austria

'Yorkshire Post' Book of the Year Award
Instituted 1964. First prize of £400 and runner-up prize of £250 for the best books published each year. Translations and works of a strictly scientific or technical nature are excluded. If the first prize is awarded to a non-fiction work, the runner-up prize goes to a fiction work and vice versa. Awarded in 1979 to Norman and Jeanne MacKenzie for *Dickens — A Life* (Oxford University Press) (first prize) and the finest fiction award to Jennifer Jones for *The Old Jest* (Hamish Hamilton). In addition there were Best First Work Awards to new authors in 1979. £300 first prize went to Mary Soames for *Clementine Churchill* (Cassells) and the runner-up prize of £200 went to Richard Morris for his *Cathedrals and Abbeys of England & Wales* (Dent). There are also special annual awards of £350 each for the book selected to advance the popular appreciation of Art. Enquiries to Secretary, Book of the Year Awards, Yorkshire Post Newspapers Ltd, PO Box 168, Wellington St, Leeds LS1 1RF, UK

Young People's Book Prize*
For an outstanding book or the collected works of a writer or illustrator in the field of juvenile literature. 3,000 Swiss francs or more. Awarded annually. Enquiries to Swiss Teachers Association, Ringstrasse 54, CH-8057 Zurich, Switzerland

The ISBN System

Background

The question of the need and feasibility of an international numbering system for books was first discussed at the third international Conference on Book Market Research and Rationalization in the Book Trade held in November 1966 in Berlin. At that time a number of publishers and book distributors in Europe were considering the use of computers in order processing and inventory control and it was evident that a pre-requisite of an efficient machine system was a unique and simple identification number for a published item.
The system which fulfilled this requirement and which became known as the International Standard Book Number (ISBN) System developed out of the book numbering system introduced into the United Kingdom in 1967.
In a report to the British Publishers Association, Professor F G Foster of the London School of Economics stated that there was '... a clear need for the introduction into the book trade of standard numbering ... and substantial benefits

would accrue to all parties therefrom'. After further study and deliberation, a detailed plan for standard numbering was produced. At the same time, the Technical Committee Documentation of the International Organization for Standardization (ISO/TC 46) set up a working party (with the British Standards Institution acting as secretariat) to investigate the possibility of adapting the British system for international use.

A meeting was held in London in 1968 with representatives from Denmark, France, Federal Republic of Germany, Eire, the Netherlands, Norway, the United Kingdom, the United States of America and an observer from UNESCO. Other countries contributed written suggestions and expressions of interest. A report of the meeting was circulated to all countries belonging to the ISO. Comments on this report and subsequent proposals were considered at meetings held in Berlin and Stockholm in 1969.

As a result of these meetings there emerged ISO Recommendation 2108 which sets out the principles and procedure for international standard book numbering. The purpose of the ISO Recommendation is to coordinate and standardize internationally the use of book numbers so that an International Standard Book Number (ISBN) identifies one title or edition of a title from one specific publisher and is unique to that edition.

The ISBN applies in the main to books — for which the system was originally created — but, by extension, it may be used for any item produced by publishers or collected by libraries.

How the International Standard Book Number (ISBN) is Built Up

Every International Standard Book Number (ISBN) consists of ten digits and whenever it is printed it is preceded by the letters ISBN. (Note: In those countries where the Latin alphabet is not used, an abbreviation in the characters of the local alphabet may be used in addition to the Latin letters ISBN.)

The ten-digit number is divided into four parts of variable length, each part when printed being separated by a hyphen or space. (Note: Experience suggests that the hyphen is preferable to the space.)

The four parts are as follows:

Part 1. Group Identifier
This part identifies the national, geographic or other similar grouping of publishers.

Part 2. Publisher's Prefix
This part identifies a particular publisher within a group.

Part 3. Title Identifier
This part identifies a particular title or edition of a title published by a particular publisher.

Part 4. Check Digit
This is a single digit at the end of the ISBN which provides an automatic check on the correctness of the ISBN.

Group identifier
Group identifiers are allocated by the International ISBN Agency and a publisher wishing to participate in the ISBN system must belong to a recognized ISBN group. Groups are determined by national, geographic, language or other pertinent considerations. Experience has shown that groups based on national or geographic considerations are the most satisfactory. The following group identifiers are in use at present:

0 and 1	Australia, English-speaking Canada, New Zealand, Republic of South Africa, UK, USA, Zimbabwe
2	France, French-speaking Belgium, French-speaking Canada, French-speaking Switzerland
3	Austria, Federal Republic of Germany, German-speaking Switzerland
4	Japan
5	Union of Soviet Socialist Republics
81	India
82	Norway
83	Poland
84	Spain, Spanish-speaking South America (partly)
85	Brazil
86	Yugoslavia
87	Denmark
88	Italy
90	Netherlands, Dutch-speaking Belgium
91	Sweden
92	United Nations
951	Finland
958	Colombia
962	Hong Kong
963	Hungary
965	Israel
968	Mexico
971	Philippines
974	Thailand
977	Egypt
978	Nigeria
9964	Ghana
9971	Singapore
99914	Suriname
99915	Trinidad and Tobago

Publisher's Prefix
The publisher's prefix designates the publisher of a given book. Publishers with a large output of books are assigned a short publisher's prefix; publishers with a small output of books are assigned a longer publisher's prefix.

Title identifier
The title identifier is assigned to a particular title or edition of a title by the publisher from within the range of numbers assigned to him and which will depend upon the length of his publisher's prefix. Title identifiers are normally assigned by the publisher himself. Publishers who assign their own title identifiers may use them to identify titles in the publishing house throughout the planning stages.

Check digit
The 'check digit' is the last digit in an ISBN and is computed as the result of an elaborate calculation on the other nine digits.

This calculation is performed almost instantaneously by an electronic computing device, and is a means of detecting incorrectly transcribed numbers. The check digit is calculated on a modulus 11 with weights 10-2, using X in lieu of 10 where ten would occur as a check digit.

This means that each of the first nine digits of the ISBN — ie excluding the check digit itself — is multiplied by a number ranging from 10 to 2 and the sum of the products thus obtained, plus the check digit, must be divisible, without remainder, by 11. For example:

	Group Identifier	Publisher's Prefix		
ISBN	0	8	4	3	6
Weight	10	9	8	7	6
Products	0 +	72+	32+	21+	36+

	Title Number			Check Digit
ISBN	1	0	7	2	7
Weight	5	4	3	2	
Products	5+	0+	21+	4 +	7

Total: 198

As 198 can be divided by 11 without remainder 0 8436 1072 7 is a valid International Standard Book Number.

The number of digits in each part; and how to recognize them in an ISBN
The number of digits in each of the identifying parts 1, 2 and 3 is variable, though the total number of digits contained in these parts is always 9. These nine digits together with the check digit bring the total number of digits in an ISBN to ten.

The number of digits in the group identifier will vary according to the likely output of books in a group. Thus groups with an expected large output will get numbers of one or two digits and publishers with an expected large output will get numbers of two or three digits.

Exceptionally, a one-digit number may be assigned to a publisher but it will be appreciated that the assignment of one-digit publisher identifiers greatly reduces the range of possible identifiers in the group. For ease of reading, the four parts of the ISBN are divided by spaces or hyphens. These spaces or hyphens, however, are not retained in a computer which depends upon the special distribution of ranges of numbers for the recognition of the parts.

Scope of the ISBN

For the purposes of the ISBN system books and other items to be numbered include:

Printed books and pamphlets

Microform publications

Braille publications

Mixed media publications

Machine-readable tapes designed to produce readable printout

Other similar media

Except:
Ephemeral printed materials such as diaries, calendars, advertising matter and the like

Art prints and art folders without title page and text

Sound recordings

Serial publications

Application of ISBN

General
A separate ISBN must be assigned to every different edition of a book, but NOT to an unchanged impression or unchanged reprint of the same book in the same format and by the same publisher. Price changes do not need new ISBN.

Facsimile reprints
A separate ISBN must be assigned to a facsimile reprint produced by a different publisher.

Books in different formats
A separate ISBN must be assigned to the different formats in which a particular title is published. For example: a hardback edition and a paperback edition each receives a separate ISBN. On the same principle, a microform edition receives a separate ISBN.

Multi-volume works
An ISBN must be assigned to the whole set of volumes of a multi-volume work as well as to each individual volume in the set.

Back stock
A publisher is required to number his back stock and publish the ISBN in his catalogues.
He must also print the ISBN in the first available reprint of an item from his back stock.

Collaborative publications
A publication issued as a coedition or joint imprint with other publishers is assigned an ISBN by the publisher in charge of distribution.

Books sold or distributed by agents
According to the principles of the ISBN system, a particular edition, published by a particular publisher receives only one ISBN and this ISBN must be retained no matter where or by whom the book is distributed or sold.
A book imported by an exclusive distributor or sole agent from an area not yet in the ISBN system and for which therefore no ISBN has been assigned, may be assigned an ISBN by the exclusive distributor.
A book imported by an exclusive distributor or sole agent to which a new title-page, bearing the imprint of the exclusive distributor, has been added in place of the title page of the original publisher, is to be given a new ISBN by the exclusive distributor or sole agent. The ISBN of the original publisher is also to be given as a related ISBN.
A book imported by several distributors from an area not yet in the ISBN system and for which, therefore, no ISBN has been assigned, may be assigned an ISBN by the group agency responsible for those distributors.

Publishers with more than one place of publication
A publisher operating in a number of places which are listed together in the imprint of a book will assign only one ISBN to the book.
A publisher operating separate and distinct offices or branches in different places may have a publisher identifier for each office or branch. Nevertheless, each book published is to be assigned only one ISBN, the assignment being made by the office or branch responsible for publication.

Register of ISBNs
Every publisher must keep a register of ISBNs that have been assigned to published and forthcoming books. The register is to be kept in numerical sequence giving ISBN, author, title and edition (where appropriate).

ISBN not to be re-used under any circumstances
An ISBN once allocated must not under any circumstances be re-used. This is of the utmost importance to avoid confusion. It is recognized that, owing to clerical errors, numbers will be incorrectly assigned. If this happens, the number must be deleted from the list of usable numbers and must not be assigned to another title. Every publisher will have sufficient numbers in his range for the loss of these numbers to be insignificant. Publishers should advise the group agency of the numbers thus deleted and of the titles to which they were erroneously assigned.

Printing of the ISBN

General
The ISBN must appear on the item itself. This is essential for the efficient running of the system.

Printing of ISBN on books
In the case of books, the ISBN must appear whenever possible: On the reverse of the title-page, or, if this is not possible, on the base of the title-page, or, if this too is not possible, at some other conspicuous location in the book. On the base of the spine.
On the back of the cover in 9-point type or larger.
On the back of the dust-jacket, and on the back of any other protective case or wrapper.
The ISBN should always be printed in type large enough to be easily legible (eg not smaller than 9 point).

Administration of the ISBN System

General
The administration of the ISBN system is carried on at three levels. These are the international, group and publisher levels.

International administration
The international administration of the system is in the hands of the International Standard Book Number Agency which has an Advisory Panel representing the ISO and the publishing and library world. The address of the International Agency is:

The International Standard Book Number Agency,
Staatsbibliothek Preussischer Kulturbesitz,
Potsdamer Str 33, Postfach 1407,
D-1000 Berlin 30, Federal Republic of Germany

The principal functions of the International Agency are:

To supervise the use of the system

To approve the definition and structure of groups

To allocate identifiers to groups

To advise groups on the setting up and functioning of group agencies

To advise group agencies on the allocation of publisher identifiers

To promote the world-wide use of the system

In addition, the International Agency also offers the following services. It will:

Provide a group agency with lists of ISBNs (with computer-generated check digits) for the use of publishers in the group.

Provide international registers of publishers, prefixes and publishers' names.

Provide from information supplied by group agencies a computer printout of lists of publishers' prefixes, names and locations.

Provide from information supplied by group agencies a computer printout of invalid or duplicate ISBNs.

Group administration
Groups are administered by Group Agencies. Within the group there may be several national agencies, eg group 0/1 has separate agencies in USA, United Kingdom, Canada, Australia etc, with the main agency for the whole group in the UK.

The functions of a group agency are:

To manage and administer the affairs of the group.

To handle relations with the International ISBN Agency on behalf of all the publishers in the group.

To decide, in consultation with trade organizations and publishers, the publisher identifier ranges required.

To allocate publishers' prefixes to publishers eligible to join the group and to maintain a register of publishers and their prefixes.

To decide, in consultation with trade organizations and publishers, which publishers shall assign numbers to their own titles and which publishers shall have numbers assigned to their titles by the group agency.

To provide technical advice and assistance to the publishers and to ensure that standards and approved procedures are observed in the group.

To make available a manual of instruction for publishers.

To make available computer printouts of ISBNs to publishers numbering their own books with check digits already calculated. (Such printouts may be obtained from the International Agency on request.)

To validate all ISBNs assigned by publishers numbering their own books and keep a register of them.

To inform publishers of any invalid or duplicate ISBNs assigned by them.

To assign numbers to all publications from those publishers who do not assign their own ISBNs and advise the publishers concerned of ISBNs assigned upon request.

To achieve, thereby, total numbering in the group.

To arrange with book listing and bibliographic agencies for the publication of ISBNs with the titles to which they refer.

To arrange with publishers for the numbering of their back lists and for the publication of these in appropriate trade lists and bibliographies.

To maintain liaison with all elements of the book trade and introduce new publishers to the system.

To assist the trade in the use of the ISBN in computer systems.

The national agencies are:

Australia
Mrs Cornell Platzer, National Library of Australia, Parkes Pl, Canberra, ACT 2600

Austria
Dr G Prosser, Hauptverband des Österreichischen Buchhandels, A-1010 Vienna 1, Grünangergasse 4

Belgium (Dutch-speaking)
Netherlands agency

Belgium (French-speaking)
French agency

Brazil
Biblioteca Nacional, Agência Brasileira do ISBN, Ave Rio Branco 219/39, 20000 Rio de Janeiro, RJ

Canada (English-speaking)
Paul McCormick, National Library of Canada, 395 Wellington St, Ottawa, Ontario K1A ON4

Canada (French-speaking)
Louise Tessier, ISBN/BNQ, Bureau de depot legal, Bibliotheque nationale du Quebec, 1700 rue St-Denis, Montreal, Quebec H2X 3K6

Colombia
Centro Regional para el Fomento del Libro en América Latina y el Caribe, Apdo Aéreo 17438, Calle 70 No 9-52, Bogotá

Denmark
Karen Lunde Christensen, Bibliothekscentralen Dansk Bogfortegnelse, Telegrafvej 5, DK-2750 Ballerup

Egypt
Dr S M El Sheniti, General Egyptian Book Organization, Boulac, Cairo

Finland
Dr Thea Aulo, Finnish ISBN Numbering Agency, Helsinki University Library, PL 312, SF-00170 Helsinki 17

France
Cécile Renault, Agence francophone pour la Numérotation internationale du Livre (AFNIL-ISBN), 117 blvd St-Germain, F-75279 Paris 6e

Federal Republic of Germany
Wilfried H Schinzel, Buchhändler-Vereinigung GmbH, Postfach 2404, D-6000 Frankfurt am Main 1

Ghana
Mr A N de Heer, Ghana Library Board, Research Library on African Affairs, PO Box 2970, Accra

Hong Kong
Timothy A Chow, Books Registration Unit, City Hall Library 6/F, Edinburgh Place, Hong Kong

Hungary
Dr Susánszky Zoltánné, Országos Széchényi Könyvtár Magyar ISBN Iroda, Pollack Mihálytér 10, H-1827 Budapest

India
Mrs Nilima Devi, Ministry of Education & Social Welfare (Department of Education), Raja Rammohun Roy National Educational Resources Centre, 1W-3, CR Barracks, Kasturba Gandhi Marg, New Delhi 1-110001

Israel
Israel ISBN Group Agency, c/o Center for Public Libraries, PO Box 242, Jerusalem

Italy
Gianni Merlini, Assoziacione Italiana Editori, Agenzia per l'Area di Lingua Italiana ISBN, Via delle Erbe 2, I-20121 Milan

Japan
Mr Shigeshi Sasaki, Japan Book Publishers Association, 6 Fukuro-machi, Shinjuku-ku, Tokyo

Mexico
Direccion General del Derecho de Autor Centro Nacional de Informacion, Mariano Escobedo 438, 5° piso, Mexico 5 DF

Netherlands
J van Leeuwan, Bureau ISBN, Centraal Boekhuis, Postbus 125, Culemborg

New Zealand
D C McIntosh, National Library of New Zealand, Private Bag, Wellington 1

Nigeria
Mrs O Omolayole, National Library of Nigeria, 4 Wesley St, PMB 12626, Lagos

Norway
May Ruth Novakowski, Norsk Boknummerkontor, Universitetsbiblioteket i Oslo, Drammensvegen 42, Oslo 2

Philippines
Lily Orbase, The National Library of the Philippines, TM Kalaw St, Manila

Poland
Bioru Miedzynarodowego Numeru Ksiazki, ul Jasna 26, 00-950 Warsaw

Singapore
Mrs Kee Yew Siew, National Library, Stamford Rd, Singapore 0617

Republic of South Africa
Dr H J Aschenborn, State Library, PO Box 397, Pretoria 0001

Spain
Instituto Nacional del Libro Español, Santiago Rusiñol 8, Madrid 3

Suriname
Dr Ellen Kensmil, Suriname Publishers' Association, Domineestr 26, Paramaribo

Sweden
Folke Hermanson-Snickars, Swedish National ISBN-Centre, Bibliographical Institute, Royal Library, PO Box 5039, S-10241 Stockholm 5

Switzerland (French-speaking)
French agency

Switzerland (German-speaking)
Peter Oprecht, Schweizerischer Buchhandler- und Verleger-Verband, Bellerivestr 3, CH-8008 Zurich

Thailand
Mrs Suwakhon Phadung-Ath, National Library, Tawasukree, Bangkok

Trinidad and Tobago
Mr S B Maharaj, The Caribbean Book Centre, 64a Independence Sq, Port-of-Spain

Union of Soviet Socialist Republics
Ju I Fartunin, Bibliograficeskij Institut SSSR, Kremlevskaja nab 1/9, 119816 Moscow G-19

UK
Standard Book Numbering Agency Ltd, 12 Dyott St, London WC1A 1DF

United Nations
Lionel Tzod, Book & International Cultural Exchange Promotions Division, UNESCO, 7 pl de Fontenoy, F-75700 Paris

USA
Emery Koltay, Standard Book Numbering Agency, 1180 Ave of the Americas, New York, NY 10036

Yugoslavia
Martin Znidersic, Cancarjeva Zalozba, YU-61001 Ljubljana, Kopitarjeva Ulica 2, Postni Predal 201-IV

Zimbabwe
National Archives of Zimbabwe, Private Bag 7729, Causeway, Salisbury

ISBN and ISSN

In addition to the International Standard Book Number System, a complementary numbering system for serial publications has also been established.
A serial is defined as any publication issued in successive parts, usually bearing numerical or chronological designations and intended to be continued indefinitely. Serials include periodicals, yearbooks and monographic series.
The International Standard Serial Number System (ISSN) is administered by the International Centre for the Registration of Serials (ISDS), whose address is:

International Serial Data System,
20 rue Bachaumont, F-75002 Paris, France

Publishers of serials should apply to the International Serials Data System or to their National Serials Data Centre, if there is one, for ISSNs for their serial publications.
Certain publications, such as yearbooks, annuals, monographic series, etc, should be assigned an ISSN for the serial title (which will remain the same for all the parts or individual volumes of the serial) and an ISBN for each individual volume.
Both ISSN and ISBN where they are assigned must be given on the publication and clearly identified.

(The above information is from the ISBN *Users' Manual*, compiled by the International ISBN Agency, Staatsbibliothek Preussischer Kulturbesitz, Berlin, Federal Republic of Germany.)

Book Trade Calendar

DATE	EVENT	CONTACT

1981

January 2-11	10th National Book Fair. Jaipur, Rajasthan, India	National Book Trust, A5 Green Park, New Delhi 110016, India *Tel:* 664667
January 29-February 9	13th Cairo International Book Fair. Cairo, Egypt	General Egyptian Book Organization, Corniche El Nil, Boulac, Cairo, Egypt *Tel:* 972649
January 31-February 5	American Library Association: Midwinter Meeting Washington DC, USA	American Library Association, 50 East Huron St, Chicago, Illinois 60611, USA *Tel:* (312) 944 6780
March 1-5	6th Ife Book Fair. Ile-Ife, Nigeria	The Fair Director, Ife Book Fair, University of Ife Bookshop Ltd, University of Ife, Ile-Ife, Nigeria
March 4-5	Book Print Fair. London, UK	Book Print Fair, 8-9 Giltspur St, London EC1A 9DE, UK *Tel:* (01) 248 7387
March 11	The London Academic Book Fair. London, UK	The London Book Fair, 16 Pembridge Rd, London W11 3HL, UK *Tel:* (01) 229 1825
March 14-22	Brussels International Book Fair. Brussels, Belgium	International Book Fair, 111 Ave du Parc, B-1060 Brussels, Belgium *Tel:* (02) 5382167
March 15-21	Leipzig International Book Fair (at Leipzig Spring Fair). Leipzig, German Democratic Republic	Leipziger Messeamt, Markt 11-15, Postfach 720, DDR-701 Leipzig, German Democratic Republic *Tel:* 71810
March 18	Publishers Association: Annual General Meeting. London, UK	The Publishers Association, 19 Bedford Sq, London WC1, UK *Tel:* (01) 580 6321
March 23-28	VI International Booksellers Congress and IBF General Assembly. Melbourne, Australia	International Booksellers Federation, Grünangergasse 4, A-1010 Vienna, Austria *Tel:* (222) 521535
March 24-28	18th Didacta Eurodidac. Basle, Switzerland	Eurodidac, Jägerstr 5, CH-4058 Basle, Switzerland *Tel:* (061) 265052
March 28-April 6	10th Thai National Book Fair. Bangkok, Thailand	Publishers' and Booksellers' Association of Thailand, 108 Sukhumvit Soi 53 (Madee Paidee), Bangkok, Thailand *Tel:* 2528759
April	Montreal International Book Fair. Montreal, Canada	Montreal International Book Fair, PO Box 596, Station N, Montreal, Quebec, Canada
April 2	International Children's Book Day. (1981 sponsor: Federal Republic of Germany)	IBBY Secretariat, Leonhardsgraben 38a, CH-4501 Basle, Switzerland
April 2-5	18th Children's Book Fair and 15th Exhibition for Illustrators. Bologna, Italy	Fiera del libro per ragazzi, Piazza della Constituzione 6, I-40128, Bologna, Italy *Tel:* (051) 503050
April 4-12	Mexico International Book Fair. Mexico	Mexico International Book Fair, Copilco 283, Apdo 20-515, Mexico 20DF, Mexico
April 5-10	10th Jerusalem International Book Fair. Jerusalem, Israel	The Jerusalem International Book Fair, 22 Jaffa Rd, Jerusalem 91000, Israel *Tel:* (02) 233720
April 5-11	National Library Week. USA	American Library Association, 50 East Huron St, Chicago, Illinois 60611, USA *Tel:* (312) 944 6780

DATE	EVENT	CONTACT

1981 (Cont'd)

April 6-9	New Zealand Booksellers 60th Annual Conference. Nelson, New Zealand	Booksellers Association of New Zealand (Inc), PO Box 11-377, Wellington, New Zealand *Tel:* Wellington 728 678
April 8-10	Book Publishers Association of New Zealand: Annual Conference. New Zealand	Book Publishers Association of New Zealand, PO Box 78-071, Grey Lynn, Auckland 2, New Zealand *Tel:* Auckland 767 251
April 9-13	Malta International Book Fair. Valletta, Malta	Malta International Book Fair, Ministry of Education, Valletta, Malta
April 11-15	International Book Festival. Nice, France	Festival International du Livre, Palais des Expositions, F-06300 Nice, France *Tel:* 551815 and 5 rue Stanislas, F-75006 Paris, France *Tel:* 544 2018
April 24-27	The Booksellers Association of Great Britain & Ireland: Annual Conference and Trade Exhibition. Eastbourne, UK	Conference Secretary, The Booksellers Association of Great Britain & Ireland, 154 Buckingham Palace Rd, London SW1W 9TZ, UK *Tel:* (01) 730 8214
April 27-May 1	International Reading Association: Annual Convention. New Orleans, Louisiana, USA	International Reading Association, 800 Barksdale Rd, PO Box 8139 Newark, Delaware 19711, USA *Tel:* (302) 731 1600
April or May	Cape Town Book Festival. Cape Town, Republic of South Africa	Associated Booksellers of Southern Africa, 1 Meerendal, Nightingale Way, Republic of South Africa *Tel:* Pinelands 7405
May 20-25	26th International Book Fair. Warsaw, Poland	Ars Polona, Sekretariat, Miedzynarodowych Targów Książki, PO Box 1001, 00-068 Warsaw, Poland *Tel:* 261201
May 20-28	Budapest Book Fair. Budapest, Hungary	Müszaki Könyvkiado, PO Box 581, H-1374 Budapest, Hungary *Tel:* 113450
May 21-25	Union internationale des industries graphiques de reproduction: Congress. Mainz, Federal Republic of Germany	Union internationale des industries graphiques de reproduction, 142 Blvd St-Germain, F-75278 Paris Cedex 06, France
May 23-26	American Booksellers Association: Annual Convention. Atlanta, USA	American Booksellers Association, 122 East 42nd St, New York, NY 10168, USA *Tel:* (212) 867 9060
June 26-July 2	American Library Association: Annual Conference. San Francisco, California, USA	American Library Association, 50 East Huron St, Chicago, Illinois 60611, USA *Tel:* (312) 944 6780
July	Canadian Booksellers Association Convention	Canadian Booksellers Association, 490 McNicoll Ave, Willowdale, Ontario, Canada
August	Colombo Children's Book Fair. Colombo, Sri Lanka	Colombo Children's Book Fair, 451 Galle Rd, Colombo 41, Sri Lanka
August	Singapore Book Fair. Republic of Singapore	Book Fair Secretariat, 428 Katon Shopping Centre, Singapore 15
August 2-5	The International Association of Printing House Craftsmen, Inc: Annual Convention. Boston, Mass, USA	The International Association of Printing House Craftsmen, Inc, 7599 Kenwood Rd, Cincinnati, Ohio 45236, USA *Tel:* (513) 891 0611 – John A Davies
August 15-22	33rd Writers' Summer School. Swanwick, Derbyshire, UK	The Secretary, Writers' Summer School, 308 Lewisham Rd, London SE13 7PA, UK

450 BOOK TRADE CALENDAR

DATE	EVENT	CONTACT
1981 (Cont'd)		
August 18-21	Annual General Meetings of: South African Publishers Association Associated Booksellers of Southern Africa Overseas Publishers Representatives Book Trade Association. Cape Town, Republic of South Africa	Associated Booksellers of Southern Africa Ltd, 1 Meerendal, Nightingale Way, Republic of South Africa *Tel:* Pinelands 7405
August 28-September 9	International Federation for Modern Languages and Literatures: XVth International Congress. Phoenix, Arizona, USA	Professor Peter Horwath, Department of Foreign Languages, Arizona State University, Tempe, Arizona, USA *Tel:* (602) 965 4727
September 2-8	Moscow International Book Fair. Moscow, USSR	General Directorate of International Book Exhibitions & Fairs of the USSR Godkomizdat, 16 Chekhov St, Moscow 103006, Union of Soviet Socialist Republics *Tel:* (299) 4034
September 15-21	14th Sofia International Book Fair. Sofia, Bulgaria	International Book Fair, Department for Exhibitions & Fairs, 11 Slaveikov Sq, Sofia, Bulgaria *Tel:* 87 9111
September 20-26	P E N 45th International Congress. Lyons and Paris, France	International PEN, 7 Dilke St, London SW3 4JE, UK *Tel:* (01) 352 9549
September 22-25	Aslib 54th Annual Conference. Oxford, UK	Conference Organizer, Aslib, 3 Belgrave Sq, London SW1X 8PL, UK *Tel:* (01) 235 5050
Autumn	International Association of Literary Critics: Annual Congress. Warsaw, Poland	Association internationale des critiques litteraires, 38 rue du Faubourg St-Jacques, F-75014 Paris, France *Tel:* 587 3876
October	New Zealand Book Month. New Zealand	Book Publishers Association of New Zealand, PO Box 78-071, Grey Lynn, Auckland 2, New Zealand *Tel:* Auckland 549-293
October 3-10	National Children's Book Week. UK	Children's Book Officer, The Publishers Association, 19 Bedford Sq, London WC1, UK *Tel:* (01) 580 6321
October 4-9	Distripress Annual Congress. Rome, Italy	Distripress, Beethovenstr 20, CH-8002, Zurich, Switzerland *Tel:* (01) 202 4121
October 14-19	33rd Frankfurt Book Fair. Frankfurt am Main, Federal Republic of Germany	Ausstellungs- und Messe-GmbH des Börsenvereins des deutschen Buchhandels, Postfach 2404, D-6000 Frankfurt am Main 1, Federal Republic of Germany *Tel:* (0611) 13061
November 1-4	Book Manufacturers' Institute: Annual Conference. Marco Island, Florida, USA	Book Manufacturers' Institute Inc, 111 Prospect St, Stamford, Connecticut 06901, USA *Tel:* (203) 324 9670
November 16-22	National Children's Book Week. USA	The Children's Book Council, 67 Irving Pl, New York, NY 10003, USA *Tel:* (212) 254 2666
November 20- December 20	The Jewish Book Month. USA	The Jewish Book Council of the National Jewish Welfare Board, 15 East 26th St, New York, NY 10010, USA *Tel:* (212) 532 4949
November 30- December 7	UNESCO Intergovernmental Copyright Committee: 4th Session. New Delhi, India	Copyright Division, UNESCO, 7 Pl de Fontenoy, F-75700 Paris, France *Tel:* 577 1610, ex. 62-11
December 27-30	Modern Language Association of America: Annual Convention. New York, USA	Modern Language Association of America, 62 Fifth Ave, New York, NY 10011, USA *Tel:* (212) 741 5588

BOOK TRADE CALENDAR

DATE	EVENT	CONTACT
1982		
February 5-15	5th World Book Fair. New Delhi, India	National Book Trust, A5 Green Park, New Delhi 110016, India *Tel:* 664667
March	Book Print Fair. London, UK	Book Print Fair, 8-9 Giltspur St, London EC1A 9DE, UK *Tel:* (01) 248 7387
March	Brussels International Book Fair. Brussels, Belgium	International Book Fair, 111 Ave du Parc, B-1060 Brussels, Belgium *Tel:* (02) 5382167
March (provisionally)	EURIM 5	The Conference Organizer, Aslib, 3 Belgrave Sq, London SW1X 8PL, UK *Tel:* (01) 235 5050
March 3-12	1982 Writers' Week. Adelaide Festival of Arts, Adelaide, Australia	Writers' Week Committee, Adelaide Festival, Adelaide Festival Centre, King William Rd, Adelaide, South Australia 5000, Australia *Tel:* 51 0121
March 14-21	Leipzig International Book Fair (at Leipzig Spring Fair). Leipzig, German Democratic Republic	Leipziger Messeamt, Markt 11-15, Postfach 720, DDR-701 Leipzig, German Democratic Republic *Tel:* 71810
March or April	19th Children's Book Fair and 16th Exhibition for Illustrators. Bologna, Italy	Fiera del libro per ragazzi, Piazza della Constituzione 6, I-40128, Bologna, Italy *Tel:* (051) 503050
March or April	The Publishers Association: Annual General Meeting. London, UK	The Publishers Association, 19 Bedford Sq, London WC1, UK *Tel:* (01) 580 6321
April	Book Publishers Association of New Zealand: Annual Conference. New Zealand	Book Publishers Association of New Zealand, PO Box 78-071, Grey Lynn, Auckland 2, New Zealand *Tel:* Auckland 767 251
April 2	International Children's Book Day	IBBY Secretariat, Leonhardsgraben 38a, CH-4051 Basle, Switzerland
April 5-7	The London Book Fair. London, UK	The London Book Fair, 16 Pembridge Rd, London W11 3HL, UK *Tel:* (01) 229 1825
April 26-30	International Reading Association: Annual Convention. Chicago, Illinois, USA	International Reading Association, 800 Barksdale Rd, PO Box 8139, Newark, Delaware 19711, USA *Tel:* (302) 731 1600
April or May	International Book Festival. Nice, France	Festival International du Livre, Palais des Expositions, F-06300 Nice, France *Tel:* 551855 and 5 rue Stanislas, F-75006 Paris, France *Tel:* 544 2018
May 19-24	27th International Book Fair. Warsaw, Poland	Ars Polona, Sekretariat, Miedzynarodowych Targów Książki, PO Box 1001, 00-068 Warsaw, Poland *Tel:* 261201
May 29-June 1	American Booksellers Association: Annual Convention. Anaheim, California, USA	American Booksellers Association, 122 East 42nd St, New York, NY 10168, USA *Tel:* (212) 867 9060
June	P E N 46th International Congress. Belgrade, Yugoslavia	International PEN, 7 Dilke St, London SW3 4JE, UK *Tel:* (01) 352 9549
July 27-29	International Reading Association: 9th World Congress. Dublin, Republic of Ireland	International Reading Association, 800 Barksdale Rd, PO Box 8139, Newark, Delaware 19711, USA *Tel:* (302) 731 1600

452 BOOK TRADE CALENDAR

DATE	EVENT	CONTACT
1982 (Cont'd)		
August 22-25	The International Association of Printing House Craftsmen, Inc: Annual Convention. Lancaster, PA, USA	The International Association of Printing House Craftsmen, Inc, 7599 Kenwood Rd, Cincinnati, Ohio 45236, USA *Tel:* (513) 819 0611 – John A Davies
September 6-10	International Board on Books for Young People: Biennial Congress. Cambridge, UK	British IBBY, Ms B Mathias, National Book League, Book House, East Hill, Wandsworth, London SW18 2HZ, UK *Tel:* (01) 870 9055
September 10-16	Federation Internationale de Documentation (FID): 41st Conference and Congress. Hong Kong	Federation Internationale de Documentation, Hofweg 7, The Hague, Netherlands
September 27-October 2	Distripress Annual Congress. Lisbon, Portugal	Distripress, Beethovenstr 20, CH-8002 Zurich, Switzerland *Tel:* (01) 202 4121
September (end)	The International League of Antiquarian Booksellers: International Congress. Paris, France	The International League of Antiquarian Booksellers, Poststr 14-16, D-2 Hamburg 36, Federal Republic of Germany *Tel:* (040) 343236
September (end)	International Antiquarian Book Fair. Paris, France	The International League of Antiquarian Booksellers, Poststr 14-16, D-2 Hamburg 36, Federal Republic of Germany *Tel:* (040) 343236
October 6-11	34th Frankfurt Book Fair. Frankfurt am Main, Federal Republic of Germany	Ausstellungs- und Messe-GmbH des Börsenvereins des deutschen Buchhandels, Postfach 2404, D-6000 Frankfurt am Main 1, Federal Republic of Germany *Tel:* (0611) 13061
November 15-21	National Children's Book Week. USA	The Children's Book Council, 67 Irving Pl, New York, NY 10003, USA *Tel:* (212) 254 2666
December 27-30	Modern Language Association of America: Annual Convention. Los Angeles, USA	Modern Language Association of America, 62 Fifth Ave, New York, NY 10011, USA *Tel:* (212) 741 5588
Date unknown at time of going to press	19th Didacta Eurodidac. Hanover, Federal Republic of Germany	Eurodidac, Jägerstr 5, CH-4058 Basle, Switzerland *Tel:* (061) 265052
Date unknown at time of going to press	International Association of Literary Critics: Annual Congress. Warsaw, Poland	Association internationale des critiques litteraires, 38 rue du Faubourg St-Jaques, F-75014 Paris, France *Tel:* 587 3876
Date unknown at time of going to press	International Booksellers Federation: General Assembly. Netherlands	International Booksellers Federation, Grünangergasse 4, A-1010 Vienna, Austria *Tel:* (222) 521535
1983		
March	Brussels International Book Fair. Brussels, Belgium	International Book Fair, 111 Ave du Parc, B-1060 Brussels, Belgium *Tel:* (02) 5382167
March 13-19	Leipzig International Book Fair (at Leipzig Spring Fair). Leipzig, German Democratic Republic	Leipziger Messeamt, Markt 11-15, Postfach 720, DDR-701 Leipzig, German Democratic Republic *Tel:* 71810
April 2	International Children's Book Day	IBBY Secretariat, Leonhardsgraben 38a, CH-4051 Basle, Switzerland
May 2-6	International Reading Association: Annual Convention. Anaheim, California, USA	International Reading Association, 800 Barksdale Rd, PO Box 8139 Newark, Delaware 19711, USA *Tel:* (302) 731 1600

DATE	EVENT	CONTACT
1983 (Cont'd)		
June 4-7	American Booksellers Association: Annual Convention. Dallas, Texas, USA	American Booksellers Association, 122 East 42nd St, New York, NY 10168, USA *Tel:* (212) 867 9060
August	The International Association of Printing House Craftsmen, Inc: Annual Convention. Calgary, Canada	The International Association of Printing House Craftsmen, Inc, 7599 Kenwood Rd, Cincinnati, Ohio 45236, USA *Tel:* (513) 891 0611 – John A Davies
October 2-7	Distripress Annual Congress. Berlin, Germany	Distripress, Beethovenstr 20, CH-8002 Zurich, Switzerland *Tel:* (01) 202 4121
November	National Children's Book Week. USA	The Children's Book Council, 67 Irving Pl, New York, NY 10003, USA *Tel:* (212) 254 2666
December 27-30	Modern Language Association of America: Annual Convention. New York, USA	Modern Language Association of America, 62 Fifth Ave, New York, NY 10011, USA *Tel:* (212) 741 5588

Index

The order of the index is word by word so that, for example, Alpha Literatur comes before Alphabet & Image.

Some words at the beginning of names are ignored when indexing. These include initials and forenames of personal names (so Jonathan Cape Ltd is listed under C) and words which simply mean 'publisher', 'bookseller' or 'company' (so Editions Arcade is listed under A). In the text the first word of a name that is counted when indexing is printed in bold type.

Names which start with numbers written as numerals are put before A in the index (so Edition No 1 is the first entry in the index, while Les Editions des Deux Coqs d'Or is listed under D).

1. Edition No. (France) 88
2. Edition der, (Federal Republic of Germany) 120
3 Arches (Belgium) 33
'8' Nentori Publishing House (Albania) 1
'13 Calle', Librería, (Guatemala) 173
14th October Corporation (People's Democratic Republic of Yemen) 421
20th Century Classics (New Zealand) 271
20th Century Classics (United Kingdom) 409
24 Heures, Editions, (Switzerland) 337
29, Ediciones, (Spain) 314
62, Edicions, SA (Spain) 314
70, Edições, Lda (Portugal) 295
99, Ediciones, SA (Spain) 314

A B C (Aurelia Book Club) (Belgium) 43
A B C Bookshop (New Zealand) 272
A B C Bookstore Ltd (Israel) 210
A B C Buchklub GmbH & Co KG (Austria) 29
A B C D Group (United Kingdom) 365
A B C, Editions, Jeunesse SARL (Belgium) 33
A B C Kitabevi (Turkey) 359
A B C, Librería, (Argentina) 8
A B C, Librerías, SA (Peru) 286
A B C, Librerías, SA (Peru) 287
A B C Verlag (Switzerland) 337
A B C Yayinevi (Turkey) 358
A B E F (France) 109
A B G R A (Asociación de Bibliotecarios Graduados de la República Argentina) (Argentina) 8
A B I C Publishers (Nigeria) 274
A B M, Librairie, (Benin) 45
A B M, Librairie-Papetiere, (Benin) 45
A B P (NZ) Ltd (New Zealand) 269
A B, The, Book Club (Iceland) 180
A C E R (Spain) 323
A C U R I L (International Organizations) 431
A D A C Verlag (Federal Republic of Germany) 120
A D A Edita Tokyo Co Ltd (Japan) 224
A D I S Press Australasia Pty Limited (Australia) 10
A D I S Press International Ltd (Hong Kong) 175
A D L A F (Federal Republic of Germany) 120
A E D O S, Editorial, Consejo de (Spain) 314
A E G - Telefunken Zentralabteilung Firmenverlag (Federal Republic of Germany) 120
A E I International (Portugal) 295
A E I International (Portugal) 297
A G I R (Artes Graficas Industrias Reunidas SA) (Brazil) 48
A G P O L (Przedsiebiorstwo Reklamy i Wydawnictw Handlu Zagranicznego) (Poland) 290
A H I Literary Research Award (New Zealand) 272
A L A Verlag (Switzerland) 337
A L F A — Radna organizacija za izdavačku djelatnost (Yugoslavia) 421

A M B (Arbeitsgemeinschaft mitteleuropäischer Bibelwerke), Association of Mid-European Biblical Presses (Federal Republic of Germany) 120
A M Z Editrice sas di Mario Abriani e C (Italy) 212
A N B A D S (Senegal) 303
A N Z (Australia) 10
A N Z Local History Award (Australia) 21
A O V, Edições, (Portugal) 295
A P A (Academic Publishers Associated) (Netherlands) 256
A P C K (Republic of Ireland) 202
A P C O L (Australia) 10
'A' Publishing Institute (Israel) 206
A R E D I P (Agence Recherches Droits Internationaux et Promotion) (France) 88
A R E S, Edizioni, (Italy) 212
A R L I S (The Art Libraries Society) (United Kingdom) 411
A R P L E (Association romande du Personnel de la Librairie et de l'Edition) (Switzerland) 336
a s p b (Federal Republic of Germany) 166
A U Press & Publications (India) 181
Aadab, Al-, Bookshop (Bahrain) 31
Aadiesh Book Depot (India) 182
Aane-Adab (Pakistan) 282
Aar-Verlag (Federal Republic of Germany) 120
Aare-Verlag (Switzerland) 337
Aarestrup, Emil, Prize (Denmark) 79
Aargauer Tagblatt (AT) Verlag AG (Switzerland) 337
Abaco, Editorial, de Rodolfo Depalma SRL (Argentina) 3
Abacus (United Kingdom) 365
Abacus Press (United Kingdom) 365
Abadia, Publicacions de l', de Montserrat (Spain) 314
Abakon Verlagsgesellschaft mbH (Federal Republic of Germany) 120
Abakus Schallplatten Barbara Fietz (Federal Republic of Germany) 120
Abbeville Press (United Kingdom) 365
Abbey (United Kingdom) 365
Abbey's Bookshop (Australia) 19
Abdulghani, Abdulla, & Sons Co (Qatar) 300
Abelard-Schuman Ltd (United Kingdom) 365
Abeledo, Editorial, Perrot SAEeI (Argentina) 3
Abercromby Bookshop (Trinidad and Tobago) 356
Aberdeen University Press Ltd (United Kingdom) 366
Abhinav Publications (India) 182
Abhishek Publications (India) 182
Abiva Publishing House Inc (Philippines) 288
Abril SA Cultural e Industrial (Brazil) 48
Abson Books (United Kingdom) 366
Abtour, Georges, SA, Librairie-Papeterie (Chad) 61
Academi, Yr, Gymreig (The Welsh Academy) (United Kingdom) 412
Academia (Czechoslovakia) 69
Academia Amazonense de Letras (Brazil) 56
Academia Argentina de Letras (Argentina) 8
Academia, Biblioteca da, das Ciências de Lisboa (Portugal) 298
Academia Cachoeirense de Letras (Brazil) 56
Academia Catarinense de Letras (Brazil) 56
Academia Cearense de Letras (Brazil) 56
Academia de Buenas Letras de Barcelona (Spain) 325
Academia de Ciencias de la República de Cuba (Cuba) 68
Academia de Letras (Brazil) 56
Academia de Letras da Bahia (Brazil) 56
Academia de Letras de Piauí (Brazil) 56
Academia Feminina Espírito Santense de Letras (Brazil) 56
Academia Matogrossense de Letras (Brazil) 56
Academia Mineira de Letras (Brazil) 56
Academia Nacional de Letras (Uruguay) 417
Academia Nicaragüense de la Lengua (Nicaragua) 273
Academia Paranaense de Letras (Brazil) 56
Academia Paulista de Letras (Brazil) 56
Academia Pernambucana de Letras (Brazil) 56
Academia Publications P Ltd (Malaysia) 244
Academia Riograndense de Letras (Brazil) 56
Academia Sinica, The Library of, (People's Republic of China) 63
Academic Press Inc (London) Ltd (United Kingdom) 366
Academic Press, The, (India) 182

Academic Publications (United Kingdom) 366
Academic Publishers (India) 182
Academic Publishers Associated (Netherlands) 256
Academica Lda (Mozambique) 254
Académie des Lettres et des Arts (France) 109
Académie Goncourt (France) 109
Académie Internationale de Tourisme (Monaco) 253
Académie, L', du Livre SA (Belgium) 43
Académie mauricienne de Langue et de Littérature (Mauritius) 248
Académie Montaigne (France) 109
Académie royale de Langue et de Littérature françaises (Belgium) 44
Académie royale des Sciences, des Lettres et des Beaux-Arts de Belgique (Belgium) 44
Academiei, Editura, Republicii Socialiste România (Romania) 300
Academiei Republicii Socialiste România, Biblioteca, (Romania) 301
Academiei Republicii Socialiste România, Biblioteca Filialei Cluj a, (The Library of the Cluj Branch of the Academy of the RSR) (Romania) 301
Academon (The Hebrew University Students' Printing and Publishing House) (Israel) 206
Academy, Council on Libraries of the, of Sciences of the USSR (Union of Soviet Socialist Republics) 363
Academy Editions (France) 88
Academy Editions (United Kingdom) 366
Academy, Fundamental Library of the, of Medical Sciences (Union of Soviet Socialist Republics) 362
Academy of Comparative Philosophy & Religion (India) 182
Academy of Islamic Research and Publications (India) 182
Academy of Sciences Publishing House (Democratic People's Republic of Korea) 236
Academy of Social Sciences Publishing House (Democratic People's Republic of Korea) 236
Academy of the Hebrew Language (Israel) 206
Academy of Thirteen Prize (France) 110
Academy, The, Press (Republic of Ireland) 202
Academy Press Ltd (Nigeria) 274
Accademia di Scienze, Lettere ed Arti (Italy) 221
Accademia Ligure di Scienze e Lettere (Italy) 221
Accademia Nazionale di Scienze, Lettere ed Arti (Italy) 221
Accademia Petrarca di Lettere, Arti e Scienze (Italy) 221
Accademia Toscana di Scienze e Lettere la Colombaria (Italy) 222
Accademia Virgiliana di Scienze, Lettere ed Arti di Mantova (Italy) 222
Accidentia Druck- und Verlagsgesellschaft mbH (Federal Republic of Germany) 121
Acco SV (Belgium) 33
Acervo, Ediciones, (Spain) 314
Acervo, Ediciones, de Argentina SRL (Argentina) 3
Achberger Verlag GmbH (Federal Republic of Germany) 121
Achenbach, Verlag Andreas, (Federal Republic of Germany) 121
Achiasaf Publishing House Ltd (Israel) 206
Achiever (Israel) 206
Ackermanns, F A, Kunstverlag (Federal Republic of Germany) 121
Acme Books (Australia) 10
Acme, Editorial, SA (Argentina) 3
Aconcagua Edic y Pub SA (Mexico) 248
Acribia, Editorial, (Spain) 315
Acropole (France) 88
Acrópole, Edições, (Portugal) 295
Acrópolis, Librería, (Guatemala) 173
Acta Medica Belgica ASBL (Belgium) 33
Acta Universitatis Gothoburgensis (Sweden) 328
Actinic Press Ltd (United Kingdom) 366
Action Publications (New Zealand) 269
Adab, Al-, Bookshop (Saudi Arabia) 302
Adab, Dar al, (Lebanon) 239
Adam, R P, (Denmark) 77
Adam Publishers (Israel) 206
Adamjee Prize (Pakistan) 284
Adams & Co Ltd (Republic of South Africa) 312

INDEX 455

Addams, Jane, Children's Book Award (International Literary Prizes) 439
Addis Ababa University Library (Ethiopia) 83
Addis Ababa University Press (Ethiopia) 83
Addison-Wesley Publishers Ltd (United Kingdom) 366
Addison-Wesley Publishing Co (Australia) 10
Addison-Wesley Publishing Co Inc (Philippines) 288
Addison-Wesley Publishing Group (Netherlands) 256
Addison-Wesley Singapore (Pte) Ltd (Republic of Singapore) 305
Adelaide University Union Press (Australia) 10
Adelphi Edizioni SpA (Italy) 212
Adeyle Brothers (Bangladesh) 32
Adeylebros & Co (Bangladesh) 31
Adkinson Parrish Ltd (United Kingdom) 366
Adlard Coles Ltd (United Kingdom) 366
Administracion, Archivo General de la, Civil del Estado (Spain) 324
Adonais Prize (Spain) 325
Adult, Directorate of, Education (India) 182
Advaita Ashrama (India) 182
Advance Publishing Co Ltd (Ghana) 169
Advanced Teacher Training College Library (Ghana) 170
Adventist Book Centre (Zimbabwe) 429
Adversaires, Editions, (Switzerland) 337
Advisory Committee on the Selection of Low-Priced Books for Overseas (United Kingdom) 364
Adyar-Verlag (Austria) 24
Æskunnar, Bókaútgáfa, (Iceland) 179
Aesopus Verlag GmbH (Switzerland) 337
Affiliated East-West Press Pvt Ltd (India) 182
Afghan Kitab (Afghanistan) 1
Afha Internacional SA (Spain) 315
Afram Publications (Ghana) Ltd (Ghana) 169
Africa Agency (Nigeria) 276
Africa Christian Press (Ghana) 169
Africa Editions (Senegal) 303
Africa Educational Representatives (Kenya) 235
Africa Literature Centre (Zambia) 428
African Book Centre (Zimbabwe) 429
African Library Association of South Africa (Republic of South Africa) 312
African Resources Publishing Co (Nigeria) 274
African Universities Press (Nigeria) 274
Africana Book Society Ltd (Republic of South Africa) 311
Africana Book Society (Pty) Ltd (Republic of South Africa) 307
Africana Educational Publishers (Nig) Ltd (Nigeria) 274
Africani Agency (Nigeria) 274
Afrikaans Literature Society (ALV) (Republic of South Africa) 313
Afrikaans Literature Society Prize (Republic of South Africa) 313
Afrique-Levant (Senegal) 303
Afrique-Levant, Edition, (Senegal) 303
Afriscope/University of Ife Bookshop Ltd Prize (International Literary Prizes) 439
Afro-Asian Writers' Bureau (Sri Lanka) 326
Afro-Asian Writers' Permanent Bureau (International Organizations) 431
Afro-Asian Writers, Permanent Bureau of, (Egypt) 81
Afrontamento, Ediçoes, (Portugal) 295
Agam Kala Prakashan (India) 182
Agathon (Netherlands) 256
'Age' Book of the Year (Australia) 21
Age d'Homme, Editions L', — La Cité (Switzerland) 337
Agence belge des grandes Editions SA (Belgium) 33
Agence belge des grandes Editions SA (Belgium) 42
Agence de Distribution de Presse (Senegal) 303
Agence de Distribution de Presse (Senegal) 303
Agence francophone pour la Numération internationale du Livre (AFNIL-ISBN) (France) 87
Agence Parisienne de Distribution Sarl (France) 88
Agência Brasileira do ISBN (Brazil) 47
Agencja Autorska (Poland) 291
Agencja Autorska (Poland) 293
Agents Editores Ltda (Brazil) 48
Agenzia Letteraria Internazionale (Italy) 220
Agenzia per l'Area di Lingua Italiana ISBN (Italy) 211
Agir, Livraria, (Brazil) 55
Agis Verlag GmbH (Federal Republic of Germany) 121
Agnelli, Giacomo, Editore (Italy) 212
Agora-Verlag (Federal Republic of Germany) 121
Agricultural Books Publishing House (Democratic People's Republic of Korea) 236
Agricultural Experiment Station Library (Puerto Rico) 299
Agricultural Library (Nigeria) 277
Agricultural Science, Central Library of, (Israel) 210
Agriculture University Library (Pakistan) 283
Agrupación Bibliotecológica del Uruguay (Uruguay) 417
Agrupación de Bibliotecas para la Integración de la Información Socio-Económica (ABIISE) (Peru) 287
Agudat Harashash (Israel) 206
Aguilar, M (Spain) 323
Aguilar Argentina SA de Ediciones (Argentina) 3
Aguilar Chilena de Ediciones (Chile) 61

Aguilar Colombiana de Ediciones (Colombia) 65
Aguilar, M, Editor SA (Mexico) 248
Aguilar, Editôra Nova, S/A (Brazil) 48
Aguilar Peruana de Ediciones SA (Peru) 286
Aguilar SA de Ediciones (Spain) 315
Aguilar Venezolana SA de Ediciones (Venezuela) 418
Aguirre, Librería, (Colombia) 66
Ahd, Al, Al Gadeed Bookstore (Egypt) 82
Ahlvwalia Book Depot (India) 182
Ahmadu Bello University Bookshop (Nigeria) 277
Ahmadu Bello University Library (Nigeria) 277
Ahmadu Bello University Press Ltd (Nigeria) 274
Ahmedabad Publishers' & Booksellers' Association (India) 181
Ahnert, L B, -Verlag (Federal Republic of Germany) 121
Ahora, Publicaciones, C por A (Dominican Republic) 79
Ahram, Al-, (Egypt) 82
Ahram, Al-, Establishment (Egypt) 81
Ahram, Al-, Establishment (Egypt) 82
Ahsan Brothers (Pakistan) 282
Aiken, Alex, (United Kingdom) 366
Airlife Publications (Shrewsbury) Ltd (United Kingdom) 366
Airport Bookshop (Republic of Korea) 238
Ajanta Books International (India) 182
Ajuda, Biblioteca da, (Portugal) 298
Akadémiai Kiadó (Publishing House of the Hungarian Academy of Sciences) (Hungary) 177
Akademie der Wissenschaften und der Literatur (Academy of Sciences, Arts and Literature) (Federal Republic of Germany) 167
Akademie-Verlag (German Democratic Republic) 115
Akademiförlaget (Sweden) 328
Akademii Nauk SSSR, Biblioteka, (Union of Soviet Socialist Republics) 362
Akademii Nauk SSSR, Gosudarstvennaya publichnaya nauchno-tekhnicheskaya biblioteka Sibirskogo otdeleniya, (Union of Soviet Socialist Republics) 362
Akademii Nauk SSSR, Institut nauchnoy informatsii po obschestvennym naukam, (Union of Soviet Socialist Republics) 362
Akademii Nauk USSR, Tsentral'nava nauchnaya biblioteka, (Union of Soviet Socialist Republics) 362
Akademilitteratur Förlaget AB (Sweden) 328
Akademische Druck- und Verlagsanstalt (Austria) 24
Akademische Verlagsgesellschaft (Federal Republic of Germany) 121
Akademische Verlagsgesellschaft Athenaion (Federal Republic of Germany) 121
Akademisk Boghandel (Denmark) 77
Akademisk Forlag (Denmark) 74
Akadia, Librería, Editorial (Argentina) 3
Akadoma (Indonesia) 198
Akane Shobo Co Ltd (Japan) 224
Akateeminen Kirjakauppa (Finland) 86
Akateeminen Kustannusliike Oy (Finland) 84
Åkerbloms, Johan, Universitetsbokhandel (Sweden) 334
Akhil Bhartiya Hindi Prakashak Sangh (India) 181
Akhila Bharatiya Sanskrit Parishad (India) 182
Akita Shoten Publishing Co Ltd (Japan) 224
Akros Publications (United Kingdom) 366
Aksorn Charerntat (Thailand) 354
Aksorn Charoen Tasna Ltd (Thailand) 354
Aktuell-Verlag (Austria) 24
Akutagawa Prize (Japan) 232
Al Book Co (Pvt) Ltd (India) 195
Aladdin Books Ltd (United Kingdom) 366
'Alas', Editorial, Valencia 234, (Spain) 315
Alba AB (Sweden) 328
Alba Buchverlag GmbH und Co KG (Federal Republic of Germany) 121
Alba Publikation Alf Teloeken GmbH und Co KG (Federal Republic of Germany) 121
Albanus Verlag (Switzerland) 337
Albatros (Czechoslovakia) 70
Albatros, Editorial, SRL (Argentina) 3
Albatros, Editura, (Romania) 300
Albatros Verlag AG (Switzerland) 337
Albe Soc Com (Uruguay) 417
Albêr, Verlag Karl, GmbH (Federal Republic of Germany) 121
Albert I, Koninklijke Bibliotheek, (Belgium) 43
Albin, Editions, Michel (France) 88
Albyn Press Ltd (United Kingdom) 366
Alcheh, Librarie, (Israel) 210
Alda, B P, (Indonesia) 198
Alden & Mowbray Ltd (United Kingdom) 366
Aldine Paperbacks (United Kingdom) 366
Aldus Books Ltd (United Kingdom) 366
Aldwych Press (United Kingdom) 366
Alekh Prakashan (India) 182
Aleko International Competition Awards in Comic Short Story (International Literary Prizes) 439
Alemana, Editorial, (Nicaragua) 273
Alemany, Juan Max, (Dominican Republic) 79
Alemar-Phoenix Publishing House Inc (Philippines) 288
Alemar's (Philippines) 289
Aleph Publishers Ltd (Israel) 206

Alexander Prize (International Literary Prizes) 439
Alexandria Municipal Library (Egypt) 82
Alfa, Editorial, Argentina SA (Argentina) 3
Alfa, Editorial, SA (Uruguay) 417
Alfa Edizioni e Rappresentanze Editoriali (Italy) 212
Alfa — Vydavatel'stvo technickej a ekonomickej literatúry (Czechoslovakia) 70
Alfa y Omega, Editora, (Dominican Republic) 79
Alfaguara, Ediciones, SA (Spain) 315
Alfieri Edizioni d'Arte (Italy) 212
Algamiia Almasriia Lilmaktabat Almadrasiia (Egypt) 82
Algemene Nederlandse Bond van Leesbibliotheekhouders (Netherlands) 266
Algemene Vlaamse Boekverkopersbond (Belgium) 33
Algona Publications Pty Ltd (Australia) 10
Alhambra, Editorial, SA (Spain) 315
Ali Publications (Bangladesh) 32
Alianza Editorial Mexicana (Mexico) 248
Alianza Editorial SA (Spain) 315
Alice, The, Literary Award (Australia) 21
Alinari Fratelli SpA Istituto di Edizioni Artistiche (Italy) 212
Alip & Sons Publishing Inc (Philippines) 288
Alison Press (United Kingdom) 366
Alkaios-Tropaiatis (Greece) 171
All India Booksellers' & Publishers' Association (India) 181
All-Union Patent and Technical Library (Union of Soviet Socialist Republics) 362
Állami könyvterjesztö vállalat (Hungary) 178
Állami könyvterjesztö vállalat orzágos antikvár (Hungary) 178
Allan, Ian, Ltd (United Kingdom) 366
Allan, Philip, Publishers Ltd (United Kingdom) 366
Allara Publishing (Australia) 10
Allen, J A, & Co Ltd (United Kingdom) 366
Allen & Unwin, George, Australia Pty Ltd (Australia) 10
Allen & Unwin, George, (Publishers) Ltd (United Kingdom) 367
Allen, W H, & Co Ltd (United Kingdom) 367
Allhems Förlag AB (Sweden) 328
Alliance, L', française (Senegal) 303
Alliance française (Zaire) 427
Alliance West African Publishers & Co (Nigeria) 274
Allied Irish Banks' Awards for Literature (Republic of Ireland) 205
Allied Publishers Private Ltd (India) 182
Allison & Busby Ltd (United Kingdom) 367
Allman & Son (Publishers) Ltd (United Kingdom) 367
Allmänna, AB, Förlaget (Sweden) 328
Allot, Librairie, (Mauritius) 248
Alma Mater, Librería, Inc (Puerto Rico) 299
Alma'Arif (Indonesia) 198
Almenna Bókafélagid (Iceland) 179
Almqvist och Wiksell Bokhandel AB (Sweden) 334
Almqvist och Wiksell Förlag AB (Sweden) 328
Almqvist och Wiksell International (Sweden) 328
Almqvist och Wiksell Läromedel AB (Sweden) 328
Alonso, Editorial Rodolfo, SRL (Argentina) 3
Alpha 9 GmbH (Federal Republic of Germany) 121
Alpha-Beta Publications Ltd (India) 182
Alpha Books (Australia) 10
Alpha Books (Zimbabwe) 429
Alpha Literatur Verlag (Federal Republic of Germany) 121
Alphabet & Image Ltd (United Kingdom) 367
Alphabooks (United Kingdom) 367
Alphonsiana, Bibliotheca, VZW (Belgium) 33
Alpina, Editions, (France) 88
Alpine Books (United Kingdom) 367
Alsatia SA (France) 88
Alta, Editions, (France) 88
Altea, Ediciones, SA (Spain) 315
Alternative Editions (United Kingdom) 367
Alternative Publishing Co-operative Ltd (Australia) 10
Alternative Verlag GmbH (Federal Republic of Germany) 121
Althea's Pet Series (United Kingdom) 367
Altiora NV (Belgium) 33
Alumni Press (Indonesia) 198
Álvarez, Librería Anibal, (Venezuela) 419
Alves, Livraria Francisco, Editôra SA (Brazil) 48
Alviella, Goblet d', Prize (Belgium) 44
Am Hasefer (Israel) 206
Am Oved Publishers Ltd (Israel) 206
Amade Prize (International Literary Prizes) 439
Amado, Armênio, Editor Suc (Portugal) 295
Amalthea-Verlag (Austria) 24
Aman, Pustaka, Press Sdn Bhd (Malaysia) 244
Amar Prakashan (India) 182
Amarko Book Agency (India) 182
Amazonen Frauenverlag GmbH (Federal Republic of Germany) 121
Ambika Publications (India) 182
Ambo, Uitgeverij, BV (Netherlands) 256
Ambro Lacus (Federal Republic of Germany) 121
Ambrosiana, Biblioteca, (Italy) 221
America, Casa, (Netherlands Antilles) 268

America Latina (Uruguay) 417
América, Librería, (Colombia) 66
América, Librería, (Nicaragua) 273
América Norildis Editores SA (Argentina) 3
Américalee, Editorial, SRL (Argentina) 3
American Book Store SA (Mexico) 252
American Books (Argentina) 8
American Bookstore (Greece) 172
American Center Library (Ghana) 170
American Center Library (India) 196
American Cultural Center Library (Libya) 241
American Cultural Center Library (Sudan) 327
American Cultural Center Library (Togo) 356
American Cultural Center Library (Upper Volta) 416
American-Israel Publishing Co Ltd (Israel) 206
American Library (Ethiopia) 83
American Library (Jordan) 233
American Library (Nepal) 255
American Library Resource Center (Republic of Singapore) 306
American-Scandinavian Foundation/PEN Translation Prizes (International Literary Prizes) 439
American University in Cairo Library (Egypt) 82
American University in Cairo Press (Egypt) 81
American University, Library of, of Beirut (Lebanon) 240
American University Publishers Group Ltd (United Kingdom) 367
Americana, Editorial, (Argentina) 3
Américas, Casa de las, (Cuba) 68
Americas, Editôra Das, SA Edameris (Brazil) 48
Amerind Publishing Co (P) Ltd (India) 182
Amerind Publishing Co (P) Ltd (India) 198
Amichai Publishing House Ltd (Israel) 206
Amigo, El, de Todos (Venezuela) 419
Amigos del Libro, Ediciones los, (Bolivia) 46
Amigos del Libro, Editorial los, (Bolivia) 46
Amigos do Livro (Portugal) 298
Amigos, Librería Los, del Libro (Bolivia) 46
Amikam (Israel) 206
Amina Book Stall (India) 182
Amir Kabir Publishing & Distributing Corporation (Iran) 201
Amir Publishing-Japheth Press Ltd (Israel) 206
Amis de Milosz, Les, (France) 88
Amis, Les, de Franco Maria Ricci (France) 107
Amitié, Editions de l', (France) 89
Amitié, L', par le Livre (France) 108
Amitié par le Livre, L', (France) 89
Amman Public Library (Jordan) 233
Amorrortu Editores SA (Argentina) 3
Amphora, Editions, SA (France) 89
Amsterdam Boek BV (Netherlands) 256
Amsterdam Prizes (Netherlands) 267
Amudha Nilayam Ltd (India) 182
Anabas-Verlag Günter Kämpf KG (Federal Republic of Germany) 121
Anagrama, Editorial, (Spain) 315
Anambra/Imo States School Libraries Association (Nigeria) 277
Anand Book Club (India) 195
Anand Paperbacks (India) 182
Anaya, Ediciones, SA (Spain) 315
Anceau, Annuaires Ravet, (France) 89
Anchor (United Kingdom) 367
Ancient History Book Club (United Kingdom) 409
Ancora, Editrice, Milano (Italy) 212
Ancora y Delfín, Librería, (Spain) 323
Andersen, Hans Christian, Awards (International Literary Prizes) 439
Andersen, Hans Christian, Prize (Denmark) 79
Andersen Press Ltd (United Kingdom) 367
Andersen Prize (Italy) 222
Andhra Pradesh Sahitya Akademi Awards (India) 197
Andreas, Jörn, Verlag (Austria) 24
Andreas und Andreas Verlagsbuchhandel (Austria) 24
Andrei, Organização, Editôra SA (Brazil) 48
Andres Kalender und Buch Verlag GmbH (Federal Republic of Germany) 121
Andromeda, Ediciones, (Argentina) 3
Angelet (Belgium) 33
Angeli, Franco, Editore (Italy) 212
Angelica, Biblioteca, (Italy) 221
Angkasa (Indonesia) 198
Anglo American, The, Bookshop (Egypt) 82
Anglo-Chinese Textbook Publishers Organization Ltd (Hong Kong) 175
Anglo Egyptian, The, Bookshop (Egypt) 82
Anglo-Hellenic Agency (Greece) 172
Anglo-Hellenic Publishing (Greece) 171
Angolana, Nova Editorial, SARL (Angola) 2
Angst, Verlag Roland, (Federal Republic of Germany) 121
Angus & Robertson Bookshops (Australia) 19
Angus & Robertson Publishers (Australia) 10
Angus & Robertson (South-East Asia) Ltd (Republic of Singapore) 305
Angus & Robertson (UK) Ltd (United Kingdom) 367
Angus & Robertson Writers' Fellowship (Australia) 21

Angyra Ekdotikos Oikos (Greece) 171
Anjuman Kitab-Khana-I-Afghanistan (Afghanistan) 1
Anjuman Taraqqi-e-Urdu Pakistan (Pakistan) 284
Ankara University Library (Turkey) 359
Ankh-Hermes BV (Netherlands) 256
Ankur Publishing House (India) 182
Anowuo Educational Publications (Ghana) 169
Anrich, Neithard, Verlag (Federal Republic of Germany) 121
Ansata-Verlag (Switzerland) 337
Ansay Pty Ltd (Australia) 10
Ansgar Forlag A/S (Norway) 278
Antara, Pustaka, (Indonesia) 198
Antara, Pustaka, (Malaysia) 244
Antenna Edições Técnicas Ltda (Brazil) 48
Anthonian Store Sdn Bhd (Malaysia) 245
Anthonian Stores Sdn Bhd (Malaysia) 244
Anthropos, Editions, SA (France) 89
Anthroposophiques Romandes, Editions, (Switzerland) 337
Antipodean Publishers Pty Ltd (Australia) 11
Antiquarian Booksellers' Association (United Kingdom) 364
Antiquarian Booksellers' Association of Japan (Japan) 224
Antoine, Editions Jacques, SPRL (Belgium) 33
Antoine, Librairies, (Lebanon) 239
Antonius-Verlag (Switzerland) 337
'Antso', Maison d'Edition Protestante, (Democratic Republic of Madagascar) 242
Antwerpse Lloyd NV (Belgium) 33
Anvil Books Ltd (Republic of Ireland) 202
Anwari Publications (Bangladesh) 31
Ao Livro Técnico (Brazil) 55
Ao Livro Técnico SA Industria a Comércio (Brazil) 48
Aoki Shoten Co Ltd (Japan) 224
Aowa Press & Publications (Nigeria) 274
Apa Productions (Pte) Ltd (Republic of Singapore) 305
Apaya, The, Bookshop (Sudan) 327
Apec Editôra SA (Brazil) 48
Apostolado, Livraria, da Imprensa (Portugal) 295
Apostolica Vaticana, Biblioteca, (Vatican City State) 418
Apoteksbolaget AB (Sweden) 328
Apple Paperbacks (Australia) 11
Appletree, The, Press Ltd (United Kingdom) 367
Applied Science Publishers Ltd (United Kingdom) 367
Aprile, Ruggero, (Italy) 212
Apuntes, Librería Los, (Uruguay) 417
Aquarian Press Ltd (United Kingdom) 367
Aquarius Editôra e Distribuidora de Livros Ltda (Brazil) 48
Aquila Publishing (United Kingdom) 367
Aquilina, A C, & Co (Malta) 246
Aquilina, A C, & Co (Malta) 246
Arab Advertising Organization (Syria) 352
Arab Archivists Institute (Iraq) 202
Arab, Al, Bookshop (Egypt) 82
Arab Institute for Research and Publishing (Lebanon) 239
Arab Library (Mauritania) 247
Arab Publishing, Al, House (Egypt) 81
Arab Regional Branch of the International Council on Archives (International Organizations) 431
Arab University Library Association (International Organizations) 431
Arador (Syria) 352
Arango, Biblioteca Luis-Angel, (Colombia) 66
Aranha, Graca, Prize (Brazil) 57
Arani-Verlag GmbH (Federal Republic of Germany) 121
Aranzadi, Editorial, (Spain) 315
Ararat Verlag GmbH (Federal Republic of Germany) 121
Arbalète, L', (France) 89
Arbeiderspers, BV Uitgeverij de, (Netherlands) 256
Arbeiterbewegung und Gesellschaftswissenschaft, Verlag, (Federal Republic of Germany) 121
Arbeitsgemeinschaft Buchgemeinschaften und verwandte Unternehmen im Börsenverein des Deutschen Buchhandels eV (Federal Republic of Germany) 118
Arbeitsgemeinschaft der Archive und Bibliotheken in der evangelischen Kirche (Federal Republic of Germany) 166
Arbeitsgemeinschaft der Hochschulbibliotheken (Federal Republic of Germany) 166
Arbeitsgemeinschaft der kirchlichen Büchereiverbände Deutschlands (Federal Republic of Germany) 166
Arbeitsgemeinschaft der Kunstbibliotheken (Federal Republic of Germany) 166
Arbeitsgemeinschaft der Parlaments- und Behördenbibliotheken (Federal Republic of Germany) 166
Arbeitsgemeinschaft der Regionalbibliotheken (Federal Republic of Germany) 166
Arbeitsgemeinschaft der Spezialbibliotheken eV (Federal Republic of Germany) 166
Arbeitsgemeinschaft der Vertriebsfachverbände (Federal Republic of Germany) 119
Arbeitsgemeinschaft Deutsche Lateinamerika-Forschung (ADLAF) (Federal Republic of Germany) 121

Arbeitsgemeinschaft für juristische Bibliotheks- und Dokumentationswesen (Federal Republic of Germany) 166
Arbeitsgemeinschaft für medizinisches Bibliothekswesen (Federal Republic of Germany) 166
Arbeitsgemeinschaft katholischtheologischer Bibliotheken (Federal Republic of Germany) 166
Arbeitsgemeinschaft Literarische und Sachbuchverlage (Federal Republic of Germany) 119
Arbeitsgemeinschaft mitteleuropäischer Bibelwerke (Federal Republic of Germany) 122
Arbeitsgemeinschaft rechts- und staatswissenschaftlicher Verleger (Federal Republic of Germany) 119
Arbeitsgemeinschaft sozialistischer und demokratischer Verleger und Buchhändler (Co-operative of Socialist and Democratic Publishing Houses and Bookshops) (Federal Republic of Germany) 122
Arbeitsgemeinschaft von Jugendbuchverlegern in der Bundesrepublik Deutschland eV (Federal Republic of Germany) 119
Arbeitsgemeinschaft wissenschaftliche Literatur eV (Federal Republic of Germany) 119
Arbeitskreis für Jugendliteratur eV (Federal Republic of Germany) 119
Arbeitsstelle für das Bibliothekswesen (Federal Republic of Germany) 166
Arbeitswelt, Verlag Die, GmbH (Federal Republic of Germany) 122
Arbetarkultur, Förlagsaktiebolaget, (Sweden) 328
Arbó SACeI (Argentina) 3
Arborio, Maria-Pia D', (Italy) 220
Arca, Editorial, SRL (Uruguay) 417
Arcade-Fonds Mercator, Editions, (Belgium) 33
Arcádia, Editora, Sarl (Portugal) 295
Arcana Editrice Srl (Italy) 212
Arcane Bookshop (Cyprus) 69
Arcanum, AB, (Sweden) 328
Archaeological Survey of India (India) 182
Archbishopric, Library of the, (Cyprus) 69
Arche, Verlag der, Peter Schifferli AG (Switzerland) 337
Archibald Brothers (Zimbabwe) 429
Archiginnasio, Biblioteca Comunale dell', (Italy) 221
Archimedes Verlag (Switzerland) 337
Archipel, Uitgeverij, (Netherlands) 256
Architectural Press Ltd (United Kingdom) 367
Architecture & Arts Publications Co (Sri Lanka) 325
Architektur, Verlag für, (Federal Republic of Germany) 122
Architektur, Verlag für, (Switzerland) 337
Archiv der Universität Wien (Austria) 29
Archival Institution (Bahamas) 31
Archivele Statului (National Archives) (Romania) 301
Archives, Central Historical, (Bulgaria) 58
Archives, Direction des, de France (France) 109
Archives, Direction des Services d', de la Martinique (Martinique) 247
Archives de l'Etat (Luxembourg) 242
Archives de Madagascar (Democratic Republic of Madagascar) 243
Archives de Sénégal (Senegal) 303
Archives départementales de la Réunion (Réunion) 300
Archives et Bibliothèque nationale (National Library and Archives) (Gabon) 113
Archives fédérales (Switzerland) 351
Archives, The Central, for the History of the Jewish People (formerly Jewish Historical General Archives) (Israel) 210
Archives générales du Royaume (Belgium) 43
Archives, Inspection des, Musées et Bibliothèques du Mali (Mali) 246
Archives nationales (Algeria) 2
Archives nationales (France) 108
Archives nationales (Niger) 274
Archives nationales (Tunisia) 357
Archives nationales de la République Populaire du Benin (Benin) 46
Archives nationales, Direction des, (Laos) 239
Archives nationales du Cameroun (United Republic of Cameroun) 60
Archives nationales du Mali (Mali) 246
Archives nationales du Zaïre (Zaire) 427
Archives of Early Russian Historical Records, Central State, (Union of Soviet Socialist Republics) 362
Archives, Public, of Sierra Leone (Sierra Leone) 304
Archives of the October Revolution, Central State, and Higher State Bodies (Union of Soviet Socialist Republics) 362
Archives, Central, of the People's Republic of Bulgaria (Bulgaria) 58
Archives of the RSFSR, Central State, (Union of Soviet Socialist Republics) 362
Archives of the USSR, Central State Historical, (Union of Soviet Socialist Republics) 362
Archives of the USSR, Central State Literature and Art, (Union of Soviet Socialist Republics) 362
Archives Service, The, of the Prime Minister's Office of the Socialist Republic of Viet Nam (Socialist Republic of Viet Nam) 420

Archivio Centrale dello Stato (Italy) 221
Archivio Storico, Biblioteca dell', Civico e Biblioteca Trivulziana (Italy) 221
Archivo General de Centro (Guatemala) 173
Archivo General de Indias (Spain) 324
Archivo General de la Nación (Dominican Republic) 80
Archivo General de la Nación (Mexico) 252
Archivo General de la Nación (Nicaragua) 273
Archivo General de la Nación (Peru) 287
Archivo General de la Nación (Uruguay) 417
Archivo General de la Nación (Venezuela) 419
Archivo General de Puerto Rico (Puerto Rico) 299
Archivo Histórico Municipal de la Habana (Cuba) 68
Archivo Historico Nacional (Spain) 324
Archivo Nacional de Colombia, Biblioteca Nacional (Colombia) 66
Archivo Nacional de Historia (Ecuador) 81
Archivo y Biblioteca Capitulares (Spain) 324
Archivos Históricos y Bibliotecas (Mexico) 252
Archiwów Państwowych, Naczelna Dyrekcja, (Main Directorate of the Polish State Archives) (Poland) 293
Archiwum Akt Nowych (Centre for Recent Documents) (Poland) 293
Archiwum Główne Akt Dawnych (Central Archives for Historical Documents) (Poland) 293
Archon, The, Press Ltd (United Kingdom) 368
Aredit, Publications, (France) 89
Arena (United Kingdom) 368
Arena-Verlag Georg Popp (Federal Republic of Germany) 122
Argente, Sentos & Cia Lda (Angola) 2
Argentine Authors Society Medal of Honour (International Literary Prizes) 439
Argentine National Prize for Literature (Argentina) 9
Argos, Editorial, Vergara SA (Spain) 315
Argos, Librería Editorial, SA (Spain) 323
Argosy, Librería, (Panama) 285
Arguedas, Premio José María, (Peru) 287
Argus Books Ltd (United Kingdom) 368
Argus Communications (UK Division) (United Kingdom) 368
Argus Elsevier BV (Netherlands) 256
Arhiv Hrvatske (Yugoslavia) 425
Arhiv na SR Makedonija (Yugoslavia) 425
Arhiv SR Slovenije (Yugoslavia) 425
Arhiv Srbije (Yugoslavia) 425
Århus Kommunes Biblioteker (Denmark) 78
Arica, Editorial, SA (Peru) 286
Arica, Librería, (Peru) 287
Ariel, Editorial, SA (Spain) 315
Ariel Publishing House (Israel) 206
Ariel-Seix Barral SA (Mexico) 248
Aries Lima (Indonesia) 198
Arinos, Afonso, Prize (Brazil) 57
Aris & Phillips Ltd (United Kingdom) 368
Ariston Verlag (formerly Ramòn F Keller) (Switzerland) 337
Ark (United Kingdom) 368
Arkady Publishing House (Poland) 291
Arkana-Verlag (Federal Republic of Germany) 122
Arkın Kitabevi (Turkey) 358
Arkistoyhdistys ry (Finland) 86
Arkivarforeningen (Norway) 281
Arkivforeningen (Denmark) 78
Arlecchino Teaterförlag (Sweden) 334
Arlen House Ltd (Republic of Ireland) 202
Arlington Books (Publishers) Ltd (United Kingdom) 368
Armada Books (United Kingdom) 368
Armando, Editore Armando, (Italy) 212
Armazens Distribuidores Lta (Mozambique) 254
Armed Forces Library Service (Ghana) 170
Armée, Editions Populaires de l', (Algeria) 2
Armitano, Ernesto, (Venezuela) 418
Armon Publishing House Ltd (Israel) 206
Arms & Armour Press (United Kingdom) 368
Arnado, Livraria, Lda (Portugal) 295
Arndt, Ernst-Moritz-, Universität Universitatsbibliothek (German Democratic Republic) 117
Arnkrone Forlaget A/S (Denmark) 74
Arnold & Son, E J, Ltd (United Kingdom) 368
Arnold, Edward, (Australia) Pty Ltd (Australia) 11
Arnold-Heinemann Publishers (India) Pvt Ltd (India) 182
Arnold (Publishers), Edward, Ltd (United Kingdom) 368
Aromolaran Publishing Co Ltd (Nigeria) 274
Arquivo Historico de Moçambique (Mozambique) 254
Arquivo Nacional (Brazil) 55
Arquivo Nacional da Torre do Tombo (Portugal) 298
Arrow (Australia) 19
Arrow Books Ltd (United Kingdom) 368
Arrow Co (Israel) 206
Ars Christiana (Poland) 291
Ars Polona (Poland) 293
Ars Polona, Foreign Trade Enterprise, (Poland) 290
Ars, Verlag, Sacra Josef Müller (Federal Republic of Germany) 122
Arscia, Editions, SA (Belgium) 33
Arsenal, Bibliothèque de l', (France) 108
Arsenides, John, Ekdotis (Greece) 171

Arsip Nasional Republik Indonesia (Indonesia) 200
Art Address Verlag Müller GmbH und Co KG (Federal Republic of Germany) 122
Art, Bibliothèque d', et d'Archéologie (France) 108
Art Heritage (United Kingdom) 368
Art, The, Publisher (Hong Kong) 175
Arte, Editorial, y Literatura (Cuba) 68
Arted (Editions d'Art) (France) 89
Artel Publishing & Commercial Organization Co Ltd (Turkey) 358
Artemis Press Ltd (United Kingdom) 368
Artemis und Winkler Verlag (Federal Republic of Germany) 122
Artemis Verlags AG (Switzerland) 337
Artenova, Editôra, Ltda (Brazil) 48
Artes, Livraría Editôra, Medicas Ltda (Brazil) 48
Arthaud, Editions, SA (France) 89
Arti Grafiche della Venezie SpA (Italy) 212
Artia (Czechoslovakia) 70
Artia (Czechoslovakia) 72
Artibus et Literis (Federal Republic of Germany) 165
Artigas-Washington, Biblioteca, (ICA) (Uruguay) 417
Artis-Historia, SC, (Belgium) 33
Artisan du Livre (Guérin et Cie) (France) 89
Artisjus (Hungary) 178
Artists' and Writers' Guild of South Africa (Republic of South Africa) 313
Artists', The, Book Club (United Kingdom) 409
Artists House (United Kingdom) 368
Arts and Crafts School Library (Libya) 241
Arts & Science University Library (Burma) 59
Arts Book Society (United Kingdom) 409
Arts Council Awards and Bursaries (International Literary Prizes) 439
Arts et Métiers Graphiques (France) 89
Arts et Voyages, Editions, (Belgium) 33
Arts Graphiques, Compagnie Française des, SA (France) 89
Arts Guild (United Kingdom) 409
Artystyczne i Filmowe, Wydawnictwa, (Poland) 291
Aruba Boekhandel (Netherlands Antilles) 268
Arusha Public Library (Tanzania) 353
Asahiya Shoten Ltd (Booksellers) (Japan) 231
Asakura Publishing Co Ltd (Japan) 224
Ascent Books Ltd (United Kingdom) 368
Aschehoug, H, & Co (W Nygaard) A/S (Norway) 278
Aschehoug Dansk Forlag A/S (Denmark) 74
Aschendorffsche Verlagsbuchhandlung (Federal Republic of Germany) 122
Asesoría Técnica de Ediciones SA (Spain) 315
Asgar Ali Book Centre (Trinidad and Tobago) 356
Asher, A, & Co, BV (Netherlands) 256
Ashish Publishing House (India) 182
Ashmolean Museum Publications (United Kingdom) 368
Ashraf, Shaikh Muhammad, (Pakistan) 282
Ashton, H J, Co Ltd (New Zealand) 269
Ashton Scholastic (Australia) 11
Asia Afrika (Indonesia) 198
Asia Book Co (Republic of Singapore) 306
Asia Book Co Ltd (Thailand) 355
Asia Pacific Research Unit Ltd (New Zealand) 269
Asia Press Bookstore Ltd (Hong Kong) 176
Asia Press Ltd (Hong Kong) 175
Asia Publishing Co (India) 182
Asia Publishing House (P) Ltd (India) 183
Asian Educational Services (India) 183
Asian Publishers (India) 183
Asian Publishers (India) 183
Asian Trading Corporation (India) 183
Asiathèque, L', (France) 89
Asiatic Society Library (India) 196
Askild och Kärnekull Förlag AB (Sweden) 328
Aslan Publishing Services Ltd (United Kingdom) 368
Aslib (United Kingdom) 411
Asmara Public Library (Ethiopia) 83
Asociación Argentina de Bibliotecas y Centros de Información Cientificos y Tecnicos (Argentina) 8
Asociación Bibliotecologica Guatemalteca (Library Association of Guatemala) (Guatemala) 173
Asociación Boliviana de Bibliotecarios (A.B.B.) (Bolivia) 47
Asociación Colombiana de Bibliotecarios (Colombia) 66
Asociación Costarricense de Bibliotecarios (Costa Rica) 67
Asociación de Bibliotecarios de El Salvador (El Salvador) 83
Asociación de Bibliotecarios de Instituciones de Enseñanza Superior e Investigación (ABIESI) (Mexico) 252
Asociación de Bibliotecarios del Paraguay (Paraguay) 286
Asociación de Bibliotecarios del Uruguay (Uruguay) 417
Asociación de Bibliotecarios Universitarios del Paraguay (Paraguay) 286
Asociación de Bibliotecarios y Archiveros de Honduras (Association of Librarians and Archivists of Honduras) (Honduras) 175
Asociación de Bibliotecas Agricolas (Peru) 287
Asociación de Bibliotecas Universitarias y Especializadas de Nicaragua (Nicaragua) 273

Asociación de Escritores de Colombia (Colombia) 64
Asociación de Escritores y Artistas Españoles (Spain) 314
Asociación de Ex-Alumnos de la Escuela Nacional de Bibliotecarios (Argentina) 8
Asociación de Libreros del Uruguay (Uruguay) 416
Asociación Dominicana de Bibliotecarios (ASODOBI) (Dominican Republic) 80
Asociación Ecuatoriana de Bibliotecarios (AEB) (Ecuador) 81
Asociación Educacionista Argentina (Argentina) 3
Asociacion Española de Editores de Musica (AEDEM) (Spain) 314
Asociación General de Archivistas de El Salvador (El Salvador) 83
Asociación Interamericana de Bibliotecarios y Documentalistas Agrícolas, IICA-CIDIA (International Organizations) 431
Asociación Interamericana de Escritores (International Organizations) 431
Asociación Latinoamericana de Escuelas de Bibliotecologia y Ciencias de la Información (ALEBCI) (International Organizations) 431
Asociación Mexicana de Bibliotecarios AC (AMBAC) (Mexico) 252
Asociación Nacional de Autores de Obras Didacticas (AUCOLDI) (Colombia) 64
Asociación Nacional de Bibliotecarios, Archiveros y Arqueólogos, (National Association of Librarians, Archivists and Archaeologists (Spain) 324
Asociación Nacional de Escritores Venezolanos (Venezuela) 418
Asociación Nacional de Escritores y Artistas (ANEA) (Peru) 286
Asociación Nicaraguense de Bibliotecarios (ASNIBI) (Nicaragua) 273
Asociación Panameña de Bibliotecarios (Panama) 285
Asociación para el Progresso de la Dirección (APD) (Spain) 315
Asociación Peruana de Archiveros (Peru) 287
Asociación Peruana de Bibliotecarios (Peru) 287
Asociación Uruguaya de Escritores (Uruguay) 416
Asociatia Bibliotecarilor din RSR (Librarians' Association of Romania) (Romania) 301
Asociation di Biblioteka i Archivo di Korsow (Carbidor) (Netherlands Antilles) 286
Aspekte Verlag GmbH (Federal Republic of Germany) 122
Aspioti-Elka SA (Greece) 171
Assam Publishers' & Booksellers' Association (India) 181
Assayad, Dar, (Lebanon) 239
Assimakopouli (Greece) 171
Assimil, Editions, SA (France) 89
Assimil, Uitgaven Nelis PVBA (Belgium) 33
Assimil-Verlag KG (Federal Republic of Germany) 122
Asso Verlag Anneliese Althoff (Federal Republic of Germany) 122
Associação Brasileira de Bibliotecarios (Brazil) 56
Associação Brasileira de Livreiros Antiquaries (Brazil) 47
Associação Brasileira do Livro (Brazil) 47
Associação dos Arquivistas Brasileiros (Brazil) 56
Associação Paulista de Bibliotecarios (Brazil) 56
Associação Portuguesa de Bibliotecários Arquivistas e Documentalistas (Portugal) 298
Associação Portuguesa dos Editores e Livreiros (Portugal) 295
Associação Profissional de Bibliotecários do Estado do Rio de Janeiro (APBERJ) (Brazil) 56
Associação Rio-Grandense de Bibliotecarios (Brazil) 56
Associació de Bibliotecaries (Spain) 324
Asociación de Bibliotecapios Graduados del Istmo de Panamá (Panama) 285
Associated Book Clubs (Republic of South Africa) 311
Associated Book Publishers (Aust) Ltd (Australia) 11
Associated Book Publishers Ltd (United Kingdom) 368
Associated Book Publishers (NZ) Ltd (New Zealand) 269
Associated Booksellers of Southern Africa Ltd (Republic of South Africa) 307
Associated Business Press (United Kingdom) 368
Associated Publishers Amsterdam (Netherlands) 256
Associated Publishers Inc (Philippines) 288
Associated Publishing House (India) 183
Associated University Presses (United Kingdom) 368
Association belge de Documentation (Belgium) 43
Association belge des Editeurs de Langue française (ABELF) (Belgium) 33
Association de l'Ecole nationale supérieure de Bibliothécaires (France) 109
Association de l'Institut national des Techniques de la Documentation (France) 109
Association des Amis du Livre (Association of Book Lovers) (French Guiana) 113
Association des Archivistes et Bibliothécaires de Belgique (Belgium) 43
Association des Archivistes français (France) 109
Association des Bibliothécaires, Archivistes, Documentalistes et Muséographes du Cameroun (ABADCAM) (United Republic of Cameroun) 61

Association des Bibliothécaires-Documentalistes de l'Institut d'Etudes sociales de l'Etat (Belgium) 43
Association des Bibliothécaires et du Personnel des Bibliothèques des Ministères de Belgique (Belgium) 43
Association des Bibliothécaires français (France) 109
Association des Bibliothécaires Laotiens (Laos) 239
Association des Bibliothécaires Suisses (Vereinigung Schweizerischer Bibliothekare) (Switzerland) 352
Association des Bibliothèques ecclésiastiques de France (ABEF) (France) 109
Association des Bibliothèques Internationales (International Organizations) 431
Association des Consommateurs, Editions de, ASBL (Belgium) 33
Association des Diplômés de l'Ecole de Bibliothécaires-Documentalistes (France) 109
Association des Ecrivains belges de langue française (Belgium) 44
Association des Ecrivains combattants (France) 109
Association des Sociétés scientifiques médicales belges (ASBL) (Belgium) 33
Association européenne des Editeurs de Publications pour la Jeunesse (EUROPRESS-JUNIOR) (International Organizations) 431
Association for Scottish Literary Studies (United Kingdom) 412
Association for the Promotion of the International Circulation of the Press (International Organizations) 431
Association française des Documentalistes et Bibliothécaires spécialisés (France) 109
Association internationale de Bibliophilie (International Organizations) 431
Association internationale des Documentalistes et Techniciens de l'Information AID (International Organizations) 431
Association internationale pour le Développement de la Documentation, des Bibliothèques et des Archives en Afrique (International Organizations) 431
Association littéraire et artistique internationale (ALAI) (International Organizations) 432
Association nationale des Bibliothécaires, Archivistes et Documentalistes sénégalais (Senegal) 303
Association nationale des Bibliothécaires d'Expression française (Belgium) 43
Association nationale des Bibliothécaires Municipaux (France) 109
Association nationale des Poètes et Ecrivains camerounais (APEC) (United Republic of Cameroun) 60
Association of Arts and Letters (Greece) 173
Association of Assistant Librarians (United Kingdom) 411
Association of Australian University Presses (Australia) 9
Association of Authors' Agents (United Kingdom) 364
Association of British Book Publishers Representatives in Australia (Australia) 9
Association of British Directory Publishers (United Kingdom) 364
Association of British Library and Information Studies Schools (ABLISS) (United Kingdom) 411
Association of British Science Writers (United Kingdom) 364
Association of British Theological and Philosophical Libraries (United Kingdom) 411
Association of Hebrew Writers (Israel) 205
Association of Learned & Professional Society Publishers (United Kingdom) 364
Association of Libraries of Judaica and Hebraica in Europe (International Organizations) 432
Association of London Chief Librarians (United Kingdom) 411
Association of Mail Order Publishers (United Kingdom) 364
Association of Publishers' Educational Representatives (United Kingdom) 364
Association of Registered Archivists of Iran Secretariat (Iran) 201
Association of Scottish Health Sciences Librarians (United Kingdom) 411
Association of South-East Asian Publishers (ASEAP) (International Organizations) 432
Association of Special Libraries of the Philippines (ASLP) (Philippines) 289
Association of Translators (Denmark) 79
Association of Yorkshire Bookmen (United Kingdom) 412
Association of Yugoslav Publishers and Booksellers (Yugoslavia) 421
Association pour la Médiathèque publique (AMP) (France) 109
Association pour le Développement de la Documentation, des Bibliothèques et Archives de la Côte d'Ivoire (ADBACI) (Ivory Coast) 223
Association suisse des Bibliothèques d'Hôpitaux (Switzerland) 352
Association suisse des Editeurs de Langue française (Switzerland) 336
Association suisse des Libraires de Langue française (Switzerland) 336

Association suisse romande des Diffuseurs de Livres (Switzerland) 336
Association togolaise pour le Développement de la Documentation, des Bibliothèques, Archives et Musées (Togo) 356
Association tunisienne de Documentalistes, Bibliothécaires et Archivistes (Tunisia) 357
Association, Verlag, GmbH & Co (Federal Republic of Germany) 122
Association voltaïque pour le Développement des Bibliothèques, des Archives et de la Documentation (AVDBAD) (Upper Volta) 416
Association Zaïroise des Archivistes, Bibliothécaires et Documentalistes (Zaire) 427
Associazione dei Libraii della Svizzera Italiana (ALSI) (Switzerland) 336
Associazione Italiana Biblioteche (Italy) 221
Associazione Italiana Editori (Italy) 211
Associazione Italiana per la Documentazione e Informazione (Italy) 221
Associazione Italiana Traduttori e Interpreti (AITI) (Italy) 222
Associazione Librai Antiquari d'Italia (Italy) 211
Associazione Librai Italiani (Italy) 211
Associazione Nazionale Archivistica Italiana (Italy) 221
Astab Books Ltd (Ghana) 169
Astaneh Razavy Library (Iran) 201
Aster, Editorial, (Portugal) 295
Asthetik und Kommunikation Verlags-GmbH (Federal Republic of Germany) 122
Astir (Greece) 171
Astragal Books (United Kingdom) 368
Astrea, Editorial, de Alfredo y Ricardo Depalma SRL (Argentina) 3
ASTRID (Belgium) 33
Astrolabe, L', (France) 89
Atelier (Egypt) 82
Atelier-Handpresse Verlag H Hoffmann (Federal Republic of Germany) 122
Atelier im Bauernhaus, Verlag, (Federal Republic of Germany) 122
Atelier Verlag Andernach (AVA) (Federal Republic of Germany) 122
Atenas, Sociedad de Educación, SA (Spain) 315
Ateneo Científico, Literario y Artístico (Spain) 325
Ateneo Científico, Literario y Artístico (Spain) 325
Ateneo de Barcelona, Biblioteca del, (Spain) 324
Ateneo de Madrid, Biblioteca del, (Spain) 324
Ateneo de Manila University Libraries (Philippines) 289
Ateneo, Editorial, de Caracas (Venezuela) 418
Ateneo, Editorial El, (Argentina) 3
Ateneo, Edizioni Dell', e Bizzarri SRL (Italy) 212
Ateneo, El, (Argentina) 8
Ateneo, Librería El, (Paraguay) 286
Ateneo Mercantil, Biblioteca del, Valenciano (Spain) 324
Atha, Antony, Publishers Ltd (United Kingdom) 368
Athena-Verlag AG (Switzerland) 351
Athenaeum Boekhandel (Netherlands) 266
Athenaeum Verlag AG (Switzerland) 338
Athenaion (Federal Republic of Germany) 122
Athenäum Verlag GmbH (Federal Republic of Germany) 122
Athene Publishing Co (United Kingdom) 368
Atheneu, Livraria, Ltda (Brazil) 48
Athenon, Ekdotike, SA (Greece) 171
Athens Academy Library (Greece) 172
Athens College Library (Greece) 172
Athens Union (Greece) 172
Athesia, Verlagsanstalt, (Italy) 212
Athlone, The, Press (United Kingdom) 368
Atica, Editôra, SA (Brazil) 48
Atika SA (Spain) 315
Atlanta NV (Belgium) 43
Atlantic (United Kingdom) 368
Atlantic Communications Ltd (United Kingdom) 368
Atlantica (Iceland) 179
Atlántida, Editorial, SA (Argentina) 3
Atlântida, Livraria Editora, Ltda (Portugal) 295
Atlantis, Bokförlaget, AB (Sweden) 328
Atlantis M Pechlivanides & Co SA (Greece) 171
Atlantis NV (Belgium) 33
Atlantis Verlag AG (Switzerland) 338
Atlantis-Verlag GmbH & Co Kg (Federal Republic of Germany) 122
Atlas-Diagoras (Greece) 171
Atlas, Editôra, SA (Brazil) 48
Atlas, The, Bookshop Ltd (Ghana) 169
Atma Ram & Sons (India) 183
Atma Ram & Sons (India) 195
Atomizdat (Union of Soviet Socialist Republics) 360
Atrium Verlag AG (Switzerland) 338
Attié, Librairie, (Upper Volta) 416
Attila, Jozsef, Prize (Hungary) 179
Atual Editôra Ltda (Brazil) 48
Au Messager (Central African Republic) 61
Au Ping-Pong, Librairie, (French Polynesia) 113
Aubanel SA (France) 89
Aubier-Montaigne, Editions, SA (France) 89

Auckland Public Library (New Zealand) 272
Auckland University Press (New Zealand) 269
Audiffred, Francois-Joseph, Prize (France) 110
Audivox (Belgium) 34
Audivox (Belgium) 43
Auer, Verlag Ludwig, (Federal Republic of Germany) 122
Aufbau-Verlag Berlin und Weimar (German Democratic Republic) 115
Augener (United Kingdom) 369
August Cesarec (Yugoslavia) 421
Augustin-Verlag (Switzerland) 338
Augustiniennes, Etudes, (France) 89
Augustinus, Librería, (Spain) 323
Aujourd'hui, Editions d', (France) 89
Aujourd'hui Prize (France) 110
Aulis Verlag Deubner & Co KG (Federal Republic of Germany) 122
Aurelia Books (Belgium) 34
Auria, M d', Editore (Italy) 212
Aurobindo, Sri, Books Distribution Agency (SABDA) (India) 183
Aurora, Asociación Ediciones La, (Argentina) 3
Aurora Art Publishers (Union of Soviet Socialist Republics) 360
Aurora, Gráfica Editôra, Ltda (Brazil) 49
Aurum Press Ltd (United Kingdom) 369
Aurum Verlag GmbH & Co KG (Federal Republic of Germany) 122
Aussaat-und-Schriftenmissions-Verlag GmbH (Federal Republic of Germany) 123
Aussenhandels-Ausschuss (Federal Republic of Germany) 119
Austick's Headrow Bookshop (United Kingdom) 410
Australasian Book Society Ltd (Australia) 11
Australasian Book Society Ltd (Australia) 19
Australasian Publishing Co Pty Ltd (Australia) 11
Australia & New Zealand Book Co Pty Ltd (Australia) 11
Australian Academy of Science (Australia) 11
Australian Advisory Council on Bibliographical Services (AACOBS) (Australia) 20
Australian Archives (Australia) 19
Australian Book Publishers Association (Australia) 9
Australian Booksellers Association (Australia) 9
Australian Copyright Council (Australia) 9
Australian Council, The, for Educational Research Ltd (Australia) 11
Australian Encyclopaedia Pty Ltd (Australia) 11
Australian Government Publications (Australia) 19
Australian Government Publishing Service (Australia) 11
Australian Independent Publishers' Association (Australia) 9
Australian Industry Awards for Young Writers (Australia) 21
Australian Institute of Aboriginal Studies (Australia) 11
Australian Institute of Criminology (Australia) 11
Australian Jewish Book Club Pty Ltd (Australia) 19
Australian Law Librarians' Group (Australia) 20
Australian Library Promotion Council (Australia) 20
Australian Library Technicians' Association (Australia) 20
Australian Literature Society (Australia) 20
Australian Literature Society Gold Medal (Australia) 21
Australian National University Library (Australia) 19
Australian National University Press (Australia) 11
Australian Natives' Association Literature Award (Australia) 21
Australian School Library Association (Australia) 20
Australian Society of Archivists (Australia) 20
Australian Society of Authors (Australia) 9
Australian Society of Indexers (Australia) 9
Australian Standard Book Numbering Agency (Australia) 9
Australian Universities Press Pty Ltd (Australia) 11
Australian Writers' Guild (Australia) 9
Austrian Appreciation Prize for Literature for Children and Young People (Austria) 30
Austrian State Prize for European Literature (International Literary Prizes) 439
Authors' Club (United Kingdom) 412
Authors' Club First Novel Award (United Kingdom) 413
Authors' Club Sir Banister Fletcher Prize Trust (United Kingdom) 413
Authors' Guild of India (India) 181
Authors' Lending & Copyright Society (United Kingdom) 364
Autobooks Ltd (United Kingdom) 369
Automobile Association (United Kingdom) 369
Autoren-und Verlagsgesellschaft, Syndikat, (Federal Republic of Germany) 123
Autoren, Verlag der, GmbH & Co KG (Federal Republic of Germany) 123
Autores, Biblioteca de, Cristianos (Spain) 315
Autran, Joseph, Prize (France) 110
'Aux Belles Images', Librairie, (Morocco) 254
'Aux Frères Réunis', Librairie, (United Republic of Cameroun) 60
Auxilium Verlag (Federal Republic of Germany) 123
Auzou, Editions Philippe, (France) 89
Ava Bookshop (Government Bookshop) (Burma) 59

Avant-Scène, L', Théâtre, Cinéma et Opéra (France) 89
'Avante!', Editorial, (Portugal) 295
Avebury Publishing Co Ltd (United Kingdom) 369
Avele College Library (Western Samoa) 421
Avery, Thomas, & Sons Ltd (New Zealand) 269
Avicenum, zdravotnické nakladatelství (Czechoslovakia) 70
Award for Achievement (New Zealand) 272
Award for Literature and Scientific Publications (Turkey) 359
Awqaf, Al-, (Iraq) 202
Axel-Juncker Verlag Jacobi KG (Federal Republic of Germany) 123
Ayacucho, Biblioteca, (Venezuela) 418
Ayam, Al-, Press Co Ltd (Sudan) 326
Aydinlik Yayinlari (Turkey) 358
Aymá SA Editora (& Edicions Proa) (Spain) 315
Ayuso, Editorial, (Spain) 315
Azerbaidzhanskaya gosudarstvennaya respublikanskaya biblioteka im. M F Akhundova (Union of Soviet Socialist Republics) 362
Azhar, Al-, University Library (Egypt) 82
Azim Publishing House (Pakistan) 282
Azteca, Editorial, SA (Mexico) 248

B A E S A (Buenos Aires Edita SA) (Argentina) 3
B A G Buchhändler-Abrechnungs-Gesellschaft mbH (Federal Republic of Germany) 119
B A L Milap (India) 195
B A S H (United Kingdom) 364
B A Service House Ltd (BASH) (United Kingdom) 364
B & T Directories (Pvt) Ltd (Zimbabwe) 429
B B C Publications (United Kingdom) 369
B C W (United Kingdom) 369
B H R A Fluid Engineering (United Kingdom) 369
B L A C Publishing House (Republic of South Africa) 307
B L V Verlagsgesellschaft mbH (Federal Republic of Germany) 123
B N V (Bohmann-Noltemeyer Verlag) (Federal Republic of Germany) 123
B O D (United Kingdom) 364
B P C Ltd (formerly British Printing Corporation Ltd) (United Kingdom) 369
B P I, Editions, (Bureau de Presse et d'Informations) (France) 89
B R E S (Netherlands) 256
B R G M, Editions, (France) 89
B R Publishing Corporation (India) 183
B S C Books Ltd (United Kingdom) 369
B S C Books Ltd (United Kingdom) 408
B S-Verlag Manfred Kerler (Federal Republic of Germany) 123
B V B (Federal Republic of Germany) 123
Baars-Jelgersma, Auteursbureau Greta, (Netherlands) 266
Babani, Bernard, (Publishing) Ltd (United Kingdom) 369
Babylon Übersetzungen (Federal Republic of Germany) 164
Babylon Übersetzungen (Federal Republic of Germany) 168
Bacchus Books (Australia) 11
Bachem, J P, Verlag GmbH (Federal Republic of Germany) 123
Bachman & Turner Ltd (United Kingdom) 369
Backer, De, Publishers PVBA (Belgium) 34
Bäckman, Ida, Prize (Sweden) 335
Backpacker's Guides Series (United Kingdom) 369
Bacon, Francis, Society Inc (United Kingdom) 412
Bacon, S John, Pty Ltd (Australia) 11
Baconnière, Editions de la, SA (Switzerland) 338
Baedeker, Buchhandlung G D, (Federal Republic of Germany) 165
Baedeker, Karl, (Federal Republic of Germany) 123
Baedeker voor de Vrouw (Netherlands) 256
Baedekers Autoführer-Verlag GmbH (Federal Republic of Germany) 123
Baekelmans, Lode, Prize (Belgium) 44
Baensch, Hans A, (Federal Republic of Germany) 123
Bagchi, K P, & Co (India) 183
Bagster, Samuel, & Sons Ltd (United Kingdom) 369
Bagutta Prize (Italy) 222
Baha'i Publishing Trust (India) 183
Baha'i Verlag GmbH (Federal Republic of Germany) 123
Baha'ies, Maison d'Editions, ASBL (Belgium) 34
Bahamas Anglo American Book Store (Bahamas) 31
Bahamas Book & Bible House (Bahamas) 31
Bahn, Friedrich, Verlag GmbH (Federal Republic of Germany) 123
Bahrain Bookshop (Bahrain) 31
Bahrain Writers and Literators Association (Bahrain) 31
Baifukan Co Ltd (Japan) 225
Bailey Brothers & Swinfen Ltd (United Kingdom) 369
Baillière, Editions J-B, (France) 89

Baillière Tindall (United Kingdom) 369
Bak Yung Sa (Republic of Korea) 236
Bakalov, Knigoizdatelstvo 'Georgi,' (Bulgaria) 57
Baker, John, (Publishers) Ltd (United Kingdom) 369
Bakewell, Michael, & Associates Ltd (United Kingdom) 408
Bakker, Bert, BV (Netherlands) 256
Balai, PN, Pustaka (Indonesia) 198
Balcells, Carmen, Agencia Literaria (Brazil) 55
Balcells, Carmen, Agencia Literaria (Spain) 323
Balding & Mansell (United Kingdom) 369
Baldini e Castoldi (Italy) 212
Bale Bandung — Sumur Bandung (Indonesia) 198
Balkan-Press (Federal Republic of Germany) 164
Balkema, A A, (Netherlands) 256
Balkema, A A, Publishers (Republic of South Africa) 307
Ball, Jonathan, Publishers (Pty) Ltd (Republic of South Africa) 308
Balland, André, (France) 89
Ballantine (United Kingdom) 369
Balmer, H R, AG Verlag (Switzerland) 338
Banana Press NV (Belgium) 34
Banca y Comercio, Editorial, SA (Mexico) 248
Bancarella Prize (Italy) 222
Bancarellino Prize (Italy) 222
Banco, Biblioteca del, Central de la República Argentina (Argentina) 8
Banda, Ediciones de la, Oriental SRL (Uruguay) 417
Bandarnsarn (Thailand) 354
Banga Sahitya Bhavan (Bangladesh) 31
Bangalore Book Bureau (India) 195
Bangalore, The, Printing & Publishing Co Ltd (India) 183
Bangkok Central Book Depot (Thailand) 355
Bangladesh Books International Ltd (Bangladesh) 31
Bangladesh Granthagar Samity (Bangladesh) 32
Bangladesh Institute of Development Studies Library (Bangladesh) 32
Bangladesh Pustak Prokashak o Bikreta Samity (Bangladesh) 31
Bani Mandir (India) 183
Bani Publications (India) 183
Bank of New Zealand Young Writers' Awards (New Zealand) 272
Banmai (Thailand) 354
Bansal and Co (India) 183
Baptist Book Centre (Zimbabwe) 429
Bar-David Literary Agency (Israel) 210
Bar Ilan University, Book Publishing Committee (Israel) 206
Bar-Ilan University Library (Israel) 210
Bar Urian Publishing House (Israel) 206
Bär, U, Verlag (Switzerland) 338
Barbera, Giunti, Editore (Italy) 212
Barbiaux (Drukkerij G — Uitgeverij de Garve) PVBA (Belgium) 34
Barblan et Saladin, Librairie, (Switzerland) 338
Barblan et Saladin, Librairie, (Switzerland) 351
Bardet, René, Prize (France) 110
Bärenreiter Verlag, Karl Vötterle KG (Federal Republic of Germany) 123
Bargezzi-Verlag AG (Switzerland) 338
Barjes, Edizioni Oreste, (Italy) 212
Barker, Arthur, Ltd (United Kingdom) 369
Barlevi (Israel) 206
Barn, Bokklubbens, (Norway) 280
Barnakarn (Thailand) 354
Barnakieh Trading (Thailand) 354
Barnasilpa (Thailand) 354
Barnes & Noble (United Kingdom) 369
Barque & Co (Pakistan) 282
Barr Smith, The, Library (Australia) 19
Barracuda Books Ltd (United Kingdom) 369
Barral Editores SA (Spain) 315
Barrau (New Caledonia) 268
Barre, André, Prize (France) 110
Barreiro y Ramos SA (Uruguay) 417
Barreiro y Ramos SA (Uruguay) 417
Barrie & Jenkins (United Kingdom) 369
Barrikaden, Förlaget, AB (Sweden) 328
Barry, Editorial Com Ind, SRL (Argentina) 3
Bartels und Wernitz, Verlag, KG (Federal Republic of Germany) 123
Barth, Otto Wilhelm, -Verlag KG (Federal Republic of Germany) 123
Barth, Johann Ambrosius, Verlagsbuchhandlung (German Democratic Republic) 115
Bartholomew & Son, John, Ltd (United Kingdom) 369
Bartholomew Books (United Kingdom) 369
Barthou, Alice Louis, Prize (France) 110
Barthou, Louis, Prize (France) 110
Barthou, Max, Prize (France) 110
Bartlett, Alice Hunt, Prize (International Literary Prizes) 439
Barudio & Hess Verlag (Federal Republic of Germany) 123
Baschet et Cie, Editeurs (France) 89
Baseball Magazine Sha (Japan) 225
Bashir, Al, Bookshop (Sudan) 327

Basic Books (United Kingdom) 370
Basileia Verlag (Switzerland) 338
Basilisk, The, Press Ltd (United Kingdom) 370
Basilius Presse (Switzerland) 338
Basis (Netherlands) 256
Basis-Verlag (Federal Republic of Germany) 123
Bassermann'sche Verlagsbuchhandlung, Friedrich, im Falken-Verlag Erich Sicker KG (Federal Republic of Germany) 123
Bastei-Verlag Gustav H Lübbe (Federal Republic of Germany) 123
Bastian, W E, & Co (Sri Lanka) 325
Bastian Prize (Norway) 281
Bastilla, Ediciones la, (Argentina) 3
Bastinos, Librería, (Spain) 324
Bataille, Agence, (France) 107
Bateleur Press (Republic of South Africa) 308
Bateman, David, Ltd (New Zealand) 269
Batsford, B T, Ltd (United Kingdom) 370
Battenberg, Ernst, Verlag (Federal Republic of Germany) 123
Bättre Ledarskap (Sweden) 334
Baudelaire, Charles, Poetry Prize (International Literary Prizes) 439
Bauer, Hermann, Verlag KG (Federal Republic of Germany) 123
Baufachverlag AG (Switzerland) 338
Bautista, Asociacion, Argentina de Publicaciones (Argentina) 3
Bautista, Centro Cultural, (Nicaragua) 273
Bauverlag GmbH (Federal Republic of Germany) 123
Bauwesen, VEB Verlag für, (German Democratic Republic) 115
Baxters (Bermuda) 46
Bayard-Presse SA (France) 89
Bayerische Staatsbibliothek (Federal Republic of Germany) 166
Bayerische Verlagsanstalt Bamberg (B V B) (Federal Republic of Germany) 124
Bayerischer Schulbuch-Verlag (Federal Republic of Germany) 124
Bayly, A W, & Co Lda (Mozambique) 254
Beatty, The Chester, Library and Gallery of Oriental Art (Republic of Ireland) 204
Beauchesne, Editions, (France) 89
Beaufort, Mme, (French Guiana) 113
Beaux Arts Ltd (New Zealand) 269
Beaux Livres, Les, (Monaco) 253
Beaver Books (United Kingdom) 370
Becher, Institut für Literatur Johannes R, (German Democratic Republic) 118
Becher, Johannes R, Prize (German Democratic Republic) 118
Bechtle (Federal Republic of Germany) 124
Becht's, H J W, Uitgeversmij bv/Uitgeverij H J de Bussy BV (Netherlands) 256
Beck, Edition Monika, (Federal Republic of Germany) 124
Beck, Verlag C H, (Federal Republic of Germany) 124
Becker, Reinhard, Verlag (Federal Republic of Germany) 124
Beckers Groep (Belgium) 34
Beckers NV Uitgeverij (Belgium) 43
Beckers SA Editions (Belgium) 34
Beckmans Bokförlag AB (Sweden) 328
Bedford Square Press of the National Council for Voluntary Organizations (United Kingdom) 370
Bedout, Editorial, SA (Colombia) 65
Beernhaert Prize (Belgium) 44
Behzad Bookshop (Afghanistan) 1
Behzad Bookstore (Afghanistan) 1
Beijing Tu Shu Guan (People's Republic of China) 63
Beirut Arab University, Library of, (Lebanon) 240
Beit Lochamei Hagetha'ot (Israel) 206
Belaieff, M P, (Federal Republic of Germany) 124
Belfast Public Library (United Kingdom) 410
Belfond, Editions Pierre, (France) 89
Belgian Government Prizes for Literature (Ministry of Flemish Culture) (Belgium) 44
Belgian Government Prizes for Literature (Ministry of French Culture) (Belgium) 44
Belgisch Instituut voor Voorlichting en Documentatie (INBEL) (Belgium) 34
Belier-Prisma, Editions le, SA (France) 89
Belin, Librairie Classique Eugène, (France) 89
Belis-Vinck, Boekhandel, (Belgium) 43
Belize Book Shop (Anglican Diocese) (Belize) 45
Belize Library Association (Belize) 45
Bell & Hyman Ltd (United Kingdom) 370
Bell, SA Editorial, (Argentina) 3
Bellas Artes, Librería, (Mexico) 252
Bellaterra, Ediciones, SA (Spain) 315
Belle, Uitgeverij van, PVBA (Belgium) 34
Bellens, Librairie, (Belgium) 43
Belles Images, Editions Les, (France) 89
Belles Lettres, Société d'Edition 'Les,' (France) 90
Bellew & Higton Publishers Ltd (United Kingdom) 370
Bellmans Prize (Sweden) 335

Bello, Andres, Prize (Chile) 63
Bello, Biblioteca de la Universidad Catolica 'Andres, (Venezuela) 419
Bello, Club de Lectores 'Andres, ' (Chile) 62
Bello, Editorial Andrés, /Juridica de Chile (Chile) 61
Bello, Librería Andrés, (Chile) 62
Bellona Publications (United Kingdom) 370
Belmont Press (Zimbabwe) 429
Belser, Chr, AG für Verlagsgeschäfte und Co KG (Federal Republic of Germany) 124
Belton Books (United Kingdom) 370
Beltz (Switzerland) 338
Beltz Verlag (Federal Republic of Germany) 124
Bemrose UK Ltd (United Kingdom) 370
Ben-Gurion University of the Negev Library (Israel) 210
Ben-Zvi Institute (Israel) 206
Bendel State Library (Nigeria) 277
Benediktinerklosters, Bibliothek des, Melk in Niederösterreich (Austria) 29
Bengali Academy Literary Awards (Bangladesh) 32
Benibengor Book Agency (Ghana) 169
Benin University Bookshop (Nigeria) 277
Benin University Library (Nigeria) 277
Benjamin/Cummings Inc (United Kingdom) 370
Benjamins, John, BV (Netherlands) 256
Benn, Ernest, Ltd (United Kingdom) 370
Bennett, G H, & Co Ltd (New Zealand) 272
Bennett Award (International Literary Prizes) 439
Benson Medal (United Kingdom) 413
Benteli Verlag (Switzerland) 338
Benziger AG (Switzerland) 338
Benziger Verlag (Federal Republic of Germany) 124
Beogradski Izdavačko-Grafički Zabod (Yugoslavia) 421
Berchmans, Johannes, Verlag GmbH (Federal Republic of Germany) 124
Berchtold-Haller-Verlag (Switzerland) 338
Berg International Editeurs (France) 90
Bergadi Editions (Greece) 171
Bergen offentlige Bibliotek Horda land Fylkesbibliotek (Norway) 281
Berger, Ferdinand, und Söhne (Austria) 24
Berger-Levrault (France) 90
Bergh, Edition Sven Erik, (Federal Republic of Germany) 124
Bergh, Edition Sven Erik, im Europabuch AG (Switzerland) 338
Berghaus Verlag (Federal Republic of Germany) 124
Berghs Bokklub (Sweden) 334
Berghs Förlag AB (Sweden) 328
Bergland-Buch, Verlag 'Das, ' (R Kiesel GmbH) (Austria) 24
Bergland Verlag (Austria) 24
Bergmann, J F, (Federal Republic of Germany) 124
Bergmann, Anton, Prize (International Literary Prizes) 439
Bergs, H M, Forlag ApS (Denmark) 74
Bergström & Boyle Books Ltd (United Kingdom) 370
Bergverlag Rudolf Rother GmbH (Federal Republic of Germany) 124
Berhan Bookshop and Stationery (Ethiopia) 83
Berichthaus Verlag, Dr Conrad Ulrich (Switzerland) 338
Berlin Verlag (Federal Republic of Germany) 124
Berliner Handpresse Wolfgang Joerg und Erich Schoenig (Federal Republic of Germany) 124
Berliner Stadtbibliothek (German Democratic Republic) 117
Berliner Union GmbH (Federal Republic of Germany) 124
Berliner Verleger- und Buchhändlervereinigung eV (Federal Republic of Germany) 119
Berlingske Forlag A/S (Denmark) 74
Berlitz, Editions, (Switzerland) 338
Berlitz, Société Internationale des Ecoles, SA (France) 90
Bermuda Archives (Bermuda) 46
Bermuda Book Store Ltd (Bermuda) 46
Bermuda Library (Bermuda) 46
Bermuda Press Ltd (Bermuda) 46
Bermudian Publishing Co (Bermuda) 46
Bernard, Librería Claudio, (El Salvador) 83
Bernard & Graefe Verlag (Federal Republic of Germany) 124
Bernards (Publishers) Ltd (United Kingdom) 370
Bernces Forlag AB (Sweden) 329
Bernhardt, Verlag Alexander, (Austria) 24
Bernheim, Bibliothèque, Bibliothèque territoriale de la Nouvelle-Caledonie (New Caledonia) 268
Beroukhim, Y, & Sons, Booksellers (Iran) 201
Berry, David, Prize (International Literary Prizes) 439
Bertelsmann de Mexico SA (Mexico) 251
Bertelsmann, C, GmbH (Federal Republic of Germany) 124
Bertelsmann GmbH, Verlagsgruppe, (Federal Republic of Germany) 124
Bertelsmann International, Verlagsgruppe, GmbH (Federal Republic of Germany) 125
Bertelsmann Lesering (Federal Republic of Germany) 165
Bertrand, Livraria, (Portugal) 298
Bertrand, Livraria, SARL (Portugal) 295

Beskow Prize (Sweden) 335
Best Book of the Sea Award (International Literary Prizes) 439
Best First Book of Poetry Award (incorporating the Jessie Mackay Award) (New Zealand) 273
Best First Book of Prose Award (Incorporating the Hubert Church Award) (New Zealand) 273
Beste, Det, A/S (Norway) 280
Besterman Medal (United Kingdom) 413
Bestetti, Edizioni d'Arte Carlo, (Italy) 212
Bestseller, The, Universal Distributors Ltd (Nigeria) 277
Beta, Editôra, Ltda (Brazil) 49
Beta, Editorial, SRL (Argentina) 3
Betis, Ediciones, (Spain) 315
Beton-Verlag (Concrete Publishing) GmbH (Federal Republic of Germany) 125
Better Books (United Kingdom) 370
Better Yourself Books (India) 183
Betz, Annette, Verlag (Austria) 24
Betz, Annette, Verlag (Federal Republic of Germany) 125
Betzel, Elke, Verlag (Federal Republic of Germany) 125
Beuhler's Shoppe (Belize) 45
Beupmun Sa Publishing Co (Republic of Korea) 236
Beuroner Kunstverlag GmbH (Federal Republic of Germany) 125
Beurs, De, NV (Belgium) 34
Beuth Verlag GmbH (Federal Republic of Germany) 125
Beyazit, The, State Library (Turkey) 359
Beyeler Editions Basel (Switzerland) 338
Beyer, Atelier, (France) 90
Beyer, F, Bok-Og Papirhandel A/S (Norway) 280
Bezige, De, Bij (Netherlands) 257
Bhai Santokh Singh Prize (India) 197
Bhaimi Prakashan (India) 183
Bhakti, P T, Centra Baru (Indonesia) 198
Bhaktivedanta Book Trust (India) 183
Bhaktivedanta, The, Book Trust (Switzerland) 338
Bharat-Bharati (India) 183
Bharat Law House (India) 183
Bharati Sahitya Sadan Sales (India) 183
Bharatiya Jnanpith (India) 183
Bharatiya Publishing House (India) 183
Bharatiya Vidya Bhavan (India) 184
Bhratara Karya Aksara (Indonesia) 199
Bialik, The, Institute (Israel) 206
Bialik Prize for Literature (Israel) 211
Bianchi, Alfredo A, Essay Prize (Argentina) 9
Bianco, Del, Editore (Italy) 212
Bias Editora (Argentina) 3
Bias Editora (Libros Jurídicos) (Argentina) 8
Bias (Société Nouvelle des Editions) SA (France) 90
Bibellesebund eV (Federal Republic of Germany) 125
Biblarte Lda (Portugal) 298
Bible Churchmen's Missionary Society (Ethiopia) 83
Bible Society of South Africa (Namibia) 255
Bible Society of South Africa (Republic of South Africa) 308
Biblical Institute Press (Pontificio Istituto Biblico) (Italy) 212
Bibliofiilien Seura (Finland) 87
Bibliographical Society (United Kingdom) 411
Bibliographical Society of Australia and New Zealand (Australia) 20
Bibliographical Society of Australia and New Zealand (Australia) 20
Bibliographical Society of Australia and New Zealand (New Zealand) 272
Bibliographical Society of Australia and New Zealand (New Zealand) 272
Bibliographical Society of Australia and New Zealand (BSANZ) (International Organizations) 432
Bibliographical Society of the Philippines (Philippines) 289
Bibliographisches Institut AG (Federal Republic of Germany) 125
Bibliographisches Institut AG (Switzerland) 338
Bibliographisches Institut GmbH (Austria) 24
Bibliographisches Institut, VEB, (German Democratic Republic) 115
Bibliomad (Democratic Republic of Madagascar) 243
Bibliophile Drucke, Verlag, von Josef Stocker AG (Switzerland) 338
Bibliophile, Le, (The Book Lover) (Haiti) 174
Bibliopolis—Edizioni di Filosofia e Scienze SpA (Italy) 212
Biblioteca Central (Mexico) 252
Biblioteca Central de Educación básica, secundaria y superior (Uruguay) 417
Biblioteca Centrala de Stat a Republicii Socialiste România (Central State Library) (Romania) 301
Biblioteca Centrala Universitara (Romania) 301
Biblioteca Centrala Universitara (Romania) 301
Biblioteca Centrala Universitara 'Mihail Eminescu' (Romania) 301
Biblioteca de la Asociación Argentina de Cultura Inglesa (Argentina) 8
Biblioteca de México (Mexico) 252
Biblioteca del Congreso (Venezuela) 419

Biblioteca dell' Universita Nazionale della Somalia (Somalia) 307
Biblioteca Dominicana (Dominican Republic) 80
Biblioteca Ecuatoriana 'Aurelio Espinosa Pólit' (Ecuador) 81
Biblioteca, Editorial, Nueva SL (Spain) 316
Biblioteca Estadual (Brazil) 55
Biblioteca General de Puerto Rico (General Library) (Puerto Rico) 299
Biblioteca Histórica Cubana y Americana (Cuba) 68
Biblioteca Judeteana Mures (Romania) 301
Biblioteca Judeteana Timis (Romania) 301
Biblioteca Municipal (Mozambique) 254
Biblioteca Municipal Central (Portugal) 298
Biblioteca Municipal Mário de Andrade (Brazil) 55
Biblioteca Nacional (Argentina) 8
Biblioteca Nacional (Brazil) 55
Biblioteca Nacional (Chile) 62
Biblioteca Nacional (Costa Rica) 67
Biblioteca Nacional (Dominican Republic) 80
Biblioteca Nacional (El Salvador) 83
Biblioteca Nacional (Nicaragua) 273
Biblioteca Nacional (Panama) 285
Biblioteca Nacional (Peru) 287
Biblioteca Nacional (Spain) 324
Biblioteca Nacional (Venezuela) 419
Biblioteca Nacional de Agricultura (Mexico) 252
Biblioteca Nacional de Angola (Angola) 2
Biblioteca Nacional de Antropología e Historia (Mexico) 252
Biblioteca Nacional de Chile de la Dirección de Bibliotecas, Archivos y Museos (Chile) 62
Biblioteca Nacional de Colombia (Colombia) 66
Biblioteca Nacional de Guatemala (National Library) (Guatemala) 173
Biblioteca Nacional de Honduras (Honduras) 175
Biblioteca Nacional de Lisboa (Portugal) 298
Biblioteca Nacional de Macau (Macau) 242
Biblioteca Nacional de Maestros (Argentina) 8
Biblioteca Nacional de México (Mexico) 252
Biblioteca Nacional de Moçambique (Mozambique) 254
Biblioteca Nacional del Ecuador (Ecuador) 81
Biblioteca Nacional del Uruguay (Uruguay) 417
Biblioteca Nacional José Martí (Cuba) 68
Biblioteca Nazionale Braidense (Italy) 221
Biblioteca Nazionale Centrale (Italy) 221
Biblioteca Nazionale Centrale (Italy) 221
Biblioteca Nazionale Marciana (Italy) 221
Biblioteca Nazionale Vittorio Emanuele III (Italy) 221
Biblioteca Popular de Lisboa (Portugal) 298
Biblioteca Pública de Ponta Delgada (Portugal) 298
Biblioteca Publica do Estado do Rio de Janeiro (Brazil) 55
Biblioteca Pública e Arquivo Distrital de Braga (Portugal) 298
Biblioteca Pública e Arquivo Distrital de Évora (Portugal) 298
Biblioteca Pública Municipal do Porto (Portugal) 298
Biblioteca Publico Central (Argentina) 8
Biblioteca Universitaria (Italy) 221
Biblioteca y Archivo Nacional de Bolivia (Bolivia) 46
Biblioteca y Archivo Nacionales (Paraguay) 286
Biblioteca y Centro Nacional de Documentación Pedagógica, Sección de Servicios Bibliotecarios (Colombia) 66
Bibliotecarios Agricolas Colombianos (Colombia) 66
Bibliotecas Municipales, Dirección de, (Argentina) 8
Biblioteka Jagiellońska (Poland) 293
Biblioteka Kombëtare (Albania) 1
Biblioteka Narodowa (Poland) 293
Biblioteka Publiczna m st Warszawy (Poland) 293
Biblioteka Śląska (Poland) 293
Bibliotekarforbundet (Denmark) 78
Biblioteksboghandelen ApS (Denmark) 77
Bibliotekscentralen (Denmark) 78
Bibliotekscentralens Forlag (Denmark) 74
Biblioteksförlaget AB (Sweden) 329
Bibliotekstjänst AB (Sweden) 329
Bibliotheca Bogoriensis (Indonesia) 200
Bibliotheca, Verlag, Christiana (Federal Republic of Germany) 165
Bibliotheek CCS (Suriname) 327
Bibliothek für Zeitgeschichte (Federal Republic of Germany) 166
Bibliotheksverband der Deutschen Demokratischen Republik (German Democratic Republic) 118
Bibliothèque cantonale et universitaire de Lausanne (Switzerland) 338
Bibliothèque cantonale et universitaire de Lausanne (Switzerland) 351
Bibliothèque cantonale et universitaire (Kantons- und Universitätsbibliothek) (Switzerland) 351
Bibliothèque centrale de la Côte d'Ivoire (Ivory Coast) 223
Bibliothèque centrale de Prêt (Réunion) 300
Bibliotheque, Centre, d'Information (Gabon) 113
Bibliothèque de Gouvernement (Luxembourg) 242
Bibliothèque de la Ville (Luxembourg) 242
Bibliothèque de la Ville (Switzerland) 351

INDEX 461

Bibliothèque de l'Université du Benin (Togo) 356
Bibliothèque de l'Université nationale de Côte d'Ivoire (Ivory Coast) 223
Bibliothèque de Monaco (Monaco) 253
Bibliothèque départementale (Réunion) 300
Bibliothèque du petit Séminaire (Haiti) 174
Bibliothèque Franconie (French Guiana) 113
Bibliothèque générale et Archives (Morocco) 254
Bibliothèque générale et Archives du Maroc (Morocco) 254
Bibliothèque mazarine (France) 108
Bibliothèque municipale (Algeria) 2
Bibliothèque municipale (France) 108
Bibliothèque municipale (France) 108
Bibliothèque municipale (France) 108
Bibliothèque municipale (Ivory Coast) 223
Bibliothèque municipale (Democratic Republic of Madagascar) 243
Bibliothèque municipale (Mali) 246
Bibliothèque municipale (Morocco) 254
Bibliothèque municipale (Réunion) 300
Bibliothèque municipale de la Ville de Lyon (France) 108
Bibliothèque nationale (Algeria) 2
Bibliothèque nationale (Benin) 46
Bibliothèque nationale (France) 108
Bibliothèque nationale (Ivory Coast) 223
Bibliothèque nationale (Laos) 239
Bibliotheque nationale (Democratic Republic of Madagascar) 243
Bibliothèque nationale (Mali) 246
Bibliothèque nationale (Mauritania) 247
Bibliothèque nationale (Togo) 356
Bibliothèque nationale (Tunisia) 357
Bibliothèque nationale (Zaire) 427
Bibliothèque nationale d'Haiti (National Library) (Haiti) 174
Bibliothèque nationale du Cameroun (United Republic of Cameroun) 60
Bibliothèque nationale du Grand-Duché de Luxembourg (Luxembourg) 242
Bibliothèque nationale du Liban (Lebanon) 240
Bibliothèque nationale et universitaire de Strasbourg (France) 108
Bibliothèque nationale (National Library) (Guinea) 174
Bibliothèque nationale populaire (Popular Republic of Congo) 67
Bibliothèque Nationale Suisse (Switzerland) 352
Bibliothèque orientale (Lebanon) 240
Bibliothèque paroissiale (Chad) 61
Bibliothèque publique (Burundi) 60
Bibliothèque publique (Zaire) 427
Bibliothèque publique centrale (Mauritania) 247
Bibliothèque publique et universitaire de Genève (Switzerland) 352
Bibliothèque universitaire (Democratic Republic of Madagascar) 243
Bibliothèque universitaire (Réunion) 300
Bibliothèque universitaire (Upper Volta) 416
Bibliothèque universitaire, Université d'Alger (Algeria) 2
Biblique, Société, Française (France) 90
Biblograf, Editorial, SA (Spain) 316
Biblos (Israel) 206
Bidang Bibliografi dan Deposit, Pusat Pembinaan Perpustakaan (Indonesia) 200
Biederstein Verlag (Federal Republic of Germany) 125
Bielmas Librairie-Papeterie (Chad) 61
Biennial International Art Book Prize (International Literary Prizes) 439
Bierman og Bierman (Denmark) 77
Bierman og Bierman A/S (Denmark) 74
Bietti SpA (Italy) 212
Big O Publishing Ltd (United Kingdom) 370
Bigot en Van Rossum BV (Netherlands) 257
Bihar Hindi Granth Akademi (India) 184
Bihar Pustak Vyayasayi Szangh (India) 181
Bihar State, The, Textbook Publishing Corporation Ltd (India) 184
Bijleveld, Erven J, (Netherlands) 257
Bijutsu Shuppan-Sha (Japan) 225
Bilac, Olavo, Prize (Brazil) 57
Bilderbuchstudio Neugebauer (Austria) 24
Bilgi Yayinevi (Turkey) 359
Billeret, Librairie, (Chad) 61
Bina Ilmu (Indonesia) 199
Binacipta (Indonesia) 199
Bingley, Clive, Ltd (United Kingdom) 370
Biography Book Club (United Kingdom) 409
Bioru Miedzynarodowego Numeru Ksiazki (Poland) 290
Bir Library (Nepal) 255
Birchalls (Australia) 19
Birkhäuser Verlag (Federal Republic of Germany) 125
Birkhäuser Verlag (Switzerland) 338
Birmingham Museums and Art Gallery (United Kingdom) 370
Birmingham Public Libraries (United Kingdom) 410
Biro, Perpustakaan, Pusat Statistik (Indonesia) 200
Birografika (Yugoslavia) 422
Bisat-e-Adab (Pakistan) 282
Bison Books Ltd (United Kingdom) 370

Biswakosh (Bangladesh) 31
Bitan (Israel) 206
Bitter, Georg, Verlag (Federal Republic of Germany) 125
Bjarnarsonar, Bókaútgáfa Thórhalls, (Iceland) 179
Björk, Bókaútgáfan, (Iceland) 179
Björnssonar, Bokaforlag Odds, (Iceland) 179
Black, A & C, (Publishers) Ltd (United Kingdom) 370
Black Academy Press (Nigeria) 274
Black Apple (New Zealand) 269
Black Community Programmes Ltd (Republic of South Africa) 308
Black, James Tait, Memorial Prizes (United Kingdom) 414
Black Pig Press (United Kingdom) 370
Black, Stephen, Prize for Drama (Republic of South Africa) 313
Blacker Calmann Cooper Ltd (United Kingdom) 370
Blackie & Son Ltd (United Kingdom) 370
Blacklock Farries & Sons (United Kingdom) 371
Blackstaff Press Ltd (United Kingdom) 371
Blackwater, The, Press (Republic of Ireland) 202
Blackwell, B H, Ltd (United Kingdom) 410
Blackwell Publisher, Basil, Ltd (United Kingdom) 371
Blackwell Scientific Publications Ltd (United Kingdom) 371
Blackwood, William, & Sons Ltd (United Kingdom) 371
Bladkompaniet A/S (Norway) 278
Blanc, Charles, Prize (France) 110
Blanchart, Editions Gérard, & Cie SA (Belgium) 34
Blandford Books Ltd (United Kingdom) 371
Blandon, Librería, (Nicaragua) 273
Blanvalet Verlag (Federal Republic of Germany) 125
Blas de la Rosa (Dominican Republic) 79
Blaukreuz-Verlag Bern (Switzerland) 338
Blaukreuz-Verlag Wuppertal (Federal Republic of Germany) 125
Blazek und Bergmann (Federal Republic of Germany) 165
Bleicher Verlags-KG (Federal Republic of Germany) 125
Blémont, Emile, Prize (France) 110
Bles, Geoffrey, (United Kingdom) 371
Blewett, Dorothy, Associates (Australia) 19
Blish, James, Award (International Literary Prizes) 439
Blitz, Andries, BV (Netherlands) 257
Bloch, Dr J E, and Mrs Karin Schindler (Brazil) 55
Bloch Editores SA (Brazil) 49
Blok, Nakladatelství, (Czechoslovakia) 70
Blok, H W, Uitgeverij NV (Netherlands) 257
Blom Prize (Sweden) 335
Blond & Briggs Ltd (United Kingdom) 371
Blondel La Rougery SA (France) 90
Bloom, Roy, Ltd (United Kingdom) 408
Blotzheim, P Stephan, Ostasiatischer Kunstverlag (Federal Republic of Germany) 125
Bloud et Gay (Librairie) SA (France) 90
Blücher, Editôra Edgard, Ltda (Brazil) 49
Blume, Editorial, (Spain) 316
Bluth, Winfried, Literary Agency (Federal Republic of Germany) 164
Blyden, Edward Wilmot, Prize (Liberia) 240
Boccard, Editions E de, (France) 90
Bodleian Library (United Kingdom) 410
Bodley Head, The, Ltd (United Kingdom) 371
Bodmer, Fondation Martin, Bibliotheca Bodmeriana (Switzerland) 352
Bodmer, Les Editions de la Fondation Martin, (Switzerland) 339
Boeck, Maison d'Edition A de, SA (Belgium) 34
Boek Promotions bv (Netherlands) 257
Boekencentrum BV (Netherlands) 257
Boekerij, De, (Netherlands) 257
Boer, de, Maritiem (Netherlands) 257
Boersig Verlag AG (Switzerland) 339
Boesen, Borge, (Denmark) 77
Bog- og Papirbranchens Kreditor-Udvalg (Denmark) 73
Bogans Forlag (Denmark) 74
Bogaziçi University Library (formerly Robert College Library) (Turkey) 359
Bøger, Clemens, og Papir I/S (Denmark) 77
Boggero, B, Editore (Italy) 212
Boghallen (Denmark) 77
Bogvennerne (Denmark) 79
Bohem Press Kinderbuchverlag (Switzerland) 339
Böhlau-Verlag GmbH (Federal Republic of Germany) 125
Böhlaus, Hermann, Nachfolger (German Democratic Republic) 115
Böhlaus, Verlag Hermann, Nachf GmbH (Austria) 24
Bohmann Druck und Verlag AG (Austria) 24
Bohn, Scheltema & Holkema (Netherlands) 257
Boighar (Bangladesh) 31
Boje-Verlag (Federal Republic of Germany) 125
Bok-, Pappers- och Kontorsvarufôrbundet (Sweden) 327
Bokas hf (Iceland) 179
Bókavardafélag Islands (Iceland) 180
Bokbranschens Finansierings-institut AB (Book Trade Finance Institute) (Sweden) 327
Bokbranschens Marknadsinstitut AB (Sweden) 327
Bokhandelsrådet (Sweden) 327

Boldt, Harald, Verlag GmbH (Federal Republic of Germany) 125
Bolivar Bookshop (Jamaica) 223
Bolivian Grand Prize for Literature (Bolivia) 47
Bollmann-Bildverlag-Verlag GmbH & Co KG (Federal Republic of Germany) 125
Bologna Fair Budding Critics' Prize (International Literary Prizes) 439
Bologna Fair Graphic Prize for Children and Youth (International Literary Prizes) 439
Bolt & Watson Ltd (United Kingdom) 408
Bombay Booksellers' and Publishers' Association (India) 181
Bombay University Library (India) 196
Bompiani, Casa Editrice Valentino, & C SpA (Italy) 212
Bon Pasteur, Librairie du, (Togo) 356
Bonacci-Libreria Editrice (Italy) 212
Bonanza, Librairie, (Mauritius) 248
Bond Alleenverkopers van Nederlandstalige Boeken (BANB) (Belgium) 33
Bonechi, Casa Editrice, (Italy) 212
Bonetti, Pascal, Grand Prize (France) 110
Bonfini (United Kingdom) 371
Bongers, Verlag Aurel, KG (Federal Republic of Germany) 125
Bonn Aktuell GmbH (Federal Republic of Germany) 125
Bonne, Editions André, (France) 90
Bonner Buchgemeinde (BBG) (Federal Republic of Germany) 165
Bonniers, Albert, Förlag AB (Sweden) 329
Bonniers Bokklubb (Sweden) 334
Bonniers Juniorförlag AB (Sweden) 329
Bonum, Librería, SACI (Argentina) 3
Bonz, Verlag Adolf, GmbH (Federal Republic of Germany) 125
Book and Printing Center — Israel Export Institute (Israel) 205
Book Association of Ireland (Republic of Ireland) 202
Book Centre, The, (Gibraltar) 170
Book Centre (Zimbabwe) 429
Book Centre Ltd (United Kingdom) 364
Book Club, The, (United Kingdom) 409
Book Club Associates (United Kingdom) 409
Book Collectors' Society of Australia (Australia) 21
Book Design Awards (Australia) 21
Book Development, The, Council (United Kingdom) 364
Book Distributors Sdn Bhd (Malaysia) 244
Book Exchange, The, (Zimbabwe) 429
Book Field Centre (India) 184
Book, The, House (Pakistan) 282
Book Lovers (United Kingdom) 409
Book Marketing, The, Council (United Kingdom) 364
Book Marketing Ltd (Hong Kong) 175
Book of the Month Club (United Kingdom) 409
Book Publishers' Association (Republic of Singapore) 304
Book Publishers' Association of Israel (Israel) 205
Book, The, Publishers' Association of Israel, International Promotion and Literary Rights Department (Israel) 210
Book Publishers Association of New Zealand (New Zealand) 268
Book Publishers' Representatives' Association (United Kingdom) 364
Book Publishing Institute (Afghanistan) 1
Book Representation Co Ltd (Nigeria) 277
Book Sales Ltd (United Kingdom) 371
Book Society of Persia (Iran) 201
Book Tokens Ltd (United Kingdom) 364
Book Trade Association of South Africa (Republic of South Africa) 307
Book Trade, The, Benevolent Society (United Kingdom) 364
Book Trade Group (New South Wales) (Australia) 9
Book Trade Group (Queensland) (Australia) 9
Book Trade Group Secretary (Victoria) (Australia) 9
Bookcentre (Pakistan) 283
Booker McConnell Prize (International Literary Prizes) 439
Booklinks Corporation (India) 184
Bookman, A/S, (Denmark) 77
Bookman of the Year Award (Australia) 21
Bookman Publishing House (Philippines) 288
Bookmark Inc (Philippines) 289
Bookmart, The, (Bermuda) 46
Books Abroad/English-Speaking Union of the United States Best Book of Belles Lettres (International Literary Prizes) 439
Books Across the Sea (United Kingdom) 412
Books for Asia (Hong Kong) 175
Books for Asia (Singapore) Pte Ltd (Republic of Singapore) 306
Books for Neoliterates Prizes (India) 197
Books for Pleasure (Australia) 11
Books in Progress (International Organizations) 432
Books of Africa (Republic of South Africa) 308
Books of Zimbabwe Book club (Zimbabwe) 429
Books of Zimbabwe Publishing Co (Pvt) Ltd (Zimbabwe) 429
Books-on-Japan-in-English Club (Japan) 231

Books Registration Unit (Hong Kong) 175
Booksellers' and Publishers' Association of South India (India) 181
Booksellers' and Publishers' Association of Zambia (Zambia) 428
Booksellers Association of Great Britain and Ireland (United Kingdom) 364
Booksellers Association of Great Britain & Ireland (Republic of Ireland) 202
Booksellers' Association of Jamaica (Jamaica) 223
Booksellers' Association of New Zealand (Inc) (New Zealand) 268
Booksellers' Association of Trinidad and Tobago (Trinidad and Tobago) 356
Booksellers' Association of Zimbabwe (Zimbabwe) 428
Booksellers Clearing House (United Kingdom) 364
Booksellers' Order Distribution Ltd (BOD) (United Kingdom) 364
Bookshelf, The, (Zambia) 428
Bookshop, The, (Namibia) 255
Bookshop, The, Ltd (Kenya) 235
Booksmith, The, (United Kingdom) 371
Bookventure (India) 184
Bookwise (Australia) Pty Ltd (Australia) 11
Bookwise Service Ltd (United Kingdom) 410
Bookworm, The, Club (United Kingdom) 409
Boolarong Publications (Australia) 11
Boom-Pers Boeken-en Tijdschriftenuitg BV (Netherlands) 257
Boosey & Hawkes (France) 90
Boosey & Hawkes Music Publishers Ltd (United Kingdom) 371
Boostan Publishing House (Israel) 206
Booth, Michael, Publications (Australia) 12
Borak, Al-, SA (Spain) 316
Borba (Yugoslavia) 422
Bordas-Dunod Bruxelles SA (Belgium) 34
Bordas, Editions, (France) 90
Bordewijk, F, Prize (Netherlands) 267
Bordin Prize (France) 110
Borgarbókasafn (Iceland) 180
Borgens Forlag A/S (Denmark) 74
Boringhieri, Editore, SpA (Italy) 212
Borla, SIL Srl Edizioni, (Italy) 212
Born NV Uitgeversmaatschappij (Netherlands) 257
Bornemann, Editions, (France) 90
Borntraeger, Gebrüder, Verlagsbuchhandlung (Federal Republic of Germany) 125
Borotha-Schoeler, Verlag Dr Gerda, (Austria) 24
Boroukhim (Iran) 201
Børsen Forlaget A/S (Denmark) 74
Börsenverein der Deutschen Buchhändler zu Leipzig (German Democratic Republic) 114
Börsenverein des deutschen Buchhandels eV (Federal Republic of Germany) 119
Bosch, Libreria, (Spain) 324
Bosch Casa Editorial SA (Spain) 316
Bosch en Keuning NV (Netherlands) 257
Boscher-Chapron (France) 90
Boscq, Jean-Pierre, (France) 107
Bosse, Gustav, Verlag (Federal Republic of Germany) 125
Botas, Libreria y Ediciones, SA (Mexico) 248
Botella, Ediciones, al Mar (Argentina) 3
Botev, Christo, International Prize for Revolutionary Poetry (International Literary Prizes) 440
Botswana Book Centre (Botswana) 47
Botswana Library Association (Botswana) 47
Botswana National Archives (Botswana) 47
Botswana National Library Service (Botswana) 47
Bottega d'Erasmo (Italy) 213
Boubée, Editions N, et Cie (France) 90
Boukoumanis' Editions (Greece) 171
Bourbon, Librairie, (Mauritius) 248
Bourcy, Librairie De, Lucien (Luxembourg) 242
Bourdeaux-Capelle SA (Belgium) 34
Bourgois, Christian, (France) 90
Bourrelier, Editions Colin, (France) 90
Boutique, La, Bleue (French Guiana) 113
Bouvier-Parviliez, Ernest, Prize (Belgium) 44
Bouvier, Universitätsbuchhandlung, GmbH (Federal Republic of Germany) 165
Bowen, Arnold Vincent, Competition (United Kingdom) 414
Bowen, D Richard, (Sweden) 334
Bowes & Bowes Books (United Kingdom) 410
Bowker and Bertram Ltd (Marine Publishers) (United Kingdom) 371
Bowker Publishing Co (United Kingdom) 371
Boxerbooks Inc (Switzerland) 351
Boyars, Marion, Publishers Ltd (United Kingdom) 371
Boyce, David, Publishing & Associates (Australia) 12
Boydell & Brewer Ltd (United Kingdom) 371
Bozzi, Ugo, Editore (Italy) 213
Bra, Bokförlaget, Böcker AB (Sweden) 329
Bra, Bokklubben, Böcker (Sweden) 334
Braby, A C, (Zimbabwe) (Pvt) Ltd (Zimbabwe) 429
Bracciodieta Editore (Italy) 213
Bradley, Mrs W A, (France) 107

Bradt Enterprises (United Kingdom) 371
Bragi, Bókaútgáfan, (Iceland) 179
Brain Anatomy Institute (Switzerland) 339
Bramante Editrice SpA (Italy) 213
Branch Line (United Kingdom) 371
Branding, De, NV (Belgium) 34
Brandstetter, Oscar, Verlag (Federal Republic of Germany) 126
Branner og Korch's Forlag A/S (Denmark) 74
Brash, Graham, Pte Ltd (Republic of Singapore) 305
Brash, Graham, Pte Ltd (Republic of Singapore) 306
Brasil-América, Editôra, (EBAL) SA (Brazil) 49
Brasil, Editôra do, SA (Brazil) 49
Brasília (J Carvalho Branco & Cia Lda) (Portugal) 295
Brasília Editôra Ltda (Brazil) 49
Brasília, Editôra, Rio Ltda (Brazil) 49
Brasília Prize for Poetry (International Literary Prizes) 440
Brasiliense, Editôra, SA (Brazil) 49
Brasiliense, Editôra, SA (Brazil) 55
Brassey's Publishers Ltd (United Kingdom) 371
Bratislava Literary Prize (Czechoslovakia) 73
Bratsvo-Jedinstvo (Yugoslavia) 422
Braumüller, Wilhelm, Universitätsverlag GmbH (Austria) 24
Braun, Literarischer Verlag Helmut, KG (Federal Republic of Germany) 126
Braun und Schneider, Verlag, (Federal Republic of Germany) 126
Braun, Verlag G, GmbH (Federal Republic of Germany) 126
Braunkohle, Verlag die, (Federal Republic of Germany) 126
Brazil Theatre Prize (International Literary Prizes) 440
Bréa Éditions (France) 90
Bread and Cheese Club (Australia) 21
Breitenbrunn, Galerie und Werkstatt, (Austria) 24
Breitenbrunn, Werkstatt und Galerie, (Federal Republic of Germany) 126
Breitkopf und Härtel (Federal Republic of Germany) 126
Breitkopf und Härtel, VEB, Musikverlag (German Democratic Republic) 115
Breitschopf, Julius, KG (Federal Republic of Germany) 126
Breitschopf, Verlagsbuchhandlung Julius, (Austria) 24
Breklumer Verlag (Federal Republic of Germany) 126
Bremen Literature Encouragement Prize (International Literary Prizes) 440
Bremen Literature Prize (International Literary Prizes) 440
Brendow-Verlag (Federal Republic of Germany) 126
Brennan, Christopher, Award (Australia) 21
Brenner Prize (Israel) 211
Brentano's (France) 108
Brenthurst, The, Press (Pty) Ltd (Republic of South Africa) 308
Brepols, Editions, SA (France) 90
Brepols IGP (Belgium) 34
Bres, Redactie, (Netherlands) 257
Bresboek (Netherlands) 257
Bretschneider, Dr Giorgio, Publisher & Bookseller (Italy) 213
Bretschneider, L'Erma di, SpA (Italy) 213
Brewer, D S, Ltd (United Kingdom) 371
Brick Row Publishing Co Ltd (New Zealand) 269
Bridge Book Co Ltd (United Kingdom) 408
Brigg Verlag GmbH (formerly Verlag die Brigg) (Federal Republic of Germany) 126
Bright Advertising and Publishing Ltd (Bahamas) 31
Bright Careers Institute (India) 184
Brill, NV Boekhandel & Drukkerij voorheen E J, (Netherlands) 257
Brimax Books (United Kingdom) 371
Brink, Educatieve Uitgeverij Ten, BV (Netherlands) 257
British and Irish Association of Law Librarians (United Kingdom) 411
British Council, The, (United Kingdom) 372
British Council Educational Resource Centre (Lesotho) 240
British Council Libraries (Iran) 201
British Council Libraries (Pakistan) 283
British Council Libraries (Sri Lanka) 326
British Council Library (Argentina) 8
British Council Library (Bangladesh) 32
British Council Library (United Republic of Cameroun) 60
British Council Library (Colombia) 66
British Council Library (Cyprus) 69
British Council Library (Ethiopia) 83
British Council Library (Ghana) 170
British Council Library (Greece) 172
British Council Library (Hong Kong) 176
British Council Library (India) 196
British Council Library (Jordan) 233
British Council Library (Malawi) 243
British Council Library (Malaysia) 245
British Council Library (Mauritius) 248

British Council Library (Morocco) 254
British Council Library (Nepal) 255
British Council Library (Sierra Leone) 304
British Council Library (Sudan) 327
British Council Library (Tanzania) 353
British Council Library (Thailand) 355
British Council Library (Tunisia) 357
British Council Library (Yemen Arab Republic) 421
British & Foreign Bible Society (United Kingdom) 372
British Heritage (United Kingdom) 409
British Horse, The, Society (United Kingdom) 372
British Library, The, (India) 196
British Library (United Kingdom) 372
British Library, Bibliographic Services Division (United Kingdom) 410
British Library Lending Division (United Kingdom) 410
British Library of Political and Economic Science (United Kingdom) 410
British Library Reference Division (United Kingdom) 410
British Library, Science Reference Library (United Kingdom) 410
British Museum (Natural History) (United Kingdom) 372
British Museum Publications Ltd (United Kingdom) 372
British Printing Corporation Ltd (United Kingdom) 372
British Science Fiction, The, Association Ltd (United Kingdom) 412
British Science Fiction Award (United Kingdom) 414
Brno Literary Prize (Czechoslovakia) 73
Brockhaus, F A, (Federal Republic of Germany) 126
Brockhaus, VEB F A, Verlag, Leipzig (German Democratic Republic) 115
Brockhaus, R, Verlag (Federal Republic of Germany) 126
Brodie, James, Ltd (United Kingdom) 372
Brodies Notes (United Kingdom) 372
Broele, Vanden, PVBA (Belgium) 34
Broese-Kemink BV (Netherlands) 266
Brombergs Bokförlag Scientia (Sweden) 329
Bronfman's Agency Ltd (Israel) 206
Bronfman's Agency Ltd (Israel) 210
Brönner Verlag Breidenstein GmbH (Federal Republic of Germany) 126
Brontë, The Incorporated, Society (United Kingdom) 412
Bronze Swagman Award (Australia) 21
Broomsleigh Press (United Kingdom) 372
Broquette-Gonin Grand Prize (France) 110
Broschek Druck GmbH & Co KG (Federal Republic of Germany) 126
Broschek Verlag (Federal Republic of Germany) 126
Broutta, Michèle, Oeuvres Graphiques Contemporaines (France) 90
Brown, Emanuel, (Israel) 210
Brown Watson Ltd & Brown Watson Juvenile (United Kingdom) 372
Bruck, Librairie Paul, (Luxembourg) 242
Brücken-Verlag GmbH Literaturvertrieb Import-Export (Federal Republic of Germany) 126
Bruckmann Kunst, Studio, im Druck Fine Art GmbH (Federal Republic of Germany) 126
Bruckmann, Verlag F, KG (Federal Republic of Germany) 126
Bruggen, Jochem van, prys vir Prosa (Republic of South Africa) 313
Bruguera, Editorial, Argentina (Argentina) 4
Bruguera, Editorial, Colombiana Ltda (Colombia) 65
Bruguera, Editorial, Mexicana SA (Mexico) 248
Bruguera, Editorial, SA (Spain) 316
Bruguera, Editorial, Venezolana SA (Venezuela) 418
Bruna, A W, & Zoon NV (Belgium) 34
Bruna, A W, & Zoon's Uitgeversmaatschappij BV (Netherlands) 257
Brunei, The, Press (Brunei) 57
Brunnen-Verlag (Switzerland) 339
Brunnen-Verlag GmbH (Federal Republic of Germany) 126
Brunner, Ing Johann, (Austria) 29
Brunner Verlagsgesellschaft (Federal Republic of Germany) 126
Brunnquell-Verlag der Bibel-und Missions-Stiftung Metzingen (Federal Republic of Germany) 126
Bruño, Asociación Editorial, (Peru) 286
Bruño, Editorial, (Spain) 316
Bruns, F, Bokhandel (Norway) 280
Bruns, F, Bokhandels Forlag A/S (Norway) 278
Bruylant, Etablissements Emile, SA (Belgium) 34
Bubenberg Verlag AG (Switzerland) 339
Buch- und Bibliothekswesen, VEB Verlag für, (German Democratic Republic) 115
Buch und Verlagsdruckerei AG (Liechtenstein) 241
Buch und Werburg — Helmut Krüger GmbH (Federal Republic of Germany) 126
Buchagentur München (Federal Republic of Germany) 164
buchclub 65 (German Democratic Republic) 117
Buchclub 69 GmbH (Federal Republic of Germany) 165
Buchdruckerei, Verlag der, Ostschweiz AG (Switzerland) 339
Bucheli, Verlag Alfred, (Switzerland) 339
Bücher, C J, GmbH (Federal Republic of Germany) 126

INDEX 463

Bücher, Verlag C J, AG (Switzerland) 339
Bücherbund Buch- und Schallplattenhandel Verlagsgesellschaft mbH (Austria) 29
Buchet/Chastel, Editions, (France) 90
Buchexport — Volkseigener Aussenhandelsbetrieb der Deutschen Demokratischen Republik, (German Democratic Republic) 114
Buchhandlung b Theater a d Wien (Austria) 29
Buchhandlung im Stadtle (Liechtenstein) 241
Buchhaus AG (Switzerland) 339
Buchholz, Librería, (Colombia) 66
Buchholz Verlag für Spiele und Freizeit (Federal Republic of Germany) 126
Buchklub der Schüler (German Democratic Republic) 117
Büchler-Verlag (Switzerland) 339
Buchmarkt- und Medien-Forschung, Verlag für, (Federal Republic of Germany) 126
Büchner, Georg, Prize (Federal Republic of Germany) 168
Buchner, Rudolf, (Austria) 29
Bucholz, Livraria, (Portugal) 298
Büchse, Verlag, der Pandora GmbH (Federal Republic of Germany) 127
Buchser, Hugo, SA (Switzerland) 339
Buckland Literary Award (New Zealand) 273
Budapesti Műszaki Egyetem Központi Könyvtára (Hungary) 178
Buena Prensa AC (Mexico) 248
Buenos Aires Literary Prizes (Argentina) 9
Buijten en Schipperheijn BV Drukkerij en Uitg Mij v/h (Netherlands) 257
Bulan Bintang, Penerbit & Pustake NV (Indonesia) 199
Bulawayo Public Library (Zimbabwe) 429
Bulgarian Academy of Sciences, Central Library, (Bulgaria) 58
Bulgarian Academy of Sciences, Institute of Literature (Bulgaria) 58
Bulgarian Publishing Award (Bulgaria) 59
Bulgarian Union of Public Libraries (Bulgaria) 58
Bulgarskata Akademia, Izdatelstvo na, na Naukite (Bulgaria) 57
Bulgarskata Komunisticheska Partiya, Izdatelstvo na, (Bulgaria) 57
Bulgarski Houdozhnik (Bulgaria) 57
Bulgarski Pissatel (Bulgaria) 58
Bulgarskiya Zemedelski Naroden Suyuz, Izdatelstvo na, (Bulgaria) 58
Bulpin, T V, (Pty) Ltd (Republic of South Africa) 308
Bulwer-Lytton Circle (United Kingdom) 412
Bulzoni Editore SRL (Italy) 213
Bumi Restu (Indonesia) 199
Bunch Books (United Kingdom) 372
Bund-Verlag GmbH (Federal Republic of Germany) 127
Bundesamt für Landestopographie (Switzerland) 339
Bundesarbeitsgemeinschaft der katholisch-kirchlichen Büchereiarbeit (Federal Republic of Germany) 166
Bundesarchiv (National Archives) (Federal Republic of Germany) 166
Bundesgremium des Handels mit Büchern, Kunstblättern und Musikalien, Zeitungen und Zeitschriften (Austria) 23
Bundeskanzleramt, Administrative Bibliothek und österreichische Rechtsdokumentation im, (Austria) 29
Bundesverband der deutschen Verlagsvertreter eV (Federal Republic of Germany) 119
Bundesverband der deutschen Versandbuchhändler eV (Federal Republic of Germany) 119
Bundesverband der Dolmetscher und Übersetzer eV (BDÜ) (Federal Republic of Germany) 168
Bundesverband des werbenden Buch- und Zeitschriftenhandels eV (Federal Republic of Germany) 119
Bungeishunju Ltd (Japan) 225
Burckhardthaus-Laetare Verlag GmbH (Federal Republic of Germany) 127
Burda, Verlag Aenne, (Federal Republic of Germany) 127
Bureau de l'union internationale pour la protection des oeuvres littéraires et artistiques (International Organizations) 432
Bureau de Presse et d'Information (France) 90
Bureau de Recherches Géologiques et Minières (France) 90
Bureau des Documentations Syriennes et Arabes (Syria) 352
Bureau d'Etudes et de Recherches pour la Promotion de la Sante (Zaire) 427
Bureau International du Travail (Switzerland) 352
Bureau of Ghana Languages (Ghana) 169
Bureau of Ghana Languages (Ghana) 170
Bureau of Statistics, Central, (Ghana) 170
Burgert Handpresse (Federal Republic of Germany) 127
Burke Enterprises (Pvt) Ltd (Zimbabwe) 429
Burke Publishing Co Ltd (United Kingdom) 372
Burke's Peerage Ltd (United Kingdom) 372
Burma Library Association (Burma) 59
Burmese Publishers' Union (Burma) 59
Burnett Books (United Kingdom) 372
Burns & Oates Ltd (United Kingdom) 372
Burns Philp (NG) Ltd (Papua New Guinea) 285

Büro für Urheberrechte (German Democratic Republic) 117
Burulan, SA de Ediciones (Spain) 316
Busche, Kartographischer Verlag, GmbH (Federal Republic of Germany) 127
Buschmann, J E, PVBA (Belgium) 34
Busck, Arnold, International Boghandel A/S (Denmark) 77
Busck, Nyt Nordisk Forlag Arnold, A/S (Denmark) 74
Bush Press Communications Ltd (New Zealand) 269
Bushatsky, Livraria e Editôra Juridica José, Ltda (Brazil) 49
Business Books Ltd (United Kingdom) 372
Business Information Establishment SA (Belgium) 34
Business Promotion Bureau (India) 184
Business Publications Ltd (China (Taiwan)) 63
Busse Kunstdokumentation GmbH (Federal Republic of Germany) 127
Bussesche Verlagshandlung GmbH (Federal Republic of Germany) 127
Bustamente Press Inc (Philippines) 288
Butler, Dorothy, Ltd (New Zealand) 272
Butler Richards Agency (New Zealand) 271
Butterbach, Christian, (Luxembourg) 242
Butterworth & Co (Publishers) Ltd (United Kingdom) 372
Butterworth & Co (SA) (Pty) Ltd (Republic of South Africa) 308
Butterworths of New Zealand Ltd (New Zealand) 269
Butterworths Pty Ltd (Australia) 12
Butzon und Bercker, Verlag, GmbH (Federal Republic of Germany) 127
Buzby Books Ltd (United Kingdom) 372
Bwrdd Croeso Cymru (United Kingdom) 372
By & Bygd, Förlaget, (Sweden) 329

C A L (Culture Art Loisirs SA) (France) 108
C A L/Retz (France) 90
C B D Research Ltd (United Kingdom) 372
C C J Ltd (United Kingdom) 373
C D D (Centar društvenih djelatnosti Saveza socijalističke omladine Hrvatske) (Yugoslavia) 422
C D L (Central Distribuidora Livreira) SARL (Portugal) 298
C D R (France) 90
C E D A M (Casa Editrice Dr A Milani) (Italy) 213
C E D A R, The, Press (Barbados) 32
C E D E L, Editorial, (Centro de Difusión del Libro) (Spain) 316
C E D I Bookshop (Zaire) 427
C E D S (France) 90
C E D-Samsom NV (Belgium) 34
C E E B A Publications (Zaire) 427
C E E L (Centre Expérimental pour l'Enseignement des Langues) (Switzerland) 339
C E E S, Librería, (Guatemala) 173
C E F A, Editions, (Centre d'Éducation à la Famille et à l'Amour) (Belgium) 34
C E F A G (France) 90
C E L I (Edizioni) (Italy) 213
C E L S E (Compagnie d'Editions Libres, Sociales et Economiques SA) (France) 90
C E P A (Brazil) 49
C E P A D (France) 90
C E P I M, Edizioni, (Italy) 213
C E P L (Centre d'Etude et de Promotion de la Lecture) (France) 90
C I E S P A L, Fondo Editorial de, (Centro Internacional de Estudios Superiores de Comunicación para América Latina) (Ecuador) 80
C K P (Clenská knižnica Pravdy) (Czechoslovakia) 72
C L A I M Bookshop (Malawi) 243
C L D (France) 91
C L E, Editions, (United Republic of Cameroun) 60
C N A (Republic of South Africa) 308
C N A Literary Award (Republic of South Africa) 313
C N R S, Editions du, (Centre national de la recherche scientifique) (France) 91
C N R S, Laboratoire Intergeo (France) 91
C O R, Ediciones, (Cuba) 68
C P S A (Republic of South Africa) 308
C R E R (France) 91
C S I R Central Reference and Research Library (Ghana) 170
C S I R O (Commonwealth Scientific and Industrial Research Organization) (Australia) 12
C S I R O (Commonwealth Scientific and Industrial Research Organization) (Australia) 19
C S S Bookshops, Agency and Publishing Division (Nigeria) 274
C S S (Nigeria) Bookshops Ltd (Nigeria) 277
C U M (Republic of South Africa) 308
C V B Buch und Druck (Switzerland) 339
Caann Verlag GmbH (Federal Republic of Germany) 127
Cacoulides, Librairie, (T Cacoulides & Co) (Greece) 172

Cadernos Didáticos, Livros Cadernos Ltda (Brazil) 49
Caffrey, Smith Publishing Co (United Kingdom) 373
Cahiers d'Art, Editions, (France) 91
Cahiers de la Renaissance Vaudoise (Switzerland) 339
Cahiers Fiscaux, Les, Européens Sàrl (France) 91
Cairo University Press (Egypt) 81
Cajica, Editorial, (Mexico) 248
Calder, John, (Publishers) Ltd (United Kingdom) 373
Calderini, Edizioni, (Italy) 213
Calicanto, Editorial, (Argentina) 4
Calinescu, Institutul de Istorie si Teorie Literara 'George, (Romania) 302
Callenbach, Uitgeverij G F, BV (Netherlands) 257
Callwey, Verlag Georg D W, (Federal Republic of Germany) 127
Calmann & Cooper, John, Ltd (United Kingdom) 373
Calmann-Lévy, Editions, Sàrl (France) 91
Calozet, Editions, SPRL (Belgium) 34
Calvyn Jubileum Boekefonds (Republic of South Africa) 308
Calwer Verlag (Federal Republic of Germany) 127
Calypso Distributors Ltd (Bahamas) 31
Cámara Argentina de Editores de Libros (Argentina) 2
Cámara Argentina de Editoriales Tecnicas (Argentina) 2
Cámara Argentina de Publicaciones (Argentina) 2
Cámara Argentina del Libro (Argentina) 2
Cámara, Biblioteca de la, Oficial de Comercio, Agricultura e Industria del Distrito Nacional (Dominican Republic) 80
Cámara Boliviana del Libro (Bolivia) 46
Câmara Brasileira do Livro (Brazil) 47
Cámara Chilena del Libro (Chile) 61
Cámara Colombiana de la Industria Editorial (Colombia) 65
Cámara Colombiana del Libro (Colombia) 65
Cámara de Editores (Venezuela) 418
Cámara Nacional de Comercio, Sección de Librerías (Mexico) 248
Cámara Nacional de la Industria Editorial (Mexico) 248
Cámara Paraguaya del Liibro (Paraguay) 286
Cámara Peruana del Libro (Peru) 286
Cámara Uruguaya del Libro (Uruguay) 416
Cámara Venezolana del Libro (Venezuela) 418
Cambridge Bibliographical Society (United Kingdom) 411
Cambridge Information and Research Services Ltd (United Kingdom) 373
Cambridge University Library (United Kingdom) 410
Cambridge University Press (New Zealand) 269
Cambridge University Press (United Kingdom) 373
Cambridge University Press (Australia) Pty Ltd (Australia) 12
Camera-Verlag (Switzerland) 339
Cameron & Tayleur (Books) Ltd (United Kingdom) 373
Cameroun Book Centre (United Republic of Cameroun) 60
Caminho, Editorial, SARL (Portugal) 295
Campbell, John W, Memorial Award (International Literary Prizes) 440
Campbell, Killie, Africana Library (Republic of South Africa) 308
Campbell, Roy, Prize for Poetry (Republic of South Africa) 313
Campert, Jan, Prize (Netherlands) 267
Campiello Prize (Italy) 222
Campos, Academia de Letras 'Humberto de, ' (Brazil) 56
Campus Corner Ltd (Trinidad and Tobago) 356
Campus, Editôra, Ltda (Brazil) 49
Campus Verlag GmbH (Federal Republic of Germany) 127
Camugli (France) 91
Camus, Bibliothèque du Centre culturel 'Albert, ' (Democratic Republic of Madagascar) 243
'Canberra Times' Short Story Award (Australia) 21
Cangallo, Editorial, SACI (Argentina) 4
Cankarjeva Založba (Yugoslavia) 422
Cankarjeva Zalozba (Yugoslavia) 425
Canongate Publishing Ltd (United Kingdom) 373
Cantabrica, Editorial, SA (Spain) 316
Cantecleer, Uitgeverij, BV (Netherlands) 257
Canterbury Public Library (New Zealand) 272
Canterbury University Library (New Zealand) 272
Cantonetto, Edizioni del Prof Mario Agliati, (Switzerland) 339
Cantor, Editio, (Federal Republic of Germany) 127
Canuto, Livraría, Ltda (Brazil) 55
Cape Catley Ltd (New Zealand) 269
Cape Coast University Bookshop (Ghana) 169
Cape, Jonathan, Ltd (United Kingdom) 373
Cape Town City Libraries (Republic of South Africa) 312
Capendu, Editions, (France) 91
Capitol Editrice Dischi CEB (Italy) 213
Capitol Publishing House Inc (Philippines) 288
Cappelens, J W, Forlag A/S (Norway) 278
Cappelli, Nuova Casa Editrice Licinio, SpA (Italy) 213
Capper Press Ltd (New Zealand) 269
Caputo, Ursula, (Italy) 220
Caralt, Luis de, Editor SA (Spain) 316
Caravelle, La, Librairie (Tunisia) 357

Carcanet Press Ltd (United Kingdom) 373
Cardeñoso, Cecilio, (Spain) 323
Carducci Prize (International Literary Prizes) 440
Caribbean Regional Library (Puerto Rico) 299
Caribbean Universities Press (Barbados) 32
Caribbean Universities Press Ltd (Jamaica) 223
Caribe, Editora El, (Dominican Republic) 79
Caribe Grolier Inc (Dominican Republic) 80
Carinthia, Verlag, (Austria) 24
Carit Andersens Forlag I/S (Denmark) 74
Caritas, Librairie, (Rwanda) 302
Caritas-Verlag (Switzerland) 339
Carl, Verlag Hans, KG (Federal Republic of Germany) 127
Carlsen/if AB (Sweden) 329
Carlsen if International Publishers A/S (Denmark) 74
Carlsen Verlag GmbH (Federal Republic of Germany) 127
Carmelitana VZW ('De Karmelieten') (Belgium) 34
Carmina, Bokförlaget, (Sweden) 329
Carnegie Free Library (Trinidad and Tobago) 356
Carnegie Library (Mauritius) 248
Carnegie Medal (United Kingdom) 414
Carnell, E J, Literary Agency (United Kingdom) 408
Caro y Cuervo, Instituto, (Colombia) 65
Carousel Books Ltd (United Kingdom) 373
Carrefour, Librairie, (Ivory Coast) 223
Carroll's Pty Ltd (Australia) 12
Carson-Gold, Ronald, Memorial Short Story Competition (Australia) 21
Carta, Lüthi und Ramseier (Switzerland) 339
Carta, The Israel Map and Publishing Co Ltd (Israel) 206
Cartago, Editorial, (Argentina) 4
'Cartea Românesca', Editura, (Publishing House of 'The Romanian Book') (Romania) 300
Carter Nash Cameron Ltd (United Kingdom) 373
Carto PVBA (Belgium) 34
Cärtögraphia (Hungary) 177
Caruana, Francis, (Gibraltar) 170
Carvajal SA (Colombia) 65
Carvan Book House (Pakistan) 282
Casa de la Cultura Ecuatoriana, Biblioteca de la, (Ecuador) 81
Casa del Libro, Librería, (Colombia) 66
Casa del Libro SA (Spain) 324
Casagrande, Edizioni, SA (Switzerland) 339
Casalini Libri (Italy) 213
Casalini Libri (Italy) 220
Casavalle, Carlos, Prize (Argentina) 9
Cass, Frank, & Co Ltd (United Kingdom) 373
Cassell Australia Ltd (Australia) 12
Cassell Ltd (New Zealand) 269
Cassell Ltd (United Kingdom) 373
Cassia House Bookshop (Trinidad and Tobago) 356
Castaigne, Librairie, (Belgium) 43
Castalia, Editorial, (Spain) 316
Casteilla, Editions André, (France) 91
Castello-Sanguinetto Prize (Italy) 222
Casterman (Belgium) 34
Casterman, Editions, (France) 91
Castex, Louis, Prize (France) 110
Castiau, Adelson, Prize (Belgium) 44
Castle (United Kingdom) 373
Castle House Publications Ltd (United Kingdom) 373
Castro e Silva, Livraria, (Portugal) 298
Castrum Peregrini Presse (Netherlands) 257
Cat and Fiddle Press (Australia) 12
Catalanes, Editions, de Paris (France) 91
Catalogue de l'Edition Française (France) 91
Catalunya, Biblioteca de, Diputación de Barcelona (Spain) 324
Cátedra, Ediciones, SA (Spain) 316
Cátedra, Livraría Editôra, Ltda (Brazil) 49
Catenacci, Hercule, Prize (France) 110
Cathasia (France) 91
Cathay (United Kingdom) 373
Cathedral Book Center (Belize) 45
Cathedral, The, Bookshop (Tanzania) 353
Catholic Book Club (United Kingdom) 409
Catholic Book Depot (Lesotho) 240
Catholic, Central, Library (Republic of Ireland) 204
Catholic, Central, Library Association Inc (Republic of Ireland) 204
Catholic, The, Bookshop Ltd (Kenya) 235
Católica, La Editorial, SA (Spain) 316
Caux, Editions de, (Switzerland) 339
Caux Verlag-, Theater- & Film-AG (Switzerland) 339
Cave, H W, & Co (Sri Lanka) 325
Cavefors, Bo, Klassiker och Förlag AB (Sweden) 329
Caveman Publications Ltd (New Zealand) 269
Caxton Publications Ltd (United Kingdom) 373
Caxton, The, Press (New Zealand) 269
Caymi, Editorial, (Argentina) 4
Ceac, Ediciones, SA (Spain) 316
Cedar Books (United Kingdom) 374
Cedibra Editôra Brasileira Ltda (Brazil) 49
Cedic, Editions, (France) 91
Cedilivre SA (Switzerland) 339
Cèdre, Editions, (France) 91

Celcius — J J Vallory (Argentina) 4
Celtic Educational Ltd (United Kingdom) 374
Celuc Libri (Italy) 213
Cement & Concrete Association (United Kingdom) 374
Cemerlang (Indonesia) 199
Centaur, De, (Netherlands) 257
Centaur Press Ltd (United Kingdom) 374
Centraal Boekhuis BV (Netherlands) 255
Centraal Bureau, Bibliotheek van het, voor de Statistiek (Netherlands) 266
Central Agricultural Library (Republic of South Africa) 312
Central Book Depot (Publishers) (India) 184
Central Bookshop Ltd (Malawi) 243
Central de Publicaciones (Mexico) 252
Central Department Store (Thailand) 355
Central Hindi Directorate (India) 184
Central Institute of Indian Languages (India) 184
Central Library (India) 196
Central Library (India) 196
Central Medical Library (Bulgaria) 58
Central News Agency (Namibia) 255
Central News Agency Ltd (Republic of South Africa) 308
Central News Agency Ltd (Republic of South Africa) 312
Central Secretariat Library (India) 196
Central Secretariat Library (Pakistan) 283
Central Tanganyika Press (Tanzania) 353
Centrala Cartii (Book Centre) (Romania) 300
Centrala Editoriala (Publishing Centre) (Romania) 300
Centrale de l'Industrie du Livre (Belgium) 33
Centralnej Rady Związków Zawodowych, Instytut Wydawniczy, (Publishing House of the Central Council of Trade Unions) (Poland) 291
Centre Africain de Formation et de Recherche administrative pour le Développement (Morocco) 254
Centre belge de Traduction (Belgium) 45
Centre culturel américain (Gabon) 113
Centre culturel américain (Ivory Coast) 223
Centre culturel américain (Senegal) 303
Centre culturel américain, Bibliothèque (Chad) 61
Centre culturel américain, Bibliothèque de Prêt (United Republic of Cameroun) 60
Centre culturel du Burundi (Burundi) 60
Centre culturel français (Central African Republic) 61
Centre culturel français (Ivory Coast) 223
Centre culturel français (Senegal) 303
Centre culturel français, Bibliothèque (United Republic of Cameroun) 60
Centre culturel français, Bibliothèque (Chad) 61
Centre culturel français, Bibliothèque (Popular Republic of Congo) 67
Centre culturel français, Bibliothèque (Togo) 356
Centre culturel français, Bibliothèques (Zaire) 427
Centre culturel français St-Exupéry (Gabon) 113
Centre d'Archives et de Documentation politiques et sociales (France) 109
Centre de Documentation (Haiti) 174
Centre de Documentation (Niger) 274
Centre de Documentation economique et sociale africaine (CEDESA) (International Organizations) 432
Centre de Documentation Pédagogique, Bibliothèque (Chad) 61
Centre de Documentation Universitaire et Société d'Edition d'Enseignement Supérieur Réunis (CDU & SEDES) (France) 91
Centre de Littérature Chrétienne (Benin) 45
Centre de Littérature Evangélique (Gabon) 113
Centre de Publications Evangeliques (Ivory Coast) 223
Centre de Recherches et de Documentation du Sénégal (CRDS) (Senegal) 303
Centre d'Edition et de Diffusion africaines (Ivory Coast) 223
Centre d'Edition et de Diffusion africaines (Ivory Coast) 223
Centre d'Edition et de Production de Manuels scolaires de l'UNESCO (United Republic of Cameroun) 60
Centre d'Edition et de Production pour l'Enseignement et la Recherche (CEPER) (United Republic of Cameroun) 60
Centre d'Education à la Famille et à l'Amour (Belgium) 34
Centre d'Enseignement supérieur de Niamey (Niger) 274
Centre d'Etude et de Promotion de la Lecture (France) 91
Centre d'Etude et d'Edition Conjugale et Familiale ASBL (Belgium) 34
Centre d'Etudes et de Documentation, Editions du, Scientifiques (CEDS Editions) (France) 91
Centre d'Etudes et Fabrication Arts Graphiques (CEFAG) (France) 91
Centre Expérimental pour l'Enseignement des Langues (Centre for the Experimentation and Evaluation of Language Learning Techniques) (Switzerland) 339
Centre for Academic Publications Japan (Japan) 225
Centre for Documentation and Research (United Arab Emirates) 363
Centre for Investment Studies (United Kingdom) 374
Centre for Pedagogical Information and Documentation (Bulgaria) 58
Centre for Public Libraries (Israel) 210

Centre for Scientific and Technical Information (Republic of South Africa) 312
Centre français de Documentation (Mali) 246
Centre International de Sémiologie (Zaire) 427
Centre international d'Etudes de la Formation religieuse Lumen Vitae ASBL (Belgium) 34
Centre, Librairie du, (Luxembourg) 242
Centre national d'Art et de Culture Georges Pompidou (France) 91
Centre national de Documentation (Laos) 239
Centre national de Documentation (Morocco) 254
Centre national de Documentation scientifique et technique (Belgium) 43
Centre national de la Recherche Scientifique (France) 91
Centre national de Recherches 'Primitifs Flamands' ASBL (Belgium) 35
Centre national des Académies et Associations littéraires et savantes des Provinces françaises (France) 109
Centre national des Lettres (France) 109
Centre national d'Etudes et de Recherches socio-économiques (CERSE) ASBL (Belgium) 35
Centre Protestant d'Editions et de Diffusion (CEDI) (Zaire) 427
Centre Publications (Australia) 12
Centre régional de Promotion du Livre en Afrique (International Organizations) 432
Centre Sénégalaise d'Editions et de Diffusion (Senegal) 303
Centro, Biblioteca del, Cultural Costarricense-Norteamericano (Costa Rica) 67
Centro de Documentación Científica e Técnica (Portugal) 298
Centro de Documentação e Informaçao da Camara dos Deputados (Brazil) 55
Centro De Documentación Bibliotecológica (Argentina) 8
Centro de Estudios Monetarios Latinoamericanos (CEMLA) (Mexico) 248
Centro de Investigação e Documentação (Brazil) 56
Centro Di (Italy) 213
Centro Di (International Documentation Centre) (International Organizations) 432
Centro do Livro Brasileiro (Portugal) 295
Centro Editor de America Latina SA (Argentina) 4
Centro Editor de Psicologia Aplicada Ltda (CEPA) (Brazil) 49
Centro Filosófico-Literario (Colombia) 66
Centro, Fundación, de Investigación ed Educación Popular (CINEP) (Colombia) 65
Centro Internazionale del Libro (Italy) 213
Centro Latinoamericano de Demografia (CELADE) (Chile) 61
Centro Mexicano de Escritores AC (Mexico) 248
Centro Nacional de Documentación e Información Educativa (Bolivia) 47
Centro Nacional de Información y Documentación (Uruguay) 417
Centro Nacional de Información y Documentación (CENID) (Chile) 62
Centro Regional para el Fomento del Libro en América Latina y el Caribe (CERLAL) (International Organizations) 432
Centrul de Lingvistica Istorie Literara si Folclor (Romania) 302
Centrum Informacji Naukowej, Technicznej i Ekonomicznej (National Centre for Scientific, Technical and Economic Information) (Poland) 293
Centrum voor Literatuuronderzoekers (Netherlands) 266
Centurion, Editions du, (France) 91
Cepadues Editions (CEPAD) SA (France) 91
Cercle Belge de la Librairie (Belgium) 33
Cercle d'Art, Editions, SA (France) 91
Cercle de la Librairie (Syndicat des Industries et Commerce du Livre (France) 87
Cercle du Bibliophile (France) 108
Cerdas (Indonesia) 199
Ceres (Belgium) 35
Ceres, Editura, (Romania) 300
Ceres Productions (Tunisia) 357
Ceres-Verlag Rudolf-August Oetker KG (Federal Republic of Germany) 127
Cerf, Editions du, (France) 91
Certificate of Honour (India) 197
Cervantes, Librería, (Ecuador) 80
Cervantes, Libreria, — Libroclub de Guatemala (Guatemala) 173
Cervantes, Miguel de, Prize (Spain) 325
České socialistické republiky, Státní knihovna, (Czechoslovakia) 72
Českého fondu, Výtvarná služba, výtvarných umělcu, sekee krasne knihy a grafiky (Czechoslovakia) 69
Československé akademie, Základní knihovna — ústředí vědeckých informací, věd (Czechoslovakia) 72
Československý spisovatel (Czechoslovakia) 70
Ceylon Institute of Scientific and Industrial Research Library (Sri Lanka) 326
Ceylon Printers Ltd (Sri Lanka) 326
Chadwyck-Healey Ltd (United Kingdom) 374
Chaix, Editions R, (France) 91

INDEX 465

Chalantika (Bangladesh) 31
Chalermnit Bookshop (Thailand) 355
Chalermnit Press (Thailand) 354
Chalet, Editions du, (France) 91
Challenge (Australia) 12
Challenge Bookshops (Nigeria) 277
Chambers, W & R, Ltd (United Kingdom) 374
Chambre syndicale des Editeurs d'Annuaires et de Publications similaires (France) 87
Champ Libre, Editions, (France) 91
Champs-Elysées, Librairie des, SA (France) 92
Chancerel Editions SA (France) 92
Chancerel Publishers Ltd (United Kingdom) 374
Chand, S, & Co Ltd (India) 184
Chandigarh Booksellers' Association (India) 181
Changjak Kwa Pipyung Sa (Republic of Korea) 236
Changjo Sa (Republic of Korea) 236
Chanlis (Belgium) 35
Chantecler, Editions, (Belgium) 35
Chantereine, Les Editions, (France) 92
Chaplin, Sid, Literary Award (United Kingdom) 414
Chapman, Geoffrey, (United Kingdom) 374
Chapman & Hall Ltd (United Kingdom) 374
Charotar Book Stall (India) 184
Charran Educational Publishers (Trinidad and Tobago) 356
Charran's Bookshop (1978) (Trinidad and Tobago) 356
Charte, La, NV (Belgium) 35
Charter Books Pty Ltd (Australia) 19
Chat, Editions du, Perché (France) 92
Chatam Sofer Institute (Israel) 206
Chateauneuf-du-Pape Grand Prize (France) 110
Chatto, Bodley Head & Jonathan Cape Australia Pty Ltd (Australia) 12
Chatto, Bodley Head & Jonathan Cape Ltd (United Kingdom) 374
Chatto & Windus Ltd (United Kingdom) 374
Chaukhambha Orientalia (India) 184
Chauveau, Pierre, Medal (International Literary Prizes) 440
Chavée, Honoré, Prize (France) 110
Chekiang Library (People's Republic of China) 63
Cheltenham Festival of Literature Poetry Competition (International Literary Prizes) 440
Chemical Society, The, (United Kingdom) 374
Chemie, VC Verlag, AG (Switzerland) 339
Chemie, Verlag, GmbH (Federal Republic of Germany) 127
Chêne, Editions du, (France) 92
Cheng Chung Book Co (China (Taiwan)) 64
Ch'eng Wen Publishing Company (China (Taiwan)) 64
Cherche-Midi, Le, Éditeur (France) 92
Cheshire (Australia) 12
Chetana Publishers Pvt Ltd (India) 184
Chevalier Press (Australia) 12
Chez Nanon (Seychelles) 304
Chiangmai Book Centre (Thailand) 354
Chiendent, Editions du, (France) 92
Chiessi-Morra, Verlag, (Italy) 213
Chikuma Shobo Publishing Co Ltd (Japan) 225
Child-Honsha Co Ltd (Japan) 225
Childerset Pty Ltd (Australia) 12
Children Book House (India) 184
Children's and Juvenile Literature Prize (Portugal) 298
Children's Book Award (International Literary Prizes) 440
Children's Book Club (United Kingdom) 409
Children's Book Council of Australia (Australia) 9
Children's Book of the Year Awards (Australia) 21
Children's Book Prize (Norway) 281
Children's Book Trust (India) 184
Children's Writers' Group (United Kingdom) 364
Child's Play (International) Ltd (United Kingdom) 374
Chile, Editorial (Nicaragua) 273
China National Association of Literature and the Arts (China (Taiwan)) 64
China Studien- und Verlagsgesellschaft mbH (Federal Republic of Germany) 128
China Youth Publishing House (People's Republic of China) 63
Chindwin Book Distributors (Burma) 59
Chinese Language and Literary Society (Republic of Singapore) 307
Chinese Language and Literature Association (Hong Kong) 176
Chinese Materials Center Inc (China (Taiwan)) 64
Chinese University of Hong Kong Library System (Hong Kong) 176
Chinese University Press, The, (Hong Kong) 175
Chinmaya Mission (India) 184
Chip Book Club (United Kingdom) 409
Chiré, Editions de, (France) 92
Chiron, Editions, (France) 92
Chispa, Editorial La, Ltda (Colombia) 65
Chivers Press Publishers (United Kingdom) 374
Cholmondeley Award for Poets (International Literary Prizes) 440
Chopmen Bookshop (Republic of Singapore) 306
Chopmen Enterprises (Republic of Singapore) 305

Chopmen Enterprises (Republic of Singapore) 306
Chopsticks Cooking Centre (CCC) (Hong Kong) 175
Chotard et Associés (France) 92
Chowkhamba, The, Sanskrit Series Office (India) 184
Choysa Bursary for Children's Writers (New Zealand) 273
Chrissi Penna — Les Editions de la Plume d'Or (Greece) 171
Christian Book Shop (Bahamas) 31
Christian Book, The, Centre (Papua New Guinea) 285
Christian Booksellers' Association (NZ Chapter) (New Zealand) 268
Christian Bookselling Association of Australia (Australia) 9
Christian Bookshop (Zambia) 428
Christian Bookstore (Thailand) 355
Christian Community, The, Press (United Kingdom) 374
Christian Council of Zambia (Zambia) 428
Christian Journals Ltd (United Kingdom) 374
Christian Literature (Belize) 45
Christian Literature Association in Malawi (Malawi) 243
Christian Literature Crusade (Barbados) 32
Christian Literature, The, Society of Korea (Republic of Korea) 236
Christian, Office of, Education and Literature (Thailand) 354
Christian Publishing Co — Newman Art (Republic of South Africa) 308
Christian, The, Literature Society (India) 184
Christian-Verlag (Federal Republic of Germany) 128
Christiana-Verlag (Switzerland) 339
Christians, Hans, Druckerei und Verlag (Federal Republic of Germany) 128
Christliche Verlagsanstalt GmbH (Federal Republic of Germany) 128
Christliche Verlagsgessellschaft mbH (Federal Republic of Germany) 128
Christlicher Bildungskreis Verlags GmbH (Federal Republic of Germany) 165
Christliches Verlagshaus GmbH (Federal Republic of Germany) 128
Christophorus-Verlag Herder GmbH (Federal Republic of Germany) 128
Chronique, Editions de la, des Lettres Françaises (France) 92
Chryssos Typos (Greece) 171
Chulalongkorn University Library, Academic Resource Center (Thailand) 355
Chung Hua Book Co (People's Republic of China) 63
Chung Hwa Book Co Ltd (China (Taiwan)) 64
Chung-kuo k'o hsueh yuan t'u shu kuan (People's Republic of China) 63
Chungking Library (People's Republic of China) 63
Chungshan Library of Kwangtung Province (People's Republic of China) 63
Chuo-Tosho Shuppan-Sha (Japan) 225
Chuokoron-Sha Inc (Japan) 225
Chur, Verlag Ernst, (Federal Republic of Germany) 128
Church Book Room Press (United Kingdom) 374
Church Pastoral Aid Society (United Kingdom) 374
Church Publishing Trust (Republic of South Africa) 308
Church, The, Bookshop (Sudan) 327
Church World Service (Niger) 274
Churchill-Livingstone (Australia) 12
Churchill Livingstone (United Kingdom) 374
Cia Internacional de Publicaciones SA de CV (Mexico) 252
Ciarrapico Editore (Italy) 213
Cicero verlagsgesellschaft mbH (Federal Republic of Germany) 128
Cid, El, Editor SAE (Spain) 316
Cid, El, Editor SRL (Argentina) 4
Ciencias Sociales, Editorial, (Cuba) 68
Científica Argentina, Editorial, (Argentina) 4
Científica Técnica, Livraría, (Brazil) 55
Científico, Editorial, Técnica (Cuba) 68
Científico Médica, Editorial, Vía (Spain) 316
Cima, Distribuidora, Inc (Puerto Rico) 299
Cima, Librería, (Ecuador) 80
Cinc d'Oros — Jaime Farrás Solé (Spain) 324
Ciordia, Editorial, SRL (Argentina) 4
Circle of Greek Children's Books Prizes (Greece) 173
Circle of State Librarians (United Kingdom) 411
Circle, The, of Greek Children's Books (Greece) 171
Círculo de Amigos de la Historia (Spain) 323
Círculo de Lectores (Colombia) 66
Círculo de Lectores Argentina SA (Argentina) 8
Círculo de Lectores SA (Spain) 323
Círculo de Leitores (Portugal) 298
Círculo do Livro SA (Brazil) 55
Círculo Mexicano de Lectores (Mexico) 251
Circus Books (Australia) 12
Citadel (United Kingdom) 374
Città Armoniosa (Italy) 213
Città Nuova Editrice (Italy) 213
Cittadella Editrice (Italy) 213
City Library (Mauritius) 248
City, The, Bookshop (Ethiopia) 83
Civilização, Editôra, Brasileira SA (Brazil) 49

Civilização, Livraria, (Américo Fraga Lamares 8 Ca Lda) (Portugal) 296
Civilização, Livraria, Brasileira (Brazil) 55
Claassen-Verlag GmbH (Federal Republic of Germany) 128
Clarendon Press (United Kingdom) 374
Claretiana, Editorial, (Argentina) 4
Claridad, Editorial, SA (Argentina) 4
Clarion Book Club (India) 195
Clark, Robin, Ltd (United Kingdom) 374
Clark, Russell, Award (New Zealand) 273
Clark, T & T, Ltd (United Kingdom) 374
Clarke, Anthony, Books (United Kingdom) 374
Clarke, James, & Co Ltd (United Kingdom) 374
Clasicos Roxsil (El Salvador) 83
Classen, Werner, Verlag (Switzerland) 339
Classey, E W, (United Kingdom) 375
Classic (Pakistan) 282
Classification Research Group (United Kingdom) 411
Claudius Verlag GmbH (Federal Republic of Germany) 128
Clausens, J Fr, Forlag (Denmark) 74
Clauwaert, Boekengilde de, (Belgium) 43
Clauwaert, De, (Belgium) 35
Clé International (France) 92
Clearway (Australia) 12
Cleary, R J, Pty Ltd (Australia) 12
Clematis Press Ltd (United Kingdom) 375
Clifford, The, Press (Australia) 12
Clivo, De, Press (Switzerland) 339
Clócomhar, An, TTA (Republic of Ireland) 202
Clódhanna Teo (Republic of Ireland) 202
Cloister Book Store Ltd (Barbados) 32
Close Up, Editora, SA (Argentina) 4
Clowes, William, (Publishers) Ltd (United Kingdom) 375
Club Bibliophile de France SA (France) 108
Club de Amigos del Libro (Spain) 323
Club de Lectores (Argentina) 4
Club de Lectores Extemporaneos (Mexico) 251
Club Degli Editori (Italy) 220
Club dei Bibliofili (Italy) 220
Club del Libro Nuevo (Argentina) 8
Club des Aventures de Guerre (France) 108
Club du Livre d'Art (France) 108
Club du Livre SA (France) 108
Club du Livre technique (France) 108
Club du Roman féminin (France) 108
Club, Editorial, de la Prensa (Puerto Rico) 299
Club 'El Libro del Mes' (Argentina) 8
Club for Bibliophiles (Hungary) 178
Club Français des Bibliophiles (France) 108
Club Français du Livre (France) 108
Club Leabhar (United Kingdom) 375
Club, Librería, de Lectores (Nicaragua) 273
Club of Mining Books (Poland) 293
Club of Twentieth Century Poetry (Poland) 293
Club of Young Readers (Czechoslovakia) 72
Co-chuideachd Leabhneachean Gaidhlig (United Kingdom) 375
Co-op Books (Publishing) Ltd (Republic of Ireland) 202
Cocco, Libreria Internazionale Fratelli, (Italy) 220
Codco Est (Qatar) 300
Codeceri, Editôra, Ltda (Brazil) 49
Codices Selecti (Austria) 24
Coebergh, H (Netherlands) 266
Coeckelberghs, René, Bokförlag AB (Sweden) 329
Cogedi SA (Belgium) 35
Coines Edizioni (Italy) 213
Cole and Yancy Bookshop Ltd (Liberia) 240
Cole Publications (Australia) 12
Cole & Yancy (Liberia) 240
Colediciones, Colombiana de Ediciones SA, (Colombia) 65
Colegial Bolivariana CA (Venezuela) 418
Colegio de Belén, Biblioteca del, (Cuba) 68
Colegio de Bibliotecarios Colombianos (Colombia) 66
Colegio de Bibliotecarios de Chile (Chile) 62
Colegio de Bibliotecarios de Costa Rica (Costa Rica) 68
Colegio de Bibliotecarios de la Provincia de Buenos Aires (Argentina) 8
Colegio de Bibliotecólogos y Archivólogos de Venezuela (Venezuela) 419
Colegio, El, de México (Mexico) 248
Colegio, El, SA (Paraguay) 286
Colegio, Libreria del, SA (Argentina) 4
Colegio Nacional de Bibliotecarios Universitarios (Cuba) 68
Colibri, Librairie Le, (Mauritius) 248
Colin, Librairie Armand, (France) 92
Collectieve Propaganda van het Nederlandse Boek (CPNB) (Netherlands) 255
Collectors Club of Franco Maria Ricci (Italy) 220
Collectors' Editions Book Club (United Kingdom) 409
College Book House (India) 184
Collège camerounais des Arts, des Sciences et de la Technologie, Bibliothèque (United Republic of Cameroun) 60
Collège Jésus Marie (Gabon) 113

College of Agriculture Library, University of Baghdad (Iraq) 202
College of Careers (Pty) Ltd (Republic of South Africa) 308
College of Our Lady of Fatima Library (Liberia) 240
College of the Bahamas Library (Bahamas) 31
Collège rural d'Ambatobe (Democratic Republic of Madagascar) 243
Collet's Holdings Ltd (United Kingdom) 375
Collier Macmillan Australia (Australia) 12
Collier Macmillan Ltd (United Kingdom) 375
Collier-Macmillan South Africa (Pty) Ltd (Republic of South Africa) 308
Collingridge (United Kingdom) 375
Collings, Rex, Ltd (United Kingdom) 375
Collins Booksellers Pty Ltd (Australia) 19
Collins, M O, (Pvt) Ltd (Zimbabwe) 429
Collins Religious Book Award (International Literary Prizes) 440
Collins, Tom, Poetry Prize (Australia) 21
Collins, William, Pty Ltd (Australia) 12
Collins, William, Publishers Ltd (New Zealand) 269
Collins, William, & Sangster (Jamaica) Ltd (Jamaica) 223
Collins, William, Sons & Co Ltd (United Kingdom) 375
Colloquium Verlag Otto H Hess (Federal Republic of Germany) 128
Colmegna SA (Argentina) 4
Colmena, La, SA (Paraguay) 286
Colomb, Verlag W A, (Federal Republic of Germany) 128
Colombian Novel Contest Awards (Colombia) 66
Colombo Catholic Press (Sri Lanka) 325
Colombo Public Library System (Sri Lanka) 326
Colonial, Editora, (Dominican Republic) 79
Colonnade (United Kingdom) 375
Colonnes, Librairie des, (Morocco) 254
Colour Library International Ltd (United Kingdom) 375
Columba, Editorial, SA (Argentina) 4
Columbia University Press (United Kingdom) 375
Columbus Publishers Ltd (Trinidad and Tobago) 356
Columbus Verlag Paul Oestergaard GmbH (Federal Republic of Germany) 128
Comb Books (Kenya) 234
Combat Prize (France) 110
Combi International AB (Sweden) 329
Combined Literary Societies (Australia) (Australia) 21
Combo Uitgeversgroep (Netherlands) 257
Comindus, Editions, (France) 92
Comisión Paraguaya Documentación e Información (Paraguay) 286
Comissao Brasileira de Documentaçao Agricola (CBDA) (Brazil) 56
Comitetul National pentru Literatura Comparata (National Committee for Comparative Literature) (Romania) 302
Commercial Press (People's Republic of China) 63
Commission belge de Bibliographie (Belgium) 44
Commission de l'Education chrétienne (Zaire) 427
Commission des Bibliothèques de l'ASDBAM (Association Senegalaise pour le Développement de la Documentation, des Bibliothèques, des Archives et des Musées) (Senegal) 304
Commission for Scientific and Technical Terminology Prizes (India) 197
Committee for Postgraduate Awards in Librarianship and Information Work (United Kingdom) 411
Common Ground (United Kingdom) 375
Commonwealth Agricultural Bureaux (International Organizations) 435
Commonwealth Library Association (International Organizations) 432
Commonwealth Patents, Trade Marks and Designs Offices Library (Australia) 19
Commonwealth Poetry Prize (International Literary Prizes) 440
Communication Foundation for Asia (Philippines) 288
Community Language Children's Books (Australia) 12
Compagnie belge d'Editions (Belgium) 35
Compagnie d'Editions Libres, Sociales et Economiques (France) 92
Compagnie Française d'Editions SA (France) 92
Companía Bibliográfica Española SA (Spain) 316
Compañía General de Ediciones SA (Mexico) 249
Compañia Impresora Argentina SA (Argentina) 4
Companion Book Club (United Kingdom) 409
Compass Verlagsgesellschaft Rudolf Hanel und Sohn (Austria) 24
Compendium Pty Ltd (Australia) 12
Complexe, Editions, (Diffusion-Promotion-Information) (Belgium) 35
Comuneros, Editorial, (Paraguay) 286
Comuneros, Librería, (Paraguay) 286
Comunità, Edizioni di, SpA (Italy) 213
Concept Publishing Co (India) 184
Concepto, Editorial, SA (Mexico) 249
Concert Verlag G Kowalski (Federal Republic of Germany) 128
Concertina Publications Ltd (United Kingdom) 375
Conch Magazine Ltd (Nigeria) 275
Concorde, Imprimerie La, (Switzerland) 339

Concordia SA—Artes Gráficas e Embalagens (Brazil) 49
Concours, Le, Médical (France) 92
Concurso Literario Municipal (Municipal Literary Competition) (Uruguay) 417
Condor Books (United Kingdom) 375
Conference of European Churches (International Organizations) 435
Confraria dos Amigos do Livro Ltda (Brazil) 49
Congreso, Biblioteca del, de la Nación (Argentina) 8
Congreso, Biblioteca del, Nacional (Bolivia) 46
Congreso, Biblioteca del, Nacional (Chile) 62
Congreso de Poesia de Puerto Rico (Puerto Rican Congress of Poetry) (Puerto Rico) 299
Congress of South-East Asian Librarians IV (CONSAL IV) (International Organizations) 432
Congresso de la Unión, Biblioteca del, (Mexico) 252
Conjunta, Editorial, SRL (Argentina) 4
Connemara (State Central) Public Library (India) 196
Connoisseur Carbooks (United Kingdom) 375
Connoisseur, The, (United Kingdom) 375
Conquista, Empress de Publicações Ltda (Brazil) 49
Conseil International des Associations de Bibliothèques de Théologie (International Organizations) 432
Conseil national des Bibliothèques d'Hôpitaux (Belgium) 43
Consejo, Biblioteca del, Superior de Investigaciones Científicas (Spain) 324
Consejo Nacional de Cultura (Cuba) 68
Conselho Federal de Biblioteconomia (CFB) (Brazil) 56
Conservative Political Centre (United Kingdom) 375
Conservatorio di Musica, Biblioteca Musicale Governativa del, S Cecilia (Italy) 221
Consolidated Labor Institute (Japan) (Japan) 225
Constable & Co Ltd (United Kingdom) 375
Construction Press Ltd (United Kingdom) 375
Contabilidad, Ediciones, Moderna SACIC (Argentina) 4
Contables y Administrativas, Ediciones, SA (Mexico) 249
Contact NV (Belgium) 35
Contact, Uitgeverij, BV (Netherlands) 257
Contempa Publications (Australia) 12
Contempora, Editorial, SRL (Argentina) 4
Continental, Cía Editorial, SA (CESCA) (Mexico) 249
Continental Publications (Bangladesh) 31
Continua Productions Ltd (United Kingdom) 375
Controinformazione (Italy) 213
Convent van Universiteitsbibliothekarissen in Nederland (Association of University Librarians in the Netherlands) (Netherlands) 266
Conway Maritime Press Ltd (United Kingdom) 375
Conzett und Huber, Manesse-Verlag, (Switzerland) 339
Cook, Albert, Library (Uganda) 359
Cook, James, Australian Literary Studies Award (Australia) 21
Cooper, Leo, Ltd (United Kingdom) 375
Cooperativa del Libro (Chile) 62
Cooperative das Casas (Mozambique) 254
Coopérative Régionale de l'Enseignement Religieux (CRER) (France) 92
Copernic (France) 92
Coppée, François, Prize (France) 110
Coppenrath, Verlag F, (Federal Republic of Germany) 128
Copplestone, Trewin, Publishing Ltd (United Kingdom) 375
Copress-Verlag (Federal Republic of Germany) 128
Copyright Agency Ltd (Australia) 9
Coquito, Ediciones, (Dominican Republic) 80
Corazón, Alberto, Editor (Spain) 316
Cordillera, Editorial, Inc (Puerto Rico) 299
Cordoba Stories Prizes (Colombia) 67
Core Libraries (Australia) 12
Corgi Books (United Kingdom) 375
Cork University Press (Republic of Ireland) 202
Cornell University Press (United Kingdom) 376
Cornelsen und Oxford University Press GmbH (Federal Republic of Germany) 128
Cornelsen-Velhagen und Klasing GmbH & Co Verlag für Lehrmedien KG (Federal Republic of Germany) 128
Cornelsen-Velhagen und Klasing Verlagsgesellschaft (Federal Republic of Germany) 128
Cornfeld, Gaalyah, (Israel) 206
Corniche, Edition, AB (Sweden) 329
Corona, Archivo de la, de Aragon (Spain) 324
Corona, Bokforlaget, AB (Sweden) 329
Corona Publishing Co (Japan) 225
Corona Verlag KG (Federal Republic of Germany) 129
Coronet (United Kingdom) 376
Corporan, Rafael, de los Santos (Dominican Republic) 79
Correa, Viriato, Prize (Brazil) 57
Corregidor, Ediciones, SAICI & E (Argentina) 4
Corvina (United Kingdom) 376
Corvina Press (Hungary) 177
Corvus Verlag (Federal Republic of Germany) 129
Cosdel (Singapore) Pte Ltd (Malaysia) 245
Cosmopolita SRL (Argentina) 4
Cosmos, Edições, (Portugal) 296
Cosmos, Editora, (Dominican Republic) 79
Cosmos, Librería, (Mexico) 252

Cosmos, Publicaciones, (Mexico) 249
Cosmos-Verlag AG (Switzerland) 340
Costa Amic, B, (Mexico) 249
Costa, Livraria Sá da, (Portugal) 298
Costa Rica, Editorial, (Costa Rica) 67
Costa, Sá da, Editora (Portugal) 296
Costello, David, Ltd (United Kingdom) 376
Cotman Colour and Cotman House (United Kingdom) 376
Coulouma, L'Imprimerie, (United Republic of Cameroun) 60
Council of Europe, Publications Section (International Organizations) 436
Council of Libraries (Albania) 1
Counson, Albert, Prize (International Literary Prizes) 440
Count of Cartagena Prizes (International Literary Prizes) 440
Country Book Club (United Kingdom) 409
Country Book Society (United Kingdom) 409
Country Life Books (United Kingdom) 376
Courrier du Livre Sàrl (France) 92
Courteline Prize (France) 110
Courtille, Editions de la, (France) 92
Couto, Editôra e Gráfica Miguel, SA (Brazil) 49
Coventure Ltd (United Kingdom) 376
Coverdale House Publishers Ltd (United Kingdom) 376
Cracow City Literary Prize (Poland) 294
Craft Book Society (United Kingdom) 409
Crafts, The, Council (United Kingdom) 376
Cramer, J (Federal Republic of Germany) 129
Cranwell Publishing Co Ltd (New Zealand) 269
Cratander AG (Switzerland) 340
Crawshay, The Rose Mary, Prizes (International Literary Prizes) 440
Crea, Editorial, SA (Argentina) 4
Creadif (Belgium) 35
Creanga, Editure Ion, (Romania) 300
Creasey, John, Memorial Award (United Kingdom) 414
Crédit Communal de Belgique—Centre Culturel (Belgium) 35
Cremers (Schoollandkaarten) PVBA (Belgium) 35
Cremonese, Edizioni, SpA (Italy) 213
Crépin-Leblond, Editeurs, et Cie SA (France) 92
Crescent Publications (Pakistan) 282
Crescent Publishers (Bangladesh) 31
Crescent Publishing Co (India) 184
Crespillo, Editorial, SA (Argentina) 4
Cressrelles Publishing Co Ltd (United Kingdom) 376
Crime Writers' Association (United Kingdom) 364
Crisp (Belgium) 35
Cristal, Librerías de, (Mexico) 252
Cristiandad, Ediciones, (Spain) 316
Critica, Editorial, SA (Spain) 316
Crnogorska akademija nauka i umjetnosti (Yugoslavia) 426
Croft Press (Australia) 12
Croix, Editions, de Sud (Mauritius) 247
Cromograf SA (Ecuador) 80
Cromphout, Van, Frères & Soeurs Imprimerie (Belgium) 35
Crompton, Paul H, Ltd (United Kingdom) 376
Croner Publications Ltd (United Kingdom) 376
Croom Helm Ltd (United Kingdom) 376
Cross Continent Press Ltd (Nigeria) 275
Cuala Press (Republic of Ireland) 203
Cubanas, Ediciones, (Cuba) 68
Cuello, Casa, (Dominican Republic) 80
Cujas, Editions, (France) 92
Cultrix, Editôra, (Brazil) 49
Cultura 70 Livraría e Editôra SA (Brazil) 55
Cultura, Casa de la, Ecuatoriana (Ecuador) 80
Cultura, Ediciones, Hispánica (Spain) 316
Cultura, Fondation, -Stichting Cultura (Belgium) 35
Cultura, Librería La, (Paraguay) 286
Cultura, Librería y Editorial, (Chile) 62
Cultura-Maroc (Morocco) 254
Cultura Médica, Editôra, Ltda (Brazil) 49
Cultura, Premio Nacional de, (Bolivia) 47
Cultural Centre, Library of the, Surinam (Bibliotheek CCS) (Suriname) 327
Cultural Centre of the Philippines Literary Awards (Philippines) 290
Cultural Colombiana Ltda (Colombia) 65
Cultural Council, Book Club of the, of Sri Lanka (Sri Lanka) 326
Cultural Council of Sri Lanka (Sri Lanka) 325
Cultural, Librería, Salvadoreña SA de CV (El Salvador) 83
Cultural Supplies, The, Co (Malaysia) 244
Culture Art Loisirs/Retz (France) 92
Culture et Civilisation, Editions, (Belgium) 35
Culture Prize (Japan) 232
Cumann Leabharfhoilsitheoirí Éireann (CLÉ) (Republic of Ireland) 202
Cumann Leabharlann na h-Éireann (Republic of Ireland) 204

Cumann Leabharlannaithe Scoile (CLS) (Republic of Ireland) 205
Cumont, Franz, Prize (International Literary Prizes) 440
Cura Verlag GmbH (Austria) 24
Curaçao Plaza Hotel (Netherlands Antilles) 268
Curaçaosche Drukkerij en Uitgevers Maatschappij (Netherlands Antilles) 268
Curci, Edizioni, SRL (Italy) 214
Curcio, Armando, Editore SpA (Italy) 214
Currawong Press Pty Ltd (Australia) 12
Currency Press Pty Ltd (Australia) 13
Current Books (India) 185
Current Technical Literature Co (Pvt) Ltd (India) 195
Currey, John, O'Neil Publishers Pty Ltd (Australia) 13
Curriculum Development Centre (Australia) 13
Curtis Brown Academic Ltd (United Kingdom) 408
Curtis Brown (Australia) Pty Ltd (Australia) 19
Curtis Brown Group Ltd (United Kingdom) 408
Curzon Press Ltd (United Kingdom) 376
Cuspide, Distribuidora, (Argentina) 8
Cut & Colour Books (United Kingdom) 376
Cuttington College and Divinity School Library (Liberia) 240
Cygne, Librairie Le, (Mauritius) 248
Cyngor Llyfrau Cymraeg (United Kingdom) 364
Cynthia, J, Co Ltd (China (Taiwan)) 64
Cypress Books (Australia) 13
Cyprus Booksellers Association (Cyprus) 69
Cyprus Library Association (Cyprus) 69
Cyprus Museum, Library of the, (Cyprus) 69
Cyril and Methodius National Library (Bulgaria) 58
Cyril and Methodius Prize (International Literary Prizes) 440
Czwiklitzer, Editions d'Art — Christophe, (France) 92
'Czytelnik', Spółdzielnia Wydawnicza, (Poland) 291

D A F S A (France) 92
D B V-Verlag (Federal Republic of Germany) 129
D C Book Club (India) 195
D C Books (India) 185
d e b Verlag (das europäische buch Literaturvertrieb GmbH) (Federal Republic of Germany) 129
D I F E L (Brazil) 49
D I G Ldá (Distribuidora Geral de Informação) (Portugal) 298
D I L I A (Czechoslovakia) 72
D J O, Federatie, (de jonge onderzoekers) (Netherlands) 257
D K F Trust (India) 185
D K Publications (India) 185
D K Publishers' Distributors (India) 195
D O P E S A, Editorial, (Documentacion Periodistica SA) (Spain) 316
D P Publications (United Kingdom) 376
D R W-Verlag Weinbrenner-KG (Federal Republic of Germany) 129
D T V (Federal Republic of Germany) 129
D und C, Verlag, (Federal Republic of Germany) 129
D V A (Federal Republic of Germany) 129
Dabbous Stores (Saudi Arabia) 302
Dacca Book Mart (Bangladesh) 32
Dacca University Library (Bangladesh) 32
Dacia, Editura, (Romania) 300
Dacosta, Les Editions Roger, (France) 92
Dado, Editoriale, (Italy) 214
Dadò, Edizioni Armando, Tipografia Stazione (Switzerland) 340
Dagbreek, Klub, (Republic of South Africa) 311
Dagen, Tidnings AB, (Sweden) 329
Dageraad, De, PVBA (Belgium) 35
Dahl, Gösta, och Son AB (Sweden) 334
Dahlia Books (Sweden) 329
Daiichi Shuppan Co Ltd (Japan) 225
Daily Times of Nigeria Ltd (Nigeria) 275
Daimon, Ediciones, — Manuel Tamayo (Spain) 316
Dais Literary Agency (Italy) 220
Dalén-Engqvists Prize, The, (Sweden) 335
Dall'Oglio Editore SpA (Italy) 214
Dalloz, Jurisprudence Générale, (France) 92
Dalton, Gilbert, Ltd (Republic of Ireland) 203
Daman, Librairie R, (Luxembourg) 242
Damascus University Library (Syria) 353
Damascus University Press (Syria) 352
Dami, Piero, Editore SpA (Italy) 214
Damm, N W, og Søn A/S (Norway) 279
Damnitz Verlag GmbH (Federal Republic of Germany) 129
Danae, Ediciones, SA (Spain) 317
Daneshdjou Bookstore (Iran) 201
Dangles, Editions, SA (France) 93
Daniel, The C W, Co Ltd (United Kingdom) 376
Danish Academy Prize for Literature (Denmark) 79
Danish Authors' Colleagues Prize (Denmark) 79

Danish Authors' Lyric Prize (Denmark) 79
Danish Critics Literary Prize (Denmark) 79
Danish Prize for Children's Literature (Denmark) 79
Danish Translations Centre (DTC) (Denmark) 79
Danmark Book Club (Denmark) 77
Danmark, Forlaget, A/S (Denmark) 74
Danmarks Biblioteksforening (Denmark) 78
Danmarks Forskningsbiblioteksforening (Denmark) 78
Danmarks Skolebibliotekarforening (Denmark) 78
Danmarks Skolebiblioteksforening (Denmark) 78
Danmarks Tekniske Bibliotek (Denmark) 78
Danov, Darzhavno Izdatelstov 'Christo G, ' (Bulgaria) 58
Dansk Boghandlermedhjaelperforening (Denmark) 73
Dansk Bogtjeneste (Denmark) 73
Dansk Central-Boghandel (Denmark) 78
Dansk Exlibris Selskab (Denmark) 79
Dansk Forfatterforening (Denmark) 73
Dansk Historisk Haandbogsforlag Ltd (Denmark) 74
Dansk Litteraturselskab, Nyt, (Denmark) 79
Dansk Musikbibliotekforening (Denmark) 78
Dansk Teknisk Litteraturselskab (Denmark) 78
Dansk Videnskabs Forlag ApS (Denmark) 74
Danske Antikvarboghandlerforening (Denmark) 73
Danske Boghandleres Bogimport A/S (Denmark) 73
Danske Boghandleres Importørforening (DANBIF) (Denmark) 73
Danske Boghandleres Kommissionsanstalt (DBK) (Denmark) 73
Danske Boghandlerforening, Den, (Denmark) 73
Danske Bogsamleres Klub (Denmark) 77
Danske Forlaeggerforening, Den, (Denmark) 73
Danske Forlag, Det, (Denmark) 74
Danske Sprog-og Litteraturselskab (Denmark) 79
Dap-Reinaert Uitgaven (Belgium) 43
Dap-Reinart, Uitgeverij, SV (Belgium) 35
Daphins-Verlag (Switzerland) 340
Daphne Diffusion SPRL (Belgium) 35
Daphne, Editions, (Belgium) 35
Dar al-Kutub al-Wataniah (National Library) (Syria) 353
Dar Arabia Lil Kitab (Tunisia) 357
Dar es Salaam Bookshop, The, (Tanzania) 353
Dar es Salaam Technical College Library (Tanzania) 353
Dar es Salaam University (Tanzania) 353
Dar es Salaam University Bookshop (Tanzania) 353
Dar Libya Publishing House (Libya) 241
Dar-ul-Kutub (Egypt) 82
Dardalet, Editions, SA (France) 93
Dardanos, G, — H Karakatsanis and Co Ltd — Gutenberg (Greece) 171
Dargaud Editeur (France) 93
Dario, Librería Recinto 'Ruben, ' (Nicaragua) 273
Dark Star (United Kingdom) 376
Darmstädter Blätter, Verlag, Schwarz und Co (Federal Republic of Germany) 129
Darton, Longman & Todd Ltd (United Kingdom) 376
Darwen Finlayson Ltd (United Kingdom) 376
Darzhavno Obedinenie 'Bulgarska Kniga' (Bulgaria) 57
Dastane Ramchandra and Co (India) 185
Daude, Librairie, (Réunion) 300
Dauguet, Constant, Endowment (France) 110
Dauphin, Editions du, (France) 93
Dausien, Werner, (Federal Republic of Germany) 129
Dauzat, Albert, Prize (France) 110
Davar (Israel) 206
David & Charles (United Kingdom) 376
Davidsfonds VZW (Belgium) 35
Davies, D J, (Australia) 13
Davies, Peter, Ltd (United Kingdom) 376
Davies Publishers, Christopher, Ltd (United Kingdom) 376
Davis-Poynter Ltd (United Kingdom) 376
Davison Publishing Ltd (United Kingdom) 376
Dawood, Abdullah, (Saudi Arabia) 302
Dawood Prize for Literature (Pakistan) 284
Dawson Publishing (United Kingdom) 376
Daystar Press (Publishers) (Nigeria) 275
Daystar Publications (India) 185
Daystar Publications (India) 195
De Donato Editore (Italy) 214
De Vecchi, Éditions, SA (France) 93
De Vecchi, Editorial, SA (Spain) 317
De Vecchi, Giovanni, Editore SpA (Italy) 214
De Wit Stores NV (Netherlands Antilles) 268
Dean and Chapter, The, Library (United Kingdom) 410
Dean & Son (United Kingdom) 377
Dearlove, Peter, Publishers (Zimbabwe) 429
Debard, Editions, (France) 93
Debooks (India) 185
Debresse, Nouvelles Editions, (France) 93
Dečje Novine (Yugoslavia) 422
Decker's, R v, Verlag G Schenck GmbH (Federal Republic of Germany) 129
Declés, Librairie, (Zaire) 427
Decomble, Librairie Générale de l'Enseignement Mme, (France) 93
Dedalo, Edizioni, (Italy) 214
Deep & Deep Publications (India) 185
Défense de l'Occident (France) 93

Dehoniane, Edizioni, Bologna (EDB) (Italy) 214
Deichmanske Bibliotek (Norway) 281
Deild bokavarda i islenskum rannsoknarbokasofnum (Iceland) 180
Dejaie, Maison d'Editions Cl, (Belgium) 35
Dekker en Nordemann BV/Meulenhoff-bruna (Netherlands) 266
Dekker en Van de Vegt (Netherlands) 257
Dekker en Van de Vegt (Netherlands) 266
Delachaux et Niestlé, Editions, SA (Switzerland) 340
Delachaux & Niestlé Spes, Editions, (France) 93
Delacroix, Eve, Prize (France) 110
Delafosse, Lycée technique Maurice, (Senegal) 303
Delagrave, Librairie, Sàrl (France) 93
Delarge, Jean-Pierre, SA (France) 93
Delattre, Mlle Sabine, (France) 107
Deldebat de Gonzalva Prize (France) 110
Delft University Press (Netherlands) 257
Delhi Library Association (India) 196
Delhi Public Library (India) 196
Delhi State Booksellers' and Publishers' Association (India) 181
Delhi University Library (India) 196
Delightful Books (United Kingdom) 377
Delius, Klasing und Co (Federal Republic of Germany) 129
Delmar (United Kingdom) 377
Delmas, Editions J, et Cie (France) 93
Delmas, Imprimeries, (France) 93
Delphin Verlag (Switzerland) 340
Delphin Verlag GmbH (Federal Republic of Germany) 129
Delpire, Editions Robert, SA (France) 93
Delp'sche Verlagsbuchhandlung (Federal Republic of Germany) 129
Delsa, Importadora de Publicaciones SA (Spain) 324
Delta, Editions, (Belgium) 35
Delta Editrice SpA (Italy) 214
Delta Förlags AB (Sweden) 329
Delta Press (Yugoslavia) 422
Delta SA (Switzerland) 340
Delta Science Fiction Bok Klubb (Sweden) 334
Deltas (Belgium) 35
Dempsey & Squires Publishers Ltd (United Kingdom) 377
Démuth, Dr rer pol Dr Julius, (Federal Republic of Germany) 164
Denayer, Felix, Prize (Belgium) 44
Denholm House Press (United Kingdom) 377
Denis & Co PVBA (Belgium) 35
Denis, Firma, & Co PVBA (Belgium) 42
Dennis, C J, Award (Australia) 22
Denoël, Editions, Sàrl (France) 93
Dent, J M, & Sons Ltd (United Kingdom) 377
Denzel Verlag Auto-und Wander Führer (Austria) 24
Depalma SRL (Argentina) 4
Departamento de Bibliotecas (Colombia) 66
Departamento de Bibliotecas y Publicaciones (Mexico) 252
Departamento de Documentación y Biblioteca (Uruguay) 417
Department of Information, Central Library of the, (Socialist Republic of Viet Nam) 420
Department of National Education Library (Republic of South Africa) 312
Department of National Education Literary Prizes (Republic of South Africa) 313
Department of Publicity (Nepal) 255
Department of Science Library (Thailand) 355
der 2, edition, Gerald Fritsch und Stefan Fritsch Buchverlag GmbH (Federal Republic of Germany) 129
Derecho Financiero, Editorial de, (Spain) 317
Derecho Privado, Editorial Revista de, (Spain) 317
Dergâh kitabevi (Turkey) 358
Dergâh kitabevi (Turkey) 358
Dergâh Yayinlari AS (Turkey) 358
D'Erlanger Prize (France) 110
Desai Bookshops (Fiji) 84
Desarrollo, Editorial, SA (Peru) 286
Desbordes-Valmore, Marceline, Prize (France) 110
Deschamps (Haiti) 174
Desclée de Brouwer SA (Belgium) 35
Desclée, De Brouwer SA (France) 93
Desclée, Editeurs (Belgium) 35
Desclée, Editions, et Cie (France) 93
Desertina Verlag (Switzerland) 340
Desforges, Librairie, (France) 93
Design Council Books (United Kingdom) 377
Desmet-Huysmans PVBA (Belgium) 35
Desoer, Editions, SA (Belgium) 35
Dessain et Tolra (France) 93
Dessain NV, H, (Belgium) 36
Dessain, F, SPRL (Belgium) 36
Dessart, Engelbert, Verlag KG (Federal Republic of Germany) 129
Destino, Ediciones, SL (Spain) 317
Desvigne, Librairie André, (France) 93
Detskaya Entsiklopediya (Union of Soviet Socialist Republics) 360

Detskaya Literatura, Izdatelstvo, (Union of Soviet Socialist Republics) 360
Deubner, Dr Peter, Verlag GmbH (Federal Republic of Germany) 129
Deuticke, Verlag Franz, (Austria) 24
Deutsch, André, Ltd (United Kingdom) 377
Deutsch, Verlag Harri, (Federal Republic of Germany) 129
Deutsch, Verlag Harri, (Switzerland) 340
Deutsche Akademie für Sprache und Dichtung (Federal Republic of Germany) 167
Deutsche Bibelstiftung (Federal Republic of Germany) 129
Deutsche Bibliothek — Goethe Institut Brüssel (Belgium) 43
Deutsche Bibliothek (National Library) (Federal Republic of Germany) 166
Deutsche Buch-Gemeinschaft C A Koch's Verlag Nachfolger (Austria) 29
Deutsche Buch-Gemeinschaft C A Koch's Verlag Nachfolger (Federal Republic of Germany) 129
Deutsche Buch-Gemeinschaft C A Koch's Verlag Nachfolger (Federal Republic of Germany) 165
Deutsche Bücherei (German Democratic Republic) 117
Deutsche Gesellschaft für Dokumentation eV (Federal Republic of Germany) 166
Deutsche Hausbücherei GmbH (Federal Republic of Germany) 165
Deutsche Jugend-Presse-Agentur KG (Federal Republic of Germany) 129
Deutsche Philips GmbH (Federal Republic of Germany) 129
Deutsche Shakespeare-Gesellschaft West eV (Federal Republic of Germany) 167
Deutsche Staatsbibliothek (German Democratic Republic) 117
Deutsche Verlags-Anstalt GmbH (DVA) (Federal Republic of Germany) 129
Deutscher Apotheker Verlag Dr Roland Schmiedel GmbH und Co (Federal Republic of Germany) 129
Deutscher Betriebswirte-Verlag GmbH (Federal Republic of Germany) 129
Deutscher Bücherbund GmbH (Federal Republic of Germany) 165
Deutscher Buchkreis (Federal Republic of Germany) 165
Deutscher Eichverlag (Federal Republic of Germany) 130
Deutscher Fachschriften-Verlag Braun GmbH & Co KG (Federal Republic of Germany) 130
Deutscher Fachverlag GmbH (Federal Republic of Germany) 130
Deutscher Gemeindeverlag GmbH (Federal Republic of Germany) 130
Deutscher Instituts-Verlag GmbH (Federal Republic of Germany) 130
Deutscher, Isaac, Memorial Prize (International Literary Prizes) 440
Deutscher Kunstverlag GmbH (Federal Republic of Germany) 130
Deutscher Landwirtschaftsverlag, VEB, (German Democratic Republic) 115
Deutscher Leihbuchhändler-Verband eV (Federal Republic of Germany) 167
Deutscher Taschenbuch Verlag GmbH & Co KG (Federal Republic of Germany) 130
Deutscher Verband evangelischer Büchereien eV (Federal Republic of Germany) 167
Deutscher Verlag der Wissenschaften, VEB, (German Democratic Republic) 115
Deutscher Verlag für Grundstoffindustrie, VEB, (German Democratic Republic) 115
Deutscher Verlag für Kunstwissenschaft GmbH (Federal Republic of Germany) 130
Deutscher Verlag für Musik, VEB, (German Democratic Republic) 115
Deutscher Wirtschaftsdienst John von Freyend GmbH (Federal Republic of Germany) 130
Deutsches Bibliotheksinstitut (Federal Republic of Germany) 167
Deutsches Jugendschriftenwerk (Federal Republic of Germany) 119
Deux Coqs d'Or, Les Editions des, (France) 93
Deux Magots Prize (France) 111
Deves et Chaumet, Librairie, (Mali) 246
Devlin, Denis, Memorial Award for Poetry (Republic of Ireland) 205
Dewallens, A (Belgium) 36
Dewan Bahasa dan Pustaka (Malaysia) 244
Dewan Bahasa dan Pustaka (Malaysia) 246
Dewan, Perpustakaan, Perwakilan Rakjat Gotong Rojong (Indonesia) 200
Dey Sahitya Kutir (P) Ltd (India) 185
Dhammabucha (Thailand) 354
Dhanani's Ltd (Kenya) 235
Dhanpat Rai & Sons (India) 185
Dheerasarn Ltd (Thailand) 355
Diafora SA (Spain) 317
Diagne, Lycée Blaise, (Senegal) 303
Diagram Visual Information Ltd (United Kingdom) 377

Diálogo, Ediciones, (Paraguay) 286
Diamond Comics (India) 185
Diamond Inc (Japan) 225
Dian Rakyat (Indonesia) 199
Diana, Editorial, (Mexico) 249
Diana-Verlag AG (Switzerland) 340
Díaz, Librería, de Santos (Spain) 324
Dickens, The, Fellowship (Argentina) 9
Dickens, The, Fellowship (Australia) 21
Dickens, The, Fellowship (Belgium) 44
Dickens, The, Fellowship (Japan) 232
Dickens, The, Fellowship (Netherlands) 267
Dickens, The, Fellowship (New Zealand) 272
Dickens, The, Fellowship (Sri Lanka) 326
Dickens, The, Fellowship (United Kingdom) 412
Dictionnaire, La Maison du, (France) 93
Didactica si Pedagogica, Editura, (Romania) 300
Didax (Switzerland) 340
Diderich, Librairie, Sàrl (Luxembourg) 242
Diderot, Livre Club, (France) 108
Didier, Editions Marcel, SA (Belgium) 36
Didier et Richard, Editions, (France) 93
Didier, John, Editions (France) 93
Didier, Librairie Marcel, SA (France) 93
Didot-Bottin, Société, SA (France) 94
Diederichs, Eugen, Verlag (Federal Republic of Germany) 130
Diesterweg, Verlag Moritz, /Otto Salle Verlag (Federal Republic of Germany) 130
Dieterich'sche Verlagsbuchhandlung (German Democratic Republic) 115
Dietz Verlag (German Democratic Republic) 115
Dietz, Verlag J H W, Nachf GmbH (Federal Republic of Germany) 130
Diffusion de la Presse (Zaire) 427
Diffusion Scientifique, Editions la, (France) 94
Difros (Greece) 171
Difusão Editorial SA (DIFEL) (Brazil) 49
Difusión, Centro de, del Libro (Spain) 317
Difusión, Editorial, (Bolivia) 46
Difusión, Editorial, SA (Argentina) 4
Difusión, Libreria, (Bolivia) 46
Dijkstra's Uitg Mij, Jacob, BV (Netherlands) 257
Dijkstra's Uitgeverij Zeist BV (Netherlands) 258
Diki-Books Srl (Italy) 214
Dilagro SA (Spain) 317
Diligentia BV (Netherlands) 258
Diligentia-Uitgeverij (Belgium) 36
Dillon's University Bookshop Ltd (United Kingdom) 410
Dimashk, Dar, (Adib Tunbakji) Bookshop (Syria) 353
Dimitrov' Academy, Central Agricultural Library of the 'G, of Agricultural Sciences (Bulgaria) 58
Dini Book Depot (India) 185
Dinosaur Publications Ltd (United Kingdom) 377
Diogenes,, Editorial, SA (Mexico) 249
Diogenes Verlag AG (Switzerland) 340
Dipa-Verlag und Druck GmbH & Co (Federal Republic of Germany) 130
Diponegoro, C V, (Indonesia) 199
Dirección de Cultura, Biblioteca de la, (Bolivia) 46
Dirección de Estadistica y Censo (Panama) 284
Directorate of Archives and Libraries (Bangladesh) 32
Directorate of Libraries (Pakistan) 284
Directorate of Publications (Republic of South Africa) 307
Directory Publishers of Zambia Ltd (Zambia) 428
Direkt Verlag (Federal Republic of Germany) 130
Discailles, Ernest, Prize (International Literary Prizes) 440
'Discovering' Books (United Kingdom) 377
Disesa (Dominican Republic) 80
Dishoeck, van, (Netherlands) 258
Distasa (Argentina) 4
Distein, Grupo Editorial, -CEAC-Timun Mas (Spain) 317
Distri BD SPRL (Belgium) 36
Distribuidora de Libros (Guatemala) 173
Distribuidora de Libros Inc (Puerto Rico) 299
Distribuidora Escolar SA (Dominican Republic) 80
Distributors' Centre for Israeli Books Ltd (Israel) 210
Distripress (International Organizations) 432
Diwan, The, Library, Ministry of Education (Iraq) 202
Djambatan BV (Netherlands) 258
Djambatan, P T, Penerbit NV (Indonesia) 199
Doaba House (India) 185
Doblinger, Ludwig, (Bernard Herzmansky) Musikverlag (Austria) 24
Dobloug Prize (Sweden) 335
Dobloug Prize (International Literary Prizes) 440
Dobson, Dennis, (Dobson Books Ltd) (United Kingdom) 377
Documentário, Editôra, Ltda (Brazil) 50
Documentation, Bibliothèque de, Internationale Contemporaine (France) 108
Documentation et d'Analyses, Société de, Financières (France) 94
Documentation Française, La, (France) 94
Documentation, La, Cistercienne (Belgium) 36
Documentation Research and Training Centre (India) 196
Dodoni (Greece) 171

Doepgen, Edition, Verlag (Belgium) 36
Dogan Kardes Matbaacilik SAS (Turkey) 358
Doin Editeurs (France) 94
Dokumentasi Ilmiah Nasional, Pusat, (Indonesia) 200
Dokumentation, Verlag, Saur KG (Federal Republic of Germany) 130
Dokumentationsstelle für neuere österreichische Literatur (Austria) 30
Dollar Books (Australia) 13
Dolmen, The, Press Ltd (Republic of Ireland) 203
Dolphin (United Kingdom) 377
Dolphin Books (United Kingdom) 377
Dom Ksiazki (Poland) 293
Dom Ksiazki (Poland) 293
Dom Quixote, Publicações, (Portugal) 296
Domi, Ekdoseis, AE (Greece) 171
Dominican Publications (Republic of Ireland) 203
Dominion Press (Pvt) Ltd (Zimbabwe) 429
Domino (France) 94
Domus Editoriale (Italy) 214
Don Bosco, Ecole Technique officielle, Bibliothèque (Rwanda) 302
Don Bosco, Ediciones, (Spain) 317
Don Bosco, Editorial y Librería, (Bolivia) 46
Don Bosco, Librería, (Bolivia) 46
Don Bosco Verlag der Gesellschaft der Salesianer (Federal Republic of Germany) 130
Donald, John, Publishers Ltd (United Kingdom) 377
Donauland, Buchgemeinschaft, (Austria) 29
Doncel (Spain) 317
Dongguk University Library (Republic of Korea) 238
Dongwha Publishing Co (Republic of Korea) 236
Donker, Ad, Ltd (United Kingdom) 377
Donker, Ad, (Pty) Ltd (Republic of South Africa) 308
Donker, Uitgeversmaatschappij Ad, BV (Netherlands) 258
Dopravy, Nakladatelství, a spoju (Czechoslovakia) 70
Dorikos Makridis (Greece) 171
Dorling Kindersley Ltd (United Kingdom) 377
Dorp Aruba, Van, NV (Netherlands Antilles) 268
Dorp Eddine, Van, NV (Netherlands Antilles) 268
Dosaaf, Znak Pochyota Order, Publishing House (Union of Soviet Socialist Republics) 360
Dossat, Editorial, SA (Spain) 317
Dossche, Editions Irène, SPRL (Belgium) 36
Doubleday Australia Pty Ltd (Australia) 13
Doubleday Australia Pty Ltd, Book Club Associates Division (Australia) 19
Doubleday Book Club (Australia) 19
Doubleday Book Club (New Zealand) 271
Doubleday & Co Inc (United Kingdom) 377
Doubleday-France (France) 94
Doubleday History Book Club (Australia) 19
Doubleday History Book Club (New Zealand) 271
Doubleday New Zealand Ltd (New Zealand) 269
Doubleday New Zealand Ltd, Book Club Associates Division (New Zealand) 272
Doucet, Bibliothèque d'Art et d'Archéologie (Fondation Jacques,) (France) 108
Doucet, Bibliothèque littéraire Jacques, (France) 108
Dove Communications Pty Ltd (Australia) 13
Draeger Editeur (France) 94
Dragon Books (United Kingdom) 377
Dragon's Dream (Netherlands) 258
Dragon's Dream Ltd (France) 94
Dragon's World Ltd (United Kingdom) 377
Drammen Folkebibliotek (Norway) 281
Drei Eichen Verlag AG (Switzerland) 340
Drei Eidgenossen Verlag (Switzerland) 340
Dreisam-Verlag (Federal Republic of Germany) 130
Dreiseitel, Galerie, (Federal Republic of Germany) 130
Drejtoria Qëndrore e Përhapjes dhe e Propagandimit të Librit (Albania) 1
Dressler, Cecilie, Verlag (Federal Republic of Germany) 130
Dreyers Forlag (Norway) 279
Driehoek, De, BV (Netherlands) 258
Droemersche Verlagsanstalt AG (Switzerland) 340
Droemersche Verlagsanstalt Th Knaur Nachf (Federal Republic of Germany) 130
Droguet et Ardant (France) 94
Droit et de Jurisprudence, Librairie Générale de, (France) 94
Dronte, Ediciones, Argentina SRL (Argentina) 4
Droste Verlag GmbH (Federal Republic of Germany) 131
Drouot, Librairie, (Ets Robert Drouot) (Benin) 45
Droz, Librairie, SA (Switzerland) 340
Druckenmüller Verlag (Federal Republic of Germany) 131
Druffel-Verlag (Federal Republic of Germany) 131
Drukarnia Narodowa (Poland) 291
Drukkerij de Stad NV (Netherlands Antilles) 268
Drummond Publishing (Australia) 13
Društvo bibliotekara Bosne i Hercegovine (Yugoslavia) 426
Društvo bibliotekarjev Slovenije (Yugoslavia) 426
Društvo na arhivskite rabotnici i arhivite na SRM (Yugoslavia) 426
Društvo na bibliotekarite na Makedonija (Yugoslavia) 426

Društvo na literaturnite preveduvači na SRM (Yugoslavia) 426
Društvo na pisatelite na SRM (Yugoslavia) 426
Društvo za srpski jezik i književnost (Yugoslavia) 426
Državna Založba Slovenije (Yugoslavia) 422
Državna Založba Slovenije (Yugoslavia) 425
Duang Kamol (Thailand) 354
Duas Cidades, Livraría, (Brazil) 55
Duas Cidades, Livraría, (Brazil) 55
Duas Cidades, Livraría, Ltda (Brazil) 50
Dublin Institute for Advanced Studies (Republic of Ireland) 203
Dublin Public Libraries (Republic of Ireland) 204
Duckworth, Gerald, & Co Ltd (United Kingdom) 377
Duculot, Editions et Imprimerie J, SA (Belgium) 36
Duculot, Jules, Prize (Belgium) 44
Duden, Konrad, Prize (Federal Republic of Germany) 168
Duff Cooper Memorial Prize (International Literary Prizes) 440
Dufour, Henry-Robert (Switzerland) 340
Duke of Alba Prize (Spain) 325
Dülk, Monika, Verlag (Federal Republic of Germany) 131
Dumas-Millier Prize (France) 111
Dumjahn, Horst-Werner, Verlag (Federal Republic of Germany) 131
Dummar & Mowakadeh & Co (Syria) 353
Dummer, Wolfgang, und Co (Federal Republic of Germany) 131
Dümmlers, Ferd, Verlag (Federal Republic of Germany) 131
Dumreicher, Edition, (Austria) 24
Duncker und Humblot (Federal Republic of Germany) 131
Dunedin Public Library (New Zealand) 272
Dunia, P T, Pustaka Jaya (Indonesia) 199
Dunitz, Martin, Ltd (United Kingdom) 377
Dunmore Press Ltd (New Zealand) 270
Dunod (France) 94
Dupuch, Etienne, Jr Publications Ltd (Bahamas) 31
Dupuis, Editions Jean, SA (Belgium) 36
Dupuis, Maison d'Editions J, Fils et Cie SA (France) 94
Durban Municipal Library (Republic of South Africa) 312
Duret, Miguel Lanz, Prize (Mexico) 253
Durham University Library (United Kingdom) 410
Durvan SA de Ediciones (Spain) 317
Dustri-Verlag Dr Karl Feistle (Federal Republic of Germany) 131
Dutch (Flemish) Literature Grand Prizes (Netherlands) 267
Dutch Literature Prize (International Literary Prizes) 440
Dutch Prize for the Best Children's Book (Netherlands) 267
Dutch Reformed Church Publishers (Republic of South Africa) 308
Dutens, Alfred, Prize (France) 111
Dutton, The, Animal Book Award (International Literary Prizes) 440
Duttweiler, Gottlieb, Institute for Economic & Social Studies (Switzerland) 340
Duvivier, Charles, Prize (Belgium) 44
'Dvir Bialik' Municipal Central Public Library (Israel) 210
Dvir, The, Publishing Co Ltd (Israel) 206
Dwyer, E J, (Australia) Pty Ltd (Australia) 13
Dymock's Book Arcade Ltd (Australia) 19
Dynamis Verlag (Switzerland) 340

E B A L (Brazil) 50
E C A Bookshop Co-op Society (Ethiopia) 83
E C A (Ediciones Culturales Argentinas) (Argentina) 4
E C I voor Boeken en Grammofoonplaten BV (Netherlands) 266
E C P Förlags AB (Sweden) 329
E C W A Productions Ltd (Nigeria) 275
E D A M E X (Mexico) 249
E D B (Italy) 214
E D E R S A (Editoriales de Derecho Reunidas SA) (Spain) 317
E D H A S A (Editora y Distribuidora Hispano-Americana SA) (Spain) 317
E D I 3 (Italy) 214
E D I M E (Venezuela) 418
E F S-förlaget (Sweden) 329
E L D Trust (Republic of South Africa) 308
E M B L A (Norway) 280
E M E S C O Book Club (India) 195
E O S Verlag, Erzabtei Sankt Ottilien (Federal Republic of Germany) 131
E P A (France) 94
E P Book Depot (Ghana) 169
E P O (Belgium) 36
E P Publishing Ltd (United Kingdom) 377
E P U (Brazil) 50

E R B (Czechoslovakia) 72
E R I — Edizioni R A I Radiotelevisione Italiana SpA (Italy) 214
E R Verlags GmbH (Federal Republic of Germany) 131
E S A Bookshop (Kenya) 235
E S A Bookshop (Uganda) 359
E S A Creative Learning Ltd (United Kingdom) 378
E S C Publishing Ltd (United Kingdom) 378
E S D U C K (Egypt) 81
E S F, Editions, (Editions Sociales Françaises) (France) 94
E S H (English for Speakers of Hebrew) (Israel) 206
E T A (Editôra Técnica de Aviação Ltda (Brazil) 50
E T H Bibliothek (Eidgenossische Technische Hochschule Bibliothek) (Switzerland) 352
E T P (Editions Techniques Professionnelles et Régies Audiovisuelles) (France) 94
E T S F (France) 94
E U D E B A (Editorial Universitaria de Buenos Aires) (Argentina) 4
E U N S A (Ediciones Universidad de Navarra SA) (Spain) 317
E U R E D I F (France) 94
Early English Text Society (United Kingdom) 413
Eason & Son Ltd (Republic of Ireland) 203
Eason & Son Ltd (Republic of Ireland) 204
East African Directory Co (Kenya) 234
East African Literature Bureau (Kenya) 234
East African Literature Bureau (Tanzania) 353
East African Literature Bureau (Tanzania) 354
East African Literature Bureau (Uganda) 359
East African Literature Bureau (Uganda) 360
East African Publishing House (Kenya) 234
East African Statistical Department Library (Kenya) 235
East and Central Africa Regional Branch of the International Council of Archives (ECARBICA) (International Organizations) 432
East and West Centre Pte Ltd (Republic of Singapore) 306
East and West Publishing Co (Pakistan) 282
East Anglian Writers (United Kingdom) 413
East Asia Book Co (Hong Kong) 176
East-West Publications Fonds BV (Netherlands) 258
East-West Publications (UK) Ltd (United Kingdom) 378
Eastern Book Co (India) 185
Eastern Book Service Corp (Philippines) 289
Eastern Book Service Ltd (Hong Kong) 176
Eastern Book Service Pte Ltd (Republic of Singapore) 306
Eastern Book Service Sdn Bhd (wholesalers) (Malaysia) 245
Eastern Cultural Organizations Sdn Bhd (Malaysia) 244
Eastern Law House Pvt Ltd (India) 185
Eastern Publishing Co Ltd (China (Taiwan)) 64
Eastern Universities Press (Malaysia) 244
Eastern Universities Press Sdn Bhd (Republic of Singapore) 305
Ebeling, Hasso, (Luxembourg) 242
Ebeling, Hasso, Verlag (Luxembourg) 242
Ebeling Verlag GmbH (Federal Republic of Germany) 131
Eblana, The, Bookshop (Republic of Ireland) 204
Ebraesp Editorial Ltda (Brazil) 50
Ebury Press (United Kingdom) 378
Ecart Publications (Switzerland) 340
Ecclesia Press (Republic of Ireland) 203
Echavarría', Biblioteca 'José Antonio, (Cuba) 68
Echeverria, Aquileo T, Prize (Costa Rica) 68
Echter-Seelsorge Verlag (Federal Republic of Germany) 131
Eckersteins Universitetsbokhandel AB (Sweden) 334
École, Bibliothèque de l', des Langues orientales (France) 108
Ecole, Bibliothèque de l', royale de Médecine (Laos) 239
Ecole, Bibliothèque de l', supérieure des Lettres (Lebanon) 240
Ecole, L', /L'Ecole des Loisirs (France) 94
Ecole Mohammedia d'Ingénieurs (Morocco) 254
Ecole nationale d'Administration Bibliothèque (Tunisia) 357
Ecole nationale polytechnique, Bibliothèque (Algeria) 2
Ecole normale supérieure (Gabon) 113
Ecole normale supérieure (Mali) 246
Ecole normale supérieure, Bibliothèque (Burundi) 60
Ecole normale supérieure de l'Afrique centrale, Bibliothèque (Popular Republic of Congo) 67
Ecole Professionelle de la Mission Catholique (Togo) 356
Ecoles, Librairie des, (Morocco) 254
Ecoma, Editorial, SA (Peru) 286
Econ-Verlag GmbH (Austria) 24
Econ Verlagsgruppe (Federal Republic of Germany) 131
Economic and Industrial Publications (Pakistan) 282
Economic Council for Israel Printing & Publishing Committee (Israel) 205
Economic Publishing House (Democratic People's Republic of Korea) 236
Economische Voorlichtingsdienst, Bibliotheek- en Documentatie-centrum van de, (Netherlands) 266
Economist, The, Newspaper Ltd (United Kingdom) 378

Ecumenical Literature, The, Distribution Trust (Republic of South Africa) 308
Edaf Ediciones y Distribuciones SA (Spain) 317
Edagricole (Edizioni Agricole) (Italy) 214
Edameris (Brazil) 50
Edanim Publishers (Israel) 206
Edart (São Paulo Livraría Editôra Ltda) (Brazil) 50
Eddison Press Ltd (United Kingdom) 378
Edekes Bookshop Stores Ltd (Nigeria) 277
Edelcid Libros Cientificos (Guatemala) 173
Edhis (France) 94
Edi-Art (Belgium) 36
Edibimbi SRL (Italy) 214
Edica SA (Spain) 317
Edicient SAIC (Argentina) 4
Ediciones de la Biblioteca (EBCV) (Venezuela) 418
Ediciones Iberoamericanas SA (EISA) (Spain) 317
Ediciones Instituto Nacional de Cultura (Panama) 284
Ediciones Pedagógicas Dominicanas C por A (Dominican Republic) 79
Ediciones Populares (Netherlands Antilles) 268
Edicom NV (Netherlands) 258
Edigraf, Editorial Vilcar y Gráficas Hamburg SA (Spain) 317
Edil, Editorial, Inc (Puerto Rico) 299
Edilec, Les Editions, SA (France) 94
Edinburgh Bibliographical Society (United Kingdom) 413
Edinburgh University Library (United Kingdom) 411
Edinburgh University Press (United Kingdom) 378
Edinburgh University Student Publications Board (United Kingdom) 378
Edinorma Ltda y Cia SCA (Colombia) 65
Edipem SpA (Italy) 214
Ediscience (France) 94
Edisud (France) 94
Edit, NiP, (Yugoslavia) 422
Edita SA (Switzerland) 340
Editalia (Edizioni d'Italia) (Italy) 214
Editart, Société, Quatre Chemins (France) 94
Editeurs Associes SA (Switzerland) 340
Editeurs de Litterature Biblique (Belgium) 36
Editeurs Français, Les, Réunis (France) 94
Editeurs Réunis, Les, (France) 94
Edition der 2 (Federal Republic of Germany) 131
Editions interuniversitaires (Belgium) 36
Editions Maritimes et d'Outre-Mer SA (France) 94
Editions Modernes Média (France) 94
Editions Mondiales, Les, SA (France) 94
Editions Sociales Françaises (France) 95
Editions Sociales, Les, (France) 94
Editions Techniques des Industries de la Fonderie (France) 95
Editions Techniques et Scientifiques Françaises (France) 95
Editions techniques et scientifiques SPRL (Belgium) 36
Editions Techniques Professionnelles (France) 95
Editions Techniques SA (France) 95
Editions Universelles, Les, Sàrl (France) 95
Éditions Universitaires-Éditions du Jour SA (France) 95
Editions universitaires, Les, d'Egypte (Egypt) 81
Editions universitaires SA (Belgium) 36
Editions Universitaires (Universitätsverlag) (Switzerland) 340
Editnemo (Italy) 214
Edito-Service SA (Switzerland) 340
Editogo (Togo) 356
Editora Cultural Dominicana (Dominican Republic) 79
Editora Educativa Dominicana (Dominican Republic) 79
Editôra Interamericana do Brasil Ltda (Brazil) 50
Editora Internacional (Dominican Republic) 79
Editôra Moderna Ltda (Brazil) 50
Editora Nacional (Mexico) 249
Editora Nacional (Spain) 317
Editôra Nacional, Cía, (Brazil) 50
Editôra Pedagogica e Universitaria Ltda (EPU) (Brazil) 50
Editora y Distribuidora Nacional de Libros (Dominican Republic) 79
Editorama, SA (Dominican Republic) 80
Editores Asociados Mexicanos SA (EDAMEX) (Mexico) 249
Editori, Associazione Italiana degli, di Musica (AIDEM) (Italy) 211
Editorial and Publishing Services (Ghana) 169
Editorial Consultancy & Agency Services (Nigeria) 276
Editorial Cultural (Puerto Rico) 299
Editorial Interamericana del Ecuador CA (Ecuador) 80
Editorial Interamericana SA (Peru) 287
Editorial Librería Dominicana (Dominican Republic) 80
Editorial Nicaragüense (Nicaragua) 273
Editorial Sudamericana SA (Argentina) 4
Editorial Universidad SRL (Argentina) 4
Editorial Universitaria (Honduras) 174
Editorial Universitariá (Panama) 284
Editorial Universitaria Centroamericana (EDUCA) (Costa Rica) 67
Editorial Universitaria de Buenos Aires (Argentina) 4

470 INDEX

Editorial Universitaria de la Universidad de El Salvador (El Salvador) 82
Editorialebari (Italy) 214
Editrice Bibliografica (Italy) 214
Educaboek BV (Netherlands) 258
Education et Culture (France) 108
Educational Aids Production Co Pte Ltd (Republic of Singapore) 306
Educational Book Centre (Republic of Singapore) 306
Educational Book Centre (The Modern Library) (Israel) 210
Educational Book Promotions (United Kingdom) 378
Educational Books Publishing House (Democratic People's Republic of Korea) 236
Educational Company (Greece) 171
Educational Company of Ireland (Republic of Ireland) 203
Educational Enterprise (Nepal) 255
Educational Enterprises (India) 185
Educational Enterprises (Pvt) Ltd (Nepal) 255
Educational Explorers Ltd (United Kingdom) 378
Educational Library (Saudi Arabia) 303
Educational Material Aid (Australia) 13
Educational Productions Ltd (United Kingdom) 378
Educational Publishers' Association (India) 181
Educational Publishers' Council (United Kingdom) 364
Educational Publishing, The, House Ltd (Hong Kong) 175
Educational Research Institute (Nigeria) 275
Educational Systems Ltd (United Kingdom) 378
Educational Writers' Group (United Kingdom) 364
Educmeds Pty Ltd (Namibia) 255
Educum Uitgewers Beperk (Republic of South Africa) 308
Eduskunnan Kirjasto (Finland) 86
Edwardian Studies Association (United Kingdom) 413
Edwards & Shaw Pty Ltd (Australia) 13
Eel Pie Publishing (United Kingdom) 378
Effendi Harahap Bookstore (Indonesia) 200
Efstathiadis, P, & Sons SA (Greece) 171
Efstathiadis, P, & Sons SA (Greece) 172
Egan, Wm, & Sons (Republic of Ireland) 204
Egerton College Library (Kenya) 235
Eghbal Co (Iran) 201
Egoist-Verlag (Federal Republic of Germany) 131
Egyptian Association for Archives and Librarianship (Egypt) 82
Egyptian Society, The, for the Dissemination of Universal Culture and Knowledge (ESDUCK) (Egypt) 81
Egyptian Society, The, for the Dissemination of Universal Culture and Knowledge (ESDUCK) (Egypt) 82
Egyptian Society, The, for the Dissemination of Universal Culture and Knowledge (ESDUCK) (Egypt) 82
Ehapa Verlag GmbH (Federal Republic of Germany) 131
Ehon Library (Japan) 231
Ehrenwirth Verlag GmbH (Federal Republic of Germany) 131
Ehrlingförlagen AB (Sweden) 329
Eibel, Alfred, (France) 95
Eibel, Alfred, Editeur (Switzerland) 340
Eide, J W, Forlag A/S (Norway) 279
Eike-Boekklub (Republic of South Africa) 311
Einaudi, Giulio, Editore SpA (Italy) 214
Eindhovensche Drukkerij BV (Netherlands) 258
Eiselé, André, (Switzerland) 340
Eisenbahn, Verlag, R Jeanmaire & Co (Switzerland) 340
Ejlers', Christian, Forlag A/S (Denmark) 74
Ekblad-Eldhs, Signe, Prize (Sweden) 335
Eked Publishing House (Israel) 206
Ekenäs Tryckeri AB (Finland) 84
Ekonomiczne, Państwowe Wydawnictwo, (State Economic Publishers) (Poland) 291
'Ekonomika', Izdatelstvo, (Union of Soviet Socialist Republics) 360
El-Am Publishing (Israel) Ltd (Israel) 207
Eldec SpA Edizioni Pregiate (Italy) 214
Elder, Anne, Poetry Fund Award (Australia) 22
Eldorado, A Casa do Livro, Ltda (Brazil) 55
Eldra Taschenbuchverlag (Federal Republic of Germany) 131
Electa Editrice (Italy) 214
Electrónicas Editôra, Seleções, Ltda (Brazil) 50
Eleftheroudakis, G C, Co Ltd (Greece) 172
Eleftheroudakis, G C, SA (Greece) 171
Elek, Paul, Ltd (United Kingdom) 378
Elektrowirtschaft (Switzerland) 341
Elgin, Mary, Prize (International Literary Prizes) 440
Elif Kitabevi (Turkey) 358
Elingaard Forlag A/S (Norway) 279
Elisas Sourasky Central Library, Tel Aviv University (Israel) 210
Elitera Verlag GmbH (Federal Republic of Germany) 131
Elizabethan Publishing House (Nigeria) 275
Elkan och Schildknecht (Sweden) 329
Ellenberg Verlag (Federal Republic of Germany) 131
Ellermann, Verlag Heinrich, KG (Federal Republic of Germany) 131
Elliot Right Way Books (United Kingdom) 378

Ellis, Aidan, Publishing Ltd (United Kingdom) 378
Elm Tree Books Ltd (United Kingdom) 378
Elmar BV (Netherlands) 258
Elmfield Press (United Kingdom) 378
Elpis Verlag GmbH (Federal Republic of Germany) 131
Elron Press Ltd (United Kingdom) 378
Elsässer, Buchhandlung zum, AG (Switzerland) 351
Elsevier Boekerij, BV Uitgeversmaatschappij, (Netherlands) 258
Elsevier, Editions, Séquoia Sàrl (France) 95
Elsevier-NDU nv (Netherlands) 258
Elsevier/North Holland Biomedical Press (Netherlands) 258
Elsevier Oxford Ltd (United Kingdom) 378
Elsevier-Phaidon (United Kingdom) 378
Elsevier Séquoia (Belgium) 36
Elsevier Sequoia SA (Switzerland) 341
Elsevier's Wetenschappelijke Uitgeverij (Elsevier Scientific Publishing Co) BV (Netherlands) 259
Elsner, Otto, Verlagsgesellschaft mbH & Co KG (Federal Republic of Germany) 131
'Elvetica' Edizioni SA (Switzerland) 341
Elwert, N G, Verlag (Federal Republic of Germany) 131
Elwert und Meurer GmbH (Federal Republic of Germany) 131
Elwert und Meurer GmbH, Buchhandlung, (Federal Republic of Germany) 165
Emblem (United Kingdom) 378
Embryo (United Kingdom) 378
Emecé Editores SA (Argentina) 4
Emecé, Premio, Annual Prize (Argentina) 9
Eminescu, Editura, (Romania) 300
Emmaus-Desclée de Brouwer NV (Belgium) 36
Emme Edizioni (Italy) 214
Emmentaler Druck AG (Switzerland) 341
Emograph (Spain) 317
Emotan Publishing Co (Nigeria) Ltd (Nigeria) 275
Empire Shop (Montserrat) 253
Emporium, The, (Belize) 45
Empresa Moderna Lda (Mozambique) 254
Empresas Editoriales SA (Mexico) 249
En-Najah (Tunisia) 357
En-Najah, Librairie, (Tunisia) 357
Enciclopédia, Editorial, Lda (Portugal) 296
Encounters (United Kingdom) 409
'Encouragement Prize' (Austria) 30
'Encouragement Prizes' for Books for Children and Young People (Austria) 30
Encre, Editions, (France) 95
Encyclopaedia Africana Project (Ghana) 169
Encyclopaedia Britannica (Federal Republic of Germany) 131
Encyclopaedia Britannica (Australia) Inc (Australia) 13
Encyclopaedia Britannica de Venezuela SA (Dominican Republic) 80
Encyclopaedia Britannica International Ltd (United Kingdom) 378
Encyclopaedia Judaica (Israel) 207
Encyclopaedia Universalis France SA (France) 95
'Energiya', Izdatelstvo, (Union of Soviet Socialist Republics) 361
Engel, Friedemann von, Verlag (Federal Republic of Germany) 131
Engelbert-Verlag Zimmermann KG (Federal Republic of Germany) 132
Engelman, Camille, Prize (International Literary Prizes) 441
Engels, Carl, Musikverlag (Federal Republic of Germany) 132
Englind, Teaterförlag Arvid, AB (Sweden) 334
Englisch, F, Verlag GmbH (Federal Republic of Germany) 132
English Agency, The, (Japan) 230
English Association (United Kingdom) 413
English Association (South African Branch) Literary Prize (Republic of South Africa) 313
English Book, The, Club (Denmark) 77
English Book Club (Netherlands) 266
English Book Store (India) 195
English Bookshop, The, (Denmark) 78
English Bookshop, The, (Iceland) 180
English-Speaking Union Book Award (International Literary Prizes) 441
Enke, Ferdinand, Verlag (Federal Republic of Germany) 132
Ennsthaler, Wilhelm, (Austria) 24
Enossis Ellenon Bibliothakarion (Greece) 172
Enriquillo, Editora, (Dominican Republic) 80
Enschede en Zonen Grafische Inrichting BV (Netherlands) 259
Enseignement, Librairie Générale de l', Sàrl (France) 95
Ensslin Jugendbuchverlag (Federal Republic of Germany) 132
Ensslin und Laiblin Verlag GmbH & Co KG (Federal Republic of Germany) 132
Ente Nazionale per le Biblioteche Popolari e Scolastiche (Italy) 221
Entente, Editions, (France) 95
Entreprise Moderne d'Edition (France) 95

Enzyklopädie, VEB Verlag, (German Democratic Republic) 115
Eötvös Loránd Tudományegyetem Egyetemi Könyvtár (Hungary) 178
Epargne, Les Editions de l', (France) 95
Epi SA Editeurs (France) 95
Epoca, Editorial, SA (Mexico) 249
Epoca, Librería, (Peru) 287
'Epoka', Wydawnictwo, (Poland) 291
Eppinger, Hans P, (Federal Republic of Germany) 132
Epworth Press (United Kingdom) 378
Equatoriale, La Librairie L', (United Republic of Cameroun) 60
Era Book Enterprises (India) 185
Era, Ediciones, SA (Mexico) 249
Era Publications (Australia) 13
Erasme, Editions, (NV Scriptoria) (Belgium) 36
Erdmann, Horst, Verlag für Internationalen Kulturaustausch (Federal Republic of Germany) 132
Erehwon Publishing House (Philippines) 288
Erel (Belgium) 36
Eremiten, Verlag, -Presse Hülsmanns & Reske GmbH (Federal Republic of Germany) 132
Eres, Edition, Horst Schubert Musikverlag (Federal Republic of Germany) 132
Eresco (Indonesia) 199
Erhvervsarkivet-Statens Erhvervshistoriske Arkiv (Denmark) 78
Erichsens, Chr, Forlag A/S (Denmark) 74
Erikssons, The Lydia and Herman, Prize (Sweden) 335
Erker-Galerie AG (Switzerland) 341
Erlangga (Indonesia) 199
Ermis (Greece) 171
Ernst, Wilhelm, und Sohn Verlag für Architektur und Technische Wissenschaften (Federal Republic of Germany) 132
Ernster, Librairie Pierre, (Luxembourg) 242
Erota-Press (Federal Republic of Germany) 132
Erster Moderner Lesezirkel Kreith & Schram (Austria) 29
Erster Wiener Lesezirkel Gebrüder Kreith (Austria) 29
Erudita Publications (Pty) Ltd (Republic of South Africa) 308
Escobo (Dominican Republic) 80
Escolar, Livraria, Infante (Portugal) 296
Escorial, Librería, (Puerto Rico) 299
Escorts Book Award (India) 197
Escuela Nacional de Biblioteconomía y Archivonomía (Mexico) 252
Esfinge, Editorial, SA (Mexico) 249
Eshkol-Haifa (Israel) 207
Eshkol-Jerusalem (Israel) 207
Eska (Netherlands) 259
Espacio Editora SA (Argentina) 5
Española, Librería, (Argentina) 8
Espasa-Calpe, Casa del Libro, SA (Spain) 324
Espasa-Calpe, Editorial, SA (Spain) 317
Espaxs, Editorial, SA (Spain) 317
Espinosa, Manuel, y Cortina Prize (Spain) 325
Espiritualista, Editôra, (Brazil) 50
Esquire (Lebanon) 239
Ess Ess Publications (India) 185
Esselte Förlag AB (Sweden) 329
Esselte Herzogs AB (Sweden) 329
Esselte Map Service (Sweden) 330
Esselte Studium AB (Sweden) 330
Est-Ouest, Editions, (Belgium) 36
Este, Librería del, (Venezuela) 419
Estense, Biblioteca, (Italy) 221
Estoup et Roy, Publications, Sàrl (France) 95
Estrada, Angel, y Cía SA (Argentina) 5
Estúdios, Editorial, Cor Sarl (Portugal) 296
Etablissements Généraux d'Imprimerie SA (Belgium) 36
Etairia Ellinon Logotechnon (Greece) 171
Etcetera, Edition, (Switzerland) 341
Etelä-Suomen Kustannus Oy (Finland) 84
Eteria Ellinikon Ekdoseon (Greece) 171
Ethiope Publishing Corporation (Nigeria) 275
Ethiopian Library Association (Ethiopia) 83
Ethiopian Manuscript Microfilm Library (Ethiopia) 83
Ethnographica Ltd (United Kingdom) 378
Etna-Taormina International Poetry Prize (International Literary Prizes) 441
Etudes Augustiniennes (France) 95
Etudes, Librairie des, (Morocco) 254
Eulama (Italy) 222
Eulama SA (Italy) 214
Eulama SA (Italy) 220
Eulenburg Edition GmbH (Switzerland) 341
Eulenspiegel Verlag für Satir und Humor (German Democratic Republic) 115
Eulyoo Publishing Co Ltd (Republic of Korea) 236
Euphorion, Freundeskreis des, Verlags (Federal Republic of Germany) 165
Euphorion Verlag (Federal Republic of Germany) 132
Eurasia Publishing House Pvt Ltd (India) 185
Eurédif (Société Européenne d'Edition et de Diffusion) (France) 95
Euroamericanas, Ediciones, (Mexico) 249

INDEX 471

Eurobook Ltd (United Kingdom) 378
Euromonitor Publications Ltd (United Kingdom) 379
Europa (Belgium) 36
Europa-America, Publicações, Lda (Portugal) 296
Európa Könyvkiadó (Europa Publishing House) (Hungary) 177
Europa-Lehrmittel, Verlag, Nourney, Vollmer & Co OHG (Federal Republic of Germany) 132
Europa Publications Ltd (United Kingdom) 379
Europa-Verlag AG (Switzerland) 341
Europa Verlags-GmbH (Austria) 25
Europabuch AG (Switzerland) 341
Europäische Bildungsgemeinschaft Verlags GmbH (Federal Republic of Germany) 165
Europäische Buch, Das, (Federal Republic of Germany) 132
Europäische Gemeinschaften (European Communities) (Federal Republic of Germany) 132
europäische Ideen, Verlag, (Federal Republic of Germany) 132
Europäische Verlagsanstalt GmbH (Federal Republic of Germany) 132
Europaring der Buch- & Schallplattenfreunde (Switzerland) 351
Europarings der Buch- und Schallplattenfreunde (Federal Republic of Germany) 165
European Association of Directory Publishers (International Organizations) 432
European Cortina-Ulisse Prize (International Literary Prizes) 441
European Press Scientific Publisher (Belgium) 36
European Schoolbooks Ltd (United Kingdom) 379
European University Institute Library (Italy) 221
Europese Bibliotheek Uitgeverij Boekhandel Antiquariaat (Netherlands) 259
Europress NV (Belgium) 36
Europrisma-Verlag (Federal Republic of Germany) 132
Evangel Publishing House (Kenya) 234
Evangelical Press and Services Ltd (United Kingdom) 379
Évangélique, Librairie, (Togo) 356
Évangélique, Librairie, (Upper Volta) 416
Evangelisch Lutherischen Mission, Verlag der, (Federal Republic of Germany) 132
Evangelische Buchgemeinde GmbH (Federal Republic of Germany) 165
Evangelische Verlagsanstalt GmbH (German Democratic Republic) 115
Evangelischer Gesellschaft, Verlag und Schriftenmission der, für Deutschland GmbH (Federal Republic of Germany) 132
Evangelischer Missionsverlag (Federal Republic of Germany) 132
Evangelischer Presseverband für Bayern eV (Federal Republic of Germany) 132
Evangelischer Pressverband in Österreich (Austria) 25
Evangelischer Schriften Verlag Schwengler (Switzerland) 341
Evangelisches Verlagswerk GmbH (Federal Republic of Germany) 132
Evangeliska Fosterlands-Stiftelsens Förlag (Sweden) 330
Evans Brothers Ltd (United Kingdom) 379
Evans Brothers (Nigeria Publishers) Ltd (Nigeria) 275
Evans Shepherd (Zimbabwe) 429
Evelyn, Hugh, Ltd (United Kingdom) 379
Everest Books Ltd (United Kingdom) 379
Everest, Editorial, SA (Spain) 317
Everymans Library, Reference Library and University Library (United Kingdom) 379
Ewald, Johannes, Prize (Denmark) 79
Ewart-Biggs, Christopher, Memorial Prize (International Literary Prizes) 441
Ewha Woman's University Library (Republic of Korea) 238
Ewha Woman's University Press (Republic of Korea) 236
Ewing Memorial Library (Pakistan) 283
Ex Libris (Switzerland) 341
Ex Libris (Switzerland) 351
Exclusive Books (Pty) Ltd (Republic of South Africa) 312
Exley Publications Ltd (United Kingdom) 379
Expanded Media Editions (Federal Republic of Germany) 132
Expansion, L', Scientifique Française (France) 95
Exped-Expansaõ Editorial Ltda (Brazil) 50
Export-Press (Yugoslavia) 425
Express Logic Ltd (United Kingdom) 379
Expresso (Portugal) 298
Extemporaneos, Editorial, SA (Mexico) 249
Eymundssonar, Bókaverslun Sigfusar, (Iceland) 179
Eyre Methuen Ltd (United Kingdom) 379
Eyre & Spottiswoode (Publishers) Ltd (United Kingdom) 379
Eyrolles, Éditions, (France) 95

F A D L Forlag (Foreningen af danske Laegestuderendes Forlag) (Denmark) 74
F A W-Barbara Ramsden Award (Australia) 22
F A W-Christopher Brennan Award (Australia) 22
F A W-John Shaw Neilson Poetry Award (Australia) 22
F A W Regional Branch Awards (Australia) 22
F B V Frauenbuchvertrieb GmbH (Federal Republic of Germany) 165
F E D , Uitgeverij, BV (Netherlands) 259
F E N A M E — Fundação Nacional de Material Escolar (Brazil) 50
F E P International (HK) Ltd (Hong Kong) 175
F E P International Private Ltd (Republic of Singapore) 305
F E P International Sdn Bhd (Far Eastern Publishers) (Malaysia) 244
F I D (International Organizations) 432
F N A C (France) 108
F T D, Editôra, SA (Brazil) 50
F W M Books Ltd (Trinidad and Tobago) 356
Fabbri Editori SpA (Italy) 214
Faber & Faber Ltd (United Kingdom) 379
Faber, The Geoffrey, Memorial Prize (International Literary Prizes) 441
Fabien Prize (France) 111
Fabril Editora SA (Argentina) 5
Fabritius Forlagshus (Norway) 279
Fachbuchverlag, VEB, (German Democratic Republic) 115
Fackel-Buchklub, Verlags- und Vertriebs GmbH (Federal Republic of Germany) 165
Fackelträger-Verlag Schmidt-Küster GmbH (Federal Republic of Germany) 133
Fackelverlag G Bowitz GmbH (Federal Republic of Germany) 133
Facla, Editura, (Romania) 301
Facsimile Uitgaven Nederland BV (FUN) (Netherlands) 259
Facultas Verlag (Austria) 25
Facultatii, Biblioteca, de Medicina din Bucuresti (Romania) 301
Faculté des Lettres et Sciences Humaines de Tunis (Tunisia) 357
Faculty of Agriculture, Forestry and Veterinary Science (Tanzania) 353
Faculty of Engineering, Library of the, (Lebanon) 240
Faculty of Law, Library of the, (Lebanon) 240
Faculty of Medicine Library (Tanzania) 353
Fællesekspeditionen (Denmark) 73
Faenza Editrice SpA (Italy) 214
Fagbamigbe, Olaiya, Ltd (Publishers) (Nigeria) 275
Faglitteratur, Forlaget for, A/S (Denmark) 74
Faik, Sait, Prize (Turkey) 359
Fairmount Press (United Kingdom) 379
Fajar, Penerbit, Bakti Sdn Bhd (Malaysia) 244
Falcon Books (United Kingdom) 379
Falk- Verlag für Landkarten & Stadtpläne Gerhard Falk GmbH (Federal Republic of Germany) 133
Falken-Verlag GmbH (Federal Republic of Germany) 133
Falkplan, NV, /CIB (Netherlands) 259
Fall, Lycée de Jeunes Filles Ameth, (Senegal) 303
Fallon, C J, Ltd (Republic of Ireland) 203
Faltermaier, Dr Martin, (Federal Republic of Germany) 133
Familia 2000 (Portugal) 296
Familia et Patria PVBA (Belgium) 37
Familia, Librerías La, (Peru) 287
Family Book Club (United Kingdom) 409
Family Bookshop (Qatar) 300
Family Bookshop (United Arab Emirates) 363
Family Bookshop (Bahrain) WLL (Bahrain) 31
Fantasia Prize (France) 111
Fantasy Library (United Kingdom) 379
Far East Book Co (China (Taiwan)) 64
Far East Book Co (Republic of Singapore) 306
Far East Publications Ltd (Hong Kong) 176
Far Eastern University Library (Philippines) 289
Farairre, Librairie, (Morocco) 254
Farandole, Editions La, (France) 95
Farjeon, Eleanor, Award (United Kingdom) 414
Farmer, Prudence, Poetry Prize (United Kingdom) 414
Farquharson, John, Ltd (United Kingdom) 408
Fastenrath Prize (Spain) 325
Fateh, al-, University, The Central Library (Libya) 241
Fausto, Ediciones Librerías, (Argentina) 5
Fausto, Librerías, (Argentina) 8
Favorit-Verlag Huntemann & Co (Federal Republic of Germany) 133
Favre, Jules, Prize (France) 111
Favre, Pierre Marcel, (Switzerland) 341
Fayard, Librairie Arthème, (France) 95
Fazer, Edition, (Finland) 84
Febres Cordero, Biblioteca Central 'Tulio, (Venezuela) 419
Federação Brasileira de Associações de Bibliotecários — Comissão Brasileira de Documentação Jurídica (FEBAB/CBDJ) (Brazil) 56

Federação Brasileira de Associações de Bibliotecários (FEBAB) (Brazil) 56
Federación Argentina de Librerías, Papelerías y Actividades Afines (Argentina) 2
Federación de Gremios de Editores de España (Spain) 314
Federal Library Association (Pakistan) 284
Federal Publications (HK) (Hong Kong) 175
Federal Publications (S) Pte Ltd (Republic of Singapore) 305
Federal Publications Sdn Bhd (Malaysia) 244
Federatie van Organisaties van Bibliotheek-, Informatie-, Dokumentatiewezen (FOBID) (Netherlands) 266
Fédération des Amicales de Documentalistes et Bibliothécaires de l'Education nationale (France) 109
Fédération des Commerçants, Groupement Papetiers-Libraires, Journaux, Editeurs et Galeries d'Art (Luxembourg) 241
Fédération des Editeurs belges (Belgium) 33
Fédération française des Syndicate de Libraires (France) 87
Fédération Internationale des Libraires (FIL) (International Organizations) 432
Fédération Internationale des Traducteurs (FIT) (International Organizations) 432
Fédération luxembourgeoise des Travailleurs du Livre (Luxembourg) 242
Fédération nationale des Bibliothèques Catholiques (Belgium) 43
Federation of Booksellers and Publishers Association in Gujarat (India) 181
Federation of Children's Book Groups (United Kingdom) 364
Federation of Indian Library Associations (India) 196
Federation of Indian Publishers (India) 181
Federation of Printing and Bookbinding Enterprises (Greece) 171
Federation of Publishers and Booksellers Associations in India (India) 181
Fédération panhellénique des Editeurs et Libraires (Greece) 171
Federazione Italiana delle Biblioteche Popolari (Italy) 221
Federspiel, Librería Universal Carlos, (Costa Rica) 67
Fehling, Willy F P, GmbH (Federal Republic of Germany) 133
Fehmers, Frank, Productions (Netherlands) 259
Fehr'sche Buchhandlung AG (Switzerland) 341
Fehr'sche Buchhandlung AG (Switzerland) 351
Feij, François, (Switzerland) 341
Feistle, Dr Karl, (Federal Republic of Germany) 133
Félag Islenskra Bókaútgefenda (Iceland) 179
Félag Islenzkra Bókaverzlana (Iceland) 179
Feldheim Publishers Ltd (Israel) 207
Fellicelli & Poli, Librairie, (Niger) 274
Fellowship of Australian Writers NSW (Australia) 21
Feltrinelli, Antonio, Prize (International Literary Prizes) 441
Feltrinelli, Giangiacomo, SpA (Italy) 215
Feltrinelli, Libreria, (Italy) 220
Fémina Prize (France) 111
Femmes d'aujourd'hui, Groupe, (France) 95
Femmes, Des, (France) 95
Fénéon Prize (France) 111
Ferenczy Verlag AG (Switzerland) 341
Ferguson, John, Pty Ltd (Australia) 13
Feria Chilena del Libro (Chile) 62
Feria del Libro (Uruguay) 417
Feria, Librería, del Libro (Guatemala) 173
Ferin, Livraria, Lda (Portugal) 296
Fernández Editores SA (Mexico) 249
Fernández, Editorial y Librería Juridica Amalio M, (Uruguay) 417
Fernández, Librería Amalio M, (Uruguay) 417
Ferozsons Ltd (Pakistan) 282
Ferozsons Ltd (Pakistan) 283
Ferro, Edizioni, SpA (Italy) 215
Fersobe, Papeleria, Hnos (Dominican Republic) 80
Festungsverlag (Austria) 29
Feu, Editions du, Nouveau (France) 95
Feuervogel-Verlag GmbH (Federal Republic of Germany) 133
'Feuilles familiales', Les, ASBL (Belgium) 37
Fher, Editorial, SA (Spain) 317
Fib's Lyrikklub (Sweden) 330
Fibula van Dishoek (Netherlands) 259
Fierro', Librería 'Martín, (Argentina) 8
Fietkau, Wolfgang, Verlag (Federal Republic of Germany) 133
Figgis, Allen, & Co Ltd (Republic of Ireland) 203
Figueirinhas, Livraria Editora, Lda (Portugal) 296
Fiji Library Association (FLA) (Fiji) 84
Fikentscher und Co (Federal Republic of Germany) 133
Fikr, Dar Al-, (Salem & Zu'bi) Bookshop (Syria) 353
Filadelfia AB, Förlaget, (Sweden) 330
Filipacchi, Editions, (France) 96
Film buchhandlung Hans Rohr (Switzerland) 351

472 INDEX

Filon, Ekdoseis, (Greece) 171
Financial Times, The, Business Publishing Ltd (United Kingdom) 379
Financial Training Publications Ltd (United Kingdom) 379
'Finansy', Izdatelstvo, (Union of Soviet Socialist Republics) 361
Findhorn Publications (United Kingdom) 379
Fine Arts Press Pty Ltd (Australia) 13
Fink, Emil, Verlag (Federal Republic of Germany) 133
Fink-Kümmerly, J, und Frey Verlag GmbH (Federal Republic of Germany) 133
Fink, Wilhelm, Verlag KG (Federal Republic of Germany) 133
Finken-Verlag (Federal Republic of Germany) 133
Finlands Svenska Författareförening (Finland) 87
Finot, Jean, Prize (France) 111
Fiorentina, Libreria Editrice, di Vittorio e Valerio Zani snc (Italy) 215
Firecrest Publishing Ltd (United Kingdom) 379
Firma KLM Private Ltd (Incorporating Firma KL Mukhopadhyay) (India) 185
Firmin-Didot et Cie (France) 96
First Book Prize (Argentina) 9
Fiscado, Editions, (France) 96
Fischbacher, Librairie, International Art Book Distribution (import-export) (France) 96
Fischer, Gustav, Verlag (Federal Republic of Germany) 133
Fischer, Rita G, Verlag (Federal Republic of Germany) 133
Fischer Taschenbuch Verlag GmbH (Federal Republic of Germany) 133
Fischer, VEB Gustav, Verlag, Jena (German Democratic Republic) 115
Fischer, W, Verlag (Federal Republic of Germany) 133
Fischer, S, Verlag GmbH (Federal Republic of Germany) 133
Fisher, H, (Israel) 207
Fishing Book Club (United Kingdom) 409
Fishing News Books Ltd (United Kingdom) 379
Fitzpatrick, Percy, Medal (Republic of South Africa) 313
Fitzwilliam Museum (United Kingdom) 379
Five Lamps, The, Press (Republic of Ireland) 203
Fix, Verlag Johannes, (Federal Republic of Germany) 133
'Fizkultura i Sport', Izdatelstvo, (Union of Soviet Socialist Republics) 361
Flaccovio, Libreria SF, (Italy) 220
Flaccovio, S F, Editore (Italy) 215
Flame Lily (Zimbabwe) 429
Flammarion (France) 108
Flammarion et Cie (France) 96
Flare Books (United Kingdom) 380
Flat, Paul, Prize (France) 111
Fleischhauer und Spohn Verlag (Federal Republic of Germany) 133
Flesch Financial Publications (Pty) Ltd (Republic of South Africa) 308
Fletcher, Authors' Club Sir Bannister, Prize Trust (United Kingdom) 414
Fleurus, Editions, SA (France) 96
Fleury, Ernest, Prize (France) 111
Fleuve, Editions, Noir (France) 96
Flor, Ediciones de la, SRL (Argentina) 5
Florence, City of, International Poetry Prize (International Literary Prizes) 441
Florio, John, Prize (United Kingdom) 414
Floris Books (United Kingdom) 380
Focal Press Ltd (United Kingdom) 380
Foch, Marshal, (France) 111
Focus Elsevier BV (Netherlands) 259
Focus Uppslagsböcker AB (Focus International Book Production AB) (Sweden) 330
Focus-Verlag (Federal Republic of Germany) 133
Foetisch, Maurice & Pierre, SA (Switzerland) 341
Fogarty's Bookshop (Republic of South Africa) 312
Fogtdal, Palle, A/S (Denmark) 74
Foilseacháin Náisiúnta Tta (Republic of Ireland) 203
Folens and Co Ltd (Republic of Ireland) 203
Folio, The, Society Ltd (United Kingdom) 380
Folio, The, Society Ltd (United Kingdom) 409
Folklore Prize (Brazil) 57
Foma, Editions, SA (Switzerland) 341
Fondeur d'Aujourd'hui (France) 96
Fondo de Cultura Económica (Mexico) 249
Fondo Editorial Común SC (Venezuela) 418
Fondo Educativo Interamericano (Mexico) 249
Fondo Educativo Interamericano CA (Venezuela) 418
Fondo Educativo Interamericano SA (Colombia) 65
Fonds, Bibliothèque, Quetelet (Belgium) 43
Fonds Mercator SA (Belgium) 37
Fonna Forlag L/L (Norway) 279
Font, Librería, (Mexico) 252
Font, Librería, SA (Mexico) 252
Fontainemore, Editions de, (Switzerland) 341
Fontana Books (United Kingdom) 380
Fontane, Theodor, Prize (Federal Republic of Germany) 168

Fontanella, Editorial, SA (Spain) 317
Fontein, Uitgeverij De, BV (Netherlands) 259
Fontes Pers (APA) (Netherlands) 259
Fonteyn, G A , Medical Books NV (Belgium) 37
Food and Agriculture Organization of the United Nations (FAO) (International Organizations) 434
Foras, An, Forbartha (Republic of Ireland) 203
Forbes Publications Ltd (United Kingdom) 380
Ford Award (Australia) 22
Foreign Affairs Publishing Co Ltd (United Kingdom) 380
Foreign Language Bookshop (Australia) 19
Foreign Languages Press (People's Republic of China) 63
Foreign Languages Publishing House (Democratic People's Republic of Korea) 236
Foreign Languages Publishing House (Socialist Republic of Viet Nam) 420
Foreign Poetry Prize (International Literary Prizes) 441
Forening for Boghaandvaerk (Denmark) 73
Forening for Forlagsfolk (Denmark) 73
Foreningen af Medarbejdere ved Danmarks Forskningsbiblioteker (Denmark) 78
Forense, Editôra, —Universitaria Ltda (Brazil) 50
Författares Bokmaskin (Sweden) 330
Förg, Alfred, GmbH & Co KG (Federal Republic of Germany) 133
Foris Publications (Netherlands) 259
Forja Editora SARL (Portugal) 296
Forkel-Verlag GmbH (Federal Republic of Germany) 133
Formar, Editôra e Encadernadora, Ltda (Brazil) 50
Formentor, Ediciones, SRL (Argentina) 5
Formentor, Ediciones, SRL (Venezuela) 418
Formentor Prize (International Literary Prizes) 441
Formgebung, Rat für, (Federal Republic of Germany) 134
Formichiere, Il, (Italy) 215
Forsamlingsforbundets Forlags AB (Finland) 84
Forsbergs, Bengt, Förlag AB (Sweden) 330
Fortschritt für alle-Verlag (Federal Republic of Germany) 134
Fortuna-Verlag W Heidelberger (Switzerland) 341
Fortune Press (United Kingdom) 380
Fortuny Prize (France) 111
Forum (New Zealand) 270
Forum (Yugoslavia) 422
Forum (Yugoslavia) 425
Forum, Bokförlaget, AB (Sweden) 330
Forum littéraire camerounais (United Republic of Cameroun) 9
Forum Publishers Ltd (Denmark) 74
Forum Verlag GmbH (Austria) 25
Főszékesegyházi könyvtár (Hungary) 178
Foto und Schmalfilm-Verlag (Switzerland) 341
Fotokinoverlag, VEB, (German Democratic Republic) 115
Fotomatic Philippines Inc (Philippines) 288
Foucher, Les Editions, (France) 96
Foulis Books (United Kingdom) 380
Foulsham & Co Ltd (United Kingdom) 380
Foundation Book Club (Philippines) 289
Foundation Books (Kenya) 234
Foundation for the Promotion of the Translation of Dutch Literature (Netherlands) 267
Foundational, The, Book Co Ltd (United Kingdom) 380
Fountain Press (United Kingdom) 380
Four Courts Press (Republic of Ireland) 203
Fourah Bay College Bookshop Ltd (Sierra Leone) 304
Fourah Bay College Library (Sierra Leone) 304
Fouraignan Prize (France) 111
Fournier, Heraclio, SA (Spain) 317
Fourth Estate Books Ltd (New Zealand) 270
Fox produktionen traude Aubeck (Federal Republic of Germany) 134
Foxcub (United Kingdom) 380
Foxwood Publishing Ltd (United Kingdom) 380
Foyer, Editions, Notre-Dame (Belgium) 37
Foyle, W & G, Ltd (United Kingdom) 410
Foyle, W & G, Ltd & John Gifford Ltd (United Kingdom) 380
Foyles Book Clubs (United Kingdom) 409
Fragua Editorial (Spain) 318
Frahm, Carlota, Literary Agency (Norway) 280
Fralit-F K Albrecht (Federal Republic of Germany) 164
Française, Librairie, (Luxembourg) 242
France-Caraïbes (France) 96
France Empire, Editions, (France) 96
France Expansion (France) 96
France, Librairie de, (Ivory Coast) 223
France, Librairie de, (Morocco) 254
France, Librairie de, (Upper Volta) 416
France-Loisirs (France) 96
Francesa, Librería, (Spain) 324
Franciscaines, Les Editions, SA (France) 96
Franciscan Printing Press (Israel) 207
Franciscana, Editorial, (Portugal) 296
Francité, Editions de la, (Imprimeries Havaux) (Belgium) 37
Francke, Buchhandlung A, AG (Switzerland) 351
Francke Buchhandlung, Verlag der, GmbH (Federal Republic of Germany) 134
Francke, A, GmbH (Federal Republic of Germany) 134

Francke Verlag (Switzerland) 341
Franckh'sche Verlagshandlung W Keller & Co (Federal Republic of Germany) 134
Franco-German Friendship Prize (International Literary Prizes) 441
François, Le, (France) 96
Franjas Prizes (Bolivia) 47
Frank Bros & Co (India) 185
Frank Publishing Ltd (Ghana) 169
Frankfurter Bücher, Verlag, (Federal Republic of Germany) 134
Frankfurter Fachverlag Michael Kohl GmbH & Co KG (Federal Republic of Germany) 134
Frankfurter Kinderbücher, Verlag, GmbH (Federal Republic of Germany) 134
Fränkische Gesellschafts-Druckerei Würzburg/Echter Verlag (Federal Republic of Germany) 134
Franklin, Biblioteca 'Benjamin, ' (USICA) (Mexico) 252
Franklin Book Programs Inc (Afghanistan) 1
Franklin Book Programs Inc (Iran) 201
Franklin, Miles, Award (Australia) 22
Frankonius Verlag GmbH (Federal Republic of Germany) 134
Franz, Verlag Ernst, und Sternberg-Verlag (Federal Republic of Germany) 134
Franzis-Verlag (Federal Republic of Germany) 134
Fraser, Gordon, Gallery Ltd (United Kingdom) 380
Frau, Verlag für die, (German Democratic Republic) 115
Frauen-Selbstverlag (Federal Republic of Germany) 134
Frauenbuchverlag (Federal Republic of Germany) 134
Frauenkalender Selbstverlag (Federal Republic of Germany) 134
Frauenoffensive, Verlag, (Federal Republic of Germany) 134
Frauenpolitik, Verlag, (Federal Republic of Germany) 134
Fréal, Editions, (France) 96
Frech-Verlag GmbH und Co Druck KG (Federal Republic of Germany) 134
Freelance Writing, Committee for, (Australia) 9
Freeland, Editorial, (Argentina) 5
Freeland Press Ltd (United Kingdom) 380
Freeman, W H, & Co Ltd (United Kingdom) 380
freies Geistesleben, Verlag, (Federal Republic of Germany) 134
Freihofer AG (Switzerland) 341
Freitas, Livraria, Bastos (Brazil) 55
Freitas, Livraria, Bastos SA (Brazil) 50
Fremad (Denmark) 74
French Academy, Foreigner's Book Award (International Literary Prizes) 441
French Book Club (United Kingdom) 409
French Catholic Grand Prize for Literature (France) 111
French Faculty of Medicine, Library of the, (Lebanon) 240
French Grand Prize for Humour (France) 111
French Language Prize (International Literary Prizes) 441
French, Samuel, Ltd (United Kingdom) 380
Fretz und Wasmuth Verlag AG (Switzerland) 341
Fretz, Verlag Gebrüder, AG (Switzerland) 341
Freud, Sigmund, Prize (Federal Republic of Germany) 168
Freund Publishing House Ltd (Israel) 207
Freytag-Berndt und Artaria, Kartographische Anstalt (Austria) 25
Frías, Universidad Boliviana Tomás, Div de Extensión Universitaria (Bolivia) 46
Fricke, Verlag Dieter, GmbH (Federal Republic of Germany) 134
Friedenauer Presse (Federal Republic of Germany) 134
Friedman, S, (Israel) 207
Friedmann, Julian, Literary Agency Ltd (United Kingdom) 408
Friedmann, Julian, Publishers Ltd (United Kingdom) 380
Friedrich, Erhard, Verlag (Federal Republic of Germany) 134
Friends of Antiquity (Czechoslovakia) 72
Friends of the National Libraries (United Kingdom) 411
Frimodts, J, Forlag (Denmark) 74
Frisia-Verlag GmbH (Federal Republic of Germany) 134
Fritsch, Edition der 2 Gerald, und Stephan Fritsch (Federal Republic of Germany) 134
Fritzes, AB C E, Kungl Hovbokhandel (Sweden) 334
Frobenius AG (Switzerland) 341
Froebel-Kan Co Ltd (Japan) 225
Fromm, Verlag A, GmbH & Co (Federal Republic of Germany) 134
Frommann-Holzboog (Friedrich Frommann Verlag, Günther Holzboog GmbH & Co) (Federal Republic of Germany) 134
Fromme, Georg, und Co (Austria) 25
Frontier Publishing Co (Pakistan) 282
Frossard, Henri, (France) 96
Frost, Robert, Award (Australia) 22
Fu-Hsing Book Co (China (Taiwan)) 64
Fu Ssu-Nien Library Institute of History and Philology (China (Taiwan)) 64
Fuchs, Dr Heinrich, (Austria) 25
Fuchsbichler, Reinfried, (Austria) 29

INDEX 473

Fudge & Co Ltd (United Kingdom) 380
Fukuinkan Shoten Publishers (Japan) 225
Fullerton, Leonard, Ltd (New Zealand) 270
Fundação Instituto Brasileiro de Geografia e Estatística (Brazil) 50
Fundação Nacional de Material Escolar (Brazil) 50
Fundación de Cultura Universitaria (Uruguay) 417
Fundamentos, Editorial, (Spain) 318
Fundepar Prize (Brazil) 57
'Furet du Nord', Librairie, (France) 108
Fürstelberger, Hans, (Austria) 29
Futura, Editorial, (Portugal) 296
Futura Publications Ltd (United Kingdom) 380
Fuzambo Publishing Co (Japan) 225
Fytrakis, Chr, (Greece) 171

G D K Publications (India) 185
G E C T I (Gabinete de Especializacão e Cooperacão Tecnica Internacional L) (Portugal) 296
G I A SA (Belgium) 37
G M T, Forlaget, (Denmark) 75
G S Verlag Basle (Switzerland) 341
Gaade, W, BV (Netherlands) 259
Gaba Publications (AFER) (Kenya) 234
Gabalda, J, et Cie (Librairie Lecoffre) SA (France) 96
Gaber, Verlag Franz-Joachim, (Federal Republic of Germany) 135
Gaberbocchus Press Ltd (United Kingdom) 380
Gabinete de Especializacão e Cooperacão Tecnica Internacional (Portugal) 296
Gabler, Betriebswirtschaftlicher Verlag Dr Theodor, (Federal Republic of Germany) 135
Gad, G E C, Dansk og Udenlandsk Boghandel A/S (Denmark) 78
Gads, G E C, Forlag (Denmark) 75
Gaehme, Verlag, (Federal Republic of Germany) 135
Gaisa, Ediciones, SL (Spain) 318
Gakken Co Ltd (Japan) 225
Gakujutsu Bunken Fukyu-Kai (Japan) 231
Gakuseisha Publishing Co Ltd (Japan) 225
Galaxia (Venezuela) 420
Galaxie Press (Pvt) Ltd (Zimbabwe) 429
Galera, La, SA Editorial (Spain) 318
Galería, Librería, Castro Soto (Peru) 287
Galerna, Editorial, SA (Argentina) 5
Galgotia, E D, & Sons (India) 196
Galgotia Publications (India) 185
Galilée, Editions, (France) 96
Gall & Inglis (United Kingdom) 380
Galland, Editions Bertil, (Switzerland) 341
Gallegos, Rómulo, International Novel Prize (International Literary Prizes) 441
Gallery, The, Press (Republic of Ireland) 203
Galley Club of Sydney (Australia) 9
Galliard (United Kingdom) 380
Gallimard, Editions, (France) 96
Galliner, Peter, Associates Ltd (United Kingdom) 408
Gama, Da, Publishers (Pty) Ltd (Republic of South Africa) 309
Gambia National Library (The Gambia) 114
Gambia, The, Methodist Bookshop Ltd (The Gambia) 114
Gamma, Editions, (Belgium) 37
Gamma, Editions, (France) 96
Gammalibri, Editrice, (Italy) 215
Gamsberg Publishers (Namibia) 255
Ganesh & Co (India) 186
Gangaram Book Bureau (India) 195
Gans en Rombach Auteursagenten (Netherlands) 266
Gantner, A R, Verlag KG (Liechtenstein) 241
García Cambeiro, Fernando, (Argentina) 5
García, Libreria y Papelería Casa, SA (Argentina) 5
Garcia, R M, Publishing House (Philippines) 288
Garden Book Club (United Kingdom) 409
Gardeners Book Society (United Kingdom) 409
Gardet, Imprimerie Librairie, (France) 96
Gardum (Norway) 280
Garnier, Éditions, Frères (France) 96
Garnier-Flammarion (France) 96
Garnstone Press Ltd (United Kingdom) 380
Garriga, Ediciones, Argentinas SA (Argentina) 8
Garriga, Ediciones, SA (Spain) 318
Garve, De, PVBA (Belgium) 37
Garzanti Editore (Italy) 215
Gauthier-Villars, Société, (France) 96
Gautier-Languereau, Les Editions, (France) 97
Gaya, P T, Favorit Press, Book Division (Indonesia) 199
Gazelle Publications Pty Ltd (Australia) 13
Gazit (Israel) 207
Gebühr, Verlag Werner, (Federal Republic of Germany) 135
Gedin, Mrs Lena I, (Sweden) 334
Gedit SA (Belgium) 37
Geering, Rudolf, Verlag (Switzerland) 341

Geest und Portig, Akademische Verlagsgesellschaft, KG (German Democratic Republic) 115
Geetha Book House (India) 186
Geetha, M S, Publishers (Malaysia) 244
Geetha Prize (India) 197
Gegner Prize (France) 111
Gehlen, Dr Max, Verlagsbuch-handlung (Federal Republic of Germany) 135
Gehrmans, AB Carl, Musikförlag (Sweden) 330
Geisenheyner und Crone (Federal Republic of Germany) 164
Gelisim Publishing (Turkey) 358
Gemeentebibliotheek Rotterdam (Netherlands) 266
Gemini Awards (Australia) 22
Gemini Publishing (United Kingdom) 380
Géminis, Editorial, SRL (Argentina) 5
Gemsberg-Verlag (Switzerland) 341
Gençlik Kitabevi (Turkey) 359
General Assembly Library (New Zealand) 272
General Company for Publishing, Advertising and Distribution (Libya) 241
General Egyptian Book Organization (Egypt) 81
General Egyptian Book Organization (Egypt) 81
General Federation of Literary and Art Unions, Publishing House of the, (Democratic People's Republic of Korea) 236
General Organization, The, for Government Press Affairs (Egypt) 81
General Press Corporation (Libya) 241
Générale des Carrières et des Mines, La, (GECAMINES) (Zaire) 427
Generalstabens Litografiska Anstalts Förlag (Sweden) 330
Genfer Bibelgesellschaft (Switzerland) 341
Genillard, Pierre, (Switzerland) 342
Genin, Editions M Th, (France) 97
Gennadius Library (Greece) 172
Gennep, Van, Ltd (Netherlands) 259
Gennotte, Librairie A, & Fils (Burundi) 60
Gensy, Creazioni, (Italy) 215
Gente Nueva, Editorial, (Cuba) 68
Gentofte Kommunebibliotek (Denmark) 78
Gentry Books Ltd (United Kingdom) 380
Geo Center Internationales Landkartenhaus GmbH (Federal Republic of Germany) 135
Geocolor SA (Spain) 318
Geographia Ltd (United Kingdom) 381
Géographie, Bibliothèque de, (France) 108
Geographische Verlagsgesellschaft Velhagen und Klasing und Hermann Schroedel GmbH & Co KG (Federal Republic of Germany) 135
Geological Survey of India (India) 186
Geologiczne, Wydawnictwa, (Poland) 291
Geoprojects Sàrl (Lebanon) 239
Georg et Cie SA (Switzerland) 342
Georg et Cie SA (Switzerland) 351
Georges, Félix, Prize (France) 111
George's, William, Sons Ltd (United Kingdom) 410
Georgi Publishing Company/Editions Georgi (Switzerland) 342
Georgi, Verlag Dr Rudolf, (Federal Republic of Germany) 135
Georgian House Pty Ltd (Australia) 13
Geraldine, The, Press (Republic of Ireland) 203
Gérard, Editions, et Cie SPRL (Belgium) 37
Gerber, Carl, Verlag (Federal Republic of Germany) 135
Gerhardt Verlag (Federal Republic of Germany) 135
Gerlach & Wiedling Buch und Kunstverlag (Austria) 25
Germain, Mme Françoise, (France) 107
German Book Club (United Kingdom) 409
German Peace Prize (International Literary Prizes) 441
German Youth, The, Book Award (International Literary Prizes) 441
Gerold & Co (Austria) 25
Gerold & Co (Austria) 29
Gerstenberg Verlag (Federal Republic of Germany) 135
Gerth, Musikverlag Klaus, (Federal Republic of Germany) 135
Geschichte und Politik, Verlag für, (Austria) 25
Gesellschaft für Bibliothekswesen und Dokumentation des Landbaues (GBDL) (Federal Republic of Germany) 167
Gesellschaft für deutsche Sprache und Literatur in Zürich (Switzerland) 352
Gesellschaft für Information und Dokumentation mbH (GID) (Federal Republic of Germany) 167
Gesellschaft für Verlagswerte GmbH (Switzerland) 351
Gesellschaft für Volkskunde (Switzerland) 342
Geschäftsstelle der Schweiz (Switzerland) 342
Geuthner, Librairie Orientaliste Paul, SA (France) 97
Ghana Association of Writers (Ghana) 169
Ghana Booksellers' Association (Ghana) 169
Ghana Institute of Management and Public Administration, Library and Documentation Centre (Ghana) 170
Ghana Library Association (Ghana) 170
Ghana Library Board (Ghana) 170
Ghana National Book Development Council (Ghana) 169
Ghana Publishing Corporation (Ghana) 169
Ghana Publishing Corporation, Distribution and Sales Division (Ghana) 169

Ghana Universities Press (Ghana) 169
Ghaqda Bibliotekarji/Library Association Valetta (Malta) 247
Gharelu Library Yojna (India) 195
Gheorghiu-Dej, Biblioteca Institutului Politehnic 'Gheorge,' Bucuresti (Romania) 301
Ghetto Fighters' House Publishers (Israel) 207
Ghost Hunters' Library (United Kingdom) 381
Ghulam, Sh, Ali & Sons (Pakistan) 282
Gianotten, Boekhandel, BV (Netherlands) 266
Giao Duc Publishing House (Socialist Republic of Viet Nam) 420
Giappichelli, Giorgio, (Italy) 215
Gibbons, Stanley, (Publications) Ltd (United Kingdom) 381
Gibert Jeune Sàrl (France) 97
Gibert, Librairie Joseph, (France) 108
Gibraltar Bookshop (Gibraltar) 170
Gibraltar Garrison Library (Gibraltar) 170
Gibraltar Junior Bookshop (Gibraltar) 170
Gibraltar Library Service (Gibraltar) 170
Gibralter Book Store (Jordan) 233
Gidlunds Förlag (Sweden) 330
Gidrometeorizdat (Union of Soviet Socialist Republics) 361
Gierows, Karin, Prizes (Sweden) 335
Giertsen, Ed B, A/S (Norway) 280
Gieseking, Verlag Ernst und Werner, (Federal Republic of Germany) 135
Giesserei-Verlag GmbH (Federal Republic of Germany) 135
Gifford & Craven (Republic of Ireland) 203
Gifford, John, Ltd (United Kingdom) 381
Gigord, Editions De, (France) 97
Gilbert, Girault, SPRL (Belgium) 37
Giles Prize (France) 111
Gili, Ediciones G, SA (Argentina) 5
Gili, Editôra Gustavo, do Brasil SA (Brazil) 50
Gili, Editorial Gustavo, de Mexico Sa (Mexico) 249
Gili, Editorial Gustavo, Ltda (Chile) 61
Gili, Editorial Gustavo, SA (Spain) 318
Gill & Macmillan Ltd (Republic of Ireland) 203
Gillani, S I, (Pakistan) 283
Gilles und Francke Verlag (Federal Republic of Germany) 135
Gilmore, Mary, Award (Australia) 22
Ginn & Co Ltd (United Kingdom) 381
Ginsberg Univ Boekhandel (Netherlands) 266
Giovanis (Greece) 171
Girardet, Verlag W, (Federal Republic of Germany) 135
Gisbert y Cía SA (Bolivia) 46
Gisbert y Cia SA (Bolivia) 46
Gitanjali Prakashan (India) 186
Giuffrè, A, Editore SpA (Italy) 215
Giunti Publishing Group (Italy) 215
Gjellerup, Jul, Forlagsaktieselskab (Denmark) 75
Gjellerups Boghandel ApS (Denmark) 78
Gjellerups Forlag A/S (Denmark) 75
Glas (Yugoslavia) 422
Glasgow, Mary, Publications Ltd (United Kingdom) 381
Glaven (United Kingdom) 381
Glaxo Travelling Fellowships for Science Writers (United Kingdom) 414
Gleerup, AB C W K, Bokförlag (Sweden) 330
Gleerupska, AB, Universitetsbokhandeln (Sweden) 334
Glem, Editorial, SACIF (Argentina) 5
Glen, Esther, Award (New Zealand) 273
Gleniffer Press (United Kingdom) 381
Global Book Resources Ltd (United Kingdom) 381
Global Editôra e Distribuidora Ltda (Brazil) 50
Globetrotter-Verlag (Federal Republic of Germany) 135
Globi Verlag AG (Switzerland) 342
Globo, Editôra, SA (Brazil) 50
Globo, Livraría do, (Brazil) 55
Globus (Yugoslavia) 422
'Globus' Zeitungs-, Druck- und Verlagsanstalt GmbH (Austria) 25
Glock und Lutz Verlag Heroldsberg (Federal Republic of Germany) 135
Glombig, PR Verlag Kurt, (Federal Republic of Germany) 135
Glöss, Verlagsgesellschaft R, und Co (Federal Republic of Germany) 135
Główna Biblioteka Lekarska (Poland) 293
Główna Politechniki, Biblioteka, Warszawskiej (Poland) 293
Główna Uniwersytetu, Biblioteka, im Adama Mickiewicza (Library of Adam Mickiewicz University) (Poland) 293
Głównego Urzedu Statystycznego, Zarzad Wydawnictw, (Publishers of the Central Statistical Office) (Poland) 291
Gluck, Felix, Press Ltd (United Kingdom) 381
Goddard's Bookshop Ltd (New Zealand) 272
Godwin, George, Ltd (United Kingdom) 381
Goede Boek, BV Uitgeversbedryf Het, (Netherlands) 259
Goel Publishing House (India) 186
Goethe Book Dealers Inc (Japan) 231
Goethe Prize (Federal Republic of Germany) 168

Gold Dagger Award (United Kingdom) 414
Golden Book House (Bangladesh) 32
Golden Book Prize (Italy) 222
Golden Eagle Award of the Festival International du Livre (International Literary Prizes) 441
Golden Eagle Books Ltd (Republic of Ireland) 203
Golden Feather of the 'Figaro littéraire' (France) 111
Golden Pen Prize (Italy) 222
Golden Pleasure Books Ltd (United Kingdom) 381
Golden Press Pty Ltd (Australia) 13
Golden Press Pty Ltd (New Zealand) 270
Goldex (United Kingdom) 381
Goldmann, Wilhelm, Verlag GmbH (Federal Republic of Germany) 135
Goldschmidt, Viktor, Verlagsbuchhandlung (Switzerland) 342
Goldsmith, The, Press (Republic of Ireland) 203
Goldstadtverlag (Federal Republic of Germany) 135
Gollancz, Victor, Ltd (United Kingdom) 381
Gomer Press (J D Lewis & Sons Ltd) (United Kingdom) 381
Gómez, P A, (Dominican Republic) 80
Goncourt, Editorial y Librería, (Argentina) 5
Goncourt Prize (France) 111
Gondolat Könyvkiadó (Hungary) 177
Gondrom Verlag GmbH & Co Kg (Federal Republic of Germany) 135
Gondu (Burma) 59
Gonin, André et Pierre, (Switzerland) 342
Gonski, Buchhandlung Heinrich, (Federal Republic of Germany) 165
Gonthier, Société Nouvelle des Editions, Sàrl (France) 97
Gonvill, Librerías, de Guadalajara (Mexico) 252
Good Companions (India) 186
Good Earth Publishing Co (Hong Kong) 175
Good Reading (United Kingdom) 381
Goodwill Trading Co Inc (Philippines) 289
Gooise, de, (Netherlands) 259
Goor Jeugdboeken, van, (Netherlands) 259
Gorachek, V, KG (Federal Republic of Germany) 135
Gorcum, Van, BV (Netherlands) 259
Gordon and Breach Science Publishers Ltd (United Kingdom) 381
Gordon and Gotch (PNG) Pty Ltd (Papua New Guinea) 285
Gordon & Cremonesi (United Kingdom) 381
Gorgas, Biblioteca Bio-Médica del Laboratorio Conmemorativo, (Panama) 285
Gor'kogo Moskovskogo, Nauchnaya biblioteka im A M, gos universiteta im M V Lomonosova (Union of Soviet Socialist Republics) 362
Gor'kovo Leningradskovo, Nauchnaya biblioteka im A M, gosudarstvennovo universiteta im A A Zhdanova (Union of Soviet Socialist Republics) 362
Göschl, Alois, & Co (Austria) 25
gosudarstvennaya ordena Trudovogo Krasnogo Znameni biblioteka, Vsesoyuznaya, inostrannoi literatury (Union of Soviet Socialist Republics) 362
Gosudarstvennaya publichnaya istoricheskaya biblioteka RSFSR (Union of Soviet Socialist Republics) 362
Gosudarstvennaya publichnaya nauchno-tekhnicheskaya biblioteka SSSR (Union of Soviet Socialist Republics) 363
Göteborgs Stadsbibliotek (City Library and County Library) (Sweden) 334
Göteborgs Universitetsbibliotek (Sweden) 334
Gotthelf-Verlag (Switzerland) 342
Gottlob, Adam, Oehlenschläger Prize (Denmark) 79
Gottmer Publishers, J H, (Netherlands) 259
Gottmer's, BV v/hB, Uitgeversbedrijf (Netherlands) 259
Gouda, S, Quint (Netherlands) 259
Gouden, Uitgeverij het, Spoor (Belgium) 37
Goudvink, De, NV (Belgium) 37
Goulden, Henry, Ltd (United Kingdom) 381
Government Archives (Namibia) 255
Government Archives, Cape Archives Depot, Library (Republic of South Africa) 312
Government Archives, Natal Archives Depot, Library (Republic of South Africa) 312
Government Archives, Orange Free State Archives Depot, Library (Republic of South Africa) 312
Government Archives, Transvaal Archives Depot, Library (Republic of South Africa) 312
Government College Library (Tanzania) 283
Government, Directorate of, Publications (India) 186
Government Library (Libya) 241
Government of India Librarians Association (India) 196
Government Press (Afghanistan) 1
Government Press, The, (The Gambia) 114
Government Printer (Algeria) 2
Government Printer (Benin) 45
Government Printer (Botswana) 47
Government Printer (Burundi) 59
Government Printer (United Republic of Cameroun) 60
Government Printer (Chad) 61
Government Printer (Popular Republic of Congo) 67
Government Printer (Egypt) 81
Government Printer (Ethiopia) 83

Government Printer (Finland) 85
Government Printer (Ivory Coast) 223
Government Printer (Kenya) 234
Government Printer (Liberia) 240
Government Printer (Lesotho) 240
Government Printer (Libya) 241
Government Printer (Democratic Republic of Madagascar) 242
Government Printer (Sierra Leone) 304
Government Printer (Somalia) 307
Government Printer (Republic of South Africa) 309
Government Printer (Sudan) 327
Government Printer (Tanzania) 353
Government Printer (Uganda) 359
Government Printer (Zambia) 428
Government Printer (Zimbabwe) 429
Government Printer (Impressa Nacional de Moçambique) (Mozambique) 254
Government Printer (Imprimerie Centrale d'Afrique) (Central African Republic) 61
Government Printer (Imprimerie Centrale d'Afrique) (Gabon) 113
Government Printer (Imprimerie de Kabgayi) (Rwanda) 302
Government Printer (Imprimerie du Gouvernement) (Senegal) 303
Government Printer (Imprimerie du Gouvernement Central) (Zaire) 427
Government Printer (Imprimerie Générale du Niger) (Niger) 274
Government Printer (Imprimerie National) (Malawi) 243
Government Printer (Imprimerie National) (Mauritius) 247
Government Printer (Imprimerie National du Rwanda) (Rwanda) 302
Government Printer (Imprimerie Nationale) (Mali) 246
Government Printer (Imprimerie Nationale) (Mauritania) 247
Government Printer, Imprimerie Nationale (Upper Volta) 416
Government Printer (Imprimerie Officielle) (Morocco) 254
Government Printer (Imprimerie Officielle de la République Tunisienne) (Tunisia) 357
Government Printer, The, (Ghana Publishing Corporation, Printing Division) (Ghana) 169
Government Printing Office (Jamaica) 223
Government Public Library (Liberia) 240
Government Publications (Pakistan) 282
Gower Press (United Kingdom) 381
Gower Publishing Co Ltd (United Kingdom) 381
Goyanarte Editor SA (Argentina) 5
Gozo Public Library (Malta) 246
Graaf, De, Publishers (Netherlands) 259
Graal, Edições, Lda (Brazil) 50
Graal, Ordem do, na Terra (Brazil) 51
Grabert-Verlag (Federal Republic of Germany) 135
Gradina, Izdavačka ustanova, (Yugoslavia) 422
Gradjevinska Knjiga (Yugoslavia) 422
Gräfe und Unzer GmbH (Federal Republic of Germany) 135
Grafia Galaxias (Greece) 171
Grafički zavod Hrvatske (Yugoslavia) 422
Grafisk Forlag A/S (Denmark) 75
Grafos (Yugoslavia) 422
Grafton Books (United Kingdom) 381
Graham & Trotman Ltd (United Kingdom) 381
Grahame Book Co (Australia) 19
Gralsbotschaft, Verlag der Stiftung, GmbH (Federal Republic of Germany) 135
Gram Editora (Argentina) 5
Gramedia, PT, (Indonesia) 199
Gramedia (Indonesia) 200
Gran Colombia, Librería La, (Colombia) 66
Gran Premio Nacional de Literatura (Uruguay) 418
Granada Publishing Australia Pty Ltd (Australia) 13
Granada Publishing Ltd (United Kingdom) 381
Grancher, Jacques, Editeur (France) 97
Grand Franco-Belgian Literary Prize (Belgium) 45
Grand Franco-Belgian Literary Prize (France) 111
Grand National Assembly, Library of the, (Turkey) 359
Grand-Pont, Editions du, (Switzerland) 342
Grand Prize (Sweden) 335
Grand Prize for a Book of Poetry (Sweden) 335
Grand Prize for a Novel (Sweden) 335
Grand Prize for Children's Literature (International Literary Prizes) 441
Grand Prize for Literature (France) 111
Grand Prize for Poetry Criticism (France) 111
Grand Prize for the Dissemination of the French Language (International Literary Prizes) 441
Grand Prize of French Poets (France) 111
Granda, Editorial Juan Carlos, (Argentina) 5
Grange Batelière SA (France) 97
Granica Editor SA (Argentina) 5
Grant Educational Co Ltd (United Kingdom) 410
Grant McIntyre Ltd (United Kingdom) 382
Grasset et Fasquelle, Société des Editions, (France) 97

Grasshopper Books (United Kingdom) 382
Grassin, Jean, Editeur (France) 97
Grassroots Books (Nigeria) 275
Gratien, Emilio, (French Guiana) 113
Gravensande, The G H 's-, Prize (Netherlands) 267
Graziano, Librería Alfa, (Argentina) 8
Graziano, Librería & Editorial Alfa, SACI (Argentina) 5
Great Austrian State Prize (Austria) 30
Great China Book Corporation (China (Taiwan)) 64
Great English Classics (United Kingdom) 409
Great Mosque of Sana'a, Library of the, (Yemen Arab Republic) 421
Great Publications Co Ltd (China (Taiwan)) 64
Gredos, Editorial, SA (Spain) 318
Green Book House Limited (Bangladesh) 32
Green, W, & Son Ltd (United Kingdom) 382
Greenaway, Kate, Medal (United Kingdom) 414
Greene & Co (Republic of Ireland) 204
Greenhouse Publications (Australia) 13
Greens, E, Forlag (Norway) 279
Greenwood Press (Hong Kong) 175
Gregg International (United Kingdom) 382
Gregorian University Press (Universitá Gregoriana Editrice) (Italy) 215
Gregoriana, Libreria, (Italy) 220
Gregoriana, Libreria Editrice, (Italy) 215
Gregory, Eric, Trust Fund Awards (United Kingdom) 414
Gregory Medal (Republic of Ireland) 205
Gremial de Libreros de Guatemala (Guatemala) 173
Gremio Sindical de Libreros de Barcelona (Association of Barcelona Booksellers) (Spain) 314
Grenfell 'Henry Lawson' Festival Prizes (Australia) 22
Gresham Books Ltd (United Kingdom) 382
Gresham, John, (United Kingdom) 382
Greshoff, J, Prize (Netherlands) 267
Grevas Forlag (Denmark) 75
Greve, Gustav, (Federal Republic of Germany) 164
Greven Verlag Köln GmbH & Co (Federal Republic of Germany) 135
Gribaudi, Piero, Editore (Italy) 215
Griegs, John, Forlag (Norway) 279
Griff, Ukvary, Verlag Kiado (Federal Republic of Germany) 135
Griffin, Charles, & Co Ltd (United Kingdom) 382
Griffon, Editions du, (Switzerland) 342
Griggs, T W, & Co (Pty) Ltd (Republic of South Africa) 309
Grigoris, Kass M, (Greece) 172
Grigoris, Kassandra M, (Greece) 171
Grijalbo Bolivia Ltda (Bolivia) 46
Grijalbo, Distribuidora exclusivo, SA (Peru) 286
Grijalbo, Ediciones, SA (Spain) 318
Grijalbo, Editorial, Ltda (Brazil) 51
Grijalbo, Editorial, SA (Mexico) 249
Grijalbo SA (Argentina) 5
Grijalbo SA (Venezuela) 419
Grijalbo y Cía Ltda (Chile) 62
Grijelmo, Artes Gráficas, SA (Spain) 318
Grip, PT, (Indonesia) 199
Grisewood & Dempsey Ltd (United Kingdom) 382
Grolier de Venezuela (Venezuela) 419
Grolier, The, Society of Australia Pty Ltd (Australia) 13
Grøndahl og Søn Forlag A/S (Norway) 279
Grønlandske Forlag, Det, (Denmark) 75
Groos, Julius, Verlag KG (Federal Republic of Germany) 135
Grösschen, Verlag und Landkartenhaus W, KG (Federal Republic of Germany) 136
Grosskopf, J W F, prys vir Drama (Republic of South Africa) 313
Grossman, David, Literary Agency Ltd (United Kingdom) 408
Grossohaus Wegner und Co (Federal Republic of Germany) 165
Grosvenor Books (The Good Road Ltd) (United Kingdom) 382
Groszer, Altberliner Verlag Lucie, (German Democratic Republic) 115
Grote'sche Verlagsbuch-handlung KG (Federal Republic of Germany) 136
Grounauer, Editions François, (Switzerland) 342
Ground Informação, Editôra, Ltda (Brazil) 51
Groupe des Editeurs de Livres de la CEE (International Organizations) 432
Groupe Expansion (France) 97
Gruenwald, F G Neuer Verlag, GmbH (Federal Republic of Germany) 136
Gründ, Librairie, (France) 97
Grundlagen, Verlag, und Praxis GmbH & Co (Federal Republic of Germany) 136
Grundt, Johan, Tanun A/S (Norway) 280
Grüner, B R, BV (Netherlands) 259
Grünewald, Matthias-, -Verlag (Federal Republic of Germany) 136
Grupo Bibliografico Nacional de la Republica Dominicana (Dominican Republic) 80
Gruyter, Walter de, & Co, Mouton Publishers (Federal Republic of Germany) 136

INDEX 475

Gryphius-Verlag (Federal Republic of Germany) 136
Gryphon Books Pty Ltd (Australia) 13
Guadagni, L'Editrice Scientifica SaS di L G, (Italy) 215
Guadalupe, Editorial, Mansilla 386 (Argentina) 5
Guadarrama, Ediciones, (Spain) 318
Guadiana, Grupo Editorial, SA (Spain) 318
Guanabara, Editôra, Koogan SA (Brazil) 51
Guanda Editore SRL (Italy) 215
Guaraldi Editore SpA (Italy) 215
Guardian Award, The, for Children's Fiction (International Literary Prizes) 442
Guardian Fiction, The, Prize (International Literary Prizes) 442
Guazzelli, Livraria Pioneira Editôra Enio Matheus, e Cia Ltda (Brazil) 51
Gubblecote, The, Press (United Kingdom) 382
Gudjónssonar, Bókaútgáfa Gudjóns Ó, (Iceland) 179
Guénégaud, Librairie, (France) 97
Guérin et Cie (France) 97
Guhl, Verlag Klaus, (Federal Republic of Germany) 136
Guida Editori SRL (Italy) 215
Guild of Travel Writers (United Kingdom) 364
Guild Publishing (United Kingdom) 382
Guildhall Library (United Kingdom) 411
Guillot, Editions d'Art Albert, (France) 97
Guinness Superlatives Ltd (United Kingdom) 382
Guitarra Facil (Colombia) 66
Gujarat State English Language Booksellers' Association, Academic Book Centre (India) 181
Gujarat Textbook, The, Publishers' Association (India) 181
Gujarat Vidyapith Granthalaya (India) 196
Gullers International AB (Sweden) 330
Gummeruksen Kirjakauppa (Finland) 86
Gummerus, K J, Osakeyhtiö (Finland) 85
Gummessons Bokförlag (Sweden) 330
Gumperts Universitetsbokhandel AB (Sweden) 334
Gunasena, M D, & Co Ltd (Sri Lanka) 326
Gundert, D, Verlag (Federal Republic of Germany) 136
Gundolf, Friedrich, Prize for Germanistics abroad (Federal Republic of Germany) 168
Gunung Agung, P T, (Indonesia) 200
Gunung Agung, PT (Indonesia) 199
Gunung Mulia, B P K, (Indonesia) 199
Gunung Mulia, Toko Buku BPK (Indonesia) 200
Guozi Shudian, China Publications Centre (People's Republic of China) 63
Güse, Verlag August, (Federal Republic of Germany) 136
Gut, Th, & Co Verlag (Switzerland) 342
Gute Schriften Verein, Basel (Switzerland) 342
Gutenberg (Belgium) 37
Gutenberg, Büchergilde, (Switzerland) 351
Gutenberg, Büchergilde, Verlagsgesellschaft mbH (Federal Republic of Germany) 136
Gutenberg, Dardanos, (Greece) 171
Gutenberg-Gesellschaft (Federal Republic of Germany) 136
Gutenberg-Gesellschaft (Gutenberg Society) (Federal Republic of Germany) 167
Gutenberghus Publishing Service (Denmark) 75
Gütersloher Verlagshaus Gerd Mohn (Federal Republic of Germany) 136
Guttentag, Premio de Novela 'Erich' (Bolivia) 47
Guyana Library Association (Guyana) 174
Guyana Medical Science Library (Guyana) 174
Guyana National Trading Corporation (GNTC) (Guyana) 174
Guyana Printers Ltd (Guyana) 174
Guyana Society Library (Guyana) 174
Guyra Publishing Co Pty Ltd (Australia) 13
Gwasg Gomer (United Kingdom) 382
Gwasg Prifysgol Cymru (United Kingdom) 382
Gwasg y Dref Wen (United Kingdom) 382
Gyan Bharati (India) 186
Gyldendal Norsk Forlag (Norway) 279
Gyldendal, Søren, Prize (Denmark) 79
Gyldendals Bogklub (Denmark) 77
Gyldendals Børnebogklub (Denmark) 77
Gyldendalske Boghandel — Nordisk Forlag A/S (Denmark) 75

H A D U - Hagemann Lehrmittel- und Verlagsgesellschaft mbH (Federal Republic of Germany) 136
H & R Academica (Republic of South Africa) 309
H A U M Academic Bookshop (Republic of South Africa) 312
H A U M Booksellers (Republic of South Africa) 312
H A U M (Hollandsch Afrikaansche Uitgevers Maatschappij) (Republic of South Africa) 309
H F L (Publishers) Ltd (United Kingdom) 382
H K Health Knowledge Publication (Hong Kong) 175
H M & M Publishers Ltd (United Kingdom) 382
H M S O (United Kingdom) 382

H U C I T E C Ltda — Editôra de Humanismo, Ciência e Tecnologia (Brazil) 51
Haack, VEB Hermann, (German Democratic Republic) 115
Haag und Herchen Verlag (Federal Republic of Germany) 136
Haan, de, (Netherlands) 259
Haase, P, & Søns Forlag A/S (Denmark) 75
Habbel, Verlag Josef, (Federal Republic of Germany) 136
Habegger, Verlag, AG (Switzerland) 342
Habelt, Rudolf, Verlag GmbH (Federal Republic of Germany) 136
Habib Bank Prize for Literature (Pakistan) 284
Hachette/Enseignement (Hachette Educational) (France) 97
Hachette, Groupe International, (France) 97
Hachette Guides Bleus (France) 97
Hachette International (Belgium) 37
Hachette-Jeunesse (France) 97
Hachette, Librairie, (Central African Republic) 61
Hachette, Librairie, (Popular Republic of Congo) 67
Hachette, Librairie, (Egypt) 82
Hachette, Librairie, (France) 97
Hachette, Librairie, (Gabon) 113
Hachette, Librairie, SA do Brasil (Brazil) 55
Hachette, Librería, (Argentina) 8
Hachette, Librería, SA (Argentina) 5
Hachette-Littérature (France) 97
Hachette Pacifique SA, Librairie, (French Polynesia) 113
Hachette Pratique (France) 97
Hachette-Réalités (France) 97
Hachette, Société congolaise, (Popular Republic of Congo) 67
Hadar (Israel) 207
Haddock, Peter, Ltd (United Kingdom) 382
Hädecke, Walter, Verlag (Federal Republic of Germany) 136
Hadwiger, Anna, (Austria) 29
Haeschel-Dufey, F (Switzerland) 342
Hagedorn, Hans Hermann, (Federal Republic of Germany) 164
Hageland, A van, (Belgium) 42
Hagemann, Lehrmittelverlag Wilhelm, (Federal Republic of Germany) 136
Hagen, Ten, BV (Netherlands) 259
Hager, Buchvertrieb, GmbH (Federal Republic of Germany) 136
Hagerups, H, Forlag (Denmark) 75
Hahn's, Mary, Kochbuchverlag (Federal Republic of Germany) 136
Haigh & Hochland Ltd (United Kingdom) 410
Hain, Dr Franz, (Austria) 25
Hain, Dr Franz, (Austria) 29
Hain, Verlag Anton, KG (Federal Republic of Germany) 136
Haji Hashim bin Haji Abdullah (Republic of Singapore) 306
Hak Won Sa (Republic of Korea) 236
Hakibbutz Hameuchad Publishing House Ltd (Israel) 207
Hakki Bigeç (Turkey) 359
Hakkim's Bookshop (Bangladesh) 32
Hakusui-Sha (Japan) 225
Hakuyu-Sha (Japan) 225
Halban, Peter, Literary Agency (Israel) 210
Halbart, Librairie, (Belgium) 43
Hale, Robert, Ltd (United Kingdom) 382
Halévy, Editions Dominique, (France) 97
Hali Prize (India) 197
Halk Kütüphanesi, Il, (Turkey) 359
Haller, Berchtold, Verlag (Switzerland) 342
Hallwag Verlag AG (Switzerland) 342
Hallwag Verlagsgesellschaft mbH (Federal Republic of Germany) 137
Hälsaböcker/Allt om Hälsa AB (Sweden) 330
Hamar, Haraldur J, (Iceland) 179
Hamburger Fremdenblatt Broschek und Co (Federal Republic of Germany) 137
Hamburger Kommissionsbuchhandlung GmbH (Federal Republic of Germany) 165
Hamburger Lesehefte Verlag Iselt und Co Nfl mbH (Federal Republic of Germany) 137
Hamburgo, Librería, Antonio Navarrete (Mexico) 252
Hamdard National Foundation (Pakistan) 282
Hameau, Le, Editeur (France) 97
Hamenorah Publishers Ltd (Israel) 207
Hamidia Library (Bangladesh) 32
Hamilton, Hamish, Ltd (United Kingdom) 382
Hamlyn Paperbacks (United Kingdom) 382
Hamlyn, Paul, Pty Ltd (Australia) 13
Hamlyn Publishing, The, Group Ltd (United Kingdom) 382
Hammer, Peter, Verlag GmbH (Federal Republic of Germany) 137
Hammicks Wholesale (United Kingdom) 410
Hampton House Productions Ltd (United Kingdom) 383
Hampton Press Features Syndicate (Australia) 19
Hamrelius & Stenvall Förlag AB (Sweden) 330
Hamrun Library (Malta) 246

Hanau, Heinrich, Publications Ltd (United Kingdom) 383
Handsel, The, Press (United Kingdom) 383
Hanguk Seoji Hakhoe (Republic of Korea) 238
Hanguk Tosogwan Hakhoe (Republic of Korea) 238
Hanna, Fred, Ltd (Republic of Ireland) 204
Hannon, J, & Co (Publishers) Oxford (United Kingdom) 383
Hans Prakashan (India) 186
Hans Publishers (India) 186
Hansa Publishers Ltd (Sri Lanka) 326
Hansa Verlag Heinz W Hass (Federal Republic of Germany) 137
Hanse Production AB (Sweden) 330
Hansen, Edition Wilhelm, (Denmark) 75
Hansen House (London) Ltd (United Kingdom) 383
Hansen Teaterförlag, Folmer, (Sweden) 334
Hanser, Carl, Verlag (Federal Republic of Germany) 137
Hänssler-Verlag (Federal Republic of Germany) 137
Hansson och Bruce, Söderbokhandeln, AB (Sweden) 334
Hanssons, Kalleberger Foundation — The Tekla, and Gösta Ronnströms Prize (Sweden) 336
Hanstein, Peter, Verlag GmbH (Federal Republic of Germany) 137
Hanthawaddy Book House (Burma) 59
Hanthawaddy Bookshop (Burma) 59
Haraucourt, Edmond, Prize (France) 111
Harbra (Brazil) 51
Harcourt Brace Jovanovich Group (Australia) Pty Ltd (Australia) 13
Harcourt Brace Jovanovich Ltd (United Kingdom) 383
Hardy, Thomas, Society Ltd (United Kingdom) 413
Hargreen Publishing Co (Australia) 14
Harjeet & Co (India) 186
Harla (Brazil) 51
Harla (Mexico) 249
Harlekin-Presse (Federal Republic of Germany) 137
Harley & Jones (United Kingdom) 383
Harleyford Publications (United Kingdom) 383
Harmonie, De, (Netherlands) 259
Harper & Row (Australasia) Pty Ltd (Australia) 14
Harper & Row, Editora, do Brasil Ltda (Brazil) 51
Harper & Row Latinoamericana-Harla, SA de CV (Mexico) 249
Harper & Row Ltd (United Kingdom) 383
Harrach und Sabrow (Federal Republic of Germany) 137
Harrap, George G, & Co Ltd (United Kingdom) 383
Harrassowitz, Otto, (Federal Republic of Germany) 165
Harrassowitz, Verlag Otto, (Federal Republic of Germany) 137
Harriers Bokforlag AB (Sweden) 330
Harris, Firma, (Indonesia) 199
Harris, Katrine, Award (Republic of South Africa) 313
Harris, Paul, Publishing (United Kingdom) 383
Harrods Ltd (United Kingdom) 410
Harrow House Editions Ltd (United Kingdom) 383
Hart-Davis Educational Ltd (United Kingdom) 383
Hart Mossman & Co Ltd (Nigeria) 277
Hartmann, Verlag Karlheinz, (Federal Republic of Germany) 137
Harvard Business Review Library (United Kingdom) 383
Harvard, John, Lending Library (Bahamas) 31
Harvard University Press (United Kingdom) 383
Harvester, The, Press Ltd (United Kingdom) 383
Harvill Press Ltd (United Kingdom) 383
Harwalik, Verlag, KG (Federal Republic of Germany) 137
Harwood Academic Publishers GmbH (Switzerland) 342
Haryana Sahitya Prize (India) 197
Hasanuddin University, Library of, (Indonesia) 200
Hasbach, A L, (Austria) 29
Haset Kitabevi AS (Turkey) 359
Háskólabókasafn (Iceland) 180
Hatchards Ltd (United Kingdom) 410
Hatier, Librairie, SA (France) 98
Hatje, Verlag Gerd, (Federal Republic of Germany) 137
Hatta, Perpustakaan Jajasan, (Indonesia) 200
Haude und Spener Verlag (Federal Republic of Germany) 137
Haufe, Rudolf, Verlag (Federal Republic of Germany) 137
Haug, Karl F, Verlag GmbH & Co KG (Federal Republic of Germany) 137
Haupt, Paul, Bern (Switzerland) 342
Hauptverband der graphischen Unternehmungen Österreichs (Austria) 23
Hauptverband des österreichischen Buchhandels (Austria) 23
Haus der Bibel (Switzerland) 342
Haus, Volksbuchhandlung, des Buches (German Democratic Republic) 117
Hauschild, Verlag H M, GmbH (Federal Republic of Germany) 137
Hauswedell, Dr Ernst, und Co Verlag (Federal Republic of Germany) 137
Hautot, Pierre, SA (France) 98
Havaux, Imprimeries, (Belgium) 37
Have, Uitgeverij ten, NV (Netherlands) 259
Havez-Planque, Marie, Prize (France) 111
Hawthorn, The, Press Pty Ltd (Australia) 14
Hawthornden Prize (United Kingdom) 414

Hayakawa Publishing Inc (Japan) 225
Hayez, Imprimerie, SPRL (Belgium) 37
Haynes Publishing Group (United Kingdom) 383
Hazan, Fernand, Editeur SA (France) 98
Health Science Press (Leslie J Speight Ltd) (United Kingdom) 383
Heath, A M, & Co Ltd (United Kingdom) 408
Heatherbank Press (United Kingdom) 383
Heckners Verlag (Federal Republic of Germany) 137
Heenemann, H, Verlagsgesellschaft mbH (Federal Republic of Germany) 137
Heering-Verlag GmbH (Federal Republic of Germany) 137
Heffers Booksellers (United Kingdom) 410
Heibonsha Ltd, Publishers (Japan) 225
Heibrand (Belgium) 37
Heideland, Boekhandel, (Belgium) 43
Heideland NV (Belgium) 37
Heideland-Orbis NV (Belgium) 37
Heideland PVBA (Belgium) 37
Heidelberger, W (Switzerland) 342
Heidmük-Verlag Günther U Müller (Federal Republic of Germany) 137
Heidrich, Leopold, (Austria) 29
Heima er Bezt Book Club (Iceland) 180
Heimatland Verlag (Austria) 25
Heimeran, Ernst, Verlag (Federal Republic of Germany) 138
Heimskringla (Iceland) 179
Heinemann, Verlag Egon, (Federal Republic of Germany) 138
Heinemann, William, Australia Pty Ltd (Australia) 14
Heinemann Award for Literature (United Kingdom) 414
Heinemann Educational Australia Pty Ltd (Australia) 14
Heinemann Educational Books (Asia) Ltd (Hong Kong) 175
Heinemann Educational Books (Asia) Ltd (Malaysia) 244
Heinemann Educational Books (East Africa) Ltd (Kenya) 234
Heinemann Educational Books (International) Ltd (United Kingdom) 384
Heinemann Educational Books Ltd (United Kingdom) 384
Heinemann Educational Books (Nigeria) Limited (Nigeria) 275
Heinemann Group, The, of Publishers Ltd (United Kingdom) 384
Heinemann, William, (International) Ltd (United Kingdom) 383
Heinemann Medical Books, William, Ltd (United Kingdom) 384
Heinemann/Octopus (United Kingdom) 384
Heinemann Publishers (New Zealand) Ltd (New Zealand) 270
Heinrichshofen's Verlag (Federal Republic of Germany) 138
Heintz, Verlag Georg, (Federal Republic of Germany) 138
Heinzle's, Gebhard, Erben (Austria) 29
Helbing und Lichtenhahn Verlag AG (Switzerland) 342
Helgafell, Bókábudin, (Iceland) 180
Helgafell, Bókaútgáfan, (Iceland) 179
Helicon Press (United Kingdom) 384
Héliographia, Arts Graphiques, SA (Switzerland) 342
Helios, Uitgeverij, (Belgium) 37
Hellenic Distribution Agency (Cyprus) Ltd (Cyprus) 69
Helmond (Netherlands) 259
Help Bookshop (Lebanon) 239
Helsingin Kaupunginkirjasto (Finland) 86
Helsingin Teknillisen Korkeakoulun Kirjasto (Finland) 86
Helsingin Yliopiston Kirjasto (Finland) 86
Helsinki Prize (Finland) 87
Helvetica Chimica Acta-Verlag (Switzerland) 342
Hemans, Felicia, Prize for Lyrical Poetry (United Kingdom) 414
Hemeroteca Municipal de Madrid (Spain) 324
Hemeroteca Nacional de México (Mexico) 252
Hemisferio, Editorial, Sur SA (Argentina) 5
Hemkunt Publishers Pvt Ltd (India) 186
Hemma, Editions, (Belgium) 37
Hemmets Journal AB (Sweden) 330
'Hemus' Foreign Trade Company (Bulgaria) 58
Hemus-Livraria Editôra Ltda (Brazil) 51
Henderson's Book Store (Jamaica) 223
Henle, G, Verlag (Federal Republic of Germany) 138
Henne, Dagmar, (Federal Republic of Germany) 164
Henny's Forlag (Norway) 279
Henry, Ian, Publications Ltd (United Kingdom) 384
Henschelverlag Kunst und Gesellschaf (German Democratic Republic) 115
Henssel Verlag (Federal Republic of Germany) 138
Her Majesty's Stationery Office (United Kingdom) 384
'Herald', The, Short Story Award (Australia) 22
Herbert, The, Press Ltd (United Kingdom) 384
Herbig, F A, Verlagsbuchhandlung (Federal Republic of Germany) 138
Herdeg:, Walter, The Graphis Press (Switzerland) 342
Herder AG (Switzerland) 342
Herder Buchgemeinde (Federal Republic of Germany) 165

Herder, Editorial, SA (Spain) 318
Herder Editrice e Libreria (Italy) 215
Herder, Librería, (Spain) 324
Herder und Co (Austria) 29
Herder und Herder GmbH (Federal Republic of Germany) 138
Herder, Verlag, GmbH & Co, KG (Federal Republic of Germany) 138
Herder, Verlag, und Co (Austria) 25
Heredia Prize (International Literary Prizes) 442
Heritage (Australia) 14
Heritage (Israel) 207
Heritage Publishers (India) 186
Hermann (Editeurs des Sciences et des Arts) SA (France) 98
Hermes, Editorial, SA (Mexico) 250
Hermes Prize (France) 111
Hermods Publishing House (Sweden) 330
Herne, Editions de l', (France) 98
Hernieuwen-Uitgaven PVBA (Belgium) 37
Hernovs Book Club (Denmark) 77
Hernovs Forlag (Denmark) 75
Herold Buch-Club (Federal Republic of Germany) 165
Herold Druck- und Verlagsgesellschaft mbH (Austria) 25
Herold Neue Verlagsgesellschaft GmbH (Federal Republic of Germany) 138
Herold Verlag Brück KG (Federal Republic of Germany) 138
Herold Verlage, Vereinigte, GmbH (Federal Republic of Germany) 138
Heron Books (United Kingdom) 409
Herrera, Casa, (Dominican Republic) 80
Herrera, Febio, (Dominican Republic) 80
Herrero, Editorial, SA (Mexico) 250
Herrero Hermanos Sucesores SA (Mexico) 250
Hertenstein-Presse (Federal Republic of Germany) 138
Hertoghs, Drukkerij-Uitgeverij, (Belgium) 37
Hertzog Prize (Republic of South Africa) 313
Herzen, Alexander, Foundation (Netherlands) 259
Herzmansky, Bernhard, (Austria) 25
Herzog August Bibliothek (Federal Republic of Germany) 166
Hessische Landes- und Hoch-schulbibliothek Darmstadt (Federal Republic of Germany) 166
Hessischer Verleger- und Buchhandler-Verband e V (Federal Republic of Germany) 119
Hessling, Bruno, Verlag (Federal Republic of Germany) 138
Hestia Bookstore (Greece) 172
Hestia-Verlag GmbH (Federal Republic of Germany) 138
Heuff, Uitgeverij, (Netherlands) 259
Heureka, Uitgeverij, (Netherlands) 260
Heures Claires, Editions d'Art Les, SA (France) 98
Heusden, Gérard Th van, (APA) (Netherlands) 260
Heyden & Son Ltd (United Kingdom) 384
Heyer, The Georgette, Historical Novel Prize (International Literary Prizes) 442
Heymann, B, Verlag (Federal Republic of Germany) 138
Heymanns, Carl, Verlag KG (Federal Republic of Germany) 138
Heyn, Johannes, (Austria) 25
Heyn, Johannes, (Austria) 29
Heyne, Rolf, Verlag (Switzerland) 342
Heyne, Wilhelm, Verlag (Federal Republic of Germany) 138
Hichtum, Nienke van, Prize (Netherlands) 267
Hicks Smith & Sons Pty Ltd (Australia) 14
Hidakarya Agung (Indonesia) 199
Hier et Demain, Editions, (France) 98
Hiersemann, Anton, Verlag (Federal Republic of Germany) 138
Higginbothams Ltd (India) 196
High Council of Arts & Literature (Egypt) 82
High Court of Australia Library (Australia) 20
Higham, David, Associates Ltd (United Kingdom) 408
Higham, David, Prize for Fiction (International Literary Prizes) 442
Higher Educational Books Publishing House (Democratic People's Republic of Korea) 236
Higher Teachers' Training Institute Library (Sudan) 327
Hikarinokuni Co Ltd (Japan) 226
Hilal, Dar Al, Publishing Institution (Egypt) 81
Hildur, Bókaútgáfan, (Iceland) 179
Hilger, Adam, Ltd (United Kingdom) 384
Hilger, Edition E, (Austria) 25
Hill, Leonard, (United Kingdom) 384
Hill of Content Publishing Co Ltd (Australia) 14
Hilleförlaget (Sweden) 330
Himachal Publishers' & Booksellers' Association (India) 181
Himalaya Prakashan (India) 186
Himalaya Publishing House (India) 186
Himpunan Masyarakat Penainta Buku (Indonesia) 200
Hind Pocket Books Private Ltd (India) 186
Hinder und Deelmann, Verlag, (Federal Republic of Germany) 138
Hindi Book Centre (India) 186
Hindi Pracharak Sansthan (India) 186

Hindustan Publishing Corporation (India) (India) 186
Hinstorff, VEB, Verlag (German Democratic Republic) 116
Hinterhaus, Gruppe, (Federal Republic of Germany) 138
Hinzelin, Emile, Prize (France) 111
Hippoboek/Studio de Zuid (Netherlands) 260
Hippokrates Verlag GmbH (Federal Republic of Germany) 139
Hirmer Verlag, Gesellschaft für Wissenschaftliches Lichtbild GmbH (Federal Republic of Germany) 139
Hirokawa Publishing Co (Japan) 226
Hirsch, Axel, Prize (Sweden) 336
Hirsch, Carlos, SRL (Argentina) 8
Hirschsprungs, H, Forlag (Denmark) 75
Hirt, Ferdinand, (Federal Republic of Germany) 139
Hirt, Ferdinand, mbH & Co KG (Austria) 25
Hirzel, S, Verlag GmbH und Co (Federal Republic of Germany) 139
Hispanas, Ediciones, (Guatemala) 173
Hispano Americana, Librería, (Spain) 324
Hispano Europea, Editorial, (Spain) 318
Hispanoamericana, Librería, (Puerto Rico) 299
Hissink, G W, & Co (APA) (Netherlands) 260
Histoire et d'Art, Editions d', J & R Wittman (France) 98
Histoire Sociale, Editions d', EDHIS (France) 98
Historical Society of Afghanistan (Afghanistan) 1
History Guild (United Kingdom) 409
Hjemmenes Forlag A/S (Norway) 279
Hjemmet A/ß (Norway) 279
Hjorts Forlag ApS (Denmark) 75
Hladbúd hf (Iceland) 179
Hlidskjálf, Bókaútgáfan, (Iceland) 179
Hna Lon Hla (Burma) 59
Hobbit Presse (Federal Republic of Germany) 139
Hobby Centre (Trinidad and Tobago) 356
Hobby, Editorial, (Argentina) 5
Hobsons Press (Cambridge) Ltd (United Kingdom) 384
Hoch-Verlag (Federal Republic of Germany) 139
Hodder & Stoughton (Australia) Pty Ltd (Australia) 14
Hodder & Stoughton Children's Books (United Kingdom) 384
Hodder & Stoughton Ltd (New Zealand) 270
Hodder & Stoughton Ltd (United Kingdom) 384
Hodemacher, Münchner Verlagsbüro Horst, -Axel Poldner GmbH & Co KG (Federal Republic of Germany) 164
Hodge, Alison, (United Kingdom) 384
Hodges Figgis & Co Ltd (Republic of Ireland) 204
Hodgson, Francis, (United Kingdom) 384
Hoepli, Casa Editrice Libraria Ulrico, SpA (Italy) 215
Hoepli, Ulrico, Libreria Internazionale (Italy) 220
Hoernle, Volksbuchhandlung Edwin, (German Democratic Republic) 117
Hofacker Ing W GmbH Verlag (Federal Republic of Germany) 139
Hofbauer, Buchhandlung Karl, (Austria) 29
Hoffman, Agence, (France) 107
Hoffman, Agence, (Federal Republic of Germany) 164
Hoffmann, Dieter, Verlag (Federal Republic of Germany) 139
Hoffmann, Julius, Verlag (Federal Republic of Germany) 139
Hoffmann und Campe Verlag (Federal Republic of Germany) 139
Hofmann, Verlag Karl, (Federal Republic of Germany) 139
Hofmeister, VEB Friedrich, Musikverlag (German Democratic Republic) 116
Hofmeyr, W A, Prize (Republic of South Africa) 313
Hogar del Libro (Spain) 324
Hogar del Libro — Nova Terra (Spain) 318
Hogarth, The, Press Ltd (United Kingdom) 384
Hogrefe, Verlag für Psychologie Dr C J, (Switzerland) 342
Hohenloher Druck- und Verlagshaus (Federal Republic of Germany) 139
Hohenstaufen Verlag Schumann KG (Federal Republic of Germany) 139
Hoi Ming Book Store (Hong Kong) 176
Hôi Thu-Viên Viet Nam (Socialist Republic of Viet Nam) 420
Hoikusha Publishing Co Ltd (Japan) 226
Hökerbergs, Lars, Bokförlag (Sweden) 330
Hokkaido University Library (Japan) 231
Hokuryukan Co Ltd (Japan) 226
Hokuseido, The, Press (Japan) 226
Holberg Medal (Denmark) 79
Holgersson, Nils, Plaque (Sweden) 336
Holkema, Van, en Warendorf (Netherlands) 260
Hölker, Verlag Wolfgang, (Federal Republic of Germany) 139
Holland (Netherlands) 260
Holland, The, Press (United Kingdom) 385
Holland University Press BV (APA) (Netherlands) 260
Hoilandia BV (Netherlands) 260
Hollandsche Boekhandel (Netherlands Antilles) 268
Holle Verlag GmbH (Federal Republic of Germany) 139
Hollinek, Brüder, und Co GmbH (Austria) 25
Hollis & Carter (United Kingdom) 385

INDEX 477

Hollriegl, Eduard, (Austria) 29
Hollym Corporation (Republic of Korea) 236
Holmes McDougall Ltd (United Kingdom) 385
Holmes, The Sherlock, Society of London (United Kingdom) 413
Holon Literary Prize (Israel) 211
Holp Book Co Ltd (Japan) 226
Holsten Verlag Wolf Schenke KG (Federal Republic of Germany) 139
Holt-Blond Ltd (United Kingdom) 385
Holt-Saunders Ltd (United Kingdom) 385
Holt-Saunders Pty Ltd (Australia) 14
Holt-Saunders Pty Ltd (New Zealand) 270
Holtby, Winifred, Memorial Prize (United Kingdom) 414
Holy Land Map Co Ltd (Israel) 207
Holzapfel, Verlag Gebr, (Federal Republic of Germany) 139
Holzboog, Gunther, GmbH & Co (Federal Republic of Germany) 139
Holzmann, Hans, Verlag GmbH und Co KG (Federal Republic of Germany) 139
Home and Garden Guild (United Kingdom) 409
Home Health Education Service (United Kingdom) 385
Home Library Plan (India) 195
Home Products Ltd (Fiji) 84
Hommes et Techniques, Editions, (France) 98
Hone, Evelyn, College Library (Zambia) 428
Hong Kong Book Centre (Hong Kong) 176
Hong Kong Booksellers' & Stationers' Association (Hong Kong) 175
Hong Kong Cultural Press Ltd (Hong Kong) 175
Hong Kong Educational Publishers Association Ltd (Hong Kong) 175
Hong Kong Junior Chamber of Commerce Libraries (Hong Kong) 176
Hong Kong Library Association (Hong Kong) 176
Hong Kong Polytechnic Library (Hong Kong) 176
Hong Kong Publishers' & Distributors' Association (Hong Kong) 175
Hong Kong University Press (Hong Kong) 175
Hong Kong Witman Publishing Co (Hong Kong) 175
Hönsetryk, Forlaget, (Denmark) 75
Hoogenhout, C P, Award (Republic of South Africa) 313
Hoogt, Lucy B en C W van der, Prize (Netherlands) 267
Hoorick, Van, Verlag (Switzerland) 342
Hope Leresche & Sayle (United Kingdom) 408
Hopkins, The, Society (United Kingdom) 413
Hor Samut Klang (Thailand) 354
Horatio-verlag und Agentur (Federal Republic of Germany) 139
Horay, Pierre, Editeur (France) 98
Horizon Bookshop Ltd (New Zealand) 272
Horizons, Editions, de France (France) 98
Horizonte, Editorial, (Peru) 286
Horizonte, Editorial, (Peru) 287
Horizonte, Livros, Lda (Portugal) 296
Horizontes, Editora, de América (Dominican Republic) 80
Hörnemann, Werner, Verlag (Federal Republic of Germany) 139
Horseman's Bookclub (United Kingdom) 409
Horst-Werner Dumjahn Verlag (Federal Republic of Germany) 139
Horwitz Grahame Books Pty Ltd (Australia) 14
Horwood, Ellis, Ltd (United Kingdom) 385
'Horyzonty', Wydawnictwo Harcerskie, (Poland) 291
Høst og Søns Forlag (Denmark) 75
Hour-Glass Press (United Kingdom) 385
Hove, M van, DPN (Belgium) 37
Høvring's, Birgitte, Icelandic World Literature (Denmark) 75
How & Why Books (United Kingdom) 385
Howard Book Co (Hong Kong) 176
Howard & Wyndham Ltd (United Kingdom) 385
Hraundragni Book Club (Iceland) 180
Hrvatska Revija (Spain) 318
Hrvatsko bibliotekarsko društvo (Yugoslavia) 426
Hsinhua New China Book Agency (People's Republic of China) 63
Hua Kuo Publishing Co (China (Taiwan)) 64
Huber, Edition Volker, (Federal Republic of Germany) 139
Huber, Hans, (Switzerland) 351
Huber, Hans, AG (Switzerland) 342
Huber, Verlag, & Co AG (Switzerland) 342
Hudsons Bookshops Ltd (United Kingdom) 410
Hueber-Holzmann Pädagogischer Verlag (Federal Republic of Germany) 139
Hueber, Max, Verlag (Federal Republic of Germany) 139
Huemul, Editorial, SA (Argentina) 5
Huemul, Librería, (Argentina) 5
Huemul, Libreria, (Argentina) 8
Hugendubel, Buchhandlung H, (Federal Republic of Germany) 165
Hughes Massie Ltd (United Kingdom) 408
Hugo, The, Awards (International Literary Prizes) 442
Hugo's Language Books Ltd (United Kingdom) 385
Hugues, Clovis, Prize (France) 111

Hulsmanns & Reske GmbH (Federal Republic of Germany) 139
Hulton Educational Publications Ltd (United Kingdom) 385
Human & Rousseau Publishers (Pty) Ltd (Republic of South Africa) 309
Humanismo, Editôra de, Ciência e Tecnologia (Brazil) 51
Humanitas, Editorial, (Argentina) 5
Humanoïdes, Les, Associés (France) 98
Humata Verlag Harold S Blume (Switzerland) 343
Humboldt-Buchhandlung (German Democratic Republic) 117
Humboldt-Taschenbuchverlag Jacobi KG (Federal Republic of Germany) 139
Humboldt Universität zu Berlin (German Democratic Republic) 117
Humboldt, Volksbuchhandlung Alexander von, (German Democratic Republic) 117
Hundertmark, Edition, (Federal Republic of Germany) 140
Hune, La, (France) 98
Hune, Librairie La, (France) 108
Hung Fung Book Co (Hong Kong) 175
Hungarian Foreign Trade Organization (Hungary) 178
Hür Yayin ve Ticaret (Turkey) 358
Hürriyet Yayinlari (Hür Yayin) (Turkey) 358
Hurst, C, & Co (Publisher's) Ltd (United Kingdom) 385
Husain, Dr Mahmud, Library (Pakistan) 283
Husum Druck- und Verlagsgesellschaft mbH und Co KG (Federal Republic of Germany) 140
Hutchinson Educational (United Kingdom) 385
Hutchinson General Books Ltd (United Kingdom) 385
Hutchinson Group (Australia) Ltd (Australia) 14
Hutchinson Group (NZ) Ltd (New Zealand) 270
Hutchinson Group (SA) (Pty) Ltd (Republic of South Africa) 309
Hutchinson Junior Books (United Kingdom) 385
Hutchinson Publishing Group, The, Ltd (United Kingdom) 385
Hutchinson Technical Books (United Kingdom) 385
Hutchinson University Library (United Kingdom) 385
Hüthig, Dr Alfred, Verlag GmbH (Federal Republic of Germany) 140
Hüthig und Pflaum Verlag GmbH & Co KG (Federal Republic of Germany) 140
Huthig und Wepf Verlag (Switzerland) 343
Hutten, Ulrich v, Volksbuchhandlung (German Democratic Republic) 117
Huygens, Constantijn, Prize (Netherlands) 267
Hviezdoslavova knižnica (Czechoslovakia) 72
Hwimoon Publishing Co (Republic of Korea) 236
Hyangmun Sa (Republic of Korea) 236
Hyderabad, The, & Secunderabad Publishers' & Booksellers' Association (India) 181
Hyfte, Van, -De Coninck (Belgium) 37
Hyland House Publishing Pty Ltd (Australia) 14
Hylton Lacy Publishers (United Kingdom) 385
Hyoronsha Publishing Co Ltd (Japan) 226
Hyun Am Sa (Republic of Korea) 236
Hyun Dae Mun Hak (Republic of Korea) 238
Hyun Dae Mun Hak Prize (Republic of Korea) 238

I B A M (Brazil) 51
I B E P (Brazil) 51
I B I (India) 186
I B I C T (Brazil) 51
I B I S (United Kingdom) 364
I B I S Information Services Ltd (Australia) 9
I B R A S A (Instituição Brasileira de Difusão Cultural SA) (Brazil) 51
I B R E X - Distribuidora de Livros e Material de Escritório Ltda (Brazil) 55
I C A-Förlaget AB (Sweden) 330
I C C E, Publicaciones, (Spain) 318
I C I C (Directory Publishers) Ltd (Nigeria) 275
I C I Writing Bursary (New Zealand) 273
I C Magazines Ltd (United Kingdom) 385
I C S Izdavačko Informativni Centar Studenata (Yugoslavia) 422
I C U-België, NV, (Belgium) 37
I C U, NV, (Informatie en Communicatie Unie NV) (Netherlands) 260
I D E P (Senegal) 303
I d W-Verlag GmbH (Federal Republic of Germany) 140
I G A, Distribuidora Cultural, (Guatemala) 173
I L A (International Literary Agency) (Italy) 220
I L E X I M — Foreign Trade Enterprise (Romania) 301
I L S (Institut für Lernsysteme) GmbH (Federal Republic of Germany) 140
I M S F (Federal Republic of Germany) 140
I N A D E S — Edition (Institut africain pour le developpement économique et social) (Ivory Coast) 223

I N A D E S (Institut africain pour le Développement économique et social) Documentation (Ivory Coast) 223
I N B E L (Belgium) 37
I N I D (Romania) 301
I P C (United Kingdom) 385
I P E A (Instituto de Planejamento Econômico e Social) Servico Editorial (Brazil) 51
I P L (Istituto Propaganda Libraria) (Italy) 211
I S B N, Bureau, (Netherlands) 255
I S P-Verlag (Internationale Sozialistische Publikationen) (Federal Republic of Germany) 140
I T A U, Edições, (Instituto Tecnico de Alimentaçao Humana) Lda (Portugal) 296
I T V Books (United Kingdom) 385
I V A C (Belgium) 37
I V A Verlag Bernd Polke GmbH (Federal Republic of Germany) 140
I V I O, Stichting, (Netherlands) 260
Ibadan University Library (Nigeria) 277
Ibadan University Press (Nigeria) 275
Ibana, SA (Uruguay) 417
Ibérico Europea de Ediciones SA (Spain) 318
Iberlibros — Unidad de Exportación (Spain) 318
Ibero-Americano, Livro, (Brazil) 55
Ibero-Americano, Livro, Ltda (Brazil) 51
Ibero-Amerikanisches Institut (Federal Republic of Germany) 166
Ibn-Sina Publishers (Iran) 201
Ibnassus Presse (Federal Republic of Germany) 140
Iceland Review (Iceland) 179
Iceland Travel Books (Iceland) 179
Icelandic Libertarians', The, Book Club (Iceland) 180
Icelandic Libertarians', The, Bookshop (Iceland) 180
Ichtiar Baru (Indonesia) 199
Icob cv (Netherlands) 266
Icob cv Uitgeverij (Netherlands) 260
Icon (Belgium) 44
Icthus, Librería, (Bolivia) 46
Idara-e-Faroghe-Undu (Pakistan) 282
Idara Siqafat-e-Islamia (Pakistan) 282
Idarah-I-Adabiyat-I-Delli (India) 186
Idea Books Distribution SA (France) 98
Idea Editions (Italy) 215
Idea Editions (Switzerland) 343
Idea Editions Distribution (United Kingdom) 385
Ideal Leather, The, Store Ltd (Trinidad and Tobago) 356
Ideal, The, Bookshop (Malta) 246
Ideeboek BV (Netherlands) 260
Ides et Calendes SA (Switzerland) 343
Idion Verlag (Federal Republic of Germany) 140
Idunn (Iceland) 179
Ie-No-Hikari Association (Japan) 226
Ife Book Fair Prizes (Nigeria) 278
Igaku-Shoin Ltd (Japan) 226
Igbo Language Translation Agency (Nigeria) 278
Ikaros Ekdotiki (Greece) 171
Ikatan Pustakawan Indonesia (Indonesia) 200
Ikhwan, PD & I, (Indonesia) 199
Ikubundo Publishers Co (Japan) 231
Il Cho Kak (Republic of Korea) 236
Il Ji Sa (Republic of Korea) 237
Il Shinsa (Republic of Korea) 237
Ilesanmi Press & Sons (N) Ltd (Nigeria) 275
Ilidio da Fonseca Matos (Portugal) 298
Illustration, Editions de l', (France) 98
Ilm, Dar al-, Bookshop (Saudi Arabia) 302
Ilm, Dar el-, Lilmalayin (Lebanon) 239
Ilmi Kitab Khana (Pakistan) 282
Image (United Kingdom) 386
Imba Verlag (Switzerland) 343
Imha (Greece) 171
Impact (Australia) 14
Impacto, Editõrial e Serviços Ltda (Brazil) 51
Imparudi (Burundi) 60
Imperial Library (Iran) 201
Imperial News Agency and Bookshop (Gibraltar) 170
Imprensa Nacional-Casa da Moeda (Portugal) 296
Impressum Verlag AG (Switzerland) 343
Imprimerie Commerciale et Administrative de Mauritanie (Mauritania) 247
Imprimerie, Editions, Fédérative SA Berne (Switzerland) 343
Imprint Academic (United Kingdom) 386
Imprint Editions Ltd (United Kingdom) 386
Imprint Society (Australia) 9
Impulso (Mexico) 250
In den Toren, Uitgeverij, (Netherlands) 260
In, Uitgeverij J van, (Belgium) 37
Inba Nilayam (India) 186
Inca, Promotion Editorial, SA (Peru) 286
Incafo, Editorial, SA (Spain) 318
Independent Publishers Guild (United Kingdom) 364
Independent Television Books Ltd (United Kingdom) 386
Index, Editorial, (Tormes, SL) (Spain) 318
Index eV (Federal Republic of Germany) 140
India Book House (India) 186
India Book House (India) 196
India Book House Education Trust (India) 186

478 INDEX

India Book House (P) Ltd (India) 186
India Office Library and Records (United Kingdom) 411
Indian Association of Academic Librarians (India) 196
Indian Association of Special Libraries and Information Centres (India) 196
Indian Council for Cultural Relations (India) 186
Indian Council of Agricultural Research (India) 186
Indian Council of Medical Research (India) 186
Indian Council of Social Science Research (India) 186
Indian Council of Social Science Research Library (India) 196
Indian Council of World Affairs Library (India) 196
Indian Documentation Service (India) 187
Indian Institute of Advanced Study (India) 187
Indian Institute of Technology Central Library (India) 196
Indian Institute of World Culture (India) 187
Indian Library Association (India) 196
Indian Museum (India) 187
Indian National Academy of Letters (Sahitya Akademi) Awards (India) 197
Indian National Scientific Documentation Centre (India) 198
Indian Press (Publications) Pvt Ltd (India) 187
Indian Printing and Publishing Co (Fiji) 84
Indian Publications (India) 187
Indian Publishing House (India) 187
Indian Society for Promoting Christian Knowledge (I S P C K) (India) 187
Indira, P T, (Indonesia) 199
Indira, P T, (Indonesia) 200
Indrajaya (Indonesia) 199
Industrias ABC (Angola) 2
Industrias ABC (Angola) 2
Industrielle Organisation, Verlag, (Switzerland) 343
Industrielle Rettsvern, Styret for det, Bibliotek (Norway) 281
Industry Publishing House (Democratic People's Republic of Korea) 236
Industry & Trade Publishers (Philippines) 288
Info Book (Sweden) 334
Infoboek (Belgium) 37
Información, La, (Dominican Republic) 80
Informare si Documentare, Institutul National de, (INID) (Romania) 301
Information Processing Association of Israel (Israel) 210
Informations Forlag ApS (Denmark) 75
Informations-Zentrum Buch (Federal Republic of Germany) 119
Informator (Yugoslavia) 422
Ingeniero, Librería del, (Colombia) 66
Ingenjörsvetenskapsakademien (I V A) (Sweden) 330
Initial Teaching, The, Alphabet Foundation (United Kingdom) 386
Ink Links Ltd (United Kingdom) 386
Inkata Press Pty Ltd (Australia) 14
Inkilâp Ve Aka Kitabevleri (Turkey) 358
Inland Publishers (Tanzania) 353
Inn-Verlag (Austria) 25
Innkaupasamband Boksala (Booksellers' Import Union Ltd) (Iceland) 179
Innovacion, Editorial, SA (Mexico) 250
Inpra International Press Agency (United Kingdom) 408
Inquérito, Editorial, Lda (Portugal) 296
Insel, Inform-Verlag (Federal Republic of Germany) 140
Insel Verlag (Federal Republic of Germany) 140
Insel-Verlag Anton Kippenberg (German Democratic Republic) 116
Instituição Brasileira de Difusão Cultural SA (Brazil) 51
Institut africain de Développement économique et de Planification (IDEP) (Senegal) 303
Institut belge d'Information et de Documentation (INBEL) (Belgium) 38
Institut belge d'Information et de Documentation (INBEL) (Belgium) 43
Institut, Bibliothèque de l', français d'Archéologie (Lebanon) 240
Institut Culturel Français Bibliothèque (Libya) 241
Institut Dagang Muchtar (Indonesia) 199
Institut de Bibliothéconomie et des Sciences Documentaires (Algeria) 2
Institut de France, Bibliotheque de l', (France) 108
Institut d'Egypte Library (Egypt) 82
Institut des Belles Lettres arabes (Tunisia) 357
Institut fondamental d'Afrique noire (Senegal) 303
Institut français d'Archéologie orientale (Egypt) 82
Institut für Heilpäcagogik Verlag (Switzerland) 343
Institut für Jugendbuchforschung der J W Goethe-Universität (Federal Republic of Germany) 167
Institut für Lernsysteme (ILS) (Federal Republic of Germany) 140
Institut für Marxistische Studien und Forschungen eV (IMSF) Frankfurt am Main (Federal Republic of Germany) 140
Institut Murundi d'Information et de Documentation (IMIDOC) (Burundi) 60
Institut national de Recherches et Documentation (National Research and Documentation Institute) (Guinea) 174
Institut national de Sténodactylographie (Belgium) 38
Institut national, Librairie de l', d'Etudes politiques (Zaire) 427
Institut pédagogique national (Zaire) 427
Institut, Perpustakaan Pusat, Teknologi Bandung (Indonesia) 200
Institut polytechnique de Conakry (Guinea) 174
Institut polytechnique de l'Afrique centrale (Gabon) 113
Institut royal des Relations internationales (Belgium) 38
Institut royal des Sciences naturelles de Belgique, Service de Documentation (Belgium) 43
Institut scientifique chérifien (Morocco) 254
Institut Universitaire de Hautes Etudes Internationales (Switzerland) 343
Institute, Central, for Scientific and Technical Information (of the State Committee for Science, Technical Progress and Higher Education) (Bulgaria) 58
Institute for Palestine Studies, Publishing and Research Organization (Lebanon) 239
Institute for Scientific and Technical Documentation and Information (Yugoslavia) 425
Institute for the Talmudic Encyclopaedia and Complete Israeli Talmud (Israel) 207
Institute of Arab Research & Studies Library (Egypt) 82
Institute of Economics Library (Burma) 59
Institute of Education Library (Burma) 59
Institute of Education Library, Kabul University (Afghanistan) 1
Institute of Information Scientists (United Kingdom) 411
Institute of Personnel Management (United Kingdom) 386
Institute of Petroleum (United Kingdom) 386
Institute of Physics, The, (United Kingdom) 386
Institute of Public Administration (Republic of Ireland) 203
Institute of Public Administration Library (Saudi Arabia) 303
Institute of Pyramidology (United Kingdom) 386
Institute of Reprographic Technology (United Kingdom) 411
Institute of Southeast Asian Studies (Republic of Singapore) 305
Institute of Technology, Rangoon, Library (Burma) 59
Institute, The, for the Translation of Hebrew Literature Ltd (Israel) 205
Institute, The, for the Translation of Hebrew Literature Ltd (Israel) 211
Institution of Civil Engineers, The, (Publications Division) (United Kingdom) 386
Institution of Electrical Engineers (United Kingdom) 386
Instituto Anglo-Mexicano de Cultura, Biblioteca del, (Mexico) 252
Instituto Autónomo Biblioteca Nacional y de Servicios de Bibliotecas (Venezuela) 419
Instituto Bibliográfico Hispánico (Spain) 324
Instituto, Biblioteca del, Chileno-Británico de Cultura (Chile) 62
Instituto Brasileiro de Administraçao Municipal (IBAM) (Brazil) 51
Instituto Brasileiro de Edições Pedagógicas (IBEP) (Brazil) 51
Instituto Brasileiro de Geografia, Fundação, e Estatística (Brazil) 51
Instituto Brasileiro de Informação em Ciência e Tecnologia (IBICT) (Brazil) 51
Instituto Brasileiro de Informação em Ciência e Tecnologia (IBICT) (Brazil) 56
Instituto Campineiro de Ensino Agrícola (Brazil) 51
Instituto Centro Americano de Administración Pública (ICAP) (Costa Rica) 67
Instituto Cubano del Libro (Cuba) 68
Instituto Cultural, Biblioteca del, Anglo-Uruguayo (Uruguay) 417
Instituto de Bibliográfia del Ministerio de Educación de la Provincia de Buenos Aires (Argentina) 8
Instituto de Cultura, Biblioteca del, Hispánica (Spain) 324
Instituto de Cultura Puertorriqueña (Puerto Rico) 299
Instituto de Estudios de Administración Local, Publicaciones (Spain) 318
Instituto de Estudios Peruanos (Peru) 286
Instituto de Estudios Politicos (Spain) 318
Instituto de Investigaciones Bibliográficas (Mexico) 252
Instituto de Investigaciones Sociales — Universidad Nacional Autonoma de Mexico (Mexico) 250
Instituto de Literatura (Argentina) 9
Instituto de Literatura, Biblioteca del, y Linguistica (Cuba) 68
Instituto de Planejamento Econômico e Social (Brazil) 51
Instituto de Publicaciones Navales (Argentina) 5
Instituto Indigenista Interamericano (Mexico) 250
Instituto Interamericano de Ciencias Agricolas (IICA) (Costa Rica) 67
Instituto Mexicano del Libro, AC (Mexico) 248
Instituto Nacional, Biblioteca del, del Libro Español (Spain) 324
Instituto Nacional de Antropologia e Historia (Mexico) 250
Instituto Nacional de Bellas Artes (Mexico) 250
Instituto Nacional del Libro Español (Spain) 314
Instituto Nacional del Libro Español, Delegación de Barcelona (Spain) 314
Instituto Nacional do Livro (Brazil) 47
Instituto Nacional do Livro e do Disco (Mozambique) 254
Instituto Panamericano de Geografía, Biblioteca del, e Historia (Mexico) 252
Instituto Panamericano de Geografía e Historia (Mexico) 250
Instituto Pontificio, Ediciones, San Pío X (Spain) 319
Instituto Português da Sociedade Científica de Goerres (Portuguese Institute of the Goerres Research Society) (Portugal) 298
Instituto Pre-universitario, Biblioteca del, de la Habana (Cuba) 68
Instituto Tecnico de Alimentaçao Humana (Portugal) 296
Instituto Tecnológico, Biblioteca del, y de Estudios Superiores de Monterrey (Mexico) 252
Instituto Venezolano, Biblioteca del, de Investigaciones Científicas (Venezuela) 419
Instituts für Weltwirtschaft, Bibliothek des, — Zentralbibliothek der Wirtschaftswissenschaften (Federal Republic of Germany) 166
Instytut Badań Literackich (Poland) 294
Instytut Bibliograficzny (Poland) 293
Instytut, Państwowy, Wydawniczy (Poland) 291
Insula (Spain) 324
Insula, Ediciones y Publicaciones de, (Spain) 319
Intellectual Publishing House (India) 187
Intellectual Society of Libya (Libya) 241
Inter American University of Puerto Rico Library (Puerto Rico) 299
Inter Documentation Co AG (Switzerland) 343
Inter-European Editions (Netherlands) 260
Inter-Governmental Maritime Consultative Organization (IMCO) (International Organizations) 434
Inter-India Publications (India) 187
Inter-Kunst und Buch GmbH (Federal Republic of Germany) 140
Inter-Médica, Editorial, SAICI (Argentina) 5
Inter-Varsity Press (United Kingdom) 386
Interallié Prize (France) 111
Interamericana de Venezuela, Editorial, CA (Venezuela) 419
Interamericana del Uruguay, Editorial, SA (Uruguay) 417
'Interavia' SA (Société anonyme d'Editions aéronautiques internationales) (Switzerland) 343
Interbankendienst, Uitgaven van, NV (Belgium) 38
Interbooks (Belgium) 43
Interciencia, Livraria, Ltda (Brazil) 51
Intercontinental Book Productions Ltd (United Kingdom) 386
Intercontinental Literary Agency (United Kingdom) 408
InterEditions Paris (France) 98
Interessengemeinschaft Musikwissenschaftlicher Herausgeber und Verleger (IHMV) (Federal Republic of Germany) 119
Interfrom, Edition, (Switzerland) 343
Intergéo, CNRS Laboratoire, (France) 98
Intergovernmental Copyright Committee (International Organizations) 432
Interkerklike Uitgewerstrust (Republic of South Africa) 309
Internationaal Instituut, Bibliotheek van het, voor Sociale Geschiedenis (Netherlands) 266
International African Institute (International Organizations) 436
International Association for Mass Communication Research (International Organizations) 432
International Association of Agricultural Librarians and Documentalists — IAALD (International Organizations) 432
International Association of Law Libraries (IALL) (International Organizations) 432
International Association of Literary Critics (International Organizations) 432
International Association of Metropolitan City Libraries (INTAMEL) (International Organizations) 432
International Association of Music Libraries (International Organizations) 432
International Association of Music Libraries, Australia/New Zealand Branch (New Zealand) 272
International Association of Music Libraries, Australia/New Zealand Branch (IAMLANZ) (Australia) 20
International Association of Music Libraries (UK Branch) (United Kingdom) 411
International Association of Orientalist Librarians (International Organizations) 432
International Association of Scholarly Publishers (IASP) (International Organizations) 432
International Association of School Librarianship (International Organizations) 432
International Association of Sound Archives (International Organizations) 432
International Association of Technological University Libraries (IATUL) (International Organizations) 432
International Atomic Energy Agency (IAEA) (International Organizations) 434

INDEX 479

International Bible Reading Association (United Kingdom) 386
International Biographical Centre (United Kingdom) 386
International Board on Books for Young People (IBBY) (International Organizations) 433
International Book Distributors Co Ltd (Thailand) 355
International Book House (Pvt) Ltd (India) 196
International Book Information Services (United Kingdom) 364
International Book Traders (India) 196
International Booksellers Federation (IBF) (International Organizations) 433
International Bookshop (Tanzania) 353
International Bookshop, The, (Iceland) 180
International Bureau of Education (International Organizations) 434
International Bureau voor Auteursrecht BV (Netherlands) 266
International Children's Book Service (Denmark) 77
International Communication Agency Library (Guinea) 174
International Communication Agency Library (Republic of Korea) 238
International Communication Agency Library (Liberia) 240
International Communication Agency Library (Democratic Republic of Madagascar) 243
International Communication Agency Library (Sierra Leone) 304
International Communication Agency Library (Tanzania) 353
International Communication Agency Library (Uganda) 359
International Communications (United Kingdom) 386
International Comparative Literature Association (International Organizations) 433
International Confederation of Societies of Authors and Composers (International Organizations) 433
International Copyright Union for the Protection of Literary and Artistic Works (International Organizations) 433
International Correspondence Schools Ltd (United Kingdom) 386
International Council of Theological Library Associations (International Organizations) 433
International Council on Archives (International Organizations) 433
International Documentary, The, Centre of Arab Manuscripts (Lebanon) 239
International Editors' Co (Argentina) 8
International Editors' Co (Brazil) 55
International Editors' Co SA (Spain) 323
International Federation for Documentation (FID) (International Organizations) 433
International Federation of Film Archives (International Organizations) 433
International Federation of Library Associations and Institutions (IFLA) (International Organizations) 433
International Fiction Association (International Organizations) 433
International Grand Prize for Poetry (International Literary Prizes) 442
International Group of Scientific, Technical and Medical Publishers (STM) (International Organizations) 433
International Institute for Children's Literature and Reading Research, UNESCO category C (International Organizations) 433
International Institute for Educational Planning (IIEP) (International Organizations) 434
International Institute of Advanced Buddhistic Studies Library (Burma) 59
International Institute of Iberoamerican Literature (International Organizations) 433
International Institute of Tropical Agriculture Library (Nigeria) 277
International Labour Office Library (ILO) (Switzerland) 352
International Labour Organisation (ILO) (International Organizations) 434
International League of Antiquarian Booksellers (International Organizations) 433
International Literary Braille Competition Awards (International Literary Prizes) 442
International Literatuur Bureau BV (Netherlands) 266
International Nursing, The, Foundation of Japan (Japan) 226
International Press Agency (Ethiopia) 83
International Press, The, Agency (Pty) Ltd (Republic of South Africa) 311
International Prize for the First Novel (International Literary Prizes) 442
International Prize of French Friendship (International Literary Prizes) 442
International Progressive Books and Periodicals Store (Nepal) 255
International Publication Cultural Award (International Literary Prizes) 442

International Publications Cultural Prize (International Literary Prizes) 442
International Publishers' Aid (IPA) (Belgium) 38
International Publishers Association (International Organizations) 433
International Publishing Corporation Ltd (United Kingdom) 386
International Reading Association (International Organizations) 433
International Science Service (Israel) 207
International Scientific Film Library (ISFL) (International Organizations) 433
International Society for Educational Information Inc (Japan) 226
International Study Group of Restorers of Archives, Libraries and Graphic Reproductions (International Organizations) 433
International Telecommunication Union (ITU) (International Organizations) 435
International Textbook Co Ltd (United Kingdom) 386
International Translations Centre (International Organizations) 433
International Union for Conservation of Nature and Natural Resources (IUCN) (International Organizations) 436
International Union of Geological Sciences (IUGS) (International Organizations) 436
International Who's Who in Poetry Awards (International Literary Prizes) 442
International Writers Workshop New Zealand Inc (New Zealand) 272
International Youth Library (International Organizations) 433
Internationale Buchhändler-Vereinigung (IBV) (International Organizations) 433
Internationale Pers, De, (Belgium) 38
Internationale Presse, Import- und Export GmbH (Federal Republic of Germany) 165
Internationale Solidarität, Verlag, Verlagsgesellschaft mbH (Federal Republic of Germany) 140
Internationale Vereinigung der Musikbibliotheken, Deutsche Gruppe BRD (Federal Republic of Germany) 167
'Interpress', Wydawnictwo, (Poland) 291
Interpresse, A/S, (Denmark) 75
Interprint (India) 187
Interpublishing AB Rahm and Stenström (Sweden) 330
Intersea (Argentina) 5
Interskrift Publishing House (Sweden) 330
Intertrade Publications (India) Pvt Ltd (India) 187
Ipler, Editorial, Ltda (Colombia) 65
Iranian Documentation Centre (IRANDOC) (Iran) 201
Iranian Publishers' Association (Iran) 201
Iraq Library Association (Iraq) 202
Iraq Museum, Library of the, (Iraq) 202
Iraq Natural History, Library of the, Research Centre and Museum (Iraq) 202
Iris Verlag AG (Switzerland) 343
Irish Academic Press (Republic of Ireland) 203
Irish Academy of Letters (Republic of Ireland) 205
Irish-American Cultural Institute Literary Awards (International Literary Prizes) 442
Irish Association for Documentation and Information Services (IADIS), The National Library of Ireland (Republic of Ireland) 205
Irish Book Publishers' Association (Republic of Ireland) 202
Irish Educational Publishers' Association (Republic of Ireland) 202
Irish Heritage Series (Republic of Ireland) 203
Irish Humanities Centre and Keohanes (Republic of Ireland) 203
Irish Management Institute (Republic of Ireland) 203
Irish Microforms (Republic of Ireland) 203
Irish Society for Archives (Republic of Ireland) 205
Irish Times, The, Ltd (Republic of Ireland) 203
Irish University Press (Republic of Ireland) 203
Irisiana Druck und Verlag (Federal Republic of Germany) 140
Ísafoldar, Bókaverzlun, (Iceland) 180
Ísafoldarprentsmidja hf (Iceland) 179
Iselt und Co Nfl mbH (Federal Republic of Germany) 140
Ishiyaku Publishers Inc (Japan) 226
Isis, Edition, (Federal Republic of Germany) 140
'Iskry', Państwowe Wydawnictwo, (Poland) 291
Iskusstvo, Izdatelstvo, (Union of Soviet Socialist Republics) 361
Islam, Perpustakaan, (Indonesia) 200
Islam, Verlag der, (Federal Republic of Germany) 140
Islamabad University Library (Pakistan) 283
Islami Kitab Khana (Pakistan) 282
Islamia Library (Bangladesh) 32
Islamic Book Centre (Pakistan) 282
Islamic Cultural Bookshop (Bahrain) 31
Islamic Culture, Institute of, (Pakistan) 282
Islamic Foundation, The, (United Kingdom) 386
Islamic Publications Bureau (Nigeria) 275
Islamic Publications Ltd (Pakistan) 282

Islamic Research Institute (Pakistan) 282
Islamic Research Institute Library (Pakistan) 283
Islamic University Library (Saudi Arabia) 303
Islamiyah (Indonesia) 199
Island Press (Australia) 14
Island, The, Shop (Bahamas) 31
Íslenzka bókmenntafélag (Iceland) 180
Íslenzka Bókmenntafélag, Hid, (Iceland) 179
Isopang Publishing Pty Ltd (Papua New Guinea) 285
Israbook (Israel) 210
Israel Academy, The, of Sciences & Humanities (Israel) 207
Israel, B M, BV (Netherlands) 260
Israel Book Importers' Association (Israel) 205
Israel Exploration Society (Israel) 207
Israel ISBN Group Agency (Israel) 205
Israel Library Association (Israel) 210
Israel, Nico, (Netherlands) 260
Israel Program for Scientific Translations (Israel) 207
Israel Society of Special Libraries and Information Centres (ISLIC) (Israel) 210
Israel State Archives (Israel) 210
Israel Universities Press (Israel) 207
Israel Yearbook Publications (Israel) 207
Israeli Music Publications Ltd (Israel) 207
Israeli Prize in Humanities and Social Sciences (Israel) 211
Israeli Prize in Jewish Studies, Hebrew Literature and Education (Israel) 211
Israeli Prize in the Arts (Israel) 211
Istanbul Üniversitesi Merkez Kütüphanesi (Turkey) 359
Istiklal, Al, Library (Jordan) 233
Istituto Centrale di Statistica (Italy) 215
Istituto Centrale per il Catalogo Unico delle Biblioteche Italiane e per le Informazioni Bibliografiche (Italy) 221
Istituto Centrale per la Patologia del Libro (Italy) 221
Istituto della Enciclopedia Italiana (Italy) 215
Istituto Editoriale Italiano SpA (Italy) 215
Istituto Geografico de Agostini SpA (Italy) 215
Istituto Italiano D'Arti Grafiche (Italy) 215
Istituto Lombardo Accademia di Scienze e Lettere (Italy) 222
Istituto Poligrafico e Zecca dello Stato (Italy) 215
Istmo, Ediciones, (Spain) 319
Istra, Librairie, Sàrl (France) 98
Italian Book Club (United Kingdom) 409
Ittihad, Al, Bookstore (Egypt) 82
Iwanami Shoten (Japan) 226
Iwasaki Shoten Co Ltd (Japan) 226
Izmir General Library (Turkey) 359
Izrael Publishing House Ltd (Israel) 207
Iztaccihuatl, Editorial, SA (Mexico) 250
Iztaccihuatl, Librerías, (Mexico) 252
Izvestiya Publishing House (Union of Soviet Socialist Republics) 361

J A, Groupe, (Editions J A) (France) 98
J B, Taller Ediciones, (Spain) 319
J K Export House (India) 196
J R O-Kartografische Verlagsgesellschaft mbH (Federal Republic of Germany) 140
Jaca Book Edizioni (Italy) 215
Jacaranda Wiley Ltd (Australia) 14
Jacaranda Wiley Ltd (New Zealand) 270
Jackdaw Publications Ltd (United Kingdom) 386
Jacobi Verlag GmbH (Federal Republic of Germany) 140
Jaeger, H-K de, Publications (ASTRID) (Belgium) 38
Jaeger und Waldmann (Federal Republic of Germany) 140
Jafet, Nami C, Memorial Library (Lebanon) 240
Jaffe Books (India) 187
Jaffe Books (India) 195
Jaffe Books (India) 196
Jäggi, Buchhandlung, AG (Switzerland) 351
Jahreszeitenverlag (Federal Republic of Germany) 140
J'ai Lu, Editions, (France) 98
Jaico Book Shop (India) 196
Jaico Publishing House (India) 187
Jain Publishers, B (India) 187
Jain Publishing Co (India) 187
Jaipur Publishing House (India) 187
Jakobsohn, Verlag Eduard, (Federal Republic of Germany) 140
Jaktjournalens Bokklubb (Sweden) 334
Jal-Verlag/Jal-Reprint Arnulf Liebing (Federal Republic of Germany) 140
Jamaica Archives (Jamaica) 224
Jamaica Library Association (Jamaica) 224
Jamaica Library Service (Jamaica) 224
Jamaica Publishing House Ltd (Jamaica) 223
James, Arthur, Ltd (United Kingdom) 386
Jamjoom, Mohamed Noor Salah, & Bros (Saudi Arabia) 302

Jane's Publishing Company Ltd (United Kingdom) 386
Jannersten Förlag AB (Sweden) 331
Janssen, Stern-Verlag, und Co (Federal Republic of Germany) 140
Janssens, J, (Belgium) 38
Januka Pustak Bhandar (Nepal) 255
Japadre, L U, Editore (Italy) 216
Japan Book Importers' Association (Japan) 224
Japan Book Publishers' Association (Japan) 224
Japan Broadcast Publishing Co Ltd (Japan) 226
Japan Contemporary Poets' Society (Japan) 232
Japan Essayists' Club (Japan) 232
Japan Essayists' Club Prize (Japan) 232
Japan Poet Club (Japan) 232
Japan Poet Club Prize (Japan) 233
Japan Publications Inc (Japan) 231
Japan Publications Trading Co Ltd (Import and Export) (Japan) 231
Japan Society of Translators (Japan) 233
Japan Times (Japan) 226
Japan Translation Prize (International Literary Prizes) 442
Japan Translation Prize for Publisher (Japan) 233
Japan Travel Bureau Inc (Japan) 226
Japan Uni Agency Inc (Japan) 230
Japan Woman Writer Prize (Japan) 233
Japan Women Writers' Literary Prizes (Japan) 233
Jarrold Colour Publications (United Kingdom) 386
Jasomirgott-Verlag (Austria) 25
Jason Publishing Co Ltd (New Zealand) 270
Jaspert, Reinhard, (Federal Republic of Germany) 140
Jaya Baya, Yayasan, (Indonesia) 199
Jaya Murni (Indonesia) 199
Jaya, Penerbit, (Malaysia) 244
Jayawardena, J K G, & Co (Sri Lanka) 326
Jaypee Brothers (India) 187
Jazirah, Al, Organization for Press, Printing, Publishing (Saudi Arabia) 302
Jean-Charles, A (Martinique) 247
Jean-Christophe Prize (France) 111
Jecta (Belgium) 38
Jedinstvo (Yugoslavia) 422
Jeffers Bookstore (Trinidad and Tobago) 356
Jeheber, J H, SA (Switzerland) 343
Jeng's Bookshop (The Gambia) 114
Jeongeumsa Publishing Co (Republic of Korea) 237
Jerusalem City (Public) Library (Israel) 210
Jerusalem Publishing House Ltd (Israel) 207
Jerusalem, The, Prize (International Literary Prizes) 442
Jespersen og Pios Forlag (Denmark) 75
Jeune Afrique, Editions, (France) 98
Jeune France Prize (France) 111
Jeunesse d'Afrique, Librairie, (Upper Volta) 416
'Jeunesse et Afrique', Librairie, (Upper Volta) 416
Jeunesse et Poésie Prize (France) 111
Jeunesses littéraires de France (France) 109
Jewish Agency, The, (Israel) 207
Jewish Book Club, The, (United Kingdom) 409
Jewish Chronicle — Harold H Wingate Book Awards (International Literary Prizes) 442
Jewish National and University Library (Israel) 210
Jhanada Prakashan (India) 187
Jims, Editorial, SA (Spain) 319
Jing Kung Book Store (Hong Kong) 176
Jing Kung Educational Press (Hong Kong) 175
Jisik Sanup Sa (Republic of Korea) 237
Jnanpith Literary Award (India) 197
Joannides, A, & Co (Cyprus) 69
Johanesburgse Boekwinkel (Republic of South Africa) 312
Johannesburg Public Library (Republic of South Africa) 312
Johannesverlag Einsiedeln (Switzerland) 343
Johns Hopkins, The, University Press (United Kingdom) 387
Johnson Publications Ltd (United Kingdom) 387
Johnson Society of London (United Kingdom) 413
Johnston & Bacon Publishers (United Kingdom) 387
Joho Shori Gakkai (Japan) 231
Johore Central Store Sdn Bhd (Malaysia) 245
Jonckheere, Tobie, Prize (Belgium) 45
Jonef Publications (Philippines) 288
Jonge, Stichting De, Onderzoekers (Netherlands) 260
Jonker, Ingrid, Prize (Republic of South Africa) 313
Jonsson, Snaebjörn, & Co HF (The English Bookshop) (Iceland) 180
Jonsson, Sveinbjörn, (Iceland) 180
Jónssonar, Bókaútgáfa Thorsteins M, (Iceland) 180
Jordan Distribution Agency (Jordan) 233
Jordan Library Association (Jordan) 233
Jordan Press and Publishing Co Ltd (Jordan) 233
Jordan & Sons Ltd (United Kingdom) 387
Joseph, F (Haiti) 174
Joseph, Michael, Ltd (United Kingdom) 387
Journal des Notaires et des Avocats SA (France) 98
Journeyman, The, Press (United Kingdom) 387
Jovene, Casa Editrice Dr Eugenio, SpA (Italy) 216
Jover, Editorial, SA (Spain) 319

József Attila Tudományegyetem Központi Könyvtára (Hungary) 178
Jubilee Library Association (Burma) 59
Judía, Biblioteca Popular, (Argentina) 5
Judogi, Edition, (France) 98
Jugend und Volk Verlag GmbH (Federal Republic of Germany) 140
Jugend und Volk Verlagsgesellschaft mbH (Austria) 25
Jugenddienst-Verlag (Federal Republic of Germany) 140
Jugoreklam (Yugoslavia) 422
Jugoslavenske Academije, Izdavački Zavod, Znanosti i Umjetnosti (Yugoslavia) 422
Jugoslavenski Leksikografski Zavod (Yugoslavia) 422
Jugoslavija (Yugoslavia) 422
Jugoslovenska Autorska Agencija (Yugoslavia) 425
Jugoslovenska Knjiga (Yugoslavia) 425
Jugoslovenska Revija (Yugoslavia) 422
Jugoslovenski bibliografski institut (Yugoslavia) 426
Jugoslovenski centar za tehničku i naučnu dokumentaciju (Yugoslavia) 425
Julien, Stanislas, Prize (International Literary Prizes) 442
Julliard, Editions René, (France) 98
Jumsai, M (Laos) 239
Juncker, Axel-, -Verlag Jacobi KG (Federal Republic of Germany) 140
Jungbrunnen, Verlag, (Austria) 25
Junge Welt, Verlag, (German Democratic Republic) 116
Junimea, Editura, (Romania) 301
Junior International (Federal Republic of Germany) 141
Junior Puffin Club (United Kingdom) 409
Junk, Dr W, BV (Netherlands) 260
Junpa Kwahak Sa (Republic of Korea) 237
Junta de Educação Religiosa e Publicações da Convenção Batista Brasileira (Brazil) 51
Jupiter Books (London) Ltd (United Kingdom) 387
Jupiter, Editions, Sàrl (France) 98
Jurídica, Ediciones & Librería, (Argentina) 5
Jurídica, Editorial, de Chile (Chile) 62
Juridica-Verlag GmbH (Austria) 25
Jurif (Société d'Etudes Juridiques Internationales et Fiscales) (France) 99
Juris Druck & Verlag AG (Switzerland) 343
Jus, Editorial, SA (Mexico) 250
Jusautor (Bulgaria) 58
Just, Gertraude, (Austria) 29
Juta & Co Ltd (Republic of South Africa) 309
Juta & Co Ltd (Republic of South Africa) 312
Juteau-Duvigneaux Prize (France) 111
Juventa Verlag, Dr Martin Faltermaier (Federal Republic of Germany) 141
Juventud, Editorial, Argentina (Argentina) 6
Juventud, Editorial, Ltda (Colombia) 65
Juventud, Librería, (Bolivia) 46
Juventud, Librería y Editorial, (Bolivia) 46
Jyväskylän Yliopiston Kirjasto (Finland) 86

K & R Books Ltd (United Kingdom) 387
K B S (Netherlands) 260
K M C (Czechoslovakia) 72
K M P (Kruh milovníkov poézie) (Czechoslovakia) 72
Kabarole Public Library (Uganda) 359
Kabete Library (Kenya) 235
Kabul University, Institute of Geography (Afghanistan) 1
Kadokawa Shoten (Japan) 227
Kaduna, Library Board of, State (Nigeria) 277
Kaffke, Verlag Gerhard, (Federal Republic of Germany) 141
Kahn & Averill (United Kingdom) 387
Kahn, Lonnie, and Co Ltd (Israel) 210
Kaibundo Publishing Co Ltd (Japan) 227
Kairali Mudralayam (India) 187
Kairos, Editorial, SA (Spain) 319
Kairyudo Publishing Co Ltd (Japan) 227
Kaisei-Sha (Japan) 227
Kaiser, Buchhandlung Christian, (Federal Republic of Germany) 165
Kaiser, Chr, Verlag (Federal Republic of Germany) 141
Kaiser, Eduard, (Austria) 29
Kaitaku-Sha (Japan) 227
Kajima Institute Publishing Co Ltd (Japan) 227
Kakoulides, C (Greece) 172
Kalinga Prize (International Literary Prizes) 442
Kalleberger Foundation (Sweden) 336
Kaloudis, Gr, (Greece) 172
Kalyani Publishers (India) 187
Kamp, Verlag Ferdinand, GmbH & Co KG (Federal Republic of Germany) 141
Kampen, Uitgeverij Van, BV (Netherlands) 260
Kampen & Zoon, PN Van, BV (Netherlands) 260
Kanehara & Co Ltd (Japan) 227
Kanisius Verlag (Switzerland) 343
Kanisius, Yayasan, (Indonesia) 199

Kano State Library (Nigeria) 277
Kantonale Kommission für Jugend- und Volksbibliotheken, Zurich (Switzerland) 352
Kapelusz, Editorial, SA (Argentina) 6
Kapelusz, Editorial, Venezolana SA (Venezuela) 419
Kapur Publications (India) 187
Kara, Ismail, /Dergâh Yayinlari AS Müessese Müdürü (Turkey) 358
Karachi University Library Science Alumni Association (Pakistan) 284
Karas-Sana Oy (Finland) 85
Karavias, Athanassios, (Greece) 171
Karavias, Nikolaos, (Greece) 171
Karger, S, AG, Medical and Scientific Publishers (Switzerland) 343
Karger, S, GmbH (Federal Republic of Germany) 141
Karilas, Tauno, Prize (Finland) 87
Karisto, Arvi A, Oy (Finland) 85
Karl-Marx-Universität (German Democratic Republic) 117
Karl Wenschow GmbH (Federal Republic of Germany) 163
Karnataka Cooperative Publishing House Ltd (India) 187
Karnataka Publishers' and Booksellers' Association (India) 181
Karni Publishers Ltd (Israel) 207
Karo-Bücher (Federal Republic of Germany) 141
Kartograficznych, Państwowe Przedsiebiorstwo Wydawnictw, (Poland) 291
Kartografie NP (Czechoslovakia) 70
Kartographisches Institut Bertelsmann (Federal Republic of Germany) 141
Karunaratne & Co (Sri Lanka) 326
Karunia (Indonesia) 199
Kasetsart University, Main Library, (Thailand) 355
Kash'shaf, Dar al, (Lebanon) 239
Katalogów i Cenników, Wydawnictwo, (Catalogue and Price List Publishers) (Poland) 291
Kataria, B D, & Sons (India) 187
Katholieke Bijbelstichting (Netherlands) 260
Katholieke Universiteit Leuven (Belgium) 43
Katholisches Bibelwerk, Verlag, GmbH (Federal Republic of Germany) 141
Katzmann-Verlag KG (Federal Republic of Germany) 141
Kaufmann (Greece) 172
Kaufmann, Verlag Ernst, (Federal Republic of Germany) 141
Kawade Shobo Shinsha (Japan) 227
Kawanku, Yayasan, (Indonesia) 199
Kawika (Philippines) 290
Kaye Ando Technical Services (Laos) 239
Kaye & Ward Ltd (United Kingdom) 387
Keats-Shelley Memorial Association (Italy) 222
Kedros (Greece) 171
Keesing — Internationale Drukkerij en Uitgeverij NV (Belgium) 38
Keimer, Verlag und Buchvertrieb E, (Federal Republic of Germany) 141
Keip, Verlag, KG Antiquariat (Federal Republic of Germany) 141
Keller, Franckh'sche Verlagshandlung, W , & Co (Federal Republic of Germany) 141
Keller, Verlag Ramon F, (Switzerland) 343
Kelly Books (Australia) 15
Kelly's Directories Ltd (United Kingdom) 387
Kemal, Orhan, Award (Turkey) 359
Kemps Group (Printers & Publishers) Ltd (United Kingdom) 387
Kendriya Hindi Sansthan (India) 187
Kenkyusha Ltd (Japan) 227
Kennedy, Albertine, Publishing (Republic of Ireland) 203
Kennedy Prize (Thailand) 356
Kent-Segep SA (France) 99
Kentavros Ekdoseis OE (Greece) 172
Kentron Ekdoseos Ellinon Syngrafeon (Greece) 173
Kenya Booksellers' and Stationers' Association (Kenya) 234
Kenya Library Association (Kenya) 235
Kenya Literature Bureau (Kenya) 234
Kenya Literature Bureau (Kenya) 235
Kenya National Archives (Kenya) 235
Kenya National Library Service (Kenya) 235
Kenya Polytechnic Library (Kenya) 235
Kenya Publishers' Association (Kenya) 234
Kenya Technical Teachers' College Library (Kenya) 235
Kenyatta, Jomo, Prize for Literature (International Literary Prizes) 442
Kenyatta, The Jomo, Foundation (Kenya) 234
Kenyatta University College Library (Kenya) 235
Keppe, Norberto R, (Brazil) 51
Képzömüvészeti Alap Kiadóvállalata (Hungary) 177
Kerala Publishers & Booksellers Association (India) 181
Kerala Sahitya Akademi (India) 187
Kerala Sahitya Akademi Awards (India) 197
Kerala University, Department of Publications (India) 187
Kerle, Verlag F H, (Federal Republic of Germany) 141
Kern Associates (Japan) 231

Kerr, The Alfred, Prize for Literary Criticism (Federal Republic of Germany) 168
Kershaw Publishing Co Ltd (United Kingdom) 387
Kesari Award (India) 197
Kesim, Nurcihan, (Turkey) 358
Kestrel Books (United Kingdom) 387
Keswick (United Kingdom) 387
Keswick Book Society (Kenya) 235
Keter-Li (Israel) 207
Keter Publishing House Ltd (Israel) 207
Keurbiblioteek (Republic of South Africa) 311
Keure, Die, NV (Belgium) 38
Keysersche Buchhandlung (German Democratic Republic) 117
Keysersche Verlagsbuchhandlung GmbH (Federal Republic of Germany) 141
Khanna Publishers (India) 187
Khartoum Polytechnic Library (Sudan) 327
Khartoum, The, Bookshop (Sudan) 327
Khartoum University Press (Sudan) 327
Khaya, Tahseen S, (Kuwait) 238
Khayat Book and Publishing Co SAL (Lebanon) 239
Khayat, Tahseen S, (Lebanon) 239
Khayat, Tahseen S, (United Arab Emirates) 363
'Khimiya', Izdatelstvo, (Union of Soviet Socialist Republics) 361
Khoa Hoc (Social Sciences) Publishing House (Socialist Republic of Viet Nam) 420
'Khudozhestvennaya Literatura', Izdatelstvo, (Union of Soviet Socialist Republics) 361
Khudozhnik RSFSR Publishers (Union of Soviet Socialist Republics) 361
Kibaha Public Library (Tanzania) 353
Kibu-Verlag GmbH (Federal Republic of Germany) 141
Kiefel, Johannes, Verlag (Federal Republic of Germany) 141
Kiehl, Friedrich, Verlag GmbH (Federal Republic of Germany) 141
Kienreich, Jos A, (Austria) 29
Kienreich, Jos A, (Austria) 29
Kiepenheuer, Gustav, Verlag (German Democratic Republic) 116
Kiepenheuer und Witsch, Verlag, (Federal Republic of Germany) 141
Kier, Editorial, SACIFI (Argentina) 6
Kier, Librería, (Argentina) 8
Kiilerich, Edith, Fiolstr 12, (Denmark) 77
Kiilerich, Edith, (Finland) 86
Kiilerich, Edith, (Denmark) 77
Kiilerich, Edith, (Sweden) 334
Kikuchi Prize (Japan) 233
Kilda Verlag (Federal Republic of Germany) 141
Kilkenny, The, Bookshop Ltd (Republic of Ireland) 204
Kimber, William, & Co Ltd (United Kingdom) 387
Kimpton, Henry, (Publishers) Ltd (United Kingdom) 387
Kina Italia SpA (Italy) 216
Kinderbuchverlag, Der, Berlin (German Democratic Republic) 116
Kinderbuchverlag Reich Luzern AG (Switzerland) 343
Kinderpers, Die, Van SA (Republic of South Africa) 309
Kindler Verlag AG (Switzerland) 343
Kindler Verlag GmbH (Federal Republic of Germany) 141
King Abdulaziz University Library (Saudi Arabia) 303
King, Martin Luther, Memorial Prize (United Kingdom) 414
King Paul National Foundation Prize (Greece) 173
King Shing Publishing Co (Hong Kong) 175
Kingfisher Books (United Kingdom) 387
Kings & Queens of England (United Kingdom) 409
Kingsmead Press (United Kingdom) 387
Kingston Bookshop (Jamaica) 223
Kingston Publishers Ltd (Jamaica) 223
Kingston's Literary Awards (Zimbabwe) 430
Kingstons Ltd (Zimbabwe) 429
Kingstons (Zambia) Ltd (Zambia) 428
Kingsway Publications Ltd (United Kingdom) 387
Kingsway Stores (Nigeria) 277
Kingsway Stores, Books and Periodicals Department (Ghana) 169
Kinokuniya Bookstore Co Ltd (Japan) 231
Kinokuniya Bookstore Co Ltd (Publishing Department) (Japan) 231
Kinta (Indonesia) 199
Kipling Society (United Kingdom) 413
Kirja-ja Paperikauppiasliitto (Finland) 84
Kirjallisuudentutkijain Seura (Finland) 87
Kirjaneliö, Kustannusliike, (Finland) 85
Kirjapalvelu (Book Service) (Finland) 84
Kirjastonhoitajien Keskusliitto-Bibliotekariernas Centralförbund ry (Finland) 86
Kirjastovirkailijat-Biblioteksanstallda ry (Finland) 86
Kirjayhtymä Oy (Finland) 85
Kiryat Sefer Ltd (Israel) 207
Kishida Prize for Drama (Japan) 233
Kister, Editions, SA (Switzerland) 343
Kitab, Dar Al-, Allubnani (Lebanon) 239
Kitab, Dar El, (Morocco) 254
Kitab Ghar (India) 187

Kitab Mahal (W D) Pvt Ltd (India) 188
Kitabastan (India) 188
Kitabi Dunya (Pakistan) 282
Kitaplar, Altin, Publishing Co (Turkey) 358
Kitri (Israel) 207
Kitwe Public Library (Zambia) 428
Klang Vidhya (Thailand) 354
Klang Vidhya (Thailand) 355
Klasing und Co GmbH (Federal Republic of Germany) 141
Klein, Kunstverlag Woldemar, (Federal Republic of Germany) 141
Klein, Preben, (Denmark) 77
Klens Verlag GmbH (Federal Republic of Germany) 141
Klett-Cotta Verlag (Federal Republic of Germany) 142
Klett, Ernst, (Federal Republic of Germany) 141
Klett und Balmer, Verlag, & Co (Switzerland) 343
Klima, La Boutique R, (French Polynesia) 113
Klincksieck, Editions, (France) 99
Klinkhardt und Biermann Richard Carl Schmidt Co (Federal Republic of Germany) 142
Klopp, Erika, Verlag GmbH (Federal Republic of Germany) 142
Klostermann, Vittorio, (Federal Republic of Germany) 142
Klotz, Ehrenfried, Verlag (Federal Republic of Germany) 142
Klub 42 (Yugoslavia) 425
Klub 707 (Republic of South Africa) 311
Klub čitalaca (Yugoslavia) 425
Klub čtenářů technické literatury (Czechoslovakia) 72
Klub přátel poézie (Czechoslovakia) 72
Kluitman, Uitgeverij, Alkmaar BV (Netherlands) 260
Kluwer Algemene Boeken BV (Netherlands) 260
Kluwer Fiscale en Juridische Boeken en Tijdschriften (Netherlands) 260
Kluwer Group (Netherlands) 260
Kluwer, NV Uitgeverij, (Belgium) 38
Kluwer Publishing Ltd (United Kingdom) 388
Kluwer Sociaal-Wetenschappelijke Boeken en Tijdschriften (Netherlands) 261
Kluwer Technische Boeken BV (Netherlands) 261
Kluwers Couranten Bedrijf (Netherlands) 261
Kluwer's, Maarten, Internationale Uitgeversonderneming NV (Belgium) 38
Knapp, Fritz, Verlag GmbH (Federal Republic of Germany) 142
Knapp, Wilhelm, Verlag (Federal Republic of Germany) 142
Knaus, Albrecht, Verlag (Federal Republic of Germany) 142
Knecht, Verlag Josef, -Carolus Druckerei GmbH (Federal Republic of Germany) 142
Knesset Library (Israel) 210
'Kniga', Izdatelstvo, (Union of Soviet Socialist Republics) 361
Knight (United Kingdom) 388
Knight, Charles, (United Kingdom) 388
Kniha (The Book) (Czechoslovakia) 72
Knihovna Národního muzea (Czechoslovakia) 72
Knorr und Hirth GmbH (Federal Republic of Germany) 142
Knowledge Book House (Burma) 59
Knowledge Printing & Publishing House (Burma) 59
Knuf, F, Publishers (Netherlands) 261
Københavns Kommunes Biblioteker (Denmark) 78
Københavns Stadsarkiv (Denmark) 78
Kober'sche Verlagsbuchhandlung AG (Switzerland) 343
Koch, Hanna-Kirsti, (Norway) 280
Koch, Neff und Oetinger und Co (Federal Republic of Germany) 165
Koch, Verlagsanstalt Alexander, GmbH (Federal Republic of Germany) 142
Koch, Volksbuchhandlung Robert, (German Democratic Republic) 117
Kochbuchverlag Heimeran KG (Federal Republic of Germany) 142
Koch's, C A, Verlag Nachfolger (Federal Republic of Germany) 142
Kodansha Disney Children's Book Club (Japan) 231
Kodansha International Ltd (Japan) 227
Kodansha Ltd (Japan) 227
Kodansha Scientific Ltd (Japan) 227
Koehler, K F, Verlag (Federal Republic of Germany) 142
Koehler und Amelang (VOB) (German Democratic Republic) 116
Koehlers Verlagsgesellschaft (Federal Republic of Germany) 142
Koerner, Verlag Valentin, GmbH (Federal Republic of Germany) 142
Kogan Page Ltd (United Kingdom) 388
Kohlhammer, Unternehmensgruppe Verlag W, GmbH (Federal Republic of Germany) 142
Kohl's Technischer Verlag Erwin Kohl GmbH & Co KG (Federal Republic of Germany) 142
Kohrtz, Ilona, Prize (Sweden) 336
Koivu, Rudolf, Prize (Finland) 87
Kok, Uitgeversmaatschappij J H, BV (Netherlands) 261

Kokuritsu Kobunshokan (Japan) 231
Kolasanya Publishing Enterprise (Nigeria) 275
Kolibri-Verlag (Federal Republic of Germany) 142
Kollaros, I D, & Co Corporation (Greece) 172
'Kolos', Izdatelstvo, (Union of Soviet Socialist Republics) 361
Kolumbus-Verlag (Switzerland) 343
Komar (Federal Republic of Germany) 142
Kometförlaget AB (Sweden) 331
Komine Shoten Publishing Co Ltd (Japan) 227
Komitet po pechati pri Sovete Ministrov SSSR (Union of Soviet Socialist Republics) 360
Komitet za Izkoustvo i Koultoura (Bulgaria) 58
Kommentator, Verlag, GmbH (Federal Republic of Germany) 142
Kommunale Bibliotekarbeiderers Forening (Norway) 281
Kompass, Etas, (Italy) 216
Komunikacji i Łączności, Wydawnictwa, (Poland) 291
Komunist, Izdavački Centar, (Yugoslavia) 422
Kongelige Bibliotek, Det, (Denmark) 78
Kongelige Danske Videnskabernes Selskab (Denmark) 79
Koninklijke Academie voor Nederlandse Taal- en Letterkunde (Belgium) 44
Koninklijke Academie voor Nederlandse TaalS en Letterkunde (Belgium) 44
Koninklijke Academie voor Wetenschappen, Letteren en Schone Kunsten van België (Belgium) 44
Koninklijke Bibliotheek (Netherlands) 266
Koninklijke Nederlandse Akademie, Bibliotheek der, van Wetenschappen (Netherlands) 266
Koninklijke Nederlandse Uitgeversbond (Netherlands) 255
Konkani Bhasha Mandal (India) 188
Konkordia AG für Druck und Verlag (Federal Republic of Germany) 143
Konrad, Anton H, Verlag (Federal Republic of Germany) 143
Könyvértékesítő Vállalat (Hungary) 178
Könyvtártudományi és módszertani központ (Hungary) 178
Konzepte der Humanwissenschaften (Federal Republic of Germany) 143
Kookaburra Technical Publications Pty Ltd (Australia) 15
Kooyker, C, BV (Netherlands) 266
Kooyker Scientific Publications BV (Netherlands) 261
Korea Book Club (Republic of Korea) 238
Korea Britannica Corp (Republic of Korea) 237
Korea Directory Co (Republic of Korea) 237
Korea Publications Export and Import Corporation (Democratic People's Republic of Korea) 236
Korea University Library (Republic of Korea) 238
Korea University Press (Republic of Korea) 237
Korean Library Association (Republic of Korea) 238
Korean Micro-Library Association (Republic of Korea) 238
Korean Publishers Association (Republic of Korea) 236
Korean Workers' Party Publishing House (Democratic People's Republic of Korea) 236
Koren Publishers (Israel) 207
Kornfeld & Co (Switzerland) 343
Koro, George Y, (Jordan) 233
Kosei Publishing Co Ltd (Japan) 227
Koseisha-Koseikaku Co Ltd (Japan) 227
Kösel-Verlag GmbH & Co (Federal Republic of Germany) 143
Koshal Book Depot (India) 195
Kosi Books (India) 188
Koska, Karl F, (Austria) 25
Kosmo Uitgewery Beperk (Republic of South Africa) 309
Kosmos BV (Netherlands) 261
Kosmos Gesellschaft (Federal Republic of Germany) 165
Kosmos, Livraría, (Brazil) 55
Kosmos, Livraría, Editôra (Brazil) 51
Kossodo Verlag AG (Switzerland) 343
Kossuth Könyvkiadó (Hungary) 177
Kossuth Lajos Tudományegyetem Egyetemi Könyvtár (Hungary) 178
Kothari Publications (India) 188
Kowalski, G, (Federal Republic of Germany) 143
Kowalski, Gerhard, (Federal Republic of Germany) 164
Koymantereas (Greece) 172
Közgazdasági és Jogi Könyvkiadó (Publishing House for Economics & Law) (Hungary) 177
Központi statisztikai hivatal könyvtár és dokumentációs szolgálat (Hungary) 178
Kraft Prize (Argentina) 7
Krains, Hubert, Prize (Belgium) 45
Krajowa Agencja Wydawnicza (KAW) (Poland) 291
Kral, Frantz, Prize (Czechoslovakia) 73
Kramer, Andrés de, (Spain) 323
Kramer, Dr Waldemar, Verlagsbuchhandlung (Federal Republic of Germany) 143
Kramer, Karin, Verlag (Federal Republic of Germany) 143
Krämer, Karl, Verlag GmbH und Co (Federal Republic of Germany) 143
Krämer, Verlag Karl, & Co (Switzerland) 344
Kramer, Verlag René, AG (Switzerland) 344
Kraus, Librairie des Messageries Paul, (Luxembourg) 242

482 INDEX

Kraus Reprint (Liechtenstein) 241
Kraus-Thomson Organization Ltd (Liechtenstein) 241
Krausskopf Verlag GmbH (Federal Republic of Germany) 143
Krebs, Verlag G, AG (Switzerland) 344
Kremayr und Scheriau, Verlag, (Austria) 25
Kremnitz, Buch- und Bildverlag W, (Federal Republic of Germany) 143
Kreuz Verlag (Federal Republic of Germany) 143
Krieg, Walter, (Austria) 29
Kriegsarchivs Wien, Bibliothek des, (Austria) 29
Kriminalistik Verlag GmbH (Federal Republic of Germany) 143
Krippler-Muller, Publisher, (Luxembourg) 242
Krishna Brothers (India) 188
Krishna Prakasman Mandir (India) 188
Kristiansand Folkebibliotek (Norway) 281
Kristna Bokförläggareföreningen (Sweden) 327
Kristna Bokringen, Den, (Sweden) 334
Kritak uitgeverij (Belgium) 38
Kriterion, Editura, (Romania) 301
Kröner, Alfred, Verlag (Federal Republic of Germany) 143
Krščanska sadašnjost (Yugoslavia) 422
Krüger, Buch und Werburg-Helmut, GmbH (Federal Republic of Germany) 143
Kruger, Wolfgang, Verlag (Federal Republic of Germany) 143
Kruh (Czechoslovakia) 70
Kruh priatelov detskej knihy (Czechoslovakia) 72
'Ksiazka i Wiedza', Wydawnictwo, (Poland) 291
Kuai-Mare, Librerías, (Venezuela) 419
Kuala Lumpur Public Library (Malaysia) 245
Kübler Verlag KG (Federal Republic of Germany) 143
Kubon und Sagner (Federal Republic of Germany) 143
Kugler Publications BV (Netherlands) 261
Kühl KG, Verlagsgesellschaft (Federal Republic of Germany) 143
Kultura (Hungary) 178
Kultura (Yugoslavia) 425
Kultura (Izdavačko Pretprijatie) (Yugoslavia) 422
Kumar, C B, Prize (India) 197
Kumkuman Award (India) 197
Kumm, Wilhelm, Verlag (Federal Republic of Germany) 143
Kümmerly und Frey (Geographischer Verlag) (Switzerland) 344
Kummerly und Frey Verlags GmbH (Austria) 25
Kundalini Research and Publication Trust (India) 188
Kündig, Imprimerie Albert, SA (Switzerland) 344
Kungl Vitterhets Historie och Antikvitets Akademien (Sweden) 335
Kungliga Biblioteket (Sweden) 334
Kungliga Svenska Vetenskapsakademiens Bibliotek (Sweden) 334
Kunnskapsforlaget (Norway) 279
Kunnuparampil Books (India) 188
Kunst und Wissen Erich Bieber OHG (Federal Republic of Germany) 143
Kunst und Wohnen Verlag (Federal Republic of Germany) 143
Kunst, VEB Verlag der, (German Democratic Republic) 116
Kunstkreis, Edition, im Ex Libris Verlag (Switzerland) 351
Kunstkreis für Bibliophile Mappen (Federal Republic of Germany) 165
Kunstkreis, Verlag, (Switzerland) 344
Kuomintang Central Committee Library (China (Taiwan)) 64
Kupferberg, Florian, Verlag (Federal Republic of Germany) 143
Kurita Shuppan Hanbai Co Ltd (Japan) 231
Kurnia Esa (Indonesia) 199
Kursverksamhetens Förlag (Sweden) 331
Kutter, Edouard, (Luxembourg) 242
Kutub, Dar Al, Al Hadeetha (Egypt) 82
Kutub, Dar al, al-Wataniya (Saudi Arabia) 303
Kutub Khana Ishayat-ul-Islam (India) 188
Kutubi Moh'd Nihad Hashem (Syria) 353
Kuwait Central Library (Kuwait) 238
Kuwait Publishing House (Kuwait) 238
Kuwait University Central Library (Kuwait) 238
Kuwait University Libraries Department (Kuwait) 238
Kwan Dong Publishing Co (Republic of Korea) 237
Kwang Hwa Bookstore Pte Ltd (Malaysia) 245
Kwang Hwa, Sharikat Toko Buku, (Brunei) 57
Kwangmyong Printing & Publishing Co Ltd (Republic of Korea) 237
Kwaratech Bookshop (Nigeria) 277
Kwong Hin Bookstore (Hong Kong) 176
Kyemong-sa (Republic of Korea) 237
Kyi-Pwar-Ye Book House (Burma) 59
Kynning Ltd, (Iceland) 180
Kyo Bun Kwan Inc (Japan) 227
Kyohak Sa (Republic of Korea) 237
Kyoritsu Shuppan Co Ltd (Japan) 227
Kyoto Sangyo University Library (Japan) 231

Kyriakou, K P, (Books — Stationery) Ltd (Cyprus) 69
Kyrios-Verlag GmbH (Federal Republic of Germany) 143
Kyung In Munwha Sa (Republic of Korea) 237
Kyungpook National University Central Library (Republic of Korea) 238
Kyushu University Library (Japan) 231

L & S Publishing Co Pty Ltd (Australia) 15
L A S I E Australia Co Ltd (Australia) 20
L E D A (Las Ediciones de Arte) (Spain) 319
L E R, Livraria, (Brazil) 55
L I C —Förlag (Sweden) 331
L I S A (Livros Irradiantes SA) (Brazil) 52
L I T A (Czechoslovakia) 72
L I T E C - Livraria Editôra Tècnica Ltda (Brazil) 55
L J Productions (France) 99
L K G (German Democratic Republic) 117
L N-Verlag Lübeck, Lübecker Nachrichten GmbH (Federal Republic of Germany) 143
L P3 E S (Lembaga Penelitian Pendidikan Dan Penerangan Ekonomi Dan Social) (Indonesia) 199
L S P Books Ltd (United Kingdom) 388
L T r Editôra Ltda (Brazil) 52
L Ts Förlag AB (Lantbrukarnas Riksförbund och Studieförbundet Vuxenskolan) (Sweden) 331
La Fontaine Prize (France) 111
La Joie par les Livres (France) 109
La Paz, Librería, (Bolivia) 46
Lääketieteellinen Keskuskirjasto (Finland) 86
Labbé-Vauquelin, Paul, Prize (France) 111
Labor, Editions, (Belgium) 38
Labor, Editorial, Argentina SA (Argentina) 6
Labor, Editorial, Colombiana Ltda (Colombia) 65
Labor, Editorial, de Venezuela SA (Venezuela) 419
Labor, Editorial, del Ecuador SA (Ecuador) 80
Labor, Editorial, do Brasil SA (Brazil) 52
Labor et Fides (Switzerland) 344
Labor, Editorial, SA (Spain) 319
Lacayo, Editorial, (Nicaragua) 273
Lachispa (Colombia) 65
Laconti, Imprimerie, SA (Belgium) 38
Lacus, Ambro, Buch- und Bildvalag W Kremnitz (Federal Republic of Germany) 143
Lademann Ltd, Publishers (Denmark) 75
Ladybird (Australia) 15
Ladybird Books Ltd (United Kingdom) 388
Laetare (Federal Republic of Germany) 143
Lafenestre, Georges, Prize (France) 111
Laffitte, Librairie, (France) 108
Laffont, Les Editions Robert, (France) 99
Lafite, Elisabeth, (Austria) 26
Lafolye et Lamarzelle Editeurs Sàrl (France) 99
Laget, Librairie Léonce, (France) 99
Lagos City Council Libraries (Nigeria) 277
Lahn-Verlag (Federal Republic of Germany) 143
Lahumière, Editions, (France) 99
Laia, Editorial, (Spain) 319
Laissue, Francisco J, (Brazil) 52
Lake House Investments Ltd (Sri Lanka) 326
Lakeland Paperbacks (United Kingdom) 388
Lakoul Press (Nepal) 255
Lakshmi Narain Agarwal (India) 188
Lalit Kala Akademi (National Academy of Art) (India) 188
Lalvani Brothers (India) 188
Lamares, Americo Fraga, & Ca Lda (Portugal) 296
Lamarre-Poinat, Editions, SA (France) 99
Lamb, Charles, Society (United Kingdom) 413
Lambert Prize (France) 112
Lambertus Verlag GmbH (Federal Republic of Germany) 143
Lameere, Eugène, Prize (Belgium) 45
Lampe, Editions, d'Or ASBL (Belgium) 38
Lamy SA (France) 99
Lancashire Authors' Association (United Kingdom) 364
Lancaster Publishing (New Zealand) 270
Lanchester, The, Prize (International Literary Prizes) 442
Landbouwhogeschool, Bibliotheek der, (Netherlands) 266
Landbuch-Verlag GmbH (Federal Republic of Germany) 143
Landesgremium Kärnten des Handels mit Büchern, Kunstblättern, Musikalien, Zeitungen und Zeitschriften (Austria) 23
Landesgremium Niederösterreich des Handels mit Büchern, Kunstblättern, Musikalien, Zeitungen und Zeitschriften (Austria) 23
Landesgremium Oberösterreich des Handels mit Büchern, Kunstblättern, Musikalien, Zeitungen und Zeitschriften (Austria) 23
Landesgremium Salzburg des Handels mit Büchern, Kunstblättern, Musikalien, Zeitungen und Zeitschriften (Austria) 23

Landesgremium Steiermark des Handels mit Büchern, Kunstblättern, Musikalien, Zeitungen und Zeitschriften (Austria) 23
Landesgremium Tirol des Handels mit Büchern, Kunstblättern, Musikalien, Zeitungen und Zeitschriften (Austria) 23
Landesgremium Vorarlberg des Handels mit Büchern und Musikalien (Austria) 23
Landesgremium Wien des Handels mit Büchern, Kunstblättern, Musikalien, Zeitungen und Zeitschriften (Austria) 23
Landesman, Jay, Ltd (United Kingdom) 388
Landestopographie, Bundesamt für, (Switzerland) 344
Landesverband der Buchhändler und Verleger in Niedersachsen eV (Federal Republic of Germany) 119
Landesverband der Verleger und Buchhändler Bremen-Unterweser eV (Federal Republic of Germany) 119
Landesverband der Verleger und Buchhändler Rheinland-Pfalz eV (Federal Republic of Germany) 119
Landesverband der Verleger und Buchhändler Saar eV (LVBS) (Federal Republic of Germany) 119
Landesverband des werbenden Buch- und Zeitschriftenhandels von Südwestdeutschland eV (Federal Republic of Germany) 119
Landsberger Verlagsanstalt Martin Neumeyer (Federal Republic of Germany) 144
Landsbókasafn Islands (Iceland) 180
Landwirtschaftliche Zentralbibliothek (German Democratic Republic) 117
Landwirtschaftlicher Staatsverlag (Agricultural Publishing House) (Czechoslovakia) 70
Landy, Livraria D, (Brazil) 55
Lane, Allen, (Australia) 15
Lane, Allen, (United Kingdom) 388
Lang, Herbert, & Cie AG (Switzerland) 344
Lang, Verlag Peter, AG (Switzerland) 344
Lange, Allert de, BV (Netherlands) 261
Langen, Albert, -Georg Müller Verlag (Federal Republic of Germany) 144
Langen-Müller, Verlagsgruppe, / Herbig (Federal Republic of Germany) 144
Langenhoven, C J, Prize (Republic of South Africa) 313
Langenscheidt KG (Federal Republic of Germany) 144
Langenscheidt AG (Switzerland) 344
Langenscheidt Group, The, (Federal Republic of Germany) 144
Langenscheidt-Hachette GmbH (Federal Republic of Germany) 144
Langenscheidt-Longman GmbH (Federal Republic of Germany) 144
Langenscheidt-Verlag GmbH (Austria) 26
Langewiesche-Brandt KG (Federal Republic of Germany) 144
Langewiesche, Karl Robert, Nachfolger Hans Koester KG (Federal Republic of Germany) 144
Langlois Prize (France) 112
Language and Literature Bureau Library (Brunei) 57
Language Book Centre (Australia) 19
Language, The, Library (United Kingdom) 388
Languages School (Thailand) 354
Lanka Booksellers' Association (India) 181
Lannoo (Belgium) 38
Lannoo, Uitgeverij, (Netherlands) 261
Lanore, Editions J, C L T (France) 99
Lanore, Librairie Fernand, Sàrl (France) 99
Lansdowne Editions (Australia) 15
Lansdowne Press (Australia) 15
Lanterna, Editrice, (Italy) 216
Lao Dong (Labour) Publishing House (Socialist Republic of Viet Nam) 420
Lao-phanit (Laos) 239
Lapautre, Mme Michelle, (France) 107
Lappeenrannan Kirjakauppa Oy (Finland) 86
Lärarbokklubben (Sweden) 334
Larcier, Maison Ferdinand, SA (Belgium) 38
Larese, Franz, und Jürg Janett (Switzerland) 344
Larousse, Ediciones, Argentina SA (Argentina) 6
Larousse, Librairie, (France) 99
Larousse, Librairie, Centrafrique (Burundi) 60
Larousse (Suisse) SA (Switzerland) 344
Larson, Bokförlaget Robert, AB (Sweden) 331
Lasser Press Mexicana, SA (Mexico) 250
Lasserre, Luis, y Cia, SACIFI (Argentina) 6
Lasten Keskus Oy (Finland) 85
Laterna Magica, Verlag, Joachim F Richter (Federal Republic of Germany) 144
Laterza, Giuseppe, e Figli SpA (Italy) 216
Latimer House Ltd (United Kingdom) 388
Latin Friendship Prize (International Literary Prizes) 442
Latina SCA (Argentina) 6
Latino Americana, Editora, SA (Mexico) 250
Latomus ASBL (Belgium) 38
Lattès, Editions Jean-Claude, (France) 99
Laudes, Editôra, SA (Brazil) 52
Laupp'sche, H, Buchhandlung (Federal Republic of Germany) 144
Laurens, Editions Henri, Successeurs Sàrl (France) 99
Laurenziana, Biblioteca Medicea, (Italy) 221

INDEX 483

Laurie, T Werner, (United Kingdom) 388
Lavauzelle, Charles, (France) 99
Lavigerie, Les Presses, (Burundi) 60
Laville, Diffusion Bernard, (France) 99
Law Books in Hindi Prize (India) 197
Law Books in Hindi Publishers (India) 188
Law Publishers (India) 188
Law, The, Book Co Ltd (Australia) 15
Lawrence & Wishart (United Kingdom) 388
Lawyers' Co-operative Publishing Co (Philippines) Inc (Philippines) 288
Lax, August, (Federal Republic of Germany) 144
Layraud, J-P, (New Caledonia) 268
Lazarillo Prize (International Literary Prizes) 442
Le Bayon, Alice, (France) 107
Le Moël, Eugène, Prize (France) 112
Le Monnier, Casa Editrice Felice, (Italy) 216
Le Prat, Editions Guy, (France) 99
Lebanese Library, The, Association (Lebanon) 240
Lebanon Bookshop (Lebanon) 239
Lechevalier, Editions, Sàrl (France) 99
Lecomte, Pierre, du Nouy Award (International Literary Prizes) 442
Leconte, Sébastien-Charles, Prize (France) 112
Lector-Verlag GmbH (Switzerland) 344
Lectura, Librería, (Venezuela) 419
Lecture Publique, Direction de la, (Tunisia) 357
Ledori (Israel) 207
Lee, T H, & Co Ltd (Hong Kong) 175
Leeds University Library (United Kingdom) 411
Leemann AG, Buchdruckerei und Verlag (Switzerland) 344
Leer, The Van, Jerusalem Foundation (Israel) 207
Lee's Book Centre (Bahamas) 31
Lefebvre, Francis, (France) 99
Léger, Editions Robert, et Cie (France) 99
Legislación Económica Ltda (Colombia) 65
'Legkaya Industriya', Izdatelstvo, (Union of Soviet Socialist Republics) 361
Legrain, Editions Paul, (Belgium) 38
Legrand, Editions, (Belgium) 38
Lehmann, Librería Imprenta y Litografía, SA (Costa Rica) 67
Lehmann, Librería Imprenta y Litografía, SA (Costa Rica) 67
Lehmanns, J F, Verlag (Federal Republic of Germany) 144
Lehnert & Landrock (Egypt) 82
Lehr- und Lernmittel, Verlag für, (Federal Republic of Germany) 165
Leibniz-Volksbuchhandlung (German Democratic Republic) 117
Leicester University Press (United Kingdom) 388
Leiden University Press (Netherlands) 261
Leiftur hf (Iceland) 180
Leins, Verlag Hermann, (Federal Republic of Germany) 144
Leipholdt, Louis, prys vir Poesie (Republic of South Africa) 313
Leipzig, Edition, (German Democratic Republic) 116
Leipziger Kommissions- und Grossbuchhandel (LKG) (German Democratic Republic) 117
Leisure Arts Ltd (United Kingdom) 388
Leisure Circle, The, Ltd (United Kingdom) 409
Leitfadenverlag Dieter Sudholt (Federal Republic of Germany) 144
Lekarskie, Państwowy Zaklad Wydawnictw, (Poland) 291
Lekha Prokashani (Bangladesh) 31
Lello & Cia Lda (Angola) 2
Lello & Cia Lda (Angola) 2
Lello e Cia Lda (Portugal) 296
Lello e Irmão (Portugal) 296
Lembeck, Verlag Otto, (Federal Republic of Germany) 144
Lemniscaat (Netherlands) 261
Lenclud, Anne, Pierre Lenclud (France) 107
Lenina, Gosudarstvennaya ordena Lenina biblioteka SSSR imeni V I, (Union of Soviet Socialist Republics) 363
'Lenizdat', Izdatelstvo, (Union of Soviet Socialist Republics) 361
Lenos Verlag (Switzerland) 344
Lensing, Verlag Lambert, GmbH (Federal Republic of Germany) 144
Lentz, Georg, Verlag (Federal Republic of Germany) 144
Lentz og Jenssens Forlag ApS (Denmark) 76
Leo, Franz, & Comp KG (Austria) 29
Leobuchhandlung (Switzerland) 344
Leobuchhandlung, Verlag der Quellenbändchen (Switzerland) 344
Leonardo da Vinci, Livraria, (Brazil) 55
Leong Brothers (Brunei) 57
Leonhardt, Albrecht, ApS (Denmark) 77
Leonhardt, Karl Ludwig, (Federal Republic of Germany) 164
Leonis Verlag (Switzerland) 344
Leopard (United Kingdom) 388

Leopold, Uitgeverij, BV (Netherlands) 261
Lepus Books (United Kingdom) 388
Lerberghe, Van, Prize (France) 112
Lerner, Ediciones, Ltda (Colombia) 65
Lerner, Librería, (Colombia) 66
Lerú, Editorial Victor, SA (Argentina) 6
Leschiera Valerio (Italy) 216
Lesigne, Editions, (Belgium) 38
Leske Verlag und Budrich GmbH (Federal Republic of Germany) 144
'Lesnaya Promyshlennost', Izdatelstvo, (Union of Soviet Socialist Republics) 361
Lesoli, Uitgavenfonds Leon, V Z W (Belgium) 38
Lesot, Editions André, Sàrl (France) 99
Lesotho Book Centre (Lesotho) 240
Lesotho National Library Service (Lesotho) 240
Lesourd, Editions Olivier, (France) 99
Lessing Prize der Freien und Hansestadt Hamburg (Federal Republic of Germany) 168
Letouzey, Société Nouvelle des Editions, et Ané Sàrl (France) 99
Letrán, Librería, (Mexico) 252
Letras Cubanas, Editorial, (Cuba) 68
Lettres Modernes Minard (France) 99
Letts, Charles, & Co Ltd (United Kingdom) 388
Leu, Edition, Verlag für nichtkommerzielle Kunst und Literatur (Switzerland) 344
Leuchter-Verlag AG (Federal Republic of Germany) 144
Leuchtturm-Verlag (Federal Republic of Germany) 144
Leuven University Press (Belgium) 38
Levéltári Osztaly, Kulturális Minisztévium, (Hungary) 178
Leven, The Grace, Prize for Poetry (Australia) 22
Leventhal, Lionel, Ltd (United Kingdom) 388
Leviathan House Ltd (United Kingdom) 388
Lewin-Epstein Ltd (Israel) 207
Lewin-Epstein-Modan, A, Ltd (Israel) 207
Lewis, A, (United Kingdom) 388
Lewis, F, (Publishers) Ltd (United Kingdom) 388
Lewis H K, & Co Ltd (United Kingdom) 388
Lewis, J D, & Sons Ltd (United Kingdom) 388
Lex Editôra SA (Brazil) 52
Lexika-Verlag (Federal Republic of Germany) 144
Lexikothek Verlag GmbH (Federal Republic of Germany) 144
Ley, La, SA Editora e Impresora (Argentina) 6
Leykam AG (Austria) 26
Lia Rumantscha (Ligia Romontscha) (Switzerland) 344
Liaoning Library (People's Republic of China) 63
Liaquat Memorial Library (Pakistan) 283
Liban, Librairie du, (Lebanon) 239
Liber Grafiska AB (Sweden) 331
Liber Juris, Editôra, Ltda (Brazil) 52
Liber, Sveučilišna Naklada, (Yugoslavia) 422
Liber Tryck (Sweden) 331
Liber Verlag GmbH (Federal Republic of Germany) 145
LiberFörlag (Sweden) 331
LiberHermods (Sweden) 331
Liberian Educational Materials Supply Corporation (Liberia) 240
Liberian Literary & Educational Publications (Liberia) 240
LiberKartor (Svensk Karttjänst AB, Swedish Map Service) (Sweden) 331
LiberLäromedel (Sweden) 331
Liberma, Libreria, (Italy) 220
Libertador, Editorial, (Venezuela) 419
Libertatea (Yugoslavia) 422
Liberty Bookstall (Pakistan) 283
Libra Books Pty Ltd (Australia) 15
Librah (Netherlands) 266
Librairie afrique (Senegal) 303
Librairie clairafrique (Senegal) 303
Librairie Commerciale et Technique (Licet) Sàrl (France) 99
Librairie de Madagascar (Democratic Republic of Madagascar) 243
Librairie du Liban (Lebanon) 239
Librairie du Liban (Lebanon) 240
Librairie encyclopédique, Editions de la, (Belgium) 38
Librairie évangélique (Chad) 61
Librairie évangélique (Central African Republic) 61
Librairie évangélique (Zaire) 423
Librairie Générale de Droit et de Jurisprudence (France) 99
Librairie Générale Française SA (France) 99
Librairie générale SA (Belgium) 38
Librairie lutherienne (Democratic Republic of Madagascar) 243
Librairie mixte Sàrl (Democratic Republic of Madagascar) 243
Librairie Nationale (Mauritius) 248
Librairie nationale (Morocco) 254
Librairie nouvelle de l'Ouest Africain (LINOA) (Senegal) 303
Librairie-Papeterie Moderne (United Republic of Cameroun) 60
Librairie-Papeterie Protestante CEBEC (United Republic of Cameroun) 60

Librairie-Papeterie Universelle (French Guiana) 113
Librairie Populaire (Popular Republic of Congo) 67
Librairie populaire de Mali (Mali) 246
Librairie universitaire (Democratic Republic of Madagascar) 243
Librairie Universitaire de la Réunion (Réunion) 300
Librairie universitaire et technique (Senegal) 303
Librairies Techniques SA (France) 99
Libraport (Guinea) 174
Library Advisory Council for England (United Kingdom) 411
Library Advisory Council for Wales (United Kingdom) 411
Library Association of Australia (Australia) 20
Library Association of Barbados (Barbados) 32
Library Association of China (China (Taiwan)) 64
Library Association of Singapore (Republic of Singapore) 306
Library Association of the Democratic People's Republic of Korea (Democratic People's Republic of Korea) 236
Library Association, The, (United Kingdom) 411
Library Automated Systems, The, Information Exchange (Australia) 20
Library Board of Western Australia, The, (Australia) 20
Library of Parliament (Republic of South Africa) 312
Library Promotion Bureau (Pakistan) 284
Library, School of, and Information Science (Japan) 231
Library Science Society (China (Taiwan)) 64
Library Science Society (Pakistan) 284
Library Service of Fiji (Fiji) 84
Library Services for South West Africa (Namibia) 255
Library, The, Shop (Republic of Ireland) 204
Librería Central (Colombia) 66
Librería Científica (Ecuador) 80
Librería Contemporanea (Puerto Rico) 299
Librería Continental (Colombia) 66
Librería Cultural (Puerto Rico) 299
Librería Cultural (Venezuela) 419
Librería Cultural Colombiana (Colombia) 66
Librería Cultural Nicaraguense (Nicaragua) 273
Librería Cultural Panameña, Ediciones, SA (Panama) 284
Librería Cultural Panameña, SA (Panama) 285
Librería Cultural Puertorriqueña Inc (Puerto Rico) 299
Librería Cultural Venezolana (Venezuela) 419
Librería Española (Ecuador) 80
Librería Inglesa (Uruguay) 417
Librería Intercontinental SA (Mexico) 252
Librería Internacional (Paraguay) 286
Librería Internacional del Perú (Peru) 287
Librería Internacional SA (Mexico) 252
Librería Nacional (Colombia) 66
Librería Tecno-Ciencia (Chile) 62
Librería Tecnológica Universitaria (Nicaragua) 273
Librería Tecnológico SA (Mexico) 252
Librería (The Bookstore) (Honduras) 174
Librería Universal (Guatemala) 173
Librería Universal (Paraguay) 286
Librería Universitaria (Chile) 62
Librería Universitaria (Ecuador) 81
Librería Universitaria (Mexico) 252
Librería Universitaria (Nicaragua) 273
Librería Universitaria de Puerto Rico (Puerto Rico) 299
Librex, Edizioni, (Italy) 216
Libri, Etas, SpA (Italy) 216
Libris Bookclub (Sweden) 334
Libris Publishing House (Sweden) 331
Libro de la Naturaleza, Club del, (Spain) 323
Libroclub de Guatemala (Guatemala) 173
Librolandia del Centro SA (Mexico) 252
Licet (France) 99
Lichtenberg Verlag GmbH (Federal Republic of Germany) 145
Lichtkreis Christi (Federal Republic of Germany) 145
Licorne, Editions de la, (France) 99
Licosa SpA (Italy) 216
Lidador, Editôra, Ltda (Brazil) 52
Lidis, Editions, SA (France) 99
Lidis, Librairie, (France) 108
Lidman Production AB (Sweden) 331
Lidové nakladatelstvi (Czechoslovakia) 70
Liebenzeller Mission, Verlag der, (Federal Republic of Germany) 145
Liebing, Arnulf, (Federal Republic of Germany) 145
Liebing, Rudolf, (Federal Republic of Germany) 145
Liechtenstein Verlag AG (Liechtenstein) 241
Liechtenstein Verlag AG (Liechtenstein) 241
Liechtensteinische Landesbibliothek (Liechtenstein) 241
Liepman, Dr Ruth, (Switzerland) 351
Lietzow, Edition/Galerie, (Federal Republic of Germany) 145
Ligel, Editions, (France) 99
Light & Life Publishers (India) 188
Ligue des Bibliothèques Européenes de Recherche (LIBER) (International Organizations) 433
Liguori Editore SRL (Italy) 216
Lile, Editions Michel de, et Philippe Auzou (France) 100
Lilja, Bókagerdin, (Iceland) 180
Lima, Waldyr, Editôra (Brazil) 52

484 INDEX

Limes Verlag (Federal Republic of Germany) 145
Limmat Verlag Genossenschaft (Switzerland) 344
Limonad, Editôra Max, Ltda (Brazil) 52
Limpert Verlag (Federal Republic of Germany) 145
Limusa, Editorial, SA (Mexico) 250
Linardi, Librería Adolfo, (Uruguay) 417
Lincoln, Biblioteca, (Argentina) 8
Lincoln Cultural Center (Malaysia) 245
Lincoln, Frances, Publishers Ltd (United Kingdom) 388
Lindblads, J A, Bokförlag AB (Sweden) 331
Linden Press (United Kingdom) 388
Linder AG Literary Agency (Switzerland) 351
Lindhardt og Ringhof (Denmark) 76
Ling, H C, Book Store & Co Ltd (China (Taiwan)) 64
Ling Kee Bookstore (Hong Kong) 176
Ling Kee Publishing Co (Hong Kong) 175
Lingen Verlag (Federal Republic of Germany) 145
Lingenbrink, Barsortiment Georg, (Wholesale Bookseller) (Federal Republic of Germany) 165
Linguaphone Institute Ltd (United Kingdom) 388
Linguaphone Institutet AB (Sweden) 331
Linosa-Linomonograph, Editorial, SA (Spain) 319
Lion Publishing (United Kingdom) 389
Lionarons Drukkerij NV (Suriname) 327
Lipi Prakashan (India) 188
Lisieux, Office Central de, SA (France) 100
List, Paul, Verlag (German Democratic Republic) 116
List, Paul, Verlag KG (Federal Republic of Germany) 145
Listín, Editora, Diario (Dominican Republic) 80
Litchfield, Jessie, Memorial Award (Australia) 22
Literackie, Wydawnictwo, (Poland) 291
Literar-Mechana, Wahrnehmungsgesellschaft für Urheberrechte mbH (Austria) 23
Literarische Agentur und Verlagsgesellschaft (Liechtenstein) 241
Literarischer Verein in Stuttgart eV (Federal Republic of Germany) 168
Literarischer Verlag Steinhausen (Federal Republic of Germany) 145
Literarisches Colloquium Berlin (Federal Republic of Germany) 145
Literary Award (Romania) 302
Literary Club of Monrovia (Liberia) 240
Literary Critics' Grand Prize (France) 112
Literary Guild (United Kingdom) 409
Literary Guild, The, (Australia) 19
Literary Guild, The, (New Zealand) 272
Literary Market Review (India) 188
Literary Prize (Republic of Korea) 238
Literary Prize (Panama) 285
Literary Prize of the Resistance (France) 112
Literary Prizes for Sinhala Literature (Sri Lanka) 326
Literary Prizes for Tamil Literature (Sri Lanka) 326
Literary Services (Pty) Ltd (Republic of South Africa) 312
Literary Supplies (Jamaica) 223
Literature Board of the Australia Council (Australia) 9
Literature Board of the Australia Council (Australia) 22
Literature Bureau, The, (Zimbabwe) 429
Literature Bureau, The, (Zimbabwe) 429
Literature Bureau, The, Annual Literary Award (Zimbabwe) 430
Literature House Ltd (China (Taiwan)) 64
Literature Prize (Federal Republic of Germany) 168
Literature Prize (Democratic Republic of Madagascar) 243
Literatury Gorniczej, Klub Czytelnikow, (Poland) 293
Literatury Hutniczej, Klub Czytelnikow, (Poland) 293
Lito, Editions, (France) 100
Litolff's, Henry, Verlag (Federal Republic of Germany) 145
Litor Publishers (United Kingdom) 389
Litpress (Switzerland) 351
Littera Scripta Manet (Netherlands) 261
Littérature, Editeurs de, biblique (Belgium) 38
Litteraturfrämjandet (Sweden) 335
Little Flower, The, Co (India) 188
Little Swan (India) 188
Liverpool City Libraries (United Kingdom) 411
Liverpool University Press (United Kingdom) 389
Living Literary Agency Elfriede Pexa (Italy) 220
Livraria Editôra Tecnica Ltda (LITEC) (Brazil) 52
Livre de Paris, Le, (France) 100
Livre de Poche, Le, (France) 100
Livres de France (Egypt) 82
Livro Científico, Estante do, (Brazil) 55
Livro Político, Clube do, (Brazil) 55
Livros, Editora, do Brasil Sarl (Portugal) 296
Livros Irradiantes SA (Brazil) 52
Lloyd, Editions du, Anversois SA (Antwerpse Lloyd NV) (Belgium) 38
Lloyd-Luke (Medical Books) Ltd (United Kingdom) 389
Llyfrgell Genedlaethol Cymru (National Library of Wales) (United Kingdom) 411
Lobato, Monteiro, Prize (Brazil) 57
Löcker Verlag (Austria) 26
Locomotive Publishing Co Ltd (United Kingdom) 389
Lodzkie, Wydawnictwo, (Lodz Publishing House) (Poland) 291

Loeb Classical Library (United Kingdom) 389
Loeff, Uitg Mij van der, BV (Netherlands) 261
Loescher Editore SpA (Italy) 216
Loewes Verlag KG (Federal Republic of Germany) 145
Lofler, Paul, Prize (France) 112
Logans University Bookshop (Pty) Ltd (Republic of South Africa) 312
Loghum, Van, Slaterus (Netherlands) 261
Logos Consorcio Editorial, SA (Mexico) 250
Logos-Verlag (Switzerland) 344
Logosófica, Editôra, (Brazil) 52
Lohlé, Carlos, SA (Argentina) 6
Lohses Forlag (Denmark) 76
Lok Vangmaya Griha (Pvt) Ltd (India) 188
Lokole, Editions, (Zaire) 427
Lomagundi Printing (Pvt) Ltd (Zimbabwe) 429
Lombard SA (Belgium) 38
London Bookshops Ltd (New Zealand) 272
London Editions Ltd (United Kingdom) 389
London Independent Books (United Kingdom) 408
London Magazine Editions (United Kingdom) 389
London Syndication (United Kingdom) 408
London Writer Circle (United Kingdom) 413
Lonely Planet Publications Pty Ltd (Australia) 15
Longanesi e C (Italy) 216
Longbow (United Kingdom) 389
Longman Arab World Centre (Lebanon) 239
Longman Caribbean Ltd (Trinidad and Tobago) 356
Longman Cheshire Pty Ltd (Australia) 15
Longman Group (Far East) Ltd (Hong Kong) 175
Longman Group Ltd (United Kingdom) 389
Longman Italia SRL (Italy) 216
Longman Kenya Ltd (Kenya) 234
Longman Malaysia Sdn Bhd (Malaysia) 244
Longman Malaysia Sdn Bhd (Republic of Singapore) 305
Longman Nigeria Ltd (Nigeria) 275
Longman Paul Ltd (New Zealand) 270
Longman Penguin Southern Africa (Pty) Ltd (Republic of South Africa) 309
Longman Publishers (Pvt) Ltd (Zimbabwe) 429
Longman Tanzania Ltd (Tanzania) 353
Longman Uganda Ltd (Uganda) 359
Longo Editore (Italy) 216
Longo, Libreria A, (Italy) 220
Look-In Books (United Kingdom) 389
Lope, Librería y Papeleria, de Vega (Dominican Republic) 80
Lopes Da Silva, Livraria, -Editôra de M Moreira Soares Rocha Lda (Portugal) 296
Lopes, Julia, de Ameida Prize (Brazil) 57
López Libreros y Editores (Argentina) 6
Löpfe-Benz, E, AG Rorschach, Graphische Anstalt und Verlag (Switzerland) 344
Lorber-Verlag (Federal Republic of Germany) 145
Lorch-Verlag GmbH (Federal Republic of Germany) 145
Lord International (India) 188
Lorrimer Books (United Kingdom) 389
Losada, Editorial, SA (Argentina) 6
Lothian Publishing Company Pty Ltd (Australia) 15
Lothian, Thomas C, Pty Ltd (New Zealand) 270
Lotu Pasifika Productions (Fiji) 84
Lotus, Uitgeverij, /Editions Lotus (Belgium) 38
Lovedale Press (Republic of South Africa) 309
Lowden Publishing Co (Australia) 15
Lowe, Peter, (United Kingdom) 389
Lowe, Robson, Ltd (United Kingdom) 389
Loyola, Edições, SA (Brazil) 52
Lübbe, Gustav, Verlag GmbH (Federal Republic of Germany) 145
Lubelskie, Wydawnictwo, (Lublin Publishers) (Poland) 291
Luchterhand, Hermann, Verlag GmbH & Co KG (Federal Republic of Germany) 145
Lucis Press Ltd (United Kingdom) 389
Lucky (Australia) 19
Lucky Book Club (United Kingdom) 409
Luctor Publishing — Stadler & Sauerbier BV (Netherlands) 261
Ludowa Spóldzielnia Wydawnicza (Poland) 291
Ludwig, Verlag W, (Federal Republic of Germany) 145
Luitingh, Uitgeverij, BV (Netherlands) 261
'Lumen Christi', Edições, (Brazil) 52
Lumen, Editions, Vitae ASBL (Belgium) 39
Lumen, Editorial, (Spain) 319
Lumiere Biblique (France) 100
Luna, Libreria G, (Italy) 220
Lund Humphries Publishers Ltd (United Kingdom) 389
Lund Universitetsbibliotek (Sweden) 335
Lunde Forlag og Bokhandel A/S (Norway) 279
Lundequistska Bokhandeln, AB, (Sweden) 334
Lundgrens, AB Edvin, Bokhandel (Sweden) 334
Lundqvists, Abr, Musikförlag AB (Sweden) 331
Lusaka City Libraries (Zambia) 428
Luscombe, William, (United Kingdom) 389
Luso-Espanhola, Livraria, Lda (Portugal) 296
Luther Forlag A/S (Norway) 279
Luther-Verlag GmbH (Federal Republic of Germany) 145

Lutherisches Verlagshaus (Federal Republic of Germany) 145
Lutterworth Press (United Kingdom) 389
Lutz, Hans-Rudolf, (Switzerland) 344
Lux Press (Malta) 246
Luxor Press (United Kingdom) 389
Lyche, Harald, og Co A/S (Norway) 279
Lydecken, Arvid, Prize (Finland) 87
Lyle Publications Ltd (United Kingdom) 389
Lyngs Bokhandel A/S (Norway) 280
Lyrikkvaennene, Bokklubbens, (Norway) 280
Lythway Press Ltd (United Kingdom) 389

M A M (Cyprus) 69
M A M (Cyprus) 69
M B A Literary Agents Ltd (United Kingdom) 408
M C A (Australia) 15
M C L (France) 100
M C S Enterprises Inc (Philippines) 288
M D I, Editions, (La Maison des Instituteurs) (France) 100
M E/D I Sviluppo (Italy) 216
M F B (Phono- und Schriftenmission des missionstrupps frohe botschaft eV) (Federal Republic of Germany) 145
M I M (Belgium) 39
M I T, The, Press (United Kingdom) 389
M P H Distributors Sdn Bhd (Malaysia) 245
M P H Pte Ltd (Republic of Singapore) 306
M P Text Book Corporation (India) 188
M R P (United Kingdom) 389
M S A (Republic of South Africa) 309
M T P Press Ltd (United Kingdom) 389
M W H London Publishers (United Kingdom) 389
Ma'alot (Israel) 207
Ma'arachot (Israel) 208
Ma'aref, Al, Library (Jordan) 233
Maaref, Dar Al, (Egypt) 81
Maaref, Dar Al-, Liban SAL (Lebanon) 239
Ma'arif, Al, Ltd (Iraq) 202
Ma'ariv Book Guild (Sifriat Ma'ariv) (Israel) 208
Maatschappij der Nederlandse Letterkunde (Netherlands) 267
Mabrochi International Co (Nigeria) 277
Mac Purcell (Lebanon) 239
Macaraig Publishing Co (Philippines) 288
Macaulay Fellowships (Republic of Ireland) 205
Macchi, Ediciones, (Argentina) 6
Macdonald (United Kingdom) 389
Macdonald Educational Ltd (United Kingdom) 390
Macdonald & Evans Ltd (United Kingdom) 389
Macdonald/Futura Publishers Ltd (United Kingdom) 390
Macdonald Guidelines, Macdonald Starters, Macdonald 3/4/5 (United Kingdom) 390
Macdonald Publishers (Edinburgh) (United Kingdom) 390
Macdonald's (Kenya) 235
Mace, Jean, Prize (France) 112
Machado de Assis Prize (Brazil) 57
Machado, Fernando, e Co Ltd (Portugal) 297
Machbarot lesifrut (Israel) 208
MacKern, Librerías, SA (Argentina) 8
Mackintosh Hall, John, Library (Gibraltar) 170
Maclellan, William, (United Kingdom) 390
Macmillan Children's Books (United Kingdom) 390
Macmillan Education Ltd (United Kingdom) 390
Macmillan London Ltd (United Kingdom) 390
Macmillan Malaysia (Malaysia) 244
Macmillan Nigeria Publishers Ltd (Nigeria) 275
Macmillan Press, The, Ltd (United Kingdom) 390
Macmillan Publishers (HK) Ltd (Hong Kong) 175
Macmillan Publishers Ltd (United Kingdom) 390
Macmillan SA (Switzerland) 344
Macmillan South Africa Publishers (Pty) Ltd (Republic of South Africa) 309
Macmillan Southeast Asia Pte Ltd (Republic of Singapore) 305
Macmillan, The, Co of Australia Pty Ltd (Australia) 15
Macmillan, The, Co of India Ltd (India) 188
Macondo Ediciones SRL (Argentina) 6
MacRae, Julia, Books (United Kingdom) 391
Madáh (Czechoslovakia) 70
Madarali, Fikret, Prize (Turkey) 359
Made Simple Books (United Kingdom) 391
Madhyo Pradesh Hindi Granth Academy (India) 188
Madju (Indonesia) 199
Madras Literary Society and Auxiliary of the Royal Asiatic Society (India) 197
Madras Literary Society Library (India) 196
Maeght Editeur (France) 100
Magasin du Nord A/S (Denmark) 78
Maghreb Livres (Morocco) 254
Maghrebines, Les Editions, (Morocco) 254
Magic-Strip SPRL (Belgium) 39
Magisterio, Editorial, Español SA (Spain) 319

INDEX 485

Magna Print Books (United Kingdom) 391
Magnard, Les Editions, Sàrl (France) 100
Magnes, The, Press (Israel) 208
Magnum Books (United Kingdom) 391
Magnus Verlag (Federal Republic of Germany) 145
Magvető Könyvkiadó (Publishing House of Belles Lettres) (Hungary) 177
Magwe College Library (Burma) 59
Magyar Bibliofil társaság (Hungary) 178
Magyar Irodalomtörténeti Társaság (Hungary) 178
Magyar Írók Szövetsége (Association of Hungarian Writers) (Hungary) 179
Magyar Könyvkiadók és Könyvterjesztők Egyesülése (Hungary) 176
Magyar Könyvtárosok Egyesülete (Hungary) 178
Magyar Központi Levéltár, Uj, (New Central Archives of Hungary) (Hungary) 178
Magyar országos levéltár (Hungary) 178
Magyar Tudományos Akadémia Irodalomtudományi Intézete (Hungary) 178
Magyar Tudományos Akadémia Könyvtára (Hungary) 178
Mahabir Singh Chiniya Main (Nepal) 255
Mahajan Brothers (India) 188
Mahligai, Pustaka, Press (Malaysia) 244
Maier, Otto, Benelux BV (Netherlands) 261
Maier, Otto, Verlag (Federal Republic of Germany) 145
Maille-Latour-Landry Prize (France) 112
Mainichi Publishing Culture Prize (Japan) 233
Mainstream Book Club (United Kingdom) 409
Mainstream Publishing Co (Edinburgh) Ltd (United Kingdom) 391
Mairs Geographischer Verlag (Federal Republic of Germany) 146
Mai's Reiseführer Verlag (Federal Republic of Germany) 146
Maison de la Presse, Société congolaise Hachette (Popular Republic of Congo) 67
Maison de Poésie (Fondation Emile Blémont) (France) 109
Maison des Instituteurs, La, (France) 100
Maison des Livres (Ivory Coast) 223
'Maison des Livres', Librairie, (Algeria) 2
Maison du Dictionnaire, La, (France) 100
Maison, La, de la Bible (Switzerland) 344
Maison, La, du Livre (Benin) 45
Maison, La, du Livre (Senegal) 303
Maison, La, Rustique SA (France) 100
Maison Tunisienne d'Edition (Tunisia) 357
Maisondieu Prize (France) 112
Maisonneuve et Larose, Editions G P, (France) 100
Maisonneuve-Librairie d'Amérique et d'Orient, Adrien, (France) 100
Máj (Czechoslovakia) 72
Majerove, Marie, Prize (Czechoslovakia) 73
Majlis Press (Iran) 201
Makedonska Knjiga (Yugoslavia) 425
Makedonska Knjiga (Knigoizdatelstvo) (Yugoslavia) 423
Makerere Institute of Social Research Library (Uganda) 359
Makerere University Bookshop (Uganda) 359
Makerere University Library (Uganda) 360
Makor Publishing Ltd (Israel) 208
Maktaba, Al-, (Saudi Arabia) 302
Maktaba Ishaat-e-Adab (Pakistan) 283
Maktaba Jadeed (Pakistan) 282
Maktaba Meri Library (Pakistan) 282
Maktaba Shahkar (Pakistan) 282
Maktabah, Al, Al Wataniah (National Library) (Syria) 353
Mál og menning (Iceland) 180
Mal Og Menning (Iceland) 180
Malabar, Toko Buku, (Indonesia) 200
Malaby Press (United Kingdom) 391
Malacorda, Marika, Editions (Switzerland) 344
Maladá fronta Award (Czechoslovakia) 73
Malan, H R, Prize (Republic of South Africa) 313
Malatestiana, Biblioteca Comunale, (Italy) 221
Malawi Book Service (Malawi) 243
Malawi Library Association, The, (Malawi) 243
Malawi National Library Service (Malawi) 243
Malawi Polytechnic, The, Library (Malawi) 243
Malaya Books Suppliers Co (Malaysia) 244
Malaya Educational Supplies Sdn Bhd (Malaysia) 244
Malaya Press, The, Sdn Bhd (Malaysia) 244
Malayan Law Journal (Pte) Ltd (Republic of Singapore) 305
Malaysia Press Sdn Bhd (Republic of Singapore) 305
Malaysian Book Publishers' Association (Malaysia) 244
Malherbe, John, (Pty) Ltd (Republic of South Africa) 309
Mali, Editions Imprimeries du, (Mali) 246
Malik Din Mohammad & Sons (Pakistan) 282
Malik Sirajuddin & Sons (Pakistan) 282
Malik Sirajuddin & Sons (Pakistan) 283
Malipiero SpA (Italy) 216
Mallings ApS (Denmark) 76
Mallinson Rendel Publishers Ltd (New Zealand) 270
Malmberg BV (Netherlands) 261

Malmö Stadsbibliotek (Sweden) 335
Maloine, Librairie, (France) 100
Malpertuis Prize (Belgium) 45
Máls og Menningar, Bókabúd, (Iceland) 180
Malsa Book Service Ltd (Zambia) 428
'Malysh', Izdatelstvo, (Union of Soviet Socialist Republics) 361
Mamadou Traoré Ray Autra (Senegal) 303
Mambo Press (Zimbabwe) 429
Mambo Press Bookshop (Zimbabwe) 429
Mame, Nouvelles Editions, (France) 100
Man in His Environment, The, Book Award (International Literary Prizes) 443
Månadens Bok (Sweden) 334
Manar, Imprimerie/Librairie Al, (Tunisia) 357
Manar, Librairie Al, (Tunisia) 357
Manchester Odd Fellows Social Concern Annual Book Awards (International Literary Prizes) 443
Manchester University Press (United Kingdom) 391
Mandarino, Editôra, Ltda (Brazil) 52
Mandas Sugatdas (Nepal) 255
Mandat des Poètes Prize (International Literary Prizes) 443
Manesse und Morgarten Verlag (Switzerland) 345
Manesse-Verlag (Switzerland) 345
Mangold, Paul, Verlag (Austria) 26
Manhin, Victor, Ltd (Trinidad and Tobago) 356
Manila City Library (Philippines) 289
Mann, Gebr, Verlag GmbH & Co (Federal Republic of Germany) 146
Mann, Thomas, Prize (Federal Republic of Germany) 168
Mann, Volksbuchhandlung Thomas, (German Democratic Republic) 117
Manohar Publications (India) 189
Manoharlal, Munshiram, Publishers Pvt Ltd (India) 189
Manole, Editôra, Ltda (Brazil) 52
Manor Press (Philippines) 288
Manosabdam Books (India) 189
Mansell Publishing (United Kingdom) 391
Mansfield, Katherine, Memorial Award (New Zealand) 273
Mansfield, Katherine, Menton Memorial Prize (International Literary Prizes) 443
Mansour, S J, (Israel) 208
Manteau (Netherlands) 261
Manteau, Uitgeversmaatschappij A, NV (Belgium) 39
Manual, El, Moderno, SA (Mexico) 250
Manutiuspresse Wulf Stratowa Verlag (Austria) 26
Manxman Publications (United Kingdom) 391
Manz Verlag (Federal Republic of Germany) 146
Manz'sche Verlags- und Universitätsbuchhandlung (Austria) 26
Manz'sche Verlags und Universitätsbuchhandlung (Austria) 29
Map Productions Ltd (United Kingdom) 391
Mapa Fiscal Editôra Ltda (Brazil) 52
Maqbool Academy (Pakistan) 282
Marabout, Les Nouvelles Editions, SA (Belgium) 39
Marais, Eugène, Prize (Republic of South Africa) 313
Marangu College of National Education Library (Tanzania) 353
Marbán, Editorial, (Spain) 319
Marchal, Joseph-Edmond, Prize (Belgium) 45
Marcombo SA de Boixareu Editores (Spain) 319
Marcus, Y, & Co Ltd (Israel) 208
Marczell, Tibor, (Federal Republic of Germany) 146
Mardaga, Pierre, SA (Belgium) 39
Maredsous ASBL (Belgium) 39
Marfiah (Indonesia) 199
Marfil, Editorial, SA (Spain) 319
Marg Publications (India) 189
Margai, Milton, Teachers' College Library (Sierra Leone) 304
Marguerat, Librairie-Editions J, (Switzerland) 345
Marhold, Carl, Verlagsbuchhandlung (Federal Republic of Germany) 146
Maria-Verlag (Federal Republic of Germany) 146
Marican & Sons (M) Sdn Bhd (Malaysia) 245
Marie-Médiatrice, Editions, ASBL (Belgium) 39
Marietti Editori SpA (Italy) 216
Marin, Editorial, SA (Spain) 319
Maritim, Edition, (Federal Republic of Germany) 146
Maritime Book Society (United Kingdom) 409
Markazi Maktaba Islami (India) 189
Markham, Arthur, Memorial Prize (United Kingdom) 415
Markovič, Univerzitetska biblioteka 'Svetozar, ' (Yugoslavia) 425
Marksa, Gosudarstvennaya Respublikanskaya biblioteka Gruzinskoi SSR im K, (Union of Soviet Socialist Republics) 363
Markus, Editions, (Belgium) 39
Maro Verlag (Federal Republic of Germany) 146
Marotta, Alberto, Editore SpA (Italy) 216
Marova, Ediciones, SL (Spain) 319
Marques of Cerralbo XVII Prize (Spain) 325
Marrimpouey, Éditions, Jeune et Cie (France) 100
Marshall, Alan, Award (Australia) 22
Marshall Cavendish Books Ltd (United Kingdom) 391

Marshall Editions Ltd (United Kingdom) 391
Marshall, Morgan & Scott Publications Ltd (United Kingdom) 391
Marshall, Muir, Ltd (Trinidad and Tobago) 356
Marsiega, Editorial, SA (Spain) 319
Marsilio Editori (Italy) 216
Marsland Press (United Kingdom) 391
Martello, Giunti, Editore (Italy) 216
Martin Books (United Kingdom) 391
Martin Educational (Australia) 16
Martin Robertson & Co Ltd (United Kingdom) 391
Martindale Press (Australia) 16
Martínez, Ediciones, Roca SA (Spain) 319
Martínez, H F, de Murguía (Argentina) 8
Martínez, H F, de Murguía (Spain) 324
Martins Forlag (Denmark) 76
Martins, Livraria, Editôra SA (Brazil) 52
Martins, Livraria Tavares, (Portugal) 297
Martinsart, Editions, (France) 100
Maruzen Asia (Pte) Ltd (Republic of Singapore) 305
Maruzen Co Ltd (Japan) 227
Maruzen Co Ltd (Japan) 231
Marva (Switzerland) 345
Marwah Publications (India) 189
Marxistische Blätter, Verlag, GmbH (Federal Republic of Germany) 146
Marymar Ediciones SA (Argentina) 6
Marzocco, Editrice Giunti, (Italy) 216
Marzorati Editore SRL (Italy) 216
Masa Baru (Indonesia) 199
Mascareignes, Librairie des, (Mauritius) 248
Masereel, Frans, Fonds VZW (Belgium) 39
'Mashinostroenie', Izdatelstvo, (Union of Soviet Socialist Republics) 361
Mashreq, Dar-el, (Lebanon) 239
Mason, Kenneth, Publications Ltd (United Kingdom) 391
Masout (Israel) 208
Maspero, François, Editeur (France) 100
Masri, Dar Al-Kitab Al-, (Egypt) 81
Mass Culture Publishing House (Democratic People's Republic of Korea) 236
Mass, Rubin, (Israel) 208
Massada Press Ltd (Israel) 208
Massada Press Ltd (Israel) 210
Massada Publishing Ltd (Israel) 208
Massimo, Editrice, (Italy) 216
Massin, Editions Charles, et Cie (France) 100
Masson Editeur (France) 100
Masson, Editôra, do Brasil (Brazil) 52
Masson Editores (Mexico) 250
Master Storytellers (United Kingdom) 409
Matica Slovenská (Czechoslovakia) 72
Matice Moravská (Czechoslovakia) 72
Matopo Book Centre (Zimbabwe) 429
Matthaes, Hugo, Druckerei und Verlag GmbH & Co KG (Federal Republic of Germany) 146
Matthes und Seitz Verlag GmbH (Federal Republic of Germany) 146
Matthias-Estienne (France) 107
Matthias-Grünewald-Verlag (Federal Republic of Germany) 146
Matthiesen Verlag Ingwert Paulsen Jr (Federal Republic of Germany) 146
Matze, Editions la, (Switzerland) 345
Mauclert, Librairie, (Niger) 274
Maudrich, Verlag Wilhelm, (Austria) 26
Maudrich, Wilhelm, (Austria) 29
Maugham, Somerset, Award (United Kingdom) 415
Maupetit, Librairie, (France) 108
Mauritanie, Librairie-Papeterie, Nouvelle (Mauritania) 247
Mauritius Archives (Mauritius) 248
Mauritius Institute Public Library (Mauritius) 248
Mauritius Library Association (Mauritius) 248
Maximilian-Verlag (Federal Republic of Germany) 146
Maximilian-Verlagsgruppe (Federal Republic of Germany) 146
May, Franca, Edizioni SRL (Italy) 216
May, Karl, -Verlag, Joachim Schmid & Co (Federal Republic of Germany) 146
May, Verlag A & G de, (Switzerland) 345
Mayela, Librería Editorial Gerardo, (Mexico) 252
Mayer, Edition Hansjörg, (Federal Republic of Germany) 146
Mayer, Ludwig, Ltd (Israel) 210
Mayer'sche Buchhandlung, J A, (Federal Republic of Germany) 165
Mayer'sche, J A, Buchhandlung (Federal Republic of Germany) 146
Mayfair Paperbacks (India) 189
Mayflower Books Ltd (United Kingdom) 391
Mayhew, Kevin, Ltd (United Kingdom) 391
Mayhew-McCrimmon Ltd (United Kingdom) 391
Mayoor Paperbacks (India) 189
Mazarde, Fernand, Prize (France) 112
Mazarine, Editions, (France) 100
Mazenod Book Centre (Lesotho) 240
Mazenod, Editions d'Art Lucien, (France) 100

486 INDEX

Mazenod Institute (Lesotho) 240
Mazzotta, Gabriele, Editore SpA (Italy) 216
McColvin Medal (United Kingdom) 415
McGraw-Hill Book Co (Switzerland) 344
McGraw-Hill Book Co Australia Pty Ltd (Australia) 15
McGraw-Hill Book Co GmbH (Federal Republic of Germany) 145
McGraw-Hill Book Co, New Zealand Ltd (New Zealand) 270
McGraw-Hill Book Co (South Africa) (Pty) Ltd (Republic of South Africa) 309
McGraw-Hill Book Co (UK) Ltd (United Kingdom) 390
McGraw-Hill, Editôra, do Brasil Ltda (Brazil) 52
McGraw-Hill, Editorial, Latino-Americana SA (Panama) 285
McGraw-Hill, Editorial, Latinoamerica SA (Puerto Rico) 299
McGraw-Hill, Editorial, Latinoamericana SA (Colombia) 65
McGraw-Hill Inc (France) 100
McGraw-Hill International Book Co (Republic of Singapore) 305
McGraw-Hill, Libros, de Mexico SA de CV (Mexico) 250
McIndoe, John, Ltd (New Zealand) 270
McIntyre, Grant, Ltd (United Kingdom) 390
McKee et Mouche (France) 107
McMillan Memorial Library (Kenya) 235
McNamara's Books (Australia) 15
McPhee Gribble Publishers Pty Ltd (Australia) 16
Mead & Beckett Publishing (Australia) 16
Meadowfield Press Ltd (United Kingdom) 391
Mebso Bookshop (Iran) 201
Meca, Editôra, Ltda (Brazil) 52
Meddens, Les Ateliers d'Art graphique, SA (Belgium) 39
Médecine, Bibliothèque Interuniversitaire de, (France) 108
Médecine & Hygiène (Switzerland) 345
Médica, Editorial, Panamericana SA (Argentina) 6
Medica, Librería, Paris (Venezuela) 419
Médica, Librería y Editorial La, (Argentina) 6
Medical Friend Co Ltd (Japan) 227
Medical Librarians' Group (Australia) 20
Medical Science Publishing House (Democratic People's Republic of Korea) 236
Medical World Book Co Pte Ltd (Republic of Singapore) 305
Medicala, Editura, (Medical Publishing House) (Romania) 301
Medici, The, Society Ltd (United Kingdom) 391
Medicina Könyvkiadó (Hungary) 177
medicina si farmacie, Institutul de, din Bucuresti Biblioteca Centrala (Romania) 301
Medicinsk Forlag ApS (Denmark) 76
Medicinska Knjiga (Yugoslavia) 423
Medicinska Naklada (Yugoslavia) 423
Medicis Foreign Prize (International Literary Prizes) 443
Médicis Prize (France) 112
Medico Farmaceutica, Organizzazione Editoriale, SRL (Italy) 217
Medina, Editorial, SRL (Uruguay) 417
Mediterranea, Librería, (Spain) 324
Mediterranee, Edizioni, SRL (Italy) 217
Meditsina i Fizkultura (Bulgaria) 58
'Meditsina', Izdatelstvo, (Union of Soviet Socialist Republics) 361
Medium, Bokförlaget, AB (Sweden) 331
Medizin, Buchhandlung für, (German Democratic Republic) 117
Medizin, Verlag für, Dr Ewald Fischer GmbH (Federal Republic of Germany) 146
Medizinisch-Literarische Verlagsgesellschaft mbH (Federal Republic of Germany) 146
Meenakshi Prakashan (India) 189
Meera Memorial Award (India) 198
Meerut Publishers' Association (India) 181
Meerwein, Rose M, (Federal Republic of Germany) 164
megapress-Verlag Franz-Joachim Gaber KG (Federal Republic of Germany) 146
Megiddo Publishing Co (Israel) 208
Mehran Library Association (Pakistan) 284
Mei Ya Publications Inc (Sueling, Inc) (China (Taiwan)) 64
Meijer Pers BV (Netherlands) 261
Meili, Buchhandlung, & Co (Switzerland) 351
Meili, Peter, & Co (Switzerland) 345
Meinema/Waltman (Netherlands) 261
Meiner, Felix, Verlag (Federal Republic of Germany) 146
Meisenheim, Verlag Anton, GmbH (Federal Republic of Germany) 146
Meissner, Otto, Verlag (Federal Republic of Germany) 146
Meixner, Friedrich, (Austria) 29
Mejía, Librería-Editorial Juan, Baca (Peru) 286
Mejía, Librería Juan, Baca (Peru) 287
Mekise Nirdamin Society (Israel) 211
Melanchthon Verlag (Federal Republic of Germany) 147
Melantrich (Czechoslovakia) 70
Melawai, Toko Buku, (Indonesia) 200
Melayu, Pustaka, Baru (Malaysia) 244

Melbourne House (Publishers) Ltd (United Kingdom) 391
Melbourne University Press (Australia) 16
Melhoramentos, Companhia, de São Paulo SP (Brazil) 52
Melins, Gustav, AB (Sweden) 331
Melissa Publishing House (Greece) 172
Mella (Dominican Republic) 80
Mellinger, J CH, Verlag GmbH; Wolfgang Militz und Co KG (Federal Republic of Germany) 147
Melrose Press Ltd (United Kingdom) 391
Melzer, Verlag Abi, GmbH (Federal Republic of Germany) 147
Melzer Verlag KG (Federal Republic of Germany) 147
Mendes, Odorico, Prize (Brazil) 57
Menéndez, Librería, (Panama) 285
Menéndez Pelayo, Biblioteca de, (Spain) 324
Menéndez, Ramón, Pidal Prize (International Literary Prizes) 443
Mengès, Editions, (France) 100
Menningarsjóds, Bókaútgáfa, og Thjód vinafélagsins (Iceland) 180
Menno Bookstore (Etiiopia) 83
Mensajero, Ediciones, (Spain) 319
Mensch und Arbeit, Verlag, Robert Pfützner GmbH (Federal Republic of Germany) 147
Mentor (United Kingdom) 391
Mentor-Verlag Dr Ramdohr KG (Federal Republic of Germany) 147
Menzies, John, (Holdings) Ltd (United Kingdom) 410
Merbabu, Toko Buku, (Indonesia) 200
Mercantile Guardian Press and Publishers (Pakistan) 282
Mercat Press (United Kingdom) 391
Mercatorfonds Arcade (Belgium) 39
Mercatorfonds SA (Belgium) 39
Mercier, The, Bookshop Ltd (Republic of Ireland) 204
Mercier, The, Press Ltd (Republic of Ireland) 203
Merck, Johann Heinrich, Prize (Federal Republic of Germany) 168
Merckx, Editeur Paul F, (Belgium) 39
Mercure de France SA (France) 100
Mercurius PVBA (Belgium) 39
Mergus Verlag Hans A Baensch (Federal Republic of Germany) 147
Merian, Christoph, Verlag (Switzerland) 345
Meribérica — Editorial e Comercialização de Direitos Lda (Portugal) 297
Meridiane, Editura, (Romania) 301
Merkaz Le-Chinuch Torani (Israel) 208
Merlin Book Club (United Kingdom) 409
Merlin Library Ltd (Malta) 246
Merlin, The, Press Ltd (United Kingdom) 392
Merlin Verlag Andreas Meyer Verlags GmbH und Co KG (Federal Republic of Germany) 147
Merrill, Charles E, Publishing Co (United Kingdom) 392
Merrion, The, Press (United Kingdom) 392
Merrow Publishing Co Ltd (United Kingdom) 392
Merve Verlag (Federal Republic of Germany) 147
Messageries Centrales du Livre (France) 100
Messeiller, Henri, (Switzerland) 345
Messepublikationen, Verlag für, (Federal Republic of Germany) 147
Mestre Jou SA (Brazil) 52
Mestre Jou SA (Brazil) 55
Městská knihovna v Praze (Czechoslovakia) 72
Metal Bulletin Books Ltd (United Kingdom) 392
'Metallurgiya', Izdatelstvo, (Union of Soviet Socialist Republics) 361
Methodik-Verlag Manfred Helfrecht (Federal Republic of Germany) 147
Methodist Book Depot Ltd (Ghana) 169
Methodist Publishing House (United Kingdom) 392
Methodist, The, Publishing House and Book Depot (Republic of South Africa) 309
Methuen Australia Pty Ltd (Australia) 16
Methuen Children's Books Ltd (United Kingdom) 392
Methuen & Co Ltd (United Kingdom) 392
Methuen New Zealand (New Zealand) 270
Methuen/Walker Books (United Kingdom) 392
Metodistkyrkans Förlag (Sweden) 331
Metropolitan Book Suppliers Ltd (Trinidad and Tobago) 356
Metz, Max S, Verlag AG (Switzerland) 345
Metzlersche Verlagsbuchhandlung, J B, (Federal Republic of Germany) 147
Metzner, Alfred, Verlag GmbH (Federal Republic of Germany) 147
Meulenhoff Bruna BV (Netherlands) 266
Meulenhoff Educatief BV (Netherlands) 261
Meulenhoff Informatief BV (Netherlands) 262
Meulenhoff International BV (Netherlands) 262
Meulenhoff Nederland BV (Netherlands) 262
Mexicana, Editorial, (Mexico) 250
Mexicanos, Editores, Unidos (Mexico) 252
Mexicanos Unidos, Editores, (Edimex) (Mexico) 250
Meyer, Editions d'Art Lucien de, ASBL (Belgium) 39
Meyers-Trefois, D (Belgium) 39
Meysmans (Belgium) 39
Meyster Verlag (Austria) 26
Meyster Verlag (Federal Republic of Germany) 147

Mezhdunarodnaya Kniga (Union of Soviet Socialist Republics) 362
'Mezhdunarodnye Otnosheniya', Izdatelstvo, (Union of Soviet Socialist Republics) 361
Mezögazdasági Könyvkiadó Vállalat (Hungary) 177
Michael, Maurice, (United Kingdom) 392
Michaelmark Books Ltd (Israel) 208
Michael's Bookshop (Republic of Singapore) 306
Michaels og Licht (Denmark) 77
Michaut, Narcisse, Prize (France) 112
Michelin (Département Cartes & Guides) SA (Belgium) 39
Michelin et Cie (Services de Tourisme) (France) 100
Michelin Tyre Co Ltd (United Kingdom) 392
Micolini's, Progress-Verlag Dr, Wtw (Austria) 26
Microfilm Association of Great Britain (United Kingdom) 411
Microshur Ltd (Israel) 208
Midas Books (United Kingdom) 392
Middelhauve, Gertraud, Verlag (Federal Republic of Germany) 147
Middle East Book Centre (Egypt) 81
Middle East Librarians Association (International Organizations) 433
Middle East Publishing Co (Lebanon) 239
Middle East Technical University Library (Turkey) 359
Miessner Libreros (Spain) 324
Mifalei Tarbut Vehinuch (Israel) 208
Mihalopoulos, John, & Son (Greece) 172
Miland Publishers (Netherlands) 262
Milano Libri Edizioni (Italy) 217
Militara, Editura, (Romania) 301
Militärverlag, VEB, der DDR (German Democratic Republic) 116
Military Book Society (United Kingdom) 409
Military Guild (United Kingdom) 409
Militz, Wolfgang, und Co KG (Federal Republic of Germany) 147
Millas-Martin, José, (France) 101
Miller, Harvey, Publishers (United Kingdom) 392
Miller, J Garnet, Ltd (United Kingdom) 392
Miller, Louis P, Prize (France) 112
Miller, Maskew, Ltd (Republic of South Africa) 309
Miller, Maskew, Ltd (Republic of South Africa) 312
Millet Library (Turkey) 359
Millî Kütüphane (Turkey) 359
Millier, Marcelle, Prize (France) 112
Millington Books (United Kingdom) 392
Milliyet Yaynlari AS (Turkey) 358
Mills & Boon Ltd (United Kingdom) 392
Millwood Press Ltd (New Zealand) 270
Mimbar, Toko Buku Pustaka, (Indonesia) 200
Min Eum Sa (Republic of Korea) 237
Minard, Lettres Modernes, (France) 101
Minard, Librairie, (France) 101
Mindolo Ecumenical Foundation, Hammarskjold Memorial Library (Zambia) 428
Mineral Research and Exploration Institute, Library of the, (Turkey) 359
'Minerva' (Yugoslavia) 423
Minerva Associates (Publications) Pvt Ltd (India) 189
Minerva Bookshop Ltd (New Zealand) 270
Minerva Central (Mozambique) 254
Minerva, Editor, (Hungary) 177
Minerva, Editora, Central (Mozambique) 254
Minerva, Editorial, (Portugal) 297
Minerva, Editura, (Romania) 301
Minerva Italica SpA (Italy) 217
Minerva, Libreria Editrice, (Italy) 220
Minerva Publishing, The, House (India) 189
Minerva Shobo Co Ltd (Japan) 227
Minerva, The, Press Ltd (United Kingdom) 392
Minerva's Express (Australia) 16
Ministère de l'Education, Bibliothèque centrale du, nationale (Belgium) 43
Ministerio das Relações Exteriores, Biblioteca do, (Brazil) 56
Ministerio de Cultura (Costa Rica) 67
Ministerio de Educación (El Salvador) 82
Ministerio de Educacion, Editorial del, 'Jose de Pineda Ibarra' (Guatemala) 173
Ministerio de Información y Turismo, Biblioteca del, (Spain) 324
Ministerrat der Deutschen Demokratischen Republik, Ministerium für Kultur, Hauptverwaltung Verlage und Buchhandel (German Democratic Republic) 114
Ministerstvo kultury CSR, Odbor knižní kultury (Czechoslovakia) 69
Ministerstwa Obrony Narodowej, Wydawnictwo, (Poland) 291
Ministry of Agriculture Library (Malaysia) 245
Ministry of Culture and Information, Book Publishing Department (Afghanistan) 1
Ministry of Culture, Department of Ancient Literature and Culture, (Burma) 59
Ministry of Defence Publishing House (Israel) 208
Ministry of Education, Department of Educational Publications (Afghanistan) 1
Ministry of Education Library (Afghanistan) 1

INDEX 487

Ministry of Education Library (Cyprus) 69
Ministry of Information (Kuwait) 238
Ministry of Information & Broadcasting (India) 189
Ministry of Justice Library (Egypt) 82
Minjungseogwan (Republic of Korea) 237
Minjungseokim Publishing Co (Republic of Korea) 237
Minkoff, Editions, Reprint (Switzerland) 345
Minoas (Greece) 172
Minoas (Greece) 172
'Mintis', Leidykla, (Union of Soviet Socialist Republics) 361
Minuit, Les Editions de, SA (France) 101
Mir, Izdatelstvo, (Union of Soviet Socialist Republics) 361
Mir, S M, (Pakistan) 283
Miracle, Editorial Luis, SA (Spain) 319
Mirananda Publishers BV (Netherlands) 262
Miranda, G, & Sons (Philippines) 289
Mirror Books Ltd (United Kingdom) 392
Mirza Book Agency (Pakistan) 283
Misla (Yugoslavia) 423
Misr Bookshop (Egypt) 82
Misr Import & Export Co (Egypt) 82
Misr, Maktabet, (Egypt) 81
Misrachi, Galeria de Arte, SA (Mexico) 250
Missionstruppe Frohe Botschaft (Federal Republic of Germany) 147
Mistral, Editora Nacional Gabriela, Ltda (Chile) 62
Misuzu Shobo Publishing Co Ltd (Japan) 227
Miswat Library (People's Democratic Republic of Yemen) 421
Mitchell Beazley London Ltd (United Kingdom) 392
Mitchell, The, Library (Glasgow District Libraries) (United Kingdom) 411
Mitra & Ghosh Publishers Pvt Ltd (India) 189
Mitre, Editorial Libreria, SRL (Argentina) 6
Mitteldeutscher Verlag Halle-Leipzig (German Democratic Republic) 116
Mittler, E S, und Sohn GmbH (Federal Republic of Germany) 147
Mizrachi, M, Publishers (Israel) 208
Mladá fronta (Czechoslovakia) 70
Mladé letá (Czechoslovakia) 70
Mladé letá Prize (Czechoslovakia) 73
Mladinska Knjiga (Yugoslavia) 423
Mladinska Knjiga (Yugoslavia) 425
Mladost (Yugoslavia) 423
Mladost (Yugoslavia) 423
Mladost (Yugoslavia) 425
Mladost's Book Fans Club (Yugoslavia) 425
Mlodziezowa Agencja Wydawnicza (Poland) 291
Mlodziezowa Agencja Wydawnicza — Polish Youth Publishing Agency (Poland) 293
Moa Publications (New Zealand) 270
Moadim (Israel) 210
Mockel, Albert, Grand Prize for Poetry (Belgium) 45
Model & Allied Publications Ltd (United Kingdom) 392
Modern Book Agency Private Ltd (India) 189
Modern Book Co Inc (Philippines) 289
Modern Book Company Inc (Philippines) 288
Modern Book Store (Republic of Singapore) 306
Modern Cairo Bookshop (Egypt) 82
Modern Teaching Aids Pty Ltd (Australia) 16
Modern Transport (United Kingdom) 392
Moderne Industrie AG (Switzerland) 345
Moderne Industrie, Verlag, Wolfgang Dummer und Co (Federal Republic of Germany) 147
Moderne Instructie Methoden (MIM) PVBA (Belgium) 39
Moderne Verlags GmbH (MVG) (Federal Republic of Germany) 147
Modernix (New Caledonia) 268
Modtryk, Forlaget, AMBA (Denmark) 76
Modulverlag GmbH (Austria) 26
Mofolo-Plomer Prize (Republic of South Africa) 313
Mohammadi Library (Bangladesh) 32
Mohler, Alfred, Verlag (Switzerland) 345
Mohn, Gütersloher Verlagshaus Gerd, (Federal Republic of Germany) 147
Mohn, Vereinigte Verlagsauslieferung R, oHG (Federal Republic of Germany) 165
Mohr, J C B, (Paul Siebeck) (Federal Republic of Germany) 147
Mohr, Robert, (Austria) 29
Mohrbooks Literary Agency (Switzerland) 351
Moizzi (Italy) 217
Molcho, Solomon, (Greece) 172
Molden, Verlag Fritz, (Austria) 26
Molden, Verlag Fritz (Federal Republic of Germany) 147
Molendinar, The, Press (United Kingdom) 392
Molino, Editorial, (Spain) 320
Moll, Editorial, (Spain) 320
Mollat, Librairie, (France) 108
Molodaya Gvardiya, Izdatelstvo, (Union of Soviet Socialist Republics) 361
Mombasa Polytechnic Library (Kenya) 235
Mon Village, Club, SA (Switzerland) 351
Mon Village, Editions, SA (Switzerland) 345
Monas Hieroglyphica Inc Cooperativa Editrice (Italy) 217

Monastery of St-Saviour, Library of the, (Basilian Missionary Order of St-Saviour) (Lebanon) 240
Mönch-Verlag GmbH & Co (Federal Republic of Germany) 147
Mondadori, Arnoldo, Editore (Italy) 217
Mondadori, Edizioni Scolastiche Bruno, (Italy) 217
Mondadori Ragazzi (Italy) 217
Mondo, Edizioni del, (Federal Republic of Germany) 147
Mondo SA (Switzerland) 345
Mondoperaio edizioni Avanti SpA (Italy) 217
Mondrup, Svend, International Literary Agency (Denmark) 77
Monfort, Gérard, (France) 101
Mongolsknigotorg (Mongolian People's Republic) 253
Moniteur, Editions du, (France) 101
Monitor Verlag (Federal Republic of Germany) 147
Monselet, Charles, Prize (France) 112
Mont-Blanc, Les Editions du, SA (Switzerland) 345
Mont, Du, Buchverlag GmbH und Co KG (Federal Republic of Germany) 148
Mont Noir, Editions du, (Zaire) 427
Montaigne (New Caledonia) 268
Montaigne, Librairie, (France) 108
Montaner y Simon SA (Spain) 320
Montchrestien, Editions, Sàrl (France) 101
Monte Avila Editores CA (Venezuela) 419
Montel, Publications Photo-Cinema Paul, (France) 101
Monterrey, Editôra, Ltda (Brazil) 53
Montesó, José, — Editor (Spain) 320
Monteverde, A, y Cia SA (Uruguay) 417
Monthly Review Press (United Kingdom) 393
Montparnasse-Diffusion (France) 101
Montparnasse, Librairie, Edition (France) 108
Montserrat Public Library (Montserrat) 253
Montsouris, Editions de, SA (France) 101
Montyon Prize (France) 112
Moonlight Publishing (United Kingdom) 393
Moonraker Press (United Kingdom) 393
Moonye Publishing Co (Republic of Korea) 237
Moore, G W, Ltd (New Zealand) 270
Moore, S J, Ltd (Kenya) 235
Moorland Publishing Company Ltd (United Kingdom) 393
Moos, Heinz, Verlag Munich (Federal Republic of Germany) 148
Mor-Carmi, M C, Ltd (Israel) 208
Móra Ferenc Ifjúsági Könyvkiadó (Hungary) 177
Mora, Marie, OHG (Austria) 29
Moraes, Editôra, Ltda (Brazil) 53
Moraes Editores (Portugal) 297
Morancé, Editions Albert, (France) 101
Morata, Ediciones, SA (Spain) 320
Morawa & Co (Austria) 26
Morawa & Co (Austria) 29
Morcelliana, Editrice, SpA (Italy) 217
Moreau, Editions Alain, (France) 101
Morel Editeurs (France) 101
Morena, Libreria, (Argentina) 8
Moreno, Fernando, Poetry Prize (Argentina) 9
Moreshet (Israel) 208
Moreton, Ediciones, SA (Spain) 320
Moretus Plantin, Bibliothèque Universitaire, (Belgium) 43
Morgan-Grampian Book Publishing Co Ltd (United Kingdom) 393
Morgarten-Verlag (Switzerland) 345
Morgen, Buchverlag Der, (German Democratic Republic) 116
Morija Sesuto Book Depot (Lesotho) 240
Morija Sesuto Book Depot (Lesotho) 240
Morikita Shuppan Co Ltd (Japan) 228
Morison Arnold Ltd (Nigeria) 277
Morra, Verlag, (Italy) 217
Morris, William, Organization SpA (Italy) 220
Morsak Verlag (Federal Republic of Germany) 148
Morskie, Wydawnictwo, (Poland) 292
Mortensens, Ernst G, Forlag (Norway) 279
Mortiz, Editorial Joaquín, SA (Mexico) 250
Morus-Verlag (Federal Republic of Germany) 148
Mosaik Verlag (Federal Republic of Germany) 148
Mosca Azul Editores SRL (Peru) 287
Mosca Hnos (Uruguay) 417
Mosca Hnos SA (Uruguay) 417
'Moskovskii Rabochiy', Izdatelstvo, (Union of Soviet Socialist Republics) 361
Moskovskogo Universiteta, Izdatelstvo, (Union of Soviet Socialist Republics) 361
Mossad Harav Kook (Israel) 208
Mosse-Ars, Verlag, Medici (Switzerland) 345
Mosul Museum, Library of the, (Iraq) 202
Mosul Public Library (Iraq) 202
Motilal Banarsidass (India) 189
Motilal Banarsidass (India) 196
Motive (United Kingdom) 393
Motor Racing Publications Ltd (United Kingdom) 393
Motorbuch-Verlag (Federal Republic of Germany) 148
Motta, Federico, Editore (Italy) 217
Mouj Prakashan Griha (India) 189
Mount Kenya Bookshop Ltd (Kenya) 235

Moussault's Uitgeverij BV (Netherlands) 262
Mouton Publishers (Netherlands) 262
Mowbray, A R, & Co Ltd (United Kingdom) 393
Moxon Paperbacks Ltd (Ghana) 169
Moya, José, und Ute Körner de Moya (Spain) 323
Mphala Creative Society (Zambia) 428
Mr H's Prize (Japan) 233
Mühlemann, Verlag Rudolf, (Switzerland) 345
Muhlethaler, Jacques, (Switzerland) 345
Muiderkring, De, BV (Netherlands) 262
Mukherjee, A, & Co Pvt Ltd (India) 189
Mukherji Book House (India) 189
Mulder en Co (Netherlands) 262
Mulder Holland BV (Netherlands) 262
Mulino, Società Editrice Il, (Italy) 217
Mullaya Publications (Australia) 16
Müller, Albert, Verlag AG (Switzerland) 345
Muller, Frederick, Ltd (United Kingdom) 393
Muller-Groff, Librairie, (Luxembourg) 242
Müller Jüristischer, C F, Verlag GmbH (Federal Republic of Germany) 148
Müller, Otto, Verlag KG (Austria) 26
Müller, Rudolf, International Booksellers BV (Netherlands) 266
Müller und Kiepenheuer, Verlag (Federal Republic of Germany) 148
Müller und Schindler, Verlag, (Federal Republic of Germany) 148
Müller und Steinicke, Rudolf, Verlag (Federal Republic of Germany) 148
Müller, Verlag C F, (Federal Republic of Germany) 148
Müller, Verlag Josef, (Federal Republic of Germany) 148
Müller, Verlagsgesellschaft Rudolf, GmbH (Federal Republic of Germany) 148
Mullick Bros (Bangladesh) 31
Mullick Brothers (Bangladesh) 32
Multiling Verlag AG (Switzerland) 345
Multimedia Zambia (Zambia) 428
Mun Woon Dang (Republic of Korea) 237
Munch Bunch (United Kingdom) 393
Munchner Arbeitsgemeinschaft der Verlagshersteller (Federal Republic of Germany) 119
Münchner Verlagsbüro, Horst Hodemacher-Axel Poldner (Federal Republic of Germany) 164
Mundi, Editorial, SAIC y F (Argentina) 6
Mundi-Prensa, Libreria, (Spain) 324
Mundi-Prensa Libros SA (Spain) 320
Mundial, Libreria, (Venezuela) 419
Mundo, Editorial, Técnico SRL (Argentina) 6
Mundo Nuevo, Editorial, (Chile) 62
Mundus, Österreichische Verlagsgesellschaft mbH (Austria) 26
Municipal Library (Bulgaria) 58
Municipal Library (Cyprus) 69
Municipal Library (Cyprus) 69
Municipal Library (Israel) 210
Municipal Library (Socialist Republic of Viet Nam) 420
Municipal Prize for Prose and Poetry (Venezuela) 420
Munin Verlag GmbH (Federal Republic of Germany) 148
Munksgaard Export & Subscription Service (Denmark) 78
Munksgaard, International Booksellers & Publishers Ltd (Denmark) 76
Münster Verlag (Federal Republic of Germany) 148
Muralla, Editorial La, (Spain) 320
Murby, Thomas, & Co (United Kingdom) 393
Murr, Georges, (Lebanon) 240
Murray, Donald, (Ramboro Books) (United Kingdom) 393
Murray, Donald, (Ramboro Books) (United Kingdom) 408
Murray, John, (Publishers) Ltd (United Kingdom) 393
Murrays Childrens Books (United Kingdom) 393
Murrays Remainder Books (United Kingdom) 408
Murrays Remainder Books Ltd (United Kingdom) 393
Mursia, Ugo, Editore SpA (Italy) 217
Muscat, Giov, & Co Ltd (Malta) 246
Musée de l'Affiche, Publications du, et du Tract (France) 101
Musée de l'Homme, Bibliothèque du, (France) 108
Musée royal de Mariemont, Bibliothèque du, (Belgium) 43
Musées Nationaux, Editions de la Réunion des, (France) 101
Museo, Biblioteca del, Histórico Nacional (Uruguay) 417
Museo de Zoologia, Biblioteca del, (Cuba) 68
Museo y Biblioteca Municipal (Ecuador) 81
Muséum national, Bibliothèque centrale du, d'Histoire naturelle (France) 108
Muséum national, Editions du, d'Histoire naturelle (France) 101
Museum, Perpustakaan, Nasional, Departemen Pendidikan dan Kebudayaan (Indonesia) 200
Museum Plantin-Moretus (Belgium) 43
Music Sales Ltd (United Kingdom) 393
Musica, Editio, (Hungary) 177
Musica, Editorial, Moderna (Spain) 320
Musikverleger Union Österreich (Austria) 23
Musin, Louis, Editeur (Belgium) 39

Müskaki Könyvklub (Hungary)   178
Muskett, Netta, Award (Isle of Man)   247
Muskett, Netta, Award (United Kingdom)   415
Muslim Welfare House (United Kingdom)   393
Muster-Schmidt Verlag (Federal Republic of Germany)   148
Műszaki Könyvkiadó (Hungary)   177
Mutiara (Indonesia)   199
Mutual Books Inc (Philippines)   288
Mutualidad Laboral de Escritores de Libros (Spain)   325
Muusses, J, BV (Netherlands)   262
Művelt nép könyvterjesztő vállalat (Hungarian Educated People Book-Distributing Enterprise) (Hungary)   178
'Muzica', Darzhavno Izdatelstvo, (Bulgaria)   58
Muzicala, Editura, (Romania)   301
Muzička Naklada (Yugoslavia)   423
Muzyczne, Polskie Wydawnictwo, (Poland)   292
'Muzyka', Izdatelstvo, (Union of Soviet Socialist Republics)   361
Myna Press (India)   189
Mysl, Izdatelstvo, (Union of Soviet Socialist Republics)   361
Mystery Guild (United Kingdom)   409

N A G Press (United Kingdom)   393
N C C Publications (United Kingdom)   393
N D V (Neue Darmstädter Verlagsanstalt) (Federal Republic of Germany)   148
N E C Z A M Library (Zambia)   428
N E L (United Kingdom)   393
N F E R Publishing Co Ltd (United Kingdom)   393
N F F (Nouvelles Feuilles Familiales) (Belgium)   39
N G Kerk Jeugboekhandel (Republic of South Africa)   309
N G Kerkboekhandel Transvaal (Republic of South Africa)   312
N G Kerkboekhandel Transvaal (DRC Publishers) (Republic of South Africa)   309
N I B, Uitgeverij, (Netherlands)   262
N I S H Shtypshkronjave 'Mihal Duri' (Albania)   1
N K I Educational Services Ltd (United Kingdom)   393
N K I-forlaget (Norway)   279
N O E (France)   101
N S T (Nová sovietska tvorba) (Czechoslovakia)   72
N Z E I (New Zealand)   270
N Z N-Buchverlag AG (Switzerland)   345
Nå Forlag A/S (formerly Elingaard Forlag) (Norway)   279
Nabco Pendidekan Sdn Bhd (Malaysia)   245
Nachrichten-Verlags-GmbH (Federal Republic of Germany)   148
Nación, Premio de 'La,' Prize (Argentina)   9
Nacional, El, Annual Story Award (Venezuela)   420
Nacionalna i Sveučilišna Biblioteka (Yugoslavia)   425
Nadal, Eugenio, Prize (Spain)   325
Nadjuri Australia (Australia)   16
Nafees Academy (Pakistan)   282
Nagai Shoten Co Ltd (Japan)   228
Nagel, Les Editions, SA (Switzerland)   345
Nagin, S, & Co (India)   189
Nagoya University Library (Japan)   231
Nah Shperndarjes Të Librit (NST) (Albania)   1
Nahda, Dar al-, al Arabia (Egypt)   81
Naim Frasheri (Albania)   1
Nairoshni (Pakistan)   282
Nakamori Prize (Japan)   233
Nakladni Zavod Matice Hrvatske (Yugoslavia)   423
Nalanda Books (India)   189
Nalanda Co Ltd (Mauritius)   248
Namboodiri, K R, Award (India)   198
Nan-ching t'u shu kuan (People's Republic of China)   63
Nankodo Co Ltd (Japan)   228
Nanyang University Library (Republic of Singapore)   306
Nanzando Co Ltd (Japan)   228
Naoki Prize (Japan)   233
Napoletana, Società Editrice, SRL (Italy)   217
Naprijed (Yugoslavia)   423
Naranco, Ediciones, SA (Spain)   320
Narcea SA de Ediciones (Spain)   320
Nardini Editore — Centro Internazionale del Libro SpA (Italy)   217
narodna biblioteka, Centralna, SR Crne Gore (Yugoslavia)   425
Narodna biblioteka NR Bosne i Hercegovine (Yugoslavia)   425
Narodna biblioteka SR Srbije (Yugoslavia)   425
Narodna Biblioteka Srbije (Yugoslavia)   425
Narodna in univerzitetna knjižnica (Ljubljana) (Yugoslavia)   425
Narodna Knjiga (Yugoslavia)   423
Narodna Kultura (Bulgaria)   58
Narodna Mladezh (Bulgaria)   58
'Narodna Prosveta', Darzhavno Izdatelstvo, (Bulgaria)   58
Narodne Novine (Yugoslavia)   423
Narongsarn (Thailand)   354

Narosa Publishing House (India)   189
Narr, Gunter, Verlag (Federal Republic of Germany)   148
Naša Djeca (Yugoslavia)   423
Naša Kniga (Yugoslavia)   423
Nascimento, Editorial, SA (Chile)   62
Naše Vojsko, Nakladatelství a distribuce knih, (Czechoslovakia)   70
Naše vojsko Prizes (Czechoslovakia)   73
Nasional, Pustaka, Pte Ltd (Republic of Singapore)   305
Nasional, Pustaka, Pte Ltd (Republic of Singapore)   306
Nasionale Boekhandel Ltd (Republic of South Africa)   309
Nasionale Boekhandel (SWA) (Pty) Ltd (Namibia)   255
Nasionale Boekwinkels Bpk (Republic of South Africa)   312
Nasou Ltd (Republic of South Africa)   310
Nassau, Editions, (Mauritius)   247
Nassau Public Library (Bahamas)   31
'Nasza Ksiegarnia', Instytut Wydawniczy, (Poland)   292
Nateev-Printing and Publishing Enterprises Ltd (Israel)   208
Nathan, Fernand, Editeur (France)   101
Nation, Verlag der, (German Democratic Republic)   116
National Academy of Letters (Sahitya Akademi) Rabindra Bhavan (India)   197
National Archives (Egypt)   82
National Archives (Libya)   241
National Archives (New Zealand)   272
National Archives (Sri Lanka)   326
National Archives (Trinidad and Tobago)   356
National Archives (Zimbabwe)   429
National Archives and Records Centre (Republic of Singapore)   306
National Archives Division (Thailand)   355
National Archives of Fiji (Fiji)   84
National Archives of India (India)   196
National Archives of Malawi (Malawi)   243
National Archives of Malaysia (Malaysia)   245
National Archives of Nigeria Library (Nigeria)   277
National Archives of Pakistan (Pakistan)   283
National Archives of Tanzania (Tanzania)   353
National Archives of Zambia (Zambia)   428
National Assembly Library (Egypt)   82
National Assembly Library (Republic of Korea)   238
National Award for Poetry and the Novel (Portugal)   298
National Bank, Library of the, (Afghanistan)   1
National Bank of Pakistan Prize for Literature (Pakistan)   284
National Book Agency (P) Ltd (India)   189
National Book Centre of Bangladesh (Bangladesh)   31
National Book, The, Co (China (Taiwan))   64
National Book Council (Australia)   10
National Book Council Awards (Australia)   22
National Book Council of Pakistan (Pakistan)   281
National Book Development Council of Singapore (Republic of Singapore)   304
National Book Development Council of Singapore Book Awards (Republic of Singapore)   307
National Book Institute Prizes (Brazil)   57
National Book, The, League (United Kingdom)   413
National Book Store (Philippines)   288
National Book Store (Philippines)   289
National Book Store (Republic of Singapore)   306
National Book Trust (India)   189
National Bookshop and Branches (Bahrain)   31
National Central Library (China (Taiwan))   64
National Centre of Archives (Iraq)   202
National Christian Education Council (United Kingdom)   393
National Computing Centre (United Kingdom)   393
National Council for Voluntary Organizations (United Kingdom)   393
National Council of Applied Economic Research, Publications Division (India)   189
National Council of Educational Research & Training, Publication Department (India)   189
National Council of Ethnographic Arts and Literature of China (China (Taiwan))   64
National Cultural Awards (Brazil)   57
National Diet Library (Japan)   231
National Educational Company of Zambia Ltd (Zambia)   428
National Essay Award (Portugal)   298
National Federation of Retail Newsagents (Republic of Ireland)   202
National Federation of Retail Newsagents (United Kingdom)   364
National Foundation for Educational Research in England & Wales (United Kingdom)   393
National Free Library Service (Zimbabwe)   429
National Grand Prize of Letters (France)   112
National House for Distributing and Advertising (Iraq)   202
National Information and Documentation Centre (Egypt)   82
National Information and Documentation Centre (Egypt)   82
National Institute, Division of Documentation, of Science and Technology (Philippines)   289

National Institute for Compilation and Translation (China (Taiwan))   64
National Institute of Administration Library (Socialist Republic of Viet Nam)   420
National Institute of Education Library (Uganda)   360
National Library (Burma)   59
National Library (Guyana)   174
National Library (Iran)   201
National Library (Iraq)   202
National Library (Libya)   241
National Library (Nepal)   255
National Library (Pakistan)   283
National Library (Qatar)   300
National Library (Saudi Arabia)   303
National Library (Republic of Singapore)   306
National Library and Archives of Ethiopia (Ethiopia)   83
National Library, Central, (Republic of Korea)   238
National Library 'Ivan Vazov' (Bulgaria)   58
National Library of Australia (Australia)   16
National Library of Australia (Australia)   20
National Library of Greece (Greece)   172
National Library of Higher Education and Culture (Somalia)   307
National Library of Ireland (Republic of Ireland)   204
National Library of Ireland Society (Republic of Ireland)   205
National Library of Jamaica, Institute of Jamaica (Jamaica)   224
National Library of Latakia (Syria)   353
National Library of Malaysia (Malaysia)   245
National Library of Malta (Malta)   246
National Library of New Zealand (New Zealand)   272
National Library of Nigeria (Nigeria)   277
National Library of Scotland (United Kingdom)   411
National Library of Thailand, The, (Thailand)   355
National Library Service (Belize)   45
National Library, The, Government of India (India)   196
National Library, The, of the Philippines (Philippines)   289
National Literary Awards (Burma)   59
National Literary Awards (Malaysia)   246
National Magazine Co Ltd (United Kingdom)   393
National Minorities Publishing House (People's Republic of China)   63
National Museum (India)   189
National Museum Library (India)   196
National Museum Library (Sri Lanka)   326
National Museums, Department of, (Sri Lanka)   326
National Portrait Gallery (Publications Dept) (United Kingdom)   393
National Press Library (Jordan)   233
National Press, The, (Republic of Ireland)   204
National Prize for Literature (Mexico)   253
National Prize for Literature (Venezuela)   420
National Publishing House (India)   189
National Story Prize (Colombia)   67
National Technological University, Library of the, of Athens (Greece)   172
National Trust Children's Series (United Kingdom)   394
National University of Lesotho Library (Lesotho)   240
National University of Malaysia Library (Malaysia)   245
National University of Singapore Library (Republic of Singapore)   306
National War College Library (China (Taiwan))   64
Nationale Forschungs- und Gedenkstätten der klassischen deutschen Literatur — Zentralbibliothek der deutschen Klassik (German Democratic Republic)   117
Nationale, Librairie, (Ministère Education National) (Benin)   45
Nationwide Book Services (United Kingdom)   409
Native Language Bureau (Namibia)   255
Native Language Bureau (Namibia)   255
Natoli and Stefan Literary Agency (Italy)   220
Natsionalniya Savet, Izdatelstvo na, na Otetchestveniya Front (Bulgaria)   58
Natur och Kultur, Bokförlaget, (Sweden)   331
Natura, Editorial, SRL (Venezuela)   419
Natura-Verlag (Switzerland)   345
Natural History Museum (United Kingdom)   394
Natural Resources Development College Library (Zambia)   428
Naučna biblioteka (Yugoslavia)   425
Naučna Knjiga (Yugoslavia)   423
Nauka, Darzhavno Izdatelstvo, i Izkustvo (Bulgaria)   58
'Nauka', Izdatelstvo, (Union of Soviet Socialist Republics)   361
Naukowe, Państwowe Wydawnictwo, (Poland)   292
Naukowo-Techniczne, Wydawnictwa, (Poland)   292
Naumann, Ulrich, (Republic of South Africa)   312
Nauta, Ediciones, SA (Spain)   320
Nautic, AB, (Sweden)   332
Nautical Publishing Co Ltd (United Kingdom)   394
Nautiska Förlaget Sjökortshallen AB (Sweden)   332
Nauwelaerts, NV Uitgeverij, Edition SA (Belgium)   39
Navajivan Trust (India)   190
Navers, Rasmus, Forlag (Denmark)   76
Naville & Cie SA (Switzerland)   345
Navoi, Gosudarstvennaya biblioteka UzSSR im Alishera, (Union of Soviet Socialist Republics)   363

Navyug Publishers (India) 190
Naya Prokash (India) 190
Ndanda Mission Press (Tanzania) 353
Ndebele Readers' Book Club (Zimbabwe) 429
Ndërmarrja e Botimeve Ushtarake (Albania) 1
Ndërmarrja e Librit (Albania) 1
Ndola Public Library (Zambia) 428
Near East School, Library of the, of Theology (Lebanon) 240
Nebelspalter Verlag (Switzerland) 345
Nederlands Bibliotheek en Lektuurcentrum (NBLC) (Netherlands) 267
Nederland's Boekhuis BV (Netherlands) 262
Nederlandsche Boekhandel, Uitgeverij De, (Belgium) 39
Nederlandsche Vereeniging voor Druk- en Boekkunst (Netherlands) 255
Nederlandsche Vereniging van Antiquaren (Netherlands) 255
Nederlandsche Zondagsschool Vereeniging (Netherlands) 262
Nederlandse Boekenclub (Netherlands Book Club) (Netherlands) 266
Nederlandse Boekverkopersbond (Netherlands) 255
Nederlandse Lezerskring (Netherlands) 266
Nederlandse Lezerskring Boek en Plaat BV (Netherlands) 262
Nederlandse Vereniging van Bedrijfsarchivarissen (Netherlands) 267
Nederlandse Vereniging van Bibliothecarissen, Documentalisten en literatuuronderzoekers (NVB) (Netherlands) 267
'Nedra', Izdatelstvo, (Union of Soviet Socialist Republics) 361
Née, Alfred, Prize (France) 112
Neff, Paul, Verlag KG (Austria) 26
Neff, Paul, Verlag KG (Federal Republic of Germany) 148
Negara, Perpustakaan, (Indonesia) 200
Nègre, Librairie SA Gaston, (Benin) 45
Neguri Editorial SA (Spain) 320
Nehru Memorial Museum Library (India) 196
Neilson, John Shaw, Poetry Award (Australia) 22
Nejat Yalki Kitabevi (Turkey) 359
Nelissen, Uitgeverij H, BV (Netherlands) 262
Nelson Memorial Public Library (Western Samoa) 421
Nelson, Thomas, Australia (Australia) 16
Nelson, Thomas, (Nigeria) Ltd (Nigeria) 275
Nelson, Thomas, & Sons Ltd (United Kingdom) 394
Nem Chand & Brothers (India) 190
Nena, Librería La, (Argentina) 8
Nepal Academy (Nepal) 255
Nepal-Bharat Sanskritik Kendra Pustakalay (Nepal) 255
Nepal Booksellers (Nepal) 255
Nepal Library Association (Nepal) 255
Neptun-Verlag (Switzerland) 345
Neruda, Librería e Importadora, (El Salvador) 83
Nerva-Verlag (Federal Republic of Germany) 148
Neske, Verlag Günther, (Federal Republic of Germany) 148
Netzach (Israel) 208
Neue Berlin, Verlag das, (German Democratic Republic) 116
Neue Darmstädter Verlagsanstalt (Federal Republic of Germany) 148
Neue Diana Press AG (Switzerland) 345
Neue Gesellschaft, Verlag, GmbH (Federal Republic of Germany) 148
Neue Kommentare (Federal Republic of Germany) 148
Neue Kritik, Verlag, KG (Federal Republic of Germany) 148
Neue Mitte, Edition, (Austria) 26
Neue Presse Agentur (NPA) (Switzerland) 351
Neue Schulmann, Verlag Der, (Federal Republic of Germany) 148
Neue Schweizer Bibliothek (Switzerland) 351
Neue Stadt, Verlag, (Switzerland) 345
Neue Stadt, Verlag, GmbH (Federal Republic of Germany) 148
Neue Wirtschafts-Briefe, Verlag, GmbH (Federal Republic of Germany) 149
Neue Zürcher Zeitung (Switzerland) 345
Neuer Jugendschriften-Verlag (Federal Republic of Germany) 149
Neuer Weg, Verlag, (Federal Republic of Germany) 149
Neues Leben, Verlag, (German Democratic Republic) 116
Neufeld-Verlag und Galerie (Austria) 26
Neufeld Verlag und Galerie (Switzerland) 345
Neugebauer, Buchhandlung W, GmbH und Co KG (Austria) 29
Neugebauer Press Verlag für bibliophile Drucke (Austria) 26
Neugebauer, Wolfgang, (Austria) 26
Neugebauer, Wolfgang, (Austria) 26
Neukirchener Verlag des Erziehungvereins GmbH (Federal Republic of Germany) 149
Neumann-Neudamm, Verlag J, KG (Federal Republic of Germany) 149
Neureuter, Verlag für Messepublikationen Thomas, KG (Federal Republic of Germany) 149

Neustadt International Prize for Literature (International Literary Prizes) 443
New Africa Booksellers (Somalia) 307
New Aqua, P T, Press/Aries Lima (Indonesia) 199
New Australian Library Pty Ltd (Australia) 16
New Book Centre (India) 190
New Cavendish Books (United Kingdom) 394
New Caxton Library Service Ltd (United Kingdom) 394
New City, London (United Kingdom) 394
New Countryside Book Club (Poland) 293
New Educational Press (United Kingdom) 394
New English Library, The, Ltd (United Kingdom) 394
New Fiction, The, Society (United Kingdom) 410
New Horn Press Ltd (Nigeria) 276
New Interlitho SpA (Italy) 217
New Leaf Books Ltd (United Kingdom) 394
New Left Books (United Kingdom) 394
New Light Publishers (India) 190
New Order Book Co (India) 190
New Portway (United Kingdom) 394
New South Wales Booksellers' Association (Australia) 10
New South Wales University Press Ltd (Australia) 16
New University Education (United Kingdom) 394
New Writers' Press (Republic of Ireland) 204
New Writers Stipendium for Literature (Austria) 30
New Zealand Anzac Fellowships (Australia) 22
New Zealand Authors, The, Fund (New Zealand) 268
New Zealand Book Awards (New Zealand) 273
New Zealand Book Council (New Zealand) 268
New Zealand Book Trade Organization (New Zealand) 268
New Zealand Council for Educational Research (New Zealand) 270
New Zealand Educational Institute (NZEI) (New Zealand) 270
New Zealand Government Printing Office (New Zealand) 270
New Zealand Library Association (New Zealand) 272
New Zealand Library Committee (New Zealand) 272
New Zealand Literary Fund (New Zealand) 273
New Zealand Maori Artists & Writers Society Inc (New Zealand) 272
New Zealand Playwrights Association (New Zealand) 272
New Zealand Women Writers' Society (New Zealand) 272
New Zealand Writers Guild (New Zealand) 272
Newdigate, Sir Roger, Prize for English Verse (United Kingdom) 415
Newman, M, (Israel) 208
Newman Art (Republic of South Africa) 310
Newnes Books (United Kingdom) 394
Newnes-Butterworths (United Kingdom) 394
Newnes-Technical (United Kingdom) 394
Newrick Associates Ltd (New Zealand) 270
Newservice Ltd (Seychelles) 304
Newspread International (Kenya) 234
Newton Compton Editori SRL (Italy) 217
Nexus Books (New Zealand) 270
Ney's Libros and Revistas (Honduras) 174
Nha Xuat Ban Van Hoc (Literature Publishing House) (Socialist Republic of Viet Nam) 420
Nibondh (Thailand) 354
Nibondh (Gaysorn) (Thailand) 355
Nicholson, Robert, Publications Ltd (United Kingdom) 394
Nici (Belgium) 39
Nicolai, M (Laos) 239
Nicolaische Verlagsbuchhandlung GmbH und Co KG (Federal Republic of Germany) 149
Niederösterreichisches Pressehaus, Verlag, mbH (Austria) 26
Niedersächsische Staats- und Universitätsbibliothek (Federal Republic of Germany) 166
Niedieck Linder AG (Switzerland) 351
Niemeyer, Max, Verlag (Federal Republic of Germany) 149
Niemeyer, VEB Max, Verlag (German Democratic Republic) 116
Niemeyer, Verlag C W, (Federal Republic of Germany) 149
Nieuwe Wieken (Netherlands) 262
Nigar, Libreria y Editorial, SRL (Argentina) 6
Niger (Acada) Bookshop Ltd (Nigeria) 277
Nigeria Educational Research, The, Council (Nigeria) 278
Nigerian Baptist Book Stores (Nigeria) 277
Nigerian Book Suppliers Ltd (Nigeria) 277
Nigerian Booksellers' Association (Nigeria) 274
Nigerian Broadcasting Corporation (Nigeria) 278
Nigerian Library Association (Nigeria) 277
Nigerian Publishers' Association (Nigeria) 274
Nigerian Trade Review (Nigeria) 276
Niggli, Verlag Arthur, AG (Switzerland) 345
Nihon Bunka Kagakusha Co Ltd (Japan) 228
Nihon Eibungakkai (Japan) 232
Nihon Shoten Kumiai Rengokai (Japan) 224
Nihon Vogue (Publishing) Co Ltd (Japan) 228
Nijgh en Van Ditmar, BV Uitgeverij, (Netherlands) 262
Nijhoff, Martinus, BV (Netherlands) 266

Nijhoff, Martinus, Prize (International Literary Prizes) 443
Nijhoff, Martinus, Publishers (Netherlands) 262
Nikas (Greece) 172
Nile & Mackenzie Ltd (United Kingdom) 394
Niloe, Bokforlaget, AB (Sweden) 332
Nimaroo Publishers (Australia) 16
'Nine', The, Prize (Sweden) 336
Niove (Dominican Republic) 80
Nippon Bungaku Kyokai (Japan) 232
Nippon Dokubungakkai (Japan) 232
Nippon Dokumentesyon Kyokai (Japan) 231
Nippon Furansu-go Furansu-bungaku Kai (Japan) 232
Nippon Hikaku Bungakukai (Japan) 232
Nippon Igaku Toshokan Kyokai (Japan) 231
Nippon Nogaku Toshokan Kyogikai (JAALD) (Japan) 231
Nippon Romazikai (Japan) 232
Nippon Rosiya Bungakkai (Japan) 232
Nippon Shuppan Hanbai KK (Japan) 231
Nippon Toshokan Gakkai (Japan) 232
Nippon Toshokan Kyokai (Japan) 232
Nippon Yakugaku Toshokan Kyogikai (Japan) 232
Nirmal Book Agency (India) 190
Nisbet, James, & Co Ltd (United Kingdom) 394
Nitzaninn (Israel) 208
Niven, Frederick, Literary Award (United Kingdom) 415
Niyom Vidhya (Thailand) 354
Nizet, Librairie A-G, (France) 101
Nizza, Agencia de Librerías, (Paraguay) 286
Nizza, Ediciones, (Paraguay) 286
Njala University College Bookshop (Sierra Leone) 304
Njala University College Library (University of Sierra Leone) (Sierra Leone) 304
Njala University Publishing Centre (Sierra Leone) 304
Njogu Gitene Publications (Kenya) 234
Nkrumah Teachers' College Library (Zambia) 428
Nnamdi Azikiwe Library (Nigeria) 277
Nobel, Livraria, (Brazil) 55
Nobel, Livraria, SA Editôra (Brazil) 53
Nobel Prize for Literature (International Literary Prizes) 443
Nobel Prize, The, Library (United Kingdom) 410
Nobele, F De, (France) 101
Noblet Editôra e Distribuidora Ltda (Brazil) 53
Noguer, Editorial, SA (Spain) 320
Nolit (Yugoslavia) 425
Nolit Publishing House (Yugoslavia) 423
Nolte, Verlag Friedrich, (Federal Republic of Germany) 149
Noma Prize for Juvenile Novel (Japan) 233
Noma Prize for Literature (Japan) 233
Nomath (Belgium) 39
Nomos Verlagsgesellschaft mbH und Co KG (Federal Republic of Germany) 149
Nonesuch, The, Library (United Kingdom) 394
Noord-Hollandsche Uitgeversmaatschappij, BV, (North Holland Publishing Company) (Netherlands) 262
Noordhoff International Publishing (Netherlands) 262
Noordnederlands Boekbedrijf, Het, NV (Belgium) 39
Noorduijn BV (Netherlands) 262
Nord, Editrice, Sdf (Italy) 217
Nord-Süd Verlag (Switzerland) 346
Nordbok, AB, (Sweden) 332
Norddeutscher Verleger- und Buchhändler-Verband eV (Federal Republic of Germany) 119
Norden, Förlagshuset, AB (Sweden) 332
Nordic Council Literary Prize (International Literary Prizes) 443
Nórdica, Editorial, Ltda (Brazil) 53
Nordisk Boghandel (Denmark) 78
Nordisk Kolportage Forlag A/S (Denmark) 76
Nordisk Musikforleggerunion (International Organizations) 433
Nordisk Romanforlag A/S (Denmark) 76
Nordiska Bokhandeln, AB, (Sweden) 332
Nordiska Bokhandeln, AB, (Sweden) 334
Nordiska Musikförlaget, AB, (Edition Wilhelm Hansen Stockholm) (Sweden) 332
Nordiska Teaterforlaget Edition Wilhelm Hansen (Denmark) 77
Nordiska Teaterförlaget/Edition Wilhelm Hansen (Sweden) 334
Nordiska Vetenskapliga Bibliotekarieförbundet (International Organizations) 433
Nordjyske Landsbibliotek, Det, (Denmark) 78
Noregs Boklag (Norway) 279
Norfolk Press (United Kingdom) 394
Norges Landbrukshøgskoles Bibliotek (Norway) 281
Noria, Editions La, (France) 101
Norlis, Olaf, Bokhandel A/S (Norway) 280
Norlis, Olaf, Forlag A/S (Norway) 279
Norma, Editorial, y Cia SCA (Colombia) 65
Norma PVBA (Belgium) 39
Normalizacyjne, Wydawnictwa, (Poland) 292
Norman, Jill, Ltd (United Kingdom) 394
Normanns, M, Forlag A/S (Denmark) 76
Normans Förlag AB (Sweden) 332

490 INDEX

Norn (Thailand) 354
Norsk Antikvarbokhandlerforening (Norway) 278
Norsk Bibliotekarlag (Norway) 281
Norsk Bibliotekforening (Norway) 281
Norsk Bokhandler Medhjelper Forening (Norway) 278
Norsk Bokhandlersamband (Norway) 278
Norsk Bokimport A/S (Norway) 278
Norsk Bokimport A/S (Norway) 280
Norsk Boknummerkontor (Norway) 278
Norsk Dokumentasjonsgruppe (Norway) 281
Norsk Forleggersamband (Norway) 278
Norsk Kunstforlag A/S (Norway) 279
Norsk Musikkforleggerforening (Norway) 278
Norske Akademi for Sprog og Litteratur (Norway) 281
Norske Bokhandlerforening (Norway) 278
Norske Bokklubben, Den, A/S (Norway) 280
Norske Deitidsbibliotekarers Yrkeslag (Norway) 281
Norske Forfatterforening (Norway) 278
Norske Forleggerforening, Den, (Norway) 278
Norske Forskningsbibliotekarers Forening (Norway) 281
Norske Samlaget, Det, (Norway) 279
Norske Videnskaps-Akademi, Det, (Norway) 281
Norstedt, AB P A, och Söners Förlag (Sweden) 332
Norte, Editorial, SAIC (Argentina) 6
Norte, Librería, (Argentina) 8
North Light (United Kingdom) 394
Northern Nigerian Publishing Co Ltd (Nigeria) 276
Northern Technical College Library (Zambia) 428
Northwood Books (United Kingdom) 394
Norwegian Association of Children's and Young People's Authors (Norway) 278
Norwegian Association of Translators (Norway) 281
Nostrand, Van, Reinhold Australia Pty Ltd (Australia) 16
Nota, Mip, (Yugoslavia) 423
Notre Dame, Librairie, (Benin) 45
Notre Dame, Librairie, (Chad) 61
Nottbeck, Verlag Wissenschaft und Politik, Berend von, (Federal Republic of Germany) 149
Nouveau Cercle parisien du Livre (France) 108
Nouveautés de l'Enseignement-éditions andré casteilla (France) 101
Nouvel Office d'Edition et de Diffusion (Les Productions de Paris — NOE) (France) 101
Nouvelle Agence, La, (France) 107
Nouvelle Cité (France) 101
Nouvelle Diffusion (Belgium) 39
Nouvelle, Librairie, (Gabon) 113
Nouvelles Editions Françaises (France) 101
Nouvelles Editions Latines (France) 101
Nouvelles Editions, Les, Africaines (Ivory Coast) 223
Nouvelles Editions, Les, Africaines (Senegal) 303
Nouvelles Editions, Les, Africaines (NEA) (Togo) 356
Nouvelles Editions Marabout, Les, SA (Belgium) 39
Nouvelles Editions Rationalistes SA (France) 101
Nouvelles Editions Vokaer SA (Belgium) 39
Nouvelles Feuilles Familiales (Belgium) 39
Nova Aguilar, Editôra, SA (Brazil) 53
Nova, Editorial, SACI (Argentina) 6
Nova Epoca Editorial Ltda (Brazil) 53
Nova Fronteira, Editôra, (Brazil) 53
Nova Hrvatska Ltd (United Kingdom) 394
Nova Knjiga (Yugoslavia) 423
Nova-Press International Publishers Ltd (Switzerland) 346
Nova Terra (Spain) 320
Novalis Verlag AG (Switzerland) 346
NovaPart Verlag GmbH (Federal Republic of Germany) 149
Novaro, Organización Editorial, SA (Mexico) 250
Novel Prize (France) 112
Novel Prize (Republic of Ireland) 205
Novello & Co Ltd (United Kingdom) 394
Novelty Trading Co (Jamaica) 223
Novissima, Edizioni di, (Italy) 217
Novos, Editions, SA (Switzerland) 346
'Novosti', Agentstvo Pechati, (Apn) (Union of Soviet Socialist Republics) 361
Novus Forlag A/S (Norway) 279
Nüchtern, Verlag Monika, (Federal Republic of Germany) 149
Nuestra Tierra, Editorial, (Uruguay) 417
Nueva Editorial Interamericana SA de CV (Mexico) 250
Nueva Imagen, Editorial, SA (Mexico) 250
Nueva Visión (Argentina) 8
Nueva Visión, Ediciones, SAIC (Argentina) 6
Nuevo, Editorial, Continente (Honduras) 174
Nuevos Horizontes, Editorial, (Nicaragua) 273
Numismatischer Verlag P N Schulten (Federal Republic of Germany) 149
Nunes, Livraria, (Portugal) 298
Nuova Foglio, La, SpA (Italy) 217
Nuova Italia, La, Editrice (Italy) 217
Nuova Vallecchi Editore SpA (Italy) 217
Nurnberg, Andrew, Associates Ltd (United Kingdom) 408
Nusa Indah (Indonesia) 199
Nusser Verlag (Federal Republic of Germany) 149
Nwamife Publishers Ltd (Nigeria) 276
Nyatsime College Library (Zimbabwe) 430

Nybloms Förlag (Sweden) 332
Nye Bøker, Bokklubben, (New Book Club) (Norway) 280
Nymphenburger Verlagshandlung GmbH (Federal Republic of Germany) 149

O N K Copyright Agency (Turkey) 358
O R S T O M (France) 101
O S (Organizzazioni Speciali SRL) (Italy) 217
Oasis Books (United Kingdom) 394
Oasis, Ediciones, SA (Mexico) 251
Obelisk, Nakladatelství, (Czechoslovakia) 70
Obelisk-Verlag (Austria) 26
Oberbaumverlag (Federal Republic of Germany) 149
Oberösterreichischer Landesverlag (Austria) 26
Obod (Yugoslavia) 423
Obra, La, (Argentina) 6
O'Brien Educational (Republic of Ireland) 204
O'Brien, The, Press (Republic of Ireland) 204
Obunsha Co Ltd (Japan) 228
Obzor (Yugoslavia) 423
Obzor, vydavatel'stvo knih a casopisov národní podnik (Czechoslovakia) 70
Oceania Printers Ltd (Fiji) 84
Octagon, The, Press Ltd (United Kingdom) 394
Octopus Books Ltd (United Kingdom) 394
Octopus Verlag (Austria) 26
Odense Centralbibliotek (Denmark) 78
Odense Universitetsbibliotek (Denmark) 78
Odeon (United Kingdom) 395
Odeon Book Club (Czechoslovakia) 72
Odeon, nakladatelství krásné literatury a umění (Czechoslovakia) 70
Odeon Store LP (Thailand) 354
Odhams Books (United Kingdom) 395
O'Donovan, Anne, Pty Ltd (Australia) 16
Odörfer-Verlags GmbH (Federal Republic of Germany) 149
Odusote Bookstores Ltd (Nigeria) 277
Oeil, L', Ouvert (France) 108
Oekumenischer Verlag Dr R-F Edel (Federal Republic of Germany) 149
Oesch, Emil, Verlag AG (Switzerland) 346
Oestergaard, Paul, GmbH (Federal Republic of Germany) 149
Oetinger, Verlag Friedrich, (Federal Republic of Germany) 149
Oetker, August, (Federal Republic of Germany) 150
Oeuvre Gravée, L', (Switzerland) 346
Ofer Publishing House (Israel) 208
Offene Worte, Verlag, (Federal Republic of Germany) 150
Office Arabe de Presse et de Documentation (Syria) 352
Office Central de Librairie Sàrl (France) 101
Office Central de Lisieux SA (France) 101
Office de Documentation Bibliographique et de Diffusion (France) 102
Office de la Recherche Scientifique et Technique Outre-Mer (French Guiana) 113
Office de la Recherche Scientifique et Technique Outre Mer (ORSTOM) (France) 102
Office de Promotion de L'Edition Française (France) 87
Office du Livre Malagasy (OLM) (Democratic Republic of Madagascar) 242
Office du Livre SA (Buchhaus AG) (Switzerland) 346
Office international de Librairie (Belgium) 43
Office national des Libraries (Popular Republic of Congo) 67
Oficiul de Informare Documentara in Stiintele Sociale si Politice (Office of Information and Documentation in Social and Political Sciences) (Romania) 301
Ofiria, Edizioni, (Italy) 217
Ogbalu, F C, (Nigeria) 276
Ogunsanya Press, Publishers and Bookstores Ltd (Nigeria) 276
Ohlssons, AB Håkan, Förlag (Sweden) 332
Ohm, Karl, Verlag (Federal Republic of Germany) 150
Ohmsha Ltd (Japan) 228
Ohridski, Narodna i univerzitetska biblioteka 'Kliment, ' (Yugoslavia) 425
Oikos-Tau SA Ediciones (Spain) 320
Oireachtas Library (Republic of Ireland) 204
Oiseau-Lyre, Editions de l', (Monaco) 253
Oisterwijk (Netherlands) 262
Ojeda Fierro, Nicolas, e Hijos (Peru) 287
Okapi Centre de Diffusion (Zaire) 427
'Oktobar', Literary Club, (Yugoslavia) 426
Oktoberförlaget AB (Sweden) 332
Olamenu (Israel) 208
Oldenbourg, Verlag, (Austria) 26
Oldenbourg, R, Verlag GmbH (Federal Republic of Germany) 150
Oleander, The, Press (United Kingdom) 395
Oliphants (United Kingdom) 395
Olive Books of Israel (Israel) 208

Oliver & Boyd (Australia) 16
Oliver & Boyd (United Kingdom) 395
Olle und Wolter, Verlag, (Federal Republic of Germany) 150
Olms, Edition, AG (Switzerland) 346
Olms, Georg, Verlag (Federal Republic of Germany) 150
Olschki, Leo S, (Italy) 217
Ölschläger, Verlag für Wirtschaftsskripten, Dipl Kfm C, GmbH (Federal Republic of Germany) 150
Ölschläger, Verlag, GmbH (Federal Republic of Germany) 150
Olympia, Nakladatelství CSTV, (Czechoslovakia) 70
Olympia Press Italia (Italy) 217
Olympio, Livraría José, Editôra SA (Brazil) 53
Olzog, Günter, Verlag GmbH (Federal Republic of Germany) 150
O'Mahony & Co Ltd (Republic of Ireland) 204
Omega (United Kingdom) 395
Omega Boek BV (Netherlands) 262
Omega, Ediciones, SA (Spain) 320
Omnia, Edizioni, Medica (Italy) 218
Omniboek, Uitgeverij, (Netherlands) 263
Omun Kak (Republic of Korea) 237
Oncken Verlag KG (Federal Republic of Germany) 150
O'Neil, Lloyd, Pty Ltd (Australia) 16
Ongaku No Tomo Sha Corporation (Japan) 228
Onibonoje Book Club (Nigeria) 277
Onibonoje Press & Book Industries (Nigeria) Ltd (Nigeria) 277
Önskeboken (Sweden) 334
Ontwikkeling, Uitgeverij S V, (Belgium) 39
Oosthoek (Netherlands) 263
Opal, Bokförlaget, AB (Sweden) 332
Opdebeek, Uitgeverij, (Belgium) 39
Open Books Publishing Ltd (United Kingdom) 395
Open University, The, Press (Open University Educational Enterprises Ltd) (United Kingdom) 395
Openbare Bibliotheek (Netherlands) 266
Openbare Leeszaal en Bibliotheek (Netherlands Antilles) 268
Openbare Leeszaal en Boekerij (Netherlands Antilles) 268
Opera Mundi SA (France) 102
Operaie, Nuove Edizioni, SRL (Italy) 218
Ophrys, Editions, (France) 102
Oppersdorff, Inigo von, Verlag (Switzerland) 346
Opta Editions (France) 108
Optimum (United Kingdom) 395
Opus Records and Publishing House (Czechoslovakia) 70
Orac, Verlag, (Austria) 27
Orangerie Galerie und Verlag, Gerhard F Reinz (Federal Republic of Germany) 150
Orante, Editions de l', (France) 102
Orban, Editions Oliver, (France) 102
Orbe, Editorial, (Cuba) 68
Orbis Boekhandel NV (Belgium) 40
Orbis, Nakladatelství, (Czechoslovakia) 70
Orbis Publishing Ltd (United Kingdom) 395
Orbit (United Kingdom) 395
Orbit NV (Netherlands) 263
Orders Clearing (United Kingdom) 364
Ordfront tryckeri & förlag AB (Sweden) 332
Ordina Editions (Belgium) 40
Ordnance Survey (United Kingdom) 395
Orell Füssli (Switzerland) 351
Orell Füssli Verlag (Switzerland) 346
Orellana, Librería, (Chile) 62
Oresko Books (United Kingdom) 395
Organisation, Les Editions d', (France) 102
Organisator, Verlag, AG (Switzerland) 346
Organización Bienestar Estudiantes (OBE) (Venezuela) 419
Organization for African Unity Library (Ethiopia) 83
Organizzazioni Speciali SRL (Italy) 218
Orhan Özsisman (Turkey) 359
Oriel Press Ltd (United Kingdom) 395
Orient Book Club (India) 195
Orient Longman Ltd (India) 190
Orient Paperbacks (Division of Vision Books) (India) 190
Oriental Book Service (Bangladesh) 32
Oriental Books Reprint Corporation (India) 190
Oriental Economist Ltd (K K Toyo Keizai Shimposha) (Japan) 228
Oriental Press BV (APA) (Netherlands) 263
Oriental & Religious, The, Publishing Corp Ltd (Pakistan) 282
Orientalia Christiana, Edizioni, (Italy) 218
Orientalia Publishers (Pakistan) 282
Orientaliste, Uitgeverij, PVBA (Belgium) 40
Oriente, Editorial, (Cuba) 68
Origo-Verlag (Switzerland) 346
Orion, Ediciones, (Argentina) 6
Orion, Editorial, (Mexico) 251
Orion-Heimreiter Verlag GmbH (Federal Republic of Germany) 150
Orion Press (Japan) 231
Orion, Uitgeverij, (Belgium) 40
Orissa Sahitya Akademi Award (India) 198

INDEX 491

Orisun Editions (Nigeria) 276
Ormeraie, Michel de l', (France) 102
Örn og Örlygur HF (Iceland) 180
Orpan Export (Poland) 293
Országos Müszaki Könyvtár és Dokumentációs Központ (Hungary) 178
Országos Széchényi Könyvtár (Hungary) 178
Országos Széchényi Könyvtár Magyar ISBN Iroda (Hungary) 176
Orte-Verlag (Switzerland) 346
Ortells, Alfredo, Ferriz (Spain) 320
Orvieto, Laura, Prize (Italy) 222
Orwell, George, Memorial Prize (United Kingdom) 415
Osaka Gakuin University Library (Japan) 231
Osaka Prefectural Nakanoshima Library (Japan) 231
Oslobodenje, NIP, (Yugoslavia) 423
Osprey Publishing Ltd (United Kingdom) 395
Ossolińskich Biblioteka, Zaklad Narodowy im, Polska Akademia Nauk (Library of the Ossoliński National Institute of the Polish Academy of Science) (Poland) 294
Ossolińskich, Zaklad Narodowy im, Wydawnictwo Polskiej Akademii Nauk (Poland) 292
Österreichische Exlibris-Gesellschaft (Austria) 30
Österreichische Gesellschaft für Dokumentation und Information (Austria) 30
Österreichische Gesellschaft für Literatur (Austria) 30
Österreichische Nationalbibliothek (Austria) 29
Österreichische Verlagsanstalt GmbH (Austria) 27
Österreichischen Akademie der Wissenschaften, Bibliothek der, (Austria) 29
österreichischen Akademie der Wissenschaften, Verlag der, (Austria) 27
österreichischen Gewerkschaftsbundes, Verlag des, GmbH (Austria) 27
Österreichischen Patentamtes, Bucherei des, (Austria) 29
Österreichischer Agrarverlag, Druck- und Verlags- GmbH (Austria) 27
Österreichischer Buchklub der Jugend (Austria) 29
Österreichischer Bundesverlag GmbH (Austria) 27
Österreichischer Schriftstellerverband (Austria) 23
Österreichischer Verlegerverband (Austria) 23
Österreichisches Institut für Bibliographie (Austria) 30
Österreichisches Institut für Bibliotheksforschung, Dokumentations- und Informationswesen (Austria) 30
Österreichisches Katholisches Bibelwerk (Austria) 27
Österreichisches Staatsarchiv (Austria) 29
Osterrieth, Verlag, (Federal Republic of Germany) 150
Ostrowiak, Rebecca, School of Reading (Republic of South Africa) 310
Osveta (Czechoslovakia) 70
Oswald, Editions Pierre Jean, (France) 102
Otago University Library (New Zealand) 272
Otava Kustannusosakeyhtiö (Finland) 85
Other, The, Award (United Kingdom) 415
Otokar Keršovani-Rijeka (Yugoslavia) 423
Otpaz (Israel) 208
Otsuki Shoten Publishers (Japan) 228
Ott Verlag AG Thun (Switzerland) 346
Ottaviano, Edizioni, (Italy) 218
Otzar Hamoreh (Israel) 208
Oude, De, Linden NV (Belgium) 40
Oudiovista Productions (Pty) Ltd (Republic of South Africa) 310
Oulun Yliopiston Kirjasto (Finland) 86
Outback Press Pty Ltd (Australia) 16
Outrigger Publishers (New Zealand) 270
Ouvrières, Les Editions, SA (France) 102
Overseas Publications Interchange Ltd (United Kingdom) 395
Overseas Publishers Association Amsterdam BV (Netherlands) 263
Overseas Publishers' Representatives Association of Southern Africa (Republic of South Africa) 307
Owen, Peter, Ltd (United Kingdom) 395
Owlet (United Kingdom) 395
Oxford Bibliographical Society (United Kingdom) 412
Oxford Book and Stationery Co (India) 196
Oxford & I B H Publishing Co (India) 190
Oxford Illustrated Press Ltd (United Kingdom) 395
Oxford Microform Publications Ltd (United Kingdom) 395
Oxford Polytechnic Press (United Kingdom) 395
Oxford Railway, The, Publishing Co Ltd (United Kingdom) 395
Oxford University (United Kingdom) 411
Oxford University Press (Australia) 16
Oxford University Press (Hong Kong) 176
Oxford University Press (India) 190
Oxford University Press (Kenya) 234
Oxford University Press (Malaysia) 244
Oxford University Press (New Zealand) 271
Oxford University Press (Pakistan) 282
Oxford University Press (Pakistan) 283
Oxford University Press (Republic of Singapore) 305
Oxford University Press (Tanzania) 353
Oxford University Press (United Kingdom) 395

Oxford University Press Southern Africa (Republic of South Africa) 310
Oxford University Press Southern Africa (Zimbabwe) 429
Oxonian Press (P) Ltd (India) 190
Oya Soichi Nonfiction Prize (Japan) 233
Oyez Publishing Ltd (United Kingdom) 396

P A C, Editions, (Presse-Auto-Conseil) (France) 102
P B D S (United Kingdom) 364
P E N All—India Centre (India) 197
P E N Centre (Greece) 173
P E N Centre (Liechtenstein) 241
P E N Centre of Zimbabwe (Zimbabwe) 430
P E N, Centro del, Internacional (Peru) 287
P E N Club (Jamaica) 224
P E N Club (Monaco) 253
P E N Club (Romania) 302
P E N Club Award, Yugoslav, (International Literary Prizes) 443
P E N Club, Belgian French Centre, International, (Belgium) 44
P E N Club de Bolivia (Centro Internacional de Escritores) (Bolivia) 47
P E N Club de la Argentina (Argentina) 9
P E N Club de Puerto Rico (Puerto Rico) 299
P E N Club de Suisse romande (Switzerland) 352
P E N Club di Italian Romansch (Switzerland) 352
P E N Club, Flemish Centre, International, (Belgium) 44
P E N Club Français (France) 109
P E N Club International Centre de Côte d'Ivoire (Ivory Coast) 223
P E N Club Medal, Hungarian, (International Literary Prizes) 443
P E N Club of Iran (Iran) 201
P E N-Club, Österreichischer, (Austria) 30
P E N Club Prizes, Polish, (International Literary Prizes) 443
P E N Club, Yugoslav, (Yugoslavia) 426
P E N Clube do Brasil (Associação Universal de Escritores) (Brazil) 56
P E N, Dacca Centre for International, Madhura (Bangladesh) 32
P E N English Centre (United Kingdom) 413
P E N, Hong Kong Chinese, Centre (Hong Kong) 176
P E N, Hong Kong English, Centre (Hong Kong) 176
P E N Internacional de Escritores de Colombia (Colombia) 66
P E N, International (International Organizations) 433
P E N, International, Centre (Iceland) 180
P E N International Centre (Italy) 222
P E N, International, Centre (Philippines) 290
P E N, International, Centre (Venezuela) 420
P E N, International, (Melbourne Centre) (Australia) 21
P E N International New Zealand Centre (New Zealand) 272
P E N, International, (Sydney Centre) (Australia) 21
P E N International-Thailand Centre (Thailand) 355
P E N, Irish, (Republic of Ireland) 205
P E N, Israeli, Centre (Israel) 211
P E N, Japan, Club (Japan) 232
P E N-Klubb, Den Norske, (Norway) 281
P E N, Korean, Centre (Republic of Korea) 238
P E N, Lebanese, Club (Lebanon) 240
P E N, Magyar, Club (Hungary) 179
P E N, Mexican, Club (Mexico) 252
P E N Netherlands Centre of the International, (Netherlands) 267
P E N, Polish, Club (Poland) 294
P E N, Portuguese, Centre (Portugal) 298
P E N Scottish Centre (United Kingdom) 413
P E N, Senegal, Centre (Senegal) 304
P E N, South African, Centre (Cape) (Republic of South Africa) 313
P E N, Spanish, Club (Spain) 325
P E N, Spanish, Club (Cataluña) (Spain) 325
P E N, Svenska Pennklubben (Swedish Centre of International,) (Sweden) 335
P E N Yazarlar Dernegi (Turkey) 359
P E N Zentrum Bundesrepublik Deutschland (Federal Republic of Germany) 168
P E N Zentrum, Deutsche Demokratische Republik (German Democratic Republic) 118
P F B (Malaysia) 244
P G Medical Books (Republic of Singapore) 305
P I A G (Federal Republic of Germany) 150
P I C S (United Kingdom) 364
P O F (France) 102
P P C, Librerías, (Promoción Popular Cristiana) (Spain) 324
P P C Ltd (Barbados) 32
P P C (Promoción Popular Cristiana) (Spain) 320
P R O N I (Public Record Office of Northern Ireland) (United Kingdom) 411

P R Verlag Wiesbaden, H G Schwieger (Federal Republic of Germany) 150
P S A (Republic of South Africa) 310
P U F (France) 102
P U L (France) 102
P W N (Panstwowe Wydawnictwo Naukowe) (Poland) 292
P Y C Edition (France) 102
Pacific Book Centre (Republic of Singapore) 306
Pacific Publications (Australia) Pty Ltd (Australia) 16
Pacifica Ltd (Japan) 228
Pacifico, Editorial del, SA (Chile) 62
Pacifique, Les Editions du, (France) 102
Pacifique, Les Editions du, (French Polynesia) 113
Packard Publishing Ltd (United Kingdom) 396
Päd extra buchverlag in der Pädex Verlags GmbH (Federal Republic of Germany) 150
Pädagogischer Verlag Schwann GmbH (Federal Republic of Germany) 150
Padilla, Editorial, (Dominican Republic) 80
Padilla, Editorial, (Dominican Republic) 80
Paedagogiki Academia, Library of the, (Cyprus) 69
Paes Barreto, Rômulo, (Brazil) 55
Pagan Publishing House (Burma) 59
Pahl-Rugenstein Verlag (Federal Republic of Germany) 150
Pahlavi Library (Iran) 201
Pahlavi University Libraries (Iran) 201
Paico Ltd (Nigeria) 276
Paico Publishing House (India) 190
Paideia Editrice (Italy) 218
Paidós, Editorial, (Argentina) 6
Paintaway (United Kingdom) 396
Pak American Commercial Inc (Pakistan) 283
Pak Book Corporation (Pakistan) 283
Pak Kitab Ghar (Bangladesh) 31
Pak Publishers (Pakistan) 283
Pakistan Board for Advancement of Literature (Pakistan) 284
Pakistan Board for Advancement of Literature Awards (Pakistan) 284
Pakistan Forest Institute, Central Forest Library (Pakistan) 283
Pakistan Institute of Nuclear Science & Technology Library (Pakistan) 283
Pakistan Law Times Publications (Pakistan) 283
Pakistan Library Association (Pakistan) 284
Pakistan Publications (Pakistan) 283
Pakistan Publishers' and Booksellers' Association (Pakistan) 281
Pakistan Publishing Co Ltd (Pakistan) 283
Pakistan Publishing House (Pakistan) 283
Pakistan Scientific and Technological Information Centre (PASTIC) (Pakistan) 283
Pakistan Writers' Guild (Pakistan) 282
Pakistan Writers' Guild (Pakistan) 284
Pakpassak Kanphin (Laos) 239
Pala SA (Spain) 320
Palacio, Biblioteca del, Real (Spain) 324
Palácio, Biblioteca do, Nacional de Mafra (Portugal) 298
Palacio del Libro (Uruguay) 417
Palacio, El, del Libro (Venezuela) 419
Paladin Books (United Kingdom) 396
Palanca, Carlos, Memorial Awards for Literature (Philippines) 290
Palatina, Biblioteca, (Italy) 221
Pallas SA (Brazil) 53
Pallas, Vydavatel'stvo SFVU, (Czechoslovakia) 70
'Pallottinum' Wydawnictwo Stowarzyszenia Apolstolstwa Katolickiego (Poland) 292
Palmerston North Public Library (New Zealand) 272
Paludans, Erik, Boghandel (Denmark) 78
Paludans, Jörgen, Forlag A/S (Denmark) 76
Palumbo, G B, e C Editore SpA (Italy) 218
Památník národního písemnictví, Strahovská knihovna (Czechoslovakia) 72
Pamplona and its Culture Prize (Colombia) 67
Pan Books (Australia) Pty Ltd (Australia) 16
Pan Books Ltd (United Kingdom) 396
Pan Library ('Circle of the Friends of Progress') (Greece) 172
Pan Malayan Publishing Co Sdn Bhd (Malaysia) 244
Pan Pacific Book Distributors (S) Pte Ltd (Republic of Singapore) 306
Pancaldi, Libreria Commissionaria Internazionale di Raffaele, (Italy) 220
Panchasheel Prakashan (India) 190
Panda Press SRL (Italy) 218
Panero, Leopoldo, Prize (International Literary Prizes) 443
Panini, Edizioni, SpA (Italy) 218
Panjab University Publication Bureau (India) 190
Panmun Book Co Ltd (Republic of Korea) 237
Panmun Book Co Ltd (Republic of Korea) 238
Pannedille, Ediciones, (Argentina) 6
Panorama, Editions du, (Switzerland) 346
Panorama, Nakladatelství a vydavatelství, (Czechoslovakia) 70

Pansegrau, Wilhelm, Verlag (Federal Republic of Germany) 150
Pantarei, Edizioni, (Switzerland) 346
Pantelides (Greece) 172
Panther (United Kingdom) 396
Panther Books Ltd (United Kingdom) 396
Panther, Penerbitan Buku, (Panther Books Malaysia) (Malaysia) 244
Panton (Czechoslovakia) 70
Paoline, Edizioni, (Italy) 218
Papachrysanthou Chryss SA (Greece) 172
Papacito, Ediciones, (Uruguay) 417
Papacito, Librerías, (Uruguay) 417
Papaioannou (Greece) 172
Papazissis Publishers SA (Greece) 172
Paper Tiger (United Kingdom) 396
Paperback Centre (Republic of Ireland) 204
Paperfronts (United Kingdom) 396
Papeterie Centrale (Central African Republic) 61
Papua New Guinea Book Depot (Papua New Guinea) 285
Papua New Guinea Library Association (Papua New Guinea) 285
Papusa Ltda (Colombia) 65
Papyros Press (Greece) 172
'Papyrus' (Central African Republic) 61
Parabel Verlag GmbH und Co KG (Federal Republic of Germany) 150
Paracelsus Verlag GmbH (Federal Republic of Germany) 150
Paradise Book Stall (Pakistan) 283
Parag Prakashan (India) 190
Paramount Book Corporation (Bangladesh) 31
Paramount Book Stall (Pakistan) 283
Paraninfo, Editorial, SA (Spain) 320
Pardo, Casa, SAC (Argentina) 6
Pardo, Librería General de Tomas, (Argentina) 8
Parera, Librería, (Chile) 62
Parey, Verlag Paul, (Federal Republic of Germany) 150
Parimal Prakashan (India) 190
Paris-Caraïbes (France) 102
Paris Grand Prize for Literature (France) 112
Paris Prize (France) 112
Parissianos, Grigorios, 'Epistemonikai Ekdoseis' (Greece) 172
Park and Roche Establishment (Switzerland) 346
Park & Roche Establishment (Liechtenstein) 241
Parkash Brothers (India) 190
Parker & Son Ltd (United Kingdom) 410
Parkland Verlag GmbH und Co Verlags- & Vertriebs-KG (Federal Republic of Germany) 150
Parlement, Bibliothèque du, (Belgium) 43
Parliament Library (Greece) 172
Parliament Library (Iran) 201
Parma (Brazil) 53
Parnfah Pittaya (Thailand) 354
Parramon, Instituto, Ediciones SA (Spain) 320
Parrish, Walter, Ltd (United Kingdom) 396
Parry's Book Center (Sri Abdul Wahab Sdn Bhd) (Malaysia) 245
Parsons, Roy, (New Zealand) 272
Partenon, Ediciones, (Spain) 320
Parthenón, Livraria, (Brazil) 55
Passavia, Verlag, (Federal Republic of Germany) 150
Passim, Librería, (Spain) 324
Paternoster, The, Press Ltd (United Kingdom) 396
Paterson, Banjo, Awards (Australia) 22
Paterson, Mark, & Associates (United Kingdom) 408
Path Publishers (India) 190
Patio, Galerie, Verlag (Federal Republic of Germany) 151
Patmos, Uitgeverij, (Belgium) 40
Patmos Verlag GmbH (Federal Republic of Germany) 151
Patria, Editorial, SA (Mexico) 251
Patria, Librería, (Mexico) 252
Patria, Librería, SA (Mexico) 251
Pàtron, Casa Editrice, SAS (Italy) 218
Pàtron, Libreria Internazionale, (Italy) 221
Pattloch, Paul, Buchhandlung und Verlag GmbH & Co KG (Federal Republic of Germany) 151
Patwa (Embakasi) Ltd (Kenya) 235
Paul, M P, Award (India) 198
Paul, M P, Prize (India) 198
Paul, Stanley, & Co Ltd (United Kingdom) 396
Pauli SA (Belgium) 40
Paulinas, Ediciones, (Argentina) 6
Paulinas, Ediciones, (Chile) 62
Paulinas, Ediciones, (Spain) 320
Paulinas, Ediciones, SA (Mexico) 251
Paulinas, Edicões, (Brazil) 53
Paulinus Verlag (Federal Republic of Germany) 151
Pauls University Bookshop Ltd (New Zealand) 272
Paulusverlag (Switzerland) 346
Pause, Firmin, (Réunion) 300
Pauvert, Jean-Jacques, Editeur (France) 102
Pavillon, Le, Roger Maria Editeur (France) 102
Pawel Pan Presse (Federal Republic of Germany) 151
Pawlak, Manfred, Grossantiquariat und Verlagsgesellschaft mbH (Federal Republic of Germany) 151
Pax (Norway) 279

Pax, Editorial, México (Mexico) 251
Pax Forlag A/S (Norway) 280
Pax, Instytut Wydawniczy, (Poland) 292
Pax, Librería, Carlos Cesarman Ltda (Chile) 62
Pax, Livraria Editora, Lda (Portugal) 297
Payot, Editions (France) 102
Payot, Librairie, SA (Switzerland) 346
Payot, Librairie, SA (Switzerland) 351
Paz e Terra, Editôra, (Brazil) 53
Paz, Editorial, Montalvo (Spain) 320
Peace and Socialism International Publishers (Czechoslovakia) 70
Pearl Publishers (India) 190
Pearson (United Kingdom) 396
Pédagogie Moderne (France) 102
Pedagogika (Union of Soviet Socialist Republics) 361
Pedagogisk Forlag A/S (Norway) 280
Pedagoško-književni zbor, pedagoško društvo SR Hrvatske (Yugoslavia) 426
Pediátrica, Editorial, (Spain) 320
Pédone, Editions, (France) 102
Pedrazzini Tipografia (Switzerland) 346
Pedrick, Don, Memorial Literary Award (Sri Lanka) 326
Pe'er Hatora (Israel) 208
Peeters SPRL (Belgium) 40
Pegaso, Ediciones, (Spain) 321
Pegasus Books (Australia) 16
Pegasus Press Ltd (New Zealand) 271
Pei-ching ta hsueh t'u shu kuan (People's Republic of China) 63
Peiffer, Librairie Armand, (Luxembourg) 242
Peisa, Ediciones, (Promoción Editorial Inca SA) (Peru) 287
Pelajar (Indonesia) 199
Pelham Books Ltd (United Kingdom) 396
Peli, Alexander, Ltd (Israel) 208
Pelican (Australia) 17
Pelican (United Kingdom) 396
Pelita Masa (Indonesia) 199
Pelmas (Israel) 208
Pembangunan (Indonesia) 199
Pemberton Publishing Co Ltd (United Kingdom) 396
Pembimbing Masa (Indonesia) 199
Pembimbing, P T, Masa (Indonesia) 200
Pembinaan, Pusat, Perpustakaan, Departemen P dan K Bidang, Bibliografi dan Deposit (Indonesia) 200
Peña, A, Lillo SA (Argentina) 6
Pendidekan, Pustaka, Sdn Bhd (Malaysia) 245
Pendo-Verlag (Switzerland) 346
Penguin Books Australia Ltd (Australia) 17
Penguin Books Ltd (United Kingdom) 396
Penguin Books (NZ) Ltd (New Zealand) 271
Peninsula, Ediciones, (Spain) 321
Penman, The, Club (International Organizations) 433
Pensamento, Editôra, (Brazil) 53
Pensée Moderne Jacques Grancher (France) 102
'Pensiero Scientifico' SRL (Italy) 218
Pentecost (New Caledonia) 268
Pentos Ltd (United Kingdom) 396
People's Literature Publishing House (People's Republic of China) 63
People's Publishing Co Ltd (Nigeria) 276
People's Publishing House (Pakistan) 283
People's Publishing House (P) Ltd (India) 191
People's Sports Publishing House (People's Republic of China) 63
Pepper Press (United Kingdom) 396
Pequeña, Una, Librería (Ecuador) 81
Père Castor (France) 102
Peregrine Books (United Kingdom) 396
Pereira, Parceria A M, Lda (Portugal) 297
Peretz, Y L, Publishing Co (Israel) 209
Perfecting Press (Hong Kong) 176
Pergamon Press (Australia) Pty Ltd (Australia) 17
Pergamon Press Ltd (United Kingdom) 396
Periféria, Ediciones, SRL (Argentina) 7
Périodiques, Les, Parisiens (France) 102
Permanent Press (United Kingdom) 396
Perpétuo, Editorial, Socorro (Portugal) 297
Perrin, Editions G M, SA (France) 102
Perrin, Librairie Académique, (France) 102
Persatuan Perpustakaan Malaysia (Malaysia) 246
Perskor Books (Pty) Ltd (Republic of South Africa) 310
Perskor Bookshop (Republic of South Africa) 312
Perskor Prize for Literature (Republic of South Africa) 313
Perskor Prize for Youth Literature (Republic of South Africa) 313
Perspectiva, Editôra, (Brazil) 53
Perspektiv (Norway) 280
Peryer, N M, Ltd (New Zealand) 271
Pestalozzi-Verlag graphische Gesellschaft mbH (Federal Republic of Germany) 151
'Petar Kočić' (Yugoslavia) 423
Peter, Verlag J P, Gebr Holstein (Federal Republic of Germany) 151
Peterborough Literary Agency (United Kingdom) 408
Peters, A D, & Co Ltd (United Kingdom) 409

Peters, C F, Musikverlag GmbH und Co KG (Federal Republic of Germany) 151
Peters, Dr Hans, Verlag (Federal Republic of Germany) 151
Petersen, Hans Heinrich, Buchimport GmbH (Federal Republic of Germany) 165
Petitdidier Prize (France) 112
Petiwala Corporation (Pakistan) 283
Pevsner Public Library (Israel) 210
Pfanneberg, Fachbuchverlag Dr, & Co (Federal Republic of Germany) 151
Pfeiffer, Verlag J, (Federal Republic of Germany) 151
Pfister, E, GmbH (Federal Republic of Germany) 151
Pflaum, Richard, Verlag KG (Federal Republic of Germany) 151
Pfriem, Engelbert, Verlag (Federal Republic of Germany) 151
Pfriemer, Udo, Verlag GmbH (Federal Republic of Germany) 151
Pfützner, Robert, GmbH (Federal Republic of Germany) 151
Phaethon, The, Press (United Kingdom) 396
Phaidon Press Ltd (United Kingdom) 396
Phaneromeni, Library of, (Cyprus) 69
Pharmacie, Bibliothèque Interuniversitaire de, (France) 108
Pharos Books (United Kingdom) 396
Pharos-Verlag (Switzerland) 346
Phébus, Editions, (France) 102
Philip, David-, Publisher (Pty) Ltd (Republic of South Africa) 310
Philip & Son, George, Ltd (United Kingdom) 396
Philip & Tacey Ltd (United Kingdom) 396
Philippine Arts and Architecture (Philippines) 288
Philippine Book Co (Philippines) 288
Philippine Book Co (Philippines) 289
Philippine Book Dealers' Association (Philippines) 288
Philippine Education Co Inc (Philippines) 289
Philippine Education Co Inc (Philippines) 289
Philippine Educational Publishers' Association (Philippines) 288
Philippine International Publishing Co (Philippines) 289
Philippine Library Association (Philippines) 289
Philips GmbH, Fachbuch-Verlag (Federal Republic of Germany) 151
Phillimore & Co Ltd (United Kingdom) 396
Philo Press-van Heusden-Hissink & Co CV (APA) (Netherlands) 263
Philograph Publications Ltd (United Kingdom) 397
Philosophisch-Anthroposophischer Verlag (Switzerland) 346
Philpott & Collins (1978) (Pvt) Ltd (Zimbabwe) 429
Pho Thong (Popularization) Publishing House (Socialist Republic of Viet Nam) 420
Phoebus Publishing Co (United Kingdom) 397
Phoebus-Verlag GmbH (Switzerland) 347
Phoenix Book Society (United Kingdom) 410
Phoenix Verlag AG (Switzerland) 347
Physica-Verlag Rudolf Liebing GmbH und Co (Federal Republic of Germany) 151
Physik Verlag GmbH (Federal Republic of Germany) 151
Piatkus Books (United Kingdom) 397
Picador (Australia) 17
Picador (United Kingdom) 397
Picard, Editions A & J, Sàrl (France) 102
Piccin Editore sas (Italy) 218
Piccoli, Editrice, SpA (Italy) 218
Piccolo (Australia) 17
Piccolo (United Kingdom) 397
Pickering & Inglis Ltd (United Kingdom) 397
Pied Piper (United Kingdom) 397
Piedra Santa (Guatemala) 173
Piedra Santa (Guatemala) 173
Pierce, Lorne, Medal (International Literary Prizes) 443
Pierron, Editions, (France) 102
Pierrot, Editions, SA (Switzerland) 347
Pierrot Publishing Ltd (United Kingdom) 397
Pietra, La, (Italy) 218
Pietsch, Buch- & Verlagshaus Paul, GmbH & Co KG (Federal Republic of Germany) 151
Pigmalión (Argentina) 8
Pike, James, Ltd (EJP Publications) (United Kingdom) 397
Pikkhanet (Thailand) 354
Pilgrim Award (International Literary Prizes) 443
Pilgrim Books Ltd (Nigeria) 276
Pilgrim Publishers (India) 191
Pilgrims Booksellers (Pty) (Republic of South Africa) 312
Pimodan, De, Prize (France) 112
Pinchgut Press (Australia) 17
Pineda Libros (Chile) 62
Pinguin-Verlag, Pawlowski KG (Austria) 27
Pink and Blue Editôra Ltda (Brazil) 53
Pink Editions & Productions (Belgium) 40
Pinter, Frances, Ltd (United Kingdom) 397
Pinx-Verlag Kurt Glombig (Federal Republic of Germany) 151
Pioneer Design Studio Pty Ltd (Australia) 17

INDEX 493

Piper, R, & Co Verlag GmbH (Switzerland) 347
Piper, R, und Co Verlag (Federal Republic of Germany) 151
Pirámide, Ediciones, SA (Spain) 321
'Pishchevaya Promyshlennost', Izdatelstvo, (Union of Soviet Socialist Republics) 361
Pitambar Publishing Co (India) 191
Pitkin Pictorials Ltd (United Kingdom) 397
Pitman Books Ltd (United Kingdom) 397
Pitman Medical Publishing Co Ltd (United Kingdom) 397
Pitman Publishing Co SA (Pty) Ltd (Republic of South Africa) 310
Pitman Publishing NZ Ltd (New Zealand) 271
Pitman Publishing Pty Ltd (Australia) 17
Pitou, Charles, Prize (France) 112
Pittayakarn (Thailand) 354
Pizzi, Amilcare, SpA (Italy) 218
Place, Editions Jean-Michel, (France) 102
Plambeck & Co, Druck und Verlag GmbH (Federal Republic of Germany) 152
Planeta, Editorial, SA (Spain) 321
Planeta Prize (International Literary Prizes) 443
Planeta Publishers (Union of Soviet Socialist Republics) 361
Planning Commission Library (Pakistan) 283
Plantyn, Editions, SA (France) 103
Plantyn, Uitgeverij, SA NV (Belgium) 40
Plata, Editorial, SA (Peru) 287
Plata, Editorial, SA (Venezuela) 419
Platano Editora SARL (Portugal) 297
Play to Learn (Australia) 17
Playfair (United Kingdom) 397
Playor (Spain) 321
Plaza & Janés, Editorial Argentina, SA (Argentina) 7
Plaza y Janés SA (Spain) 321
Pleamar, Editorial, (Argentina) 7
Plessl, Gerd, Agency (Federal Republic of Germany) 164
Plexus Publishing Ltd (United Kingdom) 397
Ploegsma, Uitgeverij, (Netherlands) 263
Ploetz, Ernst, (Austria) 27
Ploetz GmbH und Co KG (Federal Republic of Germany) 152
Plon, Librairie, SA (France) 103
Plough Publishing House (United Kingdom) 397
Pluim Book Club (Republic of South Africa) 311
Pluma, Editorial, Ltda (Colombia) 65
Plume (United Kingdom) 397
Plus, Bokförlaget, AB (Sweden) 332
Plus Ultra, Editorial, SAI & C (Argentina) 7
Pluto Press (United Kingdom) 397
Pobjeda (Yugoslavia) 423
Pochinjae (Republic of Korea) 237
Pock, Max, Universitätsbuchhandlung (Austria) 29
Pocket, Presses, (France) 103
Poder, Biblioteca del, Legislativo (Uruguay) 417
Podzun-Pallas Verlag GmbH (Federal Republic of Germany) 152
Poe, Edgar, Prize (International Literary Prizes) 443
Poeschel, C E, Verlag (Federal Republic of Germany) 152
Poètes Présents (France) 108
Poetry Book Society (United Kingdom) 410
Poetry in Irish Award (International Literary Prizes) 443
Poetry Society (United Kingdom) 413
Poetry Society of Australia (Australia) 21
Pohjalainen Kirjakauppa Oy (Finland) 86
Pohl Druckerei und Verlagsanstalt Otto Pohl (Federal Republic of Germany) 152
Poincaré, Raymond, Prize (France) 112
Point d'Interrogation, Librairie du, (Senegal) 303
'Pojezierze', Wydawnictwo Stowarzyszenia Społeczno-Kulturalnego, (Poland) 292
Polak, Emil, Prize (Belgium) 45
Polak en Van Gennep Uitg Mij BV (Netherlands) 263
Polana AG (Switzerland) 347
Polding, The, Press (Australia) 17
Poldner, Axel, (Federal Republic of Germany) 164
Policy Studies Institute (United Kingdom) 397
Poligrafa, Ediciones, SA (Spain) 321
Poligraficheskata Promishlenost i Kulturnite Instituti, Sekciya na Bibliotechnite Rabotnitsi pri Centralniya Komitet na Profesionalniya Sŭyuz na Rabotnitsite ot, (Bulgaria) 58
Polish Academy of Sciences (Poland) 294
Polish Authors' Society (Zaiks) Prizes (International Literary Prizes) 443
Polish Bibliography, Editorial Office for, (formerly Karol Estreicher Republication Centre of Polish 19th Century Bibliography) (Poland) 290
Polish Ministry of National Defence Prize (Poland) 294
Polish Prime Minister Award for Literature for Children and Youth (Poland) 294
Polish Union of Socialist Youth Prose Award (Poland) 294
Politécnica Moulines, Librería, (Venezuela) 419
Politica, Editura, (Romania) 301
Political and Social History, Library of, (Indonesia) 200
Politikens Forlag A/S (Denmark) 76
Politizdat (Union of Soviet Socialist Republics) 361

polizeiliches Fachschrifttum, Verlag für, (Federal Republic of Germany) 152
Polke, Bernd, GmbH (Federal Republic of Germany) 152
Pollinger, Laurence, Ltd (United Kingdom) 409
Polskie Towarzystwo Wydawców Ksiazek (Poland) 290
Polybooks Ltd (United Kingdom) 397
Polyglott-Verlag Dr Bolte KG (Federal Republic of Germany) 152
Polyglotte Buch- und Schallplatten-Verlag und Vertrieb (Federal Republic of Germany) 152
Polygraph Verlag GmbH (Federal Republic of Germany) 152
Polytantric Press (United Kingdom) 397
Polytechnic Institute Library (Ethiopia) 83
Polyteknisk Boghandel og Forlag (Denmark) 78
Pomaire, Editorial, Ltda (Chile) 62
Pomaire, Editorial, Ltda (Uruguay) 417
Pomaire, Editorial, SA (Colombia) 66
Pomaire, Editorial, SA (Mexico) 251
Pomaire, Editorial, SA (Spain) 321
Pomaire SA (Argentina) 7
Pomaire Venezuela (Venezuela) 419
Pompidou, Centre Georges, Edition (France) 103
Pomso Publishers (Republic of Korea) 237
Pomurska zalozba (Yugoslavia) 423
Pond Press (United Kingdom) 397
Pontificia Universidad Nacional, Biblioteca Central de la, Católica del Perú (Peru) 287
Pool Editora Ltda (Brazil) 53
Poolbeg Press Ltd (Republic of Ireland) 204
Poona Booksellers' & Publishers' Association (India) 181
Poplar Publishing Co Ltd (Japan) 228
Popp, Edition Georg, (Federal Republic of Germany) 152
Populaires (Switzerland) 347
Popular Army Publishing House (Socialist Republic of Viet Nam) 420
Popular Book Depot (India) 196
Popular Book Store (Philippines) 289
Popular Dogs Publishing Co Ltd (United Kingdom) 397
Popular Prakashan Pvt Ltd (India) 191
Popular Publications (Malawi) 243
Pordes, H (United Kingdom) 397
Pordes, H (United Kingdom) 408
Porrúa, Ediciones José, Turanzas SA (Spain) 321
Porrúa, Editorial, SA (Mexico) 251
Porrúa, Librería de, Hnos y Cía (Mexico) 252
Porrúa, Librería de Manuel, (Mexico) 251
Porrúa, Librería José, Turanzas SA (Spain) 324
Porte, Editions La, (Morocco) 254
Porter-Libros (Spain) 324
Pòrtic, Editorial, (Spain) 321
Portico, Editorial, (Portugal) 297
Porto Editôra Lda (Portugal) 297
Portugal, Livraria, Dias e Andrade Lda (Portugal) 298
Portugalia Editôra Lda (Portugal) 297
Possev-Verlag V Gorachek KG (Federal Republic of Germany) 152
Powszechna Ksiegarnia Wysyłkowa (Poland) 293
Poyser, T & A D, Ltd (United Kingdom) 397
Poznan Poetical November Prize (Poland) 294
Poznańskie, Wydawnictwo, (Poznań Publishers) (Poland) 292
Pozza, Neri, (Italy) 218
Pra Cha Chang & Co Ltd (Thailand) 354
Prabhat Prakashan (India) 191
'Práca', Vydavateľstvo ROH, (Czechoslovakia) 71
Práce (Czechoslovakia) 71
Pracharak Book Club (India) 195
Prachi Prakashan (India) 191
Prachner, Georg, (Austria) 27
Prachner, Georg, KG (Austria) 29
Pradnya Paramita (Indonesia) 199
Pradnya Paramita (Indonesia) 200
Prae Pittaya Ltd (Thailand) 354
Praepittaya Ltd (Thailand) 355
Praesentverlag Heinz Peter (Federal Republic of Germany) 152
Pragati Prakashan (India) 191
Pragopress (Czechoslovakia) 71
Prague Literary Prize (Czechoslovakia) 73
Prakash Prakashan (India) 191
Prakasham Publications (India) 191
Pramual Sarn Book Centre Ltd (Thailand) 355
Pramuansarn Publishing House (Thailand) 354
Praphansarn Book Centre (Thailand) 354
Prasarnmitr (Thailand) 354
Präsenz-Verlag der Jesus Bruderschaft (Federal Republic of Germany) 152
Pravda, Nakladatelstvo, (Czechoslovakia) 71
Pravda Publishing House (Union of Soviet Socialist Republics) 361
Prawnicze, Wydawnictwo, (Poland) 292
Praxis Libros (Spain) 324
Prayer Books (India) 191
Pre-School Publishing Co (United Kingdom) 397
Preduzeće Matice Srpske, Izdavačko, (Yugoslavia) 423
Preduzeće Sloboda, Izdavačko, (Yugoslavia) 423
Prélat, Julien, Sàrl (France) 103

Preller, Gustav, Prize (Republic of South Africa) 313
Prelo Editora Sarl (Portugal) 297
Premier Book House (Pakistan) 283
Premier, Librerías, (Argentina) 8
Premio de Remuneraciones Literarias (Uruguay) 418
Premio Nacional de Literatura (Uruguay) 418
Prensa, Biblioteca Pública Gratuita de 'La, ' (Argentina) 8
Prensa Editora, La, de Periodicos SCL (Mexico) 251
Prensa, Editorial, Española (Spain) 321
Prensa Médica, La, Mexicana (Mexico) 251
Prentice-Hall International (United Kingdom) 397
Prentice-Hall of Australia Pty Limited (Australia) 17
Prentice-Hall of India Pvt Ltd (India) 191
Prentice-Hall of Japan Inc (Japan) 228
Prentice-Hall of Southeast Asia Pte Ltd (Republic of Singapore) 306
Presbiteriana, Casa Editôra, (Brazil) 53
Presbyterian Book Depot and Printing Press Ltd (PRESBOOK) (United Republic of Cameroun) 60
Presbyterian Book Depot Ltd (Ghana) 169
Presbyterian Book Depot Ltd (Ghana) 170
Presença, Editorial, (Portugal) 297
Présence Africaine, Société Nouvelle, (France) 103
Presencia, Editorial, Ltda (Colombia) 66
President Publishers (Republic of South Africa) 310
President's Award for Pride of Performance (Pakistan) 284
Press Agency (Kuwait) 238
Press Department, Library of the, (Afghanistan) 1
Press' Förlag AB (Sweden) 332
Presse-Auto-Conseil (France) 103
Presse, La, Internationale (Belgium) 40
Presse, Verlag, Informations Agentur GmbH (PIAG) (Federal Republic of Germany) 152
Presses Africaines, Les, (Zaire) 427
Presses agronomiques de Gembloux ASBL (Belgium) 40
Presses Centrales Lausanne SA (Switzerland) 347
Presses de la Cité, Les, (France) 103
Presses de la Connaissance, Les, (Switzerland) 347
Presses de la Fondation Nationale des Sciences Politiques (France) 103
Presses de la Renaissance (France) 103
Presses d'Ile-de-France, Les, Sàrl (France) 103
Presses d'Or (France) 108
Presses, Les, Africaines (Upper Volta) 416
Presses, Librairie des, universitaires (Zaire) 427
Presses Monastiques, Les, (France) 103
Presses Polytechniques Romandes (Switzerland) 347
Presses universitaires de Bruxelles ASBL (Belgium) 40
Presses universitaires de France (France) 108
Presses Universitaires de France (PUF) (France) 103
Presses Universitaires de Grenoble (France) 103
Presses universitaires de Liège ASBL (Belgium) 40
Presses Universitaires de Lille (PUL) (France) 103
Presses Universitaires de Lyon (France) 103
Presses universitaires de Namur (Belgium) 40
Presses universitaires du Zaire et l'Office du Livre (PUZ) (Zaire) 427
Pressler, Guido, Verlag (Federal Republic of Germany) 152
Prestel Verlag (Federal Republic of Germany) 152
Prestige Booksellers (Kenya) 235
Preston Corporation Ltd (Malaysia) 245
Preston-Times Printing & Publishing (Malaysia) 245
Pretoria Boekhandel Ltd (Republic of South Africa) 310
Preussler, Helmut, Verlag (Federal Republic of Germany) 152
Price Milburn & Co Ltd (New Zealand) 271
Pride (Republic of South Africa) 310
Primary Education (Publishing) Pty Ltd (Australia) 17
Primavera (Denmark) 77
Primor, Editôra, Ltda (Brazil) 53
Primor, Gráfica Editôra, SA (Brazil) 53
Primorski Tisk (Yugoslavia) 424
Prince Pierre de Monaco Prize for Literature (International Literary Prizes) 443
Princeton University Press (United Kingdom) 398
Prins en Prins (Netherlands) 266
Prinsen-Geerlings, Reina, Prize (Netherlands) 267
Prinsen, Reina, -Geerlings Prize for South Africa (Republic of South Africa) 313
Printing and Publishing Industry Training Board (United Kingdom) 364
Printox (India) 191
Prior, George, Associated Publishers Ltd (United Kingdom) 398
Priory Press Ltd (United Kingdom) 398
Príroda, vydavateľ stvo kníh a časopisov (Czechoslovakia) 71
Prism Books (Poetry Society of Australia) (Australia) 17
Prism Press (United Kingdom) 398
Prisma, Bokförlaget, AB (Sweden) 332
Prisma, Het, NV (Belgium) 40
Prisma Verlag GmbH (Federal Republic of Germany) 152
Prisma-Verlag Zenner und Gürchott (German Democratic Republic) 116
Prithviraj Memorial Award (India) 198
Priuli e Verlucca, Editori (Italy) 218

Privat, Editions Edouard, SA (France) 103
Private Libraries Association (PLA) (International Organizations) 433
Privredni Pregled (Yugoslavia) 424
Prix des Sept (International Literary Prizes) 443
Prix Internationale des Editeurs (Prix des Sept) (International Literary Prizes) 443
Prize for Non-Hindi Speaking Area Writers (India) 198
Prizes for Manuscripts for Juveniles (Pakistan) 284
Pro Civitate (Belgium) 40
Pro Juventute Verlag (Switzerland) 347
Pro Media Literaturvertrieb GmbH (Federal Republic of Germany) 165
Pro Rege Press Ltd (Republic of South Africa) 310
Pro Schola, Editions, (Switzerland) 347
Pro Schule Verlag GmbH (Federal Republic of Germany) 152
Proa, Edicions, (Spain) 321
Problem-Verlag (Switzerland) 347
Procure, La, (Belgium) 40
Procure scolaire (Zaire) 427
Prodim SPRL (Belgium) 40
Production AB (Sweden) 332
Production et Diffusion medico-techniques SPRL (Belgium) 40
Productions de Paris, Les, (France) 103
Professional Publications (New Zealand) 271
Profil, Nakladatelství, (Czechoslovakia) 71
Profile Books Ltd (United Kingdom) 398
Profizdat (Union of Soviet Socialist Republics) 361
Profizdat, Izdatelstvo, (Bulgaria) 58
Progrès, Editions le, (Egypt) 81
Progreso, Editorial, SA (Mexico) 251
Progress (Thailand) 354
Progress Press (Malta) 246
Progress Publishers (Union of Soviet Socialist Republics) 361
Progressive Corporation Pvt Ltd (India) 191
Prolam SRL (Ediciones Economia y Empresa) (Argentina) 7
Prometeo, Editorial (Spain) 321
Prometheus Publishing Co (Zambia) 428
Promocion Cultural, Ediciones de, SA (Spain) 321
Promocion Popular Cristiana (Spain) 321
Promoculture, Librairie, (Luxembourg) 242
Promotion Littéraire (France) 107
Proost, Henri, & Co (Belgium) 40
Pröpster, Albert, (Federal Republic of Germany) 152
Propyläen Verlag (Federal Republic of Germany) 152
Prospice (United Kingdom) 398
'Prosveshchenie', Izdatelstvo, (Union of Soviet Socialist Republics) 361
Prosveta (Yugoslavia) 424
Prosveta (Yugoslavia) 425
Prosvetno Delo (Yugoslavia) 424
Prosvjeta (Yugoslavia) 424
Prosvjeta (Novinsko-izdavačko i Štamparsko) (Yugoslavia) 424
Protestante, Librairie, (Benin) 45
Protestantse Stichting tot Bevordering van het Bibliotheekwezen en de Lectuurvoorlichting in Nederland (Netherlands) 267
Proteus (Publishing) Ltd (United Kingdom) 398
Provence, Librairie de, (France) 108
Provincial Book Depot (Bangladesh) 32
Provincial Booksellers Fairs Association Annual Book Awards (United Kingdom) 415
Provincial Library (Bangladesh) 32
Proyección, Editorial, SRL (Argentina) 7
Prugg Verlag (Austria) 27
Prva Književna Komuna (Yugoslavia) 424
Psyche, Bookclub, (Japan) 231
Psychic Press Ltd (United Kingdom) 398
Psychologie, Verlag für, Dr C J Hogrefe (Federal Republic of Germany) 152
Psychologie, Verlag fur, Dr C J Hogrefe (Switzerland) 347
Psychosophische Gesellschaft (Switzerland) 347
Psykologiförlaget AB (Sweden) 332
Publi-Union (France) 103
Public Lending Right Committee (Australia) 20
Public Lending Right Committee of Australia Council (Australia) 10
Public Libraries Board (Uganda) 360
Public Library (Afghanistan) 1
Public Library (Barbados) 32
Public Library (Jordan) 233
Public Library (Jordan) 233
Public Library (Libya) 241
Public Library, Central, Dacca (Bangladesh) 32
Public Organization, The, for Books and Scientific Appliances (Egypt) 81
Public Organization, The, for Books and Scientific Appliances, Cairo University (Egypt) 81
Public Record Office (United Kingdom) 411
Public Record Office of Ireland (Republic of Ireland) 204
Publica (Sweden) 332
Publicaciones Cultural SA (Mexico) 251
Publicaciones Españolas SA (Venezuela) 419

Publicações Científicas, Editôra de, Ltda (Brazil) 54
Publication Board (India) 191
Publications Appeal Board (Republic of South Africa) 307
Publications Central Africa (Zimbabwe) 429
Publications Filmées d'Art et d'Histoire (France) 103
Publications & Information Directorate (India) 191
Publications International (Nigeria) Ltd (Nigeria) 276
Publications Orientalistes de France (POF) (France) 103
Publishers' and Booksellers' Association of Bengal (India) 181
Publishers' and Booksellers' Association of Thailand (Thailand) 354
Publishers' and Booksellers' Guild (India) 181
Publishers Association (United Kingdom) 364
Publishers' Association for Cultural Exchange (Japan) 224
Publishers' Association of South India (India) 181
Publishers' & Booksellers' Association of Andhra Pradesh (India) 181
Publishers/Booksellers Delivery Service (PBDS) (United Kingdom) 364
Publisher's Bookshop (Poland) 293
Publisher's Club (Poland) 293
Publishers' Information Card Services (United Kingdom) 364
Publishers International (Pakistan) 283
Publishers' Overseas Circle (United Kingdom) 364
Publishers Publicity Circle (United Kingdom) 364
Publishers United Ltd (Pakistan) 283
Publishing Council of the Academy of Sciences of the USSR (Union of Soviet Socialist Republics) 360
Publishing Department (People's Republic of China) 63
Pucci, Christa, (Italy) 220
Pudoc, Centre for Agricultural Publishing and Documentation (Netherlands) 263
Pueblo, Editorial, y Educación (Cuba) 68
Pueyo, Librería Pedro, (Spain) 324
Puffin (Australia) 17
Puffin Books (United Kingdom) 398
Puffin, The, Club (United Kingdom) 410
Pula Press (Republic of South Africa) 310
Punjab Advisory Board for Books Prizes (Pakistan) 284
Punjab Public Library (Pakistan) 283
Punjab State University Textbook Board (India) 191
Punjab Text Board (Pakistan) 284
Punjab University Library (Pakistan) 283
Punjabi Publishers' Association (India) 181
Punjabi Pustak Bhandar (India) 191
Punktum (Switzerland) 351
Punnoose, Kunnuparampil P, (India) 195
Purnell Books (United Kingdom) 398
Purnell & Sons (SA) (Pty) Ltd (Republic of South Africa) 310
Pushtu Toulana, Afghan Academy (Afghanistan) 1
Pustet, Anton, (Federal Republic of Germany) 152
Pustet, Universitätsverlag Anton, (Austria) 27
Pustet, Verlag Friedrich, (Federal Republic of Germany) 152
Puthigar Limited (Bangladesh) 32
Putnam Awards (International Literary Prizes) 444
Putnam & Co Ltd (United Kingdom) 398
Putsj Publications Antwerpen (Netherlands) 263
Pygmalion, Editions, — Gérard Watelet (France) 103

Q E D Publishing Ltd (United Kingdom) 398
Q Press Ltd (United Kingdom) 398
Qaumi Kutab Khana (Pakistan) 283
Qinghua Daxue Tushuguan (People's Republic of China) 63
Quadragono Libri (Italy) 218
Quality Book Club (United Kingdom) 410
Quartet Books Australia Pty Ltd (Australia) 17
Quartet Books Ltd (United Kingdom) 398
Quartier-Latin (Monaco) 253
Quartier-Latin, Librairie, (French Polynesia) 113
Quarto Press (Liechtenstein) 241
Quarto Publishing (United Kingdom) 398
Queen Anne Press Ltd (United Kingdom) 398
Queen Victoria Memorial Library (Zimbabwe) 430
Queen's, The, Gold Medal for Poetry (United Kingdom) 415
Queensland Book Depot (Australia) 19
Queensland Booksellers' Association (Australia) 10
Queensway Bookshop and Stores (Ghana) 170
Quell-Verlag (Federal Republic of Germany) 153
Quelle Press (Federal Republic of Germany) 165
Quelle und Meyer Verlag (Federal Republic of Germany) 153
Quentin Press Ltd (United Kingdom) 398
Querido's, Em, Uitgeverij BV (Netherlands) 263
Queriniana, Editrice, (Italy) 218
Queromón Editores SA (Mexico) 251

Quet, Mme Janine, (France) 107
Quevedo, Ediciones, Sacif (Argentina) 7
Quill Publishing Ltd (United Kingdom) 398
Quillet, Librairie Aristide, SA (France) 104
Quintero, Alvarez, Prize (Spain) 325
Quisqueyana, Editora Colegial, SA (Dominican Republic) 80
Quisqueyana, Editora Colegial, SA (Dominican Republic) 80
Qurinna Library (Libya) 241
Qvist, Erik, Bokhandel A/S (Norway) 280

'R', Editions, (France) 104
R A I, Edizioni, Radiotelevisione Italiana (ERI) SpA (Italy) 218
R A Verlag (Switzerland) 347
R C P (Private) Ltd (Zimbabwe) 429
R E C T A Foldex (France) 104
R Editore (Italy) 218
R E M I (France) 104
R I B A Publications Ltd (United Kingdom) 398
R N A Major Award (Isle of Man) 247
R N A Major Award (United Kingdom) 415
R S T, Editions, (France) 104
R S W (Robotnicza Spóldzielnia Wydawnicza) (Poland) 290
R V (Federal Republic of Germany) 153
Rabaul Newsagency (Papua New Guinea) 285
Rabe Verlag Zurich (Switzerland) 347
rabe verlag zürich (Switzerland) 351
Rabèn och Sjörgen, AB, Bokförlag (Sweden) 332
Rache, André De, (Belgium) 40
Racine Prize (France) 112
Rad, Izdavačka Organizacija, (Yugoslavia) 424
Radha Krishna Prakashan (India) 191
Radha Soami Satsang Beas (India) 191
Radia i Telewizji, Wydawnictwo, (Poland) 292
Radiant Publishers (India) 191
Radical Book Club (India) 195
Radical Reprints (United Kingdom) 398
Radio, Société des Editions, (France) 104
Radius-Verlag GmbH (Federal Republic of Germany) 153
Radnička Štampa (Yugoslavia) 424
Raeber AG Luzern (Switzerland) 347
Ragman Productions (Australia) 17
Rahman Brothers (Bangladesh) 31
Railway Publications Ltd (United Kingdom) 398
Railway, The, Book Club (United Kingdom) 410
Rainbird, The, Publishing Group (United Kingdom) 398
Rainbow Books (United Kingdom) 398
Rainbow Photo & Book Store (Brunei) 57
Rainer Verlag (Federal Republic of Germany) 153
Raio, Editôra, X Ltda (Brazil) 54
Rajasthan Hindi Granth Academy (India) 191
Rajasthan Pustak Vyavasayee Sangh (India) 181
Rajasthan Sahitya Akademi Awards (India) 198
Rajesh Publications (India) 191
Rajhans Prakashan Mandir (India) 191
Rajkamal Prakashan Pvt Ltd (India) 191
Rajneesh Foundation (India) 191
Rajpal & Sons (India) 191
Rakennuskirja Oy (Finland) 85
Ram Prasad & Sons (India) 191
Ramakrishna, Sri, Math (India) 192
Ramboro Enterprises Ltd (United Kingdom) 398
Ramboro Enterprises Ltd (United Kingdom) 408
Ramdor Publishing Co Ltd (Israel) 209
Ramos, Edicões António, (Portugal) 297
Ramsay, Editions, (France) 104
Ramsay, The, Head Press (United Kingdom) 399
Ramsden, Barbara, Award (Australia) 22
Randi, Libreria all' Accademia SNC di, Pietro (Italy) 221
Random, Dokument und Analyse Verlag Bogislaw von, (Federal Republic of Germany) 153
Ranelagh Editions (United Kingdom) 399
Ranner, Verlag Dr Herta, (Austria) 27
'Rast Gufter' Press (Pakistan) 283
Rastogi Publications (India) 192
Rathgeber Verlag (Federal Republic of Germany) 153
Rational Bookshops (Nigeria) (Nigeria) 277
Rationalisierungs-Kuratorium der Deutschen Wirtschaft eV (RKW) (Federal Republic of Germany) 153
Rationalist Press Association (United Kingdom) 399
Ratna Pustak Bhandar (Nepal) 255
Ratna Pustak Bhandar (Nepal) 255
Ratnabharati (India) 192
Ratnakara Press Ltd (Sri Lanka) 326
Rau, Walter, Verlag (Federal Republic of Germany) 153
Rauch, Felizian, Verlagsbuchhandlung (Austria) 27
Rauch, Karl, Verlag KG (Federal Republic of Germany) 153
Rauhen Hauses, Agentur des, GmbH (Federal Republic of Germany) 153

INDEX 495

Rautenberg, Gerhard, Druckerei und Verlag GmbH & Co KG (Federal Republic of Germany) 153
Rav Kook Institute (Israel) 209
Ravan Press (Pty) Ltd (Republic of South Africa) 310
Ravensburger Graphische Betriebe Otto Maier GmbH (Federal Republic of Germany) 153
Ravensburger Verlag GmbH (Federal Republic of Germany) 153
Ravenstein Verlag GmbH (Federal Republic of Germany) 153
Rayas, G (Greece) 172
Razon, Editora La, (Dominican Republic) 80
Read It Again (Australia) 17
Readers' Book Shop (Jamaica) 223
Readers Choice (United Kingdom) 410
Reader's Choice (Australiana Book Club) (Australia) 19
Readers' Digest AB (Sweden) 334
Reader's Digest Condensed Book Services Pty Ltd (Australia) 19
Reader's Digest, Det Bedste fra, A/S (Denmark) 77
Reader's Digest NV, Uitgeversmaatschappij, (Netherlands) 266
Reader's Digest SA (Belgium) 40
Reader's Digest, Selecciones del, (Iberia) SA (Spain) 321
Reader's Digest, Sélection du, Sàrl (France) 104
Reader's Digest Services Pty Ltd (Australia) 17
Reader's Digest, The, Association Ltd (United Kingdom) 399
Reader's Digest, The, of Japan Limited (Japan) 228
Reader's Digest, Verlag Das Beste GmbH, (Federal Republic of Germany) 165
Readers Union Book Club (United Kingdom) 410
Readers Union Ltd (United Kingdom) 410
Real Academia de Ciencias, Bellas Letras y Nobles Artes (Spain) 325
Real Academia Sevillana de Buenas Letras (Spain) 325
Real Biblioteca de San Lorenzo de El Escorial (Spain) 324
Real life (Australia) 17
Réalisations pour l'Enseignement Multilingue International (France) 104
Realizações Artis Lda (Portugal) 297
Recalde, Librería, (Nicaragua) 273
Recht und Gesellschaft, Verlag für, AG (Switzerland) 347
Recht und Wirtschaft, Verlagsgesellschaft, mbH (Federal Republic of Germany) 153
Reclam, Philipp, Jun (Federal Republic of Germany) 153
Reclam, Verlag Philipp, jun (German Democratic Republic) 116
'Recognition Prize' (Austria) 30
Record, Distribuidora, de Serviços de Imprensa SA (Brazil) 54
Redhouse Kitabevi (Turkey) 359
Redhouse Press (Turkey) 358
Rediviva, Bokförlaget, Facsimileförlaget (Sweden) 332
Reed, A H & A W, Ltd Publishers (New Zealand) 271
Reed, A H & A W, Pty Ltd (Australia) 17
Reemst, van, (Netherlands) 263
Reference International Publishers Ltd (United Kingdom) 399
Reforma, Editorial y Librería La, (Puerto Rico) 299
Regain, Editions, (Monaco) 253
Regal Publishing Co (Philippines) 289
Regenbogen-Verlag (Switzerland) 347
Regimprensa (Portugal) 298
Regina Medal (International Literary Prizes) 444
Regional Literature Awards (Pakistan) 284
Regra, R, do Jogo (Portugal) 297
Reich, Kinderbuchverlag, Luzern AG (Switzerland) 347
Reich Verlag AG (Switzerland) 347
Reichert, Dr Ludwig, Verlag (Federal Republic of Germany) 153
Reichl, Otto, Verlag (Federal Republic of Germany) 153
Reichman, Livraria Científica Ernesto, (Brazil) 55
Reidel, D, Publishing Co (Netherlands) 263
Reim, Verlag Knut, (Federal Republic of Germany) 153
Reinaert Uitgaven (Belgium) 40
Reinhardt, Ernst, GmbH & Co Verlag (Federal Republic of Germany) 153
Reinhardt, Max, Ltd (United Kingdom) 399
Reinhardt, Verlag Friedrich, AG (Switzerland) 347
Reinheimer, Verlag Wilhelm G, (Federal Republic of Germany) 153
Reise- und Verkehrsverlag GmbH (RV) (Federal Republic of Germany) 153
Reiter, Elisabeth, (Austria) 29
Reitzels, C A, Forlag (Denmark) 76
Reitzels, Hans, Forlag A/S (Denmark) 76
Reka-Or Production and Publishing Ltd (Israel) 209
Rekha Prakashan (India) 192
Rekreaboek (Netherlands) 263
Relief-Verlag-Eilers (Federal Republic of Germany) 153
Religious Education Press (United Kingdom) 399
Religious Revival Organization (Thailand) 354
Remaja Karya (Indonesia) 199
Rembrandt Verlag GmbH (Federal Republic of Germany) 153
Remembrance Award (International Literary Prizes) 444
Remzi Kitabevi (Turkey) 358

Renacimiento, Editorial, SA (Mexico) 251
Renacimiento, Librería, SA de CV (El Salvador) 83
Renaissance, La, du Livre SA (Belgium) 40
Renaitour, J-M, Prize (France) 112
Renard, Fondation André, (Belgium) 40
Rénaudot, Théophraste, Prize (France) 112
Rencontre, Editions, SA (Switzerland) 347
Renmin-Jiyou-Chuban-She (People's Republic of China) 63
Renner, Verlag Klaus G, (Federal Republic of Germany) 153
Rentsch, Eugen, Verlag AG (Switzerland) 347
Representaciones y Servicios de Ingeniería SA (Mexico) 251
Representative Church Body Library (Republic of Ireland) 204
Reprographia (United Kingdom) 399
Republički Zavod za Unapredivanje Školstva (Yugoslavia) 424
Research Library on African Affairs (Ghana) 170
Research Publishing Co (United Kingdom) 399
Resenha, Editôra, Tributaria Ltda (Brazil) 54
Residenz Verlag (Austria) 27
Restrepo, Felix, Prize (International Literary Prizes) 444
Retail Book, Stationery and Allied Trades Employees' Association (United Kingdom) 364
Retail Bookselling and Stationery Wages Council (Great Britain) (United Kingdom) 364
Retz (France) 104
Réunies, Imprimeries, SA (Switzerland) 347
Reus, Editorial, SA (Spain) 321
Revelation Awards (Poetry and Prose) (Portugal) 298
Reverté, Editôra, Ltda (Brazil) 54
Reverté, Editorial, Mexicana SA (Mexico) 251
Reverté, Editorial, SA (Spain) 321
Reverté, Editorial, Venezolana SA (Venezuela) 419
Review Publications Pty Ltd (Australia) 17
Revisematic (France) 104
Revista de Occidente SA (Spain) 321
Revista, Editôra, dos Tribunais Ltda (Brazil) 54
Revolución, Ediciones, (Cuba) 68
Revue, La, nouvelle ASBL (Belgium) 40
Rex (United Kingdom) 399
Rex Book Store (Malaysia) 245
Rex Bookstore (Brunei) 57
Rex-Verlag (Switzerland) 347
Reyes, Librería Universitaria Jose T, (Honduras) 174
Rezzonico, Edizioni Raimondo, (Switzerland) 347
Rheingauer Verlagsgesellschaft mbH (Federal Republic of Germany) 153
Rheinland-Palatinate Prize (Federal Republic of Germany) 168
Rheinland-Verlag GmbH (Federal Republic of Germany) 154
Rhodesian Christian Press (Zimbabwe) 429
Rhodos, International Science and Art Publishers (Denmark) 76
Rhombus-Verlag, Edition Dumreicher (Austria) 27
Rhys, John Llewelyn, Memorial Prize (International Literary Prizes) 444
Rialp, Ediciones, SA (Spain) 321
Riband Books (United Kingdom) 399
Riber, Editions Scientifiques, Sàrl (France) 104
Riccardiana, Biblioteca, (Italy) 221
Ricci, Franco Maria, (France) 104
Ricci, Franco Maria, Editore (Italy) 218
Ricciardi, Riccardo, Editore SRL (Italy) 218
Richards Publishing (New Zealand) 271
Richards Publishing Consultants (New Zealand) 271
Richmond Hill Press (Australia) 17
Richmond, The, Publishing Co Ltd (United Kingdom) 399
Rico SpA (Italy) 218
Ricordi Americana SAEC (Argentina) 7
Ricordi, Arti Grafiche, SpA (Italy) 218
Ricordi, G e C, SpA (Italy) 218
Ridder, Peter de, Press BV (Netherlands) 263
Rideel, Editôra, Ltda (Brazil) 54
Rider & Co (United Kingdom) 399
Riederer, Dr, Verlag GmbH (Federal Republic of Germany) 154
Riemaecker, De, Uitgeverij (Belgium) 40
Rigby Bookshops (Australia) 19
Rigby Publishers Ltd (Australia) 17
Right Way Books (United Kingdom) 399
Rigmarole of the Hours (Australia) 17
Rigsarkivet (Denmark) 78
Rijksmuseum Meermanno-Westreenianum/Museum van het Boek (Netherlands) 266
Rijksuniversiteit, Bibliotheek der, (Netherlands) 266
Rijksuniversiteit te Gent, Bibliotheek van de, (Belgium) 43
Rijksuniversiteit te Groningen, Bibliotheek der, (Netherlands) 266
Rijksuniversiteit te Leiden, Bibliotheek der, (Netherlands) 266
Ríkisútgáfa Námsbóka (Iceland) 180
Riksarkivet (Norway) 281
Riksarkivet (National Record Office) (Sweden) 335

Riksbibliotektjenesten (Norway) 281
Rilindja (Yugoslavia) 424
Ringier & Co AG (Switzerland) 347
Rio Grafica e Editôra SA (Brazil) 54
Riomar Editores y Distribuidores S de CV (Mexico) 251
Riotor, Léon, Prize (France) 112
Risosha Ltd (Japan) 228
Ristin Voitto ry (Finland) 85
Ristin Voitto ry (Finland) 86
Rithöfundasamband Íslands (Iceland) 179
Ritter Verlag GmbH (Federal Republic of Germany) 154
Ritzau KG Verlag Zeit und Eisenbahn (Federal Republic of Germany) 154
Riunti, Editori, (Italy) 218
Rivadeneyra Prizes (Spain) 325
River Niger Commission, Documentation and Analysis Centre (Niger) 274
Rivers Press (United Kingdom) 399
Rivière, Librairie Marcel, et Cie (France) 104
Rivingtons (Publishers) Ltd (United Kingdom) 399
Riyadh Modern Bookshop (Saudi Arabia) 302
Rizzoli Editore SpA (Italy) 218
Rizzoli Editore SpA (Italy) 220
Rizzoli, Libreria, (Italy) 221
Roberge Prizes (France) 112
Robert, Dictionnaire Le, (France) 104
Robert, Editions E, (France) 104
Roberts Stationery Ltd (Barbados) 32
Robertson, Martin, (United Kingdom) 399
Robin Books (Australia) 17
Robinson, J, & Co (Israel) 210
Robinson & Watkins Books Ltd (United Kingdom) 399
Robson Books Ltd (United Kingdom) 399
Rocha, M Moreira Soares, Lda (Portugal) 297
'Roche', Editiones, (Switzerland) 347
Rocher, Les Editions du, (Monaco) 253
Rochus-Verlag (Federal Republic of Germany) 154
Rocom (Switzerland) 347
Rodana Verlag (Switzerland) 347
Rodas, Ediciones, SA (Spain) 321
Röderberg-Verlag GmbH (Federal Republic of Germany) 154
Rodopi, Editions, NV (Netherlands) 263
Rodríguez, Librería, (Argentina) 8
Roebuck Books (Australia) 17
Roeland Kamer Fonds VZW (Belgium) 40
Roerdomp, De, (Belgium) 40
Rogan, Barbara, Literary Agency (Israel) 210
Rogers, Deborah, Ltd (United Kingdom) 409
Rogner und Bernhard GmbH & Co Verlags KG (Federal Republic of Germany) 154
Rohr, Buchhandlung Hans, (Switzerland) 351
Rohr, Hans, (Switzerland) 347
Rojas, Pablo, Paz Prize (Argentina) 9
Rojas, Ricardo, Prize (Argentina) 9
Rökkur, bókaútgáfan (Iceland) 180
Rolfs, Rudolf, (Federal Republic of Germany) 154
Roli Books International (India) 192
Rolnicze i Leśne, Państwowe Wydawnictwo, (Poland) 292
Romance Book Club (United Kingdom) 410
Romantic Novelists' Association (Isle of Man) 247
Rombach und Co GmbH, Verlag & Buchdruckerei (Federal Republic of Germany) 154
Rombaldi, Ediclub, (France) 108
Rombaldi, Éditions, SA (France) 104
Romen (Netherlands) 263
Romero, Litografia A, SA (Spain) 321
Ronald, George, (United Kingdom) 399
Roorkee Press (India) 192
Rosa, Editôra Ana, (Brazil) 54
Rosda (Indonesia) 199
Rose, Barry, (Publishers) Ltd (United Kingdom) 399
Rose-Jordan Ltd (United Kingdom) 399
Rose of French Poets Prize (International Literary Prizes) 444
Rose-Verlag und Edition Rose-Verlag (Federal Republic of Germany) 154
Rosenberg e Sellier Editori in Torino (Italy) 218
Rosenberg e Sellier SRL (Italy) 221
Rosenheimer Verlagshaus Alfred Förg GmbH & Co KG (Federal Republic of Germany) 154
Rosenkilde og Bagger (Denmark) 76
Rosenwald, E S F, (France) 104
Rosepierre SA (Switzerland) 347
Rösler und Zimmer Verlag (Federal Republic of Germany) 154
Rosmini, Libreria, di R Maly (Italy) 221
Ross, Librería, (Argentina) 8
Rossel Edition (France) 104
Rossel Edition SA (Belgium) 40
Rossel, Victor, Prize (Belgium) 45
Rostock, Wilhelm-Pieck-Universität, Universitätsbibliothek (German Democratic Republic) 117
Rotapfel-Verlag AG (Switzerland) 347
Rotbuch Verlag GmbH (Federal Republic of Germany) 154
Rotep, Edições, (Portugal) 297

Roter Morgen, Verlag, (Federal Republic of Germany) 154
Roter Stern, Verlag, (Federal Republic of Germany) 154
Róth, Erich, -Verlag, Kassel (Federal Republic of Germany) 154
Roth et Sauter SA (Switzerland) 348
Rother, Bergverlag Rudolf, (Federal Republic of Germany) 154
Rotten-Verlags AG (Switzerland) 348
Rotterdam University Press (Netherlands) 263
Rötzer, E, Verlag (Austria) 27
Roucoules Foundation Grand Prize for Poetry (France) 112
Roudil, Editions, (France) 104
Rouff, Editions, SA (France) 104
Rouge et Or, G P, (France) 104
Rougery, La, (France) 104
Roulet, Editions, & Cie (Switzerland) 348
Roundwood, The, Press (1978) Ltd (United Kingdom) 399
Routledge & Kegan Paul Ltd (United Kingdom) 399
Rowohlt Taschenbuch Verlag GmbH (Federal Republic of Germany) 154
Rowohlt Taschenbuch Verlag GmbH (Federal Republic of Germany) 154
Roxby Press Ltd (United Kingdom) 399
Roy, K K, (Pvt) Ltd (India) 192
Roy, Publications, (France) 104
Roya Boudewijn (Belgium) 40
Royal Afghanistan Press Department (Afghanistan) 1
Royal Book Co (Pakistan) 283
Royal Book Co (Pakistan) 283
Royal College of Surgeons in Ireland Library (Republic of Ireland) 204
Royal Dublin Society Library (Republic of Ireland) 204
Royal Gazette Ltd (Bermuda) 46
Royal Literary Fund (United Kingdom) 413
Royal Palace, Library of the, (Afghanistan) 1
Royal Prize (Sweden) 336
Royal Society of Literature of the United Kingdom (United Kingdom) 413
Royal Society of South Africa Library (Republic of South Africa) 312
Ruamsarn (1977) Co Ltd (Thailand) 354
Ruamsarn (1977) Co Ltd (Thailand) 355
Rubber Research Institute of Malaysia Library (Malaysia) 245
Rubens (Belgium) 40
Rubinstein, E, (Israel) 209
Rubsamen, Verlag Wilhelm, (Federal Republic of Germany) 165
Ruedo Ibérico (France) 104
Ruhland Verlag (Federal Republic of Germany) 154
Ruiz, Editorial, Romero (Portugal) 297
Runa Press (Republic of Ireland) 204
Rune Forlag (Norway) 280
Runge, W, Verlag (Federal Republic of Germany) 154
Rungvit Sawarn-Apichon (Thailand) 354
Rupa & Co (India) 192
Rupa & Co (India) 196
Rusbet, Ediciones, (Mexico) 251
Rusconi Editore (Italy) 219
Russell, George, (AE) Memorial Award (Republic of Ireland) 205
Russky Yazyk (Union of Soviet Socialist Republics) 361
Rustem, K, & Bro (Cyprus) 69
Rütten und Loening, Verlag, Berlin (German Democratic Republic) 116
Rütten und Loening Verlag GmbH (Switzerland) 348
Ruy Diaz SAEIC (Argentina) 7
ruže, Nakladatelství, (Czechoslovakia) 71
Rwandaises, Editions, (Rwanda) 302
Ryborsch, VWK, GmbH (Federal Republic of Germany) 154
Rylands, John, University Library of Manchester (United Kingdom) 411
Ryosho-Fukyu-Kai Co Ltd (Japan) 228

S A Cultural Holdings (Pty) Ltd (Republic of South Africa) 310
S A D E, Medalla de Oro de la, (Sociedad Argentina de Escritores) (Argentina) 9
S A D E (Sociedad Argentina de Escritores) (Argentina) 3
S A G E P (Italy) 219
S A G E Publications Ltd (United Kingdom) 399
S A I E Editrice (Italy) 219
S A Kultuurbeleggings (Republic of South Africa) 310
S A M-förlaget (Sweden) 332
S A S S-Verlagsgesellschaft mbH und Co KG (Federal Republic of Germany) 154
S B I (Switzerland) 336
S C E M I (Société Continentale d'Editions Modernes Illustrées) Sàrl (France) 104
S C M Press Ltd (United Kingdom) 399

S C O D E (Italy) 219
S E C A (Société d'Exploitation et de Diffusion des Codes Rousseau Sàrl) (France) 104
S E D E S (France) 104
S E D E (Société d'Edition de Dictionnaires et d'Encyclopédies) (France) 104
S E I (Società Editrice Internationale) (Italy) 219
S E M I C Förlags AB (Sweden) 332
S I M E P SA (France) 104
S I S A R Edizioni (Società italiana stampati affini reclame) SpA (Italy) 219
S K E A B Förlag AB (Sweden) 332
S M D, Uitgeverij, BV (Spruyt, Van Mantgem en De Does) (Netherlands) 263
S N E D, Librairie, (Societe nationale d'Edition et de Diffusion) (Algeria) 2
S N L (France) 104
S N T L Nakladatelství technické literatury (Czechoslovakia) 71
S N-Verlag, Salzburger Nachrichten Verlags GmbH & Co KG (Austria) 27
S O I, Verlag, (Schweizerisches Ost-Institut) (Switzerland) 348
S O S, Editions, (Editions du Secours Catholique) (France) 104
S P C K (The Society for Promoting Christian Knowledge) (United Kingdom) 399
S P E L D (France) 104
S P K K (Spoločnosť priateľov krásnych kníh) (Czechoslovakia) 72
S R A (Société de Recherche appliquée à l'Education) (France) 104
S T E M-Mucchi (Società Tipografica Editrice Modenese) (Italy) 219
S T L Books (United Kingdom) 399
S T M (International Organizations) 433
S T P Distributors Sdn Bhd (Republic of Singapore) 306
s t v (Federal Republic of Germany) 154
S U D E L (Société Universitaire d'Editions et de Librairie) (France) 105
S U N socialistische Uitgeverij Nijmegen (Netherlands) 263
Sa Tu-Thu Dich-Thuat Va An-Loat (Socialist Republic of Viet Nam) 420
Saar SRL (Italy) 219
Sabah State Library (Malaysia) 245
Sabe U (Burma) 59
Sabzerou, Shahrokh, (Iran) 201
Sachs, Nelly, Prize (Federal Republic of Germany) 168
Sächsische Landesbibliothek (German Democratic Republic) 117
Sadan Publishing House Ltd (Israel) 209
Sadko SA (Spain) 321
Sadoveanu', Biblioteca Municipala 'Mihail, (Romania) 301
Saeed, H M, Co (Pakistan) 283
Saeftinge (Belgium) 40
Saera Shobo (Librairie Çà et Là) (Japan) 228
Safari Verlag (Reinhard Jaspert) (Federal Republic of Germany) 154
Saffier, Klub, (Republic of South Africa) 311
Safran, Sheri, Associates Ltd (United Kingdom) 409
Saga Literaria SL (Spain) 323
Saga Publishing Co (Iceland) 180
Sageret, Editions, (France) 105
Saggiatore, Il, SpA (Italy) 219
Sagi, Victor, Servicios Editoriales (Spain) 321
Sagittaire, Les Editions du, — Union des Techniques d'Editions (France) 105
Sagittaire, Librairie du, (French Polynesia) 113
Sagner, Verlag Otto, (Federal Republic of Germany) 154
Sahayogi Prakashan (Nepal) 255
Sahitya Akademi Award (India) 198
Sahitya Akademi Library (India) 196
Sahitya Bhawan Pvt Ltd (India) 192
Sahitya Pravarthaka Benefit Fund Awards (India) 198
Sahitya Pravarthaka Co-operative Society Ltd (India) 192
Sahitya Samsad (India) 192
Saiful (Indonesia) 199
Saint-André, Publications de, (Belgium) 40
Saint Andrew Press (United Kingdom) 399
Saint-Augustin, Société de l'Oeuvre, (Switzerland) 348
Saint-Genois Prize (Belgium) 45
Saint-Germain-des-Prés, Editions, SA (France) 105
Saint James Press (United Kingdom) 399
Saint-Joseph (Gabon) 113
Saint Louis de Gonzague, Bibliothèque, (Haiti) 174
Saint Louis, Publications des Facultés universitaires, (Belgium) 40
Saint Michael's Mission (Lesotho) 240
Saint-Paul (Switzerland) 348
Saint Paul Book Centre (Uganda) 359
Saint-Paul, Departement Les Classiques Africains, Editions, (France) 105
Saint Paul, Editions, (Zaire) 427
Saint-Paul, Editions, SA (France) 105
Saint-Paul, Imprimerie, SA (Luxembourg) 242

Saint Paul, Librairie, (United Republic of Cameroun) 60
Saint Paul, Librairie, (Burundi) 60
Saint Paul, Librairie, (Zaire) 427
Saint Paul, Librairie/Imprimerie, (United Republic of Cameroun) 60
Saint Paul Publications (India) 192
Saint Paul Publications (United Kingdom) 400
Sainte-Devote (Monaco) 253
Sainte-Geneviève, Bibliothèque, (France) 108
Saintour Prize (France) 112
Sajha Prakashan, Co-operative Publishing Organization (Nepal) 255
Sal Terrae, Editorial, (Spain) 321
Saladdine Publications & Distributors (Egypt) 82
Salama Publications Ltd (Kenya) 235
Salamander Books Ltd (United Kingdom) 400
Salamander Paperbacks (Netherlands) 263
Salamandra, La, (Italy) 219
Salamon e Agustoni Editori (Italy) 219
Salani, Adriano, SpA (Italy) 219
Salesian Publications & Don Bosco Film Strips (United Kingdom) 400
Salesianas, Edicões, (Portugal) 297
Salisbury Polytechnic Library (Zimbabwe) 430
Salle, Otto, Verlag (Federal Republic of Germany) 154
Salterain, Biblioteca Municipal 'Dr Joaquín de,' (Uruguay) 417
Saltire, The, Society (United Kingdom) 400
Saltykova-Schedrina, Gosudarstvennaya publichnaya biblioteka im M E, (Union of Soviet Socialist Republics) 363
Salutiste, Librairie, (Zaire) 427
Salvadoreña, Distribuidora, (El Salvador) 83
Salvat Editores SA (Spain) 321
Salvat SA de Ediciones (Spain) 322
Salvatella, Editorial Miguel A, (Spain) 322
Salvationist Publishing & Supplies Ltd (United Kingdom) 400
Salvator, Editions, Sàrl (France) 105
Salvator Verlag GmbH (Federal Republic of Germany) 154
Salvioni & Co (Switzerland) 348
Salzburger Druckerei, Verlag der, (Austria) 27
Salzer, Eugen, Verlag (Federal Republic of Germany) 154
Sam Carlos, Livraria, (Portugal) 298
Sam Joong Dang Publishing Co (Republic of Korea) 237
Sam-sung Publishing Co (Republic of Korea) 237
Saman Publishers Ltd (Sri Lanka) 326
Samfund til Udgivelse af Gammel Nordisk Litteratur (Denmark) 79
Samfundet de Nio (Sweden) 335
Samlerens Bogklub (Denmark) 77
Samlerens Forlag A/S (Denmark) 76
Sammensiutningen af Danmarks Forskningsbiblioteker (Denmark) 78
Sammler, Verlag für, (Austria) 27
'Samopomoc Chlopska', Zakład Wydawnictw CRS, (Poland) 292
Samouhos, A, Bookstore (Greece) 172
Sampson Low (United Kingdom) 400
Samsom (CED) (Belgium) 40
Samsom Uitgeverij BV (Netherlands) 263
Samwha Publishing Co (Republic of Korea) 237
San José, Editorial, (Nicaragua) 273
San Martin, Editorial, (Spain) 322
San Min Book Co (China (Taiwan)) 64
San Pablo, Librería, (Chile) 62
San Pablo, Librería, (Colombia) 66
Sanchi Prakashan (India) 192
Sanctus, Förlaget, (Sweden) 333
Sandbergs, AB, Bokhandel (Sweden) 334
Sander Kitabevi (Turkey) 359
Sander Yayınları (Turkey) 358
Sanderus PVBA (Belgium) 40
Sandesa Ltd (Sri Lanka) 326
Sändig, Dr Martin, GmbH (Federal Republic of Germany) 154
Sandkühler, Martin, (Federal Republic of Germany) 165
Sandy Beach Book Store (Barbados) 32
Sane, Lennart, Agency (Sweden) 334
Sang-e-Meel Publications (Pakistan) 283
Sangam Books (India) 192
Sangam Sarada Printing Press (Fiji) 84
Sangna Vuddhichai Saranonda (Thailand) 354
Sangster's Book Stores Ltd (Jamaica) 223
Sanguily, Biblioteca 'Manuel,' (Cuba) 68
Sangyo Tosho Publishing Co Ltd (Japan) 228
Sankei Juvenile Literature Prize (Japan) 233
Sankei, The, Shimbun Shuppankyoku Co (Japan) 228
Sanket Library Yojna (India) 195
Sankore, Librairie, (Senegal) 303
Sankt-Benno Verlag GmbH (German Democratic Republic) 116
Sankt Gabriel, Verlag, (Austria) 27
Sankt-Johannis-Druckerei, Verlag der, C Schweickhardt (Federal Republic of Germany) 155
Sankt Otto Verlag GmbH (Federal Republic of Germany) 155

Sankt Peter, Verlag, (Austria) 27
'Sanlian Shudian' Publishing House (People's Republic of China) 63
Sanseido Co Ltd (Japan) 228
Sanskrit Pustak Bhandar (India) 192
Sanskriti (India) 192
Sansoni, Casa Editrice G C, SpA (Italy) 219
Sanssouci Verlag (Switzerland) 348
Sansyusya Publishing Co Ltd (Japan) 228
Santa, Librería, Fe (Argentina) 8
Santiago, Editorial, Rueda SRL (Argentina) 7
Santillana SA de Ediciones (Spain) 322
Säntis Verlag (Switzerland) 348
Santo Domingo, Biblioteca Municipal de, (Dominican Republic) 80
Sanyo Shuppan Boeki Co Inc (Japan) 229
São Paulo Editora (Brazil) 54
Sapienza's Library (Malta) 246
Sapphire Books Pty Ltd (Australia) 18
Sappl, Paul, Schulbuch- und Lehrmittelverlag (Austria) 27
Saraiva SA, Livreiros Editores (Brazil) 54
Saraswat Library (India) 192
Sarawak State Library (Malaysia) 245
Sari Agung, Toko Buku, (Indonesia) 200
Sarita Prakashan (India) 192
Sarkar, M C, & Sons (P) Ltd (India) 192
Sarma, Librairie, (Zaire) 427
Sarmiento, Libreria, (Argentina) 8
Sarmiento Prize (Argentina) 9
Sarpay Beikman Best Manuscripts Awards (Burma) 59
Sarpay Beikman Board (Burma) 59
Sarpay Beikman Book Club (Burma) 59
Sarpay Beikman Bookshop (Burma) 59
Sarpay Lawka (Burma) 59
Sarvier — Editôra de Livros Medicos Ltda (Brazil) 54
Sassafras Verlag (Federal Republic of Germany) 155
Sasta Sahitya Mandal (India) 192
Sastra Hudaya (Indonesia) 199
Satellite Books Publishers (United Kingdom) 400
Satire Verlag GmbH (Federal Republic of Germany) 155
Satya Press (India) 192
Saudi Library (Saudi Arabia) 303
Saudi Publishing and Distributing House (Saudi Arabia) 302
Sauer, I H, Verlag GmbH (Federal Republic of Germany) 155
Sauerländer AG (Switzerland) 348
Sauerländer, H R, und Co (Federal Republic of Germany) 155
Sauerländer's, J D, Verlag (Federal Republic of Germany) 155
Saunders, W B, Co Ltd (United Kingdom) 400
Saur, K G, Editeur Sàrl (France) 105
Saur, K G, Verlag KG (Federal Republic of Germany) 155
Sauramps, Librairie, (France) 108
Sauret, Editions du Livre André, (Monaco) 253
Sautoy, De, College Library (United Republic of Cameroun) 60
Savez bibliotečkih radnika Srbije (Yugoslavia) 426
Savez društava bibliotekara Jugoslavije (Serbo-Croatian) (Yugoslavia) 426
Savez Inženjera i Tehničara Jugoslavije (Yugoslavia) 424
Savolan Kirjakauppa Oy (Finland) 86
Savremena Administracija (Yugoslavia) 424
Sawan Kirpal Publications (India) 192
Saxon House (United Kingdom) 400
Sayam Paritat (Thailand) 354
Scala Istituto Fotografico Editoriale (Italy) 219
Scene Book Club (United Kingdom) 410
Schäfer, Karl A, Buch-und Offsetdruckerei-Goldstadtverlag (Federal Republic of Germany) 155
Schäfer und Brandt (Federal Republic of Germany) 155
Schaffstein, Hermann, Verlag (Federal Republic of Germany) 155
Schaik, J L van, (Pty) Ltd (Republic of South Africa) 310
Schaik's, Van, Bookstore (Pty) Ltd (Republic of South Africa) 312
Schapire Editor SRL (Argentina) 7
Schattauer, F K, Verlag GmbH (Federal Republic of Germany) 155
Schaubroeck PVBA (Belgium) 41
Schauenburg, Moritz, Verlag GmbH und Co KG (Federal Republic of Germany) 155
Schaum (Federal Republic of Germany) 155
Scheepers Prize (Republic of South Africa) 313
Scheffler, Verlag Heinrich, part of Societäts (Federal Republic of Germany) 155
Scheidegger, Dr A, (Switzerland) 351
Scheltema, Boekhandel, Holkema Vermeulen BV (Netherlands) 266
Schendl, Dr A, GmbH & Co KG (Austria) 27
Scherpe Verlag (Federal Republic of Germany) 155
Scherz, Buchhandlung, AG (Switzerland) 351
Scherz Verlag AG (Switzerland) 348
Scherz Verlag GmbH (Federal Republic of Germany) 155
Scheuerer, Gertrud E, Verlag (Federal Republic of Germany) 155

Schibsteds, Chr, Forlag (Norway) 280
Schiele und Schön, Fachverlag, GmbH (Federal Republic of Germany) 155
Schifferli, Verlag der Arche Peter, (Switzerland) 348
Schildts, Holger, Förlagsaktiebolag (Finland) 85
Schiller Prize (Federal Republic of Germany) 168
Schilling, Kurt, (Federal Republic of Germany) 155
Schindele, G, Verlag GmbH (Federal Republic of Germany) 155
Schipper (Netherlands) 263
Schirmer/Mosel Verlag GmbH (Federal Republic of Germany) 155
Schlaefli, Otto, Verlag (Switzerland) 348
Schläpfer & Co AG (Switzerland) 348
Schlegel-Tieck Prize (United Kingdom) 415
Schlender, Verlag Bert, (Federal Republic of Germany) 155
Schlueck, Thomas, (Federal Republic of Germany) 165
Schmid, Joachim, und Co (Karl-May Verlag) (Federal Republic of Germany) 155
Schmidt, Erich, Verlag (Federal Republic of Germany) 155
Schmidt, Richard Carl, und Co (Federal Republic of Germany) 156
Schmidt-Römhild, Max, Verlag (Federal Republic of Germany) 156
Schmidt-Römhild, Verlag für polizeiliches Fachschrifttum Georg, (Federal Republic of Germany) 156
Schmidt, Verlag Dr Otto, KG (Federal Republic of Germany) 155
Schmiedel, Dr Roland, (Federal Republic of Germany) 156
Schmiere, Die, — Rudolf Rolfs (Federal Republic of Germany) 156
Schmitz, Wilhelm, Verlag (Federal Republic of Germany) 156
Schmücking, Galerie, Verlag (Federal Republic of Germany) 156
Schneekluth, Franz, Verlag (Federal Republic of Germany) 156
Schneider, Franz, Verlag GmbH und Co KG (Federal Republic of Germany) 156
Schneider, Verlag Lambert, GmbH (Federal Republic of Germany) 156
Schnell und Steiner, Verlag, GmbH und Co (Federal Republic of Germany) 156
Schocken Publishing House Ltd (Israel) 209
Schoelcher, Bibliothèque Victor, (Martinique) 247
Schoenbergske Forlag , Det, A/S (Nyt Nordisk Forlag Arnold Busck A/S) (Denmark) 76
Schofield & Sims Ltd (United Kingdom) 400
Scholar Publications International (Nigeria) Ltd (Nigeria) 276
Scholarship, The, in Letters (New Zealand) 273
Scholastic Publications (United Kingdom) 400
Schöldström, Birger, Prize (Sweden) 336
Scholtens en Zoon BV (Netherlands) 266
Schönbrunn-Verlag GmbH (Austria) 27
Schöne Wissenschaften, Verlag fur, (Belles Lettres Publishing Co — Albert Steffen Foundation) (Switzerland) 348
Schönen Bücher, Verlag Die, Dr Wolf Strache KG (Federal Republic of Germany) 156
Schöningh, Ferdinand, Verlag (Federal Republic of Germany) 156
School Bookshop Association (United Kingdom) 364
School Library Association (United Kingdom) 412
School Library Association of Papua New Guinea (Papua New Guinea) 285
School of Oriental & African Studies (United Kingdom) 400
School of Oriental and African Studies Library (United Kingdom) 411
School Supplies Ltd (New Zealand) 272
Schoolpers (Netherlands) 263
Schott Frères Sàrl (France) 105
Schott Frères SPRL (Éditeurs de Musique) (Belgium) 41
Schottentor (Austria) 29
Schott's, B, Söhne, Musikverlag (Federal Republic of Germany) 156
Schreiber, Verlag J F, GmbH (Federal Republic of Germany) 156
Schreiner, Olive, Prize for English Literature (Republic of South Africa) 314
Schriftenmission, Verlag und, der Ev Ges für Deutschland GmbH (Federal Republic of Germany) 156
Schriftenmissions-Verlag (Federal Republic of Germany) 156
Schroedel, Hermann, Verlag AG (Switzerland) 348
Schroedel, Hermann, Verlag KG (Federal Republic of Germany) 156
Schroeder, Kurt, Verlag (Federal Republic of Germany) 156
Schroeder, Marion von, Verlag GmbH (Federal Republic of Germany) 156
Schroll, Anton, & Co (Austria) 27
Schroll, Anton, und Co GmbH (Federal Republic of Germany) 156

Schubiger Verlag AG (Switzerland) 348
Schück, Henrik, Prize (Sweden) 336
Schule und Elternhaus, Verlag, (Federal Republic of Germany) 156
Schuler, F (Switzerland) 348
Schuler Verlagsgesellschaft mbH (Federal Republic of Germany) 157
Schulfernsehen, Verlagsgesellschaft, mbH & Co KG (Federal Republic of Germany) 157
Schulte, Verlag, und Gerth GmbH & Co KG (Federal Republic of Germany) 157
Schulten, P N, (Federal Republic of Germany) 157
Schultheis, Ludwig, Verlag Haus und Heim (Federal Republic of Germany) 157
Schulthess Polygraphischer Verlag AG (Switzerland) 348
Schultz, A/S J H, Forlag (Denmark) 76
Schulverlag Vieweg GmbH (Federal Republic of Germany) 157
Schulz, Verlag R S, (Federal Republic of Germany) 157
Schünemann, Carl Ed, KG (Federal Republic of Germany) 157
Schutter, De, SA (Belgium) 41
Schütz, Verlag K W, KG (Federal Republic of Germany) 157
Schuyt en Co CV (Netherlands) 263
Schwabe & Co AG (Switzerland) 348
Schwabe und Co GmbH Verlag (Federal Republic of Germany) 157
Schwabenverlag AG (Federal Republic of Germany) 157
Schwalbach, Verlag Haus, (Federal Republic of Germany) 157
Schwaneberger Verlag GmbH (Federal Republic of Germany) 157
Schwann, Edition, (Federal Republic of Germany) 157
Schwann, Pädagogischer Verlag, GmbH (Federal Republic of Germany) 157
Schwartz Publishing Group (Victoria) Pty Ltd (Australia) 18
Schwartz, Uitgeverij Gary, (Netherlands) 263
Schwartz, Verlag Otto, und Co (Federal Republic of Germany) 157
Schwarz Bildbücher (Federal Republic of Germany) 157
Schwarz, Verlag, GmbH (Federal Republic of Germany) 157
Schwarze, Dr Wolfgang, Verlag (Federal Republic of Germany) 157
Schwarzer, Verlagsbüro Karl, (Austria) 27
Schweickhardt, Verlag der Sankt-Johannis-Druckerei G, (Federal Republic of Germany) 157
Schweitzer, J, Verlag (Federal Republic of Germany) 157
Schweiz Verlag Arbeitsgemeinschaft für die Bergbevölkerung (SAB) (Switzerland) 348
Schweizer Buchwerbung und -Information (S B I) (Switzerland) 336
Schweizer Buchzentrum (Switzerland) 336
Schweizer Jugend, Aare-Verlag/, -Verlag (Switzerland) 348
Schweizer Spiegel Verlag AG & Rodana Verlag (Switzerland) 348
Schweizer Verband der Musikalienhändler und Verleger (Switzerland) 336
Schweizer Verlagshaus AG (Switzerland) 348
Schweizer Volksbuchgemeinde AG (Switzerland) 351
Schweizerbart'sche Verlagsbuchhandlung, E (Federal Republic of Germany) 157
Schweizerische Bibliophilen-Gesellschaft (Switzerland) 352
Schweizerische Landesbibliothek (Bibliothèque nationale suisse) (Switzerland) 352
Schweizerische Stiftung für Alpine Forschungen (Switzerland) 348
Schweizerische Zentralstelle für Stahlbau (Switzerland) 348
Schweizerischen Schallplattenmission, Verlag der, (Switzerland) 348
Schweizerischer Adressbuchverleger-Verband (Switzerland) 336
Schweizerischer Buchhändler- und Verleger-Verband (SBVV) (Switzerland) 336
Schweizerischer Bühnenverleger-Verband (Switzerland) 336
Schweizerischer Schriftsteller-Verband (Switzerland) 336
Schweizerisches Jugendschriftenwerk (Switzerland) 348
Schweizerisches katholisches Bibelwerk, Verlag, (Switzerland) 348
Schweizerisches Ost-Institut (Switzerland) 348
Schweizerisches Wirtschaftsarchiv (Archives économiques suisses) (Switzerland) 352
Schwengeler-Verlag (Switzerland) 348
Schwieger, H G, (Federal Republic of Germany) 157
Schwinghammer, Verlag Junge Gemeinde E, KG (Federal Republic of Germany) 157
Schwitter Edition GmbH (Switzerland) 349
Schwitter Holding, F P, Inc (Switzerland) 349
Scialtiel, Bureau littéraire international Marguerite, (France) 107
Sciascia, Salvatore, (Italy) 219
Science Fiction Book Club (United Kingdom) 410

498 INDEX

Science Publications Centre (Republic of Korea) 238
Science Research Associates Ltd (United Kingdom) 400
Science Research Associates Pty Ltd (Australia) 18
Sciences et Lettres, Editions, SA (Belgium) 41
Scientechnica (Publishers) Ltd (United Kingdom) 400
Scientia Verlag und Antiquariat Kurt Schilling (Federal Republic of Germany) 157
Scientific Book Agency (India) 192
Scientific Book Club (United Kingdom) 410
Scientific Documentation Centre (Iraq) 202
Scientific Library and Documentation Division (Philippines) 289
Scientific Publishing House (Socialist Republic of Viet Nam) 420
Scientific Translations International Ltd (Israel) 211
Scientifica Editrice, Libreria, (Italy) 219
Scientifiche Italiane, Edizioni, (Italy) 219
Scientology Publications Organization ApS (Denmark) 76
Scipione Autores Editores Ltda (Brazil) 54
Scolar Press (United Kingdom) 400
Scolastiche, Edizioni, APE SpA (Italy) 219
Scolavox (France) 105
Scorpion Publications Ltd (United Kingdom) 400
Scott, John, Educational Books Supply (Australia) 19
Scott-Moncrieff Prize (United Kingdom) 415
Scottish Academic Press Ltd (United Kingdom) 400
Scottish Arts Council Book Awards (United Kingdom) 415
Scottish Library Association (United Kingdom) 412
Scottish Publishers' Association (United Kingdom) 365
Scottish Record Office (United Kingdom) 411
Scribae-Uitgevers VZW (Belgium) 41
Scriptar, Editions, SA (Switzerland) 349
Scriptor Verlag (Federal Republic of Germany) 157
Scripts Publications (Australia) 18
Scripture Union (United Kingdom) 400
'Scrisul Românesc', Editura, ('Romanian Writing' Publishing House) (Romania) 301
Scuola, Editrice La, SpA (Italy) 219
Se Kwang Musical Publication Co (Republic of Korea) 237
Seafarer Books (United Kingdom) 400
Seale, Patrick, Books Ltd (United Kingdom) 409
Sealy, J C (Trinidad and Tobago) 356
Seara, Empresa de Publicidade, Nova SARL (Portugal) 297
Search Press Ltd (United Kingdom) 400
Secker & Warburg, Martin, Ltd (United Kingdom) 400
Second Back Row Press Pty Ltd (Australia) 18
Secours, Editions du, Catholique (France) 105
Secretaría de Estado de Relaciones Exteriores, Biblioteca de la, (Dominican Republic) 80
Século, Editorial o, (Portugal) 298
Sécuritas, La Société, SA (France) 105
Seditas (Société d'Editions et de Diffusion Tambourinaire-Sofradel) (France) 105
Sedmay Ediciones SA (Spain) 322
See-saw Book Club (United Kingdom) 410
Seeber, Libreria, (Italy) 221
Seefeld, Edition, (Switzerland) 349
Seeley, Service & Co Ltd (United Kingdom) 401
Seelig, AB, och Co (Sweden) 334
Seemann, E A, Verlag (Federal Republic of Germany) 157
Seemann, VEB E A, Buch- und Kunstverlag (German Democratic Republic) 116
Seemant Prakashan (India) 192
Seewald Verlag GmbH & Co (Federal Republic of Germany) 157
Seghers, Les Editions, SA (France) 105
Seibundo Shinkosha Publishing Co Ltd (Japan) 229
Seiwa Shoten Co Ltd (Japan) 229
Seix, Editorial, Barral SA (Spain) 322
Seizando-Shoten Publishing Co Ltd (Japan) 229
Seizoenen, De, PVBA (Belgium) 41
Sejong Daewang Kinyom Saophoe (Republic of Korea) 237
Sekai Bunka Publishing Inc (Japan) 229
Selangor Public Library (Malaysia) 245
Selcon SAEC & I (Selección Contable) (Argentina) 7
Selecciones, Biblioteca de, (Spain) 323
Selecciones Editoriales SA (Spain) 322
Selecciones, Librería, (Ecuador) 81
Selecciones, Librería, SRL (Bolivia) 46
Selecciones SA Comercial (Paraguay) 286
Seleções Editôra Ltda (Brazil) 54
Selecta, Librería, (Venezuela) 419
Sélection, Editions, J Jacobs SA (France) 105
Selimiye Library (Turkey) 359
Selina Publishers (India) 192
Sella, Shalom, (Israel) 210
Sellerio Editore (Italy) 219
Sellevolds Bokhandel A/S (Norway) 280
Sellier Verlag GmbH (Federal Republic of Germany) 157
Sembrador, Editorial El, (Chile) 62
Sembrador, Librería El, (Chile) 62
Semences, Editions, Africaines (United Republic of Cameroun) 60
Semic Press (Netherlands) 263

Seminar on the Acquisition of Latin American Library Materials (SALALM) (International Organizations) 433
Seminario de Integración Social Guatemalteca (Guatemala) 173
Seminario, Librería del, (Colombia) 66
Semper, Uitgeverij, Agendo BV (Netherlands) 263
Senate Library (Ketabkhaneh Majles Sena) (Iran) 201
Sénevé, Les Editions du, (France) 105
Senmon Toshokan Kyogikai (SENTOKYO) (Japan) 232
Senouhy Publishers (Egypt) 82
Sentis, Santiago, Melendo (Argentina) 7
Sentral Bokhandel A/S (Norway) 278
Sentral Bokhandel a/s (Norway) 280
Seomun Dang (Republic of Korea) 237
Seonjin Publishing Co (Republic of Korea) 237
Seoul National University Library (Republic of Korea) 238
Sept Couleurs, Les, (France) 105
Septuaginta BV Uitgeverij (Netherlands) 263
Sermwit Barnakarn (Thailand) 354
Service des Bibliothèques, Ministère des Universités (France) 109
Service SC (Belgium) 41
Service Technique pour l'Education (Fonds Social Juif Unifié) (France) 105
Services, Direction générale des, de Bibliothèques, Archives et Documentation (Popular Republic of Congo) 67
Services interbancaires SA (Belgium) 41
Servicio Continental de Publicaciones (Panama) 285
Servicio de Bibliotecas Populares de la Diputación Provincial de Barcelona (Spain) 324
Servicio de Documentación y Biblioteca (Dominican Republic) 80
Servicio de Lewis (Panama) 285
Servire BV Uitgevers (Netherlands) 263
Servire BV Uitgevers (Netherlands) 266
Setberg (Iceland) 180
Settern, Bokförlaget, (Sweden) 333
Seuil, Editions du, (France) 105
Seungmun-gak (Republic of Korea) 238
Seven Seas Publishers (German Democratic Republic) 116
Sevenseas Publishing Pty Ltd (New Zealand) 271
Severin Presse (Austria) 27
Severn House Publishers Ltd (United Kingdom) 401
Severoceské nakladatelství (Czechoslovakia) 71
Sha'b, Al-, Bookshop (Saudi Arabia) 302
Shadeed's Educational & General Supplies (Jamaica) 223
Shakai Shiso-Sha (Japan) 229
Shaker, Ahmed, Al Ansary (Egypt) 82
Shakespeare Head Press (Australia) 18
Shakespeare Head Press (United Kingdom) 401
Shakespearean Authorship Society (United Kingdom) 413
Shanghai Book Co Ltd (Hong Kong) 176
Shanghai Book Co Pte Ltd (Republic of Singapore) 306
Shanghai Library (People's Republic of China) 63
Sharbain's Bookshop (Israel) 210
Sharda Prakashan (India) 192
Shaw Centre, Bernard, (United Kingdom) 413
Shaw, Pat, Associates (formerly EMBLA) (Norway) 280
Shaw Society, Bernard, (United Kingdom) 413
Shazar Prize (Israel) 211
Shearwater Press Limited (Isle of Man) 247
Sheed & Ward Ltd (United Kingdom) 401
Sheil, Anthony, Associates Ltd (United Kingdom) 409
Sheldon Press (United Kingdom) 401
Shell Book of the Year Award (Australia) 22
Shepheard-Walwyn (Publishers) Ltd (United Kingdom) 401
Sheppard Press Ltd (United Kingdom) 401
Sherratt & Hughes (Bowes & Bowes) (United Kingdom) 410
Sheth, R R, and Co (India) 192
Sheth, R R, & Co (India) 196
Shikmona Publishing Co Ltd (Israel) 209
Shiko-Sha Co Ltd (Japan) 229
Shiksha Bharati (India) 193
Shimoni, Joseph, (Israel) 209
Shincho Prizes (Japan) 233
Shinchosha Co (Japan) 229
Shindan to Chiryo Co Ltd (Japan) 229
Shinkenchiku-Sha Co Ltd (Japan) 229
Shire Publications Ltd (United Kingdom) 401
Shishu Sahitya Samsad Pvt Ltd (India) 193
Shkencore e Universitetit Shtetëror të Tiranës, Biblioteka, (Albania) 1
Shkodër Public Library (Albania) 1
Shmulik (Israel) 209
Shogakukan Literary Prize (Japan) 233
Shogakukan Publishing Co Ltd (Japan) 229
Shokabo Publishing Co Ltd (Japan) 229
Shokoku-Sha Publishing Co Ltd (Japan) 229
Shona/Ndebele Writers' Association (Zimbabwe) 430
Shona Readers' Book Club (Zimbabwe) 429
Shortland Educational Publications (New Zealand) 271
Shree Mahavir Book Depot (Publishers) (India) 193
Shree Saraswati Sadan (India) 193
Shri Ram Centre for Industrial Relations and Human Resources (India) 193

Shueisha Publishing Co Ltd (Japan) 229
Shufu-to-Seikatsu Sha Ltd (Japan) 229
Shufunotomo Co Ltd (Japan) 229
Shumawa Book House (Burma) 59
Shumawa Publishing House (Burma) 59
Shuter and Shooter (Pty) (Republic of South Africa) 312
Shuter & Shooter (Pty) Ltd (Republic of South Africa) 310
Shwepyidan Printing & Publishing House (Burma) 59
Si-Sa-Yong-O-Sa (Republic of Korea) 237
Siam Book House (Thailand) 355
Siam Directory (Thailand) 354
Siam, The, Society (Thailand) 355
Siamandas (Greece) 172
Sibelius-Akatemian Kirjasto (Finland) 86
Sideris, J, OE Ekdoseis (Greece) 172
Sidgwick & Jackson Ltd (United Kingdom) 401
Siebdruck Süd GmbH, Druck und Verlagshaus (Federal Republic of Germany) 157
Sieber, Wilfried Th, (Federal Republic of Germany) 165
Siebert und Engelbert Dessart Verlag GmbH (Federal Republic of Germany) 157
Siebert Verlag GmbH (Federal Republic of Germany) 157
Siemens AG — ZVW 5 Verlag (Federal Republic of Germany) 158
Sierra Leone Library Association (Sierra Leone) 304
Sierra Leone Library Board (Sierra Leone) 302
Sierra Leone, The, Diocesan Bookshops Ltd (Sierra Leone) 304
Sierra Leone University Press (Sierra Leone) 304
Sifriat Poalim Ltd (Israel) 209
Sifriat Poalim Ltd (Israel) 210
Siglo XX, Club del Libro Nicaragüense, Librería y Editorial, (Nicaragua) 273
Siglo XX, Ediciones, SAC & I (Argentina) 7
Siglo XXI Editores de Colombia Ltda (Colombia) 66
Siglo XXI Editores de España SA (Spain) 322
Siglo XXI Editores SA (Mexico) 251
Siglos, Editorial V, SA (Mexico) 251
Sigmar, Editorial, SACI (Argentina) 7
Signal-Verlag Hans Frevert (Federal Republic of Germany) 158
Sigueme, Ediciones, SA (Spain) 322
Sijthoff en Noordhoff International Publishers (Netherlands) 263
Sijthoff's Uitg, A W, Mij BV (Netherlands) 264
Sikkel, Uitgeverij De, NV (Belgium) 41
Silex (Spain) 322
Silliman University Library (Philippines) 289
Sillon, Editions Le, d'Or (Belgium) 41
Siloé, Editions, Sàrl (France) 105
Silogos Ecdoton Bibliopolon (Greek Publishers' Association) (Greece) 171
Silva, K V G De, & Sons (Kandy) (Sri Lanka) 326
Silvaire, Editions André, (France) 105
Silvana Editoriale Srl (Italy) 219
Silver Dagger Award (United Kingdom) 415
Silvio Romero Prize (Brazil) 57
Sima, Ediciones, (Spain) 322
Siman Krai (Israel) 209
Símbolo, Edições, (Brazil) 54
Simmat, S (Federal Republic of Germany) 158
Simon Stevin NV (Belgium) 41
Simon, Verlag Ludwig, (Federal Republic of Germany) 158
Simondium Publishers (Pty) Ltd (Republic of South Africa) 310
Simson, Samuel, Ltd (Israel) 209
Simul, The, Press Inc (Japan) 229
Sinag-Tala Publishers Inc (Philippines) 289
Sinai Publishing Co (Israel) 209
Sind University Central Library (Pakistan) 283
Sindbad (France) 105
Sindhi Adabi Board (Pakistan) 284
Sindicato Nacional dos Editores de Livros (Brazil) 47
Singapore Book Store (Republic of Singapore) 306
Singapore Booksellers' Association (Republic of Singapore) 304
Singapore Chinese Booksellers' Association (Republic of Singapore) 304
Singapore University Press Pte Ltd (Republic of Singapore) 306
Singer, BP, Features Inc (Federal Republic of Germany) 165
Singu Munwha Sa (Republic of Korea) 237
Sinite Parvulos VBVB (Belgium) 41
Sino-Malay Publishing Co (Malaysia) 245
Sinodalno Izdatelstvo (Bulgaria) 58
Sinpattana (Thailand) 354
Sint-Ignatius, Bibliotheek der Universitaire Faculteiten, (Belgium) 43
Sintal (Belgium) 41
Sintes, Editorial, SA (Spain) 322
Sinwel-Buchhandlung Verlag (Switzerland) 349
Sir Robert Ho Tung, Biblioteca, (Macau) 242
Sirey, Editions, (France) 105
Siriraj Medical Library (Thailand) 355
Sistem, Pustaka, Palajaran (Malaysia) 245

INDEX 499

Sistema Bibliotecario (Librarians' System) (Honduras) 175
Sitti, A B, Syamsiyah (Indonesia) 200
Sjöstrands Förlag (Sweden) 333
Skalholt (Iceland) 180
Skandinavia Verlag (Federal Republic of Germany) 165
Skarabee, Uitgeverij, BV (Netherlands) 264
Skarv-Nature Publications ApS (Denmark) 76
Skattekartoteket, A/S, (Denmark) 76
Sketch Publishing Co Ltd (Nigeria) 276
Skilton & Shaw (United Kingdom) 401
Skilton, Charles, Ltd (United Kingdom) 401
Skinner, Thomas, Directories (United Kingdom) 401
Skira, Editions D'Art Albert, SA (Switzerland) 349
Skjaldborg, Bókaútgáfan, sf (Iceland) 180
'Skladnica Ksiegarska', Państwowe, Przedsiębiorstwo, (Poland) 293
Škola za Strane Jezike (Yugoslavia) 424
Skolförlaget Gävle AB (Sweden) 333
'Školska knjiga' (Yugoslavia) 424
Sktachnica Ksiegarska (Poland) 293
Skuggsja bókaforlag (Iceland) 180
Skylark Children's Book Club (United Kingdom) 410
Skyline Publishing House (India) 193
Skypress International (Federal Republic of Germany) 158
'Slask', Wydawnictwo, (Poland) 292
Slaska kjiegarnia Techniczna (Poland) 292
Slatkine Reprints (Switzerland) 349
Slavika (Federal Republic of Germany) 158
Slezak, Josef Otto, (Austria) 27
Sloboda (Yugoslavia) 424
Slovart Ltd (Czechoslovakia) 72
Slovenská kartografia NP (Czechoslovakia) 71
Slovenská knižničná (Czechoslovakia) 72
Slovenská technická knižnica (Czechoslovakia) 72
Slovenské pedagogické nakladateľstvo (Czechoslovakia) 71
Slovenské ústredie knižnej kultúry (Czechoslovakia) 69
Slovenské vydavateľstvo podohospodarskej literatúry (Czechoslovakia) 71
Slovenskej Akademie Vied, Vydavateľstvo, (Czechoslovakia) 71
Slovenský spisovateľ (Czechoslovakia) 71
Slovo Ljubve (Yugoslavia) 424
Službeni List (Yugoslavia) 424
Smålänningens Forlag AB (Sweden) 333
Smart & Mookerdum (Burma) 59
Smeets Illustrated Projects (Netherlands) 264
Smena (Czechoslovakia) 71
Smith, John, & Son (Glasgow) Ltd (United Kingdom) 410
Smith, Lawrence, (Argentina) 8
Smith, Pauline, Prize for Prose (Republic of South Africa) 314
Smith & Son Children's Literary Competition, W H, (United Kingdom) 415
Smith & Son Literary Award, W H, (United Kingdom) 415
Smith, W H, & Son Ltd (United Kingdom) 410
Smriti Prakashan (India) 193
Smythe, Colin, Ltd (United Kingdom) 401
Snaefell, Bókaútgáfan, (Iceland) 180
Snoeck-Ducaju & Zoon NV (Belgium) 41
Snøfugl Forlag (Norway) 280
Sober Förlags AB (Sweden) 333
Sobrier-Arnould Prize (France) 112
Social Science Association Press (Thailand) 355
Social Sciences Library (Socialist Republic of Viet Nam) 420
Socialistisk Bogklub ApS (Denmark) 77
Sociedad Cientifica, Biblioteca de la, del Paraguay (Paraguay) 286
Sociedad de Bibliófilos Chilenos (Chile) 63
Sociedad de Bibliotecarios de Puerto Rico (Puerto Rico) 299
Sociedad de Ciencias, Letras y Artes (Spain) 325
Sociedad de Libreros del Ecuador (Ecuador) 80
Sociedad General de Autores de España (Spain) 314
Sociedad General de Autores de la Argentina (Argentina) 3
Sociedad General Española de Librería (Spain) 314
Sociedad Mexicana de Bibliografía (Mexico) 252
Sociedad Puertorriqueña de Escritores (Puerto Rico) 299
Sociedade Brasileira, Biblioteca da, de Cultura Inglesa (Brazil) 56
Società Dante Alighieri (Italy) 222
Società Dantesca Italiana (Italy) 222
Societa Editori della Svizzera Italiana (SESI) (Switzerland) 336
Società Letteraria (Italy) 222
Societäts-Verlag (Federal Republic of Germany) 158
Société africaine de Librairie-Papeterie (SALP) (International Organizations) 433
Société Africaine d'Edition (Senegal) 303
Société belge des Auteurs, Compositeurs et Editeurs (SABAM) (Belgium) 44
Société Biblique belge ASBL (Belgium) 41
Société Continentale d'Editions Modernes Illustrées (France) 105

Société de Langue et de Littérature wallones ASBL (Belgium) 44
Société de Presse et d'Edition de Madagascar (Democratic Republic of Madagascar) 242
Société de Recherche appliquée à l'Education (France) 105
Société d'Edition d'Afrique Nouvelle (Senegal) 303
Société d'Edition d'Annuaires Professionnels (France) 105
Société d'Edition de Dictionnaires et d'Encyclopédies (France) 105
Société d'Edition, de Publicité, de Radio et Télévision (France) 105
Société d'Edition d'Enseignement Supérieur (France) 105
Société d'Editions Scientifiques, Dimedia (France) 105
Société des anciens Textes Français (France) 109
Société des Bibliophiles (France) 108
Société des Gens de Lettres (France) 109
Société des Libraires et Editeurs de la Suisse romande (SLESR) (Switzerland) 336
Société des Poètes français (France) 110
Société d'Etudes dantesques (France) 109
Société d'Exploitation et de Diffusion des Codes Rousseau (France) 105
Société d'Histoire littéraire de la France (France) 109
Société d'Information médicale et d'enseignement post-universitaire (France) 105
Société du Nouveau Littré (SNL) Dictionnaire 'Le Robert' (France) 105
Société du Vieux Montmartre (France) 110
Société Editions Internationales Sàrl (France) 108
Société Encyclopédique Française (SEF) (France) 105
Société française des Traducteurs (French Union of Translators) (France) 113
Société internationale de Bibliographie classique (International Organizations) 434
Société internationale des Bibliothèques-Musées des Arts du Spectacle (SIBMAS) (International Organizations) 434
Société Kenkoson d'Etudes Africaines (United Republic of Cameroun) 60
Société Librairie nouvelle (Tunisia) 357
Société Malgache d'Edition (Democratic Republic of Madagascar) 242
Société Malgache d'Edition (Democratic Republic of Madagascar) 243
Société nationale d'Edition et de Diffusion (Tunisia) 357
Société nationale d'Edition et de Diffusion (Tunisia) 357
Société nationale d'Edition et de Diffusion (SNED) (Algeria) 2
Société Nouvelle de l'Imprimerie Centrale (Democratic Republic of Madagascar) 242
Société royale des Bibliophiles et Iconophiles de Belgique (Belgium) 44
Société Universitaire d'Editions et de Librairie (France) 105
Society for the Promotion and Improvement of Libraries (Pakistan) 284
Society for the Promotion of Japanese Literature (Japan) 232
Society for the Study of Medieval Languages and Literature (United Kingdom) 413
Society of Aesthetes, Art and Literary Critics (Bulgaria) 58
Society of Archivists (United Kingdom) 412
Society of Arts, Literature and Welfare (Bangladesh) 32
Society of Australian Writers (Australia) 21
Society of Australian Writers (United Kingdom) 413
Society of Authors (United Kingdom) 365
Society of County Librarians (United Kingdom) 412
Society of Editors (Australia) 10
Society of Indexers, The, (United Kingdom) 365
Society of Metropolitan & County Chief Librarians (United Kingdom) 412
Society of Women Writers (Australia) 10
Society of Young Publishers (United Kingdom) 365
Society, The, for Promoting Christian Knowledge (United Kingdom) 401
Sodel (Editeur) SA (France) 105
Söderström ja Co Förlagsaktiebolag (Finland) 85
Sodexport-Grem (France) 108
Sodimca, Librairies, (Zaire) 427
Soeroengan (Indonesia) 200
Soethoudt, Walter, (Belgium) 41
Sofia City and District State Archives (Bulgaria) 58
Sofia Press Agency (Bulgaria) 58
Sofiac (Société Française des Imprimeries Administratives Centrales) (France) 105
Sofiiski Universitet 'Kliment Ohridsky' Biblioteka (Bulgaria) 58
Sofradel-Seditas (France) 106
Sofradif Editions Philippe Auzou (France) 106
Sogalivre, Librairie, (Gabon) 113
Sogensha Publishing Co Ltd (Japan) 229
Sohlmans Förlag AB (Sweden) 333
Sojuz na društvata na bibliotekarite na Jugoslavija (Macedonian) (Yugoslavia) 426
Sojuz na društvata za makedonski jazik i literatura (Yugoslavia) 426
Sol, Ediciones del, SA (Argentina) 7

Solar (France) 106
Soledi (Imprimeur-Editeur) SA (Belgium) 41
Soleil Noir, Editions, (France) 106
Solicitors' Law, The, Stationery Society Ltd (United Kingdom) 401
Solidaridad Publishing House (Philippines) 289
Solum Forlag A/S (Norway) 280
Somaiya Publications Pvt Ltd (India) 193
Somalia d'Oggi (Somalia) 307
Somec-Rwanda (Rwanda) 302
Sommai Press (Thailand) 355
Sommer og Sörensen Forlag ApS (Denmark) 76
Somogy, Editions d'Art Aimery, (France) 106
Soncino Press Ltd (United Kingdom) 401
Sondagskool Boekhandel (Republic of South Africa) 310
Sonnenweg-Verlag Schäfer und Brandt (Federal Republic of Germany) 158
Sonneville Press (Uitgeversmij) PVBA (Belgium) 41
Sonrisa, 'La, Vertical' Prize (International Literary Prizes) 444
Sonzé, Editions, (France) 106
Sonzogno SpA (Italy) 219
Sopena, Editorial, Argentina SACI e I (Argentina) 7
Sopena, Editorial, Colombiana SA (Mexico) 251
Sopena, Ramón, SA (Spain) 322
Sopena Venezolana, Editorial Ramón, SA (Venezuela) 419
Soprep (Editions de Bussac) (France) 106
Soprode (France) 106
Sorbonne, Bibliothèque de la, (France) 109
Sorgente, La, Srl (Italy) 219
Sorrett Publishing Pty Ltd (Australia) 18
Sotano, Librería del, (Mexico) 252
Sotheby Parke Bernet Publications (United Kingdom) 401
Soulanges, Editions Louis, 'Le Livre Ouvert' (France) 106
Source, Les Editions de la, SA (France) 106
Sousa e Almeida, Livraria, (Portugal) 298
Sousa, Luisa Claudio de, Prize (Brazil) 57
South African Academy of Science and Arts Prizes (Republic of South Africa) 314
South African Library (Republic of South Africa) 312
South African Library Association (Republic of South Africa) 312
South African Natural History Publications Co (Republic of South Africa) 310
South African Publishers' Association (Republic of South Africa) 310
South Asian Publishers Pvt Ltd (India) 193
South Australia Biennial Literature Prize (Australia) 22
South Australia Booksellers' Association (Australia) 10
South Australian Government Literature Prize (Australia) 22
South East Asian Regional Branch of the International Council on Archives (SARBICA) (International Organizations) 434
South Head Press (Australia) 18
South Pacific Commission Library (New Caledonia) 268
Southeast Asian Ministers of Education Organization (SEAMEO) (Republic of Singapore) 306
Southeast Book Co (China (Taiwan)) 64
Southside (United Kingdom) 401
Souvenir Press Ltd (United Kingdom) 401
'Sovetskaya Entsiklopediya', Izdatelstvo, (Union of Soviet Socialist Republics) 362
'Sovetskaya Rossiya', Izdatelstvo, (Union of Soviet Socialist Republics) 362
'Sovetskii Khudozhnik', Izdatelstvo, (Union of Soviet Socialist Republics) 362
'Sovetskii Kompozitor', Izdatelstvo, (Union of Soviet Socialist Republics) 362
'Sovetskoe Radio', Izdatelstvo, Glavnyi Pochtamt p/ya693 (Union of Soviet Socialist Republics) 362
Soviet Land Nehru Awards (India) 198
Sovietskii Pisatel, Izdatelstvo, (Union of Soviet Socialist Republics) 362
Sovremennik Publishers (Union of Soviet Socialist Republics) 362
Spangenberg (Federal Republic of Germany) 158
Spanish Book Center (Spain) 314
Spanish Book Club (United Kingdom) 410
Spanos, Costas, (Greece) 172
Sparevirke, A/S, (Denmark) 76
Sparfrämjandet, Förlagsaktiebolag (Sweden) 333
Spearman, Neville, (United Kingdom) 401
Spectrum, Scherz Taschenbuch Verlag, (Switzerland) 349
Spectrum, Uitgeverij Het, BV (Netherlands) 264
Spectrum, Het, NV (Belgium) 41
Spectrum Publications (India) 193
Spectrum Publications Pty Ltd (Australia) 18
Spectrum Verlag Stuttgart GmbH (Federal Republic of Germany) 158
Spee — Buchverlag GmbH (Federal Republic of Germany) 158
Speer-Verlag (Switzerland) 349
Spektra, Bokförlaget, AB (Sweden) 333
Spemann, W, Verlag (Federal Republic of Germany) 158
Sperling e Kupfer Editori SpA (Italy) 219
Sperling & Kupfer, Libreria, (Italy) 221

Spes SA (Switzerland) 349
Sphere Books Ltd (United Kingdom) 401
Sphinx, The, (Egypt) 82
Sphinx, Le, SA (Belgium) 41
Sphinx Verlag (Switzerland) 349
Spiegelserie Boekenclub (Netherlands) 266
Spiess, Verlag Volker, (Federal Republic of Germany) 158
Splichal, Anciens Etablissements, SA (Belgium) 41
Společnost přátel knihy pro mládež (Czechoslovakia) 72
Společnost pro Československou literaturu, Index-, v zahraničí (Czechoslovakia) 72
Společnost pro krásné písmo a typografii (Czechoslovakia) 69
Spolek Českých bibliofilu (Czechoslovakia) 73
Spon, E & F N, Ltd (United Kingdom) 401
Sponholtz, Adolf, Verlag (Federal Republic of Germany) 158
Sport (Czechoslovakia) 71
Sport i Turystyka, Wydawnictwo, (Poland) 292
Sport Verlags AG (Switzerland) 349
Sporting and Leisure Press (United Kingdom) 402
Sporting Handbooks Ltd (United Kingdom) 402
Sportska Knjiga (Yugoslavia) 424
Sportsman's Book Club (United Kingdom) 410
Sportverlag (German Democratic Republic) 116
Spotlight Publications (Israel) 209
Sprachmethodik, Verlag für, (Federal Republic of Germany) 158
Språkförlaget Skriptor AB (Sweden) 333
Språktjänst (Sweden) 336
Spring Books (United Kingdom) 402
Springer-Verlag Berlin-Heidelberg-New York (Federal Republic of Germany) 158
Springer-Verlag KG (Austria) 27
Springwood Books Ltd (United Kingdom) 402
Spruyt, van Mantgem en de Does BV (Netherlands) 264
Spurbooks Ltd (United Kingdom) 402
Sreberk, J (Israel) 209
Sree Rama Publishers (India) 193
Sri Jaya, Pustaka, Sdn Bhd (Malaysia) 245
Sri Lanka, Booksellers' Association of, (Sri Lanka) 325
Sri Lanka Library Association (Sri Lanka) 326
Sri Lanka National Library Services Board (Sri Lanka) 326
Sri Lanka Publishers' Association (Sri Lanka) 325
Sri Lanka Publishing Co (Sri Lanka) 326
Sri Nakharinwirot University Library (Thailand) 355
Srpska Književna Zadruga (Yugoslavia) 424
Srpske, Biblioteka, Akademije Nauka i Umetnosti (Yugoslavia) 425
Staackmann, L, Verlag KG (Federal Republic of Germany) 158
Staatlich Genehmigte Gesellschaft der Autoren, Komponisten und Musikverleger (AKM) reg Gen mbH (Austria) 23
Staatlich genehmigte Literarische Verwertungsgesellschaft (LVG) reg Gen mbH (Austria) 23
Staats- und Universitätsbibliothek (Federal Republic of Germany) 166
Staatsarchiv, Zentrales, (German Democratic Republic) 118
Staatsbibliothek Bamberg (Federal Republic of Germany) 166
Staatsbibliothek Preussischer Kulturbesitz (Federal Republic of Germany) 166
Staatsdrukkerij en Uitgeverijbedrijf (Netherlands) 264
Staatsverlag der Deutschen Demokratischen Republik (German Democratic Republic) 116
Stabenfeldt Forlag (Norway) 280
Stacey International (United Kingdom) 402
Stadion, Editura, (Romania) 301
Stadsbibliotheek (Belgium) 43
Stadt- und Bezirksbibliothek Leipzig (German Democratic Republic) 118
Stadt- und Universitätsbibliothek (Federal Republic of Germany) 166
Stadt- und Universitätsbibliothek (Switzerland) 352
Städte-Verlag, E v Wagner und J Mitterhuber (Federal Republic of Germany) 158
Stafleu's Wetenschappelijke Uitgeversmaatschappij BV en Stafleu en Tholen BV (Netherlands) 264
Stage 1 (United Kingdom) 402
Stäheli, Buchhandlung Kurt, & Co (Switzerland) 351
Stähle und Friedel Verlagsgesellschaft mbH und Co (Federal Republic of Germany) 158
Stahleisen, Verlag, mbH (Federal Republic of Germany) 158
Stainer & Bell Ltd (United Kingdom) 402
Stalling Verlag GmbH, Druck und Verlagshaus (Federal Republic of Germany) 158
Stam Press Ltd (United Kingdom) 402
Stam/Robijns (Netherlands) 264
Stam Technische Boeken (Netherlands) 264
Stam Tijdschriften BV (Netherlands) 264
Stamford College Publishers (Republic of Singapore) 306
Stämpfli, Verlag, & Cie AG (Switzerland) 349
Standaard Hoofdstadboekhandel (Belgium) 43
Standaard Uitgeverij en Distributie BV (Netherlands) 264

Standaard Uitgeverij (NV Scriptoria) (Belgium) 41
Standard Book Numbering Agency (Australia) 10
Standard Book Numbering Agency (Austria) 23
Standard Book Numbering Agency (Belgium) 33
Standard Book Numbering Agency (Brazil) 47
Standard Book Numbering Agency (Colombia) 65
Standard Book Numbering Agency (Denmark) 73
Standard Book Numbering Agency (Egypt) 81
Standard Book Numbering Agency (Finland) 84
Standard Book Numbering Agency (France) 87
Standard Book Numbering Agency (Federal Republic of Germany) 119
Standard Book Numbering Agency (Ghana) 169
Standard Book Numbering Agency (Hong Kong) 175
Standard Book Numbering Agency (Hungary) 176
Standard Book Numbering Agency (India) 181
Standard Book Numbering Agency (Israel) 205
Standard Book Numbering Agency (Italy) 211
Standard Book Numbering Agency (Japan) 224
Standard Book Numbering Agency (Mexico) 248
Standard Book Numbering Agency (Netherlands) 256
Standard Book Numbering Agency (New Zealand) 268
Standard Book Numbering Agency (Nigeria) 274
Standard Book Numbering Agency (Norway) 278
Standard Book Numbering Agency (Philippines) 288
Standard Book Numbering Agency (Poland) 290
Standard Book Numbering Agency (Republic of Singapore) 304
Standard Book Numbering Agency (Republic of South Africa) 307
Standard Book Numbering Agency (Spain) 314
Standard Book Numbering Agency (Suriname) 327
Standard Book Numbering Agency (Sweden) 327
Standard Book Numbering Agency (Switzerland) 336
Standard Book Numbering Agency (Switzerland) 336
Standard Book Numbering Agency (Thailand) 354
Standard Book Numbering Agency (Trinidad and Tobago) 356
Standard Book Numbering Agency (Union of Soviet Socialist Republics) 360
Standard Book Numbering Agency (Yugoslavia) 421
Standard Book Numbering Agency (Zimbabwe) 428
Standard Book Numbering Agency Ltd (United Kingdom) 365
Standard Books Ltd (Zambia) 428
Standard, The, Book Depot (India) 193
Standard, The, Bookshop (Tanzania) 353
Standartov, Znak Pochyota Order Izdatelstvo, (Union of Soviet Socialist Republics) 362
Standing Conference of African Library Schools (SCALS) (International Organizations) 434
Standing Conference of African University Libraries (SCAUL) (International Organizations) 434
Standing Conference of National and University Libraries (SCONUL) (United Kingdom) 412
Standing Conference on Library Materials on Africa (SCOLMA) (International Organizations) 434
Stanford Maritime Ltd (United Kingdom) 402
Stanké, Les Editions Internationales Alain, (France) 106
Stanton, Ernest, Publishers (Pty) Ltd (Republic of South Africa) 310
Stapp Verlag Wolfgang Stapp (Federal Republic of Germany) 158
Stappaerts, NV Uitgeverij, (Belgium) 41
Star (United Kingdom) 402
Star Book Bank (India) 195
Star Book Club (India) 195
Star Publications (P) Ltd (India) 193
Star Publications (P) Ltd (India) 196
Star, Pustaka, (Indonesia) 200
Star, The, Press (Brunei) 57
Starczewski, Hanns-Joachim, Verlag/Künstlerhof-Galerie (Federal Republic of Germany) 158
Starke, Harold, Ltd (United Kingdom) 402
State Archives (Mongolian People's Republic) 253
State Book Trading Office (Mongolian People's Republic) 253
State Central Library (India) 196
State Central Library (Democratic People's Republic of Korea) 236
State Institute of Languages (India) 193
State Librarians' Council (Australia) 20
State Library (Burma) 59
State Library (Republic of South Africa) 312
State Library of New South Wales, The, (Australia) 20
State Library of Queensland (Australia) 20
State Library of South Australia (Australia) 20
State Library of Tasmania (Australia) 20
State Library of Victoria (Australia) 20
State of Victoria Short Story Awards (Australia) 22
State Press (Mongolian People's Republic) 253
State Prize for Children's and Youth Literature (Netherlands) 268
State Prize for Literature, the P C Hooft Prize (Netherlands) 268
State Prizes for Literature (Finland) 87
State Stipendium for Literature (Austria) 30
Stationery & Educational Book Centre (Jamaica) 224

Stationery Office (Oifig an tSolathair) (Republic of Ireland) 204
Statistical Publications and Printing Board of the Central Statistical Office (Poland) 292
Statisticke a evidencni vydavatelství tiskopisu (Czechoslovakia) 71
Statistics Library (Finland) 86
Statistika (Union of Soviet Socialist Republics) 362
Statistisk Sentralbyras Bibliotek (Norway) 281
Statistiska Centralbyråns Bibliotek (Sweden) 335
Statisztikai Kiadó Vállalat (Hungary) 177
Státní pedagogické nakladatelství (Czechoslovakia) 71
Státní technická knihovna (Czechoslovakia) 72
Státní technická knihovna v Brně (Czechoslovakia) 72
Státní vědecka knihovna (Czechoslovakia) 72
Státní vědecka knihovna (Czechoslovakia) 72
Státní zemědělské nakladatelství (Czechoslovakia) 71
Statsbiblioteket (Denmark) 78
Stauda, Johannes, Verlag (Federal Republic of Germany) 158
Stavanger Bibliotek (Norway) 281
Steamships Trading Co (Papua New Guinea) 285
Steensballes, P F, Boghandels Eftg (Norway) 280
Stegeland, Leif, Förlag AB (Sweden) 333
Steimatzky's Agency Ltd (Israel) 209
Steimatzky's Agency Ltd (Israel) 210
Steindecker, Editions Robert, (Editions RST) (France) 106
Steiner, Franz, Verlag GmbH (Federal Republic of Germany) 158
Steiner, Rudolf, Press (United Kingdom) 402
Steiner, Rudolf, Verlag (Switzerland) 349
Steinhausen, Literarischer Verlag, GmbH (Federal Republic of Germany) 159
Steinhauser, Dr Karl, (Austria) 28
Steinkopf, J F, Verlag GmbH (Federal Republic of Germany) 159
Steinkopff, Dr Dietrich, Verlag (Federal Republic of Germany) 159
Steintor Verlag, Rudolf Jüdes (Federal Republic of Germany) 159
Stella, Editorial, (Argentina) 7
Stella, Editorial, (Dominican Republic) 80
Stelle, Le, SpA (Italy) 219
Stenersen, Rolf, Prize (Norway) 281
Stenvalls, Frank, Förlag (Sweden) 333
Stenvert, Uitgeverij M, en Zoon BV (Netherlands) 264
Stephanus Edition Verlags GmbH (Federal Republic of Germany) 159
Stephens Book Department (Trinidad and Tobago) 356
Stephens, Patrick, Ltd (United Kingdom) 402
Stephenson, Carl, Verlag (Federal Republic of Germany) 159
Steppe (Belgium) 41
Ster, De, PVBA (Belgium) 41
Sterling Book Club (India) 195
Sterling Publishers Pvt Ltd (India) 193
Stern-Verlag Janssen und Co (Federal Republic of Germany) 159
Stern-Verlag Janssen und Co (Federal Republic of Germany) 166
Sternberg-Verlag (Federal Republic of Germany) 159
Stevens & Sons Ltd (United Kingdom) 402
Steyler Verlag (Federal Republic of Germany) 159
Stichting Bibliotheek en Documentatieacademies (Netherlands) 256
Stichting Speurwerk betreffende het Boek (Netherlands) 256
Stiehm, Lothar, Verlag GmbH (Federal Republic of Germany) 159
Stiftelsen Kursverksamhetens Förlag (Sweden) 333
Stiftelsen Svenska Barnboksinstitutet (Sweden) 335
Stiftsbibliothek (Switzerland) 352
Stiintifică si Enciclopedică, Editura, (Romania) 301
Stillitron (United Kingdom) 402
Stimme-Verlag GmbH (Federal Republic of Germany) 159
Stobart & Son Ltd (United Kingdom) 402
Stock, Editions, (France) 106
Stocker, Josef, AG (Switzerland) 349
Stocker, Leopold, Verlag (Austria) 28
Stocker-Schmid, Verlag, AG (Switzerland) 349
Stockholm Universitets Bibliotek (Stockholm University Library) (Sweden) 335
Stockholms Stadsbibliotek (Sweden) 335
Stockton House (New Zealand) 271
Stockum, Uitgeverij W P Van, en Zoon NV (Netherlands) 264
Stollfuss Verlag Bonn GmbH & Co KG (Federal Republic of Germany) 159
Stora Romanbokklubben (Sweden) 334
Story, E, -Scientia PVBA (Belgium) 43
Story, E,-Scientia PVBA (Belgium) 43
Stowarzyszenie Autorow Zaiks (Poland) 290
Stowarzyszenie Bibliotekarzy Polskich (Poland) 294
Stowarzyszenie Ksiegarzy Polskich (Poland) 290
Strakosch, Carl, & Olaf Nordgreen (Denmark) 77
Strandbergs Forlag (Denmark) 76

Strassova, Mme Greta, (France) 107
Středočeské nakladatelství knihkupectví (Czechoslovakia) 71
Strega Prize (Italy) 222
Strengholt's, A J G, Boeken Anno 1928 BV (Netherlands) 264
Strom-Verlag (Switzerland) 349
Stroyizdat Publishing House (Union of Soviet Socialist Republics) 362
Strubes Forlag og Boghandel A/S (Denmark) 76
Stručna Štampa (Yugoslavia) 424
Struik (Pty) Ltd (Republic of South Africa) 311
Struik, C, (Pty) Ltd (Republic of South Africa) 312
Student Christian Movement Press (United Kingdom) 402
Studentlitteratur AB (Sweden) 333
Students', The, Book Co (India) 193
Studia Croatica (Argentina) 7
Studia, Editions, SA (France) 106
Studio Book Club (Chile) 62
Studio Editoriale (Italy) 220
Studio, Librería, (Chile) 62
Studio, Librería, (Mexico) 252
Studio Publications (Ipswich) Ltd (United Kingdom) 402
Studio Vista (United Kingdom) 402
Studium Ediciones (Spain) 322
Studium, Edizioni, (Vita Nova SpA) (Italy) 220
Studium, Librería, SA (Peru) 287
Studium, Librería, SA (Peru) 287
Studium, Verlag für das, der Arbeiterbewegung (Federal Republic of Germany) 159
Stürtz Verlag (Federal Republic of Germany) 159
Stvarnost (Yugoslavia) 424
Styria (Austria) 29
Styria, Verlag, (Austria) 28
Su Hoc (Historical) Publishing House (Socialist Republic of Viet Nam) 420
Su Librería (Ecuador) 81
Su That (Truth) Publishing House (Socialist Republic of Viet Nam) 420
Subodh Pocket Books (India) 193
Succes BV (Netherlands) 264
Success Publications (Kenya) 235
Sud Editions (Tunisia) 357
Sudan Library Association (Sudan) 327
Sudan, The, Bookshop Ltd (Sudan) 327
Südbuch Vertriebsgesellschaft mbH (Federal Republic of Germany) 159
Süddeutsche Verlagsgesellschaft Ulm (Federal Republic of Germany) 159
Süddeutscher Verlag Buchverlag (Federal Republic of Germany) 159
Sudha Publications Pvt Ltd (India) 193
'Sudostroenie', Izdatelstvo, (Union of Soviet Socialist Republics) 362
Sudri, Bókaútgáfan, (Iceland) 180
Südwest Verlag GmbH und Co KG (Federal Republic of Germany) 159
Suenson, Finn, Forlag (Denmark) 77
Sugar and Snails Books (Australia) 18
Sugarco Edizioni SRL (Italy) 220
Suhrkamp Verlag KG (Federal Republic of Germany) 159
Suksapan Panich (Business Organization of Teachers' Institute) (Thailand) 355
Suksit Siam Co Ltd (Thailand) 355
Suksit Siam Co Ltd (Thailand) 355
Süleymaniye Kütüphanesi Müdürlüğü (Turkey) 359
Sulina, Livraria, (Brazil) 55
Sulina, Livraria, Editôra (Brazil) 54
Sultan Chand and Sons (India) 194
Sultan's Library (Cyprus) 69
Suma, Librería, (Venezuela) 419
Suman Prakashan (P) Ltd (India) 194
Sumatera (Indonesia) 200
Summit Books (Australia) 18
Sumur Bandung (Indonesia) 200
Sumus Verlag Jutta Gütermann (Switzerland) 349
Sun Books Pty Ltd (Australia) 18
Sun Yat-Sen Library (Hong Kong) 176
Sundems, H, Bokhandel A/S (Norway) 280
Sundial (United Kingdom) 402
Suomalainen Kirjakauppa Oy (Finland) 86
Suomalainen Tiedeakatemia (Finland) 87
Suomalaisen Kirjallisuuden Seura (Finland) 85
Suomalaisen Kirjallisuuden Seura (Finland) 87
Suomen Antikvariaattiyhdistys-Finska Antikvariatföreningen (Finland) 84
Suomen Arvostelijain Liitto (Finland) 87
Suomen Kääntäjäin Yhdists (Finland) 87
Suomen Kirjailijaliitto (Finland) 84
Suomen Kirjallisuuspalvelun Seura (Finland) 86
Suomen Kirjastonhoitajat — Finlands Bibliotekarier ry (Finland) 86
Suomen Kirjastoseura (Finland) 86
Suomen Kustannusyhdistys (Finland) 84
Suomen Nuortenkirjaneuvosto ry (Finland) 84
Suomen Tieteellinen Kirjastoseura (Finland) 86
Supraphon (Czechoslovakia) 71
Sur, Editorial, SA (Argentina) 7

Sur Prize (India) 198
Suriname Publishers' Association (Suriname) 327
Suriwongs Book Centre (Thailand) 355
Suriyaban Bookstore (Thailand) 355
Suriyaban Publishers (Thailand) 355
Surjeet Book Depot (India) 194
Surrey University Press (United Kingdom) 402
Susaeta, Ediciones, SA (Spain) 322
Sussex University Press (United Kingdom) 402
Sussex Video Ltd (United Kingdom) 402
Sutpaisarn (Thailand) 355
Suuri Suomalainen Kirjakerho Oy (Finland) 86
Suva Book Shop (Fiji) 84
Suva City Library (Fiji) 84
Suyuz Knigoizdatelite i Knizharite (Bulgaria) 57
Svalan, Bokklubben, (Sweden) 334
Svaz českých spisovatelu (Czechoslovakia) 69
Svensk Kartjänst AB (Sweden) 333
Svenska Antikvariatföreningen (Sweden) 327
Svenska Arkivsamfundet (Sweden) 335
Svenska Bibliotekariesamfundet (Sweden) 335
Svenska Bokförläggareföreningen (Sweden) 328
Svenska Bokhandels-Medhjälpare-Föreningen (Sweden) 328
Svenska Bokhandlareföreningen (Sweden) 328
Svenska Folkbibliotekarieförbundet (Sweden) 335
Svenska Litteratursällskapet i Finland (Finland) 87
Svenska Musikförläggareföreningen UPA (Swedish Music Publishers' Association) (Sweden) 328
Svenska Österbottens Litteraturförening (Finland) 87
Svenska Österbottens Litteraturförening (Sweden) 335
Svenska Utbildningsförlaget Liber AB (Sweden) 333
Svepomoc (Czechoslovakia) 71
Sveriges Allmänna Biblioteksförening (Sweden) 335
Sveriges B-Bokhandlareförbund (Swedish Association of Smaller Booksellers) (Sweden) 328
Sveriges Exportrads Förlag (Sweden) 333
Sveriges Författarförbund (Sweden) 328
Sveriges Lantbruksuniversitets Bibliotek (Sweden) 335
Sveriges Radios Förlag (Sweden) 333
Sveriges Vetenskapliga Specialbiblioteks Förening (Sweden) 335
Svet Knjige (Yugoslavia) 425
Svjetlost (Yugoslavia) 424
Svjetlost (Yugoslavia) 425
Svoboda (Czechoslovakia) 71
Svoboda Book Club (Czechoslovakia) 72
'Svyaz', Izdatelstvo, (Union of Soviet Socialist Republics) 362
Św Wojciecha, Ksiegarnia, (Poland) 293
Swan (India) 194
Swan, Anni, Prize (Finland) 87
Swan Book Store (Brunei) 57
Swaziland National Library Service (Swaziland) 327
Swaziland News Agency (Swaziland) 327
Swedenborg Institut (Switzerland) 349
Swedish Academy Prizes (Sweden) 336
Swedish into Foreign Language Translation Prize (Sweden) 336
Swedish Linguistics Prize (Sweden) 336
Swedish National ISBN Centre (Sweden) 328
Sweet and Maxwell (NZ) Ltd (New Zealand) 271
Sweet & Maxwell Ltd (United Kingdom) 402
Swets en Zeitlinger BV (Netherlands) 264
Swindon Book Co (Hong Kong) 176
Syarikat Cultural Supplies Sdn Bhd (Malaysia) 245
Syarikat Dian Sdn Bhd (Malaysia) 245
Syarikat United Book Sdn Bhd (Malaysia) 245
Sydney University Press (Australia) 18
Symposion-Verlag GmbH (Federal Republic of Germany) 159
Syndicat belge de la Librairie ancienne et moderne (Belgium) 33
Syndicat de la Librairie ancienne et du Commerce de l'Estampe en Suisse (Vereinigung der Buchantiquare und Kupferstichhändler in der Schweiz) (Switzerland) 336
Syndicat des Critiques littéraires (France) 110
Syndicat des Editeurs du Maroc (Morocco) 254
Syndicat des Libraires (Socialist Republic of Viet Nam) 420
Syndicat des Librairies d'Algérie (Algeria) 2
Syndicat des Librairies de Tunisie (Tunisia) 357
Syndicat des Librairies du Moroc (Morocco) 254
Syndicat des Représentants littéraires français (France) 88
Syndicat national de la Librairie ancienne et moderne (France) 88
Syndicat national de l'Edition (France) 88
Syndicat national des Annuaires et Supports divers de Publicité (France) 88
Syndicat national des Importateurs et Exportateurs de Livres (France) 88
Syndicat Romand des employés du Livre (Switzerland) 337
Syndikat Autoren- und Verlagsgesellschaft (Federal Republic of Germany) 159
Syokabo Publishing Co Ltd (Japan) 229
Syrian Documentation Papers (Syria) 352

Syrian Patriarchal Seminary, Library of the, (Lebanon) 240
Syropoulos Adelfoi OE Ekdotikos Oikos (Greece) 172
Systems Publications Ltd (United Kingdom) 402
Szabó, Fővárosi, Ervin Könyvtár (Hungary) 178
Szent benedekrend (Hungary) 178
Szépirodalmi Kiadó (Publishing House of Belles Lettres) (Hungary) 177
Szkolne i Pedagogiczne, Wydawnictwa, (The Publishing House for School and Pedagogical Books) (Poland) 293
Szot Literary Prizes (Hungary) 179

T B L (Tübinger Beiträge zur Linguistik) Verlag (Federal Republic of Germany) 159
T E A (Tipográfica Editora Argentina) (Argentina) 7
T E B R O C (Tehran Book Processing Centre) (Iran) 201
T M P Book Department (Tanzania) 353
T M P Book Department (Tanzania) 353
T R-Verlagsunion GmbH (Federal Republic of Germany) 159
T V F (Switzerland) 349
Tabajara, Ediçoes, (Brazil) 54
Tabard Press Ltd (United Kingdom) 402
Table, Les Editions de la, Ronde (France) 106
Tabor Publications (United Kingdom) 403
Taeguk Publishing Co (Republic of Korea) 237
Tafelberg Publishers Ltd (Republic of South Africa) 311
Tages-Nachrichten (Switzerland) 349
Tagore Award (India) 198
Tah Chung Book Co (China (Taiwan)) 64
Tai Kuen Book Co (Hong Kong) 176
Taipei Municipal Library (China (Taiwan)) 64
Taipei Publications Trading Co (China (Taiwan)) 64
Taishukan Publishing Co Ltd (Taishukan Shoten) (Japan) 229
Taiwan Branch Library, National Central Library (China (Taiwan)) 64
Taizé, Les Presses de, (France) 106
Taj Co Ltd (Pakistan) 283
Tájékoztatási tudományos társaság (Hungary) 178
Takahashi Shoten Co Ltd (Japan) 229
Takariva, Imprimerie, (Democratic Republic of Madagascar) 242
Talbot Press Ltd (Republic of Ireland) 204
Tallandier, Librairie Jules, (France) 106
Tallboy Publications (Australia) 18
Taller Ediciones JB (Spain) 322
Tallis Press Ltd (United Kingdom) 403
Talmudic Encyclopaedia Publications (Israel) 209
Talmy, Franklin Ltd (United Kingdom) 403
Tamaraw Publishing Co (Philippines) 289
Tamayo, Franz, Prize (Bolivia) 47
Tamburini Editore SpA (Italy) 220
Tamgu Dang Book Centre (Republic of Korea) 237
Tamil Puthakalayam (India) 194
Tammi Kustannusosakeyhtiö (Finland) 85
Tampere Prize (Finland) 87
Tampereen Kirjakauppa Oy (Finland) 86
Tampereen Yliopiston Kirjasto (Finland) 86
Táncsics Szakszervezeti Kiadó (Publishing House of the Trade Union Movement) (Hungary) 177
Tanden (United Kingdom) 403
Tanizaki Junichiro Prize (Japan) 233
Tanko-Sha Publishing Co Ltd (Japan) 229
Tankönyvkiadó Vállalat (Hungary) 177
Tansy Books (Republic of Ireland) 204
Tantivy Press (United Kingdom) 403
Tanum-Norli (Johan Grundt Tanum Forlag og Olaf Norlis Forlag A/S) (Norway) 280
Tanzania Elimu Supplies (Tanzania) 353
Tanzania Library Association (Tanzania) 353
Tanzania Library Service (Tanzania) 353
Tanzania Library Service (Tanzania) 353
Tanzania Library Service (Tanzania) 353
Tanzania Mission Press (Tanzania) 353
Tanzania Mission Press (Tanzania) 353
Tanzania Publishing House (Tanzania) 353
Tapir (Norway) 280
Tara Press (Fiji) 84
Taraporevala Publishing Industries Pvt Ltd (India) 194
Taraporevala Sons & Co Pvt Ltd (India) 194
Tarate (Indonesia) 200
Tarbut Vehinuch (Israel) 209
Tardy, Editions, SA (France) 106
Target (United Kingdom) 403
Target Publishers (Edms) Bpk (Republic of South Africa) 311
Taride, Editions, Sàrl (France) 106
Tarshish Books (Israel) 209
Tartu Riikliku Ulikooli Teaduslik Raamatükogu (Union of Soviet Socialist Republics) 363
Tasmanian Booksellers' Association (Australia) 10
Tassier, Suzanne, Prize (Belgium) 45

Tata McGraw-Hill Publishing Co Ltd (India) 194
Tate Gallery Publications (United Kingdom) 403
Tatran (Czechoslovakia) 71
Taurus Ediciones SA (Spain) 322
Tavistock Publications Ltd (United Kingdom) 403
Tawjih, al-, Press (Syria) 352
Taxation (Pakistan) 283
Taylor, Alister, Publishers (New Zealand) 271
Taylor & Francis Ltd (United Kingdom) 403
Taylor, Peter, & Co Ltd (Guyana) 174
Taylor, Reginald, Prize (United Kingdom) 415
Taylor-Whitehead, W J, (France) 107
Taylorix Fachverlag Stiegler und Co (Federal Republic of Germany) 159
Tcherikover Publishers Ltd (Israel) 209
Tchernichowsky Prize (Israel) 211
Tchou, Claude, Editeur (France) 106
Teach Yourself Books (United Kingdom) 403
Teacher Publishing Co Ltd (United Kingdom) 403
Teachers' Book Centre Ltd (Jamaica) 224
Teacher's Bookshelf (Australia) 19
Teachers' Club Library (People's Democratic Republic of Yemen) 421
Teachers' Union (Israel) 209
Teakfield Ltd (United Kingdom) 403
Technica (Bulgaria) 58
Technical Chamber, Library of the, of Greece (Greece) 172
Technical Chamber of Greece (Greece) 172
Technical High School Library (Namibia) 255
Technical Institutes, Central Library of the Higher, (Bulgaria) 58
Technical Library, Central, (Bulgaria) 58
Technical, The, Press Ltd (United Kingdom) 403
Technical University Library (Turkey) 359
Techniek, De, (Belgium) 41
Technik Tabellen Verlag Fikentscher und Co (Federal Republic of Germany) 159
Technik, VEB Verlag, (German Democratic Republic) 116
Technip, Société des Éditions, (France) 106
Technique et Documentation (Librairie Lavoisier) (France) 106
Technique et Vulgarisation SA (France) 106
Techniques de l'Ingénieur Sàrl (France) 106
Techniques Professionels, Editions, (France) 106
Technitrain (Pty) Ltd (Republic of South Africa) 311
Tecni Ciencia Libros (Venezuela) 419
Técnicos Asociados, Editores, SA (Spain) 322
Tecnicos e Cientificos, Livros, Editôra SA (Brazil) 54
Tecnoprint, Editôra, Ltda (Brazil) 54
Tecnos, Editorial, SA (Spain) 322
Teduca, Técnicas Educativas, CA (Venezuela) 419
Teenage (Australia) 19
Tegopoulos (Greece) 172
Tehnica, Editura, (Romania) 301
Tehnička Knjiga (Yugoslavia) 424
Tehnička Knjiga (Yugoslavia) 424
Tehnička Knjiga (Yugoslavia) 425
Tehnika (Yugoslavia) 424
Tehran Book Processing Centre (TEBROC) (Iran) 201
Tehran, Central Library and Documentation Centre of, University (Iran) 201
Tehran Economist (Iran) 201
Tehran University Press (Iran) 201
Teide, Editorial SA (Spain) 322
Teikoku-Shoin Co Ltd (Japan) 230
Teirlinck, Auguste, Prize (Belgium) 45
Teissonnière, Paul, Prize (France) 112
Teixeira, A M, e Cia (Filhos) Lda (Livraria Classica Editora) (Portugal) 297
Tejerina, Alfonso, Ltda (Bolivia) 46
Tek Translation & International Print Ltd (United Kingdom) 416
Teknisk Forlag A/S (Denmark) 77
Tekniska Litteratursällskapet (Sweden) 335
Teknografiska Institutet AB (Sweden) 333
Teknologisk Forlag (Norway) 280
Teknologisk Instituts Forlag (Denmark) 77
Tel Aviv University Library (Israel) 210
Tel Aviv University, Publications Sales Division (Israel) 209
Téléscope, Le, (France) 107
Telex-Verlag Jaeger Waldmann (Federal Republic of Germany) 159
Telford, Thomas, Ltd (United Kingdom) 403
Tella, Instituto Torcuato di, (Argentina) 7
Teloeken, Alf, Verlag KG (Federal Republic of Germany) 160
Telos series of Paperbacks (Federal Republic of Germany) 160
Telstar, Ediciones, (Spain) 323
Temco Publishing Ltd (Zambia) 428
Temis, Editorial, Ltda (Colombia) 66
Temis, Librería, Ltda (Colombia) 66
Tempel, Uitgeverij De, (Belgium) 41
Temple Press (United Kingdom) 403
Temple Smith, Maurice, Ltd (United Kingdom) 403
Tengler, A & G, (Austria) 29

Tenri Central Library (Japan) 231
Tequi, Librairie Pierre, et Editions Tequi (France) 106
Tercer, Ediciones, Mundo Ltda (Colombia) 66
Tercer Mundo, Librería, (Colombia) 66
Teredo Books Ltd (United Kingdom) 403
Terra Sancta Arts (Israel) 209
Tertulia, Librería La, (Puerto Rico) 299
Tessloff, Ernst, Verlag (Federal Republic of Germany) 160
Tests, Editions, (France) 106
Teti, Nicola, e C Editore SRL (Italy) 220
Tetrad Press (United Kingdom) 403
Teubner, B G, GmbH (Federal Republic of Germany) 160
Teubner, BSB B G, Verlagsgesellschaft (German Democratic Republic) 116
Text Book Centre Ltd (Kenya) 235
Text Books Malaysia Sdn Bhd (Malaysia) 245
Text und Kritik, Edition, GmbH (Federal Republic of Germany) 160
Textbook Publishers' Association of Japan (Kyokasho Kyokai) (Japan) 224
Textbook, The, Centre Ltd (Kenya) 235
Thacker & Co Ltd (India) 194
Thai Commercial Printing Press (Thailand) 355
Thai Inc (Thailand) 355
Thai Library Association (Thailand) 355
Thai National Documentation Centre (TNDC) (Thailand) 355
Thai Watana Panich (Thailand) 355
Thames & Hudson Ltd (United Kingdom) 403
Thames Translations (United Kingdom) 416
Thammasat University Library (Thailand) 355
Than Myit Baho Publishing House (Burma) 59
Thaning og Appels Forlag (Denmark) 77
Theatrum Orbis Terrarum (Netherlands) 264
Theiss, Konrad, Verlag GmbH (Federal Republic of Germany) 160
Thekes, Librería, (Puerto Rico) 299
Theodor (Haiti) 174
Theologischer Verlag AG (Switzerland) 349
Theologischer Verlag R Brockhaus (Federal Republic of Germany) 160
Theologischer Verlag (wholesaler) (Switzerland) 351
Theoria, Ediciones, SRL (Argentina) 7
Theosophical Publishing, The, House (India) 194
Thesen Verlag Vowinckel und Co (Federal Republic of Germany) 160
Theseus Verlag AG (Switzerland) 349
Thiele und Schwarz, Druck- und Verlagshaus, (Federal Republic of Germany) 160
Thielen, Verlag-Buchhandlung Joseph, (Luxembourg) 242
Thieme, BV Uitgeverij en Boekhandel W J, & Cie (Netherlands) 264
Thieme, Georg, Verlag KG (Federal Republic of Germany) 160
Thieme, VEB Georg, Leipzig (German Democratic Republic) 116
Thiemig, Verlag Karl, AG (Federal Republic of Germany) 160
Thienemanns, K, Verlag (Federal Republic of Germany) 160
Thin, James, Bookseller (United Kingdom) 410
Third World First Publications (Nigeria) 276
Thjódsaga, Bókaútgáfan, (Iceland) 180
Thjodskjalasafn (National Archives) (Iceland) 180
Thomas, A (United Kingdom) 403
Thomas-Verlag (Switzerland) 349
Thomasons, Joseph, & Co (India) 194
Thompson, Henry, Ltd (United Kingdom) 403
Thomson Books Ltd (United Kingdom) 403
Thomson Press (India) Ltd (India) 194
Thomson Publications South Africa (Pty) Ltd (Republic of South Africa) 311
Thone, Imprimerie-Editions Georges, Sciences et Lettres (Belgium) 41
Thorbecke, Jan, Verlag KG (Federal Republic of Germany) 160
Thornes, Stanley, (Publishers) Ltd (United Kingdom) 403
Thornhill Press Ltd (United Kingdom) 403
Thornton Cox Ltd (United Kingdom) 403
Thorpe, D W, Pty Ltd (Australia) 18
Thorpe, F A, (Publishing) Ltd (United Kingdom) 403
Thorsons Publishers Ltd (United Kingdom) 403
Three Hierarchs, Library of the, (Greece) 172
Thriller Book Club (United Kingdom) 410
Thu Viên Quôc Gia Viet Nam (Socialist Republic of Viet Nam) 420
Thudhammawaddy Press (Burma) 59
Thule, The, Press (United Kingdom) 404
Thun, Verlags und Versandbuchhandlung, AG (Switzerland) 349
Thurman Publishing Ltd (United Kingdom) 404
Thwe Thauk (Burma) 59
Tibetan, Central, Secretariat (India) 194
Tiden, Bokförlags AB, (Sweden) 333
Tiden Norsk Forlag (Norway) 280
Tidnings AB Dagen (Sweden) 333
Tiempo Contemporaneo, Editorial, (Argentina) 7
Tiempo de Hoy, Ediciones, (Argentina) 7

Tiempo, Editorial, Nuevo SA (Venezuela) 419
Tiers Monde, Librairie du, (Algeria) 2
Tieteellisen Informoinnin Neuvosto (Finland) 86
Tieteellisten Kirjastojen Virkailijat — Vetenskapliga Bibliotekens Tjänstemannaförening ry (Finland) 86
Tietoteos Publishing Co (Finland) 85
Tiger (United Kingdom) 404
Tijdstroom, Uitgeversmaatschappij de, BV (Netherlands) 264
Timbro, AB, (Sweden) 333
Time-Life Books (Netherlands) 264
Time-Life International de México, SA (Mexico) 251
Times Book Centre (Hong Kong) 176
Times Book Club (Nigeria) 277
Times Books Ltd (United Kingdom) 404
Times Bookshop Ltd (Malawi) 243
Times Distributors Sdn Bhd (Malaysia) 245
Times Educational Co Ltd (Hong Kong) 176
Times Educational Co Ltd (Malaysia) 245
'Times Educational Supplement', The, Information Book Awards (International Literary Prizes) 444
Times Stores Ltd (Jamaica) 224
Timmins, Howard B, (Pty) Ltd (Republic of South Africa) 311
Timun, Editorial, Mas SA (Spain) 323
Tin Fung Book Co (Hong Kong) 176
Tintamas Indonesia PT (Indonesia) 200
Tipografia Nacional (Netherlands Antilles) 268
Tipografia Poliglotta Vaticana (Vatican City State) 418
Tipografia Stazionne SA (Switzerland) 349
Tips für Trips (Federal Republic of Germany) 160
Tiranti, Alec, Ltd (United Kingdom) 404
Tirona, Ramona S, Memorial Library (Philippines) 289
Tiskarna Ljudske Pravice (Yugoslavia) 424
Tisserand, Lucien, Prize (France) 112
Tiszáninneni Református Egyházkerület Nagykönyvtára (Hungary) 178
Titania-Verlag (Federal Republic of Germany) 160
Tjeenk Willink, H D, BV (Netherlands) 264
Tjeenk Willink-Noorduijn BV (Netherlands) 265
Tjeenk Willink, W E J, BV (Netherlands) 264
Tman Batjean dan Perpustakaan Umum (Indonesia) 200
Tobin Music Books (United Kingdom) 404
Toeche-Mittler, S, Verlag (Federal Republic of Germany) 160
Togolaise, Nouvelle Librairie, (Togo) 356
Tohoku University Library (Japan) 231
Toison, Libris, d'Or SA (Belgium) 43
Tokai University Press (Japan) 230
Toko Messir (Indonesia) 200
Tokuma-Shoten (Japan) 230
Tokyo Kagaku Dozin Co Ltd (Japan) 230
Tokyo Metropolitan Central Library (Japan) 231
Tokyo News Service Ltd (Japan) 230
Tokyo Shuppan Hanbai Co Ltd (Distributors) (Japan) 231
Tokyo Sogensha Co Ltd (Japan) 230
Tokyo Tosho Co Ltd (Japan) 230
Tolkien, The, Society (United Kingdom) 413
Tolly Publishing Co (United Kingdom) 404
Tom-Gallon Trust Award (United Kingdom) 415
Tomas Förlag AB (Sweden) 333
Tomus Verlag GmbH (Federal Republic of Germany) 160
Tong-In Sunsawat (Thailand) 355
Tonger, P J, Musikverlag GmbH & Co (Federal Republic of Germany) 160
Toonder, Marten, Award (Republic of Ireland) 205
Toorts, Uitgeverij De, (Netherlands) 265
Top Stone Books (United Kingdom) 404
Topaz Publishing Ltd (United Kingdom) 404
Topelius Prize (Finland) 87
Topi, Edizioni Giulio, (Switzerland) 349
Topos Verlag AG (Liechtenstein) 241
Toppan Co Ltd (Japan) 230
Toppan Co Ltd (Japan) 231
Toppan Co (Singapore) Private Ltd (Republic of Singapore) 306
Tops'l Books (United Kingdom) 404
Tor (Israel) 209
Toray, Ediciones, SA (Spain) 323
Toray-Masson SA (Spain) 323
Tormargana Prize (Italy) 222
Toro, G del, Editor (Spain) 323
Torpis Publishing Co (Republic of South Africa) 311
Torres, João Romano, & Cia Lda (Portugal) 297
Torroja, Instituto Eduardo, (Spain) 323
Totius, Editio, Mundi E E Maenner (Austria) 28
Toulon (Belgium) 41
Touret, Editions, SA (France) 106
Touropa-Urlaubsberater (Federal Republic of Germany) 160
'Tout pour l'Ecole', Librairie, (Democratic Republic of Madagascar) 243
Towarzystwo Literackie im Mickiewicza (The Mickiewicz Literary Society) (Poland) 294
Towarzystwo Przyjaciól Ksiazki (Society of Friends of Books) (Poland) 294
Towarzystwo Przyjaciól Ksiazki (TPK) (Poland) 293

Towarzystwo Przyjaciół Nauk w Przemyślu (Poland) 294
Town & Gown Press (Nigeria) 276
Townsend & Co (Pvt) Ltd (Zimbabwe) 429
Townson, Editions, (Switzerland) 349
Townsville Foundation for Australian Literary Studies Award (Australia) 22
Toyo Keizai Shinposha Ltd (Japan) 230
Toyo, The, Bunko (Japan) 231
Trachsel Verlag (Switzerland) 349
Tradexim SA (Switzerland) 349
Tradis Verlag und Vertrieb GmbH (Federal Republic of Germany) 160
Trano Printy Loterana (Democratic Republic of Madagascar) 243
Trano Printy Loterana-Trano Printy Fiangonana Loterana Malagasy (TPFLM)-(Imprimerie Luthérienne) (Democratic Republic of Madagascar) 243
Trans-Pacific Publishers (Fiji) 84
Trans Tech Publications SA (Switzerland) 349
Transafrica (Italy) 220
Transafrica (Italy) 222
Transafrica Book Distributors (Kenya) 235
Transatlantik Verlags- und Vertriebsgesellschaft mbH (Federal Republic of Germany) 160
Translation into Swedish Prize (Sweden) 336
Translation Prize (Norway) 281
Translation Prize (Republic of South Africa) 314
Translation Prize (International Literary Prizes) 444
Translatørforeningen (Denmark) 79
Translators Association (United Kingdom) 416
Translators' Guild Ltd (United Kingdom) 416
'Transport', Izdatelstvo, (Union of Soviet Socialist Republics) 362
Transport Library (Republic of Korea) 238
Transportation Publishing House (Democratic People's Republic of Korea) 236
Transpress, VEB Verlag für Verkehrswesen (German Democratic Republic) 116
Transworld Publishers (Australia) Pty Ltd (Australia) 18
Transworld Publishers Ltd (United Kingdom) 404
Trauner, Rudolf, Verlag (Austria) 28
Trautvetter und Fischer Nachf (Federal Republic of Germany) 160
Travancore Law House (India) 194
Travel Book Club (United Kingdom) 410
Travelaid Publishing (United Kingdom) 404
Tre Böcker, Bokklubben, (Finland) 86
Trec Edizioni Pregiate (Italy) 220
Treffer-Boekklub (Republic of South Africa) 312
Treffer Uitgewers (Edms) Ltd (Republic of South Africa) 311
Trèfle, Librairie du, (Mauritius) 248
Trejos, Librería, (Costa Rica) 67
Trelingue, Edizioni, Luigi Rusconi (Switzerland) 349
Tres Américas Libros (Argentina) 8
Tres Tiempos, Ediciones, SRL (Argentina) 7
trèves, éditions, (Federal Republic of Germany) 160
Trevi, Bokförlaget, AB (Sweden) 333
Trévise, Editions de, (France) 106
Triangulo, Livraria, Ltda (Brazil) 55
Trianon Press (France) 106
Tribhuvan University Library (Nepal) 255
Tribune Editions (Switzerland) 349
Tricorne, Editions du, (Switzerland) 350
Triennial Prize for Bibliography (International Literary Prizes) 444
Trigon Press (United Kingdom) 404
Trikont Verlag GmbH (Federal Republic of Germany) 160
Trillas, Editorial, SA (Mexico) 251
Trimurti Publications Pvt Ltd (India) 194
Trinidad and Tobago, Central Library of, (County Library Department of the Government) (Trinidad and Tobago) 356
Trinidad and Tobago, Library Association of, (Trinidad and Tobago) 357
Trinidad Public Library (Trinidad and Tobago) 356
Trinidad Publishing Co (Trinidad and Tobago) 356
Trinity College Library (Republic of Ireland) 204
Trinity College Library (United Kingdom) 411
Tripathi, N M, Pvt Ltd (India) 194
Tripathi, N M, Pvt Ltd (India) 196
Triple Crown Club (Malaysia) 245
Tripode, Edizioni Il, SRL (Italy) 220
Triton Pers (Netherlands) 265
Trobisch, Editions, KG (Federal Republic of Germany) 160
Trois Arches (Belgium) 41
Trois Collines, Editions des, (Switzerland) 350
Trois Continents, Editions des, (Switzerland) 350
Trois Fleuves, Editions des, (Senegal) 303
Tropen, CV Toko Buku, (Indonesia) 200
Troquel, Editorial, SA (Argentina) 7
Troubador (United Kingdom) 404
Trubert, Maurice, Prize (France) 112
Trung-Tam San Xuat Hoc-Lieu (Socialist Republic of Viet Nam) 420
Tryma Book Shop (Bahamas) 31

Tsakalos Prize (Greece) 173
Tsuru-Shobo Co Ltd (Japan) 230
Tübinger Vereinigung für Volkskunde eV (Federal Republic of Germany) 160
tuduv Verlagsgesellschaft mbH (Federal Republic of Germany) 161
Tun Razak Library (Malaysia) 245
Tuncho, Librería, Granados G (Guatemala) 173
Turismo Editorial (Argentina) 7
Turistička Štampa (Yugoslavia) 424
Türk Editörler Dernegi (Turkey) 358
Türk Kütuphaneciler Dernegi (Turkey) 359
Turkish Public Library (Cyprus) 69
Turm-Verlag (Federal Republic of Germany) 161
Turmberg-Verlag (Musikverlag Klaus Gerth) (Federal Republic of Germany) 161
Turnbull, Alexander, Library (New Zealand) 272
Turner Ediciones SRL (Argentina) 7
Turner Memorial Library (Zimbabwe) 430
Turnstone Press Ltd (United Kingdom) 404
Turoe Press (Republic of Ireland) 204
Turtledove Publishing Ltd (Israel) 209
Turton and Armstrong (Australia) 18
Turun Kansallinen (Finland) 86
Turun Yliopiston Kirjasto (Finland) 86
Tusch, Edition, (Austria) 28
Tusquets Editores (Spain) 323
Tuttle, Charles E, Co Inc (Japan) 230
Tuttle, Charles E, Co Inc (Japan) 231
Tuttle-Mori Agency Inc (Japan) 231
Twentieth Century Classics (Australia) 19
Two Tone Poetry Awards (Zimbabwe) 430
Txertoa, Editorial, (Spain) 323
Tyndale Press (United Kingdom) 404
Typos (Greece) 172
Tyrolia (Austria) 29
Tyrolia, Verlagsanstalt, (Austria) 28

U B S Publisher's Distributors Ltd (India) 196
U Bar Verlag (Switzerland) 350
U C A Editores (El Salvador) 82
U D E F (France) 88
U G A, Editions, (Uitgeverij voor Gemeente-Administratie) (Belgium) 41
U G E (France) 107
U K B (Samenwerkingsverband van de Universiteits- en Hogeschoolbibliotheken en de Koninklijke Bibliotheek) (Netherlands) 267
U K National Serials Data Centre (United Kingdom) 365
U N A C Tokyo (Japan) 230
U N C T A D (International Organizations) 435
U N E S C O (International Organizations) 435
U N E S C O Institute for Education (UIE) (International Organizations) 435
U N Economic Commission for Africa Library (Ethiopia) 83
U O P C (Belgium) 41
U O P C (Belgium) 43
U P Indonesia (Indonesia) 200
U P L (Bangladesh) 32
U P N-Volksverlag (Federal Republic of Germany) 161
U R G S, Editôra da, (Universidade Federal do Rio Grande do Sul) (Brazil) 54
U S S R Library Council (Union of Soviet Socialist Republics) 363
U S S R Union of Writers (Union of Soviet Socialist Republics) 360
U T B (Federal Republic of Germany) 161
U T E T (Unione Tipografico-Editrice Torinese) (Italy) 220
Überreuter, Verlag Carl, (Austria) 28
Uffici (United Kingdom) 404
Uganda Bookshop (Uganda) 359
Uganda Library Association (Uganda) 360
Uganda Publishing House (Uganda) 359
Uganda Schools Library Association (Uganda) 360
Uganda Special Library Association (Uganda) 360
Uganda Technical College Library (Uganda) 360
Uhl, Verlag Dr Alfons, (Federal Republic of Germany) 161
Ullstein, Verlag, GmbH (Federal Republic of Germany) 161
Ulmer, Verlag Eugen, GmbH & Co (Federal Republic of Germany) 161
Ultima Hora (Dominican Republic) 80
Ultramar Editores SA (Spain) 323
Ulverscroft Large Print Books Ltd (United Kingdom) 404
Umschau Verlag Breidenstein GmbH (Federal Republic of Germany) 161
Underhållnings-bokklubben (Sweden) 334
Ungarischer Kultureller und Sozialer Fonds eV in der B R D (Federal Republic of Germany) 161

Ungdommens Forlag & Aamodts Forlag A/S (Denmark) 77
Unges, De, Forlag, Unitas Forlag (Denmark) 77
Uni Books (United Kingdom) 404
Uni-Oyez SA (Belgium) 41
Uni-Taschenbücher (UTB) GmbH (Federal Republic of Germany) 161
Uni-Text Book Company (Malaysia) 245
União Gráfica Sarl (Portugal) 297
Unicart Kartografisk Produktion AB (Sweden) 333
Unicorn Books (Australia) 18
Unieboek NV (Netherlands) 265
Unión, Editorial, (Nicaragua) 273
Union Book Club (Denmark) 77
Union Classics Library (Denmark) 77
Union Continentale d'Editions SA (Monaco) 253
Union Crime Club (Denmark) 77
Union dals Grischs (Switzerland) 350
Unión de Escritores y Artistas de Cuba (Cuba) 68
Union d'Editeurs Français (France) 88
Union des Ecrivains algériens (Algeria) 2
Union des Ecrivains algériens (Algeria) 2
Union des Ecrivains et Artistes latins (France) 110
Union des Editeurs de Langue française (International Organizations) 434
Union des Industries graphiques et du Livre (UNIGRA) (Belgium) 33
Union et Orientation de Presse et de Culture (UOPC) SA (Belgium) 41
Union Harlekin Library (Denmark) 77
Union Helvetia Fachbuchverlag (Switzerland) 350
Union Latine d'Editions SA (France) 107
Union Novel Library (Denmark) 77
Union of Bulgarian Writers (Bulgaria) 57
Union of Welsh Publishers and Booksellers (United Kingdom) 365
Union of Writers and Artists of Albania (Albania) 1
Union of Writers of the African Peoples (International Organizations) 434
Union Press Ltd (Hong Kong) 176
Union, The, Press (Sri Lanka) 326
Union tunisienne des Ecrivains (Tunisia) 357
Union Verlag Berlin VOB (German Democratic Republic) 117
Union Verlag Stuttgart (Federal Republic of Germany) 161
Unione Editori di Musica Italiani (UNEMI) (Italy) 211
Unionsverlag (Switzerland) 350
Unipax (Norway) 280
Unipress (France) 88
United Africa Press Ltd (Kenya) 235
United Bank Prize for Literature (Pakistan) 284
United Book Distributors (Pty) Ltd (Republic of South Africa) 312
United Book Shop & Stationers (Bahamas) 31
United Christian Council Literature Bureau (Sierra Leone) 304
United Nations (International Organizations) 435
United Nations Conference on Trade and Development (UNCTAD) (International Organizations) 435
United Nations Depository Library (Republic of Korea) 238
United Nations, Economic and Social Commission for Asia and the Pacific Library (Thailand) 355
United Nations Educational, Scientific and Cultural Organization (UNESCO) (International Organizations) 435
United Nations Institute for Training and Research (UNITAR) (International Organizations) 435
United Nations Library (Switzerland) 352
United Nations Research Institute for Social Development (UNRISD) (International Organizations) 435
United Protestant Publishers (Pty) Ltd (Republic of South Africa) 311
United Publishers (India) 196
United Publishers Services Ltd (Japan) 231
United Publishers Services Ltd (Japan) 231
United Publishers Services (M) Sdn Bhd (Malaysia) 245
United Publishing House and Stationers Sdn Bhd (Malaysia) 245
United States Book Association (Australia) 10
Unites SRL, Annuario Politecnico Italiano (Italy) 220
Unity Books Ltd (New Zealand) 272
Uniunea Scriitorilor din Republica Socialistă România (Romania) 300
Univers, Editura, (Romania) 301
Universa PVBA (Belgium) 42
Universal Book Distributors (India) 196
Universal Books (Australia) 18
Universal Books (Australia) 19
Universal Buchhandlung AG (Austria) 28
Universal Library (Israel) 210
Universal Libreria, Imprenta y Fotolitografia (Carlos Federspiel & Co) SA (Costa Rica) 67
Universal Postal Union (UPU) (International Organizations) 435
Universal Publications Agency Ltd (Republic of Korea) 237

Universal Publications Agency Ltd (Republic of Korea) 238
Universal Publications Sdn Bhd (Malaysia) 245
Universidad Autónoma, Biblioteca de la, de Santo Domingo (Dominican Republic) 80
Universidad Autónoma, Biblioteca General, de Barcelona (Spain) 324
Universidad Autónoma de Santo Domingo, Ciudad Universitaria (Dominican Republic) 80
Universidad Boliviana, Biblioteca Universitaria, Departamento de Bibliotecas, Tomás Frías (Bolivia) 47
Universidad Católica de Chile, Biblioteca Central de la, (Chile) 62
Universidad Católica de Valparaiso, Biblioteca de la, (Chile) 62
Universidad Católica, Fondo Editorial de la, (Peru) 287
Universidad Católica Madre y Maestra (Dominican Republic) 80
Universidad Católica, Pontificia, de Ecuador (Ecuador) 80
Universidad Central, Biblioteca Central de la, de Venezuela (Venezuela) 419
Universidad Central, Biblioteca General de la, de las Villas (Cuba) 68
Universidad Central de Ecuador, Biblioteca de la, (Ecuador) 81
Universidad Central de la Villas, Carretera de Camajuani (Cuba) 68
Universidad Central del Ecuador (Ecuador) 80
Universidad Centroamericana, Biblioteca de la, José Simeón Cañas (El Salvador) 83
Universidad Complutense, Biblioteca de la, de Madrid (Spain) 324
Universidad de Buenos Aires, Instituto Bibliotecológico, (Argentina) 8
Universidad de Chile, Biblioteca Central de la, (Chile) 62
Universidad de Concepción, Biblioteca Central de la, (Chile) 62
Universidad de Costa Rica, Biblioteca de la, (Costa Rica) 67
Universidad de El Salvador, Biblioteca Central de la, (El Salvador) 83
Universidad de Granada (Spain) 323
Universidad de Guayaquil (Ecuador) 80
Universidad de Guayaquil, Biblioteca General, (Ecuador) 81
Universidad de la Habana (Cuba) 68
Universidad de la Habana, Biblioteca Central 'Rubén Martínez Villena' de la, (Cuba) 68
Universidad de los Andes (Colombia) 66
Universidad de Malaga (Spain) 323
Universidad de Navarra, Ediciones, SA (Spain) 323
Universidad de Oriente, Biblioteca Central de la, (Cuba) 68
Universidad de Panama, Biblioteca Interamericana Simón Bolívar (Panama) 285
Universidad de Panama, Escuela de Bibliotecologia (Panama) 285
Universidad de San Carlos (Guatemala) 173
Universidad de San Carlos, Biblioteca Central de la, (Guatemala) 173
Universidad de Zulia, Biblioteca Central de la, (Venezuela) 419
Universidad del Salvador, Biblioteca de la, (Argentina) 8
Universidad, Editorial, de Costa Rica (Costa Rica) 67
Universidad Iberoamericana, Biblioteca de la, (Mexico) 252
Universidad, Librería 'La, ', Nicolas Ojeda Fierro e Hijos SRL Ltda (Peru) 287
Universidad Mayor de San Andres (Bolivia) 46
Universidad Mayor de San Andrés, Biblioteca Central de la, (Bolivia) 47
Universidad Mayor de San Francisco Xavier, Biblioteca Central de la, (Bolivia) 47
Universidad Mayor de San Simón, Biblioteca Central de la, (Bolivia) 47
Universidad Nacional Autónoma de México (Mexico) 251
Universidad Nacional, Biblioteca Central del, de Nicaragua (Nicaragua) 273
Universidad Nacional de Colombia, Biblioteca Central (Colombia) 66
Universidad Nacional de Córdoba, Biblioteca Mayor de la, (Argentina) 8
Universidad Nacional de Cuzeco, Biblioteca Central de la, (Peru) 287
Universidad Nacional de La Plata, Biblioteca Pública de la, (Argentina) 8
Universidad Nacional de San Agustín, Biblioteca Central de la, (Peru) 287
Universidad Nacional, Librería y Editorial, de Nicaragua (Nicaragua) 273
Universidad Nacional Mayor de San Marcos (Peru) 287
Universidad Nacional Mayor de San Marcos, Biblioteca Central de la, (Peru) 287
Universidad Nacional Mayor de San Marcos, Librería de la, (Peru) 287
Universidad Pontificia, Biblioteca Universitaria, de Salamanca (Spain) 324
Universidade de Brasília, Biblioteca Central (Brazil) 56

Universidade de Brasília, Editôra, (Brazil) 54
Universidade de Coimbra, Biblioteca Geral da, (Portugal) 298
Universidade de Luanda Biblioteca (Angola) 2
Universidade de São Paulo, Divisão de Biblioteca e Documentação da, (Brazil) 56
Universidade de São Paulo, Editôra da, (Brazil) 54
Universidade Eduardo Mondlane (Mozambique) 254
Universidade Federal do Rio de Janeiro, Centro de Ciências da Saŕde, (Brazil) 56
Universidade Federal do Rio Grande do Sul (Brazil) 54
Universidade Federal do Rio Grande do Sul, Biblioteca Central (Brazil) 56
Università degli Studi di Firenze, Biblioteca della Facolta di Lettere e Filosofia (Italy) 221
Universitaire Boekhandel Nederland (Netherlands) 266
Universitaire Boekhandel NV (Belgium) 42
Universitaire Pers Leuven (Belgium) 42
Universitaires, Editions, (Belgium) 42
Universitaires, Presses, de Bruxelles, de Liège, de Namur (Belgium) 42
Universitaires, Presses, de France, de Grenoble, de Lille, de Lyon (France) 107
Universitaires, Publications des Facultés, Saint Louis (Belgium) 42
Universitaria de Barcelona, Biblioteca, (Spain) 324
Universitária de Direito, Livraria e Editôra, Ltda (Brazil) 54
Universitaria, Editorial, (Chile) 61
Universitaria, Editorial, (Chile) 62
Universitaria, Editrice, (Italy) 220
Universitaria, Librería, de la Universidad de El Salvador (El Salvador) 83
Universitaria, Librería, UCA (El Salvador) 83
Universitarias de Valparaiso, Ediciones, (Chile) 62
Universitarie Pers Leiden (Netherlands) 265
Universitas Books (Pty) Ltd (Republic of South Africa) 312
Universitas Verlag (Federal Republic of Germany) 161
Universität Basel, Öffentliche Bibliothek der, (Switzerland) 352
Universitäts- und Landesbibliothek Sachsen-Anhalt (German Democratic Republic) 118
Universitäts- und Stadtbibliothek (Federal Republic of Germany) 166
Universitätsbibliothek (German Democratic Republic) 118
Universitätsbibliothek (Federal Republic of Germany) 166
Universitätsbibliothek der Eberhard-Karls-Universität (Federal Republic of Germany) 166
Universitätsbibliothek der Technischen Universität (German Democratic Republic) 118
Universitätsbibliothek Erlangen-Nürnberg (Federal Republic of Germany) 166
Universitätsbibliothek Graz (Austria) 29
Universitätsbibliothek Heidelberg (Federal Republic of Germany) 166
Universitätsbibliothek Innsbruck (Austria) 30
Universitätsbibliothek Wien (Austria) 30
Universitätsbuchhandlung (German Democratic Republic) 117
Universitätsbuchhandlung (German Democratic Republic) 117
Universitätsbuchhandlung (German Democratic Republic) 117
Universitätsverlag (Switzerland) 350
Université Al Quarawiyin, Bibliothèque de l', (Morocco) 254
Université Catholique de Leuven, Bibliothèque centrale de l', (Belgium) 43
Université de Constantine, Bibliothèque de l', (Algeria) 2
Université de Dakar, Bibliothèque (Senegal) 303
Université de Liège, Bibliothèque générale de l', (Belgium) 43
Université de Niamey, Bibliothèque de l', (Niger) 274
Université de Strasbourg, Bibliothèque de l', (France) 108
Université de Tunis, Bibliothèque de l', (Tunisia) 357
Université de Yaoundé, Bibliothèque (United Republic of Cameroun) 60
Université d'Oran, Bibliothèque (Algeria) 2
Université du Benin, Bibliothèque de l', (Benin) 46
Université du Burundi, Bibliothèque de l', (Burundi) 60
Université du Tchad, Bibliothèque de l', (Chad) 61
Université, Editions de l', de Bruxelles (Belgium) 42
Université Jean-Bédel Bokassa, Bibliothèque de l', (Central African Republic) 61
Université, Librairie de l', (France) 108
Université libre de Bruxelles, Bibliothèques de l', (Belgium) 43
Université Marien Ngouabi, Bibliothèque universitaire, (Popular Republic of Congo) 67
Université Mohammed V, Bibliothèque de l', (Morocco) 254
Université nationale, Bibliothèque de l', du Gabon (Gabon) 113
Université nationale, Campus de Kisangani, Bibliothèque centrale de l', (Zaire) 427
Université nationale, Campus de Lubumbashi, Bibliothèque centrale de l', (Zaire) 427

Université Nationale de Côte d'Ivoire (Ivory Coast) 223
Université Nationale du Rwanda, Bibliothèque de l', (Rwanda) 302
Université nationale du Zaire, Bibliothèque centrale de l', (Zaire) 427
Université Omar Bongo, Bibliothèque Centrale de l', (Gabon) 114
Universiteit voor Zelfstudie (Netherlands) 265
Universiteits-Bibliothek, Universiteit van de Nederlandse Antillen (Netherlands Antilles) 268
Universiteitsbibliotheek van Amsterdam (Netherlands) 266
Universités de Paris, Bibliothèques des, (Paris University Libraries) (France) 108
Universitetsbibliotek, Odense, (Denmark) 78
Universitetsbiblioteket, 1 afd (Denmark) 78
Universitetsbiblioteket, 2 afd (Denmark) 78
Universitetsbiblioteket i Bergen (Norway) 281
Universitetsbiblioteket i Oslo (Norway) 281
Universitetsbiblioteket i Trondheim, Avd B (Kongelige Norske Videnskabers Selskab Biblioteket) (Norway) 281
Universitetsbogladen (Panumbogladen/Naturfagsbogladen/Latinerbogladen) (Denmark) 78
Universitetsbokhandeln (Norway) 280
Universitetsforlaget (Norway) 280
Universities Administration Office (Burma) 59
Universities' Central Library (Burma) 59
Universitná knižnica (Czechoslovakia) 72
University (United Kingdom) 404
University Book Agency (Pakistan) 283
University Book Shop (Papua New Guinea) 285
University Book Shop (Auckland) Ltd (New Zealand) 272
University Book Shop (Canterbury) Ltd (New Zealand) 272
University Book Shop (Otago) Ltd (New Zealand) 272
University Book Store (Hong Kong) 176
University Bookshop (Ghana) 170
University Bookshop (Ghana) 170
University Bookshop (Zambia) 428
University Bookshop (Nigeria) Ltd (Nigeria) 277
University Bookstore (Liberia) 240
University Bookstore (Republic of Singapore) 306
University College Cork Library (Republic of Ireland) 204
University College Dublin Library (Republic of Ireland) 204
University College Galway Library (Republic of Ireland) 204
University College of Botswana Library (Botswana) 47
University College of Swaziland Library (Swaziland) 327
University Co-op Bookshop Ltd (Australia) 19
University Education Press (Republic of Singapore) 306
University Karlovy, Knihovny fakult a ústavu, (Czechoslovakia) 72
University Libraries, Finland (Finland) 86
University Libraries (Japan) 231
University Libraries (Romania) 301
University Libraries (Saudi Arabia) 303
University Libraries (Sweden) 335
University Libraries (United Kingdom) 411
University Library (Afghanistan) 1
University Library (Honduras) 174
University Library (Iceland) 180
University Microfilms International (United Kingdom) 404
University of Agriculture Malaysia Library (Malaysia) 245
University of Alexandria Library (Egypt) 82
University of Asmara Library (Ethiopia) 83
University of Auckland Library (New Zealand) 272
University of Baghdad, Central Library of the, (Iraq) 202
University of Baluchistan Library (Pakistan) 283
University of Cairo (Sudan) 327
University of Cairo Library (Egypt) 82
University of California Press (United Kingdom) 404
University of Canterbury Publications (New Zealand) 271
University of Cape Coast Library (Ghana) 170
University of Cape Town Libraries (Republic of South Africa) 312
University of Chicago Press Ltd (United Kingdom) 404
University of Dar es Salaam Library (Tanzania) 353
University of Engineering and Technology (Pakistan) 283
University of Ferdowsi Library (Iran) 201
University of Garyounis Library (Libya) 241
University of Ghana Library (Ghana) 170
University of Haifa Library (Israel) 210
University of Hong Kong Main Library (Hong Kong) 176
University of Ife Bookshop Ltd (Nigeria) 277
University of Ife Library (Nigeria) 277
University of Ife Press (Nigeria) 276
University of Isfahan Library (Iran) 201
University of Jordan Library (Jordan) 233
University of Kabul Bookstores (Afghanistan) 1
University of Karachi Library (Pakistan) 283
University of Khartoum Bookshop (Sudan) 327
University of Khartoum Library (Sudan) 327
University of Lagos Bookshop (Nigeria) 277
University of Lagos Library (Nigeria) 277
University of Lagos Press (Nigeria) 276

INDEX 505

University of Liberia Libraries (Liberia) 240
University of Libya (Libya) 241
University of London Library (United Kingdom) 411
University of London Press (Nigeria) 276
University of London Press Ltd (United Kingdom) 404
University of Loránd Eötvös Central Library (Hungary) 178
University of Malawi Library (Malawi) 243
University of Malaya Co-operative Bookshop Ltd (Malaysia) 245
University of Malaya Library (Malaysia) 245
University of Malaya Press Ltd (Malaysia) 245
University of Malta Library (Malta) 246
University of Manila Central Library (Philippines) 289
University of Mauritius Library (Mauritius) 248
University of Melbourne Library (Australia) 20
University of Nairobi Bookshop (Kenya) 235
University of Nairobi Library (Kenya) 235
University of Natal Library (Republic of South Africa) 312
University of Natal Press (Republic of South Africa) 311
University of New South Wales (Australia) 18
University of New South Wales Library (Australia) 20
University of Nigeria Bookshop Ltd (Nigeria) 277
University of Otago Press (New Zealand) 271
University of Papua New Guinea Library (Papua New Guinea) 285
University of Peradeniya Library (Sri Lanka) 326
University of Peshawar Library (Pakistan) 283
University of Pretoria, Merensky Library (Republic of South Africa) 312
University of Puerto Rico, General Library, Mayaguez Campus (Puerto Rico) 299
University of Puerto Rico, General Library, Río Piedras Campus (Puerto Rico) 299
University of Puerto Rico, Medical Sciences Campus Library (Puerto Rico) 299
University of Puerto Rico Press (UPRED) (Puerto Rico) 299
University of Queensland Library (Australia) 20
University of Queensland Press (Australia) 18
University of Rajshahi Library (Bangladesh) 32
University of Salonika, Library of the, (Greece) 172
University of San Carlos Library (Philippines) 289
University of Santo Tomas Library (Philippines) 289
University of Science and Technology Library (Ghana) 170
University of Science Malaysia Library (Malaysia) 246
University of Sierra Leone (Sierra Leone) 304
University of Sofia Library (Bulgaria) 58
University of South Africa (Republic of South Africa) 311
University of South Africa Library (Republic of South Africa) 312
University of Sydney Library (Australia) 20
University of Tabriz, Central Library, (Iran) 201
University of Technology Malaysia Library (Malaysia) 246
University of the East Library (Philippines) 289
University of the Philippines (Philippines) 289
University of the Philippines Library (Philippines) 289
University of the Philippines Press (Philippines) 289
University of the West Indies (Barbados) 32
University of the West Indies Library (Jamaica) 224
University of the West Indies Library (Trinidad and Tobago) 356
University of the Witwatersrand Library (Republic of South Africa) 312
University of Tokyo Library (Japan) 231
University of Tokyo Press (Japan) 230
University of Trondheim, The, The Norwegian Institute of Technology (Norway) 281
University of Wales Press (United Kingdom) 404
University of Western Australia Library (Australia) 20
University of Western Australia Press (Australia) 18
University of Zambia Library (Zambia) 428
University of Zimbabwe (Zimbabwe) 429
University of Zimbabwe Library (Zimbabwe) 430
University Press Amsterdam BV (APA) (Netherlands) 265
University Press Ltd (Nigeria) 276
University Press Ltd (UPL) (Bangladesh) 32
University Press of Africa Ltd (Kenya) 235
University Presses of Columbia and Princeton (United Kingdom) 404
University Publishers (India) 194
University Publishers & Booksellers (Pty) Ltd (Republic of South Africa) 311
University Publishing Co (Israel) 209
University Publishing Co (Nigeria) 276
University Publishing Co (Philippines) 289
University Tutorial Press Ltd (United Kingdom) 404
Universo, Editorial, SA (Peru) 287
Universo, Premio, (Peru) 287
Universo, Società Editrice, (Italy) 220
Uniwersytecka w Toruniu, Biblioteka, (Poland) 294
Uniwersytecka w Warszawie, Biblioteka, (Poland) 294
Uniwersytecka w Wroclawiu, Biblioteka, (Library of the University of Wroclaw) (Poland) 294
Unwin Paperbacks (United Kingdom) 404

Update Books Ltd (United Kingdom) 404
Upkar Prakashan (India) 194
Upper India, The, Publishing House Pvt Ltd (India) 194
Uppsala Universitetsbibliotek (Sweden) 335
Urachhaus, Verlag, Johannes M Mayer GmbH und Co KG (Federal Republic of Germany) 161
Uraki, Mitsusato, (Japan) 230
Urania-Verlag (German Democratic Republic) 117
Uranium Verlag (Switzerland) 350
Urban Council Libraries (Hong Kong) 176
Urban und Schwarzenberg (Austria) 28
Urban und Schwarzenberg (Austria) 29
Urban und Schwarzenberg, Verlag, (Medical Publishers) (Federal Republic of Germany) 161
Urdang, Laurence, Associates Ltd (United Kingdom) 405
Urdu Academy Sind (Pakistan) 283
Urdu Akademy Awards (India) 198
Urmo SA de Ediciones (Spain) 323
Urs Graf-Verlag GmbH (Switzerland) 350
Usborne Publishing Ltd (United Kingdom) 405
Ústřední knihovnická rada ČSSR (Czechoslovakia) 72
Utbildningsbolaget M M AB (Sweden) 333
Utusan Publications and Distributions Sdn Bhd (Malaysia) 245
Uusi Kirjakerho Oy (Finland) 86
Uusi Tie, Kustannus Oy, (Finland) 85
Uzima Press Ltd (Kenya) 235

V A A P (Union of Soviet Socialist Republics) 362
V A M, Stichting, (Netherlands) 265
V A P Verlag (Federal Republic of Germany) 161
V C L (Netherlands) 266
V C T A Publishing Pty Ltd (Australia) 18
V D D (Federal Republic of Germany) 167
V D E-Verlag GmbH (Federal Republic of Germany) 161
V D I-Verlag GmbH (Verlag des Vereins Deutscher Ingenieure) (Federal Republic of Germany) 161
V-Dia-Verlag GmbH (Federal Republic of Germany) 161
V E D A, vydavatel'stvo Slovenskej akadémie vied (Czechoslovakia) 71
V F P (Verlag Frauenpolitik) GmbH (Federal Republic of Germany) 161
V M B (Federal Republic of Germany) 162
V N U Business Press Group (Netherlands) 265
V N U Verenigde Nederlandse Uitgeversbedrijven BV (Netherlands) 265
V P A (Vjesnikova Press Agencija) (Yugoslavia) 425
V S A (Verlag für das Studium der Arbeiterbewegung GmbH) (Federal Republic of Germany) 162
V V A (Vereinigte Verlagsauslieferung) Reinhard Mohn (Federal Republic of Germany) 166
V W K (Verlag für Wirtschafts-und-Kartographie Publikationen) Ryborsch GmbH (Federal Republic of Germany) 162
Vaad Hayeshivot Be'eretz Israel (Israel) 209
Vaar, De, bv Dordrecht (Netherlands) 265
Vaco NV (Suriname) 327
Vaco NV (Suriname) 327
Vademecum de Pharmacie (Belgium) 42
Vadhana Panich (Thailand) 355
Vahlen, Franz, GmbH (Federal Republic of Germany) 162
Vaillant Carmanne, Imprimerie H, SA (Belgium) 42
Vaillant, Editions de, — IGO (France) 107
Vajarindra (Thailand) 355
Vakils Feffer & Simons Ltd (India) 194
Valabrègue, Antony, Prize (France) 112
Valafell, Bókaútgáfan, (Iceland) 180
Vale, The Helen, Foundation (Australia) 18
Valiant Publishers (Pty) Ltd (Republic of South Africa) 311
Vallardi, Antonio, Editore (Italy) 220
Vallardi Industrie Grafiche (Italy) 220
Vallentine, Mitchell & Co Ltd (United Kingdom) 405
Vallerini, Augusto, Editore di Alberto Vallerini (Italy) 220
Valtionarkisto (Finland) 86
Van Nostrand Reinhold Co Ltd (United Kingdom) 405
Vandenhoeck und Ruprecht (Federal Republic of Germany) 162
Vander-Oyez SA (France) 107
Vander Publishing (Belgium) 42
Vanderlinden, Librairie, (Belgium) 43
Vanderlinden, Librairie, SA (Belgium) 42
Vani Prakashan (India) 194
Vanmelle, L, (Drukkerij) NV (Belgium) 42
Vannini, Società Editrice, (Italy) 220
Vår Bok AB (Sweden) 334
Vår Skola Förlag AB (Sweden) 333
Vargas, Fundação Getúlio, (Brazil) 54
Variorum (United Kingdom) 405
Varsity (United Kingdom) 405
Varsity Book Club (Nigeria) 277
Varsity Industrial Press (Nigeria) 276

Vasco, Editorial, Americana SA (EVA) (Spain) 323
Vasiliou, J, Bibliopoleion (Greece) 172
Vassallo, A, and Sons Ltd (Malta) 246
Västra, Förlagsaktiebolaget, Sverige (Sweden) 333
Vatan Library (Turkey) 359
Vaticana, Libreria Editrice, (Vatican City State) 418
Vavrín (Czechoslovakia) 72
Vecchi, Editions de, (France) 107
Vecchi, Editôra, SA (Brazil) 54
Vecchi, Editorial De, (Spain) 323
Vecchi, Giovanni de, Editore SpA (Italy) 220
Veen, Uitgeverij L J, BV (Netherlands) 265
Vega, Ediciones, SRL (Venezuela) 419
Vega, Librería Técnica, (Venezuela) 419
Velber Verlag GmbH (Federal Republic of Germany) 162
Velde, Editions Francis Van de, (France) 107
Velde, Editions Van de, (France) 107
Velhagen und Klasing (Federal Republic of Germany) 162
Venceremos, Edition, (Federal Republic of Germany) 162
Ventura Publishing Ltd (United Kingdom) 405
Venus Press & Book Depot (India) 194
Vera-Reyes Inc (Philippines) 289
Verband bayerischer Buch- und Zeitschriftenhändler eV (Federal Republic of Germany) 119
Verband bayerischer Verlage und Buchhandlungen eV (Federal Republic of Germany) 119
Verband der Antiquare Österreichs (Austria) 23
Verband der Bibliotheken des Landes Nordrhein-Westfalen (Federal Republic of Germany) 167
Verband der Bühnenverleger Österreichs (Austria) 23
Verband der Schulbuchverlage eV (Federal Republic of Germany) 119
Verband der Verlage und Buchhandlungen in Baden-Württemberg eV (Federal Republic of Germany) 119
Verband der Verlage und Buchhandlungen in Nordrhein-Westfalen eV (Federal Republic of Germany) 119
Verband der wissenschaftlichen Gesellschaften Österreichs (Austria) 28
Verband des werbenden Buch- und Zeitschriftenhandels Gross-Berlin eV (Federal Republic of Germany) 119
Verband deutscher Adressbuchverleger eV (Federal Republic of Germany) 119
Verband deutscher Antiquare eV (Federal Republic of Germany) 119
Verband deutscher Bahnhofsbuchhändler (Federal Republic of Germany) 119
Verband deutscher Buch-Zeitungs- und Zeitschriften-Grossisten eV (Federal Republic of Germany) 119
Verband deutscher Bühnenverleger eV (Federal Republic of Germany) 119
Verband deutscher Schulbuchhändler eV (Federal Republic of Germany) 119
Verband deutscher Werkbibliotheken eV (Federal Republic of Germany) 167
Verband deutschsprachiger Übersetzer literarischer und wissenschaftlicher Werke eV (VDU) (Federal Republic of Germany) 119
Verband evangelischer Buchhandlungen und Verlage der Schweiz (Switzerland) 337
Verband katholischer Verleger und Buchhändler eV (Federal Republic of Germany) 119
Verband norddeutscher Buch- und Zeitschriftenhändler eV (Federal Republic of Germany) 119
Verband österreichischer Archivare (Austria) 30
Verband österreichischer Kommissionäre, Grossobuchhändler und Auslieferer (Austria) 23
Verband österreichischer Volksbüchereien und Volksbibliothekare (Austria) 30
Verband schweizerischer Antiquare und Kunsthändler (Switzerland) 337
Verband schweizerischer Schreinermeister und Möbelfabrikanten Verlag und Fachbüchervertrieb (Switzerland) 350
Verband schweizerischer Zeitungsagenturen und Büchergrossisten (Union d'Agences suisses de Journaux et Livres en Gros) (Switzerland) 337
Verband westdeutscher Buch- und Zeitschriftenhändler eV (Federal Republic of Germany) 119
Verbandsdruckerei, Buchverlag der, /Editions Imprimerie Fédérative SA Berne (Switzerland) 350
Verbo, Editôra, Ltda (Brazil) 55
Verbo, Editorial, Divino (Spain) 323
Verbo Sarl (Portugal) 297
Verbruikersunie, Uitgaven van de, VZW (Editions de Association des Consommateurs ASBL) (Belgium) 42
Verbum (Sweden) 333
Verdade e Vida, Livraria, Editora (Portugal) 297
Vereeniging der Antwerpsche Bibliophielen (Belgium) 44
Vereeniging ter bevordering van de belangen des Boekhandels (Netherlands) 256
Verein Angehörige des mittleren und nichtdiplomierten Bibliotheksdienstes eV (Association of Nonprofessional Librarians) (Federal Republic of Germany) 167
Verein der Bibliothekare an öffentlichen Büchereien eV (Federal Republic of Germany) 167
Verein der Diplom-Bibliothekare an Wissenschaftlichen Bibliotheken eV (Federal Republic of Germany) 167

506 INDEX

Verein Deutscher Archivare (VdA) (Federal Republic of Germany) 167
Verein Deutscher Bibliothekare eV (Federal Republic of Germany) 167
Verein Deutscher Dokumentare eV (VDD) (Federal Republic of Germany) 167
Verein für Verkehrsordnung im Buchhandel (Federal Republic of Germany) 120
Vereinigung der Schweizerischen Buchgemeinschaften (Switzerland) 337
Vereinigung katholischer Buchhändler und Verleger der Schweiz (Switzerland) 337
Vereinigung österreichischer Bibliothekare (Austria) 30
Vereinigung Schweizerischer Archivare (Association of Swiss Archivists) (Switzerland) 352
Vereinigung selbständiger Verlagsvertreter (Federal Republic of Germany) 120
Verenigde Protestantse Uitgewers (Edms) Bpk (Republic of South Africa) 311
Vereniging ter Bevordering van het Vlaamse Boekwezen (Belgium) 33
Vereniging van Archivarissen in Nederland (Netherlands) 267
Vereniging van de belgische medische Wetenschappelijke Genootschappen VZW (Belgium) 42
Vereniging van Religieus-Wetenschappelijke Bibliothecarissen (Belgium) 43
Vereniging van Uitgevers van Nederlandstalige Boeken (Belgium) 33
Vereniging van Uitgeversvertegenwoordigers (Netherlands) 256
Vereniging voor het Theologisch Bibliothecariaat (Netherlands) 267
Vergadis, M (Greece) 172
Vergara, Javier, Editor SRL (Argentina) 7
Vergara, José Ma, y Vergara Prize (Colombia) 67
Verissimo, José, Prize (Brazil) 57
Veritas Publications (Republic of Ireland) 204
Veritas-Verlag (Austria) 28
Verkehrshaus der Schweiz (Switzerland) 350
Verlagsgenossenschaft (Switzerland) 350
Verlain, Valentine Abraham, Prize (France) 112
Verlaine, Paul, Prize (France) 112
Verlegervereinigung Rechtsinformatik eV (Federal Republic of Germany) 120
Verne, Jules, Circle (United Kingdom) 413
Veron Editor (Spain) 323
Verrycken, Editions, (Belgium) 42
Verseau, Editions du, (Switzerland) 350
Versluys', W, Uitg Mij BV (Netherlands) 265
Verso Editions (United Kingdom) 405
Vertente Editôra Ltda (Brazil) 55
Vertice Ltda (Colombia) 66
Verve, Editions de la Revue, Sàrl (France) 107
Vervuert, Klaus Dieter, Buchhandel und Verlag (Federal Republic of Germany) 162
Verzekeringswereld, De, PVBA (Belgium) 42
Vesaas, Tarjei, Debutant Prize (Norway) 281
Veselin Masleša (Yugoslavia) 424
Veselin Masleša (Yugoslavia) 425
Vesti (Yugoslavia) 425
Vetenskapliga Bibliotekens Tjänstemannaförening VBT (Sweden) 335
Vetter, Verlag Alfred F, (Switzerland) 350
Veyrier (France) 107
Via Afrika Book Store (Republic of South Africa) 312
Via Afrika Botswana Ltd (Botswana) 47
Via Afrika Ltd (Republic of South Africa) 311
Vial, Editions André, (France) 107
Vialetay, Editions, Sàrl (France) 107
Viareggio Prizes (Italy) 222
Vicaire, Gabriel, Prize (France) 113
Vicens-Vives, Editorial, (Spain) 323
Victor, Leo, (Suriname) 327
Victoria Booksellers' Association (Australia) 10
Victoria University Press (New Zealand) 271
Victory Press (United Kingdom) 405
Vidhi Sahitva Prakashan (India) 194
Vidyapuri (India) 194
Vidyarthi Mithram Book Depot (India) 196
Vidyarthi Mithram Novel Club (India) 195
Vidyarthi Mithram Press & Book Depot (India) 194
Vie, Les Editions, ouvrière ASBL (Belgium) 42
Vieng Krung (Laos) 239
Vienna Art Foundation (Wiener Kunstfonds) (Austria) 30
Vienna Prize for children's and young people's literature (Austria) 30
Vienna Übersetzungsbüro und Sprachinstitut (Austria) 31
Vietnamese Publishing House (Socialist Republic of Viet Nam) 420
Vieweg, Friedr, und Sohn Verlagsgesellschaft mbH (Federal Republic of Germany) 162
Vieweg, Schulverlag, (Federal Republic of Germany) 162
Viewpoint (United Kingdom) 405
Vigilia, Editôra, Ltda (Brazil) 55
Vigot, Editions, Frères (France) 107
Vijverberg Prize (Netherlands) 268
Vikas Publishing House Pvt Ltd (India) 194

Viking Sevenseas Ltd (New Zealand) 271
Viktoria Verlag (Switzerland) 350
Villa Benia Prize (Italy) 222
Villa Books Ltd (Republic of Ireland) 204
Villaurrutia Prize (Mexico) 253
Ville de Paris, Service des Travaux Historiques de la, et Bibliothèque historique de la Ville de Paris (France) 109
Villepastour, Librairie, (Ivory Coast) 223
Vilnius, The Scientific Library of the, Vincas Kapsukas State University (Union of Soviet Socialist Republics) 363
Vilo, Editions, SA (France) 107
Vincent, Dominique, et Cie (France) 107
Vincentz, Curt R, Verlag (Federal Republic of Germany) 162
Vindrose, Forlaget, ApS (Denmark) 77
Vine Books Ltd (United Kingdom) 405
Vingtième Siècle (France) 107
Vinten's Forlag (Denmark) 77
Vipopremo Agencies (Kenya) 235
Virago Ltd (United Kingdom) 405
Viratham (Thailand) 355
Virdi, Major Tek Singh, Literary Prizes (India) 198
Virenque, Claire, Prize (France) 113
Virtue & Co Ltd (United Kingdom) 405
Visa Books (Australia) 18
Visão, Editôra, Ltda (Brazil) 55
Visentini, Olga, Prize (Italy) 222
Vishal Publications (India) 195
Vision Books Pvt Ltd (India) 195
Vision Press Ltd (United Kingdom) 405
Vision Publishing Corporation (Philippines) 289
Visscher, Albert de, Editeur (Belgium) 42
Visuals of the Australian Environment (Australia) 18
Vives, Editorial Luis, (Edelvives) (Spain) 323
Vivliofilia (Greece) 172
Vivliografiki Etaireia tis Ellados (Bibliographical Society of Greece) (Greece) 173
Vlaams Ekonomisch Verbond VZW (Belgium) 42
Vlaamse Bijbelstichting (Belgium) 42
Vlaamse Toeristenbond VZW (Belgium) 42
Vlaamse Vereniging van Bibliotheek-, Archief en Documentatie-Personeel (Belgium) 43
Vlasis, Frères, (Greece) 172
Vlijt, De, NV (Belgium) 42
'Vneshtorgizdat', Vsesoyuznoe Obyedineniye, (Union of Soviet Socialist Republics) 362
Voenno Izdatelstvo (Bulgaria) 58
Vogel, Buchhandlung W, (Switzerland) 351
Vogel-Verlag KG (Federal Republic of Germany) 162
Vogt-Schild AG Druck & Verlag (Switzerland) 350
Voix, Editions La, de l'Ain (France) 107
Vojnoizdavački Zavod (Yugoslavia) 425
Vokaer, Nouvelles Editions, SA (Belgium) 42
Volcans, Librairie Les, (Zaire) 427
Volcans, Librairie Les, (Zaire) 427
Volk, Boekhandel het, (Belgium) 43
Volk, Het, NV (Belgium) 42
Volk und Gesundheit, VEB Verlag, (German Democratic Republic) 117
Volk und Welt, Verlag, (German Democratic Republic) 117
Volk und Wissen Volkseigener Verlag Berlin (German Democratic Republic) 117
Volksbuchverlag GmbH (Austria) 29
Volksverband der Bücherfreunde Verlag GmbH (Federal Republic of Germany) 165
Vollmer, Emil, Verlag (Federal Republic of Germany) 162
Vollmer/Löwit Verlagsgruppe (Federal Republic of Germany) 162
Volney Press (France) 113
Voltaire Foundation (United Kingdom) 405
Volturna Press (United Kingdom) 405
Voluntad Editores Ltda y Cía SCA (Colombia) 66
Voluntary Health Association of India (India) 195
Voorhoeve, J N, (Netherlands) 265
Vora & Co Publishers Pvt Ltd (India) 195
Vorarlberger Verlagsanstalt GmbH (Austria) 28
Voss, Hartfrid, Verlag (Federal Republic of Germany) 162
Voss, Johann Heinrich, Translation Prize (Federal Republic of Germany) 168
Vowinckel, Kurt, Verlag (Federal Republic of Germany) 162
Voyenizdat (Union of Soviet Socialist Republics) 362
Vozes Editôra Ltda (Brazil) 55
Vries, C De, Brouwers PVBA (Belgium) 42
Vrin, Librairie Philosophique J, (France) 107
Vroente, De, (Belgium) 42
Vsesoyuznaya Knichnaya Palata (Union of Soviet Socialist Republics) 360
Vsesoyuznoe agentstvo po avtorskim pravam (VAAP) (Union of Soviet Socialist Republics) 362
Vuibert, Librairie, SA (France) 107
Vuk Karadžic (Yugoslavia) 425
Vuk Karadžic (Yugoslavia) 425
Východoslovenské vydavateľstvo np (Czechoslovakia) 71
Vyncke, PVBA Imprimerie-Editions, (Belgium) 42
Vyšehrad (Czechoslovakia) 72

'Vysshaya Shkola', Izdatelstvo, (Union of Soviet Socialist Republics) 362

W R S — Verlag (Wirtschaft, Recht und Steuern) (Federal Republic of Germany) 162
Waage, Verlag Die, Zurich (Switzerland) 350
Wachholtz, Karl, Verlag (Federal Republic of Germany) 162
Wadih M Captan Bookstores (Liberia) 240
Wagenbach, Verlag Klaus, (Federal Republic of Germany) 162
Wagner, Gebrüder, & Co Verlag (Switzerland) 350
Wagner, Universitätsverlag, GmbH (Austria) 28
Wagner'sche Universitätsbuchhandlung (Austria) 29
Wahab, Dakr Abdul, (Syria) 353
Wahbah, Ali, Bookshop (Saudi Arabia) 302
Wahle, Eugène, (Belgium) 42
Wahlström och Widstrand, AB, (Sweden) 333
Wahlströms, B, Bokförlag AB (Sweden) 333
Waiwen Shudian (People's Republic of China) 63
Walburg, De, Pers (Netherlands) 265
Waldia, AB, Förlag (Sweden) 333
Wales Tourist Board (United Kingdom) 405
Walker Books Ltd (United Kingdom) 405
Walmap Prize (International Literary Prizes) 444
Walraven, Uitgeverij Van, BV (Netherlands) 265
Walsingham (United Kingdom) 405
Walt Disney, Clube, (Portugal) 298
Walt Disney Wonderful World of Reading (Denmark) 77
Walt, J P van der, & Seun (Pty) Ltd (Republic of South Africa) 311
Walter, Henry E, Ltd (United Kingdom) 405
Walter Verlag AG (Switzerland) 350
Walter-Verlag GmbH (Federal Republic of Germany) 162
Wangels Forlag A/S (Denmark) 77
Wanyee Bookshop Ltd (Kenya) 235
Warana Writers' Awards (Australia) 22
Warburg, The, Institute (United Kingdom) 405
Ward Lock Educational Ltd (United Kingdom) 405
Ward Lock Ltd (United Kingdom) 405
Ward River (Republic of Ireland) 204
Warga (Indonesia) 200
Warne, Frederick, (Publishers) Ltd (United Kingdom) 406
Warsaw City Prize (Poland) 294
Warsaw City Prize for Young Poets (Poland) 294
Was Is Press (Australia) 18
Waseda University Library (Japan) 231
Wasmuth, Ernst, Verlagsbuchhandlung KG (Federal Republic of Germany) 162
Wastiau-Jeukens (Belgium) 42
Watelet, Gerard, (France) 107
Waterlow (London) Ltd (United Kingdom) 406
Waterville Publishing House (Ghana) 169
Watkins Publishing (United Kingdom) 406
'Watra', Wydawnictwa Kultura Zycia Codziennego, (Poland) 293
Watson, W, & Co (United Kingdom) 406
Watt, A P, Ltd (United Kingdom) 409
Wattana Panich (Thailand) 355
Wattie, Sir James, Book of the Year Award (New Zealand) 273
Watts, Franklin, Ltd (United Kingdom) 406
Wayfarer Book Store Ltd (Barbados) 32
Wayland Publishers Ltd (United Kingdom) 406
Wayzgoose, The, Press (United Kingdom) 406
Weatherhill, John, Inc (Japan) 230
Webb & Bower (Publishers) Ltd (United Kingdom) 406
Weber (France) 107
Weber, Anna, (Austria) 29
Weber SA d'Editions (Switzerland) 350
Weber-Stumfohl, Herta, (Federal Republic of Germany) 165
Weekes, A (United Kingdom) 406
Wehr und Wissen Verlagsgesellschaft mbH (Federal Republic of Germany) 162
Wehrenalp, v, & Co (Switzerland) 350
Weichert, A, Verlag (Federal Republic of Germany) 162
Weickhardt, Con, Award (Australia) 22
Weickhardt, Patricia, Award (Australia) 22
Weidenfeld & Nicolson, George, Ltd (United Kingdom) 406
Weidlich, Wolfgang, Verlag (Federal Republic of Germany) 163
Weilburg-Verlag (Austria) 28
Weilin + Göös, Amer-yhtymä Oy, (Finland) 85
Weill, Galerie Lucie, (France) 107
Weill Publishers Ltd (Israel) 209
Weinert, Erich-, -Buchhandlung (German Democratic Republic) 117
Weinmann, Verlag, (Federal Republic of Germany) 163
Weis, Rupertusbuchhandlung Augustin, und Söhne KG (Austria) 29

Weismann Verlag-Frauenbuchverlag GmbH (Federal Republic of Germany) 163
Weiss, Gebrüder, Verlag (Federal Republic of Germany) 163
Weiss, J J, Prize (France) 113
Weitbrecht GmbH (Federal Republic of Germany) 163
Weizmann Institute of Science Libraries (Israel) 210
Weizmann, The, Science Press of Israel (Israel) 209
Wellcome Institute for the History of Medicine Library (United Kingdom) 411
Wellington Public Library (New Zealand) 272
Wells, H G, Society (United Kingdom) 413
Wellsiana—The World of Wells (United Kingdom) 413
Welsermühl, Verlag, (Federal Republic of Germany) 163
Welsh Arts Council Awards to Writers (United Kingdom) 415
Welsh Books Council (Cyngor Llyfrau Cymraeg) (United Kingdom) 365
Welsh Library Association (United Kingdom) 412
Welt im Heim Morawa & Co (Austria) 29
Weltforum Verlags GmbH (Federal Republic of Germany) 163
Weltkreis-Verlags-GmbH (Federal Republic of Germany) 163
Weltrundschau Verlag AG (Switzerland) 350
Welz, Verlag Galerie, Salzburg (Austria) 28
'Wema', Wydawnictwa Przemyslu Maszynowego, (Poland) 293
Wendelin, Buchhandlung, Niedlich KG (Federal Republic of Germany) 166
Wentworth Books Pty Ltd (Australia) 18
Wepf & Co Buchhandlung und Antiquariat (Switzerland) 351
Wepf, Verlag, & Co (Switzerland) 350
Wereldbibliotheek BV (Netherlands) 265
Wereldbibliotheek NV (Belgium) 42
Wereldvenster, Het, BV Internationale Uitg Mij (Netherlands) 265
Werner & Bischoff AG (Switzerland) 350
Werner Söderström Osakeyhtiö (WSOY) (Finland) 85
Werner Söderström Osakeyhtiö (WSOY) (Finland) 86
Werner Verlag GmbH (Federal Republic of Germany) 163
Wesmael-Charlier, Maison d'Editions Ad, SA (Belgium) 42
West African Book Publishers Ltd (Nigeria) 276
West African Library Association (WALA) (International Organizations) 434
'West-Friesland', Uit-Mij, (Netherlands) 265
West Pakistan Publishing Co Ltd (Pakistan) 283
West, John, Publications Ltd (Nigeria) 276
Westbooks Pty Ltd (Australia) 18
Westdeutscher Verlag GmbH (Federal Republic of Germany) 163
Westerbergs, Ernst, Förlags AB (Sweden) 334
Westermann, Georg, Verlag, Druckerei & Kartographische Anstalt GmbH & Co (Federal Republic of Germany) 163
Western Australian Booksellers' Association (Australia) 10
Western Book Club (United Kingdom) 410
Westers, Uitgeverij, (Netherlands) 265
Westminster City Libraries (United Kingdom) 411
Wetenschappelijke Uitgeverij (Netherlands) 265
Wettergrens Bokhandel AB (Sweden) 334
Wetzikon, Buchverlag der Druckerei, AG (Switzerland) 350
Wever, Uitgeverij, BV (Netherlands) 265
Wewel, Erich, Verlag (Federal Republic of Germany) 163
Wezäta Förlag (Sweden) 334
Wheatley Medal (United Kingdom) 416
Wheaton, A, & Co Ltd (United Kingdom) 406
Wheeler-Pitman Publishing Co Pvt Ltd (India) 195
Whitaker, J, & Sons Ltd (United Kingdom) 406
Whitbread Literary Awards (United Kingdom) 416
Whitcombe & Tombs Pty Ltd (Australia) 18
Whitcombe & Tombs Pty Ltd (Australia) 19
Whitcoulls Ltd (New Zealand) 272
Whitcoulls Publishers (New Zealand) 271
White Eagle Publishing Trust (United Kingdom) 406
White Horse Books (United Kingdom) 406
White Lion Publishers Ltd (United Kingdom) 406
White, Patrick, Award (Australia) 23
White, Sir Thomas, Memorial Prize (Australia) 23
Whitman (New Zealand) 271
Whitman, Australia Pty Ltd (Australia) 19
Whittet Books Ltd (United Kingdom) 406
Wholesale Book Distributors (New Zealand) 272
Who's Who — Book & Publishing Company (Federal Republic of Germany) 163
Who's Who of Southern Africa (Republic of South Africa) 311
Wiart, Carton de, Prize (Belgium) 45
Wichmann, Herbert, Verlag GmbH (Federal Republic of Germany) 163
Widescope International Publishers Pty Ltd (Australia) 19
Widjaja (Indonesia) 200
'Wiedza Powszechna' Państwowe Wydawnictwo (Poland) 293

Wieland, Richard Rudolf, (Switzerland) 350
Wiener Bibliophilen-Gesellschaft (Austria) 30
Wiener Dom-Verlag (Austria) 28
Wiener Goethe-Verein (Austria) 30
Wiener Stadt- und Landesarchiv (Austria) 30
Wiener Stadt und Landesbibliothek (Austria) 30
Wiener Urtext Edition-Musikverlag GmbH & Co KG (Austria) 28
Wilco Publishing House (India) 195
Wild, Verlag Alexander, (Switzerland) 350
Wild & Woolley Pty Ltd (Australia) 19
Wildgans, Anton, Prize of Austrian Industry (Austria) 31
Wildwood House Ltd (United Kingdom) 406
Wiley, John, & Sons (Australia) 19
Wiley, John, & Sons Ltd (United Kingdom) 406
Wiley Eastern Ltd (India) 195
Wilfion Books Publishers (United Kingdom) 406
Wilke Literary Award (Australia) 23
Wilkenschildts Forlag (Denmark) 77
Williams, Joseph, (United Kingdom) 406
Williams & Norgate (United Kingdom) 406
Williams Book Illustration Award, Francis, (United Kingdom) 416
Williams Memorial Prize, Griffith John, (Gwobr Goffa Griffith John Williams) (United Kingdom) 416
Willis Bookshops (Republic of Ireland) 204
Wilson & Horton Ltd (New Zealand) 271
Wilson, John Rowan, Award (International Literary Prizes) 444
Wilson, Philip, Publishers (United Kingdom) 406
Wilton Publications (United Kingdom) 407
Wimmer, J, Druckerei und Zeitungshaus GmbH & Co (Austria) 28
Win Join Book Co Ltd (China (Taiwan)) 64
Windhoek Public Library (Namibia) 255
Wine & Spirit Publications Ltd (United Kingdom) 407
Wine, The, Book Club (United Kingdom) 410
Wingate, Allan, (Publishers) Ltd (United Kingdom) 407
Wingate Series (United Kingdom) 407
Winkel, Rosa, Verlags-und-Versand GmbH (Federal Republic of Germany) 163
Winkelhaak PVBA (Belgium) 42
Winkler-Verlag (Federal Republic of Germany) 163
Winter, Alfred, Verlag (Austria) 28
Winter, Carl, Universitätsverlag GmbH (Federal Republic of Germany) 163
Winter, Herta, (Austria) 29
Winthers Forlag ApS (Denmark) 77
Wirtschaft, Verlag Die, (German Democratic Republic) 117
Wirtschaft, Recht, Steuern (Federal Republic of Germany) 163
Wirtschaft und Recht, Fachbuchhandlung für, (Austria) 29
Wirtschafts- und Kartographie, Verlag für, -Publikationen, Ryborsch (Federal Republic of Germany) 163
Wirtschaftsskripten, Verlag für, (Federal Republic of Germany) 163
Wirtschaftsverlag (Federal Republic of Germany) 163
Wison Verlag GmbH (Federal Republic of Germany) 163
Wissen Verlag GmbH (Federal Republic of Germany) 163
Wissenschaft und Politik, Verlag, (Federal Republic of Germany) 163
Wissenschaft, Wirtschaft und Technik, Verlag für, GmbH und Co KG (Federal Republic of Germany) 164
Wissenschaftliche Buchgesellschaft (Federal Republic of Germany) 164
Wissenschaftliche Buchgesellschaft (Federal Republic of Germany) 165
Wissenschaftliche Verlagsgesellschaft mbH (Federal Republic of Germany) 164
Witherby, H F & G, Ltd and Witherby & Co Ltd (United Kingdom) 407
Wittig, Friedrich, Verlag (Federal Republic of Germany) 164
Wittwer, Buchhandlung Konrad, KG (Federal Republic of Germany) 166
Wittwer, Verlag Konrad, KG (Federal Republic of Germany) 164
Witwatersrand University Press (Republic of South Africa) 311
Witzstrock, Gerhard, GmbH (Federal Republic of Germany) 164
Wkallat Matbouat (Kuwait) 238
Wobbledagger (Australia) 19
Woburn, The, Press (United Kingdom) 407
Wöldikes Forlag (Denmark) 77
Wolfe Medical Publications Ltd (United Kingdom) 407
Wolfe Publishing Ltd (United Kingdom) 407
Wolff, Oswald, (Publishers) Ltd (United Kingdom) 407
Wolfhound Press (Republic of Ireland) 204
Wolfrum, Kunstverlag, (Austria) 28
Wolfrum, Kunstverlag, (Austria) 29
Wolfsbergdrucke, Verlag der, (Switzerland) 350
Wolfson History Awards (United Kingdom) 416
Wolmar, Valentine de, Prize (France) 113
Wolters Leuven, J B, NV (Belgium) 42
Wolters-Noordhoff BV (Netherlands) 265

Wolters Noordhoff Longman BV (Netherlands) 265
Women Writers' Association (Japan) 224
Women's Literary Society (Greece) 173
Women's Literary Society Prizes (Greece) 173
Women's Movement Children's Literature Co-op Ltd (Australia) 19
Women's, The, Press (Republic of Ireland) 204
Women's, The, Press Book Club (United Kingdom) 410
Women's, The, Press Ltd (United Kingdom) 407
Womm-Press (Federal Republic of Germany) 164
Woodhead-Faulkner (Publishers) Ltd (United Kingdom) 407
Word and Vision Ltd (Greece) 172
Word Books (Word (UK) Ltd) (United Kingdom) 407
Workers' Press (People's Republic of China) 63
Workshop Press Ltd (United Kingdom) 407
World Book—Childcraft International Inc (United Kingdom) 407
World Book Co (China (Taiwan)) 64
World Book Co (Hong Kong) 176
World Books (United Kingdom) 410
World Council of Churches (WCC) (International Organizations) 436
World Festival of Negro Arts Literary Prizes (International Literary Prizes) 444
World Health Organization (WHO) (International Organizations) 435
World Homoeopathic Links (India) 195
World Intellectual Property Organization (WIPO) (International Organizations) 436
World International Publishing Ltd (United Kingdom) 407
World Meteorological Organization (WMO) (International Organizations) 435
World Microfilms Publications Ltd (United Kingdom) 407
World of Information (United Kingdom) 407
World of Islam Festival Trust (United Kingdom) 407
World of Nature (United Kingdom) 410
World Press, The, Pvt Ltd (India) 195
World, The, Book Company (Macau) 242
World, The, Book Company Pte Ltd (Republic of Singapore) 306
World University Library (United Kingdom) 407
World's Work Ltd (United Kingdom) 407
Wort und Welt Verlag (Austria) 28
Woursell, Abraham, Prize (University of Vienna) (International Literary Prizes) 444
Wren Publishing Pty Ltd (Australia) 19
Wright, Mme Ellen, (France) 107
Wright Publishing, Gordon, (United Kingdom) 407
Wright & Sons, John, Ltd (United Kingdom) 407
Writers and Readers Publishing Co-operative (United Kingdom) 408
Writers' Guild of Great Britain (United Kingdom) 365
Writers' Guild Publishing House (Pakistan) 283
Writers' Publishing House (People's Republic of China) 63
Writers', The, Group (Malawi) 243
Writers' Union Prize (Romania) 302
Writers Workshop (India) 195
'Wspólna Sprawa', Wydawniczo Oświatowa Spółdzielnia Inwalidów, (Educational Publishing Cooperative of the Disabled) (Poland) 293
Wunderlich, Rainer, Verlag Hermann Leins (Federal Republic of Germany) 164
Württembergische Bibliotheksgesellschaft (Federal Republic of Germany) 167
Württembergische Landesbibliothek (Federal Republic of Germany) 166
Wykeham Publications (London) Ltd (United Kingdom) 408
Wyss, K J, Erben AG (Switzerland) 350

Xarait Ediciones (Spain) 323
Xarait Libros (Spain) 324
Xenos Verlagsgesellschaft mbH & Co (Federal Republic of Germany) 164
Xerox Publishing Group Ltd (United Kingdom) 408
Xunhasoba (Socialist Republic of Viet Nam) 420

Y Hoc Publishing House (Socialist Republic of Viet Nam) 420
Y M C A-Press (France) 107
Yachdav, United Publishers Co Ltd (Israel) 209
Yad Eliahu Chitov (Israel) 209
Yad Vashem — Martyrs' and Heroes' Remembrance Authority (Israel) 209
Yaffa Syndicate Pty Ltd (Australia) 19

Yale University Press Ltd (United Kingdom) 408
Yama-Kei (Publishers) Co Ltd (Japan) 230
Yamada Shoin (Yamada Publishing Co) (Japan) 230
Yañez, J F, Agencia Literaria (Universitas) (Spain) 323
Yarmouk University Bookshop (Jordan) 233
Yarmouk University Library (Jordan) 233
Yasaguna, C V, (Indonesia) 200
Yavneh Ltd (Israel) 209
Yayasan Buku (Malaysia) 245
Yedioth Ahronoth Enterprises (Book Dept) (Israel) 209
Yee Wen Publishing Co Ltd (China (Taiwan)) 64
Yeshurun (Israel) 209
Yesod (Israel) 209
Yiannakis, Iakovou, (Cyprus) 69
Yliopistokirjakauppa Oy (Finland) 86
Yoga Life (India) 195
Yohan Publications Inc (Japan) 230
Yohan (Western Publications Distribution Agency) (Japan) 231
Yokendo Ltd (Japan) 230
Yomiuri Literature Prize (Japan) 233
Yonsei University Library (Republic of Korea) 238
Yonsei University Press (Republic of Korea) 238
Yorkshire Arts Association Literary Awards (United Kingdom) 416
'Yorkshire Post' Book of the Year Award (International Literary Prizes) 444
Yoruba (Barbados) 32
Yoseloff, Thomas, Ltd (United Kingdom) 408
Yoshikawa Prize for Popular Novel (Japan) 233
Young People's Book Prize (International Literary Prizes) 444
Young Writers' Incentive Awards (New Zealand) 273
Youth Publishing House (People's Republic of China) 63
Youth's Library Mohamad Ahmed Sharareh (Jordan) 233
Yritystieto Oy — Foretagsdata HAb (Finland) 85
Yuhikaku Publishing Co Ltd (Japan) 230
Yulwha Dang (Republic of Korea) 238
Yundum College Library (The Gambia) 114
Yunnan Provincial Library (People's Republic of China) 63
'Yuridicheskaya Literatura', Izdatelstvo, (Union of Soviet Socialist Republics) 362
Yushodo Booksellers Ltd (Japan) 230
Yuval (Israel) 210
Yvert et Tellier, Editions Philateliques, (France) 107

Z A Reprints (German Democratic Republic) 117
Z I R A L (Zajednica Izdanja Ranjeni Labud) (Italy) 220
Z O E (Greece) 172
Z-Verlag, Genossenschaft, (Switzerland) 351

Zahar Editores (Brazil) 55
Zahiriah, Al, (National Library) (Syria) 353
Zaire, Librairie du, (Zaire) 427
Zak, S, & Co (Israel) 210
Založba Obzorja (Yugoslavia) 425
Zambia Catholic Bookshop (Zambia) 428
Zambia Institute of Technology Library (Zambia) 428
Zambia Library Association (Zambia) 428
Zambia Library Service (Zambia) 428
Zambon, Dr, (Federal Republic of Germany) 164
Zanichelli, Nicola, SpA (Italy) 220
Žanzibar Government Archives (Tanzania) 353
Západočeské nakladatelství (Czechoslovakia) 72
Zaruski, Mariusz, Literary Prize (Poland) 294
Zattera, Casa Editrice La, (Italy) 220
Zauho, The, Press (Japan) 230
Zavalia, Victor P de, Editor (Argentina) 8
Zavod za Izdavanje Udžbenika (Yugoslavia) 425
Zavod za obrazovanje kadrova za administrativne poslove SR Srbije (Yugoslavia) 425
Zavod za udžbenike i nastavna sredstva (Yugoslavia) 425
Zavod za Udžbenike i Nastavna Sredstva Sap Kosovo (Yugoslavia) 425
Zbinden Druck und Verlag AG (Switzerland) 351
Zebra Books for Children (India) 195
Zechner und Hüthig Verlag GmbH (Federal Republic of Germany) 164
Zed Press (United Kingdom) 408
Zeit, Verlag, im Bild (German Democratic Republic) 117
Zelkowitz (Israel) 210
Zell, Hans, (Publishers) Ltd (United Kingdom) 408
Zemizdat, Darzhavno Izdatelstvo, (Bulgaria) 58
Zeneműkiadó, Editio Musica Budapest, (Hungary) 178
Zeno Booksellers & Publishers (United Kingdom) 408
Zentralantiquariat der DDR — Reprintabteilung (ZA Reprints) (German Democratic Republic) 117
Zentralbibliothek der deutschen Klassik (German Democratic Republic) 118
Zentralbibliothek Zürich (Switzerland) 352
Zentralgesellschaft für buchgewerbliche und graphische Betraiebe (Austria) 29
Zentralinstitut für Bibliothekswesen (German Democratic Republic) 118
Zentralinstitut für Information und Dokumentation (German Democratic Republic) 118
Zentralstelle für maschinelle Dokumentation (Federal Republic of Germany) 167
Zero SA (Spain) 323
Zero-Zyx, Editorial, SA (Spain) 323
Zettner, Verlag Andreas, KG (Federal Republic of Germany) 164
Zibet Prize (Sweden) 336
Zig-Zag, Empressa Editora, SA (Chile) 62
Zimbabwe Library Association (Zimbabwe) 430
Zimbabwean Publications (Zimbabwe) 429

Zimmer, Verlag Wolfgang, (Federal Republic of Germany) 164
Zimmermann KG (Federal Republic of Germany) 164
Zindermans Förlag (Sweden) 334
Zip Editôra Ltda (Brazil) 55
Zjednoczenie Ksiegarstwa (Poland) 293
Zjednoczenie Przedsiebiorstw Wydawniczych Naczelny Zarzad Wydawnictw (United Publishers — Central Publishing Board) (Poland) 290
Zluhan, Verlagsgemeinschaft Friedrich, (Federal Republic of Germany) 164
Zmora, Bitan, Modan-Publishers (Israel) 210
'Znak', Spoleczny Instytut Wydawniczy, (Social Publishing Institute) (Poland) 293
Znanie (Union of Soviet Socialist Republics) 362
'Znanje', Nakladni Zavod, (Yugoslavia) 425
Zodiaque (France) 107
Zodiaque, La Pierre-qui-Vire (Switzerland) 351
Zolindakis, Har, (Greece) 172
Zollikofer Fachverlag AG (Switzerland) 351
Zomer en Keuning Boeken BV (Netherlands) 265
Zorn Prize (Sweden) 336
Zoshindo Juken-Kenkyusha (Japan) 230
Zrinyi Katonai Kiadó (Publishing House of the Hungarian Army) (Hungary) 178
Zsolnay, Paul, Verlag GmbH (Austria) 28
Zsolnay, Paul, Verlag GmbH (Federal Republic of Germany) 164
Zuckmayer, Carl, Medal (Federal Republic of Germany) 68
Zuid-Hollandsche UM (Netherlands) 265
Zuidgroep BV (formerly Hippobook/Studio de Zuid) (Netherlands) 265
Zuidnederlandse Uitgeverij NV (Belgium) 42
Zumstein & Cie (Switzerland) 351
Zur & Zur Ltd (Israel) 210
Zuri Book Shop (Afghanistan) 1
Zväz slovenskych knihovníkov a informatikov (Czechoslovakia) 72
Zväz slovenských spisovateľov (Czechoslovakia) 69
Zveza društev bibliotekarjev Jugoslavije (Slovene) (Yugoslavia) 426
Zwei-Bären Verlag der VDB (Switzerland) 351
Zwelpunkt Verlag KG (Federal Republic of Germany) 164
Zweitausendeins Versand (Federal Republic of Germany) 164
Zwemmer, A, Ltd (United Kingdom) 408
Zwiazek Literatów Poliskich (Union of Polish Writers) (Poland) 290
Zwijsen, Uitgeverij, BV (Netherlands) 266
Zwimpfer, Adolf, (Switzerland) 351
'Zycie Literackie' Prize (Poland) 294
Zytglogge Verlag (Switzerland) 351

Ref
Z
291.5
I 5
1981/82

1. Ref
2. Stacks

MAY 1 2 1981